W9-AGT-583

LEARNING IS
JUST A CLICK AWAY

The **Espaces Supersite**—everything you need to motivate students and support language learning.

- Engages and focuses students
- Improves student performance
- Saves you time with auto-grading, quick setup, and reporting tools
- Provides flexibility to personalize your course
- Offers cost-saving digital options
- Includes vText—the online, interactive Student Edition

 Go to VHLcentral.com to get started

On the cover: Notre-Dame cathedral as seen through Pont de la Tournelle, Paris, France.

Publisher: José A. Blanco

Editorial Development: Judith Bach, Deborah Coffey, Jo Hanna Kurth

Project Management: Sally Giangrande, Faith Ryan

Rights Management: Annie Fuller, Ashley Poreda

Technology Production: Kamila Caicedo, Egle Gutiérrez, Paola Ríos Schaaf

Design: Radoslav Mateev, Gabriel Noreña, Andrés Vanegas

Production: Oscar Díez, Sebastián Díez Pérez, Erik Restrepo

© 2019 by Vista Higher Learning, Inc. All rights reserved.

No part of this work may be reproduced or distributed in any form or by any means, electronic or mechanical, including photocopying and recording, or by any information storage or retrieval system without prior written permission from Vista Higher Learning, 500 Boylston Street, Suite 620, Boston, MA 02116-3736.

Student Text (Casebound): 978-1-68005-648-8
Student Text (Loose-Leaf): 978-1-68005-649-5
Instructor's Annotated Edition ISBN: 978-1-68005-650-1

Library of Congress Control Number: 2017949819

1 2 3 4 5 6 7 8 9 TC 22 21 20 19 18 17

Printed in Canada.

INSTRUCTOR'S ANNOTATED EDITION   FOURTH EDITION

ESPACES

Rendez-vous avec le monde francophone

James G. Mitchell

Cheryl Tano

VISTA®
HIGHER LEARNING

Boston, Massachusetts

Instructor's Annotated Edition

Table of Contents

THE VISTA HIGHER LEARNING STORY
Your Specialized World Language Publisher

Independent, specialized, and privately owned, Vista Higher Learning was founded in 2000 with one mission: to raise the teaching and learning of world languages to a higher level. This mission is based on the following beliefs:

- It is essential to prepare students for a world in which learning another language is a necessity, not a luxury.
- Language learning should be fun and rewarding, and all students should have the tools necessary for achieving success.
- Students who experience success learning a language will be more likely to continue their language studies both inside and outside the classroom.

With this in mind, we decided to take a fresh look at all aspects of language instructional materials. Because we are specialized, we dedicate 100 percent of our resources to this goal and base every decision on how well it supports language learning.

That is where you come in. Since our founding in 2000, we have relied on the continuous and invaluable feedback from language instructors and students nationwide. This partnership has proved to be the cornerstone of our success by allowing us to constantly improve our programs to meet your instructional needs.

The result? Programs that make language learning exciting, relevant, and effective through:

- an unprecedented access to resources
- a wide variety of contemporary, authentic materials
- the integration of text, technology, and media, and
- a bold and engaging textbook design

By focusing on our singular passion, we let you focus on yours.

The Vista Higher Learning Team

VISTA®
HIGHER LEARNING

500 Boylston Street, Suite 620 Boston, MA 02116-3736 TOLLFREE: 800-618-7375
TELEPHONE: 617-426-4910 FAX: 617-426-5209 www.vistahigherlearning.com

Getting to Know ESPACES, Fourth Edition

Vibrant and original, **ESPACES**, **Fourth Edition**, takes a fresh, student-friendly approach to introductory French aimed at making students' learning and instructors' teaching easier, more enjoyable, and more successful. **ESPACES** develops students' speaking, listening, reading, and writing skills so that they will be able to express their own ideas and interact with others meaningfully and for real-life purposes.

NEW to the Fourth Edition

- Redistributed and updated **Panorama** pages for more coverage of the Francophone world
- Redesigned vocabulary pages to reflect the A and B lesson vocabulary
- **Vocabulary Tools:** customizable word lists with multiple practice modes, and flashcards with audio and options for English translations
- Task-based activities—for use in class or for assessment
- Illustration bank for use with instructor-created activities
- Redesigned textbook icons, including easy-to-identify chat activities
- Oral testing suggestions now assignable online as chat activities
- 4 new authentic **Le Zapping** TV clips, and a new short film in Unit 15
- New **Flash culture** page, which alternates with **Le Zapping** page in A lesson of every unit
- New **Musique à fond** feature on **Espace culture** pages in B lesson of every unit
- New **Lecture** readings in Units 14 and 15

Plus, the original hallmark features of ESPACES

- Distinctive and cohesive integration of video—from a specially shot **Roman-photo** dramatic series to **Flash culture** videos to authentic TV clips and short films
- A unique four-part practice sequence for every grammar point, moving from form-focused **Essayez!** activities to directed, yet meaningful, **Mise en pratique** activities, to communicative, interactive **Communication** activities, and cumulative, open-ended **Synthèse** activities
- A unique, easy-to-navigate design with textbook pages that are visually engaging, with photos, drawings, realia, and charts designed for instructional impact and visual appeal
- Systematic development of reading and writing skills, incorporating learning strategies and a process approach
- A rich, contemporary cultural presentation of the everyday life of French speakers and the diverse cultures of the entire French-speaking world
- Groundbreaking, text-specific technology specially designed to expand students' learning and instructors' teaching options
- vText—the interactive, online text—perfect for hybrid courses

Le professeur, host of the interactive grammar tutorials

TABLE OF CONTENTS

espace contextes	espace roman-photo	espace culture

espace structures	espace synthèse	savoir-faire

TABLE OF CONTENTS

espace contextes	espace roman-photo	espace culture

TABLE OF CONTENTS

espace contextes	espace roman-photo	espace culture

TABLE OF CONTENTS

	espace contextes	espace roman-photo	espace culture

The ESPACES Supersite

The **ESPACES** Supersite is your online source for integrating text and technology resources. The Supersite enhances language learning and facilitates simple course management. With powerful functionality, a focus on language learning, and a simplified user experience, the Supersite offers features based directly on feedback from thousands of users.

- **An End to Student Frustration:** Make it a cinch for students to track due dates, save work, and access all assignments and resources.
- **Set-Up Ease:** Customize your course and section settings, create your own grading categories, plus copy previous settings to save time.
- **All-in-One Gradebook:** Add your own activities or use the new grade adjustment tool for a true, cumulative grade.
- **Grading Options:** Choose to grade student-by-student, question-by-question, or spot check. Plus, give targeted feedback via in-line editing and voice comments.
- **Accessible Student Data:** Conveniently share information one-on-one, or issue class reports in the formats that best fit you and your department.

For Instructors

- A gradebook to manage rosters, assignments, and grades
- Time-saving auto-graded activities, plus question-by-question and automated spot-checking
- A communication center for announcements, notifications, and help requests
- Downloadable Digital Image Bank (PDF), pre-made syllabi and sample lesson plan (RTF), and Testing Program (RTF)
- Instructor Resources (answer keys, audio-video scripts, translations, grammar slides)
- Online administration of quizzes, tests, and exams, now with time limits and password protection
- Tools to add your own content to the Supersite
    - Create and assign Partner Chat and open-ended activities
    - Upload and assign videos and outside resources
- Single sign-on feature for integration with your LMS
- Activity Pack (PDF) with additional activities for every lesson
- MP3 files of the complete Textbook, Lab Manual, and Testing Audio Programs
- Live Chat for video chat, audio chat, and instant messaging
- Forums for oral assignments, group discussions, and projects

Each section of your textbook comes with activities on the **ESPACES** Supersite, many of which are auto-graded for immediate feedback. Plus, the Supersite is iPad®-friendly*, so it can be accessed on the go! Visit **vhlcentral.com** to explore this wealth of exciting resources.

ESPACE CONTEXTES	• Audio for **Espace contextes** listening activity • Image-based vocabulary activity • Textbook and extra practice activities • Chat activities for conversational skill-building and oral practice • Audio recording of **Les sons et les lettres** presentation • Record-and-compare audio activities
ESPACE ROMAN-PHOTO	• Streaming video of **Roman-photo** episodes, with instructor-managed options for subtitles and transcripts in French and English • Textbook and extra practice activities
ESPACE CULTURE	• **Culture à la loupe** reading • Streaming video of **Flash culture** episodes, with instructor-managed options for subtitles and transcripts in French and English • **Musique à fond** information and activities • Textbook and extra practice activities
ESPACE STRUCTURES	• Grammar presentations • Interactive grammar tutorials • Textbook and extra practice activities • Chat activities for conversational skill-building and oral practice
SYNTHÈSE	• Chat activities for conversational skill-building and oral practice • Streaming video of **Le Zapping** TV clips and short films as well as **Flash culture** episodes • Audio for **À l'écoute** • Textbook and extra practice activities
SAVOIR-FAIRE	• Interactive map • **Sur Internet** research activity • Textbook and extra practice activities • Audio-sync **Lecture** readings • Composition engine for **Écriture**
VOCABULAIRE	• Vocabulary list with audio • Vocabulary Tools: customizable word lists, flashcards with audio

Plus! Also found on the Supersite:

- All textbook and lab audio MP3 files
- Communication center for instructor notifications and feedback
- Live Chat tool for video chat, audio chat, and instant messaging without leaving your browser
- A single gradebook for all Supersite activities
- WebSAM online Student Activities Manual
- **v̂Text** online, interactive student edition with access to Supersite activities, audio, and video

Supersite features vary by access level.

* Students must use a computer for audio recording and select presentations.

PROGRAM COMPONENTS

- **Student Edition (SE)**
  The SE is available in hardcover, loose-leaf, and digital formats.

- **Student Activities Manual (Workbook, Video Manual, and Lab Manual)**
  Workbook activities provide additional practice of the vocabulary and grammar in each textbook lesson and the cultural information in each unit's **Panorama** section. The Video Manual includes pre-viewing, viewing, and post-viewing activities for the **Roman-photo** and **Flash culture** videos. The Lab Manual contains activities for each textbook lesson that build listening comprehension, speaking, and pronunciation skills in French.

- **Lab Audio**
  The Lab Program MP3s provide the recordings to be used in conjunction with the activities in the Lab Manual.

- **Textbook Audio**
  The Textbook MP3s contain the recordings for the listening activities in **Espace contextes**, **Les sons et les lettres**, **À l'écoute**, and **Vocabulaire** sections.

- **Grammar Tutorials**
  Interactive, animated grammar tutorials pair grammar rules with fun examples and interactive questions to check understanding of concepts.

- **Online Student Activities Manual (WebSAM)**
  Incorporating the **Roman-photo** and **Flash culture** videos, as well as the complete Lab Program, this component delivers the Workbook, Video Manual, and Lab Manual online with automatic scoring. Instructors have access to the powerful Supersite classroom management and gradebook tools that allow in-depth tracking of students' scores.

- **ESPACES, Fourth Edition, Supersite**
  Your passcode to the Supersite (**vhlcentral.com**) gives you access to a wide variety of interactive activities for each section of every lesson of the student text; auto-graded exercises for extra practice of vocabulary, grammar, video, and cultural content; reference tools; **Le Zapping** TV clips and short films; the complete **Roman-photo** and **Flash culture** Video Program; the Textbook MP3s; and the Lab Program MP3s.

- **vText Virtual Interactive Text**
  Provides the entire student edition textbook with note-taking and highlighting capabilities. It is fully integrated with Supersite and other online resources.

INSTRUCTOR RESOURCES

INSTRUCTOR RESOURCES

- **Instructor's Annotated Edition (IAE)**
  The unique format of the IAE provides comprehensive support for classroom teaching: expansions, variations, teaching tips, cultural information, additional activities, scripts, and the answer key to the textbook activities.

- **Student Activities Manual Answer Key**

- **Digital Image Bank**
  The Digital Image Bank consists of Textbook Illustrations— maps of the French-speaking world, the **Contextes** illustrations, and additional images —as well as an Illustration Bank of drawings organized thematically.

- **Grammar Slides**
  The Grammar Slides are presentations of each **Structures** grammar point.

- **ESPACES Supersite**
  In addition to access to the student site, the password-protected instructor site offers a robust course management system that allows instructors to assign and track student progress, as well as instructor resources including the Textbook and Lab Audioscripts, French and English videoscripts, Supplementary Vocabulary lists, and answers to **Mise en pratique** and **Essayez!** exercises.

- **Testing Program**
  This contains two versions of tests for each textbook lesson, quarter and semester exams, listening scripts, answer keys, and optional reading, cultural, and video test items. The Testing Program also includes two versions of short quizzes for every vocabulary and grammar presentation and two versions of tests for each unit. All assessments are provided in ready-to-print RTF word processing files for ease of editing.

- **Testing Program MP3s**
  These audio files provide recordings of the Testing Program's listening sections.

- **vText Virtual Interactive Text**
  The entire student edition textbook links directly with Supersite practice activities, audio, and video. Scores for activities completed are automatically recorded to the instructor gradebook.

- **Activity Pack**
  The Activity Pack provides additional discrete and communicative practice for every **Contextes** section and every grammar point and includes handouts for the **Feuilles d'activités** and information gap activities found in the textbook. NEW! to the Fourth Edition, the Activity Pack also includes task-based activities—for use in class or for assessment.

ICONS

ICONS

These icons in the Fourth Edition of **ESPACES** alert you to the type of activity or section involved.

Icons legend			
🔊	Listening activity/section	Ⓢ	Additional content found on the Supersite: audio, video, and presentations
👓	Activity also on the Supersite	Ⓢ	Additional practice on the Supersite
👥	Pair activity	🧩	Information Gap activity
👥	Group activity	📝	Feuille d'activités
🔁	Recycling activity	👥	Chat activity

- The Information Gap activities and those involving **Feuilles d'activités** (*activity sheets*) require handouts from the instructor.
- The audio icon appears in **Contextes**, **Les sons et les lettres**, **À l'écoute**, and **Vocabulaire** sections.
- The recycling icon tells you that to complete a specific activity you will need to use vocabulary and/or grammar learned in previous lessons.

RESSOURCES BOXES

Ressources boxes let you know exactly which program components you can use to reinforce and expand on every section of every lesson in your textbook. They even include page numbers when applicable.

Ressources boxes legend			
WB pp. 29–30	Workbook	Ⓢ vhlcentral	ESPACES, Supersite
LM pp. 17	Lab Manual		
VM pp. 219–220	Video Manual		

UNIT OPENERS
outline the content and features of each unit.

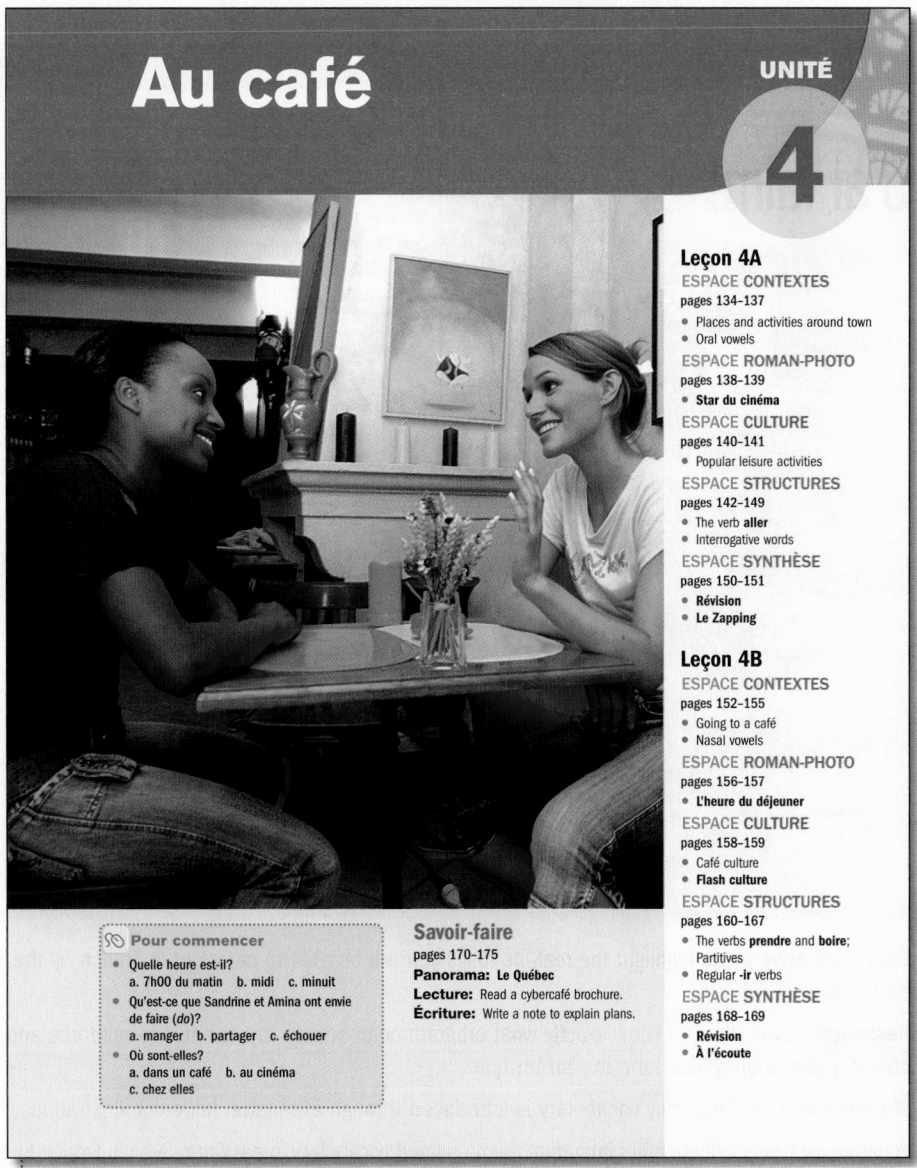

Au café

UNITÉ 4

Leçon 4A

ESPACE CONTEXTES
pages 134–137
- Places and activities around town
- Oral vowels

ESPACE ROMAN-PHOTO
pages 138–139
- Star du cinéma

ESPACE CULTURE
pages 140–141
- Popular leisure activities

ESPACE STRUCTURES
pages 142–149
- The verb **aller**
- Interrogative words

ESPACE SYNTHÈSE
pages 150–151
- Révision
- Le Zapping

Leçon 4B

ESPACE CONTEXTES
pages 152–155
- Going to a café
- Nasal vowels

ESPACE ROMAN-PHOTO
pages 156–157
- L'heure du déjeuner

ESPACE CULTURE
pages 158–159
- Café culture
- Flash culture

ESPACE STRUCTURES
pages 160–167
- The verbs **prendre** and **boire**; Partitives
- Regular -**ir** verbs

ESPACE SYNTHÈSE
pages 168–169
- Révision
- À l'écoute

Pour commencer
- Quelle heure est-il?
  a. 7h00 du matin   b. midi   c. minuit
- Qu'est-ce que Sandrine et Amina ont envie de faire (*do*)?
  a. manger   b. partager   c. échouer
- Où sont-elles?
  a. dans un café   b. au cinéma
  c. chez elles

Savoir-faire
pages 170–175
Panorama: Le Québec
Lecture: Read a cybercafé brochure.
Écriture: Write a note to explain plans.

Pour commencer activities jump-start the units, allowing you to use the French you know to talk about the photos.

Content thumbnails break down each unit into its two lessons (A and B) and one **Savoir-faire** section, giving you an at-a-glance summary of the vocabulary, grammar, cultural topics, and language skills on which you will focus.

Ⓢupersite

Supersite resources are available for every section of the unit at **vhlcentral.com.** Icons show you which textbook activities are also available online, and where additional practice activities are available. The description next to the Ⓢ icon indicates what additional resources are available for each section: videos, audio recordings, readings, presentations, and more!

Supersite features vary by access level.

ESPACE CONTEXTES
presents and practices vocabulary in meaningful contexts.

Communicative goals highlight the real-life tasks you will be able to carry out in French by the end of each lesson.

Ressources boxes let you know exactly what program components you can use to reinforce and expand on every strand of every lesson in your textbook.

Illustrations High-frequency vocabulary is introduced through expansive, full-color illustrations.

Vocabulaire boxes call out other important theme-related vocabulary in easy-to-reference French-English lists.

Mise en pratique always includes a listening activity, as well as other activities that practice the new vocabulary in meaningful contexts.

Supersite

- Audio for **Contextes** listening activity
- Textbook activities
- Additional activities for extra practice

Supersite features vary by access level.

ESPACE CONTEXTES

has a page devoted to communication activities. **Les sons et les lettres** presents the rules of French pronunciation and spelling.

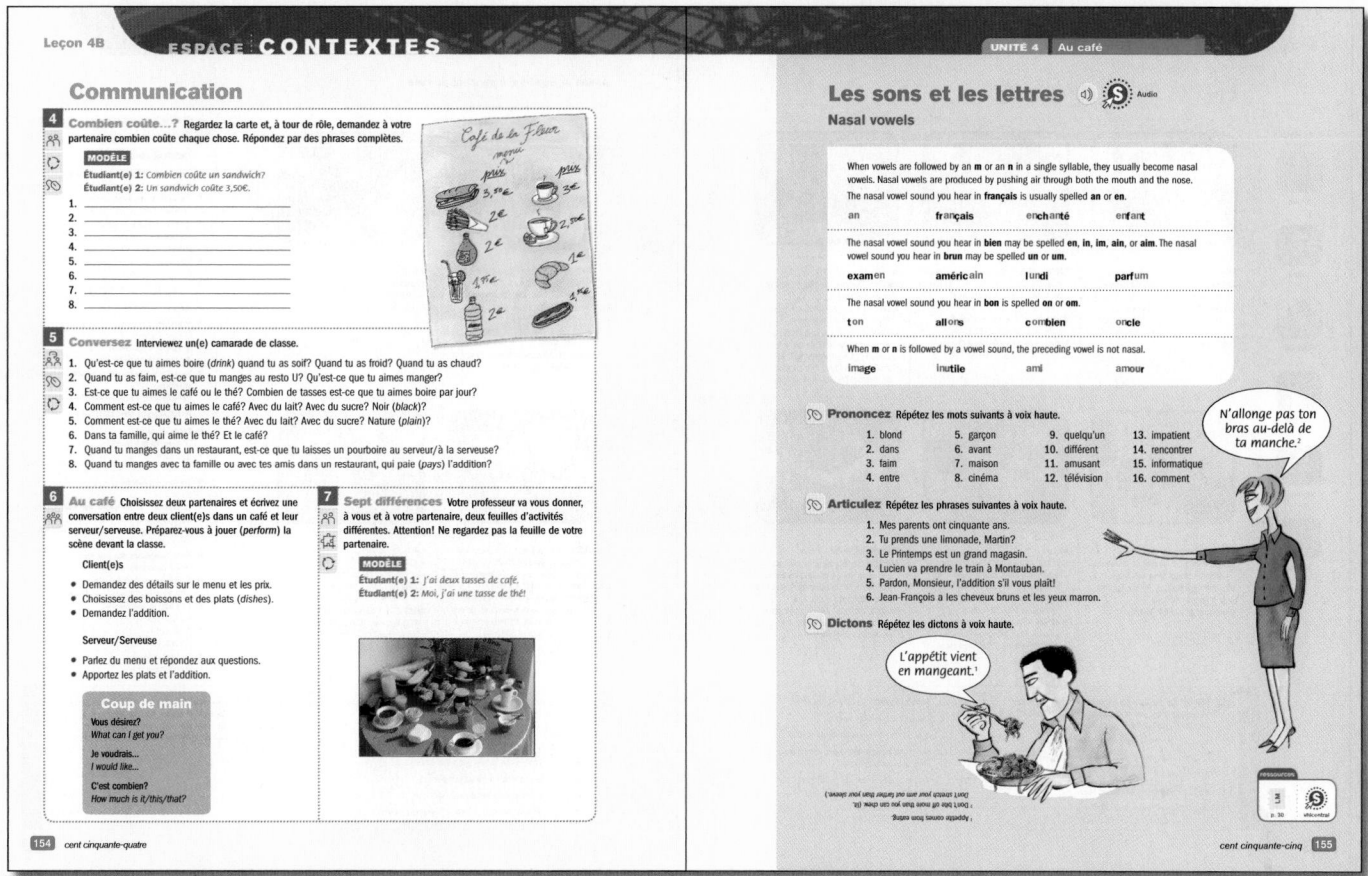

Communication activities allow you to use the vocabulary creatively in interactions with a partner, a small group, or the entire class.

Coup de main provides handy, on-the-spot information that helps you complete the activities.

The audio icon at the top of the page indicates when an explanation and activities are recorded for convenient use in or outside of class.

Explanation Rules and tips to help you learn French pronunciation and spelling are presented clearly with abundant model words and phrases.

Practice Pronunciation and spelling practice is provided at the word and sentence levels. The final activity features illustrated sayings and proverbs so that you can practice the pronunciation or spelling point in an entertaining cultural context.

Supersite

- Chat activities for conversational skill-building and oral practice
- Audio recording of **Les sons et les lettres** presentation
- Record-and-compare audio activities

Supersite features vary by access level.

ESPACE ROMAN-PHOTO
tells the story of a group of students living in Aix-en-Provence, France.

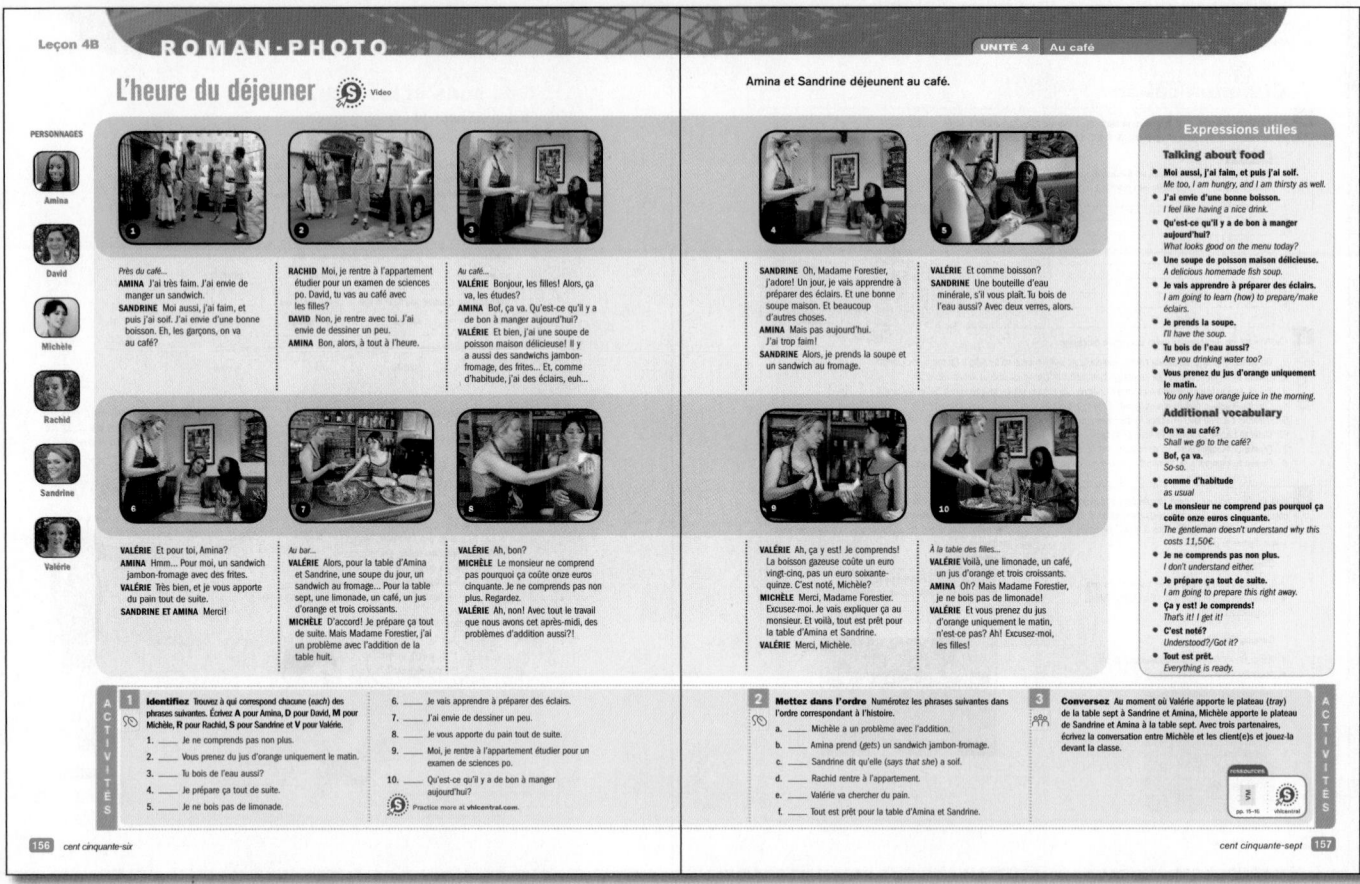

Personnages The photo-based conversations take place among a cast of recurring characters—four college students, their landlady (who owns the café downstairs), and her teenage son.

Roman-photo video episodes The **Roman-photo** episode appears in the **Roman-photo** part of the Video Program.

Conversations The conversations reinforce vocabulary from **Espace contextes**. They also preview structures from the upcoming **Espace structures** section in context and in a comprehensible way.

Expressions utiles organizes new, active words and expressions by language function so that you can focus on using them for real-life, practical purposes.

Ⓢupersite

- Streaming video of the **Roman-photo**
- End-of-video **Reprise** section where key vocabulary and grammar from the episode are called out
- Record-and-compare activities
- Textbook activities
- Additional activities for extra practice

Supersite features vary by access level.

ESPACE CULTURE

explores cultural themes introduced in **ESPACE CONTEXTES** and **ESPACE ROMAN-PHOTO**.

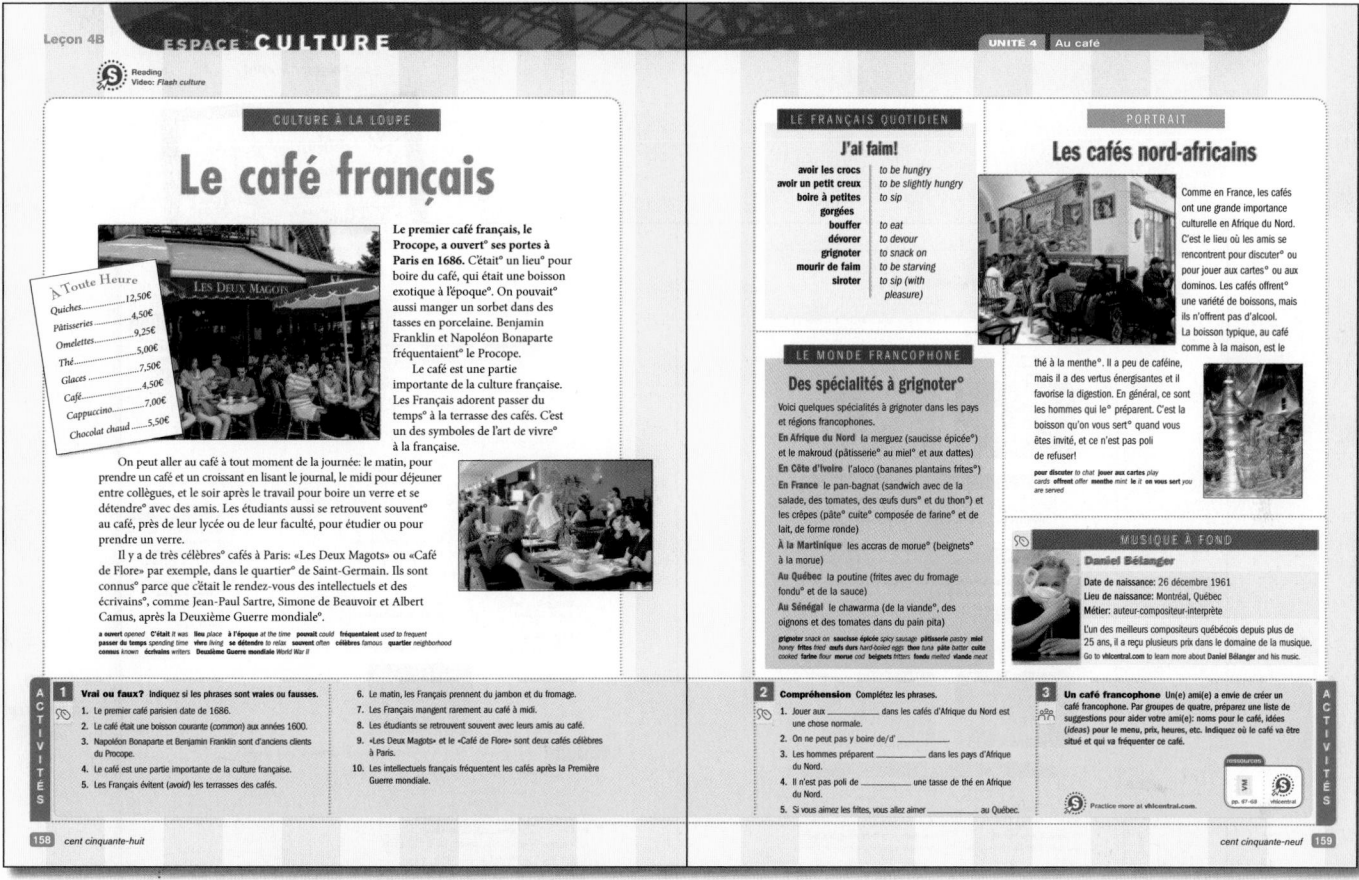

Culture à la loupe presents a main, in-depth reading about the lesson's cultural theme. Full-color photos bring to life important aspects of the topic, while charts with statistics and/or intriguing facts support and extend the information.

Le français quotidien exposes you to current, contemporary language by presenting familiar words and phrases related to the lesson's theme that are used in everyday spoken French.

Le monde francophone puts the spotlight on the people, places, and traditions of the countries and areas of the French-speaking world.

Portrait profiles people, places, and events throughout the French-speaking world, highlighting their importance, accomplishments, and/or contributions to the cultures of the French-speaking people and the global community. **Musique à fond** (in B lesson) profiles musicians of the French-speaking world.

Supersite

- Main cultural reading
- *Flash culture* streaming video (every other unit)
- **Musique à fond** information and activities
- Textbook activities
- Additional activities for extra practice

Supersite features vary by access level.

ESPACE STRUCTURES

presents French grammar in a graphic-intensive format.

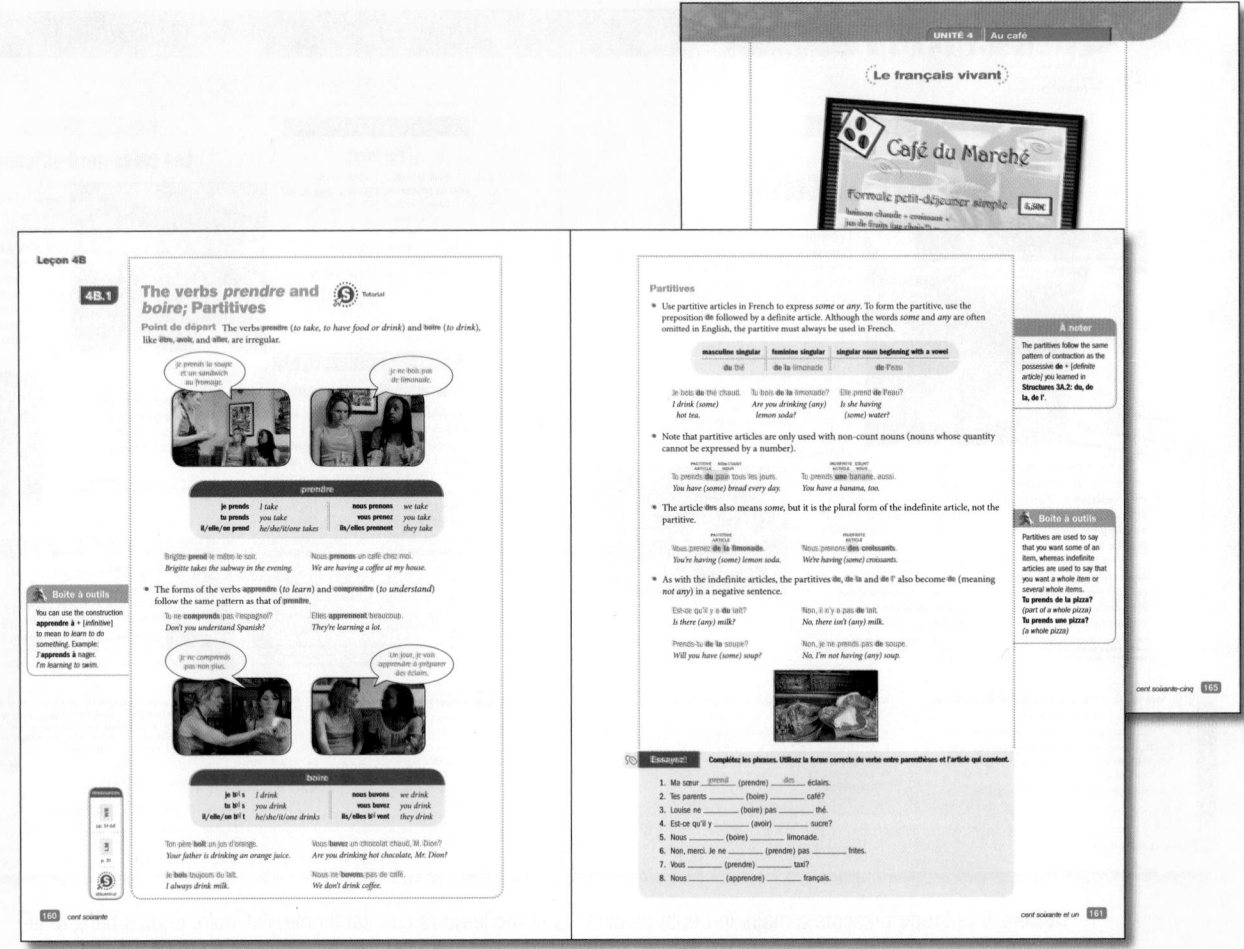

Grammar explanations Two full pages are devoted to most grammar points, allowing for presentations that are thorough and intuitive.

Le français vivant pages appear with select grammar points and feature a print ad for a product related to the lesson's theme.

Graphic-intensive design Photos from the **ESPACES**, Video Program consistently integrate the lesson's video episode and **Roman-photo** strand with the grammar explanations. Additional photos, drawings, and graphic devices liven up activities and heighten visual interest.

Sidebars The **À noter** sidebars cross-reference related grammar content in both previous and upcoming lessons. The **Boîte à outils** sidebars alert you to other important aspects of the grammar point.

Essayez! offers you your first practice of each new grammar point. It gets you working with the grammar point right away in simple, easy-to-understand formats.

ⓢupersite

- Grammar presentation
- Interactive, animated grammar tutorials
- **Essayez!** activities with auto-grading

Supersite features vary by access level.

ESPACE STRUCTURES
provides directed and communicative practice.

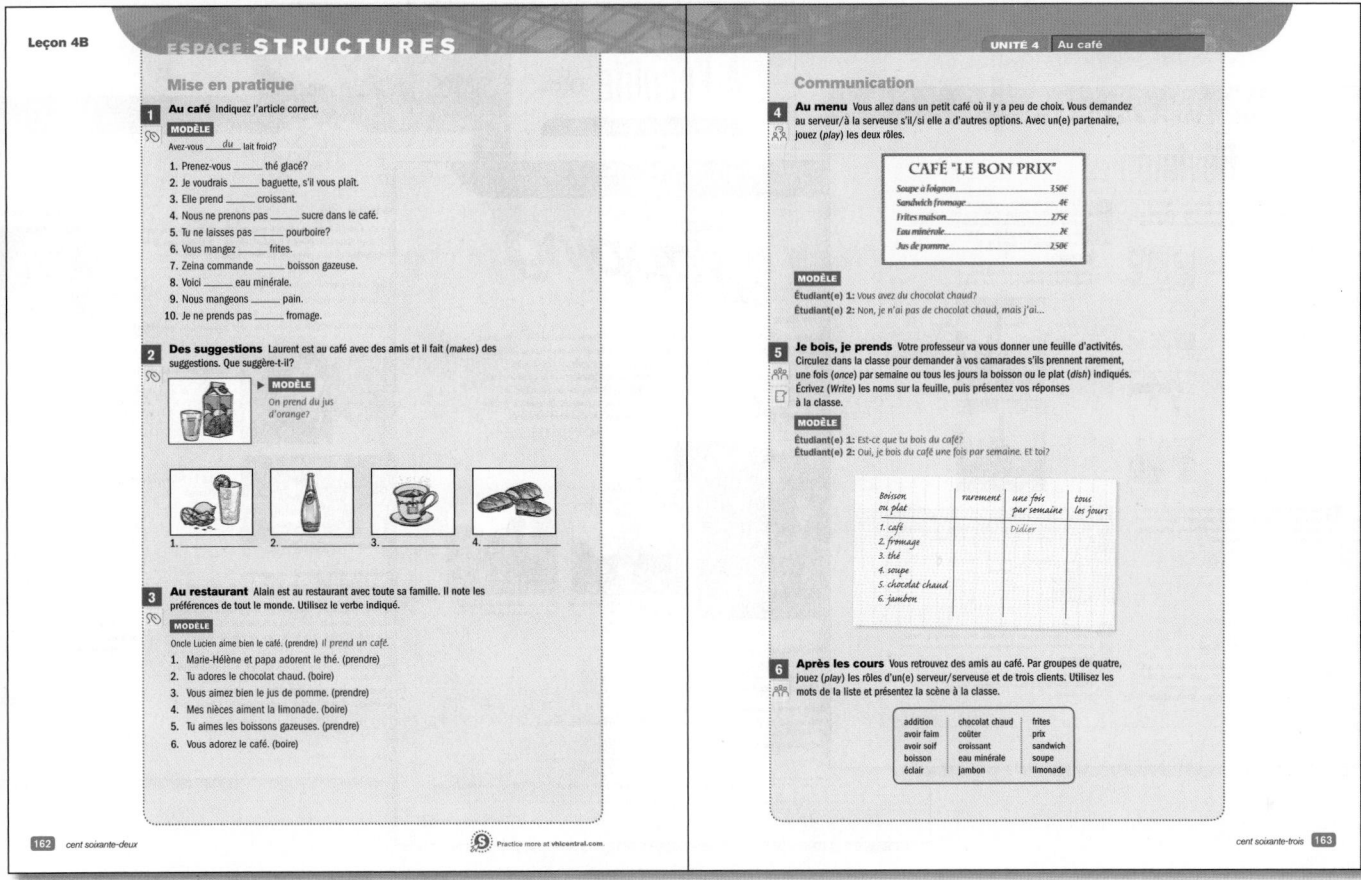

Grammar activities Two full pages are devoted to grammar activities, allowing for more practice and better transitions between activities.

Mise en pratique activities provide a wide range of guided exercises in contexts that combine current and previously learned vocabulary with the current grammar point.

Additional activities The Activity Pack provides additional discrete and communicative practice for every grammar point. It also includes handouts for the **Feuilles d'activités** and information gap activities presented in the textbook. Your instructor will distribute these handouts for review and extra practice.

Communication activities offer opportunities for creative expression using the lesson's grammar and vocabulary. You do these activities with a partner, in small groups, or with the whole class.

Supersite

- Textbook activities
- Additional activities for extra practice
- Chat activities for conversational skill-building and oral practice

Supersite features vary by access level.

ESPACE SYNTHÈSE

pulls the lesson together with cumulative practice in **Révision**. The second page of the section alternates between **Le Zapping/Flash culture** and **À l'écoute**.

Révision activities integrate the lesson's two grammar points with previously learned vocabulary and structures, providing consistent, built-in review as you progress through the text.

Pair and group icons call out the communicative nature of the activities. Situations, role-plays, games, personal questions, interviews, and surveys are just some of the types of activities that you will engage in.

Information gap activities, identified by the interlocking puzzle pieces, engage you and a partner in problem-solving situations. You and your partner each have only half of the information you need, so you must work together to accomplish the task at hand.

NEW! Flash culture (in A lessons of most odd-numbered units) This page has activities related to the cultural video.

Le Zapping (in A lessons of most even-numbered units) features television clips and short films—supported by background information, images, and activities to help you understand and check your comprehension.

À l'écoute (in all B lessons) presents a recorded conversation or narration to develop your listening skills in French. **Stratégie** and **Préparation** prepare you for listening to the recorded passage.

À vous d'écouter takes you through the recorded passage, and **Compréhension** checks your understanding of what you heard.

Ⓢupersite

- Chat activities for conversational skill-building and oral practice
- Streaming video of **Le Zapping** TV clips and short films as well as **Flash culture** episodes
- Audio for **À l'écoute**
- Textbook and extra practice activities

Supersite features vary by access level.

ESPACE SYNTHÈSE
Le Zapping court métrage
Units 12 and 15 feature short films
by contemporary French filmmakers.

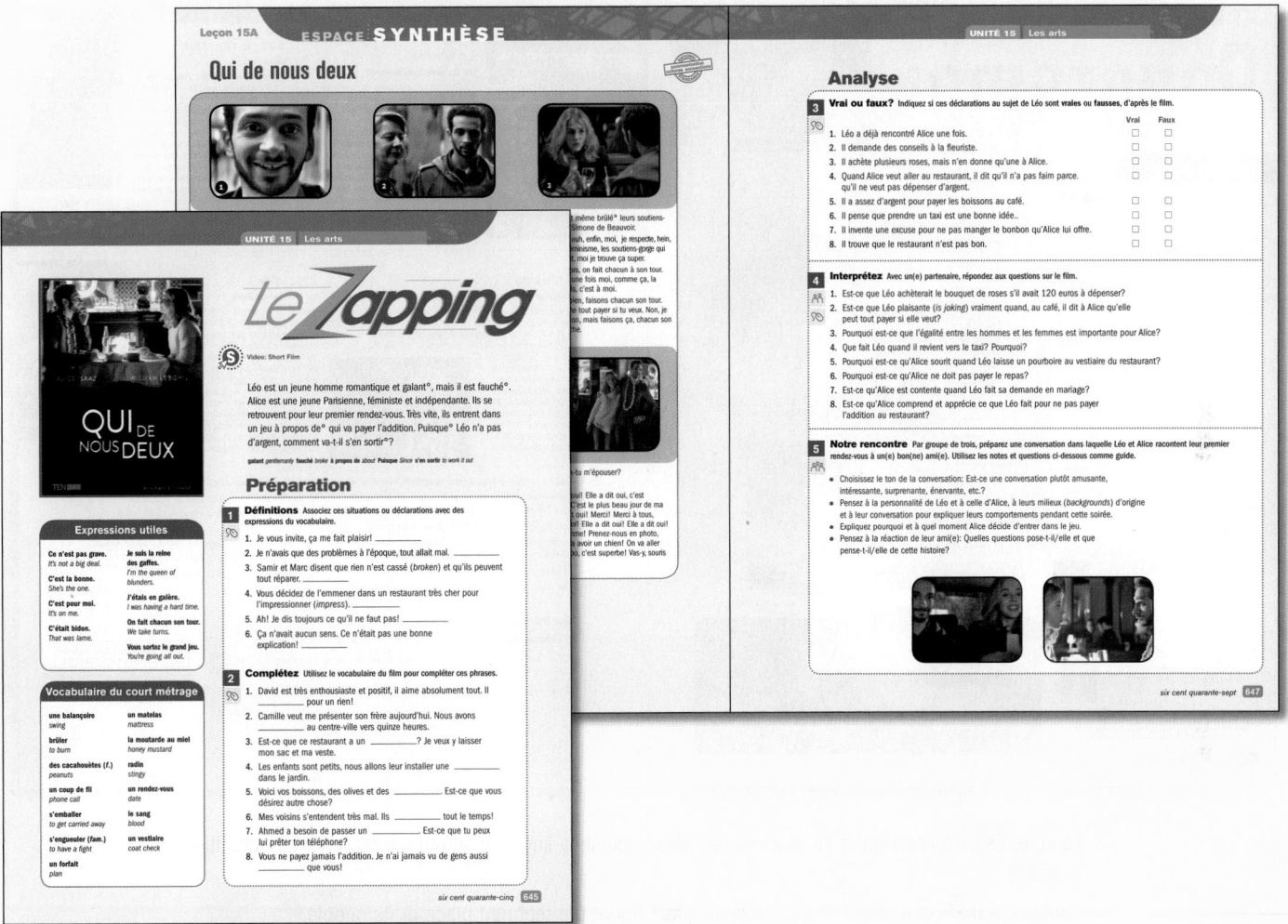

Expressions utiles highlight phrases and expressions useful in understanding the film.

Vocabulaire du court métrage features the words that you will encounter and use while doing the activities in the short film section.

Préparation Pre-viewing exercises set the stage for the short film and provide key background information, facilitating comprehension.

Scène A synopsis of the film's plot with captioned video stills prepares you visually for the film.

Analyse Post-viewing activities go beyond checking comprehension, allowing you to discover broader themes.

Supersite

- Streaming video of **Le Zapping** short films
- Textbook and extra practice activities

Supersite features vary by access level.

SAVOIR-FAIRE

Panorama presents the French-speaking world.

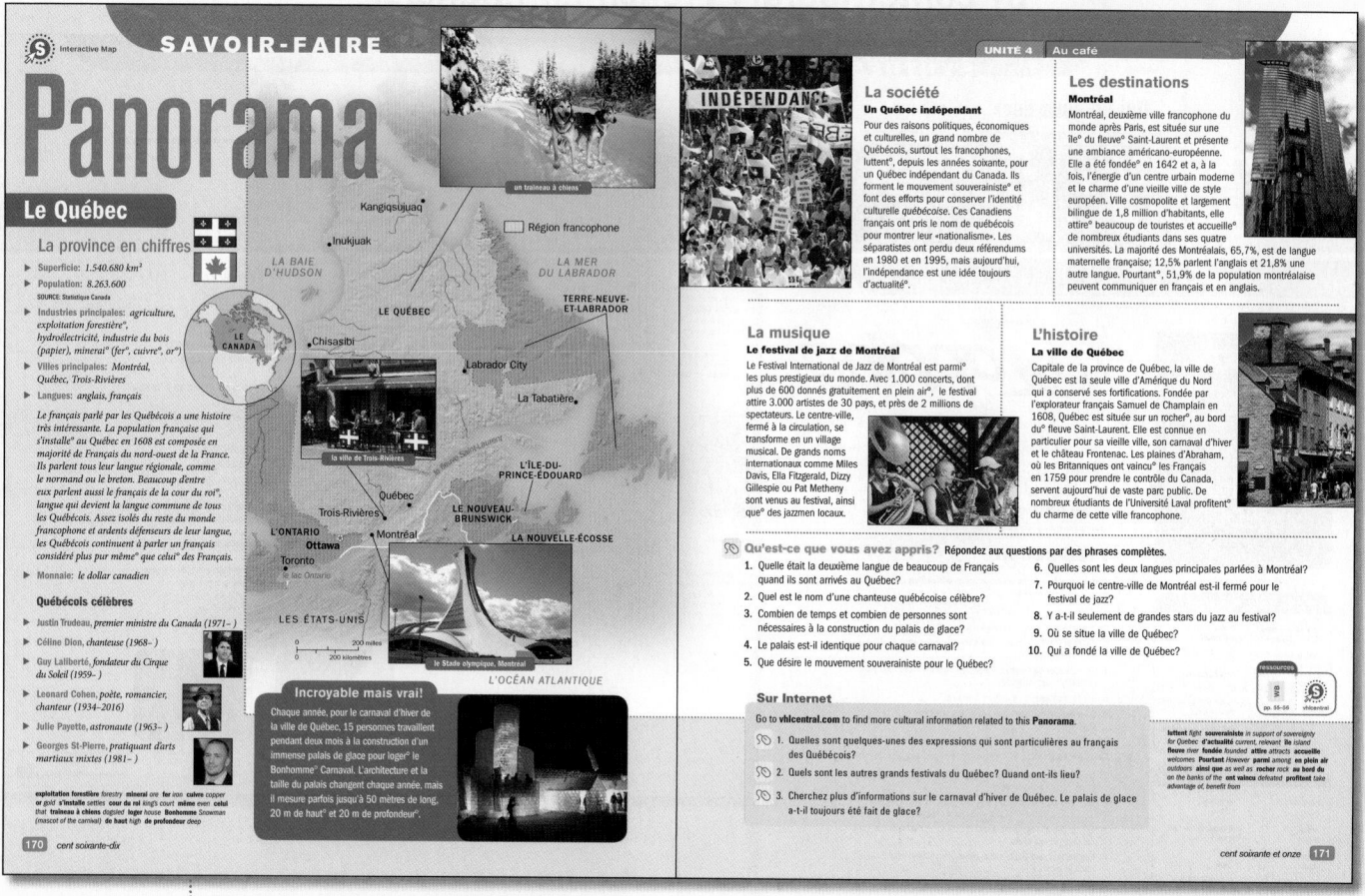

La ville/Le pays/La région en chiffres provides interesting key facts about the featured city, country, or region.

Incroyable mais vrai! highlights an intriguing fact about the featured place or its people.

Maps point out major cities, rivers, and other geographical features and situate the featured place in the context of its immediate surroundings and the world.

Qu'est-ce que vous avez appris? exercises check your understanding of key ideas, and **ressources** boxes reference the two pages of additional activities in the **ESPACES** Workbook.

Readings A series of brief paragraphs explores different facets of the featured location's culture such as history, landmarks, fine art, literature, and aspects of everyday life.

Supersite

- Interactive map
- **Sur Internet** research activity
- Textbook activities
- Additional activities for extra practice

Supersite features vary by access level.

SAVOIR-FAIRE

Lecture develops reading skills in the context of the unit's theme.

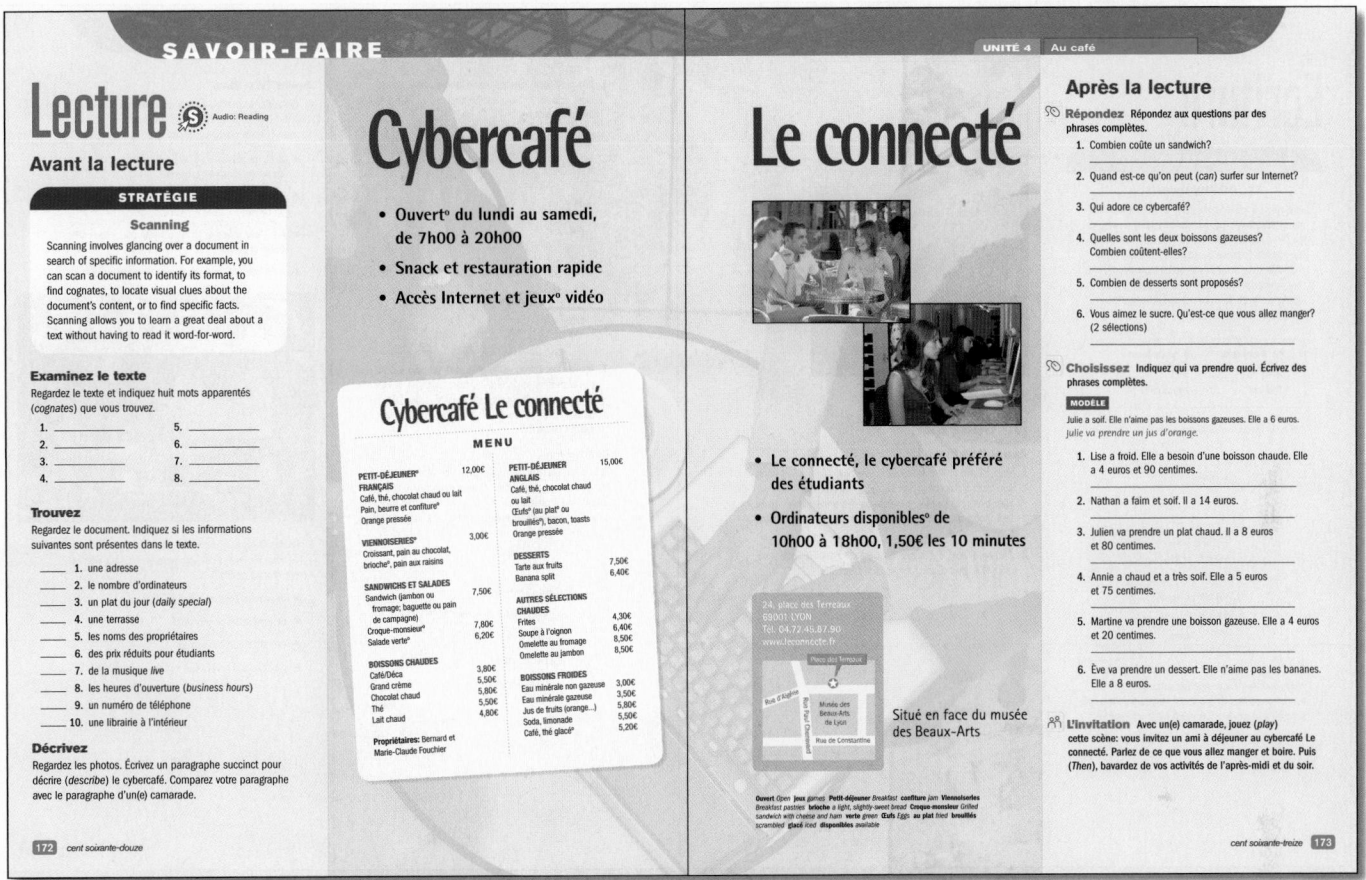

Readings are directly tied to the unit theme and recycle vocabulary and grammar you have learned. The selections in Units 1–11 are cultural texts, while those in Units 12–15 are literary pieces.

Avant la lecture presents valuable reading strategies and pre-reading activities that strengthen your reading abilities in French.

Après la lecture includes post-reading activities that check your comprehension of the reading.

Supersite

- Textbook activities
- Audio-sync technology for all readings

Supersite features vary by access level.

SAVOIR-FAIRE
Écriture develops writing skills in the context of the unit's theme.

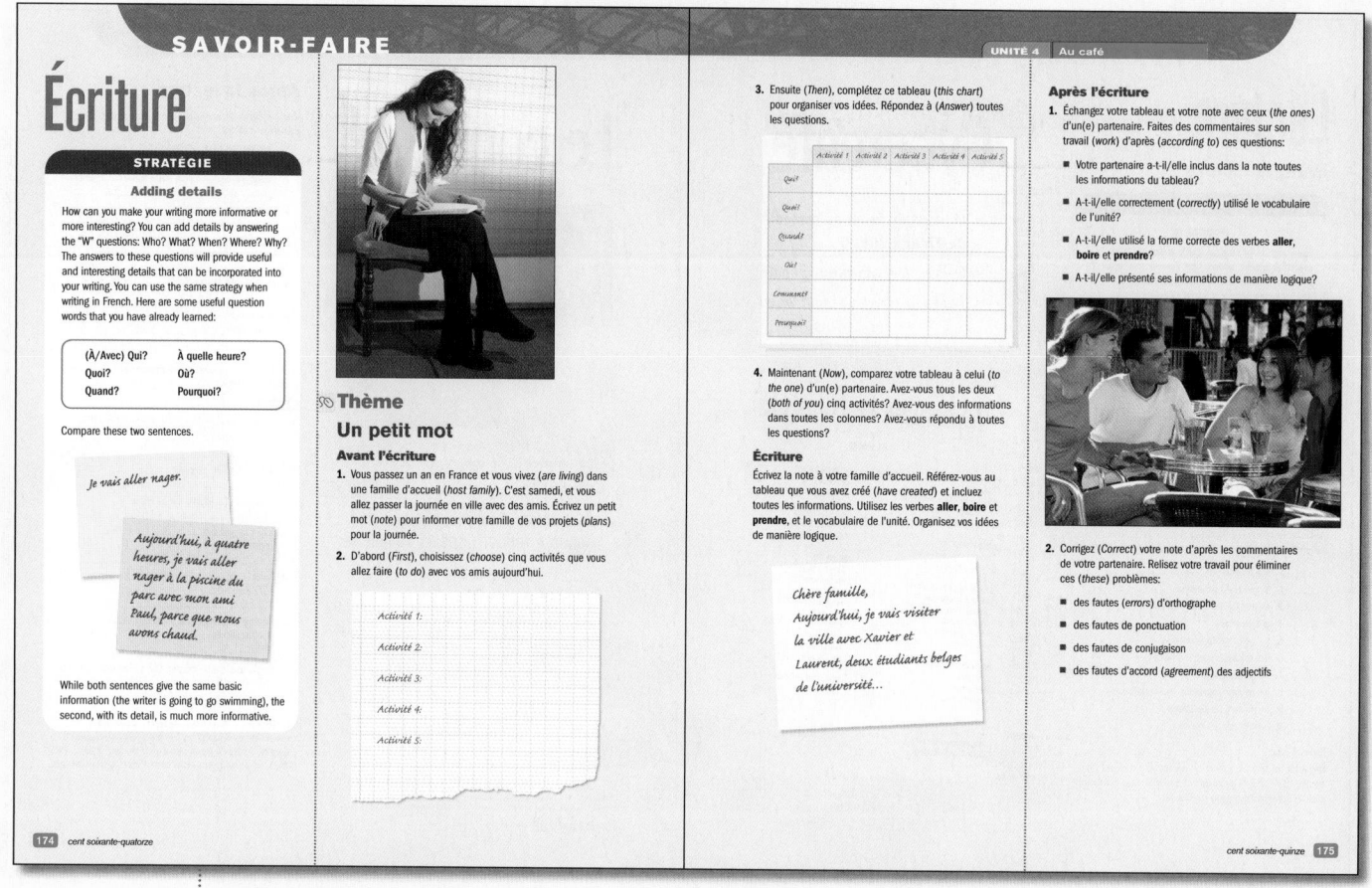

SAVOIR-FAIRE

Écriture

STRATÉGIE

Adding details

How can you make your writing more informative or more interesting? You can add details by answering the "W" questions: Who? What? When? Where? Why? The answers to these questions will provide useful and interesting details that can be incorporated into your writing. You can use the same strategy when writing in French. Here are some useful question words that you have already learned:

(À/Avec) Qui?	À quelle heure?
Quoi?	Où?
Quand?	Pourquoi?

Compare these two sentences.

> *Je vais aller nager.*

> *Aujourd'hui, à quatre heures, je vais aller nager à la piscine du parc avec mon ami Paul, parce que nous avons chaud.*

While both sentences give the same basic information (the writer is going to go swimming), the second, with its detail, is much more informative.

Thème
Un petit mot

Avant l'écriture

1. Vous passez un an en France et vous vivez (*are living*) dans une famille d'accueil (*host family*). C'est samedi, et vous allez passer la journée en ville avec des amis. Écrivez un petit mot (*note*) pour informer votre famille de vos projets (*plans*) pour la journée.

2. D'abord (*First*), choisissez (*choose*) cinq activités que vous allez faire (*to do*) avec vos amis aujourd'hui.

> Activité 1:
> Activité 2:
> Activité 3:
> Activité 4:
> Activité 5:

3. Ensuite (*Then*), complétez ce tableau (*this chart*) pour organiser vos idées. Répondez à (*Answer*) toutes les questions.

	Activité 1	Activité 2	Activité 3	Activité 4	Activité 5
Qui?					
Quoi?					
Quand?					
Où?					
Comment?					
Pourquoi?					

4. Maintenant (*Now*), comparez votre tableau à celui (*to the one*) d'un(e) partenaire. Avez-vous tous les deux (*both of you*) cinq activités? Avez-vous des informations dans toutes les colonnes? Avez-vous répondu à toutes les questions?

Écriture

Écrivez la note à votre famille d'accueil. Référez-vous au tableau que vous avez créé (*have created*) et incluez toutes les informations. Utilisez les verbes **aller**, **boire** et **prendre**, et le vocabulaire de l'unité. Organisez vos idées de manière logique.

> *Chère famille,*
> *Aujourd'hui, je vais visiter*
> *la ville avec Xavier et*
> *Laurent, deux étudiants belges*
> *de l'université...*

Après l'écriture

1. Échangez votre tableau et votre note avec ceux (*the ones*) d'un(e) partenaire. Faites des commentaires sur son travail (*work*) d'après (*according to*) ces questions:

   - Votre partenaire a-t-il/elle inclus dans la note toutes les informations du tableau?
   - A-t-il/elle correctement (*correctly*) utilisé le vocabulaire de l'unité?
   - A-t-il/elle utilisé la forme correcte des verbes **aller**, **boire** et **prendre**?
   - A-t-il/elle présenté ses informations de manière logique?

2. Corrigez (*Correct*) votre note d'après les commentaires de votre partenaire. Relisez votre travail pour éliminer ces (*these*) problèmes:

   - des fautes (*errors*) d'orthographe
   - des fautes de ponctuation
   - des fautes de conjugaison
   - des fautes d'accord (*agreement*) des adjectifs

Process approach Like **À l'écoute** and **Lecture**, **Écriture** is a skill-building feature. It was developed using a process approach in order to guide your writing efforts. It has pre-writing tasks (**Avant l'écriture**), a writing assignment (**Écriture**), and post-writing tasks (**Après l'écriture**).

Stratégie provides useful strategies that prepare you for the writing task presented in **Thème**.

Thème describes the writing topic and includes suggestions for approaching it.

Supersite

- Composition engine

Supersite features vary by access level.

VOCABULAIRE
summarizes all the active vocabulary of the unit.

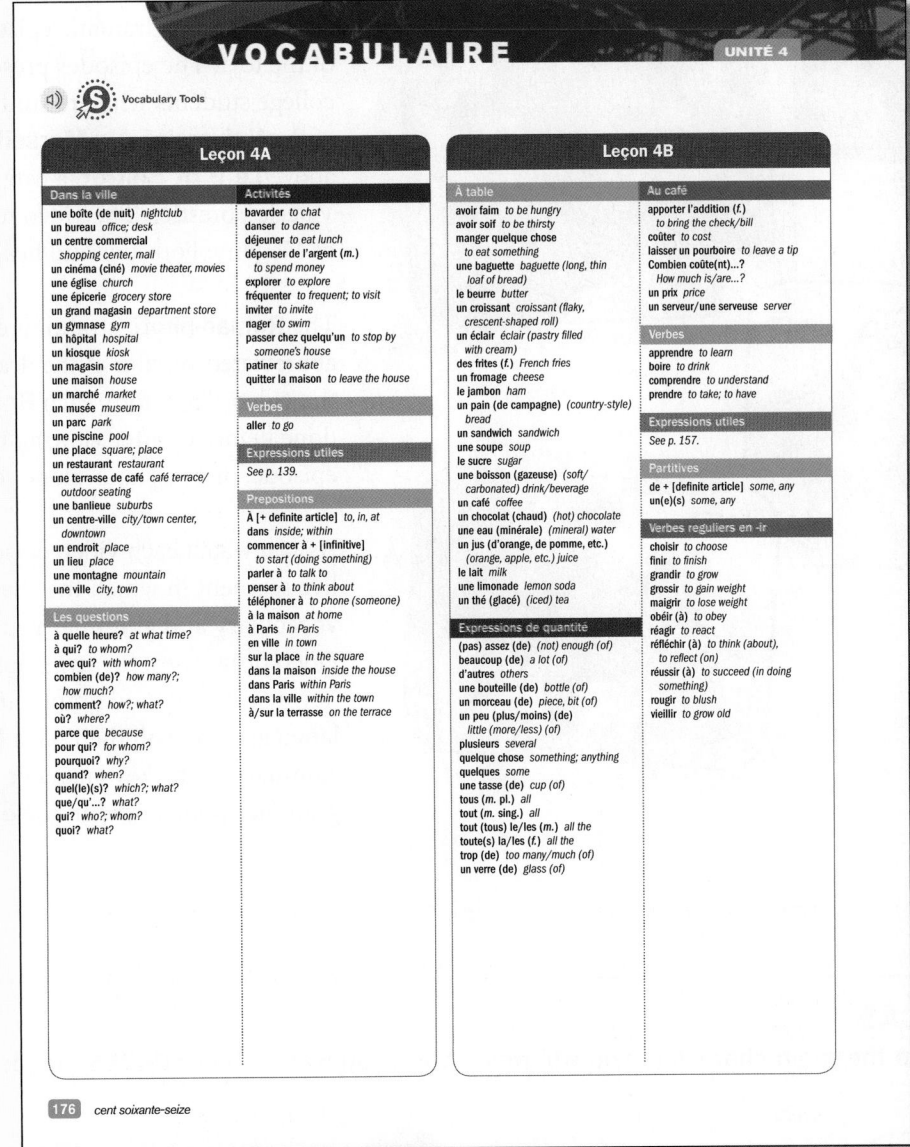

VOCABULAIRE UNITÉ 4

Vocabulary Tools

Leçon 4A

Dans la ville
une boîte (de nuit) *nightclub*
un bureau *office; desk*
un centre commercial
  shopping center, mall
un cinéma (ciné) *movie theater, movies*
une église *church*
une épicerie *grocery store*
un grand magasin *department store*
un gymnase *gym*
un hôpital *hospital*
un kiosque *kiosk*
un magasin *store*
une maison *house*
un marché *market*
un musée *museum*
un parc *park*
une piscine *pool*
une place *square; place*
un restaurant *restaurant*
une terrasse de café *café terrace/*
  outdoor seating
une banlieue *suburbs*
un centre-ville *city/town center,*
  downtown
un endroit *place*
un lieu *place*
une montagne *mountain*
une ville *city, town*

Les questions
à quelle heure? *at what time?*
à qui? *to whom?*
avec qui? *with whom?*
combien (de)? *how many?;*
  how much?
comment? *how?; what?*
où? *where?*
parce que *because*
pour qui? *for whom?*
pourquoi? *why?*
quand? *when?*
quel(le)(s)? *which?; what?*
que/qu'...? *what?*
qui? *who?; whom?*
quoi? *what?*

Activités
bavarder *to chat*
danser *to dance*
déjeuner *to eat lunch*
dépenser de l'argent (m.)
  to spend money
explorer *to explore*
fréquenter *to frequent; to visit*
inviter *to invite*
nager *to swim*
passer chez quelqu'un *to stop by*
  someone's house
patiner *to skate*
quitter la maison *to leave the house*

Verbes
aller *to go*

Expressions utiles
See p. 139.

Prepositions
À [+ definite article] *to, in, at*
dans *inside; within*
commencer à + [infinitive]
  to start (doing something)
parler à *to talk to*
penser à *to think about*
téléphoner à *to phone (someone)*
à la maison *at home*
à Paris *in Paris*
en ville *in town*
sur la place *in the square*
dans la maison *inside the house*
dans Paris *within Paris*
dans la ville *within the town*
à/sur la terrasse *on the terrace*

Leçon 4B

À table
avoir faim *to be hungry*
avoir soif *to be thirsty*
manger quelque chose
  to eat something
une baguette *baguette (long, thin*
  loaf of bread)
le beurre *butter*
un croissant *croissant (flaky,*
  crescent-shaped roll)
un éclair *éclair (pastry filled*
  with cream)
des frites (f.) *French fries*
un fromage *cheese*
le jambon *ham*
un pain (de campagne) *(country-style)*
  bread
un sandwich *sandwich*
une soupe *soup*
le sucre *sugar*
une boisson (gazeuse) *(soft/*
  carbonated) drink/beverage
un café *coffee*
un chocolat (chaud) *(hot) chocolate*
une eau (minérale) *(mineral) water*
un jus (d'orange, de pomme, etc.)
  (orange, apple, etc.) juice
le lait *milk*
une limonade *lemon soda*
un thé (glacé) *(iced) tea*

Expressions de quantité
(pas) assez (de) *(not) enough (of)*
beaucoup (de) *a lot (of)*
d'autres *others*
une bouteille (de) *bottle (of)*
un morceau (de) *piece, bit (of)*
un peu (plus/moins) (de)
  little (more/less) (of)
plusieurs *several*
quelque chose *something; anything*
quelques *some*
une tasse (de) *cup (of)*
tous (m. pl.) *all*
tout (m. sing.) *all*
tout (tous) le/les (m.) *all the*
toute(s) la/les (f.) *all the*
trop (de) *too many/much (of)*
un verre (de) *glass (of)*

Au café
apporter l'addition (f.)
  to bring the check/bill
coûter *to cost*
laisser un pourboire *to leave a tip*
Combien coûte(nt)...?
  How much is/are...?
un prix *price*
un serveur/une serveuse *server*

Verbes
apprendre *to learn*
boire *to drink*
comprendre *to understand*
prendre *to take; to have*

Expressions utiles
See p. 157.

Partitives
de + [definite article] *some, any*
un(e)(s) *some, any*

Verbes reguliers en -ir
choisir *to choose*
finir *to finish*
grandir *to grow*
grossir *to gain weight*
maigrir *to lose weight*
obéir (à) *to obey*
réagir *to react*
réfléchir (à) *to think (about),*
  to reflect (on)
réussir (à) *to succeed (in doing*
  something)
rougir *to blush*
vieillir *to grow old*

Vocabulary Active vocabulary from the unit is brought together, now grouped by lesson into easy-to-study thematic lists.

⑤upersite

- Audio recordings of all vocabulary items
- Vocabulary Tools: customizable word lists, flashcards with audio

Supersite features vary by access level.

THE *ROMAN-PHOTO* EPISODES

Fully integrated with your textbook, the **ESPACES** Video contains thirty dramatic episodes, one for each lesson of the text. The episodes present the adventures of four college students who are studying in the south of France at the **Université Aix-Marseille**. They live in apartments above **Le P'tit Bistrot**, a café owned by their landlady, Valérie Forestier. The video tells their story and the story of Madame Forestier and her teenage son, Stéphane.

The **Roman-photo** strand in each textbook lesson is an abbreviated version of the dramatic episode featured in the video. Therefore, each **Roman-photo** strand can be done before or after viewing the corresponding video episode, or as a stand-alone section.

As you watch each video episode, you will first see a live segment in which the characters interact using vocabulary and grammar you are studying. As the video progresses, the live segments carefully combine new vocabulary and grammar with previously taught language. You will then see a **Reprise** segment that summarizes the key language functions and/or grammar points used in the dramatic episode.

THE CAST

Here are the main characters you will meet when you watch the **ESPACES** Video:

Of Senegalese heritage
Amina Mbaye

From Washington, D.C.
David Duchesne

From Paris
Sandrine Aubry

From Aix-en-Provence
Valérie Forestier

Of Algerian heritage
Rachid Khalil

And, also from
Aix-en-Provence
Stéphane Forestier

THE *FLASH CULTURE* SEGMENTS

For one lesson of each unit, a **Flash culture** segment allows you to experience the sights and sounds of France, the French-speaking world, and the daily life of French speakers. Each segment is two to three minutes long. The A lesson of each odd-numbered unit features a **Flash culture** page with pre- and post-viewing activities. References to online and Video Manual activities on the **Espace culture** pages guide you to activities on the Supersite in even-numbered units.

Hosted by the **ESPACES** narrators, Csilla and Benjamin, these segments transport you to a variety of venues: schools, parks, public squares, cafés, stores, cinemas, outdoor markets, city streets, festivals, and more. They also incorporate mini-interviews with French speakers in various walks of life.

The footage was filmed to capture rich, vibrant images that will expand your cultural perspectives with information directly related to the content of your textbook. In addition, the narrations were carefully written to reflect the vocabulary and grammar covered in **ESPACES**.

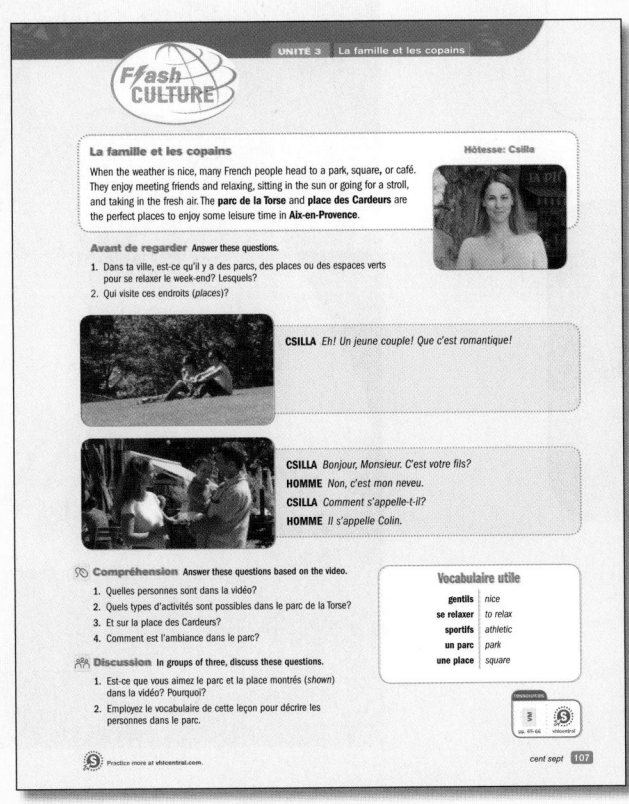

VIDEO PROGRAM

ABOUT *LE ZAPPING* TV CLIPS AND SHORT FILMS

A TV clip or short film from the French-speaking world appears in eight units. The purpose of this feature is to expose you to the language and culture contained in authentic media pieces.

Unité 2
Vie étudiante Université de Moncton

Unité 4
Une semaine sur les toits de Paris

Unité 6
Les marchés de Noël

Unité 8
Créatrice de meubles

Unité 10
Avant j'étais timide

Unité 12
Le Boucher (short film)

Unité 14
Des poules pour l'environnement

Unité 15
Qui de nous deux (short film)

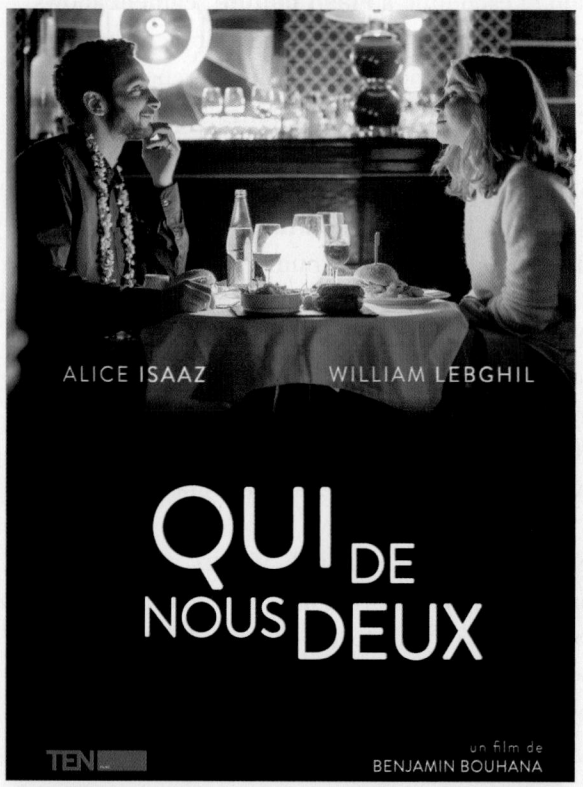

COURSE PLANNING

The entire **ESPACES** program was developed with an eye to flexibility and ease of use in a wide variety of course configurations. The following sample course plans illustrate how **ESPACES, Fourth Edition,** can be used in courses taught in semester or quarter systems, and in courses that complete the book in two to four semesters. You should, of course, feel free to organize your courses in the way that best suits your students' needs and your instructional objectives.

Lesson Plans

A sample lesson plan for **ESPACES** is available on the instructor's part of the **ESPACES** Supersite at **vhlcentral.com**, along with a sample syllabus. They are not prescriptive. You should feel free to present lesson materials as you see fit, tailoring them to your own teaching preferences and to your students' learning styles. It is our hope that you will find the **ESPACES** program very flexible: simply pick and choose from its array of instructional resources and sequence them in the way that makes the most sense for your course.

Two-Semester System

The following chart illustrates how **ESPACES** can be completed in a two-semester course. This division of material allows the present tense, the near future, the **passé composé** with **avoir** and **être**, and the imperative to be presented in the first semester; the second semester focuses on the **passé composé** vs. the imperfect, the conditional, the future, and the present subjunctive.

Semester 1	Semester 2
Units 1–7	Units 8–15

Three-Semester or Quarter System

This chart shows how **ESPACES** can be used in a three-semester or quarter course. The units are equally divided over each semester/quarter, allowing students to absorb the material at a steady pace.

Semester/Quarter 1	Semester/Quarter 2	Semester/Quarter 3
Units 1–5	Units 6–10	Units 11–15

Four-Semester System

This chart illustrates how **ESPACES** can be used in a four-semester course.

Semester 1	Semester 2	Semester 3	Semester 4
Units 1–4	Units 5–8	Units 9–12	Units 13–15

ESPACES and the *World-Readiness Standards for Learning Languages*

Since 1982, when the *ACTFL Proficiency Guidelines* were first published, that seminal document and its subsequent revisions have influenced the teaching of modern languages in the United States. **ESPACES** was written with the concerns and philosophy of the *ACTFL Proficiency Guidelines* in mind, incorporating a proficiency-oriented approach from its planning stages.

ESPACES' pedagogy was also informed from its inception by the *Standards for Foreign Language Learning in the 21st Century*. First published in 1996 under the auspices of the National Standards in Foreign Language Education Project, the Standards are organized into five goal areas, often called the Five Cs: Communication, Cultures, Connections, Comparisons, and Communities.

Since **ESPACES** takes a communicative approach to the teaching and learning of French, the Communication goal is central to the student text. For example, the diverse formats used in the **Communication** and **Révision** activities in each lesson—pair work, small-group work, class circulation, information gap, task-based, and so forth—engage students in communicative exchanges, providing and obtaining information, and expressing feelings and emotions. The **À l'écoute** and **Écriture** sections also develop students' communication skills using listening prompts and writing tasks.

The Cultures goal is most overtly evident on four pages of each lesson: the **Espace roman-photo** and the **Espace culture** sections. The **Flash culture** page, NEW to the Fourth Edition, addresses this goal in most odd-numbered units. It is also covered in the **Panorama** section at the end of each unit. However, **ESPACES** also weaves culture into virtually every page, exposing students to the multiple facets of practices, products, and perspectives of the French-speaking world. In keeping with the Connections goal, students can connect with other disciplines such as communications, business, geography, history, fine arts, and science in the **Le Zapping** and **Panorama** sections; they can acquire information and recognize distinctive cultural viewpoints in the non-literary and literary texts of the **Lecture** sections. Moreover, **Sur Internet** boxes in **Panorama** support the Connections and Communities goals as students work through those sections and complete the related activities on the **ESPACES** Supersite. As for the Comparisons goal, it is reflected in **Les sons et les lettres** pronunciation and spelling sections and the **Structures** sections.

Special Standards icons also appear on the student text pages of your Instructor's Annotated Edition to call out sections that have a particularly strong relationship with the Standards. These are a few examples of how **ESPACES** was written with the Standards firmly in mind, but you will find many more as you work with the student textbook and its ancillaries.

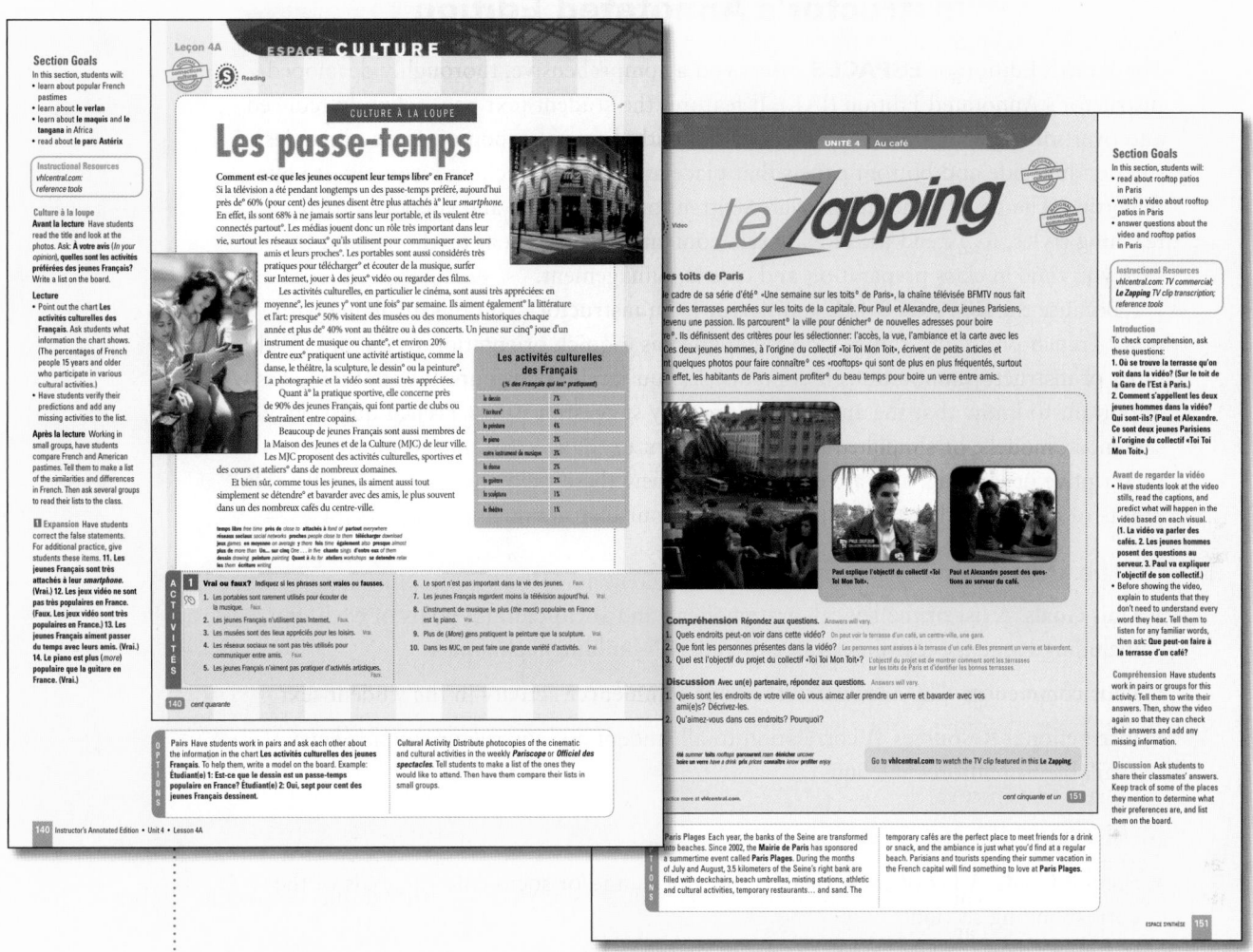

Communication Understand and be understood: read and listen to understand the French-speaking world, converse with others, and share your thoughts clearly through speaking and writing.

Cultures Experience French-speaking cultures through their own viewpoints, in the places, objects, behaviors, and beliefs important to the people who live them.

Connections Apply what you learn in your French course to your other studies; apply what you know from other courses to your French studies.

Comparisons Discover in which ways the French language and French-speaking cultures are like your own—and how they differ.

Communities Engage with French-speaking communities locally, nationally, and internationally both in your courses and beyond—for life.

Learning to Use Your Instructor's Annotated Edition

The Fourth Edition of **ESPACES** offers you a comprehensive, thoroughly developed Instructor's Annotated Edition (IAE). It features the student text pages slightly reduced and overprinted with answers to all activities with discrete responses. It also includes surrounding side and bottom panels that place a wealth of teaching resources at your fingertips. The panel annotations were written to complement and support varied teaching styles, to extend the already rich contents of the student textbook, and to save you time in class preparation and course management.

Because the **ESPACES** IAE is different from instructor's editions available with other French programs, this section is designed as a quick orientation to the principal types of instructor annotations it contains. As you familiarize yourself with them, it is important to know that the annotations are only suggestions. Any French questions, sentences, models, or simulated instructor-student exchanges are not meant to be prescriptive or limiting. You are encouraged to view these suggested "scripts" as flexible points of departure that will help you achieve your instructional goals.

On the Unit Opening Page

- **Unit Goals** A list of the lexical, grammatical, and socio-cultural goals of each unit, including language-learning strategies and skill-building techniques

- **Pour commencer** The answers to the **Pour commencer** activity in the student text

- **Instructional Resources** A correlation to all student and instructor supplements available to reinforce the unit

In the Side Panels

- **Section Goals** A list of the lexical, grammatical, and/or socio-cultural goals of the corresponding section

- **Instructional Resources** A correlation to all program components

- **Suggestion** Teaching suggestions for leading into the corresponding section, working with on-page materials, and carrying out specific activities, as well as quick ways for starting classes or activities by recycling language or ideas

- **Expansion** Expansions and variations on activities

- **Script** Printed transcripts of the Textbook MP3 recordings for the **Mise en pratique** audio activity in each **Contextes** section and the **Stratégie** and **À vous d'écouter** features in each **À l'écoute** section

- **Video Recap** Questions or a true/false activity to help students recall the events of the previous lesson's **Roman-photo** episode

- **Video Synopsis** Summaries of the **Roman-photo** sections that recap that lesson's video module

- **Expressions utiles** Suggestions for introducing upcoming **Structures** grammar points incorporated into the **Roman-photo** episode

- **Stratégie** Suggestions for working with the listening, reading, and writing strategies presented in the **À l'écoute, Lecture,** and **Écriture** sections, respectively

- **Thème** Ideas for presenting and expanding the writing assignment topic in **Écriture**

- **Map-related Annotations** Suggestions for working with the maps in the **Panorama** sections

- **Le pays, la région, la province, l'archipel en chiffres** Additional information expanding on the data presented for each French-speaking area or country featured in the **Panorama** sections

- **Incroyable mais vrai!** Curious facts about a lesser-known aspect of the area or country featured in the **Panorama** sections

- **Section-specific Annotations** Suggestions for presenting, expanding, varying, and reinforcing individual instructional elements

- **Successful Language Learning** Tips and strategies to enhance students' language-learning experience

- **Proofreading Activity** Activities exclusive to the **Écriture** sections that guide students in the development of good proofreading skills. Each item contains errors related to a structure taught in the unit's **Structures** sections and/or a spelling rule taught in its **Les sons et les lettres** sections

- **Evaluation** Suggested rubrics in **Écriture** for grading students' writing efforts

In the Options Boxes

- **Content-based Annotations with French Titles** More detailed information about an interesting aspect of the history, geography, culture, or peoples of the French-speaking world

- **Extra Practice, Pairs, and Small Groups** Activities in addition to those already in the student textbook

- **Game** Games that practice the language of the section and/or recycle previously learned language

- **TPR** Total Physical Response activities that engage students physically in learning French

- **Cultural Comparison** Suggestions to help students compare the culture they are learning with their own culture

- **Avant de regarder la vidéo/Regarder la vidéo** Techniques and activities that can be used to prepare the students to view and work with the dramatic episodes of the **ESPACES** Video in the **Roman-photo** sections

- **Video** Suggestions for using the dramatic episodes of the **ESPACES** Video in the **Structures** sections

TEACHING WITH ESPACES

Orienting Students to the Student Textbook

Because the Fourth Edition of **ESPACES** treats interior and graphic design as an integral part of students' language-learning experience, you may want to take a few minutes to orient students to the student textbook. Have them flip through one unit, and point out that they are all organized exactly the same way with two short lessons and a concluding **Savoir-faire** section. Also point out how the major sections of each lesson are color-coded for easy navigation: blue for **Espace contextes**, green for **Espace roman-photo**, purple for **Espace culture**, orange for **Espace structures**, teal for **Espace synthèse**, red for **Savoir-faire**, and dark blue for **Vocabulaire**. Let them know that, because of these design elements, they can be confident that they will always know "where they are" in their textbook.

Emphasize that sections are self-contained, occupying either a full page or a spread of two facing pages, thereby eliminating "bad breaks" and the need to flip back and forth to do activities or to work with explanatory material. Finally, call students' attention to the use of color to highlight key information in elements such as charts, diagrams, word lists, activity models, titles, and help boxes such as **Attention!**, **Coup de main**, **Boîte à outils**, and **À noter**.

Flexible Lesson Organization

ESPACES, **Fourth Edition**, uses a flexible lesson organization designed to meet the needs of diverse teaching styles, instructional goals, and institutional requirements. For example, you can begin with the unit opening page and progress sequentially through a unit. If you do not want to devote class time to grammar, you can assign the **Structures** explanations for outside study, freeing up class time for other purposes like developing oral communication skills; increasing awareness of Francophone television broadcasts; building listening, reading, or writing skills; learning more about the French-speaking world; or working with the video program. You might decide to work extensively with the **Savoir-faire** section in order to focus on students' reading and writing skills and their knowledge of the French-speaking world. On the other hand, you might prefer to skip these sections entirely, exploiting them periodically in response to your students' interests as the opportunity arises. If you plan on using the **ESPACES**, **Fourth Edition**, Testing Program, however, be aware that its quizzes, tests, and exams check language presented in **Contextes**, **Structures**, and the **Expressions utiles** boxes of **Roman-photo**.

Identifying Active Vocabulary

All words and expressions taught in the illustrations, **Vocabulaire** lists, and **Attention!** boxes in **Contextes** are considered active, testable vocabulary. The words and expressions in the **Expressions utiles** boxes in **Roman-photo**, as well as words in charts, word lists, and sample sentences in **Structures** are also part of the active vocabulary load. At the end of each unit, **Vocabulaire** provides a convenient one-page summary of the items students should know and that may appear on tests and exams. You will want to point this out to students. You might also tell them that an easy way to study from **Vocabulaire** is to cover up the French half of each section, leaving only the English equivalents exposed. They can then quiz themselves on the French items. To focus on the English equivalents of the French entries, they simply reverse this process.

Taking into Account the Affective Dimension

While many factors contribute to the quality and success rate of learning experiences, two factors are particularly germane to language learning. One is students' beliefs about how language is learned; the other is language-learning anxiety.

As studies show and experienced instructors know, students often come to modern languages courses either with a lack of knowledge about how to approach language learning or with mistaken notions about how to do so. For example, many students believe that making mistakes when speaking the target language must be avoided because doing so will lead to permanent errors. Others are convinced that learning another language is like learning any other academic subject. In other words, they believe that success is guaranteed, provided they attend class regularly, learn the assigned vocabulary words and grammar rules, and study for exams. In fact, in a study of college-level beginning language learners in the United States, over one-third of the participants thought that they could become fluent if they studied the language for only one hour a day for two years or less. Mistaken and unrealistic beliefs such as these can cause frustration and ultimately demotivation, thereby significantly undermining students' ability to achieve a successful language-learning experience.

Another factor that can negatively impact students' language-learning experiences is language-learning anxiety. As Professor Elaine K. Horwitz of The University of Texas at Austin and Senior Consulting Editor of VISTAS, First Edition, wrote, "Surveys indicate that up to one-third of American foreign language students feel moderately to highly anxious about studying another language. Physical symptoms of foreign language anxiety can include heart-pounding or palpitations, sweating, trembling, fast breathing, and general feelings of unease." The late Dr. Philip Redwine Donley, VISTAS co-author and author of articles on language-learning anxiety, spoke with many students who reported feeling nervous or apprehensive in their classes. They mentioned freezing when called on by their instructors or going inexplicably blank when taking tests. Some so dreaded their classes that they skipped them or dropped the course.

Based on what Vista Higher Learning learned from instructors and students using **ESPACES, Third Edition,** and its other successful introductory language programs, **ESPACES, Fourth Edition,** contains several features aimed at reducing students' language anxiety and supporting their successful language learning. First of all, the highly structured, visually dramatic interior design of the **ESPACES** student text was conceived as a learning tool to make students feel comfortable with the content and confident about navigating the lessons. The Instructor's Annotated Edition also includes *Successful Language Learning* annotations with suggestions for managing and/or reducing language-learning anxieties and for enhancing students' learning experiences. In addition, the student text provides on-the-spot **Attention!, Coup de main, Boîte à outils,** and **À noter** boxes that assist students by making immediately relevant connections with new information or reminding them of previously learned concepts.

Suggestions for Using the ESPACES
Roman-photo Video Episodes

The **Roman-photo** section in each of the student textbook's lessons and the **ESPACES** Video were created as interlocking pieces. All photos in **Roman-photo** are actual video stills from the corresponding video episode, while the printed conversations are abbreviated versions of the dramatic segment. Both the **Roman-photo** conversations and their expanded video versions represent comprehensible input at the discourse level; they were purposefully written to use language from the corresponding lesson's **Contextes** and **Structures** sections. Thus, as of **Leçon 1A**, they recycle known language, preview grammar points students will study later in the lesson, and, in keeping with Krashen's concept of "i + 1," contain a small amount of unknown language.

Because the **Roman-photo** textbook sections and the dramatic episodes of the **ESPACES** Video are so closely connected, you may use them in many different ways. For instance, you can use **Roman-photo** as an advance organizer, presenting it before showing the video episode. You can also show the video episode first and follow up with **Roman-photo**. You can even use **Roman-photo** as a stand-alone, video-independent section.

Depending on your teaching preferences and campus facilities, you might decide to show all video episodes in class or to assign them solely for viewing outside of the classroom. You could begin by showing the first one or two episodes in class to familiarize yourself and students with the characters,

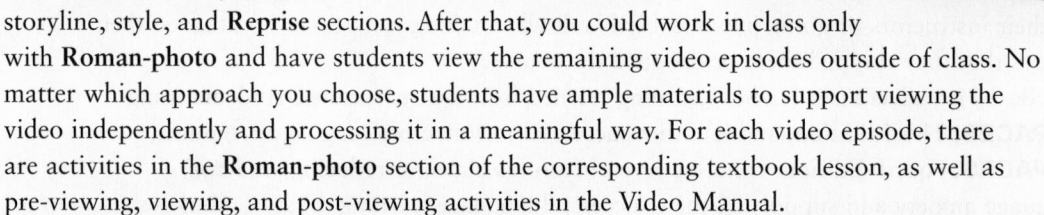

storyline, style, and **Reprise** sections. After that, you could work in class only with **Roman-photo** and have students view the remaining video episodes outside of class. No matter which approach you choose, students have ample materials to support viewing the video independently and processing it in a meaningful way. For each video episode, there are activities in the **Roman-photo** section of the corresponding textbook lesson, as well as pre-viewing, viewing, and post-viewing activities in the Video Manual.

You might also want to use the **ESPACES** Video in class when working with the **Structures** sections. You could show selected scenes and ask students to identify certain grammar points.

You could also focus on the **Reprise** sections that appear at the end of each lesson's dramatic episode to summarize the key language functions and grammar points used. In class, you could play the parts of the **Reprise** section that exemplify individual grammar points as you progress through each **Structures** section. You could also wait until you complete a **Structures** section and review it and the lesson's **Contextes** section by showing the corresponding **Reprise** section in its entirety.

Suggestions for Using the ESPACES
Flash culture Video Episodes

The **Flash culture** video segments were specially planned and shot for **ESPACES** to bring France and the French-speaking world "alive" within the context of the themes in the textbook's units. The footage was selected for visual appeal and information of interest that both reinforces content presented in the textbook's lessons and goes beyond it. The segments are hosted by the **ESPACES** narrators, Csilla and Benjamin, who alternate between odd-numbered and even-numbered segments, respectively. Csilla and Benjamin introduce each segment, provide transitions between topics, and, as appropriate, hold micro-interviews with French speakers whom they encounter as they visit parks, public squares, schools, stores, cafés, markets, and more.

Like the conversations in the **Roman-photo** dramatic episodes, the **Flash culture** narrations represent comprehensible input. Each was written to make the most of the vocabulary and grammar students learned in the corresponding and previous units while still providing a small amount of unknown language and/or cognates. In Units 1–7, the narrators begin the segments in English, but, as much as possible, use French that will be comprehensible to students to explain and describe the images shown. As of Unit 8, the **Flash culture** segments are entirely in French.

Each segment is approximately two to three minutes long and is correlated in the TOC of the **ESPACES** student text to the appropriate **Espace culture** section of most of the even-numbered units or featured on its own page in the **Synthèse** section of the A lesson of most odd-numbered units.

Flash culture Video Segments Table of Contents

Unité 1: greetings and farewells
Unité 2: colleges, universities, and school life
Unité 3: family and friends
Unité 4: cafés, food, and drink
Unité 5: leisure-time activities and sports
Unité 6: holidays and festivals
Unité 7: travel and vacation-related activities
Unité 8: apartments, homes, and other types of housing

Unité 9: an open-air food market
Unité 10: a pharmacy and other health-related locations
Unité 11: cars, transportation, and traffic-related items
Unité 12: the post office, banks, small and large stores
Unité 13: jobs, professions, and careers
Unité 14: parts of France and French-speaking countries
Unité 15: films, documentaries, books, magazines, and newspapers

---

Activities for the **Flash culture** video are located in the Video Manual section of the **ESPACES** Student Activities Manual. They follow a process approach of pre-viewing, viewing, and post-viewing and use a variety of formats to prepare students for watching the video segments, to focus them while watching, and to check comprehension after they have watched the footage.

When showing the **Flash culture** video segments in your classes, you might also want to implement a process approach. You could start with an activity that prepares students for the video segment by taking advantage of what they learned in the lesson. This could be followed by an activity that students do while you play parts of or the entire video segment.

The final activity, done in the same class period or in the next one as warm-up, could recap what students saw and heard and move beyond the video segment's topic. The following suggestions for working with the **Flash culture** video segments in class, which are in addition to those on the individual pages of the Instructor's Annotated Edition, can be carried out as described or expanded upon in any number of ways.

Before viewing

- Ask students to guess what the segment might be about based on what they've learned about the lesson's theme, especially in the **Contextes**, **Roman-photo**, and **Culture** sections.

- Have pairs make a list of the unit vocabulary they expect to hear in the video segment.

- Read a list of true-false or multiple-choice questions about the video to the class. Students must use what they learned over the lesson to guess the answers. Confirm their guesses after watching the segment.

While viewing

- Show the video segment with the audio turned off and ask students to use unit vocabulary and structures to describe what they see. Have them confirm their guesses by showing the segment again with the audio on.

- Have students refer to the list of words they brainstormed before viewing the video and put a check in front of any words they actually hear or see in the segment.

- First, have students simply watch the video. Then, show it again and ask students to take notes on what they see and hear. Finally, have them compare their notes in pairs or groups for confirmation.

- Download and print the segment's videoscript from Instructor Resources found on the Supersite and white out words and expressions related to the lesson theme. Distribute the scripts for pairs or groups to complete as cloze paragraphs.

- Show the video segment before moving on to **Contextes** to jump-start the lesson's vocabulary, grammar, and cultural focus. Have students tell you what vocabulary and grammar they recognize from previous lessons.

After viewing

- Have students say what aspects of the information presented in the corresponding textbook lesson are observable in the video segment.

- Ask groups to write a brief summary of the content of the video segment. Have them exchange papers with another group for peer editing.

- Have students pick one new aspect of the corresponding textbook lesson's cultural theme that they learned about from watching the video segment. Have them research more about that topic and write a list or paragraph to expand on it.

About strategies in À l'écoute, Lecture, and Écriture

The Fourth Edition of **ESPACES** takes a process approach to the development of listening, reading, and writing skills. These are lists of the different strategies taught in each unit so that you may refer to them in one convenient place.

À l'écoute

Unité 1	**Leçon 1B**	Listening for words you know
Unité 2	**Leçon 2B**	Listening for cognates
Unité 3	**Leçon 3B**	Asking for repetition / Replaying the recording
Unité 4	**Leçon 4B**	Listening for the gist
Unité 5	**Leçon 5B**	Listening for key words
Unité 6	**Leçon 6B**	Listening for linguistic cues
Unité 7	**Leçon 7B**	Recognizing the genre of spoken discourse
Unité 8	**Leçon 8B**	Using visual cues
Unité 9	**Leçon 9B**	Jotting down notes as you listen
Unité 10	**Leçon 10B**	Listening for specific information
Unité 11	**Leçon 11B**	Guessing the meaning of words through context
Unité 12	**Leçon 12B**	Using background information
Unité 13	**Leçon 13B**	Using background knowledge / Listening for specific information
Unité 14	**Leçon 14B**	Listening for the gist / Listening for cognates
Unité 15	**Leçon 15B**	Listening for key words / Using the context

Lecture

Unité 1	Recognizing cognates
Unité 2	Predicting content through formats
Unité 3	Predicting content from visuals
Unité 4	Scanning
Unité 5	Skimming
Unité 6	Recognizing word families
Unité 7	Predicting content from the title
Unité 8	Guessing meaning from context
Unité 9	Reading for the main idea
Unité 10	Activating background knowledge
Unité 11	Recognizing the purpose of a text
Unité 12	Identifying point of view
Unité 13	Summarizing a text in your own words
Unité 14	Recognizing personification
Unité 15	Contextualizing

Écriture

Unité 1	Writing in French
Unité 2	Brainstorming
Unité 3	Using idea maps
Unité 4	Adding details
Unité 5	Using a dictionary
Unité 6	How to report an interview
Unité 7	Making an outline
Unité 8	Mastering the simple past tenses
Unité 9	Expressing and supporting opinions
Unité 10	Sequencing events
Unité 11	Listing key words
Unité 12	Using linking words
Unité 13	Using note cards
Unité 14	Considering audience and purpose
Unité 15	Writing strong introductions and conclusions

ACKNOWLEDGMENTS

On behalf of its authors and editors, Vista Higher Learning expresses its sincere appreciation to the instructors nationwide who reviewed materials from **ESPACES**, Third Edition. Their input and suggestions were vitally helpful in forming and shaping the Fourth Edition in its final, published form.

Reviewers

Mariolina Agnolini Mousaw
The College of Saint Rose, NY

Olga Amarie
Georgia Southern University, GA

Dr. Vanessa Arnaud
California State University, Sacramento, CA

Mariana Bahtchevanova
Arizona State University, AZ

Anna Brichko
West Valley College, CA

Cary Campbell, PhD
Antioch College, OH

Gilles Colin
Muhlenberg College, PA

Dr. Dah Sansan
Southeastern University, FL

Rachele C. DeMeo
MiraCosta College, CA

Wendy E. Drought
Kennesaw State University, GA

Elizabeth Dyer
Culver-Stockton College, MO

Dr. Vicki Earnest
Calhoun Community College, AL

Eduardo A. Febles, PhD
Simmons College, MA

Dr. Carlo Ferguson-McIntyre
Truckee Meadows Community College, NV

Lisa Danielle Gonzales
Monterey Peninsula College, CA

Jennifer L. Holm
The University of Virginia's College at Wise, VA

Martha Hughes
Georgia Southern University, GA

Francis V. Ialenti
Stonehill College, MA

Edwin L. Isley, PhD
Western Carolina University, NC

E. Joe Johnson
Clayton State University, GA

Ann Kirkland
Hanover College, IN

Laurence Lambert
Sierra College, CA

John C. Lawrence
Chattanooga State Community College, TN

María José Maguire
Flagler College, FL

Mary McCullough
Samford University, AL

Heather McCoy
Pennsylvania State University, PA

C. Mennear
Wake Technical Community College, NC

Esther Mesquita
Lake Tahoe Community College, CA

Barbara Michael
Monterey Peninsula College, CA

Mihai Miroiu, PhD
Elmira College, NY

Dr. Christine Mohanty
Suffolk County Community College, NY

Claire Moisan
Grinnell College, IA

Lisa M. Noetzel, PhD
College of Coastal Georgia, GA

Maria O'Brien
University of Central Florida, FL

Dr. Philip Ojo
Agnes Scott College, GA

Helene Pafundi
Hudson Valley Community College, NY

Mary Phuong Nguyen
Greenville Technical College, SC

Julie Pomerleau
University of Central Florida, FL

Amy Sawyer
Clemson University, SC

Maryann Seeley
State University of New York Adirondack, NY

Patricia S. Seuchie
Christopher Newport University, VA

Pascale Sharpe
San Jacinto College Central, TX

Peter S. Thompson
Roger Williams University, RI

Jane E. Thornburg
San Jacinto College Central, TX

Joalyn Walker
College of Southern Nevada, NV

Dr. Lisa Wolffe
Northwestern State University, LA

Salut!

Unit Goals

Leçon 1A

In this lesson, students will learn:

- terms for greetings, farewells, and introductions
- expressions of courtesy
- the French alphabet and the names of accent marks
- about shaking hands and **bises**
- gender of nouns
- articles (definite and indefinite)
- the numbers 0–60
- the expression **il y a**
- more about greetings and farewells through specially shot video footage

Leçon 1B

In this lesson, students will learn:

- terms to identify people
- terms for objects in the classroom
- rules for silent letters
- about France's multicultural society
- about francophone singer and songwriter Stromae
- subject pronouns
- the present tense of **être**
- **c'est** and **il/elle est**
- adjective agreement
- some descriptive adjectives and adjectives of nationality
- to listen for familiar words

Savoir-faire

In this section, students will learn:

- cultural, linguistic, and historical information about the francophone world
- to recognize cognates
- strategies for writing in French
- to compile a telephone/address book

Pour commencer

- b. Bonjour!
- b. deux
- c. Mademoiselle

Pour commencer

- What are these young women saying?
  a. Excusez-moi.   b. Bonjour!   c. Merci.
- How many women are there in the photo?
  a. une   b. deux   c. trois
- What do you think is an appropriate title for either of these women?
  a. Monsieur   b. Madame   c. Mademoiselle

RESOURCES

Student Activities Manual (SAM):
Workbook Activities, pp. 1–14;
Lab Activities, pp. 1–8;
Video Activities, pp. 1–4; pp. 61–62
SAM Answer Key

vhlcentral.com: Textbook MP3s; Lab MP3s;
Textbook Audioscript; Lab Audioscript; Video;
Videoscript; **Roman-photo** Translations;
Vocabulaire supplémentaire; Activity Pack
(including **Feuilles d'activités**, Info Gap Activities,
and Task-based Activities);

Flash culture video transcription; **Essayez!** and
Mise en pratique answers; Digital Image Bank
Testing Program; Testing Program MP3s

Section Goals

In this section, students will learn and practice vocabulary related to:
- basic greetings and farewells
- introductions
- courtesy expressions

Instructional Resources

vhlcentral.com: Digital Image Bank (including vocabulary illustrations from the textbook, theme-based illustrations); Activity Pack; **Vocabulaire supplémentaire; Mise en pratique** answers; Textbook Audioscript; Lab Audioscript; Textbook MP3s; Lab MP3s; SAM Answer Key; reference tools

Suggestions

- Use the Vocabulary illustrations and the Personal interactions illustrations from the Digital Image Bank to help students familiarize themselves with different courtesy expressions.
- To familiarize students with the meanings of headings used in the lessons and important vocabulary for classroom interactions, pass out **Vocabulaire supplémentaire: vocabulaire pour la classe de français** from the Supersite.
- For a sample lesson plan, go to **vhlcentral.com** to access the instructor's part of the **ESPACES** companion Supersite.
- With student books closed, write a few greetings, farewells, and courtesy expressions on the board, explain their meaning, and model their pronunciation. Circulate around the room, greeting students, making introductions, and encouraging responses. Then, have students open their books to pages 2–3. Ask them to identify which conversations are exchanges between friends and which seem more formal. Then point out the use of **vous** vs. **tu** in each conversation. Give examples of different situations in which each form would be appropriate.

Successful Language Learning Encourage students to make flash cards to help them memorize or review vocabulary.

Leçon 1A

You will learn how to...
- greet people in French
- say good-bye

Ça va?

Vocabulaire

Bonsoir.	Good evening.; Hello.
À bientôt.	See you soon.
À demain.	See you tomorrow.
Bonne journée!	Have a good day!
Au revoir.	Good-bye.
Comme ci, comme ça.	So-so.
Je vais bien/mal.	I am doing well/badly.
Moi aussi.	Me too.
Comment t'appelles-tu? (fam.)	What is your name?
Je vous/te présente... (form./fam.)	I would like to introduce (name) to you.
De rien.	You're welcome.
Excusez-moi. (form.)	Excuse me.
Excuse-moi. (fam.)	Excuse me.
Merci beaucoup.	Thanks a lot.
Pardon.	Pardon (me).
S'il vous/te plaît. (form./fam.)	Please.
Je vous en prie. (form.)	Please.; You're welcome.
Monsieur (M.)	Sir (Mr.)
Madame (Mme)	Ma'am (Mrs.)
Mademoiselle (Mlle)	Miss
ici	here
là	there
là-bas	over there

ressources

WB pp. 1-2 | LM p. 1 | vhlcentral

GEORGES Ça va, Henri?
HENRI Oui, ça va très bien, merci. Et vous, comment allez-vous?
GEORGES Je vais bien, merci.

PAUL Merci!
JEAN Il n'y a pas de quoi.

MARIE À plus tard, Guillaume!
GUILLAUME À tout à l'heure, Marie!

JACQUES Bonjour, Monsieur Boniface. Je vous présente Thérèse Lemaire.
M. BONIFACE Bonjour, Mademoiselle.
THÉRÈSE Enchantée.

OPTIONS

Language Notes Point out that **Salut** and **À plus**, the shortened form of **À plus tard**, are familiar expressions. Explain that the translation of **Je vais bien/mal** is not literal. **Je vais** means *I go*, but **je vais bien** means *I am doing well*.

Game Divide the class into two teams. Create sentences and questions based on the **Vocabulaire** and the illustrated conversations. Choose one person at a time, alternating between teams. Tell students to respond logically to your statement or question. Award a point for each correct response. The team with the most points at the end of the game wins.

Attention!

In French, people can be addressed formally or informally. Use the **tu/toi** forms with close friends or someone younger than you. Use the **vous** forms with groups, a boss, someone older than you, or someone you do not know.

MARC Bonjour, je m'appelle Marc, et vous, comment vous appelez-vous?
ANNIE Je m'appelle Annie.
MARC Enchanté.

SOPHIE Bonjour, Catherine!
CATHERINE Salut, Sophie!
SOPHIE Ça va?
CATHERINE Oui, ça va bien, merci. Et toi, comment vas-tu?
SOPHIE Pas mal.

Mise en pratique

1 Écoutez Listen to each of these questions or statements and select the most appropriate response.

1. Enchanté.	☐	Je m'appelle Thérèse.	☑
2. Merci beaucoup.	☐	Je vous en prie.	☑
3. Comme ci, comme ça.	☑	De rien.	☐
4. Bonsoir, Madame.	☑	Moi aussi.	☐
5. Enchanté.	☑	Et toi?	☐
6. Bonjour.	☐	À demain.	☑
7. Pas mal.	☑	Pardon.	☐
8. Il n'y a pas de quoi.	☑	Moi aussi.	☐
9. Enchanté.	☐	Très bien. Et vous?	☑
10. À bientôt.	☑	Mal.	☐

2 Chassez l'intrus Circle the word or expression that does not belong.

1. a. Bonjour.
   b. Bonsoir.
   c. Salut.
   d. **Pardon.**

2. a. Bien.
   b. Très bien.
   c. **De rien.**
   d. Comme ci, comme ça.

3. a. À bientôt.
   b. À demain.
   c. À tout à l'heure.
   d. **Enchanté.**

4. a. Comment allez-vous?
   b. **Comment vous appelez-vous?**
   c. Ça va?
   d. Comment vas-tu?

5. a. **Pas mal.**
   b. Excuse-moi.
   c. Je vous en prie.
   d. Il n'y a pas de quoi.

6. a. Comment vous appelez-vous?
   b. Je vous présente Dominique.
   c. Enchanté.
   d. **Comment allez-vous?**

7. a. Pas mal.
   b. Très bien.
   c. Mal.
   d. **Et vous?**

8. a. Comment allez-vous?
   b. Comment vous appelez-vous?
   c. **Et toi?**
   d. Je vous en prie.

3 Conversez Madeleine is introducing her classmate Khaled to Libby, an American exchange student. Complete their conversation, using a different expression from **CONTEXTES** in each blank. Answers will vary.

MADELEINE (1) _Bonjour/Salut_ !
KHALED Salut, Madeleine. (2) _Comment vas-tu/ Comment ça va_ ?
MADELEINE Pas mal. (3) _Et toi, comment vas-tu/ Et toi, ça va_ ?
KHALED (4) _Je vais (très) bien/ (Très) bien_ , merci.
MADELEINE (5) _Je te présente_ Libby. Elle est de (*She is from*) Boston.
KHALED (6) _Enchanté_ , Libby. (7) _Je m'appelle_ Khaled.
(8) _Comment vas-tu/Ça va_ ?
LIBBY (9) _Je vais (très) bien/Ça va (très) bien_ , merci.
KHALED Oh, là, là. Je vais rater (*I am going to miss*) le bus. À bientôt.
MADELEINE (10) _Au revoir/À bientôt_ .
LIBBY (11) _Au revoir/À bientôt_ .

S Practice more at vhlcentral.com.

trois **3**

1 Audioscript
1. Comment vous appelez-vous?
2. Excusez-moi.
3. Comment allez-vous?
4. Bonsoir, Mademoiselle.
5. Je te présente Thérèse.
6. À bientôt.
7. Comment vas-tu?
8. Merci.
9. Bonjour, comment allez-vous?
10. Au revoir.
(On Textbook MP3s)

1 Suggestion Before students listen, tell them to read the possible responses provided and write down the questions or statements that they think would elicit each response. After completing the listening activity, go over the answers to check whether students' predictions were accurate.

2 Suggestion Go over the answers with the class and have students explain why each expression does not belong.

3 Suggestion Have students work in groups of three on the activity. Tell them to choose a role and complete the conversation. Then ask groups to act out their conversation for the class.

OPTIONS

Pairs Have students work in pairs. Tell them to write an original conversation with six to eight lines. After completing this task, they should rewrite the conversation and scramble the order of the sentences. Have pairs exchange their scrambled conversations and put them in a logical order. Remind students that they should verify the answers.

Small Groups Have small groups role-play a conversation in which other adults, children, and college-age people interact. Remind students to use formal and informal expressions in the appropriate situations. Give them time to prepare, and then have a few groups present their conversations to the class.

Communication

4 Suggestions
- Before beginning the activity, encourage students to use as many different words and expressions as they can from the **Vocabulaire** on page 2 rather than repeating the same expressions in each conversation.
- Have a few volunteers write their conversations on the board. Ask the class to identify, correct, and explain any errors.

4 Expansion Have students rewrite **Conversation 1** in the formal register, and **Conversations 2** and **3** in the informal register.

5 Suggestions
- Before beginning this activity, ask students if they would use **tu** or **vous** in each situation.
- If class time is limited, assign a specific situation to each pair.
- Call on volunteers to act out their conversations for the class.

6 Suggestion Have two volunteers read the **modèle** aloud. Remind students to use **vous** when addressing more than one classmate at a time.

4 **Conversez** With a partner, complete these conversations. Then act them out. Answers will vary.

Conversation 1 Salut! Je m'appelle François. Et toi, comment t'appelles-tu?

_____

Ça va?

_____

Conversation 2 _____

Comme ci, comme ça. Et vous?

_____

À demain, alors (then).

_____

Conversation 3 Bonsoir, je vous présente Mademoiselle Barnard.

_____

Enchanté(e).

_____

Très bien, merci. Et vous?

_____

5 **C'est à vous!** How would you greet these people, ask them for their names, and ask them how they are doing? With a partner, write a short dialogue for each item and act them out. Pay attention to the use of **tu** and **vous.** Answers will vary.

1. Madame Colombier

2. Mademoiselle Estèves

3. Monsieur Marchand

4. Marie, Guillaume et Geneviève

6 **Présentations** Form groups of three. Introduce yourself, and ask your partners their names and how they are doing. Then, join another group and take turns introducing your partners. Answers will vary.

MODÈLE

Étudiant(e) 1: *Bonjour. Je m'appelle Fatima. Et vous?*
Étudiant(e) 2: *Je m'appelle Fabienne.*
Étudiant(e) 3: *Et moi, je m'appelle Antoine. Ça va?*
Étudiant(e) 1: *Ça va bien, merci. Et toi?*
Étudiant(e) 3: *Comme ci, comme ça.*

4 *quatre*

OPTIONS

Extra Practice Read some sentences to the class and ask if they would use them with another student of the same age or an older person. Examples: **1. Je te présente Guillaume.** (student) **2. Merci beaucoup, Monsieur.** (older person) **3. Comment vas-tu?** (student) **4. Bonjour, professeur ____.** (older person) **5. Comment vous appelez-vous?** (older person)

Extra Practice Have students circulate around the classroom and conduct mini-conversations in French with other students, using the words and expressions they learned on pages 2–3. As students are carrying out the activity, move around the room, monitoring their work and offering assistance if requested.

Les sons et les lettres  Audio

The French alphabet

NATIONAL comparisons STANDARDS

The French alphabet is made up of the same 26 letters as the English alphabet. While they look the same, some letters are pronounced differently. Here is the French name of each letter.

lettre	exemple	lettre	exemple	lettre	exemple
a (a)	**a**dresse	j (ji)	**j**ustice	s (esse)	**s**pécial
b (bé)	**b**anane	k (ka)	**k**ilomètre	t (té)	**t**able
c (cé)	**c**arotte	l (elle)	**l**ion	u (u)	**u**nique
d (dé)	**d**essert	m (emme)	**m**ariage	v (vé)	**v**idéo
e (e)	**e**uro	n (enne)	**n**ature	w (double vé)	**w**agon
f (effe)	**f**ragile	o (o)	**o**live	x (iks)	**x**ylophone
g (gé)	**g**enre	p (pé)	**p**ersonne	y (i grec)	**y**oga
h (hache)	**h**éritage	q (ku)	**q**uiche	z (zède)	**z**éro
i (i)	**i**nnocent	r (erre)	**r**adio		

Notice that some letters in French words have accents. You'll learn how they influence pronunciation in later lessons. Whenever you spell a word in French, include the name of the accent after the letter.

accent	nom	exemple	orthographe
´	accent aigu	identité	I-D-E-N-T-I-T-E-accent aigu
`	accent grave	problème	P-R-O-B-L-E-accent grave-M-E
^	accent circonflexe	hôpital	H-O-accent circonflexe-P-I-T-A-L
¨	tréma	naïve	N-A-I-tréma-V-E
¸	cédille	ça	C-cédille-A

L'alphabet Practice saying the French alphabet and example words aloud.

Ça s'écrit comment? Spell these words aloud in French. For double letters, use **deux: ss=deux s.**

1. judo
2. yacht
3. forêt
4. zèbre
5. existe
6. clown
7. numéro
8. français
9. musique
10. favorite
11. kangourou
12. parachute
13. différence
14. intelligent
15. dictionnaire
16. alphabet

Dictons Practice reading these sayings aloud.

Grande invitation, petites portions.[1]

Tout est bien qui finit bien.[2]

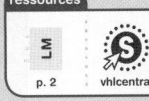

Lundi Mardi

ressources

LM
p. 2

vhlcentral

¹ Great boast, small roast.
² All's well that ends well.

cinq **5**

Section Goals

In this section, students will learn about:
• the French alphabet and how it contrasts with the English alphabet
• the names of the letters
• the names of the accent marks

Instructional Resources
vhlcentral.com:
Textbook MP3s; Lab MP3s; SAM Answer Key; Textbook Audioscript; Lab Audioscript; reference tools

Suggestions
• Model the pronunciation of the French alphabet and the example words. Have students repeat.
• Point out that vowel sounds can have many different pronunciations when combined with other vowels or when spelled with accents, particularly the **e**.
• Point out the different diacritical marks and model their pronunciation. For a detailed explanation of **l'accent aigu** and **l'accent grave**, see **Leçon 3A**, page 93. For an explanation of **l'accent circonflexe**, **le tréma**, and **la cédille**, see **Leçon 3B**, page 111.
• Draw attention to any posters, signs, or maps in the classroom. Point out individual letters, and ask the class to identify them in French.
• Write on the board the French abbreviations of several famous organizations (Examples: **ONU, OPEP**), and have students spell them in French. Explain what each abbreviation represents: **ONU** = **l'Organisation des Nations Unies** (United Nations, UN); **OPEP** = **l'Organisation des pays exportateurs de pétrole** (Organization of Petroleum-Exporting Countries, OPEC).
• Have students work on the **Ça s'écrit comment?** activity in pairs.
• The explanation and exercises are available on the **ESPACES** Supersite. You may want to play them in class so students hear French speakers other than yourself.

Extra Practice Do a dictation activity in which you spell out a list of words in French to the class. Spell each word twice to allow students sufficient time to write. After you have finished, write your list on the board or project it on a transparency and have students check their work.

Extra Practice Tell students to greet two classmates that they haven't met yet, ask each person his or her name, and ask the person to spell the last name as they write it down. Tell them to verify the spelling with the person to make sure it is correct. Before beginning the activity, write this question on the board and model the pronunciation: **Comment s'écrit** _last name_?

Section Goals

In this section, students will learn functional phrases for making introductions and speaking on the telephone through comprehensible input.

Instructional Resources
vhlcentral.com:
Roman-photo *Video, Videoscript, and Translation; SAM Answer Key; reference tools*

Video Synopsis Sandrine buys a magazine at Monsieur Hulot's newsstand. At **Le P'tit Bistrot**, Rachid introduces David, his American friend, to Sandrine and Amina. Madame Forestier (Valérie), who owns the café, gets a phone call from her son's high school French teacher because he didn't do well on his French exam. Stéphane tells Rachid to introduce David to his mother so he can avoid talking to her.

Suggestions

- Have students cover the French captions and guess the plot based only on the video stills. Write their predictions on the board.
- Have students volunteer to read the characters' parts in the **Roman-photo** aloud. Then have them get together in groups of eight to act out the episode.
- After students have read the **Roman-photo**, quickly review their predictions, and ask them which ones were correct.
- Point out that **100 centimes = 1 euro**, the monetary unit of the European Union, which includes France.

Au café

PERSONNAGES

Amina

David

Monsieur Hulot

Michèle

Rachid

Sandrine

Stéphane

Valérie

Au kiosque...
SANDRINE Bonjour, Monsieur Hulot!
M. HULOT Bonjour, Mademoiselle Aubry! Comment allez-vous?
SANDRINE Très bien, merci! Et vous?
M. HULOT Euh, ça va. Voici 45 (quarante-cinq) centimes. Bonne journée!
SANDRINE Merci, au revoir!

À la terrasse du café...
AMINA Salut!
SANDRINE Bonjour, Amina. Ça va?
AMINA Ben... ça va. Et toi?
SANDRINE Oui, je vais bien, merci.
AMINA Regarde! Voilà Rachid et... un ami?

RACHID Bonjour!
AMINA ET SANDRINE Salut!
RACHID Je vous présente un ami, David Duchesne.
SANDRINE Je m'appelle Sandrine.
DAVID Enchanté.

STÉPHANE Oh, non! Madame Richard! Le professeur de français!
DAVID Il y a un problème?

STÉPHANE Oui! L'examen de français! Présentez-vous, je vous en prie!

VALÉRIE Oh... l'examen de français! Oui, merci, merci, Madame Richard, merci beaucoup! De rien, au revoir!

ACTIVITÉS

1 **Vrai ou faux?** Choose whether each statement is vrai or faux.

1. Sandrine va (*is doing*) bien. Vrai.
2. Sandrine et Amina sont (*are*) amies. Vrai.
3. David est français. Faux.
4. David est de Washington. Vrai.
5. Rachid présente son frère (*his brother*) David à Sandrine et Amina. Faux.
6. Stéphane est étudiant à l'université. Faux.
7. Il y a un problème avec l'examen de sciences politiques. Faux.
8. Amina, Rachid et Sandrine sont (*are*) à Paris. Faux.
9. Michèle est au P'tit Bistrot. Vrai.
10. Madame Richard est le professeur de Stéphane. Vrai.
11. Madame Forestier va mal. Vrai.
12. Rachid a (*has*) cours de français dans 30 minutes. Faux.

 Practice more at **vhlcentral.com.**

OPTIONS

Video Tips General suggestions for using video clips in the classroom can be found in the front matter of this Instructor's Annotated Edition.
Avant de regarder la vidéo Before showing the video episode, have students brainstorm some greetings and some other expressions that they might hear in an episode in which some of the characters meet each other for the first time.

Regarder la vidéo Play the episode once and tell the class to listen for basic greetings. After the video is over, have students recall the greetings they heard and write them on the board. Show the episode again and ask the class to write down all of the courtesy expressions that they hear, including ways to say *pleased to meet you.*

Les étudiants se retrouvent (*meet*) au café.

DAVID Et toi..., comment t'appelles-tu?
AMINA Je m'appelle Amina.
RACHID David est un étudiant américain. Il est de Washington, la capitale des États-Unis.
AMINA Ah, oui! Bienvenue à Aix-en-Provence.
RACHID Bon..., à tout à l'heure.
SANDRINE À bientôt, David.

À l'intérieur (*inside*) du café...
MICHÈLE Allô. Le P'tit Bistrot. Oui, un moment, s'il vous plaît. Madame Forestier! Le lycée de Stéphane.
VALÉRIE Allô. Oui. Bonjour, Madame Richard. Oui. Oui. Stéphane? Il y a un problème au lycée?

RACHID Bonjour, Madame Forestier. Comment allez-vous?
VALÉRIE Ah, ça va mal.
RACHID Oui? Moi, je vais bien. Je vous présente David Duchesne, étudiant américain de Washington.

DAVID Bonjour, Madame. Enchanté!
RACHID Ah, j'ai cours de sciences politiques dans 30 (trente) minutes. Au revoir, Madame Forestier. À tout à l'heure, David.

Expressions utiles

Introductions

- **David est un étudiant américain. Il est de Washington.**
  David is an American student. He's from Washington.
- **Présentez-vous, je vous en prie!**
  Introduce yourselves, please!
- **Il/Elle s'appelle...**
  His/Her name is...
- **Bienvenue à Aix-en-Provence.**
  Welcome to Aix-en-Provence.

Speaking on the telephone

- **Allô.**
  Hello.
- **Un moment, s'il vous plaît.**
  One moment, please.

Additional vocabulary

- **Regarde! Voilà Rachid et... un ami?**
  Look! There's Rachid and... a friend?
- **J'ai cours de sciences politiques dans 30 (trente) minutes.**
  I have Political Science class in thirty minutes.
- **Il y a un problème au lycée?**
  Is there a problem at the high school?
- **Il y a...**   **euh**
  There is/are...   *um*
- **Il/Elle est**   **bon**
  He/She is...   *well; good*
- **Voici...**   **centimes**
  Here's...   *cents*
- **Voilà...**
  There's...

Successful Language Learning Tell your students that their conversational skills will grow more quickly as they learn each lesson's **Expressions utiles**. This feature is designed to teach phrases that will be useful in conversation, and it will also help students understand key phrases in each **Roman-photo**.

Expressions utiles
- Tell students that all the items in **Expressions utiles** are active vocabulary for which they are responsible. Model the pronunciation of the words and expressions and have the class repeat.
- As you work through the list, point out examples of nouns with indefinite articles (**un étudiant, un moment, un ami, un problème**). Tell students that nouns and articles will be formally presented in the **Espace structures** section.
- Explain to students that although **bon** means *well; good*, it is not an appropriate answer to the question **Ça va?**

1 Suggestion Have students correct the false statements.

2 Expansion Tell students to write three additional fill-in-the-blank statements based on the **Roman-photo**. Then have them exchange papers with a classmate and complete the sentences.

3 Suggestion Have volunteers act out their conversations for the class or another group.

2   **Complétez** Fill in the blanks with the words from the list. Refer to the video scenes as necessary.

ai	est
bienvenue	voici
capitale	

1. _____Bienvenue_____ à Aix-en-Provence.
2. Il est de Washington, la _____capitale_____ des États-Unis.
3. _____Voici_____ 45 (quarante-cinq) centimes. Bonne journée!
4. J'_____ai_____ cours de sciences politiques.
5. David _____est_____ un étudiant américain.

3   **Conversez** In groups of three, write a conversation where you introduce an exchange student to a friend. Be prepared to present your conversation to the class.

ressources

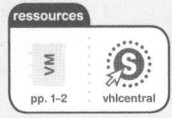
VM
pp. 1–2

vhlcentral

ACTIVITÉS

sept   **7**

OPTIONS

Extra Practice Choose four or five lines of the **Roman-photo** to use as a dictation. Read each line twice, pausing after each line so that students have time to write. Have students check their own work by comparing it with the **Roman-photo** text.

Cultural Comparison Have students make observations about the places and people they saw in the video. Ask what was surprising or different about any of the scenes or the characters' mannerisms. Did they notice anything different about the way that the American student, David, introduced himself compared to the others?

Point out that greeting friends, family members, and loved ones with a kiss on both cheeks is not unique to the French-speaking world. This custom is common throughout Europe and in other parts of the world.

Section Goals

In this section, students will:
• learn about gestures used with greetings
• learn some familiar greetings and farewells
• learn some tips about good manners in different francophone countries
• read about Aix-en-Provence

Instructional Resources
vhlcentral.com:
SAM Answer Key;
reference tools

Culture à la loupe
Avant la lecture Ask students how they greet their friends, family members, fellow students, co-workers, and people they meet for the first time. Ask them for some examples of regional variations in greetings in the United States (e.g., Howdy, Hiya, Yo).

Lecture
• Ask students what information the map on this page shows. (It shows the number of kisses traditionally given by region.)
• Explain that **faire la bise** does not actually mean to kiss another's cheek, but rather to kiss parallel to the other person's face, so that physical contact is limited to a grazing of cheeks.

Après la lecture Have students compare French and American greetings or any other method of greeting with which they are familiar.

1 Expansion Have students work in pairs. Tell them to role-play the situations in items 1–6. Example: 1. Students give each other four kisses because they are in northwestern France.

  S Reading

CULTURE À LA LOUPE

La poignée de main ou la bise?

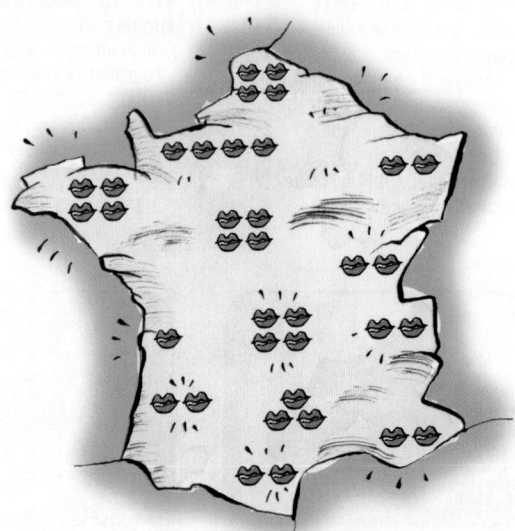

Combien de° bises?

French friends and relatives usually exchange a kiss (la bise) on alternating cheeks whenever they meet and again when they say good-bye. Friends of friends may also kiss when introduced, even though they have just met. This is particularly true among students and young adults. It is not unusual for men of the same family to exchange **la bise**; otherwise, men generally greet one another with a handshake (**la poignée de main**). As the map shows, the number of kisses varies from place to place in France. In some regions, two kisses (one on each cheek) is the standard while in others, people may exchange as many as four kisses. Whatever the number, each kiss is accompanied by a slight kissing sound.

Unless they are also friends, business acquaintances and co-workers usually shake hands each time they meet and do so again upon leaving. A French handshake is brief and firm, with a single downward motion.

Combien de How many

Coup de main

If you are not sure whether you should shake hands or kiss someone, or if you don't know which side to start on, you can always follow the other person's lead. When in doubt, start on your right.

A C T I V I T É S

1 **Vrai ou faux?** Indicate whether each statement is **vrai** or **faux**. Correct any false statements.

1. In northwestern France, giving four kisses is common. Vrai.
2. Business acquaintances usually kiss one another on the cheek. Faux. They usually shake hands.
3. French people may give someone they've just met **la bise**. Vrai.
4. **Bises** exchanged between French men at a family gathering are common. Vrai.
5. In a business setting, French people often shake hands when they meet each day and again when they leave. Vrai.
6. When shaking hands, French people prefer a long and soft handshake. Faux. A French handshake is brief and firm.
7. The number of kisses given can vary from one region to another. Vrai.
8. It is customary for kisses to be given silently. Faux. Each kiss is accompanied by a slight kissing sound.

OPTIONS

La bise Tell students that, although people in some social circles in the United States commonly kiss each other on the cheek once, this is not common practice in France. It could be considered impolite to give only one **bise** since the other person would be waiting for the second kiss. In some regions of France and Switzerland, people may even give three **bises**, but just one is rare.

Game Divide the class into two teams. Indicate one team member at a time, alternating between teams. Give situations in which people are greeting each other. Students should say if the people should greet each other with **la poignée de main** or **la bise**. Examples: female friends (**la bise**); male and female business associates (**la poignée de main**). Give a point for each correct answer. The team with the most points at the end of the game wins.

LE FRANÇAIS QUOTIDIEN

Les salutations

À la prochaine!	*Until next time!*
À plus!	*See you later!*
Ciao!	*Bye!*
Coucou!	*Hi there!/Hey!*
Pas grand-chose.	*Nothing much.*
Quoi de neuf?	*What's new?*
Rien de nouveau.	*Nothing new.*

LE MONDE FRANCOPHONE

Les bonnes manières

In the francophone world, making an effort to speak in French is important. Respecting cultural norms and using polite expressions, such as **excusez-moi**, **s'il vous plaît**, and **merci**, goes a long way when conversing with locals.

Dos and don'ts in the francophone world:

France Always greet shopkeepers upon entering a store and say good-bye upon leaving.

Cambodia Greet others traditionally with your palms together and raised in front of you.

French Polynesia/Tahiti Shake hands with everyone in a room, unless the group is large.

Viêt-Nam Remove your hat in the presence of older people and monks to show respect.

Ivory Coast Avoid making eye contact, as it is considered rude to stare.

PORTRAIT

Aix-en-Provence: ville d'eau, ville d'art

Aix-en-Provence is a vibrant university town that welcomes international students. Its main boulevard, **le cours Mirabeau**, is great for people-watching or just relaxing at a sidewalk café. One can see many beautiful fountains, traditional and ethnic restaurants, and the daily vegetable and flower market among the winding, narrow streets of **la vieille ville** (*old town*).

Aix is also renowned for its dedication to the arts, hosting numerous cultural festivals every year such as **le Festival International d'Art Lyrique, Aix en Musique**, and **Danse à Aix**. For centuries, artists have been drawn to Provence for its natural beauty and the unique quality of light there. Paul Cézanne, artist and native son of Provence, spent his days painting the surrounding countryside.

Founded in 122 BC by the Romans, Aix was once an important spa town called **Aquae Sextiae** (*The Waters of Sextius*). The city's long history is preserved in its architectural treasures, which have been carefully restored. The **Pays d'Aix** (*Aix Region*) is equally historic, housing chapels, castles, shrines, and charming hilltop villages. From the top of **la Montagne Sainte-Victoire**, hikers have an expansive view of the region's forested landscape.

ville d'eau, ville d'art *city of water, city of art*

---

2 **Les bonnes manières** In which places might these behaviors be particularly offensive?

1. making direct eye contact   Ivory Coast
2. greeting someone with a **bise** when introduced   Cambodia
3. wearing a hat in the presence of older people   Viêt-Nam
4. failing to greet a salesperson   France
5. failing to greet everyone in a room   French Polynesia/Tahiti

3 **À vous** With a partner, practice meeting and greeting people in French in various social situations.

1. Your good friend from Provence introduces you to her close friend.
2. You walk into your neighborhood bakery.
3. You arrive for an interview with a prospective employer.

S Practice more at **vhlcentral.com.**

A C T I V I T É S

Le français quotidien
- Model the pronunciation of each expression and have students repeat.
- Tell students to list all the situations they can think of in which they could use these expressions. Then have them compare their lists in pairs or small groups.

Portrait Mention that Aix-en-Provence is often referred to simply as Aix. Ask students why they think Aix is called **ville d'eau, ville d'art** in the title. Then ask if they would like to visit Aix, and which aspects of the town attract them the most.

Le monde francophone Ask students which dos and don'ts in the francophone world should be followed in the anglophone world, too. Have the class think of logical reasons for following each custom or social convention, especially for North Africa and Sub-Saharan Africa. Example: In North Africa, the left hand is reserved for using the toilets.

Suggestion Point out to students that they will find supporting activities and more information related to this **Espace culture** at **vhlcentral.com.**

2 **Suggestion** Have students check their answers with a partner.

3 **Suggestion** Before beginning this activity, ask students if they would use **tu** or **vous** in each situation. Remind them to use appropriate gestures and manners.

OPTIONS

Cultural Activity Have students choose one of these topics to research on the Internet: **Aix-en-Provence, le Festival International d'Art Lyrique, Aix en Musique,** or **Paul Cézanne.** Tell them to come to the next class with printouts of two photos illustrating their topic and a sentence or two in French, if possible, about each photo. Divide the class into groups of three or four students so that they can present the material to one another while looking at the images.

Small Groups Have students work in groups of three or four. Tell them to create an informal conversation using the expressions in **Le français quotidien** and appropriate gestures. Have a few groups act out their conversations for the class.

ESPACE STRUCTURES

Section Goals

In this section, students will learn:
- gender and number of nouns
- definite and indefinite articles

Instructional Resources
vhlcentral.com:
Activity Pack; Lab MP3s;
SAM Answer Key; **Essayez!**
and **Mise en pratique**
answers; Lab Audioscript;
reference tools

Suggestions
- Explain what a noun is by giving examples of people (**professeur**), places (**café**), things (**examen**), and ideas (**problème**). Then write these nouns on the board: **ami, amie, cours, télévision**. Point out the gender of each noun. Explain that nouns for male beings are usually masculine, and nouns for female beings are usually feminine. All other nouns can be either masculine or feminine. Tell students that they should memorize the gender of a noun along with the word.
- Write these nouns on the board: **professeur, professeurs, étudiante, étudiantes**. Ask students to point out the singular and plural nouns and to explain why. Then have students pronounce the words. Point out that the **-s** is not pronounced in French.
- Write **bureau** and **bureaux** on the board. Explain that words ending in **-eau** add **-x** to form the plural.

1A.1

Nouns and articles (S) Tutorial

Point de départ A noun designates a person, place, or thing. As in English, nouns in French have number (singular or plural). However, French nouns also have gender (masculine or feminine).

masculine singular	masculine plural	feminine singular	feminine plural
le café	**les cafés**	**la bibliothèque**	**les bibliothèques**
the café	*the cafés*	*the library*	*the libraries*

- Nouns that designate a male are usually masculine. Nouns that designate a female are usually feminine.

masculine		feminine	
l'acteur	*the actor*	**l'actrice**	*the actress*
l'ami	*the (male) friend*	**l'amie**	*the (female) friend*
le chanteur	*the (male) singer*	**la chanteuse**	*the (female) singer*
l'étudiant	*the (male) student*	**l'étudiante**	*the (female) student*
le petit ami	*the boyfriend*	**la petite amie**	*the girlfriend*

- Some nouns can designate either a male or a female regardless of their grammatical gender; in other words, whether the word itself is masculine or feminine.

un professeur
a (male or female) professor

une personne
a (male or female) person

- Nouns for objects that have no natural gender can be either masculine or feminine.

masculine		feminine	
le bureau	*the office; desk*	**la chose**	*the thing*
le lycée	*the high school*	**la différence**	*the difference*
l'examen	*the test, exam*	**la faculté**	*the faculty*
l'objet	*the object*	**la littérature**	*literature*
l'ordinateur	*the computer*	**la sociologie**	*sociology*
le problème	*the problem*	**l'université**	*the university*

🏃 Boîte à outils

As you learn new nouns, study them with their corresponding articles. This will help you remember their gender.

🏃 Boîte à outils

The final **-s** in the plural form of a noun is not pronounced. Therefore **ami** and **amis** sound the same. You can determine whether the word you're hearing is singular or plural by the article that comes before it.

- You can usually form the plural of a noun by adding **-s**.

	singular		plural	
typical masculine noun	**l'objet**	*the object*	**les objets**	*the objects*
typical feminine noun	**la télévision**	*the television*	**les télévisions**	*the televisions*

- However, in the case of words that end in **-eau** in the singular, add **-x** to the end to form the plural. For most nouns ending in **-al**, drop the **-al** and add **-aux**.

le bureau → **les bureaux**
the office *the offices*

l'animal → **les animaux**
the animal *the animals*

- When you have a group composed of males and females, use the masculine plural noun to refer to it.

les amis
the (male and female) friends

les étudiants
the (male and female) students

- The English definite article *the* never varies with number or gender of the noun it modifies. However, in French the definite article takes four different forms depending on the gender and number of the noun that it accompanies: **le, la, l'** or **les**.

	singular noun beginning with a consonant		singular noun beginning with a vowel sound		plural noun	
masculine	**le tableau**	*the painting/ blackboard*	**l'ami**	*the (male) friend*	**les cafés**	*the cafés*
feminine	**la librairie**	*the bookstore*	**l'université**	*the university*	**les télévisions**	*the televisions*

- In English, the singular indefinite article is *a/an*, and the plural indefinite article is *some*. In French, the singular indefinite articles are **un** and **une**, and the plural indefinite article is **des**. Unlike in English, the indefinite article **des** cannot be omitted in French.

	singular		plural	
masculine	**un instrument**	*an instrument*	**des instruments**	*(some) instruments*
feminine	**une table**	*a table*	**des tables**	*(some) tables*

Il y a **un ordinateur** ici.
There's a computer here.

Il y a **des ordinateurs** ici.
There are (some) computers here.

Il y a **une université** ici.
There's a university here.

Il y a **des universités** ici.
There are (some) universities here.

- Use **c'est** followed by a singular article and noun or **ce sont** followed by a plural article and noun to identify people and objects.

Qu'est-ce que **c'est**?
What is that?

C'est une librairie.
It's a bookstore.

Ce sont des bureaux.
They're offices.

Boîte à outils

In English, you sometimes omit the definite article when making general statements.

I love French.

Literature is difficult.

In French, you must always use the definite article in such cases.

J'adore le français.

La littérature est difficile.

Essayez!   Select the correct article for each noun.

le, la, l' ou les?

1. ___le___ café
2. ___la___ bibliothèque
3. ___l'___ acteur
4. ___l'___ amie
5. ___les___ problèmes
6. ___le___ lycée
7. ___les___ examens
8. ___la___ littérature

un, une ou des?

1. ___un___ bureau
2. ___une___ différence
3. ___un___ objet
4. ___des___ amis
5. ___des___ amies
6. ___une___ université
7. ___un___ ordinateur
8. ___des___ tableaux

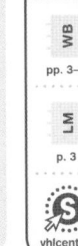

ressources

WB
pp. 3–4

LM
p. 3

S
vhlcentral

Suggestions
- Write these words on the board: **le café, les cafés, l'ami, les amis, la personne, les personnes**. Explain the use of the definite article. Point out that singular nouns beginning with a vowel or silent **h** use **l'**.
- Follow the same procedure for indefinite articles using these words: **un café, des cafés, un ami, des amis, une personne, des personnes**. Point out that the **-n** of **un** is pronounced before a vowel.
- Model how to pronounce **les** and **des** before words beginning with a consonant and a vowel.
- Consider giving your students some pointers to help them guess the gender of a noun. Words ending in **-al, -age, -eau, -et, -isme** or in a consonant are often masculine while those ending in **-ence, -ance,** or **-ie** are often feminine. However, be sure to caution your students that these are only general guidelines and there are always exceptions. Have students find words they have learned in this lesson that fit these guidelines and also find any exceptions.
- Tell students they will learn more about **c'est/ce sont** in **1B.1**.

Essayez! Have students change the singular nouns and articles to the plural and vice versa.

Video Show the video episode again to offer more input on singular and plural nouns and their articles. With their books closed, have students write down every noun and article that they hear. After viewing the video, ask volunteers to list the nouns and articles they heard.

TPR Distribute cards preprinted with articles and nouns to each of four students. Then line up ten students, each of whom is assigned a noun. Include a mix of masculine, feminine, singular, and plural nouns. Say one of the nouns (without the article), and that student must step forward. The student assigned the corresponding article has five seconds to join the student with the noun.

ESPACE **STRUCTURES**

1 Suggestion To check students' answers, have volunteers write them on the board or spell out the nouns orally.

1 Expansion Have students close their books. Tell them to change the plural nouns they hear to the singular and vice versa. Then randomly give them the answers to the items in the activity.

2 Suggestion Have volunteers read the words in the list aloud. Tell students to read all three items before attempting to start filling in blanks.

3 Suggestion This activity can also be done in pairs or groups.

Mise en pratique

1 **Les singuliers et les pluriels** Make the singular nouns plural, and vice versa.

1. l'actrice   les actrices
2. les lycées   le lycée
3. les différences   la différence
4. la chose   les choses
5. le bureau   les bureaux
6. le café   les cafés
7. les librairies   la librairie

8. la faculté   les facultés
9. les acteurs   l'acteur
10. l'ami   les amis
11. l'université   les universités
12. les tableaux   le tableau
13. le problème   les problèmes
14. les bibliothèques   la bibliothèque

2 **L'université** Complete the sentences with an appropriate word from the list. Don't forget to provide the missing articles.   Answers may slightly vary. Suggested answers below.

| bibliothèque | examen | ordinateurs | sociologie |
| bureau | faculté | petit ami | |

1. À (a) _____ la faculté _____, les tableaux et (b) _____ les ordinateurs _____ sont (are) modernes.
2. Marc, c'est (c) _____ le petit ami _____ de (of) Marie. Marc étudie (studies) la littérature.
3. Marie étudie (d) _____ la sociologie _____. Elle (She) est à (e) _____ la bibliothèque _____ de l'université.
4. Sylvie étudie pour (for) (f) _____ l'examen _____ de français.

3 **Les mots** Find ten words (mots) hidden in this word jumble. Then, provide the corresponding indefinite articles.   une amie; des bureaux; un café; une chose; une faculté; un lycée; des objets; des ordinateurs; une librairie; un tableau

 Practice more at **vhlcentral.com.**

Communication

 NATIONAL communication STANDARDS

4 Qu'est-ce que c'est? In pairs, take turns identifying each image.

▶ **MODÈLE**

Étudiant(e) 1:
Qu'est-ce que c'est?

Étudiant(e) 2: *C'est un ordinateur.*

1. Ce sont des tables.

2. Ce sont des étudiants.

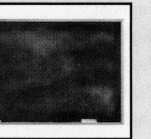

3. C'est un tableau.

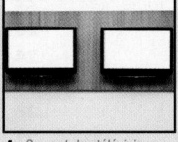

4. Ce sont des télévisions.

5. C'est une bibliothèque.

6. C'est un café.

5 Identifiez In pairs, take turns providing a category for each item.

MODÈLE

Michigan, UCLA, Rutgers, Duke
Ce sont des universités.

1. saxophone   C'est un instrument.
2. Ross, Rachel, Joey, Monica, Chandler, Phoebe   Ce sont des amis.
3. SAT   C'est un examen.
4. Library of Congress   C'est une bibliothèque.
5. Sharon Stone, Debra Messing, Catherine Deneuve   Ce sont des actrices.
6. Céline Dion, Bruce Springsteen   Ce sont des chanteurs.

6 Le français Your partner gets French words mixed up. Correct your partner as he or she points to various people and objects in the illustration and names them. When you're done, switch roles.   Answers will vary.

MODÈLE

Étudiant(e) 1: *C'est une personne.*

Étudiant(e) 2: *Non, c'est un objet.*

7 Pictogrammes In groups of four, someone draws a person, object, or concept for the others to guess. Whoever guesses correctly draws next. Continue until everyone has drawn at least once.   Answers will vary.

---

4 Suggestion Before beginning this activity, have students identify the objects in the photos. Then read the **modèle** aloud with a volunteer. Remind them that **Ce sont** is used with plural nouns.

5 Expansion Have students work in pairs. Tell them to write two more items for the activity. Example: GRE, GMAT, LSAT (**Ce sont des examens.**) Then have volunteers read their items aloud, while the rest of the class guesses the category.

7 Suggestion Before beginning the activity, remind students that they must choose something the class knows how to say in French, and that to guess what the picture is, they should say: **C'est un(e) _____?** or **Ce sont des _____?**

OPTIONS

Game Divide the class into groups of three to four students. Bring in photos or magazine pictures, point to various objects or people, and say the French word without saying the article. Call on groups to indicate the person's or object's gender. Give a point for each correct answer. Deduct a point for each wrong answer. The group with the most points at the end wins.

Extra Practice Write ten singular nouns on the board. In a rapid-response drill, call on students to give the appropriate gender. Examples: **bureau** (masculine), **étudiante** (feminine). You may also do this activity without writing the words on the board.

ESPACE STRUCTURES

1A.2

Numbers 0–60  Tutorial

Point de départ Numbers in French follow patterns, as they do in English. First, learn the numbers **0–30**. The patterns they follow will help you learn the numbers **31–60**.

Numbers 0–30					
0–10		**11–20**		**21–30**	
0	zéro				
1	un	11	onze	21	vingt et un
2	deux	12	douze	22	vingt-deux
3	trois	13	treize	23	vingt-trois
4	quatre	14	quatorze	24	vingt-quatre
5	cinq	15	quinze	25	vingt-cinq
6	six	16	seize	26	vingt-six
7	sept	17	dix-sept	27	vingt-sept
8	huit	18	dix-huit	28	vingt-huit
9	neuf	19	dix-neuf	29	vingt-neuf
10	dix	20	vingt	30	trente

- When counting a series of numbers, use **un** for *one.*

  un, deux, trois, quatre...
  one, two, three, four...

- When *one* is followed by a noun, use **un** or **une** depending on whether the noun is masculine or feminine.

  un objet   **une** télévision
  an/one object   *a/one television*

- Note that the number **21** (**vingt et un**) follows a different pattern than the numbers **22–30**. When **vingt et un** precedes a feminine noun, add **-e** to the end of it: **vingt et une.**

  vingt et un objets   **vingt et une** choses
  twenty-one objects   *twenty-one things*

- Notice that the numbers **31–39, 41–49,** and **51–59** follow the same pattern as the numbers **21–29.**

Numbers 31–60					
31–34		**35–38**		**39, 40, 50, 60**	
31	trente et un	35	trente-cinq	39	trente-neuf
32	trente-deux	36	trente-six	40	quarante
33	trente-trois	37	trente-sept	50	cinquante
34	trente-quatre	38	trente-huit	60	soixante

- As with the number **21**, to indicate a count of **31, 41,** or **51** for a feminine noun, change the **un** to **une.**

  trente et **un** objets   trente et **une** choses
  thirty-one objects   *thirty-one things*

  cinquante et **un** objets   cinquante et **une** choses
  fifty-one objects   *fifty-one things*

Section Goals

In this section, students will learn:
- numbers 0–60
- the expression **il y a**

Instructional Resources
vhlcentral.com:
Activity Pack; Lab MP3s;
*SAM Answer Key; **Essayez!***
*and **Mise en pratique***
answers; Lab Audioscript;
reference tools

Suggestions
- Introduce numbers by asking students how many of them can count to ten in French. Hold up varying numbers of fingers and ask students to shout out the corresponding number in French.
- Consider demonstrating how the French count numbers on their fingers, starting with the thumb for *one*; the thumb and index finger for *two*; the thumb, index, and middle fingers for *three*; and so on. Ask if other cultures have a different way of counting with their fingers.
- Go through the numbers, modeling the pronunciation of each. Write individual numbers on the board and call on students at random to say each number as you point to it.

- Use **il y a** to say *there is* or *there are* in French. This expression doesn't change, even if the noun that follows it is plural.

Il y a un ordinateur dans le bureau.
There is a computer in the office.

Il y a des tables dans le café.
There are tables in the café.

Il y a une table dans le café.
There is one table in the café.

Il y a dix-huit objets sur le bureau.
There are eighteen objects on the desk.

Il y a deux amies.

Il y a trois étudiants.

- In most cases, the indefinite article (**un**, **une**, or **des**) is used with **il y a**, rather than the definite article (**le**, **la**, **l'**, or **les**).

Il y a un professeur de biologie américain.
There's an American biology professor.

Il y a des étudiants français et anglais.
There are French and English students.

- Use the expression **il n'y a pas de/d'** followed by a noun to express *there isn't a...* or *there aren't any....* Note that no article (definite or indefinite) is used in this case. Use **de** before a consonant sound and **d'** before a vowel sound.

before a consonant

before a vowel sound

Il n'y a pas de tables dans le café.
There aren't any tables in the café.

Il n'y a pas d'ordinateur dans le bureau.
There isn't a computer in the office.

- Use **combien de/d'** to ask how many of something there are.

Il y a **combien de tables**?
How many tables are there?

Il y a **combien d'ordinateurs**?
How many computers are there?

Il y a **combien de librairies**?
How many bookstores are there?

Il y a **combien d'étudiants**?
How many students are there?

Essayez! Write out or say the French word for each number below.

1. 15 _quinze_
2. 6 _six_
3. 22 _vingt-deux_
4. 5 _cinq_
5. 12 _douze_
6. 8 _six_
7. 30 _trente_
8. 21 _vingt et un_
9. 1 _un_
10. 17 _dix-sept_
11. 44 _quarante-quatre_
12. 14 _quatorze_
13. 38 _trente-huit_
14. 56 _cinquante-six_
15. 19 _dix-neuf_

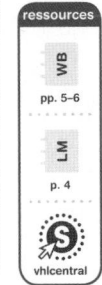

ressources
WB
pp. 5–6
LM
p. 4
vhlcentral

quinze 15

Suggestions
- Assign each student a number at random that they must remember. When finished, have the student assigned **un** say his or her number aloud, then **deux**, **trois**, etc. Help anyone who struggles with his or her number.
- Emphasize the variable forms of **un** and **une**, **vingt et un**, and **vingt et une**, giving examples of each. Examples: **vingt et un étudiants, vingt et une personnes.**
- Ask questions like the following: **Il y a combien d'étudiants dans la classe? (Il y a seize étudiants dans la classe.)**

Essayez! Have students write four more numbers from 0–60. Tell them to exchange papers with a classmate and write the numbers as words.

Game Hand out Bingo cards with B-I-N-G-O across the top of five columns. The 25 squares underneath will contain random numbers. From a hat, draw letters and numbers and call them out in French. The first student that can fill in a number in each one of the lettered columns yells "Bingo!" and wins.

TPR Assign ten students a number from 0–60 and line them up in front of the class. Call out one of the numbers at random and have the student assigned to that number take a step forward. When two students have stepped forward, ask them to repeat their numbers. Then ask individuals to add (say: **plus**) or subtract (say: **moins**) the two numbers.

1 Suggestion Once students have filled in the missing numbers, have volunteers read each series aloud.

1 Expansion Ask the class to list the prime numbers (**les nombres premiers**) up to 30. Explain that a prime number is any number that can only be divided by itself and 1. Prime numbers to 30 are: 1, 2, 3, 5, 7, 11, 13, 17, 19, 23, 29.

2 Suggestion Have students form complete sentences using **Il y a** when answering. Example: **Il y a douze mois dans une année.**

2 Expansion For additional practice, give students these items. **7. jours: semaine (sept) 8. jours: novembre (trente) 9. minutes: heure** (*hour*) **(soixante) 10. saisons** (*seasons*): **année (quatre)**

3 Expansion Write on the board three more telephone numbers for real places on campus or in town with their area codes, using double digits as in the activity. Call on volunteers to read the numbers aloud. Permit students to say the digits one by one if the numbers exceed 60.

Mise en pratique

1 **Logique** Provide the number that completes each series. Then, write out the number in French.

MODÈLE

2, 4, ___6___, 8, 10; ___six___

1. 9, 12, ___15___, 18, 21; _____quinze_____
2. 15, 20, ___25___, 30, 35; _____vingt-cinq_____
3. 2, 9, ___16___, 23, 30; _____seize_____
4. 0, 10, 20, ___30___, 40; _____trente_____
5. 15, ___17___, 19, 21, 23; _____dix-sept_____
6. 29, 26, ___23___, 20, 17; _____vingt-trois_____
7. 2, 5, 9, ___14___, 20, 27; _____quatorze_____
8. 30, 22, 16, 12, ___10___; _____dix_____

2 **Il y a combien de...?** Provide the number that you associate with these pairs of words.

MODÈLE

lettres: l'alphabet *vingt-six*

1. mois (*months*): année (*year*)   douze
2. états (*states*): USA   cinquante
3. semaines (*weeks*): année   cinquante-deux
4. jours (*days*): octobre   trente et un
5. âge: le vote   dix-huit
6. Noël: décembre   vingt-cinq

3 **Numéros de téléphone** Your roommate left behind a list of phone numbers to call today. Now he or she calls you and asks you to read them off. (Note that French phone numbers are read as double, not single, digits.)

MODÈLE

Le bureau, c'est le zéro un, vingt-trois, quarante-cinq, vingt-six, dix-neuf.

1. *bureau: 01.23.45.26.19*

2. *bibliothèque: 01.47.15.54.17*
   La bibliothèque, c'est le zéro un, quarante-sept, quinze, cinquante-quatre, dix-sept.

3. *café: 01.41.38.16.29*
   Le café, c'est le zéro un, quarante et un, trente-huit, seize, vingt-neuf.

4. *librairie: 01.10.13.60.23*
   La librairie, c'est le zéro un, dix, treize, soixante, vingt-trois.

5. *faculté: 01.58.36.14.12*
   La faculté, c'est le zéro un, cinquante-huit, trente-six, quatorze, douze.

 Practice more at **vhlcentral.com**.

Communication

4 Contradiction Thierry is describing the new Internet café in the neighborhood, but Paul is in a bad mood and contradicts everything he says. In pairs, act out the roles using words from the list. Be sure to pay attention to whether the word is singular (use **un/une**) or plural (use **des**). *Answers will vary.*

MODÈLE

Étudiant(e) 1: *Dans (In) le café, il y a des tables.*
Étudiant(e) 2: *Non, il n'y a pas de tables.*

actrices	professeurs
bureau	tableau
étudiants	tables
ordinateur	télévision

5 Sur le campus Nathalie's inquisitive best friend wants to know everything about her new campus. In pairs, take turns acting out the roles.

MODÈLE

bibliothèques: 3
Étudiant(e) 1: *Il y a combien de bibliothèques?*
Étudiant(e) 2: *Il y a trois bibliothèques.*

1. professeurs de littérature: 22   Il y a vingt-deux professeurs de littérature.
2. étudiants dans (*in*) la classe de français: 15   Il y a quinze étudiants dans la classe de français.
3. télévision dans la classe de sociologie: 0   Il n'y a pas de télévision dans la classe de sociologie.
4. ordinateurs dans le café: 8   Il y a huit ordinateurs dans le café.
5. employés dans la librairie: 51   Il y a cinquante et un employés dans la librairie.
6. tables dans le café: 21   Il y a vingt et une tables dans le café.
7. tableaux dans la bibliothèque: 47   Il y a quarante-sept tableaux dans la bibliothèque.
8. personne dans le bureau: 1   Il y a une personne dans le bureau.

6 Choses et personnes In groups of three, make a list of ten things or people that you see or don't see in the classroom. Use **il y a** and **il n'y a pas de**, and specify the number of items you can find. Then, compare your list with that of another group. *Answers will vary.*

MODÈLE

Étudiant(e) 1: *Il y a un étudiant français.*
Étudiant(e) 2: *Il n'y a pas de télévision.*
Étudiant(e) 3: *Il y a...*

4 Suggestion Have two volunteers read the **modèle** aloud. Remind students that they shouldn't use any article (definite or indefinite) after **Il n'y a pas de/d'**.

5 Suggestion Have two volunteers read the **modèle** aloud. Remind students to use **combien d'** before a noun that begins with a vowel sound.

6 Expansion After groups have compared their answers, convert the statements into questions. Example: **Il y a combien d'étudiants?**

OPTIONS

Extra Practice Ask questions about the university and the town or city in which it is located. Examples: **Il y a combien de professeurs dans le département de français? Il y a combien de bibliothèques sur le campus? Il y a combien d'universités à ____?** Encourage students to guess the number if they don't know it.

TPR Give ten students a card with a number from 0–60. (You may want to assign numbers in fives to simplify the activity.) The card must be visible to the other students. Then call out simple math problems (addition or subtraction) involving the assigned numbers. When the first two numbers are called, each student steps forward. The student whose assigned number completes the math problem has five seconds to join them.

ESPACE SYNTHÈSE

Révision

Suggestion Tell students that this section reviews and recycles the lesson vocabulary and grammar points.

Instructional Resources
vhlcentral.com:
Activity Pack (Info Gap Activities); Testing Program; Testing Program MP3s; reference tools

1 Suggestion Before beginning this activity, you may wish to review the alphabet and how to say the accent marks.

2 Suggestion Tell students not to accept a guess if the letter is not pronounced correctly in French.

3 Suggestion Before beginning the activity, have two volunteers read the **modèle** aloud.

4 Suggestion Remind students to use appropriate gestures and encourage them to add information to the introduction, such as the person's hometown.

5 Suggestions
• Before beginning this activity, quickly review the numbers 0–60. Hold up cards with various numbers, and have the class or individuals say them in French.
• Read the **modèle** aloud with a volunteer.

6 Suggestion Divide the class into pairs and distribute the Info Gap Handouts for this activity, found in the Activity Pack on the Supersite. Give students ten minutes to complete the activity.

1 Des lettres In pairs, take turns choosing nouns. One partner chooses only masculine nouns, while the other chooses only feminine. Slowly spell each noun for your partner, who will guess the word. Find out who can give the quickest answers. Answers will vary.

2 Le pendu In groups of four, play hangman (**le pendu**). Form two teams of two partners each. Take turns choosing a French word or expression you learned in this lesson for the other team to guess. Continue to play until your team guesses at least one word or expression from each category. Answers will vary.

1. un nom féminin
2. un nom masculin
3. un nombre entre (*number between*) 0 et 30
4. un nombre entre 31 et 60
5. une expression

3 C'est… Ce sont… Doug is spending a week in Paris with his French e-mail pal, Marc. As Doug points out what he sees, Marc corrects him sometimes. In pairs, act out the roles. Doug should be right half the time. Answers will vary.

MODÈLE
Étudiant(e) 1: *C'est une bibliothèque?*
Étudiant(e) 2: *Non, c'est une librairie.*

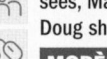

1. C'est une bibliothèque. _____

2. Ce sont des acteurs. _____

3. C'est un café. _____

4. C'est un professeur. / Ce sont des étudiants. _____

5. C'est une actrice. _____

6. Ce sont des amies. _____

4 Les présentations In pairs, introduce yourselves. Together, meet another pair. One person per pair should introduce him or herself and his or her partner. Use the items from the list in your conversations. Switch roles until you have met all of the other pairs in the class. Answers will vary.

ami	étudiant
c'est	petit(e) ami(e)
ce sont	professeur

5 S'il te plaît You are new on campus and ask another student for help finding these places. He or she gives you the building (**le bâtiment**) and room (**la salle**) number and you thank him or her. Then, switch roles and repeat with another place from the list. Answers will vary.

MODÈLE
Étudiant(e) 1: *Pardon… l'examen de sociologie, s'il te plaît?*
Étudiant(e) 2: *Ah oui… le bâtiment E, la salle dix-sept.*
Étudiant(e) 1: *Merci beaucoup!*
Étudiant(e) 2: *De rien.*

Bibliothèque d'anglais	Bâtiment C Salle 11
Bureau de Mme Girard	Bâtiment A Salle 35
Bureau de M. Brachet	Bâtiment J Salle 42
Café	Bâtiment H Salle 59
Littérature française	Bâtiment B Salle 46
Examen de littérature	Bâtiment E Salle 24
Examen de sociologie	Bâtiment E Salle 17
Salle de télévision	Bâtiment F Salle 33
Salle des ordinateurs	Bâtiment D Salle 40

6 Mots mélangés You and a partner each have half the words of a wordsearch (**des mots mélangés**). Pick a number and a letter and say them to your partner, who must tell you if he or she has a letter in the corresponding space. Do not look at each other's worksheets. Answers will vary.

Extra Practice Bring in pictures from newspapers, magazines, or the Internet of nouns that students have learned, and ask them to identify the people or objects. Examples: **C'est un(e) _____? Ce sont des _____? Qu'est-ce que c'est?** You might also ask how many people or objects are in the picture if there are more than one. Example: **Il y a combien de(d') _____?**

Small Groups Bring in family photos or magazine pictures showing people greeting or introducing each other in different situations. Assign a photo to each group or allow them to choose one. Tell students to write a brief conversation based on the photo. Remind the class to use formal and informal expressions as appropriate.

Flash CULTURE

Salut!

Meet Csilla. In this episode she visits a French city and shows us different ways of greeting people. You will see people greet one another by kissing or shaking hands and saying **Salut!**, **Bonjour!**, and **Ça va?** At the end of the video, you will see how they say good-bye with a kiss or handshake and by saying **À bientôt!**

Hôtesse: Csilla

Avant de regarder Before watching the video, discuss these questions in pairs.
Answers will vary.

1. How do you greet people in your country?
2. How do you say goodbye?

Ces deux garçons se serrent la main pour se dire bonjour.

Ces deux filles se font la bise pour se saluer.

Compréhension Use the **Vocabulaire utile** to answer the questions. *Answers will vary.*

1. What are the different gestures for greeting someone in France? *se faire la bise, se serrer la main*
2. How do women generally greet each other? *se faire la bise*
3. How do men generally greet each other? *se serrer la main*
4. What does one often say after **bonjour** or **salut**? *Ça va?*

Discussion In groups of three, discuss these questions. Use as much French as you can. *Answers will vary.*

1. Are the ways of greeting people in France similar to or different from those in your country?
2. How do you usually greet your friends? And your parents?

Vocabulaire utile

Salut!	*Hi!*
se faire la bise	*to kiss on one or both cheeks*
se serrer la main	*to shake hands*
À bientôt!	*See you soon!*

ressources

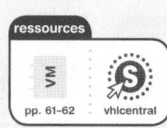

VM
pp. 61–62

vhlcentral

Practice more at **vhlcentral.com**.

dix-neuf 19

Section Goals

In this section, students will:
• read about the different ways French people greet each other
• watch a video about greetings in France
• answer questions about the video and make comparisons about the way people greet each other in different situations

Instructional Resources
vhlcentral.com: Flash culture;
Flash culture *transcription;*
reference tools

Avant de regarder la vidéo
• Have students look at the video stills, read the captions, and describe what they think the video is about.
• Before showing the video, explain to students that they don't need to understand every word they hear.

Compréhension Have students work in pairs or groups for this activity. Tell them to write their answers. Then, show the video again so that they can check their answers and add any missing information.

Discussion Have volunteers share their answers with the class.

OPTIONS

Small Groups Have students work in groups of three to prepare and role-play a scene in which two of them are at a park and a third person, who is friends with one of them, arrives. The friend should greet the newcomer and introduce him or her to the other student.

Cultural Note Many Americans find the **bise** awkward, but for the French it is an integral part of greeting others. In fact, the American practice of greeting friends and family with a hug is less common in France, and some French people find hugging just as awkward as Americans find the **bise**!

20 Instructor's Annotated Edition • Unit 1 • Lesson 1B

Section Goals

In this section, students will learn and practice vocabulary related to:
• objects in the classroom
• identifying people

Instructional Resources

vhlcentral.com:
Digital Image Bank (including vocabulary illustrations from the textbook, theme based-illustrations); Activity Pack;
Vocabulaire supplémentaire;
Mise en pratique *answers; Textbook Audioscript; Lab Audioscript; Activity Pack (Info Gap Activities); Textbook MP3s; Lab MP3s; SAM Answer Key; reference tools*

Suggestions

• Introduce vocabulary for classroom objects, such as **un cahier, une carte, un dictionnaire, un stylo.** Hold up or point to an object and say: **C'est un stylo.**
• Hold up or point to an object and ask either/or questions. Examples: **C'est un crayon ou un stylo? C'est une porte ou une fenêtre?**
• Using either objects in the classroom or the **Contextes** illustration from the Digital Image Bank, point to items or people and ask questions, such as **Qu'est-ce que c'est? Qui est-ce? C'est un stylo? C'est un professeur?**
• Have students pick up or point out objects you name. You might want to teach them the expression **Montrez-moi un/une ____.**
• Use the Vocabulary illustrations and the School and university illustrations from the Digital Image Bank to help students familiarize themselves with objects in the classroom.
• Additional vocabulary for this lesson can be found in the **Vocabulaire supplémentaire** on the Supersite.

Leçon 1B

You will learn how to...
▪ **identify yourself and others**
▪ **talk about items in the classroom**

Vocabulary Tools

En classe

Vocabulaire

Qui est-ce?	Who is it?
Quoi?	What?
une calculatrice	calculator
une montre	watch
une porte	door
un résultat	result
une salle de classe	classroom
un(e) camarade de chambre	roommate
un(e) camarade de classe	classmate
une classe	class (group of students)
un copain/ une copine (fam.)	friend
un(e) élève	pupil, student
une femme	woman
une fille	girl
un garçon	boy
un homme	man

ressources

WB	LM	S
pp. 7–8	p. 5	vhlcentral

20 *vingt*

une horloge
un crayon
un sac à dos
une fenêtre
un livre
un cahier
un dictionnaire
un stylo
une feuille de papier
une corbeille à papier

O P T I O N S

Pairs Have students work in pairs and take an inventory of all the people and items in the classroom. Tell them to write their list in French using the expression **Il y a ____.** After students have finished, tell them to compare their lists with another pair to see if they are the same.

Game Divide the class into teams. Then, in English, say the name of a classroom object and ask one of the teams to provide the French equivalent. If the team provides the correct term, it gets a point. If not, the second team gets a chance to give the correct term. Alternate giving items to the two teams. The team with the most points at the end of the game wins.

Mise en pratique

1 **Écoutez** Listen to Madame Arnaud as she describes her French classroom, then check the items she mentions.

1. une porte ☑
2. un professeur ☐
3. une feuille de papier ☐
4. un dictionnaire ☑
5. une carte ☑
6. vingt-quatre cahiers ☐
7. une calculatrice ☐
8. vingt-sept chaises ☑
9. une corbeille à papier ☑
10. un stylo ☑

2 **Chassez l'intrus** Circle the word that does not belong.

1. étudiants, élèves, (professeur)
2. un stylo, un crayon, (un cahier)
3. un livre, un dictionnaire, (un stylo)
4. un homme, (un crayon), un garçon
5. une copine, (une carte), une femme
6. une porte, une fenêtre, (une chaise)
7. une chaise, (un professeur), une fenêtre
8. (un crayon), une feuille de papier, un cahier
9. une calculatrice, une montre, (une copine)
10. une fille, (un sac à dos,) un garçon

3 **C'est...** Work with a partner to identify the items you see in the image.

MODÈLE

Étudiant(e) 1: *Qu'est-ce que c'est?*
Étudiant(e) 2: *C'est un tableau.*

1. un tableau
2. une porte
3. un crayon/stylo
4. un livre
5. une calculatrice
6. un stylo/crayon
7. une feuille
8. un bureau
9. un dictionnaire
10. une corbeille à papier
11. une chaise
12. un professeur

une carte

une chaise

FRANCE

S Practice more at **vhlcentral.com**.

vingt et un **21**

1 **Audioscript** Bonjour! Dans la salle de classe, il y a beaucoup de choses! Il y a trois fenêtres, une porte, une carte, un tableau, vingt-sept chaises et une corbeille à papier. Il y a aussi vingt-quatre étudiants et vingt-quatre sacs à dos. Dans les sacs à dos, il y a généralement un cahier, un crayon ou un stylo, un livre et un dictionnaire pour le cours de français.
(On Textbook MP3s)

1 **Suggestion** Have students check their answers by going over **Activité 2** with the whole class. Repeat any sections of the recording that the students missed or did not understand.

2 **Suggestion** Have students compare their answers in pairs or small groups. Tell them to explain why a word does not belong if they don't have the same answer.

2 **Expansion** For additional practice, read these items aloud or write them on the board.
11. une calculatrice, un étudiant, un professeur (une calculatrice)
12. une femme, un garçon, une fille (un garçon)
13. un cahier, un copain, un camarade de chambre (un cahier)

3 **Suggestion** Remind students to use the appropriate form of the indefinite article when doing this activity.

3 **Expansion** In pairs, tell students to take turns pointing to the items in the drawing and asking: **C'est un(e) ____?** If it's correct, the other person says: **Oui, c'est un(e) ____.** If it is not correct, the persons says: **Non, c'est un(e) ____.**

OPTIONS

Extra Practice Review numbers and practice vocabulary for classroom objects using printouts of advertisements in French from stores that sell school supplies, such as Monoprix. Make sure the ads include prices. As you show the pictures, ask students about the prices. Examples: **La corbeille à papier est à 15 euros ou à 20 euros? C'est combien, la calculatrice?**

Game Have the class do a chain activity in which the first student says a word in French, for example, **chaise**. The next student has to think of a word that begins with the last letter of the first person's word, such as **étudiant**. If a student can't think of a word, he or she is out of the game, and it's the next person's turn. The last student left in the game is the winner.

NATIONAL communication STANDARDS

Communication

4 Expansion For additional practice, point to different students' desks that have objects on them and ask: **Qu'est ce qu'il y a sur le bureau de ____?** You might also ask: **Qu'est-ce qu'il y a sur mon bureau?**

5 Suggestion Before beginning the activity, have a few volunteers demonstrate what students should do using the **modèle**.

6 Expansion Have students describe the people and objects in the photo using **Il y a.**

6 Suggestions
- Divide the class into pairs and distribute the Info Gap Handouts for this activity, found in the Activity Pack on the Supersite. Give students ten minutes to complete the activity.
- Have two volunteers read the **modèle** aloud.

7 Suggestion Before beginning the activity, remind students that to guess what the drawing represents they should say: **C'est un(e) ____?** or **Ce sont des ____?**

Successful Language Learning Remind the class that errors are a natural part of language learning. Point out that it is impossible to speak "perfectly" in any language. Emphasize that their spoken and written French will improve if they make an effort to practice.

---

4 Qu'est-ce qu'il y a dans mon sac à dos? Make a list of six different items that you have in your backpack, then work with a partner to compare your answers.   Answers will vary.

Dans mon (*my*) sac à dos, il y a

1. _____
2. _____
3. _____
4. _____
5. _____
6. _____

Dans le sac à dos de ____nom____, il y a

1. _____
2. _____
3. _____
4. _____
5. _____
6. _____

---

5 Qu'est-ce que c'est? Point to eight different items around the classroom and ask a classmate to identify them. Write your partner's responses in the spaces provided below.   Answers will vary.

MODÈLE
Étudiant(e) 1: *Qu'est-ce que c'est?*
Étudiant(e) 2: *C'est un stylo.*

1. _____
2. _____
3. _____
4. _____

5. _____
6. _____
7. _____
8. _____

---

6 Sept différences Your instructor will give you and a partner two different drawings of a classroom. Do not look at each other's worksheets. Find seven differences between your picture and your partner's by asking each other questions and describing what you see.   Answers will vary.

MODÈLE
Étudiant(e) 1: *Il y a une fenêtre dans ma (my) salle de classe.*
Étudiant(e) 2: *Oh! Il n'y a pas de fenêtre dans ma salle de classe.*

---

7 Pictogrammes As a class, play pictionary.   Answers will vary.
- Take turns going to the board and drawing words you learned on pp. 20–21.
- The person drawing may not speak and may not write any letters or numbers.
- The person who guesses correctly in French what the **grand(e) artiste** is drawing will go next.
- Your instructor will time each turn and tell you if your time runs out.

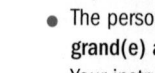

---

22   *vingt-deux*

O P T I O N S

Game Divide the class into two teams. Put labels of classroom vocabulary in a box. Alternating between teams, one person picks a label out of the box without showing it to anyone. This person must place the label on the correct person or object in the classroom and say the word aloud. Each player is allowed only 15 seconds and one guess per turn. Award a point for a correct response. If a player is incorrect, the next player on the opposing team may "steal" the point by placing the label on the correct person or object. The team with the most points at the end of the game wins.

Les sons et les lettres   Audio

Silent letters

Final consonants of French words are usually silent.

français	spor~~t~~	vous	salu~~t~~

An unaccented **-e** (or **-es**) at the end of a word is silent, but the preceding consonant *is* pronounced.

français~~e~~	américain~~e~~	orang~~es~~	japonais~~es~~

The consonants **-c**, **-r**, **-f**, and **-l** are usually pronounced at the ends of words. To remember these exceptions, think of the consonants in the word **careful**.

par**c**	bonjou**r**	acti**f**	anima**l**
la**c**	professeu**r**	naï**f**	ma**l**

🔊 **Prononcez** Practice saying these words aloud.

1. traditionnel
2. étudiante
3. généreuse
4. téléphones
5. chocolat
6. Monsieur
7. journalistes
8. hôtel
9. sac
10. concert
11. timide
12. sénégalais
13. objet
14. normal
15. importante

🔊 **Articulez** Practice saying these sentences aloud.

1. Au revoir, Paul. À plus tard!
2. Je vais très bien. Et vous, Monsieur Dubois?
3. Qu'est-ce que c'est? C'est une calculatrice.
4. Il y a un ordinateur, une table et une chaise.
5. Frédéric et Chantal, je vous présente Michel et Éric.
6. Voici un sac à dos, des crayons et des feuilles de papier.

🔊 **Dictons** Practice reading these sayings aloud.

Mieux vaut tard que jamais.[1]

Aussitôt dit, aussitôt fait.[2]

[1] Better late than never. [2] No sooner said than done.

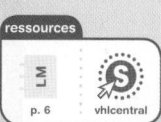

vingt-trois **23**

Section Goals

In this section, students will learn about:
- silent letters
- a strategy for remembering which consonants are pronounced at the end of words

Instructional Resources

vhlcentral.com:
Textbook MP3s; Lab MP3s; SAM Answer Key; Textbook Audioscript; Lab Audioscript; reference tools

Suggestions

- Write the sentences below on the board or a transparency. Then say each sentence and ask students which letters are silent. Draw a slash through the silent letters as students say them. **Qui est-ce? C'est Gilbert. Il est français. Qu'est-ce que c'est? C'est un éléphant.**
- Work through the example words. Model the pronunciation of each word and have students repeat after you.
- Tell students that the final consonants of a few words that end in **c, r, f,** or **l** are silent. Examples: **porc** (*pork*), **blanc** (*white*), **nerf** (*nerve*), and **gentil** (*nice*).
- Point out that the letters **-er** at the end of a word are pronounced like the vowel sound in the English word *say*. Examples: **cahier** and **papier.**
- Explain that numbers are exceptions to pronunciation rules. When counting, some final consonants are pronounced. Have students compare the pronunciation of the following: **six, sept, huit; six cahiers, sept stylos, huit crayons.**
- Tell students that the final consonants of words borrowed from other languages are often pronounced. Examples: **snob, autobus,** and **club.** This topic will be presented in **Leçon 11A.**
- The explanations and activities are available on the **ESPACES** Supersite. You may want to play them in class so students hear French speakers other than yourself.

Extra Practice Write on the board or an overhead transparency a list of words that have silent letters. Call on volunteers to spell each word in French and then pronounce it. Examples: **art, comment, sont, est, intelligent, sac à dos,** and **résultat.**

Small Groups Working in groups of three or four, have students practice pronunciation by reading the vocabulary words aloud on pages 20–21. Circulate among the groups and model correct pronunciation as needed. When they have finished, ask them if they discovered any exceptions to the pronunciation rules. **(cahier, papier)**

Section Goals

In this section, students will learn functional phrases for describing people's character traits and talking about their nationalities through comprehensible input.

Instructional Resources
vhlcentral.com:
Roman-photo *Video, Videoscript, and Translation; SAM Answer Key; reference tools*

Video Recap: Leçon 1A
Before doing this **Roman-photo**, review the previous one. Write the names of the main characters on the board and ask students with whom they associate the following people, places, or objects.
1. un étudiant américain (David)
2. Le P'tit Bistrot (Valérie et Stéphane)
3. un magazine (Sandrine)
4. un examen de français (Stéphane)
5. un cours de sciences politiques (Rachid)
6. le lycée (Stéphane)

Video Synopsis
At the café, Valérie waits on some tourists. Valérie argues with Stéphane about his failed math test. While Michèle and Valérie prepare the tourists' orders, Michèle advises Valérie to be patient with her son. At another table, David asks Amina about herself, Rachid, and Sandrine. David repeats his questions about the others to Valérie, who warns him not to get involved with Sandrine because she is seeing Pascal.

Suggestions
- Have students scan the captions and find six adjectives of nationality plus five phrases that describe people's personality or character. Call on volunteers to read the adjectives or phrases they found aloud.
- Have students volunteer to read the characters' parts in the **Roman-photo** aloud.

Les copains  Video

PERSONNAGES

 Amina

 David

 Michèle

 Stéphane

 Touriste

 Valérie

À la terrasse du café...
VALÉRIE Alors, un croissant, une crêpe et trois cafés.
TOURISTE Merci, Madame.
VALÉRIE Ah, vous êtes... américain?
TOURISTE Um, non, je suis anglais. Il est canadien et elle est italienne.
VALÉRIE Moi, je suis française.

À l'intérieur du café...
VALÉRIE Stéphane!!!
STÉPHANE Quoi?! Qu'est-ce que c'est?
VALÉRIE Qu'est-ce que c'est! Qu'est-ce que c'est! Une feuille de papier! C'est l'examen de maths! Qu'est-ce que c'est?
STÉPHANE Oui, euh, les maths, c'est difficile.

VALÉRIE Stéphane, tu es intelligent, mais tu n'es pas brillant! En classe, on fait attention au professeur, au cahier et au livre! Pas aux fenêtres. Et. Pas. Aux. Filles!
STÉPHANE Oh, oh, ça va!!

À la table d'Amina et de David...
DAVID Et Rachid, mon colocataire? Comment est-il?
AMINA Il est agréable et très poli... plutôt réservé mais c'est un étudiant brillant. Il est d'origine algérienne.

DAVID Et toi, Amina. Tu es de quelle origine?
AMINA D'origine sénégalaise.
DAVID Et Sandrine?

AMINA Sandrine? Elle est française.
DAVID Mais non... Comment est-elle?
AMINA Bon, elle est chanteuse, alors elle est un peu égoïste. Mais elle est très sociable. Et charmante. Mais attention! Elle est avec Pascal.
DAVID Pfft, Pascal, Pascal...

ACTIVITÉS

1 **Identifiez** Indicate which character would make each statement: Amina (**A**), David (**D**), Michèle (**M**), Sandrine (**S**), Stéphane (**St**), or Valérie (**V**).

1. Les maths, c'est difficile. St
2. En classe, on fait attention au professeur! V
3. Michèle, les trois cafés sont pour les trois touristes. V
4. Ah, Madame, du calme! M

5. Ma mère est très impatiente! St
6. J'ai (*I have*) de la famille au Sénégal. A
7. Je suis une grande chanteuse! S
8. Mon colocataire est très poli et intelligent. D
9. Pfft, Pascal, Pascal... D
10. Attention, David! Sandrine est avec Pascal. A/V

 Practice more at **vhlcentral.com**.

OPTIONS

Video Tips General suggestions for using video clips in the classroom can be found on page IAE-11 of the Instructor's Annotated Edition.

Avant de regarder la vidéo Before showing the video episode, have students brainstorm the type of information they might give when describing people.

Regarder la vidéo Show the video episode and have students give you a play-by-play description of the action. Write their descriptions on the board. Then show the episode a second time so students can add details if necessary, or simply consolidate information. Finally, discuss the material on the board and call attention to any incorrect information. Help students prepare a brief plot summary.

Amina, David et Stéphane passent la matinée (*spend the morning*) au café.

Au bar...

VALÉRIE Le croissant, c'est pour l'Anglais, et la crêpe, c'est pour l'Italienne.

MICHÈLE Mais, Madame. Ça va? Qu'est-ce qu'il y a?

VALÉRIE Ben, c'est Stéphane. Des résultats d'examens, des professeurs... des problèmes!

MICHÈLE Ah, Madame, du calme! Je suis optimiste. C'est un garçon intelligent. Et vous, êtes-vous une femme patiente?

VALÉRIE Oui... oui, je suis patiente. Mais le Canadien, l'Anglais et l'Italienne sont impatients. Allez! Vite!

VALÉRIE Alors, ça va bien?

AMINA Ah, oui, merci.

DAVID Amina est une fille élégante et sincère.

VALÉRIE Oui! Elle est charmante.

DAVID Et Rachid, comment est-il?

VALÉRIE Oh! Rachid! C'est un ange! Il est intelligent, poli et modeste. Un excellent camarade de chambre.

DAVID Et Sandrine? Comment est-elle?

VALÉRIE Sandrine?! Oh, là, là. Non, non, non. Elle est avec Pascal.

Expressions utiles

Describing people

- **Vous êtes/Tu es américain?**
  You're American?
- **Je suis anglais. Il est canadien et elle est italienne.**
  I'm English. He's Canadian, and she's Italian.
- **Et Rachid, mon colocataire? Comment est-il?**
  And Rachid, my roommate (in an apartment)? What's he like?
- **Il est agréable et très poli... plutôt réservé mais c'est un étudiant brillant.**
  He's nice and very polite... rather reserved, but a brilliant student.
- **Tu es de quelle origine?**
  (Of) What heritage are you?
- **Je suis d'origine algérienne/sénégalaise.**
  I'm of Algerian/Senegalese heritage.
- **Elle est avec Pascal.**
  She's with (dating) Pascal.
- **Rachid! C'est un ange!**
  Rachid! He's an angel!

Asking questions

- **Ça va? Qu'est-ce qu'il y a?**
  Are you OK? What is it?/What's wrong?

Additional vocabulary

- **Ah, Madame, du calme!**
  Oh, ma'am, calm down!
- **On fait attention à...**
  One pays attention to...
- **Mais attention!** | **alors**
  But watch out! | *so*
- **Allez! Vite!** | **mais**
  Go! Quickly! | *but*
- **Mais non...** | **un peu**
  Of course not... | *a little*

Expressions utiles
- Model the pronunciation of the **Expressions utiles** and have students repeat after you.
- Point out forms of the verb **être** and adjective agreement in the captions and in the **Expressions utiles**. Tell students that this material will be formally presented in the **Structures** section.
- Ask a few questions based on the **Expressions utiles**. Examples: **Et _____, vous êtes américain(e) [canadien(ne)/italien(ne)]? Ça va? Qu'est-ce qu'il y a?**

1 Expansion For additional practice, read these items aloud or write them on the board.
11. Je suis optimiste. (Michèle)
12. Je suis anglais. (le touriste)
13. Rachid! C'est un ange! (Valérie)

2 Expansion Write the following adjectives on the board and ask students which video character they describe.
1. sénégalais(e) (Amina)
2. algérien(ne) (Rachid)
3. français(e) (Sandrine, Stéphane, Valérie, Michèle)
4. charmant(e) (Sandrine)
5. réservé (Rachid)

3 Expansion After the students complete the activity, tell them to write a brief description of themselves using **Je suis _____**. Read some of the descriptions aloud and have the class guess who wrote them.

2 Complétez Use words from the list to describe these people in French. Refer to the video scenes and a dictionary as necessary.

1. Michèle always looks on the bright side. ___optimiste___
2. Rachid gets great grades. ___intelligent___
3. Amina is very honest. ___sincère___
4. Sandrine thinks about herself a lot. ___égoïste___
5. Sandrine has a lot of friends. ___sociable___

égoïste	
intelligent	
optimiste	
sincère	
sociable	

3 Conversez In pairs, choose the words from this list you would use to describe yourselves. What personality traits do you have in common? Be prepared to share your answers with the class.

brillant	modeste
charmant	optimiste
égoïste	patient
élégant	sincère
intelligent	sociable

ressources

VM
pp. 3–4

vhlcentral

A C T I V I T É S

O P T I O N S

Extra Practice Choose four or five lines of the **Roman-photo** to use as a dictation. Read each line twice, pausing after each line so that students have time to write. Have students check their own work by comparing it with the **Roman-photo** text.

Pairs Have students work in pairs. Tell them to look at video stills 2–3 and 6–8, and choose a situation to ad-lib. Assure them that it is not necessary to follow or memorize the **Roman-photo** word for word. Students should be creative while getting the general meaning across with the vocabulary and expressions they know.

S Reading

Section Goals

In this section, students will:
- learn about France's multicultural society
- learn some familiar terms for identifying people
- read about languages spoken in some francophone countries
- read about **Superdupont**, a popular comic-strip character

Instructional Resources
vhlcentral.com: reference tools

Culture à la loupe
Avant la lecture Have students discuss what their idea of a typical French person is.

Lecture
- Point out the regions where Provençal (**Provence**), Breton (**Bretagne**), and Basque (**Le Pays basque**) are spoken on the map of France in **Appendice A**.
- Explain that there are other regional languages not mentioned in the text: Alsatian, Caribbean Creole, Catalan, Corsican, Dutch, Gascon, Lorraine German dialect, and Occitan.
- Explain to students that "Other European countries" in the first row of the table includes both EU and non-EU countries but excludes Portugal, Italy, and Spain, which are listed separately.

Après la lecture Ask students what facts in this reading are interesting or surprising to them.

1 Expansion For additional practice, give students these items: 11. There are several official languages in France. (**Faux.** French is the only official language.) 12. South Africans represent a significant immigrant population in France. (**Faux.** North and West Africans represent significant immigrant populations.) 13. There are more immigrants in France from both Italy and Spain than from Tunisia. (**Vrai.**) 14. There aren't many Asians in France. (**Faux.** There are significant Indo-Chinese populations.)

CULTURE À LA LOUPE

Qu'est-ce qu'un Français typique?

What is your idea of a typical Frenchman?
Do you picture a man wearing a **béret**? How about French women? Are they all fashionable and stylish? Do you picture what is shown in these photos? While real French people fitting one aspect or another of these cultural stereotypes do exist, rarely do you find individuals who fit all aspects.

France is a multicultural society with no single, national ethnicity. While the majority of French people are of Celtic or Latin descent, France has significant North and West African (e.g., Algeria, Morocco, Senegal) and Indo-Chinese (e.g., Vietnam, Laos, Cambodia) populations as well. Long a **terre d'accueil°**, France today has over eleven million foreigners and immigrants. Even as France has maintained a strong concept of its culture through the preservation of its language, history, and traditions, French culture has been enriched by the contributions of its immigrant populations. Each region of the country also has its own traditions, folklore, and, often, its own language. Regional languages, such as Provençal, Breton, and Basque, are still spoken in some areas, but the official language is, of course, French.

terre d'accueil *a land welcoming of newcomers*

Immigrants in France, by country of birth

COUNTRY NAME	NUMBER OF PEOPLE
Other European countries	811,421
Algeria	748,034
Morocco	692,923
Sub-Saharan Africa	655,460
Portugal	599,333
Other Asian countries	447,149
Italy	292,592
Spain	245,077
Turkey	248,159
Tunisia	251,220
Cambodia, Laos, Vietnam	127,641
UK	152,786

A C T I V I T É S

1

Vrai ou faux? Indicate whether each statement is **vrai** or **faux**. Correct any false statements.

1. Cultural stereotypes are generally true for most people in France.
   Faux. Rarely do you find individuals who fit all aspects of a stereotype.
2. People in France no longer speak regional languages.
   Faux. Regional languages are still spoken in some areas.
3. Many immigrants from North Africa live in France. Vrai.
4. More immigrants in France come from Portugal than from Morocco. Faux. More immigrants in France come from Morocco than from Portugal.
5. Algerians and Moroccans represent the largest immigrant populations in France. Vrai.

6. Immigrant cultures have little impact on French culture.
   Faux. French culture has been enriched by immigrant cultures.
7. Because of immigration, France is losing its cultural identity.
   Faux. France has maintained its culture.
8. French culture differs from region to region. Vrai.
9. Most French people are of Anglo-Saxon heritage.
   Faux. The majority of French people are of Celtic or Latin descent.
10. For many years, France has received immigrants from many countries. Vrai.

O P T I O N S

Cultural Activity Ask students what stereotypical ideas a French person might have of Americans. If students have difficulty answering, then give them a few examples of American stereotypes and ask them if they are true or valid. Examples: Americans are loud and obnoxious. Americans only speak English. Americans are overweight.

Small Groups Divide the class into groups of three or four. Give groups five minutes to brainstorm names of cities, states, lakes, rivers, mountain ranges, and so forth in the United States that have French origins. One member of each group should write down the names. Then have groups share their lists with the class.

Le français quotidien
- Point out that these are slang terms typically used by young people in informal contexts.
- Model the pronunciation of each term and have students repeat.
- Have students brainstorm words that they use in a similar way when talking to their peers.

Portrait
- Explain that this political comic strip is not unique and that **la bande dessinée (B.D.)** represents serious reading for young and old alike in France. An international comic-book festival takes place every year in the small town of Angoulême, France.
- Ask students why they think **Superdupont** is so popular in France.

Le monde francophone
- Have students locate the countries mentioned here on the world map in **Appendice A**.
- To check comprehension, ask these questions. 1. What is the most commonly spoken language in each country? (German in Switzerland, Flemish in Belgium, and Moroccan Arabic in Morocco.) 2. Which country has the most official languages? (Switzerland) 3. In which country is French not an official language? (Morocco.)

Musique à fond Point out to students that they will find supporting activities and information at **vhlcentral.com**.

2 Expansion Have students write four more fill-in-the-blank statements based on the information on this page. Then tell them to exchange papers with a classmate and complete the activity.

3 Expansion Have students draw a picture of their comic-book character or find a photo in a newspaper or magazine to illustrate the character's profile.

LE FRANÇAIS QUOTIDIEN

Les gens

ado (*m./f.*)	*adolescent, teen*
bonhomme (*m.*)	*fellow*
gars (*m.*)	*guy*
mec (*m.*)	*guy*
minette (*f.*)	*young woman, sweetie*
nana (*f.*)	*young woman, girl*
pote (*m.*)	*buddy*
type (*m.*)	*guy*

LE MONDE FRANCOPHONE

Les langues

Many francophone countries are multilingual, some with several official languages.

Switzerland German, French, Italian, and Romansh are all official languages. German is spoken by about 64% of the population and French by about 23%. Italian and Romansh speakers together account for about 8% of the country's population.

Belgium There are three official languages: French, Dutch, and German. Wallon, the local variety of French, is used by one-third of the population. Flemish, spoken primarily in the north, is used by roughly two-thirds of Belgians.

Morocco Classical Arabic is the official language, but most people speak the Moroccan dialect of Arabic. Berber is spoken by about 15 million people, and French remains Morocco's unofficial third language.

PORTRAIT

Superdupont

Superdupont is an ultra-French superhero in a popular comic strip parodying French nationalism. The protector of all things French, he battles the secret enemy organization **Anti-France**, whose agents speak **anti-français**, a mixture of English, Spanish, Italian, Russian, and German. *Superdupont* embodies just about every French stereotype imaginable. For example, the name Dupont, much like Smith in the United States, is extremely common in France. In addition to his **béret** and moustache, he wears a blue, white, and red belt around his waist representing **le drapeau français** (*the French flag*). Physically, he is overweight and has a red nose—signs that he appreciates rich French food and wine. Finally, on his arm is **un coq** (*a rooster*), the national symbol of France. The Latin word for rooster (*gallus*) also means "inhabitant of Gaul," as France used to be called.

MUSIQUE À FOND

Stromae

Birthdate: March 12, 1985
Birthplace: Brussels, Belgium
Occupation: composer-singer

Awards:
2016 D6Bels Music Awards:
Concert of the year

His songs address current topics with humor and irony. His real name is Paul Van Haver.

Go to **vhlcentral.com** to find out more about **Stromae** and his music.

---

2 **Complétez** Provide responses to these questions.

1. France is often symbolized by this bird: _____the rooster_____
2. _____Blue, white, and red_____ are the colors of the French flag.
3. France was once named _____Gaul_____
4. There are _____four_____ official languages in Switzerland.
5. In Belgium, _____Flemish_____ is spoken by 60% of the population.

3 **Et les Américains?** What might a comic-book character based on a "typical American" be like? With a partner, brainstorm a list of stereotypes to create a profile for such a character. Compare the profile you create with your classmates'. Do they fairly represent Americans? Why or why not?

ACTIVITÉS

ressources
vhlcentral

OPTIONS

Cultural Comparison Have students compare *Superdupont* to American comic-book superheroes, such as Superman, Batman, and Wonder Woman. Bring in pictures of these comic-book characters, if possible, to facilitate the discussion. Have students discuss the following aspects: their clothing and general appearance, the reason for their existence or purpose, what they represent, and why they are so popular.

Small Groups Have students work in groups of three or four. Tell them to create an informal conversation using the expressions in **Le français quotidien**. Have a few groups act out their conversations for the class.

1B.1

ESPACE STRUCTURES

Subject pronouns and the verb *être*  Tutorial

Point de départ In French, as in English, the subject of a verb is the person or thing that carries out the action. The verb expresses the action itself.

SUBJECT ⟷ VERB
Le professeur   parle français.
The professor   speaks French.

Subject pronouns

- Subject pronouns replace a noun that is the subject of a verb.

SUBJECT PRONOUN ⟷ VERB
Il   parle français.
He   speaks French.

French subject pronouns				
	singular		**plural**	
first person	**je**	*I*	**nous**	*we*
second person	**tu**	*you*	**vous**	*you*
third person	**il**	*he/it (masc.)*	**ils**	*they (masc.)*
	elle	*she/it (fem.)*	**elles**	*they (fem.)*
	on	*one*		

- Subject pronouns in French show number (singular vs. plural) and gender (masculine vs. feminine). When a subject consists of both males and females, use the masculine form of the pronoun to replace it.

Rémy et Marie dansent très bien.
Ils dansent très bien.
They dance very well.

M. et Mme Diop sont de Dakar.
Ils sont de Dakar.
They are from Dakar.

- Use **tu** for informal address and **vous** for formal. **Vous** is also the plural form of *you*, both informal and formal.

Comment vas-**tu**?
How's it going?

Comment allez-**vous**?
How are you?

Comment t'appelles-**tu**?
What's your name?

Comment vous appelez-**vous**?
What is/What are your name(s)?

- The subject pronoun **on** refers to people in general, just as the English subject pronouns *one*, *they*, or *you* sometimes do. **On** can also mean *we* in a casual style. **On** always takes the same verb form as **il** and **elle**.

En France, **on** parle français.
In France, they speak French.

On est au café.
We are at the coffee shop.

Section Goals

In this section, students will learn:
- subject pronouns
- the verb **être**
- **c'est** and **il/elle est**

Instructional Resources
vhlcentral.com:
Activity Pack; Lab MP3s;
SAM Answer Key; **Essayez!**
and **Mise en pratique**
answers; Lab Audioscript;
reference tools

Suggestions
- Point to yourself and say: **Je suis professeur.** Then walk up to a student and say: **Tu es...** The student should say: **étudiant(e).** Once the pattern has been established, include other subject pronouns and forms of **être** while pointing to other students. Examples: **Il est étudiant. Elle est étudiante. Elles sont étudiantes.**
- Ask students a few simple questions and tell them to respond **Oui** or **Non.** Examples: **Brad Pitt est acteur? Angelina Jolie est chanteuse?**
- Point out that in French you do not use an article before a profession after **il/elle est** and **ils/elles sont.** You say: **Il est acteur,** not **Il est un acteur.**
- Remind students that in **Leçon 1A,** they learned that the noun **personne** is always feminine regardless of the gender of the subject. So **une/la personne** will be replaced by the pronoun **elle** even though it might refer to a male.

🏃 Boîte à outils

In English, you sometimes use the pronoun *it* to replace certain nouns.
The exam is long.
It is long.

In French, there is no equivalent neuter pronoun. You must use **il** or **elle** depending on the gender of the noun it is replacing.
L'examen est long.
Il est long.

Extra Practice As a rapid-response drill, call out subject pronouns and have students respond with the correct form of **être.** Examples: **tu (es)** and **vous (êtes).** Then reverse the drill; say the forms of **être** and have students give the subject pronouns. Accept multiple answers for **est** and **sont.**

Extra Practice Ask students to indicate whether the following people would be addressed as **vous** or **tu.** Examples: a roommate, a friend's grandmother, a doctor, and a neighbor's child.

The verb *être*

- Être (*to be*) is an irregular verb; its conjugation (set of forms for different subjects) does not follow a pattern. The form **être** is called the infinitive; it does not correspond to any particular subject.

être (to be)			
je suis	*I am*	**nous sommes**	*we are*
tu es	*you are*	**vous êtes**	*you are*
il/elle est	*he/she/it is*	**ils/elles sont**	*they are*
on est	*one is*		

- Note that the **-s** of the subject pronoun **vous** is pronounced as an English *z* in the phrase **vous êtes**.

Vous êtes à Paris.
You are in Paris.

Vous êtes M. Leclerc? Enchantée.
Are you Mr. Leclerc? Pleased to meet you.

C'est and *il/elle est*

- Use **c'est** or its plural form **ce sont** plus a noun to identify who or what someone or something is. Remember to use an article before the noun.

C'est un téléphone.
That's a phone.

Ce sont des photos.
Those are pictures.

- When the expressions **c'est** and **ce sont** are followed by proper names, don't use an article before the names.

C'est Amina.
That's Amina.

Ce sont Amélie et Anne.
That's Amélie and Anne.

- Use **il/elle est** and **ils/elles sont** to refer to someone or something previously mentioned.

La bibliothèque? **Elle est** moderne.
The library? It's modern.

Nathalie et Félix? **Ils sont** intelligents.
Nathalie and Félix? They are intelligent.

- Use the phrases **il/elle est** and **ils/elles sont** to tell someone's profession. Note that in French, you do not use the article before the profession.

Voilà M. Richard. **Il est** acteur.
There's Mr. Richard. He's an actor.

Elles sont chanteuses.
They are singers.

Essayez! Fill in the blanks with the correct forms of the verb **être**.

1. Je _____suis_____ ici.
2. Ils _____sont_____ intelligents.
3. Tu _____es_____ étudiante.
4. Nous _____sommes_____ à Québec.
5. Vous _____êtes_____ Mme Lacroix?
6. Marie _____est_____ chanteuse.

Boîte à outils

Use **c'est** or **ce sont** instead of **il/elle est** and **ils/elles sont** when you have an adjective qualifying the noun that follows:

C'est un professeur intelligent.
He is an intelligent professor.

Ce sont des actrices élégantes.
Those are elegant actresses.

ressources

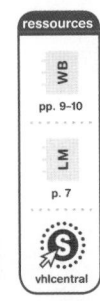

WB
pp. 9-10

LM
p. 7

vhlcentral

Suggestions
- Ask students to give examples of situations in which they would use the **tu** and **vous** forms of **être**.
- Give examples of how **on** can mean *we* in casual conversation: **On est copains.** *We are friends.*
- Point out the liaison in **vous êtes**. Also point out that the **-n** in **on est** is pronounced. Have students practice pronouncing these phrases.
- When teaching the difference between **c'est/ce sont** and **il(s)/elle(s) est/sont**, explain that **c'est/ce sont** is most often followed by a noun and **il(s)/elle(s) est/sont** is most often followed by an adjective. Point out the exceptions: **C'est très bien. Elle est chanteuse.**
- Tell students that the term **la photo**, which appears in the example **Ce sont des photos**, comes from the word **la photographie**.

Essayez! Have students create additional simple sentences using the verb **être**.

OPTIONS

Video Replay the video episode, having students focus on subject pronouns and the verb **être**. Ask them to write down as many examples of sentences that use forms of **être** as they can. Stop the video where appropriate to ask comprehension questions about what the characters said.

ESPACE **STRUCTURES**

1 Suggestion Have students work on this activity in pairs. Tell them to switch roles for items 5–8.

2 Suggestion To check students' answers, call on volunteers to read the sentences aloud or write them on the board.

3 Suggestion Before beginning the activity, have students quickly identify the items or people in the photos.

Mise en pratique

1 **Pascal répète** Pascal repeats everything his older sister Odile says. Give his response after each statement, using subject pronouns.

MODÈLE

Chantal est étudiante.
Elle est étudiante.

1. Les professeurs sont en Tunisie. Ils sont en Tunisie.
2. Mon (*My*) petit ami Charles n'est pas ici. Il n'est pas ici.
3. Moi, je suis chanteuse. Tu es chanteuse.
4. Nadège et moi, nous sommes à l'université. Vous êtes à l'université.
5. Tu es un ami. Je suis un ami.
6. L'ordinateur est dans (*in*) la chambre. Il est dans la chambre.
7. Claude et Charles sont là. Ils sont là.
8. Lucien et toi (*you*), vous êtes copains. Nous sommes copains.

2 **Où sont-ils?** Thérèse wants to know where all her friends are. Tell her by completing the sentences with the appropriate subject pronouns and the correct forms of **être**.

MODÈLE

Sylvie / au café
Elle est au café.

1. Georges / à la faculté de médecine Il est à la faculté de médecine.
2. Marie et moi / dans (*in*) la salle de classe Nous sommes dans la salle de classe.
3. Christine et Anne / à la bibliothèque Elles sont à la bibliothèque.
4. Richard et Vincent / là-bas Ils sont là-bas.
5. Véronique, Marc et Anne / à la librairie Ils sont à la librairie.
6. Jeanne / au bureau Elle est au bureau.
7. Hugo et Isabelle / au lycée Ils sont au lycée.
8. Martin / au bureau Il est au bureau.

3 **Identifiez** Describe these photos using **c'est, ce sont, il/elle est,** or **ils/elles sont.**

1. ___C'est___ un acteur. 2. ___Il est___ ici. 3. ___Elles sont___ copines.

4. ___Elle est___ chanteuse. 5. ___Elle est___ là. 6. ___Ce sont___ des montres.

 Practice more at **vhlcentral.com.**

Communication

4 **Assemblez** In pairs, take turns using the verb **être** to combine elements from both columns. Talk about yourselves and people you know. *Answers will vary.*

A	B
Singulier:	
Je	agréable
Tu	d'origine française
Mon (*My*, masc.) prof	difficile
Mon/Ma (*My*, fem.)	étudiant(e)
camarade de chambre	sincère
Mon cours	sociable
_____	_____
Pluriel:	
Nous	agréables
Mes (*My*) profs	copains/copines
Mes camarades de	difficiles
chambre	étudiant(e)s
Mes cours	sincères

5 **Qui est-ce?** In pairs, identify who or what is in each picture. If possible, use **il/elle est** or **ils/elles sont** to add something else about each person or place. *Answers will vary.*

▶ **MODÈLE**
C'est Céline Dion. Elle est chanteuse.

1. _____ 2. _____

3. _____ 4. _____ 5. _____ 6. _____

6 **On est comment?** In pairs, take turns describing these famous people using the phrases **C'est, Ce sont, Il/Elle est,** or **Ils/Elles sont** and words from the box. You can also use negative phrases to describe them. *Answers will vary.*

professeur(s)	actrice(s)	chanteuse(s)
chanteur(s)	adorable(s)	élégant(e)
pessimiste(s)	timide(s)	acteur(s)

1. Justin Bieber
2. Rihanna et Gwen Stefani
3. Barack Obama
4. Johnny Depp
5. Lucille Ball et Desi Arnaz
6. Meryl Streep

7 **Enchanté** You and your roommate are in a campus bookstore. You run into one of his or her classmates, whom you've never met. In a brief conversation, introduce yourselves, ask how you are, and say something about yourselves using a form of **être**. *Answers will vary.*

4 Suggestion Tell students to add two questions of their own to the list and to jot down notes during their interviews.

5 Suggestion Tell students to write down their descriptions. After they have completed the activity, call on volunteers to read their descriptions.

7 Suggestion Have volunteers act out their conversations for the class.

OPTIONS

Small Groups Working in small groups, have students invent a story about the people in the photos for **Activité 5**. Tell them to include who the people are, where they are from, and what they do in the story. Circulate around the room and assist with unfamiliar vocabulary as necessary, but encourage students to use terms they already know.

Extra Practice Bring in pictures of people and objects and ask students to describe them using **c'est, ce sont, il/elle est,** or **ils/elles sont.**

Section Goals

In this section, students will learn:
- forms, agreement, and position of adjectives
- some descriptive adjectives
- adjectives of nationality

Instructional Resources
vhlcentral.com:
Activity Pack; Lab MP3s;
SAM Answer Key; **Essayez!**
and **Mise en pratique**
answers; Lab Audioscript;
reference tools

Suggestions

- Write these adjectives on the board: **impatient**, **impatiente**, **impatients**, **impatientes**. Model each adjective in a sentence and ask volunteers to tell you whether it is masculine or feminine and singular or plural.
- Model the pronunciation of adjectives of nationality and have students repeat them. Point out that the feminine forms ending in -**ienne**.

1B.2

Adjective agreement

 Tutorial

Point de départ Adjectives are words that describe people, places, and things. In French, adjectives are often used with the verb **être** to point out the qualities of nouns or pronouns.

*Le cours est **difficile**.*

*Je suis **optimiste**.*

- Many adjectives in French are cognates; that is, they have the same or similar spellings and meanings in French and English.

Cognate descriptive adjectives

agréable	*pleasant*	**intelligent(e)**	*intelligent*
amusant(e)	*fun*	**intéressant(e)**	*interesting*
brillant(e)	*brilliant*	**occupé(e)**	*busy*
charmant(e)	*charming*	**optimiste**	*optimistic*
désagréable	*unpleasant*	**patient(e)**	*patient*
différent(e)	*different*	**pessimiste**	*pessimistic*
difficile	*difficult*	**poli(e)**	*polite*
égoïste	*selfish*	**réservé(e)**	*reserved*
élégant(e)	*elegant*	**sincère**	*sincere*
impatient(e)	*impatient*	**sociable**	*sociable*
important(e)	*important*	**sympathique (sympa)**	*nice*
indépendant(e)	*independent*	**timide**	*shy*

![Boîte à outils]

Boîte à outils

Use the masculine plural form of an adjective to describe a group composed of masculine and feminine nouns: **Henri et Patricia sont élégants.**

- In French, most adjectives agree in number and gender with the nouns they describe. Most adjectives form the feminine by adding a silent -**e** (no accent) to the end of the masculine form. Adding a silent -**s** to the end of masculine and feminine forms gives you the plural forms of both.

	masculine	feminine
singular	*patient*	*patiente*
plural	*patients*	*patientes*

Henri est **élégant.**   **Claire et Lise** sont **élégantes.**
Henri is elegant.   *Claire and Lise are elegant.*

- If the masculine form of the adjective already ends in an unaccented -**e**, do not add another one for the feminine form.

MASCULINE SINGULAR	NO CHANGE	FEMININE SINGULAR
optimiste	⟷	**optimiste**

- French adjectives are usually placed after the noun they modify when they don't directly follow a form of **être**.

  Ce sont des **étudiantes brillantes**.
  They're brilliant students.

  Bernard est un homme **agréable et poli**.
  Bernard is a pleasant and polite man.

- Here are some adjectives of nationality. Note that the **-n** of adjectives that end in **-ien** doubles before the final **-e** of the feminine form: **algérienne, canadienne, italienne, vietnamienne**.

Adjectives of nationality

algérien(ne)	*Algerian*	**japonais(e)**	*Japanese*
allemand(e)	*German*	**marocain(e)**	*Moroccan*
anglais(e)	*English*	**martiniquais(e)**	*from Martinique*
américain(e)	*American*	**mexicain(e)**	*Mexican*
canadien(ne)	*Canadian*	**québécois(e)**	*from Quebec*
espagnol(e)	*Spanish*	**sénégalais(e)**	*Senegalese*
français(e)	*French*	**suisse**	*Swiss*
italien(ne)	*Italian*	**vietnamien(ne)**	*Vietnamese*

- The first letter of adjectives of nationality is not capitalized.

Il est américain.

Elle est française.

- An adjective whose masculine singular form already ends in **-s** keeps the identical form in the masculine plural.

  Pierre est **un ami sénégalais**.
  Pierre is a Senegalese friend.

  Pierre et Yves sont **des amis sénégalais**.
  Pierre and Yves are Senegalese friends.

- To ask someone's nationality or heritage, use **Quelle est ta/votre nationalité?** or **Tu es/Vous êtes de quelle origine?**

  Quelle est votre nationalité?
  What is your nationality?

  Je suis de nationalité canadienne.
  I'm Canadian.

  Tu es de quelle origine?
  What is your heritage?

  Je suis d'origine italienne.
  I'm of Italian heritage.

Essayez! Write in the correct forms of the adjectives.

1. Marc est ___timide___ (timide).
2. Ils sont ___anglais___ (anglais).
3. Elle adore la littérature ___française___ (français).
4. Ce sont des actrices ___suisses___ (suisse).
5. Marie n'est pas ___mexicaine___ (mexicain).
6. Les actrices sont ___impatientes___ (impatient).
7. Elles sont ___réservées___ (réservé).
8. Il y a des universités ___importantes___ (important).
9. Christelle est ___amusante___ (amusant).
10. Les étudiants sont ___polis___ (poli) en cours.
11. Mme Castillion est très ___occupée___ (occupé).
12. Luc et moi, nous sommes ___sincères___ (sincère).

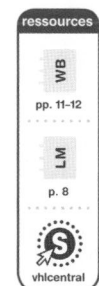

ressources

WB
pp. 11-12

LM
p. 8

S
vhlcentral

Suggestions
- Go around the room asking **Quelle est votre nationalité?** Also have a few students ask each other their nationalities.
- Use pictures and the names of celebrities to practice other adjectives of nationality. Examples: **Le prince William est-il canadien? (Non, il est anglais.) Julia Roberts est-elle française? (Non, elle est américaine.)**
- Explain that adjectives of nationality can be used as nouns as well. Examples: **La femme anglaise est réservée. L'Anglaise est réservée.** Point out that nouns of nationality are capitalized, while adjectives of nationality are not.
- Point out that in English most adjectives are placed before the noun, but in French they are placed after the noun. Write the following example on the board, circle the adjective, and draw an arrow pointing to the noun. Example: **C'est un examen difficile.**
- At this point you may want to present the adjectives in the **Vocabulaire supplémentaire** on the Supersite.

OPTIONS

Extra Practice Have students collect several interesting pictures of people from magazines or newspapers. Have them prepare a description of one of the pictures ahead of time. Invite them to show the pictures to the class and then give their descriptions orally without indicating which picture they are talking about. The class will guess which of the pictures is being described.

Extra Practice Do a quick class survey to find out how many nationalities are represented in your class. As students respond, write the nationality and number of students on the board. Ask: **Combien d'étudiants sont d'origine américaine? Mexicaine? Vietnamienne?** If students ask, clarify that the gender of the adjective of nationality agrees with the word **origine**, which is feminine.

ESPACE STRUCTURES

1 Suggestion Before beginning the activity, make sure students understand that they should use feminine plural forms of the adjectives. For each item, call on one student to read the sentence in the book and another student to respond.

2 Expansion For additional practice, change the subject of the sentence and have students restate or write the sentences. Examples: **1. Kazumi est de Tokyo. (Il est japonais.) 2. Gerta et Katarina sont de Berlin. (Elles sont allemandes.) 3. Carmen est de Guadalajara. (Elle est mexicaine.) 4. Tom et Susan sont de Londres. (Ils sont anglais.) 5. Linda est de San Francisco. (Elle est américaine.) 6. Luciano et Gino sont de Rome. (Ils sont italiens.) 7. Fatima est de Casablanca. (Elle est marocaine.) 8. Denise et Monique sont de Québec. (Elles sont canadiennes/québécoises.)**

3 Expansion Have students say what each person in the drawing is not. Example: **Madame Malbon n'est pas sociable.**

Mise en pratique

1 **Nous aussi!** Jean-Paul is bragging about himself, but his younger sisters Stéphanie and Gisèle believe they possess the same attributes. Provide their responses.

MODÈLE

Je suis amusant.
Nous aussi, nous sommes amusantes.

1. Je suis intelligent. Nous aussi, nous sommes intelligentes.
2. Je suis sincère. Nous aussi, nous sommes sincères.
3. Je suis élégant. Nous aussi, nous sommes élégantes.
4. Je suis patient. Nous aussi, nous sommes patientes.
5. Je suis sociable. Nous aussi, nous sommes sociables.
6. Je suis poli. Nous aussi, nous sommes polies.
7. Je suis charmant. Nous aussi, nous sommes charmantes.
8. Je suis optimiste. Nous aussi, nous sommes optimistes.

2 **Les nationalités** You are with a group of students from all over the world. Indicate their nationalities according to the cities they come from.

MODÈLE

Monique est de *(from)* Paris.
Elle est française.

1. Les amies Fumiko et Keiko sont de Tokyo. Elles sont japonaises.
2. Hans est de Berlin. Il est allemand.
3. Juan et Pablo sont de Guadalajara. Ils sont mexicains.
4. Wendy est de Londres. Elle est anglaise.
5. Jared est de San Francisco. Il est américain.
6. Francesca est de Rome. Elle est italienne.
7. Aboud et Moustafa sont de Casablanca. Ils sont marocains.
8. Jean-Pierre et Mario sont de Québec. Ils sont québécois.

3 **Voilà Mme...** Your parents are having a party and you point out different people to your friend. Use one of the adjectives you just learned each time. Answers will vary.

MODÈLE

Voilà M. Duval. Il est sénégalais.
C'est un ami.

M. Duval
Catherine et Jeanne
M. Forestier
Georges et Denise
Mme Malbon

 Practice more at **vhlcentral.com.**

Communication

4 Interview You are looking for a roommate and interview someone to see what he or she is like. In pairs, play both roles. Are you compatible roommates? *Answers will vary.*

MODÈLE

pessimiste
Étudiant(e) 1: *Tu es pessimiste?*
Étudiant(e) 2: *Non, je suis optimiste.*

1. impatient
2. modeste
3. timide
4. sincère

5. égoïste
6. sociable
7. indépendant
8. amusant

5 Ils sont comment? In pairs, take turns describing each item below. Tell your partner whether you agree (**C'est vrai**) or disagree (**C'est faux**) with the descriptions. *Answers will vary.*

MODÈLE

Johnny Depp
Étudiant(e) 1: *C'est un acteur désagréable.*
Étudiant(e) 2: *C'est faux. Il est charmant.*

1. Beyoncé et Céline Dion
2. les étudiants de Harvard
3. Usher
4. la classe de français
5. le président des États-Unis (*United States*)
6. Tom Hanks et Gérard Depardieu
7. le prof de français
8. Steven Spielberg
9. notre (*our*) université
10. Kate Winslet et Julia Roberts

6 Au café You and two classmates are talking about your new bosses (**patrons**), each of whom is very different from the other two. In groups of three, create a dialogue in which you greet one another and describe your bosses. *Answers will vary.*

---

4 Suggestions
• Have students add two more qualities to the list that are important to them.
• After students have completed the activity, ask them if they are compatible roommates and to explain why or why not.

5 Suggestion Have two volunteers read the **modèle** aloud.

5 Expansion Have small groups brainstorm names of famous people, places, and things not found in the activity and write them in a list. Tell them to include some plural items. Then ask the groups to exchange lists and describe the people, places, and things on that list.

6 Suggestion Tell students to give their bosses a name so that it is obvious if they are male or female. Also encourage students to ask each other questions about their bosses during the conversation.

OPTIONS

Extra Practice Write each descriptive adjective on two cards or slips of paper and put them in two separate piles in random order. Hand out one card to each student. Tell students they have to find the person who has the same adjective as they do. Example: **Étudiant(e) 1: Tu es optimiste? Étudiant(e) 2: Oui, je suis optimiste./Non, je suis sociable.** For variation, this activity can also be used to practice adjectives of nationality.

Extra Practice As a rapid-response drill, say the name of a country and have students respond with the appropriate adjective of nationality. For variation, have students write the adjective on the board or tell them to spell the adjective after they say it.

Instructional Resources
vhlcentral.com:
Activity Pack (Feuilles d'activités; Info Gap Activities; Task-based Activity); Testing Program; Testing Program MP3s; reference tools

1 Suggestion Have pairs act out their conversations for the rest of the class.

2 Suggestion Before students begin to make corrections on their classmates' papers, tell them to check the following: correct use of articles and subject pronouns, subject-verb agreement, and adjective agreement.

3 Expansion Have students repeat the activity and describe their differences this time.

4 Suggestion Distribute the **Feuilles d'activités**, found in the Activity Pack on the Supersite. Because this is the first activity in which the **Feuilles d'activités** are used, tell students that they use the **feuilles** to complete the corresponding activity. Explain that they must approach their classmates with their paper in hand and ask questions following the **modèle**. When they find someone who answers affirmatively, that student signs his or her name.

5 Expansion Have a few volunteers read their descriptions to the class. Then ask the class to point out the differences between the various descriptions.

6 Suggestions
• Divide the class into pairs and distribute the Info Gap Handouts for this activity, found in the Activity Pack on the Supersite. Give students ten minutes to complete the activity.
• Have two volunteers read the **modèle** aloud.

Révision

1 Festival francophone With a partner, choose two characters from the list and act out a conversation between them. The people are meeting for the first time at a francophone festival. Then, change characters and repeat. Answers will vary.

Angélique, Sénégal

Abdel, Algérie

Laurent, Martinique

Sylvain, Suisse

Hélène, Canada

Daniel, France

Mai, Viêt-Nam

Nora, Maroc

2 Tu ou vous? How would the conversations between the characters in **Activité 1** differ if they were all 19-year-old students at a university orientation? Write out what you would have said differently. Then, exchange papers with a new partner and make corrections. Return the paper to your partner and act out the conversation using a different character from last time. Answers will vary.

3 En commun In pairs, tell your partner the name of a friend. Use adjectives to say what you both (**tous les deux**) have in common. Then, share with the class what you learned about your partner and his or her friend. Answers will vary.

MODÈLE

Charles est un ami. Nous sommes tous les deux amusants. Nous sommes patients aussi.

4 Comment es-tu? Your instructor will give you a worksheet. Survey as many classmates as possible to ask if they would use the adjectives listed to describe themselves. Then, decide which two students in the class are most similar. Answers will vary.

MODÈLE

Étudiant(e) 1: *Tu es timide?*
Étudiant(e) 2: *Non. Je suis sociable.*

Adjectifs	Nom
1. timide	Éric
2. impatient (e)	
3. optimiste	
4. réservé (e)	
5. charmant (e)	
6. poli (e)	
7. agréable	
8. amusant (e)	

5 Mes camarades de classe Write a brief description of the students in your French class. What are their names? What are their personalities like? What is their heritage? Use all the French you have learned so far. Your paragraph should be at least eight sentences long. Remember, be complimentary! Answers will vary.

6 Les descriptions Your instructor will give you one set of drawings of eight people and a different set to your partner. Each person in your drawings has something in common with a person in your partner's drawings. Find out what it is without looking at your partner's sheet. Answers will vary.

MODÈLE

Étudiant(e) 1: *Jean est à la bibliothèque.*
Étudiant(e) 2: *Gina est à la bibliothèque.*
Étudiant(e) 1: *Jean et Gina sont à la bibliothèque.*

36 *trente-six*

OPTIONS

Small Groups Have students work in groups of three or four. Tell them to prepare a skit on any situation they wish, provided that they use material presented in this lesson. Possible situations can include meeting at a café (as in **Roman-photo**), meeting in between classes, and introducing friends to professors. Remind them to use as many adjectives as possible. Encourage students to have fun with the skit and be creative.

Extra Practice To practice **vous**, have students ask you yes/no questions. First, have them guess your nationality. Example: **Vous êtes français(e)?** Then have them ask you about your personality. Example: **Vous êtes impatient(e)?**

À l'écoute

Audio: Activities

NATIONAL communication STANDARDS

STRATÉGIE

Listening for words you know

You can get the gist of a conversation by listening for words and phrases you already know.

To help you practice this strategy, listen to this sentence and make a list of the words you have already learned.

_____ _____

_____ _____

Préparation

Look at the photograph. Where are these people? What are they doing? In your opinion, do they know one another? Why or why not? What do you think they're talking about?

À vous d'écouter

As you listen, circle the items you associate with Hervé and those you associate with Laure and Lucas.

HERVÉ	LAURE ET LUCAS
la littérature	le café
l'examen	la littérature
le bureau	la sociologie
le café	la librairie
la bibliothèque	le lycée
la librairie	l'examen
le tableau	l'université

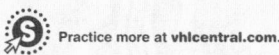

Practice more at **vhlcentral.com**.

Compréhension

Vrai ou faux? Based on the conversation you heard, indicate whether each of the following statements is **vrai** or **faux**.

	Vrai	Faux
1. Lucas and Hervé are good friends.	☐	☑
2. Hervé is preparing for an exam.	☑	☐
3. Laure and Lucas know each other from school.	☑	☐
4. Hervé is on his way to the library.	☐	☑
5. Lucas and Laure are going to a café.	☑	☐
6. Lucas studies literature.	☐	☑
7. Laure is in high school.	☐	☑
8. Laure is not feeling well today.	☐	☑

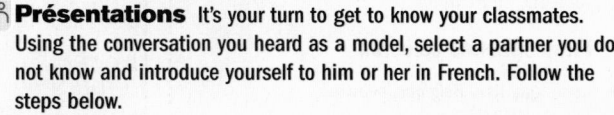

Présentations It's your turn to get to know your classmates. Using the conversation you heard as a model, select a partner you do not know and introduce yourself to him or her in French. Follow the steps below.

- Greet your partner.
- Find out his or her name.
- Ask how he or she is doing.
- Introduce your partner to another student.
- Say good-bye.

Section Goals

In this section, students will:
- learn to listen for known vocabulary
- listen to sentences containing familiar and unfamiliar vocabulary
- listen to a conversation and complete several activities

Instructional Resources
vhlcentral.com: Textbook MP3s; Textbook Audioscript; reference tools

Stratégie
Audioscript Je vous présente une amie, Juliette Lenormand. Elle étudie la sociologie à la faculté.

Successful Language Learning Reassure your students that many people feel nervous about their ability to understand what they hear in a foreign language. Tell them that following the advice in the **Stratégie** sections will help to increase their listening comprehension.

Préparation Have students look at the photo and describe what they see. Ask them to justify their responses based on the visual clues.

À vous d'écouter Audioscript
HERVÉ: Salut, Laure! Ça va?
LAURE: Bonjour, Hervé. Ça va bien. Et toi?
HERVÉ: Pas mal, merci.
LAURE: Je te présente un copain de l'université. Lucas, Hervé. Hervé, Lucas.
LUCAS: Enchanté.
H: Bonjour, Lucas. Comment vas-tu?
LU: Très bien, merci.
LA: Qu'est-ce que tu fais, Hervé?
H: Je vais à la librairie pour acheter un livre sur la littérature.
LA: Pour un examen?
H: Oui, pour un examen. Et vous?
LA: Nous, on va au café.
H: Alors, à plus tard.
LA: Oui, salut.
LU: Au revoir, Hervé.
H: À bientôt.

Section Goals

In this section, students will:
- read statistics and cultural information about the French language and the francophone world
- learn historical and cultural information about Québec, Louisiana, and Algeria

Instructional Resources
vhlcentral.com; Digital Image Bank; SAM Answer Key; reference tools

Carte du monde francophone
Have students look at the map in their books, or display the map from the Digital Image Bank. Ask students to identify the continents where French is spoken. Then ask them to make inferences about why French is spoken in these regions.

Les pays en chiffres
- Call on volunteers to read the sections. Point out cognates and clarify unfamiliar words.
- After reading **Francophones célèbres**, ask students if they know any additional information about these people.

Francophones célèbres
Ask students if they know of other Francophone celebrities, e.g. Édith Piaf, Chopin, Jacques Brel.

Incroyable mais vrai!
French is one of the official languages of UNESCO, which is the United Nations Educational, Scientific and Cultural Organization. UNESCO not only builds classrooms in impoverished countries, but it also brings nations together on social issues.

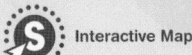

Interactive Map

SAVOIR-FAIRE

Panorama

Le monde francophone

Les pays en chiffres°

Organisation internationale de la Francophonie

▶ Nombre de pays° où le français est langue° officielle: *29*

▶ Nombre de pays où le français est parlé°: *plus de° 60*

▶ Nombre de francophones dans le monde°: *274.000.000 (deux cent soixante-quatorze millions)*

SOURCE: Organisation internationale de la Francophonie

Les pays francophones

▶ **Amérique du Nord:** *Canada (La Province de Québec), Haïti*

▶ **Europe:** *France, Belgique, Luxembourg, Monaco, Suisse*

▶ **Afrique:** *Maroc, Algérie, Tunisie, Bénin, Burkina-Faso, Côte-d'Ivoire, Guinée, Mali, Mauritanie, Niger, Sénégal, Togo, Burundi, Cameroun, Congo, Gabon, République centrafricaine, République démocratique du Congo (RDC), Rwanda, Tchad, Madagascar*

▶ **Asie:** *Laos, Viêt-Nam, Cambodge*

▶ **Océanie:** *Îles Australes, Îles de la Société, Îles Gambier, Îles Marquises, Îles Tuamotu*

▶ **Les départements et régions d'outre-mer:** *Guadeloupe, Guyane française, Martinique, Mayotte, La Réunion*

Francophones célèbres

▶ René Magritte, *Belgique, peintre° (1898–1967)*

▶ Jean Reno, *Maroc, acteur (1948–)*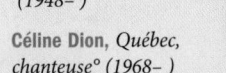

▶ 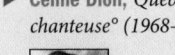 Céline Dion, *Québec, chanteuse° (1968–)*

▶  Marie-José Pérec, *Guadeloupe, coureuse° olympique (1968–)*

chiffres *numbers* **pays** *countries* **langue** *language* **parlé** *spoken* **plus de** *more than* **monde** *world* **peintre** *painter* **chanteuse** *singer* **coureuse** *runner* **sur** *on* **comme** *such as* **l'OTAN** *NATO* **Jeux** *Games* **deuxième** *second* **enseignée** *taught* **Heiva** *an annual Tahitian festival*

38 *trente-huit*

Heiva°, Papeete, Tahiti

L'AMÉRIQUE DU NORD

L'EUROPE

LA FRANCE

L'ASIE

L'OCÉAN ATLANTIQUE

L'AFRIQUE

L'OCÉAN PACIFIQUE

L'AMÉRIQUE DU SUD

L'OCÉAN INDIEN

PAYS FRANCOPHONES EN ASIE

LE LAOS

LE CAMBODGE

L'OCÉAN INDIEN

LE VIÊT-NAM

la mosquée de la plage d'Ouakam, Dakar, Sénégal

0 ———— 3,000 miles
0 ———— 3,000 kilomètres

■ Pays et régions francophones

Incroyable mais vrai!

La langue française est une des rares langues à être parlées sur° cinq continents. C'est aussi la langue officielle de beaucoup d'organisations internationales comme° l'OTAN°, les Nations unies, l'Union européenne, et aussi des Jeux° Olympiques! Le français est la deuxième° langue enseignée° dans le monde, après l'anglais.

OPTIONS

Francophones célèbres René Magritte was one of the most prominent surrealist painters. His work had a major impact on other artists and artistic movements, and remains influential today. **Jean Reno** has played a variety of roles in French and American films.

Céline Dion has received Grammy awards in the U.S., Juno and Felix awards in Canada, and World Music Awards in Europe for her vocal talents. **Marie-José Pérec** is the first sprinter to win consecutive gold medals in the 400-meter dash.

La société

Le français au Québec

Au Québec, province du Canada, le français est la langue officielle, parlée par° 82% (quatre-vingt-deux pour cent) de la population. Les Québécois, pour° préserver l'usage de la langue, ont° une loi° qui oblige l'affichage° en français dans les lieux° publics. Le français est aussi la langue co-officielle du Canada: les employés du gouvernement doivent° être bilingues.

Les gens

Les francophones d'Algérie

Depuis° 1830 (mille huit cent trente), date de l'acquisition de l'Algérie par la France, l'influence culturelle française y° est très importante. À présent ancienne° colonie, l'Algérie est un des plus grands° pays francophones au monde. L'arabe est la langue officielle, mais le français est la deuxième langue parlée et est compris° par la majorité de la population algérienne.

Les destinations

La Louisiane

Ce territoire au sud° des États-Unis a été nommé° «Louisiane» en l'honneur du Roi° de France Louis XIV. En 1803 (mille huit cent trois), Napoléon Bonaparte vend° la colonie aux États-Unis pour 15 millions de dollars, pour empêcher° son acquisition par les Britanniques. Aujourd'hui° en Louisiane, 200.000 (deux cent mille) personnes parlent° le français cajun. La Louisiane est connue° pour sa° cuisine cajun, comme° le jambalaya, ici sur° la photo avec le chef Paul Prudhomme, qui était très célèbre pour ses livres de cuisine cajun et qui est mort en 2015.

Les traditions

La Journée internationale de la Francophonie

Chaque année°, l'Organisation internationale de la Francophonie (O.I.F.) coordonne la Journée internationale de la Francophonie. Dans plus de° 100 (cent) pays et sur cinq continents, on célèbre la langue française et la diversité culturelle francophone avec des festivals de musique, de gastronomie, de théâtre, de danse et de cinéma. Le rôle principal de l'O.I.F. est la promotion de la langue française et la défense de la diversité culturelle et linguistique du monde francophone.

LE POUVOIR DES MOTS

Journée internationale de la Francophonie
20 mars 2016

Libres ensemble
Respect
Solidarité
Diversité

www.20mars.francophonie.org

ORGANISATION INTERNATIONALE DE la francophonie

Qu'est-ce que vous avez appris? Complete the sentences.

1. __René Magritte__ est un peintre belge.
2. __274 millions__ de personnes parlent français dans le monde.
3. __L'Organisation internationale de la Francophonie__ est responsable de la promotion de la diversité culturelle francophone.
4. Les employés du gouvernement du Canada parlent __anglais et français__.
5. En Algérie, la langue officielle est __l'arabe__.

6. Une majorité d'Algériens comprend (*understands*) __le français__.
7. Le nom «Louisiane» vient du (*comes from the*) nom de __Louis XIV__.
8. Plus de 100 pays célèbrent __la Journée internationale de la Francophonie__.
9. Le français est parlé sur __cinq__ continents.
10. En 1803, Napoléon Bonaparte vend __la Louisiane__ aux États-Unis.

Sur Internet

Go to **vhlcentral.com** to find more cultural information related to this **Panorama**.

1. Les États-Unis célèbrent la Journée internationale de la Francophonie. Faites (*Make*) une liste de trois événements (*events*) et dites (*say*) où ils ont lieu (*take place*).
2. Trouvez des informations sur un(e) chanteur/chanteuse francophone célèbre aux États-Unis. Citez (*Cite*) trois titres de chanson (*song titles*).

ressources

WB
pp. 13–14

vhlcentral

parlée par *spoken by* pour *in order to* ont *have* loi *law* affichage *posting* lieux *places* doivent *must* Depuis *Since* y *there* ancienne *former* un des plus grands *one of the largest* compris *understood* au sud *in the South* a été nommé *was named* Roi *King* vend *sells* empêcher *to prevent* Aujourd'hui *Today* parlent *speak* connue *known* sa *its* comme *such as* sur *in* Chaque année *Each year* Dans plus de *In more than*

trente-neuf **39**

Le français au Québec Since Jacques Cartier first arrived in the Gaspé and claimed the land for the French king in 1534, the people of Quebec have maintained their language and culture, despite being outnumbered and surrounded by English speakers. French became an official language of Canada in 1867. Ask students if they know of any places in the United States where people speak two languages or there are bilingual signs.

Les francophones d'Algérie Algeria gained its independence from France in 1962, but French is still taught from primary school through high school. French is principally used in business relations, some social situations, and in the information industries. Some newspapers, as well as several television and radio broadcasts, are produced in French.

La Louisiane The early settlers of Louisiana came from France and Acadia (now Nova Scotia and adjacent areas) during the seventeenth and eighteenth centuries. The Acadian settlers were descendents of French Canadians who were exiled from Acadia by the English and eventually settled in the bayou region. Cajun French evolved over time, borrowing terms from American Indian and African languages, and German, English, and Spanish speakers.

La Journée internationale de la Francophonie
- The members of **l'Organisation internationale de la Francophonie** comprise 63 states and governments. The celebrations in the various Francophone regions take place throughout the month of March. The name **20 mars** was chosen to commemorate the signature of a treaty which created **l'Agence intergouvernementale de la Francophonie**.
- Point out the symbol of **l'Organisation internationale de la Francophonie** on page 38 next to the heading **Les pays en chiffres**.

O P T I O N S

Pairs Have students work in pairs. Tell them to look at the maps in **Appendice A**, choose 2 countries from each continent in the **Les pays francophones** list, and look for their capital cities.

Cultural Comparison In groups of three, have students compare **la Journée internationale de la Francophonie** to a cultural celebration held in their town, city, or country. Tell them to discuss the purpose of each celebration, the reasons why people attend them, and the types of events or activities that are part of the celebration.

Section Goals

In this section, students will:
• learn to recognize cognates
• use context to guess the meaning of new words
• read some pages from an address book in French

Stratégie Tell students that cognates are words in one language that have identical or similar counterparts in another language. True cognates are close in meaning, so recognizing French words that are cognates of English words can help them read French. To help students recognize cognates, write these common correspondences between French and English on the board: -ie = -y (**sociologie**); -ique = -ic (**fantastique**); -if(-ive) = -ive (**active**).

Successful Language Learning Tell students that reading in French will be less anxiety provoking if they follow the advice in the **Stratégie** sections, which are designed to reinforce and improve reading comprehension skills.

Examinez le texte Ask students to tell you what type of text this is and how they can tell. (It's an excerpt from an address book. You can tell because it contains names and telephone numbers.)

Mots apparentés
• Check to see if students found all of the cognates from the **Stratégie** box in the reading: **pharmacie, dentiste, télévision, médecin, banque,** and **restaurant**.
• If students are having trouble finding other cognates in the reading, point out a few to get them started: **route** (route), **avenue** (avenue), **boulevard** (boulevard), **théâtre** (theater), **comédie** (comedy), **dîner** (dinner), and **municipale** (municipal).
• Point out false cognates like **librairie** (bookstore).

Devinez Ask volunteers to share their responses with the class. Find out how many were able to guess the meanings correctly: **horaires** (schedule [hours open]), **lundi** (Monday), **ouvert** (open), **soirs** (evenings; nights), and **tous** (all; every).

Lecture

S Audio: Reading

Avant la lecture

STRATÉGIE

Recognizing cognates

Cognates are words that share similar meanings and spellings in two or more languages. When reading in French, it's helpful to look for cognates and use them to guess the meaning of what you're reading. However, watch out for false cognates. For example, **librairie** means *bookstore*, not *library*, and **coin** means *corner*, not *coin*. Look at this list of French words. Can you guess the meaning of each word?

important	banque
pharmacie	culture
intelligent	actif
dentiste	sociologie
décision	fantastique
télévision	restaurant
médecine	police

Examinez le texte

Briefly look at the document. What kind of information is listed? In what order is it listed? Where do you usually find such information? Can you guess what this document is?

Mots apparentés

Read the list of cognates in the **Stratégie** box again. How many cognates can you find in the reading selection? Are there additional cognates in the reading? Which ones? Can you guess their English equivalents?

Devinez

In addition to using cognates and words you already know, you can also use context to guess the meaning of words you do not know. Find the following words in the reading selection and try to guess what they mean. Compare your answers with those of a classmate.

horaires	lundi	ouvert	soirs	tous

40 *quarante*

Carnet d'adresses

Carnet d'adresses

Recherche ▶

A B C D E F G H I J K

☑ **DAMERY Jean-Claude**
dentiste
✉ 18, rue des Lilas   02 38 23 45 46
45000 Orléans

☐ **Café de la Poste**
Ouvert° tous les jours°, de 7h00° à 22h00
✉ 25, place de la Poste   02 38 27 18 00
45000 Orléans

☐ **Librairie Balzac**
Horaires: 9h00–12h00 et 14h00–18h00
✉ 18, route de Lorient   02 38 18 60 36
45000 Orléans

☐ **DANTEC Pierre-Henri**
médecin généraliste
✉ 23, rue du Lac   02 38 47 34 20
45000 Orléans

☑ **Banque du Centre**
Ouvert de 9h00 à 17h00 du lundi° au vendredi°
✉ 17, boulevard Giroud   02 38 58 35 00
45000 Orléans

Dîner vendredi 8h00
Restaurant du Chat qui dort

O P T I O N S

Extra Practice Write these words on the board and have students guess the English meaning: **un agent** (agent), **un concert** (concert), **la géographie** (geography), **une guitare** (guitar), **la musique** (music), **un réfrigérateur** (refrigerator), **confortable** (comfortable), **courageux** (courageous), **riche** (rich), and **typique** (typical). Then have them look at the **Vocabulaire** on page 44 and identify all the cognates they have learned.

Small Groups Have students work in groups of three or four. Assign four letters of the alphabet to each group. (Adjust the number of letters according to your class size so that the entire alphabet is covered.) Tell students to use a French-English dictionary and make a list of all the cognates they find beginning with their assigned letters. Have groups read their list of cognates to the rest of the class.

Après la lecture

Où aller? Tell where each of these people should go based on what they need or want to do.

MODÈLE

Camille's daughter is starting high school.
Lycée Molière

1. Mrs. Leroy needs to deposit her paycheck.
   Banque du Centre

2. Laurent would like to take his girlfriend out for a special dinner.
   Restaurant du Chat qui dort

3. Marc has a toothache.
   DAMERY Jean-Claude, dentiste

4. Céleste would like to go see a play tonight.
   Théâtre de la Comédie

5. Pauline's computer is broken.
   Messier et fils, Réparations ordinateurs et télévisions

6. Mr. Duchemin needs to buy some aspirin for his son.
   Pharmacie Vidal

7. Jean-Marie needs a book on French history but he doesn't want to buy one.
   Bibliothèque municipale

8. Noémie thinks she has the flu.
   DANTEC Pierre-Henri, médecin généraliste

9. Mr. and Mrs. Prudhomme want to go out for breakfast this morning.
   Café de la Poste

10. Jonathan wants to buy a new book for his sister's birthday.
    Librairie Balzac

Notre annuaire With a classmate, select three of the listings from the reading and use them as models to create similar listings in French advertising places or services in your area.

MODÈLE

Restaurant du Chat qui dort
Ouvert tous les soirs pour le dîner
Horaires: 19h00 à 23h00
29, avenue des Rosiers
45000 Orléans
02 38 45 35 08

Always Good Eats Restaurant
Ouvert tous les jours
Horaires: 6h00 à 19h00
1250 9th Avenue
San Diego, CA 92108
224-0932

11:29 AM ?

Contacts | **Éditer**

Q R S T U V W X Y Z

☐ **Messier et fils°**
Réparations ordinateurs et télévisions
✉ 56, boulevard Henri IV   02 38 44 42 59
45000 Orléans

☐ **Théâtre de la Comédie**
✉ 11, place de la Comédie   02 38 45 32 11
45000 Orléans

☐ **Pharmacie Vidal**
✉ 45, rue des Acacias   02 38 13 57 53
45000 Orléans

☐ **Restaurant du Chat qui dort°**
Ouvert tous les soirs pour le dîner / Horaires: 19h00 à 23h00
✉ 29, avenue des Rosiers   02 38 45 35 08
45000 Orléans

☑ **Bibliothèque municipale**
✉ Place de la gare   02 38 56 43 22
45000 Orléans

☑ **Lycée Molière**
✉ 15, rue Molière   02 38 29 23 04
45000 Orléans

Ouvert *Open* **tous les jours** *every day* **7h00 (sept heures)** *7:00* **lundi** *Monday* **vendredi** *Friday* **fils** *son(s)* **Chat qui dort** *Sleeping cat*

Où aller? Go over the activity with the class. If students have trouble inferring the answer to any question, help them identify the cognate or provide additional context clues.

Notre annuaire
- Before beginning the activity, have students brainstorm places and services in the area, and write a list on the board. You might also want to bring in a few local telephone books for students to use as references for addresses and phone numbers.
- You may wish to have students include e-mail addresses (**les adresses e-mail**) in their lists.

OPTIONS

Pairs To review numbers 0–60, have students work in pairs and take turns asking each other the phone numbers and addresses of the people and places listed in the reading. Example:
Étudiant(e) 1: Le numéro de téléphone du dentiste Jean-Claude DAMERY? Étudiant(e) 2: C'est le zéro deux, trente-huit, vingt-trois, quarante-cinq, quarante-six. Étudiant(e) 1: Et l'adresse? Étudiant(e) 2: Dix-huit, rue des Lilas, Orléans.

Extra Practice Have several students select one of the three listings they created for the **Notre annuaire** activity to read aloud. Instruct the rest of the class to write down the information they hear. To check students' work, have the students who read the listings write the information on the board.

Section Goals

In this section, students will:
- learn strategies for writing in French
- learn to write a telephone/address book in French
- integrate vocabulary and structures taught in **Leçons 1A–1B**

Stratégie Have students focus on the final point under the "Do" section. Ask them to think about the types of writing that most interests them as readers. Why? Is it that the writer supplies vivid detail? Interesting anecdotes? An easy-to-read style? Is it simply that the subject is important to them? This shows the value of putting themselves in their reader's place.

Thème Introduce students to standard headings used in a telephone/address list: **Nom**, **Adresse**, **Numéro de téléphone**, **Numéro de portable**, and **Adresse e-mail**. Students may wish to add notes pertaining to home (**Numéro de domicile**) or office (**Numéro de bureau**) telephone numbers, fax numbers (**Numéro de fax**), or office hours (**Horaires de bureau**).

Écriture

STRATÉGIE

Writing in French

Why do we write? All writing has a purpose. For example, we may write a poem to reveal our innermost feelings, a letter to impart information, or an essay to persuade others to accept a point of view. Proficient writers are not born, however. Writing requires time, thought, effort, and a lot of practice. Here are some tips to help you write more effectively in French.

DO

▶ Write your ideas in French.

▶ Make an outline of your ideas.

▶ Decide what the purpose of your writing will be.

▶ Use the grammar and vocabulary that you know.

▶ Use your textbook for examples of style, format, and expressions in French.

▶ Use your imagination and creativity to make your writing more interesting.

▶ Put yourself in your reader's place to determine if your writing is interesting.

DON'T

▶ Translate your ideas from English to French.

▶ Repeat what is in the textbook or on a web page.

▶ Use a bilingual dictionary until you have learned how to use one effectively.

Thème

Faites une liste!

Avant l'écriture

1. Imagine that several students from a French-speaking country will be spending a year at your school. You've been asked to put together a list of people and places that might be useful and of interest to them. Your list should include:

   - Your name, address, phone number(s) (home and/or cell), and e-mail address

   - The names of four other students in your French class, their addresses, phone numbers, and e-mail addresses

   - Your French teacher's name, office and/or cell phone number(s), e-mail address, as well as his or her office hours

   - Your school library's phone number and hours

   - The names, addresses, and phone numbers of three places near your school where students like to go

2. Write down the names of the classmates you want to include.

3. Interview your classmates and your teacher to find out the information you need to include. Use the following questions and write down their responses.

Informal	Formal
Comment t'appelles-tu?	Comment vous appelez-vous?
Quel est ton numéro de téléphone?	Quel est votre numéro de téléphone?
Quelle est ton adresse e-mail?	Quelle est votre adresse e-mail?

OPTIONS

Stratégie Review the **Do** list with students. Ask them if they have tried any of these tips. Tell them that they should refer back to this list as they complete the **Écriture** tasks in each lesson. Students may also find it helpful to keep track of which tips work best for them.

Avant l'écriture Before students begin writing, brainstorm a list of popular places where students frequently go. Group them by name in different categories, such as **bibliothèques, cafés, restaurants, magasins, théâtres, parcs, librairies**, and so on. Encourage students to incorporate these category headings into their lists, along with the specific names of different businesses that fall into the categories.

4. Think of three places in your community that a group of students from a French-speaking country would enjoy visiting. They could be a library, a bookstore, a coffee shop, a restaurant, a theater, or a park. Find out their e-mail addresses, telephone numbers, and URLs and write them down.

5. Go online and do a search for two websites that promote your town or area's history, culture, and attractions. Write down their URLs.

Écriture

Write your complete list, making sure it includes all the relevant information. It should include at least five people (with their phone numbers and e-mail addresses), four places (with phone numbers and e-mail addresses), and two websites (with URLs). Avoid using a dictionary and just write what you can in French.

Après l'écriture

1. Exchange your list with a partner's. Comment on his or her work by answering these questions.

   - Did your partner include the correct number of people, places, and websites?

   - Did your partner include the pertinent information for each?

NOM: _Madame Smith (professeur de français)_ ☎

ADRESSE: _McNeil University_ ✉

NUMÉRO DE TÉLÉPHONE: _645-3458 (bureau)_
NUMÉRO DE PORTABLE: _919-0040_
ADRESSE E-MAIL: _absmith@yahoo.com_
NOTES: _Heures de bureau: 8h00–9h00_

NOM: _Skate World_
ADRESSE: _8970 McNeil Road_

NUMÉRO DE TÉLÉPHONE: _658-0349_
NUMÉRO DE PORTABLE: _–_
ADRESSE E-MAIL: _skate@skateworld.com_
NOTES: _—_

2. Edit your partner's work, pointing out any spelling or content errors. Notice the use of these editing symbols:

   ℐ   delete

   ∧   insert letter or word(s) written in margin

   | replace letter or word(s) with one(s) in margin

   ≡   change to uppercase

   /   change to lowercase

   ∿   transpose indicated letters or words

Now look at this model of what an edited draft looks like:

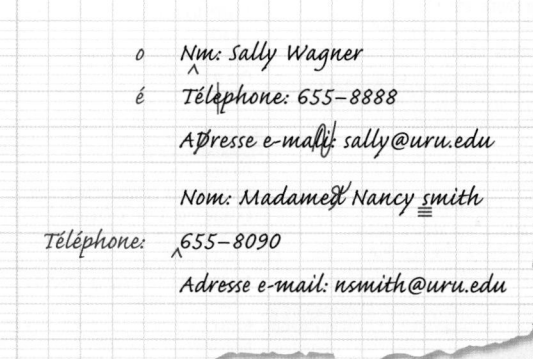

3. Revise your list according to your partner's comments and corrections. After writing the final version, read it one more time to eliminate these kinds of problems:

   - spelling errors
   - punctuation errors
   - capitalization errors
   - use of incorrect verb forms
   - use of incorrect adjective agreement
   - use of incorrect definite and indefinite articles

EVALUATION

Criteria

Content Includes all the information mentioned in the five parts of the task description.
Scale: 1 2 3 4 5

Organization Organizes the list similarly to the model provided.
Scale: 1 2 3 4 5

Accuracy Spells the French words used to designate the list categories correctly, including correct accentuation.
Scale: 1 2 3 4 5

Creativity Includes extra information (such as home, office, and fax numbers), more than three students, more than three places.
Scale: 1 2 3 4 5

Scoring

Excellent	18–20 points
Good	14–17 points
Satisfactory	10–13 points
Unsatisfactory	< 10 points

O P T I O N S

Après l'écriture Share the evaluation rubric with students before they begin writing. Tell them that you will use these criteria to evaluate their work. Be sure you do this for each **Écriture** task in subsequent units so students will have a clear understanding of your expectations for their work before they undertake the writing task.

Extra practice Ask the class to come up with other categories, such as **postes, banques, docteurs, pharmacies**. Then have them complete their address book list with new items falling into these categories.

🔊 Ⓢ Vocabulary Tools

Instructional Resources
vhlcentral.com: Textbook MP3s; Textbook Audioscript; reference tools

Suggestions
- Tell students that this is active vocabulary for which they are responsible and that it will appear on tests and exams.
- Tell them that an easy way to study from **Vocabulaire** is to cover up the French half of each section, leaving only the English equivalents exposed. They can then quiz themselves on the French items. To focus on the English equivalents of the French entries, they simply reverse this process.
- Point out to students that they can use the Vocabulary Tools at **vhlcentral.com** for reference and extra vocabulary practice.

Leçon 1A

Le campus
une bibliothèque *library*
un café *café*
une faculté *university; faculty*
une librairie *bookstore*
un lycée *high school*
une université *university*
une différence *difference*
un examen *exam, test*
la littérature *literature*
un problème *problem*
la sociologie *sociology*
un bureau *desk; office*
un ordinateur *computer*
une table *table*
un tableau *blackboard; painting*
la télévision *television*
une chose *thing*
un instrument *instrument*
un objet *object*

Les personnes
un(e) ami(e) *friend*
un(e) étudiant(e) *student*
un(e) petit(e) ami(e) *boyfriend/ girlfriend*
une personne *person*
un acteur/une actrice *actor*
un chanteur/une chanteuse *singer*
un professeur *teacher, professor*

Les présentations
Comment vous appelez-vous? (*form.*)
    What is your name?
Comment t'appelles-tu? (*fam.*)
    What is your name?
Enchanté(e). *Delighted.*
Et vous/toi? (*form./fam.*) *And you?*
Je m'appelle... *My name is...*
Je vous/te présente... (*form./fam.*) *I would like to introduce (name) to you.*

Identifier
c'est/ce sont *it's/they are*
Combien...? *How much/many...?*
ici *here*
là *there*
là-bas *over there*
Il y a... *There is/are...*
Qu'est-ce que c'est? *What is it?*
voici *here is/are*
voilà *there is/are*

Bonjour et au revoir
À bientôt. *See you soon.*
À demain. *See you tomorrow.*
À plus tard. *See you later.*
À tout à l'heure. *See you later.*
Au revoir. *Good-bye.*
Bonne journée! *Have a good day!*
Bonjour. *Good morning.; Hello.*
Bonsoir. *Good evening.; Hello.*
Salut! *Hi!; Bye!*

Comment ça va?
Ça va? *What's up?; How are things?*
Comment allez-vous? (*form.*) *How are you?*
Comment vas-tu? (*fam.*) *How are you?*
Comme ci, comme ça. *So-so.*
Je vais bien/mal. *I am doing well/ badly.*
Moi aussi. *Me too.*
Pas mal. *Not badly.*
Très bien. *Very well.*

Expressions de politesse
De rien. *You're welcome.*
Excusez-moi. (*form.*) *Excuse me.*
Excuse-moi. (*fam.*) *Excuse me.*
Il n'y a pas de quoi. *It's nothing ; You're welcome.*
Je vous en prie. (*form.*) *Please.; You're welcome.*
Merci beaucoup. *Thank you very much.*
Monsieur (M.) *Sir (Mr.)*
Madame (Mme) *Ma'am (Mrs.)*
Mademoiselle (Mlle) *Miss*
Pardon. *Pardon (me).*
S'il vous/te plaît. (*form./fam.*) *Please.*

Expressions utiles
See p. 7.

Numbers 0–60
See p. 14.

Leçon 1B

Le campus
une salle de classe *classroom*
un dictionnaire *dictionary*
un livre *book*
un résultat *result*
une carte *map*
une chaise *chair*
une fenêtre *window*
une horloge *clock*
une porte *door*
un cahier *notebook*
une calculatrice *calculator*
une corbeille (à papier) *wastebasket*
un crayon *pencil*
une feuille de papier *sheet of paper*
une montre *watch*
un sac à dos *backpack*
un stylo *pen*

Les personnes
un(e) camarade de chambre *roommate*
un(e) camarade de classe *classmate*
une classe *class (group of students)*
un copain/une copine (*fam.*) *friend*
un(e) élève *pupil, student*
une femme *woman*
une fille *girl*
un garçon *boy*
un homme *man*

Identifier
Qui est-ce? *Who is it?*
Quoi? *What?*

Expressions utiles
See p. 25.

Subject pronouns
je *I*
tu *you*
il *he/it (masc.)*
elle *she/it (fem.)*
on *one*
nous *we*
vous *you*
ils *they (masc.)*
elles *they (fem.)*

Être
je suis *I am*
tu es *you are*
il/elle est *he/she/it is*
on est *one is*
nous sommes *we are*
vous êtes *you are*
ils/elles sont *they are*

Descriptive adjectives
agréable *pleasant*
amusant(e) *fun*
brillant(e) *brilliant*
charmant(e) *charming*
désagréable *unpleasant*
différent(e) *different*
difficile *difficult*
égoïste *selfish*
élégante(e) *elegant*
impatient(e) *impatient*
important(e) *important*
indépendant(e) *independent*
intelligent(e) *intelligent*
intéressant(e) *interesting*
occupé(e) *busy*
optimiste *optimistic*
patient(e) *patient*
pessimiste *pessimistic*
poli(e) *polite*
réservé(e) *reserved*
sincère *sincere*
sociable *sociable*
sympathique (sympa) *nice*
timide *shy*

Adjectives of nationality
algérien(ne) *Algerian*
allemand(e) *German*
américain(e) *American*
anglais(e) *English*
canadien(ne) *Canadian*
espagnol(e) *Spanish*
français(e) *French*
italien(ne) *Italian*
japonais(e) *Japanese*
marocain(e) *Moroccan*
martiniquais(e) *from Martinique*
mexicain(e) *Mexican*
québécois(e) *from Quebec*
sénégalais(e) *Senegalese*
suisse *Swiss*
vietnamien(ne) *Vietnamese*

44 *quarante-quatre*

À la fac

Unit Goals

Leçon 2A

In this lesson, students will learn:

- terms for courses and places at the university
- to express likes and dislikes
- about liaisons
- about the French university system and **l'Université Laval**
- more about university life through specially shot video footage
- the present tense of regular -er verbs
- about spelling changes in -cer and -ger verbs
- to ask questions and express negation
- about the University of Moncton in Canada

Leçon 2B

In this lesson, students will learn:

- terms for talking about schedules and when things happen
- to pronounce the French r
- about university courses and **le bac** in France
- about famous French singer and songwriter Francis Cabrel
- the present tense of **avoir**
- some expressions with **avoir**
- to tell time
- to listen for cognates

Savoir-faire

In this section, students will learn:

- cultural, economic, geographical, and historical information about France
- to use text formats to predict content
- to brainstorm before writing
- to write a personal description

Pour commencer

- b. un stylo
- b. un ordinateur
- a. intelligent
- c. étudier

Pour commencer

- What object is on the table?
  a. une montre   b. un stylo   c. un tableau
- What is Rachid looking at?
  a. un cahier   b. un ordinateur   c. un livre
- How does Rachid look in this photo?
  a. intelligent   b. sociable   c. égoïste
- Which word describes what he is doing?
  a. arriver   b. voyager   c. étudier

RESOURCES

Student Activities Manual (SAM):
Workbook Activities, pp. 15–28;
Lab Activities, pp. 9–16;
Video Activities, pp. 5–8; pp. 63–64
SAM Answer Key

vhlcentral.com: Textbook MP3s; Lab MP3s;
Textbook Audioscript; Lab Audioscript; Video;
Videoscript; **Roman-photo** Translations;
Vocabulaire supplémentaire; Activity Pack
(including **Feuilles d'activités**, Info Gap Activities,
and Task-based Activities);

Le Zapping TV clip transcription; **Essayez!** and
Mise en pratique answers; Digital Image Bank;
Testing Program; Testing Program MP3s

Section Goals

In this section, students will learn and practice vocabulary related to:

- courses and fields of study
- places at the university
- expressing likes and dislikes

Instructional Resources

*vhlcentral.com: Digital Image Bank (including vocabulary illustrations from the textbook, theme-based illustrations); **Vocabulaire supplémentaire; Mise en pratique** answers, Textbook Audioscript; Lab Audioscript; Activity Pack (**Feuilles d'activités**); Textbook MP3s; Lab MP3s; SAM Answer Key; reference tools*

Suggestions

- Have students look at the new vocabulary and identify cognates. Say the words and have students guess the meaning. Point out that the words **lettres** and **note** are **faux amis** in this context.
- Call students' attention to the pronunciation of **ps** in **psychologie**.
- Point out that abbreviations, such as **sciences po** and **resto U**, are common. For more examples, see **Le français quotidien** on page 53.
- Explain that many of the adjectives they learned for nationalities in **Leçon 1B** are also used for languages and language classes. Examples: **le cours de français (d'anglais, d'italien)**
- Introduce vocabulary for expressing likes and dislikes by talking about your own. Use facial and hand gestures to convey meaning. Examples: **J'adore la littérature française. J'aime bien l'histoire. Je n'aime pas tellement la biologie. Je déteste l'informatique.**
- Use the Vocabulary illustrations and the School and university illustrations from the Digital Image Bank to help students familiarize themselves with courses and fields of study, places at the university, and expressing likes and dislikes.
- Additional vocabulary for this lesson can be found in the **Vocabulaire supplémentaire** on the Supersite.

Leçon 2A

You will learn how to...

- talk about your classes
- ask questions and express negation

🅢 Vocabulary Tools

Les cours

Vocabulaire

J'aime bien...	I like...
Je n'aime pas tellement...	I don't like... very much
être reçu(e) à un examen	to pass an exam
l'art (*m.*)	art
la chimie	chemistry
le droit	law
l'éducation physique (*f.*)	physical education
la géographie	geography
la gestion	business administration
les lettres (*f.*)	humanities
la philosophie	philosophy
les sciences (politiques/po) (*f.*)	(political) science
une bourse	scholarship, grant
un cours	class, course
un devoir; les devoirs	homework
un diplôme	diploma, degree
l'école (*f.*)	school
les études (supérieures) (*f.*)	(higher) education; studies
le gymnase	gymnasium
une note	grade
un restaurant universitaire (un resto U)	university cafeteria
difficile	difficult
facile	easy
inutile	useless
utile	useful
surtout	especially; above all

ressources

WB pp. 15–16 | LM p. 9 | 🅢 vhlcentral

OPTIONS

Extra Practice Ask students questions using the new vocabulary words. Examples: **La physique, c'est facile ou difficile? Une bourse, c'est utile ou inutile?**

Extra Practice Have them brainstorm adjectives that can describe their courses: **facile, difficile, utile, inutile, intéressant, amusant, agréable, différent,** and **important**. Ask students to describe various courses. Example: **Le cours de philosophie est difficile.**

Game Divide the class into teams. Say the name of a course in English and ask one team to say it in French. If the team is correct, it gets a point. If not, the other team gets a chance to say it and "steal" the point. Alternate giving words to the two teams.

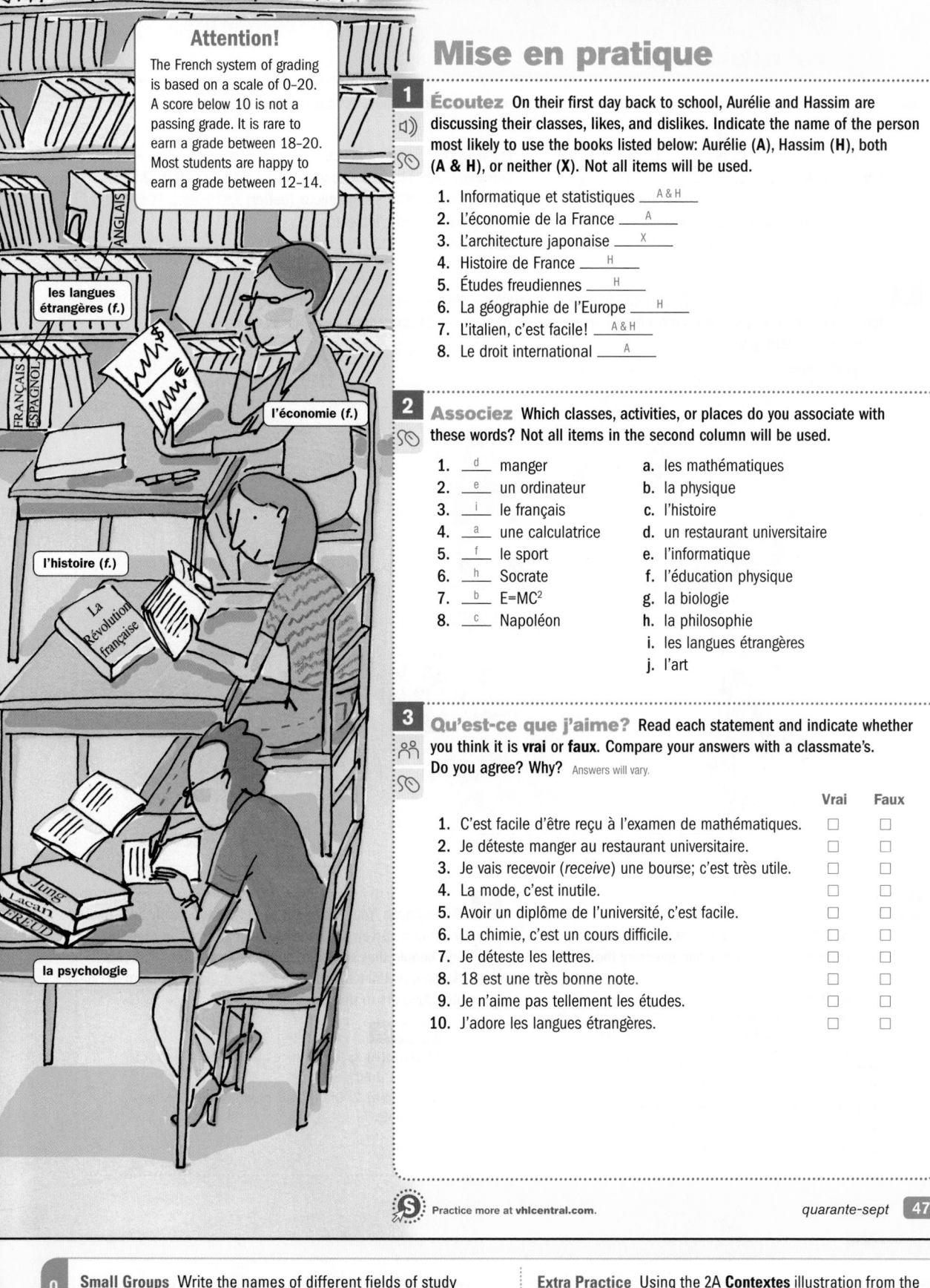

Attention!

The French system of grading is based on a scale of 0–20. A score below 10 is not a passing grade. It is rare to earn a grade between 18–20. Most students are happy to earn a grade between 12–14.

les langues étrangères (f.)

l'économie (f.)

l'histoire (f.)

la psychologie

Mise en pratique

1 Écoutez On their first day back to school, Aurélie and Hassim are discussing their classes, likes, and dislikes. Indicate the name of the person most likely to use the books listed below: Aurélie (**A**), Hassim (**H**), both (**A & H**), or neither (**X**). Not all items will be used.

1. Informatique et statistiques ___A & H___
2. L'économie de la France ___A___
3. L'architecture japonaise ___X___
4. Histoire de France ___H___
5. Études freudiennes ___H___
6. La géographie de l'Europe ___H___
7. L'italien, c'est facile! ___A & H___
8. Le droit international ___A___

2 Associez Which classes, activities, or places do you associate with these words? Not all items in the second column will be used.

1. _d_ manger
2. _e_ un ordinateur
3. _i_ le français
4. _a_ une calculatrice
5. _f_ le sport
6. _h_ Socrate
7. _b_ E=MC²
8. _c_ Napoléon

  a. les mathématiques
  b. la physique
  c. l'histoire
  d. un restaurant universitaire
  e. l'informatique
  f. l'éducation physique
  g. la biologie
  h. la philosophie
  i. les langues étrangères
  j. l'art

3 Qu'est-ce que j'aime? Read each statement and indicate whether you think it is **vrai** or **faux**. Compare your answers with a classmate's. Do you agree? Why? Answers will vary.

	Vrai	Faux
1. C'est facile d'être reçu à l'examen de mathématiques.	☐	☐
2. Je déteste manger au restaurant universitaire.	☐	☐
3. Je vais recevoir (receive) une bourse; c'est très utile.	☐	☐
4. La mode, c'est inutile.	☐	☐
5. Avoir un diplôme de l'université, c'est facile.	☐	☐
6. La chimie, c'est un cours difficile.	☐	☐
7. Je déteste les lettres.	☐	☐
8. 18 est une très bonne note.	☐	☐
9. Je n'aime pas tellement les études.	☐	☐
10. J'adore les langues étrangères.	☐	☐

Ⓢ Practice more at **vhlcentral.com**.

quarante-sept **47**

1 Audioscript AURÉLIE: Bonjour, Hassim. Comment ça va?
HASSIM: Bien. Et toi?
A: Pas mal, merci.
H: Tu aimes le cours d'informatique?
A: Oui, j'adore et j'aime bien l'économie et le droit aussi.
H: Moi, je n'aime pas tellement l'informatique, c'est difficile. J'aime l'histoire, la géographie et la psychologie. C'est très intéressant.
A: Tu aimes la gestion?
H: Ah non, je déteste!
A: Mais c'est très utile!
H: Mais non! Les langues, oui, sont utiles. J'aime bien l'italien.
A: Oui, j'adore l'italien, moi aussi!
H: Bon, à tout à l'heure, Aurélie!
A: Oui, à bientôt!
(On Textbook MP3s)

1 Expansion Play the recording again and ask students these true/false statements or write them on the board. 1. **Aurélie n'aime pas le cours d'économie. (Faux.) 2. Hassim déteste le cours de gestion. (Vrai.) 3. Pour Hassim, le cours d'informatique est facile. (Faux.) 4. Hassim aime la psychologie et la géographie. (Vrai.) 5. Aurélie et Hassim aiment bien l'italien. (Vrai.)**

2 Expansion
- Items g. and j. were not used. Ask the class what words they associate with **la biologie** and **l'art**.
- Have students brainstorm a list of famous people that they associate with the following fields: **le stylisme** (Ralph Lauren, Vera Wang); **l'informatique** (Bill Gates, Michael Dell); and **la gestion** (Donald Trump, Lee Iacocca). Then have the class guess the field associated with each of the following people: Louis Pasteur (**la biologie**), Alan Greenspan (**l'économie**), and Maya Angelou (**les lettres**).

3 Expansion Take a class survey of students' responses to each question and tally the results on the board. Ask students which questions are most controversial. Then ask them on which questions they agree. You might want to introduce the expression **être d'accord**, which will be presented later in **Leçon 2A**.

O P T I O N S

Small Groups Write the names of different fields of study across the board (for example, **les langues**, **les sciences naturelles**, **les sciences humaines**, **les cours techniques**). Working in groups of three or four, have students list the courses under the appropriate category.

Extra Practice Using the 2A **Contextes** illustration from the Digital Image Bank, point to various people in the drawing and ask general questions about them. Examples: **Les étudiants sont au resto U? Il aime la physique?**

Communication

NATIONAL communication STANDARDS

4 Suggestion Before doing this activity, complete a similar exchange; scramble the order of the sentences and write them on the board or on a transparency. Tell students to put the sentences in order to make a logical conversation.

5 Suggestion Have several volunteers write their captions on the board.

6 Suggestion For more practice, come up with other names.

7 Suggestions
• Read the **modèle** aloud with a volunteer. Then distribute the **Feuilles d'activités**, found in the Activity Pack on the Supersite.
• Have volunteers share their findings with the class.

4 Conversez In pairs, fill in the blanks according to your own situations. Then, act out the conversation for the class. _Answers will vary._

Étudiant(e) A: ___Salut/Bonjour___, comment ça va?
Étudiant(e) B: ___Ça va (très) bien/Pas mal___. Et toi?
Étudiant(e) A: ___Ça va (très) bien/Pas mal___, merci.
Étudiant(e) B: Est-ce que tu aimes le cours de ___chimie/physique/droit...___?

Étudiant(e) A: J'adore le cours de ___chimie/physique/droit...___
Étudiant(e) B: Moi aussi. Tu aimes ___l'économie/le droit/l'histoire...___?
Étudiant(e) A: Non, j'aime mieux (_better_) ___l'économie/le droit/l'histoire...___
Étudiant(e) B: Bon, à bientôt.
Étudiant(e) A: À ___tout à l'heure/bientôt/plus tard...___

5 Qu'est-ce que c'est? Write a caption for each image, stating where the students are and how they feel about their classes. Then, work with a partner, taking turns to read your captions and guess which image he or she is referring to. _Answers will vary. Suggested answers._

> **MODÈLE**
> C'est le cours de français.
> Le français, c'est facile.

1. C'est le cours d'informatique. L'informatique, je déteste.

2. Être reçu à l'examen / Avoir le diplôme de l'université, c'est difficile.

3. C'est la philosophie. La philosophie, j'adore.

Nietzsche, philosophe allemand...

4. C'est le cours de chimie. La chimie, c'est facile.

5. C'est le cours d'éducation physique / le restaurant universitaire. L'éducation physique / Le restaurant universitaire, je n'aime pas tellement...

6. C'est un devoir d'architecture / de stylisme de mode. L'architecture / Le stylisme de mode, j'aime bien...

6 Vous êtes... Imagine what subjects these celebrities liked and disliked as students. In pairs, take turns playing the role of each one and guessing the answer. _Answers will vary._

> **MODÈLE**
> **Étudiant(e) 1:** J'aime la physique et la chimie, mais je n'aime pas tellement les cours d'économie.
> **Étudiant(e) 2:** Vous êtes Albert Einstein!

• Albert Einstein
• Louis Pasteur
• Barack Obama
• Bill Clinton
• Christian Dior
• Le docteur Phil
• Bill Gates
• Frank Lloyd Wright

7 Sondage Your instructor will give you a worksheet to conduct a survey (**un sondage**). Go around the room to find people that study the subjects listed. Ask what your classmates think about their subjects. Keep a record of their answers to discuss with the class. _Answers will vary._

> **MODÈLE**
> **Étudiant(e) 1:** Jean, est-ce que tu étudies (_do you study_) le droit?
> **Étudiant(e) 2:** Oui. J'aime bien le droit. C'est un cours utile.

OPTIONS

Game Divide the class into two teams. Write names of courses or people on index cards and tape them face down on the board. Play a game of Concentration in which students match courses with an expert in the field. Examples: **le stylisme**/Jean-Paul Gaultier, **l'art**/Claude Monet, and **la philosophie**/Jean-Paul Sartre. As students turn over a card, they must read it aloud. If a player has a match, that player's team collects those cards. When all the cards have been matched, the team with the most cards wins.

Extra Practice To practice expressing likes and dislikes, ask students yes/no and either/or questions. Examples: **Vous aimez bien la psychologie? Vous détestez la géographie? Vous adorez les lettres ou les sciences?**

Les sons et les lettres   Audio

Liaisons

In French, the final sound of a word sometimes links with the first letter of the following word. Consonants at the end of French words are generally silent but are usually pronounced when the word that follows begins with a vowel sound. This linking of sounds is called a liaison.

À tout à l'heure!　　　　　　　**Comment allez-vous?**

An **s** or an **x** in a liaison sounds like the letter **z**.

les étudiants　　**trois élèves**　　**six élèves**　　**deux hommes**

Always make a liaison between a subject pronoun and a verb that begins with a vowel sound; always make a liaison between an article and a noun that begins with a vowel sound.

nous aimons　　**ils ont**　　　　**un étudiant**　　**les ordinateurs**

Always make a liaison between **est** (a form of **être**) and a word that begins with a vowel or a vowel sound. Never make a liaison with the final consonant of a proper name.

Robert est anglais.　　　　　　**Paris est exceptionnelle.**

Never make a liaison with the conjunction **et** (and).

Carole et Hélène　　　　　　**Jacques et Antoinette**

Never make a liaison between a singular noun and an adjective that follows it.

un cours horrible　　　　　　**un instrument élégant**

Prononcez Practice saying these words and expressions aloud.

1. un examen
2. des étudiants
3. les hôtels
4. dix acteurs
5. Paul et Yvette
6. cours important
7. des informations
8. les études
9. deux hommes
10. Bernard aime
11. chocolat italien
12. Louis est

Articulez Practice saying these sentences aloud.

1. Nous aimons les arts.
2. Albert habite à Paris.
3. C'est un objet intéressant.
4. Sylvie est avec Anne.
5. Ils adorent les deux universités.

Dictons Practice reading these sayings aloud.

Les amis de nos amis sont nos amis.[1]

Un hôte non invité doit apporter son siège.[2]

[1] Friends of our friends are our friends.
[2] An uninvited guest must bring his own chair.

ressources

LM p. 10　　vhlcentral

quarante-neuf **49**

Section Goals
In this section, students will learn about liaisons.

Instructional Resources
vhlcentral.com:
Textbook MP3s; Lab MP3s;
SAM Answer Key; Textbook
Audioscript; Lab Audioscript;
reference tools

Suggestions
- Model the pronunciation of each phrase and have students repeat. Explain the liaison for each case.
- Point out expressions with liaison in **Espace contextes** or ask students to find them. Have them repeat after you. Example: **les études**.
- Ask students to provide expressions from **Leçons 1A–1B** that contain a liaison. Examples: **les États-Unis** and **Comment allez-vous?**
- Write the sentences in **Articulez** on the board or on a transparency. Have students listen to the recording and tell you where they hear liaisons. Alternately, have students write the sentences on a sheet of paper, draw lines linking letters that form liaisons, and cross out silent final consonants.
- **Liaisons obligatoires** and **liaisons interdites** will be formally presented in **Leçon 15A**.
- The explanation and exercises are available on the **ESPACES** Supersite. You may want to play them in class so students practice listening to French speakers other than yourself.

Dictons Tell students to pronounce the liaison between **n** and **in** in **non invité**. Have students compare the saying **«Un hôte non invité doit apporter son siège»** with its literal translation. Ask what they think it means figuratively. (Possible answer: People who show up unexpectedly have no right to complain about the service.) Ask: What do the two sayings in this section reveal about French culture?

OPTIONS

Extra Practice Dictate the following phrases with liaisons, saying each one at least two times. Then write them on the board or on a transparency and have students check what they wrote. **1. dix-huit étudiants 2. les mathématiques 3. un cours utile 4. la chimie et l'architecture 5. les langues étrangères**

Extra Practice Here are additional sentences with liaisons to use for oral practice or dictation. **1. Robert et Alex sont anglais. 2. C'est un film très intéressant. 3. Il y a trois enfants. 4. C'est un restaurant italien.**

ESPACE ROMAN-PHOTO

Section Goals

In this section, students will learn functional phrases for talking about their courses.

Instructional Resources
vhlcentral.com:
Roman-photo Video, Videoscript, and Translation; SAM Answer Key; reference tools

Video Recap: Leçon 1B
Ask questions to review the previous **Roman-photo**.
1. Le cours d'histoire est difficile pour Stéphane, n'est-ce pas? (Non, les maths et le français sont difficiles pour Stéphane.)
2. Comment est Sandrine? (égoïste, sociable et charmante)
3. De quelle origine est Amina? (sénégalaise) Et Rachid? (algérienne)
4. Comment est Amina? (charmante, sincère et élégante)
5. Comment est Rachid? (intelligent, poli, modeste, réservé et brillant)

Video Synopsis Rachid and Antoine discuss their political science class. As they are walking, David joins them, and Rachid introduces him. Then Antoine leaves. When the two roommates get to Rachid's car, Sandrine and Amina are waiting for them. The girls ask David about school and his classes. Later, at **Le P'tit Bistrot**, Stéphane joins the four friends and they continue their discussion about classes. Stéphane hates all of his courses.

Suggestions
• Have students predict what they think the episode will be about. Record predictions on the board.
• Have students work in groups of six. Tell them to choose a role and read the **Roman-photo** conversation aloud. Ask one or two groups to act out the conversation for the class.
• After students read the **Roman-photo**, review their predictions and ask which ones were correct. Then ask a few questions to guide them in summarizing this episode.

Trop de devoirs! Video

PERSONNAGES

Amina

Antoine

David

Rachid

Sandrine

Stéphane

ANTOINE Je déteste le cours de sciences po.
RACHID Oh? Mais pourquoi? Je n'aime pas tellement le prof, Monsieur Dupré, mais c'est un cours intéressant et utile!
ANTOINE Tu crois? Moi, je pense que c'est très difficile, et il y a beaucoup de devoirs. Avec Dupré, je travaille, mais je n'ai pas de bons résultats.

RACHID Si on est optimiste et si on travaille, on est reçu à l'examen.
ANTOINE Toi, oui, mais pas moi! Toi, tu es un étudiant brillant! Mais moi, les études, oh, là, là.
DAVID Eh! Rachid! Oh! Est-ce que tu oublies ton coloc?

RACHID Pas du tout, pas du tout. Antoine, voilà, je te présente David, mon colocataire américain.
DAVID Nous partageons un des appartements du P'tit Bistrot.
ANTOINE Le P'tit Bistrot? Sympa!

SANDRINE Salut! Alors, ça va l'université française?
DAVID Bien, oui. C'est différent de l'université américaine, mais c'est intéressant.
AMINA Tu aimes les cours?
DAVID J'aime bien les cours de littérature et d'histoire françaises. Demain on étudie Les Trois Mousquetaires d'Alexandre Dumas.

SANDRINE J'adore Dumas. Mon livre préféré, c'est Le Comte de Monte-Cristo.
RACHID Sandrine! S'il te plaît! Le Comte de Monte-Cristo?
SANDRINE Pourquoi pas? Je suis chanteuse, mais j'adore les classiques de la littérature.
DAVID Donne-moi le sac à dos, Sandrine.

Au P'tit Bistrot...
RACHID Moi, j'aime le cours de sciences po, mais Antoine n'aime pas Dupré. Il pense qu'il donne trop de devoirs.

A C T I V I T É S

1 **Vrai ou faux?** Choose whether each statement is **vrai** or **faux**.

1. Rachid et Antoine n'aiment pas le professeur Dupré. Vrai.
2. Antoine aime bien le cours de sciences po. Faux.
3. Rachid et Antoine partagent (share) un appartement. Faux.
4. David et Rachid cherchent (look for) Amina et Sandrine après (after) les cours. Vrai.
5. Le livre préféré de Sandrine est Le Comte de Monte-Cristo. Vrai.

6. L'université française est très différente de l'université américaine. Vrai.
7. Stéphane aime la chimie. Faux.
8. Monsieur Dupré est professeur de maths. Faux.
9. Antoine a (has) beaucoup de devoirs. Vrai.
10. Stéphane adore l'anglais. Faux.

 Practice more at **vhlcentral.com.**

Avant de regarder la vidéo Before showing the video episode, have students brainstorm some expressions people might use when talking about their classes and professors.

Regarder la vidéo Download and print the videoscript and white out ten words or expressions in order to create a master for a cloze activity. Hand out the photocopies and tell students to fill in the missing words as they watch the video episode. You may want to show the episode twice if students have difficulty with the activity. Then have students compare their answers in small groups.

Antoine, David, Rachid et Stéphane parlent (*talk*) de leurs (*their*) cours.

RACHID Ah... on a rendez-vous avec Amina et Sandrine. On y va?

DAVID Ah, oui, bon, ben, salut, Antoine!

ANTOINE Salut, David. À demain, Rachid!

SANDRINE Bon, Pascal, au revoir, chéri.

RACHID Bonjour, chérie. Comme j'adore parler avec toi au téléphone! Comme j'adore penser à toi!

STÉPHANE Dupré? Ha! C'est Madame Richard, mon prof de français. Elle, elle donne trop de devoirs.

AMINA Bonjour, comment ça va?

STÉPHANE Plutôt mal. Je n'aime pas Madame Richard. Je déteste les maths. La chimie n'est pas intéressante. L'histoire-géo, c'est l'horreur. Les études, c'est le désastre!

DAVID Le français, les maths, la chimie, l'histoire-géo... mais on n'étudie pas les langues étrangères au lycée en France?

STÉPHANE Si, malheureusement! Moi, j'étudie l'anglais. C'est une langue très désagréable! Oh, non, non, ha, ha, c'est une blague, ha, ha. L'anglais, j'adore l'anglais. C'est une langue charmante....

Expressions utiles

Talking about classes

- **Tu aimes les cours?**
  Do you like the classes?
- **Antoine n'aime pas Dupré.**
  Antoine doesn't like Dupré.
- **Il pense qu'il donne trop de devoirs.**
  He thinks he gives too much homework.
- **Tu crois? Mais pourquoi?**
  You think? But why?
- **Avec Dupré, je travaille, mais je n'ai pas de bons résultats.**
  With Dupré, I work, but I don't get good results (grades).
- **Demain on étudie *Les Trois Mousquetaires*.**
  Tomorrow we're studying The Three Musketeers.
- **C'est mon livre préféré.**
  It's my favorite book.

Additional vocabulary

- **On a rendez-vous.**
  We have a meeting.
- **Comme j'adore...**
  How I love...
- **parler au téléphone**
  to talk on the phone
- **C'est une blague.**
  It's a joke.
- **Si, malheureusement!**
  Yes, unfortunately!
- **On y va?**
  Let's go?
- **Eh!**
  Hey!
- **pas du tout**
  not at all
- **chéri(e)**
  darling

Expressions utiles
- Model the pronunciation of the **Expressions utiles** and have students repeat after you.
- As you work through the list, point out forms of -er verbs. Also identify examples of negation. Tell students that -er verbs and negation will be formally presented in **Espace structures**.
- Ask students a few questions about their classes and professors. Examples: **Vous aimez le cours de sciences po? Comment s'appelle le prof de sciences po? Est-ce que _____ donne trop de devoirs?**
- Point out that **si** is used instead of **oui** to contradict a negative statement or question. Example: **Si, malheureusement!**

1 Suggestion Have students correct the false statements.

1 Expansion For additional practice, give students these items. **11. Rachid pense que le cours de sciences po est inutile. (Faux.) 12. Madame Richard est prof de français. (Vrai.) 13. Pour Stéphane, les études, c'est le désastre. (Vrai.)**

2 Expansion Write these verbs on the board: **aimer, détester, adorer,** and **penser.** Have students create additional statements about the video characters that relate to each verb.

3 Suggestion Encourage students to express their opinions in simple French. Write a few sentence starters on the board. Example: **Comme Stéphane, je n'aime pas...**

2 Complétez

Match the people in the second column with the verbs in the first. Refer to a dictionary, the dialogue, and the video stills as necessary. Use each option once.

1. __b/e__ travailler   a. Sandrine is very forgetful.
2. __c__ partager   b. Rachid is very studious.
3. __a__ oublier   c. David can't afford his own apartment.
4. __b/e__ étudier   d. Amina is very generous.
5. __d__ donner   e. Stéphane needs to get good grades.

3 Conversez

In this episode, Rachid, Antoine, David, and Stéphane talk about the subjects they are studying. Get together with a partner. Do any of the characters' complaints or preferences remind you of your own? Whose opinions do you agree with? Whom do you disagree with?

ressources

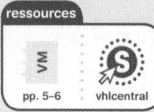

VM pp. 5–6   vhlcentral

A C T I V I T É S

OPTIONS

Alexandre Dumas Alexandre Dumas (**père**) (1802–1870) was a prolific French novelist and dramatist. With the assistance of a group of collaborators, he wrote almost 300 works. *Les Trois Mousquetaires* (The Three Musketeers), *Le Comte de Monte-Cristo* (The Count of Monte Cristo), and *La Tulipe noire* (The Black Tulip) are among his most famous and popular novels. These historical romances feature swashbuckling characters.

Ask students if they have read any of these books or seen any movies based on them.

Small Groups Working in groups of four, have students create a short skit similar to the scenes in video stills 6–10 in which some students are talking about their classes and professors. Give students about ten minutes to prepare, and then call on groups to perform their skits for the class.

Section Goals

In this section, students will:
- learn about French universities and **les grandes écoles**
- learn some familiar terms for talking about academic courses
- learn the names of some well-known universities in the francophone world
- read about **l'Université Laval**
- view authentic video footage

Instructional Resources
vhlcentral.com:
Video; SAM Answer Key;
Videoscript; reference tools

Culture à la loupe
Avant la lecture Have the class brainstorm and make a list of the different types of educational institutions that exist in the United States.

Lecture
- Point out the chart **Les étudiants en France**. Ask students what information the chart shows. (The percentages of students enrolled at different types of educational institutions in France.) Then ask them to name the types of institutions that exist.
- Tell students that an urban university system may have many individual campuses that operate autonomously. The **Université de Paris**, for example, comprises 13 campuses that are located within the city and in its suburbs.

Après la lecture Have small groups compare French and American universities. Tell them to make a list of the similarities and differences. Then ask several groups to read their lists to the class.

1 **Expansion** For additional practice, give students these items. 11. Students need to pass an exam in order to advance to a university. (**Vrai.**) 12. France changed its university system in 1998. (**Faux.** France changed its university system in 2005.) 13. A **Master** is the highest degree awarded at a French university. (**Faux.** A **Doctorat** is the highest degree awarded.)

Reading
Video: *Flash culture*

CULTURE À LA LOUPE

À l'université

French students who pass le bac° may continue on to study in a university. By American standards, university tuition is low. In 1999, 29 European countries, including France, decided to reform their university systems in order to create a more uniform European system. France began implementing these reforms in 2005. As a result, French students' degrees (**diplômes**) are now accepted in most European countries. It is also easier for French students to study in other European countries for a semester, and for other European students to study in France, because studies are now organized by semesters. Students are awarded a **Licence°** after six semesters (usually three years). If they continue their studies, they can earn a **Master°** after the fifth year and then proceed to a **Doctorat°**. If students choose technical studies, they receive a **BTS (Brevet de Technicien Supérieur)** after two years.

In addition to universities, France has an extremely competitive, elite branch of higher education called **les grandes écoles°**. These schools train most of the high-level administrators, scientists, businesspeople, and engineers in the country. There are about 300 of them, including **ENA (École Nationale d'Administration)**, **HEC (Hautes° Études Commerciales)**, and **IEP (Institut d'Études Politiques, «Sciences Po»)**.

Some French universities are city-based, lacking campuses and offering few extra-curricular activities like organized sports. Others boast both a more defined campus and a great number of student **associations**. Many students live with their families, but others live in a **résidence universitaire**, or in an apartment.

Les étudiants en France	
Universités	56,1%
Sections de Techniciens Supérieurs°	10,3%
Autres Écoles ou Formations	8,3%
Formation d'Ingénieurs	5,7%
Écoles de Commerce°	5,4%
Écoles Paramédicales et Sociales	5,4%
Instituts Universitaires de Formation de Maîtres°	5,3%
Instituts Universitaires de Technologie	4,7%
Classes Préparatoires aux Grandes Écoles	3,8%

SOURCE: Ministère de l'Éducation nationale

bac *exit exam taken after high school* **Licence** *the equivalent of a Bachelor's degree* **Master** *Master's degree* **Doctorat** *Ph.D.* **grandes écoles** *competitive, prestigious university-level schools* **Hautes** *High* **Formation de Maîtres** *teacher training* **Écoles de Commerce** *business schools*

A C T I V I T É S

1 **Vrai ou faux?** Indicate whether each statement is **vrai** or **faux**. Correct the false statements. Answers may vary slightly.

1. French university students can earn a **Licence** after only three years of study.
   Vrai.
2. It takes five years to earn a **BTS**.
   Faux. It takes two years to earn a BTS.
3. Entry into the **grandes écoles** is not competitive.
   Faux. Entry into the grandes écoles is extremely competitive.
4. The **grandes écoles** train high-level engineers.
   Vrai.
5. Some French universities lack campuses.
   Vrai.

6. Extra-curricular activities are uncommon in some French universities.
   Vrai.
7. All French students live at home with their families.
   Faux. Some students also live in résidences universitaires or in an apartment.
8. Most French students choose not to attend university.
   Faux. Most French students choose to attend university.
9. More French students study business than engineering.
   Faux. More French students study engineering.
10. Some French students are studying for a teaching degree. Vrai.

 Practice more at **vhlcentral.com**.

O P T I O N S

Pairs Explain how to read percentages so students can quiz each other in pairs about the information in the chart **Les étudiants en France**. Model how to say percentages. Example: 62,1% (**soixante-deux virgule un pour cent**). To help students, write some sample questions on the board. Examples: **Il y a plus** (*more*) **d'étudiants dans les universités ou dans les écoles de commerce? Il y a moins** (*less*) **d'étudiants dans les instituts de technologie ou dans les écoles vétérinaires?**

À l'université Despite France's longstanding low fees for a university education, tuition has increased rapidly. France has only recently needed seriously to consider a federal program of low-interest student loans to offset rising tuition costs since it is unusual for students to work while studying.

LE FRANÇAIS QUOTIDIEN

Les études

être fort(e) en...	to be good at...
être nul(le) en...	to be bad at...
bio	biology
éco	economics
géo	geography
maths	math
philo	philosophy
psycho	psychology

LE MONDE FRANCOPHONE

Des universités francophones

Voici quelques-unes° des universités du monde francophone où vous pouvez étudier°.

En Belgique Université Libre de Bruxelles

En Côte d'Ivoire Université d'Abobo-Adjamé

En France Université de Paris

Au Maroc Université Mohammed V Souissi à Rabat

En Polynésie française Université de la Polynésie française, à Faa'a, à Tahiti

Au Québec Université de Montréal

Au Sénégal Université Cheikh Anta Diop de Dakar

En Suisse Université de Genève

En Tunisie Université Libre de Tunis

quelques-unes some **où vous pouvez étudier** where you can study

PORTRAIT

L'Université Laval

Un cours de français au Québec, ça vous dit?° Avec le programme «Français pour non-francophones», les étudiants étrangers peuvent apprendre° le français. Ce programme est ouvert toute l'année: des sessions en automne, en hiver et même en été, de juin à août. À la fin du programme, les étudiants pourront° communiquer en français dans des situations courantes° de la vie quotidienne°. En arrivant à l'Université Laval, on peut être parrainé°

par un étudiant déjà° inscrit. Cela permet de mieux s'adapter et s'intégrer à la communauté universitaire et à la vie au Canada. C'est aussi un échange interculturel. Fondée° au XVIIe (dix-septième) siècle° à Québec, l'Université Laval est l'université francophone la plus ancienne° du continent américain. De plus°, elle est l'une des plus importantes du Canada. Elle compte° 17 facultés avec plus de 500 programmes d'études diverses et d'excellente qualité: les sciences humaines, la littérature, la musique, la foresterie, les technologies, les sciences. Laval est un grand centre universitaire canadien pour la recherche° scientifique. Il existe même° un astéroïde dans le système solaire qui porte le nom de° l'université!

ça vous dit? what do you think? **peuvent apprendre** can learn **pourront** will be able to **courantes** common **vie quotidienne** everyday life **parrainé** supported **déjà** already **Fondée** Founded **siècle** century **la plus ancienne** the oldest **De plus** Moreover **compte** features **dénombre** counts **dont** of which **recherche** research **même** even **porte le nom de** is named after

Coup de main

In French, a superscript $^{-e}$ following a numeral tells you that it is an ordinal number. It is the equivalent of a $^{-th}$ after a numeral in English: 4e (quatrième) = 4th.

2

Vrai ou faux? Indicate whether each statement is **vrai** or **faux**.

1. Les étudiants étrangers peuvent étudier le français à l'Université Laval. *Vrai.*

2. À la fin du programme de français, les étudiants étrangers parleront parfaitement français. *Faux.*

3. Laval offre une grande diversité de cours. *Vrai.*

4. Laval est un grand centre universitaire de recherche artistique. *Faux.*

5. Une planète porte le nom de l'université. *Faux.*

3 **Les cours** Research two of the universities mentioned in **Le monde francophone** and make a list in French of at least five courses taught at each. You may search in your library or online.

ressources

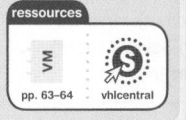

VM
pp. 63–64   vhlcentral

Practice more at **vhlcentral.com**.

A C T I V I T É S

Teacher notes (right column)

Le français quotidien Have students work in pairs. Tell them to take turns describing the courses they are good and bad at using the vocabulary in this section. Examples: **Je suis nul(le) en maths. Je suis fort(e) en géo.**

Portrait
- Show the class a photo of **l'Université Laval**. Ask: **Qu'est-ce que c'est?** (une université) **Comment s'appelle-t-elle?** Then ask students if they know why it is well known.
- Point out the **Coup de main** box. Say the ordinal numbers in French and have volunteers write them on the board using a superscript.

Le monde francophone Have students read the list. Ask: What do you notice about the names of these schools? (All include the name of the city in which they are located, except for two. **L'Université Mohammed V Souissi** in Rabat is named after the king of Morocco from 1957–1961, and **l'Université d'Adobo-Adjamé** is named after two of the ten municipalities in the city of Abidjan.)

Suggestion Point out to students that they will find supporting activities and more information related to this **Espace culture** at **vhlcentral.com**.

2 Suggestion Have students compare their answers with a classmate.

3 Expansion Have students find out the following information as part of their research: when the universities were founded, how many languages are taught, and whether or not they have programs for foreign students and study abroad programs.

Flash culture Tell students that they will learn more about classes and university life by watching a variety of real-life images narrated by Benjamin. Show the video segment, then have students jot down in French at least three examples of people or things they saw. You can also use the activities in the video manual in class to reinforce this **Flash culture** or assign them as homework.

OPTIONS

Cultural Comparison Have students compare their university to **l'Université Laval**. Begin by having students look at the photo and discuss the architecture and campus. Then have them compare other aspects mentioned in the reading, such as fields of study, number of campuses or universities, and courses for foreign students.

Des universités francophones Tell students to imagine that they have the opportunity to go on a study abroad program at one of the universities listed in **Le monde francophone**. Have them choose a location and explain why they would like to attend that particular school.

Section Goals

In this section, students will learn:
- the present tense of regular -er verbs
- spelling changes in -cer and -ger verbs

Instructional Resources
vhlcentral.com:
Activity Pack; Lab MP3s; SAM Answer Key; **Mise en pratique** *answers; Lab Audioscript; reference tools*

Suggestions
- Point out that students have been using verbs from the start: **Comment t'appelles-tu?, il y a**, forms of **être**, etc. Ask the class: **Quels cours aimez-vous?** Model the response **J'aime….** Ask a student: _____ **aime quels cours?** Model **Il/Elle aime….** Give other subjects.
- Introduce the idea of a "boot verb." Write the conjugation of a common -er verb on the board with the singular forms in the first column and the plural forms in the second column. Draw a line around **je, tu, il/elle/on**, and **ils/elles**, forming the shape of a boot. The four verb forms inside the "boot" are pronounced alike.
- Model the pronunciation of each infinitive, having students repeat. Create sentences with **j'aime…** and **j'adore…** followed by infinitives. Stress that **je** changes to **j'** before verbs starting with a vowel and most verbs starting with **h**. Ask if students like some of the activities. Example: **Vous aimez voyager?**
- Consider explaining to students that the adverb **assez** can also mean *rather* when placed before an adjective.

2A.1 Present tense of regular -er verbs 🔊 Tutorial

- The infinitives of most French verbs end in **-er**. To form the present tense of regular -er verbs, drop the **-er** from the infinitive and add the corresponding endings for the different subject pronouns. This chart demonstrates how to conjugate regular -er verbs.

parler (to speak)			
je parle	*I speak*	**nous parlons**	*we speak*
tu parles	*you speak*	**vous parlez**	*you speak*
il/elle/on parle	*he/she/it/one speaks*	**ils/elles parlent**	*they speak*

- Here are some other verbs that are conjugated the same way as **parler**.

Common -er verbs			
adorer	*to love; to adore*	**habiter (à)**	*to live (in)*
aimer	*to like; to love*	**manger**	*to eat*
aimer mieux	*to prefer (to like better)*	**oublier**	*to forget*
		partager	*to share*
arriver	*to arrive*	**penser (que/qu'…)**	*to think (that…)*
chercher	*to look for*	**regarder**	*to look (at)*
commencer	*to begin, to start*	**rencontrer**	*to meet*
dessiner	*to draw; to design*	**retrouver**	*to meet up with; to find (again)*
détester	*to hate*	**travailler**	*to work*
donner	*to give*	**voyager**	*to travel*
étudier	*to study*		

- Note that **je** becomes **j'** when it appears before a verb that begins with a vowel sound.

  J'habite à Bruxelles.
  I live in Brussels.

  J'étudie la psychologie.
  I study psychology.

- With the verbs **adorer**, **aimer**, and **détester**, use the definite article before a noun to tell what someone loves, likes, prefers, or hates.

  J'aime mieux **l'**art.
  I prefer art.

  Marine déteste **les** devoirs.
  Marine hates homework.

- Use infinitive forms after the verbs **adorer**, **aimer**, and **détester** to say that you like (or hate, etc.) to do something. Only the first verb should be conjugated.

  Ils **adorent travailler** ici.
  They love to work here.

  Ils **détestent étudier** ensemble.
  They hate to study together.

- The present tense in French can be translated in different ways in English. The English equivalent for a sentence depends on its context.

  Éric et Nadine **étudient** le droit.
  Éric and Nadine study law.

  Éric and Nadine are studying law.

  Éric and Nadine do study law.

  Nous **travaillons** à Paris.
  We work in Paris.

  We are working in Paris.

  We do work in Paris.

- Sometimes the present tense can be used to indicate an event in the near future, in which case it can be translated using *will* in English.

  Je **retrouve** le professeur demain.
  I will meet up with the professor tomorrow.

  Elles **arrivent** à Dijon demain.
  They will arrive in Dijon tomorrow.

🏃 Boîte à outils

To express yourself with greater accuracy, use these adverbs: **assez** (*enough*), **d'habitude** (*usually*), **de temps en temps** (*from time to time*), **parfois** (*sometimes*), **quelquefois** (*sometimes*), **rarement** (*rarely*), **souvent** (*often*), **toujours** (*always*).

- Verbs ending in **-ger** (**manger**, **partager**, **voyager**) and **-cer** (**commencer**) have a spelling change in the **nous** form. All the other forms are the same as regular **-er** verbs.

manger
je mange
tu manges
il/elle/on mange
nous mangeons
vous mangez
ils/elles mangent

commencer
je commence
tu commences
il/elle/on commence
nous commençons
vous commencez
ils/elles commencent

Nous **voyageons** avec une amie.
We are traveling with a friend.

Nous **commençons** les devoirs.
We are starting the homework.

- Unlike the English *to look for*, the French **chercher** requires no preposition before the noun that follows it.

Nous **cherchons les stylos**.
We are looking for the pens.

Vous **cherchez la montre**?
Are you looking for the watch?

Est-ce que tu oublies ton coloc?

Nous partageons un des appartements du P'tit Bistrot.

Boîte à outils

The spelling change in the **nous** form is made in order to maintain the same sound that the **c** and the **g** make in the infinitives **commencer** and **manger**.

Suggestions
- Explain that the French present tense equals four English present tenses. Ask volunteers to translate examples like these: **À l'université, je mange bien.** (*At college, I eat well.*) **Excusez-moi, je mange.** (*Excuse me, I'm eating.*)
- Point out that verbs ending in **-cer** and **-ger** have a spelling change in the **nous** form. Write **commençons** and **mangeons** on the board, and circle the change.
- Model the pronunciation of adverbs in **Boîte à outils.** Have students repeat. Ask volunteers for sentences using each word.

Essayez! Have students create new sentences orally or in writing by changing the subject of the sentence.

Essayez!   Complete the sentences with the correct present tense forms of the verbs.

1. Je ___parle___ (parler) français en classe.
2. Nous ___habitons___ (habiter) près de (*near*) l'université.
3. Ils ___aiment___ (aimer) le cours de sciences politiques.
4. Vous ___mangez___ (manger) en classe?!
5. Le cours ___commence___ (commencer) à huit heures (*at eight o'clock*).
6. Marie-Claire ___cherche___ (chercher) un stylo.
7. Nous ___partageons___ (partager) un crayon en cours de maths.
8. Tu ___étudies___ (étudier) l'économie.
9. Les élèves ___voyagent___ (voyager) en France.
10. Nous ___adorons___ (adorer) le prof d'anglais.
11. Je ___rencontre___ (rencontrer) Laure parfois au gymnase.
12. Tu ___donnes___ (donner) des cours de musique?

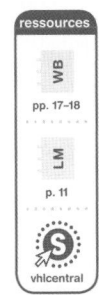

ressources

WB
pp. 17–18

LM
p. 11

S
vhlcentral

Video Show the video episode again to give students additional input on verbs. Pause the video where appropriate to discuss how certain verbs were used and to ask comprehension questions.

Extra Practice Do a rapid-response drill. Write an infinitive from the list of **-er** verbs on the board. Call out subject pronouns and/or names, and have students respond with the correct verb form. Then reverse the drill; write a verb form on the board and have students say the subject pronouns.

1 Suggestion Go over the answers quickly in class, then ask several pairs of students to act out the conversation and add at least two lines of their own at the end.

2 Suggestion To check students' answers, have volunteers write the sentences on the board and read them aloud.

2 Expansion For additional practice, change the subjects of the sentences and have students restate or write the sentences. Examples: **1. Tu (Tu oublies le devoir de littérature.) 2. Chantal (Chantal commence des études supérieures.) 3. Je (Je rencontre des amis à la fac.) 4. Les étudiants (Les étudiants détestent travailler.) 5. Nous (Nous cherchons un cours facile.) 6. Pascale (Pascale arrive avec des dictionnaires.)**

3 Expansion Have students add additional sentences to the captions below the drawings. Example: **1. Il étudie l'histoire. Il y a un examen.**

3 Expansion Have students redo the activity using **aimer** + [*infinitive*] to tell what Stéphanie's friends like to do after school.

Mise en pratique

1 **Complétez** Complete the conversation with the correct forms of the verbs.

ARTHUR Tu (1) ____parles____ (parler) bien français!

OLIVIER Mon colocataire Marc et moi, nous (2) ____retrouvons____ (retrouver) un professeur de français et nous (3) ____étudions____ (étudier) ensemble. Et toi, tu (4) ____travailles____ (travailler)?

ARTHUR Non, j' (5) ____étudie____ (étudier) l'art et l'économie. Je (6) ____dessine____ (dessiner) bien et j' (7) ____aime____ (aimer) beaucoup l'art moderne. Marc et toi, vous (8) ____habitez____ (habiter) à Paris?

2 **Phrases** Form sentences using the words provided. Conjugate the verbs and add any necessary words.

1. je / oublier / devoir de littérature   J'oublie le devoir de littérature.
2. nous / commencer / études supérieures   Nous commençons des études supérieures.
3. vous / rencontrer / amis / à / fac   Vous rencontrez des amis à la fac.
4. Hélène / détester / travailler   Hélène déteste travailler.
5. tu / chercher / cours / facile   Tu cherches un cours facile.
6. élèves / arriver / avec / dictionnaires   Les élèves arrivent avec des dictionnaires.

3 **Après l'école** Say what Stéphanie and her friends are doing after (**après**) school. Answers may vary.

▶ **MODÈLE**
Nathalie _cherche_ un livre.

1. André ____travaille____ à la bibliothèque.

2. Édouard ____retrouve____ Caroline au café.

3. Jérôme et moi, nous ____dessinons____.

4. Julien et Audrey ____parlent____ avec Simon.

5. Robin et toi, vous ____voyagez____ avec la classe.

6. Je ____mange____.

4 **Le verbe logique** Complete the following sentences logically with the correct form of an -er verb. Suggested answers.

1. La gestion, c'est très difficile. Je ____déteste____!
2. Qu'est-ce que tu ____cherches____ dans le sac à dos?
3. Nous ____mangeons____ souvent au resto U.
4. Tristan et Irène ____oublient____ toujours les clés (*keys*).
5. Le film ____commence____ dans dix minutes.
6. Yves et toi, vous ____pensez____ que Martine est charmante?
7. M. et Mme Legrand ____habitent____ à Paris.
8. On n'aime pas ____regarder____ la télévision.

Practice more at **vhlcentral.com**.

Communication

5 Activités In pairs, tell your partner which of these activities you and your roommate both do. Then, share your partner's answers with the class. Later, get together with a second partner and report to the class again. *Answers will vary.*

MODÈLE

Étudiant(e) 1: Nous parlons au téléphone, nous...
Étudiant(e) 2: Nous partageons un appartement, nous...
Étudiant(e) 1: Ils/Elles partagent un appartment, ils/elles...
Étudiant(e) 2: Ils/Elles parlent au téléphone, ils/elles...

manger au resto U	étudier une langue étrangère
partager un appartement	commencer les devoirs
retrouver des amis au café	arriver en classe
travailler	voyager

6 Les études In pairs, take turns asking your partner if he or she likes one academic subject or another. If you don't like a subject, mention one you do like. Then, use **tous** (*m.*)/**toutes** (*f.*) **les deux** (*both of us*) to tell the class what subjects both of you like or hate. *Answers will vary.*

MODÈLE

Étudiant(e) 1: Tu aimes la chimie?
Étudiant(e) 2: Non, je déteste la chimie. J'aime mieux les langues.
Étudiant(e) 1: Moi aussi... Nous adorons tous/toutes les deux les langues.

7 Un sondage In groups of three, survey your partners to find out how frequently they do certain activities. First, prepare a chart with a list of eight activities. Then take turns asking your partners how often they do each one, and record each person's response. *Answers will vary.*

MODÈLE

Étudiant(e) 1: Moi, je dessine rarement. Et toi?
Étudiant(e) 2: Moi aussi, je dessine rarement.
Étudiant(e) 3: Moi, je dessine parfois.

Activité	souvent	parfois	rarement
dessiner		Sara	David / Clara
voyager	Clara / David / Sara		

8 Adorer, aimer, détester In groups of four, ask each other if you like to do these activities. Then, use adjectives to tell why you like them or not and say whether you do them often (**souvent**), sometimes (**parfois**), or rarely (**rarement**). *Answers will vary.*

MODÈLE

Étudiant(e) 1: Tu aimes voyager?
Étudiant(e) 2: Oui, j'adore voyager. C'est amusant! Je voyage souvent.
Étudiant(e) 3: Moi, je déteste voyager. C'est désagréable! Je voyage rarement.

dessiner	partager
étudier le week-end	un appartement
manger au restaurant	retrouver des amis
oublier les devoirs	travailler à
parler avec	la bibliothèque
les professeurs	voyager

5 Suggestion Encourage students to personalize the information and to add additional information. Examples: **étudier** *a different subject*, **travailler dans** *a place*, and **regarder la télé**.

6 Suggestion Before beginning the activity, tell students to jot down a list of academic subjects that they can ask their partner about and to note their partner's responses. Examples: **Il/Elle aime** or **Il/Elle déteste**.

7 Expansion Have students share with the class which activity most people in their group do often and which one most do rarely.

8 Suggestion Before beginning the activity, have students brainstorm adjectives they can use and write them on the board.

OPTIONS

Game Divide the class into two teams. Choose one team member at a time to go to the board, alternating between teams. Say an infinitive and a subject pronoun. The person at the board must write and say the correct present tense form. Example: **parler: vous (vous parlez).** Give a point for each correct answer. The team with the most points at the end of the game wins.

Game Have students play a game of pantomime in groups of four or five. Tell students to pick a verb from the list on page 54 and act out the word. The other members of the group have to guess what the person is doing. Example: **Tu travailles?** The first person to guess correctly acts out the next pantomime.

NATIONAL comparisons STANDARDS

2A.2

Forming questions and expressing negation

Point de départ You have already learned how to make statements about yourself and others. Now you will learn how to ask questions, which are important for gathering information, and how to make statements and questions negative.

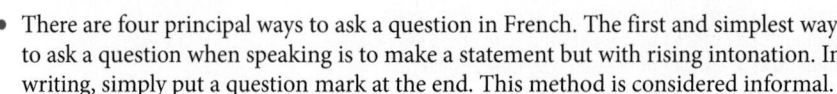 Tutorial

Section Goals

In this section, students will learn:
• to form questions
• to express negation
• expressions for agreeing and disagreeing

Instructional Resources
vhlcentral.com:
Activity Pack; Lab MP3s;
SAM Answer Key; **Mise**
en pratique *answers; Lab*
Audioscript; reference tools

Suggestions
• Model the pronunciation and intonation of the different types of example questions. Point out that the questions on page 58 elicit yes/no responses.
• Explain how to form inverted questions. Point out that inversion is usually used in written and formal language. Inversion with **je** is rare in spoken French, but seen in literary language, especially questions. Examples: **Ai-je le droit? Qui suis-je?**
• Point out that any question word can go before **est-ce que**. Example: **Que** as in **Qu'est-ce que c'est?**

 Boîte à outils

Note the statements that correspond to the questions on the right:
Vous habitez à Bordeaux.

Tu aimes le cours de français.

Forming questions

• There are four principal ways to ask a question in French. The first and simplest way to ask a question when speaking is to make a statement but with rising intonation. In writing, simply put a question mark at the end. This method is considered informal.

Vous habitez à Bordeaux?
You live in Bordeaux?

Tu aimes le cours de français?
You like French class?

• A second way is to place the phrase **Est-ce que...** directly before a statement. This turns it into a question. If the next word begins with a vowel sound, use **Est-ce qu'**. Questions with **est-ce que** are somewhat formal.

Est-ce que vous parlez français?
Do you speak French?

Est-ce qu'il aime dessiner?
Does he like to draw?

• A third way is to end a statement with a tag question, such as **n'est-ce pas?** (*isn't that right?*) or **d'accord?** (*OK?*). This method can be formal or informal.

Nous mangeons à midi, **n'est-ce pas**?
We eat at noon, don't we?

On commence à deux heures, **d'accord**?
We're starting at two o'clock, OK?

 Boîte à outils

Note the statements that correspond to the questions on the right:
Vous parlez français.

Il mange à midi.

Elle est étudiante.

• A fourth way is to invert the order of the subject pronoun and the verb and place a hyphen between them. If the verb ends in a vowel and the subject pronoun begins with one (e.g., **il, elle,** or **on**), insert **-t-** between the verb and the pronoun to make pronunciation easier. Inversion is considered more formal.

Parlez-vous français?
Do you speak French?

Mange-t-il à midi?
Does he eat at noon?

Est-elle étudiante?
Is she a student?

• If the subject is a noun rather than a pronoun, place the noun at the beginning of the question followed by the inverted verb and pronoun.

 Boîte à outils

Note the statements that correspond to the questions on the right:
Le professeur parle français.

Nina arrive demain.

Les étudiants mangent au resto U.

Rachid et toi, vous étudiez l'économie.

Le professeur parle-t-il français?
Does the professor speak French?

Nina arrive-t-elle demain?
Does Nina arrive tomorrow?

Les étudiants mangent-ils au resto U?
Do the students eat at the university?

Rachid et toi étudiez-vous l'économie?
Do you and Rachid study Economics?

• The inverted form of **il y a** is **y a-t-il**. **C'est** becomes **est-ce**.

Y a-t-il une horloge dans la classe?
Is there a clock in the class?

Est-ce le professeur de lettres?
Is he the humanities professor?

• Use **pourquoi** to ask *why?* Use **parce que** (**parce qu'** before a vowel sound) to answer *because*.

Pourquoi retrouves-tu Sophie ici?
Why are you meeting Sophie here?

Parce qu'elle habite près d'ici.
Because she lives near here.

Boîte à outils

You can use any question word before **est-ce que**. Example: **Que** as in **Qu'est-ce que c'est?**

• You can use **est-ce que** after **pourquoi** to form a question. With **est-ce que**, you don't use inversion.

Pourquoi détestes-tu la chimie?
Why do you hate Chemistry?

Pourquoi est-ce que tu détestes la chimie?
Why do you hate Chemistry?

58 *cinquante-huit*

Expressing negation

- To make a sentence negative in French, place **ne** (**n'** before a vowel sound) before the conjugated verb and **pas** after it.

Je **ne dessine pas** bien.	Elles **n'étudient pas** la chimie.
I don't draw well.	*They don't study chemistry.*

- In the construction [*conjugated verb + infinitive*], **ne** (**n'**) comes before the conjugated verb and **pas** after it.

Abdel **n'aime pas étudier**.	Vous **ne détestez pas travailler**?
Abdel doesn't like to study.	*You don't hate to work?*

- In questions with inversion, place **ne** before the inversion and **pas** after it.

Abdel **n'aime-t-il pas** étudier?	**Ne détestez-vous pas** travailler?
Doesn't Abdel like to study?	*Don't you hate to work?*

- Use these expressions to respond to a statement or a question that requires a *yes* or *no* answer.

Expressions of agreement and disagreement

oui	*yes*	**(mais) non**	*no (but of course not)*
bien sûr	*of course*	**pas du tout**	*not at all*
moi/toi non plus	*me/you neither*	**peut-être**	*maybe, perhaps*

Vous mangez souvent au resto U?	**Non, pas du tout.**
Do you eat often in the cafeteria?	*No, not at all.*

- Use **si** instead of **oui** to contradict a negative question.

Parles-tu à Daniel?	Oui.
Are you talking to Daniel?	*Yes.*
Ne parles-tu pas à Daniel?	**Si!**
Aren't you talking to Daniel?	*Yes (I am)!*

Boîte à outils

Note the affirmative statements that correspond to the negative ones on the left:

Je dessine bien.

Elles étudient la chimie.

Essayez! Make questions out of these statements. Use **est-ce que/qu'** in items 1–6 and inversion in 7–12.

	Statement	Question
1.	Vous mangez au resto U.	*Est-ce que vous mangez au resto U?*
2.	Ils adorent les devoirs.	Est-ce qu'ils adorent les devoirs?
3.	La biologie est difficile.	Est-ce que la biologie est difficile?
4.	Tu travailles.	Est-ce que tu travailles?
5.	Elles cherchent le prof.	Est-ce qu'elles cherchent le prof?
6.	Aude voyage beaucoup.	Est-ce qu'Aude voyage beaucoup?
7.	Vous arrivez demain.	*Arrivez-vous demain?*
8.	L'étudiante oublie le livre.	L'étudiante oublie-t-elle le livre?
9.	La physique est utile.	La physique est-elle utile?
10.	Il y a deux salles de classe.	Y a-t-il deux salles de classe?
11.	Ils n'habitent pas à Québec.	N'habitent-ils pas à Québec?
12.	C'est le professeur de gestion.	Est-ce le professeur de gestion?

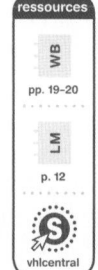

ressources

WB
pp. 19–20

LM
p. 12

vhlcentral

Suggestions

- Explain the positions of **ne (n')** and **pas** in negative phrases and in inverted questions. If an infinitive follows a conjugated verb, **ne (n')** and **pas** surround the conjugated verb. Example: **Tu n'aimes pas regarder la vidéo?**
- Tell students that **ne (n')** in negative sentences is sometimes dropped in informal speech.
- Model the expressions indicating agreement and disagreement. Show how **mais** can precede **oui** as well as **non** if you want to say yes or no more emphatically.
- Make sure students grasp when to say **si** instead of **oui** by asking questions like these: **Tu n'étudies pas le français? (Si, j'étudie le français.) Je ne suis pas le professeur? (Si, vous êtes le professeur.)** Choose two students that are friends and ask: _____ et _____ ne sont pas copains/copines? (Si, nous sommes copains/copines.)** Tell students to say, **Mais si!** if they want to contradict a negative question more forcefully.
- Consider further practicing the concept of **oui** versus **si** by asking students affirmative and negative questions and having them respond appropriately.

Essayez! Have students repeat using inversion for items 1–6 and **est-ce que/qu'** in 7–12.

OPTIONS

Pairs Write ten statements on the board or a transparency. Have students work in pairs. Tell them to convert the statements into questions by inverting the subject and verb. When they have finished writing the questions, call on volunteers to read their questions aloud. This activity can also be done orally with the class.

Extra Practice Using the same ten statements from the previous activity, ask students to form tag questions. Encourage them to use both **d'accord?** and **n'est-ce pas?** Have students answer some of the questions. Then add a few negative statements so that students will have to respond with **si**.

1 Expansion Have students work in pairs, and take turns asking and answering the questions in the negative.

2 Expansion Have students write two additional statements. Tell them to exchange papers with a partner who will ask the questions that would elicit those statements.

3 Expansion Have pairs of students create a similar conversation, replacing the answers and some of the questions with information that is true for them. Then have volunteers act out their conversations for the class.

Mise en pratique

1 **L'inversion** Restate the questions using inversion.

1. Est-ce que vous parlez espagnol?   Parlez-vous espagnol?
2. Est-ce qu'il étudie à Paris?   Étudie-t-il à Paris?
3. Est-ce qu'ils voyagent avec des amis?   Voyagent-ils avec des amis?
4. Est-ce que tu aimes les cours de langues?   Aimes-tu les cours de langues?
5. Est-ce que le professeur parle anglais?   Le professeur parle-t-il anglais?
6. Est-ce que les étudiants aiment dessiner?   Les étudiants aiment-ils dessiner?

2 **Les questions** Ask the questions that correspond to the answers. Use **est-ce que/qu'** and inversion for each item.

MODÈLE

Nous habitons sur le campus.
Est-ce que vous habitez sur le campus? / Habitez-vous sur le campus?

1. Il mange au resto U.   Est-ce qu'il mange au resto U? / Mange-t-il au resto U?
2. J'oublie les examens.   Est-ce que tu oublies les examens? / Oublies-tu les examens?
3. François déteste les maths.   Est-ce que François déteste les maths? / François déteste-t-il les maths?
4. Nous adorons voyager.   Est-ce que vous adorez voyager? / Adorez-vous voyager?
5. Les cours ne commencent pas demain.   Est-ce que les cours ne commencent pas demain? / Les cours ne commencent-ils pas demain?
6. Les étudiantes arrivent en classe.   Est-ce que les étudiantes arrivent en classe? / Les étudiantes arrivent-elles en classe?

3 **Complétez** Complete the conversation with the correct questions for the answers given. Act it out with a partner.   Suggested answers.

MYLÈNE   Salut, Arnaud. Ça va?

ARNAUD   Oui, ça va. Alors (So)... (1) __Tu aimes les cours?__

MYLÈNE   J'adore le cours de sciences po, mais je déteste l'informatique.

ARNAUD   (2) __Pourquoi est-ce que tu détestes l'informatique?__

MYLÈNE   Parce que la prof est très stricte.

ARNAUD   (3) __Il y a des étudiants sympathiques, n'est-ce pas?__

MYLÈNE   Oui, il y a des étudiants sympathiques... Et demain? (4) __Tu retrouves Béatrice?__

ARNAUD   Peut-être, mais demain je retrouve aussi Dominique.

MYLÈNE   (5) __Tu cherches une petite amie?__

ARNAUD   Pas du tout!

 Practice more at **vhlcentral.com**.

Communication

4 Au café In pairs, take turns asking each other questions about the drawing. Use verbs from the list. *Answers will vary.*

MODÈLE

Étudiant(e) 1: *Monsieur Laurent parle à Madame Martin, n'est-ce pas?*
Étudiant(e) 2: *Mais non. Il déteste parler!*

arriver	dessiner	manger	partager
chercher	étudier	oublier	rencontrer

Anne et Sylvie   Didier   André
Madame Martin   Monsieur Laurent

5 Questions You and your partner want to get to know each other better. Take turns asking each other questions. Modify or add elements as needed. *Some answers will vary.*

MODÈLE aimer / l'art
Étudiant(e) 1: *Est-ce que tu aimes l'art?*
Étudiant(e) 2: *Oui, j'adore l'art.*

1. habiter / à l'université   Est-ce que tu habites à l'université?
2. étudier / avec / amis   Est-ce que tu étudies avec des amis?
3. penser qu'il y a / cours / intéressant / à la fac   Est-ce que tu penses qu'il y a des cours intéressants à la fac?
4. cours de sciences / être / facile   Est-ce que les cours de sciences sont faciles?
5. aimer mieux / biologie / ou / physique   Est-ce que tu aimes mieux la biologie ou la physique?
6. retrouver / copains / au resto U   Est-ce que tu retrouves des copains au resto U?

6 Confirmez In groups of three, confirm whether the statements are true of your school. Correct any untrue statements by making them negative. *Answers will vary.*

MODÈLE

Les profs sont désagréables.
Pas du tout, les profs ne sont pas désagréables.

1. Les cours d'informatique sont inutiles.
2. Il y a des étudiants de nationalité allemande.
3. Nous mangeons une cuisine excellente au resto U.
4. Tous (*All*) les étudiants habitent sur le campus.
5. Les cours de chimie sont faciles.
6. Nous travaillons pour obtenir un diplôme.

soixante et un **61**

4 Suggestion Tell students to vary the method of asking questions instead of always using a tag question as in the **modèle**.

5 Suggestions
• Have two volunteers read the **modèle** aloud.
• After students have completed the activity, ask volunteers to report what they learned about their partner.

6 Suggestion Encourage students to use as many expressions indicating agreement or disagreement as they can.

6 Expansion Have groups write three additional true/false statements about their school. Ask several groups to read their statements and have the class respond to them. Encourage students to respond with **Mais oui!** or **Mais non!** where appropriate.

OPTIONS

Extra Practice Prepare eight questions. Write their answers on the board in random order. Then read your questions aloud, having students match the question to the appropriate answer. Make sure that only one of the possible answers corresponds logically to the questions you ask. Example: **Pourquoi _____ déteste-t-il les maths? (Il n'aime pas le prof.)**

Video Replay the video episode, having students focus on the different forms of questions used. Tell them to write down each question they hear. Stop the video where suitable to give students time to write and to discuss what was heard.

ESPACE STRUCTURES **61**

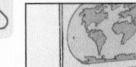

Révision

Instructional Resources
vhlcentral.com: Activity Pack (Info Gap Activities); Testing Program, Testing Program MP3s; reference tools

1 Expansion Have students compare two of their own classes that are very different, such as a large lecture and a small class, and explain which one they prefer. This activity can be done orally or in writing.

2 Suggestion Have two volunteers read the **modèle** aloud. Tell students to add at least two more items to the list, one that applies to both of them and one that does not.

3 Suggestion As students share their responses with the class, make a list of their likes and dislikes on the board under the headings **Nous aimons** and **Nous n'aimons pas.**

4 Suggestion Tell students they may use adjectives that are not in the list.

5 Suggestion Before beginning the activity, have the class decide on names for the people in the drawings. Also have them brainstorm possible relationships between the people, for example, strangers meeting for the first time or classmates.

6 Suggestion Divide the class into pairs and distribute the Info Gap Handouts, found in the Activity Pack on the Supersite for this activity. Give students ten minutes to complete the activity.

6 Expansion Have pairs compare their answers with another pair to confirm the people's likes and dislikes. Then ask a few groups to share some of their sentences with the class.

---

1 Des styles différents In pairs, compare these two very different classes. Then, tell your partner which class you prefer and why. Answers will vary.

2 Les activités In pairs, discuss whether these expressions apply to both of you. React to every answer you hear. Answers will vary.

MODÈLE

Étudiant(e) 1: Est-ce que tu étudies le week-end?
Étudiant(e) 2: Non! Je n'aime pas travailler le week-end.
Étudiant(e) 1: Moi non plus. J'aime mieux travailler le soir.

1. adorer le resto U
2. être reçu(e) à un examen difficile
3. étudier au café
4. manger souvent (often) des sushis
5. oublier les devoirs
6. parler espagnol
7. travailler le soir à la bibliothèque
8. voyager souvent

3 Le campus In pairs, prepare ten questions inspired by the list and what you know about your campus. Together, survey as many classmates as possible to find out what they like and dislike on campus. Answers will vary.

MODÈLE

Étudiant(e) 1: Est-ce que tu aimes travailler à la bibliothèque?
Étudiant(e) 2: Non, pas trop. Je travaille plutôt au café.

bibliothèque	étudiant	resto U
bureau	gymnase	salle de classe
cours	librairie	salle d'ordinateurs

4 Pourquoi? Survey as many classmates as possible to find out if they like these academic subjects and why. Ask what adjectives they would pick to describe them. Tally the most popular answers for each subject. Answers will vary.

MODÈLE

Étudiant(e) 1: Est-ce que tu aimes la philosophie?
Étudiant(e) 2: Pas tellement.
Étudiant(e) 1: Pourquoi?
Étudiant(e) 2: Parce que c'est trop difficile.

1. la biologie
2. la chimie
3. l'histoire de l'art
4. l'économie
5. la gestion
6. les langues
7. les mathématiques
8. la psychologie

   a. agréable
   b. amusant
   c. désagréable
   d. difficile
   e. facile
   f. important
   g. inutile
   h. utile

5 Les conversations In pairs, act out a short conversation between the people shown in each drawing. They should greet each other, describe what they are doing, and discuss their likes or dislikes. Choose your favorite skit and role-play it for another pair. Answers will vary.

MODÈLE

Étudiant(e) 1: Bonjour, Aurélie.
Étudiant(e) 2: Salut! Tu travailles, n'est-ce pas?

6 Les portraits Your instructor will give you and a partner a set of drawings showing the likes and dislikes of eight people. Discuss each person's tastes. Do not look at each other's worksheet. Answers will vary.

MODÈLE

Étudiant(e) 1: Sarah n'aime pas travailler.
Étudiant(e) 2: Mais elle adore manger.

OPTIONS

Extra Practice Have students write a brief paragraph describing the activities they like or don't like to do. Collect the descriptions and read a few of them to the class. Have the class guess who wrote each description by asking: **Est-ce que c'est...?**

Small Groups Tell students to turn to the **Roman-photo** on pages 50–51 and write five comprehension questions based on the dialogue. Then have them get together in groups of three or four, and take turns asking and answering each other's questions.

Video

Le Zapping

NATIONAL
communication
cultures
STANDARDS

NATIONAL
connections
communities
STANDARDS

À vos marques, prêts°... étudiez!

The University of Moncton was founded in 1963 and is the largest French-speaking university in Canada outside Quebec. Its three campuses of Edmunston, Moncton, and Shippagan are located in New Brunswick. Students come from the local francophone region of Acadia, from other Canadian provinces, and from countries around the world such as Guinea, Haiti, and Morocco.

The mission of the University of Moncton is not only to foster the academic development of these students but also to offer them a nurturing environment that will encourage their personal and social growth.

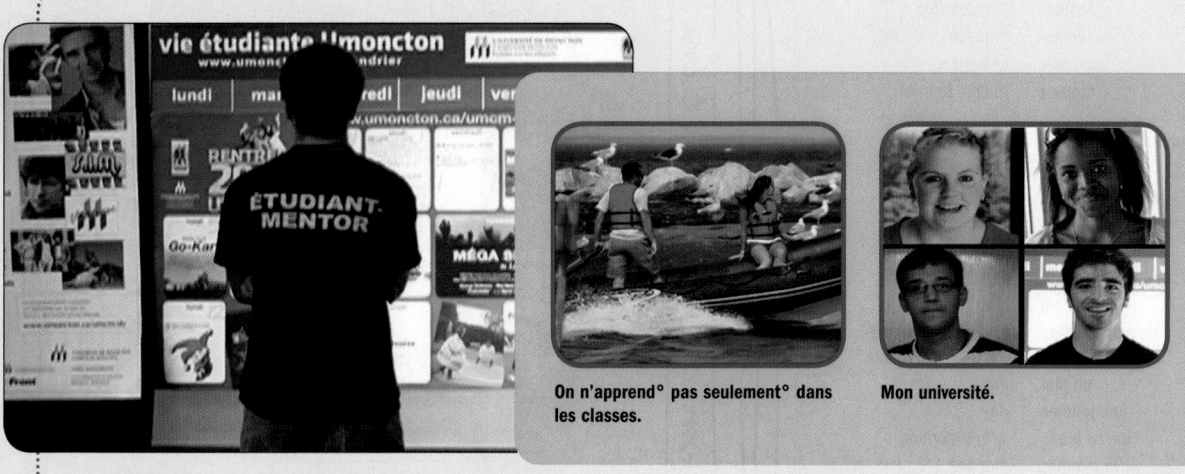

On n'apprend° pas seulement° dans les classes.

Mon université.

Comprehension Answer these questions.

1. What are the three kinds of activities offered at the University of Moncton?
Suggested answer: social activities, cultural activities, and sports.
2. Give examples of each type of activity. Answers will vary.
3. Where does learning take place at the University of Moncton?
Suggested answer: in class, in labs, and in the field.
4. Do students receive a lot of attention from their professors? Explain.
Suggested answer: The professors use a personalized approach and spend a lot of time working with their students.

Discussion In pairs, discuss the answers to these questions. Answers will vary.

1. What are the University of Moncton's strengths?
2. Would you like to study there? Explain.

À vos marques, prêts Ready, set apprend learn seulement only

Go to **vhlcentral.com** to watch the TV clip featured in this **Le Zapping**.

 Practice more at vhlcentral.com.

soixante-trois 63

Section Goals

In this section, students will:
• read about the University of Moncton
• watch an advertisement for the University of Moncton
• answer questions about the University of Moncton

Instructional Resources
vhlcentral.com:
TV commercial; *Le Zapping*
TV clip transcription;
reference tools

Avant de regarder la vidéo
• Have students look at the video stills, read the captions, and predict what the commercial will be about.
• Before showing the video, explain to students that they do not need to understand every word they hear. Tell them to listen for cognates and school-related vocabulary.

Compréhension
• Have students work in pairs or groups for this activity. Tell them to write their answers. Then show the video again so that they can check their work and add any missing information.
• Have pairs come up with a slogan for the University of Moncton. Then, ask the class to choose the best slogans.

Discussion After discussing the questions, ask volunteers to report their comments and ideas to the class.

OPTIONS

Small Groups Have students compare the University of Moncton to their own school and come up with a list of four differences and/or similarities between the two institutions. Examples: **À l'université de Moncton, il y a... et ici aussi. À l'université de Moncton, ils étudient... et ici, on n'étudie pas...**

Expansion In small groups, have students prepare a similar commercial to encourage francophone students to study at their own school. Have the groups perform their ads for the class.

Section Goals

In this section, students will learn and practice vocabulary related to:
• talking about schedules
• the days of the week
• sequencing events

Instructional Resources

vhlcentral.com: Digital Image Bank (including vocabulary illustrations from the textbook, theme-based illustrations); **Vocabulaire supplémentaire; Mise en pratique** *answers; Textbook Audioscript; Lab Audioscript; Activity Pack (***Feuilles d'activités***); Textbook MP3s; Lab MP3s; SAM Answer Key; reference tools*

Suggestions

• Write days of the week across the board and present them like this: **Aujourd'hui, c'est ____. Demain, c'est ____. Après-demain, c'est ____?**
• Write the following questions and answers on the board, explaining their meaning:
  —**Quel jour sommes-nous?**
  —**Nous sommes ____.**
  —**C'est quand l'examen?**
  —**L'examen est ____.**
Ask students the questions.
• Point out that days of the week are masculine and lowercase.
• Explain the differences between **le matin/la matinée, le soir/la soirée,** and **le jour/ la journée.**
• Introduce new vocabulary using the 2B **Contextes** illustration from the Digital Image Bank. Give the student a name, for example, Henri. Ask students picture-based questions. Examples: **Quel jour Henri assiste-t-il au cours d'économie? Il assiste au cours d'économie le matin ou le soir? Quels jours visite-t-il Paris avec Annette?**
• Use the Vocabulary illustrations and the School and university illustrations from the Digital Image Bank to help students familiarize themselves with schedules, days of the week, and sequencing events.
• Additional vocabulary for this lesson can be found in the **Vocabulaire supplémentaire** on the Supersite.

Leçon 2B

Vocabulary Tools

You will learn how to...
▪ say when things happen
▪ discuss your schedule

Une semaine à la fac

Vocabulaire

demander	to ask
échouer	to fail
écouter	to listen (to)
enseigner	to teach
expliquer	to explain
trouver	to find; to think
Quel jour sommes-nous?	What day is it?
un an	year
une/cette année	one/this year
après	after
après-demain	day after tomorrow
un/cet après-midi	a/this afternoon
aujourd'hui	today
demain (matin/ après-midi/soir)	tomorrow (morning/ afternoon/evening)
un jour	day
une journée	day
un/ce matin	a/this morning
la matinée	morning
un mois/ce mois-ci	month/this month
une/cette nuit	a/this night
une/cette semaine	a/this week
un/ce soir	an/this evening
une soirée	evening
un/le/ce week-end	a/the/this weekend
dernier/dernière	last
premier/première	first
prochain(e)	next

ressources

WB pp. 21–22 | LM p. 13 | (S) vhlcentral

semaine

lundi | mardi | mercredi | jeudi | vendredi

matin

assister au cours d'économie

passer l'examen de maths

téléphoner à Marc

après-midi

préparer l'examen de maths

soir

dîner avec Annette

O P T I O N S

Extra Practice Write **le matin, l'après-midi,** and **le soir** on the board or a transparency. Have your students tell when they do various activities, such as **préparer les cours, assister aux cours, téléphoner à des amis, écouter de la musique, regarder la télévision, rentrer à la maison,** and **dîner.**

Pairs Have the class brainstorm a list of nouns associated with verbs from **Espace contextes.** For example, for the verb **regarder,** students might think of **télévision** or **vidéo.** Write the verbs and nouns on the board as students say them. Then have students work in pairs. Give them five minutes to write original sentences using these words. Ask volunteers to write their sentences on the board.

Mise en pratique

1 Écoutez You will hear Lorraine describing her schedule. Listen carefully and indicate whether the statements are **vrai** or **faux**.

	Vrai	Faux
1. Lorraine étudie à l'université le soir.	☐	☑
2. Elle trouve le cours de mathématiques facile.	☐	☑
3. Elle étudie le week-end.	☐	☑
4. Lorraine étudie la chimie le mardi et le jeudi matin.	☐	☑
5. Le professeur de mathématiques explique bien.	☐	☑
6. Lorraine regarde la télévision, écoute de la musique ou téléphone à Claire et Anne le soir.	☑	☐
7. Lorraine travaille dans (in) une librairie.	☐	☑
8. Elle étudie l'histoire le mardi et le jeudi matin.	☑	☐
9. Lorraine adore dîner avec sa famille le week-end.	☑	☐
10. Lorraine rentre à la maison le soir.	☐	☑

2 La classe de Mme Arnaud Complete this paragraph by selecting the correct verb from the list below. Make sure to conjugate the verb. Some verbs will not be used.

demander	expliquer	rentrer
écouter	passer un examen	travailler
enseigner	préparer	trouver
étudier	regarder	visiter

Madame Arnaud (1) _____travaille_____ à l'université. Elle (2) _____enseigne_____ un cours de français. Elle (3) _____explique_____ les verbes et la grammaire aux étudiants. Le vendredi, en classe, les étudiants (4) _____regardent_____ une vidéo en français ou (or) (5) _____écoutent_____ de la musique française. Ce week-end, ils (6) _____étudient_____ pour (for) (7) _____préparer_____ un examen très difficile lundi matin. Je (8) _____travaille_____ beaucoup pour ce cours, mais mes (my) amis et moi, nous (9) _____trouvons_____ la classe sympa.

3 Quel jour sommes-nous? Complete each statement with the correct day of the week.

1. Aujourd'hui, c'est _____Answers will vary._____.
2. Demain, c'est _____Answers will vary._____.
3. Après-demain, c'est _____Answers will vary._____.
4. Le week-end, c'est le _____samedi et le dimanche_____.
5. Le premier jour de la semaine en France, c'est le _____lundi_____.
6. Les jours du cours de français sont _____Answers will vary._____.
7. Mon (My) jour préféré de la semaine, c'est le _____Answers will vary._____.
8. Je travaille à la bibliothèque le _____Answers will vary._____.

Practice more at **vhlcentral.com**.

soixante-cinq **65**

Attention!

Use the masculine definite article **le** + [day of the week] when an activity is done on a weekly basis. Omit **le** when it is done on a specific day.
Le prof enseigne le lundi.
The professor teaches on Mondays.
Je passe un examen lundi.
I'm taking a test on Monday.

samedi | dimanche

visiter Paris avec Annette

rentrer à la maison

---

1 Audioscript Cette année à l'université j'étudie: la chimie, le lundi et le mercredi matin; l'histoire, le mardi et le jeudi matin; l'art, le vendredi matin et les mathématiques, le lundi et le mercredi après-midi. Je déteste les mathématiques; le professeur n'explique pas bien et je trouve le cours difficile. J'étudie l'après-midi quand je rentre à la maison. Le soir, je ne travaille pas, alors je regarde la télévision, j'écoute de la musique ou je téléphone à mes amies, Claire et Anne. Le week-end, j'adore rendre visite à ma famille pour dîner!
(On Textbook MP3s)

1 Suggestions
- Before playing the recording, have students read the statements and identify the expressions that describe when things occur. Examples: **le soir**, **le week-end**, and **le jeudi matin**.
- Go over the answers with the class. If students have difficulty, replay the recording.

2 Expansion Have pairs write original sentences about Madame Arnaud and her class using the verbs that weren't in this paragraph. Ask volunteers to read their sentences aloud.

3 Expansions
- Give these items for more practice. **9. Le jour après lundi, c'est _____. 10. Il n'y a pas de cours de français le _____.**
- Have students repeat items 1–5 from the perspective of a different day of the week.

TPR Create a schedule for an imaginary student using the whole class. Assign each day of the week to a different student and assign each of the remaining students a different activity. As you describe the schedule, students arrange themselves as a page in a weekly day-planner, starting with the day of the week and then each activity you mention. Example: **Le lundi matin, j'assiste au cours. L'après-midi, je passe un examen de français. Le soir, je dîne au resto U.**

Extra Practice Have students write a paragraph similar to the one in **Activité 2** describing your French class or a different class. They should use as many verbs from the list as possible. Ask volunteers to read their paragraph aloud.

4 Suggestion Before doing this activity, you may want to write a short list of musical genres on the board for item 5. Also tell students that **quand** means *when*.

4 Expansions
• Have volunteers report what they learned about their classmate.
• To practice the **nous** forms, ask students what they have in common with their partner.

5 Suggestion Tell students to switch roles after completing the conversation so that both students have the opportunity to ask and answer questions.

6 Suggestions
• Have two volunteers read the **modèle** aloud. Make sure students understand the directions. Then distribute the **Feuilles d'activités**, found in the Activity Pack on the Supersite.
• Have students repeat the activity with a different partner.

7 Suggestion To save time in class, assign the written part of this activity the day before as homework.

Communication

4 Conversez Interview a classmate. Answers will vary.

1. Quel jour sommes-nous?
2. Quand est le prochain cours de français?
3. Quand rentres-tu à la maison? Demain soir? Après-demain?
4. Est-ce que tu prépares un examen cette année?
5. Est-ce que tu écoutes la radio? Quel genre de musique aimes-tu?
6. Quand téléphones-tu à des amis?
7. Est-ce que tu regardes la télévision le matin, l'après-midi ou (*or*) le soir?
8. Est-ce que tu dînes dans un restaurant ce mois-ci?

5 Le premier jour à la fac You make a new friend in your French class and want to know what his or her class schedule is like this semester. With a partner, prepare a conversation to perform for the class where you: Answers will vary.

• ask his or her name
• ask what classes he or she is taking
• ask on which days of the week he or she has class
• ask at which times of day (morning, afternoon, or evening) he or she has class

6 Bataille navale Your instructor will give you a worksheet. Choose four spaces on your chart and mark them with a battleship. In pairs, formulate questions by using the subjects in the first column and the verbs in the first row to find out where your partner has placed his or her battleships. Whoever "sinks" the most battleships wins. Answers will vary.

MODÈLE

Étudiant(e) 1: Est-ce que Luc et Sabine travaillent le week-end?
Étudiant(e) 2: Oui, ils travaillent le week-end.
(*if you marked that square*)
Non, ils ne travaillent pas le week-end.
(*if you didn't mark that square*)

	enseigner	travailler
Marie		
Luc et Sabine		🚢

7 Le week-end Fill out the schedule below with your typical weekend activities. Use the verbs you know. Compare your schedule with a classmate's, and talk about the different activities that you do and when. Be prepared to discuss your results with the class. Answers will vary.

	Moi	Nom
Le vendredi soir 🌙		
Le samedi matin ☀		
Le samedi après-midi ☀		
Le samedi soir 🌙		
Le dimanche matin ☀		
Le dimanche après-midi ☀		
Le dimanche soir 🌙		

66   *soixante-six*

Game Play a memory game in which the first player says one activity he or she does on a particular day of the week. The next player repeats what the first person said, then adds what he or she does on the following day. The third player must remember what the first two people said before saying what he or she does on the next day. Continue until the end of a week. If someone makes a mistake, then choose another student to continue.

Small Groups Have students work in groups of three. Tell them to take turns asking what days of the week TV shows are on and answering. Example: **Quel(s) jour(s) est la série *CSI*?**

Les sons et les lettres  Audio

The letter r

The French **r** is very different from the English *r*. In English, an *r* is pronounced in the middle and toward the front of the mouth. The French **r** is pronounced in the throat.

You have seen that an **-er** at the end of a word is usually pronounced **-ay**, as in the English word *way*, but without the glide sound.

| chant**er** | mang**er** | expliqu**er** | aim**er** |

In most other circumstances, the French **r** has a very different sound. Pronunciation of the French **r** varies according to its position in a word. Note the different ways the **r** is pronounced in these words.

| **r**ivière | litté**r**ature | ordinateu**r** | devoi**r** |

If an **r** falls between two vowels or before a vowel, it is pronounced with slightly more friction.

| **r**are | ga**r**age | Eu**r**ope | **r**ose |

An **r** sound before a consonant or at the end of a word is pronounced with slightly less friction.

| po**r**te | bou**r**se | ado**r**e | jou**r** |

Prononcez Practice saying the following words aloud.

1. crayon
2. professeur
3. plaisir
4. différent
5. terrible
6. architecture
7. trouver
8. restaurant
9. rentrer
10. regarder
11. lettres
12. réservé
13. être
14. dernière
15. arriver
16. après

Articulez Practice saying the following sentences aloud.

1. Au revoir, Professeur Colbert!
2. Rose arrive en retard mardi.
3. Mercredi, c'est le dernier jour des cours.
4. Robert et Roger adorent écouter la radio.
5. La corbeille à papier, c'est quarante-quatre euros!
6. Les parents de Richard sont brillants et très agréables.

Dictons Practice reading these sayings aloud.

Quand le renard prêche, gare aux oies.[2]

Qui ne risque rien n'a rien.[1]

[1] Nothing ventured, nothing gained.
[2] When the fox preaches, watch your geese.

ressources

LM
p. 14

S
vhlcentral

soixante-sept **67**

Section Goals
In this section, students will learn about the letter **r**.

Instructional Resources
vhlcentral.com:
Textbook MP3s; Lab MP3s; SAM Answer Key; Textbook Audioscript; Lab Audioscript; reference tools

Suggestions
• Model the pronunciation of words and expressions with **r** from **Espace contextes**. Then have students repeat. Examples: **regarder, préparer un examen**, etc.
• Explain that the French **r** has more in common with a **k** sound than it does with the English *r*. The **k** sound is velar, produced when the back of the tongue touches the soft palate. The French **r** is uvular, produced a bit farther back in the mouth with the back of the tongue and the uvula.
• Model the pronunciation of each example word and have students repeat.
• Ask students to provide words or expressions from previous lessons that contain the letter **r**. Examples: **au revoir, très bien, professeur**, and **merci**.
• The explanation and exercises are available on the **ESPACES** Supersite. You may want to play them in class so students hear French speakers other than yourself.

Dictons Ask students if they can think of an English saying that is similar to «**Quand le renard prêche, gare aux oies.**» (*Don't let a fox guard the hen house.*)

OPTIONS

Extra Practice Dictate five familiar words with the **r** in different places, saying each one at least two times. Examples: **librairie, résultat, jour, chercher,** and **montre**. Then write them on the board or a transparency and have students check their spelling.

Extra Practice Use these sentences with the letter **r** for additional oral practice or dictation. **1. Renée regarde un garçon américain. 2. Le colocataire de Grégoire est réservé. 3. Je travaille le mercredi après-midi et le vendredi soir. 4. Nous trouvons le cours d'histoire très intéressant.**

ESPACE CONTEXTES **67**

On trouve une solution. Video

NATIONAL
communication
cultures
STANDARDS

PERSONNAGES

Amina

Astrid

David

Rachid

Sandrine

Stéphane

À la terrasse du café...

RACHID Alors, on a rendez-vous avec David demain à cinq heures moins le quart, pour rentrer chez nous.

SANDRINE Aujourd'hui, c'est mercredi. Demain... jeudi. Le mardi et le jeudi j'ai cours de chant de trois heures vingt à quatre heures et demie. C'est parfait!

AMINA Pas de problème. J'ai cours de stylisme...

AMINA Salut, Astrid!
ASTRID Bonjour.
RACHID Astrid, je te présente David, mon (*my*) coloc américain.
DAVID Alors, cette année, tu as des cours très difficiles, n'est-ce pas?

ASTRID Oui? Pourquoi?
DAVID Ben, Stéphane pense que les cours sont très difficiles.
ASTRID Ouais, Stéphane, il assiste au cours mais... il ne fait pas ses (*his*) devoirs et il n'écoute pas les profs. Cette année est très importante, parce que nous avons le bac...
DAVID Ah, le bac...

Au parc...

ASTRID Stéphane! Quelle heure est-il? Tu n'as pas de montre?
STÉPHANE Oh, Astrid, excuse-moi! Le mercredi, je travaille avec Astrid au café sur le cours de maths...
ASTRID Et le mercredi après-midi, il oublie! Tu n'as pas peur du bac, toi!

STÉPHANE Tu as tort, j'ai très peur du bac! Mais je n'ai pas envie de passer mes (*my*) journées, mes soirées et mes week-ends avec des livres!
ASTRID Je suis d'accord avec toi, Stéphane! J'ai envie de passer les week-ends avec mes copains... des copains qui n'oublient pas les rendez-vous!

RACHID Écoute, Stéphane, tu as des problèmes avec ta (*your*) mère, avec Astrid aussi.
STÉPHANE Oui, et j'ai d'énormes problèmes au lycée. Je déteste le bac.
RACHID Il n'est pas tard pour commencer à travailler pour être reçu au bac.
STÉPHANE Tu crois, Rachid?

A C T I V I T É S

1 **Vrai ou faux?** Choose whether each statement is vrai or faux.

1. Le mardi et le mercredi, Sandrine a (*has*) cours de chant. Faux.
2. Le jeudi, Amina a cours de stylisme. Vrai.
3. Astrid pense que le bac est impossible. Faux.
4. La famille de David est allemande. Faux.
5. Le mercredi, Stéphane travaille avec Astrid au café sur le cours de maths. Vrai.

6. Stéphane a beaucoup de problèmes. Vrai.
7. Rachid est optimiste. Vrai.
8. Stéphane dîne chez Rachid samedi. Faux.
9. Le sport est très important pour Stéphane. Vrai.
10. Astrid est fâchée (*angry*) contre Stéphane. Vrai.

Practice more at vhlcentral.com.

Section Goals

In this section, students will learn functional phrases for talking about their schedules and classes and telling time.

Instructional Resources
vhlcentral.com:
Roman-photo Video, Videoscript, and Translation; SAM Answer Key; reference tools

Video Recap: Leçon 2A
Ask questions to review the previous **Roman-photo** with students.

1. Comment est-ce que Rachid trouve le cours de sciences po? (intéressant et utile)
2. Comment s'appelle le colocataire de Rachid? (David)
3. Comment est-ce que David trouve l'université française? (C'est différent de l'université américaine, mais c'est intéressant.)
4. Quels cours est-ce que David aime? (littérature et histoire françaises)
5. Stéphane a des problèmes dans quels cours? (français, maths, chimie et histoire-géo)

Video Synopsis At **Le P'tit Bistrot**, Rachid, Sandrine, Amina and David discuss their schedules. Astrid arrives; she is supposed to study with Stéphane. While she waits, Astrid talks about **le bac** and how Stéphane never does his homework. Rachid and Astrid decide to go to the park because they think Stéphane is there. At the park, Astrid and Stéphane argue. When Stéphane complains about his problems at school, Rachid offers to help him study.

Suggestions
- Have volunteers play the roles of Rachid, Sandrine, Amina, David, and Astrid in the scenes that match video stills 1–5.
- Have the class predict what will happen in scenes 6–10. Write predictions on the board.
- Read remaining scenes correcting the predictions. Ask questions to help students summarize this episode.

O P T I O N S

Avant de regarder la vidéo Write the title **On trouve une solution** on the board. Ask the class: Who has a problem in the video? What is it? Then ask the class to predict how the problem will be solved.

Regarder la vidéo Show the video episode and have students give you a play-by-play description of the action. Write their descriptions on the board. Then show the episode again so students can add more details to the description.

Les amis organisent des rendez-vous.

RACHID C'est un examen très important que les élèves français passent la dernière année de lycée pour continuer en études supérieures.

DAVID Euh, n'oublie pas, je suis de famille française.

ASTRID Oui, et c'est difficile, mais ce n'est pas impossible. Stéphane trouve que les études ne sont pas intéressantes. Le sport, oui, mais pas les études.

RACHID Le sport? Tu cherches Stéphane, n'est-ce pas? On trouve Stéphane au parc! Allons-y, Astrid.

ASTRID D'accord. À demain!

RACHID Oui. Mais le sport, c'est la dernière des priorités. Écoute, dimanche prochain, tu dînes chez moi et on trouve une solution.

STÉPHANE Rachid, tu n'as pas envie de donner des cours à un lycéen nul comme moi!

RACHID Mais si, j'ai très envie d'enseigner les maths...

STÉPHANE Bon, j'accepte. Merci, Rachid. C'est sympa.

RACHID De rien. À plus tard!

Expressions utiles

Talking about your schedule

- **Alors, on a rendez-vous demain à cinq heures moins le quart pour rentrer chez nous.**
  So, we're meeting tomorrow at quarter to five to go home (our home).

- **J'ai cours de chant de trois heures vingt à quatre heures et demie.**
  I have voice (singing) class from three-twenty to four-thirty.

- **J'ai cours de stylisme de deux heures à quatre heures vingt.**
  I have fashion design class from two o'clock to four-twenty.

- **Quelle heure est-il?** • **Tu n'as pas de montre?**
  What time is it?   *You don't have a watch?*

Talking about school

- **Nous avons le bac.**
  We have the bac.

- **Il ne fait pas ses devoirs.**
  He doesn't do his homework.

- **Tu n'as pas peur du bac!**
  You're not afraid of the bac!

- **Tu as tort, j'ai très peur du bac!**
  You're wrong, I'm very afraid of the bac!

- **Je suis d'accord avec toi.**
  I agree with you.

- **J'ai d'énormes problèmes.**
  I have big/enormous problems.

- **Tu n'as pas envie de donner des cours à un(e) lycéen(ne) nul(le) comme moi.**
  You don't want to teach a high school student as bad as myself.

Useful expressions

- **C'est parfait!** • **Ouais.**
  That's perfect!   *Yeah.*

- **Allons-y!** • **C'est sympa.**
  Let's go!   *That's nice/fun.*

- **D'accord.**
  OK, all right.

Expressions utiles
- Model the pronunciation of the **Expressions utiles** and have students repeat after you.
- As you work through the list, point out forms of **avoir**, idiomatic expressions with **avoir**, and expressions for telling time. Tell students that these concepts will be formally presented in **Espace structures**.
- Respond briefly to questions about **avoir** and reinforce correct forms, but do not expect students to produce them consistently at this time.
- Ask students a few questions based on the **Expressions utiles**. Examples: Tu as cours de chant aujourd'hui? Tu as cours de stylisme?
- Have students scan the video-still captions for phrases or sentences that show a sequence of time or events. Examples: **Aujourd'hui, c'est mercredi. Demain jeudi, ...**

1 Suggestion Have students correct the false statements.

2 Expansion For additional practice, ask these questions. **4. Où est-ce que tu as envie de dîner? 5. À qui est-ce que tu as envie de téléphoner? 6. Est-ce que tu as peur de regarder les films d'horreur?**

3 Suggestion Before beginning the activity, tell pairs to brainstorm and write a list of adjectives or phrases that describe Rachid and Stéphane.

2 Répondez Answer these questions. Refer to the video scenes and a dictionary as necessary. You do not have to answer in complete sentences. *Answers will vary.*

1. Où est-ce que tu as envie de voyager?
2. Est-ce que tu as peur de quelque chose? De quoi?
3. Qu'est-ce que tu dis (*say*) quand tu as tort?

3 À vous! With a partner, describe someone you know whose personality, likes, or dislikes resemble those of Rachid or Stéphane.

MODÈLE

Paul est comme (like) Rachid... il est sérieux.

ressources

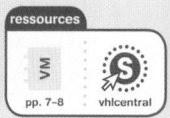

VM
pp. 7–8

vhlcentral

A C T I V I T É S

O P T I O N S

Small Groups Working in groups of three, have students create a short skit similar to the scenes in video stills 6–10 in which one of the students forgets to show up for a study session or a meeting. Give students ten minutes to prepare, then call on groups to perform their skits for the class.

Pairs Have students work in pairs. Tell them to create two-line conversations using as many of the **Expressions utiles** as they can. Example:
—**Alors, on a rendez-vous à cinq heures?**
—**Ouais! C'est parfait!**

ESPACE ROMAN-PHOTO **69**

Section Goals

In this section, students will:
• learn about university courses in France
• learn familiar terms for talking about classes and exams
• learn the names of some universities with French programs for foreigners
• read about **le bac**

Instructional Resources
vhlcentral.com: reference tools

Culture à la loupe

Avant la lecture Ask students: What would you want to know about classes at a French university of your choice if you were going there to study for a year?

Lecture
• Tell students that the word **amphi** is often used instead of **amphithéâtre**. Similarly, the word **fac** (for **faculté**) is used more often than **université**. The start of the school year is also known as the **rentrée scolaire.**
• Point out the **Coup de main**. Explain that commas are used instead of periods in percentages.
• Explain that French students rarely get praise from teachers. While American teachers are trained to encourage students for effort, the French typically reserve approbation for only truly excellent work.

Après la lecture Ask students if they prefer the French or American university system and have them explain why.

1 Expansion For extra practice, give students these items. 11. Lecture courses are rare in France. (**Faux.** They are common.) 12. The French discourage open debate. (**Faux.**) 13. The French university system relies heavily on exams for assessment. (**Vrai.**) 14. After studying abroad in France, a student needs to make sure that the overseas university provides information about grade conversion to the home institution. (**Vrai.**)

CULTURE À LA LOUPE

Les cours universitaires

French university courses often consist of lectures in large halls called **amphithéâtres.** Some also include discussion-based sessions with fewer students. Other than in the **grandes écoles** and specialized schools, class attendance is not mandatory in most universities. Students are motivated to attend by their desire to pass. Course grades may be based upon only one or two exams or term papers, so students generally take their studies seriously. They often form study groups to discuss the lectures and share class notes. This practice encourages open exchange of ideas and debate, a tradition that continues well past university life in France.

The start of classes each year is known as the **rentrée universitaire** and takes place at the beginning of October. The academic year is divided into two semesters. Four to six classes each semester is typical.

Students take exams throughout the semester, a practice known as **contrôle continu°**. At final exams in May or June, they can retake other exams they might have failed during that year or the preceding year. French grades range from 0–20, rather than from 0–100. Scores over 17 or 18 are rare and even the best students do not expect to score consistently in the near-perfect range. A grade of 10 is a passing grade, and is therefore not the equivalent of a 50 in the American system. If you plan to study abroad for credit, ask the foreign institution to provide your school with grade equivalents.

contrôle continu *continuous assessment*

Système français de notation

NOTE FRANÇAISE	NOTE AMÉRICAINE	%	NOTE FRANÇAISE	NOTE AMÉRICAINE	%
0	F	0	11	A-	85
2	F	3	12	A	90
3	F	8	13	A	93
4	F	18	14	A+	96
5	F	28	15	A+	99
6	F	38	16	A+	99.5
7	D-	50	17	A+	99.7
8	C-	60	18	A+	99.9
9	B-	70	19	A+	99.99
10	B	78	20	A+	over 99.99

Coup de main

To read decimal places in French, use the French word **virgule** (*comma*) where you would normally say *point* in English. To say *percent*, use **pour cent.**

60,4% soixante virgule quatre pour cent
sixty point four percent

A C T I V I T É S

1 Vrai ou faux? Indicate whether each statement is **vrai** or **faux**. Correct the false statements.

1. Class attendance is optional in some French universities.
   Vrai.
2. Final course grades are usually based on several exam grades and class participation.
   Faux. Grades may be based upon only one or two exams or papers.
3. The French university system discourages note sharing.
   Faux. Note sharing is completely normal.
4. The French grading system is similar to the American system.
   Faux. The French and American grading systems are very different.
5. The **rentrée universitaire** happens each year in August.
   Faux. The rentrée happens in October.

6. A grade of 11 is not a passing grade.
   Faux. A grade of 11 is equal to an A- in the United States.
7. The academic year in France is typically divided into trimesters.
   Faux. The academic year is divided into two semesters.
8. Scores of 18 or 19 are very rare.
   Vrai.
9. French students typically take three classes each semester.
   Faux. They typically take four to six classes.
10. The final exams in May or June are called the **contrôle continu**.
    Faux. The exams given throughout the semester are called the contrôle continu.

O P T I O N S

Pairs To review numbers and the alphabet, have students take turns making true/false statements about the French and American grading systems based on the information in the chart. Write on the board: a plus sign = **plus**; a minus sign = **moins**. Example: **Un vingt en France est un A plus plus plus plus plus plus aux États-Unis. (Vrai.)**

Small Groups Working in groups of three, have students describe the photos on this page. Tell them to create as many sentences in French as they can about the people, what they are doing, and why they are there. Then have volunteers read their descriptions to the class.

LE FRANÇAIS QUOTIDIEN

Les cours et les examens

cours (m.) magistral	lecture
cours (m.) de rattrapage	remedial class
bosser	to work hard
cartonner à un examen	to ace an exam
potasser	to cram
rater (un examen)	to fail (an exam)
sécher un cours	to skip a class

LE MONDE FRANCOPHONE

Le français langue étrangère

Voici quelques° écoles du monde francophone où vous pouvez aller° pour étudier le français.

En Belgique Université de Liège

En France Université de Franche-Comté–Centre de linguistique appliquée, Université de Grenoble, Université de Paris IV–Sorbonne

À la Martinique Institut Supérieur d'Études Francophones, à Schoelcher

En Nouvelle-Calédonie Centre de Rencontres et d'Échanges Internationaux du Pacifique, à Nouméa

Au Québec Université Laval, Université de Montréal

Aux îles Saint-Pierre et Miquelon Le FrancoForum, à Saint-Pierre

En Suisse Université Populaire de Lausanne, Université de Neuchâtel

quelques some **pouvez aller** can go

PORTRAIT

Le bac

Au lycée, les élèves ont des cours communs, comme le français, l'histoire et les maths, et aussi un choix° de spécialisation. À la fin° du lycée, à l'âge de dix-sept ou dix-huit ans, les jeunes Français passent un examen très important: le baccalauréat. Le bac est nécessaire pour continuer des études supérieures.

Les lycéens° passent des bacs différents: le bac L (littéraire), le bac ES (économique et social) et le bac S (scientifique) sont des bacs généraux. Il y a aussi des bacs techniques et des bacs technologiques, comme° le bac STI (sciences et technologies industrielles) ou le bac SMS (sciences et techniques médico-sociales). Il y a même° un bac technique de la musique et de la danse et un bac hôtellerie°! Entre 70 (soixante-dix) et 80 (quatre-vingts) pour cent des élèves passent le bac avec succès.

choix choice **À la fin** At the end **lycéens** high school students **comme** such as **même** even **hôtellerie** hotel trade

MUSIQUE À FOND

Francis Cabrel

Date de naissance: 23 novembre 1953
Lieu de naissance: Agen, France
Métier: auteur-compositeur-interprète

Francis Cabrel est très connu en France et ses ventes de disques sont évaluées à plus de 25 millions d'exemplaires.

Go to vhlcentral.com to find out more about **Francis Cabrel** and his music.

---

2 **Quel bac?** Which bac best fits the following interests?

1. le ballet   le bac technique de la musique et de la danse
2. la littérature   le bac littéraire
3. la médecine   le bac sciences et techniques médico-sociales
4. le tourisme   le bac hôtellerie
5. la technologie   le bac sciences et technologies industrielles
6. le piano et la flûte   le bac technique de la musique et de la danse

3 **Et les cours?** In French, name two courses you might take in preparation for each of these baccalauréat exams.

Answers will vary. Possible answers shown.

1. un bac L   le français et la philosophie
2. un bac SMS   la biologie et la psychologie
3. un bac ES   l'économie et la sociologie
4. un bac STI   la physique et les maths

 Practice more at **vhlcentral.com**.

 **ressources**

vhlcentral

ACTIVITÉS

Le français quotidien Model the pronunciation of each term and have students repeat it. You might also add these words to this list: **une dissert(ation)** (*writing assignment*), **réussir à un examen** (*to pass an exam*), **recaler** (*to fail*), and **les travaux pratiques (TP)** (*labs*).

Portrait Explain that, if a student fails the **bac**, he or she must pass an **examen de rattrapage** or repeat **terminale** and retake the exam the next year in order to pursue further study.

Le monde francophone Have students read the list. Use this as an opportunity to explain the importance of language immersion in a French-speaking country and to encourage students to start thinking about study abroad. If possible, bring in brochures or refer students to websites for study abroad programs.

Musique à fond Point out to students that they will find supporting activities and information at **vhlcentral.com**.

2 Expansion For additional practice, give students these items. 7. **l'histoire (le bac littéraire)** 8. **la biologie (le bac scientifique)** 9. **l'informatique (le bac sciences et technologies industrielles)** 10. **les sciences po (le bac économique et social)**

3 Expansion Tell students to imagine that they are in high school. Given their interests or major, ask them which **bac** they are preparing for. Example: **Quel bac est-ce que vous préparez? (Je prépare le bac S parce que j'étudie la chimie et la physique.)**

OPTIONS

Cultural Comparison Have students compare the French **lycée** to an American high school. Have them discuss the differences between the two educational systems. Then ask them what determines a student's ability to enroll in a university in France versus in the United States.

Pairs Have students work in pairs. Tell them to take turns asking and answering questions using the expressions in **Le français quotidien**. Examples: **Tu bosses pour le cours de français? Tu aimes les cours magistraux?**

Section Goals

In this section, students will learn:
- the verb **avoir**
- some common expressions with **avoir**

Instructional Resources
vhlcentral.com:
Lab MP3s; SAM Answer Key;
Mise en pratique answers;
Lab Audioscript; Activity
Pack (*Feuilles d'activités*);
reference tools

Suggestions

- Model **avoir** by asking questions such as: **Avez-vous un examen cette semaine? Avez-vous une calculatrice? ____ a-t-il/elle/on une calculatrice?** Point out that forms of **avoir** were in the **Roman-photo.**
- Explain that **avoir** is irregular and must be memorized. Begin a paradigm for **avoir** by writing **j'ai** on the board and asking volunteers questions that elicit **j'ai.** Examples: **J'ai un stylo. Qui a un crayon?**
- Add **tu as** and **il/elle a/on** to the paradigm on the board. Point out that **as** and **a** are pronounced alike. Tell students that **avoir** has no real stem apart from the letter **a.**
- Write **nous avons** and **vous avez.** Point out that **-ons** and **-ez** are the same endings as in **-er** verbs. Add **ils/elles ont.**
- Remind students of liaisons in the plural forms of **avoir** and have them pronounce these forms.

2B.1

Present tense of *avoir* Tutorial

Point de départ The verb **avoir** (*to have*) is used frequently. You will have to memorize each of its present tense forms because they are irregular.

Present tense of *avoir*			
j'ai	*I have*	**nous avons**	*we have*
tu as	*you have*	**vous avez**	*you have*
il/elle/on a	*he/she/it/one has*	**ils/elles ont**	*they have*

On a rendez-vous avec David demain.

Cette année, nous avons le bac.

- Liaison is required between the final consonants of **on, nous, vous, ils,** and **elles** and the first vowel of forms of **avoir** that follow them. When the final consonant is an **-s,** pronounce it as a *z* before the verb forms.

On a un prof sympa.
We have a nice professor.

Nous avons un cours d'art.
We have an art class.

Vous avez deux stylos.
You have two pens.

Elles ont un examen de psychologie.
They have a Psychology exam.

- Keep in mind that an indefinite article, whether singular or plural, usually becomes **de/d'** after a negation.

J'ai **un** cours difficile.
I have a difficult class.

Je n'ai pas **de** cours difficile.
I do not have a difficult class.

Il a **des** examens.
He has exams.

Il n'a pas **d'**examens.
He does not have exams.

- The verb **avoir** is used in certain idiomatic or set expressions where English generally uses *to be* or *to feel*.

Expressions with *avoir*

avoir... ans	to be... years old	avoir froid	to be cold
avoir besoin (de)	to need	avoir honte (de)	to be ashamed (of)
avoir de la chance	to be lucky	avoir l'air	to look like, to seem
		avoir peur (de)	to be afraid (of)
avoir chaud	to be hot	avoir raison	to be right
avoir envie (de)	to feel like	avoir sommeil	to be sleepy
		avoir tort	to be wrong

🏃 **Boîte à outils**

In the expression **avoir l'air** + [*adjective*], the adjective does not change to agree with the subject. It is always masculine singular, because it agrees with **air**. Examples:

Elle a l'air charmant.
She looks charming.

Ils ont l'air content.
They look happy.

Il a chaud.

Ils ont froid.

Elle a sommeil.

Il a de la chance.

- The expressions **avoir besoin de, avoir honte de, avoir peur de,** and **avoir envie de** can be followed by either a noun or a verb.

J'**ai besoin d'**une calculatrice.
I need a calculator.

J'**ai besoin d'**étudier.
I need to study.

Laure **a peur des** serpents.
Laure is afraid of snakes.

Laure **a peur de** parler au professeur.
Laure is afraid to talk to the professor.

Essayez!   Complete the sentences with the correct forms of **avoir**.

1. La température est de 35 degrés Celsius. Nous __avons__ chaud.

2. En Alaska, en décembre, vous __avez__ froid.

3. Martine écoute la radio et elle __a__ envie de danser.

4. Ils __ont__ besoin d'une calculatrice pour le devoir.

5. Est-ce que tu __as__ peur des insectes?

6. Sébastien pense que je travaille aujourd'hui. Il __a__ raison.

7. J'__ai__ cours d'économie le lundi et le mercredi.

8. Mes amis voyagent beaucoup. Ils __ont__ de la chance.

9. Mohammed __a__ deux cousins à Marseille.

10. Vous __avez__ un grand appartement.

ressources

WB
pp. 23–24

LM
p. 15

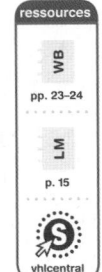
vhlcentral

Suggestions
- Tell the class that many French expressions use **avoir** + [*noun*] instead of **être** to say *to be* + [*adjective*] in English. Tell students to use **avoir envie de** + [*infinitive*] to ask people if they feel like doing something.
- Model the use of the expressions by talking about yourself while gesturing and asking students questions about themselves. Examples: **J'ai froid ce matin/cet après-midi. Vous avez froid aussi ou vous avez chaud? J'ai besoin d'un dictionnaire. Avez-vous un dictionnaire?**

Essayez! Ask students to identify the idiomatic expressions in the sentences. (All are idiomatic expressions, except items 7, 9, and 10.)

OPTIONS

Extra Practice Do a quick substitution drill with **avoir**. Write a sentence on the board and have students read it aloud. Then say a new subject and have students repeat the sentence, substituting the new subject. Examples: **1. J'ai des problèmes. (Éric et moi, tu, Stéphane, vous, les hommes) 2. Pierre a cours de chimie le mardi et le jeudi. (Pierre et Julie, nous, je, vous, tu)**

TPR Assign gestures to expressions with **avoir**. Examples: **avoir chaud**: *wipe brow*, **avoir froid**: *wrap arms around oneself and shiver*, **avoir peur**: *hold one's hand over mouth in fear*, **avoir faim**: *rub stomach*; **avoir sommeil**: *yawn and stretch*. Have students stand. Say an expression at random as you point to a student who performs the appropriate gesture. Vary by indicating more than one student at a time.

1 **Suggestion** This activity can be done in pairs. Tell students to alternate asking and answering the questions.

2 **Expansion** For each drawing, ask students how many people there are, their names, and their ages. Example: **Combien de personnes y a-t-il sur le dessin numéro 1? Comment s'appellent-elles? Quel âge a _____?**

3 **Suggestion** This activity can be done orally or in writing, in pairs or groups.

Mise en pratique

1 **On a...** Use the correct forms of **avoir** to form questions from these elements. Use inversion and provide an affirmative or negative answer as indicated.

MODÈLE

tu / bourse (oui)
As-tu une bourse? Oui, j'ai une bourse.

1. nous / dictionnaire (oui) Avons-nous un dictionnaire? Oui, nous avons un dictionnaire.
2. Luc / diplôme (non) Luc a-t-il un diplôme? Non, il n'a pas de diplôme.
3. elles / montres (non) Ont-elles des montres? Non, elles n'ont pas de montres.
4. vous / copains (oui) Avez-vous des copains? Oui, j'ai/nous avons des copains.
5. Thérèse / téléphone (oui) Thérèse a-t-elle un téléphone? Oui, elle a un téléphone.
6. Charles et Jacques / calculatrice (non) Charles et Jacques ont-ils une calculatrice? Non, ils n'ont pas de calculatrice.
7. on / examen (non) A-t-on un examen? Non, on n'a pas d'examen.
8. tu / livres de français (non) As-tu des livres de français? Non, je n'ai pas de livres de français.

2 **C'est évident** Describe these people using expressions with **avoir**.

1. J' __ai besoin d'__ étudier.

2. Vous __avez froid__ .

3. Tu __as honte__ .

4. Elles __ont sommeil__ .

3 **Assemblez** Use the verb **avoir** and combine elements from the two columns to create sentences about yourself, your class, and your school. Make any necessary changes or additions. Answers will vary.

A	B
Je	cours utiles
L'université	bourses importantes
Les profs	professeurs brillants
Mon (*My*) petit ami	ami(e) mexicain(e)
	/ anglais(e)
Ma (*My*) petite amie	/ canadien(ne)
	/ vietnamien(ne)
Nous	étudiants intéressants
	resto U agréable
	école de droit

 Practice more at **vhlcentral.com**.

Communication

4 Besoins Your instructor will give you a worksheet. Ask different classmates if they need to do these activities. Find at least one person to answer **Oui** and at least one to answer **Non** for each item. Answers will vary.

MODÈLE

regarder la télé
Étudiant(e) 1: *Tu as besoin de regarder la télé?*
Étudiant(e) 2: *Oui, j'ai besoin de regarder la télé.*
Étudiant(e) 3: *Non, je n'ai pas besoin de regarder la télé.*

Activités	Oui	Non
1. regarder la télé	Anne	Louis
2. étudier ce soir		
3. passer un examen cette semaine		
4. trouver un cours d'informatique		
5. travailler à la bibliothèque		
6. commencer un devoir important		
7. téléphoner à un(e) copain/copine ce week-end		
8. parler avec le professeur		

5 C'est vrai? Interview a classmate by transforming each of these statements into a question. Be prepared to report the results of your interview to the class. Answers will vary.

MODÈLE J'ai deux ordinateurs.

Étudiant(e) 1: *Tu as deux ordinateurs?*
Étudiant(e) 2: *Non, je n'ai pas deux ordinateurs.*

1. J'ai peur des examens.
2. J'ai vingt et un ans.
3. J'ai envie de visiter Montréal.
4. J'ai un cours de biologie.
5. J'ai sommeil le lundi matin.
6. J'ai un(e) petit(e) ami(e) égoïste.

6 Interview You are talking to the campus housing advisor. Answer his or her questions. In pairs, practice the scene and role-play it for the class. Answers will vary.

1. Qu'est-ce que (*What*) vous étudiez?
2. Est-ce que vous avez d'excellentes notes?
3. Est-ce que vous avez envie de partager la chambre?
4. Est-ce que vous mangez au resto U?
5. Est-ce que vous avez un ordinateur?
6. Est-ce que vous retrouvez des amis à la fac?
7. Est-ce que vous écoutez de la musique?
8. Est-ce que vous avez des cours le matin?
9. Est-ce que vous aimez habiter sur le campus?

soixante-quinze **75**

4 Suggestions
- Have three volunteers read the **modèle** aloud. Then distribute the **Feuilles d'activités**, found in the Activity Pack on the Supersite.
- Have students add at least two activities of their own.

5 Suggestion Have two volunteers read the **modèle** aloud. Remind students that an indefinite article becomes **de (d')** if it follows **avoir** in the negative.

6 Suggestions
- Remind students to do the interview twice so each person asks and answers the questions.
- Ask volunteers to summarize their partners' responses. Record the responses on the board as a survey (**un sondage**) about the class' characteristics. Then ask questions like this: **Combien d'étudiants dans la classe étudient l'économie?**

OPTIONS

Game Divide the class into two teams. Choose one team member at a time to go to the board, alternating between teams. Say a subject pronoun. The person at the board must write and say the correct form of **avoir**. Example: **elle (elle a)**. Give a point for each correct answer. The team with the most points at the end of the game wins.

Small Groups Have students work in groups of three. Tell them to write nine sentences, each of which uses a different expression with **avoir**. Call on volunteers to write some of their group's best sentences on the board. Have the class read the sentences aloud and correct any errors.

Section Goals

In this section, students will learn:
- to tell time
- some time expressions
- the 24-hour system of telling time

Instructional Resources
vhlcentral.com:
Activity Pack; Lab MP3s;
SAM Answer Key; Digital
*Image Bank; **Essayez!***
*and **Mise en pratique***
answers; Lab Audioscript;
reference tools

Suggestions

- To prepare for telling time, review the meanings of **il est** and numbers 0–60.
- Introduce: **Il est sept heures (huit heures, neuf heures…).**
- Explain to students that **heures** refers to *hours* when telling time, but can also mean *o'clock*.
- Introduce: **Il est _____ heure(s) cinq, dix, et quart,** and **et demie.**
- Using a paper plate clock, display various times on the hour. Ask: **Quelle heure est-il?**
- Introduce and explain: **Il est _____ heure(s) moins cinq, moins dix, moins le quart,** and **moins vingt.** Repeat the procedure above using your movable-hands clock.
- Explain that the French view times of day differently from Americans. In France, they say «**bonjour**» until about 4:00 or 5:00 p.m. After that, they use the greeting «**bonsoir**». They say «**bonne nuit**» only when going to sleep.

2B.2

Telling time  Tutorial

Point de départ Use the verb **être** with numbers to tell time.

- There are two ways to ask what time it is.

  Quelle heure est-il?
  What time is it?

  Quelle heure avez-vous / as-tu?
  What time do you have?

- Use **heures** by itself to express time on the hour. Use **une heure** for one o'clock.

Il est **six heures**.   Il est **une heure**.

- Express time from the hour to the half-hour by stating the number of minutes it is past the hour.

Il est quatre heures **cinq**.   Il est onze heures **vingt**.

- Use **et quart** to say that it is fifteen minutes past the hour. Use **et demie** to say that it is thirty minutes past the hour.

Il est une heure **et quart**.   Il est sept heures **et demie**.

- To express time from the half hour to the hour, subtract the number of minutes or the portion of an hour from the next hour.

Il est trois heures **moins dix**.   Il est une heure **moins le quart**.

- To express at what time something happens, use the preposition **à**.

  Céline travaille **à sept heures moins vingt**.
  Céline works at 6:40.

  On passe un examen **à une heure**.
  We take a test at one o'clock.

Boîte à outils

In English, you often leave out the word *o'clock* when telling time. You might say "The class starts at eleven" or "I arrive at seven." In French, however, you must always include the word **heure(s)**.

- In French, the hour and minutes are separated by the letter **h**, which stands for **heure**, whereas in English a colon is used.

  3:25 = **3h25**   11:10 = **11h10**   5:15 = **5h15**

- **Liaison** occurs between numbers and the word **heure(s)**. Final **-s** and **-x** in **deux**, **trois**, **six**, and **dix** are pronounced like a *z*. The final **-f** of **neuf** is pronounced like a *v*.

  Il est **deux heures**.   Il est **neuf heures** et quart.
  It's two o'clock.   *It's 9:15.*

- You do not usually make a **liaison** between the verb form **est** and a following number that starts with a vowel sound.

  Il est onze heures.   Il est une heure vingt.   Il est huit heures et demie.
  It's eleven o'clock.   *It's 1:20.*   *It's 8:30.*

Expressions for telling time

À quelle heure?	*(At) what time/ when?*	**midi**	*noon*
de l'après-midi	*in the afternoon*	**minuit**	*midnight*
du matin	*in the morning*	**pile**	*sharp, on the dot*
du soir	*in the evening*	**presque**	*almost*
en avance	*early*	**tard**	*late*
en retard	*late*	**tôt**	*early*
		vers	*about*

Il est **minuit** à Paris.   Il est six heures **du soir** à New York.
It's midnight in Paris.   *It's six o'clock in the evening in New York.*

- The 24-hour clock is often used to express official time. Departure times, movie times, and store hours are expressed in this fashion. Only numbers are used to tell time this way. Expressions like **et demie**, **moins le quart**, etc. are not used.

  Le train arrive à **dix-sept heures six**.   Le film est à **vingt-deux heures trente-sept**.
  The train arrives at 5:06 p.m.   *The film is at 10:37 p.m.*

J'ai cours de trois heures vingt à quatre heures et demie.

Stéphane! Quelle heure est-il?

🏃 **Boîte à outils**

In French, there are no words for *a.m.* and *p.m.* You can use **du matin** for *a.m.*, **de l'après-midi** from noon until about 6 p.m., and **du soir** from about 6 p.m. until midnight. When you use the 24-hour clock, it becomes obvious whether you're referring to *a.m.* or *p.m.*

À noter

As you learned in **Leçon 1A**, when you say 21, 31, 41, etc. in French, the *one* agrees with the gender of the noun that follows. Therefore, **21h00** is **vingt et une heures**.

Suggestions
- Explain the use of the 24-hour clock. Have students practice saying times this way by adding 12.
- Model the pronunciation of the time expressions in the box and have students repeat. Point out that a.m. and p.m. are not used in France or most francophone regions. Instead, they use **du matin**, **de l'après midi**, and **du soir**.
- Tell students that **et demi(e)** agrees in gender with the noun it follows, but not in number. After **midi** and **minuit**, both **et demi** and **et demie** are accepted.

Essayez! For additional practice, give students these items.
11. 6:20 p.m.
12. 9:10 a.m.
13. 2:15 p.m.
14. 10:35 a.m.
15. 12:00 a.m.
16. 9:55 p.m.

✏ **Essayez!**   Complete the sentences by writing out the correct times according to the cues.

1. (1:00 a.m.) Il est ___une heure___ du matin.
2. (2:50 a.m.) Il est ___trois heures moins dix___ du matin.
3. (8:30 p.m.) Il est ___huit heures et demie___ du soir.
4. (10:08 a.m.) Il est ___dix heures huit___ du matin.
5. (7:15 p.m.) Il est ___sept heures et quart___ du soir.
6. (12:00 p.m.) Il est ___midi___ .
7. (4:05 p.m.) Il est ___quatre heures cinq___ de l'après-midi.
8. (4:45 a.m.) Il est ___cinq heures moins le quart___ du matin.
9. (3:20 a.m.) Il est ___trois heures vingt___ du matin.
10. (12:00 a.m.) Il est ___minuit___ .

ressources
WB
pp. 25–26

LM
p. 16

S
vhlcentral

OPTIONS

Extra Practice Draw a large clock face on the board with its numbers but without the hands. Say a time and ask a volunteer to come up and draw the hands to indicate that time. The rest of the class verifies whether or not the person has written the correct time, saying: **Il/Elle a raison/tort**. Repeat this procedure a number of times.

Video Play the video episode again to give students additional input on telling time and the verb **avoir**. Pause the video where appropriate to discuss how time or **avoir** were used and to ask comprehension questions. Example: **Est-ce que Stéphane a peur de parler à Astrid? (Mais non, il a peur du bac.)**

ESPACE STRUCTURES **77**

ESPACE STRUCTURES

1 Expansion At random, say the times shown and have students say the number of the clock or watch described. Example: **Il est sept heures cinq. (C'est le numéro six.)**

2 Suggestion Read the **modèle** aloud with a volunteer. Working in pairs, have students take turns asking and answering the questions.

3 Expansion Create a train schedule and write it on the board or use photocopies of a real one. Ask students questions based on the schedule. Example: **À quelle heure est le train Paris-Bordeaux le vendredi soir?**

Mise en pratique

1 **Quelle heure est-il?** Give the time shown on each clock or watch.

> **MODÈLE**
> Il est quatre heures et quart de l'après-midi.

1. Il est midi/minuit et demi(e). / Il est douze heures trente.
2. Il est une heure du matin.
3. Il est huit heures dix.
4. Il est onze heures moins le quart.

5. Il est deux heures douze.
6. Il est sept heures cinq.
7. Il est quatre heures moins cinq.
8. Il est minuit moins vingt-cinq.

2 **À quelle heure?** Find out when you and your friends are going to do certain things.

> **MODÈLE**
> À quelle heure est-ce qu'on étudie? (about 8 p.m.)
> On étudie vers huit heures du soir.

À quelle heure...

1. ...est-ce qu'on arrive au café? (at 10:30 a.m.) On arrive au café à dix heures et demie du matin.
2. ...est-ce que vous parlez avec le professeur? (at noon) Nous parlons avec le professeur à midi.
3. ...est-ce que tu travailles? (late, at 11:15 p.m.) Je travaille tard, à onze heures et quart du soir.
4. ...est-ce qu'on regarde la télé? (at 9:00 p.m.) On regarde la télé à neuf heures du soir.
5. ...est-ce que Marlène et Nadine mangent? (around 1:45 p.m.) Elles mangent vers deux heures moins le quart de l'après-midi.
6. ...est-ce que le cours commence? (very early, at 8:20 a.m.) Il commence très tôt, à huit heures vingt du matin.

3 **Départ à...** Tell what each of these times would be on a 24-hour clock.

> **MODÈLE**
> Il est trois heures vingt de l'après-midi.
> Il est quinze heures vingt.

1. Il est dix heures et demie du soir. Il est vingt-deux heures trente.
2. Il est deux heures de l'après-midi. Il est quatorze heures.
3. Il est huit heures et quart du soir. Il est vingt heures quinze.
4. Il est minuit moins le quart. Il est vingt-trois heures quarante-cinq.
5. Il est six heures vingt-cinq du soir. Il est dix-huit heures vingt-cinq.
6. Il est trois heures moins cinq du matin. Il est deux heures cinquante-cinq.
7. Il est six heures moins le quart de l'après-midi. Il est dix-sept heures quarante-cinq.
8. Il est une heure et quart de l'après-midi. Il est treize heures quinze.
9. Il est neuf heures dix du soir. Il est vingt et une heures dix.
10. Il est sept heures quarante du soir. Il est dix-neuf heures quarante.

 Practice more at **vhlcentral.com**.

Communication

4 Télémonde Look at this French TV guide. In pairs, ask questions about program start times. *Answers will vary.*

MODÈLE

Étudiant(e) 1: *À quelle heure commence Télé-ciné sur Antenne 4?*
Étudiant(e) 2: *Télé-ciné commence à dix heures dix du soir.*

dessins animés	*cartoons*
feuilleton télévisé	*soap opera*
film policier	*detective film*
informations	*news*
jeu télévisé	*game show*

VENDREDI

Antenne 2	Antenne 4	Antenne 5
15h30 Pomme d'Api (dessins animés)	**14h00** Football: match France-Italie	**18h25** Montréal: une ville à visiter
17h35 Reportage spécial: le sport dans les lycées	**19h45** Les informations	**19h30** Des chiffres et des lettres (jeu télévisé)
20h15 La famille Menet (feuilleton télévisé)	**20h30** Concert: orchestre de Nice	**21h05** Reportage spécial: les Sénégalais
21h35 Télé-ciné: L'inspecteur Duval (film policier)	**22h10** Télé-ciné: Une chose difficile (comédie dramatique)	**22h05** Les informations

5 Où es-tu? In pairs, take turns asking where (**où**) your partner usually is on these days at these times. Choose from the places listed. *Answers will vary.*

au lit (*bed*)	**chez mes** (*at my*) **parents**
au resto U	
à la bibliothèque	**chez mes copains**
en ville (*town*)	**chez mon** (*my*) **petit ami**
au parc	
en cours	**chez ma** (*my*) **petite amie**

1. Le samedi: à 8h00 du matin; à midi; à minuit

2. En semaine: à 9h00 du matin; à 3h00 de l'après-midi; à 7h00 du soir

3. Le dimanche: à 4h00 de l'après-midi; à 6h30 du soir; à 10h00 du soir

4. Le vendredi: à 11h00 du matin; à 5h00 de l'après-midi; à 11h00 du soir

6 Le suspect A student on campus is a suspect in a crime. You and a partner are detectives. Keeping a log of the student's activities, use the 24-hour clock to say what he or she is doing when. *Answers will vary.*

MODÈLE

À vingt-deux heures trente-trois, il parle au téléphone.

---

4 Suggestion Before starting this activity, have students read the TV guide, point out cognates, and predict their meaning. Provide examples for non-cognate categories so students can guess their meaning. Examples: **dessins animés, feuilleton télévisé,** and **jeu télévisé.**

4 Expansion Have pairs ask each other additional questions based on the TV guide. Examples: **Est-ce qu'il y a un reportage à vingt heures dix? (Non, les reportages sont à dix-sept heures trente-cinq et à vingt et une heures cinq.) J'ai envie de regarder le film policier. À quelle heure est-il? (Le film policier est à vingt et une heures trente-cinq.)**

5 Suggestion Before beginning the activity, provide students with a model. Example: **Étudiant(e) 1: Où es-tu le samedi à midi? Étudiant(e) 2: Le samedi à midi, je suis au resto U.**

6 Expansion After completing the activity, ask students if the suspect has an alibi at certain times. Tell them to respond using the information on their logs. Example: **Le suspect a-t-il un alibi à vingt-trois heures? (Oui, à vingt-trois heures il étudie avec un ami.)**

OPTIONS

Pairs Have pairs take turns telling each other what time their classes are this semester/trimester/term. Example: **J'ai un cours à ____ heures….** For each time given, the other student draws a clock face with the corresponding time. The first student verifies if the clock is correct.

Small Groups Have students work in groups of three. Tell them to take turns asking what time various TV shows start and answering. Example: **À quelle heure est *60 Minutes*? (C'est à dix-neuf heures.)** Remind students to use the 24-hour system when talking about TV shows.

Révision

Instructional Resources
vhlcentral.com:
*Activity Pack (Info Gap
Activities; Task-based Activity);
Testing Program; Testing
Program MP3s; reference tools*

1 Suggestion Have two
volunteers read the **modèle**
aloud. Encourage students to
add other items to the list.

2 Suggestion Before
beginning the activity, tell
students to choose two language
classes, a science class, and an
elective in the list. Then read the
modèle aloud with a volunteer.

3 Expansion Have volunteers
report their findings to the
class. Then do a quick class
survey to find out how many
students are taking the same
courses. Example: **Combien
d'étudiants ont sciences
politiques ce semestre?**

4 Suggestion Before doing
the activity, point out the use
of the construction **avoir envie
de** + [*infinitive*]. Encourage
students to add activities to the
list. Examples: **regarder un film,
manger/partager une pizza,
parler au téléphone,** and
voyager en France/Europe.

5 Suggestion Ask what
expressions express likes
and dislikes, and write them
on the board before assigning
this activity.

6 Suggestions
• Divide the class into pairs
and distribute the Info Gap
Handouts, found in the Activity
Pack on the Supersite for this
activity. Have two volunteers
read the **modèle**. Give students
ten minutes to complete the
activity.
• After completing the activity, ask
students what activities Patrick
would like to do this weekend.

---

1 J'ai besoin de… In pairs, take turns saying which items
you need. Your partner will guess why you need them. How
many times did each of you guess correctly? Answers will vary.

MODÈLE

Étudiant(e) 1: *J'ai besoin d'un cahier et d'un dictionnaire
pour demain.*
Étudiant(e) 2: *Est-ce que tu as un cours de français?*
Étudiant(e) 1: *Non. J'ai un examen d'anglais.*

un cahier	un livre de physique
une calculatrice	une montre
une carte	un ordinateur
un dictionnaire	un stylo
une feuille de papier	un téléphone

2 À l'université française To complete your degree, you
need two language classes, a science class, and an elective.
Take turns deciding what classes you need or want to take.
Your partner will tell you the days and times so you can set up
your schedule. Answers will vary.

MODÈLE

Étudiant(e) 1: *J'ai besoin d'un cours de maths, peut-être
«Initiation aux maths».*
Étudiant(e) 2: *C'est le mardi et le jeudi après-midi, de deux
heures à trois heures et demie.*
Étudiant(e) 1: *J'ai aussi besoin d'un cours de langue…*

Les cours	Jours et heures
Allemand	mardi, jeudi; 14h00-15h30
Biologie II	mardi, jeudi; 9h00-10h30
Chimie générale	lundi, mercredi; 11h00-12h30
Espagnol	lundi, mercredi; 11h00-12h30
Gestion	mercredi; 13h00-14h30
Histoire des États-Unis	jeudi; 12h15-14h15
Initiation à la physique	lundi, mercredi; 12h00-13h30
Initiation aux maths	mardi, jeudi; 14h00-15h30
Italien	lundi, mercredi; 12h00-13h30
Japonais	mardi, jeudi; 9h00-10h30
Les philosophes grecs	lundi; 15h15-16h45
Littérature moderne	mardi; 10h15-11h15

3 Les cours Your partner will tell you what classes he or she
is currently taking. Make a list, including the times and days
of the week. Then, talk to as many classmates as you can, and
find at least two students who take at least two of the same
classes as your partner. Answers will vary.

4 On y va? Walk around the room and find at least one
classmate who feels like doing each of these activities with you.
For every affirmative answer, record the name of your classmate
and agree on a time and date. Do not speak to the same
classmate twice. Answers will vary.

MODÈLE

Étudiant(e) 1: *Tu as envie de retrouver des amis avec moi?*
Étudiant(e) 2: *Oui, pourquoi pas? Samedi, à huit heures
du soir, peut-être?*
Étudiant(e) 1: *D'accord!*

chercher un café sympa	regarder la télé française
dîner au resto U	retrouver des amis
écouter de la musique	travailler à la bibliothèque
étudier le français	visiter un musée
cette semaine	

5 Au téléphone Two high school friends are attending
different universities. In pairs, imagine a conversation where
they discuss the time, their classes, and likes or dislikes about
campus life. Then, role-play the conversation for the class and
vote for the best skit. Answers will vary.

MODÈLE

Étudiant(e) 1: *J'ai cours de chimie à dix heures et demie.*
Étudiant(e) 2: *Je n'ai pas de cours de chimie cette année.*
Étudiant(e) 1: *N'aimes-tu pas les sciences?*
Étudiant(e) 2: *Si, mais…*

6 La semaine de Patrick Your instructor will give you
and a partner different incomplete pages from Patrick's day
planner. Do not look at each other's worksheet. Answers will vary.

MODÈLE

Étudiant(e) 1: *Lundi matin, Patrick a cours de géographie à
dix heures et demie.*
Étudiant(e) 2: *Lundi, il a cours de sciences po à deux heures
de l'après-midi.*

O P T I O N S

Small Groups Working in groups of three or four, have students
create a short skit similar to the scene in video still 1 of the
Roman-photo. Tell them that they have to decide on a day, time,
and place to meet for a study session in order to prepare for the
next French test. Have groups perform their skits for the class.

Extra Practice Have students make a list of six items that
students normally carry in their backpacks to class. Then tell
them to circulate around the room asking their classmates if
they have those items in their backpacks. Also tell them to ask
how many they have. Example: **As-tu un cahier dans le sac à
dos? Combien de cahiers as-tu?**

À l'écoute

Audio: Activities

Section Goals

In this section, students will:
- learn to listen for cognates
- listen to sentences containing familiar and unfamiliar vocabulary
- listen to a conversation, complete a schedule, and answer true/false questions

Instructional Resources
vhlcentral.com:
Textbook MP3s; Textbook Audioscript; reference tools

STRATÉGIE

Listening for cognates

You already know that cognates are words that have similar spellings and meanings in two or more languages: for example *group* and **groupe** or *activity* and **activité**. Listen for cognates to increase your comprehension of spoken French.

 To help you practice this strategy, you will listen to two sentences. Make a list of all the cognates you hear.

Préparation

Based on the photograph, who do you think Marie-France and Dominique are? Do you think they know each other well? Where are they? Where are they probably going this morning? What do you think they are talking about?

À vous d'écouter

Listen to the conversation and list any cognates you hear. Listen again and complete the highlighted portions of Marie-France's schedule.

28 OCTOBRE	lundi		
8H00	*jogging*	14H00	psychologie
8H30		14H30	
9H00		15H00	
9H30	biologie	15H30	physique
10H00		16H00	
10H30		16H30	
11H00	chimie	17H00	
11H30		17H30	*étudier*
12H00	resto U	18H00	
12H30		18H30	
13H00	*bibliothèque*	19H00	*téléphoner à papa*
13H30		19H30	*Sophie:* restaurant vietnamien

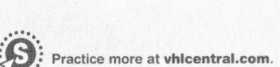 Practice more at **vhlcentral.com**.

Compréhension

Vrai ou faux? Indicate whether each statement is **vrai** or **faux**. Then correct the false statements.

1. D'après Marie-France, la biologie est facile.
   Vrai.

2. Marie-France adore la chimie.
   Faux. Marie-France déteste la chimie.

3. Marie-France et Dominique mangent au restaurant vietnamien à midi.
   Faux. Marie-France et Dominique mangent au restaurant vietnamien à sept heures et demie du soir.

4. Dominique aime son cours de sciences politiques.
   Faux. Dominique aime son cours d'informatique.

5. Monsieur Meyer est professeur de physique.
   Vrai.

6. Monsieur Meyer donne des devoirs faciles.
   Faux. Monsieur Meyer donne des devoirs très difficiles.

7. Le lundi après-midi, Marie-France a psychologie et physique.
   Vrai.

8. Aujourd'hui, Dominique mange au resto U.
   Faux. Aujourd'hui, Marie-France mange au resto U.

Votre emploi du temps With a partner, discuss the classes you're taking this semester. Be sure to say when you have each one, and give your opinion of at least three courses.

Stratégie
Audioscript 1. Dans certaines institutions d'études supérieures, les étudiants reçoivent un salaire. 2. Ma cousine étudie la médecine vétérinaire. C'est sa passion!

Préparation Have students describe the photo. Ask them to justify their descriptions based on the visual clues.

Suggestion To check answers for the **À vous d'écouter** activity, have students work in pairs and take turns asking questions about Marie-France's schedule. Example: **Est-ce que Marie-France a cours de biologie à 14h00? (Non, elle a cours de biologie à 9h30.)**

À vous d'écouter
Audioscript DOMINIQUE: Tiens, bonjour, Marie-France. Comment ça va?
MARIE-FRANCE: Salut, Dominique. Ça va bien. Et toi?
D: Très bien, merci. Tu vas en cours?
M: Oui, j'ai cours toute la journée, le lundi. Ce matin, j'ai biologie à neuf heures et demie.
D: Tu aimes la biologie?
M: Oui, j'aime bien. C'est facile. Après, à onze heures, j'ai chimie. Ça, je déteste! C'est difficile! À midi, je mange au resto U avec des copains.
D: Et cet après-midi?
M: Alors, à deux heures, j'ai psychologie et à trois heures et demie, j'ai physique.
D: Est-ce que tu aimes ça, la physique?
M: Oui, mais cette année, le prof n'est pas très intéressant.
D: Ah bon? Qui est-ce?
M: Monsieur Meyer.

D: Ah oui! Tu as raison. Il n'est pas très intéressant. Et il donne des devoirs et des examens très difficiles.
M: C'est vrai. Et toi, tu aimes tes cours cette année?
D: Oui, beaucoup. J'adore l'informatique. Le prof est amusant et il explique bien.
M: Tu as de la chance! Dis, est-ce que tu as envie de dîner au restaurant avec Sophie et moi ce soir? On va au restaurant vietnamien près de l'université.
D: Oui, avec plaisir. À quelle heure?
M: À sept heures et demie.
D: Bon, d'accord. À ce soir.
M: Salut.

Panorama

connections
cultures
NATIONAL
STANDARDS

LA FRANCE

La France

Le pays en chiffres

▶ **Superficie:** 549.000 km²
(*cinq cent quarante-neuf mille kilomètres carrés°*)

▶ **Population:** 64.395.000 (*soixante-quatre millions trois cent quatre-vingt-quinze mille*)
SOURCE: Population Division, UN Secrétariat

▶ **Industries principales:** *agro-alimentaires°, assurance°, banques, énergie, produits pharmaceutiques, produits de luxe, télécommunications, tourisme, transports*

La France est le pays° le plus° visité du monde° avec plus de° 83 millions de touristes chaque° année. Son histoire, sa culture et ses monuments– plus de 43.000 (*quarante-trois mille*)–et musées– plus de 1.200 (*mille deux cents*)–attirent° des touristes de partout° dans le monde.

▶ **Villes principales:** *Paris, Lille, Lyon, Marseille, Toulouse*

▶ **Monnaie°:** *l'euro*
La France est un pays membre de l'Union européenne et, en 2002, l'euro a remplacé° le franc français comme° monnaie nationale.

Français célèbres

▶ Jeanne d'Arc, *héroïne française (1412–1431)*

▶ Émile Zola, *écrivain° (1840–1902)*

▶ Pierre-Auguste Renoir, *peintre° (1841–1919)*

▶ Claude Debussy, *compositeur et musicien (1862–1918)*

▶ Camille Claudel, *sculptrice (1864–1943)*

▶ Claudie André-Deshays, *médecin, première astronaute française (1957–)*

carrés *square* agro-alimentaires *food processing* assurance *insurance* pays *country* le plus *the most* monde *world* plus de *more than* chaque *each* attirent *attract* partout *everywhere* Monnaie *Currency* a remplacé *replaced* comme *as* écrivain *writer* peintre *painter* élus à vie *elected for life* Depuis *Since* mots *words* courrier *mail* pont *bridge*

un bateau-mouche sur la Seine

LE ROYAUME-UNI

LA MER DU NORD

LA MANCHE

LA BELGIQUE · L'ALLEMAGNE

Lille · LE LUXEMBOURG · LES ARDENNES

Le Havre · Rouen · la Seine · la Marne · Strasbourg

Caen · Versailles · **Paris** · LES VOSGES · le Rhin

le Mont-St-Michel · Rennes

Nantes · la Loire

L'OCÉAN ATLANTIQUE

Bourges · la Saône · LE JURA · LA SUISSE

Poitiers

Limoges · Lyon

Clermont-Ferrand · LES ALPES · L'ITALIE

Bordeaux · la Garonne · LE MASSIF CENTRAL · le Rhône

Toulouse · Aix-en-Provence

Nîmes · Marseille · MONACO

LES PYRÉNÉES · LA CORSE

ANDORRE · LA MER MÉDITERRANÉE

L'ESPAGNE

le château de Chenonceau

0 — 100 milles
0 — 100 kilomètres

le pont° du Gard

Incroyable mais vrai!

Être «immortel», c'est réguler et défendre le bon usage du français! Les Académiciens de l'Académie française sont élus à vie° et s'appellent les «Immortels». Depuis° 1635 (*mille six cent trente-cinq*), ils décident de l'orthographe correcte des mots° et publient un dictionnaire. Attention, c'est «courrier° électronique», pas «e-mail»!

Section Goals
In this section, students will learn historical, cultural, and geographical information about France.

Instructional Resources
vhlcentral.com:
Digital Image Bank; SAM Answer Key; reference tools

Carte de la France
• Have students look at the map of France in their books, or display the **Panorama** map from the Digital Image Bank. Ask volunteers to read the cities' names aloud.
• Have students identify the location of the place or object in each photo.

Le pays en chiffres
• Have students read the section headings. Point out the type of information contained in each section and clarify unfamiliar words.
• Have volunteers read the sections aloud. After each section, ask questions about the content.
• Ask students to share any additional information they might know about the people in **Français célèbres.**

Incroyable mais vrai!
L'Académie française was founded by Cardinal Richelieu during the reign of Louis XIII. In the beginning, the Academy's primary role was to standardize the language for French-speaking people by establishing rules to make it pure, eloquent, and capable of dealing with the arts and sciences.

O P T I O N S

Le pays en chiffres France is the third largest country in Europe. It is divided into 13 **régions** (*regions*), which include **la Corse** (*Corsica*). The **régions** are divided into 95 **départements** (*departments*). France also has five overseas **Départements-Régions d'Outre-Mer (DROM): la Guadeloupe, la Guyane française, la Réunion, Mayotte,** and **la Martinique.** Using the map of France in **Appendix A** that shows the **régions** and **départements,** have students locate various cities as

you say the names. Example: **Marseille (C'est dans le département des Bouches-du-Rhône.)**

Oral Presentation If a student has visited France (preferably outside Paris), ask him or her to prepare a short presentation about his or her experiences there. Encourage the student to bring in photos and souvenirs of France.

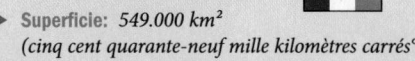

La géographie

L'Hexagone

Surnommé «l'Hexagone» à cause de° sa forme géométrique, le territoire français a trois fronts maritimes: l'océan Atlantique, la mer° Méditerranée et la Manche°; et trois frontières° naturelles: les Pyrénées, les Ardennes et les Alpes et le Jura. À l'intérieur du pays°, le Massif central et les Vosges ponctuent° un relief composé de vastes plaines et de forêts. La Loire, la Seine, la Garonne, le Rhin et le Rhône sont les fleuves° principaux de l'Hexagone.

La technologie

Le Train à Grande Vitesse

Le chemin de fer° existe en France depuis° 1827 (mille huit cent vingt-sept). Aujourd'hui, la SNCF (Société nationale des chemins de fer français) offre la possibilité aux voyageurs de se déplacer° dans tout° le pays et propose des tarifs° avantageux aux étudiants et aux moins de 25 ans°. Le TGV (Train à Grande Vitesse°) roule° à plus de 300 (trois cents) km/h (kilomètres/heure) et emmène° même° les voyageurs jusqu'à° Londres et Bruxelles.

Les arts

Le cinéma, le 7e art!

L'invention du cinématographe par les frères° Lumière en 1895 (mille huit cent quatre-vingt-quinze) marque le début° du «7e (septième) art». Le cinéma français donne naissance° aux prestigieux César° en 1976 (mille neuf cent soixante-seize), à des cinéastes talentueux comme° Jean Renoir, François Truffaut et Luc Besson, et à des acteurs mémorables comme Brigitte Bardot, Catherine Deneuve, Olivier Martinez et Audrey Tautou.

L'économie

L'industrie

Avec la richesse de la culture française, il est facile d'oublier que l'économie en France n'est pas limitée à l'artisanat°, à la gastronomie ou à la haute couture°. En fait°, la France est une véritable puissance° industrielle et se classe° parmi° les économies les plus° importantes du monde. Ses° activités dans des secteurs comme la construction automobile (par exemple, Peugeot, Citroën, Renault), l'industrie aérospatiale (avec Airbus) et l'énergie nucléaire (avec Électricité de France) sont considérables.

Qu'est-ce que vous avez appris? Complete these sentences.

1. __Camille Claudel__ est une sculptrice française.
2. Les Académiciens sont élus __à vie__.
3. Le mot correct en français pour «e-mail», c'est __courrier électronique__
4. À cause de sa forme, la France s'appelle aussi __«l'Hexagone»__.
5. La __SNCF__ offre la possibilité de voyager dans tout le pays.
6. Avec le __TGV__, on voyage de Paris à Londres.
7. Les __frères Lumière__ sont les inventeurs du cinéma.
8. __Answers will vary.__ est un grand cinéaste français.
   Possible answer: Jean Renoir
9. La France est une grande puissance __industrielle__.
10. Électricité de France produit (*produces*) __l'énergie nucléaire__.

Sur Internet

Go to **vhlcentral.com** to find more cultural information related to this **Panorama**.

1. Cherchez des informations sur l'Académie française. Faites (*Make*) une liste de mots ajoutés à la dernière édition du dictionnaire de l'Académie française.

2. Cherchez des informations sur l'actrice Catherine Deneuve. Quand a-t-elle commencé (*did she begin*) sa (*her*) carrière? Trouvez ses (*her*) trois derniers films.

ressources

WB
pp. 27–28

S
vhlcentral

à cause de *because of* mer *sea* Manche *English Channel* frontières *borders* pays *country* ponctuent *punctuate* fleuves *rivers* chemin de fer *railroad* depuis *since* se déplacer *travel* dans tout *throughout* tarifs *fares* moins de 25 ans *people under 25* Train à Grande Vitesse *high speed train* roule *rolls, travels* emmène *takes* même *even* jusqu'à *to* frères *brothers* début *beginning* donne naissance *gives birth* César *equivalent of the Oscars in France* comme *such as* artisanat *craft industry* haute couture *high fashion* En fait *In fact* puissance *power* se classe *ranks* parmi *among* les plus *the most* Ses *Its*

quatre-vingt-trois **83**

L'Hexagone Have students locate the geographical features mentioned on the map or point them out on the **Panorama** map from the Digital Image Bank.

Le Train à Grande Vitesse
- The first **TGV** service was from Paris to Lyon in 1981. Since then, its service has expanded. Presently, the high-speed network has over 30,000 kilometers of track that connect over 150 cities and towns in France.
- Have students look at the photo and compare the **TGV** to the trains they have traveled on or seen in the United States. Then have them figure out the speed of the **TGV** in miles per hour (1 km = 0.62 mile). (300 km/h = 186 mph)

Le cinéma, le 7e art!
- Each year the members of **l'Académie des Arts et Techniques du Cinéma** choose the actors, actresses, directors, and others involved in film-making to receive the **César** awards for their outstanding achievements. The ceremony was named after the artist who designed the award trophies.
- The six traditional arts are **architecture**, **sculpture**, **peinture** (*painting*), **littérature**, **musique**, and **danse**.

L'industrie
- The craft industry, **l'Artisanat**, can be found throughout France. Using traditional methods that are centuries old, French artisans craft products, such as pottery and figurines, but also work as bakers, carpenters, confectioners, butchers, or masons. Each region's products reflect the history and culture of that particular area.
- Bring in some French craft items or magazine photos of items to show the class.

O P T I O N S

Game Create categories for the newly learned information on France: **Géographie**, **Français célèbres**, **Technologie**, etc. Make index cards with a question on one side and category on the other. Tape cards to the board under the appropriate categories with questions face down. Teams take turns picking a card and answering the question. Give a point for each right answer. The team with the most points at the end wins.

Cultural Comparison Distribute a list in French of the award categories for the **César** from the website of **l'Académie des Arts et Techniques du Cinéma** (www.lescesarducinema.com). Ask if the same categories exist for the Oscars. Show them pictures of a **César** and an Oscar. Have students compare the trophies. Ask what other film festivals occur in France. (Cannes Film Festival and the American Film Festival)

Section Goals

In this section, students will:
- learn to use text formats to predict content
- read a brochure for a French language school

Stratégie Tell students that many documents have easily identifiable formats that can help them predict the content. Have them look at the document in the **Stratégie** box and ask them to identify the recognizable elements:
- days of the week
- times
- classes

Ask what kind of document it is. (a student's weekly schedule)

Examinez le texte Have students look at the headings and ask them what type of information is contained in **École de français (pour étrangers) de Lille**. (lists of courses by level and specialization, a list of supplementary activities, and a list of types of housing available) Then ask students what types of documents contain these elements. (brochures)

Mots apparentés

- In pairs, have students scan the brochure, identify cognates, and guess their meanings.
- Ask students what this document is and its purpose. (It's a brochure. It's advertising a French language and culture immersion program. Its purpose is to attract students.)

Lecture

S Audio: Reading

communication / cultures / NATIONAL STANDARDS

Avant la lecture

STRATÉGIE

Predicting content through formats

Recognizing the format of a document can help you to predict its content. For instance, invitations, greeting cards, and classified ads follow an easily identifiable format, which usually gives you an idea of the information they contain. Look at the text and identify it based on its format.

	lundi	mardi	mercredi	jeudi	vendredi
8h30	biologie		biologie		biologie
9h00		histoire		histoire	
9h30	anglais		anglais		anglais
10h00					
10h30					
11h00					
11h30					
12h00					
12h30					
1h00	art		art		art

If you guessed that this is a page from a student's schedule, you are correct. You can infer that the document contains information about a student's weekly schedule, including days, times, and activities.

Examinez le texte

Briefly look at the document. What is its format? What kind of information is given? How is it organized? Are there any visuals? What kind? What type(s) of documents usually contain these elements?

Mots apparentés

As you have already learned, in addition to format, you can use cognates to help you predict the content of a document. With a classmate, make a list of all the cognates you find in the reading selection. Based on these cognates and the format of the document, can you guess what this document is and what it's for?

ÉCOLE DE FRANÇAIS
(pour étrangers°) DE LILLE

COURS DE FRANÇAIS POUR TOUS°	COURS DE SPÉCIALISATION
Niveau° débutant°	Français pour enfants°
Niveau élémentaire	Français des affaires°
Niveau intermédiaire	Droit° français
Niveau avancé	Français pour le tourisme
Conversation	Culture et civilisation
Grammaire française	Histoire de France
	Art et littérature
	Arts culinaires

26, place d'Arsonval • 59000 Lille
Tél. 03.20.52.48.17 • Fax. 03.20.52.48.18 • www.efpelille.fr

O P T I O N S

Extra Practice Have students write a friend's or family member's weekly schedule as homework. Tell them to label the days of the week in French and add notes for that person's appointments and activities. In class, ask students questions about the schedules they wrote. Examples: **Quel cours est-ce que _____ a aujourd'hui? Combien de jours est-ce que _____ travaille cette semaine?**

Cultural Activity Ask students what aspects of this school they find appealing or interesting: **Qu'est-ce que vous trouvez intéressant à l'école?** Jot down their responses on the board. Then do a quick class survey to find out which aspect is the most appealing.

Programmes de 2 à 8 semaines,

4 à 8 heures par jour

Immersion totale

Professeurs diplômés

le Musée des Beaux-Arts, Lille

GRAND CHOIX° D'ACTIVITÉS SUPPLÉMENTAIRES

- Excursions à la journée dans la région
- Visites de monuments et autres sites touristiques
- Sorties° culturelles (théâtre, concert, opéra et autres spectacles°)
- Sports et autres activités de loisir°

HÉBERGEMENT°

- En cité universitaire°
- Dans° une famille française
- À l'hôtel

pour étrangers for foreigners **tous** all **Niveau** Level **débutant** beginner **enfants** children **affaires** business **Droit** Law **choix** choice **Sorties** Outings **spectacles** shows **loisir** leisure **hébergement** lodging **cité universitaire** university dormitories (on campus) **Dans** In

Après la lecture

∞ **Répondez** Select the correct response or completion to each question or statement, based on the reading selection.

1. C'est une brochure pour...
   a. des cours de français pour étrangers.
   b. une université française.
   c. des études supérieures en Belgique.

2. «Histoire de France» est...
   a. un cours pour les professeurs diplômés.
   b. un cours de spécialisation.
   c. un cours pour les enfants.

3. Le cours de «Français pour le tourisme» est utile pour...
   a. une étudiante qui (who) étudie les sciences po.
   b. une femme qui travaille dans un hôtel de luxe.
   c. un professeur d'administration des affaires.

4. Un étudiant étranger qui commence le français assiste probablement à quel (which) cours?
   a. Cours de français pour tous, Niveau avancé
   b. Cours de spécialisation, Art et littérature
   c. Cours de français pour tous, Niveau débutant

5. Quel cours est utile pour un homme qui parle assez bien français et qui travaille dans l'économie?
   a. Cours de spécialisation, Français des affaires
   b. Cours de spécialisation, Arts culinaires
   c. Cours de spécialisation, Culture et civilisation

6. Le week-end, les étudiants...
   a. passent des examens.
   b. travaillent dans des hôtels.
   c. visitent la ville et la région.

7. Les étudiants qui habitent dans une famille...
   a. ont envie de rencontrer des Français.
   b. ont des bourses.
   c. ne sont pas reçus aux examens.

8. Un étudiant en architecture va aimer...
   a. le cours de droit français.
   b. les visites de monuments et de sites touristiques.
   c. les activités sportives.

∞ **Complétez** Complete these sentences.

1. Le numéro de téléphone est le ____03.20.52.48.17____.

2. Le numéro de fax est le ____03.20.52.48.18____.

3. L'adresse de l'école est ___26, place d'Arsonval, 59000 Lille___

4. L'école offre des programmes de Français de ___2 à 8___ semaines et de ___4 à 8 heures___ par jour.

Répondez Go over the answers with the whole class or have students check their answers in pairs.

Complétez For additional practice, give students these items.
5. L'école est à____. (Lille)
6. L'adresse Internet de l'école est ____. (www.efpelille.fr)
7. «Grammaire française» est un cours de ____. (français pour tous) 8. Les professeurs de l'école sont ____. (diplômés) 9. On habite en cité universitaire, ____ ou à l'hôtel. (dans une famille française)

Suggestion Encourage students to record unfamiliar words and phrases that they learn in **Lecture** in their notebooks.

O P T I O N S

Small Groups Provide students with magazines and newspapers in French. Have groups of three or four students work together to look for documents in French with easily recognizable formats, such as classified ads or other advertisements. Ask them to use cognates and other context clues to predict the content. Then have groups present their examples and findings to the class.

Oral Presentation Invite a student who has studied abroad to come and speak to the class about the school he or she attended, the classes, and any interesting experiences he or she had there. Encourage the class to ask questions.

Section Goals

In this section, students will:

- learn to brainstorm and organize their ideas for writing
- learn to write a description of themselves
- integrate vocabulary and structures taught in **Leçon 2B** and previous lessons

Stratégie Discuss information students might want to include in a self-description, recording their suggestions on the board in French. Quickly review structures students will include in their writing, such as **j'aime** and **je n'aime pas** as well as the first person singular of several verbs. Examples: **je m'appelle, je suis, j'étudie, j'ai cours de…,** and **je travaille**.

Thème Copy on the board the brief chat room description for Xavier Dupré, leaving blanks where his name, nationality, course of study, and university name appear. At the end, add the sentences **J'aime _____.** and **Je n'aime pas _____.** Model completing the description orally with your own information and then ask volunteers to complete it with their own information.

Écriture

STRATÉGIE

Brainstorming

In the early stages of writing, brainstorming can help you generate ideas on a specific topic. You should spend ten to fifteen minutes brainstorming and jotting down any ideas about the topic that occur to you. Whenever possible, try to write down your ideas in French. Express your ideas in single words or phrases, and jot them down in any order. While brainstorming, do not worry about whether your ideas are good or bad. Selecting and organizing ideas should be the second stage of your writing. Remember that the more ideas you write down while brainstorming, the more options you will have to choose from later when you start to organize your ideas.

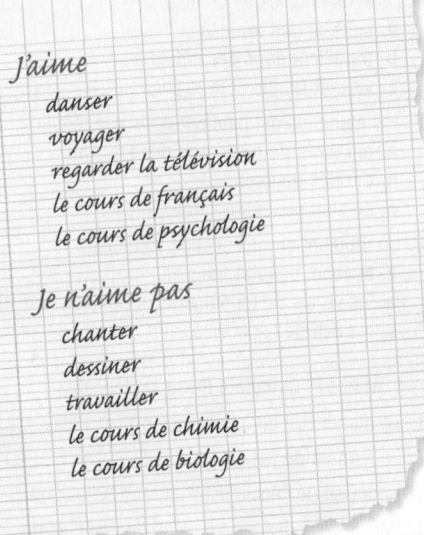

J'aime
danser
voyager
regarder la télévision
le cours de français
le cours de psychologie

Je n'aime pas
chanter
dessiner
travailler
le cours de chimie
le cours de biologie

∞ Thème

Une description personnelle

Avant l'écriture

1. Write a description of yourself to post on a website in order to find a francophone e-pal. Your description should include:

- your name and where you are from

- the name of your school and where it is located

- the courses you are currently taking and your opinion of each one

- some of your likes and dislikes

- where you work if you have a job

- any other information you would like to include

Use a chart like this one to brainstorm information about your likes and dislikes.

J'aime	Je n'aime pas

O P T I O N S

Avant l'écriture Demonstrate how to brainstorm ideas about a topic. Choose a celebrity everyone knows and use a word web to brainstorm ideas about what that person likes and dislikes. Once you have generated 10-12 ideas, choose one of them and brainstorm words related to it.

Have pairs ask each other questions about their likes and dislikes using **j'aime** and **je n'aime pas**. Each student writes down the other's answers, then they exchange their lists in order to use them as a basis for the writing task. Before students begin writing, help them personalize their lists by supplying any unknown vocabulary they may need.

2. Now take the information about your likes and dislikes and fill out this new chart to help you organize the content of your description.

Je m'appelle...	(name).
Je suis de...	(where you are from).
J'étudie...	(names of classes) à/au/à la (name of school).
Je ne travaille pas./ Je travaille à/au/ à la/chez...	(place where you work).
J'aime...	(activities you like).
Je n'aime pas...	(activities you dislike).

Écriture

Use the information from the second chart to write a paragraph describing yourself. Make sure you include all the information from the chart in your paragraph. Use the structures provided for each topic.

Bonjour!

Je m'appelle Michael Adams. Je suis américain. J'étudie le droit à l'Université de Chicago. Je travaille au restaurant Students' Corner. J'aime parler avec des amis, lire (*read*), écouter de la musique et voyager, parce que j'aime rencontrer des gens. Par contre, je n'aime pas le sport...

Après l'écriture

1. Exchange a rough draft of your description with a partner. Comment on his or her work by answering these questions:

- Did your partner include all the necessary information (at least six facts)?

- Did your partner use the structures provided in the chart?

- Did your partner use the vocabulary of the unit?

- Did your partner use the grammar of the unit?

2. Revise your description according to your partner's comments. After writing the final version, read it one more time to eliminate these kinds of problems:

- spelling errors

- punctuation errors

- capitalization errors

- use of incorrect verb forms

- use of incorrect adjective agreement

- use of incorrect definite and indefinite articles

EVALUATION

Criteria

Content Includes all the information mentioned in the six bulleted items in the description of the task.
Scale: 1 2 3 4 5

Organization Organizes the description similarly to the model provided.
Scale: 1 2 3 4 5

Accuracy Uses **j'aime/je n'aime pas**, regular **-er** verbs, and negation patterns correctly. Words are spelled correctly and adjectives agree with the nouns they modify.
Scale: 1 2 3 4 5

Creativity Includes additional information that is not specified in the task and makes an effort to create longer sentences with a number of items.
Scale: 1 2 3 4 5

Scoring

Excellent	18–20 points
Good	14–17 points
Satisfactory	10–13 points
Unsatisfactory	< 10 points

O P T I O N S

Écriture Before students begin writing, give them some transition words they may want to incorporate into their descriptions. Words and expressions such as **mais**, **parce que**, **alors**, **pourtant**, **par contre**, **ou**, and **et** can be used to make sentences longer and to make transitions between them.

Après l'écriture Once students have written their descriptions, choose several among those and ask the authors for their permission to read them aloud. As you read each one, see if the class can guess whom it is describing, based on the likes, dislikes, and other information included.

Instructional Resources
vhlcentral.com:
Textbook MP3s; Textbook
Audioscript; reference tools

Suggestions
- Tell students that an easy way to study from **Vocabulaire** is to cover up the French half of each section, leaving only the English equivalents exposed. They can then quiz themselves on the French items. To focus on the English equivalents of the French entries, they simply reverse this process.
- Point out to students that they can use the Vocabulary Tools at **vhlcentral.com** for reference and extra vocabulary practice.

◁)) Ⓢ Vocabulary Tools

Leçon 2A

Verbes

adorer *to love; to adore*
aimer *to like; to love*
aimer mieux *to prefer*
arriver *to arrive*
chercher *to look for*
commencer *to begin, to start*
dessiner *to draw; to design*
détester *to hate*
donner *to give*
étudier *to study*
habiter (à) *to live (in)*
manger *to eat*
oublier *to forget*
parler (au téléphone) *to speak (on the phone)*
partager *to share*
penser (que/qu') *to think (that)*
regarder *to look (at), to watch*
rencontrer *to meet*
retrouver *to meet up with; to find (again)*
travailler *to work*
voyager *to travel*

Vocabulaire utile

J'adore... *I love...*
J'aime bien... *I like...*
Je n'aime pas tellement... *I don't like... very much.*
Je déteste... *I hate...*
être reçu(e) à un examen *to pass an exam*

Des questions et des opinions

bien sûr *of course*
d'accord *OK, all right*
Est-ce que/qu'...? *Question phrase*
(mais) non *no (but of course not)*
moi/toi non plus *me/you neither*
ne... pas *no, not*
n'est-ce pas? *isn't that right?*
oui/si *yes*
parce que *because*
pas du tout *not at all*
peut-être *maybe, perhaps*
Pourquoi? *Why?*

L'université

l'architecture (f.) *architecture*
l'art (m.) *art*
la biologie *biology*
la chimie *chemistry*
le droit *law*
l'économie (f.) *economics*
l'éducation physique (f.) *physical education*
la géographie *geography*
la gestion *business administration*
l'histoire (f.) *history*
l'informatique (f.) *computer science*
les langues (étrangères) (f.) *(foreign) languages*
les lettres (f.) *humanities*
les mathématiques (maths) (f.) *mathematics*
la philosophie *philosophy*
la physique *physics*
la psychologie *psychology*
les sciences (politiques/po) (f.) *(political) science*
le stylisme de mode (m.) *fashion design*
une bourse *scholarhip, grant*
un cours *class, course*
un devoir; les devoirs *homework*
un diplôme *diploma, degree*
l'école (f.) *school*
les études (supérieures) (f.) *(higher) education; studies*
le gymnase *gymnasium*
une note *grade*
un restaurant universitaire (un resto U) *university cafeteria*

Adjectifs et adverbes

difficile *difficult*
facile *easy*
inutile *useless*
utile *useful*
surtout *especially; above all*

Expressions utiles

See p. 51.

Leçon 2B

L'université

assister à *to attend*
demander *to ask*
dîner *to have dinner*
échouer *to fail*
écouter *to listen (to)*
enseigner *to teach*
expliquer *to explain*
passer un examen *to take an exam*
préparer *to prepare (for)*
rentrer (à la maison) *to return (home)*
téléphoner à *to telephone*
trouver *to find; to think*
visiter *to visit (a place)*

Expressions de temps

Quel jour sommes-nous? *What day is it?*
un an *a year*
une/cette année *one/this year*
après *after*
après-demain *day after tomorrow*
un/cet après-midi *an/this afternoon*
aujourd'hui *today*
demain (matin/après-midi/soir) *tomorrow (morning/afternoon/evening)*
un jour *a day*
une journée *a day*
(le) lundi, mardi, mercredi, jeudi, vendredi, samedi, dimanche *(on) Monday(s), Tuesday(s), Wednesday(s), Thursday(s), Friday(s), Saturday(s), Sunday(s)*
un/ce matin *a/this morning*
la matinée *morning*
un mois/ce mois-ci *a month/this month*
une/cette nuit *a/this night*
une/cette semaine *a/this week*
un/ce soir *an/this evening*
une soirée *an evening*
un/le/ce week-end *a/the/this weekend*
dernier/dernière *last*
premier/première *first*
prochain(e) *next*

Expressions avec avoir

avoir *to have*
avoir... ans *to be... years old*
avoir besoin (de) *to need*
avoir chaud *to be hot*
avoir de la chance *to be lucky*
avoir envie (de) *to feel like*
avoir froid *to be cold*
avoir honte (de) *to be ashamed (of)*
avoir l'air *to look like, to seem*
avoir peur (de) *to be afraid (of)*
avoir raison *to be right*
avoir sommeil *to be sleepy*
avoir tort *to be wrong*

Expressions utiles

See p. 69.

Telling time

Quelle heure est-il? *What time is it?*
Quelle heure avez-vous/as-tu? *What time do you have?*
Il est... heures. *It is... o'clock.*
une heure *one o'clock*
et quart *fifteen minutes past the hour*
et demie *thirty minutes past the hour*
moins dix *ten minutes before the hour*
Moins le quart *fifteen minutes before the hour*
À quelle heure? *(At) what time/when?*
de l'après-midi *in the afternoon*
du matin *in the morning*
du soir *in the evening*
en avance *early*
en retard *late*
midi *noon*
minuit *midnight*
pile *sharp, on the dot*
presque *almost*
tard *late*
tôt *early*
vers *about*

88 *quatre-vingt-huit*

La famille et les copains

Unit Goals

Leçon 3A

In this lesson, students will learn:
- words for family members and marital status
- some words for pets
- usage of **l'accent aigu** and **l'accent grave**
- about families in France
- descriptive adjectives
- possessive adjectives
- more about families and friends through specially shot video footage

Leçon 3B

In this lesson, students will learn:
- words for some professions and occupations
- about famous Swiss singer Stephan Eicher
- more descriptive adjectives
- usage of **l'accent circonflexe, la cédille,** and **le tréma**
- about different types of friendships and relationships
- the numbers 61–100
- some prepositions of location
- disjunctive pronouns
- to ask for repetition in oral communication

Savoir-faire

In this section, students will learn:
- historical and cultural information about Switzerland and Belgium
- to use visuals and graphic elements to predict content
- to use idea maps to organize information
- to write an informal letter

Pour commencer
- Il y a trois personnes.
- Elles sont dans un café.
- Elles ne mangent pas. Elles parlent.
- Elles ont l'air agréables.

Pour commencer
- Combien de personnes y a-t-il?
- Où sont ces personnes?
- Que font-elles?
- Ont-elles l'air agréables ou désagréables?

RESOURCES

Student Activities Manual (SAM):
Workbook Activities, pp. 29–42;
Lab Activities, pp. 17–24;
Video Activities, pp. 9–12; pp. 65–66
SAM Answer Key

vhlcentral.com: Textbook MP3s; Lab MP3s;
Textbook Audioscript; Lab Audioscript; Video;
Videoscript; **Roman-photo** Translations;
Vocabulaire supplémentaire; Activity Pack
(including **Feuilles d'activités**, Info Gap Activities,
and Task-based Activities);

Flash culture video transcription; **Essayez!** and
Mise en pratique answers; Digital Image Bank;
Testing Program;
Testing Program MP3s

Section Goals

In this section, students will learn and practice vocabulary related to:
• family members
• some pets
• marital status

Instructional Resources

vhlcentral.com:
Digital Image Bank (including vocabulary illustrations from the textbook, theme-based illustrations);
Vocabulaire supplémentaire;
Mise en pratique *answers;*
Textbook Audioscript;
Lab Audioscript; Activity Pack
(Feuilles d'activités); *Textbook MP3s; Lab MP3s; SAM Answer Key; reference tools*

Suggestions

• Introduce active lesson vocabulary with questions and gestures. Ask: **Comment s'appelle ton frère?** Ask a different student: **Comment s'appelle le frère de _____?** Work your way through various family relationships.

• Point out the meanings of plural family terms so students understand that the masculine plural forms can refer to mixed groups of males and females:
les enfants *male children; male and female children*
les cousins *male cousins; male and female cousins*
les petits-enfants *male grandchildren; male and female grandchildren*

• Point out the difference in meaning between the noun **mari** (*husband*) and the adjective **marié(e)** (*married*).

• Use the 3A **Contextes** illustration from the Digital Image Bank. Point out that the family tree is drawn from the point of view of Marie Laval. Have students refer to the family tree to answer your questions about it. Example: **Comment s'appelle la mère de Marie?**

• Use the Family illustrations from the Digital Image Bank to help students familiarize themselves with family members, pets, and marital status.

• Additional vocabulary for this lesson can be found in the **Vocabulaire supplémentaire** on the Supersite.

Leçon 3A

You will learn how to...
▪ discuss family, friends, and pets
▪ express ownership

S Vocabulary Tools

La famille de Marie Laval

Luc Garneau

mon grand-père (*my grandfather*)

Sophie Garneau

Marc Garneau

ma tante (*aunt*), femme (*wife*) de Marc

mon oncle (*uncle*), fils (*son*) de Luc et d'Hélène

Jean Garneau

Isabelle Garneau

Virginie Garneau

mon cousin, petit-fils (*grandson*) de Luc et d'Hélène frère (*brother*) d'Isabelle et de Virginie

ma cousine, sœur (*sister*) de Jean et de Virginie, petite-fille (*granddaughter*) de Luc et d'Hélène

ma cousine, sœur de Jean et d'Isabelle, petite-fille de Luc et d'Hélène

Bambou

le chien (*dog*) de mes (*my*) cousins

Vocabulaire

divorcer	to divorce
épouser	to marry
aîné(e)	elder
cadet(te)	younger
un beau-frère	brother-in-law
un beau-père	father-in-law; stepfather
une belle-mère	mother-in-law; stepmother
un demi-frère	half-brother; stepbrother
une demi-sœur	half-sister; stepsister
les enfants (*m., f.*)	children
un(e) époux/épouse	husband/wife
une famille	family
une femme	wife; woman
une fille	daughter; girl
les grands-parents (*m.*)	grandparents
les parents (*m.*)	parents
un(e) voisin(e)	neighbor
un chat	cat
un oiseau	bird
un poisson	fish
célibataire	single
divorcé(e)	divorced
fiancé(e)	engaged
marié(e)	married
séparé(e)	separated
veuf/veuve	widowed

ressources

WB	LM	S
pp. 29–30	p. 17	vhlcentral

90 *quatre-vingt-dix*

OPTIONS

Extra Practice Draw your own family tree on a transparency or the board and label it with names. Ask students questions about it. Examples: **Est-ce que _____ est ma sœur ou ma tante? Comment s'appelle ma grand-mère? _____ est le neveu ou le frère de _____ ? Qui est le grand-père de _____ ?** Help them identify the relationships between members. Then invite them to ask you questions.

Les noms de famille français Ask for a show of hands to see if any students' last names are French in origin. Examples: names that begin with **Le____** or **La____** such as **Leblanc** or **Larose**, or even names such as **Fitzgerald** or **Fitzpatrick (Fitz- = fils de).** Ask these students what they know about their French heritage or family history.

Mise en pratique

Hélène Garneau

ma grand-mère
(*my grandmother*)

Juliette Laval

ma mère (*mother*),
fille (*daughter*) de
Luc et d'Hélène

Robert Laval

mon père (*father*),
mari (*husband*)
de Juliette

Véronique Laval   **Guillaume Laval**   **Marie Laval**

ma belle-sœur
(*sister-in-law*)

mon frère
(*brother*)

**Marie Laval,
fille de Juliette
et de Robert**

Matthieu Laval   **Émilie Laval**

mon neveu
(*nephew*)

ma nièce
(*niece*)

petits-enfants (*grandchildren*)
de mes parents

---

1 **Écoutez** Listen to each statement made by Marie Laval, and then indicate whether it is **vrai** or **faux**, based on her family tree.

	Vrai	Faux			Vrai	Faux
1.	☑	☐		6.	☐	☑
2.	☐	☑		7.	☐	☑
3.	☑	☐		8.	☑	☐
4.	☐	☑		9.	☑	☐
5.	☐	☑		10.	☑	☐

2 **Qui est-ce?** Match the definition in the first list with the correct item from the second list. Not all the items will be used.

1. __d__ le frère de ma cousine
2. __g__ le père de mon cousin
3. __a__ le mari de ma grand-mère
4. __e__ le fils de mon frère
5. __c__ la fille de mon grand-père
6. __i__ le fils de ma mère
7. __h__ la fille de mon fils
8. __f__ le fils de ma belle-mère

a. mon grand-père   f. mon demi-frère
b. ma sœur   g. mon oncle
c. ma tante   h. ma petite-fille
d. mon cousin   i. mon frère
e. mon neveu

3 **Choisissez** Fill in the blank by selecting the most appropriate answer.

1. Voici le frère de mon père. C'est mon ___oncle___ (oncle, neveu, fiancé).
2. Voici la mère de ma cousine. C'est ma ___tante___ (grand-mère, voisine, tante).
3. Voici la petite-fille de ma grand-mère. C'est ma ___cousine___ (cousine, nièce, épouse).
4. Voici le père de ma mère. C'est mon ___grand-père___ (grand-père, oncle, cousin).
5. Voici le fils de mon père, mais ce n'est pas le fils de ma mère. C'est mon ___demi-frère___ (petit-fils, demi-frère, voisin).
6. Voici ma nièce. C'est la ___petite-fille___ (cousine, fille, petite-fille) de ma mère.
7. Voici la mère de ma tante. C'est ma ___grand-mère___ (cousine, grand-mère, nièce).
8. Voici la sœur de mon oncle. C'est ma ___tante___ (tante, belle-mère, belle-sœur).
9. Voici la fille de ma mère, mais pas de mon père. C'est ma ___demi-sœur___ (belle-sœur, demi-sœur, sœur).
10. Voici le mari de ma mère, mais ce n'est pas mon père. C'est mon ___beau-père___ (beau-frère, grand-père, beau-père).

Successful Language Learning
Tell students that it isn't necessary to understand every word they hear in French. They will feel less anxious if they listen for general meaning.

1 **Audioscript**
1. Marc est mon oncle.
2. Émilie est la nièce de Véronique.
3. Jean est le petit-fils d'Hélène.
4. Robert est mon grand-père.
5. Luc est le père de Sophie.
6. Isabelle est ma tante.
7. Matthieu est le fils de Jean.
8. Émilie est la fille de Guillaume.
9. Juliette est ma mère.
10. Virginie est ma cousine.
(*On Textbook MP3s*)

1 **Expansion** Play Marie's statements again, stopping at the end of each. Where the statements are true, have students repeat. Where the statements are false, have students correct them by referring to Marie Laval's family tree.

2 **Suggestion** Mention that adjectives such as **beau** and **petit** in hyphenated family terms must agree in gender. Exceptions: **la grand-mère**, **la demi-sœur**.

3 **Expansion** Have students provide additional examples for the class to identify.

OPTIONS

Game As a class or group activity, have students state the relationship between people on Marie Laval's family tree. Their classmates will guess which person on the family tree they are describing. Example: **C'est la sœur de Jean et la fille de Sophie. (Isabelle ou Véronique)** Take turns until each member of the class or group has had a chance to state a relationship.

Extra Practice Have students draw their own family tree as homework. Tell them to label each position on the tree with the appropriate French term and the person's name. Also tell them to write five fill-in-the-blank statements based on their family tree. Examples: **Je suis la fille de ____. Mon frère s'appelle ____.** In the next class, have students exchange papers with a classmate and complete the activity.

4 Suggestion Use the **arbre généalogique** illustration from the Digital Image Bank for this activity.

5 Suggestion Tell students to jot down their partner's responses.

5 Expansion After they have finished the interview, ask students questions about their partner's answers. Examples: **Combien de personnes y a-t-il dans la famille de ____? Comment s'appellent les parents de ____?**

6 Suggestion Have two volunteers read the **modèle**. Then distribute the **Feuilles d'activités** found in the Activity Pack on the Supersite.

6 Expansion After students have finished, ask true/false questions. Example: **Est-ce que ____ est marié(e)?**

Communication

4 L'arbre généalogique With a classmate, identify the members of the family by asking questions about how each member is related to Anne Durand. *Answers will vary.*

MODÈLE

Étudiant(e) 1: *Qui est Louis Durand?*
Étudiant(e) 2: *C'est le grand-père d'Anne.*

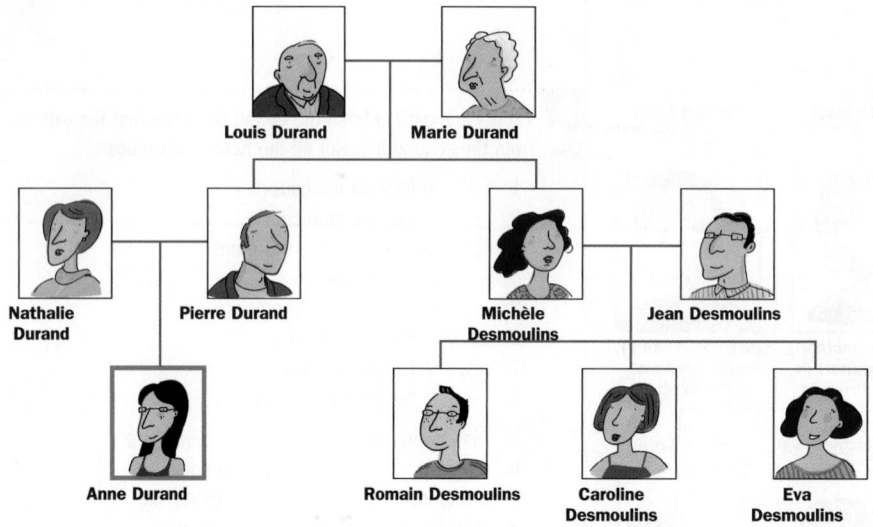

Louis Durand — Marie Durand

Nathalie Durand — Pierre Durand

Michèle Desmoulins — Jean Desmoulins

Anne Durand

Romain Desmoulins

Caroline Desmoulins

Eva Desmoulins

---

5 Entrevue With a classmate, take turns asking each other these questions. *Answers will vary.*

1. Combien de personnes y a-t-il dans ta famille?
2. Comment s'appellent tes parents?
3. As-tu des frères ou des sœurs?
4. Combien de cousins/cousines as-tu? Comment s'appellent-ils/elles? Où habitent-ils/elles?
5. Quel(le) (*Which*) est ton cousin préféré/ta cousine préférée?
6. As-tu des neveux/des nièces?
7. Comment s'appellent tes grands-parents? Où habitent-ils?
8. Combien de petits-enfants ont tes grands-parents?

Coup de main

Use these words to help you complete this activity.

ton *your (m.)*	→	mon *my (m.)*
ta *your (f.)*	→	ma *my (f.)*
tes *your (pl.)*	→	mes *my (pl.)*

6 Qui suis-je? Your instructor will give you a worksheet. Walk around the class and ask your classmates questions about their families. When a classmate gives one of the answers on the worksheet, write his or her name in the corresponding space. Be prepared to discuss the results with the class. *Answers will vary.*

MODÈLE Je suis marié(e).

Paul: *Est-ce que tu es mariée?*
Jacqueline: *Oui, je suis mariée. (You write "Jacqueline".)/ Non, je ne suis pas mariée. (You ask another classmate.)*

OPTIONS

Extra Practice Have students bring in some family photos. In pairs, tell them to take turns pointing to people in their partner's photo and asking who it is. Example: **Qui est-ce? (C'est mon/ma ____.)** Model a few examples. If necessary, write the question and a sample response on the board.

TPR Make a family tree using the whole class. Have each student write down the family designation you assign him or her on a note card or sheet of paper, then arrange students as in a family tree with each one displaying the note card. Then, ask questions about relationships. Examples: **Qui est la mère de ____? Comment s'appelle l'oncle de ____?** Give students the opportunity to ask questions by switching roles with them.

Les sons et les lettres  Audio

L'accent aigu and l'accent grave

In French, diacritical marks (*accents*) are an essential part of a word's spelling. They indicate how vowels are pronounced or distinguish between words with similar spellings but different meanings. **L'accent aigu** (´) appears only over the vowel **e**. It indicates that the **e** is pronounced similarly to the vowel *a* in the English word *cake*, but shorter and crisper. The French **é** lacks the *y* glide heard in English words like *day* and *late*.

| **é**tudier | **ré**servé | **é**légant | **té**léphone |

L'accent aigu also signals some similarities between French words and English words. Often, an **e** with **l'accent aigu** at the beginning of a French word marks the place where the letter *s* would appear at the beginning of the English equivalent.

| **é**ponge | **é**pouse | **é**tat | **é**tudiante |
| *sponge* | *spouse* | *state* | *student* |

L'accent grave (`) over the vowel **e** indicates that the **e** is pronounced like the vowel *e* in the English word *pet*.

| très | après | mère | nièce |

Although **l'accent grave** does not change the pronunciation of the vowels **a** or **u**, it distinguishes words that have a similar spelling but different meanings.

| la | là | ou | où |
| *the* | *there* | *or* | *where* |

Prononcez Practice saying these words aloud.

1. agréable
2. sincère
3. voilà
4. faculté
5. frère
6. à
7. déjà
8. éléphant
9. lycée
10. poème
11. là
12. élève

Articulez Practice saying these sentences aloud.

1. À tout à l'heure!
2. Thérèse, je te présente Michèle.
3. Hélène est très sérieuse et réservée.
4. Voilà mon père, Frédéric et ma mère, Ségolène.
5. Tu préfères étudier à la fac demain après-midi?

Dictons Practice reading these sayings aloud.

Tel père, tel fils.[1]

À vieille mule, frein doré.[2]

[1] Like father, like son.
[2] For an old mule, a golden bit.

ressources

LM p. 18   vhlcentral

quatre-vingt-treize **93**

Section Goals

In this section, students will learn about:
- l'accent aigu
- l'accent grave
- a strategy for recognizing cognates

Instructional Resources
vhlcentral.com:
Textbook MP3s; Lab MP3s; SAM Answer Key; Textbook Audioscript; Lab Audioscript; reference tools

Suggestions
- Write **é** on the board. Tell students to watch your mouth as you pronounce the sound. Explain that when **é** appears at the beginning of a word, the corners of your mouth are slightly turned up and your tongue is low behind your bottom teeth. Have students repeat **é** after you several times.
- Write words and/or French names from the Laval family with **l'accent aigu** on the board. Pronounce each word as you point to it and have students repeat it after you. Examples: **époux, célibataire, fiancé, séparé, Émilie,** and **Véronique.**
- Give students some sample sentences with **la, là, ou,** or **où** and ask them what the words mean to demonstrate how context clarifies meaning. Examples: **1. Où est la fille? 2. La fille est là. 3. Est-ce que Sophie est la tante ou la grand-mère de Marie Laval?**
- Ask students to provide more examples of words they know with these accents.
- The explanation and exercises are available on the **ESPACES** Supersite. You may want to play them in class so students hear French speakers besides yourself.

Dictons Explain to students that the saying **«À vieille mule, frein doré»** applies to a situation in which someone tries to sell something old by dressing it up or decorating it. For example, to have a better chance at selling an old car, give it a new paint job.

OPTIONS

Extra Practice Here are additional sentences to use for extra practice with **l'accent aigu** and **l'accent grave**. 1. Étienne est mon frère préféré. 2. Ma sœur aînée est très occupée avec les études. 3. André et Geneviève sont séparés. 4. Vous êtes marié ou célibataire? 5. Éric et Sabine sont fiancés.

Game Have a spelling bee using words with **l'accent aigu** and/or **l'accent grave** from **Leçon 3A** or previous lessons. Divide the class into two teams. Call on one team member at a time, alternating between teams. Give a point for each correct answer. The team with the most points at the end of the game wins. Before students begin, remind them that they must indicate the accent marks in the words. Give them an example: **très T-R-E accent grave-S.**

Section Goals

In this section, students will learn functional phrases for talking about their families and describing people through comprehensible input.

Instructional Resources
vhlcentral.com:
Roman-photo *Video, Videoscript, and Translation; SAM Answer Key; reference tools*

Video Recap: Leçon 2B
Review the previous **Roman-photo** with this activity.
1. Comment s'appelle la copine de Stéphane? (Astrid)
2. Qu'est-ce qu'elle pense de Stéphane? (Answers will vary. **Elle pense qu'il n'est pas sérieux, qu'il ne fait pas ses devoirs et qu'il n'écoute pas en classe.**)
3. Qui téléphone à Sandrine? (Pascal)
4. Comment Stéphane prépare-t-il le bac? (Il étudie les maths avec Rachid.)

Video Synopsis Michèle wants to know what Amina's friend, Cyberhomme, looks like. Valérie describes her brother's family as she, Stéphane, and Amina look at their photos. Valérie keeps pointing out all the people who have their **bac** because she thinks Stéphane is not studying enough to pass his **bac**. To ease his mother's mind, Stéphane finally tells her that Rachid is helping him study.

Suggestions
• Ask students to read the title, glance at the video stills, and predict what they think the episode will be about. Record their predictions.
• Have students work in groups of four. Tell them to choose a role and read the **Roman-photo** conversation aloud.
• After students have read the **Roman-photo**, quickly review their predictions and ask them which ones were correct. Then ask a few questions to help guide students in summarizing this episode.
• Explain that, in Video Still 1, the adjectives **marron** and **bleue** refer to **couleur**, a feminine noun, and not **les yeux**.

L'album de photos  Video

PERSONNAGES

Amina

Michèle

Stéphane

Valérie

MICHÈLE Mais, qui c'est? C'est ta sœur? Tes parents?
AMINA C'est mon ami Cyberhomme.
MICHÈLE Comment est-il? Est-ce qu'il est beau? Il a les yeux de quelle couleur? Marron ou bleue? Et ses cheveux? Ils sont blonds ou châtains?
AMINA Je ne sais pas.
MICHÈLE Toi, tu es timide.

VALÉRIE Stéphane, tu as dix-sept ans. Cette année, tu passes le bac, mais tu ne travailles pas!
STÉPHANE Écoute, ce n'est pas vrai, je déteste mes cours, mais je travaille beaucoup. Regarde, mon cahier de chimie, mes livres de français, ma calculatrice pour le cours de maths, mon dictionnaire anglais-français...

STÉPHANE Oh, et qu'est-ce que c'est? Ah, oui, les photos de tante Françoise.
VALÉRIE Des photos? Mais où?
STÉPHANE Ici! Amina, on peut regarder des photos de ma tante sur ton ordinateur, s'il te plaît?

AMINA Ah, et ça, c'est toute la famille, n'est-ce pas?
VALÉRIE Oui, ça c'est Henri, sa femme Françoise et leurs enfants: le fils aîné Bernard, et puis son frère Charles, sa sœur Sophie et leur chien Socrate.
STÉPHANE J'aime bien Socrate. Il est vieux, mais il est amusant!

VALÉRIE Ah! Et Bernard, il a son bac aussi et sa mère est très heureuse.
STÉPHANE Moi, j'ai envie d'habiter avec oncle Henri et tante Françoise. Comme ça, pas de problème pour le bac!

STÉPHANE Pardon, maman. Je suis très heureux ici avec toi. Ah, au fait, Rachid travaille avec moi pour préparer le bac.
VALÉRIE Ah, bon? Rachid est très intelligent... un étudiant sérieux.

A C T I V I T É S

1 **Vrai ou faux?** Are the sentences **vrai** or **faux**?

1. Amina communique avec sa (*her*) tante par ordinateur. Faux.
2. Stéphane n'aime pas ses (*his*) cours au lycée. Vrai.
3. Ils regardent des photos de vacances. Faux.
4. Henri est le frère aîné de Valérie. Vrai.
5. Bernard est le cousin de Stéphane. Vrai.

6. Charles a déjà son bac. Vrai.
7. La tante de Stéphane s'appelle Françoise. Vrai.
8. Stéphane travaille avec Amina pour préparer le bac. Faux.
9. Socrate est le fils d'Henri et de Françoise. Faux.
10. Rachid n'est pas un bon étudiant. Faux.

 Practice more at **vhlcentral.com.**

O P T I O N S

Avant de regarder la vidéo Before students view the video episode **L'album de photos**, ask them to brainstorm a list of things someone might say when describing his or her family photos.

Regarder la vidéo Play the first half of the video episode and have students describe what happened. Write their observations on the board. Then ask them to guess what will happen in the second half of the episode. Write their ideas on the board. Play the entire video episode; then help the class summarize the plot.

Stéphane et Valérie regardent des photos de famille avec Amina.

À la table d'Amina...

AMINA Alors, voilà vos photos. Qui est-ce?

VALÉRIE Oh, c'est Henri, mon frère aîné!

AMINA Quel âge a-t-il?

VALÉRIE Il a cinquante ans. Il est très sociable et c'est un très bon père.

VALÉRIE Ah! Et ça c'est ma nièce Sophie et mon neveu Charles! Regarde, Stéphane, tes cousins!

STÉPHANE Je n'aime pas Charles. Il est tellement sérieux.

VALÉRIE Il est peut-être trop sérieux, mais, lui, il a son bac!

AMINA Et Sophie, qu'elle est jolie!

VALÉRIE ... et elle a déjà son bac.

AMINA Ça oui, préparer le bac avec Rachid, c'est une idée géniale!

VALÉRIE Oui, c'est vrai. En théorie, c'est une excellente idée. Mais tu prépares le bac avec Rachid, hein? Pas le prochain match de foot!

Expressions utiles

Talking about your family

- **C'est ta sœur? Tes parents?**
  Is that your sister? Your parents?
- **C'est mon ami.**
  That's my friend.
- **Ça c'est Henri, sa femme Françoise et leurs enfants.**
  That's Henri, his wife Françoise, and their kids.

Describing people

- **Il a les yeux de quelle couleur? Marron ou bleue?**
  What color are his eyes? Brown or blue?
- **Il a les yeux bleus.**
  He has blue eyes.
- **Et ses cheveux? Ils sont blonds ou châtains? Frisés ou raides?**
  And his hair? Is it blond or brown? Curly or straight?
- **Il a les cheveux châtains et frisés.**
  He has curly brown hair.

Additional vocabulary

- **On peut regarder des photos de ma tante sur ton ordinateur?**
  Can/May we look at some photos from my aunt on your computer?
- **C'est toute la famille, n'est-ce pas?**
  That's the whole family, right?
- **Je ne sais pas (encore).**
  I (still) don't know.
- **Alors...**
  So...
- **vrai**
  true
- **une photo(graphie)**
  a photo(graph)
- **une idée**
  an idea
- **peut-être**
  maybe
- **au fait**
  by the way
- **Hein?**
  Alright?
- **déjà**
  already

---

2 **Vocabulaire** Describe how Stéphane would be on the occasions listed. Refer to a dictionary as necessary.

1. on his 87th birthday _____ vieux
2. after finding 20€ _____ heureux
3. while taking the bac _____ sérieux
4. after getting a good grade _____ heureux
5. after dressing for a party _____ beau

> beau
> heureux
> sérieux
> vieux

3 **Conversez** In pairs, describe which member of your family is most like Stéphane. How are they alike? Do they both like sports? Do they take similar classes? How do they like school? What are their personalities like? Be prepared to describe your partner's "Stéphane" to the class.

ressources

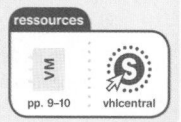

VM
pp. 9–10

vhlcentral

A C T I V I T É S

Expressions utiles

- Point out the various forms of possessive adjectives and descriptive adjectives in the captions and the **Expressions utiles**. Tell students that this material will be formally presented in the **Structures** section. Do not expect students to produce the forms correctly at this time.
- Model the pronunciation of the **Expressions utiles** and have students repeat them.
- To practice new vocabulary, ask students to describe their classmates' eyes and hair. Examples: _____ **a les yeux de quelle couleur? Marron ou bleue? Avez-vous les yeux bleus?** _____ **a-t-il/elle les cheveux blonds ou châtains? Qui a les cheveux blonds/châtains dans la classe? Est-ce que les cheveux de** _____ **sont frisés ou raides?**

1 **Suggestion** Have students correct the false statements.

1 **Expansion** For additional practice, give students these items. **11. Valérie n'aime pas son frère, Henri. (Faux.) 12. Stéphane aime les gens très sérieux. (Faux.) 13. Socrate est un chien. (Vrai.) 14. Stéphane et Rachid préparent le prochain match de foot. (Faux.)**

2 **Suggestion** Before students begin the activity, you might want to introduce the adjectives in the word list using pictures or people in the video stills, rather than having students look them up in the dictionary.

2 **Expansion** Have students describe Rachid, Charles, and Henri using the adjectives in the word list. At this point, avoid asking students to describe people that would require a feminine or plural form of these adjectives.

3 **Suggestion** If time is limited, this activity may be assigned as a written composition for homework.

O P T I O N S

Pairs Working in pairs, have students draw a family tree based on Valérie's description of her brother's family. Tell them to use the family tree on pages 90–91 as a model. Remind them to include Valérie and Stéphane. Then have them get together with another pair of students and compare their drawings.

Small Groups Have students write four questions about Henri's family based on the conversation and video still #6. Then have them get together in groups of three and take turns asking and answering each other's questions. Examples: **Combien de personnes y a-t-il dans la famille d'Henri? Comment s'appelle le fils aîné? Combien de frères a Sophie?**

  S Reading

Section Goals

In this section, students will:

- learn about different types of families in France
- learn some informal terms for family members
- find out when Mother's Day and Father's Day are celebrated in various French-speaking regions
- read about Yannick Noah and his family

Instructional Resources
vhlcentral.com:
SAM Answer Key;
reference tools

Culture à la loupe
Avant la lecture
- Have students look at the photo and describe the family there. Ask: **La famille est-elle traditionnelle ou non-conventionnelle? (Elle est traditionnelle.)**
- Tell students to scan the reading, identify the cognates, and guess their meanings.

Lecture Point out the statistics chart. Tell students that this data refers to Metropolitan France. Ask them what information this chart shows. (The percentages of different types of French families by age group.) Ask students to name the types of families. **(Célibataires, couples sans enfants, couples avec enfants, and familles monoparentales)**

Après la lecture
- Ask students what facts about families in France are new or surprising to them.
- Have students compare French and American families. Ask: **Est-ce qu'il y a des similitudes (similarities) entre la famille française et la famille américaine? Et des différences?**

🔢 **Suggestion** If students have difficulty filling in the blanks, provide them with a word bank.

🔢 **Expansion** Have pairs write four more fill-in-the-blank statements. Tell them to exchange papers with another pair and complete the sentences.

CULTURE À LA LOUPE

La famille en France

Comment est la famille française? Est-elle différente de la famille américaine? La majorité des Français sont-ils mariés, divorcés ou célibataires?

Il n'y a pas de réponse simple à ces questions. Les familles françaises sont très diverses. Le mariage est toujours° très populaire: la majorité des hommes et des femmes sont mariés. Mais attention! Les nombres° de personnes divorcées et de personnes célibataires augmentent chaque° année.

La structure familiale traditionnelle existe toujours en France, mais il y a des structures moins traditionnelles, comme les familles monoparentales, où° l'unique parent est divorcé, séparé ou veuf. Il y a aussi des familles recomposées qui combinent deux familles, avec un beau-père, une belle-mère, des demi-frères ou des demi-sœurs. Certains couples choisissent° le Pacte Civil de Solidarité (PACS), qui offre certains droits° et protections aux couples non-mariés. Depuis 2013, la France autorise également le mariage homosexuel.

Géographiquement, les membres d'une famille d'immigrés peuvent° habiter près ou loin° les uns des autres°. Mais en général, ils préfèrent habiter les uns près des autres parce que l'intégration est parfois° difficile. Il existe aussi des familles d'immigrés séparées entre° la France et le pays d'origine.

Alors, oubliez les stéréotypes des familles en France. Elles sont grandes et petites, traditionnelles et non-conventionnelles; elles changent et sont toujours les mêmes°.

Coup de main

Remember to read decimal places in French using the French word **virgule** (*comma*) where you would normally say *point* in English. To say *percent*, use **pour cent**.

64,3% soixante-quatre virgule trois pour cent

sixty-four point three percent

La situation familiale des Français
(par tranche° d'âge)

ÂGE	CÉLIBATAIRE	EN COUPLE SANS ENFANTS	EN COUPLE AVEC ENFANTS	PARENT D'UNE FAMILLE MONOPARENTALE
< 25 ans	8%	3,5%	1,3%	0,4%
25–29 ans	1,9%	16,8%	49,4%	5,9%
30–44 ans	17%	17%	54%	9,4%
45–59 ans	23%	54%	17,9%	3,9%
> 60 ans	38%	54,3%	4,7%	2,9%

SOURCE: Institut national de la statistique et des études économiques INSEE

toujours *still* **nombres** *numbers* **chaque** *each* **où** *where* **choisissent** *choose* **droits** *rights* **peuvent** *can* **près ou loin** *near or far* **les uns des autres** *from one another* **parfois** *sometimes* **entre** *between* **mêmes** *same* **tranche** *bracket*

A C T I V I T É S

1 **Complétez** Provide logical answers.

1. Si on regarde la population française d'aujourd'hui, on observe que les familles françaises sont très ___diverses___.
2. Le ___mariage___ est toujours très populaire en France.
3. La majorité des hommes et des femmes sont ___mariés___.
4. Le nombre de Français qui sont ___célibataires___ augmente.
5. Dans les familles ___monoparentales___, l'unique parent est divorcé, séparé ou veuf.
6. Il y a des familles qui combinent ___deux___ familles.
7. Le ___PACS___ offre certains droits et protections aux couples qui ne sont pas mariés.
8. Les immigrés aiment ___habiter___ les uns près des autres.
9. La France ___autorise___ le mariage homosexuel depuis 2013.
10. Les familles changent et sont toujours ___les mêmes___.

O P T I O N S

La famille française Explain to students that the concept of family is changing in France. In the past, extended families (grandparents, parents, and children) often lived in the same dwelling. Today fewer grandparents live with their children, and the number of traditional nuclear families (mother, father, and children) as well as non-traditional families is increasing.

In spite of these changes, family life is still an important social institution in French culture. When people say **la famille**, the majority of them are referring to their extended family. Most holidays are spent with family, and students often choose a university near their home so that they can spend the weekends with their family.

LE FRANÇAIS QUOTIDIEN

La famille

un frangin	*brother*
une frangine	*sister*
maman	*Mom*
mamie	*Nana, Grandma*
un minou	*kitty*
papa	*Dad*
papi	*Grandpa*
tata	*Auntie*
tonton	*Uncle*
un toutou	*doggy*

LE MONDE FRANCOPHONE

Les fêtes et la famille

Les États-Unis ont quelques fêtes° en commun avec le monde francophone, mais les dates et les traditions de ces fêtes diffèrent d'un pays° à l'autre°. Voici deux fêtes associées à la famille.

La Fête des mères
En France le dernier° dimanche de mai ou le premier° dimanche de juin
En Belgique le deuxième° dimanche de mai
À l'île Maurice le dernier dimanche de mai
Au Canada le deuxième dimanche de mai

La Fête des pères
En France le troisième° dimanche de juin
En Belgique le deuxième dimanche de juin
Au Canada le troisième dimanche de juin

quelques fêtes *some holidays* **pays** *country* **autre** *other* **dernier** *last* **premier** *first* **deuxième** *second* **troisième** *third*

PORTRAIT

Les Noah

Dans° la famille Noah, le sport est héréditaire. À chacun son° sport: pour° Yannick, né° en France, c'est le tennis; pour son père, Zacharie, né à Yaoundé, au Cameroun, c'est le football°; pour le fils de Yannick, Joakim, né aux États-Unis, c'est le basket-ball. Yannick est champion junior à Wimbledon en 1977 et participe aux championnats° du Grand Chelem° dans les années 1980. Son fils, Joakim, est joueur° de basket-ball aux États-Unis. Il

gagne° le *Final Four NCAA* en 2006 et en 2007 avec les Florida Gators. Il est aujourd'hui joueur professionnel dans l'équipe° des Chicago Bulls. Le sport est dans le sang° chez les Noah! Mais Yannick, le plus célèbre de la famille en France, est aussi chanteur. À partir de 1990, même s'il continue à participer à la vie sportive du tennis français comme entraîneur° de l'équipe de France, il décide de vivre sa seconde passion: la musique. Yannick Noah va se trouver un style: un mélange° soul et pop avec des rythmes afro. Sa musique remporte un franc° succès dans les années 2000. Il a aussi été la personnalité préférée des Français pendant plus de° quatre ans.

Dans *In* **À chacun son** *To each his* **pour** *for* **né** *born* **football** *soccer* **championnats** *championships* **Chelem** *Slam* **joueur** *player* **gagne** *wins* **équipe** *team* **sang** *blood* **entraîneur** *coach* **mélange** *mix* **franc** *clear* **plus de** *more than*

ACTIVITÉS

2 **Vrai ou faux?** Indicate if these statements are **vrai** or **faux**. Correct the false statements.

1. Le tennis est héréditaire chez les Noah.
2. Zacharie Noah est né au Cameroun.
3. Zacharie Noah était (*was*) un joueur de basket-ball.
4. Yannick gagne à l'US Open.
5. Joakim est aussi chanteur.
6. Au Canada, la Fête des mères est en mai.

3 **À vous...** With a partner, write six sentences describing another famous family whose members all share a common field or profession. Be prepared to share them with your classmates.

S Practice more at **vhlcentral.com**.

Le français quotidien Point out that these words are usually used in informal conversations with family members, children, and close friends, not in formal writing or speech.

Portrait Show the class a photo of Yannick Noah. Ask: **Qui est-ce? Comment s'appelle-t-il?** Ask students what they know about him. Explain that thanks to his active involvement in charity work, Noah is often referred to as **Tonton Yannick**.

Le monde francophone Explain that Mother's Day and Father's Day did not originate in France. The first **Journée des mères** took place in France in 1926; it became an official holiday, **La Fête des mères**, in 1950.

Suggestion Point out to students that they will find supporting activities and more information related to this **Espace culture** at **vhlcentral.com**.

2 Suggestion Have students correct the false statements.

2 Expansion Have students write three more true/false statements based on **Portrait** and **Le monde francophone**. Then have them work in groups of three and take turns reading their statements while the other group members respond **vrai** or **faux**.

3 Expansion Have students work in pairs. Tell them to create a brief conversation in which they talk about their families and pets, using vocabulary in **Le français quotidien**. Example: **Est-ce que tu as un minou? Non, mais ma tata, elle a des minous.** Remind students that this level of language is only appropriate when talking to small children.

Les fêtes de la famille Explain to students that many countries around the world have a special day to honor mothers. **La Fête des mères** and **La Fête des pères** are celebrated somewhat similarly in France, Belgium, and Canada to the way Mother's Day and Father's Day are celebrated in the United States. Children create cards, write poems, and make handicrafts in school to give to their parents on these holidays. Older sons and daughters often give a small gift. On **l'île Maurice**, they do not officially celebrate Father's Day. In other francophone regions, such as North and West Africa, there is no official holiday for either Mother's or Father's Day.

Section Goals

In this section, students will learn:
- forms, agreement, and position of adjectives
- high-frequency descriptive adjectives and some irregular adjectives

Instructional Resources
vhlcentral.com:
Activity Pack; Lab MP3s;
*SAM Answer Key; **Essayez!***
*and **Mise en pratique***
answers; Lab Audioscript;
reference tools

Suggestions
- Consider reviewing previously learned adjectives by calling out names of celebrities or school subjects and having students give a sentence to describe them. Examples: **Léonard de Vinci: Il est italien. La biologie: C'est facile.**
- Write these adjectives on the board: **américain, amusant, intelligent, timide, aînée.** Say each word and ask students if it is masculine or feminine. Model one of the adjectives in a sentence and ask volunteers to use the others in sentences.
- Work through the discussion of adjective forms point by point, writing examples on the board. Remind students that grammatical gender doesn't necessarily reflect the actual gender. Example: **Charles est une personne nerveuse.**
- Use magazine pictures and the names of celebrities to teach or practice descriptive adjectives in semantic pairs. Use either/or questions, yes/no questions, or a combination. Examples: **Tiger Woods est-il grand ou petit? (Il est grand.) Jessica Simpson est-elle brune? (Non, elle est blonde.)**
- Point out the adjectives that have the same masculine and feminine form.

Language Note Point out that the adjective **châtain** comes from the noun **une châtaigne**, which is a type of sweet chestnut. The adjective **marron** is also a noun; **un marron** means *horse chestnut.*

Leçon 3A

3A.1

Descriptive adjectives  Tutorial

Point de départ As you learned in **Leçon 1B**, adjectives describe people, places, and things. In French, unlike English, the forms of most adjectives will vary depending on whether the nouns they describe are masculine or feminine, singular or plural. Furthermore, French adjectives are usually placed after the noun they modify when they don't directly follow a form of **être**.

SINGULAR MASCULINE NOUN ⟷ SINGULAR MASCULINE ADJECTIVE	PLURAL MASCULINE NOUN ⟷ PLURAL MASCULINE ADJECTIVE
Le **père** est **américain**.	As-tu des **cours** **faciles**?
The father is American.	*Do you have easy classes?*

- You've already learned several adjectives of nationality and some adjectives to describe your classes. Here are some adjectives used to describe physical characteristics.

Adjectives of physical description

bleu(e)	*blue*	**joli(e)**	*pretty*
blond(e)	*blond*	**laid(e)**	*ugly*
brun(e)	*dark (hair)*	**marron**	*brown (not for hair)*
châtain	*brown (hair)*	**noir(e)**	*black*
court(e)	*short*	**petit(e)**	*small, short (stature)*
grand(e)	*tall, big*	**raide**	*straight (hair)*
jeune	*young*	**vert(e)**	*green*

- Notice that, in the examples below, the adjectives agree in gender (masculine or feminine) and number (singular or plural) with the subjects. Generally add -e to make an adjective feminine. If an adjective already ends in an unaccented -e, add nothing. To make an adjective plural, generally add -s. If an adjective already ends in an -s, add nothing.

Elles sont **blondes** et **petites**.
They are blond and short.

L'examen est **long**.
The exam is long.

Je n'aime pas **les cheveux raides**.
I don't like straight hair.

Les tableaux sont **laids**.
The paintings are ugly.

- Use the expression **de taille moyenne** to describe someone or something of medium size.

Victor est un homme **de taille moyenne**.
Victor is a man of medium height.

C'est une université **de taille moyenne**.
It's a medium-sized university.

- The adjective **marron** is invariable; in other words, it does not agree in gender and number with the noun it modifies. The adjective **châtain** is almost exclusively used to describe hair color.

Mon neveu a les **yeux marron**.
My nephew has brown eyes.

Ma nièce a les **cheveux châtains**.
My niece has brown hair.

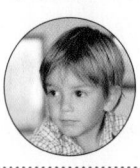

Some irregular adjectives

masculine singular	feminine singular	masculine plural	feminine plural	
beau	belle	beaux	belles	*beautiful; handsome*
bon	bonne	bons	bonnes	*good; kind*
fier	fière	fiers	fières	*proud*
gros	grosse	gros	grosses	*fat*
heureux	heureuse	heureux	heureuses	*happy*
intellectuel	intellectuelle	intellectuels	intellectuelles	*intellectual*
long	longue	longs	longues	*long*
naïf	naïve	naïfs	naïves	*naive*
roux	rousse	roux	rousses	*red-haired*
vieux	vieille	vieux	vieilles	*old*

- The forms of the adjective **nouveau** (*new*) follow the same pattern as those of **beau**.

MASCULINE PLURAL
J'ai trois **nouveaux** stylos.
I have three new pens.

FEMININE SINGULAR
Tu aimes la **nouvelle** horloge?
Do you like the new clock?

- Other adjectives that follow the pattern of **heureux** are **curieux** (*curious*), **malheureux** (*unhappy*), **nerveux** (*nervous*), and **sérieux** (*serious*).

Position of certain adjectives

- Certain adjectives are usually placed *before* the noun they modify. These include: **beau, bon, grand, gros, jeune, joli, long, nouveau, petit,** and **vieux**.

J'aime bien les **grandes** familles.
I like large families.

Joël est un **vieux** copain.
Joël is an old friend.

- Other adjectives that are also generally placed before a noun are: **mauvais(e)** (*bad*), **pauvre** (*poor as in unfortunate*), **vrai(e)** (*true, real*).

Ça, c'est un **pauvre** homme.
That is an unfortunate man.

C'est une **vraie** catastrophe!
This is a real disaster!

- When placed before a *masculine singular noun that begins with a vowel sound*, these adjectives have a special form.

beau	>	bel	>	un **bel** appartement
vieux		vieil		un **vieil** homme
nouveau		nouvel		un **nouvel** ami

- The plural indefinite article **des** changes to **de** when the adjective comes before the noun.

ADJECTIVE BEFORE NOUN
↓   ↓
J'habite avec **de bons** amis.
I live with good friends.

ADJECTIVE AFTER NOUN
↓   ↓
J'habite avec **des amis sympathiques**.
I live with nice friends.

Essayez! Provide all four forms of the adjectives.

1. grand *grand, grande, grands, grandes*
2. nerveux nerveux, nerveuse, nerveux, nerveuses
3. roux roux, rousse, roux, rousses
4. bleu bleu, bleue, bleus, bleues
5. naïf naïf, naïve, naïfs, naïves
6. gros gros, grosse, gros, grosses
7. long long, longue, longs, longues
8. fier fier, fière, fiers, fières

À noter

In **Leçon 1B,** you learned that if the masculine singular form of an adjective already ends in **-s (sénégalais)**, you don't add another one to form the plural. The same is also true for words that end in **-x (roux, vieux)**.

🏃 **Boîte à outils**

When **pauvre** and **vrai(e)** are placed after the noun, they have a slightly different meaning: **pauvre** means *poor* as in *not rich*, and **vrai(e)** means *true*.

Ça, c'est un homme **pauvre**.
That is a poor man.

C'est une histoire **vraie**.
This is a true story.

ressources

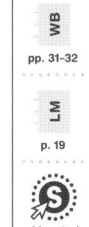

WB
pp. 31–32

LM
p. 19

vhlcentral

Suggestions
- Teach students the mnemonic device **BAGS** (beauty, age, goodness, size) to help them remember which adjectives generally precede the nouns they modify. Give examples for each category: beauty (**beau, joli**), age (**jeune, vieux**), goodness (**bon, mauvais**), size (**grand, petit**).
- Point out that the endings of adjectives patterned after **beau, bon, heureux, intellectuel,** and **naïf** are predictable. Students can apply these patterns when learning new adjectives. Ex: **affreux, affreuse, affreux, affreuses; professionnel, professionnelle, professionnels, professionnelles; actif, active, actifs, actives**.
- You may want to tell your students about other adjectives that behave like **pauvre** and **vrai**. Here are some adjectives that have different meanings based on their position before or after the noun: **nouveau, drôle, cher, brave, propre, sale**.

Essayez! Have students create sentences using these adjectives. Examples: **La tour Eiffel est grande. Les étudiants ne sont pas naïfs.**

OPTIONS

Extra Practice Have students brainstorm and make a list of adjectives in French that describe their ideal friend (**Mon copain idéal/Ma copine idéale**). Tell them to rank each adjective in terms of its importance to them. Then take a quick class survey to find out what the most important and least important qualities are in the ideal friend. Tally the results on the board.

Extra Practice Have pairs of students write sentences using adjectives such as **jeune, grand, joli,** and **petit**. When they have finished, ask volunteers to dictate their sentences to you to write on the board. After you have written a sentence and corrected any errors, ask volunteers to suggest a sentence that uses the antonym of the adjective.

ESPACE STRUCTURES

1 Expansion Have students restate the answers, except #3, #7, #8 and #9, using the phrase **les deux** to practice plural forms. Example: **1. Les deux sont curieux.**

2 Suggestion To check students' work, have volunteers write their sentences on the board and read them aloud.

2 Expansion For additional practice, change the adjective(s) and have students restate or write the sentences. Examples: **1. bon (Elle a de bons amis.) 2. beau (Elle habite dans un bel appartement.) 3. agréable (Son mari a un travail agréable.) 4. bon (Ses filles sont de bonnes étudiantes.) 5. indépendant/élégant (Christine est indépendante et élégante.) 6. fier (Son mari est un homme fier.) 7. poli (Elle a des collègues polis.) 8. joli/intelligent (Sa secrétaire est une jolie fille intelligente.)**

Mise en pratique

1 **Ressemblances** Family members often look and behave alike. Describe them.

MODÈLE

Caroline est intelligente. Elle a un frère.
Il est intelligent aussi.

1. Jean est curieux. Il a une sœur. Elle est curieuse aussi.
2. Carole est blonde. Elle a un cousin. Il est blond aussi.
3. Albert est gros. Il a trois tantes. Elles sont grosses aussi.
4. Sylvie est fière et heureuse. Elle a un fils. Il est fier et heureux aussi.
5. Christophe est vieux. Il a une demi-sœur. Elle est vieille aussi.
6. Martin est laid. Il a une petite-fille. Elle est laide aussi.
7. Sophie est intellectuelle. Elle a deux grands-pères. Ils sont intellectuels aussi.
8. Céline est naïve. Elle a deux frères. Ils sont naïfs aussi.
9. Anne est belle. Elle a cinq neveux. Ils sont beaux aussi.
10. Anissa est rousse. Elle a un mari. Il est roux aussi.

2 **Une femme heureuse** Complete these sentences about Christine. Remember: some adjectives precede and some follow the nouns they modify.

MODÈLE

Christine / avoir / trois enfants (beau)
Christine a trois beaux enfants.

1. Elle / avoir / des amis (sympathique)
   Elle a des amis sympathiques.

2. Elle / habiter / dans un appartement (nouveau)
   Elle habite dans un nouvel appartement.

3. Son (*Her*) mari / avoir / un travail (bon)
   Son mari a un bon travail.

4. Ses (*Her*) filles / être / des étudiantes (sérieux)
   Ses filles sont des étudiantes sérieuses.

5. Christine / être / une femme (heureux)
   Christine est une femme heureuse.

6. Son mari / être / un homme (beau)
   Son mari est un bel homme.

7. Elle / avoir / des collègues amusant(e)s
   Elle a des collègues amusant(e)s.

8. Sa (*Her*) secrétaire / être / une fille (jeune/intellectuel)
   Sa secrétaire est une jeune fille intellectuelle.

9. Elle / avoir / des chiens (bon)
   Elle a de bons chiens.

10. Ses voisins / être (poli)
    Ses voisins sont polis.

Practice more at **vhlcentral.com**.

Communication

3 Descriptions In pairs, take turns describing these people and things using the expressions **C'est** or **Ce sont.** Answers will vary.

MODÈLE

C'est un cours difficile.

1. _____ 2. _____ 3. _____

4. _____ 5. _____ 6. _____

4 Comparaisons In pairs, take turns comparing these brothers and their sister. Make as many comparisons as possible, then share them with the class to see which pair is most perceptive. Answers will vary.

MODÈLE

Géraldine et Jean-Paul sont grands mais Tristan est petit.

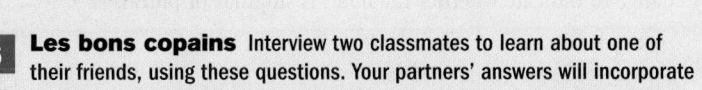

Jean-Paul   Tristan   Géraldine

5 Qui est-ce? Choose the name of a classmate. Your partner must guess the person by asking up to 10 **oui** or **non** questions. Then, switch roles. Answers will vary.

MODÈLE

Étudiant(e) 1: *C'est un homme?*
Étudiant(e) 2: *Oui.*
Étudiant(e) 1: *Il est de taille moyenne?*
Étudiant(e) 2: *Non.*

6 Les bons copains Interview two classmates to learn about one of their friends, using these questions. Your partners' answers will incorporate descriptive adjectives. Be prepared to report to the class what you learned. Answers will vary.

- Est-ce que tu as un(e) bon(ne) copain/copine?
- Comment est-ce qu'il/elle s'appelle?
- Quel âge est-ce qu'il/elle a?
- Comment est-ce qu'il/elle est?
- Il/Elle est de quelle origine?
- Quels cours est-ce qu'il/elle aime?
- Quels cours est-ce qu'il/elle déteste?

cent un **101**

---

3 Expansion Students could also describe an image and have their partner guess which one they are describing. Example:
Étudiant(e) 1: Elles sont belles.
Étudiant(e) 2: C'est la photo numéro un!

4 Expansion To practice negation, have students say what the people in the drawings are not. Example: **Géraldine et Jean-Paul ne sont pas petits.**

5 Suggestion This activity can also be done in small groups or with the whole class.

6 Suggestions
- To model this activity, have students respond as you ask the interview questions. Tell them to invent answers, where necessary.
- Tell students to add two questions of their own to the list and to take notes during their interviews.
- If time is limited, have students write a description of one of their classmates' friends as written homework.

OPTIONS

Extra Practice Prepare short descriptions of five easily recognizable people. Write their names on the board in random order. Tell students to write your descriptions as you dictate them. Then have them match the description to the appropriate name. Example: **Elle est jeune, brune, athlétique et intellectuelle. (Serena Williams)**

Game Divide the class into two teams. Call on one team member at a time, alternating between teams. Give a certain form of an adjective and name another form that the person must say and write on the board. Example: **beau**; feminine plural (**belles**). Give a point for each correct answer. The team with the most points at the end of the game wins.

3A.2

Section Goals

In this section, students will learn:
- possessive adjectives
- to express possession and relationships with **de**

Instructional Resources
vhlcentral.com:
Activity Pack; Lab MP3s;
SAM Answer Key; Essayez!
and Mise en pratique
answers; Lab Audioscript;
reference tools

Suggestions

- Introduce the concept of possessive adjectives. Ask volunteers questions, such as: **Est-ce que votre mère est heureuse? Comment est votre oncle préféré?** Point out the possessive adjectives in questions and responses.
- List the possessive adjectives on the board. Use each with a noun to illustrate agreement. Point out that all possessive adjectives agree in number with the noun they modify, but that all singular possessives must agree in gender and number. Examples: **son cousin, sa cousine, ses cousin(e)s; leur cousin, leur cousine, leurs cousin(e)s.** Also point out that **mon, ton,** and **son** are used before feminine singular nouns beginning with a vowel sound or silent **h.** Examples: **mon épouse, ton idée, son université.**
- Have students give the plural or singular of possessive adjectives with nouns. Say: **Donnez le pluriel: mon étudiant, ton examen, notre cours.** Say: **Donnez le singulier: mes sœurs, nos frères, leurs chiens, ses enfants.**

 Boîte à outils

In **Contextes**, you learned a few possessive adjectives with family vocabulary: **mon grand-père, ma sœur, mes cousins**.

Possessive adjectives  Tutorial

Point de départ In both English and French, possessive adjectives express ownership or possession.

Possessive adjectives			
masculine singular	**feminine singular**	**plural**	
mon	ma	mes	*my*
ton	ta	tes	*your (fam. and sing.)*
son	sa	ses	*his, her, its*
notre	notre	nos	*our*
votre	votre	vos	*your (form. or pl.)*
leur	leur	leurs	*their*

- Possessive adjectives are always placed before the nouns they modify.

C'est **ton** père?	Non, c'est **mon** oncle.
Is that your father?	*No, that's my uncle.*
Voici **notre** mère.	Ce sont **tes** livres?
Here's our mother.	*Are these your books?*

- In French, unlike English, possessive adjectives agree in gender and number with the nouns they modify.

mon frère	**ma** sœur	**mes** grands-parents
my brother	*my sister*	*my grandparents*
ton chat	**ta** nièce	**tes** chiens
your cat	*your niece*	*your dogs*

- Note that the forms **notre, votre,** and **leur** are the same for both masculine and feminine nouns. They only change to indicate whether the noun is singular or plural.

notre neveu	**notre** famille	**nos** enfants
our nephew	*our family*	*our children*
leur cousin	**leur** cousine	**leurs** cousins
their cousin	*their cousin*	*their cousins*

- The masculine singular forms **mon, ton,** and **son** are used with all singular nouns that begin with a vowel *even if they are feminine.*

mon amie	**ton** école	**son** histoire
my friend	*your school*	*his story*

 Boîte à outils

You already know that there are two ways to express *you* in French: **tu** (informal and singular) and **vous** (formal or plural). Remember that the possessive adjective must always correspond to the form of *you* that is used.

Tu parles à **tes** amis?

Vous parlez à **vos** amis?

O
P
T
I
O
N
S

Video Replay the video episode, having students focus on possessive adjectives. Tell them to write down each one they hear with the noun it modifies. Afterward, ask the class to describe Valérie and Stéphane's family. Remind them to use definite articles and **de** if necessary.

Suggestions
• Point out that all possessive adjectives agree in number with the noun they modify, but that all singular possessives must agree in gender and number.
• To introduce possession with **de**, write the following phrases in a list on the board: **l'ordinateur de Monique, l'ordinateur d'Alain, l'ordinateur du professeur, les ordinateurs des professeurs.** Explain the use of the contractions **d', du (de + le),** and **des (de + les)**.
• Ask students these questions. **C'est mon stylo? C'est votre amie? Ce sont leurs devoirs? C'est sa feuille de papier? Ce sont nos livres de français? C'est l'ordinateur de ____? C'est le sac à dos de ____?**

Essayez! Have students create sentences using these phrases. Examples: **C'est mon livre. Mes professeurs sont patients.**

• In English, the owner's gender is indicated by the use of the possessive adjectives *his* or *her*. In French however, the choice of **son**, **sa**, and **ses** depends on the gender and number of the noun possessed, *not* the gender and number of the owner.

> **son** frère = *his/her brother*   **sa** sœur = *his/her sister*   **ses** parents = *his/her parents*

Context will usually help to clarify the meaning of the possessive adjective.

> J'aime **Nadine** mais je n'aime pas **son** frère.   **Rémy** et **son** frère sont trop sérieux.
> *I like Nadine but I don't like her brother.*   *Rémy and his brother are too serious.*

Possession with *de*

• In English, you use *'s* to express relationships or ownership. In French, use **de (d')** + [*the noun or proper name*] instead.

> C'est le petit ami **d'Élisabeth**.   C'est le petit ami **de ma sœur**.
> *That's Élisabeth's boyfriend.*   *That's my sister's boyfriend.*

> Tu aimes la cousine **de Thierry**?   J'ai l'adresse **de ses parents**.
> *Do you like Thierry's cousin?*   *I have his parents' address.*

• When the preposition **de** is followed by the definite articles **le** and **les**, they contract to form **du** and **des**, respectively. There is no contraction when **de** is followed by **la** and **l'**.

> de + le ▶ du   de + les ▶ des

> L'opinion **du** grand-père est importante.   La fille **des** voisins a les cheveux châtains.
> *The grandfather's opinion is important.*   *The neighbors' daughter has brown hair.*

> Le nom **de l'**oiseau, c'est Lulu.   J'ai le nouvel album **de la** chanteuse française.
> *The bird's name is Lulu.*   *I have the French singer's new album.*

On peut regarder des photos de ma tante?

Elle a déjà son bac.

Essayez!   Provide the appropriate form of each possessive adjective.

mon, ma, mes
1. _mon_ livre
2. _ma_ librairie
3. _mes_ professeurs

ton, ta, tes
4. _tes_ ordinateurs
5. _ta_ télévision
6. _ton_ stylo

son, sa, ses
7. _sa_ table
8. _ses_ problèmes
9. _son_ école

notre, nos
10. _notre_ cahier
11. _nos_ études
12. _notre_ bourse

votre, vos
13. _vos_ soirées
14. _votre_ resto U
15. _vos_ devoirs

leur, leurs
16. _leur_ résultat
17. _leur_ classe
18. _leurs_ notes

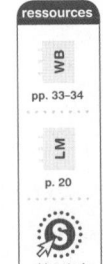

ressources

WB
pp. 33–34

LM
p. 20

vhlcentral

OPTIONS

Pairs To practice plural possessive adjectives, have pairs describe the family on pages 90–91 from the point of view of Luc and Hélène Garneau. Encourage them to include descriptive adjectives and be creative in their sentences. You might want to introduce the term **les arrière-petits-enfants** (*great-grandchildren*) for this activity. Examples: **Juliette et Marc sont nos enfants. Juliette est blonde, mais Marc est brun. Juliette et son époux, Robert, ont trois enfants. Leurs enfants s'appellent Véronique, Guillaume et Marie.**

1 Suggestion To check answers, call on volunteers to read the completed sentences aloud.

1 Expansion For additional practice, give students these items. **11. Est-ce que ____** (*your, form.*) **famille est française? (votre) 12. ____** (*My*) **femme est italienne. (Ma) 13. ____** (*Our*) **professeur est américain. (Notre) 14. Est-ce que ____** (*her*) **cousins sont espagnols? (ses) 15. ____** (*Their*) **parents sont canadiens. (Leurs) 16. ____** (*Your, fam.*) **amis sont anglais? (Tes)**

2 Suggestion Have students work in pairs. Tell them to take turns identifying the owners of the items.

2 Expansion To reinforce the relationship between possessive adjectives and possession with **de**, have students restate the answers using **son, sa,** or **ses.** Example: **C'est sa télévision.**

3 Expansion Have students come up with more combinations of family members and have volunteers tell the relationships between them.

Mise en pratique

1 **Complétez** Complete the sentences with the correct possessive adjectives.

> **MODÈLE**
>
> Karine et Léo, vous avez ____VOS____ (*your*) stylos?

1. ____Ma____ (*My*) sœur est très patiente.
2. Marc et Julien adorent ____leurs____ (*their*) cours de philosophie et de maths.
3. Nadine et Gisèle, qui est ____votre____ (*your*) amie?
4. C'est une belle photo de ____leur____ (*their*) grand-mère.
5. Nous voyageons en France avec ____nos____ (*our*) enfants.
6. Est-ce que tu travailles beaucoup sur ____ton____ (*your*) ordinateur?
7. ____Ses____ (*Her*) cousins habitent à Paris.

2 **Identifiez** Identify the owner(s) of each object.

 ▶ **MODÈLE**

Ce sont les cahiers de Sophie.

Sophie

Christophe

1. C'est la télévision de Christophe.

Paul

2. C'est l'ordinateur de Paul.

Stéphanie

3. C'est la calculatrice de Stéphanie.

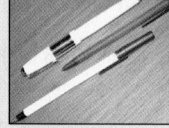

Georgette

4. Ce sont les stylos de Georgette.

Jacqueline

5. C'est l'université/la bibliothèque/ le lycée de Jacqueline.

Christine

6. Ce sont les dictionnaires de Christine.

3 **Qui est-ce?** Look at the Mercier family tree and explain the relationships between these people.

> **MODÈLE**
>
> Hubert → Marie et Fabien
> C'est leur père.

1. Marie → Guy C'est sa femme. C'est son épouse.
2. Agnès et Hubert → Thomas et Mégane Ce sont leurs grands-parents.
3. Thomas et Daniel → Yvette Ce sont ses fils.
4. Fabien → Guy C'est son beau-frère.
5. Claire → Thomas et Daniel C'est leur cousine.
6. Thomas → Marie C'est son neveu.

Hubert   Agnès

Yvette   Fabien   Marie   Guy

Thomas   Lucie   Daniel   Mégane   Claire

 Practice more at **vhlcentral.com.**

Communication

4 **Ma famille** Use these cues to interview as many classmates as you can to learn about their family members. Then, tell the class what you found out. Answers will vary.

MODÈLE

mère / parler / espagnol
Étudiant(e) 1: Est-ce que ta mère parle espagnol?
Étudiant(e) 2: Oui, ma mère parle espagnol.

1. sœur / travailler / en Californie
   _____
2. frère / être / célibataire
   _____
3. cousins / avoir / un chien
   _____
4. cousin / voyager / beaucoup
   _____
5. père / adorer / les ordinateurs
   _____
6. parents / être / divorcés
   _____
7. tante / avoir / les yeux marron
   _____
8. grands-parents / habiter / en Floride
   _____

5 **Tu connais?** In pairs, take turns telling your partner if someone among your family or friends has these characteristics. Be sure to use a possessive adjective or **de** in your responses. Answers will vary.

MODÈLE

français
Mes cousins sont français.

1. naïf
2. beau
3. petit
4. sympathique
5. optimiste
6. grand
7. blond
8. mauvais
9. curieux
10. vieux
11. roux
12. intellectuel

6 **Portrait de famille** In groups of three, take turns describing your family. Listen carefully to your partners' descriptions without taking notes. After everyone has spoken, two of you describe the other's family to see how well you remember. Answers will vary.

MODÈLE

Étudiant(e) 1: *Sa mère est sociable.*
Étudiant(e) 2: *Sa mère est blonde.*
Étudiant(e) 3: *Mais non! Ma mère est timide et elle a les cheveux châtains.*

cent cinq **105**

4 Suggestion Have two volunteers read the **modèle**. Explain to students that they use the cues to create the questions.

4 Expansion To practice asking questions with the formal *you* forms, tell students that they are going to interview the head of the French Department about his or her family. Then have students restate the questions.

5 Expansion Have students take notes on what their partner says and share them with the rest of the class. Example:
Étudiant(e) 1: Mon cousin est beau.
Étudiant(e) 2: Son cousin est beau.

6 Suggestion Before students begin the activity, tell them to make a list of the family members they plan to describe. Call on three volunteers to read the **modèle**. Explain that one student will describe his or her own family (using **mon, ma, mes**) and then the other two will describe the first student's family (using **son, sa, ses**).

OPTIONS

Small Groups Give small groups three minutes to brainstorm how many words they can associate with the phrases **notre université** and **notre cours de français**. Have them model their responses on **Dans notre cours, nous avons un(e), des ____** and **Notre université est ____**. Have the groups share their associations with the rest of the class.

Extra Practice To practice **votre** and **vos**, have students ask you questions about your family. Examples: **Comment s'appellent vos parents? Est-ce que vous avez des enfants? Comment s'appellent-ils? Est-ce que vous avez des neveux ou des nièces? Comment s'appellent-ils?**

ESPACE **SYNTHÈSE**

Révision

Instructional Resources
vhlcentral.com: Activity Pack
(Info Gap Activities); Testing
Program; Testing Program
MP3s; reference tools

1 Suggestion You may also do
this activity with the whole class
using the 3A **Contextes** illustration
from the Digital Image Bank. Have
two students do the **modèle**. The
first student will read **Étudiant(e) 1**.
The second student [**Étudiant(e)
2**] will point to the people in the
illustration as he or she states
the relationship. Continue calling
on different students to name
the family members and other
students to state the relationship.

2 Suggestion Have students
brainstorm a list of adjectives
that describe personality traits
and write them on the board.

3 Suggestion Before students
begin the activity, show them
pictures of the families listed for
identification purposes. You might
also wish to add a few names.
Examples: **la famille Noah, la
famille Clinton,** or **la famille
Kardashian.**

4 Expansion Survey students
about whether they think a large
or small family is ideal and what
they think is the ideal number of
children. Ask: **La famille idéale
est grande? Petite? Combien
d'enfants a la famille idéale?
Un? Deux? Trois? Plus?** Tally the
results.

5 Suggestion Before students
begin the activity, have two
volunteers read the **modèle**.
Make sure students understand
that **Étudiant(e) 1** is the agent
and **Étudiant(e) 2** is the casting
director. Then ask students
to describe the family in the
comedy. Example: **Comment est
le fils? (Il est brun et grand.)**

6 Suggestion Divide the class
into pairs and distribute the
Info Gap Handouts found in the
Activity Pack on the Supersite.

6 Expansion Ask students
questions based on the artwork.
Examples: **Le grand-père est-
il grand? Les filles sont-elles
heureuses?**

1 Expliquez In pairs, take turns randomly calling out one
person from column A and one from column B. Your partner
will explain how they are related. Answers will vary.

MODÈLE

Étudiant(e) 1: *ta sœur et ta mère*
Étudiant(e) 2: *Ma sœur est la fille de ma mère.*

A	B
1. sœur	a. cousine
2. tante	b. mère
3. cousins	c. grand-père
4. demi-frère	d. neveu
5. père	e. oncle

2 Les yeux de ma mère List five physical (hair, eyes, and
height) or personality traits that you share with other members
of your family. Be specific. Then, in pairs, compare your lists.
Take notes so you can present your partner's list to the class.
Answers will vary.

MODÈLE

Étudiant(e) 1: *J'ai les yeux bleus de mon père et je suis
fier/fière comme mon grand-père.*
Étudiant(e) 2: *Moi, je suis impatient(e) comme ma mère.*

3 Les familles célèbres In groups of four, play a
guessing game. Imagine that you belong to one of these
famous families or a famous family of your choice. Start
describing your new family to your partners. The first person
who guesses which family you are describing and where you
fit in is the winner. He or she should describe another family.
Answers will vary.

> La famille Addams
> La famille Obama
> La famille Kennedy
> La famille Windsor
> La famille Simpson

4 La famille idéale Survey your classmates. Ask them to
describe their ideal family. Record their answers. Then, in pairs,
compare your results. Answers will vary.

MODÈLE

Étudiant(e) 1: *Comment est ta famille idéale?*
Étudiant(e) 2: *Ma famille idéale est petite, avec deux
enfants et beaucoup de chiens et de chats.*

5 Le casting A casting director is on the phone with an
agent to find actors for a new comedy about a strange family.
In pairs, act out their conversation and find an actor to play
each character. Answers will vary.

MODÈLE

Étudiant(e) 1: *Pour la mère, il y a Émilie. Elle est rousse et
elle a les cheveux courts.*
Étudiant(e) 2: *Ah, non. La mère est brune et elle a les
cheveux longs. Avez-vous une actrice brune?*

La famille

le fils   la fille   le père   la mère   le cousin

Les acteurs et les actrices

Michelle
Annick   Patrick
Julie
Laurent
Émilie
Stéphane   Robert

6 Les différences Your instructor will give you and a
partner each a drawing of a family. Find the six differences
between your picture and your partner's. Answers will vary.

MODÈLE

Étudiant(e) 1: *La mère est blonde.*
Étudiant(e) 2: *Non, la mère est brune.*

OPTIONS

Extra Practice Use this paragraph as a dictation. Read each
sentence twice, pausing to give students time to write.
**Ma famille est très grande. Mes parents sont divorcés. Mon
beau-père a une fille. La mère de mon demi-frère cadet est
française. Leur père est américain. Leurs enfants sont
franco-américains. Ma demi-sœur et son frère sont blonds,**
**grands et beaux. Il y a aussi ma sœur aînée. Elle est jolie et de
taille moyenne. Notre mère est très fière.**

Call on volunteers to write the sentences on the board. Then ask
students to draw a family tree based on this description. You can
also ask a few comprehension questions. Examples: **Combien de
filles a son beau-père? (Il a une fille.) Qui est franco-américain?
(la demi-sœur et le demi-frère)**

La famille et les copains

Hôtesse: Csilla

When the weather is nice, many French people head to a park, square, or café. They enjoy meeting friends and relaxing, sitting in the sun or going for a stroll, and taking in the fresh air. The **parc de la Torse** and **place des Cardeurs** are the perfect places to enjoy some leisure time in **Aix-en-Provence**.

Avant de regarder Answer these questions. Answers will vary.

1. Dans ta ville, est-ce qu'il y a des parcs, des places ou des espaces verts pour se relaxer le week-end? Lesquels?
2. Qui visite ces endroits (*places*)?

CSILLA *Eh! Un jeune couple! Que c'est romantique!*

CSILLA *Bonjour, Monsieur. C'est votre fils?*

HOMME *Non, c'est mon neveu.*

CSILLA *Comment s'appelle-t-il?*

HOMME *Il s'appelle Colin.*

Compréhension Answer these questions based on the video.
Answers will vary.

1. Quelles personnes sont dans la vidéo?
Des familles, des copains, des couples, des enfants.
2. Quels types d'activités sont possibles dans le parc de la Torse?
manger, retrouver des amis
3. Et sur la place des Cardeurs?
manger, retrouver des amis
4. Comment est l'ambiance dans le parc?
L'ambiance est agréable, sympathique.

Discussion In groups of three, discuss these questions. Answers will vary.

1. Est-ce que vous aimez le parc et la place montrés (*shown*) dans la vidéo? Pourquoi?
2. Employez le vocabulaire de cette leçon pour décrire les personnes dans le parc.

Vocabulaire utile

gentils	nice
se relaxer	to relax
sportifs	athletic
un parc	park
une place	square

ressources

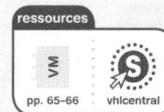
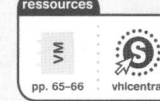
VM
pp. 65–66   vhlcentral

 Practice more at **vhlcentral.com**.

cent sept 107

Le parc de la Torse Located in the eastern part of the city, on the banks of the Torse River, the **parc de la Torse** was created in 1984. Its pathways follow and sometimes cross the river, and its trees and vegetation provide locals with a natural space to enjoy.

La place des Cardeurs The name **place des Cardeurs** refers to **cardeurs**, whose job was to smooth natural fibers such as wool by carding them. They worked outdoors because of the dust released in the process.

Section Goals

In this section, students will:
• watch a video about parks and squares in France and the people who visit them
• answer questions about the video and make comparisons about public spaces in France and in the United States

Instructional Resources
vhlcentral.com: *Flash culture*; *Flash culture* transcription; reference tools

Avant de regarder la vidéo
• Have students look at the video stills, read the captions, and predict what will happen in the episode.
• Before showing the video, explain to students that they don't need to understand every word they hear. Tell them to listen for the text in the captions and for cognates or any familiar words from this lesson.

Compréhension Have students work in pairs or groups. Tell them to write down their answers. Then, show the video again so that they can check their answers and add any missing information.

Discussion Ask volunteers to share their group's answers to the first item with the class. Write the students' descriptions of the people in the video on the board.

Section Goals

In this section, students will learn and practice vocabulary related to:
- professions and occupations
- character traits and emotional states

Instructional Resources

vhlcentral.com:
Digital Image Bank (including vocabulary illustrations from the textbook, theme-based illustrations); **Vocabulaire supplémentaire; Mise en pratique** *answers; Textbook Audioscript; Lab Audioscript; Activity Pack; Textbook MP3s; Lab MP3s; SAM Answer Key; reference tools*

Suggestions

- To introduce the adjectives, pantomime the emotions or character traits using facial expressions and/or body language. Example: **Je suis triste.** (Make a sad face.) Then ask a few students if they feel or are the same way. Example: **_____, êtes-vous triste aujourd'hui?**
- Point out that **paresseux** and **travailleur** follow the patterns of **généreux** and **coiffeur**, respectively, to form the feminine **paresseuse** and **travailleuse**.
- Point out that the masculine noun **médecin** is also used to refer to a female doctor. The expression **une femme médecin** is also common.
- Display the 3B **Contextes** illustration from the Digital Image Bank. Ask students yes/no or either/or questions using the new vocabulary. Examples: **Est-ce que la petite fille est drôle? (Non, elle n'est pas drôle.) Le petit garçon est-il heureux ou triste? (Il est triste.)**
- Use the Vocabulary illustrations and the Personality traits and Jobs illustrations from the Digital Image Bank to help students familiarize themselves with professions and occupations, character traits and emotional states.
- Additional vocabulary for this lesson can be found in the **Vocabulaire supplémentaire** on the Supersite.

Leçon 3B

You will learn how to...
- describe people
- describe locations

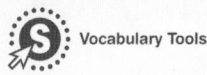
Vocabulary Tools

Comment sont-ils?

Ils sont paresseux.

Il est rapide.

Il est fort.

Il est travailleur.

le propriétaire

discrète (discret *m.*)

fatiguée (fatigué *m.*)

jaloux (jalouse *f.*)

inquiète (inquiet *m.*)

triste

Vocabulaire

actif/active	active
antipathique	unpleasant
courageux/courageuse	brave
cruel(le)	cruel
doux/douce	sweet; soft
ennuyeux/ennuyeuse	boring
étranger/étrangère	foreign
faible	weak
favori(te)	favorite
fou/folle	crazy
généreux/généreuse	generous
génial(e) (géniaux *m., pl.*)	great
gentil(le)	nice
lent(e)	slow
méchant(e)	mean
modeste	modest
pénible	annoying
prêt(e)	ready
sportif/sportive	athletic
un(e) architecte	architect
un(e) artiste	artist
un(e) athlète	athlete
un(e) avocat(e)	lawyer
un(e) dentiste	dentist
un homme/une femme d'affaires	businessman/woman
un ingénieur	engineer
un(e) journaliste	journalist
un médecin	doctor

ressources

WB	LM	
pp. 35–36	p. 21	vhlcentral

108 *cent-huit*

OPTIONS

Game Have students play a miming game in groups of four or five. Tell them that each person should think of an adjective presented in this lesson and act out the word. The first person to guess correctly acts out the next one. Example: **Es-tu fatigué(e)?** Then have each group pick out the best mime. Ask students to act out their mimes while the class guesses what they are doing.

Extra Practice Say the French term for a profession, for example, **un médecin.** Tell students to write down as many words as possible, especially the new adjectives, that they associate with this job. Then call on volunteers to read their lists as you write the words on the board, or have students compare their lists in pairs.

Mise en pratique

1 Écoutez You will hear descriptions of three people. Listen carefully and indicate whether the statements about them are **vrai** or **faux**.

Nora

Ahmed

Françoise

	Vrai	Faux
1. L'architecte aime le sport.	☐	☑
2. L'artiste est paresseuse.	☐	☑
3. L'artiste aime son travail.	☑	☐
4. Ahmed est médecin.	☐	☑
5. Françoise est gentille.	☑	☐
6. Nora est avocate.	☐	☑
7. Nora habite au Québec.	☐	☑
8. Ahmed est travailleur.	☑	☐
9. Françoise est mère de famille.	☑	☐
10. Ahmed habite avec sa femme.	☐	☑

2 Les contraires Complete each sentence with the opposite adjective.

1. Ma grand-mère n'est pas cruelle, elle est _douce/gentille_.
2. Mon frère n'est pas travailleur, il est _paresseux_.
3. Mes cousines ne sont pas faibles, elles sont _fortes_.
4. Ma tante n'est pas drôle, elle est _ennuyeuse_.
5. Mon oncle n'est pas lent, il est _rapide_.
6. Ma famille et moi, nous ne sommes pas antipathiques, nous sommes _sympathiques_.
7. Mes parents ne sont pas méchants, ils sont _gentils/doux_.
8. Mon oncle n'est pas heureux, il est _triste_.

3 Les célébrités Match these famous people with their professions. Not all of the professions will be used.

_h_	1. Bill Gates	a. médecin
_e_	2. Claude Monet	b. journaliste
_d_	3. Paul Mitchell	c. musicien(ne)
_a_	4. Dr. Phil C. McGraw	d. coiffeur/coiffeuse
_i_	5. Serena Williams	e. artiste
_b_	6. Barbara Walters	f. architecte
_c_	7. Beethoven	g. avocat(e)
_g_	8. Johnny Cochran	h. homme/femme d'affaires
		i. athlète
		j. dentiste

S Practice more at **vhlcentral.com**.

cent neuf **109**

la coiffeuse (coiffeur m.)

Il est drôle.

un musicien (musicienne f.)

---

1 Audioscript NORA: Moi, c'est Nora. J'ai 27 ans. Je suis artiste. Je suis mexicaine et j'habite à Paris. Je ne suis pas paresseuse. Je suis active, sportive et sympa. J'adore les animaux et l'art, bien sûr!
AHMED: Moi, je m'appelle Ahmed. J'ai 30 ans. Je suis architecte. Je suis discret, travailleur et un peu jaloux. Je ne suis pas sportif; je trouve le sport ennuyeux. J'habite avec mes parents au Québec.
FRANÇOISE: Moi, c'est Françoise. J'ai 51 ans. Je suis médecin. Je suis généreuse et gentille. Je travaille dans un hôpital. J'ai deux enfants, une fille et un fils. Les deux sont étudiants à l'université.
(On Textbook MP3s)

1 Suggestions
• Before students begin the activity, have them describe the people in the photos.
• To check students' answers, call on volunteers to read the sentences and answers.

2 Expansion Ask students to write two more fill-in-the-blank statements modeled on the activity. Then have them exchange papers with a classmate and complete the sentences.

3 Suggestion To check students' answers, tell them to form complete sentences using the verb **être**. Example: **Bill Gates est un homme d'affaires.** You might also have them include the person's nationality. Example: **Claude Monet est un artiste français.**

3 Expansion Have students provide additional names of famous people for each profession listed. Example: **Henri Matisse est un artiste.**

OPTIONS

Game Divide the class into two teams. Indicate one team member at a time, alternating between teams. Give a certain form of an adjective and name another form which the team member should say. Example: **fou**; feminine singular (**folle**). Give a point for each correct answer. Deduct a point for each wrong answer. The team with the most points at the end of the game wins.

Small Groups Have students work in groups of three. Tell them to decide which of the character traits presented in **Contextes** are positive qualities and which ones are negative or undesirable qualities. Have groups list the adjectives under the headings **Qualités** and **Défauts**.

Communication

4 Expansion Ask the class questions about the photos. Examples: **Qui est artiste?** (Édouard est artiste.) **Qui travaille avec un ordinateur?** (Charles travaille avec un ordinateur.) **Qui est coiffeur?** (Jean est coiffeur.) **Est-il un bon coiffeur?** (Oui, il est un bon coiffeur./Non, il est un mauvais coiffeur.) **Qui est actif?** (Jacques et Brigitte sont actifs.)

5 Suggestions
• Tell students to add at least two more questions to the list and to jot down their partner's responses.
• After completing the interviews, have volunteers report to the class what their partner said.

6 Suggestions
• Give pairs a few minutes to decide which role they are going to play and to plan what they are going to say. Have them role-play their conversation and then change partners and repeat.
• Ask a few pairs to present their conversations to the class.

7 Suggestions
• Provide students with a few models by passing out copies of authentic French personal ads or using transparencies of personal ads.
• Have students divide a sheet of paper into two columns, labeling one **Moi** and the other **Mon petit ami idéal/Ma petite amie idéale**. Have them brainstorm French adjectives for each column. Ask them to rank each adjective in the second column in terms of its importance to them.

Leçon 3B ESPACE CONTEXTES

4 Les professions In pairs, say what the true professions of these people are. Alternate reading and answering the questions.

MODÈLE
Étudiant(e) 1: *Est-ce que Sabine et Sarah sont femmes d'affaires?*
Étudiant(e) 2: *Non, elles sont avocates.*

1. Est-ce que Louis est athlète? Non, il est dentiste.
2. Est-ce que Jean est professeur? Non, il est coiffeur.
3. Est-ce que Juliette est ingénieur? Non, elle est journaliste.
4. Est-ce que Charles est médecin? Non, il est homme d'affaires.

5. Est-ce que Pauline est musicienne? Non, elle est architecte.
6. Est-ce que Jacques et Brigitte sont avocats? Non, ils sont athlètes.
7. Est-ce qu'Édouard est dentiste? Non, il est artiste.
8. Est-ce que Martine et Sophie sont propriétaires? Non, elles sont musiciennes.

5 Conversez Interview a classmate. When asked **pourquoi**, answer with **parce que** (*because*). Answers will vary.
1. Quel âge ont tes parents? Comment sont-ils?
2. Y a-t-il un(e) avocat(e) dans ta famille? Qui (*Who*)?
3. Qui est ton/ta cousin(e) préféré(e)? Pourquoi?
4. Qui n'est pas ton/ta cousin(e) préféré(e)? Pourquoi?
5. As-tu des animaux familiers (*pets*)? Quel est ton animal familier favori? Pourquoi?
6. Qui est ton professeur préféré? Pourquoi?
7. Qui est gentil dans la classe? Pourquoi?
8. Quelles professions aimes-tu? Pourquoi?

6 Quelle surprise! You run into your French instructor ten years after you graduated and want to know what his or her life is like today. With a partner, prepare a conversation where you: Answers will vary.
• greet each other
• ask each other's ages
• ask what each other's professions are
• ask about marital status and for a description of your significant others
• ask each other if you have children, and if so, describe them

7 Les petites annonces Write a **petite annonce** (*personal ad*) where you describe yourself and your ideal boyfriend or girlfriend. Include details such as profession, age, physical characteristics, and personality. Your instructor will post the ads. In groups, take turns guessing who wrote them. Answers will vary.

110 *cent dix*

OPTIONS

Extra Practice For homework, have students write a short composition about a person they admire. Tell them to include the reasons why they admire that person. Provide them with the opening statement: **J'admire _____ parce que…** On the following day, ask a few volunteers to read their compositions aloud to the class.

Game Play a game of **Dix questions**. Have a volunteer think of a profession and have the class take turns asking yes/no questions until someone guesses the profession. Limit attempts to ten questions per item instead of twenty.

Les sons et les lettres   Audio

L'accent circonflexe, la cédille, and le tréma

L'accent circonflexe (^) can appear over any vowel.

aîné	drôle	diplôme	pâté

L'accent circonflexe indicates that a letter, frequently an **s**, has been dropped from an older spelling. For this reason, **l'accent circonflexe** can be used to identify similarities between French and English words.

hospital → hôpital   forest → forêt

L'accent circonflexe is also used to distinguish between words with similar spellings but different meanings.

mûr	mur	sûr	sur
ripe	*wall*	*sure*	*on*

La cédille (̧) is only used with the letter **c**. It is always pronounced with a soft **c** sound, like the s in the English word yes. Use a **cédille** to retain the soft **c** sound before an **a**, **o**, or **u**. Before an **e** or an **i**, the letter **c** is always soft, so a **cédille** is not necessary.

garçon	français	ça	leçon

Le tréma (¨) is used to indicate that two vowel sounds are pronounced separately. It is always placed over the second vowel.

égoïste	naïve	Noël	Haïti

🔊 Prononcez Practice saying these words aloud.

1. naïf
2. reçu
3. châtain
4. âge
5. français
6. fenêtre
7. théâtre
8. garçon
9. égoïste
10. château

🔊 Articulez Practice saying these sentences aloud.

1. Comment ça va?
2. Comme ci, comme ça.
3. Vous êtes française, Madame?
4. C'est un garçon cruel et égoïste.
5. J'ai besoin d'être reçu à l'examen.
6. Caroline, ma sœur aînée, est très drôle.

🔊 Dictons Practice reading these sayings aloud.

Impossible n'est pas français.[1]

Plus ça change, plus c'est la même chose.[2]

[1] There's no such thing as "can't". (lit. Impossible is not French.)
[2] The more things change, the more they stay the same.

ressources

| LM | Ⓢ |
| p. 22 | vhlcentral |

ESPACE CONTEXTES 111

Section Goals

In this section, students will learn about:
• l'accent circonflexe
• la cédille
• le tréma
• a strategy for recognizing cognates

Instructional Resources
vhlcentral.com:
Textbook MP3s; Lab MP3s; SAM Answer Key; Textbook Audioscript; Lab Audioscript; reference tools

Suggestions

• Write the words **pâté, prêt, aîné, drôle,** and **croûton** on the board. Model the pronunciations and have students repeat. Explain that **l'accent circonflexe** can appear over any vowel. Repeat using examples with **la cédille** and **le tréma**.

• Have volunteers write **hôpital** and **forêt** on the board. Ask students what each means in English. As they respond, insert an **s** in the appropriate place above the French word. Then write these words and have students guess their meaning: **arrêter** (*to arrest*), **bête** (*beast*), **coûte** (*cost*), **île** (*isle, island*), and **Côte d'Ivoire** (*Ivory Coast*).

• Model the pronunciation of **mûr, mur,** and **sûr, sur**. Give students sentences with **mûr, mur, sûr,** or **sur** and ask them what the words mean based on the context. Examples: **1. Une grande carte est sur le mur. 2. J'ai raison; je suis sûr. 3. Les tomates ne sont pas mûres.**

• Write **comme ça** on the board and have students pronounce the words. Ask why **ça** needs **la cédille** and **comme** does not.

• The explanation and exercises are available on the **ESPACES** Supersite. You may want to play them in class so students hear French speakers besides yourself.

Dictons «**Impossible n'est pas français**» is a quote from Napoléon Bonaparte (1769–1821).

Extra Practice Write the names of French personalities on the board. Pronounce them and have the class repeat after you. Then show students each celebrity's photo and say his or her name. Show the photos a second time and ask the class to call out each name. Examples: **François Mitterrand (ancien président), Marie Laforêt (chanteuse), Jérôme Rothen (footballeur), Loïc Herbreteau (cycliste)**

Pairs Have students work in pairs. Tell them to write three sentences using as many words as possible on this page with **l'accent circonflexe, la cédille,** and **le tréma**. Encourage students to be creative and even humorous. Then ask volunteers to share their sentences with the class.

Section Goals

In this section, students will learn through comprehensible input functional phrases for making complaints, expressing location, and reading numbers.

Instructional Resources
vhlcentral.com:
Roman-photo *Video, Videoscript, and Translation; SAM Answer Key; reference tools*

Video Recap: Leçon 3A
Review the previous **Roman-photo** with this activity.
1. Qui a un ami Cyberhomme sur Internet? (Amina)
2. Pourquoi est-ce que Valérie est très inquiète? (Parce que Stéphane ne travaille pas pour le bac.)
3. Qu'est-ce que Stéphane, Valérie et Amina regardent sur l'ordinateur portable? (les photos de la famille de Valérie et de Stéphane)
4. Qui travaille avec Stéphane pour préparer le bac? (Rachid)

Video Synopsis In the café, Sandrine searches frantically for her ringing cell phone, only to find that Stéphane is playing a joke on her. Rachid and Stéphane leave to go study. At Rachid's and David's apartment, Stéphane and Rachid complain about how tiresome it is to hear David constantly talk about Sandrine. They also look at photos of Rachid's parents. Finally, they start studying math. Stéphane says he wants to be an architect.

Suggestions
• Have students scan the captions under the video stills and find four phrases with descriptive adjectives and two that mention professions.
• Have the class read through the scenes that correspond to video stills 1–4 with volunteers playing character roles. Then have small groups read scenes 5–10.
• Have students locate **Algérie** on the world map in **Appendice A**.

On travaille chez moi!  Video

PERSONNAGES

 Amina

 David

 Rachid

 Sandrine

 Stéphane

 Valérie

SANDRINE Alors, Rachid, où est David?
Un téléphone portable sonne (a cell phone rings)...
VALÉRIE Allô.
RACHID Allô.
AMINA Allô.

SANDRINE C'est Pascal! Je ne trouve pas mon téléphone!
AMINA Il n'est pas dans ton sac à dos?
SANDRINE Non!
RACHID Ben, il est sous tes cahiers.
SANDRINE Non plus!
AMINA Il est peut-être derrière ton livre... ou à gauche.

SANDRINE Mais non! Pas derrière! Pas à gauche! Pas à droite! Et pas devant!
RACHID Non! Il est là... sur la table. Mais non! La table à côté de la porte.
SANDRINE Ce n'est pas vrai! Ce n'est pas Pascal! Numéro de téléphone 06.62.70.94.87. Mais qui est-ce?

DAVID Sandrine? Elle est au café?
RACHID Oui... pourquoi?
DAVID Ben, j'ai besoin d'un bon café, oui, d'un café très fort. D'un espresso! À plus tard!
RACHID Tu sais, David, lui aussi, est pénible. Il parle de Sandrine. Sandrine, Sandrine, Sandrine.
RACHID ET STÉPHANE C'est barbant!

STÉPHANE C'est ta famille? C'est où?
RACHID En Algérie, l'année dernière chez mes grands-parents. Le reste de ma famille — mes parents, mes sœurs et mon frère, habitent à Marseille.
STÉPHANE C'est ton père, là?
RACHID Oui. Il est médecin. Il travaille beaucoup.

RACHID Et là, c'est ma mère. Elle, elle est avocate. Elle est très active... et très travailleuse aussi.

A C T I V I T É S

1 **Identifiez** Indicate which character would make each statement. The names may be used more than once. Write **D** for David, **R** for Rachid, **S** for Sandrine, and **St** for Stéphane.

1. J'ai envie d'être architecte. __St__
2. Numéro de téléphone 06.62.70.94.87. __S__
3. David est un colocataire pénible. __R__
4. Stéphane! Tu n'es pas drôle! __S__

5. Que c'est ennuyeux! __St__
6. On travaille chez moi! __R__
7. Sandrine, elle est tellement pénible. __St__
8. Sandrine? Elle est au café? __D__
9. J'ai besoin d'un café très fort. __D__
10. C'est pour ça qu'on prépare le bac. __R__

 Practice more at **vhlcentral.com**.

Avant de regarder la vidéo Write the episode title **On travaille chez moi!** on the board and have students guess its meaning. Then ask them to predict who might say this phrase in the video and to explain their reasons. Also ask them to guess in what context or situation the person might say this phrase.

Regarder la vidéo Show the video episode and have students give you a play-by-play description of the action. Write their descriptions on the board. Then show the episode again so students can add more details to the description.

Sandrine perd (*loses*) son téléphone.
Rachid aide Stéphane à préparer le bac.

STÉPHANE Qui est-ce? C'est moi!

SANDRINE Stéphane! Tu n'es pas drôle!

AMINA Oui, Stéphane. C'est cruel.

STÉPHANE C'est génial...

RACHID Bon, tu es prêt? On travaille chez moi!

À l'appartement de Rachid et de David...

STÉPHANE Sandrine, elle est tellement pénible. Elle parle de Pascal, elle téléphone à Pascal... Pascal, Pascal, Pascal! Que c'est ennuyeux!

RACHID Moi aussi, j'en ai marre.

STÉPHANE Avocate? Moi, j'ai envie d'être architecte.

RACHID Architecte? Alors, c'est pour ça qu'on prépare le bac.

Rachid et Stéphane au travail...

RACHID Allez, si *x* égale 83 et *y* égale 90, la réponse c'est...

STÉPHANE Euh... 100?

RACHID Oui! Bravo!

Expressions utiles

Making complaints

- **Sandrine, elle est tellement pénible.**
  Sandrine is such a pain.
- **J'en ai marre.**
  I'm fed up.
- **Tu sais, David, lui aussi, est pénible.**
  You know, David's a pain, too.
- **C'est barbant!/C'est la barbe!**
  What a drag!

Reading numbers

- **Numéro de téléphone 06.62.70.94.87**
  (zéro six, soixante-deux, soixante-dix, quatre-vingt-quatorze, quatre-vingt-sept).
  Phone number 06.62.70.94.87.
- **Si *x* égale 83 (quatre-vingt-trois) et *y* égale 90 (quatre-vingt-dix)...**
  If x equals 83 and y equals 90...
- **La réponse, c'est 100 (cent).**
  The answer is 100.

Expressing location

- **Où est le téléphone de Sandrine?**
  Where is Sandrine's telephone?
- **Il n'est pas dans son sac à dos.**
  It's not in her backpack.
- **Il est sous ses cahiers.**
  It's under her notebooks.
- **Il est derrière son livre, pas devant.**
  It's behind her book, not in front.
- **Il est à droite ou à gauche?**
  Is it to the right or to the left?
- **Il est sur la table à côté de la porte.**
  It's on the table next to the door.

Expressions utiles
- Point out any numbers between 61–100 and prepositions of location in the captions in the **Expressions utiles**. Tell students that this material will be formally presented in the **Structures** section.
- Model the pronunciation of the **Expressions utiles** and have students repeat after you. If available, use a cell phone to model the phrases that express location.
- To practice expressing location, point to different objects in the room and ask students where they are located. Examples: **Le livre de _____ est-il sur ou sous le bureau? Où est le sac à dos de _____?**

1 **Expansion** Give students these additional items: **11. Ce n'est pas Pascal! (Sandrine) 12. Elle est avocate. (Rachid) 13. Si *x* égale 83 et *y* égale 90, la réponse, c'est... (Rachid)**

2 **Suggestion** To check students' answers, have them form complete sentences using **être**. Examples: **Le téléphone de Sandrine est sur la table. L'ordinateur de Rachid est sur la table.**

3 **Suggestions**
- Tell pairs to choose a video character and brainstorm a list of adjectives that describe the person before they begin to write their descriptions. Remind them that they can include information from previous episodes.
- Have volunteers read their descriptions and ask the class to guess who it is. Alternatively, you can have students read their descriptions in small groups.

2 **Vocabulaire** Refer to the video stills and dialogues to match these people and objects with their locations.

a/c/e	1. sur la table	a. le téléphone de Sandrine
a	2. pas sous les cahiers	b. Sandrine
b/c/e	3. devant Rachid	c. l'ordinateur de Rachid
a/b/e/f	4. au café	d. la famille de Rachid
a/f	5. à côté de la porte	e. le café de Rachid
d	6. en Algérie	f. la table

3 **Écrivez** In pairs, write a brief description in French of one of the video characters. Do not mention the character's name. Describe his or her personality traits, physical characteristics, and career path. Be prepared to read your description aloud to your classmates, who will guess the identity of the character.

ressources
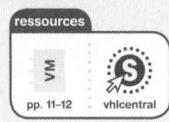
VM
pp. 11–12
vhlcentral

A C T I V I T É S

cent treize **113**

OPTIONS

Extra Practice To practice the terms **à droite** and **à gauche**, ask students to describe the people's positions in reference to each other in the video stills of the **Roman-photo**. Example: **1. Amina est à droite de Sandrine.**

Small Groups Have groups create a short skit similar to the scenes in video stills 1–4 in which someone is searching for a lost object. Provide suggestions for objects. Examples: a notebook (**un cahier**), their homework (**leurs devoirs**), a calculator (**une calculatrice**), a dictionary (**un dictionnaire**), a pen (**un stylo**), and a pencil (**un crayon**). Give students ten minutes to prepare, then call on groups to act out their skits for the class.

Section Goals

In this section, students will:
- learn to distinguish between different types of friendships
- learn some commonly used adjectives to describe people
- learn about some marriage traditions in the francophone world
- read about the Depardieu family

Instructional Resources
vhlcentral.com: reference tools

Culture à la loupe
Avant la lecture
- Introduce the reading topic by asking: **Qu'est-ce qui est important en amitié pour vous? Quelle est la différence entre un copain et un ami? Avez-vous beaucoup de copains? Combien d'amis avez-vous? De quoi parlez-vous avec vos copains? Et avec vos amis?**
- Have students look at the photos and describe the people.
- Tell students to scan the reading, identify the cognates, and guess their meanings.

Lecture
- Tell students that **un(e) petit(e) ami(e)** is the main term for boyfriend and girlfriend, but **mon ami(e)** or **mon copain/ma copine** alone without **petit(e)** can also imply a romantic relationship. Context determines the meaning.
- Tell students that it is not uncommon to hear people describe their significant others as **fiancé(e)** even if they are not officially engaged.

Après la lecture
- Have students classify the following people as **copains, amis, petits amis,** or **fiancés**.
  1. two classmates (**copains**) 2. an engaged couple (**fiancés**) 3. two coworkers (**copains**) 4. you and your best friend (**ami[e]s**) 5. a boyfriend and girlfriend in junior high (**petits amis**)
- Have students compare their view of friendship with the French view of friendship, as described in the reading. **Quelles sont les différences entre les coutumes françaises et américaines des jeunes groupes d'amis?**

1 Expansion Have students write two more true/false statements. Then tell them to exchange their papers with a classmate and complete the activity.

CULTURE À LA LOUPE

L'amitié

Pour les Français, l'amitié est une valeur sûre. En effet, plus de 95% d'entre eux estiment° que l'amitié est importante pour leur équilibre personnel°, et les amis sont considérés par beaucoup comme une deuxième famille.

Quand on demande aux Français de décrire leurs amis, ils sont nombreux à dire que ceux-ci leur ressemblent. On les choisit selon son milieu°, ses valeurs, sa culture ou son mode de vie°.

Pour les Français, l'amitié ne doit pas être confondue° avec le copinage. Les copains, ce sont des gens que l'on voit de temps en temps, avec lesquels on passe un bon moment, mais qu'on ne considère pas comme des intimes. Il peut s'agir de relations professionnelles ou de personnes qu'on fréquente° dans le cadre d'une activité commune: clubs sportifs, associations, etc. Quant aux° «vrais» amis, les Français disent en avoir seulement entre cinq et six.

Pour 6 Français sur 10, le facteur le plus important en amitié est la notion d'entraide°: on est prêt à presque tout pour aider ses amis. Viennent ensuite la fidélité et la communication. Mais attention, même si on se confie à ses amis en cas de problèmes, les amis ne sont pas là pour servir de psychologues.

Les Français considèrent aussi que l'amitié prend du temps et qu'elle est fragile. En effet, l'éloignement° et le manque de temps° peuvent lui nuire°. Mais c'est la trahison° que les Français jugent comme la première cause responsable de la fin d'une amitié.

estiment *consider* équilibre personnel *personal well-being* milieu *backgound, social standing* mode de vie *lifestyle*
confondue *confused* fréquente *see* Quant aux *As for* entraide *mutual assistance* éloignement *distance*
manque de temps *lack of time* nuire *to be detrimental* trahison *disloyalty*

Coup de main

To ask *what is* or *what are*, you can use **quel** and a form of the verb **être**. The different forms of **quel** agree in gender and number with the nouns to which they refer:

Quel / Quelle est...?
What is...?

Quels / Quelles sont...?
What are...?

A C T I V I T É S

1 **Vrai ou faux?** Are these statements **vrai** or **faux**?

1. Un copain est un très bon ami. Faux.
2. En général, les Français ont des amis très différents d'eux. Faux.
3. Les Français ont plus d'amis que de copains. Faux.
4. Un ami est une personne avec qui on a une relation très solide. Vrai.
5. Les Français pensent qu'on doit toujours aider ses amis. Vrai.

6. Un ami vous écoute quand vous avez un problème. Vrai.
7. Pour les Français, rester amis est toujours facile. Faux.
8. Il est bon de parler de tous ses problèmes à ses amis. Faux.
9. Les Français pensent que les amis sont comme une deuxième famille. Vrai.
10. Une trahison peut détruire une amitié. Vrai.

114 *cent quatorze*

OPTIONS

Extra Practice In small groups, have students draw a chart with two columns. Tell them to label the columns with the two main types of relationships between people: fellow students or coworkers (**les copains, les collègues**) and intimate, platonic friends (**les amis**). Then have students list at least five words in each column in French that apply to the people in that type of relationship. Tell them that they can use words from the reading or others that they know. Examples: **intimes, relations professionnelles, clubs sportifs, entraide, fidélité, communication** and **deuxième famille**. When students have finished, ask different groups to read their lists of words and compile the results on the board.

LE FRANÇAIS QUOTIDIEN

Pour décrire les gens

bête	*stupid*
borné(e)	*narrow-minded*
canon	*good-looking*
coincé(e)	*inhibited*
cool	*relaxed*
dingue	*crazy*
malin/maligne	*clever*
marrant(e)	*funny*
mignon(ne)	*cute*
zarbi	*weird*

LE MONDE FRANCOPHONE

Le mariage: Qu'est-ce qui est différent?

En France Les mariages sont toujours à la mairie°, en général le samedi après-midi. Beaucoup de couples vont° à l'église° juste après. Il y a un grand dîner le soir. Tous les amis et la famille sont invités.

En Belgique Les homosexuels ont le droit° de se marier depuis° 2004. Ils peuvent° aussi adopter des enfants légalement depuis 2006.

En Suisse Il n'y a pas de *bridesmaids* comme aux États-Unis mais il y a deux témoins°. En Suisse romande, la partie francophone du pays°, les traditions pour le mariage sont assez° similaires aux traditions en France.

mairie *city hall* **vont** *go* **église** *church* **droit** *right* **depuis** *since* **peuvent** *can* **témoins** *witnesses* **pays** *country* **assez** *rather*

PORTRAIT

Les Depardieu

Gérard

Les Depardieu sont une famille d'acteurs français. Gérard, le père, est l'acteur le plus célèbre° de France. Lauréat° de deux Césars°, un pour *Le Dernier Métro*° et l'autre° pour *Cyrano de Bergerac*, et d'un Golden Globe pour le film américain *Green Card*, il joue depuis trente ans° et a tourné dans° plus de 120 (cent vingt) films. Guillaume, son fils, a une carrière fulgurante° avant de décéder° prématurément à l'âge de 37 ans. Il a joué° dans beaucoup de films, y compris° *Tous les matins du monde*° avec son père. Julie, la fille de Gérard Depardieu, a déjà° deux Césars et a joué avec son père dans *Le Comte de Monte-Cristo*.

Guillaume

Julie

le plus célèbre *most famous* **Lauréat** *Winner* **Césars** *César awards (the equivalent of the Oscars in France)* **Le Dernier Métro** *The Last Metro* **l'autre** *the other* **il joue depuis trente ans** *he has been acting for thirty years* **a tourné dans** *has been in* **fulgurante** *dazzling* **avant de décéder** *before he passed away* **a joué** *acted* **y compris** *including* **Tous les matins du monde** *All the Mornings of the World* **déjà** *already*

MUSIQUE À FOND

Stephan Eicher

Date de naissance: 17 août 1960
Lieu de naissance: Münchenbuchsee, Suisse
Métier: compositeur-interprète

Stephan Eicher est un artiste reconnu en France, mais il chante aussi en anglais, en allemand et en italien.

Go to vhlcentral.com to find out more about **Stephan Eicher** and his music.

---

2 **Les Depardieu** Complete these statements with the correct information.

1. Gérard Depardieu a joué dans plus de ___120___ films.
2. Guillaume était (*was*) ___le fils___ de Gérard Depardieu.
3. Julie est ___la fille___ de Gérard Depardieu.
4. Julie joue avec Gérard dans ___Le Comte de Monte-Cristo___.
5. Guillaume joue avec Gérard dans ___Tous les matins du monde___.
6. Julie a déjà ___deux___ Césars.

3 **Comment sont-ils?** Look at the photos of the Depardieu family. With a partner, take turns describing each person in detail in French. How old do you think they are? What do you think their personalities are like? Do you see any family resemblances?

ressources

vhlcentral

Practice more at **vhlcentral.com**.

ACTIVITÉS

OPTIONS

Le mariage et les traditions Here are some other wedding customs or traditions.

- A traditional Moroccan wedding ceremony lasts from four to seven days. After the couple exchanges vows, the bride walks around the exterior of her new home three times.

- In Belgium, wedding invitations are traditionally printed on two sheets of paper—one sheet is from the bride's family and the other sheet is from the groom's family. The two sheets of paper symbolize the union of two families.

Le français quotidien Have students work in pairs. Tell them to take turns describing their friends or classmates using these words. You may want to point out that **zarbi** is **bizarre** in **verlan**. Students will learn more about **le verlan** in the 4A **français quotidien** section.

Portrait Show the class a photo of Gérard Depardieu. Ask: **Qui est-ce? Comment s'appelle-t-il? Quelle est sa profession?** Repeat the questions with a photo of his son and/or daughter. Then ask students to name any movies starring one or more of the Depardieus that they have seen, for example, *Jean de Florette* (1986), *The Man in the Iron Mask* (1998), *Last Holiday* (2006), or one of the *Astérix* movies.

Le monde francophone Ask students which differences they find most interesting. Point out that, as in the United States, the wedding traditions a couple chooses to follow often depend upon their religion. For example, a Jewish couple might observe Jewish traditions at their wedding, and an Algerian or Moroccan couple might follow Islamic traditions.

Musique à fond Point out to students that they will find supporting activities and information at **vhlcentral.com**.

2 Expansion To check students' answers, have them work in pairs. Tell students to take turns asking the questions that would elicit each statement and responding with the completed sentence.

3 Expansions
- Give students these dates of birth and have them calculate each person's age: Gérard (1948), Julie (1973)
- You might want to tell students that Gérard was born in Châteauroux, France, and that Depardieu is a typical name from the center of France.
- In October 2008, Guillaume Depardieu passed away in France after contracting severe pneumonia in Romania on the set of a new film.

ESPACE CULTURE **115**

3B.1

Numbers 61–100

 Tutorial

Section Goals

In this section, students will learn numbers 61–100.

Instructional Resources
vhlcentral.com:
Activity Pack; Lab MP3s;
*SAM Answer Key; **Essayez!***
*and **Mise en pratique***
answers; Lab Audioscript;
reference tools

Suggestions

- Review numbers 0–20 by having the class count with you. Then have them count by tens to 60.
- Model the pronunciation of numbers 61–100 and have students repeat them.
- Explain that the numbers 70–99 follow a slightly different pattern than the numbers 21–69. Point out that 61 and 71 use the conjunction **et**, while 81 and 91 need hyphens.
- Write a few numbers on the board, such as 68, 72, 85, and 99. Have students say each number in French as you point to it. Then have students count by fives from 60–100.

Essayez! Have students write five more numbers between 61–100. Then tell them to get together with a classmate and take turns dictating their numbers to each other and writing them down. Remind students to check each other's answers.

Boîte à outils

Study tip: To say numbers **70–99**, remember the arithmetic behind them. For example, **quatre-vingt-douze (92)** is **4 (quatre)** x **20 (vingt)** + **12 (douze)**.

À noter

Numbers 101 and greater are presented in **Leçon 5B**.

Numbers 61–100			
61–69		**80–89**	
61 soixante et un		80 quatre-vingts	
62 soixante-deux		81 quatre-vingt-un	
63 soixante-trois		82 quatre-vingt-deux	
64 soixante-quatre		83 quatre-vingt-trois	
65 soixante-cinq		84 quatre-vingt-quatre	
66 soixante-six		85 quatre-vingt-cinq	
67 soixante-sept		86 quatre-vingt-six	
68 soixante-huit		87 quatre-vingt-sept	
69 soixante-neuf		88 quatre-vingt-huit	
		89 quatre-vingt-neuf	
70–79		**90–100**	
70 soixante-dix		90 quatre-vingt-dix	
71 soixante et onze		91 quatre-vingt-onze	
72 soixante-douze		92 quatre-vingt-douze	
73 soixante-treize		93 quatre-vingt-treize	
74 soixante-quatorze		94 quatre-vingt-quatorze	
75 soixante-quinze		95 quatre-vingt-quinze	
76 soixante-seize		96 quatre-vingt-seize	
77 soixante-dix-sept		97 quatre-vingt-dix-sept	
78 soixante-dix-huit		98 quatre-vingt-dix-huit	
79 soixante-dix-neuf		99 quatre-vingt-dix-neuf	
		100 cent	

- Numbers that end in the digit **1** are not usually hyphenated. They use the conjunction **et** instead.

  (trente et un) (cinquante et un) (soixante et un)

- Note that **81** and **91** are exceptions:

  (quatre-vingt-un) (quatre-vingt-onze)

- The number **quatre-vingts** ends in -s, but there is no -s when it is followed by another number.

  (quatre-vingts) (quatre-vingt-cinq) (quatre-vingt-dix-huit)

ressources

WB
pp. 37–38

LM
p. 23

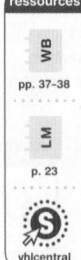
vhlcentral

Essayez! What are these numbers in French?

1. 67 _____ soixante-sept
2. 75 _____ soixante-quinze
3. 99 _____ quatre-vingt-dix-neuf
4. 70 _____ soixante-dix
5. 82 _____ quatre-vingt-deux
6. 91 _____ quatre-vingt-onze
7. 66 _____ soixante-six
8. 87 _____ quatre-vingt-sept
9. 52 _____ cinquante-deux
10. 60 _____ soixante

Le français vivant
- Call on a volunteer to read the catalogue page aloud. Point out the prices in euros.
- Ask students: **Combien d'objets y a-t-il sur la photo?**

Le français vivant

As-tu envie d'être
ingénieur, musicien, architecte, professeur?

le sac à dos 70€

le bureau 96€

la chaise 82€

la calculatrice 61€

Tu as besoin d'une calculatrice intelligente, d'un beau bureau, d'une chaise confortable et d'un bon sac à dos.

Tu trouves tout dans le **Catalogue AAZ!**

Identifiez Scan this catalogue page, and identify the instances where the numbers 61–100 are used. Answers will vary.

 Questions Answers will vary.

1. Qui sont les personnes sur la photo?
2. Où est-ce qu'elles habitent?
3. Qu'est-ce qu'elles ont dans leur maison?
4. Quels autres (*other*) objets trouve-t-on dans le Catalogue AAZ? (Imaginez.)
5. Quels sont leurs prix (*prices*)?

cent dix-sept **117**

OPTIONS

Game Ask for two volunteers and station them at opposite ends of the board so neither one can see what the other is writing. Say a number from 0–100 and tell them to write it on the board. If both students are correct, continue to give numbers until one writes an incorrect number. The winner continues on to play against another student.

TPR Assign ten students a number from 0–100 and line them up in front of the class. As you call out a number at random, that student should take a step forward. When two students have stepped forward, ask them to repeat their numbers. Then ask volunteers to add or subtract the two numbers given. Make sure the resulting sum is not greater than 100.

Expansions

• Model the question: **Quel est ton numéro de téléphone?** Then have students circulate around the room asking each other their phone numbers. Tell them to write the person's number next to his or her name and have the person verify it.

• Dictate actual phone numbers to the class and tell them to write the numerals. Examples: your office number, the department's number, etc.

2 Expansion Have each student write five more addition or subtraction problems. Then have students work in pairs and take turns reading their problems aloud while the other person says the answer.

3 Expansion Tell students to write three additional series of numbers. Then have them exchange papers with a classmate and take turns reading the series and filling in the numbers.

Mise en pratique

1 **Les numéros de téléphone** Write down these phone numbers, then read them aloud in French.

MODÈLE

C'est le zéro un, quarante-trois, soixante-quinze, quatre-vingt-trois, seize.
01.43.75.83.16

1. C'est le zéro deux, soixante-cinq, trente-trois, quatre-vingt-quinze, zéro six.
   02.65.33.95.06

2. C'est le zéro un, quatre-vingt-dix-neuf, soixante-quatorze, quinze, vingt-cinq.
   01.99.74.15.25

3. C'est le zéro cinq, soixante-cinq, onze, zéro huit, quatre-vingts.
   05.65.11.08.80

4. C'est le zéro trois, quatre-vingt-dix-sept, soixante-dix-neuf, cinquante-quatre, vingt-sept.
   03.97.79.54.27

5. C'est le zéro quatre, quatre-vingt-cinq, soixante-neuf, quatre-vingt-dix-neuf, quatre-vingt-onze.
   04.85.69.99.91

6. C'est le zéro un, vingt-quatre, quatre-vingt-trois, zéro un, quatre-vingt-neuf.
   01.24.83.01.89

7. C'est le zéro deux, quarante et un, soixante et onze, douze, soixante.
   02.41.71.12.60

8. C'est le zéro quatre, cinquante-huit, zéro neuf, quatre-vingt-dix-sept, treize.
   04.58.09.97.13

2 **Les maths** Read these math problems aloud, then write out each answer in words.

MODÈLE

$65 + 3 =$ _soixante-huit_

Soixante-cinq plus trois font (*equals*) soixante-huit.

1. $70 + 15 =$ _quatre-vingt-cinq_
2. $82 + 10 =$ _quatre-vingt-douze_
3. $76 + 3 \ =$ _soixante-dix-neuf_
4. $88 + 12 =$ _cent_
5. $40 + 27 =$ _soixante-sept_
6. $67 + 6 \ =$ _soixante-treize_
7. $43 + 54 =$ _quatre-vingt-dix-sept_
8. $78 + 5 \ =$ _quatre-vingt-trois_
9. $70 + 20 =$ _quatre-vingt-dix_
10. $64 + 16 =$ _quatre-vingts_

3 **Comptez** Read the following numbers aloud in French, then follow the pattern to provide the missing numbers.

1. 60, 62, 64, ... 80   66, 68, 70, 72, 74, 76, 78
2. 76, 80, 84, ... 100   88, 92, 96
3. 10, 20, 30, ... 90   40, 50, 60, 70, 80
4. 81, 83, 85, ... 99   87, 89, 91, 93, 95, 97
5. 62, 63, 65, 68, ... 98   72, 77, 83, 90
6. 55, 57, 59, ... 73   61, 63, 65, 67, 69, 71
7. 100, 95, 90, ... 60   85, 80, 75, 70, 65
8. 99, 96, 93, ... 69   90, 87, 84, 81, 78, 75, 72

 Practice more at **vhlcentral.com.**

Communication

4 **Questions indiscrètes** With a partner, take turns asking how old these people are. Answers will vary.

M. Hubert
Mme Hubert
M. Moreau
Mme Moreau
M. Durand
Mme Durand

MODÈLE

Étudiant(e) 1: *Madame Hubert a quel âge?*
Étudiant(e) 2: *Elle a 70 ans.*

5 **Qui est-ce?** Interview as many classmates as you can in five minutes to find out the name, relationship, and age of their oldest family member. Identify the student with the oldest family member to the class. Answers will vary.

MODÈLE

Étudiant(e) 1: *Qui est le plus vieux (the oldest) dans ta famille?*
Étudiant(e) 2: *C'est ma tante Julie. Elle a soixante-dix ans.*

6 **Fournitures scolaires** Take turns playing the role of a store employee ordering the school supplies (**fournitures scolaires**) below. Tell how many of each item you need. Your partner will write down the number of items ordered. Switch roles when you're done. Answers will vary.

MODÈLE

Étudiant(e) 1: *Vous avez besoin de combien de crayons?*
Étudiant(e) 2: *J'ai besoin de soixante-dix crayons.*

1. _____

2. _____

3. _____

4. _____

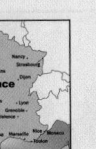

5. _____

6. _____

7. _____

8. _____

4 **Expansion** To review descriptive adjectives, have students describe the people in the drawing.

5 **Suggestions**
• Have two volunteers read the **modèle**.
• You may wish to provide a few supplementary terms for family members, such as **l'arrière-grand-mère** and **l'arrière-grand-père**.
• Ask various students to identify the person who has the oldest family member from their interviews. Continue until students identify the oldest person among all the families.

OPTIONS

Extra Practice Ask students to write down their university mailbox numbers on a slip of paper. Collect the papers. Tell students to say **«C'est ma boîte aux lettres!»** when they hear their mailbox number. Then proceed to read the numbers aloud at random.

Game Play a game of Bingo. Have students draw a square on a sheet of paper with three horizontal and three vertical rows. Tell them to write nine different numbers between 61–100 in the boxes. Explain that they should cross out the numbers as they hear them and that they should say "Bingo!" if they have three numbers in a horizontal, vertical, or diagonal row. Then call out numbers at random and write them down to verify.

3B.2

Prepositions of location and disjunctive pronouns

 Tutorial

Section Goals

In this section, students will learn:
• prepositions of location
• disjunctive pronouns

Instructional Resources
vhlcentral.com:
Activity Pack; Lab MP3s;
*SAM Answer Key; **Essayez!***
*and **Mise en pratique***
answers; Lab Audioscript;
reference tools

Suggestions

• Explain that prepositions typically indicate where one thing or person is in relation to another: *near, far, on, between, under.* Model the pronunciation of the prepositions and have students repeat.

• Remind students that they may need to use the contractions **du** and **des**.

• Take a book or other object and place it in various locations in relation to your desk or a student's desk as you ask individual students about its location. Examples: **Où est le livre? Est-ce qu'il est derrière le bureau? Quel objet est à côté du livre?** Work through various locations, eliciting all prepositions of location.

• Ask where different students are in relation to one another. Example: ____, où est ____? (Il/Elle est à côté de [à droite de, à gauche de, derrière] ____.)

À noter

In **Leçon 7A**, you will learn more names of countries and their corresponding prepositions.

Point de départ You have already learned expressions in French containing prepositions like **à**, **de**, and **en**. Prepositions of location describe the location of something or someone in relation to something or someone else.

• Use the preposition **à** before the name of any city to express *in, to*. The preposition that accompanies the name of a country varies, but you can use **en** in many cases.

Il étudie **à Nice**.	Je voyage **en France** et **en Belgique**.
He studies in Nice.	*I'm traveling in France and Belgium.*

Prepositions of location

à côté de	*next to*	**en face de**	*facing, across from*
à droite de	*to the right of*	**entre**	*between*
à gauche de	*to the left of*	**loin de**	*far from*
dans	*in*	**par**	*by*
derrière	*behind*	**près de**	*close to, near*
devant	*in front of*	**sous**	*under*
en	*in*	**sur**	*on*

• Use the forms **du, de la, de l'** and **des** in prepositional expressions when they are appropriate.

Le resto U est **à côté du** gymnase.	Mes grands-parents habitent **près des** Alpes.
The cafeteria is next to the gym.	*My grandparents live near the Alps.*
Ils sont **devant** la bibliothèque.	L'université est **à droite de** l'hôtel.
They are in front of the library.	*The university is to the right of the hotel.*

• You can further modify prepositions of location by using intensifiers such as **tout** (*very, really*) and **juste** (*just, right*).

Ma sœur habite **juste en face de** l'université.	Le lycée est **juste derrière** son appartement.
My sister lives right across from the university.	*The high school is just behind his apartment.*
Jules et Alain travaillent **tout près de** la fac.	La librairie est **tout à côté du** café.
Jules and Alain work really close to campus.	*The bookstore is right next to the café.*

Boîte à outils

You can also use the prepositions **derrière** and **devant** without a following noun.

Le chien habite derrière.
The dog lives out back.

However, a noun must always follow the prepositions **dans, en, entre, par, sous,** and **sur.**

• You may use a preposition without the word **de** if it is not followed by a noun.

Ma sœur habite **juste à côté**.	Elle travaille **tout près**.
My sister lives right next door.	*She works really close by.*

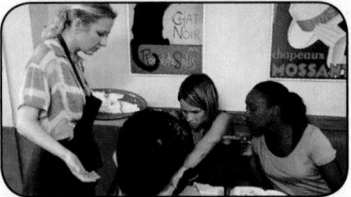

Il n'est pas sous les cahiers.	Pas derrière! Pas à droite!

120 *cent vingt*

- The preposition **chez** has no exact English equivalent. It expresses the idea of *at* or *to someone's house* or *place*.

Louise n'aime pas étudier **chez Arnaud** parce qu'il parle beaucoup.
Louise doesn't like studying at Arnaud's because he talks a lot.

Ce matin, elle n'étudie pas parce qu'elle est **chez sa cousine**.
This morning she's not studying because she's at her cousin's.

- The preposition **chez** is also used to express the idea of *at* or *to a professional's office* or *business*.

chez le docteur
at the doctor's

chez la coiffeuse
to the hairdresser's

On travaille chez moi!

Stéphane est chez Rachid.

- When you want to use a pronoun that refers to a person after any type of preposition, you don't use a subject pronoun. Instead, you use what are called disjunctive pronouns.

Disjunctive pronouns

singular		plural	
je →	moi	nous →	nous
tu →	toi	vous →	vous
il →	lui	ils →	eux
elle →	elle	elles →	elles

Maryse travaille **à côté de moi**.
Maryse is working next to me.

Est-ce qu'il y a un coiffeur près de **chez vous**?
Is there a hairdresser near where you live?

Nous pensons **à toi**.
We're thinking about you.

Voilà ma cousine Lise, **devant nous**.
There's my cousin Lise, in front of us.

Tu as besoin **d'elle** aujourd'hui?
Do you need her today?

Vous n'avez pas peur **d'eux**.
You're not afraid of them.

Essayez! Complete each sentence with the equivalent of the expression in parentheses.

1. La librairie est __derrière__ (*behind*) le resto U.
2. J'habite __près de__ (*close to*) leur lycée.
3. Le laboratoire est __à côté de__ (*next to*) ma résidence.
4. Tu retournes __chez__ (*to the house of*) tes parents ce week-end?
5. La fenêtre est __en face de__ (*across from*) la porte.
6. Mon sac à dos est __sous__ (*under*) la chaise.
7. Ses crayons sont __sur__ (*on*) la table.
8. Votre ordinateur est __dans__ (*in*) la corbeille!
9. Il n'y a pas de secrets __entre__ (*between*) amis.
10. Le professeur est __devant__ (*in front of*) les étudiants.

ressources

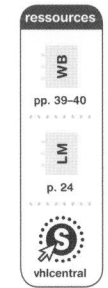

WB
pp. 39–40

LM
p. 24

vhlcentral

cent vingt et un **121**

Suggestions
- Model the pronunciation of the disjunctive pronouns and have students repeat them. Explain that these pronouns are used in prepositional phrases. Examples: **1. Ma famille vient** (*comes*) **souvent chez moi. 2. Je suis en face de toi.** Then ask volunteers for examples.
- Write the following in a column on the board and explain each usage of **chez**: chez + *person's name or person* (**chez Rachid, chez des amis**); **chez** + *professional's office or business* (**chez le docteur**); and **chez** + *disjunctive pronoun* (**chez toi**).
- Compare sentences with subject pronouns and disjunctive pronouns to help students understand when to use each. On the board, write: **Mon ami est français. —— parle français. Je travaille chez —— le week-end.** Ask students to fill in the blanks. Highlight that the first blank, which precedes a verb, requires a subject pronoun while the second, which follows a preposition, must be filled with a disjunctive pronoun. Give other examples.

Essayez! Have students write three more fill-in-the-blank sentences describing where certain objects are located in their dorm room or apartment. Then tell them to exchange papers with a classmate and complete the sentences.

O P T I O N S

TPR Have one student start with a small beanbag or rubber ball. You call out another student identified only by his or her location with reference to other students. Example: **C'est la personne derrière ____.** The student with the beanbag or ball has to throw it to the student identified. The latter student must then throw the object to the next person you identify.

Video Show the video episode again to give students more input using prepositions and disjunctive pronouns. Stop the video where appropriate to discuss how the prepositions of location and disjunctive pronouns were used. Ask comprehension questions.

1 **Suggestion** To check students' answers, have them work in pairs and take turns asking the completed questions and answering them in the affirmative or negative.

2 **Suggestion** Before students begin the activity, have them identify the people, places, and other objects in the drawing. Example: **Il y a un oiseau.**

2 **Expansion** Have students create additional sentences about the location of the people or objects in the drawing. To practice negation, have students describe where the people and other objects are not located. Example: **La famille n'est pas devant la bibliothèque.**

Mise en pratique

1 **Où est ma montre?** Claude has lost her watch. Choose the appropriate prepositions to complete her friend Pauline's questions.

> **MODÈLE**
>
> Elle est (*à gauche du* / entre le) livre?

1. Elle est (sur / entre) le bureau? sur
2. Elle est (par / derrière) la télévision? derrière
3. Elle est (entre / dans) le lit et la table? entre
4. Elle est (en / sous) la chaise? sous
5. Elle est (sur / à côté de) la fenêtre? à côté de
6. Elle est (près du / entre le) sac à dos? près du
7. Elle est (devant / sur) la porte? devant
8. Elle est (dans / sous) la corbeille? dans

2 **Complétez** Look at the drawing, and complete these sentences with the appropriate prepositions. Suggested answers

> **MODÈLE**
>
> Nous sommes _chez_ nos cousins.

1. Nous sommes __devant__ la maison de notre tante.
2. Michel est __loin de__ Béatrice.
3. __Entre__ Jasmine et Laure, il y a le petit cousin, Adrien.
4. Béatrice est __à côté de__ Jasmine.
5. Jasmine est tout __près de__ Béatrice.
6. Michel est __derrière__ Laure.
7. Un oiseau est __sur__ la maison.
8. Laure est __à droite d'__ Adrien.

Michel
Laure
Adrien
Jasmine
Béatrice

3 **Où est-on?** Tell where these people, animals, and things are in relation to each other. Replace the second noun or pronoun with the appropriate disjunctive pronoun. Suggested answers

> **MODÈLE**
>
> Alex / Anne
> Alex est à droite d'elle.

1. _____
2. _____

3. _____
4. _____
5. _____
6. _____

1. l'oiseau / je L'oiseau est loin de moi.
2. le chien / Gabrielle et Emma Le chien est entre elles.
3. le monument / tu Le monument est en face de toi.
4. l'ordinateur / Ousmane L'ordinateur est devant lui.
5. Mme Fleury / Max et Élodie Mme Fleury est derrière eux.
6. les enfants / la grand-mère Les enfants sont près d'elle.

 Practice more at vhlcentral.com.

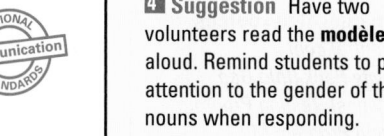

Communication

4 **Où est l'objet?** In pairs, take turns asking where these items are in the classroom. Use prepositions of location. Answers will vary.

MODÈLE la carte

Étudiant(e) 1: *Où est la carte?*
Étudiant(e) 2: *Elle est devant la classe.*

1. l'horloge
2. l'ordinateur
3. le tableau
4. la fenêtre
5. le bureau du professeur
6. ton livre de français
7. la corbeille
8. la porte

5 **Qui est-ce?** Choose someone in the room. The rest of the class will guess whom you chose by asking yes/no questions that use prepositions of location. Answers will vary.

MODÈLE

Est-ce qu'il/elle est derrière Dominique?
Est-ce qu'il/elle est entre Jean-Pierre et Suzanne?

6 **S'il vous plaît...?** A tourist stops someone on the street to ask where certain places are located. In pairs, play these roles using the map to locate the places. Answers will vary.

MODÈLE

Étudiant(e) 1: *La banque, s'il vous plaît?*
Étudiant(e) 2: *Elle est en face de l'hôpital.*

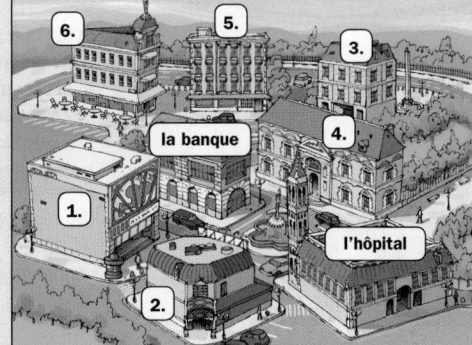

1. le cinéma Ambassadeur
2. le restaurant Chez Marlène
3. la librairie Antoine
4. le lycée Camus
5. l'hôtel Royal
6. le café de la Place

7 **Ma ville** In pairs, take turns telling your partner where the places below are located in your town or neighborhood. You may use your campus as a reference point. Correct your partner when you disagree. Answers will vary.

MODÈLE

la banque
La banque est tout près de la fac.

1. le café
2. la librairie
3. l'université
4. le gymnase
5. l'hôtel
6. la bibliothèque
7. l'hôpital
8. le restaurant italien

cent vingt-trois **123**

4 Suggestion Have two volunteers read the **modèle** aloud. Remind students to pay attention to the gender of the nouns when responding.

4 Expansion For additional practice, give students these items if they are present in the classroom. **9. le dictionnaire de français 10. la calculatrice 11. les examens**

5 Suggestion To continue this activity, allow the student who guessed the correct person to choose another person and have the class ask the student yes/no questions.

6 Suggestion Before students begin this activity, make sure they understand that the numbers on the illustration correspond to the places on the list. Have two volunteers read the **modèle** aloud.

7 Suggestion Students could even draw a rough map of the town based on their partner's description. They should first situate the campus before they draw the other places.

OPTIONS

Small Groups In groups of three or four, have students think of a city or town within a 100-mile radius of your campus. They need to figure out how many miles away it is and what other cities or towns are nearby (**La ville est près de...**). Then have them get together with another group and read their descriptions. The other group has to guess which city or town is being described.

Extra Practice Have students look at the world map in **Appendice A** or use maps of the French-speaking world from the Digital Image Bank. Make true/false statements about the locations of various countries. Examples: **1. La Chine est près des États-Unis. (Faux.) 2. Le Luxembourg est entre la France et l'Allemagne. (Vrai.)** For variation, you can make statements or ask true/false questions about the location of various cities in France.

Révision

Instructional Resources
vhlcentral.com:
Activity Pack (Info Gap Activities); Testing Program; Testing Program MP3s; reference tools

1 Suggestion Point out that in France and most francophone countries (except Canada) it is not common for universities to have sports teams. If they do, their fans are usually limited to university students. The general public doesn't usually follow college sports.

2 Expansion To review descriptive adjectives, ask students to give physical descriptions of the people.

3 Suggestion You might want to make photocopies of your campus map and distribute them to the class for this activity since some students might not know the campus well.

4 Suggestion To practice listening skills, tell students to cover the phone numbers with one hand and write the phone numbers down as their partner says them.

5 Suggestion Encourage students to ask questions when they are playing the role of the customer. For example, they can ask if the store has certain brands of an item, backpacks and notebooks in certain colors, or a specific type of dictionary.

6 Suggestion Divide the class into pairs and distribute the Info Gap Handouts found in the Activity Pack on the Supersite. Give students ten minutes to complete the activity.

6 Expansion Ask students questions based on the artwork. Example: **Est-ce que le neveu est à côté de la mère?**

---

1 Le basket These basketball rivals are competing for the title. In pairs, predict the missing playoff scores. Then, compare your predictions with those of another pair. Be prepared to share your predictions with the class. Answers will vary.

1. Ohio State 76, Michigan _____
2. Florida _____, Florida State 84
3. Stanford _____, UCLA 79
4. Purdue 81, Indiana _____
5. Duke 100, Virginia _____
6. Kansas 95, Colorado _____
7. Texas _____, Oklahoma 88
8. Kentucky 98, Tennessee _____

2 La famille d'Édouard In pairs, take turns guessing where Édouard's family members are in the photo using prepositions to describe their locations. Compare your answers with those of another pair. Answers will vary.

Édouard

MODÈLE

Son père est derrière sa mère.

3 À la fac In pairs, take turns describing the location of a building (**un bâtiment**) on your campus. Your partner must guess which building you are describing in three tries. Keep score to determine the winner after several rounds. Answers will vary.

MODÈLE

Étudiant(e) 1: *C'est un bâtiment entre la bibliothèque et Sherman Hall.*
Étudiant(e) 2: *C'est le resto U?*
Étudiant(e) 1: *C'est ça!*

4 C'est quel numéro? What courses would you take if you were studying at a French university? Take turns deciding and having your partner give you the phone number for enrollment information. Answers will vary.

MODÈLE

Étudiant(e) 1: *Je cherche un cours de philosophie.*
Étudiant(e) 2: *C'est le zéro quatre...*

Architecture	04.76.65.74.92
Biologie	04.76.72.63.85
Chimie	04.76.84.79.64
Littérature anglaise	04.76.99.90.82
Mathématiques	04.76.86.66.93
Philosophie	04.76.75.99.80
Psychologie	04.76.61.88.91
Sciences politiques	04.76.68.96.81
Sociologie	04.76.70.83.97

5 À la librairie In pairs, role-play a conversation between a customer at a campus bookstore and a clerk who points out where supplies are located. Then, switch roles. Each turn, the customer picks four items from the list. Use the drawing to find the supplies. Answers will vary.

MODÈLE

Étudiant(e) 1:
Je cherche des stylos.
Étudiant(e) 2: *Ils sont à côté des cahiers.*

des cahiers	un dictionnaire
une calculatrice	un iPhone®
une carte	du papier
des crayons	un sac à dos

6 Trouvez Your instructor will give you and your partner each a drawing of a family picnic. Ask each other questions to find out where all of the family members are located. Answers will vary.

MODÈLE

Étudiant(e) 1: *Qui est à côté du père?*
Étudiant(e) 2: *Le neveu est à côté du père.*

OPTIONS

Game Divide the class into two teams. Select a student from the first team to choose an item in the classroom and to write it down. Call on five students from the other team one at a time to ask questions in French about where this item is. The first student can respond only with **oui**, **non**, **chaud** (*hot*), or **froid** (*cold*). If a team guesses the item within five tries, give them a point. The team with the most points wins.

Extra Practice Have students work in pairs. Tell them to take turns reading phone numbers at random from the list in **Activité 4** without mentioning the department. The person who responds should say the name of the department. Example: **Étudiant(e) 1: 04.76.65.74.92 Étudiant(e) 2: C'est le département d'architecture.**

À l'écoute

NATIONAL communication STANDARDS

STRATÉGIE

Asking for repetition/ Replaying the recording

Sometimes it is difficult to understand what people are saying, especially in a noisy environment. In a conversation, you can use the questions **Comment?** (*What?*) or **Pardon?** (*Pardon me?*) to ask someone to repeat what they've just said. In class, you can ask your instructor to repeat by saying, **Répétez, s'il vous plaît** (*Repeat, please*).

🔊 To help you practice this strategy, you will listen to a short paragraph. Ask your instructor to repeat it or replay the recording, and then summarize what you heard.

Préparation

Based on the photograph, where do you think Suzanne and Diane are? What do you think they are talking about?

À vous d'écouter

Now you are going to hear Suzanne and Diane's conversation. Use **R** to indicate adjectives that describe Suzanne's boyfriend, Robert. Use **E** for adjectives that describe Diane's boyfriend, Édouard. Some adjectives will not be used.

E	brun	R	optimiste
___	laid	E	intelligent
E	grand	___	blond
E	intéressant	E	beau
E	gentil	R	sympathique
R	drôle	R	patient

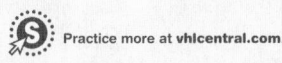

Ⓢ Practice more at **vhlcentral.com.**

Compréhension

Identifiez-les Whom do these statements describe?

1. Elle a un problème avec un garçon. Diane _____
2. Il ne parle pas à Diane. Édouard _____
3. Elle a de la chance. Suzanne _____
4. Ils parlent souvent. Suzanne et Robert _____
5. Il est sympa. Robert _____
6. Il est timide. Édouard _____

Vrai ou faux? Indicate whether each statement is **vrai** or **faux**, then correct any false statements.

1. Édouard est un garçon très patient et optimiste.
   Faux. Robert est très patient et optimiste.

2. Diane pense que Suzanne a de la chance.
   Vrai.

3. Suzanne et son petit ami parlent de tout.
   Vrai.

4. Édouard parle souvent à Diane.
   Faux. Édouard ne parle pas à Diane.

5. Robert est peut-être un peu timide.
   Faux. Édouard est peut-être un peu timide.

6. Suzanne parle de beaucoup de choses avec Robert.
   Vrai.

Section Goals

In this section, students will:
• learn to ask for repetition in oral communication
• listen to and summarize a short paragraph
• listen to a conversation and complete several activities

Instructional Resources
vhlcentral.com: Textbook MP3s; Textbook Audioscript; reference tools

Stratégie
Audioscript Bonjour, je m'appelle Christine Dupont. Je suis médecin et mère de famille. Mon mari, Richard, est ingénieur. Il est intelligent et très drôle aussi. Nous avons trois enfants charmants: deux fils et une fille. Les garçons sont roux et notre fille est blonde. Notre fils aîné, Marc, a 17 ans. Le cadet, Pascal, a 15 ans. Leur petite sœur, Véronique, a 12 ans.

Préparation Before students do the activity, tell them to look at the photo and describe what they see. Ask students to justify their responses based on visual clues in the photo.

Suggestion To check students' answers for the **À vous d'écouter** activity, have them work in pairs and take turns asking and answering questions using the adjectives listed. Example: **Est-ce que Robert est brun? Non, Édouard est brun.**

À vous d'écouter
Audioscript
SUZANNE: Salut, Diane. Est-ce que ça va?
DIANE: Oh, comme ci, comme ça. J'ai un petit problème. Ce n'est pas grand-chose, mais...
S: Quel genre de problème?
D: Tu sais que j'aime bien Édouard.

S: Oui.
D: Le problème, c'est qu'il ne me parle pas!
S: Il t'aime bien aussi. Il est peut-être un peu timide?
D: Tu crois? ...Il est si beau! Grand, brun... Et puis, il est gentil, très intelligent et aussi très intéressant. Et Robert et toi, comment ça va?
S: Euh... plutôt bien. Robert est sympa. Je l'aime

beaucoup. Il est patient, optimiste et très drôle.
D: Vous parlez souvent?
S: Oui. Nous parlons deux à trois heures par jour. Nous parlons de beaucoup de choses! De nos cours, de nos amis, de nos familles... de tout.
D: C'est super! Tu as de la chance.

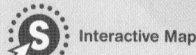
SAVOIR-FAIRE

Panorama

Section Goals

In this section, students will learn historical and cultural information about Belgium and Switzerland.

Instructional Resources
vhlcentral.com:
Digital Image Bank; SAM Answer Key; reference tools

Carte de la Belgique et la Suisse
• Have students look at the map in their books, or use the **Panorama** map from the Digital Image Bank. Ask volunteers to read aloud the names of cities and geographical features. Model the pronunciation as necessary.
• Point out the francophone regions in each country and have students name the cities that are French-speaking.
• Have students identify the countries that border Belgium and Switzerland.

Le pays en chiffres
• Point out the flag of Belgium. Point out the flag of Switzerland. Ask students to share any information they know about the two countries.
• Call on volunteers to read the sections. After each section, ask questions about content.
• Point out that one-tenth of Belgians speak both French and Flemish. In Switzerland, 64% of the population speaks German, 23% speak French, 8% speak Italian, and less than 1% speak Romansh.
• Tell students that Belgium is a kingdom. Explain that many products in Switzerland have information written in French, German, Italian, and even English.

Incroyable mais vrai! The Swiss play a major role in humanitarian peacekeeping efforts.

La Belgique

Le pays en chiffres

▶ **Superficie:** 30.528 km²
▶ **Population:** 11.299.000
SOURCE: Population Division, UN Secretariat
▶ **Industries principales:** *agroalimentaire°, chimie, textile*
▶ **Ville capitale:** *Bruxelles*
▶ **Monnaie:** *l'euro*
▶ **Langues:** *français, flamand°*

Environ° 60% de la population belge parle flamand et habite dans la partie nord°. Le français est parlé surtout dans le sud°, par environ 40% des Belges.

La Suisse

Le pays en chiffres

▶ **Superficie:** 41.285 km²
▶ **Population:** 8.299.000
SOURCE: Population Division, UN Secretariat
▶ **Industries principales:** *activités financières, agroalimentaire°, horlogerie°*
▶ **Ville capitale:** *Berne*
▶ **Monnaie:** *le franc suisse*
▶ **Langues:** *allemand, français, italien, romanche*

L'allemand, le français et l'italien sont les langues officielles. Le romanche, langue d'origine latine, est parlé dans l'est° du pays.

Personnages célèbres

▶ Jean-Luc Godard, *Suisse, cinéaste (1930–)*
▶ Amélie Nothomb, *Belgique, écrivaine (1966–)*

agroalimentaire *food processing*
horlogerie *watch and clock making*
est *east* **flamand** *Flemish* **Environ** *About*
nord *north* **sud** *south*

le château de Chillon sur le lac Léman

Bruges

Régions francophones

Incroyable mais vrai!

La Suisse n'a pas connu de guerres° depuis le 16e siècle! Battue° par la France en 1515, elle signe une paix° perpétuelle avec ce pays et inaugure donc sa période de neutralité. Ce statut° est reconnu par les autres pays européens en 1815 et, depuis, la Suisse ne peut participer à aucune guerre ni° être membre d'alliances militaires comme l'OTAN°.

O P T I O N S

Suisses célèbres **Jean-Luc Godard** was born in Paris, but grew up on the Swiss side of Lake Geneva. He is known for his independent vision and his unconventional, often controversial, films.

Belges célèbres **Amélie Nothomb** was born in Etterbeek, a municipality of Brussels. She has published one book every year since 1992. In 2015, she became a member of Belgium's Royal Academy of French Language and Literature. Her novels have been translated into several languages, and she is well-known outside the francophone world.

Les destinations

Bruxelles, capitale de l'Europe

Fondée au septième siècle, la ville de Bruxelles a été choisie en 1958, en partie pour sa situation géographique centrale, comme siège° de la C.E.E.° Aujourd'hui, elle reste encore le siège de l'Union européenne (l'U.E.), lieu central des institutions et des décisions européennes. On y trouve le Parlement européen, organe législatif de l'U.E., et depuis 1967, le siège de l'OTAN°. Bruxelles est une ville très cosmopolite, avec un grand nombre d'habitants étrangers. Elle est aussi touristique, renommée pour sa Grand-Place, ses nombreux chocolatiers et la grande qualité de sa cuisine.

Les traditions

La bande dessinée

Les dessinateurs° de bandes dessinées (BD) sont très nombreux en Belgique. À Bruxelles, il y a de nombreuses peintures murales° et statues de BD. Le dessinateur Peyo est devenu célèbre avec la création des Schtroumpfs° en 1958, mais le père de la BD belge est Hergé, dessinateur qui a créé Tintin et Milou en 1929. Tintin est un reporter qui a des aventures partout dans° le monde. En 1953, il devient le premier homme, avant Neil Armstrong, à marcher sur la Lune° dans *On a marché sur la Lune*. La BD de Tintin est traduite en 45 langues.

L'économie

Des montres et des banques

L'économie suisse se caractérise par la présence de grandes entreprises° multinationales et par son secteur financier. Les multinationales sont particulièrement actives dans le domaine des banques, des assurances, de l'agroalimentaire (Nestlé), de l'industrie pharmaceutique et de l'horlogerie (Longines, Rolex, Swatch). Cinquante pour cent de la production mondiale° d'articles° d'horlogerie viennent de Suisse. Le franc suisse est une des monnaies les plus stables du monde et les banques suisses ont la réputation de bien gérer° les fortunes de leurs clients.

Les gens

Jean-Jacques Rousseau (1712–1778)

Né à Genève, Jean-Jacques Rousseau a passé sa vie entre la France et la Suisse. Vagabond et autodidacte°, Rousseau est devenu écrivain, philosophe, théoricien politique et musicien. Il a comme principe° que l'homme naît bon et que c'est la société qui le corrompt°. Défenseur de la tolérance religieuse et de la liberté de pensée, les idées de Rousseau, exprimées° principalement dans son œuvre° *Du contrat social*, se retrouvent° dans la Révolution française. À la fin de sa vie, il écrit *Les Confessions*, son autobiographie, un genre nouveau pour l'époque°.

Qu'est-ce que vous avez appris? Répondez aux questions par des phrases complètes.

1. Quelles sont les langues officielles de la Suisse?
L'allemand, le français et l'italien sont les langues officielles de la Suisse.
2. Quels sont les secteurs importants de l'économie suisse?
Les activités financières (banques et assurances), l'agroalimentaire, l'industrie pharmaceutique et l'horlogerie.
3. Quel est le principe fondamental de la philosophie de Rousseau? L'homme naît bon, mais c'est la société qui le corrompt.
4. Quel événement a été influencé par les idées de Rousseau?
La Révolution française a été influencée par les idées de Rousseau.
5. Quelle est la langue la plus parlée en Belgique?
Le flamand est la langue la plus parlée.

6. Pourquoi Bruxelles a-t-elle été choisie comme capitale de l'Europe? Elle a été choisie en partie pour sa situation géographique centrale en Europe.
7. Quelles institutions importantes trouve-t-on à Bruxelles?
On y trouve le Parlement européen et le siège de l'OTAN.
8. Qui est le père de la bande dessinée belge?
C'est Hergé.
9. Qui est allé sur la Lune avant Armstrong?
Tintin est allé sur la Lune avant Armstrong.
10. Quelle bande dessinée a été créée (*created*) par Peyo?
Les Schtroumpfs ont été créés par Peyo.

Sur Internet

Go to **vhlcentral.com** to find more cultural information related to this **Panorama**.

1. Cherchez plus d'informations sur les œuvres de Rousseau. Quelles autres œuvres a-t-il écrites?

2. Quels sont les noms de trois autres personnages de bandes dessinées belges?

3. Cherchez des informations sur la ville de Bruges. Combien de kilomètres de canaux (*canals*) y a-t-il?

ressources

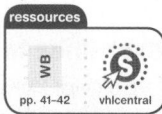

pp. 41–42   vhlcentral

entreprises *companies* mondiale *worldwide* articles *products* gérer *manage* autodidacte *self-taught* comme principe *as a principle* corrompt *corrupts* exprimées *expressed* œuvre *work* se retrouvent *are found* époque *time* siège *headquarters (lit. seat)* C.E.E *European Economic Community (predecessor of the European Union)* OTAN *NATO* dessinateurs *artists* peintures murales *murals* Schtroumpfs *Smurfs* partout dans *all over* Lune *moon*

Bruxelles, capitale de l'Europe
The city square, **la Grand-Place**, hosts concerts, festivals, and a flower market during the warmer months. Featuring baroque and gothic guild architecture, **la Grand-Place** was used as a merchant's market during the thirteenth century.

La bande dessinée
- In Brussels, one can learn about the creation of comic strips, such as **Tintin** and the **Schtroumpfs**, as well as 670 others, at the **Centre Belge de la Bande Dessinée**.
- *Smurfs: The Lost Village* movie was released in the United States in 2017. Ask students: **Combien d'étudiants connaissent les Schtroumpfs? Qui sont-ils? Décrivez-les.**

Des montres et des banques
- Located in Zurich, Crédit Suisse and UBS AG are Switzerland's largest international banks. Swiss banks are known for their discretion, confidentiality, and secrecy. Clients are protected through the use of numbered accounts, and only a few top managers actually know who owns a particular account.
- Have students look at the photo and describe what they see. Then ask: **Combien d'étudiants portent une Swatch? Pourquoi ces montres sont-elles populaires? Connaissez-vous quelqu'un qui a une Rolex?**
- Ask students to name some Nestlé products. **Citez quelques produits Nestlé (le chocolat, la nourriture pour bébés, etc.)**

Jean-Jacques Rousseau
People's views of society, family values, and political and ethical thinking were directly affected by Rousseau's writings. Through his involvement with the **Philosophes** and Diderot's *Encyclopédie*, Rousseau influenced society's taste in music, arguing for freedom of expression rather than strict adherence to rules and traditions.

Cultural Comparison Working in small groups, have students compare Belgium to Switzerland. Tell them to list the similarities and differences in a two-column chart under the headings **Similitudes** and **Différences**. After they complete their charts, call on volunteers to read their lists.

Le chocolat belge Belgium produces 172,000 tons of chocolate per year and has 2,130 chocolate shops. Godiva, Côte d'Or, Callebaut, and Nirvana are just a few of the many famous Belgian brands.
Les montres suisses Watches, clocks, and alarm clocks manufactured in Switzerland must carry the designation "Swiss made" or "Swiss."

Section Goals

In this section, students will:
• learn to use visuals and graphic elements to predict content
• read an article about pets in France

Stratégie Tell students that they can infer a great deal of information about the content of an article or text by examining the visual and graphic elements. Some items they should look at are:
• titles and headings
• photos
• photo captions
• graphs, tables, and diagrams
To practice this strategy, have students read the headings in the chart **Le Top 10 des chiens de race**. Ask: What information does this chart contain? (It lists the top ten dog breeds and the percentage of households that owns each breed.)

Examinez le texte After students have finished the activity, tell them to look at the visual elements in the article again. Then ask them the following questions and have them explain their answers.
1. What is the article about? (It is about dogs as family pets. The title of the article and the photos of dogs indicate the main topic.)
2. What information does the table on page 129 contain? (It lists the reasons why people have pets and shows the percentages of people who own dogs, cats, birds, and fish for each reason.)
3. What can you learn from the photo on page 129? (Answers will vary.)

Lecture

 Audio: Reading

Avant la lecture

STRATÉGIE

Predicting content from visuals

When you are reading in French, look for visual clues that will orient you as to the content and purpose of what you are reading. Photos and illustrations, for example, will often give you a good idea of the main points that the reading covers. You may also encounter helpful visuals that summarize large amounts of data in a way that is easy to comprehend; these visuals include bar graphs, pie charts, flow charts, lists of percentages, and other diagrams.

Le Top 10 des chiens de race°
% DE FOYERS° POSSESSEURS
les caniches° **9,3%**
les labradors **7,8%**
les yorkshires **5,6%**
les épagneuls bretons° **4,6%**
les bergers allemands° **4,1%**
les autres bergers **3,3%**
les bichons **2,7%**
les cockers/fox-terriers **2,2%**
les boxers **2%**
les colleys **1,6%**

Examinez le texte

Take a quick look at the visual elements of the article in order to generate a list of ideas about its content. Then, compare your list with a classmate's. Are your lists the same or are they different? Discuss your lists and make any changes needed to produce a final list of ideas.

race *breed* **foyers** *households* **caniches** *poodles* **épagneuls bretons** *Brittany Spaniels* **bergers allemands** *German Shepherds*

Fido

Les Français adorent les animaux. Plus de la moitié° des foyers en France ont un chien, un chat ou un autre animal de compagnie°. Les chiens sont particulièrement appréciés et intégrés dans la famille et la société françaises.

Qui possède un chien en France et pourquoi? Souvent°, la présence d'un chien en famille suit l'arrivée° d'enfants, parce que les parents pensent qu'un chien contribue positivement à leur développement. Il est aussi commun de trouver deux chiens ou plus dans le même° foyer.

Les chiens sont d'excellents compagnons. Leurs maîtres° sont moins seuls° et déclarent avoir moins de stress. Certaines personnes possèdent un chien pour avoir plus d'exercice

---

OPTIONS

Pairs Working in pairs, students should read the article aloud and write four questions about it. After they have finished, tell them to exchange their papers with another pair and answer the questions.

Extra Practice Tell students to read the chart **Le Top 10 des chiens de race**. Then pronounce the name of each dog breed and have students repeat it after you. To check comprehension, give students these true/false statements. **1. Le caniche est la race de chien la plus populaire. (Vrai.) 2. Les boxers n'existent pas en France. (Faux.) 3. Les labradors sont moins populaires que les épagneuls. (Faux.) 4. Les Français aiment mieux les yorkshires que les bergers. (Faux.) 5. Les colleys sont le numéro dix sur la liste. (Vrai.)**

en famille

physique. Et il y a aussi des personnes qui possèdent un chien parce qu'elles en ont toujours eu un° et n'imaginent pas une vie° sans° chien.

Les chiens ont parfois° les mêmes droits° que les autres membres de la famille, et parfois des droits spéciaux. Bien sûr, ils accompagnent leurs maîtres pour les courses en ville° et les promenades dans le parc, et ils entrent même dans certains magasins°. Ne trouvez-vous pas parfois un caniche ou un labrador, les deux races les plus° populaires en France, avec son maître dans un restaurant?

En France, il n'est pas difficile d'observer que les chiens ont une place privilégiée au sein de° la famille.

Pourquoi avoir un animal de compagnie?

RAISON	CHIENS	CHATS	OISEAUX	POISSONS
Pour l'amour des animaux	61,4%	60,5%	61%	33%
Pour avoir de la compagnie	43,5%	38,2%	37%	10%
Pour s'occuper*	40,4%	37,7%	0%	0%
Parce que j'en ai toujours eu un*	31,8%	28,9%	0%	0%
Pour le bien-être* personnel	29,2%	26,2%	0%	0%
Pour les enfants	23,7%	21,3%	30%	48%

Plus de la moitié *More than half* animal de compagnie *pet* Souvent *Often* suit l'arrivée *follows the arrival* même *same* maîtres *owners* moins seuls *less lonely* en ont toujours eu un *have always had one* vie *life* sans *without* parfois *sometimes* droits *rights* courses en ville *errands in town* magasins *stores* les plus *the most* au sein de *in the heart of* s'occuper *keep busy* Parce que j'en ai toujours eu un *Because I've always had one* bien-être *well-being*

Après la lecture

Vrai ou faux? Indicate whether these statements are **vrai** or **faux**, based on the reading. Correct the false statements.

	Vrai	Faux
1. Les chiens accompagnent leurs maîtres pour les promenades dans le parc.	☑	☐
2. Parfois, les chiens accompagnent leurs maîtres dans les restaurants.	☑	☐
3. Le chat n'est pas un animal apprécié en France. *En France, plus de la moitié des foyers ont un chien, un chat ou un autre animal de compagnie.*	☐	☑
4. Certaines personnes déclarent posséder un chien pour avoir plus d'exercice physique.	☑	☐
5. Certaines personnes déclarent posséder un chien pour avoir plus de stress. *Certaines personnes déclarent avoir moins de stress avec un chien.*	☐	☑
6. En France, les familles avec enfants n'ont pas de chien. *Souvent, la présence d'un chien dans une famille suit l'arrivée d'enfants.*	☐	☑

Fido en famille Choose the correct response according to the article.

1. Combien de foyers en France ont au moins (*at least*) un animal de compagnie?
   a. 20%–25%
   b. 40%–45%
   c. 50%–55%

2. Pourquoi est-ce une bonne idée d'avoir un chien?
   a. pour plus de compagnie et plus de stress
   b. pour l'exercice physique et être seul
   c. pour la compagnie et le développement des enfants

3. Que pensent les familles françaises de leurs chiens?
   a. Les chiens sont plus importants que les enfants.
   b. Les chiens font partie (*are part*) de la famille et participent aux activités quotidiennes (*daily*).
   c. Le rôle des chiens est limité aux promenades.

4. Quelles races de chien les Français préfèrent-ils?
   a. les caniches et les oiseaux
   b. les labradors et les bergers allemands
   c. les caniches et les labradors

5. Y a-t-il des familles avec plus d'un chien?
   a. non
   b. oui
   c. les caniches et les labradors

Mes animaux In groups of three, say why you own or someone you know owns a pet. Give one of the reasons listed in the table on the left or a different one. Use the verb **avoir** and possessive adjectives.

MODÈLE

Mon grand-père a un chien pour son bien-être personnel.

Vrai ou faux? Have students correct the false statements and check their answers with a partner.

Fido en famille Go over the answers with the class. Ask students to read the corresponding line(s) of the text that contain the answer to each question.

Suggestion Encourage students to record unfamiliar words and phrases that they learn in **Lecture** in their notebooks.

Expansions
• Ask students to describe their pets. If they don't own a pet, then tell them to describe someone else's pet. Example: **Mon chat s'appelle Tyler. Il est très gentil avec tout le monde. Il est noir et c'est un bon copain.**
• Write these headings on the board: **animaux de compagnie, chiens, chats, oiseaux, poissons**, and **autres animaux**. Do a quick class survey to find out how many have pets in general and how many have dogs, cats, birds, fish, and other animals. Record the results on the board. Then ask them why they have a pet. If students need help expressing their reasons, tell them to look at the reasons in the chart on this page.

Mes animaux Ask students to report their partners' answers to the class.

OPTIONS

Cultural Comparison Have students work in pairs or groups of three. Tell them to draw a two-column chart and write the headings **Similitudes** (*Similarities*) and **Différences** (*Differences*). Then, tell them to list the similarities and differences between the French and American attitudes toward dogs based on the facts in the reading and what they know about Americans and their pets. Allow students to use their books for this activity. After pairs have completed their charts, call on volunteers to read their lists. Ask the class if they agree or disagree with the similarities.

Section Goals

In this section, students will:
- learn to use idea maps to organize information
- learn to write an informal letter in French

Stratégie Tell students that they might find it helpful to use note cards to create idea maps. Writing each detail on a separate card will allow them to rearrange ideas and experiment with organization. Remind students to write their ideas in French, since they may not have the vocabulary or structures for some English terms they generate.

Thème Introduce the common salutations and closings used in informal letters in French. Point out the difference between **cher** (masculine) and **chère** (feminine). Model the pronunciation to show students that the two words sound the same.

Écriture

STRATÉGIE

Using idea maps

How do you organize ideas for a first draft? Often, the organization of ideas represents the most challenging part of the writing process. Idea maps are useful for organizing pertinent information. Here is an example of an idea map you can use when writing.

SCHÉMA D'IDÉES

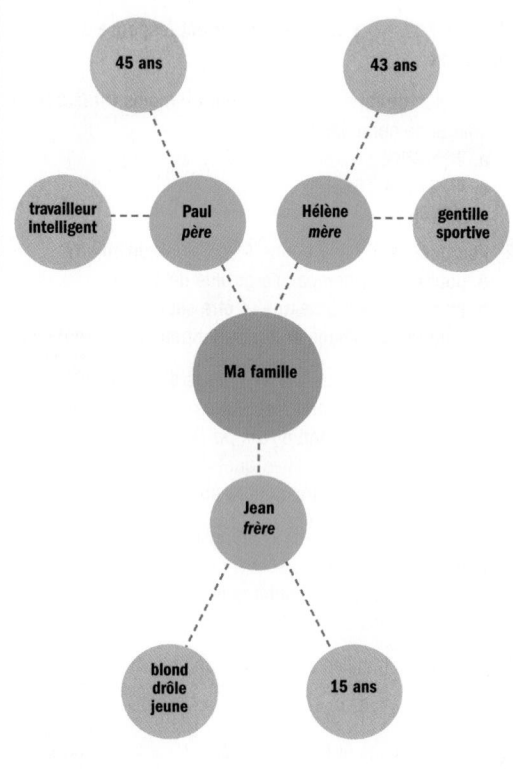

∞ Thème

Écrivez une lettre

Avant l'écriture

1. A French-speaking friend wants to know about your family. Using some of the verbs and adjectives you learned in this lesson, write a brief letter describing your own family or an imaginary one. Be sure to include information from each of these categories for each family member:

   - Names, ages, and relationships
   - Physical characteristics
   - Hobbies and interests

   Before you begin, create an idea map like the one on the left, with a circle for each member of your family.

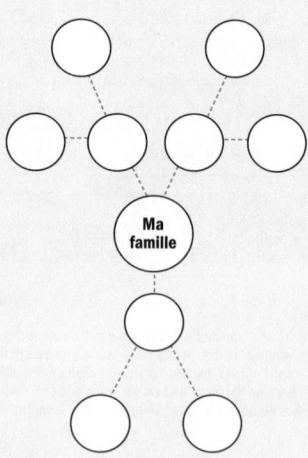

OPTIONS

Avant l'écriture Remind students that they used a word web to brainstorm ideas in Unit 2. Tell them that an idea map is similar, but that it links various ideas to a central topic and breaks those ideas down into smaller categories. Point out the colors used in the idea map on page 130 and how they are used to group similar levels of information.

Help students create an outline for a typical letter: a salutation, an introductory paragraph with greetings, a second paragraph with the family description, a third paragraph with a request for a response, a closing, and a signature. Tell them their first paragraph should include an inquiry into how the person is doing, along with a similar comment about themselves.

2. Once you have completed your idea map, compare it with the one created by a classmate. Did you both include the same kind of information? Did you list all your family members? Did you include information from each of the three categories for each person?

3. Here are some useful expressions for writing a letter in French:

Salutations	
Cher Fabien,	*Dear Fabien,*
Chère Joëlle,	*Dear Joëlle,*

Asking for a response	
Réponds-moi vite.	*Write back soon.*
Donne-moi de tes nouvelles.	*Tell me all your news.*

Closings	
Grosses bises!	*Big kisses!*
Je t'embrasse!	*Kisses!*
Bisous!	*Kisses!*
À bientôt!	*See you soon!*
Amitiés,	*In friendship,*
Cordialement,	*Cordially,*
À plus (tard),	*Until later,*

Écriture

Use your idea map and the list of letter-writing expressions to write a letter that describes your family to a friend. Be sure to include some of the verbs and adjectives you have learned in this lesson.

Cher Christophe,

Mon père s'appelle Gabriel. Il a 52 ans. Il est grand, a les cheveux châtains et les yeux marron. Il est architecte et travaille à Paris. Il aime dessiner, lire (to read) et voyager. Ma mère, Nicole, a 47 ans. Elle est petite, blonde et a les yeux bleus. Elle est professeur d'anglais à l'université. Comme mon père, elle aime voyager. Elle aime aussi faire (to do) du sport. Ma sœur, Élodie, a 17 ans. Elle est grande, a les cheveux châtains et les yeux verts. Elle est encore au lycée. Elle adore écouter de la musique et aller au (to go to) cinéma. Mon oncle, ...
Et ta famille, comment est-elle? Donne-moi vite de tes nouvelles!
À bientôt!
Caroline

Après l'écriture

1. Exchange rough drafts with a partner. Comment on his or her work by answering these questions:

- Did your partner make the adjectives agree with the person described?

- Did your partner include the age, family relationship, physical characteristics, and hobbies and interests of each family member?

- Did your partner use verb forms correctly?

- Did your partner use the letter-writing expressions correctly?

2. Revise your description according to your partner's comments. After writing the final version, read it once more to eliminate these kinds of problems:

- spelling errors

- punctuation errors

- capitalization errors

- use of incorrect verb forms

- adjectives that do not agree with the nouns they modify

EVALUATION

Criteria

Content Includes all the information mentioned in the three bulleted items in the task description as well as some of the expressions in the list of salutations, requests for response, and closings.
Scale: 1 2 3 4 5

Organization Organizes the letter into a salutation, a family description, a request for a response, and a closing.
Scale: 1 2 3 4 5

Accuracy Uses possessive and descriptive adjectives and modifies them accordingly. Spells words and conjugates verbs correctly throughout.
Scale: 1 2 3 4 5

Creativity The student includes additional information that is not included in the task and/or provides detailed information about numerous family members.
Scale: 1 2 3 4 5

Scoring
Excellent	18–20 points
Good	14–17 points
Satisfactory	10–13 points
Unsatisfactory	< 10 points

OPTIONS

Écriture Remind students of the **-er** verbs that they can use to talk about family members' hobbies and interests: **adorer, aimer,** and **détester.** Encourage them to go beyond the task to talk about what their family members dislike as well. Brainstorm a list of possible interests and hobbies that students can draw upon as they write.

Clarify the cultural differences among the closing expressions shown. **Grosses bises, Bisous,** and **À plus** are used with close friends. Where the relationship is informal but the person is not a close friend, **À plus tard** is a better choice. **Amitiés** and **Cordialement** are more formal and often used when addressing an older person or a business associate.

Instructional Resources
*vhlcentral.com: Textbook
MP3s; Textbook Audioscript;
reference tools*

Suggestions

- Tell students that an easy way
to study from **Vocabulaire** is
to cover up the French half of
each section, leaving only the
English equivalents exposed.
They can then quiz themselves
on the French items. To focus
on the English equivalents of
the French entries, they simply
reverse this process.
- Point out to students that they
can use the Vocabulary Tools
at **vhlcentral.com** for reference
and extra vocabulary practice.

🔊 Ⓢ Vocabulary Tools

Leçon 3A

La famille

aîné(e) *elder*
cadet(te) *younger*
un beau-frère *brother-in-law*
un beau-père *father-in-law; stepfather*
une belle-mère *mother-in-law; stepmother*
une belle-sœur *sister-in-law*
un(e) cousin(e) *cousin*
un demi-frère *half-brother; stepbrother*
une demi-sœur *half-sister; stepsister*
les enfants (*m., f.*) *children*
un époux/une épouse *husband/wife*
une famille *family*
une femme *wife; woman*
une fille *daughter; girl*
un fils *son*
un frère *brother*
une grand-mère *grandmother*
un grand-père *grandfather*
les grands-parents (*m.*) *grandparents*
un mari *husband*
une mère *mother*
un neveu *nephew*
une nièce *niece*
un oncle *uncle*
les parents (*m.*) *parents*
un père *father*
une petite-fille *granddaughter*
un petit-fils *grandson*
les petits-enfants (*m.*) *grandchildren*
une sœur *sister*
une tante *aunt*
un chat *cat*
un chien *dog*
un oiseau *bird*
un poisson *fish*

Adjectifs descriptifs

bleu(e) *blue*
blond(e) *blond*
brun(e) *dark (hair)*
court(e) *short*
frisé(e) *curly*
grand(e) *big; tall*
jeune *young*
joli(e) *pretty*
laid(e) *ugly*
mauvais(e) *bad*
noir(e) *black*
pauvre *poor; unfortunate*
petit(e) *small, short (stature)*
raide *straight (hair)*
vert(e) *green*
vrai(e) *true; real*
de taille moyenne *medium-sized*

Vocabulaire utile

divorcer *to divorce*
épouser *to marry*
célibataire *single*
divorcé(e) *divorced*
fiancé(e) *engaged*
marié(e) *married*
séparé(e) *separated*
veuf/veuve *widowed*
un(e) voisin(e) *neighbor*

Adjectifs irréguliers

beau/belle *beautiful; handsome*
bon(ne) *kind; good*
châtain *brown (hair)*
curieux/curieuse *curious*
fier/fière *proud*
gros(se) *fat*
intellectuel(le) *intellectual*
long(ue) *long*
(mal)heureux/(mal)heureuse *(un)happy*
marron *brown (not for hair)*
naïf/naïve *naive*
nerveux/nerveuse *nervous*
nouveau/nouvelle *new*
roux/rousse *red-haired*
sérieux/sérieuse *serious*
vieux/vieille *old*

Expressions utiles

See p. 95.

Possessive adjetives

mon, ma, mes *my*
ton, ta, tes *your (fam. and sing.)*
son, sa, ses *his, her, its*
notre, notre, nos *our*
votre, votre, vos *your (form. or pl.)*
leur, leur, leurs *their*

Leçon 3B

Adjectifs descriptifs

antipathique *unpleasant*
drôle *funny*
faible *weak*
fatigué(e) *tired*
fort(e) *strong*
génial(e) (géniaux *m.*, pl.) *great*
lent(e) *slow*
méchant(e) *mean*
modeste *modest*
pénible *annoying*
prêt(e) *ready*
rapide *fast*
triste *sad*

Professions et occupations

un(e) architecte *architect*
un(e) artiste *artist*
un(e) athlète *athlete*
un(e) avocat(e) *lawyer*
un coiffeur/une coiffeuse *hairdresser*
un(e) dentiste *dentist*
un homme/une femme
  d'affaires *businessman/woman*
un ingénieur *engineer*
un(e) journaliste *journalist*
un médecin *doctor*
un(e) musicien(ne) *musician*
un(e) propriétaire *owner; landlord/lady*

Adjectifs irréguliers

actif/active *active*
courageux/courageuse *brave*
cruel(le) *cruel*
discret/discrète *discreet; unassuming*
doux/douce *sweet; soft*
ennuyeux/ennuyeuse *boring*
étranger/étrangère *foreign*
favori(te) *favorite*
fou/folle *crazy*
généreux/généreuse *generous*
gentil(le) *nice*
inquiet/inquiète *worried*
jaloux/jalouse *jealous*
paresseux/paresseuse *lazy*
sportif/sportive *athletic*
travailleur/travailleuse *hard-working*

Expressions utiles

See p. 113.

Numbers 61–100

See p. 116.

Disjunctive pronouns

See p. 121.

Prepositions of location

à côté de *next to*
à droite de *to the right of*
à gauche de *to the left of*
dans *in*
derrière *behind*
devant *in front of*
en *in*
en face de *facing, across from*
entre *between*
loin de *far from*
par *by*
près de *close to, near*
sous *under*
sur *on*

Au café

Unit Goals

Leçon 4A

In this lesson, students will learn:
- names for places around town
- terms for activities around town
- to pronounce oral vowels
- about pastimes of young French people and **le verlan**
- the verb **aller** and using **aller** to express future actions
- the preposition **à** and contractions with **à**
- interrogative words
- about rooftop patios in Paris

Leçon 4B

In this lesson, students will learn:
- terms for food items at a café
- expressions of quantity
- to pronounce nasal vowels
- about the role of the café in France and the cafés of North Africa
- about famous Quebecker singer and songwriter Daniel Bélanger
- more about cafés and food items through specially shot video footage
- the present tense of **prendre** and **boire**
- the formation and use of partitive articles
- regular **-ir** verbs
- to listen for the gist in oral communication

Savoir-faire

In this section, students will learn:
- cultural and historical information about the Canadian province of **Québec**
- to scan a text to improve comprehension
- to add details in French to make writing more interesting

Pour commencer
- b. midi
- a. manger
- a. dans un café

Pour commencer
- Quelle heure est-il?
  a. 7h00 du matin   b. midi   c. minuit
- Qu'est-ce que Sandrine et Amina ont envie de faire (do)?
  a. manger   b. partager   c. échouer
- Où sont-elles?
  a. dans un café   b. au cinéma
  c. chez elles

RESOURCES

Student Activities Manual (SAM):
Workbook Activities, pp. 43–56;
Lab Activities, pp. 25–32;
Video Activities, pp. 13–16; pp. 67–68
SAM Answer Key

vhlcentral.com: Textbook MP3s; Lab MP3s;
Textbook Audioscript; Lab Audioscript; Video;
Videoscript; **Roman-photo** Translations;
Vocabulaire supplémentaire; Activity Pack
(including **Feuilles d'activités**, Info Gap Activities,
and Task-based Activities);

Le Zapping TV clip transcription; **Essayez!** and
Mise en pratique answers; Digital Image Bank;
Testing Program;
Testing Program MP3s

Section Goals

In this section, students will learn and practice vocabulary related to:
- places in a city
- pastimes

Instructional Resources
vhlcentral.com: Digital Image Bank (including vocabulary illustrations from the textbook, theme-based illustrations); **Vocabulaire supplémentaire; Mise en pratique** *answers; Textbook Audioscript; Lab Audioscript; Activity Pack (Info Gap Activities); Textbook MP3s; Lab MP3s; SAM Answer Key; reference tools*

Suggestions

- Have students look at the new vocabulary and identify the cognates.
- Display the **4A Contextes** illustration from the Digital Image Bank. As you point to different people, describe where they are and what they are doing. Examples: **Ils sont à la terrasse d'un café. Elles bavardent.** Follow up with simple questions based on your narrative.
- Ask students yes/no and either/or questions about their preferences using the new vocabulary. Examples: **Aimez-vous nager? Préférez-vous regarder un film au cinéma ou à la maison?**
- Tell students that proper names of places, like adjectives, usually follow generic nouns. Examples: **le cinéma Rex** and **le parc Monceau.**
- Point out that the term **une boîte de nuit** is informal and usually used among young people. **Une discothèque** is the more formal word for *nightclub*.
- Point out that **un gymnase** in France generally has a track, exercise equipment, basketball or tennis courts, and showers, but no pool.
- Use the Vocabulary illustrations and the City life illustrations from the Digital Image Bank to help students familiarize themselves with places in a city and pastimes.
- Additional vocabulary for this lesson can be found in the **Vocabulaire supplémentaire** on the Supersite.

Leçon 4A

You will learn how to...
- say where you are going
- say what you are going to do

Ou allons-nous?

S Vocabulary Tools

Vocabulaire

danser	to dance
explorer	to explore
fréquenter	to frequent; to visit
inviter	to invite
nager	to swim
patiner	to skate
une banlieue	suburbs
une boîte (de nuit)	nightclub
un bureau	office; desk
un centre commercial	shopping center, mall
un centre-ville	city/town center, downtown
un cinéma (ciné)	movie theater, movies
un endroit	place
un grand magasin	department store
un gymnase	gym
un hôpital	hospital
un lieu	place
un magasin	store
un marché	market
un musée	museum
un parc	park
une piscine	pool
un restaurant	restaurant
une ville	city, town

ressources

WB pp. 43–44 | LM p. 25 | S vhlcentral

une montagne

une maison

Il passe chez quelqu'un. (passer)

Elle quitte la maison. (quitter)

Ils déjeunent. (déjeuner)

Poissonnerie

Café

une place

une terrasse de café

Elles bavardent. (bavarder)

134 *cent trente-quatre*

Game Divide the class into two teams. Put objects related to different places in a box (for example, movie ticket stubs, sunglasses, and a coffee cup). Without looking, have a student reach into the box and pick out an object. The next player on that person's team has five seconds to name a place associated with the object. If the person cannot do so within the time limit, the other team may "steal" the point by giving a correct response. When the box is empty, the team with the most points wins.

Extra Practice Use magazine photos or clip art from the Internet to make flash cards representing places in and around town. As you show each image, students should say the name of the place and as many activities associated with it as they can think of.

Attention!

Remember that nouns that end in -al have an irregular plural. Replace -al with -aux.

un hôpital → deux hôpitaux

À (to, at) before le or les makes these contractions:
à + le = au   à + les = aux
À does NOT contract with l' or la.

une église

une épicerie

euromarché

JOURNAUX

un kiosque

Il dépense de l'argent (m.).
(dépenser)

Mise en pratique

1 Écoutez Jamila parle de sa journée à son amie Samira. Écoutez la conversation et mettez (*put*) les lieux listés dans l'ordre chronologique. Il y a deux lieux en trop (*extra*).

- _3_ a. à l'hôpital
- _8_ b. à la maison
- _1_ c. à la piscine
- _5_ d. au centre commercial
- _6_ e. au cinéma
- _NA_ f. à l'église
- _2_ g. au musée
- _7_ h. au bureau
- _NA_ i. au parc
- _4_ j. au restaurant

Coup de main

Note that the French **Je vais à...** is the equivalent of the English *I am going to...*

2 Associez Quels lieux associez-vous à ces activités?

1. nager _____une piscine_____
2. danser _____une boîte (de nuit)_____
3. dîner _____un restaurant_____
4. travailler _____un bureau_____
5. habiter _____une maison_____
6. épouser _____une église_____
7. regarder un film _____un cinéma_____
8. acheter des fruits _____un marché, une épicerie_____

3 Logique ou illogique Lisez chaque phrase et déterminez si l'action est **logique** ou **illogique. Corrigez** si nécessaire. Suggested answers.

	Logique	Illogique
1. Maurice invite Delphine à l'épicerie.	☐	☑
Maurice invite Delphine au musée.		
2. Caroline et Aurélie bavardent au marché.	☑	☐
3. Nous déjeunons à l'épicerie.	☐	☑
Nous déjeunons au restaurant.		
4. Ils dépensent beaucoup d'argent au centre commercial.	☑	☐
5. Vous explorez une ville.	☑	☐
6. Vous escaladez (*climb*) une montagne.	☑	☐
7. J'habite en banlieue.	☑	☐
8. Tu danses dans un marché.	☐	☑
Tu danses dans une boîte (de nuit).		

S Practice more at vhlcentral.com.

cent trente-cinq **135**

1 Audioscript DJAMILA: Allô, Samira. Comment ça va? SAMIRA: Très bien, et toi? D: Aujourd'hui, très bien, mais alors demain, quelle journée! S: Comment ça? D: Eh bien… demain matin, je vais à la piscine avec mon frère, Hassan, à 8h00. À 10h00, je vais au musée Rodin avec ma classe. À 11h00, je passe un moment avec grand-mère à l'hôpital. À midi, je vais au restaurant Chez Benoît, près de la place Carnot. L'après-midi, je vais au centre commercial et au cinéma voir le dernier film de Jean Reno. Pour terminer, à 17h00, je vais au bureau de maman pour travailler un peu et nous rentrons à la maison ensemble. S: Quel programme! Bon, courage Jamila et à bientôt. D: Merci, bonne soirée. *(On Textbook MP3s)*

1 Suggestion Before beginning the activity, have students read the list of places and the **Coup de main**.

2 Expansions
- For additional practice, give students these items.
  9. chanter (une église)
  10. manger (un restaurant/un café) 11. dessiner (un musée)
- Do this activity in reverse. Name places and have students say what activities can be done there.

3 Suggestion Tell students to write their corrections. Then have volunteers write their sentences on the board.

3 Expansion For additional practice, give students these items. **9. Vous dansez au magasin. (illogique) 10. Je nage au musée. (illogique) 11. Madame Ducharme habite dans une maison. (logique)**

OPTIONS

TPR Have students represent various stores and places in town by giving them signs to hold. Ask them where one does various activities. Examples: **Où est-ce qu'on regarde un film/ mange/nage?** The student with the appropriate sign should step forward and answer. Examples: **On regarde un film au cinéma. On mange au restaurant. On nage à la piscine.**

Extra Practice Ask students about their favorite places. Tell them to use generic place names in front of proper nouns, such as **le parc Zilker** and **le musée du Louvre**. Ask: **Quel(le) est votre restaurant/musée/épicerie préféré(e)?**

Communication

4 Suggestion Have two volunteers read the **modèle** aloud.

4 Expansion After completing the activity, have students share their partner's opinions with the rest of the class.

5 Suggestion Divide the class into pairs and distribute the Info Gap Handouts found in the Activity Pack on the Supersite. Give students ten minutes to complete the activity.

6 Suggestion Tell students that they should use the salutation **chère** if they are writing to a female. Remind them to include expressions of time, such as **le lundi après-midi** and **le samedi soir** in their letters.

Successful Language Learning Remind students that it's important to proofread their work. Have them brainstorm a checklist of potential errors, for example, accents, adjective agreement, and subject-verb agreement. Tell students to add grammar points to their checklists as they learn new structures and make mistakes.

4   Conversez Avec un(e) partenaire, échangez vos opinions sur ces activités. Utilisez un élément de chaque colonne dans vos réponses. Answers will vary.

MODÈLE

Étudiant(e) 1: Moi, j'adore bavarder au restaurant, mais je déteste parler au musée.
Étudiant(e) 2: Moi aussi, j'adore bavarder au restaurant. Je ne déteste pas parler au musée, mais j'aime mieux bavarder au parc.

Opinion	Activité	Lieu
adorer	bavarder	au bureau
aimer (mieux)	danser	au centre commercial
ne pas tellement aimer	déjeuner	au centre-ville
détester	dépenser de l'argent	au cinéma
	étudier	au gymnase
	inviter	au musée
	nager	au parc
	parler	à la piscine
	patiner	au restaurant

5   La journée d'Anne Votre professeur va vous donner, à vous et à votre partenaire, une feuille partielle d'activités. À tour de rôle, posez-vous des questions pour compléter vos feuilles. Utilisez le vocabulaire de la leçon. Attention! Ne regardez pas la feuille de votre partenaire. Answers will vary.

MODÈLE

Étudiant(e) 1: À 7h30, Anne quitte la maison. Qu'est-ce qu'elle fait ensuite (do next)?
Étudiant(e) 2: À 8h00, elle...

Anne

6   Une lettre Écrivez une lettre à un(e) ami(e) dans laquelle (in which) vous décrivez vos activités de la semaine. Utilisez les expressions suivantes. Answers will vary.

bavarder	passer chez quelqu'un
déjeuner	travailler
dépenser de l'argent	quitter la maison
étudier	un centre commercial
manger au restaurant	une boîte de nuit

Cher Paul,

Comment vas-tu? Moi, tout va bien. Je suis très actif/active à l'université. Je travaille beaucoup et j'ai beaucoup d'amis. En général, le samedi à midi, je déjeune au restaurant Le Lion d'Or avec mes copains. L'après-midi, je bavarde avec mes amis...

Extra Practice On a sheet of paper, have students write down six places they like to go and what they like to do there. Tell them to circulate around the room trying to find other students who also like to go to those places or do those things. Remind them to jot down the names of people who share something in common with them. Then have them report what they have in common with their classmates.

Small Groups Have small groups plan and design an ideal town or neighborhood. Have them draw the plan, label each place, and list fun activities to do at each one. One person from each group should present the plan to the class. Hold a secret vote and give prizes for the best plan in various categories, such as **le plus amusant**, **le plus créateur**, and **le plus réaliste**.

Les sons et les lettres  Audio

Oral vowels

French has two basic kinds of vowel sounds: oral vowels, the subject of this discussion, and nasal vowels, presented in **Leçon 4B**. Oral vowels are produced by releasing air through the mouth. The pronunciation of French vowels is consistent and predictable.

In short words (usually two-letter words), **e** is pronounced similarly to the *a* in the English word *about*.

l**e**	qu**e**	c**e**	d**e**

The letter **a** alone is pronounced like the *a* in *father*.

l**a**	ç**a**	m**a**	t**a**

The letter **i** by itself and the letter **y** are pronounced like the vowel sound in the word *bee*.

ic**i**	l**i**vre	st**y**lo	l**y**cée

The letter combination **ou** sounds like the vowel sound in the English word *who*.

v**ou**s	n**ou**s	**ou**blier	éc**ou**ter

The French **u** sound does not exist in English. To produce this sound, say *ee* with your lips rounded.

t**u**	d**u**	**u**ne	ét**u**dier

Prononcez Répétez les mots suivants à voix haute.

1. je
2. chat
3. fou
4. ville
5. utile
6. place
7. jour
8. triste
9. mari
10. active
11. Sylvie
12. rapide
13. gymnase
14. antipathique
15. calculatrice
16. piscine

Articulez Répétez les phrases suivantes à voix haute.

1. Salut, Luc. Ça va?
2. La philosophie est difficile.
3. Brigitte est une actrice fantastique.
4. Suzanne va à son cours de physique.
5. Tu trouves le cours de maths facile?
6. Viviane a une bourse universitaire.

Dictons Répétez les dictons à voix haute.

Plus on est de fous, plus on rit.²

Qui va à la chasse perd sa place.¹

¹ He who steps out of line loses his place.
² The more the merrier.

ressources

LM p. 26   vhlcentral

cent trente-sept 137

Section Goals
In this section, students will learn about oral vowels.

Instructional Resources
vhlcentral.com:
Textbook MP3s;
Lab MP3s; SAM Answer Key;
Textbook Audioscript;
Lab Audioscript;
reference tools

Suggestions
• Point out that although the pronunciation of the French **e caduc** and that of the *a* in the English word *about* are close, they are not identical. There is a difference in vowel quality and articulation.
• Model the pronunciation of each vowel sound. Have students watch the shape of your mouth, then repeat the sound after you. Pronounce each of the example words and have students repeat them.
• Tell students that an unaccented **e** at the end of a word is silent, but will cause a consonant that precedes it to be pronounced. Example: **petit/petite**.
• Contrast the pronunciation of words containing **u** and **ou**. Examples: **vous/vu** and **tous/tu**.
• Point out that this lesson primarily addresses the pronunciation of single oral vowels. Tell them that like **ou**, various vowel pairs create different sounds when combined. They will learn about these letter combinations in other lessons.
• Dictate five familiar words containing oral vowels to the class, repeating each one at least two times. Then write them on the board or on a transparency and have students check their spelling.

Dictons Ask students if they can think of a saying in English that is similar to **«Qui va à la chasse perd sa place.»** (*You snooze, you lose.*)

Game Have a spelling bee using vocabulary words from **Leçons 1A-4A** that contain oral vowel sounds. Pronounce each word, use it in a sentence, and then say the individual word again. Tell students that they must spell the words in French and include the diacritical marks.

Extra Practice Use these sentences with oral vowels for additional practice or dictation. **1. Madame Duclos et son mari sont séparés. 2. Marianne prépare le bac. 3. Tu aimes mieux le parc ou le gymnase? 4. Coralie nage à la piscine.**

OPTIONS

Star du cinéma  Video

Section Goals

In this section, students will learn functional phrases for talking about their plans through comprehensible input.

Instructional Resources
vhlcentral.com:
Roman-photo *Video, Videoscript, and Translation; SAM Answer Key; reference tools*

Video Recap: Leçon 3B
Review the previous **Roman-photo** with this activity.
1. De qui Sandrine parle-t-elle souvent? (de Pascal)
2. Où Rachid et Stéphane travaillent-ils? (chez Rachid)
3. Quelle est la profession du père de Rachid? (médecin)
4. Quelle est la profession de la mère de Rachid? (avocate)
5. Qui a envie d'être architecte? (Stéphane)

Video Synopsis David thinks he sees the actress Juliette Binoche in a grocery store. He runs to tell Sandrine. At the café, Sandrine is on the phone with Pascal; he wants to know her weekend plans. David arrives with his news. He, Sandrine, and Amina rush off to try to catch a glimpse of the actress, but have difficulty locating the correct store. At the store, they discover that David saw a store clerk, not Juliette Binoche.

Suggestions
• Ask students to read the title, glance at the video stills, and predict what they think the episode will be about. Record their predictions.
• Have students work in groups and read the **Roman-photo** conversation aloud.
• After students have read the **Roman-photo**, review their predictions and ask them which ones were correct. Then ask a few questions to help them summarize this episode.

PERSONNAGES

Amina

David

Pascal

Sandrine

À l'épicerie...
DAVID Juliette Binoche? Pas possible! Je vais chercher Sandrine!

Au café...
PASCAL Alors chérie, tu vas faire quoi de ton week-end?
SANDRINE Euh, demain je vais déjeuner au centre-ville.
PASCAL Bon... et quand est-ce que tu vas rentrer?
SANDRINE Euh, je ne sais pas. Pourquoi?

PASCAL Pour rien. Et demain soir, tu vas danser?
SANDRINE Ça dépend. Je vais passer chez Amina pour bavarder avec elle.
PASCAL Combien d'amis as-tu à Aix-en-Provence?
SANDRINE Oh, Pascal...
PASCAL Bon, moi, je vais continuer à penser à toi jour et nuit.

DAVID Mais l'actrice! Juliette Binoche!
SANDRINE Allons-y! Vite! C'est une de mes actrices préférées! J'adore le film *Chocolat*!
AMINA Et comme elle est chic! C'est une vraie star!
DAVID Elle est à l'épicerie! Ce n'est pas loin d'ici!

Dans la rue...
AMINA Mais elle est où, cette épicerie? Nous allons explorer toute la ville pour rencontrer Juliette Binoche?
SANDRINE C'est là, l'épicerie Pierre Dubois à côté du cinéma.
DAVID Mais non, elle n'est pas à l'épicerie Pierre Dubois, elle est à l'épicerie près de l'église, en face du parc.

AMINA Et combien d'églises est-ce qu'il y a à Aix?
SANDRINE Il n'y a pas d'église en face du parc!
DAVID Bon, hum, l'église sur la place.
AMINA D'accord, et ton église sur la place, elle est ici au centre-ville ou en banlieue?

ACTIVITÉS

1 **Vrai ou faux?** Indiquez pour chaque phrase si l'affirmation est **vraie** ou **fausse** et corrigez si nécessaire.

1. David va chercher Pascal. *Faux. David va chercher Sandrine.*
2. Sandrine va déjeuner au centre-ville. *Vrai.*
3. Pascal va passer chez Amina. *Faux. Sandrine va passer chez Amina.*
4. Pascal va continuer à penser à Sandrine jour et nuit. *Vrai.*
5. Pascal va bien. *Vrai.*

6. Juliette Binoche est l'actrice préférée de Sandrine. *Vrai.*
7. L'épicerie est loin du café. *Faux. L'épicerie n'est pas loin.*
8. L'épicerie Pierre Dubois est à côté de l'église.
Faux. L'épicerie Pierre Dubois est à côté du cinéma.
9. Il n'y a pas d'église en face du parc. *Vrai.*
10. Juliette Binoche fréquente le P'tit Bistrot.
Faux. Juliette Binoche ne fréquente pas le P'tit Bistrot.

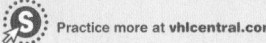 Practice more at **vhlcentral.com**.

138 *cent trente-huit*

OPTIONS

Avant de regarder la vidéo Before viewing the video, have students brainstorm possible activities that Sandrine might include in her weekend plans. Write their predictions on the board.

Regarder la vidéo Photocopy the videoscript and white out ten key words or phrases to create a master for a cloze activity. Hand out photocopies and tell students to fill in the missing words as they watch the video episode. You may want to show the episode twice if students have difficulty with the activity. Then have students compare their answers in small groups.

David et les filles à la recherche de (*in search of*) leur actrice préférée.

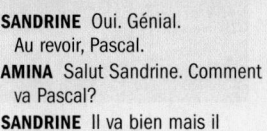

SANDRINE Oui. Génial.
Au revoir, Pascal.
AMINA Salut Sandrine. Comment va Pascal?
SANDRINE Il va bien mais il adore bavarder.

DAVID Elle est là, elle est là!
SANDRINE Mais, qui est là?
AMINA Et c'est où, «là»?
DAVID Juliette Binoche! Mais non, pas ici!
SANDRINE ET AMINA Quoi? Qui? Où?

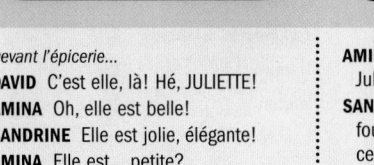

Devant l'épicerie...
DAVID C'est elle, là! Hé, JULIETTE!
AMINA Oh, elle est belle!
SANDRINE Elle est jolie, élégante!
AMINA Elle est... petite?
DAVID Elle, elle... est... vieille?!?

AMINA Ce n'est pas du tout Juliette Binoche!
SANDRINE David, tu es complètement fou! Juliette Binoche, au centre-ville d'Aix?
AMINA Pourquoi est-ce qu'elle ne fréquente pas le P'tit Bistrot?

Expressions utiles

Talking about your plans

- **Tu vas faire quoi de ton week-end?**
  What are you doing this weekend?
- **Je vais déjeuner au centre-ville.**
  I'm going to have lunch downtown.
- **Quand est-ce que tu vas rentrer?**
  When are you coming back?
- **Je ne sais pas.**
  I don't know.
- **Je vais passer chez Amina.**
  I am going to stop by Amina's (house).
- **Nous allons explorer toute la ville.**
  We're going to explore the whole city.

Additional vocabulary

- **C'est une de mes actrices préférées.**
  She's one of my favorite actresses.
- **Comme elle est chic!**
  She is so chic!
- **Ce n'est pas loin d'ici!**
  It's not far from here!
- **Ce n'est pas du tout...**
  It's not... at all.
- **Ça dépend.**
  It depends.
- **Pour rien.**
  No reason.
- **Vite!**
  Quick!, Hurry!

---

2 Questions À l'aide (*the help*) d'un dictionnaire, choisissez le bon mot pour chaque question.

1. (Avec qui, Quoi) Sandrine parle-t-elle au téléphone?
2. (Où, Parce que) Sandrine va-t-elle déjeuner?
3. (Qui, Pourquoi) Pascal demande-t-il à Sandrine quand elle va rentrer?
4. (Combien, Comment) d'amis Sandrine a-t-elle?
5. (Combien, À qui) Amina demande-t-elle comment va Pascal?
6. (Quand, Où) est Juliette Binoche?

3 Écrivez Pensez à votre acteur ou actrice préféré(e) et préparez un paragraphe où vous décrivez son apparence, sa personnalité et sa carrière. Comment est-il/elle? Dans quel(s) (*which*) film(s) joue-t-il/elle? Si un jour vous rencontrez cet acteur/cette actrice, qu'est-ce que vous allez lui dire (*say to him or her*)?

ressources

VM
pp. 13–14

vhlcentral

A C T I V I T É S

Expressions utiles
- Model the pronunciation of the **Expressions utiles** and have students repeat after you.
- As you work through the list, point out forms of **aller** and the interrogative words. Tell students that these concepts will be formally presented in **Espace structures**.
- Point out that, like the English verb *to go*, the verb **aller** is used to express future actions.
- Write **je vais** and **tu vas** on the board. Ask students the questions in the **Expressions utiles** and have them respond. Examples: **Tu vas faire quoi de ton week-end? Quand est-ce que tu vas rentrer?**
- Have students scan the video-still captions for interrogative words that are not in the list and read the sentences. Examples: **combien de, comment, qui, où,** and **pourquoi.**

1 Suggestion Have students write the correct answers to the false statements on the board.

1 Expansion For additional practice, give students these items. **11. Juliette Binoche est vieille. (Faux. Elle n'est pas vieille.) 12. Amina pense que Juliette Binoche est chic. (Vrai.)**

2 Expansion
- For additional practice, give students these items. **7. (Qui, Comment) est-ce que David voit (*see*) à l'épicerie? (Qui) 8. (Pourquoi, Comment) est Juliette Binoche? (Comment) 9. (Quand, Où) est-ce que Pascal va penser à Sandrine? (Quand)**
- Have students answer the questions.

3 Suggestion Have students exchange papers for peer editing. Remind them to pay particular attention to adjective agreement and subject-verb agreement.

O P T I O N S

Juliette Binoche Juliette Binoche (1964–), often referred to by the French press simply as "La Binoche," was born in Paris. In addition to being an actress, she is a poster designer and avid painter. Her first film was *Liberty Belle* (1983). She has now acted in more that 30 films. She won a César for "Best actress" in *Bleu* (1983) and an Oscar for "Best Supporting Actress" in *The English Patient* (1996). *Chocolat* (2000) is the film version of the novel *Chocolat* by Joanne Harris.

Small Groups Working in groups of three, have students create a short skit similar to the scenes in video stills 5–10 in which someone thinks they have seen a famous person. Give students ten minutes to prepare, then call on groups to perform their skits for the class.

Reading

CULTURE À LA LOUPE

Les passe-temps

Comment est-ce que les jeunes occupent leur temps libre° en France?
Si la télévision a été pendant longtemps un des passe-temps préféré, aujourd'hui près de° 60% (pour cent) des jeunes disent être plus attachés à° leur *smartphone*. En effet, ils sont 68% à ne jamais sortir sans leur portable, et ils veulent être connectés partout°. Les médias jouent donc un rôle très important dans leur vie, surtout les réseaux sociaux° qu'ils utilisent pour communiquer avec leurs amis et leurs proches°. Les portables sont aussi considérés très pratiques pour télécharger° et écouter de la musique, surfer sur Internet, jouer à des jeux° vidéo ou regarder des films.

Les activités culturelles, en particulier le cinéma, sont aussi très appréciées: en moyenne°, les jeunes y° vont une fois° par semaine. Ils aiment également° la littérature et l'art: presque° 50% visitent des musées ou des monuments historiques chaque année et plus de° 40% vont au théâtre ou à des concerts. Un jeune sur cinq° joue d'un instrument de musique ou chante°, et environ 20% d'entre eux° pratiquent une activité artistique, comme la danse, le théâtre, la sculpture, le dessin° ou la peinture°. La photographie et la vidéo sont aussi très appréciées.

Quant à° la pratique sportive, elle concerne près de 90% des jeunes Français, qui font partie de clubs ou s'entraînent entre copains.

Beaucoup de jeunes Français sont aussi membres de la Maison des Jeunes et de la Culture (MJC) de leur ville. Les MJC proposent des activités culturelles, sportives et des cours et ateliers° dans de nombreux domaines.

Et bien sûr, comme tous les jeunes, ils aiment aussi tout simplement se détendre° et bavarder avec des amis, le plus souvent dans un des nombreux cafés du centre-ville.

Les activités culturelles des Français
(% des Français qui les° pratiquent)

le dessin	7%
l'écriture°	4%
la peinture	4%
le piano	3%
autre instrument de musique	3%
la danse	2%
la guitare	2%
la sculpture	1%
le théâtre	1%

temps libre *free time* **près de** *close to* **attachés à** *fond of* **partout** *everywhere*
réseaux sociaux *social networks* **proches** *people close to them* **télécharger** *download*
jeux *games* **en moyenne** *on average* **y** *there* **fois** *time* **également** *also* **presque** *almost*
plus de *more than* **Un... sur cinq** *One . . . in five* **chante** *sings* **d'entre eux** *of them*
dessin *drawing* **peinture** *painting* **Quant à** *As for* **ateliers** *workshops* **se detendre** *relax*
les *them* **écriture** *writing*

ACTIVITÉS

1 Vrai ou faux? Indiquez si les phrases sont **vraies** ou **fausses**.

1. Les portables sont rarement utilisés pour écouter de la musique. Faux.
2. Les jeunes Français n'utilisent pas Internet. Faux.
3. Les musées sont des lieux appréciés pour les loisirs. Vrai.
4. Les réseaux sociaux ne sont pas très utilisés pour communiquer entre amis. Faux.
5. Les jeunes Français n'aiment pas pratiquer d'activités artistiques. Faux.

6. Le sport n'est pas important dans la vie des jeunes. Faux.
7. Les jeunes Français regardent moins la télévision aujourd'hui. Vrai.
8. L'instrument de musique le plus (*the most*) populaire en France est le piano. Vrai.
9. Plus de (*More*) gens pratiquent la peinture que la sculpture. Vrai.
10. Dans les MJC, on peut faire une grande variété d'activités. Vrai.

Section Goals

In this section, students will:
- learn about popular French pastimes
- learn about **le verlan**
- learn about **le maquis** and **le tangana** in Africa
- read about **le parc Astérix**

Instructional Resources
vhlcentral.com:
reference tools

Culture à la loupe
Avant la lecture Have students read the title and look at the photos. Ask: **À votre avis** (*In your opinion*), **quelles sont les activités préférées des jeunes Français?** Write a list on the board.

Lecture
- Point out the chart **Les activités culturelles des Français**. Ask students what information the chart shows. (The percentages of French people 15 years and older who participate in various cultural activities.)
- Have students verify their predictions and add any missing activities to the list.

Après la lecture Working in small groups, have students compare French and American pastimes. Tell them to make a list of the similarities and differences in French. Then ask several groups to read their lists to the class.

1 Expansion Have students correct the false statements. For additional practice, give students these items. **11. Les jeunes Français sont très attachés à leur** *smartphone*. **(Vrai.) 12. Les jeux vidéo ne sont pas très populaires en France. (Faux. Les jeux vidéo sont très populaires en France.) 13. Les jeunes Français aiment passer du temps avec leurs amis. (Vrai.) 14. Le piano est plus (*more*) populaire que la guitare en France. (Vrai.)**

OPTIONS

Pairs Have students work in pairs and ask each other about the information in the chart **Les activités culturelles des jeunes Français**. To help them, write a model on the board. Example: **Étudiant(e) 1: Est-ce que le dessin est un passe-temps populaire en France? Étudiant(e) 2: Oui, sept pour cent des jeunes Français dessinent.**

Cultural Activity Distribute photocopies of the cinematic and cultural activities in the weekly *Pariscope* or *Officiel des spectacles*. Tell students to make a list of the ones they would like to attend. Then have them compare their lists in small groups.

LE FRANÇAIS QUOTIDIEN

Le verlan

En France, on entend parfois° des jeunes parler en **verlan**. En verlan, les syllabes des mots sont inversées°:

l'envers° → vers–l'en → verlan.

Voici quelques exemples:

français	verlan	anglais
louche	chelou	*shady*
café	féca	*café*
mec	keum	*guy*
femme	meuf	*woman*

parfois *sometimes* **inversées** *inverted* **l'envers** *the reverse*

LE MONDE FRANCOPHONE

Où passer le temps

Voici quelques endroits typiques où les jeunes francophones aiment se restaurer° et passer du temps.

En Afrique de l'Ouest

Le maquis Commun dans beaucoup de pays° d'Afrique de l'Ouest°, le maquis est un restaurant où on peut manger à bas prix°. Situé en ville ou en bord de route°, le maquis est typiquement en plein air°.

Au Sénégal

Le tangana Le terme «tang» signifie «chaud» en wolof, une des langues nationales du Sénégal. Le tangana est un lieu populaire pour se restaurer. On trouve souvent les tanganas au coin de la rue°, en plein air, avec des tables et des bancs°.

se restaurer *have something to eat* **pays** *countries* **l'Ouest** *West* **à bas prix** *inexpensively* **en bord de route** *on the side of the road* **en plein air** *outdoors* **coin de la rue** *street corner* **bancs** *benches*

PORTRAIT

Le parc Astérix

Situé° à 30 kilomètres de Paris, en Picardie, le parc Astérix est le premier parc à thème français. Le parc d'attractions°, ouvert° en 1989, est basé sur la bande dessinée° française *Astérix le Gaulois*. Création de René Goscinny et d'Albert Uderzo, Astérix est un guerrier gaulois° qui lutte° contre l'invasion des Romains. Au parc Astérix, il y a des montagnes russes°, des petits trains et des spectacles, tous° basés sur les aventures d'Astérix et de son meilleur ami, Obélix. Entrez dans le Laboratoire de Panoramix, druide de la tribu° des Gaulois pour vivre l'expérience des potions magiques et de l'illusion. Une des attractions, *Le Tonnerre° de Zeus*, est la plus grande° montagne russe en bois° d'Europe, avec ses 30 mètres de haut°. Sa vitesse° est de plus de 80 kilomètres/heure. À l'intérieur du parc, de nombreux° restaurants, comme par exemple Le Relais Gaulois, vous proposent un grand choix° de restauration°. Si vous avez envie de passer plusieurs jours au parc Astérix, vous pouvez dormir° à l'Hôtel des Trois Hiboux, qui offre des chambres familiales, un petit-déjeuner° complet, le Wifi gratuit et surtout une rencontre° avec Astérix et Obélix...

Albert Uderzo

Situé *Located* **parc d'attractions** *amusement park* **ouvert** *opened* **bande dessinée** *comic strip* **guerrier gaulois** *Gallic warrior* **lutte** *fights* **montagnes russes** *roller coasters* **tous** *all* **tribu** *tribe* **Tonnerre** *Thunder* **la plus grande** *the largest* **en bois** *wooden* **de haut** *high* **vitesse** *speed* **de nombreux** *many* **choix** *choice* **restauration** *food* **dormir** *sleep* **petit-déjeuner** *breakfast* **rencontre** *encounter*

---

2 **Compréhension** Complétez les phrases.

1. Le parc Astérix est basé sur *Astérix le Gaulois*, une ___bande dessinée___.
2. Astérix le Gaulois est une ___création___ de René Goscinny et d'Albert Uderzo.
3. Le parc Astérix est près de la ville de ___Paris___.
4. Astérix est un ___guerrier___ gaulois.
5. On mange à bas prix dans un ___maquis___.
6. Au Sénégal, on parle aussi le ___wolof___.

3 **Vos activités préférées** Posez des questions à trois ou quatre de vos camarades de classe à propos de leurs activités favorites. Comparez vos résultats avec ceux (*those*) d'un autre groupe.

Practice more at **vhlcentral.com**.

ressources

vhlcentral

ACTIVITÉS

OPTIONS

Le verlan Write on the board: **1. une bande 2. la musique 3. le métro 4. manger 5. bonjour 6. fou** Have students work in pairs. Tell them to copy the words and write the equivalents in **verlan**. Answers: **1. une deban 2. la siquemu/sicmu 3. le tromé 4. géman 5. jourbon 6. ouf**

Le parc Astérix Some other popular attractions at the park are **La Galère** (a giant swinging ship), **Les Chaises Volantes** (flying chairs), **Le Cheval de Troie** (the Trojan horse), and **Transdemonium** (a ghost train through a castle dungeon). Have students take a virtual tour of the park by going to **www.parcasterix.com**.

Le français quotidien Model the pronunciation of each term and have students repeat it. Ask students what language or jargon in English is similar to **verlan**. (pig latin)

Portrait Point out Astérix and Obélix in the photo. If possible, bring in an Astérix comic strip to show students.

Le monde francophone Have students read the text. Then ask a few comprehension questions. Examples: **1. Pourquoi les jeunes fréquentent-ils les maquis et les tanganas? (pour manger et passer le temps) 2. On trouve les maquis en ville ou en bord de route? (les deux) Et les tanganas? (Ils sont souvent au coin d'une rue.) 3. On mange à l'intérieur ou en plein air dans le maquis et le tangana? (en plein air)**

Suggestion Point out to students that they will find supporting activities and more information related to this **Espace culture** at vhlcentral.com.

2 Expansion For additional practice, give students these items. **7. Le parc Astérix est le premier ____ à thème français. (parc) 8. Astérix lutte (*fights*) contre les ____. (Romains) 9. Au parc Astérix, il y a des montagnes ____. (russes) 10. L'ami d'Astérix s'appelle ____. (Obélix)**

3 Expansion Do a quick class survey to find out how many students like each activity and which one is the most popular. Tally the results on the board. Example: **Combien d'étudiants surfent sur Internet?**

Section Goals

In this section, students will learn:
- the verb **aller**
- the **futur proche** with **aller**
- the preposition **à**

Instructional Resources
vhlcentral.com:
Lab MP3s; SAM Answer Key;
Essayez!** and **Mise en pratique
answers; Lab Audioscript;
Activity Pack (Info Gap
Activities); reference tools

Suggestions
- Write the paradigm of **aller** on the board and model the pronunciation. Ask students what forms of **aller** are irregular.
- Write your next day's schedule on the board using infinitives and nouns. Examples: **8h00: bibliothèque; 10h00: cours de français; 12h00: déjeuner** Explain what you are going to do using the verb **aller**. Examples: **Je vais (aller) à la bibliothèque à huit heures. Je vais déjeuner à midi.** Ask students questions about their schedules using forms of **aller**.
- Ask individual students questions about their future plans using **aller**. Examples: **Allez-vous chez vos parents ce week-end? Allez-vous manger avec des copains vendredi soir?**

4A.1

The verb *aller* Tutorial

Point de départ In **Leçon 1A**, you saw a form of the verb **aller** (*to go*) in the expression **ça va**. Now you will use this verb, first, to talk about going places and, second, to express actions that take place in the immediate future.

aller			
je vais	*I go*	**nous allons**	*we go*
tu vas	*you go*	**vous allez**	*you go*
il/elle/on va	*he/she/it/one goes*	**ils/elles vont**	*they go*

- The verb **aller** is irregular. Only the **nous** and **vous** forms resemble the infinitive.

  Tu **vas** souvent au cinéma?
  Do you go to the movies often?

  Je **vais** à la piscine.
  I'm going to the pool.

  Nous **allons** au marché le samedi.
  We go to the market on Saturdays.

  Vous **allez** au parc?
  Are you going to the park?

- **Aller** can also be used with another verb to tell what is going to happen. This construction is called **le futur proche** (*the immediate future*). Conjugate **aller** in the present tense and place the other verb's infinitive form directly after it.

  Nous **allons déjeuner** sur la terrasse.
  We're going to eat lunch on the terrace.

  Je **vais partager** la pizza avec ma copine.
  I'm going to share the pizza with my friend.

  Marc et Julie **vont explorer** le centre-ville.
  Marc and Julie are going to explore downtown.

  Elles **vont retrouver** Guillaume à la boîte de nuit.
  They're going to meet Guillaume at the nightclub.

Demain, je vais déjeuner au centre-ville.

Et quand est-ce que tu vas rentrer?

À noter

In **Leçon 2A**, you learned how to form questions with inversion when you have a conjugated verb + infinitive. Follow the same pattern for **le futur proche**. Example: **Théo va-t-il déjeuner à midi?**

- To negate an expression in **le futur proche**, place **ne/n'** before the conjugated form of **aller** and **pas** after it.

  Je **ne vais pas** oublier la date.
  I'm not going to forget the date.

  Tu **ne vas pas** manger au café?
  Aren't you going to eat at the café?

  Nous **n'allons pas** quitter la maison.
  We're not going to leave the house.

  Ousmane **ne va pas** retrouver Salima au parc.
  Ousmane is not going to meet Salima at the park.

- Note that **le futur proche** can be used with the infinitive of **aller** to mean *going to go (somewhere)*.

  Elle **va aller** à la piscine.
  She's going to go to the pool.

  Vous **allez aller** au gymnase ce soir?
  Are you going to go to the gym tonight?

142 *cent quarante-deux*

The preposition à

- The preposition **à** can be translated in various ways in English: *to, in, at*. When followed by the definite article **le** or **les**, the preposition **à** and the definite article contract into one word.

à + le ▶ au	à + les ▶ aux
Nous allons **au** magasin.	Ils parlent **aux** profs.
We're going to the store.	*They speak to the professors.*

- The preposition **à** does not contract with **la** or **l'**.

à + la ▶ à la	à + l' ▶ à l'
Je rentre **à la** maison.	Il va **à l'**épicerie.
I'm going back home.	*He's going to the grocery store.*

- The preposition **à** often indicates a physical location, as with **aller à** and **habiter à**. However, it can have other meanings depending on the verb used.

Verbs with the preposition à

commencer à + [*infinitive*]	to start (doing something)	penser à	to think about
parler à	to talk to	téléphoner à	to phone (someone)

Elle va **parler au** professeur.	Il **commence à travailler** demain.
She's going to talk to the professor.	*He starts working tomorrow.*

- In general, **à** is used to mean *at* or *in*, whereas **dans** is used to mean *inside* or *within*. When learning a place name in French, learn the preposition that accompanies it.

Prepositions with place names

à la maison	at home	dans la maison	inside the house
à Paris	in Paris	dans Paris	within Paris
en ville	in town	dans la ville	within the town
sur la place	in the square	à/sur la terrasse	on the terrace

Tu travailles **à la maison**?	On mange **dans la maison**.
Are you working at home?	*We'll eat inside the house.*

Essayez! Utilisez la forme correcte du verbe **aller**.

1. Comment ça ___va___?
2. Tu ___vas___ à la piscine pour nager.
3. Ils ___vont___ au centre-ville.
4. Nous ___allons___ bavarder au café.
5. Vous ___allez___ aller au restaurant ce soir?
6. Elle ___va___ aller à l'église dimanche matin.
7. Ce soir, je ___vais___ danser en boîte.
8. On ne ___va___ pas passer par l'épicerie cet après-midi.

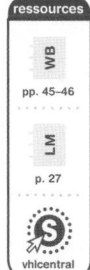

ressources

WB
pp. 45–46

LM
p. 27

S
vhlcentral

Suggestions
- Bring in pictures of people dressed for different activities. Describe them to the class using the verb **aller**. Example: Showing a picture of a swimmer, say: **Il/Elle va à la piscine.** Then explain the contractions **à + le = au** and **à + les = aux**.
- Tell students that, when followed by another verb (in the infinitive), **penser** doesn't take a preposition. Example: **Je pense aller au café après les cours**.
- Model the pronunciation of the list of prepositions with places. Tell students that they should memorize these phrases.

Essayez! Have students create a few additional sentences using the verb **aller**.

OPTIONS

Video Show the video episode again to give students additional input on the verb **aller**. Pause the video where appropriate to discuss how **aller** was used and to ask comprehension questions.

TPR Invent gestures to pantomime some activities taught in **Leçon 2B**. Examples: **nager:** *move arms as if swimming;* **bavarder:** *make talking gestures with hands;* **dépenser de l'argent:** *turn pockets inside out.* Signal individuals to gesture appropriately as you cue activities by saying: **Nous allons…** or **On va…**.

1 Suggestion To check students' answers, have a volunteer say the question, then call on another student to answer it.

2 Expansion For additional practice, give students these items. **7. Nous passons chez Martine. (Samedi prochain aussi, nous allons passer chez Martine.) 8. André travaille le matin. (... André va travailler le matin.) 9. Je dîne avec un ami. (... je vais dîner avec un ami.)**

3 Suggestion Have students take turns asking where the people in the drawings are going and answering the questions. Example: **Où va Henri? (Henri va au cinéma.)**

3 Expansion Have students redo the activity using **le futur proche** to ask questions about each image. Example: **Henri va-t-il aller au cinéma?**

Mise en pratique

1 Questions parentales Votre père est très curieux. Trouvez les questions qu'il pose.

MODÈLE

tes frères / piscine
Tes frères vont à la piscine?

1. tu / cinéma / ce soir Tu vas au cinéma ce soir?
2. tes amis et toi, vous / boîte Tes amis et toi, vous allez en boîte?
3. ta mère et moi, nous / ville / vendredi Ta mère et moi, nous allons en ville vendredi?
4. ta petite amie / souvent / marché Ta petite amie va souvent au marché?
5. je / musée / avec toi / demain Je vais au musée avec toi demain?
6. tes amis / parc Tes amis vont au parc?
7. on / église / dimanche On va à l'église dimanche?
8. ta petite amie et toi, vous / parfois / gymnase Ta petite amie et toi, vous allez parfois au gymnase?

2 Samedi prochain Voici ce que (*what*) vous et vos amis faites (*are doing*) aujourd'hui. Indiquez que vous allez faire les mêmes (*same*) choses samedi prochain.

MODÈLE

Je nage.
Samedi prochain aussi, je vais nager.

1. Paul bavarde avec ses copains. Samedi prochain aussi, Paul va bavarder avec ses copains.
2. Nous dansons. ... nous allons danser.
3. Je dépense de l'argent dans un magasin. ... je vais dépenser de l'argent dans un magasin.
4. Luc et Sylvie déjeunent au restaurant. ... Luc et Sylvie vont déjeuner au restaurant.
5. Vous explorez le centre-ville. ... vous allez explorer le centre-ville.
6. Tu patines. ... tu vas patiner.
7. Amélie nage à la piscine. ... Amélie va nager à la piscine.
8. Lucas et Sabrina téléphonent à leurs grands-parents. ... Lucas et Sabrina vont téléphoner à leurs grands-parents.

3 Où vont-ils? Avec un(e) partenaire, indiquez où vont les personnages. Answers will vary.

▶ **MODÈLE**

Henri va au cinéma.

Henri

1. tu   2. nous   3. Paul et Luc   4. vous

 Practice more at **vhlcentral.com**.

Communication

4

Activités du week-end Avec un(e) partenaire, assemblez les éléments des colonnes pour poser des questions. Rajoutez (*Add*) d'autres éléments utiles.   Answers will vary.

MODÈLE

Étudiant(e) 1: Est-ce que tu vas déjeuner aves tes copains?
Étudiant(e) 2: Oui, je vais déjeuner avec mes copains.

A	B	C	D
ta sœur	aller	voyager	professeur
vous		aller	cinéma
tes copains		déjeuner	boîte de nuit
nous		bavarder	piscine
tu		nager	centre
ton petit ami		danser	commercial
ta petite amie		parler	café
tes		inviter	parents
grands-parents		téléphoner	copains
		visiter	petit(e) ami(e)
		patiner	camarades de
			classe
			musée
			cousin(e)s

5

Le grand voyage Vous avez gagné (*have won*) un voyage. Par groupes de trois, expliquez à vos camarades ce que vous allez faire pendant (*during*) le voyage. Vos camarades vont deviner (*to guess*) où vous allez.   Answers will vary.

MODÈLE

Étudiant(e) 1: Je vais visiter le musée du Louvre.
Étudiant(e) 2: Est-ce que tu vas aller à Paris?

6

À Deauville Votre professeur va vous donner, à vous et à votre partenaire, un plan (*map*) de Deauville. Attention! Ne regardez pas la feuille de votre partenaire.   Answers will vary.

MODÈLE

Étudiant(e) 1: Où va Simon?
Étudiant(e) 2: Il va au kiosque.

---

4 Suggestion Have two volunteers read the **modèle**. Remind students that they can answer in the negative. Encourage them to expand on their answers. Examples: **Oui, je vais déjeuner avec mes copains au Petit Croissant./Non, je ne vais pas déjeuner avec mes copains, mais je vais aller au centre commercial avec ma mère.**

5 Suggestion Have two volunteers read the **modèle**. Encourage students to choose famous places in the francophone world.

6 Suggestions
• Tell students that Deauville is a fashionable seaside resort in Normandy frequented by the rich and famous.
• Divide the class into pairs and distribute the Info Gap Handouts found in the Activity Pack on the Supersite. Give students ten minutes to complete the activity.

OPTIONS

Extra Practice Do a quick substitution drill to practice **aller**. Write a sentence on the board and have students read it aloud. Then say a new subject and have students repeat the sentence, substituting the new subject. Examples: **1. Tu vas à l'hôpital. (nous, mon frère, vous, mes parents, je) 2. Il va aller au kiosque. (je, Claudine, nous, tu, les enfants, vous)**

Game Divide the class into four-member teams. Using the immediate future, each team will write a description of tomorrow's events for a well-known fictional character. Teams take turns reading and/or writing the description on the board without giving the character's name. The other teams will guess the identity. Each correct guess earns a point. If a team fools the others, it earns two points. The team with the most points wins.

Section Goals

In this section, students will learn interrogative words.

Instructional Resources
vhlcentral.com:
Activity Pack; Lab MP3s;
*SAM Answer Key; **Essayez!***
*and **Mise en pratique***
answers; Lab Audioscript;
reference tools

Suggestions

- Write the interrogative words on the board. Have students identify the words they know. Examples: **comment?**, **combien?**, **pourquoi?**, **qui?**, and **quel(s)/quelle(s)?** Model the pronunciation of the new words and have students repeat.
- Point out that in informal conversation interrogative words can be placed after the verb. Examples: **Tu vas où? Il s'appelle comment?**
- Remind students that they learned the expressions **Quelle heure est-il?** and **Quelle heure avez-vous?** in **2B.2**.
- Point out that **que?** and **quoi?** are used to ask about things. A preposition usually precedes **quoi?** or the word appears at the end of an informal question. Examples: **De quoi parlez-vous? Tu manges quoi?**
- Point out that **qui?** is used to ask about people. **Qui?** takes the third person singular verb form. You may also wish to introduce the expression **Qui est-ce qui…?**
- Emphasize to students that ending a question with **quoi** is more common in informal speech.

🏃 Boîte à outils

If a question word is followed immediately by the verb **être**, you don't use **est-ce que**.

Où est mon sac à dos?
Where is my backpack?
Comment est ta petite amie?
What is your girlfriend like?

À noter

Refer to **Structures 2A.2** to review how to answer a question with **pourquoi** using **parce que/qu'**.

Interrogative words  Tutorial

Point de départ In **Leçon 2A**, you learned four ways to formulate yes or no questions in French. However, many questions seek information that can't be provided by a simple yes or no answer.

- Use these words with **est-ce que** or inversion.

Interrogative words			
à quelle heure?	*at what time?*	**quand?**	*when?*
combien (de)?	*how many?; how much?*	**que/qu'…?**	*what?*
comment?	*how?; what?*	**quel(le)(s)?**	*which?; what?*
où?	*where?*	**(à/avec/pour) qui?**	*(to/with/for) who(m)?*
pourquoi?	*why?*	**quoi?**	*what?*

À qui est-ce que tu penses?
Whom are you thinking about?

Combien de villes y a-t-il en Suisse?
How many cities are there in Switzerland?

Pourquoi est-ce que tu danses?
Why are you dancing?

Que vas-tu manger?
What are you going to eat?

- When the question word **qui** (*who*) is the subject of a sentence, it is followed directly by a verb. The verb in this case is always in the third person singular form.

Qui invite Patrice à dîner?
Who is inviting Patrice to dinner?

Qui n'aime pas danser?
Who doesn't like to dance?

- When the question word **qui** (*whom*) is the object of a sentence, it is followed by **est-ce que** or inversion.

Qui est-ce que tu regardes?
Whom are you looking at?

Qui regardes-tu?
Whom are you looking at?

- Although **quand?** and **à quelle heure?** can be translated as *when?* in English, they are not interchangeable in French. Use **quand** to talk about a day or date, and **à quelle heure** to talk about a specific time of day.

Quand est-ce que le cours commence?
When does the class start?

À quelle heure est-ce qu'il commence?
At what time does it begin?

Il commence **le lundi 28 août**.
It starts Monday, August 28.

Il commence **à dix heures et demie**.
It starts at 10:30.

- Another way to formulate questions with most interrogative words is by placing them after a verb. This kind of formulation is very informal but very common.

Tu t'appelles **comment**?
What's your name?

Tu habites **où**?
Where do you live?

- Note that **quoi?** (*what?*) must immediately follow a preposition in order to be used with **est-ce que** or **inversion**. If no preposition is necessary, place **quoi** after the verb.

À quoi pensez-vous?
What are you thinking about?

Elle étudie **quoi**?
What does she study?

De quoi est-ce qu'il parle?
What is he talking about?

Tu regardes **quoi**?
What are you looking at?

- Use **Comment?** or **Pardon?** to indicate that you don't understand what's being said. You may also use **Quoi?** but only in informal situations with friends.

Vous allez voyager cette année?
Are you going to travel this year?

Comment?
I beg your pardon?

The interrogative adjective *quel(le)(s)*

- The interrogative adjective **quel** means *what* or *which*. The form of **quel** varies in gender and number with the noun it modifies.

The interrogative adjective *quel(le)(s)*			
	singular		**plural**
masculine	**Quel** *restaurant?*	**Quels** *cours?*	
feminine	**Quelle** *montre?*	**Quelles** *filles?*	

Quel restaurant aimes-tu?
Which restaurant do you like?

Quels cours commencent à dix heures?
What classes start at ten o'clock?

Quelle montre a-t-il?
What watch does he have?

Quelles filles vont à la boîte de nuit?
Which girls are going to the nightclub?

Boîte à outils sidebar

> **Boîte à outils**
>
> You can also use a form of **quel** as an exclamation.
> **Quel beau garçon!**
> *What a handsome boy!*
> **Quelles grandes maisons!**
> *What big houses!*

- **Qu'est-ce que** and **quel** both mean *what*, but they are used differently. Use a form of **quel** to ask *What is/are...?* if you want to know specific information about a noun. **Quel(le)(s)** may be followed directly by a form of **être** and a noun, in which case the form of **quel(le)(s)** agrees with that noun.

Quel est ton numéro de téléphone?
What is your phone number?

Quels sont tes problèmes?
What are your problems?

Quelles amies invites-tu?
What friends are you inviting?

Quel étudiant est intelligent?
What student is intelligent?

- Use **qu'est-ce que** in most other cases.

Qu'est-ce que tu vas manger?
What are you going to eat?

Qu'est-ce que Sandrine étudie?
What is Sandrine studying?

Tu es de quelle origine?

Quel jour sommes-nous?

Essayez!   Donnez les mots (*words*) interrogatifs.

1. _Comment_ allez-vous?
2. _Qu'_ est-ce que vous allez faire après le cours?
3. Le cours de français commence à _quelle_ heure?
4. _Pourquoi_ est-ce que tu ne travailles pas?
5. Avec _qui_ est-ce qu'on va au cinéma ce soir?
6. _Combien_ d'étudiants y a-t-il dans la salle de classe?
7. _Quels_ musées vas-tu visiter?
8. _Quand_ est-ce que tes parents arrivent?
9. _Qui_ n'aime pas voyager?
10. _Où_ est-ce qu'on dîne ce soir?

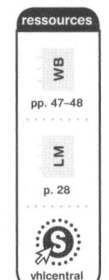

> **ressources**
> WB
> pp. 47–48
> LM
> p. 28
> vhlcentral

Suggestion Explain that **que/qu'...?**, **quel(le)(s)?**, and **quoi?** cannot be used interchangeably. **Que?** is often used in more formal questions or with **est-ce que**. Examples: **Que cherchez-vous? Qu'est-ce que vous cherchez?**

Essayez! Have one student read the question aloud, then call on another student to respond.

Extra Practice Bring in pictures or magazine photos of people doing various activities. Have students, as a class, create as many questions as they can about the pictures. Also, call on individuals to answer each question.

Extra Practice Divide the class in two. Give a strip of paper with a question on it to each member of one group. Example: **Où va-t-on pour dépenser de l'argent?** Give an answer to each member of the other group. Example: **On va au centre commercial.** Have students circulate around the room asking their questions until they find the person with the appropriate response. Write only one possible answer for each question.

1 Suggestion Have one student ask the question and call on another student to answer it.

1 Expansion Have students compare their answers with a classmate's.

2 Suggestion Have one student say the question and call on another student to answer it.

3 Suggestion Before beginning the activity, point out that there is more than one way to form some of the questions. Have students work in pairs. Tell them to take turns asking and answering the questions.

Mise en pratique

1 **Le français familier** Utilisez l'inversion pour reformuler les questions.

MODÈLE

Tu t'appelles comment?
Comment t'appelles-tu?

1. Tu habites où? <u>Où habites-tu?</u>
2. Le film commence à quelle heure? <u>À quelle heure le film commence-t-il?</u>
3. Il est quelle heure? <u>Quelle heure est-il?</u>
4. Tu as combien de frères? <u>Combien de frères as-tu?</u>
5. Le prof parle quand? <u>Quand le prof parle-t-il?</u>
6. Vous aimez quoi? <u>Qu'aimez-vous?</u>
7. Elle téléphone à qui? <u>À qui téléphone-t-elle?</u>
8. Il étudie comment? <u>Comment étudie-t-il?</u>
9. Il y a combien d'enfants? <u>Combien d'enfants y a-t-il?</u>
10. Elle aime qui? <u>Qui aime-t-elle?</u>

2 **La paire** Trouvez la paire et formez des phrases complètes. Utilisez chaque (*each*) option une seule fois (*only once*). Answers may vary.

1. À quelle heure d	a. est-ce que tu regardes?
2. Comment f	b. habitent-ils?
3. Combien de g	c. est-ce que tu habites dans le centre-ville?
4. Avec qui h	d. est-ce que le cours commence?
5. Où b	e. heure est-il?
6. Pourquoi c	f. vous appelez-vous?
7. Qu' a	g. villes est-ce qu'il y a aux États-Unis?
8. Quelle e	h. parlez-vous?

3 **La question** Vous avez les réponses. Quelles sont les questions? Some answers will vary.

MODÈLE

Il est midi.
Quelle heure est-il?

1. Les cours commencent à huit heures. <u>À quelle heure est-ce que les cours commencent?</u>
2. Stéphanie habite à Paris. <u>Où est-ce que Stéphanie habite?</u>
3. Julien danse avec Caroline. <u>Avec qui est-ce que Julien danse?</u>
4. Elle s'appelle Julie. <u>Comment s'appelle-t-elle?</u>
5. Laetitia a deux chiens. <u>Combien de chiens Laetitia a-t-elle?</u>
6. Elle déjeune dans ce restaurant parce qu'il est à côté de son bureau. <u>Pourquoi déjeune-t-elle dans ce restaurant?</u>
7. Nous allons bien, merci. <u>Comment allez-vous?</u>
8. Je vais au marché mardi. <u>Quand est-ce que tu vas au marché?</u>
9. Simon aime danser. <u>Qui aime danser?</u>
10. Brigitte pense à ses études. <u>À quoi Brigitte pense-t-elle?</u>

 Practice more at **vhlcentral.com**.

Communication

4 **Questions et réponses** À tour de rôle, posez une question à un(e) partenaire au sujet de chaque (*each*) thème de la liste. Posez une seconde question basée sur sa réponse. Answers will vary.

MODÈLE

Étudiant(e) 1: *Où est-ce que tu habites?*
Étudiant(e) 2: *J'habite chez mes parents.*
Étudiant(e) 1: *Pourquoi est-ce que tu habites chez tes parents?*

Thèmes

- où vous habitez
- ce que vous faites le week-end
- à qui vous téléphonez
- combien de frères et sœurs vous avez
- les endroits que vous fréquentez avec vos copains
- comment sont vos camarades de classe
- quels cours vous aimez

5 **La montagne** Par groupes de quatre, lisez (*read*) avec attention la lettre de Céline. Fermez votre livre. Une personne du groupe va poser une question basée sur l'information donnée. La personne qui répond pose une autre question au groupe, etc. Answers will vary.

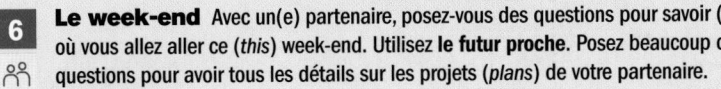

> Bonjour. Je m'appelle Céline. J'ai 20 ans. Je suis grande, mince et sportive. J'habite à Grenoble dans une maison agréable. Je suis étudiante à l'université. J'adore la montagne.
>
> Tous les week-ends, je vais skier à Chamrousse avec mes trois amis Alain, Catherine et Pascal. Nous skions de midi à cinq heures. À six heures, nous prenons un chocolat chaud à la terrasse d'un café ou nous allons manger des crêpes dans un restaurant. Nous rencontrons souvent d'autres étudiants et nous allons en boîte tous ensemble.

6 **Le week-end** Avec un(e) partenaire, posez-vous des questions pour savoir (*know*) où vous allez aller ce (*this*) week-end. Utilisez **le futur proche**. Posez beaucoup de questions pour avoir tous les détails sur les projets (*plans*) de votre partenaire. Answers will vary.

MODÈLE

Étudiant(e) 1: *Où est-ce que tu vas aller samedi?*
Étudiant(e) 2: *Je vais aller au centre commercial.*
Étudiant(e) 1: *Avec qui?*

---

4 Suggestion Have two volunteers read the **modèle** aloud. Tell students to jot down their partner's responses.

5 Suggestion Circulate among the groups, providing help where necessary. You might want to have one person in each group keep the book open to verify answers.

6 Suggestion Tell students to jot down notes on their partner's plans. Have them report to the class what their partners will be doing next weekend in as much detail as possible.

Extra Practice Tell students to write a simple statement about something they like, love, or hate. Have the first student say the statement. The next student asks **Pourquoi?** and the first student answers. Then the second student says his or her statement, and a third student asks why. Examples: **Étudiant(e) 1: Je déteste étudier le samedi soir. Étudiant(e) 2: Pourquoi? Étudiant(e) 1: Parce que c'est la barbe/barbant!**

Extra Practice Have students turn to the **Roman-photo** on pages 138–139. Tell them to write as many questions as they can based on the photos. Example: **Où est David? (Il est à l'épicerie.)** Ask volunteers to read their questions aloud and then call other students to answer them. You may also have students ask their questions in pairs.

Révision

Instructional Resources
vhlcentral.com:
Activity Pack (Info Gap Activities); Testing Program; Testing Program MP3s; reference tools

1 Suggestion Model the activity with a volunteer by asking questions about **le café**. Tell students to jot down notes during the interviews. Encourage them to add other places to the list.

2 Suggestion Photocopy and distribute a page from a French day planner so that students can make a note of the activities in the appropriate place. To review telling time, tell students to say the time at which they do the activities as well as the day.

3 Suggestion Before beginning the activity, have students make a list of possible activities for the weekend.

4 Suggestion Before beginning the activity, give students a few minutes to make a list of possible activities in their hometown to discuss.

5 Suggestion Have two volunteers read the **modèle** aloud. Then have students brainstorm places they could go and things they could do in each city. Write their suggestions on the board.

6 Suggestion Divide the class into pairs and distribute the Info Gap Handouts found in the Activity Pack on the Supersite. Give students ten minutes to complete the activity.

6 Expansion Call on volunteers to read their descriptions aloud and have the class compare them.

1 En ville Par groupes de trois, interviewez vos camarades. Où allez-vous en ville? Quand vos camarades mentionnent un endroit de la liste, demandez des détails (quand? avec qui? pourquoi? etc.). Présentez les réponses à la classe. Answers will vary.

le café	le musée
le centre commercial	le parc
le cinéma	la piscine
le marché	le restaurant

2 La semaine prochaine Voici votre agenda (*day planner*). Parlez de votre semaine avec un(e) partenaire. Mentionnez trois activités associées au travail, trois d'un autre type, et deux activités à faire en groupe. Answers will vary.

MODÈLE

Lundi je vais préparer un examen, mais samedi je vais danser en boîte.

	L	M	M	J	V	S	D
8h30							
9h00							
9h30							
10h00							
10h30							
11h00							
11h30							
12h00							
12h30							

3 Le week-end Par groupes de trois, posez-vous des questions sur vos projets pour le week-end prochain. Donnez des détails. Mentionnez aussi des activités qu'on fait avec des amis. Answers will vary.

MODÈLE

Étudiant(e) 1: *Quels projets avez-vous pour ce week-end?*
Étudiant(e) 2: *Nous allons aller au marché samedi.*
Étudiant(e) 3: *Et nous allons aller au café dimanche.*

4 Ma ville À tour de rôle, vous invitez votre partenaire dans votre ville d'origine pour une visite d'une semaine. Proposez des activités variées et préparez une liste. Ensuite (*Then*), comparez vos projets avec ceux (*those*) d'un autre groupe. Answers will vary.

MODÈLE

Étudiant(e) 1: *Samedi, on va au centre-ville.*
Étudiant(e) 2: *Nous allons dépenser de l'argent!*

5 Où passer un long week-end? Vous et votre partenaire avez la possibilité de passer un long week-end à Montréal ou à La Nouvelle-Orléans, mais vous préférez chacun(e) (*each one*) une ville différente. Jouez la conversation pour la classe. Answers will vary.

MODÈLE

Étudiant(e) 1: *À Montréal, on va visiter les sites!*
Étudiant(e) 2: *Oui, mais à La Nouvelle-Orléans, on va danser dans les boîtes cajuns!*

Montréal
- le Jardin botanique
- le Musée des Beaux-Arts
- le Parc du Mont-Royal
- le Vieux-Montréal

La Nouvelle-Orléans
- le Café du Monde
- la Cathédrale Saint-Louis
- la route des plantations
- le Vieux Carré (quartier français)

6 La semaine de Martine Votre professeur va vous donner, à vous et à votre partenaire, des informations sur la semaine de Martine. Attention! Ne regardez pas la feuille de votre partenaire. Answers will vary.

MODÈLE

Lundi matin, Martine va dessiner au parc.

O P T I O N S

Cultural Activity Invite a native French speaker to class. Before the person arrives, have students prepare a list of questions that they would like to ask this person. For example, they could ask about the person's job, family, leisure-time activities, weekend plans, and the places he or she frequents. Have students use their questions to interview the person.

Pairs Give pairs three minutes to write as many questions as they can using interrogative words. Then have them get together with another pair and take turns asking and answering the questions.

Video

 *Le Zapping*

Sur les toits de Paris

Dans le cadre de sa série d'été° «Une semaine sur les toits° de Paris», la chaîne télévisée BFMTV nous fait découvrir des terrasses perchées sur les toits de la capitale. Pour Paul et Alexandre, deux jeunes Parisiens, c'est devenu une passion. Ils parcourent° la ville pour dénicher° de nouvelles adresses pour boire un verre°. Ils définissent des critères pour les sélectionner: l'accès, la vue, l'ambiance et la carte avec les prix°. Ces deux jeunes hommes, à l'origine du collectif «Toi Toi Mon Toit», écrivent de petits articles et publient quelques photos pour faire connaître° ces «rooftops» qui sont de plus en plus fréquentés, surtout l'été. En effet, les habitants de Paris aiment profiter° du beau temps pour boire un verre entre amis.

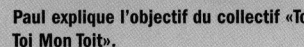
Paul explique l'objectif du collectif «Toi Toi Mon Toit».

Paul et Alexandre posent des questions au serveur du café.

Compréhension Répondez aux questions. Answers will vary.

1. Quels endroits peut-on voir dans cette vidéo? On peut voir la terrasse d'un café, un centre-ville, une gare.
2. Que font les personnes présentes dans la vidéo? Les personnes sont assises à la terrasse d'un café. Elles prennent un verre et bavardent.
3. Quel est l'objectif du projet du collectif «Toi Toi Mon Toit»? L'objectif du projet est de montrer comment sont les terrasses sur les toits de Paris et d'identifier les bonnes terrasses.

Discussion Avec un(e) partenaire, répondez aux questions. Answers will vary.

1. Quels sont les endroits de votre ville où vous aimez aller prendre un verre et bavarder avec vos ami(e)s? Décrivez-les.
2. Qu'aimez-vous dans ces endroits? Pourquoi?

été *summer* toits *rooftops* parcourent *roam* dénicher *uncover* boire un verre *have a drink* prix *prices* connaître *know* profiter *enjoy*

Go to **vhlcentral.com** to watch the TV clip featured in this **Le Zapping**.

 Practice more at **vhlcentral.com**.

cent cinquante et un 151

Section Goals
In this section, students will:
• read about rooftop patios in Paris
• watch a video about rooftop patios in Paris
• answer questions about the video and rooftop patios in Paris

Instructional Resources
*vhlcentral.com: TV commercial;
Le Zapping TV clip transcription;
reference tools*

Introduction
To check comprehension, ask these questions:
**1. Où se trouve la terrasse qu'on voit dans la vidéo? (Sur le toit de la Gare de l'Est à Paris.)
2. Comment s'appellent les deux jeunes hommes dans la vidéo? Qui sont-ils? (Paul et Alexandre. Ce sont deux jeunes Parisiens à l'origine du collectif «Toi Toi Mon Toit».)**

Avant de regarder la vidéo
• Have students look at the video stills, read the captions, and predict what will happen in the video based on each visual. **(1. La vidéo va parler des cafés. 2. Les jeunes hommes posent des questions au serveur. 3. Paul va expliquer l'objectif de son collectif.)**
• Before showing the video, explain to students that they don't need to understand every word they hear. Tell them to listen for any familiar words, then ask: **Que peut-on faire à la terrasse d'un café?**

Compréhension Have students work in pairs or groups for this activity. Tell them to write their answers. Then, show the video again so that they can check their answers and add any missing information.

Discussion Ask students to share their classmates' answers. Keep track of some of the places they mention to determine what their preferences are, and list them on the board.

OPTIONS

Paris Plages Each year, the banks of the Seine are transformed into beaches. Since 2002, the **Mairie de Paris** has sponsored a summertime event called **Paris Plages**. During the months of July and August, 3.5 kilometers of the Seine's right bank are filled with deckchairs, beach umbrellas, misting stations, athletic and cultural activities, temporary restaurants… and sand. The temporary cafés are the perfect place to meet friends for a drink or snack, and the ambiance is just what you'd find at a regular beach. Parisians and tourists spending their summer vacation in the French capital will find something to love at **Paris Plages**.

Section Goals

In this section, students will learn and practice vocabulary related to:
• foods and beverages
• eating at a café or restaurant

Instructional Resources
vhlcentral.com:
Digital Image Bank (including vocabulary illustrations from the textbook, theme-based illustrations); **Vocabulaire supplémentaire; Mise en pratique** *answers; Textbook Audioscript; Lab Audioscript; Activity Pack (Info Gap Activities); Textbook MP3s; Lab MP3s; SAM Answer Key; reference tools*

Suggestions

• Use the 4B **Contextes** illustration from the Digital Image Bank. Ask students to describe where the scene takes place and what people are doing. Have students identify items they know.

• Have students look at the new vocabulary and identify the cognates.

• Model the pronunciation of the words and have students repeat after you. Then ask students a few questions about the people in the drawing. Examples: **Qui a faim? Que mange l'homme? Qui a soif?**

• Point out the menu in the illustration. Explain the difference between **un menu** and **une carte**. Ask students what **soupe du jour** and **plat du jour** mean. Then ask: **Combien coûte le plat du jour? Et la soupe du jour?**

• Tell students that a 15% tip is usually included in the price of a meal in a café or restaurant. If the service is particularly good, it is customary to leave a little bit extra.

• Use the Vocabulary illustrations and the Food and Restaurant dining illustrations from the Digital Image Bank to help students familiarize themselves with foods and beverages and eating at a café or restaurant.

• Additional vocabulary for this lesson can be found in the **Vocabulaire supplémentaire** on the Supersite.

Leçon 4B

You will learn how to...
▪ order food and beverages
▪ ask for your check

 Vocabulary Tools

J'ai faim!

un serveur (serveuse f.)

le prix

une bouteille d'eau

l'addition (f.)

une soupe

les croissants (m.)

Elle laisse un pourboire. (laisser)

Il a faim. (avoir)

ressources

WB	LM	S
pp. 49–50	p. 29	vhlcentral

Vocabulaire

apporter l'addition	to bring the check/bill
coûter	to cost
Combien coûte(nt)...?	How much is/are...?
une baguette	baguette (long, thin loaf of bread)
le beurre	butter
des frites (f.)	French fries
un fromage	cheese
le jambon	ham
un pain (de campagne)	(country-style) bread
un sandwich	sandwich
une boisson (gazeuse)	(soft/carbonated) drink/beverage
un chocolat (chaud)	(hot) chocolate
une eau (minérale)	(mineral) water
un jus (d'orange, de pomme, etc.)	(orange, apple, etc.) juice
le lait	milk
une limonade	lemon soda
un thé (glacé)	(iced) tea
(pas) assez (de)	(not) enough (of)
beaucoup (de)	a lot (of)
d'autres	others
un morceau (de)	piece, bit (of)
un peu (plus/moins) (de)	a little (more/less) (of)
plusieurs	several
quelque chose	something; anything
quelques	some
tous (m. pl.)	all
tout (m. sing.)	all
tout (tous) le/les (m.)	all the
toute(s) la/les (f.)	all the
trop (de)	too many/much (of)
un verre (de)	glass (of)

152 *cent cinquante-deux*

O P T I O N S

Extra Practice Write **le matin**, **à midi**, and **le soir** on the board or on a transparency. Then ask students when they prefer to have various foods and beverages. Example: **Préférez-vous manger des frites le matin ou à midi?** Other items you can mention are **un éclair**, **un sandwich**, **une soupe**, and **un croissant**.

Pairs Have students work in pairs. Tell them to classify the foods and drinks under the headings **Manger** and **Boire** (*To drink*). After pairs have completed the activity, tell them to compare their lists with another pair and to resolve any differences.

Mise en pratique

Attention!

To read prices in French, say the number of euros (**euros**) followed by the number of cents (**centimes**). French decimals are marked with a comma, not a period.

8,10€ = huit euros dix (centimes)

le sucre

Il a soif. (avoir)

le thé

une tasse

Il mange quelque chose. (manger)

un café

un éclair

1 Écoutez Écoutez la conversation entre André et le serveur du café Gide, et décidez si les phrases sont **vraies** ou **fausses**.

	Vrai	Faux
1. André n'a pas très soif.	☑	☐
2. André n'a pas faim.	☐	☑
3. Au café, on peut commander (*one may order*) un jus d'orange, une limonade, un café ou une boisson gazeuse.	☑	☐
4. André commande un sandwich au jambon avec du fromage.	☐	☑
5. André commande un chocolat chaud.	☐	☑
6. André déteste le lait et le sucre.	☐	☑
7. André n'a pas beaucoup d'argent.	☑	☐
8. André ne laisse pas de pourboire.	☑	☐

2 Chassez l'intrus Trouvez le mot qui ne va pas avec les autres.

1. un croissant, le pain, le fromage, une baguette
2. une limonade, un jus de pomme, un jus d'orange, le beurre
3. des frites, un sandwich, le sucre, le jambon
4. le jambon, un éclair, un croissant, une baguette
5. l'eau, la boisson, l'eau minérale, la soupe
6. l'addition, un chocolat, le pourboire, coûter
7. apporter, d'autres, plusieurs, quelques
8. un morceau, une bouteille, un verre, une tasse

3 Reliez Reliez (*Connect*) correctement les expressions de quantité suivantes aux produits de la liste.

un morceau de	une bouteille de
un verre de	une tasse de

MODÈLE

un morceau de baguette

1. _____une bouteille d'_____ eau
2. _____un morceau de_____ quiche
3. _____un morceau de_____ fromage
4. _____une tasse de_____ chocolat chaud
5. _____une tasse de_____ café
6. _____un verre de_____ jus de pomme
7. _____une tasse de_____ thé
8. _____un verre de_____ limonade

---

1 Audioscript SERVEUR: Bonjour, Monsieur! Vous désirez?
ANDRÉ: Bonjour! Combien coûtent les sandwichs?
S: Ça dépend. Un sandwich au jambon coûte 3€, mais un sandwich au jambon avec du fromage et des frites coûtent 5,50€.
A: Et combien coûte le café?
S: Une tasse de café coûte 3€ et avec du lait 3,50€.
A: Y a-t-il d'autres boissons?
S: Bien sûr, il y a du jus d'orange, des boissons gazeuses, de la limonade et de l'eau.
A: Je n'ai pas beaucoup d'argent sur moi, mais j'ai très faim. J'ai envie d'un sandwich au jambon. Je n'ai pas très soif, alors une tasse de café au lait avec un peu de sucre, s'il vous plaît.
S: Très bien, Monsieur.
A: Excusez-moi, c'est combien?
S: C'est 6,50€.
A: Voici. Merci et bonne journée!
S: Merci, Monsieur, au revoir. Oh là là! Pas de pourboire!
(On Textbook MP3s)

1 Suggestion Have students correct the false items.

2 Expansion For additional practice, give students these items. **9. beaucoup de, un verre de, assez de, un peu de (un verre de) 10. le café, le jus, le thé, le chocolat chaud (le jus) 11. l'addition, le prix, le serveur, le pourboire (le serveur)**

3 Suggestion You may wish to introduce words for other types of containers, such as **une assiette, un bol,** and **un paquet.**

3 Expansion For additional practice, give students these items. **9. lait (une bouteille de, un verre de) 10. beurre (un morceau de)**

OPTIONS

Game Write these categories on the board: **Boissons froides / chaudes** and **Nourriture froide / chaude**. Toss a beanbag to a student at random and call out a category. The student has four seconds to name a food or beverage that fits the category. He or she then tosses the beanbag to another student and calls out a category. Players who cannot think of an item in time or repeat an item are eliminated. The last person standing wins.

Extra Practice For additional practice, ask students questions about their food and drink preferences. Examples: **Préférez-vous le thé ou le chocolat? Le lait ou l'eau minérale? Le jus d'orange ou le jus de pomme? Le jambon ou le fromage? Les sandwichs ou les éclairs? La soupe ou les frites? Les baguettes ou les croissants?**

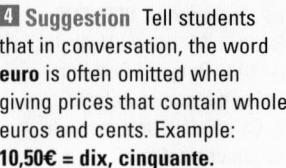

4 Suggestion Tell students that in conversation, the word **euro** is often omitted when giving prices that contain whole euros and cents. Example: **10,50€ = dix, cinquante.**

5 Suggestion Tell students to take notes during their interviews. Then have volunteers report their findings to the class.

6 Suggestion Distribute photocopies of actual café menus for students to use or have students base their conversation on the menu in **Activité 4.**

7 Suggestion Divide the class into pairs and distribute the Info Gap Handouts found in the Activity Pack on the Supersite.

Communication

4 **Combien coûte...?** Regardez la carte et, à tour de rôle, demandez à votre partenaire combien coûte chaque chose. Répondez par des phrases complètes.

> **MODÈLE**
> **Étudiant(e) 1:** *Combien coûte un sandwich?*
> **Étudiant(e) 2:** *Un sandwich coûte 3,50€.*

1. Combien coûtent les frites? Les frites coûtent 2€.
2. Combien coûte une boisson gazeuse? Une boisson gazeuse coûte 2€.
3. Combien coûte une limonade? Une limonade coûte 1,75€.
4. Combien coûte une bouteille d'eau? Une bouteille d'eau coûte 2€.
5. Combien coûte une tasse de café? Une tasse de café coûte 3€.
6. Combien coûte une tasse de thé? Une tasse de thé coûte 2,50€.
7. Combien coûte un croissant? Un croissant coûte 1€.
8. Combien coûte un éclair? Un éclair coûte 1,95€.

5 **Conversez** Interviewez un(e) camarade de classe. Answers will vary.

1. Qu'est-ce que tu aimes boire (*drink*) quand tu as soif? Quand tu as froid? Quand tu as chaud?
2. Quand tu as faim, est-ce que tu manges au resto U? Qu'est-ce que tu aimes manger?
3. Est-ce que tu aimes le café ou le thé? Combien de tasses est-ce que tu aimes boire par jour?
4. Comment est-ce que tu aimes le café? Avec du lait? Avec du sucre? Noir (*black*)?
5. Comment est-ce que tu aimes le thé? Avec du lait? Avec du sucre? Nature (*plain*)?
6. Dans ta famille, qui aime le thé? Et le café?
7. Quand tu manges dans un restaurant, est-ce que tu laisses un pourboire au serveur/à la serveuse?
8. Quand tu manges avec ta famille ou avec tes amis dans un restaurant, qui paie (*pays*) l'addition?

6 **Au café** Choisissez deux partenaires et écrivez une conversation entre deux client(e)s dans un café et leur serveur/serveuse. Préparez-vous à jouer (*perform*) la scène devant la classe. Answers will vary.

Client(e)s

- Demandez des détails sur le menu et les prix.
- Choisissez des boissons et des plats (*dishes*).
- Demandez l'addition.

Serveur/Serveuse

- Parlez du menu et répondez aux questions.
- Apportez les plats et l'addition.

> **Coup de main**
>
> **Vous désirez?**
> *What can I get you?*
>
> **Je voudrais...**
> *I would like...*
>
> **C'est combien?**
> *How much is it/this/that?*

7 **Sept différences** Votre professeur va vous donner, à vous et à votre partenaire, deux feuilles d'activités différentes. Attention! Ne regardez pas la feuille de votre partenaire. Answers will vary.

> **MODÈLE**
> **Étudiant(e) 1:** *J'ai deux tasses de café.*
> **Étudiant(e) 2:** *Moi, j'ai une tasse de thé!*

O P T I O N S

Game Divide the class into two teams. At the same time, give one person on each team a set of scrambled words that form a sentence about foods and/or beverages. The first person to unscramble the words and write the sentence on the board correctly scores a point for his or her team. The team with the most points at the end of the game wins.

Extra Practice To review vocabulary, bring in pictures or magazine photos of the foods and drinks listed. Ask students to identify the items. Example: **Qu'est-ce que c'est? (C'est _____.)** Or you can make false statements about the pictures and have students correct them. Example: **C'est un(e) _____, n'est-ce pas? (Non, c'est _____.)** For plural nouns, remind students to say **Ce sont _____.**

Les sons et les lettres   Audio

Nasal vowels

When vowels are followed by an **m** or an **n** in a single syllable, they usually become nasal vowels. Nasal vowels are produced by pushing air through both the mouth and the nose.

The nasal vowel sound you hear in **français** is usually spelled **an** or **en**.

an	fra**n**çais	e**n**chanté	e**n**fant

The nasal vowel sound you hear in **bien** may be spelled **en**, **in**, **im**, **ain**, or **aim**. The nasal vowel sound you hear in **brun** may be spelled **un** or **um**.

exam**en**	améric**ain**	l**un**di	parf**um**

The nasal vowel sound you hear in **bon** is spelled **on** or **om**.

t**on**	all**on**s	c**om**bien	**on**cle

When **m** or **n** is followed by a vowel sound, the preceding vowel is not nasal.

i**m**age	i**n**utile	a**m**i	a**m**our

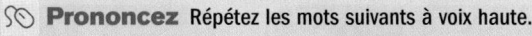 **Prononcez** Répétez les mots suivants à voix haute.

1. blond
2. dans
3. faim
4. entre
5. garçon
6. avant
7. maison
8. cinéma
9. quelqu'un
10. différent
11. amusant
12. télévision
13. impatient
14. rencontrer
15. informatique
16. comment

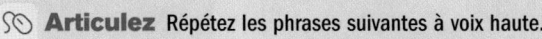 **Articulez** Répétez les phrases suivantes à voix haute.

1. Mes parents ont cinquante ans.
2. Tu prends une limonade, Martin?
3. Le Printemps est un grand magasin.
4. Lucien va prendre le train à Montauban.
5. Pardon, Monsieur, l'addition s'il vous plaît!
6. Jean-François a les cheveux bruns et les yeux marron.

Dictons Répétez les dictons à voix haute.

> L'appétit vient en mangeant.[1]

> N'allonge pas ton bras au-delà de ta manche.[2]

[1] Appetite comes from eating.
[2] Don't bite off more than you can chew. (lit. Don't stretch your arm out farther than your sleeve.)

ressources

LM
p. 30

vhlcentral

Section Goals
In this section, students will learn about nasal vowels.

Instructional Resources
vhlcentral.com:
Textbook MP3s; Lab MP3s;
SAM Answer Key;
Textbook Audioscript;
Lab Audioscript;
reference tools

Suggestions
- Model the pronunciation of each nasal vowel sound and have students repeat after you. Then pronounce each of the example words and have students repeat them.
- Tell students that when an **m** or an **n** is followed by an unaccented **e** at the end of a word, the preceding vowel is not nasalized. Have them compare these words: **un/une**, **brun/brune**, and **faim/femme**.
- Ask students to provide more examples of words they know with nasal vowels. Examples: **croissant**, **boisson**, **jambon**, **inviter**, **quand**, **dépenser**, and **danser**.
- Dictate five simple sentences with words containing nasal vowels to the class, repeating each one at least two times. Then write them on the board or on a transparency and have students check their spelling.

Dictons Ask students if they can think of a saying in English that is similar to **«L'appétit vient en mangeant.»** (*The more one has, the more one wants.*)

O P T I O N S

Extra Practice Teach students these French tongue-twisters that contain nasal vowel sounds. **1.** Son chat chante sa chanson. **2.** Un chasseur sachant chasser sait chasser sans son chien de chasse. **3.** Dans la gendarmerie, quand un gendarme rit, tous les gendarmes rient dans la gendarmerie.

Extra Practice Use these sentences with nasal vowels for additional practice or dictation. **1.** Raymond mange un sandwich au jambon. **2.** Martin invite ses cousins au restaurant. **3.** Tante Blanche a soixante-cinq ans. **4.** Mon oncle Quentin a envie de danser.

L'heure du déjeuner Video

NATIONAL
communication
cultures
STANDARDS

Section Goals

In this section, students will learn functional phrases for ordering foods and drinks and talking about food through comprehensible input.

Instructional Resources
vhlcentral.com:
Roman-photo *Video, Videoscript, and Translation; SAM Answer Key; reference tools*

Video Recap: Leçon 4A
Review the previous **Roman-photo** with this activity.
1. David pense qu'il y a une femme célèbre à l'épicerie. Qui est-ce? (Juliette Binoche)
2. À qui Sandrine parle-t-elle au téléphone? (à Pascal)
3. Les jeunes trouvent-ils facilement l'épicerie? (non)
4. Comment est la femme à l'épicerie? (belle, jolie, élégante, petite et vieille)
5. En réalité, qui est la femme? (quelqu'un qui travaille à l'épicerie)

Video Synopsis As the four friends approach **Le P'tit Bistrot**, Amina and Sandrine are hungry and want to go eat. Rachid and David decide to go back to their apartment. Valérie tells Amina and Sandrine what she is serving for lunch that day, and they place their order. Michèle makes a mistake on a customer's check, and Valérie serves the wrong food and drinks to Amina and Sandrine.

Suggestions
- Ask students to read the title, glance at the video stills, and predict what the episode will be about. Record their predictions.
- Have students volunteer to read the characters' parts in the **Roman-photo** aloud.
- After reading the **Roman-photo**, review students' predictions and ask them which ones are correct. Then help them summarize this episode.

PERSONNAGES

Amina

David

Michèle

Rachid

Sandrine

Valérie

Près du café...
AMINA J'ai très faim. J'ai envie de manger un sandwich.
SANDRINE Moi aussi, j'ai faim, et puis j'ai soif. J'ai envie d'une bonne boisson. Eh, les garçons, on va au café?

RACHID Moi, je rentre à l'appartement étudier pour un examen de sciences po. David, tu vas au café avec les filles?
DAVID Non, je rentre avec toi. J'ai envie de dessiner un peu.
AMINA Bon, alors, à tout à l'heure.

Au café...
VALÉRIE Bonjour, les filles! Alors, ça va, les études?
AMINA Bof, ça va. Qu'est-ce qu'il y a de bon à manger aujourd'hui?
VALÉRIE Et bien, j'ai une soupe de poisson maison délicieuse! Il y a aussi des sandwichs jambon-fromage, des frites... Et, comme d'habitude, j'ai des éclairs, euh...

VALÉRIE Et pour toi, Amina?
AMINA Hmm... Pour moi, un sandwich jambon-fromage avec des frites.
VALÉRIE Très bien, et je vous apporte du pain tout de suite.
SANDRINE ET AMINA Merci!

Au bar...
VALÉRIE Alors, pour la table d'Amina et Sandrine, une soupe du jour, un sandwich au fromage... Pour la table sept, une limonade, un café, un jus d'orange et trois croissants.
MICHÈLE D'accord! Je prépare ça tout de suite. Mais Madame Forestier, j'ai un problème avec l'addition de la table huit.

VALÉRIE Ah, bon?
MICHÈLE Le monsieur ne comprend pas pourquoi ça coûte onze euros cinquante. Je ne comprends pas non plus. Regardez.
VALÉRIE Ah, non! Avec tout le travail que nous avons cet après-midi, des problèmes d'addition aussi?!

ACTIVITÉS

1 **Identifiez** Trouvez à qui correspond chacune (*each*) des phrases suivantes. Écrivez **A** pour Amina, **D** pour David, **M** pour Michèle, **R** pour Rachid, **S** pour Sandrine et **V** pour Valérie.

1. _M_ Je ne comprends pas non plus.
2. _V_ Vous prenez du jus d'orange uniquement le matin.
3. _S_ Tu bois de l'eau aussi?
4. _M_ Je prépare ça tout de suite.
5. _A_ Je ne bois pas de limonade.

6. _S_ Je vais apprendre à préparer des éclairs.
7. _D_ J'ai envie de dessiner un peu.
8. _V_ Je vous apporte du pain tout de suite.
9. _R_ Moi, je rentre à l'appartement étudier pour un examen de sciences po.
10. _A_ Qu'est-ce qu'il y a de bon à manger aujourd'hui?

Practice more at **vhlcentral.com**.

OPTIONS

Avant de regarder la vidéo Before viewing the video, have students work in pairs and write a list of words and expressions that they might hear in a video episode entitled **L'heure du déjeuner**.

Regarder la vidéo Show the video episode and tell students to check off the words or expressions they hear on their lists. Then show the episode again and have students give you a play-by-play description of the action. Write their descriptions on the board.

Amina et Sandrine déjeunent au café.

SANDRINE Oh, Madame Forestier, j'adore! Un jour, je vais apprendre à préparer des éclairs. Et une bonne soupe maison. Et beaucoup d'autres choses.
AMINA Mais pas aujourd'hui. J'ai trop faim!
SANDRINE Alors, je prends la soupe et un sandwich au fromage.

VALÉRIE Et comme boisson?
SANDRINE Une bouteille d'eau minérale, s'il vous plaît. Tu bois de l'eau aussi? Avec deux verres, alors.

VALÉRIE Ah, ça y est! Je comprends! La boisson gazeuse coûte un euro vingt-cinq, pas un euro soixante-quinze. C'est noté, Michèle?
MICHÈLE Merci, Madame Forestier. Excusez-moi. Je vais expliquer ça au monsieur. Et voilà, tout est prêt pour la table d'Amina et Sandrine.
VALÉRIE Merci, Michèle.

À la table des filles...
VALÉRIE Voilà, une limonade, un café, un jus d'orange et trois croissants.
AMINA Oh? Mais Madame Forestier, je ne bois pas de limonade.
VALÉRIE Et vous prenez du jus d'orange uniquement le matin, n'est-ce pas? Ah! Excusez-moi, les filles!

Expressions utiles

Talking about food

- **Moi aussi, j'ai faim, et puis j'ai soif.**
  Me too, I am hungry, and I am thirsty as well.
- **J'ai envie d'une bonne boisson.**
  I feel like having a nice drink.
- **Qu'est-ce qu'il y a de bon à manger aujourd'hui?**
  What looks good on the menu today?
- **Une soupe de poisson maison délicieuse.**
  A delicious homemade fish soup.
- **Je vais apprendre à préparer des éclairs.**
  I am going to learn (how) to prepare/make éclairs.
- **Je prends la soupe.**
  I'll have the soup.
- **Tu bois de l'eau aussi?**
  Are you drinking water too?
- **Vous prenez du jus d'orange uniquement le matin.**
  You only have orange juice in the morning.

Additional vocabulary

- **On va au café?**
  Shall we go to the café?
- **Bof, ça va.**
  So-so.
- **comme d'habitude**
  as usual
- **Le monsieur ne comprend pas pourquoi ça coûte onze euros cinquante.**
  The gentleman doesn't understand why this costs 11,50€.
- **Je ne comprends pas non plus.**
  I don't understand either.
- **Je prépare ça tout de suite.**
  I am going to prepare this right away.
- **Ça y est! Je comprends!**
  That's it! I get it!
- **C'est noté?**
  Understood?/Got it?
- **Tout est prêt.**
  Everything is ready.

Expressions utiles
- Model the pronunciation of the **Expressions utiles** and have students repeat after you.
- As you work through the list, point out the forms of the verbs **prendre** and **boire** and the partitive articles. Tell students that these verbs and the partitive articles will be formally presented in the **Structures** section.
- Ask students questions about foods and beverages using the vocabulary in the **Expressions utiles**. Examples: **Vous prenez du jus d'orange uniquement le matin? Quand est-ce que vous avez envie de boire de l'eau?**

1 Expansions
- For additional practice, give students these items. **11. Le monsieur ne comprend pas pourquoi ça coûte 11,50€. (M) 12. J'ai faim et puis j'ai soif. (S) 13. Mais pas aujourd'hui. J'ai trop faim! (A) 14. Non, je rentre avec toi. (D)**
- Write these adverbial expressions on the board: **non plus, aussi,** and **tout de suite.** Have students create sentences with them.

2 Suggestion Have students work in groups of six. Write each sentence on a strip of paper. Make a set of sentences for each group, then distribute them to students. Tell them to read their sentences aloud and arrange them in the proper order.

2 Expansion Have students create sentences to fill in the missing parts of the story.

3 Suggestion Before doing this activity, have the class brainstorm vocabulary and expressions they might use in this activity and write their ideas on the board.

2 Mettez dans l'ordre Numérotez les phrases suivantes dans l'ordre correspondant à l'histoire.

- a. __5__ Michèle a un problème avec l'addition.
- b. __3__ Amina prend (*gets*) un sandwich jambon-fromage.
- c. __1__ Sandrine dit qu'elle (*says that she*) a soif.
- d. __2__ Rachid rentre à l'appartement.
- e. __4__ Valérie va chercher du pain.
- f. __6__ Tout est prêt pour la table d'Amina et Sandrine.

3 Conversez Au moment où Valérie apporte le plateau (*tray*) de la table sept à Sandrine et Amina, Michèle apporte le plateau de Sandrine et Amina à la table sept. Avec trois partenaires, écrivez la conversation entre Michèle et les client(e)s et jouez-la devant la classe.

ressources

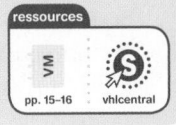

VM
pp. 15–16

vhlcentral

A C T I V I T É S

O P T I O N S

Pairs Have students work in pairs. Tell them to combine sentences in **Expressions utiles** with other words and expressions they know to create mini-dialogues. Example:
—**Qu'est-ce qu'il y a de bon aujourd'hui?**
—**Il y a une soupe de poisson maison délicieuse.**

Extra Practice Ask volunteers to act out the **Roman-photo** episode for the class. Tell them that it is not necessary to memorize the episode or to stick strictly to its content. They should try to get the general meaning across with the vocabulary and expressions they know, and they should also feel free to be creative. Give them time to prepare.

ESPACE ROMAN-PHOTO **157**

Reading
Video: *Flash culture*

Section Goals

In this section, students will:
- learn about the role of the café in French life
- learn some terms for describing how people eat and drink
- learn about some common snacks in different francophone countries
- read about the cafés of **North Africa**
- view authentic cultural footage

> **Instructional Resources**
> vhlcentral.com: Video;
> SAM Answer Key;
> Videoscript; reference tools

Culture à la loupe

Avant la lecture Have students look at the photos and describe what they see. Then ask: **Allez-vous au café? Où? Quand?**

Lecture Point out that you can order a drink or food at the bar (**le bar**) and pay less than sitting at a table. Sitting on the **terrasse** is even more expensive. The menu posted outside a café usually indicates the different **tarifs**.

Après la lecture Ask students what aspects of French cafés they find interesting or appealing.

1 Expansion Have students correct the false statements. For additional practice, give students these items. **11. Aller au café est une tradition récente en France. (Faux.) 12. Les étudiants et les adultes fréquentent les cafés en France. (Vrai.)**

CULTURE À LA LOUPE

Le café français

À Toute Heure

Quiches	12,50€
Pâtisseries	4,50€
Omelettes	9,25€
Thé	5,00€
Glaces	7,50€
Café	4,50€
Cappuccino	7,00€
Chocolat chaud	5,50€

Le premier café français, le Procope, a ouvert° ses portes à Paris en 1686. C'était° un lieu° pour boire du café, qui était une boisson exotique à l'époque°. On pouvait° aussi manger un sorbet dans des tasses en porcelaine. Benjamin Franklin et Napoléon Bonaparte fréquentaient° le Procope.

Le café est une partie importante de la culture française. Les Français adorent passer du temps° à la terrasse des cafés. C'est un des symboles de l'art de vivre° à la française.

On peut aller au café à tout moment de la journée: le matin, pour prendre un café et un croissant en lisant le journal, le midi pour déjeuner entre collègues, et le soir après le travail pour boire un verre et se détendre° avec des amis. Les étudiants aussi se retrouvent souvent° au café, près de leur lycée ou de leur faculté, pour étudier ou pour prendre un verre.

Il y a de très célèbres° cafés à Paris: «Les Deux Magots» ou «Café de Flore» par exemple, dans le quartier° de Saint-Germain. Ils sont connus° parce que c'était le rendez-vous des intellectuels et des écrivains°, comme Jean-Paul Sartre, Simone de Beauvoir et Albert Camus, après la Deuxième Guerre mondiale°.

a ouvert *opened*   **C'était** *It was*   **lieu** *place*   **à l'époque** *at the time*   **pouvait** *could*   **fréquentaient** *used to frequent*
passer du temps *spending time*   **vivre** *living*   **se détendre** *to relax*   **souvent** *often*   **célèbres** *famous*   **quartier** *neighborhood*
connus *known*   **écrivains** *writers*   **Deuxième Guerre mondiale** *World War II*

A C T I V I T É S

1   **Vrai ou faux?** Indiquez si les phrases sont **vraies** ou **fausses**.

1. Le premier café parisien date de 1686.   Vrai.
2. Le café était une boisson courante (*common*) aux années 1600.   Faux.
3. Napoléon Bonaparte et Benjamin Franklin sont d'anciens clients du Procope.   Vrai.
4. Le café est une partie importante de la culture française.   Vrai.
5. Les Français évitent (*avoid*) les terrasses des cafés.   Faux.

6. Le matin, les Français prennent du jambon et du fromage.   Faux.
7. Les Français mangent rarement au café à midi.   Faux.
8. Les étudiants se retrouvent souvent avec leurs amis au café.   Vrai.
9. «Les Deux Magots» et le «Café de Flore» sont deux cafés célèbres à Paris.   Vrai.
10. Les intellectuels français fréquentent les cafés après la Première Guerre mondiale.   Faux.

O P T I O N S

Cultural Comparison Have students work in groups of three and compare French cafés to the cafés they frequent. Tell them to list the similarities and differences in a two-column chart under the headings **Similitudes** and **Différences**. Have two groups get together and compare their lists.

Extra Practice Have students look at the **À Toute Heure** menu. Ask them what they are having and how much it costs. Examples: **Qu'est-ce que vous prenez? Combien coûte le chocolat chaud?** Alternatively, this activity can be done in pairs.

LE FRANÇAIS QUOTIDIEN

J'ai faim!

avoir les crocs	*to be hungry*
avoir un petit creux	*to be slightly hungry*
boire à petites gorgées	*to sip*
bouffer	*to eat*
dévorer	*to devour*
grignoter	*to snack on*
mourir de faim	*to be starving*
siroter	*to sip (with pleasure)*

LE MONDE FRANCOPHONE

Des spécialités à grignoter°

Voici quelques spécialités à grignoter dans les pays et régions francophones.

En Afrique du Nord la merguez (saucisse épicée°) et le makroud (pâtisserie° au miel° et aux dattes)

En Côte d'Ivoire l'aloco (bananes plantains frites°)

En France le pan-bagnat (sandwich avec de la salade, des tomates, des œufs durs° et du thon°) et les crêpes (pâte° cuite° composée de farine° et de lait, de forme ronde)

À la Martinique les accras de morue° (beignets° à la morue)

Au Québec la poutine (frites avec du fromage fondu° et de la sauce)

Au Sénégal le chawarma (de la viande°, des oignons et des tomates dans du pain pita)

grignoter snack on saucisse épicée spicy sausage pâtisserie pastry miel honey frites fried œufs durs hard-boiled eggs thon tuna pâte batter cuite cooked farine flour morue cod beignets fritters fondu melted viande meat

PORTRAIT

Les cafés nord-africains

Comme en France, les cafés ont une grande importance culturelle en Afrique du Nord. C'est le lieu où les amis se rencontrent pour discuter° ou pour jouer aux cartes° ou aux dominos. Les cafés offrent° une variété de boissons, mais ils n'offrent pas d'alcool. La boisson typique, au café comme à la maison, est le

thé à la menthe°. Il a peu de caféine, mais il a des vertus énergisantes et il favorise la digestion. En général, ce sont les hommes qui le° préparent. C'est la boisson qu'on vous sert° quand vous êtes invité, et ce n'est pas poli de refuser!

pour discuter to chat jouer aux cartes play cards offrent offer menthe mint le it on vous sert you are served

MUSIQUE À FOND

Daniel Bélanger

Date de naissance: 26 décembre 1961
Lieu de naissance: Montréal, Québec
Métier: auteur-compositeur-interprète

L'un des meilleurs compositeurs québécois depuis plus de 25 ans, il a reçu plusieurs prix dans le domaine de la musique.
Go to vhlcentral.com to learn more about **Daniel Bélanger** and his music.

2 Compréhension Complétez les phrases.

1. Jouer aux ___cartes/dominos___ dans les cafés d'Afrique du Nord est une chose normale.
2. On ne peut pas y boire de/d' ___alcool___.
3. Les hommes préparent ___le thé à la menthe___ dans les pays d'Afrique du Nord.
4. Il n'est pas poli de ___refuser___ une tasse de thé en Afrique du Nord.
5. Si vous aimez les frites, vous allez aimer ___la poutine___ au Québec.

3 Un café francophone
Un(e) ami(e) a envie de créer un café francophone. Par groupes de quatre, préparez une liste de suggestions pour aider votre ami(e): noms pour le café, idées (*ideas*) pour le menu, prix, heures, etc. Indiquez où le café va être situé et qui va fréquenter ce café.

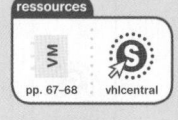

ressources

VM pp. 67–68 vhlcentral

Practice more at **vhlcentral.com**.

ACTIVITÉS

Le français quotidien Model the pronunciation of each term and have students repeat it. Then ask questions based on the vocabulary. Examples: **Avez-vous les crocs? Vous mangez quoi quand vous avez les crocs? Vous dévorez votre déjeuner?**

Portrait Coffee was first consumed in Ethiopia in the ninth century, and it became controversial in the Islamic world during the beverage's early history. Many regarded it with suspicion and blamed its stimulating properties for inviting subversive thought and tempting drinkers away from religious observance.

Le monde francophone Have students read the text. Tell them to choose a specialty they would like to eat from the list. Then ask: **Quelle spécialité préférez-vous manger? Pourquoi?**

Musique à fond Point out to students that they will find supporting activities and information at **vhlcentral.com**.

2 Expansion Have students write three more fill-in-the-blank statements based on **Portrait** and **Le monde francophone**. Then have them work in groups of three and take turns reading their statements while the other group members respond.

3 Expansion Have groups present their suggestions to the class. Then have the class discuss the role that the country's culture played in forming their ideas. For example, did it affect the name, the hours of operation, the menu, or the prices?

Flash culture Tell students that they will learn more about French cafés by watching a variety of real-life images narrated by Benjamin. Show the video segment, then have students jot down at least three examples of things they see. You can also use the activities in the video manual in class to reinforce this **Flash culture** or assign them as homework.

Pairs Have students work in pairs. Tell them to take turns stating that they like one of the specialties in the list **Des spécialités à grignoter** at their house. The other person should guess where they live based on the snack named. Example: **Étudiant(e) 1: Chez moi, on aime les accras de morue. Étudiant(e) 2: Alors tu habites à la Martinique, n'est-ce pas?**

Extra Practice Have students write five true/false statements based on the information in the **J'ai faim!** and **Des spécialités à grignoter** sections. Then tell them to exchange papers with a classmate and complete the activity. Remind them to verify their answers.

ESPACE CULTURE **159**

4B.1

Section Goals

In this section, students will learn:
- the verbs **prendre**, **apprendre**, and **comprendre**
- the verb **boire**
- partitive articles

Instructional Resources
vhlcentral.com: Lab MP3s; SAM Answer Key; ***Essayez!*** and ***Mise en pratique*** answers; Lab Audioscript; Activity Pack (***Feuilles d'activités***); reference tools

Suggestions

- Point out that **prendre** means *to have* when saying what one is having to eat or drink, but it cannot be used to express possession. For possession, **avoir** must be used.
- Point out to students that all the singular forms of **prendre** sound the same. Make sure that students pronounce the **n** sound in **prennent**.
- Ask students if they can think of any English words related to **apprendre** (*apprentice*) and **comprendre** (*comprehend*).
- Work through the forms of **boire**, asking students what they drink most often or rarely. Model a response by first saying what you drink: **Je bois souvent ____. Qu'est-ce que vous buvez?**
- Write the conjugation of **boire** on the board with the singular forms in one column and the plural forms in another column. Draw a line around the forms that have **oi**. Tell students that **boire** is a "boot verb."

Boîte à outils

You can use the construction **apprendre à** + [*infinitive*] to mean *to learn to do something.* Example: J'**apprends à** nager. *I'm learning to swim.*

ressources

WB
pp. 51–52

LM
p. 31

vhlcentral

The verbs *prendre* and *boire*; Partitives

Tutorial

Point de départ The verbs **prendre** (*to take, to have food or drink*) and **boire** (*to drink*), like **être, avoir,** and **aller,** are irregular.

Je prends la soupe et un sandwich au fromage.

Je ne bois pas de limonade.

prendre			
je prends	*I take*	**nous prenons**	*we take*
tu prends	*you take*	**vous prenez**	*you take*
il/elle/on prend	*he/she/it/one takes*	**ils/elles prennent**	*they take*

Brigitte **prend** le métro le soir.
Brigitte takes the subway in the evening.

Nous **prenons** un café chez moi.
We are having a coffee at my house.

- The forms of the verbs **apprendre** (*to learn*) and **comprendre** (*to understand*) follow the same pattern as that of **prendre**.

Tu ne **comprends** pas l'espagnol?
Don't you understand Spanish?

Elles **apprennent** beaucoup.
They're learning a lot.

Je ne comprends pas non plus.

Un jour, je vais apprendre à préparer des éclairs.

boire			
je bois	*I drink*	**nous buvons**	*we drink*
tu bois	*you drink*	**vous buvez**	*you drink*
il/elle/on boit	*he/she/it/one drinks*	**ils/elles boivent**	*they drink*

Ton père **boit** un jus d'orange.
Your father is drinking an orange juice.

Vous **buvez** un chocolat chaud, M. Dion?
Are you drinking hot chocolate, Mr. Dion?

Je **bois** toujours du lait.
I always drink milk.

Nous ne **buvons** pas de café.
We don't drink coffee.

160 *cent soixante*

Partitives

- Use partitive articles in French to express *some* or *any*. To form the partitive, use the preposition **de** followed by a definite article. Although the words *some* and *any* are often omitted in English, the partitive must always be used in French.

masculine singular	feminine singular	singular noun beginning with a vowel
du thé	**de la** limonade	**de l'**eau

Je bois **du** thé chaud.
I drink (some) hot tea.

Tu bois **de la** limonade?
Are you drinking (any) lemon soda?

Elle prend **de l'**eau?
Is she having (some) water?

- Note that partitive articles are only used with non-count nouns (nouns whose quantity cannot be expressed by a number).

PARTITIVE NON-COUNT
ARTICLE   NOUN
Tu prends **du** pain tous les jours.
You have (some) bread every day.

INDEFINITE COUNT
ARTICLE   NOUN
Tu prends **une** banane, aussi.
You have a banana, too.

- The article **des** also means *some*, but it is the plural form of the indefinite article, not the partitive.

PARTITIVE
ARTICLE
Vous prenez **de la limonade**.
You're having (some) lemon soda.

INDEFINITE
ARTICLE
Nous prenons **des croissants**.
We're having (some) croissants.

- As with the indefinite articles, the partitives **du**, **de la** and **de l'** also become **de** (meaning *not any*) in a negative sentence.

Est-ce qu'il y a **du** lait?
Is there (any) milk?

Non, il n'y a pas **de** lait.
No, there isn't (any) milk.

Prends-tu **de la** soupe?
Will you have (some) soup?

Non, je ne prends pas **de** soupe.
No, I'm not having (any) soup.

À noter

The partitives follow the same pattern of contraction as the possessive **de** + [*definite article*] you learned in **Structures 3A.2: du, de la, de l'**.

Boîte à outils

Partitives are used to say that you want *some* of an item, whereas indefinite articles are used to say that you want *a whole item* or *several whole items*.
Tu prends de la pizza?
(part of a whole pizza)
Tu prends une pizza?
(a whole pizza)

Suggestions
- Write a summary chart of the articles on the board with these headings: Definite Articles, Indefinite Articles, and Partitive Articles. Briefly review definite and indefinite articles.
- Model the pronunciation of the example sentences and have students repeat them.
- Make sure students understand the idea of count nouns and non-count nouns. Have students classify vocabulary from **Espace contextes**.
- Point out that some nouns can be both count and non-count, depending on context.
- Point out that the use of partitives differs whether you are at home or in a café/restaurant. It is preferable to use **de** + [definite article] when at home or at someone's house, and indefinite articles when in a restaurant. Examples: **Bois-tu du café?** (at home) **Je prends un café.** (in a restaurant)

Essayez! Have students create new sentences orally or in writing by changing the subjects of the sentences.

Essayez! *Complétez les phrases. Utilisez la forme correcte du verbe entre parenthèses et l'article qui convient.*

1. Ma sœur ___prend___ (prendre) ___des___ éclairs.
2. Tes parents ___boivent___ (boire) ___du___ café?
3. Louise ne ___boit___ (boire) pas ___de___ thé.
4. Est-ce qu'il y ___a___ (avoir) ___du___ sucre?
5. Nous ___buvons___ (boire) ___de la___ limonade.
6. Non, merci. Je ne ___prends___ (prendre) pas ___de___ frites.
7. Vous ___prenez___ (prendre) ___un___ taxi?
8. Nous ___apprenons___ (apprendre) ___le___ français.

OPTIONS

Extra Practice Distribute empty food and drink containers with labels or pictures of items to groups of three students. Call out the items saying: **du lait**, **des frites**, etc. The group with the item should hold up the package or photo and say: **Voici/Nous avons du lait!** To practice negative partitives, have them say: **Il n'y a pas de ____.**

Extra Practice Arrange students in rows of six. The first person in each row has a piece of paper. Call out the infinitive of **boire**, **prendre**, **apprendre**, or **comprendre**. Silently, the first student writes the **je** form and passes the paper to the student behind him or her. That student writes the **tu** form and passes the paper on. The last person holds up the completed paper. Have students rotate places before the next verb.

1 **Expansion** Have students write two more fill-in-the-blank sentences. Tell them to exchange papers with a partner and complete the sentences.

2 **Suggestion** Have students ask the questions, then call on other individuals to answer them. Examples: **Oui, on prend ____.** **Non, on ne prend pas de/d' ____.**

3 **Suggestion** This activity can also be done in pairs. One person should say the sentence and the other person responds. Remind students to switch roles after items 1–3.

Mise en pratique

1 **Au café** Indiquez l'article correct.

MODÈLE

Avez-vous ___*du*___ lait froid?

1. Prenez-vous ___du/un___ thé glacé?
2. Je voudrais ___une___ baguette, s'il vous plaît.
3. Elle prend ___un___ croissant.
4. Nous ne prenons pas ___de___ sucre dans le café.
5. Tu ne laisses pas ___de___ pourboire?
6. Vous mangez ___des___ frites.
7. Zeina commande ___une___ boisson gazeuse.
8. Voici ___de l'/une___ eau minérale.
9. Nous mangeons ___du___ pain.
10. Je ne prends pas ___de___ fromage.

2 **Des suggestions** Laurent est au café avec des amis et il fait (*makes*) des suggestions. Que suggère-t-il?

▶ **MODÈLE**

On prend du jus d'orange?

1. On prend de la limonade?   **2.** On prend de l'eau minérale?   **3.** On prend du thé?   **4.** On prend des sandwichs?

3 **Au restaurant** Alain est au restaurant avec toute sa famille. Il note les préférences de tout le monde. Utilisez le verbe indiqué.

MODÈLE

Oncle Lucien aime bien le café. (prendre) *Il prend un café.*

1. Marie-Hélène et papa adorent le thé. (prendre)
   Ils prennent un thé.
2. Tu adores le chocolat chaud. (boire)
   Tu bois un chocolat chaud.
3. Vous aimez bien le jus de pomme. (prendre)
   Vous prenez un jus de pomme.
4. Mes nièces aiment la limonade. (boire)
   Elles boivent une limonade.
5. Tu aimes les boissons gazeuses. (prendre)
   Tu prends une boisson gazeuse.
6. Vous adorez le café. (boire)
   Vous buvez un café.

 Practice more at **vhlcentral.com**.

Communication

4 Au menu Vous allez dans un petit café où il y a peu de choix. Vous demandez au serveur/à la serveuse s'il/si elle a d'autres options. Avec un(e) partenaire, jouez (*play*) les deux rôles. Answers will vary.

CAFÉ "LE BON PRIX"

Soupe à l'oignon..............................3,50€
Sandwich fromage..............................4€
Frites maison..............................2,75€
Eau minérale..............................2€
Jus de pomme..............................2,50€

MODÈLE

Étudiant(e) 1: *Vous avez du chocolat chaud?*
Étudiant(e) 2: *Non, je n'ai pas de chocolat chaud, mais j'ai...*

5 Je bois, je prends Votre professeur va vous donner une feuille d'activités. Circulez dans la classe pour demander à vos camarades s'ils prennent rarement, une fois (*once*) par semaine ou tous les jours la boisson ou le plat (*dish*) indiqués. Écrivez (*Write*) les noms sur la feuille, puis présentez vos réponses à la classe. Answers will vary.

MODÈLE

Étudiant(e) 1: *Est-ce que tu bois du café?*
Étudiant(e) 2: *Oui, je bois du café une fois par semaine. Et toi?*

Boisson ou plat	rarement	une fois par semaine	tous les jours
1. café		Didier	
2. fromage			
3. thé			
4. soupe			
5. chocolat chaud			
6. jambon			

6 Après les cours Vous retrouvez des amis au café. Par groupes de quatre, jouez (*play*) les rôles d'un(e) serveur/serveuse et de trois clients. Utilisez les mots de la liste et présentez la scène à la classe. Answers will vary.

addition	chocolat chaud	frites
avoir faim	coûter	prix
avoir soif	croissant	sandwich
boisson	eau minérale	soupe
éclair	jambon	limonade

---

2 Suggestion You may want to point out that it is sometimes possible to use either a partitive or an indefinite article. The choice depends on whether the speaker interprets the noun as count (e.g., a glass of iced tea, a bottle of mineral water) or non-count (e.g., some iced tea, some mineral water).

4 Suggestion Encourage students to also use the verbs **boire**, **apprendre**, **prendre**, and **comprendre** in their dialogues.

5 Suggestion Have two volunteers read the **modèle** aloud. Then distribute the **Feuilles d'activités** found in the Activity Pack on the Supersite.

6 Suggestions
• Bring in a few props, such as cups, bottles, and plates, for students to use in their role-plays.
• Have volunteers perform their role-plays for the class, then vote on the best one.

OPTIONS

Extra Practice Write this activity on the board. Tell students to add the missing words and form complete sentences.
1. Marc / boire / eau / et / prendre / sandwich / jambon
2. Solange / prendre / soupe / et / boire / boisson gazeuse
3. Nous / boire / café / lait / et / prendre / éclairs
4. Henri et Paul / prendre / hot-dogs / et / frites
5. Anne / prendre / soupe / poisson / et / verre / thé glacé

Extra Practice Bring in pictures or magazine photos of people consuming food, drink, or taking various things. Have students describe what the people in the pictures are doing using **boire**, **prendre**, and partitive articles.

4B.2

Section Goals

In this section, students will learn regular -ir verbs.

Instructional Resources
vhlcentral.com:
Activity Pack; Lab MP3s;
SAM Answer Key; **Essayez!**
and **Mise en pratique**
answers; Lab Audioscript;
reference tools

Suggestions

• Model the pronunciation of -ir verbs and have students repeat them.
• Introduce the verbs by saying what time you finish teaching today and asking students what time they finish classes. Examples: **Aujourd'hui, je finis d'enseigner à cinq heures. Et vous, à quelle heure finissez-vous les cours?** Then ask students to ask a classmate: **Et toi, à quelle heure finis-tu, aujourd'hui?**
• Point out that the singular forms of -ir verbs all sound the same.
• Call students' attention to the -iss- in the plural forms of -ir verbs.
• Remind students that -ss- sounds like an *s*, but a single **s** between vowels is pronounced like a *z*.
• Tell students that many -ir verbs are derived from adjectives, such as **grand, rouge, gros,** or **vieux.**
• Ask students questions using -ir verbs in the present and also with the **futur proche.** Examples: **Quand allez-vous finir vos études? Réussissez-vous vos examens?**

Essayez! For additional practice, give students these items. **9. Comment _____ (réagir)-vous quand vous avez peur? (réagissez) 10. Vos grands-parents _____ (vieillir) ensemble. (vieillissent)**

Regular -ir verbs

 Tutorial

Point de départ In **Leçon 2A,** you learned the pattern of -er verbs. Verbs that end in -ir follow a different pattern.

finir	
je fin**is**	nous fin**issons**
tu fin**is**	vous fin**issez**
il/elle/on fin**it**	ils/elles fin**issent**

Je **finis** mes devoirs.
I'm finishing my homework.

Alain et Chloé **finissent** leurs sandwichs.
Alain and Chloé are finishing their sandwiches.

• Here are some other verbs that follow the same pattern as **finir.**

Other regular -ir verbs			
choisir	to choose	réfléchir (à)	to think (about), to reflect (on)
grandir	to grow		
grossir	to gain weight	réussir (à)	to succeed (in doing something)
maigrir	to lose weight		
obéir (à)	to obey	rougir	to blush
réagir	to react	vieillir	to grow old

Marc **grossit** pendant les vacances.
Marc gains weight on vacation.

Tu **réagis** vite!
You react quickly!

Je **choisis** un chocolat chaud.
I choose a hot chocolate.

Vous **réfléchissez** à ma question?
Are you thinking about my question?

Une minute... je réfléchis.

Je choisis un sandwich.

Boîte à outils

Use the constructions **finir de** + [*infinitive*] and **choisir de** + [*infinitive*] to mean *to finish doing* and *to choose to do something.*

Je **finis de manger.**
I'm finishing eating.

Nous **choisissons de rester** ici.
We choose to stay here.

À noter

In **Leçon 2A,** you learned the phrase **être reçu(e) à un examen.** You can also use the phrase **réussir un examen** to mean *to pass a test or exam.*

ressources

WB
pp. 51-52

LM
p. 32

vhlcentral

Essayez! **Complétez les phrases.**

1. Quand on ne mange pas beaucoup, on ___maigrit___ (maigrir).
2. Il ___réussit___ (réussir) son examen.
3. Vous ___finissez___ (finir) vos devoirs?
4. Lundi prochain nous ___finissons___ (finir) le livre.

5. Les enfants ___grandissent___ (grandir) très vite (*fast*).
6. Vous ___choisissez___ (choisir) le fromage?
7. Ils n' ___obéissent___ (obéir) pas à leur parents.
8. Je ___réfléchis___ (réfléchir) beaucoup à ce problème.

Le français vivant

Café du Marché

Formule petit-déjeuner simple   5,50€

boisson chaude + croissant +
jus de fruits (au choix°) ou
boisson chaude + mini-baguette avec
du beurre + jus de fruits (au choix)

❀❀❀

Formule petit-déjeuner complet   7,50€

boisson chaude +
sandwich jambon-fromage +
jus de fruits (au choix)

Boissons

Café .... 1,50€
Café déca .... 1,60€
Café crème .... 2,00€
Chocolat chaud ..... 2,20€
Thé .... 2,20€

Eau minérale .... 2,50€
Jus de fruits .... 2,80€
Limonade .... 2,80€

au choix *your choice of*

 Répondez Avec un(e) partenaire, discutez de la carte et de ces (*these*) situations. Utilisez des verbes en **-ir**.

1. Je prends quatre croissants.
2. J'ai très faim.
3. Je ne mange pas beaucoup.
4. Je ne commande pas encore.
5. Je bois toute la bouteille d'eau minérale.

O P T I O N S

Pairs List various categories of things on the board, such as classes, foods, and beverages, and have students discuss their preferences using the verb **choisir**. Example: **Boissons: je choisis un jus d'orange**. Then have them guess other people's preferences in the same categories.

Game Divide the class into two teams. Choose one team member at a time to go to the board, alternating between teams. Say a subject pronoun and an infinitive. The person at the board must write and say the correct verb form. Example: **tu: choisir (tu choisis)**. Give a point for each correct answer. The team with the most points at the end of the game wins.

Le français vivant
• Ask volunteers to share their responses with the class.
• Have students act out a scene in which they order from the café menu. Encourage them to use as many **-ir** verbs as possible. Ask volunteers to perform their scene for the class.

ESPACE STRUCTURES

2 Suggestion Go over the correct answers with the class. Then ask two volunteers to act out the conversation.

3 Expansion Have students create additional sentences using these verbs with different subjects.

Mise en pratique

1 **On fait quoi?** Choisissez la forme correcte du verbe en **-ir**.

1. Nous (finissons / grandissons) nos devoirs avant le dîner.
2. Ursula (choisis / choisit) un croissant.
3. Eva et Léo (rougissent / réussissent) à faire un gâteau.
4. Omar (réfléchit / réfléchis) à ses problèmes.
5. Nous essayons de ne pas (grandir / grossir).
6. Tu manges une salade parce que tu essaies de (vieillir / maigrir)?

2 **Au restaurant** Complétez le dialogue avec la forme correcte du verbe entre parenthèses.

SERVEUR   Vous désirez?

MARC   Nous (1) _____réfléchissons_____ (réfléchir) encore.

FANNY   Je pense savoir ce que je veux (*know what I want*).

SERVEUR   Que (2) _____choisissez_____ (choisir)-vous, Mademoiselle?

FANNY   Je (3) _____choisis_____ (choisir) un hamburger avec des frites. Et toi?

MARC   Euh... je (4) _____réfléchis_____ (réfléchir). La soupe ou la salade, je pense... Oui, je prends la salade.

SERVEUR   Très bien. Je vous apporte ça tout de suite (*right away*).

FANNY   Tu n'as pas très faim?

MARC   Non, pas trop. Et je suis au régime (*on a diet*). J'ai besoin de (5) _____maigrir_____ (maigrir) un peu.

FANNY   Tu (6) _____réussis_____ (réussir) déjà. Ton jean est trop grand. Tu n'as pas envie de partager mon éclair?

MARC   Mais non! Je vais (7) _____grossir_____ (grossir)!

FANNY   Alors, je (8) _____finis_____ (finir) l'éclair.

3 **Complétez** Complétez les phrases avec la forme correcte des verbes de la liste. N'utilisez les verbes qu'une seule fois.

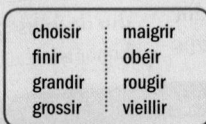

choisir	maigrir
finir	obéir
grandir	rougir
grossir	vieillir

1. Nous _____choisissons_____ l'endroit où nous allons déjeuner.
2. Corinne _____rougit_____ quand elle a honte.
3. Mes frères cadets _____grandissent_____ encore. Ils sont déjà (*already*) très grands!
4. Vous ne mangez pas assez et vous _____maigrissez_____.
5. Nous _____obéissons_____ aux profs.
6. Sylvie _____finit_____ ses études cette année.
7. Mes grands-parents _____vieillissent_____.
8. Quand on mange beaucoup de chocolat, on _____grossit_____.

Practice more at **vhlcentral.com**.

Communication

4 **Ça, c'est moi!** Avec un(e) partenaire, complétez les phrases suivantes pour parler de vous-même. Answers will vary.

1. Je ne finis jamais (de)...
2. Je grossis quand...
3. Je maigris quand...
4. Au restaurant, je choisis souvent...
5. Je réfléchis quelquefois (*sometimes*) à...
6. Je réussis toujours (à)...

5 **Assemblez** Avec un(e) partenaire, assemblez les éléments des trois colonnes pour créer des phrases. Attention! Quelques verbes sont irréguliers. Answers will vary.

A	B	C
je	choisir	aujourd'hui
tu	finir	beaucoup
le prof	grandir	cette (*this*)
mon frère	grossir	année
mes parents	maigrir	cours
ma sœur	réfléchir	devoirs
mon/ma petit(e)	réussir	diplôme
ami(e)	rougir	encore
mon/ma camarade	vieillir	problème
de chambre		vite
?		?

6 **Votre vie à la fac** Posez ces questions à un(e) partenaire puis présentez vos réponses à la classe. Answers will vary.

1. Pendant ce semestre, dans quel cours réussis-tu le mieux (*best*)?
2. Comment est-ce que tu choisis un/une camarade de chambre?
3. En général, est-ce que tu réussis aux examens de français? Comment les trouves-tu?
4. Est-ce que tu maigris ou grossis à la fac? Pourquoi?
5. À quelle heure est-ce que tes cours finissent le vendredi? Que fais-tu après les cours?
6. Que font tes parents pour toi quand tu réussis tes examens?
7. Quand fais-tu tes devoirs? À quelle heure finis-tu tes devoirs?

7 **Qui...?** Posez (*Ask*) des questions pour trouver une personne dans la classe qui fait ces (*does these*) choses. Answers will vary.

MODÈLE

Étudiant(e) 1: *Est-ce que tu rougis facilement?*
Étudiant(e) 2: *Non, je ne rougis pas facilement.*

1. rougir facilement (*easily*)
2. réagir vite
3. obéir à ses parents
4. finir toujours ses devoirs
5. choisir bien sa nourriture (*food*)

4 **Suggestion** Call on volunteers to share their information with the rest of the class.

5 **Suggestion** Give students five minutes to write as many sentences as they can using **-ir** verbs. Then have volunteers read some of their sentences aloud or write them on the board.

7 **Suggestion** Remind students to ask and answer using complete sentences. Have them write the name of the person they find for each question. Follow up with questions about what they found out. Example: **Qui finit toujours ses devoirs?**

O P T I O N S

Extra Practice Have students restate these sentences using **-ir** verbs. **1. Mes tantes sont moins jeunes qu'avant** (*than before*). **2. Cédric est moins gros qu'avant. 3. Nous sommes plus grands qu'avant. 4. Vous pensez beaucoup. 5. Je termine mes études.**

Extra Practice Have students write fill-in-the-blank or dehydrated sentences for each of the **-ir** verbs. Then tell them to exchange papers with a partner and complete the activity. Remind students to verify their answers.

ESPACE **SYNTHÈSE**

Révision

Instructional Resources
vhlcentral.com:
Activity Pack (Info Gap Activities); Testing Program; Testing Program MP3s; reference tools

1 Suggestion Have two volunteers read the **modèle** aloud.

1 Expansion Have students write three things they are learning to do. Then have them exchange papers with a partner and ask each other why they are learning to do those things.

2 Suggestions
• Tell students to jot down notes during their interviews.
• Have students report some of their findings to the rest of the class.

3 Suggestion Tell students that a few **centimes** are almost always added to the price of each item if the people sit on the **terrasse**.

4 Suggestion After completing the activity, call on volunteers to state one difference until all options are exhausted.

5 Suggestion Give students five minutes to work with a partner. Then ask volunteers to share their responses with the class.

6 Suggestion Divide the class into pairs and distribute the Info Gap Handouts found in the Activity Pack on the Supersite. Give students ten minutes to complete the activity.

---

1 Ils aiment apprendre Vous demandez à Sylvie et à Jérôme pourquoi ils aiment apprendre. Un(e) partenaire va poser des questions et l'autre partenaire va jouer les rôles de Jérôme et de Sylvie. Answers will vary.

MODÈLE

Étudiant(e) 1: *Pourquoi est-ce que tu apprends à travailler sur l'ordinateur?*
Étudiant(e) 2: *J'apprends parce que j'aime les ordinateurs.*

1.

2.

3.

4.

5.

6.

2 Quelle boisson? Interviewez une personne de votre classe. Que boit-on dans ces circonstances? Ensuite (*Then*), posez les questions à une personne différente. Utilisez des articles partitifs dans vos réponses. Answers will vary.

1. au café
2. au cinéma
3. en classe
4. le dimanche matin
5. le matin très tôt
6. quand il/elle passe des examens
7. quand il/elle a très soif
8. quand il/elle étudie toute la nuit

3 Notre café Vous et votre partenaire allez créer un café français. Choisissez le nom du café et huit boissons. Pour chaque (*each*) boisson, inventez deux prix, un pour le comptoir (*bar*) et un pour la terrasse. Comparez votre café au café d'un autre groupe. Answers will vary.

---

4 La terrasse du café Avec un(e) partenaire, observez les deux dessins et trouvez au minimum quatre différences. Comparez votre liste à la liste d'un autre groupe. Ensuite, écrivez (*write*) un paragraphe sur ces trois personnages en utilisant (*by using*) des verbes en **-ir**. Answers will vary.

MODÈLE

Étudiant(e) 1: *Mylène prend une limonade.*
Étudiant(e) 2: *Mylène prend de la soupe.*

Patrick   Mylène   Djamel

5 Elle prend... Vous êtes dans un café avec cinq membres de votre famille. Quelles boissons et quels plats (*dishes*) de la liste prennent-ils? Parlez avec un(e) partenaire. Les membres de sa famille prennent-ils les mêmes (*same*) choses? Answers will vary.

boisson gazeuse	frites	limonade
café	fromage	pain
chocolat chaud	jambon	sandwich au...
croissant	jus de...	soupe
eau minérale	lait	thé

6 La famille Arnal au café Votre professeur va vous donner, à vous et à votre partenaire, des photos de la famille Arnal. Attention! Ne regardez pas la feuille de votre partenaire. Answers will vary.

MODÈLE

Étudiant(e) 1: *Qui prend un sandwich?*
Étudiant(e) 2: *La grand-mère prend un sandwich.*

OPTIONS

Extra Practice Have students write a brief story about inviting some friends or a date to go to a café and what happens when they are at the café. Tell students that the story can be real or imaginary. Encourage them to be creative.

Extra Practice Have students write five questions that they would like to ask you using the verbs **apprendre**, **comprendre**, **boire**, **prendre**, and **-ir** verbs. Then allow each student the opportunity to ask you one question.

À l'écoute

Audio: Activities

STRATÉGIE

Listening for the gist

Listening for the general idea, or gist, can help you follow what someone is saying even if you can't hear or understand some of the words. When you listen for the gist, you try to capture the essence of what you hear without focusing on individual words.

To help you practice this strategy, you will listen to three sentences. Jot down a brief summary of what you hear.

Préparation

Regardez la photo. Combien de personnes y a-t-il? Où sont Charles et Gina? Qu'est-ce qu'ils vont manger? Boire? Quelle heure est-il? Qu'est-ce qu'ils vont faire (*to do*) cet après-midi?

À vous d'écouter

Écoutez la conversation entre Charles, Gina et leur serveur. Écoutez une deuxième fois (*a second time*) et indiquez quelles activités ils vont faire.

- ✓ 1. acheter un livre
- ✓ 2. aller à la librairie
- ___ 3. aller à l'église
- ✓ 4. aller chez des grands-parents
- ___ 5. boire un coca
- ✓ 6. danser
- ✓ 7. dépenser de l'argent
- ___ 8. étudier
- ✓ 9. manger au restaurant
- ✓ 10. manger un sandwich

Practice more at **vhlcentral.com**.

Compréhension

Un résumé Complétez ce résumé (*summary*) de la conversation entre Charles et Gina avec des mots et expressions de la liste.

aller au cinéma	une eau minérale
aller au gymnase	en boîte de nuit
avec son frère	faim
café	un jus d'orange
chez ses grands-parents	manger au restaurant
des copains	du pain
un croissant	soif

Charles et Gina sont au (1) ___café___. Charles va boire (2) ___une eau minérale___. Gina n'a pas très (3) ___faim___. Elle va manger (4) ___un croissant___. Cet après-midi, Charles va (5) ___aller au gymnase___. Ce soir, il va (6) ___manger au restaurant___ avec (7) ___des copains___. Cet après-midi, Gina va peut-être (8) ___aller au cinéma___. Ce soir, elle va manger (9) ___chez ses grands-parents___. À onze heures, elle va aller (10) ___en boîte de nuit___ avec Charles.

Et vous? Avec un(e) camarade, discutez de vos projets (*plans*) pour ce week-end. Où est-ce que vous allez aller? Qu'est-ce que vous allez faire (*to do*)?

Section Goals

In this section, students will:
- learn to listen for the gist
- listen to and summarize a short paragraph
- listen to a conversation and complete several activities

Instructional Resources
vhlcentral.com: Textbook MP3s; Textbook Audioscript; reference tools

Stratégie
Audioscript Aujourd'hui, c'est dimanche. Ce matin, Marie va aller au café avec une copine. Cet après-midi, elle va aller au centre commercial et ce soir, elle va aller danser.

Préparation Have students look at the photo and describe what they see. Ask them to justify their responses based on visual clues. Then have them guess what they might order at the café and what they might do this afternoon.

À vous d'écouter
Audioscript CHARLES: Alors, Gina, où est-ce que tu vas cet après-midi? Au centre-ville pour du shopping?
GINA: Eh bien, oui. Je cherche un livre pour mon frère. Je vais aller à la librairie Monet, près de l'hôpital. Il y a beaucoup de livres intéressants là-bas.
C: Et après, où vas-tu?
G: Euh... Je vais peut-être aller au cinéma...
SERVEUR: Bonjour. Vous désirez?
C: Pour moi, un sandwich au jambon et une eau minérale, s'il vous plaît.
S: Pour le sandwich, de la baguette ou du pain de campagne?
C: De la baguette, s'il vous plaît.
S: Très bien. Et pour vous, Mademoiselle?
G: Euh... Je ne sais pas... euh... un café, s'il vous plaît. Et un croissant. Je n'ai pas très faim ce midi.
S: D'accord. Merci.
G: Et toi, tu vas où cet après-midi?
C: Je vais aller au gymnase avec Pierre. Et ce soir, je vais manger au restaurant avec des copains et après, on va aller danser.
G: Ah oui? Où ça? En banlieue, près du centre commercial?
C: Non, à la nouvelle boîte de nuit, au centre-ville, près du parc. Tu as envie d'y aller?
G: Au restaurant, non. Je vais

manger chez mes grands-parents ce soir, mais en boîte de nuit, oui, pourquoi pas. À quelle heure?
C: Ben, je passe chez toi après le restaurant, vers onze heures, d'accord?
G: D'accord.
C: Excusez-moi, Monsieur, l'addition, s'il vous plaît.

S: Voilà.
G: C'est combien, pour mon croissant et mon café?
C: Alors, c'est 2,50 pour le croissant et pour le café, c'est... Oh, allez, je t'invite.
G: Merci. C'est gentil.

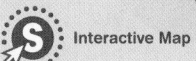
Panorama

un traîneau à chiens*

Section Goals

In this section, students will learn historical and cultural information about Quebec.

Instructional Resources
vhlcentral.com: Digital Image Bank; SAM Answer Key; reference tools

Carte du Québec

- Have students look at the map or use the **Panorama** map from the Digital Image Bank. Ask volunteers to read the names of cities and other geographical features aloud. Model pronunciation as necessary.
- Point out the St. Lawrence River and have students locate the three major cities on its banks.

La province en chiffres

- Point out the flag of Québec province.
- Have volunteers read the sections aloud. After each section, ask students questions about the content.
- Explain that the people of France began using Bourgeois French instead of the King's French after the French Revolution. From then on, the language evolved differently in France and in Québec.

Incroyable mais vrai! Ice bricks are used to build the snow palace. The palace has electrical installations for lighting displays and special effects for the festival.

Le Québec

La province en chiffres

▶ **Superficie:** *1.540.680 km²*

▶ **Population:** *8.263.600*
SOURCE: Statistique Canada

▶ **Industries principales:** *agriculture, exploitation forestière°, hydroélectricité, industrie du bois (papier), minerai° (fer°, cuivre°, or°)*

▶ **Villes principales:** *Montréal, Québec, Trois-Rivières*

▶ **Langues:** *anglais, français*

Le français parlé par les Québécois a une histoire très intéressante. La population française qui s'installe° au Québec en 1608 est composée en majorité de Français du nord-ouest de la France. Ils parlent tous leur langue régionale, comme le normand ou le breton. Beaucoup d'entre eux parlent aussi le français de la cour du roi°, langue qui devient la langue commune de tous les Québécois. Assez isolés du reste du monde francophone et ardents défenseurs de leur langue, les Québécois continuent à parler un français considéré plus pur même° que celui° des Français.

▶ **Monnaie:** *le dollar canadien*

Québécois célèbres

▶ **Justin Trudeau,** *premier ministre du Canada (1971–)*

▶ **Céline Dion,** *chanteuse (1968–)*

▶ **Guy Laliberté,** *fondateur du Cirque du Soleil (1959–)*

▶ **Leonard Cohen,** *poète, romancier, chanteur (1934–2016)*

▶ **Julie Payette,** *astronaute (1963–)*

▶ **Georges St-Pierre,** *pratiquant d'arts martiaux mixtes (1981–)*

exploitation forestière *forestry* **minerai** *ore* **fer** *iron* **cuivre** *copper* **or** *gold* **s'installe** *settles* **cour du roi** *king's court* **même** *even* **celui** *that* **traîneau à chiens** *dogsled* **loger** *house* **Bonhomme** *Snowman (mascot of the carnival)* **de haut** *high* **de profondeur** *deep*

LA BAIE D'HUDSON

LA MER DU LABRADOR

Kangiqsujuaq

Inukjuak

□ Région francophone

LE QUÉBEC

LE CANADA

Chisasibi

TERRE-NEUVE-ET-LABRADOR

Labrador City

La Tabatière

le fleuve Saint-Laurent

la ville de Trois-Rivières

L'ÎLE-DU-PRINCE-ÉDOUARD

Québec

Trois-Rivières

LE NOUVEAU-BRUNSWICK

L'ONTARIO

Ottawa

Montréal

LA NOUVELLE-ÉCOSSE

Toronto

le lac Ontario

LES ÉTATS-UNIS

| 0 | 200 milles |
| 0 | 200 kilomètres |

le Stade olympique, Montréal

L'OCÉAN ATLANTIQUE

Incroyable mais vrai!

Chaque année, pour le carnaval d'hiver de la ville de Québec, 15 personnes travaillent pendant deux mois à la construction d'un immense palais de glace pour loger° le Bonhomme° Carnaval. L'architecture et la taille du palais changent chaque année, mais il mesure parfois jusqu'à 50 mètres de long, 20 m de haut° et 20 m de profondeur°.

OPTIONS

Québécois célèbres Justin Trudeau is the second-youngest Prime Minister of Canada. His father was Pierre Elliott Trudeau, a highly respected Canadian Prime Minister. **Céline Dion** is an internationally famous singer and businesswoman. She records in French and in English, and has also sung in Chinese, Japanese, Italian, German, Spanish, and Latin. **Guy Laliberté** became the first Canadian space tourist in 2011. He also owns an atoll in French Polynesia.

Leonard Cohen received the Prince of Asturias Award in 2011. He was a prolific writer of songs and music, as well as poetry and novels. **Julie Payette** is the chief astronaut for the Canadian Space Agency. She was the first **Québécoise** woman in space and the first Canadian to participate in an International Space Station assembly mission. **Georges St-Pierre** is also an actor; he has made incursions into Hollywood.

La société

Un Québec indépendant

Pour des raisons politiques, économiques et culturelles, un grand nombre de Québécois, surtout les francophones, luttent°, depuis les années soixante, pour un Québec indépendant du Canada. Ils forment le mouvement souverainiste° et font des efforts pour conserver l'identité culturelle *québécoise*. Ces Canadiens français ont pris le nom de québécois pour montrer leur «nationalisme». Les séparatistes ont perdu deux référendums en 1980 et en 1995, mais aujourd'hui, l'indépendance est une idée toujours d'actualité°.

Les destinations

Montréal

Montréal, deuxième ville francophone du monde après Paris, est située sur une île° du fleuve° Saint-Laurent et présente une ambiance américano-européenne. Elle a été fondée° en 1642 et a, à la fois, l'énergie d'un centre urbain moderne et le charme d'une vieille ville de style européen. Ville cosmopolite et largement bilingue de 1,8 million d'habitants, elle attire° beaucoup de touristes et accueille° de nombreux étudiants dans ses quatre universités. La majorité des Montréalais, 65,7%, est de langue maternelle française; 12,5% parlent l'anglais et 21,8% une autre langue. Pourtant°, 51,9% de la population montréalaise peuvent communiquer en français et en anglais.

La musique

Le festival de jazz de Montréal

Le Festival International de Jazz de Montréal est parmi° les plus prestigieux du monde. Avec 1.000 concerts, dont plus de 600 donnés gratuitement en plein air°, le festival attire 3.000 artistes de 30 pays, et près de 2 millions de spectateurs. Le centre-ville, fermé à la circulation, se transforme en un village musical. De grands noms internationaux comme Miles Davis, Ella Fitzgerald, Dizzy Gillespie ou Pat Metheny sont venus au festival, ainsi que° des jazzmen locaux.

L'histoire

La ville de Québec

Capitale de la province de Québec, la ville de Québec est la seule ville d'Amérique du Nord qui a conservé ses fortifications. Fondée par l'explorateur français Samuel de Champlain en 1608, Québec est située sur un rocher°, au bord du° fleuve Saint-Laurent. Elle est connue en particulier pour sa vieille ville, son carnaval d'hiver et le château Frontenac. Les plaines d'Abraham, où les Britanniques ont vaincu° les Français en 1759 pour prendre le contrôle du Canada, servent aujourd'hui de vaste parc public. De nombreux étudiants de l'Université Laval profitent° du charme de cette ville francophone.

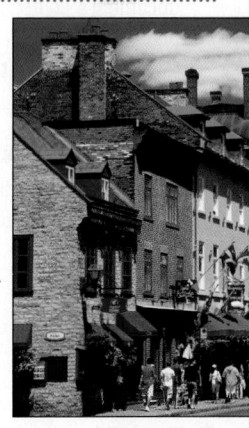

🐍 **Qu'est-ce que vous avez appris?** Répondez aux questions par des phrases complètes.

1. Quelle était la deuxième langue de beaucoup de Français quand ils sont arrivés au Québec?
   La deuxième langue de beaucoup de Français était le français de la cour du roi.
2. Quel est le nom d'une chanteuse québécoise célèbre?
   Céline Dion est une chanteuse québécoise célèbre.
3. Combien de temps et combien de personnes sont nécessaires à la construction du palais de glace?
   Quinze personnes construisent le palais pendant deux mois.
4. Le palais est-il identique pour chaque carnaval?
   Non, son architecture change chaque année.
5. Que désire le mouvement souverainiste pour le Québec?
   Il désire un Québec indépendant.
6. Quelles sont les deux langues principales parlées à Montréal?
   Ce sont le français et l'anglais.
7. Pourquoi le centre-ville de Montréal est-il fermé pour le festival de jazz?
   Il est transformé en village musical où il y a de nombreux concerts de jazz en plein air.
8. Y a-t-il seulement de grandes stars du jazz au festival?
   Non, il y a aussi des musiciens locaux.
9. Où se situe la ville de Québec?
   Elle se situe sur un rocher, au bord du fleuve Saint-Laurent.
10. Qui a fondé la ville de Québec?
    Samuel de Champlain a fondé la ville de Québec.

ressources

WB
pp. 55–56

vhlcentral

Sur Internet

Go to **vhlcentral.com** to find more cultural information related to this **Panorama**.

🐍 1. Quelles sont quelques-unes des expressions qui sont particulières au français des Québécois?

🐍 2. Quels sont les autres grands festivals du Québec? Quand ont-ils lieu?

🐍 3. Cherchez plus d'informations sur le carnaval d'hiver de Québec. Le palais de glace a-t-il toujours été fait de glace?

luttent *fight* **souverainiste** *in support of sovereignty for Quebec* **d'actualité** *current, relevant* **île** *island* **fleuve** *river* **fondée** *founded* **attire** *attracts* **accueille** *welcomes* **Pourtant** *However* **parmi** *among* **en plein air** *outdoors* **ainsi que** *as well as* **rocher** *rock* **au bord du** *on the banks of the* **ont vaincu** *defeated* **profitent** *take advantage of, benefit from*

Un Québec indépendant
- The Quebec flag and its saying **«Je me souviens»**, which appears on Quebec license plates, are symbols of Quebec's nationalism and reflect its French heritage.
- Ask students: **Quels sont les avantages et les inconvénients d'un Québec indépendant?**

Montréal Montreal's name is derived from the name of the mountain on which it is built, Mont-Royal. Due to the fur trade, Montreal grew rapidly in the eighteenth century. The majority of the population was French until around 1830. Between 1830 and 1865, the British became the majority as a result of immigration. Today, Montreal is one of Canada's chief ports.

Le festival de jazz de Montréal The festival has taken place for over 25 years. It is a non-profit event; any surplus funds are used to promote local and international jazz year-round.

La ville de Québec
- The historic district of Old Quebec has been designated a World Heritage City by UNESCO. **Vieux Québec** is surrounded by 4.6 kilometers (3 miles) of ramparts. Inside the walls are museums, shops, restaurants, buildings, churches, monuments, museums, and **la Citadelle**.

OPTIONS

Game Create categories for the information on Quebec, for example, **Québécois célèbres, La ville de Québec, Montréal,** and **Culture.** For each category, make index cards with a question on one side. Tape the cards to the board under the appropriate category. Divide the class into two teams, and have them take turns selecting a card and answering the question. Teams receive a point for each correct answer. The team with the most points at the end of the game wins.

Pairs Have students work in pairs. Tell them to make a list of reasons why a tourist should visit Quebec and Montreal. After students have completed their lists, call on volunteers to read one item from their list until all options are exhausted.

Section Goals

In this section, students will:
- learn to scan a text for specific information
- read an advertisement for a cybercafé

Stratégie Tell students that a good way to get an idea of what an article or other text is about is to scan it before reading. Scanning means running one's eyes over a text in search of specific information that can be used to infer the text's content. Explain that scanning a text before reading it is a good way to improve reading comprehension.

Examinez le texte Call on volunteers to identify the cognates. Then ask the class what the text is about. (a cybercafé)

Trouvez Have students give details about the information they found in the document. Examples: **une adresse (24 place Joliet 69006 LYON), les noms des propriétaires (Bernard et Marie-Claude Fouchier), les heures d'ouverture (7h à 20h), and le numéro de téléphone (04.72.45.87.90).**

Décrivez Tell students to proofread each other's descriptions for spelling, verb agreement, and accuracy of information.

Lecture  Audio: Reading

Avant la lecture

STRATÉGIE

Scanning

Scanning involves glancing over a document in search of specific information. For example, you can scan a document to identify its format, to find cognates, to locate visual clues about the document's content, or to find specific facts. Scanning allows you to learn a great deal about a text without having to read it word-for-word.

Examinez le texte

Regardez le texte et indiquez huit mots apparentés (*cognates*) que vous trouvez. Answers may vary.

1. Chocolat
2. Cybercafé
3. Accès Internet
4. Omelette
5. Salade
6. Tarte
7. Soupe
8. Snack

Trouvez

Regardez le document. Indiquez si les informations suivantes sont présentes dans le texte.

✓ 1. une adresse
___ 2. le nombre d'ordinateurs
___ 3. un plat du jour (*daily special*)
✓ 4. une terrasse
✓ 5. les noms des propriétaires
___ 6. des prix réduits pour étudiants
___ 7. de la musique *live*
✓ 8. les heures d'ouverture (*business hours*)
✓ 9. un numéro de téléphone
___ 10. une librairie à l'intérieur

Décrivez

Regardez les photos. Écrivez un paragraphe succinct pour décrire (*describe*) le cybercafé. Comparez votre paragraphe avec le paragraphe d'un(e) camarade.

Cybercafé

- Ouvert° du lundi au samedi, de 7h00 à 20h00
- Snack et restauration rapide
- Accès Internet et jeux° vidéo

Cybercafé Le connecté

MENU

PETIT-DÉJEUNER° FRANÇAIS	12,00€	**PETIT-DÉJEUNER ANGLAIS**	15,00€
Café, thé, chocolat chaud ou lait Pain, beurre et confiture° Orange pressée		Café, thé, chocolat chaud ou lait Œufs° (au plat° ou brouillés°), bacon, toasts Orange pressée	
VIENNOISERIES°	3,00€		
Croissant, pain au chocolat, brioche°, pain aux raisins		**DESSERTS**	
		Tarte aux fruits	7,50€
SANDWICHS ET SALADES		Banana split	6,40€
Sandwich (jambon ou fromage; baguette ou pain de campagne)	7,50€	**AUTRES SÉLECTIONS CHAUDES**	
Croque-monsieur°	7,80€	Frites	4,30€
Salade verte°	6,20€	Soupe à l'oignon	6,40€
		Omelette au fromage	8,50€
BOISSONS CHAUDES		Omelette au jambon	8,50€
Café/Déca	3,80€		
Grand crème	5,50€	**BOISSONS FROIDES**	
Chocolat chaud	5,80€	Eau minérale non gazeuse	3,00€
Thé	5,50€	Eau minérale gazeuse	3,50€
Lait chaud	4,80€	Jus de fruits (orange...)	5,80€
		Soda, limonade	5,50€
		Café, thé glacé°	5,20€
Propriétaires: Bernard et Marie-Claude Fouchier			

O P T I O N S

Game Have students work in pairs and play a game of **Dix questions**. The first person thinks of a food or beverage listed in the **Cybercafé Le connecté** menu. The second person must guess the item by asking yes/no questions. Remind students that they may only ask ten questions.

Small Groups Have students work in groups of three or four. Tell them that they are going to open up a new cybercafé and they need to create a "must-have" list of services and foods for their establishment. After groups have completed their lists, have them describe their café to the class. Then have the class vote on the cybercafé with the best features.

Le connecté

- **Le connecté, le cybercafé préféré des étudiants**

- **Ordinateurs disponibles° de 10h00 à 18h00, 1,50€ les 10 minutes**

24, place des Terreaux
69001 LYON
Tél. 04.72.45.87.90
www.leconnecte.fr

Place des Terreaux

Rue d'Algérie

Rue Paul Chenavard

Musée des
Beaux-Arts
de Lyon

Rue de Constantine

Situé en face du musée des Beaux–Arts

Ouvert *Open* **jeux** *games* **Petit-déjeuner** *Breakfast* **confiture** *jam* **Viennoiseries** *Breakfast pastries* **brioche** *a light, slightly-sweet bread* **Croque-monsieur** *Grilled sandwich with cheese and ham* **verte** *green* **Œufs** *Eggs* **au plat** *fried* **brouillés** *scrambled* **glacé** *iced* **disponibles** *available*

Après la lecture

Répondez Répondez aux questions par des phrases complètes.

1. Combien coûte un sandwich?
   Un sandwich coûte 7,50€.

2. Quand est-ce qu'on peut (*can*) surfer sur Internet?
   On peut surfer sur Internet de 10h00 à 18h00.

3. Qui adore ce cybercafé?
   Les étudiants adorent ce cybercafé.

4. Quelles sont les deux boissons gazeuses? Combien coûtent-elles?
   L'eau minérale gazeuse coûte 3,50€. Un soda coûte 5,50€.

5. Combien de desserts sont proposés?
   Deux desserts sont proposés.

6. Vous aimez le sucre. Qu'est-ce que vous allez manger?
   (2 sélections) Answers may vary. Je vais manger... Any two of the following: un croissant, un pain au chocolat, une brioche, un pain aux raisins, une tarte aux fruits, un banana split.

Choisissez Indiquez qui va prendre quoi. Écrivez des phrases complètes. Answers may vary. Possible answers provided.

MODÈLE

Julie a soif. Elle n'aime pas les boissons gazeuses. Elle a 6 euros.
Julie va prendre un jus d'orange.

1. Lise a froid. Elle a besoin d'une boisson chaude. Elle a 4 euros et 90 centimes.
   Lise va prendre un café.

2. Nathan a faim et soif. Il a 14 euros.
   Nathan va prendre un croque-monsieur et un soda.

3. Julien va prendre un plat chaud. Il a 8 euros et 80 centimes.
   Julien va prendre une omelette au jambon.

4. Annie a chaud et a très soif. Elle a 5 euros et 75 centimes.
   Annie va prendre un thé glacé.

5. Martine va prendre une boisson gazeuse. Elle a 4 euros et 20 centimes.
   Martine va prendre une eau minérale gazeuse.

6. Ève va prendre un dessert. Elle n'aime pas les bananes. Elle a 8 euros.
   Ève va prendre une tarte aux fruits.

L'invitation Avec un(e) camarade, jouez (*play*) cette scène: vous invitez un ami à déjeuner au cybercafé Le connecté. Parlez de ce que vous allez manger et boire. Puis (*Then*), bavardez de vos activités de l'après-midi et du soir.

cent soixante-treize **173**

Répondez Go over the answers with the class. Take a quick class poll to find out what is the most popular food chosen for question 6.

Choisissez Have students write two more situations similar to those in the activity. Then tell them to exchange papers with a partner, write the answers, and verify the answers.

L'invitation Before beginning the activity, tell students that they only have 20€ to spend at the **Cybercafé Le connecté**.

O P T I O N S

Cultural Comparison Working in groups of three, have students compare the **Cybercafé Le connecté** menu to a typical menu found at an American Internet café. Tell them to list the similarities and differences in a two-column chart under the headings **Similitudes** and **Différences**. After completing their charts, call on volunteers to read their lists.

Extra Practice To practice scanning written material, bring in short, simple French-language magazine or newspaper articles you have read. Have pairs or small groups scan the articles to determine what they are about. Have them write down all the clues that help them. When each group has come to a decision, ask it to present its findings to the class. Confirm the accuracy of their inferences.

Section Goals

In this section, students will:
• learn to add informative details
• learn to write an informative note

Stratégie Discuss the importance of being informative when writing a note and answering the "W" questions. For example, someone calls while you are out, and your roommate answers the phone. If your note has enough information, your roommate can answer the person's questions about where you are or when you will return.

Thème Have students read the model note and identify the details. (**aujourd'hui; avec Xavier et Laurent, deux étudiants belges de l'université**)

Proofreading Activity Have the class correct these sentences. **1. Ou est-ce que tu va après le cours? 2. Il vont à le magasin cet après-midi. 3. Est-ce que tu prend de le sucre dans le café? 4. Dominique bois de la thé avec le petit-déjeuner.**

Écriture

STRATÉGIE

Adding details

How can you make your writing more informative or more interesting? You can add details by answering the "W" questions: Who? What? When? Where? Why? The answers to these questions will provide useful and interesting details that can be incorporated into your writing. You can use the same strategy when writing in French. Here are some useful question words that you have already learned:

(À/Avec) Qui?	À quelle heure?
Quoi?	Où?
Quand?	Pourquoi?

Compare these two sentences.

> Je vais aller nager.

> Aujourd'hui, à quatre heures, je vais aller nager à la piscine du parc avec mon ami Paul, parce que nous avons chaud.

While both sentences give the same basic information (the writer is going to go swimming), the second, with its detail, is much more informative.

∽ Thème

Un petit mot

Avant l'écriture

1. Vous passez un an en France et vous vivez (*are living*) dans une famille d'accueil (*host family*). C'est samedi, et vous allez passer la journée en ville avec des amis. Écrivez un petit mot (*note*) pour informer votre famille de vos projets (*plans*) pour la journée.

2. D'abord (*First*), choisissez (*choose*) cinq activités que vous allez faire (*to do*) avec vos amis aujourd'hui.

Activité 1:
Activité 2:
Activité 3:
Activité 4:
Activité 5:

OPTIONS

Avant l'écriture Discuss the importance of facts when writing a note and answering the "W" questions. Encourage students to identify a note's purpose (to provide specific information and instructions). Point out that if a note is not complete enough, it fails to serve its purpose. Redundancies can also detract from the message.

Demonstrate how the question strategy works by choosing a general topic and then, as a class, asking and answering the questions in the box. Put students in pairs and have them try it out on their own, using the questions provided to narrow their topic and add details while avoiding redundancies.

3. Ensuite (*Then*), complétez ce tableau (*this chart*) pour organiser vos idées. Répondez à (*Answer*) toutes les questions.

	Activité 1	Activité 2	Activité 3	Activité 4	Activité 5
Qui?					
Quoi?					
Quand?					
Où?					
Comment?					
Pourquoi?					

4. Maintenant (*Now*), comparez votre tableau à celui (*to the one*) d'un(e) partenaire. Avez-vous tous les deux (*both of you*) cinq activités? Avez-vous des informations dans toutes les colonnes? Avez-vous répondu à toutes les questions?

Écriture

Écrivez la note à votre famille d'accueil. Référez-vous au tableau que vous avez créé (*have created*) et incluez toutes les informations. Utilisez les verbes **aller**, **boire** et **prendre**, et le vocabulaire de l'unité. Organisez vos idées de manière logique.

Chère famille,
Aujourd'hui, je vais visiter
la ville avec Xavier et
Laurent, deux étudiants belges
de l'université...

Après l'écriture

1. Échangez votre tableau et votre note avec ceux (*the ones*) d'un(e) partenaire. Faites des commentaires sur son travail (*work*) d'après (*according to*) ces questions:

■ Votre partenaire a-t-il/elle inclus dans la note toutes les informations du tableau?

■ A-t-il/elle correctement (*correctly*) utilisé le vocabulaire de l'unité?

■ A-t-il/elle utilisé la forme correcte des verbes **aller**, **boire** et **prendre**?

■ A-t-il/elle présenté ses informations de manière logique?

2. Corrigez (*Correct*) votre note d'après les commentaires de votre partenaire. Relisez votre travail pour éliminer ces (*these*) problèmes:

■ des fautes (*errors*) d'orthographe

■ des fautes de ponctuation

■ des fautes de conjugaison

■ des fautes d'accord (*agreement*) des adjectifs

cent soixante-quinze **175**

EVALUATION

Criteria
Content Contains a greeting, describes the five planned activities, answers the questions: **qui? quoi? quand? où? pourquoi?**, and includes supporting detail without redundancy.
Scale: 1 2 3 4 5

Organization Organizes the note into a salutation, a description, and a signature.
Scale: 1 2 3 4 5

Accuracy Uses forms of **aller** and places in town correctly. Spells words, conjugates verbs, and modifies adjectives correctly throughout. Avoids redundant language.
Scale: 1 2 3 4 5

Creativity The student includes additional information that is not included in the task, mentions more than five activities and/or includes a closing (not shown in the model).
Scale: 1 2 3 4 5

Scoring
Excellent	18–20 points
Good	14–17 points
Satisfactory	10–13 points
Unsatisfactory	< 10 points

O P T I O N S

Écriture Ask for other details that could be added, such as departure and return times, activities in the town, its name and the students' ages. Finally, have them analyze these extra details to see which are useful for the note's message and which are extraneous or redundant.

Show students how to avoid redundancies by combining similar sentences. Compare **Je vais en ville**. **Je vais avec mes amis**. **Je vais lundi matin.** with **Je vais en ville avec mes amis lundi matin.** Tell them to look for ways to condense language when they edit their work.

Instructional Resources
*vhlcentral.com: Textbook
MP3s; Textbook Audioscript;
reference tools*

🔊 🅢 Vocabulary Tools

Suggestions

- Tell students that an easy way to study from **Vocabulaire** is to cover up the French half of each section, leaving only the English equivalents exposed. They can then quiz themselves on the French items. To focus on the English equivalents of the French entries, they simply reverse this process.
- Point out to students that they can use the Vocabulary Tools at **vhlcentral.com** for reference and extra vocabulary practice.

Leçon 4A

Dans la ville

une boîte (de nuit)	nightclub
un bureau	office; desk
un centre commercial	shopping center, mall
un cinéma (ciné)	movie theater, movies
une église	church
une épicerie	grocery store
un grand magasin	department store
un gymnase	gym
un hôpital	hospital
un kiosque	kiosk
un magasin	store
une maison	house
un marché	market
un musée	museum
un parc	park
une piscine	pool
une place	square; place
un restaurant	restaurant
une terrasse de café	café terrace/ outdoor seating
une banlieue	suburbs
un centre-ville	city/town center, downtown
un endroit	place
un lieu	place
une montagne	mountain
une ville	city, town

Les questions

à quelle heure?	at what time?
à qui?	to whom?
avec qui?	with whom?
combien (de)?	how many?; how much?
comment?	how?; what?
où?	where?
parce que	because
pour qui?	for whom?
pourquoi?	why?
quand?	when?
quel(le)(s)?	which?; what?
que/qu'...?	what?
qui?	who?; whom?
quoi?	what?

Activités

bavarder	to chat
danser	to dance
déjeuner	to eat lunch
dépenser de l'argent (m.)	to spend money
explorer	to explore
fréquenter	to frequent; to visit
inviter	to invite
nager	to swim
passer chez quelqu'un	to stop by someone's house
patiner	to skate
quitter la maison	to leave the house

Verbes

aller	to go

Expressions utiles

See p. 139.

Prepositions

À [+ definite article]	to, in, at
dans	inside; within
commencer à + [infinitive]	to start (doing something)
parler à	to talk to
penser à	to think about
téléphoner à	to phone (someone)
à la maison	at home
à Paris	in Paris
en ville	in town
sur la place	in the square
dans la maison	inside the house
dans Paris	within Paris
dans la ville	within the town
à/sur la terrasse	on the terrace

Leçon 4B

À table

avoir faim	to be hungry
avoir soif	to be thirsty
manger quelque chose	to eat something
une baguette	baguette (long, thin loaf of bread)
le beurre	butter
un croissant	croissant (flaky, crescent-shaped roll)
un éclair	éclair (pastry filled with cream)
des frites (f.)	French fries
un fromage	cheese
le jambon	ham
un pain (de campagne)	(country-style) bread
un sandwich	sandwich
une soupe	soup
le sucre	sugar
une boisson (gazeuse)	(soft/ carbonated) drink/beverage
un café	coffee
un chocolat (chaud)	(hot) chocolate
une eau (minérale)	(mineral) water
un jus (d'orange, de pomme, etc.)	(orange, apple, etc.) juice
le lait	milk
une limonade	lemon soda
un thé (glacé)	(iced) tea

Expressions de quantité

(pas) assez (de)	(not) enough (of)
beaucoup (de)	a lot (of)
d'autres	others
une bouteille (de)	bottle (of)
un morceau (de)	piece, bit (of)
un peu (plus/moins) (de)	little (more/less) (of)
plusieurs	several
quelque chose	something; anything
quelques	some
une tasse (de)	cup (of)
tous (m. pl.)	all
tout (m. sing.)	all
tout (tous) le/les (m.)	all the
toute(s) la/les (f.)	all the
trop (de)	too many/much (of)
un verre (de)	glass (of)

Au café

apporter l'addition (f.)	to bring the check/bill
coûter	to cost
laisser un pourboire	to leave a tip
Combien coûte(nt)...?	How much is/are...?
un prix	price
un serveur/une serveuse	server

Verbes

apprendre	to learn
boire	to drink
comprendre	to understand
prendre	to take; to have

Expressions utiles

See p. 157.

Partitives

de + [definite article]	some, any
un(e)(s)	some, any

Verbes reguliers en -ir

choisir	to choose
finir	to finish
grandir	to grow
grossir	to gain weight
maigrir	to lose weight
obéir (à)	to obey
réagir	to react
réfléchir (à)	to think (about), to reflect (on)
réussir (à)	to succeed (in doing something)
rougir	to blush
vieillir	to grow old

Les loisirs

Unit Goals

Leçon 5A

In this lesson, students will learn:
- terms for sports and leisure activities
- adverbs of frequency
- about intonation
- about **le football**
- the verb **faire**
- expressions with **faire**
- the expression **il faut**
- irregular **-ir** verbs
- more about sports and leisure activities through specially shot video footage

Leçon 5B

In this lesson, students will learn:
- terms for seasons and months
- weather expressions
- to tell the date
- differences between open and closed vowels
- about public gardens and parks in the francophone world
- about Malian musical duo Amadou & Mariam
- the numbers 101 and higher
- **-er** verbs with spelling changes
- to listen for key words in oral communication

Savoir-faire

In this section, students will learn:
- cultural and historical information about **l'Afrique de l'Ouest et l'Afrique centrale**
- to skim a text
- to use a French-English dictionary

Pour commencer

- Il est dans le parc.
- Il dessine.
- Oui, je pense qu'il aime l'art.
- Il dessine un être humain.

Pour commencer
- Où est David?
- Qu'est-ce qu'il fait?
- Pensez-vous qu'il aime l'art?
- Il dessine un être humain ou un animal?

RESOURCES

Student Activities Manual (SAM):
Workbook Activities, pp. 57–72;
Lab Activities, pp. 33–40;
Video Activities, pp. 17–20; pp. 69–70
SAM Answer Key

vhlcentral.com: Textbook MP3s; Lab MP3s;
Textbook Audioscript; Lab Audioscript Video;
Videoscript; **Roman-photo** Translations;
Vocabulaire supplémentaire; Activity Pack
(including **Feuilles d'activités,** Info Gap Activities,
and Task-based Activities);

Flash culture video transcription; **Essayez!** and
Mise en pratique answers; Digital Image Bank;
Testing Program; Testing Program MP3s

Section Goals

In this section, students will learn and practice vocabulary related to:
• sports and leisure activities
• adverbs of frequency

Instructional Resources
vhlcentral.com:
*Digital Image Bank (including vocabulary illustrations from the textbook, theme-based illustrations); **Vocabulaire supplémentaire; Mise en pratique** answers; Textbook Audioscript; Lab Audioscript; Activity Pack (**Feuilles d'activités**); Textbook MP3s; Lab MP3s; SAM Answer Key; reference tools*

Suggestions

• Use the 5A **Contextes** illustration from the Digital Image Bank to describe what people are doing. Examples: **Ils jouent au football. Elles jouent au tennis.** Encourage students to add their remarks.
• Teach students the expression **aider quelqu'un à... (étudier, bricoler, travailler)**. Pointing to the person toward the right helping his injured friend, say: **Il aide son copain à marcher.**
• Point out the differences between the words **un jeu, jouer, un joueur,** and **une joueuse.**
• Ask students closed-ended questions about their favorite activities: **Tu préfères jouer au tennis ou aller à la pêche? Aller à un spectacle ou jouer au golf?**
• Call out sports and other activities from this section and have students classify them as either **un sport** or **un loisir**. List them on the board in two columns.
• Use the Leisure, Sports, and arts illustrations from the Digital Image Bank to help students familiarize themselves with talking about activities and telling how often and how well they do things.
• Additional vocabulary for this lesson can be found in the **Vocabulaire supplémentaire** on the Supersite.

Leçon 5A

You will learn how to...
▪ talk about activities
▪ tell how often and how well you do things

Ⓢ **Vocabulary Tools**

Le temps libre

Vocabulaire

aller à la pêche	to go fishing
bricoler	to tinker; to do odd jobs
désirer	to want
jouer (à/de)	to play
pratiquer	to play regularly, to practice
skier	to ski
le baseball	baseball
le cinéma	movies
le foot(ball)	soccer
le football américain	football
le golf	golf
un jeu	game
un loisir	leisure activity
un passe-temps	pastime, hobby
un spectacle	show
un stade	stadium
le temps libre	free time
le volley(-ball)	volleyball
une/deux fois	one/two time(s)
par jour, semaine, mois, an, etc.	per day, week, month, year, etc.
déjà	already
encore	again, still
jamais	never
longtemps	long time
maintenant	now
parfois	sometimes
rarement	rarely
souvent	often

ressources

WB	LM	Ⓢ
pp. 57–58	p. 33	vhlcentral

178 *cent soixante-dix-huit*

les joueuses (f.)

un match de tennis (m.)

Elle marche. (marcher)

le sport

une équipe

les joueurs (m.)

Il joue au foot. (jouer)

Il gagne. (gagner)

les cartes (f.)

une bande dessinée (B.D.)

OPTIONS

Extra Practice Have students give their opinions about activities in **Espace contextes**. Brainstorm pairs of adjectives that apply to activities and write them on the board or on a transparency. Examples: **agréable/désagréable, intéressant/ennuyeux, utile/inutile, génial/nul, facile/difficile**. Then ask questions like these: **Le football, c'est intéressant ou c'est ennuyeux? Les échecs, c'est facile ou difficile?**

Game Play a game of **Jacques a dit** (*Simon says*) using the activities in this section. Tell students to mime each activity only if they hear the words **Jacques a dit**. If a student mimes an activity not preceded by **Jacques a dit**, he or she is eliminated from the game. The last person standing wins. You might want students to take turns calling out activities.

Attention!

Use **jouer à** with games and sports.

Elle joue aux cartes/au baseball.
She plays cards/baseball.

Use **jouer de** with musical instruments.

Vous jouez de la guitare/du piano.
You play the guitar/piano.

le basket(-ball)

Il aide le joueur.
(aider)

Il chante.
(chanter)

Il indique.
(indiquer)

les échecs (m.)

Mise en pratique

1 **Écoutez** Écoutez Sabine et Marc parler de leurs passe-temps préférés. Dans le tableau suivant, écrivez un **S** pour Sabine et un **M** pour Marc pour indiquer s'ils pratiquent ces activités **souvent**, **parfois**, **rarement** ou **jamais**. Attention, toutes les activités ne sont pas utilisées.

Activités	Souvent	Parfois	Rarement	Jamais
1. chanter	S			
2. le basket	S	M		
3. les cartes				
4. le tennis	M	S		
5. aller à la pêche			M	S
6. le golf				M
7. le cinéma	M, S			
8. le spectacle	M		S	

2 **Remplissez** Choisissez dans la liste le mot qui convient (*the word that fits*) pour compléter les phrases. N'oubliez pas de conjuguer les verbes.

aider	jeu	pratiquer
bande dessinée	jouer	skier
bricoler	marcher	sport
équipe		

1. Notre ___équipe___ joue un match cet après-midi.
2. Le tarot est un ___jeu___ de cartes.
3. Mon livre préféré, c'est une ___bande dessinée___ de Tintin, *Le sceptre d'Ottokar*.
4. J'aime ___jouer___ aux cartes avec ma grand-mère.
5. Pour devenir (*To become*) champion de volley, je ___pratique___ tous les jours.
6. Le dimanche, nous ___marchons___ beaucoup, environ (*about*) cinq kilomètres.
7. Mon ___sport___ préféré, c'est le foot.
8. Mon père ___aide___ mon frère à préparer son match de tennis.
9. J'aime mieux ___skier___ dans les Alpes que dans le Colorado.
10. Il faut réparer la table, mais je n'aime pas ___bricoler___.

3 **Les loisirs** Utilisez un élément de chaque colonne pour former huit phrases au sujet des loisirs de ces personnes. N'oubliez pas les accords (*agreements*). Answers will vary.

Personnes	Activités	Fréquence
Je	jouer aux échecs	maintenant
Ma sœur	chanter	parfois
Mes parents	jouer au tennis	rarement
Christian	gagner le match	souvent
Sandrine et Cédric	skier	déjà
Les étudiants	regarder un spectacle	une fois par semaine
Élise	jouer au basket	une fois par mois
Mon ami(e)	aller à la pêche	encore

Ⓢ Practice more at **vhlcentral.com**.

cent soixante-dix-neuf   **179**

1 **Audioscript** SABINE: Bonjour, Marc, comment ça va?
MARC: Pas mal. Et toi?
S: Très bien, merci. Est-ce que tu joues au golf?
M: Non, jamais. Je n'aime pas ce sport. Je préfère jouer au tennis. En général, je joue au tennis trois fois par semaine. Et toi?
S: Moi? Jouer au tennis? Oui, parfois, mais j'aime mieux le basket. C'est un sport que je pratique souvent.
M: Ah le basket, je n'aime pas tellement. Je joue parfois avec des amis, mais ce n'est pas mon sport préféré. Le soir, j'aime bien aller au spectacle ou au cinéma. Et toi, qu'est-ce que tu aimes faire le soir?
S: Oh, je vais rarement au spectacle mais j'adore aller au cinéma. J'y vais très souvent.
M: C'est quoi, ton passe-temps préféré?
S: Mon passe-temps préféré, c'est le chant. J'aime chanter tous les jours.
M: Moi, j'adore aller à la pêche quand j'ai du temps libre, mais ce n'est que très rarement.
S: La pêche? Oh, moi, jamais. Je trouve ça ennuyeux.
M: Et est-ce que tu aimes le baseball?
S: Je ne sais pas; je n'ai jamais regardé un match de baseball.
M: Il y a un match toutes les semaines. C'est très intéressant.
(On Textbook MP3s)

1 **Expansion** Have students tell a partner how often they, themselves, do these activities.

2 **Suggestions**
• To review **-er** verb forms, conjugate on the board one of the verbs from the list.
• Tell students to use each item in the word box only once.

3 **Suggestion** Ask volunteers to write one of their sentences on the board, making sure to have one example sentence for each of the verbs listed in this activity.

3 **Expansion** Ask students how frequently they do each of the activities listed. Encourage them to use as many different adverbial expressions as possible.

O P T I O N S

Extra Practice Call out names of famous athletes and have students say: **Ils jouent au _sport_**. Examples: Tiger Woods, Arnold Palmer (**golf**), David Beckham, Zinédine Zidane (**football**), Serena Williams, André Agassi (**tennis**), Donovan McNabb, Troy Aikman (**football américain**), Shaquille O'Neal, Larry Bird (**basket-ball**), and Babe Ruth, Mark McGwire (**baseball**).

Game Write each of the words or expressions in **Activité 3** on an index card. Label three boxes **Personnes**, **Activités**, and **Fréquence**. Then place the cards in their respective boxes. Divide the class into two teams. Students take turns drawing one card from each box. Each player has five seconds to form a sentence using all of the words on the three cards. If they do not make a mistake, they score a point for their team.

Communication

4 Suggestion Follow up this activity by asking students about their partners' favorite sports and activities. Examples: **Est-ce que _____ est sportif/sportive? Quel sport pratique-t-il/elle? Combien de fois par mois est-ce que _____ va au cinéma?**

4 Expansion Have students conduct an informal survey by circulating around the room and asking these questions to five other students. Tell them to write down all of the responses for each question. As a class, share and compare students' findings.

5 Suggestions
- Have two volunteers read the **modèle** aloud to make sure students understand the directions. Then distribute the **Feuilles d'activités** found in the Activity Pack on the Supersite.
- Combine pairs of students to form groups of four. Have students share with the other pair what they learned about their partner.

5 Expansion Tally the results of the survey to determine the most and least popular activities among your students.

6 Suggestion Call on two students to read the **modèle** before assigning this activity.

7 Suggestion Have students exchange letters with a classmate. Remind them to begin the letter with **chère** if they are writing to a woman.

Successful Language Learning Suggest that students use mnemonics devices to memorize vocabulary. Examples: Use alliteration for interrogative words like **qui**, **quand**, and **quoi**. Group words in categories, such as team sports (**football**, **basket-ball**, **volley-ball**) versus those that are usually played one-on-one (**échecs**, **cartes**, **tennis**). Learn word "families," such as **un jeu**, **jouer**, **un joueur**, and **une joueuse**.

4 Répondez Avec un(e) partenaire, posez-vous (*ask each other*) ces (*these*) questions et répondez (*answer*) à tour de rôle. Answers will vary.

1. Quel est votre loisir préféré?
2. Quel est votre sport préféré à la télévision?
3. Êtes-vous sportif/sportive? Si oui, quel sport pratiquez-vous?
4. Qu'est-ce que vous désirez faire (*to do*) ce week-end?
5. Combien de fois par mois allez-vous au cinéma?
6. Que faites-vous (*do you do*) quand vous avez du temps libre?
7. Est-ce que vous aidez quelqu'un? Qui? À faire quoi? Comment?
8. Quel est votre jeu de société (*board game*) préféré? Pourquoi?

5 Sondage Avec la feuille d'activités que votre professeur va vous donner, circulez dans la classe et demandez à vos camarades s'ils pratiquent ces activités et si oui (*if so*), à quelle fréquence. Quelle est l'activité la plus pratiquée (*the most practiced*) de la classe? Answers will vary.

MODÈLE

aller à la pêche

Étudiant(e) 1: *Est-ce que tu vas à la pêche?*
Étudiant(e) 2: *Oui, je vais parfois à la pêche.*

Activités	Noms	Fréquence
1. aller à la pêche	François	parfois
2. jouer au tennis		
3. jouer au foot		
4. skier		

6 Conversez Avec un(e) partenaire, utilisez les expressions de la liste et les mots d'**ESPACE CONTEXTES** et écrivez une conversation au sujet de vos loisirs. Présentez votre travail au reste de la classe. Answers will vary.

MODÈLE

Étudiant(e) 1: *Que fais-tu (do you do) comme sport?*
Étudiant(e) 2: *Je joue au volley.*
Étudiant(e) 1: *Tu joues souvent?*
Étudiant(e) 2: *Oui, trois fois par semaine, avec mon amie Julie. C'est un sport que j'adore. Et toi, quel est ton passe-temps préféré?*

Avec qui?	Pourquoi?
Combien de fois par...?	Quand?
Comment?	Quel(le)(s)?
Où?	Quoi?

7 La lettre Écrivez une lettre à un(e) ami(e). Dites ce que vous faites (*do*) pendant vos loisirs, quand, avec qui et à quelle fréquence. Answers will vary.

Cher Marc,
Pendant (During) mon temps libre, j'aime bien jouer au basket et au tennis. J'aime gagner, mais ça n'arrive pas souvent! Je joue au tennis avec mes amis deux fois par semaine, le mardi et le vendredi, et au basket le samedi. J'adore les films et je vais souvent au cinéma avec ma sœur ou mes amis. Le soir...

OPTIONS

Extra Practice Give students five minutes to jot down a description of their typical weekend, including what they do, where they go, and with whom they spend time. Circulate around the class to help with unfamiliar vocabulary. Then have volunteers share their information with the rest of the class. The class decides whether or not each volunteer represents a "typical" student.

Game Play a game of **Dix questions**. Ask a volunteer to think of a sport, activity, person, or place from the vocabulary drawing or list. Other students get one chance to ask a yes/no question and make a guess until someone guesses the word. Limit attempts to 10 questions per word. You may want to write some phrases on the board to cue students' questions.

Les sons et les lettres  Audio

Intonation

In short, declarative sentences, the pitch of your voice, or intonation, falls on the final word or syllable.

Nathalie est française.   **Hector joue au football.**

In longer, declarative sentences, intonation rises, then falls.

À trois heures et demie, j'ai sciences politiques.

In sentences containing lists, intonation rises for each item in the list and falls on the last syllable of the last one.

Martine est jeune, blonde et jolie.

In long, declarative sentences, such as those containing clauses, intonation may rise several times, falling on the final syllable.

Le samedi, à dix heures du matin, je vais au centre commercial.

Questions that require a yes or no answer have rising intonation. Information questions have falling intonation.

C'est ta mère?   **Est-ce qu'elle joue au tennis?**

Quelle heure est-il?   **Quand est-ce que tu arrives?**

Prononcez Répétez les phrases suivantes à voix haute.

1. J'ai dix-neuf ans.
2. Tu fais du sport?
3. Quel jour sommes-nous?
4. Sandrine n'habite pas à Paris.
5. Quand est-ce que Marc arrive?
6. Charlotte est sérieuse et intellectuelle.

Articulez Répétez les dialogues à voix haute.

1. —Qu'est-ce que c'est?
   —C'est un ordinateur.
2. —Tu es américaine?
   —Non, je suis canadienne.
3. —Qu'est-ce que Christine étudie?
   —Elle étudie l'anglais et l'espagnol.
4. —Où est le musée?
   —Il est en face de l'église.

Dictons Répétez les dictons à voix haute.

Petit à petit, l'oiseau fait son nid.[2]

Si le renard court, le poulet a des ailes.[1]

[1] Though the fox runs, the chicken has wings.
[2] Little by little, a bird builds its nest.

ressources

LM
p. 34

vhlcentral

Section Goals

In this section, students will learn about using intonation.

Instructional Resources
vhlcentral.com:
Textbook MP3s;
Lab MP3s; SAM Answer Key;
Textbook Audioscript;
Lab Audioscript;
reference tools

Suggestions

- Model the intonation of each of the example sentences and have students repeat them after you.
- Make sure students can recognize an information question. Tell them that information questions contain question words: **qui**, **qu'est-ce que**, **quand**, **comment**, **pourquoi**, etc. Remind students that the question word is not always the first word of the sentence. Examples: **À qui parles-tu? Ils arrivent quand?**
- Contrast the intonation of various types of declarative sentences (short, long, and those containing lists).
- Point out that the sentences without question words in the **Prononcez** activity (all except items 3 and 5) can be changed from a question to a statement and vice-versa simply by changing the intonation.

Dictons

- Ask students if they can think of sayings in English that are similar to «**Petit à petit, l'oiseau fait son nid.**» (*Slow and steady wins the race.*)
- Have students discuss the meaning of «**Si le renard court, le poulet a des ailes.**»

OPTIONS

Extra Practice Here are some sentences to use for additional practice with intonation: **1. Il a deux frères? 2. Il a deux frères. 3. Combien de frères est-ce qu'il a? 4. Vous jouez au tennis? 5. Vous jouez au tennis. 6. Avec qui est-ce que vous jouez au tennis?** Make sure students hear the difference between declarative and interrogative statements.

Game Divide the class into small groups. Pronounce ten phrases based on those in the examples and in **Prononcez**. Have students silently pass one piece of paper, numbered 1–10, around their group. Members of each group take turns recording whether the statements are declarative or interrogative. Collect the papers, one per group, when you finish saying the phrases. The group with the most correct answers wins.

Section Goals

In this section, students will learn functional phrases for talking about leisure activities through comprehensible input.

Instructional Resources
vhlcentral.com:
Roman-photo *Video, Videoscript, and Translation; SAM Answer Key; reference tools*

Video Recap: Leçon 4B
Use prompts to review the previous **Roman-photo** episode.
1. Amina et Sandrine vont au café, mais David et Rachid… (rentrent à l'appartement/chez eux)
2. Rachid va étudier et David a envie de… (dessiner un peu)
3. Sandrine a envie d'apprendre à… (préparer des éclairs)
4. Amina commande… (un sandwich jambon-fromage et des frites)

Video Synopsis In a park, Rachid, David, and Sandrine talk about their favorite pastimes. David likes to draw; Rachid plays soccer. They run into Stéphane. He and Rachid talk about Stéphane's studies. Stéphane doesn't like his classes; he prefers sports. Sandrine tells David she doesn't like sports, but prefers movies and concerts. She also wants to be singer.

Suggestions
• Ask students to predict what the episode will be about.
• Have pairs of students list words they expect to hear in a video about sports and activities. As they watch, have them mark the words and expressions they hear.
• Have students scan the captions to find phrases used to talk about sports and activities. Examples: **Rachid, lui, c'est un grand sportif. Je fais du ski, de la planche à voile, du vélo… et j'adore nager.**
• Ask students to read the **Roman-photo** in groups of four. Ask groups to present their dramatic readings to the class.
• Review the predictions and confirm the correct ones. Have students summarize this episode.

Au parc

PERSONNAGES

 David
 Rachid
 Sandrine
 Stéphane

DAVID Oh là là… On fait du sport aujourd'hui!
RACHID C'est normal! On est dimanche. Tous les week-ends à Aix, on fait du vélo, on joue au foot…
SANDRINE Oh, quelle belle journée! Faisons une promenade!
DAVID D'accord.

DAVID Moi, le week-end, je sors souvent. Mon passe-temps favori, c'est de dessiner la nature et les belles femmes. Mais Rachid, lui, c'est un grand sportif.
RACHID Oui, je joue au foot très souvent et j'adore.

RACHID Tiens, Stéphane! Déjà? Il est en avance.
SANDRINE Salut.
STÉPHANE Salut. Ça va?
DAVID Ça va.
STÉPHANE Salut.
RACHID Salut.

STÉPHANE Pfft! Je n'aime pas l'histoire-géo.
RACHID Mais, qu'est-ce que tu aimes alors, à part le foot?
STÉPHANE Moi? J'aime presque tous les sports. Je fais du ski, de la planche à voile, du vélo… et j'adore nager.
RACHID Oui, mais tu sais, le sport ne joue pas un grand rôle au bac.

RACHID Et puis, les études, c'est comme le sport. Pour être bon, il faut travailler!
STÉPHANE Ouais, ouais.
RACHID Allez, commençons. En quelle année Napoléon a-t-il…

SANDRINE Dis-moi David, c'est comment chez toi, aux États-Unis? Quels sont les sports favoris des Américains?
DAVID Euh… chez moi? Beaucoup pratiquent le baseball ou le basket et surtout, on adore regarder le football américain. Mais toi, Sandrine, qu'est-ce que tu fais de tes loisirs? Tu aimes le sport? Tu sors?

1 Les événements Mettez ces (*these*) événements dans l'ordre chronologique.

10 a. David dessine un portrait de Sandrine.
6 b. Stéphane se plaint (*complains*) de ses cours.
4 c. Rachid parle du match de foot.
9 d. David complimente Sandrine.
2 e. David mentionne une activité que Rachid aime faire.
7 f. Sandrine est curieuse de savoir (*to know*) quels sont les sports favoris des Américains.
5 g. Stéphane dit (*says*) qu'il ne sait (*knows*) pas s'il va gagner son prochain match.
3 h. Stéphane arrive.
1 i. David parle de son passe-temps favori.
8 j. Sandrine parle de sa passion.

Practice more at **vhlcentral.com.**

Avant de regarder la vidéo Before viewing the **Au parc** episode, ask students to consider both the title and video still 1. Then brainstorm what David, Sandrine, and Rachid might talk about in an episode set in a park. Examples: sports and activities: **On fait du sport aujourd'hui!** or the weather: **Quelle belle journée!**

Regarder la vidéo Play the video episode once without sound and have the class create a plot summary based on the visual cues. Afterward, show the video with sound and have the class correct any mistaken guesses and fill in any gaps in the plot summary they created.

Les amis parlent de leurs loisirs.

RACHID Alors, Stéphane, tu crois que tu vas gagner ton prochain match?
STÉPHANE Hmm, ce n'est pas garanti! L'équipe de Marseille est très forte.
RACHID C'est vrai, mais tu es très motivé, n'est-ce pas?
STÉPHANE Bien sûr.

RACHID Et, pour les études, tu es motivé? Qu'est-ce que vous faites en histoire-géo en ce moment?
STÉPHANE Oh, on étudie Napoléon.
RACHID C'est intéressant! Les cent jours, la bataille de Waterloo...

SANDRINE Bof, je n'aime pas tellement le sport, mais j'aime bien sortir le week-end. Je vais au cinéma ou à des concerts avec mes amis. Ma vraie passion, c'est la musique. Je désire être chanteuse professionnelle.

DAVID Mais tu es déjà une chanteuse extraordinaire! Eh! J'ai une idée. Je peux faire un portrait de toi?
SANDRINE De moi? Vraiment? Oui, si tu insistes!

Expressions utiles

Talking about your activities

- **Qu'est-ce que tu fais de tes loisirs? Tu sors?**
  What do you do in your free time? Do you go out?
- **Le week-end, je sors souvent.**
  On weekends I often go out.
- **J'aime bien sortir.**
  I like to go out.
- **Tous les week-ends, on/tout le monde fait du sport.**
  Every weekend, people play/everyone plays sports.
- **Qu'est-ce que tu aimes alors, à part le foot?**
  What else do you like then, besides soccer?
- **J'aime presque tous les sports.**
  I like almost all sports.
- **Je peux faire un portrait de toi?**
  Can I do a portrait of you?
- **Qu'est-ce que vous faites en histoire-géo en ce moment?**
  What are you doing in history-geography at the moment?
- **Les études, c'est comme le sport. Pour être bon, il faut travailler!**
  Studies are like sports. To be good, you have to work!
- **Faisons une promenade!**
  Let's take a walk!

Additional vocabulary

- **Dis-moi.**
  Tell me.
- **Tu sais.**
  You know.
- **Ce n'est pas garanti!**
  It's not guaranteed!
- **Vraiment?**
  Really?
- **Bien sûr.**
  Of course.
- **Tiens.**
  Hey, look./Here you are.

O P T I O N S

2 **Questions** Choisissez la traduction (*translation*) qui convient pour chaque activité. Essayez de ne pas utiliser de dictionnaire. Combien de traductions y a-t-il pour le verbe **faire**?

_c_ 1. faire du ski
_d_ 2. faire une promenade
_b_ 3. faire du vélo
_a_ 4. faire du sport

a. to play sports
b. to go biking
c. to ski
d. to take a walk

3 **À vous!** David et Rachid parlent de faire des projets (*plans*) pour le week-end, mais les loisirs qu'ils aiment sont très différents. Ils discutent de leurs préférences et finalement choisissent (*choose*) une activité qu'ils vont pratiquer ensemble (*together*). Avec un(e) partenaire, écrivez la conversation et jouez la scène devant la classe.

ressources
VM pp. 17-18 vhlcentral

A C T I V I T É S

cent quatre-vingt-trois **183**

Expressions utiles
- Draw attention to the forms of the verb **faire** and irregular **-ir** verbs in the captions, in the **Expressions utiles** box, and as they occur in your conversation with students. Tell students that this material will be presented in **Structures**.
- Respond briefly to questions about **faire** and irregular **-ir** verbs. Reinforce correct forms, but do not expect students to produce them consistently at this time.
- Work through the **Expressions utiles** by asking students about their activities. As you do, respond to the content of their responses and ask other students questions about their classmates' answers. Example: **Qu'est-ce que tu fais de tes loisirs? Tu sors?**
- Remind students that the **nous** form of a verb can be used to say *Let's...* Example: **Faisons une promenade!** = *Let's take a walk!*

1 **Suggestion** Form several groups of eight students. Write each of these sentences on individual strips of paper and distribute them among the students in each group. Make a set of sentences for each group. Have students read their sentences aloud in the correct order.

1 **Expansion** Have students make sentences to fill in parts of the story not mentioned in this activity.

2 **Suggestion** Remind students that **faire** has several English translations.

3 **Suggestion** Remind students of expressions like **On...?** for suggesting activities and **D'accord** and **Non, je préfère...** for accepting or rejecting suggestions. As students write their scenes, circulate around the room to help with unfamiliar vocabulary and expressions.

Pairs Have pairs of students create two-line mini-conversations using as many **Expressions utiles** as they can. Example:
—**Qu'est-ce que tu aimes alors, à part le foot?**
—**J'aime presque tous les sports.**
Then have them use the vocabulary in this section to talk about their own activities and those of their friends and family.

Extra Practice Ask volunteers to act out the **Roman-photo** episode for the class. Assure them that it is not necessary to memorize the episode or to stick strictly to its content. They should try to get the general meaning across with the vocabulary and expressions they know. Encourage creativity. Give them time to prepare. You may want to assign this as homework and do it the next class period as a review activity.

ESPACE **CULTURE**

NATIONAL STANDARDS connections cultures

Ⓢ Reading

Section Goals

In this section, students will:
• learn about a popular sport
• learn sports terms
• learn names of champions from French-speaking regions
• read about two celebrated French athletes

Instructional Resources
vhlcentral.com:
SAM Answer Key;
reference tools

Culture à la loupe
Avant la lecture Before opening their books, ask students to call out as many sports-related words as they can remember in French. Ask them to name the most popular sports in the United States and those that they associate with the French.

Lecture
• Point out the chart **Nombre de membres des fédérations sportives en France**. Ask students what information the chart shows. (The number of members of athletic federations in France for each sport listed.)
• Point out that the term **le foot** is a common abbreviation for **le football**. Make sure your class understands that **le football américain** is *football* and **le foot** is *soccer*.

Après la lecture Have students prepare a list of questions with **jouer** and frequency expressions to ask a classmate. Have them present the other person's preferences to the class. Example: **Étudiant(e) 1: Est-ce que tu joues parfois au volley-ball? Étudiant(e) 2: Non, je joue rarement au volley-ball.**

1 Expansion Continue the activity with these true/false statements.
11. En France, le basket-ball est plus populaire que la natation. (Vrai.) 12. On fait moins de rugby que de vélo en France. (Faux.) 13. L'équipe de foot de Marseille est très populaire. (Vrai.)

CULTURE À LA LOUPE

Le football

Nombre° de membres des fédérations sportives en France	
Football	2.002.400
Tennis	1.103.500
Judo-jujitsu	634.900
Basket-ball	536.900
Rugby	447.500
Golf	414.200
Natation°	304.000
Ski	136.100
Vélo°	119.200
Danse	84.000

Le football est le sport le plus° populaire dans la majorité des pays° francophones. Tous les quatre ans°, des centaines de milliers de° fans, ou «supporters», regardent la Coupe du Monde°: le championnat de foot(ball) le plus important du monde. En 1998 (mille neuf cent quatre-vingt-dix-huit), l'équipe de France gagne la Coupe du Monde et en 2000 (deux mille), elle gagne la Coupe d'Europe, autre championnat important.

Le Cameroun a aussi une grande équipe de football. «Les Lions Indomptables°» gagnent la médaille d'or° aux Jeux Olympiques de Sydney en 2000. En 2007, l'équipe camerounaise est la première équipe africaine à être dans le classement mondial° de la FIFA (Fédération Internationale de Football Association). Certains «Lions» jouent dans les clubs français et européens.

les Lions Indomptables

En France, il y a deux ligues professionnelles de vingt équipes chacune°. Ça fait° quarante équipes professionnelles de football pour un pays plus petit que° le Texas! Certaines équipes, comme le Paris Saint-Germain («le P.S.G.») ou l'Olympique de Marseille («l'O.M.»), ont beaucoup de supporters.

Les Français, comme les Camerounais, adorent regarder le football, mais ils sont aussi des joueurs très sérieux: aujourd'hui en France, il y a plus de 17.000 (dix-sept mille) clubs amateurs de football et plus de deux millions de joueurs.

le plus *the most* **pays** *countries* **Tous les quatre ans** *Every four years* **centaines de milliers de** *hundreds of thousands of* **Coupe du Monde** *World Cup* **Indomptables** *Untamable* **or** *gold* **classement mondial** *world ranking* **chacune** *each* **Ça fait** *That makes* **un pays plus petit que** *a country smaller than* **Nombre** *Number* **Natation** *Swimming* **Vélo** *Cycling*

A C T I V I T É S

1 🖊 **Vrai ou faux?** Indiquez si ces phrases sont **vraies** ou **fausses**.

1. Le football est le sport le plus populaire en France. Vrai.
2. La Coupe du Monde a lieu (*takes place*) tous les deux ans. Faux.
3. En 2000, l'équipe de France gagne la Coupe du Monde. Faux.
4. Le Cameroun gagne le tournoi de football aux Jeux Olympiques de Sydney. Vrai.
5. Le Cameroun est la première équipe européenne à être au classement mondial de la FIFA. Faux.
6. Certains «Tigres Indomptables» jouent dans des clubs français et européens. Faux.
7. En France, il y a vingt équipes professionnelles de football. Faux.
8. La France est plus petite que le Texas. Vrai.
9. L'Olympique de Marseille est un stade de football célèbre. Faux.
10. Les Français aiment jouer au football. Vrai.

O P T I O N S

Extra Practice Provide groups of three students with a list of words that are relevant to **Le football** like **gagner**, **longtemps**, **courir** from the **Leçon 5A** vocabulary list. Ask them to work together to create sentences about the reading by incorporating the lexical items you have prompted. Example: **gagner (En 1998, la France gagne la Coupe du Monde.)** Answers will vary in an open-ended activity like this, but remind the class to stick to learned material. Follow up by creating a column on the board for each word that you prompted so students can share sentences they consider successful. After at least one student has written a response for each word, correct the sentences as a class.

LE FRANÇAIS QUOTIDIEN

Le sport

arbitre (*m./f.*)	*referee*
ballon (*m.*)	*ball*
coup de sifflet (*m.*)	*whistle*
entraîneur	*coach*
maillot (*m.*)	*jersey*
terrain (*m.*)	*playing field*
hors-jeu	*off-side*
marquer	*to score*

LE MONDE FRANCOPHONE

Des champions

Voici quelques champions olympiques récents.

Algérie Taoufik Makhloufi, athlétisme°, argent°, Rio, 2016

Burundi Francine Niyonsaba, athlétisme, argent, Rio, 2016

Cameroun Françoise Mbango Etone, athlétisme, or°, Pékin, 2008

Canada Équipe de football féminin, bronze, Rio, 2016

France Émilie Andéol, judo, or, Rio 2016

Maroc Hicham El Guerrouj, athlétisme, or, Athènes, 2004

Suisse Dominique Gisin, ski alpin°, or, Sotchi, 2014

Tunisie Inès Boubakri, escrime°, bronze, Rio, 2016

athlétisme *track and field* **argent** *silver* **or** *gold* **ski alpin** *downhill skiing*

PORTRAIT

Zinédine Zidane et Laura Flessel

Zinédine Zidane, ou «Zizou», est un footballeur français. Né° à Marseille de parents algériens, il joue dans différentes équipes françaises. Nommé trois fois «Joueur de l'année» par la FIFA, il gagne la Coupe du Monde avec l'équipe de France en 1998 (mille neuf cent quatre-vingt-dix huit). Il est aujourd'hui entraîneur du Real Madrid, en Espagne°.

Née à la Guadeloupe, **Laura Flessel** commence l'escrime° à l'âge de sept ans. Après plusieurs titres° de championne de Guadeloupe, elle va en France pour continuer sa carrière. En 1991 (mille neuf cent quatre-vingt-onze), à 20 ans, elle est championne de France et cinq ans plus tard, elle est double championne olympique à Atlanta en 1996 (mille neuf centquatre-vingt-seize). En 2007 (deuxmille sept), elle remporte aussi la médaille d'or aux Championnats d'Europe en  individuel. Et en 2017 (deux mille dix-sept), elle devient Ministre des Sports du gouvernement français.

Ces deux sportifs ont un engagement° dans des causes humanitaires. C'est une mission, pour Zinédine Zidane, de soutenir° ceux qui en ont besoin. Pour Laura, il est très important de combattre les inégalités: elle se bat pour l'égalité et contre les violences faites aux femmes.

Né *Born* **Espagne** *Spain* **escrime** *fencing* **plusieurs titres** *several titles* **engagement** *involvement* **prend part** *participates* **soutenir** *support* **courses** *run*

---

2 **Zinédine ou Laura?** Indiquez de qui on parle.

1. _Zinédine_ est de France métropolitaine (*mainland France*).
2. _Laura_ est née à la Guadeloupe.
3. _Zinédine_ gagne la Coupe du Monde pour la France en 1998.
4. _Zinédine_ a été trois fois «Joueur de l'année».
5. _Zinédine_ soutient ceux qui en ont besoin.
6. _Laura_ est engagée contre les violences faites aux femmes.

3 **Une interview** Avec un(e) partenaire, préparez une interview entre un(e) journaliste et un(e) athlète que vous aimez. Jouez la scène devant la classe. Est-ce que vos camarades peuvent deviner (*can guess*) le nom de l'athlète?

Practice more at **vhlcentral.com**.

ACTIVITÉS

Le français quotidien You might extend this list to include **le poteau de but** (*goalpost*), **le coup d'envoi** (*kickoff*), **un penalty** (*penalty kick*), and **une faute** (*foul*).

Portrait Zinédine Zidane became the most expensive player in the history of soccer when Real Madrid acquired him for the equivalent of about $66 million American dollars. «Zizou» also made history as Christian Dior's first male model. Laura Flessel is a left-handed fencer called «**la Guêpe**» (*Wasp*) because of her competitive and dangerous attack.

Le monde francophone Model the pronunciation of names and places in this box. Then ask students if they know of any other athletes from the francophone world.

Suggestion Point out to students that they will find supporting activities and more information related to this **Espace culture** at **vhlcentral.com**.

2 Expansion Continue the activity with additional fill-in-the-blank statements such as these.
7. _____ est entraîneur d'une équipe espagnole. (Zinédine)
8. _____ est championne aux Jeux Olympiques de 1996. (Laura)

3 Expansion Have students prepare five sentences in the first person for homework, describing themselves as a well-known athlete. Ask students to introduce themselves to the class. The class tries to guess the presenter's identity.

OPTIONS

Des champions Look at the map of the world in **Appendice A** to remind students where francophone countries featured in **Le monde francophone** are located. Ask students to pick one of the athletes from this list to research for homework. They should come to the next class with five French sentences about that athlete's life and career. You may want to have students bring an image from the Internet of the athlete they chose to research. Collect the photos and gather different images of the same athlete. Have students who researched the same champion work together as a group to present that athlete while the rest of the class looks at the images they found.

Section Goals

In this section, students will learn:
• the verb **faire**
• expressions with **faire**
• the expression **il faut**

Instructional Resources
vhlcentral.com: Lab MP3s; SAM Answer Key; Digital Image Bank; Essayez! and Mise en pratique answers; Lab Audioscript; Activity Pack (Feuilles d'activités); reference tools

Suggestions

• Point out that students have seen **faire** in previous lessons. Example: **faire ses devoirs** in **Leçon 2B Roman-photo.**
• Model **faire** with the whole class by asking: **Qu'est-ce que vous faites? Je fais...** Then, using the 5A **Contextes** illustration from the Digital Image Bank, ask what people in the image are doing.
• Write the forms of **faire** on the board as students hear them in your questions. If **tu** and **nous** forms are missing, complete the conjugation by asking a student: **Tu fais attention?** Then ask: **Qu'est-ce que nous faisons? (Nous apprenons/ faisons attention.)**
• Point out that **fai-** in **nous faisons** is pronounced differently than **fai-** in all other forms. Underline the first syllable of the **nous** form and have students repeat.
• Ask students where they have seen the **-s, -s, -t** pattern. (**boire: je bois, tu bois, il/elle boit**)

5A.1

The verb *faire*  Tutorial

Point de départ Like other commonly used verbs, the verb **faire** (*to do, to make*) is irregular in the present tense.

faire (to do, to make)	
je fais	nous faisons
tu fais	vous faites
il/elle/on fait	ils/elles font

Il ne **fait** pas ses devoirs.
He doesn't do his homework.

Tes parents **font**-ils quelque chose vendredi?
Are your parents doing anything Friday?

Qu'est-ce que vous **faites** ce soir?
What are you doing this evening?

Nous **faisons** une sculpture dans mon cours d'art.
We're making a sculpture in my art class.

On fait du sport aujourd'hui!

Qu'est-ce que vous faites en histoire-géo?

• Use the verb **faire** in these idiomatic expressions. Note that it is not always translated into English as *to do* or *to make*.

Boîte à outils

The verb **faire** is also used in idiomatic expressions relating to math. Example:

Trois et quatre **font** sept.
Three plus four equals (makes) seven.

Expressions with *faire*			
faire de l'aérobic	to do aerobics	faire de la planche à voile	to go wind-surfing
faire attention (à)	to pay attention (to)	faire une promenade	to go for a walk
faire du camping	to go camping	faire une randonnée	to go for a hike
faire du cheval	to go horseback riding	faire du ski	to go skiing
faire la connaissance de...	to meet (someone) for the first time	faire du sport	to play sports
faire la cuisine	to cook	faire un tour (en voiture)	to go for a walk (drive)
faire de la gym	to work out	faire du vélo	to go bike riding
faire du jogging	to go jogging		

Tu **fais** souvent **du sport**?
Do you play sports often?

Elles **font du camping**.
They go camping.

Je **fais de la gym**.
I'm working out.

Nous **faisons attention** en classe.
We pay attention in class.

Yves **fait la cuisine**.
Yves is cooking.

Faites-vous **une promenade**?
Are you going for a walk?

186 *cent quatre-vingt-six*

• Make sure to learn the correct article with each **faire** expression that calls for one. For **faire** expressions requiring a partitive or indefinite article (**un, une, du, de la**), the article is replaced with **de** when the expression is negated.

Elles font **de la** gym trois fois par semaine.
They work out three times a week.

Elles ne font pas **de** gym le dimanche.
They don't work out on Sundays.

Fais-tu **du** ski?
Do you ski?

Non, je ne fais pas **de** ski.
No, I don't ski.

• Use **faire la connaissance de** before someone's name or another noun that identifies a person you do not know.

Je vais enfin **faire la connaissance de Martin**.
I'm finally going to meet Martin.

Je vais **faire la connaissance des joueurs**.
I'm going to meet the players.

The expression *il faut*

Pour être bon, il faut travailler!

Il ne faut pas regarder la télé.

• When followed by a verb in the infinitive, the expression **il faut...** means *it is necessary to...* or *one must...*

Il faut faire attention en cours de maths.
It is necessary to pay attention in math class.

Il ne faut pas manger après dix heures.
One must not eat after 10 o'clock.

Faut-il laisser un pourboire?
Is it necessary to leave a tip?

Il faut gagner le match!
We must win the game!

 Essayez! Complétez chaque phrase avec la forme correcte du verbe **faire** au présent.

1. Tu ___*fais*___ tes devoirs le samedi?
2. Vous ne ___faites___ pas attention au professeur.
3. Nous ___faisons___ du camping.
4. Ils ___font___ du jogging.
5. On ___fait___ une promenade au parc.
6. Il ___fait___ du ski en montagne.
7. Je ___fais___ de l'aérobic.
8. Elles ___font___ un tour en voiture.
9. Est-ce que vous ___faites___ la cuisine?
10. Nous ne ___faisons___ pas de sport.
11. Je ne ___fais___ pas de planche à voile.
12. Irène et Sandrine ___font___ une randonnée avec leurs copines.

Suggestions
• To facilitate memorization, have students compare **faire** with **aller**, **avoir**, and **être**, noting similarities in the forms. Examples: **tu fais, vas, as, es**; **nous faisons, avons, allons**; **vous êtes, faites**; etc.
• Explain that **il faut** is a very common expression in French even though its English translations are not as widely used in everyday language.
• Consider explaining to students that the negative form of the expression, **il ne faut pas**, is most often used to mean *one must not* rather than *it is not necessary*.

Essayez!
• Draw students' attention to the the use of **de** in items 10 and 11.
• Have students check each other's answers.

Boîte à outils

Be careful not to confuse **il faut** and **il fait**. The infinitive of **fait** is **faire**.

The infinitive of **faut**, however, is **falloir**. Falloir is an irregular impersonal verb, which means that it only has one conjugated form in every tense: the third person singular. The verbs **pleuvoir** (*to rain*) and **neiger** (*to snow*), which you will learn in **Leçon 5B**, work the same way.

ressources

WB
pp. 59–60

LM
p. 35

vhlcentral

Game Divide the class into two teams. Pick one team member at a time to go to the board, alternating between teams. Give a subject pronoun that the team member must write and say aloud with the correct form of **faire**. Example: **vous (vous faites)**. Give a point for each correct answer. The game ends when all students have had a chance to go to the board. The team with the most points at the end of the game wins.

Extra Practice Have students study the captions from **Roman-photo**. In small groups, tell them to think of additional phrases containing **faire** expressions and **il faut** that the characters would likely say. Write the main characters' names on the board in a row and have volunteers put their ideas underneath. Ask what can be concluded about each character. Example: **Rachid donne beaucoup de conseils.**

ESPACE STRUCTURES

Leçon 5A

Mise en pratique

1 Que font-ils? Regardez les dessins. Que font les personnages?

Julien

▶ **MODÈLE**

Julien fait du jogging.

1. Je
Je fais du cheval.

2. tu
Tu fais de la planche à voile.

3. Anne
Anne fait de l'aérobic.

4. Louis et Paul
Louis et Paul font du camping.

      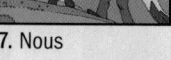 

5. Vous
Vous faites la cuisine.

6. Denis
Denis fait du ski.

7. Nous
Nous faisons une randonnée.

8. Elles
Elles font du vélo.

2 Chassez l'intrus Quelle activité ne fait pas partie du groupe?

1. a. faire du jogging   b. faire une randonnée   ⓒ faire de la planche à voile

2. a. faire du vélo   ⓑ faire du camping   c. faire du jogging

3. a. faire une promenade   ⓑ faire la cuisine   c. faire un tour

4. a. faire du sport   b. faire du vélo   ⓒ faire la connaissance

5. ⓐ faire ses devoirs   b. faire du ski   c. faire du camping

6. ⓐ faire la cuisine   b. faire du sport   c. faire de la planche à voile

3 La paire Faites correspondre (*Match*) les éléments des deux colonnes et rajoutez (*add*) la forme correcte du verbe **faire**.

1. Elle aime courir
(*to run*), alors elle...   e. fait du jogging.

2. Ils adorent les
animaux. Ils...   d. font du cheval.

3. Quand j'ai faim, je...   b. fais la cuisine.

4. L'hiver, vous...   g. faites du ski.

5. Pour marcher, nous...   f. faisons une promenade.

6. Tiger Woods...   a. fait du golf.

a. du golf.

b. la cuisine.

c. les devoirs.

d. du cheval.

e. du jogging.

f. une promenade.

g. du ski.

h. de l'aérobic.

 Practice more at **vhlcentral.com**.

1 Suggestion Bring in images of people doing other activities with **faire** expressions. Ask: **Que fait-il/elle?**

2 Suggestion Have pairs of students drill each other on the meanings of expressions with **faire** (that are not cognates). Then tell them to cover that half of the page with paper or a book before doing this activity.

3 Suggestion Have students check their answers with a partner. If partners disagree, have them say: **Mais non, il ne fait pas...** Remind students that any expression with the partitive must use **pas de** when negative.

Communication

4 Ce week-end Que faites-vous ce week-end? Avec un(e) partenaire, posez les questions à tour de rôle. *Answers will vary.*

MODÈLE

tu / jogging
Étudiant(e) 1: Est-ce que tu fais du jogging ce week-end?
Étudiant(e) 2: Non, je ne fais pas de jogging. Je fais un tour en voiture.

1. tu / le vélo   Est-ce que tu fais du vélo ce week-end?
2. tes amis / la cuisine   Est-ce que tes amis font la cuisine ce week-end?
3. ton/ta petit(e) ami(e) et toi, vous / le jogging   Est-ce que ton/ta petit(e) ami(e) et toi, vous faites du jogging ce week-end?
4. toi et moi, nous / une randonnée   Est-ce que toi et moi, nous faisons une randonnée ce week-end?
5. tu / la gym   Est-ce que tu fais de la gym ce week-end?
6. ton/ta camarade de chambre / le sport   Est-ce que ton/ta camarade de chambre fait du sport ce week-end?
7. on / faire de la planche à voile   Est-ce qu'on fait de la planche à voile ce week-end?
8. tes parents et toi, vous / un tour au parc   Est-ce que tes parents et toi, vous faites un tour au parc ce week-end?

5 De bons conseils Avec un(e) partenaire, donnez de bons conseils (*advice*). À tour de rôle, posez des questions et utilisez les éléments de la liste. Présentez vos idées à la classe. *Answers will vary.*

MODÈLE

Étudiant(e) 1: Qu'est-ce qu'il faut faire pour avoir de bonnes notes?
Étudiant(e) 2: Il faut étudier jour et nuit.

être en pleine forme (*great shape*)	avoir de bonnes notes
avoir de l'argent	gagner une course (*race*)
avoir beaucoup d'amis	bien manger
être champion de ski	réussir (*succeed*) aux examens

6 Les sportifs Votre professeur va vous donner une feuille d'activités. Faites une enquête sur le nombre d'étudiants qui pratiquent certains sports et activités dans votre classe. Présentez les résultats à la classe. *Answers will vary.*

MODÈLE

Étudiant(e) 1: Est-ce que tu fais du jogging?
Étudiant(e) 2: Oui, je fais du jogging.

Sport	Nom
1. jogging	Carole
2. vélo	
3. planche à voile	
4. cuisine	
5. camping	
6. cheval	
7. aérobic	
8. ski	

4 Expansion Have students come up with four more activities using expressions with **faire** that they would like to ask their partner about. Encourage students to include adverbs or other logical additions in their answers.

5 Expansion Write **Qu'est-ce qu'il faut faire pour...** on the board followed by a few of the most talked about expressions from the box. Have volunteers write their ideas under each expression, forming columns of categories. Accept several answers for each. Ask: **Êtes-vous d'accord? Pourquoi?**

5 Suggestion Consider asking students to give advice about what *not* to do using the expression **il ne faut pas**.

6 Suggestions
• Read the **modèle** aloud with a volunteer. Then distribute the **Feuilles d'activités** found in the Activity Pack on the Supersite.
• Have students say how popular these activities are among classmates. Tell them to be prepared to justify their statements by citing how many students participate in each. Example: **Faire du jogging, c'est très populaire. Quinze étudiants de notre classe font du jogging.**

OPTIONS

TPR Assign gestures to pantomime some of the expressions with **faire**. Examples: **faire de l'aérobic, la connaissance de...,** **du jogging, du ski.** Signal to individuals or pairs to gesture appropriately as you cue activities by saying: **Vous faites...** _____ **fait...** Then ask for a few volunteers to take your place calling out the activities.

Extra Practice Write on the board two headings: **Il faut...** and **Il ne faut pas...** Have students think of as many general pieces of advice (**les conseils**) as possible. Tell them to use **être**, any **-er** verbs, **avoir** and expressions with **avoir, aller, prendre, boire,** and **faire** to formulate the sentences. Examples: **Il faut souvent boire de l'eau. Il ne faut pas manger trop de sucre.** See how many sentences the class can write.

Section Goals

In this section, students will learn:
• the verbs **sortir** and **partir**
• other irregular **-ir** verbs

Instructional Resources
vhlcentral.com:
Activity Pack; Lab MP3s;
SAM Answer Key; **Essayez!**
and **Mise en pratique**
answers; Lab Audioscript;
reference tools

Suggestions

• Ask students where they have heard irregular **-ir** verbs before. (They heard **sortir** in this lesson's **Roman-photo**. If students have been to French-speaking places, they may have noticed the noun derived from **sortir**, **la sortie**, on **SORTIE** signs.)
• Model the pronunciation of forms for **sortir** and **partir**. Ask students simple questions. Example: **Je sors d'habitude le vendredi soir. Quand sortez-vous? (Je sors le samedi soir.)** As you elicit responses, write the present-tense forms of **sortir** on the board until the conjugation is complete. Underline the endings.
• Point out the recurrence of the **-s, -s, -t** pattern in singular forms.

Leçon 5A

5A.2

Irregular *-ir* verbs

 Tutorial

Point de départ In **Leçon 4B**, you learned to conjugate regular **-ir** verbs. However, some of the most commonly used **-ir** verbs are irregular in their conjugation.

• **Sortir** is used to express leaving a room or a building. It also expresses the idea of going out, as with friends or on a date.

sortir	
je sors	nous sortons
tu sors	vous sortez
il/elle/on sort	ils/elles sortent

Tu **sors** souvent avec tes copains?
Do you go out often with your friends?

Quand **sortez**-vous?
When are you going out?

Mon frère n'aime pas **sortir** avec Chloé.
My brother doesn't like to go out with Chloé.

Mes parents ne **sortent** pas lundi.
My parents aren't going out Monday.

• Use the preposition **de** after **sortir** when the place someone is leaving is mentioned.

L'étudiant **sort de** la salle de classe.
The student is leaving the classroom.

Nous **sortons du** restaurant vers vingt heures.
We're leaving the restaurant around 8:00 p.m.

Le week-end, je sors souvent.

Ils partent pour la fac.

Boîte à outils

As you learned in **Leçon 4A**, **quitter** is used to say that someone is leaving a place or another person: **Tu quittes Montréal?** (*Are you leaving Montréal?*)

• **Partir** is generally used to say someone is leaving a large place such as a city, country, or region. Often, a form of **partir** is accompanied by the preposition **pour** and the name of a destination.

partir	
je pars	nous partons
tu pars	vous partez
il/elle/on part	ils/elles partent

Je **pars pour** l'Algérie.
I'm leaving for Algeria.

Ils **partent pour** Genève demain.
They're leaving for Geneva tomorrow.

À quelle heure **partez**-vous?
At what time are you leaving?

Nous **partons** à midi.
We're leaving at noon.

190 *cent quatre-vingt-dix*

Other irregular -ir verbs

	dormir (to sleep)	servir (to serve)	sentir (to feel)	courir (to run)
je	dors	sers	sens	cours
tu	dors	sers	sens	cours
il/elle/on	dort	sert	sent	court
nous	dormons	servons	sentons	courons
vous	dormez	servez	sentez	courez
ils/elles	dorment	servent	sentent	courent

Rachid dort.

Nous courons.

Elles **dorment** jusqu'à midi.
They sleep until noon.

Je **sers** du fromage à la fête.
I'm serving cheese at the party.

Vous **courez** vite!
You run fast!

Nous **servons** du thé glacé.
We are serving iced tea.

- **Sentir** can mean *to feel, to smell,* or *to sense.*

  Je **sens** que l'examen va être difficile.
  I sense that the exam is going to be difficult.

  Ça **sent** bon!
  That smells good!

  Vous **sentez** le café?
  Do you smell the coffee?

  Ils **sentent** sa présence.
  They feel his presence.

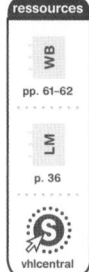

Essayez! Complétez les phrases avec la forme correcte du verbe.

1. Nous __sortons__ (sortir) vers neuf heures.
2. Je __sers__ (servir) des boissons gazeuses aux invités.
3. Tu __pars__ (partir) quand pour le Canada?
4. Nous ne __dormons__ (dormir) pas en cours.
5. Ils __courent__ (courir) pour attraper (*to catch*) le bus.
6. Tu manges des oignons? Ça __sent__ (sentir) mauvais.
7. Vous __sortez__ (sortir) avec des copains ce soir.
8. Elle __part__ (partir) pour Dijon ce week-end.

ressources

WB
pp. 61–62

LM
p. 36

vhlcentral

Suggestions
- Reiterate that **sortir** is used as *to go out* or *to exit* while **partir** means *to leave.* Ask students to think of more examples comparing the two verbs. Point out the note about **quitter** in the **Boîte à outils** on page 190. Using ideas from students, write on the board a short paragraph (two to three sentences) that contains at least one form of each of the three verbs mentioned above. Make sure the context defines the meanings well.
- Go over other irregular -**ir** verbs, pointing out that they are all in the same grammatical "verb family" as **sortir** and **partir.** Note that all verbs of this type have two stems: **sortir:** singular stem **sor-** and plural stem **sort-.** Point out that **courir** does not follow exactly the same pattern as the other verbs in the singular forms.

Essayez! Give these items for additional practice, having students choose which -**ir** verb(s) to use. **1. J'adore _____. (courir) Je _____ vingt à trente kilomètres par semaine. (cours) 2. Les enfants ne _____ pas parce qu'ils ne sont pas fatigués. (dorment) 3. Qu'est-ce qu'on _____ au café en face de chez toi? (sert) 4. Merci pour les fleurs. Elles _____ très bon. (sentent)**

TPR Tell students that they will act out the appropriate gestures when you say what certain people in the class are doing. Examples: _____ **dort.** (The student gestures sleeping.) _____ **et** _____ **courent.** (The two students indicated run in place briefly.) Repeat verbs and vary forms as much as possible.

Extra Practice Dictate sentences like these to the class, saying each one twice and pausing between. **1. Je pars pour la France la semaine prochaine. 2. Mon copain et moi, nous sortons ce soir. 3. Les étudiants ne dorment jamais en classe. 4. Le café sent bon. 5. Tu cours vite. 6. Que servez-vous au restaurant?** Advise students to pay attention to the verbs.

OPTIONS

1 Suggestion Give a tip on how to choose between **sortir** and **partir**. Remind students that **partir** is often followed by the preposition **pour**.

2 Suggestions
• Have students write at least five sentences describing their family's and friends' habits.
• In pairs, have students compare the information. Example: **Étudiant(e) 1: Est-ce que tu dors jusqu'à midi? Étudiant(e) 2: Oui, mais rarement. Étudiant(e) 1: Moi, jamais!**
• Ask for volunteers to share some of their sentences with the class.

3 Expansion Ask students to imagine they are on the telephone and a classmate can overhear them. Have students write three answers to say in front of a partner who will guess the questions. Example: **Non, maman, on ne sort pas trop souvent. Je fais mes devoirs tous les soirs. (Tu ne sors pas trop souvent avec tes copains?)**

Mise en pratique

1 **Choisissez** Monique et ses amis aiment bien sortir. Choisissez la forme correcte des verbes **partir** ou **sortir** pour compléter la description de leurs activités.

1. Samedi soir, je ___sors___ avec mes copains.
2. Mes copines Magali et Anissa ___partent___ pour New York.
3. Nous ___sortons___ du cinéma.
4. Nicolas ___part___ pour Dakar vers dix heures du soir.
5. À minuit, vous ___partez___ pour la boîte.
6. Je ___pars___ pour le Maroc dans une semaine.
7. Tu ___sors/pars___ avec ton petit ami ce week-end.
8. Olivier et Bernard ___sortent___ tard du bureau.
9. Lucien et moi, nous ___partons___ pour l'Algérie.
10. Thomas ___sort___ du stade à deux heures de l'après-midi.

2 **Vos habitudes** Utilisez les éléments des colonnes pour décrire (*describe*) les habitudes de votre famille et de vos amis. Answers will vary.

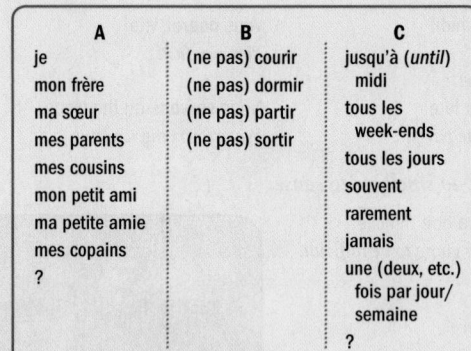

A	B	C
je	(ne pas) courir	jusqu'à (*until*) midi
mon frère	(ne pas) dormir	tous les week-ends
ma sœur	(ne pas) partir	tous les jours
mes parents	(ne pas) sortir	souvent
mes cousins		rarement
mon petit ami		jamais
ma petite amie		une (deux, etc.) fois par jour/ semaine
mes copains		
?		?

3 **La question** Vincent parle au téléphone avec sa mère. Vous entendez (*hear*) ses réponses, mais pas les questions. Avec un(e) partenaire, reconstruisez la conversation. Answers will vary.

MODÈLE

Comment vas-tu? Ça va bien, merci.

1. _____ Oui, je sors ce soir.
2. _____ Je sors avec Marc et Audrey.
3. _____ Nous partons à six heures.
4. _____ Oui, nous allons jouer au tennis.
5. _____ Après, nous allons au restaurant.
6. _____ Nous sortons du restaurant à neuf heures.
7. _____ Marc et Audrey partent pour Nice le week-end prochain.
8. _____ Non. Moi, je pars dans deux semaines.

 Practice more at **vhlcentral.com**.

Communication

4 **Descriptions** Avec un(e) partenaire, complétez les phrases avec la forme correcte d'un verbe de la liste.

courir	dormir	partir	sentir	servir	sortir

1. Véronique / _____ / tard   Véronique dort tard.

2. je / _____ / sandwichs   Je sers des sandwichs.

3. les enfants / _____ / le chocolat chaud   Les enfants sentent le chocolat chaud.

4. nous / _____ / souvent   Nous courons souvent.

5. tu / _____ / de l'hôpital   Tu sors de l'hôpital.

6. vous / _____ / pour la France demain   Vous partez pour la France demain.

5 **Indiscrétions** Votre partenaire est curieux/curieuse et désire savoir (*to know*) ce que vous faites chez vous. Répondez à ses questions.   Answers will vary.

1. Jusqu'à (*Until*) quelle heure dors-tu le week-end?
2. Dors-tu pendant (*during*) les cours à la fac? Pendant quels cours? Pourquoi?
3. À quelle heure sors-tu le samedi soir?
4. Avec qui sors-tu le samedi soir?
5. Est-ce que tu sors souvent avec des copains pendant la semaine?
6. Que sers-tu quand tu as des invités à la maison?
7. Pars-tu bientôt en vacances (*vacation*)? Où?

6 **Dispute** Laëtitia est très active. Son petit ami Bertrand ne sort pas beaucoup, alors ils ont souvent des disputes. Avec un(e) partenaire, jouez les deux rôles. Utilisez les mots et les expressions de la liste.   Answers will vary.

dormir	partir
faire des promenades	un passe-temps
	sentir
faire un tour (en voiture)	sortir
	rarement
par semaine	souvent

4 **Expansion** Find a photo to use for a **modèle**. Example: Write **Les chats** and **beaucoup** on the board. Between the two words, insert an image of cats sleeping.

4 **Suggestion** Have students ask **Que fait Véronique?** (item 1), **Qu'est-ce que je fais?** (item 2), etc. before partners answer.

5 **Suggestion** Remind students to answer in complete sentences.

6 **Suggestion** Have a couple of volunteer pairs act out their conversations for the class.

OPTIONS

Game Divide the class into two teams. Announce an infinitive and a subject pronoun. Example: **dormir; elle**. At the board, have the first member of Team A say and write down the given subject and the conjugated form of the verb. If the team member answers correctly, Team A gets one point. If not, give the first member of Team B the same example. The team with the most points at the end of the game wins.

Small Groups Have small groups of students create a short story in the present tense or a conversation in which they logically mention as many verb forms as possible of **sortir**, **partir**, **dormir**, **servir**, **sentir**, and **courir**. If the class is advanced, add **mentir**. Call on groups to tell their story to the class or act out their conversation. Have students vote on the best story or conversation.

Révision

Instructional Resources
vhlcentral.com:
Activity Pack (Info Gap
Activities); Testing Program;
Testing Program MP3s;
reference tools

1 Suggestion After the groups have collaborated, ask them how many activities they described. Have the group with most sentences share them with the class.

2 Suggestion Remind students that adverbs like **rarement**, **souvent**, and **toujours** should be placed immediately after the verb, not at the end of a sentence or elsewhere as in English. Example: **Je fais rarement du cheval.** They should never say: **je fais du cheval rarement** or **je rarement fais du cheval.**

3 Suggestion Have students say what their partners are going to do on vacation, when, where, and with whom.

4 Suggestion Call on two volunteers to read the **modèle**.

4 Expansion Have students continue the activity with additional places, such as **à la faculté, au resto U, au centre-ville**, etc.

5 Suggestion Tell students to use as many irregular **-ir** verbs and **faire** expressions as possible.

6 Suggestion Divide the class into pairs and distribute the Info Gap Handouts found in the Activity Pack on the Supersite. Give students ten minutes to complete the activity.

---

1 Au parc C'est dimanche. Avec un(e) partenaire, décrivez les activités de tous les personnages. Comparez vos observations avec les observations d'un autre groupe pour compléter votre description. *Answers will vary.*

2 Mes habitudes Avec un(e) partenaire, parlez de vos habitudes de la semaine. Que faites-vous régulièrement? Utilisez tous les mots de la liste. *Answers will vary.*

 **MODÈLE**

Étudiant(e) 1: *Je fais parfois de la gym le lundi. Et toi?*
Étudiant(e) 2: *Moi, je fais parfois la cuisine le lundi.*

parfois le lundi	souvent à midi
le mercredi à midi	toujours le vendredi
le jeudi soir	tous les jours
le vendredi matin	trois fois par semaine
rarement le matin	une fois par semaine

3 Mes vacances Parlez de vos prochaines vacances (*vacation*) avec un(e) partenaire. Mentionnez cinq de vos passe-temps habituels en vacances et cinq nouvelles activités que vous allez essayer (*to try*). Comparez votre liste avec la liste de votre partenaire, puis présentez les réponses à la classe. *Answers will vary.*

---

4 Que faire ici? Avec un(e) partenaire, trouvez au minimum quatre choses à faire dans chaque (*each*) endroit. Quel endroit préférez-vous et pourquoi? Comparez votre liste avec un autre groupe et parlez de vos préférences avec la classe. *Answers will vary.*

MODÈLE

Étudiant(e) 1: *À la campagne, on fait des randonnées à cheval.*
Étudiant(e) 2: *Oui, et il faut marcher.*

1. à la campagne

2. au parc

3. à la plage

4. au gymnase

5 Le conseiller Un(e) conseiller/conseillère à la fac suggère des stratégies à un(e) étudiant(e) pour l'aider (*help him or her*) à préparer les examens. Avec un(e) partenaire, jouez les deux rôles. Vos camarades vont sélectionner les meilleurs conseils (*best advice*).

 MODÈLE

Il faut faire tous ses devoirs.

6 Quelles activités? Votre professeur va vous donner, à vous et à votre partenaire, deux feuilles d'activités différentes pour le week-end. Attention! Ne regardez pas la feuille de votre partenaire. *Answers will vary.*

 MODÈLE

Étudiant(e) 1: *Est-ce que tu fais une randonnée dimanche après-midi?*
Étudiant(e) 2: *Oui, je fais une randonnée dimanche après-midi.*

OPTIONS

Extra Practice Ask students to write five sentences individually, at least two with **faire**, at least one with **il faut**, and at least three with different irregular **-ir** verbs. Tell them to try to include more than one requirement in each sentence. Have students dictate their sentences to their partner. After both students in each pair have finished dictating their sentences, have them exchange papers for correction.

Pairs Have students take turns telling their partners about a memorable vacation experience, who they were with, what they did, etc. Encourage students to express themselves using as much variety as possible in terms of vocabulary and grammar structures. Have students take notes as their partner narrates to share later with the class.

Les loisirs

Hôtesse: Csilla

Csilla est à Aix-en-Provence et nous montre° des sports pratiqués dans la région et en France, en général. Ensuite°, elle va à la Maison des Jeunes et de la Culture (MJC), où on peut faire différents types d'activités.

Avant de regarder Répondez aux questions. *Answers will vary.*

1. Est-ce que vous aimez le sport? Pourquoi ou pourquoi pas?
2. Quels sports est-ce que les habitants de votre ville aiment faire?
3. Quelles sont les activités sportives qu'on peut pratiquer dans votre région?

CSILLA *On fait du jogging.*

CSILLA *En France, et surtout dans le sud, on adore jouer à la pétanque.*

Compréhension Répondez aux questions. *Some answers will vary.*

1. Quelles sont les deux activités aquatiques présentées dans la vidéo?
   Ce sont la planche à voile et le canoë.
2. Mentionnez quelques sports pratiqués en extérieur dans la vidéo.
   On fait du jogging; on joue au football, au tennis, au basket; on court.
3. Quels sont les loisirs qu'on peut pratiquer à la MJC? *On peut faire de*
   la gym, de la sculpture (ou de la poterie), de la peinture, de l'aérobic, de la danse et de la musique.
4. À la fin de la vidéo, Csilla parle d'une autre activité culturelle. Qu'est-ce que c'est?
   Csilla parle du cinéma. Elle adore aller au cinéma.

Discussion Par groupes de trois, discutez des sports présentés dans la vidéo. *Answers will vary.*

1. Faites-vous les mêmes sports qu'on fait à Aix-en-Provence?
2. Faites-vous d'autres types de sports pendant votre temps libre?

Vocabulaire utile

en extérieur/en intérieur	outdoors/indoors
faire du canoë	to go canoeing
la Maison des Jeunes et de la Culture	Youth and Cultural Center
la peinture	painting
on court	we run

ressources

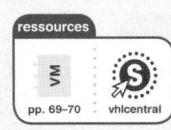

VM pp. 69–70   vhlcentral

montre *shows* Ensuite *Then, Next*

Practice more at **vhlcentral.com**.

cent quatre-vingt-quinze **195**

Section Goals

In this section, students will:
- watch a video about sports and leisure activities in Aix-en-Provence
- answer questions about the video and compare sports and leisure activities in France with those in their hometown

Instructional Resources
vhlcentral.com: **Flash culture**; **Flash culture** *transcription; reference tools*

Avant de regarder
Have students look at the video stills, read the captions, and predict what types of activities the video will show. Before showing the video, explain to students that they don't need to understand every word they hear. Tell them to listen for vocabulary from this lesson as well as cognates for sports and leisure activities.

Compréhension Have students work in pairs or groups for this activity. Tell them to write their answers. Then, show the video again so that they can check their answers and add any missing information.

Discussion Ask volunteers to share their group's answers with the class. Take a quick class survey to find out if students practice the same sports shown in the video.

La pétanque **Pétanque** is a sport traditionally associated with Provence, but it is also popular in the rest of France and internationally. Many amateur players enjoy playing the sport with friends in their free time or during summer vacation, but there are also more than 300,000 licensed **pétanque** players in France. These players take the game seriously, competing in local and regional competitions, as well as in the international competitions held each year, such as the European Championship and the World Cup.

Section Goals

In this section, students will learn and practice vocabulary related to:
• the weather
• seasons and dates

Instructional Resources

vhlcentral.com:
Digital Image Bank (including vocabulary illustrations from the textbook, theme-based illustrations); **Vocabulaire supplémentaire; Mise en pratique** *answers; Textbook Audioscript; Lab Audioscript; Activity Pack (Info Gap Activities); Textbook MP3s; Lab MP3s; SAM Answer Key; reference tools*

Suggestions

• Introduce weather-related vocabulary by describing the weather in your area today. Example: **Aujourd'hui, il pleut et il fait du vent.**
• Use the **5B Contextes** illustration from the Digital Image Bank to present new vocabulary. See how many of the words and expressions your students can understand without looking at their translations.
• Tell students that most weather expressions use the verb **faire**, but **neiger** and **pleuvoir** stand alone. Point out that these verbs are only used in the third person singular.
• Point out that the expressions **avoir froid** and **avoir chaud** refer to people, but **faire froid** and **faire chaud** describe weather. Bring in photos that include people to illustrate this distinction.
• Using magazine photos of weather conditions and seasons, describe each image. Show photos again one at a time. Then ask: **En quelle saison sommes-nous? Quel temps fait-il?**
• Use the Vocabulary illustrations and the Weather and seasons illustrations from the Digital Image Bank to help students familiarize themselves with talking about seasons, the date, and the weather.
• Additional terms for this lesson can be found in the **Vocabulaire supplémentaire** on the Supersite.

Leçon 5B

You will learn how to...
▪ **talk about seasons and the date**
▪ **discuss the weather**

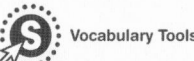 Vocabulary Tools

Quel temps fait-il?

Vocabulaire

Il fait 18 degrés.	*It is 18 degrees.*
Il fait beau.	*The weather is nice.*
Il fait bon.	*The weather is good/warm.*
Il fait mauvais.	*The weather is bad.*
Il fait un temps épouvantable.	*The weather is dreadful.*
Le temps est orageux.	*It is stormy.*
Quel temps fait-il?	*What is the weather like?*
Quelle température fait-il?	*What is the temperature?*
une saison	*season*
en automne	*in the fall*
en été	*in the summer*
en hiver	*in the winter*
au printemps	*in the spring*
Quelle est la date?	*What's the date?*
C'est le 1er (premier) octobre.	*It's the first of October.*
C'est quand votre/ton anniversaire?	*When is your birthday?*
C'est le 2 mai.	*It's the second of May.*
C'est quand l'anniversaire de Paul?	*When is Paul's birthday?*
C'est le 15 mars.	*It's March 15th.*
un anniversaire	*birthday*

ressources

| WB pp. 63–64 | LM p. 37 | vhlcentral |

Il neige. (neiger)

Il fait froid.

L'hiver (*m.*): décembre, janvier, février

Il fait (du) soleil.

Bal du 14 juillet

Quelle est la date d'aujourd'hui? C'est le 14 juillet.

Il fait chaud.

L'été (*m.*): juin, juillet, août

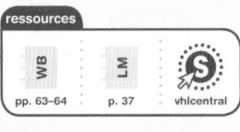

Pairs Distribute a set of illustrations of various weather conditions to pairs of students. Choose images with variety and have students write detailed descriptions of each one. They should describe the weather, the season, and any activities represented.

Extra Practice Distribute a calendar that shows **les fêtes**. First, call out dates and have students give the corresponding name on the calendar. Then call out names on the calendar and have students provide the date. Example: **la Saint-Valentin (le 14 février).**

Attention!

In France and in most of the francophone world, temperature is given in Celsius. Convert from Celsius to Fahrenheit with this formula: $F = (C \times 1.8) + 32$. Convert from Fahrenheit to Celsius with this formula: $C = (F - 32) \times 0.56$.
$11°C = 52°F$ $78°F = 26°C$

Il pleut. (pleuvoir)

un parapluie

un imperméable

Le printemps (*m.*): mars, avril, mai

Le temps est nuageux.

Il fait frais.

Il fait du vent.

L'automne (*m.*): septembre, octobre, novembre

Mise en pratique

1 Écoutez Écoutez le bulletin météorologique et répondez aux questions suivantes.

	Vrai	Faux
1. C'est l'été.	☐	☑
2. Le printemps commence le 21 mars.	☑	☐
3. Il fait 11 degrés vendredi.	☑	☐
4. Il fait du vent vendredi.	☐	☑
5. Il va faire soleil samedi.	☐	☑
6. Il faut utiliser le parapluie et l'imperméable vendredi.	☐	☑
7. Il va faire un temps épouvantable dimanche.	☑	☐
8. Il ne va pas faire chaud samedi.	☑	☐

2 Les fêtes et les jours fériés Indiquez la date et la saison de chaque fête et jour férié (*holidays*).

		Date	Saison
1.	la fête nationale française	le 14 juillet	l'été
2.	l'indépendance des États-Unis	le 4 juillet	l'été
3.	Poisson d'avril (*April Fool's Day*)	le 1er avril	le printemps
4.	Noël	le 25 décembre	l'hiver
5.	la Saint-Valentin	le 14 février	l'hiver
6.	le Nouvel An	le 1er janvier	l'hiver
7.	Halloween	le 31 octobre	l'automne
8.	l'anniversaire de Washington	le 22 février	l'hiver

3 Quel temps fait-il? Répondez aux questions par des phrases complètes. *Answers will vary.*

1. Quel temps fait-il en été?
2. Quel temps fait-il en automne?
3. Quel temps fait-il au printemps?
4. Quel temps fait-il en hiver?
5. Où est-ce qu'il neige?
6. Quel est votre mois préféré de l'année? Pourquoi?
7. Quand est-ce qu'il pleut où vous habitez?
8. Quand est-ce que le temps est orageux où vous habitez?

Practice more at vhlcentral.com.

cent quatre-vingt-dix-sept **197**

1 Audioscript Aujourd'hui, vendredi 21 mars, nous commençons le printemps avec une température de 11 degrés; il n'y a pas de vent, mais il y a quelques nuages.
Votre météo du week-end: samedi, il ne va pas faire soleil; il va faire frais avec une température de 13 degrés; dimanche, encore 13 degrés, mais il va faire un temps épouvantable; il va pleuvoir toute la journée, alors, n'oubliez pas votre parapluie et votre imperméable!
(*On Textbook MP3s*)

1 Suggestion Have students correct the false items.

2 Suggestions
• Remind students to give the date in the correct order (day before month) and to include **le** before the day.
• Point out that the day always precedes the month in French when the date is written with numbers. Examples: **14 avril 2011, 14/04/2011**

2 Expansion Using this year's calendar, have students find the dates of these holidays. **9. la fête du travail aux États-Unis 10.** *Thanksgiving* **11.** *Easter* (*Pâques*) **12.** *Memorial Day* You may ask students to look up dates of other secular celebrations or religious holidays from various faiths. Answers will vary from year to year.

3 Suggestions
• Have students work in pairs or small groups to answer these questions.
• Tell students they may also encounter the phrase **à l'automne**, meaning *this fall*. For other seasons, make sure they know to use **en** before those starting with a vowel sound and **au** with **printemps**, as it starts with a consonant.

OPTIONS

Le calendrier républicain During the French Revolution, the official calendar was changed. The New Year began on September 22 (the autumnal equinox), and the year was divided into 30-day months named as follows: **Vendémiaire** (*Vintage*), **Brumaire** (*Mist*), **Frimaire** (*Frost*), **Nivôse** (*Snow*), **Pluviôse** (*Rain*), **Ventôse** (*Wind*), **Germinal** (*Seed time*), **Floréal** (*Flower*), **Prairial** (*Meadow*), **Messidor** (*Harvest*), **Thermidor** (*Heat*), and **Fructidor** (*Fruits*).

Game Have students take turns guessing another student's birthday. He or she responds by saying **avant** or **après** until someone guesses correctly. The class then tries to guess the winning student's birthday. Play several rounds of this game to give all students as many opportunities as possible to guess.

Communication

4 **Suggestion** Have students share what they've learned about their partners with another pair of students or with the rest of the class.

5 **Suggestion** Encourage students to use a wide variety of expressions for seasons and activities. Have them exchange papers for peer editing.

6 **Suggestions**
• Divide the class into pairs and distribute the Info Gap Handouts found in the Activity Pack on the Supersite for this activity. Give students ten minutes to complete the activity.
• Have two volunteers read the **modèle**.

7 **Expansion** Assign a different francophone location to each pair of students and have them research its weather forecast on the Internet. Hold a vote without revealing names of students, and give prizes for the best presentation in various categories (**le plus amusant, créateur, utile,** and so on).

Successful Language Learning Tell students that when looking at materials intended for native speakers like weather forecasts, they should pay attention to visual cues and use their background knowledge about the subject to help them understand. They should try to anticipate vocabulary they might hear, listen for familiar sounding words, and make intelligent guesses.

4 **Conversez** Interviewez un(e) camarade de classe. Answers will vary.

1. C'est quand ton anniversaire? C'est quand l'anniversaire de ton père? Et de ta mère?
2. En quelle saison est ton anniversaire? Quel temps fait-il?
3. Quelle est ta saison préférée? Pourquoi? Quelles activités aimes-tu pratiquer?
4. En quelles saisons utilises-tu un parapluie et un imperméable? Pourquoi?
5. À quel moment de l'année es-tu en vacances? Précise les mois. Pendant (*During*) quels mois de l'année préfères-tu voyager? Pourquoi?
6. À quelle période de l'année étudies-tu? Précise les mois.
7. Quelle saison détestes-tu le plus (*the most*)? Pourquoi?
8. Quand est l'anniversaire de mariage de tes parents?

5 **Une lettre** Vous avez un(e) correspondant(e) (*pen pal*) en France qui veut (*wants*) vous rendre visite (*to visit you*). Écrivez (*Write*) une lettre à votre ami(e) où vous décrivez (*describe*) le temps qu'il fait à chaque saison et les activités que vous pouvez (*can*) pratiquer ensemble (*together*). Comparez votre lettre avec la lettre d'un(e) camarade de classe. Answers will vary.

> Cher Thomas,
>
> Ici à Boston, il fait très froid en hiver et il neige souvent. Est-ce que tu aimes la neige? Moi, j'adore parce que je fais du ski tous les week-ends.
>
> Et toi, tu fais du ski? ...

6 **Quel temps fait-il en France?** Votre professeur va vous donner, à vous et à votre partenaire, deux feuilles d'activités différentes. Attention! Ne regardez pas la feuille de votre partenaire. Answers will vary.

MODÈLE
Étudiant(e) 1: *Quel temps fait-il à Paris?*
Étudiant(e) 2: *À Paris, le temps est nuageux et la température est de dix degrés.*

7 **La météo** Préparez avec un(e) camarade de classe une présentation où vous: Answers will vary.

• mentionnez le jour, la date et la saison.
• présentez la météo d'une ville francophone.
• présentez les prévisions météo (*weather forecasts*) pour le reste de la semaine.
• préparez une affiche pour illustrer votre présentation.

La météo d'Haïti en juillet — Port-au-Prince

samedi 23	dimanche 24	lundi 25
27°C	35°C	37°C
☀	⛅	⛈
soleil	nuageux	orageux

Aujourd'hui samedi, c'est le 23 juillet.
C'est l'été. Il va faire soleil...

OPTIONS

TPR Write **C'est quand ton anniversaire?** on the board or on a transparency. Make a "human calendar" using students to represent various days. Have them form 12 rows (one for each month) and put themselves in order according to their birthdays by asking and answering the question. Give the person with the first birthday in each month a sign for that month. Call out each month and have students give their birthdays in order.

Small Groups Have students form groups of two to four. Hand out cards with the name of a holiday or other annual event. Instruct each group to hide their card from other groups. Groups come up with three sentences to describe the holiday or occasion without mentioning its name. They can mention the season. The other groups must first guess the month and day on which the event takes place, then name the event itself.

Les sons et les lettres   Audio

Open vs. closed vowels: Part 1

You have already learned that **é** is pronounced like the vowel *a* in the English word *cake*. This is a closed **e** sound.

étudiant	agré**a**ble	nationalit**é**	enchant**é**

The letter combinations **-er** and **-ez** at the end of a word are pronounced the same way, as is the vowel sound in single-syllable words ending in **-es**.

travaill**er**	av**ez**	m**es**	l**es**

The vowels spelled **è** and **ê** are pronounced like the vowel in the English word *pet*, as is an **e** followed by a double consonant. These are open **e** sounds.

rép**è**te	prem**iè**re	p**ê**che	itali**e**nne

The vowel sound in *pet* may also be spelled **et**, **ai**, or **ei**.

secr**et**	fran**çai**s	f**ai**t	s**ei**ze

Compare these pairs of words. To make the vowel sound in *cake*, your mouth should be slightly more closed than when you make the vowel sound in *pet*.

m**es** m**ai**s		c**es** c**e**tte		th**éâ**tre th**è**me

🔊 **Prononcez** Répétez les mots suivants à voix haute.

1. thé		4. été		7. degrés		10. discret
2. lait		5. neige		8. anglais		11. treize
3. belle		6. aider		9. cassette		12. mauvais

🔊 **Articulez** Répétez les phrases suivantes à voix haute.

1. Hélène est très discrète.
2. Céleste achète un vélo laid.
3. Il neige souvent en février et en décembre.
4. Désirée est canadienne; elle n'est pas française.

🔊 **Dictons** Répétez les dictons à voix haute.

Qui sème le vent récolte la tempête.[2]

Péché avoué est à demi pardonné.[1]

[1] An offense admitted is half pardoned.

[2] You reap what you sow. (lit. He who sows the wind reaps a storm.)

ressources

LM p. 38

vhlcentral

cent quatre-vingt-dix-neuf **199**

Section Goals

In this section, students will learn about open and closed vowels.

Instructional Resources
vhlcentral.com:
Textbook MP3s; Lab MP3s; SAM Answer Key; Textbook Audioscript; Lab Audioscript; reference tools

Suggestions

• Model the pronunciation of these open and closed vowel sounds and have students watch the shape of your mouth, then repeat each sound after you. Then pronounce each of the example words and have students repeat them.

• Mention words and expressions from the **Vocabulaire** on page 222 that contain the open and closed vowels presented on this page. Alternately, ask students to recall such vocabulary. Then have them repeat after you. Examples: **février**, **Il fait frais**, etc. See if a volunteer is able to recall any expression from previous lessons. Examples: **seize**, **vélo**, **aérobic**.

• Dictate five familiar words containing the open and closed vowels presented on this page, repeating each one at least two times. Then write them on the board or on a transparency and have students check and correct their spelling.

• Remind students that **ai** and **ei** are nasalized when followed by **m** or **n**. Compare the following words: **français / faim**, **seize / hein**.

• Point out that, unlike English, there is no diphthong or glide in these vowel sounds. To illustrate this, contrast the pronunciation of the English word *may* with that of the French word **mai**.

OPTIONS

Extra Practice Here are some sentences to use for additional practice with these open and closed vowel sounds. **1. Il fait soleil. 2. En janvier, il neige et il fait mauvais. 3. Toute la journée, j'aide ma mère. 4. Didier est français, mais Hélène est belge.**

Game Have a spelling bee using vocabulary words from **Leçons 1A–5B** that contain the two open and closed vowel sounds featured on this page. Pronounce each word, use it in a sentence, and then say the individual word again. Tell students that they must spell the words in French and include all diacritical marks.

Section Goals

In this section, students will learn functional phrases for talking about seasons, the weather, and birthdays through comprehensible input.

Instructional Resources

vhlcentral.com:
Roman-photo *Video, Videoscript, and Translation; SAM Answer Key; reference tools*

Video Recap: Leçon 5A
Review the previous **Roman-photo** with this activity.
1. Où sont les jeunes dans cet épisode? (Ils sont au parc.)
2. Que font Rachid et Stéphane? (Ils jouent au football.)
3. Qu'est-ce que Stéphane étudie? (de l'histoire-géo, Napoléon)
4. Qu'est-ce que Sandrine aime faire de ses loisirs? (aller au cinéma ou à des concerts)

Video Synopsis Rachid and Stéphane are in the park playing soccer. They talk about the weather. Meanwhile, David is sketching Sandrine at his apartment. They talk about the weather in Washington and things they like to do. Sandrine tells David that Stéphane's 18th birthday is next Saturday and invites him to the surprise party. Rachid arrives home and admires the portrait. Sandrine offers to make them all dinner.

Suggestions
• Ask students to predict what the episode will be about.
• Have students make a list of vocabulary they expect to see in an episode about weather and seasons.
• Ask students to read the **Roman-photo** conversation in groups of four. Ask one or two groups to present their dramatic readings to the class.
• Quickly review the predictions and confirm the correct ones.

Quel temps!  Video

PERSONNAGES

David

Rachid

Sandrine

Stéphane

Au parc...

RACHID Napoléon établit le Premier Empire en quelle année?
STÉPHANE Euh... mille huit cent quatre?
RACHID Exact! On est au mois de novembre et il fait toujours chaud.
STÉPHANE Oui, il fait bon!... dix-neuf, dix-huit degrés!

RACHID Et on a chaud aussi parce qu'on court.
STÉPHANE Bon, allez, je rentre faire mes devoirs d'histoire-géo.
RACHID Et moi, je rentre boire une grande bouteille d'eau.

RACHID À demain, Stéph! Et n'oublie pas: le cours du jeudi avec ton professeur, Monsieur Rachid Kahlid, commence à dix-huit heures, pas à dix-huit heures vingt!
STÉPHANE Pas de problème! Merci et à demain!

SANDRINE Et puis, en juillet, le Tour de France commence. J'aime bien le regarder à la télévision. Et après, c'est mon anniversaire, le 20. Cette année, je fête mes vingt et un ans. Tous les ans, pour célébrer mon anniversaire, j'invite mes amis et je prépare une super soirée. J'adore faire la cuisine, c'est une vraie passion!
DAVID Ah, oui?

SANDRINE En parlant d'anniversaire, Stéphane célèbre ses dix-huit ans samedi prochain. C'est un anniversaire important. ...On organise une surprise. Tu es invité!
DAVID Hmm, c'est très gentil, mais... Tu essaies de ne pas parler deux minutes, s'il te plaît? Parfait!

SANDRINE Pascal! Qu'est-ce que tu fais aujourd'hui? Il fait beau à Paris?
DAVID Encore un peu de patience! Allez, encore dix secondes... Voilà!

A C T I V I T É S

1 **Qui?** Identifiez les personnages pour chaque phrase. Écrivez **D** pour David, **R** pour Rachid, **S** pour Sandrine et **St** pour Stéphane.

1. Cette personne aime faire la cuisine.   S
2. Cette personne sort quand il fait froid.   D
3. Cette personne aime le Tour de France.   S
4. Cette personne n'aime pas la pluie.   S

5. Cette personne va boire de l'eau.   R
6. Ces personnes ont rendez-vous tous les jeudis.   R, St
7. Cette personne fête son anniversaire en janvier.   D
8. Ces personnes célèbrent un joli portrait.   D, R, S
9. Cette personne fête ses dix-huit ans samedi prochain.   St
10. Cette personne prépare des crêpes pour le dîner.   S

 Practice more at **vhlcentral.com**.

O P T I O N S

Avant de regarder la vidéo Before showing the video, show students individual photos and have them write their own captions. Ask volunteers to write their captions on the board.

Regarder la vidéo Download and print the videoscript found on the Supersite, and white out months, seasons, weather-related expressions, and other new vocabulary items. Distribute the scripts for pairs or groups to complete as cloze paragraphs as they watch the video.

Les anniversaires à travers (*through*) les saisons

À l'appartement de David et de Rachid...

SANDRINE C'est quand, ton anniversaire?

DAVID Qui, moi? Oh, c'est le quinze janvier.

SANDRINE Il neige en janvier, à Washington?

DAVID Parfois... et il pleut souvent à l'automne et en hiver.

SANDRINE Je déteste la pluie. C'est pénible. Qu'est-ce que tu aimes faire quand il pleut, toi?

DAVID Oh, beaucoup de choses! Dessiner, écouter de la musique. J'aime tellement la nature, je sors même quand il fait très froid.

SANDRINE Moi, je préfère l'été. Il fait chaud. On fait des promenades.

RACHID Oh là là, j'ai soif! Mais... qu'est-ce que vous faites, tous les deux?

DAVID Oh, rien! Je fais juste un portrait de Sandrine.

RACHID Bravo, c'est pas mal du tout! Hmm, mais quelque chose ne va pas, David. Sandrine n'a pas de téléphone dans la main!

SANDRINE Oh, Rachid, ça suffit! C'est vrai, tu as vraiment du talent, David. Pourquoi ne pas célébrer mon joli portrait? Vous avez faim, les garçons?

RACHID ET DAVID Oui!

SANDRINE Je prépare le dîner. Vous aimez les crêpes ou vous préférez une omelette?

RACHID ET DAVID Des crêpes... Miam!

Expressions utiles

Talking about birthdays

- **Cette année, je fête mes vingt et un ans.**
  This year, I celebrate my twenty-first birthday.
- **Pour célébrer mon anniversaire, je prépare une super soirée.**
  To celebrate my birthday, I'm planning a great party.
- **Stéphane célèbre ses dix-huit ans samedi prochain.**
  Stéphane celebrates his eighteenth birthday next Saturday.
- **On organise une surprise.**
  We are planning a surprise.

Talking about hopes and preferences

- **Tu essaies de ne pas parler deux minutes, s'il te plaît?**
  Could you try not to talk for two minutes, please?
- **J'aime tellement la nature, je sors même quand il fait très froid.**
  I like nature so much, I go out even when it's very cold.
- **Moi, je préfère l'été.**
  Me, I prefer summer.
- **Vous aimez les crêpes ou vous préférez une omelette?**
  Do you like crêpes or do you prefer an omelette?

Additional vocabulary

- **encore un peu**
  a little more
- **Quelque chose ne va pas.**
  Something's not right/working.
- **Allez.**
  Come on.
- **main**
  hand
- **Ça suffit!**
  That's enough!
- **Miam!**
  Yum!

2

Faux! Toutes ces phrases contiennent une information qui est fausse. Corrigez chaque phrase. Answers will vary. Suggested answers below.

1. Stéphane a dix-huit ans. Stéphane a dix-sept ans.

2. David et Rachid préfèrent une omelette. Ils préfèrent des crêpes.

3. Il fait froid et il pleut. Il fait beau/bon.

4. On n'organise rien (*anything*) pour l'anniversaire de Stéphane. On organise une surprise pour l'anniversaire de Stéphane.

5. L'anniversaire de Stéphane est au printemps. L'anniversaire de Stéphane est en automne.

6. Rachid et Stéphane ont froid. Ils ont chaud.

3

Conversez Parlez avec vos camarades de classe pour découvrir (*find out*) qui a l'anniversaire le plus proche du vôtre (*closest to yours*). Qui est-ce? Quand est son anniversaire? En quelle saison? Quel mois? En général, quel temps fait-il le jour de son anniversaire?

ressources

VM
pp. 19–20

vhlcentral

A C T I V I T É S

Expressions utiles

- Draw attention to numbers 101 and higher and spelling-change **-er** verbs in the video-still captions, in the **Expressions utiles** box, and as they occur in your conversation with students.
- Have students scan the video-still captions and the **Expressions utiles** box for expressions related to hopes and preferences.
- Ask students about their own preferences. You might ask questions like: **Vous préférez l'été ou l'hiver? l'automne ou le printemps? janvier ou juillet? regarder la télé ou aller au cinéma?** For a more challenging activity, follow up by asking **Pourquoi?**

1 Expansions
- Continue the activity with more statements like these. **11. Cette personne fête son anniversaire samedi prochain. (St) 12. Cette personne parle souvent au téléphone. (S) 13. Cette personne aime écouter de la musique. (D)**
- Assign one of the four main characters in this episode to a small group. Each group should write a brief description of their character's likes, dislikes, and preferences.

2 Suggestion Have students correct false statements on the board.

2 Expansion Give these false items for extra practice. **1. Sandrine n'aime pas parler au téléphone (Faux.) 2. Stéphane et Rachid étudient la psychologie aujourd'hui. (Faux.) 3. Sandrine n'aime pas regarder la télé. (Faux.) 4. Sur son portrait, Sandrine a un téléphone dans la main. (Faux.)**

3 Suggestion Brainstorm questions students might ask to find the person whose birthday is closest to their own. Once they have found that person, have them do this activity in pairs. Ask volunteers to tell the class what they learned about their partner.

O P T I O N S

Extra Practice Ask volunteers to act out the episode for the class. Assure them that it is not necessary to memorize the episode or to stick strictly to its content. They should try to get the general meaning across with the vocabulary and expressions they know, and they should feel free to be creative. Give them time to prepare. You may want to assign this as homework and do it the next class period as a review activity.

Game Play a memory game. The first player tells his or her birthday. The next player repeats what the first said, then adds his or her birthday. The third player must state the first two birthdays, then his or her own. Continue until someone makes an error. Replay the game until everyone has had a turn. Or, form teams and alternate sides. If a player makes a mistake, that team gets a strike. After three strikes, the game is over.

Section Goals

In this section, students will:
• learn about French public gardens
• learn terms for natural disasters
• learn names of public gardens and parks in various French-speaking regions
• read about cycling in France

Instructional Resources
vhlcentral.com: reference tools

Culture à la loupe
Avant la lecture
• Take a poll of students to find out how many of them come from towns or cities with public parks.
• Ask if students know of any French parks or if they have visited a park in Paris. If so, ask what they remember about these parks.

Lecture
• Point out the chart comparing **Le bois de Vincennes et le bois de Boulogne**. Ask students what information is shown. Have them compare details about the two parks.
• Look at a detailed map of Paris with the class, so students visualize where **le bois de Vincennes** and **le bois de Boulogne** are located. Point out **le jardin des Plantes**, **le parc Monceau**, **le parc Montsouris**, and **le parc des Buttes Chaumont**.

Après la lecture Have students think of the role parks play in the United States. Have them compare the level of popularity of French and American parks.

1 Expansion Continue the activity with additional questions like these.
11. Quelles activités y a-t-il pour les adultes au bois de Boulogne? 12. Quels sont les quatre parcs parisiens dans ce texte? 13. Dans quel parc trouve-t-on une cascade?

CULTURE À LA LOUPE

Les jardins publics français

le jardin du Luxembourg

Dans toutes les villes françaises, la plupart° du temps au centre-ville, on trouve des jardins° publics. Les jardins à la française ou jardins classiques sont très célèbres° depuis° le 17e (dix-septième) siècle°. Les jardins de Versailles, créés° pour Louis XIV, le roi° Soleil, vont être copiés par toutes les cours° d'Europe. Dans le jardin à la française, l'ordre et la symétrie dominent: Il faut dompter° la nature «sauvage». La perspective et l'harmonie donnent une notion de grandeur absolue. De façon° très symbolique, la géométrie présente un monde° ordré où le contrôle règne°. Il y a beaucoup de châteaux qui ont de très beaux jardins.

À Paris, le jardin des Tuileries et le jardin du Luxembourg sont deux jardins publics de style classique. Il y a des parterres de fleurs° extraordinaires avec de savants° agencements° de couleurs. Dans les deux jardins, il n'y a pas de bancs° mais des chaises, où on peut° se reposer tranquillement à l'endroit de son choix, sous un arbre° ou près d'un bassin°. Il y a aussi deux grands parcs à côté de Paris: le bois° de Vincennes, qui a un zoo, et le bois de Boulogne, qui a un parc d'attractions° pour les enfants.

Le bois de Vincennes et le bois de Boulogne	
VINCENNES	**BOULOGNE**
• une superficie° totale de 995 hectares	• une superficie totale de 863 hectares
• un zoo de 14,5 hectares	• cinq entrées°
• 19 km de sentiers pour les promenades à cheval et à vélo	• 95 km d'allées
• 32 km d'allées pour le jogging	• une cascade° de 10 mètres de large° et 14 mètres de haut°
• la Ferme° de Paris, une ferme de 5 hectares	• deux hippodromes°

En général, les villes de France sont très fleuries°. Il y a même° des concours° pour la ville la plus° fleurie. Le concours des villes et villages fleuris a lieu° depuis 1959. Il est organisé pour promouvoir° le développement des espaces verts dans les villes.

la plupart *most* jardins *gardens, parks* célèbres *famous* depuis *since* siècle *century* créés *created* roi *king* cours *courts* dompter *to tame* façon *way* monde *world* règne *reigns* parterres de fleurs *flower beds* savants *clever* agencements *schemes* bancs *benches* peut *can* arbre *tree* bassin *fountain, pond* bois *forest, wooded park* parc d'attractions *amusement park* fleuries *decorated with flowers* même *even* concours *competitions* la plus *the most* a lieu *takes place* promouvoir *to promote* superficie *area* entrées *entrances* cascade *waterfall* de haut *high* ferme *farm* hippodromes *racetracks*

Coup de main

In France and elsewhere, units of measurement are different than those used in the United States.

1 hectare = *2.47 acres*

1 kilomètre = *0.62 mile*

1 mètre = *approximately 1 yard (3 feet)*

A C T I V I T É S

1 **Répondez** Répondez aux questions par des phrases complètes.

1. Où trouve-t-on, en général, des jardins publics? En général, on trouve des jardins publics dans toutes les villes françaises, la plupart du temps au centre-ville.
2. Les jardins de Versailles sont créés pour quel roi? Les jardins de Versailles sont créés pour Louis XIV.
3. Qu'est-ce qui domine dans le jardin à la française? L'ordre et la symétrie dominent.
4. Quelle est la fonction de la perspective et de l'harmonie? La perspective et l'harmonie donnent une notion de grandeur absolue.
5. Qu'est-ce qu'il y a dans le jardin des Tuileries? Il y a des parterres de fleurs extraordinaires.

6. Que peut-on faire au jardin du Luxembourg grâce (*thanks*) aux chaises? On peut se reposer tranquillement à l'endroit de son choix.
7. Quels deux grands parcs y a-t-il à côté de Paris? Il y a le bois de Vincennes et le bois de Boulogne.
8. Que peut-on faire au bois de Vincennes? On peut visiter un zoo.
9. Comment les villes françaises sont-elles en général? Answers will vary.
10. Pourquoi les concours sont-ils organisés? Ils sont organisés pour promouvoir le développement des espaces verts.

O P T I O N S

Les jardins publics français Explain the longstanding reputations of **le bois de Vincennes** and **le bois de Boulogne**. **Le bois de Vincennes** was a working-class destination where marginal characters did business. **Le bois de Boulogne** was a place where the well-heeled hoped to be seen. Eighteenth-century associations say it all: **le Marquis de Sade** was imprisoned at **le bois de Vincennes**, and **Marie-Antoinette** lived in **le château de Bagatelle**, which she commissioned at the western end of **le bois de Boulogne**. There is no longer a socio-economic status attached to each of these green spaces, but many Parisians are familiar with their reputations.

LE FRANÇAIS QUOTIDIEN

Les catastrophes naturelles

tempête (f.) de neige	blizzard
canicule (f.)	heat wave
inondation (f.)	flood
ouragan (m.)	hurricane
raz-de-marée (m.)	tidal wave, tsunami
sécheresse (f.)	drought
tornade (f.)	tornado
tremblement (m.) de terre	earthquake

LE MONDE FRANCOPHONE

Des parcs publics

Voici quelques parcs publics du monde francophone.

Bruxelles, Belgique
le bois de la Cambre 123 hectares, un lac° avec une île° au centre

Casablanca, Maroc
le parc de la Ligue Arabe des palmiers°, un parc d'attractions pour enfants, des cafés et restaurants

Québec, Canada
le parc des Champs de Batailles («Plaines d'Abraham») 107 hectares, 6.000 arbres°

Tunis, Tunisie
le parc du Belvédère 110 hectares, un zoo de 12 hectares, 230.000 arbres (80 espèces° différentes), situé° sur une colline°

lac lake île island palmiers palm trees arbres trees espèces species situé located colline hill

PORTRAIT

Les Français et le vélo

Tous les étés, la course° cycliste du Tour de France attire° un grand nombre de spectateurs, Français et étrangers, surtout lors de° son arrivée sur les Champs-Élysées, à Paris. C'est le grand événement° sportif de l'année pour les amoureux du cyclisme. Les Français adorent aussi faire du vélo pendant° leur temps libre. Beaucoup de clubs organisent des randonnées en vélo de course° le week-end. Pour les personnes qui préfèrent le vélo tout terrain (VTT)°, il y a des sentiers° adaptés dans les parcs régionaux et nationaux. Certaines agences de voyages proposent aussi des vacances «vélo» en France ou à l'étranger°.

course race attire attracts lors de at the time of événement event pendant during vélo de course road bike vélo tout terrain (VTT) mountain biking sentiers paths à l'étranger abroad

le Tour de France sur les Champs-Élysées

MUSIQUE À FOND

Amadou et Mariam

Lieu de naissance: Bamako, Mali
Métier: musiciens-interprètes

Les deux musiciens sont aveugles (blind) et se sont rencontrés dans un institut pour jeunes aveugles. Ils se sont mariés en 1980.

Go to vhlcentral.com to find out more about **Amadou et Mariam** and their music.

---

2 **Vrai ou faux?** Indiquez si les phrases sont **vraies** ou **fausses**. Corrigez les phrases fausses.

1. Les Français ne font pas de vélo. Faux. Les Français adorent faire du vélo pendant leur temps libre.
2. Les membres de clubs de vélo font des promenades le week-end. Vrai.
3. Les agences de voyages offrent des vacances «vélo». Vrai.
4. On utilise un VTT quand on fait du vélo sur la route. Faux. On utilise un vélo de course.
5. Le Tour de France arrive sur les Champs-Élysées à Paris. Vrai.

3 **Les parcs publics** Avec un(e) partenaire, parlez des parcs publics du monde francophone. Quel temps fait-il dans les parcs pendant (during) les différentes saisons de l'année? Choisissez un parc et décrivez-le à vos camarades. Peuvent-ils deviner (Can they guess) de quel parc vous parlez?

Practice more at vhlcentral.com.

ressources
vhlcentral

A C T I V I T É S

OPTIONS

Des parcs publics Assign a francophone country to several students in class. Have everyone do individual research on gardens or a park in the country he or she has been assigned. Students should be prepared to present their findings about the park in at least three clear sentences in French and an image from the Internet, if possible.

Les Français et le vélo Bring in an example of francophone music or film about cycling. For example, play the song *Mon vélo est blanc* by Anne Sylvestre, or screen part of the Belgian film *Le vélo de Ghislain Lambert*. There are also scenes with Charlotte Gainsbourg riding a bicycle in *La petite voleuse*.

Le français quotidien After studying the vocabulary, have students close their books and write the numbers one to five on a piece of paper. Describe five **catastrophes naturelles** with new lexical items from **Leçon 5B**. Have the class write down the event you are describing. Go over the answers as a class.

Portrait
- Ask students what they know about the **Tour de France**. They may mention Lance Armstrong, **le maillot jaune** (*yellow jersey*), etc.
- Find out if the class has heard of stereotypes about the French and cycling. Have them list ideas in small groups.
- Urban bicycling is increasingly popular. Cities like Paris, Lyon, and Nantes have responded to environmental issues by increasing the number of bike paths (**pistes cyclables**) and by creating **vélopartage** systems, where city-dwellers can rent bikes at stations across the city.

Le monde francophone
- Have students look at the francophone world map in **Appendice A** to remind them where these countries are located.
- Practice pronunciation with the descriptions of these parks.

Musique à fond Point out to students that they will find supporting activities and information at **vhlcentral.com**.

2 Expansion Continue the activity with more true/false statements like these.
6. Le Tour de France est une grande course cycliste. (Vrai.)
7. Le Tour de France est au printemps. (Faux, en été)
8. Les Français et les étrangers sont spectateurs du Tour de France. (Vrai.)

3 Expansion Students can use this as an opportunity to practice contradicting while quizzing each other about weather in the context of these new expressions. Example: **Étudiant(e) 1: Quand il y a un ouragan, fait-il soleil? Étudiant(e) 2: Pas du tout! Il pleut beaucoup.**

ESPACE STRUCTURES

Numbers 101 and higher  Tutorial

Section Goals

In this section, students will learn:
• numbers 101 and higher
• mathematical terms

Instructional Resources
vhlcentral.com:
Activity Pack; Lab MP3s;
SAM Answer Key; **Essayez!**
and **Mise en pratique**
answers; Lab Audioscript;
reference tools

Suggestions

• Review numbers 0–100 by asking students questions that call for a number in the answer. Examples: **Combien d'étudiants y a-t-il dans la classe? Quel âge avez-vous? Quel âge a votre grand-mère? Anne a trois crayons. J'ai quatre boîtes de vingt crayons. Combien de crayons avons-nous? (quatre-vingt-trois)**
• Write on the board: **quatre cents étudiants, neuf cents personnes, deux mille livres, onze millions de voyageurs.** Help students deduce the meanings of the numbers.
• Model pronunciation of example numbers. Write other three- to seven-digit numbers on the board and have students read them.
• Go over the example sentences containing **cent, mille,** and **million.** Explain that the rules for when to pluralize are different from English.
• Point out that a space may be used instead of a period to indicate thousands and millions.

Numbers 101 and higher	
101 cent un	800 huit cents
125 cent vingt-cinq	900 neuf cents
198 cent quatre-vingt-dix-huit	1.000 mille
200 deux cents	1.100 mille cent
245 deux cent quarante-cinq	2.000 deux mille
300 trois cents	5.000 cinq mille
400 quatre cents	100.000 cent mille
500 cinq cents	550.000 cinq cent cinquante mille
600 six cents	1.000.000 un million
700 sept cents	8.000.000 huit millions

• Note that French uses a period, rather than a comma, to indicate thousands and millions.

• In multiples of one hundred, the word **cent** takes a final **-s.** However, if it is followed by another number, **cent** drops the **-s.**

J'ai **quatre cents** bandes dessinées. *I have 400 comic books.*	**but**	Cette bibliothèque a **neuf cent vingt** livres. *This library has 920 books.*
Il y a **cinq cents** animaux dans le zoo. *There are 500 animals in the zoo.*	**but**	Nous allons inviter **trois cent trente-huit** personnes. *We're going to invite 338 people.*

• The number **un** is not used before the word **mille** to mean *a/one thousand*. It is used, however, before **million** to say *a/one million*.

Mille personnes habitent le village. *One thousand people live in the village.*	**but**	**Un million** de personnes habitent la région. *One million people live in the region.*

À noter

As you learned in **Leçon 3B,** **cent** does *not* take the number **un** before it to mean *one hundred*.

• **Mille,** unlike **cent** and **million,** is invariable. It never takes an **-s.**

Aimez-vous *Les* **Mille** *et Une Nuits*? *Do you like "The Thousand and One Nights"?*	**Onze mille** étudiants sont inscrits. *Eleven thousand students are registered.*

• Before a noun, **million** and **millions** are followed by **de/d'.**

Un million de personnes sont ici. *One million people are here.*	Il y a **seize millions d'habitants** dans la capitale. *There are 16,000,000 inhabitants in the capital.*

• When writing out years, the word **mille** is usually shortened to **mil.**

mil huit cent soixante-cinq
eighteen (hundred) sixty-five

• In French, years before 2000 may be written out in two ways. Notice that in English, the word *hundred* can be omitted, but in French, the word **cent** is required.

mil neuf cent treize *one thousand nine hundred (and) thirteen.*	*or*	**dix-neuf cent treize** *nineteen (hundred) thirteen*

ressources

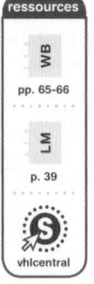

WB
pp. 65-66

LM
p. 39

vhlcentral

- You can talk about mathematical operations both formally and informally.

Mathematical terms

	informal	formal
plus	et	plus
minus	moins	moins
multiplied by	fois	multiplié par
divided by	sur	divisé par
equals	font	égale

- The verb **égaler** (*to equal*) is expressed in the singular, but the verb **faire** is plural.

110 et 205 font 315
110 + 205 = 315

110 plus 205 égale 315
110 + 205 = 315

60 fois 3 font 180
60 × 3 = 180

60 multiplié par 3 égale 180
60 × 3 = 180

999 sur 9 font 111
999 ÷ 9 = 111

999 divisé par 9 égale 111
999 ÷ 9 = 111

- In French, decimal punctuation is inverted. Use **une virgule** (*comma*) instead of **un point** (*period*).

5.419,32
5,419.32

cinq mille quatre cent dix-neuf virgule trente-deux
five thousand four hundred nineteen point thirty-two

- The expression **pour cent** (*percent*) is two words, not one.

Le magasin offre une réduction de cinquante **pour cent**.
The store is offering a fifty percent discount.

Essayez!   Écrivez les nombres en toutes lettres. (*Write out the numbers.*)

1. 10.000 dix mille
2. 620 six cent vingt
3. 365 trois cent soixante-cinq
4. 42.000 quarante-deux mille
5. 1.392.000 un million trois cent quatre-vingt-douze mille
6. 171 cent soixante et onze
7. 200.000.000 deux cents millions
8. 480 quatre cent quatre-vingts
9. 1.789 mille sept cent quatre-vingt-neuf
10. 400 quatre cents
11. 8.000.000 huit millions
12. 5.053 cinq mille cinquante-trois

deux cent cinq **205**

Suggestions
- Tell students that when writing out the year 1000, the word **mille** is not shortened to **mil**: **l'an mille**.
- You may also want to teach your students these mathematical terms:
  la différence *difference*
  le produit *product*
  le quotient *quotient*
  la somme *sum*

Successful Language Learning Tell students that to count from 101–199, they should say **cent** followed by 1–99. So, 101: **cent un**, 102: **cent deux**, 103: **cent trois**, and so forth up to 199: **cent quatre-vingt-dix-neuf**. Tell them to use the same strategy after **deux cents**, **trois cents**, etc.

Essayez! Have students write four more numbers and exchange papers with a classmate, who will write out the numbers.

OPTIONS

Extra Practice Have small groups of students work together to create a worksheet consisting of five math word problems for their classmates to complete. Have students take turns reading problems to the class or one of the other small groups, who, in turn, will solve the problems. Have groups include an answer key with their worksheets.

Groups Divide the class into groups of ten. Give a flashcard with a number from 0–9 to each person in each group. If one group is smaller, distribute extra numbers to group members, as needed, so some students have more than one card. Call out a three- to nine-digit number in which none of the digits is repeated. Students arrange themselves, showing their flashcard(s) to reflect the number. Repeat with other numbers.

ESPACE STRUCTURES

1 **Suggestion** For listening comprehension, have students read numbers from the activity to a partner.

1 **Expansion** Give students these real addresses in regions **Centre** and **Pays de la Loire**. Model how to pronounce the postal codes. Example: 45000: **quarante-cinq mille**. (1) **Préfecture de la Région Centre et du Loiret: 181, rue de Bourgogne - 45042 ORLÉANS** (2) **Espace Région Centre de Tours: 1, rue des Ursulines - 37000 TOURS** (3) **Auberge de Jeunesse: 23, Avenue Neigre - 28000 CHARTRES** (4) **Médiathèque Louis Aragon: 54, rue du Port - 72015 LE MANS**

2 **Suggestions**
• Call on pairs of students to say some of the calculations aloud.
• Give additional math problems if more practice is needed.

2 **Expansion** Have pairs convert a **calcul** into a word problem. Example: **J'ai deux cents dollars. Ma sœur a trois cents dollars. Combien de dollars avons-nous?**

3 **Expansion** Write on the board some well-known American cities and the city or town where your school is located. Ask students: **Combien d'habitants…?** Have them guess if they don't know. Then write the accurate number next to each city. Have students come to the board to write out the populations in French.

Mise en pratique

1 **Quelle adresse?** Vous allez distribuer des journaux (*newspapers*) et vous téléphonez aux clients pour avoir leur adresse. Écrivez les adresses.

MODÈLE

cent deux, rue Lafayette
102, rue Lafayette

1. deux cent cinquante-deux, rue de Bretagne __252, rue de Bretagne__
2. quatre cents, avenue Malbon __400, avenue Malbon__
3. cent soixante-dix-sept, rue Jeanne d'Arc __177, rue Jeanne d'Arc__
4. cinq cent quarante-six, boulevard St. Marc __546, boulevard St. Marc__
5. six cent quatre-vingt-huit, avenue des Gaulois __688, avenue des Gaulois__
6. trois cent quatre-vingt-douze, boulevard Micheline __392, boulevard Micheline__
7. cent vingt-cinq, rue des Pierres __125, rue des Pierres__
8. trois cent quatre, avenue St. Germain __304, avenue St. Germain__

2 **Faisons des calculs** Faites les additions et écrivez les réponses.

MODÈLE

200 + 300 =
Deux cents plus trois cents font cinq cents.

1. 5.000 + 3.000 = __Cinq mille plus trois mille font huit mille.__
2. 650 + 750 = __Six cent cinquante plus sept cent cinquante font mille quatre cents.__
3. 2.000.000 + 3.000.000 = __Deux millions plus trois millions font cinq millions.__
4. 4.400 + 3.600 = __Quatre mille quatre cents plus trois mille six cents font huit mille.__
5. 155 + 310 = __Cent cinquante-cinq plus trois cent dix font quatre cent soixante-cinq.__
6. 7.000 + 3.000 = __Sept mille plus trois mille font dix mille.__
7. 9.000.000 + 2.000.000 = __Neuf millions plus deux millions font onze millions.__
8. 1.250 + 2.250 = __Mille deux cent cinquante plus deux mille deux cent cinquante font trois mille cinq cents.__

3 **Combien d'habitants?** À tour de rôle, demandez à votre partenaire combien d'habitants il y a dans chaque ville d'après (*according to*) les statistiques.

MODÈLE

Dijon: 153.813
Étudiant(e) 1: *Combien d'habitants y a-t-il à Dijon?*
Étudiant(e) 2: *Il y a cent cinquante-trois mille huit cent treize habitants.*

1. Toulouse: 398.423 __Il y a trois cent quatre-vingt-dix-huit mille quatre cent vingt-trois habitants.__
2. Abidjan: 2.877.948 __Il y a deux millions huit cent soixante-dix-sept mille neuf cent quarante-huit habitants.__
3. Lyon: 453.187 __Il y a quatre cent cinquante-trois mille cent quatre-vingt-sept habitants.__
4. Québec: 510.559 __Il y a cinq cent dix mille cinq cent cinquante-neuf habitants.__
5. Marseille: 807.071 __Il y a huit cent sept mille soixante et onze habitants.__
6. Papeete: 26.181 __Il y a vingt-six mille cent quatre-vingt-un habitants.__
7. Dakar: 2.476.400 __Il y a deux millions quatre cent soixante-seize mille quatre cents habitants.__
8. Nice: 344.460 __Il y a trois cent quarante-quatre mille quatre cent soixante habitants.__

 Practice more at **vhlcentral.com**.

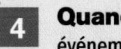

Communication

communication STANDARDS NATIONAL

4 **Quand?** Avec un(e) partenaire, regardez les dates et dites quand ces événements ont lieu (*take place*).

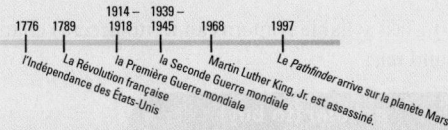

1. Le *Pathfinder* arrive sur la planète Mars. __Il arrive en mille neuf cent quatre-vingt-dix-sept.__
2. La Première Guerre mondiale commence. __Elle commence en mille neuf cent quatorze.__
3. La Seconde Guerre mondiale prend fin (*ends*). __Elle prend fin en mille neuf cent quarante-cinq.__
4. L'Amérique déclare son indépendance. __Elle déclare son indépendance en mille sept cent soixante-seize.__
5. Martin Luther King, Jr. est assassiné. __Il est assassiné en mille neuf cent soixante-huit.__
6. La Première Guerre Mondiale prend fin. __Elle prend fin en mille neuf cent dix-huit.__
7. La Révolution française a lieu (*takes place*). __Elle a lieu en mille sept cent quatre-vingt-neuf.__
8. La Seconde Guerre mondiale commence. __Elle commence en mille neuf cent trente-neuf.__

5 **Combien ça coûte?** Vous regardez un catalogue avec un(e) ami(e). À tour de rôle, demandez à votre partenaire le prix des choses.

▶ **MODÈLE**

Étudiant(e) 1: *Combien coûte l'ordinateur?*
Étudiant(e) 2: *Il coûte mille huit cents euros.*

1. É1: ... la montre?
É2: Elle ... quatre cent trente-deux ...

2. É1: ... les dictionnaires?
É2: Ils ... cent seize ...

3. É1: ... le sac à dos?
É2: Il ... cent dix-huit ...

4. É1: ... le vélo?
É2: Il ... six cent soixante-quinze ...

6 **Dépensez de l'argent** Vous et votre partenaire avez 100.000€. Décidez quels articles de la liste vous allez prendre. Expliquez vos choix à la classe. _Answers will vary._

MODÈLE

Étudiant(e) 1: *On prend un rendez-vous avec Brad Pitt parce que c'est mon acteur favori.*
Étudiant(e) 2: *Alors, nous avons encore (still) 50.000 euros. Prenons les 5 jours à Paris pour pratiquer le français.*

un ordinateur... 2.000€	des vacances à Tahiti... 7.000€
un rendez-vous avec Brad Pitt... 50.000€	un vélo... 1.000€
un rendez-vous avec Madonna... 50.000€	une voiture de luxe... 80.000€
5 jours à Paris... 8.500€	un dîner avec Justin Bieber... 45.000€
un séjour ski en Suisse... 4.200€	un jour de shopping... 10.000€
une montre 6.800€	un bateau (*boat*)... 52.000€

---

4 Expansion Ask students to brainstorm other famous years throughout history.

5 & 6 Suggestions
• Before beginning each activity, make sure students know the vocabulary.
• Do the **modèles** with a volunteer to make sure students understand the activities.

OPTIONS

Game Ask students to stand up to create a number chain. The first student states the number 25. The next student says 50. Students continue the chain, using multiples of 25. If a student misses the next number in sequence, he or she must sit down. Continue play until only one student is left standing. If a challenge is required to break a tie, play the game with multiples of 30.

Extra Practice Ask students to make a list of nine items containing the following: a variety of plural and singular nouns, three numerals in the hundreds, three in the thousands, and three in the millions. Once lists are completed, have students exchange them and read the items off their partners' lists aloud. Partners should listen for the correct number and any agreement errors.

5B.2

ESPACE STRUCTURES

Spelling-change -er verbs  Tutorial

Point de départ Some -er verbs, though regular with respect to their verb endings, have spelling changes that occur in the verb stem (what remains after the -er is dropped).

Section Goals

In this section, students will learn -er verbs with spelling changes.

Instructional Resources
vhlcentral.com:
Lab MP3s; SAM Answer Key;
Essayez! *and* ***Mise en***
pratique *answers;*
Lab Audioscript; Activity
*Pack (****Feuilles d'activités****);*
reference tools

Suggestions

• Model the pronunciation of all forms of **acheter** and **espérer**. Have students practice the difference between closed **é** and open **è**.

• Guide students to notice that, like regular -er verbs, spelling-change -er verbs are "boot verbs."

• Point out that infinitives often follow forms of **espérer**. Example: **Il espère gagner.**

• Ask questions using verbs from this section, encouraging student responses. Examples: **Où est-ce que vous achetez du pain? Quelle saison préférez-vous: l'été ou l'hiver?**

• Explain that when the letter **e** is followed by one pronounced consonant and a silent **e**, you need to add an **accent grave** over the first **e**. If the first **e** already has an **accent aigu**, it becomes an **accent grave**. This causes spelling changes in some verbs, adjectives, and nouns. Remind students to apply this rule whenever this pattern of letters occurs. Exception: **e** with an **accent circonflexe**.

• Most infinitives whose next-to-last syllable contains an **e** (no accent) change this letter to **è** in all forms except **nous** and **vous**.

acheter (to buy)	
j'achète	nous achetons
tu achètes	vous achetez
il/elle/on achète	ils/elles achètent

Où est-ce que tu **achètes** des skis?
Where do you buy skis?

Ils **achètent** beaucoup sur Internet.
They buy a lot on the Internet.

Achetez-vous une nouvelle maison?
Are you buying a new house?

Je n'**achète** pas de lait.
I'm not buying any milk.

• Infinitives whose next-to-last syllable contains an **é** change this letter to **è** in all forms except **nous** and **vous**.

espérer (to hope)	
j'espère	nous espérons
tu espères	vous espérez
il/elle/on espère	ils/elles espèrent

Elle **espère** arriver tôt aujourd'hui.
She hopes to arrive early today.

Nos profs **espèrent** avoir de bons étudiants en classe.
Our professors hope to have good students in class.

Espérez-vous faire la connaissance de Joël?
Are you hoping to meet Joël?

J'**espère** avoir de bonnes notes.
I hope I get good grades.

• Infinitives ending in -**yer** change **y** to **i** in all forms except **nous** and **vous**.

envoyer (to send)	
j'envoie	nous envoyons
tu envoies	vous envoyez
il/elle/on envoie	ils/elles envoient

J'**envoie** une lettre.
I'm sending a letter.

Tes amis **envoient** beaucoup d'e-mails.
Your friends send lots of e-mails.

Nous **envoyons** des bandes dessinées aux enfants.
We're sending the kids comic books.

Salima **envoie** un message à ses parents.
Salima is sending a message to her parents.

Boîte à outils

Use a conjugated form of **espérer** + [*infinitive*] to mean *to hope to do something.*

Tu **espères jouer** au golf samedi.
You hope to play golf on Saturday.

Elle achète quelque chose.

Ils répètent.

- The change of **y** to **i** is optional in verbs whose infinitives end in **-ayer**.

Comment est-ce que tu **payes**?
How do you pay?

Je **paie** avec une carte de crédit.
I pay with a credit card.

Other spelling change -er verbs

like espérer		like acheter	
célébrer	to celebrate	amener	to bring (someone)
considérer	to consider	emmener	to take (someone)
posséder	to possess, to own	**like envoyer**	
préférer	to prefer	employer	to use
protéger	to protect	essayer (de + [inf.])	to try (to)
répéter	to repeat; to rehearse	nettoyer	to clean
		payer	to pay

Je préfère l'été.
Il fait chaud.

Tu essaies de
ne pas parler?

- Note that the **nous** and **vous** forms of the verbs presented in this section have no spelling changes.

Vous **achetez** des sandwichs aussi.
You're buying sandwiches, too.

Nous **espérons** partir à huit heures.
We hope to leave at 8 o'clock.

Nous **envoyons** les enfants à l'école.
We're sending the children to school.

Vous **payez** avec une carte de crédit.
You pay with a credit card.

 Boîte à outils

Amener is used when you are bringing someone to the place where you are.

J'**amène** ma nièce chez moi.
I'm bringing my niece home.

Emmener is used when you are taking someone to a different location from where you are.

J'**emmène** ma grand-mère à l'hôpital.
I'm taking my grandmother to the hospital.

À noter

You learned in **Leçon 4A** that the verb **apporter** also means *to bring*. Use **apporter** instead of **amener** when you are bringing an object instead of a person or animal.

Qui **apporte** les cartes?
Who's bringing the cards?

Essayez! Complétez les phrases avec la forme correcte du verbe.

1. Les bibliothèques *emploient* (employer) beaucoup d'étudiants.
2. Vous _repétez_ (répéter) les phrases en français.
3. Nous _payons_ (payer) assez pour les livres.
4. Mon camarade de chambre ne _nettoie_ (nettoyer) pas son bureau.
5. Est-ce que tu _espères_ (espérer) gagner?
6. Vous _essayez_ (essayer) parfois d'arriver à l'heure.
7. Tu _préfères_ (préférer) prendre du thé ou du café?
8. Elle _emmène_ (emmener) sa mère au cinéma.
9. On _célèbre_ (célébrer) une occasion spéciale.
10. Les parents _protègent_ (protéger) leurs enfants?

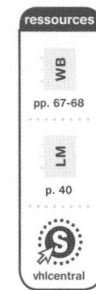

ressources

WB
pp. 67-68

LM
p. 40

vhlcentral

deux cent neuf **209**

Suggestions
- Go over the meanings of the verbs. Note the number of cognates. Make sure students understand that **amener** and **emmener** are only used for people. Ask: What verbs would you use to say *to take* and *to bring* objects? (**prendre**; **apporter**).
- Consider going over the constructions **essayer de** + [*infinitive*] and **essayer de ne pas** + [*infinitive*] with students and giving some examples.

Essayez! For additional drills with spelling-change **-er** verbs for the whole class or those who need extra practice, do this activity orally and on the board with different subjects.

OPTIONS

Game Divide the class into two teams. Announce one of the infinitives and a subject pronoun. Example: **emmener**; **ils**. At the board, have the first member of Team A say and write the given subject and the conjugated form of the verb. If the team member answers correctly, Team A gets one point. If not, give the first member of Team B the same example. The team with the most points at the end of the game wins.

Video Replay the video episode, having students focus on **-er** verbs with spelling changes. Have them note each one they hear, with subjects if conjugated. Find out how many occurrences students heard before pointing out these examples: **je préfère, célébrer, célèbre, tu essaies,** and **préférer.** Ask for remarks with spelling-change **-er** verbs that describe the characters. Example: **Rachid possède un ordinateur.**

ESPACE STRUCTURES

1 Suggestion Ask for a volunteer to read the **modèle** out loud.

1 Expansion Have students write four additional statements about their own family members.

2 Expansion Show additional pictures of people cleaning, using something, trying, sending, etc. Ask a yes/no question about each picture. Example: Showing an image of someone sending a letter, ask: **Est-ce qu'il nettoie?** Students answer: **Mais non, il envoie une lettre.**

3 Suggestion Explain that students must first choose the logical verb, then write the correct form.

Mise en pratique

1 Passe-temps Chaque membre de la famille Desrosiers a son passe-temps préféré. Utilisez les éléments pour dire comment ils préparent leur week-end.

MODÈLE

Tante Manon fait une randonnée. (acheter / sandwichs)
Elle achète des sandwichs.

1. Nous faisons du vélo. (essayer / vélo) Nous essayons le vélo.
2. Christiane aime chanter. (répéter) Elle répète.
3. Les filles jouent au foot. (espérer / gagner) Elles espèrent gagner.
4. Vous allez à la pêche. (emmener / enfants) Vous emmenez les enfants.
5. Papa fait un tour en voiture. (nettoyer / voiture) Il nettoie la voiture.
6. Mes frères font du camping. (préférer / partir tôt) Ils préfèrent partir tôt.
7. Ma petite sœur va à la piscine. (essayer de / plonger) Elle essaie de plonger.
8. Mon grand-père aime la montagne. (préférer / faire une randonnée) Il préfère faire une randonnée.
9. J'adore les chevaux. (espérer / faire du cheval) J'espère faire du cheval.
10. Mes parents vont faire un dessert. (acheter / fruits) Ils achètent des fruits.

2 Que font-ils? Dites ce que font les personnages. Answers will vary.

MODÈLE
Il achète une baguette.

acheter

1. envoyer   2. payer   3. répéter   4. nettoyer

3 Invitation au cinéma Avec un(e) partenaire, jouez les rôles de Halouk et de Thomas. Ensuite, présentez la scène à la classe.

THOMAS J'ai envie d'aller au cinéma.

HALOUK Bonne idée. Nous (1) __emmenons__ (emmener, protéger) Véronique avec nous?

THOMAS J' (2) __espère__ (acheter, espérer) qu'elle a du temps libre.

HALOUK Peut-être, mais j' (3) __envoie__ (envoyer, payer) des e-mails tous les jours et elle ne répond pas.

THOMAS Parce que son ordinateur ne fonctionne pas. Elle (4) __préfère__ (essayer, préférer) parler au téléphone.

HALOUK D'accord. Alors toi, tu (5) __achètes__ (acheter, répéter) les tickets au cinéma et moi, je vais chercher Véronique.

Communication

4 Quand? À tour de rôle, posez des questions à un(e) partenaire. Answers will vary.

1. Qu'est-ce que tu achètes tous les jours?
2. Qu'est-ce que tu achètes tous les mois?
3. Quand tu sors avec ton/ta petit(e) ami(e), qui paie?
4. Est-ce que toi et ton/ta camarade de chambre partagez les frais (*expenses*)? Qui paie quoi?
5. Est-ce que tu possèdes une voiture?
6. Qui nettoie ta chambre?
7. À qui est-ce que tu envoies des e-mails?
8. Qu'est-ce que tu espères faire cet été?
9. Qu'est-ce que tu préfères faire le vendredi soir?
10. Quand tu vas en boîte de nuit, est-ce que tu emmènes quelqu'un? Qui?
11. Est-ce que ta famille célèbre une occasion spéciale cet (*this*) été? Quand?
12. Aimes-tu essayer une nouvelle cuisine?

5 Réponses affirmatives Votre professeur va vous donner une feuille d'activités. Trouvez au moins deux camarades de classe qui répondent oui à chaque question. Et si vous aussi, vous répondez oui aux questions, écrivez votre nom. Answers will vary.

MODÈLE

Étudiant(e) 1: *Est-ce que tu achètes tes livres sur Internet?*
Étudiant(e) 2: *Oui, j'achète mes livres sur Internet.*

Questions	Noms
1. acheter ses livres sur Internet	Virginie, Éric
2. posséder un ordinateur	
3. envoyer des lettres à ses grands-parents	
4. célébrer une occasion spéciale demain	

6 E-mail à l'oncle Marcel Xavier va écrire un e-mail à son oncle pour raconter (*to tell*) ses activités de la semaine prochaine. Il prépare une liste des choses qu'il veut dire (*wants to say*). Avec un(e) partenaire, écrivez son e-mail. Answers will vary.

- lundi: emmener maman chez le médecin
- mercredi: fac envoyer notes
- jeudi: répéter rôle Roméo et Juliette
- vendredi: célébrer anniversaire papa
- vendredi: essayer faire gym
- samedi: parents acheter voiture

4 Expansion Have students write two more questions containing spelling-change **-er** verbs that they would like to ask their partner.

5 Suggestion Call on two volunteers to read the **modèle** aloud. Then distribute the **Feuilles d'activités** found in the Activity Pack on the Supersite.

6 Expansion Have students think of a family member or friend to whom they would likely write an e-mail. Tell them to first list at least five ideas using as many spelling-change **-er** verbs as possible. Then have them write an e-mail of at least five sentences.

O P T I O N S

Extra Practice Arrange students in rows of six. The first person in each row has a piece of paper. Call out an infinitive. Silently, the first student writes the **je** form and passes the paper to the student behind him or her. That student writes the **tu** form and passes the paper on. The last person in the row holds up the paper to show completion. Have students rotate places before calling out another verb.

Small Groups Have small groups write dehydrated sentences with only subjects and infinitives. Examples: **1. tu / amener / ???** **2. Sylvie et Véronique / espérer / ???** Tell groups to switch with another group, who will form a complete sentence by conjugating the verb and inventing an appropriate ending. Ask for volunteers to write one of their group's sentences on the board.

ESPACE STRUCTURES **211**

ESPACE SYNTHÈSE

Révision

Instructional Resources
vhlcentral.com:
Activity Pack (Info Gap Activities); Testing Program; Testing Program MP3s; reference tools

1 Expansion Have students write a story about their preferred sport modeled on the paragraph in this activity.

2 Suggestion Have pairs get together to form groups of four to review each others' sentences. Have students explain any corrections or suggested changes.

3 Suggestion Encourage students to choose places from the French-speaking world that they have learned about in **Espace culture** and **Panorama** sections.

3 Expansion Have students create more questions based on those in the activity to ask their partner. Guide the class to ask about where the partner hopes or prefers to go for various vacations throughout the year. Students may combine reusing weather conditions described in the box and using additional weather descriptions.

4 Expansion For additional numbers practice, have students ask each other: **Combien coûte _____ (type de voyage) avec la commission?**

5 Suggestion Ask for volunteers to do the **modèle** and auction off a few more items to set further examples.

6 Suggestions
- Divide the class into pairs and distribute the Info Gap Handouts found in the Activity Pack on the Supersite. Give students ten minutes to complete the activity.
- Act out the **modèle** with a student volunteer playing the role of **Étudiant(e) 2**.

---

1 Le basket Avec un(e) partenaire, utilisez les verbes de la liste pour compléter le paragraphe.

acheter	considérer	envoyer	essayer	préférer
amener	employer	espérer	payer	répéter

Je m'appelle Stéphanie et je joue au basket. Je/J' (1) _amène_ toujours (*always*) mes parents avec moi aux matchs le samedi. Ils (2) _considèrent_ que les filles sont de très bonnes joueuses. Mes parents font aussi du sport. Ma mère fait du vélo et mon père (3) _espère_ gagner son prochain match de foot! Le vendredi matin, je/j' (4) _envoie_ un e-mail à ma mère pour lui rappeler (*remind her of*) le match. Mais elle n'oublie jamais! Ils ne/n' (5) _achètent_ pas de tickets pour les matchs, parce que les parents des joueurs ne/n' (6) _paient_ pas. Nous (7) _essayons_ toujours d'arriver une demi-heure avant le match, parce que maman et papa (8) _préfèrent, espèrent_ s'asseoir (*to sit*) tout près du terrain (*court*). Ils sont tellement fiers!

2 Que font-ils? Avec un(e) partenaire, parlez des activités des personnages et écrivez une phrase par illustration.
Answers will vary.

1. 2. 3.

4. 5.  6.

3 Où partir? Avec un(e) partenaire, choisissez cinq endroits intéressants à visiter où il fait le temps indiqué sur la liste. Ensuite, répondez aux questions. Answers will vary.

| Il fait chaud. | Il fait soleil. | Il fait du vent. | Il neige. | Il pleut. |

1. Où essayez-vous d'aller cet été? Pourquoi?
2. Où préférez-vous partir cet hiver? Pourquoi?
3. Quelle est la première destination que vous espérez visiter? La dernière? Pourquoi?
4. Qui emmenez-vous avec vous? Pourquoi?

---

4 J'achète Vous allez payer un voyage aux membres de votre famille et à vos amis. À tour de rôle, choisissez un voyage et donnez à votre partenaire la liste des personnes qui partent. Votre partenaire va vous donner le prix à payer. Answers will vary.

MODÈLE
Étudiant(e) 1: J'achète un voyage de dix jours dans les Pays de la Loire à ma cousine Pauline et à mon frère Alexandre.
Étudiant(e) 2: D'accord. Tu paies deux mille cinq cent soixante-deux euros.

Voyages	Prix par personne	Commission
Dix jours dans les Pays de la Loire .... 1.250€ .... 62€
Deux semaines de camping .... 660€ .... 35€
Sept jours au soleil en hiver .... 2.100€ .... 78€
Trois jours à Paris en avril .... 500€ .... 55€
Trois mois en Europe en été .... 10.400€ .... 47€
Un week-end à Nice en septembre .... 350€ .... 80€
Une semaine à la montagne en juin .... 990€ .... 66€
Une semaine à la neige .... 1.800€ .... 73€

5 La vente aux enchères Par groupes de quatre, organisez une vente aux enchères (*auction*) pour vendre les affaires (*things*) du professeur. À tour de rôle, un(e) étudiant(e) joue le rôle du vendeur/de la vendeuse et les autres étudiants jouent le rôle des enchérisseurs (*bidders*). Vous avez 5.000 euros et toutes les enchères (*bids*) commencent à cent euros. Answers will vary.

MODÈLE
Étudiant(e) 1: J'ai le cahier du professeur. Qui paie cent euros?
Étudiant(e) 2: Moi, je paie cent euros.
Étudiant(e) 1: Qui paie cent cinquante euros?

6 À la bibliothèque Votre professeur va vous donner, à vous et à votre partenaire, deux feuilles d'activités différentes. Attention! Ne regardez pas la feuille de votre partenaire. Answers will vary.

MODÈLE
Étudiant(e) 1: Est-ce que tu as le livre «Candide»?
Étudiant(e) 2: Oui, son numéro de référence est P, Q, deux cent soixante-six, cent quarante-sept, cent dix.

OPTIONS

Small Groups Have students write a conversation between two friends. One friend tries to convince the other to go out. The other makes excuses to not go. Students should include as many spelling-change **-er** verbs and weather expressions as possible. Example: **Étudiant(e) 1: Faisons une randonnée! Étudiant(e) 2: Mais je nettoie ma chambre. Étudiant(e) 1: Mais il fait beau. Étudiant(e) 2: Il va pleuvoir plus tard.**

Pairs Ask students to imagine they are going on an extended trip. Have them make a list of at least five things they are to do (buy things, take someone somewhere, send mail, etc.) before leaving. Examples: **Je vais acheter un nouveau parapluie. J'espère envoyer une carte d'anniversaire.**

À l'écoute

Section Goals

In this section, students will:
• learn to listen for key words
• listen to a short paragraph and note the key words
• answer questions based on the content of a recorded weather forecast

Instructional Resources
vhlcentral.com:
Textbook MP3s;
Textbook Audioscript;
reference tools

STRATÉGIE

Listening for key words

By listening for key words (**mots-clés**) or phrases, you can identify the subject and main ideas of what you hear, as well as some of the details.

🔊 To practice this strategy, you will listen to a short paragraph. Jot down the key words that help you identify the subject of the paragraph and its main ideas.

Préparation

Regardez l'image. Où trouve-t-on ce type d'image? Manque-t-il des éléments (*Is anything missing*) sur cette carte? Faites une liste de mots-clés qui vont vous aider à trouver ces informations quand vous allez écouter la météo (*the weather*).

À vous d'écouter

Écoutez la météo. Puis, écoutez une deuxième fois et complétez le tableau. Notez la température et écrivez un **X** pour indiquer le temps qu'il fait dans chaque ville.

Ville	☀	⛅	☁	🌧	🌬	❄	Température
Paris			X				8°C
Lille				X			6°C
Strasbourg						X	5°C
Brest			X				10°C
Lyon				X			9°C
Bordeaux		X					11°C
Toulouse	X						12°C
Marseille			X				12°C
Nice					X		13°C

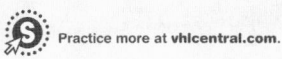

Practice more at **vhlcentral.com**.

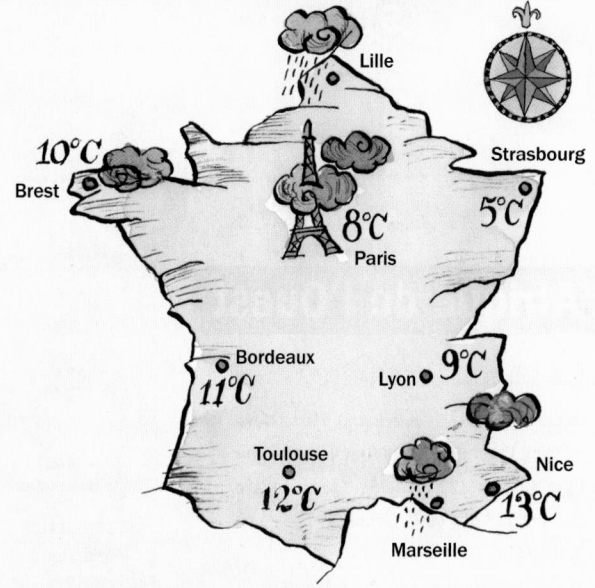

Compréhension

Probable ou improbable? Indiquez si ces (*these*) phrases sont probables ou improbables, d'après la météo d'aujourd'hui.

	Probable	Improbable
MODÈLE		
Ève va nager à Strasbourg.		✓
1. Lucie fait du vélo à Lille.		✓
2. Il fait un temps épouvantable à Toulouse.		✓
3. Émilien joue aux cartes à la maison à Lyon.	✓	
4. Il va neiger à Marseille.		✓
5. Jérome et Yves jouent au golf à Bordeaux.	✓	
6. À Lyon, on a besoin d'un imperméable.	✓	
7. Il fait froid à Strasbourg.	✓	
8. Nous allons nager à Nice cet après-midi.		✓

Quelle ville choisir? Imaginez qu'aujourd'hui vous êtes en France. Décidez dans quelle ville vous avez envie de passer la journée. Pourquoi? Décrivez le temps qu'il fait et citez des activités que vous allez peut-être faire.

MODÈLE

J'ai envie d'aller à Strasbourg parce que j'aime l'hiver et la neige. Aujourd'hui, il fait froid et il neige. Je vais faire une promenade en ville et après, je vais boire un chocolat chaud au café.

deux cent treize **213**

Stratégie
Audioscript Qu'est-ce que je fais quand j'ai du temps libre? Eh bien, l'hiver, j'aime faire du ski. Au printemps et en automne, quand il fait bon, je fais du vélo et du cheval. Et l'été, je fais de la planche à voile.

Préparation Have students look at the map and describe what they see. Guide them to think about expressions that are commonly mentioned during a weather forecast. Ask them to brainstorm and write a list of as much weather-related vocabulary as they can think of in five minutes.

À vous d'écouter
Audioscript Mesdames, Mesdemoiselles, Messieurs, bonjour et bienvenue sur Radio Satellite. Il est 10h00 et voici la météo. Aujourd'hui, sur la capitale, des nuages toute la journée. Eh oui, il fait frais à Paris ce matin, avec une température maximale de huit degrés. À Lille, on va avoir un temps épouvantable. Il fait froid avec six degrés seulement et il va pleuvoir tout l'après-midi et toute la soirée. À Strasbourg, il fait cinq degrés et il neige encore. Il fait assez frais à Brest, avec dix degrés et beaucoup de nuages. À Lyon, il fait neuf degrés aussi avec un temps très orageux, alors ne sortez pas sans votre parapluie! À Bordeaux, il fait bon, onze degrés et quelques nuages. Toulouse va avoir du soleil toute la journée et il va faire douze degrés. À Marseille, la température est de douze degrés maintenant, mais il va pleuvoir dans l'après-midi. Sur la Côte d'Azur, il fait treize degrés à Nice, et il y a beaucoup de vent. Bonne journée!

Section Goals

In this section, students will learn historical and cultural information about **l'Afrique de l'Ouest**.

Instructional Resources
vhlcentral.com:
Digital Image Bank;
SAM Answer Key;
reference tools

Carte de l'Afrique de l'Ouest
- Have students look at the map or use the map from the Digital Image Bank. Ask volunteers to read the names of countries and their capitals aloud. Model pronunciation as necessary.
- Point out the photos of Abidjan, the administrative and commercial center of **la Côte d'Ivoire**, and Tiébélé, in **Burkina Faso**. Abidjan is a major port city, whereas Tiébélé is an inland village and is home to the Kassena people.

La région en chiffres
In francophone West African countries, French is the language of administration, education, and international communication. French is the official language and may share official status with other languages native to the country.

Incroyable mais vrai!
Porto Novo means *new port* in Portuguese. The city became an important port for the slave trade during the 16th century. Cotonou is another important city in **Bénin**, and is considered the economic center of the country.

S Interactive Map

SAVOIR-FAIRE

Panorama

L'Afrique de l'Ouest

un marché en Afrique

La région en chiffres

▸ **Bénin:** *(10.880.000 habitants), Porto Novo*
▸ **Burkina-Faso:** *(18.106.000), Ouagadougou*
▸ **Côte d'Ivoire:** *(22.702.000), Yamoussoukro*
▸ **Guinée:** *(12.609.000), Conakry*
▸ **Mali:** *(17.600.000), Bamako*
▸ **Mauritanie:** *(4.068.000), Nouakchott*
▸ **Niger:** *(19.899.000), Niamey*
▸ **Sénégal:** *(15.129.000), Dakar*
▸ **Togo:** *(7.305.000), Lomé*
SOURCE: Population Division, UN Secretariat

Les peuples d'Afrique de l'Ouest ont une histoire commune. Au néolithique, ils y cultivent le millet et le sorgo. Puis, des empires centralisés y apparaissent au VIIIe siècle. Au XVIe siècle, la région connaît le commerce triangulaire, puis après 1885, la colonisation par la France. Les états modernes d'Afrique de l'Ouest naissent au XXe siècle.

Personnages célèbres

▸ **Malouma Mint El Meidah,** *Mauritanie, sénatrice et artiste (1960–)*

▸  **Didier Drogba,** *Côte d'Ivoire, footballeur (1978–)*

▸  **Angélique Kidjo,** *Bénin, chanteuse (1960–)*

la ville d'Abidjan

Tiébélé, Burkina Faso

Pays francophones

0 — 500 milles
0 — 500 kilomètres

Incroyable mais vrai!

La capitale du Bénin, Porto Novo, est connue comme° la «Ville aux trois noms». En effet°, elle est aussi appelée Adjatche, dans la langue Yoruba, et Hogbonou, dans la langue Goun. L'utilisation de ces trois noms différents reflète le côté° multiculturel de la ville.

connue comme *known as* **En effet** *Indeed* **côté** *aspect*

OPTIONS

Personnes célèbres Malouma Mint El Meidah combines traditional Mauritanian music with blues, jazz, and electro. Her music has addresses controversial topics, including poverty, inequality, and women's role in society. France named her a **Chevalier de la Légion d'honneur** in 2013. **Didier Drogba** played for various teams during his soccer career, including Chelsea, Olympique de Marseille, and the Ivory Coast national team.

Drogba has used his celebrity to advocate for peace in **la Côte d'Ivoire** after several years of civil war. **Angélique Kidjo** has been called "Africa's premier diva" and "the undisputed queen of African music." She is fluent in French, English, Fon, and Yorùbá, and sings in these languages. She is known for her colorful and creative music videos and live performances.

Les traditions

Le tissu bogolan du Mali

Le bogolan est une tradition originaire du Mali, du Burkina Faso et de Guinée. En bambara, une langue du Mali, bogo signifie «terre°» et lan, «avec». Ce tissu° en coton est fait à la main° et teint° deux fois, suivant une technique fascinante qui demande beaucoup de temps. En premier, le tissu est trempé° dans une teinture° faite avec des feuilles d'arbre écrasées° et bouillies dans de l'eau. Cela lui donne une couleur jaunâtre°. Ensuite, des motifs décoratifs sont peints° avec une préparation à base de terre. Cette terre est récoltée dans les rivières° et a besoin d'être fermentée pendant plusieurs mois avant de pouvoir être utilisée. Pour finir, on lave° le tissu, et le jaune des parties qui n'ont pas été teintes à la terre disparaît°.

La musique

Le reggae ivoirien

Alpha Blondy

La Côte d'Ivoire est un des pays d'Afrique où le reggae africain est le plus développé°. Ce type de reggae se distingue du reggae jamaïcain par les instruments de musique utilisés et les thèmes abordés°. En effet, les musiciens ivoiriens utilisent beaucoup d'instruments traditionnels d'Afrique de l'Ouest dans leurs musiques et les thèmes de leurs chansons° sont souvent très politiques. Alpha Blondy, par exemple, un chanteur célèbre dans le monde entier, fait des commentaires sociopolitiques dans beaucoup de ses chansons. Le chanteur Tiken Jah Fakoly critique souvent la politique occidentale et les gouvernants africains, et Ismaël Isaac dénonce les ventes d'armes° dans le monde. Le reggae ivoirien est chanté en français, en anglais et dans des langues africaines.

Les gens

Bineta Diop, la «vice-présidente» des femmes (Sénégal) (1950–)

Bineta Diop a appris de sa mère, Maréma Lo, une militante féministe pour le parti de Léopold Sédar Senghor au Sénégal, l'importance de la cause féminine, et elle dédie sa vie professionnelle à cette cause. En 1996, elle fonde une ONG° à Genève, Femmes Africa Solidarité, pour essayer d'encourager la solidarité entre femmes. Avec l'aide d'importantes avocates africaines, elle crée aussi un protocole pour les droits° de la femme qui naîtra° au Mozambique en 2003. Depuis janvier 2014, elle est l'envoyée spéciale pour les femmes, la paix et la sécurité à la Commission de l'Union Africaine, l'organisation principale des pays d'Afrique. Pas étonnant donc que le magazine *Times* la° nomme en 2011 l'une des cent personnalités les plus influentes au monde°!

Les arts

Le FESPACO

Le FESPACO (Festival panafricain du cinéma et de la télévision à Ouagadougou), créé en 1969 pour favoriser la promotion du cinéma africain, est le plus grand° festival de cinéma africain du monde, et c'est un événement culturel important en Afrique. Il a lieu au Burkina Faso tous les deux ans. Vingt films et vingt courts métrages° africains sont présentés en compétition officielle. Le FESPACO est aussi une fête très populaire, avec une cérémonie d'ouverture à laquelle assistent 40.000 spectateurs et des stars de la musique africaine. Ces dernières années, le festival s'est maintenu malgré° des difficultés politiques dans le pays et la menace° du virus Ebola. Il s'est aussi modernisé, avec par exemple, l'entrée en compétition de films numériques.

Le tissu bogolan du Mali
Each piece of Bogolan mud cloth is unique. The Bogolan tradition is part of the cultural identity of the Malian people.

Le reggae ivoirien
Some traditional African musical instruments are talking drums, djembe, balafone, kora, bolon, daro, and the gourd rattle. Many are made from natural materials such as seeds, grass, or wood.

Bineta Diop
The founder of **Femmes Africa Solidarité** is a guide and model for all the women in Africa who are fighting for equal rights.

Le FESPACO
- One of the objectives of **FESPACO** is to contribute to the expansion and development of African films. The festival arranges free screenings of African films in rural areas and also offers monetary prizes to its winners.
- Have students locate Ouagadougou on the map on page 214.

Qu'est-ce que vous avez appris? Répondez aux questions par des phrases complètes.

1. Qui est Didier Drogba?
   C'est un footballeur de Côte d'Ivoire.
2. Quelle est la particularité de Porto Novo, la capitale du Bénin?
   Elle a trois noms différents.
3. Que signifie «bogolan» en bambara?
   Bogo signifie «terre» et lan, «avec».
4. Avec quoi est-ce qu'on teint le bogolan? On teint le bogolan avec des feuilles d'arbres écrasées et bouillies dans de l'eau et avec une préparation à base de terre.
5. Qu'est-ce qui distingue le reggae de Côte d'Ivoire du reggae jamaïcain? Les instruments de musique et les thèmes des chansons.
6. Dans quelle langue est-ce qu'on chante le reggae en Côte d'Ivoire?
   On chante le reggae en français, en anglais et dans des langues africaines.
7. Qu'est-ce que Bineta Diop fonde à Genève en 1996?
   Elle fonde une ONG, Femmes Africa Solidarité.
8. Que fait Bineta Diop depuis janvier 2014?
   Elle est l'envoyée spéciale pour les femmes, la paix et la sécurité à la Commission de l'Union Africaine.
9. Comment s'appelle le plus grand festival de cinéma africain?
   Il s'appelle le FESPACO, ou Festival panafricain du cinéma et de la télévision à Ouagadougou.
10. Combien de films sont en compétition officielle au FESPACO?
    Vingt films sont en compétition officielle.

Sur Internet

Go to **vhlcentral.com** to find more cultural information related to this **Panorama**.

1. Trouvez des exemples de tissu bogolan. Aimez-vous ces tissus? Pourquoi ou pourquoi pas?
2. Écoutez des chansons de reggae ivoirien en français. Quels sont leurs thèmes?
3. Cherchez plus d'informations sur les films présentés au FESPACO. Est-ce qu'il y a un film que vous aimeriez voir (*would like to see*)? Lequel et pourquoi?

ressources

WB
pp. 69–70   vhlcentral

terre *dirt* tissu *fabric* fait à la main *handmade* teint *dyed* est trempé *is soaked* teinture *dye* feuilles d'arbre écrasées *crushed tree leaves* jaunâtre *yellowish* peints *painted* rivières *rivers* lave *washes* disparaît *disappears* le plus développé *the most developed* abordés *dealt with* chansons *songs* ventes d'armes *arms trade* ONG *NGO* droits *rights* naîtra *will be born* la *her* personnalités les plus influentes au monde *most influential personalities in the world* le plus grand *the largest* courts métrages *short films* malgré *despite* menace *threat*

O P T I O N S

Le reggae ivoirien Alpha Blondy, the face of African reggae in the 80s and 90s, was known for the originality of his reggae and the tonality of his lyrics. He began his career singing mostly in Dioula, a dialect from northern **Côte d'Ivoire**, and in **nouchi**, the slang of Abidjan. In 1997, Tiken Jah Fakoly, often called "**Le prophète du reggae africain**" or "**Le dauphin**," arrived on the African reggae scene singing in **Malinké**, a language spoken in several West African countries. Use of local and regional languages opened up reggae to its African audience in a new way, making the lyrics as important as or more important than the rhythms, and solidifying the pan-African identity of the genre.

Section Goals

In this section, students will learn historical and cultural information about **l'Afrique centrale**.

Instructional Resources
vhlcentral.com:
Digital Image Bank;
SAM Answer Key;
reference tools

Carte de l'Afrique centrale

- Have students look at the map or use the map from the Digital Image Bank. Ask volunteers to read the names of countries and their capitals aloud. Model pronunciation as necessary.
- Point out the photo of Kinshasa, in **la République démocratique du Congo**. Kinshasa is an inland city connected by rail to an Atlantic port city.

La région en chiffres

- In francophone Central African countries, French is the language of administration, education, and international communication. French is the official language and may share official status with English, Arabic, and other languages native to the country.
- Rwanda has three official languages, and Cameroon recognizes two official and 24 unofficial languages.

Incroyable mais vrai!

Virunga National Park was initially founded by founded in King Albert I of Belgium in 1925. Its main purpose at the time was to protect mountain gorillas.

Interactive Map

Panorama

L'Afrique centrale

La région en chiffres

▶ **Burundi:** *(11.179.000 habitants), Bujumbura*
▶ **Cameroun:** *(23.344.000), Yaoundé*
▶ **Congo:** *(4.620.000), Brazzaville*
▶ **Gabon:** *(1.725.000), Libreville*
▶ **République centrafricaine:** *(4.900.000), Bangui*
▶ **République démocratique du Congo (RDC):** *(77.267.000), Kinshasa*
▶ **Rwanda:** *(11.610.000), Kigali*
▶ **Tchad:** *(14.037.000), N'Djamena*

SOURCE: Population Division, UN Secretariat

Les premières traces humaines en Afrique centrale datent de plus de 100.000 ans. De grands empires centralisés apparaissent ensuite et pratiquent l'agriculture. La civilisation Sao, l'un des plus importants empires, perdure jusqu'au XVIe siècle. Puis, la région est dominée par la culture des Bakongo, jusqu'en 1885, date à laquelle la colonisation européenne commence.

Personnages célèbres

▶ Françoise Mbango-Etone, *Cameroun, athlète olympique (1976–)*

 Sonia Rolland, *Rwanda, actrice et réalisatrice (1981–)*

 Samuel Eto'o, *Cameroun, footballeur (1981–)*

Terre *Earth* **plus ancien** *oldest* **En plus de** *On top of* **paysages** *landscapes* **les plus actifs** *the most active*

Maisons obus en Cameroun

la place des Artistes à Kinshasa

Pays francophones

| 0 | 500 milles |
| 0 | 500 kilomètres |

Incroyable mais vrai!

Où se trouve le paradis des hippopotames sur Terre°? Dans les rivières° du plus ancien° parc d'Afrique, le parc national des Virunga, en République démocratique du Congo. En plus de° ses 20.000 hippopotames, le parc abrite une biodiversité exceptionnelle due à la variété de ses paysages°, dominés par les deux volcans les plus actifs° du continent.

Map labels: LA TUNISIE, LE MAROC, L'ALGÉRIE, LE SAHARA OCCIDENTAL, LA LYBIE, LE SAHARA, LA MAURITANIE, LE MALI, LE NIGER, LE TCHAD, LE SÉNÉGAL, LA GAMBIE, LE BURKINA-FASO, N'Djamena, LE SOUDAN, LA GUINÉE, LA GUINÉE-BISSAU, LE GHANA, LE BÉNIN, LE NIGÉRIA, LE SOUDAN DU SUD, LA SIERRA LEONE, LA CÔTE D'IVOIRE, LE TOGO, LE CAMEROUN, LA RÉPUBLIQUE CENTRAFRICAINE, LE LIBÉRIA, Yaoundé, Bangui, LE GOLFE DE GUINÉE, Libreville, L'OUGANDA, LA GUINÉE ÉQUATORIALE, LE GABON, LE CONGO, LE RWANDA, Kigali, Bujumbura, Brazzaville, LA RÉPUBLIQUE DÉMOCRATIQUE DU CONGO, LA TANZANIE, Kinshasa, L'OCÉAN ATLANTIQUE, LE BURUNDI, L'ANGOLA, LA ZAMBIE

O P T I O N S

Personnes célèbres Françoise Mbango-Etone competes in the triple jump. She was the first Cameroonian athlete to win a gold medal at the Olympics, in 2004, and won the country's second gold medal in 2008. **Sonia Rolland** grew up in Rwanda and Burundi, and moved to France with her family at age 13. She was Miss France 2000, the first African-born woman to win the pageant. She is an actress, starring in various French TV series and films, and has written two books. Her philanthropic work focuses on education in Rwanda. **Samuel Eto'o** is the most decorated African soccer player of all time. He played on the Cameroon national team during the 2000 Olympic soccer tournament, in which the team won gold. He has played for soccer clubs all over Europe, including FC Barcelona and Inter Milan. He retired in 2014.

Les destinations

Lacs d'Ounianga, Tchad

Au nord-est du Tchad, les lacs d'Ounianga occupent un large site composé de dix-huit lacs interconnectés sur 62.808 hectares. L'originalité de ce site? Ces lacs sont dans le Sahara, une région désertique et très aride, où il ne tombe que° deux millimètres d'eau par an et où l'eau s'évapore° constamment avec la chaleur°. Pourtant°, les lacs ne s'assèchent pas°. Ce phénomène est possible grâce à° une importante nappe phréatique souterraine°. Le contraste entre le désert et les lacs produit une mosaïque de couleurs: le vert des roseaux°, le bleu de l'eau, le brun du sable°... Avec le vent, la végétation ondule° à la surface des lacs, comme de véritables «vagues° d'eau flottant dans le désert».

Les traditions

Les masques du Gabon

Les masques gabonais exposés° aujourd'hui dans les musées européens ont inspiré de grands artistes du vingtième siècle, comme Matisse et Picasso. Pourtant, ces masques ne sont pas à l'origine de simples décorations ou objets d'art. Ce sont des objets rituels, utilisés par les différents groupes ethniques et sociétés initiatiques du Gabon. Chaque° société produit ses propres° masques; ils ont donc des formes très variées. Les masques sont le plus souvent° portés par les hommes, dans des cérémonies et rituels de groupe. Leurs matériaux et apparences sont donc très symboliques. Ils sont surtout faits de bois°, mais aussi de plumes°, de raphia° ou de peaux°, et ils ont des formes anthropomorphiques, zoomorphiques ou abstraites.

Les gens

La SAPE

Costumes de grands couturiers°, couleurs vives°, chaussures de marque°, sophistication et élégance, voici qui résume la SAPE, ou Société des Ambianceurs et des Personnes Élégantes. Ce concept a fait son apparition au début du XXe siècle à Brazzaville, la capitale du Congo. Aujourd'hui, la «sapologie», science de la sape°, est même plus qu'un simple mouvement de mode vestimentaire°. C'est une véritable philosophie de vie qui prône° le respect et la tolérance. En effet, les sapeurs doivent non seulement être impeccablement bien habillés en toute occasion, mais ils doivent aussi avoir un comportement irréprochable° où racisme et violence n'ont pas leur place. Et même si Brazzaville reste la capitale incontestée° de la sape, on trouve aujourd'hui des sapeurs sur tous les continents, et les grandes marques de mode n'hésitent plus à s'inspirer de ce style haut en couleurs.

Les activités sportives

Course de l'espoir°, Cameroun

La course de l'espoir est un événement sportif célèbre au Cameroun. Cette course existe depuis 1973 et a lieu près du Mont Cameroun, dans le sud-ouest du pays. Pendant la course, les participants, hommes et femmes, font l'ascension de ce mont, aller et retour, sur 42 kilomètres. À près de 4.070 mètres, le Mont Cameroun est un des plus hauts° points de la région et un de ses volcans les plus actifs. La course de l'espoir est donc très difficile, parce que c'est une épreuve de vitesse°, d'endurance et d'alpinisme°! Les meilleurs° temps sont d'environ quatre heures trente pour les hommes et d'un peu plus de cinq heures pour les femmes. La course est organisée par la Fédération camerounaise d'athlétisme, en février chaque année, et en 2016, jusqu'à° 512 athlètes ont pris le départ.

Lacs d'Ounianga
The Lakes of Ounianga became a UNESCO World Heritage site in 2012. This unique site is visited by about 500 adventurous tourists every year.

Les masques du Gabon
The Punu people of Gabon create ritual masks, many of which symbolize female ancestors. The masks are worn by dancers as part of traditional funeral rites.

La SAPE
- The clothing and lifestyle aesthetics of **la SAPE** have inspired many international musicians and writers. A good example is Solange Knowles' Losing You music video, which features African **sapeurs**.
- Ask students: **Est-ce que vous aimez le style de la SAPE? Pourquoi?**

Course de l'espoir
Volcanic Sprint is a 2007 documentary about the Race of Hope in **Cameroun**.

✍ Qu'est-ce que vous avez appris? Répondez aux questions par des phrases complètes.

1. Qui est Françoise Mbango-Etone?
   C'est une athlète olympique camerounaise.
2. Où est le paradis des hippopotames sur Terre?
   Il est dans le parc des Virunga, en République démocratique du Congo.
3. Combien y a-t-il de lacs dans la région d'Ounianga?
   Il y a dix-huit lacs.
4. Qu'est-ce qui crée une mosaïque de couleurs dans cette région?
   Le contraste entre les lacs, leur végétation et le désert.
5. Quels artistes ont été inspirés par les masques du Gabon?
   Picasso et Matisse ont été inspirés par ces masques.
6. Qui porte ces masques en général?
   Les hommes portent le plus souvent ces masques.
7. Où et quand est-ce que la SAPE a été créée?
   Au début du XXe siècle, à Brazzaville au Congo.
8. Pourquoi peut-on dire que la «sapologie» est plus qu'un simple mouvement de mode?
   Parce que les sapeurs doivent aussi prôner le respect et la tolérance.
9. Combien de kilomètres la course de l'espoir fait-elle?
   Elle fait 42 kilomètres.
10. Pourquoi est-ce que cette course est difficile?
    Elle est difficile parce que c'est une épreuve de vitesse, d'endurance et d'alpinisme.

Sur Internet

Go to **vhlcentral.com** to find more cultural information related to this **Panorama**.

✍ 1. Est-ce qu'il y a d'autres endroits sur Terre où on trouve des lacs dans le désert? Faites des recherches pour en trouver un exemple et comparez ce lieu aux lacs d'Ounianga.

✍ 2. Trouvez des exemples de masques du Gabon. Aimez-vous leurs styles? Pourquoi ou pourquoi pas?

✍ 3. Cherchez plus d'informations sur le Mont Cameroun. Pourquoi ce volcan est-il intéressant?

ressources

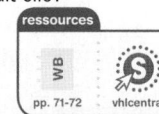

WB pp. 71-72 — vhlcentral

où il ne tombe que where it only falls **s'évapore** evaporates **chaleur** heat **Pourtant** However **ne s'assèchent pas** don't dry out **grâce à** thanks to **nappe phréatique souterraine** underground ground water **roseaux** reeds **sable** sand **ondule** moves, waves **vagues** waves **exposés** exhibited **Chaque** Each **propres** own **le plus souvent** most often **bois** wood **plumes** feathers **raphia** raffia **peaux** skins **couturiers** designers **vives** bright **marque** brand **sape** clothing **mode vestimentaire** fashion **prône** advocates **comportement irréprochable** flawless behavior **incontestée** unquestioned **Course de l'espoir** Hope race **des plus hauts** highest **épreuve de vitesse** speed test **alpinisme** mountaineering **Les meilleurs** The best **jusqu'à** up to

---

O P T I O N S

La course de l'espoir was created by Guinness Cameroun and was originally called the Guinness Mount Cameroon Race. In 1996, it was renamed **la course de l'espoir** by Colonel Kalkaba Malboum, then president of the National Olympic Committee. The race is the oldest annual marathon in Cameroon and attracts more than 20,000 spectators each year to the town of **Buea**. Additional athletic and cultural activities are offered as entertainment while spectators wait for the race participants to finish. The prizes in each category (Male, Female, Group) are up to 10 million CFA francs, which is equal to four years' annual income in Cameroon.

Section Goals

In this section, students will:
• learn to skim a text
• read a weekly city guide about Montreal

Stratégie Tell students that they can often predict the content of an unfamiliar document in French by skimming it and looking for recognizable format elements.

Examinez le texte Have students skim the text at the top of this calendar of events in and around Montreal. Point out the cognates **arts**, **culture**, **festival**, **musique classique**, and **manifestations culturelles**. Ask them to predict what type of document it is (city guide/calendar of events in a newspaper/weekly). Then ask students to scan the rest of the calendar of events.

Catégories Before students do this activity, ask them to think of three words or expressions that fit each of the three given categories (**les loisirs culturels, les activités sportives, les activités de plein air**) in English.

Trouvez Go over answers with the whole class by pointing out where in the text each piece of information is found. Expand the activity by having students write additional entries for the calendar of events that include information for the unchecked items (**où manger cette semaine, le temps qu'il va faire cette semaine, des prix d'entrée, des adresses**).

Language Note Point out that French-speaking Canadians say **la fin de semaine** instead of **le week-end**.

Lecture

 Audio: Reading

Avant la lecture

STRATÉGIE

Skimming

Skimming involves quickly reading through a document to absorb its general meaning. This allows you to understand the main ideas without having to read word for word. When you skim a text, look at its title and subtitles and read the first sentence of each paragraph.

Examinez le texte

Regardez rapidement le texte. Quel est le titre (*title*) du texte? En combien de parties le texte est-il divisé? Quels sont les titres des parties? Maintenant, regardez les photos. Quel est le sujet de l'article?

Catégories

Dans le texte, trouvez trois mots ou expressions qui représentent chaque catégorie. Answers will vary. Suggested answers below.

les loisirs culturels

| musique classique | cinéma africain | musée des Beaux-Arts |

les activités sportives

| golf | ski | tennis |

les activités de plein air (*outdoor*)

| camping | randonnées | équitation |

Trouvez

Regardez le document. Indiquez si vous trouvez ces informations.

_____ 1. où manger cette semaine
_____ 2. le temps qu'il va faire cette semaine
✓ 3. où aller à la pêche
_____ 4. des prix d'entrée (*entrance*)
✓ 5. des numéros de téléphone
✓ 6. des sports
✓ 7. des spectacles
_____ 8. des adresses

CETTE SEMAINE À MONTRÉAL ET DANS LA RÉGION

ARTS ET CULTURE

Festivals et autres manifestations culturelles à explorer:

• Festival de musique classique, samedi de 16h00 à 22h00, à la Salle de concerts Richelieu, à Montréal
• Festival du cinéma africain, dans tous les cinémas de Montréal
• Journée de la bande dessinée, samedi toute la journée, à la Librairie Rochefort, à Montréal
• Festival de reggae, dimanche tout l'après-midi, à l'Espace Lemay, à Montréal

Spectacle à voir°

• *La Cantatrice chauve*, pièce° d'Eugène Ionesco, samedi et dimanche à 20h00, au Théâtre du Chat Bleu, à Montréal

À ne pas oublier°

• Le musée des Beaux-Arts de Montréal, avec sa collection de plus de° 30.000 objets d'art du monde entier°

OPTIONS

TPR Write activities from the calendar of events (**aller à la pêche, jouer au baseball, faire de l'équitation,** etc.) on slips of paper. Divide the class into two teams. Have a member of one team draw a paper. That team member mimes the chosen activity. The other team guesses what it is. Give points for correct answers. The team with the most points wins.

Small Groups Have groups of three students work together to read aloud each section of the calendar of events (**Arts et culture, Sports et jeux, Exploration**). Each student will then write two questions about the section that he or she read. After they have finished, ask groups to exchange their questions with another group. Have groups read the questions to the class and ask volunteers to answer them.

SPORTS ET JEUX

- L'Académie de golf de Montréal organise un grand tournoi° le mois prochain. Pour plus d'informations, contactez le (514) 846-1225.
- Tous les dimanches, le Club d'échecs de Montréal organise des tournois d'échecs en plein air° dans le parc Champellier. Pour plus d'informations, appelez le (514) 846-1085.
- Skiez! Passez la fin de semaine dans les Laurentides° ou dans les Cantons-de-l'Est!
- Et pour la famille sportive: essayez le parc Lafontaine, un centre d'amusement pour tous qui offre: volley-ball, tennis, football et baseball.

PASSIONNÉ° DE PÊCHE? N'OUBLIEZ PAS LES NOMBREUX LACS° OÙ LA PÊCHE EST AUTORISÉE.

EXPLORATION

Redécouvrez la nature grâce à° ces activités à ne pas manquer°:

Visite du parc national de la Jacques-Cartier°
- Camping
- Promenades et randonnées
- Observation de la faune et de la flore

Région des Laurentides et Gaspésie°
- Équitation°
- Randonnées à cheval de 2 à 5 jours en camping

voir *see* **pièce (de théâtre)** *play* **À ne pas oublier** *Not to be forgotten* **plus de** *more than* **du monde entier** *from around the world* **tournoi** *tournament* **en plein air** *outdoor* **Laurentides** *region of eastern Quebec* **Passionné** *Enthusiast* **lacs** *lakes* **grâce à** *thanks to* **à ne pas manquer** *not to be missed* **la Jacques-Cartier** *the Jacques-Cartier river in Quebec* **Gaspésie** *peninsula of Quebec* **Équitation** *Horseback riding*

Après la lecture

Répondez Répondez aux questions avec des phrases complètes.

1. Citez deux activités sportives qu'on peut pratiquer à l'extérieur.
   Answers will vary.

2. À quel jeu est-ce qu'on joue dans le parc Champellier?
   On joue aux échecs dans le parc Champellier.

3. Où va peut-être aller un passionné de lecture et de dessin?
   Un passionné de lecture et de dessin va peut-être aller à la Journée de la bande dessinée.

4. Où pratique-t-on des sports d'équipe?
   On pratique des sports d'équipe au parc Lafontaine.

5. Où y a-t-il de la neige au Québec en cette saison?
   Il y a de la neige dans les Laurentides et dans les Cantons-de-l'Est.

6. Si on aime beaucoup la musique, où peut-on aller?
   On peut aller au Festival de musique classique ou au Festival de reggae.

Suggestions Lucille est étudiante au Québec. Ce week-end, elle invite sa famille à explorer la région. Choisissez une activité à faire ou un lieu à visiter que chaque membre de sa famille va aimer.

MODÈLE

La sœur cadette de Lucille adore le ski.
Elle va aimer les Laurentides et les Cantons-de-l'Est.

1. La mère de Lucille est artiste.
   Elle va aimer le musée des Beaux-Arts de Montréal.

2. Le frère de Lucille joue au volley-ball à l'université.
   Il va aimer le parc Lafontaine.

3. La sœur aînée de Lucille a envie de voir un film sénégalais.
   Elle va aimer le Festival du cinéma africain.

4. Le grand-père de Lucille joue souvent aux échecs.
   Il va aimer les tournois d'échecs en plein air dans le parc Champellier.

5. La grand-mère de Lucille est fan de théâtre.
   Elle va aimer *La Cantatrice chauve* au Théâtre du Chat Bleu.

6. Le père de Lucille adore la nature et les animaux, mais il n'est pas très sportif.
   Answers will vary. Possible answer: Il va aimer les promenades dans le parc national de la Jacques-Cartier.

Une invitation Vous allez passer le week-end au Québec. Qu'est-ce que vous allez faire? Par groupes de quatre, discutez des activités qui vous intéressent (*that interest you*) et essayez de trouver trois ou quatre activités que vous avez en commun. Attention! Il va peut-être pleuvoir ce week-end, alors ne choisissez pas (*don't choose*) uniquement des activités de plein air!

Répondez Present these as items 7–10. **7. Où peut-on voir des films africains? (On peut voir des films africains dans tous les cinémas de Montréal.) 8. Combien d'objets d'art y a-t-il au musée des Beaux-Arts de Montréal? (Il y a plus de 30.000 objets d'art.) 9. Quels sports pratique-t-on au parc Lafontaine? (On propose le volley-ball, le tennis, le football et le baseball.) 10. Si on aime beaucoup les animaux et les fleurs, où peut-on aller? (On peut aller au parc national de la Jacques-Cartier.)**

Suggestions Ask students to write about three more members of Lucille's family. They should model their sentences after the ones in the activity, saying what each person enjoys doing. Then have students read their sentences to a partner. The partner will come up with a suggested activity or place to visit that will suit each person.

Une invitation Give students a couple of minutes to review the **Vocabulaire** on page 178, **Expressions utiles** on page 183, and Expressions with **faire** on page 186. Add activities, such as **faire du surf des neiges, prendre des photos, faire des arts martiaux,** and **faire du skateboard.**

Expansion Have one or two groups act out their conversation from **Une invitation** for the rest of the class. Before the groups begin, have the listeners in the class write a list of ten activities that they think will be mentioned in each of the presentations. As students listen, have them check off on their list the activities they hear.

OPTIONS

Extra Practice Give students true or false statements about the **Lecture.** Example: **On peut faire des randonnées à cheval au parc national de la Jacques-Cartier. (Faux. On peut faire des randonnées à cheval en Région des Laurentides et Gaspésie.)**

Extra Practice Ask students to go through the selection and locate all of the activities that require usage of **faire.** (Encourage them to use their dictionaries, if necessary.) Then have them write sentences saying whether or not they like doing those activities. Example: **Activités avec faire: faire du vélo, faire de l'équitation,** etc. **J'aime faire du vélo. Je n'aime pas faire de l'équitation.**

Écriture

Section Goals

In this section, students will:
• learn to use a French-English dictionary
• write a brochure including weather-related information and seasonal activities

Stratégie Explain to students that when they look up a translation of an English word in a French-English dictionary, they will frequently find more than one translation. They must decide which one best fits the context. Discuss the meanings of *racket* that might be found in an entry in a French-English dictionary and the usefulness of the explanatory notes and abbreviations found in dictionary entries.

Thème Remind students of some of the common graphic features used in brochures: headings, times and places, brief descriptions of events, and prices.

STRATÉGIE

Using a dictionary

A common mistake made by beginning language learners is to embrace the dictionary as the ultimate resource for reading, writing, and speaking. While it is true that the dictionary is a useful tool that can provide valuable information about vocabulary, using the dictionary correctly requires that you understand the elements of each entry.

If you glance at a French-English dictionary, you will notice that the format is similar to that of an English dictionary. The word is listed first, usually followed by its pronunciation. Then come the definitions, organized by parts of speech. Sometimes, the most frequently used meanings are listed first.

To find the best word for your needs, you should refer to the abbreviations and the explanatory notes that appear next to the entries. For example, imagine that you are writing about your pastimes. You want to write *I want to buy a new racket for my match tomorrow*, but you don't know the French word for *racket*.

In the dictionary, you might find an entry like this one:

> **racket** n 1. boucan; 2. raquette (sport)

The abbreviation key at the front of the dictionary says that *n* corresponds to **nom** (*noun*). Then, the first word you see is **boucan**. The definition of **boucan** is *noise or racket,* so **boucan** is probably not the word you want. The second word is **raquette**, followed by the word *sport*, which indicates that it is related to **sports**. This detail indicates that the word **raquette** is the best choice for your needs.

✍ Thème

Écrire une brochure
Avant l'écriture

1. Choisissez le sujet de votre brochure:

   A. Vous travaillez à la Chambre de Commerce de votre région pour l'été. Des hommes et des femmes d'affaires québécois vont visiter votre région cette année, mais ils n'ont pas encore décidé (*have not yet decided*) quand. La Chambre de Commerce vous demande de créer (*asks you to create*) une petite brochure sur le temps qu'il fait dans votre région aux différentes saisons de l'année. Dites quelle saison, à votre avis (*in your opinion*), est idéale pour visiter votre région et expliquez pourquoi.

   B. Vous avez une réunion familiale pour décider où aller en vacances cette année, mais chaque membre de la famille suggère un endroit différent. Choisissez un lieu de vacances où vous avez envie d'aller et créez une brochure pour montrer à votre famille pourquoi vous devriez (*should*) tous y aller (*go there*). Décrivez la météo de l'endroit et indiquez les différentes activités culturelles et sportives qu'on peut y faire.

   C. Vous passez un semestre/trimestre dans le pays francophone de votre choix (*of your choice*). Deux étudiants de votre cours de français ont aussi envie de visiter ce pays. Créez une petite brochure pour partager vos impressions du pays. Présentez le pays, donnez des informations météorologiques et décrivez vos activités préférées.

OPTIONS

Avant l'écriture Reinforce to students that when they look up a word in a French-English dictionary, not all of the translations listed will have the same meaning. Tell them that a good way to check a possible translation of an English word is to look up the French word and see how it is translated back into English.

Discuss the three topics students may wish to write about. Introduce terms such as **comité**, **guide d'orientation**, and **chambre de commerce**. Evaluate the level of formality of each of the brochures described. (The chamber of commerce brochure will be more formal than the family and student brochures.) Remind students to keep this in mind when they create their brochures.

2. Choisissez le sujet de votre brochure et pensez au vocabulaire utile à son écriture. Utilisez le tableau (*chart*) pour noter tous les mots (*words*) en français qui vous viennent à l'esprit (*you can think of*). Ensuite (*Then*), revoyez (*review*) la liste de vocabulaire des unités 1–4 et ajoutez (*add*) le vocabulaire utile pour le sujet. Enfin (*Finally*), regardez votre tableau. Quels sont les mots en anglais que vous pourriez (*could*) ajouter? Créez une nouvelle liste et cherchez les mots dans un dictionnaire.

Mots en français (de moi)	Mots en français (des listes)	Mots en anglais
		anglais / français:

3. Cherchez les mots dans le dictionnaire. N'oubliez pas d'utiliser la procédure de **Stratégie**.

Écriture

Utilisez le vocabulaire du tableau pour créer votre brochure. N'oubliez pas de penser à un titre (*title*). Ensuite, créez des sections et donnez-leur (*them*) aussi un titre, comme **Printemps, Été, ...; Ville, Campagne (*Countryside*), ...; France, Tunisie, ...** Vous pouvez (*can*) utiliser des photos pour illustrer.

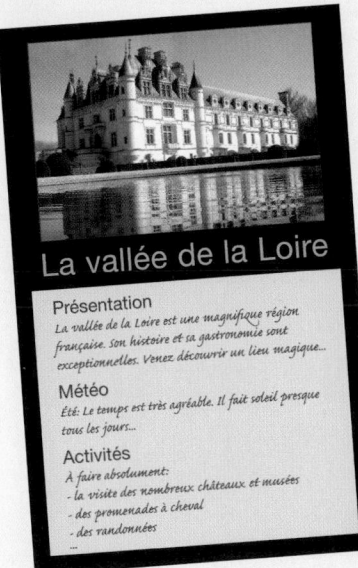

Après l'écriture

1. Échangez votre brochure avec celle (*the one*) d'un(e) partenaire. Répondez à ces questions pour commenter son travail.

- Votre partenaire a-t-il/elle couvert (*did cover*) le sujet?
- A-t-il/elle donné (*did give*) un titre à la brochure et aux sections?
- S'il (*If there*) y a des photos, illustrent-elles le texte?
- Votre partenaire a-t-il/elle utilisé (*did use*) le vocabulaire approprié?
- A-t-il/elle correctement conjugué (*did conjugate*) les verbes?

2. Corrigez votre brochure d'après (*according to*) les commentaires de votre partenaire. Relisez votre travail pour éliminer ces problèmes:

- des fautes (*errors*) d'orthographe
- des fautes de ponctuation
- des fautes de conjugaison
- des fautes d'accord (*agreement*) des adjectifs
- un mauvais emploi (*use*) de la grammaire

Criteria

Content Contains all the information included in the subject description the student chose.
Scale: 1 2 3 4 5

Organization Follows a typical brochure organization with a major head, text, and at least one visual.
Scale: 1 2 3 4 5

Accuracy Uses possessive and descriptive adjectives and modifies them accordingly. Spells words and conjugates verbs correctly throughout.
Scale: 1 2 3 4 5

Creativity The student includes additional information that is not included in the task, adds extra features to the brochure such as bulleted lists and boxed text, and/or spends extra time on design and presentation.
Scale: 1 2 3 4 5

Scoring

Excellent	18–20 points
Good	14–17 points
Satisfactory	10–13 points
Unsatisfactory	< 10 points

deux cent vingt et un **221**

OPTIONS

Avant l'écriture Group students who have chosen to work on the same brochures and encourage them to share their ideas and personalized vocabulary from step 2 before they begin writing. As a group, have them brainstorm additional vocabulary they may need to look up before they begin writing.

Before students begin writing, have the class discuss some of the features that are typically found in brochures, such as headings, schedules, lists, boxed/highlighted text, photos, graphics, and other visuals. Bring in some brochures for students to analyze before they create their own.

Instructional Resources
vhlcentral.com:
Textbook MP3s; Audioscript;
reference tools

🔊 Ⓢ Vocabulary Tools

Suggestions
• Tell students that an easy way to study from **Vocabulaire** is to cover up the French half of each section, leaving only the English equivalents exposed. They can then quiz themselves on the French items. To focus on the English equivalents of the French entries, they simply reverse this process.
• Point out to students that they can use the Vocabulary Tools at **vhlcentral.com** for reference and extra vocabulary practice.

Leçon 5A

Activités sportives et loisirs

aider *to help*
aller à la pêche *to go fishing*
bricoler *to tinker; to do odd jobs*
chanter *to sing*
désirer *to want; to desire*
gagner *to win*
indiquer *to indicate*
jouer (à/de) *to play*
marcher *to walk (person); to work (thing)*
pratiquer *to practice; to play (a sport)*
skier *to ski*
une bande dessinée (B.D.) *comic strip*
le baseball *baseball*
le basket(-ball) *basketball*
les cartes (f.) *cards*
le cinéma *movies*
les échecs (m.) *chess*
une équipe *team*
le foot(ball) *soccer*
le football américain *football*
le golf *golf*
un jeu *game*
un joueur/une joueuse *player*
un loisir *leisure activity*
un match *game*
un passe-temps *pastime, hobby*
un spectacle *show*
le sport *sport*
un stade *stadium*
le temps libre *free time*
le tennis *tennis*
le volley(-ball) *volleyball*

Verbes irréguliers en -ir

courir *to run*
dormir *to sleep*
partir *to leave*
sentir *to feel; to smell; to sense*
servir *to serve*
sortir *to go out, to leave*

La fréquence

une/deux fois *one/two time(s)*
par jour, semaine, mois, an, etc. *per day, week, month, year, etc.*
déjà *already*
encore *again; still*
jamais *never*
longtemps *a long time*
maintenant *now*
parfois *sometimes*
rarement *rarely*
souvent *often*

Expressions utiles

See p. 183.

Expressions with faire

faire de l'aérobic *to do aerobics*
faire attention (à) *to pay attention (to)*
faire du camping *to go camping*
faire du cheval *to go horseback riding*
faire la connaissance de... *to meet (someone) for the first time*
faire la cuisine *to cook*
faire de la gym *to work out*
faire du jogging *to go jogging*
faire de la planche à voile *to go windsurfing*
faire une promenade *to go for a walk*
faire une randonnée *to go for a hike*
faire du ski *to go skiing*
faire du sport *to play sports*
faire un tour (en voiture) *to go for a walk (drive)*
faire du vélo *to go bike riding*

faire

faire *to do, to make*
je fais, tu fais, il/elle/on fait, nous faisons, vous faites, ils/elles font

Il faut...

il faut... *it is necessary to...; one must...*

Leçon 5B

Le temps qu'il fait

Il fait 18 degrés. *It is 18 degrees.*
Il fait beau. *The weather is nice.*
Il fait bon. *The weather is good/warm.*
Il fait chaud. *It is hot (out).*
Il fait (du) soleil. *It is sunny.*
Il fait du vent. *It is windy.*
Il fait frais. *It is cool.*
Il fait froid. *It is cold.*
Il fait mauvais. *The weather is bad.*
Il fait un temps épouvantable. *The weather is dreadful.*
Il neige. (neiger) *It is snowing. (to snow)*
Il pleut. (pleuvoir) *It is raining. (to rain)*
Le temps est nuageux. *It is cloudy.*
Le temps est orageux. *It is stormy.*
Quel temps fait-il? *What is the weather like?*
Quelle température fait-il? *What is the temperature?*
un imperméable *rain jacket*
un parapluie *umbrella*

Verbes

acheter *to buy*
amener *to bring (someone)*
célébrer *to celebrate*
considérer *to consider*
emmener *to take (someone)*
employer *to use*
envoyer *to send*
espérer *to hope*
essayer (de + inf.) *to try (to)*
nettoyer *to clean*
payer *to pay*
posséder *to possess, to own*
préférer *to prefer*
protéger *to protect*
répéter *to repeat; to rehearse*

Les saisons, les mois, les dates

une saison *season*
l'automne (m.)/à l'automne *fall/in the fall*
l'été (m.)/en été *summer/in the summer*
l'hiver (m.)/en hiver *winter/in the winter*
le printemps (m.)/au printemps *spring/in the spring*
Quelle est la date? *What's the date?*
C'est le 1er (premier) octobre. *It's the first of October.*
C'est quand votre/ton anniversaire? *When is your birthday?*
C'est le 2 mai. *It's the second of May.*
C'est quand l'anniversaire de Paul? *When is Paul's birthday?*
C'est le 15 mars. *It's March 15th.*
un anniversaire *birthday*
janvier *January*
février *February*
mars *March*
avril *April*
mai *May*
juin *June*
juillet *July*
août *August*
septembre *September*
octobre *October*
novembre *November*
décembre *December*

Expressions utiles

See p. 201.

Numbers 101 and higher

See p. 204.

Les fêtes

Pour commencer
- Qui est l'invitée sur la photo?
- Qu'est-ce qu'Amina et Valérie vont faire?
- Qu'est-ce qu'elles vont manger? Du pain ou une mousse au chocolat?
- IDe quelle couleur est le tee-shirt d'Amina? Orange ou violet?

Unit Goals

Leçon 6A

In this lesson, students will learn:
- terms for parties and celebrations
- terms for the stages of life
- more differences between open and closed vowels
- about **carnaval** and France's Bastille Day
- more about festivals and holiday celebrations through specially shot video footage
- demonstrative adjectives
- the **passé composé** with **avoir**
- some irregular past participles
- about a traditional Christmas market in Paris

Leçon 6B

In this lesson, students will learn:
- terms for clothing, shopping, and colors
- more about open and closed vowels
- about the fashion industry in France
- about famous Algerian singer Zaho
- indirect object pronouns
- more uses of disjunctive pronouns
- regular and irregular **-re** verbs
- to listen for linguistic cues in oral communication

Savoir-faire

In this section, students will learn:
- cultural and historical information about **l'Algérie, le Maroc et la Tunisie**
- to recognize word families
- how to report an interview

Pour commencer
- Amina est l'invitée.
- Elles vont faire la fête.
- Elles vont manger une mousse au chocolat.
- Son tee-shirt est orange.

RESOURCES

Student Activities Manual (SAM): Workbook Activities, pp. 73–88; Lab Activities, pp. 41–48; Video Activities, pp. 21–24; pp. 71–72 SAM Answer Key

vhlcentral.com: Textbook MP3s; Lab MP3s; Textbook Audioscript; Lab Audioscript; Video; Videoscript; **Roman-photo** Translations; **Vocabulaire supplémentaire**; Activity Pack (including **Feuilles d'activités**, Info Gap Activities, and Task-based Activities);

Le Zapping TV clip transcription; **Essayez!** and **Mise en pratique** answers; Digital Image Bank; Testing Program; Testing Program MP3s

Section Goals

In this section, students will learn and practice vocabulary related to:
- parties and celebrations
- stages of life and interpersonal relationships

Instructional Resources

vhlcentral.com:
Digital Image Bank (including vocabulary illustrations from the textbook, theme-based illustrations); **Vocabulaire supplémentaire; Mise en pratique** *answers; Textbook Audioscript; Lab Audioscript; Activity Pack (Info Gap Activities); Textbook MP3s; Lab MP3s; SAM Answer Key; reference tools*

Suggestions

- Have students look over the new vocabulary and identify the cognates. Examples: **organiser**, **fiancé(e)**, **mariage**, and **divorce**.
- Describe what people are doing in the drawing using the **6A Contextes** illustration from the Digital Image Bank. Examples: **Ils font la fête. Ils boivent du champagne.** Follow up with simple questions based on your narrative.
- Point out the banner and the cake in the illustration. Ask students what **Bon anniversaire** and **Joyeux anniversaire** mean. *(Happy birthday)*
- Point out the similarities and differences between these related words: **aimer**, **ami(e)**, **l'amitié**, **un amour**, **amoureux**, and **amoureuse**.
- Use the Vocabulary illustrations and the Celebrations illustrations from the Digital Image Bank to help students familiarize themselves with parties and celebrations and the stages of life.
- Additional vocabulary for this lesson can be found in the **Vocabulaire supplémentaire** on the Supersite.

Leçon **6A**

You will learn how to...
- talk about celebrations
- talk about the stages of life

S Vocabulary Tools

Surprise!

Vocabulaire

faire la fête	to party
faire une surprise (à quelqu'un)	to surprise (someone)
fêter	to celebrate
organiser une fête	to organize a party
une fête	party; celebration
un jour férié	holiday
une bière	beer
le vin	wine
l'amitié	friendship
l'amour	love
le bonheur	happiness
un(e) fiancé(e)	fiancé
des jeunes mariés (m.)	newlyweds
un rendez-vous	date; appointment
l'adolescence (f.)	adolescence
l'âge adulte (m.)	adulthood
un divorce	divorce
l'enfance (f.)	childhood
une étape	stage
l'état civil (m.)	marital status
la jeunesse	youth
un mariage	marriage; wedding
la mort	death
la naissance	birth
la vie	life
la vieillesse	old age
prendre sa retraite	to retire
tomber amoureux/ amoureuse	to fall in love
ensemble	together

les invitées *(f.)*

les invités *(m.)*

l'hôte *(m.)*

l'hôtesse *(f.)*

le gâteau

la glace

les biscuits *(m.)*

les bonbons *(m.)*

le champagne

les desserts *(m.)*

les glaçons *(m.)*

ressources

WB pp. 73–74

LM p. 41

S vhlcentral

224 *deux cent vingt-quatre*

O P T I O N S

Les fêtes Point out that, in addition to celebrating birthdays, many people in French-speaking cultures celebrate **la fête**, or saint's day, which is based upon their given name. Bring in a French calendar that has the names of **fêtes** and have students find their own saint's day. You may need to help students find the name that most closely resembles their own.

Extra Practice Have students write three fill-in-the-blank sentences based on the drawing above, using the new vocabulary. Then have each student exchange papers with a classmate and complete the sentences. Remind them to verify their answers.

Mise en pratique

BON ANNIVERSAIRE, MARC!

la surprise

le couple

le cadeau

1 Écoutez
Écoutez la conversation entre Anne et Nathalie. Indiquez si les affirmations sont **vraies** ou **fausses**.

		Vrai	Faux
1.	Jean-Marc va prendre sa retraite dans six mois.	☐	☑
2.	Nathalie a l'idée d'organiser une fête pour Jean-Marc.	☐	☑
3.	Anne va acheter un gâteau.	☑	☐
4.	Nathalie va apporter de la glace.	☐	☑
5.	La fête est une surprise.	☑	☐
6.	Nathalie va envoyer les invitations par e-mail.	☑	☐
7.	La fête va avoir lieu (*take place*) dans le bureau d'Anne.	☐	☑
8.	La maison d'Anne n'est pas belle.	☐	☑
9.	Tout le monde va donner des idées pour le cadeau.	☑	☐
10.	Les invités vont acheter le cadeau.	☐	☑

2 Chassez l'intrus
Indiquez le mot ou l'expression qui n'appartient pas (*doesn't belong*) à la liste.

1. l'amour, tomber amoureux, un fiancé, (un divorce)
2. un mariage, un couple, (un jour férié,) un fiancé
3. un biscuit, (une bière,) un dessert, un gâteau
4. (une glace,) une bière, le champagne, le vin
5. (la vieillesse,) la naissance, l'enfance, la jeunesse
6. faire la fête, un hôte, des invités, (une étape)
7. fêter, un cadeau, (la vie,) une surprise
8. (l'état civil,) la naissance, la mort, l'adolescence

3 Associez
Faites correspondre les mots et expressions de la colonne de gauche avec les définitions de la colonne de droite. Notez que tous les éléments ne sont pas utilisés. Ensuite (*Then*), avec un(e) partenaire, donnez votre propre définition de quatre expressions de la première colonne. Votre partenaire doit deviner (*must guess*) de quoi vous parlez.

_b_	1. la naissance	a. C'est une date importante, comme le 4 juillet aux États-Unis.
___	2. l'enfance	b. C'est la fin de l'étape prénatale.
_c_	3. l'adolescence	c. C'est l'étape de la vie pendant laquelle (*during which*) on va au lycée.
___	4. l'âge adulte	d. C'est un événement très triste.
_e_	5. tomber amoureux	e. C'est soudain (*suddenly*) aimer une personne.
_a_	6. un jour férié	f. C'est le futur probable d'un couple qui se dispute (*fights*) tout le temps.
_g_	7. le mariage	g. C'est un jour de bonheur et de célébration de l'amour.
_f_	8. le divorce	h. C'est quand une personne décide de ne plus travailler.
_h_	9. prendre sa retraite	
_d_	10. la mort	

Ⓢ Practice more at **vhlcentral.com**.

deux cent vingt-cinq **225**

1 Audioscript ANNE: Nathalie, je vais organiser une fête pour Jean-Marc. Il va prendre sa retraite dans un mois. Ça va être une surprise. Je vais acheter un gâteau.
NATHALIE: Oh, et moi, qu'est-ce que je fais pour aider, Anne? J'apporte des biscuits?
A: Oui, c'est une bonne idée. Il faut aussi trouver un cadeau original.
N: D'accord, mais je vais avoir besoin d'un peu de temps pour y penser.
A: Qu'est-ce qu'on fait pour les invités?
N: Pour faire une vraie surprise à Jean-Marc, il faut être discrètes. Je propose d'envoyer un e-mail à tout le monde. En plus, comme ça, c'est rapide.
A: Et qu'est-ce qu'on fait pour la décoration?
N: Pourquoi ne pas fêter sa retraite chez toi? Ta maison est belle, et on n'a pas besoin de beaucoup de décoration.
A: Oui, pourquoi pas! Maintenant, il ne reste plus qu'à trouver un cadeau. Pourquoi est-ce qu'on ne demande pas aux autres de donner des idées par e-mail?
N: Oui, et quel beau cadeau pour Jean-Marc si tout le monde participe et donne un peu d'argent!
(On Textbook MP3s)

2 Suggestion Play the conversation again, stopping at the end of each sentence that contains the answer to one of these items. Have students verify true statements and correct the false ones.

2 Expansions
- For additional practice, give students these items. **9. la vieillesse, la jeunesse, la fête, l'âge adulte (la fête) 10. l'amour, le bonheur, l'amitié, la retraite (la retraite)**
- Have students create one or two additional items using at least three of the new vocabulary words in each one. Collect their papers and write some of the items on the board.

3 Suggestion Have volunteers share their definitions with the class.

O P T I O N S

Game Write vocabulary words related to celebrations on index cards. On another set of cards, draw or paste pictures to match each term. Tape them face down on the board in random order. Divide the class into two teams. Then play a game of concentration, matching words with pictures. When a player has a match, his/her team collects those cards. When all the cards have been matched, the team with the most cards wins.

Extra Practice Say vocabulary words aloud and have students write or say opposite terms. Examples: **la jeunesse (la vieillesse), le divorce (le mariage), la naissance (la mort), séparé (ensemble),** and **enfant (adulte).**

4 Suggestions
• Go over the answers to the activity with the class before students write their own sentences.
• Ask volunteers to write their sentences on the board and have the class make corrections as needed.

5 Suggestion Have two volunteers read the **modèle** aloud. Then divide the class into pairs and distribute the Info Gap Handouts found in the Activity Pack on the Supersite. Give students ten minutes to complete the activity.

6 Suggestion Tell students that they should plan the party first by answering the questions. Then they should use those answers to write the conversation discussing the details of the party.

Communication

4 Le mot juste Complétez les phrases par le mot illustré. Faites les accords nécessaires. Ensuite (*Then*), avec un(e) partenaire, créez (*create*) une phrase pour laquelle (*for which*) vous illustrez trois mots d'**ESPACE CONTEXTES**. Échangez votre phrase avec celle d'un autre groupe et résolvez le rébus.

1. Caroline est une amie d' __enfance__ 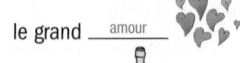. Je vais lui faire une __surprise__ samedi.

   C'est son anniversaire.

2. Marc et Sophie sont inséparables. Ils sont toujours __ensemble__ . C'est le bonheur et

   le grand __amour__ .

3. Le __vin__ rouge va bien avec les viandes rouges, alors que le __champagne__ va

   mieux (*goes better*) avec les __desserts__ 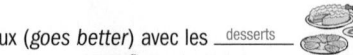 .

4. Les __(jeunes) mariés__ ont beaucoup de __cadeaux__ .

5. La __naissance__ de ma sœur est un grand __bonheur__ pour mes parents.

5 Sept différences Votre professeur va vous donner, à vous et à votre partenaire, deux feuilles d'activités différentes. À tour de rôle, posez-vous des questions pour trouver les sept différences entre les illustrations de l'anniversaire des jumeaux (*twins*) Boniface. Attention! Ne regardez pas la feuille de votre partenaire. *Answers will vary.*

MODÈLE
Étudiant(e) 1: *Sur mon image, il y a trois cadeaux. Combien de cadeaux y a-t-il sur ton image?*
Étudiant(e) 2: *Sur mon image, il y a quatre cadeaux.*

6 C'est la fête! Vous avez terminé (*have finished*) les examens de fin d'année et vous allez organiser une fête! Avec un(e) partenaire, écrivez une conversation au sujet de la préparation de cette fête. N'oubliez pas de répondre aux questions suivantes. Ensuite (*Then*), jouez (*act out*) votre dialogue devant la classe. *Answers will vary.*

1. Quand allez-vous organiser la fête?
2. Qui vont être les invités?
3. Où la fête va-t-elle avoir lieu (*take place*)?
4. Qu'allez-vous manger? Qu'allez-vous boire?
5. Qui va apporter quoi?
6. Qui est responsable de la musique? De la décoration?
7. Qu'allez-vous faire pendant (*during*) la fête?
8. Qui va nettoyer après la fête?

OPTIONS

Small Groups In groups of three or four, have students plan and perform a skit in which they depict a particular stage of life (youth, old age, etc.) or marital status (engaged, single, divorced). The rest of the class tries to guess which stage of life or marital status the skit represents.

Pairs Have students write four or five true/false statements based on the illustration on pages 224–225. Then have them get together with a partner and take turns saying their statements and responding **C'est vrai** or **C'est faux.** Call on volunteers to correct the false statements, pointing out the changes on the 6A **Contextes** illustration from the Digital Image Bank.

Les sons et les lettres   Audio

Open vs. closed vowels: Part 2

The letter combinations **au** and **eau** are pronounced like the vowel sound in the English word *coat*, but without the glide heard in English. These are closed **o** sounds.

chaud	aussi	beaucoup	tableau

When the letter **o** is followed by a consonant sound, it is usually pronounced like the vowel in the English word *raw*. This is an open **o** sound.

homme	téléphone	ordinateur	orange

When the letter **o** occurs as the last sound of a word or is followed by a *z* sound, such as a single **s** between two vowels, it is usually pronounced with the closed **o** sound.

trop	héros	rose	chose

When the letter **o** has an **accent circonflexe**, it is usually pronounced with the closed **o** sound.

drôle	bientôt	pôle	côté

Prononcez Répétez les mots suivants à voix haute.

1. rôle
2. porte
3. dos
4. chaud
5. prose
6. gros
7. oiseau
8. encore
9. mauvais
10. nouveau
11. restaurant
12. bibliothèque

Articulez Répétez les phrases suivantes à voix haute.

1. En automne, on n'a pas trop chaud.
2. Aurélie a une bonne note en biologie.
3. Votre colocataire est d'origine japonaise?
4. Sophie aime beaucoup l'informatique et la psychologie.
5. Nos copains mangent au restaurant marocain aujourd'hui.
6. Comme cadeau, Robert et Corinne vont préparer un gâteau.

Dictons Répétez les dictons à voix haute.

La fortune vient en dormant.[2]

Tout nouveau, tout beau.[1]

[1] Shiny and new.
[2] Fortune comes while you sleep.

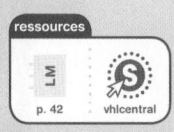

ressources

LM
p. 42

vhlcentral

deux cent vingt-sept **227**

Section Goals

In this section, students will learn more about open and closed vowels.

Instructional Resources
vhlcentral.com:
Textbook MP3s; Lab MP3s;
SAM Answer Key;
Textbook Audioscript;
Lab Audioscript;
reference tools

Suggestions
- Model the pronunciation of each open and closed vowel sound. Have students watch the shape of your mouth, then repeat the sound after you. Pronounce each of the example words and have students repeat them.
- Remind students that **o** is sometimes nasalized when followed by a single **m** or **n**. Compare the following words: **bon, nom**, and **bonne, homme**.
- Ask students to provide more examples of words from this lesson or previous lessons with these vowel sounds. Examples: **cadeau, gâteau, hôte, octobre**, and **beau**.
- Dictate five familiar words containing the open and closed vowels presented here, repeating each one at least two times. Then write them on the board or on a transparency and have students check their spelling.

Dictons Ask students if they can think of sayings in English that are similar to **«La fortune vient en dormant.»** (*Good things come to those who wait. Patience is a virtue.*)

OPTIONS

Extra Practice Use these sentences with open and closed vowel sounds for additional practice or dictation. **1. Octobre est en automne. 2. Est-ce qu'il fait mauvais aujourd'hui? 3. En août, il fait beau, mais il fait chaud. 4. Aurélie est aussi drôle que Paul.**

Extra Practice Teach students this French tongue-twister that contains a variety of vowel sounds. **Paul se pèle au pôle dans sa pile de pulls et polos pâles. Pas plus d'appel de la poule à l'Opel que d'opale dans la pelle à Paul.**

NATIONAL
communication
cultures
STANDARDS

Les cadeaux Video

Section Goals

In this section, students will learn functional phrases for talking about the past and celebrations through comprehensible input.

Instructional Resources
vhlcentral.com:
Roman-photo *Video, Videoscript, and Translation; SAM Answer Key; reference tools*

Video Recap: Leçon 5B
Review the previous **Roman-photo** with this true/false activity.
1. Rachid aime boire de l'eau. (Vrai.)
2. L'anniversaire de Stéphane est le 15 janvier. (Faux.)
3. Sandrine déteste la pluie. (Vrai.)
4. Stéphane va avoir 18 ans. (Vrai.)
5. Rachid n'aime pas le portrait de Sandrine. (Faux.)

Video Synopsis Sandrine tells Pascal about her preparations for Stéphane's party. Valérie arrives and offers to help Sandrine carry the desserts to **Le P'tit Bistrot**. Meanwhile, Astrid and Rachid are shopping for birthday gifts. They buy gag gifts and a watch. At the café, Astrid helps Valérie with decorations while Rachid goes to get Stéphane. Amina is in a good mood because her parents are coming to visit.

Suggestions
- Ask students to read the title, glance at the video stills, and predict what they think the episode will be about. Record their predictions.
- Have students scan the video-still captions and find sentences with words or expressions related to party preparations. Have volunteers read their phrases.
- After reading the **Roman-photo**, review their predictions and ask which ones were correct.

PERSONNAGES

Amina

Astrid

Rachid

Sandrine

Valérie

Vendeuse

À l'appartement de Sandrine...
SANDRINE Allô, Pascal? Tu m'as téléphoné? Écoute, je suis très occupée, là. Je prépare un gâteau d'anniversaire pour Stéphane... Il a dix-huit ans aujourd'hui... On organise une fête surprise au P'tit Bistrot.

SANDRINE J'ai fait une mousse au chocolat, comme pour ton anniversaire. Stéphane adore ça! J'ai aussi préparé des biscuits que David aime bien.

SANDRINE Quoi? David!... Mais non, il n'est pas marié. C'est un bon copain, c'est tout!... Désolée, je n'ai pas le temps de discuter. À bientôt.

RACHID Écoute, Astrid. Il faut trouver un cadeau... un *vrai* cadeau d'anniversaire.
ASTRID Excusez-moi, Madame. Combien coûte cette montre, s'il vous plaît?
VENDEUSE Quarante euros.
ASTRID Que penses-tu de cette montre, Rachid?
RACHID Bonne idée.

VENDEUSE Je fais un paquet cadeau?
ASTRID Oui, merci.
RACHID Eh, Astrid, il faut y aller!
VENDEUSE Et voilà dix euros. Merci, Mademoiselle, bonne fin de journée.

Au café...
VALÉRIE Ah, vous voilà! Astrid, aide-nous avec les décorations, s'il te plaît. La fête commence à six heures. Sandrine a tout préparé.
ASTRID Quelle heure est-il? Zut, déjà? En tout cas, on a trouvé des cadeaux.
RACHID Je vais chercher Stéphane.

A C T I V I T É S

1 **Vrai ou faux?** Indiquez si ces (*these*) affirmations sont vraies ou fausses. Corrigez les phrases fausses.

1. Sandrine prépare un gâteau d'anniversaire pour Stéphane. Vrai.
2. Sandrine est désolée parce qu'elle n'a pas le temps de discuter avec Rachid. Faux. Elle n'a pas le temps de discuter avec Pascal.
3. Rachid ne comprend pas la blague. Vrai.
4. Pour aider Sandrine, Valérie va apporter les desserts. Vrai.

5. Rachid et Astrid trouvent un cadeau pour Valérie. Faux. Ils trouvent un cadeau pour Stéphane.
6. Rachid n'aime pas l'idée de la montre pour Stéphane. Faux. Rachid aime l'idée de la montre pour Stéphane.
7. La fête d'anniversaire pour Stéphane commence à huit heures. Faux. Elle commence à six heures.
8. Sandrine va chercher Stéphane. Faux. Rachid va chercher Stéphane.
9. Amina a apporté de la glace au chocolat. Vrai.
10. Les parents d'Amina vont passer l'été en France. Vrai.

 Practice more at **vhlcentral.com.**

OPTIONS

Avant de regarder la vidéo Before playing the video, have students brainstorm a list of words or expressions that someone might say when preparing for a party and discussing gifts. Write their ideas on the board.

Regarder la vidéo Show the video in three parts, pausing the video before each location change. Have students describe what happens in each place. Write their observations on the board. Then show the entire episode again without pausing and have the class fill in any missing details to summarize the plot.

Tout le monde prépare la surprise pour Stéphane.

VALÉRIE Oh là là! Tu as fait tout ça pour Stéphane?!
SANDRINE Oh, ce n'est pas grand-chose.
VALÉRIE Tu es un ange! Stéphane va bientôt arriver. Je t'aide à apporter ces desserts?
SANDRINE Oh, merci, c'est gentil.

Dans un magasin...

ASTRID Eh Rachid, j'ai eu une idée géniale... Des cadeaux parfaits pour Stéphane. Regarde! Ce matin, j'ai acheté cette calculatrice et ces livres.
RACHID Mais enfin, Astrid, Stéphane n'aime pas les livres.
ASTRID Oh, Rachid, tu ne comprends rien. C'est une blague.

AMINA Bonjour! Désolée, je suis en retard!
VALÉRIE Ce n'est pas grave. Tu es toute belle ce soir!

AMINA Vous trouvez? J'ai acheté ce cadeau pour Stéphane. Et j'ai apporté de la glace au chocolat aussi.
VALÉRIE Oh, merci! Il faut aider Astrid avec les décorations.
ASTRID Salut, Amina. Ça va?
AMINA Oui, super. Mes parents ont téléphoné du Sénégal ce matin! Ils vont passer l'été ici. C'est le bonheur!

Expressions utiles

Talking about celebrations

- **J'ai fait une mousse au chocolat, comme pour ton anniversaire.**
  I made a chocolate mousse, (just) like for your birthday.
- **J'ai aussi préparé des biscuits que David aime bien.**
  I've also prepared some cookies that David likes.
- **Je fais un paquet cadeau?**
  Shall I wrap the present?
- **En tout cas, on a trouvé des cadeaux.**
  In any case, we've found some presents.
- **Et j'ai apporté de la glace au chocolat.**
  And I brought some chocolate ice cream.

Talking about the past

- **Tu m'as téléphoné?**
  Did you call me?
- **Tu as fait tout ça pour Stéphane?!**
  You did all that for Stéphane?!
- **J'ai eu une idée géniale.**
  I had a great idea.
- **Sandrine a tout préparé.**
  Sandrine prepared everything.

Pointing out things

- **Je t'aide à apporter ces desserts?**
  Can I help you carry these desserts?
- **J'ai acheté cette calculatrice et ces livres.**
  I bought this calculator and these books.
- **J'ai acheté ce cadeau pour Stéphane.**
  I bought this present for Stéphane.

Additional vocabulary

- **Ce n'est pas grave.**   • **discuter**
  It's okay./No problem.   *to talk*
- **Tu ne comprends rien.**   • **zut**
  You don't understand a thing.   *darn*
- **désolé(e)**
  sorry

Expressions utiles
- Model the pronunciation of the **Expressions utiles** and have students repeat them.
- As you work through the list, point out forms of the **passé composé** and demonstrative adjectives. Tell students that these grammar structures will be formally presented in the **Structures** section.
- Respond briefly to questions about the **passé composé** and demonstrative adjectives. Reinforce correct forms, but do not expect students to produce them consistently at this time.
- Say some of the **Expressions utiles** and have students react to them. Examples: 1. J'ai eu une idée géniale! (Ah oui? Quelle est ton idée?) 2. Sandrine a tout préparé. (Oh, c'est gentil!)

1 **Expansion** For additional practice, give students these items. **11. Sandrine prépare une mousse au chocolat. (Vrai.) 12. David n'aime pas les biscuits. (Faux. David aime les biscuits.) 13. Astrid achète une calculatrice pour Stéphane. (Vrai.)**

2 **Suggestion** Before beginning the activity, point out the gender of each demonstrative adjective given. Tell students that demonstrative adjectives must agree with the noun they modify just like articles and descriptive adjectives.

2 **Expansion** For additional practice, give students these items. **6. Je t'aide à apporter _____ desserts? (ces) 7. Tu es très belle _____ soir. (ce) 8. Mes parents ont téléphoné du Sénégal _____ matin. (ce)**

3 **Suggestion** If time is limited, assign students the roles of Valérie or Amina and tell them to prepare for homework a list of possible questions or responses according to their role. Then allow partners a few minutes to work together before presenting their conversations.

---

2 **Le bon mot** Choisissez le bon mot entre **ce** (*m.*), **cette** (*f.*) et **ces** (*pl.*) pour compléter les phrases. Attention, les phrases ne sont pas identiques aux dialogues!

1. Je t'aide à apporter _ce_ gâteau?
2. Ce matin, j'ai acheté _ces_ calculatrices et _ce_ livre.
3. Rachid ne comprend pas _cette_ blague.
4. Combien coûtent _ces_ montres?
5. À quelle heure commence _cette_ classe?

3 **Imaginez** Avec un(e) partenaire, imaginez qu'Amina soit (*is*) dans un grand magasin et qu'elle téléphone à Valérie pour l'aider à choisir le cadeau idéal pour Stéphane. Amina propose plusieurs possibilités de cadeaux et Valérie donne son avis (*opinion*) sur chacune d'entre elles (*each of them*).

ressources

VM
pp. 21–22   vhlcentral

A C T I V I T É S

O P T I O N S

Les cadeaux Point out the question **Je fais un paquet cadeau?** Explain that many stores gift wrap items free of charge, especially small items. The wrapping is often a simple sack sealed with a small ribbon and a sticker, which usually bears the name of the store.

L'étiquette Point out some basic etiquette regarding gifts in France. For example, if invited to eat at someone's house, one should not bring wine because the host or hostess most certainly will have chosen an appropriate wine to accompany the meal. Instead, choose candy or flowers.

Reading
Video: *Flash culture*

Section Goals

In this section, students will:
- learn about **carnaval**
- learn to express congratulations and best wishes
- learn about some festivals and holidays in various francophone regions
- read about Bastille Day
- view authentic video footage

Instructional Resources
vhlcentral.com:
SAM Answer Key;
reference tools

Culture à la loupe

Avant la lecture Ask if anyone has attended **carnaval** or **Mardi gras** or seen TV news clips of these celebrations. Then ask students to share what they know about these celebrations.

Lecture
- The word **carnaval** is from the Italian *carnevale,* an alteration of the medieval Latin *carnelevare,* meaning *removal of meat.*
- Point out that the plural of **carnaval** is **carnavals.**

Après la lecture Ask students: **Où désirez-vous assister à une célébration: à Nice, à la Nouvelle-Orléans, à Québec ou à la Martinique? Pourquoi?**

1 Expansion For additional practice, give students these items. **11. Quel événement** (*event*) **est-ce qu'on fête au carnaval?** (la fin de l'hiver et l'arrivée du printemps) **12. Où est-ce qu'il fait très froid lors du** (*during*) **carnaval?** (à Québec) **13. Combien de défilés y a-t-il pendant le carnaval de la Nouvelle-Orléans?** (plus de 70)

CULTURE À LA LOUPE

Le carnaval

le roi du carnaval de Nice

Tous les ans, beaucoup de pays° et de régions francophones célèbrent le carnaval. Cette tradition est l'occasion de fêter la fin° de l'hiver et l'arrivée° du printemps. En général, la période de fête commence la semaine avant le Carême° et se termine° le jour du Mardi gras. Le carnaval demande très souvent des mois de préparation. La ville organise des défilés° de musique, de masques, de costumes et de chars fleuris°. La fête finit souvent par la crémation du roi° Carnaval, personnage de papier qui représente le carnaval et l'hiver.

Certaines villes et certaines régions sont réputées° pour leur carnaval: Nice, en France, la ville de Québec, au Canada, La Nouvelle-Orléans, aux États-Unis et la Martinique. Chaque ville a ses traditions particulières. La ville de Nice, lieu du plus grand carnaval français, organise une grande bataille de fleurs° où des jeunes, sur des chars, envoient des milliers° de fleurs aux spectateurs. À Québec, le climat intense transforme le carnaval en une célébration de l'hiver. Le symbole officiel de la fête est le «Bonhomme» (de neige°) et les gens font du ski, de la pêche sous la glace ou des courses de traîneaux à chiens°. À la Martinique, le carnaval continue jusqu'au° mercredi des Cendres°, à minuit: les gens, tout en noir° et blanc°,

le carnaval de Québec

regardent la crémation de Vaval, le roi Carnaval. Le carnaval de La Nouvelle-Orléans est célébré avec de nombreux bals° et défilés costumés. Ses couleurs officielles sont l'or°, le vert et le violet.

pays *countries* fin *end* arrivée *arrival* Carême *Lent* se termine *ends* défilés *parades* chars fleuris *floats decorated with flowers* roi *king* réputées *famous* bataille de fleurs *flower battle* milliers *thousands* «Bonhomme» (de neige) *snowman* courses de traîneaux à chiens *dogsled races* jusqu'au *until* mercredi des Cendres *Ash Wednesday* noir *black* blanc *white* bals *balls (dances)* or *gold* choisit *chooses* reine *queen* a eu lieu *took place* pendant *during*

Le carnaval en chiffres

Martinique	Chaque ville choisit° une reine°.
Nice	La première bataille de fleurs a eu lieu° en 1876. On envoie entre 80.000 et 100.000 fleurs aux spectateurs.
La Nouvelle-Orléans	Il y a plus de 70 défilés pendant° le carnaval.
la ville de Québec	Le premier carnaval a eu lieu en 1894.

A C T I V I T É S

1 **Compréhension** Répondez par des phrases complètes.

1. En général, quel est le dernier jour du carnaval?
   En général, le dernier jour du carnaval est le jour du Mardi gras.
2. Dans quelle ville des États-Unis est-ce qu'on célèbre le carnaval?
   On célèbre le carnaval à La Nouvelle-Orléans.
3. Où a lieu le plus grand carnaval français?
   Le plus grand carnaval français a lieu à Nice.
4. Qu'est-ce que les jeunes envoient aux spectateurs du carnaval de Nice?
   Les jeunes envoient des fleurs aux spectateurs.
5. Quel est le symbole officiel du carnaval de Québec?
   Le «Bonhomme» est le symbole officiel du carnaval de Québec.

6. Que fait-on pendant (*during*) le carnaval de Québec?
   On pratique des activités d'hiver pendant le carnaval de Québec.
7. Qu'est-ce qui est différent au carnaval de la Martinique?
   Il continue jusqu'au mercredi des Cendres.
8. Qui est Vaval?
   Vaval est le roi du carnaval à la Martinique.
9. Comment est-ce qu'on célèbre le carnaval à La Nouvelle-Orléans?
   On célèbre le carnaval à La Nouvelle-Orléans avec des bals et des défilés.
10. Quelles sont les couleurs officielles du carnaval de La Nouvelle-Orléans?
    Les couleurs officielles du carnaval de La Nouvelle-Orléans sont l'or, le vert et le violet.

O P T I O N S

Small Groups Have students work in groups of three. They should choose a country, research its **carnaval**, and create an Internet home page for next year's **carnaval** in that country. Tell them that the home page should include the dates, a list of events with short descriptions, and any other important or interesting information. Have students present their home pages to the class.

Pairs Working in pairs, have students write a conversation between two people who are trying to decide if they should go to the **carnaval** in Nice or in Quebec City. After they have finished, have volunteers act out their conversations for the class.

LE FRANÇAIS QUOTIDIEN

Les vœux

À votre santé!	*To your health!*
Bonne année!	*Happy New Year!*
Bravo! Félicitations!	*Bravo! Congratulations!*
Joyeuses fêtes!	*Have a good holiday!*
Meilleurs vœux!	*Best wishes!*
Santé!	*Cheers!*
Tous mes vœux de bonheur!	*All the best!*

LE MONDE FRANCOPHONE

Fêtes et festivals

Voici d'autres fêtes et festivals francophones.

En Côte d'Ivoire

La fête des Ignames (plusieurs dates) On célèbre la fin° de la récolte° des ignames°, une ressource très importante pour les Ivoiriens.

Au Maroc

La fête du Trône (le 30 juillet) Tout le pays honore le roi° avec des parades et des spectacles.

À la Martinique/À la Guadeloupe

La fête des Cuisinières (en août) Les femmes défilent° en costumes traditionnels et présentent des spécialités locales qu'elles ont préparées pour la fête.

Dans de nombreux pays

L'Aïd el-Fitr C'est la fête musulmane° de la rupture du jeûne° à la fin du Ramadan.

fin *end* **récolte** *harvest* **ignames** *yams* **roi** *king* **défilent** *parade* **musulmane** *Muslim* **jeûne** *fast*

PORTRAIT

Le 14 juillet

Le 14 juillet 1789, sous le règne° du roi Louis XVI, les Français se sont rebellés contre° la monarchie et ont pris° la Bastille, une forteresse utilisée comme prison. Cette date est très importante dans l'histoire de France parce qu'elle représente la fin de la monarchie absolue et de la société d'ordres et de privilèges, et le début de la Révolution française. Effectivement, le 14 juillet symbolise l'union fraternelle de tous les citoyens° français dans la liberté et l'égalité, des termes utilisés dans la Déclaration des Droits de l'Homme et du Citoyen, texte fondamental de la Révolution française. Le 14 juillet symbolise aussi la fondation de la République française et a donc° été sélectionné par une loi° de 1880 comme date de la Fête nationale. Le 14 juillet est un jour férié en France: les Français ne travaillent pas. Tous les ans, il y a un grand défilé° des troupes militaires à Paris, sur les Champs-Élysées, la plus grande° avenue parisienne et, paraît-il°, la plus belle du monde. Partout° en France, les gens assistent à des défilés et à des fêtes dans les rues°. Le soir, il y a de nombreux bals populaires° où les Français dansent et célèbrent cette date historique. À minuit, on assiste aux feux d'artifices° traditionnels.

règne *reign* **se sont rebellés contre** *rebelled against* **ont pris** *stormed* **citoyens** *citizens* **donc** *therefore* **loi** *law* **défilé** *parade* **la plus grande** *the largest* **paraît-il** *it seems* **Partout** *Everywhere* **rues** *streets* **bals populaires** *street dances* **feux d'artifices** *fireworks*

---

2 **Les fêtes** Complétez les phrases.

1. Le 14 juillet 1789, c'est la date ___du début de la Révolution française___
2. Aujourd'hui, le 14 juillet, c'est la ___Fête nationale de la République française___
3. En France, les gens ne travaillent pas le 14 juillet car c'est ___un jour férié___
4. En France, le soir du 14 juillet, il y a ___des bals populaires et des feux d'artifices___
5. À plusieurs dates, les Ivoiriens fêtent ___la fin de la récolte des ignames___
6. Dans les pays musulmans, l'Aïd el-Fitr célèbre ___la fin du Ramadan___

3 **Faisons la fête ensemble!** Vous êtes en vacances dans un pays francophone et vous invitez un(e) ami(e) à aller à une fête ou à un festival francophone avec vous. Expliquez à votre partenaire ce que vous allez faire. Votre partenaire va vous poser des questions.

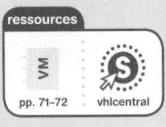

ressources

VM
pp. 71–72

S
vhlcentral

S **Practice more at vhlcentral.com.**

A C T I V I T É S

Le français quotidien
- Model the pronunciation of each expression and have students repeat it. Point out that the expression «**Tous mes vœux de bonheur!**» is used primarily at weddings. You might also give them the expression **Bonne chance!** (*Good luck!*)
- Have students identify whether they would use these expressions at **une fête d'anniversaire**, **une réception de mariage**, or **un anniversaire de mariage**.

Portrait If possible, bring in a photo of the Bastille. Then have students turn to the map of Paris on page 350. Point out that the military parade begins at **Charles de Gaulle-Étoile** and ends at the **Place de la Concorde**.

Le monde francophone After students have read the text, have them work in pairs and take turns asking each other questions about the content. Examples: **Où est la fête des Cuisinières? Comment les Marocains fêtent-ils la fête du Trône?**

Suggestion Point out to students that they will find supporting activities and more information related to this **Espace culture** at **vhlcentral.com**.

2 **Expansion** For additional practice, give students these items. **7. La Bastille était** (*was*) **une forteresse utilisée comme ____ avant la Révolution.** (prison) **8. Le défilé militaire pour le 14 juillet a lieu sur ____.** (les Champs-Élysées).

3 **Suggestion** Before beginning the activity, have students choose a holiday or festival to discuss.

Flash culture Tell students that they will learn more about French festivals and holiday celebrations by watching a variety of real-life images narrated by Benjamin. Show the video segment, and then have students jot down at least three examples of things they saw. You can also use the activities in the video manual in class to reinforce this **Flash culture** or assign them as homework.

O P T I O N S

Cultural Comparison First, ask students: **Quel jour férié aux États-Unis correspond au 14 juillet en France?** (la fête de l'indépendance américaine, le 4 juillet) Then have them work in small groups and compare the two holidays. Tell them to make a list of the similarities (**Similitudes**) and differences (**Différences**) in French. Have groups read their lists to the class.

Le 14 juillet Explain that a Bastille Day celebration would not be complete without a rendering of France's national anthem, *La Marseillaise*, composed by Claude-Joseph Rouget de Lisle in 1792. Bring the lyrics and a recording of the song for students to listen to. Alternatively, you can have students go to **www.marseillaise.org** to hear the song or read the lyrics.

Section Goals

In this section, students will learn:
• demonstrative adjectives
• to use -ci and -là to specify demonstratives

Instructional Resources
vhlcentral.com:
Activity Pack; Lab MP3s;
SAM Answer Key; **Essayez!**
and **Mise en pratique**
answers; Lab Audioscript;
reference tools

Suggestions

• Point to a book on your desk. Say: **Ce livre est sur mon bureau.** Point to a sheet of paper next to the book. Say: **Cette feuille de papier est à côté du livre.** Then point to an object in front of you and say: **Cet objet est devant moi.**
• Write **ce** and **cet** on the board. Point out that the masculine singular demonstrative adjective has two forms. Say the following words and have students give the demonstrative: **garçon**, **homme**, **biscuit**, **ordinateur**, **cadeau**, and **examen**.
• Point out that there is only one plural demonstrative adjective in French, regardless of gender: **ces**.
• Have students identify the demonstrative adjectives in the ad for **La maison Julien**. Ask them what type of store it is.

Leçon 6A

6A.1

Demonstrative adjectives Tutorial

Point de départ To identify or point out a noun with the French equivalent of *this/these* or *that/those*, use a demonstrative adjective before the noun. In French, the form of the demonstrative adjective depends on the gender and number of the noun that it goes with.

Demonstrative adjectives			
	singular		plural
	Before consonant	Before vowel sound	
masculine	**ce** café	**cet** éclair	**ces** cafés, **ces** éclairs
feminine	**cette** surprise	**cette** amie	**ces** surprises, **ces** amies

Ce copain organise une fête.
That friend is planning a party.

Cette glace est excellente.
This ice cream is excellent.

Cet hôpital est trop loin du centre-ville.
That hospital is too far from downtown.

Je préfère **ces** cadeaux.
I prefer those gifts.

Combien coûte cette montre?

J'ai ce cadeau pour Stéphane.

• Note that the forms of **ce** can refer to a noun that is near (*this/these*) or far (*that/those*). The meaning will usually be clear from context.

Ce dessert est délicieux.
This dessert is delicious.

Ils vont aimer **cette** surprise.
They're going to like this surprise.

Joël préfère **cet** éclair.
Joël prefers that éclair.

Ces glaçons sont pour la limonade.
Those ice cubes are for the lemon soda.

La maison Julien

Pour toutes ces occasions...

pour célébrer tout ce bonheur...

nous pensons à tous les détails.

- To make it especially clear that you're referring to something near versus something far, add **-ci** or **-là**, respectively, to the noun following the demonstrative adjective.

ce couple-**ci**
this couple (here)

cette invitée-**là**
that guest (there)

ces biscuits-**ci**
these cookies (here)

ces bières-**là**
those beers (there)

- Use **-ci** and **-là** in the same sentence to contrast similar items.

On prend **cette** glace-**ci**, pas **cette** glace-**là**.
We'll have this ice cream, not that ice cream.

J'aime **ce** cadeau-**ci** mais je préfère **ce** cadeau-**là**.
I like this gift, but I prefer that gift.

Tu achètes **ce** fromage-**ci** ou **ce** fromage-**là**?
Are you buying this cheese or that cheese?

Nous achetons **ces** bonbons-ci et Isabelle achète **ce** gâteau-**là**.
We're buying these candies, and Isabelle is buying that cake.

J'aime bien ces chaussures-ci.

Moi, je préfère ces chaussures-là.

Suggestions
- Hold up pictures or point to objects, saying either the singular or plural demonstrative to describe each object. Have students give the opposite. Examples: **ces baguettes (cette baguette)**, **ce stylo (ces stylos)**, and **ces invités (cet invité)**.
- Place a short pencil close to you and a long pencil far away. Say: **Ce crayon-ci est court. Ce crayon-là est long.** Continue with other objects until students grasp the concept.

Essayez! Have students create new sentences orally by changing the singular nouns to the plural or vice versa in items 1–5.

Essayez! Complétez les phrases avec la forme correcte de l'adjectif démonstratif.

1. __Cette__ glace au chocolat est très bonne!
2. Qu'est-ce que tu penses de __ce__ cadeau?
3. __Cet__ homme-là est l'hôte de la fête.
4. Tu préfères __ces__ biscuits-ci ou __ces__ biscuits-là?
5. Vous aimez mieux __ce__ dessert-ci ou __ce__ dessert-là?
6. __Cette__ année-ci, on va fêter l'anniversaire de mariage de nos parents en famille.
7. Tu achètes __cet__ éclair-là.
8. Vous achetez __cette__ montre?
9. __Cette__ surprise va être géniale!
10. __Cet__ invité-là est antipathique.
11. Ma mère fait __ces__ gâteaux pour mon anniversaire.
12. __Ce__ champagne coûte 100 euros.
13. __Ce__ divorce est très difficile pour les enfants.

ressources

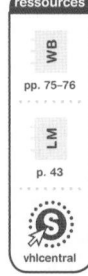

WB
pp. 75–76

LM
p. 43

vhlcentral

OPTIONS

Video Show the video episode again and have students listen for the demonstrative adjectives. Tell them to write down each demonstrative adjective they hear and the noun it modifies. Then, have students check the Videoscript to see if they were correct.

Pairs Have students turn to **Espace contextes** on pages 224–225. Working in pairs, tell them to make comments about the people and items in the illustration using demonstrative adjectives. Examples: **Ces desserts-là ont l'air délicieux, n'est-ce pas? Oui, mais je préfère ce gâteau-ci.** Use the 6A **Contextes** illustration from the Digital Image Bank when giving examples.

1 Expansion For additional practice, give students these items. **9. Ces bonbons sont trop sucrés. 10. Ces vins sont rouges. 11. J'ai besoin de ce glaçon.**

2 Suggestion Tell students to underline the nouns that will correspond to the demonstrative adjectives and identify their number and gender before they write the demonstrative adjective.

3 Suggestion Before beginning the activity, have students identify in French the items pictured.

Mise en pratique

1 Remplacez Remplacez les noms au singulier par des noms au pluriel et vice versa. Faites tous les autres changements nécessaires.

MODÈLE

J'aime mieux ce dessert.
J'aime mieux ces desserts.

1. Ces glaces au chocolat sont délicieuses. Cette glace au chocolat est délicieuse.
2. Ce gâteau est énorme. Ces gâteaux sont énormes.
3. Ces biscuits ne sont pas bons. Ce biscuit n'est pas bon.
4. Ces invitées sont gentilles. Cette invitée est gentille.
5. Ces hôtes parlent japonais. Cet hôte parle japonais.
6. Cette bière est allemande. Ces bières sont allemandes.
7. Maman achète ces imperméables pour Julie. Maman achète cet imperméable pour Julie.
8. Ces bonbons sont délicieux. Ce bonbon est délicieux.

2 Monsieur Parfait Juste avant la fête, l'hôte fait le tour de la salle et donne son opinion. Complétez ce texte avec **ce**, **cette** ou **ces**.

Mmm! (1) __Ce__ champagne est parfait. Ah! (2) __Ces__ gâteaux sont magnifiques, (3) __ces__ biscuits sont délicieux et j'adore (4) __cette__ glace. Beurk! (5) __Ces__ bonbons sont originaux, mais pas très bons. Ouvrez (*Open*) (6) __cette__ bouteille. (7) __Ce__ café sur (8) __cette__ table sent très bon. (9) __Cette__ bière n'est pas froide! (10) __Ce__ tableau n'est pas droit (*straight*)! Oh là là! Arrangez (11) __ces__ chaises autour de (*around*) (12) __ces__ trois tables!

3 Magazine Vous regardez un vieux magazine. Complétez les phrases.

▶ **MODÈLE**

<u>Ce cheval</u> est très grand.

1. <u>Ce gâteau</u> au chocolat et <u>cette glace</u> sont délicieux.
2. <u>Cette fille</u> aime beaucoup <u>ces bonbons</u>.
3. <u>Ces jeunes mariés</u> sont très heureux.
4. <u>Cet homme</u> va prendre sa retraite.

5. <u>Ce couple</u> ne sort plus (*no longer*) ensemble.
6. <u>Ces enfants</u> adorent le chocolat chaud!
7. <u>Ce garçon</u> est très méchant.
8. <u>Cette plage</u> est absolument super!

 Practice more at **vhlcentral.com**.

Communication

NATIONAL communication STANDARDS

4 Comparez Avec un(e) partenaire, regardez les illustrations. À tour de rôle, comparez les personnages et les objets. *Answers will vary.*

> **MODÈLE**
>
> **Étudiant(e) 1:** *Comment sont ces hommes?*
> **Étudiant(e) 2:** *Cet homme-ci est petit et cet homme-là est grand.*

1.　　　　2.　　　　3.　　　　4.

5 Préférences Demandez à votre partenaire ses préférences, puis donnez votre opinion. Employez des adjectifs démonstratifs et présentez vos réponses à la classe. *Answers will vary.*

> **MODÈLE**
>
> **Étudiant(e) 1:** *Quel film est-ce que tu aimes?*
> **Étudiant(e) 2:** *J'aime bien Casablanca.*
> **Étudiant(e) 1:** *Moi, je n'aime pas du tout ce vieux film.*

acteur/actrice	passe-temps
chanteur/chanteuse	restaurant
dessert	saison
film	sport
magasin	ville
?	?

6 Invitation Vous organisez une fête et vous êtes au supermarché avec un(e) ami(e). Vous n'êtes pas d'accord sur ce que (*what*) vous allez acheter. Avec un(e) partenaire, jouez les rôles. *Answers will vary.*

> **MODÈLE**
>
> **Étudiant(e) 1:** *On achète cette glace-ci?*
> **Étudiant(e) 2:** *Je n'aime pas cette glace-ci. Je préfère cette glace-là!*
> **Étudiant(e) 1:** *Mais cette glace-là coûte dix euros!*
> **Étudiant(e) 2:** *D'accord! On prend cette glace-ci.*

7 Quelle fête! Vous êtes à la fête d'un(e) ami(e) et il y a des personnes célèbres (*famous*). Avec un(e) partenaire, faites une liste des célébrités présentes et puis parlez d'elles. Employez des adjectifs démonstratifs. *Answers will vary.*

> **MODÈLE**
>
> **Étudiant(e) 1:** *Qui est cet homme-ci?*
> **Étudiant(e) 2:** *Ça, c'est Justin Timberlake. Il est sympa, mais cet homme-là est vraiment génial.*
> **Étudiant(e) 1:** *Oui, c'est...*

---

4 Suggestion Have two volunteers read the **modèle** aloud. Remind students to take turns asking and answering the questions.

5 Suggestion Have two volunteers read the **modèle** aloud. Tell students to add at least two items of their own to the list.

6 Suggestion Before beginning the activity, have students brainstorm items they might buy for the party and write them on the board.

OPTIONS

Game Divide the class into two teams. Choose one team member at a time to go to the board, alternating between teams. Say a noun. The person at the board must write and say the noun with the correct demonstrative adjective. Example: **fille** (**cette fille**). Give a point for each correct answer. The team with the most points at the end of the game wins.

Extra Practice Hold up or point to various classroom objects. Tell students to write down all forms of demonstrative adjectives that could apply. Example: **chaise** (**cette chaise, ces chaises, cette chaise-ci, cette chaise-là, ces chaises-ci, ces chaises-là**).

6A.2

ESPACE STRUCTURES

The *passé composé* with *avoir*

 Tutorial

Point de départ In order to talk about events in the past, French uses two principal tenses: the **passé composé** and the imperfect. In this lesson, you will learn how to form the **passé composé**, which is used to express actions or states completed in the past. You will learn about the imperfect in **Leçon 8A**.

- The **passé composé** is composed of two parts: the *auxiliary verb* (present tense of **avoir** or **être**) and the *past participle* of the main verb. Most verbs in French take **avoir** as the auxiliary verb in the **passé composé**.

AUXILIARY PAST
VERB PARTICIPLE
Nous **avons fêté**.
We celebrated / have celebrated.

- The past participle of a regular **-er** verb is formed by replacing the **-er** ending of the infinitive with **-é**.

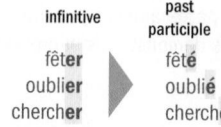

infinitive		past participle
fêt**er**		fêt**é**
oubli**er**		oubli**é**
cherch**er**		cherch**é**

- Most regular **-er** verbs are conjugated in the **passé composé** as shown below for the verb **parler**.

The *passé composé*

j'ai parlé	*I spoke/have spoken*		**nous avons parlé**	*we spoke/ have spoken*
tu as parlé	*you spoke/ have spoken*		**vous avez parlé**	*you spoke/ have spoken*
il/elle/on a parlé	*he/she/it/one spoke/ has spoken*		**ils/elles ont parlé**	*they spoke/ have spoken*

Nous **avons parlé** à l'hôtesse.
We spoke to the hostess.

J'**ai oublié** mes devoirs.
I forgot my homework.

- To make a verb negative in the **passé composé**, place **ne/n'** and **pas** around the conjugated form of **avoir**.

On **n'**a **pas** fêté mon anniversaire.
We didn't celebrate my birthday.

Elles **n'**ont **pas** acheté de biscuits hier?
They didn't buy any cookies yesterday?

- To ask questions using inversion in the **passé composé**, invert the subject pronoun and the conjugated form of **avoir**. Note that this does not apply to other types of question formation.

Avez-vous fêté votre anniversaire?
Did you celebrate your birthday?

Est-ce qu'elles **ont acheté** des biscuits?
Did they buy any cookies?

Luc **a-t-il** aimé son cadeau?
Did Luc like his gift?

Est-ce que tu **as essayé** ce vin?
Have you tried this wine?

Section Goals

In this section, students will learn:
- the **passé composé** with **avoir**
- some irregular past participles

Instructional Resources
vhlcentral.com:
Activity Pack; Lab MP3s;
SAM Answer Key; Essayez!
and Mise en pratique
answers; Lab Audioscript;
reference tools

Suggestions
- Quickly review the present tense of **avoir**.
- Introduce the **passé composé** by describing what you did yesterday. Include adverbs commonly used to indicate past actions, such as **hier** and **hier soir**. Examples: **Hier, j'ai enseigné deux cours de français. Hier soir, j'ai téléphoné à un(e) ami(e) et j'ai écouté de la musique.** Each time you say a **passé composé** form write it on the board.
- Point out that the past participles of **-er** verbs are generally pronounced the same way as their respective infinitives.

Boîte à outils

The **passé composé** has three English equivalents. Example: **Nous avons mangé.** = *We ate. We did eat. We have eaten.*

- The adverbs **hier** (*yesterday*) and **avant-hier** (*the day before yesterday*) are used often with the **passé composé**.

> Hier, Marie **a retrouvé** ses amis au stade.
> *Marie met her friends at the stadium yesterday.*

> Ses parents **ont téléphoné** avant-hier.
> *Her parents called the day before yesterday.*

- Place the adverbs **déjà**, **encore**, **bien**, **mal**, and **beaucoup** between the auxiliary verb or **pas** and the past participle.

> Tu as **déjà** mangé ta part de gâteau.
> *You already ate your piece of cake.*

> Elle n'a pas **encore** visité notre ville.
> *She hasn't visited our town yet.*

> Les filles ont **beaucoup** travaillé.
> *The girls worked a lot.*

> Je n'ai pas **bien** joué hier.
> *I didn't play well yesterday.*

- The past participles of spelling-change -er verbs have no spelling changes.

> Laurent a-t-il **acheté** le champagne?
> *Did Laurent buy the champagne?*

> Vous avez **envoyé** des bonbons.
> *You sent candy.*

- The past participle of most **-ir** verbs is formed by replacing the **-ir** ending with **-i**.

> Sylvie a **dormi** jusqu'à dix heures.
> *Sylvie slept until 10 o'clock.*

> Avez-vous **senti** ce bouquet?
> *Did you smell this bouquet?*

- The past participles of many common verbs are irregular. Learn these on a case-by-case basis.

Some irregular past participles

apprendre	appris	être	été
avoir	eu	faire	fait
boire	bu	pleuvoir	plu
comprendre	compris	prendre	pris
courir	couru	surprendre	surpris

> Nous avons **bu** du vin.
> *We drank wine.*

> Ils ont **été** très en retard.
> *They were very late.*

> A-t-il **plu** samedi?
> *Did it rain Saturday?*

> Mes sœurs ont **fait** un gâteau au chocolat.
> *My sisters made a chocolate cake.*

- The **passé composé** of **il faut** is **il a fallu**; that of **il y a** is **il y a eu**.

> **Il a fallu** passer par le supermarché.
> *It was necessary to stop by the supermarket.*

> **Il y a eu** deux fêtes hier soir.
> *There were two parties last night.*

Essayez! Indiquez les formes du passé composé des verbes.

1. j' *ai commencé, ai payé, ai bavardé* (commencer, payer, bavarder)
2. tu _as servi, as compris, as donné_ (servir, comprendre, donner)
3. on _a parlé, a eu, a dormi_ (parler, avoir, dormir)
4. nous _avons adoré, avons fait, avons amené_ (adorer, faire, amener)
5. vous _avez pris, avez employé, avez couru_ (prendre, employer, courir)
6. elles _ont espéré, ont bu, ont appris_ (espérer, boire, apprendre)
7. il _a eu, a regardé, a senti_ (avoir, regarder, sentir)
8. vous _avez essayé, avez préféré, avez surpris_ (essayer, préférer, surprendre)
9. ils _ont organisé, ont été, ont nettoyé_ (organiser, être, nettoyer)

Boîte à outils

Some verbs, like **aller**, **sortir**, and **tomber**, use **être** instead of **avoir** to form the **passé composé**. You will learn more about these verbs in **Leçon 7A**.

ressources

WB
pp. 77–78

LM
p. 44

vhlcentral

Suggestions
- Ask students some questions about their activities. Examples: **Avez-vous écouté de la musique hier? Avez-vous regardé la télé?** Ask other students about their classmates' activities. Examples: **Quelle musique est-ce que _____ a écouté hier soir? Qu'est-ce que _____ a regardé?**
- Call students' attention to the **Boîte à outils** on page 236. Point out that an example like **Vous avez envoyé des bonbons.** could be translated, depending on the context, as *You sent candy., You did send candy.,* or *You have sent candy.*

Essayez! For additional practice, have students create complete sentences orally or in writing using the subjects and verbs given.

OPTIONS

Pairs Working in pairs, have students tell each other two things they did last week, two things their best friend did, and two things they did together. Then have each student get together with another classmate and report what the first person told him or her.

Small Groups Divide the class into groups of five. Give each group a list of verbs, including some with irregular past participles. The first student chooses a verb from the list and gives the **je** form. The second student gives the **tu** form, and so on. Students work their way down the list, alternating who chooses the verb.

1 **Expansion** Ask follow-up questions about Laurent's week-end. Examples: **1. Qu'est-ce qu'ils ont mangé? 2. Qui a acheté une montre? 3. Qui a pris une glace à la terrasse d'un café? 4. Qu'est-ce que leurs parents ont célébré? 5. Quand est-ce que Laurent et sa famille ont eu sommeil?**

2 **Suggestion** To check answers, have one student ask the question and call on another student to answer it. This activity can also be done in pairs.

3 **Expansion** For additional practice, give students these items. **9. parler à ses parents (Stéphane) 10. boire du café (toi et ton copain)**

3 **Suggestion** Before beginning the activity, have students describe what the people are doing in the present tense.

Mise en pratique

1 **Qu'est-ce qu'ils ont fait?** Laurent parle de son week-end en ville avec sa famille. Complétez ses phrases avec le **passé composé** du verbe correct.

1. Nous ___avons mangé___ (nager, manger) des escargots.
2. Papa ___a acheté___ (acheter, apprendre) une nouvelle montre.
3. J' ___ai pris___ (prendre, oublier) une glace à la terrasse d'un café.
4. Vous ___avez essayé___ (enseigner, essayer) un nouveau restaurant.
5. Mes parents ___ont célébré___ (dessiner, célébrer) leur anniversaire de mariage.
6. Ils ___ont fait___ (fréquenter, faire) une promenade.
7. Ma sœur ___a bu___ (boire, nettoyer) un chocolat chaud.
8. Le soir, nous ___avons eu___ (écouter, avoir) sommeil.

2 **Pas encore** Un copain pose des questions pénibles. Écrivez ses questions puis donnez des réponses négatives.

MODÈLE

inviter vos amis (vous)
Vous avez déjà invité vos amis? Non, nous n'avons pas encore invité nos amis.

1. écouter mon CD (tu)   Tu as déjà écouté mon CD? Non, je n'ai pas encore écouté ton CD.
2. faire ses devoirs (Matthieu)   Matthieu a déjà fait ses devoirs? Non, il n'a pas encore fait ses devoirs.
3. courir dans le parc (elles)   Elles ont déjà couru dans le parc? Non, elles n'ont pas encore couru dans le parc.
4. parler aux profs (tu)   Tu as déjà parlé aux profs? Non, je n'ai pas encore parlé aux profs.
5. apprendre les verbes irréguliers (André)   André a déjà appris les verbes irréguliers? Non, il n'a pas encore appris les verbes irréguliers.
6. être à la piscine (Marie et Lise)   Marie et Lise ont déjà été à la piscine? Non, elles n'ont pas encore été à la piscine.
7. emmener Yassim au cinéma (vous)   Vous avez déjà emmené Yassim au cinéma? Non, nous n'avons pas encore emmené Yassim au cinéma.
8. avoir le temps d'étudier (tu)   Tu as déjà eu le temps d'étudier? Non, je n'ai pas encore eu le temps d'étudier.

3 **Vendredi soir** Vous et votre partenaire avez assisté à une fête vendredi soir. Parlez de la fête à tour de rôle. Qu'est-ce que les invités ont fait? Quelle a été l'occasion?   Answers will vary.

 Practice more at **vhlcentral.com**.

Communication

4 La semaine À tour de rôle, assemblez les éléments des colonnes pour raconter (*to tell*) à votre partenaire ce que (*what*) tout le monde (*everyone*) a fait cette semaine. Answers will vary.

A	B	C
je	acheter	bonbons
Luc	apprendre	café
mon prof	boire	cartes
Sylvie	enseigner	l'espagnol
mes parents	étudier	famille
mes copains et moi	faire	foot
tu	jouer	glace
vous	manger	jogging
?	parler	les maths
	prendre	promenade
	regarder	vélo
	?	?

5 L'été dernier Vous avez passé l'été dernier avec deux amis, mais vos souvenirs (*memories*) diffèrent. Par groupes de trois, utilisez les expressions de la liste et imaginez le dialogue. Answers will vary.

MODÈLE

Étudiant(e) 1: *Nous avons fait du cheval tous les matins.*
Étudiant(e) 2: *Mais non! Moi, j'ai fait du cheval. Vous deux, vous avez fait du jogging.*
Étudiant(e) 3: *Je n'ai pas fait de jogging. J'ai dormi!*

acheter	essayer	faire une promenade
courir	faire du cheval	jouer au foot
dormir	faire du jogging	jouer aux cartes
emmener	faire la fête	manger

6 Qu'est-ce que tu as fait? Avec un(e) partenaire, posez-vous les questions à tour de rôle. Ensuite, présentez vos réponses à la classe. Answers will vary.

1. As-tu fait la fête samedi dernier? Où? Avec qui?
2. Est-ce que tu as célébré une occasion importante cette année? Quelle occasion?
3. As-tu organisé une fête? Pour qui?
4. Qui est-ce que tu as invité à ta dernière fête?
5. Qu'est-ce que tu as fait pour fêter ton dernier anniversaire?
6. Est-ce que tu as préparé quelque chose à manger pour une fête ou un dîner? Quoi?

7 Ma fête Votre partenaire a organisé une fête le week-end dernier. Posez sept questions pour avoir plus de détails sur la fête. Ensuite, alternez les rôles. Answers will vary.

MODÈLE

Étudiant(e) 1: *Pour qui est-ce que tu as organisé la fête samedi dernier?*
Étudiant(e) 2: *Pour ma sœur.*

4 Suggestion Before beginning this activity, call on volunteers to give the past participles of verbs listed.

5 Suggestion Have three volunteers read the **modèle** aloud. Encourage students to be creative.

6 Suggestion Tell students to jot down notes on their partner's responses and to add two of their own questions to the list.

7 Suggestion Have students brainstorm a list of questions before they begin the activity.

deux cent trente-neuf **239**

TPR Working in groups of three, have students write three sentences in the **passé composé**, each with a different verb. After they have finished, have each group mime its sentences for the class. When someone guesses the mimed action, the group writes the sentence on the board.

Extra Practice For homework, have students write a paragraph about what they did yesterday or last weekend. Then, in class, have them exchange papers with a classmate and peer edit each other's work.

OPTIONS

Révision

Instructional Resources
vhlcentral.com:
Activity Pack (Feuilles d'activités; Info Gap Activities); Testing Program; Testing Program MP3s; reference tools

1 Suggestion Before beginning this activity, give students a few minutes to jot down some notes about the previous Thanksgiving.

2 Expansion Have a few volunteers report the places they and their partner both visited.

3 Suggestion Before beginning the activity, have students identify the items on the table.

4 Suggestion Distribute the **Feuilles d'activités** found in the Activity Pack on the Supersite.

5 Suggestion Tell students that they can talk about a real or imaginary dinner. Encourage students to be creative.

6 Suggestion Divide the class into pairs and distribute the Info Gap Handouts found in the Activity Pack on the Supersite. Give students ten minutes to complete the activity.

1 L'année dernière et cette année Décrivez vos dernières fêtes de Thanksgiving à votre partenaire. Utilisez les verbes de la liste. Parlez aussi de vos projets (*plans*) pour le prochain Thanksgiving. Answers will vary.

MODÈLE

Étudiant(e) 1: *L'année dernière, nous avons fêté Thanksgiving chez mes grands-parents. Cette année, je vais manger au restaurant avec mes parents.*

Étudiant(e) 2: *Moi, j'ai fait la fête avec mes amis l'année dernière. Cette année, je vais visiter New York avec ma sœur.*

acheter	dormir	manger	regarder
boire	faire	prendre	téléphoner
donner	fêter	préparer	visiter

2 Ce musée, cette ville Faites par écrit (*Write*) une liste de cinq lieux (villes, musées, restaurants, etc.) que vous avez visités. Avec un(e) partenaire, comparez vos listes. Utilisez des adjectifs démonstratifs dans vos phrases. Answers will vary.

MODÈLE

Étudiant(e) 1: *Ah, tu as visité Bruxelles. Moi aussi, j'ai visité cette ville. Elle est belle.*

Étudiant(e) 2: *Tu as mangé au restaurant La Douce France. Je n'aime pas du tout ce restaurant!*

3 La fête Vous et votre partenaire avez préparé une fête avec vos amis. Vous avez acheté des cadeaux, des boissons et des snacks. À tour de rôle, parlez de ce qu'il y a sur l'illustration. Answers will vary.

MODÈLE

Étudiant(e) 1: *J'aime bien ces biscuits-là.*

Étudiant(e) 2: *Moi, j'ai apporté cette glace-ci.*

4 Enquête Qu'est-ce que vos camarades ont fait de différent dans leur vie? Votre professeur va vous donner une feuille d'activités. Parlez à vos camarades pour trouver une personne différente pour chaque expérience, puis écrivez son nom. Answers will vary.

MODÈLE

Étudiant(e) 1: *As-tu parlé à un acteur?*

Étudiant(e) 2: *Oui! Une fois, j'ai parlé à Bruce Willis!*

Expérience	Noms
1. parler à un(e) acteur/actrice	Julien
2. passer une nuit entière sans dormir	
3. dépenser plus de $100 pour des CD en une fois	
4. faire la fête un lundi soir	
5. courir cinq kilomètres ou plus	
6. faire une surprise à un(e) ami(e) pour son anniversaire	

5 Conversez Avec un(e) partenaire, préparez une conversation entre deux copains/copines sur les détails d'un dîner romantique du week-end dernier. N'oubliez pas de mentionner dans la conversation: Answers will vary.

- où ils ont mangé
- les thèmes de la conversation
- qui a parlé de quoi
- qui a payé
- la date du prochain rendez-vous

6 Magali fait la fête Votre professeur va vous donner, à vous et à votre partenaire, deux feuilles d'activités différentes. Attention! Ne regardez pas la feuille de votre partenaire. Answers will vary.

MODÈLE

Étudiant(e) 1: *Magali a parlé avec un homme. Cet homme n'a pas l'air intéressant du tout!*

Étudiant(e) 2: *Après, ...*

O P T I O N S

Extra Practice Have students create a collaborative story about a person who had a very bad day. Begin the story by saying: **Hier, Robert a passé une très mauvaise journée.** Call on one student to continue the story by telling how Robert began his day. The second person tells what happened next. Students continue adding sentences until only one student remains. He or she must conclude the story.

Extra Practice Have students make a "to do" list (**à faire…**) at the beginning of their day. Then, tell students to review their list at the end of the day and write down which activities they completed and which ones they didn't complete. Example: **acheter de la nourriture: Non, je n'ai pas acheté de nourriture.**

Video

Le Zapping

Les marchés de Noël

Les marchés de Noël ont commencé en Europe centrale, dans des pays comme l'Allemagne, l'Autriche ou la Suisse. En France, traditionnellement, on ne les trouvait qu'°en Alsace. Mais depuis° quelques années, ces marchés sont arrivés dans d'autres régions ou villes, et en particulier, à Paris.

La ville a plusieurs marchés de Noël pendant les fêtes, mais celui° des Champs-Élysées est situé sur l'avenue la plus célèbre° de la capitale. Il reçoit° des milliers de visiteurs chaque année et surtout, beaucoup de touristes. Ses nombreux petits chalets° vendent toutes sortes de produits et de sa grande roue°, on a une belle vue° panoramique de l'avenue.

C'est du pain d'épices artisanal°.

À la rencontre du Père Noël°.

 Compréhension Répondez aux questions. Answers will vary. Suggested answers.

1. Quels types d'activités sont montrés ou mentionnés dans la vidéo?
le patinage, acheter des cadeaux, manger, monter dans la grande roue, faire des photos, acheter un sapin, etc.
2. Qui est-ce que le journaliste interviewe?
le Père Noël, des vendeurs
3. Que peut-on acheter sur le marché de Noël des Champs-Élysées? Donnez des exemples.
On peut acheter du pain d'épices, de la nourriture, des bonnets du Père Noël, etc.

 Discussion Avec un(e) partenaire, répondez aux questions. Answers will vary.

1. Allez-vous visiter ce marché si (if) vous êtes à Paris pendant les fêtes? Pourquoi?
2. Y a-t-il un marché de Noël dans votre ville? Avez-vous déjà visité ce marché?
3. Est-ce qu'acheter des cadeaux sur un marché de Noël est une bonne idée? Expliquez.

ne les trouvait qu' only found them **depuis** for **celui** the one **la plus célèbre** the most famous
reçoit hosts **chalets** cabins **grande roue** Ferris wheel **vue** view **artisanal** hand crafted **Père Noël** Santa

Go to **vhlcentral.com** to watch the TV clip featured in this **Le Zapping**.

 Practice more at **vhlcentral.com**.

Section Goals

In this section, students will:
• read about **les marchés de Noël**
• watch a news report on a traditional Christmas market in Paris
• answer questions about the report and about Christmas markets

Instructional Resources
vhlcentral.com:
TV news report; Le Zapping TV clip transcription; reference tools

Avant de regarder la vidéo
• Have students look at the video stills, read the captions, and predict what is happening in the report for each visual.
• Before showing the video, explain to students that they do not need to understand every word they hear. Tell them to listen for the text in the captions and for any familiar words.

Compréhension Have students work in pairs or groups for this activity. Tell them to write their answers. Then show the video again so that they can check their answers and add any missing information.

Discussion Ask students to share their partner's answers.

OPTIONS

Compréhension Ask students to name all the elements that show it is Christmastime in the video. Examples: **le Père Noël, les cadeaux, les gâteaux, les bonbons, les décorations, le temps (l'hiver), la neige.**

Discussion Ask students how they approach holiday gift shopping for their friends and family. Have volunteers share shopping or gift-making advice.

ESPACE SYNTHÈSE 241

Section Goals

In this section, students will learn and practice vocabulary related to:
- clothing and accessories
- shopping
- colors

Instructional Resources
vhlcentral.com:
Digital Image Bank (including vocabulary illustrations from the textbook, theme-based illustrations); **Vocabulaire supplémentaire; Mise en pratique** *answers; Textbook Audioscript; Lab Audioscript; Activity Pack; Textbook MP3s; Lab MP3s; SAM Answer Key; reference tools*

Suggestions

- Use the **6B Contextes** illustration from the Digital Image Bank. Point out clothing items in the store and describe what the people in the illustration are wearing. Examples: **Cette femme porte une robe. Ce tee-shirt est bon marché.**
- After presenting the new vocabulary, briefly describe what you are wearing.
- Have students name one item of clothing they are wearing today. Then ask: **Que porte ____? De quelle couleur est ____?**
- Point out the difference between **une écharpe** (a heavier scarf or wrap worn in fall or winter) and **un foulard** (a lighter scarf usually worn in spring or summer).
- Tell students that the word **taille** is used to talk about *clothing sizes.* **Pointure** refers to *shoe sizes.*
- Point out the title of this lesson. Tell students that **chic** is an invariable adjective.
- Tell students that the verb **porter** means *to wear* or *to carry.* The verb **mettre** (*to wear, to put on*) is presented on page 255.
- Use the Vocabulary illustrations and the Clothing and shopping illustrations from the Digital Image Bank to help students familiarize themselves with clothing, accessories, shopping, and colors.
- Additional vocabulary for this lesson can be found in the **Vocabulaire supplémentaire** on the Supersite.

Leçon 6B

You will learn how to...
- describe clothing
- offer and accept gifts

Vocabulary Tools

Très chic!

Vocabulaire

aller avec	to go with
un anorak	ski jacket, parka
une chaussette	sock
une chemise (à manches courtes/longues)	shirt (short-/long-sleeved)
un chemisier	blouse
un gant	glove
un jean	jeans
une jupe	skirt
un manteau	coat
un pantalon	pants
un pull	sweater
un sous-vêtement	underwear
une taille	clothing size
un tailleur	(woman's) suit; tailor
un tee-shirt	tee shirt
un vendeur/une vendeuse	salesman/saleswoman
des vêtements (*m.*)	clothing
De quelle couleur...?	In what color...?
des soldes (*m.*)	sales
chaque	each
large	loose; big
serré(e)	tight

ressources

WB pp. 79–80 | LM p. 45 | vhlcentral

OPTIONS

Game Have students stand. Toss a beanbag to a student at random and say the name of a sport, place, or activity. The person has four seconds to name a clothing item or accessory that goes with it. That person then tosses the beanbag to another student and says a sport, place, or activity. Students who cannot think of an item in time or repeat an item that has already been mentioned are eliminated. The last person standing wins.

Extra Practice Review the weather and seasons by asking students what they wear in various circumstances. Examples: **Que portez-vous quand il fait chaud/quand il fait frais/quand il neige/au printemps/en hiver?**

Mise en pratique

Attention!

Note that the adjectives **orange** and **marron** are invariable; they do not vary in gender or number to match the noun they modify.

J'aime l'anorak **orange**.

Il porte des chaussures **marron**.

1 **Écoutez** Guillaume prépare ses vacances d'hiver (*winter vacation*). Indiquez quels vêtements il va acheter pour son voyage.

		Oui	Non
1.	des baskets	☑	☐
2.	un maillot de bain	☐	☑
3.	des chemises	☐	☑
4.	un pantalon noir	☑	☐
5.	un manteau	☑	☐
6.	un anorak	☐	☑
7.	un jean	☑	☐
8.	un short	☐	☑
9.	un pull	☐	☑
10.	une robe	☐	☑

Guillaume

2 **Les vêtements** Choisissez le mot qui ne va pas avec les autres.

1. des baskets, une cravate, une chaussure
2. un jean, un pantalon, une jupe
3. un tailleur, un costume, un short
4. des lunettes, un chemisier, une chemise
5. un tee-shirt, un pull, un anorak
6. une casquette, une ceinture, un chapeau
7. un sous-vêtement, une chaussette, un sac à main
8. une jupe, une robe, une écharpe

3 **De quelle couleur?** Indiquez de quelle(s) couleur(s) sont ces choses.

MODÈLE

l'océan
Il est bleu.
la statue de la Liberté
Elle est verte.

1. le drapeau français Il est bleu, blanc et rouge.
2. les dollars américains Ils sont verts.
3. les pommes (*apples*) Answers will vary. Elles sont rouges, vertes ou jaunes.
4. le soleil Il est jaune.
5. la nuit Elle est noire.
6. le zèbre Il est blanc et noir.
7. la neige Elle est blanche.
8. les oranges Elles sont orange.
9. le café Il est marron ou noir.
10. les bananes Elles sont jaunes.

des lunettes (de soleil) (f.)

une casquette

une écharpe

un blouson

bon marché

Practice more at **vhlcentral.com**.

deux cent quarante trois **243**

1 **Audioscript** Bonjour! Je m'appelle Guillaume. Je vais aller en Suisse pour mes vacances d'hiver. J'ai besoin d'acheter un manteau parce qu'il va faire froid. J'ai déjà acheté un pull gris. J'ai aussi un bel anorak bleu qui est un peu vieux, mais chaud. Pour faire des randonnées, j'ai besoin d'un jean et de nouvelles baskets. Pour aller en boîte, je vais acheter un pantalon noir qui va aller avec toutes mes chemises: j'ai des chemises de toutes les couleurs, des chemises à manches longues, à manches courtes. Bien sûr, je ne vais pas avoir besoin d'un short parce qu'il ne va pas faire chaud.
(On Textbook MP3s)

1 **Expansion** Play the recording again. Ask students why Guillaume is not going to buy the items marked **Non**. Example: **Pourquoi Guillaume ne va-t-il pas acheter un maillot de bain? (parce qu'il va faire froid en Suisse)**

2 **Expansions**
• For additional practice, give students these items. **9. un sac à main, une ceinture, une robe (une robe) 10. un pull, un gant, un tee-shirt (un gant) 11. un pantalon, un blouson, un anorak (un pantalon) 12. des chaussettes, des baskets, un chapeau (un chapeau)**
• Have students create one or two additional items using at least three new vocabulary words in each one. Collect their papers and write some of the items on the board.

3 **Expansions**
• Point out items in the classroom and have students tell what color they are. Examples: **le tableau, ce sac à dos,** and **mon stylo**.
• Have students name items of various colors. Example: **Nommez** (*Name*) **quelque chose de rouge. (le chemisier de ____)**

TPR Play a game of **Jacques a dit** (*Simon says*). Write **asseyez-vous** and **levez-vous** on the board and model them by sitting and standing as you say them. Start by saying: **Jacques a dit: Si vous portez un jean noir, levez-vous.** Students wearing black jeans stand up and remain standing until further instruction. Work through various items of clothing. Give instructions without saying **Jacques a dit…** once in a while.

Small Groups Divide the class into small groups. Assign each group a season and a vacation destination. Have groups brainstorm a list of items to pack and write a brief explanation for each item. You might want to have groups write two lists, one for a female traveler and one for a male.

Communication

NATIONAL communication STANDARDS

4 **Qu'est-ce qu'ils portent?** Avec un(e) camarade de classe, regardez les images et à tour de rôle, décrivez ce que les personnages portent. Answers will vary.

MODÈLE

Elle porte un maillot de bain rouge.

1.   2.   3.   4.

5 **On fait du shopping** Choisissez deux partenaires et préparez une conversation. Deux client(e)s et un vendeur/une vendeuse sont dans un grand magasin; les client(e)s sont invité(e)s à un événement très chic, mais ils ou elles ne veulent pas (*don't want*) dépenser beaucoup d'argent. Answers will vary.

Client(e)s

- Décrivez l'événement auquel (*to which*) vous êtes invité(e)s.
- Parlez des vêtements que vous cherchez, de vos couleurs préférées, de votre taille. Trouvez-vous le vêtement trop large, trop serré, etc.?
- Demandez les prix et dites si vous trouvez que c'est cher, bon marché, etc.

Vendeur/Vendeuse

- Demandez les tailles, préférences, etc. des client(e)s.
- Répondez à toutes les questions de vos client(e)s.
- Suggérez des vêtements appropriés.

> ### Coup de main
> To compare French and American sizes, see the chart on p. 248.

6 **Conversez** Interviewez un(e) camarade de classe.
Answers will vary.

1. Qu'est-ce que tu portes l'hiver? Et l'été?
2. Qu'est-ce que tu portes pour aller à l'université?
3. Qu'est-ce que tu portes pour aller à la plage (*beach*)?
4. Qu'est-ce que tu portes pour faire une randonnée?
5. Qu'est-ce que tu portes pour aller en boîte de nuit?
6. Qu'est-ce que tu portes pour un entretien d'embauche (*job interview*)?
7. Quelle est ta couleur préférée? Pourquoi?
8. Qu'est-ce que tu portes pour aller dans un restaurant très élégant?
9. Où est-ce que tu achètes tes vêtements? Pourquoi?
10. Est-ce que tu prêtes (*lend*) tes vêtements à tes ami(e)s?

7 **Défilé de mode** Votre classe a organisé un défilé de mode (*fashion show*). Votre partenaire est mannequin (*model*) et vous représentez la marque (*brand*) de vêtements. Pendant que votre partenaire défile, vous décrivez à la classe les vêtements qu'il ou elle porte. Après, échangez les rôles. Answers will vary.

MODÈLE

Et voici la charmante Julie, qui porte les modèles de la dernière collection H&M®: une chemise à manches courtes et un pantalon noir, ensemble idéal pour aller en boîte de nuit. Ses chaussures blanches vont parfaitement avec l'ensemble. Cette collection H&M est très à la mode et très bon marché.

OPTIONS

Extra Practice Have students write a paragraph about a real or imaginary vacation they plan to take and the clothing they will take with them. Tell them to include what kind of weather they expect at their destination and any weather-specific clothing they will need. Ask volunteers to share their paragraphs with the class.

Extra Practice Have students write descriptions of an article of clothing or a complete outfit that best describes them without indicating who they are. Collect the papers and read the descriptions aloud. The rest of the class has to guess who wrote each one.

4 **Suggestion** Tell students to write their descriptions. Then have volunteers write a description on the board for each picture.

4 **Expansion** Have students describe what they are wearing in detail, including accessories and colors of each item.

5 **Suggestion** Remind students to include greetings and other polite expressions in their role-plays. Have volunteers perform their role-plays for the rest of the class.

6 **Expansion** Take a quick class survey to find out students' clothing preferences. Tally the results on the board.

7 **Suggestion** Have a volunteer read the **modèle** aloud.

Les sons et les lettres  Audio

Open vs. closed vowels: Part 3

The letter combination **eu** can be pronounced two different ways, open and closed. Compare the pronunciation of the vowel sounds in these words.

chev**eu**x	nev**eu**	h**eu**re	meill**eu**r

When **eu** is followed by a pronounced consonant, it has an open sound. The open **eu** sound does not exist in English. To pronounce it, say **è** with your lips only slightly rounded.

p**eu**r	j**eu**ne	chant**eu**r	b**eu**rre

The letter combination **œu** is usually pronounced with an open **eu** sound.

s**œu**r	b**œu**f	**œu**f	ch**œu**r

When **eu** is the last sound of a syllable, it has a closed vowel sound, similar to the vowel sound in the English word *full*. While this exact sound does not exist in English, you can make the closed **eu** sound by saying **é** with your lips rounded.

d**eu**x	bl**eu**	p**eu**	mi**eu**x

When **eu** is followed by a *z* sound, such as a single **s** between two vowels, it is usually pronounced with the closed **eu** sound.

chant**eu**se	génér**eu**se	séri**eu**se	curi**eu**se

Prononcez Répétez les mots suivants à voix haute.

1. leur
2. veuve
3. neuf
4. vieux
5. curieux
6. acteur
7. monsieur
8. coiffeuse
9. ordinateur
10. tailleur
11. vendeuse
12. couleur

Articulez Répétez les phrases suivantes à voix haute.

1. Le professeur Heudier a soixante-deux ans.
2. Est-ce que Matthieu est jeune ou vieux?
3. Monsieur Eustache est un chanteur fabuleux.
4. Eugène a les yeux bleus et les cheveux bruns.

Dictons Répétez les dictons à voix haute.

Les conseilleurs ne sont pas les payeurs.[2]

Qui vole un œuf, vole un bœuf.[1]

[1] He who steals an egg would steal an ox.
[2] Those who give advice are not the ones who pay the price.

ressources
LM
p. 46
vhlcentral

deux cent quarante-cinq **245**

Section Goals

In this section, students will learn about additional open and closed vowel sounds.

Instructional Resources
vhlcentral.com:
Textbook MP3s; Lab MP3s;
SAM Answer Key;
Textbook Audioscript;
Lab Audioscript;
reference tools

Suggestions
- Model the pronunciation of each open and closed vowel sound. Have students watch the shape of your mouth, then repeat each sound after you. Pronounce each of the example words and have students repeat them.
- Point out that the letters **o** and **e** together are usually written as the single character **œ**.
- Ask students to provide more examples of words from this lesson or previous lessons with these vowel sounds. Examples: **tailleur, vendeuse, ordinateur, feuille,** and **chanteuse.**
- Dictate five familiar words containing the open and closed vowels presented in this section to the class, repeating each one at least two times. Then write them on the board or on a transparency and have students check their spelling.

Dictons Ask students to explain the two sayings in their own words.

OPTIONS

Extra Practice Use these sentences with open and closed vowel sounds for additional practice or dictation. **1.** Elle a deux ordinateurs neufs. **2.** Ma sœur est jeune et sérieuse. **3.** J'aime mieux être coiffeur ou ingénieur. **4.** Tu veux ce vieux tailleur?

Extra Practice Teach students these French tongue-twisters that contain the open and closed vowel sounds on this page. **Pépé paie peu, mémé m'émeut. Je veux un feutre bleu.**

ESPACE ROMAN-PHOTO

Section Goals

In this section, students will learn functional phrases for talking about clothing and gifts through comprehensible input.

Instructional Resources
vhlcentral.com:
***Roman-photo** Video, Videoscript, and Translation; SAM Answer Key; reference tools*

Video Recap: Leçon 6A
Review the previous **Roman-photo** with this activity.
1. Qu'est-ce que Sandrine a préparé pour l'anniversaire de Stéphane? (les desserts: une mousse au chocolat, des biscuits et un gâteau)
2. Qu'est-ce que Rachid et Astrid ont acheté comme cadeaux? (une calculatrice, des livres et une montre)
3. Qui a fait la décoration au café? (Astrid, Valérie et Amina)
4. Qu'est-ce qu'Amina a apporté à la fête? (un cadeau et de la glace au chocolat)

Video Synopsis Stéphane arrives at his surprise party. Sandrine explains that David is in Paris with his parents. Sandrine admires Amina's outfit, and Stéphane opens his presents. Valérie gives him a leather jacket and gloves. When he opens the books and calculator from Rachid and Astrid, he tries to act pleased. Then he realizes they were gag gifts when he sees the watch.

Suggestions
• Have students read the title, glance at the video stills, and predict what the episode will be about. Record their predictions.
• Have students read the **Roman-photo** conversation in groups of six.
• Have students scan the captions for vocabulary related to clothing and colors.
• Review students' predictions and ask them which ones were correct.

L'anniversaire Video

PERSONNAGES

Amina

Astrid

Rachid

Sandrine

Stéphane

Valérie

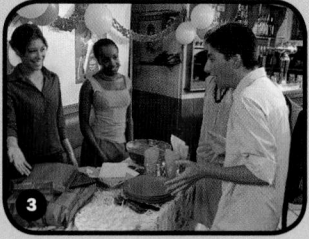

Au café...

VALÉRIE, SANDRINE, AMINA, ASTRID ET RACHID Surprise! Joyeux anniversaire, Stéphane!
STÉPHANE Alors là, je suis agréablement surpris!
VALÉRIE Bon anniversaire, mon chéri!
SANDRINE On a organisé cette surprise ensemble...

VALÉRIE Pas du tout! C'est Sandrine qui a presque tout préparé.
SANDRINE Oh, je n'ai fait que les desserts et ton gâteau d'anniversaire.
STÉPHANE Tu es un ange.
RACHID Bon anniversaire, Stéphane. Tu sais, à ton âge, il ne faut pas perdre son temps. Alors cette année, tu travailles sérieusement, c'est promis?
STÉPHANE Oui, oui.

AMINA Rachid a raison. Dix-huit ans, c'est une étape importante dans la vie! Il faut fêter ça.
ASTRID Joyeux anniversaire, Stéphane.
STÉPHANE Oh, et en plus, vous m'avez apporté des cadeaux!

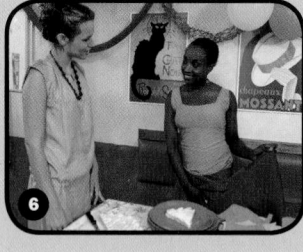

AMINA Oui. J'ai tout fait moi-même: ce tee-shirt, cette jupe et j'ai acheté ces chaussures.
SANDRINE Tu es une véritable artiste, Amina! Ta jupe est très originale! J'adore!
AMINA J'ai une idée. Tu me prêtes ta robe grise samedi et je te prête ma jupe. D'accord?
SANDRINE Bonne idée!

STÉPHANE Eh! C'est super cool, ce blouson en cuir noir. Avec des gants en plus! Merci, maman!
AMINA Ces gants vont très bien avec le blouson! Très à la mode!
STÉPHANE Tu trouves?

RACHID Tiens, Stéphane.
STÉPHANE Mais qu'est-ce que c'est? Des livres?
RACHID Oui, la littérature, c'est important pour la culture générale!
VALÉRIE Tu as raison, Rachid.
STÉPHANE Euh oui... euh... c'est gentil... euh... merci, Rachid.

A C T I V I T É S

1

Vrai ou faux? Indiquez si ces affirmations sont **vraies** ou **fausses**. Corrigez les phrases fausses.

1. David ne veut pas (*doesn't want*) aller à la fête.
   Faux. David est désolé de ne pas être là.
2. Sandrine porte une jupe bleue.
   Faux. Sandrine porte une robe grise.
3. Amina a fait sa jupe elle-même (*herself*).
   Vrai.
4. Le tee-shirt d'Amina est en soie.
   Vrai.
5. Valérie donne un blouson en cuir et une ceinture à Stéphane.
   Faux. Valérie donne un blouson en cuir et des gants à Stéphane.

6. Sandrine n'aime pas partager ses vêtements.
   Faux. Sandrine va prêter sa robe à Amina.
7. Pour Amina, 18 ans, c'est une étape importante.
   Vrai.
8. Sandrine n'a rien fait (*didn't do anything*) pour la fête.
   Faux. Sandrine a fait le gâteau et les desserts.
9. Rachid donne des livres de littérature à Stéphane.
   Vrai.
10. Stéphane pense que ses amis sont drôles.
    Faux. Stéphane pense que ses amis ne sont pas drôles.

S Practice more at **vhlcentral.com**.

O P T I O N S

Avant de regarder la vidéo Before viewing the video, have students work in pairs and make a list of words and expressions they might hear at a surprise birthday party.

Regarder la vidéo Show the video episode and tell students to check off the words or expressions they hear on their lists. Then show the episode again and have students give you a play-by-play description of the action. Write their descriptions on the board.

Les amis fêtent l'anniversaire de Stéphane.

SANDRINE Ah au fait, David est désolé de ne pas être là. Ce week-end, il visite Paris avec ses parents. Mais il pense à toi.
STÉPHANE Je comprends tout à fait. Les parents de David sont de Washington, n'est-ce pas?
SANDRINE Oui, c'est ça.

AMINA Merci, Sandrine. Je trouve que tu es très élégante dans cette robe grise! La couleur te va très bien.
SANDRINE Vraiment? Et toi, tu es très chic. C'est du coton?
AMINA Non, de la soie.
SANDRINE Cet ensemble, c'est une de tes créations, n'est-ce pas?

STÉPHANE Une calculatrice rose... pour moi?
ASTRID Oui, c'est pour t'aider à répondre à toutes les questions en maths, et avec le sourire.
STÉPHANE Euh, merci beaucoup! C'est très... utile.
ASTRID Attends! Il y a encore un cadeau pour toi...

STÉPHANE Ouah, cette montre est géniale, merci!
ASTRID Tu as aimé notre petite blague? Nous, on a bien ri.
RACHID Eh Stéphane! Tu as vraiment aimé tes livres et ta calculatrice?
STÉPHANE Ouais, vous deux, ce que vous êtes drôles.

Expressions utiles

Talking about your clothes

- **Et toi, tu es très chic. C'est du coton/ de la soie?**
  And you, you're very chic. Is it cotton/silk?
- **J'ai tout fait moi-même.**
  I did/made everything myself.
- **La couleur te va très bien.**
  The color suits you well.
- **Tu es une véritable artiste! Ta jupe est très originale!**
  You are a true artist! Your skirt is very original!
- **Tu me prêtes ta robe grise samedi et je te prête ma jupe.**
  You lend me your gray dress Saturday and I'll lend you my skirt.
- **C'est super cool, ce blouson en cuir/laine/ velours noir(e). Avec des gants en plus!**
  It's really cool, this black leather/wool/velvet jacket. With gloves as well!

Additional vocabulary

- **Vous m'avez apporté des cadeaux!**
  You brought me gifts!
- **Tu sais, à ton âge, il ne faut pas perdre son temps.**
  You know, at your age, one should not waste time.
- **C'est pour t'aider à répondre à toutes les questions en maths, et avec le sourire.**
  It's to help you answer all the questions in math, with a smile.
- **agréablement surpris(e)** *pleasantly surprised*
- **C'est promis?** *Promise?*
- **Il pense à toi.** *He's thinking of you.*
- **tout à fait** *absolutely*
- **Vraiment?** *Really?*
- **véritable** *true, genuine*
- **Pour moi?** *For me?*
- **Attends!** *Wait!*
- **On a bien ri.** *We had a good laugh.*

---

2 Identifiez Indiquez qui a dit (*said*) ces phrases: Amina (**A**), Astrid (**As**), Rachid (**R**), Sandrine (**S**), Stéphane (**St**) ou Valérie (**V**).

- S 1. Tu es une véritable artiste.
- As 2. On a bien ri.
- A 3. Très à la mode.
- St 4. Je comprends tout à fait.
- V 5. C'est Sandrine qui a presque tout préparé.
- R 6. C'est promis?

3 À vous! Ce sont les soldes. Sandrine, David et Amina vont dans un magasin pour acheter des vêtements. Ils essaient différentes choses, donnent leur avis (*opinion*) et parlent de leurs préférences, des prix et des matières (*fabrics*). Avec un(e) partenaire, écrivez la conversation et jouez la scène devant la classe.

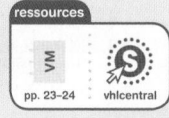
ressources

VM
pp. 23–24

vhlcentral

A C T I V I T É S

Expressions utiles
- Model the pronunciation of the **Expressions utiles** and have students repeat them.
- As you work through the list, point out expressions with indirect object pronouns, disjunctive pronouns, and **-re** verbs. Tell students that these grammar structures will be formally presented in **Espace structures**.
- Respond briefly to questions about indirect object pronouns and -re verbs. Reinforce correct forms, but do not expect students to produce them consistently at this time.
- Point out that the pronouns **tu**, **te**, and **toi** all mean *you*, but they cannot be used interchangeably because they are different parts of speech.
- To practice different fabrics and other materials, ask students yes/no and either/or questions about their clothing. Examples: _____, votre chemisier, c'est du coton ou de la soie? _____, votre blouson, c'est du cuir ou de la laine? Avez-vous des gants en cuir noir?

1 Suggestion Have students write their corrections for false statements on the board.

1 Expansion For additional practice, give students these items. **11. Stéphane n'est pas content de la fête. (Faux.) 12. David est à Paris avec ses parents (Vrai.) 13. Sandrine aime bien la jupe d'Amina. (Vrai.) 14. Stéphane n'aime pas la montre. (Faux.)**

2 Expansion In addition to identifying the speaker, have students give the name of the person to whom each one is speaking. **1. Amina 2. Stéphane 3. Stéphane 4. Sandrine 5. Stéphane 6. Stéphane**

3 Suggestion Tell students to use an idea map or outline to plan their conversation before they begin to write it.

O P T I O N S

Game Divide the class into two teams. Give one team member a card with the name of an item of clothing or an accessory. This person has 30 seconds to draw the item and one player on his or her team has to guess what it is. Give a point for each correct answer. If a player cannot guess the item within the time limit, the next player on the opposing team may "steal" the point.

Extra Practice Bring in photos from French fashion magazines or catalogues, such as *3 Suisses* or *La Redoute*, and have students give their opinions about the clothing and accessories.

Reading

Section Goals

In this section, students will:
- learn about the fashion industry in France and where to buy clothes
- learn terms related to fashion
- read about traditional clothing and fabrics in some francophone regions
- read about Coco Chanel

Instructional Resources
vhlcentral.com: reference tools

Culture à la loupe
Avant la lecture Have students read the title, look at the photos, and predict what this reading is about. Then ask them to share what they know about French fashion or the fashion industry in France.

Lecture
- Point out the **Coup de main** and have students compare the clothing sizes. Example: **Si une femme porte la taille 8 aux États-Unis, quelle taille porte-t-elle en France? (38)**
- Explain that a **hypermarché** is similar to a Wal-Mart in the United States.

Après la lecture Ask students: **Où les Français achètent-ils leurs vêtements? (dans les boutiques indépendantes, dans les chaînes de magasins spécialisés, dans les hypermarchés, dans les centres commerciaux)**

1 Suggestion Go over the answers with the class.

CULTURE À LA LOUPE

La mode en France

Pour la majorité des Français, la mode est un moyen° d'expression. Les jeunes adorent les marques°, surtout les marques américaines. Avoir un *sweatshirt* de style américain est considéré comme très chic. C'est pareil° pour les chaussures. Bien sûr, les styles varient beaucoup. Il y a le style bourgeois, par exemple, plus classique avec la prédominance de la couleur bleu marine°. Il y a aussi le style «baba cool», c'est-à-dire° *hippie*.

Les marques coûtent cher, mais en France il y a encore beaucoup de boutiques indépendantes où les vêtements ne sont pas nécessairement plus chers. Souvent les vendeurs et les vendeuses sont aussi propriétaires du magasin. Ils encouragent donc° plus les clients à acheter. Mais il y a aussi beaucoup de chaînes françaises comme Lacoste, Bensimon et Kooples. Et les chaînes américaines sont de plus en plus présentes dans les villes. Les Français achètent également° des vêtements dans les hypermarchés°, comme Auchan ou Carrefour, et dans les centres commerciaux.

L'anthropologue américain Lawrence Wylie a écrit° sur les différences entre les vêtements français et américains. Les Américains portent des vêtements plus amples et plus confortables. Pour les Français, l'aspect esthétique est plus important que le confort. Les femmes mettent des baskets uniquement pour faire du sport. Les costumes français sont plus serrés et plus près du corps° et les épaules° sont en général plus étroites°.

moyen *means* **marques** *brand names* **pareil** *the same* **marine** *navy* **c'est-à-dire** *in other words* **donc** *therefore* **également** *also* **hypermarchés** *large supermarkets* **a écrit** *wrote* **corps** *body* **épaules** *shoulders* **étroites** *narrow*

Coup de main

Comparaison des tailles°

FEMMES						
France	36	38	40	42	44	46
USA	6	8	10	12	14	16

HOMMES (PANTALONS)						
France	36	38	40	42	44	46
USA	26	28	30	32	34	36

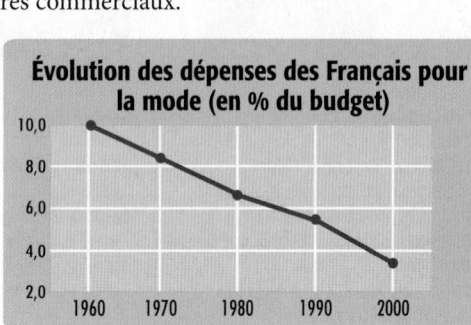

Évolution des dépenses des Français pour la mode (en % du budget)

---

1 **Vrai ou faux?** Indiquez si les phrases sont **vraies** ou **fausses**. Corrigez les phrases fausses.

1. Pour beaucoup de Français, la mode est un moyen d'expression. Vrai.
2. Un *sweatshirt* de style américain est considéré comme du mauvais goût (*taste*). Faux. C'est considéré comme très chic.
3. La couleur bleu marine prédomine dans le style bourgeois. Vrai
4. En France les boutiques indépendantes sont rares. Faux. Il y a encore beaucoup de boutiques indépendantes.

5. Les vendeurs et les vendeuses des boutiques indépendantes sont souvent aussi propriétaires. Vrai.
6. Lacoste, Bensimon et The Kooples sont des chaînes françaises. Vrai.
7. Il est possible d'acheter des vêtements dans les hypermarchés. Vrai.
8. Lawrence Wylie a écrit sur la mode italienne. Faux. Il a écrit sur les différences entre les vêtements français et américains.
9. Les Français portent des vêtements plus amples et plus confortables. Faux. Les Américains portent des vêtements plus amples et plus confortables.
10. Les costumes français sont très larges. Faux. Les costumes français sont plus serrés.

ACTIVITÉS

Cultural Comparison Have students work in groups of three and compare where French people and Americans shop for clothing. Tell them to list the similarities and differences in a two-column chart under the headings **Similitudes** and **Différences**. After they complet their charts, have two groups get together and compare their lists.

Extra Practice First, ask students what information the graph **Évolution des dépenses des Français pour la mode** shows. (The percentage of total budget that the French spent on fashion from 1960–2000.) Then ask: **Quel pourcentage de leur budget les Français ont-ils dépensé pour la mode en 1960? (10,0%) Et en 1970? (8,2%) En 1980? (6,3%) En 1990? (5,5%) En 2000? (3,7%)** (Accept approximate answers.)

OPTIONS

LE FRANÇAIS QUOTIDIEN

Les vêtements et la mode

fringues (*f.*)	clothes
look (*m.*)	style
vintage (*m.*)	vintage clothing
BCBG (bon chic bon genre)	chic and conservative
ringard(e)	out-of-style
être bien/ mal sapé(e)	to be well/ badly dressed
être sur son 31	to be well dressed

LE MONDE FRANCOPHONE

Vêtements et tissus

Voici quelques vêtements et tissus traditionnels du monde francophone.

En Afrique centrale et de l'ouest
Le boubou tunique plus ou moins° longue et souvent très colorée portée par les hommes et les femmes
Les batiks tissus° traditionnels très colorés

En Afrique du Nord
La djellaba longue tunique à capuche° portée par les hommes et les femmes
Le kaftan sorte de djellaba portée à la maison

À la Martinique
Le madras tissu typique aux couleurs vives

À Tahiti
Le paréo morceau° de tissu attaché au-dessus de la poitrine° ou à la taille°

plus ou moins more or less **tissus** fabrics **à capuche** hooded **morceau** piece **poitrine** chest **taille** waist

PORTRAIT

Coco Chanel, styliste parisienne

«La mode se démode°, le style jamais.»
—*Coco Chanel*

Coco Chanel (1883–1971) est considérée comme étant° l'icône du parfum et de la mode du vingtième siècle°. Dans les années 1910, elle a l'idée audacieuse° d'intégrer la mode «à la garçonne» dans ses créations: les lignes féminines empruntent aux° éléments de la mode masculine.

C'est la naissance du fameux tailleur Chanel. Pour «Mademoiselle Chanel», l'important dans la mode, c'est que les vêtements permettent de bouger°; ils doivent° être simples et confortables. Son invention de «la petite robe noire» illustre l'esprit° classique et élégant de ses collections. De nombreuses célébrités ont immortalisé le nom de Chanel: Jacqueline Kennedy avec le tailleur et Marilyn Monroe avec le parfum No. 5, par exemple.

se démode goes out of fashion **étant** being **vingtième siècle** twentieth century **idée audacieuse** daring idea **empruntent aux** borrow from **bouger** move **doivent** have to **esprit** spirit

MUSIQUE À FOND

Zaho

Lieu de naissance: Bab Ezzouar, Algérie
Métier: musicienne-interprète

Après avoir fait des études brillantes en informatique, elle choisit finalement de se tourner vers le monde de la musique.

Go to vhlcentral.com to find out more about **Zaho** and her music.

---

2 **Coco Chanel** Complétez les phrases.

1. Coco Chanel était (*was*) _styliste de mode_.
2. Le style Chanel est inspiré de _la mode masculine_.
3. Les vêtements Chanel sont _simples et confortables_.
4. Jacqueline Kennedy portait souvent des _tailleurs_ Chanel.
5. D'après «Mademoiselle Chanel», il est très important de pouvoir (*to be able to*) _bouger_ dans ses vêtements.
6. C'est Coco Chanel qui a inventé _la petite robe noire_.

3 **Le «relookage»** Vous êtes conseillers/conseillères en image (*image consultants*), spécialisé(es) dans le «relookage». Votre nouveau/nouvelle client(e), une célébrité, vous demande de l'aider à sélectionner un nouveau style. Discutez de ce nouveau look avec un(e) partenaire.

 ressources

 Practice more at vhlcentral.com.

ACTIVITÉS

Vêtements et tissus Have students create five true/false statements based on the content in **Le monde francophone**. Then have students get together with a classmate and take turns reading their statements and responding **vrai** or **faux**.

Les couturiers Have students research one famous French fashion designer on the Internet and write a short paragraph about the person. Tell them to include information about the person's accomplishments, type(s) of clothing he or she designs, where it is sold, and any other important details.

OPTIONS

Le français quotidien
• Model the pronunciation of each term and have students repeat it.
• Ask students to give some examples of vintage clothing.
• Have volunteers create sentences using these words.

Portrait Have students look at the photo of Coco Chanel and describe her appearance and clothing.

Le monde francophone
• Bring in photos from magazines or the Internet of people wearing these types of clothing and fabrics to show the class.
• Ask a few content questions based on the reading. Examples: **1. Comment s'appelle la tunique que les gens portent en Afrique centrale? (le boubou) 2. Qu'est-ce qu'une djellaba? (C'est une longue tunique à capuche.) 3. À la Martinique, on porte des vêtements faits de batik ou de madras? (des vêtements faits de madras) 4. Où porte-t-on le kaftan? (en Afrique du Nord)**

Musique à fond Point out to students that they will find supporting activities and information at **vhlcentral.com**.

2 Expansion For additional practice, give students these items. **7. Les collections de Chanel sont classiques et ____. (élégantes) 8. Marilyn Monroe a immortalisé ____ de Chanel. (le parfum No. 5)**

3 Suggestions
• Tell students that they can change the person's hairstyle as well as the clothing. Encourage them to include what is wrong with the person's present style in their discussion.
• Have students write their descriptions and read them aloud for the class.

Section Goals

In this section, students will learn:
- indirect object pronouns
- some additional uses of disjunctive pronouns

Instructional Resources

vhlcentral.com:
Activity Pack; Lab MP3s;
SAM Answer Key; **Essayez!**
and **Mise en pratique**
answers; Lab Audioscript;
reference tools

Suggestions

- The direct object pronouns are presented after the indirect object pronouns for two reasons: 1. Students only need to learn two third-person forms (**lui** and **leur**) now and, when they learn the direct object pronouns in **Leçon 7A,** will already be familiar with the forms the two types of object pronouns share in common (**me, te, nous, vous**). They therefore will be able to focus on the new third-person forms (**le, la, l', les**).
2. Past participle agreement with preceding direct object pronouns is a difficult concept for many students and could pose a distraction while they are still learning about the **passé composé.**
- Say and write on the board: **Valérie achète un blouson à Stéphane.** Tell students that an indirect object is a noun or pronoun that answers the question *to whom* or *for whom* an action is done. Ask them what the indirect object of the verb is in the sentence. (Stéphane) Explain that indirect object nouns are introduced by the preposition **à.** Point out that **un blouson** is the direct object of the verb.
- Write the indirect object pronouns on the board. Show students some photos and say: **Je vous montre mes photos.** Give a student an object, such as a book, and say: **Je vous prête mon livre.** Continue the same procedure with the remaining indirect object pronouns.

Leçon 6B

6B.1

À noter

In French, *direct* object pronouns follow special rules, which is why you are learning about *indirect* object pronouns first. You will learn about direct object pronouns in **Leçon 7A.**

Boîte à outils

In French, the indirect object pronouns can *only* refer to animate nouns like people or animals.

Boîte à outils

When you have a question using inversion, follow the same rules outlined on this page for the placement of the indirect object pronoun.

Lui parles-tu?

Lui as-tu parlé?

Vas-tu lui parler?

Indirect object pronouns Tutorial

- An indirect object expresses *to whom* or *for whom* an action is done. An indirect object pronoun replaces an indirect object noun. Look for the preposition à followed by a name or noun referring to a person or animal. In the example below, the indirect object answers this question: **À qui parle Gisèle?** (*To whom does Gisèle speak?*)

SUBJECT	VERB	INDIRECT OBJECT NOUN
Gisèle	**parle**	**à sa mère.**
Gisèle	*speaks*	*to her mother.*

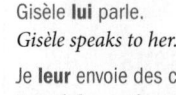

Indirect object pronouns			
me	*to/for me*	**nous**	*to/for us*
te	*to/for you*	**vous**	*to/for you*
lui	*to/for him/her*	**leur**	*to/for them*

- Indirect object pronouns replace indirect object nouns and the prepositions that precede them.

Gisèle parle **à sa mère**.
Gisèle speaks to her mother.

Gisèle **lui** parle.
Gisèle speaks to her.

J'envoie des cadeaux **à mes nièces**.
I send gifts to my nieces.

Je **leur** envoie des cadeaux.
I send them gifts.

Vous m'avez apporté des cadeaux!

Je te prête ma jupe. D'accord?

- The indirect object pronoun usually precedes the conjugated verb.

Antoine, je **te** parle.
Antoine, I'm talking to you.

Notre père **nous** a envoyé un e-mail.
Our father sent us an e-mail.

- In a negative statement, place the indirect object pronoun between **ne** and the conjugated verb.

Antoine, je **ne te parle** pas de ça.
Antoine, I'm not talking to you about that.

Notre père **ne nous a** pas envoyé d'e-mail.
Our father didn't send us an e-mail.

- When an infinitive follows a conjugated verb, the indirect object pronoun precedes the infinitive.

Nous allons **lui donner** une cravate.
We're going to give him a tie.

Il espère **vous prêter** le costume.
He's hoping to lend you the suit.

- In the **passé composé**, the indirect object pronoun comes before the auxiliary verb **avoir.**

Tu **lui** as parlé?
Did you speak to her?

Non, je ne **lui** ai pas parlé.
No, I didn't speak to her.

Verbs used with indirect object pronouns

demander à	to ask, to request	parler à	to speak/talk to
donner à	to give to	poser une question à	to pose/ask a question (to)
envoyer à	to send to	prêter à	to lend to
montrer à	to show to	téléphoner à	to phone, to call

- The indirect object pronouns **me** and **te** become **m'** and **t'** before a verb beginning with a vowel sound.

> Ton petit ami **t'**envoie des e-mails.
> *Your boyfriend sends you e-mails.*

> Isabelle **m'**a prêté son sac à main.
> *Isabelle lent me her handbag.*

> **M'**a-t-il acheté ce pull?
> *Did he buy me this sweater?*

> Elles ne **t'**ont pas téléphoné hier?
> *Didn't they call you yesterday?*

Disjunctive pronouns

- Disjunctive pronouns can be used alone or in phrases without a verb.

> Qui prend du café?
> *Who's having coffee?*

> **Moi!**
> *Me!*

> **Eux** aussi?
> *Them, too?*

- Disjunctive pronouns emphasize the person to whom they refer.

> **Moi**, je porte souvent une casquette.
> *Me, I often wear a cap.*

> Mon frère, **lui**, il déteste les casquettes.
> *My brother, he hates caps.*

- To say *myself*, *ourselves*, etc., add **-même(s)** after the disjunctive pronoun.

> Tu fais ça **toi-même**?
> *Are you doing that yourself?*

> Ils organisent la fête **eux-mêmes**.
> *They're planning the party themselves.*

- In the case of a few French verbs and expressions, you do not use the indirect object pronoun although the verb may be followed by **à** and a person or animal. Instead, use the disjunctive pronoun. One such expression is **penser à**.

> Il **pense** souvent **à** ses grands-parents, n'est-ce pas?
> *He often thinks about his grandparents, doesn't he?*

> DISJUNCTIVE PRONOUN
> Oui, il **pense** souvent **à** eux.
> *Yes, he often thinks about them.*

À noter

In **Leçon 3B**, you learned to use disjunctive pronouns (**moi, toi, lui, elle, nous, vous, eux, elles**) after prepositions: **J'ai une écharpe pour ton frère/ pour lui**. (*I have a scarf for your brother/for him.*)

Suggestions
- Explain that, in French, indirect object pronouns do not follow verbs as they do in English. The word order in French is [*subject*] + (**ne**) [*indirect object pronoun*] + [*verb or subject*] + [*conjugated verb*] + [*indirect object pronoun*] + [*infinitive*].
- Ask students to call out the disjunctive pronouns. Explain the use of **-même(s)** and provide a few examples. Then have students create some sentences with the disjunctive pronouns.
- Tell students that there are relatively few expressions followed by **à** plus a person or animal that use the disjunctive pronoun instead of the indirect object pronoun. Encourage students to keep a running list as they come across them.

Essayez! Have students restate items 1, 2, 4, 5, 6, 9, 10, 11 and 12 using the **futur proche**. Example:
1. Tu vas nous montrer tes photos?

Essayez! Complétez les phrases avec le pronom d'objet indirect approprié.

1. Tu ___nous___ montres tes photos? (*us*)
2. Luc, je ___te___ donne ma nouvelle adresse. (*you, fam.*)
3. Vous ___me___ posez de bonnes questions. (*me*)
4. Nous ___leur___ avons demandé. (*them*)
5. On ___vous___ achète une nouvelle robe. (*you, form.*)
6. Ses parents ___lui___ ont acheté un tailleur. (*her*)
7. Je vais ___lui___ téléphoner à dix heures. (*him*)
8. Elle va ___me___ prêter sa jupe. (*me*)
9. Je ___vous___ envoie des vêtements. (*you, plural*)
10. Est-ce que tu ___leur___ as apporté ces chaussures? (*them*)
11. Il ne ___te___ donne pas son anorak? (*you, fam.*)
12. Nous ne ___leur___ parlons pas! (*them*)

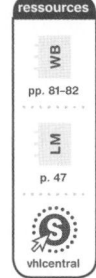

ressources

WB
pp. 81–82

LM
p. 47

vhlcentral

deux cent cinquante et un **251**

OPTIONS

Extra Practice Write sentences with indirect objects on the board. Examples: **Anne-Laure ne te donne pas de biscuits. Pierre ne me parle pas. Loïc prête de l'argent à Louise. Marie nous pose une question. Je téléphone à mes amis.** Have students come to the board and circle the indirect objects.

Small Groups Working in groups of three, the first student lends an object to the second and says: **Je te prête mon/ma….** The second student responds: **Tu me prêtes ton/ta….** The third student says: **Marc lui prête son/sa….** Groups repeat the process until everyone has begun the chain twice. To practice plural pronouns, have two groups get together. Then two students lend something to two other students.

1 **Expansion** Have students write four more sentences with indirect objects (not pronouns). Tell them to exchange papers with a classmate and rewrite the sentences, replacing the indirect object with the corresponding indirect object pronoun.

2 **Suggestion** To check students' answers, have volunteers read different roles aloud.

3 **Expansion** Have students convert three of their statements into questions for their partner, using **Qui…?** or **À qui…?** Example: **Qui te prête sa voiture?**

Mise en pratique

1 **Complétez** Corinne fait du shopping avec sa copine Célia. Trouvez le bon pronom d'objet indirect ou disjonctif pour compléter ses phrases.

1. Je ___leur___ achète des baskets. (à mes cousins)
2. Je ___te___ prends une ceinture. (à toi, Célia)
3. Nous ___lui___ achetons une jupe. (à notre copine Christelle)
4. Célia ___nous___ prend des lunettes de soleil. (à ma mère et à moi)
5. Je ___vous___ achète des gants. (à ta mère et à toi, Célia)
6. Célia ___m'___ achète un pantalon. (à moi)
7. Et, c'est l'annversaire de Magalie demain. Tu penses à ___elle___, j'espère! (à Magalie)

2 **Dialogues** Complétez les dialogues.

1. M. SAUNIER Tu m'as posé une question, chérie?
   MME SAUNIER Oui. Je ___t'___ ai demandé l'heure.
2. CLIENT Je cherche un beau pull.
   VENDEUSE Je vais ___vous___ montrer ce pull noir.
3. VALÉRIE Tu as l'air triste. Tu penses à ton petit ami?
   MÉGHANE Oui, je pense à ___lui___.
4. PROF 1 Mes étudiants ont passé l'examen.
   PROF 2 Tu ___leur___ envoies les résultats?
5. MÈRE Qu'est-ce que vous allez faire?
   ENFANTS On va aller au cinéma. Tu ___nous___ donnes de l'argent?
6. PIERRE Tu ___me___ téléphones ce soir?
   CHARLOTTE D'accord. Je te téléphone.
7. GÉRARD Christophe a oublié son pull. Il a froid!
   VALENTIN Je ___lui___ prête mon blouson.
8. MÈRE Tu ne penses pas à Théo et Sophie?
   PÈRE Mais si, je pense souvent à ___eux___.

3 **Assemblez** Avec un(e) partenaire, assemblez les éléments pour comparer vos familles et vos amis. Answers will vary.

MODÈLE

Étudiant(e) 1: *Mon père me prête souvent sa voiture.*
Étudiant(e) 2: *Mon père, lui, il nous prête de l'argent.*

A	B	C
je	acheter	argent
tu	apporter	biscuits
mon père	envoyer	cadeaux
ma mère	expliquer	devoirs
mon frère	faire	e-mails
ma sœur	montrer	problèmes
mon/ma petit(e) ami(e)	parler	vêtements
mes copains	payer	voiture
?	prêter	?
	?	

 Practice more at **vhlcentral.com**.

Communication

4 Qu'allez-vous faire? Avec un(e) partenaire, dites ce que vous allez faire dans ces situations. Employez les verbes de la liste et présentez vos réponses à la classe. *Answers will vary.*

MODÈLE

Un ami a soif.
On va lui donner de l'eau.

acheter	montrer
apporter	parler
demander	poser des questions
donner	préparer
envoyer	prêter
faire	téléphoner

1. Une personne âgée a froid.
2. Des touristes sont perdus (*lost*).
3. Un homme est sans abri (*homeless*).
4. Votre tante est à l'hôpital.
5. Des amis vous invitent à manger chez eux.
6. Vos nièces ont faim.
7. Votre petit(e) ami(e) fête son anniversaire.
8. Votre meilleur(e) (*best*) ami(e) a des problèmes.
9. Vous ne comprenez pas le prof.
10. Vos parents voyagent en France pendant (*for*) un mois.

5 Les cadeaux de l'année dernière Par groupes de trois, parlez des cadeaux que vous avez achetés à votre famille et à vos amis l'année dernière. Que vous ont-ils acheté? Présentez vos réponses à la classe. *Answers will vary.*

MODÈLE

Étudiant(e) 1: *Qu'est-ce que tu as acheté à ta mère?*
Étudiant(e) 2: *Je lui ai acheté un ordinateur.*
Étudiant(e) 3: *Ma copine Dominique m'a donné une montre.*

6 Au grand magasin Par groupes de trois, jouez les rôles de deux client(e)s et d'un(e) vendeur/vendeuse. Les client(e)s cherchent des vêtements pour faire des cadeaux. Ils parlent de ce qu'ils (*what they*) cherchent et le/la vendeur/vendeuse leur fait des suggestions. *Answers will vary.*

---

4 Suggestion Have pairs write their suggestions. Encourage them to come up with multiple responses for each item.

5 Suggestion Before students begin the activity, have them make a list of gifts they gave to family members and friends, and vice versa. Then have three volunteers read the **modèle** aloud.

6 Suggestions
• Before beginning the activity, have students describe what is happening in the photo.
• Videotape the scenes in class or have students videotape themselves outside of class. Show the videos so students can critique their role-plays.

OPTIONS

Video Have students read along as you show the video episode again. Tell them to note each time an indirect object pronoun or a disjunctive pronoun is used. After the video, ask them to read the sentences they identified and to say to whom each pronoun refers.

Pairs Have students work in pairs. Tell them to write five questions they would like to ask their partner that require an indirect object pronoun in the answer. They should then take turns asking and answering each other's questions.

 **Leçon 6B**

6B.2

Section Goals

In this section, students will learn:
• regular **-re** verbs
• irregular **-re** verbs

Instructional Resources
vhlcentral.com:
Lab MP3s; SAM Answer Key;
Essayez! *and* **Mise en pratique**
answers; Lab Audioscript;
Activity Pack (Info Gap
Activities); reference tools

Suggestions
• Model the pronunciation of the **-re** verbs and have students repeat them.
• Introduce the verbs by talking about yourself and asking students follow-up questions. Examples: **Je réponds à tous mes e-mails. Et vous, répondez-vous à tous vos e-mails? D'habitude, je mets un pantalon. Aujourd'hui, j'ai mis une jupe/un costume. Et vous, que mettez-vous, en général? Je rends visite à ma famille le week-end. Rendez-vous visite à votre famille le week-end?**
• Explain that the past participles of regular **-re** verbs add **-u** to the stem. Example: **attendre: attendu.** Then say the verbs listed and have students respond with the corresponding past participles.

Regular and irregular *-re* verbs Tutorial

Point de départ You've already seen infinitives that end in **-er** and **-ir**. The infinitive forms of a third group of French verbs end in **-re**.

• Many **-re** verbs, such as **attendre** (*to wait*), follow a regular pattern of conjugation, as shown below.

attendre	
j'attends	nous attendons
tu attends	vous attendez
il/elle/on attend	ils/elles attendent

Tu **attends** devant le café?
Are you waiting in front of the café?

Nous **attendons** dans le magasin.
We're waiting in the store.

Où **attendez**-vous?
Where are you waiting?

Il faut **attendre** dans la bibliothèque.
You have to wait in the library.

• The verb **attendre** means *to wait* or *to wait for*. Unlike English, it does not require a preposition.

Marc **attend le bus**.
Marc is waiting for the bus.

Ils **attendent Robert**.
They're waiting for Robert.

Il **attend** ses parents à l'école.
He's waiting for his parents at school.

J'**attends** les soldes.
I'm waiting for a sale.

Other regular *-re* verbs			
descendre	to go down; to take down	rendre (à)	to give back, to return (to)
entendre	to hear	rendre visite (à)	to visit someone
perdre (son temps)	to lose (to waste one's time)	répondre (à)	to answer, to respond (to)
		vendre	to sell

• To form the past participle of regular **-re** verbs, drop the **-re** from the infinitive and add **-u**.

Les étudiants ont **vendu** leurs livres.
The students sold their books.

Il a **entendu** arriver la voiture de sa femme.
He heard his wife's car arrive.

J'ai **répondu** à ton e-mail.
I answered your e-mail.

Nous avons **perdu** patience.
We lost patience.

• **Rendre visite à** means *to visit a person*, while **visiter** means *to visit a place*.

Tu **rends visite à ta grand-mère** le lundi.
You visit your grandmother on Mondays.

Cécile va **visiter le musée** aujourd'hui.
Cécile is going to visit the museum today.

Avez-vous **rendu visite à vos cousins**?
Did you visit your cousins?

Nous **avons visité Rome** l'année dernière.
We visited Rome last year.

254 *deux cent cinquante-quatre*

- Some verbs whose infinitives end in **-re** are irregular.

Irregular -re verbs

	conduire *(to drive)*	mettre *(to put (on))*	rire *(to laugh)*
je	conduis	mets	ris
tu	conduis	mets	ris
il/elle/on	conduit	met	rit
nous	conduisons	mettons	rions
vous	conduisez	mettez	riez
ils/elles	conduisent	mettent	rient

Je **conduis** la voiture.
I'm driving the car.

Thérèse **met** ses gants.
Thérèse puts on her gloves.

Elles **rient** pendant le spectacle.
They laugh during the show.

Other irregular -re verbs

like *conduire*		like *mettre*	
construire	to build, to construct	permettre	to allow
détruire	to destroy	promettre	to promise
produire	to produce	**like *rire***	
réduire	to reduce		
traduire	to translate	sourire	to smile

- The past participle of the verb **mettre** is **mis**. Verbs derived from **mettre** (**permettre**, **promettre**) follow the same pattern: **permis, promis.**

  Où est-ce que tu **as mis** mes lunettes de soleil?
  Where did you put my sunglasses?

  Je lui **ai promis** de faire la cuisine.
  I promised her that I'd cook.

- The past participle of **conduire** is **conduit**. Verbs like **conduire** follow the same pattern: **construire → construit; détruire → détruit; produire → produit; réduire → réduit; traduire → traduit.**

- The past participle of **rire** is **ri**. The past participle of **sourire** is **souri**.

 Boîte à outils

The French verbs **permettre** and **promettre** are followed by the preposition **à** and an indirect object to mean *to allow someone* or *to promise someone*: **permettre à quelqu'un** and **promettre à quelqu'un**.

Leur avez-vous permis de commencer à dix heures?
Did you allow them to start at 10 o'clock?

Je te promets de ne pas partir.
I promise you I won't leave.

Essayez! Complétez les phrases avec la forme correcte du présent du verbe.

1. Ils __attendent__ (attendre) l'arrivée du train.
2. Nous __répondons__ (répondre) aux questions du professeur.
3. Je __souris__ (sourire) quand je suis heureuse.
4. Si on __construit__ (construire) trop, on __détruit__ (détruire) la nature.
5. Quand il fait froid, vous __mettez__ (mettre) un pull.
6. Est-ce que les étudiants __entendent__ (entendre) le professeur?
7. Keiko __conduit__ (conduire) sa voiture ce week-end.
8. Si le café n'est pas bon, je __mets__ (mettre) du sucre (*sugar*).

ressources

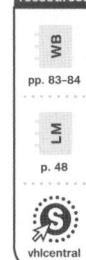

WB
pp. 83–84

LM
p. 48

vhlcentral

Suggestions
- Ask a volunteer to go to the board and write the conjugation of **donner** as you write the conjugation of **attendre**. Have students compare the endings of the two verb conjugations, noting the similarities and differences.
- Follow the same procedure with the conjugations of **conduire** and **mettre**. Point out that many irregular **-re** verbs have two stems. Examples: **conduire (condui-, conduis-)** and **mettre (met-, mett-).**
- Point out the irregular past participles.

Essayez! For additional practice, change the subjects of the sentences and have students restate them.

O P T I O N S

Extra Practice Do a rapid-response drill. Write an infinitive from the list of **-re** verbs on the board. Call out subject pronouns and/or names, and have students respond with the correct verb form. Then repeat the drill, having students respond with the correct forms of the **passé composé**.

Pairs Have students make a list of five things their parents allow them to do and five things their parents don't allow them to do. Then have them get together in pairs and compare their lists. Have volunteers report to the class the items they have in common. Example: **Mes parents ne me permettent pas de mettre des vêtements trop serrés. Ils me permettent parfois de conduire leur voiture.**

1 Suggestion Have students describe each illustration in the **passé composé**.

1 Expansion Have students create short descriptions of the people, places, and objects in the drawings by putting in additional information.

2 Expansion Ask students comprehension questions about the dialogue. Examples:
1. Pourquoi Henri n'a-t-il pas encore mangé? (Il attend Jean-Michel.) 2. Où est Jean-Michel? (Il est avec un client difficile.) 3. Pourquoi ce client est-il difficile? (parce qu'il met tout, mais il part les mains vides)

4 Expansion Have students also say what Béatrice did not do.

Mise en pratique

1 **Qui fait quoi?** Quelles phrases vont avec les illustrations?

1.   2.   3.   4.

   _3_   **a.** Martin attend ses copains.

   _4_   **b.** Nous rendons visite à notre grand-mère.

   _1_   **c.** Vous vendez de jolis vêtements.

   _2_   **d.** Je ris en regardant un film.

2 **Les clients difficiles** Henri et Gilbert travaillent pour un grand magasin. Complétez leur conversation.

GILBERT Tu n'as pas encore mangé?

HENRI Non, j' (1) _attends_ (attendre) Jean-Michel.

GILBERT Il ne (2) _descend_ (descendre) pas tout de suite. Il (3) _perd_ (perdre) son temps avec un client difficile. Il (4) _met_ (mettre) des cravates, des costumes, des chaussures...

HENRI Nous ne (5) _vendons_ (vendre) pas souvent à des clients comme ça.

GILBERT C'est vrai. Ils (6) _promettent_ (promettre) d'acheter quelque chose, puis ils partent les mains vides (*empty*).

3 **Au centre commercial** Daniel et ses copains ont passé (*spent*) la journée au centre commercial hier. Utilisez les éléments donnés pour faire des phrases complètes. Ajoutez d'autres éléments nécessaires.   Answers will vary.

1. Omar et moi / conduire / centre commercial   Omar et moi, nous avons conduit au centre commercial.
2. Guillaume / attendre / dix minutes / devant / cinéma   Guillaume a attendu dix minutes devant le cinéma.
3. Hervé et Thérèse / vendre / pulls   Hervé et Thérèse ont vendu des pulls.
4. Lise / perdre / sac à main   Lise a perdu son sac à main.
5. tu / mettre / robe / bleu   Tu as mis une robe bleue.
6. Sandrine et toi / ne pas répondre / vendeur   Sandrine et toi, vous n'avez pas répondu au vendeur.

4 **La journée de Béatrice** Hier, Béatrice a fait une liste des choses à faire. Avec un(e) partenaire, utilisez les verbes de la liste au passé composé pour dire (*to say*) tout ce qu'elle a fait.   Answers will vary.

attendre	mettre
conduire	rendre visite
entendre	traduire

1. devoir d'espagnol	*4. tante Albertine*
2. mon nouveau CD	*5. gants dans mon sac*
3. e-mail de Sébastien	*6. vieille voiture*

 Practice more at **vhlcentral.com**.

Communication

5 **Fréquence** Employez les verbes de la liste et d'autres verbes pour dire (*to tell*) à un(e) partenaire ce que (*what*) vous faites tous les jours, une fois par mois et une fois par an. Alternez les rôles. Answers will vary.

MODÈLE

Étudiant(e) 1: *J'attends mes copains au resto U tous les jours.*
Étudiant(e) 2: *Moi, je rends visite à mes grands-parents une fois par mois.*

attendre	perdre
conduire	rendre
entendre	répondre
mettre	sourire

6 **Les charades** Par groupes de quatre, jouez aux charades. Chaque étudiant(e) pense à une phrase différente avec un des verbes en **-re**. La première personne qui devine (*guesses*) propose la prochaine charade. Answers will vary.

7 **Questions personnelles** Avec un(e) partenaire, posez-vous ces questions à tour de rôle.

1. Réponds-tu tout de suite (*immediately*) à tes e-mails?
2. As-tu promis à tes parents de faire quelque chose? Quoi?
3. Que mets-tu quand tu vas à un mariage? Pour aller à l'école? Pour sortir avec des copains?
4. Tes parents te permettent-ils de sortir tard pendant la semaine?
5. Conduis-tu la voiture de tes parents? Comment conduis-tu?
6. À qui rends-tu visite pendant les vacances?
7. Quelle est la dernière fois que tu as beaucoup ri? Avec qui?
8. As-tu déjà vendu quelque chose sur Internet? Quoi?

8 **La journée des vendeuses** Votre professeur va vous donner, à vous et à votre partenaire, une série d'illustrations qui montrent la journée d'Aude et d'Aurélie. Attention! Ne regardez pas la feuille de votre partenaire. Answers will vary.

MODÈLE

Étudiant(e) 1: *Le matin, elles ont conduit pour aller au magasin.*
Étudiant(e) 2: *Après,...*

---

5 **Suggestion** Have two volunteers read the **modèle** aloud.

5 **Expansion** To practice the **passé composé**, have students specify when they did these things. Example: **J'ai rendu visite à mes grands-parents en avril.**

6 **Suggestion** This activity can also be used as a game by dividing the class into two teams with players from each team acting out the charades.

7 **Expansion** When pairs are done with the activity, have them share with the class some areas where they differ from their partner. Example: **Mes parents ne me permettent pas de sortir tard mais les parents de Gina lui permettent de sortir très tard le week-end.**

8 **Suggestion** Divide the class into pairs and distribute the Info Gap Handouts found in the Activity Pack on the instructor Supersite.

OPTIONS

Extra Practice Ask students personalized questions using **-re** verbs. Examples: **1. Comment les étudiants perdent-ils leur temps? 2. Est-ce que l'argent rend les gens heureux? 3. Que vend-on dans une boutique? 4. Vos parents vous permettent-ils d'avoir une carte de crédit à la fac? 5. Conduisez-vous rapidement? 6. Où mettez-vous vos livres en classe?**

Pairs Have students work in pairs. Tell them to write a conversation between a clerk in a clothing store and a customer who has lost some item like sunglasses, a scarf, or gloves. The customer should explain the situation, and the clerk should ask for details, such as when the item was lost and a description. Alternatively, pairs can role-play this situation.

Révision

Instructional Resources
vhlcentral.com:
Activity Pack (Info Gap
Activities); Testing Program;
Testing Program MP3s;
reference tools

1 Suggestion Have two
volunteers read the **modèle**
aloud. Remind students that
they need to use the preposition
à before the indirect object in
the questions.

2 Expansion Take a quick
class survey of students'
reactions to each type of e-mail.
Tally the results on the board.

3 Suggestion Before beginning
the activity, have students jot
down a list of objects.

4 Suggestion Before
beginning, have the class identify
the items in each **ensemble**.

4 Expansion Have students
think of two new destinations.
Tell them to switch roles and
repeat the activity.

5 Suggestion Encourage
students to use some of the
comments in the **Expressions
utiles** on page 247 in their
role-plays.

6 Suggestion Divide the class
into pairs and distribute the
Info Gap Handouts found in the
Activity Pack on the Supersite.

---

1 Je leur téléphone Par groupes de quatre, interviewez
vos camarades. Préparez dix questions avec un verbe et une
personne de la liste. Écrivez les réponses. Answers will vary.

MODÈLE

Étudiant(e) 1: *Est-ce que tu parles souvent à ton frère?*
Étudiant(e) 2: *Oui, je lui parle le lundi.*

verbes	personnes
donner un cadeau	copain ou copine d'enfance
envoyer une carte/un e-mail	cousin ou cousine
parler	grands-parents
rendre visite	petit(e) ami(e)
téléphoner	sœur ou frère

2 Mes e-mails Ces personnes vous envoient des e-mails.
Que faites-vous? Vous ne répondez pas, vous attendez
quelques jours, vous leur téléphonez? Par groupes de trois,
comparez vos réactions. Answers will vary.

MODÈLE

Étudiant(e) 1: *Ma mère m'envoie un e-mail tous les jours.*
Étudiant(e) 2: *Tu lui réponds tout de suite?*
Étudiant(e) 3: *Tu préfères lui téléphoner?*

1. un e-mail anonyme
2. un e-mail d'un(e) camarade de classe
3. un e-mail d'un professeur
4. un e-mail d'un(e) ami(e) d'enfance
5. un e-mail d'un(e) ex-petit(e) ami(e)
6. un e-mail de vos parents

3 Une liste Des membres de votre famille ou des amis vous
ont donné ou acheté des vêtements que vous n'aimez pas
du tout. Faites une liste de quatre ou cinq de ces vêtements.
Comparez votre liste à la liste d'un(e) camarade. Answers will vary.

MODÈLE

Étudiant(e) 1: *Ma soeur m'a donné une écharpe verte et
laide et mon père m'a acheté des chaussettes marron
trop petites!*
Étudiant(e) 2: *L'année dernière, mon petit ami m'a donné...*

---

4 Quoi mettre? Vous et votre partenaire allez faire des
choses différentes. Un(e) partenaire va fêter la retraite de ses
parents à Tahiti. L'autre va skier dans les Alpes. Qu'allez-vous
porter? Demandez des vêtements à votre partenaire si vous
n'aimez pas tous les vêtements de votre ensemble. Answers will vary.

MODÈLE

Étudiant(e) 1: *Est-ce que tu me prêtes ton tee-shirt violet?*
Étudiant(e) 2: *Ah non, j'ai besoin de ce tee-shirt. Tu me
prêtes ton pantalon?*

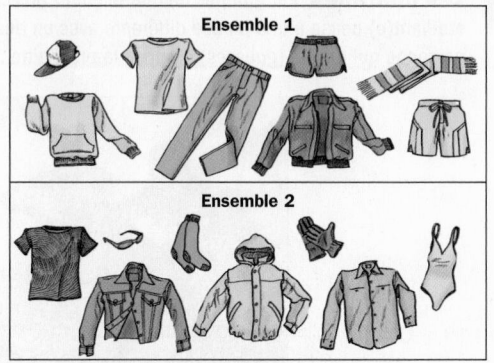

Ensemble 1

Ensemble 2

5 S'il te plaît Votre ami(e) a acheté un nouveau vêtement
que vous aimez beaucoup. Vous essayez de convaincre
(*to convince*) cet(te) ami(e) de vous prêter ce vêtement.
Préparez un dialogue avec un(e) partenaire où vous employez
tous les verbes. Jouez la scène pour la classe. Answers will vary.

aller avec	montrer
aller bien	prêter
donner	promettre
mettre	rendre

6 Bon anniversaire, Nicolas! Votre professeur va
vous donner, à vous et à votre partenaire, deux feuilles
d'activités différentes. Attention! Ne regardez pas la feuille
de votre partenaire. Answers will vary.

MODÈLE

Étudiant(e) 1: *Les amis de Nicolas lui téléphonent.*
Étudiant(e) 2: *Ensuite, ...*

OPTIONS

Small Groups Have students work in groups of three. Tell them
to imagine that it is the holiday season. They have to create a
radio commercial for a clothing store. The commercials should
include gift ideas for prospective customers, such as what they
can buy, for whom, and at what price.

Extra Practice Have students write a conversation between
two people sitting at a busy sidewalk café in the city. They are
watching the people who walk by, asking each other questions
about what the passersby are doing, and making comments
about their clothing. Tell students to use as many **-re** verbs and
verbs that take indirect object pronouns as possible.

À l'écoute

Audio: Activities

STRATÉGIE

Listening for linguistic cues

You can enhance your listening comprehension by listening for specific linguistic cues. For example, if you listen for the endings of conjugated verbs, or for familiar constructions, such as the **passé composé** with **avoir**, **avoir envie de** + [*infinitive*] or **aller** + [*infinitive*], you can find out whether a person did something in the past, wants to do something, or will do something in the future.

🔊 To practice listening for linguistic cues, you will listen to four sentences. As you listen, note whether each sentence refers to a past, present, or future action.

Préparation

Regardez la photo. Où sont Pauline et Sarah? Que font-elles? Décrivez les vêtements qu'elles regardent. À votre avis, pour quelle occasion cherchent-elles des vêtements?

À vous d'écouter

Écoutez la conversation entre Pauline et Sarah. Après une deuxième écoute, indiquez si les actions suivantes sont du **passé (p)**, du **présent (pr)** ou du **futur (f)**.

p 1. aller à la fête de la cousine de Pauline

p 2. beaucoup danser

p 3. rencontrer un musicien

f 4. déjeuner avec un garçon intéressant

pr 5. chercher de nouveaux vêtements

f 6. mettre des chaussures en cuir noir

pr 7. aimer une robe bleue

f 8. acheter la robe bleue

 Practice more at **vhlcentral.com**.

Compréhension

Complétez Complétez les phrases.

1. Pauline cherche des vêtements pour _c_.
   a. un dîner   b. une fête   c. un rendez-vous

2. Pauline va acheter un pantalon noir et _b_.
   a. un tee-shirt   b. une chemise rose   c. un maillot de bain

3. Sarah pense que _b_ ne vont pas avec les nouveaux vêtements.
   a. l'écharpe verte   b. les baskets roses   c. les lunettes de soleil

4. D'après Sarah, les chaussures _a_ sont élégantes.
   a. en cuir noir   b. roses   c. en soie

5. La couleur préférée de Sarah n'est pas le _c_.
   a. rose   b. jaune   c. vert

6. Sarah cherche un vêtement pour _b_.
   a. un déjeuner   b. la fête de retraite de son père   c. un mariage

7. Sarah va acheter une robe en soie _a_.
   a. à manches courtes   b. à manches longues   c. rouge

8. La robe existe en vert, en bleu et en _c_.
   a. noir   b. marron   c. blanc

Une occasion spéciale Décrivez la dernière fois que vous avez fêté une occasion spéciale. Qu'est-ce que vous avez fêté? Où? Comment? Avec qui? Qu'est-ce que vous avez mis comme vêtements? Et les autres?

MODÈLE

Samedi, nous avons fêté l'anniversaire de mon petit ami. Nous avons invité nos amis Paul, Marc, Julia et Naomi dans un restaurant élégant. Moi, j'ai mis une belle robe verte en coton. Mon petit ami a mis un costume gris. Paul a mis...

deux cent cinquante neuf **259**

Section Goals

In this section, students will:
• learn to listen for specific linguistic cues
• listen for temporal cues in sentences
• listen to a conversation and complete several activities

Instructional Resources
vhlcentral.com:
Textbook MP3s; Textbook Audioscript; reference tools

Stratégie
Audioscript 1. Est-ce que tu vas aller au mariage de tes cousins? (*future*) 2. Elles ont acheté dix nouveaux maillots de bain pour cet été! (*past*) 3. Noémie a envie de parler à Martha de son rendez-vous avec Julien. (*present*) 4. Vous avez vendu tous les tee-shirts? (*past*)

Préparation Have students look at the photo of Pauline and Sarah, describe what they see, and predict what they are talking about.

À vous d'écouter
Audioscript PAULINE: Tiens, bonjour, Sarah. Ça va?
SARAH: Ah, bonjour Pauline! Oui, très bien et toi?
P: Bien, merci. Dis, je t'ai cherchée hier soir à la fête de ma cousine...
S: Excuse-moi. J'ai passé une mauvaise journée hier et j'ai complètement oublié. Mais... Et toi? Tu as aimé la fête?
P: Oui, j'ai beaucoup dansé et j'ai rencontré un garçon intéressant. Il s'appelle Boris et il est musicien. Je vais déjeuner avec lui demain midi, alors je cherche de nouveaux vêtements pour notre rendez-vous. Qu'est-ce que tu penses de ce pantalon noir avec cette chemise rose?
S: Oui, c'est bien. Et qu'est-ce que tu vas mettre comme chaussures?
P: Ben, ces baskets roses, non?
S: Ah non. Des chaussures en cuir noir, c'est plus élégant.
P: Oui, tu as raison. Et toi, qu'est-ce que tu cherches?
S: Une jolie robe pas trop chère.
P: Tu as un rendez-vous, toi aussi?

S: Non, c'est pour la fête de départ en retraite de mon père. C'est samedi prochain.
P: Regarde cette robe rouge en coton. Elle est jolie, non?
S: Oui, mais elle a l'air un peu serrée. Je préfère les robes larges.

P: Et cette belle robe en soie à manches courtes?
S: Je déteste le vert. Ils l'ont en bleu?
P: Oui, et en blanc aussi.
S: Super. Je vais prendre la bleue.

Panorama

(S) Interactive Map

connections cultures
NATIONAL STANDARDS

LA FRANCE

L'OCÉAN ATLANTIQUE
LE PORTUGAL
L'ESPAGNE
LA MER MÉDITERRANÉE

Le Theatre d'O

Sétif
Alger
Oran   Constantine
Tlemecen

LES CHAÎNES DE L'ATLAS

LA TUNISIE

LE MAROC

L'ALGÉRIE

LA L

LE SAHARA OCCIDENTAL

LA MAURITANIE

LE   S A H A R A

LE MALI

L'Algérie

Le pays en chiffres

▶ **Superficie:** *2.381.741 km²*

▶ **Population:** *39.447.000*

SOURCE: Population Division, UN Secretariat

▶ **Industries principales:** *agriculture, gaz naturel, acier et métallurgie, pétrole°*

▶ **Ville capitale:** *Alger*

▶ **Monnaie:** *dinar algérien*

▶ **Langues:** *arabe, français*

L'Algérie est un paradoxe francophone. Environ la moitié des Algériens parlent français. C'est donc le second plus grand pays francophone du monde, après la France. Cependant, pour des raisons historiques datant de l'époque de la colonisation, l'Algérie n'a pas souhaité rejoindre l'Organisation internationale de la Francophonie.

Personnages célèbres

▶ Mohamed Fellag, *acteur, humoriste* (1950–)

 Khaled, *chanteur* (1960–)

 Albert Camus, *écrivain* (1913–1960)

 Hélène Cixous, *écrivaine* (1937–)

pétrole *oil* **renard** *fox* **pèse** *weighs* **chat** *cat* **oreilles** *ears* **sable** *sand*

Algeria Sahara Desert

un café à Tlemcen, en Algérie

Incroyable mais vrai!

Le fennec est un petit renard° des déserts d'Afrique du Nord: il mesure environ 20 centimètres et pèse° moins de deux kilogrammes, ce qui est plus petit qu'un chat°! Le fennec a de très longues oreilles° et une fourrure blanche et beige, comme le sable°. C'est l'animal symbolique de l'Algérie et la mascotte de son équipe de football.

Section Goals

In this section, students will learn historical, geographical, and cultural information about **l'Algérie**.

Instructional Resources
vhlcentral.com:
Digital Image Bank;
SAM Answer Key;
reference tools

Carte de l'Algérie

- Have students look at the map or use the **Panorama** map from the Digital Image Bank. Ask volunteers to read the names of the cities and geographical features aloud.
- Tell students the southern region of Algeria is sparsely populated due to the harsh conditions of the Sahara Desert, which covers about 80 percent of the territory.
- Point out that Algeria is the second largest African country.
- The word *Sahara* comes from *Sahra'*, which means *desert* in Arabic. In reality, the Sahara is not one desert but many deserts. It encompasses 3.5 million square miles and extends over portions of 11 countries.

Le pays en chiffres

- Have volunteers read the sections aloud. After each section, ask students questions about the content.
- Algeria produces large amounts of tobacco, citrus fruits, and olives.
- The **Algerian War** took place from 1954 to 1962. As a result, Algeria gained its independence from France.

Incroyable mais vrai!

The fennec fox's large ears radiate body heat and help keep it cool in its desert habitat. Thick fur protects it from cold nights and hot daytime sun, and the fur on its paws protects it from hot sand.

OPTIONS

Personnes célèbres Mohamed Fellag is known in Algeria for his work in theater and internationally for his comedy and acting. His first French-language comedy show, *Djurdjurassique Bled*, chronicled the history of Algeria. **Khaled** is the most famous singer of **raï**, the urban music developed in Oran in the 1970s. His greatest hits are "Didi" and "Aïcha." In addition to writing novels, **Albert Camus** was active in theater as a producer and a playwright. He founded the Algerian theater group **L'Équipe** in 1937. **Hélène Cixous** has written works of poetic fiction, literary theory, feminist analysis, and theater. Her work centers on ethnogrophy and **écriture féminine**.

Les arts

Assia Djebar (1936–2015)

Lauréate de nombreux prix littéraires et cinématographiques, Assia Djebar fait partie des écrivains et cinéastes algériens les plus talentueux. Dans ses œuvres°, Djebar présente le point de vue° féminin avec l'intention de donner une voix° aux femmes algériennes. *La Soif*, son premier roman°, sort en 1957. C'est plus tard, pendant qu'elle enseigne l'histoire à l'université d'Alger, qu'elle devient cinéaste et sort son premier film, *La Nouba des femmes du Mont Chenoua*, en 1979. Le film reçoit le prix de la critique internationale au festival du film de Venise. En 2005, Assia Djebar devient le premier écrivain du Maghreb, homme ou femme, à être élue° à l'Académie française.

La gastronomie

Le couscous

Le couscous est sans doute le plat d'origine berbère le plus populaire dans le monde. Le mot «couscous» désigne à la fois la semoule de blé dur° qui forme la base du plat et la préparation elle-même. Traditionnellement, on prépare le couscous dans un couscoussier: les légumes et la viande cuisent à feu doux° dans la partie inférieure et produisent de la vapeur pour la cuisson° de la semoule placée au-dessus. Il existe de nombreuses variantes de couscous. Toutes ont des légumes, mais peuvent être aussi accompagnées de différentes viandes ou de poisson. Le couscous se mange salé ou sucré, froid ou chaud. C'est l'un des trois plats préférés des Français!

Les destinations

La Casbah d'Alger

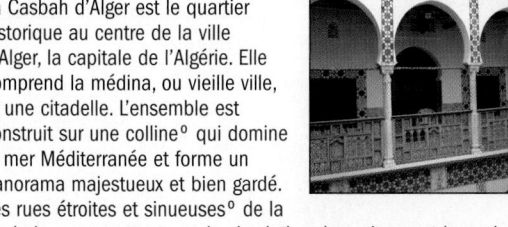

La Casbah d'Alger est le quartier historique au centre de la ville d'Alger, la capitale de l'Algérie. Elle comprend la médina, ou vieille ville, et une citadelle. L'ensemble est construit sur une colline° qui domine la mer Méditerranée et forme un panorama majestueux et bien gardé. Les rues étroites et sinueuses° de la Casbah ne permettent pas la circulation des voitures et la couleur blanche de ses maisons est devenue le symbole de la ville d'Alger. L'origine de la Casbah remonte à l'époque antique et aux Phéniciens, mais la Casbah occupe toujours une place importante dans la culture et la société algériennes modernes. C'est un port d'entrée pour les migrants ruraux et un des foyers° de la culture populaire algérienne. La Casbah est classée au patrimoine mondial de l'Unesco depuis 1992.

Les gens

Les Touareg, peuple du désert

Les Touareg sont un peuple du désert qui vit dans cinq pays africains différents. Leur territoire s'appelle «tinariwen», ce qui veut dire «les déserts», et leur mode de vie est traditionnellement nomade, c'est-à-dire qu'ils se déplacent avec les saisons et ne vivent pas toujours au même endroit. Pendant la saison des pluies, en été, ils emmènent leurs troupeaux dans les prairies° au sud du Sahara. À la saison sèche°, ils vont dans les endroits qui ont des ressources en eau permanentes et des arbres°. Les Touareg sont aussi surnommés les «hommes bleus», car ils portent souvent un turban de cette couleur qui déteint° sur leur peau°.

Qu'est-ce que vous avez appris? Répondez aux questions par des phrases complètes.

1. Quel animal symbolise l'Algérie?
   C'est le fennec.
2. Qui est le premier écrivain du Maghreb élu à l'Académie française?
   C'est l'écrivaine algérienne Assia Djebar.
3. Quelle est l'intention principale d'Assia Djebar dans ses œuvres?
   Elle veut donner une voix aux femmes algériennes.
4. Dans quoi est-ce qu'on prépare le couscous?
   On prépare le couscous dans un couscoussier.
5. Est-ce que le couscous est un plat populaire en France?
   C'est un des trois plats préférés des Français.

6. Comment est-ce qu'on mange le couscous?
   On mange le couscous salé ou sucré, et froid ou chaud.
7. Qu'est-ce que la médina à Alger?
   C'est la vieille ville.
8. De quelle couleur sont les maisons de la Casbah d'Alger?
   Les maisons de la Casbah d'Alger sont blanches.
9. Comment s'appelle le territoire des Touareg?
   Le territoire des Touareg s'appelle «tinariwen».
10. Comment est-ce qu'on surnomme les Touareg?
    On surnomme les Touareg les «hommes bleus».

ressources

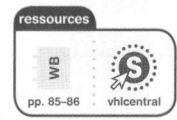

WB
pp. 85–86

vhlcentral

Sur Internet

Go to **vhlcentral.com** to find more cultural information related to this **Panorama**.

1. Trouvez une recette de couscous. Quelle est la liste des ingrédients et quelles sont les étapes de sa préparation?

2. Cherchez des informations sur le raï, un genre de musique qui vient d'Algérie. Trouvez une ou deux chanson(s) de raï. Est-ce que vous aimez ce style de musique? Pourquoi?

3. Trouvez des photos de la Casbah d'Alger. Comment sont son architecture et le style de ses maisons?

œuvres *works* **point de vue** *viewpoint* **voix** *voice* **roman** *novel* **à être élue** *to be elected* **semoule de blé dur** *hard wheat semolina* **cuisent à feux doux** *cook gently* **cuisson** *cooking* **colline** *hill* **étroites et sinueuses** *narrow and winding* **foyers** *centers* **prairies** *meadows* **sèche** *dry* **arbres** *trees* **déteint** *rubs off* **peau** *skin*

Assia Djebar (1936–2015)
Assia Djebar (whose given name was Fatima-Zohra Imalayen) is the best-known and most prolific Algerian female writer. She chronicled the complexities and evolution of life for North African women in the Muslim world. Her works have been translated into over 20 languages.

Le couscous
In Tunisia, couscous is usually served with a spicy harissa sauce. In Algeria and Morocco, a sweet version of the dish is made with almonds, cinnamon, sugar, and orange flower water.

La Casbah d'Alger
The **bataille d'Alger** in 1957 and many earthquakes have damaged many of the structures in the **Casbah d'Alger**. To return the Casbah to its original splendor, the Algerian government gives monetary grants to residents who wish to restore their homes.

O P T I O N S

Cultural Activity Assign groups of three or four students one of the UNESCO World Heritage sites in Algeria (**Tipasa, Al Qal'a of Beni Hammad, Dj'emila, M'Zab Valley, Timgad, Tassili n'Ajjer**). Have students research the site at www.unesco.org and write a brief description, including location and history. Encourage students to include photos of the site. Have the groups present their findings to the class.

Les Touaregs The **Touaregs** of Djanet, an oasis in southeastern Algeria, celebrate the annual **la Sebeiba** festival, an ancient tradition featuring jousting, dancing, music, and traditional dress. Djanet is an important stopover for **Touaregs** on the caravan route. Several thousand French visitors come to Djanet each year to explore the nearby Tassili N'Ajjer National Park.

Section Goals

In this section, students will learn historical, geographical, and cultural information about **le Maroc et la Tunisie**.

Instructional Resources
vhlcentral.com:
Digital Image Bank;
SAM Answer Key;
reference tools

Carte du Maroc et de la Tunisie
- Have students look at the map or use the **Panorama** map from the Digital Image Bank. Ask volunteers to read the names of the cities and geographical features aloud.
- Ask students to name the countries that border Morocco and Tunisia.
- Point out that Douz (see photo) is an oasis on the edge of the Sahara Desert.

Le pays en chiffres
- Point out the flag. Ask students what elements the flags of Algeria (see p. 260), Morocco, and Tunisia have in common. Then explain that the crescent, star, and color green are traditional symbols of Islam.
- Point out that Morocco is a kingdom.
- Have volunteers read the sections aloud. After each section, ask students questions about the content.
- Ask students: **Où est la Tour Hassan? (à Rabat)** Then point out that approximately 98% of the population in these countries is Muslim.

Incroyable mais vrai!
Casablanca's downtown mixes French-colonial and traditional Moroccan architecture. The Hassan-II mosque is the largest in the Maghreb, and one of the most luxurious. Casablanca houses nearly 60% of Morocco's economic activity, attracting young people from around the country. The city embraces modern European urbanism and is looking to the future.

Panorama

Interactive Map

Marché de Douz

Le Maroc

Le pays en chiffres

▶ **Superficie:** *710.850 km²*
▶ **Population:** *34.378.000*
▶ **Industries principales:** *agriculture, tourisme*
▶ **Ville capitale:** *Rabat*
▶ **Monnaie:** *dirham*
▶ **Langues:** *arabe, français*

La Tunisie

Le pays en chiffres

▶ **Superficie:** *163.610 km²*
▶ **Population:** *11.254.000*
▶ **Industries principales:** *agriculture, tourisme*
▶ **Ville capitale:** *Tunis*
▶ **Monnaie:** *dinar tunisien*
▶ **Langues:** *arabe, français*

Personnages célèbres

▶ Juliette Smaja-Zerah, *Tunisie,*
première avocate de Tunisie
(1890–1973)

▶  Nezha Chekrouni, *Maroc,*
politicienne
(1955–)

▶  Hicham El Guerrouj, *Maroc,*
athlète
(1974–)

▶  Albert Memmi, *Tunisie,*
écrivain
(1920–)

Pourtant *Yet* **tourné** *shot*

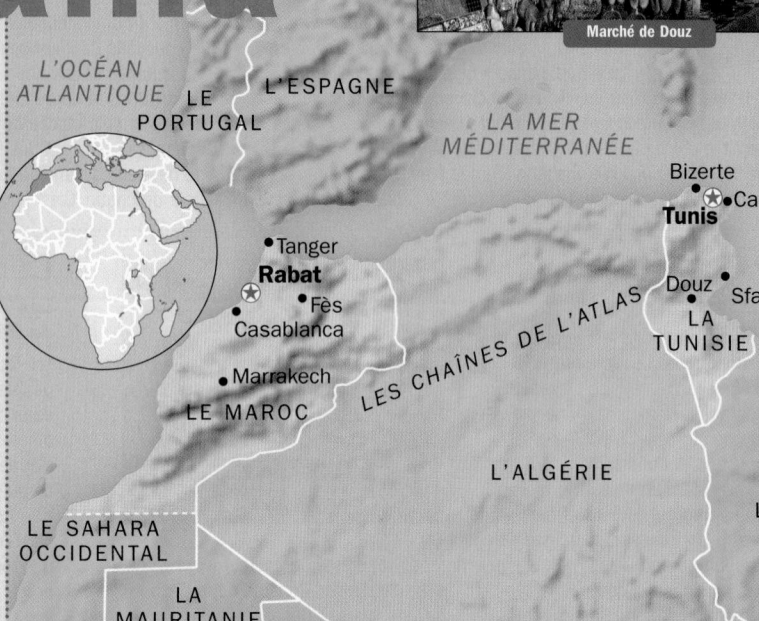

L'OCÉAN ATLANTIQUE • LE PORTUGAL • L'ESPAGNE
LA MER MÉDITERRANÉE
Bizerte
Carthag
Tunis
Tanger
Rabat
Fès
Casablanca
Douz • Sfax
LA TUNISIE
Marrakech
LES CHAÎNES DE L'ATLAS
LE MAROC
L'ALGÉRIE
LA L
LE SAHARA OCCIDENTAL
LA MAURITANIE
LE SAHARA
LE MALI

Tour Hassan, Rabat

Vieux port de Bizerte

Incroyable mais vrai!

La ville de Casablanca est associée à un grand classique du cinéma américain des années 1940, avec Humphrey Bogart et Ingrid Bergman. Pourtant°, ce film a été tourné° à 6.000 kilomètres de là, dans les studios d'Hollywood, et pas du tout à Casablanca! Cette ville est aujourd'hui la plus grande métropole du Maghreb et un des plus importants centres urbains d'Afrique.

262 *deux cent soixante-deux*

OPTIONS

Personnes célèbres **Juliette Smaja-Zerah** was the daughter of Mardoché Smadja, editor-in-chief of the newspaper *La Justice*. **Nezha Chekrouni** taught linguistics at the University of Meknès and was a fellow at Harvard University. She served as Secretary of State in Morocco and became Ambassador of Morocco to Canada in 2009. **Hicham El Guerrouj** won two gold medals in the 1500- and 5000-meter races at the 2004 Athens Olympics, the first person to do so since 1924. He is considered the greatest middle-distance runner of all time. **Albert Memmi**'s literary works address the difficulty of balancing multiple cultural identities, based on his own experiences.

Les régions

Le Maghreb

La région du Maghreb, en Afrique du Nord, est composée du Maroc, de l'Algérie et de la Tunisie. Envahis° aux VIIe et VIIIe siècles par les Arabes, les trois pays deviennent plus tard des colonies françaises avant de retrouver leur indépendance dans les années 1950–1960. La population du Maghreb est composée d'Arabes, d'Européens et de Berbères, les premiers habitants de l'Afrique du Nord. Le Grand Maghreb inclut ces trois pays, plus la Libye et la Mauritanie. En 1989, les cinq pays ont formé l'Union du Maghreb Arabe dans l'espoir° de créer une union politique et économique. Mais le projet a été ralenti° par des tensions entre l'Algérie et le Maroc à propos du Sahara occidental°.

Les gens

Gad Elmaleh

Né à Casablanca, Gad Elmaleh a commencé sa carrière d'humoriste° et d'acteur en France, après avoir fait des études de sciences politiques à Montréal. Il écrit et joue ses spectacles°, dans lesquels il incarne des personnages hilarants, dont plusieurs sont devenus des personnages cultes connus° de tous les Français. Ainsi, Chouchou, un personnage de travesti° romantique, a inspiré un film du même nom sorti en 2002 et vu par 4 millions de spectateurs°. La carrière cinématographique de Gad Elmaleh comprend° aussi des films avec Steven Spielberg et Woody Allen. En 2015, il joue à New York *Oh My Gad*, un spectacle écrit en anglais, à la suite duquel° les médias américains le décrivent comme le Jerry Seinfeld français.

Les destinations

Site archéologique de Carthage

«Il faut détruire Carthage!», une phrase célèbre prononcée par Caton l'Ancien devant le Sénat romain, est aujourd'hui le synonyme de l'idée d'acharnement°. Située sur la côte de la Tunisie actuelle, Carthage était°, dans l'Antiquité, une ville phénicienne qui menaçait° la puissance maritime, économique et militaire de Rome. Après trois guerres et un siège de quatre ans, Rome réussit enfin à atteindre son objectif et à détruire la ville. Les restes de cette époque antique dite «punique» sont dispersés à travers la Carthage moderne et forment un grand site archéologique fragmenté. Ce site est classé au patrimoine mondial de l'Unesco depuis 1989, mais il est aujourd'hui menacé par les constructions et le développement urbain.

Les traditions

Les hammams

Inventés par les Romains et adoptés par les Arabes, les hammams, ou «bains turcs», sont très nombreux et populaires en Afrique du Nord. Ce sont des bains de vapeur° composés de plusieurs pièces—souvent trois—où la chaleur est plus ou moins forte. L'architecture des hammams varie d'un endroit à un autre, mais ces bains de vapeur servent tous de lieux où se laver et de centres sociaux très importants dans la culture régionale. Les gens s'y réunissent aux grandes occasions de la vie, comme pour les mariages et les naissances, et y vont aussi de manière habituelle pour se détendre et bavarder entre amis.

Le Maghreb

In Arabic, *Maghreb* means *west*. Prior to the Arab conquest, the Maghreb region was part of the Roman Empire.

Gad Elmaleh

One of Gad Elmaleh's most famous sketches includes the phrase, "Where is Brian?" Many schoolchildren in the francophone world began learning English with an exercise based on this phrase or one similar to it.

Site archéologique de Carthage

After Rome destroyed Carthage, the Romans rebuilt the town on the ruins of the former city. Carthage was the home of Hannibal, the military genius who later crossed the Alps, as well as the navigator-explorer Hannon.

Les hammams

- The **hammams** usually offer separate quarters or special days for men and women. The experience begins with a warm steam room where people relax and socialize, then a massage and an exfoliating scrub and soak, ending with a period of relaxation.
- Ask students: **Avez-vous déjà pris un bain turc? Où? Comment vous êtes-vous senti(e)(s) après le bain?**

Qu'est-ce que vous avez appris? Répondez aux questions par des phrases complètes.

1. Où a été tourné le film *Casablanca*?
   Le film *Casablanca* a été tourné dans les studios d'Hollywood.
2. Quels sont les trois pays principaux du Maghreb?
   Ce sont le Maroc, l'Algérie et la Tunisie.
3. De quels groupes ethniques est composée la population du Maghreb?
   La population du Maghreb est composée d'Arabes, d'Européens et de Berbères.
4. Où est né Gad Elmaleh?
   Il est né à Casablanca.
5. À qui est-ce que les médias américains comparent Gad Elmaleh?
   Les médias américains comparent Gad Elmaleh à Jerry Seinfeld.

6. Quelle est la phrase célèbre prononcée par Caton devant le Sénat romain?
   «Il faut détruire Carthage!»
7. À quelle culture la ville de Carthage est-elle associée pendant l'Antiquité?
   Carthage est une ville phénicienne.
8. Où sont les restes de la ville antique de Carthage?
   Ils sont dispersés à travers la ville.
9. Qui a inventé les hammams?
   Les Romains ont inventé les hammams.
10. Combien de pièces les hammams ont-ils en général?
   Les hammams ont souvent trois pièces.

Sur Internet

Go to **vhlcentral.com** to find more cultural information related to this **Panorama**.

1. Carthage a plusieurs sites archéologiques célèbres à visiter, comme les thermes d'Antonin, le théâtre ou l'amphithéâtre. Lequel de ces lieux vous intéresse le plus et pourquoi?

2. Quel est le but de l'association L'Mdina Wel Rabtine à Tunis et quelles initiatives propose-t-elle pour sauver les hammams de la ville?

3. Qui sont les Berbères et quelle influence ont-ils eue sur l'histoire du Maghreb?

ressources

WB
pp. 87–88

vhlcentral

Envahis *Invaded* **espoir** *hope* **ralenti** *slowed down* **occidental** *Western* **humoriste** *comedian* **spectacles** *shows* **connus** *known* **travesti** *transvestite* **spectateurs** *audience* **comprend** *includes* **à la suite duquel** *after which* **acharnement** *relentlessness* **était** *was* **menaçait** *was threatening* **bains de vapeur** *steam baths*

OPTIONS

Cultural Comparison Have students work in groups of three. Tell them to compare a **hammam** to a spa in the United States. Have them list the similarities and differences in a two-column chart under the headings **Similitudes** and **Différences**. Then have two groups get together to compare their lists.

Cultural Activity Have students discuss the various elements these two countries have in common. Tell them to give specific examples. Ask: **Quels sont les éléments que ces deux pays ont en commun?** Examples: **les langues, la religion, l'histoire et la culture**.

Section Goals

In this section, students will:
- learn to recognize word families
- read an invitation to an engagement celebration

Stratégie Write **inviter** on the board and ask students what it means. Next to it, write **invitation** and **invité(e)**, then ask them the meaning of these words. Point out that all three words have the same root and belong to a word family. Explain that recognizing the relationship between a known word and unfamiliar words can help them infer the meaning of words they don't know.

Examinez le texte Tell students to scan the text for the new words and try to guess their meaning based on the root and context before they look them up in the dictionary.

Familles de mots Point out the three categories of words. You might want to tell students to look for the words in the **Vocabulaire** on page 268.

Lecture  🅢 Audio: Reading

Avant la lecture

STRATÉGIE

Recognizing word families

Recognizing related words can help you guess the meaning of words in context, ensuring better comprehension of a reading selection. Using this strategy will enrich your French vocabulary.

Examinez le texte

Voici quelques mots que vous avez déjà appris. Pour chaque mot, trouvez un terme de la même famille dans le texte et utilisez un dictionnaire pour donner son équivalent en anglais.

MODÈLE

ami	_amitié_	_friendship_
1 diplôme	diplômés	graduates
2. commencer	le commencement	beginning
3. sortir	la sortie	exit
4. timide	la timidité	shyness
5. difficile	les difficultés	difficulties
6. préférer	les préférences	preferences

👥 Familles de mots

Avec un(e) partenaire, trouvez le bon mot pour compléter chaque famille de mots. (Note: vous avez appris tous les mots qui manquent (*all the missing words*) dans cette unité et il y a un mot de chaque famille dans le texte.)

MODÈLE

attendre	_l'attente_	_attendu(e)_
VERBE	**NOM**	**ADJECTIF**
1. boire	la boisson	bu(e)
2. fêter	la fête	festif/festive
3. vivre	la vie	vif/vive
4. rajeunir	la jeunesse	jeune
5. surprendre	la surprise	surpris(e)
6. répondre	la réponse	répondu(e)

Ça y est,° c'est officie

Bravo, jeunes diplômés°! C'est le commencement d'une nouvelle vie. Il est maintenant temps de fêter ça!

Pour faire retomber la pression°, Mathilde, Christophe, Alexandre et Laurence vous invitent à fêter entre amis votre diplôme bien mérité°!

À laisser chez vous:
La timidité, la fatigue, les soucis° et les difficultés des études et de la vie quotidienne° pour une ambiance festive

Quoi d'autre?
Un groupe de musique (le frère de Mathilde et sa bande) va venir° jouer pour nous!

264 *deux cent soixante-quatre*

Extra Practice Write these words on the board. At least one form will be familiar to students. Have them discuss the relationship between the words and their meanings. **1.** idée, idéal(e), idéaliste, idéalement, idéaliser **2.** organiser, organisateur/organisatrice, organisation, organisationnel(le), **3.** chanter, chanteur/chanteuse, chansonnette, chanson, chantable

Pairs Working in pairs, have students discuss whether or not they would attend a party like the one in the selection. Tell them to talk about the aspects of the activities that they do and do not like. Afterwards, ask them if they have ever attended a similar event and what types of activities were planned for the guests.

À apporter:
Nourriture° et boissons: Chaque invité apporte quelque chose pour le buffet: salades, plats° froids/chauds, fruits, desserts, boissons
Activités: Jeux de cartes, ballons°, autres jeux selon° vos préférences, chaises pliantes°, maillot de bain (pour la piscine), crème solaire
Surprenez-nous!

Quand:
Le samedi 16 juillet (de 16h00 à minuit)

Où:
Chez les parents de Laurence, 14 route des Mines, Allouagne, Nord-Pas-de-Calais

Comment y aller°:
À la sortie d'Allouagne, prenez la route de Lozinghem. Tournez à gauche sur la route des Mines. Le numéro 14 est la grande maison sur la droite. (Nous allons mettre des ballons° de couleurs sur la route pour indiquer l'endroit.)

Au programme:
Faire la fête, bien sûr! Manger (buffet et barbecue), rire, danser et fêter la fin des cours! Attendez-vous à passer un bon moment!

Autres activités:
Activités en plein air° (football, badminton, volley, piscine... et surtout détente°!)

Pour répondre à cette invitation:
Téléphonez à Laurence (avant le 6 juillet, SVP°) au 06.14.55.85.80 ou par e-mail:
laurence@courriel.fr

Ça y est! *That's it!* diplômés *graduates* faire retomber la pression *to unwind* bien mérité *well deserved* soucis *worries* vie quotidienne *daily life* va venir *is going to come* Nourriture *Food* plats *dishes* ballons *balls* selon *depending on* pliantes *folding* y aller *get there* ballons *balloons* en plein air *outdoor* détente *relaxation* svp *please*

Après la lecture

 **Vrai ou faux?** Indiquez si les phrases sont **vraies** ou **fausses**. Corrigez les phrases fausses. *Answers may vary slightly.*

1. C'est une invitation à une fête d'anniversaire.
   Faux. C'est une invitation pour fêter le diplôme.
2. Les invités vont passer un mauvais moment.
   Faux. Les invités vont passer un bon moment.
3. On va manger des salades et des desserts.
   Vrai.
4. Les invités vont faire toutes les activités dans la maison.
   Faux. Les invités vont faire des activités en plein air.
5. Un groupe de musique va jouer à la fête.
6. La fête commence à 16h00.
   Vrai.

Conseillez Vous êtes Laurence, un des organisateurs de la fête. Les invités veulent (*want*) assister à la fête, mais ils vous contactent pour parler de leurs soucis respectifs. Donnez-leur des conseils (*advice*) pour les mettre à l'aise (*at ease*). *Answers may vary. Suggested answers:*

MODÈLE

Isabelle: J'ai beaucoup de soucis cette semaine.
Vous: *Tu vas laisser tes soucis à la maison et venir (come) à la fête.*

1. Thomas: Je ne sais (*know*) pas quoi apporter.
   Vous: Tu vas apporter des boissons gazeuses.
2. Sarah: Je me perds (*get lost*) facilement quand je conduis.
   Vous: Tu vas chercher les ballons de couleurs sur la route.
3. Sylvie: Je ne fais pas de sport.
   Vous: Tu vas jouer aux cartes et discuter.
4. Salim: Je veux (*want*) répondre à l'invitation, mais je n'ai pas d'ordinateur.
   Vous: Tu vas me téléphoner.
5. Sandra: Je n'aime pas le barbecue.
   Vous: Tu vas manger des salades.
6. Véronique: J'aime faire du sport en plein air, mais je n'aime pas le football.
   Vous: Tu vas faire du badminton et du volley.

On va à la fête? Vous êtes invité(e) à cette fête et vous allez amener un(e) ami(e). Téléphonez à cet(te) ami(e) (votre partenaire) pour l'inviter. Donnez des détails et répondez aux questions de votre ami(e) sur les hôtes, les invités, les activités de l'après-midi et de la soirée, les choses à apporter, etc.

Vrai ou faux? Go over the answers with the class. For the false items, have students point out where they found the correct answer in the text.

Conseillez
- This activity can be done in pairs. Remind students to switch roles after items 1–3.
- Have pairs write two more situations for the activity. Then have them exchange papers with another pair and complete the situations.

On va à la fête? After students have completed the activity, take a quick class poll. Ask: **Qui va assister à la fête? Qui ne va pas assister à la fête? Pourquoi?**

OPTIONS

Small Groups Have students write an invitation to a birthday party, an anniversary party, or a holiday celebration. Tell them to include the name(s) of the host(s); date, time, and place of the event; what is being celebrated; and any other important details. If possible, provide students with examples of other invitations in French to use as models.

Pairs Working in pairs, have students write three content questions based on the reading. When they have finished, have them get together with another pair and take turns asking and answering each other's questions.

Section Goals

In this section, students will:
• learn to report an interview
• learn to conduct an interview

Stratégie Play the role of an interviewee. Tell students to interview you about your clothing preferences. Allow recording so students can transcribe the interview. Then choose volunteers to report on the interview, transcribing it verbatim, summarizing it, or summarizing and quoting you occasionally.

Proofreading Activity Have the class correct these sentences.
1. Quand est-ce vous avez achete ces vetements? 2. Cette blouson-la est tres cher, mais c'est parfait. 3. Est-ce que vous déjà avez travaille comme styliste? 4. Vous allez parler moi de votre travail?

Écriture

STRATÉGIE

How to report an interview

There are several ways to prepare a written report about an interview. You can transcribe the interview verbatim, you can summarize it, or you can combine summary with direct quotations. Whatever your approach, the report should begin with an interesting title and a brief introduction including the five W's (*who, what, when, where, why*) and the H (*how*) of the interview. The report should end with an interesting conclusion. Note that when you transcribe a conversation in French, you should pay careful attention to format and punctuation.

Écrire une conversation en français

• Pour indiquer qui parle dans une conversation, on peut mettre le nom de la personne qui parle devant sa phrase.

   MONIQUE Lucie, qu'est-ce que tu vas mettre pour l'anniversaire de Julien?

   LUCIE Je vais mettre ma robe en soie bleue à manches courtes. Et toi, tu vas mettre quoi?

   MONIQUE Eh bien, une jupe en coton et un chemisier, je pense. Ou peut-être mon pantalon en cuir avec... Tiens, tu me prêtes ta chemise jaune et blanche?

   LUCIE Oui, si tu me la rends (*return it to me*) dimanche. Elle va avec le pantalon que je vais porter la semaine prochaine.

• On peut aussi commencer les phrases avec des tirets (*dashes*) pour indiquer quand une nouvelle personne parle.

   — Qu'est-ce que tu as acheté comme cadeau pour Julien?

   — Une cravate noire et violette. Elle est très jolie. Et toi?

   — Je n'ai pas encore acheté son cadeau. Des lunettes de soleil peut-être?

   — Oui, c'est une bonne idée! Et il y a des soldes à Saint-Louis Lunettes.

Thème

🔗 Écrire une interview

Avant l'écriture

1. Clarisse Deschamps est une styliste suisse. Elle dessine des vêtements pour les jeunes et va présenter sa nouvelle collection sur votre campus. Vous allez interviewer Clarisse pour le journal de votre université.

   Préparez une liste de questions à poser à Clarisse Deschamps sur sa nouvelle collection. Vous pouvez (*can*) poser des questions sur:

   ■ les types de vêtements

   ■ les couleurs

   ■ le style

   ■ les prix

Quoi?	1. 2.
Comment?	1. 2.
Pour qui?	1. 2.
Combien?	1. 2.
Pourquoi?	1. 2.
Où?	1. 2.
Quand?	1. 2.

OPTIONS

Avant l'écriture As preparation, have each student write a short paragraph or list of their ideas about Clarisse Deschamps. What is she like? What does she look like? What kinds of clothes does she like and dislike? Have them write a short profile to use when they write the answers.

Once students have written the answers, discuss various techniques they can use to organize their information. One way is to go back to the chart they used to ask their questions and add the answers to it. Another is to prioritize by level of interest, with the most interesting information first. Ask students if they have other ideas on how to organize their information.

2. Une fois que vous avez rempli (*filled out*) le tableau (*chart*), choisissez les questions à poser pendant (*during*) l'interview.

3. Une fois (*Once*) vos questions finalisées, notez les réponses. Ensuite (*Then*), organisez les informations en catégories telles que (*such as*) les types de vêtements, les couleurs et les styles, la clientèle, le prix, etc.

Écriture

Écrivez un compte rendu (*report*) de l'interview.

- Commencez par une courte introduction.

> **MODÈLE** *Voici une interview de Clarisse Deschamps, styliste suisse.*

- Résumez (*Summarize*) les informations obtenues (*obtained*) pour chaque catégorie et présentez ces éléments de manière cohérente. Citez la personne interviewée au moins deux fois (*at least twice*).

> **MODÈLE** *Je lui ai demandé: —Quel genre de vêtements préférez-vous porter pour sortir?*
> *Elle m'a répondu: —Moi, je préfère porter une robe noire. C'est très élégant.*

- Terminez par une brève (*brief*) conclusion.

> **MODÈLE** *On vend la collection de Clarisse Deschamps à Vêtements & Co à côté de l'université. Cette semaine, il y a des soldes!*

Tête-à-tête avec Clarisse Deschamps

Voici une interview de Clarisse Deschamps, styliste suisse.

Je lui ai demandé:
- Quel genre de vêtements préférez-vous porter pour sortir?
Elle m'a répondu:
- Moi, je préfère porter une robe noire. C'est très élégant...

On vend la collection de Clarisse Deschamps à Vêtements & Co à côté de l'université. Cette semaine, il y a des soldes!

Après l'écriture

1. Échangez votre compte rendu avec celui (*the one*) d'un(e) partenaire. Répondez à ces questions pour commenter son travail.

- Votre partenaire a-t-il/elle organisé les informations en plusieurs catégories?

- A-t-il/elle inclu au moins deux citations (*quotes*) dans son compte rendu?

- A-t-il/elle utilisé le bon style pour écrire les citations?

- A-t-il/elle utilisé les bonnes formes verbales?

2. Corrigez votre compte rendu d'après (*according to*) les commentaires de votre partenaire. Relisez votre travail pour éliminer ces problèmes:

- des fautes (*errors*) d'orthographe

- des fautes de ponctuation

- des fautes de conjugaison

- des fautes d'accord (*agreement*) des adjectifs

- un mauvais emploi (*use*) de la grammaire

EVALUATION

Criteria
Content Contains all the information included in bulleted list of tasks.
Scale: 1 2 3 4 5

Organization Includes a short introduction, a 10–12 line conversation that represents the interview and a brief conclusion.
Scale: 1 2 3 4 5

Accuracy Uses forms of the **passé composé** (when applicable) and new unit verbs correctly. Spells words, conjugates verbs, and modifies adjectives correctly throughout.
Scale: 1 2 3 4 5

Creativity The student includes additional information that is not included in the task and/or creates a conversation that is longer than 10–12 lines.
Scale: 1 2 3 4 5

Scoring
Excellent	18–20 points
Good	14–17 points
Satisfactory	10–13 points
Unsatisfactory	< 10 points

O P T I O N S

Écriture On the board, demonstrate other ways to report direct quotations in writing. One is the name with a colon after it, followed by the quote (dialogue style). Another is the person's name, followed by a comma and a direct quote using quotation marks (**guillemets**).

Bring in some magazines and newspapers showing how interviews are transcribed and presented. Ask students to choose one example and to follow the model.

🔊 ⓢ Vocabulary Tools

Instructional Resources
vhlcentral.com:
Textbook MP3s; Audioscript;
reference tools

Suggestions

- Tell students that an easy way to study from **Vocabulaire** is to cover up the French half of each section, leaving only the English equivalents exposed. They can then quiz themselves on the French items. To focus on the English equivalents of the French entries, they simply reverse this process.
- Point out to students that they can use the Vocabulary Tools at **vhlcentral.com** for reference and extra vocabulary practice.

Leçon 6A

Les fêtes

faire la fête *to party*
faire une surprise (à quelqu'un) *to surprise (someone)*
fêter *to celebrate*
organiser une fête *to plan a party*
une bière *beer*
un biscuit *cookie*
un bonbon *candy*
le champagne *champagne*
un dessert *dessert*
un gâteau *cake*
la glace *ice cream*
un glaçon *ice cube*
le vin *wine*
un cadeau *present, gift*
une fête *party; celebration*
un hôte/une hôtesse *host(ess)*
un(e) invité(e) *guest*
un jour férié *holiday*
une surprise *surprise*

Périodes de la vie

l'adolescence (f.) *adolescence*
l'âge adulte (m.) *adulthood*
un divorce *divorce*
l'enfance (f.) *childhood*
une étape *stage*
l'état civil (m.) *marital status*
la jeunesse *youth*
un mariage *marriage; wedding*
la mort *death*
la naissance *birth*
la vie *life*
la vieillesse *old age*
prendre sa retraite *to retire*
tomber amoureux/amoureuse *to fall in love*
avant-hier *the day before yesterday*
hier *yesterday*

Les relations

une amitié *friendship*
un amour *love*
le bonheur *happiness*
un couple *couple*
un(e) fiancé(e) *fiancé; fiancée*
des jeunes mariés (m.) *newlyweds*
un rendez-vous *date; appointment*
ensemble *together*

Expressions utiles

See p. 229.

Demonstrative adjectives

ce(t)(te)/ces *this/these; that/those*
...-ci *...here*
...-là *...there*

Leçon 6B

Les vêtements

aller avec *to go with*
porter *to wear*
un anorak *ski jacket, parka*
des baskets (f.) *sneakers, tennis shoes*
un blouson *jacket*
une casquette *(baseball) cap*
une ceinture *belt*
un chapeau *hat*
une chaussette *sock*
une chaussure *shoe*
une chemise (à manches courtes/longues) *shirt (short-/long-sleeved)*
un chemisier *blouse*
un costume *(man's) suit*
une cravate *tie*
une écharpe *scarf*
un gant *glove*
un jean *jeans*
une jupe *skirt*
des lunettes (de soleil) (f.) *(sun)glasses*
un maillot de bain *swimsuit, bathing suit*
un manteau *coat*
un pantalon *pants*
un pull *sweater*
une robe *dress*
un sac à main *purse, handbag*
un short *shorts*
un sous-vêtement *underwear*
une taille *clothing size*
un tailleur *(woman's) suit; tailor*
un tee-shirt *tee shirt*
des vêtements (m.) *clothing*
des soldes (m.) *sales*
un vendeur/une vendeuse *salesman/saleswoman*
bon marché *inexpensive*
chaque *each*
cher/chère *expensive*
large *loose; big*
serré(e) *tight*

Les couleurs

De quelle couleur...? *In what color...?*
blanc(he) *white*
bleu(e) *blue*
gris(e) *gray*
jaune *yellow*
marron *brown*
noir(e) *black*
orange *orange*
rose *pink*
rouge *red*
vert(e) *green*
violet(te) *purple; violet*

Verbes en -re

attendre *to wait*
conduire *to drive*
construire *to build; to construct*
descendre *to go down; to take down*
détruire *to destroy*
entendre *to hear*
mettre *to put (on); to place*
perdre (son temps) *to waste (one's time)*
permettre *to allow*
produire *to produce*
promettre *to promise*
réduire *to reduce*
rendre (à) *to give back; to return (to)*
rendre visite (à) *to visit someone*
répondre (à) *to respond, to answer (to)*
rire *to laugh*
sourire *to smile*
traduire *to translate*
vendre *to sell*

Expressions utiles

See p. 247.

Indirect object pronouns

me *to/for me*
te *to/for you*
lui *to/for him/her*
nous *to/for us*
vous *to/for you*
leur *to/for them*

Disjunctive pronouns

moi *me*
toi *you*
lui/elle *him/her*
nous *us*
vous *you*
eux/elles *them*
moi-même *myself*
toi-même *yourself*
lui-/elle-même *him-/herself*
nous-mêmes *ourselves*
vous-même(s) *yourself/(yourselves)*
eux-/elles-mêmes *themselves*

En vacances

Unit Goals

Leçon 7A

In this lesson, students will learn:

- terms for travel and vacation
- names of countries and nationalities
- the role of diacriticals
- about Tahiti and **le musée d'Orsay**
- the **passé composé** with **être**
- direct object pronouns
- more about transportation and lodging through specially shot video footage

Leçon 7B

In this lesson, students will learn:

- terms related to hotels and accommodations
- ordinal numbers
- expressions for sequencing events
- the pronunciation of **ti**, **sti**, and **ssi**
- how and where the French vacation
- about Guadeloupean band Kassav'
- the formation and usage of adverbs
- the **impératif**
- the verbs **dire**, **écrire**, **lire**, and **décrire**
- to recognize the genre of spoken discourse

Savoir-faire

In this section, students will learn:

- cultural and historical information about **Les Antilles et la Polynésie française**
- to predict the content of a text from its title
- to make an outline
- to write a brochure

Pour commencer

- **bleu, noir, blanc.**
- **On est en été.**
- **Il porte un maillot de bain.**
- **Il peut nager.**

Pour commencer

- ...iquez les couleurs qu'on voit (*sees*) sur ...photo.
- ...est en été ou en hiver?
- ...el(s) vêtement(s) Stéphane porte-t-il?
- ...elle(s) activité(s) Stéphane peut-il ...tiquer là où il se trouve?

RESOURCES

Student Activities Manual (SAM):
Workbook Activities, pp. 89–102;
Lab Activities, pp. 49–56;
Video Activities, pp. 25–28; pp. 73–74;
SAM Answer Key

vhlcentral.com: Textbook MP3s; Lab MP3s;
Textbook Audioscript; Lab Audioscript; Video;
Videoscript; **Roman-photo** Translations;
Vocabulaire supplémentaire; Activity Pack
(including **Feuilles d'activités**, Info Gap Activities,
and Task-based Activities);

Flash culture video transcription; **Essayez!** and **Mise en pratique** answers; Digital Image Bank;
Testing Program; Testing Program MP3s

Section Goals

In this section, students will learn and practice vocabulary related to:
• travel and vacations
• names of countries and nationalities

Instructional Resources

vhlcentral.com:
*Digital Image Bank (including vocabulary illustrations from the textbook, theme-based illustrations); **Vocabulaire supplémentaire; Mise en pratique** answers; Textbook Audioscript; Lab Audioscript; Activity Pack (Info Gap Activities); Textbook MP3s; Lab MP3s; SAM Answer Key; reference tools*

Suggestions

• Use the **7A Contextes** illustration from the Digital Image Bank and describe what the people are doing. Examples: **Cette femme achète un billet. Cet homme utilise un plan.**

• Ask students questions about travel and transportation using the vocabulary. **Aimez-vous voyager? Comment préférez-vous voyager? Aimez-vous prendre le train? Aimez-vous prendre l'avion? Préférez-vous rouler en voiture ou prendre l'autobus? Quels pays avez-vous visités?** At this time, introduce additional countries, states, provinces, and their prepositions as needed from the **Vocabulaire supplémentaire** on the Supersite.

• Point out that **faire des achats** also means *to go shopping.*

• Point out that **un (auto)bus** is a local bus; a bus that goes from town to town is **un (auto)car**. Then explain the nuance between **une station de train** and **une gare.**

• Point out that **les vacances** is always plural.

• Tell students that **un plan** is a city or town map; **une carte** is a map of a larger area, such as a region or country.

• Explain that the word **un ticket** is used for a bus, subway, or other small ticket. A plane or train ticket or a ticket to an event, such as a concert, is called **un billet.**

• Use the transportation and travel illustrations from the Digital Image Bank to help students familiarize themselves with trips, vacations, countries, and nationalities.

Leçon 7A

You will learn how to...
▪ describe trips you have taken
▪ tell where you went

Vocabulary Tools

Bon voyage!

le soleil!

Elle bronze. (bronzer)

la plage

la mer

une sortie

Il utilise un plan. (utiliser)

les gens (m.)

Le Figaro

le journal

Vocabulaire

faire du shopping	to go shopping
faire les valises	to pack one's bags
faire un séjour	to spend time (somewhere)
partir en vacances	to go on vacation
prendre un train (un taxi, un (auto)bus, un bateau)	to take a train (taxi, bus, boat)
rouler en voiture	to ride in a car
un aéroport	airport
un arrêt d'autobus (de bus)	bus stop
un billet aller-retour	round-trip ticket
un billet (d'avion, de train)	(plane, train) ticket
un (jour de) congé	day off
une douane	customs
une gare (routière)	train station (bus terminal)
une station (de métro)	(subway) station
une station de ski	ski resort
un ticket (de bus, de métro)	(bus, subway) ticket
des vacances (f.)	vacation
un vol	flight
à l'étranger	abroad, overseas
la campagne	country(side)
une capitale	capital
un pays	country
(en/l') Allemagne (f.)	(to/in) Germany
(en/l') Angleterre (f.)	(to/in) England
(en/la) Belgique (belge)	(to/in) Belgium (Belgian)
(au/le) Brésil (brésilien(ne))	(to/in) Brazil (Brazilian)
(en/la) Chine (chinois(e))	(to/in) China (Chinese)
(en/l') Irlande (irlandais(e)) (f.)	(to/in) Ireland (Irish)
(en/l') Italie (f.)	(to/in) Italy
(au/le) Japon	(to/in) Japan
(en/la) Suisse	(to/in) Switzerland

ressources

WB
pp. 89–90

LM
p. 49

vhlcentral

270 *deux cent soixante-dix*

OPTIONS

Extra Practice Call out names of countries and nationalities at random, including adjectives of nationality from previous lessons. Have students classify them as either **un pays** or **une nationalité.** You might want to list the words on the board in two columns or have students write them on the board.

Game Write vocabulary for means of transportation on index cards. On another set of cards, draw or paste pictures to match each term. Tape them face down on the board in random order. Divide the class into two teams. Play a game of Concentration in which students match words with pictures. When a match is made, that player's team collects those cards. When all pairs have been matched, the team with the most cards wins.

Mise en pratique

une arrivée
un départ
un avion
Ils vont faire un voyage.
la France (en France)
le Canada (au Canada)
les États-Unis (m.) (aux États-Unis)
Le Monde
le Mexique (au Mexique)
l'Espagne (f.) (en Espagne)

1 Écoutez Écoutez Cédric et Nathalie parler de leurs vacances. Ensuite (*Then*), complétez les phrases avec un mot ou une expression de la section **ESPACE CONTEXTES**. Notez que toutes les options ne sont pas utilisées.

_f_	1. Nathalie va partir...	a.	sont idéales pour bronzer.
_b_	2. Nathalie a déjà...	b.	son billet d'avion.
_j_	3. Nathalie va peut-être...	c.	le plan de Paris de Cédric.
_g_	4. La famille de Cédric...	d.	la capitale du Mexique.
_h_	5. Paul pense que l'Espagne est...	e.	le tour du monde.
		f.	à l'étranger.
_a_	6. Pour Cédric, les plages du Brésil...	g.	n'a pas encore décidé entre l'Espagne, le Mexique et le Brésil.
_e_	7. Un jour, Cédric va faire...	h.	un pays superbe.
_c_	8. Nathalie va utiliser...	i.	faire un séjour en Italie.

2 Chassez l'intrus Indiquez le mot ou l'expression qui ne convient pas.

1. faire un séjour, partir en vacances, un jour de congé, (une station de ski)
2. un aéroport, une station de métro, (une arrivée,) une gare routière
3. (une douane,) un départ, une arrivée, une sortie
4. le monde, un pays, (le journal,) une capitale
5. la campagne, la mer, la plage, (des gens)
6. prendre un bus, un arrêt de bus, (utiliser un plan,) une gare routière
7. (bronzer,) prendre un avion, un vol, un aéroport
8. prendre un taxi, rouler en voiture, (un vol,) une gare routière

3 Les vacances Justine va partir en vacances demain. Complétez le paragraphe avec les mots et expressions de la liste. Toutes les options ne sont pas utilisées.

aller-retour	faire ma valise	sortie
une arrivée	pays	station
faire un séjour	plage	taxi
faire du shopping	prendre un bus	vol

Demain, je pars en vacances. Je vais (1) ___faire un séjour___ avec mon frère à l'île Maurice, une petite île (*island*) tropicale dans l'océan Indien. Nous allons (2) ___prendre un bus___ pour l'aéroport à 7h00. Mon frère veut (*wants*) prendre un (3) ___taxi___, mais moi, je pense qu'il faut économiser parce que j'ai envie de (4) ___faire du shopping___ au marché et dans les boutiques de Port-Louis, la capitale. Le (5) ___vol___ est à 10h. Nous n'avons pas besoin de visa pour le voyage; pour entrer dans le (6) ___pays___, il faut seulement montrer un passeport et un billet (7) ___aller-retour___. J'ai acheté un nouveau maillot de bain pour aller à la (8) ___plage___. Et maintenant, je vais (9) ___faire ma valise___!

S Practice more at vhlcentral.com.

deux cent soixante et onze **271**

1 Audioscript CÉDRIC: Nathalie, où est-ce que tu vas aller en vacances cet été?
NATHALIE: Je vais partir à l'étranger.
C: Moi aussi. Où est-ce que tu vas?
N: Je vais en France pour quinze jours. C'est un pays tellement intéressant. J'ai déjà mon billet d'avion. J'attends le départ avec beaucoup d'impatience. Je vais aller à Paris et aussi à Nice. On va peut-être faire un court séjour en Italie. Ça va être super! Et toi, où est-ce que tu pars en vacances?
C: Moi, je vais faire un voyage mais je ne sais pas où. Ma famille n'a pas encore décidé entre l'Espagne, le Mexique et le Brésil. Qu'en penses-tu?
N: Mon frère Paul fait ses études en Espagne, à Grenade. Il trouve que c'est un pays superbe et que les gens sont très gentils.
C: Moi, je pense que le Brésil, c'est plus exotique et les plages sont idéales pour bronzer.
N: Mexico, la capitale du Mexique, a beaucoup de musées très intéressants.
C: Un jour, je vais faire le tour du monde, mais pour ça, il faut trouver un vol bon marché. Nathalie, tu as besoin de quelqu'un pour t'aider à faire tes valises et te conduire à l'aéroport?
N: Oh oui, merci. C'est vraiment gentil. Est-ce que tu as un plan de Paris à me prêter?
C: Bien sûr, pas de problème.
(On Textbook MP3s)

1 Suggestion Before students listen, have them scan the sentence fragments in this activity and pick out new words. Examples: **bronzer**, **aéroport**, **séjour**, and **pays**.

2 Suggestion Have students put **l'intrus** with other expressions like it. Example: **une station de ski** goes with item 5. If the word does not fit another set, have students create a set of at least three related words.

3 Expansion Have pairs of students add to Justine's paragraph by creating sentences using the three unused words (**arrivée, station, sortie**). Have them rewrite the paragraph, logically adding their sentences. Ask volunteers to read their paragraphs aloud.

OPTIONS

Extra Practice Ask students what means of transportation one might take to go from one place to another. Example: **Quel(s) moyen(s) de transport est-ce qu'on prend pour aller de Paris à Rome? Des États-Unis en Angleterre? De la faculté au supermarché? De la tour Eiffel à l'Arc de Triomphe?**

Game Play a game of **Dix questions**. Ask a volunteer to think of a country. Other students get one chance to ask a yes/no question and guess the country. Encourage students to ask questions about languages spoken there and location. You might want to brainstorm prepositions of location on the board. Examples: **près de**, **loin de**, **à côté de**, etc. Limit attempts to ten questions per place.

Communication

NATIONAL communication STANDARDS

4 Suggestion After completing this activity in pairs, have pairs team up to form groups of four. Have students share what they learned about their partners with the other pair.

4 Expansion Ask each student question 8: **Dans quel pays as-tu envie de voyager?** Accept simple answers like **la France.** Follow up each answer by asking **Pourquoi?**

5 Suggestion Ask volunteers to write their descriptions on the board.

6 Suggestion Before distributing the Info Gap Handouts found in the Activity Pack on the Supersite, you might want to brainstorm some questions that will elicit the missing information and write them on the board.

7 Suggestion Have students exchange letters for peer editing. Editors should make sure all required elements are included in the letter and underline, rather than correct, grammar and spelling errors.

4 **Répondez** Avec un(e) partenaire, posez-vous ces questions et répondez-y (*them*) à tour de rôle. Answers will vary.

1. Où pars-tu en vacances cette année? Quand?
2. Quand fais-tu tes valises? Avec combien de valises voyages-tu?
3. Préfères-tu la mer, la campagne ou les stations de ski?
4. Comment vas-tu à l'aéroport? Prends-tu l'autobus? Le métro?
5. Quelles sont tes vacances préférées?
6. Quand utilises-tu un plan?
7. Quel est ton pays favori? Pourquoi?
8. Dans quel(s) pays as-tu envie de voyager?

5 **Décrivez** Avec un(e) partenaire, écrivez (*write*) une description des images. Donnez autant de (*as many*) détails que possible. Ensuite (*Then*), rejoignez un autre groupe et lisez vos descriptions. L'autre groupe doit deviner (*must guess*) quelle image vous décrivez (*describe*). Answers will vary.

1.

2.

3.

4.

5.

6.

6 **Conversez** Votre professeur va vous donner, à vous et à votre partenaire, une feuille d'activités. Vous avez décidé de partir en voyage ensemble dans une région francophone. L'un(e) de vous a fait des recherches sur Internet et a trouvé trois possibilités de voyages. Travaillez à deux pour finaliser votre choix. Attention! Ne regardez pas la feuille de votre partenaire. Answers will vary.

7 **Un voyage** Vous allez faire un voyage en Europe et rendre visite à votre cousin, Jean-Marc, qui étudie en Belgique. Écrivez-lui (*Write to him*) une lettre et utilisez les mots de la liste. Answers will vary.

un aéroport	la France
la Belgique	prendre un taxi
un billet	la Suisse
faire un séjour	un vol
faire les valises	un voyage

- Parlez des détails de votre départ.
- Expliquez votre tour d'Europe.
- Organisez votre arrivée en Belgique.
- Parlez de ce que (*what*) vous allez faire ensemble.

OPTIONS

Small Groups Have students work in groups of three to write riddles about people, places, or objects from **Espace contextes.** For each riddle, the group must come up with at least three hints or descriptions. Have students from each group read hints to the rest of the class. Example: **Je suis fait de papier. Je suis souvent en noir et blanc. Je vous donne beaucoup d'informations. (Je suis un journal.)**

Game Write **Dans quel pays parle-t-on…?** on the board. Have students stand. Toss a beanbag to a student and ask where a language is spoken. The player has four seconds to name a country. He or she then tosses the beanbag to a classmate and asks where a language is spoken. Players who cannot think of a country in time are eliminated. Languages may be repeated, but countries may not. The last person standing wins.

Les sons et les lettres  Audio

Diacriticals for meaning

Some French words with different meanings have nearly identical spellings except for a diacritical mark (*accent*). Sometimes a diacritical does not affect pronunciation at all.

ou	**où**	**a**	**à**
or	*where*	*has*	*to, at*

Sometimes, you can clearly hear the difference between the words.

côte	**côté**	**sale**	**salé**
coast	*side*	*dirty*	*salty*

Very often, two similar-looking words are different parts of speech. Many similar-looking word pairs are those with and without an **-é** at the end.

âge	**âgé**	**entre**	**entré (entrer)**
age (n.)	*elderly* (adj.)	*between* (prep.)	*entered* (p.p.)

In such instances, context should make their meaning clear.

Tu as quel âge?	**C'est un homme âgé.**
How old are you? / What is your age?	*He's an elderly man.*

Prononcez Répétez les mots suivants à voix haute.

1. la (*the*) là (*there*)
2. êtes (*are*) étés (*summers*)
3. jeune (*young*) jeûne (*fasting*)
4. pêche (*peach*) pêché (*fished*)

Articulez Répétez les phrases suivantes à voix haute.

1. J'habite dans une ferme (*farm*). Le magasin est fermé (*closed*).
2. Les animaux mangent du maïs (*corn*). Je suis suisse, mais il est belge.
3. Est-ce que tu es prête? J'ai prêté ma voiture (*car*) à Marcel.
4. La lampe est à côté de la chaise. J'adore la côte ouest de la France.

Dictons Répétez les dictons à voix haute.

À vos marques, prêts, partez! [1]

C'est un prêté pour un rendu. [2]

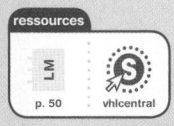

ressources

LM
p. 50

vhlcentral

[2] One good turn deserves another. (lit. It is one loaned for one returned.)
[1] On your mark, get set, go!

deux cent soixante-treize **273**

Section Goals

In this section, students will learn about the use of diacriticals to distinguish between words with the same or similar spellings.

Instructional Resources
vhlcentral.com:
Textbook MP3s; Lab MP3s;
SAM Answer Key;
Textbook Audioscript;
Lab Audioscript;
reference tools

Suggestions

- Model the pronunciation of the example words and have students repeat after you.
- Write examples of other past participles that are used as adjectives on the board. Examples: **réservé** and **préparé**. Ask students to provide more examples.
- Have students give you the English equivalents for the following words in the **Articulez** activity: **2. mais 3. prête** and **prêté 4. côté** and **côte**.
- Dictate five simple sentences with words that have diacriticals that distinguish meaning, repeating each one at least two times. Then write the sentences on the board or a transparency and have students check their spelling.

Dictons Have students compare the pronunciation and meaning of **prêts** and **prêté**. Then have them identify their parts of speech.

Extra Practice Use these sentences that contain words with and without diacriticals for additional practice or as a dictation. **1.** Quel âge a-t-il? Mon grand-père est âgé. **2.** Le bureau est entre le lit et la porte. Marcel est entré dans la salle. **3.** La ligne est occupée. Suzanne s'occupe des enfants. **4.** J'ai réservé une table au restaurant. Sylvain est réservé.

Extra Practice Teach students this French tongue-twister that contains diacriticals that affect meaning. **Un pêcheur péchait sous un pêcher, le pêcher empêchait le pêcheur de pêcher, le pêcheur coupa le pêcher, le pêcher n'empêcha plus le pêcheur de pêcher.**

Section Goals

In this section, students will learn functional phrases for talking about vacations.

Instructional Resources
vhlcentral.com:
Roman-photo *Video, Videoscript, and Translation; SAM Answer Key; reference tools*

Video Recap: Leçon 6B
Review the previous **Roman-photo** with this activity.
1. _____ a fêté ses dix-huit ans. (Stéphane)
2. _____ a fait un gâteau d'anniversaire. (Sandrine)
3. _____ a visité Paris avec ses parents. (David)
4. _____ a fait une jupe originale. (Amina)
5. _____ ont donné une montre à Stéphane. (Rachid et Astrid)
6. _____ lui a donné un blouson en cuir noir. (Valérie)

Video Synopsis At the train station, David tells Rachid about his trip to Paris. At the café, he tells Stéphane about his trip and that he loved the museums. Stéphane wants to go to Tahiti. David gives Stéphane sunglasses for his birthday. When Sandrine hears about David's trip, she remembers she needs to make reservations for her ski trip to Albertville.

Suggestions
• Ask students to read the title, glance at the video stills, and predict what the episode will be about. Record their predictions.
• Have students read the **Roman-photo** aloud in groups of four.
• Point out the expressions **bon voyage** and **bon séjour**. Explain that **un voyage** refers to travel to and from a destination; **un séjour** is extended time spent at the place itself.
• Review predictions and ask which ones were correct.

De retour au P'tit Bistrot Video

PERSONNAGES

David

Rachid

Sandrine

Stéphane

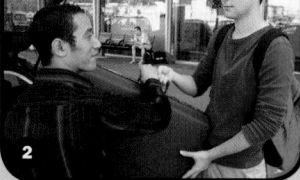

À la gare...
RACHID Tu as fait bon voyage?
DAVID Salut! Excellent, merci.
RACHID Tu es parti pour Paris avec une valise et te voici avec ces énormes sacs en plus!
DAVID Mes parents et moi sommes allés aux Galeries Lafayette. On a acheté des vêtements et des trucs pour l'appartement aussi.

RACHID Ah ouais?
DAVID Mes parents sont arrivés des États-Unis jeudi soir. Ils ont pris une chambre dans un bel hôtel, tout près de la tour Eiffel.
RACHID Génial!
DAVID Moi, je suis arrivé à la gare vendredi soir. Et nous sommes allés dîner dans une excellente brasserie. Mmm!

DAVID Samedi, on a pris un bateau-mouche sur la Seine. J'ai visité un musée différent chaque jour: le musée du Louvre, le musée d'Orsay...
RACHID En résumé, tu as passé de bonnes vacances dans la capitale... Bon, on y va?
DAVID Ah, euh, oui, allons-y!

STÉPHANE Pour moi, les vacances idéales, c'est un voyage à Tahiti. Ahhh... la plage, et moi en maillot de bain avec des lunettes de soleil... et les filles en bikini!
DAVID Au fait, je n'ai pas oublié ton anniversaire.
STÉPHANE Ouah! Super, ces lunettes de soleil! Merci, David, c'est gentil.

DAVID Désolé de ne pas avoir été là pour ton anniversaire, Stéphane. Alors, ils t'ont fait la surprise?
STÉPHANE Oui, et quelle belle surprise! J'ai reçu des cadeaux trop cool. Et le gâteau de Sandrine, je l'ai adoré.
DAVID Ah, Sandrine... elle est adorable... Euh, Stéphane, tu m'excuses une minute?

DAVID Coucou! Je suis de retour!
SANDRINE Oh! Salut, David. Alors, tu as aimé Paris?
DAVID Oui! J'ai fait plein de choses... de vraies petites vacances! On a fait...

A C T I V I T É S

1 **Les événements** Mettez ces événements dans l'ordre chronologique.

_1_ a. Rachid va chercher David.
_6_ b. Stéphane parle de son anniversaire.
_10_ c. Sandrine va faire une réservation.
_5_ d. David donne un cadeau à Stéphane.
_2_ e. Rachid mentionne que David a beaucoup de sacs.

_7_ f. Stéphane met les lunettes de soleil.
_4_ g. Stéphane décrit (*describes*) ses vacances idéales.
_8_ h. David parle avec Sandrine.
_9_ i. Sandrine pense à ses vacances.
_3_ j. Rachid et David repartent en voiture.

 Practice more at **vhlcentral.com**.

O P T I O N S

Avant de regarder la vidéo Before viewing the video episode **De retour au P'tit Bistrot**, have pairs of students make a list of things someone might say when describing a trip and talking about means of transportation.

Regarder la vidéo Download and print the videoscript on the Supersite, and white out words related to travel and transportation. Distribute the scripts to pairs or groups to complete as cloze paragraphs as they watch the video.

David parle de ses vacances.

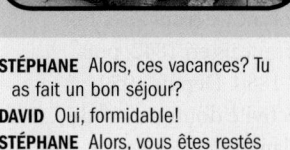

STÉPHANE Alors, ces vacances? Tu as fait un bon séjour?

DAVID Oui, formidable!

STÉPHANE Alors, vous êtes restés combien de temps à Paris?

DAVID Quatre jours. Ce n'est pas très long, mais on a visité pas mal d'endroits.

STÉPHANE Comment est-ce que vous avez visité la ville? En voiture?

DAVID En voiture!? Tu es fou! On a pris le métro, comme tout le monde.

STÉPHANE Tes parents n'aiment pas conduire?

DAVID Si, à la campagne, mais pas en ville, surtout une ville comme Paris. On a visité les monuments, les musées...

STÉPHANE Et Monsieur l'artiste a aimé les musées de Paris?

DAVID Je les ai adorés!

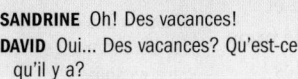

SANDRINE Oh! Des vacances!

DAVID Oui... Des vacances? Qu'est-ce qu'il y a?

SANDRINE Je vais à Albertville pour les vacances d'hiver. On va faire du ski!

SANDRINE Est-ce que tu skies?

DAVID Un peu, oui...

SANDRINE Désolée, je dois partir. J'ai une réservation à faire! Rendez-vous ici demain, David. D'accord? Ciao!

Expressions utiles

Talking about vacations

- **Tu es parti pour Paris avec une valise et te voici avec ces énormes sacs en plus!**
  You left for Paris with one suitcase and here you are with these huge extra bags!
- **Nous sommes allés aux Galeries Lafayette.**
  We went to the Galeries Lafayette.
- **On a acheté des trucs pour l'appartement aussi.**
  We also bought some things for the apartment.
- **Moi, je suis arrivé à la gare vendredi soir et nous sommes allés dîner.**
  I got to the station Friday night and we went to dinner.
- **On a pris un bateau-mouche sur la Seine.**
  We took a sightseeing boat on the Seine.
- **Vous êtes restés combien de temps à Paris?**
  How long did you stay in Paris?
- **On a pris le métro, comme tout le monde.**
  We took the subway, like everyone else.
- **J'ai fait plein de choses.**
  I did a lot of things.
- **Les musées de Paris, je les ai adorés!**
  I loved the museums in Paris!

Additional vocabulary

- **Alors, ils t'ont fait la surprise?**
  So, they surprised you?
- **J'ai reçu des cadeaux trop cool.**
  I got the coolest gifts.
- **Le gâteau, je l'ai adoré.**
  I loved the cake.
- **Tu m'excuses une minute?**
  Would you excuse me a minute?
- **Oui, formidable!**
  Yes, wonderful!
- **Qu'est-ce qu'il y a?**
  What's the matter?
- **Désolé(e), je dois partir.**
  Sorry, I have to go.

A C T I V I T É S

2 Questions Répondez aux questions. Answers may vary slightly.

1. David est parti pour Paris avec combien de valises? À son retour (*Upon his return*), est-ce qu'il a le même nombre de valises?
   Il est parti avec une valise. Non, à son retour, il a des sacs en plus.
2. Qu'est-ce que David a fait pour ses vacances?
   Il a visité Paris avec ses parents.
3. Qu'est-ce que David donne à Stéphane comme cadeau d'anniversaire? Stéphane aime-t-il le cadeau?
   Il donne des lunettes de soleil à Stéphane. Oui, Stéphane aime beaucoup le cadeau.
4. Quelles sont les vacances idéales de Stéphane? C'est un voyage à Tahiti. Stéphane est à la plage en maillot de bain avec des lunettes de soleil.
5. Qu'est-ce que Sandrine va faire pour ses vacances d'hiver?
   Elle va faire du ski à Albertville.

3 Écrivez Imaginez: vous êtes David, Stéphane ou Sandrine et vous allez en vacances à Paris, Tahiti ou Albertville. Écrivez un e-mail à Valérie. Quel temps fait-il? Où est-ce que vous restez? Quels vêtements est-ce que vous avez apportés? Qu'est-ce que vous faites chaque jour?

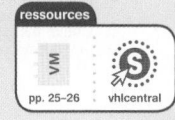

ressources

VM
pp. 25–26

vhlcentral

Expressions utiles

- Model the pronunciation of the **Expressions utiles** and have students repeat them after you.
- Draw attention to expressions with direct object pronouns and the **passé composé** with **être** in the videostill captions, in the **Expressions utiles** box, and as they occur in your conversation with students. Point out that this material will be formally presented in **Espace structures**.
- Respond briefly to questions about direct object pronouns and the **passé composé** with **être**. Reinforce correct forms, but do not expect students to produce them consistently at this time.
- Point out that **cool** is invariable since it is an adopted word.
- Point out to students that the word **formidable** is a **faux ami**, meaning *wonderful*, not *formidable*.
- Remind students that **désolée** in the last sentence is feminine because Sandrine is talking about herself. A man would say, **(je suis) désolé**.

1 Suggestion Have students form groups of five. Write each of these sentences on individual strips of paper and distribute them among the students in each group (two per student). Copy a set of sentences for each group. Have students read their sentences aloud in the proper order.

1 Expansion Have students write sentences to fill in parts of the story not mentioned in this activity.

2 Expansion Give students time to write out their answers to these questions. Then ask volunteers to write them on the board.

3 Suggestion Before starting this activity, review vocabulary for weather, clothing, and activities by asking questions. Examples: **Quel temps fait-il à Paris en été? à Albertville en hiver? Qu'est-ce que vous aimez faire à la plage? à la montagne? Qu'est-ce que vous mettez quand il fait chaud? quand il fait froid?**

O P T I O N S

Les bateaux-mouches Touring by **bateau-mouche** is an excellent way to see the famous sights along the River Seine. Tourists can listen to narrations in various languages as they pass by **la cathédrale de Notre-Dame, la Conciergerie**, under the ornate **pont Alexandre III**, under the oldest bridge in Paris **le Pont Neuf, la tour Eiffel**, and even a miniature version of the **statue de la Liberté**.

Small Groups Have students work in groups of four to prepare a skit to present to the class. In the skit, the group of friends checks into a hotel and decides what they feel like doing for the rest of the day. Tell them to describe what city they are visiting, describe the hotel and their rooms, and explain what activities they want to do while they are visiting the city.

Section Goals

In this section, students will:
- learn about Tahiti
- learn terms related to train travel
- find out some unusual facts about transportation in the francophone world
- read about **le musée d'Orsay**

Instructional Resources
vhlcentral.com:
SAM Answer Key;
reference tools

Culture à la loupe
Avant la lecture Ask students: **Où est Tahiti? Quelle(s) langue(s) parle-t-on à Tahiti?** Ask if anyone can explain Tahiti's relationship to France.

Lecture Pointing out the **Coup de main** box, explain the relationship between the verb tenses in the two clauses. Discourage students from experimenting with **si** clauses except those with both verbs in the present or one in the present and the other in **le futur proche**. **Si** clauses with the conditional are presented in **Leçon 13B, Espace structures.**

Après la lecture
- Ask students to say something they learned from the passage that makes them want to visit Tahiti or that dissuades them from visiting. Examples: **J'ai envie de visiter Tahiti parce que j'adore la montagne et la plage. Moi, je n'ai pas envie d'aller à Tahiti parce que je déteste le temps très chaud.**
- You might also ask students to identify any review vocabulary in the passage. Examples: **la pêche, la planche à voile, faire des randonnées**, etc.

1 Expansion Continue the activity with these questions.
11. Comment est le climat de Tahiti? (C'est un climat chaud.)
12. À part les plages, que peut-on visiter? (des montagnes, des lagons, des spas, Papeete)
13. Quelles attractions trouve-t-on à Papeete? (des restaurants, des boîtes de nuit, des boutiques variées et un marché)

Reading

NATIONAL connections cultures STANDARDS

CULTURE À LA LOUPE

Tahiti

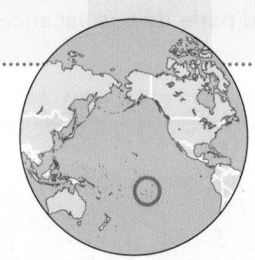

Tahiti, dans le sud° de l'océan Pacifique, est la plus grande île° de la Polynésie française. Elle devient° un protectorat français en 1842, puis° une colonie française en 1880. Depuis 1959, elle fait partie de la collectivité d'outre-mer° de Polynésie française. Les langues officielles de Tahiti sont le français et le tahitien.

Le tourisme est une activité très importante pour l'île. Ses hôtels de luxe et leurs fameux bungalows sur l'eau accueillent° près de 170.000 visiteurs par an. Les touristes apprécient Tahiti pour son climat chaud, ses superbes plages et sa culture riche en traditions. À Tahiti, il y a la possibilité de faire toutes sortes d'activités aquatiques comme du bateau, de la pêche, de la planche à voile ou de la plongée°. On peut aussi faire des randonnées en montagne ou explorer les nombreux lagons bleus de l'île. Si on n'a pas envie de faire de sport, on peut se relaxer dans un spa, bronzer à la plage ou se promener° sur l'île. Papeete, capitale de la Polynésie française et ville principale de Tahiti, offre de bons restaurants, des boîtes de nuit, des boutiques variées et un marché.

sud *south* **la plus grande île** *the largest island* **devient** *becomes* **puis** *then* **collectivité d'outre-mer** *overseas territory* **accueillent** *welcome* **plongée** *scuba diving* **se promener** *go for a walk*

Coup de main

Si introduces a hypothesis. It may come at the beginning or in the middle of a sentence.

si + [*subject*] + [*verb*] + [*subject*] + [*verb*]

Si on n'a pas envie de faire de sport, on peut se relaxer dans un spa.

[*subject*] + [*verb*] + **si** + [*subject*] + [*verb*]

On peut se relaxer dans un spa **si** on n'a pas envie de faire de sport.

A C T I V I T É S

1 **Répondez** Répondez aux questions par des phrases complètes.

1. Où est Tahiti?
   Tahiti est dans le sud de l'océan Pacifique.
2. Quand est-ce que Tahiti devient une colonie française?
   Tahiti devient une colonie en 1880.
3. De quoi fait partie Tahiti?
   Tahiti fait partie de la collectivité d'outre-mer de Polynésie française.
4. Quelles langues parle-t-on à Tahiti?
   On parle français et tahitien.
5. Quelle particularité ont les hôtels de luxe à Tahiti?
   Les hôtels de luxe ont des bungalows sur l'eau.
6. Combien de personnes visitent Tahiti chaque année?
   Près de 170.000 touristes visitent Tahiti chaque année.
7. Pourquoi est-ce que les touristes aiment visiter Tahiti? Les touristes aiment visiter Tahiti parce qu'il fait chaud et parce que les plages sont superbes.
8. Quelles sont deux activités sportives que les touristes aiment faire à Tahiti?
   Answers may vary. Possible answer: Ils aiment faire du bateau et de la plongée.
9. Comment s'appelle la ville principale de Tahiti?
   La ville principale de Tahiti s'appelle Papeete.
10. Où va-t-on à Papeete pour acheter un cadeau pour un ami?
    On va au marché ou dans les boutiques.

O P T I O N S

Pairs Have students imagine arriving in Tahiti to meet a friend who lives there. The "visitor" should ask about possible ways to spend time during the visit and the "resident" should propose activities (basing information on the reading and the vocabulary from **Espace contextes**).

Then have two pairs join together to reflect on each pair's experiences while together in Tahiti. One pair should ask the other pair what they did, using **les pronoms disjoints** for emphasis and contrast. Encourage students to use an array of verbs conjugated in the **passé composé** with **être** and **avoir.**

LE FRANÇAIS QUOTIDIEN

À la gare

contrôleur	ticket inspector
couchette	berth
guichet	ticket window
horaire	schedule
quai	train/metro platform
voie	track
wagon-lit	sleeper car
composter	to punch one's (train) ticket

LE MONDE FRANCOPHONE

Les transports

Voici quelques faits insolites° dans les transports.
Au Canada Inauguré en 1966, le métro de Montréal est le premier du monde à rouler° sur des pneus° plutôt que° sur des roues° en métal. Chaque station a été conçue° par un architecte différent.
En France L'Eurotunnel (le tunnel sous la Manche°) permet aux trains Eurostar de transporter des voyageurs et des marchandises entre la France et l'Angleterre.
En Mauritanie Le train du désert, en Mauritanie, en Afrique, est peut-être le train de marchandises le plus long° du monde. Long de 2,5 km en général, le train fait six voyages chaque jour du Sahara à la côte ouest°. C'est un voyage de plus de 600 km qui dure° 12 heures. Un des seuls moyens° de transport dans la région, ce train est aussi un train de voyageurs.

faits insolites *unusual facts* **rouler** *ride* **pneus** *tires* **plutôt que** *rather than* **roues** *wheels* **conçue** *designed* **Manche** *English Channel* **le plus long** *the longest* **côte ouest** *west coast* **dure** *lasts* **seuls moyens** *only means*

PORTRAIT

Le musée d'Orsay

Le musée d'Orsay, situé sur la rive° gauche de la Seine, est un des musées parisiens les plus° visités. Le lieu n'a pourtant° pas toujours été un musée. À l'origine, ce bâtiment° est une gare, construite par l'architecte Victor Laloux et inaugurée en 1900 à l'occasion de l'Exposition universelle. Les voies° de la gare d'Orsay deviennent° trop courtes et en 1939, on décide de limiter le service aux trains de banlieue. Plus tard, la gare sert de décor à des films, comme *Le Procès*, adapté du roman de Kafka par Orson Welles, puis° de théâtre et de salle de ventes aux enchères°. En 1986, le bâtiment est transformé et on inaugure le musée. Il est principalement dédié° à l'art du dix-neuvième siècle°, avec une collection magnifique d'art impressionniste. À Orsay, la grande diversité de l'art occidental est mise en valeur: peinture, sculpture, arts décoratifs, arts graphiques, photographie ou encore architecture. On peut y voir des chefs-d'œuvre° d'artistes comme Manet, Courbet, Cézanne, Monet ou Renoir. Il est possible de découvrir les collections grâce aux audioguides, disponibles en plusieurs langues, qui commentent plus de 300 œuvres. La boutique du musée d'Orsay propose des affiches, des livres et des accessoires de décoration ou de mode. On trouve aussi des restaurants dans le musée.

Danseuses en bleu,
Edgar Degas

rive *bank* **les plus** *the most* **pourtant** *however* **bâtiment** *building* **voies** *tracks* **deviennent** *become* **puis** *then* **ventes aux enchères** *auction* **principalement dédié** *mainly dedicated* **siècle** *century* **chefs-d'œuvre** *masterpieces* **siècle** *century*

2

Vrai ou faux? Indiquez si les phrases sont vraies ou fausses. Corrigez les phrases fausses.

1. Le musée d'Orsay a été un théâtre.
   Vrai.
2. Le musée d'Orsay a été une station de métro.
   Faux. Il a été une gare.
3. Le musée d'Orsay est dédié à la sculpture moderne.
   Faux. Le musée d'Orsay est dédié à l'art du dix-neuvième siècle.
4. Les audioguides sont seulement proposés en français.
   Faux. Ils sont disponibles en plusieurs langues.
5. Il y a un tunnel entre la France et la Guyane française.
   Faux. Il y a un tunnel entre la France et l'Angleterre.
6. Le métro de Montréal roule sur des roues en métal.
   Faux. Le métro de Montréal roule sur des pneus.

3

Comment voyager? Vous allez passer deux semaines en France. Vous avez envie de visiter Paris et deux autres régions. Par petits groupes, parlez des moyens (*means*) de transport que vous allez utiliser pendant votre voyage. Expliquez vos choix (*choices*).

 Practice more at **vhlcentral.com**.

A C T I V I T É S

Le français quotidien Explain that French people visit **la SNCF** (**Société nationale des chemins de fer français**) to get information about rates and to buy train tickets (just as Americans go to an Amtrak station). Bring in a map showing train routes, so students understand the viability of train travel to and from big cities and small towns alike. Remind students of what they learned about **le TGV** in **Unité 2, Panorama**, page 83.

Portrait Show photos of Claude Monet's train paintings **La Gare Saint-Lazare**, **Train dans la neige**, and **Train dans la campagne**, the last of which is in **le musée d'Orsay**.

Le monde francophone Have students work in pairs to ask each other content questions. Examples: **1. Quel est le nom du tunnel entre la France et l'Angleterre? (L'Eurotunnel/ le tunnel sous la Manche) 2. Quelle est une des différences entre le métro de Montréal et le métro de Paris? (Le métro de Montréal roule sur des pneus.)**

Suggestion Point out to students that they will find supporting activities and more information related to this **Espace culture** at **vhlcentral.com**.

2 Expansion Continue the activity with these true/false statements.
7. La gare d'Orsay a servi de décor à des films. (Vrai.)
8. Quand les voies deviennent trop courtes, la gare d'Orsay est limitée au métro. (Faux, aux trains de banlieue)

3 Expansion Once students have agreed on the areas they would like to visit, they should consult road and train maps to see which **moyen de transport** would work best.

OPTIONS

Cultural Comparison Bring in maps of the Paris **métro** and **RER** along with maps of a well-known American public transportation system, such as the New York City subway. Ask students: **Quel moyen de transport préférez-vous à Paris? à New York?** Then have them discuss their answers and plan mock commutes to various destinations in the two cities. Tell them to list similarities (**Similitudes**) and differences (**Différences**) between the American and French subway systems. Have groups compare lists.

Les transports You may want to supplement this section by telling students about travel between **Tanger (Maroc)** and **Algésiras (Espagne)** via hydrofoil; between **la Corse, l'Italie,** and **la Tunisie** by ferry; **le funiculaire de Montmartre**; **les canaux** in France; and **le bus amphibie** in **Montréal**.

Section Goals

In this section, students will learn the **passé composé** with **être**.

Instructional Resources
vhlcentral.com:
Lab MP3s; SAM Answer Key;
Digital Image Bank; Essayez!
and Mise en pratique
answers; Lab Audioscript;
Activity Pack (Feuilles
d'activités); reference tools

Suggestions

- Quickly review the **passé composé** with **avoir**.
- Introduce the **passé composé** with **être** by describing where you went yesterday. Example: **Hier, je suis allé(e) à la bibliothèque de la faculté. Ensuite, je suis allé(e) chez moi.** Then ask students: **Et vous, où êtes-vous allé(e) hier?**
- Write the **passé composé** of **donner** and **aller** on the board. Have students compare the forms of the **passé composé** with **avoir** and **être**.
- Explain the agreement of past participles in the **passé composé** with **être**.
- You may want to explain to students that because the pronoun **on** can represent either a singular or a plural subject, in the **passé composé**, they can use either a singular or plural past participle. Remind students, however, that **on** always takes the third person singular form of the verb. In the following example, either past participle spelling is correct. Example: **Céline et moi, on est tombé(s) du vélo.**
- Ask students to guess the gender of **je** and **tu** in the negative examples to illustrate how past participle agreement can show a subject's gender.

7A.1

The *passé composé* with *être*  Tutorial

Point de départ In **Leçon 6A**, you learned to form the **passé composé** with **avoir**. Some verbs, however, form the **passé composé** with **être**. Many such verbs involve motion. You have already learned a few of them: **aller, arriver, descendre, partir, sortir, passer, rentrer,** and **tomber**.

- To form the **passé composé** of these verbs, use a present-tense form of the auxiliary verb **être** and the past participle of the verb that expresses the action.

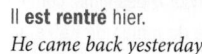

	PRESENT TENSE	PAST PARTICIPLE		PRESENT TENSE	PAST PARTICIPLE
Je	suis	allé.	Il	est	sorti.

Tu es parti pour Paris.

Mes parents sont arrivés des États-Unis.

Il **est rentré** hier.
He came back yesterday.

Je **suis tombé** de la chaise.
I fell off the chair.

- The past participles of verbs conjugated with **être** agree with their subjects in number and gender.

The *passé composé*

je suis **allé**(e)	*I went/have gone*	**nous** sommes **allé**(e)s	*we went/have gone*
tu es **allé**(e)	*you went/have gone*	**vous** êtes **allé**(e)(s)	*you went/have gone*
il/on est **allé**	*he/it/one went/has gone*	**ils** sont **allés**	*they went/have gone*
elle est **allée**	*she/it went/has gone*	**elles** sont **allées**	*they went/have gone*

Charles, tu **es allé** à Montréal?
Charles, did you go to Montreal?

Florence **est partie** en vacances.
Florence went on vacation.

Mes frères **sont rentrés**.
My brothers came back.

Elles **sont arrivées** hier soir.
They arrived last night.

- To make a verb negative in the **passé composé**, place **ne/n'** and **pas** around the auxiliary verb, in this case, **être**.

Marie-Thérèse **n'est pas sortie**?
Marie-Thérèse didn't go out?

Nous **ne sommes pas allées** à la plage.
We didn't go to the beach.

Je **ne suis pas passé** chez mon amie.
I didn't drop by my friend's house.

Tu **n'es pas rentré** à la maison hier.
You didn't come home yesterday.

- Here is a list of verbs that take **être** in the **passé composé**, including the ones you already know.

Verbs that take *être* in the *passé composé*			
aller		passer	
arriver		rentrer	
partir		sortir	
descendre		tomber	
entrer	*to enter*	rester	*to stay*
monter	*to go up; to get in/on*	retourner	*to return*
mourir	*to die*	naître	*to be born*

- These verbs have irregular past participles in the **passé composé**.

naître ▶ **né**

Mes parents **sont nés** en 1958 à Paris.
My parents were born in Paris in 1958.

mourir ▶ **mort**

Ma grand-mère **est morte** l'année dernière.
My grandmother died last year.

- Note that the verb **passer** takes **être** when it means *to pass by,* but it takes **avoir** when it means *to spend time.*

Maryse **est passée** à la douane.
Maryse passed through customs.

Maryse **a passé** trois jours à la campagne.
Maryse spent three days in the country.

- The verb **sortir** takes **être** in the **passé composé** when it means *to go out* or *to leave,* but it takes **avoir** when it means *to take someone or something out.*

Elle **est sortie** de chez elle.
She left her house.

Elle **a sorti** la voiture du garage.
She took the car out of the garage.

- To form a question using inversion in the **passé composé**, invert the subject pronoun and the conjugated form of **être**.

Est-elle restée à l'hôtel Aquabella?
Did she stay at the Aquabella Hotel?

Êtes-vous arrivée ce matin, Madame Roch?
Did you arrive this morning, Mrs. Roch?

- In affirmative statements, place short adverbs such as **déjà**, **encore**, **bien**, **mal**, and **beaucoup** between the auxiliary verb **être** and the past participle. In negative statements, place these adverbs after **pas**.

Elle **est déjà rentrée** de vacances?
She already came back from vacation?

Nous **ne sommes pas encore arrivés** à Lyon.
We haven't arrived in Lyons yet.

À noter

The verb **venir** (*to come*) also takes **être** in the **passé composé**. You will learn this verb in **Leçon 9A**.

Essayez! Choisissez le participe passé approprié.

1. Vous êtes (nés / (né)) en 1959, Monsieur?
2. Les élèves sont ((partis) / parti) le 2 juin.
3. Les filles sont ((rentrées) / rentrés) de vacances.
4. Simone de Beauvoir est-elle (mort / (morte)) en 1986?
5. Mes frères sont ((sortis) / sortie).
6. Paul n'est pas ((resté) / restée) chez sa grand-mère.
7. Tu es (arrivés / (arrivée)) avant dix heures, Sophie.
8. Jacqueline a (passée / (passé)) une semaine en Suisse.

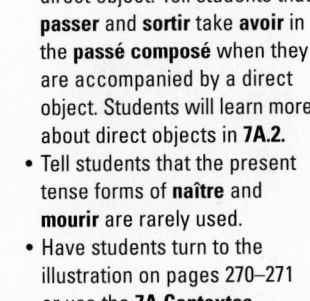

ressources

WB
pp. 91–92

LM
p. 51

vhlcentral

deux cent soixante-dix-neuf **279**

Suggestions
- Point out the verbs that form the **passé composé** with **être** as well as the irregular past participles **mort** and **né**.
- To help students remember which verbs take **être**, draw a house with doors, windows, and a staircase. Write captions that include verbs that take **être** in the **passé composé** to describe what various people are doing. Alternatively, consider giving them the mnemonic device **DR & MRS P. VANDERTRAMP**, which includes many of these verbs and their derivatives. Remind students that they will learn **venir** in Unit 9.
- You may want to explain that verbs conjugated with **être** in the **passé composé** are *intransitive*: They do not take a direct object. Tell students that **passer** and **sortir** take **avoir** in the **passé composé** when they are accompanied by a direct object. Students will learn more about direct objects in **7A.2**.
- Tell students that the present tense forms of **naître** and **mourir** are rarely used.
- Have students turn to the illustration on pages 270–271 or use the **7A Contextes** illustration from the Digital Image Bank and have them describe the scene in the past.
- Tell students they will learn about adverbs in **Espace structures 7B**.

Essayez! For additional practice, change the subjects of the sentences (except items 1 and 7), and have students restate or rewrite them.

OPTIONS

Extra Practice To practice discriminating between the **passé composé** with **être** and the **passé composé** with **avoir**, call out infinitives and have students respond with **avoir** or **être** and the past participle. Examples: **1.** voyager (avoir voyagé) **2.** entrer (être entré) **3.** aller (être allé) **4.** parler (avoir parlé) **5.** retourner (être retourné)

Game Divide the class into two teams. Choose one team member at a time to go to the board, alternating between teams. Say a subject pronoun and an infinitive. The person at the board must write and say the correct **passé composé** form. Example: **je: aller (je suis allé[e])**. Give a point for each correct answer. The team with the most points at the end of the game wins.

1 Suggestion Before beginning the activity, have students identify the past participles of the verbs in parentheses.

3 Expansion Ask students what they did last Sunday.

4 Expansion Have two volunteers play the roles of Djénaba and Safiatou. Tell the rest of the class to ask them questions about their trip. Example: **Quand êtes-vous arrivées à Dakar?**

Mise en pratique

1 **Un week-end sympa** Carole raconte son week-end à Paris. Complétez l'histoire avec les formes correctes des verbes au passé composé.

Thomas et moi, nous (1) ___sommes partis___ (partir) de Lyon samedi et nous (2) ___sommes arrivés___ (arriver) à Paris à onze heures. Nous (3) ___sommes passés___ (passer) à l'hôtel et puis je (4) ___suis allée___ (aller) au Louvre. En route, je (5) ___suis tombée___ (tomber) sur un vieil ami, et nous (6) ___sommes allés___ (aller) prendre un café. Ensuite, je (7) ___suis entrée___ (entrer) dans le musée. Samedi soir, Thomas et moi (8) ___sommes montés___ (monter) au sommet de la tour Eiffel et après nous (9) ___sommes sortis___ (sortir) en boîte. Dimanche, nous (10) ___sommes retournés___ (retourner) au Louvre. Alors aujourd'hui, je suis fatiguée.

2 **La routine** Voici ce que Nadia et Éric font aujourd'hui. Dites qu'ils ont fait les mêmes activités samedi dernier.

1. Ils vont au parc.   Ils sont allés au parc.
2. Nadia fait du cheval.   Nadia a fait du cheval.
3. Éric passe une heure à la bibliothèque.   Éric a passé une heure à la bibliothèque.
4. Nadia sort avec ses amis.   Nadia est sortie avec ses amis.
5. Ils rentrent tard le soir.   Ils sont rentrés tard le soir.
6. Ils jouent au golf.   Ils ont joué au golf.

3 **Dimanche dernier** Dites ce que (*what*) ces personnes ont fait dimanche dernier. Utilisez les verbes de la liste.   Suggested answers

Laure

▶ **MODÈLE**

Laure est allée à la piscine.

aller	rentrer
arriver	rester
monter	sortir

1. je
Je suis rentré tard.

2. tu
Tu es restée à l'hôtel.

3. nous
Nous sommes allés à l'église.

4. Pamela et Caroline
Pamela et Caroline sont sorties.

4 **L'accident** Le mois dernier, Djénaba et Safiatou sont allées au Sénégal. Avec un(e) partenaire, complétez les phrases au passé composé. Ensuite, mettez-les dans l'ordre chronologique.

___1___ **a.** les filles / partir pour Dakar en avion   Les filles sont parties pour Dakar en avion.

___5___ **b.** Djénaba / tomber de vélo   Djénaba est tombée de vélo.

___4___ **c.** elles / aller faire du vélo dimanche matin   Elles sont allées faire du vélo dimanche matin.

___2___ **d.** elles / arriver à Dakar tard le soir   Elles sont arrivées à Dakar tard le soir.

___3___ **e.** elles / rester à l'hôtel Sofitel   Elles sont restées à l'hôtel Sofitel.

___6___ **f.** elle / aller à l'hôpital   Elle est allée à l'hôpital.

 Practice more at vhlcentral.com.

5 Suggestion Have two volunteers read the **modèle** aloud.

6 Suggestion Distribute the **Feuilles d'activités** found in the Activity Pack on the Supersite.

7 Suggestion Before beginning the activity, ask the students about their travel experiences. Example: **Êtes-vous déjà allé(e)s dans un autre pays?**

Communication

5 **Les vacances de printemps** Avec un(e) partenaire, parlez de vos dernières vacances de printemps. Répondez à toutes ses questions. Answers will vary.

MODÈLE

quand / partir
Étudiant(e) 1: *Quand es-tu parti(e)?*
Étudiant(e) 2: *Je suis parti(e) vendredi soir.*

1. où / aller
2. avec qui / partir
3. comment / voyager
4. à quelle heure / arriver
5. où / dormir

6. combien de temps / rester
7. que / visiter
8. sortir / souvent le soir
9. que / acheter
10. quand / rentrer

6 **Enquête** Votre professeur va vous donner une feuille d'activités. Circulez dans la classe et demandez à différents camarades s'ils ont fait ces choses récemment (*recently*). Présentez les résultats de votre enquête à la classe. Answers will vary.

MODÈLE

Étudiant(e) 1: *Es-tu allé(e) au musée récemment?*
Étudiant(e) 2: *Oui, je suis allé(e) au musée jeudi dernier.*

Questions	Nom
1. aller au musée	François
2. passer chez ses amis	
3. sortir en boîte	
4. rester à la maison pour écouter de la musique	
5. partir en week-end avec un copain	
6. monter en avion	

7 **À l'aéroport** Par groupes de quatre, parlez d'une mauvaise expérience dans un aéroport. À tour de rôle, racontez (*tell*) vos aventures et posez le plus (*most*) de questions possible. Utilisez les expressions de la liste et d'autres aussi. Answers will vary.

MODÈLE

Étudiant(e) 1: *Quand je suis rentré(e) de la Martinique, j'ai attendu trois heures à la douane.*
Étudiant(e) 2: *Quelle horreur! Pourquoi?*

aller	passer
arriver	perdre
attendre	plan
avion	prendre un avion
billet (aller-retour)	sortir
douane	tomber
gens	valise
partir	vol

O P T I O N S

Video Show the video episode again to give students more input regarding the **passé composé** with **être** and **avoir**. Pause the video where appropriate to discuss how certain verbs were used and to ask comprehension questions.

Extra Practice Using the information in the **Roman-photo**, have students write a summary of David's trip to Paris. Then have students get together with a partner and exchange papers. Tell them to peer edit each other's work. Remind them to check for the correct usage of **avoir** and **être** in the **passé composé**, subject-verb agreement, and the correct forms of past participles.

ESPACE STRUCTURES **281**

Section Goals

In this section, students will learn direct object pronouns.

Instructional Resources

vhlcentral.com:
Activity Pack; Lab MP3s;
SAM Answer Key;
***Essayez!** and **Mise en
pratique** answers;*
Lab Audioscript; reference tools

Suggestions

- Write these sentences on the board: **Qui a les tickets? Roger les a.** Underline **les tickets** and explain that it is the direct object. Then underline **les** and explain that it is the plural direct object pronoun. Translate both sentences, pointing out the word order. Follow the same procedure with these sentences.
  —**Qui prend le bus?**
  —**Les étudiants le prennent.**
  —**Qui écrit la lettre?**
  —**Mon père l'écrit.**
- Take various objects from students' desks and ask: **Qui a _____?** Have students respond using the direct object pronoun: **Vous _____ avez.**
- Point out that direct objects are never preceded by a preposition.

Leçon 7A

7A.2

ESPACE STRUCTURES

Direct object pronouns  Tutorial

Point de départ In **Leçon 6B**, you learned about indirect objects. You are now going to learn about direct objects.

DIRECT OBJECT	INDIRECT OBJECT

J'ai fait **un cadeau à ma sœur**.
I gave a present to my sister.

- A direct object is a noun that follows a verb and answers the question *what* or *whom*. Note that a direct object receives the action of a verb directly and an indirect object receives the action of a verb indirectly. While indirect objects are frequently preceded by the preposition **à**, no preposition is needed before a direct object.

DIRECT OBJECT
J'emmène **mes parents**.
I'm taking my parents.

but

INDIRECT OBJECT
Je parle **à mes parents**.
I'm talking to my parents.

Tes parents sont allés te chercher?

Tu m'excuses une minute?

Direct object pronouns

singular		plural	
me/m'	*me*	nous	*us*
te/t'	*you*	vous	*you*
le/la/l'	*him/her/it*	les	*them*

Boîte à outils

Some French verbs do not take a preposition although their English equivalents do: **écouter** (*to listen to*), **chercher** (*to look for*) and **attendre** (*to wait for*). In deciding whether an object is direct or indirect, always check if the French verb takes the preposition **à**.

Boîte à outils

Unlike indirect object pronouns, direct object pronouns can replace a person, a place, or a thing.

- You can use a direct object pronoun in the place of a direct object noun.

Tu fais **les valises**?
Are you packing the suitcases?
► Tu **les** fais?
Are you packing them?

Ils retrouvent **Luc** à la gare.
They're meeting Luc at the train station.
► Ils **le** retrouvent à la gare.
They're meeting him at the train station.

Tu visites souvent **la Belgique**?
Do you visit Belgium often?
► Tu **la** visites souvent?
Do you visit there often?

- Place a direct object pronoun before the conjugated verb. In the **passé composé**, place a direct object pronoun before the conjugated form of the auxiliary verb **avoir**.

Les langues? Laurent et Xavier **les** étudient.
Languages? Laurent and Xavier study them.

Les étudiants **vous** ont entendu.
The students heard you.

M'attendez-vous à l'aéroport?
Are you waiting for me at the airport?

Et Daniel? **L'**as-tu retrouvé au cinéma?
And Daniel? Did you meet him at the movies?

282 *deux cent quatre-vingt-deux*

- In a negative statement, place the direct object pronoun between **ne/n'** and the conjugated verb.

    Le chinois? Je **ne le parle pas**.
    Chinese? I don't speak it.

    Elle **ne l'a pas** pris à 14 heures?
    She didn't take it at 2 o'clock?

- When an infinitive follows a conjugated verb, the direct object pronoun precedes the infinitive.

    Marcel va **nous écouter**.
    Marcel will listen to us.

    Tu ne préfères pas **la porter** demain?
    Wouldn't you rather wear it tomorrow?

Et le gâteau, je l'ai adoré!

Les musées, je les ai adorés!

- When a direct object pronoun is used with the **passé composé**, the past participle must agree with it in both gender and number.

    J'ai mis **la valise** dans la voiture ce matin.
    I put the suitcase in the car this morning.

    ▶ Je **l'ai mise** dans la voiture ce matin.
    I put it in the car this morning.

    J'ai attendu **les filles** à la gare.
    I waited for the girls at the train station.

    ▶ Je **les** ai **attendues** à la gare.
    I waited for them at the train station.

- When the gender of the direct object pronoun is ambiguous, the past participle agreement will indicate the gender of the direct object to which it refers.

    Ses copains ne **l'ont pas trouvée**.
    Her friends didn't find her.

    Mon père **nous** a **entendus**.
    My father heard us.

- In questions using **Quel(s)/Quelle(s)** and the **passé composé**, the past participle must agree with the gender and number of **Quel(s)/Quelle(s)**.

    Quel hôtel avez-vous **choisi**?
    Which hotel did you choose?

    Quels pays as-tu **visités**?
    Which countries did you visit?

    Quelle plage as-tu **préférée**?
    Which beach did you prefer?

    Quelles valises as-tu **apportées**?
    Which suitcases did you bring?

Boîte à outils

The direct object pronoun **vous** can refer to several people or to one person (formal address). Therefore, the past participle can be masculine singular or plural or feminine singular or plural. Examples:

M. Bruel, je vous ai cherché dans le bureau.

Mme Diop, je vous ai cherchée dans le parc.

Les enfants, je vous ai cherchés dans le gymnase.

Les filles, je vous ai cherchées dans la chambre.

Essayez!

Répondez aux questions en remplaçant l'objet direct par un pronom d'objet direct.

1. Thierry prend le train? Oui, il ___le___ prend.
2. Tu attends ta mère? Oui, je ___l'___ attends.
3. Vous entendez Olivier et Vincent? Oui, on ___les___ entend.
4. Le professeur te cherche? Oui, il ___me___ cherche.
5. Barbara et Caroline retrouvent Linda? Oui, elles ___la___ retrouvent.
6. Vous m'invitez? Oui, nous ___t'/vous___ invitons.
7. Tu nous comprends? Oui, je ___vous___ comprends.
8. Elles regardent la mer? Oui, elles ___la___ regardent.
9. Chloé aime la musique classique? Oui, elle ___l'___ aime.
10. Vous avez regardé le film *Chacun cherche son chat*? Oui, nous ___l'___ avons regardé.

ressources

WB
pp. 93-94

LM
p. 52

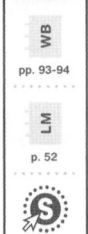

vhlcentral

Suggestions
- Continue asking questions to elicit other direct object pronouns. Examples: **M'entendez-vous?** (Oui, nous vous entendons.) **Qui achète vos vêtements?** (Je les achète.)
- Explain the agreement of past participles with direct object pronouns in the **passé composé**.
- Point out that in the second-to-last bullet, **trouvée** indicates that **l'** refers to a female, while **entendus** indicates that **nous** refers to at least two males or a mixed group of males and females. Tell students that this strategy works well for written French. In the spoken language, however, only a handful of past participles ending in a consonant, such as **fait** and **mis**, predictably reveal the gender of the direct object: **faite(s), mise(s)**.

Essayez! For additional practice, have students restate or rewrite the answers in the negative.

OPTIONS

Game Send a student out of the room. Give his or her belongings to other students to hide. Then have the person return. To get the belongings back, the person must ask students yes/no questions. They should respond using direct object pronouns. Example: **Tu as mon livre?** (Oui, je l'ai./Non, je ne l'ai pas.)

Pairs Have students work in pairs. Write the following list on the board. Tell them to take turns asking each other who does these activities: **acheter le billet, prendre le bus, aimer les sports, passer la douane,** and **étudier les mathématiques.** Example: **Qui prend le bus?** (Mon ami Patrick le prend.)

2 Suggestion Have students ask questions with a direct object pronoun for each item. Example: **Qui l'écoute?**

3 Suggestion Before beginning the activity, have students identify the direct objects.

4 Suggestion Tell students to add two of their own questions to the list.

Mise en pratique

1 À l'aéroport Jules est à l'aéroport et il parle à sa mère. Choisissez le pronom d'objet direct approprié pour compléter ses phrases.

1. Ton CD préféré? Marie (le, la, (l')) écoute.
2. Le plan? Les Cartier (la, les, (le)) regardent.
3. Notre amie? Roger et Emma (l', le, (la)) cherchent.
4. Le journal français? Papa (la, (l'), le) achète.
5. Nos billets? Coralie (le, l', (les)) a pris.

2 On fait beaucoup de choses Dites ce que (what) ces gens font le week-end. Employez des pronoms d'objet direct.

▶ **MODÈLE**

Il l'écoute.

Dominique / ce CD

1. Benoît / ses film
Il les regarde.

2. ma mère / cette robe
Elle l'admire.

3. Philippe / son gâteau
Il le mange.

4. Stéphanie et Marc / ces lunettes
Ils les achètent.

3 À la plage La famille de Dalila a passé une semaine à la mer. Dalila parle de ce que (what) chaque membre de sa famille a fait. Employez des pronoms d'objet direct.

MODÈLE

J'ai conduit Ahmed à la plage. _Je l'ai conduit à la plage._

1. Mon père a acheté le journal tous les matins. Il l'a acheté tous les matins.
2. Ma sœur a retrouvé son petit ami au café. Elle l'a retrouvé au café.
3. Mes parents ont emmené les enfants au cinéma. Ils les ont emmenés au cinéma.
4. Mon frère a invité sa fiancée au restaurant. Il l'a invitée au restaurant.
5. Anissa a porté ses lunettes de soleil. Elle les a portées.
6. Noah a pris les cartes. Il les a prises.

4 Des doutes Julien et sa petite amie Caroline sont au café. Il est inquiet et lui pose des questions sur leurs vacances avec ses parents. Avec un(e) partenaire, jouez les deux rôles. Ensuite, présentez la scène à la classe. Suggested answers

1. Tes parents m'invitent au bord de la mer? Oui, ils t'invitent au bord de la mer.
2. Tes parents vont m'écouter? Oui, ils vont t'écouter.
3. Tu vas m'attendre à l'aéroport? Oui, je vais t'attendre à l'aéroport.
4. Ton frère va nous emmener sur son bateau? Oui, il va nous emmener sur son bateau.
5. Tu penses que ta famille va m'aimer? Oui, je pense qu'elle va t'aimer.
6. Tu m'adores? Oui, je t'adore.

Communication

5

Le départ Clémentine va partir au Cameroun chez sa correspondante (*pen pal*) Léa. Sa mère veut (*wants*) être sûre qu'elle est prête, mais Clémentine n'a encore rien (*nothing*) fait. Avec un(e) partenaire, jouez leur conversation en utilisant les phrases de la liste. Answers will vary.

MODÈLE

Étudiant(e) 1: *Tu as acheté le cadeau pour ton amie?*
Étudiant(e) 2: *Non, je ne l'ai pas encore acheté.*
Étudiant(e) 1: *Quand vas-tu l'acheter?*
Étudiant(e) 2: *Je vais l'acheter cet après-midi.*

acheter ton billet d'avion	faire tes valises
avoir l'adresse de Léa	finir ton shopping
chercher un maillot de bain	prendre tes lunettes
choisir le cadeau de Léa	préparer tes vêtements
confirmer l'heure de l'arrivée	trouver ton passeport

6

À Tahiti Imaginez que vous alliez partir à Tahiti. Avec un(e) partenaire, posez-vous ces questions. Il/Elle vous répond en utilisant le pronom d'objet direct approprié. Ensuite, alternez les rôles. Answers will vary.

MODÈLE

Est-ce que tu prends le bus pour aller à la plage?
Non, je ne le prends pas.

1. Aimes-tu la mer?
2. Est-ce que tu prends l'avion?
3. Qui va t'attendre à l'aéroport?
4. Quand as-tu fait tes valises?
5. Est-ce que tu as acheté ton maillot de bain?
6. Est-ce que tu prends ton appareil photo?
7. Où as-tu acheté tes vêtements?
8. As-tu déjà choisi ton hôtel à Tahiti?
9. Est-ce que tu as réservé ta chambre d'hôtel?
10. Tu vas regarder la télévision tahitienne?
11. Vas-tu essayer les plats typiques de Tahiti?
12. As-tu regardé le plan de Tahiti?

deux cent quatre-vingt-cinq **285**

5 Suggestions
- Before beginning the activity, have students underline the direct objects in the phrases.
- Have two volunteers read the **modèle** aloud.

6 Suggestions
- Before beginning the activity, have students describe the photo.
- Tell students to add three of their own questions with direct objects to the list.

OPTIONS

Extra Practice Make a list of twenty questions requiring direct object pronouns in the answer. Arrange students in two concentric circles. Students in the inner circle ask questions from the list to those in the outer circle until you say stop (**Arrêtez-vous**). The outer circle then moves one person to the right and the questions begin again. Continue for five minutes, and then have the students in the outer circle ask the questions.

Pairs Have students work in pairs. Tell them to invent a romantic dialogue between Simone and Jean-Claude, two protagonists of a soap opera. They should include direct object pronouns in their dialogues and these verbs: **adorer, aimer, détester,** and **attendre.** Example: **Jean-Claude: Simone, je t'adore.**

Révision

Instructional Resources
vhlcentral.com:
Activity Pack (*Feuilles d'activités*; *Info Gap Activities*);
Testing Program; *Testing Program MP3s*; reference tools

1 Suggestion Have students write out the questions and answers. Check use of subject pronouns and the **imparfait** forms of **être**.

2 Suggestions
• Ask two students to read the **modèle** aloud. Then distribute the **Feuilles d'activités** found in the Activity Pack on the Supersite.
• Encourage students to add sports and leisure activities not already found in their survey.

3 Suggestion Have two volunteers model a question and answer for the class.

3 Expansion After group members finish questioning each other, have a student from each group read the answers from another student. The class will then guess which student's childhood birthday celebration was described.

4 Suggestion Before beginning the activity, have students describe what the people in the drawing are doing in the present tense.

5 Expansion Tell students to imagine they are the **ancien(ne) patron(ne)** and have decided to give the employee a second chance. It is time for the three-month review. Have them draft a brief letter to the employee discussing his or her past versus present performance on the job.

6 Suggestion Divide the class into pairs and distribute the Info Gap Handouts found in the Activity Pack on the Supersite.

---

1 Il y a dix minutes Avec un(e) partenaire, décrivez (*describe*) dans cette scène les actions qui se sont passées (*happened*) il y a dix minutes. Utilisez les verbes de la liste pour écrire (*write*) des phrases. Ensuite, comparez vos phrases avec les phrases d'un autre groupe. Answers will vary.

MODÈLE

Étudiant(e) 1: *Il y a dix minutes, M. Hamid est parti.*
Étudiant(e) 2: *Il y a dix minutes, …*

aller	partir
arriver	rentrer
descendre	sortir
monter	tomber

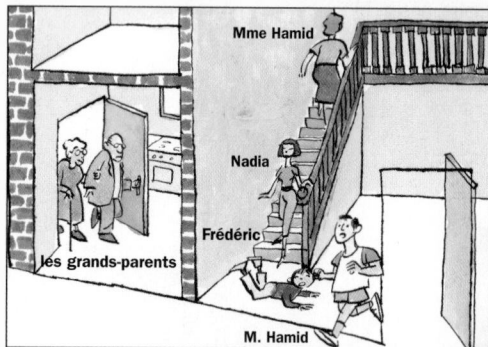

2 Qui aime quoi? Votre professeur va vous donner une feuille d'activités. Circulez dans la classe pour trouver un(e) camarade différent(e) qui aime ou qui n'aime pas chaque lieu de la liste. Answers will vary.

MODÈLE

Étudiant(e) 1: *Est-ce que tu aimes les aéroports?*
Étudiant(e) 2: *Je ne les aime pas du tout; je les déteste.*

3 À l'étranger Par groupes de quatre, interviewez vos camarades. Dans quels pays sont-ils déjà allés? Dans quelles villes? Comparez vos destinations, puis présentez toutes les réponses à la classe. N'oubliez pas de demander: Answers will vary.

• quand vos camarades sont parti(e)s
• où ils/elles sont allé(e)s
• où ils/elles sont resté(e)s
• combien de temps ils/elles ont passé là-bas

4 La valise Sandra et John sont partis en vacances. Voici leur valise. Avec un(e) partenaire, faites une description écrite (*written*) de leurs vacances. Où sont-ils allés? Comment sont-ils partis? Answers will vary.

5 Un long week-end Avec un(e) partenaire, préparez huit questions sur le dernier long week-end. Utilisez les verbes de la liste. Ensuite, par groupes de quatre, répondez à toutes les questions. Answers will vary.

MODÈLE

Étudiant(e) 1: *Où es-tu allé(e) vendredi soir?*
Étudiant(e) 2: *Vendredi soir, je suis resté(e) chez moi. Mais samedi, je suis sorti(e)!*

aller	rentrer
arriver	rester
partir	retourner
passer	sortir

6 Mireille et les Girard Votre professeur va vous donner, à vous et à votre partenaire, une feuille sur le week-end de Mireille et de la famille Girard. Attention! Ne regardez pas la feuille de votre partenaire. Answers will vary.

MODÈLE

Étudiant(e) 1: *Qu'est-ce que Mireille a fait vendredi soir?*
Étudiant(e) 2: *Elle est allée au cinéma.*

O P T I O N S

Extra Practice Use these sentences containing adverbs and regular and irregular verbs in the **imparfait** as a dictation. Read each sentence twice, pausing after the second time for students to write. **1. Heureusement, il y avait beaucoup d'étudiants dans la classe. 2. Conduisait-il vite ta voiture? 3. J'étais vraiment très heureuse de te voir. 4. Il fallait constamment travailler le samedi.**

Extra Practice Have small groups organize a skit about a birthday or other party that took place recently. Guide them to first make general comments about the party, such as **C'était vraiment amusant!** Then describe a few specific things that were going on, what people were talking about, what they were wearing, and any other appropriate details. After the skits are performed, have students vote for their favorite.

Flash CULTURE

En vacances

Hôtesse Csilla

Dans cette vidéo, on nous montre les moyens de transport qu'on peut prendre pour aller en Provence. Les gens aiment passer leurs vacances en Provence parce qu'il fait souvent très beau là-bas. Csilla nous présente plusieurs choses qu'on peut faire pendant° un séjour dans la région. Elle nous montre aussi Cassis avec sa plage et ses restaurants.

Avant de regarder Répondez aux questions. *Answers will vary.*

1. Que font les gens de votre région ou ville pendant leurs vacances?
2. Qu'est-ce que vous aimez faire pendant vos vacances?

Le TGV: *le Train à Grande Vitesse.*

Les auberges de jeunesse: *un type d'hébergement plus économique que les hôtels.*

🔊 Compréhension Répondez aux questions. *Some answers will vary.*

1. Quels sont les moyens de transport qu'on peut prendre pour arriver en Provence et pour visiter la région?
   On peut prendre l'avion, le train, l'autobus, le taxi ou la voiture.
2. Où peut-on dormir pendant des vacances en Provence?
   On peut dormir à l'hôtel. Il y a aussi des auberges de jeunesse et des campings.
3. Où se trouve Cassis?
   Cassis se trouve près d'Aix-en-Provence.
4. Qu'est-ce qui peut être très agréable à faire à Cassis?
   manger ou prendre un verre à la terrasse d'un café ou d'un restaurant, regarder les gens passer

👥 Discussion Par groupes de trois, répondez aux questions.

1. Est-ce qu'il y a des moyens de transport pour aller en Provence qui existent aussi chez vous? Quels types?
2. Où aimez-vous passer vos vacances d'été?
3. Où préférez-vous dormir quand vous voyagez? Pourquoi?

Vocabulaire utile

une auberge de jeunesse	*youth hostel*
loger	*to stay*
un moyen de transport	*means of transportation*
plus	*more*
le TGV	*high-speed train*

ressources

VM
pp. 73–74

vhlcentral

° **pendant** *during*

Practice more at **vhlcentral.com.**

O
P
T
I
O
N
S

Provence
While the French Riviera has been a popular vacation spot for over a century, Provence remained relatively unexplored by tourists until the 1980s, when the Englishman Peter Mayle published *A Year in Provence*, an account of his first year living in the area and the people and places he encountered there.

Cassis
The ambiance of the small, charming fishing village of Cassis is half-Provençal, half-Mediterranean. Visitors take advantage of the village's proximity to the **Massif des Calanques**, 20 kilometers of steep limestone inlets stretching from Cassis to Marseille. Cassis is also renowned for its wines, and is part of one of the oldest wine-growing areas of France.

Right margin:

Section Goals
In this section, students will:
• watch a video about vacationing in Aix-en-Provence
• answer questions about the video and describe personal preferences about traveling

Instructional Resources
vhlcentral.com: **Flash culture**; **Flash culture** *transcription; reference tools*

Avant de regarder
• Have students look at the video stills, read the captions, and predict what will happen in the video.
• Explain to students that they don't need to understand every word they hear. Tell them to listen for vocabulary from this lesson as well as cognates.

Compréhension Have students work in pairs or groups for this activity. Tell them to write down their answers. Then, show the video again so that they can check their answers and add any missing information.

Discussion Have students work in small groups to discuss whether they prefer organized or spontaneous travel. Ask, **Est-ce que vous aimez partir en vacances sans planifier ce que vous allez faire chaque jour, ou est-ce que vous préférez tout organiser avant de partir?** Then, have a class debate, where each group presents its best arguments.

Section Goals

In this section, students will learn and practice vocabulary related to:

- hotels
- ordinal numbers
- sequencing events

Instructional Resources
vhlcentral.com:
Digital Image Bank (including vocabulary illustrations from the textbook, theme-based illustrations); Vocabulaire supplémentaire; Mise en pratique answers; Textbook Audioscript; Lab Audioscript; Activity Pack; Textbook MP3s; Lab MP3s; SAM Answer Key; reference tools

Suggestions

- Use the **7B Contextes** illustration from the Digital Image Bank. Point out people and things in the illustration and describe what the people are doing. Example: **Ils sont à la réception d'un hôtel. Ils ont une réservation. Voici la clé de leur chambre.**
- Have students look over the new vocabulary. They should notice that many terms related to hotels and travel are cognates (**réservation, réception, passeport,** and **passager**).
- Point out that **passeport** has an **e** and **passager/passagère** have no **n**.
- Model the difference in pronunciation between **deuxième** and **douzième**, and have students repeat.
- Point out that the word **libre** means *free*, as in *available*, not *free of charge* (**gratuit(e)**).
- Emphasize that in this context, **complet/complète** means *full*, not *complete*.
- Tell students that the word **second(e)** is used instead of **deuxième** when there are only two items to list. Example: **La Seconde Guerre mondiale**.
- Additional vocabulary for this lesson can be found in the **Vocabulaire supplémentaire** on the Supersite.
- Use the Vocabulary illustrations and the travel illustrations from the Digital Image Bank to help students familiarize themselves with hotels, ordinal numbers, and sequencing events.

Leçon 7B

You will learn how to...
- make hotel reservations
- give instructions

S Vocabulary Tools

À l'hôtel

Vocabulaire

annuler une réservation	to cancel a reservation
réserver	to reserve, to book
premier/première	first
cinquième	fifth
neuvième	ninth
vingt et unième	twenty-first
vingt-deuxième	twenty-second
trente et unième	thirty-first
centième	hundredth
une agence de voyages	travel agency
un agent de voyages	travel agent
une auberge de jeunesse	youth hostel
une chambre individuelle	single room
un hôtel	hotel
un passager/une passagère	passenger
complet/complète	full (no vacancies)
libre	available
alors	so, then; at that moment
après (que)	after
avant (de)	before
d'abord	first
donc	therefore
enfin	finally, at last
ensuite	then, next
finalement	finally
pendant (que)	during, while
puis	then
tout à coup	suddenly
tout de suite	right away

la réception
le lit
l'hôtelier (m.)
l'hôtelière (f.)
le passeport
la clé
les client(e)s

Bienvenue!

ressources

WB pp. 95–96
LM p. 53
S vhlcentral

OPTIONS

TPR Ask ten volunteers to line up facing the class. Make sure students know what number they are in line. Call out ordinal numbers at random. The student whose cardinal number corresponds to the called ordinal number has three seconds to step forward. If that student is too slow, he or she sits down. The order changes for the rest of the students standing further down the line. The last students standing win.

Les étages Point out to students that a second floor in the U.S. would be called **le premier étage** in the Francophone world. Tell them that an **étage** is a floor above another floor. Elevators usually indicate the ground floor by the letter **R** (or other abbreviation of **rez-de-chaussée**) or the number **0**. Add that, in buildings with only two floors, people say **à l'étage** for *on the second floor*.

Mise en pratique

Attention!

Form ordinal numbers in French by placing –ième at the end of the cardinal number. If the cardinal number ends in an –e, drop it before adding –ième. Note the spelling changes in cinquième and neuvième. Also note that the French word for *first*, premier/première (1er/1ère), is an exception.

onze → onzième (11e)
vingt → vingtième (20e)

le premier étage

le rez-de-chaussée

l'ascenseur (m.)

les étages (m.)

le premier

le deuxième

le troisième

1er
2e   100-110
3e   200-210
4e   300-310
      400-410

le quatrième

1 Écoutez Écoutez la conversation entre Mme Renoir et un hôtelier et décidez si les phrases sont **vraies** ou **fausses**.

	Vrai	Faux
1. Mme Renoir est à l'agence de voyages.	☐	☑
2. Mme Renoir a fait une réservation.	☑	☐
3. Mme Renoir prend la chambre au cinquième étage.	☐	☑
4. Il y a un ascenseur dans l'hôtel.	☐	☑
5. Mme Renoir a réservé une chambre à deux lits.	☐	☑
6. La cliente s'appelle Margot Renoir.	☑	☐
7. L'hôtel a des chambres libres.	☐	☑
8. L'hôtelier donne à Mme Renoir la clé de la chambre 27.	☑	☐

2 Hôtel Paradis Virginie téléphone à l'hôtel Paradis pour faire une réservation. Mettez les phrases dans l'ordre chronologique.

__6__ a. Finalement, il me demande le numéro de ma carte de crédit (*credit card*) pour finaliser la réservation.

__2__ b. Pendant la conversation, je demande une chambre individuelle au troisième étage.

__1__ c. D'abord, j'appelle l'hôtel Paradis pour faire une réservation.

__4__ d. Je ne veux (*want*) pas dormir au rez-de-chaussée, donc je demande une chambre au deuxième étage.

__3__ e. Ensuite, l'hôtel me rappelle (*calls me back*) pour annoncer qu'il n'y a plus de chambre libre au troisième étage, donc ma réservation est annulée.

__5__ f. C'est alors que l'hôtelier me donne une chambre au deuxième étage à côté de l'ascenseur.

3 Remplissez Complétez les phrases avec le nombre ordinal qui convient (*fits*).

MODÈLE

B est la ___deuxième___ lettre de l'alphabet.

1. Décembre est le ___douzième___ mois de l'année.
2. Mercredi est le ___troisième___ jour de la semaine.
3. Aux États-Unis, le rez-de-chaussée est le ___premier___ étage.
4. Ma classe de français est au ___Answers will vary.___ (étage).
5. Octobre est le ___dixième___ mois de l'année.
6. Z est la ___vingt-sixième___ lettre de l'alphabet.
7. Samedi est le ___sixième___ jour de la semaine.
8. Barack Obama est le ___quarante-quatrième___ président des États-Unis.
9. Mon prénom (*first name*) commence avec la ___Answers will vary.___ lettre de l'alphabet.
10. La fête nationale américaine est le ___quatrième___ jour du mois de juillet.

Practice more at vhlcentral.com.

deux cent quatre-vingt-neuf **289**

1 Audioscript L'HÔTELIER: Bonjour, Madame. Bienvenue à l'hôtel Casablanca! Avez-vous une réservation?
LA CLIENTE: Bonjour, Monsieur. Oui, mon mari et moi avons fait une réservation.
H: Et c'est à quel nom?
C: Je l'ai faite à mon nom, Renoir.
H: Excellent! Vous avez réservé une chambre avec un grand lit. Votre chambre est la numéro 57 au cinquième étage.
C: Ah non, il y a une erreur. J'ai réservé la chambre numéro 27 au deuxième étage. Je refuse de prendre cette chambre, il n'y a pas d'ascenseur dans votre hôtel. Est-ce que vous avez une autre solution?
H: Madame Renoir, je suis désolé, mais l'hôtel est complet.
C: Oh là là. Ce n'est pas possible! Qu'est-ce que je vais faire?
H: Un instant, êtes-vous Marguerite Renoir?
C: Non, je suis Margot Renoir.
H: Madame Renoir, pardonnez-moi. Voici votre clé, chambre 27 au deuxième étage.
(On Textbook MP3s)

2 Suggestion Call students' attention to the sequencing words in these sentences. Examples: **Finalement, Pendant, D'abord,** etc.

2 Expansion Have pairs of students rewrite the story using the sequencing words, but changing the details. Example: reserve a different kind of room, encounter a different problem, and find a different solution.

3 Expansions
• Point out that the French calendar begins the week with Monday.
• Give students these items.
 11. Aujourd'hui est le _____ jour de la semaine. **12.** Ce cours est mon _____ cours aujourd'hui. **13.** Ma chambre est au _____ étage. **14.** Mon anniversaire est pendant le _____ mois de l'année. (Answers will vary.)
• Have students invent riddles using ordinal numbers. Example: **Je suis le seizième président des États-Unis. Qui suis-je?** (Abraham Lincoln)

Extra Practice Review seasons, months, and days while practicing ordinal numbers by asking questions like the following: **Quel est le septième mois de l'année? Quelle est la troisième saison de l'année? Quel est le dernier jour de la semaine?**

Extra Practice Ask questions about the **À l'hôtel** illustration. Examples: **Cet hôtel a combien d'étages? Ce monsieur a un passeport de quel pays? Qu'est-ce que l'homme à la réception donne aux clients?** Then ask students personalized questions. Examples: **Préférez-vous aller à une agence de voyages ou faire les réservations sur Internet? Aimez-vous voyager seul(e) ou en groupe? Avez-vous un hôtel préféré?**

Communication

4 Expansions
- After students have answered the questions, have them make up a conversation between a customer and a travel agent to arrange the trip.
- Ask volunteers to describe their **vacances idéales** to the class.

5 Suggestion Have students consider other details that might come up while making a hotel reservation and include them in their conversation. Examples: **Est-ce qu'il y a un ascenseur? Il y a une télévision dans la chambre?** Have them refer to the **Vocabulaire supplémentaire** from the Supersite.

6 Expansion Assign each group a different francophone location. Tell students to include any nearby attractions (**la plage, la campagne, le centre-ville**) and hotel amenities (**la piscine, le restaurant**) in their poster. For inspiration, show some French language brochures from actual hotels.

7 Suggestion Before starting this activity, have students brainstorm a list of steps involved in making a hotel reservation. If students have never reserved a room before, have them make up a scenario that includes at least one complication, for instance, their first choice of hotel is full.

Successful Language Learning Remind students to accept some corrections without explanation, especially when they are attempting to use language and structures above their current level. Tell them not to overanalyze and to trust that it will make more sense as their language skills develop.

4 Conversez Un(e) camarade passe des vacances idéales dans un hôtel. Interviewez-le/la (*him/her*). Answers will vary.

1. Quelles sont les dates de ton séjour?
2. Où vas-tu? Dans quel pays, quelle région ou quelle ville? Vas-tu à la mer, à la campagne, ...?
3. À quel hôtel descends-tu (*do you stay*)?
4. Qui fait la réservation?
5. Comment est l'hôtel? Est-ce que l'hôtel a un ascenseur, une piscine, ...?
6. À quel étage est ta chambre?
7. Combien de lits a ta chambre?
8. Laisses-tu ton passeport à la réception?

5 Notre réservation Par groupes de trois, travaillez pour préparer une présentation où deux touristes font une réservation dans un hôtel ou une auberge de jeunesse francophone. N'oubliez pas d'ajouter (*add*) les informations de la liste. Answers will vary.

- le nom de l'hôtel
- le type de chambre(s)
- l'étage
- le nombre de lits
- les dates
- le prix

6 Mon hôtel Vous allez ouvrir (*open*) votre propre hôtel. Par groupes de quatre, créez une affiche (*poster*) pour le promouvoir (*promote*) avec l'information de la liste et présentez votre hôtel au reste de la classe. Votre professeur va ensuite donner à chaque groupe un budget. Avec ce budget, vous allez faire la réservation à l'hôtel qui convient le mieux (*best suits*) à votre groupe. Answers will vary.

- le nom de votre hôtel
- le nombre d'étoiles (*stars*)
- les services offerts
- le prix pour une nuit

★	★★	★★★	★★★★	★★★★★
une étoile	deux étoiles	trois étoiles	quatre étoiles	cinq étoiles

7 Votre dernière réservation Écrivez un paragraphe où vous décrivez (*describe*) ce que vous avez fait la dernière fois que vous avez réservé une chambre. Utilisez au moins cinq mots de la liste. Échangez et comparez votre paragraphe avec celui (*the one*) d'un camarade de classe. Answers will vary.

alors	d'abord	puis
après (que)	donc	tout à coup
avant (de)	enfin	tout de suite

Extra Practice Give each student a card with either (1) a noun from the **Vocabulaire**, such as **chambre, clé,** or **passeport** or (2) a related verb, such as **réserver, prendre, oublier,** or **perdre**. Tell students to find someone whose word can be combined logically with their own. Then have them write an original sentence in the **passé composé**. Compile the sentences on the board. Then use sequencing expressions to combine them into a story.

Combien d'étoiles préférez-vous? Tell students that the French government regulates hotel ratings and requires that they be posted. Hotels must meet standards to qualify for a certain number of stars. A two-star hotel is a comfortable budget hotel. A five-star hotel is luxurious. While the level of comfort is standardized, prices are not.

Les sons et les lettres   Audio

ti, sti, and ssi

The letters **ti** followed by a consonant are pronounced like the English word *tea*, but without the puff released in the English pronunciation.

| ac**ti**f | pe**ti**t | **ti**gre | u**ti**les |

When the letter combination **ti** is followed by a vowel sound, it is often pronounced like the sound linking the English words *miss you*.

| dic**ti**onnaire | pa**ti**ent | ini**ti**al | addi**ti**on |

Regardless of whether it is followed by a consonant or a vowel, the letter combination **sti** is pronounced *stee*, as in the English word *steep*.

| ge**sti**on | que**sti**on | Séba**sti**en | arti**sti**que |

The letter combination **ssi** followed by another vowel or a consonant is usually pronounced like the sound linking the English words *miss you*.

| pa**ssi**on | expre**ssi**on | mi**ssi**on | profe**ssi**on |

Words that end in **-sion** or **-tion** are often cognates with English words, but they are pronounced quite differently. In French, these words are never pronounced with a *sh* sound.

| compre**ssi**on | na**ti**on | atten**ti**on | addi**ti**on |

Prononcez Répétez les mots suivants à voix haute.

1. artiste
2. mission
3. réservation
4. impatient
5. position
6. initiative
7. possession
8. nationalité
9. compassion
10. possible

Articulez Répétez les phrases suivantes à voix haute.

1. L'addition, s'il vous plaît.
2. Christine est optimiste et active.
3. Elle a fait une bonne première impression.
4. Laëtitia est impatiente parce qu'elle est fatiguée.
5. Tu cherches des expressions idiomatiques dans le dictionnaire.

Dictons Répétez les dictons à voix haute.

De la discussion jaillit la lumière.[1]

Il n'est de règle sans exception.[2]

[1] Discussion brings light.
[2] The exception proves the rule.

ressources
LM
p. 54
vhlcentral

deux cent quatre-vingt-onze **291**

Section Goals
In this section, students will learn about the letter combinations **ti**, **sti**, and **ssi**.

Instructional Resources
vhlcentral.com:
Textbook MP3s; Lab MP3s;
SAM Answer Key;
Textbook Audioscript;
Lab Audioscript;
reference tools

Suggestions
- Pronounce each of the example words and have students repeat them after you.
- To practice **ti**, have students put the palm of their hand in front of their lips and say the English word *tea*. Ask them if they felt the puff of air when they pronounced the letter **t**. Then have them pronounce the French word **petit** holding their hand in front of their mouth. Explain that they should not feel a puff of air when they pronounce the letters **ti** in French.
- Point out that **-sion** as in the word **télévision** has a [z] sound. Additionally, **-cia** as in the name **Patricia** has an unvoiced [s] sound
- Many words that end in **-sion**, **-ssion**, **-stion**, and **-tion** are cognates. Contrast the French and English pronunciation of words such as **attention** and **mission**.
- Mention words from the **Vocabulaire** that contain **ti**, **sti**, or **ssi**. Then have students repeat after you. Alternatively, ask students to recall such vocabulary. Examples: **réception, réservation, vingtième**. See if a volunteer is able to recall any words from previous lessons. Examples: **pessimiste, dessiner, l'addition**, and **attention**.

Dictons Tell students that the word **lumière** is used figuratively in the proverb **«De la discussion jaillit la lumière.»** Ask students what they think it means in this context (*clarity, ideas*).

OPTIONS

Extra Practice Here are some sentences to use for additional practice with these letter combinations. 1. **C'est utile d'étudier la gestion et l'informatique.** 2. **La profession de Sébastien? Il est dentiste.** 3. **Patricia utilise un plan de la station de ski.** 4. **Martine est-elle pessimiste ou optimiste?**

Extra Practice Teach your students the following French tongue-twisters that contain **ti** and **ssi**: 1. **Pauvre petit pêcheur, prend patience pour pouvoir prendre plusieurs petits poissons.** 2. **Un pâtissier qui pâtissait chez un tapissier qui tapissait, dit un jour au tapissier qui tapissait: vaut-il mieux pâtisser chez un tapissier qui tapisse ou tapisser chez un pâtissier qui pâtisse?**

ESPACE ROMAN-PHOTO

La réservation d'hôtel
 Video

NATIONAL communication cultures STANDARDS

Section Goals

In this section, students will learn functional phrases for getting help and making reservations.

Instructional Resources
vhlcentral.com:
Roman-photo Video, Videoscript, and Translation; SAM Answer Key; reference tools

Video Recap: Leçon 7A
Review the previous **Roman-photo** with this activity.
1. Où est allé David? (à Paris)
2. Avec qui a-t-il visité Paris? (avec ses parents)
3. Qu'a-t-il fait à Paris? (Il a visité les musées et les monuments. Il a pris un bateau-mouche.)
4. Qu'est-ce qu'il a apporté à Stéphane? (des lunettes de soleil)
5. Où Sandrine va-t-elle passer ses vacances d'hiver? (à Albertville)

Video Synopsis Sandrine goes to a travel agency to find a hotel in Albertville. They are all too expensive, so she leaves without making a reservation. She asks Amina to help find a cheaper hotel. Then Pascal says he can't go to Albertville after all. Disappointed, Sandrine tells Amina to cancel the reservation because she and Pascal are finished. Amina then tells Sandrine about Cyberhomme, her electronic pen pal.

Suggestions
• Ask students to read the title, glance at the video stills, and predict what the episode will be about.
• Have students read the **Roman-photo** aloud in groups of four.
• Have students scan the captions to find at least three sentences that contain words and expressions related to travel and accommodations. Examples: **Ou alors, à l'hôtel Le Mont Blanc, deux chambres individuelles pour 171 euros par personne. Les hôtels les moins chers sont déjà complets.**
• Review students' predictions and ask which ones were correct.

PERSONNAGES

Agent de voyages

Amina

Pascal

Sandrine

À l'agence de voyages...

SANDRINE J'ai besoin d'une réservation d'hôtel, s'il vous plaît. C'est pour les vacances de Noël.
AGENT Où allez-vous? En Italie?
SANDRINE Nous allons à Albertville.
AGENT Et c'est pour combien de personnes?
SANDRINE Nous sommes deux, mais il nous faut deux chambres individuelles.

AGENT Très bien. Quelles sont les dates du séjour, Mademoiselle?
SANDRINE Alors, le 25, c'est Noël, donc je fête en famille. Disons du 26 décembre au 2 janvier.
AGENT Ce n'est pas possible à Albertville, mais à Megève, j'ai deux chambres à l'hôtel Le Vieux Moulin pour 143 euros par personne. Ou alors, à l'hôtel Le Mont Blanc pour 171 euros par personne.

SANDRINE Oh non, mais Megève, ce n'est pas Albertville... et ces prix! C'est vraiment trop cher.
AGENT C'est la saison, Mademoiselle. Les hôtels les moins chers sont déjà complets.
SANDRINE Oh là là. Je ne sais pas quoi faire... J'ai besoin de réfléchir. Merci, Monsieur. Au revoir!
AGENT Au revoir, Mademoiselle.

Chez Sandrine...

SANDRINE Oui, Pascal. Amina nous a trouvé une auberge à Albertville. C'est génial, non? En plus, c'est pas cher!
PASCAL Euh, en fait... Albertville, maintenant, c'est impossible.
SANDRINE Qu'est-ce que tu dis?

PASCAL C'est que... j'ai du travail.
SANDRINE Du travail! Mais c'est Noël! On ne travaille pas à Noël! Et Amina a déjà tout réservé... Oh! C'est pas vrai!
PASCAL *(à lui-même)* Elle n'est pas très heureuse maintenant, mais quelle surprise en perspective!

Un peu plus tard...

AMINA On a réussi, Sandrine! La réservation est faite. Tu as de la chance! Mais, qu'est-ce qu'il y a?
SANDRINE Tu es super gentille, Amina, mais Pascal a annulé pour Noël. Il dit qu'il a du travail... Lui et moi, c'est fini. Tu as fait beaucoup d'efforts pour faire la réservation, je suis désolée.

1 Vrai ou faux?
Indiquez si ces affirmations sont **vraies** ou **fausses**. Corrigez les phrases fausses. Answers may vary.

1. Sandrine fait une réservation à l'agence de voyages.
Faux. Sandrine ne fait pas de réservation à l'agence de voyages.
2. Pascal dit un mensonge (*lie*).
Vrai.
3. Amina fait une réservation à l'hôtel Le Mont Blanc.
Faux. Amina fait une réservation à l'auberge de la Costaroche.
4. Il faut annuler la réservation à l'auberge de la Costaroche.
Vrai.
5. Amina est fâchée (*angry*) contre Sandrine.
Faux. Amina n'est pas fâchée contre Sandrine.
6. Pascal est fâché contre Sandrine.
Faux. Pascal n'est pas fâché contre Sandrine.
7. Sandrine est fâchée contre Pascal.
Vrai.
8. Sandrine a envie de voyager le 25 décembre.
Faux. Sandrine a envie de voyager le 26 décembre.
9. Cent soixante et onze euros, c'est beaucoup d'argent pour Sandrine.
Vrai.
10. Il y a beaucoup de touristes à Albertville en décembre.
Vrai.

 Practice more at **vhlcentral.com**.

A C T I V I T É S

O P T I O N S

Avant de regarder la vidéo Before viewing the video episode **La réservation d'hôtel**, have students brainstorm a list of things people might say when arranging a hotel reservation. For example, what questions might a travel agent ask? How might the traveler respond?

Regarder la vidéo Play the video episode once without sound and have the class create a plot summary based on the visual cues. Afterward, show the video with sound and have the class correct any mistaken guesses and fill in any gaps in the plot summary they created.

Sandrine essaie d'organiser son voyage.

Au P'tit Bistrot...

SANDRINE Amina, je n'ai pas réussi à faire une réservation pour Albertville. Tu peux m'aider?

AMINA C'est que... je suis connectée avec Cyberhomme.

SANDRINE Avec qui?

AMINA J'écris un e-mail à... Bon, je t'explique plus tard. Dis-moi, comment est-ce que je peux t'aider?

Un peu plus tard...

AMINA Bon, alors... Sandrine m'a demandé de trouver un hôtel pas cher à Albertville. Pas facile à Noël... Je vais essayer... Voilà! L'auberge de la Costaroche... 39 euros la nuit pour une chambre individuelle. L'hôtel n'est pas complet et il y a deux chambres libres. Quelle chance, cette Sandrine! Bon, nom... Sandrine Aubry...

AMINA Bon, la réservation, ce n'est pas un problème. C'est facile de l'annuler. Mais toi, Sandrine, c'est évident, ça ne va pas.

SANDRINE C'est vrai. Mais, alors, c'est qui, ce «Cyberhomme»?

AMINA Oh, c'est juste un ami virtuel. On correspond sur Internet, c'est tout. Ce soir, c'est son dixième message!

SANDRINE Lis-le-moi!

AMINA Euh non, c'est personnel...

SANDRINE Alors, dis-moi comment il est!

AMINA D'accord... Il est étudiant, sportif mais sérieux. Très intellectuel.

SANDRINE S'il te plaît, écris-lui: «Sandrine cherche aussi un cyberhomme»!

Expressions utiles

Getting help

- Je ne sais pas quoi faire... J'ai besoin de réfléchir.
  I don't know what to do... I have to think.
- Je n'ai pas réussi à faire une réservation pour Albertville.
  I didn't manage to make a reservation for Albertville.
- Tu peux m'aider?
  Can you help me?
- Dis-moi, comment est-ce que je peux t'aider?
  Tell me, how can I help you?
- Qu'est-ce que tu dis?
  What are you saying/did you say?
- On a réussi.
  We succeeded./We got it.
- S'il te plaît, écris-lui.
  Please, write to him.

Additional vocabulary

- C'est trop tard?
  Is it too late?
- Disons...
  Let's say...
- La réservation est faite.
  The reservation has been made.
- C'est fini.
  It's over.
- Je suis connectée avec...
  I am online with...
- Lis-le-moi.
  Read it to me.
- Il dit que...
  He says that...
- les moins chers
  the least expensive
- en fait
  in fact

---

2 | **Questions** Répondez aux questions.

1. Pourquoi est-il difficile de faire une réservation pour Albertville?
   C'est difficile parce que c'est Noël.
2. Pourquoi est-ce que Sandrine ne veut pas (*doesn't want*) rester à l'hôtel Le Vieux Moulin?
   L'hôtel Le Vieux Moulin est très cher.
3. Pourquoi Pascal dit-il qu'il ne peut pas (*can't*) aller à Albertville?
   Il dit qu'il a du travail.
4. Qui est Cyberhomme?
   C'est l'ami virtuel d'Amina.
5. À votre avis (*In your opinion*), Sandrine va-t-elle rester (*stay*) avec Pascal? Answers will vary.

3 | **Devinez** Inventez-vous une identité virtuelle. Écrivez un paragraphe dans lequel (*in which*) vous vous décrivez, vous et vos loisirs préférés. Donnez votre nom d'internaute (*cybername*). Votre professeur va afficher (*post*) vos messages. Devinez (*Guess*) à qui correspondent les descriptions.

ressources

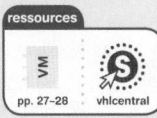

VM
pp. 27–28   vhlcentral

A C T I V I T É S

Expressions utiles

- Draw attention to -**ir** verbs and expressions used to ask for help in the captions, in the **Expressions utiles** box, and as they occur in your conversation with students. Point out that this material will be formally presented in **Espace structures**.
- Respond briefly to questions about regular and irregular -**ir** verbs. Reinforce correct forms, but do not expect students to produce them consistently at this time.
- Contrast the pronunciation of the following expressions: **en fait, on fait**.
- Point out the differences between direct and indirect discourse by writing these two sentences on the board: **Il dit qu'il a du travail. Il dit: «J'ai du travail.»**

1 **Suggestion** Have students correct the items that are false.

1 **Expansion** Give these statements to the class. **11. Sandrine a besoin de deux chambres individuelles. (Vrai.) 12. Amina ne fait pas de réservation. (Faux.) 13. Cyberhomme est l'ami virtuel de Sandrine. (Faux.)**

2 **Suggestion** Have students discuss these questions in small groups.

2 **Expansion** Discuss question #5 as a class. Have students make other predictions about what will happen. Ask what kind of surprise they think Pascal has in mind.

3 **Suggestion** Without revealing students' identities, match students with common interests and have them write back to one another.

OPTIONS

Extra Practice Ask volunteers to act out the **Roman-photo** episode for the class. Assure them that it is not necessary to memorize the episode or to stick strictly to its content. Give them time to prepare. You may want to assign this as homework and do it the next class period as a review activity.

Pairs Have students write a brief paragraph recapping the major events in this episode and using sequencing expressions, such as **d'abord, donc, ensuite, avant de, alors,** etc. Ask volunteers to read their synopses aloud.

🅢 Reading

Section Goals

In this section, students will:

- learn about how and where the French vacation
- learn some terms used in youth hostels
- find out about vacation spots in the francophone world
- read about the Alps, a popular destination for skiers

Instructional Resources
vhlcentral.com:
reference tools

Culture à la loupe

Avant la lecture Ask students how much vacation their parents can take annually, how much is typical in this country, and how much they think working people need to be happy in their work. You might also ask what vacation activities Americans enjoy and what the students imagine is popular in France.

Lecture

- Mention to students that when experts anticipate the **grands départs** on the **autoroutes**, these days are labeled **rouge** throughout France.

- Explain the **Coup de main** box on superlatives to help students understand the text.

Après la lecture Ask students to compare American and French vacation habits. Example: **Les étudiants à l'université ici commencent leurs vacances en mai, mais les étudiants en France terminent leurs études en juin.**

1 Expansion Continue the activity with these fill-in-the-blank statements.
11. Les Français d'aujourd'hui prennent des vacances qui durent ____ en moyenne. (sept jours) 12. Les vacances les moins populaires à l'étranger sont ____. (en Grèce) 13. Les étudiants commencent leurs vacances d'été en ____. (juin)

CULTURE À LA LOUPE

Les vacances des Français

une plage à Biarritz, en France

En 1936, les Français obtiennent° leurs premiers congés payés: deux semaines par an. En 1956, les congés payés passent à trois semaines, puis à quatre en 1969, et enfin à cinq semaines en 1982. Aujourd'hui, ce sont les Français qui ont le plus de vacances en Europe. Pendant longtemps, les Français prennent un mois de congés l'été, en août, et beaucoup d'entreprises°, de bureaux et de magasins ferment° tout le mois (la fermeture annuelle). Aujourd'hui, les Français ont tendance à prendre des vacances plus courtes (sept jours en moyenne°) mais plus souvent. Quant aux° destinations de vacances, 87,9% (pour cent) des Français restent en France. S'ils partent à l'étranger, leurs destinations préférées sont l'Espagne, l'Afrique et l'Italie. Environ° 46% des Français vont à la mer, 30% vont à la campagne, 25% vont en ville et 19% vont à la montagne. Ce sont les personnes âgées et les agriculteurs° qui partent le moins souvent en vacances et les étudiants qui voyagent le plus, parce qu'ils ont beaucoup de congés. Pour eux, les cours commencent en septembre ou octobre avec la rentrée des classes. Puis, il y a deux semaines de vacances plusieurs fois dans l'année: les vacances de la Toussaint en octobre-novembre, les vacances de Noël en décembre-janvier, les vacances d'hiver en février-mars et les vacances de printemps en avril-mai. L'été, les étudiants ont les grandes vacances de juin jusqu'à° la rentrée.

Les destinations de vacances des Français aujourd'hui

PAYS / CONTINENT	SÉJOURS (EN %)
France	87,9
Espagne	3,5
Italie	2,1
Amérique	1,9
Afrique	1,5
Portugal	1,2
Allemagne	0,7
Royaume-Uni	0,7
Grèce	0,5

°**obtiennent** obtain **entreprises** companies **ferment** close **en moyenne** on average **Quant aux** As for **Environ** Around **agriculteurs** farmers **jusqu'à** until

Coup de main

To form the superlative of nouns, use **le plus (de)** + [*noun*] to say *the most* and **le moins (de)** + [*noun*] to say *the least*.

Les étudiants ont le plus de congés.

Les personnes âgées prennent le moins de congés.

A C T I V I T É S

1 **Complétez** Complétez les phrases.

1. C'est en 1936 que les Français obtiennent leurs premiers __congés payés__

2. Depuis (*Since*) 1982, les Français ont __cinq semaines__ de congés payés.

3. Pendant longtemps, les Français prennent leurs vacances au mois __d'août__.

4. Pendant __la fermeture annuelle__ beaucoup de magasins sont fermés.

5. __La France__ est la destination de vacances préférée de 87,9% des Français.

6. Les destinations étrangères préférées des Français sont __l'Espagne, l'Afrique et l'Italie__

7. Le lieu de séjour favori des Français est __la mer__.

8. __Les personnes âgées et les agriculteurs__ ne partent pas souvent en vacances.

9. Ce sont __les étudiants__ qui ont le plus de vacances.

10. Les étudiants ont __deux semaines de vacances__ plusieurs fois par an.

O P T I O N S

Extra Practice Ask students what they can learn in the chart **Les destinations de vacances des Français aujourd'hui**. (percentages showing where the French spend their vacations today) Have students quiz each other on the chart, so they can practice geography and percentages.

Pairs Ask students to work with a partner to report three main points described in **Les vacances des Français** in their own words. You might brainstorm a list on the board: the history of employee vacations, the change in how the French take their vacations, and the time periods of student vacations.

LE FRANÇAIS QUOTIDIEN

À l'auberge de jeunesse

bagagerie (*f.*)	*baggage check room*
cadenas (*m.*)	*padlock*
casier (*m.*)	*locker*
couvre-feu (*m.*)	*curfew*
dortoir (*m.*)	*dormitory*
sac (*m.*) **de couchage**	*sleeping bag*
mixte	*coed*

LE MONDE FRANCOPHONE

Des vacances francophones

Si vous voulez° partir en vacances et pratiquer le français, vous pouvez° aller en France, bien sûr, mais il y a aussi beaucoup d'autres destinations.

Près des États-Unis
En hiver, dans les Antilles, il y a la Guadeloupe et la Martinique. Ces deux îles° tropicales sont des départements français. Leurs habitants ont donc des passeports français.

Dans l'océan Pacifique
De la Côte Ouest des États-Unis, au sud° de Hawaï, vous pouvez aller dans les îles de la Polynésie française: les îles Marquises; les îles du Vent, avec Tahiti; les îles Tuamotu. Au total il y a 118 îles, dont° 67 sont habitées°.

voulez *want* **pouvez** *can* **îles** *islands* **sud** *south* **dont** *of which* **habitées** *inhabited*

PORTRAIT

Les Alpes et le ski

Près de 48% des Français partent à la montagne pour deux semaines en moyenne° pendant les vacances d'hiver. Soixante-dix pour cent d'entre eux° choisissent° une station de ski des Alpes françaises. La chaîne° des Alpes est la plus grande chaîne de montagnes d'Europe. Elle fait plus de 1.000 km de long et va de la Méditerranée à l'Autriche°. Plusieurs pays la partagent: entre autres° la France, la Suisse, l'Allemagne et l'Italie. Le Mont-Blanc, le sommet° le plus haut° d'Europe occidentale°, est à 4.808 mètres d'altitude. On trouve d'excellentes pistes° de ski dans les Alpes, comme à Chamonix, Tignes, Val d'Isère et aux Trois Vallées.

en moyenne *on average* **d'entre eux** *of them* **choisissent** *choose* **chaîne** *range* **l'Autriche** *Austria* **entre autres** *among others* **sommet** *peak* **le plus haut** *the highest* **occidentale** *Western* **pistes** *trails*

MUSIQUE À FOND

Kassav'

Lieu d'origine: Guadeloupe
Métier: groupe de musique

Ce groupe de musique traditionnelle a été créé en Guadeloupe en 1979, et a popularisé le zouk (rythme typique de la Guadeloupe) en France et au Canada.

Go to vhlcentral.com to find out more about **Kassav'** and their music.

---

2 **Répondez** Répondez aux questions par des phrases complètes.

1. Quel pourcentage des Français partent à la montagne en hiver?
   40% des Français partent à la montagne en hiver.
2. Des Français qui vont à la montagne en hiver, combien choisissent les Alpes?
   70% choisissent les Alpes.
3. Qu'est-ce que c'est, les Alpes?
   C'est une grande chaîne de montagnes partagée entre plusieurs pays d'Europe.
4. Quel est le sommet le plus haut d'Europe occidentale?
   Le Mont-Blanc est le sommet le plus haut d'Europe occidentale.
5. Quelles îles des Antilles sont françaises?
   La Guadeloupe et la Martinique sont françaises.

3 **À l'agence de voyages** Vous travaillez dans une agence de voyages en France. Votre partenaire, un(e) client(e), va vous parler des activités et du climat qu'il/elle aime. Faites quelques suggestions de destinations. Votre client(e) va vous poser des questions sur les différents voyages que vous suggérez.

ressources

vhlcentral

ACTIVITÉS

 Practice more at vhlcentral.com.

Sidebar (right column)

Le français quotidien Encourage students to try an **auberge de jeunesse** if they travel overseas. They have no frills, sometimes have curfews, can be noisy, and meals (if offered) are during limited hours. **L'auberge de jeunesse** is the best deal, however, and many travelers find lifelong international friends and traveling companions there.

Portrait Explain that the Pyrenees are another important ski destination in France. Show their geographical relationship to the Alps on a map and point out that the Pyrenees create a natural border between France and Spain.

Le monde francophone Call on volunteers to read each bulleted item. Then show students the maps of the Francophone world from the Digital Image Bank, or have them consult the maps in **Appendice A**, and ask for other volunteers to point out each of the locations mentioned.

Musique à fond Point out to students that they will find supporting activities and information at **vhlcentral.com**.

2 Expansion Continue the activity with these questions. **6. Quel pourcentage des Français part pour la montagne pendant les vacances d'hiver? (près de 11%) 7. Quels pays partagent les Alpes? (la France, l'Allemagne, la Suisse, l'Autriche et l'Italie) 8. Où trouve-t-on de bonnes pistes de ski? (à Chamonix, Tignes, Val d'Isère et aux Trois Vallées)**

3 Expansion After the trip, the **client(e)** returns to the **agent** to discuss what he or she did on the trip. The **agent** asks: **Qu'est-ce que vous avez fait? Et puis, qu'est-ce que vous avez vu? Ensuite, où êtes-vous allé(e)?** The **client(e)** then volunteers as much information as possible about the trip.

Bottom options bar

OPTIONS

Pairs Have students imagine that, while studying in France, they are planning a trip for an upcoming vacation. They can speak **au présent** and **au futur proche**. Examples: **Où est-ce qu'on va aller? Qui va réserver l'hôtel/l'auberge de jeunesse? Qu'est-ce qu'on a envie de faire?** Encourage them to consult **Les vacances des Français** to plan a trip when French universities are actually on break. Then have them refer to

Le monde francophone to discuss which type of vacation they would like best, **au soleil** or **pour de l'aventure**. You might want to come up with some questions as a class before students continue in pairs. Examples: **Que préférez-vous, la plage ou le désert? Entre le Maroc et la Martinique, que préférez-vous? Moi, j'ai envie de faire une croisière, et vous?**

Section Goals

In this section, students will learn:
- the formation of adverbs using [*adjective*] + **-ment**
- irregular adverbs
- adverb placement

Instructional Resources
vhlcentral.com:
Lab MP3s; SAM Answer Key;
Essayez! *and* ***Mise en pratique***
answers; Lab Audioscript;
*Activity Pack (****Feuilles***
d'activités*); reference tools*

Suggestions

- To start the lesson, ask volunteers to give examples of adverbs already learned and use them in a sentence. Examples: **Je vais très bien/ mal. Ils ont déjà fait leurs devoirs. Elle travaille souvent le samedi**.
- Use magazine pictures of people doing various things to further review known adverbs and introduce a few new ones. Examples: **Ce chien mange beaucoup. Cette fille-ci nettoie rarement sa chambre. Cet homme-là se sent mal.**
- Brainstorm a list of masculine adjectives with the whole class. Have students write the feminine forms, reminding them that some do not change. Examples: **heureux (heureuse), facile (facile).**
- Point out that many adverbs are formed by adding **-ment** to the end of feminine forms of adjectives. Call attention to the exception for adjectives that already end in a vowel. Then ask questions with adverbs that correspond to the adjectives mentioned. Example: **Faites-vous facilement vos devoirs?**

7B.1

Adverbs  Tutorial

Point de départ Adverbs describe how, when, and where actions take place. They modify verbs, adjectives, and even other adverbs. You've already learned some adverbs such as **bien**, **déjà**, **surtout**, and **très**.

- To form an adverb from an adjective that ends in a consonant, take the feminine singular form and add **-ment**. This ending is equivalent to the English *-ly*.

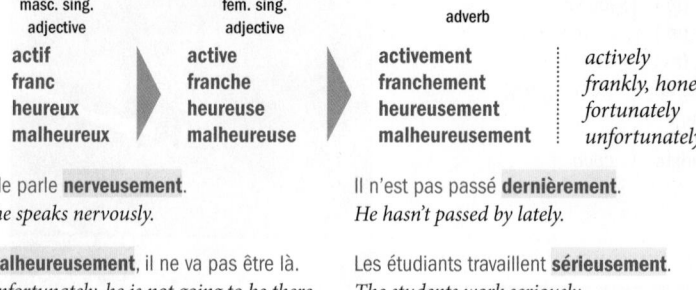

masc. sing. adjective	fem. sing. adjective	adverb	
actif	active	activement	*actively*
franc	franche	franchement	*frankly, honestly*
heureux	heureuse	heureusement	*fortunately*
malheureux	malheureuse	malheureusement	*unfortunately*

Elle parle **nerveusement**.
She speaks nervously.

Il n'est pas passé **dernièrement**.
He hasn't passed by lately.

Malheureusement, il ne va pas être là.
Unfortunately, he is not going to be there.

Les étudiants travaillent **sérieusement**.
The students work seriously.

- If the masculine singular form of an adjective already ends in a vowel, do not use the feminine form. Just add **-ment** to the end of the masculine form.

masc. sing. adjective	adverb	
absolu	absolument	*absolutely*
vrai	vraiment	*really*

Martin répond **poliment**.
Martin answers politely.

Ils apprennent **facilement** les langues.
They learn languages easily.

J'ai **vraiment** sommeil aujourd'hui.
I'm really sleepy today.

Le musée est **absolument** magnifique.
The museum is absolutely magnificent.

- To form an adverb from an adjective that ends in **-ant** or **-ent** in the masculine singular, replace the ending with **-amment** or **-emment**, respectively. Both endings are pronounced identically.

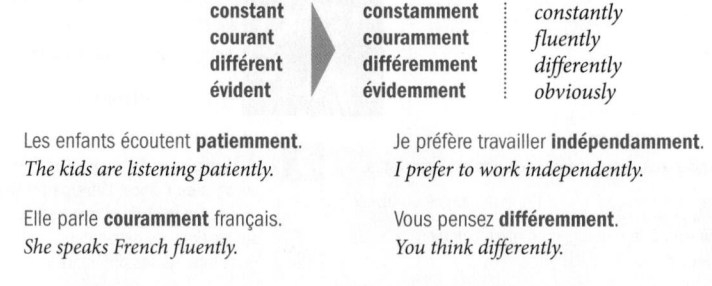

masc. sing. adjective	adverb	
constant	constamment	*constantly*
courant	couramment	*fluently*
différent	différemment	*differently*
évident	évidemment	*obviously*

Les enfants écoutent **patiemment**.
The kids are listening patiently.

Je préfère travailler **indépendamment**.
I prefer to work independently.

Elle parle **couramment** français.
She speaks French fluently.

Vous pensez **différemment**.
You think differently.

- The exception to the previous rule is the adjective **lent**. Its adverb is **lentement** (*slowly*).

Mon grand-père marche un peu **lentement**.
My grandfather walks a bit slowly.

Parlez **lentement**, s'il vous plaît.
Speak slowly, please.

ressources

WB
pp. 97-98

LM
p. 55

vhlcentral

- Some adverbs are irregular.

masculine singular adjective	adverb	
bon	bien	*well*
gentil	gentiment	*nicely*
mauvais	mal	*badly*
petit	peu	*little*

Son français est bon; il le parle **bien**.
His French is good; he speaks it well.

Leurs devoirs sont mauvais; ils écrivent **mal**.
Their homework is bad; they write badly.

- Although the adverb **rapidement** can be formed from the adjective **rapide**, you can also use the adverb **vite** to say *fast*.

Bérénice a gagné la course?
Did Bérénice win the race?

Oui, elle a couru **vite**.
Yes, she ran fast.

Tu ne comprends pas M. Bellay?
Don't you understand Mr. Bellay?

Non, il parle trop **rapidement.**
No, he speaks too quickly.

- You've learned **jamais, parfois, rarement,** and **souvent.** Here are three more adverbs of frequency: **de temps en temps** (*from time to time*), **en général** (*in general*), and **quelquefois** (*sometimes*).

Elle visite la capitale **de temps en temps**.
She visits the capital from time to time.

En général, nous prenons le bus.
In general, we take the bus.

- Place an adverb that modifies an adjective or another adverb before the word it modifies.

La chambre est **assez** grande.
The room is pretty big.

Ils courent **très** vite.
They run very fast.

- Place an adverb that modifies a verb immediately after the verb.

Elle parle **bien** le français?
Does she speak French well?

Ils parlent **constamment**.
They talk constantly.

- In the **passé composé**, short adverbs are typically placed before the past participle.

Ils sont **vite** partis.   *but*
They left quickly.

Ils ont gagné **facilement**.
They won easily.

Vous avez **bien** joué hier.   *but*
You played well yesterday.

Elle a parlé **franchement**.
She spoke frankly.

Boîte à outils

Adverbs of frequency, such as **de temps en temps, en général, quelquefois,** and **aujourd'hui,** are often placed at the beginning or end of a sentence.

À noter

See **Leçon 6A**, p. 236, for a review of the placement of short adverbs with the **passé composé**.

Essayez!   Donnez les adverbes qui correspondent à ces adjectifs.

1. complet <u>complètement</u>
2. sérieux <u>sérieusement</u>
3. séparé <u>séparément</u>
4. constant <u>constamment</u>
5. mauvais <u>mal</u>
6. actif <u>activement</u>
7. impatient <u>impatiemment</u>
8. bon <u>bien</u>
9. franc <u>franchement</u>
10. difficile <u>difficilement</u>
11. vrai <u>vraiment</u>
12. gentil <u>gentiment</u>

deux cent quatre-vingt-dix-sept **297**

Suggestions
- Write sentences using regular adverbs with **-ment** on the board. Have volunteers underline the adverb. Example: **Le professeur parle <u>rapidement</u>**.
- Tell students that most adverbs can be classified into four main categories: time, manner, frequency, and quantity. Write these categories on the board and have students list the adverbs they know under each of them.

Essayez! Make three columns on the board entitled: **l'adjectif masculin, l'adjectif féminin,** and **l'adverbe avec -ment**. Have students fill in the chart.

O P T I O N S

Video Replay the video episode, having students focus on the use of adverbs. Tell them to jot down a list of all of the adverbs they hear. Make two columns on the board, one for adverbs with **-ment** and another for all other adverbs. Have students write the adverbs under the appropriate column. Then have them create original sentences using each adverb.

Game Divide the class into small groups. Say the name of a famous person or historical figure. Give groups three minutes to write down as many short sentences as possible about that person, using adverbs and adverbial expressions. At the end of each round, have groups read their answers aloud. Award one point after each round to the group with the highest number of correct adverbs. The first group to earn five points wins.

ESPACE: STRUCTURES

1 Expansion Have students use the antonyms in a sentence using **mais**. Example: **Je vais fréquemment à la bibliothèque, mais ma camarade de chambre va rarement à la bibliothèque.**

2 Expansion Tell students to write follow-up yes/no questions about Béatrice's description of her vacation. Then have pairs ask and answer the questions. Example: **Béatrice a accepté l'invitation de sa cousine? (Oui, elle a rapidement accepté l'invitation.)**

4 Suggestion Before beginning the activity, have students identify the adjective from which the adverbs in column C are derived. Review the formation of **-amment** and **-emment** adverbs.

Mise en pratique

1 **Assemblez** Trouvez l'adverbe opposé.

_e_ 1. gentiment	a. rarement
_d_ 2. bien	b. faiblement
_f_ 3. lentement	c. impatiemment
_c_ 4. patiemment	d. mal
_a_ 5. fréquemment	e. méchamment
_b_ 6. fortement	f. vite

2 **Invitation aux vacances** Béatrice parle de ses vacances chez sa cousine. Complétez les phrases avec les adverbes qui correspondent aux adjectifs entre parenthèses.

Ma cousine Caroline m'a invitée à passer les vacances chez elle, à Nice. (1) __Évidemment__ (Évident), j'ai été très contente et j'ai (2) __rapidement__ (rapide) accepté son invitation. J'ai (3) __attentivement__ (attentif) lu les brochures touristiques et j'ai (4) __constamment__ (constant) parlé de mon voyage. (5) __Finalement__ (Final), le jour de mon départ est arrivé. J'ai (6) __prudemment__ (prudent) fait ma valise. À Paris, j'ai attendu le train très (7) __impatiemment__ (impatient). (8) __Franchement__ (Franc), j'avais hâte (*was eager*) d'arriver!

3 **On le fait comment?** Décrivez comment Gilles et ses amis font ces actions. Employez l'adverbe logique correspondant à un des adjectifs.

1. Marc et Marie dessinent. (bon, gentil)   Ils dessinent bien.
2. J'attends mon ami. (rapide, impatient)   J'attends impatiemment mon ami.
3. Ousmane court. (fréquent, intelligent)   Il court fréquemment.
4. Tu conduis ta voiture. (fort, prudent)   Tu conduis prudemment ta voiture.
5. Salima écoute le prof. (courant, attentif)   Elle écoute attentivement le prof.

4 **Les activités** Avec un(e) partenaire, assemblez les éléments des colonnes pour décrire à tour de rôle comment on fait ces activités.   Answers will vary.

MODÈLE

Étudiant(e) 1: *Je travaille sérieusement.*
Étudiant(e) 2: *Mon frère joue constamment.*

A	B	C
je	aider	constamment
mon frère	dormir	facilement
ma soeur	faire la cuisine	franchement
mon ami(e)	jouer	gentiment
mes profs	parler	patiemment
ma mère	travailler	rapidement
mon père	voyager	sérieusement
?	?	?

 Practice more at **vhlcentral.com**.

Communication

5 À l'université Vous désirez mieux connaître (*know better*) la vie universitaire. Répondez aux questions de votre partenaire avec les adverbes de la liste ou d'autres. Answers will vary.

attentivement	lentement	rapidement
bien	mal	rarement
difficilement	parfois	sérieusement
élégamment	patiemment	souvent
facilement	prudemment	quelquefois

1. Quand vas-tu à l'université?
2. Comment étudies-tu en général?
3. Quand tes amis et toi étudiez-vous ensemble?
4. Comment les étudiants écoutent-ils leur prof?
5. Comment ton prof de français parle-t-il?
6. Comment conduis-tu quand tu vas à la fac?
7. Quand ton/ta camarade de chambre fait-il/elle du sport?
8. Tes amis et toi, allez-vous souvent au cinéma?
9. Tes amis et toi, mangez-vous toujours (*always*) au resto U?
10. Comment as-tu décoré ta chambre?

6 Fréquences Votre professeur va vous donner une feuille d'activités. Circulez dans la classe et demandez à vos camarades à quelle fréquence ils/elles font ces choses. Trouvez une personne différente pour chaque réponse, puis présentez-les à la classe. Answers will vary.

MODÈLE

Étudiant(e) 1: *À quelle fréquence pars-tu en vacances?*
Étudiant(e) 2: *Je pars fréquemment en vacances.*

7 Notre classe Par groupes de quatre, choisissez les camarades de votre classe qui correspondent à ces descriptions. Trouvez le plus (*most*) de personnes possible. Answers will vary.

Qui dans la classe...
1. ... bavarde constamment avec ses voisins?
2. ... parle bien français?
3. ... chante bien?
4. ... apprend facilement les langues?
5. ... écoute attentivement le prof?
6. ... travaille sérieusement après les cours?
7. ... aime beaucoup les maths?
8. ... travaille trop?
9. ... dessine souvent pendant le cours?
10. ... dort parfois pendant le cours?
11. ... oublie fréquemment ses devoirs?
12. ... mange rarement au resto U?

5 Expansion Have students work in pairs to write three more questions like those in the activity. Students then switch questions with another pair and answer them orally.

6 Suggestions
• Have two volunteers read the **modèle** aloud, and then distribute the **Feuilles d'activités** found on the Supersite.
• If some students finish early, have them form pairs or a small group to begin comparing their findings. Teach them to ask questions, such as: **Quels camarades de classe font les choses différemment? Et semblablement** (*similarly*)?

7 Suggestion Remind the class that the adverbs in these sentences modify the verb, so they immediately follow the verb.

OPTIONS

Extra Practice Tell students to research travel to a French-speaking location. For maximum cultural variety, assign a different location to each student or simply have students select their preferred destination. Have them find information online or in the library about what there is to see and do there. After they have completed their research, have them create a brochure with images of the place and write short descriptive captions.

After that, tell students to plan an imaginary itinerary, telling what they will and won't do when they go and how often they will do each activity. Remind them to use frequency adverbs like **jamais**, **parfois**, **rarement**, **souvent**, **de temps en temps**, etc. Finally, have students present their brochures to the class and talk about their plans.

7B.2

ESPACE STRUCTURES

The *impératif*  Tutorial

Point de départ The **impératif** is the form of a verb that is used to give commands or to offer directions, hints, and suggestions. With command forms, you do not use subject pronouns.

Section Goals

In this section, students will learn:
- the imperative
- the verbs **dire, lire, écrire,** and **décrire.**

Instructional Resources
vhlcentral.com:
Lab MP3s; SAM Answer Key;
Essayez! *and **Mise en pratique*** *answers; Lab Audioscript; reference tools*

Suggestions

- Model the use of **vous** commands with simple examples using TPR and gestures. Examples: **Donnez-moi votre livre! Écoutez! Ne parlez pas! Mettez votre sac à dos sur la table.**
- Point out that the first and second person plural commands of most verbs are the same as the present tense forms without the **nous** and **vous** subject pronouns. Say a few infinitives and ask volunteers to give you the plural command forms. Examples: **manger, acheter, travailler, vendre, faire, aller,** and **attendre.**
- Introduce the **tu** commands and have students give you the **tu** commands of the verbs above.
- Explain the placement of object pronouns in affirmative and negative commands.
- Point out that **avoir** and **être** have irregular command forms.

 Boîte à outils

In French, unlike English, the command form changes depending on the person to whom it is addressed.

- Form the **tu** command form of **-er** verbs by dropping the **-s** from the present tense form. Note that **aller** also follows this pattern, even though it is irregular in the present tense.

  Réserve deux chambres.   **Travaille** vite.   **Va** au marché.
  Reserve two rooms.   *Work fast.*   *Go to the market.*

- The **nous** and **vous** command forms of **-er** verbs are the same as the present tense forms.

  Nettoyez votre chambre.   **Mangeons** au restaurant ce soir.
  Clean your room.   *Let's eat out tonight.*

- For **-ir** verbs, **-re** verbs, and most irregular verbs, the command forms are identical to the present tense forms.

  Finis la salade.   **Attendez** dix minutes.   **Faisons** du yoga.
  Finish the salad.   *Wait ten minutes.*   *Let's do yoga.*

- To make a command negative, place **ne** before the verb and **pas** after it.

  Ne regarde pas la télé.   **Ne vendons pas** la maison.   **Ne finissez pas** le jus d'orange.
  Don't watch TV.   *Let's not sell the house.*   *Don't finish the orange juice.*

The *impératif* of *avoir* and *être*

	avoir	être
(tu)	aie	sois
(nous)	ayons	soyons
(vous)	ayez	soyez

- The forms of **avoir** and **être** in the **impératif** are irregular.

  Aie confiance.   **Soyons** optimistes!
  Have confidence.   *Let's be optimistic!*

  N'ayons pas peur.   **Ne sois pas** impatient!
  Let's not be afraid.   *Don't be impatient!*

- An object pronoun can be added to the end of an affirmative command. Use a hyphen to separate them. Use **moi** and **toi** for the first- and second-person object pronouns.

  Permettez-moi de vous aider.   Achète un dictionnaire et **utilise-le.**
  Allow me to help you.   *Buy a dictionary and use it.*

À noter

You will learn more about how to use **toi** and **te** with commands when you study reflexive verbs in **Leçon 10A.**

- In negative commands, place object pronouns between **ne** and the verb. Use **me** and **te** for the first- and second-person object pronouns.

  Ne **me montre** pas les réponses.   Ma photo! Ne **la touchez** pas.
  Don't show me the answers.   *My picture! Don't touch it.*

  Ne **lui donne** pas les bonbons.   Ne **leur téléphonez** pas.
  Don't give her the candy.   *Don't phone them.*

300 *trois cents*

The verbs *dire*, *lire*, and *écrire*

	dire (to say)	lire (to read)	écrire (to write)
je/j'	dis	lis	écris
tu	dis	lis	écris
il/elle/on	dit	lit	écrit
nous	disons	lisons	écrivons
vous	dites	lisez	écrivez
ils/elles	disent	lisent	écrivent

Disons du 26 décembre au 2 janvier.

J'écris un e-mail à...

Elle m'**écrit**.
She writes to me.

Ne **dis** pas ton secret.
Don't tell your secret.

Lisez cet e-mail.
Read that e-mail.

- The verb **décrire** (*to describe*) is conjugated like **écrire**.

  Elle **décrit** l'accident.
  She's describing the accident.

  Ils **décrivent** leurs vacances.
  They're describing their vacation.

- The past participles of **dire**, **écrire**, and **décrire**, respectively, are **dit**, **écrit**, and **décrit**. The past participle of **lire** is **lu**.

  Ils l'**ont dit**.
  They said it.

  Tu l'**as écrit**.
  You wrote it.

  Nous l'**avons lu**.
  We read it.

Essayez! Employez l'impératif pour compléter ces phrases.

1. ___Envoie___ (envoyer: tu) cette lettre.
2. Ne ___quittons___ (quitter: nous) pas la maison ce soir.
3. ___Attendez___ (attendre: vous) à l'aéroport.
4. Sébastien, ___va___ (aller: tu) à la bibliothèque.
5. Christine et Serena, ne ___soyez___ (être: vous) pas impatientes.
6. ___Décrivez___ (décrire: vous) votre famille.
7. Ne ___perdons___ (perdre: nous) pas de temps.
8. Chérie, n'___aie___ (avoir: tu) pas peur.
9. ___Prenez___ (prendre: vous) des fraises.
10. ___Écris___ (écrire: tu) ton devoir pour demain.
11. Ne me ___dites___ (dire: vous) pas comment le film finit!
12. ___Lis___ (lire: tu) ce livre.
13. ___Apprends___ (apprendre: tu) une nouvelle langue.
14. ___Mettons___ (mettre: nous) un anorak.

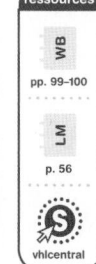

ressources

WB
pp. 99–100

LM
p. 56

vhlcentral

trois cent un **301**

Suggestions
- Introduce **dire, lire,** and **écrire** using TPR and gestures. Examples: **Je lis le livre. J'écris mon nom. Je te dis un secret.** Then ask follow-up questions to individuals. Examples: **Lisez-vous le journal? Quel journal? Écrivez-vous souvent des e-mails à vos parents? À qui écrivez-vous?**

Essayez! For additional practice, give students other subjects for command forms and have them restate the sentences.

OPTIONS

Video Show the video episode again, having students focus on the commands. Tell them to write down each command that they hear. Then form groups of three and have students compare their lists.

Extra Practice Write these three mini-conversations on the board. Tell students to fill in the blanks with **dire, écrire,** or **lire**. 1. Ève ____ que Pierre est avec Sylvie. Ses amis ____ que ce n'est pas vrai. Que ____-vous? (dit, disent, dites) 2. Avez-vous ____ à M. Gérard? Je lui ____ si vous me donnez son adresse. (écrit, écris) 3. ____-tu *Madame Bovary*? Non, je l'ai déjà ____. (Lis, lu)

1 **Expansion** Have students suggest additional commands for the little sister and roommates.

2 **Suggestion** Have students do this activity in pairs. Tell them that one person should play the role of Marilyne and Nicole while the other person plays their mother. Have them switch roles after items 1–3.

3 **Suggestion** Give students four minutes to write as many commands as they can for each illustration. Then ask volunteers to read their suggestions to the class.

Mise en pratique

1 **Dites à...** Mettez les verbes à l'impératif.

MODÈLE

Dites à votre petite sœur de nettoyer sa chambre.
Nettoie ta chambre.

Dites à votre petite sœur...

1. d'aller à l'école. Va à l'école.
2. de ne pas regarder la télé. Ne regarde pas la télé.
3. de vous attendre. Attends-moi.

Dites à vos camarades de chambre...

4. de ne pas mettre la radio. Ne mettez pas la radio.
5. d'être gentils. Soyez gentil(le)s.
6. de réfléchir avant de parler. Réfléchissez avant de parler.

2 **Écoutez** Marilyne et Nicole sont des adolescentes difficiles. Leur mère leur demande de faire le contraire de ce qu'elles (*what they*) proposent.

MODÈLE

Nous allons regarder la télé.
Ne la regardez pas.

1. Nous allons téléphoner à nos copines. Ne leur téléphonez pas.
2. Je ne vais pas parler à mon prof. Parle-lui.
3. Nous n'allons pas lire ce livre. Lisez-le.
4. Nous n'allons pas faire nos devoirs. Faites-les.
5. Je vais acheter cette nouvelle jupe. Ne l'achète pas.
6. Je ne vais pas écrire à mes grands-parents. Écris-leur.

3 **Que dites-vous?** Que dites-vous à ces personnes? Avec un(e) partenaire, employez des verbes à l'impératif. Answers will vary.

MODÈLE

Ne dormez pas tard.

1.

2.

3.

4.

 Practice more at **vhlcentral.com**.

Communication

4 **Fais-le** Dites à un(e) camarade de classe de faire certaines choses. Ensuite, changez de rôle. Utilisez ces verbes ou d'autres. *Answers will vary.*

MODÈLE

donner
Charles, donne-moi un crayon.

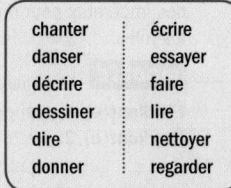

chanter	écrire
danser	essayer
décrire	faire
dessiner	lire
dire	nettoyer
donner	regarder

5 **Un voyage aux États-Unis** Un(e) étudiant(e) français(e) visite les États-Unis. Avec un(e) partenaire, suggérez des activités dans ces villes. *Answers will vary.*

MODÈLE

À New York, va à la statue de la Liberté.

villes	verbes utiles
Boston	acheter
Chicago	aller
Los Angeles	faire
Miami	manger
New York	prendre
San Francisco	regarder
Washington, D.C.	réserver
	rester
	visiter

6 **Mme Réponsatout** Vous téléphonez à l'émission (*show*) de Madame Réponsatout, qui donne des conseils (*advice*) au public. Avec un(e) partenaire, imaginez les dialogues pour les problèmes de la liste. Employez des verbes à l'impératif et alternez les rôles. *Answers will vary.*

MODÈLE

Étudiant(e) 1: *J'ai un problème d'argent.*
Étudiant(e) 2: *N'achetez pas de vêtements chers.*

- un problème d'argent
- un problème sentimental (*romantic*)
- où aller en vacances
- un(e) camarade de chambre pénible
- mauvaises notes à tous les cours
- un professeur difficile
- quoi faire après mes études
- un problème de poids (*weight*)

---

4 Suggestion Before beginning the activity, have students brainstorm a list of things they might ask their classmates to do.

4 Expansion Have volunteers report to the class what they were told to do.

5 Expansion Tell students to choose a city and write an e-mail to the French student with their recommendations.

6 Suggestions
- If time is limited, assign different situations to each pair.
- Have students vote on the best advice for each situation.

O P T I O N S

TPR Have students work in pairs and create a list of actions that can be mimed. Call on volunteers to demonstrate their actions for the class. After a repertoire of actions has been established, do a rapid-response TPR drill with the whole class using these commands and actions.

Extra Practice Write a list of situations on the board and have students respond to them with commands. Examples:
1. J'ai froid. (Mets [Mettez] un pull.) 2. Mes amis et moi, nous avons faim. (Mangez. / Faites des sandwichs.) 3. Vous avez soif. (Buvons un verre d'eau.) 4. Il pleut. (Mets [Mettez] un imperméable. / Prends [Prenez] un parapluie.)

Révision

Instructional Resources
vhlcentral.com:
Activity Pack (Info Gap Activities);
Testing Program;
Testing Program MP3s;
reference tools

1 Suggestion Distribute the **Feuilles d'activités** found in the Activity Pack on the Supersite.

1 Expansion Have students report their findings to the class.

2 Suggestion Have students write their advice.

3 Suggestion Have two volunteers read the **modèle** aloud. Point out the use of **nous** commands here. Quickly review the **nous** commands of a few verbs.

3 Expansion Take a quick class survey to find out which ideas are the best. Tally the results on the board.

4 Expansion Have volunteers present real problems they have had and ask the class for advice or a solution.

5 Suggestion
• Bring in a few travel ads from magazines or newspapers to use as models.
• Before beginning the activity, have students describe what the people in the drawing are doing.

6 Suggestion Divide the class into pairs and distribute the Info Gap Handouts found in the Activity Pack on the Supersite.

1 Oui ou non? Votre professeur va vous donner une feuille d'activités. Circulez dans la classe pour trouver deux camarades différent(e)s pour chaque situation, l'un(e) qui dit oui et l'autre qui dit non. Écrivez leur nom. Answers will vary.

MODÈLE

Étudiant(e) 1: Est-ce que tu écris des e-mails à tes grands-parents?
Étudiant(e) 2: Oui, je leur écris des e-mails parfois.

Situation	Oui	Non
1. écrire des e-mails à ses grands-parents	Lionel	
2. dire la vérité (truth) dans toutes les circonstances		
3. prendre le train de temps en temps		
4. lire le journal tous les matins		
5. partir souvent en voyage		
6. faire la fête tous les week-ends		

2 Faites attention Vous êtes médecin. Quels conseils (advice) donnez-vous à ces personnes? Employez des verbes à l'impératif. Ensuite, comparez vos suggestions aux suggestions de deux camarades. Answers will vary.

Quels conseils donnez-vous à une personne...

1. fatiguée?
2. nerveuse?
3. sans énergie?
4. faible?
5. qui ne mange pas bien

3 Apprenons le français Vous et votre partenaire cherchez à progresser en français. Trouvez huit idées d'activités à faire en français et utilisez des verbes à l'impératif avec des pronoms d'objet direct ou indirect. Ensuite, comparez votre liste avec la liste d'un autre groupe. Answers will vary.

MODÈLE

Étudiant(e) 1: Regardons le dernier film de Catherine Deneuve.

Étudiant(e) 2: Oui, regardons-le.

4 Des solutions Parlez de ces problèmes avec un(e) partenaire. Un(e) étudiant(e) présente les problèmes de la colonne A et l'autre les problèmes de la colonne B. Employez des impératifs pour répondre aux problèmes et alternez les rôles. Answers will vary.

MODÈLE J'ai perdu mon cahier de français.

Étudiant(e) 1: J'ai perdu mon cahier de français.
Étudiant(e) 2: Nettoie ta chambre et puis cherche-le.

A	B
1. Je ne trouve pas de billet aller-retour pour la Guadeloupe.	1. Mon/Ma petit(e) ami(e) est allé(e) à une fête avec une autre personne.
2. Demain c'est l'anniversaire de ma mère et je n'ai pas son cadeau.	2. Je n'ai pas acheté de billet de train pour aller à Genève demain.
3. Je n'ai pas d'argent pour payer l'addition.	3. Il est 11h00 du matin, mais j'ai déjà faim.
4. L'avion est parti sans moi.	4. Il neige et j'ai très froid.

5 La publicité Par groupes de trois, créez le texte d'une publicité pour le magazine *Mer et soleil*. Décidez quel endroit l'illustration représente, puis employez des verbes à l'impératif et des adverbes pour attirer (to attract) des touristes. Ensuite, présentez votre pub (ad) à la classe. Answers will vary.

6 Un week-end en vacances Votre professeur va vous donner, à vous et à votre partenaire, une feuille de dessins sur le week-end de M. et Mme Bardot et de leur fille Alexandra. Attention! Ne regardez pas la feuille de votre partenaire. Answers will vary.

MODÈLE

Étudiant(e) 1: D'abord, ils sont arrivés à l'hôtel.
Étudiant(e) 2: Après, …

OPTIONS

Pairs Have students work in pairs. Tell them to write a series of commands that a tour guide might give his passengers during a bus tour of Paris. Examples: **Donnez-moi vos tickets, s'il vous plaît. Retrouvez-moi à l'arrêt de bus dans une heure. Ne soyez pas en retard. N'oubliez pas vos appareils photos.**

Pairs Have students work in pairs. Tell them to imagine that they are lifeguards at a hotel pool in Nice. They have to write a list of rules telling people what they can or cannot do in the pool area. After they have completed their lists, have pairs get together with another pair and compare rules.

À l'écoute

NATIONAL communication STANDARDS

STRATÉGIE

Recognizing the genre of spoken discourse

You will encounter many different types of spoken discourse in French. For example, you may hear a political speech, a radio interview, a commercial, a message on an answering machine, or a news broadcast. Try to identify the context of what you hear so that you can activate your background knowledge about that type of discourse and identify the speaker's motives and intentions.

 To practice this strategy, you will listen to two short selections. Identify the genre of each one.

Préparation

Quand vous partez en vacances, qui décide où aller? Qui fait les réservations? Est-ce que vous utilisez les services d'une agence de voyages? Internet?

À vous d'écouter

Écoutez la publicité. Puis écoutez une deuxième fois et notez les informations qui manquent (*that are missing*). Notez aussi un détail supplémentaire pour chaque voyage.

Pays (ville/région)	Nombre de jours/semaines	Prix par personne	Détail supplémentaire
1. Italie (Venise)	3 jours	395 euros	Answers will vary.
2. Brésil	1 semaine	1.500 euros	Answers will vary.
3. Irlande (Dublin)	5 jours	575 euros	Answers will vary.
4. Amérique du Nord (États-Unis, Canada, Mexique)	14 jours	2.000 euros	Answers will vary.
5. France (Avignon)	7 jours	487 euros	Answers will vary.

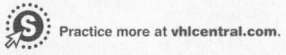 Practice more at **vhlcentral.com.**

Compréhension

Où vont-ils? Vous travaillez pour l'agence Vacances Pour Tous cet été. Indiquez où chaque personne va aller.

1. Madame Dupuis n'a pas envie d'aller à l'étranger.

   Madame Dupuis va aller à Avignon.

2. Le fils de Monsieur Girard a besoin de pratiquer son espagnol et son anglais.

   Il va aller en Amérique du Nord.

3. Madame Leroy a envie de visiter une capitale européenne.

   Elle va aller en Irlande.

4. Yves Marignaud a seulement trois jours de congés.

   Il va aller en Italie (Venise).

5. Justine adore la plage et le soleil.

   Elle va aller au Brésil.

6. La famille Abou a envie de passer ses vacances à la campagne.

   Ils vont aller à Avignon.

Votre voyage Vous avez fait un des voyages proposés par l'agence Vacances Pour Tous. C'est le dernier jour et vous écrivez une carte postale (*postcard*) à un(e) ami(e) francophone. Parlez-lui de votre séjour. Quel voyage avez-vous fait? Pourquoi? Comment avez-vous voyagé? Qu'est-ce que vous avez fait pendant votre séjour? Est-ce que vous avez aimé vos vacances? Expliquez pourquoi.

trois cent cinq **305**

Section Goals

In this section, students will:
• learn to recognize the genre of spoken discourse
• listen to a radio ad for a travel agency

Instructional Resources
vhlcentral.com:
Textbook MP3s;
Textbook Audioscript;
reference tools

Stratégie
Audioscripts 1. Bonjour et bienvenue à l'hôtel Belle Plage de Monaco. Nous sommes à quelques minutes de la plage, au 14 avenue des Anges, et nous avons des bus directs pour l'aéroport et la gare routière. Ce week-end, notre hôtel a encore six chambres libres. Si vous désirez des informations sur nos chambres, nos prix et notre hôtel en général, faites le 1. Pour faire ou confirmer une réservation, faites le 2. Pour contacter des clients de l'hôtel, faites le 3. Merci de nous avoir appelés et bonne journée. (message enregistré) **2.** Mesdames, Messieurs, nous allons bientôt arriver à notre destination. À l'arrivée à l'aéroport de Montréal, sortez vos passeports pour passer la douane. Ensuite, allez au troisième étage pour prendre vos valises. Nous espérons que vous allez passer un agréable séjour au Canada. Merci d'avoir voyagé avec Air Vacances et à bientôt. (annonce d'avion)

Préparation Have students discuss the questions in pairs or groups. Then have them describe the photo.

À vous d'écouter
Audioscript Envie de partir en vacances? Pour un petit week-end en amoureux ou pour des vacances au soleil, l'agence Vacances Pour Tous a la formule idéale!
Nos promotions de la semaine:
Week-end à Venise, en Italie. Avion au départ de Paris vendredi matin, retour dimanche soir. Logement à l'hôtel; 395 euros par personne.
Envie de mer et de plage? Séjour d'une semaine au Brésil; 1.500 euros par personne.
Découvrez la capitale irlandaise avec un séjour de 5 jours à Dublin; 575 euros par personne.

En train et bateau.
Autre super promotion pour étudiants: un voyage de deux semaines en Amérique. Une semaine aux États-Unis, quatre jours au Canada et trois jours au Mexique; 2.000 euros par personne. En avion et autobus. Logement en auberge de jeunesse.

Vous n'avez pas envie de partir à l'étranger, mais vous avez une semaine de congé? Nous avons une promotion incroyable sur la France. Sept jours à la campagne. Voyage en train. Logement dans un petit hôtel près d'Avignon; 487 euros par personne. Appelez tout de suite le 01.42.46.46.46 pour faire vos réservations!

Section Goals

In this section, students will learn historical and cultural information about the Antilles and French Polynesia.

Instructional Resources
vhlcentral.com:
Digital Image Bank;
SAM Answer Key;
reference tools

Carte des Antilles et de la Polynésie française

- Have students look at the map or use the **Panorama** map from the Digital Image Bank. Ask volunteers to read the names of countries and islands aloud.
- Point out the location of **la mer des Antilles** or **la mer des Caraïbes**.
- Give students a geographical description of a few locations and have them guess which francophone place you are describing.
- Mention that the tropical islands, which are mostly mountainous, have fertile soils that make for rich, abundant vegetation.

L'archipel en chiffres

- Have volunteers read the sections aloud. After each section, ask students questions about the content.
- Explain that an archipelago is a large group of islands. Point out that the **îles Gambier** and **îles de la Société** are composed of atolls.

Incroyable mais vrai! After the eruption, the accumulated ash and rock raised the summit of Mount Pelée from 5,000 feet to 6,000 feet. After a few more minor eruptions, the volcano now stands at 4,584 feet.

Panorama

S Interactive Map

la ville de Gustavia, à Saint-Barthélemy

Les Antilles

L'archipel en chiffres

- **Guadeloupe:** *(400.132 habitants), Pointe-à-Pitre, Basse-Terre*
- **Haïti:** *(10.711.000), Port-au-Prince*
- **Martinique:** *(396.000), Fort-de-France*
- **Saint-Barthélemy:** *(9.279), Gustavia*
- **Saint-Martin:** *(en partie) (35.594), Marigot*

SOURCE: INSEE

Antillais célèbres

- **Aimé Césaire,** *la Martinique, poète (1913–2008)*
- **Raphaël Confiant,** *la Martinique, écrivain° (1951–)*
- **Garcelle Beauvais,** *Haïti, actrice (1966–)* 
- **Wyclef Jean,** *Haïti, chanteur de rap (1969–)*

La Polynésie française

L'archipel en chiffres

- **Îles Australes:** *(6.820), Tubuai*
- **Îles de la Société:** *(235.295), Papeete*
- **Îles Gambier:** *(1.239), Mangareva*
- **Îles Marquises:** *(9.261), Nuku-Hiva*
- **Îles Tuamotu:** *(15.592), Fakarava, Rankiroa*

Polynésiens célèbres

- **Henri Hiro,** *Tahiti, îles de la Société, poète (1944–1990)*
- **Rodolphe Vinh Tung,** *Raiatea, îles de la Société, professionnel du wakeboard (1974–)*

écrivain *writer* **survivants** *survivors* **enfermé** *detained* **pirogues** *dugout canoes*

LES ÉTATS-UNIS

L'OCÉAN ATLANTIQUE

LES ANTILLES

CUBA
Porto Rico
Saint-Martin
Saint-Barthélemy
La Guadeloupe
La Martinique

LA JAMAÏQUE
HAÏTI

LE VENEZUELA
LE SURINAM

LA COLOMBIE
La Guyane française

L'OCÉAN PACIFIQUE

LA GUYANA

LA POLYNÉSIE FRANÇAISE

Les îles Marquises

L'OCÉAN PACIFIQUE

LE BRÉSIL

Les îles Tuamotu

Les îles de la Société
Tahiti

Régions francophones

0 ——— 1,000 milles
0 ——— 1,000 kilomètres

Les îles Gambier

Les îles Australes

0 ——— 500 milles
0 ——— 500 kilomètres

les courses de pirogues° en Polynésie française

Incroyable mais vrai!

Jusqu'au vingtième siècle, Saint-Pierre était le port le plus actif des Antilles et la capitale de la Martinique. Mais en 1902, son volcan, la montagne Pelée, entre en éruption. Il n'y a que deux survivants°, dont un qui a été protégé par les murs de la prison où il était enfermé°. Certains historiens doutent de l'authenticité de cette anecdote.

O P T I O N S

Antillais et Polynésiens célèbres Aimé Césaire coined the term «**Négritude**», which came from his poem «**Cahier d'un retour au pays natal**». **Raphaël Confiant** has won many literary prizes for his works, which have been published in French, Creole, and English. He has championed Creole as a literary language and has been involved in social and political activities in Martinique. **Garcelle Beauvais** is a model and actress.

She has appeared in American films and TV shows. **Wyclef Jean**'s music draws from his memories of his youth in Haiti and his multicultural experiences in a Creole environment after immigrating to the United States. **Henri Hiro** was responsible for a cultural resurgence of the traditional Polynesian customs in Tahitian theater, dance, music, and film.

Les arts

Les peintures de Gauguin

En 1891, le peintre° Paul Gauguin (1848–1903) vend ses œuvres° à Paris et déménage à Tahiti, dans les îles de la Société, pour échapper à° la vie moderne. Il y reste deux ans avant de rentrer en France et, en 1895, il retourne en Polynésie française pour y habiter jusqu'à sa mort en 1903. Inspirée par le nouvel environnement du peintre et la nature qui l'entoure°, l'œuvre «tahitienne» de Gauguin est célèbre° pour sa représentation du peuple indigène et l'emploi° de couleurs vives°. Ses peintures° de femmes font partie de ses meilleurs tableaux°.

Les destinations

Haïti, première République noire

En 1791, un ancien esclave°, Toussaint Louverture, mène° une rébellion dans la colonie française de Saint-Domingue. Après avoir gagné le combat, Louverture se proclame gouverneur de l'île et abolit l'esclavage. Il est plus tard capturé par l'armée française et exilé en France. Son successeur, Jean-Jacques Dessalines, lui-même ancien esclave, vainc° définitivement l'armée française en 1803 et proclame l'indépendance d'Haïti en 1804. Haïti est donc la première République noire du monde et le premier pays du monde occidental à abolir l'esclavage.

L'économie

La perle noire

La Polynésie française est le principal producteur de perles° noires. Dans la nature, les perles sont très rares; on en trouve dans une huître° sur 15.000. Par contre°, aujourd'hui, la Polynésie française produit plusieurs tonnes de perles noires chaque année. Des milliers de Tahitiens vivent de° l'industrie perlière. Parce qu'elle s'est développée dans les lagons, la perliculture° a même aidé à repeupler° certaines îles et certains endroits ruraux, abandonnés par les gens partis en ville. Les perles sont très variées et présentent différentes formes ou nuances de noir.

Les gens

Maryse Condé

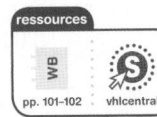

Née en Guadeloupe, puis étudiante à la Sorbonne, à Paris, Maryse Condé a vécu° huit ans en Afrique (Ghana, Sénégal, Guinée, etc.). En 1973, elle enseigne dans les universités françaises et commence sa carrière° d'écrivain°. Elle sera ensuite professeur en Californie et à l'Université de Columbia. Ses nombreux romans°, y compris° *Moi, Tituba Sorcière*, ont reçu de multiples récompenses°. Ils mêlent° souvent fiction et événements historiques pour montrer la complexité de la culture antillaise, culture liée° à l'Amérique, l'Europe et l'Afrique.

Qu'est-ce que vous avez appris? Répondez aux questions par des phrases complètes.

1. Comment s'appelle le volcan qui est entré en éruption au début du vingtième siècle?
   Le volcan s'appelle la montagne Pelée.
2. L'éruption a-t-elle tué tous les habitants de Saint-Pierre?
   Non, deux habitants n'ont pas été tués.
3. Pour quelle raison Gauguin a-t-il déménagé à Tahiti?
   Il voulait échapper à la vie moderne.
4. Pour quelles raisons l'œuvre «tahitienne» de Gauguin est-elle célèbre?
   Elle est célèbre pour sa représentation du peuple indigène et pour l'emploi de couleurs vives.
5. Quelle est la principale particularité d'Haïti?
   C'est la première République noire du monde.
6. Qui a réussi à abolir l'esclavage en Haïti?
   Toussaint Louverture a réussi à abolir l'esclavage en Haïti.
7. D'où viennent la majorité des perles noires?
   Elles viennent de Polynésie française.
8. Comment la perliculture a-t-elle changé la population de la Polynésie? Elle a aidé à repeupler certaines îles et certains endroits ruraux.
9. Où Maryse Condé a-t-elle étudié? Où est-elle née?
   Elle a fait ses études à Paris. Elle est née en Guadeloupe.
10. Ses romans sont-ils entièrement des œuvres de fiction?
    Non, ils mêlent la fiction et l'histoire.

Sur Internet

Go to **vhlcentral.com** to find more cultural information related to this **Panorama**.

1. Cherchez des informations sur Aimé Césaire. Qu'a-t-il en commun avec Léopold Sédar Senghor, poète et homme politique mentionné dans le **Panorama** précédent?

2. Trouvez des informations sur la ville de Saint-Pierre. Comment est-elle aujourd'hui?

3. Cherchez des informations sur les courses de pirogues en Polynésie française. Quelle est leur signification?

ressources
WB
pp. 101–102
vhlcentral

peintre *painter* **œuvres** *artworks* **échapper à** *escape* **entoure** *surrounds* **célèbre** *famous* **emploi** *use* **vives** *bright* **peintures** *paintings* **tableaux** *paintings* **esclave** *slave* **mène** *leads* **vainc** *defeats* **perles** *pearls* **huître** *oyster* **Par contre** *However* **vivent de** *make a living from* **perliculture** *pearl farming* **repeupler** *repopulate* **a vécu** *lived* **carrière** *career* **écrivain** *writer* **romans** *novels* **y compris** *including* **récompenses** *awards* **mêlent** *mix* **liée** *tied*

Les peintures de Gauguin
- Gauguin tried to capture authentic aspects of traditional Tahitian culture, emulated Oceanic traditions in his woodcuts, and often used the Tahitian language for titles of his works.
- Have students describe the painting. Ask: **Qui reconnaît ce tableau. Devinez comment il s'appelle.** (*Femmes de Tahiti [sur la plage]*) **Savez-vous où le tableau original se trouve aujourd'hui?** (Il est au musée d'Orsay à Paris.)

Haïti, première République noire Haitian Creole and French are the two official languages of Haiti. The grammar of Haitian Creole is similar to languages of West Africa and other Caribbean creoles. Distribute examples of Haitian Creole and have students compare the language with French.

La perle noire Baby oysters are collected from the ocean and raised in pearl farms for three years. A small round piece of mother-of-pearl is inserted into the oyster, and the oyster begins the natural process of secreting nacre in layers onto the foreign substance which becomes a pearl after several years.

Maryse Condé In her historical novels, Maryse Condé has chronicled the migration and experience of the African people from West Africa to the United States and the Caribbean. Her books explore the clash of races and cultures using personal experiences of historical characters.

Une tradition tahitienne The **Hawaiki Nui Va'a** is one of the world's premier outrigger canoe competitions, and it is an important celebration of Tahiti's traditional sports. Each year in late October or early November, canoeists compete on an 80-mile, four-island course over the span of three days.

Régions d'outre-mer Martinique and Guadeloupe are **départements** or **régions d'outre-mer** (**DOM/ROM**) of France. They have the same status and responsibilities as any other department of metropolitan France. French Polynesia is referred to as a **collectivité d'outre-mer** (previously **territoire d'outre-mer**) which is more independent, but still has some administrative ties to France.

Section Goals

In this section, students will:
• learn to predict content from a title
• read a travel brochure in French

Stratégie Tell students that they can often predict the content of a newspaper article from its headline. Display or make up several cognate-rich headlines from French newspapers. Examples: **L'ONU critique le changement de règle du vote pour le référendum en Irak; Huit clubs de football français rattrapés par la justice; À la télé américaine, le président est une femme.** Ask students to predict the content of each article.

Examinez le texte Ask volunteers to share their ideas about what type of document it is, and what information they think each section will have. Then go over the correct answers with the entire class.

Des titres Working in pairs to compare their answers, have students discuss how they are able to tell where these titles were found.

Lecture

Audio: Reading

Avant la lecture

STRATÉGIE

Predicting content from the title

Prediction is an invaluable strategy in reading for comprehension. We can usually predict the content of a newspaper article from its headline, for example. More often than not, we decide whether or not to read the article based on its headline. Predicting content from the title will help you increase your reading comprehension in French.

Examinez le texte

Regardez le titre (*title*) et les sous-titres (*subtitles*) du texte. À votre avis, quel type de document est-ce? Avec un(e) camarade, faites une liste des informations que vous allez probablement trouver dans chaque section du document.

Des titres

Regardez ces titres et indiquez en quelques mots le sujet possible du texte qui suit (*follows*) chaque titre. Où pensez-vous qu'on a trouvé ces titres (dans un journal, un magazine, une brochure, un guide, etc.)?

Cette semaine à Paris:
un journal

Encore un nouveau restaurant pour chiens
un journal, un magazine

L'Égypte des pyramides en 8 jours
une brochure, un guide

L'AÉROPORT CHARLES-DE-GAULLE A PERDU LES VALISES D'UN VOL DE TOURISTES ALLEMANDS
un journal

Plan du centre-ville
un guide

Résultats du septième match de football entre la France et l'Angleterre
un journal

Hôtel confortable près de la gare routière
une brochure

TOUR DE CORSE

Voyage organisé de 12 jours

3.000 euros tout compris°
Promotion spéciale de Vacances–Voyages, agence de voyages certifiée

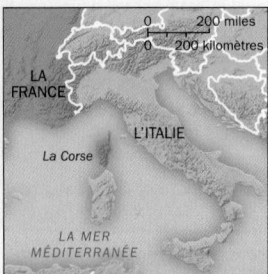

0 — 200 miles
0 — 200 kilomètres
LA FRANCE
L'ITALIE
La Corse
LA MER MÉDITERRANÉE

ITINÉRAIRE

JOUR 1   Paris–Ajaccio
Vous partez de Paris en avion pour Ajaccio, en Corse. Vous prenez tout de suite le bus pour aller à votre hôtel. Vous commencez par visiter la ville d'Ajaccio à pied°, puis vous dînez à l'hôtel.

JOUR 2   Ajaccio–Bonifacio
Le matin, vous partez en autobus pour Bonifacio, la belle ville côtière° où vous déjeunez dans un petit restaurant italien avant de visiter la ville. L'après-midi, vous montez à bord° d'un bateau pour une promenade en mer, occasion idéale pour observer les falaises rocailleuses° et les plages blanches de l'île°. Ensuite, vous rentrez à l'hôtel pour dîner et y (*there*) passer la nuit.

JOUR 3   Bonifacio–Corte
La forêt de l'Ospédale est l'endroit idéal pour une randonnée à pied. Vous pique-niquez à Zonza, petite ville montagneuse, avant de continuer vers Corte, l'ancienne° capitale de la Corse. Vous passez la soirée et la nuit à Corte.

JOUR 4   Corte–Bastia
Vous avez la journée pour visiter la ville de Bastia. Vous assistez à un spectacle de danse, puis vous passez la soirée à l'hôtel.

JOUR 5   Bastia–Calvi
Vous visitez d'abord le Cap Corse, la péninsule au nord° de la Corse. Puis, vous continuez vers le désert des Agriates, zone de montagnes désertiques où la chaleur est très forte. Ensuite, c'est l'Île-Rousse et une promenade à vélo dans la ville de Calvi. Vous dînez à votre hôtel.

OPTIONS

Small Groups Have five students work together to brainstorm a list of what would constitute an ideal vacation for them. Each student should contribute at least one idea. Opinions will vary. Ask the group to designate one student to take notes and another to present the information to the class. When each group has its list, ask the presenters to share the group's ideas.

Extra Practice Ask students if they have ever been on an organized tour. If students have not been on a tour similar to the one to Corsica described in **Lecture**, have them interview someone they know who has. Have students answer questions like these: **Où êtes-vous allé(e)? Avec quelle agence? Avez-vous aimé toutes les activités organisées? Expliquez pourquoi.**

JOUR 6 Calvi–Porto

Vous partez en bus le matin pour la vallée du Fango et le golfe de Galéria à l'ouest° de l'île. Puis, vous visitez le parc naturel régional et le golfe de Porto. Ensuite, vous faites une promenade en bateau avant de passer la soirée dans la ville de Porto.

JOUR 7 Porto–Ajaccio

En bateau, vous visitez des calanques°, particularité géographique de la région méditerranéenne, avant de retourner à Ajaccio.

JOURS 8 à 11 Ajaccio

À Ajaccio, vous avez trois jours pour explorer la ville. Vous avez la possibilité de visiter la cathédrale, la maison natale° de Napoléon ou des musées, et aussi de faire du shopping ou d'aller à la plage.

JOUR 12 Ajaccio–Paris

Vous retournez à Paris en avion.

tout compris *all-inclusive* **à pied** *on foot* **côtière** *coastal* **à bord** *aboard*
falaises rocailleuses *rocky cliffs* **île** *island* **ancienne** *former* **nord** *north*
ouest *west* **calanques** *rocky coves or creeks* **natale** *birth*

Après la lecture

Les questions du professeur Vous avez envie de faire ce voyage en Corse et vous parlez du voyage organisé avec votre professeur de français. Répondez à ses questions par des phrases complètes, d'après la brochure.

1. Comment allez-vous aller en Corse?
   Je vais prendre l'avion à Paris.

2. Où le vol arrive-t-il en Corse?
   Le vol arrive à Ajaccio.

3. Combien de temps est-ce que vous allez passer en Corse?
   Je vais passer douze jours en Corse.

4. Est-ce que vous allez dormir dans des auberges de jeunesse?
   Non. Je vais dormir à l'hôtel./dans des hôtels.

5. Qu'est-ce que vous allez faire à Bastia?
   Je vais visiter la ville, aller à un spectacle de danse, puis passer la soirée à l'hôtel.

6. Est-ce que vous retournez à Ajaccio le neuvième jour?
   Non. Je retourne à Ajaccio le septième jour.

7. Qu'est-ce que vous allez prendre comme transports en Corse?
   Je vais prendre l'autobus et des bateaux.

8. Avez-vous besoin de faire toutes les réservations?
   Non. Le voyage est organisé par une agence de voyages.

C'est sûr, je pars en Corse! Vous allez passer trois semaines en France et vous avez décidé, avec un(e) ami(e), de faire le voyage organisé en Corse au départ de Paris. Vous et votre ami(e) téléphonez à l'agence de voyages pour avoir plus de détails. Posez des questions sur le voyage et demandez des précisions sur les villes visitées, les visites et les activités au programme, les hôtels, les transports, etc.

- Vous aimez faire des randonnées, mais votre ami(e) préfère voir (*to see*) des spectacles et faire du shopping.
- L'agent va expliquer pourquoi vous allez aimer ce voyage en Corse.
- Demandez à l'agent de vous trouver un billet d'avion aller-retour pour aller de votre ville à Paris.
- Demandez aussi un hôtel à Paris pour la troisième semaine de votre séjour en France.
- L'agent va aussi suggérer des visites et des activités intéressantes à faire à Paris.
- Vous expliquez à l'agent que vous voulez (*want*) avoir du temps libre pendant le voyage.

Les questions du professeur Have students quickly review the brochure before answering the questions. Suggest that pairs take turns answering them. The student who does not answer a question should find the line of text that contains the answer.

C'est sûr, je pars en Corse! Have groups act out their conversations for the rest of the class.

Expansion Tell students that the travel agency is planning to create additional brochures to help them promote their **Tour de Corse** excursion. Their goal is to have several slightly different brochures about the same trip that may appeal to different types of people. Ask students to come up with 3 or 4 short, interesting titles for these new brochures.

OPTIONS

Pairs Have students work together in pairs. Tell them to divide the twelve-day **Tour de Corse** itinerary between them. Each student will then write at least five questions asking about their chosen parts of the trip. They will then answer each other's questions.

Pairs Bring in additional short, simple French-language magazine or newspaper articles you have read. Have pairs scan the headlines/titles of the articles to determine their content. Have them write down all the clues that help them come to these conclusions. Then ask pairs to present their findings to the class. Confirm the correct predictions.

Section Goals

In this section, students will:
• learn to make an outline
• write a travel brochure

Stratégie Explain that outlines are a great way for a writer to plan out the content of a piece of writing before expending time and effort on writing. An outline is also a great way of keeping a writer on track, and helps him or her to keep the whole writing project in mind while focusing on a specific part.

Thème Discuss the travel brochure that students are going to write. Have them brainstorm a list of information that they might include. You may want to indicate a specific number of points that should be in the brochure. Tell students that the **Tour de Corse** brochure in **Lecture**, pages 308–309, can serve as a model for their writing. Remind them that they are writing with the purpose of attracting people to a particular trip. Suggest that students brainstorm in French as many details as possible about the trip they will describe.

Écriture

STRATÉGIE

Making an outline

When we write to share information, an outline can serve to separate topics and subtopics, providing a framework for presenting the data. Consider the following excerpt from an outline of the tourist brochure on pages 308–309.

I. Itinéraire et description du voyage

  A. Jour 1
    1. ville: Ajaccio
    2. visites: visite de la ville à pied
    3. activités: dîner

  B. Jour 2
    1. ville: Bonifacio
    2. visites: la ville de Bonifacio
    3. activités: promenade en bateau, dîner

II. Description des hôtels et des transports

  A. Hôtels
  B. Transports

Schéma d'idées

Idea maps can be used to create outlines. The major sections of an idea map correspond to the Roman numerals in an outline. The minor sections correspond to the outline's capital letters, and so on. Consider the idea map that led to the outline above.

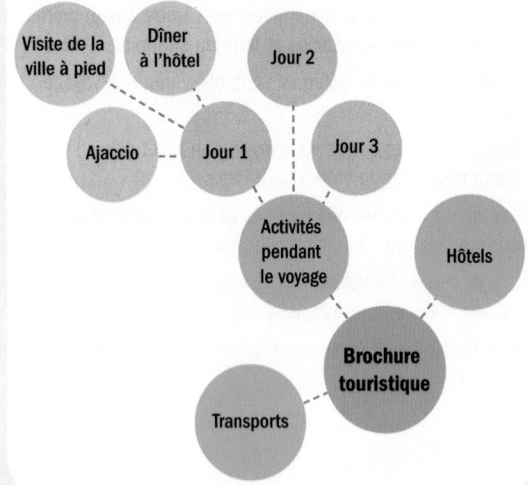

Thème

Écrivez une brochure

Avant l'écriture

1. Vous allez préparer une brochure pour un voyage organisé que vous avez fait ou que vous avez envie de faire dans un pays francophone. Utilisez un schéma d'idées pour vous aider. Voici des exemples d'informations que votre brochure peut (*can*) donner.

- le pays et la ville
- le nombre de jours
- la date et l'heure du départ et du retour
- les transports utilisés (train, avion, …) et le lieu de départ (aéroport JFK, gare de Lyon, …)
- le temps qu'il va probablement faire et quelques suggestions de vêtements à porter
- où on va dormir (hôtel, auberge de jeunesse, camping, …)
- où on va manger (restaurant, café, pique-nique dans un parc, …)
- les visites culturelles (monuments, musées, …)
- les autres activités au programme (explorer la ville, aller au marché, faire du sport, …)
- le prix du voyage par personne

OPTIONS

Avant l'écriture Show how an idea map corresponds to a numerical written outline. Use two large circles for points I and II of the outline. Use four smaller circles for the two sets of A and B points. Finally, add six smaller circles that correspond to the 1, 2, and 3 points. Challenge students to take the existing idea map and convert it to a numerical written outline.

For students who have trouble breaking larger ideas down into smaller ones, recycle the use of question words from Unit 4. Create an idea map that shows a subject in a larger circle. Spinning off from it can be smaller circles each with a different question and answer about that subject.

2. Complétez le schéma d'idées pour vous aider à visualiser ce que (*what*) vous allez présenter dans votre brochure.

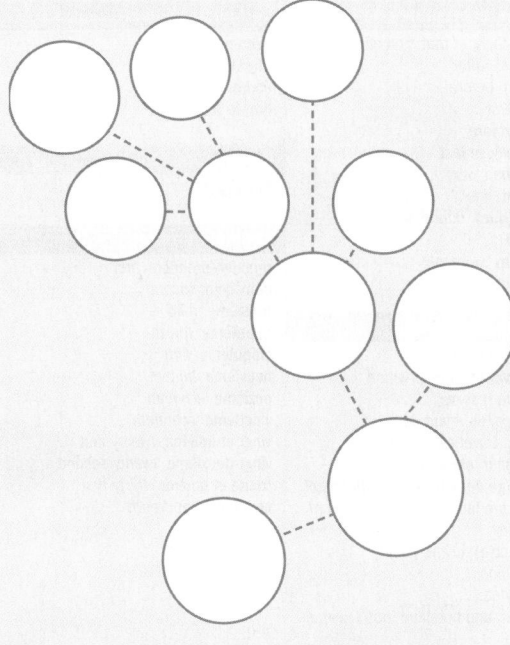

3. Une fois (*Once*) votre schéma d'idées créé, pensez à d'autres informations qui pourraient (*could*) être importantes pour la création de votre brochure.

Écriture

Utilisez votre schéma d'idées pour créer la brochure de votre voyage. Donnez un titre (*title*) à la présentation et aux différentes catégories. Chaque section et sous-section (*minor section*) doit (*must*) avoir son titre et être présentée séparément. Incorporez au moins (*at least*) quatre sous-sections. Vous pouvez inclure (*can include*) des visuels. Faites attention à bien les placer dans les sections correspondantes. Utilisez les constructions grammaticales et le vocabulaire que vous avez appris dans cette unité.

Après l'écriture

1. Échangez votre brochure avec celle (*the one*) d'un(e) partenaire. Répondez à ces questions pour commenter son travail.

- La brochure de votre partenaire correspond-elle au schéma d'idées qu'il/elle a créé?

- Votre partenaire a-t-il/elle inclu au moins quatre sections?

- Toutes les sections et sous-sections ont-elles un titre?

- Votre partenaire a-t-il/elle décrit en détail chaque catégorie?

- Chaque sous-section présente-t-elle des informations supplémentaires sur le sujet?

- Si votre partenaire a ajouté (*added*) des visuels, illustrent-ils vraiment le texte qu'ils accompagnent?

- Votre partenaire a-t-il/elle correctement utilisé les constructions grammaticales et le vocabulaire de l'unité?

2. Corrigez votre brochure d'après (*according to*) les commentaires de votre partenaire. Relisez votre travail pour éliminer ces problèmes:

- des fautes (*errors*) d'orthographe

- des fautes de ponctuation

- des fautes de conjugaison

- des fautes d'accord (*agreement*) des adjectifs

- un mauvais emploi (*use*) de la grammaire

trois cent onze **311**

EVALUATION

Criteria

Content Contains both an idea map and an outline that provide all the information requested in bulleted list of tasks.
Scale: 1 2 3 4 5

Organization An outline or idea map that is then converted into a brochure with a title and minor sections that correspond to the outline or idea map.
Scale: 1 2 3 4 5

Accuracy Uses forms of **aller** and direct object pronouns correctly. Spells words, conjugates verbs, and modifies adjectives correctly throughout.
Scale: 1 2 3 4 5

Creativity Includes additional information that is not included in the task and/or designs a brochure with photos, drawings, or extra embellishments.
Scale: 1 2 3 4 5

Scoring

Excellent	18–20 points
Good	14–17 points
Satisfactory	10–13 points
Unsatisfactory	< 10 points

O P T I O N S

Écriture Students may need help converting the bulleted information into an outline/idea map. As a class, brainstorm ways to organize the facts. For example: (1st level): **Un voyage à _____,** (2nd level): **Généralités, Que faire et voir** (to see). Then have students associate the following with one of the 2nd level categories: number of days, dates, travel times, transportation, weather, price, hotels, restaurants, cultural visits, other activities.

Review the kind of neutral and formal language typically used in a travel brochure. Remind students to use the command forms they learned in 7B. You may want to get them started with some useful expressions such as **Nous donnons...** and **Vous allez** [+ *infinitive*], along with a number of adjectives such as **fascinant(e), intéressant(e), beau/belle, historique, ancien(ne), confortable, agréable, délicieux/délicieuse,** and so on.

Instructional Resources
vhlcentral.com:
Textbook MP3s; Textbook
Audioscript; reference tools

Suggestions
- Tell students that an easy way to study from **Vocabulaire** is to cover up the French half of each section, leaving only the English equivalents exposed. They can then quiz themselves on the French items. To focus on the English equivalents of the French entries, they simply reverse this process.
- Point out to students that they can use the Vocabulary Tools at **vhlcentral.com** for reference and extra vocabulary practice.

◀)) Ⓢ Vocabulary Tools

Leçon 7A

Partir en voyage
un aéroport *airport*
un arrêt d'autobus (de bus) *bus stop*
une arrivée *arrival*
un avion *plane*
un billet aller-retour *round-trip ticket*
un billet (d'avion, de train) *(plane, train) ticket*
un départ *departure*
une douane *customs*
une gare (routière) *train station (bus station)*
une sortie *exit*
une station (de métro) *(subway) station*
une station de ski *ski resort*
un ticket de bus, de métro *bus, subway ticket*
un vol *flight*
un voyage *trip*
à l'étranger *abroad, overseas*
la campagne *country(side)*
une capitale *capital*
des gens (m.) *people*
le monde *world*
un pays *country*

Les pays
(en/l') Allemagne (f.) *(to, in) Germany*
(en/l') Angleterre (f.) *(to, in) England*
(en/la) Belgique (belge) *(to, in) Belgium (Belgian)*
(au/le) Brésil (brésilien(ne)) *(to, in) Brazil (Brazilian)*
(au/le) Canada *(to, in) Canada*
(en/la) Chine (chinois(e)) *(to, in) China (Chinese)*
(en/l') Espagne (f.) *(to, in) Spain*
(aux/les) États-Unis (m.) *(to, in) the United States*
(en/la) France *(to, in) France*
(en/l') Irlande (f.) (irlandais(e)) *(to, in) Ireland (Irish)*
(en/l') Italie (f.) *(to, in) Italy*
(au/le) Japon *(to, in) Japan*
(au/le) Mexique *(to, in) Mexico*
(en/la) Suisse *(to, in) Switzerland*

Les vacances
bronzer *to tan*
faire du shopping *to go shopping*
faire les valises *to pack one's bags*
faire un séjour *to spend time (somewhere)*
partir en vacances *to go on vacation*
prendre un train (un avion, un taxi, un (auto)bus, un bateau) *to take a train (plane, taxi, bus, boat)*
rouler en voiture *to ride in a car*
utiliser un plan *to use/read a map*
un (jour de) congé *day(s) off*
le journal *newspaper*
la mer *sea*
une plage *beach*
des vacances (f.) *vacation*

Verbes
aller *to go*
arriver *to arrive*
descendre *to go/take down*
entrer *to enter*
monter *to go/come up; to get in/on*
mourir *to die*
naître *to be born*
partir *to leave*
passer *to pass by; to spend time*
rentrer *to return*
rester *to stay*
retourner *to return*
sortir *to go out*
tomber (sur quelqu'un) *to fall (to run into somebody)*

Expressions utiles
See p. 275.

Direct object pronouns
me/m' *me*
te/t' *you*
le/la/l' *him/her/it*
nous *us*
vous *you*
les *them*

Leçon 7B

Adverbes et locutions de temps
alors *so, then; at that moment*
après (que) *after*
avant (de) *before*
d'abord *first*
donc *therefore*
enfin *finally, at last*
ensuite *then, next*
finalement *finally*
pendant (que) *during, while*
puis *then*
tout à coup *suddenly*
tout de suite *right away*

Faire une réservation
annuler *to cancel*
une réservation *a reservation*
réserver *to reserve*
une agence/un agent de voyages *travel agency/agent*
un ascenseur *elevator*
une auberge de jeunesse *youth hostel*
une chambre individuelle *single room*
une clé *key*
un(e) client(e) *client; guest*
un étage *floor*
un hôtel *hotel*
un hôtelier/une hôtelière *hotel keeper*
un lit *bed*
un passager/une passagère *passenger*
un passeport *passport*
la réception *reception desk*
le rez-de-chaussée *ground floor*
complet/complète *full (no vacancies)*
libre *available*

Adverbes
absolument *absolutely*
activement *actively*
bien *well*
constamment *constantly*
couramment *fluently*
différemment *differently*
évidemment *obviously, evidently; of course*
franchement *frankly, honestly*
gentiment *nicely*
heureusement *fortunately*
mal *badly*
malheureusement *unfortunately*
vraiment *really*

Verbes irréguliers
décrire *to describe*
dire *to say*
écrire *to write*
lire *to read*

Expressions utiles
See p. 293.

Ordinal numbers
premier/première *first*
deuxième *second*
troisième *third*
quatrième *fourth*
cinquième *fifth*
neuvième *ninth*
onzième *eleventh*
vingtième *twentieth*
vingt et unième *twenty-first*
vingt-deuxième *twenty-second*
trente et unième *thirty-first*
centième *hundredth*

Chez nous

Unit Goals

Leçon 8A

In this lesson, students will learn:
- terms for parts of the house
- terms for furniture
- the pronunciation of **s** and **ss**
- about housing in France and **le château Frontenac**
- more about housing in France through specially shot video footage
- the formation of the **imparfait**
- the uses of the **passé composé** and the **imparfait**
- about a young designer of sustainable furniture

Leçon 8B

In this lesson, students will learn:
- terms for household chores
- terms for appliances
- the pronunciation of semi-vowels
- about the interiors of French homes and the French Quarter in New Orleans
- about famous Parisian singer and songwriter Charles Aznavour
- more about the uses of the **passé composé** and the **imparfait**
- the uses of **savoir** and **connaître**
- to use visual cues to understand spoken French

Savoir-faire

In this section, students will learn:
- cultural and historical information about **Paris et l'Île-de-France**
- to guess the meaning of unknown words from context
- to write a narrative using the **passé composé** and the **imparfait**

Pour commencer
- a. dans le salon
- c. une télévision
- b. Ils passent un bon moment.

Pour commencer

Où sont David et Rachid?
a. dans le salon b. dans la cuisine
c. dans la chambre

Qu'est-ce qu'il n'y a pas sur la photo?
a. un canapé b. une table c. une télévision

Que font David et Rachid?
a. Ils étudient. b. Ils passent un bon moment.
c. Ils regardent la télé.

RESOURCES

Student Activities Manual (SAM):
Workbook Activities, pp. 103–116;
Lab Activities, pp. 57–64;
Video Activities, pp. 29–32; pp. 75–76;
SAM Answer Key

vhlcentral.com: Textbook MP3s; Lab MP3s;
Textbook Audioscript; Lab Audioscript Video;
Videoscript; **Roman-photo** Translations;
Vocabulaire supplémentaire; Activity Pack
(including **Feuilles d'activités**, Info Gap Activities,
and Task-based Activities);

Le Zapping TV clip transcription; **Essayez!** and **Mise en pratique** answers; Digital Image Bank;
Testing Program; Testing Program MP3s

Section Goals

In this section, students will learn and practice vocabulary related to:
• housing
• rooms and home furnishings

Instructional Resources
vhlcentral.com:
Digital Image Bank;
Vocabulaire supplémentaire
(including vocabulary illustrations from the textbook, theme-based illustrations);
Mise en pratique *answers;*
Textbook Audioscript; Lab Audioscript; Activity Pack (Info Gap Activities); Textbook MP3s; Lab MP3s; SAM Answer Key; reference tools

Suggestions

• Use the **8A Contextes** illustration from the Digital Image Bank. Point out rooms and furnishings in the illustration. Examples: **Ça, c'est la salle de bains. Voici un canapé.**

• Ask students questions about their homes using the new vocabulary. Examples: **Habitez-vous dans une maison, dans un appartement ou dans une résidence universitaire? Avez-vous un balcon? Un garage? Combien de salles de bains avez-vous?**

• Point out the difference between **le loyer** (*the rent*) and **louer** (*to rent*).

• Explain that **une chambre** is *a bedroom*, but **une pièce** is the generic term for *a room*.

• Explain that **un salon** is a more formal room used primarily for entertaining guests. Generally, it is not used for watching television or other leisure activities. **Une salle de séjour** is a more functional room, similar to an American family room or den.

• Point out that **un studio** is *a studio apartment*, usually equipped with a couch that converts into a bed and a kitchenette.

• Use the Vocabulary illustrations and the house and chores illustrations from the Digital Image Bank to help students familiarize themselves with housing, rooms, and home furnishings.

• Additional vocabulary for this lesson can be found in the **Vocabulaire supplémentaire** on the Supersite.

Leçon 8A

You will learn how to...
• **describe your home**
• **talk about habitual past actions**

Vocabulary Tools

La maison

Vocabulaire

déménager	to move out
emménager	to move in
louer	to rent
un appartement	apartment
une cave	cellar; basement
un couloir	hallway
une cuisine	kitchen
un escalier	staircase
un immeuble	building
un jardin	garden; yard
un logement	housing
un loyer	rent
une pièce	room
un quartier	area, neighborhood
une résidence universitaire	dorm
une salle à manger	dining room
un salon	formal living/sitting room
un studio	studio (apartment)
une armoire	armoire, wardrobe
une douche	shower
un lavabo	bathroom sink
un meuble	piece of furniture
un placard	closet, cupboard
un tiroir	drawer
un(e) propriétaire	owner

Labels in illustration: le balcon · la salle de bains · les toilettes (f.) (W.-C.) (m.) · le miroir · la lampe · la baignoire · le canapé · le tapis · une fleur · le fauteuil · le sous-sol · la salle de séjour

ressources

WB pp. 103–104 · LM p. 57 · vhlcentral

314 *trois cent quatorze*

Extra Practice Ask students what activities they do in various rooms. Examples: **Dans quelle pièce... mangez-vous? étudiez-vous? dormez-vous? faites-vous la cuisine? travaillez-vous sur l'ordinateur? parlez-vous au téléphone?**

TPR Make signs for various rooms in a house and for other parts of a home, such as **le garage** or **le balcon**. Also make several signs for bedrooms and bathrooms. Distribute the signs to students. As other students describe their homes (one floor at a time), those holding signs arrange themselves according to the descriptions. Tell students to use prepositions of location in their descriptions.

OPTIONS

les rideaux (m.)

le mur

les affiches (f.)

les étagères (f.)

la commode

la chambre

le garage

Mise en pratique

1 Écoutez Patrice cherche un appartement. Écoutez sa conversation téléphonique et dites si les affirmations sont **vraies** ou **fausses**.

	Vrai	Faux
1. Madame Dautry est la propriétaire de l'appartement.	☑	☐
2. L'appartement est au 24 rue Pasteur.	☑	☐
3. L'appartement est au cinquième étage.	☐	☑
4. L'appartement est dans un vieil immeuble.	☐	☑
5. L'appartement n'a pas de balcon, mais il a un garage.	☐	☑
6. Il y a une baignoire dans la salle de bains.	☐	☑
7. Les toilettes ne sont pas dans la salle de bains.	☑	☐
8. L'appartement est un studio.	☐	☑
9. Le loyer est de 490€.	☑	☐
10. Patrice va tout de suite emménager.	☐	☑

2 Chassez l'intrus Indiquez le mot ou l'expression qui ne va pas avec les autres (*that doesn't belong*).

1. un appartement, un quartier, un logement, un studio
2. une baignoire, une douche, un sous-sol, un lavabo
3. un salon, une salle à manger, une salle de séjour, un jardin
4. un meuble, un canapé, une armoire, une affiche
5. un placard, un balcon, un jardin, un garage
6. une chambre, une cuisine, un rideau, une pièce
7. un meuble, une commode, un couloir, un lit
8. un miroir, un tapis, une fenêtre, une affiche

3 Définitions Lisez les définitions et trouvez les mots ou expressions d'**ESPACE CONTEXTES** qui correspondent. Ensuite, avec un(e) partenaire, donnez votre propre définition de cinq mots ou expressions. Rejoignez un autre groupe et lisez vos définitions. L'autre groupe doit deviner (*must guess*) de quoi vous parlez.

1. C'est ce que (*what*) vous payez chaque mois quand vous n'êtes pas propriétaire de votre appartement. _____un loyer_____
2. Vous passez par ici pour aller d'une pièce à une autre. _____un couloir_____
3. C'est le fait de (*act of*) partir de votre appartement. _____déménager_____
4. C'est là que vous mettez vos livres. _____une étagère_____
5. En général, il y en a quatre dans une pièce et ils séparent les pièces de votre appartement. _____les murs_____
6. C'est ce que vous utilisez pour lire le soir. _____une lampe_____
7. C'est là que vous mettez votre voiture. _____un garage_____
8. C'est ce que vous utilisez pour aller du premier au deuxième étage d'un immeuble. _____un escalier/un ascenseur_____
9. Quand vous avez des invités, c'est la pièce dans laquelle (*in which*) vous dînez. _____la salle à manger_____
10. En général, il est sur le sol (*floor*) d'une pièce. _____un tapis_____

Practice more at vhlcentral.com.

trois cent quinze **315**

1 Audioscript PATRICE: Allô, Madame Dautry, s'il vous plaît.
MADAME: Oui, c'est moi. J'écoute.
P: Mon nom est Patrice Leconte. Je vous appelle au sujet de votre appartement du 24, rue Pasteur. Est-ce qu'il est toujours libre?
M: Oui, jeune homme. Il est toujours libre.
P: Parfait. Comment est-il?
M: Il est au quatrième étage d'un immeuble moderne. Il y a un balcon, mais pas de garage. La chambre est plutôt petite, mais il y a beaucoup de placards.
P: Et la salle de bains?
M: Elle est petite aussi, avec une douche, un lavabo et un grand miroir. Les toilettes sont séparées.
P: Et le salon?
M: C'est la pièce principale. Elle est plutôt grande. La cuisine est juste à côté.
P: C'est combien, le loyer?
M: Le loyer est de 490€.
P: Oh, c'est cher!
M: Mais vous êtes à côté de l'université et l'appartement est libre le premier septembre.
P: Bon, je vais y penser. Merci beaucoup. Au revoir, Madame.
M: Au revoir, Monsieur.
(On Textbook MP3s)

1 Expansion Play the recording again, stopping at the end of each sentence that contains an answer. Have students verify true statements and correct the false ones.

2 Expansion Have students create one or two additional sets using at least three of the new vocabulary words in each one. Collect their papers and write some of the items on the board.

3 Suggestion Before beginning this activity, you might want to teach your students expressions for circumlocution. Examples: **C'est un objet qu'on utilise pour... C'est une pièce où...**

OPTIONS

Game Write vocabulary words related to home furnishings on index cards. On another set of cards, draw or paste pictures to match each term. Tape them face down on the board in random order. Divide the class into two teams. Play a game of Concentration in which students match words with pictures. When a player has a match, his or her team collects those cards. When all cards are matched, the team with the most cards wins.

Extra Practice Write **Logements** and **Meubles** at the top of two columns on the board or on a transparency. Say vocabulary words and have students classify them in the correct category. Examples: **un appartement (logement), une résidence (logement), un studio (logement), un canapé (meuble), un lit (meuble),** and **une armoire (meuble).**

NATIONAL communication STANDARDS

Communication

4 Suggestion Have students take notes during their interviews. Then have them report what they learned to another pair of students.

4 Répondez À tour de rôle avec un(e) partenaire, posez-vous ces questions et répondez-y (*them*). Answers will vary.

1. Où est-ce que tu habites?
2. Quelle est la taille de ton appartement ou de ta maison? Combien de pièces y a-t-il?
3. Quand as-tu emménagé?
4. Est-ce que tu as un jardin? Un garage?
5. Combien de placards as-tu? Où sont-ils?
6. Quels meubles as-tu? Comment sont-ils?
7. Quels meubles est-ce que tu voudrais (*would like*) avoir dans ton appartement? (Répondez: Je voudrais...)
8. Qu'est-ce que tu n'aimes pas au sujet de ton appartement?

5 Suggestions
• Before beginning this activity, have students brainstorm vocabulary for furnishings and other items found in a bedroom. Write the words on the board.
• Review the prepositions in **Leçon 3B**.

5 Votre chambre Écrivez une description de votre chambre. À tour de rôle, lisez votre description à votre partenaire. Il/Elle va vous demander d'autres détails et dessiner un plan. Ensuite, regardez le dessin (*drawing*) de votre partenaire et dites s'il correspond à votre chambre ou non. N'oubliez pas d'inclure (*include*) des prépositions pour indiquer où sont certains meubles et objets. Answers will vary.

6 Suggestion Divide the class into pairs and distribute the Info Gap Handouts found in the Activity Pack on the Supersite. Have two volunteers read the **modèle** aloud.

6 Sept différences Votre professeur va vous donner, à vous et à votre partenaire, deux feuilles d'activités différentes. Il y a sept différences entre les deux images. Comparez vos dessins et faites une liste de ces différences. Quel est le groupe le plus rapide (*the quickest*) de la classe? Attention! Ne regardez pas la feuille de votre partenaire. Answers will vary.

7 Suggestion Tell students to include colors in their descriptions.

MODÈLE

Étudiant(e) 1: *Dans mon appartement, il y a un lit. Il y a une lampe à côté du lit.*
Étudiant(e) 2: *Dans mon appartement aussi, il y a un lit, mais il n'y a pas de lampe.*

7 La décoration Formez un groupe de trois. L'un de vous est un décorateur d'intérieur qui a rendez-vous avec deux clients qui veulent (*want*) redécorer leur maison. Les clients sont très difficiles. Imaginez votre conversation et jouez la scène devant la classe. Utilisez les mots de la liste. Answers will vary.

un canapé	un fauteuil
une chambre	un meuble
une cuisine	un mur
un escalier	un placard
une étagère	un tapis

Successful Language Learning Suggest to students that they study vocabulary words in varying order to avoid relying on the order itself to help them remember. Point out that words at the beginning and the end of lists tend to be easier to recall than those in the middle.

O P T I O N S

Extra Practice Call out words for furnishings and other objects, and have students write or say the room(s) where they might be found. Examples: **la télévision (la salle de séjour), le lit (la chambre),** and **la table (la salle à manger).**

TPR Have the class label various parts of the classroom with the names of rooms one would typically find in a house. Then have groups of three perform a skit in which the owner is showing the house to two exchange students who are going to be spending the semester there.

Les sons et les lettres  Audio

s and ss

Section Goals

In this section, students will learn about the sounds of **s** and **ss**.

Instructional Resources

vhlcentral.com:
Textbook MP3s; Lab MP3s;
SAM Answer Key;
Textbook Audioscript;
Lab Audioscript;
reference tools

You've already learned that an **s** at the end of a word is usually silent.

| lavabo**s** | copain**s** | va**s** | placard**s** |

An **s** at the beginning of a word, before a consonant, or after a pronounced consonant is pronounced like the *s* in the English word *set*.

| **s**oir | **s**alon | **s**tudio | ab**s**olument |

A double **s** is pronounced like the *ss* in the English word *kiss*.

| gro**ss**e | a**ss**ez | intére**ss**ant | rou**ss**e |

An **s** at the end of a word is often pronounced when the following word begins with a vowel sound. An **s** in a liaison sounds like a *z*, like the *s* in the English word *rose*.

| trè**s** élégant | troi**s** hommes |

The other instance where the French **s** has a *z* sound is when there is a single **s** between two vowels within the same word. The **s** is pronounced like the *s* in the English word *music*.

| mu**s**ée | amu**s**ant | oi**s**eau | be**s**oin |

These words look alike, but have different meanings. Compare the pronunciations of each word pair.

| poi**s**on | poi**ss**on | dé**s**ert | de**ss**ert |

Suggestions

- Model the pronunciation of the example words and have students repeat them after you.
- Ask students to provide more examples of words from this lesson or previous lessons with these sounds. Examples: **cuisine, salon, résidence,** and **expression**.
- Dictate five familiar words containing **s** and **ss**, repeating each one at least two times. Then write them on the board or on a transparency and have students check their spelling.

Prononcez Répétez les mots suivants à voix haute.

1. sac
2. triste
3. suisse
4. chose
5. bourse
6. passer
7. surprise
8. assister
9. magasin
10. expressions
11. sénégalaise
12. sérieusement

Articulez Répétez les phrases suivantes à voix haute.

1. Le spectacle est très amusant et la chanteuse est superbe.
2. Est-ce que vous habitez dans une résidence universitaire?
3. De temps en temps, Suzanne assiste à l'inauguration d'expositions au musée.
4. Heureusement, mes professeurs sont sympathiques, sociables et très sincères.

Dictons Répétez les dictons à voix haute.

Les oiseaux de même plumage s'assemblent sur le même rivage.[2]

Si jeunesse savait, si vieillesse pouvait.[1]

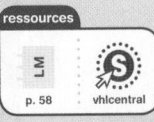

ressources

LM
p. 58

vhlcentral

[2] Birds of a feather flock together.
[1] Youth is wasted on the young. (lit. If youth but knew, if old age but could.)

trois cent dix-sept **317**

Extra Practice Use these sentences for additional practice or dictation. **1.** Serge est professeur de sociologie. **2.** Solange est paresseuse et pessimiste. **3.** Ces étudiants sénégalais sont très intelligents. **4.** Sylvain essaie les chaussures sans chaussettes.

Extra Practice Teach students these French tongue-twisters that contain the **s** and **ss** sounds. **1.** Ces six saucissons-ci sont si secs qu'on ne sait si c'en sont. **2.** Zazie causait avec sa cousine en cousant.

O P T I O N S

Section Goals

In this section, students will learn functional phrases for talking about their home.

Instructional Resources
vhlcentral.com:
Roman-photo Video, Videoscript, and Translation; SAM Answer Key; reference tools

Video Recap: Leçon 7B
Review the previous **Roman-photo** with this activity.
1. Pourquoi Sandrine est-elle allée à l'agence de voyages? (pour faire une réservation d'hôtel à Albertville)
2. Pourquoi n'a-t-elle pas fait la réservation? (Les hôtels moins chers sont complets.)
3. Comment Amina a-t-elle réussi à trouver un hôtel? (Elle a cherché sur Internet.)
4. Pourquoi Sandrine n'est-elle pas contente? (parce que Pascal ne va pas aller à Albertville)

Video Synopsis Pascal arrives in Aix-en-Provence. He runs into Rachid, who helps him pick up his flowers. He has never met Rachid before. Rachid and David then take a tour of Sandrine's apartment, which is very nice and big. Pascal shows up unexpectedly. Sandrine is not pleased by his surprise visit and breaks up with him.

Suggestions
• Have students scan the **Roman-photo** and find words related to the home.
• Have students read the **Roman-photo** conversation in groups of four.
• Review students' predictions and ask them which ones were correct.

La visite surprise  Video

PERSONNAGES

David

Pascal

Rachid

Sandrine

En ville, Pascal fait tomber (drops) ses fleurs.
PASCAL Aïe!
RACHID Tenez. (*Il aide Pascal.*)
PASCAL Oh, merci.
RACHID Aïe!
PASCAL Oh pardon, je suis vraiment désolé!
RACHID Ce n'est rien.
PASCAL Bonne journée!

Chez Sandrine...
RACHID Eh, salut, David! Dis donc, ce n'est pas un logement d'étudiants ici! C'est grand chez toi! Tu ne déménages pas, finalement?
DAVID Heureusement, Sandrine a décidé de rester.
SANDRINE Oui, je suis bien dans cet appartement. Seulement, les loyers sont très chers au centre-ville.

RACHID Oui, malheureusement! Tu as combien de pièces?
SANDRINE Il y a trois pièces: le salon, la salle à manger, ma chambre. Bien sûr, il y a une cuisine et j'ai aussi une grande salle de bains. Je te fais visiter?

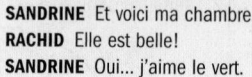

SANDRINE Et voici ma chambre.
RACHID Elle est belle!
SANDRINE Oui... j'aime le vert.

RACHID Dis, c'est vrai, Sandrine, ta salle de bains est vraiment grande.
DAVID Oui! Et elle a un beau miroir au-dessus du lavabo et une baignoire!
RACHID Chez nous, on a seulement une douche.
SANDRINE Moi, je préfère les douches, en fait.

Le téléphone sonne (rings).
RACHID Comparé à cet appartement, le nôtre, c'est une cave! Pas de décorations, juste des affiches, un canapé, des étagères et mon bureau.
DAVID C'est vrai. On n'a même pas de rideaux.

A C T I V I T É S

1

Vrai ou faux? Indiquez si ces affirmations sont **vraies** ou **fausses**. Corrigez les phrases fausses. Answers may vary.

1. C'est la première fois que Rachid visite l'appartement.
Vrai.
2. Sandrine ne déménage pas.
Vrai.
3. Les loyers au centre-ville ne sont pas chers.
Faux. Les loyers au centre-ville sont très chers.
4. Sandrine invite ses amis chez elle.
Vrai.
5. Rachid préfère son appartement à l'appartement de Sandrine. Faux. Rachid préfère l'appartement de Sandrine.

6. Chez les garçons, il y a une baignoire et des rideaux.
Faux. Les garçons ont une douche et n'ont pas de rideaux.
7. Quand Pascal arrive, Sandrine est contente (*pleased*).
Faux. Sandrine n'est pas contente.
8. Pascal doit (*must*) travailler ce week-end.
Faux. Pascal ne travaille pas ce week-end.

 Practice more at **vhlcentral.com**.

O P T I O N S

Avant de regarder la vidéo Before viewing the video, have students read the title and predict what might happen in this episode. Write their predictions on the board.

Regarder la vidéo Show the video episode without sound and have the class create a plot summary based on the visual cues. Then show the video again with sound and have the class correct any mistakes and fill in any gaps in the plot summary they created.

Pascal arrive à Aix-en-Provence.

SANDRINE Voici la salle à manger.
RACHID Ça, c'est une pièce très importante pour nous, les invités.

SANDRINE Et puis, la cuisine.
RACHID Une pièce très importante pour Sandrine...
DAVID Évidemment!

SANDRINE Mais Pascal... je pensais que tu avais du travail... Quoi? Tu es ici, maintenant? C'est une blague!
PASCAL Mais ma chérie, j'ai pris le train pour te faire une surprise...

SANDRINE Une surprise! Nous deux, c'est fini! D'abord, tu me dis que les vacances avec moi, c'est impossible et ensuite tu arrives à Aix sans me téléphoner!
PASCAL Bon, si c'est comme ça, reste où tu es. Ne descends pas. Moi, je m'en vais. Voilà tes fleurs. Tu parles d'une surprise!

Expressions utiles

Talking about your home

- Tu ne déménages pas, finalement?
  You're not moving, after all?
- Heureusement, Sandrine a décidé de rester.
  Thankfully, Sandrine has decided to stay.
- Seulement, les loyers sont très chers au centre-ville.
  However, rents are very expensive downtown.
- Je te fais visiter?
  Shall I give you a tour?
- Ta salle de bains est vraiment grande.
  Your bathroom is really big.
- Elle a un beau miroir au-dessus du lavabo.
  It has a nice mirror above the sink.
- Chez nous, on a seulement une douche.
  At our place, we only have a shower.

Additional vocabulary

- Aïe!
  Ouch!
- Tenez.
  Here.
- Je pensais que tu avais du travail.
  I thought you had work to do.
- Mais ma chérie, j'ai pris le train pour te faire une surprise.
  But sweetie, I took the train to surprise you.
- sans
  without
- Moi, je m'en vais.
  I am leaving / getting out of here.

Expressions utiles
- Model the pronunciation of the **Expressions utiles** and have students repeat them.
- As you work through the list, point out verbs in the **imparfait**. Tell them that the **imparfait** will be formally presented in the **Structures** section.
- Respond briefly to questions about the **imparfait**. Reinforce correct forms, but do not expect students to produce them consistently at this time.
- Point out that **être fâché(e) contre quelqu'un** means *to be angry with someone*, but **être fâché(e) avec quelqu'un**, means *to be no longer on speaking terms with someone*.

1 Suggestion Have students write their corrections for false statements on the board.

1 Expansion For additional practice, give students these items. 9. **Rachid et Pascal sont de bons amis. (Faux.) 10. La chambre de Sandrine est rose. (Faux.) 11. L'appartement de Sandrine est une cave. (Faux.)**

2 Expansion For additional practice, give students these items. 9. **bureau (D & R) 10. grande salle de bains (S) 11. douche (D & R)**

3 Suggestions
- Before writing the conversation, tell students that the person playing the real estate agent should make a list of questions to ask prospective clients, and the two people playing Sandrine and Amina should decide on the features they are looking for in an apartment.
- You might want to bring in some real estate ads in French from newspapers or the Internet for the agents to use.

---

2 **Quel appartement?** Indiquez si ces objets sont dans l'appartement de Sandrine **(S)** ou dans l'appartement de David et Rachid **(D & R)**.

1. baignoire   S
2. douche   D & R
3. rideaux   S
4. canapé   D & R, S
5. trois pièces   S
6. étagères   D & R
7. miroir   S
8. affiches   D & R

3 **Conversez** Sandrine décide que son loyer est vraiment trop cher. Elle cherche un appartement à partager avec Amina. Avec deux partenaires, écrivez leur conversation avec un agent immobilier *(real estate agent)*. Elles décrivent l'endroit idéal, le prix et les meubles qu'elles préfèrent. L'agent décrit plusieurs possibilités.

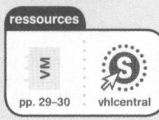

ressources

VM
pp. 29–30

vhlcentral

A C T I V I T É S

O P T I O N S

Small Groups Have groups of three interview each other about their dream houses, with one student conducting the interview, one answering, and one taking notes. At three-minute intervals, have students switch roles until each has been interviewer, interviewee, and note-taker. Then have two groups get together and take turns describing their dream houses to one another using their notes.

Pairs Have students work in pairs. Tell them to write an alternate ending to this episode, in which Sandrine is pleased to see Pascal and invites him upstairs to meet Rachid and David. Encourage students to use some of the **Expressions utiles**. Then have volunteers perform their role-plays for the class.

Section Goals

In this section, students will:
- learn about different types of housing in France
- learn terms related to renting an apartment
- read about traditional houses in various francophone regions
- read about **le château Frontenac**
- view authentic video footage

Instructional Resources
vhlcentral.com: Video; SAM Answer Key; reference tools

Culture à la loupe
Avant la lecture Have students look at the photos and describe what they see.

Lecture
- Point out the **Coup de main**.
- Point out the statistics chart. Ask students what information the chart shows. (the change in percentage between 1962 and 2005 of the size of houses as measured by number of rooms) Explain that the kitchen and bathrooms are not included when counting rooms in a French residence.

Après la lecture Ask students: **Dans quel type de logement français désirez-vous habiter? Pourquoi?**

1 Expansion For additional practice, give students these items. **11. Dans le Sud, les villas ont souvent des toits en tuiles rouges. (Vrai.) 12. Dans les banlieues, il n'y a pas de petits pavillons individuels (Faux.)**

Reading
Video: *Flash culture*

CULTURE À LA LOUPE

Le logement en France

Il y a différents types de logements. En ville, on habite dans une maison ou un appartement. À la campagne, on peut° habiter dans une villa, un château, un chalet ou un mas° provençal.

Vous avez peut-être remarqué° dans un film français qu'il y a une grande diversité de style d'habitation°. En effet°, le style et l'architecture varient d'une région à l'autre, souvent en raison° du climat et des matériaux disponibles°. Dans le Nord°, les maisons sont traditionnellement en briques° avec des toits en ardoise°. Dans l'Est°, en Alsace-Lorraine, il y a de vieilles maisons à colombages° avec des parties de mur en bois°. Dans le Sud°, il y a des villas de style méditerranéen avec des toits en tuiles° rouges et des mas provençaux (de vieilles maisons en pierre°). Dans les Alpes, en Savoie, les chalets sont en bois avec de grands balcons très fleuris°, comme en Suisse. Les maisons traditionnelles de l'Ouest° ont des toits en chaume°. Toutes les maisons françaises ont des volets° et les fenêtres sont assez différentes aussi des fenêtres aux États-Unis. Très souvent il n'y a pas de moustiquaire°, même° dans le sud de la France où il fait très chaud en été.

En France les trois quarts des gens habitent en ville. Beaucoup habitent dans la banlieue, où il y a beaucoup de grands immeubles mais aussi de petits pavillons individuels (maisons avec de petits jardins). Dans les centres-villes et dans les banlieues, il y a des HLM. Ce sont des habitations à loyer modéré°. Les HLM sont construits par l'État. Ce sont souvent des logements réservés aux familles qui ont moins d'argent.

peut *can* mas *farmhouse* remarqué *noticed* habitation *dwelling* En effet *Indeed* en raison du *due to the* disponibles *available* Nord *North* en briques *made of bricks* toits en ardoise *slate roofs* Est *East* à colombages *half-timbered* en bois *made of wood* Sud *South* en tuiles *made of tiles* en pierre *made of stone* fleuris *full of flowers* Ouest *West* en chaume *thatched* volets *shutters* moustiquaire *window screen* même *even* habitations à loyer modéré *low-cost government housing*

Coup de main

Here are some terms commonly used in statistics.

un quart = *one quarter*
un tiers = *one third*
la moitié = *half*
la plupart de = *most of*
un sur cinq = *one in five*

A C T I V I T É S

1 Vrai ou faux? Indiquez si les phrases sont **vraies** ou **fausses**. Corrigez les phrases fausses.

1. Les maisons sont similaires dans les différentes régions françaises.
   Faux. Il y a une grande diversité de style d'habitation.
2. Dans le Nord les maisons sont traditionnellement en briques.
   Vrai.
3. En Alsace-Lorraine il y a des chalets.
   Faux. Il y a de vieilles maisons à colombages.
4. Dans les Alpes il y a des mas provençaux.
   Faux. Il y a des chalets.
5. Les mas provençaux sont des maisons en bois.
   Faux. Ce sont des maisons en pierre au style méditerranéen.
6. Toutes les maisons françaises ont des volets. Vrai.

7. Les maisons françaises n'ont pas toujours des moustiquaires. Vrai.
8. La plupart (*majority*) des Français habite à la campagne. Faux. Les trois quarts des Français habitent en ville.
9. Le pavillon individuel est une sorte de grand immeuble.
   Faux. C'est une maison avec un petit jardin.
10. Les millionnaires habitent dans des HLM.
    Faux. Les HLM sont réservés aux familles qui ont moins d'argent.

---

320 *trois cent vingt*

OPTIONS

Extra Practice Write the following headings on the board and have students identify the different types of housing in each area: **Les grandes villes, La banlieue, Le Nord, L'Alsace-Lorraine, L'Ouest,** and **Le Sud**.

Cultural Comparison Have students work in groups of three to compare the types of housing in France and the United States. Tell them to list the similarities and differences in a two-column chart under the headings **Similitudes** and **Différences**. After completing their charts, have two groups get together and compare their lists.

LE FRANÇAIS QUOTIDIEN

Location d'un logement

agence (f.) de location	rental agency
bail (m.)	lease
caution (f.)	security deposit
charges (f.)	basic utilities
chauffage (m.)	heating
électricité (f.)	electricity
locataire (m./f.)	tenant
petites annonces (f.)	(rental) ads

LE MONDE FRANCOPHONE

L'architecture

Voici quelques exemples d'habitations traditionnelles.

En Afrique centrale et de l'Ouest des maisons construites sur pilotis°, avec un grenier à riz°

En Afrique du Nord des maisons en pisé (de la terre° rouge mélangée° avec de la paille°) construites autour d'un patio central et avec, souvent, une terrasse sur le toit°

Aux Antilles des maisons en bois de toutes les couleurs avec des toits en métal

En Polynésie française des bungalows, construits sur pilotis ou sur le sol, souvent en bambou avec des toits en paille ou en feuilles de cocotier°

Au Viêt-nam des maisons sur pilotis construites sur des lacs, des rivières ou simplement au-dessus du sol°

pilotis stilts **grenier à riz** rice granary **terre** clay **mélangée** mixed **paille** straw **toit** roof **feuilles de cocotier** coconut palm leaves **au-dessus du sol** off the ground

PORTRAIT

Le château Frontenac

Le château Frontenac, nommé ainsi en l'honneur° du comte de Frontenac, gouverneur de Nouvelle-France à la fin du XVIIe siècle, est un hôtel de luxe

et un des plus beaux° sites touristiques de la ville de Québec, au Canada. Construit entre la fin° du XIXe siècle et le début° du XXe siècle sur le Cap Diamant et idéalement situé à l'intérieur des fortifications dans le quartier du Vieux-Québec, le château offre une vue° spectaculaire sur la ville et sur le fleuve Saint-Laurent. Aujourd'hui, avec ses 611 chambres et suites distribuées sur 18 étages, son restaurant gastronomique, Le Champlain, ou encore son bar à vins et à fromages, Le 1608, sa piscine, son centre sportif et son spa, le château Frontenac est classé parmi° les 500 meilleurs° hôtels du monde. En famille ou en voyage d'affaires, cet hôtel vous offre le confort que vous attendez, avec entre autres, un service de gardiennage° très qualifié et bilingue pour vos enfants ou un centre d'affaires avec toutes les commodités nécessaires.

en l'honneur in honour **un des plus beaux** one of the most beautiful **fin** end **début** beginning **vue** view **classé parmi** ranked among **meilleurs** best **gardiennage** babysitting

---

2 **Répondez** D'après les informations données dans les textes, répondez aux questions.

1. Qu'est-ce que le château Frontenac?
   C'est un hôtel de luxe.
2. Quand a commencé la construction du château Frontenac?
   La construction du château Frontenac a commencé au XIXe siècle.
3. Quel est le meilleur endroit de l'hôtel pour les passionnés de vins et de fromages?
   Le meilleur endroit pour eux est Le 1608.
4. Où trouve-t-on des maisons sur pilotis? On en trouve en Afrique centrale et en Afrique de l'Ouest, au Viêt-nam et en Polynésie française.
5. Quelles sont les caractéristiques des maisons d'Afrique du Nord?
   La construction en pisé, le patio central et la terrasse sur le toit sont des caractéristiques des maisons d'Afrique du Nord.

3 **Une année en France** Vous allez habiter en France. Votre partenaire est agent immobilier (*real estate*). Expliquez-lui le type de logement que vous recherchez. Il/Elle va vous donner des renseignements sur les logements disponibles (*available*). Posez des questions pour avoir plus de détails. Voici quelques mots utiles: **le bail** (*lease*), **la caution** (*security deposit*), **les charges (f.)** (*basic utilities*), **le chauffage** (*heating*), **l'électricité (f.)** (*electricity*).

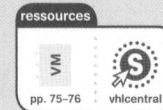

ressources

VM pp. 75–76

vhlcentral

S Practice more at **vhlcentral.com**.

A C T I V I T É S

Le français quotidien Model the pronunciation of each term and have students repeat it. Point out that the word **location** is a faux ami; it means *rental*. You might also wish to add these terms to the list: **un particulier** (*a private owner, as opposed to an agency*), **une chambre de bonne** (*a small room, usually on the top floor, to rent in someone's home; originally it was the maid's room*), **un deux-pièces** (*a two-room apartment*), and **un concierge** (*doorman*).

Portrait
• **Le château Frontenac** is located on a hill overlooking the St. Lawrence River. It is considered the symbol of Quebec City. Have students locate Quebec City on the map of North America in **Appendice A** and point out its strategic location.
• Ask students: **Désirez-vous faire un séjour au château Frontenac? Pourquoi?**

Le monde francophone Bring in photos of the various types of houses from magazines or the Internet. After students have read the text, show them the photos and have them identify the location.

Suggestion Point out to students that they will find supporting activities and more information related to this **Espace culture** at vhlcentral.com.

2 **Expansion** For additional practice, give students these items. **6. Combien de chambres y a-t-il au château? (618) 7. Où trouve-t-on les maisons en bois de toutes les couleurs? (aux Antilles)**

3 **Suggestion** Have students sit back-to-back and pretend they are holding a phone to their ear to simulate a phone conversation.

Flash culture Tell students that they will learn more about housing by watching a variety of real-life images narrated by Benjamin. Show the video segment, then have students jot down in French at least three types of residences they saw. You can also use the activities in the video manual in class to reinforce this **Flash culture** or assign them as homework.

O P T I O N S

Location d'un logement Distribute photocopies of apartment rental ads from a French newspaper or the Internet. Have students guess the meanings of abbreviations, such as **sdb**, **cuis.** and **pisc.**, and explain unfamiliar ones, such as **T3** or **m²**. Then tell students to work in pairs and write five comprehension questions based on the ads. Have volunteers read their questions aloud, and ask other students to answer them.

Cultural Comparison Have students work in groups of three and compare **le château Frontenac** to the hotels in their city or town. Tell them to list the similarities and differences in a two-column chart under the headings **Similitudes** and **Différences**. After completing their charts, have two groups get together and compare their lists.

Section Goals

In this section, students will learn:
- the imperfect tense
- **être** in the imperfect tense

Instructional Resources
vhlcentral.com:
*Activity Pack; Lab MP3s;
SAM Answer Key; **Essayez!**
and **Mise en pratique**
answers; Lab Audioscript;
reference tools*

Suggestions

- Remind students that they can already express the past using the **passé composé**. Now they will learn another tense needed to express themselves in the past. Mention that the **imparfait** expresses the past in a different way.
- Introduce the **imparfait** by describing something you used to do when you were little. Example: **Quand j'étais petit(e), je passais souvent les vacances chez mes grands-parents. Quand il faisait froid, nous jouions aux cartes à la maison. En été, ma famille louait une maison au bord de la mer.** Then ask students: **Et vous, que faisiez-vous quand vous étiez petits?**

À noter

You'll learn to distinguish the **imparfait** from the **passé composé** in **8A.2**.

🏃 Boîte à outils

Note that the forms ending in **-ais**, **-ait**, and **-aient** are all pronounced identically. To avoid confusion when writing these forms, remember that the **je** and **tu** forms never end in a **-t**.

8A.1

ESPACE STRUCTURES

The *imparfait*  Tutorial

Point de départ You've learned how the **passé composé** can express past actions. Now you'll learn another past tense, the **imparfait** (*imperfect*).

- The **imparfait** can be translated into English in several ways.

Hakim **buvait** beaucoup de thé.	Nina **chantait** sous la douche tous les matins.
Hakim drank a lot of tea.	*Nina sang in the shower every morning.*
Hakim used to drink a lot of tea.	*Nina used to sing in the shower every morning.*
Hakim would drink a lot of tea.	*Nina would sing in the shower every morning.*
Hakim was drinking a lot of tea.	*Nina was singing in the shower every morning.*

- The **imparfait** is used to talk about actions that took place repeatedly or habitually during an unspecified period of time.

Je **passais** l'hiver à Lausanne.	Vous m'**écriviez** tous les jours.
I spent the winters in Lausanne.	*You would write to me every day.*
Nous **achetions** des fleurs au marché.	Il **vendait** des meubles.
We used to buy flowers at the market.	*He used to sell furniture.*

- The **imparfait** is a simple tense, which means that it does not require an auxiliary verb. To form the **imparfait**, drop the **-ons** ending from the **nous** form of the present tense and replace it with these endings.

The *imparfait*

	parler (parlons)	finir (finissons)	vendre (vendons)	boire (buvons)
je	parl**ais**	finiss**ais**	vend**ais**	buv**ais**
tu	parl**ais**	finiss**ais**	vend**ais**	buv**ais**
il/elle/on	parl**ait**	finiss**ait**	vend**ait**	buv**ait**
nous	parl**ions**	finiss**ions**	vend**ions**	buv**ions**
vous	parl**iez**	finiss**iez**	vend**iez**	buv**iez**
ils/elles	parl**aient**	finiss**aient**	vend**aient**	buv**aient**

Il **faisait** chaud.	Nous **parlions** au prof.
It was hot.	*We were talking to the professor.*

- Verbs whose infinitives end in **-ger** add an **e** before all endings of the **imparfait** except in the **nous** and **vous** forms. Verbs whose infinitives end in **-cer** change **c** to **ç** before all endings except in the **nous** and **vous** forms.

tu **déménageais**	*but*	nous **déménagions**
les invités **commençaient**	*but*	vous **commenciez**

Mes parents **voyageaient** en Afrique.	Vous **mangiez** toujours des pâtes le soir?
My parents used to travel to Africa.	*Did you always have pasta for dinner?*
À quelle heure **commençait** l'école?	Nous **commencions** notre journée à huit heures.
What time did school start?	*We used to start our day at 8 o'clock.*

- Note that the **nous** and **vous** forms of infinitives ending in **-ier** contain a double **i** in the **imparfait**.

Vous **skiiez** dans les Alpes en janvier.
You used to ski in the Alps in January.

Nous **étudiions** parfois jusqu'à minuit.
We studied until midnight sometimes.

Je pensais que tu avais du travail.

Mais ma chérie, c'était une surprise.

- The **imparfait** is used for description, often with the verb **être**, which is irregular in this tense.

The *imparfait* of être	
j'étais	nous étions
tu étais	vous étiez
il/elle/on était	ils/elles étaient

La cuisine **était** à côté du salon.
The kitchen was next to the living room.

Les toilettes **étaient** au rez-de-chaussée.
The restrooms were on the ground floor.

Étiez-vous heureux avec Francine?
Were you happy with Francine?

Nous **étions** dans le jardin.
We were in the garden.

- Note the imperfect forms of these expressions.

Il pleuvait chaque matin.
It rained every morning.

Il neigeait parfois au printemps.
It snowed sometimes in the spring.

Il y avait deux lits et une lampe.
There were two beds and a lamp.

Il fallait payer le loyer.
We had to pay rent.

Essayez! Choisissez la réponse correcte pour compléter les phrases.

1. Muriel (louait / louais) un appartement en ville.
2. Rodrigue (partageait / partagiez) une chambre avec un autre étudiant.
3. Nous (payait / payions) notre loyer une fois par mois.
4. Il y (avait / était) des balcons au premier étage.
5. Vous (mangeait / mangiez) chez Arnaud le samedi.
6. Je n'(avais / étais) pas peur du chien.
7. Il (neigeait / fallait) mettre le chauffage (*heat*) quand il (faisaient / faisait) froid.
8. Qu'est-ce que tu (faisait / faisais) dans le couloir?
9. Vous (aimiez / aimaient) beaucoup le quartier?
10. Nous (étaient / étions) trois dans le petit studio.
11. Rémy et Nathalie (louait / louaient) leur appartement.
12. Il (avais / pleuvait) constamment en juillet.

ressources

WB
pp. 105–106

LM
p. 59

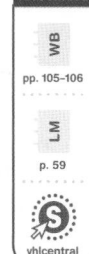
vhlcentral

Suggestions
- Ask volunteers to answer questions about their childhoods. Example: **Quand vous étiez jeune, où alliez-vous en vacances avec votre famille? Aimiez-vous aller au cinéma? Au musée?**
- Review the present-tense **nous** forms of various verbs and explain that the stem without **-ons** is also the **imparfait** stem. Mention the exception with verbs ending in **-ger** and **-cer**.

Essayez! Have students identify the infinitive of each verb in the activity. Examples: **1. louer 2. partager**

OPTIONS

Game Divide the class into two teams. Choose one team member at a time to go to the board, alternating between teams. Say a subject pronoun and an infinitive. The student at the board must write and say the correct **imparfait** form. Example: **je: parler (je parlais)**. Give a point for each correct answer. Play to five or ten points, depending on how much time you have.

Extra Practice Have students write five true/false sentences with the **imparfait** describing things they did while on vacation when they were younger. Have pairs read their descriptions aloud, one sentence at a time, listening for the **imparfait** and guessing what is true or false. Encourage follow-up discussion. Example: **L'hôtel où je suis resté avait 99 étages.** The other students might say: **Ce n'est pas vrai! Combien d'étages avait-il vraiment?**

■ **Suggestion** Before assigning this activity, review the forms of the imperfect by calling out an infinitive and a series of subject pronouns. Ask volunteers to give the corresponding forms. Example: **détester, nous (nous détestions)**.

■ **Expansion** After completing the activity, have students complete the sentences using the **passé composé** instead.

■ **Suggestion** Divide the class into two groups, **l'imparfait** and **le présent**. Have the first group give one phrase about what Emmanuel and his family used to do. The second group should describe what he and his family do differently now, using an opposite verb in the present tense.

Mise en pratique

1 **Nos déménagements** La famille d'Emmanuel déménageait souvent quand il était petit. Complétez son histoire en mettant les verbes à l'imparfait.

Quand j'étais jeune, mon père (1) ___travaillait___ (travailler) pour une société canadienne et nous (2) ___déménagions___ (déménager) souvent. Quand nous (3) ___emménagions___ (emménager), je (4) ___décorais___ (décorer) les murs de ma nouvelle chambre. Ma petite sœur (5) ___détestait___ (détester) déménager. Elle (6) ___disait___ (dire) qu'elle (7) ___perdait___ (perdre) tous ses amis et que ce n' (8) ___était___ (être) pas juste!

2 **Rien n'a changé** Laurent parle de l'école à son grand-père, qui lui explique que les choses n'ont pas changé. Employez l'imparfait pour transformer les phrases de Laurent et donner les phrases de son grand-père.

Laurent: Les cours commencent à 7h30. Je prends le bus pour aller à l'école. J'ai beaucoup d'amis. Mes copains et moi, nous mangeons à midi. Mon dernier cours finit à 16h00. Mon école est très sympa et je l'adore!

Grand-père: Les cours...

commençaient à 7h30. Je prenais le bus pour aller à l'école. J'avais beaucoup d'amis. Mes copains et moi, nous mangions à midi. Mon dernier cours finissait à 16h00. Mon école était très sympa et je l'adorais!

3 **Le samedi** Dites ce que (*what*) ces personnes faisaient habituellement le samedi. Suggested answers

▶ **MODÈLE**

Paul dormait.

Paul

1. je
Je faisais du jogging.

2. ils
Ils finissaient leurs devoirs.

3. vous
Vous mangiez des glaces.

4. tu
Tu prenais du café.

4 **Maintenant et avant** Qu'est-ce qu'Emmanuel et sa famille font différemment aujourd'hui? Écrivez des phrases à l'imparfait et trouvez les adverbes opposés. Suggested answers

MODÈLE

beaucoup travailler (je)
Maintenant je travaille beaucoup, mais avant je travaillais peu.

1. rarement déménager (je)
... je déménage rarement, ... je déménageais constamment.

2. facilement louer une grande maison (nous)
... nous louons facilement ... nous louions difficilement une grande maison.

3. souvent nettoyer ton studio (tu)
... tu nettoies souvent ton studio, ... tu nettoyais rarement ton studio.

4. parfois acheter des meubles (mes parents)
... ils achètent parfois des meubles, ... ils achetaient souvent des meubles.

5. vite conduire (vous)
... vous conduisez vite, ... vous conduisiez lentement.

6. patiemment attendre son anniversaire (ma sœur)
... elle attend patiemment ..., ... elle attendait impatiemment...

Practice more at **vhlcentral.com**.

Communication

5 **Quand tu avais seize ans** À tour de rôle, posez ces questions à votre partenaire pour savoir (*to know*) les détails de sa vie quand il/elle avait seize ans. Answers will vary.

1. Où habitais-tu?
2. Est-ce que tu conduisais déjà une voiture?
3. Où est-ce que ta famille et toi alliez en vacances?
4. Pendant combien de temps partiez-vous en vacances?
5. Est-ce que tes amis et toi, vous sortiez tard le soir?
6. Que faisaient tes parents le week-end?
7. Quels sports pratiquais-tu?
8. Quel genre de musique écoutais-tu?
9. Comment était ton école?
10. Aimais-tu l'école? Pourquoi?

6 **La chambre de Rafik** Voici la chambre de Rafik quand il était adolescent. Avec un(e) partenaire, employez des verbes à l'imparfait pour comparer la chambre de Rafik avec votre chambre quand vous aviez son âge. Answers will vary.

MODÈLE

Étudiant(e) 1: *Je n'avais pas de salle de bains à côté de ma chambre. Et toi?*
Étudiant(e) 2: *Moi, je partageais la salle de bains avec ma sœur.*

7 **Chez les grands-parents** Quand vous étiez petit(e), vous passiez toujours les vacances à la campagne chez vos grands-parents. À tour de rôle, décrivez à votre partenaire une journée typique de vacances. Answers will vary.

MODÈLE

Notre journée commençait très tôt le matin. Mémé préparait du pain...

8 **Une énigme** La nuit dernière, quelqu'un est entré dans le bureau de votre professeur et a emporté (*took away*) l'examen de français. Vous devez (*must*) trouver qui. Qu'est-ce que vos camarades de classe faisaient hier soir? Relisez vos notes et dites qui est le voleur (*thief*). Ensuite, présentez vos conclusions à la classe. Answers will vary.

5 Expansion Have students share their partner's answers with the class using the third person pronouns **il/elle**.

7 Suggestion Consider giving students the option of describing a vacation by the sea, in the mountains, or in their favorite city if they prefer.

7 Expansion Have pairs of students present their imaginary vacations to another pair or to the whole class. Using the imperfect, compile a list of activities on the board.

8 Suggestion Before doing this activity, remind students that the imperfect form of **être** is irregular.

OPTIONS

Game Label the four corners of the room with different historical periods. Examples: **la Préhistoire**, **le Moyen Âge**, **la Renaissance**, and **le Dix-Neuvième siècle**. Tell students to go to the corner that best represents the historical period they would visit if they could. Each group then discusses their reasons for picking that period using the **imparfait**. A spokesperson will summarize his or her group's responses to the class.

Extra Practice Bring in, or choose a few students to bring in, video clips from popular movies. Show clips to the class. Brainstorm important vocabulary. After viewing each clip, have students use the **imparfait** to describe what was happening and what people in the clip were doing.

Section Goals

In this section, students will learn to compare and contrast some of the basic uses and meanings of the **passé composé** and the **imparfait**:

Instructional Resources

vhlcentral.com:
Activity Pack; Lab MP3s; SAM Answer Key; Essayez! and *Mise en pratique* answers; Lab Audioscript; reference tools

Suggestions

- Draw a timeline on the board and mark events on it and label as follows: **J'ai pris mon petit-déjeuner à 7h30. J'ai quitté la maison à 8h. Je suis allé(e) au cours de biologie à 10h15. J'ai déjeuné à midi. Je suis rentré(e) à cinq heures du soir** etc. Then, write the following sentences randomly around the timeline: **Il faisait un temps épouvantable. Le cours de biologie était intéressant**. Explain to students that these sentences cannot be placed at any specific point since they express feelings, background circumstances, or events that occur over an unspecified period of time.
- Have students make two flashcards. On one they write **passé composé** and on the other they write **imparfait**. Read a short text in which both verb tenses are used. As you read each verb, students show the appropriate card. Then call on a volunteer to write the conjugated verb form on the board.

 Boîte à outils

Since the **passé composé** and **imparfait** convey different meanings, it is important to recognize the correct tense when you hear it. Also be sure to practice the pronunciation of each tense in order to make the distinction clear when speaking. Example: **je travaillais** vs. **j'ai travaillé**.

Boîte à outils

Note that the verb **avoir** has a different meaning when used in the **imparfait** versus the **passé composé**:

J'avais sommeil.
I was sleepy.

J'ai eu sommeil.
I got sleepy.

The *passé composé* vs. the *imparfait* (Part 1)

 Tutorial

Point de départ Although the **passé composé** and the **imparfait** are both past tenses, they have very distinct uses and are not interchangeable. The choice between these two tenses depends on the context and on the point of view of the speaker.

Uses of the *passé composé*	
To express specific actions that started and ended in the past and are viewed by the speaker as completed	J'**ai nettoyé** la salle de bains deux fois. *I cleaned the bathroom twice.* Nous **avons acheté** un tapis *We bought a rug.* L'enfant **est né** à la maison. *The child was born at home.* Il **a plu** hier. *It rained yesterday.*
To tell about events that happened at a specific point in time or within a specific length of time in the past	Je **suis allé** à la pêche avec papa il y a deux ans. *I went fishing with dad two years ago.* Il **est allé** au concert vendredi. *He went to the concert on Friday.* Nous **avons passé** une journée fantastique à la plage. *We spent a fantastic day at the beach.* Elle **a étudié** à Paris pendant six mois. *She studied in Paris for six months.*
To express the beginning or end of a past action	Le film **a commencé** à huit heures. *The movie began at 8 o'clock.* Ils **ont fini** leurs devoirs samedi matin. *They finished their homework Saturday morning.*
To narrate a series of past actions or events	Ce matin, j'**ai fait** du jogging, j'**ai nettoyé** la chambre et j'**ai rangé** la cuisine. *This morning, I jogged, I cleaned my bedroom, and I tidied up the kitchen.* Pour la fête d'anniversaire de papa, maman **a envoyé** les invitations, elle **a acheté** un cadeau et elle **a fait** les décorations. *For dad's birthday party, mom sent out the invitations, bought a gift, and did the decorations.*
To signal a change in someone's mental, physical, or emotional state	Il **est mort** dans un accident. *He died in an accident.* Soudain, j'**ai eu** peur. *Suddenly, I got scared.* Tout à coup, elle **a eu** soif. *All of a sudden, she felt thirsty.*

Uses of the *imparfait*

To describe an ongoing past action with no reference to its beginning or end	Vous **dormiez** sur le canapé. *You were sleeping on the couch.* Tu **attendais** dans le café? *You were waiting in the café?* Nous **regardions** la télé chez Fanny. *We were watching TV at Fanny's house.* Les enfants **lisaient** tranquillement. *The children were reading peacefully.*
To express habitual or repeated past actions and events or describe how things used to be	Nous **faisions** un tour en voiture le dimanche matin. *We used to go for a drive on Sunday mornings.* Elle **mettait** toujours la voiture dans le garage. *She always put the car in the garage.* Maman **travaillait** souvent dans le jardin. *Mom would often work in the garden.* Quand j'**étais** jeune, j'**aimais** faire du camping. *When I was young, I used to like to go camping.*
To describe an ongoing mental, physical, or emotional state or condition	Karine **était** très inquiète. *Karine was very worried.* Simon et Marion **étaient** fatigués et ils **avaient** sommeil. *Simon and Marion were tired and sleepy.* Mon ami **avait** faim et il **avait** envie de manger quelque chose. *My friend was hungry and felt like eating something.*

Essayez! Donnez les formes correctes des verbes.

passé composé

1. commencer (il) _il a commencé_
2. acheter (tu) _tu as acheté_
3. boire (nous) _nous avons bu_
4. apprendre (ils) _ils ont appris_
5. répondre (je) _j'ai répondu_
6. sortir (il) _il est sorti_
7. descendre (elles) _elles sont descendues_
8. être (vous) _vous avez été_

imparfait

1. jouer (nous) _nous jouions_
2. être (tu) _tu étais_
3. prendre (elles) _elles prenaient_
4. avoir (vous) _vous aviez_
5. conduire (il) _il conduisait_
6. falloir (il) _il fallait_
7. boire (je) _je buvais_
8. étudier (nous) _nous étudiions_

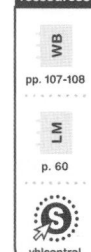

ressources

WB
pp. 107–108

LM
p. 60

vhlcentral

Suggestions

- Contrast the uses of the **passé composé** and **imparfait** by giving personalized examples of things you and/or your family did yesterday versus things you and your family used to do when you were young. Examples: **Hier soir, je suis allée au centre commercial. Quand j'étais petite, je jouais au foot.** Then make two columns on the board, one labeled **Hier, je/j'…** and the other labeled **Quand j'étais petit(e)…** Have volunteers take turns writing complete sentences about themselves under each column.
- As you are comparing the **passé composé** and the **imparfait**, have students focus on the pronunciation of these tenses, since it is very important to be able to distinguish between the respective sounds of the two tenses. You might have them practice the following sentences: **J'ai travaillé. / Je travaillais. Il parlait. / Il a parlé. Tu allais. / Tu es allé(e). Elle chantait. / Elle a chanté.** You could also add the present tense of these sentences and have them practice pronouncing all three tenses.
- Have students interview each other about their childhood activities using the following question: **Quand tu étais petit(e), qu'est-ce que tu faisais… a) après l'école? b) le week-end? c) pendant les grandes vacances** *(summer vacation)*?

Essayez! Give items like these as additional practice. For the **passé composé: 9. descendre (elle) (elle est descendue) 10. lire (je) (j'ai lu)** For the **imparfait: 9. écrire (je) (j'écrivais) 10. dire (on) (on disait)**

OPTIONS

Extra Practice Make cards that contain a verb or noun and an expression that signals a past tense. Example: **hier / parc** or **Quand j'étais jeune / voyager.** Mix them up in a hat and have each student pick a card at random. Have each student state the cues on his or her card and use them in a sentence with the **passé composé** or **imparfait.** Have the student say which tense he or she will use before formulating the sentence.

Small Groups Have students work in groups to pick a popular holiday and write a few sentences in the past tense to describe it. Students might talk about typical activities they did that day, the weather, or how they felt on that day. Then, have them share their description with the class without revealing the holiday and have their classmates guess what holiday it is.

1 **Expansion** Have volunteers explain why they chose the **passé composé** or **imparfait** in each case. Ask them to point out any words or expressions that triggered one tense or the other.

2 **Suggestion** Before assigning the activity, remind students that actions viewed as completed by the speaker take the **passé composé**. Have students give personal examples of actions in the past using this verb tense.

3 **Expansion** Have students use this activity as a model to write a short journal entry about a vacation of their own using the **passé composé** and the **imparfait**.

Mise en pratique

1 **Une surprise désagréable** Récemment, Benoît a fait un séjour à Strasbourg avec un collègue. Complétez ses phrases avec l'imparfait ou le passé composé.

Ce matin, il (1) ___faisait___ (faire) chaud. J' (2) ___étais___ (être) content de partir pour Strasbourg. Je (3) ___suis parti___ (partir) pour la gare, où j' (4) ___ai retrouvé___ (retrouver) Émile. Le train (5) ___est arrivé___ (arriver) à Strasbourg à midi. Nous (6) ___avons commencé___ (commencer) notre promenade en ville. Nous (7) ___avions___ (avoir) besoin d'un plan. J' (8) ___ai cherché___ (chercher) mon portefeuille (*wallet*), mais il (9) ___était___ (être) toujours dans le train! Émile et moi, nous (10) ___avons couru___ (courir) à la gare!

2 **Le week-end dernier** Qu'est-ce que la famille Tran a fait le week-end dernier?

MODÈLE nous / passer le week-end / chez des amis
Nous avons passé le week-end chez des amis.

1. faire / beau / quand / nous / arriver   Il faisait beau quand nous sommes arrivés.
2. nous / être / fatigué / mais content   Nous étions fatigués mais contents.
3. Audrey et son amie / aller / à la piscine   Audrey et son amie sont allées à la piscine.
4. moi, je / décider de / dormir un peu   Moi, j'ai décidé de dormir un peu.
5. samedi soir / pleuvoir / quand / nous / sortir / cinéma   Samedi soir, il pleuvait quand nous sommes sortis du cinéma.
6. nous / rire / beaucoup / parce que / film / être / amusant   Nous avons beaucoup ri parce que le film était amusant.
7. minuit / nous / rentrer / chez nous   À minuit, nous sommes rentrés chez nous.
8. Lanh / regarder / télé / quand / nous / arriver   Lanh regardait la télé quand nous sommes arrivés.
9. dimanche matin / nous / passer / chez des amis   Dimanche matin, nous sommes passés chez des amis.
10. nous / passer / cinq heures / chez eux   Nous avons passé cinq heures chez eux.
11. ce / être / très / sympa   C'était très sympa.

3 **Vacances à la montagne** Hugo raconte ses vacances. Complétez ses phrases avec un des verbes de la liste au passé composé ou à l'imparfait.

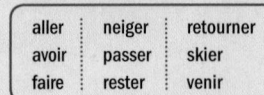

aller	neiger	retourner
avoir	passer	skier
faire	rester	venir

1. L'hiver dernier, nous ___avons passé___ les vacances à la montagne.
2. Quand nous sommes arrivés sur les pistes de ski, il ___neigeait___ beaucoup et il ___faisait___ un temps épouvantable.
3. Ce jour-là, nous ___sommes restés___ à l'hôtel tout l'après-midi.
4. Le jour suivant, nous ___sommes retournés___ sur les pistes.
5. Nous ___avons skié___ et papa ___est allé___ faire une randonnée.
6. Quand ils ___avaient___ mon âge, papa et oncle Hervé ___venaient___ tous les hivers à la montagne.

 Practice more at **vhlcentral.com**.

Communication

4 Situations Avec un(e) partenaire, parlez de ces situations en utilisant le passé composé ou l'imparfait. Comparez vos réponses, puis présentez-les à la classe. Answers will vary.

MODÈLE

Le premier jour de cours...
Étudiant(e) 1: *Le premier jour de cours, j'étais tellement nerveux/nerveuse que j'ai oublié mes livres.*
Étudiant(e) 2: *Moi, j'étais nerveux/nerveuse aussi, alors j'ai quitté ma résidence très tôt.*

1. Quand j'étais petit(e),...

2. L'été dernier,...

3. Hier soir, mon/ma petit(e) ami(e)...

4. Hier, le professeur...

5. La semaine dernière, mon/ma camarade de chambre...

6. Ce matin, au resto U,...

7. Quand j'étais au lycée,...

8. La dernière fois que j'étais en vacances,...

5 Votre premier/première petit(e) ami(e) Posez ces questions à un(e) partenaire. Ajoutez (*Add*) d'autres questions si vous le voulez (*want*). Answers will vary.

1. Qui a été ton/ta premier/première petit(e) ami(e)?

2. Quel âge avais-tu quand tu as fait sa connaissance?

3. Comment était-il/elle?

4. Est-ce que tu as fait la connaissance de sa famille?

5. Pendant combien de temps avez-vous été ensemble?

6. Où alliez-vous quand vous sortiez?

7. Aviez-vous les mêmes (*same*) centres d'intérêt?

8. Pourquoi avez-vous arrêté (*stopped*) de sortir ensemble?

6 Dialogue Jean-Michel, qui a seize ans, est sorti avec des amis hier soir. Quand il est rentré à trois heures du matin, sa mère était furieuse parce que ce n'était pas la première fois qu'il rentrait tard. Avec un(e) partenaire, préparez le dialogue entre Jean-Michel et sa mère. Answers will vary.

MODÈLE

Étudiant(e) 1: *Que faisais-tu à minuit?*
Étudiant(e) 2: *Mes copains et moi, nous sommes allés manger une pizza...*

7 Un crime Vous avez été témoin (*witness*) d'un crime dans votre quartier et la police vous pose beaucoup de questions. Avec un(e) partenaire et à tour de rôle, jouez le détective et le témoin. Answers will vary.

MODÈLE

Étudiant(e) 1: *Où étiez-vous vers huit heures hier soir?*
Étudiant(e) 2: *Chez moi.*
Étudiant(e) 1: *Avez-vous vu quelque chose?*

4 Expansion Have students choose one of these sentences to begin telling a short story in the past. Encourage students to use both the **passé composé** and the **imparfait**.

5 Expansion After completing the pair work, assign this activity as a short written composition.

6 Suggestion Act out the **modèle** with a volunteer before assigning this activity to pairs. Have pairs of students role-play their dialogues in front of the class.

trois cent vingt-neuf **329**

Pairs Have students work in pairs to write a critical review about a fashion show they attended last week. Have them give details about what the models were wearing and how they looked. They might also want to include comparisons between clothing styles they saw last week and how they were different from those in the past.

Small Groups Have students work in groups of four to write a brief account of a surprise party they organized last weekend. Have them tell how they prepared for the party, which rooms they decorated, what the weather was like, and how everyone felt after the party. Then, have them share their summary with the rest of the class.

Révision

Instructional Resources
vhlcentral.com:
Testing Program;
Testing Program MP3s;
reference tools

1 Expansion Have students add an adjective to each object they ask about. Example: **Je cherche mes nouvelles baskets. Où sont-elles? Je cherche mon pull jaune. Où est-il?**

2 Expansion You can expand this activity by having students do it in groups of three or four, where one student plays the role of the detective and the others are possible witnesses who all claim to have seen the suspects. When questioned, the witnesses give the detective conflicting information about the suspects.

3 Suggestion As the students take turns being the interviewer and interviewee, have one of them answer the questions as if he or she had a wonderful vacation, the house was lovely, the weather was great, and everything went well, while the other person had a negative experience where nothing was satisfactory.

4 Expansion Expand this activity by showing the class **avant** and **après** pictures of a person or place in a magazine. Divide the students into two groups. Have one group describe the person or place in the before picture. Have the other group describe the after picture using the present tense.

5 Suggestion Remind students that the floors are counted differently in France than in the U.S. The first floor in the U.S. would be the **rez-de-chaussée** in France while the second floor would be the **premier étage**. Ask students if they know other countries which refer to floors in the same way as the French do.

---

1 Mes affaires Vous cherchez vos affaires (*belongings*). À tour de rôle, demandez de l'aide à votre partenaire. Où étaient-elles pour la dernière fois? Utilisez l'illustration pour les trouver. Answers will vary.

MODÈLE

Étudiant(e) 1: *Je cherche mes baskets. Où sont-elles?*
Étudiant(e) 2: *Tu n'as pas cherché sur l'étagère? Elles étaient sur l'étagère.*

baskets	ordinateur
casquette	parapluie
journal	pull
livre	sac à dos

2 Un bon témoin Il y a eu un cambriolage (*burglary*) chez votre voisin M. Cachetout. Le détective vous interroge parce que vous avez vu deux personnes suspectes sortir de la maison du voisin. Avec un(e) partenaire, créez ce dialogue et jouez cette scène devant la classe. Utilisez ces éléments dans votre scène. Answers will vary.

- une description physique des suspects
- leurs attitudes
- leurs vêtements
- ce que (*what*) vous faisiez quand vous avez vu les suspects

MODÈLE

Étudiant(e) 1: *À quelle heure est-ce que vous avez vu les deux personnes sortir?*
Étudiant(e) 2: *À dix heures. Ils sont sortis du garage.*

3 Quel séjour! Le magazine *Campagne décoration* a eu un concours le mois dernier et vous avez gagné le prix, une semaine de vacances dans une maison à la campagne en France. Vous venez de retourner de (*just came back from*) vos vacances et vous donnez une interview à propos de (*about*) votre séjour. Avec un(e) partenaire, à tour de rôle, posez-vous des questions sur la maison, le temps, les activités dans la région et votre opinion de ces vacances en général. Utilisez l'imparfait et le passé composé. Answers will vary.

MODÈLE

Étudiant(e) 1: *Combien de pièces y avait-il dans cette maison?*
Étudiant(e) 2: *Il y avait six pièces dans la maison.*

4 Avant et après Voici la chambre d'Annette avant et après une visite de sa mère. Comment était sa chambre à l'origine? Avec un(e) partenaire, décrivez la pièce à tour de rôle et cherchez les différences entre les deux illustrations. Answers will vary.

MODÈLE

Avant, la lampe était à côté de l'ordinateur. Maintenant, elle est à côté du canapé.

5 La maison de mon enfance Décrivez l'appartement ou la maison de votre enfance à un(e) partenaire. Où se trouvait-il/elle? Combien de pièces y avait-il? Comment étaient-elles orientées? Y avait-il une piscine, un sous-sol? Qui vivait avec vous dans cet appartement ou cette maison? Racontez (*Tell*) des anecdotes. Donnez beaucoup de détails. Answers will vary.

MODÈLE

Ma maison se trouvait au bord de la mer. C'était une maison à deux étages (floors). Au rez-de-chaussée, il y avait...

OPTIONS

Pairs Have students work in pairs to draw the floor plan of their dream home on a sheet of paper or cardboard. Have them cut out the floor plan into pieces by individual rooms. Then have them give these pieces to their partner who will reassemble the floor plan based on their description of the house.

Extra Practice Have small groups organize a skit about a birthday or other party that took place recently. Guide them to first make general comments about the party, such as **C'était vraiment amusant!** Then describe a few specific things that were going on, what people were talking about, what they were wearing, and what happened. After the skits are performed, have students vote on their favorite one.

Video

communication cultures NATIONAL STANDARDS

connections communities NATIONAL STANDARDS

Créatrice de meubles en carton

Vu d'en haut, un court programme de la chaîne télévisée France 3, présente Caroline Martial, une femme qui, depuis° quelques années, se passionne pour le carton°. En effet, elle crée des meubles en carton et elle a décoré toute sa maison avec ses créations. Son action se trouve à mi-chemin° entre l'art et le développement durable. Cette auto-entrepreneuse a monté sa boîte° pour fabriquer des meubles sur mesure° selon les envies et les besoins. La jeune designer a trouvé dans le carton un matériau léger°, très fort, et particulièrement facile à travailler.

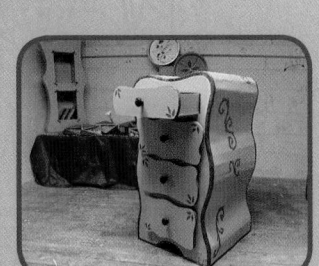

Une commode aux couleurs vives°.

Caroline, la designer de meubles en carton.

Compréhension Répondez aux questions. Suggested answers

1. Citez un élément du petit meuble en construction au début de la vidéo. Il va y avoir un tiroir et une petite niche.
2. Donnez une caractéristique du fauteuil sur lequel Caroline est assise. Le fauteuil est ultra léger.
3. Pourquoi Caroline a-t-elle choisi le carton pour fabriquer ses meubles? Parce qu'il laisse libre cours à l'imagination et à toutes les folies au niveau de la décoration.

Discussion Par groupes de trois, répondez aux questions et discutez. Answers will vary.

1. Êtes-vous créatifs/créatives? Aimez-vous l'idée de créer des meubles?
2. Pensez-vous qu'utiliser du carton pour faire des meubles est un bon concept? Pourquoi ou pourquoi pas?
3. Faites une liste d'au moins trois meubles dans votre maison dont vous avez besoin. Décrivez-les à Caroline, en incluant vos couleurs préférées, etc.

depuis *for* **carton** *cardboard* **à mi-chemin** *halfway* **a monté sa boîte** *started her business* **sur mesure** *custom-made* **léger** *light* **vives** *bright*

Go to **vhlcentral.com** to watch the TV clip featured in this **Le Zapping**.

Practice more at **vhlcentral.com**.

trois cent trente et un **331**

OPTIONS

«Le bon coin» «Le bon coin» is a classified ads website in France. It's where people go online to buy or sell used objects for economic or environmental reasons. Like many in the Internet era, the French enjoy shopping online for second-hand objects that they can update and personalize to suit their needs. Listings on leboncoin.fr also advertise vehicles, housing, multimedia, job postings, and services for today's fast-paced global needs.

Section Goals

In this section, students will:
• read about a French maker of cardboard furniture
• watch a video about this type of handicraft
• answer questions about the video and about furniture creation

Instructional Resources
vhlcentral.com:
TV commercial; **Le Zapping**
TV clip transcription;
reference tools

Introduction
To check comprehension, ask these questions: **1. Quelle est le matériau utilisé par Caroline Martial pour construire ses meubles? (Le carton.) 2. Pour qui travaille Caroline? (Pour elle-même.) 3. Où se trouvent beaucoup de ses meubles? (Chez elle.)**

Avant de regarder la vidéo
Have students look at the video stills, read the captions, and predict what will happen in the clip for each visual. **(1. On va voir comment on construit des meubles en carton. 2. On peut voir des exemples de meubles. 3. Caroline va expliquer comment et pourquoi elle réalise des meubles en carton.)**

Compréhension Have students work in pairs or groups for this activity. Tell them to write their answers. Then, show the video again so that they can check their answers and add any missing information.

Discussion For the first two questions, have students work in pairs to discuss their answers, then have some pairs present their answers to the class. For the last question, have the pairs role-play the scenario given.

Section Goals

In this section, students will learn and practice vocabulary related to:
• household chores
• home appliances

Instructional Resources
vhlcentral.com:
Digital Image Bank (including vocabulary illustrations from the textbook, theme-based illustrations); **Vocabulaire supplémentaire; Mise en pratique** answers; Textbook Audioscript; Lab Audioscript; Activity Pack (**Feuilles d'activités**); Textbook MP3s; Lab MP3s; SAM Answer Key; reference tools

Suggestions

• Use the **8B Contextes** illustration from the Digital Image Bank.
• Ask students questions about chores using the new vocabulary. Examples: **Préférez-vous balayer ou passer l'aspirateur? Faire la cuisine ou faire la lessive? Mettre la table ou sortir la poubelle?**
• Say vocabulary words and tell students to write or say the opposite terms. Examples: **sale (propre), débarrasser la table (mettre la table),** and **salir les vêtements (faire la lessive).**
• Point out the expressions that use **faire: faire la lessive, faire la poussière, faire le ménage, faire le lit,** and **faire la vaisselle.**
• Tell students that the names of several appliances are compounds of verbs and nouns. Examples: **grille-pain, lave-vaisselle,** and **sèche-linge.** Other appliances use the preposition **à: un fer à repasser, un four à micro-ondes.**
• Use the Vocabulary illustrations and the house and chores illustrations from the Digital Image Bank to help students familiarize themselves with household chores and home appliances.
• Additional vocabulary for this lesson can be found in the **Vocabulaire supplémentaire** on the Supersite.

Leçon 8B

Vocabulary Tools

You will learn how to...
▪ talk about chores
▪ talk about appliances

Les tâches ménagères

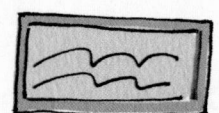

Vocabulaire

débarrasser la table	*to clear the table*
enlever/faire la poussière	*to dust*
essuyer la vaisselle/ la table	*to dry the dishes/ to wipe the table*
faire la lessive	*to do the laundry*
faire le ménage	*to do the housework*
laver	*to wash*
mettre la table	*to set the table*
passer l'aspirateur	*to vacuum*
ranger	*to tidy up; to put away*
salir	*to soil, to make dirty*
propre	*clean*
sale	*dirty*
un appareil électrique/ ménager	*electrical/household appliance*
une cafetière	*coffeemaker*
une cuisinière	*stove; female cook*
un grille-pain	*toaster*
un lave-linge	*washing machine*
un lave-vaisselle	*dishwasher*
un sèche-linge	*clothes dryer*
une tâche ménagère	*household chore*

ressources

WB	LM	S
pp. 109–110	p. 61	vhlcentral

332 · *trois cent trente-deux*

Labels in illustration:
- un évier
- un (four à) micro-ondes
- Elle fait le lit.
- un oreiller
- les draps (m.)
- Il fait la vaisselle.
- un congélateur
- un four
- une couverture
- Elle balaie. (balayer)
- un frigo
- un balai
- le linge

OPTIONS

Game Write vocabulary words for appliances on index cards. On another set of cards, draw or paste pictures to match each term. Tape them face down on the board in random order. Divide the class into two teams. Then play a game of Concentration in which students match words with pictures. When a player has a match, that player's team collects those cards. When all the cards have been matched, the team with the most cards wins.

Extra Practice Ask students what chores they do in various rooms. Examples: **Dans quelle pièce... faites-vous la vaisselle? faites-vous le lit? mettez-vous la table? passez-vous l'aspirateur? repassez-vous? balayez-vous?**

Mise en pratique

1 Écoutez Écoutez la conversation téléphonique (*phone call*) entre Édouard, un étudiant, et un conseiller (*radio psychologist*) à la radio. Ensuite, indiquez les tâches ménagères que faisaient Édouard et Paul au début du semestre.

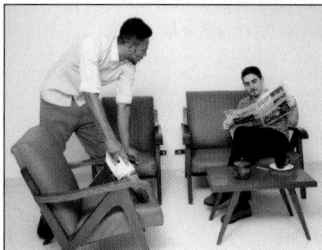

	Édouard	Paul
1. Il faisait la cuisine.	☑	☐
2. Il faisait les lits.	☐	☑
3. Il passait l'aspirateur.	☑	☐
4. Il sortait la poubelle.	☐	☑
5. Il balayait.	☐	☑
6. Il faisait la lessive.	☑	☐
7. Il faisait la vaisselle.	☐	☑
8. Il nettoyait le frigo.	☑	☐

2 On fait le ménage Complétez les phrases avec le bon mot.

1. On balaie avec _____ un balai _____.
2. On repasse le linge avec _____ un fer à repasser _____.
3. On fait la lessive avec _____ un lave-linge _____.
4. On lave la vaisselle avec _____ un lave-vaisselle _____.
5. On prépare le café avec _____ une cafetière _____.
6. On sèche les vêtements avec _____ un sèche-linge _____.
7. On met la glace dans _____ un congélateur _____.
8. Pour faire le lit, on doit arranger _____ les draps _____, _____ la couverture _____ et _____ l'oreiller/les oreillers _____.

3 Les tâches ménagères Avec un(e) partenaire, indiquez quelles tâches ménagères vous faites dans chaque pièce ou partie de votre logement. Il y a plus d'une réponse possible. *Answers will vary.*

1. La chambre: _____
2. La cuisine: _____
3. La salle de bains: _____
4. La salle à manger: _____
5. La salle de séjour: _____
6. Le garage: _____

Il sort la poubelle. (sortir)

un fer à repasser

Il repasse. (repasser)

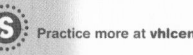
Practice more at vhlcentral.com.

trois cent trente-trois **333**

1 Audioscript J'ai un problème avec Paul, mon colocataire, parce qu'il ne m'aide pas à faire le ménage. Quand le semestre a commencé, il faisait la vaisselle, il sortait la poubelle et il balayait. Parfois, il faisait même mon lit. Paul ne faisait jamais la cuisine parce qu'il détestait ça, c'est moi qui la faisais. Je faisais aussi la lessive, je passais l'aspirateur et je nettoyais le frigo. Maintenant, Paul ne fait jamais son lit et il ne m'aide pas. C'est moi qui fais tout. Qu'est-ce que vous me suggérez de faire?
(On Textbook MP3s)

1 Suggestion After listening to the recording, have students identify Paul and Édouard in the photo and describe what they are doing.

1 Expansion Have students describe how they share household chores with their roommate(s) or others in their household.

2 Expansion Reverse this activity and ask students what each appliance is used for. Example: **Que fait-on avec une cuisinière? (On fait la cuisine.)**

3 Suggestion Have students get together with another pair and compare their answers.

OPTIONS

Extra Practice Have students complete these analogies.
1. passer l'aspirateur : tapis / lave-vaisselle : _____ (verre/tasse)
2. chaud : froid / cuisinière : _____ (congélateur)
3. ordinateur : bureau / armoire : _____ (chambre)
4. tasse : cuisine / voiture : _____ (garage)

5. café : cafetière / pain : _____ (grille-pain)
6. mauvais : bon / sale : _____ (propre)
7. chaud : four à micro-ondes / froid : _____ (frigo/congélateur)
8. arriver : partir / nettoyer : _____ (salir)
9. table : verre / lit : _____ (draps/couverture/oreiller(s))

Communication

4 Suggestion Distribute the **Feuilles d'activités** found in the Activity Pack on the Supersite. Have two volunteers read the **modèle**.

5 Suggestion Have students jot down notes during their interviews. Then ask them to report what they learned about their partners.

5 Expansion Take a quick survey about household chores using items 4 and 6. Tally the results on the board.

6 Suggestion Before beginning this activity, have students brainstorm desirable and undesirable qualities or habits of roommates. Write a list on the board.

7 Suggestion Have students exchange paragraphs for peer editing. Tell them to underline, rather than correct, grammar and spelling errors.

4 **Qui fait quoi?** Votre professeur va vous donner une feuille d'activités. Dites si vous faites les tâches indiquées en écrivant (by writing) **Oui** ou **Non** dans la première colonne. Ensuite, posez des questions à vos camarades de classe; écrivez leur nom dans la deuxième colonne quand ils répondent **Oui**. Présentez vos réponses à la classe. Answers will vary.

MODÈLE

mettre la table pour prendre le petit-déjeuner
Étudiant(e) 1: *Est-ce que tu mets la table pour prendre le petit-déjeuner?*
Étudiant(e) 2: *Oui, je mets la table chaque matin./ Non, je prends le petit-déjeuner au resto U, donc je ne mets pas la table.*

Activités	Moi	Mes camarades de classe
1. mettre la table pour prendre le petit-déjeuner		
2. passer l'aspirateur tous les jours		
3. salir ses vêtements quand on mange		
4. nettoyer les toilettes		
5. balayer la cuisine		
6. débarrasser la table après le dîner		
7. souvent enlever la poussière sur son ordinateur		
8. laver les vitres (windows)		

5 **Conversez** Interviewez un(e) camarade de classe. Answers will vary.
1. Qui fait la vaisselle chez toi?
2. Qui fait la lessive chez toi?
3. Fais-tu ton lit tous les jours?
4. Quelles tâches ménagères as-tu faites le week-end dernier?
5. Repasses-tu tous tes vêtements?
6. Quelles tâches ménagères détestes-tu faire?
7. Quels appareils électriques as-tu chez toi?
8. Ranges-tu souvent ta chambre?

6 **Camarade de chambre** Vous cherchez un(e) camarade de chambre pour votre appartement et deux personnes ont répondu à votre petite annonce (ad) dans le journal. Travaillez avec deux camarades de classe et préparez un dialogue dans lequel (in which) vous: Answers will vary.

- parlez des tâches ménagères que vous détestez/aimez faire.
- parlez des responsabilités de votre nouveau/ nouvelle camarade de chambre.
- parlez de vos passions et de vos habitudes.
- décidez quelle est la personne qui vous convient le mieux (suits you best).

7 **Écrivez** L'appartement de Martine est un désastre: la cuisine est sale et comme vous pouvez (can) l'imaginer, le reste de l'appartement est encore pire (worse). Préparez un paragraphe où vous décrivez les problèmes que vous voyez (see) et que vous imaginez. Ensuite, écrivez la liste des tâches que Martine va faire pour tout nettoyer. Answers will vary.

OPTIONS

Small Groups Have groups of three write riddles about furnishings or appliances. For each riddle, the group comes up with at least three hints. Example: **Je suis très doux. On me met sur le lit. Je vous aide à bien dormir. (Je suis un oreiller.)** Ask them to read their riddles to the class, who will guess the answer.

Extra Practice Have students complete this paragraph. **L'appartement de Roger est un désastre. Il a rarement le temps de faire le ____ (ménage). Il ____ (passe) l'aspirateur une fois par semestre et il ne/n'____ (fait/enlève) pas la poussière. Il y a des tasses et des verres dans l'____ (évier) parce qu'il oublie de les mettre dans le ____ (lave-vaisselle). L'appartement sent mauvais parce qu'il ne sort pas la ____ (poubelle).**

Les sons et les lettres   Audio

Semi-vowels

French has three semi-vowels. Semi-vowels are sounds that are produced in much the same way as vowels, but also have many properties in common with consonants. Semi-vowels are also sometimes referred to as *glides* because they glide from or into the vowel they accompany.

Luc**i**en	ch**i**en	s**oi**f	n**ui**t

The semi-vowel that occurs in the word **bien** is very much like the *y* in the English word *yes*. It is usually spelled with an **i** or a **y** (pronounced *ee*), then glides into the following sound. This semi-vowel sound is also produced when **ll** follows an **i**.

nat**i**on	bala**y**er	b**i**en	bri**ll**ant

The semi-vowel that occurs in the word **soif** is like the *w* in the English words *was* and *we*. It usually begins with **o** or **ou**, then glides into the following vowel.

tr**oi**s	fr**oi**d	**ou**i	**ou**istiti

The third semi-vowel sound occurs in the word **nuit**. It is spelled with the vowel **u**, as in the French word **tu**, then glides into the following sound.

l**u**i	s**u**is	cr**u**el	intellect**u**el

Prononcez Répétez les mots suivants à voix haute.

1. oui
2. taille
3. suisse
4. fille
5. mois
6. cruel
7. minuit
8. jouer
9. cuisine
10. juillet
11. échouer
12. croissant

Articulez Répétez les phrases suivantes à voix haute.

1. Voici trois poissons noirs.
2. Louis et sa famille sont suisses.
3. Parfois, Grégoire fait de la cuisine chinoise.
4. Aujourd'hui, Matthieu et Damien vont travailler.
5. Françoise a besoin de faire ses devoirs d'histoire.
6. La fille de Monsieur Poirot va conduire pour la première fois.

Dictons Répétez les dictons à voix haute.

La nuit, tous les chats sont gris.[1]

Vouloir, c'est pouvoir.[2]

[1] All cats are gray in the dark.
[2] Where there's a will, there's a way.

ressources

LM p. 62 | vhlcentral

trois cent trente-cinq 335

Section Goals
In this section, students will learn about semi-vowels.

Instructional Resources
vhlcentral.com:
Textbook MP3s; Lab MP3s;
SAM Answer Key;
Textbook Audioscript;
Lab Audioscript;
reference tools

Suggestions
- Model the pronunciation of the example words and have students repeat them after you.
- Ask students to provide more examples of words from this lesson or previous lessons with these sounds. Examples: **balayer, essuyer,** and **évier.**
- Dictate five familiar words containing semi-vowels, repeating each one at least two times. Then write them on the board or on a transparency and have students check their spelling.
- Remind students that many vowels combine to make a single sound with no glide. Examples: **ai** and **ou.**
- Explain that **un ouistiti** is a marmoset.

Extra Practice Use these sentences with semi-vowels for additional practice or dictation. **1. Nous balayons bien la cuisine. 2. J'ai soif, mais tu as froid. 3. Une fois, ma fille a oublié son parapluie. 4. Parfois, mon chien aime jouer entre minuit et trois heures du matin.**

Extra Practice Teach students these French tongue-twisters that contain semi-vowels. **1. Trois petites truites non cuites, trois petites truites crues. 2. Une bête noire se baigne dans une baignoire noire.**

ESPACE ROMAN-PHOTO

La vie sans Pascal  Video

NATIONAL communication cultures STANDARDS

Section Goals

In this section, students will learn functional phrases for talking about who and what they know.

Instructional Resources
vhlcentral.com:
Roman-photo *Video, Videoscript, and Translation; SAM Answer Key; reference tools*

Video Recap: Leçon 8A
Review the previous **Roman-photo** with this activity.
1. Qui a fait une visite surprise à Aix-en-Provence? (Pascal)
2. Combien de pièces y a-t-il chez Sandrine? (trois)
3. Comment est l'appartement de Sandrine? (grand et beau)
4. Comment est l'appartement de Rachid et David? (petit, pas de décorations et pas beaucoup de meubles)
5. Que pense Sandrine de la visite surprise de Pascal? (Elle n'est pas contente.)

Video Synopsis
At the café, Amina talks to Sandrine on the phone. Valérie questions Stéphane about his chores and reminds him to do the dishes before he leaves. Amina arrives at Sandrine's. As Sandrine is baking cookies, she breaks a plate. The two girls talk about how annoying Pascal is. Sandrine asks if Amina plans to meet Cyberhomme in person. Amina is not sure that's a good idea.

Suggestions
• Have students predict what the episode will be about based on the title and video stills.
• Have students scan the **Roman-photo** and find sentences related to chores.
• After reading the captions, review students' predictions.

PERSONNAGES

Amina

Michèle

Sandrine

Stéphane

Valérie

Au P'tit Bistrot...
MICHÈLE Tout va bien, Amina?
AMINA Oui, ça va, merci. *(Au téléphone)* Allô?... Qu'est-ce qu'il y a, Sandrine?... Non, je ne le savais pas, mais franchement, ça ne me surprend pas... Écoute, j'arrive chez toi dans quinze minutes, d'accord? ... À tout à l'heure!

MICHÈLE Je débarrasse la table?
AMINA Oui, merci, et apporte-moi l'addition, s'il te plaît.
MICHÈLE Tout de suite.

VALÉRIE Tu as fait ton lit, ce matin?
STÉPHANE Oui, maman.
VALÉRIE Est-ce que tu as rangé ta chambre?
STÉPHANE Euh... oui, ce matin, pendant que tu faisais la lessive.

Chez Sandrine...
SANDRINE Salut, Amina! Merci d'être venue.
AMINA Mmmm. Qu'est-ce qui sent si bon?
SANDRINE Il y a des biscuits au chocolat dans le four.
AMINA Oh, est-ce que tu les préparais quand tu m'as téléphoné?

SANDRINE Tu as soif?
AMINA Un peu, oui.
SANDRINE Sers-toi, j'ai des jus de fruits au frigo.

Sandrine casse () une assiette.
SANDRINE Et zut!
AMINA Ça va, Sandrine?
SANDRINE Oui, oui... passe-moi le balai, s'il te plaît.
AMINA N'oublie pas de balayer sous la cuisinière.
SANDRINE Je sais! Excuse-moi, Amina. Comme je t'ai dit au téléphone, Pascal et moi, c'est fini.

ACTIVITÉS

1 Questions Répondez aux questions par des phrases complètes. Answers may vary slightly.
1. Avec qui Amina parle-t-elle au téléphone? Elle parle avec Sandrine.
2. Comment va Sandrine aujourd'hui? Pourquoi? Elle est de mauvaise humeur parce que c'est fini avec Pascal.
3. Est-ce que Stéphane a fait toutes ses tâches ménagères? Non, il n'a pas fait toutes ses tâches ménagères.
4. Qu'est-ce que Sandrine préparait quand elle a téléphoné à Amina? Elle préparait des biscuits au chocolat.

5. Amina a faim et a soif. À votre avis *(opinion)*, que va-t-elle prendre? Elle va prendre un jus de fruits et elle va manger des biscuits.
6. Pourquoi Amina n'est-elle pas fâchée *(angry)* contre Sandrine? Elle comprend pourquoi Sandrine est un peu triste/de mauvaise humeur.
7. Pourquoi Amina pense-t-elle que Sandrine aimerait *(would like)* un cyberhomme américain? Amina pense que Sandrine aime David.
8. Sandrine pense qu'Amina devrait *(should)* rencontrer Cyberhomme, mais Amina pense que ce n'est pas une bonne idée. À votre avis, qui a raison? Answers will vary.

OPTIONS

Avant de regarder la vidéo Before playing the video, show students individual photos from the **Roman-photo**, #5 or #8 for example, and have them write their own captions. Ask volunteers to write their captions on the board.

Regarder la vidéo Download and print the videoscript found on the Supersite, then white out words related to household chores and other key vocabulary in order to create a master for a cloze activity. Distribute photocopies and tell students to fill in the missing information as they watch the video episode.

Amina console Sandrine.

VALÉRIE Hmm... et la vaisselle? Tu as fait la vaisselle?

STÉPHANE Non, pas encore, mais...

MICHÈLE Il me faut l'addition pour Amina.

VALÉRIE Stéphane, tu dois faire la vaisselle avant de sortir.

STÉPHANE Bon, ça va, j'y vais!

VALÉRIE Ah, Michèle, il faut sortir les poubelles pour ce soir!

MICHÈLE Oui, comptez sur moi, Madame Forestier.

VALÉRIE Très bien! Moi, je rentre, il est l'heure de préparer le dîner.

SANDRINE Il était tellement pénible. Bref, je suis de mauvaise humeur aujourd'hui.

AMINA Ne t'en fais pas, je comprends.

SANDRINE Toi, tu as de la chance.

AMINA Pourquoi tu dis ça?

SANDRINE Tu as ton Cyberhomme. Tu vas le rencontrer un de ces jours?

AMINA Oh... Je ne sais pas si c'est une bonne idée.

SANDRINE Pourquoi pas?

AMINA Sandrine, il faut être prudent dans la vie, je ne le connais pas vraiment, tu sais.

SANDRINE Comme d'habitude, tu as raison. Mais finalement, un cyberhomme, c'est peut-être mieux qu'un petit ami. Ou alors, un petit ami artistique, charmant et beau garçon.

AMINA Et américain?

Expressions utiles

Talking about what you know

- **Je ne le savais pas, mais franchement, ça ne me surprend pas.**
  I didn't know that, but frankly, I'm not surprised.
- **Je sais!**
  I know!
- **Je ne sais pas si c'est une bonne idée.**
  I don't know if that's a good idea.
- **Je ne le connais pas vraiment, tu sais.**
  I don't really know him, you know.

Additional vocabulary

- **Comptez sur moi.**
  Count on me.
- **Ne t'en fais pas.**
  Don't worry about it.
- **J'y vais!**
  I'm going there!/I'm on my way!
- **pas encore**
  not yet
- **tu dois**
  you must
- **être de bonne/mauvaise humeur**
  to be in a good/bad mood

Expressions utiles

- Model the pronunciation of the **Expressions utiles** and have students repeat them.
- As you work through the list, point out the forms of **savoir** and **connaître**. See if students can discern the difference in meaning between the two verbs from the example sentences. Respond briefly to their questions, but tell them that these verbs will be formally presented in **Espace structures 8B.2**.

1 Suggestion Have volunteers write their answers on the board. Go over them as a class.

2 Expansion Ask students who works the hardest of all these people. Have them support their opinion with details from this episode and previous ones.

3 Suggestion Have students use commands in their lists for review.

2 **Le ménage** Indiquez qui a fait ou va faire ces tâches ménagères: Amina (**A**), Michèle (**M**), Sandrine (**S**), Stéphane (**St**), Valérie (**V**) ou personne (*no one*) (**P**).

1. sortir la poubelle **M**
2. balayer **S & A**
3. passer l'aspirateur **P**
4. faire la vaisselle **St**
5. faire le lit **St**
6. débarrasser la table **M**
7. faire la lessive **V**
8. ranger sa chambre **St**

Practice more at **vhlcentral.com**.

3 **Écrivez** Vous avez gagné un pari (*bet*) avec votre colocataire et il/elle doit faire (*must do*) en conséquence toutes les tâches ménagères que vous lui indiquez pendant un mois. Écrivez une liste de dix tâches minimum. Pour chaque tâche, précisez la pièce du logement et combien de fois par semaine il/elle doit l'exécuter.

ressources

VM
pp. 31–32

vhlcentral

A C T I V I T É S

O P T I O N S

Extra Practice Divide the class into two groups based on their answers to question 8 on page 336 (whether or not Amina should meet Cyberhomme) and have a debate about who is right. Tell groups to brainstorm a list of arguments to support their point of view and anticipate rebuttals for what the other team might say.

Pairs Have students work in pairs. Tell them to reread the last lines of the **Roman-photo** and write a short paragraph predicting what will happen in future episodes. Do they think Amina will meet Cyberhomme in person? What do they think will happen in Sandrine's love life? Have volunteers read their paragraphs to the class aloud.

 Reading

Section Goals

In this section, students will:
- learn about the interior of French homes
- learn some colloquial terms for describing a home or room
- learn the names of some famous homes in the francophone world
- read about the French Quarter in New Orleans

Instructional Resources
vhlcentral.com:
reference tools

Culture à la loupe
Avant la lecture
- Have students look at the photos and describe what they see.
- Tell students to read the first sentence of the text. Then ask: **Quel est le sujet du texte?**

Lecture
- Point out the **Coup de main** and have two volunteers read the examples. Demonstrative pronouns will be presented in **Leçon 14A**.
- Point out the statistics chart. Ask students what information the chart shows. (the percentage of French residences that have the appliances listed)

Après la lecture Ask students: **Quelles sont les différences entre l'intérieur des logements français et l'intérieur des logements américains?**

1 **Suggestion** Go over the answers with the class.

CULTURE À LA LOUPE

L'intérieur des logements

L'intérieur des maisons et des appartements français est assez° différent de celui des Américains. Quand on entre dans un vieil immeuble en France, on est dans un hall° où il y a des boîtes aux lettres°. Ensuite, il y a souvent une deuxième porte. Celle-ci conduit à° l'escalier. Il n'y a pas souvent d'ascenseur, mais s'il y en a un°, en général, il est très petit et il est au milieu de° l'escalier. Le hall de l'immeuble peut aussi avoir une porte qui donne sur une cour° ou un jardin, souvent derrière le bâtiment°.

À l'intérieur des logements, les pièces sont en général plus petites que° les pièces américaines, surtout les cuisines et les salles de bains. Dans la cuisine, on trouve tous les appareils ménagers nécessaires (cuisinière, four, four à micro-ondes, frigo), mais ils sont plus petits qu'aux États-Unis. Les lave-vaisselle sont assez rares dans les appartements et plus communs dans les maisons. On a souvent une seule° salle de bains et les toilettes sont en général dans une autre petite pièce séparée°. Les lave-linge sont aussi assez petits et on les trouve dans la cuisine ou dans la salle de bains. Dans les chambres en France il n'y a pas de grands placards et les vêtements sont rangés la plupart° du temps dans une armoire. Les fenêtres s'ouvrent° sur l'intérieur, un peu comme des portes.

Combien de logements ont ces appareils ménagers?

Réfrigérateur	99,8%
Cuisinière/Four	96,4%
Lave-linge	95,6%
Congélateur	91,2%
Four à micro-ondes	88,3%
Lave-vaisselle	57,1%
Sèche-linge	28,7%

assez *rather* **hall** *entryway* **boîtes aux lettres** *mailboxes* **conduit à** *leads to* **s'il y en a un** *if there is one* **au milieu de** *in the middle of* **cour** *courtyard* **bâtiment** *building* **plus petites que** *smaller than* **une seule** *only one* **séparée** *separate* **la plupart** *most* **s'ouvrent** *open*

Coup de main

Demonstrative pronouns help to avoid repetition.

	S.	P.
M.	celui	ceux
F.	celle	celles

Ce lit est grand, mais le lit de Monique est petit.

Ce lit est grand, mais **celui** de Monique est petit.

A C T I V I T É S

1

Complétez Complétez chaque phrase logiquement.
Answers will vary. Possible answers provided.

1. Dans le hall d'un immeuble français, on trouve... *des boîtes aux lettres et des portes.*
2. Au milieu de l'escalier, dans les vieux immeubles français,... *il y a parfois un ascenseur.*
3. Derrière les vieux immeubles, on trouve souvent... *une cour ou un jardin.*
4. Les cuisines et les salles de bains françaises sont... *assez petites.*
5. Dans les appartements français, il est assez rare d'avoir... *un lave-vaisselle.*
6. Les logements français ont souvent une seule... *salle de bains.*
7. En France, les toilettes sont souvent... *dans une pièce séparée.*
8. Les Français rangent souvent leurs vêtements dans une armoire parce qu'ils... *n'ont pas de placards.*
9. On trouve souvent le lave-linge... *dans la cuisine ou dans la salle de bains.*

Cultural Comparison Take a quick class survey to find out how many students have the appliances listed in the chart in their homes. Tally the results on the board and have students calculate the percentages. Example: **Combien de personnes ont un réfrigérateur à la maison?**

Then have students compare the results of this survey with those in the chart. Examples: **Plus d'Américains ont un sèche-linge dans leur maison./Moins de Français ont un sèche-linge dans leur maison.**

LE FRANÇAIS QUOTIDIEN

Quelles conditions!

boxon (*m.*)	*mess, chaos*
gourbis (*m.*)	*pigsty*
piaule (*f.*)	*pad, room*
souk (*m.*)	*mess*
impeccable	*spic-and-span*
ringard	*cheesy, old-fashioned*
crécher	*to live*
semer la pagaille	*to make a mess*

LE MONDE FRANCOPHONE

Architecture moderne et ancienne

Architecte suisse

Le Corbusier Originaire du canton de Neuchâtel, il est l'un des principaux représentants du mouvement moderne au début° du 20e siècle. Il est connu° pour être l'inventeur de l'unité d'habitation°, concept sur les logements collectifs qui rassemblent dans un même lieu garderie° d'enfants, piscine, écoles, commerces et lieux de rencontre. Il est naturalisé français en 1930.

Architecture du Maroc

Les riads, mot° qui à l'origine signifie «jardins» en arabe, sont de superbes habitations anciennes° construites pour préserver la fraîcheur°. On les trouve au cœur° des ruelles° de la médina (quartier historique).
Les kasbah, bâtisses° de terre° dans le Sud marocain, ce sont des exemples d'un art typiquement berbère et rural.

début *beginning* **connu** *known* **unité d'habitation** *housing unit* **garderie** *nursery school* **mot** *word* **anciennes** *old* **fraîcheur** *coolness* **cœur** *heart* **ruelles** *alleyways* **bâtisses** *dwellings* **terre** *earth*

PORTRAIT

Le Vieux Carré

Le Vieux Carré, aussi appelé le Quartier Français, est le centre historique de La Nouvelle-Orléans. Il a conservé le souvenir° des époques° coloniales du 18e siècle°. La culture française est toujours présente avec des noms de rues° français comme *Toulouse* ou *Chartres*, qui sont de grandes villes françaises. Cependant° le style architectural n'est pas français; il est espagnol. Les maisons avec les beaux balcons sont l'héritage de l'occupation espagnole de la deuxième moitié° du 18e siècle.
Mardi gras, en février, est la fête la plus populaire de La Nouvelle-Orléans, qui est aussi très connue° pour son festival de jazz, en avril.

souvenir *memory* époques *times* siècle *century* noms de rues *street names* Cependant *However* moitié *half* connue *known*

MUSIQUE À FOND

Charles Aznavour

Lieu d'origine: Paris, France
Métier: chanteur et compositeur

Un des plus célèbres compositeurs français du XXe siècle, avec une carrière de plus de 70 ans et plus de 800 chansons écrites.

Go to vhlcentral.com to find out more about **Charles Aznavour** and his music.

---

2 Complétez Complétez les phrases.

1. Le Vieux Carré est aussi appelé le Quartier Français.
2. *Toulouse* et *Chartres* sont deux noms de rues français à La Nouvelle-Orléans.
3. Le style architectural du Vieux Carré n'est pas français mais espagnol.
4. La Nouvelle-Orléans est connue pour son festival de jazz.
5. Le Corbusier est l'inventeur de l'unité d'habitation.
6. On trouve les riads parmi (*among*) les ruelles de la médina.

3 C'est le désordre! Vos parents viennent vous rendre visite ce soir et c'est le désordre dans tout l'appartement. Avec un(e) partenaire, inventez une conversation où vous lui donnez cinq ordres pour nettoyer avant l'arrivée de vos parents. Jouez la scène devant la classe.

ressources

 Practice more at vhlcentral.com.

A C T I V I T É S

Le français quotidien
• Model the pronunciation of each term and have students repeat it.
• Have volunteers create sentences using these words.

Portrait Ask students: **Que désirez-vous faire ou visiter dans le Vieux Carré de la Nouvelle-Orléans?**

Le monde francophone
• Bring in photos from magazines, books, or the Internet to show examples of architecture by Le Corbusier, and of a **riad** or **kasbah** in Morocco.

2 Expansion For additional practice, give students these items. **7.** ____ est la fête la plus populaire de La Nouvelle-Orléans. (Mardi Gras) **8.** Le Corbusier est originaire de ____. (Neuchâtel)

3 Suggestion Encourage students to use terms in **Le français quotidien** in their role-plays.

3 Expansion Have some pairs pretend they live in a French apartment and others in an American apartment. They should base their conversations on what they learned in the **Culture à la loupe** article.

OPTIONS

Le Vieux Carré **Le Cabildo** was completed in 1799. The ceremonies finalizing the Louisiana Purchase were held there in 1803. Since 1903, it has been the Louisiana State Museum. The museum contains a number of objects from Napoleonic history. The present-day **cathédrale Saint-Louis** was completed in 1851. Made of bricks, the cathedral is dedicated to King Louis IX of France (1214–1270), who was canonized in 1297. His life is depicted in ten of the stained glass windows. This building is actually the third cathedral to occupy this site. The first cathedral was completed in 1727, but it burned down in 1788. The second was completed in 1794, but collapsed in 1849.

8B.1

ESPACE **STRUCTURES**

The *passé composé* vs. the *imparfait* (Part 2)

Tutorial

Section Goals

In this section, students will learn:

• the use of the **passé composé** vs. the **imparfait** in narration, to describe interrupted actions, and to express cause and effect

• common expressions indicating the past tense

• the verb **vivre**

Instructional Resources
vhlcentral.com:
Activity Pack; Lab MP3s;
SAM Answer Key;
Digital Image Bank; Essayez!
and Mise en pratique
answers; Lab Audioscript;
reference tools

Suggestions

• Tell students that the choice between the **passé composé** and the **imparfait** is very important since two tenses are used to convey different meanings. Have them explain the difference between these two sentences: **J'ai téléphoné quand ma mère est arrivée. Je téléphonais quand ma mère est arrivée.** (In the first case, I called after my mother arrived. In the second case, I was in the process of calling when my mother arrived.) Have students come up with other examples of sentences where the message changes based on which past tense form is used.

• Point out to students that if both actions in a sentence are ongoing or completed simultaneously, then both verbs can be in either the **passé composé** or the **imparfait.** Example: **Je suis sorti quand tu es entré. Je sortais quand tu entrais.** They will need to pay close attention to the meaning they want to convey.

Point de départ You have already seen some uses of the **passé composé** versus the **imparfait** for talking about things and events in the past. Here are some other contexts in which the choice of tense is important.

• The **passé composé** and the **imparfait** are often used together to narrate a story or describe an incident. The **imparfait** provides the background description, such as time, weather, and location. The **passé composé** highlights specific events foregrounded in the story.

Uses of the *passé composé* and the *imparfait*

Le passé composé	L' imparfait
is used to talk about:	*is used to describe:*
• main facts	• the framework of the story: *weather, date, time, background scenery*
• specific, completed events	• descriptions of people: *age, physical and personality traits, clothing, feelings, state of mind*
• actions that advance the plot	• background setting: *what was going on, what others were doing*

Il **était** minuit et le temps **était** orageux. J'**avais** peur parce que j'**étais** seule dans la maison. Soudain, quelqu'un a **frappé** à la porte. J'**ai regardé** par la fenêtre et j'**ai vu** un vieil homme habillé en noir...
It was midnight and the weather was stormy. I was afraid because I was home alone. Suddenly, someone knocked at the door. I looked through the window and I saw an old man dressed in black...

• When the **passé composé** and the **imparfait** occur in the same sentence, the action in the **passé composé** often interrupts the ongoing action in the **imparfait.**

J'ai rangé ma chambre pendant que tu faisais la lessive.

Tu les préparais quand tu m'as téléphoné?

ACTION IN PROGRESS   INTERRUPTING ACTION

Je **travaillais**   quand mon petit ami **est arrivé**.
I was working   *when my boyfriend arrived.*

Céline et Maxime **dormaient**   quand le téléphone **a sonné**.
Céline and Maxime were sleeping   *when the phone rang.*

340   *trois cent quarante*

O P T I O N S

Pairs Ask students to narrate an embarrassing moment. Tell them to describe what happened and how they felt, using the **passé composé** and **imparfait.** Then have volunteers retell their partner's embarrassing moment using the third person. You may want to let students make up a fake embarrassing moment.

Small Groups Have students work in groups of four to write a short article about an imaginary road trip they took last summer. Students should use the **imparfait** to set the scene and the **passé composé** to narrate events. Each student should contribute three sentences to the article. When finished, have students read their articles to the class.

- Use **pendant que** to indicate that one action was completed while another was still happening.

  Mes parents **sont arrivés** pendant que nous **répétions** dans le sous-sol.
  My parents arrived while we were rehearsing in the basement.

- Sometimes the use of the **passé composé** and the **imparfait** in the same sentence expresses a cause and effect.

  J'**avais** faim, alors j'**ai mangé** un sandwich.   Elle **est partie**, parce-qu'elle **était** fatiguée.
  I was hungry, so I ate a sandwich.   *She left because she was tired.*

- Certain adverbs often indicate a particular past tense.

Expressions that signal a past tense

passé composé		imparfait	
soudain	*suddenly*	d'habitude	*usually*
tout d'un coup/ tout à coup	*all of a sudden*	parfois	*sometimes*
une (deux, etc.) fois	*once (twice, etc.)*	souvent	*often*
un jour	*one day*	toujours	*always*
		tous les jours	*every day*

- While talking about the past or narrating a story, you might use the verb **vivre** (*to live*), which is irregular.

Vivre

je vis	nous vivons
tu vis	vous vivez
il/elle/on vit	ils/elles vivent

Les enfants **vivent** avec leurs grands-parents.   Je **vis** à Paris.
The children live with their grandparents.   *I live in Paris.*

- The past participle of **vivre** is **vécu**. The **imparfait** is formed like that of other **-re** verbs, by dropping **-ons** from the **nous** form, and adding the imperfect endings.

  Rémi a toujours **vécu** à Nice.   Nous **vivions** avec mon oncle.
  Rémi always lived in Nice.   *We used to live with my uncle.*

 **Essayez!**   Choisissez la forme correcte du verbe au passé.

1. Lise (a étudié /*étudiait*) toujours avec ses amis.
2. Maman (a fait /faisait) du yoga hier.
3. Ma grand-mère (passait /a passé) par là tous les jours.
4. D'habitude, ils (arrivaient /sont arrivés) toujours en retard.
5. Tout à coup, le professeur (entrait /est entré) dans la classe.
6. Ce matin, Camille (a lavé /lavait) le chien.

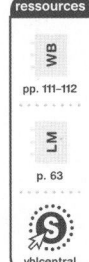

ressources

WB
pp. 111–112

LM
p. 63

vhlcentral

Suggestions
- Give personalized examples as you contrast the **passé composé** and the **imparfait**. Examples: **La semaine dernière quand je répétais dans le salon, quelqu'un m'a téléphoné. Je n'ai pas entendu le téléphone parce que je jouais du piano.**
- Give students these other expressions that signal the **imparfait**: **de temps en temps** (*from time to time*), **en général** (*in general, usually*), **quelquefois** (*sometimes*), **autrefois** (*in the past*).
- Write the following sentences on the board: **1. Je vais au cinéma avec un ami. 2. Nous prenons le bus. 3. Après le film, nous mangeons au restaurant. 4. Ensuite, nous allons danser dans une boîte de nuit. 5. Nous rentrons tard à la maison.** Have students change the sentences above first to the **passé composé** and then to the **imparfait**. Have them add adverbs or expressions they've learned that signal a past tense wherever possible.

Essayez! Give the following items as additional practice: **7. Autrefois, Nathan (a amené / amenait) sa sœur au cours de danse. (amenait) 8. Je/J' (ai parlé / parlais) deux fois à ma cousine la semaine dernière. (ai parlé) 9. Parfois, nous (faisions / avons fait) une randonnée en montagne. (faisions) 10. Elle (voyait / a vu) mes parents une fois à la mairie. (a vu)**

O P T I O N S

Extra Practice Have students recall a memorable day from their childhood. Ask them to describe this day, giving as many details as possible: the weather, who was there, what happened, how they felt etc. Alternatively, you could do this as a written activity and have students create a journal entry about their memorable day.

Pairs Distribute illustrations or photos from magazines of everyday activities and vacation activities. Have students arrange the pictures in pairs and create sentences to say that one activity was going on when the other one interrupted it. Call on pairs of students to hold up their pictures and present their sentences to the rest of the class.

ESPACE STRUCTURES

Mise en pratique

1

Pourquoi? Expliquez pourquoi Sabine a fait ou n'a pas fait ces choses.

> **MODÈLE** ne pas faire de tennis / être fatigué
> *Sabine n'a pas fait de tennis parce qu'elle était fatiguée.*

1. aller au centre commercial / aimer faire les soldes   *Sabine est allée au centre commercial parce qu'elle aimait faire les soldes.*
2. ne pas travailler / avoir sommeil   *Sabine n'a pas travaillé parce qu'elle avait sommeil.*
3. ne pas sortir / pleuvoir   *Sabine n'est pas sortie parce qu'il pleuvait.*
4. mettre un pull / faire froid   *Sabine a mis un pull parce qu'il faisait froid.*
5. manger une pizza / avoir faim   *Sabine a mangé une pizza parce qu'elle avait faim.*
6. acheter une nouvelle robe / sortir avec des amis   *Sabine a acheté une nouvelle robe parce qu'elle sortait avec des amis.*
7. vendre son fauteuil / déménager   *Sabine a vendu son fauteuil parce qu'elle déménageait.*
8. ne pas bien dormir / être inquiet   *Sabine n'a pas bien dormi parce qu'elle était inquiète.*

2

Qu'est-ce qu'ils faisaient quand...? Que faisaient ces personnes au moment de l'interruption?   Suggested answers

> **MODÈLE**
>
> *Papa débarrassait la table quand mon frère est arrivé.*

débarrasser / arriver

1. sortir / dire
Ils sortaient la poubelle quand le voisin a dit bonjour.

2. passer / tomber
Michel passait l'aspirateur quand l'enfant est tombé.

3. faire / partir
Sa mère faisait la lessive quand Anne est partie.

4. laver / commencer
Ils lavaient la voiture quand il a commencé à pleuvoir.

3

Rien d'extraordinaire Matthieu a passé une journée assez banale. Réécrivez ce paragraphe au passé.

Il est 6h30. Il pleut. Je prends mon petit-déjeuner, je mets mon imperméable et je quitte la maison. J'attends une demi-heure à l'arrêt de bus et finalement, je cours au restaurant où je travaille. J'arrive en retard. Le patron (*boss*) n'est pas content. Le soir, après mon travail, je rentre à la maison et je vais directement au lit.

Il était 6h30. Il pleuvait. J'ai pris mon petit-déjeuner, j'ai mis mon imperméable et j'ai quitté la maison. J'ai attendu une demi-heure à l'arrêt de bus et finalement, j'ai couru au restaurant où je travaillais. Je suis arrivé en retard. Le patron n'était pas content. Le soir, après mon travail, je suis rentré à la maison et je suis directement allé au lit.

 Practice more at **vhlcentral.com**.

---

1 Expansion Have students redo this activity, this time coming up with their own explanations for why Sabine did or did not do the activities.

2 Suggestion Have students come up with different sentences using the same illustrations.

2 Expansion Have students come up with a short story for each illustration.

3 Suggestion Have students compare their answers with a partner's. For sentences where their answers differ, they should explain why they chose the **passé composé** or the **imparfait** and decide which tense is appropriate.

3 Expansion Have volunteers explain why they chose the **passé composé** or **imparfait** in each sentence. Ask them to point out any words or expressions that triggered one tense or the other.

OPTIONS

Extra Practice Divide the class into teams. Make a list of all the adverbs or expressions that signal a past tense. As you read out each expression, a member from each team should come to the board and write a sentence in the past using that expression. The team that completes a correct sentence first gets a point.

Small Groups Have students work in small groups to discuss their favorite movie or book. Students should use appropriate past tense forms to describe the main characters and give a brief summary of the plot. Encourage students to ask their classmates questions about the film or text.

Communication

4 **La curiosité** Votre tante Louise veut tout savoir. Elle vous pose beaucoup de questions. Avec un(e) partenaire, répondez aux questions d'une manière logique et échangez les rôles. *Answers will vary.*

> **MODÈLE** retourner au bureau
>
> **Étudiant(e) 1:** *Pourquoi est-ce que tu es retourné(e) au bureau?*
> **Étudiant(e) 2:** *Je suis retourné(e) au bureau parce que j'avais beaucoup de travail.*

1. aller en boîte de nuit
2. aller au magasin
3. sortir avec des amis
4. téléphoner à ton cousin
5. rentrer tard
6. aller au café
7. inviter des gens
8. être triste

5 **Une entrevue** Avec un(e) partenaire, posez-vous ces questions à tour de rôle. *Answers will vary.*

1. Où allais-tu souvent quand tu étais petit(e)?
2. Qu'est-ce que tu aimais lire?
3. Est-ce que tu as vécu dans un autre pays?
4. Comment étais-tu quand tu avais dix ans?
5. Qu'est-ce que ton/ta camarade de chambre faisait quand tu es rentré(e) hier?
6. Qu'est-ce que tu as fait hier soir?
7. Qu'est-ce que tu as pris au petit-déjeuner ce matin?
8. Qu'est-ce que tu as porté aujourd'hui?

6 **Je me souviens!** Racontez à votre partenaire un événement spécial de votre vie qui s'est déjà passé. Votre partenaire vous pose des questions pour avoir plus de détails sur cet événement. Vous pouvez (*can*) parler d'un anniversaire, d'une fête familiale, d'un mariage ou d'un concert. *Answers will vary.*

> **MODÈLE**
>
> **Étudiant(e) 1:** *Nous avons fait une grande fête d'anniversaire pour ma grand-mère l'année dernière.*
> **Étudiant(e) 2:** *Quel âge a-t-elle eu?*

7 **Scénario** Par groupes de trois, créez une histoire au passé. La première personne commence par une phrase. La deuxième personne doit (*must*) continuer l'histoire. La troisième personne reprend la suite d'une manière logique. Continuez l'histoire une personne à la fois jusqu'à ce que vous ayez (*until you have*) un petit scénario. Soyez créatif! Ensuite, présentez votre scénario à la classe. *Answers will vary.*

---

4 Expansion Have students redo the activity, reframing the questions in the negative and asking why their partner did not do those activities. Example: **Pourquoi est-ce que tu n'es pas allé(e) en boîte de nuit?**

5 Suggestion Ask students some warm-up questions as a model, before they begin the activity in pairs. Examples: **Comment étaient tes profs au collège? Qu'est-ce que tu as fait le week-end dernier?**

5 Expansion Have students do questions 1, 2, 3, 6, 7, and 8 as a survey by circulating around the classroom and interviewing at least five classmates. Have them tabulate the responses of each classmate in a chart and see how similar or different the responses were.

6 Suggestions
• Act out the **modèle** with a volunteer before assigning this activity to pairs.
• Encourage students to use key adverbs to indicate the appropriate verb tenses in the dialogue. Examples: **soudain, tout à coup, autrefois,** etc.

6 Suggestion This activity can be done either orally or in writing.

O P T I O N S

Extra Practice Divide the class into groups of five. Have each group imagine that they own a household cleaning service and create a radio or TV commercial for it. Have students create a logo (if it is a TV commercial) and a slogan for their business and maybe a jingle to go with their commercial. As a part of their commercial, they should use testimonials from customers who used their service. The customers should talk in detail about everything the cleaning service did and their opinion of their work.

Pairs Have students work with a partner to write an e-mail to a friend telling about the horrible weekend they had because they had to do a lot of chores and complaining about their siblings who did not do their share of the work.

Section Goals

In this section, students will learn the uses of **savoir** and **connaître**.

Instructional Resources
vhlcentral.com:
Lab MP3s; SAM Answer Key;
Essayez! and ***Mise en pratique***
answers; Lab Audioscript;
*Activity Pack (**Feuilles***
***d'activités**); reference tools*

Suggestions

- Model **savoir** by asking several questions with it. Examples: ____, **savez-vous faire du ski? Et vous, ____, savez-vous où est la bibliothèque?** Next, write **connaître** on the board and ask questions, such as: ____, **connaissez-vous mon frère? Connaissez-vous la Nouvelle-Orléans?** Ask students further questions using both verbs to help them infer the difference in use between the two.
- Point out that the context of the phrase will indicate which verb to use. Using examples in English, have students say which verb would be used for the French translation. Examples: I know how to swim. (**savoir**) He doesn't know the president. (**connaître**)

🏃 Boîte à outils

The verb **connaître** is never followed by an infinitive. Always use the construction **savoir** + [*infinitive*] to mean *to know how to do something.*

The verbs *savoir* and *connaître* 🅢 Tutorial

Point de départ **Savoir** and **connaître** both mean *to know*. The choice of verb in French depends on the context in which it is being used.

N'oublie pas de balayer sous la cuisinière.

Je sais!

Je ne le connais pas vraiment, tu sais.

Savoir	
je	sais
tu	sais
il/elle/on	sait
nous	savons
vous	savez
ils/elles	savent

- **Savoir** means *to know a fact* or *to know how to do something.*

  Je **sais** tout sur lui.
  I know everything about him.

  Elle **sait** jouer du piano
  She knows how to play piano.

  Ils ne **savent** pas qu'il est parti.
  They don't know that he left.

  Savez-vous faire la cuisine?
  Do you know how to cook?

- The verb **savoir** is often followed by **que, qui, où, quand, comment,** or **pourquoi.**

  Nous **savons que** tu arrives mardi.
  We know that you're arriving on Tuesday.

  Je **sais où** je vais.
  I know where I am going.

  Ils **savent comment** aller à la gare.
  They know how to get to the train station.

  Tu **sais qui** a fait la lessive?
  Do you know who did the laundry?

- The past participle of **savoir** is **su.** When used in the **passé composé**, **savoir** means *found out.*

  J'**ai su** qu'il y avait une fête.
  I found out there was a party.

  Je **savais** qu'il y avait une fête.
  I knew there was a party.

Connaître

je	connais
tu	connais
il/elle/on	connaît
nous	connaissons
vous	connaissez
ils/elles	connaissent

- **Connaître** means *to know* or *be familiar with a person, place, or thing.*

Côte-Nord

Avec les sofas par **Côte-Nord**, vous connaissez le confort et la joie d'être chez vous.

Vous **connaissez** le prof.
You know the professor.

Nous **connaissons** bien Paris.
We know Paris well.

Tu **connais** ce quartier?
Do you know that neighborhood?

Je ne **connais** pas ce magasin.
I don't know this store.

- The past participle of **connaître** is **connu**. **Connaître** in the **passé composé** means *met* (*for the first time*).

Nous **avons connu** son père.
We met his father.

Nous **connaissions** son père.
We knew his father.

- **Reconnaître** means *to recognize*. It follows the same conjugation patterns as **connaître**.

Mes profs de lycée me
reconnaissent encore.
*My high school teachers still
recognize me.*

Nous **avons reconnu** vos enfants
à la soirée.
*We recognized your children
at the party.*

Essayez! Complétez les phrases avec les formes correctes des verbes **savoir** et **connaître**.

1. Je ___*connais*___ de bons restaurants.
2. Ils ne ___savent___ pas parler allemand.
3. Vous ___savez___ faire du cheval?
4. Tu ___connais___ une bonne coiffeuse?
5. Nous ne ___connaissons___ pas Jacques.
6. Claudette ___sait___ jouer aux échecs.
7. Laure et Béatrice ___connaissent___ -elles tes cousins?
8. Nous ___savons___ que vous n'aimez pas faire le ménage.

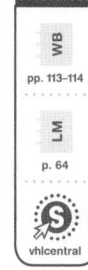

ressources

WB
pp. 113–114

LM
p. 64

S
vhlcentral

Suggestions
- Review the changes in meaning when **savoir** and **connaître** are used in the **imparfait** and **passé composé**.
- Prepare dehydrated sentences such as these: **tu / savoir / que tu / ne pas connaître / mon petit ami; nous / connaître / les nouveaux étudiants.** Write them on the board one at a time and have students complete them.
- Point out that **connaître** can also be used with feelings or emotions, as in the advertisement on this page.

Essayez! Have students change the sentences to the past tense. Examples: **1. Je connaissais de bons restaurants. 2. Ils ne savaient pas parler allemand.**

O P T I O N S

Video Replay the video episode, having students focus on forms of **savoir** and **connaître**, as well as the use of the **imparfait** and the **passé composé**. Tell them to note when each one is used. Afterward, ask the class to describe the conversations that took place and what tenses were used. Have them identify the reason for this verb choice (a series of past actions, ongoing actions in the past, etc.).

Extra Practice Ask individual students questions using **savoir** and **connaître** that are most likely not true for them. When students give a negative answer, they should indicate someone else who would answer in the affirmative. Example: ____, **connaissez-vous le président des États-Unis? (Non, je ne le connais pas, mais le Premier ministre du Canada le connaît.)**

ESPACE **STRUCTURES**

Leçon 8B

1 Expansion Ask individual students questions about what they know how to do. Example: **Savez-vous parler espagnol? (Non, je ne sais pas parler espagnol.)**

2 Suggestios
- Students might be inclined to use **savoir** for item 5. Explain that in French, one knows a phone number in the sense of being familiar with it, rather than in the sense of knowing a fact, as in English.
- Explain that **raï** (item 6) is a musical genre popular among young people that blends Algerian and Western influences.

2 Expansion Have students work in pairs to write three more sentences similar to those in the activity. Call on volunteers to present their sentences to the class.

3 Expansion Ask students questions about what certain celebrities know how to do or whom they know. Examples: **Est-ce que Brad Pitt connaît Angelina Jolie? (Oui, il la connaît.) Est-ce que Jennifer Lopez sait parler espagnol? (Oui, elle sait le parler.)**

Mise en pratique

1 **Les passe-temps** Qu'est-ce que ces personnes savent faire?

▶ **MODÈLE**
Patrick sait skier.

Patrick

1. Halima
Halima sait patiner.

2. vous
Vous savez nager.

3. tu
Tu sais jouer au tennis.

4. nous
Nous savons jouer au foot.

2 **Dialogues brefs** Complétez les conversations avec le présent du verbe **savoir** ou **connaître**.

1. Marie ____sait____ faire la cuisine?
   Oui, mais elle ne ____connaît____ pas beaucoup de recettes (*recipes*).
2. Vous ____connaissez____ les parents de François?
   Non, je ____connais____ seulement sa cousine.
3. Tes enfants ____savent____ nager dans la mer.
   Et mon fils aîné ____connaît____ toutes les espèces de poissons.
4. Je ____sais____ que le train arrive à trois heures.
   Est-ce que tu ____sais____ à quelle heure il part?
5. Vous ____connaissez____ le numéro de téléphone de Dorian?
   Oui, je le ____connais____.
6. Nous ____connaissons____ bien la musique arabe.
   Ah, bon? Tu ____sais____ qu'il y a un concert de raï en ville demain?

3 **Assemblez** Assemblez les éléments des colonnes pour construire des phrases. Answers will vary.

MODÈLE *Je sais parler une langue étrangère.*

A	B	C
Gérard Depardieu	(ne pas) connaître	des célébrités faire la cuisine
Oprah Winfrey	(ne pas) savoir	jouer dans un film
je		Julia Roberts
ton/ta camarade de chambre		parler une langue étrangère

 Practice more at **vhlcentral.com**.

Communication

4 **Enquête** Votre professeur va vous donner une feuille d'activités. Circulez dans la classe pour trouver au moins une personne différente qui répond oui à chaque question. Answers will vary.

Sujet	Nom
1. Sais-tu faire une mousse au chocolat?	Jacqueline
2. Connais-tu New York?	
3. Connais-tu le nom des sénateurs de cet état (state)?	
4. Connais-tu quelqu'un qui habite en Californie?	

5 **Je sais faire** Votre célébrité préférée cherche un(e) assistant(e) mais il y a deux candidats pour le poste. Par groupes de trois, jouez la scène. Chaque (Each) candidat essaie de montrer toutes les choses qu'il/elle sait faire. Answers will vary.

MODÈLE

Étudiant(e) 1: Alors, vous savez faire la vaisselle?
Étudiant(e) 2: Je sais faire la vaisselle, et je sais faire la cuisine aussi.
Étudiant(e) 3: Moi, je sais faire la cuisine, mais il/elle ne sait pas passer l'aspirateur.

6 **Questions** À tour de rôle, posez ces questions à un(e) partenaire. Ensuite, présentez vos réponses à la classe. Answers will vary.

1. Quel bon restaurant connais-tu près d'ici? Est-ce que tu y (there) manges souvent?
2. Dans ta famille, qui sait chanter le mieux (best)?
3. Connais-tu l'Europe? Quelles villes connais-tu?
4. Reconnais-tu toutes les chansons (songs) que tu entends à la radio?
5. Tes parents savent-ils utiliser Internet? Le font-ils bien?
6. Connais-tu un(e) acteur/actrice célèbre? Une autre personne célèbre?
7. Ton/Ta meilleur(e) (best) ami(e) sait-il/elle écouter quand tu lui racontes (tell) tes problèmes?
8. Connais-tu la date d'anniversaire de tous les membres de ta famille et de tous tes amis? Donne des exemples.
9. Connais-tu des films français? Lesquels (Which ones)? Les aimes-tu? Pourquoi?
10. Sais-tu parler une langue étrangère? Laquelle? (Which one)?

---

4 Suggestions
• Distribute the **Feuilles d'activités** found in the Activity Pack on the Supersite.
• Have students read through the list of questions using **savoir** and **connaître** for comprehension before completing the activity.

5 Suggestion Ask for three volunteers to act out the **modèle** for the class.

6 Expansion Ask these questions of the whole class. Ask students who answer in the affirmative for additional information. Examples: **Qui sait chanter? Chantez-vous bien? Chantiez-vous avec un groupe quand vous étiez plus jeune?**

OPTIONS

Extra Practice Have students write down three things they know how to do well (using **savoir bien** + [infinitive]). Collect the papers, and then read the sentences. Tell students that they must not identify themselves when they hear their sentence. The rest of the class takes turns trying to guess who wrote each sentence. Repeat this activity with **connaître**.

Pairs Ask students to write brief, but creative, paragraphs in which they use **savoir** and **connaître**. Then have them exchange their papers with a partner. Tell students to help each other, through peer editing, to make the paragraphs as error-free as possible. Collect the papers for grading.

Révision

Instructional Resources
vhlcentral.com:
Activity Pack (Feuilles d'activités; Info Gap Activities); Testing Program; Testing Program MP3s; reference tools

1 Expansion Tell students to imagine they are hosting their own dinner party. Have them make a list of tasks that must be completed before the guests arrive. Have them use the **passé composé**.

2 Suggestions
• Have two students read the **modèle** out loud before distributing the **Feuilles d'activités** found in the Activity Pack on the Supersite.
• Before doing the activity, have students practice creating sentences using **connaître** in the **passé composé** and in the **imparfait**. Example: **J'ai connu la petite amie de Jacques en 2005. Je connaissais son ancienne petite amie.**

3 Suggestion Review the **imparfait** with the verb phrases listed in this activity. Ask volunteers to supply the correct verb forms for the subjects you suggest. Example: **repasser le linge: je (je repassais le linge).**

4 Suggestion Have students bring photos from magazines or newspapers to supplement this activity. Or, students may prefer to sketch drawings of events.

5 Expansion Ask students to imagine that they are writing an e-mail home to their family expressing what they have learned and whom they have met since arriving at college. Instruct them to use sentence constructions similar to those presented in this activity.

6 Suggestion Divide the class into pairs and distribute the Info Gap Handouts found in the Activity Pack on the Supersite. Give students ten minutes to complete the activity.

---

1 Un grand dîner Émilie et son mari Vincent ont invité des amis à dîner ce soir. Qu'ont-ils fait cet après-midi pour préparer la soirée? Que vont-ils faire ce soir après le départ des invités? Conversez avec un(e) partenaire. Answers will vary.

MODÈLE

Étudiant(e) 1: *Cet après-midi, Émilie et Vincent ont mis la table.*

Étudiant(e) 2: *Ce soir, ils vont faire la vaisselle.*

2 Mes connaissances Votre professeur va vous donner une feuille d'activités. Interviewez vos camarades. Pour chaque activité, trouvez un(e) camarade différent(e) qui réponde affirmativement. Answers will vary.

Étudiant(e) 1: *Connais-tu une personne qui aime faire le ménage?*

Étudiant(e) 2: *Oui, autrefois, mon père aimait bien faire le ménage.*

Activités	Noms
1. ne pas souvent faire la vaisselle	
2. aimer faire le ménage	Farid
3. dormir avec une couverture en été	
4. faire son lit tous les jours	
5. rarement repasser ses vêtements	

3 Qui faisait le ménage? Par groupes de trois, interviewez vos camarades. Qui faisait le ménage à la maison quand ils habitaient encore chez leurs parents? Préparez des questions avec ces expressions et comparez vos réponses. Answers will vary.

balayer	mettre et débarrasser la table
faire la lessive	passer l'aspirateur
faire le lit	ranger
faire la vaisselle	repasser le linge

4 Soudain! Tout était calme quand soudain... Avec un(e) partenaire, choisissez l'une des deux photos et écrivez un texte de dix phrases. Faites cinq phrases pour décrire la photo, et cinq autres pour raconter (*to tell*) un événement qui s'est passé soudainement (*that suddenly happened*). Employez des adverbes et soyez imaginatifs. Answers will vary.

5 J'ai appris... Qu'avez-vous appris ou qui connaissez-vous depuis que (*since*) vous êtes à la fac? Avec un(e) partenaire, faites une liste de cinq choses et de cinq personnes. À chaque fois, utilisez un imparfait et un passé composé dans vos explications. Answers will vary.

MODÈLE

Étudiant(e) 1: *Avant, je ne savais pas comment dire bonjour en français, et puis j'ai commencé ce cours, et maintenant, je sais le dire.*

Étudiant(e) 2: *Avant, je ne connaissais pas tous les pays francophones, et maintenant, je les connais.*

6 Élise fait sa lessive Votre professeur va vous donner, à vous et à votre partenaire, une feuille avec des dessins représentant (*representing*) Élise et sa journée d'hier. Attention! Ne regardez pas la feuille de votre partenaire. Answers will vary.

MODÈLE

Étudiant(e) 1: *Hier matin, Élise avait besoin de faire sa lessive.*

Étudiant(e) 2: *Mais, elle...*

OPTIONS

Extra Practice Divide the class into three groups. One group is **savoir** (present tense with infinitive, **imparfait**), the second group is **connaître** (present tense, **imparfait**), and the third group is **savoir** and **connaître** (passé composé). Have each group brainstorm a list of phrases using their assigned verbs and tenses. A volunteer from each group should present their results to the class.

Example: Group 1 – **Je sais chanter. (présent) Ma mère savait parler français. (imparfait)** Group 2 – **Nous connaissons les nouveaux étudiants. (présent) Il connaissait le président des États-Unis. (imparfait)** Group 3 – **J'ai su que l'examen de français était très difficile. (passé composé) Mon père a connu mon petit ami. (passé composé)**

À l'écoute

Audio:
Activities

Section Goals

In this section, students will:
- use visual cues to understand an oral description
- listen to a conversation and complete several activities

Instructional Resources
vhlcentral.com:
Textbook MP3s; Textbook Audioscript; reference tools

STRATÉGIE

Using visual cues

Visual cues like illustrations and headings provide useful clues about what you will hear.

 To practice this strategy, you will listen to a passage related to the image. Jot down the clues the image gives you as you listen. Answers will vary.

À LOUER

Appartement en ville, moderne, avec balcon
1.200 €
(Réf. 520)

5 pièces, jardin, proche parc Victor Hugo
950 €
(Réf. 521)

Maison meublée en banlieue, grande, tt confort, cuisine équipée
1.200 €
(Réf. 522)

Préparation

Qu'est-ce qu'il y a sur les trois photos à droite? À votre avis, quel va être le sujet de la conversation entre M. Duchemin et Mme Lopez?

À vous d'écouter

Écoutez la conversation. M. Duchemin va proposer trois logements à Mme Lopez. Regardez les annonces et écrivez le numéro de référence de chaque possibilité qu'il propose.

1. Possibilité 1: _Réf. 521_
2. Possibilité 2: _Réf. 522_
3. Possibilité 3: _Réf. 520_

Compréhension

Les détails Après une deuxième écoute, complétez le tableau (*chart*) avec les informations données dans la conversation.

	Où?	Maison ou appartement?	Meublé ou non?	Nombre de chambres?	Garage?	Jardin?
Logement 1	ville	maison	non	trois	non	oui
Logement 2	banlieue	maison	oui	quatre	oui	oui
Logement 3	centre-ville	appartement	non	deux	oui	non

Quel logement pour les Lopez? Lisez cette description de la famille Lopez. Décidez quel logement cette famille va probablement choisir et expliquez votre réponse.

M. Lopez travaille au centre-ville. Le soir, il rentre tard à la maison et il est souvent fatigué parce qu'il travaille beaucoup. Il n'a pas envie de passer son temps à travailler dans le jardin. Mme Lopez adore le cinéma et le théâtre. Elle n'aime pas beaucoup faire le ménage. Les Lopez ont une fille qui a seize ans. Elle adore retrouver ses copines pour faire du shopping en ville. Les Lopez ont beaucoup de beaux meubles modernes. Ils ont aussi une nouvelle voiture: une grosse BMW qui a coûté très cher!

trois cent quarante-neuf **349**

Stratégie
Audioscript Nous avons trouvé un appartement super dans le quartier du Marais. Il est au premier étage, dans un immeuble très calme. Il y a une salle de séjour assez grande, une cuisine avec frigo, cuisinière et lave-linge, une petite salle de bains et deux chambres très jolies. Il y a aussi des placards dans toutes les pièces et un garage en sous-sol pour notre voiture. On peut emménager la semaine prochaine et le loyer n'est pas très cher. Nous sommes vraiment heureux, tu sais!

À vous d'écouter
Audioscript AGENT: Allô, bonjour. Madame Lopez, s'il vous plaît.
CLIENTE: C'est elle-même.
A: Ah, bonjour, Madame. Ici Monsieur Duchemin de l'agence immobilière. Vous cherchez un logement à louer à Avignon ou dans la banlieue, c'est bien ça?
C: Oui, Monsieur, c'est exact. Vous avez une maison à me proposer?
A: Oui, j'ai trois possibilités. La première est une maison en ville, dans un quartier calme près du parc Victor Hugo. Elle n'est pas très grande, mais elle est très jolie et elle a un petit jardin. Il y a un salon, une salle à manger, une grande cuisine avec beaucoup de placards, une salle de bains, les W.-C. et trois chambres.
C: Il y a un garage?
A: Non, Madame, mais il y a toujours des places dans le quartier.
C: Bon. Et qu'est-ce que vous avez d'autre?
A: J'ai aussi une très grande maison meublée avec jardin et garage en banlieue, à une demi-heure de la ville.
C: C'est un peu loin, mais bon...
Il y a combien de chambres?
A: Quatre chambres.
C: Et qu'est-ce qu'il y a comme meubles?
A: Un canapé, des fauteuils et des étagères dans le salon, un grand lit

et une commode dans la grande chambre... et voyons, quoi d'autre? Ah, oui! La cuisine est équipée avec tout le nécessaire: frigo, congélateur, cuisinière, four à micro-ondes, lave-linge et sèche-linge.
C: Très bien. Et la troisième possibilité?
A: C'est un grand appartement dans le centre-ville, sur la place des Halles. Il n'y a pas de jardin.
C: Et combien de chambres y a-t-il?

A: Deux chambres avec des balcons. Si vous aimez le moderne, cet appartement est parfait pour vous. Et il a un garage.
C: Bon, je vais en parler avec mon mari.
A: Très bien, Madame. Au revoir.
C: Au revoir, Monsieur Duchemin.

Section Goals

In this section, students will learn historical and cultural information about the city of Paris.

Instructional Resources
vhlcentral.com:
Digital Image Bank;
SAM Answer Key;
reference tools

Plan de Paris

- Have students look at the map of Paris in their books, or display the **Panorama** map from the Digital Image Bank. Point out that **Paris** and its surrounding areas (**la banlieue**) are called **l'Île-de-France**. This area is also known as **la Région parisienne**. Ask students to locate places mentioned in the **Panorama** on the map. Examples: **le musée du Louvre, le musée d'Orsay, l'Arc de Triomphe,** and **la tour Eiffel.**
- Point out that the Seine River (**la Seine**) divides Paris into two parts: the left bank (**la rive gauche**) to the south and the right bank (**la rive droite**) to the north.

La ville en chiffres

- Point out the city's coat of arms.
- Call on volunteers to read the sections. After each section, ask questions about content.
- Point out that the population figure for Paris does not include the suburbs.
- Tell students that there is a Rodin Museum in Paris and one in Philadelphia. If possible, show students a photo of one of Rodin's most famous sculptures: *The Thinker (le Penseur).*

Incroyable mais vrai! The miles of tunnels and catacombs under Paris used to be quarries; the city was built with much of the stone dug from them. Some of these quarries date back to Roman times. The skeletons in the catacombs are Parisians who were moved from overcrowded cemeteries in the late 1700s.

Interactive Map

SAVOIR-FAIRE

Panorama

connections
cultures

l'Arc de Triomphe

Paris

La ville en chiffres

▶ **Superficie:** *105 km²*

▶ **Population:** *2.229.621*
SOURCE: INSEE

Paris est la capitale de la France. On a l'impression que Paris est une grande ville—et c'est vrai si on compte° ses environs°. Mais Paris mesure moins de° 10 kilomètres de l'est à l'ouest°. On peut très facilement visiter la ville à pied°. Paris est divisée en 20 arrondissements°. Chaque° arrondissement a son propre maire° et son propre caractère.

▶ **Industries principales:** *haute couture, finances, transports, technologie, tourisme*

▶ **Musées°:** *plus de 150: le musée du Louvre, le musée d'Orsay, le centre Georges Pompidou et le musée Rodin*

Parisiens célèbres

▶ **Victor Hugo,** écrivain° *et activiste (1802–1885)*

▶ **Charles Baudelaire,** poète *(1821–1867)*

▶ **Auguste Rodin,** sculpteur *(1840–1917)*

▶ **Jean-Paul Sartre,** philosophe *(1905–1980)*

▶ **Simone de Beauvoir,** écrivaine *(1908–1986)*

▶ **Édith Piaf,** chanteuse *(1915–1963)*

▶   **Emmanuelle Béart,** *actrice (1965–)*

si on compte *if one counts* **environs** *surrounding areas* **moins de** *less than* **de l'est à l'ouest** *from east to west* **à pied** *on foot* **arrondissements** *districts* **Chaque** *Each* **son propre maire** *its own mayor* **plus de** *more than* **écrivain** *writer* **rues** *streets* **reposent** *lie; rest* **provenant** *from* **repos** *rest*

350 *trois cent cinquante*

(map of Paris showing:) Paris LA FRANCE, Basilique du Sacré-Cœur, Place du Tertre, Le Moulin Rouge, Parc Monceau, BOULEVARD HAUSSMANN, Opéra Garnier, BLVD. DES ITALIENS, Arc de Triomphe, AVENUE DES CHAMPS-ÉLYSÉES, La Madeleine, BLVD. DES CAPUCINES, AV. DE L'OPÉRA, BOULEVARD DE SÉBASTOPOL, Bois de Boulogne, Grand Palais, Place de la Concorde, Jeu de Paume, RUE DE RIVOLI, Les Halles, Jardins du Trocadéro, Orangerie, Jardin des Tuileries, Musée du Louvre, Beaubourg/Centre Georges Pompidou-Centre National d'Art et de Culture, Seine, QUAI D'ORSAY, Assemblée Nationale, Musée d'Orsay, RUE DE RIVOLI, Tour Eiffel, BLVD. ST. GERMAIN, Conciergerie, Hôtel de Ville, Place des Vosges, Parc du Champ de Mars, Hôtel des Invalides, Île de la Cité, Opéra de Paris Bastille, École Militaire, BOULEVARD RASPAIL, Cathédrale Notre-Dame, Île St.-Louis, BOULEVARD ST. GERMAIN, Jardin du Luxembourg, BOULEVARD SAINT-MICHEL, Sorbonne, Panthéon, Tour Montparnasse, Seine

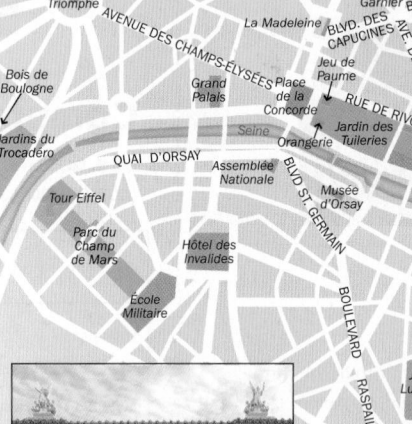

l'opéra Garnier

0   0.5 mile
0   0.5 kilomètre

une terrasse de café

Incroyable mais vrai!

Sous les rues° de Paris, il y a une autre ville: les catacombes. Ici reposent° les squelettes d'environ 7.000.000 de personnes provenant° d'anciens cimetières de Paris et de ses environs. Plus de 100.000 touristes par an visitent cette ville de repos° éternel.

OPTIONS

Oral Presentation If a student has visited Paris, ask him or her to prepare a short presentation about his or her experiences there. Encourage the student to bring in photos and souvenirs. If no students have been to Paris, then invite a French graduate student who has been there to speak to the class. Tell the presenter to include what his or her favorite place or activity is in Paris and to explain why.

Parisiens célèbres **Jean-Paul Sartre** and **Simone de Beauvoir** had a personal and professional relationship. Sartre became famous as the leader of a group of intellectuals who used to gather regularly at the **Café de Flore.** This group included **Simone de Beauvoir** and **Albert Camus.** Ask students to name some works they may have read or heard of by **Sartre, de Beauvoir,** or **Camus.**

350   Instructor's Annotated Edition • Unit 8

Les monuments

La tour Eiffel

La tour Eiffel a été construite en 1889 pour l'Exposition universelle, à l'occasion du centenaire° de la Révolution française. Elle mesure 324 mètres de haut et pèse° 10.100 tonnes. La tour attire° près de 7.000.000 de visiteurs par an. On a la possibilité de prendre l'ascenseur jusqu'au° troisième étage et les escaliers jusqu'au deuxième étage.

Les gens

Paris-Plages

Pour les Parisiens qui ne voyagent pas pendant l'été, la ville de Paris a créé° Paris-Plages pour apporter la plage aux Parisiens! Inauguré en 2001 pour la première fois sur les berges° de la Seine, puis prolongé sur le bassin de la Villette en 2007, Paris-Plages consiste en plusieurs kilomètres de sable et de pelouse°, plein° d'activités comme la natation° et le volley. Ouvert en° juillet et en août, près de 4.000.000 de personnes visitent Paris-Plages chaque année.

Les musées

Le musée du Louvre

Ancien° palais royal, le musée du Louvre est aujourd'hui un des plus grands musées du monde avec sa vaste collection de peintures°, de sculptures et d'antiquités orientales, égyptiennes, grecques et romaines. L'œuvre° la plus célèbre de la collection est *La Joconde*° de Léonard de Vinci. La pyramide de verre°, créée par l'architecte américain I.M. Pei, marque l'entrée° principale du musée.

Les transports

Le métro

L'architecte Hector Guimard a commencé à réaliser° des entrées du métro de Paris en 1898. Ces entrées sont construites dans le style Art Nouveau: en forme de plantes et de fleurs. Le métro est aujourd'hui un système très efficace° qui permet aux passagers de traverser° Paris rapidement.

Qu'est-ce que vous avez appris? Complétez les phrases.

1. La ville de Paris est divisée en vingt __arrondissements__.
2. Chaque arrondissement a ses propres __maire__ et __caractère__.
3. Charles Baudelaire est le nom d'un __poète__ français.
4. Édith Piaf est une __chanteuse__ française.
5. Plus de 500.000 personnes par an visitent __les catacombes__ sous les rues de Paris.
6. La tour Eiffel mesure __324__ mètres de haut.
7. En 2001, la ville de Paris a créé __Paris-Plages__ au bord (*banks*) de la Seine.
8. Le musée du Louvre est un ancien __palais__.
9. __La pyramide de verre__ est une création de I.M. Pei.
10. Certaines entrées du métro sont de style __Art Nouveau__.

Sur Internet

Go to **vhlcentral.com** to find more cultural information related to this **Panorama**.

1. Quels sont les monuments les plus importants à Paris? Qu'est-ce qu'on peut faire (*can one do*) dans la ville?

2. Trouvez des informations sur un des musées de Paris.

3. Recherchez (*Research*) la vie d'un(e) Parisien(ne) célèbre.

4. Cherchez un plan du métro de Paris et trouvez comment aller du Louvre à la tour Eiffel.

ressources

WB pp. 115–116

vhlcentral

centenaire *100-year anniversary* **pèse** *weighs* **attire** *attracts* **jusqu'au** *up to* **a créé** *created* **berges** *banks* **de sable et de pelouse** *of sand and grass* **plein** *full* **natation** *swimming* **Ouvert en** *Open in* **Ancien** *Former* **peintures** *paintings* **L'œuvre** *The work (of art)* **La Joconde** *The Mona Lisa* **verre** *glass* **entrée** *entrance* **réaliser** *create* **efficace** *efficient* **traverser** *to cross*

La tour Eiffel Constructed of wrought iron, the architectural design of the Eiffel Tower was an engineering masterpiece for its time. Critics of Gustave Eiffel's design said it couldn't be built, but he proved them wrong. Later, some of the engineering techniques employed would be used to build the first steel skyscrapers. The Eiffel Tower remained the world's tallest building until 1930.

Paris-Plages Paris-Plages, with its numerous organized sports activities, dances, and concerts, is one of the most popular events in Paris during the summer months. All activities, beaches, and playgrounds are open and free to the public; however, the cost to the city of Paris can reach up to 4 million euros each year. Ask students if they think that **Paris-Plages** is worth the money.

Le musée du Louvre Bring in photos or slides of the **Louvre** and some of the most famous artwork in its collection, such as the *Mona Lisa*, the *Venus de Milo*, Vermeer's *The Lacemaker*, and Delacroix's *Liberty Leading the People* (*La Liberté guidant le peuple*). Ask students to describe the woman in the *Mona Lisa*. Point out that only a fraction of the 300,000 works owned by the museum are on display.

Le métro The Paris public transportation system, **le métro** (short for **le Métropolitain**), has 14 lines. It is the most convenient and popular means of transportation in the city since every building in Paris is within 500 meters of a **métro** station. Ask students which cities in the United States have metro or subway systems.

OPTIONS

Cultural Activity Assign each student a famous site in Paris. Examples: **l'Île de la Cité, la Sainte-Chapelle, le quartier latin,** etc. Tell students to research the site and write a brief description. Encourage them to include photos from the Internet or magazines. Ask a few volunteers to share their descriptions with the class.

Pairs Have students work in pairs. Tell them that they have three days in Paris, and they have to make a list of places they want to see or visit each day so that they can make the most of their time there. Remind students that many famous sights, other than those mentioned in the text, appear on the map. Example: **Jour 1: visiter le musée du Louvre.** Ask volunteers to share their lists with the class.

Section Goals

In this section, students will learn historical and cultural information about Île-de-France

Instructional Resources
vhlcentral.com:
*Digital Image Bank;
SAM Answer Key;
reference tools*

Carte de l'Île-de-France

- Have students look at the map of **l'Île-de-France** in their book or use the **Panorama** map from the Digital Image Bank. Have volunteers read the names of cities and geographical features aloud. Model pronunciation as necessary.
- Ask students to look at the images and have volunteers read the captions aloud.
- Ask students if they recognize any of the town names and to share any prior knowledge they have about the locations.

La région en chiffres

- Point out that **Francilien(ne)s** refers to inhabitants of **Île-de-France**.
- Ask a volunteer to read the **Les impressionnistes** section aloud, then ask students what they know about impressionism and the artists involved in the movement.
- Show students Monet's painting *Le Pont d'Argenteuil* (1874) and have them compare it to the photo of the bridge on this page.

Incroyable mais vrai!

Dubuffet financed and built the **closerie** himself, and was in his seventies at the time. His style is known as **art brut**, and his collection includes sculptures, drawings, paintings, architectural constructions, and collages.

Ⓢ Interactive Map

Panorama

L'Île-de-France

La région en chiffres

▶ **Superficie:** *12.012 km²*

▶ **Population:** *12.027.565*
SOURCE: INSEE

▶ **Industries principales:** *aéronautique, automobile, énergie nucléaire, santé°, services*

▶ **Villes principales:** *Paris, Meaux, Provins, Saint-Denis, Fontainebleau, Montreuil, Nanterre, Versailles, Argenteuil*

Franciliens célèbres

▶ **Jean Cocteau,** *poète, dramaturge° et cinéaste° (1889–1963)*

▶ **Dominique Voynet,** *femme politique° (1958–)*

▶ **Thierry Henry,** *footballeur (1977–)*

▶ **Jaques Prévert,** *poète, scénariste et artiste (1900–1977)*

▶ **Omar Sy,** *acteur (1978–)*

▶ **Vanessa Paradis,** *chanteuse et actrice (1972–)*

▶ **Les impressionnistes** *Plusieurs peintres impressionnistes du 19ᵉ siècle se sont inspirés des grands espaces° de l'Île-de-France. Quand Claude Monet a habité à Argenteuil pendant sept ans, il a réalisé° près de 250 peintures, comme «La Liseuse» (1872) et «Le pont d'Argenteuil» (1874). Auvers-sur-Oise aussi a été le sujet de plusieurs œuvres° impressionnistes, y compris° soixante-dix par Vincent Van Gogh. Aujourd'hui, on peut suivre° les quatre chemins de randonnée pédestre° aux Yveliénes qui sont dédiés aux impressionnistes pour voir° les sites où les artistes ont planté leur chevalet°.*

santé *health* **dramaturge** *playwright* **femme politique** *politician* **grands espaces** *natural spaces* **réalisé** *created* **œuvres** *works of art* **y compris** *including* **suivre** *follow* **chemins de randonnée pédestre** *walking paths* **voir** *see* **chevalet** *easel* **closerie** *enclosed property* **comprend** *includes* **abrite** *houses* **pont** *bridge*

352 *trois cent cinquante-deux*

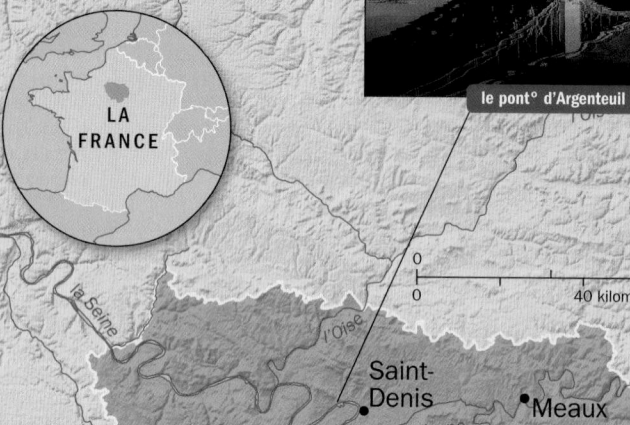
le pont° d'Argenteuil

LA FRANCE

0 — 40 miles
0 — 40 kilomètres

la Seine
l'Oise
la Marne

Saint-Denis • **Meaux**
Nanterre la Marne **Marne-la-Vallée**
Versailles • **Paris**
ÎLE-DE-FRANCE
la Seine
Provins
Melun
Fontainebleau
Nemours
la Loire
la Seine

le jardin de Versailles

un tombeau royal de la basilique Saint-Denis

Incroyable mais vrai!

La closerie° Falbala a été construite entre 1971 et 1973 par l'artiste Jean Dubuffet, qui voulait créer un «espace mental» pour son énorme œuvre d'art, *Cabinet logologique*. Située sur l'île Saint-Germain, la closerie comprend° une sorte de jardin avec, au centre, la villa Falbala qui abrite° sa création. C'est l'un des monuments historiques les plus jeunes de France.

OPTIONS

Franciliens célèbres Jean Cocteau is known for his innovative contributions to French film and literature, most notably for his novel *Les Enfants Terribles* (1929). His work influenced many **avant-garde** artists of his time. **Dominique Voynet** was the mayor of Montreuil (2008–2014) and then served as **sénatrice** of **la Seine-Saint-Denis**. She strongly supports ecological causes for the protection of the environment.

Thierry Henry is a retired international soccer player. He is the only French soccer player to have played four times in the World Cup tournament. **Jaques Prévert** was France's most popular poet of the 20th century. He also worked on classic French films of the 1930s and 1940s. **Omar Sy** is best known for his role in *Les Intouchables*, one of the highest grossing French films ever.

L'histoire

Provins

La ville de Provins a joué un rôle commercial très important en Europe au Moyen Âge. C'est ici que neuf chemins° commerciaux se croisaient. Donc, Provins est devenu la ville avec les plus grandes foires° de Champagne. Ces foires attiraient les marchands les plus important de l'Europe. Ces rassemblements, qui avaient lieu périodiquement et duraient° plusieurs semaines, permettaient les échanges internationaux. Aujourd'hui, la ville, classée au Patrimoine mondial par l'UNESCO, est toujours entourée° par des remparts° du Moyen Âge et la tradition des foires se perpétue avec des spectacles sur la thématique médiévale.

Les gens

André Le Nôtre

Né le 12 mars 1613, André Le Nôtre passe sa jeunesse à travailler avec son père, jardinier aux Tuileries. Ensuite, il suit des cours d'architecture. Il devient jardinier du roi Louis XIV en 1637. Il amasse° une fortune énorme et gagne° une réputation internationale. Considéré «architecte paysagiste°», Le Nôtre est connu pour ses «jardins de la française.» Ses œuvres les plus connus sont les jardins de Versailles, des Tuileries, et de Vaux-le-Vicomte. Ses créations précises et méticuleuses sont souvent caractérisées par des plantes en formes géométriques, ainsi que des éléments formelles et théâtrales.

Les sports

En forêt de Fontainebleau

Chaque année, des millions de visiteurs vont en forêt de Fontainebleau attirés par les plus de 1.600 kilomètres de routes et de chemins de randonnée forestiers, par le site naturel d'escalade° et par les parcours acrobatiques en hauteur, ou PAH. Souvent appelée accrobranche, l'activité consiste à explorer la forêt en hauteur sur des structures fixées entre les arbres ou entre des supports artificiels. L'escalade naturelle est une autre activité populaire. Les rochers° de faible hauteur permettent aux grimpeurs° de pratiquer un type d'escalade sans corde, appelé «le bloc». Réserve de bioshpère, la forêt de Fontainebleau offre un paysage varié et des vues exceptionnelles à ceux qui y pratiquent une activité physique.

Les destinations

Disneyland Paris

Ouvert° en 1992 sous le nom *Euro Disney Resort*, le parc d'attractions aujourd'hui appelé Disneyland Paris se trouve° à trente-deux kilomètres à l'est de° Paris. Le complexe compte° deux parcs à thèmes (un royaume° enchanté et un parc sur les thèmes du cinéma et de l'animation) et une soixantaine d'attractions. Le symbôle le plus connu du complexe, le Château de la Belle au bois dormant°, possède une particularité remarquable: son architecture est dans le style des contes de fée°, tandis que° les châteaux des autres parcs Disney représentent un style historique. Disneyland Paris est le parc d'attractions le plus visité de l'Europe, avec plus de 320 millions de visites depuis son ouverture°.

Provins The city is also known for its famous **roses de Provins**, which have been cultivated there for centuries. During the Middle Ages the roses were said to have medicinal benefits. Today they are cultivated in **roseraies** and are used in both cuisine and cosmetics.

André Le Nôtre Le Nôtre's gardens require meticulous upkeep to maintain their manicured perfection. The gardens at Versailles cover almost 2,000 acres and have undergone five major replantations.

En forêt de Fontainebleau It wasn't until the early 2000s that adventure parks featuring ropes courses became popular recreation destinations in France. There are now about 500 locations in France dedicated to the activity, including an indoor facility in downtown Lyon.

Disneyland Paris In the 1990s, Disney considered hundreds of locations for its new park, including London and Barcelona, before choosing Paris, in part because of its flat terrain and moderate climate. Disneyland Paris celebrated its twenty-fifth anniversary in 2017 by renovating and adding several attractions and shows, including a new HyperSpace Mountain ride with a *Star Wars* theme and a Disney Stars on Parade show.

Qu'est-ce que vous avez appris? Complétez les phrases.

1. __Jean Dubuffet__ était le créateur de la closerie Falbala.
2. L'artiste a construit la villa Falbala parce qu'il voulait créer un __espace mental__ pour son œuvre.
3. __Euro Disney Resort__ était le nom original de Disneyland Paris.
4. À Disneyland Paris, l'architecture du château est dans le style des __contes de fée__.
5. Au Moyen Âge, neuf chemins principaux ont croisé à __Provins__.

6. Les plus grandes __foires de Champagne__ ont eu lieu à Provins.
7. Le jardinier principal du roi Louis XIV s'appelait __André Le Nôtre__.
8. Les plantes dans les jardins de Le Nôtre sont souvent en formes __géométriques__.
9. L'acronyme PAH signifie __parcours acrobatique en hauteur__.
10. Le site d'escalade de la forêt de Fontainebleau est connu pour ses __rochers de faible hauteur__.

ressources

WB pp. 117–118

vhlcentral

Sur Internet

Go to **vhlcentral.com** to find more cultural information related to this **Panorama**.

1. Trouvez quelques images des jardins de Le Nôtre. Comment sont-ils similaires? Quel jardin est le plus visité?

2. Quelles autres particularités trouve-t-on à Disneyland Paris?

3. Trouvez un parc dans l'île-de-France où vous pouvez faire de l'accrobranche. Quels autres activités sont offertes?

chemins *routes* **foires** *fairs* **duraient** *lasted* **entourée** *surrounded* **remparts** *walls* **jardinier** *gardener* **suivi** *took* **illustre** *famed* **gagné** *earned* **architecte paysagiste** *landscape architect* **d'escalade** *rock climbing* **rochers** *boulders* **grimpeurs** *climbers* **Ouvert** *Opened* **se trouve** *is located* **à l'est de** *east of* **compte** *includes* **royaume** *kingdom* **Belle au bois dormant** *Sleeping Beauty* **contes de fée** *fairytales* **tandis que** *while* **ouverture** *opening*

OPTIONS

Cultural Comparison Have students work in pairs to find out about another Disney theme park, such as the one in California or the one in Florida, and compare it with the one in Paris. They should visit the websites and compare prices, maps, cuisine, and lodging. Have them make a chart or diagram showing the results of their research and share it with the class. If any students have been to a Disney theme park, ask them to describe the experience to the class.

Cultural Activity Have students prepare a one-minute presentation on Fontainebleau, Versailles, or Provins, in which they try to persuade their classmates to visit the location. They should include information not mentioned in the textbook, such as popular restaurants, monuments, and activities to do there. After they give their presentations, have the class vote on which location they will visit.

Section Goals

In this section, students will:
- learn to guess meaning from context
- read an article about **le château de Versailles**

Stratégie Tell students that they can often infer the meaning of an unfamiliar word by looking at the word's context and by using their common sense. Five types of context clues are:
- synonyms
- antonyms
- clarifications
- definitions
- additional details

Have students read this sentence from the letter: **Je cherchais un studio, mais j'ai trouvé un appartement plus grand: un deux-pièces près de la fac!** Point out that the meaning of **un deux-pièces** can be inferred since they already know the words **deux** and **une pièce.** The explanation that follows in the note also helps to clarify the meaning.

Examinez le texte
- Write this sentence on the board: **La pièce la plus célèbre du château de Versailles est la galerie des Glaces.** Point out the phrase **la plus célèbre** and ask a volunteer to explain how the context might give clues to its meaning.
- Go over the answers to the activity with the class.

Expérience personnelle
Before beginning the activity, have students brainstorm the names of famous or historic homes they can talk about.

SAVOIR-FAIRE

Lecture

 **Audio: Reading**

Avant la lecture

STRATÉGIE

Guessing meaning from context

As you read in French, you will often see words you have not learned. You can guess what they mean by looking at surrounding words. Read this note and guess what **un deux-pièces** means.

> Johanne,
>
> Je cherchais un studio, mais j'ai trouvé un appartement plus grand: un deux-pièces près de la fac! Le salon est grand et la chambre a deux placards. La cuisine a un frigo et une cuisinière, et la salle de bains a une baignoire. Et le loyer? Seulement 450 euros par mois!

If you guessed *a two-room apartment*, you are correct. You can conclude that someone is describing an apartment he or she will rent.

Examinez le texte

Regardez le texte et décrivez les photos. Quel va être le sujet de la lecture? Puis, trouvez ces mots et expressions dans le texte. Essayez de deviner leur sens (*to guess their meaning*).

ont été rajoutées were added	autour du around	de haut in height
de nombreux bassins numerous pools/fountains	légumes vegetables	roi King

👥 Expérience personnelle

Avez-vous visité une résidence célèbre ou historique? Où? Quand? Comment était-ce? Un personnage historique a-t-il habité là? Qui? Parlez de cette visite à un(e) camarade.

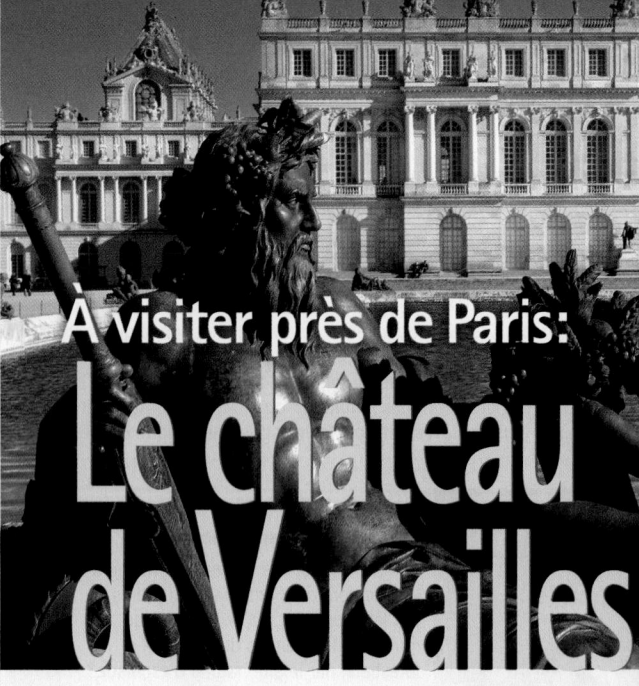

À visiter près de Paris: Le château de Versailles

La construction du célèbre° château de Versailles a commencé en 1623 sous le roi Louis XIII. Au départ, c'était un petit château où le roi logeait° quand il allait à la chasse°. Plus tard, en 1678, Louis XIV, aussi appelé le Roi-Soleil, a décidé de faire de Versailles sa résidence principale. Il a demandé à son architecte, Louis Le Vau, d'agrandir° le château, et à son premier peintre°, Charles Le Brun, de le décorer. Le Vau a fait construire, entre autres°, le Grand Appartement du Roi. La décoration de cet appartement de sept pièces était à la gloire du Roi-Soleil. La pièce la plus célèbre du château de Versailles est la galerie des Glaces°. C'est une immense pièce de 73 mètres de long, 10,50 mètres de large et 12,30 mètres de haut°. D'un côté, 17 fenêtres donnent° sur les jardins, et

de l'autre côté, il y a 17 arcades embellies de miroirs immenses. Au nord° de la galerie des Glaces, on trouve le salon de la Guerre°, et, au sud°, le salon de la Paix°. Quand on visite le château de Versailles, on peut également° voir de nombreuses autres pièces, ajoutées à différentes périodes, comme la chambre de la Reine°,

À l'intérieur du palais

OPTIONS

Le château de Versailles Located in the region **Île-de-France**, **le château de Versailles** is about twelve miles from Paris. **Le château et les jardins de Versailles** are classified as a UNESCO World Heritage Site. Hundreds of masterpieces of seventeenth-century French sculpture can be viewed in the gardens, and it is estimated that seven million people visit the gardens each year.

Extra Practice Ask students to make a list of words from the text whose meanings they guessed. Then have them work with partners and compare their lists. Students should explain to each other what clues they used in the text to help them guess the meanings. Help the class confirm the predictions, or have students confirm the meanings in a dictionary.

UNITÉ 8 Chez nous

Après la lecture

Vrai ou faux? Indiquez si les phrases sont **vraies** ou **fausses**. Corrigez les phrases fausses.

1. Louis XIII habitait à Versailles toute l'année.
Faux. Louis XIII logeait à Versailles quand il allait à la chasse.

2. Louis Le Vau est appelé le Roi-Soleil.
Faux. Louis XIV est appelé le Roi-Soleil.

3. La galerie des Glaces est une grande pièce avec beaucoup de miroirs et de fenêtres.
Vrai.

4. Il y a deux salons près de la galerie des Glaces.
Vrai.

5. Aujourd'hui, au château de Versailles, il n'y a pas de meubles.
Faux. Il y a une collection unique de meubles (lits, tables, fauteuils et chaises, bureaux, etc.).

6. Le château de Versailles n'a pas de jardins parce qu'il a été construit en ville.
Faux. Il a des jardins: l'Orangerie, le Potager et l'Arboretum de Chèvreloup.

Répondez Répondez aux questions par des phrases complètes.

1. Comment était Versailles sous Louis XIII? Quand logeait-il là?
C'était un petit château où le roi logeait quand il allait à la chasse.

2. Qu'est-ce que Louis XIV a fait du château?
Il a fait de Versailles sa résidence principale. Il l'a agrandi et l'a décoré.

3. Qu'est-ce que Louis Le Vau a fait à Versailles?
Il a construit, entre autres, le Grand Appartement du Roi.

4. Dans quelle salle Louis XVI et Marie-Antoinette ont-ils été mariés? Comment est cette salle?
Ils ont été mariés dans l'Opéra. C'est une grande salle où plus de 700 personnes assistaient souvent à divers spectacles et bals.

5. Louis XVI est-il devenu roi avant ou après son mariage?
Il est devenu roi après son mariage.

6. Le château de Versailles est-il composé d'un seul bâtiment? Expliquez.
Non, le château a aussi une chapelle et d'autres bâtiments comme le Grand et le Petit Trianon.

Les personnages célèbres de Versailles
Par groupes de trois ou quatre, choisissez une des personnes mentionnées dans la lecture et faites des recherches (*research*) à son sujet. Préparez un rapport écrit (*written report*) à présenter à la classe. Vous pouvez (*may*) utiliser les ressources de votre bibliothèque ou Internet.

Le château de Versailles et une fontaine

plusieurs cuisines et salles à manger d'hiver et d'été, des bibliothèques, divers salons et cabinets, et plus de 18.000 m²° de galeries qui racontent° l'histoire de France en images. L'opéra, une grande salle où plus de° 700 personnes assistaient souvent à divers spectacles et bals, a aussi été ajouté plus tard. C'est dans cette salle que le futur roi Louis XVI et Marie-Antoinette ont été mariés. Partout° dans le château, on peut admirer une collection unique de meubles (lits, tables, fauteuils et chaises, bureaux, etc.) et de magnifiques tissus° (tapis, rideaux et tapisseries°). Le château de Versailles a aussi une chapelle et d'autres bâtiments, comme le Grand et le Petit Trianon. Autour du château, il y a des serres° et de magnifiques jardins avec de nombreux bassins°, fontaines et statues. Dans l'Orangerie, on trouve plus de 1.000 arbres°, et de nombreux fruits et légumes sont toujours cultivés dans le Potager° du Roi. L'Arboretum de Chèvreloup était le terrain de chasse des rois et on y° trouve aujourd'hui des arbres du monde entier°.

célèbre *famous* logeait *stayed* chasse *hunting* agrandir *enlarge* peintre *painter* entre autres *among other things* Glaces *Mirrors* haut *high* donnent *open* nord *north* Guerre *War* sud *south* Paix *Peace* également *also* Reine *Queen* m² (mètres carrés) *square meters* racontent *tell* plus de *more than* Partout *Everywhere* tissus *fabrics* tapisseries *tapestries* serres *greenhouses* bassins *ponds* arbres *trees* Potager *vegetable garden* y *there* entier *entire*

trois cent cinquante-cinq 355

Vrai ou faux? Go over the answers with the class. For false items, have students point out where they found the correct information in the text.

Répondez Have students pair up to compare their answers. If they don't agree, tell them to locate the answer in the text.

Les personnages célèbres de Versailles Before assigning this activity, have students identify the people mentioned in the article and write their names on the board. To avoid duplication of efforts, you may want to assign each group a specific person. Encourage students to provide visuals with their presentations.

OPTIONS

Small Groups Working in groups of three or four, have students discuss the features that they find most interesting or appealing about **le château de Versailles** and make a list of them.

Extra Practice Tell students to skim the text and underline all of the verbs in the **passé composé** and **imparfait**. Then go through the text and ask volunteers to explain why each verb is in the **passé composé** or the **imparfait**.

Section Goals

In this section, students will:

- learn to write a narrative using the **passé composé** and the **imparfait**
- write a story about the past

Stratégie Write these sentences on the board. 1. **Le film a fini à minuit.** 2. **J'ai fait mon lit, j'ai rangé ma chambre et j'ai passé l'aspirateur.** 3. **Le bébé a dormi parce qu'il avait sommeil.** 4. **Quand nous étions au restaurant, nous avons parlé avec nos copains.** Ask volunteers to explain why the **passé composé** or **imparfait** was used in each case. Then have the class write sentences for their compositions.

Thème Explain that the story they are going to write will be about events that occurred in the past. Encourage them to brainstorm as many details as possible before they begin writing.

SAVOIR-FAIRE

Écriture

STRATÉGIE

Mastering the simple past tenses

In French, when you write about events that occurred in the past, you need to know when to use the **passé composé** and when to use the **imparfait**. A good understanding of the uses of each tense will make it much easier to determine which one to use as you write.

Look at the following summary of the uses of the **passé composé** and the **imparfait**. Write your own example sentence for each of the rules described.

Passé composé vs. imparfait

Passé composé

1. Actions viewed as completed

_____

2. Beginning or end of past actions

_____

3. Series of past actions

_____

Imparfait

1. Ongoing past actions

_____

2. Habitual past actions

_____

3. Mental, physical, and emotional states or general descriptions in the past

_____

With a partner, compare your example sentences. Use the sentences as a guide to help you decide which tense to use as you are writing a story about something that happened in the past.

Thème

Écrire une histoire

Avant l'écriture

1. Quand vous étiez petit(e), vous habitiez dans la maison ou l'appartement de vos rêves (*of your dreams*).

   - Vous allez décrire cette maison ou cet appartement.

   - Vous allez écrire sur la ville où vous habitiez et sur votre quartier.

   - Vous allez décrire les différentes pièces, les meubles et les objets décoratifs.

   - Vous allez parler de votre pièce préférée et de ce que (*what*) vous aimiez faire dans cette pièce.

Ensuite, imaginez qu'il y ait eu (*was*) un cambriolage (*burglary*) dans cette maison ou dans cet appartement. Vous allez alors décrire ce qui est arrivé (*what happened*).

Coup de main

Here are some terms that you may find useful in your narration.

le voleur	*thief*
cassé(e)	*broken*
j'ai vu	*I saw*
manquer	*to be missing*

OPTIONS

Avant l'écriture Say or read aloud some French past-tense sentences and have students identify the **passé composé** and **imparfait** forms. For each sentence, have students say why one form or the other was used. Review with them the situations and contexts that trigger the use of each tense.

Preview the use of the arrow diagram. Copy it on the board, making sure it is large enough to write inside. Start out with a description of the setting using the **imparfait** and write those sentences inside the arrow. Then have students volunteer possible completed actions using the **passé composé** and write them on the lines that intersect the arrow.

2. Utilisez le diagramme pour vous aider à analyser les éléments de votre histoire. Écrivez les éléments qui se rapportent à (*that are related to*) l'imparfait dans la partie IMPARFAIT et ceux (*the ones*) qui se rapportent au passé composé dans les parties PASSÉ COMPOSÉ.

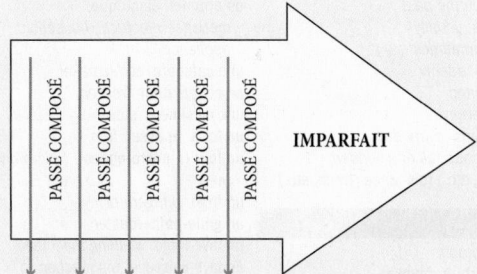

3. Après avoir complété le diagramme, échangez-le avec celui d'un(e) partenaire. Votre partenaire doit-il (*does he/she have to*) changer quelque chose? Expliquez pourquoi.

Écriture

Utilisez le diagramme pour écrire votre histoire. Écrivez trois paragraphes:

- le premier sur la présentation générale de la maison ou de l'appartement et de la ville où vous habitiez,

- le deuxième sur votre pièce préférée et la raison pour laquelle (*the reason why*) vous l'avez choisie,

- le troisième sur le cambriolage, sur ce qui s'est passé (*what happened*) et sur ce que vous avez fait (*what you did*).

> *Quand j'étais petit(e), j'habitais dans un château, en France. Le château était dans une petite ville près de Paris. Il y avait un grand jardin, avec beaucoup d'animaux. Il y avait douze pièces...*
>
> *Ma pièce préférée était la cuisine parce que j'aimais faire la cuisine et que j'aidais souvent ma mère...*
>
> *Un jour, mes parents et moi sommes rentrés de vacances...*

Après l'écriture

1. Échangez votre histoire avec celle (*the one*) d'un(e) partenaire. Répondez à ces questions pour commenter son travail.

- Votre partenaire a-t-il/elle correctement utilisé l'imparfait et le passé composé?

- A-t-il/elle écrit trois paragraphes qui correspondent aux descriptions de sa maison ou de son appartement et de la ville, de sa pièce préférée et du cambriolage?

- Quel(s) détail(s) ajouteriez-vous (*would you add*)? Lequel/Lesquels enlèveriez-vous (*Which one(s) would you delete*)? Quel(s) autre(s) commentaire(s) avez-vous pour votre partenaire?

2. Corrigez votre histoire d'après (*according to*) les commentaires de votre partenaire. Relisez votre travail pour éliminer ces problèmes:

- des fautes (*errors*) d'orthographe

- des fautes de ponctuation

- des fautes de conjugaison

- des fautes d'accord (*agreement*) des adjectifs

- un mauvais emploi (*use*) de la grammaire

EVALUATION

Criteria

Content Contains a complete description of a house or apartment, its furnishings, and the place where it was located, followed by a complete past-tense narration about a robbery that took place there.
Scale: 1 2 3 4 5

Organization Contains two parts: a complete past-tense description of a place that uses **imparfait** forms followed by a past-tense narration using the **passé composé**.
Scale: 1 2 3 4 5

Accuracy Uses **passé composé** and **imparfait** forms correctly and in the correct context. Spells words, conjugates verbs, and modifies adjectives correctly throughout.
Scale: 1 2 3 4 5

Creativity Includes additional information that is not included in the task and/or uses adjectives and descriptive verbs to make the scene more vivid.
Scale: 1 2 3 4 5

Scoring

Excellent	18–20 points
Good	14–17 points
Satisfactory	10–13 points
Unsatisfactory	< 10 points

O P T I O N S

Écriture Supply students with some useful expressions to use for their compositions: 1. Ongoing past-tense description: **toujours, tous les jours, d'habitude, normalement, en général/ généralement, chaque fois, de temps en temps** 2. Completed past actions: **tout d'un coup, tous ensemble, dans un moment, à ce moment-là, puis, ensuite, après, plus tard, enfin, finalement**

Après l'écriture When students have completed their stories, have them work in pairs or small groups to create a dramatic reenactment of the story. They can use voiceover narration for the descriptive part, then act out the completed actions that are part of the robbery and its aftermath. Encourage students to be creative and to use props and posters to set the stage and tell the story.

Instructional Resources
vhlcentral.com:
Textbook MP3s; Textbook
Audioscript; reference tools

Suggestions
- Tell students that an easy way to study from **Vocabulaire** is to cover up the French half of each section, leaving only the English equivalents exposed. They can then quiz themselves on the French items. To focus on the English equivalents of the French entries, they simply reverse this process.
- Point out to students that they can use the Vocabulary Tools at **vhlcentral.com** for reference and extra vocabulary practice.

🔊 Ⓢ Vocabulary Tools

Leçon 8A

Les parties d'une maison

un **balcon**	balcony
une **cave**	basement, cellar
une **chambre**	bedroom
un **couloir**	hallway
une **cuisine**	kitchen
un **escalier**	staircase
un **garage**	garage
un **jardin**	garden; yard
un **mur**	wall
une **pièce**	room
une **salle à manger**	dining room
une **salle de bains**	bathroom
une **salle de séjour**	living/family room
un **salon**	formal living/sitting room
un **sous-sol**	basement
un **studio**	studio (apartment)
les **toilettes/W.-C.**	restrooms/toilet

Locutions de temps

de **temps en temps**	from time to time
en **général**	in general
quelquefois	sometimes
vite	fast, quickly

Chez soi

un **appartement**	apartment
un **immeuble**	building
un **logement**	housing
un **loyer**	rent
un **quartier**	area, neighborhood
une **résidence**	residence
une **affiche**	poster
une **armoire**	armoire, wardrobe
une **baignoire**	bathtub
un **canapé**	couch
une **commode**	dresser, chest of drawers
une **douche**	shower
une **étagère**	shelf
un **fauteuil**	armchair
une **fleur**	flower
une **lampe**	lamp
un **lavabo**	bathroom sink
un **meuble**	piece of furniture
un **miroir**	mirror
un **placard**	closet, cupboard
un **rideau**	drape, curtain
un **tapis**	rug
un **tiroir**	drawer
déménager	to move out
emménager	to move in
louer	to rent

Expressions utiles

See p. 319.

Leçon 8B

Locutions de temps

autrefois	in the past
d'habitude	usually
parfois	sometimes
soudain	suddenly
souvent	often
toujours	always
tous les jours	every day
tout d'un coup	all of a sudden
une **(deux, etc.) fois**	once (twice, etc.)

Chez soi

un **balai**	broom
une **couverture**	blanket
les **draps** (m.)	sheets
un **évier**	kitchen sink
un **oreiller**	pillow

Les tâches ménagères

une **tâche ménagère**	household chore
balayer	to sweep
débarrasser la table	to clear the table
enlever/faire la poussière	to dust
essuyer la vaisselle/la table	to dry the dishes/to wipe the table
faire la lessive	to do the laundry
faire le lit	to make the bed
faire le ménage	to do the housework
faire la vaisselle	to do the dishes
laver	to wash
mettre la table	to set the table
passer l'aspirateur	to vacuum
ranger	to tidy up; to put away
repasser (le linge)	to iron (the laundry)
salir	to soil, to make dirty
sortir la/les poubelle(s)	to take out the trash
propre	clean
sale	dirty

Les appareils ménagers

un **appareil électrique/ménager**	electrical/household appliance
une **cafetière**	coffeemaker
un **congélateur**	freezer
une **cuisinière**	stove
un **fer à repasser**	iron
un **four (à micro-ondes)**	(microwave) oven
un **frigo**	refrigerator
un **grille-pain**	toaster
un **lave-linge**	washing machine
un **lave-vaisselle**	dishwasher
un **sèche-linge**	clothes dryer

Verbes

connaître	to know, to be familiar with
reconnaître	to recognize
savoir	to know (facts), to know how to do something

Expressions utiles

See p. 337.

La nourriture

Unit Goals

Leçon 9A

In this lesson, students will learn:
- terms for food and meals
- about the **e caduc** and the **e muet**
- about the **Guide Michelin**
- the verb **venir** and similar verbs
- the **passé récent**
- to use time expressions with **depuis**, **pendant**, and **il y a**
- the verbs **devoir**, **vouloir**, and **pouvoir**
- about open-air markets through specially shot video footage

Leçon 9B

In this lesson, students will learn:
- terms for eating in a restaurant
- terms for specialty food shops
- about stress and rhythm in spoken French
- about French meals and eating habits
- about the French musician Keen'V
- comparatives and superlatives of adjectives and adverbs
- irregular comparative and superlative forms
- double object pronouns
- to take notes as they listen

Savoir-faire

In this section, students will learn:
- cultural and historical information about **la Normandie, la Bretagne, les Hauts de la France, les Pays de la Loire et Centre-Val-de-Loire**
- to read for the main idea
- to express and support opinions
- to write a restaurant review

Pour commencer

- **Elle est dans un supermarché.**
- **Elle a des légumes dans la main.**
- **Elle va les servir en salade.**
- **Non, elle n'a pas encore payé.**

Pour commencer

- Où est Sandrine, dans un supermarché ou une poissonnerie?
- Qu'est-ce qu'elle a dans la main? Des légumes ou des fruits?
- Comment va-t-elle les servir, avec un steak, en salade ou en tarte?
- Est-ce qu'elle a déjà payé ou pas encore (*not yet*)?

RESOURCES

Student Activities Manual (SAM):
Workbook Activities, pp. 119–134
Laboratory Manual: Lab Activities, pp. 65–72
Workbook/Video Manual: Video Activities, pp. 33–36; pp. 77–78
WB/VM/LM Answer Key

vhlcentral.com: Textbook MP3s; Lab MP3s; Textbook Audioscript; Lab Audioscript Video; Videoscript; **Roman-photo** Translations; **Vocabulaire supplémentaire**; Activity Pack (including **Feuilles d'activités**, Info Gap Activities, and Task-based Activities);

Flash culture video transcription; **Essayez!** and **Mise en pratique** answers; Digital Image Bank; Testing Program; Testing Program MP3s

Section Goals

In this section, students will learn and practice vocabulary related to:
• foods
• meals

Instructional Resources
vhlcentral.com:
*Digital Image Bank
(including vocabulary
illustrations from the textbook,
theme-based illustrations);*
Vocabulaire supplémentaire;
Mise en pratique *answers;*
*Textbook Audioscript;
Lab Audioscript; Activity Pack*
(Feuilles d'activités); *Textbook
MP3s; Lab MP3s; SAM Answer
Key; reference tools*

Suggestions

• Use the **9A Contextes**
illustration from the Digital
Image Bank. Point out foods
as you describe the illustration.
Examples: **Voici des fraises.
Elle achète une pêche. Le
garçon a acheté des œufs, un
poivron vert et une laitue.**

• Ask students questions about
their food preferences using the
new vocabulary. **Préférez-vous
les poires ou les fraises? Les
oranges ou les bananes? Les
tomates ou les champignons?
Les escargots ou le thon? Le
porc ou le poulet? La viande ou
les fruits de mer?**

• Point out that **une cantine** is
a cafeteria in French, while
une cafétéria is a self-service
restaurant.

• Name some dishes and
have students explain what
ingredients are used to make
them. Examples: **une salade de
fruits, une salade mixte,** and
un sandwich.

• Say food items and have
students classify them in
categories under the headings:
**les fruits, les légumes, la
viande,** and **le poisson.**

• Additional vocabulary for this
lesson can be found in the
Vocabulaire supplémentaire
on the Supersite.

• Use the Food and shopping
illustrations from the Digital
Image Bank to help students
familiarize themselves with
foods, and expressing needs,
desires, and abilities.

Leçon 9A

You will learn how to...
▪ **talk about food**
▪ **express needs, desires,
and abilities**

Ⓢ Vocabulary Tools

Quel appétit!

Vocabulaire

cuisiner	to cook
faire les courses (f.)	to go (grocery) shopping
une cantine	(school) cafeteria
un supermarché	supermarket
un aliment	food item
un déjeuner	lunch
un dîner	dinner
un goûter	afternoon snack
la nourriture	food, sustenance
un petit-déjeuner	breakfast
un repas	meal
des petits pois (m.)	peas
une salade	salad
le bœuf	beef
un escargot	escargot, snail
les fruits de mer (m.)	seafood
un pâté (de campagne)	pâté
le porc	pork
un poulet	chicken
une saucisse	sausage
un steak	steak
le thon	tuna
la viande	meat
le riz	rice
des pâtes (f.)	pasta
un yaourt	yogurt

ressources

WB	LM	Ⓢ
pp. 119–120	p. 65	vhlcentral

360 *trois cent soixante*

Image labels: les poires (f.); les oranges (f.); les fruits (m.); les fraises (f.); les pêches (f.); les bananes (f.); les pommes (f.); les légumes (m.); les pommes de terre (f.); les oignons (m.); les carottes (f.); les poivrons rouges (m.); les haricots verts (m.); l'ail (m.); les champignons (m.); les tomates (f.)

O P T I O N S

Extra Practice To review colors and practice new vocabulary, ask students to name foods that are different colors. Examples: **jaune (les bananes), rouge (les pommes, les tomates, les fraises), vert (les haricots verts et les petits pois), orange (les oranges et les carottes), blanc (les oignons et le riz).**

Game Divide the class into two teams. Give one player a card with the name of a food item. That player is allowed 30 seconds to draw the item for another player on his or her team to guess. Award a point for a correct answer. If a player doesn't guess the correct answer, the next player on the opposing team may "steal" the point.

Mise en pratique

1 Écoutez Fatima et René se préparent à aller faire des courses. Ils décident de ce qu'ils vont acheter. Écoutez leur conversation. Ensuite, complétez les phrases.

Dans le frigo, il reste six (1) __carottes__, quelques (2) __champignons__, une petite (3) __laitue__ et trois (4) __tomates__. René va utiliser ce qu'il reste dans le frigo pour préparer (5) __le déjeuner/ une salade__. Fatima va acheter des (6) __pommes de terre__ et des (7) __oignons__. René va acheter des (8) __fruits__ : des (9) __fraises__, des (10) __pêches__ et quelques (11) __poires__. René va faire un bon petit repas avec des (12) __fruits de mer__.

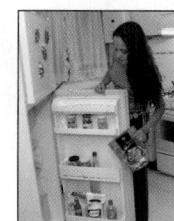

2 Les invités Vous avez invité quelques amis pour le week-end. Vous vous préparez à les accueillir (*welcome*). Complétez les phrases suivantes avec les mots ou les expressions qui conviennent le mieux (*fit the best*).

1. Au petit-déjeuner, Sébastien aime bien prendre un café et manger des croissants et __un yaourt__. (une salade, des fruits de mer, un yaourt)
2. Pour un petit-déjeuner français, il faut aussi de __la confiture__. (la confiture, l'ail, l'oignon)
3. J'adore les fruits, alors je vais acheter __des pêches__. (des petits pois, un repas, des pêches)
4. Mélanie n'aime pas trop la viande, elle va préférer manger __des fruits de mer__. (des fruits de mer, du pâté de campagne, des saucisses)
5. Je vais aussi préparer une salade pour Mélanie avec __des tomates__. (de la confiture, des tomates, du bœuf)
6. Jean-François est allergique au lait. Je ne vais donc pas lui servir de __yaourt__. (carottes, pommes de terre, yaourt)
7. Pour le dessert, je vais préparer une tarte aux fruits avec des __fraises__. (poivrons, fraises, petits pois)
8. Il faut aller au supermarché pour acheter des __oranges__ pour faire du jus pour le petit-déjeuner. (yaourts, pâtes, oranges)

3 Vos habitudes alimentaires Utilisez un élément de chaque colonne pour former des phrases au sujet de vos habitudes alimentaires. N'oubliez pas de faire les accords nécessaires. Answers will vary.

A	B	C
au petit-déjeuner	acheter	des bananes
au déjeuner	adorer	des carottes
au goûter	aimer (bien)	des fruits
au dîner	ne pas tellement	des haricots verts
à la cantine	aimer	des légumes
à la maison	détester	des œufs
au restaurant	manger	du riz
au supermarché	prendre	de la viande

Practice more at vhlcentral.com.

trois cent soixante et un **361**

la confiture de fraises

les tartes (*f.*) aux fraises

le poivron vert

la laitue

les œufs (*m.*)

1 Audioscript FATIMA: Je n'ai presque plus rien dans le frigo. Il faut aller au supermarché. RENÉ: D'accord.
F: Regardons d'abord ce qu'il nous reste. Voyons, il nous reste six carottes, quelques champignons, une petite laitue et trois tomates.
R: Parfait. Juste de quoi faire une salade pour le déjeuner. Mais il n'y a plus rien pour le dîner.
F: Dis, nous allons tout le temps au supermarché. Pourquoi ne pas aller au marché plutôt? Il y en a un place Victor Hugo aujourd'hui. Il est là deux fois par semaine: le mercredi et le dimanche. J'ai besoin d'acheter des pommes de terre et des oignons.
R: D'accord. Moi, je vais acheter des fruits: des fraises, des pêches et quelques poires. Et j'ai envie d'acheter des fruits de mer aussi. Je vais te faire un bon petit repas.
F: Alors, allons-y! Au marché!
(*On Textbook MP3s*)

1 Suggestion Play the complete conversation. Give students a few minutes to complete the paragraph, then play the recording again, stopping at the end of each sentence that contains an answer, so students can check their work or fill in any missing information.

2 Expansion Have students explain why the other items are incorrect. Example: **En général, on ne mange pas de fruits de mer au petit-déjeuner.**

3 Suggestion This activity can be done orally or in writing, in pairs or in groups.

OPTIONS

Extra Practice Have students draw food pyramids based not on what they should eat, but on what they actually do eat. Encourage them to include drawings or magazine photos to enhance their visual presentation. Then have students present their pyramids to the class.

Game Play a memory game in which the first player begins with: **Je vais au supermarché. J'ai besoin d'acheter…** and names one food item. The next player repeats what the first person said and adds another food. The third player must remember what the first two people said before adding an item.

Communication

4 Expansion Have students describe what they typically eat at each meal and for snacks.

5 Suggestion Distribute the **Feuilles d'activités** found in the Activity Pack on the Supersite. Have two volunteers read the **modèle** aloud.

6 Suggestions
• Point out the **Coup de main.**
• Encourage students to include photos or drawings to illustrate their brochures. Have students vote on the best brochure in various categories.

4 Quel repas? Regardez les dessins et pour chacun d'eux (*each one of them*), indiquez le repas qu'il représente et faites une liste de ce que (*what*) chaque personne mange. Ensuite, avec un(e) partenaire, décrivez une image à tour de rôle. Votre partenaire doit deviner (*must guess*) quel dessin vous décrivez. Answers will vary.

1. _____

2. _____

3. _____

4. _____

5 Sondage Votre professeur va vous donner une feuille d'activités. Circulez dans la classe et utilisez les éléments du tableau pour former des questions afin de savoir (*in order to find out*) ce que vos camarades de classe mangent. Quels sont les trois aliments les plus (*the most*) souvent mentionnés? Answers will vary.

MODÈLE

Étudiant(e) 1: À quelle heure est-ce que tu prends ton petit-déjeuner? Que manges-tu?
Étudiant(e) 2: Je prends mon petit-déjeuner à sept heures. Je mange du pain avec du beurre et de la confiture, et je bois un café au lait.

Questions	Noms	Réponses
1. Petit-déjeuner: Quand? Quoi?	1. ____	1. ____
2. Déjeuner: Où? Quand? Quoi?	2. ____	2. ____
3. Goûter: Quand? Quoi?	3. ____	3. ____
4. Dîner: Quand? Quoi?	4. ____	4. ____
5. Supermarché: Quoi? À quelle fréquence?	5. ____	5. ____
6. Cantine: Quoi? Quand? À quelle fréquence?	6. ____	6. ____

6 La brochure Avec un(e) partenaire, vous allez préparer une brochure pour les nouveaux étudiants français qui viennent (*are coming*) étudier dans votre université. Une partie de la brochure est consacrée (*dedicated*) aux habitudes alimentaires. Faites une comparaison entre la France et les États-Unis. Ensuite, présentez votre brochure à la classe. Answers will vary.

Coup de main

Here are some characteristics of traditional French eating habits.

Le petit-déjeuner is usually light, with bread, butter, and jam, or cereal and coffee or tea. Croissants are normally reserved for the weekend.

Le déjeuner is typically the main meal and may include a starter, a main dish (meat or fish with vegetables), cheese or yogurt, and dessert (often fruit). Lunch breaks may be a half hour to two hours (allowing people to eat at home).

Le goûter is a light afternoon snack such as cookies, French bread with chocolate, pastry, yogurt, or fruit.

Le dîner starts between 7:00 and 8:00 p.m. Foods served at lunch and dinner are similar. However, dinner is typically lighter than lunch and is usually eaten at home.

OPTIONS

Game Play a game of **Dix questions**. Ask a volunteer to think of a food from the new vocabulary. Other students get to ask one yes/no question, and then they can guess what the word is. Limit attempts to ten questions per word. You may want to provide students with some sample questions. Examples: **C'est un fruit? Est-ce qu'il est vert?**

Extra Practice Prepare descriptions of various meals, which include breakfasts, lunches, snacks, and dinners. Have students write down what you say as a dictation. Then have them guess which meal each description represents.

Les sons et les lettres   Audio

e caduc and e muet

In **Leçon 4A**, you learned that the vowel **e** in very short words is pronounced similarly to the *a* in the English word *about*. This sound is called an **e caduc**. An **e caduc** can also occur in longer words and before words beginning with vowel sounds.

rechercher	devoirs	le haricot	le onze

An **e caduc** occurs in order to break up clusters of several consonants.

appartement	quelquefois	poivre vert	gouvernement

An **e caduc** is sometimes called **e muet** (*mute*). It is often dropped in spoken French.

Tu ne sais pas.	Je veux bien!	C'est un livre intéressant.

An unaccented **e** before a single consonant sound is often silent unless its omission makes the word difficult to pronounce.

semaine	petit	finalement

An unaccented e at the end of a word is usually silent and often marks a feminine noun or adjective.

fraise	salade	intelligente	jeune

Prononcez Répétez les mots suivants à voix haute.

1. vendredi
2. logement
3. exemple
4. devenir
5. tartelette
6. finalement
7. boucherie
8. petits pois
9. pomme de terre
10. malheureusement

Articulez Répétez les phrases suivantes à voix haute.

1. Tu ne vas pas prendre de casquette?
2. J'étudie le huitième chapitre maintenant.
3. Il va passer ses vacances en Angleterre.
4. Marc me parle souvent au téléphone.
5. Mercredi, je réserve dans une auberge.
6. Finalement, ce petit logement est bien.

Dictons Répétez les dictons à voix haute.

Le soleil luit pour tout le monde.[2]

L'habit ne fait pas le moine.[1]

[1] Clothes don't make the man. (lit. The habit doesn't make the monk.)
[2] The sun shines for everyone.

ressources

LM
p. 66

vhlcentral

trois cent soixante-trois 363

Section Goals

In this section, students will learn about **e caduc** and **e muet**.

Instructional Resources
vhlcentral.com:
Textbook MP3s; Lab MP3s;
SAM Answer Key;
Textbook Audioscript;
Lab Audioscript;
reference tools

Suggestions
• Point out that although the pronunciation of the French **e caduc** and that of the *a* in the English word *about* are close, they are not identical. There is a difference in vowel quality and articulation.
• Model the pronunciation of the example words and have students repeat them after you.
• Point out that while the unaccented **e** at the end of a word is itself silent, it can influence the pronunciation of a word, often causing the final consonant to be pronounced. Example: **intelligent / intelligente.**
• Ask students to provide more examples of words from this lesson or previous lessons with **e caduc** and **e muet**. Examples: **repas, petit-déjeuner,** and **petits pois.**
• Dictate five familiar words containing **e caduc** and **e muet**, repeating each one at least two times. Then write them on the board or on a transparency and have students check their spelling.

O P T I O N S

Extra Practice Use these sentences with **e caduc** and **e muet** for additional practice or dictation. **1. Je fais mes devoirs le samedi. 2. Malheureusement, elle ne va pas descendre de son appartement. 3. Tu me fais une tartelette aux fraises, s'il te plaît? 4. La semaine dernière, Denise a acheté un immeuble en ville.**

Extra Practice Teach students these French tongue-twisters that contain **e caduc** and **e muet**. **1. Le poivre fait fièvre à la pauvre pieuvre** (*octopus*). (by Pierre Abbat) **2. Je dis que tu l'as dit à Didi ce que j'ai dit jeudi.**

Section Goals

In this section, students will learn functional phrases for discussing meetings, time, and grocery shopping.

Instructional Resources
vhlcentral.com:
Roman-photo *Video, Videoscript, and Translation; SAM Answer Key; reference tools*

Video Recap: Leçon 8B
Review the previous **Roman-photo** with this activity.
1. Quelles tâches ménagères a fait Stéphane? (Il a rangé sa chambre, il a fait son lit et il a fait la vaisselle.)
2. Que préparait Sandrine quand Amina est arrivée? (Elle préparait des biscuits au chocolat.)
3. Comment Sandrine décrit-elle Pascal? (Elle dit qu'il est pénible.)
4. Comment était Sandrine? (Elle était de mauvaise humeur.)
5. Pourquoi Sandrine dit-elle qu'Amina a de la chance? (Parce qu'elle a son Cyberhomme.)

Video Synopsis
Amina and David are at the supermarket. Sandrine finally arrives, explaining that her French teacher kept her 20 minutes late, plus she ran into Stéphane who wanted to discuss tonight's dinner. The three friends then discuss what is going to be prepared, and Sandrine picks out the ingredients she needs. At the check-out counter, Amina and David insist on buying the groceries.

Suggestions
• Have students predict what the episode will be about based on the title and video stills.
• Have students scan the captions and find sentences describing foods.
• Review predictions and have students summarize the episode.

Au supermarché  Video

PERSONNAGES

Amina

Caissière

David

Sandrine

Stéphane

Au supermarché...
AMINA Mais quelle heure est-il? Sandrine devait être là à deux heures et quart. On l'attend depuis quinze minutes!
DAVID Elle va arriver!
AMINA Mais pourquoi est-elle en retard?
DAVID Elle vient peut-être juste de sortir de la fac.

En ville...
STÉPHANE Eh! Sandrine!
SANDRINE Salut, Stéphane, je suis très pressée! David et Amina m'attendent au supermarché depuis vingt minutes.
STÉPHANE À quelle heure est-ce qu'on doit venir ce soir, ma mère et moi?
SANDRINE À sept heures et demie.

STÉPHANE D'accord. Qu'est-ce qu'on peut apporter?
SANDRINE Oh, rien, rien.
STÉPHANE Mais maman insiste.
SANDRINE Bon, une salade, si tu veux.

AMINA Alors, Sandrine. Qu'est-ce que tu vas nous préparer?
SANDRINE Un repas très français. Je pensais à des crêpes.
DAVID Génial, j'adore les crêpes!
SANDRINE Il nous faut des champignons, du jambon et du fromage. Et, bien sûr, des œufs, du lait et du beurre.

SANDRINE Et puis non! Finalement, je vous prépare un bœuf bourguignon.
AMINA Qu'est-ce qu'il nous faut alors?
SANDRINE Du bœuf, des carottes, des oignons...
DAVID Mmm... Ça va être bon!

AMINA Mais le bœuf bourguignon, c'est long à préparer, non?
SANDRINE Tu as raison. Vous ne voulez pas plutôt un poulet à la crème et aux champignons, accompagné d'un gratin de pommes de terre?
AMINA ET DAVID Mmmm!
SANDRINE Alors, c'est décidé.

A C T I V I T É S

1 **Les ingrédients** Répondez aux questions par des phrases complètes.

1. Quels ingrédients faut-il pour préparer les crêpes de Sandrine? Pour préparer ses crêpes, il faut des champignons, du jambon, du fromage, des œufs, du lait et du beurre.
2. Quels ingrédients faut-il pour préparer le bœuf bourguignon? Pour préparer le bœuf bourguignon, il faut du bœuf, des carottes et des oignons.
3. Quels ingrédients faut-il à Sandrine pour préparer le poulet et le gratin? Pour préparer le poulet et le gratin, il faut du poulet, de la crème, des champignons et des pommes de terre.

4. Quelle va être la salade de Valérie, à votre avis? Quels ingrédients va-t-elle mettre? Answers will vary. Possible answer: Ça va être une salade au thon avec des tomates.
5. À votre avis, quel(s) dessert(s) Sandrine va-t-elle préparer? Answers will vary. Possible answer: Sandrine va préparer une tarte aux fraises.
6. Après avoir lu/regardé cet ESPACE ROMAN-PHOTO, quel plat préférez-vous? Pourquoi? Answers will vary.

 Practice more at vhlcentral.com.

O P T I O N S

Avant de regarder la vidéo Before viewing the video, have students work in pairs and write a list of words and expressions that they might hear in a video episode entitled **Au supermarché**.

Regarder la vidéo Show the video episode and tell students to check off the words and expressions they hear on their lists. Then show the episode again and have students give you a play-by-play description of the action. Write their descriptions on the board.

Amina, Sandrine et David font les courses.

STÉPHANE Mais quoi, comme salade?
SANDRINE Euh, une salade de tomates ou... peut-être une salade verte... Désolée, Stéphane, je suis vraiment pressée!
STÉPHANE Une salade avec du thon, peut-être? Maman fait une salade au thon délicieuse!
SANDRINE Comme tu veux, Stéphane!

SANDRINE Je suis en retard. Je suis vraiment désolée. Je ne voulais pas vous faire attendre, mais je viens de rencontrer Stéphane et avant ça, mon prof de français m'a retenue pendant vingt minutes!
DAVID Oh, ce n'est pas grave!
AMINA Bon, on fait les courses?

SANDRINE Voilà exactement ce qu'il me faut pour commencer! Deux beaux poulets!
AMINA Tu sais, Sandrine, le chant, c'est bien, mais tu peux devenir chef de cuisine si tu veux!

CAISSIÈRE Ça vous fait 51 euros et 25 centimes, s'il vous plaît.
AMINA C'est cher!
DAVID Ah non, Sandrine, tu ne paies rien du tout. C'est pour nous!
SANDRINE Mais, c'est mon dîner et vous êtes mes invités.
AMINA Pas question, Sandrine. C'est nous qui payons!

Expressions utiles

Meeting friends

- **Sandrine devait être là à deux heures et quart.**
  Sandrine should have been here at 2:15.
- **On l'attend depuis quinze minutes!**
  We've been waiting for her for fifteen minutes!
- **Elle vient peut-être juste de sortir de la fac.**
  Maybe she just left school.
- **Je suis très pressé(e)!**
  I'm in a big hurry!
- **À quelle heure est-ce qu'on doit venir ce soir?**
  What time should we come tonight?
- **Je ne voulais pas vous faire attendre, mais je viens de rencontrer Stéphane.**
  I didn't want to make you wait, but I just ran into Stéphane.
- **Mon prof m'a retenue pendant vingt minutes!**
  My professor kept me for twenty minutes!

Additional vocabulary

- **une caissière**
  cashier
- **Vous ne voulez pas plutôt un poulet à la crème accompagné d'un gratin de pommes de terre?**
  Wouldn't you prefer chicken with cream sauce accompanied by potatoes au gratin?
- **Voilà exactement ce qu'il me faut.**
  Here's exactly what I need.
- **Tu peux devenir chef de cuisine si tu veux!**
  You could become a chef if you want!
- **Comme tu veux.**
  As you like./It's up to you./Whatever you want.
- **C'est pour nous.**
  It's on us.

Expressions utiles
- Model the pronunciation of the **Expressions utiles**.
- As you work through the list, point out forms of **devoir**, **pouvoir**, **vouloir**, **venir**, and the **passé recent**. Explain that **venir de** can be used to say what just happened or what someone just did. Then tell students that these verbs and structures will be formally presented in **Espace structures**.
- Point out that, although **là** means *there*, in some cases it can be interpreted as *here*. Example: **Sandrine devait être là à deux heures et quart**.
- Explain the difference between **il faut** + *infinitive* and **il nous faut** + *noun*.

1 **Suggestion** Have volunteers write their answers on the board. Then go over them as a class.

2 **Suggestion** Have students form small groups. Make a set of individual sentences on strips of paper for each group and distribute them. Tell students to arrange the sentences in the proper order and then read them aloud.

2 **Expansion** Have students create sentences to fill in parts of the story not mentioned in this activity.

3 **Suggestion** Tell students to refer to the **Expressions utiles** as they prepare their role-plays.

2 **Les événements** Mettez les événements dans l'ordre chronologique.

- 3 a. Sandrine décide de ne pas préparer de bœuf bourguignon.
- 1 b. Le prof de Sandrine parle avec elle après la classe.
- 4 c. Amina dit que Sandrine peut devenir chef de cuisine.
- 6 d. David et Amina paient.
- 2 e. Stéphane demande à quelle heure il doit arriver.
- 5 f. Sandrine essaie de payer.

3 **À vous!** Stéphane arrive chez lui et dit à sa mère qu'il faut préparer une salade pour le dîner de Sandrine. Avec un(e) partenaire, préparez une conversation entre Stéphane et sa mère. Parlez du dîner et décidez des ingrédients pour la salade. Présentez votre conversation à la classe.

ACTIVITÉS

ressources

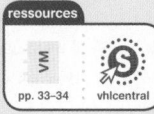

VM pp. 33–34

vhlcentral

trois cent soixante-cinq **365**

OPTIONS

Small Groups Have students work in groups of three or four. Tell them to create a menu for a classic French meal, then make a shopping list for the ingredients they need. You might want to suggest some classic dishes, such as **une tarte aux pommes**, **une soupe à l'oignon**, and **un pot-au-feu** (*beef and vegetable stew*). You can also bring in French cookbooks or simple recipes from magazines or the Internet, for students to use as reference.

Extra Practice Ask volunteers to act out the scenes in video stills 5–10 for the class. Tell them it is not necessary to memorize the episode or to stick strictly to its content. They should try to get the general meaning across with the vocabulary they know, and they should also feel free to be creative. Give them time to prepare.

Section Goals

In this section, students will:
• learn about the **Guide Michelin**
• learn some colloquial expressions related to foods and meals
• learn about some traditional foods of New Orleans
• read about French cheeses

Instructional Resources
vhlcentral.com:
SAM Answer Key;
reference tools

Culture à la loupe
Avant la lecture Have students look at the photos and describe what they see. Ask them what associations they have with the name Michelin.

Lecture
• If you have a **Guide Michelin**, bring it in to share with students.
• Ask students if they know of any Michelin-starred restaurants outside of France.

1 Expansion Have students create three more fill-in-the-blank sentences. Then tell them to exchange papers with a classmate and complete the activity.

 Reading

CULTURE À LA LOUPE

Le Guide Michelin et la gastronomie

Chaque année le Guide Michelin sélectionne les meilleurs° restaurants et hôtels dans toute la France. Ce petit guide rouge est le guide gastronomique le plus réputé° et le plus ancien°. Les gastronomes et les professionnels de l'hôtellerie attendent sa sortie° au mois de mars avec impatience. Les plus grands restaurants reçoivent° des étoiles° Michelin, avec un maximum de trois étoiles. Il n'y a que° 25 restaurants trois étoiles en France, tous très prestigieux et très chers, et 81 restaurants deux étoiles. Un repas au Plaza Athénée à Paris, célèbre° restaurant trois étoiles du chef Alain Ducasse, coûte entre 250 et 450 dollars. Un restaurant trois étoiles est une «cuisine exceptionnelle qui vaut° le voyage»; un restaurant deux étoiles, une «excellente cuisine, qui vaut le détour»; un restaurant une étoile, une «très bonne cuisine dans sa catégorie». Beaucoup de restaurants ne reçoivent pas d'étoiles mais simplement des fourchettes°. Quoi qu'il en soit°, c'est un honneur d'être sélectionné et d'apparaître° dans le Guide Michelin. Tous les restaurants sont des «bonnes tables°». Maintenant le Guide Michelin est publié pour plus de douze autres pays en Europe ainsi que° pour des villes comme New York, San Francisco et Tokyo.

Le premier Guide Michelin a été créé en 1900 par André et Édouard Michelin, propriétaires des pneus° Michelin. Il était offert° avec l'achat de pneus. À cette époque°, il n'y avait en France que 2.400 conducteurs°. Le guide leur donnait des informations précieuses sur les rares garagistes°, le plan de quelques villes et une liste des curiosités. Un peu plus tard ils ont inclus les restaurants.

La gastronomie française fait maintenant partie du patrimoine mondial° de l'humanité depuis 2010.

meilleurs *best* **le plus réputé** *most renowned* **le plus ancien** *oldest* **sortie** *release* **reçoivent** *receive* **étoiles** *stars* **Il n'y a que** *There are only* **célèbre** *famous* **vaut** *is worth* **fourchettes** *forks* **Quoi qu'il en soit** *Be that as it may* **apparaître** *appear* **bonnes tables** *good restaurants* **ainsi que** *as well as* **pneus** *tires* **offert** *offered* **époque** *time* **conducteurs** *drivers* **garagistes** *car mechanics* **patrimoine mondial** *world heritage*

A C T I V I T É S

1

Complétez Complétez les phrases.

1. Chaque année le Guide Michelin sélectionne les __meilleurs restaurants et hôtels__
2. Les __professionnels__ de l'hôtellerie attendent la sortie du Guide avec impatience.
3. Les restaurants peuvent (*can*) recevoir un maximum de __trois__ étoiles.
4. Il y a __26__ restaurants trois étoiles en France.
5. Un repas au Plaza Athénée coûte entre 250 et 450 __dollars.__

6. Un restaurant deux étoiles vaut le __détour__ .
7. Beaucoup de restaurants ne reçoivent pas d'étoiles mais des __fourchettes__ .
8. Aujourd'hui le Guide Michelin est publié pour des villes américaines comme __New York__ ou San Francisco.
9. Le premier Guide Michelin a été créé en 1900 par les __propriétaires des pneus Michelin__
10. Autrefois le Guide Michelin donnait aux conducteurs des informations sur les rares __garagistes__ .

O P T I O N S

Les Français et l'alimentation Tell students that small specialty shops (**les petits commerces**) continue to play an important role in French food culture and that many shoppers go to the **boulangerie** for bread, the **fromagerie** for cheese, the **poissonerie** for fish, etc. Nevertheless, many stores offer a variety of grocery products in a single location, including **les grandes surfaces** (**supermarchés** and **hypermarchés**) as well as the smaller **supérettes** and **épiceries**.

Faire des courses Grocery shopping in France is somewhat different from shopping in the United States. Grocery carts are usually locked together in a central place, most often in the parking lot. In order to use a cart, shoppers must insert a token. They get their money back when they return the cart. Also, customers are expected to bag their own groceries. Students will learn more about French shopping habits in **Leçon 12A**.

LE FRANÇAIS QUOTIDIEN

La nourriture

bidoche (f.)	meat
casse-croûte (m.)	snack
frometon (m.)	cheese
poiscaille (f.)	fish
faire un gueuleton	to have a large meal
faire ripaille	to feast
se faire une bouffe	to have a dinner party with friends

LE MONDE FRANCOPHONE

La cuisine de La Nouvelle-Orléans

À La Nouvelle-Orléans, la cuisine combine les influences créoles des colons° français et les influences cajuns des immigrés acadiens du Canada. Voici quelques spécialités.

le beignet un morceau de pâte frit° et recouvert de sucre, servi à toute heure du jour et de la nuit avec un café au lait et à la chicorée°

le gumbo une soupe à l'okra et aux fruits de mer, souvent accompagnée de riz

le jambalaya un riz très pimenté° préparé avec du jambon, du poulet, des tomates et parfois des saucisses et des fruits de mer

le po-boy de *poor boy* (garçon pauvre), un sandwich au poisson, aux écrevisses°, aux huîtres° ou à la viande dans un morceau de baguette

colons *colonists* **morceau de pâte frit** *fried piece of dough* **chicorée** *chicory* **pimenté** *spicy* **écrevisses** *crawfish* **huîtres** *oysters*

PORTRAIT

Les fromages français

Les Français sont très fiers de leurs fromages, et beaucoup de ces fromages sont connus dans le monde entier. La France produit près de 500 fromages dont° le type varie dans chaque région. En effet, le fromage est d'abord° un produit de terroir; c'est un emblème du pays. Chaque fromage est fabriqué selon des méthodes particulières et dans une zone géographique bien précise. Les fromages peuvent être au lait de vache°, comme le Brie ou le Camembert, au lait de chèvre°, comme le crottin de Chavignol, au lait de brebis°, comme le Roquefort, ou ils peuvent être faits d'un mélange° de plusieurs laits. Ils sont aussi classés en plusieurs catégories: cuit° ou non cuit, fermenté, fondu° ou frais°. Plus de 95% des Français mangent du fromage au moins une fois par semaine. Le fromage est présent dans approximativement 70% des repas en France et il est généralement consommé après le plat principal, avant le dessert. D'après les chiffres officiels, les Français dépensent sept milliards° d'euros par an pour le fromage. Au tout début du printemps, vers la fin du mois de mars, on célèbre la Journée nationale du fromage, à l'initiative de l'association «Fromages de terroirs», avec des débats, des conférences, des démonstrations de recettes° et des dégustations°. C'est l'occasion pour la France de mettre en avant° les produits de ses terroirs.

dont *of which* **d'abord** *first* **vache** *cow* **chèvre** *goat* **brebis** *ewe* **mélange** *mix* **cuit** *cooked* **fondu** *melted* **frais** *fresh* **milliards** *billions* **recettes** *recipes* **dégustations** *tastings* **mettre en avant** *show off*

---

2 **À table!** Répondez aux questions d'après les textes par des phrases complètes.

1. Combien de types de fromage sont produits en France?
   Près de 500 fromages différents sont produits en France.
2. Quels laits sont utilisés pour faire le fromage en France?
   Le lait de vache, le lait de chèvre et le lait de brebis sont utilisés pour faire le fromage.
3. À quel moment du repas les Français mangent-ils généralement le fromage?
   Ils mangent généralement le fromage après le plat principal, avant le dessert.
4. Comment célèbre-t-on la Journée nationale du fromage?
   Avec des débats, des conférences, des démonstrations de recettes et des dégustations.
5. Que met-on dans le jambalaya? Du riz, du piment, du jambon, du poulet, des tomates et parfois des saucisses et des fruits de mer.

3 **Le pique-nique** Vous et un(e) partenaire avez décidé de faire un pique-nique en plein air. Qu'allez-vous manger? Boire? Allez-vous apporter d'autres choses, comme des chaises ou une couverture? Parlez avec un autre groupe et échangez vos idées.

 Practice more at **vhlcentral.com**.

ACTIVITÉS

Sidebar:

Le français quotidien
- Model the pronunciation of each term and have students repeat.
- The word **poiscaille** can be masculine or feminine, but it is more commonly used as a feminine noun.

Portrait
- Explain that in a good cheese shop customers can sample the cut cheeses before purchasing them. Also, the shop clerks often give advice on selecting cheeses.
- Point out that a kind of goat cheese is generally referred to as **un chèvre**; the animal is **une chèvre**.

Le monde francophone Have students read the text. Then ask: **Avez-vous déjà mangé du gumbo? Du jambalaya? Avez-vous envie d'essayer un beignet? Pourquoi? Avez-vous envie d'essayer un po-boy au poisson, aux écrevisses, aux huîtres ou à la viande?**

Suggestion Point out to students that they will find supporting activities and more information related to this **Espace culture** at **vhlcentral.com**.

2 **Expansion** For additional practice, give students these items. **6. Dans quels pays mange-t-on du fromage français?** (dans le monde entier) **7. Combien de Français mangent du fromage?** (plus de 95%) **8. Combien les Français dépensent-ils par an pour le fromage?** (7 milliards d'euros) **9. Comment s'appelle un sandwich typique de la Nouvelle-Orléans?** (un po-boy)

3 **Suggestion** Tell students to jot down their ideas so that they will be prepared to discuss them.

Flash culture Tell students they will learn more about open-air markets by watching a variety of real-life images narrated by Csilla. Show the video segment without sound and tell students to call out what they see. Then, show the video segment again with sound. You can also use the activities in the video manual in class to reinforce this **Flash culture** or assign them as homework.

OPTIONS

La cuisine de la Nouvelle-Orléans New Orleans has many excellent chefs, but Paul Prudhomme and Emeril Lagasse are probably the most widely known. Additional specialities of the Crescent City include red beans and rice, crawfish étouffé, dirty rice, barbecued shrimp, blackened redfish, and pralines. Oysters are also popular and are featured in a number of dishes.

Les fromages français Have students go to a grocery store or an online grocery store and make a list of the different varieties or brands of French cheese they can buy there. Also have them note how much each cheese costs per pound and how long it was aged.

Section Goals

In this section, students will learn:
- the verb **venir** and similar verbs
- the **passé récent**
- time expressions with **depuis**, **pendant**, and **il y a**

Instructional Resources
vhlcentral.com:
Activity Pack; Lab MP3s;
SAM Answer Key; **Essayez!**
and **Mise en pratique**
answers; Lab Audioscript;
reference tools

Suggestions

- Model **venir** with the whole class by asking volunteers questions such as: **Venez-vous souvent au cours? Venez-vous de déjeuner? Venez-vous d'apprendre un nouveau verbe? Venez-vous me parler?** Point out that this verb has different meanings. Explain that when a form of **venir** is followed by **de** + [*infinitive*], it means the action has just happened.
- Point out that **venir, devenir,** and **revenir** always take **être** in the **passé composé**.
- Write the conjugation of **venir** on the board. Point out that the **e** changes to **ie** except in the **nous** and **vous** forms.
- Remind students of the DR & MRS P. VANDERTRAMP mnemonic for recalling verbs that take **être** in the **passé composé**. Explain that, while other verbs like **tenir, maintenir,** etc. are conjugated like **venir**, they are not verbs of motion and take **avoir** in the **passé composé**.
- To ensure that students understand the difference in meaning between the constructions **venir de** + [*infinitive*] and **venir** + [*infinitive*], write the following sentences on the board and have volunteers explain the meanings:
  Tu viens de la voir.
  Tu viens la voir.

À noter

In **Leçon 7A**, you learned about verbs that take **être** in the **passé composé**. Add the verbs **venir, devenir,** and **revenir** to that list to complete it.

ESPACE STRUCTURES

9A.1

The verb *venir* and the *passé récent* Ⓢ Tutorial

Point de départ In **Leçon 4A**, you learned the verb **aller** (*to go*). Now you will learn how to conjugate and use the irregular verb **venir** (*to come*).

venir	
je viens	nous venons
tu viens	vous venez
il/elle/on vient	ils/elles viennent

Mes tantes **viennent** de Nice.
My aunts are coming from Nice.

Viens vers huit heures du soir.
Come around 8 o'clock in the evening.

Tu **viens** avec moi au supermarché?
Are you coming with me to the supermarket?

Vous **venez** souvent au resto U?
Do you come to the dining hall often?

- **Venir** takes the auxiliary **être** in the **passé composé**. Its past participle is **venu**.

  Ils **sont venus** vendredi dernier.
  They came last Friday.

  Nadine **est venue** chez moi.
  Nadine came to my house.

  Nous **sommes venues** à la fac.
  We came to the campus.

  Es-tu **venu** trop tard?
  Did you come too late?

- **Venir** in the present tense can also be used with **de** and an infinitive to say that something has just happened. This is called the **passé récent**.

  Je **viens de prendre** mon goûter dans ma chambre.
  I just had a snack in my room.

  Nous **venons de regarder** cette émission.
  We just watched that show.

  Ma mère **vient de partir**.
  My mother just left.

  Karine **vient de manger** à la cantine.
  Karine just ate at the cafeteria.

- **Venir** can be used with an infinitive to say that someone has come to do something.

  Papa **est venu** me **chercher**.
  Dad came to pick me up.

  Elle **venait** nous **rendre** visite.
  She used to come visit us.

  Thuy et Mia **venaient répéter** avec nous.
  Thuy and Mia used to come rehearse with us.

  Ali **vient** te **parler**.
  Ali is coming to talk to you.

- The verbs **devenir** (*to become*) and **revenir** (*to come back*) are conjugated like **venir**. They, too, take **être** in the **passé composé**.

  Estelle et sa copine **sont devenues** médecins.
  Estelle and her friend became doctors.

  Il **est revenu** avec une tarte aux fraises.
  He came back with a strawberry tart.

- The verbs **tenir** (*to hold*), **maintenir** (*to maintain*), and **retenir** (*to keep, to retain*) are also conjugated like **venir**. However, they take **avoir** in the **passé composé**.

  Corinne **tient** le livre de cuisine.
  Corinne is holding the cookbook.

  On **a retenu** mon passeport à la douane.
  They kept my passport at customs.

- A command form of **tenir** is often used when handing something to someone.

  Tiens, une belle orange pour toi.
  Here, a nice orange for you.

  Votre sac est tombé! **Tenez**, Madame.
  Your bag fell! Here, ma'am.

Depuis, pendant, il y a + [*time*]

- To say that something happened at a time *ago* in the past, use **il y a** + [*time ago*].

  Il y a une heure, on était à la cantine.
  An hour ago, we were at the cafeteria.

  Il a visité Ouagadougou **il y a deux ans**.
  He visited Ouagadougou two years ago.

- To say that something happened for a particular period of time and ended in the past, use **pendant** + [*time period*]. Often the verb will be in the **passé composé**.

  Salim a fait la vaisselle **pendant deux heures**.
  Salim washed dishes for two hours.

  Ils ont voyagé **pendant un mois**.
  They traveled for one month.

- To say that something has been going on *since* a particular time and continues into the present, use **depuis** + [*time period, date, or starting point*]. Unlike its English equivalent, the verb in the French construction is usually in the present tense.

  Elle danse **depuis son arrivée** à la fête.
  She has been dancing since she got to the party.

  Nous passons l'été au Québec **depuis 1998**.
  We've been spending our summers in Quebec since 1998.

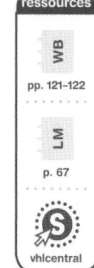
ressources

WB
pp. 121–122

LM
p. 67

vhlcentral

∞ Essayez!   Choisissez l'option correcte pour compléter chaque phrase.

1. Chloé, tu _____d_____ avec nous à la cantine?
2. Vous _____j_____ d'où, Monsieur?
3. Les Aubailly _____a_____ de dîner au café.
4. Julia Child est _____i_____ célèbre en 1961.
5. Qu'est-ce qu'ils _____g_____ dans la main?
6. Ils sont _____b_____ du supermarché à midi.
7. On allait souvent en Europe _____e_____ dix ans.
8. On mange bien _____h_____ l'arrivée de maman.
9. Le prof _____k_____ l'ordre dans la salle de classe.
10. Nous avons loué notre maison _____f_____ les vacances d'été.
11. Alex et Sylvie, _____c_____ ces valises, s'il vous plaît!

a. viennent
b. revenus
c. tenez
d. viens
e. il y a
f. pendant
g. tiennent
h. depuis
i. devenue
j. venez
k. maintient

trois cent soixante-neuf **369**

Suggestions
- Explain that, when used as an interjection, **tiens/tenez** can mean either *here, here you,* or *hey,* depending on the context.
- Tell students that **retenir** means *to remember a piece of information.* Other uses of the verb *to remember* are expressed in French by **se rappeler** or **se souvenir**.
- Ask students questions like these to practice talking about time in the past: **Que faisiez-vous il y a trois ans? (J'étudiais au lycée il y a trois ans.) Depuis quand habitez-vous sur le campus? (J'habite sur le campus depuis le semestre dernier.)**
- Point out that French speakers may use a noun phrase after **depuis** where an English speaker would use a full clause (e.g., **depuis son arrivée à la fête** *since she got to the party*).

Essayez! After completing the activity, have students invent answers to items 1, 2, and 5. Then have them write questions that elicit the responses in items 3, 4, 6, 7, and 8.

O P T I O N S

Extra Practice Do a pattern practice drill. Give an infinitive of a verb like **venir** and ask individual students to provide conjugations for the different subject pronouns and/or names you suggest. Reverse the activity by saying a conjugated form and asking students to give the appropriate subject pronoun. Try this activity with the **passé composé** as well.

Game Divide the class into two teams. Indicate one team member at a time, alternating between teams. Give a verb in its infinitive form and a subject pronoun. The team member goes to the board to write and say the correct **passé récent** form. Give one point per correct answer. Deduct a point for each wrong answer. The team with the most points at the end of play wins.

1 **Expansion** Using magazine pictures, show images similar to those in the activity. Students should create sentences using **venir de**. Have volunteers show their pictures to the class and write their sentences on the board.

2 **Expansion** Have students work in pairs and create questions that correspond to the sentences in the activity. Example:
1. Depuis quand Georges est-il revenu de vacances?

3 **Suggestion** Before beginning the activity, review the **futur proche** form **aller** + [*infinitive*], taught in **Espace structures 4A.1.**

Mise en pratique

1 **Qu'est-ce qu'ils viennent de faire?** Regardez les images et dites ce qu'ils (*what they*) viennent de faire.

Jullen

MODÈLE

Julien vient de faire du cheval.

1. M. et Mme Martin
M. et Mme Martin viennent
d'aller au concert.

2. vous
Vous venez de dîner.

3. nous
Nous venons de jouer au
tennis.

4. je
Je viens de faire des courses.

2 **Mes tantes** Tante Olga téléphone à tante Simone pour lui donner des nouvelles (*news*) de la famille. Complétez ses phrases au passé composé.

1. La semaine dernière, Georges ___est revenu___ (revenir) de vacances.
2. Marc a déménagé, mais je ___n'ai pas retenu___ (ne pas retenir) sa nouvelle adresse.
3. J'ai rencontré Martine ce matin; elle ___est devenue___ (devenir) très jolie.
4. Alfred va avoir 100 ans; c'est parce qu'il ___a maintenu___ (maintenir) un bon rythme de vie.
5. Hier midi, Charles et Antoinette ___sont venus___ (venir) déjeuner à la maison.
6. Marie-Louise et Roland ___sont devenus___ (devenir) avocats.
7. La fille d'Albert ___n'est pas venue___ (ne pas venir) le voir le mois dernier.
8. Mélanie ___a tenu___ (tenir) son chien dans ses bras parce que les enfants avaient peur.

3 **Nos activités** Avec un(e) partenaire, dites ce que (*what*) chaque personne vient de faire et ce qu'elle va faire maintenant. Answers will vary.

MODÈLE

Je viens de manger. Maintenant, je vais faire la vaisselle.

A	B	C
je	manger	emménager
tu	faire la lessive	répondre
elle	recevoir une lettre	faire un séjour
nous	acheter une maison	faire la vaisselle
vous	partir en vacances	prendre le train
ils	faire ses valises	repasser le linge
on	faire les courses	cuisiner

 Practice more at **vhlcentral.com.**

Communication

4 Préparation de la fête Marine a invité ses amis ce soir. Elle a demandé à un(e) ami(e) de l'aider. Ils/Elles sont tous/toutes les deux impatient(e)s et ont besoin de savoir si tout est prêt. Avec un(e) partenaire, jouez les rôles de Marine et de son ami(e). Alternez les rôles et utilisez **venir de, il y a, depuis** et **pendant.** Answers will vary.

> **MODÈLE**
>
> **Étudiant(e) 1:** *Étienne a téléphoné?*
> **Étudiant(e) 2:** *Oui, il a téléphoné il y a une heure.*

1. Ta mère a apporté les gâteaux?
2. Tu as mis les fleurs dans le vase?
3. Pierre et Stéphanie ont fini de faire les courses?
4. Quand est-ce que tu as sorti les boissons?
5. Il faut mettre les escargots au four pendant longtemps?
6. Les salades de fruits sont dans le frigo?
7. Tu as préparé les tartes aux poires?
8. Ton petit ami est déjà arrivé?

5 Devinez À tour de rôle avec un(e) partenaire, devinez (*guess*) ce que Floriane et ses amis viennent de faire. Answers will vary.

> **MODÈLE**
>
> Michel débarrasse la table.
> *Il vient de dîner.*

1. Malika et moi, nous n'avons pas soif.
2. Josiane n'est pas à la maison.
3. Faroukh et Alisha ont dépensé beaucoup d'argent.
4. Vous êtes tout mouillés (*wet*).
5. Tu es très fatigué.
6. Hugo a l'air content.

6 Un(e) Américain(e) à Paris Vous venez de rencontrer un(e) Américain(e) de San Francisco (votre partenaire). Vous lui demandez de vous décrire sa vie à Paris, ses voyages, ce qui (*what*) l'intéresse, etc. Utilisez **depuis, il y a** et **pendant.** Ensuite, jouez la scène pour la classe. Answers will vary.

> **MODÈLE**
>
> **Étudiant(e) 1:** *Tu habites en France depuis longtemps?*
> **Étudiant(e) 2:** *Oui, j'habite à Paris depuis 2004.*

7 De nouveaux voisins Deux policiers (*police officers*) vous interrogent sur une famille mystérieuse qui vient d'emménager dans votre quartier. Par groupes de trois, jouez les rôles. Utilisez **depuis, il y a** et **pendant** dans votre conversation. Answers will vary.

> **MODÈLE**
>
> **Étudiant(e) 1:** *Quand est-ce que les Rocher ont emménagé?*
> **Étudiant(e) 2:** *Ils ont emménagé il y a trois mois.*
> **Étudiant(e) 1:** *D'habitude, qui est à la maison pendant la journée?*

---

4 Suggestions
• Ask two students to act out the **modèle**.
• Tell pairs to feel free to create additional questions that fit in the conversation.
• Have volunteers rehearse the conversation, then present it to the class.

6 Suggestion Before beginning the activity, remind students that each expression of time takes a different verb tense when referencing the past. A sentence with **pendant** usually uses the **passé composé** while **depuis** usually uses the **présent**.

7 Suggestion Have groups perform their conversation for the class to see which group came up with the most questions using the time expressions.

OPTIONS

Extra Practice Pass out a copy of a sample French C.V. Explain that the French use this abbreviation for the Latin term *curriculum vitæ* instead of *résumé*. Remind them that **un résumé** is a false cognate meaning *a summary*. Point out differences from an American C.V., such as the incorporation of age and other personal information. Have students invent a job and work in pairs to imagine that they must interview a candidate.

They should create a list of questions about the candidate's experience and leisure activities using expressions of time. Example: **Pendant combien de temps avez-vous travaillé à Paris?** Once students have created five questions, have them switch with other pairs and come up with answers. Example: **J'ai travaillé à Paris pendant trois ans.** Finally, have students role-play their interviews in front of the class.

Section Goals

In this section, students will learn the verbs **devoir**, **vouloir**, and **pouvoir**.

Instructional Resources

vhlcentral.com:
Activity Pack; Lab MP3s;
SAM Answer Key; **Essayez!**
and **Mise en pratique**
answers; Lab Audioscript;
reference tools

Suggestions

- Introduce **devoir**, **vouloir**, and **pouvoir** by taking a survey with questions like these: **Qui doit faire les courses cette semaine? Qui veut devenir chef de cuisine? Qui peut dîner avec moi au restaurant vendredi soir?** Summarize the results on the board.

- Write the conjugation of **devoir** on the board or on a transparency and model its pronunciation. Point out the **-s, -s, -t** pattern in the singular forms. Then write the conjugations of **vouloir** and **pouvoir**, noting the **-x, -x, -t** pattern.

- Explain the differences between **devoir** and **falloir**, since they express similar ideas in different ways. The former expresses an obligation, whereas the latter expresses necessity and can be more formal. Remind students that **falloir** is an impersonal verb that takes only third-person singular forms.

Leçon 9A

9A.2

BOÎTE À OUTILS

When you ask a question using inversion, the first person singular form of **pouvoir** changes.

Est-ce que je **peux** vous parler?

but

Puis-je vous parler?

ESPACE STRUCTURES

The verbs *devoir, vouloir, pouvoir*

 Tutorial

Point de départ The verbs **devoir** (*to have to [must]; to owe*), **vouloir** (*to want*), and **pouvoir** (*to be able to [can]*) are all irregular.

devoir, vouloir, pouvoir			
	devoir	**vouloir**	**pouvoir**
je	dois	veux	peux
tu	dois	veux	peux
il/elle/on	doit	veut	peut
nous	devons	voulons	pouvons
vous	devez	voulez	pouvez
ils/elles	doivent	veulent	peuvent

Je **dois** repasser.
I have to iron.

Veut-elle des pâtes?
Does she want pasta?

Vous **pouvez** entrer.
You can come in.

- **Devoir**, **vouloir**, and **pouvoir** all take **avoir** in the **passé composé**. They have irregular past participles.

devoir	dû
vouloir	voulu
pouvoir	pu

- **Devoir** can be used with an infinitive to mean *to have to* or *must*.

On **doit** manger tous les jours.
One must eat every day.

Je **dois** faire mes devoirs.
I have to do my homework.

- When **devoir** is followed by a noun, it means *to owe*.

Tu me **dois** cinq euros.
You owe me five euros.

Il **doit** sa vie aux médecins.
He owes his life to the doctors.

- **Devoir** is often used in the **passé composé** with an infinitive to speculate on what *must have happened* or what someone *had to do*. The context will determine the meaning.

Ils ne sont pas arrivés chez eux. Ils **ont dû avoir** un accident.
They haven't arrived home. They must have had an accident.

Louise n'est pas allée à la fête parce qu'elle **a dû travailler**.
Louise didn't go to the party because she had to work.

- **Devoir** can be used with an infinitive to express *supposed to*.

Nous ne **devons** pas parler en classe.
We're not supposed to talk in class.

Vous **deviez arriver** à huit heures.
You were supposed to arrive at 8 o'clock.

- When **vouloir** is used with the infinitive **dire**, it is translated as *to mean*.

Nous **voulons dire** exactement le contraire.
We mean exactly the opposite.

Biscuit? Ça **veut dire** «cookie» en français.
Biscuit? That means "cookie" in French.

> Sandrine devait être là. Elle a dû parler à son prof.

> Enfin, j'ai pu vous retrouver.

Suggestions
- Use magazine pictures to prompt students to make sentences using **devoir**, **vouloir**, and **pouvoir**. Example: picture of someone making a meal (**Elle doit préparer le dîner.**)
- Ask volunteers to translate sentences such as: *We must study for the exam tonight.* (**Nous devons préparer l'examen ce soir.**) *Have you managed to clean your room?* (**As-tu /Avez-vous pu nettoyer ta/votre chambre?**) *My parents refused to eat the meal I prepared.* (**Mes parents n'ont pas voulu manger le repas que j'ai préparé.**)
- Practice by asking the class more questions using the different meanings of **devoir**, **vouloir**, and **pouvoir**. Examples: **Que deviez-vous faire hier soir? Qui vous doit de l'argent? Que veut dire cette phrase? Voulez-vous voyager dans un autre pays? Avez-vous pu faire vos devoirs?**

Essayez! Have students rewrite the sentences in the past using the **passé composé** or the **imparfait**. Discuss whether the meaning changes. Example: **1. Tu devais …** (The meaning changes from *You have to…* to *You were supposed to….*)

- **Vouloir bien** can be used to express willingness.

Tu veux prendre de la glace?	Oui, je **veux bien** prendre de la glace.
Do you want to have some ice cream?	*Yes, I'd really like to have some ice cream.*

Voulez-vous dîner avec nous demain soir?	Nous **voulons bien** manger avec vous demain soir.
Do you want to have dinner with us tomorrow evening?	*We'd love to eat with you tomorrow evening.*

- **Vouloir** is often used in the **passé composé** with an infinitive in negative sentences to express *refused to*.

J'ai essayé, mais il **n'a pas voulu** parler.	Elles **n'ont pas voulu** débarrasser la table.
I tried, but he refused to talk.	*They refused to clear the table.*

Nous **n'avons pas voulu** aller chez lui.	Tu **n'as pas voulu** lui dire bonjour.
We refused to go to his house.	*You refused to say hello to him.*

- **Pouvoir** can be used in the **passé composé** with an infinitive to express *managed to do something*.

Nous **avons pu** tout finir.	Fathia **a pu** nous trouver.
We managed to finish everything.	*Fathia managed to find us.*

J'**ai pu** parler à l'avocat.	Vous **avez pu** acheter les billets?
I managed to talk to the lawyer.	*Did you manage to buy the tickets?*

Boîte à outils

Vouloir often takes the **imparfait** in the past since the action of wanting does not usually have a clear beginning or end and lasts an unspecified amount of time. In cases where the beginning or end is specified, use the **passé composé**.

Je voulais rire.
I wanted to laugh.
(no beginning or end)

Tout à coup, j'ai voulu rire.
All of a sudden, I felt like laughing.
(a specific moment in time)

Essayez! Complétez ces phrases avec les formes correctes du présent des verbes.

devoir

1. Tu _____dois_____ revenir à midi?
2. Elles _____doivent_____ manger tout de suite.
3. Nous _____devons_____ encore vingt euros.
4. Je ne _____dois_____ pas assister au pique-nique.
5. Elle _____doit_____ nous téléphoner.

vouloir

6. _____Voulez_____ -vous manger sur la terrasse?
7. Tu _____veux_____ quelque chose à boire?
8. Il _____veut_____ faire la cuisine.

9. Nous ne _____voulons_____ pas prendre de dessert.
10. Ils _____veulent_____ préparer un grand repas.

pouvoir

11. Je _____peux_____ passer l'aspirateur ce soir.
12. Il _____peut_____ acheter de l'ail au marché.
13. Elles _____peuvent_____ emménager demain.
14. Vous _____pouvez_____ maigrir de quelques kilos.
15. Nous _____pouvons_____ mettre la table.

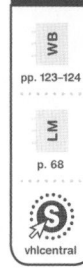

ressources

WB
pp. 123–124

LM
p. 68

vhlcentral

Video Replay the video episode, having students focus on the different uses of **devoir**, **vouloir**, and **pouvoir**. Stop the video where appropriate to discuss how they are used in the conversation and to ask comprehension questions. Example: **À quelle heure doivent-ils arriver chez Sandrine?**

Extra Practice Write a pattern sentence on the board. Example: **Nous ne voulons pas étudier.** Have students copy the model and then dictate a list of different subjects like **Charles, je, les étudiants,** etc. Have students write down the subjects and supply the correct verb form. Ask volunteers to read their answers aloud. Repeat using various forms of **devoir**, **vouloir**, and **pouvoir** expressions.

ESPACE STRUCTURES

1 Expansion Have students create three sentences modeled on those in the activity for their partner to complete. Write some on the board and have the class use the appropriate forms of **devoir**, **vouloir**, and **pouvoir** to complete the sentences.

2 Expansion Have students imagine they are planning a class party and everyone must help out. Ask the class: **Qui peut faire quoi?**

3 Suggestion Have two students act out the **modèle**.

3 Expansion Have pairs repeat this activity in the first and second person, using affirmative and negative sentences with **vouloir**.

Mise en pratique

1 **Que doit-on faire?** Qu'est-ce que ces personnes doivent faire pour avoir ce qu'elles (*what they*) veulent?

MODÈLE André ___*veut*___ courir le marathon, alors il ___*doit*___ faire du jogging.

1. Je ___*veux*___ grossir, alors je ___*dois*___ manger des frites.
2. Il ___*veut*___ être en forme, alors il ___*doit*___ aller à la gym.
3. Vous ___*voulez*___ manger des spaghettis, alors vous ___*devez*___ aller dans un resto italien.
4. Tu ___*veux*___ manger chez toi, alors tu ___*dois*___ faire la cuisine.
5. Elles ___*veulent*___ maigrir, alors elles ___*doivent*___ moins manger.
6. Nous ___*voulons*___ écouter de la musique, alors nous ___*devons*___ acheter des CD.

2 **Qui peut faire quoi?** Ève prépare un grand repas. Dites ce que (*what*) chaque personne peut faire.

MODÈLE

Joseph / faire / courses
Joseph peut faire les courses.

1. Marc / acheter / boissons   Marc peut acheter les boissons.
2. Benoît et Anne / préparer / gâteaux   Benoît et Anne peuvent préparer des gâteaux.
3. Jean et toi / décorer / salle à manger   Jean et toi pouvez décorer la salle à manger.
4. Patrick et moi / essuyer / verres   Patrick et moi pouvons essuyer les verres.
5. je / prendre / photos   Je peux prendre des photos.
6. tu / mettre / table   Tu peux mettre la table.

3 **Mes enfants** M. Dion est au restaurant avec ses enfants. Le serveur/ La serveuse lui demande ce qu'ils (*what they*) veulent prendre. Avec un(e) partenaire, posez les questions et répondez. Alternez les rôles. Answers will vary.

MODÈLE Éric: ou

Étudiant(e) 1: *Veut-il un jus d'orange ou un verre de lait?*
Étudiant(e) 2: *Il veut un jus d'orange, s'il vous plaît.*

1. Michèle:  ou

2. Stéphanie et Éric:  ou

3. Stéphanie:  ou

4. Éric: ou

 Practice more at **vhlcentral.com**.

Communication

4 **Que faire?** À tour de rôle avec un(e) partenaire, dites ce que (*what*) ces personnes peuvent, doivent ou veulent faire ou ne pas faire. Utilisez **pouvoir**, **devoir** et **vouloir** dans vos réponses. Answers will vary.

▶ **MODÈLE**

Étudiant(e) 1: *Il veut maigrir.*

Étudiant(e) 2: *Il ne peut pas manger de dessert.*

1. 2.

3. 4. 5. 6.

5 **Ce n'est pas de ma faute.** Préparez une liste de cinq choses qui vous sont arrivées (*happened to you*) par accident. Montrez la liste à un(e) partenaire, qui va deviner pourquoi. A-t-il/elle raison? Answers will vary.

MODÈLE

Étudiant(e) 1: *J'ai perdu les clés de ma maison.*
Étudiant(e) 2: *Tu as dû les laisser sur ton lit.*

6 **Ce week-end** Invitez vos camarades de classe à faire des choses avec vous le week-end prochain. S'ils refusent votre invitation, ils doivent vous donner une excuse. Quelles réponses avez-vous reçues (*received*)? Answers will vary.

MODÈLE

Étudiant(e) 1: *Tu veux jouer au tennis avec moi le week-end prochain?*
Étudiant(e) 2: *Quel jour?*
Étudiant(e) 1: *Samedi matin.*
Étudiant(e) 2: *Désolé(e), je ne peux pas. Je dois rendre visite à ma famille.*

7 **La permission** La mère de Sylvain lui permet de faire certaines choses mais pas d'autres. Avec un(e) partenaire, préparez leur dialogue. Utilisez les verbes **devoir**, **vouloir** et **pouvoir**. Answers will vary.

MODÈLE

Étudiant(e) 1: *Maman, je veux sortir avec Paul vendredi.*
Étudiant(e) 2: *Tu peux sortir, mais tu dois d'abord ranger ta chambre.*

8 **Des conseils** Votre ami(e) a beaucoup de problèmes et vous demande des conseils (*advice*). Avec un(e) partenaire, préparez le dialogue. Utilisez le verbe **devoir** pour lui faire des suggestions. Answers will vary.

MODÈLE

Étudiant(e) 1: *Je ne peux pas dormir la nuit.*
Étudiant(e) 2: *Tu ne dois pas boire de café après le dîner.*

4 **Suggestion** Call on volunteer pairs to say aloud what the people want and what they have to do to attain their goal.

4 **Expansion** Use photos or magazine pictures to extend the activity. Choose pictures that lend themselves to sentences using **devoir**, **vouloir**, and **pouvoir**.

5 **Suggestion** Have pairs form groups of four, switch lists, and discuss the reasons why each thing happened. Tell students to suggest alternate or better reasons whenever possible.

6 **Suggestions**
• Ask two students to act out the **modèle**.
• Before doing the activity, review different ways to refuse an invitation politely using **devoir**, **vouloir**, and **pouvoir**.

7 **Suggestions** Have volunteers act out their conversations for the class.

OPTIONS

Small Groups In groups of three or four, tell each student to write three sentences using different forms of **devoir**, **vouloir**, and **pouvoir**. Two of the sentences must be true, and one of them must be false. The other members of the group have to guess which of the sentences is false. This can also be done with the whole class.

Pairs Have students imagine they are going on vacation. Ask them to make a list of tasks **à faire...** (a "to do" list) using **devoir** to prepare for the trip. Example: **1. Avant de partir, je dois faire la lessive.** Then have them create a list of things they can or want to do on the trip using **pouvoir** and **vouloir**. Example: **1. On peut bronzer à la plage. 2. Je veux faire une randonnée.** Call on volunteers to present their lists to the class.

ESPACE **SYNTHÈSE**

Révision

Instructional Resources
vhlcentral.com:
Activity Pack (Info Gap
Activities); Testing Program;
Testing Program MP3s;
reference tools

1 Suggestion Before
assigning this activity, briefly
review the **passé récent** with
venir de + *infinitive.* Remind
students that this tense conveys
a different meaning than the
passé composé.

2 Expansion Have the students
state that the mother or father
refused to purchase the item
for the child using **vouloir** in
the **passé composé.** Example:
**La mère n'a pas voulu acheter
de confiture.**

3 Expansion Have volunteers
make comments to the chefs or
ask them questions about their
recipes. Example: **Je n'aime pas
les carottes. Est-ce qu'on peut
utiliser des tomates?**

4 Suggestion Before assigning
the activity, ask the students
questions using the construction
Depuis combien de temps…?
Review the different ways to
answer (**il y a** + *time period* and
depuis + *time period*).

5 Suggestion Have two
students act out the **modèle**
before assigning this activity.

5 Expansion Have pairs write
down their conversation. Call on
pairs to perform it for the class.

6 Suggestions
- Act out the **modèle** with
  a volunteer.
- Divide the class into pairs and
  distribute the Info Gap Handouts
  found in the Activity Pack on
  the Supersite. Give students ten
  minutes to complete the activity.

1 Au restaurant Avec un(e) partenaire, dites ce que
(*what*) ces personnes viennent de faire. Utilisez les verbes
de la liste et d'autres verbes. Answers will vary.

apporter	manger
arriver	parler
boire	prendre
demander	téléphoner

2 Au supermarché Un(e) enfant et son père ou sa
mère sont au supermarché. L'enfant demande ces choses à
manger, mais le père ou la mère ne veut pas les acheter et
doit lui donner des raisons. Avec un(e) partenaire, préparez
un dialogue, puis jouez-le pour la classe. Employez les verbes
devoir, vouloir et **pouvoir** et le passé récent. Answers will vary.

MODÈLE

Étudiant(e) 1: *Maman, je veux de la confiture. Achète-moi
cette confiture, s'il te plaît.*
Étudiant(e) 2: *Tu ne dois pas manger ça. Tu viens de
manger un dessert.*

du chocolat	une glace
des chips	du pâté
un coca	une saucisse
de la confiture	des yaourts aux fruits

3 Le chef de cuisine Vous et votre partenaire êtes deux
chefs. Expliquez à votre partenaire comment préparer votre
salade préférée. Donnez des conseils (*advice*) avec les verbes
devoir, vouloir et **pouvoir** et employez le passé récent.
Answers will vary.

MODÈLE

Étudiant(e) 1: *Combien de carottes doit-on utiliser?*
Étudiant(e) 2: *On peut utiliser deux ou trois carottes.*

4 Dans le frigo Vous et vos partenaires êtes colocataires
et vous nettoyez votre frigo. Qu'allez-vous mettre à la poubelle?
Par groupes de trois, regardez l'illustration et décidez. Ensuite,
présentez vos décisions à la classe. Answers will vary.

MODÈLE

Étudiant(e) 1: *Depuis combien de temps a-t-on ce fromage
dans le frigo?*
Étudiant(e) 2: *Je viens de l'acheter, nous pouvons le garder
encore un peu.*

5 Chez moi Vous et votre partenaire voulez manger ensemble
après les cours. Vous voulez manger chez vous ou chez votre
partenaire, mais pas au resto U. Que pouvez-vous préparer?
Que voulez-vous manger ou boire? Answers will vary.

MODÈLE

Étudiant(e) 1: *Chez moi, j'ai du chocolat et du lait,
et je peux te faire un chocolat chaud.*
Étudiant(e) 2: *Non merci, je veux plutôt une boisson
froide et j'ai des boissons gazeuses à la maison.*

6 Une journée bien occupée Votre professeur va vous
donner, à vous et à votre partenaire, une feuille sur les activités
d'Alexandra. Attention! Ne regardez pas la feuille de votre
partenaire. Answers will vary.

MODÈLE

Étudiant(e) 1: *À quatre heures et demie, Alexandra
a pu faire du jogging.*
Étudiant(e) 2: *Après, à cinq heures, elle…*

OPTIONS

Extra Practice Have students write a "how to" paragraph
describing a simple task without using commands, but rather
the **vous** forms of **devoir, vouloir,** and **pouvoir.** Example: **faire un
sandwich—D'abord, vous devez prendre du pain. Vous pouvez
mettre du fromage si vous voulez. Ensuite, …** The paragraph
should include five or six basic directions and use vocabulary
from this lesson and previous lessons. Then have students
exchange their papers with classmates who will ask questions
for clarification and provide suggestions for peer editing. Call on
volunteers to share their paragraphs with the class. Have one
volunteer read an instructional paragraph while another student
follows the instructions in front of the class. Encourage the use
of props. Have students explain any mistakes they notice.

Flash CULTURE

La nourriture

Hôtesse: Csilla

Csilla est au marché d'Aix-en-Provence. Comme tous les matins, il y a beaucoup de vendeurs de fruits et de légumes sur la place Richelme. On peut aussi y trouver de belles fleurs que Csilla adore. L'ambiance est calme et agréable, et les gens font leurs courses tranquillement en plein air° et mettent leurs achats dans leurs paniers°.

Avant de regarder Répondez aux questions. *Answers will vary*

1. Quels sont vos aliments préférés? Aimez-vous les légumes? Aimez-vous les fruits?

2. Où est-ce que votre famille fait les courses?

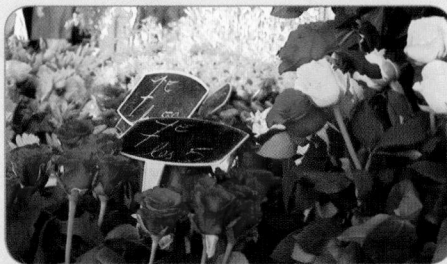

CSILLA *Sur les marchés, on vend des fleurs.*

CSILLA *Il y a des baguettes et du pain de campagne.*

Compréhension Répondez aux questions.

1. Quels sont les types d'aliments présentés par Csilla dans la vidéo?
   Csilla nous montre des légumes, des fruits, des fruits de mer, de la charcuterie, du fromage et du pain.

2. Quels sont les légumes que Csilla nous montre? *Csilla nous montre des carottes, des pommes de terre, des tomates, des haricots verts et des poivrons rouges.*

3. Qu'est-ce que Csilla pense faire avec les fraises?
   Csilla pense faire une tarte aux fraises.

4. Quel est le genre de repas que Csilla va organiser?
   Csilla va organiser un pique-nique.

Discussion Par groupes de trois, répondez aux questions.

1. Existe-t-il des marchés en plein air chez vous? Si oui, est-ce que votre famille et vous achetez vos aliments dans ces marchés?

2. Quels sont les aliments que vous aimez acheter au marché ou au supermarché?

en plein air *outdoors* **paniers** *baskets*

Vocabulaire utile

les aliments (*m.***) bio**	*organic food*
Ça sent bon!	*That smells good!*
C'est sympa, non?	*That's nice, no?*
le marché fermier	*farmer's market*

ressources

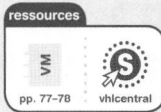

VM
pp. 77–78

vhlcentral

Practice more at **vhlcentral.com.**

trois cent soixante-dix-sept **377**

Section Goals

In this section, students will:
- watch a video about a farmers' market in Aix-en-Provence
- answer questions about the video and describe personal preferences about food shopping

Instructional Resources
vhlcentral.com: **Flash culture**;
Flash culture *transcription;
reference tools*

Avant de regarder la vidéo
- Have students look at the video stills, read the captions, and predict what will happen in this episode.
- Explain to students that they don't need to understand every word they hear. Tell them to listen for vocabulary from this lesson as well as cognates.

Compréhension Have students work in pairs or groups. Tell them to write down their answers. Then, show the video again so that they can check their answers and add any missing information.

Vocabulaire utile Tell students that **bio** is short for **biologique**. The abbreviated form is invariable: **les aliments biologiques** but **les aliments bio.**

Discussion Have students work in groups of three or four to share and compare their shopping preferences. Then, take a class survey to find out where students like to shop and what foods they like to buy.

O P T I O N S

La place Richelme
Since the 14th century, **place Richelme** has been home to markets and vendors selling fresh produce. Today, a small market is held here every morning. Originally called the **place aux Herbes**, the square was renamed **Richelme** in the 19th century in honor of Louis-Fernand Richelme, a celebrated tenor born in Aix-en-Provence.

Le Grand Marché
Three times a week, Aix-en-Provence's **Grand Marché** is held along the **cours Mirabeau**, famous for its charming fountains. On Saturdays, the city center is filled with market stalls, where shoppers can find textiles, clothing, handmade objects, antiques, flowers, and fresh produce. Artists are also on hand to promote their wares.

Section Goals

In this section, students will learn and practice vocabulary related to:

- setting the table
- eating in a restaurant
- shopping for food

Instructional Resources

vhlcentral.com:
Digital Image Bank
(including vocabulary
illustrations from the textbook,
theme-based illustrations);
Vocabulaire supplémentaire;
Mise en pratique *answers;*
Textbook Audioscript; Lab
Audioscript; Activity Pack (Info
Gap Activities); Textbook MP3s;
Lab MP3s; SAM Answer Key;
reference tools

Suggestions

- Use the **9B Contextes** illustration from the Digital Image Bank. Describe what people are doing, then point out eating utensils and other items on the tables. Examples: **Le serveur apporte la carte. La femme commande. C'est une fourchette à côté de la serviette.**
- Ask students simple questions based on your narrative. Example: **Que fait le chef?**
- Bring in items for setting the table. Hold up each one and ask: **Qu'est-ce que c'est?**
- Point out that **une entrée** is *an appetizer*, not *a main course* as in English.
- Point out that **une assiette** is *a plate*, and **un plat** is *a serving dish* or the *food on the serving dish.*
- Explain the **faux ami: commander** means *to order*, not *to command*.
- Bring in photos from magazines or the Internet to introduce the names of the shops listed. Say: **C'est une boulangerie. On vend du pain à la boulangerie.**
- Additional vocabulary for this lesson can be found in the **Vocabulaire supplémentaire** on the Supersite.
- Use the Vocabulary illustrations and the Food and restaurant dining illustrations from the Digital Image Bank to help students familiarize themselves with eating in a restaurant and shopping for food.

Leçon **9B**

S Vocabulary Tools

À table!

You will learn how to...
- describe and discuss food
- shop for food

Vocabulaire

être au régime	to be on a diet
une boîte (de conserve)	can
la crème	cream
la mayonnaise	mayonnaise
la moutarde	mustard
une tranche	slice
une entrée	appetizer, starter
un hors-d'œuvre	hors-d'oeuvre, appetizer
un plat (principal)	(main) dish
À table!	Let's eat!/Food is ready!
compris	included
une boucherie	butcher's shop
une boulangerie	bread shop, bakery
une charcuterie	delicatessen
un(e) commerçant(e)	shopkeeper
un kilo(gramme)	kilo(gram)
une pâtisserie	pastry shop, bakery; pastry
une poissonnerie	fish shop

ressources

WB	LM	S
pp. 125–126	p. 69	vhlcentral

378 *trois cent soixante-dix-huit*

Il goûte la soupe. (goûter)

l'assiette (f.)

la carte

la serviette

la fourchette

le couteau

la nappe

O P T I O N S

Game On index cards, write vocabulary words related to setting the table. On another set of cards, draw or paste pictures for each term. Tape them face down on the board. Divide the class into two teams. Then play a game of concentration in which students match words with pictures. When a player makes a match, that player's team collects those cards. The team with the most cards at the end of the game wins.

Extra Practice Say the names of foods and have students respond with the type of store that sells each item. Examples: **un steak (une boucherie), des fruits de mer (une poissonnerie), des saucisses (une charcuterie/une boucherie), du pain (une boulangerie), de la moutarde (une épicerie), un gâteau (une pâtisserie), du pâté (une charcuterie),** and **du thon (une poissonnerie).**

Mise en pratique

1 Écoutez Catherine est au régime. Elle parle de ses habitudes alimentaires. Écoutez et indiquez si les affirmations suivantes sont **vraies** ou **fausses**.

	Vrai	Faux
1. Catherine mange beaucoup de desserts.	☐	☑
2. Catherine fait les courses au supermarché.	☐	☑
3. Elle adore la viande.	☐	☑
4. Elle est au régime.	☑	☐
5. Catherine achète des fruits et des légumes au marché.	☑	☐
6. Selon (*According to*) Catherine, le service chez les commerçants est désagréable.	☐	☑
7. Elle va souvent à la boucherie et à la poissonnerie.	☐	☑
8. Elle vient de devenir végétarienne.	☑	☐

2 Le repas Mettez ces différentes étapes dans l'ordre chronologique.

_5_ a. dire «À table!»

_7_ b. servir le plat principal

_4_ c. mettre les assiettes, les fourchettes, les cuillères et les couteaux sur la table

_6_ d. servir l'entrée

_2_ e. faire les courses

_1_ f. organiser un menu

_8_ g. goûter le dessert avec les invités

_3_ h. faire la cuisine

3 Complétez Complétez ces phrases avec le bon mot.

1. Pour manger de la soupe, on utilise...
   a. un couteau.
   b. une cuillère.
   c. une fourchette.

2. On sert la soupe dans...
   a. une assiette.
   b. une carafe.
   c. un bol.

3. Au restaurant, le serveur/ la serveuse doit... la nourriture.
   a. commander
   b. apporter
   c. goûter

4. On vend des baguettes à...
   a. la boulangerie.
   b. la charcuterie.
   c. la boucherie.

5. On met... dans le café.
   a. du beurre
   b. du poivre
   c. de la crème

6. On vend des gâteaux à...
   a. la boucherie.
   b. la pâtisserie.
   c. la poissonnerie.

7. Au restaurant, on commande d'abord...
   a. une entrée.
   b. un plat principal.
   c. une serviette.

8. On vend du jambon à...
   a. la charcuterie.
   b. la boucherie.
   c. la pâtisserie.

Image labels:
- Elle commande. (commander)
- le menu
- le sel
- le poivre
- l'huile d'olive (f.)
- la carafe d'eau
- le bol
- la cuillère à soupe
- la cuillère à café

1 Audioscript Je suis au régime, alors je ne peux pas manger beaucoup de desserts, ou bien, de pain en général. Parfois, je vais à la boulangerie et j'achète des croissants pour le petit-déjeuner, mais je les prends sans confiture. Quand je mange une salade, je n'utilise jamais d'huile d'olive. Je fais très attention à ce que je mange et je ne mets pas trop de sel dans mes plats. J'utilise très peu de poivre parce que je n'aime pas beaucoup ça. Chaque semaine, quand je fais les courses, je vais à la boulangerie pour acheter du pain. Pour les fruits et les légumes, je vais au marché. Je vais rarement au supermarché; je préfère aller chez les commerçants parce que le service est très agréable. Je ne vais jamais ni à la boucherie ni à la poissonnerie parce que je viens de devenir végétarienne. *(On Textbook MP3s)*

1 Suggestion Have students read the true/false sentences before they listen to the recording.

2 Suggestion Have students form groups of eight. Make a set of individual phrases on strips of paper for each group and distribute them. Tell students to arrange the phrases in the proper order and then read them aloud.

3 Expansion For additional practice, give students these items. **9. Pour manger du bœuf, on utilise _____. (une fourchette et un couteau) 10. On sert de la salade dans _____. (un bol/une assiette) 11. Au restaurant, après l'entrée, on mange _____. (le plat principal) 12. On vend du pâté dans les _____. (charcuteries)**

OPTIONS

Mettre la table A typical French table setting in a restaurant has at least two stemmed glasses per person. If they are not the same size, the larger goblet is for water and the smaller one is for wine. In more formal table settings, there may be several glasses for different types of wine. Champagne is served in tall glasses called **flûtes** or in large shallow glasses called **coupes**; white wine may be served in smaller glasses than red wine. When placing cutlery, knives go on the right with the blade turned toward the plate, and forks go on the left, tines down. Soupspoons are placed next to the forks, on the outside. Teaspoons or dessert forks belong above the plate. A formal French place setting may also include **un porte-couteau**, which serves to protect the tablecloth.

Communication

NATIONAL communication STANDARDS

4 **Conversez** Interviewez un(e) camarade de classe. Answers will vary.

1. En général, qu'est-ce que tu commandes au restaurant comme entrée? Comme plat principal?
2. Qui fait les courses chez toi? Où? Quand?
3. Est-ce que tu préfères faire les courses au supermarché ou chez les commerçants? Pourquoi?
4. Es-tu au régime? Qu'est-ce que tu manges?
5. Quel est ton plat principal préféré?
6. Aimes-tu la moutarde? Avec quel(s) plat(s) l'utilises-tu?
7. Aimes-tu la mayonnaise? Avec quel(s) plat(s) l'utilises-tu?
8. Dans quel(s) plat(s) mets-tu de l'huile d'olive?

5 **Sept différences** Votre professeur va vous donner, à vous et à votre partenaire, deux feuilles d'activités différentes avec le dessin (*drawing*) d'un restaurant. Il y a sept différences entre les deux images. Sans regarder l'image de votre partenaire, comparez vos dessins et faites une liste de ces différences. Quel est le groupe le plus rapide de la classe? Answers will vary.

> **MODÈLE**
>
> **Étudiant(e) 1:** *Dans mon restaurant, le serveur apporte du beurre à la table.*
> **Étudiant(e) 2:** *Dans mon restaurant aussi, on apporte du beurre à la table, mais c'est une serveuse, pas un serveur.*

6 **Au restaurant** Travaillez avec deux camarades de classe pour présenter ce dialogue. Answers will vary.

- Une personne invite un(e) ami(e) à dîner au restaurant.
- Une personne est le serveur/la serveuse et décrit le menu.
- Vous parlez du menu et de vos préférences.
- Une personne est au régime et ne peut pas manger certains ingrédients.
- Vous commandez les plats.
- Vous parlez des plats que vous mangez.

7 **Écriture** Écrivez un paragraphe dans lequel vous: Answers will vary.

- parlez de la dernière fois que vous avez préparé un dîner, un déjeuner ou un petit-déjeuner pour quelqu'un.
- décrivez les ingrédients que vous avez utilisés pour préparer le(s) plat(s).
- mentionnez les endroits où vous avez acheté les ingrédients et leurs quantités.
- décrivez comment vous avez mis la table.

Instructor's sidebar (left column)

4 **Suggestions**
- Before beginning the activity, give students a few minutes to think about their responses to these questions.
- Tell students to take notes during their interviews. Then have volunteers share their partner's responses with the class.

5 **Suggestion** Have two volunteers read the **modèle** aloud. Then divide the class into pairs and distribute the Info Gap Handouts found in the Activity Pack on the Supersite. Give students ten minutes to complete the activity.

6 **Suggestion** Give each group a menu from a real French restaurant to use in their role-plays. Many restaurants include sample menus on their websites.

7 **Suggestions**
- Before beginning the activity, have students describe what they see in the drawing.
- Have students exchange paragraphs for peer editing. Students should make sure all required elements are included and underline grammar and spelling errors.

O P T I O N S

Game Toss a beanbag to a student at random and say the name of a store from this lesson or a previous one. The person has four seconds to name a food that is sold there. That person then tosses the beanbag to another student and names a store. Students who cannot think of a food in time or who repeat an item that has already been mentioned are eliminated. The last person standing wins.

Small Groups Have groups of students plan a dinner party for a group of celebrities. Tell them to decide who will attend and what foods will be served. The meal should include several courses and appropriate beverages. You might want to bring in French cookbooks or food magazines for students' reference. Have the class vote on the most delicious-sounding meal and the most interesting guest list.

Les sons et les lettres
  Audio

Stress and rhythm

In French, all syllables are pronounced with more or less equal stress, but the final syllable in a phrase is elongated slightly.

Je fais souvent du sport, mais aujourd'hui, j'ai envie de rester à la maison.

French sentences are divided into three basic kinds of rhythmic groups.

Noun phrase	*Verb phrase*	*Prepositional phrase*
Caroline et Dominique	**sont venues**	**chez moi.**

The final syllable of a rhythmic group may be slightly accentuated either by rising intonation (pitch) or elongation.

Caroline et Dominique sont venues chez moi.

In English, you can add emphasis by placing more stress on certain words. In French, you can emphasize the word by adding the corresponding pronoun or you can elongate the first consonant sound.

Je ne sais pas, moi.   **Quel idiot!**   **C'est fantastique!**

Prononcez Répétez les phrases suivantes à voix haute.

1. Ce n'est pas vrai, ça.
2. Bonjour, Mademoiselle.
3. Moi, je m'appelle Florence.
4. La clé de ma chambre, je l'ai perdue.
5. Je voudrais un grand café noir et un croissant, s'il vous plaît.
6. Nous allons tous au marché, mais Marie, elle va au centre commercial.

Articulez Répétez les phrases en mettant l'emphase (*by emphasizing*) sur les mots indiqués.

1. C'est *impossible*!
2. Le film était *super*!
3. Cette tarte est *délicieuse*!
4. Quelle idée *extraordinaire*!
5. Ma sœur parle *constamment*.

Dictons Répétez les dictons à voix haute.

> Le chat parti, les souris dansent.[2]

> Les chemins les plus courts ne sont pas toujours les meilleurs.[1]

[1] The shortest paths aren't always the best.
[2] When the cat is away, the mice will play.

ressources

LM
p. 70

S
vhlcentral

Section Goals

In this section, students will learn about:
- stress and rhythm
- a strategy for emphasizing a word

Instructional Resources
vhlcentral.com:
Textbook MP3s; Lab MP3s;
SAM Answer Key;
Textbook Audioscript;
Lab Audioscript;
reference tools

Suggestions
- Model the pronunciation of the example sentences and have students repeat after you.
- Write these sentences from the **Roman-photo** in **Leçon 9A** on the board or a transparency.
  1. **Mais quelle heure est-il?**
  2. **Bon, une salade, si tu veux.**
  3. **Mais le bœuf bourguignon, c'est long à préparer, non?**
  4. **Il nous faut des champignons, du jambon et du fromage.**
  Say the sentences and have students repeat after you. Alternately, have students read the entire video episode aloud in small groups, focusing on correct stress and rhythm.
- Have students read the sentences in the **Articulez** activity more than once, using a variety of methods to place emphasis on the appropriate words, for example, pauses before the word or between syllables.
- Prepare a handout that has several sentences with varied rhythm and stress. Tell students to draw arrows to mark rising and falling intonation as you read the sentences aloud.

OPTIONS

Extra Practice Use these sentences for additional practice with stress and rhythm or as a dictation. **1. Ils préfèrent aller au cinéma. 2. Mon anniversaire, c'est le 14 octobre. 3. Charlotte est professeur d'anglais dans un lycée en France. 4. Pour mes vacances, il me faut un maillot de bain, un short et des lunettes de soleil.**

Extra Practice To practice varying stress and rhythm, teach students these French tongue-twisters. **1. Mur pourrit, trou s'y fit, rat s'y mit; chat l'y vit, rat s'enfuit; chat suivit, rat fut pris. 2. Bonjour, Madame Sans Souci. Combien sont ces six saucissons-ci et combien sont ces six saucissons-là? Six sous, Madame, sont ces six saucissons-ci et six sous aussi sont ces six saucissons-là!**

Section Goals

In this section, students will learn functional phrases for making comparisons and discussing a meal.

Instructional Resources

vhlcentral.com:
Roman-photo Video, Videoscript, and Translation; SAM Answer Key; reference tools

Video Recap: Leçon 9A

Review the previous **Roman-photo** with this activity.
1. Pourquoi Sandrine a-t-elle retrouvé Amina et David au supermarché? (pour faire les courses pour son dîner)
2. Pourquoi Stéphane a-t-il voulu parler à Sandrine? (Il a voulu savoir à quelle heure il doit arriver chez elle et s'il doit apporter quelque chose.)
3. Qu'est-ce que Sandrine a décidé de préparer? (un poulet à la crème aux champignons avec un gratin de pommes de terre)
4. Qui a payé les courses au supermarché? (Amina et David)

Video Synopsis

David runs into Rachid in town. Rachid has bought a box of chocolates for Sandrine. David decides to buy her a bouquet of flowers. That evening, the guests arrive at Sandrine's. Sandrine is pleased with her gifts. Amina and Stéphane finish setting the table, and they all sit down to eat. The meal is a great success, and everyone compliments Sandrine on her cooking.

Suggestions

- Have students predict what the episode will be about based on the title and video stills.
- Point out that, in **que j'aie jamais reçues,** the subjunctive is used with the superlative.
- After reading the **Roman-photo**, review students' predictions and have them summarize the episode.

Le dîner Video

PERSONNAGES

 Amina

 David

 Rachid

 Sandrine

 Stéphane

 Valérie

Au centre-ville...

DAVID Qu'est-ce que tu as fait en ville?
RACHID Des courses à la boulangerie et chez le chocolatier.
DAVID Tu as acheté ces chocolats pour Sandrine?
RACHID Pourquoi? Tu es jaloux? Ne t'en fais pas! Elle nous a invités. Il est normal d'apporter quelque chose.

DAVID Je n'ai pas de cadeau pour elle. Qu'est-ce que je peux lui acheter? Je peux lui apporter des fleurs!
Chez le fleuriste...
DAVID Ces roses sont très jolies, non?
RACHID Tu es tombé amoureux?
DAVID Mais non! Pourquoi tu dis ça?
RACHID Des roses, c'est romantique.
DAVID Ah... Ces fleurs-ci sont jolies. C'est mieux?

RACHID Non, c'est pire! Les chrysanthèmes sont réservés aux funérailles.
DAVID Hmmm. Je ne savais pas que c'était aussi difficile de choisir un bouquet de fleurs!
RACHID Regarde! Celles-là sont parfaites!
DAVID Tu es sûr?
RACHID Sûr et certain, achète-les!

AMINA Sandrine, est-ce qu'on peut faire quelque chose pour t'aider?
SANDRINE Oui, euh, vous pouvez finir de mettre la table, si vous voulez.
VALÉRIE Je vais t'aider dans la cuisine.
AMINA Tiens, Stéphane. Voilà le sel et le poivre. Tu peux les mettre sur la table, s'il te plaît?
SANDRINE À table!

SANDRINE Je vous sers autre chose? Une deuxième tranche de tarte aux pommes peut-être?
VALÉRIE Merci.
AMINA Merci. Je suis au régime.
SANDRINE Et toi, David?
DAVID Oh! J'ai trop mangé. Je n'en peux plus!
STÉPHANE Moi, je veux bien...
SANDRINE Donne-moi ton assiette.

STÉPHANE Tiens, tu peux la lui passer, s'il te plaît?
VALÉRIE Quel repas fantastique, Sandrine. Tu as beaucoup de talent, tu sais.
RACHID Vous avez raison, Madame Forestier. Ton poulet aux champignons était superbe!

A C T I V I T É S

1 **Vrai ou faux?** Indiquez si ces affirmations sont **vraies** ou **fausses.** Corrigez les phrases fausses. Answers may vary.

1. Rachid est allé chez le chocolatier. Vrai.
2. Rachid et David sont arrivés en avance. Faux. Rachid et David sont arrivés en retard.
3. David n'a pas apporté de cadeau. Faux. David a apporté des fleurs.
4. Sandrine aime les fleurs de David. Vrai.
5. Personne (*Nobody*) n'aide Sandrine. Faux. Valérie, Amina et Stéphane aident Sandrine.

6. David n'a pas beaucoup mangé. Faux. David a trop mangé.
7. Stéphane n'est pas au régime. Vrai.
8. Sandrine a fait une tarte aux pêches pour le dîner. Faux. Sandrine a fait une tarte aux pommes.
9. Les plats de Sandrine ne sont pas très bons. Faux. Les plats de Sandrine sont bons.
10. Les invités ont passé une soirée très agréable. Vrai.

 Practice more at vhlcentral.com.

O P T I O N S

Avant de regarder la vidéo Before viewing the video, have students brainstorm a list of things people might say at a dinner party. What expressions might they use before, during, and after a meal? Write the list on the board.

Regarder la vidéo Download and print the videoscript found on the Supersite. Then white out words related to meals, eating, and other key vocabulary in order to create a master for a cloze activity. Distribute the photocopies and tell students to fill in the missing information as they watch the video episode.

Sandrine a préparé un repas fantastique pour ses amis.

Chez Sandrine...

SANDRINE Bonsoir... Entrez! Oh!

DAVID Tiens. C'est pour toi.

SANDRINE Oh, David! Il ne fallait pas, c'est très gentil!

DAVID Je voulais t'apporter quelque chose.

SANDRINE Ce sont les plus belles fleurs que j'aie jamais reçues! Merci!

RACHID Bonsoir, Sandrine.

SANDRINE Oh, du chocolat! Merci beaucoup.

RACHID J'espère qu'on n'est pas trop en retard.

SANDRINE Pas du tout! Venez! On est dans la salle à manger.

STÉPHANE Oui, et tes desserts sont les meilleurs! C'est la tarte la plus délicieuse du monde!

SANDRINE Vous êtes adorables, merci. Moi, je trouve que cette tarte aux pommes est meilleure que la tarte aux pêches que j'ai faite il y a quelques semaines.

AMINA Tout ce que tu prépares est bon, Sandrine.

DAVID À Sandrine, le chef de cuisine le plus génial!

TOUS À Sandrine!

Expressions utiles

Making comparisons and judgments

- **Ces fleurs-ci sont jolies. C'est mieux?**
  These flowers are pretty. Is that better?
- **C'est pire! Les chrysanthèmes sont réservés aux funérailles.**
  It's worse! Chrysanthemums are reserved for funerals.
- **Je ne savais pas que c'était aussi difficile de choisir un bouquet de fleurs!**
  I didn't know it was so hard to choose a bouquet of flowers!
- **Ce sont les plus belles fleurs que j'aie jamais reçues!**
  These are the most beautiful flowers I have ever received!
- **C'est la tarte la plus délicieuse du monde!**
  This is the most delicious tart in the world!
- **Cette tarte aux pommes est meilleure que la tarte aux pêches.**
  This apple tart is better than the peach tart.

Additional vocabulary

- **Ah, tu es jaloux? Ne t'en fais pas!**
  Are you jealous? Don't be!/Don't make anything of it!
- **sûr(e) et certain(e)**
  totally sure/completely certain
- **Il ne fallait pas.**
  You shouldn't have./It wasn't necessary.
- **J'ai trop mangé. Je n'en peux plus!**
  I ate too much. I can't fit anymore!
- **Tu peux la lui passer?**
  Can you pass it to her?

---

2 **Questions** Répondez aux questions par des phrases complètes.
Answers may vary slightly.

1. Qu'est-ce que Rachid a apporté à Sandrine?
   Il lui a apporté des chocolats.
2. Qu'a fait Amina pour aider?
   Elle a fini de mettre la table.
3. Qui mange une deuxième tranche de tarte aux pommes?
   Stéphane la mange.
4. Quel type de tarte Sandrine a-t-elle préparé il y a quelques semaines?
   Elle a préparé une tarte aux pêches.
5. Pourquoi David n'a-t-il pas acheté les roses?
   Il ne les a pas achetées parce que (Rachid lui a dit que) les roses sont romantiques.

3 **Écrivez** David veut raconter le dîner de Sandrine à sa famille. Composez un e-mail. Quels ont été les préparatifs (*preparations*)? Qui a apporté quoi? Qui est venu? Qu'est-ce qu'on a mangé? Relisez l'**ESPACE ROMAN-PHOTO** de la Leçon 9A si nécessaire.

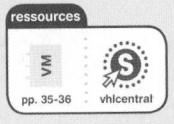

ressources

VM
pp. 35–36

vhlcentral

A C T I V I T É S

Expressions utiles

- Model the pronunciation of the **Expressions utiles** and have students repeat them after you.
- As you work through the list, point out the comparative and superlative expressions and double object pronouns. Explain that **mieux** and **meilleur** both mean *better*, but one is an adverb and the other is an adjective. Tell students that these constructions will be formally presented in the **Structures** section.
- Respond briefly to questions about the comparative, the superlative, and double object pronouns. Reinforce correct forms, but do not expect students to produce them consistently at this time.
- Tell students that the expression **je n'en peux plus** is used to say, *"I'm full."* They should not use the word **plein(e)** in this context.

1 Suggestion Have students write their corrections on the board.

1 Expansion For additional practice, give students these items. **11. David achète les roses. (Faux. Il achète d'autres fleurs.) 12. Valérie aide Sandrine dans la cuisine. (Vrai.) 13. Amina est au régime. (Vrai.) 14. Sandrine n'aime pas sa tarte aux pommes. (Faux. Elle aime sa tarte aux pommes.)**

2 Expansion For additional practice, give students these items. **6. Pourquoi est-ce que David et Rachid ont acheté des cadeaux pour Sandrine? (Ils vont dîner chez elle.) 7. Qu'est-ce que Sandrine a préparé pour le dîner? (Elle a préparé un poulet aux champignons.) 8. Pourquoi est-ce que David n'a pas acheté les chrysanthèmes? (Les chrysanthèmes sont pour les funérailles.)**

3 Suggestion Tell students to jot down the answers to the questions before they begin to compose their e-mails.

O P T I O N S

Extra Practice Using the **Roman-photo** as a model, have students write a conversation that takes place at a dinner party. The host or hostess should offer foods, which the guests politely accept or refuse. As each dish is served, guests should comment on the quality of the food. Remind students to use as many of the **Expressions utiles** as they can.

Les fleurs et les sentiments Various flowers are associated with specific sentiments. Much of the symbolism has been forgotten today, but some traditions stemming from the "language" of flowers remain in French culture. For example, red roses are romantic. Chrysanthemums bloom in the fall, so these flowers were placed on graves on Day of the Dead (November 2nd). Now they are a traditional flower for funerals.

Reading

NATIONAL
connections
cultures
STANDARDS

CULTURE À LA LOUPE

Les repas en France

En France, un grand repas traditionnel peut être composé de beaucoup de plats différents et il peut durer° plusieurs heures. Avant de passer à table, on sert des amuse-gueules° comme des biscuits salés°, des olives ou des cacahuètes°. Ensuite, on commence le repas par un hors-d'œuvre ou directement par une ou deux entrées chaudes ou froides, comme une soupe, de la charcuterie, des escargots, etc. Après l'entrée, on prend parfois un sorbet pour nettoyer le palais°. Puis, on passe au plat principal, qui est en général une viande ou un poisson servi avec des légumes. Après, on apporte la salade, puis le fromage et enfin, on sert le dessert et le café. Le repas traditionnel est souvent accompagné de vin, et dans les grandes occasions, de champagne pour le dessert. Bien sûr, tous les Français ne font pas ce genre de repas tous les jours. En général, on mange beaucoup plus simplement. Au petit-déjeuner, on boit du café au lait, du thé ou du chocolat chaud. On mange des tartines° ou du pain grillé° avec du beurre et de la confiture, et des croissants le week-end. Le déjeuner est traditionnellement le repas principal, mais aujourd'hui, les Français n'ont pas souvent le temps de rentrer à la maison. Pour cette raison, on mange de plus en plus° au travail ou au café. Après l'école, les enfants prennent parfois un goûter, par exemple du pain avec du chocolat. Et le soir, on dîne à la maison, en famille.

Les Français et les repas

- 10% des Français ne prennent pas de petit-déjeuner.
- 60% boivent du café le matin, 20% du thé, 15% du chocolat.
- 99% dînent chez eux en semaine.
- 35% dînent en famille, 30% en couple.
- 75% des dîners consistent en moins de° trois plats successifs.
- Le pain est présent dans plus de 60% des déjeuners et des dîners.

durer last **amuse-gueules** small appetizers **salés** savory **cacahuètes** peanuts **palais** palate **tartines** slices of bread **pain grillé** toast **de plus en plus** more and more **moins de** less than

Coup de main

You can use these terms to specify how you would like meat to be cooked.

bleu(e)	very rare
saignant(e)	medium rare
à point	medium
bien cuit(e)	well-done

ACTIVITÉS

1 **Vrai ou faux?** Indiquez si les phrases sont **vraies** ou **fausses**. Corrigez les phrases fausses.

1. On mange les hors-d'œuvres avant les amuse-gueules.
   Faux. On mange les amuse-gueules avant les hors-d'œuvres.
2. On prend parfois un sorbet après l'entrée.
   Vrai.
3. En France, on mange la salade en entrée.
   Faux. On mange la salade après le plat principal.
4. En général, on ne boit pas de vin pendant le repas.
   Faux. En général, on boit du vin pendant le repas.
5. On sert le fromage entre la salade et le dessert.
   Vrai.
6. Les Français mangent souvent des œufs au petit-déjeuner. Faux. Ils mangent des tartines ou du pain grillé avec du beurre et de la confiture ou des croissants le week-end.
7. Tous les Français mangent un grand repas traditionnel chaque soir. Faux. En général, on mange plus simplement.
8. Le déjeuner est traditionnellement le repas principal de la journée en France.
   Vrai.
9. À midi, les Français mangent toujours à la maison. Faux. Ils mangent de plus en plus souvent au travail ou au café.
10. Les enfants prennent parfois un goûter après l'école.
    Vrai.

Section Goals

In this section, students will:
- learn about meals and eating habits in France
- learn some terms for methods of preparing food
- learn some tips about dining manners in France and North Africa
- read about the popularity of North African food in France

Instructional Resources
vhlcentral.com:
reference tools

Culture à la loupe
Avant la lecture Have students look at the photos, identify the meals, and describe what they see.

Lecture
- Explain that large family meals consisting of many courses typically take place on Sunday afternoons and on holidays.
- Point out the **Coup de main** and model the pronunciation of the terms. Ask: **Comment préférez-vous votre steak? À point? Bien cuit?**
- Point out the chart **Les Français et les repas**. Ask students what type of information is contained in this chart. (statistics about French meals and eating habits)

Après la lecture Ask students to name the courses in a large French meal in chronological order as you write them on the board.

1 **Suggestion** Have students read out the sentences in the text where they found the correct answers.

OPTIONS

Cultural Comparison Have students work in groups of three and compare a large, traditional French meal with a typical, large American meal. Tell them to list the similarities and differences in a two-column chart under the headings **Similitudes** and **Différences**. After completing the charts, have volunteers read their lists aloud.

Les Français et les repas Have students write five true/false sentences based on the information in the chart. Then tell them to exchange papers with a classmate and complete the activity. Remind them to verify their answers.

LE FRANÇAIS QUOTIDIEN

Au menu

côtelette (f.)	*chop*
escalope (f.)	*thin slice of meat or fish*
faux-filet (m.)	*sirloin steak*
à la vapeur	*steamed*
farci(e)	*stuffed*
frit(e)	*fried*
garni(e)	*garnished*
rôti(e)	*roasted*

LE MONDE FRANCOPHONE

Si on est invité...

Voici quelques bonnes manières à observer quand on dîne chez des amis.

En Afrique du Nord

- Si quelqu'un vous invite à boire un thé à la menthe, ce n'est pas poli de refuser.
- En général, on enlève ses chaussures avant d'entrer dans une maison.
- On mange souvent avec les doigts°.

En France

- Il est poli d'apporter un petit cadeau pour les hôtes, par exemple des bonbons ou des fleurs.
- On dit parfois «Santé!°» ou «À votre santé°!» avant de boire et «Bon appétit!» avant de manger.
- On mange avec la fourchette dans la main gauche et le couteau dans la main droite et on garde toujours les deux mains sur la table.

doigts *fingers* **Santé!** *Cheers!* **santé** *health*

PORTRAIT

La couscousmania des Français

La cuisine du Maghreb est très populaire en France. Les restaurants orientaux sont nombreux et appréciés pour la qualité de leur nourriture et leur ambiance. Les merguez, des petites saucisses rouges pimentées°, sont vendues dans toutes les boucheries. Dans les grandes villes, des pâtisseries au miel° sont dégustées° au goûter. Le plat le plus célèbre reste le couscous, le quatrième plat préféré des Français, devant le steak-frites! Aujourd'hui, des restaurants trois étoiles° le proposent en plat du jour et on le sert dans les cantines. Les Français consomment 96.000 tonnes de couscous par an, une vraie couscousmania!

pimentées *spicy* **miel** *honey* **dégustées** *savored* **étoiles** *stars*

MUSIQUE À FOND

Keen'V

Lieu d'origine: Rouen, France
Métier: compositeur - interprète

Keen'V, de son vrai nom Kevin Bonnet, s'est d'abord fait connaître en discothèque en tant que disc-jockey.

Go to vhlcentral.com to find out more about **Keen'V** and his music.

---

2 **Répondez** Répondez aux questions d'après les textes.

1. Qu'est-ce qu'il est impoli de refuser en Afrique du Nord?
   Il est impoli de refuser un thé à la menthe.
2. Pourquoi les Français apprécient-ils les restaurants orientaux?
   Ils les apprécient pour leur ambiance et la qualité de leur nourriture.
3. Où sert-on le couscous aujourd'hui?
   On le sert dans les restaurants trois étoiles et les cantines.
4. Quel cadeau peut-on apporter quand on dîne chez des Français?
   On peut apporter des bonbons ou des fleurs.
5. Une fourchette et un couteau sont-ils nécessaires en Afrique du Nord? Non, on mange souvent avec les doigts.

3 **Que choisir?** Avez-vous déjà mangé dans un restaurant nord-africain? Quand? Où? Qu'avez-vous mangé? Du couscous? Si vous n'êtes jamais allé(e) dans un restaurant nord-africain, imaginez que des amis vous invitent à en essayer un. Qu'avez-vous envie de goûter? Pourquoi?

Practice more at vhlcentral.com.

ressources
vhlcentral

A C T I V I T É S

Le français quotidien
- Model the pronunciation of each term and have students repeat it.
- Have volunteers describe different dishes using these terms. Examples: **pommes frites, escalope de poulet, légumes à la vapeur**, and **côtelette de porc**.

Portrait
- Have students look at the map of the French-speaking world in **Appendice A**. Point out the proximity of France to North Africa. Explain that **le Maghreb** refers to the three French-speaking nations in North Africa (**le Maroc, l'Algérie**, and **la Tunisie**).
- Explain that couscous is steamed semolina usually served with meat and vegetables.
- Couscous is often considered the national dish of **le Maghreb**.

Le monde francophone Bring in a knife and fork. Demonstrate how Americans typically use these eating utensils, then show students how the French use them.

2 **Expansion** For additional practice, give students these items. 6. Où peut-on acheter des merguez? (dans toutes les boucheries) 7. Quel type de pâtisserie mange-t-on traditionnellement en Afrique du Nord? (les pâtisseries au miel) 8. Combien de tonnes de couscous les Français mangent-ils par an? (75.000 tonnes) 9. Quand peut-on dire «Santé!»? (avant de boire) 10. Que faut-il enlever avant d'entrer dans une maison en Afrique du Nord? (ses chaussures)

3 **Expansion** Take a quick class survey to find out how many students have tried couscous and how many like it. Ask: **Combien d'étudiants ont déjà mangé du couscous? Combien de personnes ont aimé ce plat?** Tally the results on the board.

OPTIONS

La couscousmania des Français Traditionally prepared, couscous is cooked very slowly with meat and vegetables and served on large platters made of colorful **faïence**. When preparing couscous, it is best to use a special couscous cooker called **un couscoussier**. The couscous found in stores is usually instant and requires only hot water.

Si on est invité... It is customary to drink **un thé à la menthe** in small, narrow glasses that are often decorated with faux gold leaf. It is sometimes served with pine nuts floating in the tea. Mint is sold in large bunches at Arab markets in France. For an authentic experience drinking this tea, one should go to the café near **la mosquée** in Paris.

Section Goals

In this section, students will learn:

• comparatives and superlatives of adjectives and adverbs
• irregular comparative and superlative forms

Instructional Resources
vhlcentral.com:
Lab MP3s; SAM Answer Key;
Essayez!** and **Mise en pratique
answers; Lab Audioscript;
*Activity Pack (**Feuilles**
d'activités); reference tools*

Suggestions

• Write **plus** + *adjective* + **que** and **moins** + *adjective* + **que** on the board, explaining their meaning. Illustrate with examples like this: **Cette classe est plus grande que la classe de l'année dernière.**

• Practice by asking the class questions whose responses require comparisons. Examples: **Qui est aussi jolie que Gwyneth Paltrow? Qui est aussi riche qu'Oprah Winfrey?**

• Practice superlative questions by asking students their opinions. Example: **Quel cours est le plus difficile? Le plus facile?**

• Point out that **que** and what follows it are optional if the items being compared are evident. Example: **Le steak est plus cher (que le poulet).**

• Point out that if the adjective precedes the noun, the definite article will only be used once.

Leçon 9B

9B.1

Boîte à outils

As always, the adjective in comparative phrases agrees in number and gender with the noun.

Nicole est plus **nerveuse** que Luc.

Luc est moins **nerveux** que Nicole.

Boîte à outils

The noun in a superlative construction can be omitted if it is clear to whom or what it refers. To show this, the noun **les filles** in the sample sentence appears in parentheses.

À noter

You learned many of the adjectives that precede the nouns they modify in **Leçon 3A.**

Comparatives and superlatives of adjectives and adverbs

 Tutorial

• To compare people, things, and actions, use the following expressions with adjectives and adverbs.

plus				more... than
aussi	+	[adjective/adverb]	que	as... as
moins				less... than

ADJECTIVE
Simone est **plus âgée que** son mari.
Simone is older than her husband.

ADVERB
Elle parle **plus vite que** son mari.
She speaks more quickly than her husband.

ADJECTIVE
Guillaume est **moins sportif que** son père.
Guillaume is less athletic than his father.

ADVERB
Il m'écrit **moins souvent que** son père.
He writes me less often than his father.

ADJECTIVE
Nina est **aussi indépendante qu'**Anne.
Nina is as independent as Anne.

ADVERB
Elle joue au golf **aussi bien qu'**Anne.
She plays golf as well as Anne.

• Superlatives express extremes like *the most* or *the least.* The preposition **de** often follows the superlative to express *in* or *of.*

[noun]	+	le la les	+	plus/moins	+	[adjective]	+	de

NOUN   DEFINITE COMPARATIVE
     ARTICLE
Le TGV est **le train le plus rapide du** monde.
The TGV is the fastest train in the world.

NOUN   DEFINITE   COMPARATIVE
   ARTICLE
Éva et Martine sont **(les filles) les moins réservées de la** classe.
Éva and Martine are the least reserved (girls) in class.

• The superlative construction goes before or after the noun depending on whether the adjective precedes or follows the noun. In the case of adjectives like **beau**, **bon**, **grand**, and **nouveau** that precede the nouns they modify, the superlative forms can precede or follow the nouns they modify.

SUPERLATIVE   NOUN
C'est **la plus grande ville**.
It's the largest city.

NOUN   SUPERLATIVE
C'est **la ville la plus grande**.
It's the largest city.

- Since adverbs are invariable, you always use **le** to form the superlative.

  M. Duval est le prof qui parle **le plus vite**.
  Mr. Duval is the professor who speaks the fastest.

  C'est Amandine qui écoute **le moins patiemment**.
  Amandine listens the least patiently.

- Some adjectives and adverbs have irregular comparative and superlative forms.

Irregular comparative and superlative adjectives

Adjective	Comparative	Superlative
bon(ne)(s) *good*	**meilleur(e)(s)** *better*	**le/la/les meilleur(e)(s)** *best*
mauvais(e)(s) *bad*	**pire(s)** *worse* or **plus mauvais(e)(s)**	**le/la/les pire(s)** *worst* or **le/la/les plus mauvais(e)(s)**

Irregular comparative and superlative adverbs

Adverb	Comparative	Superlative
bien *well*	**mieux** *better*	**le mieux** *best*

En été, les pêches sont **meilleures** que les pommes.
In the summer, peaches are better than apples.

Les frites sont **pires** pour la santé que les pâtes.
Fries are worse for your health than pasta.

Mon ami chante bien mais sa sœur chante **mieux** que lui.
My friend sings well, but his sister sings better than he does.

Les plats dans ce restaurant sont mauvais mais la soupe est **la pire**.
The food in this restaurant is bad, but the soup is the worst.

Voilà **la meilleure** boulangerie de la ville.
There's the best bakery in town.

Dans la classe, c'est Clémentine qui écrit **le mieux**.
In our class, it's Clémentine who writes the best.

- The other comparative and superlative forms of **bon** and **mauvais** (**aussi bon, (la) moins mauvaise**, etc.) are regular. This is also true of the other comparative and superlative forms of **bien** (**aussi bien, (le) moins bien**).

Essayez! Complétez les phrases avec le comparatif ou le superlatif.

Comparatifs

1. Les étudiants sont _moins âgés que_ (- âgés) le professeur.
2. Les plages de la Martinique sont-elles _meilleures que_ (+ bonnes) les plages de la Guadeloupe?
3. Évelyne parle _aussi poliment que_ (= poliment) Luc.
4. Les chaussettes sont _moins chères que_ (- chères) les baskets.
5. Ses sœurs sont _aussi généreuses que_ (= généreux) lui.
6. La soupe est _moins bonne que_ (- bon) la salade.

Superlatifs

7. Quelle librairie vend les livres _les plus intéressants_ (+ intéressants)?
8. Le jean est _le moins élégant_ (- élégant) de tous mes pantalons.
9. Je joue aux cartes avec ma mère. C'est elle qui joue _le mieux_ (+ bien).
10. Les fraises de son jardin sont _les moins belles_ (- belles).
11. Victor et son cousin sont _les plus beaux_ (+ beau) garçons de l'école.
12. Mme Damier a _la moins vieille_ (- vieux) maison du quartier.

Boîte à outils

Use a disjunctive pronoun (see **Leçon 3B**) rather than a subject pronoun after **que** in comparative constructions.

Gilles est plus gentil que toi.

Carole mange plus vite que lui.

Suggestions
- Use magazine pictures to practice the different irregular comparative and superlative forms, for example: uses of **meilleur(e)** (*adjective*) and **mieux** (*adverb*), **pire / plus mauvais(e)** (*adjective*) and **plus mal** (*adverb*).
- Consider mentioning to students that the adverb **mal** has the irregular comparative and superlative forms **pis** and **le pis** but that these are rarely used. The more commonly used forms are **plus mal** and **le plus mal**.
- To avoid confusion between **meilleur** and **mieux** since they are both translated as *better* in English, tell students that **meilleur** is used to compare nouns and **mieux** usually modifies a verb.
- Consider telling students that **plus, le plus, moins**, and **le moins** also serve to compare the adverbs **beaucoup** and **peu**. Examples: **1. Émilie travaille beaucoup./Thérèse travaille plus./Leur frère travaille le plus. 2. Yves dort peu./Patrick dort moins./Anne et Félix dorment le moins.**

Essayez! Give additional sentences for extra practice. Examples: **Comparatif: Les roses sentent _____ (+ bon) les chrysanthèmes. (meilleur que) Superlatif: C'est le fromage qui sent (+ mauvais) _____, mais c'est (+ bon) _____. (le plus mauvais/le meilleur)**

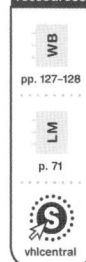

ressources

WB
pp. 127–128

LM
p. 71

vhlcentral

OPTIONS

Extra Practice Give ten comparative and superlative sentences orally to practice listening comprehension. Dictate the sentences, then give students about 30 seconds per sentence to write the direct opposite. Ask volunteers to present their opposite sentences. Example: **La fin de ce livre est meilleure que le début. (La fin de ce livre est pire que le début.)**

TPR Have two or more volunteer students stand up in front of the class with similar objects. Make a comparison between these objects. Example: **John a le cahier le plus grand.** Then call on other volunteers to make different comparisons between other objects. Then ask: **Qui a _____ le/la plus grand(e)?**

Mise en pratique

1 **Oui, mais...** Deux amis comparent deux restaurants. Complétez les phrases avec **bon, bien, meilleur** ou **mieux.**

1. J'ai bien mangé au Café du marché hier.

   Oui, mais nous avons _____mieux_____ mangé Chez Charles.

2. Le vin blanc au Café du marché est _____bon_____.

   Oui, mais le vin blanc de Chez Charles est meilleur.

3. Mes amis ont bien aimé le Café du marché.

   Oui, mais mes amis ont _____mieux_____ mangé Chez Charles.

4. Au Café du marché, le chef prépare _____bien_____ le poulet.

   Oui, mais le chef de Chez Charles le prépare mieux.

5. Les salades au Café du marché sont bonnes.

   Oui, mais elles sont _____meilleures_____ Chez Charles.

6. Tout est bon au Café du marché!

   Tout est _____meilleur_____ Chez Charles!

2 **Un nouveau quartier** Vous venez d'emménager. Assemblez les éléments des trois colonnes pour poser des questions sur le quartier à un(e) voisin(e). Answers will vary.

MODÈLE

Est-ce que le jambon est moins cher au supermarché ou à la charcuterie?

A	B	C
pain	boucherie	aussi
fruits de mer	boulangerie	meilleur(e)
faire les courses	charcuterie	mieux
dîner	pâtisserie	moins
aller	poissonnerie	pire
acheter	voisins	plus
desserts	quartier	
jambon	supermarché	

3 **Aujourd'hui et autrefois** Avec un(e) partenaire, comparez la vie domestique d'aujourd'hui et d'autrefois. Utilisez les adjectifs de la liste à tour de rôle. Ensuite, présentez vos opinions à la classe. Answers will vary.

MODÈLE

Aujourd'hui, les tâches ménagères sont moins difficiles.

bon	difficile	mauvais	poli
compliqué	grand	naturel	rapide
curieux	indépendant	occupé	sophistiqué

1. les congélateurs
2. la nourriture
3. les femmes
4. les commerçants
5. les voyages
6. les voitures
7. les enfants
8. la vie

 Practice more at **vhlcentral.com.**

1 **Expansion** In pairs, have students select two local restaurants and describe them using comparatives and superlatives modeled on those in the activity. Ask volunteers to share their sentences with the class.

2 **Suggestion** You may want to do this as a whole-class activity, giving different students the opportunity to ask and answer questions using the words in the columns.

3 **Suggestion** Remind students to use verbs in the imperfect to describe **la vie d'autrefois**. Review the imperfect tense if necessary.

3 **Expansion** After completing the activity, ask students to give their opinions about which is better: **la vie d'autrefois ou la vie moderne.** Encourage students to use superlative and comparative forms.

Communication

4 **Trouvez quelqu'un** Votre professeur va vous donner une feuille d'activités. Circulez dans la classe pour trouver des camarades différents qui correspondent aux phrases. Answers will vary.

MODÈLE

Étudiant(e) 1: *Quel âge as-tu?*
Étudiant(e) 2: *J'ai dix-neuf ans.*
Étudiant(e) 3: *Alors tu es plus jeune que moi.*

Trouvez dans la classe quelqu'un qui...	*Nom*
1. ... est plus jeune que vous.	Myriam
2. ... habite plus loin de la fac que vous.	
3. ... prend l'avion aussi souvent que vous.	
4. ... fait moins de gym que vous.	

5 **Comparaisons** Par groupes de trois, comparez les sujets présentés. Utilisez des comparatifs et des superlatifs. Answers will vary.

▶ **MODÈLE**

Étudiant(e) 1: *Les vacances à la mer sont plus amusantes que les vacances à la montagne.*

Étudiant(e) 2: *Moi, je pense que les vacances à la montagne sont plus intéressantes.*

Étudiant(e) 3: *D'accord, mais les vacances à l'étranger sont les plus amusantes.*

1.   2.   3.   4.

6 **À mon avis** À tour de rôle avec un(e) partenaire, comparez ces personnes et ces choses en utilisant des comparatifs. Answers will vary.

1. New York / Chicago
2. Ryan Reynolds / Leonardo DiCaprio
3. George W. Bush / Barack Obama
4. Tom Brady / DeMarco Murray
5. Rihanna / Katy Perry
6. le cours de français / le cours d'anglais
7. la vie à la campagne / la vie en ville
8. *Modern Family / The Big Bang Theory*

7 **Comparaisons** À tour de rôle avec un(e) partenaire, parlez de votre famille et de vos amis. Utilisez des comparatifs et des superlatifs dans vos descriptions. Answers will vary.

MODÈLE

Ma sœur Amy est plus sérieuse que moi, mais mon frère Thomas est la personne la plus sérieuse de ma famille.

---

4 Suggestions
• Before beginning the activity, have the class brainstorm additional characteristics to use in this survey. Encourage them to use other vocabulary from previous units.
• Have two students act out the **modèle**. Then distribute the **Feuilles d'activités** found in the Activity Pack on the Supersite.

5 Suggestion Act out the **modèle** with two volunteers.

5 Expansion Using magazine pictures, show images similar to those in the activity. Have students create additional sentences.

6 Expansion Have volunteers come up with more pairs for the class to comment on using comparative and superlative phrases.

7 Expansion After pairs complete the activity, ask the class questions about their conversations using comparatives and superlatives.

O P T I O N S

Extra Practice Have students write three original comparative or superlative sentences that describe themselves or compare them with a friend, family member, or famous person. Examples: **Je suis la personne la plus intelligente de l'université. Je suis moins égoïste que mon frère.** Then collect the papers and read the sentences aloud. See if the rest of the class can guess who wrote each description.

Game Divide the class into two teams, A and B. Place the names of 20 famous people into a hat. Select a member from each group to draw a name. The student from team A then has ten seconds to compare those two famous people in a complete sentence. If the student has made a logical comparison, team A gets a point. Then it's team B's turn to make a different comparison. The team with the most points at the end wins.

9B.2

Section Goals

In this section, students will learn double object pronouns.

Instructional Resources
vhlcentral.com:
*Activity Pack; Lab MP3s;
SAM Answer Key; **Essayez!**
and **Mise en pratique**
answers; Lab Audioscript;
reference tools*

Suggestions

• Briefly review indirect object pronouns (**Leçon 6B**) and direct object pronouns (**Leçon 7A**). Give sentences and have students replace objects with object pronouns. Examples: **Jean nous donne le cours. (Jean nous le donne.) Il écrit la lettre. (Il l'écrit.) Le garçon mange la tarte. (Le garçon la mange.)**

• Explain that object pronouns replace key elements in a conversation or text in order to avoid redundancy.

Double object pronouns  Tutorial

Point de départ In **Leçon 6B** and **Leçon 7A**, respectively, you learned to use indirect and direct object pronouns. Now you will learn to use these pronouns together.

DIRECT OBJECT	INDIRECT OBJECT		DIRECT OBJECT PRONOUN	INDIRECT OBJECT PRONOUN

J'ai rendu **le menu** à **la serveuse**.
I gave the menu back to the waitress.

▶ Je **le lui** ai rendu.
I gave it back to her.

Tu peux la lui passer, s'il te plaît?

Une deuxième tranche? Je te la sers.

• Use this sequence when a sentence contains both a direct and an indirect object pronoun.

me		le			
te		la		lui	
nous	*before*	l'	*before*	leur	+ [*verb*]
vous		les			

Gérard m'envoie les messages de Christiane.
Il **me les** envoie tous les jours.
Gérard sends me Christiane's messages.
He sends them to me every day.

Je lui envoie aussi les messages de Laurent.
Je **les lui** envoie tous les week-ends.
I send him Laurent's messages, too.
I send them to him every weekend.

Le chef nous prépare son meilleur plat.
Les serveurs **nous l'**apportent.
The chef prepares his best dish for us.
The waiters bring it to us.

Nous avons laissé le pourboire des serveurs sur la table. Nous **le leur** avons laissé quand nous sommes partis.
We left a tip for the waiters on the table.
We left it for them when we left.

- In an infinitive construction, the double object pronouns come after the conjugated verb and precede the infinitive, just like single object pronouns.

Mes notes de français? Je vais
vous les prêter.
*My French notes? I'm going to
lend them to you.*

Carole veut lire mon poème?
Je vais **le lui** montrer.
*Carole wants to read my poem?
I'm going to show it to her.*

- In the **passé composé** the double object pronouns precede the auxiliary verb, just like single object pronouns. The past participle agrees with the preceding direct object.

Rémi a-t-il acheté ces fleurs pour sa mère?
Did Rémi buy those flowers for his mother?

Oui, il **les lui** a **achetées**.
Yes, he bought them for her.

Vous m'avez donné la plus grande chambre?
Did you give me the biggest room?

Oui, nous **vous** l'avons **donnée**.
Yes, we gave it to you.

- In affirmative commands, the verb is followed by the direct object pronoun and then the indirect object pronoun, with hyphens in between. Remember to use **moi** and **toi** instead of **me** and **te**.

Vous avez trois voitures?
Montrez-**les-moi**.
*You have three cars?
Show them to me.*

Tu connais la réponse à la
question du prof? Dis-**la-nous**.
*You know the answer to the
professor's question? Tell it to us.*

Voici le livre. Donne-**le-leur**.
Here's the book. Give it to them.

Ce poème? Traduisons-**le-lui**.
This poem? Let's translate it for her.

 Boîte à outils

In negative commands, object pronouns come before the verb. The direct object pronoun precedes the indirect object pronoun.

Tu veux vendre la montre à ta cousine? Ne la lui vends pas!

 Essayez! **Utilisez deux pronoms pour refaire ces phrases.**

1. Le prof vous donne les résultats des examens. ___*Le prof vous les donne.*___
2. Tes parents t'achètent le billet. ___Tes parents te l'achètent.___
3. Qui t'a donné cette belle lampe bleue? ___Qui te l'a donnée?___
4. Il nous a réservé les chambres. ___Il nous les a réservées.___
5. Pose-moi tes questions. ___Pose-les-moi.___
6. Explique-leur le problème de maths. ___Explique-le-leur.___
7. Peux-tu me montrer les photos? ___Peux-tu me les montrer?___
8. Tu préfères lui prêter ton dictionnaire? ___Tu préfères le lui prêter?___
9. Dites-moi la vérité (*truth*)! ___Dites-la-moi!___
10. Nous n'avons pas apporté les couteaux à Paul. ___Nous ne les lui avons pas apportés.___

ressources

WB
pp. 129–130

LM
p. 72

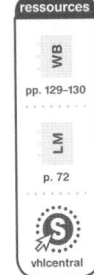
vhlcentral

Suggestions
- To help students visualize which object pronouns are indirect and which are direct, draw a Venn diagram (two intersecting circles) on the board. In the left circle, write direct object pronouns **le, la, l'**, and **les**. Where there is overlap in the circles, write direct and indirect object pronouns **me, te, nous**, and **vous**. In the right circle, write the indirect object pronouns **lui** and **leur**. Label the left circle *Direct object pronouns* and the right circle *Indirect object pronouns*.
- Ask students questions to which they respond with third-person double object pronouns. Examples: **Qui rend la monnaie à la cliente? (Le serveur/La serveuse la lui rend.) Qui donne le livre de grammaire aux étudiants? (Le professeur le leur donne.)**

Essayez! Have students rewrite the answers from **Essayez!** as negative sentences. Example:
1. Le prof ne vous les donne pas.

OPTIONS

Video Replay the video, having students focus on the use of comparatives, superlatives, and all object pronouns. Stop the video where appropriate to discuss how these forms were used and to ask questions. Ask to whom or to what each object pronoun refers. For example, when David says **Qu'est-ce que je peux lui apporter?**, have students clarify the use of **lui**.
(Il demande ce qu'il peut apporter à Sandrine.)

Pairs Have students write five sentences that contain both direct and indirect object nouns. When they are finished, have them switch papers with a partner who must restate the sentences using double object pronouns.

ESPACE STRUCTURES

1 Suggestion Have students write the answers on the board and go over them with the class.

2 Suggestion Before assigning this activity, have students underline the direct objects and circle the indirect objects in each sentence on photocopies or a transparency.

3 Expansion Have students write their own sentences using double object pronouns modeled on those in the activity. Pairs exchange papers and invent possible questions that elicit those responses.

Mise en pratique

1 **Les livres** Le père de Bertrand lui a acheté des livres. Refaites l'histoire avec deux pronoms pour chaque phrase.

1. Papa a acheté ces *livres à Bertrand*. Papa les lui a achetés.

2. Il a lu *les livres à ses petits frères*. Il les leur a lus.

3. Maintenant, ses frères veulent lire *les livres à leur père*. Maintenant, ses frères veulent les lui lire.

4. Bertrand donne *les livres à ses petits frères*. Bertrand les leur donne.

5. Les garçons montrent *les livres à leur père*. Les garçons les lui montrent.

6. Leur père préfère donner *sa place à leur mère*. Leur père préfère la lui donner.

7. Les enfants lisent *les livres à leur mère*. Les enfants les lui lisent.

8. «Maintenant, lisez *les livres à votre père*», dit-elle. «Maintenant, lisez-les-lui», dit-elle.

2 **Comment?** Un groupe d'amis parle de l'anniversaire de Claudette. Antoine n'entend pas très bien. Il répète tout ce que les gens disent. Utilisez des pronoms pour écrire ses questions.

MODÈLE

Je veux donner cette chemise noire à Claudette.
Tu veux la lui donner?

1. Son père a acheté la petite voiture bleue à Claudette. Son père la lui a achetée?

2. Nous envoyons les invitations aux amis. Vous les leur envoyez?

3. Le prof a donné la meilleure note à Claudette le jour de son anniversaire. Le prof la lui a donnée?

4. Je vais prêter mon tailleur à Claudette vendredi soir. Tu vas le lui prêter vendredi soir?

5. Est-ce que vous voulez me lire l'invitation? Est-ce que je veux / nous voulons vous la lire?

6. Nous n'avons pas envoyé la carte au professeur. Vous ne la lui avez pas envoyée?

7. Gilbert et Arthur vont nous apporter le gâteau. Gilbert et Arthur vont vous l'apporter?

8. Sa mère va payer le restaurant à sa fille. Sa mère va le lui payer?

3 **De quoi parle-t-on?** Avec un(e) partenaire, imaginez les questions qui ont donné ces réponses. Ensuite, présentez vos questions à la classe. Answers will vary.

MODÈLE

Il veut le lui vendre.
Il veut vendre son vélo à son camarade?

1. Marc va la lui donner.

2. Nous te l'avons envoyée hier.

3. Elle te les a achetés la semaine dernière.

4. Tu me les prêtes souvent.

5. Micheline ne va pas vous les prendre.

6. Tu ne nous les as pas prises.

7. Rendez-les-moi!

8. Ne le lui disons pas!

9. Vous n'allez pas le leur apporter.

Practice more at vhlcentral.com.

Communication

4 **Qui vous aide?** Avec un(e) partenaire, posez des questions avec les mots interrogatifs **qui** et **quand.** Vous pouvez choisir le présent, le passé composé ou l'imparfait. Répondez aux questions avec deux pronoms. Answers will vary.

MODÈLE prêter sa voiture
Étudiant(e) 1: *Qui te prête sa voiture?*
Étudiant(e) 2: *Ma mère me la prête.*
Étudiant(e) 1: *Quand est-ce qu'elle te la prête?*
Étudiant(e) 2: *Elle me la prête le vendredi.*

faire le lit	faire la cuisine
prêter ses livres	nettoyer la chambre
payer l'université	laver les vêtements

5 **Une entrevue** Avec un(e) partenaire, répondez aux questions sur votre enfance. Utilisez deux pronoms dans vos réponses. Answers will vary.

1. Est-ce que tes parents te montraient les films de Disney quand tu étais petit(e)?
2. Est-ce que tu vas montrer les films de Disney à tes enfants un jour?
3. Est-ce que quelqu'un te parlait français quand tu étais petit(e)?
4. Qui t'a acheté ton premier vélo?
5. Qui te faisait à dîner quand tu étais petit(e)?
6. Qui te préparait le petit-déjeuner le matin?
7. Qui t'achetait tes vêtements quand tu étais petit(e)?
8. Est-ce que quelqu'un vous lisait les livres du Dr. Seuss à toi et à tes frères et sœurs?

6 **Au marché** Avec un(e) partenaire, préparez deux dialogues basés sur deux des photos. À tour de rôle, jouez le/la client(e) et le/la marchand(e). Utilisez le vocabulaire et deux pronoms si possible dans les dialogues. Answers will vary.

commander	une entrée	une tarte
être au régime	un plat	une saucisse
cuisiner	du poulet	des croissants
les fruits de mer	un steak	du porc

---

4 Expansion Have students tell the class their partners' responses using the third person. Example: **Sa mère la lui prête le vendredi.**

5 Expansion Have two pairs get together and ask each other questions in the third person based on what they just learned about their partners.

6 Suggestions
• Go over the photos with the students so it is clear what stores are pictured.
• Make sure students include at least two affirmative commands including **s'il vous plaît** and double object pronouns in their conversations.
• Call on a few volunteer pairs to act out one of the conversations for the class.

OPTIONS

Extra Practice Here are three questions and answers containing object pronouns to use as a dictation. 1. **Qui parle aux étudiants? Le professeur leur parle.** 2. **Qui m'a invité(e) à la fête? Mon petit ami t'a invité(e) à la fête.** 3. **Prêtes-tu la voiture à ton frère? Non, je ne la lui prête pas.**

Pairs Have students brainstorm a list of people to whom they relate well. Examples: **le prof de français, les parents, les amis,** etc. Have them describe their relationships with those people to their partner. Encourage them to use object pronouns whenever possible. Example: **le prof de français (Je peux lui poser des questions, lui parler en français et lui demander une bonne note.)**

ESPACE SYNTHÈSE

Révision

NATIONAL STANDARDS communication

---

1 Fais les courses pour moi
Vous n'avez pas le temps d'aller dans tous ces magasins. Choisissez un magasin. Puis, par groupes de quatre, trouvez des camarades qui vont dans d'autres magasins. À tour de rôle, demandez-leur de faire des courses pour vous. Utilisez des pronoms doubles dans vos réponses. *Answers will vary.*

MODÈLE

Étudiant(e) 1: *J'ai besoin de deux filets de poissons. Tu peux me les prendre à la poissonnerie?*
Étudiant(e) 2: *Pas de problème. Et moi, j'ai besoin de...*

un camembert	six croissants
deux bouteilles de lait	une tarte aux pêches
deux filets de poissons	des tomates
douze œufs	une tranche de jambon
quatre côtes (*chops*) de porc	trois baguettes

BOUCHERIE BOULANGERIE CHARCUTERIE POISSONNERIE PÂTISSERIE

2 Je les leur commande
Vous êtes au restaurant. Avec un(e) partenaire, choisissez le meilleur plat pour chaque membre de votre famille. Employez des comparatifs, des superlatifs et des pronoms doubles dans vos réponses. *Answers will vary.*

MODÈLE

Étudiant(e) 1: *Et le poulet?*
Étudiant(e) 2: *Mon père mange du poulet plus souvent que ma mère. Je vais le lui commander.*

Assiette de fruits de mer	Petits pois et carottes
Bœuf avec une sauce au vin	Pizza aux quatre fromages
Hamburger et frites	Sandwich au thon
Pêches à la crème	Tarte aux pommes

3 Mes plats préférés
Par groupes de trois, interviewez vos camarades. Quels sont les plats qu'ils aiment le mieux? Quand les ont-ils mangés la dernière fois? Choisissez vos trois plats préférés, puis comparez-les avec les plats de vos camarades. Employez des comparatifs, des superlatifs et le passé récent. *Answers will vary.*

---

4 Le week-end dernier
Préparez deux listes par écrit, une pour les choses que vous avez pu faire le week-end dernier et une pour les choses que vous n'avez pas pu faire. Ensuite, avec un(e) partenaire, comparez vos listes et expliquez vos réponses. Employez les verbes **devoir**, **vouloir** et **pouvoir** au passé composé et, si possible, les pronoms doubles. *Answers will vary.*

MODÈLE

Étudiant(e) 1: *J'ai voulu envoyer un e-mail à ma cousine.*
Étudiant(e) 2: *Est-ce que tu as pu le lui envoyer?*

Choses que j'ai pu faire
_____
_____
_____

Choses que je n'ai pas pu faire
_____
_____
_____

5 C'est mieux
Par groupes de trois, donnez votre opinion sur ces sujets. Pour chaque sujet, comparez les deux options. Soyez prêts à présenter les résultats de vos discussions à la classe. *Answers will vary.*

MODÈLE apporter des fleurs ou du vin à un dîner

Étudiant(e) 1: *C'est plus sympa d'apporter des fleurs à un dîner.*
Étudiant(e) 2: *Oui, on peut les mettre sur la table. Elles sont plus jolies qu'une bouteille de vin.*
Étudiant(e) 3: *Peut-être, mais le vin est un cadeau plus généreux.*

- commencer ou finir un régime
- faire les courses ou faire la cuisine
- manger ou faire la cuisine

6 Six différences
Votre professeur va vous donner, à vous et à votre partenaire, deux feuilles d'activités différentes. Comparez les deux familles pour trouver les six différences. Attention! Ne regardez pas la feuille de votre partenaire. *Answers will vary.*

MODÈLE

Étudiant(e) 1: *Fatiha est aussi grande que Samira.*
Étudiant(e) 2: *Non, Fatiha est moins grande que Samira.*

Instructional Resources
vhlcentral.com:
Activity Pack (Info Gap Activities); Testing Program; Testing Program MP3s; reference tools

1 Suggestion Encourage students to use both familiar commands and **pouvoir** + [*infinitive*] when completing the activity.

2 Expansion You can also have students do this activity in groups of three. Have the third student imagine he or she is the server. The other students must ask questions about the food in order to make a decision. Example: **La tarte aux pommes est-elle plus fraîche que les pêches à la crème?**

3 Expansion Students should imagine they must create a restaurant ad featuring their favorite dish. Have students make up five sentences using superlatives to convince customers their restaurant is the best and to entice them to order their favorite dish.

4 Suggestion Before assigning this activity, review the different meanings the verbs **devoir**, **vouloir**, and **pouvoir** can have in the past and negative forms.

5 Suggestions
- Act out the **modèle** with two volunteers.
- Have students brainstorm a list of additional ideas with two options on the board. Example: **étudier dans une grande ou une petite université**

6 Suggestion Divide the class into pairs and distribute the Info Gap Handouts found in the Activity Pack on the Supersite. Give students ten minutes to complete the activity.

OPTIONS

Extra Practice Have students imagine that a senior from their old high school wants to attend their university the following year and wrote them an e-mail asking questions about it. Provide a brief sample message. Example: **Je suis en terminale au lycée et je veux être prêt(e) pour l'université. Le campus est plus grand ou plus petit que le lycée? Les cours au lycée sont-ils beaucoup moins difficiles que les cours à la fac?**

Quel cours est le plus intéressant? Est-ce que les repas sont meilleurs? Quelles sont les autres différences avec le lycée? Students then write a reply telling about different aspects of the university. Encourage the use of personal experience in their comparisons. Then in groups of three, have each student present his or her e-mail. Students should discuss whether they agree or disagree with their classmates.

À l'écoute

STRATÉGIE

Jotting down notes as you listen

Jotting down notes while you listen to a conversation in French can help you keep track of the important points or details. It will help you to focus actively on comprehension rather than on remembering what you have heard.

To practice this strategy, you will listen to a paragraph. Jot down the main points you hear.

Préparation

Regardez la photo et décrivez la scène. Où sont ces hommes? Que font-ils? Qui sont-ils, à votre avis? Qu'y a-t-il dans la poêle (*frying pan*)? À votre avis, que préparent-ils?

À vous d'écouter

Écoutez les instructions pour préparer une salade niçoise et notez les ingrédients nécessaires.

Pour la salade

des haricots verts	des tomates
des pommes de terre	un poivron
des œufs	du thon
de la salade	des olives noires

Pour la vinaigrette (*dressing*)

de l'huile d'olive	du sel
de la moutarde	du poivre
de l'ail	du vinaigre

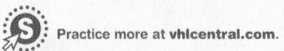
Practice more at **vhlcentral.com**.

Compréhension

Le bon ordre Mettez ces instructions simplifiées dans le bon ordre, d'après la recette de la salade niçoise.

- __7__ **a.** Mélanger (*Mix*) le vinaigre, l'huile d'olive, la moutarde et l'ail pour faire la vinaigrette.
- __6__ **b.** Mettre le thon et les olives sur la salade.
- __4__ **c.** Couper (*Cut*) les œufs et les mettre dans la salade.
- __1__ **d.** Faire cuire (*Cook*) les pommes de terre, les haricots verts et les œufs.
- __5__ **e.** Mettre les morceaux de tomates et de poivron sur la salade.
- __2__ **f.** Laver (*Wash*) la salade et la mettre dans une grande assiette.
- __3__ **g.** Mettre les haricots verts et les pommes de terre sur la salade.
- __8__ **h.** Mettre la vinaigrette sur la salade et servir.

Votre recette préférée Quel est votre plat ou dessert favori? Donnez la liste des ingrédients qu'il faut pour le préparer, puis expliquez à un groupe de camarades comment le préparer. Ne leur donnez pas le nom du plat. Ils vont prendre des notes et essayer de le deviner (*to guess*). Ensuite, changez de rôles.

trois cent quatre-vingt-quinze **395**

Section Goals

In this section, students will:
- learn to take notes as they listen
- listen to a paragraph and jot down the main points
- listen to a cooking program and complete several activities

Instructional Resources
vhlcentral.com:
Textbook MP3s; Textbook Audioscript; reference tools

Stratégie
Audioscript Bon, je vais aller faire les courses. D'abord, je vais passer à la boucherie. J'ai besoin d'un poulet et de quatre steaks. Ensuite, je vais aller à la boulangerie pour acheter du pain et des croissants. Ah oui! Il faut aussi du poisson pour ce soir. Alors, du thon à la poissonnerie. Et au supermarché, des légumes et des fruits.

Préparation Have students look at the photo and describe what they see. Then ask them to guess what dish the chef is preparing.

À vous d'écouter
Audioscript Bonjour à tous et bienvenue à «Cuisiner avec Claude». Aujourd'hui, nous allons préparer une salade bien française: la salade niçoise. C'est une salade très complète qui est parfaite pour l'été. Alors, voici ce que vous devez faire pour préparer cette salade. Tout d'abord, faites cuire les haricots verts et les pommes de terre dans de l'eau très chaude avec un peu de sel. Faites aussi cuire les œufs dans de l'eau. Lavez bien la salade et mettez-la dans une grande assiette. Mettez les pommes de terre et les haricots verts sur la salade. Coupez les œufs, quelques tomates et un poivron et mettez-les dans la salade. Ensuite, mettez du thon et des olives noires. Et maintenant, pour la vinaigrette, mélangez du vinaigre, de l'huile d'olive, de la moutarde et un peu d'ail. Mettez du sel et du poivre dans la vinaigrette et ajoutez-la à la salade. Et voilà! Votre salade est prête!

Vous pouvez la servir avec du pain ou bien des croûtons, si vous le désirez. Cette salade délicieuse est rapide à préparer et vous pouvez la servir en entrée ou bien comme plat principal. Allez! À table! Et bon appétit à tous!

SAVOIR-FAIRE

les falaises° d'Étretat

connections cultures

Panorama

Section Goals

In this section, students will read historical and cultural information about Normandy, Brittany, and Hauts-de-France.

Instructional Resources
vhlcentral.com:
*Digital Image Bank;
SAM Answer Key;
reference tools*

Carte de la Normandie, de la Bretagne et des Hauts-de-France

• Have students look at the map or use the **Panorama** map from the Digital Image Bank. Ask volunteers to read the names of cities and rivers aloud. Model the pronunciation as necessary.

• Ask students to name the country that borders Hauts-de-France. (**La Belgique**)

La région en chiffres

• Have volunteers read the sections aloud. After each section, ask students questions about the content.

• Have students compare the populations of these three regions.

• Ask students to share any information they might know about the **Personnes célèbres**.

Incroyable mais vrai! In the 1990s, workers restoring the **cathédrale d'Amiens** found that the sculptures on the western façade had once been painted with intricate colors. Rather than repainting the sculptures, a sound and light show was created to show how the façade once looked. The show is now one of the most popular attractions in Amiens.

La Normandie

La région en chiffres

▶ **Superficie:** *29.906 km²*

▶ **Population:** *3.328.364*

▶ **Industries principales:** *élevage bovin°, énergie*

▶ **Villes principales:** *Caen, Le Havre, Rouen*

Personnages célèbres

▶ **Christian Dior,** *couturier° (1905–1957)*

La Bretagne

La région en chiffres

▶ **Superficie:** *27.208 km²*

▶ **Population:** *3.237.097*

▶ **Industries principales:** *agriculture, pêche°*

▶ **Villes principales:** *Brest, Quimper, Rennes*

Personnages célèbres

▶ **Anne de Bretagne,** *reine° de France (1477–1514)*

Les Hauts-de-France

La région en chiffres

▶ **Superficie:** *31.813 km²*

▶ **Population:** *6.006.156*

▶ **Industries principales:** *agro-alimentaire, chimie*

▶ **Villes principales:** *Lille, Arras, Amiens*

Personnages célèbres

▶ **Dany Boon,** *acteur (1966–)*

élevage bovin *raising cattle* **couturier** *fashion designer* **pêche** *fishing*
reine *queen* **agro-alimentaire** *food processing* **chef-d'œuvre** *masterpiece*
restaurée *restored* **falaises** *cliffs* **moulin** *mill*

LE ROYAUME-UNI

LA MANCHE

LA FRANCE

Dunkerque
Calais
Boulogne-sur-Mer
HAUTS-DE-FRA
Dieppe · Ami
Cherbourg · Le Havre · Rouen · Compiè
la Seine
Deauville ·
Caen · NORMANDIE
Évreux
Brest · St-Brieuc · Le Mont-St-Michel
l'Aulne · Alençon
Quimper · BRETAGNE
Lorient · Rennes
Vannes · la Vilaine
Belle Île en Mer

L'OCÉAN ATLANTIQUE

le Vieux Lille

un moulin° en Bretagne

0 | 50 miles
0 | 50 kilomètres

Incroyable mais vrai!

La Région Hauts-de-France est la terre des cathédrales. La cathédrale d'Amiens, construite entre 1220 et 1269 et considérée un chef-d'œuvre° du style gothique, est la plus vaste de France. Elle est deux fois plus grande que Notre-Dame de Paris! La cathédrale a été restaurée° au dix-neuvième siècle par l'architecte Eugène Viollet-le-Duc.

O P T I O N S

Personnes célèbres After World War II, the "New Look" designs of **Chrisitan Dior** placed Paris at the center of the fashion world. The Dior fashion house was founded in 1946, and its first collection was presented in 1947. **Anne de Bretagne** was Queen of France twice by marriage. She married Charles VIII in 1491 and his successor, Louis XII, in 1499.

She devoted her life to preserving the autonomy of Brittany. **Dany Boon** is an actor and director. His most famous film is *Bienvenue chez les Ch'tis* (2008), and his films typically feature northern France in some way. He has worked on various projects with other comedians, including Kad Merad and Gad Elmaleh.

La gastronomie

Les crêpes bretonnes et le camembert normand

Les crêpes sont une des spécialités culinaires de Bretagne; en Normandie, c'est le camembert. Les crêpes sont appréciées sucrées, salées°, flambées... Dans les crêperies°, le menu est complètement composé de crêpes! Le camembert normand est un des grands symboles gastronomiques de la France. Il est vendu° dans la fameuse boîte en bois ronde° pour une bonne conservation.

Les traditions

Les géants° du Nord

D'origine médiévale, les géants sont des mannequins gigantesques portés° par une ou plusieurs personnes pendant les fêtes et les célébrations locales du Nord de la France. Fortement liés° à l'identité d'une ville, d'un quartier ou d'une association, ils représentent des héros historiques ou légendaires, des personnages locaux, des métiers ou des animaux. Chaque géant a sa vie: il naît, il se marie, il a des enfants. Et cette vie de citoyen° modèle sert d'exemple à sa communauté.

Les monuments

Les menhirs et les dolmens

À Carnac, en Bretagne, il y a 3.000 (trois mille) menhirs et dolmens. Les menhirs sont d'énormes pierres° verticales. Alignés ou en cercle, ils ont une fonction rituelle associée au culte de la fécondité ou du soleil°. Les plus

anciens° datent de 4.500 (quatre mille cinq cents) ans avant J.-C.° Les dolmens servent de° sépultures° collectives et sont peut-être utilisés dans des rites funéraires de passage de la vie° à la mort°.

Les destinations

Deauville: station balnéaire de réputation internationale

Deauville, en Normandie, est une station balnéaire° de luxe et un centre de thalassothérapie°. La ville est célèbre pour sa marina, ses courses hippiques°, son casino, ses grands hôtels et son festival du film américain. La clientèle internationale apprécie beaucoup la plage°, le polo et le golf. L'hôtel le Royal Barrière est un palace° du début° du vingtième° siècle.

Compréhension Complétez ces phrases.

1. __Christian Dior__ est un couturier normand.

2. La cathédrale d' __Amiens__ est la plus vaste de France.

3. __Les crêpes__ sont une spécialité bretonne.

4. Dans __les crêperies__, on mange uniquement des crêpes.

5. __Le camembert__ est vendu dans une boîte en bois ronde.

6. Les géants du Nord sont d'origine __médiévale__.

7. La vie de citoyen modèle des géants sert d'exemple à __sa communauté__.

8. Les menhirs ont une fonction __rituelle__.

9. Les dolmens servent de __sépultures__.

10. Deauville est une __station balnéaire__ de luxe.

Sur Internet

Go to **vhlcentral.com** to find more cultural information related to this **Panorama**.

1. Quelles sont quelques caractéristiques architecturales de la cathédrale d'Amiens?

2. Cherchez des informations sur les géants de la ville d'Arras. Comment s'appellent-ils? Dans quelles années sont-ils nés?

---

salées savory **crêperies** crêpe restaurants **vendu** sold **boîte en bois ronde** round, wooden box **géants** giants **portés** carried **liés** linked **citoyen** citizen **pierres** stones **soleil** sun **Les plus anciens** The oldest **avant J.-C.** B.C. **servent de** serve as **sépultures** graves **vie** life **mort** death **station balnéaire** seaside resort **thalassothérapie** seawater therapy **courses hippiques** horse races **plage** beach **palace** luxury hotel **début** beginning **vingtième** twentieth

ressources
WB pp. 131–132
vhlcentral

Les crêpes bretonnes et le camembert normand
- There are various types of crêpes. In Brittany, the **galettes de blé noir** (*buckwheat crêpes*) are filled with savory foods such as egg, ham and cheese, or mushrooms. The **crêpes de froment** (*wheat flour crêpes*) frequently have sweet fillings such as honey, sugar, jam, or chocolate. Normandy has been known for its cheeses since the sixteenth century. Created in 1890, the wooden container permitted Camembert to be exported worldwide.
- Ask students if they have eaten crêpes or Camembert and if they like them. Or bring in some Camembert and a baguette for students to sample.

Les géants du Nord
- There are more than 500 **géants** in the Hauts-de-France region. In 2008, the **géants** of France and Belgium were recognized as Intangible Cultural Heritage by UNESCO.
- Bring in photos of **géants** from different towns and have students briefly comment on their costumes and artistic designs, and have them guess who the **géants** represent.

Les menhirs et les dolmens
The megaliths, which are ancient granite blocks, can be found all over Brittany. The **menhir** is the most common form of megalith. The **dolmen** has two upright stones with a flat stone on top, like a table. The words **menhir** and **dolmen** come from Breton; **men** means *stone*, **hir** means *long*, and **dol** means *table*.

Deauville: station balnéaire de réputation internationale
Founded by the Duke of Normandy in the 1860s, Deauville is famous for its **Promenade des Planches**, the wooden boardwalk alongside the beach, which was created so women wouldn't have to walk in the sand. Ask students: **Avez-vous envie de visiter Deauville? Pourquoi?**

OPTIONS

Cultural Comparison Working in small groups, have students compare Deauville to a famous American seaside resort. Tell them to list the similarities and differences in a two-column chart under the headings **Similitudes** and **Différences**. After completing their charts, call on volunteers to read their lists.

La Chandeleur On February 2, friends and family gather to celebrate the holiday **la Chandeleur** by cooking and eating crêpes and hoping for a prosperous year. Originally a religious celebration, **la Chandeleur** attracted pilgrims to Rome, and according to legend, the pope gave the pilgrims crêpes. Since then, crêpes have been associated with the holiday.

Section Goals

In this section, students will read historical and cultural information about **le Pays de la Loire** and le **Centre-Val de Loire**.

> **Instructional Resources**
> vhlcentral.com:
> *Digital Image Bank;*
> *SAM Answer Key;*
> *reference tools*

Carte des Pays de la Loire et du Centre-Val de Loire

- Have students look at the map or use the **Panorama** map from the Digital Image Bank. Ask volunteers to read the names of cities and rivers aloud. Model the pronunciation as necessary.
- Ask students to name a geographical feature that was likely an asset to these regions during their development. (the many major rivers)
- Ask students if they recognize any of the town names and to share any prior knowledge they have about the locations.

La région en chiffres

- Ask volunteers to read the sections. After each section, ask other students questions about the content.
- Have students list the many cognates that appear in this section and state the likely English equivalent or what the word might relate to.

Incroyable mais vrai!
Chambord's construction began in 1519 under François Ier, continued under Henri II, and was finally completed in 1685 under Louis XIV.

 Interactive Map

Panorama

Les Pays de la Loire

La région en chiffres

- ▶ **Superficie:** *32.082 km²*
- ▶ **Population:** *3.689.465*
  SOURCE: INSEE
- ▶ **Industries principales:** *aéronautique, agriculture, informatique, tourisme*
- ▶ **Villes principales:** *Angers, Laval, Le Mans, Nantes, Saint Nazaire*

Personnages célèbres

- ▶ **Claire Bretécher,** *dessinatrice de bandes dessinées (1940–)*
- ▶ **Léon Bollée,** *inventeur d'automobiles (1870–1913)*
- ▶ **Jules Verne,** *écrivain° (1828–1905)*

Le Centre-Val de Loire

La région en chiffres

- ▶ **Superficie:** *39.152 km²*
- ▶ **Population:** *2.556.835*
- ▶ **Industrie principale:** *tourisme*
- ▶ **Villes principales:** *Bourges, Chartres, Orléans, Tours, Vierzon*

Personnages célèbres

- ▶ **Honoré de Balzac,** *écrivain (1799–1850)*
- ▶ **George Sand,** *écrivaine (1804–1876)*
- ▶ **Gérard Depardieu,** *acteur (1948–)*

écrivain writer **Construit** *Constructed* **siècle** *century* **chaque** *each*
logis *living area* **hélice** *helix* **même** *same* **ne se croisent jamais** *never cross*
pèlerinage *pilgrimage* **course** *race*

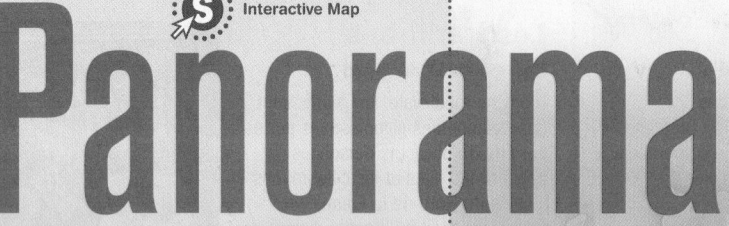
un pèlerinage° à la cathédrale de Chartres

LA FRANCE

Chartres
Laval
Le Mans
Orléans
PAYS DE LA LOIRE
St.-Nazaire
Angers
Chambord
Tours
Chenonceaux
Nantes
Saumur
Vierzon
L'île de Noirmoutier
Cholet
Bourges
L'île d'Yeu
CENTRE-VAL DE LOIRE
Châteauroux
Les Sables-d'Olonne
La Roche-sur-Yon
la Mayenne
la Sarthe
le Loir
la Loire
l'Indre
le Cher
la Vienne

L'OCÉAN ATLANTIQUE

le Vendée Globe, course° nautique

la Loire

| 0 | | 50 miles |
| 0 | | 50 kilomètres |

Incroyable mais vrai!

Construit° au XVIe (seizième) siècle°, l'architecture du château de Chambord est influencée par Léonard de Vinci. Le château a 440 pièces, 84 escaliers et 365 cheminées (une pour chaque° jour de l'année). Le logis° central a deux escaliers en forme de double hélice°. Les escaliers vont dans la même° direction, mais ne se croisent jamais°.

OPTIONS

Tours et Chartres Tours and Chartres are lively cities that have thriving industries and are considered historical, academic, and cultural centers. Tours was at one time the capital of France and the residence of kings. Built on the site of a Roman town, it has remnants of medieval architecture, such as the timber-framed houses present in **place Plumereau**, which is the pedestrian-zoned, medieval heart of the city.

Chartres was named after the Celtic tribe, the Carnutes. The city was attacked and many of its structures destroyed. However, many efforts were put into its restoration. One of the most magnificent architectural masterpieces is **la cathédrale Notre-Dame de Chartres**. The cathedral marks the high point of gothic and medieval art, featuring fine sculptures, over 170 stained-glass windows, and flying buttresses.

Les monuments

La vallée des rois

La vallée de la Loire, avec ses châteaux, est appelée la vallée des rois°. C'est au XVIe (seizième) siècle° que les Valois° quittent Paris pour habiter dans la région, où ils construisent° de nombreux° châteaux de style Renaissance. François Ier inaugure le siècle des «rois voyageurs»: ceux° qui vont d'un château à l'autre avec leur cour° et toutes leurs possessions. Chenonceau, Chambord et Amboise sont aujourd'hui les châteaux les plus° visités.

Les festivals

Le Printemps de Bourges

Le Printemps de Bourges est un festival de musique qui a lieu° chaque année, en avril. Pendant° une semaine, tous les styles de musique sont représentés: variété française, musiques du monde°, rock, musique électronique, reggae, hip-hop, etc... Il y a des dizaines° de spectacles, de nombreux artistes, des milliers de spectateurs et des noms légendaires comme Serge Gainsbourg, Yves Montand, Ray Charles et Johnny Clegg.

Les sports

Les 24 heures du Mans

Les 24 heures du Mans, c'est la course° d'endurance automobile la plus célèbre° du monde. Depuis° 1923, de prestigieuses marques° y° participent. C'est sur ce circuit de 13,6 km que Ferrari gagne neuf victoires et que Porsche détient° le record de 16 victoires avec une vitesse moyenne° de 222 km/h sur 5.335 km. Il existe aussi les 24 heures du Mans moto°.

Les destinations

La route des vins

La vallée de la Loire est réputée pour ses vignobles°, en particulier pour ses vins blancs, qui constituent environ° 75% (pour cent) de la production. La vigne est cultivée dans la vallée depuis l'an 380. Aujourd'hui, les vignerons° de la région produisent 400 millions de bouteilles par an. Pour apprécier le vin, il est nécessaire de l'observer°, de le sentir, de le goûter° et de le déguster°. C'est tout un art!

La vallée des rois

François Ier (1515–1547) and his court resided and traveled between his châteaux in Amboise, Blois, and Chambord. The castles were first built as defense structures but later evolved into decorative palaces. With less of a need for defense, elements like moats and towers remained as symbols of rank and ancestry. Other magnificent châteaux of the area are Azay-le-Rideau, Chenonceau, Villandry, Saumur, Ussé, Chaumont, and Cour-Cheverny.

Le Printemps de Bourges

This music festival has been taking place every spring since its creation in 1977. Festival goers can listen to the music of up-and-coming talent as well as world-renowned artists. Musicians play in a variety of locations on outdoor and indoor stages. Some shows are free to the public.

Les 24 heures du Mans

The biggest names in sports car racing come to test their speed, endurance, and reliability on the 13.6 km (8.5 mile) track. The driver of the car to travel the greatest distance within the 24-hour period is the champion. Over 250,000 fans and hundreds of journalists come to Le Mans in June for one of the best-known automobile races in the world.

La route des vins

The Loire River flows through the heart of the Loire Valley, connecting many of the major wine-producing towns. Nantes, home of the Muscadet grape, produces dry white wines. There is a concentration of vineyards closer to the center of the Loire Valley in Saumur, Vouvray, Azayle-Rideau, Chinon, Bourgueil, among others. Classic white wines are found further east in Pouilly-sur-Loire. The Loire Valley is known for all sorts of white wines, but also produces some red and rosé wines.

Qu'est-ce que vous avez appris? Répondez aux questions par des phrases complètes.

1. Quel événement peut-on voir aux Sables d'Olonne?
   On peut voir le Vendée Globe, une course nautique, aux Sables d'Olonne.
2. Au seizième siècle, qui influence le style de construction de Chambord?
   Léonard de Vinci influence le style de construction de Chambord.
3. Combien de cheminées y a-t-il à Chambord?
   Il y a 365 cheminées à Chambord.
4. De quel style sont les châteaux de la Loire?
   Les châteaux de la Loire sont de style Renaissance.
5. Pourquoi les Valois sont-ils «les rois voyageurs»?
   Ils sont «les rois voyageurs» parce qu'ils vont d'un château à l'autre avec toutes leurs possessions.
6. Combien de spectateurs vont au Printemps de Bourges chaque année?
   Des milliers de spectateurs vont au Printemps de Bourges chaque année.
7. Qu'est-ce que les 24 heures du Mans?
   C'est une course d'endurance automobile.
8. Quel autre type de course existe-t-il au Mans?
   Il existe aussi une course de moto.
9. Quels vins sont produits dans la vallée de la Loire?
   Les vins blancs sont principalement produits dans la vallée de la Loire.
10. Combien de bouteilles y sont produites chaque année? 400 millions de bouteilles de vin sont produites chaque année dans la vallée de la Loire.

Sur Internet

Go to **vhlcentral.com** to find more cultural information related to this **Panorama**.

1. Trouvez des informations sur le Vendée Globe. Quel est l'itinéraire de la course? Combien de bateaux (boats) y participent chaque année?

2. Qui étaient (were) les artistes invités au dernier Printemps de Bourges? En connaissez-vous quelques-uns? (Do you know some of them?)

ressources

WB

pp. 133–134 vhlcentral

ois kings siècle century les Valois name of a royal dynasty construisent build de nombreux numerous ceux those cour court les plus the most a lieu takes place dizaines dozens milliers thousands course race célèbre famous Depuis Since marques brands y there détient holds vitesse moyenne average speed moto motorcycle vignobles vineyards environ around vignerons winegrowers l'observer observe it le goûter taste it le déguster savor it

---

O P T I O N S

Cultural Activity Considering the historical, architectural, and cultural richness of the regions **Pays de la Loire** and **Centre**, it's no wonder they are part of the World Heritage List of UNESCO (United Nations Education, Scientific, and Cultural Organization). Have students explore UNESCO's website to find out more. Ask students to search the World Heritage List for other places from these regions.

Small Groups During the reign of François Ier, the Renaissance period was at its height. There was an increasing interest in arts and humanism, which was evident in the court life at the châteaux. Have small groups research various aspects of court life, such as the food they ate, activities they participated in, and what kinds of music, literature, and art were preferred. Have each group make a short presentation on their findings.

Section Goals

In this section, students will:
- learn to identify the main idea in a text
- read a menu and restaurant review

Stratégie Tell students that recognizing the main idea of a text will help them infer the meanings of unfamiliar words they encounter while reading. Tell them to check the title first because the main idea is often expressed there. Also tell them to read the topic sentence of each paragraph before they read the full text so they will get a sense of the main idea.

Examinez le texte First, have students look at the format of the two texts and ask them if the formats are similar or different. Then, tell them to get together with a partner and discuss the reading strategies they can use to identify the texts' genre.

Comparez les deux textes
- Have students look at the first text (the menu) and ask students if it has a title. Then have them identify the subtitles or subheadings and the type of vocabulary used. Finally, ask them to identify the text's genre.
- Have students look at the second text (the review) and identify the different parts of the reading. Then ask them to compare the formats and vocabulary of the two texts. Write a list of the similarities and differences on the board. Finally, have them identify the genre of the second text.

Lecture

S Audio: Reading

Avant la lecture

STRATÉGIE

Reading for the main idea

As you know, you can learn a great deal about a reading selection by looking at its format and by looking for cognates, titles, and subtitles. You can skim to get the gist of the reading selection and scan it for specific information. Reading for the main idea is another useful strategy; it involves locating the topic sentences of each paragraph to determine the author's purpose. Topic sentences can provide clues about the content of each paragraph, as well as the general organization of the reading. Your choice of which reading strategies to use will depend on the style and format of each reading selection.

Examinez le texte

Dans cette lecture, il y a deux textes différents. Regardez ces textes rapidement. Leur format est-il similaire ou différent? Quelles stratégies vont être utiles pour identifier le genre de ces textes, d'après vous? Comparez vos idées avec un(e) camarade.

Comparez les deux textes
Premier texte
Analysez le format du texte. Y a-t-il un titre? Des sous-titres? Plusieurs sections? Comment ce texte est-il organisé? Regardez rapidement le contenu (*content*) du texte. Quel genre de vocabulaire trouvez-vous dans ce texte? D'après vous, qu'est-ce que c'est?

Deuxième texte
Ce texte est-il organisé comme (*like*) le premier texte? Y a-t-il un titre, des sous-titres et plusieurs parties? Y a-t-il des informations similaires aux informations données dans le premier texte? Lesquelles? (*Which ones?*) Le vocabulaire est-il similaire au vocabulaire du premier texte? D'après vous, quel genre de texte est le deuxième texte? Les deux textes parlent-ils du même restaurant?

Chez Michel

12, rue° des Oliviers • 75006 Paris
Tél. 01.42.56.78.90
Ouvert° tous les soirs, de 19h00 à 23h30

Menu à 18 euros • Service compris

Entrée (au choix°)

Assiette de charcuterie
Escargots (1/2 douzaine°)
Salade de tomates au thon
Pâté de campagne
Soupe de légumes

Plat principal (au choix)

Poulet rôti° haricots verts
Steak au poivre pommes de terre
Thon à la moutarde (riz ou légumes au choix)
Bœuf aux carottes et aux champignons
Pâtes aux fruits de mer

Salade verte et plateau de fromages°

Dessert (au choix)

Tarte aux pommes
Tarte aux poires
Fruits de saison
Fraises à la crème Chantilly
Sorbet aux pêches
Gâteau au chocolat
Crème brûlée
Profiteroles au chocolat

OPTIONS

Small Groups Have students work in groups of three. Tell them to create a skit about a waiter or waitress and two customers at **Chez Michel**. The customers should enter the restaurant, ask for a table, order from the menu, and then ask for the check at the end of the meal. The waiter or waitress should respond appropriately and write down the customers' orders on a piece of paper.

Cultural Comparison Have students work in pairs. Tell them to compare the menu from **Chez Michel** with the menu of a restaurant that they frequent. Are they similar or different? Have them consider the format of the menu, the number of dishes and types of food served, and the prices.

À essayer: L'Huile d'Olive

Un nouveau restaurant provençal dans le quartier de Montmartre

L'Huile d'Olive
14, rue Molière
75018 Paris
01.44.53.76.35

*Ouvert tous les jours sauf° le lundi
Le midi, de 12h00 à 14h30, Menu à 12 euros
et Plat du jour
Le soir, de 19h00 à 23h00, Menus à 15 et 20
euros, Carte*

De l'extérieur, L'Huile d'Olive est un restaurant aux murs gris, dans une petite rue triste du quartier de Montmartre. Mais à l'intérieur, tout change. C'est la Provence, avec tout son soleil et toute sa beauté. Les propriétaires, Monsieur et Madame Duchesnes, ont transformé ce vieux restaurant qui est maintenant entièrement décoré dans le style provençal, en bleu et jaune. Dans ce nouveau restaurant très sympathique, les propriétaires vous proposent des plats provençaux traditionnels préparés avec soin°. Comme entrée, je vous recommande la salade de tomates à l'ail ou le carpaccio de thon à l'huile d'olive. Comme plat principal, commandez la daube° provençale, si vous aimez le bœuf, ou le poulet au pastis°. Le plateau de fruits de mer est un excellent choix pour les amoureux du poisson. Comme légumes, essayez les pommes de terre au romarin° ou les petits pois aux oignons. Pour les végétariens, Madame Duchesnes propose des pâtes aux légumes avec une sauce à la crème délicieuse ou bien une ratatouille° de légumes fantastique. À la fin° du repas, commandez le fromage de chèvre° ou si vous préférez les desserts, goûtez la tarte poires-chocolat.

À L'Huile d'Olive, tout est délicieux et le service est impeccable. Alors, n'hésitez pas! Allez à L'Huile d'Olive pour goûter la Provence! ***

rue *street* Ouvert *Open* choix *choice* douzaine *dozen* rôti *roast* plateau de
fromages *cheeseboard* sauf *except* soin *care* daube *beef stew* pastis *anise
liquor* romarin *rosemary* ratatouille *vegetable stew* fin *end* chèvre *goat*

Après la lecture

Vrai ou faux? Indiquez si les phrases au sujet du premier texte sont **vraies** ou **fausses**. Corrigez les phrases fausses.

1. On peut déjeuner au restaurant Chez Michel.
   Faux. On peut seulement dîner au restaurant Chez Michel.

2. Il n'y a pas de poisson dans les entrées.
   Faux. Il y a du poisson dans la salade de tomates au thon.

3. Comme plat principal, il y a trois viandes.
   Vrai.

4. Le poulet rôti est accompagné de légumes.
   Vrai.

5. Il y a trois plats principaux avec du bœuf.
   Faux. Il y a deux plats principaux avec du bœuf: le steak au poivre pommes de terre et le bœuf aux carottes et aux champignons.

6. On ne peut pas commander de fromage ou de dessert.
   Faux. On peut commander du fromage et des desserts.

Commandez Suggérez une entrée, un plat et un dessert pour ces personnes qui vont dîner au restaurant Chez Michel.
Answers will vary. Possible answers provided.

1. Madame Lonier est au régime et elle n'aime pas la viande.
   Elle peut prendre les escargots, le thon et les fruits de saison.

2. Monsieur Sanchez est végétarien. Il n'aime pas le thon.
   Il adore les légumes, mais il ne mange jamais de fruits.
   Il peut prendre la soupe de légumes, les pâtes aux fruits de mer et le gâteau au chocolat.

3. Madame Petit a envie de manger de la viande, mais elle n'aime pas beaucoup le bœuf. Elle n'aime ni (*neither*) les gâteaux ni (*nor*) les tartes. Elle peut prendre le pâté de campagne, le poulet rôti haricots verts et les fraises à la crème Chantilly.

4. Et vous, qu'est-ce que vous avez envie de goûter au restaurant Chez Michel? Pourquoi?

Répondez Répondez aux questions par des phrases complètes, d'après le deuxième texte.

1. Comment s'appelle le restaurant?
   Il s'appelle L'Huile d'Olive.

2. Combien coûtent les menus du soir?
   Ils coûtent 15 et 20 euros.

3. Quel est le style de cuisine du restaurant?
   Le style de cuisine est provençal.

4. Quelles viandes le critique (*critic*) recommande-t-il?
   Il recommande la daube provençale et le poulet au pastis.

5. Comment Madame Duchesnes prépare-t-elle les pâtes?
   Elle les prépare avec des légumes et une sauce à la crème délicieuse.

6. Le critique a-t-il aimé ce restaurant? Justifiez votre réponse. Answers may vary. Sample answer: Oui. Le restaurant est très sympathique. Les plats sont préparés avec soin. Tout est délicieux et le service est impeccable.

À vous Vous et votre partenaire allez sortir manger dans un de ces restaurants. Décidez quel restaurant vous préférez. Est-ce que vous allez déjeuner ou dîner? Combien d'argent allez-vous dépenser? Qu'est-ce que vous allez commander?

Vrai ou faux? Go over the answers with the class.

Commandez
• This activity can be done in pairs.
• For additional practice, give students these situations.
 5. David n'aime ni la soupe ni le poisson. Il aime les fruits.
 6. Isabelle adore la viande, mais elle n'aime pas les légumes. Elle adore les fruits, surtout les pommes.
 7. Claudine adore le thon et les tomates. Elle aime aussi le chocolat.

Répondez Have students write three more questions about the reading. Then tell them to exchange papers with a partner and answer the questions.

À vous After completing the activity, take a quick class survey to find out which restaurant was more popular among students. Ask: **Combien de personnes choisissent Chez Michel? Et L'Huile d'Olive?** Tally the results on the board. Then ask pairs to explain why they chose that particular restaurant.

OPTIONS

Montmartre **Le quartier de Montmartre**, located on a hill in Paris (**la butte Montmartre**), is the highest natural point in the city and a popular tourist site. **La Basilique du Sacré-Cœur**, with its large white dome, sits on the top of the hill. Montmartre is famous for its history of bohemian artists and its nightlife, with the **Moulin Rouge** giving it worldwide acclaim.

Extra Practice For additional practice with the restaurant review, give students these true/false items. 1. Le restaurant se trouve en Provence. (Faux.) 2. Le restaurant est fermé le samedi. (Faux.) 3. L'extérieur du restaurant n'est pas très beau. (Vrai.) 4. Il y a des choix de plats si on est végétarien. (Vrai.)

Section Goals

In this section, students will:
- learn to express and support opinions
- write a restaurant review

Stratégie Explain to students that when they write a restaurant review, it is helpful to have some way of organizing the details required to support the rating. Working in groups of three, have students write a list of questions in French that elicit information readers might want to know and use them to create a rating sheet. Tell them to refer to the list of questions in the **Thème** section as a guide. Encourage students to leave space for comments in each category so they can record details that support their opinions. Suggest that they fill out the rating sheet during the various stages of the meal.

Thème Explain that each student will rate a local restaurant and write a review of a meal there, including a recommendation for future patrons.

Écriture

STRATÉGIE

Expressing and supporting opinions

Written reviews are one of the many kinds of writing that require you to state your opinions. In order to convince your reader to take your opinions seriously, it is important to support them as thoroughly as possible, using facts, examples, and other forms of evidence. In a restaurant review, for example, it is not enough just to rate the food, service, and atmosphere. Readers will want details about the dishes you ordered, the kind of service you received, and the type of atmosphere you encountered. If you were writing a concert or album review, what kinds of details might your readers expect to find?

It is easier to include details that support your opinions if you plan ahead. Before going to a place or event that you are planning to review, write a list of questions that your readers might ask. Decide which aspects of the experience you are going to rate, and list the details that will help you decide upon a rating. You can then organize these lists into a questionnaire and a rating sheet. Bring these forms with you to remind you of the kinds of information you need to gather in order to support your opinions. Later, these forms will help you organize your review into logical categories. They can also provide the details and other evidence you need to convince your readers of your opinions.

Thème

Écrire une critique

Avant l'écriture

1. Vous allez écrire la critique d'un restaurant de votre ville pour le journal de l'université. Avant de l'écrire, vous allez d'abord créer un questionnaire et une feuille d'évaluation (*rating*) pour vous faire (*to form*) une opinion. Ces éléments vont aussi vous servir pour l'écriture de votre critique.

2. Travaillez avec un(e) partenaire pour créer le questionnaire. Vous pouvez utiliser ces questions ou en inventer (*invent some*) d'autres. Incluez les quatre catégories indiquées.

   - **Cuisine** Quel(s) type(s) de plat(s) y a-t-il au menu? Le restaurant a-t-il une spécialité? Citez quelques plats typiques (entrées et plats principaux) que vous avez goûtés et indiquez les ingrédients utilisés dans ces plats.

   - **Service** Comment est le service? Les serveurs sont-ils gentils et polis? Sont-ils lents ou rapides à apporter la carte, les boissons et les plats?

   - **Ambiance** Comment est le restaurant? Est-il beau? Grand? Bien décoré? Est-ce un restaurant simple ou élégant? Y a-t-il une terrasse? Un bar? Des musiciens?

   - **Informations pratiques** Quel est le prix moyen d'un repas dans ce restaurant (au déjeuner et/ou au dîner)? Où est le restaurant? Quelle est son adresse et comment y (*there*) va-t-on de l'université? Quels sont le numéro de téléphone du restaurant et ses heures d'ouverture (*operating hours*)?

O P T I O N S

Avant l'écriture Before students start the assignment, review the difference between fact and opinion and tell them that a good review will contain both. Make various statements and have students say whether they are **fait** (*fact*) or **opinion**: That restaurant has three function rooms. (**fait**) The rooms are beautifully decorated. (**opinion**) Everyone who dines there will have a wonderful time. (**opinion**) The entrees range between 20 and 30 euros each. (**fait**) To warm up and generate vocabulary for the writing assignment, have students work in groups of three to role-play a restaurant scene: two diners (one of whom is a restaurant reviewer) and a waiter/waitress. Have them role-play the diners' conversation with the server and then their own conversations while they wait for their food and after it arrives.

3. Après avoir écrit le questionnaire, utilisez les quatre catégories et la liste de questions pour créer une feuille d'évaluation. Un restaurant reçoit (*gets*) trois étoiles (*stars*) s'il est très bon et ne reçoit pas d'étoile s'il est mauvais.

4. Après avoir créé la feuille d'évaluation, utilisez-la pour évaluer un restaurant que vous connaissez. Si (*If*) vous le connaissez bien, peut-être n'est-il pas nécessaire d'aller y (*there*) manger pour compléter la feuille. Si vous ne le connaissez pas bien, vous devez aller l'essayer. Utilisez des comparatifs et des superlatifs quand vous écrivez vos commentaires et vos opinions.

Nom du restaurant:

Nombre d'étoiles:

1. Cuisine

    Type:

    Ingrédients:

    Qualité:

    Meilleur plat:

    Pire plat:

    Informations sur le chef:

Écriture

Utilisez la feuille d'évaluation que vous avez complétée pour écrire votre critique culinaire. Écrivez six brefs paragraphes:

1. une introduction pour indiquer votre opinion générale du restaurant et le nombre d'étoiles qu'il a reçu (*got*)

2. une description de la carte

3. une description du service

4. une description de l'ambiance (*atmosphere*)

5. un paragraphe pour donner les informations pratiques

6. une conclusion pour souligner (*to emphasize*) votre opinion et pour donner des suggestions pour améliorer (*to improve*) le restaurant

Après l'écriture

1. Échangez votre critique avec celle (*the one*) d'un(e) partenaire. Répondez à ces questions pour commenter son travail.

- Votre partenaire a-t-il/elle écrit une introduction présentant (*presenting*) une opinion générale du restaurant?

- Votre partenaire a-t-il/elle écrit quatre paragraphes sur la cuisine, le service, l'ambiance et les informations pratiques?

- Votre partenaire a-t-il/elle écrit une conclusion présentant une nouvelle fois son opinion et proposant (*suggesting*) des suggestions pour le restaurant?

- Votre partenaire a-t-il/elle utilisé des comparatifs et des superlatifs pour décrire le restaurant?

- Quel(s) détail(s) ajouteriez-vous (*would you add*)? Quel(s) détail(s) enlèveriez-vous (*would you delete*)? Quel(s) autre(s) commentaire(s) avez-vous pour votre partenaire?

2. Corrigez votre brochure d'après (*according to*) les commentaires de votre partenaire. Relisez votre travail pour éliminer ces problèmes:

- des fautes (*errors*) d'orthographe et de ponctuation

- des fautes de conjugaison

- des fautes d'accord (*agreement*) des adjectifs

- un mauvais emploi (*use*) de l'imparfait et du passé composé

- un mauvais emploi des comparatifs et des superlatifs

EVALUATION

Criteria

Content Contains a complete description of a dining experience that includes information about the food, the service, the atmosphere, and factual details about the restaurant.
Scale: 1 2 3 4 5

Organization Organized into six paragraphs: an introduction, four paragraphs corresponding to the four sections of the task, and a conclusion.
Scale: 1 2 3 4 5

Accuracy Uses forms of **devoir**, **vouloir**, and **pouvoir** correctly. Uses verb tenses correctly and in the correct context. Spells words, conjugates verbs, and modifies adjectives correctly throughout.
Scale: 1 2 3 4 5

Creativity Includes additional information that is not included in the task and/or uses adjectives and descriptive verbs to make the review more interesting and informative.
Scale: 1 2 3 4 5

Scoring

Excellent	18–20 points
Good	14–17 points
Satisfactory	10–13 points
Unsatisfactory	< 10 points

OPTIONS

Écriture Encourage students to use forms of **devoir** in their reviews to make recommendations for improvement. Point out that reviewers frequently express their preferences and opinions in a review while offering advice based on those opinions. They should use **vouloir** to express things they want to see done, **devoir** to say what should be done, and **pouvoir** to say what the restaurant can and can't do well.

Give students some helpful expressions to get them started as they begin each paragraph. Paragraph 1: **J'ai récemment dîné à...**, **La semaine dernière, j'ai eu l'opportunité d'aller à...**, **Un nouveau restaurant a ouvert** (*opened*)... Paragraphs 2-5: **Concernant** (*Regarding*)..., **Pour ce qui est de** (*When it comes to*)..., **À noter** (*Note*) **aussi que...** Paragraph 6: **En conclusion..., En résumé.../Pour résumer..., Je veux finir en disant** (*by saying*) **que...**

Instructional Resources
vhlcentral.com:
Textbook MP3s; Textbook
Audioscript; reference tools

Suggestions
• Tell students that an easy way to study from **Vocabulaire** is to cover up the French half of each section, leaving only the English equivalents exposed. They can then quiz themselves on the French items. To focus on the English equivalents of the French entries, they simply reverse this process.
• Point out to students that they can use the Vocabulary Tools at **vhlcentral.com** for reference and extra vocabulary practice.

◁)) Ⓢ Vocabulary Tools

Leçon 9A

À table!

une cantine *school cafeteria*
cuisiner *to cook*
un déjeuner *lunch*
un dîner *dinner*
un goûter *afternoon snack*
un petit-déjeuner *breakfast*
un repas *meal*

Les fruits

une banane *banana*
une fraise *strawberry*
un fruit *fruit*
une orange *orange*
une pêche *peach*
une poire *pear*
une pomme *apple*
une tomate *tomato*

Autres aliments

un aliment *food item*
la confiture *jam*
la nourriture *food, sustenance*
des pâtes (f.) *pasta*
le riz *rice*
une tarte *pie, tart*
un yaourt *yogurt*

Verbes

devenir *to become*
devoir *to have to (must); to owe*
maintenir *to maintain*
pouvoir *to be able to (can)*
retenir *to keep, to retain*
revenir *to come back*
tenir *to hold*
venir *to come*
vouloir *to want; to mean (with dire)*

Autres mots et locutions

depuis + [time] *since*
il y a + [time] *ago*
pendant + [time] *for*

Les viandes et les poissons

le bœuf *beef*
un escargot *escargot, snail*
les fruits de mer (m.) *seafood*
un œuf *egg*
un pâté (de campagne) *pâté, meat spread*
le porc *pork*
un poulet *chicken*
une saucisse *sausage*
un steak *steak*
le thon *tuna*
la viande *meat*

Les légumes

l'ail (m.) *garlic*
une aubergine *eggplant*
une carotte *carrot*
un champignon *mushroom*
des haricots verts (m.) *green beans*
une laitue *lettuce*
un légume *vegetable*
un oignon *onion*
des petits pois (m.) *peas*
un poivron (vert, rouge) *(green, red) pepper*
une pomme de terre *potato*
une salade *salad*

Les achats

faire les courses (f.) *to go (grocery) shopping*
un supermarché *supermarket*

Expressions utiles

See p. 365.

Leçon 9B

À table!

une assiette *plate*
un bol *bowl*
une carafe d'eau *pitcher of water*
une carte *menu*
un couteau *knife*
une cuillère (à soupe/à café) *spoon (soup spoon/teaspoon)*
une fourchette *fork*
un menu *menu*
une nappe *tablecloth*
une serviette *napkin*
une boîte (de conserve) *can*
la crème *cream*
l'huile (d'olive) (f.) *(olive) oil*
la mayonnaise *mayonnaise*
la moutarde *mustard*
le poivre *pepper*
le sel *salt*
une tranche *slice*
À table! *Dinner is ready!*
compris *included*

Les repas

commander *to order*
être au régime *to be on a diet*
goûter *to taste*
une entrée *appetizer, starter*
un hors-d'œuvre *hors-d'oeuvre, appetizer*
un plat (principal) *(main) dish*

Les achats

une boucherie *butcher's shop*
une boulangerie *bread shop, bakery*
une charcuterie *delicatessen*
une pâtisserie *pastry shop, bakery*
une poissonnerie *fish shop*
un(e) commerçant(e) *shopkeeper*
un kilo(gramme) *kilo(gram)*

Expressions utiles

See p. 383.

Comparatives and superlatives

plus + [adjective/adverb] + que *more... than*
aussi + [adjective/adverb] + que *as... as*
moins + [adjective/adverb] + que *less... than*
[noun] + le/la/les + plus + [adjective] + de *the most*
[noun] + le/la/les + moins + [adjective] + de *the least*
bon(ne)(s) *good*
mauvais(e)(s) *bad*
meilleur(e)(s) *better*
pire(s)/plus mauvais(e)(s) *worse*
le/la/les meilleur(e)(s) *best*
le/la/les pire(s); le/la/les plus mauvais(e)(s) *worst*
bien *well*
mieux *better*
le mieux *best*

La santé

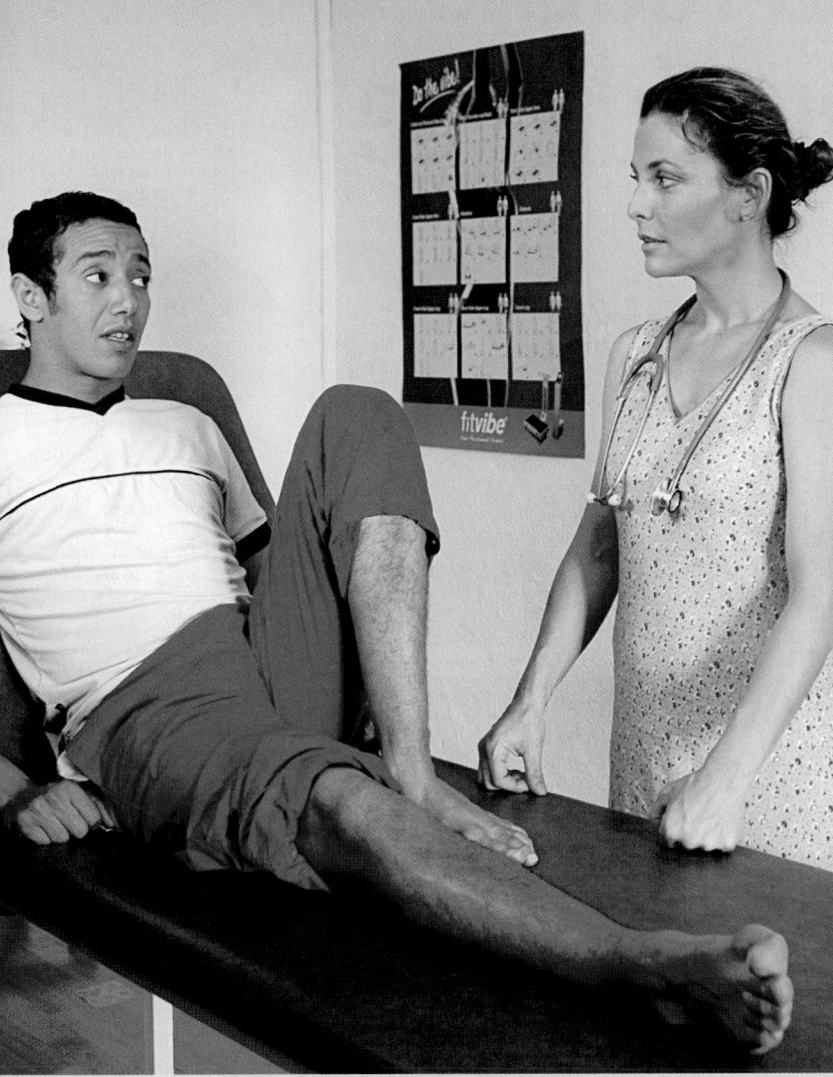

Pour commencer

- Quelle est la profession de la dame, coiffeuse ou médecin?
- Où sont Rachid et cette dame, à l'hôpital ou à l'épicerie?
- Qu'est-ce qu'il faisait avant de venir, il jouait au foot ou il faisait les courses?

Unit Goals

Leçon 10A

In this lesson, students will learn:
- terms for parts of the body
- terms to discuss one's daily routine
- the pronunciation of **ch, qu, ph, th**, and **gn**
- about healthcare in France
- reflexive verbs
- some common idiomatic reflexive verbs
- about the optical company Krys

Leçon 10B

In this lesson, students will learn:
- terms to describe one's health
- terms for illnesses and remedies
- terms related to medical visits and treatments
- the pronunciation of **p, t**, and **c**
- about the national healthcare system in France
- more information on pharmacies and health-related businesses through specially shot video footage
- about famous French singer and songwriter Pierre Bachelet
- the **passé composé** of reflexive verbs
- the pronouns **y** and **en**
- to listen for specific information

Savoir-faire

In this section, students will learn:
- cultural and historical information about **la Nouvelle-Aquitaine**
- to use background knowledge to increase reading comprehension
- to sequence events in a narration

Pour commencer
- **Elle est médecin.**
- **Ils sont à l'hôpital.**
- **Il jouait au foot.**

RESOURCES

Student Activities Manual (SAM):
Workbook Activities, pp. 135–148
Laboratory Manual: Lab Activities, pp. 73–80
Workbook/Video Manual: Video Activities, pp. 37-40; pp. 79-80
WB/VM/LM Answer Key

vhlcentral.com: Textbook MP3s; Lab MP3s; Textbook Audioscript; Lab Audioscript Video; Videoscript; **Roman-photo** Translations; **Vocabulaire supplémentaire**; Activity Pack (including **Feuilles d'activités**, Info Gap Activities, and Task-based Activities);

Le Zapping TV clip transcription; **Essayez!** and **Mise en pratique** answers; Digital Image Bank; Testing Program; Testing Program MP3s

Section Goals

In this section, students will learn and practice vocabulary related to:
• daily routines
• personal hygiene
• parts of the body

Instructional Resources
vhlcentral.com:
Digital Image Bank;
Vocabulaire supplémentaire
(including vocabulary illustrations from the textbook, theme-based illustrations);
Mise en pratique *answers;*
Textbook Audioscript;
Lab Audioscript; Activity Pack (Info Gap Activities);
Textbook MP3s; Lab MP3s;
SAM Answer Key;
reference tools

Suggestions

• Using the **10A Contexts** illustration from the Digital Image Bank, describe what the people in the illustration are doing. Then point out objects and parts of the body. Examples: **Il se rase. Elle se maquille. C'est une serviette de bain.**

• Explain the relationships between these terms: **se raser, un rasoir, une crème à raser; se réveiller, un réveil; se coiffer, un coiffeur, une coiffeuse;** and **se brosser les dents, le dentifrice.**

• Remind students that the plural of **l'œil** is **les yeux.**

• Review the use of partitives with non-count nouns using words from **Espace contextes.** Examples: **du dentifrice** and **du shampooing.**

• Keep in mind that reflexives will only be used in the infinitive and third person singular in the activities until **Espace structures 10A.1**

• Use the Vocabulary illustrations and the Daily routine illustrations from the Digital Image Bank to help students familiarize themselves with personal hygiene and parts of the body.

• Additional vocabulary for this lesson can be found in the **Vocabulaire supplémentaire** on the Supersite.

Leçon 10A

You will learn how to...
▪ describe your daily routine
▪ discuss personal hygiene

Ⓢ Vocabulary Tools

La routine quotidienne

Vocabulaire

faire sa toilette	to wash up
se brosser les cheveux	to brush one's hair
se brosser les dents	to brush one's teeth
se coiffer	to do one's hair
se coucher	to go to bed
se déshabiller	to undress oneself
s'endormir	to go to sleep, to fall asleep
s'habiller	to get dressed
se laver (les mains)	to wash oneself (one's hands)
prendre une douche	to take a shower
se regarder	to look at oneself
se réveiller	to wake up
se sécher	to dry oneself
le shampooing	shampoo
le cœur	heart
le corps	body
le dos	back
la gorge	throat
une joue	cheek
un orteil	toe
la peau	skin
la poitrine	chest
la taille	waist
le visage	face

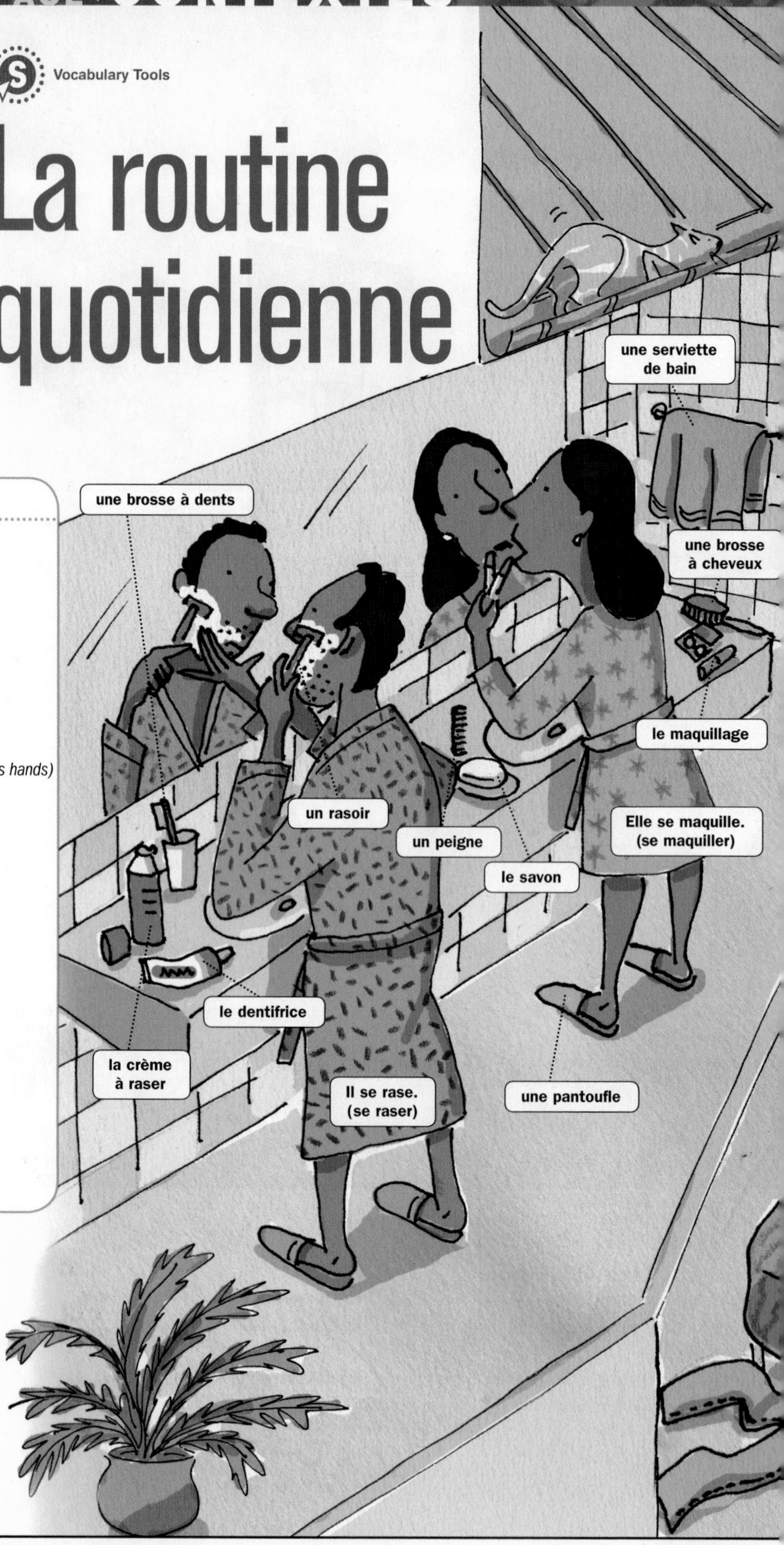

une serviette de bain

une brosse à dents

une brosse à cheveux

le maquillage

Elle se maquille. (se maquiller)

un rasoir

un peigne

le savon

le dentifrice

la crème à raser

Il se rase. (se raser)

une pantoufle

ressources

WB	LM	Ⓢ
pp. 135–136	p. 73	vhlcentral

OPTIONS

Game Write vocabulary words for parts of the body on index cards. On another set of cards, draw or paste pictures to match each term. Tape them face down on the board in random order. Divide the class into two teams. Play a game of Concentration in which students match words with pictures. When a player makes a match, that player's team collects those cards. The team with the most cards at the end of the game wins.

Extra Practice Write two columns on the board: **la routine du matin** and **la routine du soir.** Have students classify the verbs in **Espace contextes** according to whether people do the actions when they wake up in the morning or in the evening before they go to bed. Then have students order the actions logically. This activity can also be done in pairs.

Mise en pratique

1 Écoutez

Sarah, son grand frère Guillaume et leur père parlent de qui va utiliser la salle de bains en premier ce matin. Écoutez la conversation et indiquez si les affirmations suivantes sont **vraies** ou **fausses**.

	Vrai	Faux
1. Guillaume ne va pas se raser.	☐	☑
2. Guillaume doit encore prendre une douche et se brosser les dents.	☑	☐
3. Sarah n'a pas entendu son réveil.	☑	☐
4. Guillaume demande à Sarah de lui apporter de la crème à raser.	☐	☑
5. Guillaume demande un savon à Sarah.	☐	☑
6. Guillaume demande une grande serviette de bain à Sarah.	☑	☐
7. Sarah doit prendre une douche et s'habiller en moins de vingt minutes.	☑	☐
8. Sarah décide de ne pas se maquiller et de ne pas se sécher les cheveux aujourd'hui.	☑	☐

2 Association

Associez les activités de la colonne de gauche aux parties du corps correspondantes des colonnes de droite. Notez que certains éléments ne sont pas utilisés et que d'autres sont utilisés plus d'une fois.

_e_ 1. écouter	a. la bouche	f. le pied
_a/b_ 2. manger	b. la gorge	g. la taille
_f_ 3. marcher	c. l'orteil	h. la tête
_i_ 4. montrer	d. l'œil	i. le doigt
_a/b_ 5. parler	e. l'oreille	j. le nez
_h_ 6. penser		
_c/f/i/j_ 7. sentir		
_d_ 8. regarder		

3 Quel matin!

Complétez les phrases par le mot ou l'expression de la liste qui convient pour trouver ce qui est arrivé à Alexandre aujourd'hui. Notez que tous les mots et expressions ne sont pas utilisés.

le bras	se coucher	se laver	le réveil
se brosser les dents	la gorge	le peigne	le ventre
le cœur	s'habiller	le pied	les yeux

Ce matin, Alexandre n'entend pas son (1) __réveil__. Quand il se lève, il met d'abord le (2) __pied__ gauche par terre. Il entre dans la salle de bains. Là, il ne trouve pas le (3) __peigne__ pour se coiffer ni (*nor*) le dentifrice pour (4) __se brosser les dents__. Il se regarde dans le miroir. Ses (5) __yeux__ sont tout rouges. Comme il a très faim, son (6) __ventre__ commence à faire du bruit (*noise*). Il retourne ensuite dans sa chambre pour (7) __s'habiller__. Il met un pantalon noir et une chemise bleue. Puis, il descend les escaliers et tombe. Après un moment, il retourne dans sa chambre. Après un tel début (*such a beginning*) de journée, Alexandre va (8) __se coucher__.

Practice more at vhlcentral.com.

quatre cent sept **407**

Attention!
The verbs following the pronoun **se** are called reflexive verbs. You will learn more about them in **STRUCTURES**. For now, when talking about another person, place the pronoun **se** between the subject and the verb.
Il se regarde. *He looks at himself.*
Elle se réveille. *She wakes up.*

---

la tête
un œil (yeux *pl.*)
le nez
une oreille
la bouche
le cou
un bras
le réveil
un doigt
le ventre
un genou (genoux *pl.*)
une jambe
Elle se lève. (se lever)
un pied
un doigt de pied

---

1 Audioscript SARAH: Allez, Guillaume. J'ai besoin d'utiliser la salle de bains.
GUILLAUME: Une minute! Je viens juste d'y entrer.
S: Mais, je suis en retard pour mes cours. Je n'ai pas entendu mon réveil.
PÈRE: Sarah, laisse ton frère se raser, prendre une douche et se brosser les dents. Il est arrivé le premier.
G: Je fais vite. Tiens! Il n'y a plus de shampooing. Est-ce que tu peux m'apporter une nouvelle bouteille et une grande serviette de bain, s'il te plaît?
S: Et tes pantoufles aussi?
Un peu plus tard...
P: Où est ta sœur?
G: Sarah va prendre sa douche. Elle doit se brosser les dents, s'habiller et se coiffer en moins de vingt minutes. Elle a décidé de ne pas se maquiller et de ne pas se sécher les cheveux pour gagner du temps.
P: Bon, on va te préparer quelque chose à manger dans le bus.
(On Textbook MP3s)

1 Suggestion Have students correct the false statements. If necessary, play the recording again.

2 Expansions
- Have students think of other verbs to add to the list and let the class guess the body part(s) associated with them.
- Do this activity in reverse. Name various parts of the body and have students suggest verbs associated with them.

3 Expansion Ask students comprehension questions based on the paragraph. Examples: **1. Pourquoi Alexandre se lève-t-il tard?** (Il n'entend pas son réveil.) **2. Que fait-il d'abord?** (Il met le pied par terre.) **3. Où va-t-il?** (Il va à la salle de bains.) **4. Ça ne va pas bien. Pourquoi?** (Il ne peut pas se coiffer./Il ne trouve pas le dentifrice./Ses yeux sont rouges.) **5. Que met-il quand il s'habille?** (Il met un pantalon noir et une chemise bleue.) **6. Pourquoi Alexandre veut-il se coucher?** (Il veut se coucher parce qu'il est tombé dans les escaliers./La journée commence mal.)

OPTIONS

Pairs Have students write down three daily routine activities. Each partner should ask questions using words that indicate time like **pendant**, **avant**, and **après** in order to guess the activities on their partner's list. Example: **Étudiant(e) 1: C'est avant ou après le petit-déjeuner? Étudiant(e) 2: C'est après le petit-déjeuner. Étudiant(e) 1: C'est se brosser les dents? Étudiant(e) 2: Oui, c'est ça.**

Small Groups Have students work in groups of three. Tell them to draw a picture and write a description of a fantastical alien or monster. Example: **C'est un extraterrestre/un monstre. Il a trois nez, quatre yeux et huit bras.** Then have each group read their description while the class draws a picture of the alien or monster. Have students compare their drawings with the group's picture.

Communication

NATIONAL communication STANDARDS

4

Que font-ils? Écrivez ce que (*what*) font ces personnes et ce qu'elles utilisent pour le faire. Donnez autant de (*as many*) détails que possible. Ensuite, à tour de rôle avec un(e) partenaire, lisez vos descriptions. Votre partenaire doit deviner quelle image vous décrivez. Answers will vary.

1.

2.

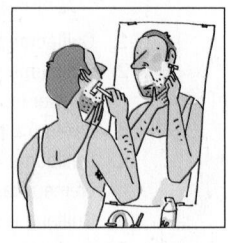
3.

4.

5.

6.

7.

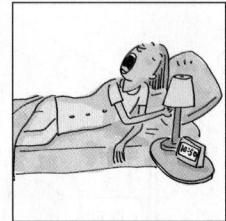
8.

5

Définition Créez votre propre définition des mots de la liste. Ensuite, à tour de rôle, lisez vos définitions à votre partenaire. Il/Elle doit deviner le mot correspondant. Answers will vary.

MODÈLE

cheveux

Étudiant(e) 1: *On utilise une brosse ou un peigne pour les coiffer. Qu'est-ce que c'est?*
Étudiant(e) 2: *Ce sont les cheveux.*

1. le cœur
2. le corps
3. le cou
4. les dents
5. le dos
6. le genou
7. la joue
8. le nez
9. l'œil
10. l'orteil
11. la poitrine
12. le visage

6

Décrivez Avec un(e) partenaire, pensez à votre acteur/actrice préféré(e). Quelle est sa routine du matin? Décrivez-la et utilisez les adjectifs de la liste et les mots et expressions d'**ESPACE CONTEXTES**. Answers will vary.

beau	gros	petit
court	heureux	sincère
égoïste	jeune	de taille moyenne
grand	long	vieux

7

Que fait-elle? Votre professeur va vous donner, à vous et à votre partenaire, deux feuilles d'activités différentes. À tour de rôle, posez-vous des questions pour savoir ce que fait Nadia chaque soir et chaque matin. Attention! Ne regardez pas la feuille de votre partenaire. Answers will vary.

MODÈLE

Étudiant(e) 1: *À vingt-trois heures, Nadia se déshabille et met son pyjama. Que fait-elle ensuite?*
Étudiant(e) 2: *Après, elle…*

---

4 Expansion Use the illustration for this activity from the Digital Image Bank. Assign names to the people in the drawings. Then ask questions about the people's actions. Examples: **Qui se lave les mains? Que fait ____?**

5 Suggestion Have two volunteers read the **modèle** aloud.

5 Expansion For additional practice, give students these items. **13. les doigts de pied 14. la tête 15. le pied**

6 Expansion Have volunteers read their descriptions to the class without saying the person's name. The class has to guess who they're describing.

7 Suggestions
- Before beginning this activity, you might want to review telling time and adverbs of time.
- Have two volunteers read the **modèle** aloud. Then divide the class into pairs and distribute the Info Gap Handouts found in the Activity Pack on the Supersite for this activity. Give students ten minutes to complete the activity.

OPTIONS

Extra Practice Have students name the body part(s) associated with each of the following objects. **1. du shampooing (les cheveux) 2. les lunettes (les yeux) 3. un rasoir (les jambes, le visage) 4. les pantoufles (les pieds) 5. un gant (la main) 6. une écharpe (le cou) 7. un pantalon (les jambes) 8. un peigne (les cheveux) 9. une radio (les oreilles)**

Extra Practice Read these statements to students and have them say whether they are **logique** or **illogique**. **1. Alain prend une douche, puis il se sèche. (logique) 2. Gilles s'habille, puis il se couche. (illogique) 3. Solange se coiffe, puis elle s'endort. (illogique) 4. Isabelle se maquille, puis elle se lave. (illogique) 5. Denis se lève, puis il fait sa toilette. (logique)**

Les sons et les lettres  Audio

ch, qu, ph, th, and gn

The letter combination **ch** is usually pronounced like the English *sh*, as in the word *shoe*.

chat	**ch**ien	**ch**ose	en**ch**anté

In words borrowed from other languages, the pronunciation of **ch** may be irregular. For example, in words of Greek origin, **ch** is pronounced **k**.

psy**ch**ologie	te**ch**nologie	ar**ch**aïque	ar**ch**éologie

The letter combination **qu** is almost always pronounced like the letter **k**.

quand	pratik**qu**er	kios**qu**e	**qu**elle

The letter combination **ph** is pronounced like an **f**.

télé**ph**one	**ph**oto	pro**ph**ète	géogra**ph**ie

The letter combination **th** is pronounced like the letter **t**. English *th* sounds, as in the words *this* and *with*, never occur in French.

thé	a**th**lète	biblio**th**èque	sympa**th**ique

The letter combination **gn** is pronounced like the sound in the middle of the English word *onion*.

monta**gn**e	espa**gn**ol	ga**gn**er	Allema**gn**e

Prononcez Répétez les mots suivants à voix haute.

1. thé
2. quart
3. chose
4. question
5. cheveux
6. parce que
7. champagne
8. casquette
9. philosophie
10. fréquenter
11. photographie
12. sympathique

Articulez Répétez les phrases suivantes à voix haute.

1. Quentin est martiniquais ou québécois?
2. Quelqu'un explique la question à Joseph.
3. Pourquoi est-ce que Philippe est inquiet?
4. Ignace prend une photo de la montagne.
5. Monique fréquente un café en Belgique.
6. Théo étudie la physique.

N'éveillez pas le chat qui dort.[2]

Dictons Répétez les dictons à voix haute.

La vache la première au pré lèche la rosée.[1]

[1] The early bird gets the worm. (lit. The cow that arrives at the pasture first licks the dew.)
[2] Let sleeping dogs lie. (lit. Don't wake a sleeping cat.)

ressources
LM
p. 74
vhlcentral

quatre cent neuf **409**

Section Goals

In this section, students will learn about the sounds **ch, qu, ph, th,** and **gn.**

Instructional Resources
vhlcentral.com:
Textbook MP3s; Lab MP3s; SAM Answer Key; Textbook Audioscript; Lab Audioscript; reference tools

Suggestions
- Model the pronunciation of each of the example words and have students repeat them.
- Mention words and expressions from the **Vocabulaire** that contain the consonant clusters presented on this page. Then have them repeat after you. Alternatively, ask students to recall such vocabulary. Examples: **se coucher, se maquiller, un peigne,** etc. See if a volunteer is able to recall any words from previous lessons. Examples: **géographie, enseigner, prochain, quatre.**
- Dictate six to eight familiar words containing these letter combinations to the class, repeating each one at least two times. Then write them on the board or on a transparency and have students check and correct their spelling.
- Explain that in the words **pourquoi** and **quoi** there is a **w** sound, which is an effect of **oi** (**moi, toi**), not **qu.**
- Tell students that the letter combination **tch** is pronounced as it is in English. Example: **Tchad.** The difference is that **ch** and **tch** are always pronounced differently in French, but often the same in English.

O P T I O N S

Extra Practice Here are some sentences to use for additional practice. **1.** Charlotte et Michèle ont de la chance. **2.** Élisabeth quitte la maison à quatre heures et quart. **3.** Chantal a visité l'Allemagne et le Mexique. **4.** Thérèse a acheté une photo d'une montagne espagnole.

Extra Practice Teach students these French tongue-twisters that contain the sounds featured on this page. **1.** Une bête noire se baigne dans une baignoire noire. **2.** Je suis ce que je suis et si je suis ce que je suis, qu'est-ce que je suis? **3.** Cinq chiens chassent six chats.

Section Goals

In this section, students will learn functional phrases for talking about daily routines and emotional states.

Instructional Resources
vhlcentral.com:
Roman-photo *Video, Videoscript, and Translation; SAM Answer Key; reference tools*

Video Recap: Leçon 9B
Review the previous **Roman-photo** with this activity.
1. Quel cadeau Rachid a-t-il apporté à Sandrine? (des chocolats)
2. Et David, qu'a-t-il apporté à Sandrine? (des fleurs)
3. Qui aide à mettre la table? (Amina et Stéphane)
4. Qui est au régime? (Amina)
5. Qu'est-ce que Sandrine a préparé comme dessert? (une tarte aux pommes)

Video Synopsis
In the bathroom, David notices a rash on his face. Rachid needs to use the bathroom, because he woke up late and doesn't want to be late for class. David is taking a long time to get ready. When David finally opens the door, Rachid tricks him into closing his eyes so that he can slip into the bathroom and lock the door. Rachid also advises David to call a doctor about his rash.

Suggestions
• Have students predict what the episode will be about based on the video stills.
• Tell students to scan the **Roman-photo** and find sentences related to daily routines.
• After reading the **Roman-photo** in pairs, have students summarize the episode.

Drôle de surprise  Video

PERSONNAGES

David

Rachid

Chez David et Rachid...

DAVID Oh là là, ça ne va pas du tout, toi!
RACHID David, tu te dépêches? Il est sept heures et quart. Je dois me préparer, moi aussi!

DAVID Ne t'inquiète pas. Je finis de me brosser les dents!
RACHID On doit partir dans moins de vingt minutes. Tu ne te rends pas compte!
DAVID Excuse-moi, mais on s'est couché tard hier soir.
RACHID Oui et on ne s'est pas réveillé à l'heure, mais mon prof de sciences po, ça ne l'intéresse pas tout ça.

DAVID Attends, je ne trouve pas le peigne... Ah, le voilà. Je me coiffe... Deux secondes!
RACHID C'était vraiment sympa hier soir... On s'entend tous super bien et on ne s'ennuie jamais ensemble... Mais enfin, qu'est-ce que tu fais? Je dois me raser, prendre une douche et m'habiller, en exactement dix-sept minutes!

RACHID Bon, tu veux bien me passer ma brosse à dents, le dentifrice et un rasoir, s'il te plaît?
DAVID Attends une minute. Je me dépêche.
RACHID Comment est-ce qu'un mec peut prendre aussi longtemps dans la salle de bains?

DAVID Euh, j'ai un petit problème...
RACHID Qu'est-ce que tu as sur le visage?
DAVID Aucune idée.
RACHID Est-ce que tu as mal à la gorge? Fais: Ah!
RACHID Et le ventre, ça va?
DAVID Oui, oui, ça va...

RACHID Attends, je vais examiner tes yeux... regarde à droite, à gauche... maintenant ferme-les. Bien. Tourne-toi...
DAVID Hé!

1 **Vrai ou faux?** Indiquez si ces affirmations sont **vraies ou fausses.** Corrigez les phrases fausses.
Some answers may vary slightly.
1. David va bien ce matin. *Faux. David ne va pas bien ce matin.*
2. Rachid est pressé ce matin. *Vrai.*
3. David se rase. *Faux. David se brosse les dents.*
4. David se maquille. *Faux. David se coiffe.*
5. Rachid doit prendre une douche. *Vrai.*

6. David ne s'est pas réveillé à l'heure. *Vrai.*
7. David s'est couché tôt hier soir. *Faux. David s'est couché tard hier soir.*
8. Tout le monde s'est bien amusé (*had a good time*) hier soir. *Vrai.*
9. Les amis se disputent ce matin. *Vrai.*
10. Rachid est très inquiet pour David. *Faux. Rachid n'est pas inquiet.*

 Practice more at **vhlcentral.com**.

Avant de regarder la vidéo Tell students to read the title and scene setter. Then have them brainstorm what two roommates might say as they are trying to get ready for class at the same time. Write their ideas on the board.

Regarder la vidéo Show the video episode once without sound and have the class create a plot summary based on the visual cues. Then show the episode with sound and have the class make corrections and fill in any gaps in the plot summary.

David et Rachid se préparent le matin.

DAVID Patience, cher ami!
RACHID Tu n'as pas encore pris ta douche?!
DAVID Ne te mets pas en colère. J'arrive, j'arrive! Voilà... un peu de crème sur le visage, sur le cou...
RACHID Tu te maquilles maintenant?

DAVID Ce n'est pas facile d'être beau, ça prend du temps, tu sais. Écoute, ça ne sert à rien de se disputer. Lis le journal si tu t'ennuies, j'ai bientôt fini.

RACHID Ne t'inquiète pas, c'est probablement une réaction allergique. Téléphone au médecin pour prendre un rendez-vous. Qu'est-ce que tu as mangé hier?
DAVID Eh ben... J'ai mangé un peu de tout! Hé! Je n'ai pas encore fini ma toilette!

RACHID Patience, cher ami!

Expressions utiles

Talking about your routine

- **Je dois me préparer.**
  I have to get (myself) ready.
- **Je finis de me brosser les dents!**
  I'm almost done brushing my teeth!
- **On s'est couché tard hier soir.**
  We went to bed late last night.
- **On ne s'est pas réveillé à l'heure.**
  We didn't wake up on time.
- **Je me coiffe.**
  I'm doing my hair.
- **Je dois me raser et m'habiller.**
  I have to shave (myself) and get dressed.
- **Tu te maquilles maintenant?**
  Are you putting makeup on now?

Talking about states of being

- **Ça ne sert à rien de se disputer.**
  It doesn't help to argue.
- **Tu te dépêches?**
  Are you hurrying?/Will you hurry?
- **Ne t'inquiète pas.**
  Don't worry.
- **Tu ne te rends pas compte!**
  You don't realize!
- **On s'entend tous super bien et on ne s'ennuie jamais ensemble.**
  We all get along really well and we never get bored with one another.
- **Ne te mets pas en colère.**
  Don't get angry.
- **Lis le journal si tu t'ennuies.**
  Read the paper if you're bored.

Additional vocabulary

- **Je me dépêche.**
  I'm hurrying.
- **un mec**
  a guy
- **Tourne-toi.**
  Turn around.
- **aucune idée**
  no idea

---

2 **Les opposés** Trouvez pour chaque verbe de la colonne de gauche son opposé dans les colonnes de droite. Utilisez un dictionnaire. Attention! Tous les mots ne sont pas utilisés.

___e___ 1. bien s'entendre   a. s'amuser   d. s'appeler
_a/b_ 2. s'ennuyer   b. s'occuper   e. se disputer
___c___ 3. se dépêcher   c. se détendre   f. se coucher
___f___ 4. se lever
___b___ 5. se reposer

3 **Écrivez** Écrivez un paragraphe dans lequel (*in which*) vous décrivez la routine du matin et du soir de David ou de Rachid. Utilisez votre imagination et ce que vous savez d'**ESPACE ROMAN-PHOTO**.

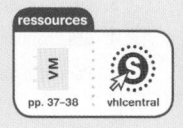
ressources
VM
pp. 37–38
vhlcentral

A C T I V I T É S

quatre cent onze **411**

Expressions utiles
- Model the pronunciation of the **Expressions utiles** and have students repeat them after you.
- As you work through the list, point out reflexive verbs and other expressions used to talk about daily routines. Explain that reflexive pronouns always correspond to their subject pronouns. Examples: **je me, tu te,** and **on se**. Point out that the phrases **On s'est couché** and **On ne s'est pas réveillé** are in the past tense. Tell students that reflexive verbs will be formally presented in **Espace structures**.
- Respond briefly to questions about reflexive verbs. Reinforce correct forms, but do not expect students to produce them consistently at this time.
- Have students combine sentences in **Expressions utiles** with known vocabulary to create mini-conversations.
- If students ask, explain that **j'ai bientôt fini** in video still #5 is an example of a particular use of the **passé composé** to express a future action. Although it is often used with the verb **finir**, they should use the **futur proche** to express an action that occurs in the near future.

1 Suggestion Have students correct the false statements.

1 Expansion For additional practice, give students these items. **11. Rachid est en retard pour son cours de maths. (Faux.) 12. Rachid ne va pas se raser. (Faux.) 13. David dit à Rachid de lire le journal. (Vrai.) 14. Rachid va téléphoner au médecin. (Faux.)**

2 Expansion For additional practice with reflexive verbs, give students these items.
**6. s'endormir (se réveiller)
7. s'habiller (se déshabiller)
8. se maquiller (se démaquiller)**

3 Suggestion Before beginning this activity, have students brainstorm vocabulary and expressions for describing daily routines and write their suggestions on the board.

O P T I O N S

Extra Practice Have students write at least five sentences telling about their roommate's or best friend's actions using the verbs in **Activité 2**. Then tell them to get together with a classmate and take turns reading their descriptions. After students read their descriptions, have them ask their partner to state two facts from the description that has just been read to them.

Extra Practice Ask volunteers to act out the scenes in video stills 6–10 for the class. Tell them it is not necessary to memorize the episode. They should try to get the general meaning across with the vocabulary they know. Give them time to prepare or have them do their skit as a review activity during the next class period.

Section Goals

In this section, students will:
- learn about medical services and pharmacies in France
- learn some colloquial expressions for parts of the body
- learn some idiomatic expressions associated with body parts
- read about the company L'Occitane

Instructional Resources
vhlcentral.com:
reference tools

Culture à la loupe
Avant la lecture Ask students: **Que faites-vous quand vous avez une réaction allergique? Et quand vous avez mal? Téléphonez-vous au médecin? Allez-vous à la pharmacie?**

Lecture
- Point out the **Coup de main**. Tell students that **°C** is read **degrés Celsius**. Have students convert the temperatures to degrees Fahrenheit using the formula $\frac{9}{5}$°C + 32 = °F.
- French prescription drug use ranks among the highest in the world, in part due to low cost and generous coverage by **la Sécurité sociale**.

Après la lecture Ask students: **Que peuvent faire les Français quand ils ne se sentent pas bien?** (aller chez le médecin, aller à la pharmacie, avoir une visite à domicile, téléphoner à SOS Médecin ou contacter le Samu)

1 Expansion Have students write two more fill-in-the-blank sentences. Collect their papers and read some of the sentences aloud. Call on volunteers to complete them.

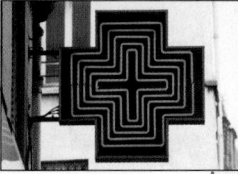

CULTURE À LA LOUPE

Les Français et la maladie

Que fait-on en France quand on ne se sent pas bien? On peut bien sûr contacter son médecin. Généralement, il vous reçoit° dans son cabinet° pour une consultation et vous donne une ordonnance. Il faut ensuite se rendre° à la pharmacie et présenter son ordonnance pour acheter ses médicaments. Beaucoup de médicaments ne sont pas en vente libre°, donc consulter un médecin est important et nécessaire.

Cependant°, pour leurs petites maladies, les Français aiment demander conseil° à leur pharmacien. Les pharmaciens en France ont un diplôme spécialisé et font six années d'études supérieures. Ils sont donc très compétents pour donner des conseils de qualité. Les pharmacies sont faciles à trouver: elles ont toutes une grande croix° verte lumineuse° suspendue° à l'extérieur. Elles sont en général ouvertes du lundi au samedi, entre 9h00 et 20h00. Pour les jours fériés et la nuit, il existe des pharmacies de garde°, dont° la liste est affichée sur la porte de chaque pharmacie.

Quand on est très malade, le médecin donne une consultation à domicile°, ce qui° est très pratique pour les enfants et les personnes âgées! En cas d'urgence, on peut appeler deux autres numéros. SOS Médecin existe dans toutes les grandes villes. Ses médecins répondent aux appels 24 heures sur 24 et font des visites à domicile. Pour les accidents et les gros problèmes, on peut contacter le Samu. C'est un service qui emmène les patients à l'hôpital si nécessaire.

Coup de main
In France, body temperature is measured in Celsius.

37°C is the normal body temperature.

Between **37°** and **38°C** is a slight fever.

For a fever above **38.5°C**, medication should be taken.

Between **39°** and **40°C** is a high fever.

Les services et les produits de santé
- 85% des Français voient° un médecin généraliste dans l'année.
- 52% vont chez le dentiste dans l'année.
- Les médecins donnent une ordonnance dans 75% des consultations.
- 57% des Français utilisent les médecines alternatives.
- 39% utilisent l'homéopathie° au moins une fois dans l'année.

reçoit *sees* cabinet *office* se rendre *to go* en vente libre *available over the counter* Cependant *However* conseil *advice* croix *cross* lumineuse *illuminated* suspendue *hung* de garde *emergency* dont *of which* à domicile *at home* ce qui *which* voient *see* homéopathie *homeopathy*

ACTIVITÉS

1 Complétez Complétez les phrases, d'après le texte et le tableau.

1. À la fin d'une consultation, le médecin vous donne parfois une ordonnance.
2. Beaucoup de médicaments en France ne sont pas en vente libre.
3. Les pharmaciens en France font six années d'études supérieures.
4. Les pharmacies sont faciles à trouver grâce à la grande croix verte lumineuse suspendue à l'extérieur.
5. Parfois, le médecin vient à domicile pour donner une consultation.
6. Quand on est très malade, on peut appeler Answers will vary. Possible answers: SOS Médecin, le Samu
7. 85% des Français voient un médecin généraliste dans l'année.
8. 39% des Français utilisent l'homéopathie au moins une fois dans l'année.
9. La température normale du corps est de 37°C.
10. On a une forte fièvre quand on a 39 ou 40°C.

OPTIONS

Cultural Comparison Have students work in pairs and compare medical services and pharmacies in France with those in the United States. Tell them to list the similarities and differences in a two-column chart under the headings **Similitudes** and **Différences**. After completing the charts, have volunteers read their lists to the class.

Les habitudes des Français et la santé Give students these true/false items based on the chart. Examples: **1. La majorité des Français n'utilisent pas de méthodes homéopathiques. (Vrai.) 2. Les Français ne vont pas fréquemment chez le médecin généraliste. (Faux.) 3. Les médecines alternatives ne sont pas populaires en France. (Faux.) 4. Plus de Français doivent aller chez le dentiste tous les ans. (Vrai.)**

LE FRANÇAIS QUOTIDIEN

Les parties du corps

bec (*m.*)	*mouth*
caboche (*f.*)	*head*
carreaux (*m.*)	*eyes*
esgourdes (*f.*)	*ears*
gosier (*m.*)	*throat*
paluche (*f.*)	*hand*
panard (*m.*)	*foot*
pif (*m.*)	*nose*
tifs (*m.*)	*hair*

LE MONDE FRANCOPHONE

Des expressions près du corps

Voici quelques expressions idiomatiques.

En France

avoir le bras long être une personne importante qui peut influencer quelqu'un

avoir un chat dans la gorge ne pas pouvoir parler

casser les pieds à quelqu'un ennuyer une personne

coûter les yeux de la tête coûter très cher

se mettre le doigt dans l'œil faire une grosse erreur

Au Québec

avoir quelqu'un dans le dos détester quelqu'un

coûter un bras coûter très cher

un froid à couper un cheveu un très grand froid

sur le bras gratuit, qu'on n'a pas besoin de payer

En Suisse

avoir des tournements de tête avoir des vertiges°

donner une bonne-main donner un pourboire

vertiges *dizziness, vertigo*

PORTRAIT

L'Occitane en Provence

En 1976, un jeune étudiant en littérature de 23 ans, Olivier Baussan, a commencé à fabriquer chez lui de l'huile de romarin° et l'a vendue sur les marchés de Provence. Son huile a été très appréciée par le public et Baussan a fondé° L'Occitane en Provence, une marque° de produits de beauté. La première boutique a ouvert ses portes dans le sud de la France en 1980 et aujourd'hui, la société a plus de 2000 boutiques dans plus de 100 pays, y compris aux États-Unis et au Canada. Les produits de L'Occitane en Provence, tous faits d'ingrédients naturels, comme la lavande° ou l'olive, s'inspirent de la Provence et sont fabriqués selon des méthodes traditionnelles. En effet, L'Occitane en Provence sélectionne des composants issus° de filières° agricoles responsables et locales. La marque propose des produits de beauté (soins du visage et du corps pour femmes et hommes), des parfums, du maquillage et des produits pour le bain, pour la douche et pour la maison. Depuis 1997, la marque se fournit° en beurre de karité° issu du commerce durable au Burkina Faso, en Afrique. Elle utilise le braille sur certains de ses produits pour garantir leur accessibilité aux personnes non-voyantes. Depuis les années 2000, L'Occitane en Provence soutient des causes humanitaires, principalement la lutte° contre la cécité évitable° dans le monde et l'émancipation économique des femmes au Burkina Faso.

huile de romarin *rosemary oil* **a fondé** *founded* **marque** *brand* **lavande** *lavender* **issus** *derived* **filières** *channels* **se fournit** *buys* **beurre de karité** *shea butter* **lutte** *fight* **cécité évitable** *preventable blindness*

---

2 Vrai ou faux? Indiquez si les phrases suivantes sont **vraies** ou **fausses**. Corrigez les phrases fausses.

1. La compagnie L'Occitane en Provence a été fondée en Provence. Vrai.
2. Le premier magasin L'Occitane a ouvert ses portes en 1976. Faux. La compagnie a été fondée en 1976, mais le premier magasin a ouvert ses portes en 1980.
3. On trouve de l'olive dans certains produits de L'Occitane. Vrai.
4. Les produits de L'Occitane en Provence utilisent des ingrédients naturels et sont fabriqués selon des méthodes traditionnelles. Vrai.
5. La société L'Occitane en Provence est engagée dans des causes humanitaires depuis 1976. Faux. Elle a commencé à s'engager dans des causes humanitaires dans les années 2000.

3 Les expressions idiomatiques Regardez bien la liste des expressions dans **Le monde francophone**. En petits groupes, discutez de ces expressions. Lesquelles (*Which*) aimez-vous? Pourquoi? Essayez de deviner l'équivalent de ces expressions en anglais.

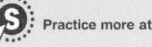 Practice more at vhlcentral.com.

ressources

vhlcentral

A C T I V I T É S

Le français quotidien

- Model the pronunciation of each term and have students repeat it.
- Say the words and have students point to the corresponding body part.

Portrait

- Have students look at the photo and identify the product. Ask students: **Avez-vous déjà utilisé un produit de L'Occitane? Quel produit?**
- These products contain oils used in homeopathic remedies, a form of alternative medicine. Some product lines are based on honey (**le miel**), verbena (**la verveine**), everlasting flower (**l'immortelle**) from Corsica, or shea (**le karité**) from Africa.

Le monde francophone Model the pronunciation of each expression and have students repeat it. You might also give them these expressions: **prendre ses jambes à son cou (partir très vite)** (France), **perdre la tête (devenir fou)** (France), **être beau/belle comme un cœur (être très beau/belle)** (France/Canada).

2 Expansion For additional practice, give students these items. **6. Les produits de L'Occitane sont vendus seulement en France. (Faux. Il y a plus de 2.000 boutiques dans plus de 100 pays.) 7. Olivier Baussan étudiait les maths avant de lancer sa compagnie. (Faux. Il étudiait la littérature.) 8. Baussan a d'abord travaillé avec l'huile de lavande. (Faux. Il a d'abord travaillé avec l'huile de romarin.)**

3 Expansion Have students write five sentences using these expressions in a specific context. Example: **Mon billet d'avion m'a coûté les yeux de la tête!**

trois cent treize **413**

OPTIONS

Cultural Activity Go to the French website for L'Occitane. Print out a few pages of gift ideas for men and women from their **Boutique cadeaux**, and make photocopies to distribute to pairs. Tell students to take turns asking each other questions about the products and deciding which ones they want to buy.

Les parties du corps Have students write four true/false statements defining the terms from **Le français quotidien**. Examples: **1. Le gosier est le pied. (Faux.) 2. La paluche veut dire la main. (Vrai.)** Then have students get together with a classmate and take turns reading their statements and responding.

Section Goals

In this section, students will learn:
- present-tense reflexive verbs
- the imperative with reflexive verbs

Instructional Resources
vhlcentral.com:
Lab MP3s; SAM Answer Key;
Essayez!** and **Mise en pratique
answers; Lab Audioscript;
*Activity Pack (**Feuilles***
***d'activités**); reference tools*

Suggestions

- Model the first person reflexive by talking about yourself. Examples: **Je me réveille très tôt. En général, je me lève à six heures du matin.**
- Model the second person by asking questions using verbs you mentioned in the first person. Examples: **À quelle heure vous réveillez-vous pendant la semaine? Vous levez-vous tôt ou tard en général?** Encourage student responses.
- Introduce the third person by making statements and asking questions about what a student has told you. Examples: ____ **se lève très tard le samedi, n'est-ce pas? (Oui, il/elle se lève entre onze heures et midi.)**
- Write the conjugation of **se laver** on the board and model its pronunciation.
- Use magazine pictures to clarify meanings between third person singular and third person plural forms. Examples: **La femme sur cette photo-ci se maquille. Sur cette photo-là, les enfants se couchent.**

10A.1

Reflexive verbs  Tutorial

Point de départ A reflexive verb usually describes what a person does to or for himself or herself. It "reflects" the action of the verb back to the subject. Reflexive verbs always use reflexive pronouns (**me, te, se, nous, vous**).

SUBJECT   REFLEXIVE VERB
André   **se rase** à huit heures.

Reflexive verbs		
se laver *(to wash oneself)*		
je	me lave	*I wash (myself)*
tu	te laves	*you wash (yourself)*
il/elle/on	se lave	*he/she/it/one washes (himself/herself/itself/oneself)*
nous	nous lavons	*we wash (ourselves)*
vous	vous lavez	*you wash (yourself/yourselves)*
ils/elles	se lavent	*they wash (themselves)*

- The pronoun **se** before an infinitive identifies the verb as reflexive: **se laver**.

Je me coiffe.

Tu te maquilles, maintenant?

- When a reflexive verb is conjugated, the reflexive pronoun agrees with the subject. Except for **se**, reflexive pronouns have the same forms as direct and indirect object pronouns (**me, te, nous, vous**); **se** is used for both singular and plural third-person subjects.

Tu **te couches**.
You're going to bed.

Les enfants **se réveillent**.
The kids are waking up.

Je **me maquille** aussi.
I put on makeup too.

Nous **nous levons** très tôt.
We get up very early.

- Note that the reflexive pronouns **nous** and **vous** are identical to the corresponding subject pronouns.

Nous **nous regardons** dans le miroir.
We look at ourselves in the mirror.

Vous habillez-vous déjà?
Are you getting dressed already?

Nous ne **nous levons** pas avant six heures.
We don't get up before six o'clock.

À quelle heure est-ce que **vous vous couchez**?
What time do you go to bed?

Common reflexive verbs

se brosser les cheveux/ les dents	*to brush one's hair/teeth*	se laver (les mains)	*to wash oneself (one's hands)*
se coiffer	*to do one's hair*	se lever	*to get up, to get out of bed*
se coucher	*to go to bed*	se maquiller	*to put on makeup*
se déshabiller	*to undress*	se raser	*to shave*
s'endormir	*to go to sleep, to fall asleep*	se regarder	*to look at oneself*
		se réveiller	*to wake up*
s'habiller	*to get dressed*	se sécher	*to dry oneself*

- **S'endormir** is conjugated like **dormir**. **Se lever** and **se sécher** follow the same spelling-change patterns as **acheter** and **espérer**, respectively.

Il **s'endort** tôt.	Tu **te lèves** à quelle heure?	Elles **se sèchent**.
He falls asleep early.	*What time do you get up?*	*They're drying off.*

- Some verbs can be used reflexively or non-reflexively. If the verb acts upon something other than the subject (for example, **son fils** in the second example below), the non-reflexive form is used.

La mère **se réveille** à sept heures.	Ensuite, elle **réveille** son fils.
The mother wakes up at 7 o'clock.	*Then, she wakes her son up.*

- When a body part is the direct object of a reflexive verb, it is usually preceded by a definite article.

Je ne **me brosse** pas **les** dents.	Vous **vous lavez les** mains.
I'm not brushing my teeth.	*You're washing your hands.*

- Form the imperative of a reflexive verb as you would that of a non-reflexive verb. Add the reflexive pronoun to the end of an affirmative command. In negative commands, place the reflexive pronoun between **ne** and the verb. (Remember to change **te** to **toi** in affirmative commands.)

Réveille-toi, Bruno!	*but*	**Ne te réveille pas!**
Wake up, Bruno!		*Don't wake up!*

- In the **futur proche** and **passé récent**, place the reflexive pronoun after the conjugated forms of **aller** and **venir** and before the infinitive. Note that although the reflexive pronoun changes according to the subject, the second verb stays in the infinitive.

Nous n'**allons** pas **nous réveiller** tôt demain.	Est-ce que tu **viens de te raser**?
We're not going to wake up early tomorrow.	*Did you just shave?*

Essayez! Complétez les phrases avec les formes correctes des verbes.

1. Ils __se brossent__ (se brosser) les dents.
2. À quelle heure est-ce que vous __vous couchez__ (se coucher)?
3. Tu __t'endors__ (s'endormir) en cours.
4. Nous __nous séchons__ (se sécher) les cheveux.
5. On __s'habille__ (s'habiller) vite! Il faut partir.
6. Les hommes __se maquillent__ (se maquiller) rarement.
7. Tu ne __te déshabilles__ (se déshabiller) pas encore.
8. Je __me lève__ (se lever) vers onze heures.

Suggestions
- Compare and contrast reflexive and non-reflexive verbs using examples like these: **Il se réveille à six heures et demie. Il réveille les enfants à sept heures.**
- Provide examples of other verbs that can be reflexive or non-reflexive, and have students create sentences using them.
- Point out that to make a question using inversion with a reflexive verb, you simply invert the placement of the subject pronoun with the reflexive verb.

Essayez! Have students say logical commands for items 2, 3, 4, and 7. (**2. Couchez-vous [de bonne heure]. 3. Ne t'endors pas en cours. 4. Séchons-nous les cheveux. 7. Ne te déshabille pas.**)

Boîte à outils

Since reflexive verbs already imply that the action is performed on the subject, French uses definite articles (**le, la, les**) with body parts, whereas English uses possessive adjectives (*my, your, his/her/its, our, their*).

Je me lave les mains.
I wash my hands.

À noter

There are some special rules for using reflexive verbs in the **passé composé**. You will learn these in **Leçon 10B**.

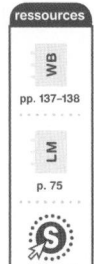

ressources

WB
pp. 137–138

LM
p. 75

vhlcentral

Extra Practice To provide oral practice with reflexive verbs, create sentences that follow the pattern of the sentences in the examples. Say each sentence, have students repeat it, and then say a different subject. Have students then say the new sentence with the new subject, changing pronouns and verb forms as necessary. Example: **Je me brosse les dents deux fois par jour.: on (On se brosse les dents deux fois par jour.)**

TPR Model gestures for a few of the reflexive verbs. Examples: **se coucher** (*lay head on folded hands*), **se coiffer** (*pretend to fix hair*). Have students stand. Begin by practicing as a class using only the **nous** form, saying an expression at random. Example: **Nous nous lavons les mains.** Then vary the verb forms and point to individuals or groups of students who should perform the appropriate gesture. Keep the pace rapid.

ESPACE **STRUCTURES**

1 Suggestion Before assigning this activity, review reflexive verbs by comparing and contrasting weekday versus weekend routines. Example: **Vous couchez-vous plus tôt pendant la semaine?**

2 Expansion Repeat the activity as a pattern drill, supplying different subjects for each drawing. Example: **1. je (Je me réveille.) 2. ils (Ils se lèvent.)**

3 Suggestion Tell students that they may vary the sequencing expressions used, such as **puis** instead of **ensuite**.

3 Expansion Have students add a third reflexive activity to their sequence and give the logical order using **d'abord**, **puis/ensuite**, and **finalement**. Example: **se lever / se laver / se maquiller (D'abord ma mère se lève, ensuite elle se lave et finalement elle se maquille.)**

Mise en pratique

1 Les habitudes Vous allez chez vos amis Frédéric et Pauline. Tout le monde a ses habitudes. Que fait-on tous les jours?

> **MODÈLE**
>
> Frédéric / se raser
> *Frédéric se rase.*

1. vous / se réveiller / à six heures   Vous vous réveillez à six heures.
2. Frédéric et Pauline / se brosser / dents   Frédéric et Pauline se brossent les dents.
3. tu / se lever / puis / prendre une douche   Tu te lèves puis tu prends une douche.
4. nous / se sécher / cheveux   Nous nous séchons les cheveux.
5. on / s'habiller / avant le petit-déjeuner   On s'habille avant le petit-déjeuner.
6. Frédéric et Pauline / se coiffer / avant / sortir   Frédéric et Pauline se coiffent avant de sortir.
7. je / se déshabiller / et après / se coucher   Je me déshabille et après, je me couche.
8. tout le monde / s'endormir / tout de suite   Tout le monde s'endort tout de suite.
9. leurs tantes / se maquiller / et après / s'habiller   Leurs tantes se maquillent et après elles s'habillent.
10. leur père / se laver / mains / avant / manger   Leur père se lave les mains avant de manger.
11. les cousins de Pauline / ne pas se raser   Les cousins de Pauline ne se rasent pas.

2 La routine Tous les matins, Juliette suit (*follows*) la même routine. Regardez les illustrations et dites ce que (*what*) fait Juliette.

1. Juliette se réveille.   **2.** Juliette se lève.   **3.** Juliette se brosse les dents.   **4.** Juliette se maquille.

3 L'ordre logique Indiquez dans quel ordre vous faites ces choses, ou dans quel ordre quelqu'un que vous connaissez les fait.   Suggested answers

> **MODÈLE**
>
> se lever / se réveiller
> *D'abord je me réveille, ensuite je me lève.*

1. se laver / se sécher   D'abord je me lave, ensuite je me sèche.
2. se maquiller / prendre une douche   D'abord ma sœur prend une douche, ensuite elle se maquille.
3. se lever / s'habiller   D'abord mon camarade de chambre se lève, ensuite il s'habille.
4. se raser / se réveiller   D'abord je me réveille, ensuite je me rase.
5. se coucher / se brosser les cheveux   D'abord nous nous brossons les cheveux, ensuite nous nous couchons.
6. s'endormir / se coucher   D'abord tu te couches, ensuite tu t'endors.
7. se coucher / se déshabiller   D'abord je me déshabille, ensuite je me couche.
8. se lever / se réveiller   D'abord le prof se réveille, ensuite il se lève.
9. se brosser les cheveux / se coiffer   D'abord ma cousine se brosse les cheveux, ensuite elle se coiffe.
10. se maquiller / se sécher   D'abord nous nous séchons et ensuite nous nous maquillons.

 Practice more at **vhlcentral.com**.

Communication

4 **Tous les jours** Que fait votre partenaire tous les jours? Posez-lui les questions et il/elle vous répond. *Some answers will vary.*

MODÈLE

se lever tôt le matin
Étudiant(e) 1: *Est-ce que tu te lèves tôt le matin?*
Étudiant(e) 2: *Non, je ne me lève pas tôt le matin.*

1. se réveiller tôt ou tard le week-end   *Est-ce que tu te réveilles tôt ou tard le week-end?*
2. se lever tout de suite   *Est-ce que tu te lèves tout de suite?*
3. se maquiller tous les matins   *Est-ce que tu te maquilles tous les matins?*
4. se laver les cheveux tous les jours   *Est-ce que tu te laves les cheveux tous les jours?*
5. se raser le soir ou le matin   *Est-ce que tu te rases le soir ou le matin?*
6. se coucher avant ou après minuit   *Est-ce que tu te couches avant ou après minuit?*
7. se brosser les dents chaque nuit   *Est-ce que tu te brosses les dents chaque nuit?*
8. s'habiller avant ou après le petit-déjeuner   *Est-ce que tu t'habilles avant ou après le petit-déjeuner?*
9. s'endormir parfois en classe   *Est-ce que tu t'endors parfois en classe?*

5 **Enquête** Votre professeur va vous donner une feuille d'activités. Circulez dans la classe et trouvez un(e) camarade différent(e) pour chaque action. Présentez les réponses à la classe. *Answers will vary.*

MODÈLE

Étudiant(e) 1: *Est-ce que tu te lèves avant six heures du matin?*
Étudiant(e) 2: *Oui, je me lève parfois à cinq heures!*

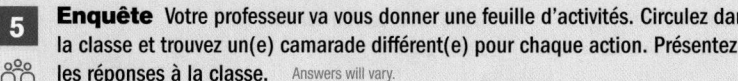

Activité	Nom
1. se lever avant six heures du matin	Carole
2. se maquiller pour venir en cours	
3. se brosser les dents trois fois par jour	
4. se laver les cheveux le soir	
5. se coiffer à la dernière mode	
6. se reposer le vendredi soir	

6 **Jacques a dit** Par groupes de quatre, un(e) étudiant(e) donne des ordres au groupe. Attention! Vous devez obéir seulement si l'ordre est précédé de **Jacques a dit...** (*Simon says...*) La personne qui se trompe devient le meneur de jeu (*leader*). Le gagnant (*winner*) est l'étudiant(e) qui n'a pas été le meneur de jeu. Utilisez les expressions de la liste puis trouvez vos propres expressions. *Answers will vary.*

se brosser les dents	se laver les mains
se coiffer	se lever
s'endormir	se maquiller
s'habiller	se sécher les cheveux

4 **Expansion** Have students come up with four additional items. Pairs then switch papers and form questions.

5 **Suggestion** Have two students demonstrate the **modèle**. Then distribute the **Feuilles d'activités** found in the Activity Pack on the Supersite.

6 **Suggestion** To give winners a chance to lead the game, have **le/la gagnant(e)** from each group come to the front of the room to take turns saying **Jacques a dit...**

Extra Practice Have students compare their own routines with Juliette's in **Activité 2** on page 416. Have them express each part of the morning routine that they have in common. Example: **Moi aussi, je me réveille, puis je me lève.** Then have them express any differences. Examples: **Je ne me maquille pas (tous les matins). Juliette ne se lave pas le visage. Moi, si, je me lave le visage.**

Small Groups Have groups of three pretend that they share an apartment with only one bathroom. Tell them to have a conversation in which they discuss their morning schedule problems. Example: **Étudiant(e) 1: J'ai cours à huit heures. Je me lève à sept heures et je me lave tout de suite. Étudiant(e) 2: Moi aussi, je dois me laver à sept heures. Étudiant(e) 3: Alors, ____, réveille-toi à sept heures moins le quart.**

Section Goals

In this section, students will learn idiomatic reflexive expressions.

Instructional Resources
vhlcentral.com:
Activity Pack; Lab MP3s;
SAM Answer Key; **Essayez!**
and **Mise en pratique**
answers; Lab Audioscript;
reference tools

Suggestions

• Remind students what idiomatic expressions are. Ask for examples of such expressions that students already know. (idiomatic expressions with **avoir** and **faire**)

• Go through the list of common idiomatic reflexives with the class, pronouncing them and having students repeat. Have them point out which verb(s) they have seen before, such as **s'appeler**.

• Ask students to study the list and note related English words. Examples: **s'amuser** *amuse*, **s'occuper** *occupy*.

• Have students pick verbs from the list that could be used non-reflexively and provide examples.

10A.2

Reflexives: *Sens idiomatique* Ⓢ Tutorial

Point de départ You've learned that reflexive verbs "reflect" the action back to the subject. Some reflexive verbs, however, do not literally express a reflexive meaning.

Common idiomatic reflexives

s'amuser	*to play; to have fun*	**s'intéresser (à)**	*to be interested (in)*
s'appeler	*to be called*	**se mettre à**	*to begin to*
s'arrêter	*to stop*	**se mettre en colère**	*to become angry*
s'asseoir	*to sit down*		
se dépêcher	*to hurry*	**s'occuper (de)**	*to take care of, to keep oneself busy*
se détendre	*to relax*		
se disputer (avec)	*to argue (with)*	**se préparer**	*to get ready*
s'énerver	*to get worked up, to become upset*	**se promener**	*to take a walk*
		se rendre compte	*to realize*
s'ennuyer	*to get bored*	**se reposer**	*to rest*
s'entendre bien (avec)	*to get along well (with)*	**se souvenir (de)**	*to remember*
		se tromper	*to be mistaken*
s'inquiéter	*to worry*	**se trouver**	*to be located*

Le marché **se trouve** derrière l'église.
The market is located behind the church.

Nous **nous amusons** bien chez Fabien.
We have fun at Fabien's house.

Mon grand-père **se repose** à la maison.
My grandfather is resting at home.

Ne **te mets** pas **en colère**.
Don't get angry.

Je **m'occupe du** linge.
I'm taking care of the laundry.

Vous devez **vous dépêcher**.
You must hurry.

Lis le journal si tu t'ennuies.

Ne t'inquiète pas.

• **Se souvenir** is conjugated like **venir**.

Souviens-toi de son anniversaire.
Remember her birthday.

Nous nous souvenons de cette date.
We remember that date.

• **S'ennuyer** has the same spelling changes as **envoyer**. **Se promener** and **s'inquiéter** have the same spelling changes as **acheter** and **espérer**, respectively.

Je **m'ennuie** à mourir aujourd'hui.
I'm bored to death today.

On **se promène** dans le parc.
We're taking a walk in the park.

Ils **s'inquiètent** plus que mes parents.
They worry more than my parents.

- Note the spelling changes of **s'appeler** in the present tense.

> **s'appeler** (to be named, to call oneself)
>
> | | |
> |---|---|
> | je m'appelle | nous nous appelons |
> | tu t'appelles | vous vous appelez |
> | il/elle/on s'appelle | ils/elles s'appellent |

> Tu **t'appelles** comment?
> *What is your name?*

> Vous **vous appelez** Laure Dubois?
> *Is your name Laure Dubois?*

- Note the irregular conjugation of the verb **s'asseoir**.

> **s'asseoir** (to be seated, to sit down)
>
> | | |
> |---|---|
> | je m'assieds | nous nous asseyons |
> | tu t'assieds | vous vous asseyez |
> | il/elle/on s'assied | ils/elles s'asseyent |

> **Asseyez-vous**, Monsieur.
> *Have a seat, sir.*

> **Assieds-toi** ici sur le canapé.
> *Sit here on the sofa.*

- Many idiomatically reflexive expressions can be used alone, with a preposition, or with the conjunction **que**.

> Tu **te trompes**.
> *You're wrong.*

> Il **se trompe** toujours **de** date.
> *He's always mixing up the date.*

> Marlène **s'énerve** facilement.
> *Marlène gets mad easily.*

> Marlène **s'énerve contre** Thierry.
> *Marlène gets mad at Thierry.*

> Ils **se souviennent de** ton anniversaire.
> *They remember your birthday.*

> Je **me souviens que** tu m'as téléphoné.
> *I remember you phoned me.*

> Vous **vous inquiétez** trop!
> *You worry too much!*

> Tu **t'inquiètes pour** tes enfants?
> *Are you worried about your children?*

Essayez!   **Complétez les phrases avec les formes correctes des verbes.**

1. Mes parents _____*s'inquiètent*_____ (s'inquiéter) beaucoup.
2. Nous _____ nous entendons _____ (s'entendre) bien, ma sœur et moi.
3. Alexis ne _____ se rend _____ (se rendre) pas compte que sa petite amie ne l'aime pas.
4. On doit _____ se dépêcher _____ (se dépêcher) pour arriver à la fac.
5. Papa _____ s'occupe _____ (s'occuper) toujours de la cuisine.
6. Tu _____ t'amuses _____ (s'amuser) quand tu vas au cinéma?
7. Vous _____ vous intéressez _____ (s'intéresser) au cours d'histoire de l'art?
8. Je ne _____ me dispute _____ (se disputer) pas souvent avec les profs.
9. Tu _____ te reposes _____ (se reposer) un peu sur le lit.
10. Angélique _____ s'assied _____ (s'asseoir) toujours près de la porte.
11. Je _____ m'appelle _____ (s'appeler) Susanne.
12. Elles _____ s'ennuient _____ (s'ennuyer) chez leurs cousins.

ressources

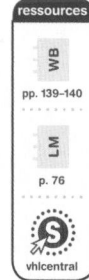

WB
pp. 139–140

LM
p. 76

S
vhlcentral

Suggestions

- Call attention to the spelling change verbs and the irregular **s'asseoir**.
- To show how **s'asseoir** can be polite or abrupt in its imperative form, tell students that **Assieds-toi/Asseyez-vous** can mean *Be seated., Have a seat.,* or *Sit down!*
- Have students practice affirmative and negative commands using as many of the reflexive verbs as possible.
- Point out that when **que** follows a verb, it means *that,* as in the example: **Je me souviens que tu m'as téléphoné.** = *I remember (that) you phoned me.* Although the word *that* is optional in English, stress that **que** is required in French.

Essayez! Give these sentences for additional practice. Tell students to choose a reflexive verb from the list. **13. La boulangerie _____ à côté de l'épicerie. (se trouve) 14. Cette fête est nulle. On _____. (s'ennuie) 15. Mes copains disent que ce cours est facile, mais je ne suis pas d'accord. Je pense qu'ils _____ (se trompent).**

OPTIONS

Pairs Have students write a short account of their own daily routine using both types of reflexives. Pairs then compare and contrast their routines using a Venn Diagram. Have the pair write one of their names in the left circle, the other in the right circle, and **les deux** where the circles overlap. They list their activities in the appropriate locations. Remind them to change the subject pronoun to **nous** in the overlapping section.

Video Replay the video episode, having students focus on reflexive verbs. Stop the video strategically to discuss how reflexives are used in various structures. Examples: **Je dois me préparer, moi aussi!** (infinitive) **Ne t'inquiète pas.** (command) **Tu ne te rends pas compte!** (present tense) Have students identify the **passé composé** of reflexive verbs, but tell them it will be formally introduced in **Espace structures 10B.1.**

ESPACE STRUCTURES

Leçon 10A

1 **Expansion** Give students related sentences like the following. **1. Stéphanie et Anne _____ (se promener) parfois le week-end. (se promènent) 2. Le soir, elles _____ (ne pas s'endormir) tout de suite parce qu'elles parlent beaucoup. (ne s'endorment pas)**

2 **Expansion** Give additional statements modeled on those in the activity. Examples: **7. Cette étudiante n'est pas très patiente et elle _____ facilement. (s'énerve) 8. Tu t'entends assez bien avec mon frère, mais quelquefois vous _____. (vous disputez)**

3 **Suggestion** Help pairs get started by asking a question or two to the whole class. Example: **Que fait Fatima? (Elle s'ennuie./ Elle ne parle pas.)**

3 **Expansion** Have students enhance their descriptions by giving reasons for what they see in the scene. Example: **Virginie s'inquiète parce que son petit ami n'est pas encore arrivé.** Then, have pairs share their descriptions with the class to find out which ones are the most creative.

Mise en pratique

1 **Ma sœur et moi** Complétez ce texte avec les formes correctes des verbes.

Je (1) __m'appelle__ (s'appeler) Anne, et j'ai une sœur, Stéphanie. Nous (2) __nous habillons__ (s'habiller) souvent de la même manière, mais nous sommes très différentes. Stéphanie (3) __s'intéresse__ (s'intéresser) à la politique et elle étudie le droit, et moi, je (4) __m'intéresse__ (s'intéresser) à la peinture et je fais de l'art. Nous habitons ensemble, et nous (5) __nous entendons bien__ (s'entendre bien). On (6) __s'assied__ (s'asseoir) souvent sur un banc (*bench*) au parc pour bavarder. Quelquefois on (7) __se met en colère__ (se mettre en colère). Heureusement, on (8) __se rend compte__ (se rendre compte) que c'est inutile et on (9) __s'arrête__ (s'arrêter). En fait, Stéphanie et moi, nous (10) __ne nous ennuyons pas__ (ne pas s'ennuyer) ensemble.

2 **Que faire?** Que font Diane et ses copains? Utilisez les verbes de la liste pour compléter les phrases. *Suggested answers*

s'amuser	se disputer	s'occuper
s'appeler	s'énerver	se préparer
s'asseoir	s'ennuyer	se promener
se dépêcher	s'entendre bien	se reposer
se détendre	s'inquiéter	se tromper

1. Si je suis en retard pour mon cours, je __me dépêche__.
2. Parfois, Toufik __se trompe__ et ne donne pas la bonne réponse.
3. Quand un cours n'est pas intéressant, nous __nous ennuyons__.
4. Le week-end, Hubert et Édith sont fatigués, alors ils __se reposent__.
5. Quand je ne comprends pas mon prof, je __m'inquiète__.
6. Quand il fait beau, vous allez dans le parc et vous __vous promenez__.
7. Quand tes parents sortent, tu __t'occupes__ de tes petites sœurs.
8. Ils __se disputent__ tout le temps. Ils vont sûrement divorcer!

3 **La fête** Marc a invité ses amis pour célébrer la fin (*end*) du semestre. Avec un(e) partenaire, décrivez la scène à tour de rôle. Utilisez tous les verbes possibles de la liste de l'**Activité 2**. *Answers will vary.*

 Practice more at **vhlcentral.com**.

Communication

4 **Se connaître** Vous voulez mieux connaître vos camarades. Par groupes de quatre, posez-vous des questions et puis présentez les réponses à la classe. *Answers will vary.*

MODÈLE

s'intéresser à la politique

Étudiant(e) 1: *Je ne m'intéresse pas à la politique. Et toi, t'intéresses-tu à la politique?*
Étudiant(e) 2: *Je m'intéresse beaucoup à la politique et je lis le journal tous les jours.*

1. s'amuser en cours de français
2. s'inquiéter pour des questions d'argent
3. s'asseoir au premier rang (*row*) dans la classe
4. s'énerver facilement
5. se mettre souvent en colère
6. se reposer le week-end
7. s'entendre bien avec ses camarades de classe
8. se promener souvent

5 **Curieux** Utilisez ces verbes et expressions pour interviewer un(e) partenaire. *Answers will vary.*

MODÈLE

avec qui / s'amuser

Étudiant(e) 1: *Avec qui est-ce que tu t'amuses?*
Étudiant(e) 2: *Je m'amuse avec mes amis.*

1. avec qui / s'entendre bien
2. à quoi / s'intéresser
3. quand, pourquoi / s'ennuyer
4. pourquoi / se mettre en colère
5. quand, comment / se détendre
6. avec qui, où, quand / se promener
7. avec qui, pourquoi / se disputer
8. quand, pourquoi / se dépêcher

6 **Une mère inquiète** La mère de Philippe lui a écrit cet e-mail. Avec un(e) partenaire, préparez par écrit la réponse de Philippe. Employez des verbes réfléchis à sens idiomatique. *Answers will vary.*

> Mon chéri,
>
> Je m'inquiète beaucoup pour toi. Je me rends compte que tu as changé. Tu ne t'amuses pas avec tes amis et tu te mets constamment en colère. Maintenant, tu restes tout le temps dans ta chambre et tu t'intéresses seulement à la télé. Est-ce que tu t'ennuies à l'école? Te souviens-tu que tu as des amis? J'espère que je me trompe.

quatre cent vingt et un **421**

---

4 Suggestions
- Have two volunteers act out the **modèle**.
- Give more topics to discuss. Examples: **s'appeler comme son père/sa mère** and **bien s'entendre avec tout le monde**.

5 Expansion Have two pairs form a group of four. Students take turns asking questions in the second person plural. Example: **Vous vous amusez bien avec vos amis? (Oui, nous nous amusons bien avec eux.)** Then have students report back to the class in the third person singular and plural. Examples: _____ s'entend bien avec sa tante. _____ et _____ s'intéressent à la médecine.

6 Suggestion Read the e-mail aloud and ask if students have any questions before assigning this activity.

OPTIONS

Extra Practice Have students think of a friend or family member to whom they are particularly close. Assign a short writing task in which students describe their relationship with this person using at least five different common idiomatic reflexives. Tell them to be creative. They may also refer to **Activité 1** on page 420 for sample sentences.

Game Have two teams write descriptions of five famous people or places, real or fictional, using idiomatic reflexives. Use **se trouver**. Team members take turns reading their descriptions while the opposing team gets three chances to guess who or what is being described. Each correct guess wins a point, while a team that fools its opponents gets two points. For a tiebreaker, you give clues to both teams. The first to guess correctly wins.

Révision

Instructional Resources
vhlcentral.com:
Activity Pack (Info Gap Activities); Testing Program; Testing Program MP3s; reference tools

1 Suggestion First, have students describe the people physically as a brief review activity. Then have them make up names for the people before describing what they are doing.

2 Suggestion Act out the **modèle** with a volunteer. Then point out the use of double object pronouns. Review the correct order if necessary.

3 Suggestion Before assigning groups, go over some of the things that men and women often do differently to get ready to go out. Examples: **Les femmes ne se rasent pas le visage. Les hommes ne se maquillent pas.**

4 Suggestion Ask students what sentence structure they will likely use most in this conversation. (commands)

5 Suggestion Have pairs compare their stories with others. Have students point out any errors or omissions. Vote on the funniest story.

6 Suggestion Divide the class into pairs and distribute the Info Gap Handouts found in the Activity Pack on the Supersite. Give students ten minutes to complete the activity.

---

1 **Les colocataires** Avec un(e) partenaire, décrivez cette maison de colocataires. Que font-ils à sept heures du matin? *Answers will vary.*

1.

2.

3.

2 **Le camping** Vous et votre partenaire faites du camping dans un endroit isolé. Malheureusement, vous avez tout oublié. À tour de rôle, parlez de ces problèmes à votre partenaire. Il/Elle va essayer de vous aider. *Answers will vary.*

MODÈLE

Étudiant(e) 1: *Je veux me laver les cheveux, mais je n'ai pas pris mon shampooing.*
Étudiant(e) 2: *Moi, j'ai apporté mon shampooing. Je te le prête.*

se brosser les cheveux	se laver le visage
se brosser les dents	prendre une douche
se coiffer	se raser
se laver les mains	se sécher les cheveux

3 **Débat** Par groupes de quatre, débattez cette question: Qui prend plus de temps pour se préparer avant de sortir, les hommes ou les femmes? Préparez une liste de raisons pour défendre votre point de vue. Présentez vos arguments à la classe. *Answers will vary.*

---

4 **Dépêchez-vous!** Avec un(e) partenaire, vous êtes les parents de trois enfants. Ils doivent partir pour l'école dans dix minutes, mais ils viennent juste de se réveiller! Que leur dites-vous? Utilisez des verbes réfléchis. *Answers will vary.*

MODÈLE

Étudiant(e) 1: *Dépêchez-vous!*
Étudiant(e) 2: *Lève-toi!*

5 **Départ en vacances** Avec un(e) partenaire, observez les images et décrivez-les. Utilisez tous les verbes de la liste. Ensuite, racontez à la classe l'histoire du départ en vacances de la famille Glassié. *Answers will vary.*

s'amuser	s'énerver
se dépêcher	se mettre en colère
se détendre	se préparer
se disputer (avec)	se rendre compte

1.   2.

3.   4.

6 **La personnalité de Martin** Votre professeur va vous donner, à vous et à votre partenaire, une feuille d'information sur Martin. Attention! Ne regardez pas la feuille de votre partenaire. *Answers will vary.*

MODÈLE

Étudiant(e) 1: *Martin s'habille élégamment.*
Étudiant(e) 2: *Mais il s'ennuie le soir.*

OPTIONS

Extra Practice Ask students to translate these sentence pairs into French using reflexive and non-reflexive forms of the same verb. 1. My dog is called Buddy. When I call him, he doesn't listen to me. (**Mon chien s'appelle Buddy. Quand je l'appelle, il ne m'écoute pas.**) 2. The children are walking the dog while their parents take a walk. (**Les enfants promènent le chien pendant que leurs parents se promènent.**) 3. We have to get ready. Why are you *(pl.)* preparing for the exam now? (**Nous devons nous préparer. Pourquoi préparez-vous l'examen maintenant?**) 4. Wash your *(sing.)* hands. Then wash your little brother. (**Lave-toi les mains. Puis lave ton petit frère.**) 5. The hairdresser does her hair in the morning. She does her clients' hair all day. (**La coiffeuse se coiffe le matin. Elle coiffe ses clients toute la journée.**)

 Video

Le Zapping

S'aimer mieux

La marque° Krys veut que la beauté soit° accessible à tous. Ses lunettes ont donc des prix raisonnables et elles sont vendues partout° en France, en Belgique et sur Internet. Ses opticiens sont des professionnels qui savent aussi donner de bons conseils° esthétiques à leurs clients.

Cette compagnie est apparue° en 1966 quand les 14 plus grands opticiens de France ont décidé de travailler ensemble. Pour choisir leur nom, ils ont pensé à la transparence et au cristal, et «Krys» est née.

Collection [K]
60€ monture + verres

...eillé pour une monture K + 2 verres organiques 1.5 blancs durcis unifocaux, corrections...

Non merci.

Jolies lunettes!

 Compréhension Répondez aux questions. Answers will vary.

1. Est-ce que le jeune homme se sentait (*felt*) bien avant? Quel était son plus gros problème?
2. Qu'est-ce qui a ensuite changé dans sa vie?

Discussion Par groupes de quatre, répondez aux questions et discutez. Answers will vary.

1. Quelle partie de votre routine matinale prend le plus de temps ou est vraiment essentielle?
2. En général, est-ce que votre *look* vous aide à vous sentir (*feel*) mieux et à passer une bonne journée, ou est-ce qu'il n'a pas d'importance?
3. Comme la jeune fille dans la pub (*ad*), avez-vous déjà essayé de faire un compliment à un(e) inconnu(e) (*stranger*) sur son *look*? Quelle réaction a eu cette personne?

marque *brand* **soit** *be* **partout** *everywhere* **conseils** *advice* **apparue** *appeared*

Go to **vhlcentral.com** to watch the TV clip featured in this **Le Zapping**.

 Practice more at **vhlcentral.com**.

quatre cent vingt-trois 423

Section Goals

In this section, students will:
- read about the optical company Krys
- watch a commercial for Krys eye-glasses
- answer questions about the commercial

Instructional Resources
vhlcentral.com: TV commercial; ***Le Zapping*** *TV clip transcription; reference tools*

Avant de regarder la vidéo
- Have students look at the video stills, read the captions, and predict what will happen in the commercial for each visual. **(1. Le jeune homme n'aime pas son *look* et il ne se sent pas bien. 2. Une jeune fille fait un compliment au jeune homme sur ses nouvelles lunettes.)**
- Before showing the video, explain to students that they do not need to understand every word they hear. Tell them to listen for cognates, the product name, and its qualities.

Compréhension Have students work in pairs or groups for this activity. Tell them to write their answers. Then show the video again so that they can check their answers and add any missing information.

Discussion
- Take a quick class survey to find out how many students wear glasses, how many wear contact lenses, and how many wear neither.
- Ask students if they have ever bought clothing or an accessory that made them feel better about themselves. Ask those who answer yes what it was and how they felt wearing it.

O P T I O N S

Krys The name Krys was chosen in 1967 to replace the name Guilde des Lunetiers de France. Today, there are over 800 Krys stores in France and Belgium. The brand's slogan is **Vous allez vous aimer**. Through its foundation, **la fondation Krys**, the brand collects, refurbishes, and provides free eyeglasses for those who need them in several regions of the world.

Pairs Ask students to imagine that the same night, the young man writes a short e-mail to a friend describing how he met the young woman. Have pairs write his e-mail and read it to the class. Then vote for the best message.

Section Goals

In this section, students will learn and practice vocabulary related to:
- illnesses and medical conditions
- accidents
- medical visits and treatments

Instructional Resources

vhlcentral.com:
Digital Image Bank;
Vocabulaire supplémentaire;
Mise en pratique answers;
Textbook Audioscript;
Lab Audioscript; Activity Pack;
Textbook MP3s; Lab MP3s;
SAM Answer Key;
reference tools

Suggestions

- Use the **10B Contextes** illustration from the Digital Image Bank. Describe the scene at this emergency room. Point out various medical conditions and treatments. Examples: **Ces personnes sont chez le médecin. Ce sont des patients. Elle est enceinte. Il a une blessure. Elle fait une piqûre.**
- Point out expressions with **avoir (avoir mal au dos, avoir mal au cœur); faire (faire mal, faire une piqûre, faire de l'exercice);** and **être (être en bonne/mauvaise santé, être malade, être en pleine forme).**
- Then point out reflexive verbs (**se fouler, se casser, se sentir**). Tell students to use **se sentir bien** to say they *feel good (feel well)* and **se sentir mal** to say they *feel bad.* **Sentir bon/mauvais** means *to smell good/bad.* Remind them to use the definite article, not a possessive adjective, when describing injuries to body parts. Example: **Il se casse le bras** (not **son** bras).
- Use the Vocabulary illustrations and the Health illustrations from the Digital Image Bank to help students familiarize themselves with illnesses, medical conditions, accidents, and medical visits and treatments.
- Additional vocabulary for this lesson can be found in the **Vocabulaire supplémentaire** on the Supersite.

Leçon 10B

You will learn how to...
- describe your health
- talk about remedies and well-being

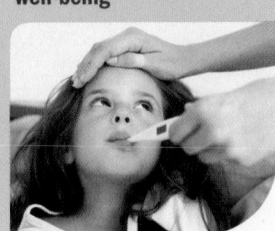

Vocabulary Tools

J'ai mal!

- Il a de la fièvre.
- Elle fait une piqûre.
- Elle tousse. (tousser)
- Elle a mal au dos.
- un patient (patiente f.)
- Elle est enceinte.
- une pilule
- Il a un rhume.
- Elle est en bonne santé.
- une blessure
- Il éternue. (éternuer)
- ATCHOUM!

Vocabulaire

aller aux urgences/ à la pharmacie	to go to the emergency room/ to the pharmacy
avoir mal	to have an ache
avoir mal au cœur	to feel nauseous
enfler	to swell
être en bonne santé	to be in good health
être en mauvaise santé	to be in bad health
être en pleine forme	to be in good shape
éviter de	to avoid
faire mal	to hurt
garder la ligne	to stay slim
guérir	to get better
se blesser	to hurt oneself
se casser (la jambe/ le bras)	to break one's (leg/ arm)
se fouler la cheville	to twist/sprain one's ankle
se porter mal/mieux	to be ill/better
se sentir	to feel
tomber/être malade	to get/to be sick
un(e) dentiste	dentist
un(e) pharmacien(ne)	pharmacist
une allergie	allergy
une douleur	pain
la grippe	flu
un symptôme	symptom
une aspirine	aspirin
un médicament (contre/pour)	medication (to prevent/for)
une ordonnance	prescription
les urgences	emergency room
déprimé(e)	depressed
grave	serious
sain(e)	healthy

ressources

WB pp. 141–142

LM p. 77

vhlcentral

OPTIONS

Extra Practice Write the following headings at the top of three columns on the board: **Les maladies, Les remèdes,** and **Les professions médicales.** Say words and expressions from the **Contextes** and have students classify them. Ask volunteers to write them in the appropriate column.

Game Have students stand. Toss a beanbag to a student at random and say the name of an illness or injury. The person has five seconds to suggest a remedy or treatment. That person then tosses the beanbag to another student and says an illness or injury. Tell students to be creative with their remedies. (**prendre un thé/de la soupe, se reposer, ne pas marcher...**) Students who cannot think of a remedy or treatment are eliminated. The last person standing wins.

Mise en pratique

1 **Écoutez** Monsieur Sebbar est tombé malade. Vous allez écouter une conversation entre lui et son médecin. Choisissez les éléments de chaque catégorie qui sont vrais.

Symptômes
1. J'ai mal à la tête. ☑
2. J'ai mal au ventre. ☐
3. J'ai mal aux yeux. ☑
4. J'ai mal à la gorge. ☐
5. J'ai mal au cœur. ☐
6. J'ai mal à la cheville. ☑
7. J'ai de la fièvre. ☑

Diagnostic
1. la grippe ☑
2. un rhume ☐
3. la cheville cassée ☐

Traitement
1. faire de l'exercice ☐
2. faire une piqûre ☑
3. prendre des médicaments ☑

2 **Chassez l'intrus** Indiquez le mot qui ne va pas avec les autres.

1. un médicament, une pilule, (une ordonnance,) une aspirine
2. un médecin, un dentiste, (un patient,) une pharmacienne
3. un rhume, (une aspirine,) la grippe, une allergie
4. (tomber malade,) guérir, être en bonne santé, se porter mieux
5. éternuer, tousser, (fumer,) avoir mal à la gorge
6. être en pleine forme, (être malade,) être en bonne santé, garder la ligne
7. se sentir bien, se porter mieux, (être en mauvaise santé,) ne pas fumer
8. une blessure, (une pharmacie,) un symptôme, une douleur

3 **Complétez** Complétez ces phrases avec le bon mot choisi dans **ESPACE CONTEXTES** pour faire des phrases logiques. _Some answers may vary._

1. Vous allez chez le médecin quand vous tombez _malade_.
2. Vous allez chez _le/la dentiste_ quand vous avez mal aux dents.
3. _L'infirmier/ière_ aide les médecins.
4. Une femme qui va avoir un bébé est _enceinte_.
5. Une personne qui a eu un grave accident est emmenée (_taken_) aux _urgences_.
6. On prend une _aspirine_ quand on a mal à la tête.
7. Pour être en forme et garder la ligne, il faut _faire de l'exercice_.
8. Si on n'est pas malade, on est _sain(e)/en bonne santé_.
9. Le médecin peut vous faire _une piqûre_.
10. _Une ordonnance_ est une liste de médicaments à prendre.
11. Être _déprimé_, c'est être tout le temps malheureux.
12. Si les fleurs vous font _éternuer_, vous avez une allergie.

 Practice more at **vhlcentral.com**.

quatre cent vingt-cinq **425**

---

un infirmier

ne pas fumer

Elle fait de l'exercice.

une infirmière

Elle a mal à la tête.

Il a mal au ventre.

---

1 Audioscript MÉDECIN: Monsieur Sebbar, qu'est-ce qui ne va pas?
MONSIEUR SEBBAR: Docteur, j'ai mal partout. J'ai mal aux yeux et j'ai mal à la tête.
M: Laissez-moi voir... je vais prendre votre température. Vous avez de la fièvre, aussi.
S: Ce n'est pas tout! Ce matin, quand je me suis levé pour aller aux toilettes, je suis tombé. J'ai peur de m'être cassé la cheville parce qu'elle me fait très mal.
M: Monsieur Sebbar, ne vous inquiétez pas. Heureusement, vous vous êtes seulement foulé la cheville. Je vais vous donner quelques médicaments contre la douleur. Quant à vos autres symptômes, vous avez la grippe. Restez au lit pendant une semaine. Buvez beaucoup d'eau. L'infirmière va vous faire une piqûre. Comme ça, vous allez guérir plus vite.
(_On Textbook MP3s_)

1 Suggestion Play the conversation again, stopping at the end of each sentence that contains an answer so students can check their work.

2 Suggestion Go over the answers with the class. Have volunteers explain why each word doesn't belong.

3 Suggestion Ask volunteers to read the completed sentences aloud.

OPTIONS

Pairs Have students work in pairs and take turns asking each other questions based on the illustration on pages 424–425. Tell them to point to the people as they ask their questions. Examples: **1. Qui travaille chez le médecin? 2. Que fait le médecin? 3. Qui prend une pilule? 4. Qu'est-ce que ce patient fait? 5. Qui se sent mal?**

Extra Practice Bring in drawings or magazine photos related to illness, medicine, and medical appointments. Have the class describe what is going on in the images or create stories about the people.

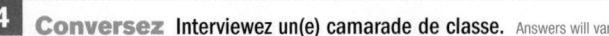

4 Suggestions
- Tell students to jot down notes during their interviews.
- After completing the interviews, have pairs get together with another pair and report what they learned about their partner.

5 Suggestion Tell students to write a description of each illustration. Then ask volunteers to read their descriptions aloud and have the class guess which illustration they are describing.

6 Suggestions
- Provide a model for students by describing an illness or accident you have had.
- For this activity, you might want to preview the **passé composé** of reflexive verbs by presenting the first person singular form of a few verbs. Example: **Je me suis foulé (cassé/blessé) la cheville (le bras/l'orteil).**

7 Suggestions
- Before beginning the activity, remind students that the doctor/patient relationship calls for the formal subject pronoun **vous**.
- Have students brainstorm a list of symptoms they might have and write them on the board.

Communication

4 Conversez Interviewez un(e) camarade de classe. Answers will vary.

1. Quand t'a-t-on fait une piqûre pour la dernière fois? Pourquoi? Et une ordonnance?
2. Est-ce que tu as souvent un rhume? Que fais-tu pour te soigner (*to treat yourself*)?
3. Quel médicament prends-tu quand tu as de la fièvre? Et quand tu as mal à la tête?
4. Es-tu allé(e) chez le médecin cette année? À l'hôpital? Pourquoi?
5. Es-tu déjà allé(e) aux urgences? Pourquoi?
6. Un membre de ta famille ou un(e) de tes ami(e)s est-il/elle à l'hôpital en ce moment? Comment se sent cette personne?
7. Est-ce une bonne idée de fumer? Pourquoi?
8. Comment te sens-tu aujourd'hui? Et comment te sentais-tu hier?

5 Qu'est-ce qui ne va pas? Travaillez avec un(e) camarade de classe et à tour de rôle, indiquez ce qui ne va pas chez chaque personne. Proposez un traitement (*treatment*). Answers will vary.

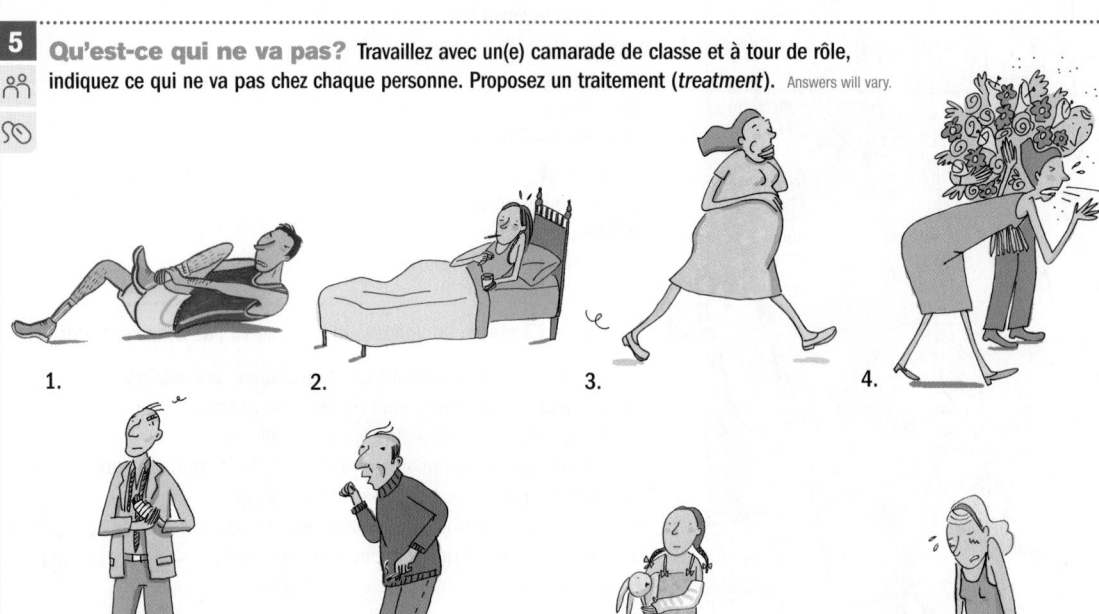

1.   2.   3.   4.

5.   6.   7.   8.

6 Écriture Suivez les instructions et composez un paragraphe. Ensuite, comparez votre paragraphe avec celui d'un(e) camarade de classe. Answers will vary.

- Décrivez la dernière fois que vous étiez malade ou la dernière fois que vous avez eu un accident.
- Dites quels étaient vos symptômes.
- Dites si vous êtes allé(e) chez le médecin ou aux urgences.
- Mentionnez si vous avez eu une ordonnance et quels médicaments vous avez pris.

7 Chez le médecin Travaillez avec un(e) camarade de classe pour présenter un dialogue dans lequel vous: Answers will vary.

- jouez le rôle d'un médecin et d'un(e) patient(e).
- parlez des symptômes du/de la patient(e).
- présentez le diagnostic (*diagnosis*) du médecin.
- proposez une ordonnance au/à la patient(e).

O P T I O N S

Pairs Have students work in pairs. Tell them to make a list of suggestions on how to prevent a cold (**un rhume**) or the flu (**la grippe**). Examples: **On doit souvent se laver les mains. On doit manger des fruits et des légumes. On doit éviter les personnes malades.** Then have pairs get together to compare their lists.

Extra Practice Have the class create a story of a very unfortunate person, **Pauvre Pierre**. The first person starts by saying what happens to him using the present tense. The next person repeats what the first one said, then adds another sentence to the story. Example: **Pauvre Pierre, quand il se réveille, il a mal à la tête.** The last student to speak concludes the story.

Les sons et les lettres   Audio

p, t, and c

Read the following English words aloud while holding your hand an inch or two in front of your mouth. You should feel a small burst of air when you pronounce each of the consonants.

pan   **top**   **cope**   **pat**

In French, the letters **p**, **t**, and **c** are not accompanied by a short burst of air. This time, try to minimize the amount of air you exhale as you pronounce these consonants. You should feel only a very small burst of air or none at all.

panne   **taupe**   **capital**   **cœur**

To minimize a t sound, touch your tongue to your teeth and gums, rather than just your gums.

taille   **tête**   **tomber**   **tousser**

Similarly, you can minimize the force of a **p** by smiling slightly as you pronounce it.

pied   **poitrine**   **pilule**   **piqûre**

When you pronounce a hard c sound, you can minimize the force by releasing it very quickly.

corps   **cou**   **casser**   **comme**

Prononcez Répétez les mots suivants à voix haute.

1. plat
2. cave
3. tort
4. timide
5. commencer
6. travailler
7. pardon
8. carotte
9. partager
10. problème
11. rencontrer
12. confiture
13. petits pois
14. colocataire
15. canadien

Articulez Répétez les phrases suivantes à voix haute.

1. Paul préfère le tennis ou les cartes?
2. Claude déteste le poisson et le café.
3. Claire et Thomas ont-ils la grippe?
4. Tu préfères les biscuits ou les gâteaux?

Dictons Répétez les dictons à voix haute.

Il n'y a que le premier pas qui coûte.[2]

Les absents ont toujours tort.[1]

[1] Those who are absent are always the ones to blame.
[2] The first step is always the hardest.

ressources

LM
p. 78

vhlcentral

quatre cent vingt-sept **427**

Section Goals

In this section, students will learn about the letters **p**, **t**, and **c**.

Instructional Resources
vhlcentral.com:
Textbook MP3s; Lab MP3s;
SAM Answer Key;
Textbook Audioscript;
Lab Audioscript;
reference tools

Suggestions
- Model the pronunciation of the example words and have students repeat them after you.
- Ask students to provide more examples of words from this lesson or previous lessons with these sounds. Examples: **ventre, pleine, patient, santé, thé, café,** and **commander**.
- Dictate five familiar words containing the consonants **p, t** and **c**, repeating each one at least two times. Then write them on the board or a transparency and have students check their spelling.

Extra Practice Use these sentences with **p, t,** and **c** for additional practice or as a dictation. **1. Carole partage son gâteau avec Paul. 2. Ta tante Thérèse nous a apporté du thé. 3. Patricia prend des pilules pour sa grippe. 4. Chloé a très mal au cou parce qu'elle est tombée.**

Extra Practice Teach students this French tongue-twister that contains plosive sounds. **Tu t'entêtes à tout tenter, tu t'uses et tu te tues à tant t'entêter. Tatie, ton thé t'a-t-il ôté ta toux, disait la tortue au tatou. Mais pas du tout, dit le tatou, je tousse tant que l'on m'entend de Tahiti à Tombouctou.**

Section Goals

In this section, students will learn functional phrases for giving instructions or suggestions and for describing ailments or injuries.

Instructional Resources
vhlcentral.com:
Roman-photo *Video, Videoscript, and Translation; SAM Answer Key; reference tools*

Video Recap: Leçon 10A
Review the previous **Roman-photo** with this activity.
1. Qui ne se sent pas bien? (David)
2. Où est David? (dans la salle de bains)
3. Qui est en retard pour son cours de sciences po? (Rachid)
4. Comment est-ce que Rachid entre enfin dans la salle de bains? (Il dit à David de fermer les yeux.)
5. À qui est-ce que David va téléphoner? (au médecin)

Video Synopsis
Rachid and Stéphane are playing soccer at the park. Rachid hurts his ankle so Amina and Stéphane take him to the doctor's. Dr. Beaumarchais says it is only sprained. Then she tells him how to treat his ankle and writes a prescription. At the apartment, David is surprised when Rachid arrives on crutches. Stéphane wants to know what happened to David. He explains that the cream is for his rash, which is an allergic reaction. They also gave him a shot and some medication.

Suggestions
- Have students predict what the episode will be about based on the video stills.
- Have students scan the captions for sentences related to injuries or illnesses.
- After reading the **Roman-photo**, have students summarize the episode.

Leçon 10B

ESPACE **ROMAN-PHOTO**

L'accident Video

PERSONNAGES

Amina

David

Dr Beaumarchais

Rachid

Stéphane

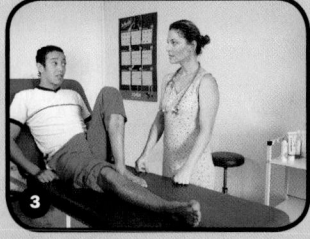

Au parc...
RACHID Comment s'appelle le parti politique qui gagne les élections en 1936?
STÉPHANE Le Front Populaire.
RACHID Exact. Qui en était le chef?
STÉPHANE Je ne m'en souviens pas.
RACHID Réfléchis. Qui est devenu président...?

AMINA Salut, vous deux!
RACHID Bonjour, Amina! (*Il tombe.*) Aïe!
STÉPHANE Tiens, donne-moi la main. Essaie de te relever.
RACHID Attends... non, je ne peux pas.
AMINA On va t'emmener chez le médecin tout de suite. Stéphane, mets-toi là, de l'autre côté. Hop là! On y va? Allons-y.

Chez le médecin...
DOCTEUR Alors, expliquez-moi ce qui s'est passé.
RACHID Eh bien, je jouais au foot quand tout à coup, je suis tombé.
DOCTEUR Et où est-ce que vous avez mal? Au genou? À la jambe? Ça ne vous fait pas mal ici?
RACHID Non, pas vraiment.

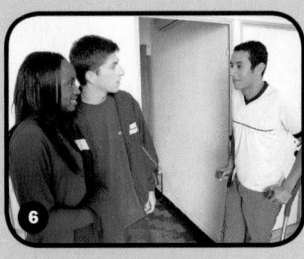

AMINA Ah, te voilà, Rachid!
STÉPHANE Alors, tu t'es cassé la jambe? Euh... tu peux toujours jouer au foot?
AMINA Stéphane!
RACHID Pas pour le moment, non; mais ne t'inquiète pas. Après quelques semaines de repos, je vais guérir rapidement et retrouver la forme.

AMINA Qu'est-ce que t'a dit le docteur?
RACHID Oh, ce n'est pas grave. Je me suis foulé la cheville. C'est tout.
AMINA Ah, c'est une bonne nouvelle. Bon, on rentre?
RACHID Oui, volontiers. Dis, est-ce qu'on peut passer par la pharmacie?
AMINA Bien sûr!

Chez David et Rachid...
DAVID Rachid! Qu'est-ce qui t'est arrivé?
RACHID On jouait au foot et je suis tombé. Je me suis foulé la cheville.
DAVID Oh! C'est idiot!
AMINA Bon, on va mettre de la glace sur ta cheville. Il y en a au congélateur?
DAVID Oui, il y en a.

A C T I V I T É S

1 **Les événements** Mettez ces événements dans l'ordre chronologique.

___7___ a. Rachid, Stéphane et Amina vont à la pharmacie.
___3___ b. Rachid tombe.
___9___ c. David explique qu'il a eu une réaction allergique.
___1___ d. Rachid et Stéphane jouent au foot.
___5___ e. Le docteur Beaumarchais explique que Rachid n'a pas la cheville cassée.

___2___ f. Stéphane ne se souvient pas de la réponse.
___4___ g. Amina et Stéphane aident Rachid.
___8___ h. Amina et Stéphane sont surpris de voir (see) comment est le visage de David.
___10___ i. David dit qu'il est allé aux urgences.
___6___ j. Le docteur Beaumarchais prépare une ordonnance.

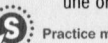 Practice more at **vhlcentral.com**.

428 *quatre cent vingt-huit*

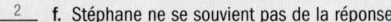

O P T I O N S

Avant de regarder la vidéo Before viewing the video, have students work in pairs and brainstorm a list of things people might say to a doctor when they get hurt. Also have them write a list of things a doctor might ask a patient who is hurt.

Regarder la vidéo Download and print the videoscript found on the Supersite. Then white out words related to injuries, illnesses, and other key vocabulary in order to create a master for a cloze activity. Distribute the photocopies and tell students to fill in the missing information as they watch the video episode.

Rachid se foule la cheville.

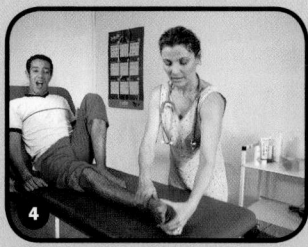

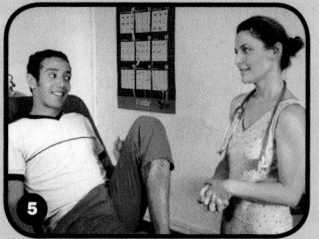

DOCTEUR Et là, à la cheville?

RACHID Aïe! Oui, c'est ça!

DOCTEUR Vous pouvez tourner le pied à droite... Et à gauche? Doucement. La bonne nouvelle, c'est que ce n'est pas cassé.

RACHID Ouf, j'ai eu peur.

DOCTEUR Vous vous êtes simplement foulé la cheville. Alors, voilà ce que vous allez faire: mettre de la glace, vous reposer. Ça veut dire: pas de foot pendant une semaine au moins et prendre des médicaments contre la douleur. Je vous prépare une ordonnance tout de suite.

RACHID Merci, Docteur Beaumarchais.

STÉPHANE Et toi, David, qu'est-ce qui t'est arrivé? Tu fais le clown ou quoi?

DAVID Ah! Ah!... Très drôle, Stéphane.

AMINA Ça te fait mal?

DAVID Non. C'est juste une allergie. Ça commence à aller mieux. Je suis allé aux urgences. On m'a fait une piqûre et on m'a donné des médicaments. Ça va passer. En attendant, je dois éviter le soleil.

STÉPHANE Vous faites vraiment la paire, tous les deux!

AMINA Allez, Stéphane. Laissons-les tranquilles. Au revoir, vous deux. Reposez-vous bien!

RACHID Merci! Au revoir!

DAVID Au revoir!

DAVID Eh! Rends-moi la télécommande! Je regardais ce film...

Expressions utiles

Giving instructions and suggestions

- **Essaie de te relever.**
  Try to get up.
- **On y va? Allons-y.**
  Ready? Let's go (there).
- **Qu'est-ce qui t'est arrivé?**
  What happened to you?
- **Laissons-les tranquilles.**
  Let's leave them alone.
- **Rends-moi la télécommande.**
  Give me back the remote.

Referring to ideas, quantities, and places

- **Qui en était le chef?**
  Who was the leader of it?
- **Je ne m'en souviens pas.**
  I don't remember it.
- **De la glace. Il y en a au congélateur?**
  Ice. Is there any in the freezer?
- **Oui, il y en a.**
  Yes, there is some (there).

Additional vocabulary

- **la bonne nouvelle**
  the good news
- **ça veut dire**
  that is to say/that means
- **volontiers**
  gladly
- **en attendant**
  in the meantime

---

 2 **À vous!** Sandrine ne sait pas encore ce qui *(what)* est arrivé à David et à Rachid. Avec deux camarades de classe, préparez une conversation dans laquelle Sandrine découvre ce qui s'est passé. Ensuite, jouez les rôles de Sandrine, David et Rachid devant la classe.

- Imaginez le contexte de la conversation: le lieu, qui fait/a fait quoi.
- Décidez si Sandrine rencontre les garçons ensemble ou séparément.
- Décrivez la surprise initiale de Sandrine. Détaillez ses questions et ses réactions.

3 **Écrivez** Rachid et David ont deux problèmes de santé très différents. Qu'est-ce que vous préférez, une cheville foulée pendant une semaine ou une réaction allergique au visage? Écrivez un paragraphe dans lequel vous comparez les deux situations. Quelle situation est la pire? Pourquoi?

ressources
VM pp. 39–40
vhlcentral

A C T I V I T É S

quatre cent vingt-neuf **429**

Expressions utiles
- Model the pronunciation of the **Expressions utiles** and have students repeat them.
- As you work through the list, point out the **passé composé** of reflexive verbs and the pronouns **y** and **en**. Tell students that these structures will be formally presented in **Espace structures**.
- Respond briefly to questions about the **passé composé** of reflexive verbs and the pronouns **y** and **en**. Reinforce correct forms, but do not expect students to produce them consistently at this time.
- Point out that the pronoun **en** is not the same as the preposition **en**. To illustrate this point, write the following sentences on the board and compare them. **Il y en a.** (*There is/are some.*) **Il est en France.** (*He is in France.*)

Successful Language Learning Tell students that before traveling to a French-speaking country, they should make a list of their allergies and medical needs and learn how to say them in French.

1 Suggestion Have students form groups of five. Make a set of individual sentences on strips of paper for each group and distribute them (two sentences per student). Tell students to arrange the sentences in the proper order and read them aloud.

1 Expansion Have students create sentences to fill in parts of the story not mentioned in this activity.

2 Suggestion Assign students a role (Sandrine, David, or Rachid). Encourage them to be creative.

3 Suggestion Before writing their paragraphs, tell students to jot down a list of positive and negative aspects of each situation so that they can make a decision.

OPTIONS

Game Play a game of **Dix questions**. Ask a volunteer to think of an ailment or illness from this lesson. Other students get to ask one yes/no question each. Then they can guess the ailment/illness. Limit attempts to ten questions per item. You may want to provide students with some sample questions. Examples: **As-tu mal à la tête? As-tu mal au cœur? Es-tu blessé(e)?**

Pairs Have students work in pairs and interview each other using these questions. **1. Est-ce que tu tombes souvent malade? 2. Est-ce que tu as souvent mal à la tête? 3. Est-ce que tu manges bien ou mal? 4. Est-ce que tu manges beaucoup de fruits et de légumes? 5. Est-ce que tu fais de l'exercice? 6. Combien de fois par an est-ce que tu vas chez le dentiste?**

Reading
Video: *Flash culture*

Section Goals

In this section, students will:
• learn about the national healthcare system in France
• learn some terms for common health problems
• learn about several francophone pioneers in medicine
• read about **Marie Curie**
• view authentic video footage

Instructional Resources
vhlcentral.com:
Video; SAM Answer Key;
reference tools

Culture à la loupe
Avant la lecture Have students look at the visuals and describe what they see. Then ask them what they think **la Sécurité sociale** in France is.

Lecture
• Point out the statistics chart. Ask students what information the chart shows. (French medical visits)
• Tell students that the French healthcare system was ranked number one by the World Health Organization in 2000 and in 2002.

Après la lecture Ask students to name the different branches of **la Sécurité sociale** and explain what they do. (**la branche «famille», la branche «vieillesse» et la branche «maladie»**)

1 Expansion Have students write two more true/false statements based on the reading. Then tell them to get into groups of three and take turns reading their sentences and responding.

CULTURE À LA LOUPE

La Sécurité sociale

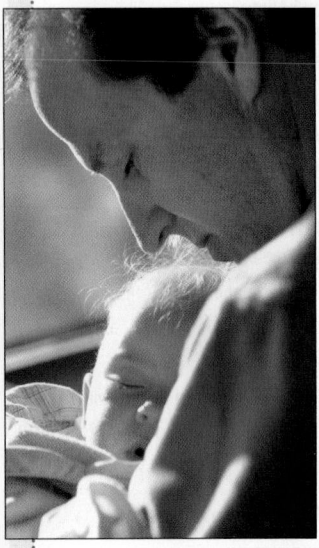

En France, presque tous les habitants sont couverts par le système national de la Sécurité sociale. La Sécurité sociale, ou «la sécu», est un organisme d'État, financé principalement par les cotisations° sociales des travailleurs, qui donne une aide financière à ses bénéficiaires dans différents domaines. La branche «famille», par exemple, s'occupe des allocations° pour la maternité et les enfants. La branche «vieillesse» paie les retraites des personnes âgées. La branche «maladie» aide les gens en cas de maladies et d'accidents du travail. Chaque personne qui bénéficie des prestations° de la Sécurité sociale a une carte Vitale qui ressemble à une carte de crédit et qui contient° toutes ses informations personnelles. La Sécurité sociale rembourse° en moyenne 75% des frais° médicaux. Les visites chez le médecin sont remboursées à 70%. Le taux° de remboursement varie entre 80 et 100% pour les séjours en clinique ou à l'hôpital et entre 70 et 100% pour les soins dentaires°. Pour les achats° en pharmacie, le taux de remboursement varie beaucoup: de 35 à 100% selon° les médicaments achetés. Beaucoup de gens ont aussi une mutuelle, une assurance santé supplémentaire qui rembourse ce que la Sécurité sociale ne rembourse pas. Ceux° qui ne peuvent pas avoir de mutuelle et ceux qui n'ont pas droit à° la Sécurité sociale traditionnelle bénéficient parfois de la Couverture Maladie Universelle (CMU). La CMU garantit le remboursement à 100% des frais médicaux aux gens qui n'ont pas beaucoup de ressources.

Les visites médicales

• En moyenne°, les Français consultent un médecin sept fois par an,
• dont° quatre fois un généraliste
• et trois fois un spécialiste.
• 70% des visites médicales ont lieu° chez le médecin.
• 20% ont lieu à la maison.
• 10% ont lieu à l'hôpital.

cotisations *contributions* **allocations** *allowances* **prestations** *benefits* **contient** *holds* **rembourse** *reimburses* **frais** *expenses* **taux** *rate* **soins dentaires** *dental care* **achats** *purchases* **selon** *depending on* **Ceux** *Those* **n'ont pas droit à** *don't qualify for* **En moyenne** *On average* **dont** *of which* **ont lieu** *take place*

A C T I V I T É S

1 Vrai ou faux? Indiquez si les phrases sont **vraies** ou **fausses.** Corrigez les phrases fausses.

1. Les cotisations des travailleurs financent la Sécurité sociale.   Vrai.
2. La Sécurité sociale a plusieurs branches.   Vrai.
3. La branche «vieillesse» s'occupe des accidents du travail.
   Faux. Elle s'occupe des retraites.
4. La carte Vitale est une assurance supplémentaire.
   Faux. C'est une carte qui contient toutes les informations personnelles d'une personne.
5. La Sécurité sociale rembourse en moyenne 100% des frais médicaux.   Faux. Elle rembourse en moyenne 75% des frais médicaux.

6. Entre 70 et 100% des soins dentaires sont remboursés par la sécu.   Vrai.
7. La Sécurité sociale ne rembourse pas les médicaments.
   Faux. Elle rembourse entre 35 et 100% du prix des médicaments.
8. En plus de la Sécurité sociale, certaines personnes ont des assurances santé supplémentaires.   Vrai.
9. Si on n'a pas beaucoup d'argent, on peut bénéficier de la CMU.   Vrai.
10. Vingt pour cent des consultations médicales ont lieu à l'hôpital.
    Faux. Dix pour cent ont lieu à l'hôpital. Vingt pour cent ont lieu à la maison.

430 *quatre cent trente*

O P T I O N S

Cultural Comparison Take a quick class survey to find out how many times students visit a doctor in a year and if they see the doctor at his or her office, if they go to the hospital, or if the doctor comes to their home. Tally the results on the board and have students figure out the percentages. Then have students compare the results of this survey with the information in the chart **Les visites médicales.**

La Sécurité sociale France offers a degree of socialized medicine, though the coverage is not as complete as in some other countries. Criticism of the system stems from abuse by those who pay little for services at the expense of those who earn the most, and thus pay the most to the government.

LE FRANÇAIS QUOTIDIEN

Des problèmes de santé

angine (*f.*)	*strep throat*
bronchite (*f.*)	*bronchitis*
carie (*f.*)	*cavity*
frissons (*m.*)	*chills*
migraine (*f.*)	*migraine*
nez bouché	*stuffy nose*
nez qui coule	*runny nose*
sinusite (*f.*)	*sinus infection*
toux (*f.*)	*cough*

LE MONDE FRANCOPHONE

Des pionniers de la médecine

Voici quelques autres pionniers francophones de la médecine.

En Belgique
Jules Bordet (1870–1961) médecin et microbiologiste qui a découvert° le microbe de la coqueluche°

En France
Bernard Kouchner (1939–) médecin, cofondateur° de Médecins sans frontières° et de Médecins du monde

En Haïti
Yvonne Sylvain (1907–1989) première femme médecin et gynécologue obstétricienne d'Haïti

Au Québec
Jeanne Mance (1606–1673) fondatrice du premier hôpital d'Amérique du Nord

En Suisse
Henri Dunant (1828–1910) fondateur de la Croix-Rouge°

a découvert *discovered* **coqueluche** *whooping cough* **cofondateur** *cofounder* **frontières** *Borders* **Croix-Rouge** *Red Cross*

PORTRAIT

Marie Curie

Grande figure féminine du 20ᵉ siècle et de l'histoire des sciences, Marie Curie reçoit° en 1903 le prix Nobel de physique avec son mari, Pierre, pour leurs travaux° sur la radioactivité. Quelques années plus tard elle reçoit le prix Nobel de chimie pour la découverte° de deux éléments radioactifs: le polonium et le radium. Pendant la Première Guerre mondiale° elle organise un service de radiologie mobile pour mieux soigner° les blessés. La lutte° contre le cancer bénéficie aussi des vertus thérapeutiques du radium. Marie Curie est la première femme à recevoir° un prix Nobel et la seule personne à en avoir reçu° deux. Elle est née Maria Sklodowska à Varsovie en Pologne. À 24 ans elle est venue à Paris pour faire des études scientifiques car° l'université de Varsovie refusait l'accès aux jeunes filles. Elle a consacré° toute sa vie aux recherches scientifiques et est morte d'une leucémie en 1934.

reçoit *receives* **travaux** *work* **découverte** *discovery* **Première Guerre mondiale** *World War I* **soigner** *treat* **lutte** *fight* **recevoir** *receive* **reçu** *received* **car** *because* **consacré** *devoted*

MUSIQUE À FOND

Pierre Bachelet

Lieu d'origine: Paris, France
Métier: auteur-compositeur-interprète

Très connu pour sa voix mélodique, il évoque le Nord dans ses chansons. Il est connu aussi pour ses musiques de films.

Go to vhlcentral.com to find out more about **Pierre Bachelet** and his music.

---

2 Répondez Répondez aux questions par des phrases complètes.

1. Quels grands prix Marie Curie a-t-elle reçus?
Elle a reçu le prix Nobel de physique et de chimie.
2. Quelles sont les implications pour la lutte contre le cancer?
La lutte contre le cancer bénéficie des vertus thérapeutiques du radium.
3. Où Marie Curie est-elle née?
Marie Curie est née à Varsovie en Pologne.
4. Pourquoi est-elle venue à Paris?
Elle est venue à Paris pour faire des études scientifiques.
5. Qui a été la première femme médecin d'Haïti?
Yvonne Sylvain a été la première femme médecin d'Haïti.

3 Problèmes de santé Avec un(e) camarade, écrivez cinq phrases où vous utilisez ce vocabulaire: **une angine** (*strep throat*), **une carie** (*cavity*), **des frissons** (*m.*) (*chills*), **le nez bouché** (*stuffy nose*), **une toux** (*cough*). Soyez prêts à les présenter devant la classe.

ressources

VM pp. 79-80 | vhlcentral

 Practice more at **vhlcentral.com.**

A C T I V I T É S

OPTIONS

Small Groups Have students work in groups of three. Tell them to make a list of symptoms and treatments for these illnesses: **l'angine, la bronchite, la migraine,** and **la sinusite.** You might want to give them the words **l'antibiotique** and **la pénicilline.** Then have two groups get together and compare their lists.

Portrait Ask students if they can think of other women who have made important contributions to scientific research.

Le français quotidien
• Model the pronunciation of each term and have students repeat it.
• Ask students questions using these terms. Examples: **1. Avez-vous déjà eu une angine (une bronchite/une migraine/une sinusite)? Quand? 2. Les frissons sont-ils un symptôme d'une migraine?**

Le monde francophone Have students write four true/false statements based on the information given in **Des pionniers de la médecine**. Then have them get together with a classmate and take turns reading their sentences and responding.

2 Expansion For additional practice, give students these items. **6. Qui a fondé** (*founded*) **la Croix-Rouge? (Henri Dunant) 7. Qui a aidé à fonder Médecins sans frontières? (Bernard Kouchner)**

3 Suggestion Have pairs get together with another pair of students and peer edit each other's sentences.

Flash culture Tell students that they will learn more about pharmacies and other health related businesses by watching a variety of real-life images narrated by Benjamin. Show the video segment, then have students jot down in French at least three examples of things they saw. You can also use the activities in the video manual in class or as homework to reinforce this **Flash culture**.

10B.1

Section Goals

In this section, students will learn:
• the **passé composé** and the **imparfait** of reflexive verbs
• past participle agreement with reflexive verbs

Instructional Resources

vhlcentral.com:
Activity Pack; Lab MP3s;
*SAM Answer Key; **Essayez!***
*and **Mise en pratique***
answers; Lab Audioscript;
reference tools

Suggestions

• Briefly review the **passé composé** with **être** and past participle agreement from **Espace structures 7A.1** and **7A.2**.

• Compare reflexive verbs in the **passé composé** and in the present tense by contrasting something out of character that you did one day with what you usually do. Example: **Hier, je me suis levé(e) à neuf heures, mais d'habitude, je me lève à six heures.** Encourage similar statements from students. Write the sentences on the board, having volunteers underline the auxiliary verbs and circle the past participle agreements.

À noter

In **Leçon 7A**, you learned about verbs that take **être** in the **passé composé** and about agreement of past participles with a preceding direct object pronoun in the **passé composé** with **avoir**. Keep these in mind as you learn how to form the **passé composé** of reflexive verbs.

🏃 Boîte à outils

Recall that some verbs can be used both reflexively and non-reflexively. In the **passé composé**, reflexive verbs take **être** as the auxiliary verb, while their non-reflexive counterparts take **avoir**.

Elle **s'est arrêtée**.
Elle **a arrêté** la voiture.

The *passé composé* of reflexive verbs

 Tutorial

Point de départ In **Leçon 10A**, you learned to form the present tense and command forms of reflexive verbs. You will now learn how to form the **passé composé** of reflexive verbs.

• Use the auxiliary verb **être** with all reflexive verbs in the **passé composé**, and place the reflexive pronoun before it.

Nous **nous sommes fait** mal hier, pendant la randonnée.
We hurt ourselves during the hike yesterday.

Il **s'est lavé** les mains avant de prendre le médicament.
He washed his hands before taking the medicine.

Où est-ce que tu **t'es blessé**?
Where did you hurt yourself?

Vous **vous êtes trompé**?
Did you make a mistake?

• If the verb is not followed by a direct object, the past participle does agree with the subject in gender and number.

SUBJECT   PAST PARTICIPLE
L'infirmier et le médecin **se sont disputés**.
The nurse and the doctor argued.

SUBJECT PAST PARTICIPLE
Elle **s'est assise** dans le fauteuil du dentiste.
She sat in the dentist's chair.

SUBJECT   PAST PARTICIPLE
Ahmed et toi, vous **vous êtes** bien **entendus**?
Did you and Ahmed get along?

• If the verb is followed by a direct object, the past participle does not agree with the subject. Use the masculine singular form.

PAST PARTICIPLE DIRECT OBJECT
Régine **s'est foulé** les deux chevilles.
Régine twisted both ankles.

PAST PARTICIPLE DIRECT OBJECT
Ils **se sont cassé** les bras.
They broke their arms.

• To make a reflexive verb negative in the **passé composé**, place **ne** before the reflexive pronoun and **pas** after the auxiliary verb.

Elles **ne se sont pas** mises en colère.
They didn't get angry.

Nous **ne nous sommes pas** sentis mieux.
We didn't feel better.

Je **ne me suis pas** rasé ce matin.
I didn't shave this morning.

Tu **ne t'es pas** coiffée.
You didn't do your hair.

- To ask a question using inversion with a reflexive verb in the **passé composé**, follow the same pattern as you would with non-reflexive verbs. Invert the subject pronoun and the auxiliary verb, and keep the reflexive pronoun before the auxiliary.

  Irène **s'est-elle** blessée au genou?
  Did Irène hurt her knee?

  Ne **vous êtes-vous** pas rendu compte de ça?
  Didn't you realize that?

- Place a direct object pronoun between the reflexive pronoun and the auxiliary verb. Make the past participle agree with the direct object pronoun that precedes it.

  Il a la cheville un peu enflée. Il **se l'**est **cassée** il y a une semaine.
  His ankle is a bit swollen. He broke it a week ago.

  Mes mains? Mais je **me les** suis déjà **lavées**.
  My hands? But I already washed them.

- The irregular past participle of the verb **s'asseoir** is **assis(e)**.

Elle **s'est assise** près de la fenêtre.
She sat near the window.

Les jeunes mariés **se sont assis** dans le salon.
The newlyweds sat in the living room.

- Form the **imparfait** of reflexive verbs exactly as you would for non-reflexive verbs. Just add the corresponding reflexive pronoun.

  Je **me brossais** les dents trois fois par jour.
  I used to brush my teeth three times a day.

  Nous **nous promenions** souvent au parc.
  We often used to take walks in the park.

 **Essayez!** **Complétez ces phrases.**

1. Natalia s'est ((foulé)/ foulée) le bras.
2. Sa jambe? Comment Robert se l'est-il (cassé / (cassée))?
3. Les deux joueurs de basket se sont (blessé / (blessés)) au genou.
4. L'infirmière s'est ((lavé)/ lavées) les mains.
5. M. Pinchon s'est ((fait)/ faite) mal à la jambe.
6. S'est-elle ((rasé)/ rasées) les jambes?
7. Elles se sont ((maquillé)/ maquillés) les yeux?
8. Nous nous les sommes (cassé / (cassés)).
9. Sandrine, tu t'es (réveillé / (réveillée)) tard ce matin.
10. Tout à coup, Omar s'est ((senti)/ sentie) mal.
11. Nous ne nous sommes pas (déshabillé / (déshabillées)) avant de nous coucher.

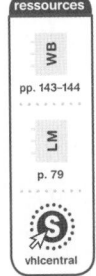

ressources

WB
pp. 143–144

LM
p. 79

vhlcentral

Suggestion
- Talk about things that happened to you and to your students in the past. Examples: **Il y a deux ans, je me suis arrêté(e) chez mes amis français pendant mon voyage en Europe**.

Essayez! Review that only direct objects preceding the **passé composé** with **être** require past participle agreement. Clarify that when a direct object comes after the verb in **passé composé** reflexive sentences, the reflexive pronoun acts as an indirect object (no agreement). Where there is no direct object after the verb, the reflexive pronoun acts as a direct object, thereby requiring past participle agreement.

OPTIONS

Extra Practice Ask students questions like the following with reflexive verbs. Examples: **Vous êtes-vous souvenu(e)s de vos cours de français pendant l'examen?** (Oui, je me suis souvenu[e] de ....) **Vous êtes-vous couché(e)s tôt ou tard hier soir?** (Je me suis couché[e] tôt/tard.) **Vous êtes-vous mis(e) en colère contre un de vos amis?** (Oui/Non, je [ne] me suis [pas] mis[e] en colère contre un de mes amis.)

Game Divide the class into two teams. Choose one student at a time to go to the board, alternating between teams. Say a subject and a reflexive verb in the infinitive. The student at the board writes and says the **passé composé** form. Example: **il: s'asseoir (il s'est assis); nous** (*fem.*): **s'inquiéter (nous nous sommes inquiétées)** Teams earn a point per correct answer. The team with the most points at the end of the game wins.

ESPACE STRUCTURES

1 **Expansion** Ask students to think of other details that Christine didn't mention. Examples: **Elle s'est habillée. Elle (ne) s'est (pas) maquillée. Elle (ne) s'est (pas) peigné les cheveux.**

2 **Expansion** Show photos or magazine pictures, having students describe what happened based on the subject (pronoun) you give. Examples: 5. a couple of young women relaxing (**nous**) (**Nous nous sommes détendues.**) 6. an elderly woman going to bed (**notre grand-mère**) (**Notre grand-mère s'est couchée.**)

3 **Suggestions**
• Have two students act out the **modèle**.
• Call on pairs to do the activity in front of the class.

Mise en pratique

1 **Une lettre** Complétez la lettre que Christine a écrite sur sa journée. Mettez les verbes au passé composé.

Hier soir, je (1) <u>me suis couchée</u> (se coucher) trop tard, et quand je (2) <u>me suis réveillée</u> (se réveiller), j'étais fatiguée. Mais je voulais jouer au basket, alors je (3) <u>me suis levée</u> (se lever) et je (4) <u>me suis brossé</u> (se brosser) les dents. Mon amie est venue me chercher et je (5) <u>me suis endormie</u> (s'endormir) dans la voiture! Je pense que mon amie (6) <u>s'est énervée</u> (s'énerver) un peu contre moi. Nous (7) <u>nous sommes préparées</u> (se préparer) pour le match et nous (8) <u>nous sommes mises</u> (se mettre) à jouer.

2 **Descriptions** Utilisez des verbes réfléchis pour décrire ce que (*what*) les personnages des illustrations ont fait ou n'ont pas fait hier. Mettez les verbes au passé composé. Suggested answers

MODÈLE
Thomas ne s'est pas lavé.

Thomas

1. mes amis
Mes amis se sont disputés.

2. tu
Tu t'es rasé.

3. je
Je me suis ennuyée.

4. vous
Vous vous êtes mise en colère.

3 **Une mauvaise journée** Hier, Djamila a eu toutes sortes de difficultés. Avec un(e) partenaire, utilisez le vocabulaire de la liste pour raconter sa mauvaise journée. Answers will vary.

MODÈLE
Étudiant(e) 1: Djamila s'est trompée.
Étudiant(e) 2: Elle s'est brossé les dents avec du savon!

se brosser	se sentir	la cheville
se casser	se tromper	la jambe
se fouler	le bras	le pied
s'habiller	les chaussures	un rhume
se laver	du dentifrice	du savon
se lever	la salle des urgences	du shampooing

 Practice more at **vhlcentral.com**.

Communication

4 **Et toi?** Avec un(e) partenaire, posez-vous ces questions. Ensuite, présentez vos réponses à la classe. Answers will vary.

1. À quelle heure t'es-tu réveillé(e) ce matin?
2. Avec quel dentifrice t'es-tu brossé les dents?
3. Avec quel shampooing t'es-tu lavé les cheveux aujourd'hui?
4. T'es-tu énervé(e) cette semaine? Pourquoi?
5. T'es-tu disputé(e) avec quelqu'un cette semaine? Avec qui?
6. T'es-tu endormi(e) facilement hier soir? Pourquoi?
7. T'es-tu promené(e) récemment? Où?
8. Comment t'es-tu détendu(e) le week-end dernier?
9. Comment t'es-tu amusé(e) le week-end dernier?
10. T'es-tu bien entendu(e) avec ton/ta camarade de chambre le premier mois?
11. T'es-tu couché(e) tard le week-end dernier? Pourquoi?
12. T'es-tu mis(e) en colère contre quelqu'un récemment? Contre qui? Pourquoi?

5 **Une enquête criminelle** Il y a eu un crime dans votre quartier et un agent de police vous pose des questions pour l'enquête (*investigation*). Avec un(e) partenaire, utilisez le vocabulaire de la liste pour créer le dialogue. Answers will vary.

se coucher	se trouver
se disputer	appartement
s'énerver	blessure
se lever	corps
se mettre en colère	quartier
se réveiller	déprimé(e)
revenir	grave
se souvenir	soudain

6 **Charades** Par groupes de quatre, pensez à une phrase au passé composé avec un verbe réfléchi et jouez-la. La première personne qui devine joue la prochaine phrase. Answers will vary.

---

4 **Expansion** Ask volunteers to share some of their answers. The class then adds information by speculating on the reason behind each answer. Have the volunteer confirm or refute the speculation. Allow students to make up answers if the questions are too personal. Example: **Tu t'es énervé(e) cette semaine parce que ton/ta copain/copine et toi vous êtes disputés.**

5 **Suggestion** Before beginning this activity, ask students warm-up questions. Examples: **Est-ce qu'il y a déjà eu un crime dans votre quartier? Est-ce que vous vous êtes blessés? Ou est-ce que quelqu'un que vous connaissez s'est blessé? Est-ce qu'il y a eu une enquête?**

6 **Suggestion** Ask each group to present their best charade to the class.

OPTIONS

TPR Have a volunteer quickly mime two or three activities in front of the class. Examples: stand up, wash hands, and do hair. Then ask: **Qu'a-t-il/elle fait?** Call on students to say what the classmate did in the **passé composé** with reflexive verbs. Example: _____ **s'est levé(e). Ensuite, il/elle s'est lavé les mains. Enfin, il/elle s'est coiffé(e).** Repeat with more than one volunteer miming the activities at the same time.

Small Groups Have groups compile a list of famous people who could be described using one of the reflexive verbs. Then group members must work together to write a sentence with a reflexive verb in the **passé composé** about each person without mentioning the person's name. Other groups guess who it is. Example: **Simone de Beauvoir s'est bien entendue avec cet auteur. (Jean-Paul Sartre)**

Section Goals

In this section, students will learn the pronouns **y** and **en**.

Instructional Resources
vhlcentral.com:
SAM Answer Key; **Essayez!**
and **Mise en pratique**
answers; Lab Audioscript;
*Activity Pack (***Feuilles
d'activités***); reference tools*

Suggestions

• Ask students to recall expressions containing pronouns **y** and **en** that they have already learned. Examples: **il y a, ne t'en fais pas,** and **je vous en prie.** Make sure they understand when **en** is a preposition instead of a pronoun.

• Have students ask you questions about various locations, first in the present tense and then in the **passé composé**. Examples: **Dînez-vous au restaurant?** (Oui, j'y dîne./Non, je n'y dîne pas.) **Êtes-vous allé(e) à l'hôtel des Invalides?** (Oui, j'y suis allé(e)./Non, je n'y suis pas allé(e).) Have them make up other questions to ask you that elicit **en** as a pronoun. Then turn the questions back to the students, encouraging their responses with **y** or **en**.

The pronouns *y* and *en*  Tutorial

Point de départ The pronoun **y** replaces a previously mentioned phrase that begins with the prepositions **à, chez, dans, en,** or **sur**. The pronoun **en** replaces a previously mentioned phrase that begins with a partitive or indefinite article, or with the preposition **de**.

PREPOSITIONAL PHRASE
Nous allons **chez le médecin**. ▶ PRONOUN Nous **y** allons.

PREPOSITIONAL PHRASE
Il était le chef **du Front Populaire**. ▶ PRONOUN Il **en** était le chef.

Allons-y!

Le Front Populaire.
Qui en était le chef?

• The pronouns **y** and **en** precede the conjugated verb.

Es-tu allée **à la plage**?
Did you go to the beach?

Oui, j'**y** suis allée.
Yes, I went there.

Achètent-elles **de la moutarde**?
Are they buying mustard?

Oui, elles **en** achètent.
Yes, they're buying some.

Tu te mets **à la danse**?
Are you taking up dancing?

Oui, je m'**y** mets.
Yes, I'm taking it up.

• Like other pronouns in an infinitive construction, **y** and **en** follow the conjugated verb and precede the infinitive.

Quand préfères-tu manger **chez Fatima**?
When do you prefer to eat at Fatima's?

Je **préfère y manger** demain soir.
I prefer to eat there tomorrow night.

Allez-vous prendre **du thé**?
Are you going to have tea?

Oui, **nous allons en prendre.**
Yes, we're going to have some.

• Never omit **y** or **en** even when the English equivalents can be omitted.

Ah, vous allez **à la boulangerie**.
Oh, you're going to the bakery.

Tu **y** vas aussi?
Are you going (there), too?

Est-ce qu'elle prend **du sucre**?
Does she take sugar?

Non, elle n'**en** prend pas.
No, she doesn't (take any).

• Use **en** to replace a prepositional phrase that begins with **de**.

Vous revenez **de vacances**?
Are you coming back from vacation?

Oui, nous **en** revenons.
Yes, we're coming back (from vacation).

- Always use **en** to replace nouns that follow a number or expression of quantity. In such cases, you must still use the number or expression of quantity in the sentence together with **en**.

  Combien **de frères** a-t-elle?
  How many brothers does she have?

  Elle **en** a **un** (**deux, trois**).
  She has one (two, three).

  Avez-vous acheté **beaucoup de pain**?
  Did you buy a lot of bread?

  Oui, j'**en** ai acheté **beaucoup**.
  Yes, I bought a lot.

- In the **passé composé**, the past participle never agrees with **y** or **en**.

  Avez-vous trouvé **des fraises**?
  Did you find some strawberries?

  Oui, nous **en** avons trouvé.
  Yes, we found some.

  A-t-elle attendu **à la salle des urgences**?
  Did she wait in the emergency room?

  Oui, elle **y** a attendu.
  Yes, she waited there.

- In an affirmative **tu** command, do not drop the **-s** when an **-er** verb is followed by **y** or **en**. Note that **aller** also follows this pattern.

  Tu vas chez le médecin? Va**s-y**!   *but*   Va chez le médecin!
  You're going to the doctor's? Go!   *Go to the doctor's!*

  Il y a des pommes. Mange**s-en**!   *but*   Mange des pommes!
  There are some apples. Eat a few!   *Eat some apples!*

- With imperatives, **moi** followed by **y** and **en** becomes **m'y** and **m'en**. **Toi** followed by **y** and **en** becomes **t'y** and **t'en**.

  Vous avez **des pêches** aujourd'hui?
  You have peaches today?

  Donnez-**m'en** dix.
  Give me ten.

- When using two pronouns in the same sentence, **y** and **en** always come in second position.

  Vous parlez **à Hélène de sa toux**?
  Are you talking to Hélène about her cough?

  Oui, nous **lui en** parlons.
  Yes, we're talking to her about it.

- When used together in the same sentence, **y** is placed before **en**.

  Il y a **de bons médecins** à l'hôpital?
  Are there good doctors at the hospital?

  Oui, il **y en** a.
  Yes, there are.

Boîte à outils

The pronoun **y** is not used to refer to people. The pronoun **en** may refer to people when the noun it refers to is preceded by the indefinite article **des**. However, in the constructions [*verb*] + **à** + [*person*] and [*verb*] + **de** + [*person*], **y** and **en** cannot be used to refer to people. Instead, use disjunctive pronouns.

Je pense **à ma mère**.
Je pense **à elle**.

Nous parlons de **notre père**.
Nous parlons de **lui**.

Suggestions

- Give contrasting pairs of examples to emphasize that **y** and **en** are not used to refer to people:
  Je parle des cours. → J'en parle.
  Je parle de mon père. → Je parle de lui.
  Je pense à mes cours. → J'y pense.
  Je pense à ma mère. → Je pense à elle.
- Tell students that they need to make the liaison in affirmative imperative commands with **y** and **en**, and have them practice the pronunciation with several examples.

Essayez! Supplement this activity with items like these:
11. Avez-vous besoin d'une aspirine? (Non, nous n'en avons pas besoin.) 12. Qui joue au foot? (J'y joue. / _____ y joue.) 13. Combien de pièces y avait-il dans la maison? (Il y en avait quatre).

Essayez! Complétez les phrases avec le(s) pronom(s) correct(s).

1. Faites-vous du sport? Oui, nous _en_ faisons.
2. Papa est au garage? Oui, il _y_ est.
3. Nous voulons des fraises. Donnez-nous- _en_ un kilo.
4. Mettez-vous du sucre dans votre café? Oui, nous _en_ mettons.
5. Est-ce que tu t'intéresses à la médecine? Oui, je _m'y_ intéresse.
6. Il est allé au cinéma? Oui, il _y_ est allé.
7. Combien de pièces y avait-il? Il y _en_ avait quatre.
8. Avez-vous des lampes? Non, nous n' _en_ avons pas.
9. Elles sont chez leur copine. Elles _y_ sont depuis samedi.
10. Êtes-vous allés en France? Oui, nous _y_ sommes déjà allés.

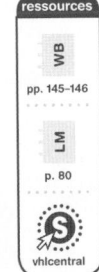

ressources

WB
pp. 145–146

LM
p. 80

vhlcentral

OPTIONS

Extra Practice Show pictures of easily identifiable places around town and/or around the world. Ask students if they go, have been, if they want to go, if they used to go, etc., to the various places. Examples: **Y allez-vous souvent? Y alliez-vous quand vous étiez petit(e)s? Voulez-vous y aller?** You could also do a similar activity without pictures. Ask questions with specific places, requiring students to use **y** in their replies.

Game Divide the class into two teams. Choose one student at a time, alternating between teams. Call out a prepositional phrase that could be replaced with **en** or **y**. The student has three seconds to choose. Examples: **chez moi (y); dans la salle de bains (y); des États-Unis (en); en France (y); du pain (en).** Teams earn a point per correct answer. The team with the most points at the end of the game wins.

1 Expansion After completing the activity, have students form the questions that would elicit the responses. Then have them take turns asking each other the questions and answering them. Example: **Combien d'enfants a-t-il?** (Il en a trois.)

2 Suggestion Have students take turns playing the roles of the nurse and the celebrity.

3 Suggestion You may want to assign this activity to groups of three. If so, call on a volunteer group to act out the completed conversation for the class.

Mise en pratique

1 **Sondage** M. Renaud répond aux questions d'un journaliste qui fait un sondage (*poll*) pour un magazine français. Utilisez **y** ou **en** pour compléter les notes du journaliste. Answers may vary slightly.

Nombre/Fréquence		Notes
1. Enfants	3	M. Renaud en a trois.
2. Chiens	0	M. Renaud n'en a pas.
3. Voiture	2	M. Renaud en a deux.
4. Cinéma	rarement	M. Renaud y va rarement.
5. Argent	peu	M. Renaud en a peu.
6. Thé/café	parfois	M. Renaud en boit parfois.
7. New York	en 2005	M. Renaud y est allé en 2005.
8. Chez le médecin	une fois par an	M. Renaud y va une fois par an.

2 **Dossier médical** Avec un(e) partenaire, choisissez une célébrité. Cette personne est allée à l'hôpital, où on lui pose ces questions. Comment répond votre célébrité? Justifiez toutes vos réponses. Utilisez les pronoms **y** et **en**. Some answers will vary.

1. Avez-vous des allergies? Oui, j'en ai. / Non, je n'en ai pas.
2. Êtes-vous allé(e) aux urgences cette année? Oui, j'y suis allé(e). / Non, je n'y suis pas allé(e).
3. Allez-vous chez le médecin régulièrement? Oui, j'y vais régulièrement. / Non, je n'y vais pas régulièrement.
4. Combien d'aspirines prenez-vous par jour? J'en prends... / Je n'en prends pas.
5. Faites-vous du sport tous les jours? Oui, j'en fais. / Non, je n'en fais pas.
6. Avez-vous des douleurs? Oui, j'en ai. / Non, je n'en ai pas.
7. Avez-vous de la fièvre? Oui, j'en ai. / Non, je n'en ai pas.
8. Vous êtes-vous blessé(e) au travail? Oui, je m'y suis blessé(e). / Non, je ne m'y suis pas blessé(e).

3 **Chez le dentiste** Mme Hanh emmène ses fils chez un nouveau dentiste. Complétez le dialogue entre le dentiste et les deux garçons. Utilisez les pronoms **y** et **en**. Suggested answers.

LE DENTISTE C'est la première fois que vous venez chez le dentiste?

FRÉDÉRIC Oui, (1) _c'est la première fois que nous y venons._

LE DENTISTE N'ayez pas peur. Alors, mangez-vous beaucoup de sucre?

HENRI (2) _Non, nous n'en mangeons pas beaucoup._

LE DENTISTE Et toi, Frédéric, utilises-tu du dentifrice?

FRÉDÉRIC (3) _Oui, j'en utilise._

HENRI Est-ce que vous allez nous faire une piqûre?

LE DENTISTE (4) _Oui, je vais vous en faire une._

HENRI Moi, je n'ai pas peur des piqûres... mais j'espère que vous n'allez pas trouver de caries (*cavities*).

LE DENTISTE (5) _Je vais peut-être en trouver une ou deux._

 Practice more at **vhlcentral.com**.

Communication

4 Trouvez quelqu'un qui… Votre professeur va vous donner une feuille d'activités. Circulez dans la classe pour trouver un(e) camarade différent(e) qui donne une réponse affirmative à chaque question. Employez les pronoms **y** et **en**. Answers will vary.

MODÈLE

Étudiant(e) 1: *Je suis né(e) à Los Angeles. Y es-tu né(e) aussi?*
Étudiant(e) 2: *Oui, j'y suis né(e) aussi!*

Qui…	Nom
1. est né(e) dans la même (same) ville que vous?	Mireille
2. a pris une aspirine aujourd'hui? Pourquoi?	
3. est allé(e) en Suisse? Quand?	
4. a mangé au resto U cette semaine? Combien de fois?	
5. est déjà allé(e) aux urgences une fois? Pourquoi?	
6. est allé(e) chez le dentiste ce mois-ci? Quand?	

5 Interview Posez ces questions à un(e) partenaire. Employez **y** ou **en** dans vos réponses, puis présentez-les à la classe. Answers will vary.

Demandez à un(e) partenaire...

1. s'il/elle va à la bibliothèque (au restaurant, à la plage, chez le dentiste) aujourd'hui. Pourquoi?
2. s'il/elle a besoin d'argent (d'une voiture, de courage, de temps libre). Pourquoi?
3. s'il/elle s'intéresse aux sports (à la littérature, au jazz, à la politique). Que préfère-t-il/elle?
4. combien de personnes il y a dans sa famille (dans la classe de français, dans sa résidence).
5. s'il/elle a un chien (beaucoup de cousins, un grand-père, un vélo, un ordinateur). Où sont-ils?
6. s'il/elle a des allergies (une blessure, un rhume). Que fait-il/elle contre les symptômes?

6 Chez le docteur Vous avez ces problèmes et vous allez chez le docteur. Votre partenaire va jouer le rôle du docteur. Parlez de vos symptômes. Que faut-il faire? Utilisez les pronoms **y** et **en**. Answers will vary.

- des allergies
- une grippe
- un rhume
- une cheville foulée
- mal à la gorge
- se sentir mal

7 Devinez! Avec un(e) partenaire, décrivez un endroit ou une chose en utilisant les pronoms **y** ou **en**. Votre partenaire va essayer de deviner (*guess*) ce que vous décrivez.

MODÈLE

Étudiant(e) 1: *J'y vais pour jouer au foot.*
Étudiant(e) 2: *Tu vas au stade?*
Étudiant(e) 1: *J'en mange deux le matin.*
Étudiant(e) 2: *Tu manges des croissants?*

4 Suggestions
- Have two volunteers act out the **modèle**.
- Distribute the **Feuilles d'activités** found in the Activity Pack on the Supersite.

5 Suggestions
- Encourage students to think of a few additional questions modeled on those in the activity.
- Have students report what they learned about their partner in small groups.

6 Suggestions
- Make sure each student plays both the doctor and patient roles.
- Tell students to feel free to talk about other symptoms learned in this lesson.

7 Suggestion
- You could also have pairs come up with descriptions and have them take turns asking another pair to guess the place or object.

OPTIONS

Video Replay the video episode, having students focus on the **passé composé** of reflexive verbs and the pronouns **y** and **en**. Pause the video where appropriate to discuss how they were used and to ask comprehension questions. Examples: **Stéphane s'est-il souvenu du nom du chef du Front Populaire?** (Non, il ne s'en est pas souvenu.) **Qui s'est blessé?** (Rachid s'est blessé.) **Va-t-il chez le médecin?** (Oui, il y va.)

Pairs Have pairs ask each other if they play sports or musical instruments, or do certain activities. Students respond yes or no in a complete sentence using **y** or **en**. If the answer is no, encourage them to say whether they used to, are going to, want to, if someone else plays, etc. Examples: **Fais-tu de l'exercice?** (Oui, j'en fais cinq fois par semaine.) **Fais-tu du golf?** (Non, je n'en fais pas, mais ma mère en fait.)

Instructional Resources
*vhlcentral.com:
Activity Pack (Info Gap
Activities); Testing Program;
Testing Program MP3s;
reference tools*

NATIONAL communication cultures STANDARDS

Révision

1 Suggestions
- Before assigning this activity, ask for a volunteer pair to complete the **modèle** for the class.
- When the activity is over, have another pair communicate their whole conversation to the class.

2 Suggestions
- To help students get started, have two volunteers act out a **modèle**. Example: **Étudiant(e) 1: Vas-tu souvent chez le médecin? Étudiant(e) 2: Non, heureusement, je n'y vais pas souvent.**
- Provide students with a word bank including expressions like these: **aller chez le docteur/ dentiste, avoir des allergies, avoir un rhume, se casser/ se fouler le/la/les + (body part), faire du sport, faire un régime, fumer, prendre des médicaments,** etc.

3 Expansion To practice more verb forms and review indirect discourse, have pairs tell each other about a minor accident they had. Tell them to say who helped them and what they said to one other.

4 Expansion Have volunteers act out their conversation for the class using props such as empty toiletry bottles and empty medication boxes.

5 Suggestions
- Before assigning this activity, ask some questions. Examples: **Êtes-vous hypocondriaque? Connaissez-vous quelqu'un qui a une maladie «imaginaire»? Que lui dites-vous?**
- Call on two students to act out the **modèle**.

6 Suggestion Divide the class into pairs and distribute the Info Gap Handouts found in the Activity Pack on the Supersite. Give students ten minutes to complete the activity.

---

1 **La salle d'attente** Observez cette salle d'attente (*waiting room*) et, avec un(e) partenaire, décrivez la situation ou la maladie de chaque personne. À tour de rôle, essayez de prescrire un remède. Utilisez les pronoms **y** ou **en** dans vos dialogues. Answers will vary.

MODÈLE

Étudiant(e) 1: *Ce garçon s'est foulé la cheville. Il doit aller aux urgences.*
Étudiant(e) 2: *Oui, et cette fille...*

2 **Êtes-vous souvent malade?** Avec un(e) partenaire, préparez huit questions pour savoir si vos camarades de classe sont en bonne ou en mauvaise santé. Ensuite, par groupes de quatre, posez les questions à vos camarades et écrivez leurs réponses. Employez des pronoms. Answers will vary.

3 **Oh! Ça va?!** Vous êtes un(e) piéton(ne) (*pedestrian*) et tout d'un coup, vous voyez (*see*) un(e) cycliste tomber de son vélo. Avec un(e) partenaire, suivez (*follow*) ces instructions et préparez la scène. Utilisez les pronoms **y** et **en**. Answers will vary.

Piéton(ne)		Cycliste
Demandez s'il/elle s'est fait mal.	▶	Dites quel est le problème.
Posez des questions sur les symptômes.	▶	Décrivez les symptômes.
Proposez de l'emmener aux urgences.	▶	Acceptez ou refusez la proposition.

4 **Pour partir loin** Vous et un(e) partenaire allez vivre (*to live*) un mois dans une région totalement isolée. Regardez l'illustration: vous pouvez mettre seulement cinq choses dans votre sac de voyage. Choisissez-les avec votre partenaire. Answers will vary.

MODÈLE

Étudiant(e) 1: *On prend du shampooing pour se laver les cheveux?*
Étudiant(e) 2: *Non, la bouteille est trop grande!*

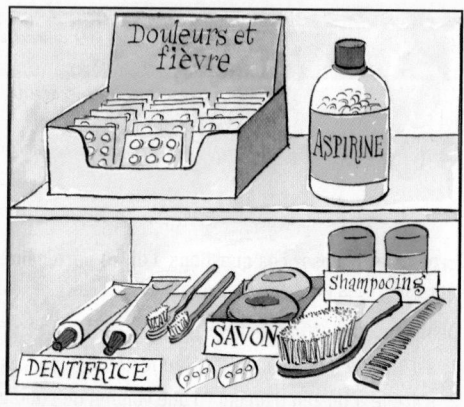

5 **Le malade imaginaire** Vous êtes hypocondriaque et vous pensez être très malade. À tour de rôle, parlez de vos peurs à votre partenaire, qui va essayer de vous rassurer. Utilisez les pronoms **y** et **en** dans votre dialogue. Answers will vary.

MODÈLE

Étudiant(e) 1: *J'ai de la fièvre, n'est-ce pas?*
Étudiant(e) 2: *Mais non, tu n'en as pas!*
Étudiant(e) 1: *J'ai besoin d'un médicament!*
Étudiant(e) 2: *Mais non, tu n'en as pas besoin!*

6 **La famille Valmont** Votre professeur va vous donner, à vous et à votre partenaire, une feuille d'informations sur la famille Valmont. Attention! Ne regardez pas la feuille de votre partenaire. Answers will vary.

MODÈLE

Étudiant(e) 1: *David jouait au baseball.*
Étudiant(e) 2: *Voilà pourquoi il s'est cassé le bras!*

OPTIONS

Game Divide the class into groups of three. Have each member tell about the strangest, funniest, worst, or most exciting thing that he or she has ever done. Require students to use the **passé composé** with as many reflexive verbs as possible and the pronouns **y** and **en** wherever appropriate to avoid redundancy. Point out that they should also use the **imparfait**. Example: **Quand j'avais seize ans, je suis allé(e) au Mexique. Un jour,** **quand je me suis réveillé(e), je ne me sentais pas très bien. J'avais mal et j'avais besoin de médicaments, mais je ne savais pas où en trouver...** The group then chooses one account to write down. Read each group's description aloud. Give the class two minutes to question the group to find out whose experience was described. A group that guesses correctly wins a point; a group that fools the class wins two points.

À l'écoute

STRATÉGIE

Listening for specific information

You can listen for specific information effectively once you identify the subject of a conversation. You can also use your background knowledge to predict what kinds of information you might hear.

 To practice this strategy, you will listen to a commercial for a flu relief medication. Before you listen, use what you already know about the flu and commercials for medications to predict the content of the commercial. Then, listen and jot down specific information the commercial provides. Compare these details to the predictions you first made.

Préparation

Regardez la photo et décrivez les deux personnes. Comment est l'homme? Est-il sportif, d'après vous? A-t-il l'air en forme? Pensez-vous qu'il a des problèmes de santé? Quels problèmes? Et la femme, comment est-elle? A-t-elle l'air en forme? De quoi parlent-ils?

À vous d'écouter

Écoutez la conversation et indiquez chaque problème que Dimitri mentionne.

1. Il est déprimé.	X
2. Il fume trop.	____
3. Il ne fait pas assez d'exercice.	X
4. Il a des douleurs à la gorge.	____
5. Il a beaucoup d'allergies.	____
6. Il a mal au dos.	X
7. Il ne mange pas sainement.	X
8. Il a de la fièvre.	____

 Practice more at **vhlcentral.com**.

Compréhension

Les conseils de Nadine Écoutez la conversation une deuxième fois. Pour chaque catégorie, donnez un des conseils (*pieces of advice*) de Nadine. Answers will vary. Possible answers provided.

1. Nutrition

   manger plus sainement; manger des fruits, des légumes et du poisson; éviter les régimes

2. Exercice

   faire du sport (de l'exercice); faire de la natation

3. Mode de vie (*Lifestyle*)

   prendre le temps de se reposer; s'amuser un peu tous les jours

Avez-vous deviné? Relisez vos notes de la Préparation. Avez-vous deviné le sujet de la conversation entre Dimitri et Nadine? Comparez avec un(e) camarade.

Un questionnaire Vous travaillez au centre médical de votre université. Il va y avoir beaucoup d'étudiants francophones ce semestre et ils doivent tous passer une visite médicale. Le directeur du centre vous a demandé de créer un questionnaire en français sur la santé et le mode de vie. Par groupes de trois ou quatre, préparez ce questionnaire (10 questions minimum) et soyez prêts à le présenter à la classe. Voici quelques thèmes à considérer:

- les maladies
- les problèmes de santé récents
- la nutrition
- l'exercice
- les régimes
- le stress et les problèmes personnels
- le repos

quatre cent quarante et un **441**

---

commencer un régime.
N: Ah non! Ce n'est pas une bonne idée. Les régimes sont mauvais pour la santé. Manger sainement, c'est simplement manger plus de fruits, de légumes et de poisson. Tu vas voir, si tu manges sainement, tu vas retrouver la ligne sans problème. Et tu ne fais pas de sport?
D: Non, j'ai souvent des douleurs dans le dos, alors le sport...

N: Fais de la natation! C'est excellent pour le dos.
D: Oui, bonne idée... Mais toi, tu as l'air d'être en forme, dis donc!
N: Oui, j'ai une forme super en ce moment. J'ai arrêté de fumer, je mange bien et je fais de l'exercice trois fois par semaine. Je me sens vraiment très bien!
D: Eh bien, bravo!

Section Goals

In this section, students will:
- learn to listen for specific information
- listen to a commercial and jot down information
- listen to a conversation and complete several activities

Instructional Resources
vhlcentral.com:
Textbook MP3s; Textbook Audioscript; reference tools

Stratégie
Audioscript Vous ne vous sentez pas bien? Vous avez mal à la tête et au dos? Tout votre corps vous fait mal? Vous éternuez et vous toussez? Vous vous sentez faible et vous n'êtes pas en forme? Vous avez probablement la grippe. Alors, n'attendez pas! Dépêchez-vous d'acheter le médicament homéopathique Grippum. Avec Grippum, la santé est retrouvée en quelques jours! Grippum, en vente chez votre pharmacien.

À vous d'écouter
Audioscript NADINE: Tiens... Dimitri? Dimitri Klein?
DIMITRI: Euh... oui?
N: C'est moi, Nadine Girardot, du cours de littérature de Madame Larose. Tu ne te souviens pas de moi?
D: Ah si, bien sûr! Excuse-moi. Je ne me sens pas très bien, aujourd'hui.
N: Oui, tu as l'air fatigué... Qu'est-ce qui ne va pas?
D: Ben, je ne sais pas trop. Je ne suis pas très en forme depuis deux mois.
N: Ah bon? Et tu es allé chez le médecin?
D: Oui, mais il dit que je ne suis pas malade. Il pense que je suis un peu déprimé parce que je m'ennuie à l'université. Et comme je ne me repose pas beaucoup, il pense aussi que je suis fatigué.
N: C'est très important de se reposer. Tu dois prendre le temps de te reposer et de t'amuser un peu tous les jours.
D: Il dit aussi que je dois manger plus sainement et faire de l'exercice.
N: C'est vrai, tu sais. On est beaucoup plus en forme quand on mange bien et quand on fait du sport.
D: Oui, je sais... Je pense

Section Goals

In this section, students will read historical and cultural information about **Nouvelle-Aquitaine**.

Instructional Resources
vhlcentral.com:
Digital Image Bank;
SAM Answer Key;
reference tools

Carte de la Nouvelle-Aquitaine
- Have students look at the map or use the **Panorama** map from the Digital Image Bank. Ask volunteers to read aloud the names of cities and geographical features. Model French pronunciation as necessary. Point out the location of Spain.
- Have students identify the locations of the places in the photos.

La région en chiffres
- Point out the Nouvelle-Aquitaine logo. Tell students that the lion's head is in the shape of the region.
- Have volunteers read the sections aloud. After each section, ask questions about the content.
- Point out that the Bordeaux region is one of the largest producers of fine wines in the world.
- Ask students to share any information they might know about the **Personnes célèbres.**

Incroyable mais vrai! The original cave at Lascaux was closed to the public in 1963 in order to save the painting from deterioration. A replica of the cave, known as Lascaux II, was built nearby and contains reproductions of the Great Hall of Bulls and the Painted Gallery.

Panorama

 Interactive Map

La Nouvelle-Aquitaine

La région en chiffres

- ▶ **Superficie:** *84.060 km²*
- ▶ **Population:** *5.879.144*
- ▶ **Industries principales:** *agriculture, bois° et industries papetières°, aéronautique et spatiale, tourisme*
- ▶ **Villes principales:** *Bordeaux, Bayonne, Poitiers, La Rochelle, Limoges, Pau*

Créée en 2016, la région Nouvelle-Aquitaine regroupe les anciennes régions Aquitaine, Limousin et Poitou-Charentes. La Nouvelle-Aquitaine est la première région agricole de France, et la première région pour les surfaces boisées° en France métropolitaine, avec 2,8 millions d'hectares de forêts.

Personnages célèbres

- ▶ **Aliénor d'Aquitaine,** *reine° de France (1122–1204)*
- ▶ **Jacques-Yves Cousteau,** *explorateur océanographique et cinéaste (1910–1997)*
- ▶ **Barbara Schulz,** *actrice (1972–)*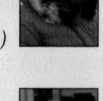
- ▶ **Henri IV,** *roi° de France (1553–1610)*
- ▶ **Jean Nouvel,** *architecte (1945–)*
- ▶ **François Mauriac,** *écrivain (1885–1970)*

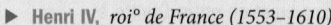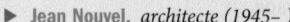
bois *wood* **industries papetières** *paper manufacturing* **boisées** *wooded*
reine *queen* **roi** *king* **grotte** *cave* **gravures** *carvings* **peintures** *paintings*
découvrent *discover*

le parc d'attractions Futuroscope

Poitiers
La Rochelle
Limoges
Angoulême
LA FRANCE
L'OCÉAN ATLANTIQUE
Périgueux
Bordeaux
NOUVELLE-AQUITAINE
la Garonne
Agen
Bayonne
Pau
LES PYRÉNÉES
la cathédrale de Périgueux
LA MER MÉDITERRA
ANDORRE
L'ESPAGNE
la dune du Pilat

0 — 80 miles
0 — 80 kilomètres

Incroyable mais vrai!

Appelée parfois «la chapelle Sixtine préhistorique», la grotte° de Lascaux, en Nouvelle-Aquitaine, est décorée de 1.500 gravures° et de 600 peintures°, vieilles de plus de 17.000 ans. En 1940, quatre garçons découvrent° ce sanctuaire. Les fresques, composées de plusieurs animaux, ont jusqu'à ce jour une signification mystérieuse.

OPTIONS

Personnes célèbres **Eleanor of Aquitaine** was one of the most powerful women in Europe during her time. Her first husband was King Louis VII of France. She later became Queen of England when she married Henry II, and was the mother of Richard the Lionheart. **Jacques-Yves Cousteau** popularized scuba diving and sparked interest in the world's oceans through his films and TV specials.

Barbara Schulz is a well-known film actress and comedian. **Henri IV** reigned as King of France from 1589–1610 and united France after the wars of religion. **Jean Nouvel** won architecture's highest honor, the Pritzker Prize, in 2008 and designed the Institut du Monde Arabe in Paris. **François Mauriac** was elected to the Académie française in 1933 and won the Nobel Prize in Literature in 1952.

La gastronomie
La truffe noire du Périgord

La truffe° noire du Périgord, dans le nord de la Nouvelle-Aquitaine, est célèbre dans le monde entier°. Les truffes poussent° dans le sol° près des arbres, et on utilise des chiens ou cochons truffiers° pour les trouver. Chaque année, la Nouvelle-Aquitaine produit entre huit et neuf tonnes de truffes, qui sont vendues aux marchés de truffes de la région. La truffe noire du Périgord coûte très cher à environ 650–700 euros le kilo, et on l'appelle «le diamant noir».

Les destinations
L'île de Ré

Cette petite île° est située sur la côte° atlantique de la France, près de La Rochelle. En 1987, un pont° a été construit pour relier° l'île au continent. Ses 18.000 habitants permanents utilisent souvent des vélos au lieu des voitures pour se promener autour de° l'île. En été, elle reçoit° le même nombre d'heures de soleil que les plages méditerranéennes et accueille° entre 102.000 et 132.000 touristes.

Le sport
La pelote basque

L'origine de la pelote est ancienne: on retrouve des versions du jeu chez les Mayas, les Grecs et les Romains. C'est au Pays Basque, à la frontière° entre la France et l'Espagne, en Nouvelle-Aquitaine, que le jeu se transforme en véritable sport.

La pelote basque existe sous sept formes différentes; le principe de base est de lancer° une balle en cuir°, la «pelote», contre un mur avec la «paleta», une raquette en bois°, et la «chistera», un grand gant en osier°.

La géographie
La forêt des Landes

Jusqu'au° 14e siècle, cette région était composée de marécages° et a été habitée principalement par des bergers°. En 1857, pour réduire la malaria et pour développer l'économie de la région, les habitants des Landes sont forcés à boiser° leurs terres. Les marécages ont disparu et la forêt des Landes, aujourd'hui la plus grande forêt artificielle de l'Europe, est créée°. La forêt est composée principalement de pins° maritimes, qui étaient déjà présents sur la côte atlantique de la région.

Qu'est-ce que vous avez appris? Répondez aux questions par des phrases complètes.

1. Qui était écrivain né en Nouvelle-Aquitaine?
   François Mauriac était écrivain né en Nouvelle-Aquitaine.
2. Quel est le surnom (*nickname*) de la grotte de Lascaux?
   Le surnom de la grotte de Lascaux est «la chapelle Sixtine préhistorique».
3. Que trouve-t-on dans la grotte de Lascaux?
   On trouve des peintures et des gravures dans la grotte de Lascaux.
4. Où trouve-t-on des truffes noires?
   On trouve des truffes noires dans le Périgord, dans le nord de la Nouvelle-Aquitaine.
5. Qu'est-ce qu'on utilise pour trouver les truffes noires?
   On utilise des chiens ou des cochons truffiers pour trouver les truffes noires.
6. Où se trouve l'île de Ré?
   L'île de Ré se trouve sur la côte atlantique de la France, près de La Rochelle.
7. Combien de touristes l'île de Ré accueille-t-elle en été?
   L'île de Ré accueille entre 102.000 et 132.000 touristes en été.
8. Quelles civilisations ont une version de la pelote?
   Les civilisations des Mayas, des Romains et des Grecs ont une version de la pelote.
9. Combien de formes différentes de pelote basque y a-t-il?
   Il y a sept formes différentes de pelote basque.
10. De quel type d'arbre se compose la forêt des Landes?
    La forêt des Landes se compose principalement de pins maritimes.

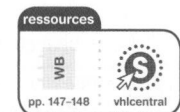
ressources

WB
pp. 147–148

vhlcentral

Sur Internet

Go to **vhlcentral.com** to find more cultural information related to this **Panorama**.

1. Il existe une forme de la pelote basque aux États-Unis. Comment s'appelle ce sport?

2. Cherchez des peintures de la grotte de Lascaux. Quelles sont vos préférées? Pourquoi?

3. Cherchez plus d'informations sur Jean Nouvel. Avez-vous déjà vu quelques-uns de ses bâtiments? Où?

truffe *truffle* **entier** *whole* **poussent** *grow* **sol** *ground*
cochons truffiers *truffle-hunting pigs* **île** *island*
côte *coast* **pont** *bridge* **relier** *connect* **autour de** *around*
reçoit *receives* **accueille** *welcomes* **frontière** *border*
lancer *throw* **cuir** *leather* **mur** *wall* **bois** *wood*
osier *wicker* **Jusqu'au** *Until the* **marécages** *marshes*
bergers *shepherds* **boiser** *plant with trees* **créée** *created*
pins *pine trees*

quatre cent quarante-trois **443**

La truffe noire du Périgord
- The truffle fly lays its eggs on the ground directly above truffles. Some truffle hunters search for the fly by gently moving a stick around an area, then dig for truffles where they find the flies.
- Truffle season lasts from December through February. Most truffles are sold at regional markets, which are controlled by truffle authorities to ensure authenticity and quality.
- Ask students whether they know of or have tried truffles.

L'île de Ré
- The donkeys of **Île de Ré** are a special breed, with a large head and ears. To protect the donkeys from the flies and mosquitoes in the island's salt marshes, their legs were covered with cloth, which makes the donkeys appear to be wearing pajama pants.
- Ask students if they know any islands similar to the **Île de Ré**.

La pelote basque
- The courts, gear, and rules for playing **pelote basque** vary from village to village, but no matter which variety of the game is played, it is always lively and fast. The speed of the **pelote** can reach 250–300 kph or about 155–186 mph.
- Ask students what sports are similar to **pelote basque**.

La forêt des Landes
- Most of the Landes forest is privately owned, and the land and the trees are passed down within families. Part of the forest, along the Atlantic coast, is natural.
- Show students pictures of the **bergers landais**, the shepherds who lived in the Landes region before the forest was planted.

O P T I O N S

La forêt des Landes The **bergers landais** who tended their sheep in the pre-forest marshland of the Landes were known for using stilts, called **échassiers**. The stilts helped them navigate the swampy ground without getting their feet wet, and allowed them to keep track of their sheep over a large area. A third wooden stick served as a staff when walking or as a prop for sitting. Postcards from the nineteenth and twentieth centuries show the shepherds wearing large **bérets** and coats made of sheep's wool. When the land was turned over to forest, the shepherds lost their pastureland, but some of them became performers instead. Their dances in traditional shepherd dress are still performed today throughout the Landes region.

SAVOIR-FAIRE **443**

Section Goals

In this section, students will:
- learn to use background knowledge when reading
- read a magazine article on combating fatigue

Stratégie Explain to students that they will find it easier to understand the content of a text if they consider their previous knowledge about the topic before they begin reading.

Examinez le texte Students should mention that the text is a magazine article written by Dr. Émilie Parmentier and published in France.

Questions personnelles
- Point out to students that by answering these **Questions personnelles** they are activating their background knowledge about health habits and fatigue. This will help them to understand the magazine article.
- Have students discuss their answers to the questions in pairs or small groups.

Lecture

Audio: Reading

Avant la lecture

STRATÉGIE

Activating background knowledge

Using what you already know about a particular subject will often help you better understand a reading selection. For example, if you read an article about a recent medical discovery, you might think about what you already know about health in order to understand unfamiliar words or concepts.

Examinez le texte

Regardez le document. Analysez le titre de la lecture. Quel est le mot-clé de ce titre? Quel est le sens (*meaning*) du titre? Quel va être le sujet du texte? Faites une liste de vos idées et comparez-les avec les idées d'un(e) camarade. Puis, avec votre partenaire, faites aussi une liste de ce que vous savez déjà sur ce sujet. Essayez de répondre aux questions.

- Quel type de texte est-ce?
- Où pensez-vous que ce texte a été publié?
- Qui a écrit ce texte?
- Quelle est la profession de l'auteur?

Questions personnelles

Répondez aux questions par des phrases complètes.

1. Vous sentez-vous parfois fatigué(e) pendant la journée? Quand? Pourquoi?
2. Êtes-vous souvent fatigué(e) quand vous avez beaucoup de devoirs ou d'examens? Et quand vous faites beaucoup de sport?
3. Dormez-vous bien, en général? Vous couchez-vous tôt ou tard? Et le matin, à quelle heure vous levez-vous, en général?
4. Prenez-vous le temps de vous détendre dans la journée? Que faites-vous pour vous détendre?
5. Mangez-vous sainement? Qu'aimez-vous manger?
6. Faites-vous du sport ou d'autres activités physiques? Lesquel(le)s (*Which ones*)?

Non à la fatigue!

Par le docteur Émilie Parmentier

Selon un sondage° récent, plus de 50% des Français se sentent souvent fatigués. Que faire pour être moins fatigué? Voici les dix conseils° du docteur Émilie Parmentier.

(1) Mangez sainement et évitez les régimes

Vous pouvez garder la ligne et la forme si vous évitez les régimes et choisissez les fruits, les légumes et le poisson au lieu de° la viande et des féculents°. Le matin, prenez le temps de vous préparer un bon petit-déjeuner, mais le soir, mangez léger°.

(2) Dormez bien

Chaque personne est différente. Certaines ont besoin de 6 heures de sommeil° par nuit, d'autres de 10 heures. Respectez vos besoins et essayez de dormir assez, mais pas trop.

(3) Essayez de respecter des horaires réguliers

Avoir des horaires réguliers°, c'est bon pour la forme. Levez-vous à la même heure chaque jour, si possible, puis le soir, essayez aussi de vous coucher toujours à la même heure.

(4) Prenez le temps de vous détendre avant de vous coucher

Le soir avant de vous coucher, prenez quelques minutes pour vous détendre et oublier vos préoccupations et vos problèmes. Essayez la méditation ou le yoga.

(5) Ne vous dépêchez pas tout le temps

Il est très important d'avoir des moments de calme tous les jours et de ne pas toujours se dépêcher. Promenez-vous dans un parc, asseyez-vous et reposez-vous quelques minutes.

OPTIONS

Small Groups Have students work in groups of three or four. Tell them to create a list of possible reasons why more than 50% of French people often feel tired. Example: **Ils travaillent beaucoup.** Then have them get together with another group and compare their lists. Record the most popular reasons on the board.

Pairs Have students work in pairs. Tell them to go through the article and find all the sentences that contain reflexive verbs. Mention that students should watch for reflexive verbs appearing in the infinitive. Example: **... prenez le temps de *vous préparer...*** Then have them point out which verbs are literally reflexive versus those with an idiomatic sense.

6 **Amusez-vous et détendez-vous avec les personnes que vous aimez**

Passez des moments en famille ou avec des amis et des personnes avec qui vous vous entendez bien. Parlez de sujets agréables, riez et amusez-vous!

7 **Faites du sport ou d'autres activités physiques**

Si on fait trop de sport, on peut être fatigué, mais quand on ne pratique pas assez d'activités physiques, on se sent fatigué aussi. Donc, pour bien vous porter, pratiquez des activités physiques plusieurs fois par semaine. Mais attention! Les activités sportives sont à éviter tard le soir parce qu'elles peuvent causer des troubles du sommeil.

8 **Évitez les discussions importantes le soir**

Il n'est pas bon de s'énerver, de se mettre en colère ou de s'inquiéter avant de se coucher parce que cela rend le sommeil difficile. Le soir, évitez donc les grandes discussions (entre époux, entre colocataires, entre petits amis, sur vos problèmes dans les études).

9 **Attention au tabac°, au café et à l'alcool**

Limitez votre consommation° de café et d'alcool. Et si vous fumez, essayez d'arrêter. Demandez à votre médecin de vous donner une ordonnance pour des médicaments qui peuvent vous aider à arrêter.

10 **Faites des petites siestes**

Parfois, quand vous êtes fatigué, même° une sieste° de vingt minutes peut vous aider à continuer la journée. Alors, quand vous avez juste° quelques minutes de libres, pensez à faire une petite sieste.

Enfin, si vous vous sentez très faible, voire° mal pendant une période de plus de deux semaines, allez voir le médecin. Consultez un médecin si vous tombez malade très souvent ou si vous vous sentez déprimé.

Selon un sondage *According to a survey* **conseils** *pieces of advice* **au lieu de** *instead of* **féculents** *starches* **léger** *light* **sommeil** *sleep* **horaires réguliers** *set schedules* **tabac** *tobacco* **consommation** *consumption* **même** *even* **sieste** *nap* **juste** *just* **voire** *or even*

Après la lecture

Complétez Complétez les phrases.

1. Pour être en bonne santé, il est nécessaire de manger __sainement__.

2. __L'alcool__ et __le tabac__ ne sont pas bons pour la santé. On ne doit donc pas beaucoup boire et on doit arrêter de fumer.

3. Il est bon de faire du yoga ou de la méditation pour __se détendre__.

4. Il est préférable d'éviter les discussions importantes ou graves __le soir__.

5. On doit prendre le temps de __s'amuser et de se détendre__ avec ses amis.

6. Si on se sent vraiment très fatigué ou si on est déprimé, c'est toujours une bonne idée d' __aller consulter un médecin__.

7. Il est bon de toujours __se lever__ et __se coucher__ à la même heure.

8. Pour être en forme, pratiquez __des activités physiques__ plusieurs fois par semaine.

Vrai ou faux? Indiquez si les phrases sont **vraies** ou **fausses**. Corrigez les phrases fausses.

1. C'est une infirmière qui donne ces conseils.
   Faux. Émilie Parmentier est médecin.

2. Les Français ne sont pas souvent fatigués.
   Faux. Plus de 50% des Français sont souvent fatigués.

3. D'après le docteur Parmentier, il est important de faire un régime pour garder la ligne.
   Faux. Il est important d'éviter les régimes et de manger des fruits, des légumes et du poisson.

4. C'est le soir qu'on doit manger le plus.
   Faux. Le soir, on doit manger léger.

5. Quand on dort trop, on peut se sentir fatigué.
   Vrai.

6. Il est bon de se lever et de se coucher à la même heure tous les jours.
   Vrai.

7. On doit se reposer au calme tous les jours.
   Vrai.

8. Il est recommandé de faire du sport le soir avant de se coucher. Faux. Il est recommandé d'éviter les activités sportives tard le soir parce qu'elles peuvent causer des troubles du sommeil.

Votre opinion compte Que pensez-vous des conseils du docteur Parmentier? A-t-elle raison ou tort, d'après vous? Avec un(e) camarade, choisissez deux de ses conseils et donnez votre opinion sur chacun (*each one*). Quels conseils allez-vous donner à votre camarade?

quatre cent quarante-cinq **445**

Complétez Go over the answers with the class. Call on volunteers to read the completed sentences aloud.

Vrai ou faux?
• Have students work in pairs. Tell them to take turns reading the statements aloud and deciding whether they are true or false. They should also locate the correct answer to the false items in the text.
• Have students write two more true/false items. Then ask volunteers to read their sentences aloud and have the class respond.

Votre opinion compte After completing the activity, take a quick class survey to find out which pieces of advice students agreed with and which ones they thought were wrong.

O P T I O N S

Extra Practice Have students write an additional piece of advice on staying healthy and fighting fatigue. Remind them to use the imperative. Then ask volunteers to read their piece of advice to the class. The class should decide if the advice is valid or not.

Small Groups Have students write the numbers from the reading that correspond to the suggestions that they already follow and the numbers of the suggestions they would like to try. Then have students form groups of four and compare their answers.

Section Goals

In this section, students will:
• learn to sequence events in a narration
• write a letter

Stratégie Discuss the importance of having an introduction (**introduction**), body (**corps**), and a conclusion (**conclusion**). Then read through the list of adverbs with the class. Point out that these words can be used to indicate a sequence of events or activities.

Thème Tell students they should answer the questions before they begin to write their letters.

Proofreading Activity To practice editing skills, have the class correct these sentences. **1. Je finis de se brosser mes dents! 2. Il s'a couchée tard hier soir. 3. On n'est pas fait de l'exercise hier. 4. Je dois me rase et m'habille. 5. Ne te met pas en colére. 6. Lisez le journal si tu t'ennuyes.**

Écriture

STRATÉGIE

Sequencing events

Paying attention to sequencing in a narrative will ensure that your writing flows logically from one part to the next. Every composition should have an introduction, a body, and a conclusion.

The introduction presents the subject, the setting, the situation, and the people involved. The body describes the events and people's reactions to these events. The conclusion brings the narrative to a close.

Adverbs and adverbial phrases are often used as transitions between the introduction, the body, and the conclusion. Here is a list of commonly used adverbs in French.

Adverbes	
(tout) d'abord	*first*
premièrement / en premier	*first*
avant (de)	*before*
après	*after*
alors	*then, at that time*
(et) puis	*(and) then*
ensuite	*then*
plus tard	*later*
bientôt	*soon*
enfin	*finally*
finalement	*finally*

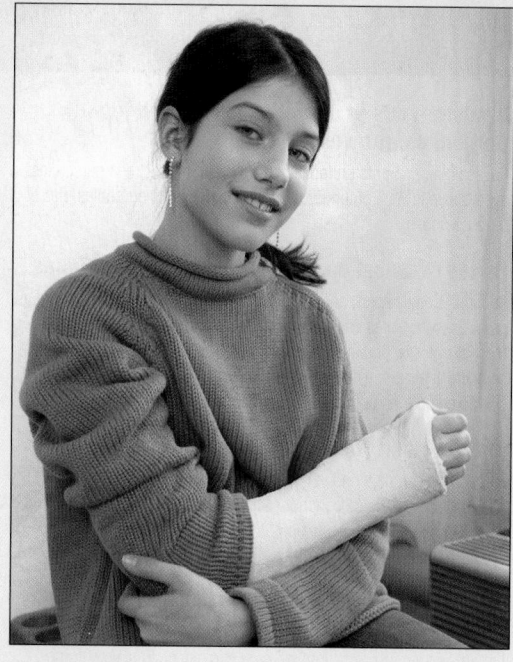

Thème

Écrire une lettre

Avant l'écriture

1. Vous avez été malade le jour du dernier examen de français et vous n'avez pas pu passer l'examen. Vous allez préparer une lettre destinée à votre professeur de français pour lui expliquer ce qui s'est passé. Pour vous y aider, répondez d'abord aux questions:

   ■ Que s'est-il passé? (maladie, accident, autre problème de santé, etc.)

   ■ Quels étaient les symptômes ou quelle blessure avez-vous eue? (avoir mal au ventre, avoir de la fièvre, avoir une jambe cassée, etc.)

   ■ Qu'est-ce qui a peut-être causé ce problème? (accident, pas assez d'exercice physique, ne pas manger sainement, etc.)

   ■ Qu'avez-vous fait? (prendre des médicaments, aller chez le docteur ou le dentiste, aller aux urgences, etc.)

   ■ Qu'est-ce qu'on vous a fait là-bas? (une piqûre, une radio [*X-ray*], une ordonnance, etc.)

   ■ Comment vous sentez-vous maintenant et qu'allez-vous faire pour rester en forme? (ne plus fumer, faire plus attention, faire de l'exercice, etc.)

O P T I O N S

Avant l'écriture Working in groups of three, have students practice the adverbs (**tout**) **d'abord, alors, (et) puis, ensuite, plus tard,** and **enfin** by telling a past-tense story. The first student begins by creating a sentence that starts with (**tout**) **d'abord.** The second student follows with a sentence that begins with **alors.** The story continues this way until all the adverbs have been used and each student has created two sentences.

Help students turn the list of tasks into an outline for their letter. Then show them how it corresponds to the eight parts of the sequence chart.
Salutation / Paragraph 1: Introduction / Paragraphs 2-7: the six bulleted items / Paragraph 8: Conclusion / Closing and signature

2. Maintenant, vous allez compléter ce schéma d'idées avec vos réponses. Il va vous servir à placer les informations dans l'ordre. Chaque cadre (*box*) représente une information. Ajoutez-y (*Add*) une introduction et une conclusion. Utilisez des verbes réfléchis.

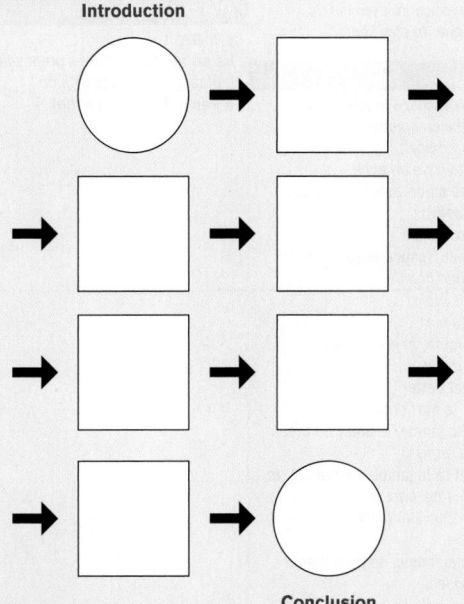

3. Regardez à nouveau (*again*) le schéma d'idées. Quels adverbes pouvez-vous y ajouter pour lier (*link*) les informations? Écrivez-les au-dessus de (*above*) chaque cadre.

Écriture

Utilisez le schéma d'idées pour écrire votre lettre au passé (passé composé et imparfait). Elle doit inclure (*include*) une introduction, une partie centrale (le corps), une conclusion et les adverbes que vous avez écrits au-dessus des cadres. À la fin (*end*) de la lettre, excusez-vous et demandez à votre professeur si (*if*) vous pouvez passer l'examen la semaine prochaine. (Attention! Cette partie de la lettre doit être au présent.)

Après l'écriture

1. Échangez votre lettre avec celle (*the one*) d'un(e) partenaire. Répondez à ces questions pour commenter son travail.

- Votre partenaire a-t-il/elle écrit une introduction et une conclusion?

- Votre partenaire a-t-il/elle écrit une partie centrale présentant (*presenting*) les raisons de son absence?

- Votre partenaire a-t-il/elle inclu les adverbes?

- Votre partenaire s'est-il/elle excusé(e) et a-t-il/elle demandé de repasser (*retake*) l'examen?

- Votre partenaire a-t-il/elle correctement utilisé les verbes réfléchis?

- Quel(s) détail(s) ajouteriez-vous (*would you add*)? Quel(s) détail(s) enlèveriez-vous (*would you delete*)? Quel(s) autre(s) commentaire(s) avez-vous pour votre partenaire?

2. Corrigez votre lettre d'après (*according to*) les commentaires de votre partenaire. Relisez votre travail pour éliminer ces problèmes:

- des fautes (*errors*) d'orthographe

- des fautes de ponctuation

- des fautes de conjugaison

- un mauvais emploi (*use*) du passé

- un mauvais emploi de la grammaire de l'unité

- des fautes d'accord (*agreement*) des adjectifs

EVALUATION

Criteria
Content Contains descriptions of each of the bulleted points of the task, as well as an appropriate introduction and conclusion.
Scale: 1 2 3 4 5

Organization Organized into an eight-paragraph letter with a salutation, an introduction, six descriptive paragraphs, a conclusion, a closing, and a signature.
Scale: 1 2 3 4 5

Accuracy Uses forms of **passé composé**, **imparfait**, and reflexive verbs correctly. Spells words, conjugates verbs, and modifies adjectives correctly throughout.
Scale: 1 2 3 4 5

Creativity Includes additional information that is not included in the task and/or uses adjectives, descriptive verbs, and additional details to make the letter more interesting and persuasive.
Scale: 1 2 3 4 5

Scoring
Excellent	18–20 points
Good	14–17 points
Satisfactory	10–13 points
Unsatisfactory	< 10 points

OPTIONS

Avant l'écriture Before students begin writing, have them jot down a word that relates to each bulleted item in the task inside the sequence diagram. (For example: **problème, symptômes, raison,** etc.) Then, next to each key word, have students indicate the tenses they are likely to use when describing it. (For example: **problème** – **passé composé** for accidents, **imparfait** for illnesses, and so on.)

Écriture Give students some formal salutations, introductions, and closings they can use in the letter to their instructor.
Salutations: **Monsieur/Madame le Professeur...**
Introductions: **Je vous prie de bien vouloir me faire savoir..., Je vous saurais gré de bien vouloir...**
Closings: **Je vous adresse mes sincères salutations..., Recevez mes cordiales salutations...**

Instructional Resources
vhlcentral.com:
Textbook MP3s; Textbook Audioscript; reference tools

Suggestions
- Tell students that an easy way to study from **Vocabulaire** is to cover up the French half of each section, leaving only the English equivalents exposed. They can then quiz themselves on the French items. To focus on the English equivalents of the French entries, they simply reverse this process.
- Point out to students that they can use the Vocabulary Tools at **vhlcentral.com** for reference and extra vocabulary practice.

🔊 Ⓢ Vocabulary Tools

Leçon 10A

La routine
faire sa toilette	to wash up
se brosser les cheveux/dents	to brush one's hair/teeth
se coiffer	to do one's hair
se coucher	to go to bed
se déshabiller	to undress
s'endormir	to go to sleep, to fall asleep
s'habiller	to get dressed
se laver (les mains)	to wash oneself (one's hands)
se lever	to get up, to get out of bed
se maquiller	to put on makeup
prendre une douche	to take a shower
se raser	to shave oneself
se regarder	to look at oneself
se réveiller	to wake up
se sécher	to dry oneself

Dans la salle de bains
un réveil	alarm clock
une brosse (à cheveux, à dents)	brush (hairbrush, toothbrush)
la crème à raser	shaving cream
le dentifrice	toothpaste
le maquillage	makeup
une pantoufle	slipper
un peigne	comb
un rasoir	razor
le savon	soap
une serviette (de bain)	(bath) towel
le shampooing	shampoo

Verbes pronominaux
s'amuser	to play, to have fun
s'appeler	to be called
s'arrêter	to stop
s'asseoir	to sit down
se dépêcher	to hurry
se détendre	to relax
se disputer (avec)	to argue (with)
s'énerver	to get worked up, to become upset
s'ennuyer	to get bored
s'entendre bien (avec)	to get along well (with)
s'inquiéter	to worry
s'intéresser (à)	to be interested (in)
se mettre à	to begin to
se mettre en colère	to become angry
s'occuper (de)	to take care of, to keep oneself busy
se préparer	to get ready
se promener	to take a walk
se rendre compte	to realize
se reposer	to rest
se souvenir (de)	to remember
se tromper	to be mistaken
se trouver	to be located

Le corps
la bouche	mouth
un bras	arm
le cœur	heart
le corps	body
le cou	neck
un doigt	finger
un doigt de pied	toe
le dos	back
un genou (genoux pl.)	knee (knees)
la gorge	throat
une jambe	leg
une joue	cheek
le nez	nose
un œil (yeux pl.)	eye (eyes)
une oreille	ear
un orteil	toe
la peau	skin
un pied	foot
la poitrine	chest
la taille	waist
la tête	head
le ventre	stomach
le visage	face

Expressions utiles
See p. 411.

Leçon 10B

La forme
être en pleine forme	to be in good shape
faire de l'exercice	to exercise
garder la ligne	to stay slim

La santé
aller aux urgences/à la pharmacie	to go to the emergency room/ to the pharmacy
avoir mal	to have an ache
avoir mal au cœur	to feel nauseous
enfler	to swell
éternuer	to sneeze
être en bonne/mauvaise santé	to be in good/bad health
éviter de	to avoid
faire mal	to hurt
faire une piqûre	to give a shot
fumer	to smoke
guérir	to get better
se blesser	to hurt oneself
se casser (la jambe/le bras)	to break one's (leg/arm)
se faire mal (à la jambe, au bras...)	to hurt one's (leg, arm...)
se fouler la cheville	to twist/sprain one's ankle
se porter mal/mieux	to be ill/better
se sentir	to feel
tomber/être malade	to get/to be sick
tousser	to cough
une allergie	allergy
une blessure	injury, wound
une douleur	pain
la fièvre (avoir de la fièvre)	fever (to have a fever)
la grippe	flu
un rhume	cold
un symptôme	symptom
une aspirine	aspirin
un médicament (contre/ pour)	medication (to prevent/for)
une ordonnance	prescription
une pilule	pill
la salle des urgences	emergency room
déprimé(e)	depressed
enceinte	pregnant
grave	serious
sain(e)	healthy
un(e) dentiste	dentist
un infirmier/une infirmière	nurse
un(e) patient(e)	patient
un(e) pharmacien(ne)	pharmacist

Expressions utiles
See p. 429.

The pronouns y and en
y	there; it
en	some; any; replaces prepositional phrases beginning with de
Il y en a	There are (some).

La technologie

Pour commencer

David et Rachid font...
a. les courses. b. la cuisine.
c. de l'ordinateur.

Quel est l'objet présent sur la photo?
a. un savon b. une télévision c. un ordinateur

Que font-ils?
a. Ils surfent sur Internet.
b. Ils font du sport. c. Ils font la fête.

Savoir-faire

Unit Goals

Leçon 11A

In this lesson, students will learn:
- terms for electronics products
- Internet terms
- the pronunciation of final consonants
- about technology in France and the Ariane rocket
- the use of prepositions with infinitives
- reciprocal reflexives
- more about city streets and driving in France through specially shot video footage

Leçon 11B

In this lesson, students will learn:
- terms for cars and driving
- terms for car maintenance and repair
- the pronunciation of the letter **x**
- about cars and driving in France and the car manufacturer Citroën
- about French singer Émilie Simon
- the verbs **ouvrir** and **offrir**
- the conditional
- to guess the meaning of words from context in spoken French

Savoir-faire

In this section, students will learn:
- cultural and historical information about **l'Occitanie**
- to recognize the purpose of a text
- to make a list of key words

Pour commencer
- c. de l'ordinateur.
- c. un ordinateur.
- a. Ils surfent sur Internet.

RESOURCES

Student Activities Manual (SAM):
Workbook Activities, pp. 149–162;
Lab Activities, pp. 81–88;
Video Activities, pp. 41–44; pp. 81–82
SAM Answer Key

vhlcentral.com: Textbook MP3s; Lab MP3s;
Textbook Audioscript; Lab Audioscript; Video;
Videoscript; **Roman-photo** Translations;
Vocabulaire supplémentaire; Activity Pack
(including **Feuilles d'activités,** Info Gap Activities,
and Task-based Activities);

Flash culture video transcription; **Essayez!** and **Mise en pratique** answers; Digital Image Bank; Testing Program; Testing Program MP3s

Leçon 11A

Section Goals

In this section, students will learn and practice vocabulary related to:
• electronics products
• the Internet

Instructional Resources
vhlcentral.com:
Digital Image Bank (including vocabulary illustrations from the textbook, theme-based illustrations);
Vocabulaire supplémentaire;
Mise en pratique *answers;*
Textbook Audioscript;
Lab Audioscript; Activity Pack (Info Gap Activities); Textbook MP3s; Lab MP3s; SAM Answer Key; reference tools

Suggestions

• Have students look over the vocabulary. Point out that many words related to electronics and the Internet are cognates.
• Use the **11A Contextes** illustration from the Digital Image Bank. Point out objects and describe what the people are doing. Examples: **C'est une imprimante. Il a un portable.**
• Ask students questions about electronics and the Internet using the new vocabulary. Examples: **Jouez-vous à des jeux vidéo? Avez-vous un smartphone? Une tablette?**
• Tell students that the official French term for *e-mail* is **la messagerie électronique**, but most people say **l'e-mail**. **Le courriel** is also used, especially in Canada.
• Point out that **marcher** is used more than **fonctionner** in everyday language.
• Additional vocabulary for this lesson can be found in the **Vocabulaire supplémentaire** on the Supersite.
• Use the Science and technology, and communications illustrations from the Digital Image Bank to help students familiarize themselves with electronics products, the Internet, and communications.

You will learn how to...
▪ **talk about communication**
▪ **talk about electronics**

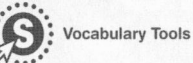
Vocabulary Tools

Le son et l'image

Vocabulaire

ajouter/supprimer un(e) ami(e)	to add/delete a friend
allumer	to turn on
brancher	to plug in; to connect
composer (un numéro)	to dial (a number)
démarrer	to start up
effacer	to erase
enregistrer	to record
éteindre	to turn off
être connecté(e) (avec)	to be connected (to)
être en ligne (avec)	to be online/on the phone (with)
fermer	to close; to shut off
fonctionner/marcher	to function, to work
imprimer	to print
prendre une photo(graphie)	to take a photo(graph)
recharger	to charge
sauvegarder	to save
surfer sur Internet	to surf the Internet
télécharger	to download
un appareil photo (numérique)	(digital) camera
une chaîne (de télévision)	(television) channel
une clé USB	USB drive
un e-mail	e-mail
un fichier	file
un jeu vidéo (jeux vidéo *pl.*)	video game(s)
un lecteur (de) DVD	DVD player
un lien	link
un logiciel	software, program
un mot de passe	password
une page d'accueil	home page
un réseau (social)	(social) network
un site Internet/web	website
un smartphone	smartphone
un texto/SMS	text message

un lecteur MP3/(de) CD

un portable

un moniteur

un écran

un casque (audio)

un disque dur

un clavier

une souris

une imprimante

une tablette (tactile)

ressources

WB
pp. 149–150

LM
p. 81

vhlcentral

OPTIONS

Extra Practice Have students make a list of six electronic devices they have or use frequently. Then tell them to circulate around the room asking others if they have or use the same items. If someone answers affirmatively, the student should ask the person to sign his or her name next to the item. Students should try to get a different signature for each item.

Game Write vocabulary words for electronic equipment on index cards. On another set of cards, draw or paste pictures to match each term. Tape them face down on the board in random order. Divide the class into two teams. Play a game of Concentration in which students match words with pictures. When a player makes a match, that player's team collects those cards. The team with the most cards at the end of the game wins.

Attention!

- The prefix **re-** in French is used much as it is in English. It expresses the idea of doing an action again.

to dial	composer
to redial	recomposer
to start	démarrer
to restart	redémarrer

- The conjugation of **éteindre** is irregular:

j'éteins	nous éteignons
tu éteins	vous éteignez
il/elle/on éteint	ils/elles éteignent

Le téléphone sonne. (sonner)

une télécommande

un poste de télévision

un enregistreur DVR

des CD/compact disc/disques compacts (m.)

Mise en pratique

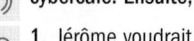

1 Écoutez Écoutez la conversation entre Jérôme et l'employée d'un cybercafé. Ensuite, complétez les phrases suivantes.

1. Jérôme voudrait (*would like*)...
   a. imprimer et envoyer ses photos.
   b. sauvegarder ses photos sur son disque dur.
   c. effacer ses photos.

2. Jérôme peut sélectionner les photos...
   a. par un clic de la souris.
   b. sur l'écran tactile.
   c. avec le clavier.

3. L'employée propose à Jérôme...
   a. de faire fonctionner le logiciel.
   b. de graver un CD.
   c. d'utiliser une imprimante noir et blanc.

4. Pour regarder les photos, Jérôme doit utiliser...
   a. une télécommande.
   b. un écran.
   c. le lecteur de CD.

5. L'adresse du site web de Jérôme est...
   a. www.email.fr.
   b. www.courriel.fr.
   c. www.courriel.com.

6. L'employée demande à Jérôme de ne pas oublier...
   a. d'éteindre.
   b. de sonner.
   c. de fermer.

Coup de main

Here are some useful terms to help you read e-mail addresses in French.

at sign (@)	**arobase** (*f.*)
dash	**tiret** (*m.*)
dot	**point** (*m.*)
underscore	**tiret bas** (*m.*)

2 Association Faites correspondre les activités de la colonne de gauche aux objets correspondants de la colonne de droite.

1. enregistrer une émission   e
2. protéger ses e-mails   c
3. parler avec un ami à tout moment   f
4. jouer sur l'ordinateur   d
5. taper (*type*) un e-mail   h
6. écouter de la musique   g
7. changer de chaîne   a
8. prendre des photos   b

a. une télécommande
b. un appareil photo
c. un mot de passe
d. un jeu vidéo
e. un enregistreur DVR
f. un portable
g. un casque (audio)
h. un clavier

3 Chassez l'intrus Choisissez le mot ou l'expression qui ne va pas avec les autres.

1. un lien, une page d'accueil, un site web, (un texto)
2. sonner, (démarrer,) un portable, un smartphone
3. une souris, un clavier, une clé USB, (un logiciel)
4. brancher, démarrer, (ajouter,) allumer
5. un fichier, sauvegarder, (une télécommande,) effacer
6. un site web, être en ligne, télécharger, (composer)

S   Practice more at **vhlcentral.com**.

quatre cent cinquante et un   **451**

---

1 Audioscript
JÉRÔME: Bonjour, Mademoiselle. J'ai besoin de votre aide, s'il vous plaît.
L'EMPLOYÉE: Oui, bien sûr, Monsieur.
J: Voilà. J'ai pris des photos avec mon appareil numérique, mais je n'ai pas de logiciel adapté pour les regarder. Je veux les imprimer et aussi les envoyer par e-mail.
E: Pour imprimer, vous n'avez qu'à utiliser cette imprimante couleur, mais d'abord, il faut télécharger vos photos. Ensuite, vous pouvez les sélectionner par un simple clic de la souris. Vous pouvez aussi les sauvegarder et les graver sur CD.
J: Parfait. Et pour les envoyer par e-mail?
E: Pour envoyer les photos, passez à votre compte d'e-mail. Attachez les photos à l'e-mail, et envoyez-le normalement.
J: C'est finalement simple.
E: Oui, c'est très simple. Avez-vous d'autres questions, Monsieur?
J: Non, c'était le seul problème que j'avais. Je vous remercie beaucoup.
E: De rien. Au revoir, Monsieur.
(On Textbook MP3s)

1 Suggestion Play the conversation again, stopping at the end of each sentence that contains the answer to one of the items so students can check their work.

2 Expansion Ask students what electronic devices are used to perform these actions. **1. imprimer un document (une imprimante) 2. composer un numéro (un téléphone/un smartphone/un portable) 3. regarder un film (un enregistreur DVR/une télévision/un lecteur [de] DVD) 4. écouter de la musique (une chaîne stéréo/une radio/un lecteur MP3/une tablette/un lecteur [de] CD)**

3 Expansion Have students create two more items using words or expressions from the new vocabulary. Collect their papers, write some of the items on the board, and have the class identify **l'intrus**.

O P T I O N S

Les adresses Internet Most Internet addresses in the United States end in the codes **.com**, **.org**, **.gov**, or **.edu**. Write the following codes on the board and have students guess which French-speaking region they refer to. **1.** .fr (France) **2.** .be (Belgique) **3.** .ch (Suisse) **4.** .ca (Canada) **5.** .ci (Côte d'Ivoire) **6.** .ma (Maroc) **7.** .sn (Sénégal) **8.** .pf (Polynésie française) **9.** .mc (Monaco) **10.** .lu (Luxembourg) **11.** .qc.ca (Québec)

Game Divide the class into two teams. Give one player a card with the name of an electronic device or technology product. That player is allowed 30 seconds to draw the item for another player on his or her team to guess. Award a point for a correct guess. If a player doesn't guess the correct answer, the next player on the opposing team may "steal" the point.

ESPACE CONTEXTES

NATIONAL
communication
STANDARDS

Communication

4 Suggestion Point out that some of the items in column C require verbs to make complete sentences. Tell students to write down their questions.

5 Suggestions
- Tell students that crossword terms can be found **horizontalement** and **verticalement**.
- Have two volunteers read the **modèle** aloud. Then divide the class into pairs and distribute the Info Gap Handouts found in the Activity Pack on the Supersite. Give students ten minutes to complete the activity.

6 Suggestion Encourage students to include drawings, clip art, or magazine photos in their brochures. You may wish to assign this activity as homework.

7 Suggestion Before beginning this activity, brainstorm famous people from the past with whom it might be interesting to have such a discussion. Examples: Benjamin Franklin, Thomas Edison, and Alexander Graham Bell.

4 Qui fait quoi? Avec un(e) partenaire, formez des questions à partir de ces listes d'expressions. Ensuite, à tour de rôle, posez vos questions à votre partenaire afin d'en (*in order to*) savoir plus sur ses habitudes par rapport à la technologie. Answers will vary.

MODÈLE

Étudiant(e) 1: À qui envoies-tu des e-mails?
Étudiant(e) 2: J'envoie des e-mails à mes professeurs pour les devoirs et à mes amis.

A	B	C
à qui	être en ligne	toi
combien de	télécharger	tes parents
comment	un e-mail	tes grands-parents
où	un texto	ton professeur de français
pour qui	un site web	ta sœur
pourquoi	graver	tes amis
quand	un appareil photo numérique	les autres étudiants
quel(le)(s)	un jeu vidéo	les enfants

5 Mots croisés Votre professeur va vous donner, à vous et à votre partenaire, deux grilles de mots croisés (*crossword puzzle*) incomplètes. Votre partenaire a les mots qui vous manquent, et vice versa. Donnez-lui une définition et des exemples pour compléter la grille. Attention! N'utilisez pas le mot recherché.

MODÈLE

Étudiant(e) 1: Horizontalement (Across), le numéro 1, c'est ce que (*what*) tu fais pour mettre ton fichier Internet sur ton disque dur.
Étudiant(e) 2: Télécharger!

6 Le cybercafé Le patron d'un cybercafé souhaite (*wishes*) avoir plus de clients et vous demande de créer une brochure. Avec un(e) partenaire, présentez les différents services offerts et tous les avantages de ce cybercafé. Incluez les informations suivantes: Answers will vary.

- nom, adresse et horaires du cybercafé
- nombre et type d'appareils (*devices*) électroniques
- description des services
- liste des prix par type de service

7 La technologie d'hier et d'aujourd'hui Avec un(e) partenaire, imaginez une conversation avec une personne célèbre du passé. Vous parlez de l'évolution de la technologie et, bien sûr, cette personne est choquée de voir (*see*) les appareils électroniques du 21e siècle (*century*). Answers will vary.

- Choisissez trois ou quatre appareils différents.
- Demandez/Donnez une définition pour chaque objet.
- Demandez/Expliquez comment utiliser chaque appareil.
- Demandez quels sont les points positifs et négatifs de chaque appareil, et expliquez-les.

OPTIONS

Pairs Have students work in pairs. Tell them to role-play a situation between a person who is computer savvy and someone who wants to learn how to use a computer and surf the Internet. If possible, have students use their laptops during the role-play to demonstrate how a computer works.

Extra Practice Stage a debate about the role of technology in today's world. Propose this question: **La technologie est-elle bonne ou mauvaise pour la société?** Divide the class into two groups, assigning each side a position. Allow groups time to plan their arguments before staging the debate. You may also divide the class into four groups and have two debates going on at the same time.

Les sons et les lettres   Audio

Final consonants

You already learned that final consonants are usually silent, except for the letters **c**, **r**, **f**, and **l**.

ave**c**	hive**r**	che**f**	hôte**l**

You've probably noticed other exceptions to this rule. Often, such exceptions are words borrowed from other languages. These final consonants are pronounced.

Latin	*English*	*Inuit*	*Latin*
foru**m**	sno**b**	anora**k**	ga**z**

Numbers, geographical directions, and proper names are common exceptions.

cin**q**	su**d**	**Agnès**	**Maghre**b

Some words with identical spellings are pronounced differently to distinguish between meanings or parts of speech.

fil**s** = *son*	fil~~s~~ = *threads*
tou**s** (pronoun) = *everyone*	tou~~s~~ (adjective) = *all*

The word **plus** can have three different pronunciations.

plu~~s~~ **de** (silent *s*)	plu**s** **que** (*s* sound)	plu**s** **ou moins** (*z* sound in liaison)

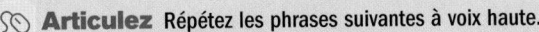

Prononcez Répétez les mots suivants à voix haute.

1. cap
2. six
3. truc
4. club
5. slip
6. actif
7. strict
8. avril
9. index
10. Alfred
11. bifteck
12. bus

Articulez Répétez les phrases suivantes à voix haute.

1. Leur fils est gentil, mais il est très snob.
2. Au restaurant, nous avons tous pris du bifteck.
3. Le sept août, David assiste au forum sur le Maghreb.
4. Alex et Ludovic jouent au tennis dans un club de sport.
5. Prosper prend le bus pour aller à l'est de la ville.

Dictons Répétez les dictons à voix haute.

Un pour tous, tous pour un![2]

Plus on boit, plus on a soif.[1]

[1] The more you drink, the thirstier you are.
[2] All for one and one for all!

ressources
LM p. 82
vhlcentral

quatre cent cinquante-trois **453**

Section Goals

In this section, students will learn about final consonants.

Instructional Resources
vhlcentral.com:
Textbook MP3s; Lab MP3s;
SAM Answer Key;
Textbook Audioscript;
Lab Audioscript;
reference tools

Suggestions

• Model the pronunciation of the examples and have students repeat them after you.

• Explain that some words with pronounced final consonants are actually abbreviated forms of longer words. Examples: **gym** (*f.*) = **gymnastique** (*f.*) and **petit-déj** = **petit-déjeuner**.

• Mention that many exceptions must be memorized.

• Dictate five familiar words containing pronounced and silent final consonants, repeating each one at least two times. Then write them on the board or a transparency and have students check their spelling.

Dictons The proverb «**Plus on boit, plus on a soif.**» is a quote from Arthur Schopenhauer. The full quote is «**La richesse est pareille à l'eau de mer: plus on en boit, plus on a soif.**» The proverb «**Un pour tous, tous pour un!**» is the motto of Switzerland.

OPTIONS

Extra Practice For additional practice with silent and pronounced final consonants, have students write sentences on individual index cards using the words below. Then collect the cards and distribute some of them (at least one for each word) for students to read aloud. 1. porc 2. concept 3. œufs 4. bol 5. appareil 6. truc 7. premier 8. four 9. hôtel 10. gentil

Extra Practice Teach students the following French tongue-twisters that contain silent and pronounced final consonants. **1. Des blancs pains, des bancs peints, des bains pleins. 2. Lily lit le livre dans le lit. 3. Si ton bec aime mon bec comme mon bec aime ton bec, donne-moi le plus gros bec de la Province de Québec!**

ESPACE ROMAN-PHOTO

Section Goals

In this section, students will learn functional phrases for talking about communication and technology.

Instructional Resources
vhlcentral.com:
Roman-photo Video, Videoscript, and Translation; SAM Answer Key; reference tools

Video Recap: Leçon 10B
Ask questions to review the previous **Roman-photo**.
1. Que faisait Rachid quand il s'est blessé? (Il jouait au foot.)
2. Qu'est-ce qui est arrivé? (Il est tombé et il s'est foulé la cheville.) 3. Que lui a dit le médecin? (Elle lui a dit de mettre de la glace, de se reposer, de prendre des médicaments contre la douleur et de ne pas jouer au football pendant une semaine).
4. Pourquoi David avait-il de la crème sur le visage? (Il a eu une réaction allergique.)

Video Synopsis
Rachid is annoyed because David is using several electronic devices at the same time. Rachid reminds him of a paper that is due in two days. Just as David finishes his paper, he has a computer problem and loses part of his work. He calls Amina for help, and she manages to retrieve his document. When Amina sees Rachid's computer screen, she realizes that he is Cyberhomme.

Suggestions
• Tell students to scan the captions for vocabulary related to electronics and technology.
• After reading the **Roman-photo**, have students summarize the episode.

C'est qui, Cyberhomme? Video

PERSONNAGES

Amina

David

Rachid

Sandrine

Valérie

Chez David et Rachid...
RACHID Dis donc, David! Un peu de silence. Je n'arrive pas à travailler!
DAVID Qu'est-ce que tu dis?
RACHID Je dis que je ne peux pas me concentrer! La télé est allumée, tu ne la regardes même pas. Et en même temps, la chaîne stéréo fonctionne et tu ne l'écoutes pas!

DAVID Oh, désolé, Rachid.
RACHID Ah, on arrive enfin à s'entendre parler et à s'entendre réfléchir! À quoi est-ce que tu joues?
DAVID Un jeu vidéo génial!
RACHID Tu n'étudies pas? Tu n'avais pas une dissertation à faire? Lundi, c'est dans deux jours!
DAVID Okay. Je la commence.

Au café...
SANDRINE Tu as un autre e-mail de Cyberhomme? Qu'est-ce qu'il dit?
AMINA Oh, il est super gentil, écoute: «Chère Technofemme, je ne sais pas comment te dire combien j'adore lire tes messages. On s'entend si bien et on a beaucoup de choses en commun. J'ai l'impression que toi et moi, on peut tout se dire.»

Chez David et Rachid...
DAVID Et voilà! J'ai fini ma dissert, Rachid.
RACHID Bravo!
DAVID Maintenant, je l'imprime.
RACHID N'oublie pas de la sauvegarder.
DAVID Oh, non!
RACHID Tu n'as pas sauvegardé?

DAVID Si, mais... Attends... le logiciel redémarre. Ce n'est pas vrai! Il a effacé les quatre derniers paragraphes! Oh non!
RACHID Téléphone à Amina. C'est une pro de l'informatique. Peut-être qu'elle peut retrouver la dernière version de ton fichier.
DAVID Au secours, Amina! J'ai besoin de tes talents.

Un peu plus tard...
AMINA Ça y est, David. Voilà ta dissertation.
DAVID Tu me sauves la vie!
AMINA Ce n'était pas grand-chose, mais tu sais, David, il faut sauvegarder au moins toutes les cinq minutes pour ne pas avoir de problème.
DAVID Oui. C'est idiot de ma part.

A C T I V I T É S

1 **Vrai ou faux?** Indiquez si ces affirmations sont **vraies** ou **fausses**. Corrigez les phrases fausses. Answers may vary.

1. Rachid est en train d'écrire (*in the process of writing*) une dissertation pour son cours de sciences po.
   Faux. Rachid est en train d'écrire à Technofemme.
2. David ne fait pas ses devoirs immédiatement; il a tendance à remettre les choses à plus tard. Vrai.
3. David aime les jeux vidéo. Vrai.
4. David regarde la télévision avec beaucoup d'attention.
   Faux. David ne regarde pas la télévision.

5. Rachid n'aime pas les distractions. Vrai.
6. Valérie s'inquiète de la sécurité d'Amina. Vrai.
7. David sauvegarde ses documents toutes les cinq minutes.
   Faux. David ne sauvegarde pas toujours ses documents.
8. David pense qu'il a perdu la totalité de son document.
   Faux. David pense qu'il a perdu les quatre derniers paragraphes.
9. Amina sait beaucoup de choses sur la technologie. Vrai.
10. Amina et Cyberhomme décident de se rencontrer.
    Faux. Amina ne veut pas rencontrer Cyberhomme.

Practice more at vhlcentral.com.

O P T I O N S

Avant de regarder la vidéo Tell students to read the title and scene setter. Then have them guess who Cyberhomme is. They should support their ideas with details from previous episodes. Write their guesses on the board.

Regarder la vidéo Show the video episode once without sound and have the class create a plot summary based on the visual cues. Then show the episode with sound and have the class make corrections and fill in any gaps in the plot summary.

Amina découvre l'identité de son ami virtuel.

SANDRINE Il est adorable, ton Cyberhomme! Continue! Est-ce qu'il veut te rencontrer en personne?
VALÉRIE Qui vas-tu rencontrer, Amina? Qui est ce Cyberhomme?
SANDRINE Amina l'a connu sur Internet. Ils s'écrivent depuis longtemps, n'est-ce pas, Amina?

AMINA Oui, mais comme je te l'ai déjà dit, je ne sais pas si c'est une bonne idée de se rencontrer en personne. S'écrire des e-mails, c'est une chose; se donner rendez-vous, ça peut être dangereux.
VALÉRIE Amina a raison, Sandrine. On ne sait jamais.
SANDRINE Mais il est si charmant et tellement romantique...

RACHID Merci, Amina. Tu me sauves la vie aussi. Peut-être que maintenant, je vais pouvoir me concentrer.
AMINA Ah? Et tu travailles sur quoi? Ce n'est pas possible!... C'est toi, Cyberhomme?!

RACHID Et toi, tu es Technofemme?!
DAVID Évidemment, tu me l'as dit toi-même: Amina est une pro de l'informatique.

Expressions utiles

Expressing how you communicate with others

- **On arrive enfin à s'entendre parler!**
  Finally we can hear each other speak!
- **On s'entend si bien.**
  We get along so well.
- **On peut tout se dire.**
  We can tell each other anything.
- **Ils s'écrivent depuis longtemps.**
  They've been writing to each other for quite a while.
- **S'écrire des e-mails, c'est une chose; se donner rendez-vous, ça peut être dangereux.**
  Writing e-mails to each other, that's one thing; arranging to meet could be dangerous.

Additional vocabulary

- **se rencontrer**
  to meet each other
- **On ne sait jamais.**
  You/One never know(s).
- **Au secours!**
  Help!
- **C'est idiot de ma part.**
  It's stupid of me.
- **une dissertation**
  paper
- **pas grand-chose**
  not much

Expressions utiles
- Model the pronunciation of the **Expressions utiles** and have students repeat them after you.
- As you work through the list, point out reciprocal verbs and prepositions used with infinitives. Explain the difference between **entendre** and **s'entendre**. Tell students that these grammar points will be formally presented in **Espace structures**.
- Respond briefly to questions about reciprocal verbs and prepositions with infinitives. Reinforce correct forms, but do not expect students to produce them consistently at this time.
- Ask students what **arriver** means. (*to arrive, to happen*) Then point out that **arriver à** + [*infinitive*] means *to be able to* or *to manage to do something.* Example: **Je n'arrive pas à travailler.**
- Explain that **une dissertation** is a *paper*, such as an essay, not a *dissertation*. The abbreviated form is **dissert**.

1 Suggestion Have students correct the false statements.

2 Suggestion Have students compare their answers in pairs or small groups.

2 Expansion For additional practice, give students these items. **6. David éteint la télé et la chaîne stéréo, puis que se met-il à faire? (Il se met à jouer à un jeu vidéo.) 7. Qu'est-ce que Cyberhomme et Technofemme ont en commun? (Ils aiment la technologie.) 8. Selon Sandrine, comment est Cyberhomme? (Il est adorable, charmant et romantique.)**

3 Suggestion Before beginning this activity, give students a few minutes to think about their study habits and jot down some ideas.

2 Questions Répondez aux questions par des phrases complètes.

1. Pourquoi Rachid se met-il en colère?
   Il se met en colère parce qu'il ne peut pas se concentrer.
2. Pourquoi y a-t-il beaucoup de bruit (*noise*) chez Rachid et David?
   Il y a beaucoup de bruit parce que la chaîne stéréo et la télévision sont allumées.
3. Est-ce qu'Amina s'entend bien avec Cyberhomme?
   Oui, elle s'entend bien avec Cyberhomme.
4. Que pense Valérie de la possibilité d'un rendez-vous avec Cyberhomme?
   Elle pense que ça peut être dangereux.
5. Qu'est-ce que Rachid fait pendant que David joue au jeu vidéo et écrit sa dissertation?
   Il écrit des e-mails à Amina/Technofemme.

3 À vous Pour ce qui est des (*With respect to*) études, David et Rachid sont très différents. David aime les distractions et Rachid a besoin de silence pour travailler. Avec un(e) camarade de classe, décrivez vos habitudes en ce qui concerne (*concerning*) les études. Avez-vous les mêmes? Pouvez-vous être de bon(ne)s colocataires? Présentez vos conclusions à la classe.

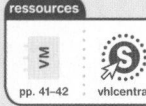

ressources

VM
pp. 41–42

vhlcentral

A C T I V I T É S

OPTIONS

Small Groups Working in groups of three, have students role-play this situation. One student is an irate customer in a cybercafé who is annoyed by something the customer seated nearby is doing: for example, playing music too loudly or making noises while playing a game. Another student is the customer who defends his or her own actions. The third student is an employee who tries to resolve the situation.

Pairs Have students work in pairs and discuss these questions. **1. Pourquoi Amina n'a-t-elle pas l'intention d'avoir un rendez-vous avec Cyberhomme? 2. Sandrine pense que Cyberhomme est romantique et elle encourage Amina à fixer un rendez-vous avec lui. Qui a raison, Amina ou Sandrine? Pourquoi?**

Reading

Section Goals

In this section, students will:
• learn about technology in France
• learn some common Internet terms
• learn about some online francophone radio stations
• read about the Ariane rocket

Instructional Resources
vhlcentral.com:
reference tools

Culture à la loupe
Avant la lecture Have students look at the photos and describe what the people are doing.

Lecture
• Tell students to make a list of new Internet terms they encounter as they read the article. Examples: **la connexion par câble/ADSL, la caméra vidéo, la tablette tactile,** and **le scanner**.
• In 2011, France was ranked number 8 in the top 20 countries for Internet usage. Canada is number 4. (Source: INSEE)
• Point out the statistics chart. Ask students what information it shows. (the percentage of French households that have the electronics devices listed)

Après la lecture Ask students: **À votre avis, pourquoi est-ce que les cybercafés sont plus populaires en France qu'aux États-Unis?**

1 Suggestion Have students get together with a classmate to check their answers.

CULTURE À LA LOUPE

La technologie et les Français

le Minitel

Pendant les années 1980, la technologie a connu une grande évolution. En France, cette révolution technologique a commencé par l'invention du Minitel, développé par France Télécom, la compagnie nationale française de téléphone, au début des années 1980. Le Minitel peut être considéré comme le prédécesseur d'Internet. C'est un petit terminal qu'on branche° sur sa ligne de téléphone et qui permet d'accéder à toutes sortes d'informations et de jeux, de faire des réservations de train ou d'hôtel, de commander des articles en ligne ou d'acheter des billets de concert, par exemple. Aujourd'hui, le Minitel n'existe plus. Internet l'a remplacé et de plus en plus de Français sont équipés chez eux d'un ordinateur et d'une connexion. Moins de 300.000 abonnés° utilisent encore une connection bas débit° et la majorité des connections se font avec le haut débit°. Les Français ont le choix, pour ce haut débit, entre la connexion par câble et la connexion ADSL°. Enfin, pour ceux° qui n'ont pas d'autre manière° de se connecter à Internet, il existe les smartphones et—beaucoup plus qu'aux États-Unis—de nombreux cybercafés.

En ce qui concerne les autres appareils électroniques à la mode, on note une augmentation des achats° de consoles de jeux vidéo, de lecteurs de CD/DVD, de caméras vidéo, de tablettes tactiles, d'appareils photos numériques ou de produits périphériques° pour les ordinateurs, comme les imprimantes ou les scanners. Mais l'appareil qui a connu le plus grand succès en France, c'est sans doute le téléphone portable. En 1996, moins de 2,5 millions de Français avaient un téléphone portable. Aujourd'hui, presque tous les Français en possèdent un.

L'équipement technologique des Français (% *de ménages*)

Télévision	97,1
Téléphone fixe	91,1
Téléphone portable	88,9
Ordinateur	76,8
Lecteur DVD	76,7
Connexion Internet	75,1

branche *connects* **abonnés** *subscribers* **bas débit** *low-speed* **haut débit** *high-speed* **ADSL** *DSL* **ceux** *those* **manière** *way* **achats** *purchases* **périphériques** *peripheral*

Coup de main

When saying an e-mail address aloud, follow this example.

claude-monet@yahoo.fr

claude tiret monet arobase yahoo point F R

A C T I V I T É S

1

Répondez Répondez par des phrases complètes.

1. Quelle invention française est le prédécesseur d'Internet? C'est le Minitel.
2. Qu'est-ce que le Minitel? C'est un petit terminal qu'on branche sur sa ligne de téléphone et qui permet d'accéder à toutes sortes d'informations.
3. Quel est le nom de la compagnie nationale française de téléphone? C'est France Télécom.
4. La connexion Internet haut débit existe-t-elle en France? Oui, la majorité des connections se font avec le haut débit.
5. Où peut-on aller si on n'a pas d'accès Internet à la maison? On peut aller dans un cybercafé.
6. Quels sont deux appareils électroniques qu'on achète souvent en France en ce moment? Answers will vary. Possible answer: Ce sont les lecteurs de CD/DVD et les consoles de jeux vidéo.
7. Quel appareil électronique a eu le plus de succès depuis 1996? C'est le téléphone portable.
8. Quel est le pourcentage de Français qui possèdent un ordinateur? Soixante-dix-huit pour cent des Français possèdent un ordinateur.
9. Est-il courant (*common*) d'avoir Internet en France? Oui, 75% des Français ont Internet chez eux et de plus en plus de gens ont des smartphones.
10. La majorité des Français ont-ils encore un Minitel? Non. Le Minitel n'existe plus.

OPTIONS

Cultural Comparison Take a quick class survey to find out how many students have the electronic devices listed in the chart in their homes. Example: **Combien d'étudiants ont un téléphone à la maison?** Tally the results on the board and have students calculate the percentages.

Then have students compare the results of this survey with the percentages in the chart. Example: **Plus d'Américains ont un ordinateur chez eux.**

LE FRANÇAIS QUOTIDIEN

Cyberespace

blog (*m.*)	blog
grimace (*f.*)	frown
message (*m.*) **instantané**	instant message
moteur (*m.*) **de recherche**	search engine
pseudo(nyme) (*m.*)	screen name
smiley (*m.*)	smiley (face)
chatter	to chat

LE MONDE FRANCOPHONE

Quelques stations de radio francophones

Voici quelques radios francophones en ligne.

En Afrique

Africa 1 radio africaine qui propose des actualités et beaucoup de musique africaine (www.africa1.com)

En Belgique

Classic 21 radio pour les jeunes qui passe° de la musique rock et propose des emplois° pour les étudiants (www.classic21.be)

En France

NRJ radio privée nationale pour les jeunes qui passe tous les grands tubes° (www.nrj.fr)

En Suisse

Fréquence Banane radio universitaire de Lausanne (www.frequencebanane.ch)

passe *plays* **emplois** *jobs* **tubes** *hits*

PORTRAIT

La fusée Ariane

Après la Seconde Guerre mondiale°, la conquête de l'espace° s'est amplifiée. Les Russes et les Américains progressent très rapidement dans leurs programmes spatiaux, ce qui leur donne accès à de nouvelles perspectives, principalement dans les domaines de la physique et de l'astronomie. En Europe, le premier programme spatial, le programme Europa, n'a pas bien marché et a été abandonné. En 1973, afin de ne pas dépendre des autres puissances spatiales pour mettre des satellites en orbite, l'Agence spatiale européenne, sur la base de travaux de scientifiques français, a proposé un nouveau programme spatial, le projet Ariane, qui a eu, lui, un succès considérable. La fusée° Ariane est un lanceur° civil européen de satellites: la première fusée du programme, Ariane 1, a été lancée en 1979 depuis la base de Kourou, en Guyane française, une région d'outre-mer° située en Amérique du Sud. Elle transporte des satellites commerciaux dans l'espace. Depuis, il y a eu plusieurs générations de fusées. Aujourd'hui, Ariane 5, un lanceur beaucoup plus puissant° que ses prédécesseurs, est utilisée. Fin 2016, Ariane 5 a connu un nouveau succès et a placé sur orbite deux satellites de télécommunication destinés à l'Inde et à l'Australie. La fusée continuera sa mission jusqu'en 2023, date à laquelle Ariane 6 devrait prendre entièrement le relais°.

Guerre mondiale *World War* **espace** *space* **fusée** *rocket* **lanceur** *launcher* **outre-mer** *overseas* **puissant** *powerful* **prendre le relais** *replace*

---

2 **Complétez** Complétez les phrases d'après les textes.

1. Africa 1, la radio africaine, propose de la musique, mais aussi ___des actualités___.

2. La radio privée nationale française destinée aux jeunes s'appelle ___NRJ___.

3. En Suisse, beaucoup d'étudiants apprécient la radio ___Fréquence Banane___.

4. Le premier programme spatial européen s'appelait ___Europa___.

5. La fusée Ariane est le ___lanceur civil de satellites___ européen.

3 **À vous...** Avec un(e) partenaire, choisissez une des stations de radio présentées dans **Le monde francophone** et écrivez six phrases où vous donnez des exemples de ce qu'on entend sur cette station. Soyez prêt(e)s à les présenter à la classe.

ressources

🅢

vhlcentral

🅢 Practice more at **vhlcentral.com**.

quatre cent cinquante-sept **457**

A C T I V I T É S

Le français quotidien
- Model the pronunciation of each term and have students repeat it.
- Ask students questions using these terms. Examples: **1. Écrivez-vous des messages instantanés? Si oui, à qui les écrivez-vous? 2. Quel moteur de recherche préférez-vous? 3. Quels sont les pseudonymes de Rachid et d'Amina dans la vidéo? (Cyberhomme et Technofemme) 4. Aimez-vous chatter en ligne? Avec qui chattez-vous?**

Portrait Point out that the space age began in 1957 with the launch of the satellite *Sputnik*. This touched off a "space race" between the United States and Russia, which culminated in the first man landing on the moon in 1969.

Le monde francophone
- You might want to tell students about **RFI (Radio France Internationale)**. **RFI** also has a music site at (**Radio France Internationale Musique**).
- After reading the text, have students search online to find the Internet addresses for various radio stations. Have them take turns reading the addresses out loud.
- Take a quick class survey to find out which radio station(s) they would be interested in listening to and have them explain why. Example: **Combien d'étudiants aimeraient** (*would like*) **écouter NRJ? Pourquoi?**

Suggestion Point out to students that they will find supporting activities and more information related to this **Espace culture** at **vhlcentral.com**.

2 **Expansion** For additional practice, give students these items. **6. Pour une réponse immédiate, on peut envoyer ____. (un message instantané) 7. Pour protéger son identité quand on chatte, on peut employer ____. (un pseudonyme) 8. La première fusée Ariane a été lancée en ____. (1979)**

3 **Suggestion** Have each pair get together with another pair of students to peer edit each other's sentences.

O P T I O N S

Quelques stations de radio francophones Have students write a brief critique of one of the radio stations in **Le monde francophone**. Assign each student a station so that all are covered. Tell them to go to the station's website, look at the features, and listen to the music. They should comment on what they like, dislike, or find interesting about the website.

Cultural Comparison Have students research and discuss the similarities and differences between **le projet Ariane** and NASA's Apollo Space Program (**le projet Apollo**), Skylab (**le projet Skylab**), and the space shuttle (**la navette spatiale**).

Section Goals

In this section, students will learn verbs that require a preposition before the infinitive.

Instructional Resources
vhlcentral.com:
Activity Pack; Lab MP3s;
SAM Answer Key; **Essayez!**
and **Mise en pratique** answers;
Lab Audioscript;
reference tools

Suggestions

• Point out that students already know how to use verbs with infinitives by asking questions with **aller, pouvoir, savoir**, etc. Examples: **Allez-vous faire une promenade après la classe? Pouvons-nous refaire la leçon? Savez-vous danser?**

• Introduce prepositions with the infinitive by using both constructions (verb + [infinitive], verb + [preposition] + [infinitive]) in the same sentence. Ask students what differences they hear. Example: **D'habitude, mon oncle déteste voyager à l'étranger, mais il a décidé d'aller à Paris cet été.**

• After presenting the use of **à** and **de** with the infinitive, write an infinitive on the board and ask volunteers to use it in a sentence with the appropriate preposition.

• Tell students about the construction **permettre à quelqu'un de faire quelque chose**, and explain the use of **à** and **de**. Example: **Ce logiciel permet à Xavier d'enregistrer des chansons.**

• To contrast the use of **à** and **de** with pronouns, review the contractions these prepositions form with definite articles: **au, aux, des**. Point out that prepositions with infinitives and pronouns do not take this form. Example: **Ce film… j'hésite à le voir.**

• Point out that the preposition **pour** + [infinitive] can mean in order to. Example: **Ils sont allés à la bibliothèque pour étudier.**

Essayez! After completing the activity, have students underline the conjugated verb and preposition (if applicable). Ask volunteers to replace the verbs and prepositions with others from the list on page 450.

Prepositions with the infinitive Tutorial

Point de départ Infinitive constructions, where the first verb is conjugated and the second verb is an infinitive, are common in French.

CONJUGATED VERB	INFINITIVE
Vous **pouvez**	**fermer** le document.
You can	*close the document.*

• Some conjugated verbs are followed directly by an infinitive. Others are followed by the preposition **à** or **de** before the infinitive.

verbs followed directly by infinitive	verbs followed by à before infinitive		verbs followed by de before infinitive	
adorer	aider à		arrêter de	*to stop*
aimer	s'amuser à	*to pass time by*	décider de	*to decide to*
aller	apprendre à		éviter de	
détester	arriver à	*to manage to*	finir de	
devoir	commencer à		s'occuper de	*to take care of, to see to*
espérer	continuer à		oublier de	
pouvoir	hésiter à	*to hesitate to*	permettre de	
préférer	se préparer à		refuser de	*to refuse to*
savoir	réussir à		rêver de	*to dream about/of*
vouloir			venir de	*to have just*

Nous **allons manger** à midi.	Elle **a appris à conduire** une voiture.	Il **rêve de visiter** l'Afrique.
We are going to eat at noon.	*She learned to drive a car.*	*He dreams of visiting Africa.*

• Place object pronouns before infinitives. Unlike definite articles, they do not contract with the prepositions **à** and **de**.

J'**ai décidé de les télécharger**.	Il **est arrivé à lui donner** l'argent.
I decided to download them.	*He managed to give him the money.*

N'**oublie** pas **de l'éteindre**.	Elle **continue à t'envoyer** des e-mails?
Don't forget to turn it off.	*Does she continue to send you e-mails?*

• The infinitive is also used after the prepositions **pour** and **sans**.

Nous sommes venus **pour t'aider**.	Elle est partie **sans manger**.
We came to help you.	*She left without eating.*

Il a téléphoné **pour dire** bonjour.	Ne fermez pas le fichier **sans le sauvegarder**.
He called to say hello.	*Don't close the file without saving it.*

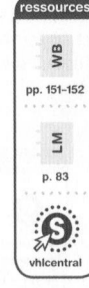

ressources

WB
pp. 151-152

LM
p. 83

vhlcentral

Essayez! Décidez s'il faut ou non une préposition. S'il en faut une, choisissez entre **à** et **de**.

1. Tu sais __Ø__ cuisiner.
2. Commencez __à__ travailler.
3. Tu veux __Ø__ goûter la soupe?
4. Il s'occupe __de__ me donner à manger.
5. J'espère __Ø__ avoir mon diplôme cette année.
6. Elles vont __Ø__ revenir.
7. Je finis __de__ mettre la table.
8. Il hésite __à__ me poser la question.
9. Marc continue __à__ lui parler.
10. Arrête __de__ m'énerver!

Le français vivant
- Ask what the ad is for, and then ask a volunteer to read it aloud.
- Have students describe what the person in the photo is doing and identify all of the objects they see.
- Ask students: **Voulez-vous acheter cet ordinateur? Expliquez.**

Le français vivant

Football? Jeux? **Musique?** Films et séries?

Vous avez toujours rêvé de posséder un ordinateur comme ça. Vous vouliez l'acheter, et vous venez de l'allumer. Maintenant, vous commencez à vous rendre compte de ses possibilités. N'hésitez pas à en profiter. En tout confort.

Identifiez Quels verbes trouvez-vous devant un infinitif dans le texte de cette publicité (*ad*)? Lesquels (*Which ones*) prennent une préposition? **Quelle préposition?**   rêver de, vouloir, venir de, commencer à, hésiter à

Questions À tour de rôle avec un(e) partenaire, posez-vous ces questions.   Answers will vary.

1. As-tu toujours rêvé de posséder quelque chose? De faire quelque chose? Explique.

2. Que veux-tu acheter en ce moment? Pourquoi?

3. D'habitude, qu'hésites-tu à faire?

4. La technologie peut-elle vraiment apporter le confort?

5. Qu'as-tu commencé à faire grâce à (*thanks to*) la technologie? Qu'as-tu arrêté de faire à cause de la technologie?

6. Y a-t-il quelqu'un dans ta famille qui évite d'utiliser la technologie? Qui? Pourquoi?

OPTIONS

Extra Practice Have students write five original sentences using verbs with prepositions and infinitives. Students should use as much active lesson vocabulary as possible. Then have students read their sentences aloud.

Game Divide the class into teams. Call out a verb from the list above. The first member of each team runs to the board and writes a sample sentence, using the verb, its corresponding preposition (if applicable), and an infinitive. If the sentence of the team finishing first is correct, the team gets a point. If not, check the next team, and so on. Practice all verbs from the chart, making sure each team member has had at least two turns. Then tally the points to see which team wins.

ESPACE STRUCTURES

Mise en pratique

1 **Les vacances** Paul veut voyager cet été. Il vous raconte ses problèmes. Complétez le paragraphe avec les prépositions **à** ou **de**, si nécessaire.

Je n'arrive pas (1) __à__ décider où partir en vacances. Je veux (2) __ø__ visiter un pays chaud et ensoleillé (*sunny*). J'espère (3) __ø__ trouver des billets d'avion pour la Martinique. Cet après-midi, je me suis amusé (4) __à__ regarder les prix des billets d'avion sur Internet. Je n'ai pas réussi (5) __à__ trouver un bon tarif (*fare*). Je vais continuer (6) __à__ chercher. J'hésite (7) __à__ payer plein tarif mais je refuse (8) __de__ voyager en stand-by.

2 **Le week-end dernier** Sophie et ses copains ont fait beaucoup de choses le week-end dernier. Regardez les illustrations et dites ce qu'ils (*what they*) ont fait. Suggested answers

▶ **MODÈLE**
J'ai décidé de conduire.

je / décider

1. nous / devoir
Nous avons dû nous réveiller tôt.

2. elles / apprendre
Elles ont appris à jouer au tennis.

3. André / refuser
André a refusé de nager.

4. vous / aider
Vous avez aidé à faire la cuisine.

5. tu / s'amuser
Tu t'es amusée à dessiner.

6. mes cousins / éviter
Mes cousins ont évité de ranger leur chambre.

7. Sébastien / continuer
Sébastien a continué à faire de la planche à voile.

8. il / finir
Il a fini de nettoyer.

3 **Questionnaire** Vous cherchez un travail d'été. Complétez les phrases avec les prépositions **à** ou **de**, quand c'est nécessaire. Ensuite, indiquez si vous êtes d'accord avec ces affirmations.

oui	non	
1. ____	____	Vous savez __ø__ parler plusieurs langues.
2. ____	____	Vous acceptez __de__ voyager souvent.
3. ____	____	Vous n'hésitez pas __à__ travailler tard.
4. ____	____	Vous oubliez __de__ répondre au téléphone.
5. ____	____	Vous pouvez __ø__ travailler le week-end.
6. ____	____	Vous commencez __à__ travailler immédiatement.

 Practice more at **vhlcentral.com**.

1 **Suggestion** Before starting, ask individual students to identify the infinitives of the conjugated verbs.

2 **Expansion** Ask volunteers to share two things they did last weekend.

3 **Expansion** Take a survey of students' responses to the statements. Examples: **Qui sait parler plusieurs langues? Qui accepte de voyager souvent? Qui hésite à travailler tard?** Have students expand on their answers. Example: **Pourquoi hésitez-vous à travailler tard?**

Communication

4 Suggestion Before dividing the class into pairs, introduce the activity using your own situation. Example: **Moi, j'aime envoyer des e-mails à mes amis. J'arrive à sauvegarder tous les messages qu'ils m'envoient.**

5 Expansion Have students continue the activity, using these items 10. arriver / utiliser un plan 11. éviter / bronzer

6 Expansion After the groups present their ads, have students from other groups imagine they are potential **École-dinateur** clients and ask questions about their services. Examples: **Est-ce que nous apprenons à naviguer un site web? Qui nous aide à télécharger des fichiers?**

4 **Assemblez** Avez-vous eu de bonnes ou de mauvaises expériences avec la technologie? À tour de rôle, avec un(e) partenaire, assemblez les éléments des colonnes pour créer des phrases logiques. *Answers will vary.*

MODÈLE

Étudiant(e) 1: *Je déteste télécharger des logiciels.*
Étudiant(e) 2: *Chez moi, ma mère n'arrive pas à envoyer des e-mails.*

A	B	C	D
mère		aimer	composer
mon père		arriver	effacer
mon frère		décider	envoyer
ma sœur		détester	éteindre
mes copains		hésiter	être en ligne
mon petit ami	(ne pas)	oublier	fermer
ma petite amie		refuser	graver
notre prof		réussir	ouvrir
nous		savoir	sauvegarder
?		?	télécharger

5 **Les voyages** Vous et votre partenaire parlez des vacances et des voyages. Utilisez ces éléments pour vous poser des questions. Justifiez vos réponses. *Answers will vary.*

MODÈLE

aimer / faire des voyage
Étudiant(e) 1: *Aimes-tu faire des voyages?*
Étudiant(e) 2: *Oui, j'aime faire des voyages. J'aime faire la connaissance de beaucoup de personnes.*

1. rêver / aller en Afrique
2. vouloir / visiter des musées
3. préférer / voyager avec un groupe ou seul(e)
4. commencer / lire des guides touristiques
5. réussir / trouver des vols bon marché
6. aimer / rencontrer des amis à l'étranger
7. hésiter / visiter un pays où on ne parle pas anglais
8. apprendre / parler des langues étrangères
9. s'occuper / faire les réservations d'hôtel

6 **Une pub** Par groupes de trois, préparez une publicité pour École-dinateur, une école qui enseigne l'informatique aux technophobes. Utilisez le plus de verbes possible de la liste avec un infinitif. *Answers will vary.*

MODÈLE

Rêvez-vous d'écrire des e-mails? Continuez-vous à travailler comme vos grands-parents? Alors...

aimer	détester	refuser
s'amuser	éviter	réussir
apprendre	espérer	rêver
arriver	hésiter	savoir
continuer	oublier	vouloir

quatre cent soixante et un **461**

Extra Practice Have students write three sentences about themselves using three different types of verbs: verbs followed directly by an infinitive, verbs followed by **à** before the infinitive, and verbs followed by **de** before the infinitive. Collect the papers and read them aloud. The rest of the class tries to guess who wrote the sentences.

Video Show the video again to give the students more input with verbs + [*infinitives*] and verbs + [*prepositions*] + [*infinitives*]. Stop the video where appropriate to discuss how these constructions were used and to ask comprehension questions.

Section Goals

In this section, students will learn reciprocal reflexives.

Instructional Resources
vhlcentral.com:
Activity Pack; Lab MP3s;
SAM Answer Key; **Essayez!**
and **Mise en pratique** *answers;*
Lab Audioscript;
reference tools

Suggestions

• Review the reflexive pronouns in the paradigm: **(je) me, (tu) te, (il/elle/on) se, (nous) nous, (vous) vous, (ils/elles) se.**

• Ask volunteers to explain what reflexive verbs are. Ask other students to provide examples. Review reflexive verbs and pronouns by asking students questions about their personal routine. Example: **Je me suis réveillé(e) à sept heures. Et vous, à quelle heure vous êtes-vous réveillé(e)?**

• Use magazine pictures to introduce the concept of reciprocal reflexive verbs.

• After going over the example sentences, ask students questions using reciprocal constructions. Examples: **Les frères s'entendent-ils bien? Vous écrivez-vous des lettres ou des e-mails? Quand vous êtes-vous rencontrés?**

Essayez! Have volunteers create sentences with the verbs in this activity.

Reciprocal reflexives  Tutorial

Point de départ In **Leçon 10A**, you learned that reflexive verbs indicate that the subject of a sentence does the action to itself. Reciprocal reflexives, on the other hand, express a shared or reciprocal action between two or more people or things. In this context, the pronoun means *(to) each other* or *(to) one another*.

Il **se regarde** dans le miroir.
He's looking at himself in the mirror.

Alain et Diane **se regardent**.
Alain and Diane are looking at each other.

Common reciprocal verbs			
s'adorer	*to adore one another*	s'entendre bien	*to get along well (with one another)*
s'aider	*to help one another*		
s'aimer (bien)	*to love (like) one another*	se parler	*to speak to one another*
se connaître	*to know one another*	se quitter	*to leave one another*
se dire	*to tell one another*	se regarder	*to look at one another*
se donner	*to give one another*	se rencontrer	*to meet one another (make an acquaintance)*
s'écrire	*to write one another*		
s'embrasser	*to kiss one another*	se retrouver	*to meet one another (planned)*
		se téléphoner	*to phone one another*

Boîte à outils

The pronouns **nous**, **vous**, and **se** are used to reflect reciprocal actions.

Annick et Joël **s'écrivent** tous les jours.
Annick and Joël write one another every day.

Vous **vous donnez** souvent rendez-vous le lundi?
Do you often arrange to meet each other on Mondays?

Nous **nous retrouvons** devant le métro à midi.
We're meeting each other in front of the subway at noon.

Vous **embrassez**-vous devant vos parents?
Do you kiss each other in front of your parents?

• The past participle of a reciprocal verb only agrees with the subject when the subject is also the direct object of the verb.

DIRECT OBJECT
Marie a aidé **son frère**.
Marie helped her brother.

DIRECT OBJECT → AGREEMENT
Marie et son frère **se sont aidés**.
Marie and her brother helped each other.

DIRECT OBJECT
Son frère a aidé **Marie**.
Her brother helped Marie.

INDIRECT OBJECT
Régine a parlé à **Sophie**.
Régine spoke to Sophie.

INDIRECT OBJECT → NO AGREEMENT
Régine et Sophie **se sont parlé**.
Régine and Sophie spoke to each other.

INDIRECT OBJECT
Sophie a parlé à **Régine**.
Sophie spoke to Régine.

ressources

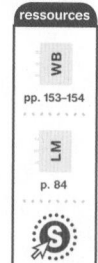

WB
pp. 153–154

LM
p. 84

vhlcentral

Essayez!   **Donnez les formes correctes des verbes.**

1. (s'embrasser) nous *nous embrassons*
2. (se quitter) vous *vous quittez*
3. (se rencontrer) ils *se rencontrent*
4. (se dire) nous *nous disons*
5. (se parler) elles *se parlent*
6. (se retrouver) ils *se retrouvent*
7. (se regarder) vous *vous regardez*
8. (s'aider) nous *nous aidons*

Le français vivant
- Have students describe what the man in the photo is doing.
- Call on a volunteer to read the ad aloud.
- Ask: **Possédez-vous un smartphone?** Have students who own a smartphone note which feature(s) in the ad they use or like most or least. Examples: **Je fais tout avec mon smartphone, mais je l'utilise surtout pour répondre à mes e-mails. / Moi, je ne me sers pas de l'agenda.**

Le français vivant

MIEUX CHERCHER ▪ MIEUX COMMUNIQUER ▪ MIEUX JOUER

▪ POUR MIEUX S'ENTENDRE ▪

Avec le smartphone, je cherche l'heure de mes cours.
Nous nous retrouvons entre amis.

Nous nous écrivons.
Nous nous entendons mieux.
Avec ce téléphone, c'est facile de se parler.

Identifiez Quels verbes réciproques avez-vous trouvés dans la publicité (*ad*)?
s'entendre, se retrouver, s'écrire, se parler

Questions À tour de rôle avec un(e) partenaire, posez-vous ces questions.   Answers will vary.

1. Tes amis et toi, vous écrivez-vous avec un téléphone? Comment vous écrivez-vous?

2. Penses-tu que les gens s'entendent mieux grâce à (*thanks to*) la technologie? Pourquoi?

3. Quels gadgets technologiques utilises-tu pour communiquer avec tes amis? Pourquoi les utilises-tu?

4. Quels gadgets technologiques utilisaient tes grands-parents pour communiquer avec leurs amis? Pourquoi les utilisaient-ils?

5. Quelles applications de ton portable utilises-tu le plus souvent?

quatre cent soixante-trois **463**

Video Ask students to write two columns on a piece of paper: Reflexive Verbs and Reciprocal Reflexive Verbs. Replay the video episode. Have students write down any examples they hear. Then form groups of three and have students compare their lists.

Extra Practice To provide oral practice with reciprocal reflexive verbs, create sentences that follow the pattern of the sentences in the examples. Say the sentence, have students repeat it, then give a different subject, varying the number. Have students then say the sentence with the new subject, changing pronouns and verbs as necessary.

ESPACE STRUCTURES

Mise en pratique

1 Suggestion Do this as a whole-class activity, giving different students the opportunity to form sentences.

1 Expansion Ask students to put each answer in the **passé composé**, paying attention to the type of pronouns (direct or indirect) used in the original sentences to decide whether the past participle will agree.

2 Expansion Have students imagine that someone from the class contradicts what is said at the reunion. Ask volunteers to change the sentences in the activity to their negative form.

3 Suggestion Remind students to pay attention to the agreement of the past participle.

3 Expansion After assigning this activity, have pairs find magazine pictures and create three more sentences using reciprocal reflexives and the **passé composé**.

1 **L'amour réciproque** Employez des verbes réciproques pour raconter l'histoire d'amour de Laure et d'Habib.

MODÈLE Laure retrouve Habib tous les jours. Habib retrouve Laure tous les jours.
Laure et Habib se retrouvent tous les jours.

1. Laure connaît bien Habib. Habib connaît bien Laure. Laure et Habib se connaissent bien.
2. Elle le regarde amoureusement. Il la regarde amoureusement. Ils se regardent amoureusement.
3. Laure écrit des SMS à Habib. Habib écrit des SMS à Laure. Laure et Habib s'écrivent des SMS.
4. Elle lui téléphone tous les soirs. Il lui téléphone tous les soirs. Ils se téléphonent tous les soirs.
5. Elle lui dit tous ses secrets. Il lui dit tous ses secrets. Ils se disent tous leurs secrets.
6. Laure aime beaucoup Habib. Habib aime beaucoup Laure. Ils s'aiment beaucoup.

2 **Souvenir** Les étudiants de votre classe se retrouvent pour fêter leur réunion. Employez l'imparfait.

MODÈLE Marie et moi / s'aider souvent
Marie et moi, nous nous aidions souvent.

1. Marc et toi / se regarder en cours Marc et toi, vous vous regardiez en cours.
2. Anne et Mouna / se téléphoner Anne et Mouna se téléphonaient.
3. François et moi / s'écrire deux fois par semaine François et moi, nous nous écrivions deux fois par semaine.
4. Paul et toi / s'entendre bien Paul et toi, vous vous entendiez bien.
5. Luc et Sylvie / s'adorer Luc et Sylvie s'adoraient.
6. Patrick et moi / se retrouver après les cours Patrick et moi, nous nous retrouvions après les cours.
7. Alisha et Malik / ne pas se connaître bien Alisha et Malik ne se connaissaient pas bien.
8. Agnès et moi / se parler à la cantine Agnès et moi, nous nous parlions à la cantine.
9. Félix et toi / se donner parfois des cadeaux Félix et toi, vous vous donniez parfois des cadeaux.

3 **Une rencontre** Regardez les illustrations. Qu'est-ce que ces personnages ont fait? Suggested answers

▶ **MODÈLE**
Ils se sont rencontrés.

ils

1. Arnaud et moi
Arnaud et moi, nous nous sommes embrassés.

2. vous
Vous vous êtes quittés.

3. elles
Elles se sont téléphoné.

4. nous
Nous nous sommes écrit.

 Practice more at **vhlcentral.com**.

Communication

4 Curieux Pensez à deux amis qui sont amoureux. Votre partenaire va vous poser beaucoup de questions pour tout savoir sur leur relation. Répondez à ses questions. *Answers will vary.*

MODÈLE

Étudiant(e) 1: Est-ce qu'ils se regardent tout le temps?
Étudiant(e) 2: Non, ils ne se regardent pas tout le temps, mais ils n'arrêtent pas de se téléphoner!

s'adorer	se retrouver	régulièrement
s'aimer	se téléphoner	souvent
s'écrire	bien	tout le temps
s'embrasser	mal	tous les jours
s'entendre	quelquefois	?

5 Un rendez-vous Avec un(e) partenaire, posez-vous des questions sur la dernière fois que vous êtes sorti(e) avec quelqu'un. *Answers will vary.*

MODÈLE

à quelle heure / se donner rendez-vous
Étudiant(e) 1: À quelle heure est-ce que vous vous êtes donné rendez-vous?
Étudiant(e) 2: Nous nous sommes donné rendez-vous à sept heures.

1. où / se retrouver
2. longtemps / se parler
3. se regarder / amoureusement
4. s'entendre / bien
5. à quelle heure / se quitter
6. s'embrasser / avant de se quitter
7. plus tard / se téléphoner
8. s'envoyer des SMS / souvent

6 On se quitte Julie a reçu (*received*) cette lettre de son petit ami Sébastien. Elle ne comprend pas du tout, mais elle doit lui répondre. Avec un(e) partenaire, employez des verbes réciproques pour écrire la réponse. *Answers will vary.*

> Chère Julie,
> Nous devons nous quitter, ma chérie. Pourquoi sommes-nous encore ensemble? Nous ne nous sommes pas vraiment aimés. Nous nous disputons tout le temps et nous ne nous parlons pas assez. Soyons réalistes. Je te quitte et j'espère que tu comprends.
> Sébastien

---

4 Expansion Have pairs use the reciprocal reflexives from the activity to create a short story about two friends falling in love. Encourage them to use the **passé composé**, the **imparfait**, and the present tense.

5 Expansion After completing the activity, have the students imagine they overheard the conversation about the date. Have pairs retell the facts of the conversation using the **passé composé** and the third person.

6 Suggestion Before assigning the activity, have volunteers identify the infinitive forms of each verb.

6 Expansion Have pairs act this out as a phone conversation where one person wants to break up with the other.

OPTIONS

Pairs Have students write and perform a conversation in which one friend discusses a misunderstanding he or she just had with his or her significant other. One student must explain the misunderstanding while the other must ask questions and offer advice. Encourage students to incorporate verbs with infinitives (and prepositions, where needed) and reciprocal reflexive verbs.

TPR Write reciprocal reflexive verbs on index cards and mix them up in a hat. Have volunteers pick a card at random and act out the reciprocal action. The class will guess the action, using the verb in a sentence.

Révision

Instructional Resources
vhlcentral.com:
Activity Pack (Feuilles d'activités; Info Gap Activities); Testing Program; Testing Program MP3s; reference tools

1 Suggestion Before starting the activity, have students brainstorm a list of reciprocal verbs to use.

2 Suggestion Call on two volunteers to act out the **modèle.** Then distribute the **Feuilles d'activités** found in the Activity Pack on the Supersite.

2 Expansion Have pairs write six original sentences with reciprocal reflexives based on the answers from the survey. Some sentences should be affirmative statements, and some should be negative.

3 Expansion Have pairs invent situations or stories about the people in the drawing.

4 Expansion Ask students questions about how they, their close friends, or their family met their significant others. Example: _____, avez-vous un(e) petit(e) ami(e)? Comment vous êtes-vous rencontrés?

5 Suggestion Before assigning the activity, have a group act out the **modèle** in front of the class. The third group member ad-libs a piece of advice.

6 Suggestion Divide the class into pairs and distribute the Info Gap Handouts found in the Activity Pack on the Supersite. Give students ten minutes to complete the activity.

---

1 **À deux** Que peuvent faire deux personnes avec chacun (*each one*) de ces objets? Avec un(e) partenaire, répondez à tour de rôle et employez des verbes réciproques. Answers will vary.

> **MODÈLE** un appareil photo numérique
>
> *Avec un appareil photo numérique, deux personnes peuvent s'envoyer des photos tout de suite.*

- un portable
- un smartphone
- du papier et un stylo
- un fax
- un ordinateur
- une tablette

2 **La communication** Votre professeur va vous donner une feuille d'activités. Circulez dans la classe pour interviewer vos camarades. Comment communiquent-ils avec leurs familles et leurs amis? Pour chaque question, parlez avec des camarades différents qui doivent justifier leurs réponses. Answers will vary.

> **MODÈLE**
>
> **Étudiant(e) 1:** *Tes amis et toi, vous écrivez-vous plus de cinq e-mails par jour?*
> **Étudiant(e) 2:** *Oui, parfois nous nous écrivons dix e-mails.*
> **Étudiant(e) 1:** *Pourquoi vous écrivez-vous tellement souvent?*

Activités	Oui	Non
1. s'écrire plus de cinq textos par jour	Théo	Corinne
2. s'envoyer des lettres par la poste		
3. se téléphoner le week-end		
4. se parler dans les couloirs		
5. se retrouver au resto U		
6. se donner rendez-vous		
7. se rencontrer sur Internet		
8. bien s'entendre		

3 **Dimanche au parc** Ces personnes sont allées au parc dimanche dernier. Avec un(e) partenaire, décrivez à tour de rôle leurs activités. Employez des verbes réciproques. Answers will vary.

4 **Leur rencontre** Comment ces couples se sont-ils rencontrés? Par groupes de trois, inventez une histoire courte pour chaque couple. Utilisez les verbes donnés (*given*) et des verbes réciproques. Answers will vary.

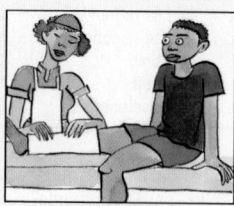
1. venir de

2. continuer à

3. commencer à

4. rêver de

5 **Les bonnes relations** Parlez avec deux camarades. Que faut-il faire pour maintenir de bonnes relations avec ses amis ou sa famille? À tour de rôle, utilisez les verbes de la liste pour donner des conseils (*advice*). Answers will vary.

> **MODÈLE**
>
> **Étudiant(e) 1:** *Dans une bonne relation, deux personnes peuvent tout se dire.*
> **Étudiant(e) 2:** *Oui, et elles apprennent à se connaître.*

s'adorer	se connaître	hésiter à
s'aider	se dire	oublier de
apprendre à	s'embrasser	pouvoir
arrêter de	espérer	refuser de
commencer à	éviter de	savoir

6 **Rencontre sur Internet** Votre professeur va vous donner, à vous et à votre partenaire, une feuille d'illustrations sur la rencontre sur Internet d'Amandine et de Christophe. Attention! Ne regardez pas la feuille de votre partenaire. Answers will vary.

Extra Practice Have students brainstorm a list of chores that must be done every week at their house using vocabulary from previous lessons. Then ask students: **Qui s'occupe de quoi?** After assigning names to each task, have students create sentences telling who forgets to do their chores (**oublier de**), who refuses to do their chores (**refuser de**), and who receives help with their chores (**aider à**).

Game Divide the class into teams of four. Write a reciprocal verb on the board. Groups have 15 seconds to come up with a sentence in the present, the **imparfait**, or the **passé composé**. All groups with correct sentences earn one point.

Flash CULTURE

La technologie

Hôtesse: Csilla

Csilla est en ville, où il y a beaucoup de circulation°. Elle nous fait découvrir différents types de voitures et d'autres véhicules. Elle nous indique aussi les limitations et les dangers de la route°. Elle nous parle des conditions nécessaires pour conduire une voiture en France et nous montre une auto-école, où on passe le permis de conduire°.

Avant de regarder Répondez aux questions. *Answers will vary.*

1. Avez-vous une voiture ou un autre véhicule? Si oui, est-ce que vous l'utilisez souvent?
2. Est-il possible de se déplacer sans voiture dans votre ville? Où peut-on aller à pied?

CSILLA *Et ça, c'est une autoroute!*

CSILLA *Voici une station-service!*

Compréhension Répondez aux questions.

1. Quels sont les différents types de véhicules que Csilla présente dans la vidéo? *Csilla présente des petites voitures, des voitures de luxe, des monospaces, des décapotables, des camions et des scooters.*
2. Que peut-on faire dans une station-service? *On peut acheter de l'essence, vérifier l'huile et la pression des pneus ou nettoyer le pare-brise.*
3. Quel âge faut-il avoir pour passer le permis de conduire en France? *Il faut avoir au moins 18 ans pour passer le permis de conduire.*
4. Pourquoi doit-on aller à l'auto-école? *On doit aller à l'auto-école pour apprendre le code de la route et pour apprendre à conduire.*

Discussion Par groupes de trois, répondez aux questions.
Answers will vary.

Quels moyens de transport en France sont similaires aux transports dans votre ville? Quels transports sont différents?

circulation *traffic* **route** *road* **permis de conduire** *driver's license*

Vocabulaire utile

l'essence (*f.*)	*gas*
nettoyer le pare-brise	*to clean the windshield*
le panneau	*sign*
le péage	*toll*
vérifier (l'huile (*f.*) / la pression des pneus)	*to check (the oil / the air pressure)*

ressources

VM pp. 81–82 vhlcentral

 Practice more at **vhlcentral.com**.

Section Goals

In this section, students will:
- watch a video about traffic, driving, and different types of vehicles in France
- answer questions about the video, compare and describe traffic, driving, and transportation in their towns

Instructional Resources
*vhlcentral.com: **Flash culture**; **Flash culture** transcription; reference tools*

Avant de regarder
- Have students look at the video stills, read the captions, and predict what happens in this episode.
- Explain to students that they don't need to understand every word they hear. Tell them to listen for vocabulary from this lesson as well as cognates.

Compréhension Have students work in pairs or groups. Tell them to write down their answers. Then, show the video again so that they can check their answers and add any missing information.

Discussion Have students work in groups of three to compare their responses. Ask volunteers to describe their preferred mode of transportation for getting around town.

OPTIONS

Vélib' **Vélib'** is Paris's bicycle-sharing system and an affordable way to move about the city. **Vélib'** has had immense popular success since it was first introduced in 2007, and it is used by students, businesspeople, and tourists alike. In 2017, when the **Vélib'** contract came up for renewal, a new operator won it with a proposal to modernize the fleet of more than 23,000 bicycles. The new models are equipped with wifi, Bluetooth, and GPS tracking, and a third of the fleet has been converted to electric.

Section Goals

In this section, students will learn and practice vocabulary related to:
• cars and driving
• car maintenance and repair

Instructional Resources
vhlcentral.com:
Digital Image Bank (including vocabulary illustrations from the textbook, theme-based illustrations); ***Vocabulaire supplémentaire;*** ***Mise en pratique*** *answers; Textbook Audioscript; Lab Audioscript; Activity Pack (Info Gap Activities); Textbook MP3s; Lab MP3s; SAM Answer Key; reference tools*

Suggestions

• Use the **11B Contextes** illustration from the Digital Image Bank. Point out objects and describe what the people are doing. Examples: **Ces personnes sont dans une station-service. C'est une voiture. Il a un pneu crevé. Il fait le plein d'essence.**

• Follow up with simple questions based on your narrative. Examples: **C'est un volant? Qu'est-ce que c'est? Le mécanicien vérifie la pression des pneus?**

• Ask students questions about cars and driving using the new vocabulary. Examples: **Avez-vous une voiture? Attachez-vous votre ceinture de sécurité quand vous conduisez? Quand vous allez à la station-service, faites-vous le plein vous-même? Combien coûte un gallon d'essence?**

• Explain that **dépasser** has two meanings: **dépasser la limitation de vitesse** means *to go over the speed limit* and **dépasser une voiture/un camion** means *to pass a car/truck.*

• Additional vocabulary for this lesson can be found in the **Vocabulaire supplémentaire** on the Supersite.

• Use the Transportation illustrations from the Digital Image Bank to help students familiarize themselves with cars and driving, and car maintenance and repair.

Leçon 11B

Vocabulary Tools

You will learn how to...
▪ talk about cars
▪ talk about traffic
▪ say what you would do

En voiture!

Vocabulaire

arrêter (de faire quelque chose)	to stop (doing something)
attacher	to buckle, to fasten
avoir un accident	to have/to be in an accident
dépasser	to go over; to pass
freiner	to brake
se garer	to park
rentrer dans	to hit
réparer	to repair
tomber en panne	to break down
vérifier (l'huile/ la pression des pneus)	to check (the oil/ the air pressure)
l'embrayage (m.)	clutch
l'essence (f.)	gas
les freins (m., pl.)	brakes
l'huile (f.)	oil
un pare-chocs (pare-chocs pl.)	bumper
un réservoir d'essence	gas tank
un rétroviseur	rearview mirror
une roue	wheel
une roue de secours	spare tire
un voyant (d'essence/ d'huile)	(gas/oil) warning light
une amende	fine
une autoroute	highway
un parking	parking lot
un permis de conduire	driver's license
une rue	street

ressources

WB pp. 155–156	LM p. 85	S vhlcentral

468 *quatre cent soixante-huit*

Game Play a game of **Dix questions**. Ask a volunteer to think of a car part from the new vocabulary. Other students get to ask one yes/no question, then they can guess what the word is. Limit attempts to ten questions per word. You might want to tell students that they can narrow down the options by asking questions about where the part is on the car and what it does.

Small Groups Distribute pictures of cars to groups of three students. Detailed photos of car interiors and exteriors are available online or from car dealerships. List parts of the car on the board, such as **volant, pneu, coffre,** and **rétroviseur**. Tell students to label the parts on the pictures. Alternatively, ask a student who can draw well to sketch a car (inside and out) on the board and have students label its parts.

Mise en pratique

1 Écoutez
Madeleine a eu une mauvaise journée. Écoutez son histoire. Ensuite, indiquez si les phrases suivantes sont **vraies** ou **fausses**.

		Vrai	Faux
Madeleine...			
1.	a oublié son permis de conduire.	☐	☑
2.	a dépassé la limitation de vitesse.	☑	☐
3.	a fait le plein avant d'aller à la fac.	☐	☑
4.	a attaché sa ceinture de sécurité.	☑	☐
5.	s'est garée à l'université.	☑	☐
6.	conduisait quand un policier l'a arrêtée.	☑	☐
Sa voiture...			
7.	a redémarré.	☐	☑
8.	avait un pneu crevé.	☐	☑
9.	n'avait pas d'essence.	☑	☐
10.	était en panne.	☑	☐

2 Les correspondances
Reliez (*Link*) les éléments des deux colonnes.

b	1. dépasser	a.	les freins
d	2. tomber en panne	b.	la limitation de vitesse
a	3. freiner	c.	la ceinture de sécurité
e	4. faire le plein	d.	une voiture
g	5. réparer une voiture	e.	l'essence
f	6. se garer	f.	un parking
c	7. attacher	g.	un mécanicien
h	8. vérifier la pression	h.	les pneus

3 Complétez
Complétez les phrases avec le bon mot de vocabulaire.

1. La personne qui répare une voiture est un _____mécanicien_____.
2. Il faut ouvrir le _____capot_____ de la voiture pour vérifier l'huile.
3. On met de l'essence dans le _____réservoir d'essence_____.
4. Le _____permis de conduire_____ est un document officiel qui vous autorise à conduire.
5. On utilise les _____phares_____ pour voir (*see*) quand on conduit la nuit.
6. On utilise les _____essuie-glaces_____ pour voir à travers (*through*) le pare-brise quand il pleut.
7. Le _____volant_____ sert à diriger (*steer*) la voiture.
8. Vous utilisez le _____rétroviseur_____ pour voir la circulation derrière vous.
9. La personne qui peut donner une amende est un _____policier/agent de police_____.
10. On peut ranger ses valises dans le _____coffre_____ de la voiture.
11. On utilise les _____freins_____ quand on veut s'arrêter.
12. Quand il y a beaucoup de voitures sur la route, il y a de la _____circulation_____.

S Practice more at **vhlcentral.com**.

quatre cent soixante-neuf **469**

Labels (illustration)
- la limitation de vitesse
- la circulation
- un agent de police/un policier (policière *f.*)
- les essuie-glaces (*m.*)
- un pare-brise (pare-brise *pl.*)
- les phares (*m.*)

---

1 Audioscript Hier, j'ai eu une journée terrible! J'avais un examen de maths à 8h00 du matin et je me suis levée en retard. J'étais très pressée, donc je conduisais très vite, quand tout à coup j'ai entendu une sirène. Quand j'ai regardé dans le rétroviseur, c'était un policier. Heureusement, j'avais mon permis de conduire avec moi et j'avais ma ceinture de sécurité attachée, mais comme je roulais plus vite que la vitesse autorisée, j'ai dû payer une amende. Finalement, je suis arrivée à l'université et j'ai trouvé une place pour me garer sans problème. J'ai passé mon examen de maths et je suis partie. Quand je suis retournée à ma voiture pour partir, elle n'a pas démarré. Un mécanicien est venu, il a vérifié la voiture et il m'a dit qu'elle ne démarrait pas parce qu'elle n'avait pas d'essence.
(On Textbook MP3s)

1 Suggestion Play the recording again, stopping at the end of each sentence that contains an answer so students can check their work.

2 Expansion For additional practice, ask students what parts of a car are associated with these activities. **1. nettoyer le pare-brise (les essuie-glaces) 2. conduire (le volant) 3. arrêter (les freins) 4. changer de vitesse (l'embrayage) 5. regarder ce qui est derrière la voiture (le rétroviseur)**

3 Suggestion Have students work in pairs on this activity. Then go over the answers with the class.

OPTIONS

Les appellations des routes en France The letter preceding the highway number indicates what type of road it is. For example, the **A-8** is **une autoroute** (*freeway*). **Une autoroute à péage** is a *toll road*. The **N-7** is **une route nationale**, a smaller highway. The **D-15** is **une route départementale**, an even smaller road. **Les autoroutes** are much faster than **les routes nationales** or **départementales**, but they are not free and usually less scenic.

Extra Practice Propose various driving situations to your students and then ask: **De quoi avez-vous besoin?** Examples: **1. Vous allez en ville en voiture pour faire vos courses. (un parking) 2. Vous êtes sur l'autoroute et vous avez un pneu crevé. (une roue de secours) 3. Vous avez 18 ans et vous voulez conduire. (un permis de conduire) 4. Vous conduisez et il commence à pleuvoir. (les essuie-glaces)**

NATIONAL communication STANDARDS

Communication

4 Suggestions
- Tell students to jot down notes during their interviews.
- After completing the interviews, ask volunteers to share their partner's responses with the class.

5 Suggestion Have two volunteers read the **modèle** aloud. Then divide the class into pairs and distribute the Info Gap Handouts found in the Activity Pack on the Supersite. Give students ten minutes to complete the activity.

6 Suggestions
- Before beginning the activity, have students look at the photo and describe what they see.
- Have the class brainstorm a list of potential problems that a car can have and write their suggestions on the board. Example: **Ma voiture consomme beaucoup d'essence.**

7 Suggestion Have students review the use of the **passé composé** and **imparfait** for narrating events in the past before they begin writing. See **Leçon 8B**, pages 340–341.

4 Conversez Interviewez un(e) camarade de classe. Answers will vary.

1. As-tu une voiture? De quelle sorte?
2. À quel âge as-tu obtenu (*obtained*) ton permis de conduire? Comment s'est passé l'examen?
3. Sais-tu comment changer un pneu crevé? En as-tu déjà changé un?
4. Ta voiture est-elle tombée en panne récemment? Qui l'a réparée?
5. Respectes-tu la limitation de vitesse sur l'autoroute? Et tes amis?
6. As-tu déjà été arrêté(e) par un policier? Pour quelle(s) raison(s)?
7. Combien de fois par mois fais-tu le plein (d'essence)? Combien paies-tu à chaque fois?
8. Quelle(s) autoroute(s) utilises-tu pour aller à l'université?
9. Sais-tu comment conduire une voiture à boîte de vitesses manuelle (*manual*)? Et tes amis?
10. As-tu eu des problèmes de pare-chocs récemment? Et des problèmes d'essuie-glaces?

5 Sept différences Votre professeur va vous donner, à vous et à votre partenaire, deux feuilles d'activités différentes. À tour de rôle, posez-vous des questions pour trouver les sept différences entre vos dessins. Attention! Ne regardez pas la feuille de votre partenaire.

MODÈLE

Étudiant(e) 1: *Ma voiture est blanche. De quelle couleur est ta voiture?*
Étudiant(e) 2: *Oh! Ma voiture est noire.*

6 Chez le mécanicien Travaillez avec un(e) camarade de classe pour présenter un dialogue dans lequel (*in which*) vous jouez les rôles d'un(e) client(e) et d'un(e) mécanicien(ne). Answers will vary.

Le/La client(e)...
- explique le problème qu'il/elle a.
- donne quelques détails sur les problèmes qu'il/elle a eus dans le passé.
- négocie le prix et la date à laquelle (*when*) il/elle peut venir chercher la voiture.

Le/La mécanicien(ne)...
- demande quand le problème a commencé et s'il y en a d'autres.
- explique le problème et donne le prix des réparations.
- accepte les conditions du/de la clien(e).

7 Écriture Écrivez un paragraphe à propos d'un (*about an*) accident de la circulation. Suivez les instructions. Answers will vary.

- Parlez d'un accident (voiture, moto [*f.*], vélo) que vous avez eu récemment. Si vous n'avez jamais eu d'accident, inventez-en un.
- Décrivez ce qui (*what*) s'est passé avant, pendant et après.
- Donnez des détails.
- Comparez votre paragraphe à celui (*that*) d'un(e) camarade de classe.

O P T I O N S

Game Write vocabulary words related to cars on index cards. On another set of cards, draw or paste pictures to match each term. Tape them face down on the board in random order. Divide the class into two teams. Play a game of Concentration in which students match words with pictures. When a player makes a match, that player's team collects those cards. The team with the most cards at the end of the game wins.

Pairs Have students work in pairs. Tell them to take turns explaining to a younger brother or sister how to drive a car. Example: **Tout d'abord, tu attaches ta ceinture de sécurité. Puis...**

Les sons et les lettres  Audio

The letter x

The letter **x** in french is sometimes pronounced -ks, like the x in the English word *axe*.

| ta**x**i | e**x**pliquer | me**x**icain | te**x**te |

Unlike English, some French words begin with a *gz-* sound.

| **x**ylophone | **x**énon | **x**énophile | **X**avière |

The letters **ex-** followed by a vowel are often pronounced like the English word *eggs*.

| e**x**emple | e**x**amen | e**x**il | e**x**act |

Sometimes an x is pronounced s, as in the following numbers.

| soi**x**ante | si**x** | di**x** |

An **x** is pronounced z in a liaison. Otherwise, an **x** at the end of a word is usually silent.

| deu**x** enfants | si**x** éléphants | mieu**x** | curieu**x** |

Prononcez Répétez les mots suivants à voix haute.

1. fax
2. eux
3. dix
4. prix
5. jeux
6. index
7. excuser
8. exercice
9. orageux
10. expression
11. contexte
12. sérieux

Articulez Répétez les phrases suivantes à voix haute.

1. Les amoureux sont devenus époux.
2. Soixante-dix euros! La note (*bill*) du taxi est exorbitante!
3. Alexandre est nerveux parce qu'il a deux examens.
4. Xavier explore le vieux quartier d'Aix-en-Provence.
5. Le professeur explique l'exercice aux étudiants exceptionnels.

Dictons Répétez les dictons à voix haute.

Les belles plumes font les beaux oiseaux.[2]

Les beaux esprits se rencontrent.[1]

Great minds think alike.
Beautiful feathers make beautiful birds.

ressources

LM p. 86 | vhlcentral

quatre cent soixante et onze **471**

Section Goals

In this section, students will learn about the letter **x**.

Instructional Resources

vhlcentral.com:
SAM Answer Key;
Textbook Audioscript;
Lab Audioscript;
reference tools

Suggestions

- Model the pronunciation of the example words and have students repeat after you.
- Have students practice saying words that contain the letter **x** in various positions. Examples: Middle: **excellent, expliquer, expérience,** and **extérieur.** End: **yeux, heureux, époux, cheveux, jeux,** and **mieux.**
- Ask students to provide more examples of words with the letter **x**.
- Dictate five simple sentences with words that have the letter **x**, repeating each one at least two times. Then write the sentences on the board or a transparency and have students check their spelling.

Dictons The saying **«Les belles plumes font les beaux oiseaux»** is a quote from the French poet Bonaventure Des Périers (1500–1544).

OPTIONS

Extra Practice For additional practice with the letter **x**, have students write sentences on individual index cards using the words below. Then collect the cards and distribute some of them (at least one for each word) for students to read aloud. 1. excuser 2. deux 3. époux 4. cheveux 5. malheureux 6. roux 7. vieux 8. ennuyeux 9. explorer 10. généreux

Extra Practice Teach students these French tongue-twisters that contain the letter **x**. 1. Le fisc fixe exprès chaque taxe fixe excessive exclusivement au luxe et à l'acquis. 2. Un taxi attaque six taxis. 3. Je veux et j'exige d'exquises excuses.

ESPACE ROMAN-PHOTO

La panne  Video

Section Goals

In this section, students will learn functional phrases for talking about dating and cars.

Instructional Resources
vhlcentral.com:
Roman-photo *Video, Videoscript, and Translation; SAM Answer Key; reference tools*

Video Recap: Leçon 11A
Review the previous **Roman-photo** with this true/false activity.
1. Rachid n'arrive pas à travailler à cause de David. (Vrai.) 2. David ne finit pas sa dissertation. (Faux.) 3. Amina n'a pas l'intention de rencontrer Cyberhomme. (Vrai.) 4. Amina retrouve la dissertation de David. (Vrai.) 5. David est Cyberhomme. (Faux.)

Video Synopsis
Rachid goes to the service station to get some gas. Amina is waiting at **Le P'tit Bistrot** for him to pick her up for a date. Rachid brings her flowers and is very attentive. In the car, Rachid notices that an indicator light is on, so he returns to the service station. The car just needs some oil. After fixing the problem, they take off again, but they don't get very far because they have a flat tire.

Suggestions
• Have students predict what the episode will be about based on the video stills.
• Tell students to scan the captions and find vocabulary related to cars and driving.
• After reading the **Roman-photo**, review students' predictions and have them summarize the episode.

PERSONNAGES

Amina

Mécanicien

Rachid

Sandrine

Valérie

À la station-service...
MÉCANICIEN Elle est belle, votre voiture! Elle est de quelle année?
RACHID Elle est de 2005.
MÉCANICIEN Je vérifie l'huile ou la pression des pneus?
RACHID Non, merci, ça va. Je suis un peu pressé, en fait. Au revoir.

Au P'tit Bistrot...
SANDRINE Ton Cyberhomme, c'est Rachid! Quelle coïncidence!
AMINA C'est incroyable, non? Je savais qu'il habitait à Aix, mais...
VALÉRIE Une vraie petite histoire d'amour, comme dans les films!
SANDRINE C'est exactement ce que je me disais!

AMINA Rachid arrive dans quelques minutes. Est-ce que cette couleur va avec ma jupe?
SANDRINE Vous l'avez entendue? Ne serait-elle pas amoureuse?
AMINA Arrête de dire des bêtises.

RACHID Oh, non!!
AMINA Qu'est-ce qu'il y a? Un problème?
RACHID Je ne sais pas. J'ai un voyant qui s'est allumé.
AMINA Allons à une station-service.
RACHID Oui... c'est une bonne idée.

De retour à la station-service...
MÉCANICIEN Ah! Vous êtes de retour. Mais que se passe-t-il? Je peux vous aider?
RACHID J'espère. Il y a quelque chose qui ne va pas, peut-être avec le moteur. Regardez, ce voyant est allumé.
MÉCANICIEN Ah, ça? C'est l'huile. Je m'en occupe tout de suite.

MÉCANICIEN Vous pouvez redémarrer? Et voilà.
RACHID Parfait. Au revoir. Bonne journée.
MÉCANICIEN Bonne route!

A C T I V I T É S

1 **Vrai ou faux?** Indiquez si ces affirmations sont **vraies** ou **fausses**. Corrigez les phrases fausses. *Answers may vary.*

1. La voiture de Rachid est neuve (*new*). Faux. Elle est de 2005.
2. Quand Rachid va à la station-service la première fois, il a beaucoup de temps. Faux. Il est un peu pressé.
3. Amina savait que Cyberhomme habitait à Aix. Vrai.
4. Sandrine trouve l'histoire de Rachid et Amina très romantique. Vrai.

5. Amina ouvre la portière de la voiture. Faux. Rachid ouvre la portière.
6. Rachid est galant (*a gentleman*). Vrai.
7. Le premier problème que Rachid rencontre est une panne d'essence. Faux. Un voyant s'est allumé.
8. Le mécanicien répare la voiture. Vrai.
9. La voiture a un pneu crevé. Vrai.
10. Rachid n'est pas très content. Vrai.

 Practice more at **vhlcentral.com**.

O P T I O N S

Avant de regarder la vidéo Tell students to read the title and scene setter. Then have them predict what might happen in this episode. Write their predictions on the board. After viewing the episode, have them confirm or correct their predictions.

Regarder la vidéo Print out the videoscript found on the Supersite. Then white out words related to cars and other key vocabulary in order to create a master for a cloze activity. Distribute photocopies and tell students to fill in the missing information as they watch the video episode.

Amina sort avec Rachid pour la première fois.

SANDRINE Oh, regarde, il lui offre des fleurs.

RACHID Bonjour, Amina. Tiens, c'est pour toi.

AMINA Bonjour, Rachid. Oh, merci, c'est très gentil.

RACHID Tu es très belle, aujourd'hui.

AMINA Merci.

RACHID Attends, laisse-moi t'ouvrir la portière.

AMINA Merci.

RACHID N'oublie pas d'attacher ta ceinture.

AMINA Oui, bien sûr.

AMINA Heureusement, ce n'était pas bien grave. À quelle heure est notre réservation?

RACHID Oh! C'est pas vrai!

AMINA Qu'est-ce que c'était?

RACHID On a un pneu crevé.

AMINA Oh, non!!

Expressions utiles

Talking about dating

- **Il lui offre des fleurs.**
  He's giving her flowers.

- **Attends, laisse-moi t'ouvrir la portière.**
  Wait, let me open the (car) door for you.

Talking about cars

- **N'oublie pas d'attacher ta ceinture.**
  Don't forget to fasten your seatbelt.

- **J'ai un voyant qui s'est allumé.**
  One of the dashboard lights came on.

- **Il y a quelque chose qui ne va pas.**
  There's something wrong.

Additional vocabulary

- **incroyable**
  incredible

---

2 **Qui?** Indiquez qui dirait (*would say*) ces affirmations: Amina (**A**), le mécanicien (**M**), Rachid (**R**), Sandrine (**S**) ou Valérie (**V**).

1. La prochaine fois, je vais suivre les conseils du mécanicien. R

2. Je suis un peu anxieuse. A

3. C'est comme dans un conte de fées (*fairy tale*)! S/V

4. Taisez-vous (*Be quiet*), s'il vous plaît! A

5. Il aurait dû (*should have*) m'écouter. M

3 **Écrivez** Que se passe-t-il pour Amina et Rachid après le deuxième incident? Utilisez votre imagination et écrivez un paragraphe qui raconte ce qu'ils ont fait. Est-ce que quelqu'un d'autre les aide? Amina est-elle fâchée? Y aura-t-il (*Will there be*) un deuxième rendez-vous pour Cyberhomme et Technofemme?

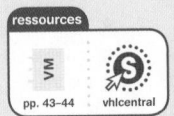

ressources
VM
pp. 43–44
vhlcentral

A C T I V I T É S

Expressions utiles

- Model the pronunciation of the **Expressions utiles** and have students repeat them after you.

- As you work through the list, point out forms of **offrir** and **ouvrir**, as well as forms of the **conditionnel**. Tell students that these verbs and structures will be formally presented in **Espace structures**.

- Respond briefly to questions about verbs like **offrir** and **ouvrir** and conditional forms. Reinforce correct forms, but do not expect students to produce them consistently at this time.

- Tell students that **un mécanicien** is a *car mechanic* and **un garagiste** is a *garage owner*.

- Explain the different words for *light*: **un voyant (lumineux)** is a *warning light* on a vehicle, **les phares** are *headlights*, and the generic term for *light* is **la lumière**.

- Point out that **une portière** is a *car door*; a door in a room or a house is **une porte**. Similarly, a *car window* is **une vitre**, not **une fenêtre**.

1 **Suggestion** Have students correct the false statements.

2 **Expansion** Have students create three more items using lines from the **Roman-photo** conversation. Collect their papers, write some of the items on the board, and ask volunteers to identify the speakers.

3 **Expansion** Have students exchange papers for peer editing. Then ask volunteers to read their paragraphs aloud.

O P T I O N S

Extra Practice Assign students a character (**Rachid, Amina,** or **le mécanicien**) and have them prepare a brief summary of the day's events from that character's point of view without saying the person's name. Ask volunteers to read their summaries to the class. Then have the class guess which character would have given each summary.

Le permis de conduire In France, the legal driving age for a regular permit is 18. In order to get a license, students take classes at an **auto-école**. Drivers must know **le code de la route** (*the driving code*) and understand how a car works. Since the lessons are very expensive, it is not unusual for young people to receive them as a gift for their eighteenth birthday.

Section Goals

In this section, students will:
- learn about cars and driving habits in France
- learn some terms for types of vehicles
- learn about the rules of the road in various francophone regions
- read about the car manufacturer Citroën
- view authentic video footage

Instructional Resources
vhlcentral.com:
reference tools

Culture à la loupe
Avant la lecture Have students look at the photos and describe what they see.

Lecture
- Explain that in Europe gas is sold in liters, not in gallons (1 gallon = 3.79 liters).
- Point out the statistics chart. Ask students what information it shows. (the percentage of French people in rural and urban areas who own a car)

Après la lecture Have students compare cars, driving habits, and car ownership in France and in the United States.

1 **Suggestion** Have students work on this activity in pairs.

 Reading

CULTURE À LA LOUPE

Les voitures

la Smart

Dans l'ensemble°, les Français utilisent moins leurs voitures que les Américains. Il n'est pas rare qu'un couple ou une famille possède une seule voiture. Dans les grandes villes, beaucoup de gens se déplacent° à pied ou utilisent les transports en commun°. Dans les villages ou à la campagne, les gens utilisent un peu plus fréquemment leurs voitures. Pour de longs voyages, pourtant°, ils ont tendance, plus que les Américains, à laisser leurs voitures chez eux et à prendre le train ou l'avion. En général, les voitures en France sont beaucoup plus petites que les voitures qu'on trouve aux États-Unis, mais on y trouve des quatre-quatre°, même dans les grandes villes. La Smart, une voiture minuscule produite par les compagnies Swatch et Mercedes-Benz, a aussi beaucoup de succès en France et en Europe.

Il y a plusieurs raisons qui expliquent ces différences. D'abord, les rues des villes françaises sont beaucoup moins larges. Au centre-ville, beaucoup de rues sont piétonnes° et d'autres sont si petites qu'il est parfois difficile de passer, même pour une petite voiture. Il y a aussi de gros problèmes de parking dans la majorité des villes françaises. Il y a peu de places de parking et elles sont en général assez petites. Il est donc nécessaire de faire un créneau° pour se garer et plus la voiture est petite, plus° on a de chance de le réussir. Les rues en dehors° des villes sont souvent plus larges. En plus, en France, l'essence est plus chère qu'aux États-Unis. Il vaut donc mieux avoir une petite voiture économique qui ne consomme pas beaucoup d'essence, ou prendre les transports en commun quand c'est possible.

Les voitures les plus vendues° en France	
Peugeot 206	700.000
Renault Clio 2	630.000
Renault Clio 3	401.000
Peugeot 207	400.500
Citroën Xsara	395.000
Renault Twingo 1	380.000

Dans l'ensemble By and large **se déplacent** get around **transports en commun** public transportation **pourtant** however **quatre-quatre** sport utility vehicles **piétonnes** reserved for pedestrians **faire un créneau** parallel park **plus..., plus...** the more..., the more... **en dehors** outside **vendues** sold

A C T I V I T É S

1 **Complétez** Donnez un début ou une suite logique à chaque phrase, d'après le texte. Answers may vary. Possible answers provided.

1. … possèdent parfois une seule voiture. Les familles françaises
2. Les Français qui habitent en ville se déplacent souvent… à pied ou ils utilisent les transports en commun.
3. Beaucoup de Français prennent le train ou l'avion… pour faire de longs voyages.
4. … sont en général plus petites qu'aux États-Unis. Les voitures en France
5. Comme aux États-Unis, même dans les grandes villes en France, on trouve… des quatre-quatre.

6. …, on peut facilement faire un créneau pour se garer. Avec la Smart
7. … sont souvent plus larges. Les rues en dehors des villes
8. Il n'est pas toujours facile de se garer dans les villes françaises… parce qu'il y a peu de places de parking et parce qu'elles sont en général assez petites.
9. … parce que l'essence coûte cher en France. Il vaut mieux avoir une petite voiture économique
10. …, la grande majorité des Français à une voiture. Dans les villages et à la campagne

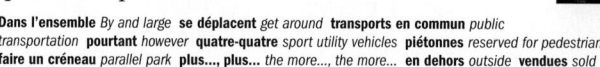

O P T I O N S

Les voitures les plus vendues en France Ask students these questions. **1. Quelle est la voiture la plus populaire en France? (la Peugeot 206) 2. Est-ce que la Peugeot 207 se vend mieux que la Peugeot 206? (Non) 3. Des trois marques représentées, laquelle vend le plus grand nombre de voitures? (Renault)**

Les parcmètres Parking meters in France are not generally located next to the parking spot. The failure to see a parking meter is not a valid excuse for an expired meter. One should look for a meter down the street to avoid getting a parking ticket and having to pay a fine.

LE FRANÇAIS QUOTIDIEN

Pour parler des voitures

bagnole (f.)	*car*
berline (f.)	*sedan*
break (m.)	*station wagon*
caisse (f.)	*car*
char (m.) (Québec)	*car*
coupé (m.)	*coupe*
décapotable (f.)	*convertible*
monospace (m.)	*minivan*
pick-up (m.)	*pickup*

LE MONDE FRANCOPHONE

Conduire une voiture

Voici quelques informations utiles.

En France Il n'existe pas de carrefours° avec quatre panneaux° de stop.

En France, en Belgique et en Suisse Il est interdit d'utiliser un téléphone portable quand on conduit et on n'a pas le droit de tourner à droite quand le feu° est rouge.

À l'île Maurice et aux Seychelles Faites attention! On conduit à gauche.

En Suisse Pour conduire sur l'autoroute, il est nécessaire d'acheter une vignette° et de la mettre sur son pare-brise. On peut l'acheter à la poste ou dans les stations-service et elle est valable° un an.

Dans l'Union européenne Le permis de conduire d'un pays de l'Union européenne est valable dans tous les autres pays de l'Union.

carrefours *intersections* **panneaux** *signs* **feu** *traffic light* **vignette** *sticker* **valable** *valid*

PORTRAIT

Le constructeur automobile Citroën

La marque° Citroën est une marque de voitures française créée° en 1919 par André Citroën, ingénieur et industriel français. La marque est réputée pour son utilisation de technologies d'avant-garde et pour ses innovations dans le domaine de l'automobile. Le premier véhicule construit par Citroën, la voiture type A, a été la première voiture européenne construite en série°. En 1924, Citroën a utilisé la première carrosserie° entièrement en acier° d'Europe. Puis, dans les années 1930, Citroën a inventé la traction avant°. Parmi les modèles de voiture les plus vendus de la marque Citroën, on compte la 2CV, ou «deux chevaux», un modèle bon marché et très apprécié des jeunes dans les années 1970 et 1980. En 1976, Citroën a fusionné° avec un autre grand constructeur automobile français, Peugeot, pour former le groupe PSA Peugeot-Citroën.

marque *make* **créée** *created* **construite en série** *mass-produced* **carrosserie** *body* **acier** *steel* **traction avant** *front-wheel drive* **a fusionné** *merged*

MUSIQUE À FOND

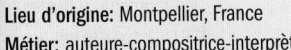

Émilie Simon

Lieu d'origine: Montpellier, France
Métier: auteure-compositrice-interprète

Elle est très douée dans la musique traditionnelle ainsi que dans la musique pop électronique.

Go to **vhlcentral.com** to find out more about **Émilie Simon** and her music.

---

2 **Répondez** Répondez par des phrases complètes.

1. Quelles sont les caractéristiques de la marque Citroën? *Elle est réputée pour son utilisation de technologies d'avant-garde et pour ses innovations.*
2. Quelle est une des innovations de la marque Citroën? *Possible answer: La construction en série d'une voiture en Europe a été une innovation.*
3. Quel modèle de voiture Citroën a eu beaucoup de succès? *La 2CV, ou «deux chevaux», a eu beaucoup de succès.*
4. Qu'a fait la compagnie Citroën en 1976? *La compagnie a fusionné avec un autre constructeur automobile français, Peugeot.*
5. Que faut-il avoir pour conduire sur l'autoroute en Suisse? *Il faut avoir une vignette sur le pare-brise.*
6. Les résidents d'autres pays de l'U.E. ont-ils le droit de conduire en France? *Oui, les permis de conduire des autres pays de l'Union européenne sont valables en France.*

3 **À vous...** Quelle est votre voiture préférée? Pourquoi? Avec un(e) partenaire, discutez de ce sujet et soyez prêt(e)s à expliquer vos raisons au reste de la classe.

 Practice more at vhlcentral.com.

ACTIVITÉS

OPTIONS

Les limitations de vitesse Speed limits are generally higher in France than in the United States. For example, speed limits are 130 km/h (about 80 mph) on **les autoroutes**, 110 km/h (about 70 mph) on **les voies** (*lanes*) **rapides**, 90 km/h (about 55 mph) on **les routes**, and 50 km/h (about 30 mph) in cities and towns.

Cultural Activity Make a color transparency of French road signs (**panneaux de signalisation/signaux routiers**), which can be reproduced from the Internet or other reference sources. Then have the class guess what the signs mean.

Le français quotidien

- Model the pronunciation of each term and have students repeat it.
- Bring in photos of the different types of vehicles from an automotive magazine and have students identify them. Ask: **Qu'est-ce que c'est? C'est un monospace?**

Portrait

- André Citroën (1878–1935) got the idea of mass producing cars when he visited Henry Ford's new Rouge River plant in Detroit. He was also a master at marketing his cars.
- Have students look at the photo of the car. Ask: **Que pensez-vous de la Citroën sur la photo? Voulez-vous en posséder une? Pourquoi?**

Le monde francophone Have students compare the information given here with driving rules in the United States. Example: **Aux États-Unis, il y a souvent des carrefours avec quatre panneaux de stop. En France, il n'y en a pas.**

2 **Expansion** For additional practice, give students these items. **7. Qu'est-ce qu'il est interdit de faire au volant dans les pays francophones d'Europe?** (utiliser un portable) **8. Dans quels lieux francophones conduit-on à gauche?** (à l'île Maurice et aux Seychelles)

3 **Suggestion** Have students bring in a photo of their favorite car to use as a visual aid during this activity. Photos can generally be found at a company's or a car dealer's website.

Section Goals

In this section, students will learn:
• the verbs **ouvrir** and **offrir**
• other verbs with the same conjugation (**couvrir**, **souffrir**, etc.)

Instructional Resources
vhlcentral.com:
Activity Pack; Lab MP3s;
SAM Answer Key; Essayez!
and Mise en pratique
answers; Lab Audioscript;
reference tools

Suggestions
• Review the conjugation of **-er** verbs.
• Write **j'ouvre, tu ouvres, il/elle ouvre** on the board. Point out that the endings are the same as **-er** verbs in the present tense.
• Follow the same procedure with **ouvrir**, but in the imperfect tense. Point out that with this tense, the verb is regular and takes **-ir** verb endings.
• Model verbs like **ouvrir** and **offrir** by asking volunteers questions. Examples: **À quelle heure la bibliothèque ouvre-t-elle? Quels services les grands magasins offrent-ils? Avez-vous souffert quand vous avez eu la varicelle** (chicken pox)?
• Tell students that **s'offrir** is typically used with a direct object to mean *to treat oneself to something.* Example: **Je m'offre une glace.**

Essayez! Give additional items such as these. **9. Qu'est-ce que je t'____ (offrir) pour ton anniversaire?** (offre) **10. Vous ____ (ouvrir) les fichiers.** (ouvrez)

Leçon 11B

11B.1

ESPACE **STRUCTURES**

The verbs *ouvrir* and *offrir*  Tutorial

Point de départ The verbs **ouvrir** (*to open*) and **offrir** (*to offer, to give as a gift*) are irregular. Although they end in **-ir**, they use the endings of regular **-er** verbs in the present tense.

Ouvrir and *offrir*		
	ouvrir	**offrir**
je/j'	ouvre	offre
tu	ouvres	offres
il/elle	ouvre	offre
nous	ouvrons	offrons
vous	ouvrez	offrez
ils/elles	ouvrent	offrent

La boutique **ouvre** à dix heures.
The shop opens at 10 o'clock.

Nous **offrons** soixante-quinze dollars.
We're offering seventy-five dollars.

• The verbs **couvrir** (*to cover*), **découvrir** (*to discover*), and **souffrir** (*to suffer*) use the same endings as **ouvrir** and **offrir**.

Elle **souffre** quand elle est chez le dentiste.
She suffers when she's at the dentist's.

Couvrez l'assiette avant de la mettre au micro-ondes.
Cover the dish before you put it in the microwave.

• The past participles of **ouvrir** and **offrir** are, respectively, **ouvert** and **offert**. Verbs like **ouvrir** and **offrir** follow this pattern.

Nous **avons découvert** un bon logiciel.
We discovered a good software program.

Il **a souffert** d'une allergie.
He suffered from an allergy.

• Verbs like **ouvrir** and **offrir** are regular in the **imparfait**.

Nous **souffrions** pendant les moments difficiles.
We suffered during the bad times.

Ils nous **offraient** de beaux cadeaux.
They used to give us nice gifts.

• The verbs **ouvrir**, **couvrir**, and **offrir** are often used reflexively.

Couvre-toi la bouche quand tu tousses.
Cover your mouth when you cough.

Le coffre ne **s'ouvre** pas!
The trunk won't open!

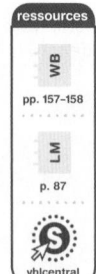

ressources
WB
pp. 157–158
LM
p. 87
vhlcentral

Essayez! Complétez les phrases avec les formes correctes du présent des verbes.

1. On _découvre_ (découvrir) beaucoup de choses quand on lit.
2. Vous _ouvrez_ (ouvrir) le livre.
3. Tu _souffres_ (souffrir) beaucoup chez le dentiste?
4. Elle _offre_ (offrir) des fleurs à ses amis.
5. Nous _offrons_ (offrir) dix mille dollars pour la voiture.
6. Les profs _couvrent_ (couvrir) les réponses.
7. J' _ouvre_ (ouvrir) le capot pour vérifier le moteur.
8. Vos parents vous _offrent_ (offrir) une voiture?

476 *quatre cent soixante-seize*

Le français vivant

À Nöel, offrez le plus beau des cadeaux.

Elle ouvre le paquet, et c'est le bonheur!

Quoi de plus beau à offrir?

Parlez-vous à cœur ouvert.

TopTel

Le français vivant
- Call on a volunteer to read the advertisement aloud.
- After pairs finish the **Questions** activity, go over the answers as a class.
- Items 5 and 6 use subjunctive forms. Supply the first person form **j'aie**, if necessary. Tell students that they will learn more about the subjunctive in units 14 and 15.

Identifiez Avez-vous trouvé des formes des verbes **ouvrir** et **offrir** dans cette publicité (*ad*)? Lesquelles (*Which ones*)? offrez, ouvre, offrir, ouvert

 Questions Posez ces questions à un(e) partenaire et répondez à tour de rôle. Answers will vary.

1. Qui offre un cadeau dans la pub? Qui reçoit (*receives*) un cadeau?
2. Quel cadeau offre-t-on?
3. Qu'est-ce que tu penses de ce cadeau?
4. D'après la publicité, comment se sent la personne qui reçoit le cadeau?
5. Quel est le plus beau cadeau qu'on t'ait (*has*) offert?
6. Quel est le plus beau cadeau que tu aies (*have*) offert à quelqu'un?
7. En général, à qui offres-tu des cadeaux, et quand?

OPTIONS

Video Play the video and have students listen for **-er** and **-ir** verbs, including verbs like **ouvrir** and **offrir**. Have them write down those they hear. Afterward, write the verbs on the board. Ask their meanings. Have students write original sentences using each verb.

Extra Practice Here are four sentences containing verbs like **ouvrir** to use as dictation. Read each twice, pausing after the second time for students to write. **1. J'ai découvert que mon frère a eu un accident! 2. Nous couvrons la piscine en hiver. 3. Mon grand-père m'offrait des bonbons après le dîner. 4. Le musée ouvre à dix heures.**

1 Suggestion Have students check their answers orally with a partner.

2 Suggestion Before assigning this activity, ask questions using **déjà**. Remind students that **déjà** is placed after the conjugated verb and before the past participle. Example: **Qui a déjà étudié la biologie à l'université?**

3 Expansion Divide the class into small groups. Have each student pick an image to present to the group as a verbal portrait. Each one should include an introductory sentence that sets the scene, a body, and a conclusion. The verbal portrait should answer the questions *who, what, where, when,* and *why* based on the image. After everyone in the group has presented an image, the group votes on which one to present to the class.

Mise en pratique

1 Mais non! Alexandra et sa copine Djamila viennent d'arriver en cours et parlent de leurs camarades. Que se disent-elles?

> **MODÈLE** Julianne souffre d'un mal de tête. (je)
> *Je souffre aussi d'un mal de tête.*

1. Sylvain ouvre son livre. (Caroline) Caroline ouvre aussi son livre.
2. Antoine souffre d'allergies. (le professeur et moi) Le professeur et moi souffrons aussi d'allergies.
3. Loïc découvre la réponse. (nous) Nous découvrons aussi la réponse.
4. Tu offres ta place à Maéva. (Théo) Théo offre aussi sa place à Maéva.
5. Je souffre beaucoup avant les examens. (nous) Nous souffrons aussi beaucoup avant les examens.
6. Vous ouvrez votre sac à dos. (Luc et Anne) Luc et Anne ouvrent aussi leur sac à dos.
7. Odile et Fatou couvrent leurs devoirs. (Lise) Lise couvre aussi ses devoirs.
8. Angèle découvre qu'elle adore les maths. (je) Je découvre aussi que j'adore les maths.

2 Je l'ai déjà fait Maya parle avec sa sœur des choses qu'elle veut faire pour organiser une fête dans leur nouvelle maison. Sophie lui dit qu'elle les a déjà faites.

> **MODÈLE** Je veux ouvrir les bouteilles.
> *Je les ai déjà ouvertes.*

1. Je veux couvrir les meubles pour les protéger. Je les ai déjà couverts.
2. Je veux ouvrir toutes les fenêtres. Je les ai déjà ouvertes.
3. Je veux découvrir le centre-ville. Je l'ai déjà découvert.
4. Je veux offrir des cadeaux aux voisins. Je leur en ai déjà offert.
5. Je veux ouvrir les nouveaux CD. Je les ai déjà ouverts.
6. Je veux couvrir les murs d'affiches. Je les ai déjà couverts.
7. Je veux découvrir ce que (*what*) nos amis vont nous offrir. Je l'ai déjà découvert.
8. Je veux offrir une fleur aux invités. Je leur en ai déjà offert une.

3 Que faisaient-ils? Qu'est-ce que ces personnages faisaient hier? Employez les verbes de la liste. Answers will vary. Sample answers provided.

| couvrir | découvrir | offrir | ouvrir | souffrir |

1. Benoît Benoît ouvrait son livre.

2. vous Vous découvriez de l'argent.

3. Thérèse Thérèse ouvrait la fenêtre.

5. tu Tu souffrais d'une grippe.

4. ils Ils offraient un cadeau.

6. je Je souffrais d'une allergie.

 Practice more at **vhlcentral.com**.

Communication

4 **Questions** Avec un(e) partenaire, posez-vous ces questions à tour de rôle. Ensuite, présentez les réponses à la classe. *Answers will vary.*

1. Qu'est-ce que tu as offert à ta mère pour la Fête des mères?

2. En quelle saison souffres-tu le plus d'allergies? Pourquoi?

3. Est-ce que tu te couvres la tête quand tu bronzes? Avec quoi?

4. Est-ce que tu ouvres la fenêtre de ta chambre quand tu dors? Pourquoi?

5. Qu'est-ce que tes amis t'ont offert pour ton dernier anniversaire?

6. Que fais-tu quand tu souffres d'une grippe?

7. As-tu découvert des sites web intéressants? Quels sites?

8. Quand tu achètes un nouveau CD, est-ce que tu l'ouvres tout de suite? Pourquoi?

5 **Une amende** Un agent de police vous arrête parce que vous n'avez pas respecté la limitation de vitesse. Vous inventez beaucoup d'excuses. Avec un(e) partenaire, créez le dialogue et utilisez ce vocabulaire. *Answers will vary.*

amende	dépasser	ouvrir
avoir	freiner	permis
un accident	freins	de conduire
circulation	se garer	pneu crevé
coffre	limitation	rentrer dans
couvrir	de vitesse	rue
découvrir	offrir	souffrir

6 **Un cadeau électronique** Vous avez de l'argent et vous voulez acheter des cadeaux à des membres de votre famille. Dites à un(e) partenaire les choses que vous voulez acheter et pourquoi. Utilisez les verbes de la liste. *Answers will vary.*

MODÈLE

Je peux acheter un jeu vidéo pour l'offrir à mon neveu.

couvrir	découvrir	offrir
ouvrir	souffrir	

7 **En panne!** Hier, vous rentriez tard avec votre frère quand votre voiture est tombée en panne sur l'autoroute. Racontez à votre partenaire ce qui s'est passé (*what happened*) avec les mots de la liste. *Answers will vary.*

capot	crevé	freins	ouvrir	roue
coffre	découvrir	moteur	phares	souffrir
couvrir	essence	offrir	pneu	station-service

4 Expansion Have pairs create two additional questions using the verbs **couvrir, découvrir, offrir, ouvrir,** and **souffrir**. Then pairs switch their questions with other pairs. Students should answer their classmates' questions in complete sentences.

5 Expansion Ask pairs to perform their conversation for the class or have them videotape it outside of class.

6 Expansion Have pairs use the sentences created in the activity to write a short conversation between two friends shopping for a gift at an electronics store. Then ask for volunteers to present their conversation to the class.

OPTIONS

Game Divide the class into two teams. Indicate one team member at a time, alternating between teams. Give a certain infinitive from the lesson (**couvrir, découvrir, offrir, ouvrir, souffrir**) and name a subject. The team member uses that subject and verb in a sentence. Give a point per correct sentence. Deduct a point for each erroneous sentence. The team with the most points at the end of play wins.

Small Groups Have small groups prepare a conversation in which two roommates borrow a third roommate's car for the weekend without asking and return it in terrible condition. Encourage groups to use vocabulary and verbs from the lesson. Give groups time to prepare and practice their skits before presenting them to the class.

11B.2

Le conditionnel  Tutorial

Point de départ The conditional expresses what you *would* do or what *would* happen under certain circumstances.

Section Goals

In this section, students will learn:
• the conditional tense
• the use of the conditional for expressing polite requests and future actions in a past tense

Instructional Resources

vhlcentral.com:
Activity Pack; Lab MP3s;
SAM Answer Key; Essayez!
and **Mise en pratique**
answers; Lab Audioscript;
reference tools

Suggestions

• The **conditionnel** is presented here before the **futur simple** since students already know the **imparfait** endings and can easily assimilate this concept.
• Read the captions of the video stills and ask volunteers to indicate the verbs in the conditional.
• After going through the conjugations, check for understanding by asking volunteers to give different forms of verbs not listed: **finir**, **rendre**, etc.

Sans réservation, nous ne mangerions pas avant minuit!

Y aurait-il une autre station-service près d'ici?

À noter

Review the **imparfait** endings you learned in **Leçon 8A**. The **conditionnel** has the same endings as the **imparfait**.

Conditional of regular verbs

	parler	réussir	attendre
je/j'	parler**ais**	réussir**ais**	attendr**ais**
tu	parler**ais**	réussir**ais**	attendr**ais**
il/elle/on	parler**ait**	réussir**ait**	attendr**ait**
nous	parler**ions**	réussir**ions**	attendr**ions**
vous	parler**iez**	réussir**iez**	attendr**iez**
ils/elles	parler**aient**	réussir**aient**	attendr**aient**

• Note that you form the conditional of **-er** and **-ir** verbs by adding the conditional endings to the infinitive. The conditional endings are the same as those of the **imparfait**. To form the conditional of **-re** verbs, drop the final **-e** and add the endings.

Boîte à outils

In English, *would* can be used instead of *used to*, to describe a past habitual action. In French, you must use the **imparfait** to express this meaning.

La vieille voiture tombait toujours en panne.
The old car would (used to) always break down.

but

Sans un bon moteur, cette voiture tomberait en panne.
Without a good engine, this car would break down.

Nous **voyagerions** cet été.	Tu ne **sortirais** pas.	Ils **attendraient** Luc.
We'd travel this summer.	*You wouldn't go out.*	*They would wait for Luc.*

• Note the conditional forms of most spelling-change **-er** verbs:

present form of je	+r	conditional forms
j'achète	achèter-	j'achèterais
je nettoie	nettoier-	je nettoierais
je paie/paye	paier-/payer-	je paierais/payerais
je m'appelle	m'appeller-	je m'appellerais

Tu te **lèverais** si tôt?	Vous **essaieriez** de vous garer.
Would you get up that early?	*You would try to park.*
Je n'**achèterais** pas cette voiture.	Il **nettoierait** le pare-brise.
I would not buy this car.	*He would clean the windshield.*

• The conditional of **-er** verbs with an **é** before the infinitive ending follows the same pattern as that of regular **-er** verbs.

Elle **répéterait** ses questions.	Elles **considéreraient** le pour et le contre.
She would repeat her questions.	*They'd consider the pros and cons.*

480 *quatre cent quatre-vingts*

- Although the conditional endings are the same for all verbs, some verbs use irregular stems.

Irregular verbs in the conditional

infinitive	stem	conditional forms
aller	ir-	j'irais
avoir	aur-	j'aurais
devoir	devr-	je devrais
envoyer	enverr-	j'enverrais
être	ser-	je serais
faire	fer-	je ferais
mourir	mourr-	je mourrais
pouvoir	pourr-	je pourrais
savoir	saur-	je saurais
venir	viendr-	je viendrais
vouloir	voudr-	je voudrais

Elles y **seraient** plus heureuses.
They'd be happier there.

Je **ferais** le plein pour toi.
I would fill the tank for you.

- The verbs **devenir**, **maintenir**, **retenir**, **revenir**, and **tenir** are patterned after **venir** in the conditional, just as they are in the present tense.

Nous **reviendrions** bientôt.
We would come back soon.

Tu **deviendrais** architecte un jour?
Would you become an architect one day?

- Use the conditional to make a polite request, soften a demand, or express what someone *could* or *should* do.

Je **voudrais** acheter une imprimante.
I would like to buy a printer.

Pourriez-vous nous dire où il est?
Could you tell us where he is?

- To express what someone at a past time thought would happen in the future, use a past tense verb before **que** and the **conditionnel** after it.

Il savait que Lucie ne **reviendrait** pas.
He knew that Lucie wouldn't come back.

Je pensais que tu **ferais** tes devoirs
I thought you'd do your homework.

- The conditional forms of **il y a**, **il faut**, and **il pleut** are, respectively, **il y aurait**, **il faudrait**, and **il pleuvrait**.

Pleuvrait-il beaucoup dans ce pays?
Would it rain a lot in that country?

Il **faudrait** apporter un parapluie.
We'd need to bring an umbrella.

À noter

The conditional is also used in *if-then* statements. You will learn more about this usage in **Leçon 13B**.

Essayez! Indiquez la forme correcte du conditionnel de ces verbes.

1. je (perdre, devoir, venir) _____ *perdrais, devrais, viendrais*
2. tu (vouloir, aller, essayer) _____ voudrais, irais, essaierais
3. Michel (dire, prendre, savoir) _____ dirait, prendrait, saurait
4. nous (préférer, nettoyer, faire) _____ préférerions, nettoierions, ferions
5. vous (être, pouvoir, avoir) _____ seriez, pourriez, auriez
6. elles (dire, espérer, amener) _____ diraient, espéreraient, amèneraient

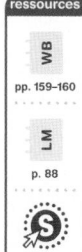

ressources

WB
pp. 159–160

LM
p. 88

vhlcentral

Suggestions
- Explain the concept of the conditional as *the future in the past*. Explain that the conditional is used to express an action that was yet to occur at some past time, and give more examples like this: **Je (ne) savais (pas) que je serais professeur de français.** Encourage students to make statements modeled on yours.
- Tell students to imagine they are shopping at the mall. Ask them what they would like to buy there. Example: **Que voudriez-vous acheter? (Je voudrais acheter _____.)** Tell students that **vouloir** in the conditional is a polite form. Emphasize how the conditional is used to make polite requests.

Essayez! Have volunteers make up stories (two or three sentences long) using each of the items.

OPTIONS

Pairs Have students take turns asking each other favors, using the conditional for courtesy. Partners respond by saying whether they will do the favor. If partners can't do it, they should make up an excuse. Example: **Pourrais-tu m'aider à faire mes devoirs ce soir? (Je suis désolé, je ne peux pas t'aider. Je dois aller chez mes parents ce soir.)**

Video Show the video again to give students more input on the use of the conditional. Stop the video where appropriate to discuss how and why the conditional was used.

ESPACE STRUCTURES

1 Suggestion Ask six volunteers to write the completed sentences on the board. Have other volunteers correct any errors.

2 Expansion Have students compose questions that would elicit the sentences from the activity as answers. Example: **Marc donnerait-il des devoirs?**

3 Suggestion Have students work in pairs on this activity.

Mise en pratique

1 **Changer de vie** Alexandre parle à son ami de ce qu'il aimerait changer dans sa vie. Complétez ses phrases avec les formes correctes du conditionnel.

MODÈLE
J' _étudierais_ (étudier) tous les week-ends.

1. Ma petite amie et moi __ferions__ (faire) des études dans la même (*same*) ville.
2. Je __vendrais__ (vendre) ma vieille voiture.
3. Nous __achèterions__ (acheter) une Porsche.
4. Je __travaillerais__ (travailler) bien.
5. Nos amis nous __rendraient__ (rendre) souvent visite.
6. Quelqu'un __nettoierait__ (nettoyer) la maison.
7. Je n' __aurais__ (avoir) pas de problèmes d'argent.
8. Ma petite ami et moi, nous __pourrions__ (pouvoir) nous retrouver tous les jours.
9. Tous mes cours __seraient__ (être) très faciles.

2 **Les professeurs** Que feraient ces personnes si (*if*) elles étaient profs de français?

MODÈLE
tu / donner / examen / difficile
Tu donnerais des examens difficiles.

1. Marc / donner / devoirs   Marc donnerait des devoirs.
2. vous / répondre / à / questions / étudiants   Vous répondriez aux questions des étudiants.
3. nous / permettre / à / étudiants / de / manger / en classe   Nous permettrions aux étudiants de manger en classe.
4. tu / parler / français / tout le temps   Tu parlerais français tout le temps.
5. tes parents / boire / café / classe   Tes parents boiraient du café en classe.
6. nous / montrer / films / français   Nous montrerions des films français.
7. je / enseigner / chansons françaises / étudiants   J'enseignerais des chansons françaises aux étudiants.
8. Guillaume et Robert / être / gentil / avec / étudiants   Guillaume et Robert seraient gentils avec les étudiants.

3 **Sur une île** Vous découvrez une île (*island*) et vous y emmenez un groupe de personnes et leurs familles. Assemblez les éléments des colonnes pour faire des phrases avec le conditionnel. Quels rôles joueraient ces personnes?   Answers will vary.

MODÈLE
Le professeur enseignerait les mathématiques aux enfants.

A	B	C
agent de police	construire	cartes
agent de voyages	découvrir	disputes
chauffeur	enseigner	enfants
dentiste	s'occuper de	logement
hôtelier/hôtelière	organiser	nourriture
infirmier/infirmière	parler	problèmes
mécanicien(ne)	préparer	réunions
professeur	servir	transports
serveur/serveuse	trouver	urgences
?	?	?

 Practice more at **vhlcentral.com**.

Communication

4 **Une grosse fortune** Avec un(e) partenaire, parlez de la façon dont (*the way in which*) vous dépenseriez l'argent si quelqu'un vous laissait une grosse fortune. Posez-vous ces questions à tour de rôle. Answers will vary.

1. Partirais-tu en voyage? Où irais-tu?
2. Quelle profession choisirais-tu?
3. Où habiterais-tu?
4. Qu'est-ce que tu achèterais? À tes amis? À ta famille?
5. Donnerais-tu de l'argent à des œuvres de charité (*charities*)? Auxquelles (*To which ones*)?
6. Qu'est-ce qui changerait dans ta vie quotidienne (*daily*)?

5 **Sans ça...** Par groupes de trois, dites ce qui (*what*) changerait dans le monde sans ces choses. Answers will vary.

> **MODÈLE** sans écoles?
> Les étudiants n'apprendraient pas.

- sans voitures?
- sans ordinateurs?
- sans télévisions?
- sans avions?
- sans téléphones?
- ?

6 **Le tour de la France** Vous aimeriez faire le tour de la France avec un(e) partenaire. Regardez la carte et discutez de l'itinéraire. Où commenceriez-vous? Que visiteriez-vous? Utilisez ces idées et trouvez-en d'autres. Answers will vary.

> **MODÈLE**
> *Nous commencerions à Paris.*

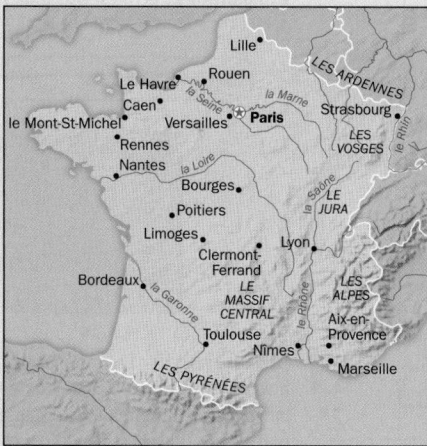

- les plages de la Côte d'Azur
- les randonnées dans le Centre
- le ski dans les Alpes
- les musées à Paris
- les châteaux (*castles*) de la Loire

Sidebar

4 **Expansion** Have volunteers use the third person to present their partner's responses to the questions.

5 **Suggestion** Before assigning the activity, have the class brainstorm other items similar to those in the activity. Ask a volunteer to write these items on the board.

6 **Expansion** Have pairs present their itinerary to the class. Ask volunteers to come up with questions for each pair.

Options

Game To prepare for a relay race, line students up in teams of six several feet from the board. Write an infinitive on the board and call out **Commencez!** The first team members go to the board and write the **je** form of the verb in the conditional, then pass the chalk to the next team member, who writes the **tu** form, and so on. The team that finishes first and has all the forms correct wins the round.

Extra Practice Ask students what they would or would not do over the next six months if they could do anything they wanted and money and time were no object. Example: **Je ferais le tour du monde.** Call on volunteers to read their sentences, and then ask the class comprehension questions about what was said. Example: **Qu'est-ce que Paula ferait?**

Révision

Instructional Resources
vhlcentral.com:
*Activity Pack (**Feuilles d'activités**; Info Gap Activities);*
Testing Program; Testing Program MP3s; reference tools

1 Suggestion Have two volunteers act out the **modèle**. Then distribute the **Feuilles d'activités** found in the Activity Pack on the Supersite.

1 Expansion Have pairs come up with additional questions related to cars and driving that they could ask their classmates.

2 Suggestion Have students compare their sentences with those of other groups. Have them vote on the most creative sentence for each image.

3 Expansion Have students reverse roles and imagine that they are going to run a marathon. Have them write a letter to a personal trainer asking five questions about what they should do to get ready for the event. Remind them to use the conditional to phrase their questions politely.

4 Expansion Invite pairs to perform their conversation for the class.

5 Expansion Using magazine and newspaper ads, have pairs invent slogans that advertise an electronic device.

6 Suggestion Divide the class into pairs and distribute the Info Gap Handouts found in the Activity Pack on the Supersite. Give students ten minutes to complete the activity.

---

1 **Dans ma famille…** Votre professeur va vous donner une feuille d'activités. Circulez dans la classe pour interviewer un(e) camarade différent(e) pour chaque question. Mentionnez un détail supplémentaire dans vos réponses. Answers will vary.

MODÈLE

Étudiant(e) 1: *Qui, dans ta famille, a peur de conduire?*
Étudiant(e) 2: *Mon oncle Olivier a peur de conduire. Il a eu trop d'accidents.*

Qui, dans ta famille, …	Noms
1. a peur de conduire?	mon oncle Olivier
2. aime l'odeur de l'essence?	
3. n'aime pas conduire vite?	
4. n'a jamais eu d'accident?	
5. ne dépasse jamais la limitation de vitesse?	
6. n'a pas son permis de conduire?	
7. ne sait pas faire le plein?	
8. sait vérifier l'huile?	

2 **Des explications** Avec un(e) partenaire, observez ces personnages et inventez une phrase au conditionnel pour décrire leur situation. Answers will vary.

MODÈLE

Elle ferait du jogging, mais elle s'est foulé la cheville.

1.

2.

3.

4.

3 **Le marathon** Votre meilleur(e) ami(e) va participer à un marathon dans six mois et il/elle veut savoir ce qu'il/elle (*what he/she*) devrait faire pour s'entraîner (*train*). Avec un(e) partenaire, écrivez un e-mail à votre ami(e) pour dire ce que vous feriez à sa place pour vous préparer. Utilisez le conditionnel. Answers will vary.

4 **La leçon de conduite** Vous êtes moniteur de conduite (*driving instructor*) et c'est la première leçon de conduite que prend votre partenaire. Inventez une scène où il/elle découvre la voiture et où vous lui expliquez la fonction des différentes commandes. Utilisez le conditionnel dans votre dialogue. Answers will vary.

MODÈLE

Étudiant(e) 1: *J'utiliserais ce bouton pour ouvrir le capot?*
Étudiant(e) 2: *Non. Tu utiliserais ce bouton pour ouvrir le coffre.*

5 **Les slogans** Avec un(e) partenaire, utilisez ces verbes dans des slogans pour vendre cette voiture. Soyez prêts à voter pour les meilleurs slogans de la classe. Answers will vary.

MODÈLE

Étudiant(e) 1: *Qu'est-ce que tu penses de: «Offrez-vous l'évasion»?*
Étudiant(e) 2: *Ce n'est pas mal, mais j'aime bien aussi: «Le monde vous découvre.»*

couvrir	découvrir	offrir	ouvrir	souffrir

6 **Mots-croisés** Votre professeur va vous donner, à vous et à votre partenaire, deux grilles de mots croisés (*crossword*) incomplètes. Attention! Ne regardez pas la feuille de votre partenaire. Utilisez le conditionnel dans vos définitions.

MODÈLE

Étudiant(e) 1: *Horizontalement, le numéro 1, tu les allumerais pour conduire la nuit.*
Étudiant(e) 2: *Les phares!*

O P T I O N S

Extra Practice Ask students to work in groups of five. One person in each group will play the role of a campus radio talk show host along the lines of "Dear Abby". The other four students will take turns calling in with various problems, and the host will give them advice. Students can perform their skits in front of the class or record it and play the "show" for the class.

Game Divide the class into several groups. Tell them to imagine that it is the year 2050. Each team has to write as many phrases as they can using the conditional to describe what the world would be like. Set a time limit for the game. At the end of the allotted time, have each team read their phrases. The team with the most grammatically correct phrases at the end of the game wins.

À l'écoute

NATIONAL communication STANDARDS

STRATÉGIE

Guessing the meaning of words through context

When you hear an unfamiliar word, you can often guess its meaning by listening to the words and phrases around it.

To practice this strategy, you will listen to a paragraph. Jot down the unfamiliar words that you hear. Then, listen to the paragraph again and jot down the word or words that are the most useful clues to the meaning of each unfamiliar word.

Préparation

Regardez la photo. Que fait la policière? Et l'homme, que fait-il? Où sont-ils? Que se passe-t-il, d'après vous?

À vous d'écouter

Écoutez la conversation entre la policière et l'homme et utilisez le contexte pour vous aider à comprendre les mots et expressions de la colonne A. Trouvez leur équivalent dans la colonne B.

A	B
__d__ 1. la moto	a. un document qui indique une infraction
__f__ 2. la loi	b. un signal pour indiquer dans quelle direction on va aller
__a__ 3. une contravention	
__c__ 4. rouler	c. conduire une voiture
__b__ 5. le clignotant	d. véhicule à deux roues
__e__ 6. être prudent	e. faire attention
	f. quelque chose qu'il faut respecter

 Practice more at **vhlcentral.com**.

Compréhension

Vrai ou faux? Indiquez si les phrases sont **vraies** ou **fausses**. Corrigez les phrases fausses.

1. L'homme a oublié son permis de conduire à l'aéroport.
   Faux. Il va chercher son fils à l'aéroport.

2. L'homme roulait trop vite.
   Vrai.

3. La vitesse est limitée à 150 km/h sur cette route.
   Faux. Elle est limitée à 130.

4. L'homme a dépassé un camion rouge.
   Faux. Il a dépassé une grosse moto.

5. L'agent de police n'accepte pas les excuses de l'homme.
   Vrai.

6. L'agent de police donne une contravention à l'homme.
   Vrai.

7. L'homme préfère payer l'amende tout de suite.
   Faux. Il pense qu'il ne va pas pouvoir payer l'amende.

8. L'agent de police demande à l'homme de faire réparer son rétroviseur avant de repartir.
   Faux. Elle lui demande de bien regarder dans son rétroviseur avant de repartir.

Racontez Choisissez un sujet et écrivez un paragraphe.

1. Avez-vous déjà eu une contravention (*ticket*)? Quand? Où? Que faisiez-vous? Si vous n'avez jamais (*never*) eu de contravention, parlez d'une personne que vous connaissez qui en a déjà eu une.

2. Avez-vous déjà eu de gros problèmes de voiture ou une panne? Quand? Où? Quel était le problème? Êtes-vous allé(e) chez un mécanicien? Qu'a-t-il fait? Est-ce que ça a coûté cher?

quatre cent quatre-vingt-cinq **485**

Section Goals

In this section, students will:
- learn to guess the meaning of words from context
- listen to a paragraph and jot down unfamiliar words plus clues to their meaning
- listen to a conversation and complete several activities

Instructional Resources
vhlcentral.com: Textbook MP3s; Textbook Audioscript; reference tools

Stratégie
Audioscript Bonjour, Monsieur. J'ai examiné votre voiture. Suite à l'accident, votre voiture a plusieurs problèmes. En particulier, la portière côté passager ne ferme pas et on ne peut plus remonter la vitre. J'ai regardé sous le capot et le moteur est en bon état. Je vais réparer la voiture et vous pouvez venir la chercher demain.

Préparation Have students look at the photo and describe what they see. Then have them guess what the police officer and the driver are talking about.

À vous d'écouter
Audioscript L'AGENT DE POLICE: Bonjour, Monsieur. Votre permis de conduire, s'il vous plaît.
L'HOMME: Oui, Madame. Voilà. Euh... Quel est le problème?
AP: Vous rouliez à 150 kilomètres/heure quand vous avez dépassé la grosse moto et la limitation de vitesse sur cette autoroute est à 130, Monsieur.
H: Vous êtes sûre que j'allais si vite?
AP: Sûre et certaine, Monsieur!
H: Euh... Je suis désolé. C'est que... je suis très, très en retard. Je dois aller chercher mon fils à l'aéroport à vingt heures et...
AP: Ce n'est pas une raison, Monsieur. Vous devez respecter la limitation de vitesse comme tout le monde...
H: Oui, je sais. Je suis vraiment désolé. Vous ne pouvez pas...
AP: Je dois vous donner une contravention.
H: Oh non! Je vous en prie... Je n'ai vraiment pas beaucoup d'argent en ce moment. Je ne sais pas comment je vais pouvoir payer une amende pareille!

AP: Désolée, Monsieur, mais c'est la loi. Tenez. Et roulez moins vite!
H: Oui, Madame.
AP: Et n'oubliez pas d'attacher votre ceinture de sécurité, de mettre votre clignotant et de bien regarder dans votre rétroviseur avant de repartir.

H: Oui, Madame. Au revoir.
AP: Au revoir, Monsieur, et soyez prudent.

SAVOIR-FAIRE

NATIONAL connections cultures STANDARDS

Panorama

Section Goals

In this section, students will read historical and cultural information about **Occitanie**.

Instructional Resources
vhlcentral.com: Digital Image Bank; SAM Answer Key; reference tools

Carte de l'Occitanie

- Have students look at the map or use the **Panorama** map from the Digital Image Bank. Ask volunteers to read aloud the names of cities and geographical features. Model French pronunciation as necessary.
- Have students identify the locations of the places in the photos.

La région en chiffres

- Point out the region's logo. Tell students that Toulouse is the region's administrative center.
- Have volunteers read the sections aloud. After each section, ask questions about the content.
- Ask students to share any information they might know about the **Personnes célèbres**.

Incroyable mais vrai! The aqueduct was closed after several hundred years of use due to buildup of calcium deposits and lack of maintenance. The calcium buildup still can be seen on the top tier of the Pont du Gard.

L'Occitanie

La région en chiffres

Occitanie

▶ **Superficie:** *72.724 km²*

▶ **Population:** *5.730.753*

▶ **Industries principales:** *aéronautique, agriculture, recherches°*

▶ **Villes principales:** *Toulouse, Montpellier, Nîmes, Perpignan*

Créée en 2016, la région Occitanie regroupe les anciennes régions Languedoc-Roussillon et Midi-Pyrénées. La région accueille° 240.000 étudiants français et internationaux chaque année, avec des universités renommées°. La Faculté de Médecine de Montpellier, créée au 12ᵉ siècle, est la plus ancienne de France.

Personnes célèbres

▶ **Jean Jaurès,** *homme politique (1859–1914)*

▶ **Henri de Toulouse-Lautrec,** *peintre et lithographe (1864–1901)*

▶ **Georges Brassens,** *chanteur (1921–1981)*

▶ **Paul Valéry,** *poète (1871–1945)*

recherches *research* **accueille** *welcomes* **renommées** *renowned*
pont *bridge* **aqueduc** *aqueduct* **jusqu'à** *to* **pèse** *weighs*
hauteur *height* **inscrit** *registered* **patrimoine mondial** *world heritage*

les gorges de l'Hérault

LA FRANCE

L'OCÉAN ATLANTIQUE

la Tarn
Albi
Nîmes
OCCITANIE
Toulouse
LES CÉVENNES
Montpelli
Béziers
la Garonne
LES PYRÉNÉES
LA MER MÉDITERRA
Perpignan
ANDORRE
L'ESPAGNE

0 ——— 80 miles
0 ——— 80 kilomètres

le Capitole

la cité de Carcassonn

Incroyable mais vrai!

Le Pont° du Gard est un monument romain qui date du 1ᵉʳ siècle. Il fait partie d'un aqueduc° de 50 kilomètres qui apportait l'eau de la ville d'Uzès jusqu'à° Nîmes. Le pont pèse° 50.400 tonnes, mesure 360 mètres de long et a 50 mètres de hauteur°. C'est le pont romain le plus haut du monde! En 1985, le site a été inscrit° au patrimoine mondial° de l'UNESCO.

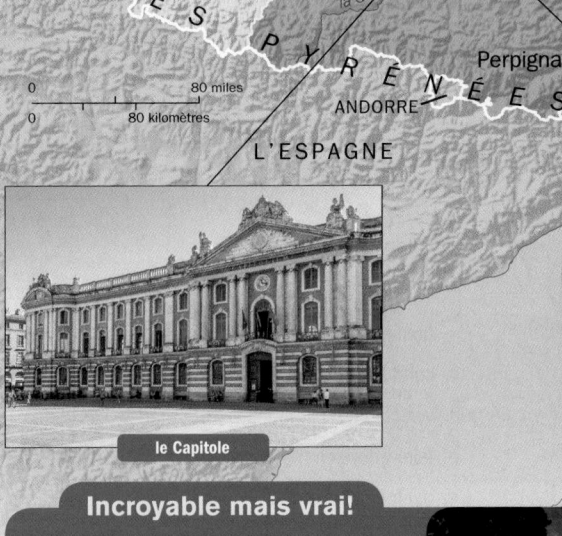

OPTIONS

Personnes célèbres **Jean Jaurès** was a leader of the French socialist movement. He was a teacher in Albi and at the University of Toulouse, and served three terms in the Chamber of Deputies. **Henri de Toulouse-Lautrec** was born in Albi. He established lithography as a major art form with his vivid posters depicting Parisian nightlife in Montmartre. **Georges Brassens** was a poetic songwriter and performer who used his lyrics to address social issues. **Paul Valéry** was born in the small port town of Sète. He studied in nearby Montpellier, whose Université Paul-Valéry, for the study of arts, letters, languages, and social and human sciences, was named in his honor. He was elected to the Académie française in 1925.

La gastronomie

Le cassoulet

Le cassoulet est une spécialité du Sud-Ouest° de la France. C'est un plat populaire, préparé à l'origine dans une «cassole°». Les ingrédients varient, mais en général cette spécialité est composée de haricots blancs, de viande de porc et de canard, de saucisses, de tomates, d'ail et d'herbes. Le cassoulet a ses origines à Castelnaudary, une ville qui se trouve entre Toulouse et Carcassonne. Les trois villes ont chacune° leur propre° version du cassoulet.

Les monuments

Les arènes de Nîmes

Inspirées du Colisée de Rome, les arènes° de Nîmes datent de la fin du premier siècle. C'est l'amphithéâtre le plus grand de France et le mieux conservé de l'ère° romaine. Les spectacles de gladiateurs, d'autrefois° appréciés par plus de 20.000 spectateurs, sont aujourd'hui remplacés° par des corridas° et des spectacles musicaux. Chaque année, la ville de Nîmes accueille plus de 500.000 visiteurs.

L'architecture

Les bastides

Les bastides° sont plus de 300 villes créées en Occitanie au 13e et 14e siècles par les comtes° de Toulouse et les rois° de France. Elles sont composées de groupes de maisons et de rues aux angles droites organisées autour d'°une place centrale. Les bastides ont été construites pour des raisons politiques, économiques et de sécurité. La plus ancienne bastide est la ville de Montauban, construite en 1144, et la plus récente est la ville de Revel, construite en 1342.

Les traditions

La langue d'Oc

La langue d'Oc (l'occitan) est une langue romane° développée dans le sud de la France. Cette langue a donné son nom à la région: Occitanie. La poésie lyrique occitane et la philosophie des troubadours° du Moyen Âge° influencent les valeurs° culturelles et intellectuelles européennes. Il existe plusieurs dialectes de l'occitan. «Los cats fan pas de chins» (les chats ne font pas des chiens) et «la bornicarié porta pas pa a casa» (la beauté n'apporte pas de pain à la maison) sont deux proverbes occitans connus.

Qu'est-ce que vous avez appris? Répondez aux questions par des phrases complètes.

1. Qui était peintre et lithographe d'origine occitane?
   Henri de Toulouse-Lautrec était peintre et lithographe d'origine occitane.
2. De quel siècle date le Pont du Gard?
   Le Pont du Gard date du 1er siècle.
3. Combien pèse le Pont du Gard?
   Le Pont du Gard pèse 50.400 tonnes.
4. Quelles sont les trois villes connues pour le cassoulet?
   Les trois villes connues pour le cassoulet sont Castelnaudary, Toulouse et Carcassonne.
5. Quels ingrédients utilise-t-on pour le cassoulet?
   On utilise des haricots blancs, de la viande, des saucisses, des tomates, de l'ail et des herbes.
6. De quand datent les arènes de Nîmes?
   Les arènes de Nîmes datent de la fin du 1er siècle.
7. Combien de visiteurs la ville de Nîmes accueille-t-elle chaque année?
   La ville de Nîmes accueille plus de 500.000 visiteurs chaque année.
8. Combien de bastides y a-t-il en Occitanie?
   Il y a plus de 300 bastides en Occitanie.
9. Qui a construit les bastides?
   Les comtes de Toulouse et les rois de France ont construit les bastides.
10. Qu'est-ce qui influence les valeurs culturelles et intellectuelles européennes? Ce sont la poésie occitane et la philosophie des troubadours du Moyen Âge.

Sur Internet

Go to **vhlcentral.com** to find more cultural information related to this **Panorama**.

1. Vous savez que Montauban et Revel sont deux bastides. Trouvez trois autres bastides en Occitanie et citez-en le nom et les dates de construction.

2. Cherchez plus d'informations sur le Pont du Gard et son aqueduc.

3. Cherchez plus d'informations sur Henri de Toulouse-Lautrec. Avez-vous déjà vu quelques-unes de ses peintures? Où?

ressources

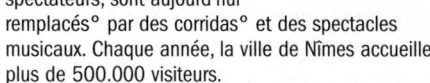

WB
pp. 161–162 | vhlcentral

Sud-Ouest Southwest **cassole** pottery dish **chacune** each **propre** own **arènes** amphitheater **ère** era **autrefois** long ago **remplacés** replaced **corridas** bullfights **bastides** fortified towns **comtes** counts **rois** kings **autour d'** around **langue romane** Romance language **troubadours** minstrels **Moyen Âge** Middle Ages **valeurs** values

Le cassoulet
- The differences in varieties of **cassoulet** occur primarily in the types of meat and beans used.
- The **Grande Confrérie du Cassoulet** defends the quality and reputation of **cassoulet** in Castelnaudary. Its members conduct surprise taste tests of local chefs' **cassoulets**. The **Académie Universelle du Cassoulet** promotes the dish and its cultural heritage.
- Ask students to name some regional dishes in their country. Also ask if they know of a dish similar to **cassoulet**.

Les arènes de Nîmes
- The amphitheater has always remained in use. At one time, residences were built within the arena, and during another period it was used as a fortress and refuge. In 1909, it was restored to its original design and is used today as an arena for entertainment.
- Have students compare today's amphitheaters or arenas to those of the Romans.

Les bastides
- One of the most famous and most visited **bastides** is the **cité de Carcassonne**.
- The word **bastide** originally referred to a construction of some importance. In the 13th century, in Southwest France, the word came to mean a new town with a new population.

La langue d'Oc
La langue d'Oc is spoken by over a million people in the south of France. Although the Occitan dialects have been influenced by modern French, they still strongly resemble dialects of the Middle Ages in which the phonology and grammar are more closely related to Spanish.

OPTIONS

La langue d'Oc The troubadours of southern France were traveling poet-musicians. They wrote and performed courtly love poems or songs for the ladies of the courts in the Occitan dialect Provençal. Eleanor of Aquitaine, a patron of troubadours, used her influence to introduce Provençal poetry at the courts in northern France. This type of poetry thrived in the 12th and 13th centuries and had a great influence on later lyric poetry.

Cultural Activity Have students work in groups of three to make a list of the political, economic, and security reasons for building **bastides**. Circulate to provide support as needed. Write each group's reasons on the board and discuss as a class.

Section Goals

In this section, students will:
• learn to recognize the purpose of a text
• read some cartoons and jokes

Stratégie Tell students that recognizing the writer's purpose will help them understand an unfamiliar text.

Examinez le texte Students should infer that the illustrations are cartoons, the short texts are jokes, the writer's purpose is to make people laugh or to make fun of something or someone, and the language is colloquial.

À propos de l'auteur After reading the text, ask students these comprehension questions.
1. D'où vient Lévy? (Québec)
2. À quel âge a-t-elle commencé à dessiner? (à trois ans)
3. Qui l'a encouragée à être artiste? (son père)
4. Quels sont les sujets de ses dessins humoristiques? (la vie de tous les jours, le travail, les animaux et la politique)

Lecture Audio: Reading

Les Technoblagues

Avant la lecture

STRATÉGIE

Recognizing the purpose of a text

When you are faced with an unfamiliar text, it is important to determine the writer's purpose. If you are reading an editorial in a newspaper, for example, you know that the journalist's objective is to persuade you of his or her point of view. Identifying the purpose of a text will help you better comprehend its meaning.

Examinez le texte

Examinez les illustrations. Quel est le genre de ce texte? Décrivez ce qu'il y a dans chaque illustration. Puis, regardez les trois textes courts. Quel est le genre de ces textes? Quel est leur but (*purpose*)? D'après vous, quel genre de vocabulaire allez-vous trouver dans ces textes?

À propos de l'auteur
Renée Lévy

Renée Lévy est une artiste québécoise. Son père, artiste lui aussi, lui a expliqué les principes du dessin et l'a encouragée à dessiner. Au lycée, Renée Lévy amusait ses camarades de classe avec ses caricatures de professeurs. Ses dessins humoristiques traitent de° nombreux sujets, comme la vie de tous les jours, le travail, les animaux et la politique. On peut voir ses caricatures et ses dessins humoristiques dans plusieurs publications et sur son site Internet: http://www.reneelevy.com. Renée Lévy est l'auteur des deux dessins que vous allez voir°.

Dessin 1

C'EST UN LECTEUR DE MP3, DE CD ET DE DVD. C'EST AUSSI UN TÉLÉPHONE, UN APPAREIL PHOTO ET UN ORDINATEUR. IL PEUT NUMÉRISER°, TÉLÉCOPIER° ET IMPRIMER.

IL VERROUILLE° MON AUTO, ALLUME MON FOUR ET MESURE MON DIABÈTE. IL ME SERT DE BROSSE À DENTS, D'ASPIRATEUR ET DE RASOIR.

IL M'INDIQUE AUSSI LE MAGASIN DE BATTERIES LE PLUS PROCHE°!

BATTERIES BATTERIES BATTERIES

© www.reneelevy.c

Blague 1

Dans un magasin d'ordinateurs, un père se plaint° du manque d'intérêt° de son fils pour le sport. «Il passe son temps devant son écran, avec ses jeux vidéo», explique le père découragé à l'employé. «Tenez, l'autre jour, je lui ai proposé un match de tennis. Savez-vous ce que mon fils m'a répondu? "Quand tu veux, papa, je vais chercher la disquette."»

traitent de *deal with* **voir** *see*

OPTIONS

Language Notes Point out that several words in the cartoons are specific to **Québécois** French. In the first cartoon, the word **batterie(s)** is used for *battery*, instead of **pile(s)**. In the second cartoon, **V.U.S.** is used for *SUV*, instead of **4x4 (quatre-quatre)**.

Pairs Have students work in pairs. Tell them to go through the cartoons and jokes, and make a list of all the words they can find in the text related to technology. Then have them get together with another pair and verify their answers.

Blague 2

La maîtresse°, absente de sa classe pendant dix minutes, y retourne et entend un véritable vacarme°. «Quand je suis partie, dit-elle, sévèrement, je vous ai interdit° de bavarder entre vous.» «Mais, dit un élève, on ne s'est pas adressé la parole°. Seulement, pour s'occuper, on a tous sorti nos portables et on a passé un coup de fil° à nos parents.»

Dessin 2

L'ESSENCE COÛTE TRÈS CHER. JE REMPLACE LE MOTEUR DE MON V.U.S° ...

PAR LE MOTEUR ÉLECTRIQUE DE MA MACHINE À COUDRE°!

SAUF°QU'IL ME FAUDRA° UN PLUS LONG FIL° ...

www.reneelévy.com

Blague 3

Un homme vient d'acheter une nouvelle voiture, mais il est obligé de la laisser dans la rue la nuit. Comme il sait que les voleurs° d'autoradios° n'hésitent pas à fracturer° les portières, il met sur son pare-brise la note suivante: IL N'Y A PAS DE RADIO DANS CETTE VOITURE. Le jour d'après, plus de° voiture. À la place où elle se trouvait, il y a seulement la note sur laquelle° on a écrit: *Ce n'est pas grave, on en fera mettre une°.*

numériser *scan* **télécopier** *fax* **verrouille** *locks* **le plus proche** *the closest* **se plaint** *complains* **manque d'intérêt** *lack of interest* **maîtresse** *school teacher* **vacarme** *racket* **interdit** *forbade* **on ne s'est pas adressé la parole** *we didn't speak to each other* **a passé un coup de fil** *made a call* **V.U.S.** *S.U.V.* **machine à coudre** *sewing machine* **sauf** *except* **il me faudra** *I will need* **fil** *cord* **voleurs** *thieves* **autoradios** *car radios* **fracturer** *break* **plus de** *no more* **sur laquelle** *on which* **on en fera mettre une** *we'll have one installed*

Après la lecture

🔗 **Répondez** Répondez aux questions par des phrases complètes.

1. Quelles sont trois des fonctions de l'appareil du **dessin 1**?
   Answers will vary. Possible answer: C'est un lecteur de MP3, un téléphone et un aspirateur.

2. De quoi l'appareil du **dessin 1** a-t-il beaucoup besoin?
   L'appareil a besoin de beaucoup de batteries.

3. Pour jouer au tennis, on a besoin d'une raquette. Dans la **blague 1**, quel mot (*word*) le garçon utilise-t-il au lieu de (*instead of*) «raquette»?
   Il utilise le mot «disquette».

4. Dans la **blague 1**, pourquoi le père est-il découragé?
   Il est découragé parce que son fils ne s'intéresse pas au sport et passe son temps devant son écran d'ordinateur, avec ses jeux vidéo.

5. Dans la **blague 2**, qu'est-ce que la maîtresse a demandé aux élèves?
   Elle a demandé aux élèves de ne pas bavarder entre eux.

6. Qu'ont fait les élèves de la **blague 2** quand la maîtresse est partie?
   Ils ont téléphoné à leurs parents avec leur portable.

7. Pourquoi faut-il remplacer le moteur du V.U.S. dans le **dessin 2**?
   Il faut le remplacer parce que l'essence coûte très cher.

8. De quoi le personnage a-t-il besoin après dans le **dessin 2**?
   Il a besoin d'un fil plus long.

9. Dans la **blague 3**, qu'est-ce que l'homme écrit sur la note qu'il met sur le pare-brise de sa voiture? Pourquoi?
   Il écrit qu'il n'y a pas de radio dans sa voiture. Il pense que les voleurs d'autoradios ne vont pas fracturer les portières s'il n'y a pas de radio dans la voiture.

10. À la fin de la **blague 3**, qu'ont pris les voleurs? Que vont-ils faire?
    Ils ont pris la voiture et vont faire installer un autoradio.

Des inventions L'appareil du **dessin 1** a beaucoup de fonctions. D'après vous, quelle invention de la liste est la plus utile et pourquoi? Soyez prêt à expliquer votre décision à la classe.

appareil photo	lecteur CD
aspirateur	lecteur DVD
fax	lecteur MP3
imprimante	téléphone

Inventez Électropuissance, une compagnie d'équipement électronique, vous demande d'inventer l'appareil idéal pour la vie de tous les jours. Dites comment votre invention va vous aider à la maison, à l'école, dans la voiture, en voyage et pour rester en bonne santé.

Répondez
- Go over the answers with the class.
- Ask various students: **À votre avis, quelle blague est la plus drôle? Quel dessin est le plus drôle? Pourquoi?** Then take a quick poll to find out which cartoon or joke the class considers the funniest. Tally the results on the board.

Des inventions
- Give students a few minutes to choose an invention and jot down their reasons before discussing them.
- For each invention listed, ask: **Combien d'étudiants ont choisi _____? Pourquoi?**

Inventez
- If time is limited, you may want to assign this activity as written homework. Then have volunteers present their devices during the next class period. Encourage students to make a drawing of their device so the class can see what it looks like.
- Have the class vote on the most useful invention.

O P T I O N S

Pairs Have students work in pairs. Tell them to create a cartoon or write a joke similar to the ones in this reading. They should brainstorm a list of topics first. You might want to suggest that they be related to technology. Then have students present their cartoons or jokes to the class. Have the class vote on the most humorous cartoon and joke.

Cultural Activity Have students go to Renée Lévy's web site to view more of her work. Tell them to find out what other types of artwork she creates, decide which style they prefer, and explain their reasons. Alternatively, you can have them find another cartoon about technology to bring in and share with the class.

Section Goals

In this section, students will:

- learn to make a list of key words before writing
- write a composition about their past and present communication habits

Stratégie Explain that having a list of key words will allow students to maintain their writing flow rather than stopping every few minutes to try and think of a specific word to use.

Thème Tell students to answer the questions first. Then they should make a list of people they communicate with regularly and the means they use to communicate before they begin writing their compositions.

Écriture

STRATÉGIE

Listing key words

Once you have determined the purpose for a piece of writing and identified your audience, it is helpful to make a list of key words you can use while writing. If you were to write a description of your campus, for example, you would probably need a list of prepositions that describe location, such as **devant**, **à côté de**, and **derrière**. Likewise, a list of descriptive adjectives would be useful if you were writing about the people and places of your childhood.

By preparing a list of potential words ahead of time, you will find it easier to avoid using the dictionary while writing your first draft. You will probably also learn a few new words in French while preparing your list of key words.

Listing useful vocabulary is also a valuable organizational strategy since the act of brainstorming key words will help you form ideas about your topic. In addition, a list of key words can help you avoid redundancy when you write.

If you were going to write a composition about your communication habits with your friends, what words would be the most helpful to you? Jot a few of them down and compare your list with a partner's. Did you choose the same words? Would you choose any different or additional words, based on what your partner wrote?

_____

_____

_____

_____

_____

_____

_____

_____

∾ Thème

Écrire une dissertation

Avant l'écriture

1. Vous allez écrire une dissertation pour décrire vos préférences et vos habitudes en ce qui concerne (*regarding*) les moyens (*means*) de communication d'hier et d'aujourd'hui.

2. D'abord, répondez en quelques mots à ces questions pour vous faire une idée de ce que (*what*) doit inclure votre dissertation.

   - Quel est votre moyen de communication préféré (e-mail, téléphone, lettre, ...)? Pourquoi?

   - En général, comment communiquez-vous avec les gens que vous connaissez? Pourquoi? Avez-vous toujours communiqué avec eux de cette manière (*in this way*)?

   - Communiquez-vous avec tout le monde de la même manière ou cela dépend-il des personnes? Par exemple, restez-vous en contact avec vos grands-parents de la même manière qu'avec votre professeur de français? Expliquez.

   - Comment restez-vous en contact avec les membres de votre famille? Et avec vos amis et vos camarades de classe?

   - Communiquez-vous avec certaines personnes tous les jours? Avec qui? Comment?

OPTIONS

Stratégie Encourage students to rely primarily on known vocabulary when preparing their lists. They should consult a dictionary only if they need a word that is central to their topic and they can't think of it on their own.

Review other strategies for creating a list of useful vocabulary.
- Two or more students can work together to brainstorm a list of words.
- Students can list antonyms for key words related to the topic.
- If necessary, students can look up key words in a bilingual dictionary or a thesaurus and review the entries for related words and synonyms.

3. Ensuite, complétez ce tableau pour faire une liste des personnes avec qui vous communiquez régulièrement, et pour donner le moyen de communication que vous avez utilisé dans le passé et que vous utilisez aujourd'hui. Utilisez aussi votre liste de mots-clés comme point de départ pour votre dissertation.

Personnes	Moyen de communication du passé	Moyen de communication d'aujourd'hui
Personne 1		
Personne 2		
Personne 3		
Personne 4		
Personne 5		

Écriture

1. Servez-vous de la liste de mots-clés que vous avez créée, de vos réponses aux questions et du tableau pour écrire votre dissertation. Utilisez le vocabulaire et la grammaire de l'unité.

2. N'oubliez pas d'inclure ces informations:

- Toutes les personnes avec qui vous communiquez souvent

- Les moyens de communications que vous utilisiez avant

- Les moyens de communications que vous utilisez maintenant

- La raison pour laquelle vous avez changé de moyen de communication

Après l'écriture

1. Échangez votre dissertation avec celle (*the one*) d'un(e) partenaire. Répondez à ces questions pour commenter son travail.

- Votre partenaire a-t-il/elle inclu toutes les personnes citées dans le tableau?

- A-t-il/elle mentionné tous les moyens de communications qu'il/elle utilisait avant?

- A-t-il/elle mentionné tous les moyens de communications qu'il/elle utilise maintenant?

- A-t-il/elle mentionné la raison pour laquelle il/elle a changé de moyen de communication?

- A-t-il/elle utilisé le vocabulaire et la grammaire de l'unité?

- Quel(s) détail(s) ajouteriez-vous (*would you add*)? Quel(s) détail(s) enlèveriez-vous (*would you delete*)? Quel(s) autre(s) commentaire(s) avez-vous pour votre partenaire?

2. Corrigez votre dissertation d'après (*according to*) les commentaires de votre partenaire. Relisez votre travail pour éliminer ces problèmes:

- des fautes (*errors*) d'orthographe

- des fautes de ponctuation

- des fautes de conjugaison

- un mauvais emploi (*use*) de la grammaire de l'unité

- des fautes d'accord (*agreement*) des adjectifs

quatre cent quatre-vingt-onze **491**

EVALUATION

Criteria

Content Contains answers to each set of questions called out in the bulleted points of the task, as well as a preliminary list of people and means of communication.
Scale: 1 2 3 4 5

Organization Organized into logical paragraphs that begin with a topic sentence and contain appropriate supporting details.
Scale: 1 2 3 4 5

Accuracy Uses prepositions with the infinitive and conditional forms correctly. Spells words, conjugates verbs, and modifies adjectives correctly throughout.
Scale: 1 2 3 4 5

Creativity Includes additional information that is not included in the task and/or uses adjectives, descriptive verbs, and additional details to make the composition more interesting.
Scale: 1 2 3 4 5

Scoring

Excellent	18–20 points
Good	14–17 points
Satisfactory	10–13 points
Unsatisfactory	< 10 points

O P T I O N S

Avant l'écriture   Have students create the list of persons on their own. Then tally the results as a class to see how many people the average student is in touch with, as well as what means of communication he or she used five years ago and what he or she uses today. Create a summary that lists the different means of communication in order of popularity, now and five years ago.

Tell students that they should organize their information around the questions called out by the five bulleted items in the writing task. Here are some transitional phrases they may find useful for moving from one bulleted category to the next: **À mon avis…, Concernant/À propos de/Au sujet de…, Quand il s'agit de…, En général/Généralement, Normalement, D'habitude.**

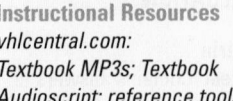 Vocabulary Tools

Instructional Resources
vhlcentral.com:
Textbook MP3s; Textbook
Audioscript; reference tools

Suggestions
- Tell students that an easy way to study from **Vocabulaire** is to cover up the French half of each section, leaving only the English equivalents exposed. They can then quiz themselves on the French items. To focus on the English equivalents of the French entries, they simply reverse this process.
- Point out to students that they can use the Vocabulary Tools at **vhlcentral.com** for reference and extra vocabulary practice.

Leçon 11A

L'ordinateur

un clavier *keyboard*
une clé USB *USB drive*
un disque dur *hard drive*
un écran *screen*
un e-mail *e-mail*
un fichier *file*
une imprimante *printer*
un jeu vidéo (jeux vidéo *pl.*) *video game(s)*
un logiciel *software, program*
un mot de passe *password*
une page d'accueil *home page*
un site Internet/web *website*
une souris *mouse*
démarrer *to start up*
être connecté(e) (avec) *to be connected (to)*
être en ligne (avec) *to be online/on the phone (with)*
imprimer *to print*
sauvegarder *to save*
télécharger *to download*

Verbes pronominaux réciproques

s'adorer *to adore one another*
s'aider *to help one another*
s'aimer (bien) *to love (like) one another*
se connaître *to know one another*
se dire *to tell one another*
se donner *to give one another*
s'écrire *to write one another*
s'embrasser *to kiss one another*
s'entendre bien (avec) *to get along well (with one another)*
se parler *to speak to one another*
se quitter *to leave one another*
se regarder *to look at one another*
se rencontrer *to meet one another (make an acquaintance)*
se retrouver *to meet one another (planned)*
se téléphoner *to phone one another*

L'électronique

un appareil photo (numérique) *(digital) camera*
un casque (audio) *headphones*
une chaîne (de télévision) *(television) channel*
un enregistreur DVR *DVR*
un lien *link*
un portable *cell phone*
un réseau (social) *(social) network*
un smartphone *smartphone*
une tablette (tactile) *tablet*
une télécommande *remote control*
un texto/SMS *text message*
ajouter/supprimer un(e) ami(e) *to add/delete a friend*
allumer *to turn on*
brancher *to plug in; to connect*
composer (un numéro) *to dial (a number)*
effacer *to erase*
enregistrer *to record*
éteindre *to turn off*
fermer *to close; to shut off*
fonctionner/marcher *to work; to function*
prendre une photo(graphie) *to take a photo(graph)*
recharger *to recharge*
sonner *to ring*

Expressions utiles

See p. 455.

Prepositions with the infinitive

See p. 458.

Leçon 11B

Verbes

couvrir *to cover*
découvrir *to discover*
offrir *to offer, to give something*
ouvrir *to open*
souffrir *to suffer*

La voiture

arrêter (de faire quelque chose) *to stop (doing something)*
attacher sa ceinture de sécurité (f.) *to buckle one's seatbelt*
avoir un accident *to have/to be in an accident*
dépasser *to go over; to pass*
faire le plein *to fill the tank*
freiner *to brake*
se garer *to park*
rentrer (dans) *to hit (another car)*
réparer *to repair*
tomber en panne *to break down*
vérifier (l'huile/la pression des pneus) *to check (the oil/the air pressure)*
un capot *hood*
un coffre *trunk*
l'embrayage (m.) *clutch*
l'essence (f.) *gas*
un essuie-glace (des essuie-glaces) *windshield wiper(s)*
les freins (m.) *brakes*
l'huile (f.) *oil*
un moteur *engine*
un pare-brise (pare-brise pl.) *windshield*
un pare-chocs (pare-chocs pl.) *bumper*
les phares (m.) *headlights*
un pneu (crevé) *(flat) tire*
une portière *car door*
un réservoir d'essence *gas tank*
un rétroviseur *rearview mirror*
une roue (de secours) *(emergency) tire*
une voiture *car*
un volant *steering wheel*
un voyant d'essence/d'huile *(gas/oil) warning light*
un agent de police/un(e) policier/policière *police officer*
une amende *fine*
une autoroute *highway*
la circulation *traffic*
la limitation de vitesse *speed limit*
un(e) mécanicien(ne) *mechanic*
un parking *parking lot*
un permis de conduire *driver's license*
une rue *street*
une station-service *service station*

Expressions utiles

See p. 473.

En ville

Unit Goals

Leçon 12A

In this lesson, students will learn:
- terms for banking
- terms for business establishments
- terms for the post office
- the pronunciation of the letter **h**
- about small shops and businesses in France
- more about businesses and small shops through specially shot video footage
- the verbs **voir, croire, recevoir,** and **apercevoir**
- negative and affirmative expressions

Leçon 12B

In this lesson, students will learn:
- terms for asking for and giving directions
- rules of French capitalization
- about the centers of French cities and towns
- about French reggae music band Massilia Sound System
- the formation and usage of **le futur simple**
- irregular future tense forms
- to use background information to understand spoken French

Savoir-faire

In this section, students will learn:
- cultural and historical information about the French regions of **Provence-Alpes-Côte d'Azur** and **Corsica**
- to identify the narrator's point of view
- to use linking words when writing

Pour commencer
- b. une carte
- a. dans un parc
- c. Il fait beau.

Pour commencer

Qu'est-ce que David a dans la main?
a. une lettre b. une carte c. une photo

Où sont-ils?
a. dans un parc b. à la maison
c. au restaurant

Quel temps fait-il?
a. Il fait froid. b. Il pleut. c. Il fait beau.

RESOURCES

Student Activities Manual (SAM): Workbook Activities, pp. 163–176; Lab Activities, pp. 89–96; Video Activities, pp. 45–48; pp. 83–84 SAM Answer Key

vhlcentral.com: Textbook MP3s; Lab MP3s; Textbook Audioscript; Lab Audioscript Video; Videoscript; **Roman-photo** Translations; **Vocabulaire supplémentaire**; Activity Pack (including **Feuilles d'activités**, Info Gap Activities, and Task-based Activities);

Le Zapping short film transcription; **Essayez!** and **Mise en pratique** answers; Digital Image Bank; Testing Program; Testing Program MP3s

Section Goals

In this section, students will learn and practice vocabulary related to:
- banking
- the post office
- business establishments

Instructional Resources

vhlcentral.com:
Digital Image Bank;
Vocabulaire supplémentaire
(including vocabulary illustrations from the textbook, theme-based illustrations); **Mise en pratique**
answers; Textbook Audioscript; Lab Audioscript; Activity Pack; Textbook MP3s; Lab MP3s; SAM Answer Key; reference tools

Suggestions

- Use the **12A Contextes** illustration from the Digital Image Bank. Describe what people are doing. Examples: **Elle poste une lettre. Il retire de l'argent.** Then point out the various stores and other businesses. Have students identify the types of business based on the signs.

- Ask students questions using the new vocabulary. Examples: **Que fait le facteur? Que fait l'homme au distributeur automatique? Que vend-on dans une papeterie? Qu'achète-t-on chez le marchand de journaux? Où est le cybercafé?**

- To introduce banking terms, mime several transactions. Say: **Quand j'ai besoin d'argent, je vais au distributeur.** Follow the same procedure with the post office vocabulary.

- Use the Vocabulary illustrations and the City life and shopping illustrations from the Digital Image Bank to help students familiarize themselves with making business transactions and getting around town.

- Additional vocabulary for this lesson can be found in the **Vocabulaire supplémentaire** on the Supersite.

Leçon **12A**

S Vocabulary Tools

You will learn how to...
- make business transactions
- get around town

Les courses

Vocabulaire

accompagner	to accompany
avoir un compte bancaire	to have a bank account
déposer de l'argent	to deposit money
emprunter	to borrow
payer par carte (de crédit)	to pay by credit card
payer en liquide	to pay in cash
payer par chèque	to pay by check
remplir un formulaire	to fill out a form
retirer de l'argent	to withdraw money
signer	to sign
une adresse	address
une carte postale	postcard
une enveloppe	envelope
un timbre	stamp
une boutique	boutique, store
une brasserie	café, restaurant
un commissariat de police	police station
une laverie	laundromat
une mairie	town/city hall; mayor's office
un compte-chèques	checking account
un compte d'épargne	savings account
une dépense	expenditure, expense
des pièces de monnaie	coins
de la monnaie	change
fermé(e)	closed
ouvert(e)	open

Labels in illustration:
une papeterie — La Maison du Papier — SOLDES — une bijouterie — un cybercafé — un bureau de poste — un colis — Elle poste une lettre. (poster) — une boîte aux lettres — un marchand de journaux

ressources

WB	LM	S
pp. 163–164	p. 89	vhlcentral

O P T I O N S

Extra Practice For additional practice, ask these questions.
1. Avez-vous un compte-chèques? 2. Avez-vous un compte d'épargne? 3. Où y a-t-il un distributeur automatique? 4. Où y a-t-il un bureau de poste? 5. Où y a-t-il une banque? 6. Quelle est votre marchand de journaux préféré? 7. Quelle est votre boutique préférée?

Game Play a game of **Dix questions**. Ask a volunteer to think of a place listed in the new vocabulary. Other students get to ask one yes/no question, then they can guess what the word is. Limit attempts to ten questions per word. You might want to tell students that they can narrow down their options by asking questions about what can be done at the location.

Mise en pratique

1 Écoutez Écoutez la conversation entre Jean-Pierre et Carole. Ensuite, complétez les phrases avec le bon mot.

1. Carole demande à Jean-Pierre d'acheter des timbres et de _____poster_____ un colis. (déposer, poster, retirer)
2. Le __bureau de poste__ se trouve sur la route de Jean-Pierre. (bureau de poste, papeterie, laverie)
3. Jean-Pierre veut _____déposer_____ de l'argent à la banque. (retirer, déposer, emprunter)
4. Jean-Pierre doit _____remplir_____ et signer des formulaires. (accompagner, remplir, payer)
5. Jean-Pierre a acheté le journal chez le __marchand de journaux__. (papeterie, marchand de journaux, bureau de poste)
6. Jean-Pierre n'avait pas assez de _____liquide_____ sur lui. (compte-chèques, carte de crédit, liquide)

2 Associez Associez chaque activité de la colonne de gauche avec le lieu qui correspond dans la colonne de droite.

_d_ 1. acheter un chemisier	a. un bureau de poste
_j_ 2. acheter du maquillage	b. une banque
_i_ 3. acheter un magazine	c. une bijouterie
_c_ 4. acheter une montre	d. une boutique
_e_ 5. boire un café	e. une brasserie
_a_ 6. envoyer une carte	f. un commissariat de police
_g_ 7. envoyer un e-mail	g. un cybercafé
_h_ 8. faire la lessive	h. une laverie
_b_ 9. ouvrir un compte	i. un marchand de journaux
_f_ 10. payer une amende	j. un salon de beauté

3 Complétez Complétez ces phrases avec le mot ou l'expression qui convient le mieux. N'oubliez pas de faire les accords nécessaires.

1. __Le facteur__ apporte le courrier tous les jours à la même heure.
2. Quand les magasins sont _____fermés_____, on ne peut pas faire de courses.
3. Pour poster une lettre, on peut simplement la mettre dans __une boîte aux lettres__.
4. Quand on n'a pas beaucoup d'argent, il faut faire attention à ses _____dépenses_____.
5. Si la banque n'est pas ouverte, on peut toujours __retirer de l'argent__ au distributeur automatique.
6. Quand on envoie une lettre, il ne faut pas oublier d'écrire _____l'adresse_____ et de mettre __un timbre__.
7. Pour acheter une voiture, il faut souvent _____emprunter_____ de l'argent.
8. Si on n'a pas de lave-linge à la maison, il faut aller à __la laverie__.

S Practice more at vhlcentral.com.

quatre cent quatre-vingt-quinze **495**

Image labels: un salon de beauté / Salon de Beauté Claude / le facteur / le courrier / BANQUE / une banque / guichet / les billets (m.) / un distributeur (automatique/de billets) / Elle fait la queue.

1 Audioscript JEAN-PIERRE: Carole, je vais aller à la banque. Est-ce que tu as besoin de quelque chose en ville?
CAROLE: Oui. Est-ce que tu peux aller faire des courses pour moi? Tu peux prendre le journal chez le marchand de journaux? J'ai aussi un colis à poster et j'ai besoin de timbres.
J-P: Pas de problème. Le bureau de poste et le marchand de journaux sont sur ma route. *Jean-Pierre est maintenant à la banque.*
J-P: Bonjour, Monsieur. J'ai de l'argent à déposer sur mon compte-chèques et sur mon compte d'épargne, s'il vous plaît.
L'EMPLOYÉ: Oui, bien sûr, Monsieur. Voici les formulaires à remplir et à signer. Si vous avez besoin de liquide pendant le week-end, nous avons un nouveau distributeur de billets à l'extérieur.
J-P: Très bien, je vous remercie. *Plus tard, à la maison…*
C: Alors, tu as fait mes courses?
J-P: Oui, voici le journal, mais je n'ai pas envoyé le colis. La machine ne fonctionnait pas. Je n'ai pas pu payer avec ma carte de crédit et je n'avais pas assez de liquide sur moi. Je suis désolé.
C: Ce n'est pas grave. Je dois aller à la papeterie plus tard, je peux passer à la poste après.
(On Textbook MP3s)

1 Suggestion Have volunteers read the completed sentences aloud.

2 Suggestion Ask students what one does at each place listed. They should respond with the activity. Example: **Que fait-on dans un bureau de poste? (On envoie une lettre/carte.)**

2 Expansion For additional practice, ask students where they might do these activities.
1. poster un colis (au bureau de poste) 2. retirer de l'argent (à la banque/au distributeur automatique) 3. manger quelque chose (dans une brasserie) 4. acheter un cadeau (dans une boutique/dans une bijouterie)

3 Suggestion Have students check their answers with a classmate.

OPTIONS

Game Toss a beanbag to a student at random and call out the name of a place. You may want to include places from **Leçon 4A**. The student has four seconds to name an activity that goes with it. That student then tosses the beanbag to another student and says another place. Students who cannot think of an activity or repeat one that has already been mentioned are eliminated. The last person standing wins.

Small Groups Have students work in groups of four or five. Give each group a different list of errands. Tell them to create a story in which someone goes to various places to complete the errands. Remind them to use sequencing expressions, such as **d'abord, puis**, and **après ça**.

ESPACE CONTEXTES

Communication

4 Suggestion Encourage students to provide as many details as possible about each photo.

5 Suggestion Tell students to jot down notes during their interviews so that they will remember their partner's responses.

6 Suggestion Encourage students to brainstorm words and expressions they might want to use in their dialogue before they begin writing.

4 Décrivez Avec un(e) partenaire, regardez les photos et décrivez où et comment Annick et Charles ont passé la journée samedi dernier. Donnez l'heure exacte pour chaque endroit. Answers will vary.

1.

2.

3.

4.

5.

6.

5 Répondez Avec un(e) partenaire, posez ces questions et répondez-y à tour de rôle. Ensuite, comparez vos réponses avec celles (*the ones*) d'un autre groupe. Answers will vary.

1. Vas-tu souvent au bureau de poste? Pour quoi faire?

2. Quel genre de courses fais-tu le week-end?

3. Où est-ce que tu fais souvent la queue? Pourquoi?

4. Y a-t-il une laverie près de chez toi? Combien de fois par mois y vas-tu?

5. Comment préfères-tu payer tes achats (*purchases*)? Pourquoi?

6. Combien de fois par semaine utilises-tu un distributeur de billets?

6 À vous de jouer Par petits groupes, choisissez une de ces situations et écrivez un dialogue. Ensuite, jouez la scène. Answers will vary.

1. À la banque, un(e) étudiant(e) veut ouvrir un compte bancaire et connaître les services offerts.

2. À la poste, une vieille dame (*lady*) veut envoyer un colis, acheter des timbres et faire un changement d'adresse. Il y a la queue derrière elle.

3. Dans un salon de beauté, deux femmes discutent de leurs courses à la mairie, à la papeterie et chez le marchand de journaux.

4. Dans un cybercafé, des étudiants font des achats en ligne sur différents sites.

OPTIONS

Extra Practice Have students make signs and set up various businesses around the classroom, such as a bank and a post office. Then give students detailed errands to run and have them role-play the situations at the locations. Example: Go to the bank and withdraw 20 euros, then go to the post office and buy six stamps. Tell students to alternate playing employees and customers.

Game Divide the class into two teams. Have a spelling bee using vocabulary words from **Espace contextes**. Pronounce each word, use it in a sentence, and then say the word again. Tell students that they must spell the words in French and include all diacritical marks.

Les sons et les lettres   Audio

The letter h

You already know that the letter **h** is silent in French, and you are familiar with many French words that begin with an **h muet**. In such words, the letter **h** is treated as if it were a vowel. For example, the articles **le** and **la** become **l'** and there is a liaison between the final consonant of a preceding word and the vowel following the **h**.

l'heure   l'homme   des hôtels   des hommes

Some words begin with an **h aspiré**. In such words, the **h** is still silent, but it is not treated like a vowel. Words beginning with **h aspiré**, like these you've already learned, are not preceded by **l'** and there no liaison.

la honte   les haricots verts   le huit mars   les hors-d'œuvre

Words that begin with an **h aspiré** are normally indicated in dictionaries by some kind of symbol, usually an asterisk (*).

Prononcez Répétez les mots suivants à voix haute.

1. le hall
2. la hi-fi
3. l'humeur
4. la honte
5. le héron
6. l'horloge
7. l'horizon
8. le hippie
9. l'hilarité
10. la Hongrie
11. l'hélicoptère
12. les hamburgers
13. les hiéroglyphes
14. les hors-d'œuvre
15. les hippopotames
16. l'hiver

Articulez Répétez les phrases suivantes à voix haute.

1. Hélène joue de la harpe.
2. Hier, Honorine est allée à l'hôpital.
3. Le hamster d'Hervé s'appelle Henri.
4. La Havane est la capitale de Cuba.
5. L'anniversaire d'Héloïse est le huit mars.
6. Le hockey et le handball sont mes sports préférés.

Dictons Répétez les dictons à voix haute.

La honte n'est pas d'être inférieur à l'adversaire, c'est d'être inférieur à soi-même.[1]

L'heure, c'est l'heure; avant l'heure, c'est pas l'heure; après l'heure, c'est plus l'heure.[2]

[1] Shame is not being inferior to an adversary; it's being inferior to oneself.

[2] On time is on time; before the hour is not on time; after the hour is no longer on time.

p. 90   vhlcentral

Section Goals

In this section, students will learn about the letter **h**.

Instructional Resources
vhlcentral.com:
Textbook MP3s; Lab MP3s; SAM Answer Key; Textbook Audioscript; Lab Audioscript; reference tools

Suggestions

- Model the pronunciation of the example words and have students repeat them after you.
- Remind students that **h** often combines with other consonants to make different sounds. Examples: **ch** (**chat, chose**) and **ph** (**téléphone**). The **h** is silent when it combines with the letter **t**. Examples: **thé** and **théâtre**.
- Point out that many words beginning with an **h aspiré** are borrowed from other languages. Examples: **le hall, les hamburgers, le handball,** and **la Hollande**.
- Ask students to provide more examples of words that begin with the letter **h**. Examples: **l'huile, l'hôte, l'hôtesse, des habitants,** and **l'hôtel**.
- Dictate five familiar words containing the letter **h**, repeating each one at least two times. Then write them on the board or a transparency and have students check their spelling.

Dictons The saying «**La honte n'est pas d'être inférieur à l'adversaire, c'est d'être inférieur à soi-même**» is a Manchurian proverb. The saying «**L'heure, c'est l'heure; avant l'heure, c'est pas l'heure; après l'heure, c'est plus l'heure**» is a quote from Jules Jouy.

Extra Practice Use these sentences with the letter **h** for additional practice or dictation. **1. En hiver, Henri va en Hongrie. 2. Horace a honte d'habiter dans cette habitation. 3. Hélène est heureuse de fêter ses huit ans. 4. Notre hôte Hubert sert des huîtres à l'huile d'olive comme hors-d'œuvre.**

Extra Practice Teach students this French tongue-twister that contains the letter **h**. **La pie niche en haut, l'oie niche en bas, le hibou niche ni haut ni bas.**

ESPACE ROMAN-PHOTO

Section Goals

In this section, students will learn functional phrases for talking about errands and money and expressing negation.

Instructional Resources
vhlcentral.com: **Roman-photo** Video, Videoscript, and Translation; SAM Answer Key; reference tools

Video Recap: Leçon 11B
Review the previous **Roman-photo** with this activity.
1. Où est Rachid quand l'épisode commence? (Il est à une station-service.)
2. Pourquoi y va-t-il? (Il y va pour faire le plein.)
3. Qui attend Rachid au P'tit Bistrot? (Amina l'attend.)
4. Qu'est-ce que Rachid donne à Amina? (Il lui donne des fleurs.)
5. Qu'est-ce qui se passe en route? (Un voyant s'allume. Ils ont un pneu crevé.)

Video Synopsis
Rachid and Amina are buying some food at a **charcuterie** for a picnic. Rachid needs some cash, so they head for an ATM. As they are walking, Amina says she has to go to the post office, the jewelry store, and a boutique that afternoon. David invites Sandrine to eat at a **brasserie**. On the way, they run into Rachid and Amina at the ATM. Sandrine and Amina discuss their new relationships.

Suggestions
• Have students predict what the episode will be about based on the video stills.
• Have students scan the captions for sentences related to places in a city.
• After reading the **Roman-photo**, have students summarize the episode.
• Point out that Amina can buy stamps from a machine even when the post office is closed.

On fait des courses. Video

PERSONNAGES

Amina

David

Employée

Rachid

Sandrine

À la charcuterie...
EMPLOYÉE Bonjour, Mademoiselle, Monsieur. Qu'est-ce que je vous sers?
RACHID Bonjour, Madame. Quatre tranches de pâté et de la salade de carottes pour deux personnes, s'il vous plaît.
EMPLOYÉE Et avec ça?
RACHID Deux tranches de jambon, s'il vous plaît.

RACHID Vous prenez les cartes de crédit?
EMPLOYÉE Ah, désolée, Monsieur. Nous n'acceptons que les paiements en liquide ou par chèque.
RACHID Amina, je viens de m'apercevoir que je n'ai pas de liquide sur moi!
AMINA Ce n'est pas grave, j'en ai assez. Tiens.

Dans la rue...
RACHID Merci, chérie. Passons à la banque avant d'aller au parc.
AMINA Mais, nous sommes samedi midi, la banque est fermée.
RACHID Peut-être, mais il y a toujours le distributeur automatique.
AMINA Bon, d'accord... J'ai quelques courses à faire plus tard cet après-midi. Tu veux m'accompagner?

Dans une autre partie de la ville...
DAVID Tu aimes la cuisine alsacienne?
SANDRINE Oui, j'adore la choucroute!
DAVID Tu veux aller à la brasserie La Petite France? C'est moi qui t'invite.
SANDRINE D'accord, avec plaisir.
DAVID Excellent! Avant d'y aller, il faut trouver un distributeur automatique.
SANDRINE Il y en a un à côté de la banque.

Au distributeur automatique...
SANDRINE Eh, regarde qui fait la queue!
RACHID Tiens, salut, qu'est-ce que vous faites de beau, vous deux?
SANDRINE On va à la brasserie. Vous voulez venir avec nous?

AMINA Non non! Euh... je veux dire... Rachid et moi, on va faire un pique-nique dans le parc.
RACHID Oui, et après ça, Amina a des courses importantes à faire.
SANDRINE Je comprends, pas de problème... David et moi, nous avons aussi des choses à faire cet après-midi.

ACTIVITÉS

1

Vrai ou faux? Indiquez si ces affirmations sont vraies ou fausses. Corrigez les phrases fausses. Answers may vary.

1. Aujourd'hui, la banque est ouverte. Faux. Le samedi midi, la banque est fermée.
2. Amina doit aller à la poste pour envoyer un colis. Faux. Elle doit envoyer des cartes postales.
3. Amina doit aller à la poste pour acheter des timbres. Vrai.
4. Amina va mettre ses cartes postales dans une boîte aux lettres à côté de la banque. Faux. Elle va les mettre dans une boîte aux lettres à côté de la poste.
5. Sandrine n'aime pas la cuisine alsacienne. Faux. Elle adore la cuisine alsacienne.
6. David et Rachid vont retirer de l'argent. Vrai.
7. Il n'y a pas de queue au distributeur automatique. Faux. Il y a la queue au distributeur automatique.
8. David et Sandrine invitent Amina et Rachid à la brasserie. Vrai.
9. Amina et Rachid vont à la brasserie. Faux. Ils vont faire un pique-nique dans le parc.
10. Amina va faire ses courses après le pique-nique. Vrai.

 Practice more at vhlcentral.com.

OPTIONS

Avant de regarder la vidéo Tell students to read the title and the scene setter. Then have them predict what might happen in this episode. Write their predictions on the board. After viewing the episode, have them confirm or correct their predictions.

Regarder la vidéo Show the video in four parts, pausing the video before each location change. Have students describe what happens in each place. Write their observations on the board. Then show the entire episode again without pausing and have the class fill in any missing details to summarize the plot.

RACHID Volontiers. Où est-ce que tu vas?

AMINA Je dois aller à la poste pour acheter des timbres et envoyer quelques cartes postales, et puis je voudrais aller à la bijouterie. J'ai reçu un e-mail de la bijouterie qui vend les bijoux que je fais. Regarde.

RACHID Très joli!

AMINA Oui, tu aimes? Et après ça, je dois passer à la boutique Olivia où l'on vend mes vêtements.

RACHID Tu vends aussi des vêtements dans une boutique?

AMINA Oui, mes créations! J'étudie le stylisme de mode, tu ne t'en souviens pas?

RACHID Si, bien sûr, mais... Tu as vraiment du talent.

AMINA Alors! On n'a plus besoin de chercher un cyberhomme?

SANDRINE Pour le moment, je ne cherche personne. David est super.

DAVID De quoi parlez-vous?

SANDRINE Oh, rien d'important.

RACHID Bon, Amina. On y va?

AMINA Oui. Passez un bon après-midi.

SANDRINE Vous aussi.

Expressions utiles

Dealing with money

- **Nous n'acceptons que les paiements en liquide.**
  We only accept payment in cash.
- **Je viens de m'apercevoir que je n'ai pas de liquide.**
  I just noticed/realized I don't have any cash.
- **Il y a toujours le distributeur automatique.**
  There's always the ATM.

Running errands

- **J'ai quelques courses à faire plus tard cet après-midi.**
  I have a few/some errands to run later this afternoon.
- **Je voudrais aller à la bijouterie qui vend les bijoux que je fais.**
  I would like to go to the jewelry shop that sells the jewelry I make.

Expressing negation

- **Pas de problème.**
  No problem.
- **On n'a plus besoin de chercher un cyberhomme?**
  We no longer need to look for a cyberhomme?
- **Pour le moment, je ne cherche personne.**
  For the time being/the moment, I'm not looking for anyone.
- **Rien d'important.**
  Nothing important.

Additional vocabulary

- **J'ai reçu un e-mail.**
  I received an e-mail.
- **Qu'est-ce que vous faites de beau?**
  What are you up to?

Expressions utiles
- Model the pronunciation of the **Expressions utiles** and have students repeat them.
- As you work through the list, point out the forms of **recevoir** and **apercevoir**, and negative expressions. Tell students that these verbs and constructions will be formally presented in **Espace structures**.
- Respond briefly to questions about **recevoir**, **apercevoir**, and negative expressions. Reinforce correct forms, but do not expect students to produce them consistently at this time.
- Point out that **les brasseries** usually offer quick, hearty meals. They often specialize in Alsatian dishes, such as **la choucroute**.

1 Suggestion Have students correct the false statements.

1 Expansion For additional practice, give students these items. **11. La charcuterie accepte les cartes de crédit. (Faux. Elle n'accepte que les paiements en liquide ou par chèque.) 12. À la charcuterie, Rachid paie par chèque. (Faux. Amina paie en liquide.) 13. Rachid va accompagner Amina cet après-midi. (Vrai.) 14. Sandrine cherche toujours un cyberhomme. (Faux. Sandrine n'a plus besoin de chercher un cyberhomme.)**

2 Suggestion Have volunteers read the completed sentences aloud.

3 Suggestion Tell students to choose a situation and brainstorm ideas before writing their conversations. Encourage them to be creative.

2 **Complétez** Complétez ces phrases.

1. La charcuterie accepte les paiements en liquide et par chèque.
2. Amina veut aller à la poste, à la boutique de vêtements et à la bijouterie.
3. À côté de la banque, il y a un distributeur automatique.
4. Amina paie avec des pièces de monnaie et des billets.
5. Amina a des courses à faire cet après-midi.

3 **À vous!** Que se passe-t-il au pique-nique ou à la brasserie? Avec un(e) camarade de classe, écrivez une conversation entre Amina et Sandrine ou Rachid et David, dans laquelle elles/ils se racontent ce qu'ils ont fait. Qu'ont-ils mangé? Se sont-ils amusés? Était-ce romantique? Jouez la scène devant la classe.

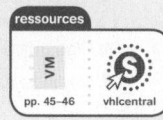

ressources
VM pp. 45–46
vhlcentral

A C T I V I T É S

quatre cent quatre-vingt-dix-neuf **499**

OPTIONS

Les heures d'ouverture Many small shops close for an hour or two between 12:00 p.m. and 2:00 p.m. It is common to reopen in the afternoon and stay open until around 7:00 p.m. Most stores are not open late in the evening or on Sundays except around the holidays. Stores near popular tourist attractions are exceptions. For example, many businesses along the Champs-Élysées in Paris are open until midnight.

Extra Practice Ask volunteers to act out the scenes in video stills 5–10 for the class. Tell them it is not necessary to memorize the episode. They should just try to get the general meaning across with the vocabulary they know. Give them time to prepare or have them do their skit as a review activity during the next class period.

S Reading
Video: *Flash culture*

Section Goals

In this section, students will:
- learn about small businesses and specialty shops in France
- learn some terms to talk about the **métro**
- learn about some interesting places to shop in the francophone world
- read about Alain Robert, the French "Spiderman"
- view authentic video footage

Instructional Resources
vhlcentral.com:
Video; SAM Answer Key;
Videoscript; reference tools

Culture à la loupe
Avant la lecture Have students look at the visuals and describe what they see.

Lecture
- Point out that supermarkets in France usually close no later than 8 or 9 p.m., and that they are typically closed on Sundays. Small shops, on the other hand, are often open on Sunday mornings.
- Give students the names of these additional small shops: **la charcuterie, le traiteur, la fromagerie, la confiserie.**

Après la lecture Ask students: **Où est-ce qu'on va pour la viande en France? (à la boucherie) Et pour le poisson? (à la poissonnerie) Quel petit commerce français est le plus fréquenté? (la boulangerie)**

1 Suggestion Have volunteers write the answers on the board. Then go over them with the class.

CULTURE À LA LOUPE

Les petits commerces

Dans beaucoup de pays francophones, on fait toujours les courses chez les petits commerçants, même° s'il est plus pratique d'aller au supermarché.
On allie° modernité et tradition: on fait souvent les courses une fois par semaine au supermarché mais quand on a plus de temps, on se rend° dans les petits commerces où on achète des produits plus authentiques et parfois plus proches° de son domicile°.

Pour le fromage, par exemple, on va à la crémerie; pour la viande, on va à la boucherie; pour le poisson, à la poissonnerie. Dans les épiceries de quartier, on trouve aussi toutes sortes de produits, par exemple des fruits et des légumes, des produits frais°, des boîtes de conserve°, des produits surgelés°, etc. Les épiceries fines se spécialisent dans les produits de luxe et parfois, dans les plats préparés.

En France, la boulangerie reste le petit commerce le plus fréquenté. Le pain artisanal, les croissants et les brioches au beurre ont aussi un goût° bien différent des produits industriels. Chaque quartier, chaque village a au minimum une boulangerie. Dans certaines rues des grandes villes françaises (Paris, Lyon, Marseille, Bordeaux, etc.) il y en a parfois quatre ou cinq proches les unes des autres. Les pâtisseries aussi sont très nombreuses°.

Les petits commerces ont survécu° en France grâce à° une volonté° politique. Pour les sauvegarder°, les pouvoirs° publics des années 1980 ont limité les autorisations de constructions des supermarchés et hypermarchés dans la périphérie° des villes. Avec la présence des petits commerces, vie et activités dans les centres-villes ont ainsi° été préservés.

même *even* **allie** *combines* **se rend** *goes* **proches** *close* **domicile** *home* **frais** *fresh* **boîtes de conserve** *canned goods* **surgelés** *frozen* **goût** *flavor* **nombreuses** *numerous* **survécu** *survived* **grâce à** *thanks to* **volonté** *will* **sauvegarder** *save* **pouvoirs** *authorities* **périphérie** *outskirts* **ainsi** *thus*

A C T I V I T É S

1 Complétez Complétez les phrases.

1. Dans beaucoup de pays francophones, on fait les courses au supermarché ou chez <u>les petits commerçants</u>.
2. On fait souvent les courses une fois par semaine <u>au supermarché</u>.
3. Dans les petits commerces on achète des produits plus <u>authentiques / proches de son domicile</u>.
4. Pour acheter du fromage, on peut aller à <u>la crémerie</u>.
5. Dans <u>les épiceries de quartier</u>, on peut acheter des produits frais et surgelés.
6. On peut acheter des plats préparés et des produits de luxe dans certaines <u>épiceries fines</u>.
7. Le pain artisanal des boulangeries a <u>un goût</u> très différent des produits industriels.
8. Dans certaines rues <u>des grandes villes françaises</u>, il y a parfois cinq boulangeries.
9. Les petits commerces français ont survécu grâce à une volonté <u>politique</u>.
10. Les pouvoirs publics en France ont limité la construction des supermarchés dans <u>la périphérie</u> des villes.

O P T I O N S

Cultural Comparison Have students work in groups of three. Tell them to compare French and American shopping habits. Have them list the similarities and differences in a two-column chart under the headings **Similitudes** and **Différences**. Also tell them to discuss where they like to shop for groceries.

Les marchés en France In addition to supermarkets and small shops, most French cities, towns, and villages also have a weekly outdoor market, where shoppers can find food items, as well as a variety of other things (clothing and shoes, housewares, flowers and plants, books, etc.). In some French cities and towns, people can also do their grocery shopping at a daily indoor market called **les Halles.**

LE FRANÇAIS QUOTIDIEN

Le vocabulaire du métro

bouche (f.) **de métro**	subway station entrance
correspondance (f.)	connection
ligne (f.) **de métro**	subway line
rame (f.) **de métro**	subway train
strapontin (m.)	foldaway seat
changer	to change (subway line)
monter/descendre	to get on/to get off
prendre la direction	to go in the direction

LE MONDE FRANCOPHONE

Où faire des courses?

Voici quelques endroits où faire des courses.

En Afrique du Nord les souks, quartiers des vieilles villes où il y a une grande concentration de magasins et de stands

En Côte d'Ivoire le marché de Cocody à Abidjan où on trouve des tissus° et des objets locaux

À la Martinique le grand marché de Fort-de-France, un marché couvert°, ouvert tous les jours, qui offre toutes sortes de produits

À Montréal la ville souterraine°, un district du centre-ville où il y a de nombreux centres commerciaux reliés° entre eux par des tunnels

À Paris le marché aux puces° de Saint-Ouen où on trouve des antiquités et des objets divers

À Tahiti le marché couvert de Papeete où on offre des produits pour les touristes et pour les Tahitiens

tissus fabrics **couvert** covered **souterraine** underground **reliés** connected **marché aux puces** flea market

PORTRAIT

Le «Spiderman» français

Alain Robert, surnommé° le «Spiderman» français, découvre l'escalade° quand il est enfant et devient un des meilleurs grimpeurs° de falaises° du monde. Dès l'adolescence, il pratique le solo intégral en escalade: c'est un style d'escalade libre et en solitaire sans aucun système de sécurité (pas de corde°, pas d'équipements de protection spécialisés). Au début des années 90, il est médiatisé et admiré par le monde de l'escalade. Malgré° deux accidents qui l'ont laissé invalide à 60%°, avec des problèmes de vertige°, il commence sa carrière de grimpeur «urbain» et escalade son premier gratte-ciel° à Chicago, en 1994. Depuis, il a escaladé plus de 70 gratte-ciel et autres structures du monde, dont la tour Eiffel à Paris et la Sears Tower à Chicago. En 1997, il a été arrêté par la police pendant son ascension de l'un des plus grands bâtiments du monde, les tours Petronas en Malaisie. Parfois en costume de Spiderman, mais toujours sans corde et à mains nues°, Alain Robert fait souvent des escalades pour collecter des dons° et il attire° parfois des milliers de spectateurs. Sur sa page Facebook ou son site web, on peut suivre ses engagements et ses exploits: il est entré dans le livre Guinness des Records en 2012 pour la plus rapide ascension de l'Aspire Tower au Qatar. Il assure que «l'escalade est une passion», «une philosophie de vie».

surnommé nicknamed **escalade** climbing **grimpeurs** climbers **falaises** cliffs **corde** rope **Malgré** In spite of **invalide à 60%** 60% disabled **vertiges** vertigo **gratte-ciel** skyscraper **nues** bare **dons** charitable donations **attire** attracts

---

2 Vrai ou faux? Indiquez si les phrases sont vraies ou fausses.

1. Alain Robert escalade seulement des falaises.
   Faux. Il escalade aussi des gratte-ciel et d'autres structures.
2. Alain Robert escalade avec des protections et un équipement de sécurité. Faux. Il escalade à mains nues, sans corde et en solo.
3. Alain Robert n'a jamais eu de problèmes de santé dans sa carrière de grimpeur. Faux. Il a eu deux accidents graves et il a des problèmes de vertiges.
4. À Montréal, il y a un quartier souterrain.
   Vrai.
5. Il y a des souks dans les marchés d'Abidjan.
   Faux. Il y a des souks dans les vieilles villes d'Afrique du Nord.

3 Le marchandage

En Afrique du Nord, il est très courant de marchander ou de discuter avec un vendeur pour obtenir un meilleur prix. Avez-vous déjà eu l'occasion de marchander? Où? Quand? Qu'avez-vous acheté? Avez-vous obtenu un bon prix? Discutez de ce sujet avec un(e) partenaire.

ressources

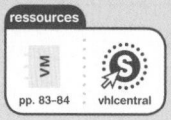

VM pp. 83–84 | vhlcentral

Practice more at vhlcentral.com.

A C T I V I T É S

Sidebar

Le français quotidien
- Model the pronunciation of each term and have students repeat it.
- Point out that you say **prendre une correspondance**. Remind students that a subway ticket is **un ticket**. In some cities it is possible to purchase **un carnet** or **une carte** for unlimited monthly access.

Portrait
- After two accidents while training in 1982, Robert hasn't suffered any more climbing injuries. He trained mostly on cliffs before starting to climb skyscrapers, which he is now paid to do.
- Ask students: **À votre avis, quel type d'homme est Alain Robert? Avez-vous envie d'escalader un gratte-ciel? Pourquoi?**

Le monde francophone After students have read the text, ask: **Où voulez-vous faire des courses dans le monde francophone? Pourquoi?**

2 Expansion For additional practice, give students these items. **6. Alain Robert escalade les bâtiments en France aussi bien qu'à l'étranger. (Vrai.) 7. Robert réussit à escalader les tours Petronas. (Faux. Il est arrêté par la police.) 8. Le public ne s'intéresse pas à Robert. (Faux. Il attire parfois des milliers de spectateurs.)**

3 Expansion Bring in pictures of objects one might find at a market, such as vegetables, pottery, rugs, and shirts. Have students work in pairs and practice bargaining for the objects pictured. They should take turns playing the customer and the vendor.

Flash culture Tell students that they will learn more about businesses and small shops by watching a variety of real-life images narrated by Benjamin. Show the video segment, then have students jot down in French at least three examples of people or things they saw. You can also use the activities in the video manual in class to reinforce this **Flash culture** or assign them as homework.

OPTIONS

Où faire des courses? Bargaining (**le marchandage**) is a common practice in Arab markets in France and throughout the Arab world. If visiting a souk in North Africa, it is best to go with someone who speaks Arabic. If that isn't possible, it's better to speak French than English, since Americans have a reputation for being wealthy.

Pairs Have students work in pairs. Tell them to write a conversation between two tourists who are taking the **métro** in Paris from the Bastille stop to the Franklin D. Roosevelt stop (line 1) to the Trocadéro stop (line 9), using the vocabulary in **Le français quotidien**. Then have pairs role-play their conversations for the class.

Section Goals

In this section, students will learn:
- the verbs **voir, croire, recevoir,** and **apercevoir**
- the meaning of **revoir** and **s'apercevoir**

Instructional Resources
vhlcentral.com:
Lab MP3s; SAM Answer Key;
Essayez! *and* ***Mise en pratique***
answers; Lab Audioscript;
reference tools

Suggestions
- Point out the **-s,-s,-t,-ons,-ez, -ent** endings of both **voir** and **croire** seen before in irregular verbs. Then note that the **nous** and **vous** forms have irregular stems **voy-** and **croy-**.
- Tell students that, just as in English, the verb **voir** is commonly used to mean *to understand.* Examples: **Ah, je vois!** *Ah, I see (understand)!* **Je ne vois pas le problème.** *I don't see (understand) the problem.*
- Have a volunteer write the conjugation of **revoir** on the board and model its pronunciation. Point out that students have already encountered this verb in the phrase **Au revoir!**

12A.1

Voir, croire, recevoir, and apercevoir

Tutorial

Je m'aperçois que je n'ai pas d'argent.

On vous a vus devant le distributeur!

Boîte à outils

The verb **revoir** (*to see again*) is derived from **voir** and is conjugated in the same way.

On se revoit mercredi?
Will we see each other again on Wednesday?

On a revu nos camarades à la papeterie.
We saw our classmates again at the stationery store.

Boîte à outils

You can use the expression **aller voir** to mean *to go (and) see/visit.*

On va voir les ruines.
We're going to see (visit) the ruins.

Se voir can be used either reflexively or reciprocally.

Je me vois dans le miroir.
(reflexive)
Dorian et Lise se voient.
(reciprocal)

The verb *voir* (to see)

je vois	nous voyons
tu vois	vous voyez
il/elle/on voit	ils/elles voient

Nous **voyons** le nouveau
bureau de poste.
We see the new post office.

Tu **vois** les cartes postales
sur la table?
Do you see the postcards on the table?

- **Voir** takes **avoir** as an auxiliary verb in the **passé composé**, and its past participle is **vu.**

Tu **as vu** le nouveau facteur?
Did you see the new mailman?

Ils **ont vu** *Un air de famille* en DVD.
They saw Un air de famille *on DVD.*

- The **conditionnel** of **voir** is formed with the stem **verr-.**

S'ils pouvaient, ils **verraient**
le film ce week-end.
*If they could, they would see
the film this weekend.*

Elle **verrait** mieux si elle portait
des lunettes.
*She would see better if she
wore glasses.*

- The verb **croire** (*to believe, to think*) follows the same conjugation pattern as **voir.**

croire

je crois	nous croyons
tu crois	vous croyez
il/elle/on croit	ils/elles croient

Tu **crois** qu'il est innocent?
Do you believe that he's innocent?

Elle **croit** que la boutique est fermée.
She thinks the store is closed.

- **Croire** takes **avoir** as an auxiliary verb in the **passé composé**, and its past participle is **cru.**

J'**ai cru** qu'elle y était
I thought she was there.

Vous **avez cru** à son histoire?
Did you believe his story?

- The **conditionnel** of **croire** is formed with the stem **croir-.**

Nous le **croirions** si nous le voyions.
We would believe it if we saw it.

On **croirait** que c'est facile à faire.
One would think it's easy to do.

---

502 *cinq cent deux*

- In **Leçon 9A**, you learned to conjugate **devoir**. **Recevoir** and **apercevoir** are conjugated similarly.

recevoir and apercevoir

	recevoir *(to get, to receive)*	**apercevoir** *(to catch sight of, to see)*
je/j'	reçois	aperçois
tu	reçois	aperçois
il/elle/on	reçoit	aperçoit
nous	recevons	apercevons
vous	recevez	apercevez
ils/elles	reçoivent	aperçoivent

Je **reçois** des lettres de mon copain.
I get letters from my friend.

Vous **recevez** le courrier à la même heure tous les après-midi.
You get the mail at the same time every afternoon.

Les policiers **aperçoivent** le criminel.
The police officers see the criminal.

Le chien **aperçoit** le facteur quand il s'approche.
The dog sees the mailman when he approaches.

- **Recevoir** and **apercevoir** take **avoir** as the auxiliary verb in the **passé composé**. Their past participles are, respectively, **reçu** and **aperçu**.

Guillaume **a reçu** une carte postale.
Guillaume received a postcard.

J'**ai aperçu** un distributeur automatique au coin.
I saw an ATM at the corner.

À noter

In **Leçon 2A**, you learned the expression **être reçu(e) à un examen** (*to pass an exam*).

- The **conditionnel** of **recevoir** and **apercevoir** is formed with the stems **recevr-** and **apercevr-**, respectively.

Nous **recevrions** des colis de nos grands-parents.
We would get packages from our grandparents.

De là-bas, on **apercevrait** le commissariat de police.
From over there, you would catch sight of the police station.

- The verb **s'apercevoir** (**de**) means *to notice* or *to realize*.

Elle **s'est aperçue** qu'il fallait faire la queue.
She realized she had to wait in line.

Nous **nous sommes aperçus** du problème hier.
We noticed the problem yesterday.

Essayez!   Complétez les phrases avec les formes correctes des verbes au présent.

1. Je ne _____vois_____ (voir) pas la banque d'ici.
2. Vous _____croyez_____ (croire) à son histoire (*story*)?
3. Mes amis _____croient_____ (croire) que je dors.
4. Nous _____voyons_____ (voir) encore nos amis d'enfance.
5. Le prof _____reçoit_____ (recevoir) un cadeau des étudiants.
6. Tu _____aperçois_____ (apercevoir) le marchand de journaux?

ressources

WB
pp. 165–166

LM
p. 91

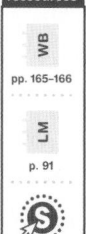
vhlcentral

OPTIONS

Small Groups Ask small groups of students to compose sentences with **s'apercevoir**. Give them a point for each sentence in which the verb is used and conjugated correctly, and a prize to the group with the most points.

Game Divide the class into teams of three. Each team has a piece of paper. Call out a subject, an infinitive, and a verb tense. Example: **je / voir (conditionnel)**. Each team composes a sentence with the given elements. As soon as a team finishes their sentence, one team member should run to the board and write it out. The first team to write a correct sentence on the board wins. Team members should take turns going to the board.

Suggestions

- Ask students why they think some forms of **recevoir** and **apercevoir** are spelled with a **cédille**. (It tells the reader to pronounce the sound as [s]. Remind them that the letter **c** is pronounced [s] in front of the letters **e** and **i**, and [k] in front of the letters **a, o,** and **u**.)
- Ask questions to practice **voir, croire, recevoir,** and **apercevoir** in the present and the **passé composé**. Examples: Qui a vu un film au cinéma récemment? Qui a reçu le prix Nobel de la paix l'année dernière? Qui croit aux fantômes?
- Test comprehension of the conditional forms of all four verbs by asking volunteers to supply the correct verb form for the subjects you suggest. Example: **tu / voir (tu verrais)**
- You may want to teach the class the verb **décevoir** and the adjective **déçu** along with **recevoir** and **apercevoir**.
- Point out that **s'apercevoir** is followed by **que/qu'** + [*another verb*] or by **de** + [*noun*].

Essayez! Have students create sentences in the **passé composé** and the **conditionnel**.

ESPACE **STRUCTURES**

1 **Suggestion** If students find this first activity difficult, provide a list of the conjugated verbs in random order and ask them to pick the correct verb for each sentence.

2 **Expansion** Change the subjects of the dehydrated sentences in the activity and have students write or say the new sentences.

3 **Suggestions**
• Model the activity by talking about a set of your own vacation photos
• Remind students that the conditional forms of **voir** and **revoir** are spelled with **rr**.

3 **Expansion** Have students create additional sentences using **croire**, **recevoir**, and **apercevoir**. Tell them that they can illustrate the sentences if they wish.

Mise en pratique

1 **Sur le campus** Vous parlez avec un(e) ami(e) de votre vie sur le campus. Complétez les phrases avec les verbes appropriés au présent.

1. De sa chambre, mon ami Marc __voit/aperçoit__ le campus.
2. Mon camarade de chambre et moi, nous ne __recevons__ pas de visites pendant la semaine.
3. Je __crois__ que la vie universitaire peut être difficile quelquefois.
4. Ma petite amie et sa sœur __reçoivent__ souvent des colis de leurs parents.
5. Quand il fait beau, nous __apercevons/voyons__ les montagnes derrière le stade.
6. Ton meilleur ami et toi, vous __recevez__ de bonnes notes aux examens?

2 **À Nice** Mélanie a passé une semaine à Nice avec sa famille. Elle en parle avec son petit ami. Utilisez les verbes donnés au passé composé.

> **MODÈLE**
> mon frère Paul / voir / le musée Matisse
> *Mon frère Paul a vu le musée Matisse.*

1. nous / recevoir / journal / à sept heures / du matin
   Nous avons reçu le journal à sept heures du matin.
2. papa et Fabrice / apercevoir / la Promenade des Anglais / de l'avion
   Papa et Fabrice ont aperçu la Promenade des Anglais de l'avion.
3. papa et maman / recevoir / des cadeaux / de leurs amis
   Papa et maman ont reçu des cadeaux de leurs amis.
4. je / voir / beaucoup / de spectacles
   J'ai vu beaucoup de spectacles.
5. Simon / croire / à la vieille légende / de Nice
   Simon a cru à la vieille légende de Nice.
6. ta sœur et toi / recevoir / ma carte postale / ?
   Ta sœur et toi avez reçu ma carte postale?

3 **Revoir** Alain et Chantal ont beaucoup aimé leur séjour à la Martinique et ils disent à une amie qu'ils ont déjà vu ces endroits et qu'ils les reverraient volontiers.

la montagne Pelée (nous)

> **MODÈLE**
> *Nous avons vu la montagne Pelée et nous la reverrions volontiers.*

1. d'énormes poissons (tu)
Tu as vu d'énormes poissons et tu les reverrais volontiers.

2. la forêt tropicale (je)
J'ai vu la forêt tropicale et je la reverrais volontiers.

3. le marché (Alain)
Alain a vu le marché et il le reverrait volontiers.

4. les plages (vous)
Vous avez vu les plages et vous les reverriez volontiers.

 Practice more at **vhlcentral.com**.

Communication

4 **Curieux!** Avec un(e) partenaire, posez-vous ces questions à tour de rôle.   Answers will vary.

1. Reçois-tu souvent des lettres? De qui? Quand?

2. As-tu vu un bon film récemment? Quel film?

3. Tes parents recevaient-ils souvent des amis quand tu étais petit(e)? Aimais-tu leurs amis?

4. Voyais-tu tes camarades pendant les vacances d'été? Pourquoi?

5. Qu'aperçois-tu de ta chambre? Que préférerais-tu apercevoir?

6. Crois-tu aux extraterrestres? Pourquoi?

7. D'habitude, quand est-ce que tu vois tes cousins?

8. Reçois-tu toujours de bonnes notes? Dans quels cours?

9. Que ferais-tu si tu apercevais un crime sur le campus?

5 **Assemblez** Achetez-vous sur Internet? Avec un(e) partenaire, assemblez les éléments des colonnes pour raconter vos expériences. Utilisez les verbes **voir**, **recevoir**, **apercevoir** et **s'apercevoir** dans votre conversation.   Answers will vary.

MODÈLE

Étudiant(e) 1: *Je commande parfois des livres sur Internet. Une fois, je n'ai pas reçu mes livres!*
Étudiant(e) 2: *Mon père adore acheter sur Internet. Il voit souvent des objets qui l'intéressent.*

A	B	C
je	apercevoir	billets d'avion
tu	s'apercevoir	billets de concert
un(e) ami(e)	commander	colis
nous	croire	CD
vous	poster	DVD
tes parents	recevoir	livres
tes profs	voir	vêtements
?	?	?

6 **Enquête** Votre professeur va vous donner une feuille d'activités. Circulez dans la classe et demandez à vos camarades s'ils connaissent quelqu'un qui pratique chaque activité de la liste. S'ils répondent par l'affirmative, demandez-leur qui est la personne et écrivez la réponse. Ensuite, présentez vos réponses à la classe.   Answers will vary.

MODÈLE

Étudiant(e) 1: *Connais-tu quelqu'un qui reçoit rarement des e-mails?*
Étudiant(e) 2: *Oui, mon frère aîné reçoit très peu d'e-mails.*

Activités	Nom	Réponses
1. recevoir / rarement / e-mails	Quang	son frère aîné
2. s'inquiéter / quand / ne pas / recevoir / e-mails		
3. apercevoir / e-mail bizarre / le / ouvrir		

4 **Expansion** Have students retell their partner's answers using third person subjects. Example: **Nathalie a récemment reçu une lettre de son copain du Canada.**

5 **Suggestion** Tell students to use each expression in the columns at least once.

6 **Suggestion** Call on volunteers to do the **modèle**. Then distribute the **Feuilles d'activités** found in the Activity Pack on the Supersite.

6 **Expansion** Ask students questions about themselves based on the sentence fragments given for the activity. Examples: **Qui reçoit rarement des e-mails? Vous inquiétez-vous quand vous ne recevez pas d'e-mails?** You may want to let students invent answers.

Extra Practice Briefly show the class a picture or drawing with numerous objects displayed: for example, a photo of a messy or cluttered room. Ask students to study the objects they see in the photo. Then remove the picture from view and ask students what they remember seeing and what they did not see, using **croire** and/or the **passé composé** of **voir**. Examples: **J'ai vu un lit. Je crois avoir vu…**

Game Tell pairs of students to write an obviously illogical sentence with **recevoir** or **apercevoir**. Example: **J'ai reçu une mauvaise note pour mon anniversaire.** Have students read their sentences aloud while their classmates correct the sentences so that they are logical. Then award prizes for the funniest, most ridiculous, and most creative sentences.

Section Goals

In this section, students will learn negative and affirmative expressions.

Instructional Resources
vhlcentral.com:
Activity Pack; Lab MP3s;
*SAM Answer Key; **Essayez!***
*and **Mise en pratique***
answers; Lab Audioscript;
reference tools

Suggestions

- To help students distinguish between the negative expressions on this page, make a transparency with a set of six fill-in-the-blank sentences with only the second negative particle (**personne, rien,** etc.) missing from each one. Examples: **Je n'ai** _____ **d'argent!** (pas) **Il n'y a** _____ **dans le couloir.** (personne)
- Point out to students that when **personne** and **rien** are used as subjects, the verbs that accompany them are singular. You could also point out that when **de** + [adjective] is used to modify **personne, rien, quelque chose,** and **quelqu'un,** the adjective is a masculine singular form.
- Explain to students that the expressions **jamais, rien,** and **personne** can also be used alone as a one-word answer to a question.

12A.2

NATIONAL comparisons STANDARDS

À noter

In the **Leçon 8B Roman-photo,** you learned the negative expression **ne... pas encore** (not yet). It works the same way as the negative expressions in this lesson.

🏃 Boîte à outils

The expression **ne... que** does not really express negation although it contains **ne.** Therefore, you use an indefinite article rather than **de** after this expression.

Je n'ai qu'un compte de chèques.
I only have one checking account.

Use **de** in all other negative constructions.

Il n'y a plus de billets dans le distributeur.
There aren't any more bills in the ATM.

Personne ne poste de lettre le dimanche.
No one mails letters on Sundays.

ESPACE STRUCTURES

Negative/affirmative expressions  Tutorial

Point de départ In **Leçon 2A,** you learned how to negate verbs with **ne... pas,** which is used to make a general negation. In French, as in English, you can also use a variety of expressions that add a more specific meaning to the negation.

- The other negative expressions are also made up of two parts: **ne** and a second negative word. The verb is placed between these two parts.

Negative expressions			
ne... aucun(e)	*none (not any)*	**ne... plus**	*no more (not anymore)*
ne... jamais	*never (not ever)*	**ne... que**	*only*
ne... ni... ni	*neither... nor*	**ne... rien**	*nothing (not anything)*
ne... personne	*nobody, no one*		

Je **n**'ai **aucune** envie de manger.
I have no desire to eat.

Le bureau de poste **n**'est **jamais** ouvert.
The post office is never open.

Elle **ne** parle à **personne**.
She doesn't talk to anyone.

Il **n**'a **plus** faim.
He's not hungry anymore.

Ils **n**'ont **que** des timbres de la poste aérienne.
They only have airmail stamps.

Le facteur **n**'avait **rien** pour nous.
The mailman had nothing for us.

- To negate the expression **il y a**, place **n'** before **y** and the second negative word after the form of **avoir**.

Il **n**'y a **aucune** banque près d'ici?
Aren't there any banks nearby?

Il **n**'y avait **rien** sur mon compte.
There wasn't anything in my account.

- The negative words **personne** and **rien** can be the subject of a verb, in which case they are placed before a third-person singular verb with **ne** following them.

Personne n'était là.
No one was there.

Rien n'est arrivé dans le courrier.
Nothing arrived in the mail.

- Note that **aucun(e)** can be either an adjective or a pronoun. Therefore, it must agree with the noun it modifies or replaces. It is always used in the singular.

Tu **ne** trouves **aucune boîte aux lettres**?
Can't you find any mailboxes?

Il **n**'a choisi **aucun** de ces pulls?
Didn't he pick any of these sweaters?

Je **n**'en trouve **aucune** par ici.
I can't find any around here.

Non, il **n**'en a aimé **aucun**.
No, he didn't like any of them.

- **Jamais, personne, plus,** and **rien** can be doubled up with **ne**.

Elle **ne** parle **jamais** à **personne**.
She never talks to anyone.

Elle **ne** dit **jamais rien**.
She never says anything.

Il **n**'y a **plus personne** ici.
There isn't anyone here anymore.

Il **n**'y a **plus rien** ici.
There isn't anything here anymore.

- To say *neither... nor*, you use three negative words: **ne... ni... ni**. Note that partitive and indefinite articles are usually omitted.

    Je **n'**ai **ni** frères **ni** sœurs.
    I have neither brothers nor sisters.

    Il **ne** paie **ni** par carte **ni** par chèque.
    He doesn't pay either by card or by check.

- Note that in the **passé composé**, the words **jamais**, **plus**, and **rien** are placed between the auxiliary verb and the past participle. **Aucun(e)**, **personne**, and **que** follow the past participle.

    Elle **n'**est **jamais** revenue.
    She's never returned.

    Nous **n'**avons **plus** emprunté d'argent.
    We haven't borrowed any more money.

    Je **n'**ai **rien** dit aujourd'hui.
    I didn't say anything today.

    Vous **n'**avez signé **aucun** papier.
    You didn't sign any papers.

    Il **n'**a parlé à **personne**.
    He didn't speak to anyone.

    Ils **n'**en ont posté **que** deux.
    They only mailed two.

- These expressions can be used in affirmative phrases. Note that when **jamais** is not accompanied by **ne**, it can mean *ever*.

jamais	*ever*	quelqu'un	*someone*
quelque chose	*something*	toujours	*always; still*

    As-tu **jamais** été à cette brasserie?
    Have you ever been to that brasserie?

    Il y a **quelqu'un**?
    Is someone there?

    Vous cherchez **quelque chose**?
    Are you looking for something?

    Il est **toujours** aussi réservé?
    Is he still so reserved?

- Note that **personne**, **quelque chose**, **quelqu'un**, and **rien** can be modified with an adjective after **de**.

    Nous cherchons **quelque chose de joli**.
    We're looking for something pretty.

    Ce n'est **rien de nouveau**.
    It's nothing new.

    Il y a **quelqu'un de célèbre** dans ta famille?
    Are there any famous people in your family?

    Je ne connais **personne de plus intelligent** que lui.
    I don't know anyone more intelligent than him.

Essayez! Choisissez l'expression correcte.

1. (Jamais / Personne) ne trouve cet homme agréable.
2. Je ne veux (rien / jamais) faire aujourd'hui.
3. Y a-t-il (quelqu'un / personne) à la banque?
4. Je n'ai reçu (pas de / aucun) colis.
5. Il n'y avait (ne / ni) lettres ni colis dans la boîte aux lettres.
6. Il n'y a (plus / aucun) d'argent à la banque?
7. Jérôme ne va (toujours / jamais) à la poste.
8. Le facteur n'arrive (toujours / qu') à trois heures.

Boîte à outils

Pay attention to the affirmative expressions used in questions to decide which negative expression is appropriate in the response.

quelqu'un (*someone*) →
ne... personne (*no one*)

quelquefois / toujours
(*sometimes / always*) →
ne... jamais (*never*)

quelque chose / tout
(*something / everything*) →
ne... rien (*nothing*)

toujours (*still*) → **ne... plus**
(*anymore*)

déjà (*already*) → **ne... pas
encore** (*not yet*)

Suggestions
- You might give students some more sentences with several negative particles so that they get a feel for those kinds of emphatic constructions. Examples: **Je n'ai jamais rien dit à personne! Il n'y a plus rien sur mon compte en banque.**
- Point out that while double negatives are grammatically incorrect in English, they are perfectly acceptable in French.
- To practice adverb placement in the **passé composé**, write sentences on sets of index cards, so that a word is on each card. Give out the cards for a sentence to a group of students and have them put the cards in order.

Essayez! Go over the answers to this activity with the class and have students with the correct responses explain them to the class.

---

ressources

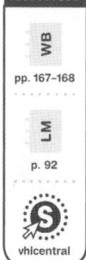

WB
pp. 167–168

LM
p. 92

vhlcentral

---

cinq cent sept **507**

Video Replay the video episode while students listen for negative expressions in the last scene. Tell them to raise their hands when they hear one. Then replay the video, pausing each time a negative expression is used for students to say it aloud or write it down.

Pairs Give pairs of students a set of negative sentences and have them give you an affirmative version of each sentence. Example: **Il n'y a personne à la porte. (Il y a quelqu'un à la porte.)** Go over the sentences with the class, asking students to give all the different positive sentences possible.

OPTIONS

ESPACE STRUCTURES

Mise en pratique

1 Expansion Ask students to give additional negative sentences for the activity. Example: **3. Anaïs ne voit jamais ses amies d'enfance.**

2 Suggestion After students have completed item 6, you may wish to teach them the expression **personne d'autre** (*no one else*): **Non, personne d'autre ne peut retirer d'argent de votre compte bancaire.**

3 Suggestion Have pairs of students complete this activity and act it out in front of the class. One student plays Tristan and one plays his friend.

1 **Les jumelles** Olivia et Anaïs sont des jumelles (*twin sisters*) bien différentes. Expliquez comment.

MODÈLE

Olivia est toujours heureuse.
Anaïs n'est jamais heureuse.

1. Olivia rit tout le temps.   Anaïs ne rit jamais.
2. Olivia remarque (*notices*) tout.   Anaïs ne remarque rien.
3. Olivia voit encore ses amies d'enfance.   Anaïs ne voit plus /aucune de ses amies d'enfance.
4. Olivia aime le chocolat et la glace.   Anaïs n'aime ni le chocolat ni la glace.
5. Olivia connaît beaucoup de monde.   Anaïs ne connaît personne.
6. Olivia reçoit beaucoup de colis.   Anaïs ne reçoit aucun colis.
7. Olivia est toujours étudiante.   Anaïs n'est plus étudiante.

2 **À la banque** Vous voulez ouvrir un nouveau compte et vous posez des questions au banquier. Écrivez ses réponses à la forme négative.

MODÈLE

La banque ferme-t-elle à midi? (jamais)
Non, la banque ne ferme jamais à midi.

1. La banque est-elle ouverte le samedi? (jamais)   Non, la banque n'est jamais ouverte le samedi.
2. Peut-on ouvrir un compte sans papier d'identité?
   (personne)   Non, personne ne peut ouvrir de compte sans papier d'identité.
3. Avez-vous des distributeurs automatiques dans les supermarchés?
   (aucun)   Non, nous n'avons aucun distributeur automatique dans les supermarchés.
4. Pour retirer de l'argent, avons-nous encore besoin de remplir ce document?
   (plus)   Non, vous n'avez plus besoin de remplir ce document.
5. Avez-vous des billets et des pièces dans vos distributeurs automatiques?
   (que)   Non, nous n'avons que des billets dans nos distributeurs automatiques.
6. Est-ce que tout le monde peut retirer de l'argent de mon compte bancaire?
   (personne)   Non, personne ne peut retirer d'argent de votre compte bancaire.

3 **Pas exactement** Tristan exagère souvent. Il a écrit cet e-mail et vous lui répondez pour dire que les choses ne sont pas arrivées exactement comme ça. Mettez toutes ses phrases à la forme négative dans votre réponse.

MODÈLE

Tu n'es pas arrivé tard à la banque...

> Je suis arrivé tard à la banque. Quelqu'un m'a ouvert la porte. J'ai regardé les affiches et les brochures. J'ai demandé quelque chose. Il y avait encore beaucoup d'argent sur mon compte. Je vais souvent revenir dans cette banque.

Tu n'es pas arrivé tard à la banque. Personne ne t'a ouvert la porte. Tu n'as regardé ni les affiches ni les brochures. Tu n'as rien demandé. Il n'y avait plus d'argent sur ton compte. Tu ne vas jamais revenir dans cette banque.

Communication

4 **De mauvaise humeur** Aujourd'hui, Anne-Marie est très négative. Elle répond négativement à toutes les questions. Avec un(e) partenaire, jouez les rôles d'Anne-Marie et de son amie. Rajoutez (*Add*) deux lignes supplémentaires de dialogue à la fin. Answers will vary.

MODÈLE

tu / sortir avec quelqu'un en ce moment
Étudiant(e) 1: *Est-ce que tu sors avec quelqu'un en ce moment?*
Étudiant(e) 2: *Non, je ne sors avec personne.*

1. tu / faire quelque chose ce soir
2. tes parents / déjà venir chez toi le week-end
3. ton frère / avoir encore sa vieille voiture
4. tes amis et toi / aller toujours au Canada en été
5. quelqu'un / habiter dans ta maison cet été
6. tu / prendre quelquefois des vacances
7. ?
8. ?

5 **Activités dangereuses** Avec un(e) partenaire, faites une liste de dix activités dangereuses. Ensuite, travaillez avec un autre groupe et demandez à vos camarades s'ils pratiquent ces activités. Répondent-ils toujours par des phrases négatives? Answers will vary.

MODÈLE

Étudiant(e) 1: *Fais-tu du jogging la nuit?*
Étudiant(e) 2: *Non! Je ne fais jamais de jogging la nuit.*

6 **Quel désastre!** En vacances, vous vous apercevez que votre valise a disparu (*disappeared*) avec votre argent liquide, vos papiers et vos cartes de crédit. Vous avez besoin de retirer de l'argent à la banque. Préparez un dialogue entre vous et deux employés de banque. Utilisez les expressions de la liste. Answers will vary.

jamais	ne... que	quelqu'un
ne... aucun(e)	ne... rien	rien
ne... ni... ni...	quelque chose	toujours
ne... plus		

4 **Expansion** Once students have written two additional lines of dialogue, alternately call on pairs of students to share the questions they composed and call on other pairs to answer those questions in the negative.

5 **Suggestion** To get students warmed up for this activity, ask them if they do some unsafe things. Examples: **Vous retirez de l'argent du distributeur automatique à deux heures du matin? Vous ne fermez pas la porte quand vous quittez la maison?**

6 **Suggestion** Tell students that each member should write the lines for one of the characters (the traveler and the two bank employees). Help them as they collaborate on the dialogue, and encourage them to be as creative as possible.

OPTIONS

Extra Practice Have the class collaborate on a description of a ghost town or a haunted house using expressions from pages 506–507. Write the sentences on the board or on a transparency as they are said and make sure that all seven negative expressions (including **ne... ni... ni...**) are used.

Game Give students index cards with one negative expression from pages 506–507 and another expression that could be used with it on each card. Then tell the students to produce sentences. Example: (*on the card*) **ne... personne + l'école (Personne ne va à l'école le dimanche.)**

ESPACE SYNTHÈSE

Révision

Instructional Resources
vhlcentral.com:
Activity Pack (Feuilles d'activités; Info Gap Activities); Testing Program; Testing Program MP3s; reference tools

1 Suggestion Have two volunteers read the **modèle** aloud. Then distribute the **Feuilles d'activités** found in the Activity Pack on the Supersite.

2 Expansion Once students have completed this activity, ask them the following questions about other students. **Qu'est-ce que _____ reçoit dans son courrier? Est-ce que _____ envoie des lettres par la poste de temps en temps? Des colis?**

3 Suggestion To get the class started, have students read the instructions and then make up different kinds of questions. Examples: **Y a-t-il un(e) _____ près d'ici? Où se trouve le/la _____ ?**

4 Suggestion Have students formulate **vrai** or **faux** statements about any subject using the negative expressions listed for the activity.

5 Expansion Remind students of the difference in meaning between **apercevoir** and **s'apercevoir**. Then ask them to make up a couple of sentences with the phrases **s'est aperçu(e) de/que** and **sans m'en apercevoir**.

6 Suggestion Divide the class into pairs and distribute the Info Gap Handouts found in the Activity Pack on the Supersite. Give students ten minutes to complete the activity.

1 Je ne vais jamais… Votre professeur va vous donner une feuille d'activités. Circulez dans la classe pour trouver un(e) camarade différent(e) qui fait ses courses à ces endroits. Où ne vont-ils jamais? Où ne vont-ils plus? Justifiez toutes vos réponses. *Answers will vary.*

MODÈLE

Étudiant(e) 1: Vas-tu à la laverie?
Étudiant(e) 2: Non, je n'y vais plus parce que j'ai acheté un lave-linge. Mais, je vais toujours à la banque le lundi.

Endroits	Noms
1. banque	Sabrina
2. bijouterie	
3. boutique de vêtements	
4. cybercafé	
5. laverie	

2 Le courrier Avec un(e) partenaire, préparez six questions pour interviewer vos camarades. Que reçoivent-ils dans leur courrier? Qu'envoient-ils? Utilisez les expressions négatives et les verbes **recevoir** et **envoyer**. Ensuite, par groupes de quatre, posez vos questions et écrivez les réponses. *Answers will vary.*

MODÈLE

Étudiant(e) 1: Est-ce que tu ne reçois que des lettres dans ton courrier?
Étudiant(e) 2: Non, je reçois des cadeaux parfois, mais je n'en envoie jamais.

3 Au village Vous visitez un petit village pour la première fois. Malheureusement, tout y est fermé. Vous posez des questions à un(e) habitant(e) sur les endroits de la liste et il/elle vous répond par des expressions négatives. Préparez le dialogue avec un(e) partenaire. *Answers will vary.*

MODÈLE

Étudiant(e) 1: À quelle heure le bureau de poste ouvre-t-il aujourd'hui?
Étudiant(e) 2: Malheureusement, le bureau de poste n'existe plus, Monsieur!

banque	laverie
bureau de poste	mairie
commissariat de police	salon de beauté

4 Vrai ou faux? Par groupes de quatre, travaillez avec un(e) partenaire pour préparer huit phrases au sujet des deux autres partenaires de votre groupe. Essayez de deviner ce qu'ils/elles (*what they*) ont fait et n'ont pas fait. Utilisez dans vos phrases le passé composé et les expressions négatives indiquées. Ensuite, lisez les phrases à vos deux camarades, qui vont vous dire si elles sont vraies ou fausses. *Answers will vary.*

MODÈLE

Étudiant(e) 1: Tu n'es jamais allé(e) dans le bureau du prof.
Étudiant(e) 2: C'est faux. J'ai dû y aller hier pour lui poser une question.

- ne… aucun(e)
- ne… jamais
- ne… personne
- ne… plus
- ne… que
- ne… rien

5 Au secours! Avec un(e) partenaire, préparez un dialogue pour représenter la scène de cette illustration. Utilisez les verbes **s'apercevoir**, **voir** et **croire** et des expressions négatives et affirmatives. *Answers will vary.*

6 Dix ans plus tard Votre professeur va vous donner, à vous et à votre partenaire, deux plans d'une ville. Attention! Ne regardez pas la feuille de votre partenaire. *Answers will vary.*

MODÈLE

Étudiant(e) 1: Il y a dix ans, la laverie avait beaucoup de clients.
Étudiant(e) 2: Aujourd'hui, il n'y a personne dans la laverie.

510 *cinq cent dix*

OPTIONS

Extra Practice State that someone is wearing a certain article of clothing and then ask students who it is. Example: **Est-ce que vous voyez quelqu'un dans la classe qui porte un tee-shirt rouge? Qui?** In some cases, name an article not present in the classroom so that students will answer negatively: **Personne ne porte de jupe.**

Extra Practice Read a series of logical and illogical statements that use the verbs **voir**, **recevoir**, **croire**, **apercevoir**, and **s'apercevoir**. Tell students to raise their right hand and say **logique** for logical ones, and to raise their left hand and say **illogique** for illogical ones. Example: **Je reçois toujours de mauvaises notes quand je fais tous mes devoirs. (illogique)**

Le Zapping

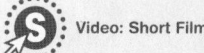
Video: Short Film

Mimoun tient une boucherie halal à Noisy-le-Grand, en banlieue parisienne. Son commerce connaît des difficultés financières, ce qui l'oblige à augmenter ses prix. Les clients se font rares, et Mimoun doit faire un choix. Va-t-il accepter une proposition commerciale alléchante° ou demeurer° le pauvre boucher de quartier?

alléchante tempting **demeurer** *remain*

Préparation

1 Synonymes Remplacez les termes soulignés par des synonymes appropriés du vocabulaire.

1. Tu dois porter <u>un uniforme pour travailler</u>. Sinon, tu vas salir tes vêtements. *une blouse*
2. Marie est <u>très fatiguée</u>. Elle a passé la journée au bureau. *épuisée*
3. Viens <u>voir</u>, j'ai trouvé l'adresse que l'on cherchait! *jeter un œil/ jeter un coup d'œil*
4. <u>Nous nous promenions dans le quartier</u> quand nous sommes tombés sur ce magasin. *Nous passions dans le coin*
5. Si vous continuez à dépenser comme ça, vous n'aurez plus d'<u>argent</u>! *un sou*

2 Réactions Avec un(e) partenaire, complétez ces dialogues avec des mots et expressions du vocabulaire.

1. —S'il te plaît! Pardonne-moi, c'est la dernière fois!
   —Non, c'est trop tard! Je ne veux plus te voir! __Va-t-en/Fous-__ __moi le camp__!
2. —Votre père et moi, nous allons au cinéma ce soir. Alors vous écoutez ce que la baby-sitter vous dit, d'accord? __Pas de bêtises__!
   —Oui, promis!
3. —Ce soir, nous allons cuisiner des hamburgers.
   —En ce cas, il faudra acheter de la __viande hachée__.
4. —Pourquoi est-ce que Gisèle appelle le plombier (*plumber*)?
   —Parce qu'il y a __une fuite__ dans sa salle de bains.
5. —Avec quel type de farine est-ce que le pain est préparé?
   —Avec de la farine de __blé__!
6. —Tout est en solde dans ce magasin.
   —Oui, ils ont vraiment __écrasé les prix__!

Expressions utiles

Je passais dans le coin...
I was passing by...

jeter un (coup d')œil
to take a look at

Va-t-en!
Get out!

écraser les prix
to slash prices

Je m'en fous. (fam.)
I don't care.

Pas de bêtises!
Behave yourself!

Foutez-moi le camp! (fam.)
Get lost!

tout compte fait
all things considered

Vocabulaire du court métrage

un agent matrimonial
matchmaker

épuisé(e)
exhausted, drained

des ailes/cuisses de poulet
chicken wings/legs

une fuite
leak

le blé
wheat

un sou
penny; small amount of money

une blouse
work apron

la viande hachée
ground beef

enfermé(e)
locked up

Introduction To check comprehension, ask these questions:
1. D'après l'introduction, quel est le sujet du court métrage que vous allez regarder?
2. Pourquoi le boucher doit-t-il faire un choix?
3. À votre avis, qu'est-ce qu'il va choisir?

Préparation Have students look at the poster and predict what the short film will be about.

1 Expansion Write all the vocabulary words and expressions on strips of paper and have students pick one. Ask them to create logical sentences in which they use the words or expressions they picked.

2 Expansion Ask students if they currently have or if they have ever had a part time job. Have volunteers share their experiences with their classmates. Ask them what problems they think immigrants might face when they move to another country in search of work.

OPTIONS

Note culturelle When looking for work, French people can turn to **Pôle Emploi**, formed in 2008 from two older job-search and benefits agencies. Its goal is to help job seekers find jobs, help companies recruit new employees, and fight against discrimination in the labor market.

Note culturelle The **SMIC (salaire minimum interprofessionnel de croissance)** is the French equivalent of the US minimum wage. It is currently € 9,76 per hour. The **SMIC** is reevaluated every year on January 1st.

Le Boucher

NATIONAL communication cultures STANDARDS

Avant de regarder le film Give students a moment to look at the images and scan the captions. Then, have them predict what they think will happen in the film.

Suggestion Stop after each segment and ask students to summarize what happened using their own words. After each segment, ask students to try and guess what might happen in the next segment.

Compréhension Have students look at the stills and read the dialogues. Then ask these questions: 1. Qui est François? Est-il un ami de Mimoun, à votre avis? Comment le savez-vous? 2. Que voudrait Anna? Pourquoi? 3. Est-ce que Mimoun va l'aider? 4. Comment Mimoun réagit-il quand Anna lui demande quel est son problème? 5. De quoi Mimoun et François discutent-ils à la fin?

MIMOUN Qu'est-ce que tu veux?

FRANÇOIS Je passais dans le coin, je me suis dit que ça serait gentil de venir faire un petit coucou° à mon ami Mimoun.

MIMOUN Dis-moi qu'est-ce que tu veux et va-t'en!

FRANÇOIS On raconte que votre petite affaire° n'est plus aussi florissante° qu'à ses débuts. Voici ce que je vous offre.

FRANÇOIS Tenez, jetez un œil, c'est intéressant.

ANNA C'est ma cousine. Tu ne la connais pas. Ça fait des mois qu'elle reste enfermée, elle n'arrête pas de regarder la télé et de manger.

ANNA Au début je pensais qu'elle était paresseuse, mais en fait, j'ai compris qu'elle était très déprimée°... Elle doit se marier. Tu ne connais pas quelqu'un?

MIMOUN Je suis boucher, pas agent matrimonial... Dis-lui qu'un homme a vu sa photo et qu'il la trouve la femme de sa vie. Et tu dis à cet homme que ta cousine le regarde par la fenêtre. Et ça va passer.

MIMOUN Tu as une copine?

SOFIAN Quelques-unes, ouais. Pourquoi?

MIMOUN Il y a une fille qui te trouve beau... J'ai promis de ne pas dire qui elle est.

SOFIAN Écoute, je l'appellerai moi-même! Je veux juste savoir qui c'est, s'il te plaît! Dis-moi!

MIMOUN Attention! Pas de bêtises! C'est une fille sérieuse, hein!

ANNA Qu'est-ce que tu as?

MIMOUN Rien.

ANNA Rien? Ça veut dire quoi, "rien"?

MIMOUN Je dois toujours être excité? Je suis simplement fatigué, laisse-moi tranquille.

ANNA Fatigué? C'est quoi ton problème?

MIMOUN Ce magasin me fatigue! Ce voisinage° m'épuise! J'ai soixante ans! Je dois écouter vos histoires et régler vos problèmes! Vous ne me laissez pas gagner un sou!

SOFIAN Bonsoir! On est venus par ici et on s'était dits que voilà on aurait un petit peu plus faim dans la nuit.

MIMOUN Je suis fermé... Bon. Qu'est-ce que tu veux?

SOFIAN Cinq cents grammes de viande hachée, s'il te plaît.

MIMOUN Bon, c'est cadeau pour les nouveaux mariés. Foutez-moi le camp, je dois fermer.

SOFIAN Merci beaucoup.

FRANÇOIS Voici la somme convenue°.

MIMOUN Mais qui va me remplacer?

FRANÇOIS Oh, sûrement pas moi! Mais ce ne sera pas difficile à trouver. Et pour être tout à fait honnête avec vous, j'ai déjà des candidats...

FRANÇOIS N'ayez aucun regret. Vous n'êtes plus tout jeune maintenant, il est temps de penser à la retraite. Et puis, ce n'est pas plus mal, moins de soucis°, plus d'argent! Tenez, signez.

coucou (fam.) hello **affaire** business **florissante** successful **déprimée** depressed
voisinage neighborhood **la somme convenue** the amount we agreed on **soucis** worries

 Practice more at **vhlcentral.com**.

O P T I O N S

Noisy-le-Grand Tell students that Noisy-le-Grand is a large, mainly working-class, eastern municipality of Paris, with a large and diverse immigrant community, including many people with Arab, Asian, and African roots.

Extra Practice Once students have viewed the various segments, ask them to describe and contrast Mimoun's interactions with the following characters: François, Anna,

Sofian, and Ammar (the teenage boy). What does each character want from Mimoun and what (if anything) do they offer in return? Ask students about Mimoun's actions at the end of the film. Why do they think he acted the way he did? Do they agree with his decision?

3 Expansion Have students justify their answers by quoting relevant sentences from the film.

4 Expansion Have students consider the predictions they made in the **Avant de regarder** activity. Have them compare their predictions with the actual events of the film.

5 Suggestion Before pairs begin work on this activity, brainstorm ideas to incorporate in the dialogues. Have students make a list of the characters in the film and consider how each one might react to Mimoun's announcement.

Analyse

3 Associez D'abord, faites correspondre les images aux phrases. Ensuite, mettez les images dans l'ordre chronologique.

_a_ 1. Il y a une fuite dans la boucherie de Mimoun.

_c_ 2. Mimoun demande à Sofian s'il a une copine.

_d_ 3. Mimoun rend le contrat signé à François.

_f_ 4. Anna explique que sa cousine a besoin de trouver un mari.

_e_ 5. Mimoun écoute la proposition de François.

_b_ 6. Mimoun regarde un documentaire sur la colonisation.

a. __2__   b. __5__   c. __4__

d. __6__   e. __1__   f. __3__

4 Mimoun et son entourage Avec un(e) partenaire, répondez à ces questions sur le film. Answers will vary.

1. Expliquez la citation au début du film. Est-ce qu'elle correspond bien à l'histoire de Mimoun?

2. Comment est-ce qu'Anna explique l'attitude paresseuse de sa cousine? Pourquoi veut-elle que sa cousine trouve un mari? Pensez-vous que c'est une bonne solution?

3. Qui est la femme avec Sofian? Que demande Sofian à Mimoun? Que pensez-vous du comportement (*behavior*) de Sofian? Auriez-vous été aussi généreux(se) que Mimoun?

4. Pourquoi Mimoun s'énerve-t-il quand Anna lui demande quel est son problème? Sa réaction est-elle légitime?

5. Quel genre de vie Mimoun a-t-il? Utilisez des adjectifs pour décrire sa routine.

6. Qu'auriez-vous fait à la place de Mimoun? Auriez-vous signé le contrat que François propose? Pourquoi?

5 LChez Mimoun Par groupes de trois, préparez une scène dans laquelle Mimoun explique à deux autres personnages (*characters*) du film qu'il va relancer (*revive*) sa boucherie. Servez-vous de ces questions pour créer leur conversation. Answers will vary.

- Qui sont les deux autres personnages?
- Comment Mimoun va-t-il attirer (*attract*) de nouveaux clients?
- À qui va-t-il demander de l'aide?
- Va-t-il proposer des promotions sur ses produits?
- Comment est-ce que les deux autres personnages réagissent?

cinq cent treize 513

OPTIONS

Small Groups Have students write a brief character study of Mimoun. What role does he serve in his community? What would happen to the other characters if he chose to close his shop or move away? Encourage them to use elements from the film to make inferences and draw conclusions.

Extra Practice Have students imagine they are employees at Mimoun's butcher shop. Ask them to write a paragraph explaining what their daily routine is like and describing their interactions with Mimoun.

Section Goals

In this section, students will learn and practice vocabulary related to:
- asking for and giving directions
- landmarks

Instructional Resources
vhlcentral.com:
Digital Image Bank;
Vocabulaire supplémentaire;
Mise en pratique *answers;*
Textbook Audioscript;
Lab Audioscript; Activity Pack;
Textbook MP3s; Lab MP3s;
SAM Answer Key;
reference tools

Suggestions

- Tell students to look over the new vocabulary and identify the cognates.
- Use the **12B Contextes** illustration from the Digital Image Bank. Point out objects and describe what the people are doing. Examples: **Il est perdu. C'est une statue. Il y a deux feux de signalisation au carrefour.**
- Define and contrast the words for types of roads: **une rue, une autoroute, un boulevard, une avenue,** and **un chemin.** Also give examples using local roads students know.
- Point out that **coin** and **angle** both mean *corner.*
- Point out the difference between **tout droit** (*straight ahead*) and **à droite** (*to the right*).
- You might want to teach students the expression **point de repère** (*landmark; point of reference*).
- Use the Vocabulary illustrations and the City life illustrations from the Digital Image Bank to help students familiarize themselves asking for and giving directions, and landmarks.
- Additional vocabulary for this lesson can be found in the **Vocabulaire supplémentaire** on the Supersite.

Leçon 12B

You will learn how to...
- ask for directions
- tell what you will do

Vocabulary Tools

Où se trouve...?

Vocabulaire

continuer	to continue
se déplacer	to move (change location)
suivre	to follow
tourner	to turn
traverser	to cross
un angle	corner
une avenue	avenue
un bâtiment	building
un boulevard	boulevard
un chemin	way; path
un coin	corner
des indications (f.)	directions
un office du tourisme	tourist office
au bout (de)	at the end (of)
au coin (de)	at the corner (of)
autour (de)	around
jusqu'à	until
(tout) près (de)	(very) close (to)
tout droit	straight ahead

un pont

Elle monte les escaliers. (monter)

une statue

Il descend les escaliers. (descendre)

une fontaine

OUEST   NORD   SUD   EST

Il est perdu. (perdue f.)

Elle s'oriente. (s'orienter)

ressources

WB	LM	vhlcentral
pp. 169–170	p. 93	

Extra Practice Ask students which vocabulary words they associate with these verbs. **1.** descendre (rue/escalier) **2.** suivre (rue/boulevard/chemin) **3.** tourner (gauche/droite) **4.** demander (indications) **5.** monter (escaliers) **6.** traverser (un pont/une rue) **7.** regarder (une statue) **8.** boire (une fontaine) **9.** téléphoner (une cabine téléphonique) **10.** s'arrêter (un feu de signalisation)

TPR Label four points in your classroom with the cardinal directions. Play a game of **Jacques a dit** (*Simon says*) in which students respond to commands using the four directions. Example: **Regardez vers le nord.** Tell students to respond only if they hear the words **Jacques a dit.** If a student responds to a command not preceded by **Jacques a dit**, he or she is eliminated. The last person standing wins.

O P T I O N S

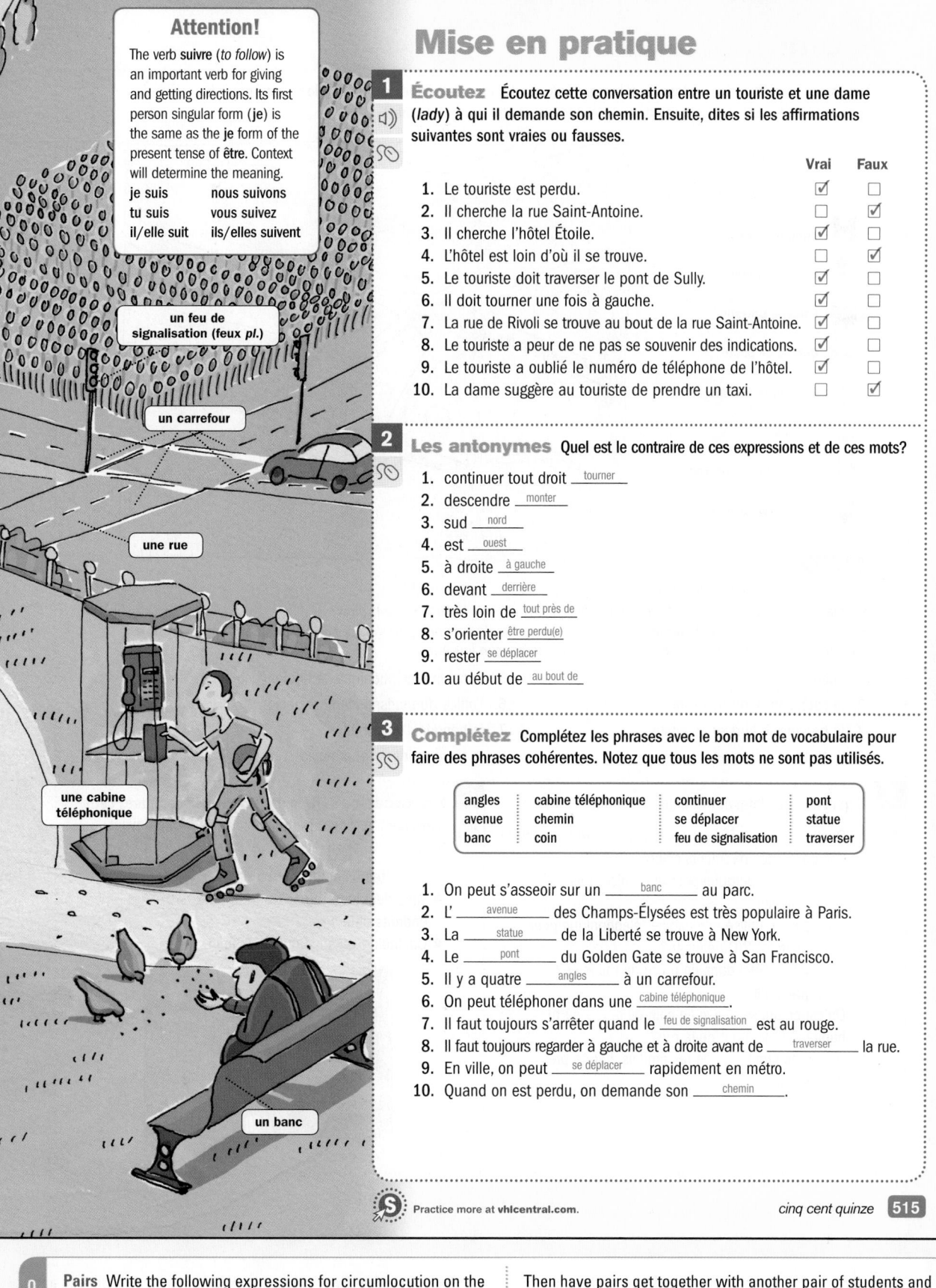

Attention!

The verb **suivre** (*to follow*) is an important verb for giving and getting directions. Its first person singular form (**je**) is the same as the **je** form of the present tense of **être**. Context will determine the meaning.

je suis	nous suivons
tu suis	vous suivez
il/elle suit	ils/elles suivent

un feu de signalisation (feux _pl._)

un carrefour

une rue

une cabine téléphonique

un banc

Mise en pratique

1 Écoutez Écoutez cette conversation entre un touriste et une dame (*lady*) à qui il demande son chemin. Ensuite, dites si les affirmations suivantes sont vraies ou fausses.

	Vrai	Faux
1. Le touriste est perdu.	☑	☐
2. Il cherche la rue Saint-Antoine.	☐	☑
3. Il cherche l'hôtel Étoile.	☑	☐
4. L'hôtel est loin d'où il se trouve.	☐	☑
5. Le touriste doit traverser le pont de Sully.	☑	☐
6. Il doit tourner une fois à gauche.	☑	☐
7. La rue de Rivoli se trouve au bout de la rue Saint-Antoine.	☑	☐
8. Le touriste a peur de ne pas se souvenir des indications.	☑	☐
9. Le touriste a oublié le numéro de téléphone de l'hôtel.	☑	☐
10. La dame suggère au touriste de prendre un taxi.	☐	☑

2 Les antonymes Quel est le contraire de ces expressions et de ces mots?

1. continuer tout droit ___tourner___
2. descendre ___monter___
3. sud ___nord___
4. est ___ouest___
5. à droite ___à gauche___
6. devant ___derrière___
7. très loin de ___tout près de___
8. s'orienter ___être perdu(e)___
9. rester ___se déplacer___
10. au début de ___au bout de___

3 Complétez Complétez les phrases avec le bon mot de vocabulaire pour faire des phrases cohérentes. Notez que tous les mots ne sont pas utilisés.

angles	cabine téléphonique	continuer	pont
avenue	chemin	se déplacer	statue
banc	coin	feu de signalisation	traverser

1. On peut s'asseoir sur un ___banc___ au parc.
2. L' ___avenue___ des Champs-Élysées est très populaire à Paris.
3. La ___statue___ de la Liberté se trouve à New York.
4. Le ___pont___ du Golden Gate se trouve à San Francisco.
5. Il y a quatre ___angles___ à un carrefour.
6. On peut téléphoner dans une ___cabine téléphonique___.
7. Il faut toujours s'arrêter quand le ___feu de signalisation___ est au rouge.
8. Il faut toujours regarder à gauche et à droite avant de ___traverser___ la rue.
9. En ville, on peut ___se déplacer___ rapidement en métro.
10. Quand on est perdu, on demande son ___chemin___.

S Practice more at vhlcentral.com.

cinq cent quinze **515**

1 Audioscript TOURISTE: Pardon, Madame, je suis perdu. Où se trouve l'hôtel Étoile, s'il vous plaît?
FEMME: L'hôtel Étoile? Désolée, Monsieur, je ne sais pas. Avez-vous l'adresse?
T: Oui, c'est 37 rue de Rivoli.
F: Ah, ce n'est pas loin d'ici. Suivez cette avenue tout droit jusqu'au pont de Sully. Traversez le pont et continuez sur le boulevard Henri IV. Tournez à gauche sur la rue Saint-Antoine et tout au bout, c'est la rue de Rivoli.
T: Merci, Madame. J'espère pouvoir me souvenir de vos indications.
F: Voulez-vous appeler l'hôtel? Il y a une cabine téléphonique devant nous. Peut-être que quelqu'un peut venir vous chercher?
T: Non, je n'ai pas leur numéro de téléphone. Je l'ai oublié à l'hôtel, mais, merci.
(On Textbook MP3s)

1 Suggestion Have students correct the false statements.

2 Expansions
- Have volunteers create sentences with the words in the activity.
- For additional practice, have students give synonyms for these words. **1.** angle (coin) **2.** chemin (rue) **3.** un grand boulevard (une avenue) **4.** un immeuble (un bâtiment)

3 Suggestion Have volunteers read the completed sentences aloud.

OPTIONS

Pairs Write the following expressions for circumlocution on the board: **C'est un endroit où…, Ça sert à…, C'est où on va pour…, C'est le contraire de…, C'est un synonyme de…, C'est une sorte de….** Tell students to work in pairs and write definitions for these vocabulary words. **1.** un boulevard **2.** un pont **3.** une fontaine **4.** des escaliers **5.** un bâtiment **6.** un office du tourisme **7.** une cabine téléphonique

Then have pairs get together with another pair of students and take turns reading their definitions and guessing the word. Ask each group to choose their best definition and write it on the board for the whole class to guess.

4 Suggestions
• Model the pronunciation of the roads on the map and have students repeat after you.
• Have two volunteers read the **modèle** aloud. Make sure students understand that they are supposed to give directions to the first place from the second place.

5 Expansion Have volunteers report what they learned about their partner to the class.

6 Suggestion Distribute real maps of French towns for students to use in their conversations. Such maps are available through tourist offices and online.

Communication

4 Le plan de la ville À tour de rôle avec un(e) partenaire, demandez des indications pour pouvoir vous rendre (to get) aux endroits de la liste. Indiquez votre point de départ. Answers will vary.

 Café de la Gare

 Boulangerie Le Pain Chaud

 H Hôpital St-Jean

 i Office du tourisme

 Épicerie Bresson

 Bureau de poste

 Pharmacie Molière

 € Banque

 U Université Joseph Fourier

 Cabine téléphonique

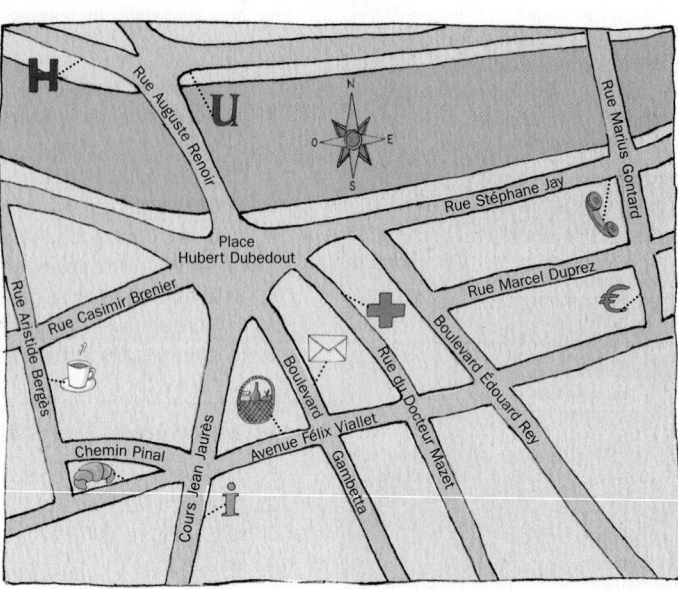

MODÈLE

la boulangerie Le Pain Chaud, le bureau de poste
Étudiant(e) 1: Excusez-moi, où se trouve la boulangerie Le Pain Chaud, s'il vous plaît?
Étudiant(e) 2: Du bureau de poste, suivez le boulevard jusqu'à l'avenue Félix Viallet, ensuite prenez à droite, continuez tout droit, la boulangerie est à droite, juste après le cours Jean Jaurès.

1. l'hôpital, la pharmacie
2. le café, l'office du tourisme
3. la banque, le bureau de poste
4. l'université, l'épicerie
5. la cabine téléphonique, la boulangerie
6. l'office du tourisme, la pharmacie
7. la banque, l'université
8. la boulangerie, la pharmacie

5 Conversez Interviewez un(e) camarade de classe. Answers will vary.

1. Quelles statues célèbres connais-tu? Connais-tu aussi des ponts, des bâtiments célèbres?
2. Quand t'es-tu perdu(e) pour la dernière fois? Où? Qui t'a aidé(e)?
3. Quand as-tu utilisé une cabine téléphonique pour la dernière fois? Où étais-tu?
4. Es-tu déjà allé(e) dans un office du tourisme? Pour quoi faire?
5. Qu'est-ce qui se trouve au coin de la rue où tu habites? Et au bout de la rue?
6. Qui, de ta famille ou de tes ami(e)s, habite près de chez toi?

6 En vacances Avec un(e) partenaire, préparez cette conversation. Soyez prêt(e)s à jouer la scène devant la classe. Answers will vary.

• Vous êtes un(e) touriste perdu(e) en ville.
• Vous demandez où se trouvent deux endroits différents.
• Quelqu'un vous indique le chemin.

OPTIONS

Game Arrange furniture to form meandering pathways around the classroom. Blindfold a student and point out to the class a destination somewhere in the room. Have the class give the blindfolded student directions to arrive at the destination. Example: **Tourne(z) à gauche/à droite.** To make this a competitive game, divide the class into two teams. Blindfold two students and have them race to different destinations.

Extra Practice Have students ask for and give directions to and from specific places on campus. Example: **Comment va-t-on du resto U à la bibliothèque?** Other campus landmarks can include: **la librairie, la statue de _____, la fontaine, l'amphithéâtre, le stade,** and **la piscine.**

Les sons et les lettres   Audio

Les majuscules et les minuscules

Some of the rules governing capitalization are the same in French as they are in English. However, many words that are capitalized in English are not capitalized in French. For example, the French pronoun **je** is never capitalized except when it is the first word in a sentence.

Aujourd'hui, je vais au marché.   *Today, I am going to the market.*

Days of the week, months, and geographical terms are not capitalized in French.

Qu'est-ce que tu fais lundi après-midi?   **Mon anniversaire, c'est le 14 octobre.**
Cette ville est au bord de la mer Méditerranée.

Languages are not capitalized in French, nor are adjectives of nationality. However, if the word is a noun that refers to a person or people of a particular nationality, it is capitalized.

Tu apprends le français.   **C'est une voiture allemande.**
You are learning French.   *It's a German car.*

Elle s'est mariée avec un Italien.   **Les Français adorent le foot.**
She married an Italian.   *The French love soccer.*

As a general rule, you should write capital letters with their accents. Diacritical marks can change the meaning of words, so not including them can create ambiguities.

LES AVOCATS SERONT JUGÉS.   **LES AVOCATS SERONT JUGES.**
Lawyers will be judged.   *Lawyers will be the judges.*

Corrigez Corrigez la capitalisation des mots suivants.

1. MAI mai
2. QUÉBEC Québec
3. VENDREDI vendredi
4. ALLEMAND allemand
5. L'OCÉAN PACIFIQUE l'océan Pacifique
6. LE BOULEVARD ST-MICHEL le boulevard St-Michel

Écrivez Écrivez correctement les phrases en utilisant *(by writing)* les minuscules et les majuscules.

1. LE LUNDI ET LE MERCREDI, J'AI MON COURS D'ITALIEN.
   Le lundi et le mercredi, j'ai mon cours d'italien.
2. CHARLES BAUDELAIRE ÉTAIT UN POÈTE FRANÇAIS.
   Charles Baudelaire était un poète français.
3. LES AMÉRICAINS AIMENT BEAUCOUP LE LAC MICHIGAN.
   Les Américains aiment beaucoup le lac Michigan.
4. UN MONUMENT SE TROUVE SUR L'AVENUE DES CHAMPS-ÉLYSÉES.
   Un monument se trouve sur l'avenue des Champs-Élysées.

Dictons Répétez les dictons à voix haute.

Si le Français est «tout yeux», l'Anglais est «tout oreilles».[2]

La France, c'est le français quand il est bien écrit.[1]

ressources

LM
p. 94

vhlcentral

[1] France is French (when it is) well written.
[2] If the Frenchman is all eyes, the Englishman is all ears.

cinq cent dix-sept **517**

Section Goals

In this section, students will learn about French capitalization.

Instructional Resources
vhlcentral.com:
Lab MP3s; SAM Answer Key;
Textbook Audioscript;
Lab Audioscript;
reference tools

Suggestions
• Model the pronunciation of the example sentences and have students repeat them after you.
• Have students translate the sentences in the second set of examples into English and compare capitalization rules in the two languages.
• You might want to tell students that diacritical marks are sometimes omitted on capital letters in French, especially on signs or headlines. In such cases, they should use the context to ascertain meaning.
• You might want to tell students that the names of religions are not capitalized in French. Example: **Paul est catholique.**
• Dictate three sentences that contain days of the week, months, countries, nationalities or languages, repeating each one at least two times. Then write them on the board or a transparency and have students check their spelling.

Dictons The saying **«La France, c'est le français quand il est bien écrit.»** is a quote from Napoléon Bonaparte. The saying **«Si le Français est "tout yeux", l'Anglais est "tout oreilles".»** is a quote from Jules Verne.

Extra Practice Use these sentences for additional practice with capitalization. **1. EN FÉVRIER, LISE VA EN ITALIE. 2. LOUIS A UNE VOITURE JAPONAISE. 3. MA COUSINE LAURE S'EST MARIÉE AVEC UN ESPAGNOL. 4. EUGÈNE HABITE AU 28 AVENUE GEORGE V. 5. LES TOURISTES BELGES ONT VISITÉ LA CATHÉDRALE DE NOTRE-DAME DE PARIS.**

Extra Practice Teach students these French tongue-twisters that model French capitalization conventions. **1. Je suis ce que je suis et si je suis ce que je suis, qu'est-ce que je suis? 2. Je dis que tu l'as dit à Didi ce que j'ai dit jeudi.**

ESPACE ROMAN-PHOTO

NATIONAL STANDARDS
communication cultures

Chercher son chemin Video

Section Goals

In this section, students will learn functional phrases for giving directions and talking about weekend plans.

Instructional Resources
vhlcentral.com:
Roman-photo Video, Videoscript, and Translation; SAM Answer Key; reference tools

Video Recap: Leçon 12A
Review the previous **Roman-photo** with this activity.
1. Pourquoi Rachid et Amina sont-ils à la charcuterie? (Ils achètent de la nourriture pour un pique-nique.)
2. Pourquoi Amina paie-t-elle? (Rachid n'a pas de liquide et la charcuterie n'accepte pas les cartes de crédit.)
3. Où Amina invite-t-elle Rachid à l'accompagner pendant l'après-midi? (dans une boutique et dans une bijouterie)
4. Où David invite-t-il Sandrine à aller avec lui? (dans une brasserie)

Video Synopsis
A tourist asks Monsieur Hulot for directions to the post office. He doesn't know, so he sends him to **Le P'tit Bistrot**. At the café, the four friends are discussing their weekend plans. When the tourist asks for directions, Rachid and David give him conflicting information. Stéphane asks the tourist, more confused than ever, if he can help and then proceeds to give him clear directions.

Suggestions
• Have students predict what the episode will be about based on the video stills.
• Have students scan the captions, and identify places and landmarks in a city.
• After reading the **Roman-photo**, have students summarize the episode.

PERSONNAGES

Amina

David

M. Hulot

Rachid

Sandrine

Stéphane

Touriste

Au kiosque de M. Hulot...
M. HULOT Bonjour, Monsieur.
TOURISTE Bonjour.
M. HULOT Trois euros, s'il vous plaît.
TOURISTE Je n'ai pas de monnaie.
M. HULOT Voici cinq, six, sept euros qui font dix. Merci.
TOURISTE Excusez-moi, où est le bureau de poste, s'il vous plaît?

M. HULOT Euh... c'est par là... Ah... non... euh... voyons... vous prenez cette rue, là et... euh, non non... je ne sais pas vraiment comment vous expliquer... Attendez, vous voyez le café qui est juste là? Il y aura certainement quelqu'un qui saura vous dire comment y aller.
TOURISTE Ah, merci, Monsieur. Au revoir!

Au P'tit Bistrot...
SANDRINE Qu'est-ce que vous allez faire le week-end prochain?
RACHID Je pense que nous irons faire une randonnée à la Sainte-Victoire.
AMINA Oui, j'espère qu'il fera beau!
DAVID S'il ne pleut pas, nous irons au concert en plein air de Pauline Ester. C'est la chanteuse préférée de Sandrine, n'est-ce pas, chérie?

DAVID Non! À droite!
RACHID Non, à gauche! Puis, vous continuez tout droit, vous traversez le cours Mirabeau et c'est juste là, en face de la fontaine de La Rotonde, à côté de la gare.
DAVID Non, c'est à côté de l'office du tourisme.

TOURISTE Euh merci, je... je vais le trouver tout seul. Au revoir.
TOUS Bonne journée, Monsieur.

À la terrasse...
STÉPHANE Bonjour, je peux vous aider?
TOURISTE J'espère que oui.
STÉPHANE Vous êtes perdu?
TOURISTE Exactement. Je cherche le bureau de poste.

A | 1 | **Questions** Répondez par des phrases complètes.
C
T
I
V
I
T
É
S

1. Qu'est-ce que Rachid et Amina vont faire ce week-end?
   Ils vont faire une randonnée à la Sainte-Victoire.
2. Qu'est-ce que Sandrine et David vont faire ce week-end?
   Ils vont aller à un concert en plein air.
3. Quels points de repères (*landmarks*) Stéphane donne-t-il au touriste?
   Il mentionne le cours Mirabeau, La Rotonde et la fontaine.
4. Est-ce que vous pensez que la musique de Pauline Ester est très appréciée aujourd'hui? Pourquoi?
   Answers will vary.

5. Est-ce que vous pensez que les choses vont bien entre Amina et Rachid? Pourquoi? Answers will vary.
6. Est-ce que vous pensez que les choses vont bien entre Sandrine et David? Pourquoi? Answers will vary.
7. Comment pensez-vous que le touriste se sent quand il sort du P'tit Bistrot? Answers will vary.
8. Qui avait raison, à votre avis (*in your opinion*), David ou Rachid? Answers will vary.

O
P
T
I
O
N
S

Avant de regarder la vidéo Before viewing the video, have students work in pairs and brainstorm a list of words and expressions they might hear in an episode involving people asking for directions.

Regarder la vidéo Show the video episode and tell students to check off the words or expressions they hear on their lists. Then show the episode again and have students give you a play-by-play description of the action. Write their descriptions on the board.

Un touriste se perd à Aix… heureusement, il y a Stéphane!

SANDRINE Absolument! «Oui, je l'adore, c'est mon amour, mon trésor...»
AMINA Pauline Ester! Tu aimes la musique des années quatre-vingt-dix?
SANDRINE Pas tous les styles de musique, mais Pauline Ester, oui.
AMINA Comme on dit, les goûts et les couleurs, ça ne se discute pas!
RACHID Tu n'aimes pas Pauline Ester, mon cœur?

TOURISTE Excusez-moi, est-ce que vous savez où se trouve le bureau de poste, s'il vous plaît?
RACHID Oui, ce n'est pas loin d'ici. Vous descendez la rue, juste là, ensuite vous continuez jusqu'au feu rouge et vous tournez à gauche.

STÉPHANE Le bureau de poste? C'est très simple.
TOURISTE Ah bon! C'est loin d'ici?
STÉPHANE Non, pas du tout. C'est tout près. Vous prenez cette rue, là, à gauche. Vous continuez jusqu'au cours Mirabeau. Vous le connaissez?
TOURISTE Non, je ne suis pas d'ici.
STÉPHANE Bon... Le cours Mirabeau, c'est le boulevard principal de la ville.

STÉPHANE Alors, une fois que vous serez sur le cours Mirabeau, vous tournerez à gauche et suivrez le cours jusqu'à La Rotonde. Vous la verrez... Il y a une grande fontaine. Derrière la fontaine, vous trouverez le bureau de poste, et voilà!
TOURISTE Merci beaucoup.
STÉPHANE De rien. Au revoir!

Expressions utiles

Giving directions

- **Attendez, vous voyez le café qui est juste là?**
  Wait, do you see the café right over there?
- **Il y aura certainement quelqu'un qui saura vous dire comment y aller.**
  There will surely be someone there who'll know how to tell you how to get there.
- **Vous tournerez à gauche et suivrez le cours jusqu'à La Rotonde.**
  You'll turn left and follow the street until the Rotunda.
- **Vous la verrez.**
  You will see it.
- **Derrière la fontaine, vous trouverez le bureau de poste.**
  Behind the fountain, you will find the post office.

Talking about the weekend

- **Je pense que nous irons faire une randonnée.**
  I think we'll go for a hike.
- **J'espère qu'il fera beau!**
  I hope it will be nice/the weather will be good!
- **Nous irons au concert en plein air.**
  We'll go to the outdoor concert.

Additional vocabulary

- **voyons**
  let's see
- **le boulevard principal**
  the main drag/principal thoroughfare

---

2 **Comment y aller?** Remettez les indications pour aller du P'tit Bistrot au bureau de poste dans l'ordre. Écrivez un **X** à côté de l'indication qu'on ne doit pas suivre.

- _3_ a. Suivez le cours Mirabeau jusqu'à la fontaine.
- _4_ b. Le bureau de poste se trouve derrière la fontaine.
- _2_ c. Tournez à gauche.
- _X_ d. Tournez à droite au feu rouge.
- _1_ e. Prenez cette rue à gauche jusqu'au boulevard principal.

3 **Écrivez** Le touriste est soulagé (relieved) d'enfin arriver au bureau de poste. Il était très découragé; presque personne ne savait lui expliquer comment y aller. Il écrit une carte postale à sa petite amie pour lui raconter son aventure . Composez son message.

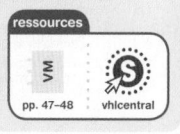
ressources
VM
pp. 47–48
vhlcentral

A C T I V I T É S

Expressions utiles
- Model the pronunciation of the **Expressions utiles** and have students repeat them after you.
- As you work through the list, point out forms of **le futur simple**. Tell students that this tense will be formally presented in **Espace structures**.
- Respond briefly to questions about **le futur**. Reinforce correct forms, but do not expect students to produce them consistently at this time.
- Point out in caption 4 where Amina says: **Les goûts et les couleurs, ça ne se discute pas**. Ask students to interpret it. Then point out that English expresses the same idea with the saying "*To each his own.*"

1 **Suggestions**
- Go over the answers with the class.
- For item 4, point out that Pauline Ester recorded the song *Oui, je l'adore* in 1989, and it remained popular in the 1990s. In this episode, Amina is surprised that Sandrine likes such an old song.

1 **Expansion** For additional practice, give students these questions. **9. Où va le touriste pour demander son chemin? (Il va chez le marchand de journaux et au café.) 10. Que cherche le touriste? (Il cherche le bureau de poste.) 11. Est-ce que le bureau de poste est loin du P'tit Bistrot? (Non, il est tout près.)**

2 **Suggestion** Have students form groups of five. Make a set of individual sentences on strips of paper for each group and distribute them. Tell students to arrange the sentences in the proper order and then read them aloud. The person who receives the sentence that does not fit should read that sentence last.

3 **Suggestions**
- Remind students to use appropriate salutations and closings. (See page 131.)
- If time is limited, this activity may be assigned as homework.

O P T I O N S

La Rotonde The large fountain located at one end of **le cours Mirabeau** is called **La Rotonde**. Built in 1860, it features bronze lions and stone cherubs riding swans. The source of the water is the city's underground springs. Every evening, this beautiful fountain is illuminated. If possible, bring in photos of **La Rotonde** to show the class.

Extra Practice Have students find the verbs used to give directions in this episode and list them on the board. Examples: **prendre, tourner, descendre, traverser,** and **continuer.** Then have students write directions from campus to various places in town using as many of these verbs as possible. You may wish to assign students different locations.

ESPACE ROMAN-PHOTO   **519**

Reading

Section Goals

In this section, students will:
- learn about main squares in French cities and towns
- learn more terms for small shops or businesses
- learn the names of famous areas in the heart of several francophone cities
- read about the Baron Georges Eugène Haussmann

Instructional Resources
vhlcentral.com: reference tools

Culture à la loupe

Avant la lecture Have students read the first sentence of the text. Then ask: **Votre ville natale a-t-elle une place principale ou un centre-ville? Quels bâtiments trouvez-vous souvent dans ces endroits?**

Lecture
- Point out the **Coup de main**. Explain that people in Paris customarily refer to a locale as **le 1ᵉʳ** or **le 13ᵉᵐᵉ**, without using the word **arrondissement**. Paris has 20 **arrondissements**.
- Explain that the term **la mairie** is related to the title of the person who works there, **le maire**.

Après la lecture Have students describe what they see in the photos. Then ask: **Pensez-vous que c'est une photo d'un village, d'une petite ville ou d'une grande ville? Pourquoi?**

1 Suggestion Have students work in pairs on this activity.

CULTURE À LA LOUPE

Villes et villages

Quand on regarde le plan d'un village, d'une petite ville ou celui d'un quartier dans une grande ville, on remarque qu'il y a souvent une place au centre, autour de laquelle° la vie urbaine s'organise. C'est un peu comme «le cœur» de la ville ou du quartier.

Sur la place principale des villes et villages français, on trouve souvent une église. Il peut aussi y avoir l'hôtel de ville (la mairie), ainsi que° d'autres bâtiments administratifs comme la poste, le commissariat de police ou l'office du tourisme. Autour de cette grande place se trouve le centre-ville où beaucoup de gens vont pour faire leurs courses dans les magasins ou pour se détendre dans un café, restaurant ou cinéma. Parfois, on y trouve aussi un musée ou un théâtre. La place principale peut être piétonne° ou ouverte à la circulation, mais dans les deux cas, elle est souvent très animée°.

En général, cette place est bien entretenue° et décorée d'une fontaine, d'un parterre de fleurs° ou d'une statue. La majorité des rues principales de la ville ou du quartier y sont connectées. Le nom de cette place reflète ce qui s'y trouve, par exemple place de l'Église, place de la Mairie ou place de la Comédie. Les rues, elles, portent souvent le nom d'un écrivain ou d'un personnage célèbre de l'histoire de France, par exemple rue Victor Hugo ou avenue du général de Gaulle. Au centre-ville, les rues sont souvent très étroites et beaucoup sont à sens unique°.

laquelle *which* **ainsi que** *as well as* **piétonne** *pedestrian* **animée** *busy* **entretenue** *cared for* **parterre de fleurs** *flower bed* **à sens unique** *one-way*

Coup de main

Some major cities in France, such as Paris, Lyon, and Marseille, are divided into **arrondissements**, or districts. You can determine in which **arrondissement** something is located by the final numbers of its zip code. For example, 75011 indicates the 11ᵗʰ **arrondissement** in Paris and 13001 is the 1ˢᵗ **arrondissement** in Marseille.

A C T I V I T É S

1

Complétez Donnez un début logique à chaque phrase, d'après le texte. Answers will vary. Possible answers provided.

1. ... au centre de la majorité des petites villes françaises.
   Il y a une place
2. ... autour de sa grande place.
   Une petite ville française s'organise
3. ... se situe souvent sur la place principale d'une ville française.
   Une église
4. ... pour faire leurs courses ou pour se détendre.
   Beaucoup de gens vont au centre-ville
5. ... décorent souvent les places.
   Une fontaine, une statue ou un parterre de fleurs
6. ... sont réservées exclusivement aux piétons.
   Les places piétonnes
7. ... détermine souvent le nom d'une place.
   Un bâtiment
8. ... donnent souvent leur nom aux rues françaises.
   Des écrivains ou d'autres personnages célèbres
9. ... sont souvent à sens unique.
   Les rues du centre-ville
10. ... sont parfois divisées en arrondissements.
   Les grandes villes françaises

O P T I O N S

Cultural Comparison Have students work in groups of three. Tell them to compare the center of French towns and cities with the center of the town or city in which their campus is located. Have them list the similarities and differences in a two-column chart under the headings **Similitudes** and **Différences**. Alternatively, you can let students choose another location to compare.

Villes et villages Having a book of maps (**un plan détaillé**) is essential when visiting a French city because roads are often short, narrow, and organized on uneven grids or no grids at all. Even many lifelong residents of Paris and Lyon keep their maps with them.

LE FRANÇAIS QUOTIDIEN

Des magasins

cordonnerie (*f.*)	*cobbler's*
disquaire (*m.*)	*music store*
fleuriste (*m.*)	*florist*
parfumerie (*f.*)	*perfume/beauty shop*
photographe (*m.*)	*photo shop*
quincaillerie (*f.*)	*hardware store*
tailleur (*m.*)	*tailor's*
pressing (*m.*)	*dry cleaner's*
vidéoclub (*m.*)	*video store*

LE MONDE FRANCOPHONE

Le centre des villes

Les places centrales reflètent le cœur des centres-villes.

En Belgique
La Grand-Place à Bruxelles est bordée de superbes bâtiments ornés aux riches architectures néo-gothiques et baroques du 17e siècle. Énorme, elle est considérée comme une des plus belles places du monde.

Au Maroc
La place Djemaa El Fna à Marrakesh est immense et débordante° d'activités. Et quelles activités! On y trouve des acrobates, des charmeurs de serpents, des danseurs, des groupes de musique, des conteurs° et beaucoup de restaurants ambulants°.

Ces deux places sont inscrites° au patrimoine mondial° de l'UNESCO.

débordante *overflowing* **conteurs** *storytellers* **restaurants ambulants** *food stalls* **inscrites** *registered* **patrimoine mondial** *world heritage*

PORTRAIT

Le baron Haussmann

En 1853, Napoléon III demande au baron Georges Eugène Haussmann (1809-1891) de moderniser Paris. Le baron imagine alors un programme de transformation de la ville entière°. Il en est le premier vrai urbaniste. Il multiplie sa surface par deux. Pour améliorer° la circulation, il ouvre de larges avenues et des boulevards, comme le boulevard Haussmann, qu'il borde° d'immeubles bourgeois. Il crée de grands carrefours, comme l'Étoile ou la place de

la Concorde, et de nombreux parcs et jardins. Plus de 600 km d'égouts° sont construits. Parce qu'il a aussi détruit beaucoup de bâtiments historiques, les Français ont longtemps détesté le baron Haussmann. Pourtant°, son influence a été remarquable.

entière *entire* **améliorer** *improve* **borde** *lines with* **égouts** *sewers* **Pourtant** *However*

MUSIQUE À FOND

Massilia Sound System

Lieu d'origine: Marseille, France
Métier: groupe de musique

Ce groupe de reggae français a commencé à jouer en 1984 Ils sont connus pour chanter des thèmes français avec le rythme jamaïcain. Ils chantent aussi en occitan ou langue d'oc.

Go to vhlcentral.com to find out more about **Massilia Sound System.**

---

2 **Complétez** Donnez une suite logique à chaque phrase.

1. En 1853, Napoléon III demande à Haussmann... *de moderniser Paris.*
2. Pour améliorer la circulation dans Paris, le baron Haussmann a créé... *de larges avenues et des boulevards.*
3. Les Français ont longtemps détesté le baron Haussmann... *parce qu'il a détruit beaucoup de bâtiments historiques.*
4. La Grand-Place est bordée de bâtiments ornés aux riches architectures... *néo-gothiques et baroques du 17e siècle.*
5. Sur la place Djemaa El Fna, on peut trouver des restaurants... *ambulants.*

3 **Une école de langues** Vous et un(e) partenaire dirigez une école de langues située en plein centre-ville. Préparez une petite présentation de votre école où vous expliquez où elle se situe, les choses à faire au centre-ville, etc. Vos camarades ont-ils envie de s'y inscrire (*enroll*)?

 ressources

 **vhlcentral**

 Practice more at **vhlcentral.com.**

ACTIVITÉS

OPTIONS

Le baron Haussmann Have students turn to the map of Paris on page 350. Tell them to find **le boulevard Haussmann, la place de la Concorde,** and **l'Étoile (l'Arc de Triomphe)** and describe each location. Then have them find other boulevards and describe the locations of various parks and gardens.

Small Groups Have students work in groups of three or four. Tell them to discuss these topics: **Les Français ont-ils eu raison de détester Haussmann? Faut-il détruire des bâtiments historiques au nom du progrès?** Then ask volunteers to report the results of their discussion to the class.

Le français quotidien
- Model the pronunciation of each term and have students repeat it.
- Have volunteers explain what service(s) each store offers or what product(s) each one sells. Example: **Chez le fleuriste, on vend des fleurs.** Alternatively, you can have them write definitions in French. Then tell them to get together with a partner, and take turns reading their definitions and guessing the kind of shop.

Portrait
- Haussmann was born in Paris and began his **carrière préfectorale** in 1831, working in several regions of France before being asked to modernize Paris. The transformation of Paris took place in three stages between 1858 and 1870. The city's sewer system was rebuilt to help prevent disease after a cholera epidemic.
- Have students describe the photos of **le boulevard Haussmann** and **la place de la Concorde**.

Le monde francophone
- After reading the text, ask students in what countries or cities these places are located. Examples: **1. Dans quel pays est la Grand-Place? (en Belgique) 2. Où est la place Djemaa El Fna? (Elle est à Marrakesh.)**
- Then ask questions about the individual places. Examples: **1. Dans quels endroits pouvez-vous manger? (sur la Grand-Place) 2. Où pouvez-vous trouver des objets artisanaux? (dans la médina de Fès) 3. Où pouvez-vous voir des monuments et des bâtiments historiques? (sur la Grand-Place, à la médina et sur la Place-Royale)**

2 Expansion For additional practice, give students these items. **6. Haussmann est le premier vrai... (urbaniste de Paris.) 7. Pour rendre Paris plus belle, Haussmann a créé... (de nombreux parcs et jardins.) 8. Le marché municipal de Nouméa est ouvert... (tous les jours.)**

3 Expansion After the presentations have been completed, have students vote on the school they most wish to attend.

 12B.1

Le futur simple

Point de départ In **Leçon 4A**, you learned to use **aller** + [*infinitive*] to express actions that are going to happen in the immediate future (**le futur proche**). You will now learn the future tense to say what *will happen*.

- The future uses the same verb stems as the conditional.

Future tense of regular verbs			
	parler	réussir	attendre
je/j'	parlerai	réussirai	attendrai
tu	parleras	réussiras	attendras
il/elle/on	parlera	réussira	attendra
nous	parlerons	réussirons	attendrons
vous	parlerez	réussirez	attendrez
ils/elles	parleront	réussiront	attendront

Au Québec, nous **parlerons** français.
In Quebec, we will speak French.

Je **suivrai** le chemin autour du parc.
I'll follow the path around the park.

- The same patterns that you learned for forming the conditional of spelling-change **-er** verbs also apply to the future.

Vous m'**emmènerez** avec vous?
Will you take me with you?

Tu **répéteras** les indications?
Will you repeat the directions?

Nous **achèterons** une maison dans deux ans.
We'll buy a house in two years.

Mes parents t'**appelleront** demain.
My parents will call you tomorrow.

- The same irregular stems you learned for the conditional are used for the future.

J'**irai** chez toi, mais pas aujourd'hui.
I'll go to your house, but not today.

À l'angle, tu **devras** tourner à gauche.
At the corner, you'll have to turn left.

- The words **le futur** and **l'avenir** (*m.*) both mean *the future*. Use the first word when referring to the grammatical tense; use the second word when referring to events that haven't occurred yet.

On étudie **le futur** en cours.
We're studying the future tense in class.

Je parlerai de **mon avenir** au prof.
I'll speak to the professor about my future.

Essayez! Complétez les phrases avec la forme correcte du futur des verbes.

1. je _____*mangerai*_____ (manger)
2. il _____prendra_____ (prendre)
3. on _____boira_____ (boire)
4. elles _____partiront_____ (partir)
5. ils _____achèteront_____ (acheter)
6. vous _____choisirez_____ (choisir)
7. tu _____connaîtras_____ (connaître)
8. nous _____suivrons_____ (suivre)

À noter

See **Leçon 11B** for the explanation of how to form the conditional of spelling-change verbs and for the list of verbs with irregular conditional stems. Irregular stems will be reviewed in **12B.2**.

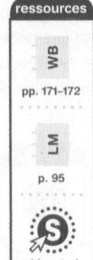

ressources

WB
pp. 171–172

LM
p. 95

vhlcentral

Section Goals

In this section, students will learn:
- the **futur simple** of regular verbs
- the **futur simple** with spelling-change **-er** verbs

Instructional Resources

vhlcentral.com:
Activity Pack; Lab MP3s; SAM Answer Key; **Essayez!** *and* **Mise en pratique** *answers; Lab Audioscript; reference tools*

Suggestions

- Before introducing the **futur simple**, review **futur proche** constructions by asking students questions about their plans for the upcoming weekend. Examples: **Qui va sortir ce week-end? Vous allez faire quoi ce week-end, _____ ?**
- Go over the pronunciation of spelling-change **-er** verbs in the table. Then ask students for other verbs they've learned that end in **-yer** (**employer, essayer, balayer, essuyer,** and **s'ennuyer**).
- You might want to teach the expressions **à l'avenir** and **dans l'avenir** (*in the future*) to the class. In addition, consider giving students a list of other adverbial expressions to use with the **futur simple: l'année/la semaine/le mois prochain(e)**; [*day of the week*] **+ prochain; dans … ans/mois/ semaines; en** + [*name of month or year*]; etc.

Essayez! Have students create sentences using these phrases.

Le français vivant Ask students to find New Brunswick on the map on page 170. Point out that it is an officially bilingual province whose languages are French and English, and that it borders Quebec and Maine.

Le français vivant

Le Nouveau-Brunswick vous enchantera!

Le Nouveau-Brunswick vous habitera pour toujours.
Vous aimerez ses villes cosmopolites et historiques,
au style jeune et moderne. Venez faire un tour.

Identifiez Quelles formes de verbes au futur trouvez-vous dans cette publicité (*ad*)?
enchantera, habitera, aimerez

Questions À tour de rôle, avec un(e) partenaire, posez-vous ces questions et répondez.
Some answers will vary.

1. Que veut dire «Le Nouveau-Brunswick vous habitera pour toujours»?
   a. Vous habiterez toujours au Nouveau-Brunswick.
   b. Vous penserez toujours au Nouveau-Brunswick.
   c. Le Nouveau-Brunswick existera toujours.

2. Pourquoi le touriste aimera-t-il le Nouveau-Brunswick?

3. Dans quel pays se trouve le Nouveau-Brunswick? au Canada

4. Dans quelle région du monde veux-tu voyager? Cette région t'enchantera-t-elle?

5. Voyageras-tu un jour au Nouveau-Brunswick? Pourquoi?

cinq cent vingt-trois **523**

OPTIONS

Extra Practice Write the following on the board: **L'année prochaine, je/j'...**. Then ask students to complete the sentence using a verb in the **futur simple**. If they wish to use a verb with an irregular stem, give them the form and tell them that they'll review irregular stems in **Espace structures 12B.2**.

Extra Practice Read predictions about the future while students react by saying **Oui, c'est probable** or **Non, c'est peu probable**. Write the two phrases on the board before you get started. Example: **En l'an 3000, personne ne parlera ni français ni anglais.**

1 **Suggestion** Have students do this activity in pairs. One student should read items 1–3, and the other one should restate the sentence using the **futur simple**. Then they should switch roles.

2 **Suggestion** Students could complete this activity in phases, first writing out the sentences in the present tense and then changing the verbs from the present to the future tense.

3 **Expansion** When students have finished, have them write an ad for their ideal job and write sentences about it based on the activity's questions. Allow them to create humorous job descriptions, such as for TV watchers.

Mise en pratique

1 **Projets** Cécile et ses amis parlent de leurs projets (*plans*) d'avenir. Employez le futur pour refaire ses phrases.

> **MODÈLE** Je vais chercher une belle maison.
> *Je chercherai une belle maison.*

1. Je vais finir mes études.   Je finirai mes études.
2. Philippe va me dire où trouver un travail.   Philippe me dira où trouver un travail.
3. Tu vas gagner beaucoup d'argent.   Tu gagneras beaucoup d'argent.
4. Mes amis vont habiter près de chez moi.   Mes amis habiteront près de chez moi.
5. Mon petit ami et moi, nous allons acheter un chien.   Mon petit ami et moi, nous achèterons un chien.
6. Vous allez nous rendre visite de temps en temps.   Vous nous rendrez visite de temps en temps.

2 **Dans l'avenir** Qu'est-ce qu'Habib et sa famille vont faire cet été?

> **MODÈLE** mon cousin / lire / dix livres
> *Mon cousin lira dix livres.*

1. mon neveu / apprendre / nager   Mon neveu apprendra à nager.
2. mes grands-parents / voyager / en voiture   Mes grands-parents voyageront en voiture.
3. en août / je / conduire / ma nouvelle voiture   En août, je conduirai ma nouvelle voiture.
4. mon père / écrire / cartes postales   Mon père écrira des cartes postales.
5. tante Yamina / maigrir   Tante Yamina maigrira.
6. nous / vendre / notre vieille voiture   Nous vendrons notre vieille voiture.

3 **Je cherche du travail** Regardez ces deux annonces (*ads*). Ensuite, avec un(e) partenaire, posez-vous ces questions et parlez du travail que vous préférez.   Answers will vary.

NOUVEAU RESTAURANT CHERCHE SERVEUR/ SERVEUSE	**TRAVAILLEZ COMME COIFFEUR/ COIFFEUSE**
Cinq ans d'expérience minimum. Cuisine française. Du mardi au samedi de 16h30 à 23h30; le dimanche de 11h30 à 22h30 Salaire 1.200 euros par mois, avec une augmentation après six mois Métro: Goncourt Téléphonez au: 01.40.96.31.15	Excellent salaire: 1.000 euros par mois Deux ans d'expérience Pour commencer immédiatement Horaires: mardi, mercredi, jeudi, de 9h00 à 15h00 Téléphonez pour rendez-vous au: 01.38.18.42.90

1. Quel emploi préfères-tu? Pourquoi?
2. À quelle heure arriveras-tu au travail? À quelle heure sortiras-tu?
3. T'amuseras-tu au travail? Pourquoi?
4. Combien gagneras-tu?
5. Prendras-tu le métro? Conduiras-tu? Pourquoi?
6. Chercheras-tu un autre emploi l'année prochaine? Pourquoi?

 Practice more at **vhlcentral.com**.

Communication

4 **Chez la voyante** Vous voulez savoir ce qui (*what*) vous attend dans l'avenir. Vous allez chez une voyante (*fortune-teller*) et vous lui posez ces questions. Jouez les deux rôles avec un partenaire, puis échangez les rôles. Answers will vary.

1. Où est-ce que je travaillerai après l'université?
2. Où est-ce que j'habiterai dans 20 ans?
3. Avec qui est-ce que je partagerai ma vie?
4. Quelle voiture est-ce que je conduirai?
5. Est-ce que je m'occuperai de ma santé?
6. Qu'est-ce que j'aimerai faire pour m'amuser?
7. Où est-ce que je passerai mes vacances?
8. Où est-ce que je dépenserai mon argent?

5 **L'horoscope** Avec un(e) partenaire, préparez par écrit l'horoscope d'une célébrité. Ensuite, par groupes de quatre, lisez cet horoscope à vos camarades qui essaieront de découvrir l'identité de la personne. Answers will vary.

MODÈLE

Vous travaillerez comme acteur de cinéma. Vous jouerez dans beaucoup de films français et américains. Vous jouerez des rôles divers dans des films comiques comme Last Holiday *et dans des films classiques comme* Jean de Florette. *(réponse: Gérard Depardieu)*

6 **Partir très loin** Vous et votre partenaire avez décidé de prendre des vacances très loin de chez vous. Regardez les photos et choisissez deux endroits où vous voulez aller, puis comparez-les. Utilisez ces questions pour vous guider. Ensuite, présentez vos réponses à la classe. Answers will vary.

- Qu'apporterez-vous?
- Quand partirez-vous?
- Que ferez-vous?
- Comment vous détendrez-vous? (*relax*)
- Combien de temps y resterez-vous?
- Quand rentrerez-vous?

7 **Faites des projets** Travaillez avec un(e) camarade de classe pour faire des projets (*plans*) pour ces événements qui auront lieu dans l'avenir. Answers will vary.

MODÈLE

Étudiant(e) 1: *Après l'université, je chercherai un travail à San Diego. J'enseignerai dans un lycée.*
Étudiant(e) 2: *Moi, après l'université, j'irai en Europe. Je travaillerai comme serveuse dans un café.*

1. Samedi soir: Décidez où vous irez et comment vous y arriverez.
2. Les prochaines vacances: Parlez de ce que (*what*) vous ferez. Que visiterez-vous?
3. Votre prochain anniversaire: Quel âge aurez-vous? Que ferez-vous? Avec qui ferez-vous la fête?
4. À 65 ans: Où serez-vous? Que ferez-vous? Avec qui partagerez-vous votre vie?

cinq cent vingt-cinq **525**

---

4 Expansion Have fortune-tellers record predictions. Then ask volunteers to read the most interesting predictions to the class.

5 Suggestion Discreetly assign a picture of a celebrity from magazines or the Internet to each pair.

6 Suggestion You might suggest that students use **on** rather than **nous** in their sentences so that they are typical of informal, everyday speech.

OPTIONS

Extra Practice Read a set of statements about what will happen in the future with some good events and some bad ones. Students should react to the statements by giving a thumbs-up (for good events) or a thumbs-down (for bad events). Example: **On gagnera des millions à la loterie.** (thumbs-up)

Small Groups Have students write a half-page description of a place in the future. It can be a utopia or a dystopia. You might suggest that they use ideas from science fiction. You may need to give them forms for some verbs with irregular stems in the future.

Section Goals

In this section, students will learn irregular forms of the **futur simple**.

Instructional Resources
vhlcentral.com:
Activity Pack; Lab MP3s;
SAM Answer Key; **Essayez!**
and **Mise en pratique**
answers; Lab Audioscript;
reference tools

Suggestions

• Ask students if they'll be doing certain things this coming year. Example: **Irez-vous à l'étranger?** As they give you their answers, write the subject pronoun and verb for each statement on the board and have the class repeat the combination after you.

• Ask students: **Que ferez-vous cet été?** As they tell you what they'll be doing, ask the other students if they'll be doing the same thing. Example: **Qui d'autre habitera à New York?**

• Make index cards with future forms of some of the verbs on this page (**j'irai, ils voudront**) and divide them equally between small groups of students. Have the groups formulate a sentence for each verb form with a statement about what will happen in the future. Example: **Rico deviendra médecin.**

• Have the class make a set of resolutions for the new year using the future tense. Write the resolutions on the board. Example: **Je ferai mes devoirs tous les jours.**

Essayez! If students are struggling to remember endings, write a paradigm for a verb in the future tense on the board and underline the endings. Then ask the class what the endings remind them of. (They resemble the present tense of **avoir**.)

12B.2

Irregular future forms  Tutorial

Point de départ In the previous grammar point, you learned how to form the future tense. Although the future endings are the same for all verbs, some verbs use irregular stems in the future tense. You learned to use many of these stems with the conditional in **Leçon 11B**.

Irregular verbs in the future		
infinitive	stem	future forms
aller	ir-	j'irai
apercevoir	apercevr-	j'apercevrai
avoir	aur-	j'aurai
devoir	devr-	je devrai
envoyer	enverr-	j'enverrai
être	ser-	je serai
faire	fer-	je ferai
pouvoir	pourr-	je pourrai
recevoir	recevr-	je recevrai
savoir	saur-	je saurai
venir	viendr-	je viendrai
vouloir	voudr-	je voudrai

Vous **aurez** des vacances?
Will you have vacation?

Nous **irons** en Tunisie.
We will go to Tunisia.

Il **enverra** des cartes postales.
He will send postcards.

Tu les **recevras** dans une semaine.
You will receive them in a week.

• The verbs **devenir, maintenir, retenir, revenir,** and **tenir** are patterned after **venir** in the future tense, just as they are in the present tense.

Nous **reviendrons** bientôt.
We will come back soon.

Tu **deviendras** architecte un jour?
Will you become an architect one day?

Qu'est-ce que vous **tiendrez** à la main?
What will you be holding in your hand?

Mme Tissot **retiendra** les enfants après l'école.
Mrs. Tissot will keep the children after school.

• The future forms of **il y a, il faut,** and **il pleut** are, respectively, **il y aura, il faudra,** and **il pleuvra.**

Il **faudra** apporter le parapluie.
We'll need to bring the umbrella.

Tu penses qu'il **pleuvra** ce week-end?
Do you think it will rain this weekend?

 Essayez! Conjuguez ces verbes au futur.

1. je/j' (aller, vouloir, savoir) ___irai, voudrai, saurai___
2. tu (faire, pouvoir, envoyer) ___feras, pourras, enverras___
3. Marc (venir, être, apercevoir) ___viendra, sera, apercevra___
4. nous (avoir, devoir, faire) ___aurons, devrons, ferons___
5. vous (recevoir, tenir, aller) ___recevrez, tiendrez, irez___
6. elles (vouloir, faire, être) ___voudront, feront, seront___
7. je/j' (devenir, pouvoir, envoyer) ___deviendrai, pourrai, enverrai___
8. elle (aller, avoir, vouloir) ___ira, aura, voudra___

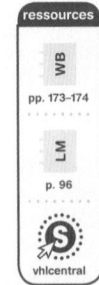
ressources

WB
pp. 173–174

LM
p. 96

vhlcentral

Le français vivant

Un emplacement unique, près du parc Vendôme

Le Voltaire à Nice

À 500 mètres du magnifique parc Vendôme, il y aura bientôt la Villa Adriana: une belle architecture, de grands appartements, avec terrasses et balcons. Vous viendrez visiter et vous ne voudrez plus repartir. Vous serez charmé.

AGENCE IMMO

Identifiez Quelles formes de verbes au futur trouvez-vous dans cette publicité (*ad*)?
aura, viendrez, voudrez, serez

 Questions À tour de rôle, avec un(e) partenaire, posez-vous ces questions et répondez.
Some answers will vary.

1. Où se trouvera bientôt le Voltaire?
Il se trouvera à 500 mètres du magnifique parc Vendôme.
2. Quelle sera l'architecture des appartements?
L'architecture sera belle avec de grands appartements, avec terrasses et balcons.
3. D'après (*According to*) la pub, quel effet une visite au Voltaire peut-elle avoir?
Vous ne voudrez plus repartir. Vous serez charmé.
4. As-tu été dans un appartement que tu n'as pas voulu quitter? Habiteras-tu un jour dans un appartement comme ça?
5. Est-ce que tu penses qu'un appartement à la Villa Adriana sera bon marché?
6. À ton avis, quelles boutiques et quels bureaux y aura-t-il autour du Voltaire?

OPTIONS

Extra Practice Make up a transparency with a set of **si** clauses, each beginning a sentence. Allow students to complete the sentences by supplying clauses with the verb in the future tense. Example: **S'il pleut cet après-midi, ... (je resterai à la maison avec mon chat.)**

Pairs Teach the expression **Quand les poules auront des dents** and then add ellipses (...) after it and tell the class to complete the thought by describing an improbable scenario with a partner. Example: **... moi, j'irai à la bibliothèque le samedi soir.** When students have completed their work in pairs, have them share it with the class.

1 Expansion Have students create a series of illustrations accompanied by text telling what they'll be doing next week.

2 Suggestion To make sure that students understand the passage they just completed, read each sentence back to them and ask the class if their dream life would be similar. Example: **Et vous? Est-ce que vous rêvez d'avoir une grande maison?**

3 Suggestion Write this paradigm on the board to help students with the activity: **si** + *present tense verb* → *future tense verb*. Tell students they will learn more about **si** clauses in **Leçon 13B**.

Mise en pratique

1 **Que ferai-je?** Que feront ces personnes la semaine prochaine?

MODÈLE

J'étudierai.

je / étudier

1. nous / faire
Nous ferons du shopping.

2. vous / aller
Vous irez au cinéma.

3. Anne et Sara / acheter
Anne et Sara achèteront des fleurs.

4. tu / être
Tu seras à la plage.

5. Yves / devoir
Yves devra travailler.

6. Rachid / envoyer
Rachid enverra une lettre.

2 **Le rêve de Stéphanie** Complétez les phrases pour décrire le rêve (*dream*) de Stéphanie. Employez le futur des verbes.

Quand j' (1) ___aurai___ (avoir) 26 ans, j' (2) ___irai___ (aller) habiter au bord de la mer. Mon beau mari (3) ___sera___ (être) avec moi et nous (4) ___aurons___ (avoir) une grande maison. Je ne (5) ___ferai___ (faire) rien à la maison. Nos amis (6) ___viendront___ (venir) nous rendre visite tous les week-ends. On (7) ___mangera___ (manger) bien et on (8) ___s'amusera___ (s'amuser) beaucoup!

3 **Si...** Avec un(e) partenaire, finissez ces phrases à tour de rôle. Employez le futur des verbes de la liste dans toutes vos réponses.   Answers will vary.

MODÈLE   Si (*If*) mon ami(e) ne me téléphone pas ce soir, ...

Si mon amie ne me téléphone pas ce soir,
je ne ferai pas de gym demain.

aller	devoir	faire	venir
avoir	être	pouvoir	vouloir

1. Si on m'invite à une fête samedi soir, ...
2. Si mes parents me donnent $1.000, ...
3. Si mon ami(e) me prête sa voiture, ...
4. Si le temps est mauvais, ...
5. Si je suis fatigué(e) vendredi, ...
6. Si ma famille me rend visite, ...
7. Si j'ai de bonnes notes ce semestre, ...
8. Si je ne dors pas bien cette nuit, ...
9. Si on a des difficultés en cours, ...

 Practice more at **vhlcentral.com**.

Communication

4 **Faites des projets** Travaillez avec un(e) camarade de classe pour faire des projets (*plans*) pour ces événements qui auront lieu dans l'avenir. Answers will vary.

MODÈLE

Étudiant(e) 1: *Après l'université, je chercherai un travail à San Diego. J'enseignerai dans un lycée où je pourrai travailler avec les adolescents.*
Étudiant(e) 2: *Moi, après l'université, j'irai en Europe. Je travaillerai comme serveuse dans un café.*

1. Samedi soir: Décidez où vous irez et comment vous y arriverez.
2. Les prochaines vacances: Parlez de ce que (*what*) vous ferez. Que visiterez-vous?
3. Votre prochain anniversaire: Quel âge aurez-vous? Que ferez-vous? Avec qui ferez-vous la fête?
4. Votre première voiture: Quelle voiture achèterez-vous? De quelle couleur sera-t-elle? Sera-t-elle chère?
5. Votre vie professionnelle: Que ferez-vous après l'université? Où irez-vous?
6. Votre famille: Serez-vous marié(e)? Aurez-vous des enfants? Où habiterez-vous?
7. Votre maison idéale: Sera-t-elle près du centre-ville ou en banlieue? Combien de pièces aura-t-elle?
8. À 65 ans: Où serez-vous? Que ferez-vous? Avec qui partagerez-vous votre vie?

5 **Prédictions** Par groupes de trois, parlez de comment sera le monde en 2020, 2050 et 2100. Utilisez votre imagination. Answers will vary.

6 **Demain** Avec un(e) partenaire, parlez de ce que (*what*) vous, votre famille et vos amis ferez demain. Answers will vary.

MODÈLE

Étudiant(e) 1: *Que feras-tu demain à midi?*
Étudiant(e) 2: *Demain à midi, j'irai poster une lettre. Mon camarade de chambre fera ses devoirs.*

vendredi	samedi
8h00	8h00
	10h00
10h00	12h00
	14h00
12h00	16h00
	18h00
14h00	20h00
	22h00
16h00	**dimanche**
	8h00
18h00	10h00
	12h00
20h00	14h00
	16h00
22h00	18h00
	20h00
	22h00

7 **Bonnes résolutions!** C'est bientôt le nouvel an et vous faites des résolutions. Avec un(e) partenaire, parlez à tour de rôle de cinq choses que vous changerez dans votre vie l'année prochaine. Answers will vary.

MODÈLE

Étudiant(e) 1: *L'année prochaine, je mangerai moins de pizzas et je perdrai cinq kilos.*
Étudiant(e) 2: *Moi, je ferai plus attention en classe et j'aurai de meilleures notes.*

---

4 **Suggestion** If students aren't comfortable sharing personal information, tell them that they can answer the questions in the activity for a well-known person or a fictional character (Rambo, Barbie, etc.).

5 **Expansion** For the presentation part of this activity, you might write a few reactions on the board for students to repeat. Examples: **Ah, oui, c'est sûr! Mais non! C'est une blague ou quoi?**

6 **Suggestion** To simplify the presentations, have students present only their partner's plans for tomorrow.

7 **Expansion** Have students provide encouragement to their partner by using the construction **Si** + *present tense verb* → *future tense verb* . Example: **Si tu manges moins de pizzas, tu maigriras sûrement!**

OPTIONS

Video Replay the video episode, having students focus on the conversation at the café. Afterwards, ask them questions about it. Examples: **Pourquoi Amina dit-elle qu'elle espère qu'il fera beau ce week-end? Que feront David et Sandrine ce week-end?**

Game Play a game of Bingo. Distribute Bingo cards with infinitives of verbs written in the squares. Then read aloud sentences, each with a future form of one of the verbs in it. Students should block out the verbs they recognize with tokens or scraps of paper and call Bingo! when they've blocked out a whole row.

Révision

Instructional Resources
vhlcentral.com:
*Activity Pack (Info Gap
Activities); Testing Program;
Testing Program MP3s;
reference tools*

1 Suggestion You might wish to hand out campus maps as a visual aid to help students complete this activity. Students with difficulty visualizing space could trace the routes their partner describes to them on their maps. You could mark the classroom with an X and the words **Vous êtes ici.**

2 Suggestion Tell students to include a time reference (**le matin, jeudi soir,** etc.) in each sentence.

3 Suggestion Before students begin this activity, you may wish to review the vocabulary for houses in **Leçon 8A.**

4 Suggestion So that students have a point of reference to verify the original instructions, have the student who first gives directions write them down. Then he or she can read the directions aloud to the first person and verify them while the second person recalls what he or she heard.

5 Suggestion To get the class warmed up for this activity, read a set of logical and illogical statements about what you will do given certain weather conditions. Tell students to qualify each statement as **logique** or **illogique.** Examples: **Il pleuvra samedi, donc j'irai à la plage. (illogique) S'il fait beau dimanche, on ira au parc. (logique)**

6 Suggestion Divide the class into pairs and distribute the Info Gap Handouts found in the Activity Pack on the Supersite. Give students ten minutes to complete the activity.

1 **Le campus** À tour de rôle, donnez des indications à un(e) partenaire pour aller d'où vous vous trouvez en ce moment jusqu'à d'autres endroits sur le campus. Employez le futur. Answers will vary.

> **MODÈLE**
>
> **Étudiant(e) 1:** *Tu sortiras du bâtiment et tu tourneras à gauche. Ensuite, tu traverseras la rue. Où seras-tu?*
> **Étudiant(e) 2:** *Je serai à la bibliothèque.*

2 **La visite de Québec** Avec un(e) partenaire, vous visitez la ville de Calvi, en Corse. Préparez un itinéraire de votre visite où vous vous arrêterez souvent pour visiter ou acheter quelque chose, manger, boire, etc. Soyez prêts à présenter votre itinéraire à la classe. Answers will vary.

> **MODÈLE**
>
> **Étudiant(e) 1:** *Le matin, nous prendrons le petit-déjeuner dans l'hôtel.*
> **Étudiant(e) 2:** *Ensuite, nous irons visiter la citadelle.*

Calvi vous attend!
Visitez
la citadelle
le phare de la Revellata
l'église Sainte-Marie-Majeure
le village d'Occi
l'ancien palais des Gouverneurs
et beaucoup plus!

3 **Ma future maison** Avec un(e) partenaire, parlez de votre future maison et de ses pièces, de son jardin, du quartier et de vos voisins. Utilisez le futur et ces prépositions pour les décrire. Ensuite, présentez les projets (*plans*) de votre partenaire à la classe. Answers will vary.

> **MODÈLE**
>
> **Étudiant(e) 1:** *Il y aura un énorme jardin devant ma future maison.*
> **Étudiant(e) 2:** *Je n'aurai aucun voisin en face de ma future maison.*

à droite (de)	autour (de)	en face (de)
à gauche (de)	derrière	loin (de)
au bout (de)	devant	(tout) près (de)
au milieu de		

4 **Ma ville** Vous invitez votre partenaire à venir vous rendre visite dans votre ville d'origine. Expliquez-lui le chemin de l'aéroport jusqu'à votre maison. Ensuite, votre partenaire donnera ces indications à un(e) autre camarade, qui vous les répétera. Les indications sont-elles toujours correctes? Utilisez le futur et alternez les rôles. Answers will vary.

> **MODÈLE**
>
> **Étudiant(e) 1:** *Tu sortiras de l'aéroport, tu iras jusqu'au centre-ville et tu passeras la mairie où tu tourneras à droite.*
> **Étudiant(e) 2:** *D'accord, à droite à la mairie. Et après, j'irai où?*

5 **Des prévisions météo** Avec un(e) partenaire, parlez des prévisions météo pour le week-end prochain. Chacun (*Each one*) doit faire cinq prévisions et dire ce qu'on (*what one*) peut faire par ce temps. Soyez prêts à parler de vos prévisions et des possibilités pour le week-end devant la classe. Answers will vary.

> **MODÈLE**
>
> **Étudiant(e) 1:** *Samedi, il fera beau dans le nord. On pourra faire une promenade.*
> **Étudiant(e) 2:** *Dimanche, il pleuvra dans l'ouest. On devra passer la journée dans l'appartement.*

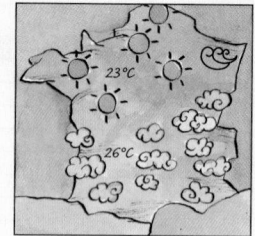 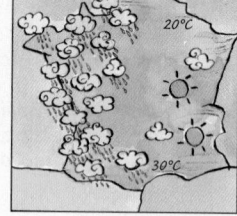

samedi   dimanche

6 **La vie de Gaëlle et de Marc** Votre professeur va vous donner, à vous et à votre partenaire, deux feuilles d'activités différentes sur l'avenir de Gaëlle et de Marc. Attention! Ne regardez pas la feuille de votre partenaire. Answers will vary.

> **MODÈLE**
>
> **Étudiant(e) 1:** *Marc et Gaëlle finiront leurs études au lycée.*
> **Étudiant(e) 2:** *Ensuite, ...*

Extra Practice Read answers and have students produce questions that could have prompted the responses. The answers should contain verbs in the future tense. Challenge the class to come up with as many different questions as possible. Example: **J'habiterai une maison au bord de la mer. (Qu'est-ce que vous ferez après la retraite?)**

Game Make two oversized dice out of paper. Stick labels with subject pronouns on all the facets of one die. Then label the facets of the other die with infinitives of verbs with irregular future stems. Have students take turns rolling the dice so that they know which future-tense verb form to produce for their classmates. Example: **nous + avoir (nous aurons)**

À l'écoute

Section Goals

In this section, students will:
• learn to use background information
• listen for the subject and main points in a paragraph
• listen to a conversation and complete several activities

STRATÉGIE

Using background information

Once you discern the topic of a conversation, take a minute to think about what you already know about the subject. Using this background information will help you guess the meaning of unknown words or linguistic structures.

 To help you practice this strategy, you will listen to a short paragraph. Jot down the subject of the paragraph, and then use your knowledge of the subject to listen for and write down the paragraph's main points.

Compréhension

Vrai ou faux? Indiquez si les phrases sont **vraies** ou **fausses**. Corrigez les phrases fausses.

1. Amélie habite cette ville depuis toujours.
   Faux. Elle habite cette ville depuis un mois.
2. Amélie ne connaît pas bien la ville.
   Vrai.
3. Christophe recommande la Banque de l'Ouest parce qu'il aime beaucoup son architecture. Faux. Il la recommande parce qu'elle est tout près et parce qu'il y a un distributeur automatique ouvert 24 heures sur 24.
4. La Banque de l'Ouest est en face d'une bijouterie.
   Faux. Elle est en face d'une pharmacie.
5. Amélie a besoin d'emprunter de l'argent à la banque.
   Faux. Elle veut ouvrir un compte en banque.
6. Amélie veut aller à la bibliothèque pour chercher des livres.
   Faux. Elle veut aller à une librairie pour acheter des livres.
7. La librairie Molière est près d'un jardin public.
   Vrai.
8. Christophe demande à Amélie si elle peut aller chercher un colis à la poste.
   Faux. Il lui demande de déposer un formulaire à la mairie.
9. Pour aller à la mairie, on doit traverser un pont.
   Vrai.
10. Ce matin, Christophe doit aller à la papeterie.
    Faux. Il doit aller à la laverie.

Dans votre ville Amélie passe un semestre à votre université. Elle vous pose les mêmes questions qu'elle a posées à Christophe. Écrivez-lui un petit mot pour lui expliquer comment aller, d'abord, de l'université à une banque qui se trouve dans le quartier universitaire. Puis, expliquez-lui comment aller de cette banque à un supermarché où les étudiants de votre université font souvent leurs courses. Demandez aussi à Amélie si elle peut faire une petite course pour vous et expliquez-lui où se trouve l'endroit où elle devra aller.

Préparation

Regardez la photo. Combien de personnes y a-t-il? Où sont-elles? Que font-elles? D'après vous, de quoi parlent-elles?

À vous d'écouter

Écoutez la conversation entre Amélie et Christophe. Puis, écoutez une deuxième fois et notez les quatre choses qu'ils vont faire ce matin. Comparez vos notes avec celles d'un(e) camarade.

ouvrir un compte en banque

acheter des livres à la librairie

aller à la mairie

aller à la laverie

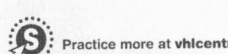 Practice more at **vhlcentral.com**.

Instructional Resources
vhlcentral.com:
Textbook MP3s; Textbook
Audioscript; reference tools

Stratégie
Audioscript La nuit dernière, il y a eu un cambriolage à la Banque Monet. Le directeur, Monsieur Dumais, a appelé le commissariat de police aussitôt qu'il est arrivé à la banque, vers huit heures trente ce matin. Pour l'instant, on ne sait pas encore combien d'argent a été volé.

Préparation Tell students to describe the photo. Then have them guess what the people are talking about.

À vous d'écouter
Audioscript AMÉLIE: Dis, Christophe, j'habite ici depuis un mois et je n'ai pas encore ouvert de compte en banque. Quelle banque est-ce que tu me recommandes?
CHRISTOPHE: La Banque de l'Ouest. Elle est tout près d'ici et il y a un distributeur automatique ouvert 24 heures sur 24. Tu sais où elle se trouve?
A: Non. Elle est où?
C: Dans la rue Flaubert. Pour y aller, tu prends le boulevard Jean Jaurès et au carrefour, tu tournes à droite. La banque est à l'angle de la rue Victor Hugo, en face de la pharmacie.
A: D'accord. Et je dois aussi acheter des livres pour la fac. Tu connais une bonne librairie?
C: Oui, la meilleure, c'est la librairie Molière, dans l'avenue de la République. Alors, pour y aller de la banque, tu prends la rue du Ménil et au bout de la rue, tu traverses la place d'Armes. Ensuite, tu descends l'avenue Girard et tu tournes à droite dans l'avenue de la République. Là-bas, tu trouveras la librairie, près du jardin public. Dis, est-ce que tu voudras bien faire une petite course pour moi?
A: Oui, bien sûr.
C: C'est dans le quartier. J'ai besoin

de déposer ce formulaire à la mairie.
A: OK. Elle est où, la mairie?
C: Alors, la mairie est sur la place Bellevue. De la librairie, tu continues tout droit dans l'avenue de la République. Ensuite, tu prends à gauche sur le boulevard Henri IV. Tu prends le pont Alexandre Dumas et la mairie sera juste là, de l'autre côté du pont, sur la place Bellevue.
A: Bon, d'accord, pas de problème. Et toi, qu'est-ce que tu vas faire ce matin?
C: Je vais aller à la laverie. J'ai plein de lessive à faire.
A: Eh bien bon courage, alors! À tout à l'heure.
C: Salut!

Panorama

la promenade des Anglais à Nice

Section Goals

In this section, students will read historical and cultural information **Provence-Alpes-Côte d'Azur** and **Corse**.

> **Instructional Resources**
> *vhlcentral.com; Digital Image Bank; SAM Answer Key; reference tools*

Carte de Provence-Alpes-Côte d'Azur et de la Corse

- Have students look at the map or use the **Panorama** map from the Digital Image Bank. Ask volunteers to read the names of cities and other geographical features aloud. Model the pronunciation as necessary.
- Point out that both regions are popular tourist destinations. Have students identify the geographical features that make these regions desirable vacation spots.

Les régions en chiffres

- Have volunteers read the sections aloud. After each section, ask students questions about the content.
- Point out cognates and clarify unfamiliar words.
- Point out Corsica's flag with the Moor's head (**testa mora**). Tell students that on the original flag, the bandana covered the man's eyes. However, when Pasquale Paoli established the Corsican Republic in 1755, the bandana was moved to above the eyes to symbolize the people's liberation.

Incroyable mais vrai! Have students locate **la Camargue** on the map. Tell them that a reserve was created to protect the flora and fauna found in the 211,740-acre park.

Provence-Alpes-Côte d'Azur

La région en chiffres

▶ **Superficie:** *31.400 km²*

▶ **Population:** *4.989.435*
SOURCE: INSEE

▶ **Industries principales:** *agriculture, industries agro-alimentaires°, métallurgiques et mécaniques, parfumerie, tourisme*

▶ **Villes principales:** *Avignon, Gap, Marseille, Nice, Toulon*

Personnes célèbres

▶ **Nostradamus,** *astrologue et médecin (1503–1566)*

▶ **Marcel Pagnol,** *cinéaste° et écrivain (1895–1974)*

▶ **Surya Bonaly,** *athlète olympique (1973–)*

La Corse

La région en chiffres

▶ **Superficie:** *8.680 km²*

▶ **Population:** *330.354*
SOURCE: ADEC

▶ **Industries principales:** *agriculture, tourisme*

▶ **Villes principales:** *Ajaccio, Bastia, Porto-Vecchio, Calvi, Corte*

Personnes célèbres

▶ **Pasquale Paoli,** *homme politique et philosophe, (1725–1807)*

▶ **Tino Rossi,** *chanteur, (1907–1983)*

▶ **Marie-Josée Nat,** *actrice, (1940–)*

agro-alimentaires *food-processing* **cinéaste** *filmmaker* **confrérie** *brotherhood* **gardians** *herdsmen* **taureaux** *bulls* **flamants** *flamingos* **Montés sur** *Riding* **Papes** *Popes* **falaises** *cliffs*

Map labels: LA FRANCE · L'ITALIE · LES ALPES · Gap · la Durance · le Rhône · PROVENCE-ALPES-CÔTE D'AZUR (PACA) · Avignon · MONACO · Arles · LA CAMARGUE · la Durance · le Verdon · Grasse · Nice · Antibes · Cannes · Aix-en-Provence · le Var · Marseille · Toulon · LA MER MÉDITERRANÉE · Les îles d'Hyères · 0 80 miles · 0 80 kilomètres · Bastia · Calvi · Corte · CORSE · Ajaccio · Porto-Vecchio · Bonifacio · LA SARDAIGNE

le palais des Papes° à Avignon

les falaises° de Bonifacio

Incroyable mais vrai!

Tous les cow-boys ne sont pas américains. En Camargue, la confrérie° des gardians° perpétue depuis 1512 les traditions des cow-boys français. C'est dans le sud que cohabitent les chevaux blancs camarguais, des taureaux° noirs et des flamants° roses. Montés sur° des chevaux blancs, les gardians gardent les taureaux noirs.

OPTIONS

Personnages célèbres **Nostradamus** was a physician and astrologer best known for his predictions of the future. **Marcel Pagnol** was the first filmmaker to be elected to the **Académie française.** **Surya Bonaly** has competed in three Olympic Games and won medals in many national and international figure skating competitions. **Pasquale Paoli** led a rebellion in 1755 to create the first democratic state in Europe, **la République de Corse.** **Tino Rossi** was a popular singer in the 20th century and best known for his Christmas song **Petit papa Noël.** Cannes Film Festival award-winner, **Marie-Josée Nat (née Benhalassa),** has performed on stage, screen, and in theater.

Les destinations

La réserve naturelle de Scandola

La réserve naturelle de Scandola en Corse a été l'un des premiers sites français à être classé réserve du patrimoine° naturel terrestre et marin. La réserve fait partie° d'un ancien complexe volcanique connu au niveau international pour sa biodiversité. Des scientifiques viennent y étudier le corail° rouge, des espèces marines qui ont disparu ailleurs° dans la Méditerranée, et des espèces inconnues jusqu'à présent. La réserve abrite° aussi une population importante de balbuzards pêcheurs°, une espèce de rapace° qui a été très menacée dans les années 1970.

Les arts

Le festival de Cannes

Chaque année depuis 1946, au mois de mai, de nombreux acteurs, réalisateurs° et journalistes viennent à Cannes, sur la Côte d'Azur, pour le Festival International du Film. Avec la présence de plus de 4.000 journalistes et de nombreux pays représentés, c'est la manifestation cinématographique annuelle la plus médiatisée°. Après deux semaines de projections, de fêtes, d'expositions et de concerts, le jury international du festival choisit le meilleur d'une vingtaine de films présentés en compétition officielle.

Les personnages

Napoléon Bonaparte

Né en 1769 à Ajaccio en Corse, Napoléon Bonaparte devient général à un très jeune âge. Ses succès militaires l'ont rendu° très populaire en France, ce qui lui a permis d'organiser un coup d'État en 1799. Il s'est déclaré Empereur en 1804. Pendant son règne°, il a fondé plusieurs institutions qui forment la base de la société française d'aujourd'hui: la Banque de France, le Code civil et le système éducatif, entre d'autres. Il a aussi cherché à conquérir° l'Europe. Il a obtenu de grandes victoires, mais en 1815, il subit° son ultime défaite à la bataille de Waterloo. Il est capturé et expatrié° à l'île d'Elbe où il meurt en 1821.

Les traditions

Grasse, France

La ville de Grasse, sur la Côte d'Azur, est le centre de la parfumerie° française. Cette «capitale mondiale du parfum» cultive les fleurs depuis le Moyen Âge°: violette, lavande, rose, plantes aromatiques, etc. Au dix-neuvième siècle, ses parfumeurs, comme Molinard, ont conquis° les marchés du monde grâce à° la fabrication industrielle.

La réserve naturelle de Scandola

Located on the western coast of Corsica, the reserve covers over 900 **hectares** (1 **hectare** = 2.47 acres) of land and around 1000 **hectares** of water. The only ways to reach it are by boat or by crossing high mountains on foot.

Le festival de Cannes

Only accredited film industry professionals can attend **le festival de Cannes**. Those not involved in the film industry can obtain invitations to the **Cinéma de la Plage** where films not in the running for the **Palme d'Or** (the highest award) may be viewed on an open-air screen.

Napoléon Bonaparte

Many consider **Napoléon** one of the greatest leaders in military history, but he was also a reformer. He created a tax system, central banking system, sewer system, and a system of higher education. The Napoleonic Code, a code of basic civil laws, is perhaps one of his most lasting reforms. In fact, this code is still followed not only in France but also in the State of Louisiana. Have students research the Napoleonic Code to find out how it is different from the Common Law code followed in the rest of the United States.

Grasse, France

Each summer, people in Grasse celebrate the **Fête du Jasmin**. Over 150,000 flowers are used in the Battle of the Flowers parade. Women throw flowers from the floats and spray the audience with jasmine water.

Qu'est-ce que vous avez appris? Répondez aux questions par des phrases complètes.

1. Comment s'appelle la région où les gardians perpétuent les traditions des cow-boys français?
   La région s'appelle la Camargue.
2. Quel est le rôle des gardians?
   Ils gardent les taureaux noirs.
3. Pour quelle caractéristique la réserve naturelle Scandola est-elle connue au niveau international?
   Elle est connue pour sa biodiversité.
4. Qu'est-ce que les scientifiques étudient dans la réserve naturelle Scandola?
   Ils étudient le corail rouge et des espèces marines.

5. Depuis quand le festival de Cannes existe-il?
   Le festival de Cannes existe depuis 1946.
6. Qui choisit le meilleur film au festival de Cannes?
   Le jury international choisit le meilleur film.
7. Quelle était la profession de Napoléon avant de devenir Empereur?
   Il était général (militaire).
8. Quelles institutions Napoléon a-t-il fondé?
   Il a fondé la Banque de France, le Code civil et le système éducatif.
9. Quelle ville est le centre de la parfumerie française?
   La ville de Grasse est le centre de la parfumerie française.
10. Pourquoi cette ville est-elle le centre de la parfumerie française?
    Grasse est le centre de la parfumerie française parce que la ville cultive les fleurs / grâce à la fabrication industrielle.

Sur Internet

Go to **vhlcentral.com** to find more cultural information related to this **Panorama**.

1. Quels films étaient (*were*) en compétition au dernier festival de Cannes? Qui composait (*made up*) le jury?

2. Trouvez des informations sur une parfumerie de Grasse. Quelles sont deux autres parfumeries qu'on trouve à Grasse?

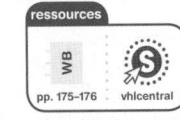

ressources

WB
pp. 175–176   vhlcentral

patrimoine *heritage* **fait partie** *is part* **corail** *coral* **ailleurs** *elsewhere* **abrite** *shelters* **balbuzards pêcheurs** *osprey* **rapace** *bird of prey* **réalisateurs** *filmmakers* **médiatisée** *publicized* **ont rendu** *made* **règne** *reign* **conquérir** *to conquer* **subit** *suffers* **expatrié** *exiled* **parfumerie** *perfume industry* **Moyen Âge** *Middle Ages* **ont conquis** *conquered* **grâce à** *thanks to*

OPTIONS

Cultural Activity Have students look at the web sites for **le festival de Cannes**, **les César du Cinéma**, and a major award show or film festival from their region. Ask them to compare and contrast the award categories, the selection process, the event, and the winners. Have each student share his or her findings with the class.

Pairs Have students imagine that they have gone on vacation in **Provence-Alpes-Côte d'Azur** or **Corse**. Students will work with a partner to talk about their experiences. Have students say where they went, describe at least two activities they did there, and say what the weather was like. The partner should then ask a question about the trip and share information about his or her vacation.

Section Goals

In this section, students will:
- learn to identify the narrator's point of view
- read a poem in French

Stratégie Tell students that recognizing the point of view from which a text is written will help them comprehend it. On the board, write the following two excerpts from texts by Jacques Prévert and Alain Robbe-Grillet. Ask students to identify the points of view.

En sortant de l'école
Nous avons rencontré
Un grand chemin de fer
(first person)

Trois enfants marchant le long d'une grève (*seashore*). **[...] Ils ont sensiblement la même taille, et sans doute aussi le même âge: une douzaine d'années.**
(omniscient narrator)

Examinez le texte Students should infer that the poem is about a city and that it concerns a woman named Barbara.

À propos de l'auteur Tell students that Neuilly-sur-Seine is a wealthy suburb of Paris. You may want to play students a recording of one of Prévert's poems set to music, such as **«Les feuilles mortes»** or **«Les bruits de la nuit»**.

Lecture

Audio: Reading

Avant la lecture

STRATÉGIE

Identifying point of view

You can understand a text more completely if you identify the point of view of the narrator. You can do this by simply asking yourself from whose perspective the story is being told. Some stories are narrated in the first person. That is, the narrator is a character in the story, and everything you read is filtered through that person's thoughts, emotions, and opinions. Other texts have an omniscient narrator who is not a character in the story but who reports the thoughts and actions of the story's characters.

Examinez le texte

Regardez le titre du texte et l'image. De quoi va parler ce texte, à votre avis? Décrivez l'image.

À propos de l'auteur
Jacques Prévert (1900–1977)

Jacques Prévert est un poète, artiste et dramaturge° français né le 4 février 1900 à Neuilly-sur-Seine. Sa passion pour la lecture, la poésie et le spectacle était évidente dès son enfance. Dans les années 1920, Prévert participe au mouvement surréaliste. Par la suite, il écrit les scénarios et les dialogues de films, dont certains° sont des chefs-d'œuvre° du cinéma français. Pacifiste et viscéralement opposé à la guerre, il n'hésite pas à en dénoncer  l'horreur et l'absurdité dans ses écrits et apparitions télévisées. Son œuvre poétique atteint son paroxysme° avec le succès de *Paroles* en 1946. Le 11 avril 1977, il décède d'un cancer du poumon°. Sa poésie est marquée par les jeux de mots°, mais aussi par certains poèmes aux thèmes sombres, tel que Barbara, où le narrateur nous révèle ses peines et sa nostalgie, après les 165 bombardements de Brest pendant la Seconde Guerre mondiale.

dramaturge *playwright* **dont certains** *some of which* **chefs-d'œuvre** *masterpieces* **atteint son paroxysme** *reaches its height* **poumon** *lung* **jeux de mots** *wordplay*

Barbara
JACQUES PRÉVERT

1 Rappelle-toi Barbara,
Il pleuvait sans cesse sur Brest ce jour-là
Et tu marchais souriante
Épanouie° ravie° ruisselante°
5 Sous la pluie
Rappelle-toi Barbara
Il pleuvait sans cesse sur Brest
Et je t'ai croisée rue de Siam
Tu souriais
10 Et moi je souriais de même
Rappelle-toi Barbara
Toi que je ne connaissais pas
Toi qui ne me connaissais pas
Rappelle-toi
15 Rappelle-toi quand même ce jour-là
N'oublie pas
Un homme sous un porche s'abritait°
Et il a crié ton nom
Barbara
20 Et tu as couru vers lui sous la pluie
Ruisselante ravie épanouie
Et tu t'es jetée dans ses bras
Rappelle-toi cela Barbara
Et ne m'en veux pas° si je te tutoie
25 Je dis tu à tous ceux que j'aime
Même si je ne les ai vus qu'une seule fois
Je dis tu à tous ceux qui s'aiment
Même si je ne les connais pas
Rappelle-toi Barbara
30 N'oublie pas
Cette pluie sage° et heureuse
Sur ton visage heureux
Sur cette ville heureuse
Cette pluie sur la mer

Épanouie *Radiant* **ravie** *delighted* **ruisselante** *dripping* **s'abritait** *took shelter* **ne m'en veux pas** *don't hold it against me* **sage** *well-behaved* **arsenal** *dockyard* **Ouessant** *the island of Ushant* **connerie** (*fam.*) *stupidity* **acier** *steel* **sang** *blood* **vivant** *living* **abîmé** *ruined* **deuil** *mourning* **crèvent** *die* **pourrir** *to rot*

O P T I O N S

Extra Practice Ask students these questions based on the author's biography. **1. Où est né Jacques Prévert?** (à Neuilly-sur-Seine) **2. En plus d'être poète, quelles autres professions avait-il?** (Il était artiste et dramaturge.) **4. Quel est le nom de son recueil de poèmes?** (*Paroles*)

Pairs Remind students that they can appreciate the lyrical nature of poetry by reading a poem aloud. Have partners read **«Barbara»** to each other. Tell them to pay close attention to the repetition of words and sounds.

35 Sur l'arsenal°
    Sur le bateau d'Ouessant°
    Oh Barbara
    Quelle connerie° la guerre
    Qu'es-tu devenue maintenant
40 Sous cette pluie de fer
    De feu d'acier° de sang°
    Et celui qui te serrait dans ses bras
    Amoureusement
    Est-il mort disparu ou bien encore vivant°
45 Oh Barbara
    Il pleut sans cesse sur Brest
    Comme il pleuvait avant
    Mais ce n'est plus pareil et tout est abimé°
    C'est une pluie de deuil° terrible et désolée
50 Ce n'est même plus l'orage
    De fer d'acier de sang
    Tout simplement des nuages
    Qui crèvent° comme des chiens
    Des chiens qui disparaissent
55 Au fil de l'eau sur Brest
    Et vont pourrir au loin
    Au loin très loin de Brest
    Dont il ne reste rien.

Après la lecture

Vrai ou faux? Indiquez si les phrases sont **vraies** ou **fausses**. Citez les lignes du texte pour justifier vos réponses.

Answers may vary slightly.

	Vrai	Faux
1. Le narrateur connaît Barbara depuis son enfance. *Lignes 12-13 et 25-26.*	☐	☑
2. Le narrateur déteste Brest. *Ligne 33.*	☐	☑
3. Dans le poème, il pleut beaucoup sur Brest. *Lignes 2, 7, 46.*	☑	☐
4. Le narrateur a croisé Barbara rue de Priam. *Ligne 8.*	☐	☑
5. Le narrateur dit «Je t'aime.» à tous ceux qu'il tutoie. *Ligne 25, 27.*	☐	☑
6. Il tutoie même ceux qu'il n'a vus qu'une fois. *Ligne 26.*	☑	☐
7. Le narrateur ne sait pas ce que Barbara est devenue. *Ligne 39.*	☑	☐
9. Il ne reste rien de Brest. *Ligne 58.*	☑	☐

Le message poétique Répondez aux questions suivantes sur la structure et le sens du poème.

1. À quel évènement historique le poème fait-il référence?
   Aux 165 bombardements de Brest pendant la Seconde Guerre mondiale.
2. Quels sont les différents thèmes du poème?
   Answers will vary.
3. Comment peut-on décrire le ton (*tone*) du narrateur? Trouvez des mots qui expriment sa colère, son pessimisme et son amour. *Answers will vary.*
4. D'après vous, qui est le narrateur? Est-ce le poète lui-même? *Answers will vary.*
5. Y a-t-il des métaphores dans le poème? Donnez des exemples. *Answers will vary.*

Sous la pluie Barbara et son amant se retrouvent sous la pluie de Brest. Avec un(e) partenaire, imaginez leur conversation. Que vont-ils se dire ? Soyez prêt(e)s à présenter votre dialogue à la classe.

Vrai ou faux? Have volunteers write the answers and supporting quotes from the text on the board. Then go over them with the class.

Suggestion Take a class survey to find out how many students think that the narrator is the poet himself. Have students justify their answers.

Le message poétique Have students discuss these questions in small groups.

O P T I O N S

Le cadavre exquis Have students play a version of **le cadavre exquis**, a surrealist game that Jacques Prévert helped to invent. The object of the game is to create a sentence by having each participant contribute a word without knowing what words the others have chosen, as in the famous example «**Le cadavre – exquis – boira – le vin – nouveau**». Have students work in groups of four or five. Assign each group member a different sentence element: **sujet – (adjectif) – verbe – complément – (adjectif)**, and have each student choose a corresponding word from Prévert's poem or from the lesson vocabulary, then have a volunteer read the entire sentence out loud.

Section Goals

In this section, students will:
• learn to use linking words
• write a description of a new business

Stratégie Review the list of linking words with the class and have volunteers create sentences with the words.

Thème Tell students to answer the questions first. Remind them to use linking words so that their descriptions won't sound like the first paragraph in the **Stratégie**.

Proofreading Activity Have the class correct these sentences. **1. Je vens de m'apercevoir que je n'ai pas liquide. 2. Il y est toujours le distributeur automatic. 3. Vous tournerez à gauche et suivez le cours jusque à la rotonde. 4. Derriere la fontaine, vous trouverez la bureau poste.**

Écriture

STRATÉGIE

Using linking words

You can make your writing more sophisticated by using linking words to connect simple sentences or ideas in order to create more complex sentences. Consider these passages that illustrate this effect:

Without linking words

Aujourd'hui, j'ai fait beaucoup de courses. Je suis allé à la poste. J'ai fait la queue pendant une demi-heure. J'ai acheté des timbres. J'ai aussi posté un colis. Je suis allé à la banque. La banque est rue Girardeau. J'ai perdu ma carte de crédit hier. Je devais aussi retirer de l'argent. Je suis allé à la brasserie pour déjeuner avec un ami. Cet ami s'appelle Marc. Je suis rentré à la maison. Ma mère rentrait du travail.

With linking words

Aujourd'hui, j'ai fait beaucoup de courses. D'abord, je suis allé à la poste où j'ai fait la queue pendant une demi-heure. J'ai acheté des timbres et j'ai aussi posté un colis. Après, je suis allé à la banque qui est rue Girardeau, parce que j'ai perdu ma carte de crédit hier et parce que je devais aussi retirer de l'argent. Ensuite, je suis allé à la brasserie pour déjeuner avec un ami qui s'appelle Marc. Finalement, je suis rentré à la maison alors que ma mère rentrait du travail.

Linking words			
alors	*then*	mais	*but*
alors que	*as*	ou	*or*
après	*then, after that*	où	*where*
d'abord	*first*	parce que	*because*
donc	*so*	pendant (que)	*while*
dont	*of which*	(et) puis	*(and) then*
enfin	*finally*	puisque	*since*
ensuite	*then, after that*	quand	*when*
et	*and*	que	*that, which*
finalement	*finally*	qui	*who, that*

Thème

Faire la description d'un nouveau commerce

Avant l'écriture

1. Avec des amis, vous allez ouvrir un commerce (*business*) dans le quartier de votre université. Vous voulez créer quelque chose d'original qui n'existe pas encore et qui sera très utile aux étudiants: un endroit où ils pourront faire plusieurs choses en même temps (par exemple, une laverie/salon de coiffure).

2. Lisez ces questions et utilisez votre imagination comme point de départ de votre description.

   ■ Quel sera le nom du commerce?

   ■ Quel type de commerce voulez-vous ouvrir?

   ■ Quels seront les produits (*products*) que vous vendrez? Quels seront les prix? Donnez quelques détails sur l'activité commerciale.

   ■ Où se trouvera le commerce?

   ■ Comment sera l'intérieur du commerce (style, décoration, etc.)?

   ■ Quels seront ses jours et heures d'ouverture (*business hours*)?

   ■ En quoi consistera l'originalité de votre commerce? Expliquez pourquoi votre commerce sera unique et donnez les raisons pour lesquelles (*which*) des étudiants fréquenteront votre commerce.

OPTIONS

Stratégie Review the linking words with students. Point out that they have seen some of these words in the **Écriture** section of previous units, in particular Unit 8, which involved narration in the past, and Unit 10, which focused on sequencing events. If needed, refer them back to the explanation and practice in these units.

Have students analyze the two sample paragraphs and comment on the writing style used in each. Which sounds less sophisticated? Which sounds more sophisticated? How does the use of linking words affect style? Tell students that as they begin to master accuracy in their writing, they need to develop their writing style, which is an important part of the writing process because of the subtle messages it conveys.

3. Avant d'écrire votre description détaillée, complétez ce tableau par des phrases complètes, à l'aide (*with the help*) des questions que vous venez de lire. Vous devez inventer les détails (le nom du commerce, les produits, les prix...).

Le commerce	1. le nom: 2. le type:
Les produits	1. le type: 2. le prix: 3. détails:
L'endroit	1. l'adresse: 2. près de (monument, grand magasin, ...):
L'intérieur	1. le style: 2. la décoration: 3. autre information:
Les jours et heures d'ouverture	1. les horaires: 2. les jours d'ouverture:
L'originalité	1. le style: 2. détails:
...?	

4. Après avoir complété le tableau, regardez les phrases que vous avez écrites. Est-il possible de les combiner avec des mots de liaison (*linking words*) de la liste de **Stratégie**? Regardez cet exemple:

Le commerce est une laverie, mais aussi un salon de coiffure, parce que nous savons que les étudiants aiment pouvoir faire plusieurs choses en même temps.

5. Réécrivez les phrases que vous pouvez combiner.

Écriture

1. Utilisez les phrases du tableau et celles (*the ones*) que vous venez de combiner pour écrire la description de votre commerce.

2. Pendant que vous écrivez, trouvez d'autres phrases à combiner avec des mots de liaison.

3. Utilisez le vocabulaire de l'unité.

4. Utilisez les verbes voir, recevoir, apercevoir et croire, des expressions négatives et le futur simple.

Après l'écriture

1. Échangez votre description avec celle (*the one*) d'un(e) partenaire. Répondez à ces questions pour commenter son travail.

■ Votre partenaire a-t-il/elle inclu toutes les informations du tableau?

■ A-t-il/elle utilisé des mots de liaison pour combiner les phrases?

■ A-t-il/elle utilisé le vocabulaire de l'unité?

■ A-t-il/elle utilisé les verbes voir, recevoir, apercevoir et croire, des expressions négatives et le futur simple?

■ A-t-il/elle utilisé le conditionnel?

■ Quel(s) détail(s) ajouteriez-vous (*would you add*)? Quel(s) détail(s) enlèveriez-vous (*would you delete*)? Quel(s) autre(s) commentaire(s) avez-vous pour votre partenaire?

2. Corrigez votre description d'après (*according to*) les commentaires de votre partenaire. Relisez votre travail pour éliminer ces problèmes:

■ des fautes (*errors*) d'orthographe

■ des fautes de ponctuation

■ des fautes de conjugaison

■ des fautes d'accord (*agreement*) des adjectifs

■ un mauvais emploi (*use*) de la grammaire

cinq cent trente-sept **537**

EVALUATION

Criteria

Content Contains answers to each question called out in the bulleted points of the task.
Scale: 1 2 3 4 5

Organization Organized into logical paragraphs that begin with a topic sentence and contain appropriate supporting details.
Scale: 1 2 3 4 5

Accuracy Uses the simple future tense and linking words correctly. Spells words, conjugates verbs, and modifies adjectives correctly throughout.
Scale: 1 2 3 4 5

Creativity Includes additional information that is not included in the task and/or uses adjectives, descriptive verbs, and additional details to make the composition more interesting.
Scale: 1 2 3 4 5

Scoring
Excellent	18–20 points
Good	14–17 points
Satisfactory	10–13 points
Unsatisfactory	< 10 points

OPTIONS

Stratégie Have students practice the linking words by writing a sentence on the board. Ask students to think of a linking word and a second sentence that could be joined to the first. Once you have tried this several times as a class, put students in pairs and have each write single sentences individually and then try to combine them using different linking words.

Point out to students that although the strategy they are practicing is the use of linking words, the writing task itself calls for use of the simple future tense. Have them look carefully at the words used in the questions and review the future tense forms of those verbs in particular before they begin writing.

🔊 ⓢ **Audio: Vocabulary Flashcards**

Instructional Resources
vhlcentral.com:
Textbook MP3s; Textbook
Audioscript; reference tools

Suggestions
- Tell students that an easy way to study from **Vocabulaire** is to cover up the French half of each section, leaving only the English equivalents exposed. They can then quiz themselves on the French items. To focus on the English equivalents of the French entries, they simply reverse this process.
- Point out to students that they can use the Vocabulary Tools at **vhlcentral.com** for reference and extra vocabulary practice.

Leçon 12A

À la poste

poster une lettre	*to mail a letter*
une adresse	*address*
une boîte aux lettres	*mailbox*
une carte postale	*postcard*
un colis	*package*
le courrier	*mail*
une enveloppe	*envelope*
un facteur	*mailman*
un timbre	*stamp*

À la banque

avoir un compte bancaire	*to have a bank account*
déposer de l'argent	*to deposit money*
emprunter	*to borrow*
payer avec une carte de crédit	*to pay with a credit card*
payer en liquide	*to pay in cash*
payer par chèque	*to pay by check*
retirer de l'argent	*to withdraw money*
les billets (*m.*)	*bills, notes*
un compte de chèques	*checking account*
un compte d'épargne	*savings account*
une dépense	*expenditure, expense*
un distributeur automatique/de billets	*ATM*
les pièces de monnaie (*f.*)/**de la monnaie**	*coins/change*

En ville

accompagner	*to accompany*
faire la queue	*to wait in line*
remplir un formulaire	*to fill out a form*
signer	*to sign*
une banque	*bank*
une bijouterie	*jewelry store*
une boutique	*boutique, store*
une brasserie	*café, restaurant*
un bureau de poste	*post office*
un cybercafé	*cybercafé*
une laverie	*laundromat*
un marchand de journaux	*newsstand*
une papeterie	*stationery store*
un salon de beauté	*beauty salon*
un commissariat de police	*police station*
une mairie	*town/city hall; mayor's office*
fermé(e)	*closed*
ouvert(e)	*open*

La négation

jamais	*never; ever*
ne... aucun(e)	*none (not any)*
ne... jamais	*never (not ever)*
ne... ni... ni...	*neither... nor*
ne... personne	*nobody, no one*
ne... plus	*no more (not anymore)*
ne... que	*only*
ne... rien	*nothing (not anything)*
pas (de)	*no, none*
personne	*no one*
quelque chose	*something*
quelqu'un	*someone*
rien	*nothing*
toujours	*always; still*

Verbes

apercevoir	*to catch sight of, to see*
s'apercevoir	*to notice; to realize*
recevoir	*to receive*
voir	*to see*

Expressions utiles

See p. 499.

Leçon 12B

Retrouver son chemin

continuer	*to continue*
se déplacer	*to move (change location)*
descendre	*to go/come down*
être perdu(e)	*to be lost*
monter	*to go up/come up*
s'orienter	*to get one's bearings*
suivre	*to follow*
tourner	*to turn*
traverser	*to cross*
un angle	*corner*
une avenue	*avenue*
un banc	*bench*
un bâtiment	*building*
un boulevard	*boulevard*
une cabine téléphonique	*phone booth*
un carrefour	*intersection*
un chemin	*way; path*
un coin	*corner*
des indications (*f.*)	*directions*
un feu de signalisation (**feux** pl.)	*traffic light(s)*
une fontaine	*fountain*
un office du tourisme	*tourist office*
un pont	*bridge*
une rue	*street*
une statue	*statue*
est	*east*
nord	*north*
ouest	*west*
sud	*south*

Pour donner des indications

au bout (de)	*at the end (of)*
au coin (de)	*at the corner (of)*
autour (de)	*around*
jusqu'à	*until*
(tout) près (de)	*(very) close (to)*
tout droit	*straight ahead*

Vocabulaire supplémentaire

dès que	*as soon as*
quand	*when*

Expressions utiles

See p. 519.

Le futur simple

See pp. 522.

L'avenir et les métiers

Unit Goals

Leçon 13A

In this lesson, students will learn:
- terms for the workplace
- terms for job interviews
- terms for making and receiving phone calls
- rules of punctuation in French
- about telephones, text messages, and **les artisans**
- the future tense with **quand** and **dès que**
- interrogative pronouns **lequel**, **laquelle**, **lesquels**, and **lesquelles**
- more about professions and work through specially shot video footage

Leçon 13B

In this lesson, students will learn:
- terms for professions
- more terms for discussing one's work
- about neologisms and **franglais**
- about labor unions, strikes, and civil servants
- about French singer and musician **Tino Rossi**
- **si** clauses
- the relative pronouns **qui**, **que**, **dont**, and **où**
- to use background knowledge and listen for specific information

Savoir-faire

In this section, students will learn:
- cultural, geographical, and historical information about **Auvergne-Rhône-Alpes**
- to summarize a text in their own words
- to use note cards to organize their writing

Pour commencer
- Elle fera du stylisme de mode.
- Answers will vary.
- Oui, elle l'aimera beaucoup.
- Elle porte une robe rose.

Pour commencer

Quel genre de travail Amina fera-t-elle?
Est-ce qu'elle travaillera dans un bureau?
Est-ce qu'elle aimera son travail?
Que porte-t-elle aujourd'hui?

RESOURCES

Student Activities Manual (SAM):
Workbook Activities, pp. 175–188;
Lab Activities, pp. 97–104;
Video Activities, pp. 49–52; pp. 85–86
SAM Answer Key

vhlcentral.com: Textbook MP3s; Lab MP3s;
Textbook Audioscript; Lab Audioscript Video;
Videoscript; **Roman-photo** Translations;
Vocabulaire supplémentaire; Activity Pack
(including **Feuilles d'activités**, Info Gap Activities,
and Task-based Activities);

Flash culture video transcription; **Essayez!** and
Mise en pratique answers; Digital Image Bank;
Testing Program; Testing Program MP3s

Section Goals

In this section, students will learn and practice vocabulary related to:
- the workplace
- job interviews
- phone calls

Instructional Resources

vhlcentral.com:
Digital Image Bank (including vocabulary illustrations from the textbook, theme-based illustrations); **Vocabulaire supplémentaire; Mise en pratique** *answers; Textbook Audioscript; Lab Audioscript; Activity Pack; Textbook MP3s; Lab MP3s; SAM Answer Key; reference tools*

Suggestions

- Tell students to look over the new vocabulary and identify the cognates.
- Use the **13A Contextes** illustration from the Digital Image Bank. Point out objects and describe what the people are doing. Examples: **Il patiente. C'est une employée. Il passe un entretien.**
- Point out that **un salaire modeste** is a figurative rather than literal equivalent of *low salary.* One might also say **un bas salaire.**
- Explain that **une lettre de motivation** is a letter a job candidate writes in response to a want ad or when introducing him or herself to a prospective employer.
- Point out the **Attention!** box. Explain that **chercher** is a general term, while **rechercher** refers to more thorough, methodical research.
- Tell students that **les petites annonces** are short, telegraphic-style ads, usually for low-level or temporary jobs rather than career positions.
- Additional vocabulary for this lesson can be found in the **Vocabulaire supplémentaire** on the Supersite.
- Use the Jobs illustrations from the Digital Image Bank to help students familiarize themselves with the workplace, job interviews, and phone calls.

Leçon 13A

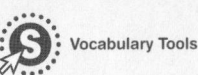
Vocabulary Tools

Au bureau

You will learn how to...
- make and receive phone calls
- talk about your goals

Vocabulaire

chercher un/du travail	to look for work
embaucher	to hire
faire des projets	to make plans
obtenir	to get, to obtain
postuler	to apply
prendre (un) rendez-vous	to make an appointment
trouver un/du travail	to find a job
un(e) candidat(e)	candidate, applicant
un conseil	advice
un domaine	field
une entreprise	firm, business
une expérience professionnelle	professional experience
une formation	education; training
une lettre de recommandation	letter of reference/ recommendation
une lettre de motivation	letter of application
une mention	distinction
un métier	profession
un poste	position
une référence	reference
un salaire (élevé, modeste)	(high, low) salary
un(e) spécialiste	specialist
un stage	internship; professional training
appeler	to call
laisser un message	to leave a message
l'appareil (m.)	telephone
une télécarte	phone card
Qui est à l'appareil?	Who's calling please?
C'est de la part de qui?	On behalf of whom?
C'est M./Mme/Mlle... (à l'appareil.)	It's Mr./Mrs./Miss... (on the phone.)
Ne quittez pas.	Please hold.

ressources

WB pp. 175–176   LM p. 97   vhlcentral

540 *cinq cent quarante*

Extra Practice For additional practice, ask students these questions. **1. Quel est votre numéro de téléphone? 2. Quels projets avez-vous faits pour votre carrière? 3. Préférez-vous travailler dans une grande entreprise ou dans une petite compagnie? Pourquoi? 4. Est-il plus important d'avoir un salaire élevé ou un métier qu'on aime bien? 5. Avez-vous déjà écrit une lettre de motivation?**

Game Divide the class into two teams. Have a spelling bee using vocabulary words from **Espace contextes**. Pronounce each word, use it in a sentence, and then say the word again. Tell students that they must spell the words in French and include all diacritical marks.

1 Audioscript MICHEL: Alors Armand, est-ce que tu as trouvé un travail pour l'été?
ARMAND: Chut, je suis au téléphone!
M: Oh, je suis désolé.
A: Allô. Oui, bonjour, Madame. C'est Armand Lemaire à l'appareil. Je vous appelle au sujet de l'annonce que j'ai lue dans le journal ce matin.
LA SECRÉTAIRE: Oui, très bien. Pour le stage, il faut envoyer votre CV accompagné d'une lettre de motivation.
A: En fait, je n'appelle pas pour le stage, mais pour le poste d'assistant.
S: Oh, excusez-moi. Dans ce cas, il vous faut appeler Monsieur Dupont, notre chef du personnel, pour prendre un rendez-vous et obtenir un entretien. Ne quittez pas. Je vous le passe. (*Musique*) Je suis désolée, mais ça ne répond pas. Je vous passe sa messagerie. Vous pouvez laisser un message avec votre numéro de téléphone.
A: Je vous remercie, Madame. *Plus tard…*
M: Voilà, tu n'as plus besoin de chercher du travail! Je suis sûr qu'ils vont t'embaucher!
A: Je préfère attendre. Et toi, comment ça va, ta recherche de travail?
M: Je ne sais pas vraiment où postuler et je ne sais pas comment obtenir un entretien.
A: Avec ta formation et ton expérience professionnelle, je pense que tu trouveras facilement un travail dans l'informatique. Tiens, regarde le journal, cette compagnie et cette autre entreprise-là recherchent des spécialistes dans ton domaine. En plus, je suis certain qu'elles offrent un bon salaire. Tiens, prends le combiné et appelle-les.
(*On Textbook MP3s*)

Attention!

Note the difference in the usage and meaning of **chercher** and **rechercher**.
Il cherche du travail.
He is looking for work.
Cette compagnie recherche un chef du personnel.
This company is looking for a human resources director.

Mise en pratique

1 **Écoutez** Armand et Michel cherchent du travail. Écoutez leur conversation et répondez ensuite aux questions.

1. Quel genre de travail Armand recherche-t-il?
   Armand recherche un travail d'assistant.
2. Où est-ce qu'Armand a lu l'annonce?
   Armand a lu l'annonce dans le journal ce matin.
3. Quel(s) document(s) faut-il envoyer pour le stage?
   Il faut envoyer un CV accompagné d'une lettre de motivation.
4. Qui est M. Dupont?
   M. Dupont est le chef du personnel.
5. Que doit faire Armand pour obtenir un entretien?
   Armand doit appeler M. Dupont pour prendre un rendez-vous.
6. Quel est le domaine professionnel de Michel?
   Son domaine professionnel est l'informatique.
7. Pourquoi Michel a-t-il des difficultés à trouver du travail?
   Michel a des difficultés à trouver du travail parce qu'il ne sait pas où postuler ni comment obtenir un entretien.
8. Comment est-ce qu'Armand aide Michel?
   Armand trouve deux entreprises qui recherchent des spécialistes dans le domaine de Michel.

2 **Complétez** Complétez ces phrases avec le verbe de la liste qui convient le mieux. N'oubliez pas de faire les accords nécessaires.

appeler	lire les annonces	postuler
décrocher	métier	prendre (un) rendez-vous
conseil	obtenir	raccrocher
embaucher	passer un entretien	salaire
laisser des messages	patienter	trouver un/du travail

1. Quand on cherche du travail, il faut ___lire les annonces___ tous les jours.
2. Il est toujours plus facile de trouver un ___métier___ intéressant quand on a une bonne formation.
3. Le téléphone sonne. Est-ce que tu peux ___décrocher___, s'il te plaît?
4. Il y a peu d'entreprises qui ___embauchent___ en ce moment. L'économie ne va pas très bien.
5. —Bonjour, Madame. Je vous ___appelle___ pour ___prendre (un) rendez-vous___.
   —Vous pouvez venir lundi 15, à 16h00?
6. J'ai envoyé mon CV. J'espère qu'ils vont m'appeler pour ___passer un entretien___.
7. ___Patientez___ quelques minutes, s'il vous plaît. Madame Benoît va bientôt arriver.
8. Il ___a raccroché___ parce que la ligne n'était pas bonne.
9. Sophie vient juste de ___trouver un travail___. Elle va organiser une petite fête vendredi pour célébrer son nouveau poste.
10. Une messagerie permet de ___laisser des messages___.

3 **Corrigez** Lisez ces phrases et dites si elles sont **vraies** ou **fausses**. Corrigez les phrases qui ne sont pas cohérentes.

1. Il faut décrocher le combiné avant de composer un numéro de téléphone.
   Vrai.
2. Quand on appelle d'une cabine téléphonique, on utilise des billets.
   Faux. Quand on appelle d'une cabine téléphonique, on utilise une télécarte.
3. Quand on est embauché, on perd son travail.
   Faux. Quand on est embauché, on trouve un travail.
4. Quand on travaille, on reçoit un salaire à la fin de chaque mois.
   Vrai.
5. À la fin d'un CV américain, il ne faut pas oublier de mentionner ses références.
   Vrai.
6. Pour savoir qui vous appelle au téléphone, vous demandez: «Ne quittez pas.»
   Faux. Vous demandez: «Qui est à l'appareil?»
7. Un(e) patron(ne) dirige (*manages*) une entreprise ou des employés.
   Vrai.
8. Avant d'obtenir un poste, il faut souvent passer une entreprise.
   Faux. Il faut souvent passer un entretien.
9. Quand on travaille dans une entreprise, on est un(e) employé(e).
   Vrai.

un curriculum vitæ, un CV

un chef du personnel

Il passe un entretien. (passer)

Elle lit les annonces. (lire)

le combiné

la messagerie

Personnel

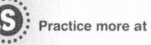

une compagnie

S Practice more at **vhlcentral.com**.

cinq cent quarante et un **541**

1 Suggestion Go over the answers with the class. If students have difficulty, play the conversation again.

2 Expansion Have students write sentences with the unused words from the list: **conseil, obtenir, postuler,** and **salaire.**

3 Suggestion Have students check their answers with a classmate.

OPTIONS
Pairs Write these expressions for circumlocution on the board: **C'est quand on…, C'est ce qu'on fait quand…, C'est un objet/ une machine qu'on utilise pour…, C'est quelqu'un qui…** Then have pairs of students write definitions for the following vocabulary words. **1. chercher du travail 2. postuler 3. un appareil 4. un patron 5. raccrocher 6. un entretien 7. une télécarte 8. un spécialiste**

Have pairs get together with another pair of students and take turns reading their definitions and guessing the words. Ask each group to choose its best definition and write it on the board for the whole class to guess.

Communication

NATIONAL
communication
STANDARDS

4 Suggestions
- Tell students to jot down notes during the interviews.
- After completing the interviews, have pairs get together with another pair and report what they learned about their partner.

5 Suggestion If time is limited, have students role-play the conversations in groups of six. Each pair will act out one of the conversations instead of all three.

6 Suggestions
- Before beginning the activity, ask volunteers to read each ad aloud.
- Have the class brainstorm questions a manager might ask. Write the questions on the board.
- Model the activity by role-playing one of the situations with a student. Remind students to use appropriate greetings.

7 Suggestions
- Before beginning this activity, write a list of professional fields on the board. Examples: **les sciences, les affaires, l'éducation,** and **le commerce**.
- Have the class brainstorm questions an advisor might ask in this situation. Write the questions on the board.

4 Répondez Avec un(e) partenaire, posez-vous ces questions à tour de rôle. Answers will vary.

1. Est-ce que tu as fait des projets d'avenir? Quels sont-ils?
2. Après tes études, dans quel domaine est-ce que tu vas chercher du travail?
3. As-tu déjà fait un stage en entreprise? Comment était-ce?
4. As-tu une expérience professionnelle? Dans quel(s) domaine(s)?
5. As-tu déjà répondu à des annonces pour trouver du travail? Est-ce qu'on t'a embauché(e)?
6. À ton avis, qu'est-ce qui est le plus important pour réussir un entretien d'embauche?
7. Pour qui imagines-tu pouvoir écrire une bonne lettre de recommandation un jour?
8. As-tu déjà préparé ton curriculum vitæ? Quels types d'informations as-tu inclus?

5 Les conversations Avec un(e) partenaire, complétez et remettez dans l'ordre ces conversations. Ensuite, jouez les scènes devant la classe.

Conversation 1

3 —C'est Mlle Grandjean à l'appareil. Est-ce que vous pouvez me passer le chef du personnel, s'il vous plaît?

1 —<u>Allô</u>. Bonjour, Monsieur.

2 —Bonjour. <u>Qui est à l'appareil?</u> ?

4 —<u>Ne quittez pas</u>. Je vous le passe.

Conversation 2

3 —Tu n'as donc pas vu <u>le poste</u> que la compagnie Petit et Fils offre.

1 —Est-ce que tu <u>as lu les annonces</u> ce matin?

4 —Non, mais je connais cette entreprise et elle n'est pas dans <u>mon domaine</u>.

2 —Non, je n'ai pas encore acheté le journal.

Conversation 3

2 —Non, appelle plutôt son portable.

4 —C'est le 06-22-28-80-83.

5 —Oh, encore sa <u>messagerie</u>! Elle ne décroche jamais.

3 —Tu as raison. Quel est son <u>numéro de téléphone</u>?

1 —Stéphanie ne <u>décroche</u> pas. Je vais lui <u>laisser un message</u>.

6 Les petites annonces Lisez ces annonces et choisissez-en une. Avec un(e) partenaire, imaginez votre conversation avec le directeur de l'entreprise que vous avez sélectionnée. Vous devez parler de votre expérience professionnelle, de votre formation et de vos projets. Ensuite, choisissez une autre annonce et changez de rôle. Answers will vary.

Nous recherchons des professionnels de la gestion. Première expérience ou expert(e) dans votre domaine, notre groupe vous offre d'intéressantes opportunités d'évolution. Retrouvez nos postes sur www.comptaparis.fr/ métiers.

France Conseil recherche un analyste financier bilingue anglais. Vous travaillez avec nos bureaux à l'étranger pour développer les projets du département. De formation supérieure, vous avez une expérience de chef de projet de 2 à 4 ans. Nous contacter à: France Conseil, 80, rue du Faubourg Saint-Antoine, 75012 Paris

SARLA recherche un(e) assistant(e) commercial(e) trilingue anglais et espagnol avec expérience en informatique (logiciels et Internet). **Envoyer CV et lettre de motivation à SARLA, 155, avenue de Gerland, BP 72, 69007 Lyon**

7 Le poste idéal Vous souhaitez travailler à l'étranger pendant les vacances d'été, mais vous ne savez pas par où commencer. Vous allez donc dans un Centre d'Information Jeunesse pour rencontrer un conseiller/une conseillère (*advisor*) qui va déterminer le pays et le domaine professionnel les mieux adaptés. Travaillez à deux et échangez les rôles avec votre partenaire. Answers will vary.

O P T I O N S

Extra Practice Brainstorm a list of professions learned in earlier lessons. Have each student pick a profession or randomly assign one to each student. Tell students to write an advertisement in search of someone in that profession, using the ads in **Activité 6** as models.

Pairs Have students role-play a phone call. Tell pairs to sit back-to-back to simulate the phone conversation. Then give them the following situation: The person they want to speak to is not there, so the caller should leave a message. Tell students to use as much phone-related vocabulary as possible in their conversations.

Les sons et les lettres   Audio

La ponctuation française

Although French uses most of the same punctuation marks as English, their usage often varies. Unlike English, no period (**point**) is used in abbreviations of measurements in French.

200 m (*meters*) **30 min** (*minutes*) **25 cl** (*centiliters*) **500 g** (*grams*)

In other abbreviations, a period is used only if the last letter of the abbreviation is different from the last letter of the word it represents.

Mme Bonaire = Madame Bonaire **M. Bonaire = Monsieur Bonaire**

French dates are written with the day before the month, so if the month is spelled out, no punctuation is needed. When using digits only, use slashes to separate them.

le 25 février 1954 **25/2/1954** **le 15 août 2006** **15/8/2006**

Notice that a comma (**une virgule**) is not used before the last item in a series or list.

Lucie parle français, anglais et allemand. *Lucie speaks French, English, and German.*

Generally, in French, a direct quotation is enclosed in **guillemets**. Notice that a colon (**deux points**), not a comma, is used before the quotation.

Charlotte a dit: «Appelle-moi!» **Marc a demandé: «Qui est à l'appareil?»**

Réécrivez Ajoutez la ponctuation et remplacez les mots en italique par leurs abréviations.

1. Depuis le *21 mars 1964 Madame Pagny* habite à 500 *mètres* de chez moi
   Depuis le 21.03.1964, Mme Pagny habite à 500 m de chez moi.
2. Ce matin j'ai acheté 2 *kilos* de poires *Monsieur* Florent m'a dit Lucien tu as très bien fait
   Ce matin, j'ai acheté 2 kg de poires. M. Florent m'a dit: «Lucien, tu as très bien fait!»

Corrigez Lisez le paragraphe et ajoutez la bonne ponctuation et les majuscules.

hier michel le frère de ma meilleure amie sylvie m'a téléphoné il a dit carole on va fêter l'anniversaire de sylvie le samedi 13 novembre est-ce que tu peux venir téléphone-moi
Answers may vary. Possible answer: Hier, Michel, le frère de ma meilleure amie, Sylvie, m'a téléphoné. Il a dit: «Carole, on va fêter l'anniversaire de Sylvie, le samedi 13 novembre. Est-ce que tu peux venir? Téléphone-moi!»

Dictons Répétez les dictons à voix haute.

Le temps, c'est de l'argent.[1]

Ne parle jamais des princes: si tu en dis du bien, tu mens; si tu en dis du mal, tu t'exposes.[2]

ressources

LM

p. 98 vhlcentral

[1] Time is money.
[2] Never talk about princes. If you talk nicely about them, you lie. If you say bad things about them, you reveal yourself.

Section Goals

In this section, students will learn about French punctuation.

Instructional Resources
vhlcentral.com:
Textbook MP3s; Lab MP3s; SAM Answer Key; Textbook Audioscript; Lab Audioscript; reference tools

Suggestions

- Tell students that the semi-colon (**le point-virgule**) is used much more often in French than in English. They will also see a space before a colon (**deux-points**), a question mark (**un point d'interrogation**), an exclamation mark (**un point d'exclamation**), a semi-colon (**un point-virgule**), or between a word and quotation marks (**guillemets**).
- Remind students that phone numbers are written in sets of two digits separated by periods or spaces in French. Examples: **01.23.45.67.99** or **01 23 45 67 99**.
- Review the use of a comma (**une virgule**) for decimals and the use of a period or a space instead of a comma to separate groups of three digits. Examples: **10,5** = 10.5, **1.000.000** or **1 000 000** = 1,000,000.
- Explain that the lines of different speakers in a dialogue may be preceded by an em dash (**un tiret**):
  —**Tu viens avec moi?**
  —**Non, je reste chez moi.**
  —**Avez-vous déjà parlé à la patronne?**
  —**Oui, j'ai un rendez-vous avec elle demain.**

Dictons The saying «**Le temps, c'est de l'argent**» is based on an English proverb (*Time is money*).

Extra Practice Use these sentences for additional practice with French punctuation and have students replace the italicized words with abbreviations. **1. Mon anniversaire c'est le *17 avril 1988* 2. Est-ce que vous avez bu 75 *centilitres* de lait 3. Caroline a visité le musée du Louvre l'Arc de Triomphe et la tour Eiffel 4. L'homme a crié (*shouted*) Au secours**

Extra Practice Teach students this French tongue-twister that models some French punctuation conventions.
—**Ta tante t'attend.**
—**J'ai tant de tantes. Quelle tante m'attend?**
—**Ta tante Antoinette t'attend.**

Section Goals

In this section, students will learn functional phrases for talking about tests, future plans, and successes.

Instructional Resources
Roman-photo Video, Videoscript, and Translation; SAM Answer Key; reference tools

Video Recap: Leçon 12B
Review the previous **Roman-photo** with this activity.
1. Que cherche le touriste? (le bureau de poste)
2. À qui demande-t-il des indications? (d'abord à M. Hulot, puis à David et à Rachid et finalement à Stéphane)
3. Qui lui donne de bonnes indications? (Stéphane)
4. Où est le bureau de poste? (derrière la fontaine, la Rotonde)

Video Synopsis
Stéphane and Astrid just took their **bac**. Stéphane tells Astrid he wants to study architecture at the **Université de Marseille**. She plans to study medicine at the **Université de Bordeaux**. Stéphane calls his mother to tell her the exam is over. At **Le P'tit Bistrot**, a young woman inquires about a job. Unbeknownst to Valérie, Michèle has an interview for a receptionist's job at Dupont.

Suggestions
• Have students predict what the episode will be about based on the video stills.
• Have students scan the captions to find sentences related to jobs and future plans.
• After reading the **Roman-photo**, have students summarize the episode.

Le bac

PERSONNAGES

 Astrid
 Jeune femme
 Michèle
 Stéphane
 Valérie

Après le bac...
STÉPHANE Alors, Astrid, tu penses avoir réussi le bac?
ASTRID Franchement, je crois que oui. Et toi?
STÉPHANE Je ne sais pas, c'était plutôt difficile. Mais au moins, c'est fini, et ça, c'est le plus important pour moi!

ASTRID Qu'est-ce que tu vas faire une fois que tu auras le bac?
STÉPHANE Aucune idée, Astrid. J'ai fait une demande à l'université pour étudier l'architecture.
ASTRID Vraiment? Laquelle?
STÉPHANE L'université de Marseille, mais je n'ai pas encore de réponse. Alors, Mademoiselle Je-pense-à-tout, tu sais déjà ce que tu feras?

ASTRID Bien sûr! J'irai à l'université de Bordeaux et dès que je réussirai l'examen de première année, je continuerai en médecine.
STÉPHANE Ah oui? Pour moi, les études, c'est fini pour l'instant. On vient juste de passer le bac, il faut fêter ça! C'est loin, la rentrée.

VALÉRIE Mais bien sûr que je m'inquiète! C'est normal.
STÉPHANE Tu sais, finalement, ce n'était pas si difficile.
VALÉRIE Ah bon? Tu sais quand tu auras les résultats?
STÉPHANE Ils seront affichés dans deux semaines.
VALÉRIE En attendant, il faut prendre des décisions pour préparer l'avenir.

STÉPHANE L'avenir! L'avenir! Vous n'avez que ce mot à la bouche, Astrid et toi. Oh maman, je suis tellement content aujourd'hui. Pour le moment, je voudrais juste faire des projets pour le week-end.
VALÉRIE D'accord, Stéphane. Je comprends. Tu rentres maintenant?
STÉPHANE Oui, maman. J'arrive dans quinze minutes.

Au P'tit Bistrot...
JEUNE FEMME Bonjour, Madame. Je cherche un travail pour cet été. Est-ce que vous embauchez en ce moment?
VALÉRIE Eh bien, c'est possible. L'été en général nous avons beaucoup de clients étrangers. Est-ce que vous parlez anglais?
JEUNE FEMME Oui, c'est ce que j'étudie à l'université.

ACTIVITÉS

1 Complétez Complétez les phrases suivantes.
1. Stéphane et Astrid viennent de passer _le bac_.
2. Stéphane doit téléphoner à _sa mère/Valérie_.
3. Astrid prête une _télécarte_ à Stéphane.
4. Aujourd'hui, Stéphane est très _content/heureux_.
5. Il aura les résultats du bac dans _deux semaines_.
6. Stéphane ne veut pas parler de l' _avenir_.
7. La jeune femme étudie _l'anglais_ à l'université.
8. Valérie dit que de nombreux clients du P'tit Bistrot sont _étrangers_.
9. _Michèle_ est en train (*in the process*) de chercher un nouveau travail.
10. Elle ne veut pas demander _une lettre de recommandation_ à Valérie.

 Practice more at **vhlcentral.com**.

Avant de regarder la vidéo Before viewing the video, have students work in pairs and brainstorm a list of things a student might say after taking a difficult exam and what a parent might say to a son or daughter after the exam.

Regarder la vidéo Download and print the videoscript from the Supersite. Then white out words related to tests, jobs, and other key vocabulary in order to create a master for a cloze activity. Distribute the photocopies and tell students to fill in the missing information as they watch the video.

544 Instructor's Annotated Edition • Unit 13 • Lesson 13A

Stéphane et Astrid ont passé l'examen.

STÉPHANE Écoute, je dois téléphoner à ma mère. Je peux emprunter ta télécarte, s'il te plaît?
ASTRID Oui, bien sûr. Tiens.
STÉPHANE Merci.
ASTRID Bon... Je dois rentrer chez moi. Ma famille m'attend. Au revoir.
STÉPHANE Salut.

Stéphane appelle sa mère...
VALÉRIE Le P'tit Bistrot. Bonjour.
STÉPHANE Allô.
VALÉRIE Allô. Qui est à l'appareil?
STÉPHANE Maman, c'est moi!
VALÉRIE Stéphane! Alors, comment ça a été? Tu penses avoir réussi?
STÉPHANE Oui, bien sûr, maman. Ne t'inquiète pas!

VALÉRIE Et vous avez déjà travaillé dans un café?
JEUNE FEMME Eh bien, l'été dernier j'ai travaillé à la brasserie les Deux Escargots. Vous pouvez les appeler pour obtenir une référence si vous le désirez. Voici leur numéro de téléphone.
VALÉRIE Au revoir, et peut-être à bientôt!

Près de la terrasse...
MICHÈLE J'ai un rendez-vous pour passer un entretien avec l'entreprise Dupont... C'est la compagnie qui offre ce poste de réceptionniste... Tu es fou, je ne peux pas demander une lettre de recommandation à Madame Forestier... Bien sûr, nous irons dîner pour fêter ça dès que j'aurai un nouveau travail.

Expressions utiles

Talking about tests

- **Tu penses avoir réussi le bac?**
  Do you think you passed the bac?
- **Je crois que oui.**
  I think so.
- **Qu'est-ce que tu vas faire une fois que tu auras le bac?**
  What are you going to do once you have the bac?
- **Tu sais quand tu auras les résultats?**
  Do you know when you will have the results?
- **Ils seront affichés dans deux semaines.**
  They will be posted in two weeks.

Enjoying successes

- **L'avenir! Vous n'avez que ce mot à la bouche.**
  The future! That's all you talk about.
- **Je suis tellement content(e) aujourd'hui.**
  I am so happy today.
- **Pour le moment, je voudrais juste faire des projets pour le week-end.**
  For the time being, I would only like to make plans for the weekend.
- **Nous irons dîner pour fêter ça dès que j'aurai un nouveau travail.**
  We will go to dinner to celebrate as soon as I have a new job.

Additional vocabulary

- **Laquelle?**
  Which one (f.)?

Expressions utiles
- Model the pronunciation of the **Expressions utiles** and have students repeat them.
- As you work through the list, point out **le futur** with **dès que** and **quand**. Also point out the use of the interrogative pronoun **laquelle** in caption 2. Tell students that these grammar points will be formally presented in **Espace structures**.
- Respond briefly to students' questions about these points.
- Remind students that **le futur** is a grammatical term referring to the future tense. To talk about the future in the context of time, they should use **l'avenir**.

1 **Suggestion** Have volunteers read the completed sentences aloud.

1 **Expansion** Have students write additional sentences to fill in the gaps in the storyline.

2 **Suggestion** Have volunteers write the answers to the questions on the board. Then go over them with the class.

2 **Expansion** Ask students personalized questions. Allow students to invent answers if they prefer. Examples: **1. Quels sont vos projets d'avenir? 2. Que voulez-vous faire l'année prochaine? 3. Est-ce que vos projets sont sûrs?**

3 **Suggestion** If time is limited, this activity may be assigned as homework. Assign each student a role (Michèle or the young woman). Have partners prepare their parts at home, then allow them a few minutes to rehearse before presenting their conversation to the class.

2 **Répondez** Répondez aux questions suivantes par des phrases complètes.

1. Quels sont les projets d'avenir d'Astrid?
   Elle ira à l'université de Bordeaux et étudiera la médecine.
2. Qu'est-ce que Stéphane veut faire l'année prochaine?
   Il veut étudier l'architecture à l'université de Marseille.
3. Est-ce que les projets d'Astrid et de Stéphane sont certains?
   (Supposez que les deux auront le bac.) Les projets d'Astrid sont certains, mais Stéphane n'a pas encore de réponse de l'université de Marseille.
4. Quel est le projet de Michèle pour l'avenir?
   Michèle veut travailler comme réceptionniste pour une compagnie.
5. Son projet est-il certain? Non, son projet n'est pas certain: elle doit passer l'entretien d'embauche d'abord. Elle ne sait pas encore s'ils vont lui donner le poste.

3 **À vous!** La jeune femme qui veut travailler au P'tit Bistrot rencontre Michèle. Elle veut savoir comment est le travail et comment est Valérie comme patronne. Michèle, qui n'est pas vraiment heureuse au P'tit Bistrot en ce moment, lui raconte tout. Avec un(e) camarade de classe, composez le dialogue et jouez la scène devant la classe.

ressources

VM
pp. 49–50

vhlcentral

A C T I V I T É S

O P T I O N S

Extra Practice Ask students yes/no questions based on the **Roman-photo**. Tell them to answer **Je crois que oui** or **Je crois que non**. Examples: **1. Stéphane a-t-il réussi au bac? 2. Stéphane va-t-il étudier l'architecture à l'université? 3. Astrid va-t-elle étudier la médecine? 4. La jeune femme va-t-elle être embauchée au P'tit Bistrot? 5. Michèle va-t-elle trouver un autre travail?**

Small Groups Have students work in groups of three. Tell them to write a résumé for a famous person. Write this format on the board for students to follow: **Objectif(s) professionnel(s), Formation, Expérience professionnelle,** and **Références.** Then have volunteers read the résumé to the class without saying the person's name. The class should try to guess whose résumé it is.

Section Goals

In this section, students will:
• learn about phone usage in France
• learn some common terms used in text messages
• read about well-paying jobs in the francophone world
• read about **les artisans** in France

Instructional Resources
vhlcentral.com;
reference tools

Culture à la loupe
Avant la lecture
• Have students look at the photos and describe what they see.
• Take a quick class survey to find out how many students use public phones, phone cards, cell phones, smartphones, and text messaging. Tally the results on the board.

Lecture
• Point out the **Coup de main**. Tell students that the commonly used term **SMS** stands for *short message service.*
• Point out the statistics chart. Ask students what information it shows. (the percentage of French people who had mobile subscriptions from 2000–2012)

Après la lecture Have students compare the French usage of telephones and phone cards with their own usage based on the results in the survey in **Avant la lecture**.

1 Suggestion Have students read the completed sentences aloud.

CULTURE À LA LOUPE

Le téléphone en France

Les Français sont très accros° à leur téléphone portable. Aujourd'hui, il y a plus de 73 millions d'abonnements°. Certains abonnés° choisissent le forfait° et payent un tarif mensuel°. Ce type d'abonnement exige° d'avoir un compte bancaire en France. Sinon, on a la possibilité de choisir des cartes prépayées ou de louer un portable pour une courte période.

Les gens utilisent aussi beaucoup leurs mobiles et smartphones pour communiquer par SMS°. En moyenne, chaque abonné envoie plus de 200 SMS par mois. Ces messages sont écrits dans un langage particulier, qui permet de taper° plus vite.

Le langage SMS est très phonétique et joue avec le son des lettres et des chiffres°. Tous les jeunes l'utilisent. Les jeunes aiment aussi beaucoup télécharger les logos et sonneries° du moment. En France, le marché de la téléphonie mobile se porte très bien!

Si on n'a pas de portable, on peut téléphoner avec une télécarte d'une cabine publique, mais il y en a de moins en moins. Les télécartes sont vendues dans les bureaux de tabac°, à la poste et dans tous les endroits qui affichent° «Télécartes en vente ici».

> **Coup de main**
>
> A mobile phone has many names in French: **téléphone, portable, GSM, mobile, smartphone.**
>
> A text message may be called an **SMS** or a **texto.**

accros *addicted* **abonnements** *subscriptions* **abonnés** *subscribers*
forfait *package* **tarif mensuel** *monthly fee* **exige** *requires*
SMS *text message* **taper** *type* **chiffres** *numbers* **sonneries** *ringtones*
bureaux de tabac *tobacco shops* **affichent** *post*

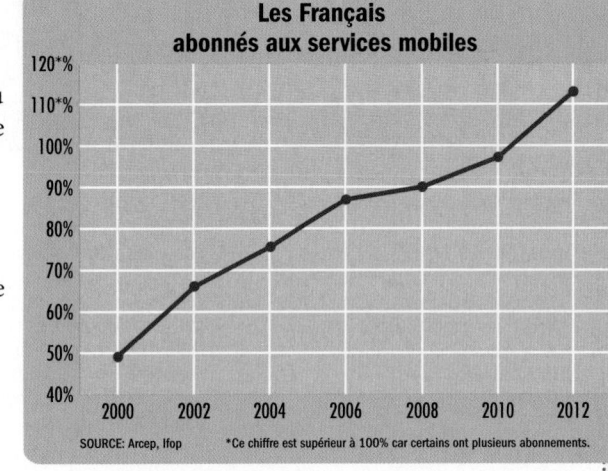

Les Français abonnés aux services mobiles

SOURCE: Arcep, Ifop   *Ce chiffre est supérieur à 100% car certains ont plusieurs abonnements.

---

1 Complétez Donnez le début ou la suite de chaque phrase, d'après le texte et le tableau. Answers may vary. Possible answers provided.

1. … des Français ont un abonnement mobile en 2012.
   112%
2. Si on a un compte bancaire, on peut choisir…
   un forfait.
3. En moyenne, chaque abonné envoie…
   plus de 200 SMS par mois.
4. … joue avec le son des lettres et des chiffres.
   Le langage SMS
5. Les jeunes aiment aussi…
   télécharger des logos et des sonneries.

6. En 2000, 49% seulement des Français…
   étaient abonnés aux services mobiles.
7. … sont d'autres noms pour désigner le portable.
   Téléphone, GSM, smartphone et mobil
8. Un SMS s'appelle aussi…
   un texto.
9. Pour téléphoner en France si on n'a pas de portable, on peut utiliser…
   une cabine publique avec une télécarte.
10. … dans les bureaux de tabac, à la poste et dans tous les endroits qui affichent «Télécartes en vente ici».
    Les télécartes sont vendues

O P T I O N S

La télécarte When purchasing **une télécarte**, it is less expensive per unit (**unité**) to buy **une grande** for 120 units than **une petite** for 50 units. The disposable **télécarte** works without a code. The French phone booth has two advantages: the quick, efficient insertion system for **la télécarte** and the caller's ability to view the remaining units on the phone card while talking on the phone.

Pairs Have students work in pairs. Tell them to take turns quizzing each other about the information on cell phones in the chart. Write a sample question on the board for students to use as a model. Example: **En quelle année est-ce que 65 pour cent des Français étaient équipés d'un portable? (2002)**

Le français quotidien
- Model the pronunciation of both columns so students can hear the sound-symbol correspondence between the abbreviations and the actual expressions.
- Point out that **après-midi** is one of the few words in French that can be either masculine or feminine. This book refers to it as masculine.

Portrait
- It is a point of pride in France to work as an **artisan** and to sell something that can be labeled **artisanal**.
- Ask students: **Considérez-vous qu'un plombier est un artisan? Pourquoi? Et un fleuriste? Un boucher? Un bijoutier?**

Le monde francophone Ask students: **Quels métiers ou secteurs de la liste sont bien/mal payés aux États-Unis? Pourquoi?**

2 Expansion For additional practice, give students these items. **7. Au Québec _____ est un secteur lucratif. (l'industrie du papier) 8. Si on veut bien gagner sa vie en tant que prêtre, on peut vivre _____. (en Haïti)**

3 Expansion Collect the text messages, choose a few, and write them on the board or a transparency. Tell the class to write the messages in standard French.

LE FRANÇAIS QUOTIDIEN

Le SMS, C pratik!

A+	À plus (tard).
Bap	Bon après-midi.
C pa 5pa	C'est pas sympa!
Dak	D'accord.
GT o 6né	J'étais au ciné.
Je t'M	Je t'aime.
Jenémar	J'en ai marre!
Kestufé	Qu'est-ce que tu fais?
Komencava	Comment ça va?
MDR	Mort de rire!

LE MONDE FRANCOPHONE

Comment gagner sa vie

Voici des métiers et des secteurs où on peut gagner sa vie dans le monde francophone.

Quelques exemples de métiers bien payés

En France avocat(e)
En Haïti prêtre°
Au Sénégal joueur de football professionnel
En Suisse banquier d'affaires

Quelques exemples de secteurs lucratifs

En Belgique l'industrie chimique, du pétrole
Au Québec l'industrie du papier
En Suisse les banques et les assurances
En Tunisie le tourisme

prêtre priest

PORTRAIT

Les artisans

L'artisanat en France emploie environ 3 millions de personnes. On le décrit souvent comme «la plus grande entreprise de France». C'est aujourd'hui, partout° en France, plus d'un million d'entreprises présentes dans différents secteurs: bouchers, plombiers, fleuristes, bijoutiers... La grande diversité des activités de l'artisanat favorise la construction d'un avenir à sa mesure. Les artisans travaillent dans plus de 500 activités différentes et occupent une place importante dans l'économie française. C'est un secteur créateur et générateur d'emplois. Les entreprises artisanales sont de petite taille, avec généralement moins de dix employés. Les artisans sont plus nombreux dans les villes, mais ils jouent aussi un rôle important en milieu rural (environ 30% des entreprises sont des entreprises artisanales). En plus d'°y apporter les services nécessaires, ils aident à créer le «lien social°». Ces chefs d'entreprise indépendants sont à l'origine d'initiatives et d'innovations. Ils sont toujours à la recherche d'une qualité excellente, de la satisfaction du client et du respect de l'environnement. Artisans et artisans d'art sont considérés comme les gardiens° de la tradition française et de son savoir-faire°, qu'ils se transmettent depuis des générations, grâce au° système de l'apprentissage°.

partout everywhere **En plus de** In addition to **lien social** social cohesion **gardiens** guardians
savoir-faire expertise **grâce au** thanks to **apprentissage** apprenticeship

---

2 Complétez Complétez les phrases.

1. L'artisanat en France emploie _environ 3 millions de personnes_.
2. _Answer will vary. Possible answer: Bouchers, plombiers, fleuristes, bijoutiers_ sont des exemples d'artisans.
3. Les artisans sont à la recherche de _la satisfaction du client, de la qualité et du respect de l'environnement_.
4. Le savoir-faire des artisans est transmis _grâce au système de l'apprentissage_.
5. Au Sénégal, _joueur de football professionnel_ est un métier bien payé.
6. En Tunisie, _le tourisme_ est un secteur lucratif.

3 Échange de textos Vous et un(e) partenaire allez faire connaissance par SMS. Préparez un dialogue en français facile, puis transformez-le en messages SMS. Comparez ensuite votre conversation SMS à la conversation d'un autre groupe. Présentez-la devant la classe.

S Practice more at **vhlcentral.com**.

ressources

vhlcentral

A C T I V I T É S

O P T I O N S

Les artisans The French government supports small family businesses. Also, the general public is accustomed to walking from shop to shop to do errands for services and products that may cost more than in chain stores, but are consistently of higher quality.

Extra Practice Have students write five true/false statements based on the information on this page. Then have them get together with a classmate, and take turns reading their statements aloud and responding.

13A.1

Le futur simple with quand and dès que

 Tutorial

Point de départ In **Leçon 12B**, you learned how to form **le futur simple**. You will now learn how to use **le futur simple** where English uses the present tense.

FUTURE   FUTURE
Je me **mettrai** à chercher du travail, quand je n'**aurai** plus d'argent.
*I **will start** looking for work when I **don't have** any more money.*

Dès que je réussirai l'examen de première année, je continuerai en médecine.

Nous irons dîner pour célébrer dès que j'aurai un nouveau travail.

- In English, you use the present tense after words like *when* or *as soon as*, even if you're talking about an action that takes place in the future. However, in French, you use the future tense after **quand** or **dès que** (*as soon as*) if the clause describes an event that will happen in the future.

Il **enverra** son CV **quand il aura** le temps.
He will send his résumé when he has time.

Je **posterai** les lettres **dès que je pourrai**.
I will mail the letters as soon as I can.

Quand j'**arriverai** à Lyon, je **prendrai** un taxi pour aller à l'hôtel.
When I get to Lyons, I'll take a taxi to the hotel.

Dès qu'on **finira** nos études, on **voyagera**.
As soon as we finish our studies, we'll travel.

- If a clause with **quand** or **dès que** does not describe a future action, another tense may be used for the verb.

Quand avez-vous fait le stage?
When did you do the internship?

La patronne nous parle **dès qu'elle arrive**.
The boss talks to us as soon as she arrives.

 **Essayez!**   Écrivez la forme correcte des verbes indiqués.

1. On l'embauchera dès qu'on _____aura_____ (avoir) de l'argent.
2. Nous commencerons le stage quand nous _____connaîtrons_____ (connaître) les résultats.
3. Il a téléphoné dès qu'il _____a reçu_____ (recevoir) la lettre.
4. On a envie de sortir quand il _____fait_____ (faire) beau.
5. Dès que vous _____prendrez_____ (prendre) rendez-vous, on vous indiquera le salaire.
6. Ils enverront leurs CV dès qu'ils _____achèteront_____ (acheter) l'ordinateur.
7. Nous passerons un entretien quand il _____reviendra_____ (revenir) de vacances.
8. Je décroche quand le téléphone _____sonne_____ (sonner).

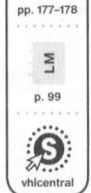

ressources

WB
pp. 177-178

LM
p. 99

vhlcentral

Section Goals

In this section, students will learn the future tense with **quand** and **dès que**.

Instructional Resources
vhlcentral.com:
Lab MP3s; SAM Answer Key;
Essayez! *and* ***Mise en pratique***
answers; Activity Pack
*(**Feuilles d'activités**); Lab*
Audioscript; reference tools

Suggestions

- Quickly review the **futur simple**.
- Explain that the future tense with **quand** and **dès que** is for expressing an act that has not yet taken place. Point out that in English one usually uses the present tense after *when* or *as soon as*. Check comprehension by asking students to supply the future tense of phrases using **quand** and **dès que**. Example: **Quand je ____ (voyager) en Europe, je ____ (louer) une voiture. (voyagerai; louerai)** Contrast with the English equivalent *When I travel to Europe, I will rent a car.*
- Explain that expressions with **quand** and **dès que** that express generalities do not use the future tense. Example: **Quand on veut trouver un travail, on doit écrire une lettre de motivation.**
- Write two columns on the board: **quand** and **dès que**. Have students give example sentences using each clause in the present and future tenses.
- Model the use of **quand** and **dès que** by asking questions about what others will do when they begin looking for a job. Examples: **Où habiterez-vous quand vous chercherez un travail? Dès que vous obtiendrez un travail, que ferez-vous?**

Essayez! Before assigning this activity, have students underline the verbs in the sentences and identify their tense. Example:
1. on l'embauchera (*future*)

Le français vivant

SALON DES JEUNES **PROFESSIONNELS**

Prenez en main votre avenir!

Vous prendrez en main votre avenir quand vous irez à ce salon. Dès que vous entrerez, vous rencontrerez des gens qui vous aideront à rencontrer d'autres gens, à trouver un emploi.

JEUNES PROFESSIONNELS

Identifiez Quelles formes de verbes au futur trouvez-vous après quand et dès que dans cette publicité (*ad*)? Quels autres verbes au futur trouvez-vous?

prendrez, irez, entrerez, rencontrerez, aideront

 Questions À tour de rôle, avec un(e) partenaire, posez-vous ces questions. Answers will vary.

1. Qui assistera au Salon des jeunes professionnels? Pourquoi?
2. Que trouvera-t-on au Salon des jeunes professionnels? Que fera-t-on?
3. Que feras-tu dès que tu finiras tes études universitaires?
4. Que penses-tu faire pour trouver un emploi quand tu seras prêt(e) à travailler?

Le français vivant Call on a volunteer to read the ad aloud. Ask students: **Quelles sont les questions qu'on doit poser à un forum pour l'emploi?** Encourage students to use the future tense with **quand** and **dès que**.

OPTIONS

Extra Practice Write these statements on the board, then ask students to finish them using the appropriate verb tense. **1. Quand on a envie de passer un entretien… 2. Dès qu'il a trouvé un travail… 3. Quand je voyagerai à Paris… 4. Quand je recevrai un salaire élevé… 5. Dès que je parlerai avec mon patron…**

Game Have students write three important things they will or will not do when they graduate on a slip of paper and put it in a box. Example: **Quand j'obtiendrai le diplôme, je n'habiterai plus chez mes parents.** Have students draw a paper from the box, then walk around the room, asking others if they will do what is listed, until they find the person who wrote the prediction. The first person to find a match wins.

1 Expansion Have pairs model the activity and write three more sentences expressing generalities. Then have students switch their sentences with other pairs.

2 Suggestion Have volunteers write each sentence with the future tense on the board. Ask other volunteers to change the sentences into the present or the past tense and discuss how the meanings change.

3 Suggestion Before beginning the activity, have students talk about the last job they had. Encourage them to use **quand** and **dès que** with the past tense.

Mise en pratique

1 **Projets** Nathalie et Brigitte discutent des problèmes de travail. Nathalie explique ce qu'elle fait quand elle est sans travail. Brigitte approuve.

MODÈLE

Je lis les annonces quand je cherche un travail.
Moi aussi, je lirai les annonces quand je chercherai un travail.

1. J'envoie mon CV quand je cherche du travail.   Moi aussi, j'enverrai mon CV quand je chercherai du travail.
2. Mon mari lit mon CV dès qu'il a le temps.   Mon mari aussi lira mon CV dès qu'il aura le temps.
3. Je suis contente quand tu passes un entretien.   Moi aussi, je serai contente quand tu passeras un entretien.
4. Je prends rendez-vous dès que je reçois une lettre d'une compagnie.   Mes amis habiteront près de chez moi.
5. Mon petit ami et moi, nous allons acheter un chien.   Moi aussi, je prendrai rendez-vous dès que je recevrai une lettre d'une compagnie.
6. Je fais des projets quand j'ai un travail.   Moi aussi, je ferai des projets quand j'aurai un travail.

2 **Plus tard** Aurélien parle de ses projets et des projets de sa famille et de ses amis. Mettez les verbes au futur.

MODÈLE

dès que / je / avoir / le bac / je / aller / à l'université
Dès que j'aurai le bac, j'irai à l'université.

1. quand / je / être / à l'université / ma sœur
   et moi / habiter ensemble   Quand je serai à l'université, ma sœur et moi habiterons ensemble.
2. quand / ma sœur / étudier plus / elle / réussir   Quand ma sœur étudiera plus, elle réussira.
3. quand / mes parents / être / à la retraite / je /
   emprunter pour payer mes études   Quand mes parents seront à la retraite, j'emprunterai pour payer mes études.
4. dès que / vous / finir vos études / vous / envoyer
   vos CV / tout / entreprises de la ville   Dès que vous finirez vos études, vous enverrez vos CV à toutes les entreprises de la ville.
5. quand / tu / travailler / tu / acheter une voiture   Quand tu travailleras, tu achèteras une voiture.
6. quand / nous / trouver / nouveau travail /
   nous / ne plus lire / les annonces   Quand nous trouverons un nouveau travail, nous ne lirons plus les annonces.

3 **Conseils** Quels conseils pouvez-vous donner à un(e) ami(e) qui cherche du travail? Avec un(e) partenaire, assemblez les éléments des colonnes pour formuler vos conseils. Utilisez **quand** ou **dès que**.   Answers will vary.

MODÈLE

Quand tu auras ton diplôme, tu chercheras un travail.

A	B
avoir son diplôme	s'amuser
avoir un métier	chercher un travail
passer un entretien	être riche
réussir ses examens	gagner beaucoup d'argent
trouver un emploi	lire les annonces
	se marier
	parler de son expérience professionnelle

 Practice more at **vhlcentral.com.**

Communication

4 **L'avenir** Qu'est-ce que l'avenir nous réserve? Avec un(e) partenaire, complétez ces phrases. Ensuite, présentez vos réponses à la classe. Answers will vary.

1. Dès que je réussirai mes examens, je...
2. Ton ami(e) et toi, vous lirez les annonces quand...
3. Mon/Ma meilleur(e) ami(e) travaillera dès que...
4. Tu enverras ton CV quand...
5. Mes amis se marieront dès que...
6. Quand nous aurons beaucoup d'argent, nous...

5 **Content(e)** Votre professeur va vous donner une feuille d'activités. Circulez dans la classe pour trouver une personne qui réponde oui et une qui réponde non à chaque question. Justifiez toutes vos réponses. Answers will vary.

> **MODÈLE**
>
> **Étudiant(e) 1:** Est-ce que tu seras plus content(e) quand tu auras du temps libre?
> **Étudiant(e) 2:** Oui, je serai plus content(e) dès que j'aurai du temps libre, parce que je ferai plus souvent de la gym.

6 **Les métiers** Vous allez bientôt exercer ces métiers (*have these jobs*). Dites à un(e) partenaire ce qui (*what*) sera possible et ce qui ne sera pas possible quand vous commencerez votre nouveau poste. Alternez les rôles. Answers will vary.

> **MODÈLE**
>
> **Étudiant(e) 1:** Dès que je commencerai ce travail, je chercherai un nouvel appartement.
> **Étudiant(e) 2:** Je n'aurai plus le temps de sortir quand j'aurai ce poste.

1.

2.

3.

4.

5.

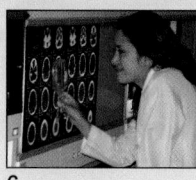
6.

7 **Un autre monde** Vous espérez devenir homme ou femme politique à l'avenir. Que ferez-vous pour changer le monde? Précisez au moins (*at least*) cinq choses qui seront différentes. Avec un(e) partenaire, discutez de ce sujet à tour de rôle. Answers will vary.

> **MODÈLE**
>
> Quand je deviendrai homme/femme politique, il n'y aura plus d'enfants pauvres.

cinq cent cinquante et un **551**

---

4 Expansion Have students write three original sentences modeled on the sentences from this activity. Then ask volunteers to share their sentences with the class.

5 Suggestion Have two volunteers act out the **modèle**. Then hand out the **Feuilles d'activités** from the Activity Pack on the Supersite.

6 Expansion Ask volunteers to tell you the job of their dreams. Modeling the activity, have them talk about what will and will not be possible once they have begun their job.

7 Suggestion Have students share what they will change with the rest of the class and have the class vote on which changes they like the most.

O P T I O N S

Extra Practice Have students imagine they are taking a vacation to Europe. Ask them to write six things they will do when they arrive. Then in pairs have students imagine they are calling home after their first few days of vacation. Have one student ask questions about what they did upon arrival. The second student should answer the questions using **quand** and **dès que**.

Video Show the video episode again to give students more input on the use of the future tense. Ask the students to write down all the examples of the future tense they hear in the conversation. When the video has finished, review the lists as a class. Discuss the use of **quand**, **dès que**, and **une fois que**.

Section Goals

In this section, students will learn:

- interrogative pronouns **lequel**, **laquelle**, **lesquels**, and **lesquelles**
- contractions with prepositions and forms of **lequel**

Instructional Resources
vhlcentral.com:
Activity Pack; Lab MP3s; SAM Answer Key; **Essayez!** *and* **Mise en pratique** *answers; Activity Pack* **(Feuilles d'activités);** *Lab Audioscript; reference tools*

Suggestions

- Review the use and forms of **quel: quel(s), quelle(s).** Remind students that **quel** agrees with the noun it modifies.
- Point out that students already use other interrogative pronouns (**qui, que**). **Lequel** differs in that it has a specific antecedent (a person or thing already mentioned).
- Brainstorm a list of movies and write them on the board. Demonstrate the use of **lequel** by pointing to the list and asking students: **Lequel préférez-vous?**
- Practice **de + lequel** and **à + lequel** by asking students questions that elicit their use. Examples: **Je parle des films étrangers avec mes amis. Desquels parlez-vous? Je m'intéresse à l'histoire américaine. À laquelle vous intéressez-vous?**

Essayez! Before assigning this activity, have students underline the noun (and preposition, if applicable) that the appropriate form of **lequel** should replace.

Leçon 13A

13A.2

À noter

Review the interrogative adjective **quel** and its forms, which you learned in **Leçon 4A**.

The interrogative pronoun *lequel* Ⓢ Tutorial

Point de départ The different forms of the interrogative pronoun **lequel** (*which one*) are used to ask about a person or thing previously mentioned. They replace the forms of the interrogative adjective **quel** + [*noun*].

Quel métier choisirez-vous?	**Lequel** choisirez-vous?
Which profession will you choose?	*Which one will you choose?*

- The interrogative pronoun agrees in gender and number with the noun to which it refers.

	singular	plural
masculine	**lequel**	**lesquels**
feminine	**laquelle**	**lesquelles**

Quelle entreprise l'a embauché?	**Laquelle** l'a embauché?
Which company hired him?	*Which one hired him?*
Quelles entreprises embaucheront de nouveaux employés?	**Lesquelles** embaucheront de nouveaux employés?
Which businesses will hire new employees?	*Which ones will hire new employees?*

- Place the form of **lequel** wherever you would place **quel(le)(s)** + [*noun*] in a question.

Dans **quel domaine** travaille-t-elle?	Dans **lequel** travaille-t-elle?
Which field does she work in?	*Which one does she work in?*
Pour **quelle compagnie** travaillez-vous?	Pour **laquelle** travaillez-vous?
Which company do you work for?	*Which one do you work for?*

- Remember that past participles agree with preceding direct objects.

Laquelle avez-vous **choisie**?	**Lesquels** as-tu **faits**?
Which one did you choose?	*Which ones did you do?*

- Forms of **lequel** contract with the prepositions **à** and **de**.

à + form of *lequel*		
	singular	plural
masculine	**auquel**	**auxquels**
feminine	**à laquelle**	**auxquelles**

de + form of *lequel*		
	singular	plural
masculine	**duquel**	**desquels**
feminine	**de laquelle**	**desquelles**

Auxquels vous intéressez-vous?	Vous parlez **duquel**?
Which ones interest you?	*Which one are you talking about?*

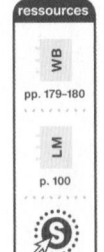

ressources

WB
pp. 179–180

LM
p. 100

Ⓢ
vhlcentral

Essayez! Réécrivez les phrases avec des formes de **lequel**.

1. Pour quelle compagnie travaillez-vous? *Pour laquelle travaillez-vous?*
2. Quel métier préférez-vous? *Lequel préférez-vous?*
3. À quel métier t'intéresses-tu? *Auquel t'intéresses-tu?*
4. De quels stages est-ce que vous parlez? *Desquels est-ce que vous parlez?*
5. Quelle entreprise as-tu choisie? *Laquelle as-tu choisie?*

552 *cinq cent cinquante-deux*

Le français vivant

Recherchons candidats avec talents particuliers.
Lequel ou laquelle choisir?

La question traditionnelle:
Lesquels ont un diplôme? Quel diplôme?

La question d'aujourd'hui:
Lequel ou laquelle a une personnalité inhabituelle?

 BANQUE COMMUNAUTAIRE DE FRANCE (BCDF)
Enfin une banque à votre écoute

Identifiez Quelles formes du pronom interrogatif **lequel** trouvez-vous dans cette publicité (*ad*)? Lequel, laquelle, Lesquels

 Questions À tour de rôle, avec un(e) partenaire, posez-vous ces questions. Answers will vary.

1. Quel est le but (*goal*) de cette pub?
2. Quelle question posait-on traditionnellement?
3. Quelle question pose-t-on aujourd'hui?
4. Les formations traditionnelles fonctionnent-elles toujours pour trouver un travail? Pourquoi?
5. Pourquoi faut-il aujourd'hui avoir une personnalité inhabituelle?

cinq cent cinquante-trois **553**

OPTIONS

Video Replay the video episode, having students focus on the use of **laquelle**. Point out that forms of **lequel** are often used in conversation to clarify a point. Stop the video where appropriate and ask students which noun each **laquelle** refers to.

Game Use a ball to play a game that practices the use of the interrogative pronoun **lequel**. Say a sentence that can be restated using a form of **lequel**. Example: **De quelle université parlez-vous?** Toss the ball to a student who must repeat the sentence using the appropriate form of **lequel**. (**De laquelle parlez-vous?**) When the student has given the appropriate form, he or she tosses the ball back to you. Include both feminine and masculine, singular and plural nouns, and the prepositions **à** and **de** with **lequel**. Keep the pace rapid.

ESPACE STRUCTURES

1 Suggestion Ask six volunteers to write the completed sentences on the board. Have other volunteers correct any spelling or grammar errors.

2 Expansion Have students work in pairs to brainstorm other nouns and verbs similar to those in the activity. Ask volunteers to write their examples on the board. Have other volunteers formulate questions aloud using **lequel.**

3 Suggestion Before assigning the activity, use magazine pictures of popular movies, TV programs, etc., to ask some general questions about students' likes and preferences.

Mise en pratique

1 **Au bureau** Hubert parle à ses collègues. Complétez ses phrases avec une forme du pronom interrogatif **lequel**.

1. J'ai deux stylos. ___Lequel___ veux-tu emprunter?
2. Voici la liste des entreprises. À ___laquelle___ devons-nous téléphoner?
3. Avez-vous contacté les employés avec ___lesquels___ il faut travailler?
4. Sais-tu le nom des stages ___auxquels___ tu as assisté?
5. ___Lesquelles___ de ces lettres avez-vous lues?
6. Je suis allé dans plusieurs bureaux. ___Desquels/Duquel___ parlez-vous?

2 **Répétez** Vous rencontrez M. Dupont pendant un dîner où il y a beaucoup de bruit (*noise*). Il vous pose des questions, mais il n'entend pas vos réponses. Avec un(e) partenaire, alternez les rôles. *Some answers will vary.*

> **MODÈLE** examen / réussir
> **Étudiant(e) 1:** *Quel examen avez-vous réussi?*
> **Étudiant(e) 2:** *L'examen de chimie.*
> **Étudiant(e) 1:** *Lequel avez-vous réussi?*

1. métier / s'intéresser à   À quel métier vous intéressez-vous? Auquel vous intéressez-vous?
2. CV / avoir envoyé   Quel CV avez-vous envoyé? Lequel avez-vous envoyé?
3. entreprise / avoir embauché   Quelle entreprise vous a embauché(e)? Laquelle vous a embauché(e)?
4. candidats / ne pas avoir obtenu de poste   Quels candidats n'ont pas obtenu de poste? Lesquels n'ont pas obtenu de poste?
5. formations / devoir suivre   Quelles formations devez-vous suivre? Lesquelles devez-vous suivre?
6. domaine / se spécialiser dans   Dans quel domaine vous spécialisez-vous? Dans lequel vous spécialisez-vous?

3 **La culture francophone** Vous voulez savoir si votre partenaire connaît la culture francophone. À tour de rôle, posez-vous ces questions et répondez-y. Ensuite, posez-vous une question avec une forme de **lequel**. *Some answers will vary.*

> **MODÈLE** Qui chante en français?
> a. Madonna   (b.) Céline Dion   c. Mariah Carey
> *Laquelle/Lesquelles de ces chanteuses aimes-tu?*

1. Qui est un acteur français?   Lequel/Lesquels de ces acteurs préfères-tu?
   (a.) Gérard Depardieu   b. Tom Hanks   c. Johnny Depp
2. Où parle-t-on français?   Laquelle/Lesquelles de ces villes voudras-tu visiter un jour?
   a. Philadelphie   (b.) Montréal   c. Athènes
3. Quelle voiture est française?   Laquelle/Lesquelles de ces voitures as-tu déjà conduite(s)?
   a. Lotus   b. Ferrari   (c.) Peugeot
4. Quelle marque (*brand*) est française?   Laquelle/Lesquelles de ces marques vas-tu essayer?
   a. Mabelle   b. Versace   (c.) L'Oréal
5. Qui est un réalisateur (*director*) français?   Lequel/Lesquels de ces réalisateurs aimes-tu?
   a. Luchino Visconti   (b.) Luc Besson   c. Steven Spielberg

 Practice more at **vhlcentral.com.**

Communication

4 **Des choix** Cet été, vous irez en vacances avec des amis et vous visiterez plusieurs endroits. Avec un(e) partenaire, parlez de vos projets et posez des questions pour demander des détails. Answers will vary.

> **MODÈLE** visiter des châteaux (castles)
>
> **Étudiant(e) 1:** *Quand je serai en Suisse, je visiterai des châteaux.*
> **Étudiant(e) 2:** *Lesquels visiteras-tu?*

aller dans des musées	marcher dans les rues
bronzer sur la plage	se promener au parc
dîner au restaurant	sortir en boîte
faire du sport	visiter des sites touristiques
?	?

5 **Enquête** Votre professeur va vous donner une feuille d'activités. Circulez dans la classe et parlez à différent(e)s camarades pour trouver, pour chaque question, une personne qui réponde oui. Demandez des détails. Answers will vary.

> **MODÈLE**
>
> **Étudiant(e) 1:** *Écoutes-tu de la musique?*
> **Étudiant(e) 2:** *Oui.*
> **Étudiant(e) 1:** *Laquelle aimes-tu?*
> **Étudiant(e) 2:** *J'écoute toujours de la musique classique.*

Activités	Noms	Réponses
1. écouter de la musique	Sam	musique classique
2. avoir des passe-temps		
3. bien s'entendre avec des membres de sa famille		
4. s'intéresser aux livres		
5. travailler avec d'autres étudiant(e)s		
6. habiter dans un appartement		

6 **Ce semestre** Avec un(e) partenaire, parlez des bons et des mauvais aspects de votre vie à la fac ce semestre. Employez des formes du pronom interrogatif **lequel**. Ensuite, présentez vos réponses à la classe. Answers will vary.

> **MODÈLE**
>
> **Étudiant(e) 1:** *J'ai des cours très difficiles ce semestre.*
> **Étudiant(e) 2:** *Lesquels?*
> **Étudiant(e) 1:** *Le cours de biologie et le cours de chimie.*

- les cours
- la résidence
- les livres
- les camarades
- les profs
- ?

---

4 Expansions
- Have students bring in photos from a past vacation. Working in pairs, students should ask questions similar to those in the activity, but using the past tense.
- Ask volunteers to present their photos to the class. Have classmates ask questions using the appropriate form of **lequel**.

5 Suggestion Have two volunteers act out the **modèle**. Then hand out the **Feuilles d'activités** from the Activity Pack on the Supersite.

6 Suggestion Brainstorm vocabulary related to university life before assigning the activity. Examples: **un emploi sur le campus, les examens**, etc.

OPTIONS

Pairs Have your students interview each other in pairs about where they want to be and what they want to be doing in five years, in ten years, in thirty years, and so forth. Encourage students to use the future tense and ask clarifying questions using the appropriate forms of **lequel**. Have each student take notes on his or her partner's plans. Then ask for a few volunteers to report on their partner's plans for the future.

Small Groups Divide the class into groups of three. Ask each group to work together to write a prediction of a classmate's future, using the future tense with **quand** and **dès que**. The group should not include the name of their subject. Then circulate the description and ask other groups to identify the name of the classmate whose future is being predicted.

Révision

Instructional Resources
vhlcentral.com:
Activity Pack (Info Gap Activities); Testing Program; Testing Program MP3s; reference tools

1 Expansion Have pairs repeat the activity referring to their budgets. Example: **Quelles choses achèterez-vous dès que vous aurez le budget nécessaire?** Give students magazine pictures to represent what items they will buy.

2 Suggestion Review the use of the relative pronoun **qui** when giving details about a person.

3 Expansion Have students write a letter to a friend giving career advice. Ask students to include the strategies they developed in the activity as part of their letter.

4 Suggestion Before assigning this activity, do the **modèle** with a volunteer. Ask students to describe any companies they have worked for. Write two of the company names and characteristics on the board.

5 Suggestion Brainstorm typical interview questions with the class before assigning groups for this activity.

6 Suggestion Divide the class into pairs and distribute the Info Gap Handouts found in the Activity Pack on the Supersite. Give students ten minutes to complete the activity.

---

1 Mon premier emploi Avec un(e) partenaire, dites ce que (*what*) vous ferez et utilisez **quand** ou **dès que**. Answers will vary.

MODÈLE

mon premier emploi
Dès que je serai embauché(e), je téléphonerai à ma mère.

1. mon premier entretien
2. mon premier jour dans l'entreprise
3. rencontrer les autres employés
4. mon premier salaire
5. travailler sur mon premier projet
6. changer de poste
7. me disputer avec le patron
8. quitter l'entreprise

2 Lequel? Avec un(e) partenaire, imaginez un dialogue entre un(e) patron(ne) et son assistant(e). L'assistant(e) demande des précisions. Alternez les rôles. Answers will vary.

MODÈLE

Étudiant(e) 1: *Vous appellerez notre client, s'il vous plaît?*
Étudiant(e) 2: *Oui, mais lequel?*
Étudiant(e) 1: *Le client qui est venu hier après-midi.*

accompagner un visiteur	envoyer un colis
appeler un client	laisser un message à un(e) employé(e)
chercher un numéro de téléphone	prendre un rendez-vous
faire une lettre de recommandation	préparer une réunion (*meeting*)

3 Mes stratégies Avec un(e) partenaire, faites une liste de dix stratégies pour bien mener (*to lead*) votre carrière. Pour chaque stratégie, utilisez **quand** ou **dès que**. Answers will vary.

MODÈLE

Étudiant(e) 1: *Dès que je m'ennuierai, je chercherai un nouveau poste.*
Étudiant(e) 2: *Quand je serai trop fatigué(e), je prendrai des vacances.*

---

4 Laquelle choisir? Deux entreprises différentes vous ont offert un travail. Avec un(e) partenaire, comparez-les. Posez des questions avec la forme correcte du pronom interrogatif **lequel** et donnez des réponses avec **quand** et **dès que**. Choisissez une entreprise et comparez vos réponses avec la classe. Answers will vary.

MODÈLE

Étudiant(e) 1: *Laquelle te propose un meilleur salaire?*
Étudiant(e) 2: *Verrin me propose un meilleur salaire, mais dès que je commencerai, je devrai travailler jusqu'à neuf heures du soir.*

5 Un entretien Par groupes de trois, jouez cette scène: un chef du personnel visite votre université et vous et un(e) ami(e) passez un entretien informel. Utilisez le pronom interrogatif **lequel** et le futur avec **quand** et **dès que**. Answer will vary.

Le chef du personnel...

- décrit le poste.
- pose des questions.
- répond aux questions des candidat(e)s.
- dit aux candidat(e)s quand il/elle va les contacter.

Les candidat(e)s...

- L'un doit donner toutes les bonnes réponses.
- L'autre ne donne que de mauvaises réponses.
- Les deux posent des questions pour en savoir plus sur l'entreprise et sur les postes.

6 Quand nous chercherons du travail... Votre professeur va vous donner, à vous et à votre partenaire, deux feuilles d'activités différentes. Attention! Ne regardez pas la feuille de votre partenaire. Answers will vary.

O P T I O N S

Extra Practice Tell students to imagine they were fired from a job. Now they must write a letter convincing their **patron(ne)** that they deserve a second chance. Give students fifteen minutes to complete this activity. Encourage the use of the lesson vocabulary and the future tense with **quand** and **dès que**. Then have students switch letters with a classmate for peer editing.

Small Groups Divide the class into groups of three. Have students take turns telling the group three things they hope will be true when they are ten years older. Example: **Quand j'aurai 30 ans, je gagnerai beaucoup d'argent.**

L'avenir et les métiers

Hôtesse: Csilla

Csilla va à la rencontre de plusieurs personnes sur la terrasse d'un café. Elle pose des questions sur les métiers de ces personnes, qui ont des professions bien différentes les unes des autres. Csilla nous présente aussi d'autres métiers, comme vétérinaire, dentiste ou encore banquier.

Avant de regarder Répondez aux questions. Answers will vary.

1. Est-ce que vous travaillez? Ou bien avez-vous déjà travaillé? Si oui, dans quel secteur?
2. Quels métiers font vos parents?
3. Aimeriez-vous faire un métier comme ceux (*those*) de vos parents?

CSILLA *Excusez-moi, Monsieur, Madame. Quelle est votre profession?*

CSILLA *Chef de cuisine.*

Compréhension Répondez aux questions.

1. Michèle aime-t-elle sa profession de serveuse? Pourquoi ou pourquoi pas? Oui, Michèle aime sa profession de serveuse, parce qu'elle est assez sociable.
2. Quelles sont les professions du couple assis à la terrasse du café? La femme est psychologue et l'homme est comptable.
3. Comment la jeune femme du couple décrit-elle sa profession? Elle dit que sa profession est exigeante mais très intéressante.
4. Quelles sont les autres professions présentées par Csilla? homme ou femme d'affaires, agent de police, pompier, chef de cuisine, infirmier ou infirmière, chauffeur de taxi, vétérinaire, dentiste et banquier

Discussion Par groupes de trois, répondez aux questions. Answers will vary.

1. Est-ce qu'un des domaines mentionnés dans la vidéo vous intéresse? Lequel?
2. Pourriez-vous faire de ce domaine votre métier? Pourquoi?
3. Quelles seraient les étapes pour y parvenir (*to get there*)?

Vocabulaire utile

Ça vous plaît?	*Do you like it?*
cette profession me convient	*this job suits me*
un laboratoire	*laboratory*

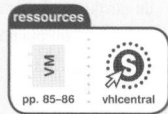

ressources
VM
pp. 85–86
vhlcentral

Section Goals

In this section, students will:
- watch a video about different types of careers
- answer questions about the video and their own working life and career aspirations

Instructional Resources
vhlcentral.com:
Flash culture; Flash culture transcription; reference tools

Avant de regarder
- Have students look at the video stills, read the captions, and predict what happens in this episode.
- Explain to students that they don't need to understand every word they hear. Tell them to listen for vocabulary from this lesson as well as cognates. They should also watch every scene carefully and jot down further examples of this lesson's vocabulary.

Compréhension Have students work in pairs or groups. Tell them to write down their answers. Then, show the video again so that they can check their answers and add any missing information.

Discussion
- Ask students what they wanted to be when they were little.
- Have volunteers share their answers to the questions in the activity.
- How do they think career choices are similar or different in France?

Pôle emploi When looking for work, French job seekers can turn to **Pôle emploi**, created in 2008 from the merger of two similar agencies in existence since 1967. The goals of **Pôle emploi** include registering job seekers and assisting them in their job search, working with employers to place job seekers in open positions, and assisting entrepreneurs who want to open their own business.

SMIC The **SMIC (salaire minimum interprofessionnel de croissance)** is the French equivalent of the U.S. minimum wage. In 2017 it was €9,76 per hour. The **SMIC** is reevaluated every year on January 1st.

Section Goals

In this section, students will learn and practice vocabulary related to:
• professions and occupations
• the workplace

Instructional Resources

vhlcentral.com:
Digital Image Bank (including vocabulary illustrations from the textbook, theme-based illustrations);
Vocabulaire supplémentaire;
Mise en pratique *answers;*
Textbook Audioscript; Lab Audioscript; Activity Pack (Info Gap Activities); Textbook MP3s; Lab MP3s; SAM Answer Key; reference tools

Suggestions

• Tell students to look over the new vocabulary and identify the cognates.

• Use the **13B Contextes** illustration from the Digital Image Bank. Identify the professions of people in the illustration. Examples: **C'est un agriculteur. C'est un banquier.**

• Explain that for the terms listed here with no feminine form (**un agriculteur/une agricultrice; un homme/une femme politique**) and no feminine article (**un/une psychologue**), the French say **elle est** followed by the masculine form of the profession. Examples: **Elle est plombier. Elle est chef d'entreprise.**

• Ask students questions using the new vocabulary. Examples: **1. Avez-vous un emploi à mi-temps? 2. Êtes-vous au chômage? 3. Avez-vous une assurance maladie? 4. Pourquoi est-il important d'avoir une assurance maladie? 5. Quelles professions sont exigeantes, à votre avis? 6. Connaissez-vous une femme politique célèbre?**

• Additional vocabulary for this lesson can be found in the **Vocabulaire supplémentaire** on the Supersite.

• Use the Jobs illustrations from the Digital Image Bank to help students familiarize themselves with professions, occupations, and the workplace.

Leçon 13B

Ⓢ **Vocabulary Tools**

Les professions

You will learn how to...
▪ discuss your work
▪ say what you would do

une chercheuse
(chercheur *m.*)

$H_2O + C$

une vétérinaire
(vétérinaire *m.*)

un chauffeur
de camion

une comptable
(comptable *m.*)

un pompier
(femme pompier *f.*)

un chauffeur
de taxi

un cuisinier
(cuisinière *f.*)

Vocabulaire

démissionner	*to resign*
diriger	*to manage*
être au chômage	*to be unemployed*
être bien/mal payé(e)	*to be well/badly paid*
gagner	*to earn; to win*
prendre un congé	*to take time off*
renvoyer	*to dismiss, to let go*
une carrière	*career*
un chômeur/une chômeuse	*unemployed person*
un emploi à mi-temps/ à temps partiel	*part-time job*
un emploi à plein temps	*full-time job*
un niveau	*level*
une profession (exigeante)	*(demanding) profession*
un(e) retraité(e)	*retired person*
une réunion	*meeting*
une réussite	*success*
un syndicat	*union*
une assurance-maladie	*health insurance*
une assurance-vie	*life insurance*
une augmentation (de salaire)	*raise (in salary)*
une promotion	*promotion*
un cadre/une femme cadre	*executive*
un chef d'entreprise	*head of a company*
un conseiller/une conseillère	*consultant; advisor*
une femme au foyer	*housewife*
un(e) gérant(e)	*manager*
un homme/une femme politique	*politician*
un ouvrier/une ouvrière	*worker, laborer*
un plombier	*plumber*

TAXI
Parisien

ressources

WB	LM	Ⓢ
pp. 181–182	p. 101	vhlcentral

OPTIONS

TPR Have students mime the work of different professionals. Write the names of professions on slips of paper or whisper them to each person. Examples: **comptable, pompier,** and **chauffeur.** The rest of the class should guess what profession the person is miming. The student who guesses correctly gets to mime the next profession.

Extra Practice Give French words that are related to a profession. Then ask students to guess the profession. Example: **la nourriture, un restaurant, cuisiner, une fourchette, un menu, le dîner (un chef de cuisine)**

Mise en pratique

1 Écoutez
Écoutez la conversation entre Henri et Margot, deux jeunes élèves, et indiquez si les phrases suivantes sont **vraies** ou **fausses**.

Henri **Margot**

1. Henri veut être comptable. Faux.
2. Il aidera ses employés. Vrai.
3. Ses employés seront bien payés. Vrai.
4. Il offrira à tous une assurance vie. Faux.
5. Margot veut être chef d'entreprise. Faux.
6. Elle aidera les femmes au foyer. Faux.
7. Margot ne parlera pas aux syndicats. Faux.
8. Une de ses priorités sera le chômage. Vrai.

2 Les professions
Pour chaque profession de la colonne de gauche, trouvez la définition qui correspond dans la colonne de droite.

g 1. un chef d'entreprise — a. travaille avec des budgets
j 2. une femme au foyer — b. est employé dans une usine (*factory*)
k 3. un chauffeur — c. répare les fuites (*leaks*) d'eau
i 4. une banquière — d. loue et vend des appartements
h 5. un cuisinier — e. travaille dans un laboratoire
a 6. une comptable — f. s'occupe de la santé des animaux
b 7. un ouvrier — g. dirige des employés
f 8. une vétérinaire — h. prépare des plats dans un restaurant
d 9. un agent immobilier — i. travaille avec de l'argent
c 10. un plombier — j. s'occupe de la maison et des enfants
k. conduit un taxi ou un camion
l. donne des conseils

3 Le monde du travail
Complétez le paragraphe en utilisant les mots de vocabulaire de la liste pour faire des phrases cohérentes.

à mi-temps	un conseil
à plein temps	mal payés
l'assurance maladie	un niveau
une augmentation	d'une promotion
leur carrière	un salaire élevé

Quand les étudiants ont un travail, en général c'est un emploi (1) à mi-temps parce qu'ils doivent aussi étudier pour préparer (2) leur carrière. Souvent, ils sont (3) mal payés. Mais avec leur diplôme, ils auront la possibilité de trouver un poste (4) à plein temps, avec (5) un salaire élevé et bien souvent (6) l'assurance maladie. Plus tard, ils pourront demander (7) une augmentation de salaire ou bien attendre l'opportunité (8) d'une promotion pour gagner plus d'argent.

 Practice more at vhlcentral.com.

cinq cent cinquante-neuf **559**

Professions illustrées: un banquier (banquière f.), un agent immobilier, un agriculteur (agricultrice f.), une électricienne (électricien m.), un psychologue

1 Audioscript HENRI: Quand je serai grand, je serai chef d'entreprise. J'aiderai mes employés. Ils auront un salaire élevé et bien sûr l'assurance maladie et les congés payés. MARGOT: Moi aussi, quand je serai grande, j'aiderai les gens, spécialement les ouvriers. Je serai femme politique. J'assisterai aux réunions des différents syndicats, j'écouterai les besoins des chômeurs et je travaillerai pour développer les emplois. (On Textbook MP3s)

1 Suggestions
- Before playing the recording, have students describe the people in the photos.
- After playing the recording, tell students to correct the false statements.

2 Expansions
- Ask students what professions item e. (**travaille dans un laboratoire**) and item l. (**donne des conseils**) describe. (item e.: **chercheur/chercheuse** and item l.: **conseiller/conseillère**)
- Have students write definitions for other professions not listed. Examples: **un agriculteur, un électricien, un psychologue.**

3 Expansion Have students write three comprehension questions based on the paragraph. Then tell them to get together in groups of three and take turns asking and answering each other's questions.

Game Brainstorm a list of professions from previous lessons and write them on the board. Distribute or have students make a Bingo card (a 5 X 5 grid of 25 squares) and write the name of a profession from this lesson or a previous one in each square. Write the name of each profession on a separate card and put the cards in a box. Draw cards one by one from the box and read the profession aloud. If students have that profession on their cards, they put a check mark in the corner of the box. To win, a student must have five professions in a row. The first person to have five in a row should say Bingo! To verify a win, have the student read the names of the professions in the winning row.

ESPACE CONTEXTES

NATIONAL
communication
STANDARDS

Communication

4 Expansion Have pairs get together with another pair and report what information they collected from their partners.

5 Suggestion Before beginning the activity, give students a few minutes to jot down some ideas about their job, boss, and/or employees.

6 Suggestion Have two volunteers read the **modèle** aloud. Then divide the class into pairs and distribute the Info Gap Handouts found in the Activity Pack on the Supersite. Give students ten minutes to complete the activity.

7 Suggestion Tell students to use the ads on page 542 as models. Encourage them to invent information for the company, such as a telephone number, a street address, or an e-mail address.

4 Conversez Interviewez un(e) camarade de classe. Les réponses peuvent être réelles ou imaginaires. *Answers will vary.*

1. Où travailles-tu en ce moment? Es-tu bien payé(e)?
2. Préfères-tu travailler à mi-temps ou à plein temps? Pourquoi?
3. Est-ce le métier que tu feras plus tard? Pourquoi?
4. Est-ce que tu as des congés payés? Une assurance maladie? Qu'en penses-tu?
5. As-tu déjà demandé une augmentation de salaire? As-tu réussi à en obtenir une? Comment?
6. As-tu déjà obtenu une promotion? Quand? Pourquoi?
7. As-tu déjà été au chômage? Pendant combien de temps? Qu'est-ce que tu as fait pendant ce temps-là?
8. Quel genre de carrière veux-tu faire? Ta profession sera-t-elle exigeante? Pourquoi?

5 Votre carrière Voilà cinq ans que vous n'avez pas vu votre ami(e) de la fac. Depuis, vous avez obtenu tous/toutes les deux votre diplôme et trouvé un travail. Travaillez avec un(e) camarade de classe pour présenter un dialogue avec ces éléments: *Answers will vary.*

- Vous vous retrouvez et vous parlez de votre métier.
- Vous décrivez votre poste.
- Vous parlez de votre patron/patronne et/ou de vos employés.
- Vous parlez des avantages et des inconvénients (*drawbacks*) de votre travail.

6 Décrivez Votre professeur va vous donner, à vous et à votre partenaire, deux feuilles d'activités différentes. À tour de rôle, posez-vous des questions pour trouver ce que font les personnages de chaque profession pendant la journée. *Answers will vary.*

MODÈLE

Étudiant(e) 1: *Sur mon dessin, j'ai un plombier qui répare une fuite (leak) d'eau sous un évier.*
Étudiant(e) 2: *Moi, j'ai un homme…*

7 L'offre d'emploi Vous êtes le chef d'entreprise de Cartalis, une agence immobilière. Vous développez votre entreprise et avez besoin de rapidement embaucher un(e) nouvel(le) employé(e). Avec deux partenaires, écrivez une annonce que vous enverrez à votre journal local. Utilisez les mots de la liste. *Answers will vary.*

agent immobilier	poste exigeant
carrière	promotion
congés payés	réussite
diriger	salaire élevé
entretien	temps partiel

OPTIONS

Extra Practice Have students categorize professions according to various paradigms. Examples: **les emplois de bureau/ les emplois en plein air; les métiers physiques/les métiers intellectuels;** and **les métiers qui exigent une longue formation/ les métiers qui n'exigent pas ou peu de formation.**

Pairs Have students work in pairs. Tell them to make a list of reasons people resign from a job (**Raisons pour démissionner d'un poste**) and a list of reasons people are let go from a job (**Raisons pour être renvoyé[e]**). Then call on volunteers to read one item from their list.

Les sons et les lettres  Audio

Les néologismes et le franglais

The use of words or neologisms of English origin in the French language is called **franglais**. These words often look identical to the English words, but they are pronounced like French words. Most of these words are masculine, and many end in -**ing**. Some of these words have long been accepted and used in French.

le sweat-shirt	le week-end	le shopping	le parking

Some words for foods and sports are very common, as are expressions in popular culture, business, and advertising.

un milk-shake	le base-ball	le top-modèle	le marketing

Many **franglais** words are recently coined terms (**néologismes**). These are common in contemporary fields, such as entertainment and technology. Some of these words do have French equivalents, but the **franglais** terms are used more often.

un e-mail = un courriel	le chat = la causette	une star = une vedette

Some **franglais** words do not exist in English at all, or they are used differently.

un brushing = *a blow-dry*   **un relooking** = *a makeover*   **le zapping** = *channel surfing*

Prononcez Répétez les mots suivants à voix haute.

1. flirter
2. un fax
3. cliquer
4. le look
5. un clown
6. le planning
7. un scanneur
8. un CD-ROM
9. le volley-ball
10. le shampooing
11. une speakerine
12. le chewing-gum

Articulez Répétez les phrases suivantes à voix haute.

1. Le cowboy porte un jean et un tee-shirt.
2. Julien joue au base-ball et il fait du footing.
3. J'ai envie d'un nouveau look, je vais faire du shopping.
4. Au snack-bar, je commande un hamburger, des chips et un milk-shake.
5. Tout ce qu'il veut faire, c'est rester devant la télé dans le living et zapper!

Dictons Répétez les dictons à voix haute.

Un gentleman est un monsieur qui se sert d'une pince à sucre, même lorsqu'il est seul.[2]

Ce n'est pas la star qui fait l'audience, mais l'audience qui fait la star.[1]

[1] It's not the star that makes the fans, it's the fans that make the star.
[2] A gentleman is a man who uses sugar tongs, even when he is alone.

ressources

LM p. 102

vhlcentral

cinq cent soixante et un **561**

Section Goals

In this section, students will learn about neologisms and **franglais**.

Instructional Resources
vhlcentral.com:
Textbook MP3s; Lab MP3s; SAM Answer Key; Textbook Audioscript; Lab Audioscript; reference tools

Suggestions
- Model the pronunciation of the example words and have students repeat after you.
- Ask students to provide more examples of words that are neologisms or **franglais**. Examples: **cool, le basket-ball, un site web, un toaster** and **surfer**.
- Dictate five familiar words that are neologisms or **franglais**, repeating each one at least two times. Then write them on the board or a transparency and have students check their spelling. Examples: **un GPS, un cowboy, un penalty, un pressing, un blog**.

Dictons The saying «**Ce n'est pas la star qui fait l'audience, mais l'audience qui fait la star**» is a quote from Noël Mamère, a journalist and politician. The saying «**Un gentleman est un monsieur qui se sert d'une pince à sucre, même lorsqu'il est seul**» is a quote from Alphonse Allais, a writer and humorist.

OPTIONS

Extra Practice Write these Internet words on the board or a transparency. Have the class guess the English equivalents.
1. arrosage (*spamming*) **2. accès** (*hit*) **3. bombardement** (*bombing*) **4. balise** (*tag*) **5. moteur de recherche** (*search engine*) **6. téléchargement** (*downloading*)

Small Groups Have the class work in groups of three or four. Tell them to write a humorous paragraph using as many neologisms or **franglais** terms as possible. Ask a few volunteers to read their paragraphs to the class.

Section Goals

In this section, students will learn functional phrases for talking about hypothetical situations and making polite requests or suggestions.

Instructional Resources
vhlcentral.com:
Roman-photo Video, Videoscript, and Translation; SAM Answer Key; reference tools

Video Recap: Leçon 13A
Review the previous **Roman-photo** with this activity.
1. Qu'est-ce que Stéphane et Astrid viennent de faire? (passer le bac)
2. Qu'est-ce que Stéphane veut étudier à l'université? (l'architecture)
3. Qu'est-ce qu'Astrid veut étudier à l'université? (la médecine)
4. Qu'est-ce que cherche la jeune femme au P'tit Bistrot? (un emploi)
5. Qu'est-ce que cherche Michèle? (un nouveau travail)

Video Synopsis
Sandrine is anxious about her first public performance as a singer. Amina offers to make her a dress to give her confidence. Stéphane and Astrid get their **bac** results. Astrid passed with honors, but Stéphane has to retake one part of the exam. At **Le P'tit Bistrot**, Michèle asks Valérie for a raise. When Valérie refuses, Michèle quits. Then Stéphane arrives and tells his mother his bad news.

Suggestions
• Tell students to scan the captions to find job-related vocabulary.
• After reading the **Roman-photo**, review students' predictions and have them summarize the episode.

Je démissionne! Video

PERSONNAGES

Amina

Astrid

Michèle

Sandrine

Stéphane

Valérie

En ville...
AMINA Alors, Sandrine, ton concert, ce sera la première fois que tu chantes en public?
SANDRINE Oui, et je suis un peu anxieuse!
AMINA Ah! Tu as le trac!
SANDRINE Un peu, oui. Toi, tu es toujours tellement chic, tu as confiance en toi, tu n'as peur de rien...

AMINA Mais Sandrine, la confiance en soi, c'est ici dans le cœur et ici dans la tête. J'ai une idée! Ce qui te donnerait du courage, c'est de porter une superbe robe.
SANDRINE Tu crois? Mais, je n'en ai pas...
AMINA Je m'en occupe. Quel style de robe est-ce que tu aimerais? Suis-moi!

Au marché...
AMINA Que penses-tu de ce tissu noir?
SANDRINE Oh! C'est ravissant!
AMINA Oui et ce serait parfait pour une robe du soir.
SANDRINE Bon, si tu le dis. Moi, si je faisais cette robe moi-même, elle finirait sans doute avec une manche courte et avec une manche longue!

STÉPHANE Attends. Forestier, Stéphane... Oh! Ce n'est pas possible!
ASTRID Quoi, qu'est-ce qu'il y a?
STÉPHANE Je dois repasser une partie de l'examen la semaine prochaine.
ASTRID Oh, ce n'est pas vrai! Il y a peut-être une erreur. Stéphane, attends!

Au P'tit Bistrot...
MICHÈLE Excusez-moi, Madame. Auriez-vous une petite minute?
VALÉRIE Oui, bien sûr!
MICHÈLE Voilà, ça fait deux ans que je travaille ici au P'tit Bistrot... Est-ce qu'il serait possible d'avoir une augmentation?

VALÉRIE Michèle, être serveuse, c'est un métier exigeant, mais les salaires sont modestes!
MICHÈLE Oui, je sais, Madame. Je ne vous demande pas un salaire très élevé, mais... c'est pour ma famille.
VALÉRIE Désolée, Michèle, j'aimerais bien le faire, mais, en ce moment, ce n'est pas possible. Peut-être dans quelques mois...

A C T I V I T É S

1 **Vrai ou faux?** Indiquez si ces affirmations sont vraies ou **fausses**. Corrigez les phrases fausses.
Answers may vary.
1. Sandrine a un peu peur avant son concert.
Vrai.
2. Amina ne sait pas comment aider Sandrine.
Faux. Amina va faire une robe pour Sandrine.
3. Amina va faire une robe de velours noir.
Faux. Amina va faire une robe en soie noire.
4. Sandrine ne sait pas faire une robe.
Vrai.
5. Pour la remercier (*To thank her*), Sandrine va préparer un dîner pour Amina.
Faux. Sandrine va préparer un gâteau pour Amina.

6. Stéphane doit repasser tout le bac.
Faux. Stéphane doit repasser une partie du bac.
7. Astrid a reçu une très bonne note.
Vrai.
8. Michèle travaille au P'tit Bistrot depuis deux ans.
Vrai.
9. Valérie offre à Michèle une toute petite augmentation de salaire.
Faux. Valérie n'offre pas d'augmentation de salaire à Michèle.
10. Michèle va retourner au P'tit Bistrot après ses vacances.
Faux. Michèle ne va pas retourner au P'tit Bistrot.

 Practice more at **vhlcentral.com**.

562 *cinq cent soixante-deux*

O P T I O N S

Avant de regarder la vidéo Tell students to look at the video stills and to read the title and the scene setter. Then have them predict what might happen in this episode. Write their predictions on the board. After viewing the episode, have them confirm or correct their predictions.

Regarder la vidéo Show the video in four parts, pausing it before each location change. Have students describe what happens in each place. Write their observations on the board. Then show the entire episode again without pausing and have the class fill in any missing details to summarize the plot.

Valérie et Stéphane rencontrent de nouveaux problèmes.

AMINA Je pourrais en faire une comme ça, si tu veux.

SANDRINE Je préférerais une de tes créations. Si tu as besoin de quoi que ce soit un jour, dis-le-moi.

AMINA Oh, Sandrine, je vais te faire une robe qui te fera plaisir.

SANDRINE Je pourrais te préparer un gâteau au chocolat?

AMINA Mmmm... Je ne dirais pas non.

Au lycée...

ASTRID Oh, Stéphane, c'est le grand jour! On va enfin connaître les résultats du bac! Je suis tellement nerveuse. Pas toi?

STÉPHANE Non, pas vraiment. Seulement si j'échoue, ma mère va m'étrangler. Eh! Félicitations, Astrid! Tu as réussi! Avec mention bien en plus!

ASTRID Et toi?

MICHÈLE Non, Madame! Dans quelques mois, je serai déjà partie. Je démissionne! Je prends le reste de mes vacances à partir d'aujourd'hui.

VALÉRIE Michèle, attendez! Mais Michèle! Ah, Stéphane, te voilà. Hé! Où vas-tu? Tu as eu les résultats du bac, non? Qu'est-ce qu'il y a?

STÉPHANE Maman, je suis désolé, mais je vais devoir repasser une partie de l'examen.

VALÉRIE Oh là là! Stéphane!

STÉPHANE Bon, écoute maman, voici ce que je vais faire: je vais étudier nuit et jour jusqu'à la semaine prochaine: pas de sports, pas de jeux vidéo, pas de télévision. J'irai à l'université, maman. Je te le promets.

Expressions utiles

Talking about hypothetical situations

- **Ce qui te donnerait du courage, c'est de porter une superbe robe.**
  Wearing a great dress would give you courage.

- **Ce serait parfait pour une robe du soir.**
  This would be perfect for an evening gown.

- **Si je faisais cette robe, elle finirait avec une manche courte et avec une manche longue!**
  If I made this dress, it would end up with one short sleeve and one long sleeve!

- **Je préférerais une de tes créations.**
  I would prefer one of your creations.

- **Je ne dirais pas non.**
  I wouldn't say no.

- **Si tu as besoin de quoi que ce soit un jour, dis-le-moi.**
  If you ever need anything someday, tell me.

- **Si j'échoue, ma mère va m'étrangler.**
  If I fail, my mother is going to strangle me.

Making polite requests and suggestions

- **Quel style de robe est-ce que tu aimerais? J'aimerais...**
  What kind of dress would you like? I would like...

- **Je pourrais en faire une comme ça, si tu veux.**
  I could make you one like this, if you'd like.

- **Auriez-vous une petite minute?**
  Would you have a minute?

- **Est-ce qu'il serait possible d'avoir une augmentation?**
  Would it be possible to get a raise?

Additional vocabulary

- **le trac**
  stage fright
- **ravissant(e)**
  beautiful; delightful
- **faire plaisir à quelqu'un**
  to make someone happy

---

2 **Les mauvaises nouvelles** Stéphane, Valérie et Michèle ont été très déçus *(disappointed)* aujourd'hui pour des raisons différentes. Avec deux partenaires, décidez qui a passé la pire journée et pourquoi. Ensuite, discutez-en avec le reste de la classe.

3 **Écrivez** Pensez à un examen très important de votre vie et écrivez un paragraphe, en répondant à *(by answering)* ces questions. Quel était l'examen? Qu'est-ce que vous avez fait pour le préparer? Comment était-ce? Comme l'histoire de Stéphane ou d'Astrid? Comment cet examen a-t-il affecté vos projets d'avenir?

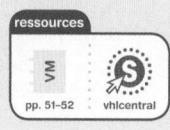

ressources

VM pp. 51–52

vhlcentral

A C T I V I T É S

Expressions utiles
- Model the pronunciation of the **Expressions utiles** and have students repeat them after you.
- As you work through the list, point out relative pronouns and forms of **le conditionnel** with **si** clauses. Tell students that these grammar points will be formally presented in **Espace structures**.
- Respond briefly to questions about relative pronouns and **si** clauses. Reinforce correct forms, but do not expect students to produce them consistently at this time.

1 Suggestion Have students correct the false statements.

1 Expansion For additional practice, give students these items. **11. Amina refuse le gâteau au chocolat parce qu'elle est au régime. (Faux.) 12. Astrid dit que la note de Stéphane est peut-être une erreur. (Vrai.) 13. Michèle veut une augmentation pour acheter une nouvelle voiture. (Faux.) 14. Stéphane promet d'étudier nuit et jour pour réussir son bac. (Vrai.)**

2 Suggestion If time is limited, this activity may be assigned as homework. Group students according to the person they believe had the worst day—Stéphane, Michèle, or Valérie. Have them prepare their arguments at home, then allow the groups a few minutes to rehearse before presenting their case to the class.

3 Expansion Have students exchange compositions for peer editing.

O P T I O N S

Pairs Working in pairs, have students write a conversation between a boss and an employee, based on the conversation between Michèle and Valérie. In the conversation, the employee should negotiate something with the boss, such as extra vacation time, permission to come in late one day, or a day off. At first, the boss refuses, but eventually the two compromise and come to an agreement.

Extra Practice Write **j'aimerais** and **vous aimeriez** on the board. Ask students variations of the question: **Quel style de robe est-ce que vous aimeriez porter?** Tell them to respond with **J'aimerais….** Examples: **1. Quelle profession est-ce que vous aimeriez avoir? 2. Quel salaire est-ce que vous aimeriez recevoir? 3. Quel film est-ce que vous aimeriez voir ce week-end?**

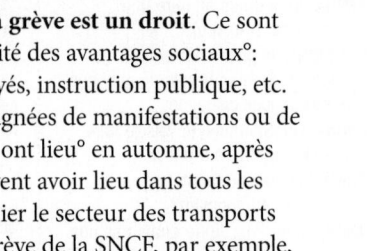

Des passagers attendent un train
pendant une grève de la SNCF.

Section Goals

In this section, students will:
- learn about unions and strikes in France
- learn some colloquial terms for talking about money
- learn about paid vacations and holidays in various francophone regions
- read about civil servants in France

Instructional Resources
vhlcentral.com:
reference tools

Culture à la loupe
Avant la lecture Have students look at the photo of the people protesting and describe what they see. Ask what they are protesting.

Lecture
- Point out the statistics chart. Ask students what information it shows. (the percentage of French people in favor of minimum service for the sectors listed) Then ask: **Pourquoi pensez-vous que tant de gens veulent un service minimum pour ces secteurs? Pourquoi ces services sont-ils très importants?**
- See **Unité 2 Panorama** on page 83 for more information on the SNCF.

Après la lecture Ask students: **Pourquoi fait-on la grève? Qu'espère-t-on obtenir quand on fait la grève?**

1 Suggestion Have volunteers write the answers to the questions on the board. Then go over the answers with the class.

CULTURE À LA LOUPE

Syndicats et grèves en France

Les gens se plaignent° souvent des grèves° en France, mais faire la grève est un droit. Ce sont les grandes grèves historiques qui ont apporté aux Français la majorité des avantages sociaux°: retraite, sécurité sociale, congés payés, instruction publique, etc. Les grèves en France sont accompagnées de manifestations ou de pétitions, et beaucoup d'entre elles ont lieu° en automne, après les vacances d'été. Des grèves peuvent avoir lieu dans tous les secteurs de l'économie, en particulier le secteur des transports et celui° de l'enseignement°. Une grève de la SNCF, par exemple, peut immobiliser tout le pays et causer des ennuis à des millions de voyageurs.

Les syndicats organisent les trois quarts° de ces mouvements sociaux. La France est pourtant° le pays industrialisé le moins syndiqué° du monde. En 2009, seulement six à huit pour cent des salariés français étaient syndiqués contre environ° 13% aux États-Unis ou 91% en Suède.

De plus en plus, des non-salariés, comme les médecins et les commerçants, font aussi la grève. Dans ce cas, ils cherchent surtout à faire changer les lois°.

En général, le public soutient° les grévistes, mais il demande aussi la création d'un service minimum obligatoire dans les transports publics et l'enseignement pour éviter la paralysie totale du pays. Ce service minimum obligerait° un petit nombre d'employés à travailler pendant chaque grève. La fréquence des grèves a diminué pendant les années 1970, 1980 et 1990, mais a vu° une certaine augmentation depuis l'année 2000.

une manifestation de la CGT, un syndicat

Les Français favorables à un service minimum

Dans le ramassage des ordures°	84%
Dans l'enseignement public	79%
Dans les transports aériens	77%
Dans les transports publics	74%

SOURCE: Francoscopie

se plaignent *complain* **grèves** *strikes* **avantages sociaux** *benefits* **ont lieu** *take place* **celui** *the one* **enseignement** *education* **trois quarts** *three quarters* **pourtant** *however* **syndiqué** *unionized* **environ** *around* **faire changer les lois** *have the laws changed* **soutient** *supports* **obligerait** *would force* **a vu** *has seen* **ramassage des ordures** *trash collection*

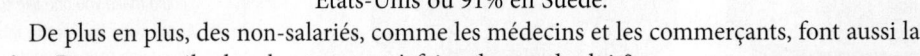

A C T I V I T É S

1

Répondez Répondez aux questions d'après les textes.

1. Quel est un des droits des Français?
Faire la grève est un des droits des Français.
2. Qu'est-ce que la grève a apporté aux Français?
Elle leur a apporté des avantages sociaux.
3. Quand ont souvent lieu les grèves?
Elles ont souvent lieu en automne.
4. Par qui la majorité des grèves sont-elles organisées?
Elles sont organisées par les syndicats.
5. Les travailleurs français sont-ils très syndiqués?
Non, la France est le pays industrialisé le moins syndiqué du monde.
6. Combien de travailleurs français étaient syndiqués en 2009?
Entre six et huit pour cent des travailleurs étaient syndiqués en 2009.

7. Pourquoi les médecins et les commerçants font-ils la grève?
Ils font la grève pour changer les lois.
8. Y a-t-il toujours eu un grand nombre de grèves en France?
Non, la fréquence des grèves a diminué pendant les années 1970, 1980 et 1990.
9. Combien de Français sont favorables au service minimum dans l'enseignement public?
79% y sont favorables.
10. À quoi sont favorables 77% des Français?
77% des Français sont favorables à un service minimum dans les transports aériens.

O P T I O N S

Les grèves In France, as in the United States, strikes may be large-scale or small. The media coverage of participants in a strike is also similar: unions consistently report a higher rate of participation than the police. In France, however, one might see police carrying body shields and using tear gas when large groups assemble to strike.

Small Groups Have students work in groups of three or four. Have them discuss the various options unions have for making their demands known: **la pétition, la grève, la manifestation,** and **le boycott**. Tell them to decide which means they think are the most and least effective and explain why.

LE FRANÇAIS QUOTIDIEN

L'argent

Voici d'autres noms familiers souvent utilisés pour parler de l'argent.

avoine (*f.*)	oseille (*f.*)
biffeton (*m.*)	pépètes (*f., pl.*)
blé (*m.*)	pèze (*m.*)
cash (*m.*)	pognon (*m.*)
flouze (*m.*)	radis (*m.*)
fric (*m.*)	rond (*m.*)
grisbi (*m.*)	thune (*f.*)

LE MONDE FRANCOPHONE

La durée des vacances et les jours fériés

Voici la durée des congés payés dans quelques pays francophones.

En Belgique 20 jours après une année de travail, plus 10 jours fériés par an

En France 25 jours et 10 jours fériés par an

Au Luxembourg 25 jours et 12 jours fériés par an

Au Maroc 18 jours par an

Au Québec 10 jours et 8 jours fériés par an

Au Sénégal un minimum de 24 jours par an, plus pour les travailleurs avec ancienneté° et pour les mères de famille

En Suisse 20 jours pour les plus de 20 ans, 25 jours pour les moins de 20 ans

En Tunisie 12 jours par an pour les plus de 20 ans, 18 jours pour les 18-20 ans et 24 jours pour les moins de 18 ans

ancienneté *seniority*

PORTRAIT

Les fonctionnaires

Avec environ six millions de fonctionnaires° dans le pays, ou 21% de la population active°, la France bat des records°. Ces fonctionnaires travaillent pour l'État (dans le gouvernement, les universités, les lycées, les compagnies nationales), pour la fonction publique territoriale (le département, la région) ou pour la fonction publique hospitalière. Ils ont de nombreux avantages: des salaires compétitifs, une bonne retraite et une grande protection de l'emploi. Pour devenir fonctionnaire, il faut passer un concours°. Chaque année, près de 40.000 emplois sont ainsi° ouverts au public.

fonctionnaires *civil servants* **population active** *working population* **bat des records** *breaks records* **concours** *competitive examination* **ainsi** *thus*

MUSIQUE À FOND

Tino Rossi

Lieu d'origine: Ajaccio, France
Métier: chanteur, interprète et acteur

Star du cinéma et de la chanson, Tino Rossi est le seul artiste français à avoir vendu plus de 500 millions de disques.

Go to vhlcentral.com to find out more about **Tino Rossi** and his music.

2 **Complétez** Donnez une suite logique à chaque phrase.

1. La France bat des records avec... environ six millions de fonctionnaires dans le pays.
2. Les fonctionnaires sont employés par... l'État.
3. Ils bénéficient de nombreux... avantages.
4. On peut devenir fonctionnaire après avoir passé... un concours.
5. Au Sénégal, on a des journées de vacances supplémentaires si on est... travailleur avec ancienneté ou mère de famille.
6. La durée des vacances dépend de l'âge en... Tunisie et en Suisse.

3 **La grève** Vous êtes journaliste et votre partenaire est un fonctionnaire en grève. Vous allez l'interviewer pour le journal télévisé de 20 heures. Préparez un dialogue où vous cherchez à comprendre pourquoi il ou elle est en grève et depuis combien de temps. Soyez prêts à jouer le dialogue devant la classe.

 Practice more at **vhlcentral.com**.

ACTIVITÉS

Le français quotidien
- Model the pronunciation of each term and have students repeat it.
- Point out that **l'avoine** literally means *oats* and **le blé** means *wheat*.

Portrait
- Point out that the **concours** mentioned here is similar to a civil service exam in the United States.
- Ask students: **Quels sont les avantages des fonctionnaires en France?** (des salaires compétitifs, une bonne retraite et une grande protection de l'emploi)

Le monde francophone
- Explain that the number of days off refers to weekdays.
- Ask students: **Dans quel pays la durée des congés payés est-elle la plus longue?** (au Luxembourg)

2 **Expansion** Have students create three more items for this activity. Then tell them to exchange papers with a classmate and complete the sentences. Remind them to verify their answers.

3 **Suggestion** If time is limited, assign this activity as homework, so students can prepare their interview questions or responses. Then allow partners a few minutes to rehearse during the next class before presenting their interviews.

OPTIONS

Extra Practice Tell students that federal civil service employees in the United States get ten paid holidays per year. Then ask these questions. **1. Quels pays ont le plus de jours fériés?** (la Belgique et le Luxembourg) **2. Quelle région a le moins de jours fériés?** (le Québec)

Pairs Have students work in pairs to make a list of the sectors in which civil servants in France work. Also tell them to list some of the occupations these sectors include. Then have them get together with another pair and compare their lists.

Section Goals

In this section, students will learn:

• the use of **si** clauses with the conditional
• **si** clauses with the present and **imparfait**

Instructional Resources
vhlcentral.com:
Activity Pack; Lab MP3s;
SAM Answer Key; **Essayez!**
and **Mise en pratique**
answers; Lab Audioscript;
reference tools

Suggestions

• To help students sort out the possibilities with **si** clauses, make a chart with these headings: Condition, **Si** clause, Main clause. Under the first column, list the three types of **si** clauses introduced in this lesson: *contrary-to-fact, possible or likely*, and *suggestion or wish*. Under the second column, write these three items in order: **si** + *[imperfect]*, **si** + *[present]*, **si** + *[imperfect]*. Under the third column, write *imperfect, future or near future*, and *N/A*.

• Compare and contrast contrary-to-fact situations (which use the imperfect and the conditional) with events that are possible or likely to occur (which use the present and future) using the example sentences. Check understanding by providing main clauses and having volunteers finish the sentence with a **si** clause. Examples: **Je n'irais pas à Paris...** (si je n'avais pas d'argent.) **Elle travaillera comme professeur...** (si elle obtient son doctorat.)

• Explain that a **si** clause in the past can also express something that was habitual in the past. In such cases, the **imparfait** is used in both the **si** clause and the result clause. Example: **Si mon amie m'invitait à une fête, j'y allais toujours.**

Essayez! Have students change the sentences from a contrary-to-fact situation to a possible or likely situation, and vice versa. Example: **1. Si on visite la Tunisie, on ira admirer les ruines.**

Si clauses Tutorial

• **Si** (*If*) clauses describe a condition or event upon which another condition or event depends. Sentences with **si** clauses consist of a **si** clause and a main (or result) clause.

Si je faisais une robe, elle serait laide.

Si j'échouais, ma mère se mettrait en colère.

• **Si** clauses can speculate or hypothesize about a current event or condition. They express what *would happen* if an event or condition *were to occur*. This is called a contrary-to-fact situation. In such instances, the verb in the **si** clause is in the **imparfait** while the verb in the main clause is in the conditional. Either clause can come first.

Si j'**étais** au chômage, je lui **enverrais** mon CV.
If I were unemployed, I'd send her my résumé.

Vous **partiriez** souvent en vacances si vous **aviez** de l'argent.
You would go on vacation often if you had money.

• **Si** clauses can also express conditions or events that are possible or likely to occur. In such instances, the **si** clause is in the present while the main clause uses the **futur** or **futur proche**.

Si le patron me **renvoie**, je **trouverai** un emploi à mi-temps.
If the boss fires me, I'll find a part-time job.

Si vous ne **signez** pas le contrat, vous **allez perdre** votre poste.
If you don't sign the contract, you're going to lose your job.

• Note that **si** and **il/ils** contract to become **s'il** and **s'ils**, respectively.

Nous **marcherions s'il** ne **pleuvait** pas.
We'd walk if it weren't raining.

S'ils étaient forts en maths, ils **deviendraient** comptables.
If they were good at math, they'd become accountants.

• Use a **si** clause alone with the **imparfait** to make a suggestion or to express a wish.

Si nous **faisions** des projets pour le week-end?
What about making plans for the weekend?

Ah! Si elle **obtenait** un meilleur travail!
Oh! If only she got a better job!

Essayez! Complétez les phrases avec la forme correcte des verbes.

1. Si on visitait la Tunisie, on ___irait___ (aller) admirer les ruines.
2. Vous ___serez___ (être) plus heureux si vous faites vos devoirs.
3. Si tu ___avais___ (avoir) la grippe, tu devrais aller chez le médecin.
4. Si elles avaient un million d'euros, que ___feraient___-elles (faire)?
5. Mes parents me ___rendront___ (rendre) visite ce week-end s'ils ont le temps.
6. J'___écrirais___ (écrire) au président si j'avais son adresse.
7. Si nous lisons, nous ___saurons___ (savoir) les réponses.
8. Il ___aurait___ (avoir) le temps s'il ne regardait pas la télé.

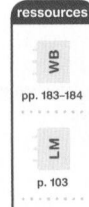

ressources

WB
pp. 183–184

LM
p. 103

vhlcentral

Le français vivant

Que trouveriez-vous si vous parliez
à une autre entreprise?

Une hôtesse d'accueil ou
une hôtesse de l'air?
Vous voudriez une hôtesse
compétente, non?

Si vous parlez à
quelqu'un d'autre,
vous risquerez
beaucoup.

INTERIM 21

Identifiez Combien de phrases avec si trouvez-vous dans cette publicité
(ad)? Lesquelles?   Three: 1. Viendriez-vous nous consulter si vous cherchiez une hôtesse?
2. Que trouveriez-vous si vous parliez à une autre entreprise? 3. Si vous
parlez à quelqu'un d'autre, vous risquerez beaucoup.

 Questions À tour de rôle, avec un(e) partenaire, posez-vous
ces questions.   Answers will vary.

1. Pourquoi irait-on chez Interim 21?

2. Quelle erreur pourrait-on éviter?

3. Comment font les conseillers d'Interim 21 pour trouver l'emploi et
l'employé(e) idéal(e) pour tous leurs clients?

4. Irais-tu consulter Interim 21 si tu étais au chômage? Pourquoi?

Le français vivant Call on a
volunteer to read the ad aloud.
Have students point out all the
si clauses and note whether the
futur or the **conditionnel** is used.

OPTIONS

Video Replay the video episode, having students focus on **si**
clauses. Ask students to write each one down as they hear it.
Afterward, have them compare their notes in groups of four.

Extra Practice Ask each student to write a question that
contains a **si** clause. Then have students walk around the room
until you signal them to stop. On your cue, each student should
turn to the nearest classmate. Give students three minutes to
ask and answer one another's question before having them
begin walking around the room again. Each time you say "stop,"
students should ask a new partner their question.

ESPACE STRUCTURES

1 **Expansion** Have students come up with three more questions for their **chef du personnel**. Then have students swap their questions with their classmates and answer their questions using **si** clauses.

2 **Expansion** Write more situations like those in the activity. Example: **Situation 3: Que feriez-vous si… 1. vous / gagner à la loterie? 2. le club de français / propose un voyage en France? 3. le professeur de français / être malade?**

3 **Suggestion** Organize the class into two groups: **si + le présent** and **si + l'imparfait**. Have each group complete the activity using the tenses according to their groups. Then discuss the different meanings of the sentences produced by each group.

Mise en pratique

1 **Questions** Vous cherchez un emploi. Indiquez vos réponses aux questions du chef du personnel.

> **MODÈLE** Quand est-ce que vous pourriez commencer? (vous / avoir besoin de moi / je / pouvoir commencer demain)
>
> *Si vous aviez besoin de moi, je pourrais commencer demain.*

1. Est-ce que vous aimeriez travailler à plein temps? *Si vous m'offriez un travail à plein temps, je l'accepterais.*
   (vous / offrir un travail à plein temps / je / l'accepter)

2. Auriez-vous besoin d'une assurance-vie? *Si j'en avais besoin d'une, je vous le dirais.*
   (je / en avoir besoin / je / vous le dire)

3. Quand prendriez-vous un congé? *Si mon/ma petit(e) ami(e) prenait un congé, nous partirions en mai.*
   (mon/ma petite ami(e) / prendre un congé / nous / partir en mai)

4. Voudriez-vous devenir cadre un jour? *Si vous le permettiez, je deviendrais cadre dans deux ans.*
   (vous / le permettre / je / devenir cadre dans deux ans)

5. Quand rentreriez-vous le soir? *Si nous devions travailler très tard, je rentrerais vers minuit.*
   (nous / devoir travailler très tard / je / rentrer vers minuit)

2 **¿Et si…** D'abord, complétez les questions. Ensuite, employez le conditionnel pour y répondre. Comparez vos réponses aux réponses d'un(e) partenaire.

> **MODÈLE** Que ferais-tu si… tu / être malade?
>
> *Que ferais-tu si tu étais malade? Si j'étais malade, je dormirais toute la journée.*

Situation 1: Que ferais-tu si…

1. tu / être fatigué(e)? *… si tu étais fatigué(e)?*
2. il / pleuvoir? *… s'il pleuvait?*
3. il / faire beau? *… s'il faisait beau?*

Situation 2: Que feraient tes parents si…

1. tu / quitter l'université? *… si tu quittais l'université?*
2. tu / choisir de devenir avocat(e)? *… si tu choisissais de devenir avocat(e)?*
3. tu / partir habiter en France? *… si tu partais habiter en France?*

3 **Des réactions** À tour de rôle avec un(e) partenaire, dites ce que (*what*) vous ferez dans ces circonstances. Answers will vary.

> **MODÈLE** Vous trouvez votre petit(e) ami(e) avec un(e) autre garçon/fille.
>
> *Si je trouve mon petit ami…, je ne lui parlerai plus.*

1. Vous n'avez pas de devoirs ce week-end.
2. Votre ami(e) organise une fête sans rien vous dire.
3. Vos parents ne vous téléphonent pas pendant un mois.
4. Le prof de français vous donne une mauvaise note.
5. Vous tombez malade.

 Practice more at **vhlcentral.com**.

Communication

4 **L'imagination** Par groupes de trois, choisissez un de ces sujets et préparez un paragraphe par écrit. Ensuite, lisez votre paragraphe à la classe. **Vos camarades décideront quel groupe est le gagnant (*winner*).** Answers will vary.

- Si je pouvais devenir invisible, ...
- Si j'étais un extraterrestre à New York, ...
- Si j'inventais une machine, ...
- Si j'étais une célébrité, ...
- Si nous pouvions prendre des vacances sur Mars, ...

5 **Le portefeuille** Vos camarades de classe trouvent un portefeuille (*wallet*) plein d'argent. Par groupes de quatre, parlez avec un(e) de vos camarades pour deviner ce que (*what*) feraient les deux autres. Ensuite, rejoignez-les pour comparer vos prédictions. Answers will vary.

MODÈLE

Étudiant(e) 1: *Si vous trouviez le portefeuille, vous le rendriez à la police*
Étudiant(e) 2: *Oui, mais nous garderions l'argent pour aller dans un bon restaurant.*

6 **Interview** Par groupes de trois, préparez cinq questions pour un(e) candidat(e) à la présidence des États-Unis. Ensuite, jouez les rôles de l'interviewer et du/de la candidat(e). Alternez les rôles. Answers will vary.

MODÈLE

Étudiant(e) 1: *Que feriez-vous au sujet du sexisme dans l'armée?*
Étudiant(e) 2: *Alors, si j'étais président(e), nous...*

---

4 Suggestion Before assigning this activity, write **Si nous pouvions prédire** (*predict*) **l'avenir...** on the board. Brainstorm possible main clauses with the whole class.

5 Expansion Have groups of four brainstorm other moral dilemmas using **Que feraient vos camarades de classe si...** Example: **...s'ils trouvaient les réponses de l'examen de français.**

6 Suggestions
- You may wish to have students pick a different prominent politician that interests them.
- Videotape the interviews and show clips from them during the next class, or post the video online for students to view outside of class.

OPTIONS

Pairs Ask students to reflect on their French study habits. Then assign them partners to write a list of eight complex sentences to express what they could do better. Example: **Si je lisais un journal français tous les jours, je pourrais mieux comprendre la langue.**

Small Groups Ask students to bring in the most outlandish tabloid news report they can find. In groups of four, have students write a list of statements that use **si** clauses about each report. Example: **Si les extraterrestres venaient à Washington, D.C. pour avoir un rendez-vous avec le président des États-Unis...**

Section Goals

In this section, students will learn the relative pronouns **qui**, **que**, **dont**, and **où**.

Instructional Resources
vhlcentral.com:
Activity Pack; Lab MP3s;
SAM Answer Key; ***Essayez!***
and ***Mise en pratique***
answers; Lab Audioscript;
reference tools

Suggestions

• Give an example of an optional relative pronoun in English. *The movie (that) we just watched was very sad.* Emphasize to students that relative pronouns are required in French. Example: **Le film que nous venons de regarder était très triste.**

• Explain that **que** can refer to both people and things. Example: **Le chanteur que tu écoutes est très populaire.**

• Point out that the relative pronoun **qui** is always followed by a conjugated verb. **Qui** acts as the subject. **Qui** can also refer to people or things. Example: **Le stylo (qui est) sur la table est vert.**

Relative pronouns *qui, que, dont, où* Tutorial

Point de départ Relative pronouns combine two sentences into one more complex sentence. The second phrase gives more information about a noun that both sentences have in common. In English, relative pronouns can be omitted, but the relative pronoun in French cannot.

Je suis allé voir **le docteur**.
I went to see the doctor.

Tu m'as parlé de **ce docteur**.
You talked to me about this doctor.

Je suis allé voir le docteur **dont** tu m'as parlé.
I went to see the doctor that you talked to me about.

Relative pronouns

qui	who, that, which	dont	of which, of whom
que	that, which	où	where

🏃 Boîte à outils

The pronoun **qui** does not drop the **i** before another vowel sound.

La femme qui ouvre la porte est ma mère.

Je préfère le café qui est au coin de cette rue.

• Use **qui** if the noun in common is the subject of the second phrase. Since **qui** is the subject, it is followed by a conjugated verb.

COMMON NOUN		SUBJECT

Il a renvoyé **la comptable**.
He fired the accountant.

La comptable travaillait à mi-temps.
The accountant worked part-time.

Il a renvoyé la comptable **qui** travaillait à mi-temps.
He fired the accountant who was working part-time.

COMMON NOUN		SUBJECT

Les étudiantes vont au **café**.
The students go to the café.

Le café se trouve près de la fac.
The café is near the university.

Les étudiantes vont au café **qui** se trouve près de la fac.
The students go to the café that is near the university.

À noter

As the last set of sample sentences on this page shows, the relative clause antecedent is not always the final noun in the first sentence.

COMMON NOUN		SUBJECT

Ta cousine travaille beaucoup.
Your cousin works a lot.

Ta cousine habite à Boston.
Your cousin lives in Boston.

Ta cousine **qui** habite à Boston travaille beaucoup.
Your cousin who lives in Boston works a lot.

570 *cinq cent soixante-dix*

- Use **que** if the noun in common is the direct object in the second phrase. If **que** is followed by the **passé composé**, the past participle should agree in gender and number with the noun that **que** represents.

ELEMENT
Le banquier a deux **voitures** bleues.
The banker has two blue cars.

DIRECT OBJECT
Il a acheté les **voitures** hier.
He bought the cars yesterday.

Le banquier a deux voitures bleues **qu'**il a acheté**es** hier.
The banker has two blue cars that he bought yesterday.

COMMON NOUN
Stéphanie arrive bientôt.
Stéphanie is arriving soon.

DIRECT OBJECT
Samir a retrouvé **Stéphanie** à la gare.
Samir met Stéphanie at the train station.

Stéphanie, **que** Samir a retrouvé**e** à la gare, arrive bientôt.
Stéphanie, who Samir met at the train station, is arriving soon.

Boîte à outils

The pronoun **que** is usually followed by a subject and a verb. **Que** becomes **qu'** if it precedes a word that begins with a vowel sound. Note that the word *that* or *whom* is often omitted in English, but **que** must always be used in French.

La fille que j'ai vue était blonde.
The girl (whom) I saw was blond.

- Use **dont**, meaning *that* or *of which*, after the noun in common if it is the object of the preposition **de** in the second phrase. There is never agreement of the past participle in the **passé composé** with **dont**.

ELEMENT
Stéphane est **pompier**.
Stéphane is a firefighter.

DIRECT OBJECT
Tu m'as parlé de **ce pompier**.
You talked to me about this firefighter.

Stéphane est le pompier **dont** tu m'as parlé?
Is Stéphane the firefighter (that) you talked to me about?

Boîte à outils

Dont (*whose*) can also indicate possession.

Voilà M. Duval. La femme de M. Duval est actrice.

Voilà M. Duval, dont la femme est actrice.

- Use **où**, meaning *where*, *when*, or *in which*, if the noun in common is a place or a period of time.

COMMON NOUN
Venez me parler à **ce moment-là**.
Come speak with me at that time.

PERIOD OF TIME
Vous arrivez à **ce moment-là**.
You arrive at that time.

Venez me parler au moment **où** vous arrivez.
Come speak with me at the time (when) you arrive.

Essayez! Complétez les phrases avec qui, que, dont, où.

1. La France est le pays ___que___ j'aime le plus.
2. Tu te souviens du jour ___où___ tu as fait ma connaissance?
3. M. Valois est le gérant ___dont___ mon employé m'a parlé.
4. C'est la voiture ___que___ vous avez louée?
5. Voici l'enveloppe ___dont___ tu as besoin.
6. Vous connaissez le plombier ___qui___ a réparé le lavabo chez Lucas?
7. On passe devant la fac ___où___ j'ai fait mes études.
8. Je reconnais le chauffeur de taxi ___qui___ a conduit Lucie à l'hôtel.

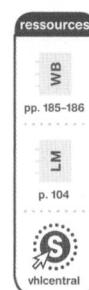

ressources

WB
pp. 185–186

LM
p. 104

vhlcentral

Suggestions
- Point out that **qui**, **que**, and **dont** are all used for both people and things.
- Emphasize that, although the interrogative word **où?** means *where?*, the relative pronoun **où** can also be translated as *when* or *in which*.
- Review verbs followed by the preposition **de** with which **dont** might be used. Examples: **avoir besoin de, avoir peur de, parler de, rêver de**, etc. Example: **C'est le voyage dont je rêvais.**

Essayez! Ask volunteers to create questions or answers that correspond to the sentences in the activity. Example: **1. Quel est le pays que tu aimes le plus?**

OPTIONS

Video Replay the video episode, having students focus on relative pronouns. Have students divide their paper into two columns: **qui** and **que**. Ask them to write down each example they hear under its appropriate column. Then form groups of three and have students compare their papers.

Extra Practice Have students make complete sentences with phrases like the following. **1. Le tennis est un sport que... 2. Le tennis est un sport qui... 3. Gwyneth Paltrow est une actrice que... 4. Gwyneth Paltrow est une actrice qui... 5.** *Le fabuleux destin d'Amélie Poulain* (*Amélie*) **est un film que... 6.** *Amélie* **est un film qui...**

1 Suggestion Ask a volunteer to read the **modèle** aloud. Ask another volunteer to explain the use of the relative pronoun in that example. (The answer is **qui** because it is a subject followed by the verb **est**.)

2 Expansion Have pairs write two or more sentences that contain relative pronouns and refer to other people in the village where Isabelle has moved.

3 Expansion Expand the activity by asking students to talk about what they prefer. Have them model their sentences on Marianne's.

Mise en pratique

1 Notre entreprise Sophie et Thierry discutent de leur bureau et de leurs collègues. Complétez leurs phrases en utilisant (*by using*) les pronoms relatifs **qui**, **que**, **dont** ou **où**.

MODÈLE

Ils ont une cafétéria ___*qui*___ n'est pas trop chère.

1. C'est une entreprise ___*où*___ les employés peuvent suivre des formations supplémentaires.
2. Nous avons une profession ___*qui*___ est exigeante.
3. Notre chef d'entreprise a commandé les nouveaux ordinateurs ___*dont*___ nous avions besoin.
4. La personne ___*qui*___ a un entretien aujourd'hui est l'ami du gérant.
5. La réunion ___*que*___ tu as ratée (*missed*) hier était vraiment intéressante.
6. La femme ___*dont*___ tu as peur est notre chef du personnel, n'est-ce pas?
7. L'homme ___*qu'*___ on a embauché est le mari de Sandra.
8. Tu te souviens du jour ___*où*___ on a fait la connaissance du patron?

2 Les villageois Isabelle vient de déménager dans un petit village et son agent immobilier lui parle des gens qui y habitent. Assemblez les deux phrases avec **qui**, **que**, **dont** ou **où** pour en faire une seule

1. Voici le bureau de M. Dantès. Vous pouvez vous adresser à ce bureau pour obtenir une assurance-vie. *Voici le bureau de M. Dantès où vous pouvez vous adresser pour obtenir une assurance-vie.*
2. Je vous ai parlé d'une banquière. La banquière s'appelle Murielle Marteau. *La banquière dont je vous ai parlé s'appelle Murielle Marteau.*
3. Vous avez vu la grande boutique. M. Descartes est le patron de cette boutique. *M. Descartes est le patron de la grande boutique que vous avez vue.*
4. Je ne connais pas le pompier. Le pompier habite en face de chez vous. *Je ne connais pas le pompier qui habite en face de chez vous.*
5. Madame Thibaut sert beaucoup de plats régionaux. Vous allez adorer ces plats. *Madame Thibaut sert beaucoup de plats régionaux que vous allez adorer.*
6. Les cuisinières travaillent à temps partiel. Vous avez rencontré les cuisinières chez moi. *Les cuisinières que vous avez rencontrées chez moi travaillent à temps partiel.*

3 Les choses que je préfère Marianne parle des choses qu'elle préfère. À tour de rôle avec un(e) partenaire, utilisez les pronoms relatifs pour écrire ses phrases. Présentez vos phrases à la classe. *Answers will vary.*

1. Marc est l'ami... (qui, dont)
2. «Chez Henri», c'est le restaurant... (où, que)
3. Ce CD est le cadeau... (que, qui)
4. Ma sœur est la personne... (dont, que)
5. Paris est la ville... (où, dont)
6. L'acteur/L'actrice... (qui, que)
7. Les livres... (dont, que)
8. J'aimerais sortir avec une personne... (qui, que)

 Practice more at **vhlcentral.com**.

Communication

4 **Des opinions** Avec un(e) partenaire, donnez votre opinion sur ces thèmes. Utilisez les pronoms relatifs **qui, que, dont** et **où**. Answers will vary.

MODÈLE

le printemps / saison
Étudiant(e) 1: Le printemps est la saison que je préfère parce que j'aime les fleurs.
Étudiant(e) 2: L'hiver est la saison que moi, je préfère, parce que j'aime la neige.

1. le petit-déjeuner / repas
2. surfer sur Internet / passe-temps
3. mon/ma camarade de chambre / personne
4. le samedi / jour
5. la chimie / cours
6. la France / pays
7. Tom Cruise / acteur
8. ? / ?

5 **Des endroits intéressants** Par groupes de trois, organisez un voyage. Parlez des endroits qui vous intéressent et expliquez pourquoi vous voulez y aller. Utilisez des pronoms relatifs dans vos réponses et décidez où vous allez. Answers will vary.

MODÈLE

Allons à Bruxelles où nous pouvons acheter des chocolats délicieux.

6 **Chère Madame** Avec un(e) partenaire, écrivez un e-mail à votre gérante dans lequel (*in which*) vous expliquez pourquoi vous n'avez pas fini le document qu'elle voulait pour la réunion. Utilisez des pronoms relatifs dans votre e-mail. Answers will vary.

De: clement@entreprise.fr
À: madame.giraud@entreprise.fr
Objet: Document

Chère Madame Giraud,

Je suis désolé, mais je n'ai pas fini le document que vous vouliez aujourd'hui. Ce matin, je suis allé à l'entreprise François et Fils où…

7 **Mes préférences** Avec un(e) partenaire, parlez de vos préférences dans chaque catégorie ci-dessous (*below*). Donnez des raisons pour vos choix (*choices*). Utilisez les pronoms relatifs **qui, que, dont** et **où** dans vos descriptions. Answers will vary.

MODÈLE

mon film préféré
Le film que j'aime le plus, c'est *Pirates des Caraïbes*. Johnny Depp, qui joue dans ce film, est super!

1. mon film préféré
2. mon roman (*novel*) préféré
3. mon chanteur/ma chanteuse préféré(e)
4. la meilleure ville pour aller en vacances

---

4 **Expansion** In addition to **surfer sur Internet** from #2, brainstorm a list of pastimes with the class. Conduct a conversation with the whole class about which pastimes they prefer and why.

5 **Expansion** Using magazine or real pictures, have students create a brief travel ad for the destination they chose. The ad should contain at least three uses of relative pronouns. Have students present their ads to the class.

6 **Suggestion** Do this activity orally, having pairs role-play the manager and the employee talking on the phone.

7 **Suggestion** Have students talk about any categories of their own and ask volunteers to share their preferences with the class.

OPTIONS

Game Ask students to bring in some interesting pictures from magazines or the Internet, but tell them not to show these photos to one another. Divide the class into groups of three. Each group should pick a picture. One student will write an accurate description of it, and the others will write imaginary descriptions. Tell them to use relative pronouns in the descriptions.

Each group will read its three descriptions aloud without showing the picture. Give the rest of the class two minutes to ask questions about the descriptions before guessing which is the accurate description. Award one point for a correct guess and two points to a team that fools the class.

Révision

Instructional Resources
vhlcentral.com:
Testing Program;
Testing Program MP3s;
reference tools

1 Suggestion Have volunteers share their list with the class.

2 Expansion Ask groups to choose a **métier** not listed in the activity. Then have them write a short paragraph describing what they would and would not do in that position. Have one volunteer from each group read the group's paragraph aloud.

3 Suggestion Point out that this activity elicits sentences that are contrary to fact. Remind students that their sentences should include the conditional tense in the main clause and the imperfect tense in the **si** clause.

4 Suggestion Before assigning the activity, identify the genre of each film. *Le dernier métro*: drama / *Les visiteurs*: comedy, sci-fi / *Toto le héros*: comedy, drama / *La chèvre*: comedy / *L'argent de poche*: documentary-style portrait / *Le professionnel*: action, thriller

5 Suggestion Before assigning the activity, ask the class polite questions using **pouvoir** in the conditional tense. Examples: **Pourriez-vous me prêter votre livre? Pourrais-je vous poser une question? Pourriez-vous m'expliquer...?**

6 Expansion Before assigning the activity, encourage students to brainstorm ideas for different people and places in the office that they are going to ask questions about.

---

1 Du changement Avec un(e) partenaire, observez ces bureaux. Faites une liste d'au minimum huit changements que les employés feraient s'ils en avaient les moyens (*means*). Answers will vary.

MODÈLE

Étudiant(e) 1: *Si ces gens pouvaient changer quelque chose, ils achèteraient de nouveaux ordinateurs.*
Étudiant(e) 2: *Si les affaires allaient mieux, ils déménageraient.*

2 Si j'étais... Par groupes de quatre, discutez et faites votre propre (*own*) portrait à travers (*through*) ces métiers. Utilisez la phrase **Si j'étais...** Comparez vos réponses et présentez le portrait d'un(e) camarade à la classe. Answers will vary.

MODÈLE

Étudiant(e) 1: *Si j'étais cuisinier/cuisinière, je ne préparerais que des desserts.*
Étudiant(e) 2: *Si je travaillais comme chauffeur, je ne conduirais que sur autoroute.*

artiste	conseiller/	médecin
chauffeur	conseillère	patron(ne)
chef d'entreprise	cuisinier/cuisinière	professeur
chercheur/chercheuse	femme au foyer	

3 Je démissionnerais... Pour quelles raisons seriez-vous prêt(e)s à démissionner de votre travail? Par groupes de trois, donnez chacun(e) (*each one*) au minimum deux raisons positives et deux raisons négatives. Answers will vary.

MODÈLE

Étudiant(e) 1: *Je démissionnerais si je devais suivre ma famille et déménager loin.*
Étudiant(e) 2: *Moi, je démissionnerais tout de suite si je m'ennuyais dans mon travail.*

---

4 C'est l'histoire de... Avec un(e) partenaire, commentez ces titres de films français et imaginez les histoires. Utilisez des pronoms relatifs. Ensuite, comparez vos histoires avec les histoires d'un autre groupe. Qui a l'histoire la plus proche (*closest*) du vrai film? Answers will vary.

MODÈLE

Étudiant(e) 1: *C'est l'histoire d'un homme qui...*
Étudiant(e) 2: *... et que la police recherche...*

- Le dernier métro
- Les visiteurs
- Toto le héros
- La chèvre (goat)
- L'argent de poche (pocket)
- Le professionnel

5 Un(e) patron(ne) poli(e) Avec un(e) partenaire, inventez un dialogue entre un(e) patron(ne) et son/sa secrétaire. Le/La patron(ne) demande plusieurs services au/à la secrétaire, qui refuse. Le/La patron(ne) recommence alors ses demandes, mais plus poliment, et le/la secrétaire accepte. Answers will vary.

MODÈLE

Étudiant(e) 1: *Apportez-moi le téléphone!*
Étudiant(e) 2: *Si vous me parlez comme ça, je ne vous apporterai rien.*
Étudiant(e) 1: *Pourriez-vous m'apporter le téléphone, s'il vous plaît?*
Étudiant(e) 2: *Avec plaisir!*

6 Il y a longtemps! Au bout de (*After*) cinq ans, vous retournez dans la ville où vous avez travaillé(e) et vous déjeunez avec un(e) ancien(ne) collègue. Jouez cette scène avec un(e) partenaire. Vous posez des questions à propos d'autres (*about other*) collègues du bureau. Utilisez autant de (*as many*) pronoms relatifs que possible dans votre dialogue. Answers will vary.

MODÈLE

Étudiant(e) 1: *Est-ce que la fille qui faisait un stage travaille toujours avec Paul?*
Étudiant(e) 2: *Ah non! La fille dont tu parles a quitté l'entreprise.*

O P T I O N S

Extra Practice Ask students to finish the following sentences logically: **1. S'il ne pleut pas demain... 2. Si j'avais assez d'argent... 3. Si mon/ma petit(e) ami(e) gagnait à la loterie... 4. Si j'étais psychologue... 5. S'il faisait beau...** Encourage them to be creative.

Pairs Have pairs write ten sentences about what they would do to improve their campus. First, ask them to list the problems they would change and how they would do so. Then have them form their sentences as contrary-to-fact statements. Example: **S'il y avait plus d'aides financières, les étudiants n'auraient pas de prêts étudiants** (*student loans*).

À l'écoute

STRATÉGIE

Using background knowledge/ Listening for specific information

If you know the subject of something you are going to listen to, your background knowledge will help you anticipate words and phrases you are going to hear. It will also help you determine important information that you should listen for.

To practice these strategies, you will listen to a radio advertisement for a culinary school. Before you listen, make a list of the things you expect the advertisement to contain. Make another list of information you would listen for if you were considering this school. After listening, look at your lists. Did they help you anticipate the content of the advertisement and focus on key information?

Préparation

Dans la conversation que vous allez entendre, un homme passe un entretien pour obtenir un nouvel emploi. De quoi cet homme et le chef du personnel discuteront-ils pendant l'entretien? Faites une liste des choses dont ils parleront probablement.

À vous d'écouter

Écoutez la conversation. Après une deuxième écoute, complétez les notes du chef du personnel.

Nom: Patrick Martin
Emploi demandé: chercheur en biologie
Diplôme en: biologie
Expérience professionnelle:
• stage (chercheur) au Laboratoire Roche
• Chercheur dans une entreprise de médicaments
• Emploi à mi-temps à l'Hôpital Saint-Jean
• Cherche un emploi à: plein temps

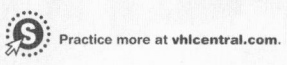
Practice more at **vhlcentral.com**.

Compréhension

Répondez Répondez aux questions d'après la conversation par des phrases complètes. Answers may vary slightly.

1. Le chef du personnel est-il un homme ou une femme?
   C'est une femme.

2. Patrick a-t-il envoyé son CV avant d'aller à l'entretien?
   Oui, il l'a envoyé.

3. Pourquoi ne travaille-t-il plus pour l'entreprise de médicaments?
   Il a perdu son emploi.

4. Où devra-t-il voyager s'il est choisi pour l'emploi de chercheur?
   Il devra voyager à l'étranger.

5. Est-il d'accord pour voyager? Pourquoi?
   Oui. Il est d'accord parce qu'il aime beaucoup voyager.

6. D'après le chef du personnel, l'emploi de chercheur est-il facile?
   Non, c'est un travail exigeant.

7. Quels sont deux des avantages (benefits) qu'on proposera à Patrick s'il est choisi pour l'emploi?
   Possible answer: On lui proposera un bon salaire et la possibilité de souvent avoir des promotions.

8. Quand Patrick commencera-t-il à travailler si on l'embauche pour cet emploi?
   Il commencera à travailler le mois prochain.

Une lettre de candidature Vous allez chercher un stage d'été dans une entreprise en France ou dans un autre pays francophone. Préparez une lettre dans laquelle vous expliquez au chef du personnel quel genre de stage vous intéresse et pourquoi vous voulez faire un stage dans cette entreprise. Parlez aussi de votre formation et de votre expérience professionnelle et expliquez comment ce stage sera utile à votre future carrière.

cinq cent soixante-quinze **575**

M: Non, pas du tout. Je suis prêt à aller à l'étranger quand cela sera nécessaire et j'aime beaucoup voyager.
C: Très bien. Vous savez, ce poste est très exigeant, mais si vous êtes travailleur, vous aurez la possibilité d'obtenir des promotions et vous serez très bien payé. Bien sûr, vous aurez cinq semaines de congés payés et la mutuelle de l'entreprise. Notre compagnie offre en plus la possibilité d'avoir une augmentation de salaire tous les six mois.

Avez-vous des questions?
M: Oui. Si je suis choisi, quand est-ce que je commencerai?
C: Le mois prochain. Je vous contacterai dans la semaine si vous êtes choisi.
M: Bon. Merci, Madame. Au revoir.
C: Au revoir.

Section Goals

In this section, students will:
• learn to use background knowledge and listen for specific information
• listen to a radio advertisement for a culinary school
• listen to a job interview and complete several activities

Instructional Resources
vhlcentral.com:
Textbook MP3s; Textbook Audioscript; reference tools

Stratégie
Audioscript Envie d'une nouvelle carrière? Notre école propose une formation exceptionnelle de cuisinier. Pendant deux ans, nos étudiants suivent des cours trois jours par semaine et les deux autres jours, ils font des stages dans de nombreux restaurants parisiens. Avec leur diplôme, tous nos étudiants trouvent un emploi bien payé, très facilement. N'hésitez pas, appelez l'École de Cuisine Rochefort au 01.42.34.67.90 pour plus d'informations.

À vous d'écouter
Audioscript CHEF DU PERSONNEL: Bonjour, Monsieur Martin. Entrez.
M. MARTIN: Bonjour, Madame.
C: Alors, voyons... C'est l'emploi de chercheur en biologie qui vous intéresse, c'est bien cela?
M: Oui, Madame, c'est exact.
C: Et vous avez une maîtrise en biologie. Avez-vous déjà de l'expérience professionnelle dans ce domaine?
M: Oui, après mon diplôme, j'ai fait un stage de six mois au Laboratoire Roche pendant lequel j'ai travaillé comme chercheur. Ensuite, j'ai encore travaillé comme chercheur pour une entreprise de médicaments, mais malheureusement, j'ai perdu mon emploi.
C: Et depuis, vous travaillez à l'Hôpital Saint-Jean?
M: Oui, j'ai été embauché en mars, mais ce travail est un emploi à mi-temps et je désire travailler à plein temps. C'est pour cette raison que je vous ai envoyé mon CV.
C: Ah, d'accord... Si vous êtes choisi, vous devrez voyager à l'étranger deux fois par mois, parce que nous avons des bureaux dans plusieurs pays d'Europe. Est-ce que cela vous posera des problèmes?

Section Goals

In this section, students will read historical and cultural information about **Auvergne-Rhône-Alpes**.

Instructional Resources
vhlcentral.com:
Digital Image Bank;
SAM Answer Key;
reference tools

Carte de l'Auvergne-Rhône-Alpes
- Have students look at the map or use the **Panorama** map from the Digital Image Bank. Ask volunteers to read the names of the cities and geographical features aloud.
- Ask students to name the bordering countries (**la Suisse, l'Italie**).
- Tell students that **Mont-Blanc**, Europe's highest mountain, reaches 15,780 feet.

La région en chiffres
- Have volunteers read the sections aloud. After each section, ask students questions about the content.
- Ask students if they have heard of any of the **personnes célèbres** and what they know about them.
- Point out that some of France's best destinations for skiing are in the **Auvergne-Rhône-Alpes** region. Grenoble was the site of the 1968 Winter Olympics and Albertville hosted the 1992 games.

Incroyable mais vrai!
- Tell students that the **Palais Idéal** is an example of naïve art and was classed as a Historic Monument in 1969.
- **Cheval** also built a villa next to the site of the palace, and he and his wife lived there during the palace's construction.
- Show the class pictures of some of the statues and other details on the **Palais Idéal**.

Panorama

L'Auvergne-Rhône-Alpes

La région en chiffres

▶ **Superficie:** *69.711 km²*

▶ **Population:** *7.874.586*
SOURCE: INSEE

▶ **Industries principales:** *industries automobile, pharmaceutique, métallurgique*

▶ **Villes principales:** *Annecy, Clermont-Ferrand, Grenoble, Lyon, Valence*

La région Auvergne-Rhône-Alpes a huit universités et 50 grandes écoles, avec 305.000 étudiants. La région est un centre de recherche et d'innovation, surtout dans les secteurs de la santé, des sciences physiques, de l'environnement, de la chimie, de l'énergie et de l'ingénierie.

Personnages célèbres

▶  **Antoine de Saint-Exupéry,** *écrivain, auteur du* Petit Prince *(1900–1944)*

▶ **André-Marie Ampère,** *mathématicien, physicien et chimiste (1775–1836)*

▶ **Jean Anthelme Brillat-Savarin,** *gastronome et écrivain (1755–1826)*

▶ **Audrey Tautou,** *actrice (1976–)*

▶ **Florence Foresti,** *humoriste, actrice (1973–)*

tournée quotidienne *daily round* **pierres** *stones* **palais féerique** *fantastical palace* **a duré** *lasted* **lentille** *lentil* **téléphérique** *cable car*

le Mont Blanc

LA FRANCE

LA SUISSE

Clermont-Ferrand

Lyon

Annecy

AUVERGNE-RHÔNE-ALPES

LES ALPES

Grenoble

L'ITALIE

Valence

la lentille° verte du Puy

le téléphérique° de Grenoble Bastille

Incroyable mais vrai!

Joseph Ferdinand Cheval (1836–1924) était facteur rural dans la campagne au sud de Lyon. Pendant sa tournée quotidienne° de 33 kilomètres, il collectionnait des pierres° pour la construction d'un palais féerique°, qu'il appellerait le «Palais Idéal». La construction du palais a commencé en 1879 et a duré° 33 ans.

OPTIONS

Personnes célèbres Antoine de Saint-Exupéry is best known for writing and illustrating *Le Petit Prince*, which has been translated into 300 languages and made into a movie. He was also a pilot and served in the French Air Force. **Ampère** was one of the founders of the branch of physics known as classical electromagnetism. The unit of measurement of electric current, the ampere, is named after him. **Brillat-Savarin** is most famous

for writing *La Physiologie du goût*, an epicurean treatise which remains the bible of amateur gastronomes. He also served as mayor of his hometown of Belley. **Audrey Tautou** is one of France's most famous actresses. She is especially known for her starring role in the 2001 film *Amélie*. **Florence Foresti** is known for her stand-up comedy. She has also appeared on television and in several films.

576 Instructor's Annotated Edition • Unit 13

La gastronomie

La raclette et la fondue

La Savoie est très riche en fromages et deux de ses spécialités sont à base de fromage. Pour la raclette, on met du fromage à raclette sur un appareil° pour le faire fondre°. Chaque personne racle° ensuite du fromage dans son assiette et le mange avec des pommes de terre et de la charcuterie°. La fondue est un mélange° de fromages fondus° comme le comté, le beaufort ou l'emmental. Avec un bâton°, on trempe° un morceau de pain dans le mélange. Ne le laissez pas tomber!

Les destinations

Grenoble

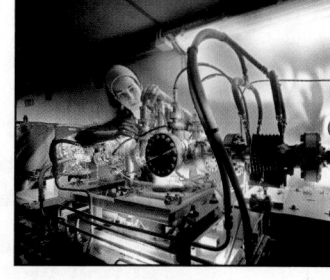

La ville de Grenoble est surnommée «Capitale des Alpes» et «Ville Technologique». Située à la porte des Alpes, elle donne accès aux grandes stations de ski alpin et est le premier centre de recherche en France après Paris, avec 25.000 emplois. Le synchrotron de Grenoble, un des plus grands accélérateurs de particules du monde, permet d'étudier la matière°. Grenoble est également° une ville universitaire, avec quatre universités et 65.500 étudiants.

Les festivals

La Fête des Lumières

Chaque année vers le 8 décembre, la ville de Lyon s'allume°. Commençant en 1852, une fois par an, les Lyonnais mettent des lumignons° à leurs fenêtres et à leurs balcons, puis sortent dans la rue pour voir leur ville illuminée. Depuis 1989, des artistes internationaux sont invités à créer des œuvres et des spectacles de lumière pour illuminer les sites patrimoniaux°, les paysages° et les quartiers de la ville.

Les sports

ViaRhôna

Un itinéraire cyclable de 815 kilomètres, cette route rejoint° les Alpes suisses et la mer Méditerranée en traversant la région Auvergne-Rhône-Alpes. La route commence au Lac Léman, en Suisse, et se termine° sur la côte° méditerranéenne française. L'Auvergne-Rhône-Alpes contient° 557 kilomètres de la route, et l'étape Genève-Lyon est inaugurée en juin 2016. Les différentes étapes sont adaptées aux sportifs, aux moins sportifs et aux familles.

Qu'est-ce que vous avez appris? Répondez aux questions par des phrases complètes.

1. Qui a écrit *Le Petit Prince*?
   Antoine de Saint-Exupéry a écrit *Le Petit Prince.*
2. Quel était le métier de Joseph Ferdinand Cheval?
   Il était facteur (rural).
3. Combien d'années la construction du Palais Idéal a-t-elle duré?
   La construction du Palais Idéal a duré 33 ans.
4. Qu'est-ce que les chercheurs viennent étudier à Grenoble?
   Ils viennent étudier la matière.
5. Quel sport peut-on faire à côté de Grenoble?
   On peut faire du ski alpin.
6. Avec quoi est-ce qu'on mange le fromage d'une raclette?
   On le mange avec des pommes de terre et de la charcuterie.
7. Où est-ce que les Lyonnais mettent des lumignons pendant la Fête des Lumières?
   Ils mettent des lumignons à leurs fenêtres et à leurs balcons.
8. Quels endroits de la ville sont illuminés?
   Les sites patrimoniaux, les paysages et les quartiers de la ville sont illuminés.
9. Combien de kilomètres de la route ViaRhôna se trouvent en Auvergne-Rhône-Alpes?
   557 kilomètres de la route se trouvent en Auvergne-Rhône-Alpes.
10. Quand est-ce que l'étape Genève-Lyon de la route ViaRhôna est inaugurée?
    Elle est inaugurée en juin 2016.

Sur Internet

Go to **vhlcentral.com** to find more cultural information related to this **Panorama**.

1. Cherchez plus d'informations sur le Palais Idéal du Facteur Cheval. Est-ce qu'on peut le visiter aujourd'hui? Quelles figures (animaux, créatures mythiques, etc.) y sont représentées?

2. Trouvez des informations sur les vacances d'hiver à Grenoble: logement, prix, activités, etc.

3. Cherchez plus d'informations sur la Fête des Lumières à Lyon. Quelles sont les dates de la fête cette année?

ressources

WB pp. 187–188   S vhlcentral

appareil *machine* **fondre** *to melt* **racle** *scrapes* **charcuterie** *cured meats* **mélange** *mix* **fondus** *melted* **bâton** *stick* **trempe** *dips* **matière** *matter* **également** *also* **s'allume** *lights up* **lumignons** *tea lights* **sites patrimoniaux** *heritage sites* **paysages** *landscapes* **rejoint** *links* **se termine** *ends* **côte** *coast* **contient** *contains*

La raclette et la fondue

Invented by the Swiss, fondue has become an international dish and has even been adapted to local tastes. In Savoie, people use **comté** and **beaufort** cheese as well as **emmental**. Both raclette and fondue are traditional winter dishes.

Grenoble There are numerous educational institutions in Grenoble. The city is considered a center for chemical, electronic, and nuclear research. Have students search Grenoble's city website for information about how many universities are located there and in what areas they specialize.

La Fête des Lumières

- The **Fête des Lumières** typically lasts for four nights, with between two and three million visitors in a given year.
- The light shows change every year, making each **Fête des Lumières** unique.
- Lyon is a leader in urban lighting. Its first lighting plan was started in 1989 and organized permanent lighting for the city's buildings, monuments, and streets. In 2004, the second lighting plan completed the first, highlighting the activities and rhythms of city life by emphasizing the city's natural features and thoroughfares.

ViaRhôna

- Tell students that 114.2 kilometers of the route are in the Provence-Alpes-Côte d'Azur region and 146.3 in Occitanie.
- The **ViaRhôna** is part of a larger bicycle route system in Europe, called EuroVelo.

O P T I O N S

Cultural Comparison Have students research Antoine de Saint-Exupéry. What were his exploits as a pilot? What other literary works did he write? Are students familiar with any of them? Ask students if they are familiar with **Le Petit Prince**, in English or French. Share a synopsis of the story or read an excerpt in class.

Group Activity Assign one of the five sections of the **ViaRhôna** route to multiple groups of three or four. Have each group identify the towns and places of interest in their section of the route and create a short presentation with the information. Have each group present to the class, then discuss which section students would most like to visit.

Lecture

🅢 Audio: Reading

La Cigale et

Avant la lecture

STRATÉGIE

Summarizing a text in your own words

Summarizing a text in your own words can help you comprehend it better. Before summarizing a text, you may find it helpful to skim it and jot down a few notes about its general meaning. You can then read the text again, writing down the important details. Your notes will help you summarize what you have read. If the text is particularly long, you may want to subdivide it into smaller segments so that you can summarize it more easily.

Examinez le texte

D'abord, regardez la forme du texte. Quel genre de texte est-ce? Puis, regardez les illustrations. Qu'y a-t-il sur ces illustrations? Qui sont les personnages de l'histoire (*story*)? Que font les insectes dans la première illustration? Et dans la deuxième?

À propos de l'auteur
Jean de La Fontaine (1621–1695)

Jean de La Fontaine est un auteur et un poète français très connu du dix-septième siècle. Né à Château-Thierry, à l'est de Paris, il a passé toute son enfance à la campagne avant de devenir avocat et de s'installer à Paris. C'est à la capitale qu'il a rencontré des écrivains célèbres et qu'il a décidé d'écrire. Il est l'auteur de poèmes, de nouvelles en vers° et de contes°, mais il est connu surtout pour ses fables, considérées comme des chefs-d'œuvre° de la littérature française. Au total, La Fontaine a publié 12 livres de fables dans lesquels il a créé des histoires autour de concepts fondamentaux de la morale qu'il a empruntés principalement aux fables d'Ésope. Les fables de La Fontaine, avec leurs animaux et leurs histoires assez simples, étaient, pour lui, une manière° subtile de critiquer la société contemporaine et la nature humaine. Deux de ses fables les plus connues sont *La Cigale et la Fourmi* et *Le Corbeau et le Renard*.

nouvelles en vers *short stories in verse* **contes** *tales* **chefs-d'œuvre** *masterpieces* **manière** *way*

578   *cinq cent soixante-dix-huit*

1   La Cigale°, ayant° chanté
    Tout l'été,
    Se trouva fort dépourvue°
    Quand la bise fut venue°:
5   Pas un seul petit morceau
    De mouche° ou de vermisseau°.
    Elle alla crier° famine
    Chez la Fourmi° sa voisine,
    La priant° de lui prêter
10 Quelque grain pour subsister°
    Jusqu'à la saison nouvelle.
    «Je vous paierai, lui dit-elle,
    Avant l'Oût°, foi d'animal°,
    Intérêt et principal.»
15 La Fourmi n'est pas prêteuse°;
    C'est là son moindre défaut°.
    «Que faisiez-vous au temps chaud?
    Dit-elle à cette emprunteuse°.
    —Nuit et jour à tout venant°
20 Je chantais, ne vous déplaise°.
    —Vous chantiez? j'en suis fort aise°.
    Eh bien! dansez maintenant.»

Section Goals

In this section, students will:
• learn to summarize a text in their own words
• read a fable in French

Stratégie Tell students that summarizing a text in their own words will help them understand it. Explain that a summary is a restatement of the main idea and major points of a text without the details. As they read a text, they should list the important points and then use linking words to join the ideas.

Examinez le texte Students should mention that the text is a poem, and the main characters are an ant and a cicada. In the first illustration, the ant is working hard, and the cicada is having fun. In the second illustration, it's winter. The cicada is cold and hungry, while the ant has food and shelter.

À propos de l'auteur
• The house in which La Fontaine was born in Château-Thierry is now the **Musée Jean de La Fontaine**.
• Ask students these comprehension questions. **1. Où est né Jean de La Fontaine? (à Château-Thierry) 2. Avant de devenir écrivain, que faisait-il? (Il était avocat.) 3. A-t-il écrit seulement des fables? (Non, il a écrit des poèmes, des nouvelles en vers et des contes.) 4. Quelles fables ont influencé La Fontaine? (les fables d'Ésope) 5. Pourquoi La Fontaine a-t-il écrit des fables? Comment les a-t-il employées? (Les fables de La Fontaine ont critiqué la société contemporaine et la nature humaine.)**

Extra Practice Have students write speech or thought balloons in French for **la cigale** and **la fourmi** in each illustration. Encourage them to use their own words. You might want to photocopy the illustrations and distribute them to the class so students can draw speech balloons and write the text in them.

Pairs Have students discuss these questions. Why did La Fontaine choose **une cigale** and **une fourmi** as the two insects in this fable? Do his choices make sense? What two insects or animals could replace **la cigale** and **la fourmi**? Tell students to justify their answers.

la Fourmi
de Jean de La Fontaine

Cigale *Cicada* **ayant** *having* **Se trouva fort dépourvue** *Found itself left without a thing* **la bise fut venue** *the cold winds of winter arrived* **mouche** *fly* **vermisseau** *small worm* **alla crier** *went crying* **Fourmi** *Ant* **La priant** *Begging her* **subsister** *survive* **Oût** *August* **foi d'animal** *on my word as an animal* **n'est pas prêteuse** *doesn't like lending things* **moindre défaut** *the least of her shortcomings* **emprunteuse** *borrower* **à tout venant** *all the time* **ne vous déplaise** *whether you like it or not* **fort aise** *overjoyed*

Après la lecture

Répondez Répondez aux questions par des phrases complètes.

1. Qu'est-ce que la Cigale a fait tout l'été?
   _____

2. Quel personnage de la fable a beaucoup travaillé pendant l'été?
   _____

3. Pourquoi la Cigale n'a-t-elle rien à manger quand l'hiver arrive?
   _____

4. Que fait la Cigale quand elle a faim?
   _____

5. Que fera la Cigale si la Fourmi lui donne à manger?
   _____

6. Qu'est-ce que la Fourmi demande à la Cigale?
   _____

7. Quel est le moindre défaut de la Fourmi?
   _____

8. La Fourmi va-t-elle donner quelque chose à manger à la Cigale? Expliquez.
   _____

Un résumé Écrivez un résumé (*summary*) de la fable de La Fontaine. Regardez le texte et prenez des notes sur ce qui se passe aux différents moments de l'histoire. Faites aussi une liste des mots importants que vous ne connaissez pas et trouvez-leur des synonymes que vous pourrez utiliser dans votre résumé. Par exemple, vous connaissez déjà le mot «vent», synonyme de «bise».

La morale de la fable Comme les fables en général, *La Cigale et la Fourmi* a une morale, mais La Fontaine ne la donne pas explicitement. À votre avis, quelle est la morale de cette fable? Êtes-vous d'accord avec cette morale? Discutez ces questions en petits groupes.

Les fables Connaissiez-vous déjà l'histoire de cette fable? Connaissez-vous d'autres fables, comme celles du Grec Ésope, de l'Américain James Thurber, de l'Allemand Gotthold Lessing ou de l'Espagnol Félix Maria Samaniego? Que pensez-vous des fables en général? Aimez-vous les lire? À quoi servent-elles? Quels thèmes trouve-t-on souvent dans les fables? Quels animaux sont souvent utilisés? Discutez ces questions en petits groupes.

Répondez Go over the answers with the class.

Un résumé After completing the activity, have students compare their summaries with a classmate or ask a few volunteers to read their summaries aloud.

La morale de la fable Ask groups to state the moral of the fable. Then ask students why animals are used as characters in fables.

Les fables Before beginning the activity, take a quick class survey to find out how many students have read fables by Thurber, Aesop, Lessing, or Samaniego.

OPTIONS

Pairs Have students work in pairs. Tell them to think of some real-life situations that would mirror the moral taught in this fable. Then have volunteers give examples and ask the class if they think the situation is appropriate or not.

Small Groups Have students work in groups of three or four. Tell them to create a fable of their own. They should decide what the purpose or moral of their fable is, what situation would illustrate it, and which animals should be the main characters. Encourage them to include an illustration. Have volunteer groups act out their fable for the class.

Section Goals

In this section, students will:
- learn to use note cards
- write a composition about their professional goals

Stratégie Explain that using note cards in preparation for writing a composition will help organize and sequence information or ideas.

Thème Tell students to answer the questions first, using note cards for each category (**Types de professions, Recherche d'un emploi,** and **Évolution de carrière**). Remind them to number the cards by category.

Proofreading Activity Have students correct these sentences. **1. Tu penses avoir reussir au bac? 2. Qu'est ce que tu allez faire une fois que tu as le bac? 3. Nous allons diner pour célébrer des que j'ai un nouveau travail. 4. Si je ferais cette robe, elle finirais avec une manche courte et avec une manche longue! 5. Si tu avoir besoin de quoi que c'est un jour, dites-le-moi.**

Écriture

STRATÉGIE

Using note cards

Note cards serve as valuable study aids in many different contexts. When you write, note cards can help you organize and sequence the information you wish to present.

If you were going to write a personal narrative about a trip you took, you would jot down notes about each part of the trip on a different note card. Then you could easily arrange them in chronological order or use a different organization, such as the best parts and the worst parts, traveling and staying, before and after, etc.

Here are some helpful techniques:

- Label the top of each card with a general subject, such as **l'avion** or **l'hôtel**.

- Number the cards in each subject category in the upper right corner to help you organize them.

- Use only the front side of each note card so that you can easily flip through them to find information.

Study this example of a note card used to prepare a composition.

> *l'avion*
>
> · *arrivée à l'aéroport de Chicago à 14h30*
> · *départ pour Paris à 16h45, Vol 47 d'Air France*
> · *arrivée à Paris (aéroport Charles-de-Gaulle) à 7h15 le lendemain matin*
> · *douane*
> · *voyage long mais agréable*

Thème

Écrire une rédaction

Avant l'écriture

1. Vous allez écrire une rédaction (*composition*) dans laquelle vous expliquez vos projets d'avenir en ce qui concerne (*concerning*) votre carrière professionnelle.

2. D'abord, préparez des petites fiches (*cards*) avec des notes pour chacune (*each*) des catégories suivantes. Vous avez trois catégories de fiches:

   - types de professions
   - recherche d'un emploi
   - évolution de carrière

3. Pour chaque catégorie, écrivez vos idées sur la fiche correspondante. Utilisez une fiche pour chaque idée. Basez-vous sur ces questions pour trouver des idées.

TYPES DE PROFESSIONS

- Quels domaines professionnels ou quelles professions vous intéressent? Pourquoi? Correspondent-ils à vos études?

- Connaissez-vous déjà des compagnies pour lesquelles vous avez envie de travailler? Lesquelles? Pourquoi?

O P T I O N S

Stratégie Have students analyze the topic, notes, and organization of the sample note card shown in the strategy box. Then, as a class, brainstorm other kinds of information you could add to it. Tell students that once they have completed each note card, they should look at it and decide which pieces of information are pertinent to their topic and which are extraneous.

Talk about different ways to organize the note cards. For example, you could organize each card chronologically. Or you could divide it in half, with one side tracking the pros of the subject and the other half indicating the cons. Another way is to record facts in one column and opinions in a second column. Reinforce that students should customize the cards to suit their particular purpose.

RECHERCHE D'UN EMPLOI

- Resterez-vous dans la région où vous habitez maintenant?

- Comment chercherez-vous du travail? Chercherez-vous dans le journal ou sur Internet?

- Chercherez-vous un emploi à temps partiel ou à plein temps? Quel salaire vous proposera-t-on, à votre avis?

ÉVOLUTION DE CARRIÈRE

- Travaillerez-vous pour la même entreprise toute votre carrière ou changerez-vous d'emploi?

- Votre emploi évoluera-t-il beaucoup (promotions, salaire et autres avantages,...), à votre avis?

- Finirez-vous par créer votre propre entreprise?

- À quel âge prendrez-vous votre retraite?

4. Regardez cet exemple pour la catégorie numéro 1.

> *Types de professions*
>
> *Je travaillerai dans le domaine de la science. Je deviendrai astronome et j'étudierai l'univers. J'ai toujours voulu savoir s'il y avait de la vie sur d'autres planètes.*

5. Avant de noter vos idées sur les fiches, organisez-les selon (*according to*) les trois catégories. Vous aurez ainsi toutes vos idées prêtes pour l'écriture de votre rédaction.

Écriture

1. Servez-vous des fiches pour écrire votre rédaction. Écrivez trois paragraphes en utilisant (*by using*) les catégories comme thèmes de chaque paragraphe.

2. Employez les points de grammaire de cette unité dans votre rédaction.

Après l'écriture

1. Échangez votre rédaction avec celle (*the one*) d'un(e) partenaire. Répondez à ces questions pour commenter son travail.

- Votre partenaire a-t-il/elle écrit trois paragraphes qui correspondent aux trois catégories d'information?

- A-t-il/elle répondu à toutes les questions de la liste qui apparaît dans **Avant l'écriture**?

- A-t-il/elle bien utilisé les points de grammaire de l'unité?

- Quel(s) détail(s) ajouteriez-vous (*would you add*)? Quel(s) détail(s) enlèveriez-vous (*would you delete*)? Quel(s) autre(s) commentaire(s) avez-vous pour votre partenaire?

2. Corrigez votre rédaction d'après (*according to*) les commentaires de votre partenaire. Relisez votre travail pour éliminer ces problèmes:

- des fautes (*errors*) d'orthographe

- des fautes de ponctuation

- des fautes de conjugaison

- un mauvais emploi (*use*) des temps

- un mauvais emploi de la grammaire de l'unité

- des fautes d'accord (*agreement*) des adjectifs

EVALUATION

Criteria

Content Contains answers to each set of questions called out in the bulleted points of the task.
Scale: 1 2 3 4 5

Organization Organized into a set of note cards with preliminary answers to the questions, followed by a composition that is organized into logical paragraphs, each of which begins with a topic sentence and contains appropriate supporting detail.
Scale: 1 2 3 4 5

Accuracy Uses the simple future tense and forms of **lequel** correctly. Spells words, conjugates verbs, and modifies adjectives correctly throughout.
Scale: 1 2 3 4 5

Creativity Includes additional information that is not specified in the task and/or uses adjectives, descriptive verbs, and additional details to make the composition more interesting.
Scale: 1 2 3 4 5

Scoring

Excellent	18–20 points
Good	14–17 points
Satisfactory	10–13 points
Unsatisfactory	< 10 points

cinq cent quatre-vingt-un **581**

OPTIONS

Avant l'écriture To activate vocabulary for the topic, have students work in pairs and role-play an interview. Students should take turns asking and answering questions from the list and taking notes on their answers and the words they use in their responses. Then, as needed, they can use a dictionary to add any specific words that will personalize these responses.

Point out that most of the questions in the writing task require answers using the simple future tense. Review its formation and the irregular forms from **Unité 12**, and its use with **quand** and **dès que** from this unit. Also review the use of **lequel** and its various combined forms. Practice by asking simple questions using these forms and calling upon individual students to respond.

Instructional Resources
vhlcentral.com:
Textbook MP3s; Textbook
Audioscript; reference tools

Suggestions
• Tell students that an easy way to study from **Vocabulaire** is to cover up the French half of each section, leaving only the English equivalents exposed. They can then quiz themselves on the French items. To focus on the English equivalents of the French entries, they simply reverse this process.
• Point out to students that they can use the Vocabulary Tools at **vhlcentral.com** for reference and extra vocabulary practice.

🔊 ⓢ **Vocabulary Tools**

Leçon 13A

La recherche d'emploi

chercher un/du travail *to look for work*
embaucher *to hire*
faire des projets *to make plans*
lire les annonces (f.) *to read the want ads*
obtenir *to get, to obtain*
passer un entretien *to have an interview*
postuler *to apply*
prendre (un) rendez-vous *to make an appointment*
trouver un/du travail *to find a job*
un(e) candidat(e) *candidate, applicant*
un chef du personnel *human resources director*
un chômeur/une chômeuse *unemployed person*
une compagnie *company*
un conseil *advice*
un curriculum vitæ (un CV) *résumé*
une entreprise *firm, business*
une lettre de motivation *letter of application*
un métier *profession*
un poste *position*
un salaire (élevé, modeste) *(high, low) salary*

Vocabulaire supplémentaire

dès que *as soon as*
quand *when*
lequel *which one (m. sing.)*
lesquels *which ones (m. pl.)*
laquelle *which one (f. sing.)*
lesquelles *which ones (f. pl.)*

Qualifications

un domaine *field*
une expérience professionnelle *professional experience*
une formation *education; training*
une lettre de recommandation *letter of reference/recommendation*
une mention *distinction*
une référence *reference*
un(e) spécialiste *specialist*
un stage *internship; professional training*

Expressions utiles

See p. 545.

Au téléphone

appeler *to call*
décrocher *to pick up*
laisser un message *to leave a message*
patienter *to wait (on the phone), to be on hold*
raccrocher *to hang up*
l'appareil (m.) *telephone*
le combiné *receiver*
la messagerie *voicemail*
un numéro de téléphone *phone number*
une télécarte *phone card*
Allô! *Hello! (on the phone)*
Qui est à l'appareil? *Who's calling please?*
C'est de la part de qui? *On behalf of whom?*
C'est M./Mme/Mlle... (à l'appareil.) *It's Mr./Mrs./Miss... (on the phone.)*
Ne quittez pas. *Please hold.*

Leçon 13B

Au travail

démissionner *to resign*
diriger *to manage*
être au chômage *to be unemployed*
être bien/mal payé(e) *to be well/badly paid*
gagner *to earn; to win*
prendre un congé *to take time off*
renvoyer *to dismiss, to let go*

une carrière *career*
un chômeur/une chômeuse *unemployed person*
un emploi à mi-temps/à temps partiel *part-time job*
un emploi à plein temps *full-time job*
un niveau *level*
une profession (exigeante) *(demanding) profession*
un(e) retraité(e) *retired person*
une réunion *meeting*
une réussite *success*
un syndicat *union*
une assurance (maladie, vie) *(health, life) insurance*
une augmentation (de salaire) *raise (in salary)*
une promotion *promotion*

Pronoms relatifs

dont *of which, of whom*
où *where*
que *that, which*
qui *who, that, which*

Expressions utiles

See p. 563.

Les métiers

un agent immobilier *real estate agent*
un agriculteur/une agricultrice *farmer*
un banquier/une banquière *banker*
un cadre/une femme cadre *executive*
un chauffeur de taxi/de camion *taxi/truck driver*
un chef d'entreprise *head of a company*
un chercheur/une chercheuse *researcher*
un(e) comptable *accountant*
un conseiller/une conseillère *consultant; advisor*
un cuisinier/une cuisinière *cook, chef*
un(e) électricien(ne) *electrician*
une femme au foyer *housewife*
un(e) gérant(e) *manager*
un homme/une femme politique *politician*
un ouvrier/une ouvrière *worker, laborer*
un plombier *plumber*
un pompier/une femme pompier *firefighter*
un(e) psychologue *psychologist*
un(e) vétérinaire *veterinarian*

L'espace vert

Pour commencer

Où est le groupe d'amis?
a. à la mer   b. à la campagne   c. en ville

Qu'est-ce qu'ils vont faire?
a. un pique-nique   b. les courses   c. du vélo

Qu'est-ce qu'il y a derrière eux?
a. une jungle   b. une montagne   c. un pont

Unit Goals

Leçon 14A

In this lesson, students will learn:
- terms related to ecology and the environment
- common differences in French and English spelling
- about the ecological movement and nuclear energy in France
- the demonstrative pronouns **celui**, **celle**, **ceux**, and **celles**
- to form **le subjonctif**
- common impersonal expressions that take the subjunctive
- about a French ecological initiative.

Leçon 14B

In this lesson, students will learn:
- terms to discuss nature and conservation
- about homophones
- about French singer and actor **Liz Van Deuq**
- about France's national park system and Madagascar
- more about the diverse geography of the francophone world through specially shot video footage
- about the subjunctive with verbs and expressions of will and emotion
- verbs with irregular subjunctive forms
- the comparative and superlative of nouns
- to listen for the gist and cognates

Savoir-faire

In this section, students will learn:
- cultural and historical information about **Bourgogne-Franche-Comté**
- to recognize personification in a text
- to consider audience and purpose when writing

Pour commencer
- b. à la campagne
- a. un pique-nique
- b. une montagne

RESOURCES

Student Activities Manual (SAM): Workbook Activities, pp. 189–202; Lab Activities, pp. 105–112; Video Activities, pp. 53–56; pp. 87–88 SAM Answer Key

vhlcentral.com: Textbook MP3s; Lab MP3s; Textbook Audioscript; Lab Audioscript; Video; Videoscript; **Roman-photo** Translations; **Vocabulaire supplémentaire**; Activity Pack (including **Feuilles d'activités**, Info Gap Activities), and Task-based Activities;

Le Zapping TV clip transcription; **Essayez!** and **Mise en pratique** answers; Digital Image Bank; Testing Program; Testing Program MP3s

Section Goals

In this section, students will learn and practice vocabulary related to:
- ecology
- the environment

Instructional Resources
vhlcentral.com:
Digital Image Bank;
Vocabulaire supplémentaire
(including vocabulary illustrations from the textbook, theme-based illustrations);
Mise en pratique *answers;*
Textbook Audioscript;
Lab Audioscript; Activity Pack;
Textbook MP3s; Lab MP3s;
SAM Answer Key;
reference tools

Suggestions
- Tell students to look over the new vocabulary and identify the cognates.
- Use the **14A Contextes** illustration from the Digital Image Bank. Point out people and things as you describe the illustration. Examples: **Elle recycle. Ils ont pollué. C'est une centrale nucléaire.**
- Point out the verb **interdire** and the sign next to it. Write on the board: **Il est interdit de...** Then have students finish the sentence with various things people might be forbidden to do, such as **gaspiller de l'énergie.**
- Ask students questions using the new vocabulary. Examples: **L'université a-t-elle un programme de recyclage? Quels objets recyclez-vous? Que faites-vous pour réduire la pollution? Quel est le plus gros problème écologique de votre région? L'énergie solaire est-elle mieux que l'énergie nucléaire? Pourquoi? Où y a-t-il souvent des glissements de terrain?**
- Additional vocabulary for this lesson can be found in the **Vocabulaire supplémentaire** on the Supersite.
- Use the Vocabulary illustrations and the Nature and the environment illustrations from the Digital Image Bank to help students familiarize themselves with ecology and the environment.

Leçon 14A

(S) Vocabulary Tools

You will learn how to...
- talk about pollution
- talk about what needs to be done

Sauvons la planète!

Vocabulaire	
abolir	to abolish
améliorer	to improve
développer	to develop
gaspiller	to waste
préserver	to preserve
prévenir l'incendie	to prevent a fire
proposer une solution	to propose a solution
sauver la planète	to save the planet
une catastrophe	catastrophe
un danger	danger, threat
des déchets toxiques (m.)	toxic waste
l'effet de serre (m.)	greenhouse effect
le gaspillage	waste
un glissement de terrain	landslide
une population croissante	growing population
le réchauffement climatique	global warming
la surpopulation	overpopulation
le trou dans la couche d'ozone	hole in the ozone layer
une usine	factory
l'écologie (f.)	ecology
un emballage en plastique	plastic wrapping/packaging
l'environnement (m.)	environment
un espace	space, area
un produit	product
la protection	protection
écologique	ecological
en plein air	outdoor, open-air
pur(e)	pure
un gouvernement	government
une loi	law

ressources

WB	LM	(S)
pp. 189–190	p. 105	vhlcentral

584 *cinq cent quatre-vingt-quatre*

O P T I O N S

Extra Practice Whisper a vocabulary word in a student's ear. That student should draw a picture or a series of pictures that represent the word on the board. The class must guess the word, then spell it in French as a volunteer writes the word on the board.

Game Divide the class into two teams. Have a spelling bee using vocabulary words from **Espace contextes**. Pronounce each word, use it in a sentence, and then say the word again. Tell students that they must spell the words in French and include all diacritical marks.

Mise en pratique

1 Écoutez Écoutez l'annonce radio suivante. Ensuite, complétez les phrases avec le mot ou l'expression qui convient le mieux.

1. C'est l'annonce radio _____
   a. d'un groupe d'étudiants.
   b. d'une entreprise commerciale.
   c. d'une agence écologiste.

2. La protection de l'environnement, c'est l'affaire _____
   a. de tous.
   b. du gouvernement.
   c. des centres de recyclage.

3. L'annonce dit qu'on peut recycler _____
   a. les emballages en plastique et en papier.
   b. les boîtes de conserve.
   c. les bouteilles en plastique.

4. Pour les déchets toxiques, il y a _____
   a. le ramassage des ordures.
   b. le centre de recyclage.
   c. l'effet de serre.

5. Pour ne pas gaspiller l'eau, on peut _____
   a. acheter des produits écologiques.
   b. développer les incendies.
   c. prendre des douches plus courtes.

2 Complétez Complétez ces phrases avec le mot ou l'expression qui convient le mieux pour parler de l'environnement. N'oubliez pas les accords.

1. Nous avons trois poubelles différentes pour pouvoir ___recycler___.
2. ___L'effet de serre___ contribue au réchauffement de la Terre.
3. ___Les centrales nucléaires___ produisent près de 80% de l'énergie en France.
4. Les pluies ont provoqué ___un glissement de terrain___. À présent, la route est fermée.
5. Chez moi, ___le ramassage___ des ordures se fait tous les lundis.
6. L'accident à l'usine chimique a provoqué un ___nuage de pollution___.

3 Composez Utilisez les éléments de chaque colonne pour former six phrases logiques au sujet de l'environnement. Vous pouvez composer des phrases affirmatives ou négatives. Answers will vary.

Les gens	Les actions	Les éléments
vous	développer	l'eau
on	gaspiller	le covoiturage
les gens	polluer	l'énergie solaire
les politiciens	préserver	l'environnement
les entreprises	proposer	la planète
les centrales nucléaires	sauver	la Terre

Practice more at vhlcentral.com.

cinq cent quatre-vingt-cinq **585**

le ramassage des ordures (f.)

Elle recycle. (recycler)

le recyclage

interdire

Ils ont pollué. (polluer)

1 Audioscript L'écologie, c'est l'affaire de tous! Aidez-nous à préserver et à améliorer l'environnement. Tout commence avec le ramassage des ordures: recyclez vos emballages en plastique et en papier! Ne polluez pas: votre centre de recyclage local est là pour s'occuper de vos déchets toxiques. Ne gaspillez pas l'eau, surtout en cette période de réchauffement de la Terre: comment? Prenez des douches plus courtes! Nous vous rappelons également qu'une loi interdit de laver sa voiture dans certaines régions de France quand il fait extrêmement chaud l'été. Ne gaspillez pas non plus l'énergie: faites attention à la consommation inutile d'énergie de vos appareils électriques. Enfin, évitez d'acheter des produits qui peuvent mettre l'environnement en danger: choisissez des produits écologiques. Ensemble, nous sommes plus forts! Nous développons et proposons des solutions simples. Alors, la prochaine fois que vous entendrez parler de pluies acides, de trou dans la couche d'ozone, de l'effet de serre, de pollution et de catastrophe écologique, vous pourrez être fier de dire que vous faites partie de la solution.

Ceci était un message de l'agence nationale pour la protection de l'environnement. (On Textbook MP3s)

1 Suggestion Go over the answers with the class. Ask volunteers to read the complete sentences.

2 Expansion For additional practice, give students these items. **7. Une nouvelle étude des Nations Unies confirme qu'il y a un risque de ____. (surpopulation) En 2050, il y aura neuf milliards (billions) de personnes sur Terre. 8. Le parti écologiste veut améliorer ____ de l'environnement. (la protection) 9. Le gouvernement vient de passer ____ sur le transport des déchets toxiques. (une loi) 10. Nous évitons de laisser ____ derrière nous quand nous mangeons dans le parc. (des ordures)**

3 Suggestion This activity can be done orally or in writing in pairs or groups.

OPTIONS

Game Play a game of **Dix questions**. Ask a volunteer to think of a word or expression from the new vocabulary. Other students get to ask one yes/no question, then they can guess what the word is. Limit attempts to ten questions per word. You may want to write some phrases on the board to cue students' questions.

Pairs Have students work in pairs. Write the following list of dangers facing our planet on the board. Tell students to rank them from the most serious to least serious and explain why. Dangers: **la surpopulation, le réchauffement de la Terre, les déchets toxiques, la pollution de l'environnement, la pluie acide, l'effet de serre, le risque d'accident dans une centrale nucléaire**, and **la crise de l'énergie**

4 Suggestion Tell students that their descriptions should include the weather, the time of day, and a possible location.

4 Expansion Bring in additional photos from magazines or the Internet that illustrate ecological problems and have students describe what they see.

5 Suggestion You may wish to assign groups specific situations so that all of them are covered.

6 Suggestion Ask a volunteer to read the **modèle** aloud. Then have students brainstorm a list of words and expressions that are used to inform, persuade, or register a complaint.

Communication

4 Décrivez Avec un(e) partenaire, décrivez ces photos et donnez autant de détails et d'informations que possible. Soyez prêt(e)s à présenter vos descriptions à la classe. Answers will vary.

1.

2.

3.

4.

5 À vous de jouer Par petits groupes, préparez une conversation au sujet d'une de ces situations. Ensuite jouez la scène devant la classe. Answers will vary.

- Un(e) employé(e) du centre de recyclage local vient dans votre université pour expliquer aux étudiants un nouveau système de recyclage. De nombreux étudiants posent des questions.
- Un groupe d'écologistes rencontre le patron d'une entreprise accusée de polluer la rivière (*river*) locale.
- Le ministre de l'environnement donne une conférence de presse au sujet d'une nouvelle loi sur la protection de l'environnement.
- Votre colocataire oublie systématiquement de recycler les emballages. Vous avez une conversation animée avec lui/elle.

6 L'article Vous êtes journaliste et vous devez écrire un article pour le journal local au sujet de la pollution. Vous en expliquez les causes et les conséquences sur l'environnement. Vous suggérez aussi des solutions pour améliorer la situation. Answers will vary.

MODÈLE

Les dangers de la pollution chimique

Les usines chimiques de notre région polluent! C'est une catastrophe pour notre environnement. Il faut leur interdire de fonctionner jusqu'à ce qu'elles améliorent leurs systèmes de recyclage...

OPTIONS

Pairs Write these expressions for circumlocution on the board: **C'est un endroit où..., Ça sert à..., C'est le contraire de..., C'est un synonyme de..., C'est quand on....** Then have pairs of students write definitions for these vocabulary words. 1. améliorer 2. un incendie 3. le recyclage 4. le covoiturage 5. la pollution 6. une catastrophe 7. une loi 8. une usine 9. le réchauffement de la Terre

Have pairs get together with another pair of students and take turns reading their definitions and guessing the word. Ask each group to choose their best definition and write it on the board for the whole class to guess.

Les sons et les lettres   Audio

French and English spelling

You have seen that many French words only differ slightly from their English counterparts. Many differ in predictable ways. English words that end in -y often end in **-ie** in French.

| biologie | psychologie | énergie | écologie |

English words that end in -ity often end in **-ité** in French.

| qualité | université | cité | nationalité |

French equivalents of English words that end in -ist often end in **-iste**.

| artiste | optimiste | pessimiste | dentiste |

French equivalents of English words that end in -or and -er often end in **-eur**. This tendency is especially common for words that refer to people.

| docteur | acteur | employeur | agriculteur |

Other English words that end in -er end in **-re** in French.

| centre | membre | litre | théâtre |

Other French words vary in ways that are less predictable, but they are still easy to recognize.

| problème | orchestre | carotte | calculatrice |

Prononcez Répétez les mots suivants à voix haute.

1. tigre
2. bleu
3. lettre
4. salade
5. poème
6. banane
7. tourisme
8. moniteur
9. pharmacie
10. écologiste
11. conducteur
12. anthropologie

Articulez Répétez les phrases suivantes à voix haute.

1. Ma cousine est vétérinaire.
2. Le moteur ne fonctionne pas.
3. À la banque, Carole paie par chèque.
4. Mon oncle écrit l'adresse sur l'enveloppe.
5. À la station-service, le mécanicien a réparé le moteur.

Dictons Répétez les dictons à voix haute.

On ne fait pas d'omelette sans casser des œufs.[2]

On reconnaît l'arbre à son fruit.[1]

[1] You can recognize a tree by its fruit.
[2] You can't make an omelet without breaking some eggs.

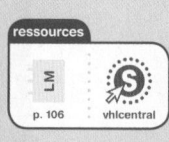

ressources

LM

p. 106 vhlcentral

cinq cent quatre-vingt-sept **587**

Section Goals

In this section, students will learn about:
- differences between French and English spelling
- various strategies for recognizing cognates

Instructional Resources
vhlcentral.com:
Textbook MP3s; Lab MP3s;
SAM Answer Key;
Textbook Audioscript;
Lab Audioscript;
reference tools

Suggestions
- Point out that all the words in the explanation section are cognates.
- Model the pronunciation of the example words and have students repeat them after you.
- Ask students to provide more examples of French words that are spelled only slightly differently from their English counterparts. Examples: **allergie, journaliste, spécialiste, géographie, économie, appartement, couleur, développer,** and **espace.**
- Point out that English adjectives ending in -ous often end in **-eux** in the masculine form and **-euse** in the feminine form in French. Examples: **nerveux/nerveuse, curieux/curieuse,** and **sérieux/sérieuse.**
- Explain that words that end in -al in English often end in **-el** in French. Examples: **naturel, personnel, culturel,** and **fraternel.**
- Explain that English words that end in -ory may end in **-oire** in French. Examples: **histoire, laboratoire,** and **victoire.**
- Ask students to think of additional French words that follow these patterns.

O P T I O N S

Extra Practice Use these words for additional practice or dictation. **1.** anxieux **2.** essentiel **3.** délicieuse **4.** environnement **5.** intellectuel **6.** serveuse **7.** journaliste **8.** développer **9.** exercice **10.** distributeur

Extra Practice Teach students these French tongue-twisters that contain French words that are similar to English words. **1.** Papier, panier, piano **2.** Un généreux déjeuner régénérerait des généraux dégénérés.

ESPACE ROMAN-PHOTO

NATIONAL communication cultures STANDARDS

Une idée de génie Video

Section Goals

In this section, students will learn functional phrases for talking about necessities, asking for opinions, and expressing denial.

Instructional Resources
vhlcentral.com:
Roman-photo Video, Videoscript, and Translation; SAM Answer Key; reference tools

Video Recap: Leçon 13B
Review the previous **Roman-photo** with this activity.
1. Pourquoi Sandrine est-elle anxieuse? (à cause de son concert)
2. Que propose Amina? (de lui faire une jolie robe)
3. Pourquoi Stéphane n'est-il pas content? (Il doit repasser une partie du bac.)
4. Qu'a demandé Michèle à Valérie? (une augmentation de salaire)
5. Qu'est-ce que Michèle a décidé de faire finalement? (Elle a démissionné.)

Video Synopsis
Valérie asks Stéphane to recycle some bottles and plastic packaging. Amina wants to know where Michèle is. Valérie explains that she quit. David announces that he has to return home to the States in three weeks. To cheer everyone up, Rachid suggests a weekend trip to **la montagne Sainte-Victoire**. They all agree that it's a great idea.

Suggestions
• Have students scan the captions to find sentences related to ecology and the environment.
• After reading the **Roman-photo**, have students summarize the episode.

PERSONNAGES

Amina

David

Rachid

Sandrine

Stéphane

Valérie

Au P'tit Bistrot...
VALÉRIE Stéphane, mon chéri, tu peux porter ces bouteilles en verre à recycler, s'il te plaît?
STÉPHANE Oui, bien sûr, maman.
VALÉRIE Oh, et puis, ces emballages en plastique aussi.
STÉPHANE Oui, je m'en occupe tout de suite.

RACHID ET AMINA Bonjour, Madame Forestier!
VALÉRIE Bonjour à vous deux.
AMINA Où est Michèle?
VALÉRIE Je n'en sais rien.
RACHID Mais elle ne travaille pas aujourd'hui?
VALÉRIE Non, elle ne vient ni aujourd'hui, ni demain, ni la semaine prochaine.

AMINA Elle est en vacances?
VALÉRIE Elle a démissionné.
RACHID Mais pourquoi?
AMINA Ça ne nous regarde pas!
VALÉRIE Oh, ça va, je peux vous le dire. Michèle voulait un autre travail.
RACHID Quelle sorte de travail?
VALÉRIE Plus celui-ci... Elle voulait une augmentation, ce n'était pas possible.

DAVID Madame Forestier, vous avez entendu la nouvelle? Je rentre aux États-Unis.
VALÉRIE Tu repars aux États-Unis?
DAVID Dans trois semaines.
VALÉRIE Il te reste très peu de temps à Aix, alors!
SANDRINE Oui. On sait.
DAVID Il faut que nous passions le reste de mon séjour de bonne humeur, hein?

RACHID Ah, mais vraiment, tout le monde a l'air triste aujourd'hui!
AMINA Oui. Pensons à quelque chose pour améliorer la situation. Tu as une idée?
RACHID Oui, peut-être.
AMINA Dis-moi! (Il lui parle à l'oreille.) Excellente idée!
RACHID Tu crois? Tu es sûre? Bon... Écoutez, j'ai une idée.

DAVID C'est quoi, ton idée?
RACHID Tout le monde a l'air triste aujourd'hui. Si on allait au mont Sainte-Victoire ce week-end. Ça vous dit?
DAVID Oui! J'aimerais bien y aller. J'adore dessiner en plein air.

ACTIVITÉS

1 **Les événements** Remettez ces événements dans l'ordre chronologique.

_6_ a. David dit qu'il part dans trois semaines.

_3_ b. Valérie explique que Michèle ne travaille plus au P'tit Bistrot.

_9_ c. Amina dit qu'elle veut aller à la montagne Sainte-Victoire ce week-end.

_1_ d. Stéphane va porter les bouteilles et les emballages à recycler.

_2_ e. Amina veut savoir où est Michèle.

_4_ f. David dit au groupe ce qu'il a lu dans le journal.

_5_ g. Sandrine semble (seems) avoir le trac.

_10_ h. Ils décident de passer le week-end tous ensemble.

_8_ i. Rachid essaie de remonter le moral à ses amis.

_7_ j. David console Sandrine.

Practice more at vhlcentral.com.

OPTIONS

Avant de regarder la vidéo Based on the title **Une idée de génie** and video still 7, have students guess what idea Rachid might be suggesting to Amina and why he is suggesting it.

Regarder la vidéo Show the first half of the video episode and have students describe what happened. Write their observations on the board. Then ask them to guess what will happen in the second half of the episode. Write their ideas on the board. Show the entire episode and have students confirm or correct their predictions.

Rachid propose une excursion en montagne.

DAVID Bonjour, tout le monde. Vous avez lu le journal ce matin? Il faut que je vous parle de cet article sur la pollution. J'ai appris beaucoup de choses au sujet des pluies acides, du trou dans la couche d'ozone, de l'effet de serre...
AMINA Oh, David, la barbe.
RACHID Allez, assieds-toi et déjeune avec nous.

Un peu plus tard...
RACHID Ton concert est dans une semaine, n'est-ce pas Sandrine?
SANDRINE Oui.
RACHID Qu'est-ce que tu vas chanter?
SANDRINE Écoute, Rachid, je n'ai pas vraiment envie de parler de ça.

SANDRINE Oui, peut-être...
AMINA Allez! Ça nous fera du bien! Adieu pollution de la ville. À nous, l'air pur de la campagne! Qu'en penses-tu, Sandrine?
SANDRINE Bon, d'accord.

AMINA Super! Et vous, Madame Forestier? Vous et Stéphane avez besoin de vous reposer aussi, vous devez absolument venir avec nous!
VALÉRIE En effet, je crois que c'est une excellente idée!

Expressions utiles

Talking about necessities
- **Il faut que je vous parle de cet article sur la pollution.**
  I have to tell you about this article on pollution.
- **Il faut que nous passions le reste de mon séjour de bonne humeur.**
  We have to spend the rest of my stay in a good mood.

Getting someone's opinion
- **Qu'en penses-tu?**
  What do you think (about that)?
- **Je pense que...**
  I think that...

Expressing denial
- **Je n'en sais rien.**
  I have no idea.
- **Ça ne nous regarde pas.**
  That's none of our business.
- **Quelle sorte de travail? Plus celui-ci.**
  What kind of job? Not this one anymore.

Additional vocabulary
- **au sujet de**
  about
- **Adieu!**
  Farewell!
- **Il te reste très peu de temps.**
  You don't have much time left.
- **en effet**
  indeed/in fact
- **je crois**
  I think/believe
- **Ça te/vous dit?**
  Does that appeal to you?

 2 **Répondez** Répondez à ces questions par des phrases complètes.

1. Que se passe-t-il avec Sandrine? Elle est nerveuse avant son concert et elle est triste parce que David part dans trois semaines.
2. Qu'est-ce qu'Amina croit (*believe*) qu'il se passe avec Michèle? Elle croit que Michèle est peut-être en vacances.
3. Pourquoi Rachid veut-il aller à la montagne Sainte-Victoire? Il trouve que ses amis ont l'air triste et il veut les aider à changer d'humeur.
4. À votre avis, qu'est-ce que David a appris après avoir lu le journal? Answers will vary.

3 **Écrivez** Imaginez comment se passera le week-end du groupe d'amis à la montagne Sainte-Victoire. Composez un paragraphe qui explique comment ils vont y aller, ce qu'ils y feront, s'ils s'amuseront...

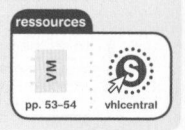
ressources
VM pp. 53–54
vhlcentral

A C T I V I T É S

Expressions utiles
- Model the pronunciation of the **Expressions utiles** and have students repeat them after you.
- As you work through the list, point out forms of the present subjunctive with impersonal expressions and demonstrative pronouns. Tell students that these grammar points will be formally presented in **Espace structures**.
- Respond briefly to questions about the present subjunctive and demonstrative pronouns. Reinforce correct forms, but do not expect students to produce them consistently at this time.
- Point out the different meanings of the word **reste**. Write these sentences and phrases on the board and have students translate them. **1. Il reste des pommes.** (*There are some apples left.*) **2. Il reste là.** (*He stays there.*) **3. Il me reste cinq euros.** (*I have five euros left.*) **4. le reste de la famille** (*the rest of the family*)

1 Suggestion Have students work in groups of five. Make a set of individual sentences on strips of paper for each group and distribute them (two sentences per student). Tell students to arrange the sentences in the proper order and read them aloud.

2 Suggestion Have volunteers write the answers on the board. Go over them with the class.

2 Expansion For additional practice, ask students: **Qu'est-ce que le groupe d'amis veut faire à la montagne Sainte-Victoire?** (David veut dessiner en plein air, Amina veut respirer l'air pur et Valérie veut se reposer.)

3 Suggestion Before beginning the activity, have students brainstorm a list of activities the group might do at **la montagne Sainte-Victoire**. Write them on the board.

OPTIONS

Extra Practice Ask volunteers to ad-lib the **Roman-photo** episode for the class. Tell them it is not necessary to memorize the episode. They should just try to get the general meaning across with the vocabulary they know. Give them time to prepare or have them do their skit as a review activity during the next class period.

Extra Practice Have students write two sentences that a character in this **Roman-photo** episode would say. Tell them they can look at the text for ideas, but they shouldn't copy sentences word for word. Then have volunteers read their sentences aloud. The class has to guess who would say them.

Section Goals

In this section, students will:
- learn about the ecological movement and environmental concerns in France
- learn some ecological terms
- learn about ecotourism in the francophone world
- read about nuclear power in France

Instructional Resources
vhlcentral.com:
reference tools

Culture à la loupe
Avant la lecture Have students look at the photo of the Green Party protest and describe what they see. Point out the words on the flag «**les verts**». Ask students to guess what it means.

Lecture
- France was a pioneer in **l'agriculture biologique** during the 1980s. Organic production in France then slowed, while it increased elsewhere in Europe. French organic production has been back on the rise since the late 1990s.
- Some of the steps the French government has taken in regard to environmental concerns are: **le Grenelle de l'environnement** (series of meetings begun in 2007 that have led to the passage of new laws), **les crédits d'impôts** (tax deduction for people who have energy-saving work done on their house), **les bonus (ou malus) écologiques** (depending on what car a person buys).
- Point out the statistics chart. Ask students what information it shows. (the percentages of French people who are concerned about the environmental problems listed)

Après la lecture Ask students: **Quelles similitudes et quelles différences pouvez-vous trouver entre l'attitude française et l'attitude américaine concernant l'environnement?**

1 **Suggestion** Have students read the completed sentences aloud.

 Reading

CULTURE À LA LOUPE

L'écologie

l'agriculture française

une manifestation° des Verts

Le mouvement écologique a commencé en France dans les années 1970, mais ne s'est réellement développé que dans les années 1980. Ce sont surtout les crises majeures comme le nuage de Tchernobyl en 1986, la destruction de la couche d'ozone, l'effet de serre et les marées noires° qui ont réveillé la conscience écologique des Français. Le désir de préserver la qualité de la vie et les espaces naturels s'est développé en même temps.

Aujourd'hui, l'environnement n'est pas le sujet d'inquiétude° numéro un des Français. L'emploi, la baisse des revenus° et l'avenir des retraites les préoccupent° plus. Pourtant, le score aux élections du parti écologique des Verts est en hausse° depuis 1999 et on considère que le parti des Verts est le deuxième parti de gauche.

De manière générale, les problèmes liés à° l'environnement qui retiennent° le plus l'attention des Français sont la pollution atmosphérique des villes, la pollution de l'eau, le réchauffement du climat et la prolifération des déchets nucléaires. Pour l'opinion publique, le plus urgent à régler est la qualité de l'eau. En effet, à cause de° l'agriculture française, les taux° de nitrates et de phosphates dans l'eau sont presque partout largement supérieurs à la normale. Depuis la crise de la vache folle°, les Français sont aussi sensibles aux menaces alimentaires°. Les cultures OGM° ont porté le débat écologique dans les assiettes.

Les inquiétudes sur l'environnement

• les Français qui s'opposent à la culture de plantes génétiquement modifiées	79%
• les Français qui sont préoccupés par la pollution de l'air et de l'eau	54%
• les Français qui s'inquiètent de plus en plus des changements climatiques	40%
• les Français qui sont préoccupés par les problèmes de qualité du cadre de vie°: urbanisation en augmentation, pollution sonore°, disparition des paysages°, etc.	37%

marées noires *oil spills* **inquiétude** *concern* **baisse des revenus** *lowering of incomes* **préoccupent** *worry* **en hausse** *on the rise* **liés à** *linked to* **retiennent** *hold* **régler** *solve* **à cause de** *because of* **taux** *levels* **vache folle** *mad cow* **menaces alimentaires** *food-related threats* **OGM (organismes génétiquement modifiés)** *GMO (genetically modified organisms)* **cadre de vie** *living environment* **pollution sonore** *noise pollution* **disparition des paysages** *changing landscapes* **manifestation** *demonstration*

A C T I V I T É S

1 **Complétez** Complétez les phrases.

1. Le mouvement écologique s'est développé _dans les années 1980_.

2. Les crises majeures comme _le nuage de Tchernobyl, la destruction de la couche d'ozone, l'effet de serre et les marées noires_ ont réveillé la conscience écologique des Français.

3. _L'environnement_ n'est pas la principale préoccupation des Français.

4. _Les problèmes d'emploi, la baisse des revenus et l'avenir des retraites_ préoccupent plus les Français.

5. Le score aux élections du parti écologique des Verts est _en hausse depuis 1999_.

6. Pour les Français, le problème écologique le plus urgent à régler est _la qualité de l'eau_.

7. À cause de l'agriculture, _les taux de nitrates et de phosphates dans l'eau_ sont presque partout largement supérieurs à la normale.

8. 70 à 80% des Français sont préoccupés _par la pollution de l'air et de l'eau_.

9. 66% des Français s'opposent _à la culture de plantes génétiquement modifiées_.

10. _40% des Français_ s'inquiètent de plus en plus des changements climatiques.

O P T I O N S

Pairs Write the following list of problems on the board: **la pollution de l'eau, la pollution de l'air, les changements climatiques, l'emploi, l'urbanisation, les cultures OGM, l'avenir des retraites**, and **les marées noires**. Tell students to take turns making comparisons based on the information in the reading. Example: **La catastrophe des marées noires est moins importante pour les Français que l'emploi.**

Extra Practice Have a class debate. Divide the class into two groups. Assign each group one of these positions: **Il est important de protéger l'environnement. / Il est important de développer l'économie et l'emploi.** Allow groups time to prepare their arguments before staging the debate. You may also divide the class into four groups and have two debates going on at the same time.

Le français quotidien
- Model the pronunciation of each term and have students repeat it. Point out that **bio** is short for **biologique**.
- Have volunteers create sentences using this vocabulary.

Portrait Ask students: **Y a-t-il une centrale nucléaire près de chez vous? Voudriez-vous habiter près d'une centrale nucléaire? Y a-t-il un problème avec les déchets nucléaires aux États-Unis?**

Le monde francophone After reading the text, take a quick class survey to find out which are the most popular ecotourism destinations. Example: **Combien d'étudiants aimeraient faire de l'écotourisme en Afrique du Nord?** Tally the results on the board.

2 Expansion For additional practice, give students these items. **6. Quand a eu lieu la catastrophe nucléaire à Tchernobyl? (en 1986) 7. Quel pourcentage des déchets nucléaires ne sont pas traitables en France? (10 pour cent) 8. Où peut-on faire de l'écotourisme en Afrique du Nord? (dans le désert du Sahara, en Algérie, au Maroc et en Tunisie) 9. Où peut-on faire de l'écotourisme dans une forêt tropicale? (à la Guadeloupe et en Guyane française)**

3 Suggestion Give students time to review the material on both pages and jot down some ideas before they begin their discussion.

LE FRANÇAIS QUOTIDIEN

L'écologie

agriculture (f.) bio	organic farming
bac (m.) de recyclage	recycling bin
écologiste (m., f.)	ecologist
énergie (f.) éolienne	wind power
énergie (f.) renouvelable	renewable energy
panneau (m.) solaire	solar panel
produit (m.) bio	organic product
seuil (m.) de tolérance	threshold

LE MONDE FRANCOPHONE

L'écotourisme

Voici quelques destinations francophones de l'écotourisme.

En Afrique du Nord avec le désert du Sahara, en Algérie, au Maroc et en Tunisie

À la Guadeloupe avec le volcan de la Soufrière, ses nombreuses cascades° et ses forêts tropicales

En Guyane française avec sa forêt tropicale humide qui couvre 90% du pays

Au Québec avec sa géographie variée, ses communautés indigènes° et ses trois réserves de biosphère

Aux Seychelles les 115 îles de l'archipel, avec leurs nombreuses réserves naturelles et leurs récifs de corail°

Au Viêt-nam le delta du Mékong, avec son paysage de canaux° et ses cultures de riz

cascades waterfalls **indigènes** native **récifs de corail** coral reefs
canaux canals

PORTRAIT

L'énergie nucléaire

En France, l'électricité d'origine nucléaire est la principale énergie produite et consommée: en effet, le nucléaire produit 75 à 80% de l'électricité. C'est EDF (Électricité de France) qui a construit les premières centrales du pays dans les années 1950. La production d'énergie d'origine nucléaire est plus largement développée à partir de 1974, au lendemain du premier choc pétrolier°. Aujourd'hui, le pays possède 58 réacteurs et une usine de traitement°, Areva NC, située à La Hague, dans le nord-ouest du pays. Les déchets radioactifs de France, d'Europe et d'Asie y sont traités°. La France est un exemple de réussite en ce qui concerne l'énergie nucléaire, mais sa population est inquiète. L'explosion de Tchernobyl en 1986 a démontré les risques d'accidents dans les centrales. Dix pour cent des déchets, dits «à vie longue»,  ne sont pas traitables° et deviennent un problème de santé publique. C'est pourquoi le rôle des énergies renouvelables ne peut donc qu'augmenter à l'avenir. Ces «énergies propres», ou «énergies vertes», proviennent° de sources que la nature renouvelle en permanence: elles sont inépuisables° à l'échelle° du temps humain. Elles sont issues de plusieurs grandes sources naturelles comme le soleil (solaire), l'eau (hydraulique), le vent (éolienne°) ou encore la terre (géothermique).

choc pétrolier oil crisis **usine de traitement** treatment plant **traités** treated
ne sont pas traitables are not treatable **proviennent** come from
inépuisables inexhaustible **à l'échelle** on the scale **éolienne** wind power

---

2 Répondez Répondez aux questions d'après les textes.

1. En France, quelle quantité d'électricité le nucléaire produit-il?
   Le nucléaire produit 75% à 80% de l'électricité en France.
2. Qui a construit les premières centrales françaises?
   EDF (Électricité de France) a construit les premières centrales françaises.
3. Les Français sont-ils satisfaits du nucléaire?
   Non, en majorité, ils sont inquiets.
4. Quelles sont les grandes sources d'énergies renouvelables? Les grandes sources d'énergies renouvelables sont le soleil, l'eau, le vent ou encore la terre.
5. Où peut-on faire de l'écotourisme au Québec?
   On peut faire de l'écotourisme dans les trois réserves de biosphère.

3 Nucléaire et environnement Vous travaillez pour Areva NC et votre partenaire est un(e) militant(e) écologiste. Imaginez ensemble un dialogue où vous parlez de vos opinions pour et contre l'usage (use) de l'énergie nucléaire en France. Soyez prêt(e)s à jouer votre dialogue devant la classe.

 Practice more at vhlcentral.com.

A C T I V I T É S

OPTIONS

Areva NC Based in La Hague (Normandy), **Areva NC** reprocesses spent power reactor fuel in order to recycle uranium and plutonium and to condition the waste. **Areva NC** has been criticized for its disposal of radioactive waste in the English Channel and in the air. The site in La Hague houses the world's largest stockpile of separated plutonium.

Les énergies renouvelables The windmill (**le moulin à vent**) has existed in Europe since the twelfth century. Today it has evolved into the powerful wind turbine (**l'éolienne moderne**), which owes its technology to the aviation industry. Other renewable energy sources include solar energy (**l'énergie solaire**), hydroelectric power (**l'énergie hydroélectrique**), and geothermal energy (**l'énergie géothermique**).

Section Goals

In this section, students will learn:

- the demonstrative pronouns **celui**, **celle**, **ceux**, and **celles**
- to use **-ci** and **-là** with forms of **celui**

Instructional Resources

vhlcentral.com:
Activity Pack; Lab MP3s;
*SAM Answer Key; **Essayez!***
*and **Mise en pratique***
answers; Lab Audioscript;
reference tools

Suggestions

- Tell the class that adjectives modifying forms of **celui** agree in gender and number. Use the **Point de départ** example. Past participles also agree in gender and number with any preceding direct object form of **celui**. Example: **La centrale nucléaire de Belleville est celle qu'on a vue à la télé cet après-midi.**
- Make sure students understand that forms of **celui** in relative clauses can be used with the relative pronoun **dont**. Example: **La voiture hybride est celle dont on parle le plus.**
- When using forms of **celui** in prepositional phrases, make sure students understand how possession can be expressed with the construction **celui de** + *a person's name*: **Quel sac cherches-tu? Celui d'Isabelle.**
- Have the class play a guessing game about articles in the classroom (such as clothing and school supplies). Say phrases with the construction **celui de** + [*a person's name*]. Students should respond with an antecedent for your statement. Examples: **Celui de Shayne est bleu. (le tee-shirt) Celles de Roger sont noires. (les lunettes)**

Essayez! Give students some additional items. For example: **9. La population de l'Inde est croissante. (Celle / Celui) de la Russie est en déclin. (Celle)**

Leçon 14A

 **ESPACE STRUCTURES**

14A.1

Demonstrative pronouns  Tutorial

Point de départ In **Leçon 6A**, you learned how to use demonstrative adjectives. Demonstrative *pronouns* refer to a person or thing that has already been mentioned. Examples of English demonstrative pronouns include *this one* and *those*.

> **Boîte à outils**
>
> Notice that adjectives agree in number and gender with the forms of **celui** they modify. Past participles also agree in number and gender with any preceding direct object form of **celui**. Example: **Cette usine est celle qu'on a vue à la télé hier.**

La voiture qui coûte moins cher est plus dangereuse pour l'environnement.
The car that costs less is more dangerous for the environment.

Celle qui coûte moins cher est plus dangereuse pour l'environnement.
The one that costs less is more dangerous for the environment.

Les produits que tu développes sont très importants.
The products that you're developing are very important.

Ceux que tu développes sont très importants.
The ones that you're developing are very important.

- Demonstrative pronouns agree in number and gender with the noun to which they refer.

Demonstrative pronouns				
	singular		**plural**	
masculine	**celui**	*this one; that one; the one*	**ceux**	*these; those; the ones*
feminine	**celle**	*this one; that one; the one*	**celles**	*these; those; the ones*

- Demonstrative pronouns must be followed by one of three constructions: **-ci** or **-là**, a relative clause, or a prepositional phrase.

-ci; -là	**Quels emballages? Ceux-ci?** *Which packages? These here?*	**Quelle bouteille? Celle-là, en verre?** *Which bottle? The glass one there?*
relative clause	**Quelle femme? Celle qui parle?** *Which woman? The one who's talking?*	**Henri Rouet? C'est celui qu'on a entendu à la radio.** *Henri Rouet? He's the one we heard on the radio.*
prepositional phrase	**Quel pull veux-tu? Celui de ton frère?** *Which sweatshirt do you want? Your brother's?*	**Ces sacs coûtent plus cher que ceux en papier.** *Those bags cost more than the paper ones.*

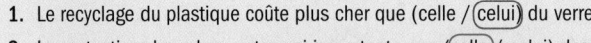 **Essayez!** **Choisissez le pronom démonstratif correct.**

1. Le recyclage du plastique coûte plus cher que (celle / (celui)) du verre.
2. La protection des arbres est aussi importante que ((celle) / celui) des animaux.
3. Les espaces verts sont ((ceux) / celles) dont on a le plus besoin en ville.
4. Les ordures les plus sales sont ((ceux) / celles) des industries.
5. De tous les problèmes écologiques, l'effet de serre est ((celui) / ceux) dont on parle le plus.
6. Quels sacs préfères-tu: ((ceux) / celui)-ci?
7. Les bouteilles en verre sont-elles plus écologiques que (ceux / (celles)) en plastique?
8. Le gaspillage de l'eau n'est pas plus excusable que ((celui) / celle) de l'électricité.

> **ressources**
>
> WB
> pp. 191–192
>
> LM
> p. 107
>
>
> vhlcentral

592 *cinq cent quatre-vingt-douze*

Le français vivant

L'île de Corse

Celle qui a les plus belles plages de la Méditerranée. Tous ceux qui habitent ce paradis sont fiers de le partager avec tous ceux qui leur rendent visite. Celui qui vient en Corse une fois y reviendra toujours.

beautécorse

Identifiez Quels pronoms démonstratifs trouvez-vous dans la publicité (*ad*)? Celle, ceux, Celui

 Questions À tour de rôle, avec un(e) partenaire, posez-vous ces questions. **Employez des pronoms démonstratifs dans vos réponses, si possible.** Some answers will vary.

1. D'après (*According to*) la pub, quelles sont les plus belles plages de la Méditerranée? celles de la Corse
2. Qui est fier de partager la Corse? tous ceux qui y habitent
3. Que veut celui qui vient une fois en Corse? Celui qui vient en Corse veut y revenir.
4. Y a-t-il un endroit dans le monde qui a eu cet effet sur toi? Lequel? Answers will vary.
5. Voudrais-tu visiter la Corse un jour? Pourquoi? Answers will vary.

cinq cent quatre-vingt-treize 593

OPTIONS

Extra Practice Have the class identify all the nouns in **Espace contextes**, pages 584–585. Then tell students to work in pairs to write a couple of sentences in which nouns from the list are replaced with forms of **celui**. Example: **des déchets toxiques (Ceux des usines de Sugar Land sont-ils dangereux?)**

Game Make up a set of enigmatic sentences using forms of **celui**. The sentences should contain enough clues to suggest an antecedent. Tell students to guess at possible antecedents for each sentence and encourage them to be creative. Example: **Ceux de Jennifer Lawrence sont blonds. (les cheveux)**

Le français vivant Hand out or have students copy the text in the advertisement. Tell them to underline the demonstrative pronouns. Then ask them what they think the antecedents are.

1 **Suggestion** You might want to have students complete items 1, 3, and 4 first. Then remind them of the suffixes **-ci** and **-là** before proceeding to the remaining items.

2 **Suggestion** Remind students that French speakers usually refer to a near object with **-ci** before referring to a far object with **-là** in the same sentence.

3 **Suggestion** Have two volunteers read the **modèle** aloud to the class. Then review forms of the relative pronoun **lequel**. Make sure students understand the different ways **lequel** and **celui** are used.

Mise en pratique

1 **Le marché aux puces** Vous êtes au marché aux puces (*flea market*) pour trouver des cadeaux. Complétez les phrases avec des pronoms démonstratifs.

1. Ce magnifique vase bleu, je pense que c'est ____celui____ que maman voulait.
2. Ces deux jolis sacs: ____celui-ci____ est pour Sylvie et ____celui-là____ est pour Soraya.
3. Cette casquette rouge est pour moi. Elle ressemble à ____celle____ de Françoise.
4. Il y avait des boîtes pleines de livres anciens. ____Ceux____ que j'ai achetés étaient les plus beaux.
5. J'adore ces deux affiches. ____Celle-ci____ est pour Julien et ____celle-là____ est pour André.
6. Nous allons acheter un nouveau vélo. ____Celui____ de Julien est trop vieux!
7. Tu aimes ces bottes-ci ou préfères-tu ____celles____ -là?
8. Ces pulls coûtent trop cher! ____Ceux____ que Stéphane a choisis sont mieux.

2 **Entretien** Camille doit passer un entretien et elle parle à sa copine Alice. Ajoutez des pronoms démonstratifs avec **-ci** et **-là**. Some answers will vary.

CAMILLE Qu'est-ce que je peux mettre pour cet entretien? J'ai plusieurs tailleurs sympas.

ALICE Ces deux tailleurs gris font sérieux. Tu devrais plutôt mettre (1) ____celui-là____. Il est élégant et classique.

CAMILLE Et comme chemisier, qu'est-ce que je mets?.

ALICE (2) ____Celui-ci____ est joli, mais (3) ____celui-là____ ira mieux avec le style de ton tailleur.

CAMILLE Tu penses que je devrais mettre ces chaussures-ci ou (4) ____celles-là____?

ALICE (5) ____Celles-ci____ sont très à la mode mais (6) ____celles-là____ sont plus classiques.

3 **Cadeau d'anniversaire** C'est bientôt l'anniversaire d'Houda et vous discutez avec un(e) partenaire des cadeaux que vous pourriez lui offrir. Refaites leur conversation. Answers will vary.

> **MODÈLE** des tee-shirts / plus joli
>
> **Étudiant(e) 1:** *Tu aimes ce tee-shirt?*
> **Étudiant(e) 2:** *Non, pas trop.*
> **Étudiant(e) 1:** *Alors, lequel préfères-tu?*
> **Étudiant(e) 2:** *Je préfère celui-ci. Il est plus joli.*

- des robes / élégant
- des lunettes de soleil / trop cher
- des CD / plus classique
- des livres / très intéressant

 Practice more at **vhlcentral.com**.

Communication

4 **Suggestion** Have students draw pictures like those in children's books to accompany their definitions.

4 **Définitions** Votre petit frère vous demande de lui expliquer ces expressions. Avec un(e) partenaire, alternez les rôles pour donner leurs définitions. Utilisez **celui qui, celle qui, ceux qui** ou **celles qui.** Answers will vary.

> **MODÈLE** un pollueur
>
> **Étudiant(e) 1:** Qu'est-ce que c'est, un pollueur?
> **Étudiant(e) 2:** C'est celui qui laisse des papiers sales dans la rue.

- les déchets toxiques
- un(e) écologiste
- un écoproduit
- l'énergie solaire
- une loi
- la pluie acide
- une usine
- les voitures hybrides

5 **Expansion** Introduce students to a concept of personal responsibility from existentialism: **la mauvaise foi.** A person that acts in **mauvaise foi** behaves in a way that is inconsistent with his or her true beliefs. Ask the class to categorize certain behaviors as a **politique de bonne foi** or a **politique de mauvaise foi** for an environmentalist. Examples: **le covoiturage (bonne foi)** and **promouvoir le covoiturage, mais aller seul(e) au travail avec une grosse voiture (mauvaise foi).**

5 **La pollution** Que pensent vos camarades de la pollution? Posez ces questions à un(e) partenaire. Ensuite, présentez les réponses à la classe. Utilisez **celui, celle, ceux** ou **celles.** Answers will vary.

1. Quelles voitures polluent le moins: les voitures hybrides ou les voitures de sport? Lesquelles préfères-tu?
2. Connais-tu quelqu'un qui fait régulièrement du covoiturage? Qui? Pourquoi le fait-il/elle?
3. Les emballages en plastique polluent-ils plus que ceux en papier? Pourquoi?
4. Est-ce que ceux qui recyclent leurs déchets aident à préserver la nature? Pourquoi?
5. Quelles usines sont mauvaises pour l'environnement? Pourquoi?
6. À votre avis, le gouvernement doit-il passer des lois pour arrêter le gaspillage? Quelles sortes de lois?
7. Quelles solutions proposez-vous pour sauver la planète?
8. Parmi (*Among*) les pays industrialisés, lesquels polluent le plus? Lesquels polluent le moins?

6 **Expansion** Have groups select a topic from the list and prepare a small debate. Regardless of their personal beliefs, one student should advocate **d'accord** and the other **pas d'accord.**

6 **D'accord, pas d'accord** Par groupes de quatre, faites ce sondage (*survey*). Qui est d'accord ou qui n'est pas d'accord avec ces phrases? Justifiez vos réponses. Ensuite, comparez-les avec celles d'un autre groupe. Answers will vary.

	D'accord	Pas d'accord
1. Les déchets toxiques d'une centrale nucléaire sont plus dangereux que ceux d'une centrale électrique.	____	____
2. Les sacs en plastique sont aussi facilement recyclables que ceux en papier.	____	____
3. En ce qui concerne la voiture du futur, la voiture hybride est celle dont on parle le plus.	____	____
4. Les déchets qui polluent le plus sont ceux des centrales nucléaires.	____	____

Extra Practice Have small groups of students prepare a fashion outlook for the season. They should make collages with pictures from magazines or the Internet of the latest styles and tell the class what they think of them, using forms of the demonstrative pronoun **celui** whenever possible. Example: **Ce jean-ci est laid! J'aime mieux celui-là.**

Extra Practice Make a set of index cards, organized in pairs with two similar objects, one on each card. Then prompt students to evaluate the objects with questions using forms of **lequel** and **celui.** Example: (*two pictures of cars*) **Laquelle pollue moins, à votre avis? Celle-ci ou celle-là? (La voiture rouge!)**

Section Goals

In this section, students will learn:
- the present subjunctive of regular verbs
- to use the subjunctive after some impersonal expressions

Instructional Resources
vhlcentral.com:
Activity Pack; Lab MP3s;
SAM Answer Key; **Essayez!**
and **Mise en pratique** *answers;*
Lab Audioscript; reference tools

Suggestion Tell the class that to negate impersonal expressions they should place the negative particles around the conjugated verb in the indicative, not around the subjunctive verb that follows in the next clause. Example: **Il ne faut pas qu'elle mette ces ordures dans le bac à recyclage.**

14A.2

The subjunctive (Part 1) Tutorial

Introduction, regular verbs, and impersonal expressions

Point de départ With the exception of commands and the conditional, the verb forms you have learned have been in the indicative mood. The indicative is used to state facts and to express actions or states that the speaker considers real and definite. In contrast, the subjunctive mood expresses the speaker's subjective attitudes toward events and actions or presents the speaker's views as uncertain or hypothetical.

Present subjunctive of one-stem verbs			
	parler	**finir**	**attendre**
que je/j'	parle	finisse	attende
que tu	parles	finisses	attendes
qu'il/elle/on	parle	finisse	attende
que nous	parlions	finissions	attendions
que vous	parliez	finissiez	attendiez
qu'ils/elles	parlent	finissent	attendent

- The **je**, **tu**, **il/elle/on**, and **ils/elles** forms of the three verb types form the subjunctive the same way. They add the subjunctive endings to the stem of the **ils/elles** form of the present indicative.

INFINITIVE	PRESENT INDICATIVE OF ILS/ELLES	PRESENT SUBJUNCTIVE
parler	**parlent**	**que je parle**
finir	**finissent**	**que je finisse**
attendre	**attendent**	**que j'attende**

Il est nécessaire qu'on **évite** le gaspillage.
It is necessary for us to avoid waste.

Il est important qu'elle **réfléchisse** aux dangers.
It's important that she thinks about the dangers.

Il faut qu'elles **finissent** leurs devoirs.
They must finish their homework.

Il est essentiel que je **vende** ma voiture.
It is essential that I sell my car.

Il est bon qu'il **attende** à l'école.
It's good that he's waiting at school.

Il est nécessaire que tu **proposes** une solution.
It's necessary for you to propose a solution.

- The **nous** and **vous** forms of the present subjunctive are the same as those of the **imparfait**.

Il vaut mieux que nous **préservions** l'environnement.
It's better that we preserve the environment.

Il est essentiel que vous **trouviez** un meilleur travail.
It is essential that you find a better job.

Il faut que nous **commencions**.
It is necessary for us to start.

Il est bon que vous **réfléchissiez**.
It's good that you're thinking.

Il est essentiel que nous lui **parlions** tout de suite.
It is essential that we talk to him immediately.

Il est dommage que vous n'**étudiiez** pas l'allemand.
It's too bad that you don't study German.

🏃 Boîte à outils

English also uses the subjunctive. It used to be very common, but now survives mostly in expressions such as *if I were you* and *be that as it may.*

À noter

Remember that verbs ending in **-ier** have a double **i** in the **nous** and **vous** forms of the present subjunctive: **étudiiez**, **skiions**, etc. You learned this in **Leçon 8A** with the **imparfait**.

Suggestions
• Emphasize to students that the expressions **il faut** and **il vaut mieux** can be followed directly by an infinitive, while the other expressions in the list are followed by **de/d'** + *infinitive.* Examples: **Il vaut mieux partager sa voiture de temps en temps. Il est nécessaire de partager sa voiture de temps en temps.**
• Read aloud a set of logical and illogical statements about environmentalism that make use of impersonal expressions and the subjunctive. Students should respond by saying **logique** or **illogique**. Example: **Pour éviter de gaspiller l'essence, il vaut mieux qu'on recycle le verre. (illogique)**

Essayez! Toss a tennis ball or a crumpled piece of paper to a student while saying a subject pronoun and the infinitive of a regular verb. He or she gives the present subjunctive form and tosses the object to another student while you call out another pronoun and infinitive.

• The verbs on the preceding page are called one-stem verbs because the same stem is used for all the endings. Two-stem verbs have a different stem for **nous** and **vous**, but their forms are still identical to those of the **imparfait**.

Present subjunctive of two-stem verbs

	acheter	venir	prendre	boire
que je/j'	achète	vienne	prenne	boive
que tu	achètes	viennes	prennes	boives
qu'il/elle/on	achète	vienne	prenne	boive
que nous	achetions	venions	prenions	buvions
que vous	achetiez	veniez	preniez	buviez
qu'ils/elles	achètent	viennent	prennent	boivent

• The subjunctive is usually used in complex sentences that consist of a main clause and a subordinate clause. The main clause contains a verb or expression that triggers the subjunctive. The word **que** connects the two clauses.

Il est important **que** nous **buvions** de l'eau propre.
It's important that we drink clean water.

Il faut **que** vous **preniez** vos médicaments.
You have to take your medicine.

• These impersonal expressions of opinion are often followed by clauses in the subjunctive. They are followed by the infinitive, without **que**, if no person or thing is specified. Add **de** before the infinitive after expressions with **être**.

Il est bon que...	*It is good that...*	**Il est indispensable que...**	*It is essential that...*
Il est dommage que...	*It is a shame that...*	**Il est nécessaire que...**	*It is necessary that...*
Il est essentiel que...	*It is essential that...*	**Il est possible que...**	*It is possible that...*
Il est important que...	*It is important that...*	**Il faut que...**	*One must.../It is necessary that...*
		Il vaut mieux que...	*It is better that...*

Il est important qu'on **réduise** le gaspillage.   *but*   **Il est important de réduire** le gaspillage.
It is important that we reduce waste.   *It is important to reduce waste.*

Il faut qu'on **ferme** l'usine.   *but*   **Il faut fermer** l'usine.
We must close the factory.   *The factory must be closed.*

Il vaut mieux qu'on **achète** des produits écologiques.   *but*   **Il vaut mieux acheter** des produits écologiques.
It's better that we buy ecological products.   *It's better to buy ecological products.*

Essayez!   Indiquez la forme correcte du présent du subjonctif de ces verbes.

1. (améliorer) que j' ___améliore___
2. (maigrir) que tu ___maigrisses___
3. (dire) qu'elle ___dise___
4. (attendre) que nous ___attendions___
5. (revenir) que nous ___revenions___
6. (apprendre) que vous ___appreniez___
7. (répéter) qu'ils ___répètent___
8. (choisir) qu'on ___choisisse___

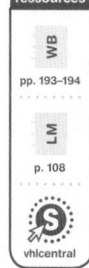

ressources
WB
pp. 193–194

LM
p. 108

vhlcentral

cinq cent quatre-vingt-dix-sept **597**

OPTIONS

Video Distribute copies of the script for the last scene of the **Leçon 14A** video and have students underline all the verbs. Ask them to identify the mood (indicative, imperative, or subjunctive) of each verb. When they realize that the subjunctive is used only rarely, point out that native speakers often avoid the subjunctive because it can be tricky for them, too.

Extra Practice Have the class make up a list of ten environmental resolutions using some of the impersonal expressions listed on this page. Help them when they need expressions such as *a recycling bin* (**un bac à recyclage**). Example: **Il est essentiel qu'on préserve la nature.**

Leçon 14A

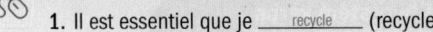

ESPACE **STRUCTURES**

Sidebar

1 Expansion To ensure students' comprehension, ask them to categorize each statement as **une responsabilité gouvernementale**, une **responsabilité personnelle**, or **les deux**.

2 Expansion Have students reformulate each answer so that the subject is **je/j'**. Then ask them **C'est vrai?** to confirm whether the statement is true for them personally. Example: **Le matin, il faut que je me lève à sept heures. (Ce n'est pas vrai! D'habitude, je me lève à neuf heures.)**

3 Suggestion Remind students to use each of the expressions in the columns at least once.

Main content

Mise en pratique

1 Prévenir et améliorer Complétez ces phrases avec la forme correcte des verbes au présent du subjonctif.

1. Il est essentiel que je ___recycle___ (recycler).
2. Il est important que nous ___réduisions___ (réduire) la pollution.
3. Il faut que le gouvernement ___interdise___ (interdire) les voitures polluantes (*polluting*).
4. Il vaut mieux que vous ___amélioriez___ (améliorer) les transports en commun (*public transportation*).
5. Il est possible que les pays ___prennent___ (prendre) des mesures pour réduire les déchets toxiques.
6. Il est indispensable que tu ___boives___ (boire) de l'eau pure.
7. Il est bon que vous ___proposiez___ (proposer) des solutions pour préserver la nature.
8. Il est dommage qu'on ___gaspille___ (gaspiller) de l'eau.

2 Sur le campus Quelles règles les étudiants qui habitent sur le campus doivent-ils suivre? Transformez ces phrases avec **il faut** et le présent du subjonctif.

MODÈLE
Vous devez vous coucher avant minuit.
Il faut que vous vous couchiez avant minuit.

1. Le matin, vous devez vous lever à sept heures.   Le matin, il faut que vous vous leviez à sept heures.
2. Ils doivent fermer leur porte avant de partir.   Il faut qu'ils ferment leur porte avant de partir.
3. Tu dois prendre le bus au coin de la rue.   Il faut que tu prennes le bus au coin de la rue.
4. Je dois déjeuner au resto U à midi.   Il faut que je déjeune au resto U à midi.
5. Nous devons rentrer tôt pendant la semaine.   Il faut que nous rentrions tôt pendant la semaine.
6. Elle doit travailler pour payer ses études.   Il faut qu'elle travaille pour payer ses études.
7. Nous devons étudier à la bibliothèque.   Il faut que nous étudiions à la bibliothèque.
8. On doit se coucher avant minuit.   Il faut qu'on se couche avant minuit.

3 Éviter une catastrophe Que devons-nous faire pour préserver notre planète? Avec un(e) partenaire, faites des phrases avec des expressions impersonnelles. Answers will vary.

MODÈLE
Il est essentiel que tu évites le gaspillage.

A	B	C
je/j'	améliorer	les écoproduits
tu	développer	les emballages
on	éviter	le gaspillage
nous	préserver	les glissements de terrain
vous	prévenir	les industries propres
le président	recycler	la nature
les pays	sauver	la pollution
?	trouver	le ramassage des ordures

598   *cinq cent quatre-vingt-dix-huit*

 Practice more at **vhlcentral.com**.

598   Instructor's Annotated Edition • Unit 14 • Lesson 14A

Communication

4 **Oui ou non?** Vous discutez avec un(e) partenaire des problèmes de l'environnement. À tour de rôle, dites si vous êtes d'accord ou non. *Answers will vary.*

MODÈLE

Étudiant(e) 1: *Il faut que les pays industrialisés réduisent les émissions de gaz à effet de serre.*
Étudiant(e) 2: *C'est vrai, il faut qu'ils réduisent les émissions de gaz à effet de serre.*

1. Il est nécessaire que tu recycles les bouteilles.
2. Il est dommage que les étudiants prennent le bus pour aller à la fac.
3. Il est bon qu'on développe des énergies propres.
4. Il est essentiel qu'on signe le protocole de Kyoto.
5. Il est indispensable que nous évitions le gaspillage.
6. Il faut que les pays développent de nouvelles technologies pour réduire les émissions toxiques.

5 **Les opinions** Vous discutez avec un(e) partenaire des problèmes de pollution. À tour de rôle, répondez à ces questions. Justifiez vos réponses. *Answers will vary.*

MODÈLE

Étudiant(e) 1: *Faut-il que nous préservions l'environnement?*
Étudiant(e) 2: *Oui, il faut que nous préservions l'environnement pour éviter le réchauffement de la Terre.*

1. Est-il important qu'on s'intéresse à l'écologie?
2. Faut-il qu'on évite de gaspiller?
3. Est-il essentiel que nous construisions des centrales nucléaires?
4. Vaut-il mieux que j'utilise des bacs (*bins*) à recyclage pour le ramassage des ordures?
5. Est-il indispensable qu'on prévienne les incendies?
6. Est-il possible qu'on développe l'énergie solaire?

6 **L'écologie** Par groupes de quatre, regardez les deux photos et parlez des problèmes écologiques qu'elles évoquent. Ensuite, préparez par écrit une liste de solutions. Comparez votre liste avec celles de la classe. *Answers will vary.*

MODÈLE

Étudiant(e) 1: *Aujourd'hui, il y a trop de centrales nucléaires.*
Étudiant(e) 2: *Il faut qu'on développe l'énergie solaire.*

cinq cent quatre-vingt-dix-neuf 599

---

4 **Expansion** When students have completed this activity, suggest that they prepare a conversation between a passionate environmentalist and an environmentalism skeptic. Encourage them to use humor and to perform their conversation for the class.

5 **Suggestion** Have students develop two responses for each question, one that begins with **oui** and one that begins with **non**. They should summarize their arguments in writing when they've completed the activity and place a check next to the argument for each topic that they find most persuasive.

5 **Expansion** Have students present their solutions in the form of slogans as part of a Green Earth campaign against pollution.

6 **Expansion** After completing the activity, write this statement on the board: **L'avenir de l'écologie, c'est les technologies**. Then ask students to find arguments that support or contradict it. You might suggest that they do Internet or library research to support their arguments.

6 **Expansion** Have students write to their city government expressing their concerns about a local environmental problem.

O P T I O N S

Extra Practice Have students complete the following sentences to practice the subjunctive with impersonal expressions.
1. Il ne faut pas qu'on _____ l'eau. (gaspille) **2.** Pour prévenir les incendies, il vaut mieux que les visiteurs du camping ne _____ pas. (fument) **3.** L'écologiste nous a dit qu'il fallait qu'on _____ la planète. (sauve)

Extra Practice Make a set of statements about the environment that use impersonal expressions and the subjunctive. Ask students to pretend that they are ecologists and to give a thumbs-up if they like what they hear or a thumbs-down if they don't. Example for thumbs-up: **Il faut qu'on réduise les déchets toxiques des usines.**

Révision

Instructional Resources

vhlcentral.com:
Activity Pack (Info Gap Activities); Testing Program; Testing Program MP3s; reference tools

1 Suggestion Tell students to complete this activity in phases. In the first phase, they describe the problem. In the second, they formulate a solution, using a sentence with the present subjunctive. In the third, they rewrite their solution using a form of **celui**.

2 Suggestion Explain to students that French speakers tend to write formal, respectful letters in these sorts of situations. Then supply them with a few of the formulas commonly used by native speakers in formal letters of complaint. Example: **Je vous prie d'agréer, Monsieur/ Madame, l'expression de mes salutations respectueuses.**

3 Expansion For an extra challenge, suggest that students also give advice telling what *not* to do. Example for **votre camarade de chambre**: **Il ne faut pas que tu t'énerves quand tu lui expliques le problème.**

4 Suggestion This activity could also be completed by groups of three, so that each student comes up with a suggestion about how to address the situation. Tell students to rotate the order in which they give their suggestions.

5 Suggestion To make sure that students understand others' suggestions, ask the class to rate each suggestion on a scale of 1 (**C'est facile à faire!**) to 5 (**C'est très difficile à faire!**).

6 Suggestion Divide the class into pairs and distribute the Info Gap Handouts found in the Activity Pack on the Supersite. Give students ten minutes to complete the activity.

1 Des solutions Avec un(e) partenaire, décrivez ces problèmes et donnez des solutions. Utilisez le présent du subjonctif et un pronom démonstratif pour chaque photo. Présentez vos solutions à la classe. Answers will vary.

MODÈLE

Étudiant(e) 1: Cette eau est sale.
Étudiant(e) 2: Il faut que celui qui a pollué cette eau paie une grosse amende.

1.

2.

3.

4.

2 Une lettre Vous habitez dans un village où les autorités veulent construire un grand aéroport. Avec un(e) partenaire, écrivez une lettre aux responsables dans laquelle vous expliquez vos inquiétudes (*worries*). Utilisez des expressions impersonnelles, puis lisez la lettre à la classe. Answers will vary.

3 Les plaintes Par groupes de trois, interviewez vos camarades à tour de rôle. Que vous conseillent-ils de faire quand vous vous plaignez (*complain*) d'une de ces personnes? Écrivez leurs réponses, puis comparez-les à celles d'un autre groupe. Answers will vary.

MODÈLE

Il est important que tu écrives une lettre au gérant.

- vos parents
- votre professeur
- votre camarade de chambre
- un(e) serveur/serveuse
- un(e) patron(ne)
- un médecin

4 Si... Avec un(e) partenaire, observez ces scènes et lisez les phrases. Pour chaque scène, faites trois phrases au présent du subjonctif, puis présentez-les à la classe. Answers will vary.

MODÈLE

Étudiant(e) 1: Si l'eau est sale, il ne faut pas que les gens mangent les poissons.
Étudiant(e) 2: Oui, il faut qu'ils les achètent à la poissonnerie.

1. Si l'eau est sale, ...

2. S'il y a un nuage de pollution, ...

3. S'il tombe une pluie acide, ...

4. S'il y a un glissement de terrain, ...

5 Des propositions Que peut-on faire pour préserver l'environnement? Avec un(e) partenaire, utilisez le présent du subjonctif et, si nécessaire, des pronoms pour faire des propositions. Ensuite, comparez-les à celles d'un autre groupe. Answers will vary.

MODÈLE

Étudiant(e) 1: Celui qui change l'huile de sa voiture? Il est essentiel qu'il recycle l'huile et qu'il l'apporte à un garagiste.
Étudiant(e) 2: Il ne faut pas qu'il change l'huile trop souvent ou qu'il utilise de l'huile de mauvaise qualité.

6 Non, Solange! Votre professeur va vous donner, à vous et à votre partenaire, deux feuilles d'activités différentes sur les mauvaises habitudes de Solange. Attention! Ne regardez pas la feuille de votre partenaire. Answers will vary.

MODÈLE

Étudiant(e) 1: Il est dommage que Solange conduise une voiture qui pollue.
Étudiant(e) 2: Il faut qu'elle conduise une voiture plus écologique.

OPTIONS

TPR Read a list of admonishments that make use of the impersonal expressions on page 597 and the present subjunctive. Ask students to pantomime what you are asking them to do. Example: **Il faut que tu passes l'aspirateur dans ta chambre cet après-midi, Mike!**

Game Make two sets of cards, one labeled with **que/qu'** + [*subject pronouns*], the other labeled with the infinitives of regular verbs. Students in small groups can "play" their hands by providing subjunctive verb forms suggested by pairs of cards. They should put down cards they've used and then draw more to collect as many as possible.

Video: Short Film

La BMCE

La Banque Marocaine du Commerce Extérieur est la deuxième plus grande banque du Maroc. Elle a des agences en Europe et en Asie et vise° constamment à étendre° les liens° entre le Maroc et le reste du monde. À travers la Fondation BMCE Éducation et Environnement, elle se soucie° aussi de la protection de l'environnement et du développement de la société marocaine. En 2000, elle a lancé le projet Medersat.com, dont un des objectifs les plus importants est la scolarisation des enfants dans les villages ruraux du Maroc.

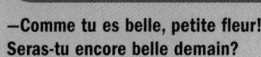

—Comme tu es belle, petite fleur! Seras-tu encore belle demain?

—Attends-moi! Moi aussi, j'ai envie d'apprendre.

 Compréhension Répondez aux questions.

1. Sur quoi le garçon est-il debout (*standing*) dans la première scène? Il est debout sur la Terre/la planète.
2. Que demande-t-il à la colombe (*dove*)? Il lui demande si elle peut lui montrer le chemin de la Liberté.
3. Où vont le garçon et sa sœur à la fin? Ils vont à l'école.

Discussion Par groupes de trois, répondez aux questions et discutez. Answers will vary.

1. Pourquoi le garçon pose-t-il des questions? Pourquoi à une fleur, aux étoiles (*stars*), à une colombe et à un arbre (*tree*)? Quels sont leurs attributs?
2. Quels messages concernant les missions de la BMCE la publicité (*commercial*) nous transmet-elle?

vise *aims* **étendre** *to extend* **liens** *links* **se soucie** *cares*

OPTIONS

La langue tamazight One of the BMCE's social missions is the promotion of the Tamazight language of Moroccan Berbers. Most Tamazight speakers today live in central Morocco, but people of Berber descent live across most of North Africa. Tamazight is only one of many Berber dialects, though the term is often used generically to denote all of its dialects, some of which are spoken as far south as Burkina Faso and as far east as Egypt. After gaining independence from France in the 1960s, several North African countries, including Morocco, instituted policies to promote the use of Arabic in schools. However, in the process they also suppressed or outright banned the teaching of Tamazight. In the case of Morocco, new policies are today reversing the trend and introducing Tamazight-language instruction in schools.

Section Goals

In this section, students will:
- read about the **Banque Marocaine du Commerce Extérieur**
- watch a commercial for the bank
- answer questions about the commercial and the BMCE

Instructional Resources
vhlcentral.com:
*TV commercial; **Le Zapping**
TV clip transcription;
reference tools*

Introduction
To check comprehension, ask these questions:
1. Que vise constamment à faire la BMCE? (Elle vise à étendre les liens entre le Maroc et le reste du monde.)
2. De quoi la banque se soucie-t-elle aussi? (Elle se soucie de la protection de l'environnement et du développement de la société marocaine.)
3. Quel est un des objectifs importants du projet Medersat. com? (Un de ses objectifs les plus importants est la scolarisation des enfants dans les villages marocains.)

Avant de regarder la vidéo
- Have students look at the video stills, read the captions, and predict what is happening in the commercial for each visual. **(1. Le garçon est sur la planète et il parle à une fleur. 2. Un groupe d'enfants court. Ils vont à l'école.)**
- Before showing the video, explain to students that they do not need to understand every word they hear. Tell them to listen for the text in the captions and jot down any familiar words.

Compréhension Have students work in pairs or groups for this activity. Tell them to write their answers. Then show the video again so that they can check their answers and add any missing information.

Discussion Ask groups to explain the connection between all the boy's questions and Medersat.com's educational objective referenced in the introductory paragraph.

Section Goals

In this section, students will learn and practice vocabulary related to:
• nature and conservation
• animals

Instructional Resources
vhlcentral.com:
Digital Image Bank;
Vocabulaire supplémentaire;
Mise en pratique answers;
Textbook Audioscript; Lab Audioscript; Activity Pack; Textbook MP3s; Lab MP3s; SAM Answer Key; reference tools

Suggestions
• Tell students to look over the new vocabulary and identify the cognates.
• Use the **14B Contextes** illustration from the Digital Image Bank. Point out people and things as you describe the illustration. Examples: **Ils voient une étoile. C'est une vache.**
• To practice the vocabulary, show drawings or magazine photos and ask students questions. Examples: **Qu'est-ce que c'est? C'est un lapin ou un écureuil? Y a-t-il un fleuve sur le dessin?**
• Explain that **jeter**, like **appeler**, doubles the stem's final consonant in all singular forms as well as the third person plural form of the present tense: **je jette, tu jettes, il/elle jette, nous jetons, vous jetez, ils/elles jettent.**
• Additional vocabulary for this lesson can be found in the **Vocabulaire supplémentaire** on the Supersite.
• Use the Vocabulary illustrations and the Nature and the environment illustrations from the Digital Image Bank to help students familiarize themselves with nature and conservation and animals.

Leçon 14B

En pleine nature

You will learn how to...
▪ discuss nature and the environment
▪ make comparisons

🖱 Vocabulary Tools

Vocabulaire

chasser	to hunt
jeter	to throw away
un animal	animal
un bois	woods
un champ	field
une côte	coast
un désert	desert
un fleuve	river
une forêt (tropicale)	(tropical) forest
la jungle	jungle
la nature	nature
une région	region
une rivière	river
un sentier	path
un volcan	volcano
la chasse	hunt
le déboisement	deforestation
l'écotourisme (m.)	ecotourism
une espèce (menacée)	(endangered) species
l'extinction (f.)	extinction
la préservation	protection
une ressource naturelle	natural resource
le sauvetage des habitats naturels	natural habitat preservation

le ciel

un arbre

une plante

Ils font un pique-nique(s). (faire)

un écureuil

une vache

l'herbe (f.)

ressources
WB pp. 195–196
LM p. 109
vhlcentral

OPTIONS

TPR Make a series of true/false statements related to the lesson theme using the new vocabulary. Tell students to remain seated if a statement is true and to stand if it is false. Examples: **Les lapins habitent dans les arbres.** (Students stand.) **On voit des étoiles dans le ciel.** (Students remain seated or sit down.)

Extra Practice Write these categories on the board: **Animaux** and **Éléments naturels** (*Natural features*). Dictate words from the vocabulary. Tell students to write the words under the correct heading on their papers. Examples: **serpent, île, désert, écureuil, volcan, falaise, vallée,** and **vache.**

Mise en pratique

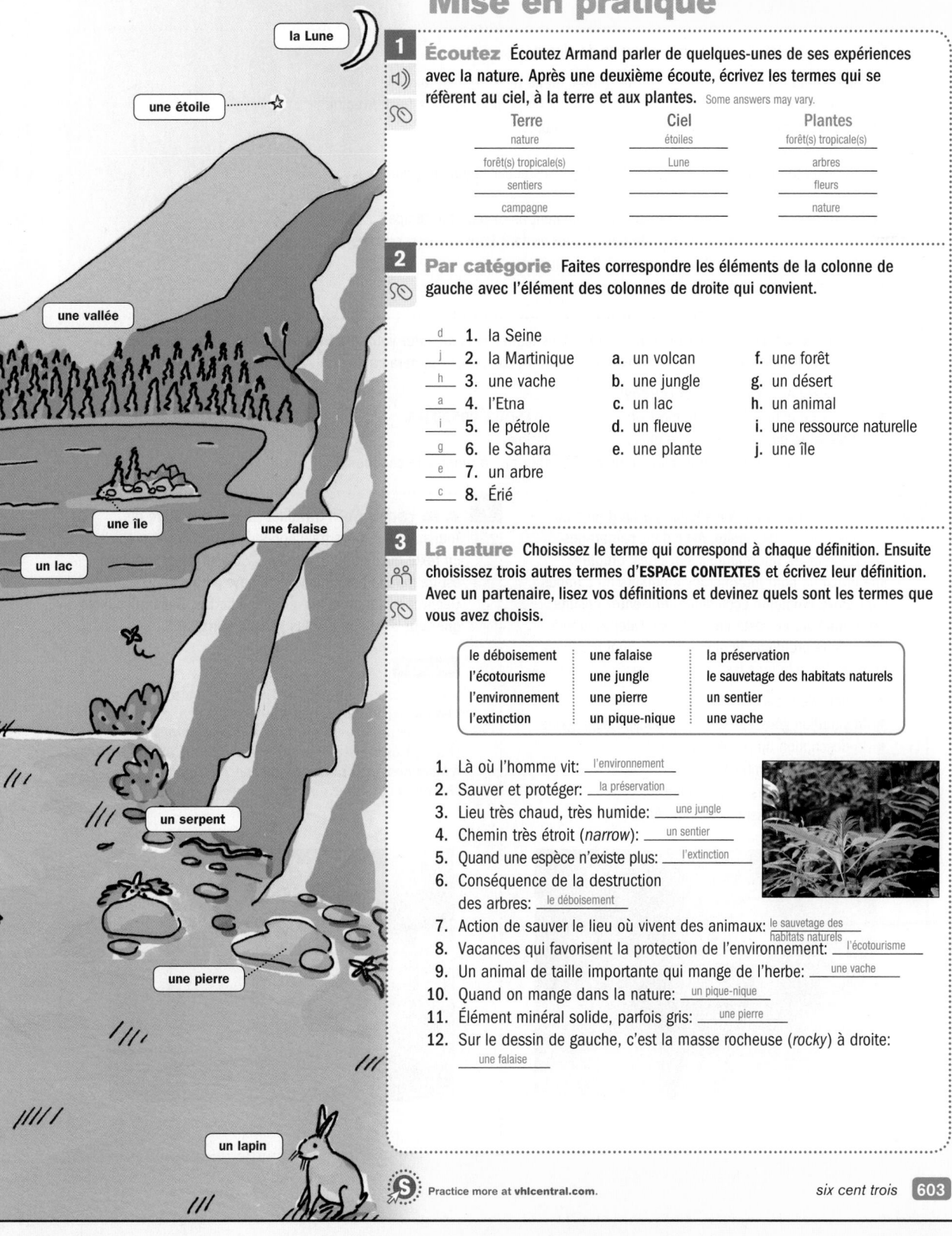

la Lune

une étoile

une vallée

une île

un lac

une falaise

un serpent

une pierre

un lapin

1 Écoutez Écoutez Armand parler de quelques-unes de ses expériences avec la nature. Après une deuxième écoute, écrivez les termes qui se réfèrent au ciel, à la terre et aux plantes. Some answers may vary.

Terre	Ciel	Plantes
nature	étoiles	forêt(s) tropicale(s)
forêt(s) tropicale(s)	Lune	arbres
sentiers		fleurs
campagne		nature

2 Par catégorie Faites correspondre les éléments de la colonne de gauche avec l'élément des colonnes de droite qui convient.

_d_ 1. la Seine
_j_ 2. la Martinique
_h_ 3. une vache
_a_ 4. l'Etna
_i_ 5. le pétrole
_g_ 6. le Sahara
_e_ 7. un arbre
_c_ 8. Érié

a. un volcan
b. une jungle
c. un lac
d. un fleuve
e. une plante

f. une forêt
g. un désert
h. un animal
i. une ressource naturelle
j. une île

3 La nature Choisissez le terme qui correspond à chaque définition. Ensuite choisissez trois autres termes d'**ESPACE CONTEXTES** et écrivez leur définition. Avec un partenaire, lisez vos définitions et devinez quels sont les termes que vous avez choisis.

le déboisement	une falaise	la préservation
l'écotourisme	une jungle	le sauvetage des habitats naturels
l'environnement	une pierre	un sentier
l'extinction	un pique-nique	une vache

1. Là où l'homme vit: _l'environnement_
2. Sauver et protéger: _la préservation_
3. Lieu très chaud, très humide: _une jungle_
4. Chemin très étroit (narrow): _un sentier_
5. Quand une espèce n'existe plus: _l'extinction_
6. Conséquence de la destruction des arbres: _le déboisement_
7. Action de sauver le lieu où vivent des animaux: _le sauvetage des habitats naturels_
8. Vacances qui favorisent la protection de l'environnement: _l'écotourisme_
9. Un animal de taille importante qui mange de l'herbe: _une vache_
10. Quand on mange dans la nature: _un pique-nique_
11. Élément minéral solide, parfois gris: _une pierre_
12. Sur le dessin de gauche, c'est la masse rocheuse (rocky) à droite: _une falaise_

Practice more at **vhlcentral.com**.

six cent trois **603**

1 Audioscript ARMAND: Moi, j'adore la nature. Quand j'ai le temps, je quitte la vie en ville et je fais de l'écotourisme. C'est l'idéal pour profiter de la nature et protéger l'environnement en même temps. Je n'aime pas aller à la pêche parce qu'il y a déjà beaucoup de poissons qui sont en danger d'extinction. J'aime beaucoup les forêts tropicales. L'année dernière, je suis allé visiter la forêt tropicale du Cameroun. C'était magnifique! Il y avait des espèces d'arbres et de fleurs variées et j'ai marché des heures dans des sentiers très différents. Aussi, quand je peux, je vais rendre visite à mon grand-père pour me reposer. Il habite à la campagne. Le soir, on peut se coucher dans l'herbe et regarder les étoiles et la Lune. (On Textbook MP3s)

1 Suggestion Go over the answers with the class.

2 Expansion Ask students questions about the location of each item in this activity. Examples: **Dans quelle grande ville se trouve la Seine? (à Paris) Où trouve-t-on des vaches? (dans les vallées/ à la campagne)**

3 Suggestions
• Tell students to compare their answers with their partner's.
• Have students describe what they see in the photo.

OPTIONS

Game Have students fold a sheet of paper into 16 squares (four folds in half) and write a new vocabulary word in each square. Say definitions for words. If students have the defined word, they mark their paper. The first student to mark four words in a row (across, down or diagonally) calls out **«gagné!»** To verify a win, the student should read the words in the row aloud.

Extra Practice To practice the new vocabulary, ask students these questions. 1. **Préférez-vous la montagne ou la mer? 2. Êtes-vous déjà allé(e) dans le désert? dans une forêt tropicale? à la montagne? dans la jungle? 3. Quel est votre animal préféré? 4. Où préféreriez-vous faire un pique-nique? 5. Est-ce que vous chassez? Pourquoi ou pourquoi pas?**

4 Expansion Have pairs get together with another pair of students and share what they learned about their partners.

5 Suggestion If time is limited, this activity may be assigned as homework. Then allow partners time to work together for peer editing in class.

6 Suggestion Encourage students to illustrate their brochures with drawings, magazine photos, or clip art.

7 Suggestion Have a volunteer read the **modèle**. You might suggest that students incorporate information from **Le monde francophone**, page 591, in their radio ads.

Communication

4 Conversez Interviewez un(e) camarade de classe. Answers will vary.

1. As-tu déjà fait de l'écotourisme? Où? Sinon, où as-tu envie d'en faire?
2. Aimes-tu les pique-niques? Quand en as-tu fait un pour la dernière fois? Avec qui?
3. Quelles activités aimes-tu pratiquer dans la nature?
4. As-tu déjà visité une forêt? Laquelle?
5. Connais-tu un lac? Quand y es-tu allé(e)? Quelles activités y as-tu pratiquées?
6. Es-tu déjà allé(e) dans un désert? Lequel?
7. Es-tu déjà allé(e) sur une île? Laquelle? Comment as-tu passé le temps?
8. Quelles sont les régions du monde que tu veux visiter? Pour quelle(s) raison(s)?
9. Si tu étais un animal, lequel serais-tu? Pourquoi?
10. Quand tu regardes le ciel, que trouves-tu de beau? Pourquoi?

5 La nature et moi Écrivez un paragraphe dans lequel vous racontez votre expérience avec la nature. Ensuite, à tour de rôle, lisez votre description à votre partenaire et comparez vos paragraphes. Answers will vary.

- Choisissez au minimum deux lieux naturels différents.
- Utilisez un minimum de huit mots de vocabulaire d'**ESPACE CONTEXTES**.
- Faites votre description avec le plus de détails possible.
- Expliquez ce que vous aimez ou ce que vous n'aimez pas à propos de chaque lieu.

6 Les écologistes Vous faites partie d'un club d'écologistes à l'université. Avec deux camarades de classe et les informations suivantes, préparez une brochure pour informer les étudiants du campus d'un grave problème écologique. Présentez ensuite votre brochure au reste de la classe. Quel groupe a présenté le problème le plus sérieux? Quel groupe a proposé les solutions les plus originales? Answers will vary.

- le nom de votre club
- la situation géographique du problème écologique
- la description du problème
- les causes du problème
- les conséquences du problème
- les solutions possibles au problème

7 À la radio Vous travaillez pour le ministère du Tourisme d'un pays francophone et vous devez préparer un texte qui sera lu à la radio. L'objectif de ce message est de faire la promotion de ce pays pour son écotourisme. Décrivez la nature et les activités offertes. Utilisez les mots que vous avez appris dans **ESPACE CONTEXTES**. Answers will vary.

MODÈLE

Venez découvrir la beauté de l'île de Madagascar. Chaque région vous offre des sentiers qui permettent d'admirer des plantes rares et des arbres magnifiques et de rencontrer des animaux extraordinaires… à Madagascar, la nature est unique, préservée. Le charme et l'exotisme sont ici!

Game Play a game of **Dix questions**. Ask a volunteer to think of a word from the new vocabulary. Other students get one chance to ask one yes/no question, then they can guess what the word is. Limit attempts to ten questions per word. You may want to write some phrases on the board to cue students' questions.

Game Write vocabulary words related to animals and nature on index cards. On another set of cards, draw or paste pictures to match each term. Tape them face down on the board in random order. Divide the class into two teams. Play a game of Concentration in which students match words with pictures. When a player makes a match, that player's team collects those cards. The team with the most cards at the end of the game wins.

Les sons et les lettres  Audio

Homophones

Many French words sound alike, but are spelled differently. As you have already learned, sometimes the only difference between two words is a diacritical mark. Other words that sound alike have more obvious differences in spelling.

a / à	ou / où	sont / son	en / an

Several forms of a single verb may sound alike. To tell which form is being used, listen for the subject or words that indicate tense.

je parle	tu parles	ils parlent
vous parlez	j'ai parlé	je vais parler

Many words that sound alike are different parts of speech. Use context to tell them apart.

VERB	POSSESSIVE ADJECTIVE	PREPOSITION	NOUN
Ils sont belges.	C'est son mari.	Tu vas en France?	Il a un an.

You may encounter multiple spellings of words that sound alike. Again, context is the key to understanding which word is being used.

je peux *I can*	elle peut *she can*	peu *a little, few*
le foie *liver*	la foi *faith*	une fois *one time*
haut *high*	l'eau *water*	au *at, to, in the*

Prononcez Répétez les paires de mots suivants à voix haute.

1. ce   se
2. leur   leurs
3. né   nez
4. foi   fois
5. ces   ses
6. vert   verre
7. au   eau
8. peut   peu
9. où   ou
10. lis   lit
11. quelle   qu'elle
12. c'est   s'est

Choisissez Choisissez le mot qui convient à chaque phrase.

1. Je (lis / lit) le journal tous les jours.
2. Son chien est sous le (lis / lit).
3. Corinne est (née / nez) à Paris.
4. Elle a mal au (née / nez).

Jeux de mots Répétez les jeux de mots à voix haute.

Le ver vert va vers le verre.[1]

Mon père est maire, mon frère est masseur.[2]

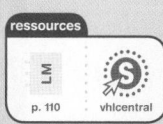
MAIRE DE PETITE VILLE

[2] My father is a mayor, my brother is a masseur.

[1] The green worm is going toward the glass.

ressources

LM
p. 110

vhlcentral

six cent cinq **605**

Section Goals

In this section, students will learn about homophones.

Instructional Resources
vhlcentral.com:
Textbook MP3s; Lab MP3s;
SAM Answer Key; Textbook
Audioscript; Lab Audioscript;
reference tools

Suggestions
• Model the pronunciation of the example words and have students repeat them after you.
• Point out these additional homophones: **là** (*there*) / **la** (*the*); **ont** (*have*) / **on** (*one*); **je vois** (*I see*) / **il voit** (*he sees*) / **une voie** (*a way*) / **une voix** (*a voice*).
• Read each sentence in the **Choisissez** activity aloud. Then have students select the correct word to complete each one.
• Have students look in the end vocabulary or verb charts in **Appendice D** and identify other homophones.
• Dictate five sentences that contain familiar homophones, repeating each one at least two times. Then write them on the board or a transparency and have students check their spelling.

Jeux de mots Make sure students understand the humor in the saying **«Mon père est maire, mon frère est masseur.»** Point out that it sounds like **«Mon père est mère, mon frère est ma sœur.»**

Extra Practice Tell students to write six pairs of sentences using words in the **Prononcez** activity. Then have volunteers write their sentences on the board and go over them with the class.

Extra Practice Teach students this French tongue-twister that contains homophones. **Si six scies scient six cyprès, six cent six scies scient six cent six cyprès.**

OPTIONS

ESPACE ROMAN-PHOTO

Section Goals

In this section, students will learn functional phrases for expressing regrets, preferences, comparisons, and suggestions.

Instructional Resources
vhlcentral.com:
Roman-photo Video, Videoscript, and Translation; SAM Answer Key; reference tools

Video Recap: Leçon 14A
Review the previous **Roman-photo**, with this activity.
1. Pourquoi Valérie est-elle de mauvaise humeur? (Michèle a démissionné. Stéphane n'a pas réussi son bac.)
2. Pourquoi Sandrine est-elle de mauvaise humeur? (Elle est/était anxieuse à cause de son concert/du départ de David.)
3. Quelle idée Rachid a-t-il eue? (d'aller à la montagne Sainte-Victoire)
4. Qui va aller à la montagne Sainte-Victoire? (Rachid, Amina, David, Sandrine, Valérie et Stéphane)

Video Synopsis
At **la montagne Sainte-Victoire**, the group visits the **Maison Sainte-Victoire**, an eco-museum. The guide explains that the mountain is a nature preserve. After a picnic, Sandrine wants David to draw her portrait. Rachid and Amina share a romantic moment, until Stéphane interrupts them.

Suggestions
• Have students predict what the episode will be about based on the video stills.
• Tell students to scan the captions for vocabulary related to nature and conservation.
• After reading the **Roman-photo**, have students summarize the episode.

La randonnée  Video

PERSONNAGES

Amina

David

Guide

Rachid

Sandrine

Stéphane

Valérie

À la montagne...
DAVID Que c'est beau!
VALÉRIE C'est la première fois que tu viens à la montagne Sainte-Victoire?
DAVID Non, en fait, je viens assez souvent pour dessiner, mais malheureusement c'est peut-être la dernière fois. C'est dommage que j'aie si peu de temps.

SANDRINE Je préférerais qu'on parle d'autre chose.
AMINA Elle a raison, nous sommes venus ici pour passer un bon moment.
STÉPHANE Tiens, et si on essayait de trouver des serpents?
AMINA Des serpents ici?
RACHID Ne t'inquiète pas, ma chérie. Par précaution, je suggère que tu restes près de moi.

RACHID Mais il ne faut pas que tu sois aussi anxieuse.
SANDRINE C'est romantique ici, n'est-ce pas?
DAVID Comment? Euh, oui, enfin...
VALÉRIE Avant de commencer notre randonnée, je propose qu'on visite la Maison Sainte-Victoire.
AMINA Bonne idée. Allons-y!

Après le pique-nique...
DAVID Mais tu avais faim, Sandrine!
SANDRINE Oui. Pourquoi?
DAVID Parce que tu as mangé autant que Stéphane!
SANDRINE C'est normal, on a beaucoup marché, ça ouvre l'appétit. En plus, ce fromage est délicieux!
DAVID Mais, tu peux manger autant de fromage que tu veux, ma chérie.

Stéphane laisse tomber une serviette...
VALÉRIE Stéphane! Mais qu'est-ce que tu jettes par terre? Il est essentiel qu'on laisse cet endroit propre!
STÉPHANE Oh, ne t'inquiète pas, maman. J'allais mettre ça à la poubelle plus tard.

SANDRINE David, j'aimerais que tu fasses un portrait de moi, ici, à la montagne. Ça te dit?
DAVID Peut-être un peu plus tard... Cette montagne est tellement belle!
VALÉRIE David, tu es comme Cézanne. Il venait ici tous les jours pour dessiner. La montagne Sainte-Victoire était un de ses sujets favoris.

A C T I V I T É S

1 **Vrai ou faux?** Indiquez si ces affirmations sont vraies ou fausses. Corrigez les phrases fausses. Answers may vary.

1. David fait un portrait de Sandrine sur-le-champ (*on the spot*).
   Faux. David ne veut pas faire un portrait de Sandrine tout de suite.
2. C'est la première fois que Stéphane visite la Maison Sainte-Victoire. Vrai.
3. Valérie traite la nature avec respect. Vrai.
4. Sandrine mange beaucoup au pique-nique. Vrai.
5. David et Sandrine passent un après-midi très romantique.
   Faux. L'après-midi de David et Sandrine n'est pas romantique.

6. Le guide confirme qu'il y a des serpents sur la montagne Sainte-Victoire. Faux. Le guide ne parle pas des serpents.
7. David est un peu triste de devoir bientôt retourner aux États-Unis. Vrai.
8. Valérie pense que David ressemble à Cézanne. Vrai.
9. Rachid est très romantique. Answers will vary.
10. Stéphane laisse Rachid et Amina tranquilles. Faux. Stéphane ne les laisse pas tranquilles.

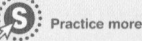 Practice more at vhlcentral.com.

O P T I O N S

Avant de regarder la vidéo Before viewing the video, have students work in pairs and brainstorm a list of words and expressions they expect to hear in an episode about a hike in the mountains.

Regarder la vidéo Show the video episode and tell students to check off the words or expressions on their lists when they hear them. Then show the episode again and have students give you a play-by-play description of the action. Write their descriptions on the board.

Les amis se promènent à la montagne Sainte-Victoire.

À la Maison Sainte-Victoire

GUIDE Mesdames, Messieurs, bonjour et bienvenue. C'est votre première visite de la Maison Sainte-Victoire?

STÉPHANE Pour moi, oui.

GUIDE La Maison Sainte-Victoire a été construite après l'incendie de 1989.

DAVID Un incendie?

GUIDE Oui, celui qui a détruit une très grande partie de la forêt.

GUIDE Maintenant, la montagne est un espace protégé.

DAVID Protégé? Comment?

GUIDE Eh bien, nous nous occupons de la gestion de la montagne et de la forêt. Notre mission est la préservation de la nature, le sauvetage des habitats naturels et la prévention des incendies. Je vous fais visiter le musée?

VALÉRIE Oui, volontiers!

RACHID Tiens, chérie.

AMINA Merci, elle est très belle cette fleur.

RACHID Oui, mais toi, tu es encore plus belle. Tu es plus belle que toutes les fleurs de la nature réunies!

AMINA Rachid...

RACHID Chut! Ne dis rien... Stéphane! Laisse-nous tranquilles.

Expressions utiles

Expressing regrets and preferences

- **C'est dommage que j'aie si peu de temps.**
  It's a shame that I have so little time.
- **Je préférerais qu'on parle d'autre chose.**
  I would prefer to talk about something else.
- **J'aimerais que tu fasses un portrait de moi.**
  I would like you to do a portrait of me.

Making suggestions

- **Par précaution, je suggère que tu restes près de moi.**
  As a precaution, I suggest that you stay close to me.
- **Il ne faut pas que tu sois si anxieuse.**
  There's no need to be so anxious.
- **Je propose qu'on visite...**
  I propose we visit...

Making comparisons

- **Tu as mangé autant que Stéphane!**
  You ate as much as Stéphane!
- **Tu peux manger autant de fromage que tu veux.**
  You can eat as much cheese as you want.

---

2   **À vous!** Imaginez que vous êtes allé(e) à la montagne Sainte-Victoire avec des amis. À l'entrée du parc, il y a une liste de règles (*rules*) à suivre pour protéger la nature. Avec un(e) camarade de classe, imaginez quelles sont ces règles et écrivez une liste. Qu'estce qu'il faut faire si vous faites un pique-nique? Une randonnée? Quelles sont les activités interdites? Présentez votre liste à la classe.

3   **Écrivez** Il y a deux couples dans notre histoire, Sandrine et David, Amina et Rachid. Composez un paragraphe dans lequel vous expliquez quel couple va rester ensemble et quel couple va se séparer. Pourquoi? Attention! Le départ de David n'entre pas en jeu (*doesn't come into play*).

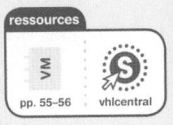

ressources

VM pp. 55–56   vhlcentral

A C T I V I T É S

Expressions utiles

- Model the pronunciation of the **Expressions utiles** and have students repeat them after you.
- As you work through the list, point out the use of the subjunctive with verbs of will and emotion as well as comparatives and superlatives of nouns. Tell students that these constructions will be formally presented in the **Structures** section.
- Respond briefly to questions about the use of the subjunctive with verbs of will and emotion, comparatives, and superlatives. Reinforce correct forms, but do not expect students to produce them consistently at this time.
- Have students scan the **Roman-photo** and find other expressions used to make comparisons. Examples: **David, tu es comme Cézanne. Tu es plus belle que toutes les fleurs....**

1 **Suggestion** Have students correct the false statements.

1 **Expansion** For additional practice, give students these items. **11. David va assez souvent à la montagne Sainte-Victoire. (Vrai.) 12. Sandrine ne veut pas parler du départ de David. (Vrai.) 13. Stéphane prend une photo de David et de Sandrine. (Faux.)**

2 **Suggestions**
- If time is limited, this activity may be assigned as homework. As an alternative, you can have students create posters instead of lists.
- Encourage students to create symbols for the forbidden activities similar to the "No littering" sign on page 585.

3 **Suggestion** As students write, circulate around the room to help with unfamiliar vocabulary and expressions.

O P T I O N S

Paul Cézanne Born in Aix-en-Provence, Paul Cézanne (1839–1906) lived much of his life as a recluse in Provence. A master of Postimpressionism, he is considered one of the greatest modern French painters. Bring in some photos of Cézanne's sketches and paintings of **la montagne Sainte-Victoire** and have students describe them.

Le mistral The south of France is at high risk for wildfires. Because of the extremely strong wind, **le mistral**, fires can get out of control and spread rapidly. **Le mistral** is caused by air that cools over the mountains and then flows into the valleys, creating a funnel effect and generating extremely strong wind currents. **Le mistral** occurs most often in the spring or winter.

Section Goals

In this section, students will:
- learn about France's national parks
- learn some conservation-related terms
- learn about some famous natural sites in the francophone world
- read about Madagascar
- view authentic video footage

Instructional Resources
vhlcentral.com:
*Video; SAM Answer Key;
Videoscript; reference tools*

Culture à la loupe
Avant la lecture
- Have students look at the photos and describe what they see.
- Ask students: **Quels parcs nationaux avez-vous déjà visités?**

Lecture
- Point out the list of French natural sites that hold records.
- Explain that Guadeloupe has been an overseas department of France since 1946. Tourism is one of the main industries.

Après la lecture Ask students: **Quel(s) parc(s) français voudriez-vous visiter? Pourquoi?**

1 Expansion For additional practice, give students these items. **11. Que trouve-t-on dans tous les parcs nationaux? (On trouve des sentiers de randonnée et des activités d'écotourisme guidées.) 12. Combien de parcs nationaux sont montagneux? (sept sur neuf) 13. Quand est-ce que le premier parc national a été créé en France? (en 1963) 14. Où peut-on trouver des bouquetins? (dans la Vanoise)**

Reading
Video: *Flash culture*

NATIONAL connections cultures STANDARDS

CULTURE À LA LOUPE

Les parcs nationaux

perroquet°, Guadeloupe

le parc de la Vanoise

Le gouvernement français protège et gère° dix parcs nationaux. Tous offrent des sentiers de randonnée et la possibilité de découvrir la nature avec de l'écotourisme guidé. Ce sont aussi souvent des endroits où les visiteurs peuvent pratiquer différentes activités sportives. Par exemple, on peut faire des sports d'hiver dans cinq des sept parcs de montagnes et dans leurs nombreux sommets° et glaciers.

Les Cévennes, en Occitanie, est le plus grand parc forestier, avec 3.200 km² de forêts, mais on y trouve aussi des montagnes et des plateaux. La Vanoise, un parc de haute montagne dans les Alpes, a été le premier parc créé° en France, en 1963. Avec ses 107 lacs et sa vingtaine° de glaciers, c'est une réserve naturelle où le bouquetin° est protégé. Deux autres parcs, les Écrins et le Mercantour, sont aussi situés dans la région des Alpes. Toujours dans les parcs montagneux, le parc national des Pyrénées est composé de six vallées principales qui sont riches en forêts, cascades° et autres formations naturelles. C'est un refuge pour de nombreuses espèces menacées, comme l'ours° et l'aigle royal°. Quand il fait beau l'été, le parc marin de Port-Cros, composé d'îles méditerranéennes, est idéal pour les activités aquatiques. Aux Antilles°, il fait chaud et humide toute l'année dans le parc national de la Guadeloupe. Les paysages° de ce parc sont très variés: forêt tropicale, volcan et paysages côtiers° ou maritimes. Ouvert depuis 2012 seulement, le parc national le plus récent est le Parc national des Calanques, dans le sud de la France.

Les records naturels de la France en Europe de l'Ouest

- Le Mont-Blanc, dans les Alpes, est la plus haute montagne d'Europe de l'Ouest. Il mesure 4.810 mètres.
- La forêt de pins des Landes, en Nouvelle-Aquitaine, est le plus grand massif forestier d'Europe. Il fait plus d'un million d'hectares.
- La dune du Pilat, en Nouvelle-Aquitaine, est la plus haute dune de sable° d'Europe. Elle mesure 110,9 mètres.
- Le cirque° de Gavarnie, dans les Pyréées, a une des plus grandes cascades de la France. Elle mesure 423 mètres.

gère *manages* **sommets** *summits* **créé** *created* **vingtaine** *about twenty* **bouquetin** *ibex, a type of wild goat* **cascades** *waterfalls* **ours** *bear* **aigle royal** *golden eagle* **Antilles** *French West Indies* **paysages** *landscapes* **côtiers** *coastal* **perroquet** *parrot* **sable** *sand* **cirque** *steep-walled, mountainous basin*

A C T I V I T É S

1

Répondez Répondez aux questions par des phrases complètes.

1. Combien de parcs nationaux français y a-t-il?
   Il y a dix parcs nationaux français.
2. Quel type de parc est le parc des Cévennes?
   Le parc des Cévennes est un parc forestier.
3. Quel parc est situé sur des îles méditerranéennes?
   Le parc marin de Port-Cros est situé sur des îles méditerranéennes.
4. Quels sont deux animaux qu'on peut trouver dans les Pyrénées?
   On peut trouver des ours et des aigles royaux dans les Pyrénées.
5. Quels sont deux types de paysages du parc de la Guadeloupe?
   Answers will vary. Possible answer: Les paysages forestiers et volcaniques sont deux types de paysages du parc de la Guadeloupe.
6. Comment s'appellent deux des parcs nationaux français et où se trouvent-ils (à la montagne, etc.)? Answers will vary. Possible answer: La Vanoise se trouve dans les montagnes et Port-Cros se trouve sur des îles.
7. Quelle est la plus haute montagne d'Europe?
   C'est le Mont-Blanc.
8. Où se trouve le plus grand massif forestier d'Europe?
   Il se trouve dans les Landes, en France.
9. Combien mesure la dune du Pilat?
   Elle mesure 110,9 mètres.
10. Combien mesure la cascade du cirque de Gavarnie?
    Elle mesure 423 mètres.

608 *six cent huit*

OPTIONS

Cultural Comparison Have the class brainstorm a list of famous national parks in the Unites States and write them on the board. Examples: Yellowstone, Yosemite, Death Valley, the Everglades, the Grand Canyon, Hawaii Volcanoes, Hot Springs, and Rocky Mountain.
Then tell students to work in groups of three and compare these national parks to those in France. They should consider geographical features and recreational activities. Have them list the similarities and differences in a two-column chart under the headings **Similitudes** and **Différences**. After completing their charts, have volunteers read their lists and ask the class if they agree or disagree with the observations.

LE FRANÇAIS QUOTIDIEN

La protection de la nature

essence (*f.*) sans plomb	*unleaded gas*
protection du littoral	*shoreline restoration*
mesures (*f.*) antipollution	*pollution control*
reboisement (*m.*)	*reforestation*
valorisation (*f.*) des terres	*land improvement*

LE MONDE FRANCOPHONE

Grands sites naturels

Voici quelques exemples d'espaces naturels remarquables du monde francophone.

En Algérie Plus de 80% de la superficie de l'Algérie, deuxième plus grand pays d'Afrique, sont occupés par le Sahara.

Au Cambodge Le lac Tonle Sap est le plus grand lac d'Asie du sud-est.

Au Cameroun La réserve Dja Faunal est l'une des plus grandes forêts tropicales d'Afrique.

À l'île Maurice L'île est presque entièrement entourée° de plus de 150 km de récifs de corail.

Au Sénégal Le parc national du Niokolo Koba, site du Patrimoine° mondial (UNESCO) et Réserve de la biosphère internationale, est l'une des réserves naturelles les plus importantes d'Afrique de l'Ouest.

Aux Seychelles L'atoll Aldabra abrite la plus grande population de tortues géantes du monde.

entièrement entourée *entirely surrounded* **Patrimoine** *Heritage*

PORTRAIT

Madagascar

Madagascar, ancienne colonie française, est la quatrième plus grande île du monde, et, avec plus de 20 parcs nationaux et réserves naturelles, elle est un paradis pour l'écotourisme. Madagascar (plus de 20 millions d'habitants) est située à 400 km à l'est du Mozambique, dans l'océan Indien. Sa faune et sa flore sont exceptionnelles avec 250.000 espèces différentes, dont 1.000 orchidées. 90% de ces espèces sont uniques au monde. Ses mangroves, rivières, lacs et récifs coralliens° offrent des milieux écologiques variés et ses forêts abritent° 90% des lémuriens° du monde. Caméléons, tortues terrestres°, tortues de mer° et baleines à bosse° sont aussi typiques de l'île.

récifs coralliens *coral reefs* **abritent** *provide a habitat for* **lémuriens** *lemurs* **tortues terrestres** *tortoises* **tortues de mer** *sea turtles* **baleines à bosse** *humpback whales*

MUSIQUE À FOND

Liz Van Deuq

Lieu d'origine: Nevers, France
Métier: musicienne-interprète

Piquante et décalée, elle se produit dans des spectacles piano-solo, où humour, funk et rock se mélangent.

Go to vhlcentral.com to find out more about **Liz Van Deuq** and her music.

---

2   **Complétez** Complétez les phrases.

1. Madagascar est une grande _____île_____ près du Mozambique.
2. Madagascar est une bonne destination pour ___l'écotourisme___.
3. À Madagascar, la majorité des espèces sont ___uniques au monde___
4. ___Caméléons, tortues___ sont des espèces typiques de l'île. terrestres, tortues de mer et baleines à bosse
5. L'une des plus grandes forêts tropicales d'Afrique se trouve ___au Cameroun___.

3   **À la découverte** Vous et deux partenaires voulez visiter ensemble plusieurs pays francophones et découvrir la nature. Quelles destinations choisissez-vous? Comparez les activités qui vous intéressent et les endroits que vous voulez visiter. Soyez prêts à présenter votre itinéraire à la classe.

ressources

VM
pp. 87–88
vhlcentral

Practice more at **vhlcentral.com.**

A C T I V I T É S

OPTIONS

Madagascar Madagascar was settled by Indonesian migrants around A.D. 700. It became **un protectorat français** in 1885, **une colonie** in 1896, and an independent state in 1960. The official languages are Malagasy (**malgache**), French, and English. More than 90 percent of the people earn their living from the forest, where most of the biodiversity can be found, but 85 percent of the country has already suffered deforestation. The island's population is also growing.

Pairs Have students write five true/false statements using the information on these pages. Then have them get together in pairs and take turns reading their statements and responding.

Le français quotidien
- Model the pronunciation of each term.
- Ask students questions using these terms. Examples: **1. Votre voiture consomme-t-elle de l'essence sans plomb? 2. Combien cela coûte-t-il par gallon? 3. Pourquoi a-t-on besoin de mesures antipollution? 4. Quand faut-il reboiser? 5. Pourquoi faut-il protéger le littoral?**

Portrait
- Have students locate the island of Madagascar on the map in **Appendice A**.
- Tell students to look at the photo and ask: **Quelle espèce d'animal est-ce? (un lémurien) Avez-vous déjà vu un lémurien? Si oui, où?**

Le monde francophone
- Have students locate the countries or islands on the map of the francophone world in **Appendice A**.
- Point out that an atoll is a ribbon of coral reef around a lagoon. Along the top there are often flat islands or strips of flat land.

2 Expansion For additional practice, give students these items. 6. Madagascar a plus de ____ parcs nationaux et réserves naturelles. (vingt) 7. Madagascar se trouve à l'est du ____. (Mozambique) 8. Dix pour cent des ____ au monde n'habitent pas à Madagascar. (lémuriens)

3 Suggestion Before beginning the activity, have the class brainstorm a list of possible destinations for ecotourism and write them on the board.

Flash culture Tell students that they will learn more about the diverse geography of France and the French-speaking world by watching a variety of real-life images narrated by Benjamin. Show the video segment. Then ask students to close their eyes and describe from memory what they saw as you write their descriptions on the board. You can also use the activities in the video manual in class to reinforce this **Flash culture** or assign them as homework.

ESPACE STRUCTURES

Section Goals

In this section, students will learn:
- to use the subjunctive to express will or emotion
- the present subjunctive forms of **avoir**, **être**, and **faire**

Instructional Resources
vhlcentral.com:
Activity Pack; Lab MP3s; SAM Answer Key; **Essayez!** *and* **Mise en pratique** *answers; Lab Audioscript; reference tools*

Suggestions
- Read these sentences to the class: **Je veux manger au resto U ce midi. Je veux que tu manges avec moi au resto U ce midi.** Ask why an infinitive is used in the first sentence and a conjugated verb in the subjunctive mood in the second. (In the first one, the subject is the same for both verbs. In the second one, there are two different subjects.)
- Point out that the subjunctive is sometimes used in English to express will. Example: *The professor demands that we pay attention in class.* **Le prof exige que nous soyons attentifs en classe.** English speakers often use an infinitive instead after a verb that expresses will, even if the subjects of the two verbs are different. Example: *I want you to get out now!* **Je veux que tu sortes d'ici tout de suite!**

14B.1

À noter

See **Leçon 14A** for an introduction to the subjunctive and the structure of clauses containing verbs in the subjunctive.

The subjunctive (Part 2)  Tutorial
Will and emotion, irregular subjunctive forms

- Use the subjunctive with verbs and expressions of will and emotion. Verbs and expressions of will are often used when someone wants to influence the actions of other people. Verbs and expressions of emotion express someone's feelings or attitude.

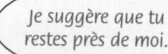

Je suggère que tu restes près de moi.

Je propose qu'on visite la Maison Sainte-Victoire.

- When the main clause contains an expression of will or emotion and the subordinate clause has a different subject, the subjunctive is required.

MAIN CLAUSE VERB OF WILL	CONNECTOR	SUBORDINATE CLAUSE SUBJUNCTIVE
Mes parents exigent *My parents demand*	**que** *that*	**je dorme** huit heures. *I sleep eight hours.*

EXPRESSION OF EMOTION	CONNECTOR	SUBJUNCTIVE
Tu es triste *You are sad*	**que** *that*	**Sophie ne vienne pas** avec nous. *Sophie isn't coming with us.*

VERB OF WILL	CONNECTOR	SUBJUNCTIVE
Je préfère *I prefer*	**que** *that*	**tu travailles** ce soir. *you work tonight.*

EXPRESSION OF EMOTION	CONNECTOR	SUBJUNCTIVE
Elle est heureuse *She is happy*	**que** *that*	**tu finisses** tes études. *you're finishing your studies.*

- Here are some verbs and expressions of will commonly followed by the subjunctive.

Verbs of will			
demander que...	*to ask that...*	**recommander que...**	*to recommend that...*
désirer que...	*to want/ desire that...*	**souhaiter que...**	*to wish that...*
exiger que...	*to demand that...*	**suggérer que...**	*to suggest that...*
préférer que...	*to prefer that...*		
proposer que...	*to propose that...*	**vouloir que...**	*to want that...*

Mon père **recommande que** nous **dînions** au restaurant français.
My father recommends that we have dinner at the French restaurant.

Le gouvernement **exige qu'**on **recycle** les produits en plastique.
The government demands that we recycle plastic products.

ressources

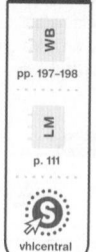

WB
pp. 197–198

LM
p. 111

vhlcentral

- These are some verbs and expressions of emotion followed by the subjunctive.

Verbs and expressions of emotion			
aimer que...	to like that...	être heureux/ heureuse que...	to be happy that...
avoir peur que...	to be afraid that...	être surpris(e) que...	to be surprised that...
être content(e) que...	to be glad that...	être triste que...	to be sad that...
être désolé(e) que...	to be sorry that...	regretter que...	to regret that...
être furieux/ furieuse que...	to be furious that...		

Martine est **surprise que** Thomas **arrive** demain.
Martine is surprised that Thomas is arriving tomorrow.

Nous sommes **furieux que** les gens **jettent** des ordures dans la rivière.
We're furious that people throw trash in the river.

> **Boîte à outils**
>
> The is no future form of the subjunctive, so use the present subjunctive even when expressing an action that is going to take place in the future. The context will clarify the meaning.
>
> **Elle est contente que tu prennes des cours de musique l'année prochaine.**
> *She's glad that you're taking music classes next year.*

- In English, the word *that* introducing the subordinate clause may sometimes be omitted. In French, never omit **que** between the two clauses.

Ils sont heureux **que** j'arrive.
They're happy (that) I'm arriving.

Elle préfère **que** tu partes.
She prefers that you leave.

- If the subject doesn't change, use the infinitive with expressions of will and emotion. In the case of **avoir peur**, **regretter**, and expressions with **être**, add **de** before the infinitive.

Tu veux faire un pique-nique?
Do you want to have a picnic?

Nous sommes tristes d'apprendre la mauvaise nouvelle.
We're sad to learn the bad news.

- Some verbs have irregular subjunctive forms.

Present subjunctive of *avoir, être, faire*			
	avoir	**être**	**faire**
que je/j'	aie	sois	fasse
que tu	aies	sois	fasses
qu'il/elle/on	ait	soit	fasse
que nous	ayons	soyons	fassions
que vous	ayez	soyez	fassiez
qu'ils/elles	aient	soient	fassent

Elle veut que je **fasse** le lit.
She wants me to make the bed.

Je suis désolé qu'elle **soit** malheureuse.
I'm sorry that she's unhappy.

Essayez!   Indiquez les formes correctes du présent du subjonctif des verbes.

1. que je ___sois___ (être)
2. qu'il ___fasse___ (faire)
3. que vous ___soyez___ (être)
4. que leur enfant ___ait___ (avoir)
5. qu'elle ___fasse___ (faire)
6. que nous ___fassions___ (faire)
7. qu'ils ___aient___ (avoir)
8. que tu ___sois___ (être)

Suggestions
- Read statements that begin with **Je propose que vous...,** **Je recommande que vous...,** and **Je suggère que vous....** Have students qualify each piece of advice you give them as **un bon conseil** or **un mauvais conseil.** Example: **Je recommande que vous ne mangiez que des gâteaux au déjeuner. (C'est un mauvais conseil.)**
- Ask students if the present subjunctive forms of the verbs **avoir** and **être** seem familiar to them. (They resemble the imperative forms for those verbs.)

Essayez!
- Assign an infinitive to each row of students. They should take turns giving present subjunctive forms for their appointed verb. The first student should give the **que je/j'...** form, the second student the **que tu...** form, and so on. Example for one row of students: (*first student*) **que je fasse,** (*second student*) **que tu fasses,** etc.
- Have volunteers make complete sentences using each item.

OPTIONS

Game Play a variation of **Jacques a dit** (*Simon Says*) with direct and indirect commands. Students should obey indirect commands that use the subjunctive and ignore all direct commands (those that use the imperative). Examples: **Jacques demande que vous vous leviez.** (*Students stand up.*) **Levez-vous!** (*Students remain seated*.)

Extra Practice Tell students to pretend that they've just seen a documentary on an environmental subject and that they should react to what they've seen using an expression of emotion from this page. Example: **Je suis contente que l'on fasse quelque chose pour protéger les espèces d'oiseaux menacées.**

ESPACE STRUCTURES   611

Mise en pratique

1 **Des réactions** Que devraient faire les personnages sur les illustrations? Employez ces expressions pour donner vos réactions. Suggested answers

vous (proposer que)

▶ **MODÈLE**

Je propose que vous mangiez quelque chose.

acheter une décapotable
  (*convertible*)
boire de l'eau
me donner de l'argent

faire une fête
garder le secret
manger quelque chose
trouver des amis

1. tu (suggérer que)
Je suggère que tu boives de l'eau.

2. mes voisins (vouloir que)
Je veux que mes voisins me donnent de l'argent.

3. vous (exiger que)
J'exige que vous gardiez le secret.

4. Yves (souhaiter que)
Je souhaite qu'Yves trouve des amis.

5. elle (recommander que)
Je recommande qu'elle achète une décapotable.

6. tu (désirer que)
Je désire que tu fasses une fête.

2 **Des opinions** Complétez ces phrases avec le présent du subjonctif. Ensuite, comparez vos réponses avec celles d'un(e) partenaire. Answers will vary.

1. Nous sommes furieux que les examens...
2. Notre prof exige que...
3. Nous aimons que le prof...
4. Je propose que... le vendredi.
5. Les étudiants veulent que les cours...
6. Je recommande que... tous les jours.
7. C'est triste que cette université...
8. Nous préférons que le resto U...
9. Mes ami(e)s suggèrent que...
10. Je souhaite que...

 Practice more at **vhlcentral.com**.

1 Suggestion Encourage students to come up with creative suggestions for the people pictured and to share the most interesting suggestions with the class.

2 Suggestion Have one pair of students share their sentences with the class. Ask their classmates to say **d'accord** if they agree or **pas d'accord** if they don't agree with the statements.v

Communication

3 **Enquête** Comparez vos idées sur la nature et l'environnement avec celles d'un(e) partenaire. Posez-vous ces questions. Answers will vary.

1. Que suggères-tu qu'on fasse pour protéger les forêts tropicales?
2. Vaut-il mieux qu'on ne chasse plus? Pourquoi?
3. Que recommandes-tu qu'on fasse pour arrêter la pollution?
4. Comment souhaites-tu que nous préservions nos ressources naturelles?
5. Quels produits recommandes-tu qu'on développe?
6. Quel problème écologique veux-tu qu'on traite tout de suite?
7. Que proposes-tu qu'on fasse pour sauver les espèces menacées?
8. Est-il important qu'on arrête le déboisement? Pourquoi?

4 **Mme Quefège** Mme Quefège donne des conseils (*advice*) à la radio. Pensez à une difficulté que vous avez et préparez par écrit un paragraphe que vous lui lirez. Elle va vous faire des recommandations. Avec un(e) partenaire, alternez les rôles pour jouer les scènes. Answers will vary.

MODÈLE

Étudiant(e) 1: *Ma petite amie fait constamment ses devoirs et elle ne quitte plus son appartement.*
Étudiant(e) 2: *Je suis désolée qu'elle n'arrête pas de travailler. Si elle ne quitte toujours pas l'appartement ce week-end, je suggère que vous écriviez à ses parents.*

5 **Il faut que...** À tour de rôle, donnez des conseils à votre partenaire pour chacune (*each one*) de ces situations. Utilisez des expressions de volonté et d'opinion avec le subjonctif. Answers will vary.

- Il/Elle voyage en Europe pour la première fois.
- Il/Elle veut rester en forme.
- Il/Elle a un mauvais rhume.
- Il/Elle ne respecte pas la nature.

6 **Les habitats naturels** Par groupes de trois, préparez le texte pour cette affiche où vous expliquez ce qu'on doit faire pour sauver les habitats naturels. Utilisez des verbes au présent du subjonctif. Answers will vary.

OPTIONS

Extra Practice Read aloud some sentence starters that refer to current events or celebrities. Each one should use an expression of emotion from page 611. Students should complete the sentences appropriately. Example: **Emeril Lagasse est furieux que...** (qu'il n'y ait plus d'ail au supermarché.)

Video As students watch the last scene of the video for **Leçon 14B** again, pause periodically and ask them these questions. **Qu'est-ce que Valérie veut que Stéphane fasse? Qu'est-ce que Sandrine veut que David fasse? Qu'est-ce que Rachid veut qu'Amina fasse? Qu'est-ce que Rachid veut que Stéphane fasse?**

---

3 Expansion Students could also answer these questions. **Avez-vous peur que des espèces soient menacées dans votre région? Que proposez-vous que l'on fasse pour éviter la destruction des habitats naturels autour des villes?**

4 Suggestion Ask students why they think the radio personality is named **Quefège.** (It sounds like the phrase **Que fais-je?**)

6 Expansion Have the class vote on the best text for the poster. Then have small groups create a television ad campaign in the same vein. They should produce a script modeled on the poster text and a storyboard that shows the visuals to appear on the screen. Remind the class that successful TV ads often use striking images and catchy slogans.

Section Goals

In this section, students will learn:
• comparatives with noun
• superlatives with nouns

Instructional Resources
vhlcentral.com:
Activity Pack; Lab MP3s;
SAM Answer Key; **Essayez!**
and **Mise en pratique**
answers; Lab Audioscript;
reference tools

Suggestions

• Ask students what words are used in comparatives and superlatives for adjectives and adverbs. You might need to remind them by asking a few questions. Example: **Qui est le plus drôle de la classe?** Once students have identified **plus/moins/aussi** + [*adjective/ adverb*] + **que**, tell them that the words used to compare quantities for nouns are similar.

• Point out that **de** is used in all the examples of comparative noun constructions just as **que** is used with comparative adjectives and adverbs. You might copy the paradigms that appear under the photos on the board, adding **+ que**.

• Make statements about things in the classroom using comparatives and superlatives of nouns while students qualify them as **vrai** or **faux**. Example: **Sean a plus de livres que Jennifer.**

• Point out that native speakers distinguish **plus de** meaning *more of* from **plus de** meaning *anymore of* by pronouncing the **s** in the former. Example: **Je n'ai plus d'argent!** (s not pronounced) **J'ai plus d'argent que toi!** (s pronounced)

Essayez! Show a transparency with false statements and have students correct them. Examples: **Il y a plus d'habitants en France qu'aux États-Unis. Il y a autant d'ail dans un gâteau que dans une pizza. Le Grand Canyon est moins grand qu'un timbre postal.**

14B.2

Comparatives and superlatives of nouns

 Tutorial

Point de départ In **Leçon 9B**, you learned how to compare nouns and verbs by using comparative and superlative forms of adjectives and adverbs. You will now learn how to compare nouns when talking about quantities.

Tu peux manger autant de fromage que tu veux.

Nous nous occupons de la forêt pour avoir moins d'incendies.

• To compare amounts of things, use these expressions:

plus de	+	[noun]	more.
moins de	+	[noun]	less; fewer
autant de	+	[noun]	as much; as many

Elle fait **plus d'heures** que sa sœur.
She works more hours than her sister (does).

Vous recevez **autant de courrier** que vos amis.
You receive as much mail as your friends (do).

Il y a **moins d'arbres** dans le jardin que dans la forêt.
There are fewer trees in the garden than in the forest.

Il n'y a pas **autant d'animaux** dans la ville que dans la jungle.
There aren't as many animals in the city as (there are) in the jungle.

• To express the superlative quantity of a noun (*the most, the least/fewest*), add the definite article **le**: **le plus de, le moins de**.

Ce sont les forêts tropicales qui ont **le plus de plantes**.
Tropical rainforests have the most plants.

Qui a vu **le plus de lapins**?
Who saw the most rabbits?

Ce sont les pays pauvres qui ont **le moins d'argent**.
Poor countries have the least money.

Dans quelle ville y a-t-il **le moins de pollution**?
Which city has the least pollution?

---

ressources

WB
pp. 199–200

LM
p. 112

vhlcentral

Essayez! Complétez les phrases avec les comparatifs ou les superlatifs corrects.

1. Mon ami n'a pas _autant de_ (*as much*) travail que moi.
2. Qui a _le moins de_ (*the fewest*) cousins?
3. La Corse a-t-elle _autant de_ (*as many*) falaises que la Sicile?
4. Il y a _moins de_ (*fewer*) déserts en Amérique du Nord qu'en Afrique.
5. Quel pays a _le plus de_ (*the most*) rivières polluées?
6. Malheureusement, on a _plus de_ (*more*) problèmes que de solutions.

Le français vivant When students are working on question 3, ask them why the last statement might strike someone as contradicting the first two. Then ask them what you call a contradictory statement that may be true nonetheless (*a paradox*/ **un paradoxe**).

Le français vivant

Le Québec

Là où il y a le plus de calme, le plus de sérénité. Moins de stress que chez vous, mais autant de confort et autant de bonheur.

Venez découvrir le Québec... pour plus d'émotions.

Identifiez Quels comparatifs et superlatifs trouvez-vous dans cette publicité (*ad*)?
le plus de calme; le plus de sérénité; Moins de stress; autant de confort; autant de bonheur; plus d'émotions

Questions Posez ces questions à un(e) partenaire et répondez à tour de rôle. Employez des comparatifs et des superlatifs dans vos réponses, si possible. Answers will vary.

1. D'après (*According to*) cette pub, que cherche le/la touriste qui voudrait passer des vacances au Québec?

2. Quelle comparaison la pub fait-elle entre le Québec et l'endroit où habite le lecteur/la lectrice (*reader*)?

3. As-tu déjà passé des vacances au Québec? Voudrais-tu y aller un jour?

4. Si tu vas ou retournes au Québec un jour, voudras-tu y faire un séjour comme celui que la pub décrit? Pourquoi?

5. Connais-tu un autre endroit qui est moins stressant que chez toi? Y vas-tu souvent? Décris-le.

OPTIONS

Extra Practice Ask students questions about themselves using comparative and superlative noun constructions. They should be able to answer each question by saying **Moi!** or remaining silent. Examples: **Qui a le plus de fichiers audio** (*audio files*) **de la classe? Qui a autant de stylos que Luan? Qui a moins de paires de chaussures que Nisha?**

Extra Practice Challenge students to formulate sentences that use comparatives and superlatives of nouns with the pronoun **en**. Ask them how they would substitute **en** for the nouns in the examples on page 614. Example: **Elle fait plus d'heures que sa sœur. (Elle en fait plus que sa sœur.)**

ESPACE STRUCTURES

Mise en pratique

1 **Avec qui sortir?** Amaia compare deux garçons pour voir avec qui elle va accepter de sortir le week-end prochain. Assemblez ses phrases.

> **MODÈLE** Kadir / avoir / plus / énergie / Jacques
> *Kadir a plus d'énergie que Jacques.*

1. Kadir / avoir / moins / problèmes / Jacques   Kadir a moins de problèmes que Jacques.
2. Jacques / avoir / plus / humour / Kadir   Jacques a plus d'humour que Kadir.
3. Kadir / donner / plus / cadeaux / Jacques   Kadir donne plus de cadeaux que Jacques.
4. Jacques / avoir / autant / amis / Kadir   Jacques a autant d'amis que Kadir.
5. Kadir / avoir / moins / patience / Jacques   Kadir a moins de patience que Jacques.
6. Jacques / avoir / plus / ambition / Kadir   Jacques a plus d'ambition que Kadir.

2 **À la campagne** Lise parle de son séjour à la campagne et compare le nombre de choses qu'elle a observées dans la nature. Que dit-elle?

> **MODÈLE**
> *J'ai observé autant de nuages blancs que de nuages gris!*

1. J'ai observé moins d'arbres que de fleurs./J'ai observé plus de fleurs que d'arbres.   **2.** J'ai observé moins d'écureuils que de lapins./J'ai observé plus de lapins que d'écureuils.   **3.** J'ai observé moins de chiens que de chats./J'ai observé plus de chats que de chiens.   **4.** J'ai observé moins de vaches que de serpents./J'ai observé plus de serpents que de vaches.

3 **Des opinions!** Ahmed donne ses opinions sur les choses suivantes. Faites des comparaisons avec les éléments donnés.   Answers may vary. Suggested answers.

1. les villages / charme / les grandes villes   Les villages ont plus de charme que les grandes villes.
2. Donald Trump / argent / Mark Zuckerberg   Donald Trump a moins d'argent que Mark Zuckerberg.
3. Paris / musées / New York   Paris a autant de musées que New York.
4. la campagne / usines / la ville   La campagne a moins d'usines que la ville.
5. Angelina Jolie / films / Anne Hathaway   Angelina Jolie a fait autant de films qu'Anne Hathaway.

4 **Combien de calories?** Vous et votre partenaire êtes au régime. Faites au moins quatre comparaisons entre ces aliments. Dites à la classe quel aliment contient le plus de calories et lequel en contient le moins.   Answers will vary.

> **MODÈLE**
> *Il y a autant de calories dans un café que dans un thé.*

banane	carotte	glace	poulet
biscuits	frites	pain	saucisses
bonbons	gâteau	porc	thon

 Practice more at **vhlcentral.com**.

---

1 **Expansion** Tell students to write down six statements in which they compare themselves to a good friend or to a sibling.

2 **Expansion** Ask students to make similar observations about the campus by looking out the window or walking around outside.

3 **Expansion** Ask students to make comparisons according to their own opinions. Then, ask their partners to contradict their statements. Example: **Étudiant(e) 1: Les villages ont plus de charme que les grandes villes. Étudiant(e) 2: Mais non! Les villages ont moins de charme que les grandes villes.**

4 **Suggestion** You can focus students' attention by grouping items from the list. Example: **gâteau / carotte (Il y a plus de calories dans un gâteau que dans une carotte.)**

Communication

5 Assemblez Posez ces questions à un(e) partenaire, puis faites une comparaison. Answers will vary.

> **MODÈLE**
>
> **Étudiant(e) 1:** *Pendant combien d'heures par jour regardes-tu la télévision?*
> **Étudiant(e) 2:** *Je regarde la télévision deux heures par jour.*
> **Étudiant(e) 1:** *Je regarde plus d'heures de télévision que toi: Je la regarde trois heures par jour.*

1. Combien de frères (sœurs, cousins) as-tu?
2. Combien d'heures par jour étudies-tu?
3. Combien d'e-mails reçois-tu par jour?
4. Combien d'heures dors-tu chaque nuit?
5. Combien de cours as-tu ce semestre?
6. Combien de cafés prends-tu par jour?
7. Combien de personnes connais-tu qui parlent une langue étrangère?
8. Combien d'examens as-tu ce mois-ci?

6 Où habiter? Avec un(e) partenaire, comparez la vie dans une résidence universitaire à la vie dans un appartement. Décidez où vous préféreriez habiter si vous aviez le choix. Utilisez le vocabulaire de la liste. Answers will vary.

> **MODÈLE**
>
> **Étudiant(e) 1:** *Dans un appartement, nous pouvons mettre plus d'affiches sur les murs.*
> **Étudiant(e) 2:** *Oui, et dans une résidence, il y a moins d'espace.*

affiches	armoire	meuble	supervision
amis	espace	protection	télé
argent	fêtes	repas	?

7 Un dialogue Par groupes de trois, vous voulez voyager dans un pays francophone. Vous consultez une agence de voyages et vous posez des questions. Préparez un dialogue où vous utilisez **autant de, moins de** et **plus de** et alternez les rôles. Answers will vary.

> **MODÈLE**
>
> **Étudiant(e) 1:** *Où y a-t-il moins de pollution, au Cameroun ou à Paris?*
> **Étudiant(e) 2:** *Il y a de la pollution aux deux endroits. Mais il y a plus de forêts tropicales au Cameroun.*
> **Étudiant(e) 3:** *Où y a-t-il plus de sentiers? On voudrait faire des randonnées.*

8 Les comparaisons Vous habitez dans une grande ville et votre cousin(e) habite à la campagne. Avec un(e) partenaire, préparez une conversation où vous discutez des différences entre vos deux environnements. Utilisez autant de comparatifs et de superlatifs que possible. Answers will vary.

> **MODÈLE**
>
> **Étudiant(e) 1:** *Il y a beaucoup de bâtiments en ville.*
> **Étudiant(e) 2:** *À la campagne, il y a moins de bâtiments, mais il y a plus d'arbres.*

six cent dix-sept **617**

5 Expansion When students have completed the activity, find out which student has the most of each item in the questions. Example: **1. Qui a le plus de frères de toute la classe?**

6 Suggestion Tally on the board how many students prefer apartments and dormitories. Then ask: **Y a-t-il plus d'étudiants qui préfèrent les appartements ou plus d'étudiants qui préfèrent les résidences universitaires?**

7 Expansion Ask students to take notes on their conversation for reference and then verify the travel agent's answers by doing some research on French-language Internet sites.

O P T I O N S

Extra Practice Ask the class questions about objects around the classroom using comparative and superlative noun constructions. Example: **Qui a plus de crayons, Max ou Lina?** Students should answer in complete sentences.

Game Tell students to write three statements about themselves using comparatives or superlatives of nouns. Suggest that they mention characteristics that would allow their classmates to identify them. Example: **J'ai moins de cheveux que Jason.** Then collect the papers and read them aloud while students guess the identity of each writer. The student with the most correct guesses wins.

Révision

Instructional Resources
vhlcentral.com:
Activity Pack (Info Gap Activities); Testing Program; Testing Program MP3s; reference tools

1 Expansion Write items like these on the board and ask students to say whether they would like more or fewer of them in town: **voitures, arrêts de bus, bars, musées, restaurants français, boutiques, prisons, commissariats de police, parcs, criminels, poubelles.** Example: **J'aimerais qu'il y ait moins de voitures dans notre ville.**

2 Suggestion Give students categories to help them think of tourist attractions to mention. Examples: restaurants, shopping, sports, museums, architecture, festivals, etc.

3 Suggestion Ask students to summarize what they said. Example: **C'est dommage qu'il n'y ait pas assez de poubelles sur le campus. Je souhaite qu'il y en ait plus à l'avenir.**

4 Suggestion Have the class identify the expressions listed on pages 597, 610, and 611 that would be useful in this activity. Examples: **Il faut que…, Je propose que… , Je regrette que…,** etc.

5 Expansion When students have finished, tell them to write a new conversation that includes a third speaker—an environmentalist hunter. Have them imagine what this person thinks about hunting while preserving animal species. (Environmental hunters tend to advocate strict controls that assure only overpopulated animal species are hunted, but not overhunted.)

6 Suggestion Divide the class into pairs and distribute the Info Gap Handouts found in the Activity Pack on the Supersite. Give students ten minutes to complete the activity.

---

1 Des changements Avec un(e) partenaire, observez ces endroits et dites, à tour de rôle, si vous aimeriez qu'il y ait **plus de** ou **moins de** certaines choses. Ensuite, comparez vos phrases à celles d'un autre groupe. *Answers will vary.*

MODÈLE

Étudiant(e) 1: *Je préférerais qu'il y ait plus d'eau dans cette rivière.*
Étudiant(e) 2: *J'aimerais mieux qu'il y ait plus d'herbe.*

 1.
 2.
 3.
 4.

2 Visite de votre région Interviewez vos camarades. Que recommandent-ils à des visiteurs qui ne connaissent pas votre région? Écrivez leurs réponses, puis comparez vos résultats à ceux d'un autre groupe. Utilisez ces expressions. *Answers will vary.*

MODÈLE

Étudiant(e) 1: *Que devraient faire les visiteurs de cette région?*
Étudiant(e) 2: *Je recommande qu'ils visitent les musées du centre-ville. Il serait bon qu'ils assistent aussi à un match de baseball.*

il est bon que	proposer que
il est indispensable que	recommander que
il faut que	suggérer que
?	?

3 Plus d'arbres Avec un(e) partenaire, pensez à votre environnement et dites si vous voulez qu'il y ait **plus de, moins de** ou **autant de** choses ou d'animaux. Quand vous n'êtes pas d'accord, justifiez vos réponses. *Answers will vary.*

MODÈLE

Étudiant(e) 1: *Je souhaite qu'il y ait plus d'arbres.*
Étudiant(e) 2: *Oui, il faut plus d'arbres sur le campus et en ville.*

4 Voyage en Afrique centrale Avec un(e) partenaire, vous voulez visiter ces endroits en Afrique centrale. Préparez un dialogue avec des verbes au présent du subjonctif et des comparatifs ou des superlatifs. Ensuite, alternez les rôles. *Answers will vary.*

MODÈLE

Étudiant(e) 1: *J'aimerais qu'on visite Kribi, au Cameroun. Il y a plus de plages.*
Étudiant(e) 2: *Il vaut mieux que nous visitions le marché, au Gabon.*

la forêt de Dzanga-Sangha (République centrafricaine)
le lac Kivu (Rwanda)
les marchés (Gabon)
le parc national de Lobéké (Cameroun)
le parc national de l'Ivindo (Congo)
les plages de Kribi (Cameroun)

5 Échange d'opinions Avec un(e) partenaire, imaginez une conversation entre un chasseur (*hunter*) et un défenseur de la nature. Préparez un dialogue où les deux se font des suggestions. Ensuite, jouez votre dialogue pour la classe. *Answers will vary.*

MODÈLE

Étudiant(e) 1: *Il est dommage que vous disiez que les chasseurs n'aiment pas la nature.*
Étudiant(e) 2: *Je souhaite que vous respectiez plus les animaux.*

6 La maman de Carine Votre professeur va vous donner, à vous et à votre partenaire, deux feuilles d'activités différentes sur Carine et sa mère. Attention! Ne regardez pas la feuille de votre partenaire. *Answers will vary.*

MODÈLE

Étudiant(e) 1: *Si Carine prend l'avion,…*
Étudiant(e) 2: *… sa mère veut qu'elle l'appelle de l'aéroport.*

OPTIONS

Game Ask small groups to write down three statements using comparative or superlative noun constructions. Two of the statements should be true; the third one should be false. Read the statements aloud. Groups identify the false statement in each set. The group with the most correct answers wins.

Extra Practice Put slips of paper, each with the names of two celebrities on it, in a bin. Have students draw slips, and then ask a question using a comparative or superlative that prompts them to identify one of the celebrities. Example: (1. Mark Zuckerberg 2. Mark Wahlberg) **C'est celui des deux qui a le plus d'argent.** (Mark Zuckerberg)

À l'écoute

STRATÉGIE

Listening for the gist/ Listening for cognates

Combining these two strategies is an easy way to get a good sense of what you hear. When you listen for the gist, you get the general idea of what you're hearing, which allows you to interpret cognates and other words in a meaningful context. Similarly, the cognates give you information about the details of the story that you might not have understood when listening for the gist.

🔊 To practice these strategies, you will listen to a short paragraph. Write down the gist of what you hear and jot down a few cognates. What conclusions can you draw about what you heard?

Préparation

Regardez la photo. Que se passe-t-il à votre avis? Combien de personnes y a-t-il? Pour quelle cause ces personnes manifestent-elles (*demonstrate*)? De quoi vont-elles parler?

À vous d'écouter

Écoutez la personne qui a organisé la manifestation (*demonstration*) et encerclez les sujets mentionnés.

la chasse	les lois sur la protection de l'environnement
(les déchets toxiques)	
l'effet de serre	la pluie acide
l'énergie nucléaire	(la pollution)
(l'extinction de certaines espèces)	(la pollution des rivières)
(le gaspillage)	(le ramassage des ordures)
	la surpopulation

 Practice more at vhlcentral.com.

Compréhension

Complétez Choisissez la bonne réponse pour terminer chaque phrase, d'après ce que vous venez d'entendre.

1. On peut recycler __a__.
   a. le verre   b. les déchets toxiques   c. tous les déchets

2. Les emballages recyclables aident à __c__.
   a. éviter le ramassage des ordures
   b. trier (*to sort*) les déchets   c. combattre la pollution de la Terre

3. Il faut __b__ le gaspillage.
   a. développer   b. éviter   c. polluer

4. Le gouvernement doit __a__.
   a. passer des lois plus strictes en ce qui concerne l'écologie
   b. éviter l'effet de serre   c. réduire le trou dans la couche d'ozone

5. Il y a beaucoup de __a__ dans les rivières.
   a. déchets toxiques   b. ressources naturelles   c. verre

6. Trop __b__ sont en train de disparaître.
   a. d'écoproduits   b. d'espèces   c. d'océans

Les lois Un(e) représentant(e) du Congrès vient à votre université pour discuter de l'environnement. Par petits groupes, choisissez un problème écologique qui est très important pour vous. Préparez des arguments à lui présenter. Vous voulez lui faire comprendre que le gouvernement doit faire plus dans le domaine que vous avez choisi. Soyez prêts à bien expliquer la situation actuelle (*today*) et les changements nécessaires pour l'améliorer. Pensez aussi à quelques nouvelles lois sur la protection de l'environnement que vous pourrez suggérer à votre représentant(e) du Congrès.

six cent dix-neuf **619**

Section Goals

In this section, students will:
- learn to listen for the gist and for cognates
- listen to a paragraph and jot down the gist and some cognates
- listen to a speech at an environmental demonstration and complete several activities

Instructional Resources
vhlcentral.com:
Textbook MP3s; Textbook Audioscript; reference tools

Stratégie
Audioscript Les Français choisissent de plus en plus de passer des vacances «vertes», c'est-à-dire des vacances qui proposent des activités d'écotourisme. Ces voyages, qui sont souvent des voyages organisés, permettent à leurs participants de passer du temps dans la nature et de découvrir ce qu'ils peuvent faire pour contribuer plus activement à la protection de notre planète.

Préparation Have students look at the photo and describe what is happening. Then have them guess what the people might be saying.

À vous d'écouter
Audioscript Bonjour à tous et merci beaucoup d'être venus participer à notre manifestation aujourd'hui. Si nous travaillons tous ensemble, nous pourrons trouver des solutions concrètes pour moins polluer notre environnement. Tout d'abord, il est essentiel que nous prenions tous l'habitude de trier nos déchets. Le verre et beaucoup d'autres emballages ménagers peuvent être recyclés. Il est aussi indispensable que vous achetiez des produits emballés dans des emballages recyclables. Ils aident à combattre la pollution de notre planète. Il est aussi nécessaire d'éviter le gaspillage. Ces suggestions sont un bon début, mais malheureusement, nous ne pouvons pas réussir seuls. Il faut absolument que notre gouvernement fasse plus d'efforts en ce qui concerne le recyclage et le ramassage des ordures. Il est également nécessaire que tous les

gouvernements d'Europe ainsi que ceux des autres pays et continents fassent passer des lois beaucoup plus strictes en ce qui concerne les déchets toxiques. Nous ne voulons plus de déchets toxiques dans nos rivières ni dans nos océans! La pollution de l'eau, comme celle du reste de la Terre, est un véritable danger qu'il faut prendre très au sérieux. Trop d'espèces aussi

sont en train de disparaître et je souhaite qu'aujourd'hui, nous promettions tous d'essayer de faire plus d'efforts pour favoriser l'écologie. Je propose en plus que nous écrivions tous au ministre de l'environnement pour demander des changements dès aujourd'hui!

Panorama

La Bourgogne-Franche-Comté

la ville d'Ornans

Section Goals

In this section, students will read historical and cultural information about **Bourgogne-Franche-Comté**.

Instructional Resources
vhlcentral.com:
Digital Image Bank;
SAM Answer Key;
reference tools

Carte de la Bourgogne-Franche-Comté

• Have students look at the map of **Bourgogne-Franche-Comté** or use the **Panorama** map from the Digital Image Bank. Ask volunteers to read the names of the cities and geographical features aloud.
• Ask students to name the bordering country (**la Suisse**).
• Tell students that the region was created in 2016 by merging former regions **la Bourgogne** and **la Franche-Comté**.

La région en chiffres

• Point out the region's logo.
• Have volunteers read the sections aloud. After each section, ask students questions about the content.
• Ask students if they have heard of the **personnes célèbres** and what they know about them.
• Point out that the vineyards of Burgundy produce some of the world's greatest wines.
• The town of Nevers is famous for its fine hand-painted decorative pottery, known as **faïence**.
• The area of **Franche-Comté** is known for handcrafted wood items, such as violins, guitars, pipes, clocks, and toys.

Incroyable mais vrai! Snails have been a source of food since at least the time of the Romans. They are a rich source of protein and supposedly prevent aging.

La région en chiffres

RÉGION BOURGOGNE FRANCHE COMTE

▶ **Superficie:** *48.800 km²*

▶ **Population:** *2.820.623*
SOURCE: INSEE

▶ **Industries principales:** *industries automobile et pharmaceutique, tourisme, viticulture°*

▶ **Villes principales:** *Auxerre, Belfort, Besançon, Chalon-sur-Saône, Dijon, Dole, Mâcon, Nevers*

La région Bourgogne-Franche-Comté offre le meilleur de la terre et de la montagne. À l'ouest, la Bourgogne compte seulement 3% du vignoble° français mais propose le plus grand nombre d'appellations° d'origine. La moutarde de Dijon est célèbre dans le monde entier, et elle est produite en Bourgogne avec des graines de moutarde et du vin de la région. À l'est, les montagnes du Jura comprennent° le Parc Naturel Régional du Haut-Jura, deux stations thermales° et trois stations de ski.

Personnages célèbres

▶ **Gustave Eiffel,** *ingénieur (la tour Eiffel) (1832–1923)*

▶ **Colette,** *écrivaine (1873–1954)*

▶ **Louis** *(1864–1948)* **et Auguste** *(1862–1954)* **Lumière,** *inventeurs du cinématographe°*

▶ **Guillaume Meurice,** *humoriste et chroniqueur° radio (1981–)*

▶ **Claude Jade,** *actrice (1948–2006)*

▶ **François Mitterrand,** *ancien Président de la République française (1916–1996)*

viticulture *grape growing* **vignoble** *wine-growing regions* **appellations** *designations* **comprennent** *consist of* **stations thermales** *spas* **cinématographe** *motion picture camera* **chroniqueur** *commentator* **persil** *parsley* **lutter contre** *fight against* **vendanges** *grape harvest*

Auxerre • **Belfort** • **BOURGOGNE-FRANCHE-COMTÉ** **Dijon** • **Besançon** • **Nevers** • **Beaune** • **Dole** • **Chalon-sur-Saône** **Pontarlier** • **LE JURA** **LA SUISSE** **Mâcon** • **LA FRANCE** L'A... L'ITA...

la Seine · la Loire · l'Yonne · la Saône · le Doubs · le Doubs · la Saône · l'Ain · le Rhône · le Rhône

0 — 80 miles
0 — 80 kilomètres

les vendanges° en Bourgogne

un marché à Dijon

Incroyable mais vrai!

Au Moyen Âge, les escargots servaient à la fabrication de sirops contre la toux. La recette bourguignonne (beurre, ail, persil°) est popularisée au 19ᵉ siècle. En France, on consomme jusqu'à 16.000 tonnes d'escargots par an. L'escargot aide à lutter contre° le mauvais cholestérol et les maladies cardio-vasculaires.

OPTIONS

Personnes célèbres **Gustave Eiffel** is famous for his contribution to the construction of the **tour Eiffel** in Paris and the Statue of Liberty in New York. **Colette** wrote novels about women; some of them were autobiographical. One of her best-known works, *Gigi* (1945), was made into a Hollywood musical in 1958. **Louis** and **Auguste Lumière** were among the first inventors to patent and improve the motion picture camera.

Guillaume Meurice is known for *Le Moment Meurice*, part of a talk show on **France Inter** radio. **Claude Jade** appeared in films directed by François Truffaut and Alfred Hitchcock. **François Mitterrand** was president of France from 1981 to 1995. His **Grands travaux** built a series of twentieth-century monuments in Paris, including the **Grande Arche de La Défense** and the **Bibliothèque nationale de France**.

Les sports

Les sports d'hiver dans le Jura

On peut pratiquer de nombreux sports d'hiver dans les montagnes du Jura, en Franche-Comté: ski alpin, surf°, monoski, planche à voile sur neige. Mais le Jura est surtout le paradis du ski de fond°. Avec des centaines de kilomètres de pistes°, on y skie de décembre à avril, y compris° la nuit, sur des pistes éclairées°. La célèbre Transjurassienne

est la deuxième course° d'endurance du monde avec un parcours° de 76 kilomètres et un de 50 kilomètres. Il y a aussi la Transjeune, un parcours de 10 kilomètres pour les jeunes de moins de 20 ans.

Les destinations

Besançon: ancienne capitale de l'horlogerie

L'artisanat de l'horlogerie commence au 16e siècle avec l'installation de grandes horloges dans les monastères. Au 18e siècle, 400 horlogers suisses viennent s'installer° en Franche-Comté. Au 19e siècle, Montbéliard comptait 5.000 horlogers. En hiver, les paysans°-horlogers s'occupaient°, dans leurs fermes°, de la finition° et de la décoration des horloges. En 1862, une école d'horlogerie est créée° et en 1900, Besançon devient le berceau° de l'horlogerie française avec 8.000 horlogers qui produisent 600.000 montres par an.

L'architecture

Les toits de Bourgogne

Les toits° en tuiles vernissées° multicolores sont typiques de la Bourgogne. Inspirés de l'architecture flamande° et d'Europe centrale, ils forment des dessins géométriques. Le plus célèbre bâtiment est l'Hôtel-Dieu° de Beaune, construit en 1443 pour accueillir° les pauvres et les victimes de la guerre° de Cent Ans (1337–1443). Aujourd'hui, l'Hôtel-Dieu organise la plus célèbre vente aux enchères° de vins du monde.

Les gens

Louis Pasteur (1822–1895)

Louis Pasteur est né à Dole, en Franche-Comté. Il découvre que les fermentations sont dues à des micro-organismes spécifiques. Dans ses recherches sur les maladies contagieuses, il montre la relation entre le microbe et l'apparition d'une maladie. Cette découverte° a des applications dans le monde hospitalier et industriel avec les méthodes de désinfection, de stérilisation et de pasteurisation. Le vaccin contre la rage° est aussi une de ses inventions. L'Institut Pasteur est créé à Paris en 1888. Aujourd'hui, il a des filiales° sur cinq continents.

Qu'est-ce que vous avez appris? Répondez aux questions par des phrases complètes.

1. Comment s'appellent les inventeurs du cinématographe?
   Ils s'appellent Louis et Auguste Lumière.
2. À quoi servaient les escargots au Moyen Âge?
   Ils servaient à fabriquer des sirops contre la toux.
3. Avec quoi sont préparés les escargots de Bourgogne?
   Ils sont préparés avec du beurre, de l'ail et du persil.
4. Quel est le sport le plus pratiqué dans le Jura?
   C'est le ski de fond.
5. Qu'est-ce que la Transjurassienne?
   C'est une course d'endurance. C'est une course d'endurance.
6. D'où viennent les horlogers au 18e siècle?
   Ils viennent de Suisse.

7. Quel style d'architecture a influencé les toits de Bourgogne?
   L'architecture flamande et d'Europe centrale les a influencés.
8. Quel est le bâtiment avec le toit le plus célèbre en Bourgogne?
   C'est l'Hôtel-Dieu de Beaune.
9. Comment les recherches de Pasteur ont-elles été utilisées par les hôpitaux et l'industrie?
   Elles ont été utilisées dans les méthodes de désinfection, de stérilisation et de pasteurisation.
10. Où trouve-t-on des Instituts Pasteur aujourd'hui?
    On trouve des Instituts Pasteur à Paris et sur cinq continents.

Sur Internet

Go to **vhlcentral.com** to find more cultural information related to this **Panorama**.

1. Cherchez trois recettes à base (*using*) d'escargots.

2. Quand ont lieu les vendanges en Bourgogne?

3. Cherchez des informations sur Louis Pasteur. Quel effet ont eu ses découvertes sur des produits alimentaires d'usage courant (*everyday use*)?

ressources

WB
pp. 201–202

vhlcentral

surf *snowboarding* **ski de fond** *cross-country skiing* **pistes** *trails* **y compris** *including* **éclairées** *lit* **course** *race* **parcours** *course* **s'installer** *settle* **paysans** *peasants* **s'occupaient** *took care* **fermes** *farms* **finition** *finishing* **créée** *created* **berceau** *cradle* **toits** *roofs* **tuiles vernissées** *glazed tiles* **flamande** *Flemish* **Hôtel-Dieu** *Hospital* **accueillir** *take care of* **guerre** *war* **vente aux enchères** *auction* **découverte** *discovery* **rage** *rabies* **filiales** *branches*

six cent vingt et un **621**

Les sports d'hiver dans le Jura
- The Jura Mountains along the Swiss-French border extend from the Rhône River to the Rhine River.
- Ask students: **Que font les gens sur la photo? (Ils font du ski de fond.) Avez-vous envie de visiter les montagnes du Jura? Pourquoi?**

Besançon: ancienne capitale de l'horlogerie
- The **musée du Temps** in the **palais Granvelle** contains all sorts of timepieces from ancient to modern times. It also chronicles the history of the measurement of time.
- Besançon is no longer the capital of watch/clockmaking. Many businesses in the industry have closed, and the region has turned to microtechnics, opticals, and electronics.

Les toits de Bourgogne
- The multicolored tiles appear mostly on buildings dating from the late Middle Ages or the Renaissance, but they were sometimes used on houses built or restored in the 19th and 20th centuries. Ask students to describe the tiles.
- Explain that the **guerre de Cent Ans** was a series of conflicts between England and France. The war, along with epidemics and civil unrest, took a heavy toll on the French population.

Louis Pasteur
- Louis Pasteur also discovered ways of preventing silkworm diseases, anthrax, and chicken cholera.
- Have students research Pasteur's contributions to science. Then discuss as a class the long-term consequences of his work.

O P T I O N S

Bourgogne The duchy of Burgundy enjoyed a golden age from the beginning of Duke Philip the Bold's reign in 1364 to the end of Duke Charles the Bold's reign in 1477. During that time Franche-Comté became part of the Burgundian duchy, as did Flanders and parts of the Netherlands. As a result, Burgundy became a powerful economic and cultural force, and it enjoyed prosperous trade in wine, wool, and grain.

Extra Practice After students have read the **Panorama**, ask them to give examples of industries in Burgundy and Franche-Comté that were influenced by the geography or location of these two regions. Examples: **la viticulture, le tourisme ou les sports d'hiver dans les montagnes du Jura, l'horlogerie (qui a commencé avec l'arrivée des horlogers suisses au 18e siècle).**

Section Goals

In this section, students will:
• learn to recognize personification in literature
• read a text by Jules Renard

Stratégie Give students a few more examples of English phrases that use personification, such as "the book flew off the shelves" and "the wind was howling." Ask them to identify the words and expressions that denote personification.

Successful Language Learning Point out that the author of the text they are going to read uses personification in this work. As a class, brainstorm words and expressions in French that could be used to describe a "family of trees."

Examinez le texte
• Have volunteers describe the image on this page spread.
• As they read, tell students to look for characteristics and qualities, used to describe the trees, that they normally associate with human beings.

À propos de l'auteur
• Ask these comprehension questions: **1. Dans quel type d'environnement est-ce que Jules Renard a passé son enfance? (dans un village à la campagne) 2. Pourquoi a-t-il quitté sa famille à l'adolescence? (il a été envoyé en pension) 3. Comment a-t-il commencé sa carrière d'écrivain? (il a commencé à écrire des articles pour des journaux et des revues) 4. De quoi parle-t-il principalement dans ses œuvres? (de ses observations des hommes et de leurs comportements) 5. Qu'est-ce qui a joué un rôle important dans sa vie? (la campagne et la nature)**
• Explain to students that Renard's writing style is often humorous and full of irony.
• Give students some additional information about *Poil de carotte*, Jules Renard's most famous novel, and ask if they would be interested in reading it.

Lecture

Audio: Dramatic Reading

Avant la lecture

STRATÉGIE

Recognizing personification

For dramatic effect and to achieve a more interesting writing style, authors rely on different literary techniques in their stories or poems.

Personification (**la personnification**) is a literary technique in which an author gives human characteristics, such as feelings, thoughts, or behaviors, to something that is not human. The phrases "Old Man Winter" and "time flies" are common examples of personification and how it makes descriptions more poetic and vivid.

Examinez le texte

Regardez l'image et lisez le titre du texte. Quel mot dans ce titre dénote un exemple de personnification? Comment imaginez-vous cette «famille d'arbres»?

À propos de l'auteur
Jules Renard (1864–1910)

Jules Renard a passé son enfance à Chitry-les-Mines, un village de campagne. Enfant mal aimé, il est envoyé en pension° pour faire ses études. Il obtient son baccalauréat à Paris, où il fréquente les cafés littéraires.
Il commence sa carrière d'écrivain en écrivant des articles pour des journaux et des revues°, puis il se tourne vers la littérature. Son œuvre, pleine d'humour et de poésie, relate ses observations des hommes et de leurs comportements°, et elle reflète son amour pour la campagne et la nature. Son roman le plus célèbre, *Poil de carotte*, est une autobiographie où il raconte son enfance malheureuse.

pension *boarding school* **revues** *magazines* **comportements** *behaviors*

Une famille d'arbres

Jules Renard

1 C'est après avoir traversé une plaine brûlée de soleil que je les rencontre.

Ils ne demeurent° pas au bord de la route, à cause du bruit°. Ils habitent les champs incultes°, sur une
5 source° connue des oiseaux seuls.

De loin, ils semblent impénétrables. Dès que j'approche, leurs troncs se desserrent°. Ils m'accueillent° avec prudence. Je peux me reposer, me rafraîchir, mais je devine qu'ils m'observent et se défient°.

10 Ils vivent en famille°, les plus âgés au milieu et les petits, ceux dont les premières feuilles viennent de naître, un peu partout, sans jamais s'écarter°.

Ils mettent longtemps à mourir, et ils gardent les morts° debout° jusqu'à la chute en poussière°.

15 Ils se flattent° de leurs longues branches, pour s'assurer qu'ils sont tous là, comme les aveugles°. Ils gesticulent de colère° si le vent s'essouffle° à les déraciner°. Mais entre eux aucune dispute. Ils ne murmurent que d'accord.

20 Je sens qu'ils doivent être ma vraie famille. J'oublierai vite l'autre. Ces arbres m'adopteront peu à peu, et pour le mériter j'apprends ce qu'il faut savoir:
Je sais déjà regarder les nuages qui passent.
Je sais aussi rester en place.
25 Et je sais presque me taire°.

O P T I O N S

Pairs Have pairs research and write a summary about an aspect of Renard's life that is not mentioned in this brief biography. Have them jot down notes and share some of their findings orally with the class.

Small Groups Tell students that Jules Renard illustrated some of his stories. Have them work in small groups to research his drawings for *Histoires naturelles*. Ask them to prepare a short presentation in which they show and describe a few of the illustrations. Encourage the class to comment on Renard's style and discuss how his drawings reflect his love for nature.

Après la lecture

Vrai ou faux? Indiquez si les phrases sont **vraies** ou **fausses**, d'après le texte. Corrigez les fausses. Some answers may vary.

1. Les arbres habitent près de la route.
   Faux. Les arbres habitent loin de la route.
2. Les arbres accueillent le narrateur avec beaucoup de joie.
   Faux. Les arbres accueillent le narrateur avec prudence.
3. Les jeunes arbres grandissent près des plus vieux.
   Vrai.
4. Il y a souvent des disputes entre les membres de cette famille d'arbres.
   Faux. Il n'y a aucune dispute entre eux.
5. Il n'est pas facile de se faire adopter par une famille d'arbres.
   Vrai.
6. Le narrateur n'apprécie pas beaucoup sa propre famille humaine.
   Vrai.

Répondez Répondez aux questions par des phrases complètes. Answers will vary. Suggested answers.

1. Où habite la famille d'arbres?
   Elle habite les champs incultes, sur une source.
2. Comment réagissent les arbres quand le narrateur s'approche d'eux?
   Ils l'accueillent avec prudence, ils l'observent et se défient.
3. Comment est-ce que les arbres vivent en famille?
   Ils vivent tous ensemble, les plus âgés au milieu.
4. Pourquoi est-ce que les arbres se mettent parfois en colère contre le vent?
   Parce qu'il essaie de les déraciner.
5. Comment est la relation entre les arbres?
   Il n'y a aucune dispute entre eux, et ils sont toujours d'accord.
6. Que doit faire le narrateur pour être accepté dans la famille d'arbres?
   Il doit regarder les nuages qui passent, rester en place et se taire.

La personnification Avez-vous trouvé des exemples de la personnification dans ce texte? Citez-en quelques-uns. Quelles sont les caractéristiques humaines présentes dans ces exemples (des émotions, des traits, des pensées, des comportements, etc.)? Answers will vary. Suggested answers.
«Ils m'accueillent avec prudence.» (émotions, comportements), «le vent s'essouffle» (comportements), etc.

À votre tour Travaillez par groupes de trois. Choisissez un élément de la nature (un animal, un endroit, etc.) que vous aimez particulièrement. Ensemble, créez-en une description. Utilisez la technique de la personnification pour rendre votre description plus intéressante.

MODÈLE

Le tournesol se réveille et sent le vent caresser ses pétales. Il passe la journée à parler avec le soleil, se tournant la tête pour le suivre.

demeurent *live, réside* bruit *noise* incultes *uncultivated* source *spring*
leurs troncs se desserrent *their trunks loosen up* m'accueillent *greet me*
se défient *are wary* vivent en famille *live as a family*
s'écarter *moving away from one another* les morts *the dead* debout *upright*
chute en poussière *fall to dust* se flattent *touch one another*
les aveugles *the blind* colère *anger* s'essouffle *exhausts itself*
déraciner *to uproot* me taire *to be quiet, silent*

Vrai ou faux? Ask for volunteers to read their corrected false statements aloud.

Répondez Have students compare their answers and discuss where they disagree.

La personnification Before students begin this activity, remind them that personification assigns human feelings, traits, thoughts, or behaviors to something that is not human. Ask students why they think Jules Renard chose to use this technique in the text. (It helps the reader relate the tree family's behavior to human behavior and emotions.)

À votre tour Have groups choose a subject for their description. Have them brainstorm words and expressions they could use, as you circulate to provide vocabulary support. Ask the groups to share their descriptions orally and have the class vote on the description that uses personification most effectively.

Extra Practice Have the class discuss these questions. For item 3, encourage students to be creative.
1. À votre avis, la famille d'arbres va-t-elle décider d'adopter le narrateur? 2. Et lui, va-t-il vraiment oublier sa famille humaine? 3. En quoi la vie du narrateur va-t-elle changer s'il devient un membre de la famille d'arbres?

Extra Practice Have students read the last 3 lines of the text again. Say: **Le narrateur mentionne qu'il doit savoir faire trois choses pour mériter d'être adopté par les arbres: savoir regarder les nuages qui passent, savoir rester en place et savoir se taire. Qu'est-ce que ces trois choses révèlent sur la personnalité de la famille d'arbres et sur leur mode de vie?** Discuss as a class.

Section Goals

In this section, students will:
- learn about a writer's audience and purpose
- write a letter or an article about an environmental issue

Stratégie Review with the class the importance of considering the purpose and audience when writing. Then go through questions 1–5. If possible, provide students with samples of persuasive letters in French, such as letters to the editor. Tell them to identify the audience and the author's purpose for each letter.

Thème Tell students to follow the steps outlined here when writing their letter or article.

Proofreading Activity Have students correct these sentences. **1. Il faut que je vous parler de cette article sur le pollution. 2. C'est dommage que j'ai si peu de temp. 3. J'aimerais que tu fasse une portraite de moi. 4. Il ne faut pas que tu être si anxieuse.**

Écriture

STRATÉGIE

Considering audience and purpose

Writing always has a purpose. During the planning stages, you must determine to whom you are addressing the piece, and what you want to express to your reader. Once you have defined both your audience and your purpose, you will be able to decide which genre, vocabulary, and grammatical structures will best serve your literary composition.

Let's say you want to share your thoughts on local traffic problems. Your audience can be either the local government or the community. You could choose to write a newspaper article, a letter to the editor, or a letter to the city's governing board. You should first ask yourself these questions:

1. Are you going to comment on traffic problems in general, or are you going to point out several specific problems?

2. Are you intending to register a complaint?

3. Are you simply intending to inform others and increase public awareness of the problems?

4. Are you hoping to persuade others to adopt your point of view?

5. Are you hoping to inspire others to take concrete actions?

The answers to these questions will help you establish the purpose of your writing and determine your audience. Of course, your writing can have more than one purpose. For example, you may intend for your writing to both inform others of a problem and inspire them to take action.

✎ Thème

Écrire une lettre ou un article
Avant l'écriture

1. Vous allez écrire au sujet d'un (*about a*) problème de l'environnement qui est important pour vous. Choisissez d'abord le problème dont vous voulez parler. Lisez les trois sujets et choisissez à propos duquel (*about which one*) vous voulez écrire.

   - Écrivez au sujet des programmes qui existent pour protéger l'environnement dans votre communauté. Sont-ils efficaces (*effective*)? Tout le monde (*Everybody*) participe-t-il? Avez-vous des doutes sur le futur de l'environnement dans votre communauté?

   - Décrivez un des attraits (*attractions*) naturels de votre région. Êtes-vous optimiste sur le futur environnemental de votre région? Que font le gouvernement et les habitants de votre région pour protéger l'environnement? Faut-il faire plus?

   - Écrivez au sujet d'un programme pour la protection de l'environnement au niveau national ou international. Est-ce un programme du/des gouvernement(s) ou d'une entreprise privée? Est-il efficace? Qui y participe? Avez-vous des doutes au sujet de ce programme? Pensez-vous qu'on devrait le changer ou l'améliorer? Comment?

2. Décidez qui sera votre public: Voulez-vous écrire une lettre à un membre du gouvernement, à une association universitaire, etc.? Préférez-vous écrire un article pour un journal, un magazine? Complétez ce tableau (*chart*).

O P T I O N S

Stratégie Review the strategy with students. Then list some possible audiences for a writing task: the general public, someone you don't know well, someone you know very well. Ask how your language would change for each audience. Then do the same thing with various purposes: to entertain, to inform, to persuade. How would your language change to reflect your purpose in writing?

If possible, provide students with samples of persuasive letters in French, such as letters to the editor from actual or digital newspapers. Ask them: Who is the intended audience for a letter to the editor? Do different newspapers have different kinds of audiences? Then have students work in pairs to analyze each letter and to identify the writer's purpose in writing.

Audience: Cochez (Select) les options qui décrivent votre audience.

_____ *un(e) ami(e) (lequel/laquelle?)*

_____ *une association universitaire (laquelle?)*

_____ *un membre du/d'un gouvernement (lequel?)*

_____ *les lecteurs (readers) d'un journal/magazine (lequel?)*

_____ *les lecteurs d'un magazine (lequel?)*

Décrivez votre audience ici.

Mots (Words) et expressions pour atteindre (reach) ces lecteurs:

3. Identifiez le but de votre lettre ou article: Voulez-vous simplement informer le public ou allez-vous aussi donner votre opinion personnelle? Complétez ce tableau.

But: Cochez toutes les options qui décrivent votre but.

_____ *informer les lecteurs* _____ *se plaindre (to complain)*

_____ *exprimer vos sentiments (feelings)* _____ *examiner différents problèmes et situations*

_____ *persuader les lecteurs* _____ *examiner un seul problème ou une seule situation*

_____ *inspirer les lecteurs*

Décrivez votre but ici.

Détails qui soutiennent (support) votre but:

4. Après avoir complété les deux tableaux, décidez quel type de rédaction vous allez écrire.

Écriture

1. Préparez une courte introduction, puis présentez le problème que vous avez choisi.

2. N'oubliez pas de répondre à toutes les questions posées dans la présentation du sujet en page précédente.

3. Utilisez le subjonctif pour exprimer la volonté et l'émotion, des comparatifs et des superlatifs, et des pronoms démonstratifs dans votre rédaction.

4. Si vous avez choisi d'exprimer votre opinion personnelle, justifiez-la pour essayer de persuader votre/vos lecteur(s).

5. Préparez la conclusion de votre lettre ou article.

Après l'écriture

1. Échangez votre lettre/article avec celle/celui d'un(e) partenaire. Répondez à ces questions pour commenter son travail.

■ Votre partenaire a-t-il/elle identifié un but et une audience spécifiques?

■ Sa lettre/Son article montre-t-elle/il clairement le but?

■ Sa lettre/Son article est-elle/il réellement destiné(e) (*aimed*) à un type de lecteurs spécifiques?

■ Votre partenaire a-t-il/elle répondu à toutes les questions posées dans la présentation du sujet?

■ A-t-il/elle utilisé les points de grammaire de l'unité?

■ Quel(s) détail(s) ajouteriez-vous (*would you add*)? Quel(s) détail(s) enlèveriez-vous (*would you delete*)? Quel(s) autre(s) commentaire(s) avez-vous pour votre partenaire?

2. Corrigez votre lettre/article d'après (*according to*) les commentaires de votre partenaire. Relisez votre travail pour éliminer ces problèmes:

■ des fautes (*errors*) d'orthographe, de ponctuation et de conjugaison

■ un mauvais emploi (*use*) des temps et de la grammaire de l'unité

■ des fautes d'accord (*agreement*) des adjectifs

EVALUATION

Criteria

Content Includes evidence of and information related to each of the numbered items in the writing task.
Scale: 1 2 3 4 5

Organization Organized into a letter or an article that contains logical paragraphs that begin with a topic sentence and contain appropriate supporting detail.
Scale: 1 2 3 4 5

Accuracy Uses the subjunctive verb forms correctly. Spells words, conjugates verbs, and modifies adjectives correctly throughout.
Scale: 1 2 3 4 5

Creativity Includes additional information that is not requested in the task and/or uses adjectives, descriptive verbs, and additional details to make the composition more interesting.
Scale: 1 2 3 4 5

Scoring

Excellent	18–20 points
Good	14–17 points
Satisfactory	10–13 points
Unsatisfactory	< 10 points

OPTIONS

Avant l'écriture Talk about persuasive language and the kinds of words that inspire people to take action. As a class, brainstorm a list of useful words and expressions that could be used in a typical letter to the editor. Possible items for inclusion: **À mon avis, Je pense que/Je crois que…, Il est urgent/nécessaire/important que…, Nous ne pouvons pas/Nous ne devrions pas…, Je vous exhorte de (***urge***)/Je vous demande de/Je vous prie de (***beg***)…**

Tell students that many of these persuasive expressions and verbs will trigger the use of the subjunctive, such as impersonal expressions with **être (Il est bon que…, etc.)**, verbs and expressions of will (**Je demande que…, etc.**), and verbs and expressions of emotion (**J'aimerais que…, etc.**). These can be found on pages 597, 610, and 611 of this unit.

Instructional Resources
vhlcentral.com:
Textbook MP3s; Textbook
Audioscript; reference tools

Suggestions
- Tell students that an easy way to study from **Vocabulaire** is to cover up the French half of each section, leaving only the English equivalents exposed. They can then quiz themselves on the French items. To focus on the English equivalents of the French entries, they simply reverse this process.
- Point out to students that they can use the Vocabulary Tools at **vhlcentral.com** for reference and extra vocabulary practice.

🔊 Ⓢ Vocabulary Tools

Leçon 14A

La nature
un espace *space, area*
en plein air *outdoor, open-air*
pur(e) *pure*

L'écologie
améliorer *to improve*
développer *to develop*
gaspiller *to waste*
polluer *to pollute*
préserver *to preserve*
prévenir l'incendie *to prevent fires*
proposer une solution *to propose a solution*
recycler *to recycle*
sauver la planète *to save the planet*
une catastrophe *catastrophe*
une centrale nucléaire *nuclear power plant*
le covoiturage *carpooling*
un danger *danger, threat*
des déchets toxiques (m.) *toxic waste*
l'écologie (f.) *ecology*
l'effet de serre (m.) *greenhouse effect*
un emballage en plastique *plastic wrapping/packaging*
l'énergie nucléaire (f.) *nuclear energy*
l'énergie solaire (f.) *solar energy*
l'environnement (m.) *environment*
le gaspillage *waste*
un glissement de terrain *landslide*
un nuage de pollution *pollution cloud*
la pluie acide *acid rain*
la pollution *pollution*
une population croissante *growing population*
un produit *product*
la protection *protection*
le ramassage des ordures *garbage collection*
le réchauffement de la Terre *global warming*
le recyclage *recycling*
la surpopulation *overpopulation*
le trou dans la couche d'ozone *hole in the ozone layer*
une usine *factory*
écologique *ecological*

Les lois et les règlements
abolir *to abolish*
interdire *to forbid, to prohibit*
un gouvernement *government*
une loi *law*

Pronoms démonstratifs
celui *this one; that one; the one (m. sing.)*
ceux *these; those; the ones (m. pl.)*
celle *this one; that one; the one (f. sing.)*
celles *these; those; the ones (f. pl.)*

Expressions utiles
See p. 589.

Expressions impersonnelles
Il est bon que... *It is good that...*
Il est dommage que... *It is a shame that...*
Il est essentiel que... *It is essential that...*
Il est important que... *It is important that...*
Il est indispensable que... *It is essential that...*
Il est nécessaire que... *It is necessary that...*
Il est possible que... *It is possible that...*
Il faut que... *One must..., It is necessary that...*
Il vaut mieux que... *It is better that...*

Leçon 14B

La nature
une espèce (menacée) *(endangered) species*
la nature *nature*
un pique-nique *picnic*
une région *region*
une ressource naturelle *natural resource*
un arbre *tree*
un bois *woods*
un champ *field*
le ciel *sky*
une côte *coast*
un désert *desert*
une étoile *star*
une falaise *cliff*
un fleuve *river*
une forêt (tropicale) *(tropical) forest*
l'herbe (f.) *grass*
une île *island*
la jungle *jungle*
un lac *lake*
la Lune *moon*
une pierre *stone*
une plante *plant*
une rivière *river*
un sentier *path*
une vallée *valley*
un volcan *volcano*

L'écologie
chasser *to hunt*
jeter *to throw away*
la chasse *hunt*
le déboisement *deforestation*
l'écotourisme (m.) *ecotourism*
l'extinction (f.) *extinction*
la préservation *protection*
le sauvetage des habitats *habitat preservation*

Les animaux
un animal *animal*
un écureuil *squirrel*
un lapin *rabbit*
un serpent *snake*
une vache *cow*

Expressions utiles
See p. 607.

Verbs of will
demander que... *to ask that...*
désirer que... *to want/desire that...*
exiger que... *to demand that...*
préférer que... *to prefer that...*
proposer que... *to propose that...*
recommander que... *to recommend that...*
souhaiter que... *to wish that...*
suggérer que... *to suggest that...*
vouloir que... *to want that...*

Verbs and expressions of emotion
aimer que... *to like that...*
avoir peur que... *to be afraid that...*
être content(e) que... *to be glad that...*
être désolé(e) que... *to be sorry that...*
être furieux/furieuse que... *to be furious that...*
être heureux/heureuse que... *to be happy that...*
être surpris(e) que... *to be surprised that...*
être triste que... *to be sad that...*
regretter que... *to regret that...*

Comparatives and superlatives of nouns
See p. 614.

Les arts

UNITÉ 15

Unit Goals

Leçon 15A

In this lesson, students will learn:
- terms related to the theater and performance arts
- rules for making liaisons and some exceptions
- about the theater in France and Molière
- about the subjunctive with expressions of doubt, disbelief, and uncertainty
- some irregular forms of the subjunctive
- the possessive pronouns
- more about movie theaters and kiosks through specially shot video footage

Leçon 15B

In this lesson, students will learn:
- terms for television and film
- terms for literature and fine arts
- about abbreviations and acronyms
- about Haitian painting and **le Cirque du Soleil**
- about French singer and musician **Patricia Kaas**
- the subjunctive with conjunctions
- to listen for key words and use context

Savoir-faire

In this section, students will learn:
- cultural, economic, and historical information about **le Grand-Est**
- to contextualize a text
- to write strong introductions and conclusions

Pour commencer
- **David est dans une classe.**
- **Il dessine des fruits.**
- **Answers may vary.**
- **Answers may vary.**

Pour commencer
Où est David? Sur une falaise? Dans une classe? Dans un champ?

Que dessine-t-il?

Est-il nécessaire qu'il ait un modèle pour dessiner?

Est-il possible qu'il soit déjà un artiste connu?

RESOURCES

Student Activities Manual (SAM): Workbook Activities, pp. 203–216; Lab Activities, pp. 113–120; Video Activities, pp. 57–60; pp. 89–90 SAM Answer Key

vhlcentral.com: Textbook MP3s; Lab MP3s; Textbook Audioscript; Lab Audioscript; Video; Videoscript; **Roman-photo** Translations; **Vocabulaire supplémentaire**; Activity Pack (including **Feuilles d'activités**, Info Gap Activities, and Task-based Activities);

Le Zapping short film transcription; **Essayez!** and **Mise en pratique** answers; Digital Image Bank; Testing Program; Testing Program MP3s

Section Goals

In this section, students will learn and practice vocabulary related to:
• theater
• performance arts

Instructional Resources

vhlcentral.com:
Digital Image Bank
(including vocabulary
illustrations from the textbook,
theme-based illustrations);
Vocabulaire supplémentaire;
Mise en pratique answers;
Textbook Audioscript;
Lab Audioscript; Activity Pack
(Info Gap Activities); Textbook
MP3s; Lab MP3s; SAM Answer
Key; reference tools

Suggestions

• Tell students to look over the new vocabulary and identify the cognates.
• Use the **15A Contextes** illustration from the Digital Image Bank. Point out people and things as you describe the illustration. Examples: **Il joue du piano. C'est un opéra. La spectatrice applaudit.**
• Point out the difference between **un personnage** and **une personne**.
• Tell students that **profiter de** does not necessarily have the negative connotation that *to take advantage of* does in English.
• Remind students to use **jouer à** with sports, but **jouer de** with musical instruments. Examples: **Il joue *au* tennis. Il joue *de* la guitare.**
• Ask students questions using the new vocabulary. Examples: **Quels réalisateurs célèbres connaissez-vous? Quelle est votre chanson préférée? Jouez-vous d'un instrument de musique? Si oui, lequel? Aimez-vous aller au théâtre? À l'opéra?**
• Additional vocabulary for this lesson can be found in the **Vocabulaire supplémentaire** on the Supersite.
• Use the Arts and culture illustrations from the Digital Image Bank to help students familiarize themselves with theater and performance arts.

Leçon 15A

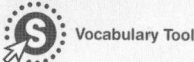 Vocabulary Tools

You will learn how to...

▪ talk about performance arts
▪ express your feelings and opinions

Que le spectacle commence!

une danseuse

une spectatrice

un danseur

Elle applaudit.
(applaudir)

un piano

La danse

une guitare

Vocabulaire

jouer un rôle	to play a role
présenter	to present
profiter de quelque chose	to take advantage of/ to enjoy something
un applaudissement	applause
une chanson	song
un chœur	choir, chorus
une comédie (musicale)	comedy (musical)
un compositeur	composer
un concert	concert
une danse	dance
un dramaturge	playwright
un entracte	intermission
un membre	member
un metteur en scène	director (of a play, a show)
un personnage (principal)	(main) character
une pièce de théâtre	play
un réalisateur/ une réalisatrice	director (of a movie)
une séance	show; screening
une troupe	company, troop
le début	beginning; debut
la fin	end
un genre	genre
une sorte	sort, kind
célèbre	famous

un orchestre

YVETTE LEBLANC & CO.

la batterie

Ils font de la musique.
(faire)

ressources

WB pp. 203–204
LM p. 113
vhlcentral

O P T I O N S

Extra Practice Have students identify familiar artists, songs, films, plays, etc., by completing your statements with vocabulary from **Espace contextes**. Examples: 1. *Carmen* est ____ de Bizet. (un opéra) 2. *La vie en rose* est ____. (une chanson) 3. *Giselle* est ____. (un ballet) 4. Steven Spielberg est ____. (un réalisateur)

Extra Practice Write or have students write the names of well-known artists on sticky notes and put them on the backs of other students. Then tell them to walk around the room asking their classmates yes/no questions to determine their identity. Examples: **Est-ce que je suis dramaturge? Est-ce que j'écris des tragédies? Est-ce que je suis William Shakespeare?**

Mise en pratique

une comédie

une tragédie

Le théâtre

un spectateur

CARMEN de Bizet

Il joue du violon. (jouer)

un opéra

une place

1 Écoutez Écoutez la conversation entre Hakim et Nadja pendant le spectacle de *Notre-Dame de Paris*, ensuite indiquez la bonne réponse.

1. Hakim et Nadja donnent leurs...
   a. places.
   b. billets.
   c. détails.

2. Leurs places sont situées...
   a. très loin de l'orchestre.
   b. au balcon.
   c. près de l'orchestre.

3. Le spectacle est...
   a. une comédie musicale.
   b. un concert.
   c. une tragédie.

4. Gilles Maheu est...
   a. un dramaturge.
   b. un metteur en scène.
   c. un personnage.

5. Hakim...
   a. n'a pas applaudi.
   b. a très peu applaudi.
   c. a beaucoup applaudi.

6. Nadja pense qu'Hakim...
   a. va devenir célèbre.
   b. n'est pas un bon danseur.
   c. est un bon compositeur.

2 Choisissez Choisissez la phrase de la colonne **B** qui complète le mieux les phrases de la colonne **A**. Notez que tous les éléments de la colonne **B** ne sont pas utilisés.

A

- a 1. Pour entrer dans une salle de spectacle,
- g 2. Georges Bizet a écrit **Carmen** en 1875;
- e 3. Au milieu d'une pièce de théâtre
- d 4. Un metteur en scène est chargé de
- h 5. La tragédie **Hamlet** est une
- b 6. Une comédie musicale est

B

a. il faut un billet.

b. un spectacle de musique et de danse.

c. un membre de la troupe.

d. guider les comédiens dans leur travail.

e. il y a souvent un entracte.

f. il faut danser à l'entracte.

g. c'est un des opéras français les plus célèbres.

h. des pièces de théâtre les plus connues de Shakespeare.

3 Associez Complétez les analogies suivantes par le mot ou l'expression d'**ESPACE CONTEXTES** qui convient le mieux.

1. chanter ⟷ chanson / applaudir ⟷ _applaudissement_
2. heureux ⟷ comédie / triste ⟷ _tragédie_
3. théâtre ⟷ pièce / cinéma ⟷ _séance_
4. concert ⟷ orchestre / chanson ⟷ _chœur_
5. film ⟷ acteur / ballet ⟷ _danseur_
6. opéra ⟷ chanter / concert ⟷ _faire de la musique_
7. livre ⟷ écrivain / musique ⟷ _compositeur_
8. classe ⟷ étudiant / troupe ⟷ _membre_
9. film ⟷ réalisateur / pièce de théâtre ⟷ _metteur en scène_
10. danse ⟷ danseur / chanson ⟷ _chanteur_

1 Audioscript L'EMPLOYÉ: Soyez les bienvenus à *Notre-Dame de Paris*. Vos billets, s'il vous plaît.
NADJA: Oui, tenez.
E: Si vous voulez bien me suivre. Voici vos places.
HAKIM: C'est parfait. On n'est pas loin de l'orchestre. On pourra profiter de tous les détails du spectacle.
N: Ce soir, c'est la première de cette comédie musicale. C'est aussi les débuts de Julie Zenatti dans un des rôles principaux.
H: Tu sais qui est le metteur en scène?
N: Oui. C'est Gilles Maheu. Pourquoi?
H: Juste pour savoir. Oh, regarde! Le spectacle va commencer. On continuera de parler à l'entracte.
Un peu plus tard...
H: Tu ne m'avais pas dit qu'en plus de chansons, il y aurait de la danse.
N: Tu n'aimes pas ce genre de spectacle?
H: Si, j'adore. J'ai même mal aux mains tellement j'ai applaudi. Ça me donne envie de faire partie de la troupe. Je pourrais peut-être jouer un petit rôle, non?
N: Je ne suis pas sûre. Tu sais, il faut être très bon danseur. Et puis, en plus, tu ne fais pas de musique...
H: Ce n'est pas vrai. Je te rappelle que je joue de la guitare.
N: Ah, oui... Tu peux toujours te présenter à une audition, mais ne t'attends pas à beaucoup d'applaudissements.
H: Eh bien, si c'est comme ça, tu n'auras pas de place pour mon premier concert!
(On Textbook MP3s)

1 Suggestion Go over the answers with the class.

2 Suggestion Write each of the phrases in column B on separate pieces of paper and distribute them. Have students read the items in column A aloud. Those with the correct ending finish the sentences.

3 Suggestion Have students explain the relationship between the first set of words, then give the answer.

Game Write words for various types of artists on index cards. On another set of cards, write words for their works. Tape them face down on the board in random order. Divide the class into two teams. Play a game of Concentration in which students match artists with their works. Example: **dramaturge/pièce de théâtre**. When a player makes a match, that player's team collects those cards. The team with the most cards wins.

Notre-Dame de Paris Gilles Maheu (from Québec) is the actual director of the musical ***Notre-Dame de Paris***, which was adapted from Victor Hugo's novel (titled *The Hunchback of Notre Dame* in English). In addition, Julie Zenatti is the actress and singer who played Fleur-de-Lys in the 1999 movie version of the musical.

O P T I O N S

4 Expansion Have pairs create two more illustrated sentences using the words from **Espace contextes**. Then tell them to exchange papers with another pair and complete the sentences.

5 Suggestions
• Tell students to jot down notes during their interviews.
• Have students add two of their own questions to the interview.

6 Suggestion Divide the class into pairs and distribute the Info Gap Handouts found in the Activity Pack on the Supersite. Give students ten minutes to complete the activity.

7 Suggestions
• If time is limited, have students write their critiques as homework.
• Give students a set amount of time to write their comments before passing the papers on to the next student.

Communication

4 **Le mot juste** Avec un(e) partenaire, remplissez les espaces par le mot qui est illustré. Faites les accords nécessaires.

1. Ma petite sœur apprend à __jouer de la batterie__ . Ça fait beaucoup de bruit (*noise*) dans la maison. Elle prépare son premier __concert__ qui sera en décembre.

2. Je dois me dépêcher de trouver une __place__ parce que la __séance__ va bientôt commencer.

3. Marie-Claude Pietragalla a été __danseuse__ étoile de l'Opéra de Paris. Je l'ai beaucoup aimée dans le __rôle__ __GISELLE__ de Giselle.

4. Je sais __jouer du piano__ et je voudrais apprendre à __jouer du violon__, mais je n'ai pas beaucoup de temps.

5 **Répondez** Avec un(e) partenaire, posez-vous les questions suivantes et répondez-y à tour de rôle. Ensuite, comparez vos réponses avec celles d'un autre groupe. Answers will vary.

1. Quelle sorte de chanson préfères-tu? Pour quelle(s) raison(s)?
2. Quel est le dernier concert auquel tu as assisté? Comment était-ce?
3. Quel est ton genre de spectacle favori? Pourquoi?
4. Quel réalisateur admires-tu le plus? Décris un de ses films.
5. Est-ce que tu fais de la musique? De quel genre?
6. Es-tu un(e) bon(ne) danseur/danseuse? Pour quelle(s) raison(s)?
7. Si tu pouvais jouer un rôle, lequel choisirais-tu? Pourquoi?
8. Est-ce que les arts sont importants pour toi? Lesquels? Pourquoi?

6 **Les sorties** Votre professeur va vous donner, à vous et à votre partenaire, une feuille d'activités. Attention! Ne regardez pas la feuille de votre partenaire. Answers will vary.

MODÈLE

Étudiant(e) 1: *Bonjour.*
Étudiant(e) 2: *Bonjour. J'aimerais voir quelques spectacles ce week-end. Pourriez-vous me dire quels sont les spectacles proposés?*
Étudiant(e) 1: *Bien sûr! Eh bien, vendredi soir...*

7 **Le blog virtuel** Formez un petit groupe. Chaque membre du groupe choisit un film ou un spectacle différent. Answers will vary.

• Écrivez une critique de ce film/spectacle.
• Passez-la à votre partenaire de gauche.
• Il/Elle écrit ensuite ses réactions.
• Continuez le processus pour faire un tour complet.
• Ensuite, discutez de tous vos commentaires.

OPTIONS

Game Have students stand. Toss a beanbag to a student at random and say the name of a famous artist or work. The player has four seconds to classify the work or artist. He or she then tosses the beanbag to another student and says a person or work. Example: *Macbeth* (**C'est une tragédie.**) Students who cannot classify the item in time or repeat one that has already been named are eliminated. The last person standing wins.

Pairs Have pairs of students create posters advertising performances or other types of artistic events on campus or in the community. To ensure variety, you might want to assign specific events. Tell students to use at least six vocabulary words in their posters. Then have students present them to the rest of the class.

Les sons et les lettres  Audio

Les liaisons obligatoires et les liaisons interdites

Rules for making liaisons are complex and have many exceptions. Generally, a liaison is made between pronouns, and between a pronoun and a verb that begins with a vowel or vowel sound.

vous en avez   **nous habitons**   **ils aiment**   **elles arrivent**

Make liaisons between articles, numbers, or the verb **est** and a noun or adjective that begins with a vowel or a vowel sound.

un éléphant   **les amis**   **dix hommes**   **Roger est enchanté.**

There is a liaison after many single-syllable adverbs, conjunctions, and prepositions.

très intéressant   **chez eux**   **quand elle**   **quand on décidera**

Many expressions have obligatory liaisons that may or may not follow these rules.

C'est-à-dire...   **Comment allez-vous?**   **plus ou moins**   **avant-hier**

Never make a liaison before or after the conjunction **et** or between a noun and a verb that follows it. Likewise, do not make a liaison between a singular noun and an adjective that follows it.

un garçon et une fille   **Gilbert adore le football.**   **un cours intéressant**

There is no liaison before **h aspiré** or before the word **oui** and before numbers.

un hamburger   **les héros**   **un oui et un non**   **mes onze animaux**

🔊 **Prononcez** Répétez les mots suivants à voix haute.

1. les héros   2. mon petit ami   3. un pays africain   4. les onze étages

🔊 **Articulez** Répétez les phrases suivantes à voix haute.

1. Ils en veulent onze.
2. Vous vous êtes bien amusés hier soir?
3. Christelle et Albert habitent en Angleterre.
4. Quand est-ce que Charles a acheté ces objets?

🔊 **Dictons** Répétez les dictons à voix haute.

Les murs ont des oreilles.[2]

Deux avis valent mieux qu'un.[1]

[1] Two heads are better than one. (lit. Two opinions are better than one.)

[2] The walls have ears.

ressources

LM
p. 114

vhlcentral

six cent trente et un **631**

Section Goals

In this section, students will learn about:
• obligatory liaisons
• exceptions to liaison rules

Instructional Resources
vhlcentral.com:
Textbook MP3s; Lab MP3s;
SAM Answer Key;
Textbook Audioscript;
Lab Audioscript;
reference tools

Suggestions
• Model the pronunciation of the example phrases and have students repeat them after you.
• Tell students to avoid making liaisons with proper names.
• Point out that liaisons are optional in certain circumstances, such as after plural nouns or within compound verb phrases. Examples: **des enfants espagnols, tu es allé**.
• Ask students to provide additional examples of each type of liaison.
• Write the phrases in the **Prononcez** activity on the board or a transparency. Have students listen to the recording and tell you where they hear liaisons. Alternately, have students rewrite the phrases on their own paper and draw lines linking letters that form liaisons and crossing out silent final consonants.

Extra Practice Write the following sentences on the board and have students copy them. Then read the sentences aloud. Tell students to mark the liaisons they hear and cross out silent letters. **1. Nous en prenons une. 2. Ils aiment bien aller aux concerts. 3. Magali et Simon ont un animal de compagnie. 4. Elles iront chercher six oranges et un gâteau pour ce soir.**

Extra Practice Teach students this French tongue-twister that contains liaisons. **Un ange qui songeait à changer de visage se trouva soudain si changé que jamais plus ange ne songea à se changer.**

ESPACE CONTEXTES **631**

ESPACE ROMAN-PHOTO

Section Goals

In this section, students will learn functional phrases for talking about a performance and for expressing certainty, doubt, necessities and desires.

Instructional Resources

vhlcentral.com:
Roman-photo *Video, Videoscript, and Translation; SAM Answer Key; reference tools*

Video Recap: Leçon 14B

Review the previous **Roman-photo** with this activity.
1. Le groupe a fait un pique-nique à ____.
(la montagne Sainte-Victoire)
2. D'abord, ils ont visité ____.
(la Maison Sainte-Victoire)
3. Sandrine voulait que David fasse ____, mais il préférait dessiner ____. (un portrait d'elle/la montagne)
4. Stéphane a essayé de prendre une photo de ____. (Rachid et Amina)

Video Synopsis

Rachid, Amina, and David discuss the musical comedy they just saw and Sandrine's performance in it. At **Le P'tit Bistrot**, Valérie wants to know about the show and Sandrine's performance. David says she's not a bad actress, but she can't sing very well. Sandrine overhears his comments and confronts him. They argue and Sandrine breaks up with him.

Suggestions

• Tell students to scan the captions for vocabulary related to shows and performances.
• After reading the **Roman-photo**, have students summarize the episode.

Après le concert

 Video

PERSONNAGES

Amina

David

Rachid

Sandrine

Valérie

Après le concert...
RACHID Bon... que pensez-vous du spectacle?
AMINA Euh... c'est ma comédie musicale préférée... Les danseurs étaient excellents.
DAVID Oui, et l'orchestre aussi!

RACHID Et les costumes, comment tu les as trouvés, Amina?
AMINA Très beaux!
RACHID Moi, je trouve que la robe que tu as faite pour Sandrine était le plus beau des costumes.
AMINA Vraiment?
DAVID Eh, voilà Sandrine.

SANDRINE Vous avez entendu ces applaudissements? Je n'arrive pas à croire que c'était pour moi... et toute la troupe, bien sûr!
DAVID Oui c'est vraiment incroyable!
SANDRINE Alors, vous avez aimé notre spectacle?
RACHID Oui! Amina vient de nous dire que c'était sa comédie musicale préférée.

VALÉRIE Et Sandrine?
DAVID Euh, comme ci, comme ça... À vrai dire, ce n'était pas terrible... C'est le moins que l'on puisse dire.
VALÉRIE Ah bon?
DAVID Comme actrice elle n'est pas mal. Elle a bien joué son rôle, mais il est évident qu'elle ne sait pas chanter.
VALÉRIE Tu ne lui as pas dit ça, j'espère!

DAVID Ben, non, mais... Je doute qu'elle devienne une chanteuse célèbre! C'est ça, son rêve. Croyez-vous que ce soit mieux qu'elle le sache?
SANDRINE Tu en as suffisamment dit...
DAVID Sandrine! Je ne savais pas que tu étais là.
SANDRINE De toute évidence! Il vaut mieux que je m'en aille.

À la terrasse...
DAVID Sandrine! Attends!
SANDRINE Pour quoi faire?
DAVID Je voudrais m'expliquer... Il est clair que...
SANDRINE Écoute, ce qui est clair, c'est que tu n'y connais rien en musique et que tu ne sais rien de moi!

ACTIVITÉS

1 **Vrai ou faux?** Indiquez si ces affirmations sont **vraies** ou **fausses**. Corrigez les phrases fausses. *Answers may vary.*

1. Le spectacle est la comédie musicale préférée de Rachid.
Faux. Rachid n'a pas aimé le spectacle.
2. Amina a beaucoup aimé les costumes. Vrai.
3. David a apporté des fleurs à Sandrine. Vrai.
4. David n'aime pas vraiment la robe de Sandrine.
Faux. David aime bien la robe de Sandrine.
5. Finalement, Sandrine a dû acheter sa robe elle-même.
Faux. Amina a fait la robe de Sandrine.

6. Valérie est surprise d'apprendre que Sandrine n'est pas une très bonne chanteuse. Vrai.
7. Sandrine est furieuse quand elle découvre la véritable opinion de David. Vrai.
8. David voulait être méchant avec Sandrine.
Faux. Il ne voulait pas être méchant avec elle.
9. Sandrine rompt (*breaks up*) avec David. Vrai.
10. David veut rompre avec Sandrine.
Faux. Sandrine veut rompre avec David.

 Practice more at vhlcentral.com.

OPTIONS

Avant de regarder la vidéo Before viewing the video, have students work in pairs and brainstorm a list of things people might say after a concert or musical. What aspects of the show might they mention? What expressions might they use to praise or criticize a performance?

Regarder la vidéo Photocopy the videoscript found under Instructor Resources on the Supersite. Then white out words related to performance arts and other important vocabulary in order to create a master for a cloze activity. Distribute photocopies and tell students to fill in the missing information as they watch the video episode.

Les amis échangent leurs opinions.

SANDRINE C'est vrai? C'est la mienne aussi. *(Elle chante.)* J'adore cette chanson!

DAVID Euh... Sandrine, que tu es ravissante dans cette robe!

SANDRINE Merci, David. Elle me va super bien, non? Et toi, Amina, merci mille fois!

Au P'tit Bistrot...

VALÉRIE Alors c'était comment, la pièce de théâtre?

DAVID C'était une comédie musicale.

VALÉRIE Oh! Alors, c'était comment?

DAVID Pas mal. Les danseurs et l'orchestre étaient formidables.

VALÉRIE Et les chanteurs?

DAVID Mmmm... pas mal.

DAVID Sandrine, je suis désolé de t'avoir blessée, mais il faut bien que quelqu'un soit honnête avec toi.

SANDRINE À quel sujet?

DAVID Eh bien..., la chanson... je doute que ce soit ta vocation.

SANDRINE Tu doutes? Eh bien, moi, je suis certaine... certaine de ne plus jamais vouloir te revoir. C'est fini, David.

DAVID Mais, Sandrine, écoute-moi! C'est pour ton bien que je dis...

SANDRINE Oh ça suffit. Toi, tu m'écoutes... Je suis vraiment heureuse que tu repartes bientôt aux États-Unis. Dommage que ce ne soit pas demain!

Expressions utiles

Talking about a performance

- **Je n'arrive pas à croire que ces applaudissements étaient pour moi!**
  I can't believe all that applause was for me!

- **À vrai dire, ce n'était pas terrible... C'est le moins que l'on puisse dire.**
  To tell the truth, it wasn't great... That's the least that you could say.

Expressing doubts

- **Je doute qu'elle devienne une chanteuse célèbre!**
  I doubt that she'll become a famous singer!

- **Croyez-vous que ce soit mieux qu'elle le sache?**
  Do you think it would be better if she knew it?

- **Je doute que ce soit ta vocation.**
  I doubt that it's your vocation/ professional calling.

Expressing certainties

- **Il est évident qu'elle ne sait pas chanter.**
  It's obvious that she doesn't know how to sing.

- **Ce qui est clair, c'est que tu n'y connais rien en musique.**
  What's clear is that you don't know anything about music.

- **Il est clair que tu ne sais rien de moi.**
  It's clear that you know nothing about me.

- **Je suis certaine de ne plus jamais vouloir te revoir.**
  I'm certain that I never want to see you again.

Talking about necessities and desires

- **Il vaut mieux que je m'en aille.**
  It's better that I go.

- **Il faut bien que quelqu'un soit honnête avec toi.**
  It's really necessary that someone be honest with you.

Expressions utiles
- Model the pronunciation of the **Expressions utiles** and have students repeat them after you.
- As you work through the list, point out the use of the subjunctive with verbs of doubt and irregular forms of the subjunctive. Tell students that these grammar points will be formally presented in the **Structures** section.
- Respond briefly to questions about the subjunctive. Reinforce correct forms, but do not expect students to produce them consistently at this time.
- Remind students that **terrible** often means *great* or *terrific*, not *terrible*. The phrase **pas terrible** (*not so great*) is an example of French understatement (**la litote**).
- Explain that **«Il vaut mieux que je m'en aille»** is a subjunctive version of **«Je m'en vais.»**

1 Suggestion Have students correct the false statements.

1 Expansion For additional practice, give students these items. **11. David pense que Sandrine est une bonne actrice. (Vrai.) 12. Amina n'aime pas les comédies musicales. (Faux.) 13. Selon Rachid, la robe de Sandrine est le plus beau des costumes. (Vrai.) 14. David repart aux États-Unis demain. (Faux.)**

2 Suggestion Remind students to use discourse connectors, such as **d'abord, puis**, and **après** in their conversations. Rachid should use a variety of structures when giving advice. Examples: **Dis-lui que...** and **À ta place je** [+ *conditional*]....

3 Expansion Have the class divide into two groups and debate whether or not David did the right thing by telling Sandrine what he thought of her singing.

2 À vous! David rentre chez lui et explique à Rachid qu'il s'est disputé avec Sandrine. Avec un(e) camarade de classe, préparez une conversation dans laquelle David dit ce qu'il a fait et explique la réaction de Sandrine. Rachid doit lui donner des conseils.

3 Écrivez Pauvre Sandrine! C'est vrai qu'elle ne chante pas bien, mais que son petit ami le dise, c'est blessant (*hurtful*). À votre avis, David a-t-il bien fait d'en parler? Pourquoi? Pour Sandrine, est-ce mieux de savoir ce que pense réellement David? Composez un paragraphe dans lequel vous expliquez votre point de vue.

A C T I V I T É S

ressources

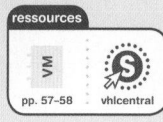

VM pp. 57–58

vhlcentral

six cent trente-trois **633**

OPTIONS

Pairs Have students work in pairs. Tell them to write predictions about what will happen in the final episode of the **Roman-photo**. Then have volunteers read their predictions aloud and ask the class if they agree or disagree.

Extra Practice Write a few expressions of doubt, certainty, and necessity from the **Roman-photo** on the board. Examples: **Je doute que..., Il est évident que...,** and **Il faut bien que...** Then have students create statements about the characters or their actions using these expressions. You might ask other students to react to their statements.

Reading
Video: *Flash culture*

la Comédie-Française

Section Goals

In this section, students will:
- learn about the theater in France
- learn some terms related to the theater
- learn about some famous francophone musicians
- read about Molière
- view authentic video footage

Instructional Resources
vhlcentral.com:
Video; SAM Answer Key;
Videoscript; reference tools

Culture à la loupe
Avant la lecture Have students describe the photo of the actors. Then ask: **Avez-vous déjà vu la représentation d'une pièce par une troupe professionnelle? Où? Quelle pièce de théâtre a-t-elle présentée?**

Lecture
- Point out the **Coup de main**. Ask: **Comment indique-t-on le début d'un spectacle aux États-Unis?**
- Explain that the word **amateur** is a cognate when it refers to a non-professional, such as an amateur actor, but it can also mean *lover of (something)*, for example, **un amateur d'art** (*art lover*).
- Point out the statistics chart. Ask students what information it shows. (key statistics about theater performances in France during three seasons)

Après la lecture Ask students: **Comment savez-vous que le théâtre est populaire en France? Quelles parties du texte soutiennent cette idée?**

1 **Suggestion** Go over the answers with the class.

CULTURE À LA LOUPE

Le théâtre, un art vivant et populaire

Les Français sont de plus en plus nombreux à fréquenter les théâtres: un Français sur trois voit° au moins une pièce par an. Ce public fréquente les théâtres privés, les théâtres municipaux et les cinq théâtres nationaux, dont le plus ancien est la Comédie-Française. Les spectacles d'amateurs sont aussi très appréciés. Les comédiens° de théâtre ont beaucoup de prestige et reçoivent des récompenses° professionnelles spéciales, les Molières. Le théâtre joue aussi un rôle social important, en particulier pour les jeunes.

Le théâtre français est né au XVIIᵉ siècle. Le roi Louis XIV était un grand amateur° de spectacles et la cour° de Versailles offrait les divertissements° les plus extravagants°. Les œuvres° d'auteurs célèbres, comme Molière ou les tragédiens Pierre Corneille et Jean Racine, datent de cette époque. En 1680, Louis XIV crée l'institution théâtrale la plus prestigieuse de France, la Comédie-Française.

Aujourd'hui, elle s'appelle aussi «Maison de Molière» ou «Théâtre-Français» et elle est toujours le symbole de la tradition théâtrale française. Elle compte parfois jusqu'à 70 comédiens et elle est subventionnée par l'État. Elle a plus de 3.000 pièces à son répertoire et ses comédiens jouent dans près de 900 représentations° par an. Ils partent aussi en tournée° en province et à l'étranger et participent à des enregistrements° pour la radio et pour la télévision.

Pour assister à un de ces spectacles, il faut prendre une réservation et retirer des billets avant le début de la représentation. Au théâtre Richelieu, on peut admirer le fauteuil dans lequel Molière a joué° il y a plus de 300 ans!

Coup de main

Les trois coups du lever de rideau°

A French tradition is to signal the beginning of a theater performance with three knocks. At the **Comédie-Française**, a six-knock signal is used instead.

Les chiffres clés du théâtre français sur trois saisons

- 2.638 textes différents ont été joués
- 7.044 mises en scène° ont été programmées
- 31.884 représentations ont été données
- il y a eu entre 1 et 323 représentations par pièce

voit *sees* **comédiens** *actors* **récompenses** *awards* **amateur** *lover* **cour** *royal court* **divertissements** *entertainment* **les plus extravagants** *wildest* **œuvres** *works* **représentations** *performances* **en tournée** *on tour* **enregistrements** *recordings* **a joué** *acted* **lever de rideau** *rise of the curtain* **mises en scène** *productions*

ACTIVITÉS

1 **Complétez** Complétez les phrases.

1. _Un Français sur trois_ voit au moins une pièce par an.
2. Les comédiens de théâtre reçoivent _des récompenses professionnelles spéciales, les Molières_
3. _Le théâtre français_ est né au XVIIᵉ siècle.
4. Trois auteurs qui datent de cette époque sont _Molière, Pierre Corneille et Jean Racine_
5. _La Comédie-Française_ a été créée par Louis XIV en 1680.
6. _Maison de Molière et Théâtre-Français_ sont deux autres noms pour la Comédie-Française.
7. La Comédie-Française a un répertoire de plus de _3.000 pièces_ .
8. Ses comédiens partent aussi _en tournée en province et à l'étranger_
9. Au théâtre Richelieu se trouve _le fauteuil dans lequel Molière a joué il y a plus de 300 ans_
10. _2.638 textes_ ont été joués en France sur trois saisons.

OPTIONS **Les dramaturges français** Pierre Corneille (1606–1684) helped shape the French classic theatre and was a master at creating tragic protagonists of heroic dimension. *Le Cid* (1637) is one of his masterpieces.

Jean Racine (1639–1699) also exemplifies French classicism and replaced Corneille as France's leading tragic dramatist. His most memorable characters are the fierce and tender women of his tragedies. Early in his career Racine became friends with Molière, who produced his first two tragedies. *Andromaque* (1667), *Bajazet* (1672), *Mithradate* (1673), *Iphigénie en Aulide* (1674), and *Phèdre* (1677) are considered his greatest plays.

Le français quotidien
• Model the pronunciation of each term and have students repeat it.
• Point out that **reprise** is a **faux ami** for the English word *reprise*.

Portrait Have students describe the theater poster. Then ask students: **Avez-vous déjà lu ou vu une comédie de Molière? Laquelle?**

Le monde francophone Have students write four true/false statements based on the information in this section. Then have them get together with a classmate and take turns reading their statements and responding.

2 Expansion For additional practice, give students these items. **7. Quel est le vrai nom de Molière? (Jean-Baptiste Poquelin) 8. Qu'a-t-il inventé avec le compositeur Lully? (la comédie-ballet) 9. Où a-t-on inventé la musique zouk? (aux Antilles)**

3 Suggestion Many festivals post their programs on the Internet. Provide students with a model of an actual program for a cultural festival to follow. Encourage them to be creative and use information they already know.

LE FRANÇAIS QUOTIDIEN

Les spectacles

billetterie (*f.*)	box office
jour (*m.*) **de relâche**	day with no performances
orchestre (*m.*)	orchestra seats
poulailler (*m.*)	gallery
rentrée (*f.*) **théâtrale**	start of theatrical season
reprise (*f.*)	revival; rerun
à l'affiche	now playing
incontournable	must-see

LE MONDE FRANCOPHONE

Des musiciens

Voici quelques musiciens francophones célèbres.

En Algérie Khaled, chanteur de raï, un mélange° de chanson arabe et d'influences occidentales

Aux Antilles le groupe Kassav, inventeur de la musique zouk

Au Cameroun Manu Dibango, célèbre joueur de saxophone

Au Mali Amadou et Mariam, couple de chanteurs aveugles°

À la Réunion Danyèl Waro, la voix° du maloya, musique typique de l'île

À Saint-Pierre-et-Miquelon Henri Lafitte, auteur, compositeur et interprète° de plus de 500 chansons

Au Sénégal Youssou N'Dour, compositeur et interprète de musique mbalax, un mélange de musique traditionnelle d'Afrique de l'Ouest et de musique occidentale

mélange *mix* **aveugles** *blind* **voix** *voice* **interprète** *performer*

PORTRAIT

Molière (1622–1673)

LE THÉÂTRE A TRAVERS LES AGES
Molière et sa troupe.

Molière, dont le vrai nom est Jean-Baptiste Poquelin, est le génie de la Comédie-Française. D'origine bourgeoise, il choisit la vie difficile du théâtre. En 1665, il obtient le soutien° de Louis XIV et devient le premier acteur comique, auteur et metteur en scène de France. Molière est un innovateur: il écrit des satires et des farces quand la mode est aux tragédies néoclassiques. Avec le compositeur Lully, il invente la comédie-ballet: genre dramatique, musical et chorégraphique qui traite° de thèmes contemporains et montre les mœurs° et les comportements de personnages ordinaires de la vie quotidienne°. Molière, interprète du rôle principal dans la plupart de ses pièces, est certainement le plus grand créateur de formes dans le théâtre français. Après une vie riche en aventures, il meurt après une représentation° du *Malade imaginaire*, dans laquelle il tenait° le rôle principal. Aujourd'hui, ses pièces sont toujours d'actualité° et Molière reste l'auteur le plus joué en France. Sa vie a inspiré de nombreux° réalisateurs et son œuvre a été adaptée au cinéma et à la télévision plusieurs fois. C'est grâce à sa place emblématique dans la culture nationale qu'on désigne souvent le français comme «la langue de Molière», comme l'anglais est «la langue de Shakespeare».

soutien *support* **traite** *discusses* **mœurs** *habits* **vie quotidienne** *daily life* **représentation** *performance* **tenait** *played* **d'actualité** *current* **de nombreux** *many*

ACTIVITÉS

2 **Répondez** Répondez aux questions par des phrases complètes.

1. Molière était-il d'origine populaire?
   Non, il était d'origine bourgeoise.
2. Pourquoi Molière est-il un innovateur?
   Il écrit des satires et des farces quand la mode est aux tragédies néoclassiques.
3. Comment Molière est-il mort?
   Il est mort sur scène, dans le rôle du *Malade imaginaire*.
4. Comment peut-on désigner la langue française?
   On peut la désigner comme «la langue de Molière».
5. Qu'est-ce que le raï?
   C'est un mélange de chanson traditionnelle arabe et d'influences occidentales.
6. De quel instrument joue Manu Dibango?
   Il joué du saxophone.

3 **Un festival** Vous et un(e) partenaire allez organiser un festival de culture francophone. Faites des recherches sur des artistes francophones et choisissez qui vous allez inviter. Où vont-ils jouer? Indiquez les genres d'œuvres. Comparez ensuite votre programme avec celui d'un autre groupe.

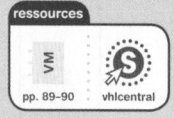
ressources
VM pp. 89–90
vhlcentral

S Practice more at vhlcentral.com.

Molière Sometimes referred to as the father of modern French comedy, Molière's plays often ridicule human vices and excesses, which are embodied in his characters. These characters encompass a broad spectrum and offer a wide view of seventeenth-century French society. *L'École des femmes* (1662), *Le Tartuffe* (1664), *Don Juan* (1665), *Le Misanthrope* (1666), *Le Bourgeois gentilhomme* (1670), and *Les Femmes savantes* (1672) are among his masterpieces.

Pairs Distribute a French theater schedule, including titles of plays, times of performances, and prices of seats. Then have students work in pairs, with one person playing the role of the theatergoer who wants to buy a ticket and the other person acting as the ticket seller.

Section Goals

In this section, students will learn:

- the subjunctive with expressions of doubt, disbelief, or uncertainty
- the subjunctive of irregular verbs **aller**, **pouvoir**, **savoir**, and **vouloir**

Instructional Resources

*vhlcentral.com:
Activity Pack; Lab MP3s;
SAM Answer Key; **Essayez!**
and **Mise en pratique**
answers; Lab Audioscript;
reference tools*

Suggestions

- Review the subjunctive verb forms from **Espace structures 14A** and **14B**. You may also want to review the conjugation of **croire**, taught in **12A**.
- Emphasize that **que** is always required in French. Example: *I doubt (that) the concert will be good.* **Je doute que le concert soit bon.**
- Emphasize that most of these expressions of doubt or uncertainty are the negative form of expressions of certainty. Therefore, they take the subjunctive only when used in the negative.
- On the board, write expressions of certainty in one column and expressions of doubt in another, and have volunteers make sentences with each of them to reinforce the use of the indicative versus the subjunctive.

15A.1

À noter

As you learned in **Structures 13B.1**, the connector *that* is often optional in English, but **que** is always required in French.

The subjunctive (Part 3) Tutorial
Verbs of doubt, disbelief, and uncertainty; more irregular subjunctive forms

Point de départ The subjunctive is used in a subordinate clause when there is a change of subject and the main clause implies doubt, disbelief, or uncertainty.

MAIN CLAUSE	CONNECTOR	SUBORDINATE CLAUSE
Je doute	**que**	le concert **soit** bon.
I doubt	*that*	*the concert will be good.*

Je doute qu'elle devienne une chanteuse célèbre!

Je suis certaine que je ne veux plus jamais te revoir!

Expressions of doubt, disbelief, and uncertainty

douter que...	*to doubt that...*	**Il est impossible que...**	*It is impossible that...*
ne pas croire que...	*not to believe that...*	**Il n'est pas certain que...**	*It is not certain that...*
ne pas penser que...	*not to think that...*	**Il n'est pas sûr que...**	*It is not sure that...*
Il est douteux que...	*It is doubtful that...*	**Il n'est pas vrai que...**	*It is not true that...*

Il n'est pas certain qu'il y **ait** un problème.
It's not certain that there is a problem.

Je ne crois pas qu'on **vende** les billets ici.
I don't believe that they sell the tickets here.

Il n'est pas vrai que Julie **sorte** avec Ahmed.
It's not true that Julie is going out with Ahmed.

Vous ne pensez pas qu'il y **ait** une séance du film ce soir?
Don't you think there's a screening of the film tonight?

- Use the indicative in a subordinate clause when the main clause expresses certainty.

Expressions of certainty

croire que...	*to believe that...*	**Il est clair que...**	*It is clear that...*
penser que...	*to think that...*	**Il est évident que...**	*It is obvious that...*
savoir que...	*to know that...*	**Il est sûr que...**	*It is sure that...*
Il est certain que...	*It is certain that...*	**Il est vrai que...**	*It is true that...*

On **sait que** l'histoire **finit** mal.
We know the story ends badly.

Il est certain qu'elle **comprend**.
It is certain that she understands.

ressources

WB
pp. 205–206

LM
p. 115

vhlcentral

636 *six cent trente-six*

Suggestions
- Check for understanding by writing on the board main clauses ending in **que** that require a subjunctive in the subordinate clause. Invite volunteers to suggest several endings for each, using verbs they have just reviewed. Example: **Il est douteux que / qu'…(qu'il y ait un examen la semaine prochaine / que j'achète une nouvelle voiture / qu'on aille à Paris).**
- Point out that the subjunctive is used when there is a change of subject as well as an expression of doubt, disbelief, or uncertainty. If the subject does not change, the infinitive is used. Example: **Jacques n'est pas sûr de pouvoir aller à Paris cet été.**

Essayez! Have students underline the main clauses in these sentences. Then have them create original sentences, using the indicative or subjunctive where appropriate.

- Sometimes a speaker may opt to use the subjunctive in a question to indicate that he or she feels doubtful or uncertain of an affirmative response.

Crois-tu que cet acteur joue bien son rôle?
Do you think that this actor plays his part well?

Est-il vrai que vous **partiez** déjà en vacances?
Is it true that you're already leaving on vacation?

Croyez-vous que ce soit mieux qu'elle le sache?

Il vaut mieux que je m'en aille.

- Here are more verbs that are irregular in the subjunctive.

Present subjunctive of *aller, pouvoir, savoir, vouloir*				
	aller	**pouvoir**	**savoir**	**vouloir**
que je/j'	aille	puisse	sache	veuille
que tu	ailles	puisses	saches	veuilles
qu'il/elle/on	aille	puisse	sache	veuille
que nous	allions	puissions	sachions	voulions
que vous	alliez	puissiez	sachiez	vouliez
qu'ils/elles	aillent	puissent	sachent	veuillent

Je doute qu'on **aille** au théâtre ce soir.
I doubt we'll go to the theater tonight.

Il n'est pas sûr qu'on **puisse** voir les acteurs.
It's not sure that we'll be able to see the actors.

Il vaut mieux qu'il **sache** la vérité.
It's better that he knows the truth.

Est-il possible qu'ils **veuillent** apprendre à jouer du violon?
Is it possible that they want to learn to play the violin?

Essayez! **Choisissez la forme correcte du verbe.**

1. Il est douteux que le metteur en scène (sait / sache) où est l'acteur.
2. Je sais que Carole Bouquet et Gérard Depardieu (sont / soient) mariés.
3. Il est impossible qu'il (est / soit) amoureux d'elle.
4. Ne crois-tu pas que l'histoire du Titanic (finit / finisse) bien?
5. Est-il vrai que les Français (font / fassent) uniquement des films intellectuels?
6. Je ne crois pas qu'il (peut / puisse) jouer le rôle du jeune prisonnier.
7. Tout le monde sait que le ballet (est / soit) d'origine française.
8. Il n'est pas certain qu'ils (peuvent / puissent) terminer le spectacle.

O P T I O N S

TPR Call out a series of sentences, using either an expression of certainty or an expression of doubt, disbelief, or uncertainty. Have students stand if they hear an expression of certainty or remain seated if they hear an expression of doubt. Example: **Il est impossible que j'apprenne une autre langue.** (Students remain seated.)

Pairs Have students write five absurd or strange sentences. Then have them switch sentences with a classmate. Students should write their reactions using a different expression of doubt, disbelief, or uncertainty. Example: **Toutes les femmes aiment bien faire le ménage. (Je ne crois pas que toutes les femmes aiment bien faire le ménage!)**

ESPACE STRUCTURES

Mise en pratique

1 Expansion Have pairs discuss why each subordinate clause is in the indicative or subjunctive. If the sentence is in the indicative, have pairs make the necessary changes in the main clause to elicit the subjunctive. Example: **1. Je ne crois pas que Fort-de-France soit plus loin de Paris que de New York.**

2 Expansion For emphasis, have **Étudiant(e) 1** counter the statement of doubt made by **Étudiant(e) 2** with another statement of certainty. Example: **Mais si! Il est sûr que le carnaval martiniquais est très populaire!**

3 Suggestion Before starting, have the class brainstorm what would be necessary for someone to do or be in order to participate successfully in the **Tour de France**. Examples: **Je sais qu'il faut être en pleine forme. Il est clair qu'on doit faire de l'exercice tous les jours avant d'y participer.**

1 Fort-de-France Vous discutez de vos projets (*plans*) avec votre ami(e) martiniquais(e). Complétez les phrases avec les formes correctes du présent de l'indicatif ou du subjonctif.

1. Je crois que Fort-de-France _____est_____ (être) plus loin de Paris que de New York.
2. Il n'est pas certain que je _____vienne_____ (venir) à Fort-de-France cet été.
3. Il n'est pas sûr que nous _____partions_____ (partir) en croisière (*cruise*) ensemble.
4. Il est clair que nous _ne partons/partirons pas_ (ne pas partir) sans toi.
5. Nous savons que ce voyage _____va_____ (aller) t'intéresser.
6. Il est douteux que le ski alpin _____soit_____ (être) un sport populaire ici.

2 Camarade pénible Vous faites une présentation sur la Martinique devant la classe. Un(e) camarade critique toutes vos idées. Avec un(e) partenaire, jouez la scène. *Answers will vary.*

MODÈLE

Étudiant(e) 1: *Le carnaval martiniquais est populaire.*
Étudiant(e) 2: *Je doute qu'il soit populaire.*

1. Les ressources naturelles sont protégées.
2. Tout le monde va se promener dans la forêt.
3. Les Martiniquais font des pique-niques tous les jours.
4. L'île a de belles plages.
5. Les enfants y font des randonnées.
6. On y boit des jus de fruits délicieux.

3 Le Tour de France Maxime veut participer un jour au Tour de France. Employez des expressions de doute et de certitude pour lui dire ce que vous pensez de ses bonnes et de ses mauvaises habitudes. *Answers will vary.*

MODÈLE

Je ne crois pas que tu puisses dormir jusqu'à midi!

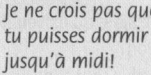

ne pas croire que...
douter que...
Il est clair que...
Il est essentiel que...

Il faut que...
penser que...
recommander que...
suggérer que...

1.

2.

3.

4.

5.

6.

 Practice more at **vhlcentral.com**.

Communication

4 Assemblez Imaginez que vous ayez l'occasion de faire un séjour aux Antilles françaises. À tour de rôle avec un(e) partenaire, assemblez les éléments de chaque colonne pour parler de ces vacances. Answers will vary.

MODÈLE

Il n'est pas certain que nous allions visiter une plantation.

A	B	C
Il est certain que	je/j'	être content(e)(s)
Il n'est pas certain que	tu	faire des excursions
Il est évident que	mon copain	faire beau temps
Il est impossible que	ma sœur	faire du bateau
Il est vrai que	mon frère	jouer sur la plage
Il n'est pas sûr que	nous	pouvoir parler créole
Je doute que	les touristes	visiter une plantation
Je crois que	mes parents	?
Je ne crois pas que	?	
?		

5 Comédie musicale Votre classe prépare une comédie musicale et vous organisez le spectacle. Votre partenaire voudrait y participer et il/elle postule pour un rôle. Alternez les rôles, puis présentez vos dialogues à la classe. Answers will vary.

MODÈLE

Étudiant(e) 1: *Est-il possible que je chante dans la chorale?*
Étudiant(e) 2: *Je doute qu'il soit possible que vous y chantiez. Il n'y a plus de place, mais je crois que...*

- acteur/actrice
- compositeur
- metteur en scène
- animateur/animatrice (emcee)
- chorale
- danseurs
- musiciens
- ouvreur/ouvreuse (usher)

6 L'avenir Vous et votre partenaire parlez de vos doutes et de vos certitudes à propos de l'avenir. À tour de rôle, complétez ces phrases pour décrire comment vous envisagez (envision) l'avenir. Answers will vary.

1. Je doute que...
2. Il est sûr que...
3. Il n'est pas certain que...
4. Il est impossible que...
5. Je ne crois pas que...
6. Je sais que...

7 Je doute Votre partenaire veut mieux vous connaître. Écrivez cinq phrases qui vous décrivent: quatre fausses et une vraie. Votre partenaire doit deviner laquelle est vraie et justifier sa réponse. Ensuite, alternez les rôles. Answers will vary.

MODÈLE

Étudiant(e) 1: *Je finis toujours mes devoirs avant de me coucher.*
Étudiant(e) 2: *Je doute que tu finisses tes devoirs avant de te coucher, parce que tu as toujours beaucoup de devoirs.*

4 Suggestion Have volunteers give sentences using elements from each of the three columns. Have other volunteers act as secretaries, writing examples on the board. Ask the class to help you correct the grammar and spelling.

5 Suggestion Ask two volunteers to read the **modèle** aloud. Correct any pronunciation errors.

7 Expansion Call on a student to read two statements about his or her partner, without revealing which one is true and which one is false. Have the class guess which statement is which, using expressions of doubt and certainty.

Video Replay the video episode, having students focus on expressions of certainty, uncertainty, doubt, and disbelief. Stop the video where appropriate and ask students to repeat any construction that includes [*main clause*] + **que** + [*subordinate clause*] and explain why the indicative or subjunctive was used in each instance.

Extra Practice Have students write sentences about three things of which they are certain and three things they doubt or cannot believe. Students should use a different expression for each of their sentences. Have students share some of their sentences with the class.

Section Goals

In this section, you will learn:
- the possessive pronouns
- the use of the expression **être à quelqu'un**

Instructional Resources

vhlcentral.com:
Activity Pack; Lab MP3s;
SAM Answer Key; **Essayez!**
and **Mise en pratique**
answers; Lab Audioscript;
reference tools

Suggestions

- You might want to quickly review the possessive adjectives and their usage from **Leçon 3A** with your students before presenting the possessive pronouns. Call out different phrases in English, for example *my hats, their dogs, his boat,* etc. and have students give the equivalent in French.

- Practice the difference in pronunciation between **notre** vs. **nôtre** and **votre** vs. **vôtre**. Be sure to stress that the possessive pronouns are pronounced with the closed **o** sound. After students practice this a few times, have them write down the four words on separate index cards. Say one of these words at a time and have them hold up the correct card to check if they are able to hear the difference.

ressources

WB
pp. 207–208

LM
p. 116

vhlcentral

Leçon 15A

15A.2

ESPACE STRUCTURES

Possessive pronouns  Tutorial

Point de départ In **Leçon 3A** , you learned how possessive adjectives function in French. You will now learn about possessive pronouns and how they differ in French and English.

- Possessive pronouns replace nouns modified by possessive adjectives. In French, the possessive pronouns have different forms depending on whether the noun is masculine or feminine, singular or plural. These are the forms of the French possessive pronouns.

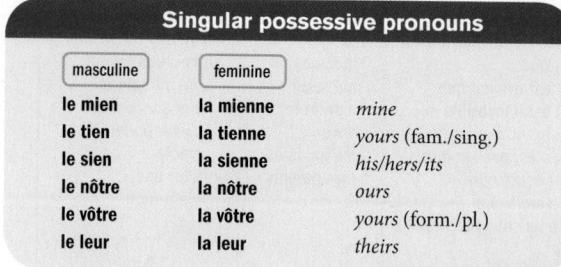

Singular possessive pronouns		
masculine	feminine	
le mien	la mienne	*mine*
le tien	la tienne	*yours (fam./sing.)*
le sien	la sienne	*his/hers/its*
le nôtre	la nôtre	*ours*
le vôtre	la vôtre	*yours (form./pl.)*
le leur	la leur	*theirs*

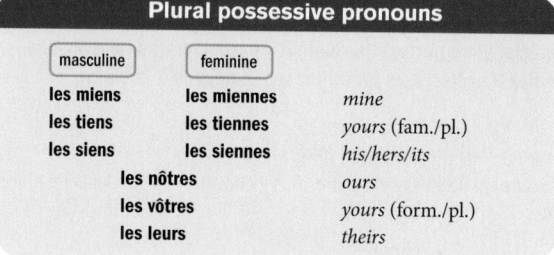

Plural possessive pronouns		
masculine	feminine	
les miens	les miennes	*mine*
les tiens	les tiennes	*yours (fam./pl.)*
les siens	les siennes	*his/hers/its*
les nôtres		*ours*
les vôtres		*yours (form./pl.)*
les leurs		*theirs*

Je connais **ton frère**, mais je ne connais pas **le sien**.
I know your brother, but I don't know hers.

Leurs chansons sont en espagnol et **les miennes** sont en français.
Their songs are in Spanish and mine are in French.

- French and English possessive pronouns are very similar in usage. They can refer to an object or a person. However, the French possessive pronouns consist of two parts: the definite article and the possessive word. Both parts must agree in number and gender with the noun to which they refer.

Ils aiment mes pièces, mais ils préfèrent **les tiennes**. (**tes pièces**)
They like my plays, but they prefer yours.

Je vois **ma voiture**, mais je ne vois pas **la vôtre**. (**votre voiture**)
I see my car, but I don't see yours.

- Possessive pronouns, like possessive adjectives, reflect the object or person possessed, *not* the possessor.

sa voiture → *his car*
sa voiture → *her car*

la sienne (*referring to the car*) → *his*
la sienne (*referring to the car*) → *hers*

640 *six cent quarante*

- Remember that the articles **le** and **les** contract with **à** when it precedes a possessive pronoun.

à + le mien	au mien
à + la mienne	à la mienne
à + les miens	aux miens
à + les miennes	aux miennes

Tu vas téléphoner **à mes amis** ou **aux tiens**?
Are you going to call my friends or yours?

Avez-vous récemment parlé **à leurs parents** ou **aux vôtres**?
Did you speak recently to their parents or yours?

- Likewise, the articles **le** and **les** contract with **de** before a possessive pronoun.

de + le mien	du mien
de + la mienne	de la mienne
de + les miens	des miens
de + les miennes	des miennes

Pourquoi t'occupes-tu **de ses problèmes** au lieu **des tiens**?
Why are you concerned with his problems instead of yours?

Les critiques parlent **de votre pièce**, pas **de la nôtre**.
The critics are talking about your play, not ours.

- With the indefinite pronoun **on**, always use the masculine possessive pronoun **le sien/les siens**.

On est fier **des siens**.
One is proud of one's own (people).

- Do not use possessive pronouns after the verb **être** in the construction [*noun/pronoun (subject)*] + **être**. Instead, use the expression **être à** + [*noun/disjunctive pronoun*].

Ce pull **est à** Nathan.
This sweater belongs to Nathan.

Ce pull **est à** lui.
This sweater is his.

Ces places **sont à** M. et Mme Ndiaye.
These seats belong to Mr. and Mrs. Ndiaye.

Ces places **sont à** eux.
These seats are theirs.

- You can, however, use the possessive pronouns after the expressions **C'est** and **Ce sont**.

C'est **la nôtre**.
It's ours.

Ce sont **les miennes**.
These are mine.

Essayez! Récrivez la phrase en utilisant le pronom possessif qui correspond.

1. Où est ma feuille d'examen? ___Où est la mienne?___
2. Ce sont tes sœurs qui reviennent de Grèce? ___Ce sont les tiennes qui reviennent de Grèce?___
3. J'ai revu mon amie d'enfance hier soir! ___J'ai revu la mienne hier soir!___
4. C'est votre lampe qui ne marche plus! ___C'est la vôtre qui ne marche plus!___
5. Ils viennent d'acheter leur piano. ___Ils viennent d'acheter le leur.___
6. Ce sont nos chansons qui passent à la radio! ___Ce sont les nôtres qui passent à la radio!___
7. Ses fauteuils sont toujours en bon état (*condition*). ___Les siens sont toujours en bon état.___
8. Quand ton concert a-t-il lieu (*takes place*)? ___Quand le tien a-t-il lieu?___

Suggestion
- Once students are comfortable with the concept of the possessive pronouns, you might want to contrast the different ways one can indicate possession using the possessive adjective, the expression **être à quelqu'un**, the possessive pronouns, and the demonstrative pronouns. Example: **C'est le piano de Didier.** (*This is Didier's piano.*) **C'est son piano.** (*It's his piano.*) **C'est le sien./Il est à lui.** (*It's his.*) **Il est meilleur que celui d'Armand.** (*It is better than Armand's.*)

Essayez! Here are some additional items that you could give the students. **9. Sa tragédie est longue. (La sienne est longue.) 10. Avez-vous écouté leur chœur? (Avez-vous écouté le leur?) 11. Notre opéra est moderne. (Le nôtre est moderne.) 12. Leurs spectateurs sont contents d'être venus. (Les leurs sont contents d'être venus.)**

Game Split the class into four teams. Using the **Essayez!** activity as a model, have each team come up with a list of additional words from the vocabulary they have learned so far and use them with different possessive adjectives. Then, have each team take turns calling out one of their words. The next team should give the corresponding possessive pronoun. The team that answers then gets a chance to call out its word. If a team gives a wrong answer, the following team gets a chance to answer and score a point. The game should proceed at a fairly fast pace. Set a time limit for the game. You could make the game more challenging by having each responding team not only give the corresponding possessive pronoun, but also use it in a logical sentence.

ESPACE **STRUCTURES**

1 Suggestion Have students do this as a written activity. Then, have them exchange their papers and correct each other's work.

2 Expansion Change the subjects of the dehydrated sentences in the activity and have students say or write the new sentences.

3 Expansion Have students redo this activity, this time saying that they have already done what their partner did. Example: **Moi, j'ai déjà écrit une carte postale aux miens.**

Mise en pratique

1 **Pas de répétitions!** Remplacez les mots indiqués par les bons pronoms possessifs.

MODÈLE

Je vois <u>mon frère</u>, mais je ne vois <u>pas ton frère</u>.
Je vois le mien, mais je ne vois pas le tien.

1. Tu préfères <u>mes chansons</u> ou <u>leurs chansons</u>? Tu préfères les miennes ou les leurs?
2. <u>Mes danseurs</u> sont arrivés, mais <u>vos danseurs</u> pas encore. Les miens sont arrivés, mais les vôtres pas encore.
3. <u>Ta comédie</u> est amusante, mais <u>sa comédie</u> est ennuyeuse. La tienne est amusante, mais la sienne est ennuyeuse.
4. <u>Mon petit ami</u> et <u>ton petit ami</u> sont allés au match ensemble. Le mien et le tien sont allés au match ensemble.
5. <u>Ma grand-mère</u> habite à Bruxelles. Et <u>leur grand-mère</u>? La mienne habite à Bruxelles. Et la leur?
6. <u>Nos chansons</u> sont meilleures que <u>vos chansons</u>. Les nôtres sont meilleures que les vôtres.
7. <u>Sa maison</u> est près de la banque. Où est <u>votre maison</u>? La sienne est près de la banque. Où est la vôtre?
8. <u>Leurs séances</u> sont moins longues que <u>tes séances</u>. Les leurs sont moins longues que les tiennes.

2 **Quel chaos!** Madame Mercier emmène ses enfants et leurs copains à la plage, mais tout le monde a oublié d'apporter quelque chose. Faites des phrases complètes pour dire qui a oublié quoi.

MODÈLE

je / serviette / David
J'ai ma serviette, mais David a oublié la sienne.

1. tu / lunettes de soleil / Marie et Claire Tu as tes lunettes de soleil, mais Marie et Claire ont oublié les leurs.
2. nous / chaussures / Christophe Nous avons nos chaussures, mais Christophe a oublié les siennes.
3. Tristan et Benjamin / casquettes / Élisa et toi Tristan et Benjamin ont leurs casquettes, mais Élisa et toi avez oublié les vôtres.
4. vous / maillot de bain / nous Vous avez votre maillot de bain, mais nous avons oublié les nôtres.
5. Thomas / crème solaire (*sunscreen*) / vous Thomas a sa crème solaire, mais vous avez oublié la vôtre.
6. je / lecteur MP3 / tu J'ai mon lecteur MP3, mais tu as oublié le tien.
7. Magalie / tee-shirt / nous Magalie a son tee-shirt, mais nous avons oublié le nôtre.
8. tu / chapeau / il Tu as ton chapeau, mais il a oublié le sien.

3 **Les mêmes choses** Votre cousin va faire exactement les mêmes choses que vous, aujourd'hui. Écrivez ses réponses avec des pronoms possessifs.

MODÈLE

Tu vas écrire une carte postale à tes grands-parents?
Alors, je vais aussi écrire une carte postale aux miens.

1. Tu vas jouer avec ton petit frère? Alors, je vais aussi jouer avec le mien.
2. Tu vas téléphoner à tes amies? Alors, je vais aussi téléphoner aux miennes.
3. Tu vas donner à manger à tes chats? Alors, je vais aussi donner à manger aux miens.
4. Tu vas dire bonjour à ton prof? Alors, je vais aussi dire bonjour au mien.
5. Tu vas prendre une photo de ta maison? Alors, je vais aussi prendre une photo de la mienne.
6. Tu vas t'occuper de tes affaires? Alors, je vais aussi m'occuper des miennes.
7. Tu vas acheter un cadeau à ta mère? Alors, je vais aussi acheter un cadeau à la mienne.
8. Tu vas aller au cinéma avec tes amis? Alors, je vais aussi aller au cinéma avec les miens.

 Practice more at **vhlcentral.com**.

Communication

4 C'est à qui? Vous êtes responsable du bureau des objets trouvés dans votre université. Avec un(e) partenaire, créez un dialogue et jouez la scène devant la classe. *Answers will vary.*

MODÈLE

Étudiant(e) 1: *Ces cahiers sont à toi?*
Étudiant(e) 2: *Non, ce ne sont pas les miens.*
Étudiant(e) 1: *Tu es sûr(e)?*
Étudiant(e) 2: *Oui, les miens sont plus grands.*

1.

2.

3.

4.

5.

6.

5 Au spectacle Catherine est au théâtre avec son ami Rémi. Elle est metteur en scène et compare la pièce qu'elle voit avec la sienne. Avec un(e) partenaire, jouez la conversation. Utilisez autant de pronoms possessifs que possible. *Answers will vary.*

MODÈLE

Étudiant(e) 1: *Le début de ma pièce est plus intéressant que le sien.*
Étudiant(e) 2: *Je ne suis pas d'accord. Le sien est aussi intéressant que le tien.*

6 Questions personnelles Vous voulez mieux connaître votre partenaire. Posez-vous ces questions à tour de rôle. Utilisez des pronoms possessifs dans vos réponses. *Answers will vary.*

1. Est-ce que tes idées (*ideas*) sont vraiment différentes de celles de tes parents?
2. Est-ce que ton style de vêtements est le même que celui de ton frère ou ta sœur?
3. D'habitude, est-ce que tu t'occupes de tes affaires ou de celles de tes amis?
4. Tu t'entends mieux avec tes parents ou avec ceux de ton/ta petit(e) ami(e)?
5. Tu aimes ton quartier ou celui de tes amis?
6. Tu préfères ta voiture ou celle d'un de tes amis?
7. Est-ce que tes goûts (*tastes*) en musique sont différents de ceux de tes grands-parents?

7 La réunion Vous avez terminé vos études universitaires il y a dix ans et vous rencontrez un(e) ami(e) que vous n'avez pas vu(e) depuis tout ce temps. Parlez de vos vies et utilisez des pronoms possessifs dans votre conversation. *Answers will vary.*

MODÈLE

Étudiant(e) 1: *Mon mari/Ma femme est professeur. Et le tien/la tienne?*
Étudiant(e) 2: *Le mien/La mienne est architecte.*

adresse e-mail	frère	parents
compagnie	maison	sœur
enfants	mari	travail
femme	numéro de téléphone	voiture

4 Suggestion Before they start this activity, have students brainstorm a variety of adjectives they could use to describe their belongings.

4 Expansions
• Students could extend the activity by using their personal belongings and asking their partners if the items belong to them.
• Have students use the third person to share their partner's response with the class. Example: **Ces cahiers ne sont pas à lui/elle. Les siens sont plus grands.**

5 Expansion Have pairs volunteer to perform this as a skit in front of the class.

6 Expansion You might have students circulate around the class and ask at least five other students these questions. Then, have them write five sentences to summarize the information obtained through the interviews.

Extra Practice Have students come up with sentences using the indefinite pronoun **on** with **le sien/les siens**. Here are some examples that you can give them. **On s'occupe du sien. On ne se fâche pas contre les siens. On s'intéresse aux siens. On se souvient des siens.**

Extra Practice Have students work in pairs to write at least eight questions on a variety of topics to ask the other. The goal is to use possessive pronouns in the questions or the answers. Ex: **1. Mes grands-parents habitent à Houston. Et les tiens? 2. Ma famille est très grande. Et la tienne? 3. Mon/Ma petit(e) ami(e) est très intelligent(e). Et le tien/la tienne? 4. J'adore mes cours. Et toi? Les miens sont trop difficiles.**

Révision

Instructional Resources
vhlcentral.com:
Activity Pack (Info Gap Activities); Testing Program; Testing Program MP3s; reference tools

1 Expansion Brainstorm other hobbies and occupations with the whole class. Then have pairs continue this activity using magazine pictures.

2 Expansion Give these additional items to the class.
• **Il n'y a pas de place pour les femmes dans les films d'action.**
• **La plupart des films américains sont violents.**
• **Les gens plus âgés n'aiment pas la musique rock.**

3 Suggestion Divide the class into pairs and distribute the Info Gap Handouts found in the Activity Pack on the Supersite. Give students ten minutes to complete the activity.

4 Expansion Have pairs create a new **annonce** for a **rôle principal**. Encourage students to be creative. Then have students exchange their **annonce** with another pair and repeat the activity.

5 Suggestion Ask a volunteer from each group to take notes on their conversations. After the groups have compared lists, have each volunteer write their group's selections on the board. Each group should take turns summarizing their selections and relating the expressions of doubt and certainty used in the activity.

6 Suggestion Before students begin this activity, have pairs make a list of university supplies they are going to ask to borrow and possible excuses. After they finish the activity, have them share their most creative excuses with the rest of the class. Students should vote for the best excuse they hear.

---

1 Il est clair que… Observez ces personnes et imaginez leurs activités artistiques préférées. Avec un(e) partenaire, utilisez des expressions de doute et de certitude pour répondre aux questions et pour décrire chaque personnage. *Answers will vary.*

chanteur de chorale ou de comédie musicale?

danseur ou acteur?

chef d'orchestre ou metteur en scène?

compositeur d'opéra ou dramaturge?

2 Je ne pense pas Que pensent vos camarades de ces affirmations? Par groupes de quatre, trouvez au moins une personne qui soit d'accord avec chaque phrase et une qui ne soit pas d'accord. Utilisez des expressions de doute et de certitude. Ensuite, présentez vos arguments à la classe. *Answers will vary.*

> **MODÈLE** La télévision fait du mal au cinéma.
>
> **Étudiant(e) 1:** *Penses-tu que la télévision fasse du mal au cinéma?*
> **Étudiant(e) 2:** *Non, je ne crois pas que ce soit vrai. Il est clair que les acteurs de cinéma sont plus célèbres que ceux de la télé.*

• Jimi Hendrix est le meilleur joueur de guitare.
• Mozart est le meilleur compositeur de musique classique.
• Personne n'aime les comédies musicales aujourd'hui.
• Un danseur est autant un sportif qu'un artiste.
• L'opéra est un genre trop ésotérique et ennuyeux.

3 Les arts Votre professeur va vous donner, à vous et à votre partenaire, deux feuilles d'activités différentes sur les arts. Attention! Ne regardez pas la feuille de votre partenaire. *Answers will vary.*

4 C'est tout moi! Avec un(e) partenaire, vous voyez ces annonces dans le journal. Vous pensez qu'un de ces rôles est pour vous. Un(e) ami(e) n'est pas du tout d'accord, mais vous insistez. Utilisez des expressions de doute et de certitude dans votre dialogue. *Answers will vary.*

Cherchons jeune homme de 27-30 ans, sportif et musclé, avec permis moto et avion, pour rôle principal. Doit être un acteur expérimenté qui sache jouer du piano comme un professionnel et qui puisse monter à cheval. Doit avoir les yeux noirs, beaucoup de charme, de la présence et un look aventurier.

Cherchons jeune femme de 18-20 ans avec beaucoup de personnalité et qui ait une formation de chanteuse classique, pour rôle dans une comédie musicale en espagnol. Doit pouvoir danser le tango, la salsa et la rumba.

Venez rencontrer le compositeur et le metteur en scène, jeudi à 20 heures, au Théâtre du Boulevard.

5 Le meilleur Avec un(e) partenaire, trouvez un exemple pour chaque catégorie de la liste. Ensuite, comparez votre liste avec celle d'un autre groupe et parlez de vos opinions. Utilisez des expressions de doute et de certitude. *Answers will vary.*

le/la meilleur(e) … en ce moment

• film
• chanson à la radio
• danseur/danseuse
• chanteur/chanteuse
• acteur/actrice

6 Mal organisé Vous étiez très pressé(e) ce matin et vous avez oublié de mettre beaucoup de choses dans votre sac à dos. Demandez à votre partenaire si vous pouvez lui emprunter cinq choses dont vous avez besoin pour l'université. Votre partenaire va vous donner des excuses pour ne pas vous les prêter. Utilisez des pronoms possessifs. Jouez votre dialogue devant la classe. *Answers will vary.*

> **MODÈLE**
>
> **Étudiant(e) 1:** *Je peux emprunter ta calculatrice?*
> **Étudiant(e) 2:** *Désolé(e). J'ai besoin de la mienne pour faire ce devoir.*

Extra Practice Have students imagine they are writing to a friend who is just about to start his or her freshman year of college. In their letter, students should give advice about the uncertainties of university life. Encourage students to use the expressions listed on page 640. You may want to collect students' papers and grade them.

Game Divide the class into two teams. One team writes sentences with expressions of certainty, while the other writes sentences with expressions of doubt, disbelief, or uncertainty. Put all the sentences in a hat. Students take turns drawing sentences for their team and stating the opposite of what the sentence says. The team with the most correct sentences wins.

Le Zapping

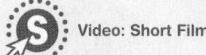 Video: Short Film

Léo est un jeune homme romantique et galant°, mais il est fauché°. Alice est une jeune Parisienne, féministe et indépendante. Ils se retrouvent pour leur premier rendez-vous. Très vite, ils entrent dans un jeu à propos de° qui va payer l'addition. Puisque° Léo n'a pas d'argent, comment va-t-il s'en sortir°?

galant *gentlemanly* **fauché** *broke* **à propos de** *about* **Puisque** *Since* **s'en sortir** *to work it out*

Préparation

1 **Définitions** Associez ces situations ou déclarations avec des expressions du vocabulaire.

1. Je vous invite, ça me fait plaisir! __C'est pour moi.__

2. Je n'avais que des problèmes à l'époque, tout allait mal. __J'étais en galère.__

3. Samir et Marc disent que rien n'est cassé (*broken*) et qu'ils peuvent tout réparer. __Ce n'est pas grave.__

4. Vous décidez de l'emmener dans un restaurant très cher pour l'impressionner (*impress*). __Vous sortez le grand__ jeu.

5. Ah! Je dis toujours ce qu'il ne faut pas! __Je suis la reine des__ gaffes.

6. Ça n'avait aucun sens. Ce n'était pas une bonne explication! __C'était bidon.__

2 **Complétez** Utilisez le vocabulaire du film pour compléter ces phrases.

1. David est très enthousiaste et positif, il aime absolument tout. Il __s'emballe__ pour un rien!

2. Camille veut me présenter son frère aujourd'hui. Nous avons __rendez-vous__ au centre-ville vers quinze heures.

3. Est-ce que ce restaurant a un __vestiaire__? Je veux y laisser mon sac et ma veste.

4. Les enfants sont petits, nous allons leur installer une __balançoire__ dans le jardin.

5. Voici vos boissons, des olives et des __cacahouètes__. Est-ce que vous désirez autre chose?

6. Mes voisins s'entendent très mal. Ils __s'engueulent__ tout le temps!

7. Ahmed a besoin de passer un __coup de fil__. Est-ce que tu peux lui prêter ton téléphone?

8. Vous ne payez jamais l'addition. Je n'ai jamais vu de gens aussi __radins__ que vous!

Expressions utiles

Ce n'est pas grave.
It's not a big deal.

C'est la bonne.
She's the one.

C'est pour moi.
It's on me.

C'était bidon.
That was lame.

Je suis la reine des gaffes.
I'm the queen of blunders.

J'étais en galère.
I was having a hard time.

On fait chacun son tour.
We take turns.

Vous sortez le grand jeu.
You're going all out.

Vocabulaire du court métrage

une balançoire
swing

brûler
to burn

des cacahouètes (f.)
peanuts

un coup de fil
phone call

s'emballer
to get carried away

s'engueuler (fam.)
to have a fight

un forfait
plan

un matelas
mattress

la moutarde au miel
honey mustard

radin
stingy

un rendez-vous
date

le sang
blood

un vestiaire
coat check

Section Goals

In this section, students will:
- watch a short film about a first date
- answer questions about the film

Instructional Resources
vhlcentral.com: short film; *Le Zapping* short film transcription; reference tools

Introduction
To check comprehension, ask these questions: **1. D'après l'introduction, qui sont les deux personnages principales du court métrage que vous allez regarder?** (Léo et Alice) **2. Est-ce que ces deux personnes se connaissent bien?** (Non. C'est leur premier rendez-vous.) **3. Pourquoi Léo veut-il éviter de payer l'addition?** (Parce qu'il est fauché. / Parce qu'il n'a pas d'argent.)

Avant de regarder le film
- Have students look at the video stills, read the captions, and predict what is happening for each visual. (**1. Ces gens ont un premier rendez-vous et ils dînent ensemble. 2. À la fin, ils sont fiancés.**)
- Before showing the video, explain to students that they do not need to understand every word they hear. Tell them to listen for the text in the captions and for vocabulary from this lesson. They should also watch every scene carefully and jot down further examples of this lesson's vocabulary.

1 **Expansion** Have students work in pairs or groups for this activity. Tell them to write their answers. Ask them to write an additional sentence for the remaining expression in the vocabulary. Then have a few volunteers share their answers with the class.

2 **Expansion** Ask students if they or someone they know have ever been on a date like the one in the short film. Have volunteers share their experiences with their classmates. How did the date end?

OPTIONS

Note culturelle In the United States, men have traditionally been the ones to pay for things on a date, but this is less frequently the case than it used to be. Nowadays, young Americans on dates will often split the bill or take turns paying for things.

The tradition of men paying for things on a date remains more prevalent in France, though young French couples who are dating are as likely to split the bill or take turns paying for things as their modern American counterparts. Among friends, however, the bill is nearly always split between the group.

ESPACE SYNTHÈSE **645**

Qui de nous deux

Avant de regarder le film
Give students a moment to look at the images and captions. Then, have them predict what they think will happen in the film.

Suggestion Stop after each segment and ask students to summarize what happened using their own words. After each segment, ask students to try and guess what might happen in the next segment.

Compréhension Have students look at the stills and read the captions. Then ask these questions: 1. Comment Léo et Alice se sont-ils rencontrés? (Ils se sont rencontrés dans la rue quand Léo avait demandé à Alice d'utiliser son portable.) 2. Pensez-vous que Léo va acheter le bouquet de roses? (Non, parce qu'il n'a pas assez d'argent.) 3. Est-ce que Léo va tout payer? (Non, ils vont partager et payer chacun à son tour.)

LÉO En fait, j'étais en galère, c'était un soir tard, j'étais dans la rue, et, j'avais absolument besoin de passer un coup de fil, mais comme j'ai un forfait bloqué... C'est à dire qu'un forfait bloqué, c'est euh... genre au bout d'une heure, ben, t'es bloqué, quoi, tu peux plus appeler. Enfin bref, elle est arrivée de nulle part, et elle m'a prêté son téléphone, et il s'est passé un truc.

FLEURISTE C'est pour une demande en mariage?

LÉO Ah non! C'est notre premier rendez-vous.

FLEURISTE Alors, ben, on a ça. Cinquante roses. Mais avec ça, vous sortez le grand jeu.

LÉO Ah oui, il est magnifique. C'est combien?

FLEURISTE Cent vingt euros.

ALICE Elles ont même brûlé° leurs soutiens-gorge° avec Simone de Beauvoir.

LÉO Oui, mais, euh, enfin, moi, je respecte, hein, la parité, le féminisme, les soutiens-gorge qui brûlent et tout, moi je trouve ça super.

ALICE Mais alors, on fait chacun à son tour. Une fois toi, une fois moi, comme ça, la prochaine fois, c'est à moi.

LÉO Oui, très bien, faisons chacun son tour. Tu peux même tout payer si tu veux. Non, je déconne°. Non, mais faisons ça, chacun son tour, ça marche.

LÉO Ça donne faim, la lutte°.

ALICE Oui. Alors, tiens, Vas-y, commence par celui-là.

LÉO Ah oui, ah oui! C'est incroyable, ça.

ALICE C'est mon préféré. Ce qui fait la différence, tu vois, c'est la moutarde au miel. Et celle-ci, enfin, moi, je la trouve juste dingue°, quoi.

LÉO Mais, merci beaucoup, c'est gentil. L'intention...

ALICE Bon ben, dommage, hein. Ce n'est pas grave. Tu prends juste la surprise!

LÉO Ah, je n'avais pas vu!

ALICE La petite surprise.

LÉO La petite surprise. Bon ben, du coup c'est à moi de... c'est à moi.

LÉO Alice, veux-tu m'épouser?

ALICE Quoi?

LÉO Elle a dit oui! Elle a dit oui, c'est formidable! C'est le plus beau jour de ma vie! Elle a dit oui! Merci! Merci à tous, c'est trop cool! Elle a dit oui! Elle a dit oui! C'est ma femme! Prenez-nous en photo, allez-y! On va avoir un chien! On va aller chez DomExpo, c'est superbe! Vas-y, souris un peu.

brûlé *burned* **soutiens-gorge** *bras* **je déconne** *I'm kidding* **lutte** *fight* **dingue** *unbelievable*

OPTIONS

Note culturelle Tell students that the man who comes to Léo and Alice's table at the restaurant is selling *maalaï*, a garland of flowers used especially in India and Thailand for celebratory and ritual purposes. The man thanks them in Urdu, a language spoken in India and Pakistan.

Expansion Have students compare "typical" first dates in the United States with the first date in the film. Are the places, food, and things talked about on the date in the film similar or different? Ask students how they think the date in the film compares to "typical" first dates in France.

Analyse

3 Vrai ou faux? Indiquez si ces déclarations au sujet de Léo sont vraies ou fausses, d'après le film.

	Vrai	Faux
1. Léo a déjà rencontré Alice une fois.	☑	☐
2. Il demande des conseils à la fleuriste.	☑	☐
3. Il achète plusieurs roses, mais n'en donne qu'une à Alice.	☐	☑
4. Quand Alice veut aller au restaurant, il dit qu'il n'a pas faim parce. qu'il ne veut pas dépenser d'argent.	☑	☐
5. Il a assez d'argent pour payer les boissons au café.	☐	☑
6. Il pense que prendre un taxi est une bonne idée..	☐	☑
7. Il invente une excuse pour ne pas manger le bonbon qu'Alice lui offre.	☑	☐
8. Il trouve que le restaurant n'est pas bon.	☐	☑

4 Interprétez Avec un(e) partenaire, répondez aux questions sur le film. Answers will vary.

1. Est-ce que Léo achèterait le bouquet de roses s'il avait 120 euros à dépenser?
2. Est-ce que Léo plaisante (is joking) vraiment quand, au café, il dit à Alice qu'elle peut tout payer si elle veut?
3. Pourquoi est-ce que l'égalité entre les hommes et les femmes est importante pour Alice?
4. Que fait Léo quand il revient vers le taxi? Pourquoi?
5. Pourquoi est-ce qu'Alice sourit quand Léo laisse un pourboire au vestiaire du restaurant?
6. Pourquoi est-ce qu'Alice ne doit pas payer le repas?
7. Est-ce qu'Alice est contente quand Léo fait sa demande en mariage?
8. Est-ce qu'Alice comprend et apprécie ce que Léo fait pour ne pas payer l'addition au restaurant?

5 Notre rencontre Par groupe de trois, préparez une conversation dans laquelle Léo et Alice racontent leur premier rendez-vous à un(e) bon(ne) ami(e). Utilisez les notes et questions ci-dessous comme guide. Answers will vary.

- Choisissez le ton de la conversation: Est-ce une conversation plutôt amusante, intéressante, surprenante, énervante, etc.?
- Pensez à la personnalité de Léo et à celle d'Alice, à leurs milieux (backgrounds) d'origine et à leur conversation pour expliquer leurs comportements pendant cette soirée.
- Expliquez pourquoi et à quel moment Alice décide d'entrer dans le jeu.
- Pensez à la réaction de leur ami(e): Quelles questions pose-t-il/elle et que pense-t-il/elle de cette histoire?

4 Expansion Have students write a brief outline of the interactions between Léo and Alice that explains what the two might be thinking as they learn about each other.

4 Expansion Have students consider the predictions they made in the **Avant de regarder le film** activity. Have them compare their predictions with the actual events of the film.

5 Suggestion Have students list the clues in the film that show that Léo has no money to spend on the date (suggesting a walk in the park, asking another customer for change, saying that he's not hungry, etc.)

OPTIONS

Small Groups Have groups of three or four students reimagine the events of the film. What do they think would happen if Léo had told Alice in the beginning that he had no money? What would happen if the restaurant owner didn't offer them their meal for free?

Cultural comparison Have students work in groups of three or four and compare the places they see in the short film to those in their town. How are they similar or different? Are there places in the film which don't exist in the students' town? Have them describe when and with whom they frequent these places.

Section Goals

In this section, students will learn and practice vocabulary related to:
• fine arts
• films and television
• books

Instructional Resources

vhlcentral.com:
Digital Image Bank (including vocabulary illustrations from the textbook, theme-based illustrations);
Vocabulaire supplémentaire;
Mise en pratique *answers; Textbook Audioscript; Lab Audioscript; Activity Pack* (***Feuilles d'activités***)*; Textbook MP3s; Lab MP3s; SAM Answer Key; reference tools*

Suggestions

• Tell students to look over the new vocabulary and identify the cognates.
• Use the **15B Contextes** illustration from the Digital Image Bank. Point out people and things as you describe the illustration. Examples: **Elle fait de la peinture. C'est un film d'horreur.**
• Point out the difference in spelling between the French word **aventure** and the English word *adventure.*
• Explain that **les beaux-arts** (*fine arts*) is a term that refers collectively to a variety of artistic fields, particularly those concerned with the creation of beautiful things, such as painting and sculpture.
• Additional vocabulary for this lesson can be found in the **Vocabulaire supplémentaire** on the Supersite.
• Use the Arts and culture illustrations from the Digital Image Bank to help students familiarize themselves with fine arts, films and television, and books.

Leçon 15B

Vocabulary Tools

Au festival d'art

You will learn how to...
▪ discuss films and television
▪ discuss books

Vocabulaire

faire les musées	to go to museums
publier	to publish
les beaux-arts (*m.*)	fine arts
un chef-d'œuvre	masterpiece
un conte	tale
une critique	review; criticism
un dessin animé	cartoon
un documentaire	documentary
un drame psychologique	psychological drama
une émission (de télévision)	(television) program
un festival (festivals *pl.*)	festival
un feuilleton	soap opera
un film (d'aventures, policier)	(adventure, crime) film
une histoire	story
les informations (infos) (*f.*)	news
un jeu télévisé	game show
la météo	weather
les nouvelles (*f.*)	news
une œuvre	artwork, piece of art
un programme	program
une publicité (pub)	advertisement
les variétés (*f.*)	popular music
ancien(ne)	ancient; old; former
doué(e)	talented, gifted
gratuit(e)	free
littéraire	literary
récent(e)	recent
à la radio	on the radio
à la télé(vision)	on television

un film de science-fiction

un sculpteur (une sculptrice *f.*)

une femme auteur/ une écrivaine

une sculpture

un auteur/ écrivain

un roman

M. Pierre LeGrand, auteur de *La plume enchantée*

O P T I O N S

Game Write types of television shows or movies on index cards and place them in a box. Divide the class into two teams. Have students draw a card and describe the genre without saying the word, but they may use French titles as clues. Award points as follows: after one clue = 3 points, after two clues = 2 points, and after three clues = 1 point. If a team does not guess the answer after three tries, the other team has one chance to "steal" the point by guessing correctly.

Extra Practice Tell students that they have just returned from an arts festival. Ask them to describe what they did, saw, and heard. Example: **J'ai vu beaucoup de beaux tableaux et j'ai parlé à deux peintres.**

Mise en pratique

un film d'horreur

1 Écoutez Écoutez la conversation entre Nora et Jeanne et indiquez si Nora (N), Armand (A), Jeanne (J) ou Charles (C) ont fait les choses suivantes.

<u>N</u>   1. s'est bien amusée au Festival des beaux-arts.
<u>N et A</u>   2. ont vu une exposition d'art contemporain.
<u>J et C</u>   3. ont vu un film d'aventures.
<u>N et A</u>   4. ont assisté à une critique littéraire sur Assia Djebar.
<u>J et C</u>   5. sont restés chez eux.
<u>N et A</u>   6. sont allés à la librairie pour acheter un roman.
<u>C</u>   7. a promis de faire les musées le week-end prochain.
<u>J</u>   8. a fait de la peinture.

une poétesse (poète m.)

un poème

un magazine

2 Vous les connaissez? Faites correspondre les œuvres, personnages et programmes télévisés de la colonne de gauche avec le mot de la colonne de droite qui convient.

<u>e</u>   1. *La Belle et la Bête*
<u>d</u>   2. *Whistler's Mother*
<u>a</u>   3. Le *David*
<u>h</u>   4. *Jeopardy*
<u>l</u>   5. Claude Monet
<u>g</u>   6. *Les Trois Mousquetaires*
<u>b</u>   7. Victor Hugo
<u>f</u>   8. *All My Children*
<u>i</u>   9. *Vogue*
<u>c</u>   10. *2001, l'Odyssée de l'espace*

a. une sculpture
b. un auteur
c. un film de science-fiction
d. une peinture
e. un conte
f. un feuilleton
g. un roman
h. un jeu télévisé
i. un magazine
j. une exposition
k. un film d'horreur
l. un peintre

un tableau

une peinture

une femme peintre (peintre m.)

Elle fait de la peinture.

une exposition

3 Complétez Complétez ces phrases avec le mot de vocabulaire d'ESPACE CONTEXTES qui convient.

1. La peinture et la sculpture font partie des <u>beaux-arts</u>.
2. Une <u>poétesse</u> est une personne qui écrit des poèmes.
3. Un <u>auteur</u> est quelqu'un qui est à l'origine d'une œuvre.
4. Art de juger (*to judge*) les créations littéraires ou artistiques: <u>une critique</u>.
5. Un <u>documentaire</u> est basé sur la réalité.
6. Une <u>publicité</u> est une activité commerciale pour vendre un produit.
7. *Bugs Bunny* et *Mickey Mouse* sont des exemples de <u>dessin animé</u>.
8. *Indiana Jones* est un exemple de film <u>d'aventures</u>.
9. Si on n'a pas besoin de payer pour entrer dans un musée, c'est <u>gratuit</u>.
10. On peut écouter les informations <u>à la radio</u>.

S Practice more at **vhlcentral.com**.

six cent quarante-neuf **649**

1 Audioscript JEANNE: Salut Nora, es-tu allée au Festival des beaux-arts et de la littérature de l'université?
NORA: Oui, j'y suis allée avec Armand. Nous nous sommes bien amusés. D'abord, nous avons vu une exposition d'art contemporain d'artistes locaux. Après, nous avons assisté à une critique des œuvres littéraires d'Assia Djebar, tu sais, l'écrivaine algérienne. À la fin de la présentation, Armand était tellement intéressé par ses œuvres que nous sommes allés à la librairie pour acheter un de ses romans. Et toi, y es-tu allée? Je ne t'ai pas vue.
J: Malheureusement, non. Tu sais que Charles n'aime pas vraiment l'art. Pour lui, c'est ennuyeux, sauf le cinéma. Nous sommes restés à la maison et nous avons regardé deux films. J'ai choisi un drame psychologique et lui, un film d'aventures. C'était bien. Après ça, j'ai fait de la peinture et Charles s'est endormi. Il m'a promis que le week-end prochain, il ferait les musées avec moi quand nous serons en Italie.
(On Textbook MP3s)

1 Expansion For review, ask students: **Qui est Assia Djebar?** Students should remember that she is an Algerian feminist author and filmmaker, and the first writer from the Maghreb to be admitted into the **Académie française** (2005). See page 261.

2 Expansion Ask students to provide additional examples for each term in the right-hand column.

3 Expansion Have students write three more fill-in-the-blank sentences. Then have them exchange papers with a classmate and fill in the missing words.

OPTIONS

Game Distribute an authentic French-language television guide. Discuss the genres of the programs listed. Then write titles of various programs from the guide on cards and place them in a hat or box. Write categories for the programs on the board or a transparency. Examples: **un dessin animé, un jeu télévisé, un drame psychologique, un feuilleton, les informations, un** **film policier**, and **un film d'aventures**. Divide the class into two teams. Have teams take turns drawing titles and classifying them according to their genres. If a player guesses incorrectly, the other team may "steal" the point. Remind students that answers called out of turn do not count. The team with the most points wins.

NATIONAL communication STANDARDS

Communication

4 Suggestions
- Tell students to jot down notes during their interviews.
- Have pairs get together with another pair of students and share what they learned about their partners.

5 Suggestions
- Distribute the **Feuilles d'activités** found in the Activity Pack on the Supersite.
- Give students three to four minutes to complete the first column before having them work in pairs. Then have two volunteers read the **modèle**.

6 Suggestion If time is limited, have students write their paragraphs as homework, then discuss their thoughts with a partner in class.

7 Expansion Have groups write a script for their program and perform it for the class.

4 Conversez Interviewez un(e) camarade de classe au sujet de l'art et des médias. Answers will vary.

1. Quel(s) genre(s) de film préfères-tu? Pourquoi?
2. Quel film récent as-tu vu? Quelle en est l'histoire?
3. As-tu un auteur favori? Lequel?
4. Quel(s) genre(s) d'œuvres littéraires aimes-tu?
5. Qu'est-ce que tu écoutes à la radio? Quand?
6. As-tu fait les musées récemment? Quelle(s) exposition(s) as-tu vue(s)?
7. Quel(s) chef(s)-d'œuvre admires-tu?
8. Qui considères-tu être un peintre doué? Pour quelle(s) raison(s)?
9. Es-tu un(e) artiste? Dans quel domaine?
10. Lis-tu des magazines? Lesquels?

5 À la télévision et à la radio Votre professeur va vous donner, à vous et à votre partenaire, une feuille d'activités. Remplissez d'abord la première colonne avec vos préférences pour chaque catégorie. Ensuite, comparez vos réponses avec celles d'un(e) camarade de classe. Answers will vary.

MODÈLE

un dessin animé
Étudiant(e) 1: *Quel est ton dessin animé préféré?*
Étudiant(e) 2: *J'adore regarder les Simpson.*

Programmes	Moi	Noms
1. un dessin animé		
2. une émission		
3. un feuilleton		

6 L'art et vous Écrivez un paragraphe d'après (*according to*) ces instructions. Ensuite, à tour de rôle, discutez-en avec un(e) camarade de classe. Answers will vary.

- Décrivez l'importance que vous donnez à l'art dans votre vie.
- Parlez de l'influence positive et/ou négative de l'art sur le monde.
- Parlez de comment vous aimeriez contribuer à cette influence.

7 Regardons la télé Avec les éléments donnés, travaillez avec trois autres partenaires pour présenter une émission pour la chaîne de télévision de votre université. Answers will vary.

- Choisissez une catégorie de programme télévisé. Chaque groupe doit choisir un genre différent, par exemple un jeu, un feuilleton, les informations, la météo, un documentaire, etc.
- Donnez un nom à votre programme et aux personnages de l'émission.
- Annoncez le contenu de votre programme.

650 *six cent cinquante*

OPTIONS

Small Groups Have students work in groups of three. Tell them to role-play a situation in which three roommates share a single television and no one can agree on which shows to watch. Students should discuss what shows are on that night, which are better and why, and so forth. Tell students to resolve the argument in their conversation.

Pairs Have students work in pairs. Give them a list of movie titles and/or TV shows to discuss. Brainstorm expressions for giving favorable and unfavorable opinions and write them in two columns on the board. Examples: **C'est très amusant. C'est trop violent. On ne s'ennuie jamais. Il n'y a pas d'histoire. Le metteur en scène est doué.**

Les sons et les lettres  Audio

Les abréviations

French speakers use many acronyms. This is especially true in newspapers, televised news programs, and in political discussions. Many stand for official organizations or large companies.

EDF = Électricité de France   **ONU** = Organisation des Nations Unies

People often use acronyms when referring to geographical place names and transportation.

É-U = États-Unis   **RF** = République Française
RN = Route Nationale   **TGV** = Train à Grande Vitesse

Many are simply shortened versions of common expressions or compound words.

SVP = S'il Vous Plaît   **RV** = Rendez-Vous   **RDC** = Rez-De-Chaussée

When speaking, some acronyms are spelled out, while others are pronounced like any other word.

Cedex = Courrier d'Entreprise à Distribution Exceptionnelle *(an overnight delivery service)*

Prononcez Répétez les abréviations suivantes à voix haute.

1. W-C = *Water-Closet*
2. HS = Hors Service *(out of order)*
3. VF = Version Française
4. CV = Curriculum Vitæ
5. TVA = Taxe à la Valeur Ajoutée *(added)*
6. DELF = Diplôme d'Études en Langue Française
7. RATP = Régie Autonome *(independent administration)* des Transports Parisiens
8. SMIC = Salaire Minimum Interprofessionnel de Croissance *(growth)*

Assortissez-les Répétez les abréviations à voix haute. Que représentent-elles?

d	1. ECP	a.	objet volant non identifié
e	2. GDF	b.	toutes taxes comprises
f	3. DEUG	c.	président-directeur général
b	4. TTC	d.	École centrale de Paris
c	5. PDG	e.	Gaz de France
a	6. OVNI	f.	diplôme d'études universitaires générales

Expressions Répétez les expressions à voix haute.

RSVP (Répondez, S'il Vous Plaît).[1]

Elle est BCBG (Bon Chic, Bon Genre).[2]

ressources
LM p. 118 — vhlcentral

[1] Please reply.
[2] She is preppy. (in a conservatively classic fashion)

Instructional Resources
vhlcentral.com:
Textbook MP3s; Lab MP3s; SAM Answer Key; Textbook Audioscript; Lab Audioscript; reference tools

Suggestions
• Model the pronunciation of the abbreviations and acronyms and have students repeat them after you.
• Explain that an **acronyme** refers to an abbreviation that can be pronounced as a word and is written without periods, such as **ONU**. A **sigle** is a set of letters forming an abbreviation that is pronounced as separate letters, for example, **RATP**. The general tendency is to omit the periods in everyday French.
• Ask students to provide additional examples of French abbreviations or acronyms they have seen or heard.
• Distribute French newspapers or magazines and tell students to find acronyms and abbreviations. Ask them to guess what words they stand for.

O P T I O N S

Language Note Tell students that French speakers use many abbreviated forms of words. Some of them are considered slang, so they should be careful about using them in formal situations. Then write the shortened forms of the words below on the board or a transparency and ask students what the original word is. **1.** métro (métropolitain) **2.** ciné (cinéma) **3.** ado (adolescent) **4.** micro (microphone) **5.** moto (motocyclette)

6. appart (appartement) **7.** frigo (réfrigérateur) **8.** pub (publicité) **9.** petit-déj (petit-déjeuner)

Extra Practice Write the following abbreviations in a column on the board and their meanings in another column. Have students match the abbreviations and words. **1.** K7 (cassette) **2.** PJ (police judiciaire) **3.** Cie (compagnie) **4.** VO (version originale) **5.** RP (relations publiques) **6.** DOM (département d'outre-mer)

ESPACE ROMAN-PHOTO

Section Goals

In this section, students will learn functional phrases for expressing conditions and possible actions.

Instructional Resources
vhlcentral.com:
Roman-photo Video, Videoscript, and Translation; SAM Answer Key; reference tools

Video Recap: Leçon 15A
Review the previous **Roman-photo**, with this true/false activity.
1. Le spectacle de Sandrine, c'est la comédie musicale préférée d'Amina. (Vrai.)
2. Rachid admire la robe qu'Amina a faite. (Vrai.)
3. Sandrine chante mal, mais elle est une assez bonne actrice. (Vrai.)
4. David dit directement à Sandrine ce qu'il pense de son concert. (Faux.)
5. Sandrine accepte gracieusement ce que David lui dit. (Faux.)

Video Synopsis
Sandrine is making a cake for David's farewell party. She tells Amina that David helped her find her true passion, cooking, and she has decided to become a professional chef. At the party, Amina explains that some of her clothes are going to be in a fashion show for young designers in Paris. Rachid announces that he got his diploma with honors. David says he plans to return next year and have an exhibit of his paintings at **Le P'tit Bistrot**.

Suggestions
• Have students predict what the episode will be about based on the video stills.
• After reading the **Roman-photo**, have students summarize the episode.

PERSONNAGES

Amina

Astrid

David

Rachid

Sandrine

Stéphane

Valérie

Au revoir, David!  Video

Chez Sandrine...
AMINA Qu'est-ce qui sent si bon?
SANDRINE C'est un gâteau pour David. Il repart demain aux États-Unis tu sais.
AMINA David et toi, vous avez décidé de ne plus vous disputer?
SANDRINE C'est de l'histoire ancienne.
AMINA C'est comme dans un feuilleton. Vous vous disputez, vous vous détestez. Vous vous réconciliez.

SANDRINE J'étais tellement en colère contre lui ce jour-là, mais depuis, j'ai beaucoup réfléchi à ce qu'il m'a dit.
AMINA Et alors...?
SANDRINE En fait, David m'a aidée.
AMINA Comment ça?
SANDRINE Ma vraie passion, ce n'est pas la musique.
AMINA Non? Mais alors, c'est quoi, ta vraie passion?

SANDRINE J'ai décidé de devenir chef de cuisine!
AMINA Ça, c'est une excellente idée.
SANDRINE N'est-ce pas? Et j'ai aussi décidé de préparer ce gâteau pour la fête de ce soir.
AMINA Et moi qui pensais que tu ne voudrais pas y aller...
SANDRINE Mais... David ne peut pas partir sans que je lui dise au revoir!

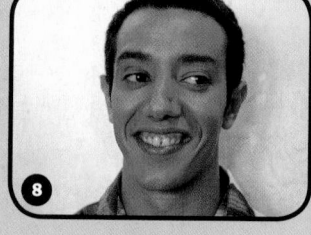

À la fête de David...
ASTRID Elle est jolie, ta jupe. C'est une de tes créations, n'est-ce pas?
SANDRINE Cet été, Amina participe à un défilé de mode à Paris.
AMINA N'exagérons rien... C'est une petite présentation des collections de plusieurs jeunes stylistes.
SANDRINE Tu vas montrer ce chef-d'œuvre?

AMINA Oui, cette jupe-ci, la robe que j'ai faite pour toi et d'autres modèles.
RACHID Elle n'est pas géniale, ma chérie? Belle, intelligente, douée...
AMINA Toi aussi, tu as de bonnes nouvelles, n'est-ce pas?
SANDRINE Ah bon?
RACHID Oh, ce n'est pas grand-chose.

AMINA Au contraire, c'est très important!
SANDRINE Vas-y, dis-nous tout, avant que je ne perde patience!
RACHID Eh bien, ça y est, j'ai mon diplôme!
AMINA Ah, mais ce n'est pas tout! Il a eu mention très bien!
SANDRINE Bravo, Rachid!
ASTRID Oui, félicitations!

A C T I V I T É S

1 **Les événements** Remettez les événements suivants dans l'ordre chronologique.

_6_ a. Rachid annonce une bonne nouvelle.
_4_ b. Stéphane veut absolument réussir son bac.
_9_ c. David promet qu'il va revenir à Aix.
_2_ d. Sandrine dit qu'elle n'est plus fâchée avec David.
_5_ e. Amina explique qu'elle va à Paris cet été.
_1_ f. Amina arrive chez Sandrine.

_10_ g. Valérie prend une photo du groupe.
_7_ h. Valérie attire (*gets*) l'attention du groupe.
_8_ i. David fait un petit discours (*speech*).
_3_ j. Sandrine annonce qu'elle souhaite devenir chef de cuisine.

 Practice more at vhlcentral.com.

O P T I O N S

Avant de regarder la vidéo Before viewing the video, have students work in pairs and brainstorm a list of things people might say at a farewell party. What questions might they ask? What might they talk about?

Regarder la vidéo Download and print the videoscript found on the Supersite. Then white out key vocabulary in order to create a master for a cloze activity. Distribute photocopies and tell students to fill in the missing information as they watch the video episode.

Les amis organisent une fête pour David.

Au P'tit Bistrot...
SANDRINE Stéphane, tu ne veux pas nous aider à préparer la fête?
STÉPHANE Une minute s'il te plaît.
SANDRINE Mais, qu'est-ce que tu lis de si intéressant? Oh là là, *L'Histoire des Républiques françaises*. Ah, oui je vois... j'ai entendu dire que tu devais repasser une partie du bac.

STÉPHANE Oui, je dois absolument réussir cette fois-ci, mais une fois l'examen passé, je retourne à mes passions—le foot, les jeux vidéo...
SANDRINE Chut... ta mère va t'entendre.
STÉPHANE *(parlant plus fort et de manière sérieuse)* Oui, je t'assure, les documentaires et les infos sont mes nouvelles passions.

VALÉRIE S'il vous plaît. Nous sommes ici ce soir pour dire au revoir et bon voyage à David, qui repart demain aux États-Unis. Alors, David, comment s'est passée ton année à Aix?
DAVID Oh ça a été fantastique! Je ne connaissais personne à mon arrivée, mais j'ai rapidement trouvé un coloc super! J'ai fait la connaissance de quelques femmes formidables.

DAVID Mais surtout, je me suis fait des amis pour la vie...
ASTRID Quand est-ce que tu vas revenir nous voir, David?
DAVID Eh bien, j'ai l'intention de revenir l'année prochaine pour organiser une exposition de tous mes tableaux au P'tit Bistrot, à condition, bien sûr, que Madame Forestier accepte!
VALÉRIE Allez, une photo. Souriez!

Expressions utiles

Relating conditions and possible actions

- **David ne peut pas partir sans que je lui dise au revoir!**
  David can't leave without my saying good-bye to him!
- **Dis-nous tout, avant que je (ne) perde patience!**
  Tell us everything, before I lose patience!
- **J'ai l'intention de revenir à condition que Madame Forestier accepte.**
  I intend to return on the condition that Madame Forestier accepts.

Additional vocabulary

- **repartir**
  to go back
- **repasser**
  to take again
- **chut**
  shh/hush
- **au contraire**
  on the contrary
- **félicitations**
  congratulations
- **se réconcilier**
  to make up

Expressions utiles
- Model the pronunciation of the **Expressions utiles** and have students repeat them after you.
- As you work through the list, point out the use of the subjunctive with conjunctions. Tell students that this construction will be formally presented in **Espace structures**.
- Have students scan the **Roman-photo** captions and find expressions used to express intentions. Example: **... une fois l'examen passé, je retourne à mes passions...**

1 Suggestion Have students form groups of five. Make a set of individual sentences on strips of paper for each group and distribute them (two per student). Tell students to arrange the sentences in the proper order and then read them aloud.

1 Expansion Have students write sentences to fill in parts of the story not mentioned in this activity.

2 Suggestion If time is limited, assign each student the role of either Sandrine or David and tell them to prepare their parts at home. Then allow partners a few minutes to rehearse before presenting their conversation to the class.

2 Expansion Have students write a conversation between Rachid and Amina in which they discuss recent events and future plans. How might their story end?

3 Suggestion Tell students to write a paragraph of at least three sentences for each character in the **Roman-photo**.

 2 **À vous!** Sandrine est bien plus calme maintenant. Elle a même dit qu'elle voulait dire au revoir à David à la fête. Avec un(e) camarade de classe, préparez une conversation entre David et Sandrine à cette occasion. Comment finit leur histoire?

3 **Écrivez** Pendant la fête de David, certains ont parlé de leurs projets d'avenir. À votre avis, qu'est-ce qui va arriver l'année prochaine? Écrivez vos prédictions pour chacun d'entre eux, au niveau professionnel et au niveau personnel.

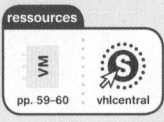
ressources
VM pp. 59–60
vhlcentral

ACTIVITÉS

OPTIONS

Game Have students fold small strips of paper in half. On the outside of the folded paper, they should write an original sentence that one of the characters might say. On the inside, they should write the name of the character. Divide the class into two teams. Put the sentences in a box and have students draw one, read it aloud, and then guess who might say it. Award a point for each correct guess.

Extra Practice Assign each student one of the characters from this **Roman-photo** and have them prepare a brief summary of the party from that character's point of view. Ask volunteers to read their summaries to the class. Then have the class guess which character would give each summary.

Reading

NATIONAL STANDARDS communication cultures

Section Goals

In this section, students will:
- learn about Haitian painting
- learn some terms for talking about books
- learn about traditional arts in the francophone world
- read about **le Cirque du Soleil**

Instructional Resources
vhlcentral.com: reference tools

Culture à la loupe
Avant la lecture Have students locate Haiti on the map on page 666. Point out that Haiti shares the island with the Dominican Republic.

Lecture
- Point out the **tréma** on the **i** of **Haïti**, a version of *Ayiti* in Creole, is the name given to the land by the original inhabitants, the Taino-Arawak peoples. It means *mountainous country*.
- The country was named Haiti after it gained its independence from France in 1804.

Après la lecture Ask students: **Quels éléments de la peinture haïtienne pouvez-vous identifier sur les tableaux? Que représentent-ils?**

1 Suggestion Go over the answers with the class.

CULTURE À LA LOUPE

La peinture haïtienne

L'art haïtien est surtout connu grâce à° sa peinture. Cette tradition artistique est très ancienne sur l'île, mais ses débuts officiels datent de 1804, quand le roi Christophe crée la première Académie de peinture. Les thèmes les plus fréquents à cette époque sont les thèmes historiques de l'émancipation° et les thèmes religieux du vaudou°.

La peinture haïtienne ne devient célèbre dans le monde qu'à partir de 1943. Cette année-là, Dewitt Peters, un professeur américain du lycée de Port-au-Prince, capitale d'Haïti, rencontre plusieurs jeunes peintres haïtiens. Il aime leurs toiles° et fonde avec eux un centre d'art et de peinture. Ce centre va donner à la majorité des peintres haïtiens les ressources nécessaires pour accéder au° succès. Aujourd'hui, on en est à la quatrième génération d'artistes. Ces peintres appartiennent à° diverses écoles d'art et leurs styles sont très variés, du plus naïf au plus sophistiqué. Ils peuvent être surréalistes, impressionnistes ou même primitifs modernes.

La peinture haïtienne est souvent très colorée et d'une grande vitalité. Quand elle n'est pas abstraite, elle illustre des scènes de la vie quotidienne°, des cérémonies religieuses et des paysages°. En Haïti, la peinture est partout. Elle décore les rues, les murs et les bus. On la trouve aussi bien sur les marchés que dans les galeries d'art. Grâce à des expositions dans le monde entier, les peintres haïtiens séduisent un public de plus en plus large.

un peintre haïtien devant son œuvre

grâce à *thanks to* émancipation *liberation* vaudou *voodoo* toiles *paintings* accéder au *achieve* appartiennent à *belong to* quotidienne *everyday* paysages *landscapes*

A C T I V I T É S

1 **Répondez** Répondez aux questions par des phrases complètes.

1. Quel est l'art le plus connu à Haïti?
   C'est la peinture.
2. Pourquoi ses débuts officiels datent-ils de 1804?
   Le roi Christophe crée la première Académie de peinture en 1804.
3. Quels sont les thèmes les plus fréquents à cette époque?
   Ce sont les thèmes historiques de l'émancipation et les thèmes religieux du vaudou.
4. À partir de quand la peinture haïtienne est-elle devenue célèbre dans le monde?
   Elle est devenue célèbre à partir de 1943.
5. Quel était le métier de Dewitt Peters?
   Il était professeur au lycée de Port-au-Prince.

6. Qu'a-t-il créé? Il a créé un centre d'art et de peinture avec des jeunes peintres haïtiens.
7. À quelles écoles d'art les peintres haïtiens appartiennent-ils et comment est leur style? Ils appartiennent à diverses écoles et leurs styles sont très variés.
8. Comment est la peinture haïtienne?
   Elle est souvent très colorée et d'une grande vitalité.
9. Quels sont les sujets les plus souvent peints? Les scènes de la vie quotidienne, les cérémonies religieuses et les paysages sont les sujets les plus souvent peints.
10. Où peut-on voir de la peinture à Haïti?
    On peut en voir dans les rues, sur les murs, sur les bus, sur les marchés et dans les galeries d'art.

OPTIONS

Haïti Haiti's official languages are French and Creole. Columbus landed on the island in 1492 and called it Española; it was later renamed Hispaniola. The island was under Spanish rule until 1697, when Haiti became a French colony and was renamed Saint-Domingue. The colony relied on African slaves to work the sugar plantations there. Today over 90% of Haiti's inhabitants are descendants of those slaves.

Small Groups Have students work in groups of three. Tell them that they are owners of a gallery specializing in Haitian art. Each student should research one Haitian painting on the Internet and print an image of the work for his or her gallery. In class, the owners of each gallery should describe the style of their paintings and what they represent to the potential buyers (the class).

LE FRANÇAIS QUOTIDIEN

Les livres

bouquin (*m.*)	book
dico (*m.*)	dictionary
lecture (*f.*)	reading
manuel (*m.*)	textbook
nouvelle (*f.*)	short story
recueil (*m.*)	collection
bouquiner	to read
feuilleter	to leaf through
parcourir	to skim

LE MONDE FRANCOPHONE

Des arts traditionnels

Voici quelques exemples d'art traditionnel du monde francophone.

Aux Antilles la fabrication de poupées° en costumes de madras° traditionnels

Au Burkina Faso les poteries en terre cuite° décorées à la teinture° végétale et la fabrication de masques traditionnels

Au Cambodge le théâtre d'ombres°, avec ses marionnettes en cuir°

Au Maroc l'art de la tapisserie° et du métal

En Polynésie française la sculpture et l'art du tatouage corporel

En Tunisie les arts céramiques et l'art de la calligraphie

Au Viêt-nam la peinture à la laque° et la peinture sur soie°

poupées *dolls* **madras** *brightly-colored cotton or silk fabric* **terre cuite** *terra-cotta* **teinture** *dye* **ombres** *shadows* **marionnettes en cuir** *leather puppets* **tapisserie** *tapestry* **laque** *lacquer* **soie** *silk*

PORTRAIT

Le Cirque du Soleil

En 1982, des saltimbanques° et des cracheurs de feu° sur échasses° se rencontrent et montent un spectacle à Baie-Saint-Paul, au Québec. En 1984, le gouvernement les embauche pour célébrer le 450e anniversaire de l'arrivée de l'explorateur Jacques Cartier. Ainsi° est né le Cirque du Soleil. Depuis, il a connu un succès international sous la direction de son fondateur principal, Guy Laliberté. Ses spectacles pleins de féerie° et de poésie ravissent° tous les publics et, à la différence de ceux du cirque traditionnel, ils n'ont aucun animal. Ils intègrent plutôt les numéros° acrobatiques de contorsionnistes, trapézistes, équilibristes° et jongleurs à ceux de danseurs et de clowns. Leur univers magique a apporté à la troupe une popularité incroyable et a transformé le monde du cirque.

saltimbanques *acrobats, performers* **cracheurs de feu** *fire-eaters* **échasses** *stilts* **Ainsi** *In this way* **féerie** *enchantment* **ravissent** *delight* **numéros** *acts* **équilibristes** *tightrope walkers*

MUSIQUE À FOND

Patricia Kaas

Lieu d'origine: Forbach, France
Métier: chanteuse – actrice

Elle est très connue en France et dans les pays germanophones, et ses albums sont commercialisés dans plus de 40 pays.

Go to vhlcentral.com to find out more about Patricia Kaas and her music.

---

2 Complétez Complétez les phrases.

1. En 1982, des saltimbanques et des cracheurs de feu sur échasses montent un spectacle au Québec.
2. Le Cirque du Soleil est né en _____1984_____.
3. Ses spectacles pleins de féerie et de poésie ravissent tous les publics.
4. Ils intègrent les numéros acrobatiques de _contorsionnistes, de trapézistes, d'équilibristes, de jongleurs, de danseurs et de clowns._
5. La fabrication de poupées en costumes de madras traditionnels est un art traditionnel _____aux Antilles_____.
6. En Polynésie française, _le tatouage corporel_ est un art.

3 Au cirque Interviewez votre partenaire. Est-il/elle déjà allé(e) au cirque? Au Cirque du Soleil? Combien de fois? Quels numéros a-t-il/elle préférés? En a-t-il/elle un souvenir particulier? A-t-il/elle envie d'y retourner? Soyez prêts à présenter vos résultats à la classe.

 Practice more at **vhlcentral.com.**

ACTIVITÉS

OPTIONS

Le Cirque du Soleil Unlike the American three-ring circus, **le Cirque du Soleil** is rooted in the European tradition of a one-ring circus. It does not show animals or freaks, but focuses instead on human skills highlighted by state-of-the-art sets, artistic costumes, and contemporary music.

Pairs Have students write five true/false statements based on the information on this page. Then have them get together with a classmate and take turns reading their sentences and responding.

Le français quotidien
- Model the pronunciation of each term and have students repeat it.
- You may wish to show photos of **les bouquinistes** and present these terms: **poche** or **broché** (*paperback*), **cartonné** (*hardback*), and **relié** (*bound*).
- Have volunteers create sentences with these terms.

Portrait
- In 2004, Guy Laliberté earned **l'Ordre du Canada** the highest distinction of its type in Canada.
- Ask students: **Les gens sur les photos sont des danseurs, des clowns, des jongleurs, des contorsionnistes, des équilibristes ou des trapézistes?** (des contorsionnistes et des trapézistes) **Voudriez-vous trouver un travail comme celui-là? Pourquoi?**

Le monde francophone Bring in some books or magazines with examples of these art forms to show students. Then have students identify the country that creates each type of art.

2 Expansion For additional practice, give students these items. **7. L'explorateur _____ arrive au Canada au seizième siècle.** (Jacques Cartier) **8. Dans les spectacles du Cirque du Soleil il n'y a aucun _____.** (animal) **9. Le théâtre _____ est bien connu au Cambodge.** (d'ombres) **10. La calligraphie est un exemple d'art traditionnel _____.** (en Tunisie)

3 Suggestion Have students jot down notes during their interviews.

Section Goals

In this section, students will learn:
• conjunctions that require the subjunctive
• when to use the infinitive instead of the subjunctive

Instructional Resources
vhlcentral.com:
*Activity Pack; Lab MP3s; SAM Answer Key; **Essayez!** and **Mise en pratique** answers; Lab Audioscript; reference tools*

Suggestions

• To introduce conjunctions that require the subjunctive, make a few statements about yourself. Examples: **Je n'arrive pas en retard au cours, à moins que ma voiture ne démarre pas. Je range mes livres avant que la classe finisse. Je vais à pied au cours, à condition qu'il ne pleuve pas.** Write each conjunction on the board as you say it.

• Have a volunteer read the example sentences. Point out that these conjunctions must be followed by a change in subject in order to elicit the subjunctive mood.

• Write sentences that use **avant de** and **pour**, and ask volunteers to rewrite them so that each ends with a subordinate clause with the subjunctive instead of a preposition and infinitive. Example: **Je vais parler avec Chantal avant d'aller au cours.** (... avant qu'elle aille au cours/... avant qu'il lui parle)

• You might want to explain the use of the **ne explétif** at this point. Example: **Je vais parler avec Chantal avant qu'elle n'achète cette voiture.**

• Write the six conjunctions on the board. Ask students to call out some main clauses and subordinate clauses in order to make six logical sentences.

Essayez! Have students form sentences with these phrases. Example: **Avant que nous partions, il faut que j'aille chercher un pull.**

The subjunctive (Part 4)  Tutorial

The subjunctive with conjunctions

Point de départ Conjunctions are words or phrases that connect two clauses in a sentence. Certain conjunctions commonly introduce adverbial clauses, which describe *how*, *why*, *when*, and *where* an action takes place.

• Conjunctions that express a condition upon which an action is dependent are followed by the subjunctive form of the verb.

Conjunctions that require the subjunctive			
à condition que...	*on the condition that..., provided that...*	**jusqu'à ce que...**	*until...*
à moins que...	*unless...*	**pour que...**	*so that...*
avant que..	*before...*	**sans que....**	*without...*

• When the main clause contains an expression of will or emotion and the subordinate clause has a different subject, the subjunctive is required.

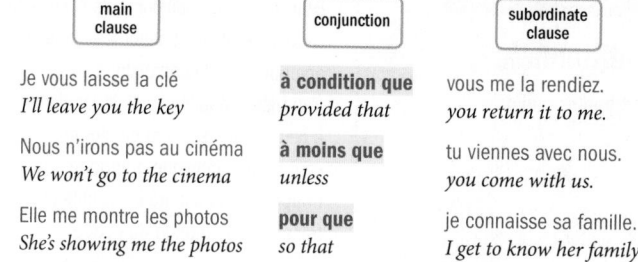

main clause	conjunction	subordinate clause
Je vous laisse la clé	à condition que	vous me la rendiez.
I'll leave you the key	*provided that*	*you return it to me.*
Nous n'irons pas au cinéma	à moins que	tu viennes avec nous.
We won't go to the cinema	*unless*	*you come with us.*
Elle me montre les photos	pour que	je connaisse sa famille.
She's showing me the photos	*so that*	*I get to know her family.*

• Remember to use an infinitive in the subordinate clause when its subject is the same as the subject of the main clause. Note the change in the form of these frequently used conjunctions when they precede an infinitive.

avant que	avant de	sans que	sans	pour que	pour

Tu feras tes devoirs **avant que** je rentre.
You'll do your homework before I get back.

Tu feras tes devoirs **avant de** sortir.
You'll do your homework before you go out.

Elle travaille **pour que** son fils puisse aller à l'université.
She's working so that her son can go to college.

Elle travaille **pour** gagner de l'argent.
She's working in order to earn some money.

Essayez! **Indiquez les formes correctes du présent du subjonctif des verbes.**

1. avant que nous ___*partions*___ (partir)
2. pour que je ne ___*me mette*___ (se mettre) pas en colère
3. à condition que nous ___*soyons*___ (être) prudents
4. à moins que tu ___*dises*___ (dire) oui
5. sans que les spectateurs les ___*applaudissent*___ (applaudir)
6. à moins qu'il ___*fasse*___ (faire) beau
7. avant que tu ___*saches*___ (savoir) conduire
8. pour que vous ___*appreniez*___ (apprendre) des choses

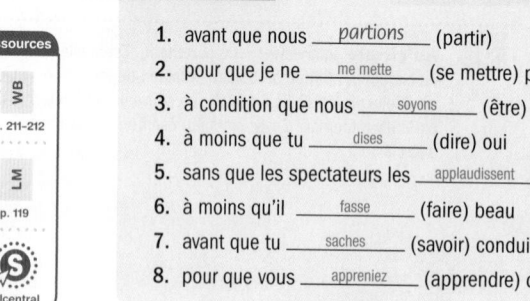

ressources

WB
pp. 211–212

LM
p. 119

S
vhlcentral

Le français vivant

Le français vivant Before reading the ad aloud, ask students to describe the image. Then ask what they think is being advertised. Say: **Regardez bien cette publicité. Que voyez-vous?**

MAURICE QUENTIN DE LA TOUR

Magnifique exposition sur ce grand peintre. Venez au château de Versailles du 2 au 29 septembre avant que ces peintures retournent dans leurs musées d'origine. Nous avons beaucoup travaillé pour que vous ayez l'occasion de voir ces superbes portraits. Venez contempler ces magnifiques tableaux qui vous feront voyager dans une autre époque... à moins que vous restiez indifférent à la beauté éternelle.

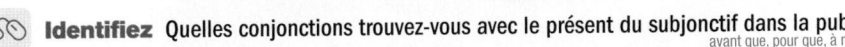

Identifiez Quelles conjonctions trouvez-vous avec le présent du subjonctif dans la publicité?
avant que, pour que, à moins que

Questions Posez ces questions à un(e) partenaire et répondez à tour de rôle.

1. Qui était Maurice Quentin de La Tour?
   un grand peintre
2. Pourquoi faut-il voir l'exposition avant le 29 septembre?
   Après cette date, les peintures retournent dans leurs musées d'origine.
3. Pourquoi a-t-on beaucoup travaillé au château de Versailles?
   pour que vous ayez l'occasion de voir ces portraits
4. Quel effet ont les magnifiques tableaux sur les visiteurs?
   Ils les font voyager dans une autre époque.
5. D'après (According to) la pub, quelle sorte de personne ne voudrait pas visiter l'exposition?
   Answers will vary.
6. Aimes-tu visiter les musées? Pourquoi? Quels musées as-tu visités?
   Answers will vary.

six cent cinquante-sept 657

OPTIONS

Extra Practice Write the following partial sentences on the board. Have students complete them with true or fictional information about their own lives. **1. Je vais finir mes études à condition que... 2. Je voudrais avoir 500 $ pour que... 3. Je peux sortir ce soir à moins que... 4. Le monde change sans que... 5. Je dois... avant que... 6. Je continuerai à travailler jusqu'à ce que...**

Video Show the video again to give students more input on the use of conjunctions with the subjunctive. Stop the video where appropriate to discuss how and why the subjunctive was used.

1 Suggestion Before assigning the activity, have students circle the conjunctions that always require the subjunctive.

2 Expansion Have students create three similar dehydrated sentences for a partner to complete.

3 Suggestion As you go through the items, ask students which conjunctions require the subjunctive and which could be followed by either the subjunctive or the indicative. For those that could take either, discuss why.

Mise en pratique

1 **Je veux bien y aller si...** Richard veut que Louise aille avec lui au cinéma ce week-end, mais elle y met plusieurs conditions. Complétez les phrases avec la forme correcte du verbe.

1. Je veux bien aller avec toi au cinéma à moins qu'il ___fasse___ (faire) beau.
2. S'il fait beau, je préfère aller à la plage pour ___bronzer___ (bronzer).
3. Regarde la météo pour que nous ___sachions___ (savoir) le temps qu'il fera.
4. S'il ne fait pas beau, j'irai avec toi à condition que ce ___ne soit pas___ (ne pas être) un film d'horreur.
5. J'aime bien les films policiers à moins qu'il y ___ait___ (avoir) trop de violence.
6. Nous pouvons voir un documentaire à condition qu'il ne ___soit___ (être) pas sur les animaux.
7. Souviens-toi que je ne vois pas de film sans ___manger___ (manger) de pop-corn.
8. Si j'ai sommeil, je veux rentrer chez moi avant que le film ___finisse___ (finir).

2 **Au musée des Beaux-Arts** Myriam et Delphine passent la journée au musée. Faites les changements nécessaires pour créer leur conversation. Suggested answers

MYRIAM (1) je / pouvoir / regarder / ce / chef-d'œuvre / jusqu'à ce que / le musée / fermer
Je pourrais regarder ce chef-d'œuvre jusqu'à ce que le musée ferme.

DELPHINE (2) le peintre / avoir / faire / ce / tableau / avant / avoir / douze ans
Le peintre a fait ce tableau avant d'avoir douze ans.

MYRIAM (3) certain / enfants / être / vraiment doué / sans que / les parents / le / savoir
Certains enfants sont vraiment doués sans que les parents le sachent.

DELPHINE (4) je / vouloir bien / voir / sculptures / Rodin / avant que / nous / partir
Je voudrais bien voir les sculptures de Rodin avant que nous partions.

MYRIAM (5) pouvoir / nous / voir / documentaire sur Rodin / avant / partir
Pouvons-nous voir le documentaire sur Rodin avant de partir?

DELPHINE (6) d'accord / je / aller / le voir / à condition que / il / ne pas être / ennuyeux
D'accord, j'irai le voir à condition qu'il ne soit pas ennuyeux.

3 **Opinions** Complétez ces phrases de manière originale. Ensuite, comparez vos réponses avec celles d'un(e) partenaire. Answers will vary.

1. J'aime les films d'horreur à moins que...
2. Les gens regardent les feuilletons pour...
3. Je ferai les musées de Paris jusqu'à ce que...
4. On fait des publicités pour que les gens...
5. Je lis des romans à condition que...
6. Je regarde la météo avant de...

4 **Votre santé** Vous êtes instructeur/instructrice à la gym et votre partenaire est un(e) client(e) qui veut être en forme et garder la ligne. Votre partenaire vous pose des questions et vous lui donnez des conseils. Utilisez les expressions de la liste. Answers will vary.

à condition que	jusqu'à ce que
à moins que	pour que/pour
avant que/avant de	sans que/sans

 Practice more at **vhlcentral.com.**

Communication

5 Questions Avec un(e) partenaire, répondez à ces questions. Ensuite, présentez vos réponses à la classe. *Answers will vary.*

1. Que fais-tu tous les soirs avant de te coucher?
2. Que font tes parents pour que tu puisses étudier à la fac?
3. Que peux-tu faire pour améliorer (*to improve*) ton français?
4. Que veux-tu faire demain à moins qu'il fasse mauvais?
5. Que fais-tu pendant les cours sans que les profs le sachent?
6. Que fais-tu seulement à condition qu'un(e) ami(e) t'accompagne?
7. Quelles stratégies utilises-tu pour avoir de bonnes notes?
8. Quelle activité pratiques-tu sans t'arrêter jusqu'à ce que tu la finisses?
9. Qu'est-ce que tes parents te laissent (*allow*) faire à condition que tu aies de bonnes notes?
10. Que peux-tu faire pendant des heures sans t'ennuyer?

6 Le week-end Avec un(e) partenaire, parlez de vos projets pour ce week-end. Utilisez ce vocabulaire. *Answers will vary.*

MODÈLE

Samedi, je vais aller à la piscine à moins que mes amis veuillent aller à la plage.

à condition que	jusqu'à ce que
à moins que	pour (que)
avant de/que	sans (que)

7 Tic-Tac-Toe Formez deux équipes. Une personne commence une phrase et une autre de son équipe la finit avec les mots de la grille. La première équipe à créer trois phrases d'affilée (*in a row*) gagne. *Answers will vary.*

MODÈLE

Étudiant(e) 1: *J'aime bien admirer un chef-d'œuvre...*
Étudiant(e) 2: *... à moins que ce soit une sculpture.*

pour que	sans que	avant que
à condition que	jusqu'à ce que	pour
à moins que	sans	avant de

5 Expansion Have students react to individual responses. Example: _____ **fait de l'exercice tous les jours avant de se coucher. Qui fait plus d'exercice? Qui regarde la télévision? Qui lit avant de s'endormir?**

6 Expansion Have partners guess what their friends and family will do for the weekend. Have them do the same with celebrities, taking guesses about their weekend plans.

7 Suggestions
- Have groups prepare tic-tac-toe cards like the one shown in the activity.
- Have the students form new groups and do a second round of tic-tac-toe.

OPTIONS

Pairs Ask partners to interview each other about what they must do today in order to reach their future goals. Students should state what their goals are, the necessary conditions to achieve them, and talk about obstacles they may encounter. They should use as many conjunctions as possible in their interviews. Have pairs present their interviews to the class.

Extra Practice Prepare several statements, some with clauses followed by the infinitive and some with the subjunctive. After each statement, hold up two flashcards, one with **I** for infinitive and one with **S** for subjunctive. Students point to the card that represents what they heard. Examples: **Le professeur parle lentement pour que les étudiants le comprennent. (S) Je n'ai pas besoin de voiture pour aller à l'université. (I)**

Section Goals

In this section, students will review the subjunctive.

Instructional Resources
vhlcentral.com:
*Activity Pack; Lab MP3s;
SAM Answer Key; Essayez!
and Mise en pratique
answers; Lab Audioscript;
reference tools*

Suggestions

• Review the subjunctive by summing up the year in statements that use the subjunctive. Example: **Je veux que vous continuiez à étudier le français. Je doute que vous oubliiez ce qu'on a appris pendant l'année scolaire. Il faut que vous parliez souvent avec vos amis francophones. Avant que nous finissions le cours, vous allez réviser les usages particuliers du subjonctif.** Ask volunteers to identify the subjunctive form in each sentence.

• Have students look over the one-stem and two-stem forms of the subjunctive of regular verbs. Ask them on which form the present subjunctive is based. (One-stem is based on present tense, third person plural **ils/elles**; two-stem is based on present tense, first person plural **nous.**) Then have them close their books. Have them give the present subjunctive of irregular verbs such as **avoir, être, faire, pouvoir, savoir,** and **vouloir.**

15B.2

Review of the subjunctive  Tutorial

Point de départ Since **Leçon 9B**, you have been learning about subjunctive verb forms. Because there is no exact English equivalent of the subjunctive in French, do not rely on translation. Learn to recognize the contexts and cues that trigger the subjunctive. The charts on this and the following page will help you review and synthesize what you have learned about the subjunctive.

D'accord, je vous dis tout avant que vous perdiez patience.

David ne peut pas partir sans que je lui dise au revoir!

Summary of subjunctive forms

one-stem

	parler	finir	attendre	partir
que je/j'	parle	finisse	attende	parte
que tu	parles	finisses	attendes	partes
qu'il/elle/on	parle	finisse	attende	parte
que nous	parlions	finissions	attendions	partions
que vous	parliez	finissiez	attendiez	partiez
qu'ils/elles	parlent	finissent	attendent	partent

two-stem   **irregular forms**

	prendre	aller	avoir	être
que je/j'	prenne	aille	aie	sois
que tu	prennes	ailles	aies	sois
qu'il/elle/on	prenne	aille	ait	soit
que nous	prenions	allions	ayons	soyons
que vous	preniez	alliez	ayez	soyez
qu'ils/elles	prennent	aillent	aient	soient

irregular forms

	faire	pouvoir	savoir	vouloir
que je	fasse	puisse	sache	veuille
que tu	fasses	puisses	saches	veuilles
qu'il/elle/on	fasse	puisse	sache	veuille
que nous	fassions	puissions	sachions	voulions
que vous	fassiez	puissiez	sachiez	vouliez
qu'ils/elles	fassent	puissent	sachent	veuillent

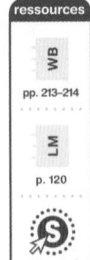

ressources

WB
pp. 213–214

LM
p. 120

S
vhlcentral

- Certain expressions trigger the subjunctive in the subordinate clause when the subject of the main clause is different.

Summary of subjunctive uses

Subjunctive trigger in main clause	Subjunctive in subordinate clause
Verb or expression of opinion	**Il est bon que Djamel sache** conduire. *It is good that Djamel knows how to drive.*
Verb or expression of necessity or obligation	**Il est essentiel que les étudiants fassent** leurs devoirs. *It's essential that students do their homework.*
Verb or expression of will or emotion	Nous **avons peur que vous ayez** trop de travail. *We're afraid (that) you have too much work.*
Verb or expression of doubt, disbelief, or uncertainty	Tu **ne crois pas que nous soyons** américaines. *You don't believe (that) we're American.*
Conjunction	Je chanterai **à condition que tu saches** jouer du piano. *I'll sing, provided that you know how to play the piano.*

- Use the indicative in the subordinate clause when there is an expression of belief, certainty, or truth in the main clause.

Je crois que nous sommes
à l'heure.
I believe (that) we're on time.

but

Je doute que nous soyons
en retard.
I doubt (that) we're late.

- Use the infinitive when the subject of the main clause is the same as that of the subordinate clause.

Préfères-tu jouer de la guitare?
Do you prefer to play the guitar?

Nous sommes ici **pour voir** l'auteur.
We're here to see the author.

Essayez!   Choisissez les formes correctes des verbes.

1. Veut-il qu'elle (vient / **vienne**) avec nous?
2. Montre-moi tes photos pour que je (vois / **voie**) les belles plages.
3. Il faut que tu (as / **aies**) de la patience.
4. Elle ne doute pas que cette pièce (**finit** / finisse) tard.
5. Il est vrai que Dahlia (**est** / soit) malade.
6. Nous sommes contents que vous (allez / **alliez**) au musée du Louvre.
7. Il est dommage que nous ne (voyons / **voyions**) pas de peintures.
8. J'espère rentrer avant que mes parents (font / **fassent**) la cuisine.

six cent soixante et un **661**

Suggestions
- Before working through the summary of subjunctive usage, review the concepts of indicative and subjunctive. Remind students that in most discourse verbs are in the indicative. Then ask volunteers to tell you when the subjunctive is used. Write their statements on the board and discuss them.
- Compare the uses of the subjunctive and indicative. When comparing the subjunctive and infinitive in expressions of emotion, doubt, and certainty, discuss cases where the infinitive is used instead of the subjunctive. Compare and contrast the use of subjunctive and indicative with conjunctions.

Essayez! Have students change the main clause from affirmative to negative, and vice versa. Discuss the impact this change has on the subordinate clause, if any.

OPTIONS

Video Have students divide a sheet of paper into four sections, labeling them *Impersonal expressions, Will and emotion, Doubt,* and *Conjunctions.* Replay the video. Have them listen for each use of the subjunctive, writing the examples they hear in the appropriate section. Play the video again, then have students write a short summary that includes each use of the subjunctive.

Extra Practice Here are four sentences to use as a dictation. Read each twice, pausing after the second time for students to write. **1. Il est important que nous regardions cette émission de télévision ce soir. 2. Je vais au mariage à condition qu'il ne pleuve pas. 3. Le patron demande que les employés travaillent plus d'heures. 4. Nathalie est en France jusqu'à ce qu'elle finisse ses études.**

ESPACE STRUCTURES

1 Expansion Ask volunteers to read the completed sentences and state their reason for choosing the infinitive, subjunctive, or indicative form.

2 Suggestion Model the activity by giving a personal example. Write, for example, **Je doute que mon frère…** on the board, then complete the sentence. (**Je doute que mon frère se souvienne de la date de mon anniversaire.**)

3 Suggestion Call on several pairs to role-play their conversation for the class.

Mise en pratique

1 **Oui, maman…** La mère de Tarik et d'Aïcha veut que ses enfants soient très instruits (*educated*) sur l'art et la musique. Mettez les verbes à l'infinitif, à l'indicatif ou au subjonctif pour compléter ses phrases.

1. Il est nécessaire de ___lire___ (lire) tous les jours.
2. Il ne faut pas que nous ___regardions___ (regarder) trop la télévision.
3. Je pense que Tarik ___ne va pas___ (ne pas aller) assez souvent au musée.
4. Je ne pense pas que vous ___fassiez___ (faire) assez de peinture.
5. Il faut que vous ___étudiiez___ (étudier) la peinture et la musique.
6. Il est impossible que vous ___puissiez___ (pouvoir) tout comprendre, bien sûr.
7. Je veux que votre père vous ___apprenne___ (apprendre) à reconnaître les chefs-d'œuvre de Van Gogh.
8. Il croit que Van Gogh ___est___ (être) le plus grand peintre du dix-neuvième siècle (*century*).

2 **Parle-moi de ta famille…** Marc, le petit ami de Marion, veut tout savoir sur sa famille. Que lui dit-elle? Complétez les phrases. Answers will vary.

1. Il est clair que mes parents…
2. Je ne pense pas que mon frère…
3. Je crois que ma grand-mère…
4. Il est possible que je…
5. Je sais que mon frère et moi, nous…
6. Il est évident que ma famille…
7. Je ne suis pas sûre que…
8. Nous avons peur que…

3 **Et nous?** Marc veut épouser Chantal, mais elle n'est pas sûre. Comment répond-elle à ses questions? Avec un(e) partenaire, jouez les rôles. Answers will vary.

1. De quoi as-tu peur, Chantal?
2. N'est-il pas clair que je t'aime?
3. Est-il possible que tu sois malheureuse avec moi?
4. Que faut-il que je fasse pour te persuader?
5. De quoi n'es-tu pas sûre?
6. De quoi doutes-tu?
7. Que pensent tes amis?
8. Et tes parents, que veulent-ils que tu fasses?

4 **Chez le médecin** Mélanie ne se sent pas bien et va voir le médecin. Avec un(e) partenaire, créez la conversation entre Mélanie et son médecin et utilisez les expressions de la liste. Answers will vary.

> Je ne crois pas que…
> Je recommande que…
> Il est douteux que…
> Il est évident que…
> Il faut que…

 Practice more at **vhlcentral.com**.

Communication

5 **Mon émission préférée** Avec un(e) partenaire, parlez de vos émissions de télévision préférées. Utilisez ces débuts de phrases dans votre conversation. *Answers will vary.*

1. Je la regarde à condition que...

2. Je suis furieux/furieuse que...

3. Tu devrais la regarder pour que...

4. Je ne suis pas sûr(e) que...

5. Il est important que...

6. Je ne pense pas que...

7. Je crois que...

8. Je souhaite que...

6 **Une pub** Par groupes de trois, inventez un produit et faites sa publicité. Utilisez autant de ces expressions que possible. Ensuite, présentez vos produits et vos pubs à la classe, qui votera pour les meilleurs. *Answers will vary.*

MODÈLE

Voulez-vous que votre maison soit propre? Il faut que vous achetiez «Nettoitou»! Il est formidable!
Utilisez-le pour que toute votre maison soit belle!

avant que	il est évident	ne pas penser
croire que	il est impossible	que
il est douteux que	que	pour que
il est essentiel	il faut que	sans que
que	jusqu'à ce que	vouloir que

7 **Vos opinions** Avec un(e) partenaire, écrivez un paragraphe pour donner votre opinion sur un de ces thèmes. Ensuite, échangez vos feuilles avec un groupe qui a choisi un thème différent et discutez de toutes les opinions. *Answers will vary.*

MODÈLE

Il est important que les profs écoutent les problèmes de leurs étudiants.

- Le coût (*cost*) élevé des études universitaires
- Les relations entre la France et les États-Unis
- Le rôle du gouvernement dans la vie privée
- La nécessité des armes et de la guerre
- La séparation de l'Église et de l'État (*State*)
- Les conséquences du réchauffement climatique
- L'assurance maladie (*health insurance*) aux États-Unis
- Les avantages (*advantages*) et les désavantages des réseaux sociaux

5 **Expansion** Write on the board all of the **émissions de télévision préférées** that the pairs discussed. Have students who chose the same program sit together. Then ask questions to elicit class discussion about the different programs. Example: **Il y a trois étudiants qui disent qu'***Entourage* **est leur émission de télévision préférée. Pourquoi? Il est important que vous la regardiez toutes les semaines?**

6 **Expansion** Give each group member a task when presenting the ad to the class. The first member should explain the target audience of the ad. The second member should read the text to the class. The third member should pretend to be a client, giving a testimonial about the product's benefits.

7 **Suggestion** Before dividing the class into groups, give individuals two minutes to choose a topic. Then have them write down three ideas about the topic. Divide the class according to the subject they chose.

OPTIONS

Game Write verbs and expressions of will or emotion on slips of paper and put them in a box or bag. On separate strips, write an equal number of infinitives and subject pronouns. Place these in a separate box or bag. Divide the class into two teams. One member of each team draws a slip of paper from each box and writes a sentence on the board using the elements on both slips. If the sentence makes sense and the grammar is correct, that team gets a point. Play until every team member has had a chance to go to the board. The team with the most points at the end of play wins.

Pairs Have students tell a partner three things they doubt and three things of which they are certain.

Révision

Instructional Resources
vhlcentral.com:
Activity Pack (Info Gap
Activities); Testing Program;
Testing Program MP3s;
reference tools

1 Suggestion Assign students to groups of three. Tell them to appoint a mediator to lead the discussion, a secretary to write out the eight phrases, and a proofreader to check what was written.

2 Expansion Ask each group to choose one art museum and exhibit that they have visited. Have students create an ad to promote the exhibit. Refer them to the ad in **Le français vivant** on page 657 or Internet sites as a resource. Students must use at least three subjunctive phrases in their ad.

3 Suggestion Before assigning this activity, remind students that **vouloir** takes the subjunctive only when there is a subject change. Ask a volunteer to give an example of a sentence with **vouloir** + **que** + [*subjunctive*]. Then have another volunteer give an example of **vouloir** + [*infinitive*].

4 Expansion Have pairs imagine that their friend needs advice about becoming a writer and draft an e-mail to their friend using the sentences created in the activity. Then have pairs exchange their letters with other groups for peer editing.

5 Suggestion Divide the class into pairs and distribute the Info Gap Handouts found in the Activity Pack on the Supersite. Give students ten minutes to complete the activity.

1 Un film d'horreur Que doit-on faire pour qu'un film d'horreur soit une réussite? Avec un(e) partenaire, faites par écrit une liste de huit phrases pour expliquer les critères. Utilisez tout ce vocabulaire. Answers will vary.

MODÈLE

Le film peut être une réussite à condition que les acteurs soient des célébrités.

PHILIPPE VERSOI   CHRISTINE MONACO

LE FANTÔME DU LAC

à condition que	jusqu'à ce que
à moins que	pour que
avant que	sans que

2 Quels artistes? Par groupes de trois, interviewez vos camarades pour leur demander quels artistes et quelles œuvres ils vous recommandent de découvrir la prochaine fois que vous visiterez un musée. Écrivez leurs réponses, puis présentez leurs recommandations à la classe. Utilisez ces expressions avec le présent du subjonctif. Answers will vary.

MODÈLE *La télévision fait du mal au cinéma.*

Je suggère que tu ailles voir les tableaux de Monet. Tu aimeras les couleurs et la représentation des personnages.

il est important que	proposer que
il est indispensable que	recommander que
(ne pas) penser que	suggérer que
?	?

3 Mes enfants Avec un(e) partenaire, préparez un dialogue où ces parents se disent ce qu'ils veulent que leurs enfants fassent plus tard. Utilisez au moins huit verbes au présent du subjonctif. Ensuite, jouez votre scène devant la classe. Answers will vary.

4 Un bon écrivain Que faut-il pour devenir un bon écrivain? Trouvez huit qualités qu'il faut avoir et utilisez l'infinitif pour faire une liste de conseils. À tour de rôle, utilisez votre liste pour donner des conseils à votre partenaire au présent du subjonctif. Answers will vary.

MODÈLE

Étudiant(e) 1: *Conseil numéro 1: Pour être un bon écrivain, il faut avoir beaucoup d'imagination.*
Étudiant(e) 2: *Si tu veux être un bon écrivain, il est essentiel que tu développes ton imagination.*

5 Au Louvre Votre professeur va vous donner, à vous et à votre partenaire, deux feuilles d'activités différentes. Attention! Ne regardez pas la feuille de votre partenaire. Answers will vary.

OPTIONS

Extra Practice Write a cloze paragraph, making remarks about the course. Give students a word bank or let them pick a logical word from the context. Example: **Il est difficile de croire que nous ____ (soyons/arrivions) déjà à la fin du semestre. Je ____ (vous) conseille de bien réviser vos cours pour le dernier examen qui ____ (sera/aura lieu) le vendredi 15 mai à 8 heures. J'espère que vous ____ (avez/aurez) beaucoup appris, non seulement en français, mais aussi à propos du monde francophone. Je souhaite que vous ____ (continuiez) à apprendre cette belle langue, à moins, bien sûr, que vous ne ____ (décidiez) d'arrêter vos études universitaires, mais ce ____ (serait) dommage! N'hésitez pas à me ____ (rendre) visite au bureau à l'avenir. ____ (Tenez)-moi au courant de vos projets!**

À l'écoute

NATIONAL communication STANDARDS

STRATÉGIE

Listening for key words/ Using the context

The comprehension of key words is vital to understanding spoken French. You can use your background knowledge of the subject to help you anticipate some key words. When you hear unfamiliar words, remember that you can use context to figure out their meaning.

 To practice these strategies, you will listen to a paragraph from a letter sent to a job applicant. Jot down key words, as well as any other words you figured out from the context.

Préparation

Regardez et décrivez la photo. Où sont ces personnes? Que font-elles? Que vont-elles aller voir, à votre avis?

À vous d'écouter

Vous êtes en France et vous voulez inviter un(e) ami(e) à sortir ce week-end. Vous écoutez la radio et vous entendez une annonce pour un spectacle qui plaira peut-être à votre ami(e). Notez les informations principales pour pouvoir ensuite décrire ce spectacle à votre ami(e) et pour lui dire quand vous pourrez aller le voir. Answers will vary.

_____
_____
_____
_____
_____
_____
_____

 Practice more at **vhlcentral.com.**

Compréhension

Complétez Complétez les phrases.

1. Molière est ___a___ de *L'Avare*.
   a. l'auteur   b. le metteur en scène   c. le personnage principal

2. *L'Avare* est ___c___.
   a. une exposition   b. un jeune comédien très dynamique
   c. une pièce de théâtre

3. *L'Avare* est drôle. C'est ___b___.
   a. une tragédie   b. une comédie   c. un drame psychologique

4. Yves Lemoîne est ___c___ de *L'Avare*.
   a. l'auteur   b. le journaliste qui a écrit la critique
   c. le metteur en scène

5. Harpagon est le nom du ___a___.
   a. personnage principal   b. spectacle   c. poète

6. Dans le journal, il y avait ___b___ positive de *L'Avare*.
   a. une pub   b. une critique   c. un applaudissement

Invitez votre ami(e)! Vous avez maintenant toutes les informations importantes nécessaires pour inviter votre ami(e) (un[e] camarade) à aller voir *L'Avare* ce week-end.

• Invitez-le/la au spectacle et dites-lui quand vous pourrez y aller.

• Il/Elle va vous poser quelques questions pour obtenir plus de détails sur le spectacle (histoire, personnages, acteurs, etc.).

• Ensuite, comme il/elle n'a pas très envie d'aller voir le spectacle, il/elle va faire plusieurs suggestions d'autres activités artistiques (films, concerts, expositions, etc.).

• Discutez de ces possibilités et choisissez-en une ensemble.

six cent soixante-cinq **665**

Section Goals

In this section, students will:
• learn to listen for key words and use context
• listen to a letter sent to a job applicant and jot down key words
• listen to a radio advertisement for a play and complete several activities

Instructional Resources
vhlcentral.com:
Textbook MP3s; Textbook Audioscript; reference tools

Stratégie
Audioscript Monsieur, Nous vous remercions de votre lettre de candidature pour le poste d'ingénieur informatique et pour l'intérêt que vous portez à notre compagnie. Malheureusement, nous regrettons de vous informer que nous avons déjà retenu un candidat pour cet emploi. Nous vous prions d'agréer, Monsieur, l'expression de nos sentiments distingués.

Préparation Have students look at the photo and describe what they see. They should mention that the people are waiting in line at a box office of a theater.

À vous d'écouter
Audioscript Les amateurs de Molière ne doivent surtout pas manquer *L'Avare* au Théâtre Monfort. Le metteur en scène, Yves Lemoîne, réinvente ce grand classique avec beaucoup de créativité. Avec dans le rôle d'Harpagon, le personnage principal qui a toujours peur qu'on lui prenne son argent, Julien Roche; un jeune comédien très talentueux qui a fait ses débuts il y a trois ans avec la troupe Comédia. *L'Avare* est une comédie très amusante et je suis certain que cette adaptation aura un grand succès. La première représentation a eu lieu hier soir et déjà les applaudissements étaient nombreux et enthousiastes. La pièce a aussi reçu une critique très positive dans le journal *Le Monde*. Si vous souhaitez voir *L'Avare* par Yves Lemoîne, les billets sont en vente au guichet du théâtre tous les jours de 10h00 à 18h00.

Successful Language Learning Ask students if they approach listening to French or English differently after using the strategies presented in **ESPACES.**

Il y a deux représentations le vendredi et le samedi, à 19h00 et à 21h30 et une à 14h00 le dimanche.

le Centre Pompidou à Metz

Panorama

Le Grand Est

La région en chiffres

Grand Est

► **Superficie:** *57.433 km²*

► **Population:** *5.554.645*

► **Industries principales:** *viticulture, exploitation forestière°, industrie automobile, tourisme, agroalimentaire°, chimie et pétrochimie, métallurgie, verre et cristal*

► **Villes principales:** *Strasbourg, Reims, Metz, Nancy*
La région Grand Est, créée en 2016, regroupe les anciennes régions Champagne-Ardenne, Alsace et Lorraine. À l'ouest, on trouve les célèbres vignobles° de la Champagne et les champs de bataille° à Verdun. À l'est, les influences germaniques se ressentent° toujours dans la langue, l'architecture et la gastronomie de l'Alsace et de la Lorraine.

Personnes célèbres

► **Patricia Kaas,** *chanteuse (1966–)*

► **Albert Uderzo,** *dessinateur et scénariste de BD°, co-créateur de la série **Astérix** (1927–)*

► **Albert Schweitzer,** *médecin, prix Nobel de la paix en 1952 (1875–1965)*

► **Marcel Marceau,** *mime et acteur (1923–2007)*

► **Pierre Hermé,** *pâtissier (1961–)*

► **Marguerite Thiébold,** *écrivaine (1908–1997)*

exploitation forestière *forestry* **agroalimentaire** *food processing*
vignobles *vineyards* **champs de bataille** *battlefields* **se ressentent** *are felt*
rois *kings* **sacrés** *crowned* **incendie** *fire* **l'endommagent** *damage it*

des vignobles en Champagne

L'ALLEMAGNE
LA BELGIQUE
LE LUXEMBOURG
Sedan
Reims
Verdun
Metz
Châlons-en-Champagne
Bar-le-Duc
Nancy
Strasbourg
GRAND EST
Troyes
Épinal
Chaumont
Colmar
Langres
Mulhouse
LA FRANCE
LA SUISSE
la Meuse
la Moselle
la Seine
le Rhin

0   80 miles
0   80 kilomètres

la ville de Colmar

Incroyable mais vrai!

La cathédrale Notre-Dame de Reims est le lieu où, entre 1027 et 1825, 29 des rois° de France sont sacrés°. Clovis, le premier roi des Francs, est baptisé sur le site à la fin du 5e siècle. La cathédrale elle-même est construite au 13e siècle. En 1914, un bombardement et un incendie° l'endommagent°, mais elle est reconstruite après la guerre.

Section Goals

In this section, students will read historical and cultural information about **Le Grand Est**.

Instructional Resources
vhlcentral.com:
Digital Image Bank;
SAM Answer Key;
reference tools

Carte du Grand Est
• Have students look at the map or use the **Panorama** map from the Digital Image Bank. Ask volunteers to read the names of the cities and geographical features aloud.
• Ask students to name the countries that border the region (**la Suisse, la Belgique, le Luxembourg, l'Allemagne**).

La région en chiffres
• Point out the region's logo.
• Have volunteers read the sections aloud. After each section, ask students questions about the content.
• Ask students if they have heard of the **personnes célèbres** and what they know about them.

Incroyable mais vrai!
• Although the cathedral was rebuilt after World War I, its stone and wall statuary still show the damage caused by the related fire's intense heat.
• Nine of the cathedral's stained glass windows were designed and made by Marc Chagall.

OPTIONS

Personnes célèbres Patricia Kaas sings in the style of the French **chanson**, mixing traditional elements with pop, jazz, and blues. **Albert Uderzo** and his collaborator René Goscinny created the comic book series *Astérix*, which has sold over 350 million copies worldwide. **Albert Schweitzer** was awarded the Nobel Prize for his medical missionary work in Africa. He was also a philosopher, musician, and theologian.

Marcel Marceau was born in Strasbourg. His most famous character is **Bip le Clown**. **Pierre Hermé** was born in Colmar. He worked at Fauchon and Ladurée before establishing his own pastry house in Paris, known for its **macarons**. **Marguerite Thiébold** wrote for adult and young adult audiences. Her most famous young adult series is titled *Lili* and is about a girl of the same name.

La gastronomie

Les dragées

En 1220, un apothicaire à Verdun décide de conserver des amandes° en les enrobant° de sucre et de miel° et en les cuisinant: la dragée est née. En 1750, un confiseur° parisien nommé Pecquet invente la dragée lisse°, forme qu'on trouve encore aujourd'hui. Les dragées font partie intégrante des célébrations familiales en France, surtout des mariages et des baptêmes°, où on offre un petit sachet de dragées aux invités.

Les gens

Jeanne d'Arc

Jeanne d'Arc est née en 1412 en Lorraine dans une famille de paysans°. En 1429, quand la France est en guerre contre l'Angleterre, elle décide de partir au combat pour libérer son pays. Elle prend la tête° d'une armée et libère la ville d'Orléans des Anglais. Cette victoire permet de sacrer° Charles VII roi de France. Plus tard, Jeanne d'Arc perd ses alliés pour des raisons politiques. Vendue aux Anglais, elle est condamnée pour hérésie. Elle est exécutée à Rouen, en Normandie, en 1431. En 1920, l'Église catholique la canonise.

Les destinations

Strasbourg

Strasbourg, chef-lieu° du Grand Est, est le siège° du Conseil de l'Europe depuis 1949 et du Parlement européen depuis 1979. Le Conseil de l'Europe est responsable de la promotion des valeurs démocratiques et de l'identité culturelle européenne et de la recherche de solutions aux problèmes de société. Les membres du Parlement sont élus° dans chaque pays de l'Union européenne. Le Parlement contribue à l'élaboration de la législation européenne et à la gestion de l'Europe.

La société

Un mélange de cultures

L'Alsace a été enrichie par de multiples courants° historiques et culturels grâce à sa position entre la France et l'Allemagne. La langue alsacienne vient d'un dialecte germanique et l'allemand est maintenant enseigné dans les écoles primaires. Quand l'Alsace est rendue à la France en 1919, les Alsaciens continuent de bénéficier des lois sociales allemandes. Le mélange° des cultures est visible à Noël avec des traditions allemandes et françaises (le sapin de Noël°, Saint Nicolas, les marchés).

Qu'est-ce que vous avez appris? Répondez aux questions par des phrases complètes.

1. Dans quelle cathédrale les rois de France ont-ils été sacrés?
   Ils ont été sacrés dans la cathédrale de Reims.
2. Qui était Clovis?
   C'était le premier roi des Francs.
3. De quels ingrédients fait-on des dragées?
   On les fait avec des amandes, du sucre et du miel.
4. Qu'est-ce que le confiseur Pecquet invente en 1750?
   Il invente la dragée lisse.
5. Pourquoi Strasbourg est-elle importante?
   C'est le siège du Conseil de l'Europe et du Parlement européen.
6. Quel est un des rôles du Conseil de l'Europe?
   Answers will vary. Suggested answer: Il est responsable de la promotion des valeurs démocratiques.
7. Contre qui Jeanne d'Arc a-t-elle défendu la France?
   Elle a défendu la France contre les Anglais.
8. Comment est-elle morte?
   Elle a été exécutée.
9. Quelle langue étrangère enseigne-t-on aux petits Alsaciens?
   On leur enseigne l'allemand.
10. À quel moment de l'année le mélange des cultures est-il particulièrement visible en Alsace?
    Il est particulièrement visible à Noël.

Sur Internet

Go to **vhlcentral.com** to find more cultural information related to this **Panorama**.

1. Quelle est la différence entre le Conseil européen et le Conseil de l'Europe?

2. Trouvez d'autres informations sur Jeanne d'Arc.

3. Cherchez des informations sur les rois sacrés à Reims. En quoi consistait la cérémonie de couronnement?

ressources

W/B
pp. 215–216

vhlcentral

amandes *almonds* enrobant *coating* miel *honey* confiseur *confectioner* lisse *smooth* baptêmes *baptisms* paysans *peasants* prend la tête *takes the lead* sacrer *crown* chef-lieu *regional seat of government* siège *headquarters* droits de l'homme *human rights* élus *elected* courants *trends, movements* mélange *mix* sapin de Noël *Christmas tree*

Les dragées
- Tell students that in the thirteenth century, apothecaries were the only people authorized to sell sugar and sugar products.
- Since 1783, the confectioner Braquier has made **dragées** and other sweet treats in Verdun.

Jeanne d'Arc
- Joan of Arc was accused of witchcraft, wantonness in cutting her hair, wearing men's clothes, and blasphemous pride. She was burned at the stake at the age of 19. In 1456, she was officially declared innocent, and later canonized for her bravery and martyrdom. Her life has been the subject of many famous literary works.
- Ask students if they think it was common for a woman to lead an army into battle in the fifteenth century. Have them explain their answers.

Strasbourg **Le Conseil de l'Europe** is Europe's oldest political organization and includes 47 member countries. Have students research the **Conseil de l'Europe** website to find out which countries were the original members and which ones are more recent members.

Un mélange de cultures
The traditional costume worn by Protestant Alsatian women has either a red or black bonnet tied with a bow. The traditional costume of Catholic Alsatian women has a white bonnet made of tulle and bordered with flowers.

OPTIONS

Cultural Activity Have students research the different possible colors of **dragées** to find out when each one is used. (White is used for marriages and first communions, blue or pink for baptisms, green for engagements, red for birthdays and graduations, etc.)

The Battle of Verdun During World War I, northern France became a battleground. In 1916 at Verdun, the French and Germans fought from February to December in what became the longest and largest battle of the war. One hundred sixty-three thousand French soldiers and 143,000 German soldiers were killed, and even more were wounded. The rain and the violent fighting turned the battleground into a field of mud. The Germans relinquished their hope of capturing Verdun in July, but the fighting didn't end until December, with the French retaining the territory.

Lecture

🅢 Audio: Dramatic Reading

Avant la lecture

STRATÉGIE

Contextualizing

To better understand an autobiographical novel it is helpful to contextualize it; that is, to take into consideration the biographical and cultural contexts that pertain to the author's experience. Doing so will allow you to recognize the differences between your experience, values, and attitudes and those presented in the text.

Examinez le texte

Regardez le texte. Est-ce un poème? Une pièce de théâtre? Un article? Un extrait de roman? Quel en est le titre? De quel point de vue le texte est-il écrit? Qu'est-ce que cela indique? Regardez aussi l'image. À votre avis, quel va être le thème de la lecture?

À propos de l'auteur
Kim Thúy (1968–)

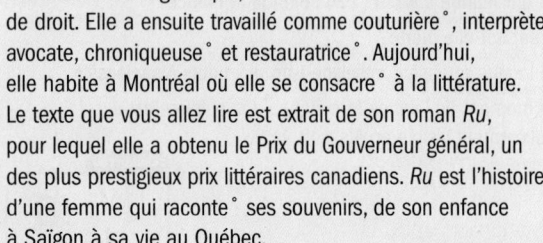

Née au Viêt-Nam en 1968 et arrivée comme réfugiée avec ses parents au Québec à l'âge de dix ans, Kim Thúy a fait des études de linguistique, de traduction et de droit. Elle a ensuite travaillé comme couturière°, interprète, avocate, chroniqueuse° et restauratrice°. Aujourd'hui, elle habite à Montréal où elle se consacre° à la littérature. Le texte que vous allez lire est extrait de son roman *Ru*, pour lequel elle a obtenu le Prix du Gouverneur général, un des plus prestigieux prix littéraires canadiens. *Ru* est l'histoire d'une femme qui raconte° ses souvenirs, de son enfance à Saïgon à sa vie au Québec.

couturière *seamstress, designer* **chroniqueuse** *columnist* **restauratrice** *restaurant owner* **se consacre** *dedicates herself* **raconte** *tells about*

Le geste d'aimer

extrait de *Ru* | Kim Thúy

1 Tout récemment, j'ai vu à Montréal une grand-mère vietnamienne demander à son petit-fils d'un an: «Thu'o'ng Bà dê dâu?» Je ne sais pas comment traduire cette phrase de seulement
5 quatre mots, mais qui contient deux verbes, «aimer» et «porter». Littéralement, c'est: «Aimer grand-mère porter où?» Le petit s'est touché la tête avec sa main. J'avais complètement oublié ce geste°, que moi-même j'ai fait mille fois
10 quand j'étais petite. J'avais oublié que l'amour vient de la tête et non pas du cœur. De tout le corps, seule la tête importe°. Il suffit° de toucher la tête d'un Vietnamien pour l'insulter, non seulement lui mais tout son arbre généalogique.
15 C'est ainsi qu'un timide Vietnamien de huit ans s'est transformé en tigre furieux quand son coéquipier° québécois a frotté le dessus° de sa tête pour le féliciter° d'avoir attrapé son premier ballon de football.

20 Si une marque d'affection peut parfois être comprise comme une offense, peut-être que le geste d'aimer n'est pas universel: il doit aussi être traduit d'une langue à l'autre, il doit être appris. Dans le cas du vietnamien, il est possible
25 de classifier, de quantifier le geste d'aimer par des mots spécifiques: aimer par goût (thích), aimer, sans être amoureux (thu'o'ng), aimer amoureusement (yêu), aimer avec ivresse° (mê), aimer aveuglément° (mù quáng), aimer par
30 gratitude (tình nghĩa). Il est donc impossible d'aimer tout court, d'aimer sans sa tête.

Section Goals

In this section, students will:
• learn how to contextualize a reading to better understand the author's experience
• read an excerpt from the novel *Ru* by Kim Thúy

Stratégie Have students look at the image and read **À propos de l'auteur** independently. Then go over the reading strategy with students and invite them to identify aspects of the author's personal life experience and culture that may have an impact on her writing.

Successful Language Learning Have students scan the text to find language elements that specifically relate to the author's biographical and cultural contexts.

Examinez le texte
• Students should mention that the text is an excerpt from a novel, that the title of the excerpt is «**Le Geste d'aimer**», and that the title of the novel is *Ru*. They should also mention that it is written in the first person, which indicates that the narrator is telling the story.
• Explain that the title of the novel, *Ru*, has significance in both French and Vietnamese. In French it means *stream* or *flow*. In Vietnamese it means *cradle* or *lullaby*. Ask students why they think the author chose a single word that has significance in both French and Vietnamese as the title.

À propos de l'auteur Give students additional information about the author. Tell them that after fleeing Vietnam's communist regime, she and her family spent time in a refugee camp in Malaysia before emigrating to Quebec. Ask students: À votre avis, qu'est-ce qui est le plus difficile quand on émigre dans un autre pays? Students will further develop this topic in the Activity 4 writing assignment.

OPTIONS

Extra Practice Have students research the following: 1. the reasons Vietnamese boat people fled their country; 2. the countries they emigrated to; and 3. the political situation in Vietnam today. Ask volunteers to share with the class interesting historical facts they uncovered.

Pairs Have pairs research information about other refugees or immigrants who, like Kim Thúy, have made contributions to the arts in their adopted country. Students could research other authors, musicians, artists, etc. Have the pairs prepare a brief presentation in which they share their findings with the class.

geste *gesture* **importe** *matters* **suffit** *suffices*
coéquipier *teammate* **a frotté le dessus** *rubbed the top* **féliciter** *to congratulate* **aimer avec ivresse** *to love with exhilaration* **aveuglément** *blindly*

Après la lecture

Le bon choix Choisissez la réponse correcte à chaque question.

1. Qui sont les deux personnes que la narratrice a observées?
   a. une mère vietnamienne et sa fille née au Québec
   (b.) une grand-mère vietnamienne et son petit-fils
   c. une Québécoise et son mari vietnamien

2. D'après la narratrice, avec quelle partie du corps ressent-on (*does one feel*) l'amour dans la culture vietnamienne?
   (a.) avec la tête
   b. avec le cœur
   c. avec l'estomac

3. Qu'est-ce qui n'est pas acceptable dans la culture vietnamienne?
   (a.) de toucher la tête à une autre personne
   b. de montrer de l'affection en public
   c. de parler de ses sentiments

4. D'après le texte, à quoi doit-on faire attention quand on est avec des personnes d'une autre culture?
   a. à bien traduire ce qu'on veut leur dire
   (b.) à ne pas les offenser par nos gestes
   c. à ne pas leur poser de questions sur leur culture

5. Quelle est la conclusion de la narratrice au sujet des mots et de la culture?
   a. L'affection est un sujet à éviter dans la culture vietnamienne.
   b. On parle de l'affection de la même façon dans toutes les cultures.
   (c.) Il y a plusieurs façons de quantifier l'affection dans la culture vietnamienne.

Répondez Répondez aux questions par des phrases complètes. Answers will vary. Suggested answers.

1. Qu'a fait le petit garçon pour répondre à la question de sa grand-mère?
   Il s'est touché la tête avec la main.
2. Que s'est-il passé quand un Québécois a touché la tête de son coéquipier d'origine vietnamienne pour le féliciter?
   Le Vietnamien est devenu furieux.
3. Pourquoi le petit Vietnamien a-t-il réagi comme il l'a fait?
   Parce que toucher la tête d'un Vietnamien l'insulte.
4. Pourquoi le geste d'aimer n'est-il pas universel, d'après la narratrice?
   Il doit être traduit d'une langue à une autre; il doit être appris.
5. Qu'est-ce qui est impossible dans la langue et la culture vietnamiennes, d'après la narratrice?
   Il est impossible d'aimer tout court, sans sa tête.

Discussion Relisez le texte et identifiez les différents types d'amour dans la culture vietnamienne cités dans le texte. Avec un(e) partenaire, décidez si ces types d'amour existent aussi dans votre culture. Créez une liste de quelques exemples concrets pour chaque type d'amour.

six cent soixante-neuf **669**

Le bon choix Have pairs work together to write two additional sets of multiple choice questions and answers about the reading or narrator. Have them exchange papers with another pair and select the correct responses.

Répondez Go over the answers with the class. You may want to introduce the verb **réagir** (*to react*).

Discussion Circulate as students discuss, providing support as needed. On the board, make six columns and title them: **aimer par goût, aimer sans être amoureux, aimer amoureusement, aimer avec ivresse, aimer aveuglément, aimer par gratitude**. Write students' examples of each type of love on the board, and discuss as a class.

OPTIONS

Groups Have small groups research additional works by Kim Thúy. Tell them to write a paragraph that includes the work's title, themes, main characters, and a brief summary of the story. Ask students to identify specific elements in the work that reflect Thúy's personal biographical and cultural contexts.

Extra Practice Conduct a class discussion on the following topic: **D'après vous, quand on émigre dans un autre pays, est-ce qu'il est important de conserver sa langue et sa culture d'origine? Ou est-ce qu'il vaut mieux essayer de s'intégrer complètement dans la nouvelle culture?**

Écriture

STRATÉGIE

Writing strong introductions and conclusions

Introductions and conclusions serve a similar purpose: both are intended to focus the reader's attention on the topic being covered. The introduction presents a brief preview of the topic. In addition, it informs your reader of the important points that will be covered in the body of your writing. The conclusion reaffirms those points and concisely sums up the information that has been provided. A compelling fact or statistic, a humorous anecdote, or a question directed to the reader are all interesting ways to begin or end your writing.

For example, if you were writing a biographical report on Voltaire, whom you learned about in **Unité 14 LECTURE**, you might start by noting that Voltaire's *Candide* is one of the most widely read books in the French literary canon. The rest of your introductory paragraph would outline the areas you would cover in the body of your paper, such as the author's life, his works, and the impact that *Candide* has had on modern literature. In your conclusion, you might sum up the most important information in the report and tie this information together in a way that would make your reader want to learn even more about the topic. You could write, for example, "Voltaire, with his imagination and unique view on the world, has created one of the most well-known and enduring characters in world literature."

Thème

🔗 Écrire la critique d'une œuvre artistique

Avant l'écriture

1. Vous allez écrire la critique d'un film, d'une pièce de théâtre ou d'un spectacle de votre choix. Votre critique doit avoir trois parties: l'introduction, le développement et la conclusion. Dans l'introduction, vous allez rapidement présenter l'œuvre. Ensuite, dans le développement, vous allez la décrire en détail. Enfin, dans la conclusion, vous allez donner votre opinion et expliquer pourquoi vous recommandez ce spectacle ou non. Utilisez ce plan pour la recherche des idées et pour leur organisation.

Introduction

- Le titre de l'œuvre et le nom de son créateur
- Description du sujet et/ou du genre de l'œuvre
- Quand et où vous l'avez vue

Développement

- Un petit résumé de l'histoire
- Les noms des personnages ou des artistes
- Description des personnages, du/des décor(s) et des costumes

---

Section Goals

In this section, students will:
- learn to write introductions and conclusions
- write a critique of a film, show, or theatrical work

Stratégie Explain that a strong introduction presents the topic and outlines the important points that will be addressed.

Thème Tell students to follow the steps outlined here when writing their critique.

Proofreading Activity Have students correct these sentences. **1. Croyez-vous que ce soit meilleur qu'elle le sache? 2. Il est évidente qu'elle ne connaît pas chanter. 3. Il est clair que tu ne saches rien de moi.**

OPTIONS

Avant l'écriture Ask students why a strong introduction to a biography of Voltaire should mention his best-known work. Explain that a strong conclusion summarizes the information given. Ask students how this conclusion could be stronger: **Voltaire était un grand écrivain.**

Tell students that the sample introduction uses a summarizing statement as a starting point. Other ways to begin an introduction are with statistics or other factual information related to your topic, with a quotation that summarizes the point of view you plan to develop, or with an anecdote that sets the stage for the rest of your evaluation.

670 Instructor's Annotated Edition • Unit 15

Conclusion

- Votre opinion de l'œuvre

- Explication des raisons pour lesquelles vous la recommandez ou non

Écriture

1. Pour vous assurer (*ensure*) que vous allez écrire une introduction et une conclusion bien développées, remplissez (*fill in*) ce diagramme. Ces deux sections doivent contenir la même information sur les idées principales de votre critique, mais doivent aussi avoir au moins (*at least*) une idée différente. Référez-vous à la stratégie, si nécessaire.

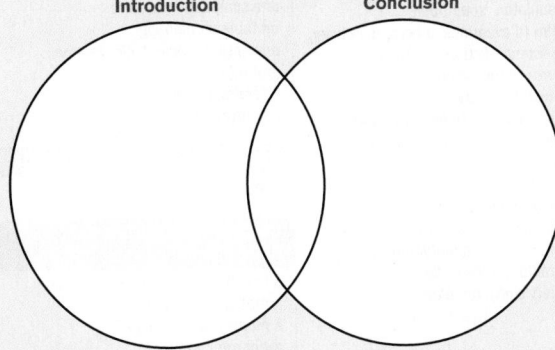

Introduction   Conclusion

2. Ensuite, utilisez vos idées de la section précédente et du diagramme pour écrire votre critique.

3. Utilisez aussi des formes du subjonctif et, si possible, des pronoms possessifs dans votre critique.

Critique d'une pièce de théâtre

Le malade imaginaire de Molière est une comédie théâtrale que j'ai eu la chance de voir hier soir au Théâtre des Capucins.

L'histoire, qui se passe au XVIIe siècle, est celle d'un vieux bourgeois, Argan, qui se croit constamment malade, alors qu'il ne l'est pas. Béline, sa femme, …

Cette pièce, qui est d'ailleurs un des nombreux chefs-d'œuvre de Molière, m'a donné l'occasion de passer un très bon moment…

Après l'écriture

1. Échangez votre critique avec celle d'un(e) partenaire. Répondez à ces questions pour commenter son travail.

- Votre partenaire a-t-il/elle inclu une introduction développée?

- A-t-il/elle écrit une partie centrale détaillée?

- A-t-il/elle écrit une conclusion bien développée et en relation avec l'introduction, mais contenant (*containing*) aussi au moins une nouvelle idée?

- A-t-il/elle présenté toutes les informations de la section **Avant l'écriture**?

- A-t-il/elle utilisé des formes du subjonctif?

- Quel(s) détail(s) ajouteriez-vous (*would you add*)? Quel(s) détail(s) enlèveriez-vous (*would you delete*)? Quel(s) autre(s) commentaire(s) avez-vous pour votre partenaire?

2. Corrigez votre lettre d'après (*according to*) les commentaires de votre partenaire. Relisez votre travail pour éliminer ces problèmes:

- des fautes (*errors*) d'orthographe

- des fautes de ponctuation

- des fautes de conjugaison

- un mauvais emploi (*use*) de la grammaire de l'unité

- des fautes d'accord (*agreement*) des adjectifs

Criteria

Content Contains a complete evaluation of a film, drama, or show that addresses all the information called out in the bulleted list.
Scale: 1 2 3 4 5

Organization Organized into a clear introduction, body, and conclusion, each of which is made up of logical paragraphs that begin with topic sentences and contain appropriate supporting detail.
Scale: 1 2 3 4 5

Accuracy Uses present and past tense forms correctly. Spells words, conjugates verbs, and modifies adjectives correctly throughout.
Scale: 1 2 3 4 5

Creativity Includes additional information that is not requested in the task and/or uses adjectives, descriptive verbs, and additional details to make the composition more interesting.
Scale: 1 2 3 4 5

Scoring

Excellent	18–20 points
Good	14–17 points
Satisfactory	10–13 points
Unsatisfactory	< 10 points

O P T I O N S

Avant l'écriture Allow students who may have difficulty with the task to watch a French movie or dramatization of a one-act play together. Give them extra support by supplying some facts about the presentation and then discussing it afterwards with the group. More advanced students who don't need this level of help may either join this group or elect to do the assignment on a piece of their own choosing.

Écriture Supply students with some useful expressions for critiquing a play or film: **À mon avis…, Beaucoup de personnes considèrent (que)/pensent que…., Comme tout le monde le sait…, D'un point de vue artistique/historique…, Selon les critiques…** etc. You may also want to supply a list of adjectives such as **brillant(e), éblouissant(e), réussi(e), avant-gardiste, innovant(e), innovateur/innovatrice, génial(e), surestimé(e), lamentable, médiocre**, and so on.

Instructional Resources
vhlcentral.com:
Textbook MP3s; Textbook
Audioscript; reference tools

Suggestions

• Tell students that an easy way to study from **Vocabulaire** is to cover up the French half of each section, leaving only the English equivalents exposed. They can then quiz themselves on the French items. To focus on the English equivalents of the French entries, they simply reverse this process.

• Point out to students that they can use the Vocabulary Tools at **vhlcentral.com** for reference and extra vocabulary practice.

🔊 Ⓢ Vocabulary Tools

Leçon 15A

Aller au spectacle

applaudir *to applaud*
présenter *to present*
profiter de quelque chose *to take advantage of/to enjoy something*
un applaudissement *applause*
une chanson *song*
un chœur *choir, chorus*
une comédie (musicale) *comedy (musical)*
un concert *concert*
une danse *dance*
le début *beginning; debut*
un entracte *intermission*
la fin *end*
un genre *genre*
un opéra *opera*
une pièce de théâtre *play*
une place *seat*
une séance *show; screening*
une sorte *sort, kind*
un spectateur/une spectatrice *spectator*
une tragédie *tragedy*

Les artistes

faire de la musique *to play music*
jouer un rôle *to play a role*
jouer de la batterie/de la guitare/du piano/du violon *to play the drums/ the guitar/the piano/the violin*
un compositeur *composer*
un danseur/une danseuse *dancer*
un dramaturge *playwright*
un membre *member*
un metteur en scène *director (of a play, a show)*
un orchestre *orchestra*
un personnage (principal) *(main) character*
un réalisateur/une réalisatrice *director (of a movie)*
une troupe *company, troop*
célèbre *famous*

Expressions utiles

See p. 633.

Expressions de doute et de certitude

douter que... *to doubt that...*
ne pas croire que... *not to believe that...*
ne pas penser que... *not to think that...*
Il est douteux que... *It is doubtful that...*
Il est impossible que... *It is impossible that...*
Il n'est pas certain que... *It is uncertain that...*
Il n'est pas sûr que... *It is not sure that...*
Il n'est pas vrai que... *It is untrue that...*
croire que... *to believe that...*
penser que... *to think that*
savoir que... *to know that...*
Il est certain que... *It is certain that...*
Il est clair que... *It is clear that...*
Il est évident que... *It is obvious that...*
Il est sûr que... *It is sure that...*
Il est vrai que... *It is true that...*

Pronoms possessifs

le mien (*m. sing.*) *mine*
la mienne (*f. sing.*) *mine*
les miens (*m. pl.*) *mine*
les miennes (*f. pl.*) *mine*
le tien (*m. sing.*) *yours*
la tienne (*f. sing.*) *yours*
les tiens (*m. pl.*) *yours*
les tiennes (*f. pl.*) *yours*
le sien (*m. sing.*) *his/hers/its*
les siens (*m. pl.*) *his/hers/its*
les siennes (*f. pl.*) *his/hers/its*
le/la nôtre (*m./f. sing.*) *ours*
les nôtres (*m./f. pl.*) *ours*
le/la vôtre (*m./f. sing.*) *yours (form./pl.)*
les vôtres (*m./f. pl.*) *yours (form./pl.)*
le/la leur (*m./f. sing.*) *theirs*
les leurs (*m./f. pl.*) *theirs*

Leçon 15B

Les artistes

un auteur/une femme auteur *author*
un écrivain/une écrivaine *writer*
un peintre/une femme peintre *painter*
un poète/une poétesse *poet*
un sculpteur/une sculptrice *sculptor*
doué(e) *talented; gifted*

Le cinéma et la télévision

un dessin animé *cartoon*
un documentaire *documentary*
un drame psychologique *psychological drama*
une émission (de télévision) *(television) program*
un feuilleton *soap opera*
un film (d'aventures, d'horreur, policier, de science-fiction) *(adventure, horror, crime, science-fiction) film*
une histoire *story*
les informations (infos) (*f.*) *news*
un jeu télévisé *game show*
la météo *weather*
les nouvelles (*f.*) *news*
un programme *program*
une publicité (pub) *advertisement*
les variétés (*f.*) *popular music*
à la radio *on the radio*
la télé(vision) *on television*

Les arts

faire les musées *to go to museums*
publier *to publish*
les beaux-arts (*m.*) *fine arts*
un chef-d'œuvre (chefs-d'œuvre *pl.*) *masterpiece*
un conte *tale*
une critique *review; criticism*
une exposition *exhibit*
un festival (festivals *pl.*) *festival*
un magazine *magazine*
une œuvre *artwork, piece of art*
une peinture *painting*
un poème *poem*
un roman *novel*
une sculpture *sculpture*
un tableau *painting*
ancien(ne) *ancient; old; former*
gratuit(e) *free*
littéraire *literary*
récent(e) *recent*

Expressions utiles

See p. 653.

Conjonctions suivies du subjonctif

à condition que... *on the condition that..., provided that...*
à moins que... *unless...*
avant que... *before...*
jusqu'à ce que... *until...*
pour que... *so that...*
sans que... *without...*

672   *six cent soixante-douze*

Le monde francophone

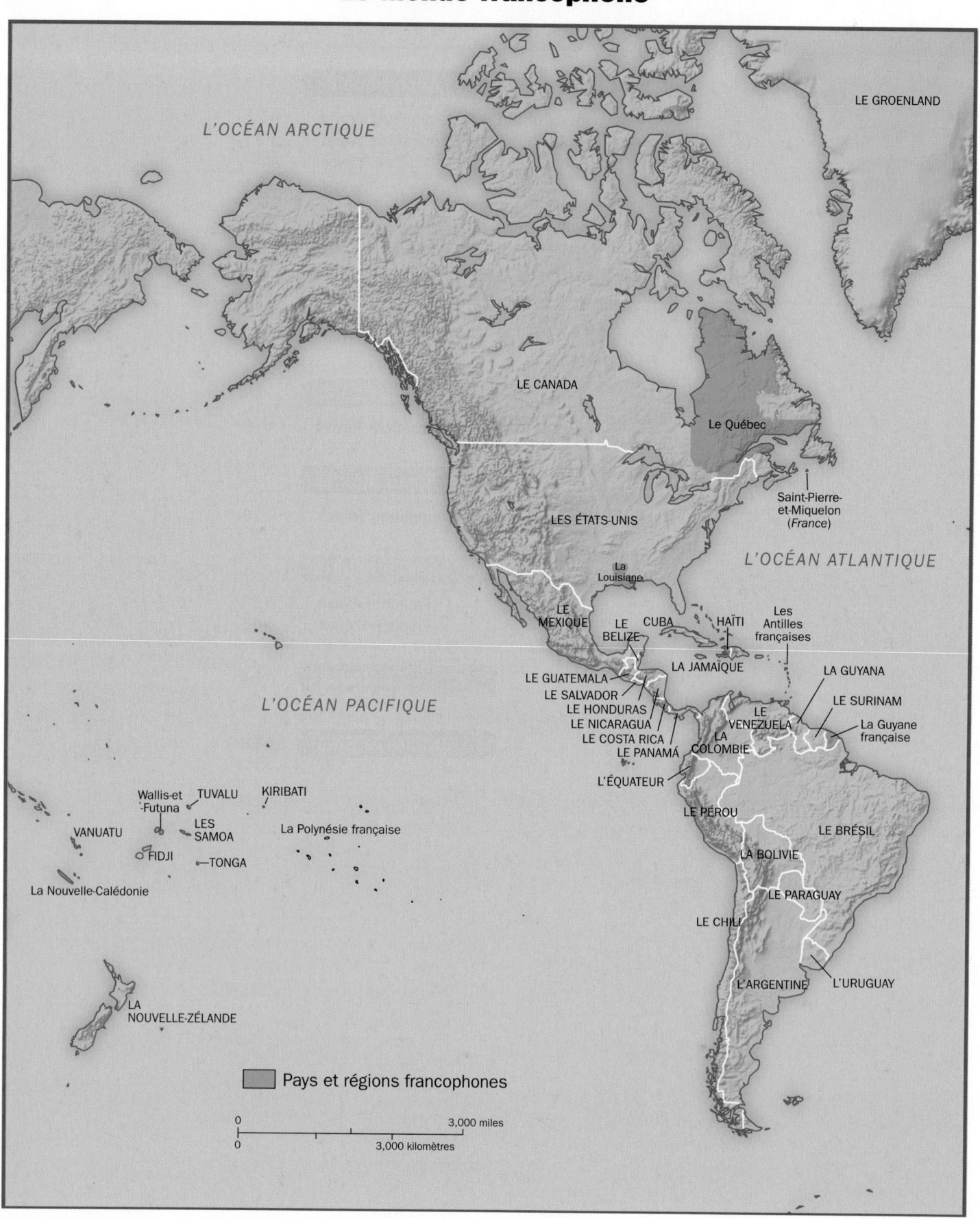

L'OCÉAN ARCTIQUE

LE GROENLAND

LE CANADA

Le Québec

Saint-Pierre-
et-Miquelon
(*France*)

LES ÉTATS-UNIS

L'OCÉAN ATLANTIQUE

La Louisiane

LE MEXIQUE

LE BELIZE

CUBA

HAÏTI

Les Antilles françaises

LA JAMAÏQUE

LA GUYANA

LE GUATEMALA

LE SALVADOR

LE SURINAM

LE HONDURAS

LE VENEZUELA

La Guyane française

LE NICARAGUA

LE COSTA RICA

LA COLOMBIE

LE PANAMÁ

L'ÉQUATEUR

L'OCÉAN PACIFIQUE

LE PÉROU

Wallis-et-Futuna

TUVALU

KIRIBATI

LE BRÉSIL

VANUATU

LES SAMOA

La Polynésie française

LA BOLIVIE

FIDJI

TONGA

LE PARAGUAY

La Nouvelle-Calédonie

LE CHILI

L'ARGENTINE

L'URUGUAY

LA NOUVELLE-ZÉLANDE

Pays et régions francophones

0   3,000 miles

0   3,000 kilomètres

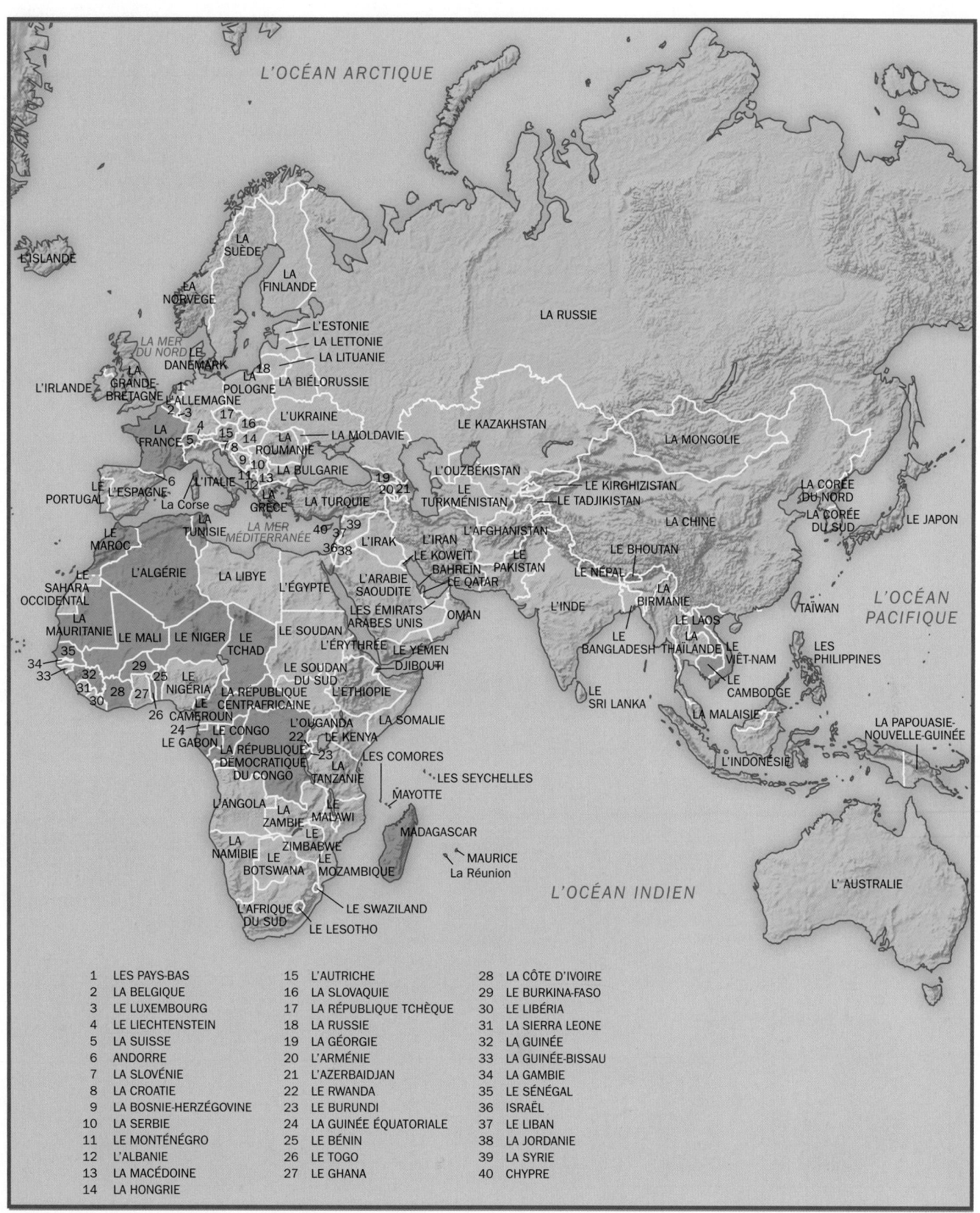

L'OCÉAN ARCTIQUE

L'ISLANDE

LA SUÈDE
LA NORVÈGE
LA FINLANDE
L'ESTONIE
LA LETTONIE
LA LITUANIE
LA MER DU NORD
LE DANEMARK
L'IRLANDE
LA GRANDE-BRETAGNE
LA POLOGNE
LA BIÉLORUSSIE
LA RUSSIE
L'ALLEMAGNE
L'UKRAINE
LA FRANCE
LA MOLDAVIE
LA ROUMANIE
LE KAZAKHSTAN
LA MONGOLIE
LA BULGARIE
LE PORTUGAL
L'ESPAGNE
L'ITALIE
La Corse
LA GRÈCE
LA TURQUIE
L'OUZBÉKISTAN
LE KIRGHIZISTAN
LA CORÉE DU NORD
LE TADJIKISTAN
LA CORÉE DU SUD
LE JAPON
LA TUNISIE
LA MER MÉDITERRANÉE
L'IRAK
L'IRAN
L'AFGHANISTAN
LA CHINE
LE MAROC
LE KOWEÏT
BAHREÏN
LE QATAR
LE PAKISTAN
LE NÉPAL
LE BHOUTAN
TAÏWAN
L'OCÉAN PACIFIQUE
LE SAHARA OCCIDENTAL
L'ALGÉRIE
LA LIBYE
L'ÉGYPTE
L'ARABIE SAOUDITE
LES ÉMIRATS ARABES UNIS
OMAN
L'INDE
LA BIRMANIE
LA MAURITANIE
LE MALI
LE NIGER
LE TCHAD
LE SOUDAN
L'ÉRYTHRÉE
LE YÉMEN
DJIBOUTI
LE BANGLADESH
LE LAOS
LA THAÏLANDE
LE VIÊT-NAM
LES PHILIPPINES
LE SOUDAN DU SUD
L'ÉTHIOPIE
LE SRI LANKA
LE CAMBODGE
LA RÉPUBLIQUE CENTRAFRICAINE
LE NIGÉRIA
LE CAMEROUN
LA SOMALIE
LE CONGO
LE GABON
L'OUGANDA
LE KENYA
LA MALAISIE
LA PAPOUASIE-NOUVELLE-GUINÉE
LA RÉPUBLIQUE DÉMOCRATIQUE DU CONGO
LA TANZANIE
LES COMORES
LES SEYCHELLES
L'INDONÉSIE
L'ANGOLA
LA ZAMBIE
LE MALAWI
MAYOTTE
LA NAMIBIE
LE ZIMBABWE
LE MOZAMBIQUE
MADAGASCAR
MAURICE
La Réunion
LE BOTSWANA
L'OCÉAN INDIEN
L'AUSTRALIE
L'AFRIQUE DU SUD
LE SWAZILAND
LE LESOTHO

1	LES PAYS-BAS	15	L'AUTRICHE	28	LA CÔTE D'IVOIRE
2	LA BELGIQUE	16	LA SLOVAQUIE	29	LE BURKINA-FASO
3	LE LUXEMBOURG	17	LA RÉPUBLIQUE TCHÈQUE	30	LE LIBÉRIA
4	LE LIECHTENSTEIN	18	LA RUSSIE	31	LA SIERRA LEONE
5	LA SUISSE	19	LA GÉORGIE	32	LA GUINÉE
6	ANDORRE	20	L'ARMÉNIE	33	LA GUINÉE-BISSAU
7	LA SLOVÉNIE	21	L'AZERBAIDJAN	34	LA GAMBIE
8	LA CROATIE	22	LE RWANDA	35	LE SÉNÉGAL
9	LA BOSNIE-HERZÉGOVINE	23	LE BURUNDI	36	ISRAËL
10	LA SERBIE	24	LA GUINÉE ÉQUATORIALE	37	LE LIBAN
11	LE MONTÉNÉGRO	25	LE BÉNIN	38	LA JORDANIE
12	L'ALBANIE	26	LE TOGO	39	LA SYRIE
13	LA MACÉDOINE	27	LE GHANA	40	CHYPRE
14	LA HONGRIE				

La France

L'ANGLETERRE

LES PAYS-BAS

LA MANCHE

LA BELGIQUE

L'ALLEMAGNE

LE LUXEMBOURG

HAUTS-DE-FRANCE

Lille
Arras
Amiens
Charleville-Mézières
Laon
Beauvais
Rouen

NORMANDIE

Saint-Lô
Caen
Évreux
Pontoise
Châlons-en-Champagne
Metz
Bar-le-Duc
Nancy
Strasbourg

Paris
ÎLE-DE-FRANCE
Versailles
Évry
Chartres
Melun

GRAND EST

Troyes
Chaumont
Épinal
Colmar

St-Brieuc
Alençon

BRETAGNE
Quimper
Rennes
Laval
Le Mans

Vannes

PAYS DE LA LOIRE
Angers
Nantes
Tours

Orléans
Blois
CENTRE-VAL DE LOIRE
Bourges
Châteauroux

Auxerre

Dijon
Besançon
Belfort
Vesoul

BOURGOGNE-FRANCHE-COMTÉ

Nevers

LA SUISSE

La-Roche-sur-Yon

Poitiers
Niort
La Rochelle

Moulins

Lons-le-Saunier

Mâcon
Bourg-en-Bresse

Annecy

Limoges
Angoulême

Guéret

NOUVELLE-AQUITAINE

Clermont-Ferrand

Lyon
St-Étienne

Chambéry

Périgueux
Tulle

AUVERGNE-RHÔNE-ALPES
Grenoble

L'ITALIE

Bordeaux
Aurillac
Le Puy-en-Velay
Privas
Valence

Gap

Cahors
Rodez
Mende

Agen
Montauban
Albi

Digne-les-Bains

Mont-de-Marsan
Auch
Toulouse

Nîmes
Avignon

PROVENCE-ALPES-CÔTE D'AZUR

Pau
Tarbes
OCCITANIE

Montpellier

Marseille
Toulon

Nice

MONACO

L'ESPAGNE
Foix
Carcassonne

Perpignan

ANDORRE

LA MER MÉDITERRANÉE

GUYANE

0 40 miles
0 40 kilomètres

L'OCÉAN ATLANTIQUE

Cayenne

LE SURINAM

LE BRÉSIL

L'OCÉAN ATLANTIQUE

la Seine
la Marne
la Loire
la Saône
la Garonne
le Rhône
le Rhin

LA RÉUNION

0 10 miles
0 10 kilomètres

L'OCÉAN INDIEN

Saint-Denis

MAYOTTE

0 5 miles
0 5 kilomètres

L'OCÉAN INDIEN

Mamoudzou
Dzaoudzi

CORSE

0 30 miles
0 30 kilomètres

Bastia
2B Haute-Corse

Ajaccio
2A Corse-du-Sud

0 100 miles
0 100 kilomètres

L'Europe

0   500 miles

0   500 kilomètres

☐ Pays francophones

LA MER DE BARENTS

L'ISLANDE
Reykjavik

LA MER DE NORVÈGE

LA SUÈDE

LA FINLANDE

LA NORVÈGE
Helsinki

LA RUSSIE

Oslo   Stockholm   Tallinn   L'ESTONIE   Moscou

LA MER DU NORD   LE DANEMARK   Copenhague   LA MER BALTIQUE   Riga   LA LETTONIE   LA LITUANIE   Vilnius   Minsk

LA RUSSIE   LA BIÉLORUSSIE

L'IRLANDE   Dublin

LA GRANDE BRETAGNE   LES PAYS-BAS   Berlin   LA POLOGNE   Varsovie   Kiev

L'OCÉAN ATLANTIQUE   Londres   La Haye   L'ALLEMAGNE   L'UKRAINE

Bruxelles   LA BELGIQUE   Prague

Paris   Luxembourg   LA RÉPUBLIQUE TCHÈQUE   LA SLOVAQUIE

LE LUXEMBOURG   LE LIECHTENSTEIN   Bratislava   LA MOLDAVIE   Chisinau

Vienne   Budapest

Berne   L'AUTRICHE   LA HONGRIE   LA ROUMANIE

LA SUISSE   Ljubljana   Zagreb   Belgrade   Bucarest   LA MER NOIRE

LA FRANCE   LA SLOVÉNIE

LA CROATIE   LA BOSNIE-HERZÉGOVINE   LA SERBIE

Monte Carlo   Sarajevo   LA BULGARIE

LE PORTUGAL   ANDORRE   Andorre-la-Vieille   MONACO   L'ITALIE   LE MONTÉNÉGRO   Podgorica   Sofia   Skopje   LA TURQUIE

La Corse   Rome   Tirana   LA MACÉDOINE

Madrid   L'ALBANIE   Nicosie

Lisbonne   L'ESPAGNE   La Sardaigne   LA GRÈCE

La Sicile   Athènes   CHYPRE

LE MAROC   MALTE   La Valette

L'ALGÉRIE   LA TUNISIE   LA MER MÉDITERRANÉE

LA LIBYE   L'ÉGYPTE

L'Afrique

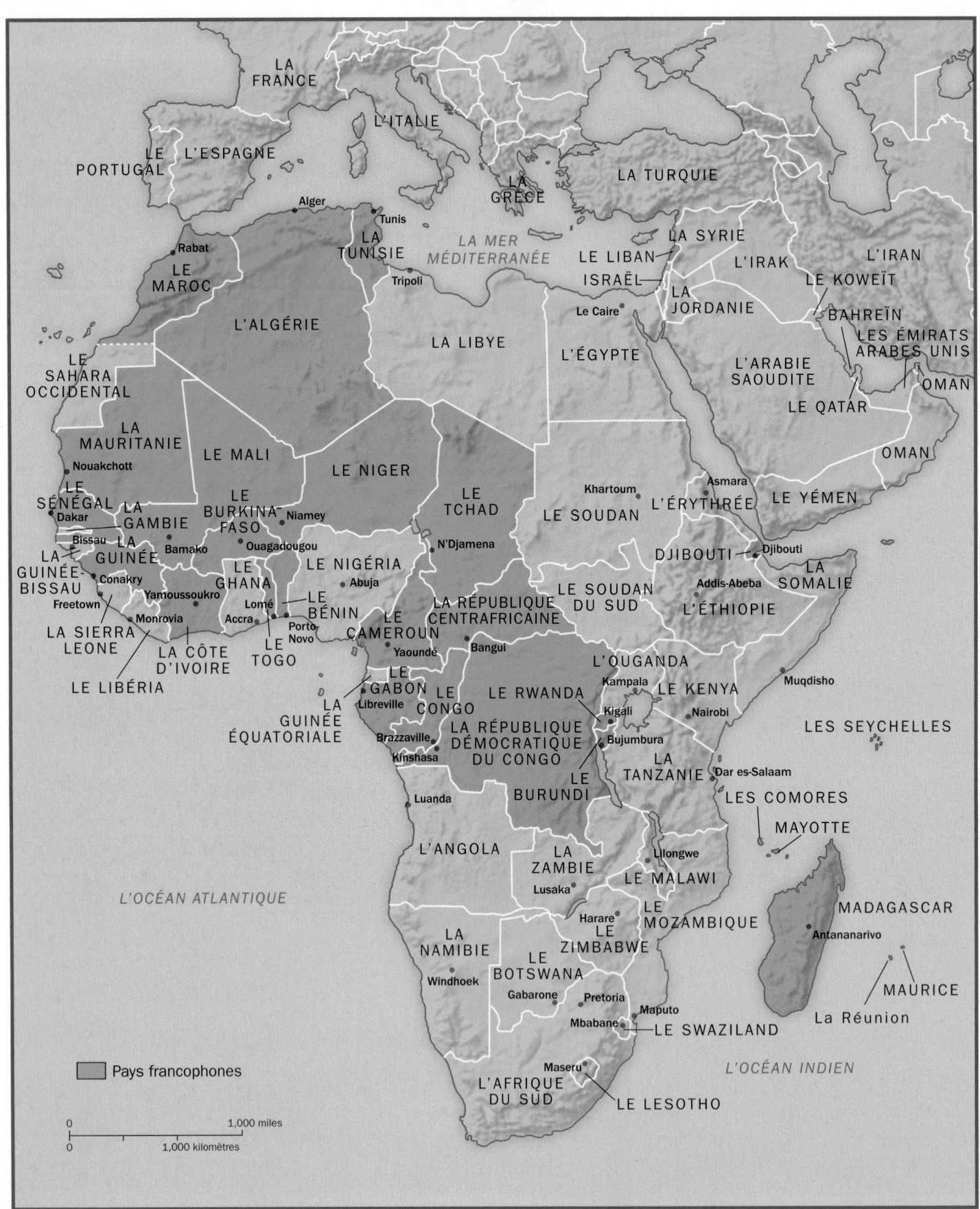

LA FRANCE

L'ITALIE

LE PORTUGAL   L'ESPAGNE

LA GRÈCE

LA TURQUIE

Alger

Tunis

LA TUNISIE

LA SYRIE

LE LIBAN

ISRAËL

L'IRAN

LA MER MÉDITERRANÉE

Rabat

LE MAROC

Tripoli

LE KOWEÏT

LA JORDANIE

BAHREÏN

LES ÉMIRATS ARABES UNIS

L'ALGÉRIE

LA LIBYE

L'ÉGYPTE

Le Caire

L'ARABIE SAOUDITE

OMAN

LE QATAR

LE SAHARA OCCIDENTAL

OMAN

LA MAURITANIE

LE MALI

Nouakchott

LE NIGER

LE TCHAD

Khartoum

LE SOUDAN

L'ÉRYTHRÉE

Asmara

LE YÉMEN

LE SÉNÉGAL   LA GAMBIE

Dakar

LE BURKINA FASO

Niamey

Bissau

Bamako

Ouagadougou

N'Djamena

DJIBOUTI

Djibouti

LA GUINÉE

LE GHANA

LE NIGÉRIA

LE SOUDAN DU SUD

Addis-Abeba

LA SOMALIE

LA GUINÉE-BISSAU

Conakry

Abuja

L'ÉTHIOPIE

Yamoussoukro

Lomé

LE BÉNIN

LA RÉPUBLIQUE CENTRAFRICAINE

Freetown

Accra

Porto-Novo

LE CAMEROUN

Monrovia

LA SIERRA LEONE

LA CÔTE D'IVOIRE

LE TOGO

Yaoundé

Bangui

L'OUGANDA

LE KENYA

Muqdisho

LE LIBÉRIA

LE GABON

LE CONGO

LE RWANDA

Kampala

Libreville

Kigali

Nairobi

LES SEYCHELLES

LA GUINÉE ÉQUATORIALE

LA RÉPUBLIQUE DÉMOCRATIQUE DU CONGO

Brazzaville

Bujumbura

Kinshasa

LE BURUNDI

LA TANZANIE

Dar es-Salaam

LES COMORES

Luanda

MAYOTTE

L'ANGOLA

LA ZAMBIE

Llongwe

Lusaka

LE MALAWI

L'OCÉAN ATLANTIQUE

MADAGASCAR

Antananarivo

Harare

LE MOZAMBIQUE

LA NAMIBIE

LE ZIMBABWE

MAURICE

LE BOTSWANA

Windhoek

Gabarone

Pretoria

Maputo

La Réunion

Mbabane

LE SWAZILAND

Pays francophones

Maseru

L'OCÉAN INDIEN

0   1,000 miles

0   1,000 kilomètres

L'AFRIQUE DU SUD

LE LESOTHO

L'Amérique du Nord et du Sud

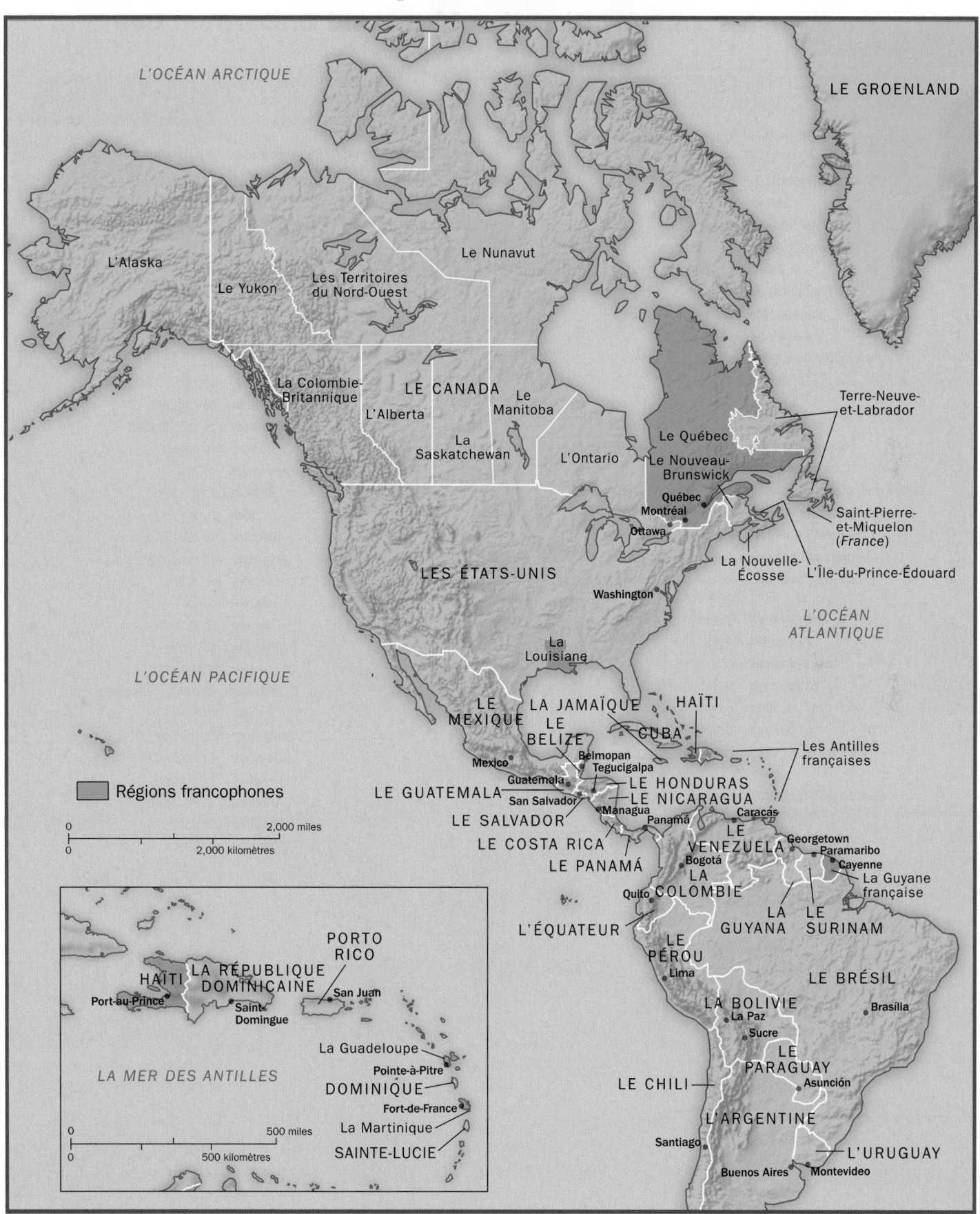

L'OCÉAN ARCTIQUE

LE GROENLAND

L'Alaska

Le Yukon

Les Territoires
du Nord-Ouest

Le Nunavut

La Colombie-
Britannique

LE CANADA

L'Alberta

Le
Manitoba

La
Saskatchewan

L'Ontario

Le Québec

Terre-Neuve-
et-Labrador

Le Nouveau-
Brunswick

Québec

Montréal

Ottawa

LES ÉTATS-UNIS

Saint-Pierre-
et-Miquelon
(France)

La Nouvelle-
Écosse

L'Île-du-Prince-Édouard

Washington

L'OCÉAN
ATLANTIQUE

L'OCÉAN PACIFIQUE

La
Louisiane

LE
MEXIQUE

LA JAMAÏQUE

LE
BELIZE

CUBA

HAÏTI

Les Antilles
françaises

Mexico

Belmopan

Tegucigalpa

LE GUATEMALA

Guatemala

San Salvador

LE HONDURAS

LE NICARAGUA

LE SALVADOR

Managua

Panamá

Caracas

LE COSTA RICA

LE PANAMÁ

LE
VENEZUELA

Georgetown

Paramaribo

Cayenne

Bogotá

LA
COLOMBIE

LA
GUYANA

LE
SURINAM

La Guyane
française

Quito

L'ÉQUATEUR

LE
PÉROU

Régions francophones

0   2,000 miles

0   2,000 kilomètres

Lima

LE BRÉSIL

LA BOLIVIE

La Paz

Sucre

Brasília

LE
PARAGUAY

PORTO
RICO

LA RÉPUBLIQUE
DOMINICAINE

HAÏTI

Port-au-Prince

Saint-
Domingue

San Juan

LE CHILI

Asunción

L'ARGENTINE

LA MER DES ANTILLES

La Guadeloupe

Pointe-à-Pitre

DOMINIQUE

Fort-de-France

La Martinique

SAINTE-LUCIE

0   500 miles

0   500 kilomètres

Santiago

Buenos Aires

Montevideo

L'URUGUAY

French Terms for Direction Lines and Classroom Use

Mots utiles *Useful words*

une affirmation	*statement, sentence*
une brochure	*brochure*
un brouillon	*draft*
un but	*purpose, goal*
le contenu	*content*
une conversation	*conversation*
le début	*beginning*
le(s) devoir(s)	*homework*
une enquête	*survey*
une étape	*step*
un indice, une piste	*clue*
la lecture	*reading*
un nom	*name*
l'orthographe	*spelling*
un(e) partenaire	*partner*
un personnage	*a character*
la/les personne(s) décrite(s)	*person (people) described*
une phrase complète	*complete sentence*
un point de départ	*starting point*
le prochain examen	*next test*
une pub/publicité	*ad/advertisement; commercial*
une question	*question*
le rapport	*report*
les ressources	*resources*
un sondage	*opinion poll*
la suite	*ending*
le tableau	*blackboard*
un thème, un sujet	*topic*
dans lequel/laquelle/ lesquel(le)s	*in which*
par exemple	*for example*
avant	*before*
chaque	*each*
d'abord	*first*
dernier	*last*
efficace	*efficient*
ensemble	*together*
maintenant	*now*

Pour parler à vos camarades de classe *To talk with your classmates*

C'est ton tour./C'est mon tour.	*It's your/my turn.*
Épelez./Épelle.	*Spell.*
Je commence./Tu commences.	*I start./You start.*
Je suis d'accord/pas d'accord avec toi.	*I agree/disagree with you.*
Ne me dis pas la réponse.	*Don't tell me the answer.*
Veux-tu travailler avec moi?	*Do you want to work with me?*

Verbes utiles *Useful verbs*

ajouter	*to add*
combiner	*to combine*
converser	*to talk; to chat*
créer	*to create*
demander	*to ask*
deviner	*to guess*
dire	*to say*
discuter	*to talk; to discuss*
échanger	*to exchange*
écrire	*to write*
essayer	*to try*
inclure	*to include*
justifier	*to justify*
noter	*to jot down*
raconter	*to tell, to relate (a story)*
relier	*to link*
remplacer	*to replace*
souligner	*to underline*
suivre	*to follow*
traduire	*to translate*
utiliser	*to use*
vérifier	*to check*

Expressions utiles *Useful expressions*

Allez à la page 2.	*Go to page 2.*
Alternez les rôles.	*Switch roles.*
À tour de rôle...	*Take turns...*
À voix haute	*Aloud*
À votre/ton avis	*In your opinion*
Après une deuxième écoute...	*After a second listening...*
Articulez.	*Enunciate.; Pronounce carefully.*
Au sujet de, À propos de	*Regarding, about*
Avec un(e) partenaire/ un(e) camarade de classe	*With a partner/a classmate*
Avez-vous/As-tu des questions?	*Do you have any questions?*
Avez-vous/As-tu fini/terminé?	*Are you done?; Have you finished?*
Chassez l'intrus.	*Choose the item that doesn't belong.*
Choisissez le bon mot.	*Choose the right word.*
Circulez dans la classe.	*Walk around the classroom.*
Comment dit-on _____ en français?	*How do you say _____ in French?*
Comment écrit-on _____ en français?	*How do you spell _____ in French?*
Corrigez les phrases fausses.	*Correct the false statements.*
Créez/Formez des phrases...	*Create/Form sentences...*
D'après vous/Selon vous...	*According to you...*
Décrivez les images/dessins...	*Describe the images/ drawings...*
Désolé(e), j'ai oublié.	*I'm sorry, I forgot.*
Déterminez si...	*Decide whether...*
Dites si vous êtes/Dis si tu es d'accord ou non.	*Say if you agree or not.*
Écrivez une lettre/une phrase.	*Write a letter/a sentence.*
Employez les verbes de la liste.	*Use the verbs from the list.*
En utilisant...	*Using...*
Est-ce que vous pouvez/ tu peux choisir un(e) autre partenaire/ quelqu'un d'autre?	*Can you please choose another partner/ someone else?*
Êtes vous prêt(e)?/ Es-tu prêt(e)?	*Are you ready?*
Excusez-moi, je suis en retard.	*Excuse me for being late.*
Faites correspondre...	*Match...*
Faites les accords nécessaires.	*Make the necessary agreements.*
Félicitations!	*Congratulations!*
Indiquez le mot qui n'appartient pas.	*Indicate the word that doesn't belong.*
Indiquez qui a dit...	*Indicate who said...*
J'ai gagné!/Nous avons gagné!	*I won!/We won!*
Je n'ai pas/Nous n'avons pas encore fini.	*I/We have not finished yet.*
Je ne comprends pas.	*I don't understand.*
Je ne sais pas.	*I don't know.*
Je ne serai pas là demain.	*I won't be here tomorrow.*
Je peux continuer?	*May I continue?*
Jouez le rôle de.../la scène...	*Play the role of.../the scene...*
Lentement, s'il vous plaît.	*Slowly, please.*
Lisez...	*Read...*
Mettez dans l'ordre...	*Put in order...*
Ouvrez/Fermez votre livre.	*Open/Close your books.*
Par groupes de trois/quatre...	*In groups of three/four...*
Partagez vos résultats...	*Share your results...*
Posez-vous les questions suivantes.	*Ask each other the following questions.*
Pour demain, faites...	*For tomorrow, do...*
Pour demain, vous allez/ tu vas faire...	*Tomorrow you are going to do...*
Prononcez.	*Pronounce.*
Qu'est-ce que _____ veut dire?	*What does _____ mean?*
Que pensez-vous/penses-tu de...	*What do you think about...*
Qui a gagné?	*Who won?*
...qui convient le mieux.	*...that best completes/is the most appropriate.*
Rejoignez un autre groupe.	*Get together with another group.*
Remplissez les espaces.	*Fill in the blanks.*
Répondez aux questions suivantes.	*Answer the following questions.*
Soyez prêt(e)s à...	*Be ready to...*
Venez/Viens au tableau.	*Come to the board.*
Vous comprenez?/ Tu comprends?	*Do you understand?*
Vous pouvez expliquer encore une fois, s'il vous plaît?	*Could you explain again, please?*
Vous pouvez répéter, s'il vous plaît?	*Could you repeat that, please?*
Vrai ou faux?	*True or false?*

Glossary of Grammatical Terms

ADJECTIVE A word that modifies, or describes, a noun or pronoun.

des livres **amusants**   un homme **grand**
*some **funny** books*   *a **tall** man*

de **jolies** fleurs
*some **pretty** flowers*

Demonstrative adjective An adjective that specifies which noun a speaker is referring to.

cette chemise   **ce** placard
***this** shirt*   ***this** closet*

cet hôtel   **ces** boîtes
***this** hotel*   ***these** boxes*

Possessive adjective An adjective that indicates ownership or possession.

ma belle montre   C'est **son** cousin.
***my** beautiful watch* *This is **his/her** cousin.*

tes crayons   Ce sont **leurs** tantes.
***your** pencils*   *Those are **their** aunts.*

ADVERB A word that modifies, or describes, a verb, adjective, or other adverb.

Michael parle **couramment** français.
*Michael speaks French **fluently**.*

Ces enfants sont **vraiment** intelligents.
*These kids are **really** smart.*

Elle lui parle **très** franchement.
*She speaks to him **very** candidly.*

ARTICLE A word that points out a noun in either a specific or a non-specific way.

Definite article An article that points out a noun in a specific way.

le marché   **la** valise
***the** market*   ***the** suitcase*

les dictionnaires   **les** mots
***the** dictionaries* ***the** words*

Indefinite article An article that points out a noun in a general, non-specific way.

un vélo   **une** fille
***a** bike*   ***a** girl*

des oiseaux   **des** affiches
***some** birds*   ***some** posters*

CLAUSE A group of words that contains both a conjugated verb and a subject, either expressed or implied.

Main (or Independent) clause A clause that can stand alone as a complete sentence.

J'ai un manteau vert.
I have a green coat.

Subordinate (or Dependent) clause A clause that does not express a complete thought and therefore cannot stand alone as a sentence.

Je travaille dans un restaurant **parce que j'ai besoin d'argent**.
*I work in a restaurant **because I need money.***

COMPARATIVE A construction used with an adjective or adverb to express a comparison between two people, places, or things.

Thomas est **plus petit** qu'Adrien.
*Thomas is **shorter than** Adrien.*

En Corse, il pleut **moins souvent qu'**en Alsace.
*In Corsica, it rains **less often than** in Alsace.*

Cette maison n'a pas **autant de fenêtres que** l'autre.
*This house does not have **as many windows as** the other one.*

CONJUGATION A set of the forms of a verb for a specific tense or mood, or the process by which these verb forms are presented.

Imparfait conjugation of **chanter**:
je chant**ais**   nous chant**ions**
tu chant**ais**   vous chant**iez**
il/elle/on chant**ait** ils/elles chant**aient**

CONJUNCTION A word used to connect words, clauses, or phrases.

Suzanne **et** Pierre habitent en Suisse.
*Suzanne **and** Pierre live in Switzerland.*

Je ne dessine pas très bien, **mais** j'aime les cours de dessin.
*I don't draw very well, **but** I like art classes.*

CONTRACTION The joining of two words into one. In French, the contractions are **au**, **aux**, **du**, and **des**.

Ma sœur est allée **au** concert hier soir.
*My sister went **to a** concert last night.*

Il a parlé **aux** voisins cet après-midi.
*He talked **to the** neighbors this afternoon.*

Je retire de l'argent **du** distributeur automatique.
*I withdraw money **from the** ATM machine.*

Nous avons campé **près du** village.
*We camped **near the** village.*

DIRECT OBJECT A noun or pronoun that directly receives the action of the verb.

Thomas lit **un livre**. Je **l'**ai vu hier.
*Thomas reads **a book**. I saw **him** yesterday.*

GENDER The grammatical categorizing of certain kinds of words, such as nouns and pronouns, as masculine, feminine, or neuter.

Masculine
articles **le, un**
pronouns **il, lui, le, celui-ci, celui-là, lequel**
adjective **élégant**

Feminine
articles **la, une**
pronouns **elle, la, celle-ci, celle-là, laquelle**
adjective **élégante**

IMPERSONAL EXPRESSION A third-person expression with no expressed or specific subject.

Il pleut. **C'est** très important.
It's raining. *It's very important.*

INDIRECT OBJECT A noun or pronoun that receives the action of the verb indirectly; the object, often a living being, to or for whom an action is performed.

Éric donne un livre **à Linda**.
*Éric gave a book **to Linda**.*

Le professeur **m'**a donné une bonne note.
*The teacher gave **me** a good mark.*

INFINITIVE The basic form of a verb. Infinitives in French end in **-er**, **-ir**, **-oir**, or **-re**.

parler	**finir**	**savoir**	**prendre**
to speak	*to finish*	*to know*	*to take*

INTERROGATIVE An adjective or pronoun used to ask a question.

Qui parle?
Who is speaking?

Combien de biscuits as-tu achetés?
How many cookies did you buy?

Que penses-tu faire aujourd'hui?
What do you plan to do today?

INVERSION Changing the word order of a sentence, often to form a question.

Statement: Elle a vendu sa voiture.

Inversion: A-t-elle vendu sa voiture?

MOOD A grammatical distinction of verbs that indicates whether the verb is intended to make a statement or command or to express a doubt, emotion, or condition contrary to fact.

Conditional mood Verb forms used to express what would be done or what would happen under certain circumstances, or to make a polite request, soften a demand, express what someone could or should do, or to state a contrary-to-fact situation.

Il irait se promener s'il avait le temps.
He would go for a walk if he had the time.

Pourrais-tu éteindre la lumière, s'il te plaît?
Would you turn off the light, please?

Je devrais lui parler gentiment.
I should talk to her nicely.

Imperative mood Verb forms used to make commands or suggestions.

Parle lentement. **Venez** avec moi.
Speak slowly. *Come with me.*

Indicative mood Verb forms used to state facts, actions, and states considered to be real.

Je sais qu'**il a** un chat.
I know that he has a cat.

Subjunctive mood Verb forms used principally in subordinate (dependent) clauses to express wishes, desires, emotions, doubts, and certain conditions, such as contrary-to-fact situations.

Il est important que **tu finisses** tes devoirs.
*It's important that **you finish** your homework.*

Je doute que **Louis ait** assez d'argent.
*I doubt that **Louis has** enough money.*

NOUN A word that identifies people, animals, places, things, and ideas.

homme	**chat**
man	*cat*
Belgique	**maison**
Belgium	*house*
amitié	**livre**
friendship	*book*

NUMBER A grammatical term that refers to singular or plural. Nouns in French and English have number. Other parts of a sentence, such as adjectives, articles, and verbs, can also have number.

Singular	Plural
une chose	**des** choses
a thing	*some things*
le professeur	**les** professeurs
the professor	*the professors*

NUMBERS Words that represent amounts.

Cardinal numbers Words that show specific amounts.

cinq minutes
five minutes

l'année **deux mille six**
the year 2006

Ordinal numbers Words that indicate the order of a noun in a series.

le **quatrième** joueur	la **dixième** fois
the **fourth** player	the **tenth** time

PAST PARTICIPLE A past form of the verb used in compound tenses. The past participle may also be used as an adjective, but it must then agree in number and gender with the word it modifies.

Ils ont beaucoup **marché**.
*They have **walked** a lot.*

Je n'ai pas **préparé** mon examen.
*I haven't **prepared** for my exam.*

Il y a une fenêtre **ouverte** dans le salon.
*There is an **open** window in the living room.*

PERSON The form of the verb or pronoun that indicates the speaker, the one spoken to, or the one spoken about. In French, as in English, there are three persons: first, second, and third.

Person	Singular		Plural	
1st	**je**	*I*	**nous**	*we*
2nd	**tu**	*you*	**vous**	*you*
3rd	**il/elle**	*he/she/it*	**ils/elles**	*they*
	on	*one*		

PREPOSITION A word or words that describe(s) the relationship, most often in time or space, between two other words.

Annie habite **loin de** Paris.
*Annie lives **far from** Paris.*

Le blouson est **dans** la voiture.
*The jacket is **in** the car.*

Martine s'est coiffée **avant de** sortir.
*Martine combed her hair **before** going out.*

PRONOUN A word that takes the place of a noun or nouns.

Demonstrative pronoun A pronoun that takes the place of a specific noun.

Je veux **celui-ci**.
*I want **this one**.*

Vas-tu acheter **celle-là**?
*Are you going to buy **that one**?*

Marc préférait **ceux-là**.
*Marc preferred **those**.*

Object pronoun A pronoun that functions as a direct or indirect object of the verb.

Elle **lui** donne un cadeau.
*She gives **him** a present.*

Frédéric **me l'**a apporté.
*Frédéric brought **it** to **me**.*

Reflexive pronoun A pronoun that indicates that the action of a verb is performed by the subject on itself. These pronouns are often expressed in English with -*self*: *myself, yourself*, etc.

Je **me lave** avant de sortir.
*I **wash (myself)** before going out.*

Marie **s'est couchée** à onze heures et demie.
*Marie **went to bed** at eleven-thirty.*

Relative pronoun A pronoun that connects a subordinate clause to a main clause.

Le garçon **qui** nous a écrit vient nous voir demain.
*The boy **who** wrote us is coming to visit tomorrow.*

Je sais **que** nous avons beaucoup de choses à faire.
*I know **that** we have a lot of things to do.*

Subject pronoun A pronoun that replaces the name or title of a person or thing, and acts as the subject of a verb.

Tu vas partir bientôt.
***You** are going to leave soon.*

Il arrive demain.
***He** arrives tomorrow.*

SUBJECT A noun or pronoun that performs the action of a verb and is often implied by the verb.

Marine va au supermarché.
***Marine** goes to the supermarket.*

Ils travaillent beaucoup.
***They** work a lot.*

Ces livres sont très chers.
***Those books** are very expensive.*

SUPERLATIVE A word or construction used with an adjective, adverb or a noun to express the highest or lowest degree of a specific quality among three or more people, places, or things.

Le cours de français est **le plus intéressant**.
*The French class is **the most interesting**.*

Romain est le garçon qui court **le moins rapidement**.
*Romain is the boy who runs **the least fast**.*

C'est son jardin qui a **le plus d'arbres**.
*It is her garden that has **the most trees**.*

TENSE A set of verb forms that indicates the time of an action or state: past, present, or future.

Compound tense A two-word tense made up of an auxiliary verb and a present or past participle. In French, there are two auxiliary verbs: **être** and **avoir**.

Le colis n'**est** pas encore **arrivé**.
*The package **has** not **arrived** yet.*

Elle **a réussi** son examen.
*She **has passed** her exam.*

Simple tense A tense expressed by a single verb form.

Timothée **jouait** au volley-ball pendant les vacances.
*Timothée **played** volleyball during his vacation.*

Joëlle **parlera** à sa mère demain.
*Joëlle **will speak** with her mom tomorrow.*

VERB A word that expresses actions or states-of-being.

Auxiliary verb A verb used with a present or past participle to form a compound tense. **Avoir** is the most commonly used auxiliary verb in French.

Les enfants **ont** vu les éléphants.
*The children **have** seen the elephants.*

J'espère que tu **as** mangé.
*I hope you **have** eaten.*

Reflexive verb A verb that describes an action performed by the subject on itself and is always used with a reflexive pronoun.

Je **me suis acheté** une voiture neuve.
*I **bought myself** a new car.*

Pierre et Adeline **se lèvent** très tôt.
*Pierre and Adeline **get (themselves) up** very early.*

Spelling-change verb A verb that undergoes a predictable change in spelling in the various conjugations.

acheter	→	e → è	nous achetons	j'achète
espérer	→	é → è	nous espérons	j'espère
appeler	→	l → ll	nous appelons	j'appelle
envoyer	→	y → i	nous envoyons	j'envoie
essayer	→	y → i	nous essayons	j'essaie/ j'essaye

Verb Conjugation Tables

The list of verbs below and the model verb tables that start on page A-17 show you how to conjugate the verbs that appear in **ESPACES**. Each verb in the list is followed by a model verb conjugated according to the same pattern. The number in parentheses indicates where in the verb tables you can find the conjugated forms of the model verb. For example, if you want to find out how to conjugate the verb **offrir**, look up number 31 to refer to its model verb, **ouvrir**. The phrase **p.c.** with **être** after a verb means that it is

conjugated with **être** in the **passé composé**. Reminder: All reflexive (pronominal) verbs use **être** as their auxiliary verb in the **passé composé**. The infinitives of reflexive verbs begin with **se** or **s'**.

In the tables you will find the infinitive, past participles, and all the forms of each model verb you have learned.

abolir like finir (2)
aborder like parler (1)
abriter like parler (1)
accepter like parler (1)
accompagner like parler (1)
accueillir like ouvrir (31)
acheter (7)
adorer like parler (1)
afficher like parler (1)
aider like parler (1)
aimer like parler (1)
aller (13); **p.c.** with **être**
allumer like parler (1)
améliorer like parler (1)
amener like acheter (7)
animer like parler (1)
apercevoir like recevoir (36)
appeler (8)
applaudir like finir (2)
apporter like parler (1)
apprendre like prendre (35)
arrêter like parler (1)
arriver like parler (1) *except* **p.c.** with **être**
assister like parler (1)

attacher like parler (1)
attendre like vendre (3)
attirer like parler (1)
avoir (4)
balayer like essayer (10)
bavarder like parler (1)
boire (15)
bricoler like parler (1)
bronzer like parler (1)
célébrer like préférer (12)
chanter like parler (1)
chasser like parler (1)
chercher like parler (1)
choisir like finir (2)
classer like parler (1)
commander like parler (1)
commencer (9)
composer like parler (1)
comprendre like prendre (35)
compter like parler (1)
conduire (16)
connaître (17)
consacrer like parler (1)
considérer like préférer (12)
construire like conduire (16)

continuer like parler (1)
courir (18)
coûter like parler (1)
couvrir like ouvrir (31)
croire (19)
cuisiner like parler (1)
danser like parler (1)
débarrasser like parler (1)
décider like parler (1)
découvrir like ouvrir (31)
décrire like écrire (22)
décrocher like parler (1)
déjeuner like parler (1)
demander like parler (1)
démarrer like parler (1)
déménager like manger (11)
démissionner like parler (1)
dépasser like parler (1)
dépendre like vendre (3)
dépenser like parler (1)
déposer like parler (1)
descendre like vendre (3) *except* **p.c.** with **être; p.c.** w/**avoir** if takes a direct object
désirer like parler (1)

dessiner like parler (1)
détester like parler (1)
détruire like conduire (16)
développer like parler (1)
devenir like venir (41); **p.c.** with **être**
devoir (20)
dîner like parler (1)
dire (21)
diriger like parler (1)
discuter like parler (1)
divorcer like commencer (9)
donner like parler (1)
dormir like partir (32) *except* **p.c.** with **avoir**
douter like parler (1)
durer like parler (1)
échapper like parler (1)
échouer like parler (1)
écouter like parler (1)
écrire (22)
effacer like commencer (9)
embaucher like parler (1)
emménager like manger (11)
emmener like acheter (7)
employer like essayer (10)

emprunter like parler (1)
enfermer like parler (1)
enfler like parler (1)
enlever like acheter (7)
enregistrer like parler (1)
enseigner like parler (1)
entendre like vendre (3)
entourer like parler (1)
entrer like parler (1)
except **p.c.** with **être**
entretenir like tenir (40)
envahir like finir (2)
envoyer like essayer (10)
épouser like parler (1)
espérer like préférer (12)
essayer (10)
essuyer like essayer (10)
éteindre (24)
éternuer like parler (1)
étrangler like parler (1)
être (5)
étudier like parler (1)
éviter like parler (1)
exiger like manger (11)
expliquer like parler (1)
explorer like parler (1)
faire (25)
falloir (26)
fermer like parler (1)
fêter like parler (1)
finir (2)
fonctionner like parler (1)
fonder like parler (1)
freiner like parler (1)
fréquenter like parler (1)
fumer like parler (1)
gagner like parler (1)
garder like parler (1)
garer like parler (1)
gaspiller like parler (1)
goûter like parler (1)
grossir like finir (2)
guérir like finir (2)
habiter like parler (1)
imprimer like parler (1)
indiquer like parler (1)
interdire like dire (21)

inviter like parler (1)
jeter like appeler (8)
jouer like parler (1)
laisser like parler (1)
laver like parler (1)
lire (27)
loger like manger (11)
louer like parler (1)
lutter like parler (1)
maigrir like finir (2)
maintenir like tenir (40)
manger (11)
marcher like parler (1)
mêler like préférer (12)
mener like parler (1)
mettre (28)
monter like parler (1)
except **p.c.** with **être**; **p.c.** w/**avoir** if takes a direct object
montrer like parler (1)
mourir (29); **p.c.** with **être**
nager like manger (11)
naître (30); **p.c.** with **être**
nettoyer like essayer (10)
noter like parler (1)
obtenir like tenir (40)
offrir like ouvrir (31)
organiser like parler (1)
oublier like parler (1)
ouvrir (31)
parler (1)
partager like manger (11)
partir (32); **p.c.** with **être**
passer like parler (1)
patienter like parler (1)
patiner like parler (1)
payer like essayer (10)
penser like parler (1)
perdre like vendre (3)
permettre like mettre (28)
pleuvoir (33)
plonger like manger (11)
polluer like parler (1)
porter like parler (1)
poser like parler (1)
posséder like préférer (12)

poster like parler (1)
pouvoir (34)
pratiquer like parler (1)
préférer (12)
prélever like parler (1)
prendre (35)
préparer like parler (1)
présenter like parler (1)
préserver like parler (1)
prêter like parler (1)
prévenir like tenir (40)
produire like conduire (16)
profiter like parler (1)
promettre like mettre (28)
proposer like parler (1)
protéger like préférer (12)
provenir like venir (41)
publier like parler (1)
quitter like parler (1)
raccrocher like parler (1)
ranger like manger (11)
réaliser like parler (1)
recevoir (36)
recommander like parler (1)
reconnaître like connaître (17)
recycler like parler (1)
réduire like conduire (16)
réfléchir like finir (2)
regarder like parler (1)
régner like préférer (12)
remplacer like parler (1)
remplir like finir (2)
rencontrer like parler (1)
rendre like vendre (3)
rentrer like parler (1)
except **p.c.** with **être**
renvoyer like essayer (10)
réparer like parler (1)
repasser like parler (1)
répéter like préférer (12)
repeupler like parler (1)
répondre like vendre (3)
réserver like parler (1)
rester like parler (1) *except* **p.c.** with **être**

retenir like tenir (40)
retirer like parler (1)
retourner like parler (1)
except **p.c.** with **être**
retrouver like parler (1)
réussir like finir (2)
revenir like venir (41); **p.c.** with **être**
revoir like voir (42)
rire (37)
rouler like parler (1)
salir like finir (2)
s'amuser like se laver (6)
s'asseoir (14)
sauvegarder like parler (1)
sauver like parler (1)
savoir (38)
se brosser like se laver (6)
se coiffer like se laver (6)
se composer like se laver (6)
se connecter like se laver (6)
se coucher like se laver (6)
se croiser like se laver (6)
se dépêcher like se laver (6)
se déplacer like se laver (6)
se déshabiller like se laver (6)
se détendre like vendre (3)
except **p.c.** with **être**
se disputer like se laver (6)
s'embrasser like se laver (6)
s'endormir like partir (32)
except **p.c.** with **être**
s'énerver like se laver (6)
s'ennuyer like essayer (10) *except* **p.c.** with **être**
s'excuser like se laver (6)
se fouler like se laver (6)
s'installer like se laver (6)
se laver (6)
se lever like se laver (6)

se maquiller like se laver (6)

se marier like se laver (6)

se promener like acheter (7) *except* **p.c.** with **être**

se rappeler like se laver (6)

se raser like se laver (6)

se rebeller like se laver (6)

se réconcilier like se laver (6)

se relever like se laver (6)

se reposer like se laver (6)

se réveiller like se laver (6)

servir like partir (32) *except* **p.c.** with **avoir**

se sécher like préférer (12) *except* **p.c.** with **être**

se souvenir like venir (41)

se tromper like se laver (6)

s'habiller like se laver (6)

sentir like partir (32) *except* **p.c.** with **avoir**

signer like parler (1)

s'inquiéter like préférer (12) *except* **p.c.** with **être**

s'intéresser like se laver (6)

skier like parler (1)

s'occuper like se laver (6)

sonner like parler (1)

s'orienter like se laver (6)

sortir like partir (32)

sourire like rire (37)

souffrir like ouvrir (31)

souhaiter like parler (1)

subvenir like venir (41) *except* **p.c.** with **avoir**

suffire like lire (27)

suggérer like préférer (12)

suivre (39)

surfer like parler (1)

surprendre like prendre (35)

télécharger like parler (1)

téléphoner like parler (1)

tenir (40)

tomber like parler (1) *except* **p.c.** with **être**

tourner like parler (1)

tousser like parler (1)

traduire like conduire (16)

travailler like parler (1)

traverser like parler (1)

trouver like parler (1)

tuer like parler (1)

utiliser like parler (1)

valoir like falloir (26)

vendre (3)

venir (41); **p.c.** with **être**

vérifier like parler (1)

visiter like parler (1)

vivre like suivre (39)

voir (42)

vouloir (43)

voyager like manger (11)

Regular verbs

Infinitive / Past participle	Subject Pronouns	INDICATIVE				CONDITIONAL	SUBJUNCTIVE	IMPERATIVE
		Present	Passé composé	Imperfect	Future	Present	Present	
1 parler (to speak) parlé	je (j')	parle	ai parlé	parlais	parlerai	parlerais	parle	
	tu	parles	as parlé	parlais	parleras	parlerais	parles	parle
	il/elle/on	parle	a parlé	parlait	parlera	parlerait	parle	
	nous	parlons	avons parlé	parlions	parlerons	parlerions	parlions	parlons
	vous	parlez	avez parlé	parliez	parlerez	parleriez	parliez	parlez
	ils/elles	parlent	ont parlé	parlaient	parleront	parleraient	parlent	
2 finir (to finish) fini	je (j')	finis	ai fini	finissais	finirai	finirais	finisse	
	tu	finis	as fini	finissais	finiras	finirais	finisses	finis
	il/elle/on	finit	a fini	finissait	finira	finirait	finisse	
	nous	finissons	avons fini	finissions	finirons	finirions	finissions	finissons
	vous	finissez	avez fini	finissiez	finirez	finiriez	finissiez	finissez
	ils/elles	finissent	ont fini	finissaient	finiront	finiraient	finissent	
3 vendre (to sell) vendu	je (j')	vends	ai vendu	vendais	vendrai	vendrais	vende	
	tu	vends	as vendu	vendais	vendras	vendrais	vendes	vends
	il/elle/on	vend	a vendu	vendait	vendra	vendrait	vende	
	nous	vendons	avons vendu	vendions	vendrons	vendrions	vendions	vendons
	vous	vendez	avez vendu	vendiez	vendrez	vendriez	vendiez	vendez
	ils/elles	vendent	ont vendu	vendaient	vendront	vendraient	vendent	

Auxiliary verbs: *avoir* and *être*

Infinitive / Past participle	Subject Pronouns	INDICATIVE Present	Passé composé	Imperfect	Future	CONDITIONAL Present	SUBJUNCTIVE Present	IMPERATIVE
4 avoir *(to have)* eu	j'	ai	ai eu	avais	aurai	aurais	aie	
	tu	as	as eu	avais	auras	aurais	aies	aie
	il/elle/on	a	a eu	avait	aura	aurait	ait	
	nous	avons	avons eu	avions	aurons	aurions	ayons	ayons
	vous	avez	avez eu	aviez	aurez	auriez	ayez	ayez
	ils/elles	ont	ont eu	avaient	auront	auraient	aient	
5 être *(to be)* été	je (j')	suis	ai été	étais	serai	serais	sois	
	tu	es	as été	étais	seras	serais	sois	sois
	il/elle/on	est	a été	était	sera	serait	soit	
	nous	sommes	avons été	étions	serons	serions	soyons	soyons
	vous	êtes	avez été	étiez	serez	seriez	soyez	soyez
	ils/elles	sont	ont été	étaient	seront	seraient	soient	

Reflexive (Pronominal)

Infinitive / Past participle	Subject Pronouns	INDICATIVE Present	Passé composé	Imperfect	Future	CONDITIONAL Present	SUBJUNCTIVE Present	IMPERATIVE
6 se laver *(to wash oneself)* lavé	je	me lave	me suis lavé(e)	me lavais	me laverai	me laverais	me lave	
	tu	te laves	t'es lavé(e)	te lavais	te laveras	te laverais	te laves	lave-toi
	il/elle/on	se lave	s'est lavé(e)	se lavait	se lavera	se laverait	se lave	
	nous	nous lavons	nous sommes lavé(e)s	nous lavions	nous laverons	nous laverions	nous lavions	lavons-nous
	vous	vous lavez	vous êtes lavé(e)s	vous laviez	vous laverez	vous laveriez	vous laviez	lavez-vous
	ils/elles	se lavent	se sont lavé(e)s	se lavaient	se laveront	se laveraient	se lavent	

Verbs with spelling changes

Infinitive Past participle	Subject Pronouns	INDICATIVE Present	Passé composé	Imperfect	Future	CONDITIONAL Present	SUBJUNCTIVE Present	IMPERATIVE
7 acheter (*to buy*) acheté	j'	achète	ai acheté	achetais	achèterai	achèterais	achète	
	tu	achètes	as acheté	achetais	achèteras	achèterais	achètes	achète
	il/elle/on	achète	a acheté	achetait	achètera	achèterait	achète	
	nous	achetons	avons acheté	achetions	achèterons	achèterions	achetions	achetons
	vous	achetez	avez acheté	achetiez	achèterez	achèteriez	achetiez	achetez
	ils/elles	achètent	ont acheté	achetaient	achèteront	achèteraient	achètent	
8 appeler (*to call*) appelé	j'	appelle	ai appelé	appelais	appellerai	appellerais	appelle	
	tu	appelles	as appelé	appelais	appelleras	appellerais	appelles	appelle
	il/elle/on	appelle	a appelé	appelait	appellera	appellerait	appelle	
	nous	appelons	avons appelé	appelions	appellerons	appellerions	appelions	appelons
	vous	appelez	avez appelé	appeliez	appellerez	appelleriez	appeliez	appelez
	ils/elles	appellent	ont appelé	appelaient	appelleront	appelleraient	appellent	
9 commencer (*to begin*) commencé	je (j')	commence	ai commencé	commençais	commencerai	commencerais	commence	
	tu	commences	as commencé	commençais	commenceras	commencerais	commences	commence
	il/elle/on	commence	a commencé	commençait	commencera	commencerait	commence	
	nous	commençons	avons commencé	commencions	commencerons	commencerions	commencions	commençons
	vous	commencez	avez commencé	commenciez	commencerez	commenceriez	commenciez	commencez
	ils/elles	commencent	ont commencé	commençaient	commenceront	commenceraient	commencent	
10 essayer (*to try*) essayé	j'	essaie	ai essayé	essayais	essaierai	essaierais	essaie	
	tu	essaies	as essayé	essayais	essaieras	essaierais	essaies	essaie
	il/elle/on	essaie	a essayé	essayait	essaiera	essaierait	essaie	
	nous	essayons	avons essayé	essayions	essaierons	essaierions	essayions	essayons
	vous	essayez	avez essayé	essayiez	essaierez	essaieriez	essayiez	essayez
	ils/elles	essayent	ont essayé	essayaient	essaieront	essaieraient	essaient	
11 manger (*to eat*) mangé	je (j')	mange	ai mangé	mangeais	mangerai	mangerais	mange	
	tu	manges	as mangé	mangeais	mangeras	mangerais	manges	mange
	il/elle/on	mange	a mangé	mangeait	mangera	mangerait	mange	
	nous	mangeons	avons mangé	mangions	mangerons	mangerions	mangions	mangeons
	vous	mangez	avez mangé	mangiez	mangerez	mangeriez	mangiez	mangez
	ils/elles	mangent	ont mangé	mangeaient	mangeront	mangeraient	mangent	

Infinitive / Past participle	Subject Pronouns	INDICATIVE Present	Passé composé	Imperfect	Future	CONDITIONAL Present	SUBJUNCTIVE Present	IMPERATIVE
12 préférer (to prefer) préféré	je (j')	préfère	ai préféré	préférais	préférerai	préférerais	préfère	
	tu	préfères	as préféré	préférais	préféreras	préférerais	préfères	préfère
	il/elle/on	préfère	a préféré	préférait	préférera	préférerait	préfère	
	nous	préférons	avons préféré	préférions	préférerons	préférerions	préférions	préférons
	vous	préférez	avez préféré	préfériez	préférerez	préféreriez	préfériez	préférez
	ils/elles	préfèrent	ont préféré	préféraient	préféreront	préféreraient	préfèrent	

Irregular verbs

Infinitive / Past participle	Subject Pronouns	INDICATIVE Present	Passé composé	Imperfect	Future	CONDITIONAL Present	SUBJUNCTIVE Present	IMPERATIVE
13 aller (to go) allé	je (j')	vais	suis allé(e)	allais	irai	irais	aille	
	tu	vas	es allé(e)	allais	iras	irais	ailles	va
	il/elle/on	va	est allé(e)	allait	ira	irait	aille	
	nous	allons	sommes allé(e)s	allions	irons	irions	allions	allons
	vous	allez	êtes allé(e)s	alliez	irez	iriez	alliez	allez
	ils/elles	vont	sont allé(e)s	allaient	iront	iraient	aillent	
14 s'asseoir (to sit down, to be seated) assis	je	m'assieds	me suis assis(e)	m'asseyais	m'assiérai	m'assiérais	m'asseye	
	tu	t'assieds	t'es assis(e)	t'asseyais	t'assiéras	t'assiérais	t'asseyes	assieds-toi
	il/elle/on	s'assied	s'est assis(e)	s'asseyait	s'assiéra	s'assiérait	s'asseye	
	nous	nous asseyons	nous sommes assis(e)s	nous asseyions	nous assiérons	nous assiérions	nous asseyions	asseyons-nous
	vous	vous asseyez	vous êtes assis(e)s	vous asseyiez	vous assiérez	vous assiériez	vous asseyiez	asseyez-vous
	ils/elles	s'asseyent	se sont assis(e)s	s'asseyaient	s'assiéront	s'assiéraient	s'asseyent	
15 boire (to drink) bu	je (j')	bois	ai bu	buvais	boirai	boirais	boive	
	tu	bois	as bu	buvais	boiras	boirais	boives	bois
	il/elle/on	boit	a bu	buvait	boira	boirait	boive	
	nous	buvons	avons bu	buvions	boirons	boirions	buvions	buvons
	vous	buvez	avez bu	buviez	boirez	boiriez	buviez	buvez
	ils/elles	boivent	ont bu	buvaient	boiront	boiraient	boivent	

Infinitive / Past participle	Subject Pronouns	INDICATIVE Present	Passé composé	Imperfect	Future	CONDITIONAL Present	SUBJUNCTIVE Present	IMPERATIVE
16 conduire (*to drive; to lead*) conduit	je (j')	conduis	ai conduit	conduisais	conduirai	conduirais	conduise	
	tu	conduis	as conduit	conduisais	conduiras	conduirais	conduises	conduis
	il/elle/on	conduit	a conduit	conduisait	conduira	conduirait	conduise	
	nous	conduisons	avons conduit	conduisions	conduirons	conduirions	conduisions	conduisons
	vous	conduisez	avez conduit	conduisiez	conduirez	conduiriez	conduisiez	conduisez
	ils/elles	conduisent	ont conduit	conduisaient	conduiront	conduiraient	conduisent	
17 connaître (*to know, to be acquainted with*) connu	je (j')	connais	ai connu	connaissais	connaîtrai	connaîtrais	connaisse	
	tu	connais	as connu	connaissais	connaîtras	connaîtrais	connaisses	connais
	il/elle/on	connaît	a connu	connaissait	connaîtra	connaîtrait	connaisse	
	nous	connaissons	avons connu	connaissions	connaîtrons	connaîtrions	connaissions	connaissons
	vous	connaissez	avez connu	connaissiez	connaîtrez	connaîtriez	connaissiez	connaissez
	ils/elles	connaissent	ont connu	connaissaient	connaîtront	connaîtraient	connaissent	
18 courir (*to run*) couru	je (j')	cours	ai couru	courais	courrai	courrais	coure	
	tu	cours	as couru	courais	courras	courrais	coures	cours
	il/elle/on	court	a couru	courait	courra	courrait	coure	
	nous	courons	avons couru	courions	courrons	courrions	courions	courons
	vous	courez	avez couru	couriez	courrez	courriez	couriez	courez
	ils/elles	courent	ont couru	couraient	courront	courraient	courent	
19 croire (*to believe*) cru	je (j')	crois	ai cru	croyais	croirai	croirais	croie	
	tu	crois	as cru	croyais	croiras	croirais	croies	crois
	il/elle/on	croit	a cru	croyait	croira	croirait	croie	
	nous	croyons	avons cru	croyions	croirons	croirions	croyions	croyons
	vous	croyez	avez cru	croyiez	croirez	croiriez	croyiez	croyez
	ils/elles	croient	ont cru	croyaient	croiront	croiraient	croient	
20 devoir (*to have to; to owe*) dû	je (j')	dois	ai dû	devais	devrai	devrais	doive	
	tu	dois	as dû	devais	devras	devrais	doives	dois
	il/elle/on	doit	a dû	devait	devra	devrait	doive	
	nous	devons	avons dû	devions	devrons	devrions	devions	devons
	vous	devez	avez dû	deviez	devrez	devriez	deviez	devez
	ils/elles	doivent	ont dû	devaient	devront	devraient	doivent	

		INDICATIVE				CONDITIONAL	SUBJUNCTIVE	IMPERATIVE
Infinitive / Past participle	Subject Pronouns	Present	Passé composé	Imperfect	Future	Present	Present	
21 dire (*to say, to tell*) / dit	je (j')	dis	ai dit	disais	dirai	dirais	dise	
	tu	dis	as dit	disais	diras	dirais	dises	dis
	il/elle/on	dit	a dit	disait	dira	dirait	dise	
	nous	disons	avons dit	disions	dirons	dirions	disions	disons
	vous	dites	avez dit	disiez	direz	diriez	disiez	dites
	ils/elles	disent	ont dit	disaient	diront	diraient	disent	
22 écrire (*to write*) / écrit	j'	écris	ai écrit	écrivais	écrirai	écrirais	écrive	
	tu	écris	as écrit	écrivais	écriras	écrirais	écrives	écris
	il/elle/on	écrit	a écrit	écrivait	écrira	écrirait	écrive	
	nous	écrivons	avons écrit	écrivions	écrirons	écririons	écrivions	écrivons
	vous	écrivez	avez écrit	écriviez	écrirez	écririez	écriviez	écrivez
	ils/elles	écrivent	ont écrit	écrivaient	écriront	écriraient	écrivent	
23 envoyer (*to send*) / envoyé	j'	envoie	ai envoyé	envoyais	enverrai	enverrais	envoie	
	tu	envoies	as envoyé	envoyais	enverras	enverrais	envoies	envoie
	il/elle/on	envoie	a envoyé	envoyait	enverra	enverrait	envoie	
	nous	envoyons	avons envoyé	envoyions	enverrons	enverrions	envoyions	envoyons
	vous	envoyez	avez envoyé	envoyiez	enverrez	enverriez	envoyiez	envoyez
	ils/elles	envoient	ont envoyé	envoyaient	enverront	enverraient	envoient	
24 éteindre (*to turn off*) / éteint	j'	éteins	ai éteint	éteignais	éteindrai	éteindrais	éteigne	
	tu	éteins	as éteint	éteignais	éteindras	éteindrais	éteignes	éteins
	il/elle/on	éteint	a éteint	éteignait	éteindra	éteindrait	éteigne	
	nous	éteignons	avons éteint	éteignions	éteindrons	éteindrions	éteignions	éteignons
	vous	éteignez	avez éteint	éteigniez	éteindrez	éteindriez	éteigniez	éteignez
	ils/elles	éteignent	ont éteint	éteignaient	éteindront	éteindraient	éteignent	
25 faire (*to do; to make*) / fait	je (j')	fais	ai fait	faisais	ferai	ferais	fasse	
	tu	fais	as fait	faisais	feras	ferais	fasses	fais
	il/elle/on	fait	a fait	faisait	fera	ferait	fasse	
	nous	faisons	avons fait	faisions	ferons	ferions	fassions	faisons
	vous	faites	avez fait	faisiez	ferez	feriez	fassiez	faites
	ils/elles	font	ont fait	faisaient	feront	feraient	fassent	
26 falloir (*to be necessary*) / fallu	il	faut	a fallu	fallait	faudra	faudrait	faille	

Infinitive / Past participle	Subject Pronouns	INDICATIVE Present	INDICATIVE Passé composé	INDICATIVE Imperfect	INDICATIVE Future	CONDITIONAL Present	SUBJUNCTIVE Present	IMPERATIVE
27 lire *(to read)* lu	je (j')	lis	ai lu	lisais	lirai	lirais	lise	
	tu	lis	as lu	lisais	liras	lirais	lises	lis
	il/elle/on	lit	a lu	lisait	lira	lirait	lise	
	nous	lisons	avons lu	lisions	lirons	lirions	lisions	lisons
	vous	lisez	avez lu	lisiez	lirez	liriez	lisiez	lisez
	ils/elles	lisent	ont lu	lisaient	liront	liraient	lisent	
28 mettre *(to put)* mis	je (j')	mets	ai mis	mettais	mettrai	mettrais	mette	
	tu	mets	as mis	mettais	mettras	mettrais	mettes	mets
	il/elle/on	met	a mis	mettait	mettra	mettrait	mette	
	nous	mettons	avons mis	mettions	mettrons	mettrions	mettions	mettons
	vous	mettez	avez mis	mettiez	mettrez	mettriez	mettiez	mettez
	ils/elles	mettent	ont mis	mettaient	mettront	mettraient	mettent	
29 mourir *(to die)* mort	je	meurs	suis mort(e)	mourais	mourrai	mourrais	meure	
	tu	meurs	es mort(e)	mourais	mourras	mourrais	meures	meurs
	il/elle/on	meurt	est mort(e)	mourait	mourra	mourrait	meure	
	nous	mourons	sommes mort(e)s	mourions	mourrons	mourrions	mourions	mourons
	vous	mourez	êtes mort(e)s	mouriez	mourrez	mourriez	mouriez	mourez
	ils/elles	meurent	sont mort(e)s	mouraient	mourront	mourraient	meurent	
30 naître *(to be born)* né	je	nais	suis né(e)	naissais	naîtrai	naîtrais	naisse	
	tu	nais	es né(e)	naissais	naîtras	naîtrais	naisses	nais
	il/elle/on	naît	est né(e)	naissait	naîtra	naîtrait	naisse	
	nous	naissons	sommes né(e)s	naissions	naîtrons	naîtrions	naissions	naissons
	vous	naissez	êtes né(e)s	naissiez	naîtrez	naîtriez	naissiez	naissez
	ils/elles	naissent	sont né(e)s	naissaient	naîtront	naîtraient	naissent	
31 ouvrir *(to open)* ouvert	j'	ouvre	ai ouvert	ouvrais	ouvrirai	ouvrirais	ouvre	
	tu	ouvres	as ouvert	ouvrais	ouvriras	ouvrirais	ouvres	ouvre
	il/elle/on	ouvre	a ouvert	ouvrait	ouvrira	ouvrirait	ouvre	
	nous	ouvrons	avons ouvert	ouvrions	ouvrirons	ouvririons	ouvrions	ouvrons
	vous	ouvrez	avez ouvert	ouvriez	ouvrirez	ouvririez	ouvriez	ouvrez
	ils/elles	ouvrent	ont ouvert	ouvraient	ouvriront	ouvriraient	ouvrent	

Infinitive / Past participle	Subject Pronouns	INDICATIVE Present	INDICATIVE Passé composé	INDICATIVE Imperfect	INDICATIVE Future	CONDITIONAL Present	SUBJUNCTIVE Present	IMPERATIVE
32 partir (to leave)	je	pars	suis parti(e)	partais	partirai	partirais	parte	
	tu	pars	es parti(e)	partais	partiras	partirais	partes	pars
parti	il/elle/on	part	est parti(e)	partait	partira	partirait	parte	
	nous	partons	sommes parti(e)s	partions	partirons	partirions	partions	partons
	vous	partez	êtes parti(e)(s)	partiez	partirez	partiriez	partiez	partez
	ils/elles	partent	sont parti(e)s	partaient	partiront	partiraient	partent	
33 pleuvoir (to rain)	il	pleut	a plu	pleuvait	pleuvra	pleuvrait	pleuve	
plu								
34 pouvoir (to be able)	je (j')	peux	ai pu	pouvais	pourrai	pourrais	puisse	
	tu	peux	as pu	pouvais	pourras	pourrais	puisses	
	il/elle/on	peut	a pu	pouvait	pourra	pourrait	puisse	
pu	nous	pouvons	avons pu	pouvions	pourrons	pourrions	puissions	
	vous	pouvez	avez pu	pouviez	pourrez	pourriez	puissiez	
	ils/elles	peuvent	ont pu	pouvaient	pourront	pourraient	puissent	
35 prendre (to take)	je (j')	prends	ai pris	prenais	prendrai	prendrais	prenne	
	tu	prends	as pris	prenais	prendras	prendrais	prennes	prends
	il/elle/on	prend	a pris	prenait	prendra	prendrait	prenne	
pris	nous	prenons	avons pris	prenions	prendrons	prendrions	prenions	prenons
	vous	prenez	avez pris	preniez	prendrez	prendriez	preniez	prenez
	ils/elles	prennent	ont pris	prenaient	prendront	prendraient	prennent	
36 recevoir (to receive)	je (j')	reçois	ai reçu	recevais	recevrai	recevrais	reçoive	
	tu	reçois	as reçu	recevais	recevras	recevrais	reçoives	reçois
	il/elle/on	reçoit	a reçu	recevait	recevra	recevrait	reçoive	
reçu	nous	recevons	avons reçu	recevions	recevrons	recevrions	recevions	recevons
	vous	recevez	avez reçu	receviez	recevrez	recevriez	receviez	recevez
	ils/elles	reçoivent	ont reçu	recevaient	recevront	recevraient	reçoivent	
37 rire (to laugh)	je (j')	ris	ai ri	riais	rirai	rirais	rie	
	tu	ris	as ri	riais	riras	rirais	ries	ris
	il/elle/on	rit	a ri	riait	rira	rirait	rie	
ri	nous	rions	avons ri	riions	rirons	ririons	riions	rions
	vous	riez	avez ri	riiez	rirez	ririez	riiez	riez
	ils/elles	rient	ont ri	riaient	riront	riraient	rient	

		INDICATIVE					CONDITIONAL	SUBJUNCTIVE	IMPERATIVE
Infinitive / Past participle	Subject Pronouns	Present	Passé composé	Imperfect	Future		Present	Present	

38 savoir (to know) / su

Subject Pronouns	Present	Passé composé	Imperfect	Future	Conditional Present	Subjunctive Present	Imperative
je (j')	sais	ai su	savais	saurai	saurais	sache	
tu	sais	as su	savais	sauras	saurais	saches	sache
il/elle/on	sait	a su	savait	saura	saurait	sache	
nous	savons	avons su	savions	saurons	saurions	sachions	sachons
vous	savez	avez su	saviez	saurez	sauriez	sachiez	sachez
ils/elles	savent	ont su	savaient	sauront	sauraient	sachent	

39 suivre (to follow) / suivi

Subject Pronouns	Present	Passé composé	Imperfect	Future	Conditional Present	Subjunctive Present	Imperative
je (j')	suis	ai suivi	suivais	suivrai	suivrais	suive	
tu	suis	as suivi	suivais	suivras	suivrais	suives	suis
il/elle/on	suit	a suivi	suivait	suivra	suivrait	suive	
nous	suivons	avons suivi	suivions	suivrons	suivrions	suivions	suivons
vous	suivez	avez suivi	suiviez	suivrez	suivriez	suiviez	suivez
ils/elles	suivent	ont suivi	suivaient	suivront	suivraient	suivent	

40 tenir (to hold) / tenu

Subject Pronouns	Present	Passé composé	Imperfect	Future	Conditional Present	Subjunctive Present	Imperative
je (j')	tiens	ai tenu	tenais	tiendrai	tiendrais	tienne	
tu	tiens	as tenu	tenais	tiendras	tiendrais	tiennes	tiens
il/elle/on	tient	a tenu	tenait	tiendra	tiendrait	tienne	
nous	tenons	avons tenu	tenions	tiendrons	tiendrions	tenions	tenons
vous	tenez	avez tenu	teniez	tiendrez	tiendriez	teniez	tenez
ils/elles	tiennent	ont tenu	tenaient	tiendront	tiendraient	tiennent	

41 venir (to come) / venu

Subject Pronouns	Present	Passé composé	Imperfect	Future	Conditional Present	Subjunctive Present	Imperative
je	viens	suis venu(e)	venais	viendrai	viendrais	vienne	
tu	viens	es venu(e)	venais	viendras	viendrais	viennes	viens
il/elle/on	vient	est venu(e)	venait	viendra	viendrait	vienne	
nous	venons	sommes venu(e)s	venions	viendrons	viendrions	venions	venons
vous	venez	êtes venu(e)(s)	veniez	viendrez	viendriez	veniez	venez
ils/elles	viennent	sont venu(e)s	venaient	viendront	viendraient	viennent	

42 voir (to see) / vu

Subject Pronouns	Present	Passé composé	Imperfect	Future	Conditional Present	Subjunctive Present	Imperative
je (j')	vois	ai vu	voyais	verrai	verrais	voie	
tu	vois	as vu	voyais	verras	verrais	voies	vois
il/elle/on	voit	a vu	voyait	verra	verrait	voie	
nous	voyons	avons vu	voyions	verrons	verrions	voyions	voyons
vous	voyez	avez vu	voyiez	verrez	verriez	voyiez	voyez
ils/elles	voient	ont vu	voyaient	verront	verraient	voient	

43 vouloir (to want, to wish) / voulu

Subject Pronouns	Present	Passé composé	Imperfect	Future	Conditional Present	Subjunctive Present	Imperative
je (j')	veux	ai voulu	voulais	voudrai	voudrais	veuille	
tu	veux	as voulu	voulais	voudras	voudrais	veuilles	veuille
il/elle/on	veut	a voulu	voulait	voudra	voudrait	veuille	
nous	voulons	avons voulu	voulions	voudrons	voudrions	voulions	veuillons
vous	voulez	avez voulu	vouliez	voudrez	voudriez	vouliez	veuillez
ils/elles	veulent	ont voulu	voulaient	voudront	voudraient	veuillent	

Guide to Vocabulary

Abbreviations used in this glossary

adj.	adjective	*form.*	formal	*p.p.*	past participle
adv.	adverb	*imp.*	imperative	*pl.*	plural
art.	article	*indef.*	indefinite	*poss.*	possessive
comp.	comparative	*interj.*	interjection	*prep.*	preposition
conj.	conjunction	*interr.*	interrogative	*pron.*	pronoun
def.	definite	*inv.*	invariable	*refl.*	reflexive
dem.	demonstrative	*i.o.*	indirect object	*rel.*	relative
disj.	disjunctive	*m.*	masculine	*sing.*	singular
d.o.	direct object	*n.*	noun	*sub.*	subject
f.	feminine	*obj.*	object	*super.*	superlative
fam.	familiar	*part.*	partitive	*v.*	verb

French-English

A

à *prep.* at; in; to 4
  À bientôt. See you soon. 1
  à condition que on the condition that, provided that 15
  à côté de *prep.* next to 3
  À demain. See you tomorrow. 1
  à droite (de) *prep.* to the right (of) 3
  à gauche (de) *prep.* to the left (of) 3
  à ... heure(s) at ... (o'clock) 4
  à la radio on the radio 15
  à la télé(vision) on television 15
  à l'étranger abroad, overseas 7
  à mi-temps half-time (*job*) 13
  à moins que unless 15
  à plein temps full-time (*job*) 13
  À plus tard. See you later. 1
  À quelle heure? What time?; When? 2
  À qui? To whom? 4
  À table! Let's eat! Food is on! 9
  à temps partiel part-time (*job*) 13
  À tout à l'heure. See you later. 1
  au bout (de) *prep.* at the end (of) 12
  au contraire on the contrary 15
  au fait *by the way* 3
  au printemps in the spring 5
  Au revoir. Good-bye. 1
  au secours help 11
  au sujet de on the subject of, about 14

abolir *v.* to abolish 14
absolument *adv.* absolutely 7
accident *m.* accident 11
  avoir un accident to have/to be in an accident 11
accompagner *v.* to accompany 12
acheter *v.* to buy 5
acteur *m.* actor 1
actif/active *adj.* active 3
activement *adv.* actively 7
actrice *f.* actress 1
addition *f.* check, bill 4
adieu farewell 14
adolescence *f.* adolescence 6
adorer *v.* to love 2
  J'adore... I love... 2
adresse *f.* address 12
aérobic *m.* aerobics 5
  faire de l'aérobic *v.* to do aerobics 5
aéroport *m.* airport 7
affaires *f., pl.* business 3
affiche *f.* poster 8
afficher *v.* to post 13
âge *m.* age 6
  âge adulte *m.* adulthood 6
agence de voyages *f.* travel agency 7
agent *m.* officer; agent 11
  agent de police *m.* police officer 11
  agent de voyages *m.* travel agent 7
  agent immobilier *m.* real estate agent 13
agréable *adj.* pleasant 1
agriculteur/agricultrice *m., f.* farmer 13
aider (à) *v.* to help (*to do something*) 5
aie (avoir) *imp. v.* have 7
ail *m.* garlic 9
aimer *v.* to like 2

aimer mieux to prefer 2
aimer que... to like that... 14
J'aime bien... I really like... 2
Je n'aime pas tellement... I don't like ... very much. 2
aîné(e) *adj.* elder 3
ajouter *v. to add* 11
  ajouter un(e) ami(e) to add a friend 11
algérien(ne) *adj.* Algerian 1
aliment *m.* food item; a food 9
Allemagne *f.* Germany 7
allemand(e) *adj.* German 1
aller *v.* to go 4
  aller à la pêche to go fishing 5
  aller aux urgences to go to the emergency room 10
  aller avec to go with 6
  aller-retour *adj.* round-trip 7
  billet aller-retour *m.* round-trip ticket 7
  Allons-y! Let's go! 2
  Ça va? What's up?; How are things? 1
  Comment allez-vous? *form.* How are you? 1
  Comment vas-tu? *fam.* How are you? 1
  Je m'en vais. I'm leaving. 8
  Je vais bien/mal. I am doing well/badly. 1
  J'y vais. I'm going/coming. 8
  Nous y allons. We're going/coming. 9
allergie *f.* allergy 10
Allez. Come on. 5
allô (*on the phone*) hello 1
allumer *v.* to turn on 11
alors *adv.* so, then; at that moment 2
améliorer *v.* to improve 13
amende *f.* fine 11
amener *v.* to bring (*someone*) 5

américain(e) *adj.* American 1
  football américain *m.*
  football 5
ami(e) *m., f.* friend 1
  petit(e) ami(e) *m., f.* boy-
  friend/girlfriend 1
amitié *f.* friendship 6
amour *m.* love 6
amoureux/amoureuse *adj.*
  in love 6
  **tomber amoureux/
  amoureuse** *v.* to fall in love 6
amusant(e) *adj.* fun 1
an *m.* year 2
ancien(ne) *adj.* ancient, old;
  former 15
ange *m.* angel 1
anglais(e) *adj.* English 1
angle *m.* corner 12
Angleterre *f.* England 7
animal *m.* animal 14
année *f.* year 2
  cette année this year 2
anniversaire *m.* birthday 5
  **C'est quand l'anniversaire
  de ... ?** When is ...'s
  birthday? 5
  **C'est quand ton/votre
  anniversaire?** When is your
  birthday? 5
annuler (une réservation) *v.*
  to cancel (a reservation) 7
anorak *m.* ski jacket, parka 6
antipathique *adj.* unpleasant 3
août *m.* August 5
apercevoir *v.* to see, to catch
  sight of 12
aperçu (apercevoir) *p.p.* seen,
  caught sight of 12
appareil *m.* (on the phone)
  telephone 13
  **appareil (électrique/
  ménager)** *m.* (electrical/
  household) appliance 8
  appareil photo (numérique)
  m. (digital) camera 11
  **C'est M./Mme/Mlle ... à
  l'appareil.** It's Mr./Mrs./
  Miss ... on the phone. 13
  Qui est à l'appareil? Who's
  calling, please? 13
appartement *m.* apartment 7
appeler *v.* to call 13
applaudir *v.* to applaud 15
applaudissement *m.*
  applause 15
apporter *v.* to bring, to carry
  (*something*) 4
apprendre (à) *v.* to teach; to
  learn (*to do something*) 4
appris (apprendre) *p.p., adj.*
  learned 6
après (que) *adv.* after 2

après-demain *adv.* day after
  tomorrow 2
après-midi *m.* afternoon 2
  cet après-midi this afternoon 2
  de l'après-midi in the afternoon 2
  demain après-midi *adv.*
  tomorrow afternoon 2
  hier après-midi *adv.* yesterday
  afternoon 7
arbre *m.* tree 14
architecte *m., f.* architect 3
architecture *f.* architecture 2
argent *m.* money 12
  dépenser de l'argent *v.* to
  spend money 4
  déposer de l'argent *v.* to
  deposit money 12
  retirer de l'argent *v.* to withdraw money 12
armoire *f.* armoire, wardrobe 8
arrêt d'autobus (de bus)
  m. bus stop 7
**arrêter (de faire quelque
  chose)** *v.* to stop (doing
  something) 11
arrivée *f.* arrival 7
arriver (à) *v.* to arrive; to manage
  (*to do something*) 2
art *m.* art 2
  beaux-arts *m., pl.* fine arts 15
artiste *m., f.* artist 3
ascenseur *m.* elevator 7
aspirateur *m.* vacuum cleaner 8
  passer l'aspirateur to
  vacuum 8
aspirine *f.* aspirin 10
Asseyez-vous! (s'asseoir) *imp.*
  v. Have a seat! 10
assez *adv.* (*before adjective or
  adverb*) pretty; quite 7
  assez (de) (*before noun*)
  enough (of) 4
  pas assez (de) not enough
  (of) 4
assiette *f.* plate 9
assis (s'asseoir) *p.p., adj.* (*used
  as past participle*) sat down;
  (*used as adjective*) sitting,
  seated 10
assister *v.* to attend 2
assurance (maladie/vie) *f.*
  (health/life) insurance 13
athlète *m., f.* athlete 3
attacher *v.* to attach 11
  **attacher sa ceinture de
  sécurité** to buckle one's
  seatbelt 11
attendre *v.* to wait 6
attention *f.* attention 5
  faire attention (à) *v.* to pay
  attention (to) 5

au (à + le) *prep.* to/at the 4
auberge de jeunesse *f.* youth
  hostel 7
aucun(e) *adj.* no; *pron.* none 10
  ne... aucun(e) none, not
  any 12
augmentation (de salaire) *f.*
  raise (in salary) 13
aujourd'hui *adv.* today 2
auquel (à + lequel) *pron., m.,
  sing.* which one 13
aussi *adv.* too, as well; as 1
  Moi aussi. Me too. 1
  aussi ... que (*used with an
  adjective*) as ... as 9
autant de ... que *adv.* (*used
  with noun to express quantity*)
  as much/as many ... as 14
auteur/femme auteur *m., f.*
  author 15
autobus *m.* bus 7
  arrêt d'autobus (de bus) *m.*
  bus stop 7
  prendre un autobus to take
  a bus 7
automne *m.* fall 5
  à l'automne in the fall 5
autoroute *f.* highway 11
autour (de) *prep.* around 12
autrefois *adv.* in the past 7
aux (à + les) to/at the 4
auxquelles (à + lesquelles)
  pron., f., pl. which ones 13
auxquels (à + lesquels) *pron.,
  m., pl.* which ones 13
avance *f.* advance 2
  en avance *adv.* early 2
avant (de/que) *adv.* before 7
avant-hier *adv.* day before
  yesterday 7
avec *prep.* with 1
  Avec qui? With whom? 4
aventure *f.* adventure 15
  film d'aventures *m.*
  adventure film 15
avenue *f.* avenue 12
avion *m.* airplane 7
  prendre un avion *v.* to take
  a plane 7
avocat(e) *m., f.* lawyer 3
avoir *v.* to have 2
  aie *imp. v.* have 2
  avoir besoin (de) to need
  (*something*) 2
  avoir chaud to be hot 2
  avoir de la chance to be
  lucky 2
  avoir envie (de) to feel like
  (*doing something*) 2
  avoir faim to be hungry 4
  avoir froid to be cold 2
  avoir honte (de) to be
  ashamed (of) 2

avoir mal to have an ache 10

avoir mal au cœur to feel nauseated 10

avoir peur (de/que) to be afraid (of/that) 2

avoir raison to be right 2

avoir soif to be thirsty 4

avoir sommeil to be sleepy 2

avoir tort to be wrong 2

avoir un accident to have/to be in an accident 11

avoir un compte bancaire to have a bank account 12

en avoir marre to be fed up 3

avril *m.* April 5

ayez (avoir) *imp. v.* have 7

ayons (avoir) *imp. v.* let's have 7

B

bac(calauréat) *m.* an important exam taken by high-school students in France 2

baguette *f.* baguette 4

baignoire *f.* bathtub 8

bain *m.* bath 6

  salle de bains *f.* bathroom 8

balai *m.* broom 8

balayer *v.* to sweep 8

balcon *m.* balcony 8

banane *f.* banana 9

banc *m.* bench 12

bancaire *adj.* banking 12

  avoir un compte bancaire *v.* to have a bank account 12

bande dessinée (B.D.) *f.* comic strip 5

banlieue *f.* suburbs 4

banque *f.* bank 12

banquier/banquière *m., f.* banker 13

barbant *adj.,* **barbe** *f.* drag 3

baseball *m.* baseball 5

basket(-ball) *m.* basketball 5

baskets *f., pl.* tennis shoes 6

bateau *m.* boat 7

  prendre un bateau *v.* to take a boat 7

bateau-mouche *m.* riverboat 7

bâtiment *m.* building 12

batterie *f.* drums 15

bavarder *v.* to chat 4

beau (belle) *adj.* handsome; beautiful 3

  faire quelque chose de beau *v.* to be up to something interesting 12

  Il fait beau. The weather is nice. 5

beaucoup (de) *adv.* a lot (of) 4

  Merci (beaucoup). Thank you (very much). 1

beau-frère *m.* brother-in-law 3

beau-père *m.* father-in-law; stepfather 3

beaux-arts *m., pl.* fine arts 15

belge *adj.* Belgian 7

Belgique *f.* Belgium 7

belle *adj., f. (feminine form of* **beau***)* beautiful 3

belle-mère *f.* mother-in-law; stepmother 3

belle-sœur *f.* sister-in-law 3

besoin *m.* need 2

  avoir besoin (de) to need (*something*) 2

beurre *m.* butter 4

bibliothèque *f.* library 1

bien *adv.* well 7

  bien sûr *adv.* of course 2

  Je vais bien. I am doing well. 1

  Très bien. Very well. 1

bientôt *adv.* soon 1

  À bientôt. See you soon. 1

bienvenu(e) *adj.* welcome 1

bière *f.* beer 6

bijouterie *f.* jewelry store 12

billet *m. (travel)* ticket 7; *(money)* bills, notes 12

  billet aller-retour *m.* round-trip ticket 7

biologie *f.* biology 2

biscuit *m.* cookie 6

blague *f.* joke 2

blanc(he) *adj.* white 6

blessure *f.* injury, wound 10

bleu(e) *adj.* blue 3

blond(e) *adj.* blonde 3

blouson *m.* jacket 6

bœuf *m.* beef 9

boire *v.* to drink 4

bois *m.* wood 14

boisson (gazeuse) *f.* (carbonated) drink/beverage 4

boîte *f.* box; can 9

  boîte aux lettres *f.* mailbox 12

  boîte de conserve *f.* can (of food) 9

  boîte de nuit *f.* nightclub 4

bol *m.* bowl 9

bon(ne) *adj.* kind; good 3

  bon marché *adj.* inexpensive 6

  Il fait bon. The weather is good/warm. 5

bonbon *m.* candy 6

bonheur *m.* happiness 6

Bonjour. Good morning.; Hello. 1

Bonsoir. Good evening.; Hello. 1

bouche *f.* mouth 10

boucherie *f.* butcher's shop 9

boulangerie *f.* bread shop, bakery 9

boulevard *m.* boulevard 12

  suivre un boulevard *v.* to follow a boulevard 12

bourse *f.* scholarship, grant 2

bout *m.* end 12

  au bout (de) *prep.* at the end (of) 12

bouteille (de) *f.* bottle (of) 4

boutique *f.* boutique, store 12

brancher *v.* to plug in 11

bras *m.* arm 10

brasserie *f.* café; restaurant 12

Brésil *m.* Brazil 7

brésilien(ne) *adj.* Brazilian 7

bricoler *v.* to tinker; to do odd jobs 5

brillant(e) *adj.* bright 1

bronzer *v.* to tan 6

brosse (à cheveux/à dents) *f.* (hair/tooth)brush 10

brun(e) *adj. (hair)* dark 3

bu (boire) *p.p.* drunk 6

bureau *m.* desk; office 1

  bureau de poste *m.* post office 12

bus *m.* bus 7

  arrêt d'autobus (de bus) *m.* bus stop 7

  prendre un bus *v.* to take a bus 7

C

ça *pron.* that; this; it 1

  Ça dépend. It depends. 4

  Ça ne nous regarde pas. That has nothing to do with us.; That is none of our business. 14

  Ça suffit. That's enough. 5

  Ça te dit? Does that appeal to you? 14

  Ça va? What's up?; How are things? 1

  ça veut dire that is to say 10

  Comme ci, comme ça. So-so. 1

cabine téléphonique *f.* phone booth 12

cadeau *m.* gift 6

  paquet cadeau wrapped gift 6

cadet(te) *adj.* younger 3

cadre/femme cadre *m., f.* executive 13

café *m.* café; coffee 1

  terrasse de café *f.* café terrace 4

  cuillère à café *f.* teaspoon 9

cafetière *f.* coffeemaker 8

cahier *m.* notebook 1

calculatrice *f.* calculator 1

calme *adj.* calm 1; *m.* calm 1

camarade *m., f.* friend 1

  camarade de chambre *m., f.* roommate 1

  camarade de classe *m., f.* classmate 1

campagne *f.* country(side) 7

pain de campagne *m.* country-style bread 4

pâté (de campagne) *m.* pâté, meat spread 9

camping *m.* camping 5

  faire du camping *v.* to go camping 5

Canada *m.* Canada 7

canadien(ne) *adj.* Canadian 1

canapé *m.* couch 8

candidat(e) *m., f.* candidate; applicant 13

cantine *f.* (school) cafeteria 9

capitale *f.* capital 7

capot *m.* hood 11

carafe (d'eau) *f.* pitcher (of water) 9

carotte *f.* carrot 9

carrefour *m.* intersection 12

carrière *f.* career 13

carte *f.* map 1; menu 9; card 12

  payer avec une carte de crédit to pay with a credit card 12

  carte postale *f.* postcard 12

  cartes *f. pl.* (*playing*) cards 5

casquette *f.* (baseball) cap 6

catastrophe *f.* catastrophe 14

cave *f.* basement, cellar 8

CD *m.* CD(s) 11

ce *dem. adj., m., sing.* this; that 6

  ce matin this morning 2

  ce mois-ci this month 2

  Ce n'est pas grave. It's no big deal. 6

  ce soir this evening 2

  ce sont... those are... 1

  ce week-end this weekend 2

ceinture *f.* belt 6

  attacher sa ceinture de sécurité *v.* to buckle one's seatbelt 11

célèbre *adj.* famous 15

célébrer *v.* to celebrate 5

célibataire *adj.* single 3

celle *pron., f., sing.* this one; that one; the one 14

celles *pron., f., pl.* these; those; the ones 14

celui *pron., m., sing.* this one; that one; the one 14

cent *m.* one hundred 3

  cent mille *m.* one hundred thousand 5

  cent un *m.* one hundred one 5

  cinq cents *m.* five hundred 5

centième *adj.* hundredth 7

centrale nucléaire *f.* nuclear plant 14

centre commercial *m.* shopping center, mall 4

centre-ville *m.* city/town center,
downtown 4

certain(e) *adj.* certain 9

  Il est certain que... It is certain that... 15

  Il n'est pas certain que... It is uncertain that... 15

ces *dem. adj., m., f., pl.* these; those 6

c'est... it/that is... 1

  C'est de la part de qui? On behalf of whom? 13

  C'est le 1er (premier) octobre. It is October first. 5

  C'est M./Mme/Mlle ... (à l'appareil). It's Mr./Mrs./Miss ... (on the phone). 13

  C'est quand l'anniversaire de... ? When is ...'s birthday? 5

  C'est quand ton/votre anniversaire? When is your birthday? 5

  Qu'est-ce que c'est? What is it? 1

cet *dem. adj., m., sing.* this; that 6

  cet après-midi this afternoon 2

cette *dem. adj., f., sing.* this; that 6

  cette année this year 2

  cette semaine this week 2

ceux *pron., m., pl.* these; those; the ones 14

chaîne (de télévision) *f.* (television) channel 11

chaîne stéréo *f.* stereo system 11

chaise *f.* chair 1

chambre *f.* bedroom 8

  chambre (individuelle) *f.* (single) room 7

  camarade de chambre *m., f.* roommate 1

champ *m.* field 14

champagne *m.* champagne 6

champignon *m.* mushroom 9

chance *f.* luck 2

  avoir de la chance *v.* to be lucky 2

chanson *f.* song 15

chanter *v.* to sing 5

chanteur/chanteuse *m., f.* singer 1

chapeau *m.* hat 6

chaque *adj.* each 6

charcuterie *f.* delicatessen 9

charmant(e) *adj.* charming 1

chasse *f.* hunt 14

chasser *v.* to hunt 14

chat *m.* cat 3

châtain *adj.* (*hair*) brown 3

chaud *m.* heat 2

  avoir chaud *v.* to be hot 2

  Il fait chaud. (*weather*) It is
hot. 5

chauffeur de taxi/de camion *m.* taxi/truck driver 13

chaussette *f.* sock 6

chaussure *f.* shoe 6

chef d'entreprise *m.* head of a company 13

chef-d'œuvre *m.* masterpiece 15

chemin *m.* path; way 12

  suivre un chemin *v.* to follow a path 12

chemise (à manches courtes/ longues) *f.* (short-/long-sleeved) shirt 6

chemisier *m.* blouse 6

chèque *m.* check 12

  compte-chèques *m.* checking account 12

  payer par chèque *v.* to pay by check 12

cher/chère *adj.* expensive 6

chercher *v.* to look for 2

  chercher un/du travail to look for work 12

chercheur/chercheuse *m., f.* researcher 13

chéri(e) *adj.* dear, beloved, darling 2

cheval *m.* horse 5

  faire du cheval *v.* to go horseback riding 5

cheveux *m., pl.* hair 9

  brosse à cheveux *f.* hairbrush 10

  cheveux blonds blond hair 3

  cheveux châtains brown hair 3

  se brosser les cheveux *v.* to brush one's hair 9

cheville *f.* ankle 10

  se fouler la cheville *v.* to twist/sprain one's ankle 10

chez *prep.* at (*someone's*) house 3, at (*a place*) 3

  passer chez quelqu'un *v.* to stop by someone's house 4

chic *adj.* chic 4

chien *m.* dog 3

chimie *f.* chemistry 2

Chine *f.* China 7

chinois(e) *adj.* Chinese 7

chocolat (chaud) *m.* (hot) chocolate 4

chœur *m.* choir, chorus 15

choisir *v.* to choose 4

chômage *m.* unemployment 13

  être au chômage *v.* to be unemployed 13

chômeur/chômeuse *m., f.* unemployed person 13

chose *f.* thing 1

  quelque chose *m.* something;

anything 4

chrysanthèmes *m., pl.* chrysanthemums 9

chut shh 15

-ci *(used with demonstrative adjective* **ce** *and noun or with demonstrative pronoun* **celui)** here 6

ce mois-ci this month 2

ciel *m.* sky 14

cinéma (ciné) *m.* movie theater, movies 4

cinq *m.* five 1

cinquante *m.* fifty 1

cinquième *adj.* fifth 7

circulation *f.* traffic 11

clair(e) *adj.* clear 15

Il est clair que... It is clear that... 15

classe *f.* (*group of students*) class 1

camarade de classe *m., f.* classmate 1

salle de classe *f.* classroom 1

clavier *m.* keyboard 11

clé *f.* key 7

clé USB *f.* USB drive 11

client(e) *m., f.* client; guest 7

cœur *m.* heart 10

avoir mal au cœur to feel nauseated 10

coffre *m.* trunk 11

coiffeur/coiffeuse *m., f.* hairdresser 3

coin *m.* corner 12

colis *m.* package 12

colocataire *m., f.* roommate (*in an apartment*) 1

Combien (de)... ? *adv.* How much/many... ? 1

Combien coûte... ? How much is... ? 4

combiné *m.* receiver 13

comédie (musicale) *f.* comedy (musical) 15

commander *v.* to order 9

comme *adv.* how; like, as 2

Comme ci, comme ça. So-so. 1

commencer (à) *v.* to begin (*to do something*) 2

comment *adv.* how 4

Comment? *adv.* What? 4

Comment allez-vous?, *form.* How are you? 1

Comment t'appelles-tu? *fam.* What is your name? 1

Comment vas-tu? *fam.* How are you? 1

Comment vous appelez-vous? *form.* What is your name? 1

commerçant(e) *m., f.* shop-

keeper 9

commissariat de police *m.* police station 12

commode *f.* dresser, chest of drawers 8

compact disque *m.* compact disc 11

complet (complète) *adj.* full (no vacancies) 7

composer (un numéro) *v.* to dial (a number) 11

compositeur *m.* composer 15

comprendre *v.* to understand 4

compris (comprendre) *p.p., adj.* understood; included 6

comptable *m., f.* accountant 13

compte *m.* account (*at a bank*) 12

avoir un compte bancaire *v.* to have a bank account 12

compte de chèques *m.* checking account 12

compte d'épargne *m.* savings account 12

se rendre compte *v.* to realize 10

compter sur quelqu'un *v.* to count on someone 8

concert *m.* concert 15

condition *f.* condition 15

à condition que on the condition that..., provided that... 15

conduire *v.* to drive 6

conduit (conduire) *p.p., adj.* driven 6

confiture *f.* jam 9

congé *m.* day off 7

jour de congé *m.* day off 7

prendre un congé *v.* to take time off 13

congélateur *m.* freezer 8

connaissance *f.* acquaintance 5

faire la connaissance de *v.* to meet (*someone*) 5

connaître *v.* to know, to be familiar with 8

connecté(e) *adj.* connected 11

être connecté(e) avec quelqu'un *v.* to be online with someone 7, 11

connu (connaître) *p.p., adj.* known; famous 8

conseil *m.* advice 13

conseiller/conseillère *m., f.* consultant; advisor 13

considérer *v.* to consider 5

constamment *adv.* constantly 7

construire *v.* to build, to construct 6

conte *m.* tale 15

content(e) *adj.* happy 13

être content(e) que... *v.* to be happy that... 14

continuer (à) *v.* to continue (*doing something*) 12

contraire *adj.* contrary 15

au contraire on the contrary 15

copain/copine *m., f.* friend 1

corbeille (à papier) *f.* wastebasket 1

corps *m.* body 10

costume *m.* (*man's*) suit 6

côte *f.* coast 14

coton *m.* cotton 12

cou *m.* neck 10

couche d'ozone *f.* ozone layer 14

trou dans la couche d'ozone *m.* hole in the ozone layer 14

couleur *f.* color 6

De quelle couleur... ? What color... ? 6

couloir *m.* hallway 8

couple *m.* couple 6

courage *m.* courage 13

courageux/courageuse *adj.* courageous, brave 3

couramment *adv.* fluently 7

courir *v.* to run 5

courrier *m.* mail 12

cours *m.* class, course 2

course *f.* errand 9

faire les courses *v.* to go (grocery) shopping 9

court(e) *adj.* short 3

chemise à manches courtes *f.* short-sleeved shirt 6

couru (courir) *p.p.* run 6

cousin(e) *m., f.* cousin 3

couteau *m.* knife 9

coûter *v.* to cost 4

Combien coûte... ? How much is... ? 4

couvert (couvrir) *p.p.* covered 11

couverture *f.* blanket 8

couvrir *v.* to cover 11

covoiturage *m.* carpooling 14

cravate *f.* tie 6

crayon *m.* pencil 1

crème *f.* cream 9

crème à raser *f.* shaving cream 10

crêpe *f.* crêpe 5

crevé(e) *adj.* deflated; blown up 11

pneu crevé *m.* flat tire 11

critique *f.* review; criticism 15

croire (que) *v.* to believe (that) 12

ne pas croire que... to not believe that... 15

croissant *m.* croissant 4

croissant(e) *adj.* growing 14

population croissante *f.* growing population 14

cru (croire) *p.p.* believed 15

cruel/cruelle *adj.* cruel 3

cuillère (à soupe/à café) *f.* (soup/tea)spoon 9
cuir *m.* leather 12
cuisine *f.* cooking; kitchen 5
  faire la cuisine *v.* to cook 5
cuisiner *v.* to cook 9
cuisinier/cuisinière *m., f.* cook 13
cuisinière *f.* stove 8
curieux/curieuse *adj.* curious 3
curriculum vitæ (C.V.) *m.* résumé 13
cybercafé *m.* cybercafé 12

D

d'abord *adv.* first 7
d'accord *(tag question)* all right? 2; *(in statement)* okay 2
  être d'accord to be in agreement 2
d'autres *m., f.* others 4
d'habitude *adv.* usually 7
danger *m.* danger, threat 14
dangereux/dangereuse *adj.* dangerous 11
dans *prep.* in 3
danse *f.* dance 15
danser *v.* to dance 4
danseur/danseuse *m., f.* dancer 15
date *f.* date 5
  Quelle est la date? What is the date? 5
de/d' *prep.* of 3; from 1
  de l'après-midi in the afternoon 2
  de laquelle *pron., f., sing.* which one 13
  De quelle couleur... ? What color... ? 6
  De rien. You're welcome. 1
  de taille moyenne of medium height 3
  de temps en temps *adv.* from time to time 7
débarrasser la table *v.* to clear the table 8
déboisement *m.* deforestation 14
début *m.* beginning; debut 15
décembre *m.* December 5
déchets toxiques *m., pl.* toxic waste 14
décider (de) *v.* to decide (*to do something*) 11
découvert (découvrir) *p.p.* discovered 11
découvrir *v.* to discover 11
décrire *v.* to describe 7
décrocher *v.* to pick up 13
décrit (décrire) *p.p., adj.* described 7
degrés *m., pl. (temperature)* degrees 5
  Il fait ... degrés. *(to describe weather)* It is ... degrees. 5
déjà *adv.* already 5

déjeuner *m.* lunch 9; *v.* to eat lunch 4
de l' *part. art., m., f., sing.* some 4
de la *part. art., f., sing.* some 4
délicieux/délicieuse delicious 8
demain *adv.* tomorrow 2
  À demain. See you tomorrow. 1
  après-demain *adv.* day after tomorrow 2
  demain matin/après-midi/ soir *adv.* tomorrow morning/ afternoon/evening 2
demander (à) *v.* to ask (*someone*), to make a request (*of someone*) 6
  demander que... *v.* to ask that... 14
démarrer *v.* to start up 11
déménager *v.* to move out 8
demie half 2
  et demie half past ... (o'clock) 2
demi-frère *m.* half-brother, stepbrother 3
demi-sœur *f.* half-sister, stepsister 3
démissionner *v.* to resign 13
dent *f.* tooth 9
  brosse à dents *f.* toothbrush 10
  se brosser les dents *v.* to brush one's teeth 9
dentifrice *m.* toothpaste 10
dentiste *m., f.* dentist 3
départ *m.* departure 7
dépasser *v.* to go over; to pass 11
dépense *f.* expenditure, expense 12
dépenser *v.* to spend 4
  dépenser de l'argent *v.* to spend money 4
déposer de l'argent *v.* to deposit money 12
déprimé(e) *adj.* depressed 10
depuis *adv.* since; for 9
dernier/dernière *adj.* last 2
dernièrement *adv.* lastly, finally 7
derrière *prep.* behind 3
des *part. art., m., f., pl.* some 4
des (de + les) *m., f., pl.* of the 3
dès que *adv.* as soon as 13
désagréable *adj.* unpleasant 1
descendre (de) *v.* to go downstairs; to get off; to take down 6
désert *m.* desert 14
désirer (que) *v.* to want (that) 5

désolé(e) *adj.* sorry 6
  être désolé(e) que... to be sorry that... 14
desquelles (de + lesquelles) *pron., f., pl.* which ones 13
desquels (de + lesquels) *pron., m., pl.* which ones 13
dessert *m.* dessert 6
dessin animé *m.* cartoon 15
dessiner *v.* to draw 2
détester *v.* to hate 2
  Je déteste... I hate... 2
détruire *v.* to destroy 6
détruit (détruire) *p.p., adj.* destroyed 6
deux *m.* two 1
deuxième *adj.* second 7
devant *prep.* in front of 3
développer *v.* to develop 14
devenir *v.* to become 9
devoir *m.* homework 2; *v.* to have to, must 9
dictionnaire *m.* dictionary 1
différemment *adv.* differently 7
différence *f.* difference 1
différent(e) *adj.* different 1
difficile *adj.* difficult 1
dimanche *m.* Sunday 2
dîner *m.* dinner 9; *v.* to have dinner 2
diplôme *m.* diploma, degree 2
dire *v.* to say 7
  Ça te dit? Does that appeal to you? 14
  ça veut dire that is to say 10
  veut dire *v.* means, signifies 9
diriger *v.* to manage 13
discret/discrète *adj.* discreet; unassuming 3
discuter *v.* discuss 6
disque *m.* disk 11
  compact disque *m.* compact disc 11
  disque dur *m.* hard drive 11
dissertation *f.* essay 11
distributeur automatique/de billets *m.* ATM 12
dit (dire) *p.p., adj.* said 7
divorce *m.* divorce 6
divorcé(e) *adj.* divorced 3
divorcer *v.* to divorce 3
dix *m.* ten 1
dix-huit *m.* eighteen 1
dixième *adj.* tenth 7
dix-neuf *m.* nineteen 1
dix-sept *m.* seventeen 1
documentaire *m.* documentary 15
doigt *m.* finger 10
doigt de pied *m.* toe 10
domaine *m.* field 13
dommage *m.* harm 14
  Il est dommage que... It's a

shame that… 14
donc *conj.* therefore 7
donner (à) *v.* to give (*to someone*) 2

dont *rel. pron.* of which; of whom; that 13
dormir *v.* to sleep 5
dos *m.* back 10
  sac à dos *m.* backpack 1
douane *f.* customs 7
douche *f.* shower 8
  prendre une douche *v.* to take a shower 10
doué(e) *adj.* talented, gifted 15
douleur *f.* pain 10
douter (que) *v.* to doubt (that) 15
douteux/douteuse *adj.* doubtful 15
  Il est douteux que… It is doubtful that… 15
doux/douce *adj.* sweet; soft 3
douze *m.* twelve 1
dramaturge *m.* playwright 15
drame (psychologique) *m.* (psychological) drama 15
draps *m., pl.* sheets 8
droit *m.* law 2
droite *f.* the right (side) 3
  à droite de *prep.* to the right of 3
drôle *adj.* funny 3
du *part. art., m., sing.* some 4
du (de + le) *m., sing.* of the 3
dû (devoir) *p.p., adj. (used with infinitive)* had to; *(used with noun)* due, owed 9
duquel (de + lequel) *pron., m., sing.* which one 13

E

eau (minérale) *f.* (mineral) water 4
  carafe d'eau *f.* pitcher of water 9
écharpe *f.* scarf 6
échecs *m., pl.* chess 5
échouer *v.* to fail 2
éclair *m.* éclair 4
école *f.* school 2
écologie *f.* ecology 14
écologique *adj.* ecological 14
économie *f.* economics 2
écotourisme *m.* ecotourism 14
écouter *v.* to listen (to) 2
écouteurs *m.* headphones 11
écran *m.* screen 11
écrire *v.* to write 7
écrivain/écrivaine *m., f.* writer 15
écrit (écrire) *p.p., adj.* written 7
écureuil *m.* squirrel 14

éducation physique *f.* physical education 2
effacer *v.* to erase 11
effet de serre *m.* greenhouse effect 14
égaler *v.* to equal 3
église *f.* church 4
égoïste *adj.* selfish 1
Eh! *interj.* Hey! 2
électrique *adj.* electric 8
  appareil électrique/ménager *m.* electrical/household appliance 8
électricien/électricienne *m., f.* electrician 13
élégant(e) *adj.* elegant 1
élevé *adj.* high 13
élève *m., f.* pupil, student 1
elle *pron., f.* she; it 1; her 3
  elle est… she/it is… 1
elles *pron., f.* they 1; them 3
  elles sont… they are… 1
e-mail *m.* e-mail 11
emballage (en plastique) *m.* (plastic) wrapping/packaging 14
embaucher *v.* to hire 13
embrayage *m. (automobile)* clutch 11
émission (de télévision) *f.* (television) program 15
emménager *v.* to move in 8
emmener *v.* to take (*someone*) 5
emploi *m.* job 13
  emploi à mi-temps/à temps partiel *m.* part-time job 13
  emploi à plein temps *m.* full-time job 13
employé(e) *m., f.* employee 25
employer *v.* to use, to employ 5
emprunter *v.* to borrow 12
en *prep.* in 3
  en automne in the fall 5
  en avance early 2
  en avoir marre to be fed up 6
  en effet indeed; in fact 14
  en été in the summer 5
  en face (de) *prep.* facing, across (from) 3
  en fait in fact 7
  en général *adv.* in general 7
  en hiver in the winter 5
  en plein air in fresh air 14
  en retard late 2
  en tout cas in any case 6
  en vacances on vacation 7
  être en ligne to be online 11
en *pron.* some of it/them; about it/them; of it/them; from it/them 10
  Je vous en prie. *form.* Please.; You're welcome. 1
  Qu'en penses-tu? What do you think about that? 14

enceinte *adj.* pregnant 10
Enchanté(e). Delighted. 1
encore *adv.* again; still 3
endroit *m.* place 4

énergie (nucléaire/solaire) *f.* (nuclear/solar) energy 14
enfance *f.* childhood 6
enfant *m., f.* child 3
enfin *adv.* finally, at last 7
enfler *v.* to swell 10
enlever la poussière *v.* to dust 8
ennuyeux/ennuyeuse *adj.* boring 3
énorme *adj.* enormous, huge 2
enregistrer *v.* to record 11
enregistreur DVR *m.* DVR 11
enseigner *v.* to teach 2
ensemble *adv.* together 6
ensuite *adv.* then, next 7
entendre *v.* to hear 6
entracte *m.* intermission 15
entre *prep.* between 3
entrée *f.* appetizer, starter 9
entreprise *f.* firm, business 13
entrer *v.* to enter 7
entretien: passer un entretien *to have an interview* 13
enveloppe *f.* envelope 12
envie *f.* desire, envy 2
  avoir envie (de) to feel like (*doing something*) 2
environnement *m.* environment 14
envoyer (à) *v.* to send (*to someone*) 5
épargne *f.* savings 12
  compte d'épargne *m.* savings account 12
épicerie *f.* grocery store 4
épouser *v.* to marry 3
épouvantable *adj.* dreadful 5
  Il fait un temps épouvantable. The weather is dreadful. 5
époux/épouse *m., f.* husband/wife 3
équipe *f.* team 5
escalier *m.* staircase 8
escargot *m.* escargot, snail 9
espace *m.* space 14
Espagne *f.* Spain 7
espagnol(e) *adj.* Spanish 1
espèce (menacée) *f.* (endangered) species 14
espérer *v.* to hope 5
essayer *v.* to try 5
essence *f.* gas 11
  réservoir d'essence *m.* gas tank 11
  voyant d'essence *m.* gas warning light 11

essentiel(le) *adj.* essential 14
  Il est essentiel que... It is essential that... 14
essuie-glace *m.* **(essuie-glaces** *pl.*) windshield wiper(s) 11
essuyer (la vaiselle/la table) *v.* to wipe (the dishes/the table) 8
est *m.* east 12
Est-ce que... ? *(used in forming questions)* 2
et *conj.* and 1
  Et toi? *fam.* And you? 1
  Et vous? *form.* And you? 1
étage *m.* floor 7
étagère *f.* shelf 8
étape *f.* stage 6
état civil *m.* marital status 6
États-Unis *m., pl.* United States 7
été *m.* summer 5
  en été in the summer 5
été (être) *p.p.* been 6
éteindre *v.* to turn off 11
éternuer *v.* to sneeze 10
étoile *f.* star 14
étranger/étrangère *adj.* foreign 2
  langues étrangères *f., pl.* foreign languages 2
étranger *m.* *(places that are)* abroad, overseas 7
  à l'étranger abroad, overseas 7
étrangler *v.* to strangle 13
être *v.* to be 1
  être bien/mal payé(e) to be well/badly paid 13
  être connecté(e) avec quelqu'un to be online with someone 7, 11
  être en ligne avec to be online with 11
  être en pleine forme to be in good shape 10
études (supérieures) *f., pl.* studies; (higher) education 2
étudiant(e) *m., f.* student 1
étudier *v.* to study 2
eu (avoir) *p.p.* had 6
eux *disj. pron., m., pl.* they, them 3
évidemment *adv.* obviously, evidently; of course 7
évident(e) *adj.* evident, obvious 15
  Il est évident que... It is evident that... 15
évier *m.* sink 8
éviter (de) *v.* to avoid *(doing something)* 10
exactement *adv.* exactly 9
examen *m.* exam; test 1
  être reçu(e) à un examen *v.* to pass an exam 2

passer un examen *v.* to take an exam 2
Excuse-moi. *fam.* Excuse me. 1
Excusez-moi. *form.* Excuse me. 1
exercice *m.* exercise 10
  faire de l'exercice *v.* to exercise 10
exigeant(e) *adj.* demanding 13
  profession (exigeante) *f.* a (demanding) profession 13
exiger (que) *v.* to demand (that) 14
expérience (professionnelle) *f.* (professional) experience 13
expliquer *v.* to explain 2
explorer *v.* to explore 4
exposition *f.* exhibit 15
extinction *f.* extinction 14

F

facile *adj.* easy 2
facilement *adv.* easily 7
facteur *m.* mailman 12
faculté *f.* university; faculty 1
faible *adj.* weak 3
faim *f.* hunger 4
  avoir faim *v.* to be hungry 4
faire *v.* to do; to make 5
  faire attention (à) *v.* to pay attention (to) 5
  faire quelque chose de beau *v.* to be up to something interesting 12
  faire de l'aérobic *v.* to do aerobics 5
  faire de la gym *v.* to work out 5
  faire de la musique *v.* to play music 13
  faire de la peinture *v.* to paint 15
  faire de la planche à voile *v.* to go windsurfing 5
  faire de l'exercice *v.* to exercise 10
  faire des projets *v.* to make plans 13
  faire du camping *v.* to go camping 5
  faire du cheval *v.* to go horseback riding 5
  faire du jogging *v.* to go jogging 5
  faire du shopping *v.* to go shopping 7
  faire du ski *v.* to go skiing 5
  faire du sport *v.* to do sports 5
  faire du vélo *v.* to go bike riding 5
  faire la connaissance de *v.* to meet *(someone)* 5

faire la cuisine *v.* to cook 5
faire la fête *v.* to party 6
faire la lessive *v.* to do the laundry 8
faire la poussière *v.* to dust 8
faire la queue *v.* to wait in line 12
faire la vaisselle *v.* to do the dishes 8
faire le lit *v.* to make the bed 8
faire le ménage *v.* to do the housework 8
faire le plein *v.* to fill the tank 11
faire les courses *v.* to run errands 9
faire les musées *v.* to go to museums 15
faire les valises *v.* to pack one's bags 7
faire mal *v.* to hurt 10
faire plaisir à quelqu'un *v.* to please someone 13
faire sa toilette *v.* to wash up 10
faire une piqûre *v.* to give a shot 10
faire une promenade *v.* to go for a walk 5
faire une randonnée *v.* to go for a hike 5
faire un séjour *v.* to spend time *(somewhere)* 7
faire un tour (en voiture) *v.* to go for a walk (drive) 5
faire visiter *v.* to give a tour 8
fait (faire) *p.p., adj.* done; made 6
falaise *f.* cliff 14
faut (falloir) *v.* *(used with infinitive)* is necessary to... 5
  Il a fallu... It was necessary to... 6
  Il fallait... One had to... 8
  Il faut que... One must.../It is necessary that... 14
fallu (falloir) *p.p.* *(used with infinitive)* had to... 6
  Il a fallu... It was necessary to... 6
famille *f.* family 3
fatigué(e) *adj.* tired 3
fauteuil *m.* armchair 8
favori/favorite *adj.* favorite 3
félicitations congratulations 15
femme *f.* woman; wife 1
  femme d'affaires businesswoman 3
  femme au foyer housewife 13
  femme auteur author 15
  femme cadre executive 13
  femme peintre painter 15
  femme politique politician 13

femme pompier firefighter 13
fenêtre *f.* window 1
fer à repasser *m.* iron 8
férié(e) *adj.* holiday 6
  jour férié *m.* holiday 6
fermé(e) *adj.* closed 12
fermer *v.* to close; to shut off 11
festival (festivals *pl.***)** *m.*
  festival 15
fête *f.* party 6; celebration 6
  faire la fête *v.* to party 6
fêter *v.* to celebrate 6
feu de signalisation *m.* traffic
  light 12
feuille de papier *f.* sheet of
  paper 1
feuilleton *m.* soap opera 15
février *m.* February 5
fiancé(e) *adj.* engaged 3
fiancé(e) *m., f.* fiancé 6
fichier *m.* file 11
fier/fière *adj.* proud 3
fièvre *f.* fever 10
  avoir de la fièvre *v.* to have a
  fever 10
fille *f.* girl; daughter 1
**film (d'aventures, d'horreur, de
  science-fiction, policier)** *m.*
  (adventure, horror, science-
  fiction, crime) film 15
fils *m.* son 3
fin *f.* end 15
finalement *adv.* finally 7
fini (finir) *p.p., adj.* finished,
  done, over 4
finir (de) *v.* to finish (*doing
  something*) 4
fleur *f.* flower 8
fleuve *m.* river 14
fois *f.* time 8
  une fois *adv.* once 7
  deux fois *adv.* twice 7
fonctionner *v.* to work, to
  function 11
fontaine *f.* fountain 12
foot(ball) *m.* soccer 5
  football américain *m.*
  football 5
forêt (tropicale) *f.* (tropical)
  forest 14
formation *f.* education; training 13
forme *f.* shape; form 10
  être en pleine forme *v.* to be
  in good shape 10
formidable *adj.* great 7
formulaire *m.* form 12
  remplir un formulaire to fill
  out a form 12
fort(e) *adj.* strong 3
fou/folle *adj.* crazy 3
four (à micro-ondes) *m.*
  (microwave) oven 8

fourchette *f.* fork 9
frais/fraîche *adj.* fresh; cool 5

  Il fait frais. (*weather*) It is
  cool. 5
fraise *f.* strawberry 9
français(e) *adj.* French 1
France *f.* France 7
franchement *adv.* frankly,
  honestly 7
freiner *v.* to brake 11
freins *m., pl.* brakes 11
fréquenter *v.* to frequent; to visit 4
frère *m.* brother 3
  beau-frère *m.* brother-in-law 3
  demi-frère *m.* half-brother,
  stepbrother 3
frigo *m.* refrigerator 8
frisé(e) *adj.* curly 3
frites *f., pl.* French fries 4
froid *m.* cold 2
  avoir froid to be cold 2
  Il fait froid. (*weather*) It is
  cold. 5
fromage *m.* cheese 4
fruit *m.* fruit 9
fruits de mer *m., pl.* seafood 9
fumer *v.* to smoke 10
funérailles *f., pl.* funeral 9
furieux/furieuse *adj.* furious 14
  être furieux/furieuse que…
  v. to be furious that… 14

G

gagner *v.* to win 5; to earn 13
gant *m.* glove 6
garage *m.* garage 8
garanti(e) *adj.* guaranteed 5
garçon *m.* boy 1
garder la ligne *v.* to stay slim 10
gare (routière) *f.* train station
  (bus station) 7
gaspillage *m.* waste 14
gaspiller *v.* to waste 14
gâteau *m.* cake 6
gauche *f.* the left (side) 3
  à gauche (de) *prep.* to the
  left (of) 3
gazeux/gazeuse *adj.* carbonated,
  fizzy 4
  boisson gazeuse *f.* carbonated
  drink/beverage 4
généreux/généreuse *adj.*
  generous 3
génial(e) *adj.* great 3
genou *m.* knee 10
genre *m.* genre 15
gens *m., pl.* people 7
gentil/gentille *adj.* nice 3
gentiment *adv.* nicely 7
géographie *f.* geography 2

gérant(e) *m., f.* manager 13
gestion *f.* business
  administration 2
glace *f.* ice cream 6
glaçon *m.* ice cube 6
glissement de terrain *m.*
  landslide 14
golf *m.* golf 5
gorge *f.* throat 10
goûter *m.* afternoon snack 9;
  v. to taste 9
gouvernement *m.* government 14
grand(e) *adj.* big 3
  grand magasin *m.* department
  store 4
grandir *v.* to grow 4
grand-mère *f.* grandmother 3
grand-père *m.* grandfather 3
grands-parents *m., pl.*
  grandparents 3
gratin *m.* gratin 9
gratuit(e) *adj.* free 15
grave *adj.* serious 10
  Ce n'est pas grave. It's
  okay.; No problem. 6
grille-pain *m.* toaster 8
grippe *f.* flu 10
gris(e) *adj.* gray 6
gros(se) *adj.* fat 3
grossir *v.* to gain weight 4
guérir *v.* to get better 10
guitare *f.* guitar 15
gym *f.* exercise 5
  faire de la gym *v.* to work out 5
gymnase *m.* gym 4

H

habitat *m.* habitat 14
  sauvetage des habitats *m.*
  habitat preservation 14
habiter (à) *v.* to live (in/at) 2
haricots verts *m., pl.* green
  beans 9
Hein? *interj.* Huh?; Right? 3
herbe *f.* grass 14
hésiter (à) *v.* to hesitate (*to do
  something*) 11
heure(s) *f.* hour, o'clock; time 2
  à … heure(s) at … (o'clock) 4
  À quelle heure? What time?;
  When? 2
  À tout à l'heure. See you
  later. 1
  Quelle heure avez-vous?
  form. What time do you have? 2
  Quelle heure est-il? What
  time is it? 2
heureusement *adv.* fortunately 7
heureux/heureuse *adj.* happy 3
  **être heureux/heureuse
  que…** to be happy that… 14

hier (matin/après-midi/soir) *adv.* yesterday (morning/afternoon/evening) 7

avant-hier *adv.* day before yesterday 7

histoire *f.* history; story 2

hiver *m.* winter 5

en hiver in the winter 5

homme *m.* man 1

homme d'affaires *m.* businessman 3

homme politique *m.* politician 13

honnête *adj.* honest 15

honte *f.* shame 2

avoir honte (de) *v.* to be ashamed (of) 2

hôpital *m.* hospital 4

horloge *f.* clock 1

hors-d'œuvre *m.* hors d'œuvre, appetizer 9

hôte/hôtesse *m., f.* host 6

hôtel *m.* hotel 7

hôtelier/hôtelière *m., f.* hotel keeper 7

huile *f.* oil 9

huile *f.* (automobile) oil 11

huile d'olive *f.* olive oil 9

vérifier l'huile to check the oil 11

voyant d'huile *m.* oil warning light 11

huit *m.* eight 1

huitième *adj.* eighth 7

humeur *f.* mood 8

être de bonne/mauvaise humeur *v.* to be in a good/bad mood 8

I

ici *adv.* here 1

idée *f.* idea 3

il *sub. pron.* he; it 1

il est... he/it is... 1

Il n'y a pas de quoi. It's nothing.; You're welcome. 1

Il vaut mieux que... It is better that... 14

Il faut (falloir) *v. (used with infinitive)* It is necessary to... 6

Il a fallu... It was necessary to... 6

Il fallait... One had to... 8

Il faut (que)... One must.../ It is necessary that... 14

il y a there is/are 1

il y a eu there was/were 6

il y avait there was/were 8

Qu'est-ce qu'il y a? What is it?; What's wrong? 1

Y a-t-il... ? Is/Are there... ? 2

il y a... *(used with an expression of time)* ... ago 9

île *f.* island 14

ils *sub. pron., m., pl.* they 1

ils sont... they are... 1

immeuble *m.* building 8

impatient(e) *adj.* impatient 1

imperméable *m.* rain jacket 5

important(e) *adj.* important 1

Il est important que... It is important that... 14

impossible *adj.* impossible 15

Il est impossible que... It is impossible that... 15

imprimante *f.* printer 11

imprimer *v.* to print 11

incendie *m.* fire 14

prévenir l'incendie to prevent a fire 14

incroyable *adj.* incredible 11

indépendamment *adv.* independently 7

indépendant(e) *adj.* independent 1

indications *f.* directions 12

indiquer *v.* to indicate 5

indispensable *adj.* essential, indispensable 14

Il est indispensable que... It is essential that... 14

individuel(le) *adj.* single, individual 7

chambre individuelle *f.* single (hotel) room 7

infirmier/infirmière *m., f.* nurse 10

informations (infos) *f., pl.* news 15

informatique *f.* computer science 2

ingénieur *m.* engineer 3

inquiet/inquiète *adj.* worried 3

instrument *m.* instrument 1

intellectuel(le) *adj.* intellectual 3

intelligent(e) *adj.* intelligent 1

interdire *v.* to forbid, to prohibit 14

intéressant(e) *adj.* interesting 1

inutile *adj.* useless 2

invité(e) *m., f.* guest 6

inviter *v.* to invite 4

irlandais(e) *adj.* Irish 7

Irlande *f.* Ireland 7

Italie *f.* Italy 7

italien(ne) *adj.* Italian 1

J

jaloux/jalouse *adj.* jealous 3

jamais *adv.* never 5

ne... jamais never, not ever 12

jambe *f.* leg 10

jambon *m.* ham 4

janvier *m.* January 5

Japon *m.* Japan 7

japonais(e) *adj.* Japanese 1

jardin *m.* garden; yard 8

jaune *adj.* yellow 6

je/j' *sub. pron.* I 1

Je vous en prie. *form.* Please.; You're welcome. 1

jean *m., sing.* jeans 6

jeter *v.* to throw away 14

jeu *m.* game 5

jeu télévisé *m.* game show 15

jeu vidéo (des jeux vidéo) *m.* video game(s) 11

jeudi *m.* Thursday 2

jeune *adj.* young 3

jeunes mariés *m., pl.* newlyweds 6

jeunesse *f.* youth 6

auberge de jeunesse *f.* youth hostel 7

jogging *m.* jogging 5

faire du jogging *v.* to go jogging 5

joli(e) *adj.* handsome; beautiful 3

joue *f.* cheek 10

jouer (à/de) *v.* to play (a sport/a musical instrument) 5

jouer un rôle *v.* to play a role 15

joueur/joueuse *m., f.* player 5

jour *m.* day 2

jour de congé *m.* day off 7

jour férié *m.* holiday 6

Quel jour sommes-nous? *What day is it?* 2

journal *m.* newspaper; journal 7

journaliste *m., f.* journalist 3

journée *f.* day 2

juillet *m.* July 5

juin *m.* June 5

jungle *f.* jungle 14

jupe *f.* skirt 6

jus (d'orange/de pomme) *m.* (orange/apple) juice 4

jusqu'à (ce que) *prep.* until 12

juste *adv.* just; right 3

juste à côté right next door 3

K

kilo(gramme) *m.* kilo(gram) 9

kiosque *m.* kiosk 4

L

l' *def. art., m., f. sing.* the 1; *d.o. pron., m., f.* him; her; it 7

la *def. art., f. sing.* the 1; *d.o. pron., f.* her; *it* 7
là(-bas) (over) there 1
-là *(used with demonstrative adjective* **ce** *and noun or with demonstrative pronoun* **celui)** there 6
lac *m.* lake 14
laid(e) *adj.* ugly 3
laine *f.* wool 12
laisser *v.* to let, to allow 11
  laisser tranquille *v.* to leave alone 10
  laisser un message *v.* to leave a message 13
  laisser un pourboire *v.* to leave a tip 4
lait *m.* milk 4
laitue *f.* lettuce 9
lampe *f.* lamp 8
langues (étrangères) *f., pl.* (foreign) languages 2
lapin *m.* rabbit 14
laquelle *pron., f., sing.* which one 13
  à laquelle *pron., f., sing.* which one 13
  de laquelle *pron., f., sing.* which one 13
large *adj.* loose; big 6
lavabo *m.* bathroom sink 8
lave-linge *m.* washing machine 8
laver *v.* to wash 8
laverie *f.* laundromat 12
lave-vaisselle *m.* dishwasher 8
le *def. art., m. sing.* the 1; *d.o. pron.* him; it 7
lecteur MP3/de CD/ DVD *m.* MP3/CD/DVD player 11
légume *m.* vegetable 9
lent(e) *adj.* slow 3
lequel *pron., m., sing.* which one 13
  auquel (à + lequel) *pron., m., sing.* which one 13
  duquel (de + lequel) *pron., m., sing.* which one 13
les *def. art., m., f., pl.* the 1; *d.o. pron., m., f., pl.* them 7
lesquelles *pron., f., pl.* which ones 13
  auxquelles (à + lesquelles) *pron., f., pl.* which ones 13
  desquelles (de + lesquelles) *pron., f., pl.* which ones 13
lesquels *pron., m., pl.* which ones 13
  auxquels (à + lesquels) *pron., m., pl.* which ones 13
  desquels (de + lesquels) *pron., m., pl.* which ones 13
lessive *f.* laundry 8

faire la lessive *v.* to do the laundry 8
lettre *f.* letter 12
  boîte aux lettres *f.* mailbox 12
  lettre de motivation *f.* letter of application 13
  lettre de recommandation *f.* letter of recommendation, reference letter 13
lettres *f., pl.* humanities 2
leur *i.o. pron., m., f., pl.* them 6
leur(s) *poss. adj., m., f.* their 3
  le leur *poss. pron.* their 15
  la leur *poss. pron.* their 15
  les leurs *poss. pron.* theirs 15
librairie *f.* bookstore 1
libre *adj.* available 7
lien *m.* link 11
lieu *m.* place 4
ligne *f.* figure, shape 10
  garder la ligne *v.* to stay slim 10
limitation de vitesse *f.* speed limit 11
limonade *f.* lemon soda 4
linge *m.* laundry 8
  lave-linge *m.* washing machine 8
  sèche-linge *m.* clothes dryer 8
liquide *m.* cash *(money)* 12
  payer en liquide *v.* to pay in cash 12
lire *v.* to read 7
lit *m.* bed 7
  faire le lit *v.* to make the bed 8
littéraire *adj.* literary 15
littérature *f.* literature 1
livre *m.* book 1
logement *m.* housing 8
logiciel *m.* software, program 11
loi *f.* law 14
loin de *prep.* far from 3
loisir *m.* leisure activity 5
long(ue) *adj.* long 3
  chemise à manches longues *f.* long-sleeved shirt 6
longtemps *adv.* a long time 5
louer *v.* to rent 8
loyer *m.* rent 8
lu (lire) *p.p.* read 7
lui *pron., sing.* he 1; him 3; *i.o. pron. (attached to imperative)* to him/her 9
l'un(e) à l'autre to one another 11
l'un(e) l'autre one another 11
lundi *m.* Monday 2
Lune *f.* moon 14
lunettes (de soleil) *f., pl.* (sun)glasses 6
lycée *m.* high school 1
lycéen(ne) *m., f.* high school student 2

M

ma *poss. adj., f., sing.* my 3
Madame *f.* Ma'am; Mrs. 1
Mademoiselle *f.* Miss 1
magasin *m.* store 4
  grand magasin *m.* department store 4
magazine *m.* magazine 15
mai *m.* May 5
maigrir *v.* to lose weight 4
maillot de bain *m.* swimsuit, bathing suit 6
main *f.* hand 5
  sac à main *m.* purse, handbag 6
maintenant *adv.* now 5
maintenir *v.* to maintain 9
mairie *f.* town/city hall; mayor's office 12
mais *conj.* but 1
  mais non (but) of course not; no 2
maison *f.* house 4
  rentrer à la maison *v.* to return home 2
mal *adv.* badly 7
  Je vais mal. I am doing badly. 1
  le plus mal *super. adv.* the worst 9
  se porter mal *v.* to be doing badly 10
mal *m.* illness; ache, pain 10
  avoir mal *v.* to have an ache 10
  avoir mal au cœur *v.* to feel nauseated 10
  faire mal *v.* to hurt 10
malade *adj.* sick, ill 10
  tomber malade *v.* to get sick 10
maladie *f.* illness 13
  assurance maladie *f.* health insurance 13
malheureusement *adv.* unfortunately 2
malheureux/malheureuse *adj.* unhappy 3
manche *f.* sleeve 6
  chemise à manches courtes/ longues *f.* short-/long-sleeved shirt 6
manger *v.* to eat 2
  salle à manger *f.* dining room 8
manteau *m.* coat 6
maquillage *m.* makeup 10
marchand de journaux *m.* newsstand 12
marché *m.* market 4
  bon marché *adj.* inexpensive 6
marcher *v.* to walk *(person)* 5; to work *(thing)* 11
mardi *m.* Tuesday 2
mari *m.* husband 3

mariage *m.* marriage; wedding (*ceremony*) 6
marié(e) *adj.* married 3
mariés *m., pl.* married couple 6
  jeunes mariés *m., pl.* newlyweds 6
marocain(e) *adj.* Moroccan 1
marron *adj., inv.* (not for hair) brown 3
mars *m.* March 5
martiniquais(e) *adj.* from Martinique 1
match *m.* game 5
mathématiques (maths) *f., pl.* mathematics 2
matin *m.* morning 2
  ce matin *adv.* this morning 2
  demain matin *adv.* tomorrow morning 2
  hier matin *adv.* yesterday morning 7
matinée *f.* morning 2
mauvais(e) *adj.* bad 3
  Il fait mauvais. The weather is bad. 5
  le/la plus mauvais(e) *super. adj.* the worst 9
mayonnaise *f.* mayonnaise 9
me/m' *pron., sing.* me; myself 6
mec *m.* guy 10
mécanicien *m.* mechanic 11
mécanicienne *f.* mechanic 11
méchant(e) *adj.* mean 3
médecin *m.* doctor 3
médicament (contre/pour) *m.* medication (against/for) 10
meilleur(e) *comp. adj.* better 9
  le/la meilleur(e) *super. adj.* the best 9
membre *m.* member 15
même *adj.* even 5; same 6
-même(s) *pron.* -self/-selves 6
menacé(e) *adj.* endangered 14
  espèce menacée *f.* endangered species 14
ménage *m.* housework 8
  faire le ménage *v.* to do housework 8
ménager/ménagère *adj.* household 8
  appareil ménager *m.* household appliance 8
  tâche ménagère *f.* household chore 8
mention *f.* distinction 13
menu *m.* menu 9
mer *f.* sea 7
Merci (beaucoup). Thank you (very much). 1
mercredi *m.* Wednesday 2

mère *f.* mother 3
  belle-mère *f.* mother-in-law; stepmother 3
mes *poss. adj., m., f., pl.* my 3
message *m.* message 13
  laisser un message *v.* to leave a message 13
messagerie *f.* voicemail 13
météo *f.* weather 15
métier *m.* profession 13
métro *m.* subway 7
  station de métro *f.* subway station 7
metteur en scène *m.* director (*of a play*) 15
mettre *v.* to put, to place 6
  mettre la table to set the table 8
meuble *m.* piece of furniture 8
mexicain(e) *adj.* Mexican 1
Mexique *m.* Mexico 7
Miam! *interj.* Yum! 5
micro-onde *m.* microwave oven 8
  four à micro-ondes *m.* microwave oven 8
midi *m.* noon 2
  après-midi *m.* afternoon 2
le mien *poss. pron.* mine 15
la mienne *poss. pron.* mine 15
les miens *poss. pron.* mine 15
les miennes *poss. pron.* mine 15
mieux *comp. adv.* better 9
  aimer mieux *v.* to prefer 2
  le mieux *super. adv.* the best 9
  se porter mieux *v.* to be doing better 10
mille *m.* one thousand 5
  cent mille *m.* one hundred thousand 5
million, un *m.* one million 5
  deux millions *m.* two million 5
minuit *m.* midnight 2
miroir *m.* mirror 8
mis (mettre) *p.p.* put, placed 6
mode *f.* fashion 2
modeste *adj.* modest 13
moi *disj. pron., sing.* I, me 3; *pron.* (attached to an imperative) to me, to myself 9
  Moi aussi. Me too. 1
  Moi non plus. Me neither. 2
moins *adv.* before ... (o'clock) 2
moins (de) *adv.* less (of); fewer 4
  le/la moins *super. adv.* (used with verb or adverb) the least 9
  le moins de... (used with noun to express quantity) the least... 14
  moins de... que... (used with noun to express quantity) less... than... 14
mois *m.* month 2
  ce mois-ci this month 2

moment *m.* moment 1
mon *poss. adj., m., sing.* my 3
monde *m.* world 7
moniteur *m.* monitor 11
monnaie *f.* change, coins; money 12
Monsieur *m.* Sir; Mr. 1
montagne *f.* mountain 4
monter *v.* to go up, to come up; to get in/on 7
montre *f.* watch 1
montrer (à) *v.* to show (*to someone*) 6
morceau (de) *m.* piece, bit (of) 4
mort *f.* death 6
mort (mourir) *p.p., adj.* (as past participle) died; (as adjective) dead 7
mot de passe *m.* password 11
moteur *m.* engine 11
mourir *v.* to die 7
moutarde *f.* mustard 9
moyen(ne) *adj.* medium 3
  de taille moyenne of medium height 3
mur *m.* wall 8
musée *m.* museum 4
  faire les musées *v.* to go to museums 15
musical(e) *adj.* musical 15
  comédie musicale *f.* musical 15
musicien(ne) *m., f.* musician 3
musique: faire de la musique *v.* to play music 15

N

nager *v.* to swim 4
naïf/naïve *adj.* naïve 3
naissance *f.* birth 6
naître *v.* to be born 7
nappe *f.* tablecloth 9
nationalité *f.* nationality 1
  Je suis de nationalité... I am of ... nationality. 1
  Quelle est ta nationalité? *fam.* What is your nationality? 1
  Quelle est votre nationalité? *fam., pl., form.* What is your nationality? 1
nature *f.* nature 14
naturel(le) *adj.* natural 14
  ressource naturelle *f.* natural resource 14
né (naître) *p.p., adj.* born 7
ne/n' no, not 1
  ne... aucun(e) none, not any 12
  ne... jamais never, not ever 12
  ne... ni... ni... neither... nor... 12

ne... pas no, not 2
ne... personne nobody, no one 12
ne... plus no more, not anymore 12
ne... que only 12
ne... rien nothing, not anything 12
N'est-ce pas? *(tag question)* Isn't it? 2
nécessaire *adj.* necessary 14
   Il est nécessaire que... It is necessary that... 14
neiger *v.* to snow 5
   Il neige. It is snowing. 5
nerveusement *adv.* nervously 7
nerveux/nerveuse *adj.* nervous 3
nettoyer *v.* to clean 5
neuf *m.* nine 1
neuvième *adj.* ninth 7
neveu *m.* nephew 3
nez *m.* nose 10
ni nor 12
   ne... ni... ni... neither... nor 12
nièce *f.* niece 3
niveau *m.* level 13
noir(e) *adj.* black 3
non no 2
   mais non (but) of course not; no 2
nord *m.* north 12
nos *poss. adj., m., f., pl.* our 3
note *f.* (academics) grade 2
notre *poss. adj., m., f., sing.* our 3
   le nôtre *poss. pron.* ours 15
   la nôtre *poss. pron.* ours 15
   les nôtres *poss. pron.* ours 15
nourriture *f.* food, sustenance 9
nous *pron.* we 1; us 3; ourselves 10
nouveau/nouvelle *adj.* new 3
nouvelles *f., pl.* news 15
novembre *m.* November 5
nuage de pollution *m.* pollution cloud 14
nuageux/nuageuse *adj.* cloudy 5
   Le temps est nuageux. It is cloudy. 5
nucléaire *adj.* nuclear 14
   centrale nucléaire *f.* nuclear plant 14
   énergie nucléaire *f.* nuclear energy 14
nuit *f.* night 2
   boîte de nuit *f.* nightclub 4
nul(le) *adj.* useless 2
numéro *m.* (telephone) number 11
   composer un numéro *v.* to dial a number 11
   recomposer un numéro *v.* to redial a number 11

O

obéir (à) *v.* to obey 4
objet *m.* object 1
obtenir *v.* to get, to obtain 13
occupé(e) *adj.* busy 1
octobre *m.* October 5
œil (les yeux) *m.* eye (eyes) 10
œuf *m.* egg 9
œuvre *f.* artwork, piece of art 15
   chef-d'œuvre *m.* masterpiece 15
   hors-d'œuvre *m.* hors d'œuvre, starter 9
offert (offrir) *p.p.* offered 11
office du tourisme *m.* tourist office 12
offrir *v.* to offer 11
oignon *m.* onion 9
oiseau *m.* bird 3
olive *f.* olive 9
   huile d'olive *f.* olive oil 9
omelette *f.* omelette 5
on *sub. pron., sing.* one (we) 1
   on y va let's go 10
oncle *m.* uncle 3
onze *m.* eleven 1
onzième *adj.* eleventh 7
opéra *m.* opera 15
optimiste *adj.* optimistic 1
orageux/orageuse *adj.* stormy 5
   Le temps est orageux. It is stormy. 5
orange *adj. inv.* orange 6; *f.* orange 9
orchestre *m.* orchestra 15
ordinateur *m.* computer 1
ordonnance *f.* prescription 10
ordures *f., pl.* trash 14
   ramassage des ordures *m.* garbage collection 14
oreille *f.* ear 10
oreiller *m.* pillow 8
organiser (une fête) *v.* to organize/to plan (a party) 6
origine *f.* heritage 1
   Je suis d'origine... I am of... heritage. 1
orteil *m.* toe 10
ou *or* 3
où *adv., rel. pron.* where 4, 13
ouais *adv.* yeah 2
oublier (de) *v.* to forget (*to do something*) 2
ouest *m.* west 12
oui *adv.* yes 2
ouvert (ouvrir) *p.p., adj. (as past participle)* opened; *(as adjective)* open 11
ouvrier/ouvrière *m., f.* worker, laborer 13
ouvrir *v.* to open 11

ozone *m.* ozone 14
   trou dans la couche d'ozone *m.* hole in the ozone layer 14

P

page d'accueil *f.* home page 11
pain (de campagne) *m.* (country-style) bread 4
panne *f.* breakdown, malfunction 11
   tomber en panne *v.* to break down 11
pantalon *m., sing.* pants 6
pantoufle *f.* slipper 10
papeterie *f.* stationery store 12
papier *m.* paper 1
   corbeille à papier *f.* wastebasket 1
   feuille de papier *f.* sheet of paper 1
paquet cadeau *m.* wrapped gift 6
par *prep.* by 3
   par jour/semaine/mois/an per day/week/month/year 5
parapluie *m.* umbrella 5
parc *m.* park 4
parce que *conj.* because 2
Pardon. Pardon (me). 1
Pardon? What? 4
pare-brise *m.* windshield 11
pare-chocs *m.* bumper 11
parents *m., pl.* parents 3
paresseux/paresseuse *adj.* lazy 3
parfait(e) *adj.* perfect 4
parfois *adv.* sometimes 5
parking *m.* parking lot 11
parler (à) *v.* to speak (to) 6
   parler (au téléphone) *v.* to speak (on the phone) 2
partager *v.* to share 2
partir *v.* to leave 5
   partir en vacances *v.* to go on vacation 7
pas (de) *adv.* no, none 12
   ne... pas no, not 2
   pas de problème no problem 12
   pas du tout not at all 2
   pas encore not yet 8
   Pas mal. Not badly. 1
passager/passagère *m., f.* passenger 7
passeport *m.* passport 7
passer *v.* to pass by; to spend time 7
   passer chez quelqu'un *v.* to stop by someone's house 4
   passer l'aspirateur *v.* to vacuum 8

passer un examen *v.* to take an exam 2

passe-temps *m.* pastime, hobby 5

pâté (de campagne) *m.* pâté, meat spread 9

pâtes *f., pl.* pasta 9

patiemment *adv.* patiently 7

patient(e) *m., f.* patient 10; *adj.* patient 1

patienter *v.* to wait (on the phone), to be on hold 13

patiner v. to skate 4

pâtisserie *f.* pastry shop, bakery, pastry 9

patron(ne) *m., f.* boss 25

pauvre *adj.* poor 3

payé (payer) *p.p., adj.* paid 13

être bien/mal payé(e) *v.* to be well/badly paid 13

payer *v.* to pay 5

payer avec une carte de crédit *v.* to pay with a credit card 12

payer en liquide *v.* to pay in cash 12

payer par chèque *v.* to pay by check 12

pays *m.* country 7

peau *f.* skin 10

pêche *f.* fishing 5; peach 9

aller à la pêche *v.* to go fishing 5

peigne *m.* comb 10

peintre/femme peintre *m., f.* painter 15

peinture *f.* painting 15

pendant (que) *prep.* during, while 7

pendant *(with time expression) prep.* for 9

pénible *adj.* tiresome 3

penser (que) *v.* to think (that) 2

ne pas penser que... to not think that... 15

Qu'en penses-tu? What do you think about that? 14

perdre *v.* to lose 6

perdre son temps *v.* to lose/ to waste time 6

perdu *p.p., adj.* lost 12

être perdu(e) to be lost 12

père *m.* father 3

beau-père *m.* father-in-law; stepfather 3

permettre (de) *v.* to allow (to do something) 6

permis *m.* permit; license 11

permis de conduire *m.* driver's license 11

permis (permettre) *p.p., adj.* permitted, allowed 6

personnage (principal) *m.* (main) character 15

personne *f.* person 1; *pron.* no one 12

ne... personne nobody, no one 12

pessimiste *adj.* pessimistic 1

petit(e) *adj.* small 3; short (*stature*) 3

petit(e) ami(e) *m., f.* boy-friend/girlfriend 1

petit-déjeuner *m.* breakfast 9

petite-fille *f.* granddaughter 3

petit-fils *m.* grandson 3

petits-enfants *m., pl.* grand-children 3

petits pois *m., pl.* peas 9

peu (de) *adv.* little; not much (of) 2

peur *f.* fear 2

avoir peur (de/que) *v.* to be afraid (of/that) 2

peut-être *adv.* maybe, perhaps 2

phares *m., pl.* headlights 11

pharmacie *f.* pharmacy 10

pharmacien(ne) *m., f.* pharmacist 10

philosophie *f.* philosophy 2

photo(graphie) *f.* photo(graph) 3

physique *f.* physics 2

piano *m.* piano 15

pièce *f.* room 8

pièce de théâtre *f.* play 15

pièces de monnaie *f., pl.* change 12

pied *m.* foot 10

pierre *f.* stone 14

pilule *f.* pill 10

pique-nique *m.* picnic 14

piqûre *f.* shot, injection 10

faire une piqûre *v.* to give a shot 10

pire *comp. adj.* worse 9

le/la pire *super. adj.* the worst 9

piscine *f.* pool 4

placard *m.* closet; cupboard 8

place *f.* square; place 4; *f.* seat 15

plage *f.* beach 7

plaisir *m.* pleasure, enjoyment 13

faire plaisir à quelqu'un *v.* to please someone 13

plan *m.* map 7

utiliser un plan *v.* to use a map 7

planche à voile *f.* windsurfing 5

faire de la planche à voile *v.* to go windsurfing 5

planète *f.* planet 14

sauver la planète *v.* to save the planet 14

plante *f.* plant 14

plastique *m.* plastic 14

emballage en plastique *m.* plastic wrapping/packaging 14

plat (principal) *m.* (main) dish 9

plein air *m.* outdoor, open-air 14

pleine forme *f.* good shape, good state of health 10

être en pleine forme *v.* to be in good shape 10

pleurer *v.* to cry

pleuvoir *v.* to rain 5

Il pleut. It is raining. 5

plombier *m.* plumber 13

plu (pleuvoir) *p.p.* rained 6

pluie acide *f.* acid rain 14

plus *adv. (used in comparatives, superlatives, and expressions of quantity)* more 4

le/la plus ... *super. adv. (used with adjective)* the most 9

le/la plus mauvais(e) *super. adj.* the worst 9

le plus *super. adv. (used with verb or adverb)* the most 9

le plus de... *(used with noun to express quantity)* the most... 14

le plus mal *super. adv.* the worst 9

plus... que *(used with adjective)* more... than 9

plus de more of 4

plus de... que *(used with noun to express quantity)* more... than 14

plus mal *comp. adv.* worse 9

plus mauvais(e) *comp. adj.* worse 9

plus *adv.* no more, not anymore 12

ne... plus no more, not any-more 12

plusieurs *adj.* several 4

plutôt *adv.* rather 2

pneu (crevé) *m.* (flat) tire 11

vérifier la pression des pneus *v.* to check the tire pressure 11

poème *m.* poem 15

poète/poétesse *m., f.* poet 15

point *m. (punctuation mark)* period 11

poire *f.* pear 9

poisson *m.* fish 3

poissonnerie *f.* fish shop 9

poitrine *f.* chest 10

poivre *m. (spice)* pepper 9

poivron *m. (vegetable)* pepper 9

poli(e) *adj.* polite 1

police *f.* police 11

agent de police *m.* police officer 11

commissariat de police *m.* police station 12

policier *m.* police officer 11

film policier *m.* detective film 15

policière *f.* police officer 11

poliment *adv.* politely 7

politique *adj.* political 2
  femme politique *f.* politician 13
  homme politique *m.*
    politician 13
  **sciences politiques (sciences
    po)** *f., pl.* political science 2
polluer *v.* to pollute 14
pollution *f.* pollution 14
  nuage de pollution *m.*
    pollution cloud 14
pomme *f.* apple 9
pomme de terre *f.* potato 9
pompier/femme pompier *m., f.*
    firefighter 13
pont *m.* bridge 12
population croissante *f.* growing
    population 14
porc *m.* pork 9
portable *m.* cell phone 11
porte *f.* door 1
porter *v.* to wear 6
portière *f.* car door 11
portrait *m.* portrait 5
poser une question (à) *v.* to
    ask (*someone*) a question 6
posséder *v.* to possess, to own 5
possible *adj.* possible 15
  Il est possible que... *It is
    possible that...* 14
poste *f.* postal service; post
    office 12
  bureau de poste *m.* post
    office 12
poste *m.* position 13
poste de télévision *m.* television
    set 11
poster une lettre *v.* to mail a
    letter 12
postuler *v.* to apply 13
poulet *m.* chicken 9
pour *prep.* for 5
  pour qui? for whom? 4
  pour rien for no reason 4
  pour que so that 15
pourboire *m.* tip 4
  laisser un pourboire *v.* to
    leave a tip 4
pourquoi? *adv.* why? 2
poussière *f.* dust 8
  enlever/faire la poussière
    v. to dust 8
pouvoir *v.* to be able to; can 9
pratiquer *v.* to play regularly, to
    practice 5
préféré(e) *adj.* favorite,
    preferred 2
préférer (que) *v.* to prefer (that) 5
premier *m.* the first (*day of the
    month*) 5
  **C'est le 1ᵉʳ (premier)
    octobre.** It is October first. 5
premier/première *adj.* first 2

prendre *v.* to take 4; to have 4
  prendre sa retraite *v.* to retire 6
  **prendre un train/avion/
    taxi/autobus/bateau** *v.* to
    take a train/plane/taxi/bus/
    boat 7
  prendre un congé *v.* to take
    time off 13
  prendre une douche *v.* to
    take a shower 10
  prendre une photo(graphie)
    v. to take a photo(graph) 11
  prendre (un) rendez-vous *v.*
    to make an appointment 13
préparer *v.* to prepare (for) 2
près (de) *prep.* close (to), near 3
  tout près (de) very close (to) 12
présenter *v.* to present, to
    introduce 15
  Je te présente... *fam.* I would
    like to introduce... to you. 1
  Je vous présente... *fam., form.*
    I would like to introduce... to
    you. 1
préservation *f.* protection 14
préserver *v.* to preserve 14
presque *adv.* almost 2
pressé(e) *adj.* hurried 9
pression *f.* pressure 11
  vérifier la pression des pneus
    to check the tire pressure 11
prêt(e) *adj.* ready 3
prêter (à) *v.* to lend (*to someone*) 6
prévenir l'incendie *v.* to prevent
    a fire 14
principal(e) *adj.* main, principal 9
  personnage principal *m.*
    main character 15
  plat principal *m.* main dish 9
printemps *m.* spring 5
  au printemps in the spring 5
pris (prendre) *p.p., adj.* taken 6
prix *m.* price 4
problème *m.* problem 1
prochain(e) *adj.* next 2
produire *v.* to produce 6
produit *m.* product 14
produit (produire) *p.p., adj.*
    produced 6
professeur *m.* teacher, professor 1
profession (exigeante) *f.*
    (demanding) profession 13
professionnel(le) *adj.*
    professional 13
  expérience professionnelle *f.*
    professional experience 13
profiter (de) *v.* to take advantage
    (of); to enjoy 15
programme *m.* program 15
projet *m.* project 13
  faire des projets *v.* to make
    plans 13

promenade *f.* walk, stroll 5
  faire une promenade *v.* to go
    for a walk 5
promettre *v.* to promise 6
promis (promettre) *p.p., adj.*
    promised 6
promotion *f.* promotion 13
proposer (que) *v.* to propose
    (that) 14
  proposer une solution *v.* to
    propose a solution 14
propre *adj.* clean 8
propriétaire *m., f.* owner 8;
    landlord/landlady 8
protection *f.* protection 14
protéger *v.* to protect 5
psychologie *f.* psychology 2
psychologique *adj.*
    psychological 15
psychologue *m., f.* psychologist 13
pu (pouvoir) *p.p. (used with
    infinitive)* was able to 9
publicité (pub) *f.* advertise-
    ment 15
publier *v.* to publish 15
puis *adv.* then 7
pull *m.* sweater 6
pur(e) *adj.* pure 14

Q

quand *adv.* when 4
  **C'est quand l'anniversaire
    de ... ?** When is ...'s birthday? 5
  **C'est quand ton/votre
    anniversaire?** When is your
    birthday? 5
quarante *m.* forty 1
quart *m.* quarter 2
  et quart a quarter after...
    (o'clock) 2
quartier *m.* area, neighbor-
    hood 8
quatorze *m.* fourteen 1
quatre *m.* four 1
quatre-vingts *m.* eighty 3
quatre-vingt-dix *m.* ninety 3
quatrième *adj.* fourth 7
que/qu' *rel. pron.* that;
    which 13; *conj.* than 9, 14
  plus/moins ... que *(used with
    adjective)* more/less ... than 9
  plus/moins de ... que *(used
    with noun to express quantity)*
    more/less ... than 14
que/qu'...? *interr. pron.* what? 4
  Qu'en penses-tu? What do
    you think about that? 14
  Qu'est-ce que c'est? What is
    it? 1
  Qu'est-ce qu'il y a? What is
    it?; What's wrong? 1

que *adv.* only 12
  ne... que only 12
québécois(e) *adj.* from Quebec 1
quel(le)(s)? *interr. adj.* which? 4;
  what? 4
  À quelle heure? What time?;
  When? 2
  Quel jour sommes-nous?
  What day is it? 2
  Quelle est la date? What is
  the date? 5
  Quelle est ta nationalité?
  fam. What is your nationality? 1
  Quelle est votre nationalité?
  form. What is your nationality? 1
  Quelle heure avez-vous?
  form. What time do you have? 2
  Quelle heure est-il? What
  time is it? 2
  Quelle température fait-il?
  (weather) What is the
  temperature? 5
  Quel temps fait-il? What is
  the weather like? 5
quelqu'un *pron.* someone 12
quelque chose *m.* something;
  anything 4
  Quelque chose ne va pas.
  Something's not right. 5
quelquefois *adv.* sometimes 7
quelques *adj.* some 4
question *f.* question 6
  poser une question (à) to ask
  (someone) a question 6
queue *f.* line 12
  faire la queue *v.* to wait in
  line 12
qui? *interr. pron.* who? 4;
  whom? 4; *rel. pron.* who, that 13
  à qui? to whom? 4
  avec qui? with whom? 4
  C'est de la part de qui? On
  behalf of whom? 13
  Qui est à l'appareil? Who's
  calling, please? 13
  Qui est-ce? Who is it? 1
quinze *m.* fifteen 1
quitter (la maison) *v.* to leave
  (the house) 4
  Ne quittez pas. Please hold. 13
quoi? *interr. pron.* what? 1
  Il n'y a pas de quoi. It's
  nothing.; You're welcome. 1
  quoi que ce soit whatever it
  may be 13

R

raccrocher *v.* to hang up 13
radio *f.* radio 15
  à la radio on the radio 15
raide *adj.* straight 3

raison *f.* reason; right 2
  avoir raison *v.* to be right 2
ramassage des ordures *m.*
  garbage collection 14
randonnée *f.* hike 5
  faire une randonnée *v.* to go
  for a hike 5
ranger *v.* to tidy up, to put away 8
rapide *adj.* fast 3
rapidement *adv.* rapidly 7
rarement *adv.* rarely 5
rasoir *m.* razor 10
ravissant(e) *adj.* beautiful;
  delightful 13
réagir *v.* to react 4
réalisateur/réalisatrice *m., f.*
  director *(of a movie)* 15
récent(e) *adj.* recent 15
réception *f.* reception desk 7
recevoir *v.* to receive 12
recharger *v.* to charge 11
réchauffement de la Terre *m.*
  global warming 14
rechercher *v.* to search for, to
  look for 13
recommandation *f.* recommendation 13
recommander (que) *v.* to
  recommend (that) 14
recomposer (un numéro) *v.* to
  redial (a number) 11
reconnaître *v.* to recognize 8
reconnu (reconnaître) *p.p., adj.*
  recognized 8
reçu *m.* receipt 12
reçu (recevoir) *p.p., adj.* received 7
  être reçu(e) à un examen
  to pass an exam 2
recyclage *m.* recycling 14
recycler *v.* to recycle 14
redémarrer *v.* to restart, to start
  again 11
réduire *v.* to reduce 6
réduit (réduire) *p.p., adj.* reduced 6
référence *f.* reference 13
réfléchir (à) *v.* to think (about),
  to reflect (on) 4
refuser (de) *v.* to refuse (*to do
  something*) 11
regarder *v.* to watch 2
  Ça ne nous regarde pas.
  That has nothing to do with us.;
  That is none of our business. 14
régime *m.* diet 10
  être au régime *v.* to be on a
  diet 9
région *f.* region 14
regretter (que) *v.* to regret
  (that) 14
remplir (un formulaire) *v.* to fill
  out (a form) 12
rencontrer *v.* to meet 2

rendez-vous *m.* date;
  appointment 6
  prendre (un) rendez-vous *v.*
  to make an appointment 13
rendre (à) *v.* to give back, to
  return (to) 6
  rendre visite (à) *v.* to visit 6
rentrer (à la maison) *v.* to
  return (home) 2
  rentrer (dans) *v.* to hit 11
renvoyer *v.* to dismiss, to let go 13
réparer *v.* to repair 11
repartir *v.* to go back 15
repas *m.* meal 9
repasser *v.* to take again 15
  repasser (le linge) *v.* to iron
  (the laundry) 8
  fer à repasser *m.* iron 8
répéter *v.* to repeat; to rehearse 5
répondre (à) *v.* to respond, to
  answer (to) 6
réseau (social) *m.* (social)
  network 11
réservation *f.* reservation 7
  annuler une réservation *v.*
  to cancel a reservation 7
réservé(e) *adj.* reserved 1
réserver *v.* to reserve 7
réservoir d'essence *m.* gas
  tank 11
résidence universitaire *f.*
  dorm 8
ressource naturelle *f.* natural
  resource 14
restaurant *m.* restaurant 4
  **restaurant universitaire
  (resto U)** *m.* university
  cafeteria 2
rester *v.* to stay 7
résultat *m.* result 2
retenir *v.* to keep, to retain 9
retirer (de l'argent) *v.* to
  withdraw (money) 12
retourner *v.* to return 7
retraite *f.* retirement 6
  prendre sa retraite *v.* to retire 6
retraité(e) *m., f.* retired person 13
retrouver *v.* to find (again); to
  meet up with 2
rétroviseur *m.* rear-view mirror 11
réunion *f.* meeting 13
réussir (à) *v.* to succeed (*in doing
  something*) 4
réussite *f.* success 13
réveil *m.* alarm clock 10
revenir *v.* to come back 9
rêver (de) *v.* to dream about 11
revoir *v.* to see again 12
  Au revoir. Good-bye. 1
revu (revoir) *p.p.* seen again 12
rez-de-chaussée *m.* ground
  floor 7

rhume *m.* cold 10
ri (rire) *p.p.* laughed 6
rideau *m.* curtain 8
rien *m.* nothing 12
  De rien. You're welcome. 1
  ne... rien nothing, not
  anything 12
  ne servir à rien *v.* to be good
  for nothing 9
rire *v.* to laugh 6
rivière *f.* river 14
riz *m.* rice 9
robe *f.* dress 6
rôle *m.* role 14
  jouer un rôle *v.* to play a
  role 15
roman *m.* novel 15
rose *adj.* pink 6
roue (de secours) *f.*
  (emergency) tire 11
rouge *adj.* red 6
rougir *v.* to blush 4
rouler en voiture *v.* to ride in
  a car 7
rue *f.* street 11
  suivre une rue *v.* to follow a
  street 12

S

s'adorer *v.* to adore one another 11
s'aider *v.* to help one another 11
s'aimer (bien) *v.* to love (like)
  one another 11
s'allumer *v.* to light up 11
s'amuser *v.* to play; to have
  fun 10
  s'amuser à *v.* to pass time by
  11
s'apercevoir *v.* to notice; to
  realize 12
s'appeler *v.* to be named, to be
  called 10
  Comment t'appelles-tu? *fam.*
  What is your name? 1
  Comment vous appelez-vous?
  form. What is your name? 1
  Je m'appelle... My name is... 1
s'arrêter *v.* to stop 10
s'asseoir *v.* to sit down 10
sa *poss. adj., f., sing.* his; her; its 3
sac *m.* bag 1
  sac à dos *m.* backpack 1
  sac à main *m.* purse, handbag 6
sain(e) *adj.* healthy 10
saison *f.* season 5
salade *f.* salad 9
salaire (élevé/modeste) *m.*
  (high/low) salary 13
  augmentation de salaire
  f. raise in salary 13

sale *adj.* dirty 8
salir *v.* to soil, to make dirty 8
salle *f.* room 8
  salle à manger *f.* dining
  room 8
  salle de bains *f.* bathroom 8
  salle de classe *f.* classroom 1
  salle de séjour *f.* living/family
  room 8
salon *m.* formal living room,
  sitting room 8
  salon de beauté *m.* beauty
  salon 12
Salut! Hi!; Bye! 1
samedi *m.* Saturday 2
sandwich *m.* sandwich 4
sans *prep.* without 8
  sans que *conj.* without 15
santé *f.* health 10
  être en bonne/mauvaise
  santé *v.* to be in good/bad
  health 10
saucisse *f.* sausage 9
sauvegarder *v.* to save 11
sauver (la planète) *v.* to save
  (the planet) 14
sauvetage des habitats *m.*
  habitat preservation 14
savoir *v.* to know (*facts*), to know
  how to do something 8
  savoir (que) *v.* to know (that)
  15
  Je n'en sais rien. I don't
  know anything about it. 14
savon *m.* soap 10
sciences *f., pl.* science 2
  sciences politiques (sciences
  po) *f., pl.* political science 2
sculpture *f.* sculpture 15
sculpteur/sculptrice
  m., f. sculptor 15
se/s' *pron., sing., pl. (used with*
  reflexive verb) himself; herself;
  itself; 10 (*used with reciprocal*
  verb) each other 11
séance *f.* show; screening 15
se blesser *v.* to hurt oneself 10
se brosser (les cheveux/les
  dents) *v.* to brush one's (hair/
  teeth) 9
se casser *v.* to break 10
sèche-linge *m.* clothes dryer 8
se coiffer *v.* to do one's hair 10
se connaître *v.* to know one
  another 11
se coucher *v.* to go to bed 10
secours *m.* help 11
  Au secours! Help! 11
s'écrire *v.* to write one
  another 11

sécurité *f.* security; safety
  attacher sa ceinture de
  sécurité *v.* to buckle one's
  seatbelt 11
se dépêcher *v.* to hurry 10
se déplacer *v.* to move, to change
  location 12
se déshabiller *v.* to undress 10
se détendre *v.* to relax 10
se dire *v.* to tell one another 11
se disputer (avec) *v.* to argue
  (with) 10
se donner *v.* to give one
  another 11
se fouler (la cheville) *v.* to
  twist/to sprain one's (ankle) 10
se garer *v.* to park 11
seize *m.* sixteen 1
séjour *m.* stay 7
  faire un séjour *v.* to spend time
  (*somewhere*) 7
  salle de séjour *f.* living room 8
sel *m.* salt 9
se laver (les mains) *v.* to wash
  oneself (one's hands) 10
se lever *v.* to get up, to get out
  of bed 10
semaine *f.* week 2
  cette semaine this week 2
s'embrasser *v.* to kiss one
  another 11
se maquiller *v.* to put on
  makeup 10
se mettre *v.* to put (*something*)
  on (yourself) 10
  se mettre à *v.* to begin to 10
  se mettre en colère *v.* to
  become angry 10
s'endormir *v.* to fall asleep, to go
  to sleep 10
s'énerver *v.* to get worked up, to
  become upset 10
sénégalais(e) *adj.* Senegalese 1
s'ennuyer *v.* to get bored 10
s'entendre bien (avec) *v.* to
  get
  along well (with one another) 10
sentier *m.* path 14
sentir *v.* to feel; to smell;
  to sense 5
séparé(e) *adj.* separated 3
se parler *v.* to speak to one
  another 11
se porter mal/mieux *v.* to be
  ill/better 10
se préparer (à) *v.* to get ready;
  to prepare (*to do something*) 10
se promener *v.* to take a walk 10
sept *m.* seven 1
septembre *m.* September 5
septième *adj.* seventh 7

se quitter *v.* to leave one another 11
se raser *v.* to shave oneself 10
se réconcilier *v.* to make up 15
se regarder *v.* to look at oneself; to look at each other 10
se relever *v.* to get up again 10
se rencontrer *v.* to meet one another, to make each other's acquaintance 11
se rendre compte *v.* to realize 10
se reposer *v.* to rest 10
se retrouver *v.* to meet one another (*as planned*) 11
se réveiller *v.* to wake up 10
se sécher *v.* to dry oneself 10
se sentir *v.* to feel 10
sérieux/sérieuse *adj.* serious 3
serpent *m.* snake 14
serre *f.* greenhouse 14
  effet de serre *m.* greenhouse effect 14
serré(e) *adj.* tight 6
serveur/serveuse *m., f.* server 4
serviette *f.* napkin 9
  serviette (de bain) *f.* (bath) towel 10
servir *v.* to serve 5
ses *poss. adj., m., f., pl.* his; her; its 3
se souvenir (de) *v.* to remember 10
se téléphoner *v.* to phone one another 11
se tourner *v.* to turn (oneself) around 10
se tromper (de) *v.* to be mistaken (about) 10
se trouver *v.* to be located 10
seulement *adv.* only 7
s'habiller *v.* to dress 10
shampooing *m.* shampoo 10
shopping *m.* shopping 7
  faire du shopping *v.* to go shopping 7
short *m., sing.* shorts 6
si *conj.* if 13
si *adv.* (*when contradicting a negative statement or question*) yes 2
le sien *poss. pron.* his/hers 15
la sienne *poss. pron.* his/hers 15
les siens *poss. pron.* his/hers 15
les siennes *poss. pron.* his/hers 15
signer *v.* to sign 12
S'il te plaît. *fam.* Please. 1
S'il vous plaît. *form.* Please. 1
sincère *adj.* sincere 1
s'inquiéter *v.* to worry 10
s'intéresser (à) *v.* to be interested (in) 10
site Internet/web *m.* web site 11

six *m.* six 1
sixième *adj.* sixth 7
ski *m.* skiing 5
  faire du ski *v.* to go skiing 5
  station de ski *f.* ski resort 7
skier *v.* to ski 5
smartphone *m.* smartphone 11
SMS *m.* text message 11
s'occuper (de) *v.* to take care (*of something*), to see to 10
sociable *adj.* sociable 1
sociologie *f.* sociology 1
sœur *f.* sister 3
  belle-sœur *f.* sister-in-law 3
  demi-sœur *f.* half-sister, stepsister 3
soie *f.* silk 12
soif *f.* thirst 4
  avoir soif *v.* to be thirsty 4
soir *m.* evening 2
  ce soir *adv.* this evening 2
  demain soir *adv.* tomorrow evening 2
  du soir *adv.* in the evening 2
  hier soir *adv.* yesterday evening 7
soirée *f.* evening 2
sois (être) *imp. v.* be 2
soixante *m.* sixty 1
soixante-dix *m.* seventy 3
solaire *adj.* solar 14
  énergie solaire *f.* solar energy 14
soldes *f., pl.* sales 6
soleil *m.* sun 5
  Il fait (du) soleil. It is sunny. 5
solution *f.* solution 14
  proposer une solution *v.* to propose a solution 14
sommeil *m.* sleep 2
  avoir sommeil *v.* to be sleepy 2
son *poss. adj., m., sing.* his; her; its 3
sonner *v.* to ring 11
s'orienter *v.* to get one's bearings 12
sorte *f.* sort, kind 15
sortie *f.* exit 7
sortir *v.* to go out, to leave 5; to take out 8
  sortir la/les poubelle(s) *v.* to take out the trash 8
soudain *adv.* suddenly 7
souffrir *v.* to suffer 11
souffert (souffrir) *p.p.* suffered 11
souhaiter (que) *v.* to wish (that) 14
soupe *f.* soup 4
  cuillère à soupe *f.* soupspoon 9
sourire *v.* to smile 6; *m.* smile 12
souris *f.* mouse 11
sous *prep.* under 3
sous-sol *m.* basement 8
sous-vêtement *m.* underwear 6

souvent *adv.* often 5
soyez (être) *imp. v.* be 7
soyons (être) *imp. v.* let's be 7
spécialiste *m., f.* specialist 13
spectacle *m.* show 5
spectateur/spectatrice *m., f.* spectator 15
sport *m.* sport(s) 5
  faire du sport *v.* to do sports 5
sportif/sportive *adj.* athletic 3
stade *m.* stadium 5
stage *m.* internship; professional training 13
station (de métro) *f.* (subway) station 7
station de ski *f.* ski resort 7
station-service *f.* service station 11
statue *f.* statue 12
steak *m.* steak 9
studio *m.* studio (*apartment*) 8
stylisme *m.* **de mode** *f.* fashion design 2
stylo *m.* pen 1
su (savoir) *p.p.* known 8
sucre *m.* sugar 4
sud *m.* south 12
suggérer (que) *v.* to suggest (that) 14
sujet *m.* subject 14
  au sujet de on the subject of; about 14
suisse *adj.* Swiss 1
Suisse *f.* Switzerland 7
suivre (un chemin/une rue/ un boulevard) *v.* to follow (a path/a street/a boulevard) 12
supermarché *m.* supermarket 9
sur *prep.* on 3
sûr(e) *adj.* sure, certain 9
  bien sûr of course 2
  Il est sûr que... It is sure that... 15
  Il n'est pas sûr que... It is not sure that... 15
surfer sur Internet *v.* to surf the Internet 11
surpopulation *f.* overpopulation 14
surpris (surprendre) *p.p., adj.* surprised 6
  être surpris(e) que... *v.* to be surprised that... 14
  faire une surprise à quelqu'un *v.* to surprise someone 6
surtout *adv.* especially; above all 2
sympa(thique) *adj.* nice 1
symptôme *m.* symptom 10
syndicat *m.* (*trade*) union 13

T

ta *poss. adj., f., sing.* your 3
table *f.* table 1
  À table! Let's eat! Food is ready! 9
  débarrasser la table *v.* to clear the table 8
  mettre la table *v.* to set the table 8
tableau *m.* blackboard; picture 1; *m.* painting 15
tablette (tactile) *f.* tablet computer 11
tâche ménagère *f.* household chore 8
taille *f.* size; waist 6
  de taille moyenne of medium height 3
tailleur *m.* (*woman's*) suit; tailor 6
tante *f.* aunt 3
tapis *m.* rug 8
tard *adv.* late 2
  À plus tard. See you later. 1
tarte *f.* pie; tart 9
tasse (de) *f.* cup (of) 4
taxi *m.* taxi 7
  prendre un taxi *v.* to take a taxi 7
te/t' *pron., sing., fam.* you 7; yourself 10
tee-shirt *m.* tee shirt 6
télécarte *f.* phone card 13
télécharger *v.* to download 11
télécommande *f.* remote control 11
téléphone *m.* telephone 2
  parler au téléphone *v.* to speak on the phone 2
téléphoner (à) *v.* to telephone (*someone*) 2
téléphonique *adj.* (*related to the*) telephone 12
  cabine téléphonique *f.* phone booth 12
télévision *f.* television 1
  à la télé(vision) on television 15
  chaîne de télévision *f.* television channel 11
tellement *adv.* so much 2
  Je n'aime pas tellement... I don't like... very much. 2
température *f.* temperature 5
  Quelle température fait-il? What is the temperature? 5
temps *m., sing.* weather 5
  Il fait un temps épouvantable. The weather is dreadful. 5
  Le temps est nuageux. It is cloudy. 5

  Le temps est orageux. It is stormy. 5
  Quel temps fait-il? What is the weather like? 5
temps *m., sing.* time 5
  de temps en temps *adv.* from time to time 7
  emploi à mi-temps/à temps partiel *m.* part-time job 13
  emploi à plein temps *m.* full-time job 13
  temps libre *m.* free time 5
Tenez! (tenir) *imp. v.* Here! 9
tenir *v.* to hold 9
tennis *m.* tennis 5
terrasse (de café) *f.* (café) terrace 4
Terre *f.* Earth 14
  réchauffement de la Terre *m.* global warming 14
tes *poss. adj., m., f., pl.* your 3
tête *f.* head 10
texto *m.* text message 11
thé *m.* tea 4
théâtre *m.* theater 15
thon *m.* tuna 9
ticket de bus/métro *m.* bus/subway ticket 7
le tien *poss. pron.* yours 15
la tienne *poss. pron.* yours 15
les tiens *poss. pron.* yours 15
les tiennes *poss. pron.* yours 15
Tiens! (tenir) *imp. v.* Here! 9
timbre *m.* stamp 12
timide *adj.* shy 1
tiret *m.* (*punctuation mark*) dash; hyphen 11
tiroir *m.* drawer 8
toi *disj. pron., sing., fam.* you 3; *refl. pron., sing., fam.* (*attached to imperative*) yourself 10
  toi non plus you neither 2
toilette *f.* washing up, grooming 10
  faire sa toilette to wash up 10
toilettes *f., pl.* restroom(s) 8
tomate *f.* tomato 9
tomber *v.* to fall 7
  tomber amoureux/amoureuse *v.* to fall in love 6
  tomber en panne *v.* to break down 11
  tomber/être malade *v.* to get/be sick 10
  tomber sur quelqu'un *v.* to run into someone 7
ton *poss. adj., m., sing.* your 3
tort *m.* wrong; harm 2
  avoir tort *v.* to be wrong 2
tôt *adv.* early 2
toujours *adv.* always 7

tour *m.* tour 5
  faire un tour (en voiture) *v.* to go for a walk (drive) 5
tourisme *m.* tourism 12
  office du tourisme *m.* tourist office 12
tourner *v.* to turn 12
tousser *v.* to cough 10
tout *m., sing.* all 4
  tous les (*used before noun*) all the... 4
  tous les jours *adv.* every day 7
  toute la *f., sing.* (*used before noun*) all the... 4
  toutes les *f., pl.* (*used before noun*) all the... 4
  tout le *m., sing.* (*used before noun*) all the... 4
  tout le monde everyone 9
tout(e) *adv.* (*before adjective or adverb*) very, really 3
  À tout à l'heure. See you later. 1
  tout à coup suddenly 7
  tout à fait absolutely; completely 12
  tout de suite right away 7
  tout droit straight ahead 12
  tout d'un coup *adv.* all of a sudden 7
  tout près (de) really close by, really close (to) 3
toxique *adj.* toxic 14
  déchets toxiques *m., pl.* toxic waste 14
trac *m.* stage fright 13
traduire *v.* to translate 6
traduit (traduire) *p.p., adj.* translated 6
tragédie *f.* tragedy 15
train *m.* train 7
tranche *f.* slice 9
tranquille *adj.* calm, serene 10
  laisser tranquille *v.* to leave alone 10
travail *m.* work 12
  chercher un/du travail *v.* to look for work 12
  trouver un/du travail *v.* to find a job 13
travailler *v.* to work 2
travailleur/travailleuse *adj.* hard-working 3
traverser *v.* to cross 12
treize *m.* thirteen 1
trente *m.* thirty 1
très *adv.* (*before adjective or adverb*) very, really 8
  Très bien. Very well. 1
triste *adj.* sad 3
  être triste que... *v.* to be sad that... 14

trois *m.* three 1
troisième *adj.* third 7
trop (de) *adv.* too many/much (of) 4
tropical(e) *adj.* tropical 14
   forêt tropicale *f.* tropical forest 14
trou (dans la couche d'ozone) *m.* hole (in the ozone layer) 14
troupe *f.* company, troupe 15
trouver *v.* to find; to think 2
   trouver un/du travail *v.* to find a job 13
truc *m.* thing 7
tu *sub. pron., sing., fam.* you 1

U

un *m.* *(number)* one 1
un(e) *indef. art.* a; an 1
universitaire *adj. (related to the)* university 1
   restaurant universitaire (resto U) *m.* university cafeteria 2
université *f.* university 1
urgences *f., pl.* emergency room 10
   aller aux urgences *v.* to go to the emergency room 10
usine *f.* factory 14
utile *adj.* useful 2
utiliser (un plan) *v.* use (a map) 7

V

vacances *f., pl.* vacation 7
   partir en vacances *v.* to go on vacation 7
vache *f.* cow 14
vaisselle *f.* dishes 8
   faire la vaisselle *v.* to do the dishes 8
   lave-vaisselle *m.* dishwasher 8
valise *f.* suitcase 7
   faire les valises *v.* to pack one's bags 7
vallée *f.* valley 14
variétés *f., pl.* popular music 15
vaut (valoir) *v.*
   Il vaut mieux que It is better that 14
vélo *m.* bicycle 5
   faire du vélo *v.* to go bike riding 5
velours *m.* velvet 12
vendeur/vendeuse *m., f.* seller 6
vendre *v.* to sell 6
vendredi *m.* Friday 2
venir *v.* to come 9
   venir de *v. (used with an infinitive)* to have just 9

vent *m.* wind 5
   Il fait du vent. It is windy. 5
ventre *m.* stomach 10
vérifier (l'huile/la pression des pneus) *v.* to check (the oil/the tire pressure) 11
véritable *adj.* true, real 12
verre (de) *m.* glass (of) 4
vers *adv.* about 2
vert(e) *adj.* green 3
   haricots verts *m., pl.* green beans 9
vêtements *m., pl.* clothing 6
   sous-vêtement *m.* underwear 6
vétérinaire *m., f.* veterinarian 13
veuf/veuve *adj.* widowed 3
veut dire (vouloir dire) *v.* means, signifies 9
viande *f.* meat 9
vie *f.* life 6
   assurance vie *f.* life insurance 13
vieille *adj., f. (feminine form of vieux)* old 3
vieillesse *f.* old age 6
vieillir *v.* to grow old 4
vietnamien(ne) *adj.* Vietnamese 1
vieux/vieille *adj.* old 3
ville *f.* city; town 4
vin *m.* wine 6
vingt *m.* twenty 1
vingtième *adj.* twentieth 7
violet(te) *adj.* purple; violet 6
violon *m.* violin 15
visage *m.* face 10
visite *f.* visit 6
   rendre visite (à) *v.* to visit (*a person or people*) 6
visiter *v.* to visit (*a place*) 2
   faire visiter *v.* to give a tour 8
vite *adv.* quickly 1; quick, hurry 4
vitesse *f.* speed 11
voici here is/are 1
voilà there is/are 1
voir *v.* to see 12
voisin(e) *m., f.* neighbor 3
voiture *f.* car 11
   faire un tour en voiture *v.* to go for a drive 5
   rouler en voiture *v.* to ride in a car 7
vol *m.* flight 7
volant *m.* steering wheel 11
volcan *m.* volcano 14
volley(-ball) *m.* volleyball 5
volontiers *adv.* willingly 10
vos *poss. adj., m., f., pl.* your 3
votre *poss. adj., m., f., sing.* your 3
   le vôtre *poss. pron.* yours 15
   la vôtre *poss. pron.* yours 15
   les vôtres *poss. pron.* yours 15

vouloir *v.* to want; to mean (*with* **dire**) 9
   ça veut dire that is to say 10
   veut dire *v.* means, signifies 9
   vouloir (que) *v.* to want (that) 14
voulu (vouloir) *p.p., adj. (used with infinitive)* wanted to… ; (*used with noun*) planned to/for 9
vous *pron., sing., pl., fam., form.* you 1; *d.o. pron.* you 7; yourself, yourselves 10
voyage *m.* trip 7
   agence de voyages *f.* travel agency 7
   agent de voyages *m.* travel agent 7
voyager *v.* to travel 2
voyant (d'essence/d'huile) *m.* (gas/oil) warning light 11
vrai(e) *adj.* true; real 3
   Il est vrai que… It is true that… 15
   Il n'est pas vrai que… It is untrue that… 15
vraiment *adv.* really, truly 5
vu (voir) *p.p.* seen 15

W

W.-C. *m., pl.* restroom(s) 8
week-end *m.* weekend 2
   ce week-end this weekend 2

Y

y *pron.* there; at (*a place*) 10
   j'y vais I'm going/coming 8
   nous y allons we're going/coming 9
   on y va let's go 10
   Y a-t-il… ? Is/Are there… ? 2
yaourt *m.* yogurt 9
yeux (œil) *m., pl.* eyes 3

Z

zéro *m.* zero 1
zut *interj.* darn 6

English-French

A

a **un(e)** *indef. art.* 1
able: to be able to **pouvoir** *v.* 9
abolish **abolir** *v.* 14
about **vers** *adv.* 2
abroad **à l'étranger** 7
absolutely **absolument** *adv.* 7;
  tout à fait *adv.* 6
accident **accident** *m.* 10
  to have/to be in an accident
  avoir un accident *v.* 11
accompany **accompagner** *v.* 12
account *(at a bank)* **compte** *m.* 12
  checking account **compte** *m.*
  de chèques 12
  to have a bank account **avoir**
  un compte bancaire *v.* 12
accountant **comptable** *m., f.* 13
acid rain **pluie acide** *f.* 14
across from **en face de** *prep.* 3
acquaintance **connaissance** *f.* 5
active **actif/active** *adj.* 3
actively **activement** *adv.* 7
actor **acteur/actrice** *m., f.* 1
add **ajouter** *v.* 11
  add a friend **ajouter un(e)**
  ami(e) 11
address **adresse** *f.* 12
administration: business
  administration **gestion** *f.* 2
adolescence **adolescence** *f.* 6
adore **adorer** 2
  I love... **J'adore...** 2
  to adore one another
  s'adorer *v.* 11
adulthood **âge adulte** *m.* 6
adventure **aventure** *f.* 15
  adventure film **film** *m.*
  d'aventures 15
advertisement **publicité (pub)** *f.* 15
advice **conseil** *m.* 13
advisor **conseiller/conseillère**
  m., f. 13
aerobics **aérobic** *m.* 5
  to do aerobics **faire de**
  l'aérobic *v.* 5
afraid: to be afraid of/that **avoir**
  peur de/que *v.* 14
after **après (que)** *adv.* 7
afternoon **après-midi** *m.* 2
  ... (o'clock) in the afternoon
  ... heure(s) de l'après-midi 2
afternoon snack **goûter** *m.* 9
again **encore** *adv.* 3
age **âge** *m.* 6
agent: travel agent **agent de**

voyages *m.* 7
  real estate agent **agent**
  immobilier *m.* 13
ago *(with an expression of time)*
  il y a... 9
agree: to agree (with) **être**
  d'accord (avec) *v.* 2
airport **aéroport** *m.* 7
alarm clock **réveil** *m.* 10
Algerian **algérien(ne)** *adj.* 1
all **tout** *m., sing.* 4
  all of a sudden **soudain** *adv.* 7;
  tout à coup *adv.*; **tout d'un**
  coup *adv.* 7
all right? *(tag question)* **d'accord?** 2
allergy **allergie** *f.* 10
allow *(to do something)* **laisser** *v.*
  11; **permettre (de)** *v.* 6
allowed **permis (permettre)**
  p.p., adj. 6
all the... *(agrees with noun that*
  follows) **tout le...** *m., sing;*
  toute la... *f., sing;* **tous les...**
  m., pl.; **toutes les...** *f., pl.* 4
almost **presque** *adv.* 5
a lot (of) **beaucoup (de)** *adv.* 4
alone: to leave alone **laisser**
  tranquille *v.* 10
already **déjà** *adv.* 3
always **toujours** *adv.* 7
American **américain(e)** *adj.* 1
an **un(e)** *indef. art.* 1
ancient *(placed after noun)*
  ancien(ne) *adj.* 15
and **et** *conj.* 1
  And you? **Et toi?**, *fam.;* **Et**
  vous? *form.* 1
angel **ange** *m.* 1
angry: to become angry
  s'énerver *v.* 10; **se mettre**
  en colère *v.* 10
animal **animal** *m.* 14
ankle **cheville** *f.* 10
apartment **appartement** *m.* 7
appetizer **entrée** *f.* 9;
  hors-d'œuvre *m.* 9
applaud **applaudir** *v.* 15
applause **applaudissement** *m.* 15
apple **pomme** *f.* 9
appliance **appareil** *m.* 8
  electrical/household appliance
  appareil *m.* **électrique/**
  ménager 8
applicant **candidat(e)** *m., f.* 13
apply **postuler** *v.* 13
appointment **rendez-vous** *m.* 13
  to make an appointment
  prendre (un) rendez-vous *v.* 13
April **avril** *m.* 5
architect **architecte** *m., f.* 3

architecture **architecture** *f.* 2
Are there... ? **Y a-t-il... ?** 2
area **quartier** *m.* 8
argue (with) **se disputer**
  (avec) *v.* 10
arm **bras** *m.* 10
armchair **fauteuil** *m.* 8
armoire **armoire** *f.* 8
around **autour (de)** *prep.* 12
arrival **arrivée** *f.* 7
arrive **arriver (à)** *v.* 2
art **art** *m.* 2
  artwork, piece of art **œuvre** *f.* 15
  fine arts **beaux-arts** *m., pl.* 15
artist **artiste** *m., f.* 3
as *(like)* **comme** *adv.* 6
  as ... as *(used with adjective to*
  compare) **aussi ... que** 9
  as much ... as *(used with noun*
  to express comparative quan-
  tity) **autant de ... que** 14
  as soon as **dès que** *adv.* 13
ashamed: to be ashamed of
  avoir honte de *v.* 2
ask **demander** *v.* 2
  to ask *(someone)* **demander**
  (à) *v.* 6
  to ask *(someone)* a question
  poser une question (à) *v.* 6
  to ask that... **demander**
  que... 14
aspirin **aspirine** *f.* 10
at **à** *prep.* 4
  at ... (o'clock) **à ... heure(s)** 4
  at the doctor's office **chez le**
  médecin *prep.* 2
  at (someone's) house **chez...**
  prep. 2
  at the end (of) **au bout (de)**
  prep. 12
  at last **enfin** *adv.* 11
athlete **athlète** *m., f.* 3
ATM **distributeur** *m.* **automa-**
  tique/de billets *m.* 12
attend **assister** *v.* 2
August **août** *m.* 5
aunt **tante** *f.* 3
author **auteur/femme auteur**
  m., f. 15
autumn **automne** *m.* 5
  in autumn **en automne** 5
available *(free)* **libre** *adj.* 7
avenue **avenue** *f.* 12
avoid **éviter de** *v.* 10

B

back **dos** *m.* 10
backpack **sac à dos** *m.* 1
bad **mauvais(e)** *adj.* 3

to be in a bad mood **être de mauvaise humeur** 8

to be in bad health **être en mauvaise santé** 10
badly **mal** *adv.* 7
I am doing badly. **Je vais mal.** 1
to be doing badly **se porter mal** *v.* 10
baguette **baguette** *f.* 4
bakery **boulangerie** *f.* 9
balcony **balcon** *m.* 8
banana **banane** *f.* 9
bank **banque** *f.* 12
to have a bank account **avoir un compte bancaire** *v.* 12
banker **banquier/banquière** *m., f.* 13
banking **bancaire** *adj.* 12
baseball **baseball** *m.* 5
baseball cap **casquette** *f.* 6
basement **sous-sol** *m.*; **cave** *f.* 8
basketball **basket(-ball)** *m.* 5
bath **bain** *m.* 6
bathing suit **maillot de bain** *m.* 6
bathroom **salle de bains** *f.* 8
bathtub **baignoire** *f.* 8
be **être** *v.* 1
sois (être) *imp. v.* 7; **soyez (être)** *imp. v.* 7
beach **plage** *f.* 7
beans **haricots** *m., pl.* 9
green beans **haricots verts** *m., pl.* 9
bearings: to get one's bearings **s'orienter** *v.* 12
beautiful **beau (belle)** *adj.* 3
beauty salon **salon** *m.* **de beauté** 12
because **parce que** *conj.* 2
become **devenir** *v.* 9
bed **lit** *m.* 7
to go to bed **se coucher** *v.* 10
bedroom **chambre** *f.* 8
beef **bœuf** *m.* 9
been **été (être)** *p.p.* 6
beer **bière** *f.* 6
before **avant (de/que)** *adv.* 7
before (o'clock) **moins** *adv.* 2
begin (to do something) **commencer (à)** *v.* 2; **se mettre à** *v.* 10
beginning **début** *m.* 15
behind **derrière** *prep.* 3
Belgian **belge** *adj.* 7
Belgium **Belgique** *f.* 7
believe (that) **croire (que)** *v.* 12
believed **cru (croire)** *p.p.* 12
belt **ceinture** *f.* 6
to buckle one's seatbelt **attacher sa ceinture de**

sécurité *v.* 11
bench **banc** *m.* 12

best: the best **le mieux** *super. adv.* 9; **le/la meilleur(e)** *super. adj.* 9
better **meilleur(e)** *comp. adj.*; **mieux** *comp. adv.* 9
It is better that… **Il vaut mieux que/qu'…** 14
to be doing better **se porter mieux** *v.* 10
to get better (from illness) **guérir** *v.* 10
between **entre** *prep.* 3
beverage (carbonated) **boisson** *f.* **(gazeuse)** 4
bicycle **vélo** *m.* 5
to go bike riding **faire du vélo** *v.* 5
big **grand(e)** *adj.* 3; (clothing) **large** *adj.* 6
bill (in a restaurant) **addition** *f.* 4
bills (money) **billets** *m., pl.* 12
biology **biologie** *f.* 2
bird **oiseau** *m.* 3
birth **naissance** *f.* 6
birthday **anniversaire** *m.* 5
bit (of) **morceau (de)** *m.* 4
black **noir(e)** *adj.* 3
blackboard **tableau** *m.* 1
blanket **couverture** *f.* 8
blonde **blond(e)** *adj.* 3
blouse **chemisier** *m.* 6
blue **bleu(e)** *adj.* 3
blush **rougir** *v.* 4
boat **bateau** *m.* 7
body **corps** *m.* 10
book **livre** *m.* 1
bookstore **librairie** *f.* 1
bored: to get bored **s'ennuyer** *v.* 10
boring **ennuyeux/ennuyeuse** *adj.* 3
born: to be born **naître** *v.* 7; **né (naître)** *p.p., adj.* 7
borrow **emprunter** *v.* 12
bottle (of) **bouteille (de)** *f.* 4
boulevard **boulevard** *m.* 12
boutique **boutique** *f.* 12
bowl **bol** *m.* 9
box **boîte** *f.* 9
boy **garçon** *m.* 1
boyfriend **petit ami** *m.* 1
brake **freiner** *v.* 11
brakes **freins** *m., pl.* 11
brave **courageux/courageuse** *adj.* 3
Brazil **Brésil** *m.* 7
Brazilian **brésilien(ne)** *adj.* 7
bread **pain** *m.* 4
country-style bread **pain** *m.* **de campagne** 4
bread shop **boulangerie** *f.* 9

break **se casser** *v.* 10
breakdown **panne** *f.* 11

break down **tomber en panne** *v.* 11
break up (to leave one another) **se quitter** *v.* 11
breakfast **petit-déjeuner** *m.* 9
bridge **pont** *m.* 12
bright **brillant(e)** *adj.* 1
bring (a person) **amener** *v.* 5; (a thing) **apporter** *v.* 4
broom **balai** *m.* 8
brother **frère** *m.* 3
brother-in-law **beau-frère** *m.* 3
brown **marron** *adj., inv.* 3
brown (hair) **châtain** *adj.* 3
brush (hair/tooth) **brosse** *f.* **(à cheveux/à dents)** 10
to brush one's hair/teeth **se brosser les cheveux/ les dents** *v.* 9
buckle: to buckle one's seatbelt **attacher sa ceinture de sécurité** *v.* 11
build **construire** *v.* 6
building **bâtiment** *m.* 12; **immeuble** *m.* 8
bumper **pare-chocs** *m.* 11
bus **autobus** *m.* 7
bus stop **arrêt d'autobus (de bus)** *m.* 7
bus terminal **gare** *f.* **routière** 7
business (profession) **affaires** *f., pl.* 3; (company) **entreprise** *f.* 13
business administration **gestion** *f.* 2
businessman **homme d'affaires** *m.* 3
businesswoman **femme d'affaires** *f.* 3
busy **occupé(e)** *adj.* 1
but **mais** *conj.* 1
butcher's shop **boucherie** *f.* 9
butter **beurre** *m.* 4
buy **acheter** *v.* 5
by **par** *prep.* 3
Bye! **Salut!** *fam.* 1

C

cabinet **placard** *m.* 8
café **café** *m.* 1; **brasserie** *f.* 12
café terrace **terrasse** *f.* **de café** 4
cybercafé **cybercafé** *m.* 12
cafeteria (school) **cantine** *f.* 9
cake **gâteau** *m.* 6
calculator **calculatrice** *f.* 1
call **appeler** *v.* 13
calm **calme** *adj.* 1; **calme** *m.* 1
camera **appareil photo** *m.* 11

digital camera **appareil photo** *m.* **numérique** 11
camping **camping** *m.* 5
   to go camping **faire du camping** *v.* 5
can (of food) **boîte (de conserve)** *f.* 9
Canada **Canada** *m.* 7
Canadian **canadien(ne)** *adj.* 1
cancel (a reservation) **annuler (une réservation)** *v.* 7
candidate **candidat(e)** *m., f.* 13
candy **bonbon** *m.* 6
cap: baseball cap **casquette** *f.* 6
capital **capitale** *f.* 7
car **voiture** *f.* 11
   to ride in a car **rouler en voiture** *v.* 7
card *(letter)* **carte postale** *f.* 12; credit card **carte** *f.* **de crédit** 12
   to pay with a credit card **payer avec une carte de crédit** *v.* 12
   cards *(playing)* **cartes** *f.* 5
carbonated drink/beverage **boisson** *f.* **gazeuse** 4
career **carrière** *f.* 13
carpooling **covoiturage** *m.* 14
carrot **carotte** *f.* 9
carry **apporter** *v.* 4
cartoon **dessin animé** *m.* 15
case: in any case **en tout cas** 6
cash **liquide** *m.* 12
   to pay in cash **payer en liquide** *v.* 12
cat **chat** *m.* 3
catastrophe **catastrophe** *f.* 14
catch sight of **apercevoir** *v.* 12
CD(s) **CD** *m.* 11
CD/DVD player **lecteur de CD/DVD** *m.* 11
celebrate **célébrer** *v.* 5; **fêter** *v.* 6
celebration **fête** *f.* 6
cellar **cave** *f.* 8
cell(ular) phone **portable** *m.* 11
center: city/town center **centre-ville** *m.* 4
certain **certain(e)** *adj.* 9; **sûr(e)** *adj.* 15
   It is certain that… **Il est certain que…** 15
   It is uncertain that… **Il n'est pas certain que…** 15
chair **chaise** *f.* 1
champagne **champagne** *m.* 6
change *(coins)* **(pièces** *f. pl.* **de) monnaie** 12
channel (television) **chaîne** *f.* **(de télévision)** 11
character **personnage** *m.* 15
   main character **personnage principal** *m.* 15
charge **recharger** *v.* 11
charming **charmant(e)** *adj.* 1

chat **bavarder** *v.* 4
check **chèque** *m.* 12; *(bill)* **addition** *f.* 4
   to pay by check **payer par chèque** *v.* 12;
   to check (the oil/the air pressure) **vérifier (l'huile/la pression des pneus)** *v.* 11
checking account **compte** *m.* **de chèques** 12
cheek **joue** *f.* 10
cheese **fromage** *m.* 4
chemistry **chimie** *f.* 2
chess **échecs** *m., pl.* 5
chest **poitrine** *f.* 10
   chest of drawers **commode** *f.* 8
chic **chic** *adj.* 4
chicken **poulet** *m.* 9
child **enfant** *m., f.* 3
childhood **enfance** *f.* 6
China **Chine** *f.* 7
Chinese **chinois(e)** *adj.* 7
choir **chœur** *m.* 15
choose **choisir** *v.* 4
chorus **chœur** *m.* 15
chrysanthemums **chrysanthèmes** *m., pl.* 9
church **église** *f.* 4
city **ville** *f.* 4
city hall **mairie** *f.* 12
city/town center **centre-ville** *m.* 4
class (group of students) **classe** *f.* 1; *(course)* **cours** *m.* 2
classmate **camarade de classe** *m., f.* 1
classroom **salle** *f.* **de classe** 1
clean **nettoyer** *v.* 5; **propre** *adj.* 8
clear **clair(e)** *adj.* 15
   It is clear that… **Il est clair que…** 15
   to clear the table **débarrasser la table** 8
client **client(e)** *m., f.* 7
cliff **falaise** *f.* 14
clock **horloge** *f.* 1
   alarm clock **réveil** *m.* 10
close (to) **près (de)** *prep.* 3
   very close (to) **tout près (de)** 12
close **fermer** *v.* 11
closed **fermé(e)** *adj.* 12
closet **placard** *m.* 8
clothes dryer **sèche-linge** *m.* 8
clothing **vêtements** *m., pl.* 6
cloudy **nuageux/nuageuse** *adj.* 5
   It is cloudy. **Le temps est nuageux.** 5
clutch **embrayage** *m.* 11
coast **côte** *f.* 14
coat **manteau** *m.* 6
coffee **café** *m.* 1
coffeemaker **cafetière** *f.* 8
coins **pièces** *f. pl.* **de monnaie** 12

cold **froid** *m.* 2
   to be cold **avoir froid** *v.* 2 *(weather)* It is cold. **Il fait froid.** 5
cold **rhume** *m.* 10
color **couleur** *f.* 6
   What color is… ? **De quelle couleur est… ?** 6
comb **peigne** *m.* 10
come **venir** *v.* 7
come back **revenir** *v.* 9
Come on. **Allez.** 2
comedy **comédie** *f.* 15
comic strip **bande dessinée (B.D.)** *f.* 5
compact disc **compact disque** *m.* 11
company *(troop)* **troupe** *f.* 15
completely **tout à fait** *adv.* 6
composer **compositeur** *m.* 15
computer **ordinateur** *m.* 1
computer science **informatique** *f.* 2
concert **concert** *m.* 15
congratulations **félicitations** 15
consider **considérer** *v.* 5
constantly **constamment** *adv.* 7
construct **construire** *v.* 6
consultant **conseiller/conseillère** *m., f.* 13
continue *(doing something)* **continuer (à)** *v.* 12
cook **cuisiner** *v.* 9; **faire la cuisine** *v.* 5; **cuisinier/cuisinière** *m., f.* 13
cookie **biscuit** *m.* 6
cooking **cuisine** *f.* 5
cool: *(weather)* It is cool. **Il fait frais.** 5
corner **angle** *m.* 12; **coin** *m.* 12
cost **coûter** *v.* 4
cotton **coton** *m.* 6
couch **canapé** *m.* 8
cough **tousser** *v.* 10
count (on someone) **compter (sur quelqu'un)** *v.* 8
country **pays** *m.* 7
   country(side) **campagne** *f.* 7
country-style **de campagne** *adj.* 4
couple **couple** *m.* 6
courage **courage** *m.* 13
courageous **courageux/courageuse** *adj.* 3
course **cours** *m.* 2
cousin **cousin(e)** *m., f.* 3
cover **couvrir** *v.* 11
covered **couvert (couvrir)** *p.p.* 11
cow **vache** *f.* 14
crazy **fou/folle** *adj.* 3
cream **crème** *f.* 9
credit card **carte** *f.* **de crédit** 12
   to pay with a credit card **payer avec une carte de crédit** *v.* 12

crêpe **crêpe** *f.* 5
crime film **film policier** *m.* 15
croissant **croissant** *m.* 4
cross **traverser** *v.* 12
cruel **cruel/cruelle** *adj.* 3
cry **pleurer** *v.*
cup (of) **tasse (de)** *f.* 4
cupboard **placard** *m.* 8
curious **curieux/**
   curieuse *adj.* 3
curly **frisé(e)** *adj.* 3
currency **monnaie** *f.* 12
curtain **rideau** *m.* 8
customs **douane** *f.* 7
cybercafé **cybercafé** *m.* 12

D

dance **danse** *f.* 15
   to dance **danser** *v.* 4
danger **danger** *m.* 14
dangerous **dangereux/**
   dangereuse *adj.* 11
dark (*hair*) **brun(e)** *adj.* 3
darling **chéri(e)** *adj.* 2
darn **zut** 11
dash (*punctuation mark*) **tiret**
   m. 11
date (*day, month, year*) **date** *f.* 5;
   (*meeting*) **rendez-vous** *m.* 6
   to make a date **prendre (un)**
   rendez-vous *v.* 13
daughter **fille** *f.* 1
day **jour** *m.* 2; **journée** *f.* 2
   day after tomorrow **après-**
   demain *adv.* 2
   day before yesterday **avant-**
   hier *adv.* 7
   day off **congé** *m.*, **jour de**
   congé 7
dear **cher/chère** *adj.* 2
death **mort** *f.* 6
December **décembre** *m.* 5
decide (*to do something*)
   décider (de) *v.* 11
deforestation **déboisement** *m.* 14
degree **diplôme** *m.* 2
degrees (*temperature*) **degrés**
   m., pl. 5
   It is... degrees. **Il fait... degrés.** 5
delicatessen **charcuterie** *f.* 9
delicious **délicieux/délicieuse**
   adj. 4
Delighted. **Enchanté(e).** *p.p.,*
   adj. 1
demand (*that*) **exiger (que)** *v.* 14
demanding **exigeant(e)** *adj.* 13
   demanding profession
   profession *f.* **exigeante** 13
dentist **dentiste** *m., f.* 3
department store **grand magasin**
   m. 4
departure **départ** *m.* 7

deposit: to deposit money
   déposer de l'argent *v.* 12
depressed **déprimé(e)** *adj.* 10
describe **décrire** *v.* 7
described **décrit (décrire)** *p.p.,*
   adj. 7
desert **désert** *m.* 14
design (*fashion*) **stylisme (de**
   mode) *m.* 2
desire **envie** *f.* 2
desk **bureau** *m.* 1
dessert **dessert** *m.* 6
destroy **détruire** *v.* 6
destroyed **détruit (détruire)**
   p.p., adj. 6
detective film **film policier** *m.* 15
detest **détester** *v.* 2
   I hate... **Je déteste...** 2
develop **développer** *v.* 14
dial (*a number*) **composer**
   (un numéro) *v.* 11
dictionary **dictionnaire** *m.* 1
die **mourir** *v.* 7
died **mort (mourir)** *p.p., adj.* 7
diet **régime** *m.* 10
   to be on a diet **être au**
   régime 9
difference **différence** *f.* 1
different **différent(e)** *adj.* 1
differently **différemment** *adv.* 7
difficult **difficile** *adj.* 1
digital camera **appareil photo**
   m. **numérique** 11
dining room **salle à manger** *f.* 8
dinner **dîner** *m.* 9
   to have dinner **dîner** *v.* 2
diploma **diplôme** *m.* 2
directions **indications** *f.* 12
director (*movie*) **réalisateur/**
   réalisatrice *m., f.;* (*play/show*)
   metteur en scène *m.* 15
dirty **sale** *adj.* 8
discover **découvrir** *v.* 11
discovered **découvert**
   (découvrir) *p.p.* 11
discreet **discret/discrète** *adj.* 3
discuss **discuter** *v.* 11
dish (*food*) **plat** *m.* 9
   to do the dishes **faire la**
   vaisselle *v.* 8
dishwasher **lave-vaisselle** *m.* 8
dismiss **renvoyer** *v.* 13
distinction **mention** *f.* 13
divorce **divorce** *m.* 6
   to divorce **divorcer** *v.* 3
divorced **divorcé(e)** *p.p., adj.* 3
do (*make*) **faire** *v.* 5
   to do odd jobs **bricoler** *v.* 5
doctor **médecin** *m.* 3
documentary **documentaire**
   m. 15
dog **chien** *m.* 3
done **fait (faire)** *p.p., adj.* 6

door (*building*) **porte** *f.* 1;
   (*automobile*) **portière** *f.* 11
dorm **résidence** *f.* **universita-**
   ire 8
doubt (*that*)... **douter (que)...**
   v. 15
doubtful **douteux/douteuse**
   adj. 15
   It is doubtful that... **Il est**
   douteux que... 15
download **télécharger** *v.* 11
downtown **centre-ville** *m.* 4
drag **barbant** *adj.* 3; **barbe** *f.* 3
drape **rideau** *m.* 8
draw **dessiner** *v.* 2
drawer **tiroir** *m.* 8
dreadful **épouvantable** *adj.* 5
dream (*about*) **rêver (de)** *v.* 11
dress **robe** *f.* 6
   to dress **s'habiller** *v.* 10
dresser **commode** *f.* 8
drink (*carbonated*)
   boisson *f.* **(gazeuse)** 4
   to drink **boire** *v.* 4
drive **conduire** *v.* 6
   to go for a drive **faire un tour**
   en voiture 5
driven **conduit (conduire)** *p.p.* 6
driver (*taxi/truck*) **chauffeur**
   (de taxi/de camion) *m.* 13
driver's license **permis** *m.* **de**
   conduire 11
drums **batterie** *f.* 15
drunk **bu (boire)** *p.p.* 6
dryer (*clothes*) **sèche-linge** *m.* 8
dry oneself **se sécher** *v.* 10
due **dû(e) (devoir)** *adj.* 9
during **pendant** *prep.* 7
dust **enlever/faire la poussière**
   v. 8

E

each **chaque** *adj.* 6
ear **oreille** *f.* 10
early **en avance** *adv.* 2; **tôt**
   adv. 2
earn **gagner** *v.* 13
Earth **Terre** *f.* 14
easily **facilement** *adv.* 7
east **est** *m.* 12
easy **facile** *adj.* 2
eat **manger** *v.* 2
   to eat lunch **déjeuner** *v.* 4
éclair **éclair** *m.* 4
ecological **écologique** *adj.* 14
ecology **écologie** *f.* 14
economics **économie** *f.* 2
ecotourism **écotourisme** *m.* 14
education **formation** *f.* 13
effect: in effect **en effet** 14
egg **œuf** *m.* 9
eight **huit** *m.* 1

eighteen **dix-huit** *m.* 1
eighth **huitième** *adj.* 7
eighty **quatre-vingts** *m.* 3
eighty-one **quatre-vingt-un** *m.* 3
elder **aîné(e)** *adj.* 3
electric **électrique** *adj.* 8
　electrical appliance **appareil** *m.* **électrique** 8
electrician **électricien/ électricienne** *m., f.* 13
elegant **élégant(e)** *adj.* 1
elevator **ascenseur** *m.* 7
eleven **onze** *m.* 1
eleventh **onzième** *adj.* 7
e-mail **e-mail** *m.* 11
emergency room **urgences** *f., pl.* 10
　to go to the emergency room **aller aux urgences** *v.* 10
employ **employer** *v.* 5
end **fin** *f.* 15
endangered **menacé(e)** *adj.* 14
　endangered species **espèce** *f.* **menacée** 14
engaged **fiancé(e)** *adj.* 3
engine **moteur** *m.* 11
engineer **ingénieur** *m.* 3
England **Angleterre** *f.* 7
English **anglais(e)** *adj.* 1
enormous **énorme** *adj.* 2
enough (of) **assez (de)** *adv.* 4
　not enough (of) **pas assez (de)** 4
enter **entrer** *v.* 7
envelope **enveloppe** *f.* 12
environment **environnement** *m.* 14
equal **égaler** *v.* 3
erase **effacer** *v.* 11
errand **course** *f.* 9
escargot **escargot** *m.* 9
especially **surtout** *adv.* 2
essay **dissertation** *f.* 11
essential **essentiel(le)** *adj.* 14
　It is essential that... **Il est essentiel/indispensable que...** 14
even **même** *adv.* 5
evening **soir** *m.;* **soirée** *f.* 2
　... (o'clock) in the evening ... **heures du soir** 2
every day **tous les jours** *adv.* 7
everyone **tout le monde** *m.* 9
evident **évident(e)** *adj.* 15
　It is evident that... **Il est évident que...** 15
evidently **évidemment** *adv.* 7
exactly **exactement** *adv.* 9
exam **examen** *m.* 1
Excuse me. **Excuse-moi.** *fam.* 1; **Excusez-moi.** *form.* 1
executive **cadre/femme cadre** *m., f.* 13

exercise **exercice** *m.* 10
　to exercise **faire de l'exercice** *v.* 10
exhibit **exposition** *f.* 15
exit **sortie** *f.* 7
expenditure **dépense** *f.* 12
expensive **cher/chère** *adj.* 6
explain **expliquer** *v.* 2
explore **explorer** *v.* 4
extinction **extinction** *f.* 14
eye (eyes) **œil (yeux)** *m.* 10

F

face **visage** *m.* 10
facing **en face (de)** *prep.* 3
fact: in fact **en fait** 7
factory **usine** *f.* 14
fail **échouer** *v.* 2
fall **automne** *m.* 5
　in the fall **en automne** 5
　to fall **tomber** *v.* 7
　to fall in love **tomber amoureux/amoureuse** *v.* 6
　to fall asleep **s'endormir** *v.* 10
family **famille** *f.* 3
famous **célèbre** *adj.* 15; **connu (connaître)** *p.p., adj.* 8
far (from) **loin (de)** *prep.* 3
farewell **adieu** *m.* 14
farmer **agriculteur/ agricultrice** *m., f.* 13
fashion **mode** *f.* 2
　fashion design **stylisme de mode** *m.* 2
fast **rapide** *adj.* 3; **vite** *adv.* 7
fat **gros(se)** *adj.* 3
father **père** *m.* 3
father-in-law **beau-père** *m.* 3
favorite **favori/favorite** *adj.* 3; **préféré(e)** *adj.* 2
fear **peur** *f.* 2
　to fear that **avoir peur que** *v.* 14
February **février** *m.* 5
fed up: to be fed up **en avoir marre** *v.* 3
feel (to sense) **sentir** *v.* 5; (state of being) **se sentir** *v.* 10
　to feel like (doing something) **avoir envie (de)** 2
　to feel nauseated **avoir mal au cœur** 10
festival (festivals) **festival (festivals)** *m.* 15
fever **fièvre** *f.* 10
　to have fever **avoir de la fièvre** *v.* 10
fiancé **fiancé(e)** *m., f.* 6
field (terrain) **champ** *m.* 14; (of study) **domaine** *m.* 13
fifteen **quinze** *m.* 1
fifth **cinquième** *adj.* 7

fifty **cinquante** *m.* 1
figure (physique) **ligne** *f.* 10
file **fichier** *m.* 11
fill: to fill out a form **remplir un formulaire** *v.* 12
　to fill the tank **faire le plein** *v.* 11
film **film** *m.* 15
　adventure/crime film **film** *m.* **d'aventures/policier** 15
finally **enfin** *adv.* 7; **finalement** *adv.* 7; **dernièrement** *adv.* 7
find (a job) **trouver (un/du travail)** *v.* 13
　to find again **retrouver** *v.* 2
fine **amende** *f.* 11
fine arts **beaux-arts** *m., pl.* 15
finger **doigt** *m.* 10
finish (doing something) **finir (de)** *v.* 4, 11
fire **incendie** *m.* 14
firefighter **pompier/femme pompier** *m., f.* 13
firm (business) **entreprise** *f.* 13;
first **d'abord** *adv.* 7; **premier/ première** *adj.* 2; **premier** *m.* 5
　It is October first. **C'est le 1ᵉʳ (premier) octobre.** 5
fish **poisson** *m.* 3
fishing **pêche** *f.* 5
　to go fishing **aller à la pêche** *v.* 5
fish shop **poissonnerie** *f.* 9
five **cinq** *m.* 1
flat tire **pneu** *m.* **crevé** 11
flight (air travel) **vol** *m.* 7
floor **étage** *m.* 7
flower **fleur** *f.* 8
flu **grippe** *f.* 10
fluently **couramment** *adv.* 7
follow (a path/a street/a boulevard) **suivre (un chemin/une rue/ un boulevard)** *v.* 12
food (item) **aliment** *m.* 9; **nourriture** *f.* 9
foot **pied** *m.* 10
football **football américain** *m.* 5
for **pour** *prep.* 5; **pendant** *prep.* 9
　For whom? **Pour qui?** 4
forbid **interdire** *v.* 14
foreign **étranger/ étrangère** *adj.* 2
　foreign languages **langues** *f., pl.* **étrangères** 2
forest **forêt** *f.* 14
　tropical forest **forêt tropicale** *f.* 14
forget (to do something) **oublier (de)** *v.* 2
fork **fourchette** *f.* 9
form **formulaire** *m.* 12
former (placed before noun) **ancien(ne)** *adj.* 15

fortunately **heureusement** *adv.* 7
forty **quarante** *m.* 1
fountain **fontaine** *f.* 12
four **quatre** *m.* 1
fourteen **quatorze** *m.* 1
fourth **quatrième** *adj.* 7
France **France** *f.* 7
frankly **franchement** *adv.* 7
free *(at no cost)* **gratuit(e)** *adj.* 15
  free time **temps libre** *m.* 5
freezer **congélateur** *m.* 8
French **français(e)** *adj.* 1
French fries **frites** *f., pl.* 4
frequent *(to visit regularly)* **fréquenter** *v.* 4
fresh **frais/fraîche** *adj.* 5
Friday **vendredi** *m.* 2
friend **ami(e)** *m., f.* 1; **copain/copine** *m., f.* 1
friendship **amitié** *f.* 6
from **de/d'** *prep.* 1
  from time to time **de temps en temps** *adv.* 7
front: in front of **devant** *prep.* 3
fruit **fruit** *m.* 9
full *(no vacancies)* **complet (complète)** *adj.* 7
full-time job **emploi** *m.* **à plein temps** 13
fun **amusant(e)** *adj.* 1
  to have fun *(doing something)* **s'amuser (à)** *v.* 11
funeral **funérailles** *f., pl.* 9
funny **drôle** *adj.* 3
furious **furieux/furieuse** *adj.* 14
  to be furious that... **être furieux/furieuse que...** *v.* 14

G

gain: gain weight **grossir** *v.* 4
game *(amusement)* **jeu** *m.* 5; *(sports)* **match** *m.* 5
game show **jeu télévisé** *m.* 15
garage **garage** *m.* 8
garbage **ordures** *f., pl.* 14
garbage collection **ramassage** *m.* **des ordures** 14
garden **jardin** *m.* 8
garlic **ail** *m.* 9
gas **essence** *f.* 11
gas tank **réservoir d'essence** *m.* 11
gas warning light **voyant** *m.* **d'essence** 11
generally **en général** *adv.* 7
generous **généreux/généreuse** *adj.* 3
genre **genre** *m.* 15
gentle **doux/douce** *adj.* 3
geography **géographie** *f.* 2
German **allemand(e)** *adj.* 1
Germany **Allemagne** *f.* 7

get *(to obtain)* **obtenir** *v.* 13
get along well (with) **s'entendre bien (avec)** *v.* 10
get off **descendre (de)** *v.* 6
get up **se lever** *v.* 10
  get up again **se relever** *v.* 10
gift **cadeau** *m.* 6
  wrapped gift **paquet cadeau** *m.* 6
gifted **doué(e)** *adj.* 15
girl **fille** *f.* 1
girlfriend **petite amie** *f.* 1
give *(to someone)* **donner (à)** *v.* 2
  to give a shot **faire une piqûre** *v.* 10
  to give a tour **faire visiter** *v.* 8
  to give back **rendre (à)** *v.* 6
  to give one another **se donner** *v.* 11
glass (of) **verre (de)** *m.* 4
glasses **lunettes** *f., pl.* 6
  sunglasses **lunettes de soleil** *f., pl.* 6
global warming **réchauffement** *m.* **de la Terre** 14
glove **gant** *m.* 6
go **aller** *v.* 4
  Let's go! **Allons-y!** 4; **On y va!** 10
  I'm going. **J'y vais.** 8
  to go back **repartir** *v.* 15
  to go downstairs **descendre** *v.* 6
  to go out **sortir** *v.* 7
  to go over **dépasser** *v.* 11
  to go up **monter** *v.* 7
  to go with **aller avec** *v.* 6
golf **golf** *m.* 5
good **bon(ne)** *adj.* 3
  Good evening. **Bonsoir.** 1
  Good morning. **Bonjour.** 1
  to be good for nothing **ne servir à rien** *v.* 9
  to be in a good mood **être de bonne humeur** *v.* 8
  to be in good health **être en bonne santé** *v.* 10
  to be in good shape **être en pleine forme** *v.* 10
  to be up to something interesting **faire quelque chose de beau** *v.* 12
  Good-bye. **Au revoir.** 1
government **gouvernement** *m.* 14
grade *(academics)* **note** *f.* 2
grandchildren **petits-enfants** *m., pl.* 3
granddaughter **petite-fille** *f.* 3
grandfather **grand-père** *m.* 3
grandmother **grand-mère** *f.* 3
grandparents **grands-parents** *m., pl.* 3
grandson **petit-fils** *m.* 3
grant **bourse** *f.* 2
grass **herbe** *f.* 14

gratin **gratin** *m.* 9
gray **gris(e)** *adj.* 6
great **formidable** *adj.* 7; **génial(e)** *adj.* 3
green **vert(e)** *adj.* 3
green beans **haricots verts** *m., pl.* 9
greenhouse **serre** *f.* 14
  greenhouse effect **effet de serre** *m.* 14
grocery store **épicerie** *f.* 4
groom: to groom oneself *(in the morning)* **faire sa toilette** *v.* 10
ground floor **rez-de-chaussée** *m.* 7
growing population **population** *f.* **croissante** 14
grow old **vieillir** *v.* 4
grow up **grandir** *v.* 4
guaranteed **garanti(e)** *p.p., adj.* 5
guest **invité(e)** *m., f.* 6; **client(e)** *m., f.* 7
guitar **guitare** *f.* 15
guy **mec** *m.* 10
gym **gymnase** *m.* 4

H

habitat **habitat** *m.* 14
  habitat preservation **sauvetage des habitats** *m.* 14
had **eu (avoir)** *p.p.* 6
  had to **dû (devoir)** *p.p.* 9
hair **cheveux** *m., pl.* 9
  to brush one's hair **se brosser les cheveux** *v.* 9
  to do one's hair **se coiffer** *v.* 10
hairbrush **brosse** *f.* **à cheveux** 10
hairdresser **coiffeur/coiffeuse** *m., f.* 3
half **demie** *f.* 2
  half past ... (o'clock) **... et demie** 2
half-brother **demi-frère** *m.* 3
half-sister **demi-sœur** *f.* 3
half-time job **emploi** *m.* **à mi-temps** 13
hallway **couloir** *m.* 8
ham **jambon** *m.* 4
hand **main** *f.* 5
handbag **sac à main** *m.* 6
handsome **beau** *adj.* 3
hang up **raccrocher** *v.* 13
happiness **bonheur** *m.* 6
happy **heureux/heureuse** *adj.*; **content(e)** 13
  to be happy that... **être content(e) que...** *v.* 14; **être heureux/heureuse que...** *v.* 14
hard drive **disque (dur)** *m.* 11
hard-working **travailleur/travailleuse** *adj.* 3

hat **chapeau** *m.* 6
hate **détester** *v.* 2
   I hate… **Je déteste…** 2
have **avoir** *v.* 2; **aie (avoir)** *imp.,*
   v. 7; **ayez (avoir)** *imp. v.* 7;
   prendre *v.* 4
   to have an ache **avoir**
   mal *v.* 10
   to have to *(must)* **devoir** *v.* 9
he **il** *sub. pron.* 1
head *(body part)* **tête** *f.* 10;
   (of a company) **chef** *m.*
   d'entreprise 13
headache: to have a headache
   avoir mal à la tête *v.* 10
headlights **phares** *m., pl.* 11
headphones **des**
   écouteurs *(m.)* 11
health **santé** *f.* 10
   to be in good health **être en**
   bonne santé *v.* 10
health insurance **assurance**
   f. **maladie** 13
healthy **sain(e)** *adj.* 10
hear **entendre** *v.* 6
heart **cœur** *m.* 10
heat **chaud** *m.* 2
hello *(on the phone)* **allô** 1; *(in the*
   evening) **Bonsoir.** 1; *(in the*
   morning or afternoon)
   Bonjour. 1
help **au secours** 11
   to help *(to do something)* **aider**
   (à) *v.* 5
   to help one another **s'aider**
   v. 11
her **la/l'** *d.o. pron.* 7; **lui** *i.o. pron.*
   6; *(attached to an imperative)*
   -lui *i.o. pron.* 9
her **sa** *poss. adj., f., sing.* 3; **ses**
   poss. adj., m., f., pl. 3; **son**
   poss. adj., m., sing. 3; **la/les**
   sienne(s) *poss. pron.* 15
Here! **Tenez!** *form., imp. v.* 9;
   Tiens! *fam., imp., v.* 9
here **ici** *adv.* 1; *(used with*
   demonstrative adjective ce *and*
   noun or with demonstrative
   pronoun celui*)*; **-ci** 6;
   Here is…. **Voici…** 1
heritage: I am of… heritage. **Je**
   suis d'origine… 1
herself *(used with reflexive verb)*
   se/s' *pron.* 10
hesitate *(to do something)*
   hésiter (à) *v.* 11
Hey! **Eh!** *interj.* 2
Hi! **Salut!** *fam.* 1
high **élevé(e)** *adj.* 13
high school **lycée** *m.* 1
   high school student **lycéen(ne)**
   m., f. 2
higher education **études**

supérieures *f., pl.* 2
highway **autoroute** *f.* 11
hike **randonnée** *f.* 5
   to go for a hike **faire une**
   randonnée *v.* 5
him **lui** *i.o. pron.* 6; **le/l'** *d.o. pron.*
   7; *(attached to imperative)* **-lui**
   i.o. pron. 9
himself *(used with reflexive verb)*
   se/s' *pron.* 10
hire **embaucher** *v.* 13
his **sa** *poss. adj., f., sing.* 3; **ses**
   poss. adj., m., f., pl. 3; **son** *poss.*
   adj., m., sing. 3; **le(s) sien(s)**
   poss. pron. 15
history **histoire** *f.* 2
hit **rentrer (dans)** *v.* 11
hold **tenir** *v.* 9
   to be on hold **patienter** *v.* 13
hole in the ozone layer **trou dans**
   la couche d'ozone *m.* 14
holiday **jour férié** *m.* 6; **férié(e)**
   adj. 6
home *(house)* **maison** *f.* 4
   at (someone's) home **chez…**
   prep. 4
home page **page d'accueil** *f.* 11
homework **devoir** *m.* 2
honest **honnête** *adj.* 15
honestly **franchement** *adv.* 7
hood **capot** *m.* 11
hope **espérer** *v.* 5
hors d'œuvre **hors-d'œuvre** *m.* 9
horse **cheval** *m.* 5
   to go horseback riding **faire**
   du cheval *v.* 5
hospital **hôpital** *m.* 4
host **hôte/hôtesse** *m., f.* 6
hot **chaud** *m.* 2
   It is hot (weather). **Il fait**
   chaud. 5
   to be hot **avoir chaud** *v.* 2
hot chocolate **chocolat chaud**
   m. 4
hotel **hôtel** *m.* 7
   (single) hotel room **chambre**
   f. **(individuelle)** 7
hotel keeper **hôtelier/**
   hôtelière *m., f.* 7
hour **heure** *f.* 2
house **maison** *f.* 4
   at (someone's) house **chez…**
   prep. 2
   to leave the house **quitter la**
   maison *v.* 4
   to stop by someone's house
   passer chez quelqu'un *v.* 4
household **ménager/ménagère**
   adj. 8
household appliance **appareil**
   m. **ménager** 8
household chore **tâche**
   ménagère *f.* 8

housewife **femme au foyer** *f.* 13
housework: to do the housework
   faire le ménage *v.* 8
housing **logement** *m.* 8
how **comme** *adv.* 2; **comment?**
   interr. adv. 4
   How are you? **Comment**
   allez-vous? *form.* 1;
   Comment vas-tu? *fam.* 1
   How many/How much (of)?
   Combien (de)? 1
   How much is… ? **Combien**
   coûte… ? 4
huge **énorme** *adj.* 2
Huh? **Hein?** *interj.* 3
humanities **lettres** *f., pl.* 2
hundred: one hundred **cent** *m.* 5
   five hundred **cinq cents** *m.* 5
   one hundred one **cent un** *m.* 5
   one hundred thousand **cent**
   mille *m.* 5
hundredth **centième** *adj.* 7
hunger **faim** *f.* 4
hungry: to be hungry **avoir faim**
   v. 4
hunt **chasse** *f.* 14
   to hunt **chasser** *v.* 14
hurried **pressé(e)** *adj.* 9
hurry **se dépêcher** *v.* 10
hurt **faire mal** *v.* 10
   to hurt oneself **se blesser**
   v. 10
husband **mari** *m.*; **époux** *m.* 3
hyphen *(punctuation mark)*
   tiret *m.* 11

I

I **je** *sub. pron.* 1; **moi** *disj. pron.,*
   sing. 3
ice cream **glace** *f.* 6
ice cube **glaçon** *m.* 6
idea **idée** *f.* 3
if **si** *conj.* 13
ill: to become ill **tomber**
   malade *v.* 10
illness **maladie** *f.* 13
immediately **tout de suite** *adv.* 4
impatient **impatient(e)** *adj.* 1
important **important(e)** *adj.* 1
   It is important that… **Il est**
   important que… 14
impossible **impossible** *adj.* 15
   It is impossible that… **Il est**
   impossible que… 15
improve **améliorer** *v.* 13
in **dans** *prep.* 3; **en** *prep.* 3; **à**
   prep. 4
included **compris (compren-**
   dre) *p.p., adj.* 6
incredible **incroyable** *adj.* 11
independent **indépendant(e)**
   adj. 1

independently **indépendamment** *adv.* 7
indicate **indiquer** *v.* 5
indispensable **indispensable**
adj. 14
inexpensive **bon marché** *adj.* 6
injection **piqûre** *f.* 10
to give an injection **faire une
piqûre** *v.* 10
injury **blessure** *f.* 10
instrument **instrument** *m.* 1
insurance (health/life) **assurance**
f. (**maladie/vie**) 13
intellectual **intellectuel(le)**
adj. 3
intelligent **intelligent(e)** *adj.* 1
interested: to be interested (in)
s'intéresser (à) *v.* 10
interesting **intéressant(e)** *adj.* 1
intermission **entracte** *m.* 15
internship **stage** *m.* 13
intersection **carrefour** *m.* 12
interview: to have an interview **passer un entretien** 13
introduce **présenter** *v.* 1
I would like to introduce
(*name*) to you. **Je te
présente…** , *fam.* 1
I would like to introduce
(*name*) to you. **Je vous
présente…** , *form.* 1
invite **inviter** *v.* 4
Ireland **Irlande** *f.* 7
Irish **irlandais(e)** *adj.* 7
iron **fer à repasser** *m.* 8
to iron (the laundry) **repasser
(le linge)** *v.* 8
isn't it? (*tag question*) **n'est-ce
pas?** 2
island **île** *f.* 14
Italian **italien(ne)** *adj.* 1
Italy **Italie** *f.* 7
it: It depends. **Ça dépend.** 4
It is… **C'est…** 1
itself (*used with reflexive verb*)
se/s' *pron.* 10

jacket **blouson** *m.* 6
jam **confiture** *f.* 9
January **janvier** *m.* 5
Japan **Japon** *m.* 7
Japanese **japonais(e)** *adj.* 1
jealous **jaloux/jalouse** *adj.* 3
jeans **jean** *m. sing.* 6
jewelry store **bijouterie** *f.* 12
jogging **jogging** *m.* 5
to go jogging **faire du
jogging** *v.* 5
joke **blague** *f.* 2
journalist **journaliste** *m., f.* 3
juice (orange/apple) **jus** *m.*

(**d'orange/de pomme**) 4
July **juillet** *m.* 5
June **juin** *m.* 5
jungle **jungle** *f.* 14
just (*barely*) **juste** *adv.* 3

keep **retenir** *v.* 9
key **clé** *f.* 7
keyboard **clavier** *m.* 11
kilo(gram) **kilo(gramme)** *m.* 9
kind **bon(ne)** *adj.* 3
kiosk **kiosque** *m.* 4
kiss one another **s'embrasser**
v. 11
kitchen **cuisine** *f.* 8
knee **genou** *m.* 10
knife **couteau** *m.* 9
know (*as a fact*) **savoir** *v.* 8; (*to
be familiar with*) **connaître** *v.* 8
to know one another **se
connaître** *v.* 11
I don't know anything about
it. **Je n'en sais rien.** 14
to know that… **savoir que…** 15
known (*as a fact*) **su (savoir)**
p.p. 8; (*famous*) **connu
(connaître)** *p.p., adj.* 8

laborer **ouvrier/ouvrière** *m.,
f.* 13
lake **lac** *m.* 14
lamp **lampe** *f.* 8
landlord **propriétaire** *m.* 3
landslide **glissement de
terrain** *m.* 14
language **langue** *f.* 2
foreign languages **langues** *f.,
pl.* **étrangères** 2
last **dernier/dernière** *adj.* 2
lastly **dernièrement** *adv.* 7
late (*when something happens late*)
en retard *adv.* 2; (*in the evening,
etc.*) **tard** *adv.* 2
laugh **rire** *v.* 6
laughed **ri (rire)** *p.p.* 6
laundromat **laverie** *f.* 12
laundry: to do the laundry **faire
la lessive** *v.* 8
law (*academic discipline*) **droit** *m.*
2; (*ordinance or rule*) **loi** *f.* 14
lawyer **avocat(e)** *m., f.* 3
lay off (*let go*) **renvoyer** *v.* 13
lazy **paresseux/paresseuse**
adj. 3
learned **appris (apprendre)** *p.p.* 6
least **moins** 9
the least… (*used with adjective*)
le/la moins… *super. adv.* 9
the least… , (*used with noun*

to express quantity) **le moins
de…** 14
the least… (*used with verb or
adverb*) **le moins…** *super. adv.* 9
leather **cuir** *m.* 6
leave **partir** *v.* 5; **quitter** *v.* 4
to leave alone **laisser tranquille**
v. 10
to leave one another **se quitter**
v. 11
I'm leaving. **Je m'en vais.** 8
left: to the left (of) **à gauche
(de)** *prep.* 3
leg **jambe** *f.* 10
leisure activity **loisir** *m.* 5
lemon soda **limonade** *f.* 4
lend (*to someone*) **prêter (à)** *v.* 6
less **moins** *adv.* 4
less of… (*used with noun
to express quantity*) **moins
de…** 4
less … than (*used with noun
to compare quantities*) **moins
de… que** 14
less… than (*used with adjective
to compare qualities*) **moins…
que** 9
let **laisser** *v.* 11
to let go (*to fire or lay off*)
renvoyer *v.* 13
Let's go! **Allons-y!** 4; **On y
va!** 10
letter **lettre** *f.* 12
letter of application **lettre** *f.*
de motivation 13
letter of recommendation/
reference **lettre** *f.* **de
recommandation** 13
lettuce **laitue** *f.* 9
level **niveau** *m.* 13
library **bibliothèque** *f.* 1
license: driver's license **permis** *m.*
de conduire 11
life **vie** *f.* 6
life insurance **assurance**
f. **vie** 13
light: warning light (*automobile*)
voyant *m.* 11
oil/gas warning light **voyant**
m. **d'huile/d'essence** 11
to light up **s'allumer** *v.* 11
like (*as*) **comme** *adv.* 6; to like
aimer *v.* 2
I don't like … very much. **Je
n'aime pas tellement…** 2
I really like… **J'aime bien…** 2
to like one another **s'aimer
bien** *v.* 11
to like that… **aimer
que…** *v.* 14
line **queue** *f.* 12
to wait in line **faire la queue**
v. 12

link **lien** *m.* 11
listen (to) **écouter** *v.* 2
literary **littéraire** *adj.* 15
literature **littérature** *f.* 1
little *(not much)* (of) **peu (de)**
　adv. 4
live (in) **habiter (à)** *v.* 2
living room *(informal room)*
　salle de séjour *f.* 8; *(formal
　room)* **salon** *m.* 8
located: to be located **se trouver**
　v. 10
long **long(ue)** *adj.* 3
　a long time **longtemps** *adv.* 5
look *(at one another)* **se regarder**
　v. 11; *(at oneself)* **se regarder**
　v. 10
look for **chercher** *v.* 2
　to look for work **chercher
　du/un travail** 12
loose *(clothing)* **large** *adj.* 6
lose: to lose (time) **perdre (son
　temps)** *v.* 6
　to lose weight **maigrir** *v.* 4
lost: to be lost **être perdu(e)** *v.* 12
lot: a lot of **beaucoup de** *adv.* 4
love **amour** *m.* 6
　to love **adorer** *v.* 2
　I love… **J'adore…** 2
　to love one another **s'aimer**
　v. 11
　to be in love **être amoureux/
　amoureuse** *v.* 6
luck **chance** *f.* 2
　to be lucky **avoir de la chance**
　v. 2
lunch **déjeuner** *m.* 9
　to eat lunch **déjeuner** *v.* 4

M

ma'am **Madame.** *f.* 1
machine: answering machine
　répondeur *m.* 11
mad: to get mad **s'énerver** *v.* 10
made **fait (faire)** *p.p., adj.* 6
magazine **magazine** *m.* 15
mail **courrier** *m.* 12
mailbox **boîte** *f.* **aux lettres** 12
mailman **facteur** *m.* 12
main character **personnage
　principal** *m.* 15
main dish **plat (principal)** *m.* 9
maintain **maintenir** *v.* 9
make **faire** *v.* 5
makeup **maquillage** *m.* 10
　to put on makeup **se
　maquiller** *v.* 10
make up **se réconcilier** *v.* 15
malfunction **panne** *f.* 11
man **homme** *m.* 1
manage *(in business)* **diriger** *v.* 13;

(to do something) **arriver à** *v.* 2
manager **gérant(e)** *m., f.* 13
many (of) **beaucoup (de)** *adv.* 4
　How many (of)? **Combien
　(de)?** 1
map *(of a city)* **plan** *m.* 7;
　(of the world) **carte** *f.* 1
March **mars** *m.* 5
marital status **état civil** *m.* 6
market **marché** *m.* 4
marriage **mariage** *m.* 6
married **marié(e)** *adj.* 3
　married couple **mariés** *m., pl.* 6
marry **épouser** *v.* 3
Martinique: from Martinique
　martiniquais(e) *adj.* 1
masterpiece **chef-d'œuvre** *m.* 15
mathematics **mathématiques
　(maths)** *f., pl.* 2
May **mai** *m.* 5
maybe **peut-être** *adv.* 2
mayonnaise **mayonnaise** *f.* 9
mayor's office **mairie** *f.* 12
me **moi** *disj. pron., sing.* 3;
　(attached to imperative) **-moi**
　pron. 9; **me/m'** *i.o. pron.* 6;
　me/m' *d.o. pron.* 7
　Me too. **Moi aussi.** 1
　Me neither. **Moi non plus.** 2
meal **repas** *m.* 9
mean **méchant(e)** *adj.* 3
　to mean *(with* dire*)* **vouloir**
　v. 9
means: that means **ça veut dire** *v.* 9
meat **viande** *f.* 9
mechanic **mécanicien/
　mécanicienne** *m., f.* 11
medication (against/for) **médica-
　ment (contre/pour)** *m., f.* 10
meet *(to encounter, to run into)*
　rencontrer *v.* 2; *(to make the
　acquaintance of)* **faire la
　connaissance de** *v.* 5, **se
　rencontrer** *v.* 11; *(planned
　encounter)* **se retrouver** *v.* 11
meeting **réunion** *f.* 13;
　rendez-vous *m.* 6
member **membre** *m.* 15
menu **menu** *m.* 9; **carte** *f.* 9
message **message** *m.* 13
　to leave a message **laisser
　un message** *v.* 13
Mexican **mexicain(e)** *adj.* 1
Mexico **Mexique** *m.* 7
microwave oven **four à micro-
　ondes** *m.* 8
midnight **minuit** *m.* 2
milk **lait** *m.* 4
mine **le(s) mien(s), la/les
　mienne(s)** *poss. pron.* 15
mineral water **eau** *f.* **minérale** 4
mirror **miroir** *m.* 8

Miss **Mademoiselle** *f.* 1
mistaken: to be mistaken *(about
　something)* **se tromper (de)**
　v. 10
modest **modeste** *adj.* 13
moment **moment** *m.* 1
Monday **lundi** *m.* 2
money **argent** *m.* 12; *(currency)*
　monnaie *f.* 12
　to deposit money **déposer de
　l'argent** *v.* 12
monitor **moniteur** *m.* 11
month **mois** *m.* 2
　this month **ce mois-ci** 2
moon **Lune** *f.* 14
more **plus** *adv.* 4
　more of **plus de** 4
　more … than *(used with noun
　to compare quantities)*
　plus de… que 14
　more … than *(used with
　adjective to compare qualities)*
　plus… que 9
morning **matin** *m.* 2; **matinée**
　f. 2
　this morning **ce matin** 2
Moroccan **marocain(e)** *adj.* 1
most **plus** 9
　the most… *(used with adjective)*
　le/la plus… *super. adv.* 9
　the most… *(used with noun to
　express quantity)* **le plus de…** 14
　the most… *(used with verb or
　adverb)* **le plus…** *super. adv.* 9
mother **mère** *f.* 3
mother-in-law **belle-mère** *f.* 3
mountain **montagne** *f.* 4
mouse **souris** *f.* 11
mouth **bouche** *f.* 10
move *(to get around)* **se déplacer**
　v. 12
　to move in **emménager** *v.* 8
　to move out **déménager** *v.* 8
movie **film** *m.* 15
　adventure/horror/science-
　fiction/crime movie **film** *m.*
　**d'aventures/d'horreur/de
　science-fiction/policier** 15
movie theater **cinéma (ciné)** *m.* 4
MP3 player **lecteur MP3** *m.* 11
much (as much … as) *(used with
　noun to express quantity)*
　autant de … que *adv.* 14
　How much (of something)?
　Combien (de)? 1
　How much is… ? **Combien
　coûte… ?** 4
museum **musée** *m.* 4
　to go to museums **faire les
　musées** *v.* 15
mushroom **champignon** *m.* 9
music: to play music **faire de la**

musique 15
musical **comédie** *f.* **musicale**
  15; **musical(e)** *adj.* 15
musician **musicien(ne)** *m., f.* 3
must (to have to) **devoir** *v.* 9
  One must **Il faut...** 5
mustard **moutarde** *f.* 9
my **ma** *poss. adj., f., sing.* 3; **mes**
  poss. adj., m., f., pl. 3; **mon**
  poss. adj., m., sing. 3
myself **me/m'** *pron., sing.* 10;
  (attached to an imperative)
  -moi *pron.* 9

N

naïve **naïf (naïve)** *adj.* 3
name: My name is... **Je**
  m'appelle... 1
named: to be named
  s'appeler *v.* 10
napkin **serviette** *f.* 9
nationality **nationalité** *f.*
  I am of ... nationality. **Je suis**
  de nationalité... 1
natural **naturel(le)** *adj.* 14
natural resource **ressource**
  naturelle *f.* 14
nature **nature** *f.* 14
nauseated: to feel nauseated
  avoir mal au cœur *v.* 10
near (to) **près (de)** *prep.* 3
  very near (to) **tout près (de)** 12
necessary **nécessaire** *adj.* 14
  It was necessary... *(followed*
  by infinitive or subjunctive)
  Il a fallu... 6
  It is necessary.... *(followed by*
  infinitive or subjunctive)
  Il faut que... 5
  It is necessary that... *(followed by*
  subjunctive) **Il est nécessaire**
  que/qu'... 14
neck **cou** *m.* 10
need **besoin** *m.* 2
  to need **avoir besoin (de)** *v.* 2
neighbor **voisin(e)** *m., f.* 3
neighborhood **quartier** *m.* 8
neither... nor **ne... ni... ni...**
  conj. 12
nephew **neveu** *m.* 3
nervous **nerveux/nerveuse** *adj.* 3
nervously **nerveusement** *adv.* 7
network **réseau** *m.* 11
never **jamais** *adv.* 5; **ne...**
  jamais *adv.* 12
new **nouveau/nouvelle** *adj.* 3
newlyweds **jeunes mariés**
  m., pl. 6
news **informations (infos)**
  f., pl. 15; **nouvelles** *f., pl.* 15
newspaper **journal** *m.* 7

newsstand **marchand de**
  journaux *m.* 12
next **ensuite** *adv.* 7;
  prochain(e) *adj.* 2
  next to **à côté de** *prep.* 3
nice **gentil/gentille** *adj.* 3;
  sympa(thique) *adj.* 1
nicely **gentiment** *adv.* 7
niece **nièce** *f.* 3
night **nuit** *f.* 2
nightclub **boîte (de nuit)** *f.* 4
nine **neuf** *m.* 1
nine hundred **neuf cents** *m.* 5
nineteen **dix-neuf** *m.* 1
ninety **quatre-vingt-dix** *m.* 3
ninth **neuvième** *adj.* 7
no *(at beginning of statement to*
  indicate disagreement)
  (mais) non 2; **aucun(e)**
  adj. 10
  no more **ne... plus** 12
  no problem **pas de prob-**
  lème 12
  no reason **pour rien** 4
  no, none **pas (de)** 12
nobody **ne... personne** 12
none (not any) **ne... aucun(e)**
  12
noon **midi** *m.* 2
no one **personne** *pron.* 12
north **nord** *m.* 12
nose **nez** *m.* 10
not **ne... pas** 2
  not at all **pas du tout** *adv.* 2
  Not badly. **Pas mal.** 1
  to not believe that **ne pas**
  croire que *v.* 15
  to not think that **ne pas**
  penser que *v.* 15
  not yet **pas encore** *adv.* 7
notebook **cahier** *m.* 1
notes **billets** *m., pl.* 11
nothing **rien** *indef. pron.* 12
  It's nothing. **Il n'y a pas de**
  quoi. 1
notice **s'apercevoir** *v.* 12
novel **roman** *m.* 15
November **novembre** *m.* 5
now **maintenant** *adv.* 5
nuclear **nucléaire** *adj.* 14
nuclear energy **énergie nucléaire**
  f. 14
nuclear plant **centrale nucléaire**
  f. 14
nurse **infirmier/infirmière**
  m., f. 10

O

obey **obéir (à)** *v.* 4
object **objet** *m.* 1

obtain **obtenir** *v.* 13
obvious **évident(e)** *adj.* 15
  It is obvious that... **Il est**
  évident que... 15
obviously **évidemment** *adv.* 7
o'clock: It's... (o'clock). **Il est...**
  heure(s). 2
  at ... (o'clock) **à ... heure(s)** 4
October **octobre** *m.* 5
of **de/d'** *prep.* 3
  of medium height **de taille**
  moyenne *adj.* 3
  of the **des (de + les)** 3
  of the **du (de + le)** 3
  of which, of whom **dont**
  rel. pron. 13
of course **bien sûr** *adv.*;
  évidemment *adv.* 2
  of course not *(at beginning*
  of statement to indicate
  disagreement) **(mais) non** 2
offer **offrir** *v.* 11
offered **offert (offrir)** *p.p.* 11
office **bureau** *m.* 4
  at the doctor's office **chez le**
  médecin *prep.* 2
often **souvent** *adv.* 5
oil **huile** *f.* 9
  automobile oil **huile** *f.* 11
  oil warning light **voyant** *m.*
  d'huile 11
  olive oil **huile** *f.* **d'olive** 9
  to check the oil **vérifier**
  l'huile *v.* 11
okay **d'accord** 2
old **vieux/vieille** *adj.*; *(placed*
  after noun) **ancien(ne)** *adj.* 3
old age **vieillesse** *f.* 6
olive **olive** *f.* 9
olive oil **huile** *f.* **d'olive** 9
omelette **omelette** *f.* 5
on **sur** *prep.* 3
  On behalf of whom? **C'est de**
  la part de qui? 13
  on the condition that... **à**
  condition que 15
  on television **à la télé(vision)**
  15
  on the contrary **au contraire** 15
  on the radio **à la radio** 15
  on the subject of **au sujet**
  de 14
  on vacation **en vacances** 7
once **une fois** *adv.* 7
one **un** *m.* 1
  one **on** *sub. pron., sing.* 1
  one another **l'un(e) à**
  l'autre 11
  one another **l'un(e) l'autre** 11
  one had to... **il fallait...** 8
  One must... **Il faut que/**
  qu'... 14

One must… **Il faut…** (*followed by infinitive or subjunctive*) 5
one million **un million** *m.* 5
  one million (*things*) **un million de…** 5
onion **oignon** *m.* 9
online **en ligne** *11*
  to be online **être en ligne** *v.* 11
  to be online (with someone) **être connecté(e) (avec quelqu'un)** *v.* 7, 11
only **ne… que** 12; **seulement** *adv.* 7
open **ouvrir** *v.* 11; **ouvert(e)** *adj.* 11
opened **ouvert (ouvrir)** *p.p.* 11
opera **opéra** *m.* 15
optimistic **optimiste** *adj.* 1
or **ou** 3
orange **orange** *f.* 9; **orange** *inv. adj.* 6
orchestra **orchestre** *m.* 15
order **commander** *v.* 9
organize (a party) **organiser (une fête)** *v.* 6
orient oneself **s'orienter** *v.* 12
others **d'autres** 4
our **nos** *poss. adj., m., f., pl.* 3; **notre** *poss. adj., m., f., sing.* 3; **le(s) nôtre(s), la/les nôtre(s)** *poss. pron.* 15
outdoor (*open-air*) **plein air** 14
over **fini** *adj., p.p.* 7
overpopulation **surpopulation** *f.* 14
overseas **à l'étranger** *adv.* 7
over there **là-bas** *adv.* 1
owed **dû (devoir)** *p.p., adj.* 9
own **posséder** *v.* 5
owner **propriétaire** *m., f.* 3
ozone **ozone** *m.* 14
  hole in the ozone layer **trou dans la couche d'ozone** *m.* 14

P

pack: to pack one's bags **faire les valises** 7
package **colis** *m.* 12
paid **payé (payer)** *p.p., adj.* 13
  to be well/badly paid **être bien/mal payé(e)** 13
pain **douleur** *f.* 10
paint **faire de la peinture** *v.* 15
painter **peintre/femme peintre** *m., f.* 15
painting **peinture** *f.* 15; **tableau** *m.* 15
pants **pantalon** *m., sing.* 6
paper **papier** *m.* 1
Pardon (me). **Pardon.** 1
parents **parents** *m., pl.* 3

park **parc** *m.* 4
  to park **se garer** *v.* 11
parka **anorak** *m.* 6
parking lot **parking** *m.* 11
part-time job **emploi** *m.* **à mi-temps/à temps partiel** *m.* 13
party **fête** *f.* 6
  to party **faire la fête** *v.* 6
pass **dépasser** *v.* 11; **passer** *v.* 7
  to pass an exam **être reçu(e) à un examen** *v.* 2
passenger **passager/passagère** *m., f.* 7
passport **passeport** *m.* 7
password **mot de passe** *m.* 11
past: in the past **autrefois** *adv.* 7
pasta **pâtes** *f., pl.* 9
pastime **passe-temps** *m.* 5
pastry **pâtisserie** *f.* 9
pastry shop **pâtisserie** *f.* 9
pâté **pâté (de campagne)** *m.* 9
path **sentier** *m.* 14; **chemin** *m.* 12
patient **patient(e)** *adj.* 1
patiently **patiemment** *adv.* 7
pay **payer** *v.* 5
  to pay by check **payer par chèque** *v.* 12
  to pay in cash **payer en liquide** *v.* 12
  to pay with a credit card **payer avec une carte de crédit** *v.* 12
  to pay attention (to) **faire attention (à)** *v.* 5
peach **pêche** *f.* 9
pear **poire** *f.* 9
peas **petits pois** *m., pl.* 9
pen **stylo** *m.* 1
pencil **crayon** *m.* 1
people **gens** *m., pl.* 7
pepper (*spice*) **poivre** *m.* 9; (*vegetable*) **poivron** *m.* 9
per day/week/month/year **par jour/semaine/mois/an** 5
perfect **parfait(e)** *adj.* 2
perhaps **peut-être** *adv.* 2
period (*punctuation mark*) **point** *m.* 11
permit **permis** *m.* 11
permitted **permis (permettre)** *p.p., adj.* 6
person **personne** *f.* 1
pessimistic **pessimiste** *adj.* 1
pharmacist **pharmacien(ne)** *m., f.* 10
pharmacy **pharmacie** *f.* 10
philosophy **philosophie** *f.* 2
phone booth **cabine téléphonique** *f.* 12
phone card **télécarte** *f.* 13
phone one another **se téléphoner** *v.* 11
photo(graph) **photo(graphie)** *f.* 3

physical education **éducation physique** *f.* 2
physics **physique** *f.* 2
piano **piano** *m.* 15
pick up **décrocher** *v.* 13
picnic **pique-nique** *m.* 14
picture **tableau** *m.* 1
pie **tarte** *f.* 9
piece (of) **morceau (de)** *m.* 4
  piece of furniture **meuble** *m.* 8
pill **pilule** *f.* 10
pillow **oreiller** *m.* 8
pink **rose** *adj.* 6
pitcher (of water) **carafe (d'eau)** *f.* 9
place **endroit** *m.* 4; **lieu** *m.* 4
planet **planète** *f.* 14
plans: to make plans **faire des projets** *v.* 13
plant **plante** *f.* 14
plastic **plastique** *m.* 14
plastic wrapping **emballage en plastique** *m.* 14
plate **assiette** *f.* 9
play **pièce de théâtre** *f.* 15
play **s'amuser** *v.* 10; (*a sport/a musical instrument*) **jouer (à/de)** *v.* 5
  to play regularly **pratiquer** *v.* 5
  to play sports **faire du sport** *v.* 5
  to play a role **jouer un rôle** *v.* 15
player **joueur/joueuse** *m., f.* 5
playwright **dramaturge** *m.* 15
pleasant **agréable** *adj.* 1
please: to please someone **faire plaisir à quelqu'un** *v.* 13
  Please. **S'il te plaît.** *fam.* 1
  Please. **S'il vous plaît.** *form.* 1
  Please. **Je vous en prie.** *form.* 1
  Please hold. **Ne quittez pas.** 13
plug in **brancher** *v.* 11
plumber **plombier** *m.* 13
poem **poème** *m.* 15
poet **poète/poétesse** *m., f.* 15
police **police** *f.* 11; **policier** *adj.* 15
police officer **agent de police** *m.* 11; **policier** *m.* 11; **policière** *f.* 11
police station **commissariat de police** *m.* 12
polite **poli(e)** *adj.* 1
politely **poliment** *adv.* 7
political science **sciences politiques (sciences po)** *f., pl.* 2
politician **homme/femme politique** *m., f.* 13
pollute **polluer** *v.* 14
pollution **pollution** *f.* 14

pollution cloud **nuage de pollution** *m.* 14
pool **piscine** *f.* 4
poor **pauvre** *adj.* 3
popular music **variétés** *f., pl.* 15
population **population** *f.* 14
  growing population **population** *f.* **croissante** 14
pork **porc** *m.* 9
portrait **portrait** *m.* 5
position (*job*) **poste** *m.* 13
possess (*to own*) **posséder** *v.* 5
possible **possible** *adj.* 15
  It is possible that… **Il est possible que…** 14
post **afficher** *v.* 13
post office **bureau de poste** *m.* 12
postal service **poste** *f.* 12
postcard **carte postale** *f.* 12
poster **affiche** *f.* 8
potato **pomme de terre** *f.* 9
practice **pratiquer** *v.* 5
prefer **aimer mieux** *v.* 2; **préférer (que)** *v.* 5
pregnant **enceinte** *adj.* 10
prepare (for) **préparer** *v.* 2
  to prepare (*to do something*) **se préparer (à)** *v.* 10
prescription **ordonnance** *f.* 10
present **présenter** *v.* 15
preservation: habitat preservation **sauvetage des habitats** *m.* 14
preserve **préserver** *v.* 14
pressure **pression** *f.* 11
  to check the tire pressure **vérifier la pression des pneus** *v.* 11
pretty **joli(e)** *adj.* 3; (*before an adjective or adverb*) **assez** *adv.* 7
prevent: to prevent a fire **prévenir l'incendie** *v.* 14
price **prix** *m.* 4
principal **principal(e)** *adj.* 12
print **imprimer** *v.* 11
printer **imprimante** *f.* 11
problem **problème** *m.* 1
produce **produire** *v.* 6
produced **produit (produire)** *p.p., adj.* 6
product **produit** *m.* 14
profession **métier** *m.* 13; **profession** *f.* 13
  demanding profession **profession** *f.* **exigeante** 13
professional **professionnel(le)** *adj.* 13
  professional experience **expérience professionnelle** *f.* 13
program **programme** *m.* 15; (*software*) **logiciel** *m.* 11; (*television*) **émission** *f.* **de télévision** 15

prohibit **interdire** *v.* 14
project **projet** *m.* 13
promise **promettre** *v.* 6
promised **promis (promettre)** *p.p., adj.* 6
promotion **promotion** *f.* 13
propose that… **proposer que…** *v.* 14
  to propose a solution **proposer une solution** *v.* 14
protect **protéger** *v.* 5
protection **préservation** *f.* 14; **protection** *f.* 14
proud **fier/fière** *adj.* 3
psychological **psychologique** *adj.* 15
psychological drama **drame psychologique** *m.* 15
psychology **psychologie** *f.* 2
psychologist **psychologue** *m., f.* 13
publish **publier** *v.* 15
pure **pur(e)** *adj.* 14
purple **violet(te)** *adj.* 6
purse **sac à main** *m.* 6
put **mettre** *v.* 6
  to put (on) (*yourself*) **se mettre** *v.* 10
  to put away **ranger** *v.* 8
  to put on makeup **se maquiller** *v.* 10
put **mis (mettre)** *p.p.* 6

Q

quarter **quart** *m.* 2
  a quarter after … (o'clock) **… et quart** 2
Quebec: from Quebec **québécois(e)** *adj.* 1
question **question** *f.* 6
  to ask (*someone*) a question **poser une question (à)** *v.* 6
quick **vite** *adv.* 4
quickly **vite** *adv.* 1
quite (*before an adjective or adverb*) **assez** *adv.* 7

R

rabbit **lapin** *m.* 14
rain **pleuvoir** *v.* 5
  acid rain **pluie** *f.* **acide** 14
  It is raining. **Il pleut.** 5
  It was raining. **Il pleuvait.** 8
rain forest **forêt tropicale** *f.* 14
rain jacket **imperméable** *m.* 5
rained **plu (pleuvoir)** *p.p.* 6
raise (in salary) **augmentation (de salaire)** *f.* 13
rapidly **rapidement** *adv.* 7
rarely **rarement** *adv.* 5
rather **plutôt** *adv.* 1

ravishing **ravissant(e)** *adj.* 13
razor **rasoir** *m.* 10
react **réagir** *v.* 4
read **lire** *v.* 7
read **lu (lire)** *p.p., adj.* 7
ready **prêt(e)** *adj.* 3
real (*true*) **vrai(e)** *adj.;* **véritable** *adj.* 3
real estate agent **agent immobilier** *m., f.* 13
realize **se rendre compte** *v.* 10
really **vraiment** *adv.* 5; (*before adjective or adverb*) **tout(e)** *adv.* 3; (*before adjective or adverb*) **très** *adv.* 7
  really close by **tout près** 3
rear-view mirror **rétroviseur** *m.* 11
reason **raison** *f.* 2
receive **recevoir** *v.* 12
received **reçu (recevoir)** *p.p., adj.* 12
receiver **combiné** *m.* 13
recent **récent(e)** *adj.* 15
reception desk **réception** *f.* 7
recognize **reconnaître** *v.* 8
recognized **reconnu (reconnaître)** *p.p., adj.* 8
recommend that… **recommander que…** *v.* 14
recommendation **recommandation** *f.* 13
record **enregistrer** *v.* 11
recycle **recycler** *v.* 14
recycling **recyclage** *m.* 14
red **rouge** *adj.* 6
redial **recomposer (un numéro)** *v.* 11
reduce **réduire** *v.* 6
reduced **réduit (réduire)** *p.p., adj.* 6
reference **référence** *f.* 13
reflect (on) **réfléchir (à)** *v.* 4
refrigerator **frigo** *m.* 8
refuse (*to do something*) **refuser (de)** *v.* 11
region **région** *f.* 14
regret that… **regretter que…** 14
relax **se détendre** *v.* 10
remember **se souvenir (de)** *v.* 10
remote control **télécommande** *f.* 11
rent **loyer** *m.* 8
  to rent **louer** *v.* 8
repair **réparer** *v.* 11
repeat **répéter** *v.* 5
research **rechercher** *v.* 13
researcher **chercheur/chercheuse** *m., f.* 13
reservation **réservation** *f.* 7
  to cancel a reservation **annuler une réservation** 7
reserve **réserver** *v.* 7
reserved **réservé(e)** *adj.* 1
resign **démissionner** *v.* 13

resort (ski) **station** *f.* **(de ski)** 7
respond **répondre (à)** *v.* 6
rest **se reposer** *v.* 10
restart **redémarrer** *v.* 11
restaurant **restaurant** *m.* 4
restroom(s) **toilettes** *f., pl.* 8;
  W.-C. *m., pl.*
result **résultat** *m.* 2
résumé **curriculum vitæ**
  (C.V.) *m.* 13
retake **repasser** *v.* 15
retire **prendre sa retraite** *v.* 6
retired person **retraité(e)** *m., f.* 13
retirement **retraite** *f.* 6
return **retourner** *v.* 7
  to return (home) **rentrer (à la**
  maison) *v.* 2
review (*criticism*) **critique** *f.* 15
rice **riz** *m.* 9
ride: to go horseback riding
  faire du cheval *v.* 5
  to ride in a car **rouler en**
  voiture *v.* 7
right **juste** *adv.* 3
  to the right (of) **à droite**
  (de) *prep.* 3
  to be right **avoir raison** 2
  right away **tout de suite** 7
  right next door **juste à côté** 3
ring **sonner** *v.* 11
river **fleuve** *m.* 14; **rivière** *f.* 14
riverboat **bateau-mouche** *m.* 7
role **rôle** *m.* 14
room **pièce** *f.* 8; **salle** *f.* 8
  bedroom **chambre** *f.* 7
  classroom **salle** *f.* **de classe** 1
  dining room **salle** *f.* **à manger** 8
  single hotel room **chambre**
  f. **individuelle** 7
roommate **camarade de**
  chambre *m., f.* 1
  (*in an apartment*) **colocataire**
  m., f. 1
round-trip **aller-retour** *adj.* 7
  round-trip ticket **billet** *m.*
  aller-retour 7
rug **tapis** *m.* 8
run **courir** *v.* 5; **couru (courir)**
  p.p., adj. 6
  to run into someone **tomber**
  sur quelqu'un *v.* 7

S

sad **triste** *adj.* 3
  to be sad that... **être triste**
  que... *v.* 14
safety **sécurité** *f.* 11
said **dit (dire)** *p.p., adj.* 7
salad **salade** *f.* 9
salary (a high, low) **salaire**

(élevé, modeste) *m.* 13
sales **soldes** *f., pl.* 6
salon: beauty salon **salon** *m.*
  de beauté 12
salt **sel** *m.* 9
sandwich **sandwich** *m.* 4
sat (down) **assis (s'asseoir)**
  p.p. 10
Saturday **samedi** *m.* 2
sausage **saucisse** *f.* 9
save **sauvegarder** *v.* 11
  save the planet **sauver la**
  planète *v.* 14
savings **épargne** *f.* 12
savings account **compte**
  d'épargne *m.* 12
say **dire** *v.* 7
scarf **écharpe** *f.* 6
scholarship **bourse** *f.* 2
school **école** *f.* 2
science **sciences** *f., pl.* 2
  political science
  sciences politiques
  (sciences po) *f., pl.* 2
screen **écran** *m.* 11
screening **séance** *f.* 15
sculpture **sculpture** *f.* 15
sculptor **sculpteur/sculptrice**
  m., f. **15**
sea **mer** *f.* 7
seafood **fruits de mer** *m., pl.* 9
search for **chercher** *v.* 2
  to search for work **chercher**
  du travail *v.* 12
season **saison** *f.* 5
seat **place** *f.* 15
seatbelt **ceinture de sécurité** *f.* 11
  to buckle one's seatbelt
  attacher sa ceinture de
  sécurité *v.* 11
seated **assis(e)** *p.p., adj.* 10
second **deuxième** *adj.* 7
security **sécurité** *f.* 11
see **voir** *v.* 12; (*catch sight*
  of) **apercevoir** *v.* 12
  to see again **revoir** *v.* 12
  See you later. **À plus tard.** 1
  See you later. **À tout à**
  l'heure. 1
  See you soon. **À bientôt.** 1
  See you tomorrow. **À demain.** 1
seen **aperçu (apercevoir)** *p.p.* 12;
  vu (voir) *p.p.* 12
  seen again **revu (revoir)** *p.p.* 12
self/-selves **même(s)** *pron.* 6
selfish **égoïste** *adj.* 1
sell **vendre** *v.* 6
seller **vendeur/vendeuse** *m., f.* 6
send **envoyer** *v.* 5
  to send (*to someone*) **envoyer**
  (à) *v.* 6
  to send a letter **poster une**

lettre 12
Senegalese **sénégalais(e)** *adj.* 1
sense **sentir** *v.* 5
separated **séparé(e)** *adj.* 3
September **septembre** *m.* 5
serious **grave** *adj.* 10; **sérieux/**
  sérieuse *adj.* 3
serve **servir** *v.* 5
server **serveur/serveuse** *m., f.* 4
service station **station-service**
  f. 11
set the table **mettre la table** *v.* 8
seven **sept** *m.* 1
seven hundred **sept cents** *m.* 5
seventeen **dix-sept** *m.* 1
seventh **septième** *adj.* 7
seventy **soixante-dix** *m.* 3
several **plusieurs** *adj.* 4
shame **honte** *f.* 2
  It's a shame that... **Il est**
  dommage que... 14
shampoo **shampooing** *m.* 10
shape (*state of health*) **forme** *f.* 10
share **partager** *v.* 2
shave (oneself) **se raser** *v.* 10
shaving cream **crème à raser** *f.* 10
she **elle** *pron.* 1
sheet of paper **feuille de papier**
  f. 1
sheets **draps** *m., pl.* 8
shelf **étagère** *f.* 8
shh **chut** 15
shirt (short-/long-sleeved)
  chemise (à manches
  courtes/longues) *f.* 6
shoe **chaussure** *f.* 6
shopkeeper **commerçant(e)**
  m., f. 9
shopping **shopping** *m.* 7
  to go shopping **faire du**
  shopping *v.* 7
  to go (grocery) shopping **faire**
  les courses *v.* 9
shopping center **centre**
  commercial *m.* 4
short **court(e)** *adj.* 3;
  (*stature*) **petit(e)** 3
shorts **short** *m.* 6
shot (*injection*) **piqûre** *f.* 10
  to give a shot **faire une piqûre**
  v. 10
show **spectacle** *m.* 5; (*movie or*
  theater) **séance** *f.* 15
  to show (*to someone*) **montrer**
  (à) *v.* 6
shower **douche** *f.* 8
shut off **fermer** *v.* 11
shy **timide** *adj.* 1
sick: to get/be sick **tomber/être**
  malade *v.* 10
sign **signer** *v.* 12
silk **soie** *f.* 6

since **depuis** *adv.* 9
sincere **sincère** *adj.* 1
sing **chanter** *v.* 5
singer **chanteur/chanteuse**
  m., f. 1
single (*marital status*) **célibataire**
  adj. 3
  single hotel room **chambre** *f.*
  individuelle 7
sink **évier** *m.* 8; (*bathroom*)
  lavabo *m.* 8
sir **Monsieur** *m.* 1
sister **sœur** *f.* 3
sister-in-law **belle-sœur** *f.* 3
sit down **s'asseoir** *v.* 10
sitting **assis(e)** *adj.* 10
six **six** *m.* 1
six hundred **six cents** *m.* 5
sixteen **seize** *m.* 1
sixth **sixième** *adj.* 7
sixty **soixante** *m.* 1
size **taille** *f.* 6
skate **patiner** *v.* 4
ski **skier** *v.* 5; **faire du ski** 5
skiing **ski** *m.* 5
ski jacket **anorak** *m.* 6
ski resort **station** *f.* **de ski** 7
skin **peau** *f.* 10
skirt **jupe** *f.* 6
sky **ciel** *m.* 14
sleep **sommeil** *m.* 2
  to sleep **dormir** *v.* 5
  to be sleepy **avoir sommeil** *v.* 2
sleeve **manche** *f.* 6
slice **tranche** *f.* 9
slipper **pantoufle** *f.* 10
slow **lent(e)** *adj.* 3
small **petit(e)** *adj.* 3
smartphone **smartphone** *m.* 11
smell **sentir** *v.* 5
smile **sourire** *m.* 6
  to smile **sourire** *v.* 6
smoke **fumer** *v.* 10
snack (*afternoon*) **goûter** *m.* 9
snake **serpent** *m.* 14
sneeze **éternuer** *v.* 10
snow **neiger** *v.* 5
  It is snowing. **Il neige.** 5
  It was snowing… **Il**
  neigeait… 8
so **si** 11; **alors** *adv.* 1
  so that **pour que** 15
soap **savon** *m.* 10
soap opera **feuilleton** *m.* 15
soccer **foot(ball)** *m.* 5
sociable **sociable** *adj.* 1
social network **réseau**
  social *m.* 11
sociology **sociologie** *f.* 1
sock **chaussette** *f.* 6
software **logiciel** *m.* 11

soil (*to make dirty*) **salir** *v.* 8
solar **solaire** *adj.* 14
solar energy **énergie solaire** *f.* 14
solution **solution** *f.* 14
some **de l'** *part. art., m., f., sing.* 4
  some **de la** *part. art., f., sing.* 4
  some **des** *part. art., m., f., pl.* 4
  some **du** *part. art., m., sing.* 4
  some **quelques** *adj.* 4
  some (of it/them) **en** *pron.* 10
someone **quelqu'un** *pron.* 12
something **quelque chose** *m.* 4
  Something's not right.
  Quelque chose ne va pas. 5
sometimes **parfois** *adv.* 5;
  quelquefois *adv.* 7
son **fils** *m.* 3
song **chanson** *f.* 15
sorry **désolé(e)** 11
  to be sorry that… **être**
  désolé(e) que… *v.* 14
sort **sorte** *f.* 15
So-so. **Comme ci, comme ça.** 1
soup **soupe** *f.* 4
soup spoon **cuillère à soupe**
  f. 9
south **sud** *m.* 12
space **espace** *m.* 14
Spain **Espagne** *f.* 7
Spanish **espagnol(e)** *adj.* 1
speak (on the phone) **parler**
  (au téléphone) *v.* 2
  to speak (to) **parler (à)** *v.* 6
  to speak to one another **se**
  parler *v.* 11
specialist **spécialiste** *m., f.* 13
species **espèce** *f.* 14
  endangered species **espèce** *f.*
  menacée 14
spectator **spectateur/**
  spectatrice *m., f.* 15
speed **vitesse** *f.* 11
speed limit **limitation de vitesse**
  f. 11
spend **dépenser** *v.* 4
  to spend money **dépenser de**
  l'argent 4
  to spend time **passer** *v.* 7
  to spend time (*somewhere*)
  faire un séjour 7
spoon **cuillère** *f.* 9
sport(s) **sport** *m.* 5
  to play sports **faire du sport**
  v. 5
sporty **sportif/sportive** *adj.* 3
sprain one's ankle **se fouler la**
  cheville 10
spring **printemps** *m.* 5
  in the spring **au printemps** 5
square (*place*) **place** *f.* 4
squirrel **écureuil** *m.* 14
stadium **stade** *m.* 5

stage (*phase*) **étape** *f.* 6
stage fright **trac** 13
staircase **escalier** *m.* 8
stamp **timbre** *m.* 12
star **étoile** *f.* 14
starter **entrée** *f.* 9
start up **démarrer** *v.* 11
station **station** *f.* 7
  subway station **station** *f.* **de**
  métro 7
  train station **gare** *f.* 7
stationery store **papeterie** *f.* 12
statue **statue** *f.* 12
stay **séjour** *m.* 7; **rester** *v.* 7
  to stay slim **garder la ligne**
  v. 10
steak **steak** *m.* 9
steering wheel **volant** *m.* 11
stepbrother **demi-frère** *m.* 3
stepfather **beau-père** *m.* 3
stepmother **belle-mère** *f.* 3
stepsister **demi-sœur** *f.* 3
stereo system **chaîne stéréo** *f.* 11
still **encore** *adv.* 3
stomach **ventre** *m.* 10
  to have a stomach ache **avoir**
  mal au ventre *v.* 10
stone **pierre** *f.* 14
stop (doing something) **arrêter**
  (de faire quelque chose) *v.;*
  (*to stop oneself*) **s'arrêter** *v.* 10
  to stop by someone's house
  passer chez quelqu'un *v.* 4
  bus stop **arrêt d'autobus (de**
  bus) *m.* 7
store **magasin** *m.;* **boutique** *f.* 12
  grocery store **épicerie** *f.* 4
stormy **orageux/orageuse** *adj.* 5
  It is stormy. **Le temps est**
  orageux. 5
story **histoire** *f.* 2
stove **cuisinière** *f.* 8
straight **raide** *adj.* 3
  straight ahead **tout droit** *adv.* 12
strangle **étrangler** *v.* 13
strawberry **fraise** *f.* 9
street **rue** *f.* 11
  to follow a street **suivre une**
  rue *v.* 12
strong **fort(e)** *adj.* 3
student **étudiant(e)** *m., f.* 1;
  élève *m., f.* 1
  high school student **lycéen(ne)**
  m., f. 2
studies **études** *f.* 2
studio (*apartment*) **studio** *m.* 8
study **étudier** *v.* 2
suburbs **banlieue** *f.* 4
subway **métro** *m.* 7
subway station **station** *f.* **de**
  métro 7
succeed (*in doing something*)

réussir (à) *v.* 4
success réussite *f.* 13
suddenly soudain *adv.* 7; tout à coup *adv.* 7.; tout d'un coup *adv.* 7
suffer souffrir *v.* 11
suffered souffert (souffrir) *p.p.* 11
sugar sucre *m.* 4
suggest (that) suggérer (que) *v.* 14
suit (*man's*) costume *m.* 6; (*woman's*) tailleur *m.* 6
suitcase valise *f.* 7
summer été *m.* 5
in the summer en été 5
sun soleil *m.* 5
It is sunny. Il fait (du) soleil. 5
Sunday dimanche *m.* 2
sunglasses lunettes de soleil *f., pl.* 6
supermarket supermarché *m.* 9
sure sûr(e) 9
It is sure that... Il est sûr que... 15
It is unsure that... Il n'est pas sûr que... 15
surf on the Internet surfer sur Internet 11
surprise (*someone*) faire une surprise (à quelqu'un) *v.* 6
surprised surpris (surprendre) *p.p., adj.* 6
to be surprised that... être surpris(e) que... *v.* 14
sweater pull *m.* 6
sweep balayer *v.* 8
swell enfler *v.* 10
swim nager *v.* 4
swimsuit maillot de bain *m.* 6
Swiss suisse *adj.* 1
Switzerland Suisse *f.* 7
symptom symptôme *m.* 10

T

table table *f.* 1
to clear the table débarrasser la table *v.* 8
tablecloth nappe *f.* 9
tablet computer tablette (tactile) *f.* 11
take prendre *v.* 4
to take a photo(graph) prendre une photo(graphie) 11
to take a shower prendre une douche 10
to take a train (plane, taxi, bus, boat) prendre un train (un avion, un taxi, un autobus, un bateau) *v.* 7
to take a walk se promener *v.* 10
to take advantage of profiter

de *v.* 15
to take an exam passer un examen *v.* 2
to take care (of something) s'occuper (de) *v.* 10
to take out the trash sortir la/les poubelle(s) *v.* 8
to take time off prendre un congé *v.* 13
to take (*someone*) emmener *v.* 5
taken pris (prendre) *p.p., adj.* 6
tale conte *m.* 15
talented (*gifted*) doué(e) *adj.* 15
tan bronzer *v.* 6
tart tarte *f.* 9
taste goûter *v.* 9
taxi taxi *m.* 7
tea thé *m.* 4
teach enseigner *v.* 2
to teach (*to do something*) apprendre (à) *v.* 4
teacher professeur *m.* 1
team équipe *f.* 5
teaspoon cuillère à café *f.* 9
tee shirt tee-shirt *m.* 6
teeth dents *f., pl.* 9
to brush one's teeth se brosser les dents *v.* 9
telephone (*receiver*) appareil *m.* 13
to telephone (*someone*) téléphoner (à) *v.* 2
It's Mr./Mrs./Miss ... (on the phone.) C'est M./Mme/Mlle ... (à l'appareil.) 13
television télévision *f.* 1
television channel chaîne *f.* de télévision 11
television program émission *f.* de télévision 15
television set poste de télévision *m.* 11
tell one another se dire *v.* 11
temperature température *f.* 5
ten dix *m.* 1
tennis tennis *m.* 5
tennis shoes baskets *f., pl.* 6
tenth dixième *adj.* 7
terminal (bus) gare *f.* routière 7
terrace (café) terrasse *f.* de café 4
test examen *m.* 1
text message SMS/texto *m.* 11
than que/qu' *conj.* 9, 14
thank: Thank you (very much). Merci (beaucoup). 1
that ce/c', ça 1; que *rel. pron.* 13
Is that... ? Est-ce... ? 2
That's enough. Ça suffit. 5
That has nothing to do with us. That is none of our business. Ça ne nous regarde pas. 14
that is... c'est... 1
that is to say ça veut dire 10

theater théâtre *m.* 15
their leur(s) *poss. adj., m., f.* 3
theirs le(s) leur(s), la/les leur(s) *poss. pron.* 15
them les *d.o. pron.* 7, leur *i.o. pron., m., f., pl.* 6
then ensuite *adv.* 7, puis *adv.* 7, puis 4; alors *adv.* 7
there là 1; y *pron.* 10
Is there... ? Y a-t-il... ? 2
over there là-bas *adv.* 1
(over) there (*used with demonstrative adjective* ce *and noun or with demonstrative pronoun* celui) -là 6
There is/There are... Il y a... 1
There is/There are.... Voilà... 1
There was... Il y a eu... 6; Il y avait... 8
therefore donc *conj.* 7
these/those ces *dem. adj., m., f., pl.* 6
these/those celles *pron., f., pl.* 14
these/those ceux *pron., m., pl.* 14
they ils *sub. pron., m.* 1; elles *sub. and disj. pron., f.* 1; eux *disj. pron., pl.* 3
thing chose *f.* 1, truc *m.* 7
think (about) réfléchir (à) *v.* 4
to think (that) penser (que) *v.* 2
third troisième *adj.* 7
thirst soif *f.* 4
to be thirsty avoir soif *v.* 4
thirteen treize *m.* 1
thirty trente *m.* 1
thirty-first trente et unième *adj.* 7
this/that ce *dem. adj., m., sing.* 6; cet *dem. adj., m., sing.* 6; cette *dem. adj., f., sing.* 6
this afternoon cet après-midi 2
this evening ce soir 2
this one/that one celle *pron., f., sing.* 14; celui *pron., m., sing.* 14
this week cette semaine 2
this weekend ce week-end 2
this year cette année 2
those are... ce sont... 1
thousand: one thousand mille *m.* 5
one hundred thousand cent mille *m.* 5
threat danger *m.* 14
three trois *m.* 1
three hundred trois cents *m.* 5
throat gorge *f.* 10
throw away jeter *v.* 14
Thursday jeudi *m.* 2
ticket billet *m.* 7
round-trip ticket billet *m.*

aller-retour 7
  bus/subway ticket **ticket de bus/de métro** m. 7
tie **cravate** f. 6
tight **serré(e)** adj. 6
time (occurence) **fois** f.; (general sense) **temps** m., sing. 5
  a long time **longtemps** adv. 5
  free time **temps libre** m. 5
  from time to time **de temps en temps** adv. 7
  to lose time **perdre son temps** v. 6
tinker **bricoler** v. 5
tip **pourboire** m. 4
  to leave a tip **laisser un pourboire** v. 4
tire **pneu** m. 11
  flat tire **pneu** m. **crevé** 11
  (emergency) tire **roue (de secours)** f. 11
  to check the tire pressure **vérifier la pression des pneus** v. 11
tired **fatigué(e)** adj. 3
tiresome **pénible** adj. 3
to **à** prep. 4; **au (à + le)** 4; **aux (à + les)** 4
toaster **grille-pain** m. 8
today **aujourd'hui** adv. 2
toe **orteil** m. 10; **doigt de pied** m. 10
together **ensemble** adv. 6
tomato **tomate** f. 9
tomorrow (morning, afternoon, evening) **demain (matin, après-midi, soir)** adv. 2
  day after tomorrow **après-demain** adv. 2
too **aussi** adv. 1
  too many/much (of) **trop (de)** 4
tooth **dent** f. 9
  to brush one's teeth **se brosser les dents** v. 9
toothbrush **brosse** f. **à dents** 10
toothpaste **dentifrice** m. 10
tour **tour** m. 5
tourism **tourisme** m. 12
tourist office **office du tourisme** m. 12
towel (bath) **serviette (de bain)** f. 10
town **ville** f. 4
town hall **mairie** f. 12
toxic **toxique** adj. 14
toxic waste **déchets toxiques** m., pl. 14
traffic **circulation** f. 11
traffic light **feu de signalisation** m. 12
tragedy **tragédie** f. 15
train **train** m. 7
train station **gare** f. 7; **station**

f. **de train** 7
training **formation** f. 13
translate **traduire** v. 6
translated **traduit (traduire)** p.p., adj. 6
trash **ordures** f., pl. 14
travel **voyager** v. 2
travel agency **agence de voyages** f. 7
travel agent **agent de voyages** m. 7
tree **arbre** m. 14
trip **voyage** m. 7
troop (company) **troupe** f. 15
tropical **tropical(e)** adj. 14
  tropical forest **forêt tropicale** f. 14
true **vrai(e)** adj. 3; **véritable** adj. 6
  It is true that… **Il est vrai que…** 15
  It is untrue that… **Il n'est pas vrai que…** 15
trunk **coffre** m. 11
try **essayer** v. 5
Tuesday **mardi** m. 2
tuna **thon** m. 9
turn **tourner** v. 12
  to turn off **éteindre** v. 11
  to turn on **allumer** v. 11
  to turn (oneself) around **se tourner** v. 10
twelve **douze** m. 1
twentieth **vingtième** adj. 7
twenty **vingt** m. 1
twenty-first **vingt et unième** adj. 7
twenty-second **vingt-deuxième** adj. 7
twice **deux fois** adv. 7
twist one's ankle **se fouler la cheville** v. 10
two **deux** m. 1
two hundred **deux cents** m. 5
two million **deux millions** m. 5
type **genre** m. 15

U

ugly **laid(e)** adj. 3
umbrella **parapluie** m. 5
uncle **oncle** m. 3
under **sous** prep. 3
understand **comprendre** v. 4
understood **compris (comprendre)** p.p., adj. 6
underwear **sous-vêtement** m. 6
undress **se déshabiller** v. 10
unemployed person **chômeur/chômeuse** m., f. 13
  to be unemployed **être au chômage** v. 13
unemployment **chômage** m. 13
unfortunately **malheureusement**

adv. 2
unhappy **malheureux/malheureuse** adj. 3
union **syndicat** m. 13
United States **États-Unis** m., pl. 7
university **faculté** f. 1; **université** f. 1
university cafeteria **restaurant universitaire (resto U)** m. 2
unless **à moins que** conj. 15
unpleasant **antipathique** adj. 3; **désagréable** adj. 1
until **jusqu'à** prep. 12; **jusqu'à ce que** conj. 15
upset: to become upset **s'énerver** v. 10
us **nous** i.o. pron. 6; **nous** d.o. pron. 7
USB drive **clé USB** f.
use **employer** v. 5
  to use a map **utiliser un plan** v. 7
useful **utile** adj. 2
useless **inutile** adj. 2; **nul(le)** adj. 2
usually **d'habitude** adv. 7

V

vacation **vacances** f., pl. 7
  vacation day **jour de congé** m. 7
vacuum **aspirateur** m. 8
  to vacuum **passer l'aspirateur** v. 8
valley **vallée** f. 14
vegetable **légume** m. 9
velvet **velours** 6
very (before adjective) **tout(e)** adv. 3; (before adverb) **très** adv. 7
  Very well. **Très bien.** 1
veterinarian **vétérinaire** m., f. 13
video game(s) **jeu vidéo (des jeux vidéo)** m. 11
Vietnamese **vietnamien(ne)** adj. 1
violet **violet(te)** adj. 6
violin **violon** m. 15
visit **visite** f. 6
  to visit (a place) **visiter** v. 2; (a person or people) **rendre vis-ite (à)** v. 6; (to visit reglarly) **fréquenter** v. 4
voicemail **messagerie** f. 13
volcano **volcan** m. 14
volleyball **volley(-ball)** m. 5

W

waist **taille** f. 6
wait **attendre** v. 6
  to wait (on the phone) **patienter** v. 13

to wait in line **faire la queue** *v.* 12
wake up **se réveiller** *v.* 10
walk **promenade** *f.* 5; **marcher** *v.* 5
    to go for a walk **faire une promenade** 5; **faire un tour** 5
wall **mur** *m.* 8
want **désirer** *v.* 5; **vouloir** *v.* 9
wardrobe **armoire** *f.* 8
warming: global warming **réchauffement de la Terre** *m.* 14
warning light (gas/oil) **voyant** *m.* **(d'essence/d'huile)** 11
wash **laver** *v.* 8
    to wash oneself (one's hands) **se laver (les mains)** *v.* 10
    to wash up (in the morning) **faire sa toilette** *v.* 10
washing machine **lave-linge** *m.* 8
waste **gaspillage** *m.* 14; **gaspiller** *v.* 14
wastebasket **corbeille (à papier)** *f.* 1
waste time **perdre son temps** *v.* 6
watch **montre** *f.* 1; **regarder** *v.* 2
water **eau** *f.* 4
    mineral water **eau** *f.* **minérale** 4
way (*by the way*) **au fait** 3; (*path*) **chemin** 12
we **nous** *pron.* 1
weak **faible** *adj.* 3
wear **porter** *v.* 6
weather **temps** *m., sing.* 5; **météo** *f.* 15
    The weather is bad. **Il fait mauvais.** 5
    The weather is dreadful. **Il fait un temps épouvantable.** 5
    The weather is good/warm. **Il fait bon.** 5
    The weather is nice. **Il fait beau.** 5
web site **site Internet/web** *m.* 11
wedding **mariage** *m.* 6
Wednesday **mercredi** *m.* 2
weekend **week-end** *m.* 2
    this weekend **ce week-end** *m.* 2
welcome **bienvenu(e)** *adj.* 1
    You're welcome. **Il n'y a pas de quoi.** 1
well **bien** *adv.* 7
    I am doing well/badly. **Je vais bien/mal.** 1
west **ouest** *m.* 12
What? **Comment?** *adv.* 4; **Pardon?** 4; **Quoi?** 1 *interr. pron.* 4
    What day is it? **Quel jour sommes-nous?** 2

What is it? **Qu'est-ce que c'est?** *prep.* 1
What is the date? **Quelle est la date?** 5
What is the temperature? **Quelle température fait-il?** 5
What is the weather like? **Quel temps fait-il?** 5
What is your name? **Comment t'appelles-tu?** *fam.* 1
What is your name? **Comment vous appelez-vous?** *form.* 1
What is your nationality? **Quelle est ta nationalité?** *sing., fam.* 1
What is your nationality? **Quelle est votre nationalité?** *sing., pl., fam., form.* 1
What time do you have? **Quelle heure avez-vous?** *form.* 2
What time is it? **Quelle heure est-il?** 2
What time? **À quelle heure?** 2
What do you think about that? **Qu'en penses-tu?** 14
What's up? **Ça va?** 1
whatever it may be **quoi que ce soit** 13
What's wrong? **Qu'est-ce qu'il y a?** 1
when **quand** *adv.* 4
    When is …'s birthday? **C'est quand l'anniversaire de …?** 5
    When is your birthday? **C'est quand ton/votre anniversaire?** 5
where **où** *adv., rel. pron.* 4, 13
which? **quel(le)(s)?** *adj.* 4
    which one **à laquelle** *pron., f., sing.* 13
    which one **auquel (à + lequel)** *pron., m., sing.* 13
    which one **de laquelle** *pron., f., sing.* 13
    which one **duquel (de + lequel)** *pron., m., sing.* 13
    which one **laquelle** *pron., f., sing.* 13
    which one **lequel** *pron., m., sing.* 13
    which ones **auxquelles (à + lesquelles)** *pron., f., pl.* 13
    which ones **auxquels (à + lesquels)** *pron., m., pl.* 13
    which ones **desquelles (de + lesquelles)** *pron., f., pl.* 13
    which ones **desquels (de + lesquels)** *pron., m., pl.* 13
    which ones **lesquelles** *pron., f., pl.* 13
    which ones **lesquels** *pron., m., pl.* 13

while **pendant que** *prep.* 7
white **blanc(he)** *adj.* 6
who? **qui?** *interr. pron.* 4; **qui** *rel. pron.* 13
    Who is it? **Qui est-ce?** 1
    Who's calling, please? **Qui est à l'appareil?** 13
whom? **qui?** *interr.* 4
    For whom? **Pour qui?** 4
    To whom? **À qui?** 4
why? **pourquoi?** *adv.* 2, 4
widowed **veuf/veuve** *adj.* 3
wife **femme** *f.* 1; **épouse** *f.* 3
willingly **volontiers** *adv.* 10
win **gagner** *v.* 5
wind **vent** *m.* 5
    It is windy. **Il fait du vent.** 5
window **fenêtre** *f.* 1
windshield **pare-brise** *m.* 11
windshield wiper(s) **essuie-glace (essuie-glaces** *pl.***)** *m.* 11
windsurfing **planche à voile** *v.* 5
    to go windsurfing **faire de la planche à voile** *v.* 5
wine **vin** *m.* 6
winter **hiver** *m.* 5
    in the winter **en hiver** 5
wipe (the dishes/the table) **essuyer (la vaisselle/la table)** *v.* 8
wish that… **souhaiter que…** *v.* 14
with **avec** *prep.* 1
    with whom? **avec qui?** 4
withdraw money **retirer de l'argent** *v.* 12
without **sans** *prep.* 8; **sans que** *conj.* 5
woman **femme** *f.* 1
wood **bois** *m.* 14
wool **laine** *f.* 6
work **travail** *m.* 12
    to work **travailler** *v.* 2; **marcher** *v.* 11; **fonctionner** *v.* 11
work out **faire de la gym** *v.* 5
worker **ouvrier/ouvrière** *m., f.* 13
world **monde** *m.* 7
worried **inquiet/inquiète** *adj.* 3
worry **s'inquiéter** *v.* 10
worse **pire** *comp. adj.* 9; **plus mal** *comp. adv.* 9; **plus mauvais(e)** *comp. adj.* 9
worst: the worst **le plus mal** *super. adv.* 9; **le/la pire** *super. adj.* 9; **le/la plus mauvais(e)** *super. adj.* 9
wound **blessure** *f.* 10
wounded: to get wounded **se blesser** *v.* 10
write **écrire** *v.* 7
    to write one another **s'écrire** *v.* 11

writer **écrivain/écrivaine** *m.,*
f. 15
written **écrit (écrire)** *p.p., adj.* 7
wrong **tort** *m.* 2
to be wrong **avoir tort** *v.* 2

Y

yeah **ouais** 2
year **an** *m.* 2; **année** *f.* 2
yellow **jaune** *adj.* 6
yes **oui** 2; *(when making a
contradiction)* **si** 2
yesterday (morning/afternoon
evening) **hier (matin/
après-midi/soir)** *adv.* 7
day before yesterday **avant-
hier** *adv.* 7
yogurt **yaourt** *m.* 9
you **toi** *disj. pron., sing., fam.*
3; **tu** *sub. pron., sing., fam.*
1; **vous** *pron., sing., pl., fam.,
form.* 1
you neither **toi non plus** 2
You're welcome. **De rien.** 1
young **jeune** *adj.* 3
younger **cadet(te)** *adj.* 3
your **ta** *poss. adj., f., sing.* 3;
tes *poss. adj., m., f., pl.* 3;
ton *poss. adj., m., sing.* 3;
vos *poss. adj., m., f., pl.* 3;
votre *poss. adj., m., f., sing.* 3;
yours **le(s) tien(s), la/les
tienne(s), le(s) vôtre(s),
la/les vôtre(s)** *poss. pron.* 15
yourself **te/t'** *refl. pron., sing.,
fam.* 10; **toi** *refl. pron., sing.,
fam.* 10; **vous** *refl. pron.,
form.* 10
youth **jeunesse** *f.* 6
youth hostel **auberge de
jeunesse** *f.* 7
Yum! **Miam!** *interj.* 5

Z

zero **zéro** *m.* 1

Index

Photography and Art Credits

All images © Vista Higher Learning unless otherwise noted.

Cover: Loic Lagarde.

Front Matter (IAE): IAE-32: (all) VHL.

Front Matter (SE): 3: Photolibrary; **xxviii:** (all) VHL.

Unit 1

1: VHL; **2:** Anne Loubet; **4:** (t) Pascal Pernix; (b) Rossy Llano; **8:** (t) Anne Loubet; (b) Paula Díez; **9:** Ian G Dagnall/Alamy; **13:** (tl) LdF/iStockphoto; (tm) Martín Bernetti; (tr) Odilon Dimier/Media Bakery; (bl) Rawpixel/Fotolia; (bml) Sami Sert/iStockphoto; (bmr) WavebreakmediaMicro/Fotolia; (br) Laura Stevens; **15:** (l) Anne Loubet; (r) Terex/Fotolia; **17:** Pascal Pernix; **20:** Martín Bernetti; **22:** Rossy Llano; **26:** (l) Andrew Bayda/Fotolia; (r) Huang Zheng/Shutterstock; **27:** (t) Extrait de Superdupont – Tome 2/Solé/Fluide Glacial; (b) Chelsea Lauren/Getty Images; **28:** (l) Anne Loubet; (r) Anne Loubet; **29:** (tl) Thaporn942/Fotolia; (tr) VHL; (bl) VHL; (br) Masson/Shutterstock; **30:** (tl) Featureflash Photo Agency/Shutterstock; (tm) BillionPhotos/Fotolia; (tr) Hongqi Zhang/Alamy; (tm) Niko Guido/iStockphoto; (tr) Michal Kowalski/Shutterstock; (br) Demidoff/Fotolia; **31:** (tl) Jstone/Shutterstock; (tm) Featureflash Photo Agency/Shutterstock; (tr) Jose Luis Pelaez/Media Bakery; (bl) Anne Loubet; (bml) Odilon Dimier/Media Bakery; (bmr) Martín Bernetti; (br) Colleen Cahill/Media Bakery; **33:** (l) VHL; (r) VHL; **35:** Paula Díez; **36:** (tl) Anne Loubet; (tr) Anne Loubet; (mtl) Robert Lerich/Fotolia; (mtr) Anne Loubet; (mbl) Rossy Llano; (mbr) Anne Loubet; (bl) Anne Loubet; (br) Anne Loubet; **37:** Pascal Pernix; **38:** (left col: t) Allstar Picture Library/Alamy; (left col: r) Eddy Lemaistre/For Picture/Getty Images; (t) Photo courtesy of www.Tahiti-Tourisme.com; (m) Lonely Planet Images/Ariadne Van Zandbergen/Getty Images; (r) Eddy Lemaistre/For Picture/Getty Images; **39:** (tl) Robert McGouey/Alamy; (tr) Nick Hannes/ZUMA Press/Newscom; (bl) Owen Franken/Getty Images: (br) Courtesy of the International Organisation of La Francophonie; **42:** Anne Loubet.

Unit 2

45: VHL; **46:** Tom Stewart/Corbis/Getty Images; **52:** (l) Pascal Pernix; (r) Martín Bernetti; **53:** Francis Vachon/Alamy; **60:** ImageSource; **64:** Rossy Llano; **66:** (l) Martín Bernetti; (r) Jupiter Images; **70:** (l) Rossy Llano; (r) Anne Loubet; **71:** (t) Pascal Pernix; (m) David Schaffer/Media Bakery; (b) Benaroch/Sipa/Newscom; **72:** (tl) VHL; (tr) VHL; (bl) VHL; (br) VHL; **73:** (tl) Anne Loubet; (tr) JGI/Jamie Grill/Media Bakery; (bl) Paula Díez; (br) Anne Loubet; **81:** Anne Loubet; **82:** (left col: t) Dante Gabriel Rossetti (1828–1882). Joan of Arc kissing the Sword of Deliverance, 1863. Oil on canvas, 61 cm x 53 cm. Inv.55.996.8.1. Location: Musee musée d'Art moderne et contemporain, Strasbourg, France. Photo credit: Christie's Images/Superstock; (left col: m) Bettmann/Getty Images; (left col: b) Antoine Gyori/Sygma/Getty Images; (t) Anne Loubet; (ml) Martine Coquilleau/Fotolia; (mr) Mddphoto/iStockphoto; (b) Anne Loubet; **83:** (tl) David Gregs/Alamy; (tr) Anne Loubet; (bl) Anne Loubet; (br) Caroline Beecham/iStockphoto; **84:** Martín Bernetti; **84-85:** Art Kowalsky/Alamy; **85:** Pascal Pernix; **86:** Pascal Pernix; **87:** (l) VHL; (r) Pressmaster/Shutterstock.

Unit 3

89: VHL; **90:** Anne Loubet; **92:** Hero/Media Bakery; **96:** Anne Loubet; **97:** (l) Alix William/SIPA/Newscom; (r) Nuccio DiNuzzo/TNS/Newscom; **98:** (l) Martín Bernetti; (r) FogStock LLC/Photolibrary; **100:** Hemera Technologies/Getty Images; **101:** (t) Tomasz Trojanowski/Shutterstock; (ml) Brian McEntire/iStockphoto; (mm) Anna Lurye/Shutterstock; (mr) RJGrant/Big Stock Photo; (bl) Linda Kloosterhof/iStockphoto; (bm) Dmitry Pistrov/Shutterstock; (br) Oliveromg/Shutterstock; **104:** (tl) Martín Bernetti; (tm) Dmitry Kutlayev/iStockphoto; (tr) Martín Bernetti; (bl) AHBE/Fotolia; (bml) VHL; (bmr) Anne Loubet; (br) Martín Bernetti; **105:** (t) Martín Bernetti; (bl) Dynamic Graphics/Jupiter Images; (br) Rossy Llano; **108:** Anne Loubet; **109:** (l) Martín Bernetti; (m) Anne Loubet; (r) Anne Loubet; **110:** (t) Anne Loubet; (ml) Hemera Technologies/Photos.com; (mml) JackF/Fotolia; (mmr) Paula Díez; (mr) Vstock, LLC/Photolibrary; (bl) Martín Bernetti; (bml) Photolibrary; (bmr) Keith Levit Photography/Photolibrary; (br) Anne Loubet; **114:** (l) Anne Loubet; (r) Anne Loubet; **115:** (tl) Anita Bugge/Getty Images; (tr) Patrick Roncen/Kipa/Getty Images; (m) Bertrand Rindoff Petroff/Getty Images; (b) Julien Reynaud/APS-Medias/Sipa/Newscom; **117:** Imagesource/123RF; (inset, t) FRSE_U01_L02ST_p024_PH06b; (inset, b) Anne Loubet; **119:** (t) Martín Bernetti; (ml) David Lee/Alamy; (mml) AKF/Fotolia; (mmr) Yay Micro/AGE Fotostock; (mr) Igor Tarasov/Fotolia; (bl) Creative Jen Designs/Shutterstock; (bml) Photofriday/Shutterstock; (bmr) F9photos/Shutterstock; (br) Martín Bernetti; **122:** (tl) Valuavital/Dreamstime; (tm) Roy Hsu/Media Bakery; (tr) Don Mason/Getty Images; (bl) Simon Kolton/Alamy; (bml) Blend Images/Ariel Skelley/Getty Images; (bmr) Jacek Chabraszewski/iStockphoto; (br) Sergei Telegin/Shutterstock; **124:** Anne Loubet; **125:** Anne Loubet; **126:** (left col) Marta Perez/EFE/Newscom; (t) Paul Springett 09/Alamy; (m) Simona Dumitru/Alamy; (b) Nicole Paton/Shutterstock; **127:** (tl) Franky DeMeyer/iStockphoto; (tr) Dave Bartruff/Danita Delimont/Alamy; (bl) Erik Tham/Alamy; (br) Portrait of Jean Jacques Rousseau by Edouard Lacretelle. Gianni Dagli Orti/The Art Archive at Art Resource, NY; **128:** (t) Juniors Bildarchiv/Alamy; (b) Martín Bernetti; **129:** Anne Loubet; **130:** Anne Loubet; **131:** Anne Loubet.

Unit 4

133: VHL; **134:** Martín Bernetti; **136:** (t) Anne Loubet; (b) Martín Bernetti; **140:** (l) Vincent Besnault/Photographer's Choice/Getty Images; (r) Directphoto Collection/Alamy; **141:** (t) Foc Kan/WireImage/Getty Images; (b) Romuald Meigneux/SIPA/Newscom; **145:** David Hughes/Photolibrary; **152:** Pascal Pernix; **153:** Pascal Pernix; **154:** Anne Loubet; **158:** (t) Carlos S. Pereyra/AGE Fotostock; (b) Pascal Pernix; **159:** (t) Yadid Levy/Alamy; (m) Kevin Foy/Alamy; (b) Audiogram; **161:** VHL; **165:** Ana Cabezas Martín; **169:** Anne Loubet; **170:** (left col: t) Art Babych/Shutterstock; (left col: m) Yoan Valat/EPA/Newscom; (left col: b) Byron Purvis/AdMedia/Newscom; (t) Carlos Sanchez Pereyra/123RF; (ml) Stephen Saks Photography/Alamy; (mr) Peter Spiro/iStockphoto; (b) Richard T. Nowitz/Corbis Documentary/Getty Images; **171:** (tl) Mike Blake/Reuters; (tr) Grafxcom/iStockphoto; (bl) Rubens Abboud/Alamy; (br) Perry Mastrovito/Getty Images; **172-173:** Anne Loubet; **173:** (t) Anne Loubet; (b) Anne Loubet; **174:** Martín Bernetti; **175:** Anne Loubet.

Unit 5

177: VHL; **178:** Anne Loubet; **180:** Martín Bernetti; **184:** (t) Michael Sohn/AP Images; (b) Neil Marchand/Liewig Media Sports/Getty Images; **185:** (t) EPP Euro Press Photo; (b) Arko Datta/Reuters; **196:** FogStock LLC/Photolibrary; **198:** Ron Koeberer/Getty Images; **202:** (l) Anne Loubet; (r) Anne Loubet; **203:** (t) Anne Loubet; (m) Reuters; (b) Ian Gavan/Zuma Press/Newscom; **205:** Vanessa Bertozzi; **214:** (left col: t) Dorn Byg/Cal Sport Media/Newscom; (left col: b) CS2/Charlie Steffens/WENN/Newscom; (t) Brianafrica/Alamy; (ml) Authors Image/Alamy; (mr) Jalvarezg/Fotolia; (b) Anton_Ivanov/Shutterstock; **215:** (tl) Morandi Bruno/ZUMA Press/Newscom; (tr) Sadaka Edmond/SIPA/Newscom; (bl) Seyllou/AFP/Getty Images; (br) Nic Bothma/EPA/Newscom; **216:** (left col: t) ATB/ATP/WENN/Newscom; (left col: b) SA Terli/Anadolu Agency/Getty Images; (tl) Anthony Asael/Corbis Documentary/Getty Images; (tr) MJ Photography/Alamy; (b) Gerard Lacz Images/SuperStock; **217:** (tl) SFM Titti Soldati/Alamy; (tr) Werner Forman Archive/Heritage Image Partnership Ltd/Alamy; (bl) Per-Anders Pettersson/Corbis Documentary/Getty Images; (br) Philippe Giraud/Corbis Sport/Getty Images; **218:** (t) Perry Mastrovito/Corbis; (b) Rossy Llano; **219:** Anne Loubet; **220:** Anne Loubet; **221:** (l) Martine Coquilleau/Fotolia; (r) Nancy Camley.

Unit 6

223: VHL; **224:** Pascal Pernix; **230:** (l) Fadi Al-barghouthy/123RF; (r) Vespasian/Alamy; **231:** (t) Mal Langsdon/Reuters; (b) Trevor Pearson/Alamy; **232:** Rachel Distler; **233:** (l) Paula Díez; (r) Paula Díez; **242:** Anne Loubet; **243:** (t) Ben Blankenburg/Corbis; (ml) Hemera Technologies/Getty Images; (mr) Purestock/Jupiter Images; (b) Ablestock.com/Getty Images; **248:** (l) Poree-Wyters/ABACA/Newscom; (r) 123RF; **249:** (t) Evening Standard/Getty Images; (m) Laurent/EPA/REX/Shutterstock; (b) Tony Barson/Getty Images; **253:** Anne Loubet; **257:** Anne Loubet; **259:** Anne Loubet; **260:** (left col: t) Criben/Shutterstock; (left col: m) AKG-Images/Newscom; (left col: b) Baltel/Sipa/Newscom; (t) Photononstop/SuperStock; (ml) Dmitry Pichugin/Fotolia; (mr) Nik Wheeler/Corbis Documentary/Getty Images; (b) Hagit Berkovich/Fotolia; **261:** (tl) Sophie Bassouls/Sygma/Corbis/Getty Images; (tr) PhotoCuisine RM/Alamy; (bl) Photononstop/SuperStock; (br) Bartosz Hadyniak/Media Bakery; **262:** (left col: t) Abdelhak Senna/AFP/Getty Images; (left col: m) Toshifumi Kitamura/AFP/Getty Images; (left col: b) Marc Gantier/Gamma-Rapho/Getty Images; (t) Idealink Photography/Alamy; (ml) Kicimici/Fotolia; (mr) Posztos/Shutterstock; (b) Philipus/123RF; **263:** (tl) Stephen Lloyd Morocco/Alamy; (tr) Maria Laura Antonelli/ZUMA Press/Newscom; (bl) Calin Stan/Fotolia; (br) Romilly Lockyer/Getty Images; **264:** The Canadian Press/Trois-Rivieres Le Nouvelliste-Sylvain Mayer; **264-265:** Corbis; **266:** Jeff Greenberg/Alamy; **267:** Karl Prouse/Catwalking/Getty Images.

Unit 7

269: VHL; **270:** Glow Images/Getty Images; **272:** Pab Map/Fotolia; **276:** (t) Photo courtesy of www.Tahiti-Tourisme.com; (b) Photo courtesy of www.Tahiti-Tourisme.com; **277:** (l) Zonesix/Shutterstock; (r) Edgar Degas (1834–1917). Danseuses bleues, Blue Dancers, c. 1890. Location: Musée d'Orsay, Paris, France. Art Resource; **285:** Photo courtesy of www.Tahiti-Tourisme.com; **288:** Anne Loubet; **289:** Photolibrary; **290:** Martín Bernetti; **294:** (t) Anne Loubet; (b) Hubert Stadler/Getty Images; **295:** (t) Johner Images/Alamy; (b) Kambou SIA/AFP/Getty Images; **305:** Anne Loubet; **306:** (left col: t) Gilbert Nencioli/Gamma/Getty Images; (left col: b) Lori Conn/ZUMA Press/Newscom; (t) Ocean/Corbis; (m) Melba Photo Agency/Alamy; (b) David Sanger/Getty Images; **307:** (tl) Tahitian Women(1891), Paul Gauguin. Oil on canvas, 69 x 91.5 cm. Musee d'Orsay, Paris, France. Laurent Lecat/Mondadori Portfolio/AGE Fotostock; (tr) Frederic/Fotolia; (bl) Photo courtesy of www.Tahiti-Tourisme.com; (br) Philippe Giraud/Sygma/Getty Images; **308-309:** Andreas Prott/Shutterstock; **310:** Pascal Pernix; **311:** Jessica Beets.

Unit 8

313: VHL; **314:** Brand X Pictures/Fotosearch; **320:** (t) Michele Molinari/Alamy; (b) Anne Loubet; **321:** Maridav/Shutterstock; **332:** Tetra Images/Alamy; **333:** Paula Díez; **334:** Anne Loubet; **338:** (l) Anne Loubet; (r) Pascal Pernix; **339:** (t) AJ Sisco/UPI/Newscom; (m) David Redfern/Redferns/Getty Images; (b) Axelle Woussen/Bauergriffin/Newscom; **345:** 290712/Fotolia; **346:** (t) Stockshot/Alamy; (bl) Ben Blankenburg/Corbis; (bml) Martín Bernetti; (bmr) Martín Bernetti; (r) Martín Bernetti; **347:** Anne Loubet; **348:** (l) Anne Loubet; (rt) Martín Bernetti; (rb) Anne Loubet; **349:** (left col) Anne Loubet; (t) Anne Loubet; (m) Anne Loubet; (b) Anne Loubet; **350:** (left col: t) Philip and Elizabeth De Bay/Corbis Historical/Getty Images; (left col: m) Keystone Pictures USA/ZUMA Press/Newscom; (left col: b) Pascal Le Segretain/Getty Images; (t) Jeremy Reddington/Shutterstock; (ml) Abadesign/Shutterstock; (mr) Pascal Pernix; (b) Benjamin Herzoq/Fotolia; **351:** (tl) Tom Delano; (tr) Images of France/Alamy; (bl) Keren Su/Corbis Documentary/Getty Images; (br) Anne Loubet; **352:** (left col, t) Aksaran/Gamma-Rapho/Getty Images; (left col, m) Stills Press/Alamy; (left col, b) AF Archive/Alamy; (t) Structurae / Nicolas Janberg; (ml) Paanna/Deposit Photos; (mr)

Sigurcamp/Shutterstock; (b) Jean Dubuffet. Closerie Falbala (1971-1973). Painted epoxy resin and sprayed concrete. Surface area: 1.610 m2. Fondation Dubuffet, Perigny-sur-Marne (France). Copyright Fondation Dubuffet / ARS 2017; **353:** (tl) Kalpana Kartik/Alamy; (tr) Josse Christophel/Alamy; (bl) Tony C. French/Getty Images; (br) Bukki88/Depositphotos; **354:** Jan Butchofsky/Getty Images; **354-355:** John Kellerman/Alamy; **355:** Directphoto/AGE Fotostock; **356:** Anne Loubet; **357:** Terry J Alcorn/iStockphoto.

Unit 9

359: VHL; **360:** Martín Bernetti; **361:** Martín Bernetti; **366:** (l) Franck Dubray/PhotoPQR/Ouest France/Newscom; (r) Gilles ROLLE/REA/Redux; **367:** VHL; **369:** (l) Jupiter Images/Thinkstock/Getty Images; (r) Jeffrey M. Frank/Shutterstock; **378:** Anne Loubet; **380:** Martín Bernetti; **384:** (l) Anne Loubet; (r) Paula Díez; **385:** (t) Sergio Pitamitz/Getty Images; (m) FoodCollection/Photolibrary; (b) Stephane Cardinale/Corbis/Getty Images; **386:** Anne Loubet; **389:** (t) Photolibrary; (bl) Jovannig/Fotolia; (bml) Design Pics Inc./Alamy; (bmr) Anne Loubet; (br) MediaPictures.pl/Shutterstock; **391:** (t) Comstock/Jupiter Images; (b) Martín Bernetti; **393:** (tl) Anne Loubet; (tr) Bold Stock/Fotosearch; (bl) Photolibrary; (br) Anne Loubet; **395:** Andersen Ross/Blend Images/Corbis; **396:** (left col: t) Hulton-Deutsch Collection/Corbis/Getty Images; (left col: b) Sonia Recchia/Getty Images; (t) Christophe Boisvieux/Corbis; (ml) David Osborne/Alamy; (mr) Hemis/Alamy; (b) Tashka/iStockphoto; **397:** (tl) Janet Dracksdorf; (tr) Hemis/Alamy; (bl) Pecold/Fotolia; (br) Walid Nohra/Shutterstock; **398:** (left col: t) Bettmann/Getty Images; (left col: b) Hulton-Deutsch Collection/Corbis/Getty Images; (t) Dean Conger/Corbis Historical/Getty Images; (ml) Daniel Joubert/Reuters; (mr) Dianne Maire/iStockphoto; (b) Pikselstock/Shutterstock; **399:** (tl) Demid Borodin/iStockphoto; (tr) Alain Jocard/AFP/Getty Images; (bl) Daniel Joubert/Reuters; (br) James Warren/iStockphoto; **402:** Pascal Pernix; **403:** José Blanco.

Unit 10

405: VHL; **406:** Martín Bernetti; **412:** (t) Max Alexander/Getty Images; (b) Pascal Pernix; **413:** (t) Janet Dracksdorf; (b) Rachel Distler; **424:** Image Source; **430:** (l) Ingram Publishing/Photolibrary; (r) Chassenet/AGE Fotostock; **431:** (t) Hulton-Deutsch Collection/Corbis/Getty Images; (b) Photo 12/Alamy; **433:** (l) Dynamic Graphics/Jupiter Images; (r) DesignPics Inc./Photolibrary; **435:** Martín Bernetti; 441: Anne Loubet; **442:** (left col: t) Bettmann/Getty Images; (left col: m) Album/Oronoz/Newscom; (left col: b) Adoc-Photos/Getty Images; (t) Gonzalo Azumendi/AGE Fotostock; (m) Sonnet Sylvain/Hemis.fr/Alamy; (bl) Kumar Sriskandan/Alamy; (br) Bettmann/Getty Images; **443:** (tl) Mauritius Images Gmbh/Alamy; (tr) Andia/Getty Images; (bl) Owen Franken/Corbis Documentary/Getty Images; (br) FreeProd/Deposit Photos; **444:** (t) Martín Bernetti; (b) Anne Loubet; **445:** Moodboard/Corbis; **446:** Ebby May/Getty Images; **447:** Commercial Eye/Getty Images.

Unit 11

449: VHL; **450:** Anne Loubet; **452:** David R. Frazier/Danita Delimont Photography/Newscom; **456:** (l) Goodshot/Jupiterimages; (r) Pascal Pernix; **457:** Alain Nogues/Sygma/Getty; **459:** DomenicoGelermo/iStockphoto; (background) Nadla/iStockphoto; **463:** Linzyslusher/iStockphoto; **468:** Anne Loubet; **470:** Anne Loubet; **474:** (all) Anne Loubet; **475:** (t) Bettmann/Getty Images; (m) ThePenguin/Shutterstock; (b) David Wolff-Patrick/Getty Images; **477:** Flashon Studio/Shutterstock; (inset) YanLev/Shutterstock; **484:** John DeCarli; **485:** Anne Loubet; **486:** (left col) Bettmann/Getty Images; (t) Sylvie Lebchek/Shutterstock; (ml) Milosk50/Shutterstock; (mr) Mikhail Lavrenov/123RF; (b) Elenathewise/Deposit Photos; **487:** (tl) Foodfolio/Alamy; (tr) Philip Lange/iStockphoto; (bl) Hamis/Alamy; (br) Troubadour Plays Six Musical Instruments. Handcoloured engraving from Pierre de la Mesangere's Le Bon Genre, Paris, 1817. Florilegius/SSPL/Getty Images; **490:** Quavondo/iStockphoto; **491:** Anne Loubet.

Unit 12

493: VHL; **494:** Hero/Corbis; **496:** (tl) Gavin Rodgers/Alamy; (tm) Pascal Pernix; (tr) Anne Loubet; (bl) Paris Metro/Alamy; (bm) Anne Loubet; (br) Anne Loubet; **500:** (l) Carole Castelli/Shutterstock; (r) Paul Warburton/Alamy; **501:** Matt Dunham/Reuters; **504:** (t) David Sanger Photography/Getty Images; (ml) Beijersbergen/Shutterstock; (mr) Szefei/Shutterstock; (bl) Bruno de Hogues/Getty Images; (br) Richard Klune/Getty Images; **514:** Rossy Llano; **516:** VHL; **520:** (t) Franck Boston/Big Stock Photo; (bl) Anne Loubet; (br) Pascal Pernix; **521:** (t) Degas Jean-Pierre/Getty Images; (m) Tom Delano; (br) Courtesy of Marcel Tessier-Caune and Manivette Records; **523:** Corbis; (inset) Richard T. Nowitz/Getty Images; **525:** (l) VHL; (ml) Elpis Ioannidis/Shutterstock; (mr) Ablestock.com/Getty Images; (r) Ingram Publishing/Photolibrary; **527:** Michał Krakowiak/iStockphoto; **528:** (t) Anne Loubet; (ml) Anne Loubet; (mm) Pascal Pernix; (mr) Ana Cabezas Martín; (bl) Anne Loubet; (bm) Anne Loubet; (br) VHL; **530:** Jan Wlodarczyk/AGE Fotostock; **531:** Rossy Llano; **532:** (left col: t) Stephane Cardinale/Corbis Entertainment/Getty Images; (left col: m) Peace PhotoHunter/Shutterstock; (left col: bl) Abaca Press/Khayat Nicolas/Sipa USA/Newscom; (left col: br) De Agostini/Getty Images; (t) Elena Elisseeva/123RF; (ml) Miloski50/Shutterstock; (mr) Pawel Kazmierczak/Shutterstock; (b) Tom Brakefield/Corbis Documentary/Getty Images; **533:** (tl) John Schults/Reuters/Alamy; (tr) KCS Presse/Splash News/Newscom; (bl) Everett-Art/Shutterstock; (br) Andreas Karelias/iStockphoto; **534:** Roger Viollet/Getty Images; **534-535:** Johner Images/Alamy; **536:** Rossy Llano; **537:** PhotoAlto/Alamy.

Unit 13

539: Pascal Pernix; **540:** Photolibrary; **542:** Martín Bernetti; **546:** (t) Rehan Qureshi/Shutterstock; (b) Elvira Ortiz; **547:** Anna Clopet/Getty Images; **549:** Image100/Alamy; **551:** (tl) Jack Hollingsworth/Corbis; (tm) Martín Bernetti; (tr) Martín Bernetti; (bl) Martín Bernetti; (bm) Anne Loubet; (br) Janet Dracksdorf; **553:** Andresr/Shutterstock; **556:** (all) Bill Lai/Index Stock Imagery/Photolibrary/Getty Images; **558:** Anne Loubet; **559:** (all) Anne Loubet; **560:** (all) Anne Loubet; **564:** (t) Peter Turnley/Getty Images; (b) Owen Franken/Getty Images; **565:** (t) Anne Loubet; (b) Sueddeutsche Zeitung Photo/Alamy; **567:** (t) Birgit Reitz-Hofmann/iStockphoto; (b) Se1ect/Shutterstock; **569:** Anne Loubet; **570:** Martín Bernetti; **575:** Anne Loubet; **576:** (left col: t) Bettmann/Getty Images; (left col: b) Dominique Charriau/WireImage/Getty Images; (t) Guenter Fischer/imagebroker/AGE Fotostock; (ml) Foodpictures/Shutterstock; (mr) SidBradypus1/Deposit Photos; (b) Milosk50/Shutterstock; **577:** (tl) Patrick

Frauchiger/Flickr Open/Getty Images; (tr) Peter Ginter/Superstock/Alamy; (bl) Sabarrere/Shutterstock; (br) France Pictures Agency/Alamy; **578:** Fine Art Images/Heritage Images/Newscom; **580:** Anne Loubet; **581:** Lofoto/Fotolia.

Unit 14

583: VHL; **584:** Art Konovalov/Shutterstock; **586:** (tl) Tomas Sereda/Shutterstock; (tr) Mny-Jhee/Fotolia; (bl) Bosca78/iStockphoto; (br) Anne Loubet; **590:** (t) Raphael Daniaud/iStockphoto; (b) Directphoto Collection/Alamy; **591:** (t) Bertrand Reiger/Hemis.fr/Alamy; (b) Nobor/Fotolia; **593:** Nancy Camley; **599:** (l) Mark Karrass/Corbis; (r) Goodshoot/Alamy; **600:** (left col: tl) Index Open/Photolibrary; (left col: tr) Pidjoe/iStockphoto; (left col: bl) FogStock LLC/Photolibrary; (left col: br) Hemera Technologies/Getty Images; (right col: tl) Index Open/Photolibrary; (right col: tr) Image Source Limited/Index Stock Imagery; (right col: bl) Ablestock.com/Getty Images; (right col: br) Index Open/Photolibrary; **602:** Keith Levit Photography/Index Open; **603:** Rafael Rios; **604:** (l) Jonathan Heger/iStockphoto; (r) William Wang/iStockphoto; **608:** (t) Vrabelpeter1/Fotolia; (r) Vincent Lowe/Alamy; **609:** (t) Gail A. Johnson/iStockphoto; (m) Thomas Pozzo Di Borgo/123RF; (b) Bertrand Rindoff Petroff/Getty Images; **613:** Jupiter Images/Getty Images; **615:** Index Open/Photolibrary; **618:** (left col: tl) Index Open/Photolibrary; (left col: tr) Juuce/iStockphoto; (left col: bl) Anastasiya Maksimenko/123RF; (left col: br) Keith Levit Photography/Photolibrary; (right col) Nick Greaves/Alamy; **619:** Jean-Michel Turpin/Gamma-Rapho/Getty Images; **620:** (left col: t) Bettmann/Getty Images; (left col: m) Science and Society/SuperStock; (left col: b) Jean_Pierre Bonnotte/Getty Images; (t) Media Bakery; (ml) SGM/AGE Fotostock; (mr) AnkNet/iStockphoto; (b) Fotosearch; **621:** (tl) Imagebroker/Alamy; (tr) Iconotec/Alamy; (bl) ImagesEurope/Alamy; (br) Everett Art/Shutterstock; **622:** Paul Fearn/Alamy; **622-623:** Ebru Sidar/Arcangel; **624:** Kevin Fleming/Getty Images; **625:** Anne Loubet.

Unit 15

627: Pascal Pernix; **628:** Michael Le Poer Trench/Getty Images; **634:** (t) Images-of-france/Alamy; (b) Marmaduke St. John/Alamy; **635:** Lebrecht Music and Arts Photo Library; **643:** (t) Martín Bernetti; (ml) Anne Loubet; (mm) Martín Bernetti; (mr) Annie Pickert Fuller; (bl) Anne Loubet; (bm) Anne Loubet; (br) F9photos/Shutterstock; **644:** (tl) Image Source; (tr) Index Open/Photolibrary; (bl) Index Open/Photolibrary; (br) Hot Ideas/Photolibrary; **648:** Anne Loubet; **649:** VHL; **650:** (l) Jeff Morgan 02/Alamy; (r) Pascal Pernix; **654:** (l) Danita Delimont/Alamy; (tr) Danita Delimont/Alamy; (br) Kelly-Mooney Photography/Getty Images; **655:** (t) Robbie Jack/Getty Images; (m) Rune Hellestad/Getty Images; (b) Ullstein Bild/Getty Images; **657:** The Gallery Collection/Newscom; **662:** Jack Hollingsworth/Brand X/Corbis; **664:** (t) Pascal Pernix; (b) Stock Connection Blue/Alamy; **665:** Images-of-france/Alamy; **666:** (left col) Stephane Cardinale/Corbis/Getty Images; (tl) Robert Harding/Alamy; (tr) Ivan Vdovin/AGE Fotostock; (m) Hiro1775/Deposit Photos; (b) CSFotoimages/iStockphoto; **667:** (tl) Courtesy of the LaLorraine Tourism office (www.tourisme-lorraine.fr); (tr) Gianni Dagli Orti/Art Resource; (bl) Thierry Tronnel/Sygma/Getty Images; (br) Hemis/Alamy; **668:** Agence Opale/Alamy; **668-669:** Simon Rawles/Getty Images; **670:** Pascal Pernix; **671:** Andrew Paradise.

Back Cover: Damaerre/iStockphoto.

Text Credits

534: Texts by Jacques Prévert : «Barbara» in Paroles (Ed. Gallimard, 1946) and «Mai 1968» in Choses et autres (Ed. Gallimard, 1972). © Fatras / Succession Jacques Prévert, electronics rights reserved.
668: Libre Expression, 2009, Montreal, Canada.

Comic Credits

488: © Renée Lévy.

TV Clip Credits

63: Courtesy of the Université de Moncton.
151: Courtesy of NextInteractive.
241: Courtesy of ResoNews.
331: Courtesy of France TV.
423: Courtesy of KRYS Group.
601: © BMCE Bank – Morocco.

Short Film Credits

511: By permission of Luminus Films Ltd.
645: Courtesy of Premium Films.

About the Authors

James G. Mitchell received his Ph.D. in Romance Studies with a specialization in Second Language Acquisition from Cornell University. Dr. Mitchell teaches French, Italian, linguistics, and applied linguistics at Salve Regina Univeristy.

Cheryl Tano received her M.A. in Spanish and French from Boston College and has also completed all course work toward a Ph.D. in Applied Linguistics with a concentration in Second Language Acquisition at Boston University. She is currently teaching French at Emmanuel College and Spanish at Tufts University.

About the Illustrators

A French Canadian living in the province of Quebec, **Sophie Casson** has been a professional illustrator for more than ten years. Her illustrations have appeared in local and national magazines throughout Canada, as well as in children's books.

Born in Caracas, Venezuela, **Hermann Mejía** studied illustration at the **Instituto de Diseño de Caracas**. Hermann currently lives and works in the United States.

Pere Virgili lives and works in Barcelona, Spain. His illustrations have appeared in textbooks, newspapers, and magazines throughout Spain and Europe.

Kent H. Redford
LE 1985
Arbor

W9-AGT-776

The Giant Pandas of Wolong

Painting by Wu Tsoren (reproduced by permission of World Wildlife Fund—Hong Kong)

卧龙大熊猫

Calligraphy by Hu Tieqin

Painting by Chiu Xiaochiu (reproduced by permission of World Wildlife Fund—Hong Kong)

The
GIANT PANDAS
of
WOLONG

George B. Schaller
Hu Jinchu · Pan Wenshi
Zhu Jing

The University of Chicago Press

Chicago and London

George B. Schaller is director of Wildlife Conservation International, a division of the New York Zoological Society, and adjunct associate professor at Rockefeller University. Hu Jinchu is associate professor in the Department of Biology at Nanchong Normal College, Sichuan. Pan Wenshi is lecturer in the Department of Zoology at Beijing University. Zhu Jing is research associate at the Institute of Zoology, Academia Sinica, Beijing.

The University of Chicago Press, Chicago 60637
The University of Chicago Press, Ltd., London
© 1985 by The University of Chicago
All rights reserved. Published 1985
Printed in the United States of America

94 93 92 91 90 89 88 87 86 85   5 4 3 2 1

Library of Congress Cataloging in Publication Data
Main entry under title:

The giant pandas of Wolong.

  Bibliography: p.
  Includes index.
  1. Giant panda. 2. Mammals—China
I. Schaller, George B.
QL737.C214G53   1985   599.74′7443   84-8807
ISBN 0-226-73643-1

The permanent field staff at Wuyipeng
helped collect the information in this report.

Peng Jiagan
Tian Zhixiang
Wang Lianke
Wang Pengyian
Zhang Xianti
Zhou Shoude

The Biochemical Laboratory of the
Northeast Forest Institute in Harbin, the
Chemistry Department of Beijing University, and the
Department of Animal Science of Cornell University
conducted the laboratory analyses.

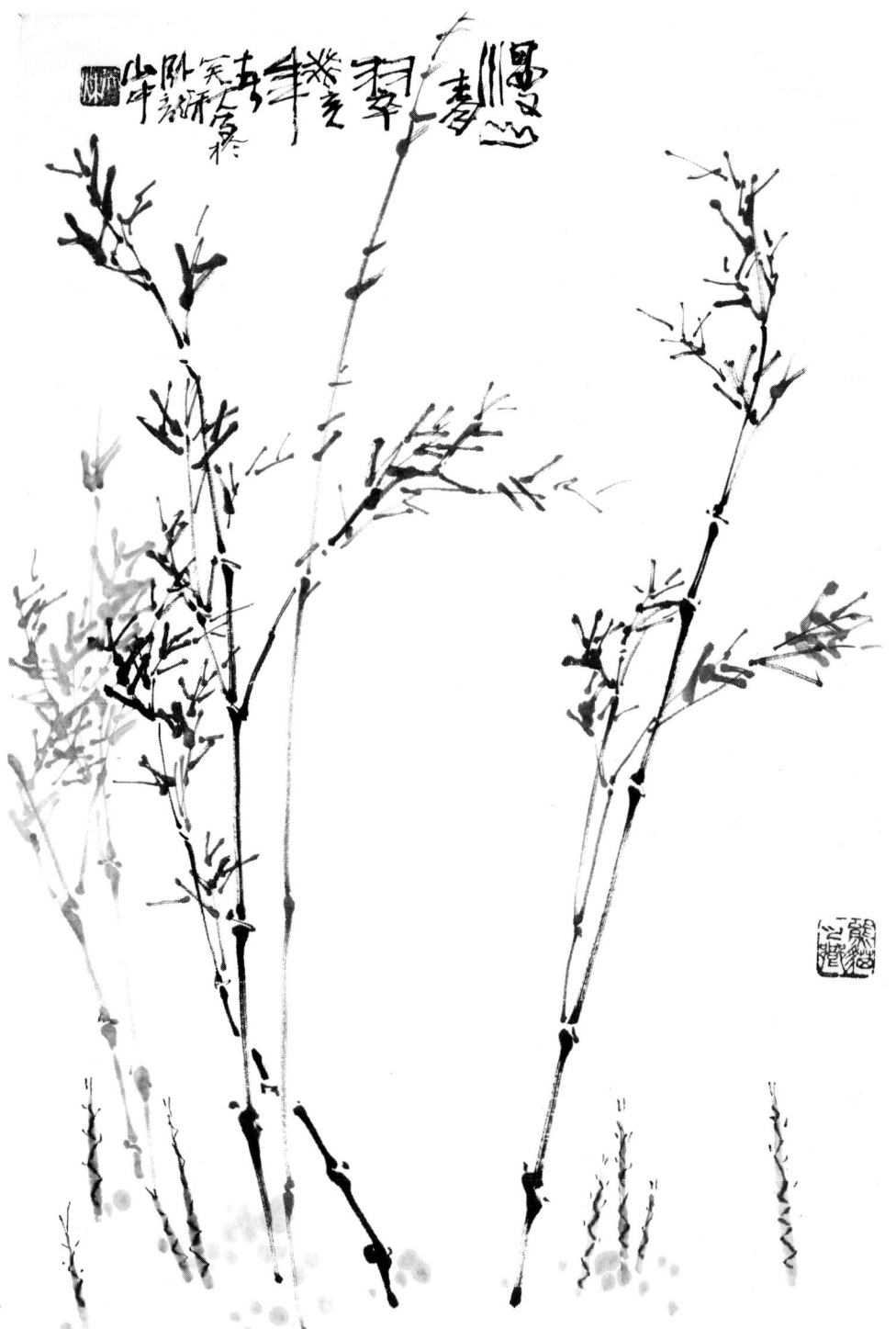

Painting by Chiu Xiaochiu

Contents

Appendixes   261

References   277
Index   289

Preface

There are two giant pandas, the one that exists in our mind and the one that lives in its wilderness home. Soft, furry, and strangely patterned in black and white, with a large, round head and a clumsy, cuddly body, a panda seems like something to play with and hug. No other animal has so entranced the public. Pandas in captivity are known by name, usually a flattering name repeated as a sign of affection, such as Mei-Mei, "Beautiful-Beautiful." Their reluctant romances, pregnancies, births, hospitalizations, and deaths receive global news coverage. China considers the panda a national treasure; World Wildlife Fund has selected it as a symbol of world conservation. This, together with the animal's remote habitat and rarity both in the wild and in captivity, has transformed the panda into an almost mythical creature in which legend and reality merge. A protocol signed by China and World Wildlife Fund described the giant panda as "not only the precious property of the Chinese people, but also a precious natural heritage of concern to people all over the world."

The real panda, however, the panda as it lives in the wild, had remained essentially a mystery. Little was known about its habits until the 1940s except that it dwelled in the densest bamboo; little was written about its life except how to hunt it and capture it for zoos. Then, in the 1950s, Chinese scientists began to make observations on the animal in several areas. In 1973, a meeting was held to plan surveys of rare wild animals throughout China. The surveys for the panda lasted from 1974 to 1977. While these were in progress, an event occurred that startled scientists and the public alike. Between 1974 and 1976, the umbrella bamboo (*Fargesia*) and other bamboos flowered, produced seeds, and died over large areas of the Min Mountains of northern Sichuan. Such flowering occurs at long intervals, in some bamboo species only every 40 or more years, the plant usually reproducing vegetatively by sending up shoots from rootlike rhizomes. Since these bamboos are the panda's main food in the Min Mountains, their death caused starvation among the animals. At least 138 pandas died (Wen and Wang 1980). And more mass-flowering in other areas was expected during the coming years.

Aware that the panda is an endangered species, the Chinese government, through the departments concerned, supervised a preliminary investigation of the panda populations to serve as a basis for a comprehensive conservation plan. To enhance this program and to initiate detailed long-term work, the relevant government departments agreed to cooperate with World Wildlife Fund in a collaborative panda research project.

In September 1979 a delegation from World Wildlife Fund, led by Sir Peter Scott, met with Chinese representatives from the Chinese Association for Environmental Sciences, the Ministry of Forestry, and Academia Sinica. One result of the meeting was the formation of a China–World Wildlife Fund Joint Committee, consisting of six members—three from the Chinese side and three from World Wildlife Fund. At a meeting of the joint committee in May 1980, a protocol and action plan were drawn up.

The program included two main parts: (1) the construction of a Research Centre for the Protection of the Giant Panda and Its Ecosystem; and (2) research on the giant panda itself. The research center has been constructed in Wolong, jointly financed by China's Ministry of Forestry and World Wildlife Fund, and consists of laboratories and a breeding facility, including a veterinary hospital and panda nursery. As stated in the action plan, the research consists of three main parts:

a. Research on the ecology and behaviour of free-living Giant Pandas, including survey and studies on population dynamics, movements, reproductive biology, and food habits, as well as the possibility of improving the feeding areas.

b. Working on Emergency Plan to deal with natural disasters. The Plan may include artificial feeding, moving pandas from disaster areas to new habitats, or putting the animals in temporary captivity, as well as other possible means.

c. Studies on pandas in captivity, including reproductive biology, nutrition, behaviour, and handrearing of newborn pandas.

After the meeting in May 1980, the World Wildlife Fund delegation briefly visited the proposed panda study area in the Wolong Natural Reserve. Chinese scientists had initiated panda research in Wolong's Choushuigou, a small valley near the reserve headquarters, in March 1978. In late December 1980, the collaborative China–World Wildlife Fund project began its work in the same valley under the leadership of Hu Jinchu from Nanchong Normal College and George B. Schaller from the New York Zoological Society on behalf of World Wildlife Fund. Research in the area has continued to the present. The first two and a half years of work have been summarized by Hu et al. (1980) and Hu (1981c). The present report covers the first one and a half years of our collaborative effort. Although most data were gathered between January 1981 and June 1982, a few relevant observations up to late 1983 have been included. To supplement our information on free-living pandas, we also observed captives at the Chengdu Zoo and at Yingxionggou, the latter being a small valley adjoining our study area where the Ministry of Forestry maintained several captives.

The primary purpose of the project is to study those aspects of the panda's life history which are most important to conservation. For example, to preserve the panda it is essential to determine the minimum population size needed for the species to persist in the small, isolated areas that now form its habitat. Such a determination requires information on birth and death rates, movement patterns, and carrying capacity. But the panda has also intrinsic biological interest. Taxonomists have debated for more than 100 years whether the panda is more closely related to bears or to racoons. Perhaps the most remarkable facet of the panda's biology is its food habits. That the panda subsists almost exclusively on bamboo has long been known. Specialization on a particular type of plant is not in itself unusual among mammals; what is unusual here is that the panda retains the simple stomach and intestines of a carnivore while leading the life of a specialized herbivore. Without physical and physiological specializations to process cellulose and other indigestible plant materials, the panda has in evolution tied itself to bamboo; it has, in fact, become so fettered by the bamboo's passive power that its fate now depends on that of the plant. Virtually all aspects of an animal's existence are influenced by the abundance, dispersion, and nutritional quality of the food it lives on. How is the giant panda adapted to bamboo? This is the main scientific question our report attempts to answer.

Painting by Lu Ling

Acknowledgments

The dedication, spirit of cooperation, and wisdom of many organizations and individuals made the collaborative panda research project possible and contributed to it during the first one and a half years of field research covered by this report.

We received constant guidance and encouragement from the six members of the China–World Wildlife Fund Committee: Zhang Shuzhong (Environmental Protection Office); Wang Menghu (Ministry of Forestry); Zhu Jing (Academia Sinica); Sir Peter Scott, Lee Talbot, and Charles de Haes (World Wildlife Fund).

The late Li Chaobo and Jin Jiaming of the Environmental Protection Office of the State Council assisted the project in important ways, and we are grateful for their efforts.

Of the many persons who helped us in Chengdu and Wolong, we would especially like to express our appreciation to Bi Fengzhou, Hu Shixiu, Fu Chengjun, Gung Tongyang, Lai Binghui, and Zhao Changgui.

World Wildlife Fund Hong Kong, under the leadership of Sir Kenneth Ping Fan Fung and Philip Kwok, has provided constant assistance and cooperation. We owe a special debt to Nancy Nash, who has participated in the project and helped guide its progress since its inception.

Interpreters are crucial to a collaborative project; we would like to thank Ma Huanqin, Shen Jiango, Liu Yanying, Xie Tsuchuan, Millicent Se Yung, Fay Loo, Yuan Haiying, Hwang Xiaoguang, Zhou Li, and especially Qiu Mingjiang.

In addition to the permanent research staff at Wolong, many scientists and technicians contributed information or assisted directly with the research. These include Wang Xuequan of the Northeast Forest Institute; Long Zhi of Academia Sinica; and Huang Lichuang, Liao Changan, Wang Chenhua, Dong Cai, Li Liang, Zhao Cannan, Teng Qitao, Qin Jian, Yong Yange, and Yang Qingan, who came from various reserves to contribute their efforts. Qin Zisheng of Nanchong Normal College, together with Julian Campbell of the University of Kentucky, studied bamboo ecology and generously provided us with the data. Howard Quigley of the University of Tennessee worked with the project for two months to help establish the radio-telemetry program. In the name of the collaborative project, we would like to express our gratitude to these workers.

The New York Zoological Society assisted the project both financially and scientifically. Several scientists came to Wolong to assist at the captive panda facility. William Conway of the New York Zoological Society contributed to the design of a new facility for captive breeding. Emil Dolensek and Janet Stover, both from the New York Zoological Society, and Steven Seager of the National Institutes of Health helped with captive management. Devra Kleiman of the National Zoological Park, Smithsonian Institution, studied reproductive behavior of captives. We are indebted to these investigators for making their observations available to us.

The Chengdu zoo kindly permitted us to observe pandas on several occasions, and the Beijing zoo provided information.

The Biochemical Laboratory of the Northeast Forest Institute, under the guidance of Zeng Kewen, conducted the proximate analysis of bamboo. The Chemistry Department of Beijing University, under the guidance of Chen Fengxiang and Yuan Hongsheng, analyzed bamboo for minerals and amino acids, and Li Ronggao examined bamboo microscopically. The Department of Animal Sciences of Cornell University, under the guidance of Peter J. Van Soest, James Robertson, and especially Ellen S. Dierenfeld, analyzed bamboo for various constituents. We are deeply grateful to these laboratories and their staffs for this important contribution to the project.

Several other institutions and persons provided valuable assistance in preparing this report, and we acknowledge our indebtedness to them. Michael Pelton of the Department of Forestry, Wildlife, and Fisheries, University of Tennessee, made the computer and library of his department available to us. Patrick Carr, University of Tennessee, computed the radio-telemetry results and analyzed some other data. Liu Wanru, Zhou Zhiying, and Quan Gaoxi of Beijing University provided mathematical and computing advice. The spectographic analyses of panda vocalizations were made with the assistance and advice of Gustav Peters of the Alexander Koenig Museum in Bonn and Devra Kleiman of the National Zoological Park, Smithsonian Institution. In addition to assisting with field work, Kay Schaller helped with the preparation of the manuscript. Martha Schwartz and Claire Belinchak assisted with typing; Wendy Mansfield prepared the maps and graphs, and Jin Xuqi contributed several photographs. Lyndal Meuli, Raymond Napolitano, and Otto Sieber provided information.

Richard Keane drew the excellent panda sketches.

Several fine examples of Chinese art enhance this report, and we are deeply grateful to Wu Tsoren, Lu Ling, and Chiu Xiaochiu for contributing the paintings, and to Hu Tieqin for the calligraphy.

Wu Baihui, Li Yuan, and especially Qiu Mingjiang translated drafts of the manuscript from Chinese into English and from English into Chinese, a difficult task which they accomplished with great diligence and dedication. Gu Xiaocheng and Joseph Chang of Beijing University generously checked the translations.

We would also like to thank several scientists for reading the manuscript and offering valuable comments and suggestions. A. R. E. Sinclair of the University of British Columbia read the whole manuscript; John Hearn, Wellcome Institute of the

Zoological Society of London, chapters 3–8; and Gustav Peters of the Alexander Koenig Museum in Bonn, chapter 8. Wang Menghu, Ministry of Forestry, patiently guided the report from inception to completion.

Other persons who contributed to the project in various ways include Mark Halle of World Wildlife Fund; Michael McCrary, Iain Orr, and Wu Taichow of Hong Kong; Wang Huenpu of the Institute of Botany, Academia Sinica; Peter White of the National Park Service, Tennessee; Charles Krebs of the University of British Columbia, and H. Dathe of the Berlin (DDR) zoo.

The project was financed through an agreement between the Ministry of Forestry of the People's Republic of China and World Wildlife Fund International. We are deeply grateful for their support.

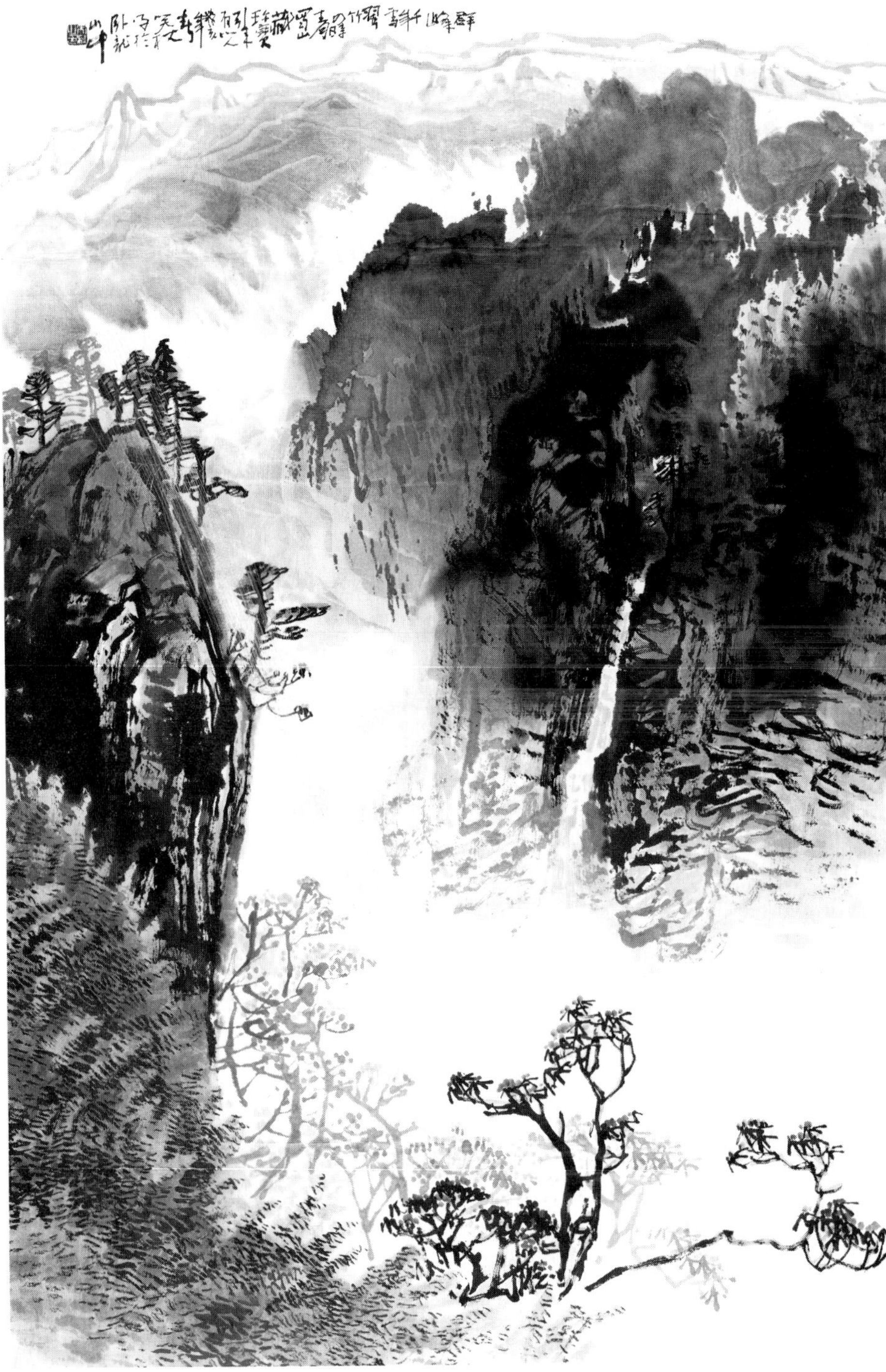

Painting by Chiu Xiaochiu

The Giant Pandas of Wolong

1

The Giant Panda, Past and Present

The giant panda requires no detailed description; its striking, black-and-white image is known throughout the world. In this chapter we discuss several of its physical adaptations to the environment. Also, to understand the panda as it lives today, to place it and our study into perspective, we briefly review the panda's past in the prehistory and history of China.

Physical characteristics

Scientifically the panda is known as *Ailuropoda melanoleuca*, the species name meaning black-and-white. The current Chinese name is *daxiongmao*, large bear-cat. Together, these names well convey the animal's appearance. The panda is bearlike with a stocky, relatively short, barrel-shaped body, about 160–180 cm in total length (table 2.4). Its legs are stout and powerful, the forelegs more so than the hindlegs, and the feet are plantigrade; it walks with its toes turned in. Although these features give the panda a clumsy appearance, they enable it to move with remarkable ease and silence over precipitous terrain and through dense bamboo. The color pattern of the panda's pelage is unique among mammals: a white face with oval, black eye patches, and erect black ears, 9–10 cm long, placed high on the head; black forelegs extending in a narrowing band over the shoulder; black hindlegs; and the rest white, except for some brownish-to-black hair on the chest. This color pattern is highly conspicuous in the forest; only in snow is it cryptic. The pelage is rather coarse and extremely dense and woolly, though somewhat sparse on the underside; it feels slightly oily. The white hairs on back and rump are about 3.5–4.5 cm long, the black ones on the shoulders 5.0–7.0 cm, and some chest and belly hairs up to 10 cm. The density of the coat keeps the animal warm, and the oiliness prevents water from penetrating—an adaptation to a cool, moist climate.

Two structures, head and forepaws, are specialized for handling bamboo stems. The head is round, broad, and massive, and the muzzle short. Looking at the skull, one notes that the zygomatic arches are spread widely, and the sagittal crest is prominent, serving as a place of attachment for the powerful jaw muscles. A typically carnivorous dentition ($I_3^3 C_1^1 P_4^4 M_3^2 = 42$, but P_1 may be absent) has been strongly modified for crushing and grinding food: not only are the molars broad and flat and heavily cusped, but the posterior premolars are too, an unusual condition, not, for example, found in bears (Ewer 1973) but superficially resembling that of ungulates. The forepaws are adapted for grasping bamboo stems with dexterity through the addition of a sixth digit, the panda's famous "thumb." Greatly enlarged, the radial sesamoid, a wrist bone, now functions as an opposable thumb, capable of independent movement which brings it into opposition with the first digit (Davis 1964). The panda can handle bamboo stems with great precision by holding them as if with forceps in the hairless groove connecting the pad of the first digit and pseudothumb.

Several inconspicuous physical traits are also of note. The pupil of the eye is a catlike vertical slit, a more efficient means of regulating light than a round pupil, suggesting the sensitive retina of a nocturnal animal. A naked, glandular region used in scent marking surrounds the anogenital area; there are, in addition, two small invaginations, the anal sacs, one on each side of the anus, which secrete a substance smelling slightly acetic. The tail is short, only 10–15 cm long, and heavily furred. Pressed close to the body, as it usually is, it supplies a protective cover for the glandular area; extended and wiped over objects, it serves as a brush, painting the animal's scent.

Head held low, the panda moves with a rolling gait in the diagonal walk typical of most mammals. When startled, it trots off rapidly; we have only once observed a gallop, a mode of locomotion unsuited to bamboo thickets. Though a panda can stand upright on its hindlegs with ease, we have not seen one walk bipedally. A panda may climb a massive tree slowly, as if slightly inept, embracing the trunk and using sharp claws and the friction of the soles to pull itself up by alternating fore- and hindpaws. When ascending a tree of moderate diameter, however, it can walk up the trunk with speed and ease. It descends rump first. While a panda does not always display the agility of a gymnast, it does have the flexibility of one. In its typical sitting posture, as when eating, the panda hunches, its back much curved, hindlegs extended. Sometimes it half sits and half lies on its back as it manipulates some item with its forepaws. From this or other positions, it can raise a foreleg straight up and scratch the top of its head or the back of its neck. One female showed her suppleness by lying on her belly, extending one hindleg forward, and using it as a pillow.

Newborn pandas are tiny, averaging only 104 g in weight (Peking zoo 1974a), but they gain rapidly so that by the age of 12 months they average about 35 kg (fig. 1.1). It is difficult to estimate age based on weight in animals older than one year. Some captive individuals gain weight rapidly and become obese, and, in general, captives are heavier than wild animals of similar age. By the age of 30 months, captives may reach a weight of 80 kg or more (fig. 1.2). Representative weights of subadults between the ages of 20 to 40 months include those in fig. 1-2 and also Qing-Qing (Yingxionggou), 40 kg at 20 months; Kang-Kang (Tokyo), 60 kg at 25 months; Bao-Bao and Tian-Tian (Berlin), 60 and 50 kg at 28 months (Frädrich 1981); Yuan Jing (Beijing), 80 kg at 36 months (Anon. 1981a); and Shao-Shao (Madrid), 71 kg at 40 months (Zhu and Li 1980). For comparison, we caught 3 subadults which, on the basis of size, dentition, and presumed birth month, we judged to be 30–33 months

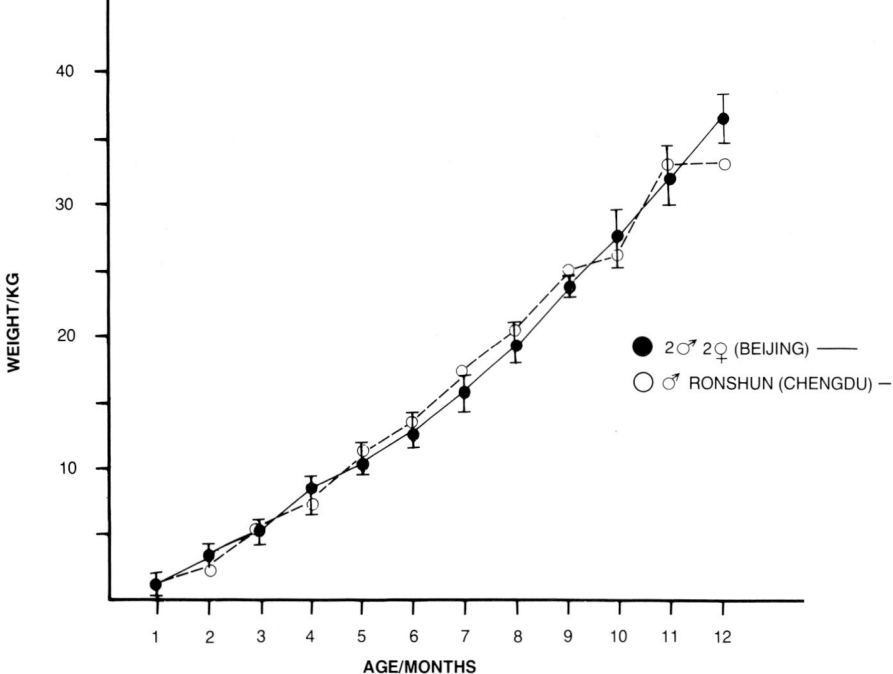

FIGURE 1.1   Weight increase of captive panda young during the first 12 months of life. (Data from Peking zoo 1974a; Xu et al. 1981.)

old, and these weighed only 52–55 kg. When two of the animals, a female and a male, were recaptured at the age of about 40 months, the former then weighed 61 kg and the latter 70 kg (table 2.4). Adults average 80–125 kg, with fat captives exceeding 150 kg (Morris and Morris 1966). Five captive adult males at Chengdu zoo and Yingxionggou averaged 117.8 kg (SD 15.2, range 100–142), and 4 females 96.8 kg (SD 11.3, range 78–108). Two wild-caught females weighed 86 and 89 kg and 2 males 97 kg and 107 kg (see table 2.4). Although adults within a sex may vary considerably in size, and some males are only as large as females, the weights indicate a sexual dimorphism, with males weighing an average of 10–20% more than females.

The panda in ancient Chinese history

Over 3000 years ago, in the Western Chou dynasty (1066–771 BC), *The Book of History* and the earliest collection of Chinese poetry, *The Book of Songs*, mentioned an animal resembling the giant panda. The former used the expression "like a tiger and a *pi*"; the latter contains the phrase "to present the pelt of a *pi*," and also notes that the animal resembles a tiger or a leopard. *Pi* or *pixiu* is an ancient name for the panda. Later, the earliest dictionary, the *Er Ya*, of the Qin dynasty (221–207 BC) explained that the *pi* is a white fox, but also describes the *mo*—another name for the panda—as a white leopard with a small head, short limbs, and black-and-white markings. The animal is said to lick and eat copper, iron, and bamboo stems; its bones are straight and hard; and its pelt is useful in controlling menses. *The Classics of Seas and Mountains*, a famous geography book dating from 770 to 256 BC, mentioned that "a bearlike, black-and-white animal that eats copper and iron lives in the Qionglai Mountains south of Yandao County" (vol 18, p. 36). The supposed propensity of the *mo* to eat metal may be based on the fact that pandas sometimes enter villages and lick and chew up cooking pots.

Similar descriptions with minor variations subsequently appeared in dozens of books; but, as is generally true of ancient natural history in any culture, writings were based on descriptions and inferences from the classics, not on actual observations. This resulted in confusing names and descriptions that may or may not refer to the panda. *The Annotated Readings of the Book of Songs*, published during the Warring States period (475–221 BC), described an animal resembling a tiger or a white bear and referred to it as *zhi yi* or *bai hu*. In the introduction to his poem "To the screen

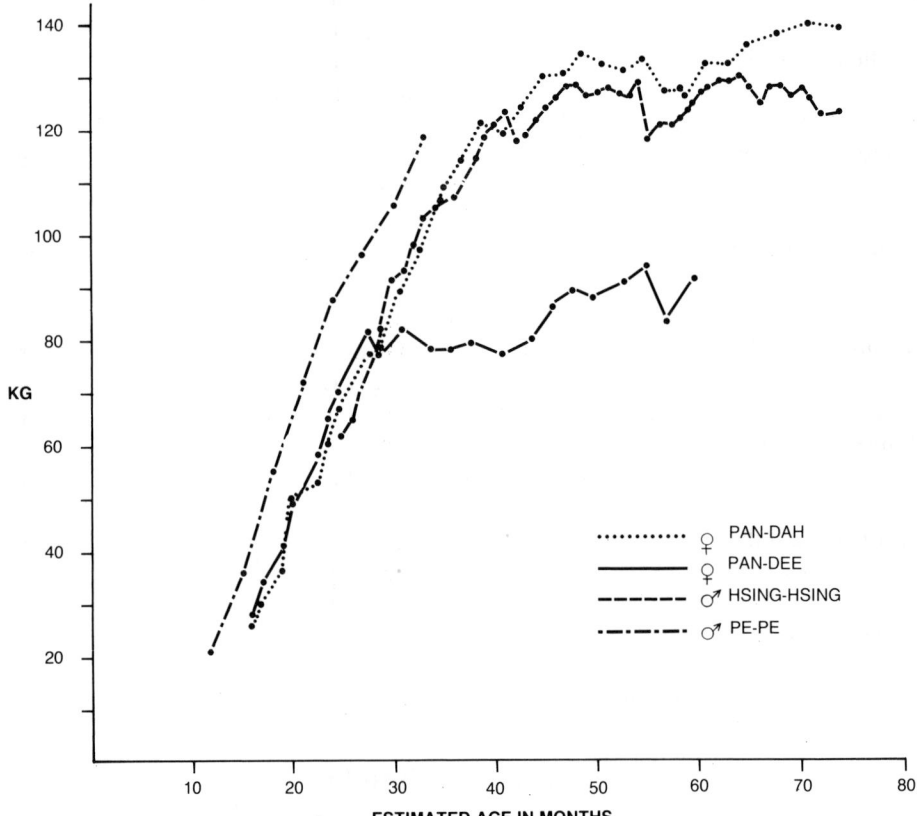

FIGURE 1.2   Weight increase of captive pandas during the first years of life. (Data from New York Zoological Park; National Zoological Park; Giron 1980.)

with a *mo* on it," Bai Juyi, a famous poet of the Tang dynasty (AD 618–907), wrote: "*Mo* has the nose of an elephant, eyes of a rhinoceros, tail of an ox, and feet of a tiger. It lives in the valleys in the south . . . According to *The Classics of Seas and Mountains* the animal eats also iron and copper." To Bai Juyi, the word *mo* meant perhaps a tapir, certainly not a panda. In the *Ben Cao Gang Mu*, a medicinal text published in 1578 during the Ming dynasty (AD 1368–1644), Li Shizhen quoted from the earlier *Shuo Wen*, a dictionary of Chinese characters from the Eastern Han Dynasty (AD 25–220), when he wrote: "*Mo* looks like a bear, has a yellowish color and lives in Sichuan. The Annals of the county Nan Zhong note that it is the size of a donkey, has a whitish color, and resembles a bear. The animal licks iron and may eat ten jin [5kg] at a time; its pelt is good for keeping warm." Also during the Ming dynasty, Cao Xue Shuan in his *Shu Zhong Guan Ji*, a history of Sichuan, used not only the name *mo* but also *meng shi shou* (beast of prey), *bai bao* (white leopard), and *shi tie shou* (iron-eating beast). The *mo* and *pixiu* are described as two different species in several books, further increasing the confusion over names. After studying this literature, some authors concluded that the panda was known as *mo* (Gao 1973), others that it was known as *pixiu* (Zhou 1956), and still others that both names applied (Hu 1981a,1981b). With about 20 possible panda names in the ancient literature, the controversy over meanings is likely to continue.

Current Chinese names for the panda are also in dispute. In China, an animal's name consists of 2 parts, the generic name preceded by a modifier. Is the panda a catlike bear (*maoxiong*), a banded bear (*huaxiong*), or a bearlike cat (*xiongmao*)? Compound names may also indicate something new, not implied by the words, and many feel that the commonly used "great bear-cat" (*daxiongmao*) suits the animal well.

Although the ancient literature contains relatively few descriptions of the panda, the animal itself was in the past considered rare and a symbol of might and bravery. In his *Shang Linfu*, the noted Western Han dynasty (206 BC–AD 24) historian Simao Xiangru noted that the emperor's garden in the capital of Xian held nearly 40 rare animal species, among which the panda was the most treasured. When Empress Dowager Bo, mother of Wen Di, fourth emperor of the Western Han dynasty, died and was buried in the Nangling mausoleum near Xian, in about 179–163 BC, the skull of a giant panda as well as the skeleton of a rhinoceros were entombed with her (Anon 1981c). It is said that Tang Taicong, first emperor of the Tang dynasty (AD 618–907), once held a grand banquet in his capital of Xian at which he honored 14 subjects by giving each a panda skin. Later, Tang Taicong's grandson may have sent two live pandas, as well as many skins, to Japan as a gesture of friendship during a period when trade relations between the two countries were close.

The panda in modern history

Numerous expeditions traveled to China during the 19th century and, impressed with the marvelous variety of plants and animals, collected many species new to Western science.

Knowledge of the panda in the Western world began on 11 March 1869, when Père Armand David, a missionary and avid collector of museum specimens, returned to his camp in the Baoxing area of Sichuan. He describes his first view of the skin of "the famous black and white bear" in his journal as follows:

> En revenant de notre excursion, nous sommes invités à nous reposer chez un certain *Li*, le principal propriétaire de cette vallée, qui me régale de thé et de sucreries. Je vois chez ce païen une peau plate du fameux ours blanc et noir, qui me paraît assez grand: c'est une espèce très-remarquable, et je me réjouis en entendant dire à mes chasseurs que j'obtiendrai certainement cet animal dans un court délai; dès demain, me dit-on, les chasseurs vont se mettre en campagne pour tuer ce carnassier qui paraît devoir constituer une nouveauté intéressante pour la science. (David 1874).

Père David's desire "to kill this carnivore" was also to become the goal of all Western hunters and museum collectors who visited the panda's range in the 70 years following the scientific discovery. The books by Roosevelt and Roosevelt (1929) and Sheldon (1975) are representative of such expeditions. Then, on 9 November 1936, Ruth Harkness obtained a live infant and exported it to the United States (Harkness 1938). Su Lin, as the panda was named, captivated Europe and North America to such an extent that emphasis changed from killing pandas to capturing them for zoos. A total of 14 pandas reached Western zoos alive between 1937 and 1946 (table B.1). By the time liberation in 1949 brought panda export under control, at least 73 pandas, dead or alive, had left China (see Morris and Morris 1966).

The Chinese people became aware that the panda's existence was threatened as early as 1946, when the newspaper *Da Gong Bao* wrote under the headline PANDA ON THE BRINK OF EXTINCTION: "Pandas living in the border areas of Sichuan and Xikang are becoming very scarce due to intensive capturing at present. Hunters have raised the price of the animal and every couple of months a panda is caught. If the situation goes on like this, the giant panda is likely to become extinct." A new era for the panda began with the Third National People's Congress in 1957, during which it was resolved to establish forest reserves. A 1962 directive from the State Council urged all provinces to "actively protect and reasonably utilize wildlife resources." Panda hunting was now completely banned. The first panda reserves were established in 1963, soon to be followed by others, until in 1983 there were 12 protected areas totaling 5927 km^2 (table 1.1; fig. 1.3), or 20% of the total range encompassed by the animal.

Although Tang (1983) took note of the panda during a mammal survey of Sichuan in 1935, and Sheldon (1937) and Schäfer (1938) published brief scientific reports based on their hunting expeditions, field research on the species began only with Pen's survey of habitats along the northern limit of the panda's range in 1940 (Pen 1943); later he helped define the southern limit as well (Pen et al. 1962). A. de Sowerby suspected the presence of pandas in the Qinling Mountains as early as 1937, but the animal's existence there was not confirmed until 1964, when a specimen was obtained (Zheng and Xu 1964; Wu 1981).

A team of scientists censused pandas and studied natural history in Wanglang

TABLE 1.1

PANDA RESERVES AND THEIR ESTIMATED PANDA POPULATIONS[a]

Number (see fig 1.3)	Name	District	Province	Year established	Area/ km²	Estimated number of pandas[b]	Km² per panda	Local residents in reserve
1	Foping[c]	Foping	Shaanxi	1978	350	100	3.5	several hundred
2	Baishuaijiang[c]	Wen	Gansu	1978	953	20–40	23.8–47.7	10,000±
3	Baihe	Nanping	Sichuan	1963	200	20	10.0	0
4	Jiuzhaigou	Nanping	Sichuan	1978	600	40	15.0	820
5	Wanglang	Pingwu	Sichuan	1965	277	10–20	13.9–27.7	0
6	Tangjiahe	Qingchuan	Sichuan	1978	400	100–140	2.9– 4.0	278
7	Xiaozhaizigou	Beichuan	Sichuan	1979	167	20	8.4	0
8	Fengtongzhai	Baoxing	Sichuan	1975	400	50	8.0	2,000±
9	Wolong[c]	Wenchuan	Sichuan	1975	2000	130–150	13.3–15.4	3,000±
10	Labaihe	Tianquan	Sichuan	1963	120	25	4.8	?
11	Dafengding	Mabian	Sichuan	1978	300	30–40	7.5–10.0	0
12	Dafengding	Meigu	Sichuan	1978	160	10	16.0	2,000±
Total					5927	555–655	9.3–10.7	

[a]Most reserve data from Wang (1980). [b]Estimates provided mainly by Hu Jinchu.
[c]Reserves under central government control; the others are under provincial control.

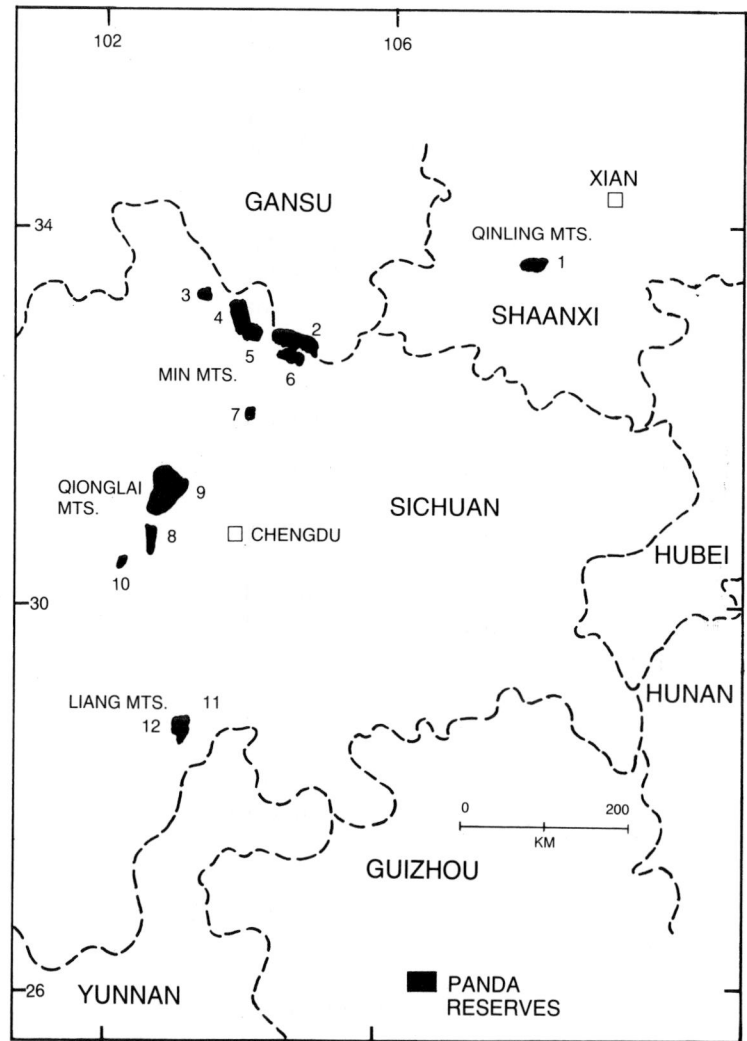

FIGURE 1.3   Location of the 12 panda reserves. The numbers correspond to those in table 1.1.

Reserve for several months in 1968 and 1969 (Giant Panda Expedition 1974), an important step in panda research. An extensive survey of panda status and distribution was conducted in the mid-1970s, providing for the first time information on the exact range and approximate number of animals (Expedition of Rare Animal Species in Sichuan 1977; Gansu Forest and Agricultural Bureau 1976; Shaanxi Biological Resources Expedition 1976). During the bamboo die-off in the Min Mountains, teams checked on the panda's fate (Investigation Team 1977; Qing 1977). The first intensive panda research began in Wolong in 1978 (Hu et al. 1980; Hu 1981c) and in Foping in 1980 (Yong 1981; Ruan and Yong 1983).

Except for two pandas which may have resided briefly in the Shanghai zoo in 1937 or 1938 (Morris and Morris 1966) and one short-lived animal in the Chengdu zoo in 1953, Chinese zoos had no pandas on exhibit until, in 1955, the Beijing zoo obtained three young animals. On 9 September 1963, Ming-Ming was born at that zoo, the first panda bred in captivity; on 8 September 1978, Yuan Jing was born there, the first panda conceived through artificial insemination. In 1982, keepers at the Beijing zoo hand-reared an infant from birth to the age of 2 months, and keepers at the Shanghai zoo hand-reared an infant successfully from the age of 14 days. All are important events for panda conservation. Morris and Morris's (1966) book on general panda behavior and the Peking zoo's (1974a) report on panda reproduction were landmarks in the study of captives.

Past and present distribution

The giant panda appeared without known precursor in the fossil record during the Early Pleistocene about 3 million years ago. Except for one site in Burma (Woodward 1915), fossils have been found only in China (fig. 1.4), where they have been discovered in 48 localities of 14 provinces and autonomous regions (Chu and Long 1983). Pandas appear so often in association with the Pleistocene elephant *Stegadon* that these two species are used to designate a distinct fossil fauna (Zhou 1964). Four species of giant panda have been recognized, but Wang (1974) reviewed the fossils and concluded that there are only 2: *Ailuropoda microta*, an animal half the size of the present-day panda from the Early Pleistocene, and *A. melanoleuca* from the Mid-Pleistocene onward.

The giant panda had a wide Pleistocene distribution, encompassing parts of Burma and much of eastern China, as far north as Choukoutien near Beijing. As figure 1.4 shows, fossil finds are confined to hills and plateaus surrounding the lowlands of the Huang and Chang Jiang rivers, at an altitude of about 500 m and above, but this may reflect poor fossilization in alluvial plains rather than a former absence of animals.

Pandas survive today only along the eastern edge of the Tibetan plateau in six small blocks of land totaling about 29,500 km^2 (fig 1.5; table 1.2). Starting in the

TABLE 1.2

TOTAL SQUARE KILOMETERS ENCOMPASSED BY THE SIX MOUNTAIN AREAS WITHIN THE PANDA'S RANGE

Number (see fig 1.5)	Province	Name of Mountains	Area/km^2	% of total area
1	Shaanxi	Qinling (south slope)	2,425	8.2
2	Gansu } Sichuan }	Min	13,300	45.1
3	Sichuan	Qionglai	10,475	35.5
4		Daxiangling	325	1.1
5		Xiaoxiangling	975	3.3
6		Liang	2,000	6.8

After Chu and Long 1983.

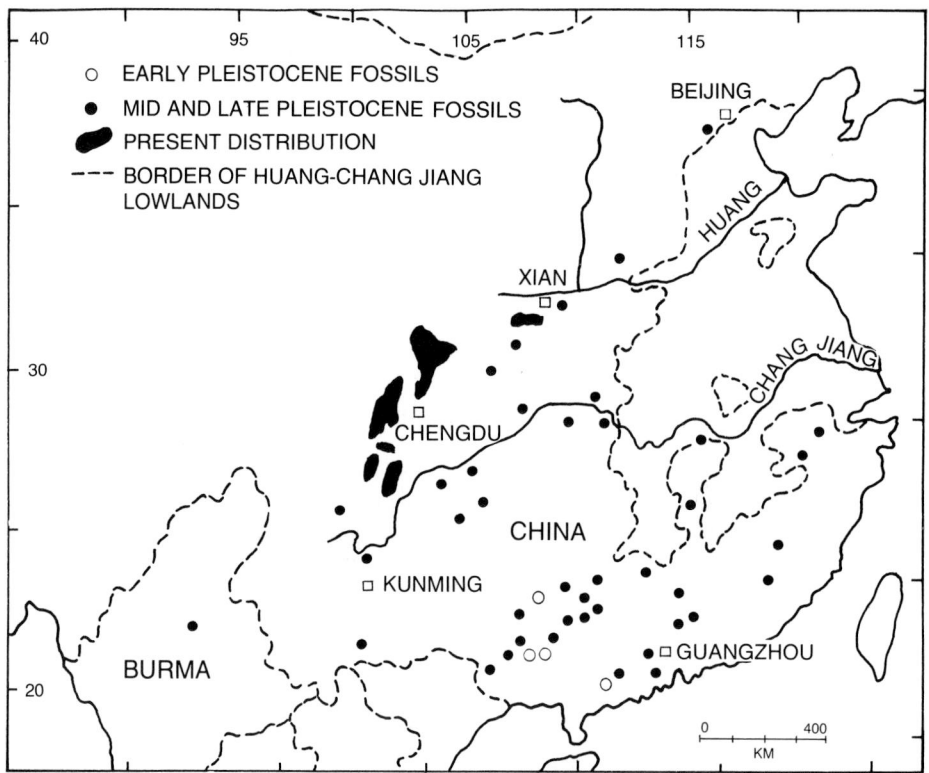

FIGURE 1.4   Pleistocene sites with panda fossils and present distribution of pandas. (After Zhu and Li 1980.)

north, pandas inhabit the southern slopes of the Qinling Mountains in Shaanxi. The largest panda area, about 13,300 km² in size, is in the Min Mountains of southern Gansu and northern Sichuan; 6 of the 12 panda reserves are found there (fig 1.3). The Qionglai Mountains, including the Balang and Jianjin ranges, form the second largest tract of panda habitat; the Wolong Natural Reserve is located in this area. The southernmost panda localities include three small ranges, the Daxiang, Xiao-xiang, and Daliang (fig. 1.5; table 1.2).

In June 1940, Pen (1943) reported seeing a female panda with two large cubs on the grasslands of the Tibetan plateau about 600 km northeast of the panda's known range. The animals were digging up and eating the bulbs of gentian, iris, and other plants. This record has often been quoted in the literature. Given the aberrant nature of the observation with respect to geographical location and habitat, the rarity with which pandas rear twins, and the unusual diet and method of obtaining it, the record is not now accepted. Pen probably observed Tibetan brown bears, which have dark legs and a light-colored crown and back.

Within each area, pandas occur only in suitable habitat. Confined to bamboo, the animal has an altitudinal limit of around 3200–3500 m—exceptionally as high as

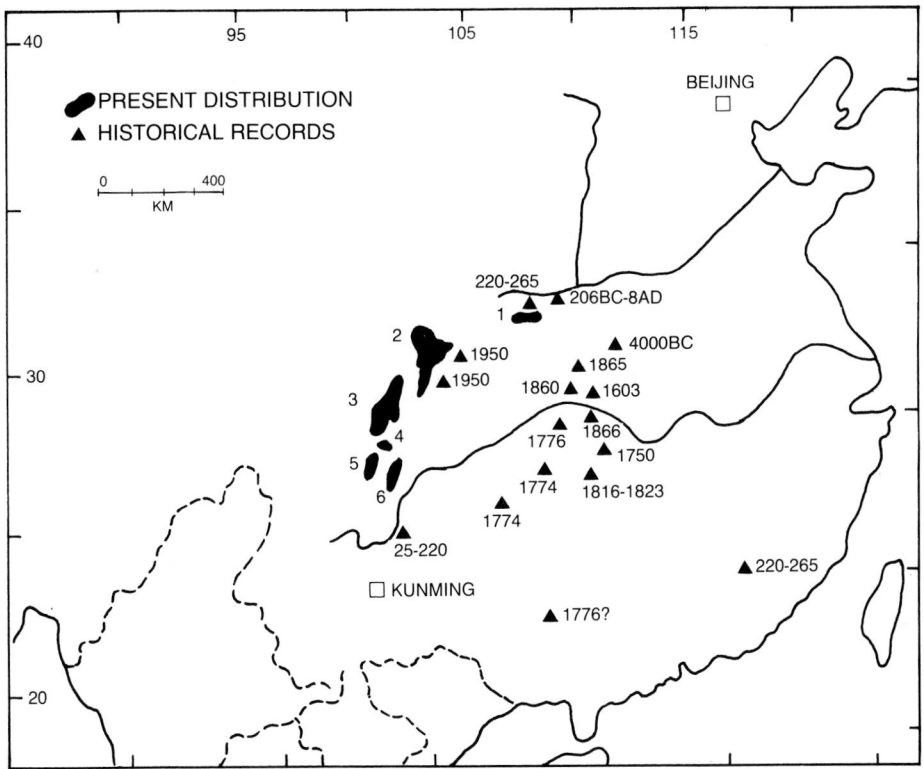

FIGURE 1.5   Historical records of pandas and present distribution of pandas. (After Chu and Long 1983).

4000 m (Giant Panda Expedition 1974). Sheldon (1937) once found droppings 1500 m above the nearest bamboo, but the animal no doubt made only a brief excursion into this alpine zone. The lower altitudinal limit is now determined by humankind, which has destroyed the forest and its bamboo to such an extent that no pandas persist below 1200–1300 m. Since most valleys are inhabited by people whose cultivation extends far up the slopes, many panda populations are isolated in narrow belts of bamboo no more than 1000–1200 m in width. The actual geographical range is therefore much smaller than indicated in figure 1.5. For example, Wolong comprises 2000 km^2, but if cultivation, alpine areas, and other unsuitable panda habitats are eliminated, only about 500 km^2 (25%) remain. Similarly, panda habitat in the Jiuzhaigou constitutes only about 15% of the total area, and Wanglang 35%. Dafending (Mabian) is exceptional in that about 80% of the reserve is suitable for pandas. Habitat destruction in these and other reserves has been less extensive than elsewhere. Although the panda's total range encompasses 29,500 km^2 (Chu and Long 1983), probably less than 20%, or 5900 km^2, represents panda habitat.

  The drastic decrease in the panda's range (figs 1.4 and 1.5) can be attributed to climatic changes during the Pleistocene and mainly to man's activities during the postglacial Holocene. All of Eurasia was affected by climatic oscillations during Pleistocene glacials and interglacials (Frenzel 1968). Judging by tooth structure of the earliest fossils, the panda had already specialized for subsisting on bamboo at the beginning of the Pleistocene; so it has long been associated with this grass. Most bamboos thrive under humid conditions with an annual precipitation exceeding 1500 mm, a habitat preference that has enabled these plants to colonize most subtropical and tropical areas of the world; none tolerate exteme cold, although a few species thrive where snow covers the ground for several months (Numata 1979).

Since many paleoclimatic questions regarding China still need answers, we can do little more than speculate about events affecting the panda during the Pleistocene. In the Late Pliocene it was warmer and moister than it is today, conditions favoring a northward extension of tropical and subtropical forests and, by implication, of pandas too. The climate became increasingly drier during the Early Pleistocene, leaving northern China arid, covered with *Artemisia* shrub and oak and spruce forest (Frenzel 1968). Further south, pollen profiles at Lantian near Xian, close to the Qinling Mountains where pandas exist today, show a temperate climate fluctuating between fir and and spruce forests and warmer periods with birch, willow, and alder as well. The Middle and Upper Pleistocene show similar oscillations in northern China, north of the Huang and Wei rivers, from forests with conifers and deciduous trees to dry temperate steppes (Wang Huenpu, pers. comm.). It is possible that pandas and bamboos expanded and contracted their ranges several times during the Pleistocene, expanding especially during warm, humid interglacials and contracting during cool, dry glacials. Habitat north of the Huang River may at best have been marginal and fragmental; but in the south, with its more moderate climate, the panda's tenure may have been prolonged, unless the Pleistocene uplift of the Himalaya affected monsoon patterns in some areas to such an extent that moisture-dependent bamboos ceased to thrive. As conditions at low altitudes deteriorated, various animals and plants remained only in mountain refuges; as conditions improved, they emerged to recolonize former terrain. So, perhaps, did the panda.

The Holocene found the panda distributed widely south of the Huang River. About 2500 to 3000 years ago it was warmer and wetter than today. In northern Henan province, tapir and elephant roamed (Wen and He 1980), and historical records speak of lush bamboo growth along the Wei River (Anon. 1981c). Although the climate has fluctuated somewhat (fig. 1.6), cooling after AD 1000 (Zhu 1973; Shen 1974), these changes cannot account for the gradual and then precipitous decline of the panda's range during historic times. Within the past 2000 years, pandas have been reported from Henan, Hubei, Hunan, Guizhou, and Yunnan, all provinces from which pandas have vanished (Jian 1977; Hu 1981b; Wen 1981). This range reduction has been well documented since the middle of the 18th century. As recently as 1850, pandas still existed in western Hubei and Hunan and in eastern Sichuan (fig 1.3). Such rapid contraction must be ascribed not to changing climate but to the growth of the human population. Forests were cut for timber and land was converted to fields and pastures. And pandas were hunted. The animal's pelt was

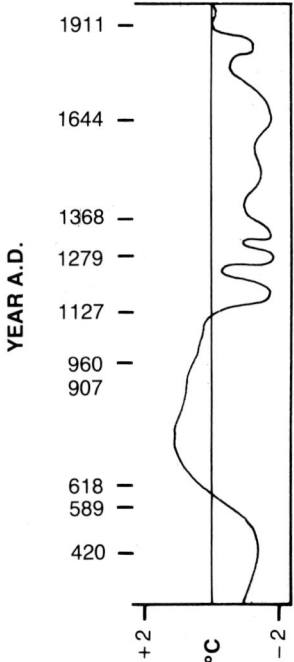

FIGURE 1.6   Mean temperature fluctuations in China during the past 1700 years. (After Zhu 1973.)

much sought as a sleeping mat, for, aside from being springy, it was said to predict the future (a peaceful sleep indicated good fortune), and it kept away ghosts.

Sichuan already had 45 million people by the year 1900. As this population grew, the panda's range continued to shrink. Pandas are now gone from several areas near the Min River where Sheldon encountered animals or their spoor in 1934 and 1935 (Sheldon 1975). Construction of the Baoji-Chengdu railway and subsequent development near the tracks in the Jiangyou and other hill areas of northern Sichuan between 1950 and 1980 pushed the panda's range almost 100 km westward. The panda now clings to a small vestige of its former range, its habitat still disappearing as settlers push ever higher up the mountain slopes.

Current status

Between 1974 and 1977, but especially in late April 1975 and early May 1976, about 3000 people took part in a panda census, during which units roamed through the panda's range and estimated numbers on the basis of sightings and spoor. The problems of censusing a silent, solitary animal confined to dense vegetation in remote mountains are immense, and the results for the three provinces provided only a rough estimate: Shaanxi 150–200, Gansu 100, and Sichuan 800—a total of

1050–1100. These figures do not include the animals that died during and after the gregarious flowering of bamboo in the eastern Min Mountains, which resulted in the death of at least 138 pandas. The flowering occurred over an area of 5250 square kilometers, but pandas were not equally affected throughout (fig 1.7). In areas where the only existing bamboo species flowered, an estimated average of 30–50%, in some cases up to 80%, of the pandas died; in areas with two or more bamboo species of which one did not flower, few starved (Investigation Team 1977). No one knows precisely how many pandas existed in the starvation areas, but that the decrease was substantial was confirmed in the Wanglang Reserve. By censusing pandas throughout the reserve, plotting approximate ranges of several individuals on the basis of

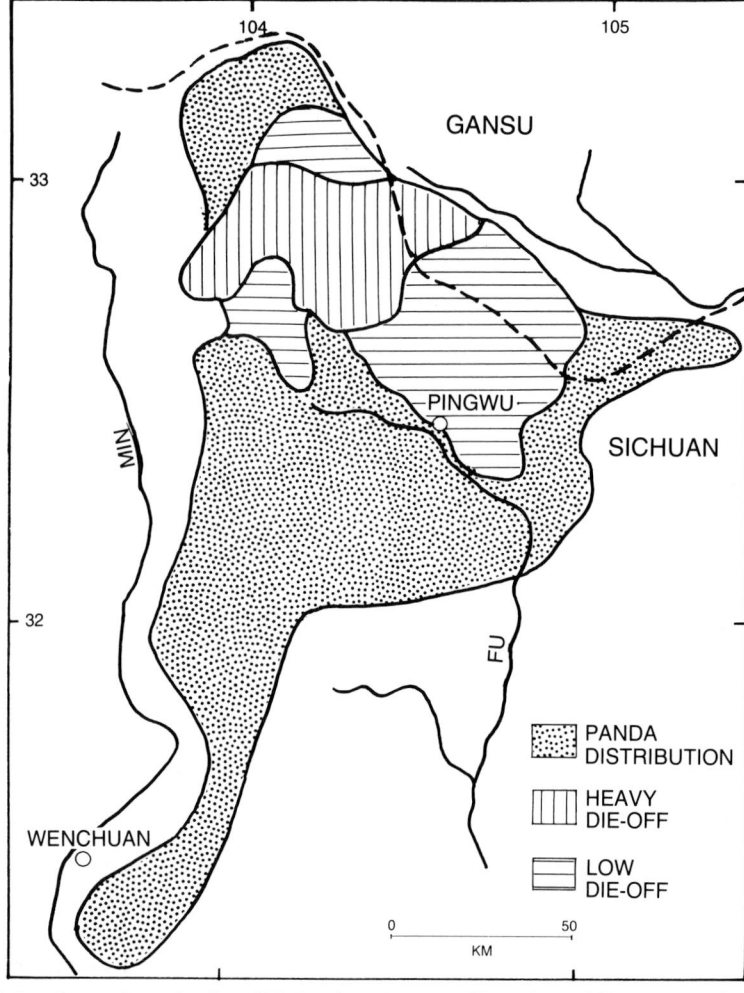

FIGURE 1.7   Area of panda die-off following the mass-flowering of *Fargesia* and other bamboos in the eastern Min Mountains, 1974–76. (After Investigation Team 1977.)

spoor, and counting animals in 2 km^2 by driving them out with dogs, the Giant Panda Expedition (1974) estimated that in 1968–69 there were 196 pandas in 122.5 km^2. Ten years later, about 10–20 pandas remained. Of those that had disappeared, some had starved, some may have emigrated during the bamboo die-off, and some may have been killed in landslides during a major earthquake in 1976.

Of the estimated 1000–1100 pandas in the wild, about 56–66% are in the 12 reserves (table 1.2). Most reserves contain fewer than 50 animals, whereas Foping, Wolong, and Tangjiahe each have a population of 100 or more, judging by personal estimates and information from local forest officials. Density of pandas within the 5927 km^2 of reserves is low, averaging one animal per 9.3–10.7 km^2. This figure is similar to the density of one animal per 6.7–10.0 km^2 calculated by Sheldon in 1934 for the Wenchuan area near Wolong (Sheldon 1975). But if only suitable habitat is considered, then, for example, Wolong has a density of one animal per 3.3–3.8 km^2, Jiuzhaigou one per 2.3 km^2, Dafending (Mabian) one per 6.0–8.0 km^2, and Wanglang one per 4.8–9.7 km^2.

Between 1957 and 1983, China gave 24 pandas to zoos in 9 different countries as an expression of friendship. Thirteen of these were still alive in 8 countries at the end of 1983. Two young have been successfully raised at the Chapultepec zoo in Mexico and one young at the Madrid zoo. There are about 60–70 captives in zoos and forest department installations within China. In 1982, Yingxionggou had 8 pandas, the Chengdu zoo 10, and the Beijing zoo about 20, to mention only the three largest captive populations. By the end of 1983, 37 litters had to our knowledge been born in China; of these 19 (30%) young survived the first months of life.

Summary

1. Pandas are robust, bearlike animals, weighing about 85–110 kg, whose specialized physical features include broad, flat molars, modified for crushing, and an enlarged wrist bone functioning as a thumb—both adaptions for eating bamboo stems.

2. The panda has been mentioned in Chinese geography and medicine books and in literature for over 2000 years. A panda skull in a royal tomb dating back to 179–163 BC reveals that the animal was prized in ancient China. The species became known to the Western world in 1869.

3. Efforts to protect the panda began in 1957, and the first reserves were established in 1963. At present, 12 reserves, totaling 5927 km^2, contain pandas. Field observations on pandas began in the 1930s; intensive research in the Wolong Natural Reserve began in March 1978. The first captive birth occured at the Beijing zoo in 1963, and the first successful artificial insemination at the same zoo in 1978.

4. During the Pleistocene, pandas occurred over much of eastern China, as far north as Beijing. In historic times they were still widespread south of the Huang River, but hunting and habitat destruction have eliminated the animal from most of its range. Today it exists in only 6 small areas, totaling 29,500 km^2, along the eastern edge of

the Tibetan highlands. Since the animal is confined to bamboo, its altitudinal distribution extends from 1200 to 3400 m. A census in the mid-1970s indicated that approximately 1050–1100 pandas survive in the wild. Of these, about 60% are in reserves. Density in reserves is low, an average of about one animal per 9–11 km^2.

2

Wolong and its Pandas

Heading northwest of Chengdu, the capital of Sichuan Province, the road passes through intensively cultivated land. A broad-leafed evergreen forest once covered the Sichuan basin. But at this altitude of 500 m the climate is so mild that 3 crops can be grown annually, and the forests have long been replaced by rice, wheat, vegetables, and other crops. Soon, mountains appear faint in the haze, evolving into a solid rampart, the eastern edge of the Tibetan highlands. There, at the town of Guanxian, the road passes the Dujiangyan irrigation system, built 2100 years ago, and then enters mountains, following the valley of the Min River. Thousands of fir, spruce, and other logs glide downriver toward the plain; severe floods in the summer of 1981 were blamed on deforestation in the mountains, for Sichuan's forests have been reduced by 30% since the 1950s (Smil 1983).

Turning up a narrow valley, the road first traces the banks of the Utze (Gengda) River and then those of its tributaries, the Zheng and the Pitiao. Here, mountain flanks are steep, often broken by cliffs, their tops obscured by clouds, and the river rushes among boulders. The elevation is 1000 m and rising. The entrance to the Wolong Reserve is about 130 km from Chengdu. Near this entrance a large hydroelectric station is under construction, one of two dams completed; fields crowd the valley floor and spread up the mountain sides, leaving forest only on the steepest pitches and highest ridges (plate 2.1). Farther into the reserve, on an ancient alluvial terrace of the Pitiao River, is Hetauping, site of the panda research laboratories and breeding station (plate 2.2). A rock face towers up behind the station; across the valley, forested slopes angle up into favored haunts of the panda. Another 5 km up-valley, approximately four hours' drive from Chengdu, lie the reserve headquarters. At 1950 m in the heart of Wolong, the headquarters consists of a cluster of buildings vacated in 1975 by a timber extraction unit when the reserve was established. The road continues, zigzaging up the side of the sharp-crested Balang Mountains, up above the last conifers and birch, until, at an elevation of over 4200 m, it dips over a pass, leaving Wolong to enter the upland habitats of the Tibetan Plateau.

19

The Wolong Natural Reserve

Wolong is 2000 km^2 in size, extending about 60 km east to west and 63 km north to south (102°52′–103°24′E, 30°45′–31°25′N), the largest of China's panda reserves. In altitude it ranges from about 1200 m to 6250 m, a vertical span encompassing several climatic zones, each with a distinctive flora and fauna.

The environment of Wolong

Lying between the Sichuan basin and the Tibetan highlands, the mountains of Wolong have been so warped, crumbled, and folded during the Tertiary, especially since the Eocene, when the uplifts of the Himalaya and neighboring ranges began, that the topography is spectacular, from glacier-capped peaks to shadowed canyons. With the Longmen Mountain fault passing through the area in a northeast-southwest

PLATE 2.1   Fields cover many slopes in Wolong's Pitiao valley. People in this area will soon be resettled and the slopes replanted with trees and bamboo.

PLATE 2.2   Forest persists on steep slopes of the Pitiao valley at Hetauping. The panda breeding station is in the foreground; the research laboratories are a short distance away.

direction, the mountains and rivers generally parallel the fault. The terrain descends progressively from the northwest to southeast, with the Pitiao River a natural dividing line. Peaks to the east of the Pitiao are usually below 3200 m in elevation and the reserve border descends close to 1200 m; the peaks to the west are usually over 4000 m and about 60 are over 5000 m, crowned by 6250 m Mt. Siguniang (see fig. 2.4).

According to the Chengdu Geographic Institute of Academia Sinica, the rock strata in Wolong consist primarily of sandstone, slate, schist, siltstone, gneiss, quartzite, dolomite, limestone, and phyllite, with the two last-named most abundant, ranging in age from Silurian to Triassic; there are also igneous intrusions of serpentine, granite, and granodiorite. Intense tectonic activity and erosion have created deep, V-shaped valleys, flanked either by cliffs or by steep riverbanks, where landslides, mudflows, and other surface slips are common. The drop in river gradient is drastic and the water turbulent, a sparkling turquoise for much of the year but often silt-laden during the height of summer rains. The river water is slightly alkaline (mean pH 8.2, range 7.7–8.6), low in salinity (mean 160.4 mg/1, range 102.0–265.7), and generally soft (mean 6.4, range 3.7–11.2 German system). On the slopes between 2000 and 3100 m are many small plateaus or stripped plains—flat-lying strata from which weaker rocks have been removed by erosion—whose thick layer of brown and dark brown soil provides excellent conditions for forest and bamboo growth. Several of the highest peaks still have glaciers. Cirques and moraines at elevations as low as 3500 m reveal that, although glaciations during the Pleistocene were more extensive than in recent times, forests could survive on the slopes below, offering refuge to panda and other species.

Wolong belongs to the Tibetan climatic belt characterized by a long winter, with snows that may last from November to March, and relatively cool summers beneath a layer of cloud. The southeast monsoon arrives from the Pacific in June without having to surmount high ranges, reaches the edge of the Sichuan basin with full force, and drives its rain clouds deep into the valleys, where, coming to a halt against the mountain ramparts, they shed their moisture until October. Although winters are cold, temperatures are not extreme, for high mountains to the north and west check the advance of cold fronts from Tibet, Xinjiang, and Mongolia. With its combination of high humidity and nonextreme temperatures, much of Wolong has a climate more typical of a coastal than of an inland region. However, the great variation in altitude gives rise to several climatic belts, a subtropical zone below 2000 m, a temperate zone from 2000 to 3600 m, a frigid zone from 3600 to 5000 m, and a zone of perpetual ice and snow above 5000 m.

Variable conditions of topography, climate, soil, and hydrology have resulted in a diverse flora. The vegetation grows in a characteristic vertical zonation, as described for western Sichuan by Wilson (1929), Chiang (1960), Wang (1961), and an anonymous study (Anon. 1980), among others, and specifically for Wolong by Hu (1981c). From the standpoint of panda ecology, 4 forest types with their associated bamboo species play a major role (figs. 2.1, 2.2, and 2.3).

1. A subtropical, evergreen broad-leafed forest grows below an elevation of 1600 m in the southeastern part and comprises only about 33 km² or 2% of the total reserve area. *Cinnamomum inunctum*, *Lithocarpus cleistocarpa*, *Lindera* sp., and *Phoebe* sp. are prominent trees; *Phyllostachys nidularia* and especially *Sinarundinaria ferax*, both bamboos up to 4–6 m tall, are found in the understory.

2. An evergreen and deciduous broad-leafed forest lies between about 1600 and 2000 m and covers 266 km² or 13% of the reserve. *Cyclobalanopsis oxyodon* and oak are common evergreens, and birch, beech, maple and *Juglans cathayensis* conspicuous deciduous trees; dogwood, *Pterocarya insignis*, *Sophora* sp., and *Tetracentron sinense* are also prominent forest trees. *Fargesia* is the most widespread bamboo.

3. Extending from 2000 to 2600 m is a mixed coniferous and deciduous broad-leafed forest comprising 284 km² or 14% of Wolong. Hemlock, spruce, and larch are the main conifers, and birch, maple, basswood, and cherry some of the most common broad-leafed trees. *Fargesia* is the dominant bamboo in this zone, with *Sinarundinaria chungii* and *S. fangiana* locally prominent.

4. The most extensive forest in Wolong is the subalpine coniferous one that lies between 2600 and 3600 m and covers 317 km² or 16% of the total area. Fir is dominant, but birch and rhododendron are also abundant. *S. fangiana* is the most widespread bamboo, with *S. chungii* contributing significantly in some areas.

From timberline, thickets of fir, juniper, oak, and rhododendron grade upward into alpine meadows. Still higher, the vegetation becomes sparse, with only isolated clumps of *Saussurea, Saxifraga, Rhodiola*, and other species growing among scree and boulders until finally plant growth ceases. About half of the reserve lies above timberline, an area unsuitable for pandas.

There are approximately 4000 species of plants in the reserve (about 40% of the total number of species in Sichuan). Some were part of an ancient ecosystem in the western Chinese mountains that remained secure and isolated while the region that is now Tibet was covered by the Tethys Sea. Among the relics of this Tertiary palaeotropical flora are *Cercidiphyllum japonicum*, dove tree, rhododendrons,

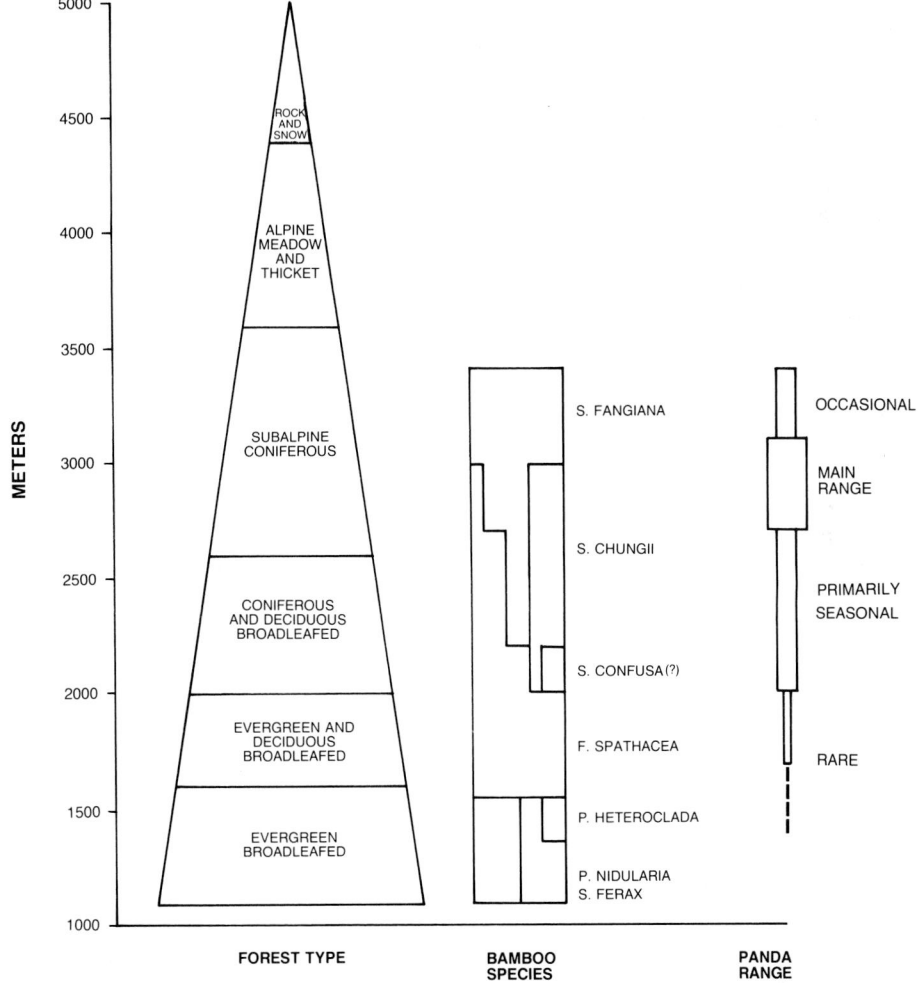

FIGURE 2.1   Vertical zonation of forest types, bamboo species, and panda habitat use in the Wolong Natural Reserve. (Data provided by Hu Jinchu.)

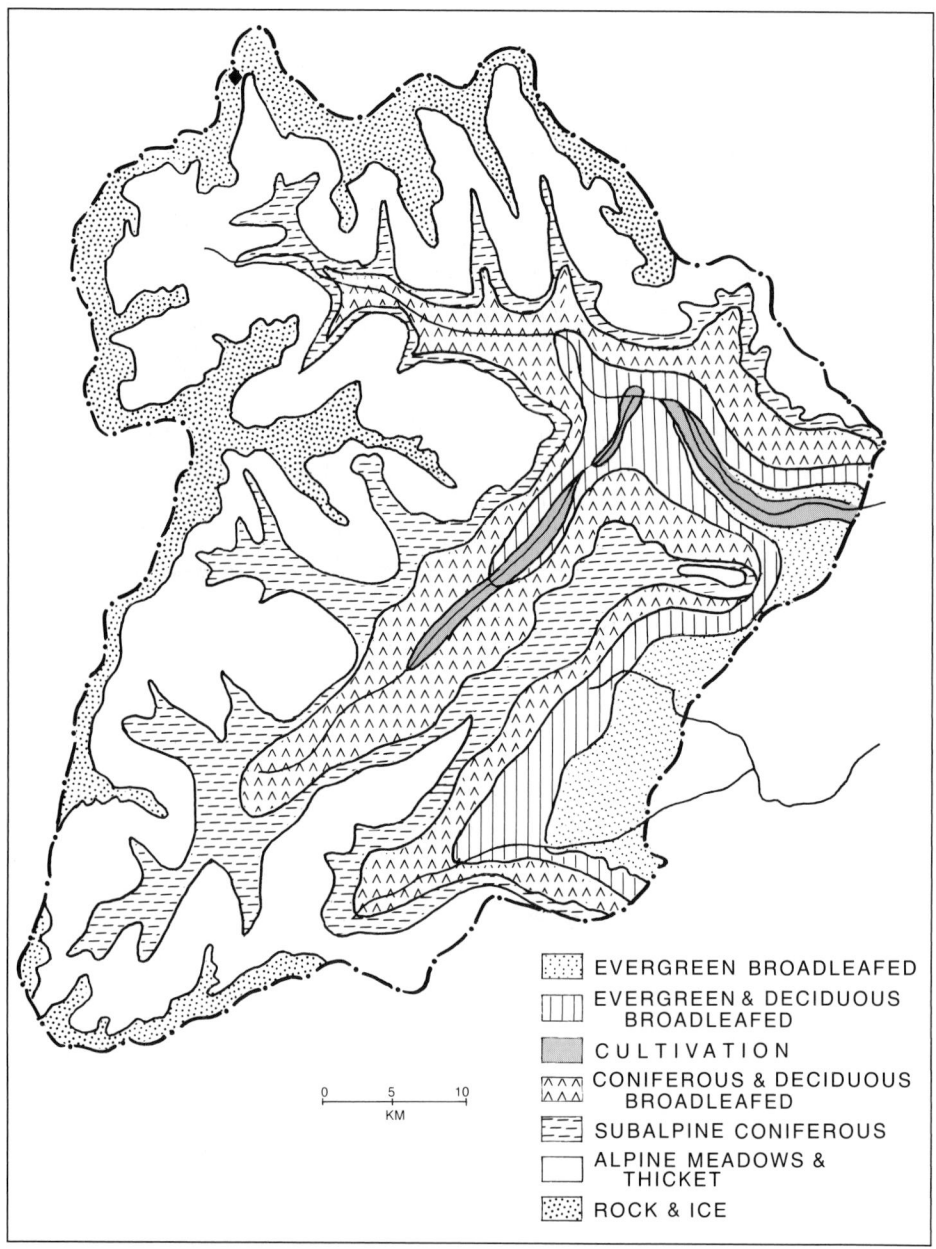

FIGURE 2.2   Approximate distribution of main vegetation types in the Wolong Natural
Reserve. (Data provided by Hu Jinchu.)

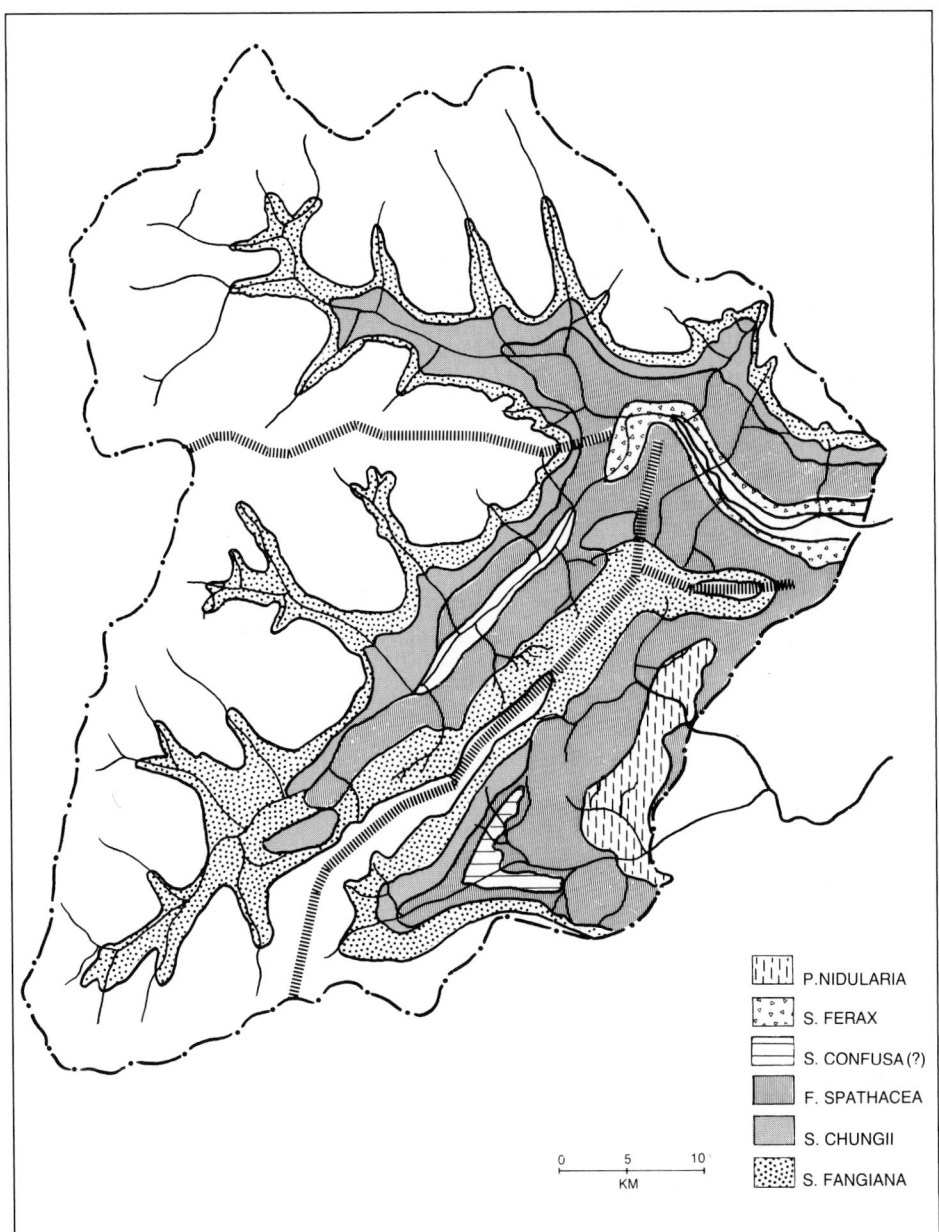

FIGURE 2.3 Approximate distribution of bamboo species in the Wolong Natural Reserve. The small area of *Phyllostachys heteroclada* in the Gengda valley is not indicated; and the extent of *Sinarundinaria confusa* (?) needs to be confirmed. (Data provided by Hu Jinchu.)

oaks, and firs. When, beginning in the early Tertiary, the vertical uplifts and horizontal thrusts moved the Tethys Sea upward to create the Tibetan highlands and later created the Himalayan system, new migration routes opened to the ancient flora. Some plants remained sedentary, among them the massive and gnarled *Tetracentron sinense*; others, such as the bamboos and oaks, emigrated far into other areas.

The reserve also supports many kinds of vertebrates, 96 species of mammals, 230 of birds, 20 of reptiles, 14 of amphibians, and 6 of fish having been noted so far. Among these animals are 30 species that China prizes and to which it has given complete legal protection, including green-tailed monal and Temminck's tragopan pheasants, golden monkey, white-lipped deer, a robust goat-antelope called the takin, snow leopard, red panda, and, of course, the giant panda, for whom the reserve was established and whose presence has assured the survival of all other species there. Wolong straddles the border between tropical lowlands and temperate uplands to the north and west; its animals are thus allied both to the Oriental and Palaearctic faunal regions. Despite considerable altitudinal overlap, forest fauna at low-to-medium altitudes is mainly Oriental in origin and includes golden pheasant, civet, stump-tailed macaque, clouded leopard, bamboo rat, tufted deer, serow, and panda, to name just a few. In subalpine coniferous forest and, especially, above timberline, Palaearctic elements occur, among them snowcock, pika, muskdeer, steppe cat, and snow leopard. Zheng et al. (1981) and Zhang and Zheng (1981) analyzed faunal affinities of birds and mammals of the Tibetan highlands and areas bordering them. The giant panda has long been associated with this fauna. Porcupine, hog badger, yellow-throated marten, wild pig, and sambar deer were all part of the *Stegodon*–giant panda fossil fauna of the Pleistocene. With climate relatively mild and glaciations in the area not extensive, forests continued to flourish and so did the animals, as noted from various fossil sites in and around the Sichuan basin, such as at Jiaoshipa in Fuli County, Yanjinggou in Wanxian, Maxiangpao in Guli, and Gelephan near the city of Chongqing. Many of the panda's associates have continued to thrive, maintaining a wide distribution in spite of humankind's encroachment. But the panda has become a relict.

Status and distribution of pandas

From April to July 1974, the Rare Animal Resources Investigation Team conducted a panda survey and census throughout Wolong. This effort, together with data accumulated later by reserve staff and researchers from Nanchong Normal College, provided the information upon which the present discussion is based. Before censusing, researchers visited various parts of the reserve to delineate the animal's range and select census routes. After that, transects were made along the main valleys, tributary valleys, and crests of the range. Since pandas are difficult to observe, indirect methods were used to estimate numbers. The location of fresh droppings, for example, was noted, and the length of stem fragments in a sample of droppings was measured. A difference in bite size can be used to distinguish age classes of animals (see table 6-2).

Evidence for 145 pandas was found during the census (fig. 2.4), of which 39 (27%) were in the Zheng-Gengda drainage, 46 (32%) in the Zhong-Xi drainage, and 60 (41%) in the Pitiao drainage (table 2.1). We believe that the census results are of the correct order of magnitude, that there are an estimated 130–150 pandas in the reserve. The Choushuigou—the valley in which we conducted our research—provided an independent check on the census results. Eighteen pandas were tallied there during the census, a figure similar to our estimate of 12–18 for 1981 (fig. 2.10).

Several factors have an influence on the abundance and distribution of pandas in

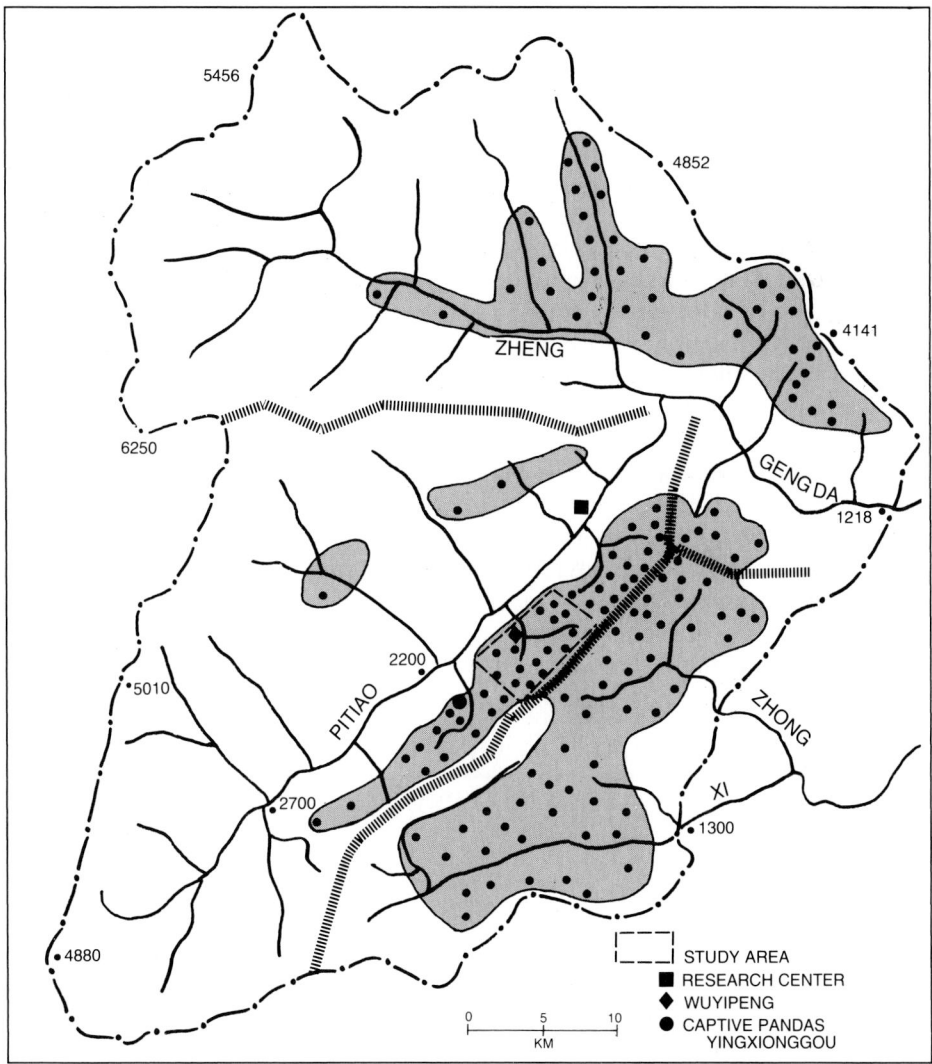

FIGURE 2.4   Distribution of pandas in the Wolong Natural Reserve during the 1974 census. Each dot represents one panda. The numbers indicate elevations (in m).

Wolong. One is obviously the availability of bamboo. Some areas within the forest are devoid of bamboo, its growth precluded by terrain, soil, and light conditions (see fig. 2.8). Ridges in the southeastern part are relatively low, receiving the full effect of the monsoon; bamboo there grows to an elevation of 3400 m. Farther north and west, as in the Zheng valley, high ridges check the monsoon force and high pressure systems from the Tibetan Plateau affect the climate; there bamboo may cease at 2800 m. The lower slopes of the Gengda and parts of the Pitiao valley, as well as several tributary valleys, have been cultivated up to an altitude of 2600–2700 m in places; no pandas were noted there below 2200 m during the census, whereas in the undisturbed Xi and Zhong drainages a number were at low elevations (table 2.1). Pandas on the southeast-facing slopes of the Pitiao valley are close to extinction because of habitat destruction. Even where bamboo is still widespread, providing a coverage of at least 50% in the understory as it does locally in all forest zones, pandas may be uncommon. Only 13% of the pandas were tallied in mixed coniferous and deciduous broadleafed forest where *Fargesia* and *Sinarundinaria chungii* predominate. This percentage might have been higher if the census had been conducted only in late May and June, when pandas often descend below 2600 m and sometimes below 2000 m to eat bamboo shoots. We are uncertain why pandas are scarce in this forest zone. In some areas, human disturbance may be a factor. Pandas favor forests with a canopy coverage of 70% or more. Logging and wood collecting have affected the canopy of these forests, which are accessible from the Pitiao and Gengda valleys. Topography may also have an influence on panda distribution. Surveys revealed that animals are most abundant on stripped plains, valley terraces, heads of streams, and just above or below cliffs, all areas that are spacious and relatively level with a gradient of 20° or less. During the census it was found that 12% of the pandas were in terrain with a gradient of 30° or more, 25% with a gradient of 20–30°, and the rest with a gradient of 20° or less. Mixed coniferous and deciduous forest grows low on the slopes—which in Wolong tend to be steep and broken by cliffs. Since the panda's water requirements exceed what bamboo can provide, the animals need to drink almost daily. Water appears plentiful in Wolong, although there may be seasonal shortages on some steep slopes, preventing pandas from ranging there. In the Jiuzhaigou Re-

TABLE 2.1

ESTIMATES OF PANDA NUMBERS IN DIFFERENT AREAS OF WOLONG NATURAL RESERVE, 1974 CENSUS

| Altitude/m | Zheng and Gengda drainage | Zhong and Xi drainage | Pitiao drainage | | |
			Choushuigou	Yingxionggou	Other
3000+	3	0	1	3	0
2800–3000	8	3	5	7	10
2600–2800	19	22	10	0	21
2400–2600	4	4	2	0	1
2200–2400	5	4	0	0	0
2000–2200	0	7	0	0	0
2000–	0	6	0	0	0
Total	39	46	18	10	32

serve, for instance, there is little water on slopes in late spring, streams vanishing into the limestone and then reappearing far below in the valley bottom.

Because of the alignment of ridges, favored panda areas are often on north- and east-facing slopes, the shady parts of a valley; 66% of the pandas in the 1974 census were in shady areas and 34% on sunny ones.

The Choushuigou study area

About 4 km up-valley from the reserve headquarters, a foot bridge spans the Pitiao River, and from there a trail angles up the northwest-facing mountainside. Fields soon give way to shrubs and saplings—*Buddleia*, hazelnut, *Daphne*, *Cotoneaster*—among which domestic sheep and goats forage. Higher up, the undergrowth becomes more dense, and clumps of *Fargesia* bamboo appear. On reaching a spur, the trail levels and enters a valley, the Choushuigou. Following the contours of the slope, the trail winds through forest to the tented camp of Wuyipeng, our research base, established here in March 1978. Climbing time from the road is about one hour; the elevation is 2520 m.

The Choushuigou comprises one drainage almost encircled by a ridge whose highest point, Mt. Qitouyan, reaches an altitude of 3624 m. Several subsidiary ridges project abruptly into this drainage, creating a complex and rugged topography encompassing 20 km^2 (plate 2.3). Slopes are steep, 20°–30°, some up to 50°, and even the ridge crests, along which pandas and people tend to travel, often rise precipitously. At elevations of 2800–2900 m are two prominent stripped plains, or plateaus—Fanzipeng on the north side of the valley and Erdaoping on the south side—which are much favored by pandas (plate 2.4). Since pandas readily move into and out of the Choushuigou, we included two small adjoining valleys, the Gangou and Zhuanjinggou, and parts of two other valleys, the Huacaodigou and Yingxiong-gou, into our study area (fig. 2.10). Although this area totaled 35 km^2, we did most research in about 15 km^2 between an altitude of 2300 and 3100 m.

Climate

We recorded weather information daily at Wuyipeng. In general, the climate is cool and wet. Snow fell at camp between late October and April, and, higher up, there was an occasional snowstorm well into May. Total snowfall in 1981 was about 573 mm. Snowfall during the winters of 1980–81 and 1981–82 was unusually light and during the winter of 1982–83 unusually heavy, according to the Wuyipeng camp staff. Most rain occurs between May and September during the height of the southeast monsoon. Total 1981 rainfall (excluding snow) was 938 mm (fig. 2.5). The average daily minimum temperature from November through March was below freezing, the coldest day registering −12.5°C. March–April and October–November are transitional months, with snow, sleet, or rain depending on the vagaries of weather. The warmest months are June, July, and August, when average daily maxima reach 16°–19°C; on rare days, when the rainclouds part and sun reaches the valley, the temperature may rise well above 20°C (fig. 2.6).

Statistics such as these fail to convey actual weather conditions. Clouds from the east and southeast collide with the Qionglai Mountains, and, unable to surmount the crest, settle into the valleys. There are 15 or more days with measurable rain every month between May and November 1981, much of it at night. Even when it did not rain, fog continued to swirl along slopes, everything remained sodden, and everywhere water trickled and dripped. The sun seldom appeared. Humidity remained above 85% (Hu 1981c), and even on sunny days it seldom dropped as low as 50%. In November, the weather began to clear; during winter and spring we sometimes had spells of a week or more during which peaks stood sharp-edged against blue sky.

Vegetation

Two major forest types—mixed coniferous and deciduous broad-leafed forest and subalpine coniferous forest—originally covered the study area, but human activities have altered these considerably on some slopes. Many conifers were logged from the

PLATE 2.3   Viewed from an altitude of 3300 m, the forested slopes of the Choushuigou study area extend northwest into the Pitiao valley.

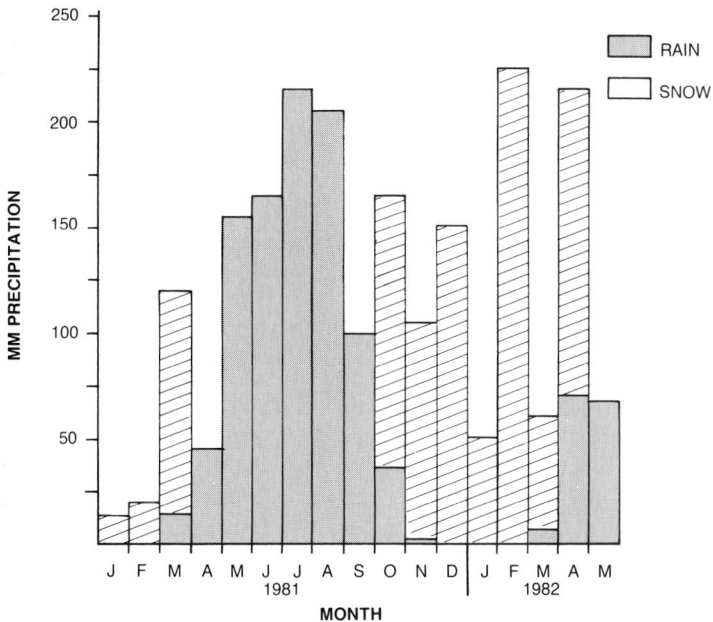

FIGURE 2.5   Monthly rainfall and snowfall at Wuyipeng during the period of study.

1930s until the 1970s, almost changing some areas, such as Fanzipeng, into deciduous broad-leafed forest. The Zhuanjinggou had been virtually denuded by the time felling ceased in 1972, and some parts of the Yingxionggou were also bare of trees when logging stopped in 1974. The slope opposite Wuyipeng was once cleared for cultivation, but later, after fields were abandoned by the 1960s, it grew over with willow, hazelnut, and other shrubs; the forest department also planted larch and spruce there. Patches of cultivation existed on the Wuyipeng side of the valley as well. Cutting of trees by villagers persists, especially in the Huacaodigou and on the slopes facing the Pitiao valley, with the result that some areas have been or are being converted from forest to secondary shrub (fig. 2.7).

In the valley bottom near the mouth of the Choushuigou is a small, degraded patch of evergreen and deciduous broad-leafed forest of oak, poplar, and *Cercidiphyllum*. Otherwise all forest below 2500–2600 m is of the coniferous and deciduous broad-leafed type. Because many larch, spruce, hemlock, and fir have been logged, deciduous trees usually predominate—among them maple, cherry, birch, basswood, *Tetracentron*, and *Pterocarya insignis*, a relative of the walnut. These trees provide a canopy density of 60–90% and form an uneven canopy up to a height of 25–30 m, except where conifers tower above to 35–40 m. Trees in the understory include willow, viburnum, hydrangea, *Litsea cubeba*, *Maddenia hypoleuco*, *Sorbus koehneana*, *S. rufipilosa*, *Lindera obtusiloba*, and several rhododendrons, especially *R. arterochnoum*, most no taller than 8–12 m. Barberry, rose, bramble, holly, and gooseberry grow in openings and along trails, and the shrubby *Rhododendron*

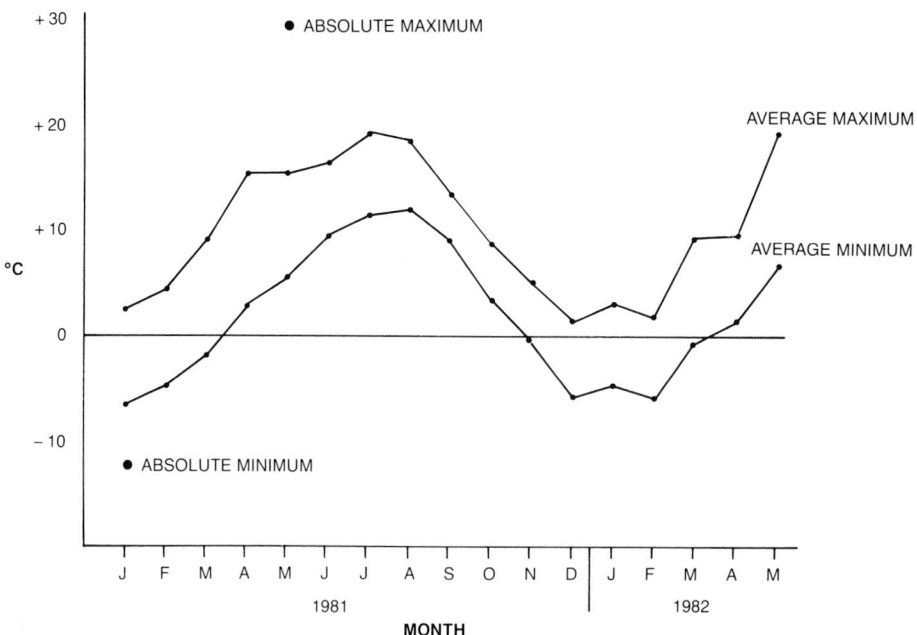

FIGURE 2.6   Average monthly minimum and maximum temperatures at Wuyipeng during the period of study.

polylepis is conspicuous. Bamboo is also pervasive in the understory, as discussed later (plate 2.5). Groundcover in deep shade consists mostly of *Sphagnum, Haplocladium* and other mosses, some ferns, and such herbs as wood sorrel, *Thalictum* sp., *Beesia calthaefolia*, and *Chrysosplenium griffithii*. Where the slope is gradual and moist, the soil is often deep: below the humus layer is a horizon of dark-brown acidic soil, 4–10 cm thick, followed by a horizon of granular yellow-brown soil, 50–80 cm thick, and finally a layer of phyllite detritus. Such places may support lush herb meadows with snakeroot, gentian, *Androsace henryi, Tiarella polyphylla*, bedstraw, nettle, *Sambucus* sp., false Solomon's seal, cowslip, *Corydalis taliensis*, grasses and sedges, and an occasional orchid, to name just a few. Slopes being steep and soils unstable, landslips occur yearly, leaving scars either bare or, later, covered sparsely with vegetation.

Large tracts along the northwestern border of the study area consist of secondary shrub—*Sorbus* sp., rose, willow, hazelnut, hawthorn, *Buddleia davidii, Syringa* sp., *Aralia chinensis, Cotoneaster horizontalis*, rhododendron, and other kinds—which form tall thickets with only occasional emergent trees to indicate what kind of forest once existed there (plate 2.6). The large-leafed *Rodgersia aesculifolia* is a characteristic herb in openings, its sprays of white flowers flamboyant in June and July.

Of the 150-odd woody species in the study area, most grow at low elevations. Between 2500 and 2600 m is a transition zone above which certain species cease abruptly or fade out gradually. *Tetracentron*, hazelnut, *Litsea*, and *Pterocarya* stop at that altitude, and *Rhododendron polylepis* and *R. lutescens* and several maples cease soon after. Extending from this elevation upward to timberline is a subalpine coniferous forest (plate 2.7). At its lower limit, this forest remains relatively diverse—hemlock, spruce, and fir being mixed with a variety of deciduous trees, especially hydrangea, cherry, viburnum, birch, and *Sorbus*, each represented by at least two species. By 2800–2900 m, only a fir (*Abies faxoniana*) and two birches remain abundant. For example, of 304 trees with a DBH of more than 5 cm tallied around one panda's maternity den at Erdaoping, 104 were fir; 142 *Betula utilis*; 36 *Betula albosinensis*; and 22 *Prunus diehlsiana*, *Sorbus* sp, rhododendron, and others. Shrubs are sparse in the forest at this altitude (there is some gooseberry and rhododendron) and herbs inconspicuous—an occasional *Beesia*, *Rubus nutans*, or lousewort with a cover of less than 10%; grasses occur in isolated tufts along trails and other openings. Ground cover consists primarily of mosses; on ridges, beneath a canopy of fir and rhododendron (*R. oreodoxa*, *R. watsonii*, *R. faberi*), mosses may

PLATE 2.4   Much of the panda research was done on this rugged, east-facing slope in the Choushuigou. The Wuyipeng camp is located on a level part of the spur on the right, and several pandas frequented the relatively gentle upper slopes. In the foreground, shrubs grow on a formerly cultivated site.

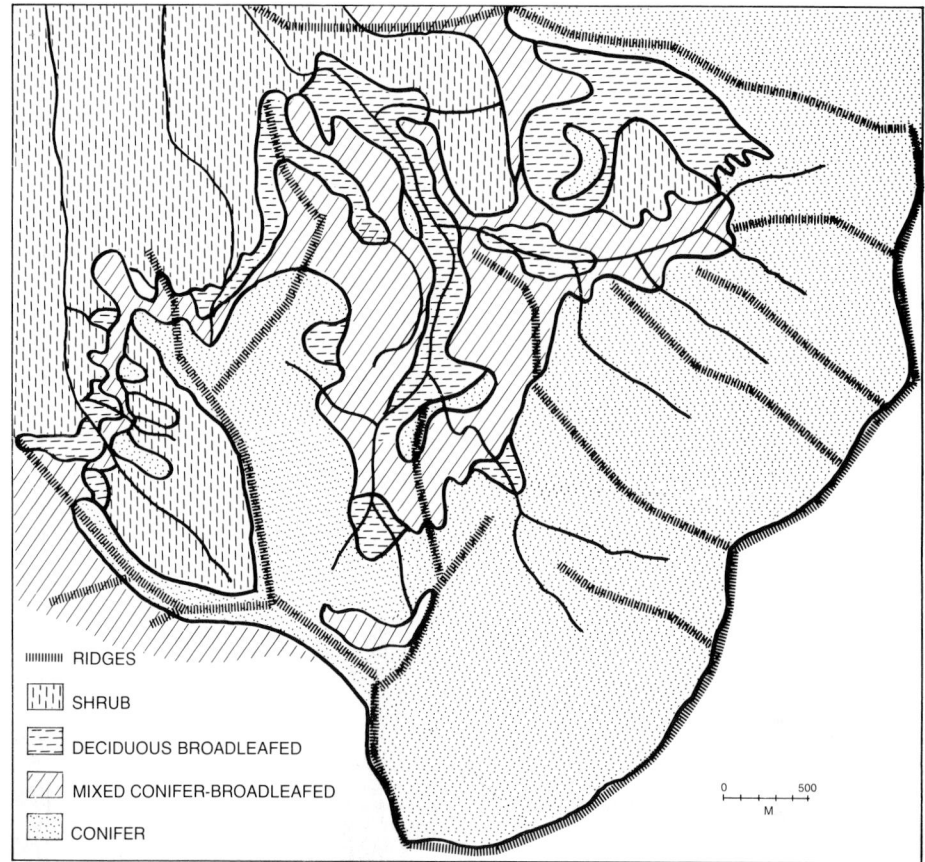

FIGURE 2.7 Distribution of main vegetation types in the study area. (See fig. 2.10 for elevations and place names.)

cushion the entire slope. Generally, conifers and rhododendrons dominate on ridges and rises and deciduous trees in between. Excluding logged areas, such as Fanzipeng, where a secondary deciduous broad-leafed forest of birch predominates, and the upper Zhuanjinggou, where only scattered trees and shrubs remain on open slopes (plates 2.8 and 2.9), about two-thirds of this forest zone has a canopy coverage of conifers. Total canopy coverage is usually 75% or more when trees are in leaf. Above 3200 m, trees become stunted; at 3600–3700 m, fir and rhododendron persist only as thickets, broken by patches of procumbent juniper and by alpine meadows of *Festuca, Polygonum, Allium, Pedicularis, Morina*, and other genera.

Using a 5-factor wedge prism at point plots to select trees at random, we measured tree diameters at three sites. The forest between 2300 and 2500 m around Wuyipeng is rather shrubby, one-third of the trees being 10 cm or less in diameter. Between 2800 and 3000 m, at Erdaoping, the forest contains few small trees but many large fir, 50 cm or more in diameter. And at Fanzipeng, which probably was similar to

Erdaoping before being logged, large firs are scarce, whereas birches, 11–30 cm in diameter, predominate (fig. 2.8). From data obtained with the wedge prism, the basal area of trees and the number of trees per hectare can be calculated (table 2.2). Basal areas at Wuyipeng and Erdaoping were similar (28–29 m²/ha), but tree density in the former is 44% greater, there being many small broad-leafed trees and few large conifers. Fanzipeng reflects the effect of logging 50 years ago in that the basal area is 35% less and tree density 28% less than at Erdaoping.

Not mentioned so far is bamboo. Of the 196 bamboo species listed in one study as occurring in China (Anon. 1974), 7 native species are known for Wolong (fig. 2.1). Of these, *Phyllostachys nidularia* and *P. heteroclada* are patchy and rare; *Sinarundinaria confusa* (?) appears to exist in only one small area of unknown extent, and its identification is open to question; and *S. ferax* has a restricted distribution low in the Gengda valley, where human disturbance is heavy. *S. chungii* is quite widespread, but barely extends into our study area, where only two species predominate: *Fargesia spathacea* Franchet and *Sinarundinaria fangiana* (A. Camus) Keng ex Keng f. The taxonomy of both is in flux. Soderstrom (1979) and Chao et al. (1980) transferred *Fargesia* to the genus *Thamnocalamus*; and *Sinarundinaria fangiana* may belong to *Arundinaria*, judging by rhizome characteristics (Anon. 1974; Chao et al.

PLATE 2.5   The Wuyipeng research camp lies at 2520 m in deciduous broad-leafed forest with an understory of *Fargesia* bamboo.

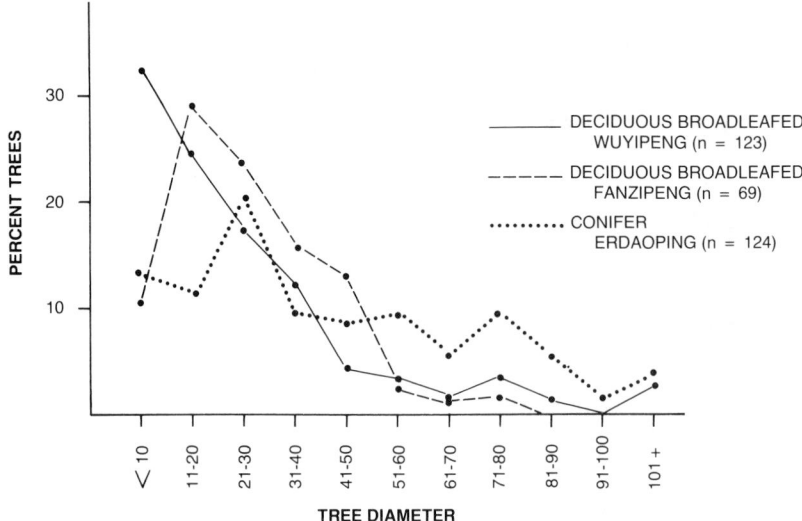

FIGURE 2.8   Percentage of trees in different diameter size classes (DBH) at 3 sites in the study area, based on a random sample in point plots with a 5-factor wedge prism.

1980). In the absence of a general agreement, we retain the old names in this report.* *Fargesia* grows at low altitudes, as low as 1600 m in Wolong, and *S. fangiana* at high ones, reaching its upper limit at around 3400 m. The transition between the two in the study area lies between 2500 and 2650 m. In other localities, as in the Min Mountains (Investigation team 1977), *Fargesia* sp. may reach an altitude of 3300 m when *S. fangiana* is absent, suggesting that two species may compete for space. *Fargesia* grows in clumps, and its short dichotomous branching rhizomes spread slowly, whereas *S. fangiana* has long rhizomes that colonize rapidly.

Bamboo occurs throughout the study area except high on the northeast-facing slopes. About 25% of the bamboo mapped in figure 2.9 is *Fargesia*, the rest *S. fangiana*. *Fargesia* is tall, stems averaging 2.5 m in height; some are 4.5 m, and rare ones over 5 m. Diameter of stems at the base averages 0.86 cm, but varies from a spindly 0.3 to a robust 2.5 cm. On the average, 30 to 40 stems of varying height grow per m^2 (see table 3.14). Tops of the stems are often permanently bent to form an interlacing tangle through which it is difficult to move. *Fargesia* distribution is patchy, the species being sparse on steep, unstable terrain (such as in gulleys), on shallow soil, and on formerly cultivated slopes, which it may not have had time to recolonize completely. No more than an estimated 40% of the area available to *Fargesia* is covered with it.

S. fangiana is thin, 0.3–0.8 (mean 0.5) cm in diameter, and short, with an average

*Yi Tongpei (pers. comm.) recently investigated bamboos in parts of Wolong and proposed the following name changes: *Fargesia angustissima* Yi instead of *Sinarundinaria ferax*, *Yushania chungii* (Keng) Wang et Yi instead of *Sinarundinaria chungii*, *Gelidocalamus fangianus* (A. Camus) Keng f. et Wen instead of *Sinarundinaria fangiana*, and *Fargesia robusta* Yi instead of *Fargesia spathacea*.

PLATE 2.6 February snows blanket a secondary shrub forest with its dense understory of *Sinarundinaria fangiana* bamboo at 2700 m.

PLATE 2.7 A subalpine coniferous forest of fir and birch covers a ridge at 3000 m. A trail winds through the expanse of *Sinarundinaria fangiana* bamboo. The forest to the left of the trail has not been logged; to the right, it has been almost clear-felled.

TABLE 2.2
DENSITY OF TREES (> 5 CM DBH) IN THREE AREAS OF THE CHOUSHUIGOU,
BASED ON MEASUREMENTS WITH A 5-FACTOR WEDGE PRISM AT POINT PLOTS

	Location		
	Fanzipeng[a]	Erdaoping	Wuyipeng
Altitude	2800–2900	2800–3000	2300–2500
Sample			
Plots (N)	13	20	21
Trees (N)	54	121	119
Conifers (%)	9.2	47.9	16.8
Broad-leafed trees (%)	90.8	52.1	83.2
Av. basal area of trees (m²/ha)	19.2	29.4	27.7
Av. tree density (trees/ha)			
Conifer	7.2 ± 17.2	154.4 ± 307.2	171.5 ± 531.2
Broad-leafed	1150.6 ± 1375.9	1449.5 ± 1492.4	2681.5 ± 2187.8
Total	1157.8	1603.9	2853.0

[a]All plots were in logged areas.

height of 1.4 m but with some stems up to 2.5 m. Stems crowd together, about 70–75 per m², double the density of *Fargesia*. Patches of *S. fangiana* may occur as low as 2350 m in shady, cold spots, where *Fargesia* thrives less well. Above 2600 m, the species is pervasive. Although it grows thinly or not at all in heavy shade, in valley bottoms, on ridge crests densely covered with mosses and rhododendron, and on steep east- and northeast-facing slopes, it usually blankets the more open and gentle terrain, its stems in dense ranks with seldom a clearing. Coverage in most areas averages at least 50–60%. At Fanzipeng, around Erdaoping, in the Zhuanjinggou, and in other localities it is as high as 80–90%. In such areas the bamboo may be so dense that little vegetation, not even much moss, grows beneath it. Above 3200 m, bamboo becomes stunted, stems only 20–50 cm tall, and between 3300 and 3400 m it ceases to grow.

The seasons

November is a month of transition. Deciduous trees are bare, or almost so, and the ground brown and yellow with leaves crisp underfoot in the morning after a night's frost. The constant fog and drizzle of summer may give way to sparkling days or to snow. An early snow melts rapidly but persists in ravines and on east- and northeast-facing slopes as the season advances. Full winter arrives in December. Water in washbasins has 10 mm of ice in the morning, and birches are heavy with frost; rhododendron leaves are tightly curled, bamboo rigid with cold. It is silent except when, or rare occasions, a mixed flock of twittering nuthatches, tits, and white-eyes passes through. Although many rivulets are frozen, valley streams continue to flow between ice-glazed boulders. After a storm, conifer branches sag and bamboo bows under the snow, but this burden is soon shed; indeed, slopes with western and southern exposures seldom have snow for long. Throughout winter the forest remains strangely verdant, for conifers, rhododendron, and bamboo retain their green leaves. Winter begins its retreat toward late February, and, by mid-March, stream banks and trails are almost free of ice. Rhododendron leaves unfurl; flocks of blood pheasant begin to break up in preparation for nesting; and the first spring flower—the lavender *Primula moupinensis*—appears. Snow may still fall, especially at night, but the day's warmth soon melts it.

April is filled with resurgent life. Rhododendron begins to flower, as do the less conspicuous anemone, wood sorrel, violet, and *Chrysosplenium*. Ferns push up through the sodden mat of dead leaves. Amber *Tetracentron* leaves shine like gold coins against the slanting light of early morning, and budding larch and maples impart a soft green sheen to slopes. Growing from underground rhizomes, the first new shoots of *Fargesia* push up through the soil by late April. Gould's sunbird, brilliant scarlet and yellow, and some other migrants return at month's end, and the forest rings to the insistent calls of hawk-cuckoos. *Apodemus* mice give birth. In May, certain trees and shrubs flower, including *Maddenia*, *Litsea*, cherry, rose, and

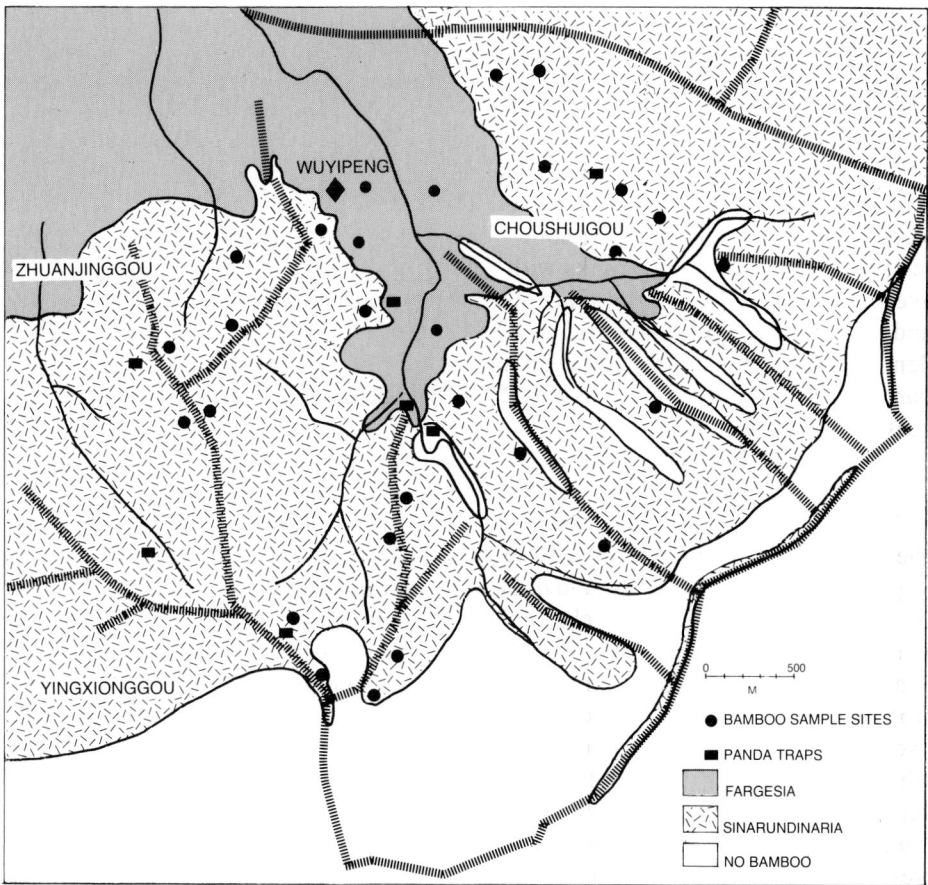

FIGURE 2.9   Distribution of *Fargesia* and *Sinarundinaria* bamboo in the study area.

PLATE 2.8   Hu Jinchu moves through *Sinarundinaria fangiana* bamboo in the birch forest of Fanzipeng at 2900 m; most conifers in the area have been logged.

PLATE 2.9   Large areas of Zhuanjinggou were clear-felled by loggers, leaving only forest patches. The open slopes are covered densely with *Sinarundinaria fangiana* bamboo. The subadult pandas Long and Ning often frequented this slope.

bramble. Herb meadows are deep green and speckled with white from the blossoms of trillium, snakeroot, *Androsace*, and *Tiarella*. Jack-in-the-pulpit, pyrola, and blue-flowered *Microula sikkimensis* bloom along trails. Land leeches make their appearance. Hidden among bamboo, tit babblers incubate blue-splotched eggs in grass nests. By late May, spring is essentially finished around Wuyipeng: leaves are out, the burst of flowering is over, many *Fargesia* shoots are more than one meter tall. Five hundred meters above, however, birches have just come into leaf and new *Sinarundinaria* shoots have only recently pierced through the moss.

Clouds usually swirl around the valleys in June, the sunny spells of April and May over as the weather deteriorates into a rainy season. Even if the clouds lift, the mountains remain brooding, as if in dark shadow, and the vegetation is wet, the trail spongy. Fog and rain continue, but the season changes almost imperceptibly from summer to autumn. Temminck's tragopan chicks, hatched as downy balls in early June, are by September transformed into plump pheasants almost as large as their mothers. Bamboo shoots have reached their full height, each having become just another stem in the crowded ranks; some birch leaves have a yellow tinge; *Sorbus hupehensis* is laden with clusters of white berries. Although there are still flowering herbs—touch-me-not, ragwort, *Cleome*—September is the month of mushrooms, white, pink, and sulfur-colored, shining in the forest. During that month too, rock squirrels feed intensively on hazelnuts in preparation for hibernation, and woodcock rest on forest paths in transit to warmer climates. Then, during October, maple leaves turn golden and viburnum scarlet. And the first snow may announce the coming of winter.

The pandas of Choushuigou

The 1974 census revealed that the southeastern slopes of the Pitiao valley harbored the densest panda population. When in 1977 it was decided to establish a research camp, another survey of this area was conducted to locate a good study site. The Choushuigou was chosen because it had a sizable panda population and was easily accessible from the reserve headquarters.

Even though 18 pandas were known to frequent the study area in 1981 (fig. 2.10), we observed them infrequently. Between March 1978 and December 1980, the research team saw pandas 16 times; between January 1980 and May 1981, our enlarged team observed them 39 times. Bamboo is usually so dense that an animal is invisible at a distance of 5–10 m. When snow lies on the slopes, panda tracks are easy to follow. But, being squat, a panda can move silently and rapidly through tunnels of bamboo and under fallen trees, whereas a field biologist progresses slowly and with much noise. With its acute sense of smell, the panda may detect a person at 40 m and respond by snorting and moving away; its hearing seems sensitive too. When disturbed, a panda does not rear up on its hindlegs to investigate in the manner of bears. These factors make direct, prolonged observations difficult. Most of our contacts were brief—a glimpse as an animal crossed an opening or ambled up a trail. Though timid, pandas are not particularly shy unless frightened, and on a number of occasions we observed them in situations with fairly good visibility (plate 2.10).

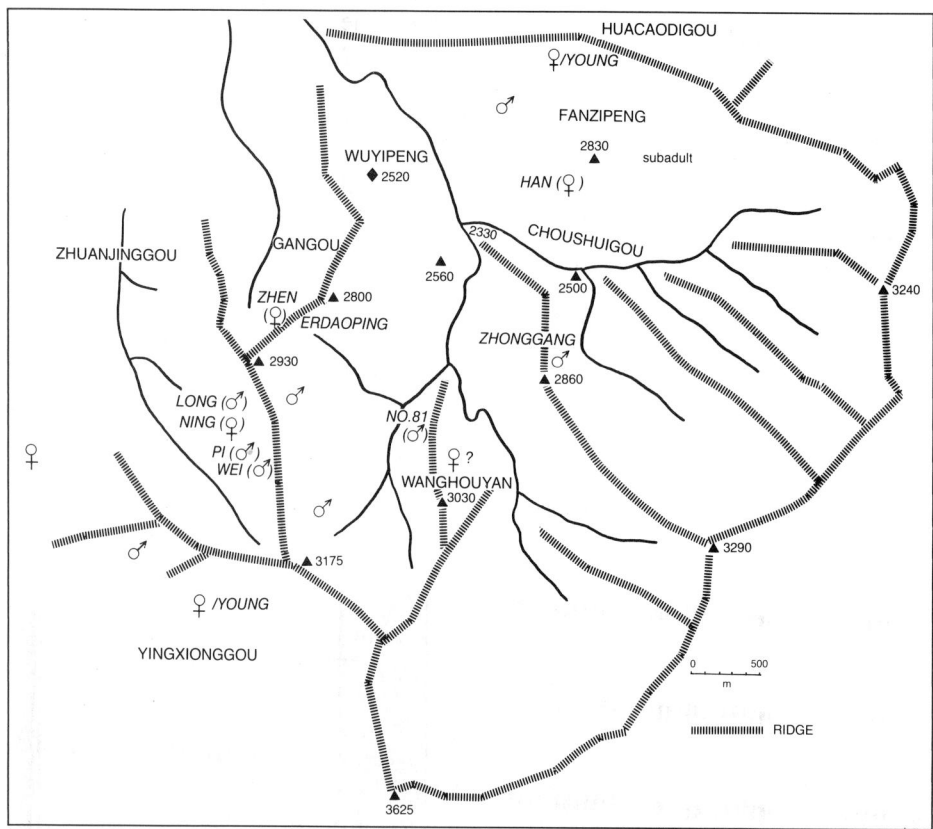

FIGURE 2.10   Approximate distribution of pandas in the study area. (See tables 2.3 and 2.4 for details concerning the named individuals.)

Zhen-Zhen, a female whose range encompassed Wuyipeng, was somewhat habituated to people, as this encounter on 27 May 1981 illustrates:

—1535 hours. Zhen walks uphill and sits in a bamboo patch, barely visible among the stems, about 25 m from the observer. She eats a *Fargesia* shoot. Standing up, she reaches for and breaks off a second shoot, which she strips of sheaths and eats as she sits. Twice she leans far to one side, collecting a shoot each time.

—1540. She snorts and honks, having sensed the observer, but she continues to forage.

—1545. Abruptly, she walks from the bamboo into a clearing, and, with nose raised high as if sniffing, she faces the observer, who sits quietly at 10 m. Then, bobbing her head up and down, she honks and snorts in agitation for 30 seconds before retreating to 19 m. But she advances once again, stopping at 12 m. Seemingly indecisive, she turns as if to move uphill, looks intently at the observer, and finally angles to a small bamboo thicket at 16 m. There she sits, honking softly, as her head sags onto her chest and she seems to doze. Once she jerks her head up, as if suddenly remembering the observer, snorts, gives the air a swat with her right forepaw, and sleeps again. After 10 minutes she awakens and sits hunched, forepaws in her lap.

—1600. Zhen yawns, scratches her ear and chin and glances toward the observer.

—1605. As she walks away, she pulls a shoot off with her teeth, carries it 13 m in her mouth, and then sits to eat it. She continues into another bamboo thicket, out of sight.

Wei-Wei, a male with little human contact, tolerated the presence of two observers near his rest site by a hollow tree on 8 September 1982, a cold, rainy day.

—1145. Wei stands and looks alertly toward the observers.

—1152. He sits, then lies briefly on his side, sits again, and reclines once more, obviously nervous.

—1156. He raises his head and looks around.

—1158. He lies facing the observers, raises his head, and then rests, though remaining alert, his ears twitching.

PLATE 2.10   The female Zhen stands in a bower of *Fargesia* bamboo staring intently at the observer.

—1225. Standing up, he looks around, and after that he reclines and apparently dozes, only occasionally lifting his head as if to check on the situation.

—1323. He stands up, sits, stands again as he defecates two droppings, and sits.

—1329. Turning over, he lies with his back toward the observers, his head inside the hollow tree.

—1339. He rolls over and looks at the observers for two minutes, licking his lips.

—1352. He honks for 3 minutes.

—1355. Standing up, he rubs his right side on a tree trunk. Afterward he lies inside the hollow tree, face toward the observers.

—1411. He raises his head, looks around, then sleeps.

The observers quietly retreat as Wei continues his rest.

Such encounters were too rare to provide much quantitative data on panda movements and activities. We therefore trapped six pandas, fitted them with radio transmitters, and released them. Table 2.3 provides background on their name, age, sex, and trapping history; and table 2.4 gives weights and measurements. By giving names to the pandas, we elevated them to living entities that became part of camp life, individuals whose doings we constantly discussed, whose successes we cheered, and whose problems we viewed with concern. On our few meetings with them, we sensed a peculiar blend of remoteness and intimacy in their responses to us. Even though we unfortunately could not know them well as individuals, some nevertheless projected distinct temperaments, never more so than when we approached while they were trapped.

Long-Long. The male Long was about 2.5 years old when first captured. Held by a foot snare, he tried to pull away but made neither sound nor aggressive gestures as he was injected with the sedating drug from a distance of one meter. The following year he was also subdued, sitting hunched in the trap, giving the impression of a gentle, uncomplicated creature that fate had placed in a situation beyond its control.

Ning-Ning. Ning, a female, was the same age as Long. Her behavior in the trap resembled that of a tame zoo animal: she reached through the bars, permitting us to hold her forepaw, and she pressed closer when we scratched her head. Given bamboo, she ate it readily. However, eight months later she merely sat, muzzle by her feet, and shivered as we approached.

No. 81. Although this 2.5-year-old male was of the same age as Long and Ning when we first captured them, his behavior was entirely different. He squealed, barked, and roared as he swatted the air in our direction. After being ear-tagged only—a yellow tag No. 81—and released, he twice more entered traps and each time clamored just as aggressively.

Zhen-Zhen. When Zhen was first trapped in 1981, the wear on her teeth was moderately heavy; the fourth premolar and first and second molars on the left side of the lower jaw were missing, and a deposit of tartar, 1 cm thick, encrusted the outside of the upper right molars. She felt lean; pelvic bones were prominent beneath her hide. We judged her to be past prime. Either honking, snorting, roaring, or chomp-

TABLE 2.3

NAME, SEX, AGE, AND CAPTURE DATES OF PANDAS IN THE STUDY AREA, 1981–82

Name of Panda	Sex	Age at first capture	Date of first capture	Subsequent captures	Comments
Long-Long (Dragon)	Male	2.5 years	10 March 1981[a]	30 Jan. 1982[b]	—
Ning-Ning (Gentle)	Female	2.5 years	19 April 1981[a]	28 Dec. 1981[b] 7 Jan. 1982	Transmission stopped 30 March 1982
No. 81	Male	2.5 years	21 Jan. 1982	16 Feb. 1982 27 Feb. 1982	—
Zhen-Zhen (Precious)	Female	Adult	13 March 1981[a]	21 March 1981 24 March 1981 25 March 1981 13 Jan. 1982 2 March 1982[b]	Panda removed collar 17 Sep. 1982
Han-Han (Lovely but Inept)	Female	Adult	11 Jan. 1982[a]	—	Died in poacher's snare 24 Jan. 1983
Wei-Wei (Grand)	Male	Adult	22 Dec. 1981[a]	6 Jan. 1982	—
Pi-Pi (Brave)	Male	Adult	5 Dec. 1982[a]	—	Pi is an ancient Chinese name for the panda

[a]First time radio-collared. [b]Collar changed.

TABLE 2.4

WEIGHTS (IN KG) AND MEASUREMENTS (IN CM) OF CAPTURED PANDAS

Name	Age and Sex	Date	Weight	Total length (over curve)	Chest circumference	Shoulder height	Tail
Long	Subadult male	10 March 1981	54.6	138	91	71	8
		30 Jan. 1982	70.0	162	—	—	15
No. 81	Subadult male	21 Jan. 1982	52.3	142	82	75	13
Wei	Adult male	22 Dec. 1981	—	176	—	84.5	10.5
		17 Oct. 1983	96.8	—	—	—	—
Pi	Adult male	5 Dec. 1981	106.7	—	—	—	16
Ning	Subadult female	19 April 1981	52.3	127±	—	—	12.5
		28 Dec. 1981	61.0	—	—	—	—
Zhen	Adult female	13 March 1981	86.4	166	104	81	13
		5 Dec. 1983	78.8	—	—	—	—
Han	Adult female	11 Jan. 1982	est. 95	165	99	86	15
—	Adult female[a]	8 April 1983	88.6	158	95	83	15

[a]Found dead in poacher's snare set for musk deer.

ing, she was vocal in the trap as well as aggressive, rearing up and at times swatting as we drew near. When caught again a year later, she seemed in better condition, and the tartar was gone from her teeth. She was more subdued then, shivering at our approach so violently that her teeth chattered. All pandas may bite at the wooden supports of the trap, but Zhen was exceptional in the diligence with which she splintered logs into chips.

Han-Han. Han was a large female in her prime, heavier than Zhen though we did not weigh her. Like Zhen, she was vocal and aggressive, but, unlike Zhen, her actions were charged with energy; she conveyed self-assurance.

Pi-Pi. Pi is the dominant male in the area, older than Wei-Wei, an impressively large animal with massive neck and shoulders. Although he roared at us a few times, he mostly sat quiet and detached in the trap.

Wei-Wei. Wei is a medium-sized male, considerably smaller than Pi and somewhat past his prime. When captured, he remained silent, cowed, sitting bowed with his muzzle tucked in by his hindfeet.

Much of the information in this report is based on these seven animals.

Summary

1. Wolong Natural Reserve comprises 2000 km^2 of rugged mountains at the eastern edge of the Tibetan highlands. Extending from an elevation of 1200 to 6250 m, the reserve supports several climatic zones. About half of the reserve lies above timberline, a habitat unsuitable for pandas. Four major forest types cover the slopes below timberline. The climate is cool and wet, with snow in winter and a monsoon from June to October.

2. About 145 pandas were found in the reserve during a 1974 census. Most animals inhabit forest between the elevation of 2600 and 3000 m, lower slopes often being avoided because of habitat destruction or steepness of terrain.

3. The study area comprises 35 km^2, covered below 2600 m with a mixed conifer and deciduous broad-leafed forest and above by a subalpine coniferous forest, both modified in many places by logging. Of the 7 native bamboo species in Wolong, only *Fargesia spathacea* and *Sinarundinaria fangiana* are common in the study area.

4. Two adult males, 2 adult females, and 2 independent subadults were captured, fitted with radio transmitters, and released. Much of the information in this report is based on these pandas.

3

Feeding Strategy

Everything an animal does requires energy. It expends energy on all basic metabolic requirements, such as digesting foods, pumping blood, and keeping warm in winter, and on its every action, whether it is standing still, scratching its head, or actively foraging. Such energy is needed just for basic maintenance. Additional energy is required for growth—growth of muscle, deposition of fat, fetal development, milk production. Balanced against these demands is the energy obtained by an animal from its food. The health of individuals and populations ultimately depends on whether energy intake is below, equal to, or above the needed expenditures. An animal's feeding adaptations and strategies determine how it meets its requirements.

Omnivores and carnivores eat meat, fruits, and seeds—all foods rich in protein, lipids, and starches. Such foods are easily broken down and assimilated by the body, and the animals therefore have simple stomachs and relatively short, unmodified intestines to process them. Herbivores, subsisting on grasses, leaves, and stems, have a diet not only relatively low in nutrients but also difficult to digest. Plants have two main components when viewed from the standpoint of herbivore digestion (Van Soest 1975, 1977): the cell content with its soluble nutrients, and the cell wall with its tough, fibrous components of cellulose, hemicellulose, and lignin. Cell content is almost all available to an animal once the cell wall has been broken down, and presents no special digestive problem. Herbivores, however, lack the enzymes necessary to break down cellulose and hemicellulose—both of them structural polysaccharides—in the cell wall. To use the structural part of the plant as food, a herbivore must form a symbiotic relationship with certain bacteria and protozoans that can degrade cellulose and hemicellulose by fermentation. Fermentation takes time, making it essential that herbivores retain food in the digestive tract. To slow food passage and to provide gastrointestinal microbes with a fermentation site are two basic requirements of an efficient herbivore. Two different systems have evolved. Horses, rhinoceroses, elephants, and hares, for example, have a modified hindgut with a saclike cecum and enlarged colon that store, ferment, and absorb nutrients. Cattle, deer, and other ruminants are even more specialized in that the foregut has, in effect, become a vat where food is fermented before passing into the stomach for further digestion by enzymes. Microbes digest cellulose and hemicellulose; and, using nitrogen, they synthesize amino acids, which a herbivore can

47

assimilate. Lignin, the third main component of plant cell wall, is indigestible (Parra 1978).

Now consider the panda's potential problems in meeting its nutritional requirements. The panda has retained the simple digestive tract of a carnivore: it lacks a special chamber to retain food, and it has no symbiotic microbes to ferment cellulose into available nutrients. The longer food remains in the digestive tract, the more fully will it be utilized; thus a long intestine, as found in herbivores, might benefit the panda. A deer, for example, has an intestine about 15 times as long as its body, and a sheep 25 times (Short 1981); a carnivore generally has intestines 4 to 8 times as long (Davis 1964). On the basis of measurements of single individuals, the panda has intestines 4.1 (Davis 1964), 5.5 (Raven 1936), 6.1 (this study), and 7.7 (Hu Jinchu, pers. obs.) times as long as its body, suggesting a short retention time of food. The length of intestinal villi—small processes that serve in the absorption of nutrients—are typically long in carnivores and short in ungulates. They may exceed 1000 μ in panda, 960 μ in cat, and 645 μ in dog, as compared with 400 μ or less in horse and cow (Wang et al. 1982). The panda's digestive tract lacks physical and physiological adaptations for processing a bulky, herbivorous diet. Unable to extract nutrients from cellulose, it has to depend mainly on cell content for needed energy.

Given such constraints, there are still ways in which an animal can adapt. Such species as koala, three-toed sloth, and domestic goat eat mainly leaves that have a high cell wall content and therefore a low available caloric density; that is, they must eat much bulk to obtain relatively little energy. They appear to have adapted to nutrient-poor foods by lowering their basal metabolic rate somewhat (McNab 1978), and we wonder whether this may also be true of pandas. Forage varies in quality throughout the year, protein and other nutrients being highest and fiber content lowest in the growing parts of the plant. An animal can select for such highly digestible and nutritious food as buds, young leaves, and shoots. But such items grow scattered and are time-consuming to pluck; a panda with its large body might be unable to collect enough food for its daily needs. Besides, there could be a paradox, for succulent food has a low retention time, and the panda, with its short digestive tract, might have to increase its consumption rate even more. An animal usually has but two options: to retain food long enough to extract the maximum amount of energy possible at the expense of food intake, or to select food of high quality at the cost of extra feeding time (Van Soest 1980).

Food intake, digestibility, nutritive value, and retention time are all related. Somehow the panda has worked out a balance between its required energy consumption and the time needed to process bulky food; it has worked out a strategy for living as a herbivore while retaining the alimentary characteristics of a carnivore. With such problems in mind, our aim was to find out how the panda achieved such a balance.

Food habits

Bamboos belong to the Gramineae family but differ from typical grasses in having woody stems, complex branching at the nodes, an extensive rhizome system, and a flowering cycle that may exceed 50 years. Although bamboos are widely distributed, especially in the tropics and subtropics, few wild mammals subsist on this locally abundant food source. Those which forage mainly on bamboo leaves or stems include an arboreal rodent (*Hapalomys longicaudatus*) and the fossorial bamboo rat (*Rhizomys*), both from Southeast Asia; an African monkey (*Cercopithecus mitis kandti*); a lemur (*Hapalemur*); the red panda; and importantly, the giant panda (Musser 1972; Schaller 1963; Petter and Peyrieras 1975). That the giant panda eats bamboo almost exclusively in the wild has been noted repeatedly (Sheldon 1937; Wang and Lu 1973; Hu 1981c). McClure (1943) lists nine bamboo species that are palatable to captives, and Chu and Long (1983) list 25 species that are eaten in the wild. Only a few species, however, are widespread at the high altitudes where pandas now survive. There are, for example, 5 common species in the Liang Mountains and only one in parts of the Min Mountains. Taking the panda's present range as a whole, *Fargesia spathacea*, *Sinarundinaria chungii*, *S. nitida*, and *S. fangiana* are the most important foods, although others, such as *Phyllostachys*, *Indocalamus*, and *Chimonobambusa*, may become locally significant. Leaves, branches, stems, and shoots provide food for pandas; rhizomes are not pulled or dug up.

Pandas occasionally eat plants other than bamboo. Animals in the Min Mountains have been reported to forage on leaves, stems, and bark of a variety of plants, especially after the bamboo die-off in the mid-1970s, including *Equisetum hiemale*; a water weed (*Potamogeton*); herbs (*Ligusticum sinense, Heracleum caudianus, Aster alpina, Allium, Saussurea, Notopterygium, Houtinyxia cordata*); a vine (*Actinidia*); shrubs (*Salix magnifica, Rubus setchuenensis*); and trees (*Juniperus, Picea asperata, Ilex franchetiana, Litsea szechuanica, Hydrangea rosthornii*) (Chu and Long 1983). In our study area, a wild parsnip (*Angelica* sp.) was eaten a number of times, and the remains of a tree fungus (*Polyporaceae*) were found in droppings. On three occasions, a panda clawed and bit bark from a conifer—a hemlock, a fir, and a pine—and perhaps ate the cambium layer, as reported for black bear (Poelker and Hartwell 1973). Such behavior has also been noted in the Min and Liang Mountains (Hu 1981c). A captive at the Chengdu zoo plucked and ate three kinds of grasses; other captives at Yingxionggou ate grass (*Deyeuxia scabrescens*) and leaves from a shrub (*Buddleia davidii*). Excluding bamboo, pandas are now known to eat over 25 wild plant species, usually only in small amounts, however. Over 99% of their food consists of bamboo.

Villagers informed the Giant Panda Expedition (1974) of having found "the remains of small rodents" in the stomachs of wild pandas. We were told in Wolong that a panda was observed as it caught a bamboo rat; and we found hair of golden monkey in one dropping. In the Wanglang reserve, we noted hair, bones, and hooves of musk deer in the droppings of one panda. The animals in our study area had an obvious predilection for the meat in our traps, consuming bones, hair, and skin, as well as flesh. Four of seven captives at Yingxionggou immediately ate some offered mutton. The panda's dentition, though apparently designed for crushing bamboo, is also well suited to crunching bones. The fact that pandas seldom catch or scavenge animals probably indicates a lack of opportunity rather than preference. Potential prey in the Choushuigou is scarce. Only the young of muskdeer, tufted deer, and other ungulates would be vulnerable to the relatively slow-moving panda. Bamboo rats are uncommon as well as being largely fossorial. Large predators are rare, leaving few kill remains to scavenge. And striped squirrels (80 g), *Rattus niviventer* (70 g), and *Apodemus* mice (20 g) offer too small a reward compared to the time and energy required to search for and capture them.

Two of Zhen's droppings contained much gray, claylike soil. At Yingxionggou, the captive Ja-Jia ate similar soil in her outdoor enclosure. Sitting or lying on her side, she raked the slope with a forepaw, then balled up the mud in her palm and ate it.

The koala and panda are often cited as examples of extreme food specialization. Indeed, the koala's physiology appears so adapted to a diet of *Eucalyptus* leaves that the animal cannot change readily to more conventional food (Eberhard 1978). Pandas have obviously specialized on bamboo in various ways, but they remain essentially omnivores; their dependence on bamboo reflects mainly the lack of a large alternative food supply, especially in winter, rather than an inability to assimilate other foods.

Feeding behavior

Since feeding techniques depend somewhat on the age of bamboo, the different age classes require brief description. *Sinarundinaria* and *Fargesia* produce shoots mainly between April and June. Growing rapidly out of the ground, shoots soon emerge from their enveloping sheaths, and most reach their full height during July or August. We refer to shoots during this growth stage as "*new* shoots." From July and August to about the following May, shoots remain easy to identify, and we refer to them as "*old* shoots." Old *Sinarundinaria* shoots consist solely of a stem with a sheath at each node and a few leaves at the top; there are no branches other than occasional short stubs. By contrast, *Fargesia* stems branch and leaf out during the first summer. These branches do not fork, the stem is dark green, and sheaths may adhere to nodes, all characters identifying this age class.

Sinarundinaria stems usually grow branches during their second season, and *Fargesia* branches fork at that time. Such two-year stems, as we called them, have few branches, and these fork less often than do those of stems older than two years. Furthermore, stems are not as yellow as old ones, and their tops are seldom broken. However, considerable error was made in distinguishing two-year from old stems in both species, as shown when various workers sampled biomass (see table 3.14). Early in 1981, a total of 11.6% of the *Sinarundinaria* stems were old shoots. These shoots would advance one age class in August. Sampling late in the year gave 26.1% two-year-olds, over double the expected figure. Consequently, this report generally uses three age categories—new shoot, old shoot, and stem. In certain instances, as in the collection of samples for nutritional analysis when unambigous stems were collected, we divide bamboo into four classes—new shoot, old shoot, two-year stem, and old stem. Two-year stems are one to two years old.

These descriptions of age categories apply only to the Choushuigou, not to other areas where bamboo may have different patterns of growth. For example, in the Jiuzhaigou and Wanglang reserves, where climatic conditions are more severe than at Wolong, most new shoots do not appear until June or later and do not branch and leaf out until the following spring.

Feeding on stems and leaves

A panda usually sits and hooks in a suitable *Sinarundinaria* stem with the curved claws of a forepaw, holds it, and, bending it sideways, bites it off, sometimes as close as 3 cm from the base. The height of the remaining stump may depend on whether it is an old shoot or stem. Generally, stump height averages 15–25 cm. But sometimes a panda concentrates on the tops of old shoots, leaving stumps averaging about 81 cm in height (table 3.1); Schäfer (1938) reported stumps of 20–40 cm.

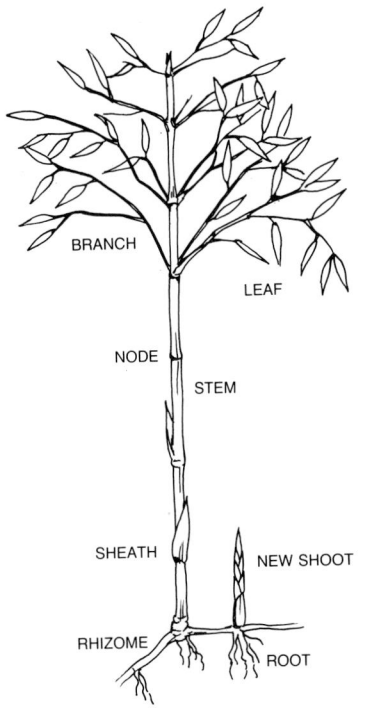

Sitting or half lying on its back, a panda pushes the stem at right angles into the corner of its mouth and takes one or more rapid bites from it (plate 3.1). The average number of such bites is 3.0 ± 1.3, as determined by observation of captives. While biting, the animal jerks the forepaw holding the stem up and down and lifts its head slightly, actions which help to sever pieces 2–5 cm long. Then it gives each mouthful an average of 6.7 ± 2.3 chews, very few considering the woodiness of the food. If a sheath adheres to a node, the panda detaches it, using incisors or premolars. Captives may pick up and eat 2 or 3 stems simultaneously; one animal we observed bit an old shoot into four sections and, holding all together in a forepaw, consumed them. A panda tends to eat a stem only up to the branches, discarding the leafy top, but once in a while it bites off branches and ingests them also. It seldom peels the tough outside of a *Sinarundinaria* stem. When it does, however, the animal bites into the base of the stem with incisors or into the side with premolars and tears off strips by simultaneously twisting paw and head in opposite directions. Canines are seldom used on the thin stems. A panda eats on the average between 25 and 30 cm of a stem, though on occasion it may eat almost all of it. In the miscellaneous January–March sample and the April samples of table 3.1, the panda ate significantly more from an old shoot than from a stem (chi-square test, $p < 0.05$), probably because the former is more nutritious and, lacking branches, easier to eat than the latter. One captive required an average of 39.1 ± 16.6 seconds to eat the selected parts of an old shoot ($N = 84$) as compared to 47.8 ± 36.2 seconds for a stem ($N = 23$), statistically an insignificant difference.

When eating leaves, the panda grabs one or more stems with a forepaw, bends them and bites off leaves and branch tips. Or it holds a stem with one paw and with the other pushes the leafy branches into its mouth. Sometimes it chews immediately; more commonly, it clips off leaves until a large bouquet has accumulated in the corner of the mouth. Then, taking these leaves with one paw, it bites off mouthfuls and chews. One captive pulled leafy tops rapidly sideways through its mouth three to six times before eating, as if ridding them of debris or concentrating leaves for easy consumption. An intensively used feeding site has a characteristic appearance: the branch tips are neatly pruned as if clipped by shears.

Since pandas frequently bite off *Fargesia* stems not to eat but to make leaves

PLATE 3.1   Half sitting and half lying, a captive subadult takes a bite from a wad of leaves in its forepaw.

TABLE 3.1

CALCULATED LENGTHS OF *Sinarundinaria* STEM EATEN BY PANDA ($\bar{x} \pm SD$)

	Date	Stump length N	Stump length cm	Top length N	Top length cm	Sample uneaten stem N	Sample uneaten stem cm	Amount eaten/cm	Remarks
Old shoot	19 Jan. 1981	70	81.3 ±24.3	—		25	137.1 ±25.4	55.8	Wei; ate tops only
	9 March 1981	43	21.7 ±10.6	49	78.1 ±23.5	19	190.1 ±22.2	90.3	Probably a subadult; ate middle of stem
	Jan.–March 1981	468	25.6 ±18.0	342	92.7 ±35.7	93	170.2 ±29.6	51.9	Miscellaneous sample
	27 April 1981	—	14.7*	12	87.3 ±23.9	6	141.0 ±25.4	39.0	Zhen feeding site
	22 April 1982	35	14.7 ± 5.9	18	85.7 ±26.2	18	136.0 ±27.3	36.2	Zhen; same site as previous year
Stem	Jan.–March 1981		as above	171	92.3 ±39.4	16	154.0 ±31.1	36.4	Miscellaneous sample
	27 April 1981		as above	20	76.1 ±23.7	15	118.7 ±20.3	27.9	Zhen feeding site
	22 April 1982		as above	71	80.2 ±25.6	40	124.0 ±20.7	29.1	Zhen; same site as previous year

*Figure for April 22 used as average stump length.

accessible, it was at times difficult for us to determine whether stem had also been consumed (plate 3.2). However, stump height generally indicated why the stem had been detached. In winter, when pandas ate mainly leaves, average stump height was 67.5 ± 29.5 ($N = 82$), whereas in May and June, when stem was the only food, it was 38.4 ± 14.1 ($N = 121$). Average stump height of *Fargesia* in spring was more than double that of *Sinarundinaria*. We doubt that this difference is related to nutrition (see table B.6 in appendix B); it may be that pandas avoid the thickest part of the *Fargesia* stem. *Fargesia* is stripped of branches, sometimes peeled, and eaten in the manner of *Sinarundinaria*. The animal takes an average of $2.3 \pm .98$ quick bites and chews these 6.8 ± 1.8 times, figures similar to those for *Sinarundinaria* in spite of the fact that most *Fargesia* stems are twice as thick. We are uncertain how much of a stem is consumed. Our calculated average length for May and June is 3 cm, probably too low a figure because *Fargesia* stems vary so much in length that our sample of

PLATE 3.2   Wang Menghu examines a panda feeding site showing *Fargesia* stumps surrounded by discarded tops.

measured stems was too small. A captive spent an average of 82.2 ± 35.8 seconds on each of 9 stems.

To reach leaves above its head, a panda either bites off the stem or bends it. Sometimes it uses both paws, hand over hand, to pull a stem over, and then lies on its back, keeping the stem from springing erect by clutching it with the hindpaws, while the forepaws manipulate the leaves into the mouth, much as described for *Sinarundinaria*. Collins and Page (1973) described how a captive subadult straddled a stem and walked along its length, bending it until it could reach the leaves. Bent *Fargesia* stems usually snap erect after a panda has fed. Since browsed stems are often scattered, there may be little evidence of foraging unless a panda bit off or splintered a stem while pulling it over. Of 590 browsed stems sampled, 18.1% had so been broken.

The amount of time a panda spends feeding at a particular site varies considerably. Sometimes it may virtually eat a swath through bamboo, its route marked without interruption by debris and browsed stems. For example, in 186 m of feeding trail, Wei in one 24-hour period during winter foraged on a calculated 3481 *Sinarundinaria* stems, or 18.7 per meter (see fig. 4.8). At times, feeding sites are well spaced, even though the panda is engulfed by potential food—leaves and stem within reach all around and above. When tracking pandas in snow, we recorded distances between 134 *Sinarundinaria* feeding sites and between 68 *Fargesia* feeding sites, arbitrarily limiting our calculations to sites 25 m or less apart. Average distance between *Sinarundinaria* sites was 6.6 ± 5.9 m, and between *Fargesia* sites 9.0 ± 6.1 m. Average number of stems eaten per site was 3.8 for both species, with many seemingly palatable stems left untouched at each site and between sites. In a day's foraging, a panda may switch repeatedly between intensive foraging in one area and sporadic foraging at well-spaced sites. One traveling subadult ate only occasionally, but then, on entering a swale with tall but relatively sparse bamboo, it consumed 78 stems in 13 m before resuming its intermittent foraging.

Pandas in the Qinling Mountains eat *Phyllostachys** much as they do *Fargesia* in our study area, judging by Yong's (1981) descriptions. Yong found that the animals bite off or bend over stems to eat leaves, plucking them with a paw or the mouth. Having collected a bunch, they eat the leaves, taking half a minute to chew a mouthful. After eating on 3–5 stems at one site, the animal moves to another.

Feeding on new *Fargesia* shoots

New shoots are available for only a short period each year. High in protein (tables B.5 and B.6), they might be expected to be a favored panda food. Yet only *Fargesia* shoots are sought, those of *Sinarundinaria* perhaps being too thin and light (4–10 g) to justify searching time. *Fargesia* shoots are at times an exclusive food, whereas *Sinarundinaria* shoots remain only a casual item.

In 1981, we noted the first new *Fargesia* shoot on 22 April. Zhen began to subsist on shoots near Wuyipeng on 28 April and continued to do so until 20 June, when she

*This identification remains uncertain; the bamboo may be *Fargesia*, according to Hu Jinchu.

<small>PLATE</small> 3.3   The female Zhen sits while she eats a new *Fargesia* shoot.

moved back up into *Sinarundinaria*; at least two other pandas foraged for shoots in the same area as Zhen. In 1982, the first new *Fargesia* shoot was seen on 17 April, but Zhen delayed her descent until 15 May. Han, Wei, and another panda were also in *Fargesia* for the shoot season, and, as in the previous year, all switched back to *Sinarundinaria* around the end of June. By then the new shoots had grown tall and hard, obviously less palatable.

Growth of new *Fargesia* shoots is rapid, up to 18 cm a day. Excluding shoots that later died of insect damage, the average growth rate of 29 shoots in 1981 was a slow 2.9 cm per day from late April to mid-May, but a rapid 7.9 cm between late May to mid-June. Growth curves of four representative shoots in figure 3.1 show that by the age of about 50 days, shoots have almost reached their final height. There was an abrupt growth spurt at one point, on days 9 and 10, two days before the onset of rain; otherwise shoots had highly individualistic growth curves.

Sitting or standing, a panda may simply break a shoot off with a forepaw, severing it at a node (plate 3.3). It may also take a shoot between its teeth, jerk up its head, and at the same time push away the shoot with a forepaw, snapping it off. As the base of a shoot becomes wooden, it breaks less readily, and the panda then bites the shoot off as it would a stem. Once Zhen leaned far back, hooked a distant tall shoot with the claws of one paw, bent it in, grabbed it with the other paw, and bit it off, all in one fluid motion.

Shoots less than about 30 cm tall may be eaten whole, hairy sheaths and all. Usually, however, the panda removes sheaths in one of two ways. Holding the shoot at a slant in the mouth, it bites into the tightly adhering sheath with the anterior premolars or, rarely, the canines and, with mouth pulling sideways and forepaw jerking down and twisting, tears away the sheath and drops it. A sheath sometimes extends over the edge of the broken node, and the panda pinches the protruding part with the incisors and jerks its head up and paw down, pulling the sheath off. Then the animal eats the shoot, much as it would a stem, taking a few rapid bites, detaching sheaths, constantly switching from one side of the mouth to the other. A captive took an average of 2.1 ± 1.4 rapid bites before chewing 4.3 ± 0.12 times and swallowing; it chewed significantly less than when eating stem (t test, $p < 0.0001$). The bites often crush rather than sever pieces of shoot, as shown by wads of fiber up to 20 cm long in droppings. We collected a random sample of 73 shoots and peeled them as a panda would. The edible portion constituted 62.8 ± 6.0% by weight.

A panda may eat a 50-cm shoot in 20 seconds, and one of 150 cm in 70 seconds. Between 18 and 20 May, we fed the captive Ping-Ping 77 shoots with an average diameter of 1.4 ± 0.21 (range 0.9–1.8) cm and average length of 63.8 ± 29.7 (range 26–156) cm, measurements typical of shoots in the wild, except that we had eliminated short and thin shoots, which pandas generally disdain. Average eating time was 36.6 ± 20.8 (range 10–110) seconds per shoot, but average total time per shoot, including activities other than preparing and eating the shoot, was 50 seconds (table 3.7). Pandas in the wild eat just as rapidly: in our study 14 shoots were consumed, on the average, in 36.5 ± 10.1 seconds. Of course, an animal must spend time searching for shoots, and it sometimes stops feeding to scratch, defecate, or just sit. On one occasion in late May, Zhen ate 65 shoots between 0630 and 0805 hours, and on another occasion 60 shoots between 0855 and 1035, or an average of one shoot every 93.6 seconds.

After eating one shoot, the panda glances around and, if another suitable one is within reach, plucks it, reaching as far as 1–1½ m without leaving its seat. At times a panda collects a shoot 2–3 m away and returns to its former place. A feeding site is characteristically littered with sheaths, pieces of tough shoot, and discarded tops, and is surrounded by stumps (plate 3.4). Stump height varies with the age of the shoot. Young shoots break near or even below ground level. When about 75–100 cm tall, the lower part of the shoot begins to emerge from the sheaths and quickly becomes hard and woody. The panda breaks off tender tops, leaving progressively taller stumps as shoots mature (fig. 3.1).

In 1982, we established 32 plots totaling 62m² in which we noted shoot emergence during May and June, the time most shoots appear and almost all feeding on shoots takes place. We checked plots at about weekly intervals. Of the 285 shoots that emerged during this period, 7.4% had appeared by 2 May, 42.8% by 9 May, 79.3% by 16 May, 93.0% by 23 May, and 97.2% by 30 May. Since pandas avoid eating very small shoots, it was only after mid-May that shoots reached maximum abundance as a food source. The average number eaten at 929 feeding sites in 1981 was 2.04 before 15 May and 2.97 after that date, suggesting greater availability later in the season. Between 17 May and 4 June 1982, pandas consumed an average of 3.6 shoots (range 1–16) at each of 186 feeding sites, as compared to 2.7 shoots for the same period a year earlier. There were also more than twice as many sites with one shoot eaten in

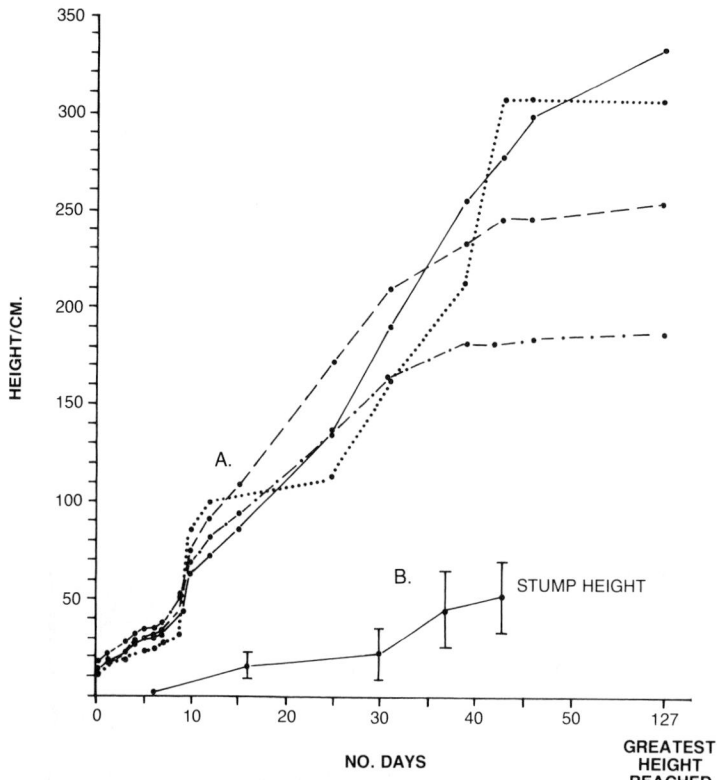

FIGURE 3.1   A. Growth rate of 4 selected new *Fargesia* shoots in 1981.   B. Average stump height of new *Fargesia* shoots after a panda has broken off the top. As the shoot grows older and more fibrous, a panda leaves a progressively taller stump.

1981 as in 1982 (fig. 3.2). These numbers reflect greater shoot abundance in the latter year. After finishing at one site, the panda shifts to another nearby. On the basis of 710 measurements, the average distance between feeding sites, including an occasional walk of up to 20 m between adjoining bamboo patches, was 2.8 ± 2.1 m in 1981 and 2.3 ± 1.6 m in 1982, showing that a panda needs to expend little energy in search of shoots.

When watching a panda eat leaves, stem or new shoots we were always impressed by its dexterity. Forepaws and mouth work together with great precision, with great economy of motion, as the food is grasped, plucked, peeled, stripped, bitten and otherwise prepared for being swallowed. Actions are fluid and rapid, as if the animal has little time—behavior true even of captives.

The question remains how a panda chooses a particular food item among the many available. Zhen obviously glanced around and then reached for shoots; and captives picked certain stems from the bundles provided them, using sight to select.

However, a panda often sniffed a new shoot or stem at one or more places before eating, and sometimes discarded it; Schneider (1939) also mentioned such
sniffing. It seems likely that scent is important in the final selection of an item,
especially at night, when in a thicket it may be difficult visually to distinguish a shoot
from a stem. One night we observed Zhen in the weak beam of a flashlight as she
foraged for new shoots. She walked slowly, moving her muzzle low among the stems
as if searching by scent, behavior different from that in daytime. Then, on finding a
shoot, she detached it in the usual manner and sat to eat. Occasionally a panda bit
into a stem before dropping it, taste or toughness probably being the final criterion in
the selection process.

Food selection

At first glance the panda's food supply appears inexhaustible, with stems and
leaves in abundance throughout the year. That a panda may consume various parts
of the plant was noted long ago by Jacobi (1923) and recently by Yong (1981). Little

PLATE 3.4   When harvesting new *Fargesia* shoots, a panda breaks off the tender tops, leaving
stumps standing, and discards the sheaths before eating the juicy center.

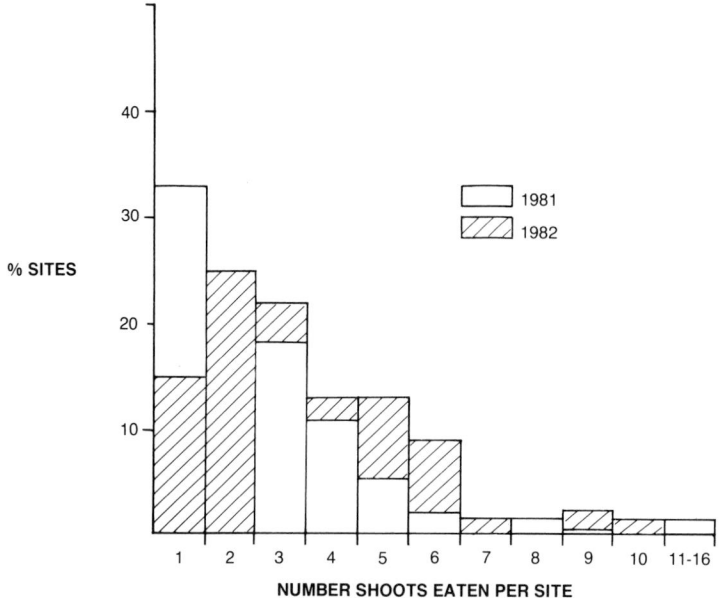

% SITES

NUMBER SHOOTS EATEN PER SITE

FIGURE 3.2   Number of new *Fargesia* shoots eaten by pandas at each feeding site. Data were collected between 17 May and 10 June and are based on 632 sites in 1981 and 186 sites in 1982.

is known, however, about how selectively pandas harvest their resources. Do they prefer one bamboo species over another? Do they select stems of a certain age? Do they take more leaf or more stem? Since such questions are basic to panda ecology, we attempted to find answers by analyzing droppings and examining feeding sites.

Both *Fargesia* and *Sinarundinaria* were easily accessible to pandas in the study area, yet the amount of time they spent in each varied greatly. All pandas confined themselves to *Sinarundinaria* for much of the year; they visited *Fargesia* only during the months when new shoots were available and in transit from one slope to another. Several pandas even remained in *Sinarundinaria* for much of the new shoot season. For instance, Ning visited *Fargesia* in the Zhuanjinggou for only about a week in June 1981, and Long did not descend at all in 1982, to our knowledge. Wei occasionally traveled through *Fargesia*, as on 22 December and 3 April, and he fed there on new shoots for 6 days in May and 8 in June 1982. Taking one 12-month period, Zhen spent 14.5% of her days in *Fargesia*, Long 4.1%, and Wei 4.9%. Zhen was in *Fargesia* more than the other two, a difference possibly related to sex and age. Judging by the radio-collared animals, adult females forage in *Fargesia* more persistently than do adult males and subadults, perhaps because, when pregnant, they seek the high level of nutrition provided by new shoots in spring. Nevertheless, the pandas spent over 85% of their time in *Sinarundinaria*, making this by far the most important food species. It remains unclear why *Fargesia* is not much used. Nutrition, physiognomy of the plant, topography, human interference (resident animals at low altitudes having been eliminated), or a combination of these factors may be involved. Certainly *Fargesia* sp. is an adequate food source, pandas in the Jiuzhaigou reserve and some other areas subsisting entirely on it.

Selection for stems and leaves

Droppings show whether a panda selects for a certain part of the plant. We collected a monthly sample of droppings, oven-dried it, separated stems (including old shoot) from leaves, and weighed each portion. Since an animal chews its food relatively little and its digestive tract cannot break down cellulose, stems and leaves pass through intact enough that we could separate most leaf from stem manually. However, a panda grinds a part of the stem into dust, which is difficult to separate from leaf fragments. Droppings containing only stem revealed that 8.6% by weight consists of such dust, and our calculations have been adjusted accordingly.

Our examination of 399 droppings revealed that, in the annual *Sinarundinaria* diet, the proportion of stem to leaf differed markedly from month to month even though both stems and leaves remained abundant throughout the year (fig. 3.3). From November to March, pandas selected both stems and leaves. Starting in late March or early April, they switched abruptly to stems and seldom ate leaves until after mid-June. By July, leaves again contributed much to the diet, and from August to October, pandas ate little else (fig. 3.4).

A total of 36 *Fargesia* droppings were collected between January and March,

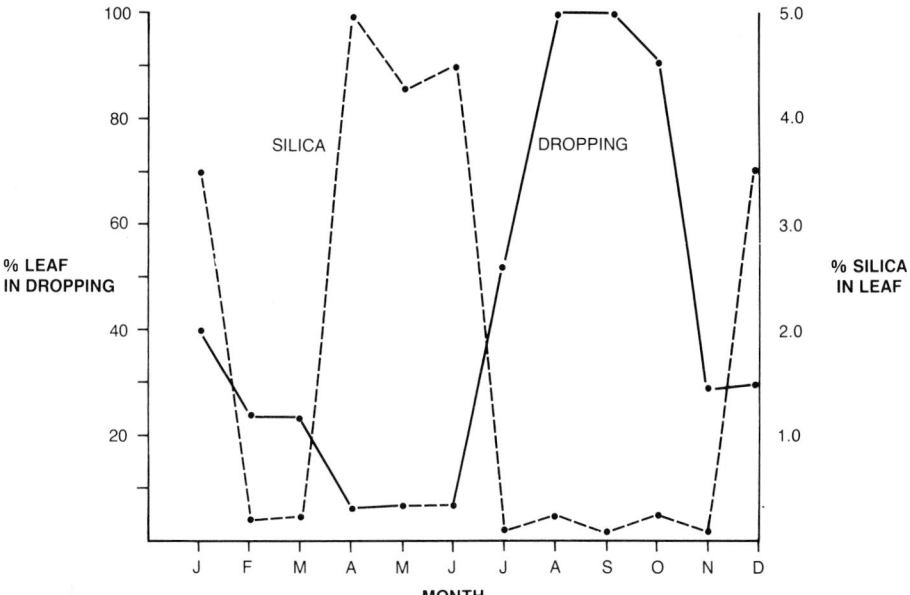

FIGURE 3.3 Percentage of *Sinarundinaria* leaves in panda droppings each month compared to the average silica content of fresh leaves that month. (The June droppings were inspected only visually—not dried and weighed as in other months—and the percentage of leaf content was estimated.)

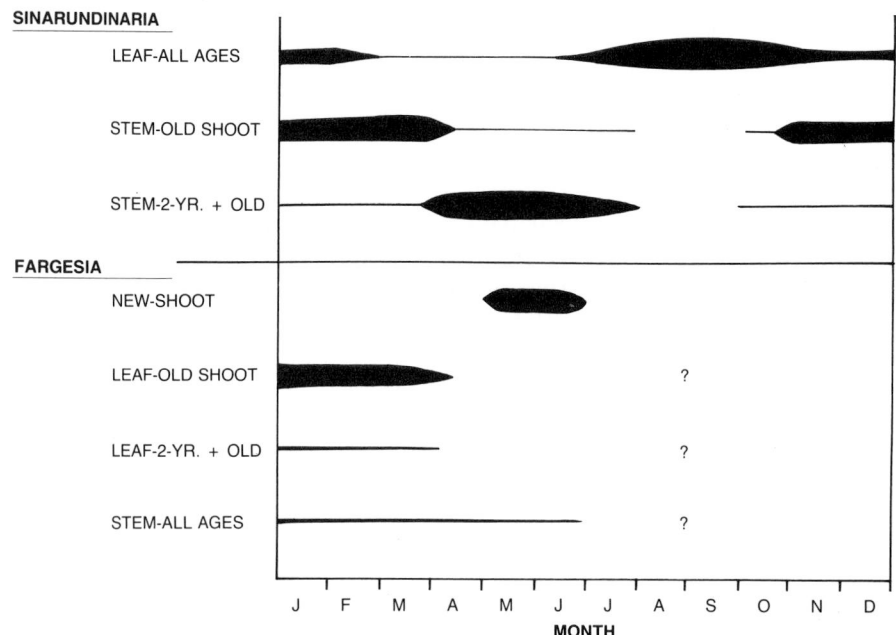

FIGURE 3.4   The different parts of *Sinarundinaria* and *Fargesia* eaten by pandas each month. The thickness of the black bars represents the relative importance of that part in the diet during the month.

containing 75.0% leaf and 25% stem, as compared with only 27.8% leaf in the droppings of *Sinarundinaria* for the same period. By late April, pandas wholly ignored leaves in favor of stems and new shoots, a preference that continued into June. Of 1001 *Fargesia* droppings examined during this period, 93.5% consisted solely of new shoot and 6.5% contained at least some stem; only 5.6% by weight of the droppings was stem. We lack information on *Fargesia* forage selection during summer and autumn.

Next, we sought to determine whether pandas prefer stems and leaves of a particular age. By examining bamboo tops discarded at feeding sites, we noted that in winter the animals favored old *Sinarundinaria* shoots (79.5%) over other stems (20.5%) (table 3.2). With only 12–15% of the available stems being old shoots (see table 3.14), selection for this age class is strong. For example, one animal ate 164 stems of all ages in a 150 m^2 area, 156 of them old shoots; and another ate 209 stems while traveling, 178 of them old shoots. We also attempted to separate two-year from older stems, and judged that 46.4% belonged in the former age class. The actual percentage of two-year-olds in the bamboo population was about 15% (Campbell et al. 1983). Even given an unknown margin of error in classification, pandas apparently ate two-year-olds in disproportionately large numbers. By mid-April, pandas had ceased to select for old shoots (table 3.2), apparently taking any stems within reach. One animal, for instance, tracked for 239 m on April 7, had eaten 128 stems of all ages, only 3 of them old shoots.

When eating *Sinarundinaria* leaves, a panda often grabbed several stems and seemed to bite off leaves indiscriminately. During September and October we classified 851 stems whose leaves had been eaten; among these were 3.1% old shoots, 24.3% two-year-olds, and 72.6% old stems, showing no striking selection.

In winter, pandas ate some *Fargesia* stem but favored leaves, harvesting 69.6% old shoots, 18% two-year stems, and 12.3% other stems as food. Since old shoots constituted about 13% of the population (table 3.14) and two-year stems around 20% (Campbell et al. 1983), pandas selected strongly for old shoots and against old stems. We estimated the percentage of leaves cropped from 166 stems—81.8 ± 14.9% from old shoots, 37.6 ± 22.7% from two-year stems, and 25.6 ± 14.9% from other stems; pandas again showed a preference for the leaves of old shoots. In April, pandas switched from old shoots to stems and at the same time ignored leaves, a change similar to that for *Sinarundinaria*; at that season, only 4.1% of the stems eaten were from old shoots.

Selection for new *Fargesia* shoots

In 1981 we noted that pandas did not select new *Fargesia* shoots randomly. They often foraged along the periphery of thickets rather than in the interior, and they left uneaten shoots behind at feeding sites. To provide an unbiased sample of shoots available to pandas, we established in 1982 a total of 83 plots—1, 2, or 2.25 m² in size—throughout the *Fargesia* zone. About one-third of the 176.75 m² total bordered an open area, such as a trail or clearing. We checked the plots at intervals in May and June, recording shoot emergence, shoot diameter at base, proximity of shoots to an open area, and causes of death. The plots had produced 723 shoots, or 4.1 per m², by the end of June. In addition, another 27 shoots, most of them thin, appeared in July, and 20 more between August and mid-September, a minor peak that raised the total to 770 shoots, or 4.4 per m² for the season (J. Campbell, pers. comm.). Since the new July–September shoots became available after pandas left the area, they are not included in the calculations except where stated.

To ascertain whether pandas select for shoots of a particular diameter, we compared uneaten shoots with those eaten by pandas and insects. In general, pandas ate fewer thin shoots, 0.9 cm or less in diameter, than expected ($p < 0.001$); disproportionately many shoots in the 1.0–1.2 cm size class ($p < 0.001$); and also

TABLE 3.2

AGE CLASSES OF STEMS (EXCLUDING LEAVES) SELECTED AS FOOD BY PANDAS AT DIFFERENT TIMES OF YEAR

Species	Months	Stems sampled	Old shoot (%)	Other stems (%)
Sinarundinaria	Nov.–March	3,295	79.5	20.5
	April–July	2,624	6.6	93.4
Fargesia	Dec.–March	107	69.6	30.4
	April–June	316	4.1	95.9

many thick ones, those 1.3 cm and above, but not in significantly larger numbers (table 3-3; fig. 3.5). It takes at least as much effort and time to remove the sheaths from a thin shoot as from a thick one but with less return in energy, probably one reason for this selectivity.

We also noticed that pandas generally do not eat short shoots, those less than 25 cm long. Length preference was tested as follows: we measured the length of all shoots not eaten by pandas within a 1 m radius of feeding sites, and then measured shoots at random in nearby places where a panda had not foraged. Three samples revealed that pandas left behind short shoots (all diameters) significantly more often than expected, and that they preferred tall shoots with a diameter of 1.0 cm or more (table 3.4). Short shoots consist almost entirely of sheath; by weighing 45 shoots we determined that the ratio of sheath to core is about 2:1 by weight in short shoots of more than 1 cm in diameter, whereas it is 1:2 in long ones. Some of the long shoots not eaten by pandas are thin, not a preferred size, but others are thick, and we can only speculate that the panda overlooked them, especially at night.

Next, we wanted to find out why pandas often forage along the edge of bamboo stands or in small patches (fig. 3.6), rather than in the interior of large thickets. Our plots showed that shoot density per m^2 within one meter of the edge was nearly

TABLE 3.3

DIAMETERS OF NEW *Fargesia* SHOOTS AVAILABLE COMPARED WITH THOSE EATEN BY PANDAS AND INSECTS, MAY–JUNE 1982

	Shoot diameter class / cm				
	< 0.6	0.7–0.9	1.0–1.2	1.3–1.5	> 1.6
Random sample	68	118	183	217	137
Eaten by pandas	4	86	388	356	240
Eaten by insects	24	89	60	27	8
Panda					
W	0.009	0.116	0.336	0.260	0.278
E	−0.911	−0.266	0.254	0.130	0.163
P	<0.001	<0.001	<0.001	<0.500	0.250
use	*np	*np	*p	p	p
Insect					
W	0.217	0.467	0.202	0.077	0.036
E	0.041	0.400	0.005	−0.444	−0.693
P	<0.950	<0.001	<0.950	<0.001	<0.001
use	p	*p	p	*np	*np

W = Vanderploeg and Scavia's selectivity coefficient with values above 0.2 indicating preference.
E = Vanderploeg and Scavia's electivity index with values on a continuum (− 1 avoidance, 0 random, + 1 prefer-
    ence).
P = probability that selection deviated from random (X^2, 4df); statistics based on Lechowicz (1982).
np = not preferred.
p = preferred.
* = Indicates statistical significance.

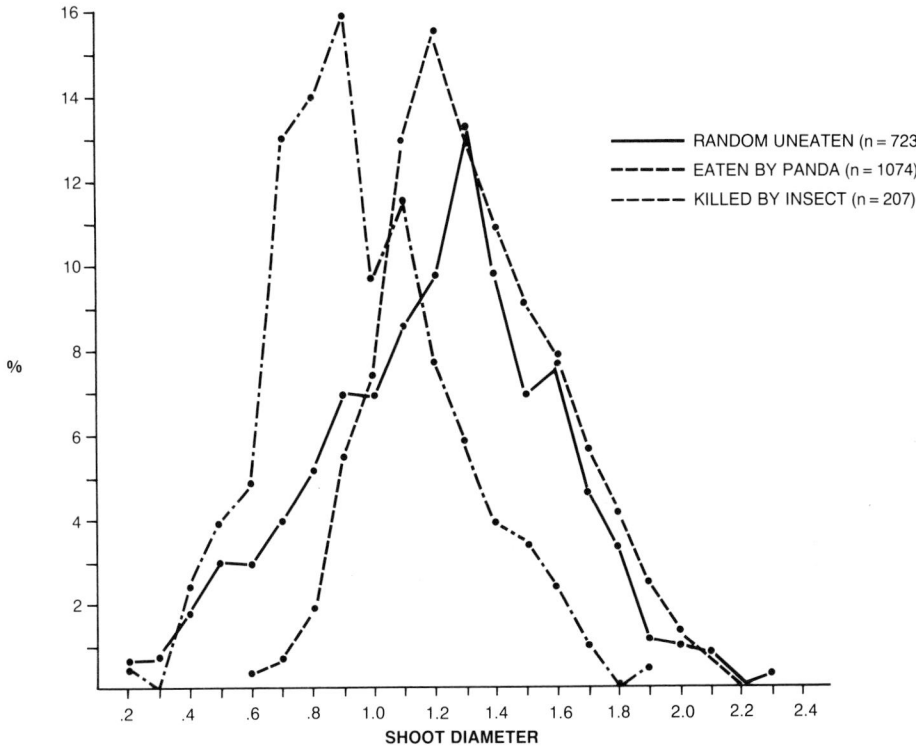

FIGURE 3.5   Diameter of new *Fargesia* shoots available compared to those eaten by pandas and insects (See also table 3.3.)

one-third greater, and that thin shoots, those 0.8 cm or less in diameter and rarely eaten by pandas, were significantly more common inside a stand than near the periphery (table 3.5). It is therefore more rewarding for a panda to forage along edges.

Food and water intake

Food intake

Unable to observe food intake in the wild, we first sought to obtain needed information by feeding Yingxionggou captives known amounts of bamboo. Most captives, however, except the male Ping-Ping, ate little bamboo once they had adapted to a diet of porridge, and he too ingested considerably less than a free-living animal would, even when deprived of supplements. Then we reasoned that weight of bamboo eaten should be proportional to the weight of droppings. To determine how much a panda defecates in a day in captivity is easy, but in the wild we seldom could determine an animal's precise route for a given period of time. Besides, defecation rates varied with the parts of bamboo eaten and also seemed to change somewhat from day to day. Consequently we derived no more than approximate figures of food intake, using several indirect methods.

The weight of droppings produced by Ping-Ping when eating *Sinarundinaria* leaves, including branchtips, averaged 14.9% more than the actual food (table 3.6), the increase being due to water content. We obtained wet and dry weights of 335

TABLE 3.4

SELECTION FOR NEW *Fargesia* SHOOTS BY PANDAS

Length and diameter class	Random sample	Not eaten by panda	W	E	P	Use
6–10 May 1981						
< 25 cm, all diameters	34	83	0.588	0.277	< 0.001	*not preferred
> 25 cm, < 1.0 cm	28	30	0.258	− 1.127	< 0.5	preferred
> 25 cm, > 1.0 cm	36	23	0.154	− 0.368	< 0.001	*preferred
Total	98	136				
14 May 1981						
< 25 cm, all diameters	15	32	0.533	0.231	< 0.001	*not preferred
> 25 cm, < 1.0 cm	9	13	0.360	0.039	$0.05 < p$ < 0.10	not preferred (borderline significance)
> 25 cm, > 1.0 cm	84	36	0.107	− 0.514	< 0.005	*preferred
Totals	108	81				
2 June 1982						
< 25 cm, all diameters	3	9	0.502	0.202	< 0.025	*not preferred
> 25 cm, < 1.0 cm	24	63	0.439	0.137	< 0.001	*not preferred
> 25 cm, > 1.0 cm	50	18	0.060	− 0.693	< 0.001	*preferred
Totals	77	90				

Note: Table compares choice of short shoots, long and thin shoots, and long and thick shoots, based on 3 samples, each consisting of measurements of shoots left uneaten at the feeding site and random measurements nearby.
W = selectivity coefficient, with values above 0.33 indicating avoidance;
E = electivity index (− 1 preference, 0 random, + 1 avoidance;
P = probability that selection deviated from random χ^2, $2df$).
*Indicates statistical significance.
See table 3.3 for sources of statistical procedures.

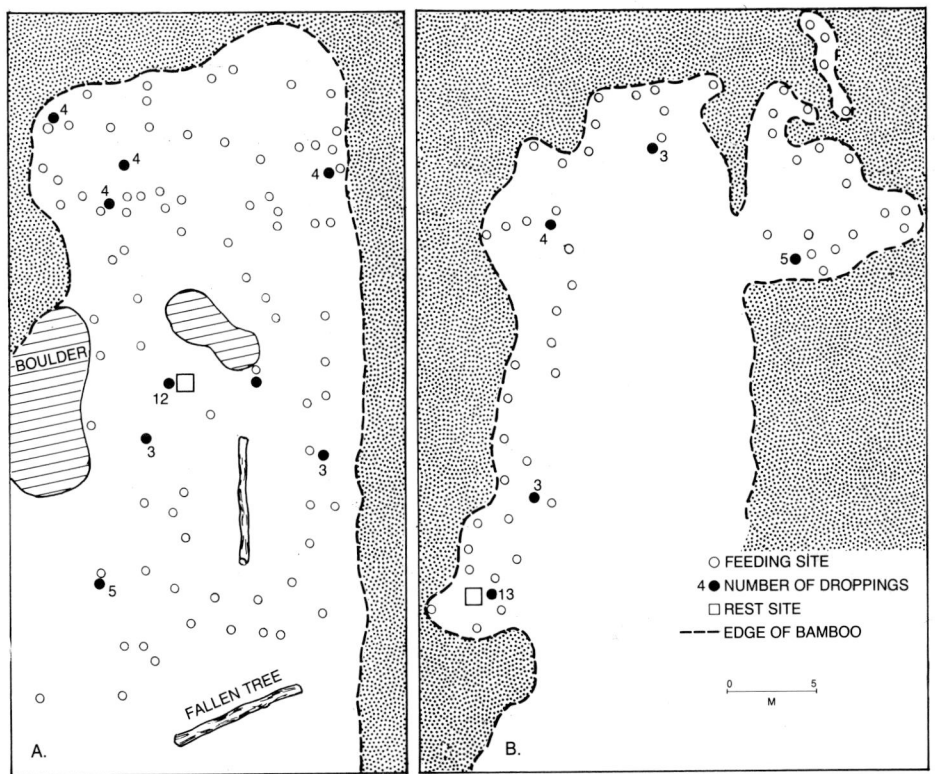

FIGURE 3.6   Foraging patterns of Zhen when eating new *Fargesia* shoots.   A. She harvests shoots intensively throughout a stand.   B. She selects shoots along the periphery of a stand.

Sinarundinaria droppings throughout the year in the wild. Although water content varied significantly from a low of 60% in May to a high of 76% in August, with an annual average of 69.9%, it showed no major fluctuations (table B.2), probably reflecting the need for coarse and poorly digested food to move smoothly through the intestines. Droppings were also coated with a thin mucus layer, which no doubt assists in the passage; indeed, Wang et al. (1982) have shown that the panda's digestive tract has a notable number of mucus cells. Water content of bamboo was consistently lower than that of droppings. Taking only the parts of *Sinarundinaria* most commonly eaten at various seasons, the mean annual water content was 51.6%, or 18.3% less than the droppings. As shown in figure 3.7, average water deficit was, for example, great from April to June (20.3%), when pandas subsisted on old stems, and small during summer (11.9%), when they ate leaves, often leaves wet from rain.

We followed Wei's trail in snow through *Sinarundinaria* for 5½ days between 17 and 22 January 1982. In that time he produced 533 droppings, or 96.9 per day, 4.0 per hour. His droppings weighed on the average 211.5g each, a total production of 112.7 kg, or 20.5 kg per day, fresh weight. Judging by dropping content, Wei's food consisted of 41% old shoot and 59% leaves and branches. The amount of water in

TABLE 3.5

EFFECT OF EDGE OF BAMBOO STAND ON DENSITY AND DIAMETER OF NEW *Fargesia* SHOOTS, MAY–JUNE 1982

	Shoots within 1m of edge	Shoots more than 1m from edge	*t*-test
Average number of shoots/m^2	5.29	3.49	$p < 0.001$
Average number thin shoots/m^2	0.66	0.83	$p < 0.001$

this food averaged 46.3% (table B.3). Since water content of Wei's droppings averaged 70.1%, Wei defecated 20.5 kg × 29.9% DM, or 6.13 kg dry matter per day. A panda digests about 18.7% of this dry matter in winter (see below), so that Wei's daily intake was 6.13(100)/100 − 18.7, or 7.54 kg dry matter, which represents 7.54 kg/100 − 46.3% or 14.04 kg fresh bamboo.

Wei's feeding sites during an estimated 24-hour period, 17–18 January, provide an independent test of the accuracy of this figure. There were 186 m of feeding trails (fig. 4.8), of which we sampled 19 m. Along this 19 m, Wei ate parts of 348 old shoots and browsed leaves from 213 stems. Assuming that he harvested similarly along his whole route, Wei consumed that day 2232 old shoots and the leaves from 1366 stems. By measuring the height of a sample of stumps and the length of the discarded portion, as well as a number of whole stems, we calculated that Wei had eaten an average of 55.9 cm from each old shoot, usually the top. The eaten portion weighed, on the average, 3.3 g, or a total of 7.4 kg, fresh weight, for the whole day's intake. In 8 feeding trials, the captive Ping-Ping required an average of 131.9 ± 23.1 stems for each kilogram of leaves eaten. If Wei harvested similarly, he ate 10.4 kg, fresh weight, of leaves. The total of 17.8 kg is somewhat higher than the average of 14.0 kg derived from droppings over a period of 5.5 days, but food intake no doubt varies from day to day.

In December we once followed Zhen's estimated one-day route in *Sinarundinaria* and tallied 100 droppings weighing 15.1 kg, fresh weight. Her food consisted of 68% stem—mostly old shoot—and 32% leaves and branches; average water content of food was 48.1%, and of droppings 72.1%. Dry matter digestibility was 18.7%. Zhen consumed 5.18 kg dry matter, or 10.0 kg of bamboo, fresh weight, that day, according to calculations like those described above.

TABLE 3.6

KILOGRAMS OF *Sinarundinaria* LEAVES EATEN AND DEFECATED BY THE CAPTIVE MALE PING-PING 1–3 SEPTEMBER 1981[a]

	Leaves eaten (kg)	Droppings		Weight increase of droppings (%)
		N	kg	
Day 1	6.66[b]	82	8.20	18.8
Day 2	7.83	76	8.75	10.5
Day 3	7.75	105	9.15	15.3
Average	7.4	87.7	8.7	14.9

[a]Data collected with the assistance of J. Stover.
[b]Some porridge also fed inadvertently by keeper.

Using another method of calculation, we noted that 5 of Zhen's rest periods in mid-April averaged 3.3 hours in duration, as revealed by radiotelemetry; and 4 of her rest sites at that time averaged 16 droppings, a defecation rate of 5 per hour, or 120 per day. With the average dropping weighing 148.4 g, total output was 17.8 kg, fresh weight, per day. April droppings contained 63.6% water and stem 44%. Dry matter digestibility was 12.5%. Hence, she ate 7.20 kg dry matter, or 12.8 kg of bamboo, fresh weight.

Pandas appear to eat many more kilograms of new *Fargesia* shoots per day than they do *Sinarundinaria* leaves and stem. We fed Ping-Ping only new shoots for two consecutive days. He ate an average of 16.4 kg per day, about double his 7.4 kg leaf intake. The first day his droppings weighed 55.7% less, and the second day 29.6% less, than the amount of shoot eaten; excess water was eliminated mostly as urine (table 3.7). Even so, droppings consisted mostly of water, the average of a sample of 24 in the wild containing 88.9 ± 1.2%.

Once Zhen spent about 10 hours within an area of 1533 m², eating in that time 281 shoots and depositing 57 droppings weighing 10.2 kg, fresh weight, based on an average weight of 179.5 g per dropping (see table 6.1). Extrapolated to a whole day, the figures would be 674 shoots and 137 droppings weighing 24.6 kg, fresh weight. Since water content of shoot and dropping is similar, food intake is, on the average, 40.8% higher, the same as the water loss, if data from Ping-Ping are typical. This would raise Zhen's consumption that day to 34.6 kg, fresh weight. On another occasion, Zhen foraged intermittently for 2.5 hours, in that time eating 65 shoots and

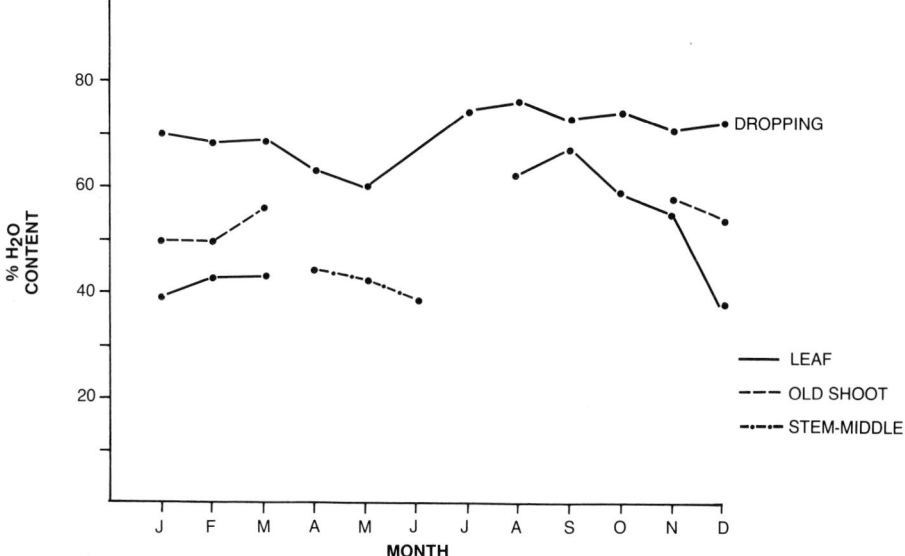

FIGURE 3.7   Average percentage of water in panda droppings compared with percentage of water in those *Sinarundinaria* parts that represent the panda's principal forage each month.

TABLE 3.7
NEW *Fargesia* SHOOTS EATEN AND DEFECATED BY THE CAPTIVE MALE PING-PING 19–21 MAY 1981[a]

	Duration of feeding (min.)	Shoots eaten (N)	Av. time per shoot (sec.)	Weight shoots eaten (kg)	Droppings (N)	Weight droppings (kg)
Day 1	50	60	50.0	3.57		
	30	35	51.4	1.73		
	45	45	60.0	2.43		
	20	30	40.0	1.61		
	110	110	60.0	4.82		
Totals	255	280	54.6	14.16	64	6.28
Day 2	60	70	51.4	3.91		
	55	70	47.1	3.38		
	—	30	—	3.12		
	40	64	37.5	3.64		
	65	82	47.6	4.67		
Totals	—	319	45.6	18.72	150	13.18

[a]Calculations exclude about 630g of leaves and stem eaten the first day and 760g the second.

eliminating 17 droppings weighing 3.0 kg, a daily rate of 624 shoots, 163 droppings, and 40.8 kg shoot intake. On yet other occasions, Zhen deposited 9 droppings (1.6 kg) in 1.6 hours, 23 droppings (3.9 kg) in 2.9 hours, and 35 droppings (5.9 kg) in 5.5 hours. Since a panda forages intermittently throughout the day and night, these samples can be converted to a daily basis, or a total of 136–189 droppings and an approximate food intake of 34.2 kg, 45.6 kg, and 36.3 kg respectively per day. The average amount eaten by Zhen in these samples was 38.3 kg, three times the amount of stem and leaves she ate at other times. Since she weighed about 86 kg, she consumed the equivalent of around 45% of her body weight per day. With shoots consisting of 90% water, her dry-matter intake would be about 4.5% of body weight, a somewhat higher figure than the 1.5–3.0% of body weight eaten by cattle and African buffalo, and 4.0% by wildebeest grazing under good feeding conditions (Sinclair 1977).

The number of shoots required to fulfill the daily weight requirement will, of course, depend on their size. The above calculations of 674 and 624 shoots are based on observations in late May and early June. On 30 May, we took the average weight of the edible portions of a random shoot sample, except that all were taller than 25 cm and thicker than 0.9 cm. Mean weight of 65 shoots was 52.5 ± 30.3 (range 13–162) g. A panda eating 650 shoots would ingest 34.1 kg, confirming our earlier calculation. Two weeks earlier, however, the average edible portion had weighed 19.7 ± 12.3 g, and the panda would then have required 1148 shoots to reach 34.1 kg.

Observations similar to ours were made by Ruan and Yong (1983) in the Qinling Mountains. Feeding on new *Phyllostachys* shoots, one adult eliminated 31 kg of droppings in 24 hours, which, using our method of calculation, indicates a food intake of 43.6 kg. Ruan and Yong also watched a panda continuously for 48 hours as it ate shoots. During this period it consumed an estimated 90.3 kg, or 45.2 kg per day;

other observations indicate that intake may reach 57 kg or more per day (Yong 1981).

A poem written in A.D. 817 by the Tang dynasty poet Bai Juyi describes the enthusiasm with which villagers harvest and eat bamboo shoots:

> Here is the home of bamboo;
> in spring, the hills
> and valleys are covered with bamboo shoots!
> . . . .
> I have long lived in Chang'an and Luoyang, yet
> I never could get enough bamboo
> shoots to eat; here now there are many;
> do not wait to eat them, for soon the south wind
> will rise and they will grow into tall bamboos.

These lines could have been written with the panda in mind.

Frequency of drinking

Throughout the year, except when eating new *Fargesia* shoots, pandas have a water imbalance because feces eliminate more water than food brings in. During rainy times of year, pandas can obtain moisture from wet bamboo; besides, virtually every gulley has water. In winter, however, pandas may lack ready access to water, for rivulets high on slopes are often frozen or covered with snow. Zhen once stopped at two such frozen rivulets as if looking for water, then walked on. Although the pandas in our study descended into valleys, it remained unclear whether they went there to drink at the perennial streams or were merely in transit to another slope. At times, tracks at the stream's edge suggested that they had stopped to drink, but more often an animal waded across seemingly without halting, or even crossed on a log bridge.

We followed panda tracks in snow for a total of 36.1 km in the winter of 1981–82 and noted 20 places, or one per 1.8 km, where an animal drank. After tracking Wei for 5½ days we noted that he drank 7 or possibly 8 times, and that he also crossed six rivulets where he could have stopped but did not. On 4 of the days he drank once, and on one day he drank 3 or 4 times. Our limited evidence suggests that pandas generally drink at least once a day, a conclusion also reached by Yong (1981). In its wet environment the panda has never needed to evolve an efficient water economy. While foraging on new *Phyllostachys* shoots, one panda did not drink but urinated 8 times during a 24-hour period (Ruan and Yong 1983), a reflection on the high water content of shoots. We found no evidence that pandas eat snow to obtain water. An animal would lose considerable energy by using body heat to melt snow in the stomach.

Retention time of food

Dierenfeld (1981) fed the Washington pandas some carrots and whole wheat and noted a passage time of 8 ± 3 hours of these particles through the digestive tract. A few observations on Ping-Ping confirm Dierenfeld's data. Seven passages of new

Fargesia shoots varied from 5.1 to 11.3 hours, with a mean of 7.9 hours from the time of eating to their first appearance in the droppings. On one of these occasions, Ping-Ping had an empty digestive tract after 7.5 hours of fasting, and when fed new shoots he defecated the first ones in 5.1 hours. One passage of leaves required 13.8 hours. Other passage times, based on observing several Yingxionggou animals, include an average of 10 hours for *Sinarundinaria* stem; 12 to 13 hours for a mixture of ground rice, maize, and beans; and 15 to 16 hours for mutton and bones.

Panda nutrition (*with Ellen S. Dierenfeld and Zeng Kewen*)

The bamboo samples on which this analysis is based were collected between April 1981 and March 1982. We collected monthly samples at two sites, one in *Sinarundinaria* at Erdaoping at 2850 m and the other in *Fargesia* below Wuyipeng at 2450 m. Taking old shoots, two-year stems, and old stems of different height and diameter, we divided each age class into several parts—lower, middle, and upper portion of stems, branches, leaves—corresponding to those parts eaten or not eaten by pandas. This provided 13 monthly *Sinarundinaria* samples (old shoots lack branches and have only a few leaves) and 15 *Fargesia* samples, excluding such special samples as new shoots, rhizomes, and bamboo in flower. Each sample was weighed when fresh, oven-dried, then weighed again, and stored in plastic bags. Fresh droppings were also collected every month, weighed and dried; and the leaf and stem remnants were retained separately for analysis.

The standard and most widely used method to determine the nutritive value of plants is proximate analysis, which provides information on ash, ether extract (crude fat), crude fiber, and nitrogen-free extract (NFE). The analysis of crude fiber—supposedly the indigestible part of the plant—is imprecise, obscuring the actual contribution made by carbohydrates to the diet of animals. In a new approach, cell wall and cell content are treated separately (Goering and Van Soest 1970, Van Soest 1982). The cell wall constituents (cellulose, hemicelluloses, and lignin) are not affected by mammalian enzymes, whereas the cell content (sugars, fats, amino acids) is available for digestion. The relative proportions of cell wall to cell content and the availability of both to the animal determine the nutritive value of a plant. To separate the digestible from the indigestible parts, the soluble cell contents are first washed out in a neutral detergent solution, leaving the cell wall as residue. After the residue is treated with an acid detergent, the difference in weight between the total cell wall and the remaining acid detergent fiber provides an estimate of hemicelluloses. The acid detergent fiber is then treated with 72% sulfuric acid to separate cellulose from lignin, the residue providing a measure for cellulose. Total ash represents the inorganic matter—salts and minerals—in the plant.

We determined nutritional content of bamboo both by the Van Soest (1982) method and by proximate analysis. Although we base our discussion of panda nutrition primarily on results derived by the former method, we also include data from proximate analysis, because they furnish a standard against which past research on herbivore food habits may be compared.

Since protein in the form of amino acids is essential for body growth and maintenance, we hypothesized that pandas may select bamboo on the basis of protein content. Protein was calculated as total Kjeldahl nitrogen $\times$ 6.25. High-pressure liquid chromatography (Beckman 121 MB Amino Acid Analyzer) was used to determine the amounts of 16 different amino acids in bamboo.

Animals require minerals for growth and various physiological functions. Minerals can be obtained from food, water, or soil. We tested bamboo and several water sources in the Choushuigou for macro and trace elements, using an atomic absorption spectrophotometer. The macro elements include calcium (Ca), phosphorus (P), potassium (K), sodium (Na), and magnesium (Mg); and the trace elements include iron (Fe), manganese (Mn), copper (Cu), boron (B), silicon (Si), titanium (Ti), aluminum (Al), lead (Pb), nickel (Ni), and zinc (Zn). (Pb, Ti, and Al are not required by the body.)

Silica (Si O_2) is a structural component of cell walls often complementing lignin. Its influence on the digestibility of the plant remains unclear, except that high levels may inhibit cell wall digestion in ruminants (Van Soest 1982). Plants differ widely in silica content, even within the same species, depending on soil type. Some plants deposit silica on the leaf surface, giving the leaf a rough, sandy feeling, which might reduce palatability. Since various grasses, including bamboo (Lanning et al. 1958), are known to contain high levels of silica, we tested specifically for this inorganic constituent using the method described by Goering and Van Soest (1970).

Organic constituents of bamboo

Tables B.5 and B.6 present the results of the Van Soest (1982) method of analysis, and table 3.8 provides a summary of those results. The monthly samples have been averaged, for there is not much variation as expressed by standard deviations, and

TABLE 3.8
CHEMICAL COMPOSITION OF *Sinarundinaria* AND *Fargesia* (IN % DRY MATTER)

		Leaf (all ages)	Branch (all ages)	Stem	
				Old shoot	Two-year and old
Crude protein	*Sinarundinaria*	15.5	6.5	4.4	2.4
	Fargesia	14.1	4.3	2.5	1.2
Hemicellulose	*Sinarundinaria*	35.5	30.0	23.6*	23.1*
	Fargesia	33.0	29.1	22.9*	22.3*
Cellulose	*Sinarundinaria*	27.8	35.3	46.7*	45.7*
	Fargesia	28.5	37.5	47.6*	47.8*
Lignin	*Sinarundinaria*	8.6	13.0*	13.6*	16.2
	Fargesia	9.7	14.4	15.3	16.4
Ash	*Sinarundinaria*	8.4	6.5	2.7	2.0
	Fargesia	8.8	4.5	2.3	1.2
Silica	*Sinarundinaria*	2.5	1.2	0.2*	0.3*
	Fargesia	2.3	1.0	0.3*	0.2*

*Within each constituent of a species, those marked with an asterisk are *not* significantly different ($p < 0.05$) from each other.

the little that does exist may have been partly due to local differences in soil composition, ages of stems sampled, and other variables. The results are expressed in percent dry matter. All values, except for crude protein, have been calculated as percent organic matter, ash excluded. The Student's *t*-test was used to determine significance.

Crude protein

Virtually all protein is available to pandas as part of the cell content. Different parts of bamboo vary greatly in protein levels. Taking *Sinarundinaria* first, leaves average 15.5% protein, branches 6.5%, old shoots 4.4%, and stems 2.4%. Two-year and old stems show little difference in protein values, except that branches and stems of the former tend to be higher (bottom n.s.; rest $p< 0.01$). Old shoots have significantly more protein, especially in the top, than do stems ($p< 0.05$).

Analyzed on a monthly basis, levels remain remarkably constant throughout the year. There is a minor peak among old shoots in August because in that month new shoots are high in protein (fig. 3.8) and advance into the old-shoot category. Leaves and branches peak in July, probably because the largest number of young growing leaves are then present. Young leaves contain more protein than do old leaves, as shown by samples collected from old shoots in May, June, and July. During those months the few leaves on old shoots are predominantly young, with an average protein content of $21.4 \pm 1.1\%$. Two-year and old stems have proportionately fewer young leaves at that season than do old shoots, and their protein levels were $17.00 \pm$

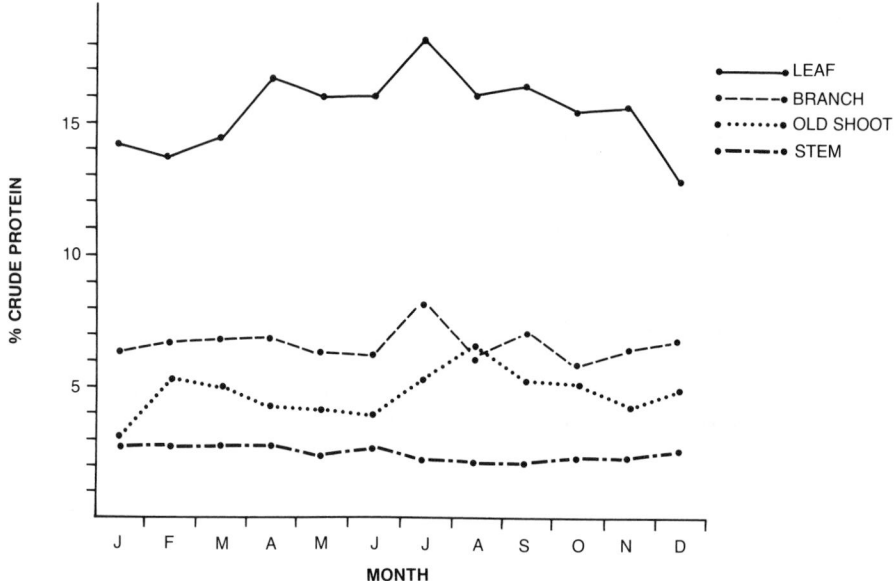

FIGURE 3.8 Percentage of crude protein in different *Sinarundinaria* parts, by month. In figures 3.8 and 3.9, two-year and old stems have been combined and the bottoms of old shoots and stems deleted.

.76% and 16.59 ± 1.38%, significantly less ($p < 0.05$). During winter, from December to March, leaves have the lowest protein content ($p < 0.05$), which can readily be explained by the annual cycle of leaf death. *Sinarundinaria* remains in green leaf all year. But by late October some leaves begin to turn yellowish and die, and by December the bamboo slopes look like dead grass from a distance. Counts of several stems showed that about one-third of the leaves were dead and still attached to the branches. In late March or early April, just before the new growing season, most dead leaves fall off. One February sample of dead leaves contained 9% protein, whereas green leaves from the same stems contained 17.5%. Therefore, dead leaves, as used in our analysis, lower the average protein level available in winter.

Fargesia shows protein values similar to those of *Sinarundinaria* (fig. 3.9). Old shoots have 15.8% protein in leaves, 5.7% in branches, and 2.5% in stems; two-year and old stems contain 13.2% protein in leaves, 3.8% in branches, and 1.2% in stems, significantly less than do old shoots in all categories ($p < 0.001$). Two-year stems are slightly richer in protein than old ones but not statistically so. Values fluctuate little from month to month, except for some minor dips and rises among leaves, for which we have no explanation. Leaves show no drop in protein level during winter (n.s. at $p < 0.05$), probably because *Fargesia* lacks a season during which leaves die in conspicuous numbers. Old shoots show a protein peak in July, the month when new shoots were first classified as old ones.

Sinarundinaria leaves, branches, old shoots, and stems have significantly more protein ($p < 0.001$) than the corresponding parts in *Fargesia*; nonetheless, the panda has a remarkably constant supply of protein available. If a panda were to select only for the most protein-rich parts, it would feed on *Sinarundinaria* leaves and the leaves of old *Fargesia* shoots. But it does not always do so (fig. 3.3).

The underground rhizomes provide an important potential food source in terms of biomass. With a protein content of 4.0–4.6%, they contain more protein than do stems; yet we saw no evidence that pandas excavate rhizomes.

New shoots may be exceptionally high in protein with 26–28% reported for *Bambusa* and 30.1% for *Phyllostachys aureosulcata* (Dierenfeld 1981). Whole new shoots of *Sinarundinaria* contained 14.8% protein. When analyzing new *Fargesia* shoots, we separated sheaths from the core in the manner of pandas. One sheath sample had 10.9% protein; and two core samples, collected in late April and early May, contained 14.8 and 20.3% protein with an average of 17.6% (table B.6). As shoots grew taller and hardened, protein levels dropped, and pandas tended to eat the soft portions, those still protected by the sheath, discarding the hard ones. The soft portions are richer in protein (8.5%) than the others (6.7%), judging by one sample from late May.

In summer, pandas in our study area occasionally ate stems of wild parsnip with a moderate protein level of 7.3%.

Amino acids (with Yuan Hongsheng)

Eight amino acids are considered to be essential for optimum growth and must be supplied by the diet. Table 3.9 shows levels of 7 amino acids in various bamboo parts

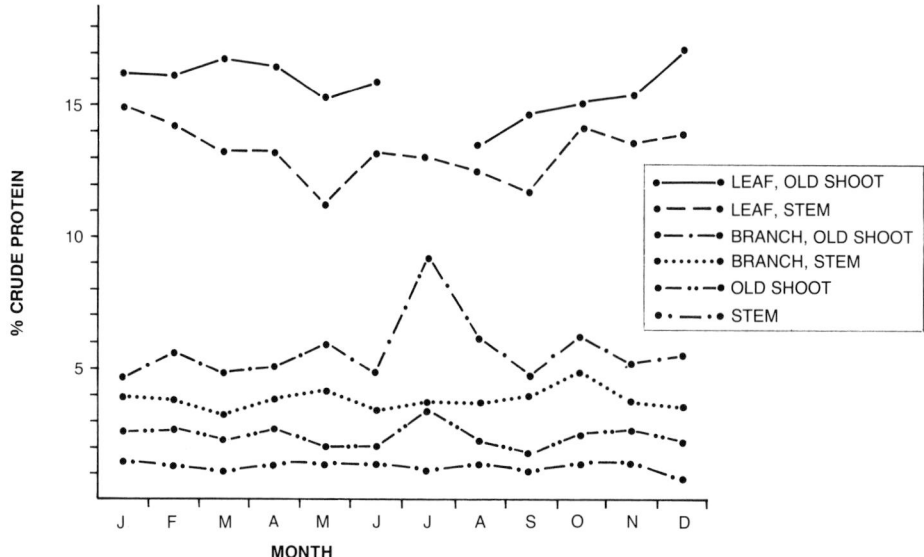

FIGURE 3.9   Percentage of crude protein in different *Fargesia* parts, by month. (See fig. 3.8.)

and compares these to levels in egg, beef, and maize; the eighth amino acid, tryptophan, was not analyzed, but new shoots are said to be rich in it (Hladik 1978). As expected from the analysis of crude protein, new *Fargesia* shoots and the leaves of both species contain higher amino acid levels than do old shoots. Leaves show peak levels in winter and old shoots in spring, trends for unexplained reasons not apparent in the crude protein analyses (figs. 3.8 and 3.9). Of the 7 amino acids, methionine is almost always present in smaller amounts than the others; it may therefore represent a limiting amino acid in the diet of pandas. Given a panda's predilection for meat, it is instructive to compare amino acids in bamboo and beef. Bamboo leaves have more leucine, phenylalanine, threonine, and valine than does beef, and new shoots have more isoleucine as well; only methionine is notably low in bamboo. The nutritional value of a protein, however, lies more in a good balance of all 8 essential amino acids than in the maximum amount of any one of them. Egg is often used as a standard for comparison because of its balanced amino acid content. If egg is given an amino acid score of 100, it outranks beef (69), maize (45), and bamboo (43 maximum). New *Fargesia* shoots, though much favored, show a poor balance (8). The bamboo parts with the best balance are old *Sinarundinaria* shoots (43) and leaves (31–40); thus it is probably not coincidental that they constitute the bulk of the panda's food (table 3.9). Bamboo seems to contain an adequate ratio of 7 essential amino acids and 9 other amino acids (table B.10); indeed, values of bamboo compare well with those of alfalfa, a good amino acid source (P. Van Soest pers. comm.).

Other cell content

The bamboo cell contains other nutrients besides protein, principally soluble carbohydrates. Stems, branches, and leaves have similar average amounts of these

TABLE 3.9
THE CONTENT OF ESSENTIAL AMINO ACIDS[a] IN VARIOUS BAMBOO PARTS AND IN SELECTED OTHER FOODS (IN MG/100G)

Season	Food	Plant part	Isoleucine	Leucine	Lysine	Phenyl-alanine	Methionine	Threonine	Valine	Amino acid score[b]
	Egg	—	.428	.565	.396	.368	.342	.310	.460	100.0
	Beef	—	.332	.515	.540	.256	.237	.275	.345	69.3
	Maize	—	.351	.834	.178	.420	.205	.223	.381	44.9
Spring	Fargesia	new shoot	.360	.739	.412	.357	.028	.362	.397	8.2
		old shoot–middle	.122	.246	.240	.014	.057	.175	.213	3.8
		leaf	.310	.613	.238	.377	.056	.495	.596	16.3
	Sinarundinaria	old shoot–middle	.529	.874	.350	.462	.146	.532	.788	42.6
		leaf	.113	.221	.149	.100	.032	.184	.202	9.3
Summer–Autumn	Fargesia	old shoot–middle	.086	.162	.255	.053	.054	.153	.189	15.9
		leaf	.345	.658	.362	.389	.056	.397	.528	16.4
	Sinarundinaria	old shoot–middle	.207	.310	.172	.088	.030	.148	.137	8.8
		leaf	.393	.729	.512	.410	.105	.478	.607	30.7
Winter	Fargesia	old shoot–middle	.146	.213	.101	.063	.035	.050	.107	10.2
		leaf	.363	.847	.459	.516	.024	.595	.632	7.0
	Sinarundinaria	old shoot–middle	.166	.302	.220	.075	.044	.145	.156	12.8
		leaf	.411	.835	.454	.469	.138	.564	.728	40.4

[a]Tryptophan not tested.
[b]The amino acid score represents the ratio of the least adequately supplied essential amino acid in a sample and a standard reference protein (egg) with the best balance of essential amino acids.

nutrients—*Sinarundinaria* about 12–14% and *Fargesia* somewhat less; the average for new *Fargesia* shoots is only about 4%, a low level (figs. 3.15 and 3.16).

Hemicelluloses

Hemicellulose is a complex polysaccharide associated with lignin and cellulose but, unlike those two components, not entirely indigestible. Acids in the stomach and to a lesser extent alkalines in the small intestine may break some of the sugar linkages, which enables the flora of the lower gut to digest a fraction by fermentation during the brief passage. Hemicellulose is therefore, the only part of the cell wall nutritionally available to pandas. *Sinarundinaria* leaves average 35.5% hemicellulose, branches 30.0%, old shoot 23.6%, and stem 23.1%, there being little monthly variation. Two-year stems tend to have slightly but not significantly higher values than old stems. The top of old shoots and stems contains more hemicellulose than do the middle and bottom ($p < 0.001$). The hemicellulose content of *Fargesia* is similar to that of *Sinarundinaria*, except that it averages about 1% lower.

Cellulose

Sinarundinaria leaves average 27.8% cellulose, branches 35.3%, and old shoot and stem 46%; the top of old shoots and stems has less cellulose than do the middle and bottom ($p < 0.001$). *Fargesia* is similar to *Sinarundinaria* in cellulose content. The bottom of old shoots and stems contains a little but not significantly more cellulose than do the middle and top. New shoots, in spite of their tenderness, contain a considerable amount of indigestible cellulose—*Sinarundinaria* 36.0% and *Fargesia* 31.5%.

Lignin

The average lignin content of *Sinarundinaria* leaves is 8.6%, branches 13.0%, old shoot 13.6%, and stem 16.2%. The bottom of old shoots and stems is highest in lignin and the top is lowest, though differences are not statistically significant. All *Fargesia* values are slightly higher than those for *Sinarundinaria*.

Vitamin C

Several fresh bamboo samples were analyzed in Wolong. Table 3.10 shows that new and old shoots contain much less vitamin C than do leaves. *Sinarundinaria* leaves from a sunny location had almost twice the vitamin level of leaves from a shady one. Pandas can probably synthesize ascorbic acid in the liver, and may at most require a supplement at certain critical times in their lives.

Standard proximate analyses of organic constituents

Table 3.11 presents the proximate analyses of old shoots and leaves by season to complement the Van Soest (1982) method of analyses discussed so far (see also Tang et al. 1983). Direct comparisons are not possible, except for crude protein, because of the differences in approach. The two independent analyses of crude protein produced similar results. Ether extract (crude fat) contains not only fatty acids but

TABLE 3.10
VITAMIN C CONTENT OF BAMBOO, SEPTEMBER 1982

	Bamboo part	Elevation (m)	Sample size	Vitamin C mg/100g
Fargesia	new shoot	2,500	12	0.47 ± 0.02
	old shoot–middle	2,500	6	0.28 ± 0.01
	leaf	2,500	8	6.54 ± 0.05
Sinarundinaria	old shoot–middle	2,800	6	0.33 ± 0.02
		2,950	8	0.37 ± 0.02
	leaf	2,800	16	5.19 ± 0.04
		2,950	8	9.74 ± 0.02

also other ether-soluble plant products such as pigments, waxes, resins, and volatile oils. Bamboo, like most plants, contains little crude fat. Leaves have more crude fat (3.3–3.4%) than do old shoots (0.36–0.59%), a result consistent with other nutrients. Theoretically, crude fiber constitutes the indigestible fraction of the food, but, in fact, it lacks lignin and some of the hemicelluloses. Instead, lignin appears in the nitrogen-free extract fraction, which by definition is highly digestible. In spite of this inherent methodological problem, the crude fiber percentages indicate that leaves contain much less indigestible material than do old shoots and that percentages in the two bamboos are similar. NFE contains about 22–33% mono and polysaccharides, which are soluble in 6 N HCL and therefore assumed to be digestible.

Inorganic constituents of bamboo

Bamboo was analyzed for total ash, representing all inorganic matter, and specifically for silica and 15 elements.

Total ash

Ash contains sodium, phosphorus, calcium, and other minerals and salts with essential functions in animal metabolism. The availability of minerals in the soil and the capacity of roots to absorb them varies with the seasons, being generally highest during growth and lowest at maturity (Van Soest 1982). Using the Van Soest (1982) method of analysis, *Sinarundinaria* leaves averaged 8.4% ash, branches 6.5%, old shoot 2.7%, and stem 2.0%; and *Fargesia* leaves 8.8% ash, branches 4.5%, old shoot 2.3%, and stem 1.2%. Percentages varied little from month to month (tables B.5 and B.6). These results are similar to those derived by standard proximate analyses (table 3.11).

Silica

Sinarundinaria leaves have the highest average silica content (2.5%), branches an intermediate amount (1.2%), and old shoots and stems the lowest (0.30%). The values for *Fargesia* were similar—2.3% for leaves, 1.0% for branches and 0.21% for stems. Silica values fluctuate markedly from month to month. *Sinarundinaria* shows a high silica level of 3.5–5.0% in December–January and April–July, and a low level,

TABLE 3.11

STANDARD PROXIMATE ANALYSES OF SELECTED BAMBOO PARTS ON A DRY MATTER BASIS

Species	Plant part	Season	Crude protein	Crude fat	Monosac-charide	Polysac-charide	NFE	Crude fiber	Total ash
Fargesia	Old shoot-middle	spring	2.15	0.15	—	—	45.81	49.82	2.09
		summer-autumn	2.48	0.46	0.38	16.02	40.43	53.90	2.73
		winter	2.53	0.48	3.00	21.78	46.71	48.18	2.12
	Leaf (all ages)	spring	14.56	3.64	—	—	48.98	22.95	9.87
		summer-autumn	13.09	3.65	1.97	20.12	49.87	24.12	9.27
		winter	12.02	2.83	4.56	26.92	49.10	27.33	7.75
	New shoot	spring	12.12	1.27	0.81	26.41	49.40	33.62	5.18
Sinarundinaria	Old shoot-middle	spring	4.88	0.47	—	—	45.57	46.28	2.80
		summer-autumn	4.25	0.76	0.65	21.33	46.71	45.88	2.40
		winter	3.95	0.55	7.77	25.06	45.76	46.92	2.51
	Leaf (2-year and older)	spring	18.19	3.18	—	—	46.69	23.74	8.22
		summer-autumn	17.85	3.65	1.06	22.70	45.26	27.03	7.43
		winter	15.88	3.01	2.42	26.31	48.20	23.50	8.65

below 0.3%, in the remaining months (see fig. 3.3); *Fargesia* levels follow a similar pattern, except that December is low (.05%), February high (5.42%), and August intermediate (2.7%). Since these values are based on averages, the changes in level appear to reflect actual conditions rather than mere sampling errors due to different local soil conditions. However, on two occasions—in the December *Sinarundinaria* sample and August *Fargesia* sample—the silica content of two-year and old stems differed, one high and one low. Both bamboos have the highest silica levels during the coldest months and during spring.

Little is known about the role of silica in the physiology of plants (Van Soest 1982), and we cannot explain these fluctuations. An accumulation of silica may make leaves less palatable to insects (Miller et al. 1960) and perhaps to other predators. A high level from April to June, the main growing season, might deter a leaf predator like the panda, but it is unclear if silica in bamboo reaches a high enough level to serve such a function.

Minerals in bamboo (with Chen Fengxiang Chen Jianwei, and Li Neng)

Figures 3.10 and 3.11 illustrate mineral levels in different bamboo parts. Phosphorus, calcium. silicon, iron, magnesium, and sodium reach high levels of a few parts per 100 to a few per 1000; manganese, aluminum, potassium, and zinc are intermediate with a few parts per 10,000 to a few per 100,000; and nickel, copper, lead, boron, and titanium have low levels, a few parts per 1,000,000. The two bamboo species contain generally similar amounts, but *Sinarundinaria* fluctuates more than *Fargesia* from one plant part to another. The levels of a few minerals (boron, copper) remain similar in the different parts, though levels tend to be lowest in stem bottom and middle and to increase in the order of stem top, branch, and leaf—the increase of calcium, aluminum, silicon, and manganese in leaves being particularly marked.That leaves are richer in minerals than are stems is also evident from figures 3.12 and 3.13, which illustrate monthly variation in *Sinarundinaria*. Levels of several minerals fluctuate over the year—aluminum, silicon, calcium, zinc, nickel, copper, and sodium, among others—reaching peaks between April or May and August. All decline, some drastically, in September, old shoots more than leaves, and then increase during subsequent months. Such a September drop was not apparent from the analysis of total ash, the fluctuation apparently masked by other inorganic matter. The low levels in September could be due to rapid growth of leaves and other plant tissues at this season and a resulting dilution of mineral reserves, especially in stems. Although the mineral requirements of pandas are not known, bamboo has adequate levels of those elements the lack of which is most likely to cause a mineral deficiency in animals. These, listed in decreasing order of such likelihood, are: sodium, chlorine, phosphorus, magnesium, calcium, sulfur, zinc, copper, cobalt, iodine, selenium, iron, potassium, managenese, molybdenum, silicon, and boron (Van Soest 1982).

Minerals in water

On 1 May 1981, we collected water samples from two streams, a rivulet, and a small pool in the Choushuigou. Pandas drink in the streams and in the rivulet but have not been noted to do so in the pool. The pH of the running water is neutral and that of the pool is slightly acidic. Calcium, magnesium, manganese, potassium, zinc, and iron show high levels in several samples (table B.7). During a hydrochemical survey, the Chengdu Geographic Institute of Academia Sinica found that the rivers of Wolong contain higher-than-average levels of manganese, zinc, copper, lead, and especially iron.

Chemical analyses of feces

The panda is unable to digest lignin, cellulose, and silica, but it can digest hemicelluloses partially and proteins almost completely (Dierenfeld et al. 1982). The chemical composition of panda feces, as well as fecal samples from other bamboo-eating mammals, are presented in tables B.8, B.9, and B.10. Fecal constituents will be discussed in the context of the panda's nutrient intake. Crude protein, however, needs comment here. Protein levels in feces are quite high, considerably higher than would be expected from the 90% digestion coefficient calculated by Dierenfeld (1981). For example, *Sinarundinaria* leaf averages 15.5% protein, of which all but 1.6% is probably absorbed, yet the feces contained 9.3% (table B.8). The extra protein derives from metabolic wastes. Fecal leaf may contain more protein than fecal stem because leaves are often more finely chewed and therefore provide more surface area for the attachment of microbes than do stems (Dierenfeld 1981). Such a protein difference is especially noticeable when comparing amino acid levels of leaves and new shoots between plant and dropping. Well-chewed leaves provide much surface area and appear to move through the digestive tract slowly, accumulating so much metabolic waste that the level of many amino acids remains high and fails to reflect whatever digestion has occurred (fig 3.14 A). By contrast, new shoots are chewed little, offering little surface area. They are moist and slippery and pass through the tract quickly; microbes have little chance to adhere. Analyses show that most amino acids of shoots have been digested (fig 3.14 B).

Microscopic examination of digested bamboo (*with Li Ronggao*)

A cross section of *Sinarundinaria* stem, sliced at the internode, shows a typical monocotyledonous arrangement with an outer layer of epidermal cells, some strengthening tissue beneath the epidermis, then vascular bundles scattered through the ground parenchyma, and finally a central pith cavity. Having been chewed and passed through the digestive tract, a piece of stem has a characteristic appearance: the tough, outer tissue of cellulose and lignin, though crushed and broken, remains relatively intact, whereas the parenchymal cells (the small cells surrounding the vascular bundles) and other thin-walled cells have been digested, leaving gaps in the tissue (plate 3.5). Most of the parenchyma in a new *Fargesia* shoot is digested too, but pandas chew shoots so little and passage through the tract is so rapid that the vascular bundles seem to be little affected (plate 3.6).

Fibrous bamboo cells are normally needle-shaped—straight, long, and thin—and arranged into adhering bundles and chains to form a protective layer. After passage through the tract, they are swollen and misshapen. We wonder whether partial digestion of the hemicelluloses not only changes the permeability of the cell wall but also causes the remaining cellulose and other structural components to warp.

Discussion

Bamboo obviously contains organic and inorganic substances in amounts and proportions adequate to sustain pandas, for, after all, the animals have depended on this plant for thousands of years. Through our analyses we have discovered a little

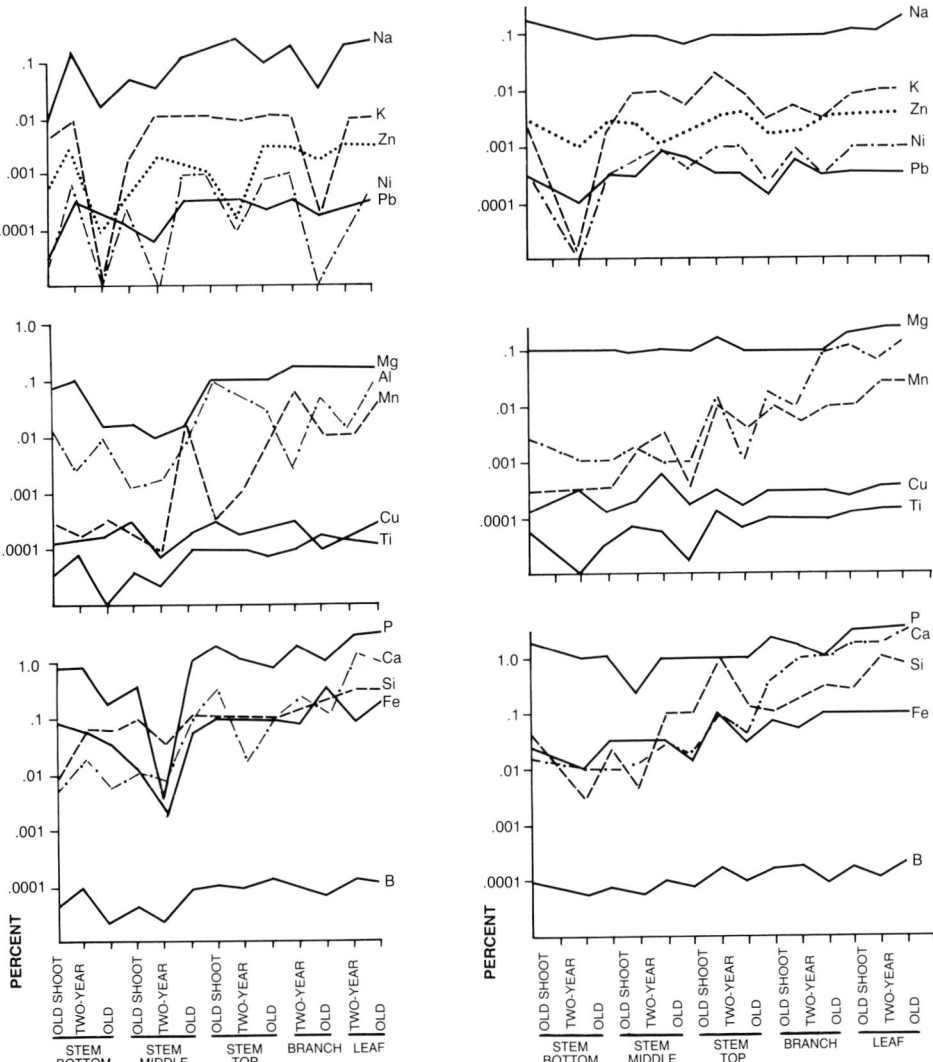

FIGURE 3.10 Percentage of 15 different minerals in various *Sinarundinaria* parts.

FIGURE 3.11 Percentage of 15 different minerals in various *Fargesia* parts.

about the nutrient content of bamboo, but a panda's actual mineral, amino acid, and other requirements remain unknown. We are also uncertain why pandas select different plant parts or even different species at certain seasons. To understand the nutrient cycles of bamboo species at various altitudes and to relate these cycles to the animal's foraging strategy is one research goal essential to conservation. As a first step, we have noted what pandas select as food in the Choushuigou and have calculated how much they eat and digest in terms of gross energy.

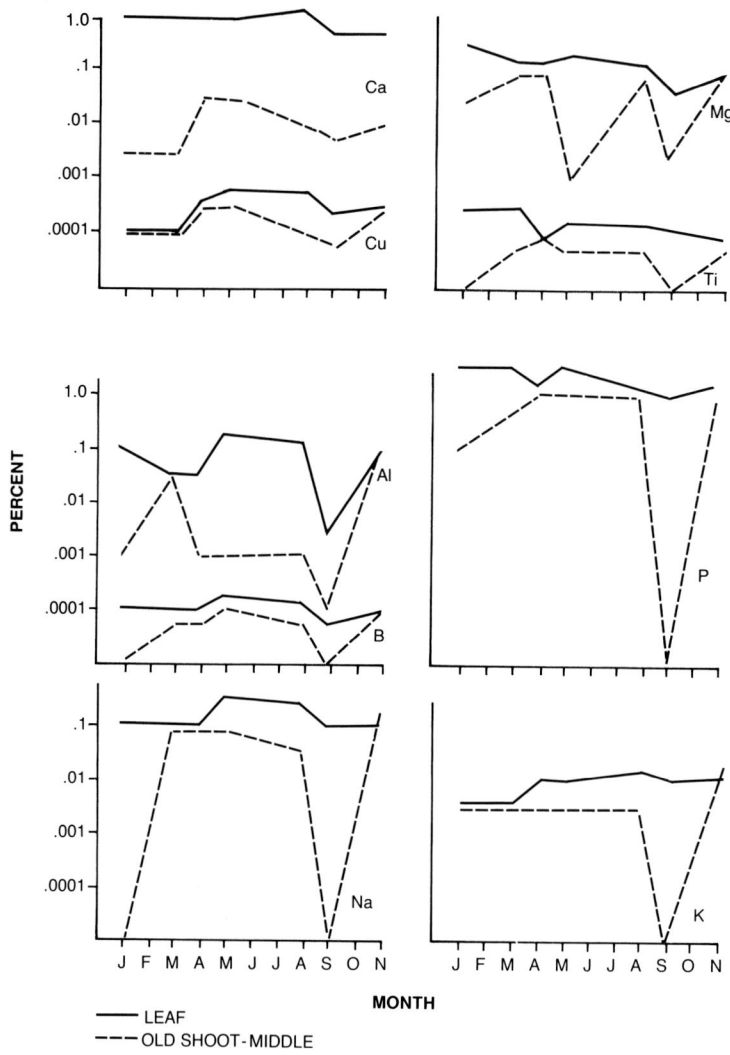

FIGURE 3.12   Percentage of 9 different minerals in leaf and old shoot (middle) of *Sinarundi-naria*, by month.

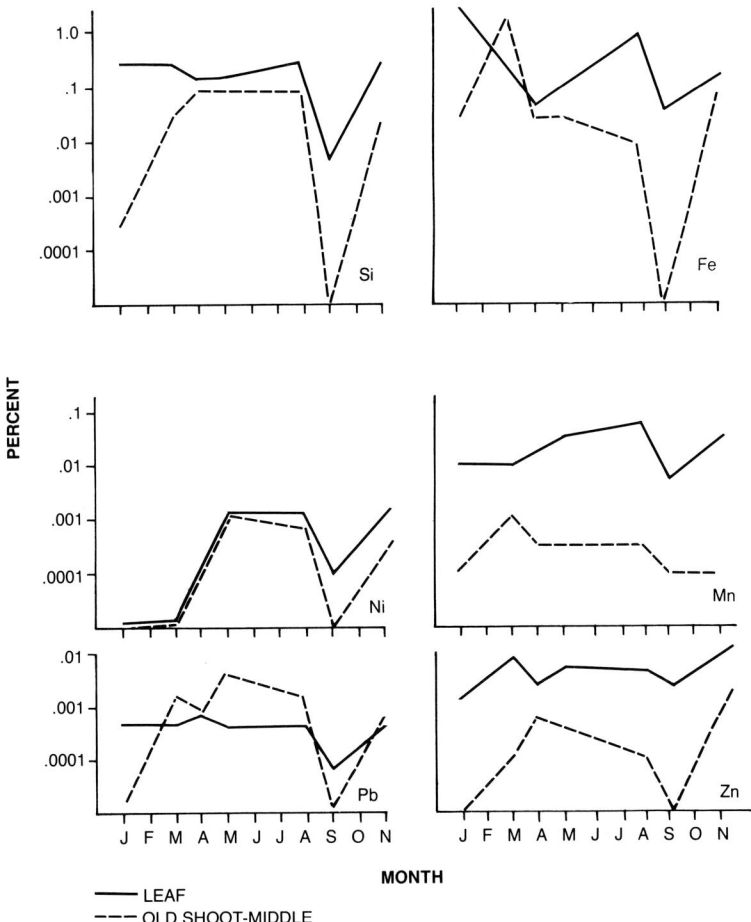

FIGURE 3.13   Percentage of 6 different minerals in leaf and old shoot (middle) of *Sinarundinaria*, by month.

Food selection

To obtain a few nutrients, mainly from cell content, a panda must also consume much cellulose and lignin, bulky material that fills the digestive tract and consequently limits the animal's food intake without contributing to maintenance. Therefore, a panda's optimum diet should consist of bamboo parts not only with the highest available nutrients but also with the lowest cellulose and lignin content. The leaves of *Sinarundinaria* and *Fargesia* have the most protein and least cellulose and lignin. Expressed as a ratio of protein to cellulose plus lignin, here termed the "nutritive quality ratio," the plant parts listed in order of decreasing food value are: leaves of *Sinarundinaria* (.432) and *Fargesia* (.368); branches of *Sinarundinaria*

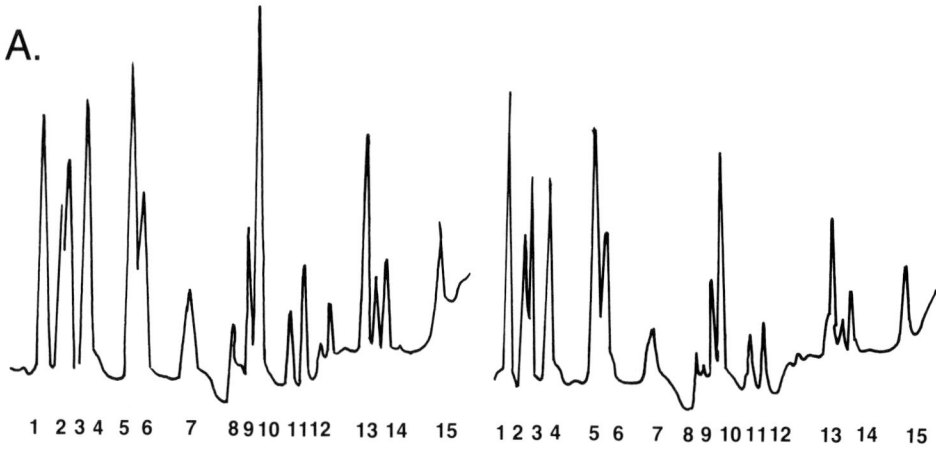

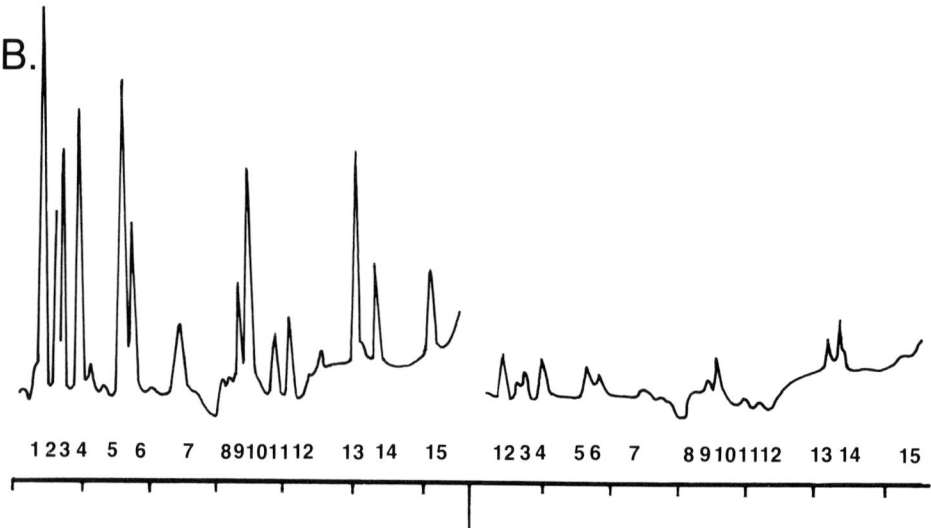

FIGURE 3.14   Amino acid content of bamboo, as determined by liquid chromatography. The relative concentration of each amino acid is determined by the height and width of peaks. A. The levels on the left represent amino acids in fresh *Sinarundinaria* leaves, and on the right, in the leaves of droppings.   B. The levels on the left represent amino acids in new *Fargesia* shoots, and on the right, in the shoots of droppings. Differential digestion and contamination with metabolic wastes account for the difference in amino acid levels of droppings. The numbers refer to the following amino acids: 1—aspartic acid; 2—threonine; 3—serine; 4—glutamic acid; 5—glycine; 6—alanine; 7—valine; 8—methionine; 9—isoleucine; 10—leucine; 11—tyrosine; 12—phenylalanine; 13—lysine; 14—histidine; 15—arginine.

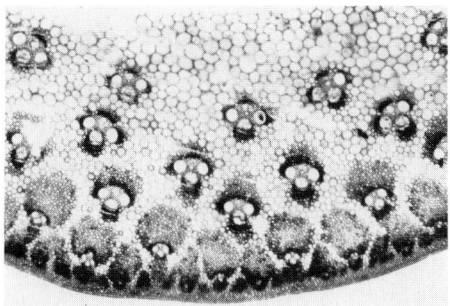 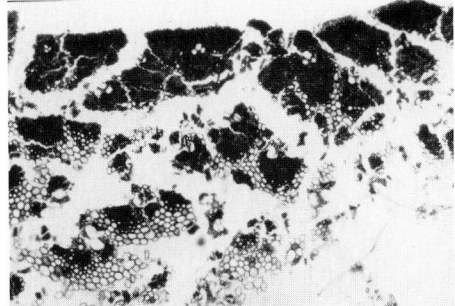

PLATE 3.5   A. A cross section through the internode of the middle part of a *Sinarundinaria fangiana* stem shows the typical monocotyledonous arrangement of cells.   B. A cross-section through a crushed and chewed piece of stem that has passed through the alimentary tract shows broken tissue and partial digestion.

(.137) and *Fargesia* (.086); old shoots of *Sinarundinaria* (.073) and *Fargesia* (.049); and stems of *Sinarundinaria* (.039) and *Fargesia* (.019). *Sinarundinaria* has a more favorable ratio in each category than *Fargesia*. Hemicellulose, partially digestible, is highest in leaves, somewhat lower in branches, and lowest in old shoots and stems; ash follows a similar pattern (figs 3.15 and 3.16). A panda would obtain the most nutrients, including minerals, and the least amount of indigestible bulk, by consuming only leaves. For a brief period each year, new *Sinarundinaria* shoots (ratio .354) and new *Fargesia* shoots (.485) also provide a food source nutritionally as good as leaves. How did the food habits of the pandas in our study conform to expectation?

Pandas favored *Sinarundinaria* over *Fargesia* perhaps because the former contains somewhat more protein and other nutrients and less cellulose and lignin, and, in addition, the balance of essential amino acids is better (table 3.9). It is known that altitude may affect nutritional levels: grasses in temperate climates tend to be more nutritious than those in tropical ones, high temperature and transpiration rates increasing lignin content (Minson and McLeod 1970). In November 1981, we collected *Phyllostachys nidularia* and *Pleioblastus armarus* growing at an altitude of only 400 m near the city of Chongqing in Sichuan, and found a protein content of 11.0% in leaves of the former and 7.7% in leaves of the latter, as compared to 14.1% for *Fargesia* in the Choushuigou. If altitudinal differences in nutrient content of bamboo are consistent, this might influence the food habits, as well as the carrying capacity and distribution, of pandas. Nutrition alone, however, probably does not explain the panda's preference for *Sinarundinaria* rather than *Fargesia*. Other factors, such as time and effort required to select, prepare, and eat the bamboo could also be involved.

When pandas do forage on *Fargesia*, they generally select leaves and branch tips, especially those of old shoots, as expected from our analyses. Stems are not much favored, hardly surprising given their low ratio, but we need to explain why pandas eat them at all. For example, in May and June, at a time when pandas select mainly new shoots, they also eat stems on occasion. Since new shoots are lower in soluble carbohydrates than are stems (fig 3.16), pandas perhaps eat the latter to supplement

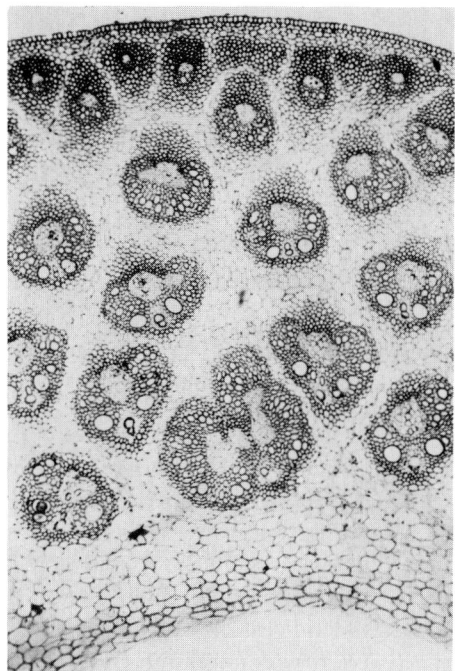 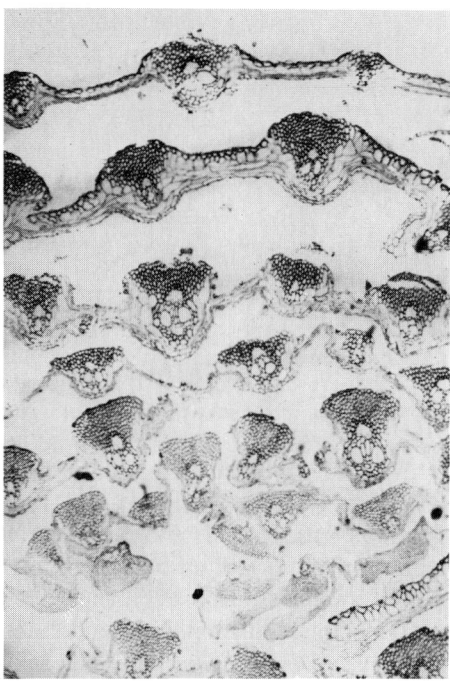

PLATE 3.6   A. A cross section through the middle of a new *Fargesia* shoot reveals the normal arrangement of cells.   B. A shoot section from a dropping indicates that many vascular bundles were little affected by digestion during the rapid passage through the alimentary tract.

energy intake. It is also possible that stems slow the rate of passage of new shoots through the digestive tract. With a passage time of as little as 5 hours, new shoots move through the tract more rapidly than stems. By increasing the retention time of shoots, which leads to more complete digestion, stems would contribute indirectly as well as directly to nutrition at this season.

Pandas eat mainly old *Sinarundinaria* shoots and leaves from November to March, primarily stems from April to June, and almost only leaves from July to October (fig 3.3). In winter, a choice of leaves is expected but a choice of old shoots puzzling because old shoots have a quality ratio below that of leaves. In spring, a choice of stems is surprising because stems have the least food value. We can only presume that leaves are in some way unpalatable or at least not favored at certain times of year, but our analyses do not give a definite indication as to which leaf constituent might cause such aversion.

Leaves have higher silica levels than do the other parts, which could make them distasteful or difficult to digest. Indeed, pandas eat proportionally the most leaves from July to October, when silica levels are lowest, and the least from April to June, when levels are highest. This inverse correlation does not extend into December and Janurary, when 30 to 40% of the panda's diet consists of leaves in spite of fairly high silica levels. One could suggest that foraging pandas select for stems that carry leaves low in silica during winter, but their unselective method of feeding by grasping handfuls argues against this, as does fecal analysis. *Sinarundinaria* fecal samples have silica values that correspond month by month to those of fresh leaves—3.0–4.2% at high levels and below 0.40% at low levels.

At times, leaves may have unacceptably low levels of certain amino acids and minerals. As shown in table 3.9, *Sinarundinaria* leaves contain higher levels of essential amino acids than do old shoots in summer, autumn, and winter; but the reverse is true in spring. This provides a tempting explanation for the panda's aversion to leaves in spring. Yet *Fargesia*, though containing more essential amino acids than do old shoots at all seasons, are also avoided in spring. None of the minerals we tested help to explain a change in diet; besides, leaves have consistently higher mineral levels, except for lead, than do old shoots. Alkaloids, tannins, and other plant toxins inhibit nutrient utilization, young leaves sometimes having higher concentrations of toxins than mature ones (Rhoades and Cates 1976). The element selenium is such a toxic substance if present at high levels. It has been found in bamboo leaves in areas where this mineral is common in the soil (McClure 1966); but, in general, grasses do not contain plant toxins.

The panda has a water imbalance for much of the year in that its food contains less water than do its feces. Possibly a panda selects for food with a high water content at a small cost in nutritional content. Although the different bamboo parts contain roughly similar percentages of water, as determined by averaging monthly samples,

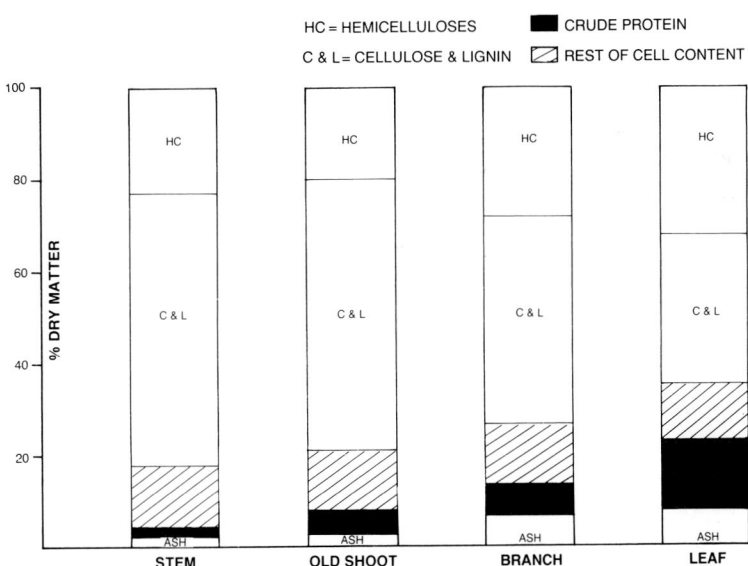

FIGURE 3.15 Nutrient content of different *Sinarundinaria* parts, expressed as percent dry matter. In figures 3.15 and 3.16, two-year and old stems have been combined, and the bottoms of old shoots and stems are excluded. Most crude protein and the rest of cell content are nutritionally available to pandas, as are 20–25% of the hemicelluloses; the cellulose and lignin are indigestible.

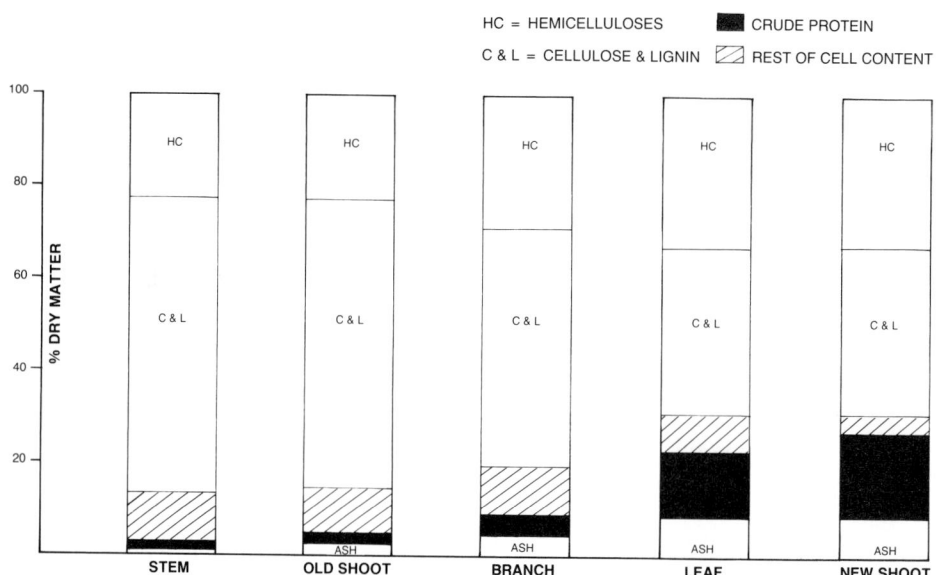

FIGURE 3.16   Nutrient content of different *Fargesia* parts, expressed as percent dry matter. (See fig. 3.15.)

some seasonal fluctuation occurs (tables B.3 and B.4). In general, *Sinarundinaria* and *Fargesia* have significantly less ($p < 0.05$) water from January to June than from July to December, and they have significantly more ($p < 0.05$) from August to October than at any other time (as determined by an inverse sine transformation of percent water followed by Duncan's multiple-range test). In winter, when surface water is most difficult to find, except as snow, old shoots contain more moisture than do leaves (fig 3.7), lending some credence to our idea. But from April to June, when pandas select stem, the leaves contain considerably more water.

If silica does affect leaf digestibility, we can suggest two reasons why pandas eat leaves in winter. First, a principal food item at this season is old shoots, which are of higher nutritional quality than other stems. Since old shoots are time-consuming to eat, a panda may devote only a certain number of hours to old shoots and then fill up on leaves, even though the nutrients in leaves are not as digestible in winter as in summer. Second, the passage rate of food through the intestines of herbivores can be speeded up by increasing particle size (Van Soest 1982). Diet selection in winter may be a compromise between two methods of increasing nutrient intake. Either an animal can increase the rate of passage by eating stems, but at a cost of feeding time, or it can decrease the rate and, at the same time, increase opportunity for digestion by eating leaves. These explanations presuppose that leaves are more palatable in winter than in spring when pandas rarely eat them.

To ascertain whether the panda's preference for certain bamboo parts is related to the level of crude protein, cell content, hemicellulose, cellulose, lignin, ash, or silica in the plant, we divided the monthly *Sinarundinaria* samples of leaves and stems (middle and top only) into 2 categories—the parts favored and the parts not favored by the animals at various times of year. Using a 3-way analysis of variance for unbalanced designs, we hoped to determine which of the 7 independent nutrient variables accounted for most of the variability observed in food selection. The results indicate that levels of crude protein ($p = 0.386$), cell content ($p = 0.687$), lignin ($p = 0.265$), ash ($p = 0.447$), and silica ($p = 0.754$) show no relation to the favored and nonfavored parts; that the hemicelluloses ($p = 0.080$) show a close but not statistically significant relation; and that cellulose ($p = 0.049$) bears a good relation. To determine whether animals indeed find cellulose important when discriminating between plant parts, a further statistical procedure was applied to the data. A stepwise discriminant analysis, using a BMD.07M computer program, indicated that cellulose was again the best single variable for discriminating between favored and nonfavored food, 76.84% of the cases we analyzed being correctly classified. Silica (73.68%) was the second best variable, but it provided no gain in our ability to classify favored and nonfavored food. A panda no doubt does select its food partly on the basis of cellulose content, disdaining those parts which are toughest to break or chew. And it probably does avoid leaves with a high silica content because of their abrasive quality. Yet, in spite of our analyses, we remain uncertain why pandas select stems rather than leaves during certain winter months.

New *Fargesia* shoots are much sought. Before eating a new shoot, however, the panda usually makes an effort to remove the sheath, even though sheaths have a quite favorable quality ratio of .262. There may be several reasons for discarding sheaths. The shoot core has an even higher ratio (.485) than the sheath, and the panda may simply be selecting for the most nutritious part. Furthermore, sheaths are hairy, perhaps making them less palatable. Dierenfeld (1981) tested *Phyllostachys* sheaths and found suggestive evidence for a tannin. When by late May many new shoots have grown tall and hard, their quality ratio drops to .168, and soon thereafter pandas switch to *Sinarundinaria* leaves.

Sinarundinaria rhizomes have a quality ratio of .075, and *Fargesia* rhizomes .100, both low values; pandas do not eat rhizomes.

At long intervals, bamboo flowers, produces seeds, and then dies. Its carbohydrates and proteins are supposedly exhausted, and all its energy is used up in reproduction (Janzen 1976). Several *Sinarundinaria* patches flowered in the study area in 1981, many did so in 1982, and the species mass-flowered in 1983. In late April 1981 we collected two-year stems and old stems in flower. The flowers had 23.4% protein, leaves 16.3%, branches 8.9%, and stems 2.7%—values similar to those of bamboo not in flower. Some stems die the same year in which they seed; others, blooming late in the season, retain the inflorescence into winter and die the following summer; and still others seed in spring but remain alive, with leaf and branch number reduced, at least through the following spring. In May 1982 we collected several living stems that had flowered in May 1981. Inflorescences were dead but the plants themselves were alive. The branches on several stems had grown grotesquely into "witch's brooms," with several dead inflorescences protruding from each. The protein content of leaves, branches (witch's broom), and stems is similar to that of bamboo that has not flowered (table B.5), as is the quality ratio of leaf (.483), branch (.155), and stem (.033). We therefore lack evidence to support the idea that flowering reduces the nutritional content of *Sinarundinaria* while it remains alive. Pandas presumably have adequate forage available during the early stages of mass-flowering.

Nutrient intake of pandas

We calculated that an adult panda in the wild ingests about 10–18 kg of *Sinarundinaria* leaves and stems per day. Lacking accurate average daily intake figures for each season, we assume an average consumption of 12.5 kg per day, or 4563 kg per year. The contents of 399 droppings provided an estimate of the percentage of leaves (including branch tips) and stem in the diet each month, figures from which we derived amounts of each consumed (table B.11). Our assumption that average food intake remains constant probably ignores certain variations. For example, pandas may consume less in April when on a stem diet than in August when on a leaf diet because stems are more time-consuming to eat. Individual differences due to size and sex no doubt exist too. However, by using one average we can obtain a first approximation of the relative amount of nutrients an animal obtains each season, and from this we can deduce which time of year is nutritionally most stressful to the panda.

CRUDE PROTEIN REQUIREMENTS. Protein is essential for maintenance and growth. The minimum daily protein requirements can be expressed as endogenous urinary nitrogen, multiplied by 6.25, a standard figure which assumes that protein contains 16% nitrogen and that all urinary nitrogen is derived from protein oxidation (Moen 1973). The requirements can be expressed by the equation $Q_{eun} = (2)(70)(W_{kg}^{0.75})(6.25)/1000$, where Q_{eun} represents the endogenous urinary nitrogen in g/day, and 2 the ratio of nitrogen in mg to kcal in the equation for basal metabolism, $70(W_{kg}^{0.75})$, a mean standard rate for mammals of 70 times the three-fourth power of their body weight. A 100 kg panda would require 27.65 g/day. This figure does not include protein lost in feces. Such loss can be calculated from the equation $Q_{mfn} = 5(F_{kg})(6.25)/6.25$, where Q_{mfn} equals the metabolic fecal nitrogen in g/day, 5 the estimated protein loss in grams per kilogram of dry matter intake per day for herbivores, and F_{kg} the dry matter intake in kg per day (Moen 1973). With a dry matter intake of 6 kg, a panda would require an additional 30 g of protein. A small amount of protein is also used for hair production. Using the equation $Q_{nh} = 0.02\ W_{kg}^{0.75}$, where Q_{nh} is the amount of nitrogen needed for hair growth in g/day (Moen 1973), a panda requires 3.94 g more protein. Assuming no gain in body weight, the total minimum requirement is 61.6 g/day. The equations are based on research with ruminants but probably apply in general terms to other large mammals as well. Bamboo contains different levels of various amino acids. A panda's daily requirements are unknown, but our calculated minimum protein intake may not contain all essential amino acids in the amounts needed daily by a panda. If we raise the protein intake by 1.5 (Crampton and Harris 1969) to a total of 92.4 g/day, then the animal will most likely obtain enough of those amino acids such as methionine in which bamboo is most deficient. Additional protein is needed for growth and reproduction.

Protein levels vary with different parts of the bamboo, and pandas select the leaves, old shoots, and stems of *Sinarundinaria* in different proportions depending on season. Taking this into account, the food of pandas in our study averaged 3.55% protein in spring (April–June), 14.49% in summer and autumn (July–October), and 7.02% in winter (November–March). Food intake was presumed to be 12.5 kg fresh weight; this figure was converted to dry weight on the basis of the data in table B.3. Dierenfeld (1981) found that protein digestibility in captive pandas is 90%. Given these figures, we calculated that pandas obtained 241.6 g of protein per day in spring, 645.6 in summer–autumn, and 401.9 g in winter. Free-living pandas often macerate bamboo poorly, and protein digestibility may at times be less than 90%. At a digestibility of 75% or even at 60%, protein intake is still above that required for maintenance if pandas consume 12.5 kg fresh weight of bamboo per day (see fig 7.2). Protein intake is lowest in spring, but during that season some animals switch to new *Fargesia* shoots. Such shoots average 17.6% protein. A panda consumes about 38.3 kg per day, providing the animal with 606.7 g protein at a 90% digestibility. Shoots enable pandas to increase their protein intake substantially for more than a month during a time of year when other forage is either unpalatable or low in protein.

HEMICELLULOSE DIGESTIBILITY. The hemicelluloses represent the only cell wall constituents that are nutritionally available to pandas. About 20–30% of bamboo (dry weight) consists of hemicelluloses. Since leaves and stems contain relatively low levels of soluble carbohydrates as part of the cell content (figs. 3.15 and 3.16), a panda benefits from any additional calories it can obtain from the hemicelluloses. Dierenfeld et al. (1982) found that the Washington pandas digested 27% of the hemicelluloses in *Phyllostachys* bamboo. To determine digestibility precisely, the amounts eaten and excreted by an animal must be known. Our figures present only estimates. There are also some differential weight changes in leaves and stems as they pass through the digestive tract—changes that introduce a bias when leaf and stem ratios are compared in food and feces.

The difference between the amount of hemicellulose ingested and excreted represents the amount digested. Based on the nutritional analyses of bamboo and feces and the ratios of leaves and stem eaten at various seasons, we derived a hemicellulose digestibility of 21.5% for spring, 26.0% for summer-autumn, and 18.2% for winter (table 3.12). One feeding trial with the captive Ping-Ping in September represents a check on the summer–autumn figure. His intake averaged 7.4 kg fresh weight or 2.93 kg dry weight of *Sinarundinaria* leaves; the hemicellulose digestibility was 29%. Our spring and summer-autumn figures appear to be of the correct order of magnitude, judging by data from captivity, but the winter figure inexplicably is several percentage points lower than we would expect. New *Fargesia* shoots have a calculated digestibility of 40%.

TABLE 3.12

HEMICELLULOSE DIGESTIBILITY BY SEASON, BASED ON A 12.5 KG (FRESH WEIGHT) BAMBOO INTAKE PER DAY

	Spring		Summer-autumn		Winter	
	Bamboo	Feces	Bamboo	Feces	Bamboo	Feces
Dry matter intake/kg[a]	7.56	6.62	4.95	3.80	6.36	5.17
Diet ratio, leaf:stem[b]	9:91	7:93	89:11	86:14	30:70	29:71
Leaf						
% Hemicellulose	34.96	31.02	36.41	35.19	34.55	32.37
Hemicellulose intake/kg	.24	.14	1.61	1.15	.66	.48
Stem[c]						
% Hemicellulose	25.64	23.44	22.47	25.10	22.27	23.78
Hemicellulose intake/kg	1.76	1.43	.12	.13	.99	.87
Total hemicellulose intake/kg	2.00	1.57	1.73	1.28	1.65	1.35
Hemicellulose digestibility (%)	21.5		26.0		18.2	

[a]Percent dry matter of bamboo in spring is 60.5, summer-autumn 39.6, and winter 50.9.
[b]For fecal ratios see table B.11.
[c]Adjusted for percent old shoot and other stem (see table 3.2).

DRY MATTER DIGESTIBILITY. Protein and hemicelluloses are just two of the constituents that provide a panda with nutrients. Dry matter digestibility is an expression of total nutrient intake. The best method of measuring dry matter digestibility, given the limitations of our data, is by using an internal indicator or marker; that is, by comparing the concentration of an indigestible constituent in food and feces, the digested material can be calculated. Lignin is such a marker in mature plants (Van Soest 1982). We first determined the percent difference in lignin between leaves in plant and leaves in feces on a monthly basis and then between stem and feces. Three lignin values—for December and January leaf and December stem—were excluded from the calculations because the digestibility had a minus value, perhaps due to a deviation in chemical analyses or digestive interference from the high levels of silica in the leaves during those months. Averaged by season and adjusted to the proportion of leaves and stems in the diet, dry matter digestibility for spring was 12.47%, summer-autumn 23.25%, and winter 18.70%. These figures follow expectation in that they are lowest in spring when pandas subsist on stem, and highest in summer-autumn when they eat leaves.

Lignin in immature plants, such as bamboo shoots, has a composition different from that of mature plants, and much of it disappears while passing through the digestive tract. The digestibility of new *Fargesia* shoots can be calculated without the use of a marker. Since new shoots and feces both contain about 90% water, and since about 40% by weight of shoots disappears in the digestive tract (table 3.7), we can assume that dry matter digestibility is also about 40%.

DIGESTIBLE ENERGY. Having estimated dry matter digestibility, we can now derive a figure for the digestible energy per day available to a panda. Using a bomb calorimeter, Dierenfeld (1981) determined that the gross energy of *Phyllostachys aureosulcata* leaves was 4800 kcal/kg, of stems 4600 kcal/kg, and of new shoots 4400 kcal/kg. The chemical composition of *Phyllostachys* (Dierenfeld et al. 1982) being similar to that of the bamboo we studied, we assume that gross energy is too. On a diet of 12.5 kg (fresh weight) of *Sinarundinaria* leaf and stem, a panda would obtain about 4354 kcal/day in spring, 5488 kcal in summer-autumn, and 5542 kcal in winter (table 3.13). Although these values are approximate, they do show that spring is nutritionally the leanest season for a panda foraging on *Sinarundinaria*. Those pandas that switch at that time to new *Fargesia* shoots, however, have for 1–1¼ months a caloric intake of 6741 kcal/day if they consume 38.3 kg (fresh weight) per day.

We still lack systematic observations on food intake of individual animals. During one winter period of 5.5 days, Wei ate an average of 6654 kcal/day; Zhen once ate 4518 kcal on a winter day and 4140 kcal on a spring one (see "Food intake," above).

The captive Ping-Ping consumed 2.93 kg *Sinarundinaria* leaves and 1.64 kg new *Fargesia* shoots, dry weight, during feeding trials (see tables 3.6 and 3.7), which provided him with 3270 and 2893 kcal/day, respectively. His intake was considerably lower than that estimated for free-living animals.

These preliminary results reveal certain trends in the nutrient intake of pandas. Although our calculations were confined to *Sinarundinaria*, our comments apply also to *Fargesia*. The animals appear to derive considerably more protein from their diet than they need for maintenance and growth. So far, we have assumed that pandas select for the protein-rich parts of the bamboo. It is likely that they do so. However, they do not need to consume as much bamboo as they do to obtain the required amount of protein. The leaves and stems of plants contain relatively small amounts of soluble carbohydrates and fats (Hladik 1978; Milton 1980), both of which an animal needs for energy. It seems likely that pandas must eat so much bamboo not to fulfill protein requirements but to obtain calories in the form of soluble carbohydrates and fats. Stems are as good as leaves in providing such energy from cell content (figs. 3.15 and 3.16)—probably one reason they are so readily eaten in winter—but leaves have the further advantage of being rich in protein. Extra protein can also be deaminated and used as an energy source, although it is a relatively poor

TABLE 3.13
Estimated total digestible energy (in kcal/day) obtained by free-living
pandas on a diet of *Sinarundinaria* and new *Fargesia* shoots

	Dry matter intake (kg)[a]	Diet ratio, Leaf:stem	Gross energy (kcal)[b]	Dry matter digestibility (%)	Digestible energy (kcal/day)
Spring					
Leaf and stem	7.56	9:91	34,912	12.47	4,354
New *Fargesia* shoot	3.83	—	16,852	40.00	6,741
Summer-autumn	4.95	89:11	23,604	23.25	5,488
Winter	6.63	30:70	29,638	18.70	5,542

[a]Based on 12.5 kg (fresh weight) intake except for 38.3 kg new *Fargesia* shoot.
[b]Based on 4,800 kcal/kg leaf, 4,600 stem, 4,400 new shoot (Dierenfeld 1981).

fuel. Only one-third can be burned for energy, the rest being excreted by the body as nitrogen. In addition, the panda partially degrades hemicellulose, a structural component abundant in all parts of the bamboo. Hemicellulose digestibility averages 22%, its sugar components thus contributing substantially to a panda's caloric intake.

Our figures for protein intake, dry matter digestibility, and digestible energy all show clearly that spring is nutritionally the poorest time of the year for the pandas that forage only on *Sinarundinaria*. With leaves apparently unpalatable, animals subsist mostly on stems, which are lowest in both protein and hemicelluloses. The actual caloric intake is possibly even lower than we calculated because pandas may not always eat the estimated 12.5 kg of stem a day. New *Fargesia* shoots provide an important alternative food source at that season. After a nutrient-poor month that includes the stresses of the mating season, pandas have the high-quality shoots of May available. For a month the caloric intake of those that descend into *Fargesia* is at least equal to that of the best time of year. And when the nutritional level of shoots begins to drop, animals can soon switch to the good leaf diet of summer.

Effects of pandas on bamboo

To measure impact of pandas on their food supply is not possible until bamboo has been studied in detail. It is particularly important to know how long stems live, what factors cause death, and to what extent reproductive and mortality rates vary from year to year. Since we lack detailed data on these topics, our observations are only preliminary.

Effect on leaves and stems

Sinarundinaria is the most important food of pandas in the study area, animals subsisting on it throughout the year, except for brief periods when some forage on *Fargesia*. To determine bamboo density and biomass available to pandas, we clipped 1 m² samples bimonthly* at 30 sites (fig. 2.8)—26 in *Sinarundinaria* and 4 in *Fargesia*—selected for differences in exposure, degree of slope, and canopy coverage. The number of dead stems, old shoots, and live stems on each plot were counted, and each category was weighed (table 3.14). In addition, we weighed leaves, branches, and stems separately in 3 plots of each species to determine how much each component contributes to total biomass. Our biomass calculations exclude roots and rhizomes, even though they constitute about one-third of the total weight of bamboo (J. Campbell, pers. comm.), because pandas do not dig them up.

Sinarundinaria

Below 3100 m, the average number of old *Sinarundinaria* shoots per m² was 10 and of stems 64, a total of 74, and the average biomass was 1.4 kg; above 3200, the

---

*The July samples have not been included in our calculations because of methodological problems in classifying stems.

average number of old shoots and stems totaled 62, and the biomass was 0.7 kg, bamboo being stunted in growth. Biomass was somewhat higher in summer than at other seasons. This was due partly to new growth and partly to a general increase in the water content of bamboo (fig. 3.17).

How much food do pandas like Wei or Long, who spend most of the year in *Sinarundinaria* below 3100 m, have available? Bamboo coverage around Erdaoping, the upper Zhuanjinggou, and Fanzipeng, where the radio-collared pandas spent most time, is about 85%, there being few clearings, landslips, or other sites devoid of bamboo. At this coverage, one km^2 would provide 8.5 million old shoots and 54.4 million stems for a total biomass of 1.19 million kg, fresh weight. Of this biomass, about 16.1% or 191,590 kg consisted of leaves, 11.5% or 136,850 kg of branches, and the rest of old shoots and other stems.

An adult panda ingested about 10 to 18 kg of *Sinarundinaria* leaves and stems per day. Taking a conservative average of 12.5 kg, an animal would require 4562.5 kg per year. On an annual basis, the panda's diet consisted of 43% leaves and branch tips and 57% stems (table B.11). An animal therefore consumed only 0.59% by weight of the available leaves and branches on 1 km^2, a small harvest. Furthermore, stems whose leaves and branch tips have been browsed are not permanently damaged; new leaves and branches sprout from the remaining branch nodes. In winter, pandas we observed ate about 80% old shoot and 20% stem, and the rest of the year 7% old shoot and 93% stem (table 3.2). On the average, 52 cm from an old shoot and 36 cm from a stem were consumed (table 3.1), the former weighing about 6.5 g and the latter 5 g. On the basis of these figures, a panda would need roughly 174,000 old shoots and 292,000 stems for a total of 466,000 in the course of a year. This translates into 2.1% of the total number of old shoots and 0.5% of other stems in 1 km^2. A

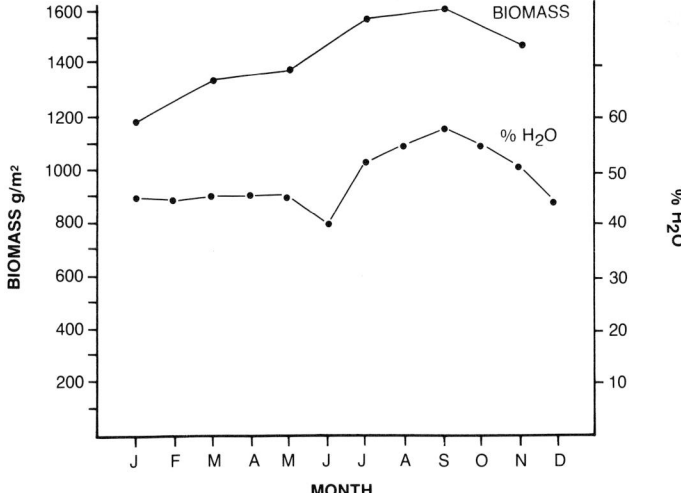

FIGURE 3.17 Average biomass (fresh weight) of *Sinarundinaria* on 1 m^2 plots below 3100 m (N = 159) at different times of year, compared with average percent water in *Sinarundinaria*.

stump seldom sprouts after a panda has bitten the top off, the stem having effectively
been destroyed. An old shoot weighs, on the average, 18.8 g and a stem 19.0 (table
3.14), so a panda destroys about 0.74% of the *Sinarundinaria* biomass on 1 km^2
annually. This figure does not include any new shoots a panda may eat or stems it
may break without eating.

The impact of such destruction depends on the annual increment of stems. In
early 1981, we established four 1 m^2 plots at Erdaoping. These plots contained a total
of 255 old shoots and stems. By early 1982, about 28 new shoots had appeared, and
21 old shoots and stems had died of causes other than panda destruction, an annual
increment in stem number for this particular year of 2.7% or 1.75 stems per
m^2—enough to support 2–3 pandas per km^2 without detriment to the food supply,
assuming that there was no other major stem predation and our sample was typical of
the area as a whole. Two factors reduce the panda's impact on *Sinarundinaria*: some
animals forage for brief periods on stunted bamboo above 3100 m, and some descend
for part of the year into *Fargesia*.

Fargesia

Density of old *Fargesia* shoots and stems averaged 37 per m^2, and the biomass was
3.01 kg per m^2 (table 3.14). This species covers an estimated 40% of its area, with
14.8 million old shoots and stems per km^2 and a biomass of 1.21 million kg. Leaves
constituted 16.2% of the total biomass, branches 14.9%, and old shoot and stem the
rest. In winter, pandas ate mainly *Fargesia* leaves, breaking or biting off only about
20% of the stems on which they browsed; in May and June they sometimes fed on
stems, but the great bulk of their food at that time consisted of new shoots. Since
pandas spent little time in *Fargesia*, they destroyed few stems.

Pandas prefer to eat the leaves of old shoots in winter. Transects showed that in
1981, a poor shoot year, only one new shoot per m^2 survived to become an old shoot
in parts of the study area, and it is possible that this favored item was in relatively
short supply. An old shoot weighs an average of 114.6 g, of which about 10.5%
consists of leaves, as determined from a sample of 20 old shoots, or 4813 kg of leaves
per km^2. During the winter of 1981–82, a panda would have had to spend more time
in search of this food than during the winter of 1982–83, when old shoots were about
twice as abundant.

In early 1981 we counted 177 stems in 4 plots totaling 5 m^2. Nineteen new shoots
appeared, of which 10 were killed by pandas and insects. Nine stems had died by
early 1982, apparently of old age. Thus, the number of stems in these plots remained
static that year.

Shoot production and stem mortality vary not only from year to year but also with
altitude, density of bamboo stands, exposure of slope, and other factors. Annual
variation in number of new shoots may lead to fluctuations in the number of stems
dying later in any one year. *Sinarundinaria* stems in our plot died at the rate of 6.7%
a year and *Fargesia* at 5.1%. Both figures are lower than an expected 10–20% if the
death rate is constant and longevity of stems only 5–10 years (McClure 1966).
Campbell et al. (1983) estimated that longevity of *Sinarundinaria* and *Fargesia* stems

TABLE 3.14
Number and biomass of bamboo stems in 1m² sample plots

| | Sinarundinaria | | | | Fargesia | |
| | Below 3100m altitude | | Above 3200 altitude | | | |
	Jan.–May	Sept.–Nov.	Jan.–May	Sept.–Nov.	Jan.–May	Sept.–Nov.
Total samples	94	46	10	6	20	8
Mean number						
Dead	26.6 ±17.6	27.9 ±20.3	15.9 ±7.2	10.3 ±6.9	10.4 ±6.3	9.0 ±6.1
Old shoot	11.6 ±7.3	8.7 ±6.4	7.5 ±2.2	8.0 ±4.4	5.3 ±3.0	4.4 ±1.4
2yr. + old	64.0 ±23.7	63.7 ±21.1	51.6 ±11.4	52.7 ±18.3	36.3 ±17.4	27.8 ±9.0
Total live stems	75.6	72.4	63.0	60.7	41.6	32.2
Mean weight (g)						
Dead	147.1 ±101.3	180.4 ±157.1	71.7 ±49.0	47.5 ±37.6	127.6 ±86.7	223.8 ±121.3
Old shoot	199.1 ±137.8	175.9 ±135.1	73.0 ±34.2	56.7 ±36.5	387.3 ±359.0	686.9 ±311.3
2yr. + old	1058.0 ±454.7	1369.2 ±589.4	684.1 ±334.6	609.2 ±211.9	2219.1 ±929.8	2735.6 ±1050.3
Total live stems	1257.5	1545.1	757.1	665.9	2606.4	3422.5

New shoots in May are excluded.
T-tests comparing the January–May and September–November biomass samples in each category show no significant differences; biomass of *Sinarundinaria* below 3100 m is significantly greater than that above 3200 m ($p<0.0001$).

is about 8 years and that most mortality occurs in the last few years. Such variation has an influence on the number of stems available to pandas and, conversely, on the impact of pandas on bamboo.

Recruitment of *Sinarundinaria* at Erdaoping and other such high-altitude sites was somewhat greater than mortality (Campbell et al. 1983), confirming our observations from the sample plots. But at low elevations, mortality may have exceeded recruitment in part because some stems flowered there in 1981 and 1982. Virtually all remaining *Sinarundinaria* blossomed in 1983. This imminent flowering may have inhibited shoot production from the late 1970s onward. *Fargesia* was not in flower, nor was there evidence that it might soon bloom, yet it had a low recruitment rate—about 4% in 1981, 7% in 1982, and 5% in 1983—largely the result of poor shoot production and survival (see below). Our observations and those of Campbell et al. (1983) indicated that the number of *Fargesia* stems was static or declining, depending on area. Any stem destruction by pandas will, therefore, further reduce the density of stands.

Other mammalian stem and leaf eaters

Mammals other than the giant panda consume bamboo, and these could have an influence on the number of pandas an area can support.

UNGULATES. Sambar deer, serow, and tufted deer forage on leaves and the tops of old shoots. In summer, a few takin enter the Choushuigou and eat the leaves of the two bamboos, as well as those of herbs, shrubs, and small trees; Hu (1981c) lists 40 takin food plants. Since these and other ungulates are scarce in the area, their impact on bamboo is negligible.

MONKEYS. Golden monkeys occur throughout the study area. From March to September most or all animals may be in one large group, numbering 200–300, which ranges out of the Choushuigou into neighboring valleys, covering an area of over 25 km². During winter, the monkeys occur in smaller units of up to 75 animals. The monkeys' main food in summer consists of leaves from shrubs and trees (Hu et al. 1980); in winter, it consists of birch buds, *Hydrangea* bark, and, most important, *Ramalina*, *Usnea* and other tree lichens. Hu Jinchu only once observed monkeys eating bamboo leaves.

RED PANDA. Red pandas were rare, but several individuals frequented Erdaoping and the slope below Wuyipeng. Droppings resembled those of the giant panda in shape but were only about 4.5 cm in length, 2.0 cm in width, and 4 to 9 g in weight. Water content of a January dropping was 71.2%. All winter droppings we examined consisted of finely chewed bamboo leaves; spring droppings consisted of new *Fargesia* shoots.

BAMBOO RAT. The bamboo rat is the only mammal, other than man, which may compete with the giant panda for bamboo stems. The genus with its three species is distributed from Assam eastward across Burma, Indochina, Malaya, and Sumatra to southern China. *Rhizomys sinense*, the species in western Sichuan, has soft, thick, gray fur; it is about 40 cm long, including the almost naked tail (Allen 1940), and weighs about 1 kg. It is heavy-bodied and short-legged with large digging claws, well adapted to subterranean life. Earthmounds, about 30–70 cm in diameter and 10–25 cm high, point to the presence of bamboo rat burrows. In the Choushuigou such burrows were usually on slightly sloping but not steep terrain in areas with few rocks and deep soil. We excavated about a third of the 207 m^2 covered by one active burrow system as well as two small, unoccupied systems.

Burrows run about 15–20 cm below the surface, just beneath the horizontally spreading bamboo rhizomes; they are 15–20 cm wide and 13–17 high, but may be wider at junctions. One nest chamber had a floor space of 35 × 46 cm and contained a bed of bamboo leaves. At certain places a burrow may be widened to serve as a latrine. Droppings measure 2.5 × 1 cm and consist of finely chewed stem. A burrow system contains some passages filled with earth and some with discarded food and feces (fig. 3.18).

Bamboo rats collect bamboo in two ways. Venturing from the burrow, an animal cuts off a stem, leaving a stump 7–17 cm high, pulls the stem underground, and closes the entrance with earth. In the security of its burrow, a bamboo rat may also cut stems where they join the rhizome or the rhizome itself; sometimes an earth mound is pushed up around the base of several stems, which are then bitten off. The large burrow we excavated had two fresh piles of *Sinarundinaria* in it, one with 11 stems, the other with about 21. A bamboo rat often eats just the bottom of a steam, however, leaving the rest standing upright in the soil, without pulling the stem into the burrow.

The animals eat mainly stem and some rhizome; leaves, branches, and roots appear not to be taken. Feeding seemed unselective in May when we excavated the burrows. Of 32 *Sinarundinaria* stems collected by the bamboo rat, 3 were old shoots and 29 other stems; of 17 stems in one *Fargesia* clump, 14 had been consumed.

By cutting stems intensively in a small area, a bamboo rat creates openings in the bamboo. A dense rat population could therefore affect the panda by eliminating habitat. On the other hand, bamboo rats may stimulate production of new shoots by thinning out dense stands—a benefit to pandas, at least with respect to *Fargesia*. The impact of the two stem-eating species on each other requires study in an area where both are more abundant than in the Choushuigou.

Janzen (1976) hypothesized that synchronous flowering and seeding of bamboo may be a means of assuring the survival of some seeds by satiating seed predators, such as rodents, with food. Since individuals that flower out of phase would increase the probability of having their seeds destroyed, selection would favor synchrony. Vertebrate seed predators may become noticeably abundant when bamboo flowers (Janzen 1976; Veblen 1982), but we have neither seen nor heard of this occurring with respect to *Fargesia* or *Sinarundinaria*. Flowering actually has an adverse effect on one rodent, the bamboo rat. In the Min Mountains, bamboo rats have been observed to migrate in large numbers out of areas with dying *Fargesia*.

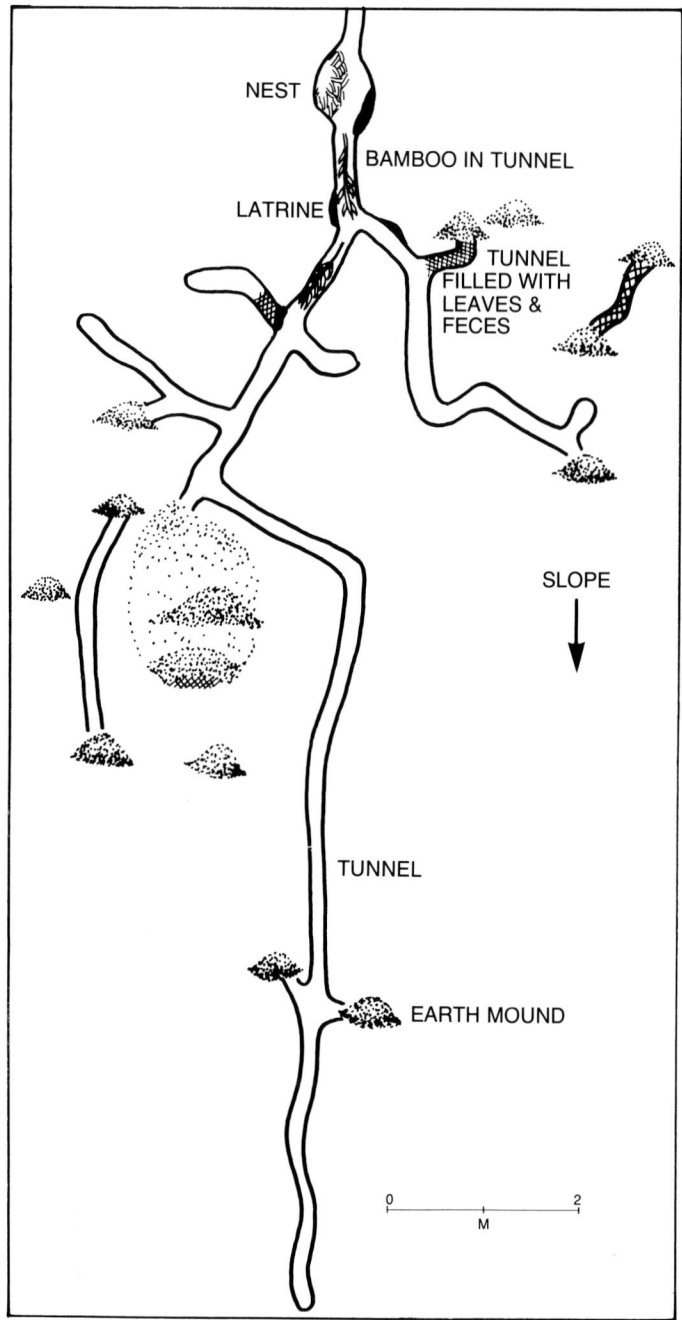

FIGURE 3.18   The tunnel system of a bamboo rat in *Sinarundinaria* habitat. We excavated only about one-third of the total system, the rest extending uphill. (Excavated with the help of J. Campbell.)

In sum, none of these mammals has an appreciable effect on bamboo, and the giant panda, in spite of its rarity, remains the most important consumer of stems and leaves in the study area.

Effect on new Fargesia shoots

When pandas forage on new *Fargesia* shoots, they select for a limited, short-term resource, taking it in prodigious amounts, an ideal situation for measuring impact.

As a first step, we needed to know how many shoots per unit area were being produced and how many survived. In spring 1982 we established 32 permanent plots totaling 62 m^2 to record shoot production. These plots contained 1.0 old shoots—the survivors of the 1981 shoot crop—per m^2. Sampling more widely in the Choushuigou, J. Campbell (pers. comm.) obtained a figure of 1.7 old shoots per m^2. A number of his plots were located in areas where pandas seldom foraged on shoots, partly explaining the difference in results. Of the new shoots produced in the 32 plots in 1982, 2.5 per m^2 survived to 1983. And of those produced in 1983, 1.3 per m^2 survived to the following year. Thus, density of surviving shoots in these plots over 3 years ranged from 1.0 to 2.5 per m^2, a variation that, if typical, may have a marked impact on *Fargesia* because feeding pressure by pandas will under normal circumstances change little from one year to the next.

Pandas often forage for an hour or more in one bamboo stand before moving to another site, and during this period they may eat most of the preferred shoots. In 1981 we measured the panda's impact by counting shoots eaten and not eaten in 5 sample areas, totaling 1068 m^2 (table 3.15). The pandas removed an average of 59.1% of the shoots. Many of the remaining shoots were of a height or diameter not preferred by pandas; of 277 shoots not eaten in the two largest sample areas, 27% belonged to the nonpreferred category.

In 1981 we tagged 37 shoots to measure growth rates, but also noted that pandas ate 24.3% of our sample during May and June that year. Wanting more information on this point, we recorded shoot mortality in sample plots during 1982 and 1983. Of the shoots produced between April and June, pandas took 12% during this period in 1982, and 24% in 1983 (table 3.16). The high rate of predation in 1983 was partly due to the small number of plots (32 versus 83), and partly because Zhen happened to plunder 32 shoots from the two most productive plots.

TABLE 3.15

PERCENTAGE OF NEW *Fargesia* SHOOTS EATEN BY A PANDA DURING A SINGLE VISIT TO SAMPLE AREAS, JUNE 1981

Area (m^2)	Shoots (m^2)	Total shoots	Shoots eaten (%)	Weight shoots not eaten (kg)
45	.64	29	72.4	.50
63	1.03	68	70.7	1.72
68	.87	59	62.7	1.68
176	.64[a]	114	35.1	—
716	.63	449	54.7	17.59

[a]The same panda also ate 30 shoots in the same area two weeks earlier.

The panda is not the only shoot predator. Takin, sambar, tufted deer, wild pig, porcupine, and, at lower elevation, badger, hog badger, and palm civet all eat shoots. One Asiatic black bear dropping in the Zhuanjinggou consisted wholly of shoots, as did all droppings in two red panda latrines. Among small mammals, we observed pikas and rock squirrels gnaw shoots; rats and mice probably do so as well. It is likely that bamboo rats took several of our tagged shoots, which vanished without trace. Greater parrotbill rip through sheaths with their strong bills and eat the tender shoot tops. The impact of all these species, however, was minor (table 3.16).

Among the most important shoot predators in the study areas were insects, particularly beetles and flies of the family Anthomyiiadae. Shoots often stopped growing, usually before reaching a height of 50 cm, and became soft and yellowish. One or more larvae, sometimes of two sizes, could be found inside the internodes, eating the interior and ultimately killing the shoot. In 1981, insects killed 29.7% of the sample; in 1982, they had killed 15.6% by the end of June and a few more by mid-September, raising total mortality for the season to 15.7%; and in 1983 they had killed 12.0% by early June (table 3.16).

Since pandas and insects both ate shoots, we needed to determine to what extent the two were competing for the same resource. Insects attacked shoots of all sizes but preferred those with a diameter of 0.7–0.9 cm ($p < 0.001$) and generally avoided those with a diameter of 1.3 cm and above ($p < 0.001$). Although predation showed some overlap, insects essentially selected for thin shoots and pandas for thick ones (fig. 3.5, table 3.3).

In spite of the fact that wildlife in the Choushuigou is now rare, with bears, wild pigs and other shoot-eating species decimated by man, pandas and insects still destroyed one-third to one-half of the new shoots. In areas with more abundant wildlife, animals could well remove much or all of the annual production in a poor shoot year. Those shoots that did survive would be further reduced the following winter because pandas select for them strongly. Since predators, except perhaps insects, cannot adjust population size to shoot abundance during the short season, *Fargesia* can compensate for its losses only with good shoot years. One 2 m² *Fargesia* plot had 92 living stems in January 1981. Five new shoots were produced that year,

TABLE 3.16
PERCENTAGE OF NEW *Fargesia* SHOOTS DESTROYED BY PREDATORS, MAY–JUNE

Predator	1981 (N = 37 shoots) %	1982 (N = 724 shoots)[a] %	1983 (N = 209 shoots)[b]
Insects	29.7	15.6	12.0
Giant panda	24.3	12.0	23.9
Rodents and Lagomorphs	2.7	3.7	6.2
Domestic goat	—	.3	—
Unknown	—	4.0	.5
Total	56.7	35.6	42.6

[a]Data collected in collaboration with J. Campbell.
[b]Observations to 8 June only.

but pandas and insects took all. Eight stems had died by January 1982, a net loss of 8 for the year. Of 19 new shoots that spring, 6 survived, but 7 stems died. Of 24 new shoots in 1983, all but 4 were taken by pandas and insects, and 7 stems died, a net loss of 12 stems in 3 years. In this plot, at least, shoot predation was responsible for the decline in stems.

Pandas, tending to select for thick shoots, often forage along the edge of thickets. Both these habits can have a long-term impact on a *Fargesia* stand. The removal of shoots from the edge prevents or slows the spread of bamboo into unoccupied areas. Consistent removal of thick shoots permits a disproportionate number of thin ones to survive, which ultimately produces low, dense thickets composed of spindly stems, leaning into each other, their tops easily broken by snow. As a stand becomes more dense, shoots grow less abundantly and are, on the average, thinner (table 3.5). As noted earlier, a second and minor peak of shoot emergence occurred between July and mid-September 1982, after pandas had ceased to forage in *Fargesia* and insect predation was negligible. Of 47 such shoots appearing in our plots, 83% were 0.8 cm or less in diameter, as compared to 18.8% during the May–June period; and 95% of these thin shoots were away from the edge, as compared to 13.4% during May–June. These late-season, thin shoots in the interior accelerate the trend toward stands composed of fragile stems and less vital reproduction. One way to reverse such a trend, to open up areas for new growth, is to remove all old bamboo. The periodic mass-flowering, seeding, and death of *Fargesia* has just this effect. Janzen (1976) discusses possible reasons for the synchronous nature of flowering, such as the need to assure widespread pollination and provide favorable environmental conditions for the new generation of seedlings.

Discussion

In the Choushuigou, pandas affect *Sinarundinaria* mainly by destroying stems, and *Fargesia* by selecting for new shoots. *Sinarundinaria* had a recruitment rate of about 1.75 stems per m^2 in the areas most favored by pandas, and we calculated that even such a small number was enough to support at least two animals per km^2 without detriment to the bamboo. About 12 pandas inhabited 15 km^2 of *Sinarundinaria* more or less permanently during 1981, or 0.8 pandas per km^2. Although many parts of the study area were less densely covered with *Sinarundinaria* than the sites at which we sampled bamboo, the panda population still appeared to be low, well below carrying capacity if only food availability is considered. Other factors, of course, such as preference for a certain type of terrain, social interactions, and mortality, keep numbers down.

Long-term research on pandas and bamboo is necessary before we can determine how many pandas even one small area can support. And the carrying capacity of every area will differ depending on stem density, percent coverage, relative palatability of leaves and stems, and the presence of food competitors. Of importance, too, is the number of bamboo species available to a panda population. With two or more species present, pandas can shift seasonally to take advantage of preferred items. For example, in the Liang Mountains, where panda habitat still extends from 1300 m to timberline, several bamboos provide succulent new shoots, among them *Qiong-zhuea* from late March into July, depending on altitude, and *Chimonobambusa* in August and September. In such a situation the bamboos not only provide pandas with nutritious food for an extended season but also serve as each other's buffers, deflecting foraging pressure on each other for part of the year.

That the panda's impact on bamboo may be more subtle and far-reaching than mere destruction of shoots and stems was shown by their choice of new *Fargesia* shoots. By selecting for new shoots of a certain size in certain locations, pandas may help to determine the height and density of stands, average stem diameter, and rate of colonization of unoccupied terrain.

The number of new shoots surviving annually, coupled with the death rate of old stems, ultimately determines panda-carrying capacity. Nonetheless, survival and mortality rates of shoots and stems vary considerably from year to year. Pandas reproduce slowly. Unable to adjust their numbers to short-term fluctuations in bamboo abundance, they depend on the vegetative vitality of the plants to compensate for any reduction of stems they may have temporarily caused. Only during the periodic mass-flowering and dying may the panda be seriously affected; to avoid possible starvation, it must be able either to switch to another bamboo species or to emigrate from the affected area.

Summary

1. Although pandas may eat various plants, as well as meat, more than 99% of their food consists of bamboo stems, branches, and leaves. In the study area, pandas spent more than 85% of the year above 2600 m in *Sinarundinaria fangiana* bamboo, frequenting *Fargesia spathacea* at low elevations mainly in May and June, the season when new shoots are a favored food. Animals are selective when eating *Sinarundinaria*: from November to March they consume mainly leaves and young stems, from April to June mainly old stems, and from July to October almost exclusively leaves. Food intake of adults was estimated at 10–18 (av. 12.5) kg, fresh weight, per day when animals were foraging on leaves and stem; and 38 kg—or about 45% of total body weight—when they were subsisting on new *Fargesia* shoots.

2. The nutrient content of bamboo fluctuates little throughout the year, an unusual situation in the food supply of a large herbivore which enables pandas to subsist on a low-quality diet. Leaves contain the highest protein levels, followed by branches and stems. *Sinarundinaria* leaves and one-year stems have the best balance of amino acids, probably an important reason why they provide the bulk of the panda's food. New *Fargesia* shoots contain much protein but have a poor amino acid balance. Leaves also contain more hemicellulose and minerals and less cellulose and lignin than do branches and stems, and they therefore represent the plant part that pandas can be expected to favor. In spring, however, leaves are for unknown reasons disdained, high silica levels possibly making them unpalatable at that time.

3. On a diet of 12.5 kg, fresh weight, per day of *Sinarundinaria*, an adult panda

ingests about 242–646 g of protein per day, the amount varying with the season, considerably more than seems needed for maintenance and growth. This suggests that the panda consumes large quantities of bamboo more to obtain calories in the form of soluble carbohydrates than to fulfill protein requirements. In terms of both total nutrient intake and digestible energy, spring was the leanest season for a panda subsisting on *Sinarundinaria*. Dry matter digestibility varied with the season, ranging from 12% to 23% with an average of 17%, exceptionally low figures for a herbivore.

4. Calculations indicate that the increment in *Sinarundinaria* stems in 1981 was large enough to support at least two pandas per km^2 without detriment to the bamboo. By contrast, the number of *Fargesia* stems was static or declining, due mainly to poor shoot production and survival. Between 1981 and 1983, insects and pandas destroyed one-third to one-half of the annual production of shoots. The pandas' selection for thick shoots, coupled with their tendency to forage along the edge of thickets, affects bamboo by slowing rate of spread and favoring the survival of spindly stems.

4

Movement Patterns

Mammals usually spend their lives within a limited area, a home range, which contains food, potential mates, and other essential resources. Range size may change considerably as an individual matures. At first a young animal has the same range as its mother; then, growing older, it may make exploratory trips into new areas; and finally it may settle into a range of its own. The size of a range depends on several factors, including the weight and sex of the animal, the number of conspecifics sharing the range, the presence of other species competing for the same resources, and the quality of the habitat. Affected by individual, social, and ecological factors, the use of space is a complex and dynamic phenomenon. Engulfed by bamboo throughout the year, a panda has no need to compete for food or to expend much energy in search of it. We would therefore expect pandas to travel little, have small ranges, and achieve high population densities.

Methods

With pandas seldom observable, we had to catch them and fit them with radio collars to provide detailed information on movements and activity patterns. We caught the first panda in an Aldrich foot snare and all others in box traps. Three traps were small and made of aluminum bars (150 long × 65 wide × 100 cm high), and 5 were large and made of logs (about 290 × 110 × 135), a total of 8 traps (see fig. 2.8). When a panda pulled at a chunk of sheep or goat meat tied to the trigger at the rear of the trap, the door descended, confining the animal. Snares were checked twice daily and traps daily. Using both snares and traps, we trapped during February and March 1981, and then again, using only traps, from December 1981 to February 1982. We kept an occasional trap open longer in an attempt to catch a particular animal.

Ketamine is usually used to tranquilize pandas in zoos (Wang 1978; Zheng 1980). To sedate a wild panda, we injected it in shoulder or thigh with a mixture of Ketamine-Rompun (ratio 10:1) or CI-744; 7 of the 9 sedations involved CI-744 with an average dose of 2.75 (range 1.90–3.43) mg/kg, a low dose with which animals usually remained inactive for 40 minutes or less. Sometimes an animal awakened before we had sufficient time to weigh and measure it adequately, but rather than give a supplementary dose we placed it back in the trap to recover (plates 4.1, 4.2, 4.3).

We collared 3 pandas during the 1980–81 winter. During the 1981–82 winter we recollared these, and caught 2 new ones; a sixth animal was collared in December 1982. The equipment, supplied by Telonics (Mesa, Arizona), functioned extremely well. Collars weigh about 650 g and operate in a 150–151 MHz band, each at a different frequency. Trapping, handling, and collaring had no obvious long-term effect on pandas; in fact, animals readily entered traps again (table 2.3).

We determined the position of radio-collared pandas from known reference points along ridges and trails. At least 3 azimuth intersections were used to locate an animal, and the position was then transcribed onto a 1:10,000 map. Most azimuths were taken with a hand-held 2-element H antenna, but some also with a fixed 8-element antenna at 2 locations. We attempted to contact all collared pandas either once daily, or at least once every 2–3 days, but a number of fixes were imprecise and could not be used for analysis. Each panda was radio-tracked from the date of initial collaring until August 1982, an arbitrary cutoff point for this report except for the males, though the monitoring itself is continuing. The radio of the subadult female Ning ceased to transmit in March 1982. A total of 452 accurate locations were

PLATE 4.1   Howard Quigley measures the sedated female Zhen, while George Schaller takes notes, and Hu Jinchu examines a tracing of the animal's hindfoot.

obtained for Long, 317 for Ning, 482 for Zhen, 98 for Han, and 212 for Wei. The bearings were plotted on a map, which was then divided with a grid overlay into 1 ha quadrats. Patrick Carr of the University of Tennessee coded the grid coordinates of each bearing into a computer for analysis (Anon. 1982a).

With the capture of Pi in December 1982, we had for the first time 2 radio-collared adult males. To show Pi's movements in relation to those of Wei, as well as of Long, we include data on range use by the 3 males from December 1982 to May 1983.

In addition to radio-locating pandas, movements were traced by following tracks in snow for a total of 55.2 km.

Home range

We calculated home range size by the convex polygon method (Garshelis and Pelton 1981, Quigley 1982). In this procedure the outermost radio locations are connected in such a way that the angle toward the inside of the polygon formed by any 3 consecutive points never exceeds 180°. The area enclosed by the polygon is then determined by using point coordinates, expressed by the formula $\frac{1}{2}[\Sigma \; x_1 (y_{i-1} - y_{i+1})]$ in which x and y are the grid coordinates (Brinker 1969).

Range size varied from 3.9 to 6.2 km^2 (table 4.1; fig. 4.1). These range sizes are based on data collected until August 1982, a period of 18 months for Long and Zhen, 11 months for Ning, 8 months for Wei, and 7 months for Han. Additional data obtained between September 1982 and May 1983 show the following changes: the

TABLE 4.1
PERCENTAGE OF TOTAL HOME RANGE USED BY PANDAS EACH MONTH

		Long	Ning	Zhen	Han	Wei
Home range size (km^2)		5.73	4.28	3.89	4.33	6.20
1981	March	8.3%		15.1%		
	April	9.2	34.6%	33.6		
	May	30.0	45.1	17.7		
	June	18.5	15.8	44.8		
	July	8.3	9.5	6.2		
	August	5.8	4.5	10.3		
	September	5.1	7.7	2.3		
	October	10.1	5.0	5.6		
	November	7.5	10.6	6.0		
	December	8.6	24.5	21.2		
1982	January	24.3	10.2	4.7		63.0%
	February	17.6	17.4	3.4	9.9%	48.7
	March	16.5		16.9	23.4	37.2
	April	43.7		24.5	26.5	63.3
	May	4.6		51.2	37.1	58.9
	June	9.6		24.2	21.3	38.5
	July	10.1		18.7		17.4
	August	24.1		10.5		5.5
Av. % Jan.–June 1982		19.3 ±12.5		20.8 ±16.0		51.6 ±10.9

PLATE 4.2   Dong Cai (left), Qiu Mingjiang, and Jilin Zhiha (right) examine subadult male No. 81, 2.5 years old, before ear-tagging him. The animal's forepaw clearly shows the five digits and the pseudothumb.

PLATE 4.3   Li Yuan (left) and Yong Tianzhong weigh subadult male Long, 3.5 years old, beside the trap in which he was caught.

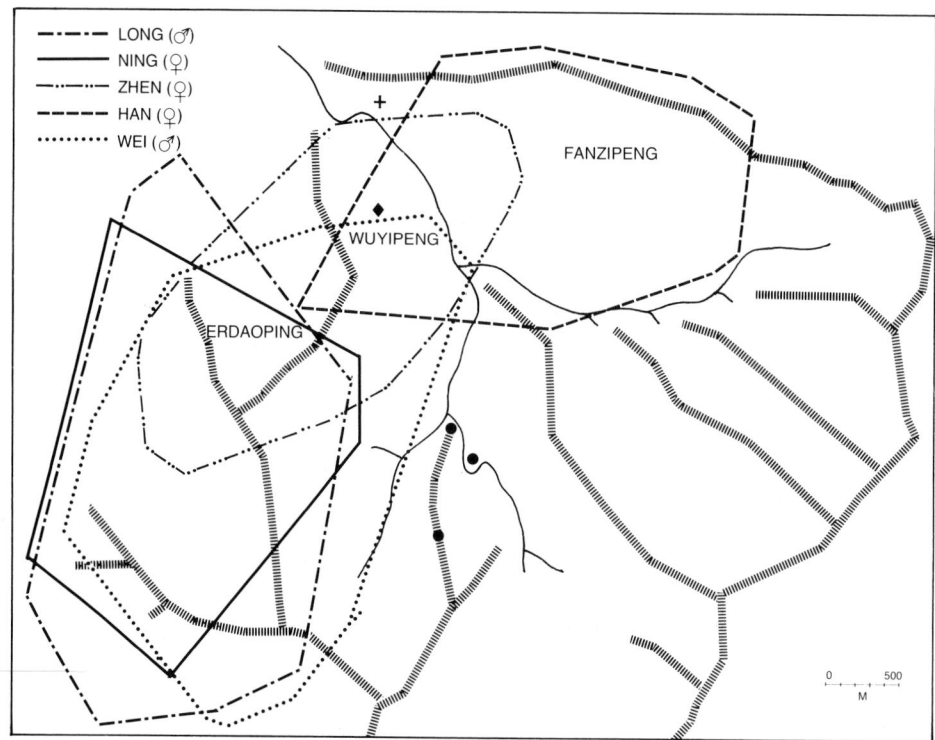

FIGURE 4.1   The home ranges of 5 radio-collared pandas, showing extent of overlap. The 3 black spots indicate where subadult male No. 81 was trapped in January and February 1982.

male Long remained within his defined range; the female Zhen removed her radio collar in September 1982, but, judging by spoor, she remained within her previous range; the male Wei traveled farther east than usual during one trip, enlarging the size of his known range from 6.2 to 6.4 km^2; and the female Han shifted to the southeast of her usual range for several days in September 1982 and to the west in January 1983, into an area where she died in a poacher's snare (marked with a + in Fig. 4.1), having during a 12-month period roamed over a total of 5.4 km^2.

With these expansions, the ranges of the 3 females averaged 4.5 km^2 and those of the 2 males 6.1 km^2. Not included is the male Pi, who had a range of about 3.1 km^2 between December 1982 and May 1983. Males may have, on the average, slightly larger ranges than females, but no firm conclusions can be drawn from our small sample of animals.

Even though we tracked 5 of the pandas for 11 months or more, range sizes may be larger than our data indicate.

1. A panda may visit certain parts of its range only at long, irregular intervals. The male Wei visited a valley along the eastern border of his range just twice in 1.5 years. The female Han centered her activity around Fanzipeng, but on 21 May 1982 she crossed to the opposite slope and for nearly 2 days roamed around Wuyipeng before

returning to her usual haunts. Whether this foray extended her range or merely was a rare visit to a part of her usual range is not known.

2. Seasonal differences in food abundance may affect extent of movement. In spring 1981, a poor season for new *Fargesia* shoots, the female Zhen crossed onto the slope opposite Wuyipeng to forage, whereas in 1982 and 1983—good shoot years— she did not visit that part of the valley.

3. A subadult panda may on occasion make what can be termed an excursion. It is probable that excursions are especially prevalent between the time a subadult leaves its mother at 1.5 years and settles into a range of its own. During the winter of 1980–81, we tracked a subadult on several occasions through a part of the valley which, we later learned, did not include the home ranges of Long and Ning (fig. 4.6). Yet Long was responsible for some of the tracks; only hours before he was first caught, he traversed the slope just above Wuyipeng, an area he never revisited during the subsequent 2.5 years. This and other excursions are not here included as part of his range. Had we caught Long a few months earlier, before he apparently became more sedentary at the age of 2.5 years, his known range would be consider- ably larger.

More important than maximum size is an animal's spatial use of its home range. A panda tends to visit only a small fraction, as little as 10%, of its total range during any one month, the amount used depending on age and sex of the individual and on the season (table 4.1). All pandas may shift into and out of *Fargesia* during spring, a seasonal movement of up to 2 km, which, for example, helps to explain the high percentage of range use by the female Zhen in April and June 1981 and in May 1982. Animals seem to be rather sedentary during summer. In November, judging by an increase of droppings on trails, scent-marked trees, and other spoor, adult males begin to roam persistently and continue to do so into the following June. Radio- telemetry data from Wei confirm these observations. Between January and June 1982, Wei used an average of 52% of his total range each month, as compared to 19–21% for Long and Zhen, a significant difference ($p < 0.05$, Duncan's multiple- range test).

Another way of showing spatial use is to count the number of times an animal was radio-located in each of the 1 ha quadrats of its range. Figures 4.2 and 4.3 illustrate the frequency distributions for Long, Ning, Zhen, and Wei by season. The two subadults were rather sedentary, spending most of their time within a small part of their range. Zhen moved little, other than to visit the *Fargesia* zone in spring. The sharp summer-autumn peak reflected her focus on a den site, and the winter peak indicated a preference for a particular area—in this instance a moderate slope with ample bamboo beneath a canopy of fir. Han revealed a movement pattern similar to that of Zhen in that she descended into *Fargesia* during spring. Wei moved widely, spending less time than the others in any particular area, except in summer and autumn when he settled down somewhat.

Ignoring the seasonal movement into and out of *Fargesia*, figures 4.2 and 4.3 also emphasize that subadult and female pandas tend to concentrate their activity in a certain part of their range, that they have core areas, to use Kaufmann's (1962) term.

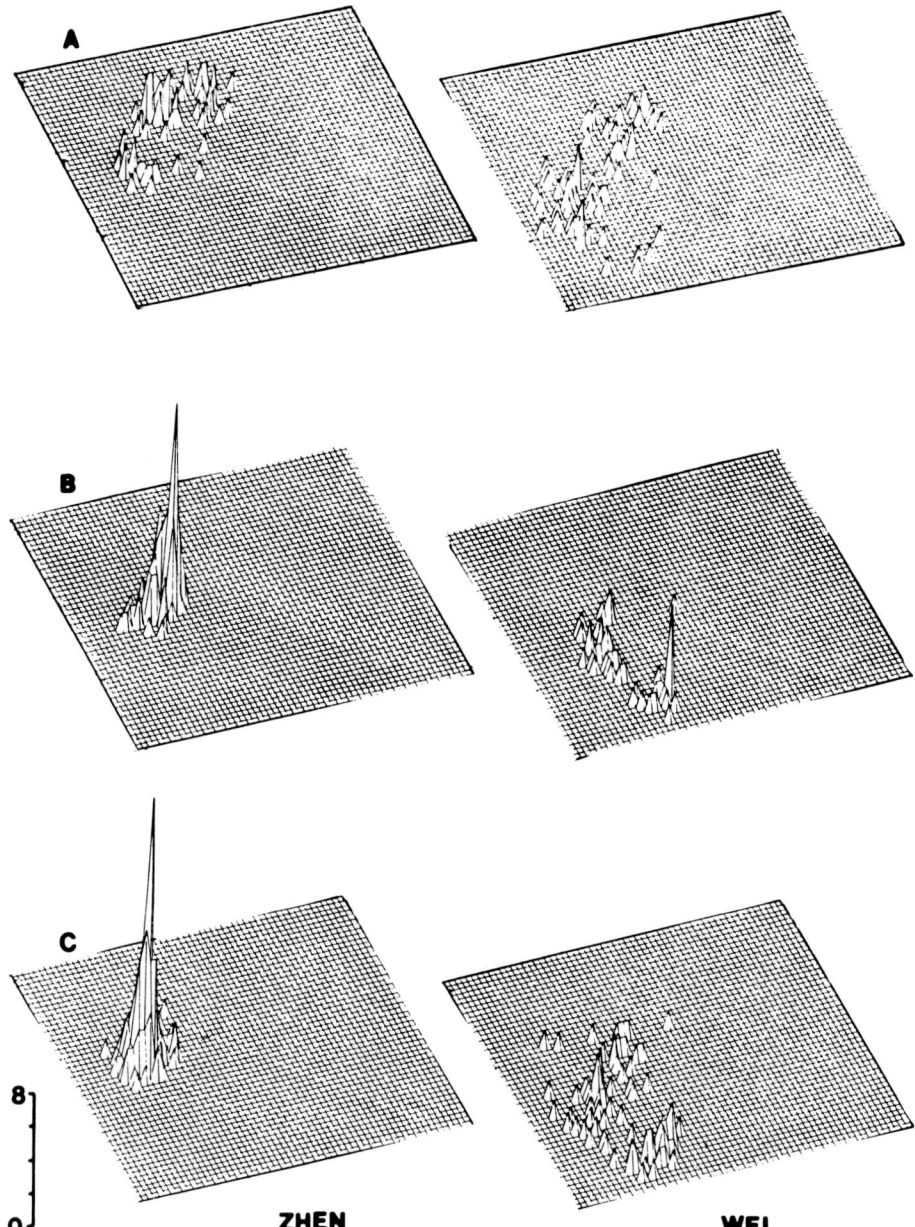

FIGURE 4.2   Frequency distribution of radio locations of Zhen and Wei.   A. Spring 1982 (Zhen N = 79; Wei N = 75);   B. Summer-autumn 1981 (Zhen N = 119) and summer 1982 (Wei N = 48);   C. Winter 1981–82 (Zhen N = 146, Wei N = 89). Zhen's summer-autumn peak represents her focus at a den site. Each square in the grids of figures 4.2 and 4.3 is 1 ha in size, and all squares have the same coordinates, making it possible to compare seasons and individuals directly. (Figures were prepared by P. Carr.)

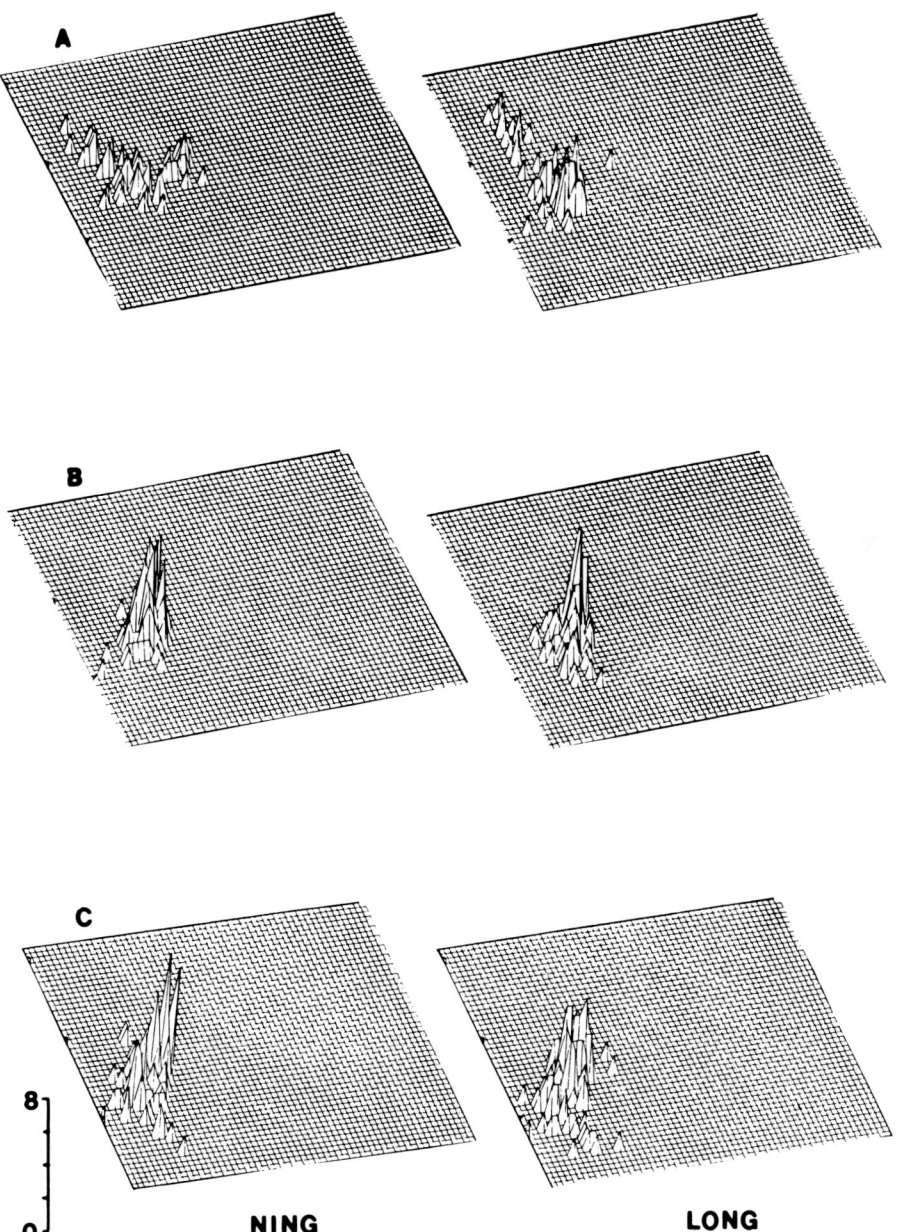

FIGURE 4.3   Frequency distribution of radio locations of Ning and Long.   A. Spring 1981 (Ning N = 64; Long N = 81);   B. Summer-autumn 1981 (Ning N = 120; Long N = 117);   C. Winter 1981–82 (Ning N = 133; Long N = 144).

Han's core area was at Fanzipeng, and Zhen's on both sides of a ridge above Erdaoping, especially on the west-facing slope. Long and Ning shared a core area in the Zhuanjinggou. Wei lacked an easily defined core area, but he often returned to the Yingxionggou, where he favored the upper slopes of a wooded valley, especially in summer.

To define the size of core areas more precisely, we tallied all 1 ha quadrats in which a panda was recorded on 1% or more of its total radio locations and plotted these on a map (fig. 4.4). Although total range size is 389 to 640 ha, each panda concentrated its activity in about 29–38 (mean 33) ha where it was radio-located on 42–66% (mean 52%) of the days. (Han was excluded from the computations because of scanty data.) Zhen's core area and Long's and Ning's shared core area are well defined and contiguous, almost without overlap; Wei's lacks a definite core area and instead seems to favor several localities.

Home ranges are not discrete but overlap extensively, several pandas frequenting the same area (figs. 4.1 and 4.4); for example, Long, Ning, Zhen, and Wei all used the ridge above Erdaoping. However, the core areas tended to reduce direct contact by spacing individuals, especially females. Zhen and Han occupied opposite sides of a valley, 3.0 km apart, and they were near each other only in spring when both descended to forage on new *Fargesia* shoots. No other adult females shared Zhen's range, to our knowledge, even though 2 inhabited areas to the south and west of her (see fig. 2.10). Han's range overlapped that of another female by an undetermined amount.

The range overlap between Long and Ning exceeded 50% in most months, and the animals were often within 200 m of each other (see table 6.12), a social attraction not evident in the other pandas. Although these subadults were frequently on the same slope as Zhen, actual range overlap with her during any one month was small, usually less than 15%, the two occupying a core area just south of hers (table 4.2).

Wei's behavior differed from that of the females and subadults in that he traveled widely, readily entering and remaining within the core areas of Long, Ning, and Zhen (fig. 4.4). His peripatetic behavior can be illustrated in another way: Erdaoping, part of Zhen's core area, and the upper slope of Yingxionggou lie 2 km apart. Between December 1981 and July 1982, Wei made at least one trip to Erdaoping every month except in February and at least one to Yingxionggou except in June. He apparently did not visit Erdaoping between August 1982 and March 1983, except once in November; instead, he settled in the Zhuanjinggou, and from there he continued to make monthly trips into the Yingxionggou.

Other pandas also entered the area shared by Long, Ning, Zhen, and Wei. The male Pi, caught on 5 December 1982, was radio-located on 166 days between his capture date and 31 May 1983. During these six months he centered his activity in the Zhuanjinggou, where his range was almost identical to Wei's range and to Long's as well (fig. 4.5). In addition, 2 other adult males—a large one like Pi and a medium-sized one like Wei—frequented the area; in April 1983 they were with Pi near an estrous female on the west side of Zhuanjinggou and later again at Erdaoping (see chapter 6). Thus, at least 7 pandas frequented Erdaoping at intervals. Similarly, at

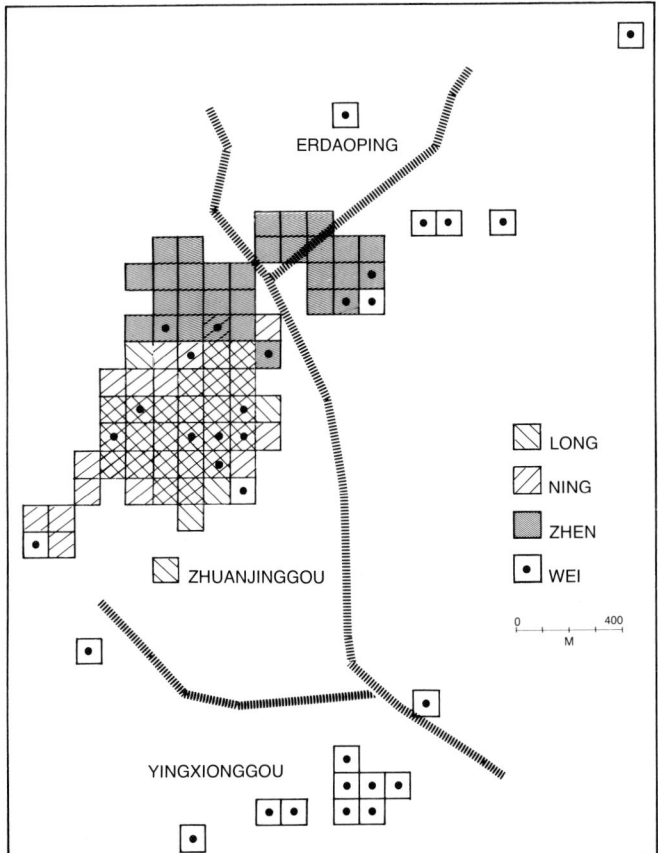

FIGURE 4.4   Core areas of several pandas occupying overlapping home ranges. Each square is 1 ha. As defined here, a core area includes all squares in which the panda was recorded on 1.0% or more of the total radio locations. Note that Wei lacks a well-defined core area and that the core areas of Long and Ning overlap.

least 2 males, a subadult, and a female shared Fanzipeng with Han. Several pandas also frequented other parts of the study area (figs. 2.10, 4.6). All suitable habitat in the Choushuigou and neighboring valleys appeared to be divided into a mosaic of overlapping ranges, animals of all ages and both sexes sharing the terrain.

Daily movements

We found it difficult to determine how far a panda travels each day. By following tracks in snow we could pace distances with fair precision, but the two winters of the study were unusually mild, so that we soon lost animals when they moved to snow-free slopes. Although we tracked pandas for 55 km, we were able to trace a route for 1 km or more on only 14 occasions, and we usually had little idea how much

TABLE 4.2

PERCENT OVERLAP OF THE HOMERANGES OF LONG, WEI, AND ZHEN WITH OTHER RADIO-COLLARED PANDAS, BY MONTH

		Percent overlap of Long's range by				Percent overlap of Zhen's range by				Percent overlap of Wei's range by		
	Zhen	Ning	Wei	Han	Long	Ning	Wei	Han	Long	Ning	Zhen	Han
1981												
March	0	—			0	—						
April	0	16.4			0	0.1						
May	0	69.6			0	0						
June	0.1	69.5			0.1	25.5						
July	4.1	69.7			8.0	9.1						
August	3.3	86.0			2.7	15.9						
September	0	58.9			0	0						
October	0	39.2			0	0						
November	0	69.4			0	0						
December	1.5	60.3			0.9	0						
1982												
January	1.9	69.3	61.3	0	14.8	0.1	100.0	0	21.8	21.6	4.6	—
February	0	32.7	85.5	0	0		100.0	0	28.5	12.3	4.9	0
March	2.7	51.1	22.3	0	3.8	19.3	0	0	9.1	4.3	0	0
April	5.8	—	71.8	0	15.3	—	64.4	0	45.8	—	15.6	0
May	0.7	—	100.0	0	0.1	—	70.1	17.5	7.3	—	38.3	8.6
June	0	—	89.1	0	0	—	25.3	34.6	20.5	—	10.0	5.6
July	6.2	—	17.3	0	4.9	—	13.7	0	9.7	—	13.6	0
August	6.1	—	25.6	0	20.5	—	0	0	99.9	—	0	0

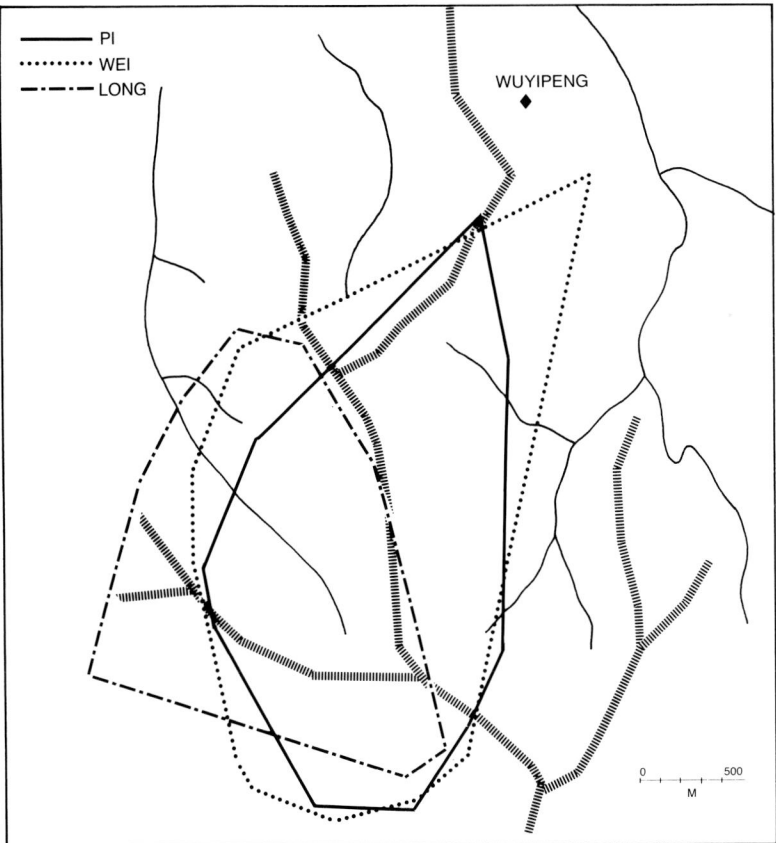

FIGURE 4.5 The home ranges of three male radio-collared pandas between December 1982 and May 1983, showing almost complete overlap.

of the total daily route our effort represented. Sedentary individuals were not tracked, for our intrusion could have disturbed them and caused them to shift to another part of their range. For example, when we entered Long's core area on 27 October, he moved 700 m up the valley. Consequently we usually tracked males when they were on a tour of their range or subadults when they were on an excursion.

Linear distances between radio locations on consecutive days provide an index of how far animals travel (table 4.3). With the exception of Wei, average daily movements did not exceed 500 m. Wei moved significantly ($p < 0.05$) less in summer than at other seasons, and moved most during spring, the mating time; Long displayed no seasonal differences except that he moved significantly more in spring 1982 than in spring 1981; Zhen traveled most in spring, when she shifted to and from the *Fargesia* zone and roamed widely in search of new shoots; and Ning, like Wei, was especially sedentary in summer. Wei moved significantly more in winter and spring than the other pandas, behavior that appears to be typical of adult males, judging by spoor and some telemetry data from Pi. Linear distances, of course, underestimate the actual distances an animal travels.

On several occasions we tracked undisturbed pandas as they moved without prolonged rest stops and with little or no feeding for 1 km or more, the longest distance 4.2 km (fig. 4.6). The animals were not radio-collared, but their behavior and other evidence indicated that most or all were either adult males or subadults. The pandas often walked steadily, covering the distance we followed them in no more than a few hours; along some routes of 1100 to 2300 m there were 6 or fewer droppings, an amount deposited usually in 2 hours or less. On one occasion, Wei remained on a snow-covered slope for 5.5 days, and we made a detailed record of his activities (fig. 4.7). His total travel distance was about 7113 m, or 1293 m per day, excluding a few detours from the main trail while he was foraging. He made 2 major stops, both lasting almost a day, during which he fed intensively; at one of these he moved only about 250 m between late afternoon and mid-morning of the following day (fig. 4.8). This pattern of movement, of remaining sedentary for several days then shifting to another part of the range, was typical of Wei. In one sample month, March 1982, Wei spent a few days in the Yingxionggou, moved for a prolonged spell

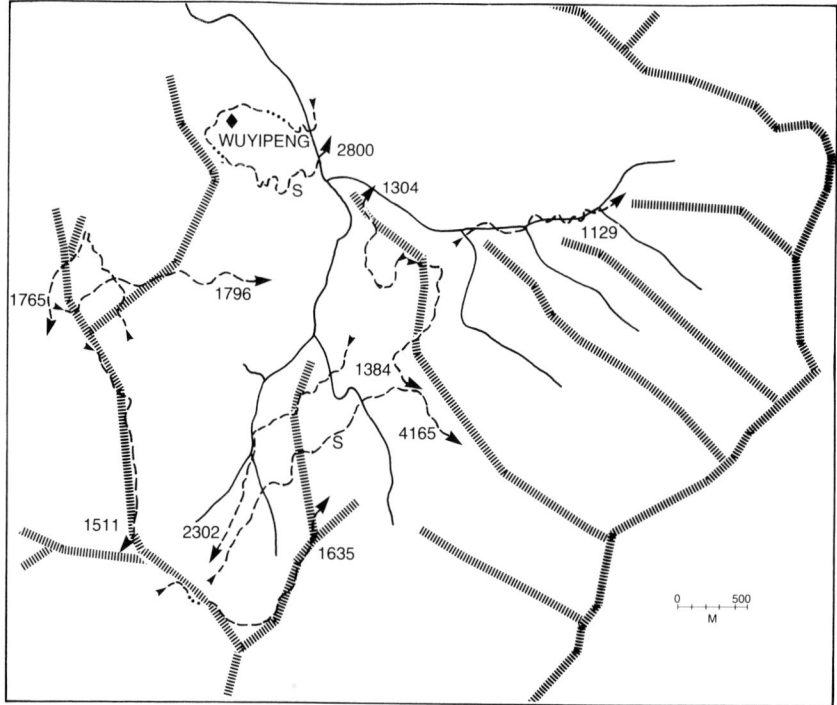

FIGURE 4.6 Representative routes and distances of travel of pandas without radio collars, based on tracking in snow. The animals traveled with little or no feeding and did not stop for a long rest. The numbers represent total travel distance (in m); the *s* indicates the route of a subadult.

TABLE 4.3
LINEAR DISTANCES (IN M) BETWEEN CONSECUTIVE DAILY RADIO-LOCATIONS

	Spring		Summer-autumn		Winter	
	N	m	N	m	N	m
Long	54 (1981)	297 ±36*	124 (both		112 (both	
	34 (1982)	441 ±45	years)	312 ±23*	years)	367 ±25*
Ning	38	459 ±42*	95	269 ±27**	79	374 ±29*
Zhen	115	280 ±24*	129	206 ±23**	98	180 ±26**
Wei	44	758 ±39*	27	333 ±50**	49	532 ±37***

Han has been excluded because samples are too small.
Within each row, distances with different number of asterisks are significantly ($p < 0.05$) different from each other.

into the Zhuanjinggou, and then visited Erdaoping before returning to the Ying-xionggou. His movements between areas was abrupt; in one instance he covered a linear distance of 2.5 km overnight (fig. 4.9). In contrast to Wei, Zhen was highly sedentary, usually spending a month or more in a limited area and seldom moving to distant points of her range. In May, when foraging on new *Fargesia* shoots, and in June, while shifting from shoots back to *Sinarundinaria*, her daily radio locations were scattered, though confined to a limited area; in summer and winter they tended to be clumped, Zhen sometimes spending a whole month within an area of 15 ha (fig. 4.10).

Wei traveled an average of about 1300 m per day during the 5.5 days we tracked

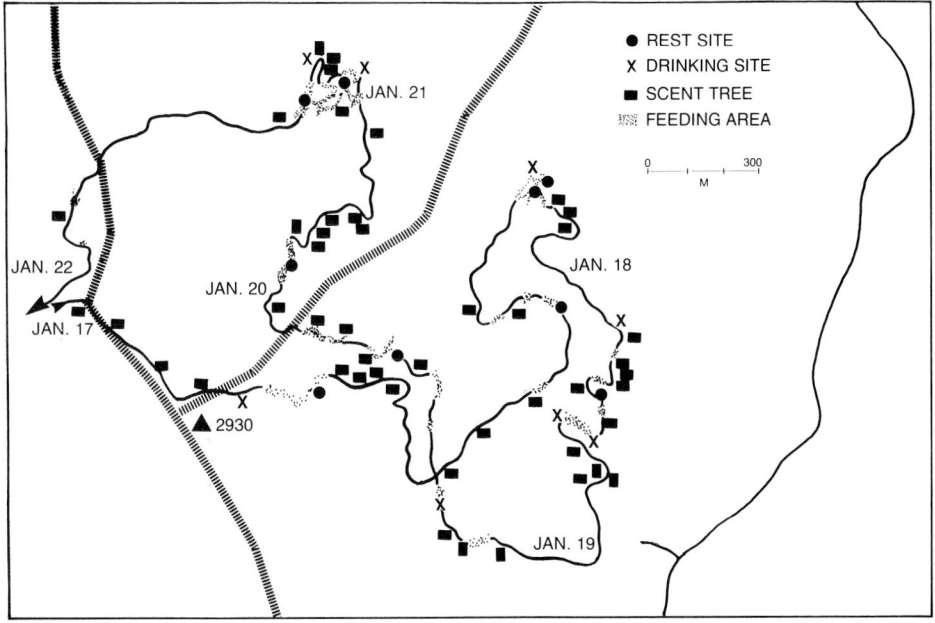

FIGURE 4.7   A 5.5 day route of the male Wei, based on tracking in snow. All rest sites, drinking places, and scent-marked trees were tallied.

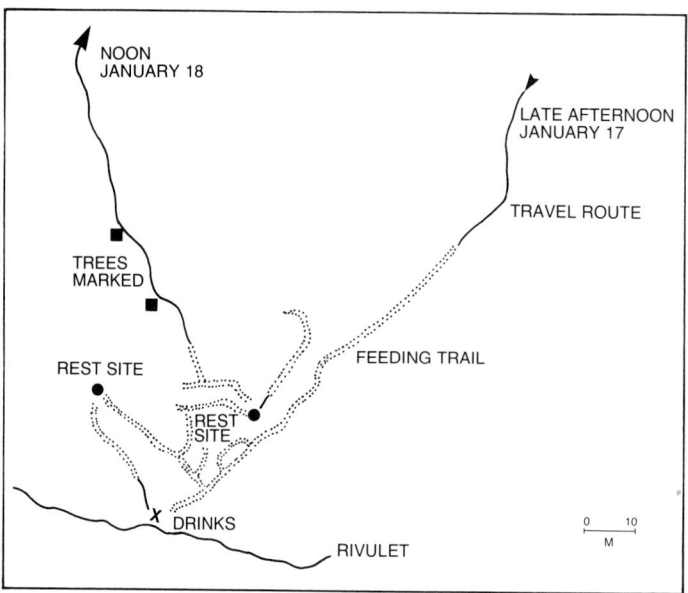

FIGURE 4.8   Wei's trail from 17 to 18 January, showing his main activities as deduced from spoor. (See also fig. 4.7.)

him in winter, a figure more than double the average calculated linear distance between consecutive radio locations (table 4.3). Going on the assumption that actual distances are about twice the linear ones, Wei averaged about 600–1500 m per day, depending on season, and females and subadults somewhat less.

Discussion

The panda population consisted of resident individuals, each living within a small, relatively stable home range, all or part of which was shared with others of all ages and both sexes. Although our sample of radio-collared animals is too small to provide much insight into the intricacies of panda land tenure, fragmentary evidence suggests that females and males have somewhat different systems.

An adult female appears to concentrate her activity in a certain part of her range, the core area, which provides most or all of her resources and is not shared with others of her sex or, apparently, with subadults. It is not known whether a female considers the core area a territory in the sense that she defends it selectively against intrusion. A female certainly does not patrol the boundaries of her core area, nor do others refrain from entering, although they do not remain long. With confrontations between individuals rare, defense of an area is difficult to distinguish from mere antagonism. Whatever the spacing mechanism, Zhen, Han, and other females were so well dispersed that their ranges overlapped little or not at all. Long and Ning centered their activity in a part of the Zhuanjinggou that neither Zhen nor the two other nearby females favored.

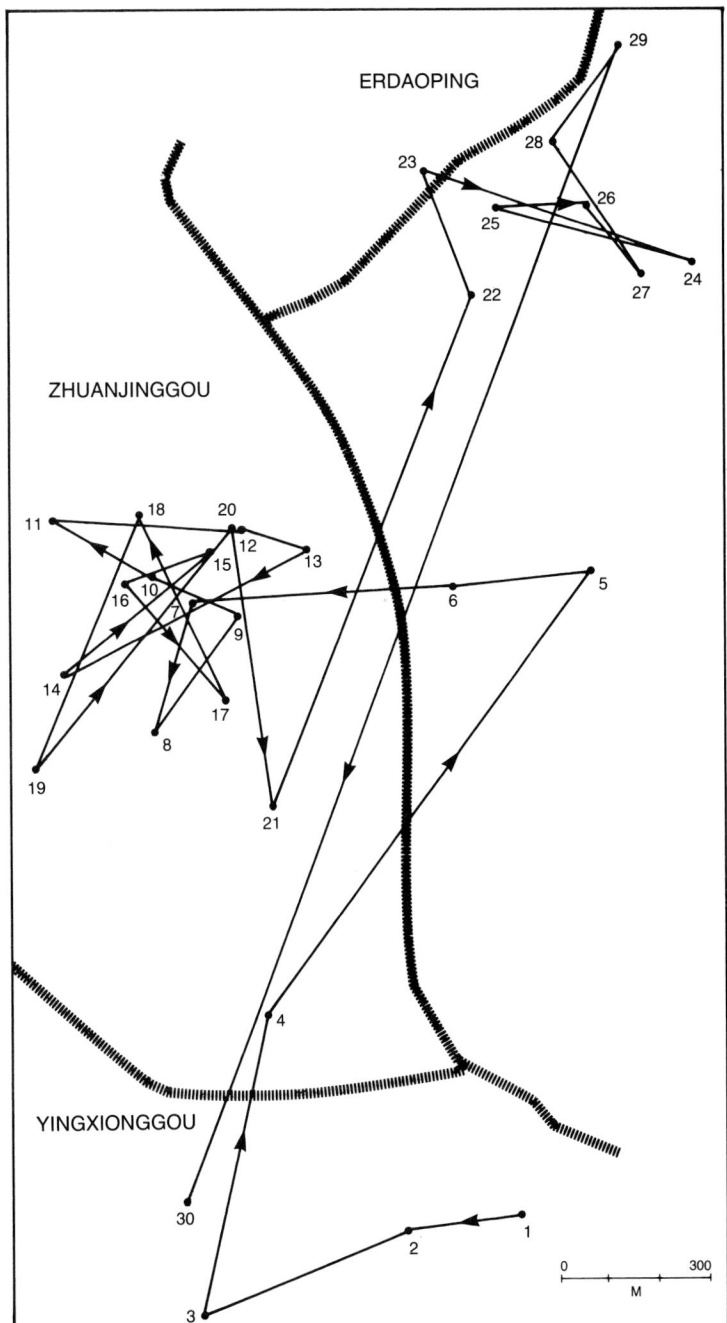

FIGURE 4.9 Daily radio locations of Wei during March 1982. His movements were characterized by sedentary phases followed by abrupt shifts.

Long and Ning shared a core area and were often near each other, showing the rudiments of a social grouping. Whether such associations are typical among subadults needs to be investigated further. Among black bears (Rogers 1977; Alt 1978) and tigers (Sunquist 1981), female offspring on reaching independence tend to establish a new home range near that of their mother, whereas male offspring often settle many kilometers away. Since a female panda seldom rears two young, we presume that Long and Ning are not siblings. If the panda's system of dispersion resembles that of black bear, Ning is possibly Zhen's daughter, born in the area, and was joined there by Long.

An adult male may have one or more favored sites within his range, but seems to lack a well-defined core area; instead, he roams widely, entering and remaining within the core areas of females and subadults. The ranges of males in an area overlap extensively (fig. 4.5). Male pandas show no exclusiveness, defense, or other indication of territoriality; nor do they patrol or scent-mark range borders at frequent intervals, as is the case among territorial male tigers (Sunquist 1981) and wolf packs (Peters and Mech 1975). Their social interactions appear to be based on rank

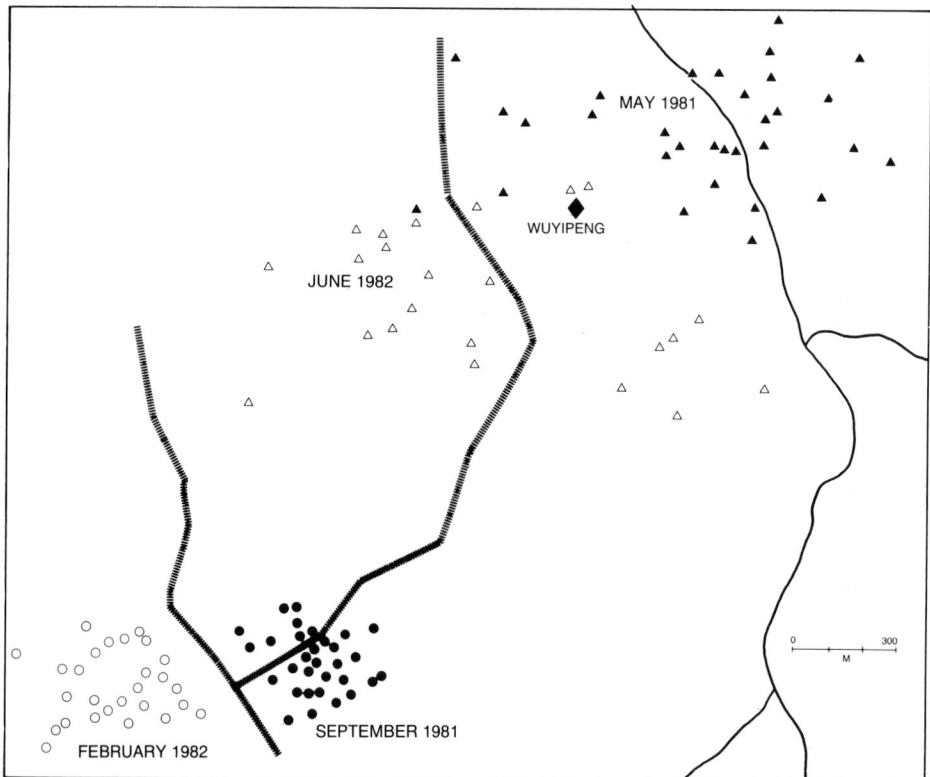

FIGURE 4.10   Radio locations of Zhen during four selected months, two in spring, one in summer, and one in winter.

mediated mainly by scent and, on rare occasions, by direct aggression (see chapter 6).

Bamboo being abundant, a panda has little need to maintain an exclusive area to ensure itself rights to this resource; home range overlap is therefore not surprising. But if, as we suspect, females discourage other females and subadults from impinging on their core areas, then these must contain resources worth claiming. In general, the pandas in our study centered their activity on ridges and upper slopes above 2700 m, where *Sinarundinaria* cover is almost continuous, and they preferred south- and west-facing exposures where snow does not persist as long as on other exposures. Females had core areas in terrain notable for its gentleness by comparison to other parts of the valley. Travel over steep terrain requires a disproportionate amount of energy (see chapter 7)—perhaps one reason pandas may not favor such areas. Females also preferred well-wooded slopes with an almost continuous forest canopy. In the open, bamboo grows more densely than beneath a canopy, the stalks seem drier and are sometimes stunted, and a larger proportion of leaves die in winter, affecting nutritional content—all factors that may influence a panda's foraging efficiency. Large trees also provide potential den sites, an important resource for a female. By contrast, Long and Ning were usually on a steep hillside cut by many ravines in a part of the Zhuanjinggou that had been almost denuded of trees during a logging operation in the early 1970s. There they concentrated their foraging in and around the remaining forest patches rather than on the open slopes. The two subadults were in habitat which seemed inferior to that occupied by the females, a further indication of a possible competitive system spacing animals.

A male's range is based on the presence of one important resource—females. Pi's and Wei's range overlapped the ranges of Zhen, Han, and two uncollared females, and the other males in the area probably had access to a similar number of females. Since a male might find it energetically too costly to maintain his range as a territory, he has little choice but to compete with other males for mating rights. He could, of course, claim a small territory. This, however, would not only reduce the number of his potential mates but also might deprive him of females entirely if a stronger rival evicted him. Competitive interference at mating time seems to be a preferable option. A male spends much of the year monitoring other pandas within his range, his travels taking him to the core areas of females and subadults (fig. 4.4) even during months when there is no sexual activity. Such movements may help maintain his social network. In this trait, panda males differ from black bear males, which are most mobile and travel most widely during the mating season in June and July (Alt et al. 1980).

If a male increases his chances of reproductive success by including as many females as possible within his domain—a reasonable assumption—then the small ranges of panda males are rather puzzling. With Han's range outside the ranges of Pi and Wei during the April mating season, these males had to our knowledge at most three females available, and they had to compete for access to them. Why did Pi not enlarge his range from 3 km^2 to 20 km^2 or more during the April mating season? Average range size of black bear males exceeds 30 km^2 (Quigley 1982; Garshelis and

Pelton 1981; Alt 1977), and the range of one male may include the ranges of 7–15 females (Rogers 1977). We can only speculate that there may be energetic limits to the amount of travel a panda male can afford, to the amount of terrain he can monitor, and to the number of competitive situations he can tolerate (see chapters 5 and 7). For a panda male, habitat quality may be measured more by the number of females inhabiting his range than by the availability of food. But, paradoxically, his foraging strategy may have bound him to a relatively sedentary life, which, under conditions existing in the Choushuigou, places constraints on his sexual imperative.

Summary

1. Home range sizes of pandas in our study varied from 3.9 to 6.4 km². The ranges of males were only as large as, or slightly larger than, those of females—a situation different from that of black and grizzly bear, in which male ranges may be several times larger than female ranges. There are possibly energetic limits to the amount of terrain a panda male can monitor on his low-nutrient diet. Even though an animal's range is small, the animal visits some parts of the range only rarely.

2. A panda population consists of several residents, each living within a small stable home range, all or part of which is shared with others. Adult males and females, however, appear to have somewhat different land tenure systems. Females are well dispersed. Although their ranges may overlap, each female spends most of her time within a discrete core area only 30–40 ha in extent. Two subadults shared a core area adjoining one occupied by a female. Males occupy greatly overlapping ranges and lack well-defined core areas; they shift frequently within their range, spending time within the core areas of females and subadults.

3. Females possibly do not tolerate other females and subadults within their core area. Males show no evidence of territorial behavior; interactions are probably based on rank, mediated mainly by scent, except during courtship when there may be confrontations over an estrous female.

4. An occasional panda may travel as much as 4 km in a day, as revealed by tracking in snow, but the animals we observed were usually sedentary. Linear distances between radio locations on consecutive days averaged less than 500 m for most animals.

5

Activity Patterns

Life for the panda represents a balance between activities to fulfill basic needs and inactivity to conserve energy. Theories of feeding strategies predict that an animal has become adapted for maximum feeding efficiency—that it obtains the greatest net energy return for the energy spent in procuring food (Schoener 1971; Westoby 1974; Krebs 1978). Other activities merely drain an animal's energy. A panda must allocate an appropriate amount of energy to each activity, depending on which confers the greatest immediate benefit. During the mating season, for example, a male not only must search for an estrous female but also must continue to forage, the actual amount of time spent on each task being perhaps a compromise between conflicting needs.

Activity cycles (*with Patrick Carr*)

The radio transmitters on the pandas contain special motion sensors that transmit a signal with a pulse rate of 75 per minute when the animal is inactive and a pulse rate of 100 when it travels, feeds, or is otherwise active. We monitored animals, from the time they were first caught, every month for one or more 24-hour periods, usually for 5 but occasionally for as long as 20 consecutive days. Activity was recorded every 15 minutes, giving 96 readings per day, except on those days when the signal faded for varying periods, transmission obscured by terrain and trees. Our data include 88 days (8285 readings) of monitoring of Long, 70 days (6539) of Ning, 99 days (9326) of Zhen, 22 days (2077) of Han, and 24 days (2223) of Wei—a total of 300 days and 28,450 readings. The analyses are based only on these 24-hour samples; we excluded brief periods of monitoring and intermittent readings obtained in the course of radio-locating animals. The motion sensor has a time lag of one or two minutes when switching from an active to inactive pulse rate. We recorded an animal as being inactive if this change occurred as we began to listen. The pandas were usually monitored from a tent on the ridge above Erdaoping at 3000 m, a location that enabled us to receive signals from most or all radio-collared animals one after another during the same sampling period. This allowed us to make direct monthly comparisons between pandas.

To determine relations between activity on the one hand and season, month, hour, weather, and other factors on the other, we used the least-squares means procedure with analysis of variance (Garshelis and Pelton 1980). This method enables us to measure the relation between activity and any one factor independent of all other factors. Activity is defined as a discrete variable with a value of 1 for active or 0 for inactive in relation to date, time of day, weather, and other factors. The results can then be expressed as a probability of activity under a given set of conditions rather than as a percentage of animals active, which facilitates statistical comparisons (Garshelis and Pelton 1980; Carr 1983). The correlation between percent activity and probability of activity is good (Pearson product-moment correlation $r = 0.99$, $p<0.001$), as shown in fig. 5.1. The t-test ($p<0.05$) was used to determine significance in most other comparisons.

Individual differences in activity

As we began to monitor pandas, we soon noted that the animals were active at any time of day or night, with active sessions interrupted by rest periods of varying length. Generally, pandas displayed a daily cycle with two activity peaks, one near dawn and one at dusk. It was also clear that animals monitored during the same time periods were sometimes active in synchrony and sometimes not. For example, the subadults Long and Ning had similar daily cycles in December 1981, whereas the females Zhen and Han did not in February 1982 (fig. 5.2). Only on rare occasions

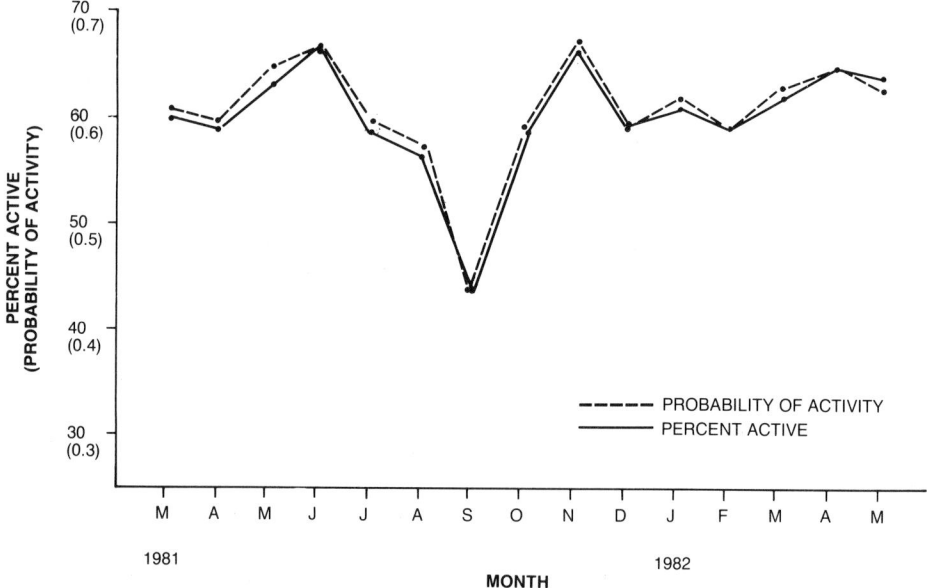

FIGURE 5.1 Average activity by month during period of study, showing close agreement between calculations based on percent activity and probability of activity. (Data from all pandas combined.)

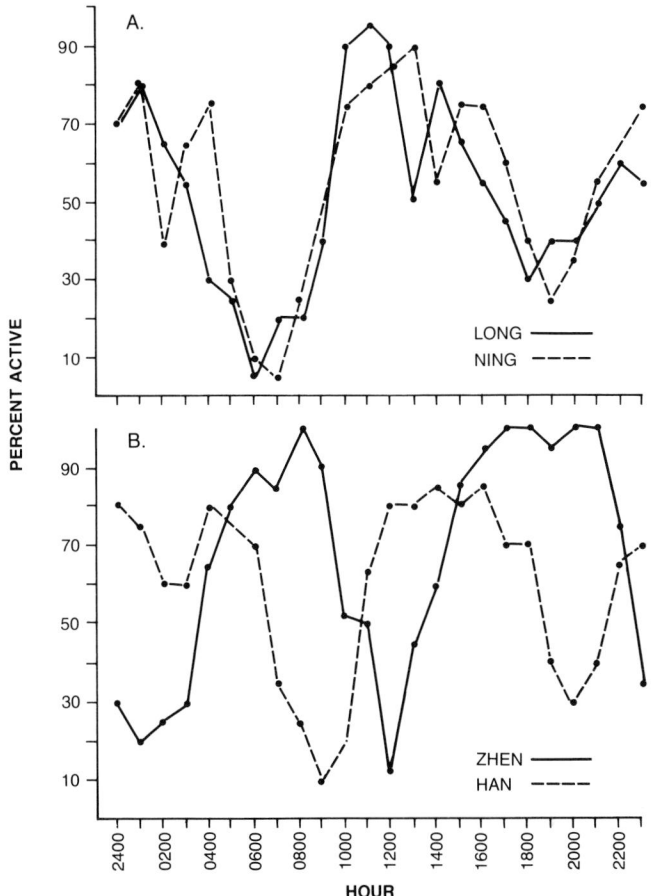

FIGURE 5.2 Synchronous and asynchronous activity patterns of pandas being monitored concurrently. Top: Long and Ning have similar patterns, December 1981 (N = 5 days). Bottom: Zhen and Han have patterns out of phase with each other, February 1982 (N = 5 days).

were we able to explain an unusual pattern. Zhen, for instance, revealed a low and rather even level of activity throughout the day in September 1981, when she was with a newborn, but then reverted to a typically bimodal pattern in October (fig. 5.3). Considerably more pandas must be monitored before such variations can be ascribed to individuality rather than to sex, age, or other factors. Although seemingly idiosynchratic patterns were evident, no significant differences in overall activity levels existed between Long, Ning, and Zhen from April 1981 to March 1982, or between Long, Zhen, Han, and Wei from January to July 1982 (inverse sine transformation of percent activity and Duncan's multiple-range test). Because of this similarity, we usually combined data from all pandas.

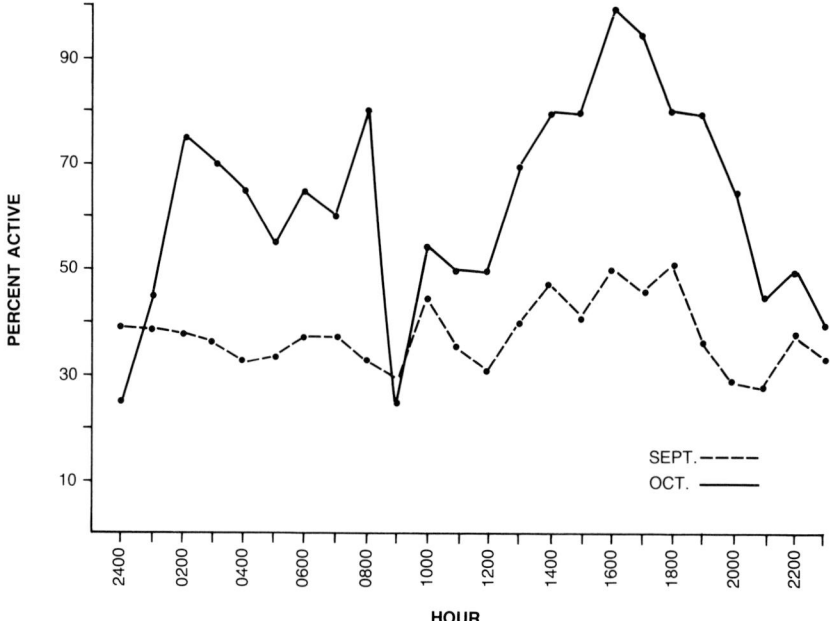

FIGURE 5.3   Changes in Zhen's activity pattern after parturition. In September 1981, when with newborn, Zhen showed a low but fairly constant level (N = 20 days); in October, when young was over a month old, she showed a typical bimodal pattern (N = 5 days).

Factors influencing activity

During an average day, pandas are usually 59% active and 41% inactive. Time of year and time of day, as well as weather, influence activity patterns.

Time of year

The probability of activity in pandas remained relatively constant from month to month at around 0.60, except for a significant rise in June 1981* and November 1981, and a major drop in September (fig. 5.1). To analyze monthly variation in more detail, we plotted activity of each individual separately (fig. 5.4). Applying Bonferroni's procedure to the normal approximation of a binomial population (Steel and Torrie 1960), the confidence limits for each monthly sample were determined. Points lying outside the confidence interval were significantly different ($p < 0.01$) from the expected average annual value of 0.584. Long, Ning, and Zhen all showed a marked September drop; Ning was notably active in June 1981 and Long moderately so in June 1982; Zhen remained highly active from November 1981 to April 1982. Long and Ning well illustrate the problems of explaining differences in activity of individual pandas on the basis of our small sample. These subadults inhabited the same

*Our analysis excludes June 1982 because only one panda was monitored for a mere 2 days.

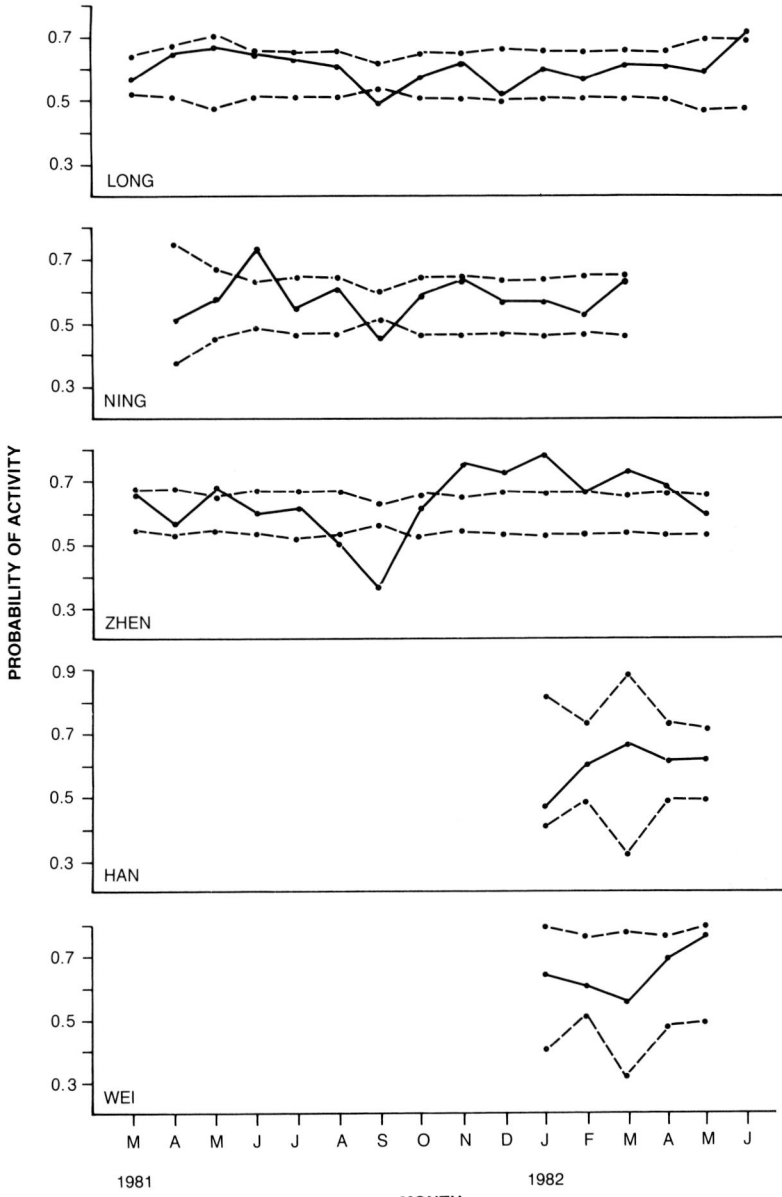

FIGURE 5.4   Probability of activity by month for each panda during period of study, showing individual variation (solid line). The confidence intervals are also indicated (broken line). Values differing significantly ($p < .01$) from the average annual probability of 0.584 lie outside the dashed lines.

slopes, ate the same food, and were, in fact, often near each other. Nonetheless, during 5 of the 6 months between April and September their activity levels differed significantly, but from October to March they were remarkably similar (table B.12).

On the basis of the panda's food habits, the year can be divided into three ecological seasons: spring, April–June, when pandas eat mainly stem; summer-autumn, July–October, when they browse primarily on leaves; and winter, November–March, when they forage on old shoots, stems, and leaves. The probability of activity for all pandas by season is 0.65 for spring, 0.52 for summer-autumn, and 0.62 for winter, levels significantly different ($p < 0.05$) from each other. Every panda's probability also differed significantly by season (table 5.1), with individual variation small, except that Zhen was unusually active in winter and the male Wei in spring.

Time of day

The effect of changing environmental factors associated with seasons are evident in the panda's daily activity cycle (figs. 5.5 and 5.6). During spring, the activity level never falls below 0.50; during winter, it is below 0.50 only from dawn at 0700 to about

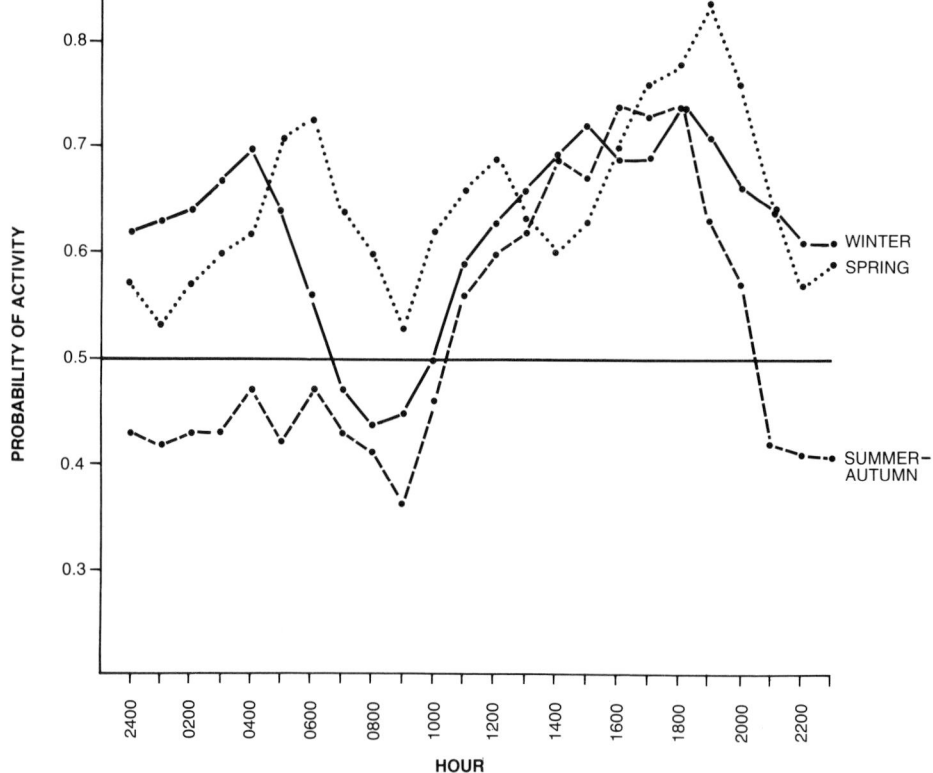

FIGURE 5.5 Probability of activity by hour of day and by season. (Data from all pandas combined.)

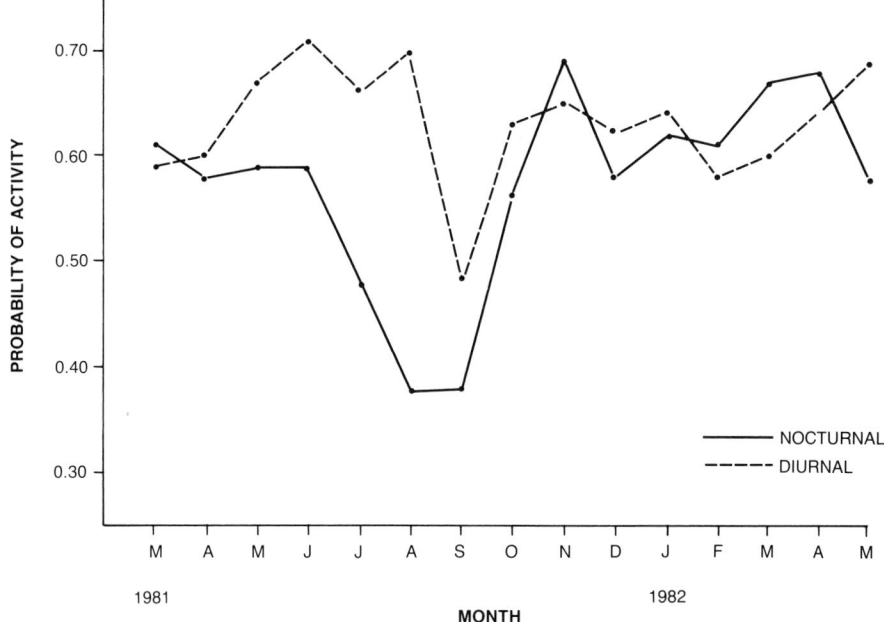

FIGURE 5.6 Probability of activity by month during period of study, comparing activity in daytime and at night. (Data from all pandas combined.)

0900; and during summer it remains below 0.50 from 2100 to 1000 hours, a significant difference ($p < 0.05$) from the level reached between 1100 and 2000 hours. The high spring level differs statistically from both summer and winter on 14 of the 24 hours (table B.13). Although these are seasonal differences, they reflect day patterns as well. Activity declines toward dawn during every season, reaching the lowest level after daylight, between 0800 and 0900 hours, and around dusk, after 1900 hours. Pandas are most active before and around dawn from 0400 to 0600 hours, and in late afternoon, from 1600 to 1900 hours. The peaks and troughs in activity remain similar at all seasons, with little apparent reference to day length. We defined dawn and dusk as the time of increasing or decreasing light when, during the monitoring period, the trees were barely distinguishable. Official sunrise and sunset times might be quite different because our data are affected by fog and rain and the shading effect of the forest canopy. In December, dawn is at about 0715 and dusk at 1815; in June, dawn is at 0515 and dusk at 2015. The morning decline in activity began in winter 2 to 3 hours before dawn, and in spring at or after dawn. This suggests that pandas do not adjust activity on the basis of light alone.

With all seasons combined, the probability of activity was 0.64 in daytime and 0.58 during nighttime. Analyzed on a monthly basis, pandas are significantly more active in daytime than at night between April and October (fig. 5.5), a difference partly due to greater day length without a compensatory shift in the animals' activity. Nevertheless, pandas do have a bimodal cycle of daily activity with peaks around dawn and dusk. To test whether the animals are crepuscular, we divided the 24 hours into night, dawn ± 1 hour, day, and dusk ± 1 hour, and compared the results by season (fig. 5.7). In winter, pandas showed a marked drop at dawn after an active night; in spring, their activity increased sharply at dawn and then did not change statistically in daytime; and in summer, they were relatively inactive at night and dawn, followed by a conspicuous rise in activity. There is a marked contrast in this variable dawn behavior with activity at dusk, when pandas during all seasons are significantly more active than at other times of day. If we further divide daytime into a morning half and an afternoon half, morning activity levels remain significantly different from one another between seasons, with pandas least active in summer and most active in spring, whereas afternoon levels are identical in every season. Such averages mask any individual variation, which may be considerable (fig. 5.8; table 5.1). In winter, for instance, Long and Wei, as well as Ning, showed a significant drop in activity at dawn, in contrast to Zhen, who at that time was very active; in summer-autumn, Long was more active at dusk than during the day, whereas Ning and Zhen continued at the same level.

Weather

Daily temperatures generally reach a maximum in early afternoon and a minimum around dawn. Spring and summer temperatures showed no particular correla-

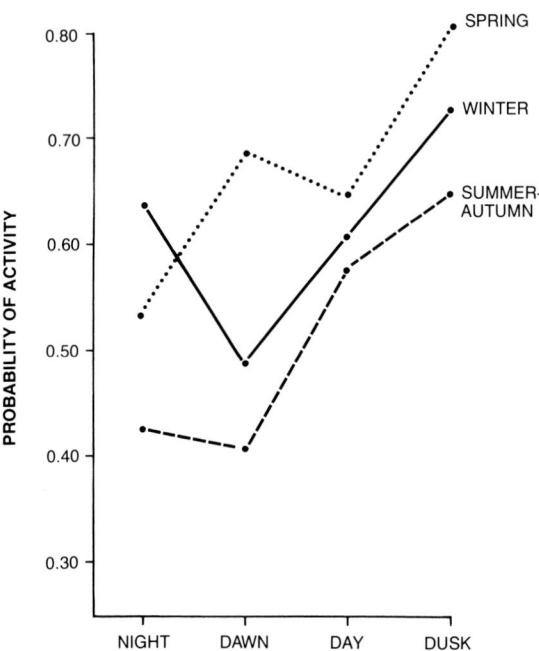

FIGURE 5.7   Probability of activity by season, comparing activity at night, dawn, in daytime, and at dusk. (Data from all pandas combined.)

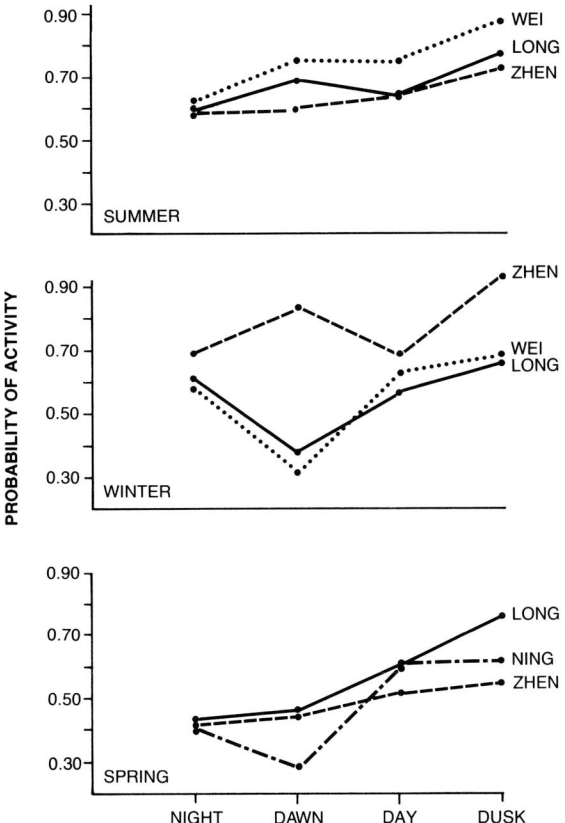

FIGURE 5.8 Probability of activity by time of day and season, showing individual variation in selected pandas.

tion with activity, but in winter there was a precipitous drop in activity at dawn (fig. 5.7), perhaps due to temperature, which is usually below freezing at that hour.

To assess the impact of cloudiness and precipitation on activity, we noted amount of cloud cover and duration of rain and snowfall. Pandas were as active on mostly-to-wholly-cloudy days (0.59) as on clear-to-partly-cloudy ones (0.60). The effects of precipitation are difficult to measure because bamboo remains wet for hours even after a brief rain, showering with drops any panda moving through it. Pandas were equally active on rainy, cloudy, or clear days, but snow appeared to induce a small but significant ($p < 0.05$) drop. On the day following a snowfall or, even more important, a rainfall, levels rose significantly (from 0.56 on a snow day to 0.62 the day after, and from 0.58 on a rain day to 0.69 the day after; $p < 0.05$), suggesting that pandas respond to improved conditions after a day or more of inclement weather.

These calculations fail to reveal certain responses of pandas to weather. During heavy continuous rain, animals occasionally seem to seek shelter. One panda, for

TABLE 5.1
PROBABILITY OF ACTIVITY FOR EACH PANDA BY SEASON

	Spring	Summer-autumn	Winter
Long	0.65	0.54	0.58
Ning	0.67	0.51	0.59
Zhen	0.64	0.48	0.72
Han	0.62	0.66[a]	0.58
Wei	0.72	0.71[a]	0.59

Every animal shows significant differences ($p < 0.05$) in its activity between seasons. Within a season, Zhen differs significantly from the others in winter, Wei in spring, and all three in summer-autumn.
[a]Sample was too small to be included in the statistical computations.

example, rested in a hollow fir on such a day on 19 July 1982, and Wei was in a similar refuge on 7 September 1982. Each remained in its shelter for at least 5 hours, judging by the 28–33 droppings there. Little snow fell during the winters of our study. In deep snow, pandas may have to forage longer to obtain food, and at such times they have been known to move to lower elevations in Wolong and elsewhere.

Restless behavior

A panda may remain active or inactive for long periods, sometimes for 6 hours or more, or it may change constantly from activity to inactivity, with a seeming restlessness. On some days it has only 4 to 6 activity changes in a day, and on others over 30, with a usual average of about 10–25. Restlessness can be expressed as the ratio of the number of instances of monitoring in which there was no change in activity to each change in activity. The lower the ratio, the greater an animal's restlessness. A panda varies considerably in its restlessness ratio from month to month, for reasons that we cannot explain in most cases (fig. 5.9). For example, Ning was exceptionally restless in July 1981; Zhen was persistent in her activities in January 1982, and so was Han in March 1982 when her ratio rose to 15.8, more than 8 points higher than in any other month. The 1981 mating and birth seasons had an influence on Zhen's restless behavior. In April she averaged 31 activity changes, with a maximum of 45 on the day of mating and three days prior to it. And in September she averaged 34.5 changes per day when she had a newborn young in the den. Yet she was considerably less restless in April and May 1982 even though she mated at some time during this period. Wei's restlessness increased during the year from a ratio of 7.1 in January and 5.1 in February to 2.9 in March, 4.0 in April, and 3.8 in May and then decreased to 4.8 in July. It is tempting to ascribe the initial rise to the approach of the mating season, except that pandas are generally less restless in winter (av. ratio 6.2) than in spring (4.1) or in summer and autumn (4.0). More monitoring is necessary before we can establish any relationship between reproductive activity and restlessness.

To test for a correlation between activity and restlessness, we plotted both by month (fig. 5.9). There were no significant correlations, but 2 trends are worthy of note. One was that the females Ning and Zhen tended to become more restless as their activity levels dropped. And the other was that the male Long became more restless as his level rose. Limited data on the female Han and male Wei, not shown in fig. 5.9, reveal similar trends. We need information on more pandas to determine whether the difference is fortuitous or based on the animal's sex.

Rest periods

A panda is, on the average, inactive for 9.8 hours every day. Sometimes it sits or lies for only a few minutes, or occasionally it remains still for an hour or two before moving on. While it rests, it continues to defecate, and the number of droppings

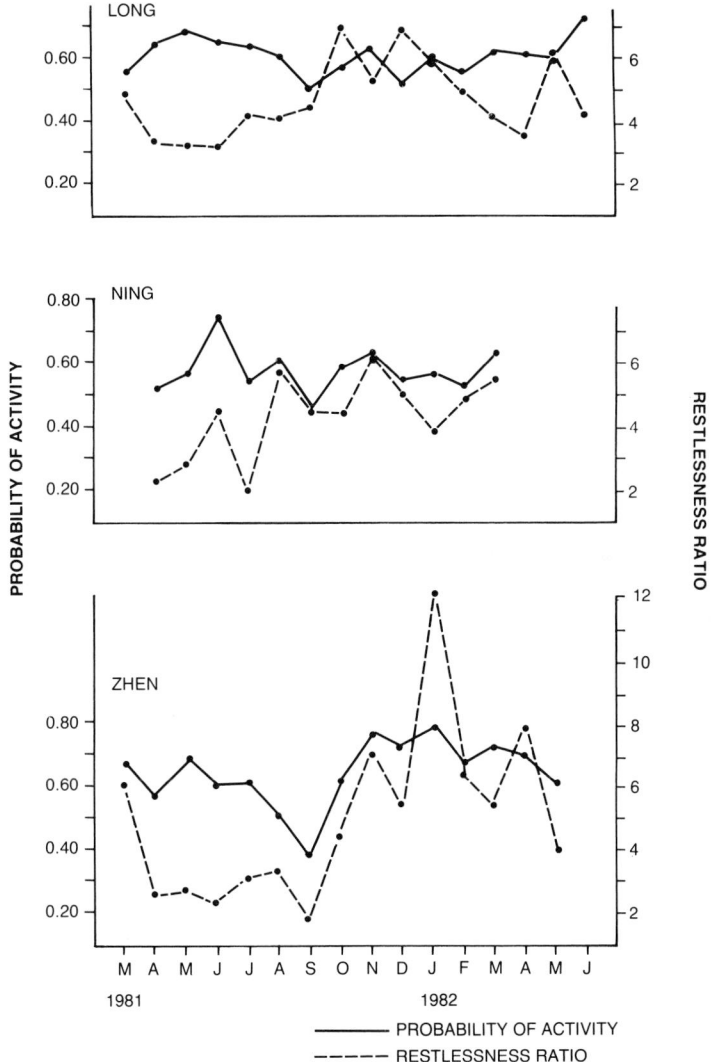

FIGURE 5.9   Comparison of probability of activity with the restlessness ratio (see text) in Long, Ning, and Zhen. The lower the ratio, the greater the animal's restlessness.

provide an estimate of the length of the rest period. During a short rest of under 2 hours, a panda usually produces 5–10 droppings, whereas during a longer rest, lasting over 2 hours, it eliminates about 11 to 25 and occasionally 40 or more droppings (fig. 5.10). In terms of bulk, 26 droppings at one site weighed 4.04 kg, 28 at another 5.05 kg, and 33 at a third 7.01 kg. Some sites had 50 or more droppings, usually an indication that a panda had rested 2 or more times there. For example, Wei rose in the morning of 21 January, having deposited 33 droppings. He then

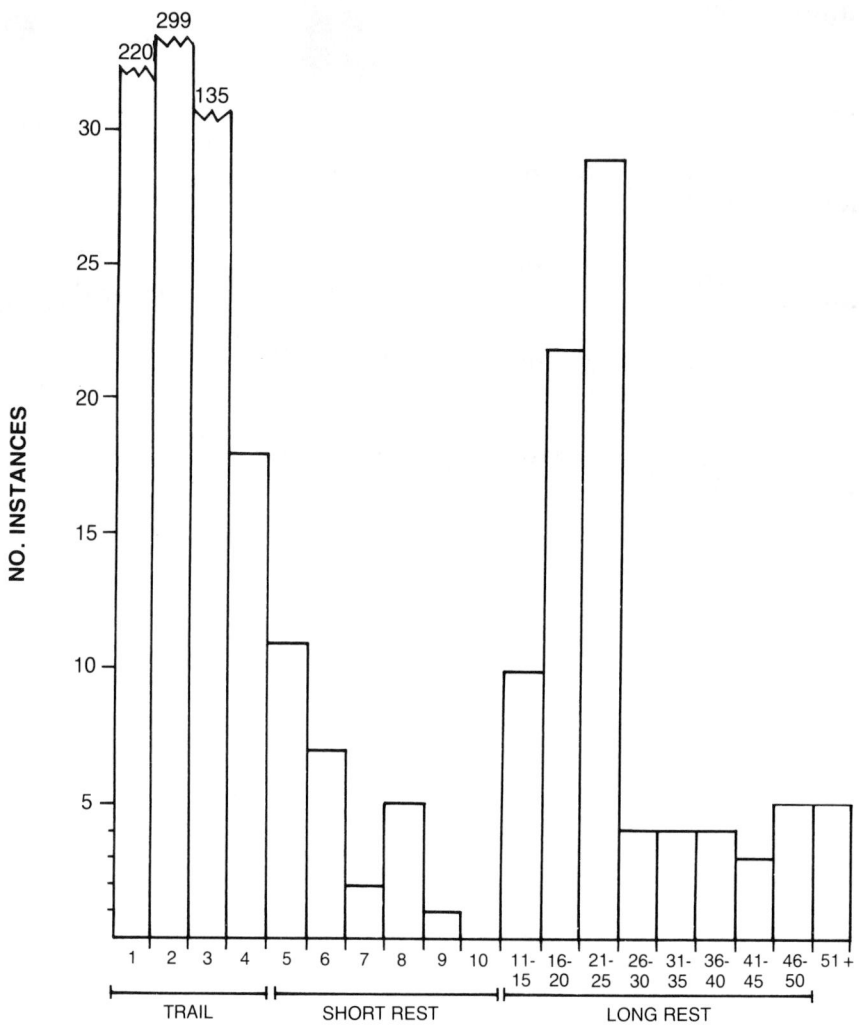

NO. DROPPINGS AT SITE

FIGURE 5.10   Number of panda droppings per site on trails and at rest places, based on 3847 droppings. Droppings containing new *Fargesia* shoots are not included.

PLATE 5.1   A panda often rests at the base of a tree. Droppings litter the perimeter of the site, as do partially eaten *Sinarundinaria fangiana* stems.

foraged nearby, rested awhile, a period during which he eliminated 14 droppings, foraged some more, and returned to his rest site of the previous night. The following morning there were 47 more droppings, a total of 80 at the site.

Although an animal sometimes rested wherever it happened to be, it more commonly selected a place with something to lean against. Of 103 sites with 11 or more droppings, 30.1% were simply in a bamboo thicket, 51.5% were at the base of a tree, 9.7% against a log, and 4.9% by a stump. Of 4 further rest sites, 2 were inside the hollow shell of an old stump, one was on top of a log, and one on a boulder. It was striking that pandas made no effort to construct nests; they merely reclined on damp earth, snow, or frozen ground. Body heat sometimes melted snow into ice. Many rest sites (42.7%) were at the base of massive conifers, perhaps partly because needles and wood dust there were soft and dry. Good sites may be used repeatedly for resting. In a one-hectare area at Wanghouyan there were 10 large firs with at least 316 droppings in rest sites at the base, and in a half-hectare area in the Zhuanjinggou there were 12 firs with at least 626 droppings. On occasion, a panda ate bamboo while sitting at a rest site, and the discarded stems inadvertently provided bedding (plate 5.1). By contrast, gorillas (Schaller 1963) and Asiatic black bears construct bamboo sleeping nests. For instance, we examined 3 black bear nests in *Fargesia*, 2 with old droppings. At one nest the bear had bent in 7 stems, at another 18 stems, and at the third 32 stems, and then had folded and broken the tops to form a springy, soft bed. A panda's coat apparently provides sufficient protection and comfort without need for padding. Nevertheless, pandas can build nests, as shown in maternity dens.

A resting panda either remains relatively motionless for lengthy periods or repeatedly shifts its position. It may lie on its back, or partly on its side, one hindleg in the air; it may recline on its belly, either sprawled or with forelegs and hindlegs tucked in; or it may rest on its side, sometimes curled up. Paws or forelegs often cover the muzzle. Frequently, a panda merely sits hunched (fig. 13).

On 25 May at 1215 hours, Zhen walked from a *Fargesia* thicket, climbed a flat, mossy boulder on a ridge covered with rhododendron and rested. Our notes describe some of her behavior:

—1220. Zhen sits, muzzle tucked into her folded forelegs. Once she scratches her head with a hindpaw. She then lies on her belly, a paw cupped over her nose.

—1230. She sits up, scratches belly with a hindpaw, and wipes a forepaw over her face as if bothered by flies. After scratching herself once more, she hunches, eyes closed, head sunk to the chest, forepaws in lap. Her breathing rate is 36 times per minute.

—1245. Zhen shifts, now resting on belly.

—1255. Sitting up, she looks around briefly, her nostrils moving as if sniffing air.

—1304. She rolls partly on her side, extends her tail and defecates. During the following 22 minutes she shifts her position 3 times, a protruding tree root at the site apparently causing discomfort.

—1331. Someone shouts near camp. Zhen raises her head, looks toward the sound, yawns, and reclines.

—1347. She sits, scratches herself, and rolls on her side, curled up.

—1410. She turns partially on her back, hindlegs extended, a forepaw thrown over her face. Her breathing rate is 24 times per minute.

—1426. Zhen sits up again, looks around, and yawns. She scratches her ear with a hindpaw. Light rain falls. Hunching over, she continues to rest.

TABLE 5.2

AVERAGE NUMBER OF LONG REST PERIODS PER DAY OF INDIVIDUAL PANDAS AT DIFFERENT SEASONS

	Spring	Summer-autumn	Winter
Long	1.2	1.5	1.6
Ning	1.1	1.3	1.7
Zhen	1.1	1.5	1.1
Han	1.9	0.3[a]	2.2
Wei	0.4[b]	0.5[a]	1.6

[a]Sample was small, only 2 to 3 days, and excluded from statistical computations.
[b]Wei has significantly ($p < 0.05$) fewer long rests in spring than in winter; other pandas show no seasonal difference.

TABLE 5.3
DURATION OF LONG REST PERIODS AT DIFFERENT SEASONS (ALL PANDAS COMBINED)

	Total days	Total rest periods	Average rest periods/day	Duration of rest periods (hours)				
				2–4	4–6	6–8	8–10	10–12
Spring	76	89	1.2	75	14	0	0	0
Summer-autumn	112	175	1.6	106	47	13	7	2
Winter	109	162	1.5	121	35	3	3	0
% of total				70.9	22.5	3.8	2.3	0.5

—1448. It begins to rain heavily. Zhen sits erect, stretches forelegs above her head and yawns. Leaving the rest site, she immediately begins to feed, consuming 13 new *Fargesia* shoots in 17 minutes.

As this example illustrates, a resting panda may change position, scratch itself, or otherwise move enough to activate the motion sensor. Animals often appear to be restless at the start and toward the end of a long rest period. Since such behavior made it difficult for us to define the actual duration of a rest period, we established several criteria for analyzing data. To eliminate brief breaks in activity, we defined a long rest period as one lasting 2 hours (9 activity readings) or more. One active reading in a series of inactive ones is disregarded as long as that active reading has been preceded by 4 consecutive inactive readings to mark the beginning of the rest and followed by at least 2 inactive ones to signify continuation of the rest.

A panda may take a long rest at any time of day or night; on some days it rests 1–4 times, and on others not at all, limiting itself to brief inactive periods. Animals averaged fewer ($p < 0.05$) long rests each day in spring (1.2) than in summer and winter (1.5, 1.6). Wei took significantly fewer rests than the others in spring, and Zhen somewhat fewer in winter, indicating some individual variation (table 5.2). Most rest periods (70.9%) were 2–4 hours in duration, some (22.5%) were 4–6 hours, and a few (6.6%) were more than 6 hours, with the majority of those more than 6 hours occurring during summer (table 5.3). The average duration of rest periods varied seasonally. Spring and winter tended to be similar, but 2 of the 3 pandas for which we have data rested significantly longer in summer than at other seasons (table 5.4). The exception was Zhen, whose restlessness while she had an infant probably lowered her average. Rain or snow could have an influence on the duration of rest periods, but our analysis in table 5.5 shows no significant response to precipitation within a season. Pandas rested for significantly shorter periods in spring (2.6 hours) than in winter (3.8 hours) only when it rained, a difference for which we lack an explanation. To find out whether pandas take long rests at a particular time of day, we calculated the average duration of rest periods at night, in daytime, and during the crepuscular hours (fig. 5.11). Analyzed by season, the results show that the length of rest periods in spring does not differ with time of day, that in winter there is a small but significant ($p < 0.05$) increase in number of hours at dawn and dusk, and that, in summer, pandas tend to have major rests, averaging 6 hours in length, starting at night and continuing far into morning.

TABLE 5.4
DURATION OF LONG REST PERIODS (IN HOURS) OF PANDAS BY SEASON

	Spring	Summer-autumn	Winter
Long	2.7*	4.3**	3.5***
Ning	2.5*	4.0**	3.4*
Zhen	3.0*	3.2*	3.4*
Han	3.2*	3.0ᵃ	3.6*
Wei	2.9*	2.5ᵃ	3.2*

An animal's rest periods are not significantly different ($p < 0.05$) by season if the number of asterisks are the same. Within a season, pandas are not significantly different from each other except Zhen in summer.
[a]Sample was too small to be included in the statistical computations.

We wondered whether length of rest periods was related to probability of activity. Using the Pearson Product Moment test, we found that all pandas, except Wei, showed a negative correlation, ranging from weak (Zhen: $r = -0.28$, $p > 0.30$) to strong (Long: $r = -0.75$, $p < 0.0007$). This means that as activity of pandas increases, the average length of rest periods also increases: the more time a panda forages during the day, the longer it rests afterward.

The same test was used to check on the relationship between rest period length and restlessness (ratio of number nonchanges to one change). The three females showed no correlation ($r = 0.09$, $p > 0.62$), Long a moderately positive one ($r = 0.42$, $p > 0.10$), and Wei a weak negative one ($r = -0.32$, $p > 0.59$). A positive correlation means that as the average length of rest periods increases, restlessness also increases; the data, however, indicate no definite relationship.

Behavioral time budget

By radio-monitoring activity, we determined that, on the average, pandas are active for 14.2 hours a day. The next step is to find out how much time a panda devotes to various types of activity. Under ideal field conditions, it is possible to watch an animal directly. Ruan and Yong (1983), for example, obtained valuable insights into panda activity while observing an adult continuously for 48 hours during May in the Qinling Mountains. The animal remained localized around a small cave in which it often rested and from which it ventured to feed on new shoots. In 48 hours, it

TABLE 5.5
AVERAGE DURATION OF LONG REST PERIODS (IN HOURS) ANALYZED BY SEASON AND WEATHER

		No precipitation	Rain	Snow
Spring	all pandas	2.9	2.6	3.1
Summer-autumn	Long and Ning	4.1	4.3	—
	Zhen only	3.3	3.0	—
Winter	all pandas	3.3	3.8	3.5

There is no significant response to precipitation within each season.

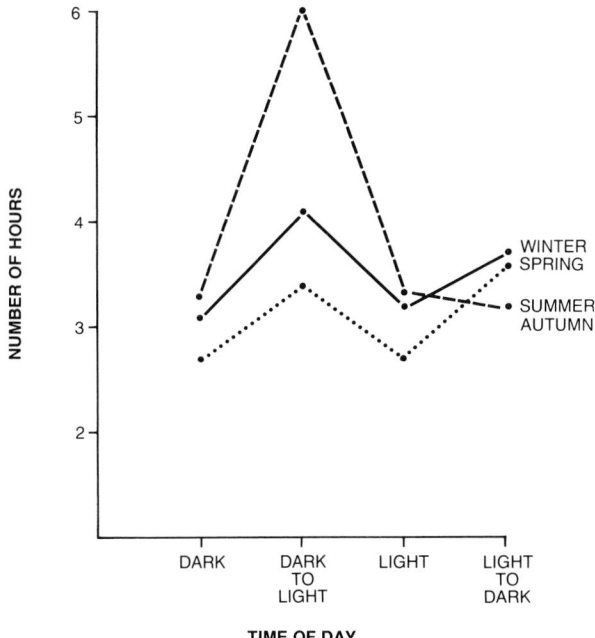

FIGURE 5.11   Duration of rest periods at various times of day during different seasons. (Data from all pandas combined.)

foraged 14 times in bouts ranging from 35 minutes to 5 hours 8 minutes (average 1 hour 34 minutes); and it also rested 14 times for periods of 28 minutes to 4 hours 7 minutes (average 1 hour 52 minutes). Other activities included drinking 5 times for 3–5 minutes each, urinating 16 times, and defecating 96 times. The panda was active for an average of 11 hours per day, with most time devoted to feeding. Since we seldom saw pandas, we had to infer behavior by examining spoor. Routes such as those in figure 5.12 are typical of many kilometers of tracking. In one, Ning meandered for 169 m in May, eating 456 *Sinarundinaria* stems of all ages and 6 new shoots at 38 feeding sites; she rested 4 times for short periods, once by a fir, once apparently up in a fir, and twice in bamboo, each time leaving 6 droppings; she defecated 5–6 times when not resting, and clawed a birch and possibly also a fir. In another example, an adult was tracked for 500 m through fresh snow in November; in a sample stretch of 122 m, it sat down to rest or eat 29 times, consuming 161 stems, most of them old shoots, and defecated about 9 times, a total of 19 droppings. Each route represents several hours in a panda's day. From such mundane data, supplemented with observations on captives, we can prepare a preliminary activity budget for the panda. Several activities, among them feeding and traveling, have been described in detail above (chapters 3 and 4) and now require only brief comment; others need description.

Feeding

For how many hours must a panda forage each day to meet its nutritional requirements? As we lack observations on rate of leaf consumption, we limit our calculations to stems and new shoots. The captive male Ping-Ping needed about 40 seconds to pick up, prepare, and eat an old shoot or stem. About 6.5 g of food are obtained from an old shoot and 5 g from a stem. In winter, a panda consumes about 12.5 kg (fresh weight) of *Sinarundinaria* of which 29.4% is leaf and 70.6% stem; 79.5% of the latter consists of old shoot (see chapter 3). Given these figures, a panda would require 12.0 hours per day to consume the old shoots and 4.0 hours for other stems. The total of 16 hours is obviously too high, for animals are active for only about 14.9 hours a day in winter, and the calculations exclude leaves. Ping-Ping may have eaten more slowly than would a free-living panda. If we allow only 30 seconds per old shoot or stem, then the numbers would be 9.7 and 3.8 hours respectively, a total of 13.5 hours.

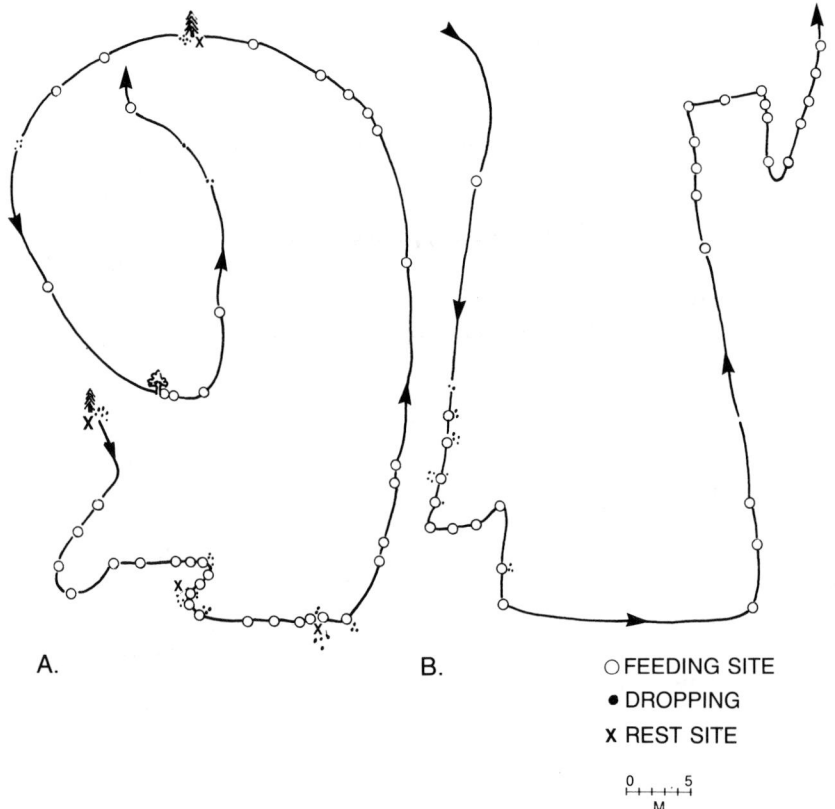

A.   B.   ○ FEEDING SITE
                                                           ● DROPPING
                                                           x REST SITE

                                                           0   5
                                                           ┝┼┼┼┼┤
                                                              M

FIGURE 5.12   Typical routes of pandas in *Sinarundinaria* showing feeding and resting sites. A. Ning, 14 May 1981.   B. Adult, 29 November 1981.

During spring, pandas eat 93% stem, most of them two-year and old. At 30 seconds per item, a panda would need 19.4 hours to consume 12.5 kg, an impossibly high total, for pandas are, on the average, active only 15.4 hours at this season. We can only conjecture why the calculated and expected number of hours fail to match. Perhaps a panda's rate of eating is higher. An animal could, for instance, save seconds by eating several stems at once, as it sometimes does, or by ingesting more of each stem, thereby reducing time spent searching and plucking. But even if a panda were to process and eat a stem every 20 seconds, an unlikely speed, it would still need its whole active period to feed. There are obvious time constraints in eating a stem: to consume a section 36 cm long requires 8 to 10 bites, not to mention time spent chewing. We suspect that total food intake may be less than 12.5 kg at this season; but, if so, then the animal's nutritional level might fall to the presumed minimum daily requirement unless it switched from *Sinarundinaria* stems to new *Fargesia* shoots (see chapter 3, "Panda Nutrition"). Until we can obtain data on possible seasonal differences in the amount of food eaten, the estimated intake of 12.5 kg per day provides a useful average on which to base comparisons. Although our calculations are crude, they raise an important issue: a panda forages with considerable constraints on its time, especially when *Sinarundinaria* stems contribute greatly to its diet. Much of a panda's active time must be devoted to keeping its digestive tract filled; the animal probably cannot increase nutrient intake by increasing feeding time because the rate of food passage limits the tract's capacity to process bamboo.

The direct observations by Ruan and Yong (1983), as well as our own on Zhen when she foraged on new *Fargesia* shoots, support our conclusion concerning a panda's time constraints. Zhen collected, peeled, and ate a shoot about every 93.6 seconds, a figure that includes short rests. We calculated that Zhen consumed about 650 shoots per day. To eat this number she would require 16.9 hours at 93.6 seconds per shoot, and 10.8 hours if she ate more rapidly at 60 seconds per shoot. Her actual active period at that season was 15.2 hours.

Drinking

Tracking pandas in snow showed that during winter the animals drink at least once a day at puddles, rivulets, and streams. Water at seepages is sometimes covered lightly with snow, ice, and gravel, and at such sites a panda may paw a shallow basin, about 25 × 20 cm in size, and drink the water that trickles in. Of 20 drinking sites investigated in winter, 6 had been excavated. A panda usually passes drinking sites in the normal course of travel. Once, however, Wei left a feeding site, walked 75 m to a rivulet, drank, and returned to foraging. Interrupting his courtship of Zhen, a male went into a shallow ravine where he drank from a puddle for 2 minutes; later the other male drank there for 3 minutes. Captives drink either by lapping or sucking.

Traveling

By radio-locating pandas on consecutive days, we found that they usually had moved a linear distance of 400 m or less (see table 4.4). And, by tracking pandas in snow, we noted that most movement was related to foraging and that the total actual travel distance was often less than 1 km per day (plate 5.2). Any panda may move without feeding, however—a female shifting to another part of her range, a subadult making an exploratory trip. Adult males travel more widely in winter and spring than do others pandas. Wei averaged 1293 m per day, as determined by following his snow trail for 5.5 days; on 2 of the days he remained localized, foraging intensively, and on the others he roamed, eating only at intervals (fig. 4.7). Since a panda walks at an estimated speed of 2–3 km per hour, it probably devotes relatively little of its daily time budget to traveling without feeding, perhaps an average of 30 minutes a day for a male and less for a female and subadult.

Tree climbing

We observed pandas in trees on 8 occasions between January 1981 and June 1982, twice or possibly 3 times when a subadult escaped from another panda, twice to avoid man, twice when Zhen retreated from a courting male (plate 5.3), and once when during the mating season a male ascended to call. One young escaped into a tree in May 1983 when harassed by roaming village dogs. Animals may occasionally rest in trees, to judge by the droppings below; and they may also sun themselves in treetops, according to Yong (1981). Pandas climb trees mainly when courting (see chapter 6) and when avoiding danger; in general, the behavior is uncommon.

PLATE 5.2   The male Wei moves through December snow from one *Fargesia* bamboo patch to another. His radio collar is clearly visible.

PLATE 5.3   The female Zhen has climbed into the low branches of a hemlock to avoid a courting male.

Grooming and other comfort movements

Pandas stretch themselves catlike by lowering their forequarters with extended forelegs while keeping the hindquarters raised. After waking, they may raise their forelegs above their head and yawn. When wet, they shake themselves like dogs. They rub neck, shoulders, back, thighs, and rump against walls, rocks, and trees; one captive female squirmed on her side in a rivulet while rubbing her head and shoulders on gravel and sod. A paw dirty with mud or porridge may be licked clean, and an animal also licks its pelage and nibbles it with teeth. Apparent itches are scratched with fore- or hindpaw (fig. 13).

In December 1980, Chengdu's Mei-Mei groomed herself for 5.4% of the time we observed her, an average of 6 bouts per hour, most lasting 15–60 seconds. She may have groomed with abnormal frequency, for she developed a skin problem within a month. Once we observed Zhen in the Zhuanjinggou. It was 22 July, a time of year when flies and mosquitoes may be bothersome. From 0950 to 1130, Zhen foraged on bamboo leaves, eating from the tops of 124 stems. Then she reclined, but insects disturbed her rest and caused her to make comfort movements:

—1209. Shakes head

—1213. Turns over

—1221. Raises head

FIGURE 5.13   Typical postures of giant pandas. Top two: scratching. Middle: resting in a sitting position. Bottom: crouching by a female in estrus when approached by a male.

—1232. Shakes head

—1237. Scratches herself with a hindpaw

—1238. Scratches face with a forepaw

—1239. Scratches face with a forepaw and back with a hindpaw

—1245. Shakes head

—1248. Shakes head

—1252. Twice swipes air with a forepaw as if driving away insects

—1254. Shakes head

—1255. Her nose twitches, and she scratches face with a forepaw

—1258. Wipes and scratches face with a forepaw

—1303. Shakes head, sits up, and continues to doze

—1307. Swipes air by her face with a forepaw, then reclines

—1313–1320. Wipes face three times with a forepaw; yawns

—1321. Departs from rest site.

On another occasion, Zhen scratched herself 5 times and wiped her muzzle with a forepaw twice during an 2.5-hour rest, a total of about one minute in grooming time. On an average, grooming uses perhaps only 10 minutes of a day.

For most (89%) grooming bouts, Chengdu's Mei-Mei used a hindpaw, even though it would seem easier to scratch foreleg, shoulder, head, or chest with a forepaw. In 5% of the bouts she licked or nibbled a part of her body, in 3% she rubbed her arm against a wall, and in 3% she used her forepaw to wipe her head. The forepaws, though dexterous, feature little in body care; the hindpaws, however, appear specially adapted for grooming in that the central three claws are close together like a comb.

Defecating and urinating

A panda defecates while squatting lightly, tail extended horizontally, or while walking. A reclining animal may simply raise its rump to drop feces along the perimeter of the rest site. It often sleeps on its feces, but these, consisting mainly of coarse bamboo fragments, do not soil the pelage. Pandas defecate prodigiously—an average of 97 droppings per day, or 4 per hour, in the case of Wei feeding on *Sinarundinaria*, as described in chapter 3. With one defecation averaging two droppings (fig. 5.10), Wei defecated about 48 times a day. One adult in the Qinling Mountains defecated 96 times in 48 hours, or also 48 times a day, on a diet of new *Phyllostachys* shoots (Ruan and Yong 1983). Since a panda may not interrupt other activities to defecate, and since, in any event, elimination requires just a few seconds, probably not more than 5–10 minutes need to be budgeted for this behavior.

Pandas urinate infrequently during winter, except in the context of scent marking. When feeding on new shoots, however, they urinate often (Ruan and Yong 1983), commonly doing so at the same time as they defecate.

Scent marking

Adult male pandas appear to mark trees more often than do animals of any other age and sex; the activity may be seasonal (see chapter 6). Wei once marked 47 trees in 5.5 days in winter, or 8.5 trees per day. We doubt that, on the average, a panda spends more than 5 minutes a day to mark and to investigate olfactory signals in the environment.

Playing

Captive pandas are playful until at least 3 years of age (Haas 1958; Wilson and Kleiman 1974; Zhu and Li 1980). They run with a high-stepping, lively gait; climb up on stumps, boulders, and trees; hang upside down from suspended ropes; roll on their backs, rocking back and forth and waving their legs and sometimes manipulating a stick or ball with jaws and all four paws. Lateral rolls and somersaults are common during exhuberant play. One subadult at Yingxionggou, on being released into an outdoor enclosure after long confinement, took several fast steps downslope and rolled over and over in a series of somersaults that sent her crashing through brush; then she walked back uphill and repeated this. An infant may play on its mother, scrambling up on her back and sliding down, and it may bite at and wrestle with one of her legs; she in turn may mouth and paw it gently.

We had no opportunity to observe play in the wild. Our only evidence of playful behavior is circumstantial and involved tobogganing in snow. One animal, probably a subadult, walked down a steep slope. Whenever it came to a forest opening where snow lay deeply, it slid downhill on chest and belly for 4 to 7 m, leaving a deep furrow. There were at least 6 such sites; at one, the panda apparently walked back uphill to repeat the slide (H. Quigley, pers. comm). Another trail showed similar furrows; and once Wei tobogganed 15 m at a place where he could more safely have walked. Murie (1981) describes similar behavior in grizzly bears.

Socializing

Excluding contact between mother and young, social interactions are uncommon. For much of the year, most pandas appear to spend days and weeks alone without meeting others, although certain individuals, such as Long and Ning, may have more frequent contact (see chapter 6). Animals associate more readily during the mating season, but even then interactions last at most a few days and occur at widely spaced intervals.

Discussion

Three ways of assessing seasonal patterns of activity reveal the same trend: pandas are least active in summer, with a marked decline in September, and they also rest most frequently and have the longest rest periods in that season; they are most active in spring, when they take both the fewest rests and the fewest long rests. Animals are almost as active at night as in daytime, with peaks before and around dawn and especially at dusk. Although a panda seems at times to adhere to some idiosynchratic pattern of its own, overall activity patterns are similar in all animals, suggesting some common influence.

Three conspicuous seasonal events could affect activity: mating, bamboo shoot availability, and birth. (1) Pandas might be expected to become particularly active during the mating season. No such trend is discernible in the females and subadults. Wei shows an increase in activity during April and May, but, as a preliminary summary of data from late 1982 shows, his July and August levels are as high as those in the mating season. There is a typical September drop in his activity and a rise in October, followed by a relatively low and constant level during winter. (2) In May and June, some pandas feed on new *Fargesia* shoots, a scattered resource that might require extra searching time. Three adults that ate shoots extensively showed no marked change in level; only Ning was highly active in June, and she was not in *Fargesia* when we monitored her. (3) When Zhen had a newborn in September, her activity level dropped for a month, but so did that of Long and Ning, though to a lesser extent. Zhen probably lost her infant in November, and she was unusually active from then until April. Possibly she needed to recover nutritionally from the energy drain of lactation, but Han, who may also have lost an infant, showed no such increase. The mating and birth seasons have a relatively small effect on overall activity levels.

The availability of nutritious forage has an important impact on activity, judging by seasonal changes. For at least part of spring, pandas subsist on stems, which are not only low in nutrients but also time-consuming to eat. Since stems maintain pandas only at subsistence level, animals must forage most actively at that season. Those pandas that switch to a diet of new *Fargesia* shoots have a nutritious food, which, however, has such a high water content that an animal must consume an inordinate amount to provide sustenance. And this takes time. By contrast, pandas browse mainly on nutritious leaves in summer and autumn. These take little time to collect and eat. Activity and nutrition levels are intermediate in winter, though daily patterns seem also to be influenced by snowfall and dawn cold.

That the nutrient content of food can influence peaks in activity is evident when comparing the sharp night peak in winter and spring to the relatively low and even level in summer and autumn, when animals are more likely to rest than to forage during the hours before dawn (fig. 5.5). Nutrients alone, however, cannot be invoked to explain the sharp dusk peak at all season. It is possible that activity is to some extent synchronized by physiological demands. With digestibility of food low and rate of passage rapid, a panda must eat often to keep its digestive tract filled. Rest sites commonly contain 16–25 droppings (fig. 5.10) weighing 2.5–4 kg and representing about 3–5 hours of inactivity. While autopsying an adult female panda, we also measured the capacity of her digestive tract. Her stomach was 74 cm long, her small intestine 727 cm, and her large intestine 125 cm, and, including the 50-cm-long esophagus, they weighed a total of 4.47 kg. Filled with water—full but not taut—the stomach held 10 liters, the small intestine 8.7, and the large intestine 4—a total of 22.7 liters. Measuring the volume of 13 droppings, we found that it was, on the average, 15% greater than the weight. The tract can therefore hold 19.3 kg, but only when stretched out, not when coiled within the body. Calculated another way, the capacity of the panda's stomach was 44% of the total capacity of the tract, a figure similar to the 47% derived by Jaczewski et al. (1960) for brown bear. On 5 occasions we fed Ping-Ping new *Fargesia* shoots until he stopped abruptly, his stomach apparently full, having consumed an average of 4.5 (3.9–5.9) kg within one hour. The capacity of his digestive tract is then 10.2 kg, fresh weight. Rate of passage averages 8 hours (see chapter 3). A panda that rests for as long as 5 hours and eliminates 4 kg or more of droppings probably has an empty stomach. Maintaining a steady flow of nutrients into its system is essential to an animal living on a diet of low quality, so that the panda must soon refill its stomach. This explains why pandas alternately feed and rest throughout the day and night and why they rarely rest for more than 6 hours. In summer, when it is not as important to keep the digestive tract filled, animals sometimes have a long rest; the 2 pandas which were inactive for 10–12 hours (table 5.3) may have had almost empty tracts when they began to forage again.

The 2 daily peaks at around 0500 and 1700 are about 12 hours apart. At first glance, it is tempting to ascribe these peaks to an endogenous rhythm cued to light change, animals stuffing themselves before a rest. Yet individual patterns are highly flexible, and the morning peak does not correlate with dawn. If pandas had a strong tendency to be crepuscular, captives might also show evidence of it. The pandas at Yingxionggou receive a diet supplement of porridge, milk, and vitamins. Confined to cages and provided with a concentrated food, the animals eat relatively little of the bamboo that is given them. In mid-March, Dong Cai and D. Kleiman monitored the

TABLE 5.6
TWENTY-FOUR HOUR ACTIVITY BUDGETS OF SELECTED LARGE MAMMALS (PERCENT)

	Rest	Feed	Travel	Hunt	Other
Giant panda (this study)	40.9	55.0	2.1	—	2.0
Grizzly bear[a] (Gebhard 1983)	36.0	49.8	2.8	8.8	2.7
Polar bear[b] (Stirling 1974)	42.0	2.3	29.0	24.6[c]	2.0
Lion (Schaller 1972)	84.0	3.1	8.3[d]		4.6±
Impala (Jarman and Jarman 1973)	41.7[e]	40.0	7.5	—	10.5
Plains zebra (Gogan 1973)	29.0±	56.0±	15.0±	—	no data
African elephant (Wyatt and Eltringham 1974)	13.2	74.2	11.3	—	1.3
Mountain gorilla (Fossey and Harcourt 1977)	76.5	12.5	7.2	—	3.8

[a]Data are based on one female with two yearlings in northern Alaska; the female hunted only ground squirrels; hibernation lasts 7 months in this area, October to May, a period not included in the activity budget.
[b]Observations were made in July and August only.
[c]Mostly still-hunting.
[d]Travel is often related to hunting.
[e]Includes much ruminating.

activity of the 8 pandas at 15-minute intervals for several days. During one typical 24-hour period, the animals were active 31.3 (26.6–38.3)% of the time, with peaks (50–72%) when fed at 0800–0900 and 1500, and also between 2400 and 0300 hours. These animals were less active, on the average, than those in the wild. They had a daily activity cycle with three peaks, two induced by the keepers and one of their own, none of which corresponded to those in the wild.

The sharp dusk peak of free-living animals could be a result of the pandas' physiological rhythm of feeding and resting only if some other factor tended to synchronize activity at a certain point. Such a factor could be an environmental one. If, for example, cool morning temperatures made it advantageous for animals to rest, they might afterward feed for 6–8 hours until tired and replete they rest again, a cycle which would tend to persist in spite of great individual variation in activity.

The amount of time a panda allots to various activities depends somewhat on its age, sex, and reproductive state. Nevertheless, all animals devote nearly the whole day to just two activities: feeding and resting. Ignoring seasonal differences, a panda forages for at least 55.0% of the day and rests for 40.9%; all other activities require no more than an average of 4.1%, or one hour per day. Carnivores usually spend little time feeding and considerable time hunting, or, if food is abundant, much of the day resting (table 5.6). Ruminants, such as the impala, forage for about 40% of the day, there being little need to travel far in search of food; they then spend rest periods chewing cud. Zebras, elephants, and other nonruminant herbivores have less efficient digestive systems than ruminants; they must therefore eat more to compensate for the reduced extraction of nutrients (Van Soest 1982). The greater quantity is reflected in feeding time, which may reach 74% of the day in elephants (table 5.6). The time budget of giant pandas most closely resembles that of nonruminant herbivores in that more than 50% of the day is usually devoted to foraging.

Summary

1. Life for a panda represents a balance between activities to fulfill basic needs, and inactivity to conserve energy. An animal is active for about 60% of the day, a figure that remains quite constant from month to month except for a drop in September. Daily activity reaches its lowest levels between 0800 and 0900 and after 1900 hours, and its highest levels between 0400 and 0600 and between 1600 and 1900 hours. The bimodal peaks and troughs remain similar all year, regardless of length of daylight.

2. A panda is inactive for an average of 9.8 hours a day. Some of this time is devoted to rest periods lasting 2 hours or more. Animals averaged 1.2 such long rests per day in spring and 1.5–1.6 at other seasons. Most rests were 2–4 hours long, and few more than 6 hours.

3. A panda is, on the average, active for 14.2 hours per day. Most of a panda's active period is devoted to collecting, preparing, and eating bamboo; other activities, such as traveling, scent marking, and grooming, use only a small fraction of the

day. A panda forages with considerable time constraints: much of its active time must be devoted to keeping its digestive tract filled. An animal probably cannot increase nutrient intake by increasing feeding time because rate of food passage limits the tract's capacity to process bamboo. A panda's time budget most closely resembles that of a nonruminant herbivore in that more than 50% of the day is spent foraging.

4. Various ways of assessing activity all reveal the same trend: pandas are most active in spring and also rest less often and for shorter periods at that season than during others. In spring, pandas either eat stems or new shoots, both of which are time-consuming to collect and eat.

6

Population Dynamics and Social Behavior

Pandas are generally considered to be solitary. Of course, every mammal has at least two social imperatives: when young, it depends on prolonged contact with its mother for survival; and later it must at intervals find a mate. If, as with pandas, home ranges of solitary individuals overlap, occasional meetings are almost inevitable. The outcome of encounters will then depend on the age and sex of the individuals as well as on such factors as genetic relationship and the results of previous contacts. There is little question that even solitary individuals have organized societies based on personal alliances. Social traits are labile, however, readily adapted to local conditions, affected by, for instance, population density and food distribution (Wilson 1975). Social structure depends on communication, on a system of visual, vocal, and olfactory signals. The results from a study of one population do not necessarily apply to all populations—a point to remember with respect to the small panda society in the Choushuigou.

Population dynamics

To preserve and possibly manage the panda, detailed knowledge of its population dynamics is necessary; yet this is the topic for which it is most difficult to obtain unbiased, quantitative information. To estimate population size is a major task in itself, and to determine age at sexual maturity, reproductive and mortality rates, and longevity requires years of sustained effort. At present we can do little more than summarize our few data and draw conclusions from available information on captives.

Population size and composition

It would be fortunate if individuals could be identified from spoor. An infant following its mother presents no problem, for its small tracks and droppings are distinctive. Spoor of subadults, however, may resemble that of adults. For instance, the hindfoot of Long (subadult) at 2.5 years was 20.5 cm long and toe pad 9 cm wide, whereas those of Zhen (adult) were 18 cm long and 9.5 cm wide. Also, tracks in snow are usually too blurred, because of the animal's hairy soles, to provide precise

155

measurements. Droppings may vary considerably in size and weight, both in one individual and from one individual to another. Zhen's droppings were on the average bigger than Long's (table 6.1), but large samples are required to detect such differences. The length of stem fragments in droppings provides perhaps the most reliable indicator of an animal's general age class. The pandas in the study area could be divided into 3 bite-size classes: large infant (1.25–1.5 years old) 2.7 cm; small subadult (2.5–3.5 years old) 3.5 cm; large subadult plus adult 3.8–4.1 cm (table 6.2).

All resident pandas extended their movements beyond the Choushuigou, and others drifted into it. On seeing a panda, we usually could not sex it, much less identify it individually, and bite size of stems in droppings could not be used with precision to distinguish individuals. Using various means, direct and indirect, we knew or inferred the presence of the following animals in the study area during 1981 and early 1982 (see fig. 2.10):

There were 7 marked individuals. Long (subadult male), Ning (subadult female), Zhen and Han (adult females), and Wei and Pi (adult males) were radio-collared; No. 81 (subadult male) was ear-tagged.

Two adult males—one large and one medium-sized—frequented Erdaoping and the Zhuanjinggou, and at least one of them used the Wanghouyan ridge as well. Another medium-sized male appeared to remain at the periphery of the study area in the Yingxionggou. We saw these three males together in April 1983. There were probably 2 males around Fanzipeng: one a large, seemingly elderly animal, observed by us several times, which often stayed on a ridge across the valley from Fanzipeng at Zhonggang; and the other a medium-sized animal, which ranged widely between the Huacaodigou and Chouchuigou.

On 30 October, 1981 we startled a year-old infant on the ridge separating Yingxionggou and Zhuanjinggou. Its mother was not observed at that time, but a month later we found fresh droppings there of an adult and infant together at a rest site. This female was trapped in the Zhuanjinggou in early 1983, but escaped before she could be radio-collared. Another female apparently ranged along the west side of the Zhuanjinggou and adjoining slopes at the periphery of the study area. She was seen with a small infant in December 1982. In autumn 1980, a female was observed in a tree den at Wanghouyan, and it was thought that she would soon give birth. We found no definite sign of this female in 1981 even though we visited the area often. In February 1982, we discovered month-old droppings of a female with large infant at Fanzipeng. Since the droppings remained our only evidence of this pair, we inferred

TABLE 6.1
WEIGHT AND DIMENSIONS OF PANDA DROPPINGS, $\bar{x} \pm SD$

	All droppings[a] N = 317	New *Fargesia* shoot only N = 28	Zhen N = 33	Long and Ning N = 40	15–17 mo. infant N = 6
Length	147.2 ±28.5	151.0 ±25.9	139.3 ±24.1	115.7 ±23.8	100.0 ±16.1
Width	59.1 ±6.5	54.1 ±5.0	57.3 ±5.1	52.5 ±4.0	36.5 ±4.6
Weight	153.3 ±54.7	179.5 ±69.7	131.4 ±39.7	98.5 ±27.9	39.5 ±11.2

[a]Excludes infants and new *Fargesia* shoots.

TABLE 6.2
BITE SIZES (IN CM) OF *Sinarundinaria* STEMS EATEN BY PANDAS

Panda	Approximate age	Sample size	Length of bite		
			Mean	± SD	range
Infant	15 mo.	25	2.74	± .29	2.2–3.2
Infant	17½ mo.	25	2.68	± .38	1.8–3.4
No. 81	2 yrs. 5 mo.	56	3.49	± .31	2.8–4.0
Ning	3 yrs. 4 mo.	50	3.52	± .36	2.6–4.3
Long	3 yrs. 5 mo.	63	3.48	± .33	2.7–4.2
Zhen	adult	72	4.05	± .40	2.5–4.8
Han	adult	98	4.14	± .49	2.9–5.3
Wei	adult	71	3.77	± .42	2.6–4.6
Pi	adult	155	4.04	± .50	2.6–5.5

Infant bite size is significantly smaller than subadult bite size, and subadult than adult ($p < 0.05$).

that its activity centered near the edge of the study area in the Huacaodigou. A female was found dead there on 8 April 1983.

At Fanzipeng, we occasionally picked up droppings of a subadult with a bite size of 3.5 cm, but could not determine whether these belonged to No. 81 or to a different animal. Wei treed a subadult, about 2.7 years old, on 8 May 1982. We could not detect an ear tag, and it is probable that a fourth subadult frequented the study area.

Not counting infants that died and possible transients, the population at the end of 1981 consisted of 2 large infants (sex unknown), 4 subadults (2 males, 1 female, 1 sex unknown), 7 adult males, and 5 or possibly 6 adult females—a total of 18–19. Six (33%) of the 18 animals thought to be present were below breeding age. Long and Ning were born in late 1978, No.81 in late 1979, and the two infants in late 1980, showing steady recruitment in this small population. Chu and Long (1983) obtained 53 skulls from the Min Mountains, most of them from animals that had died of starvation in the mid-1970s. They estimated that 13 (24.5%) of the skulls belonged to animals less than 5 years old, below breeding age.

Panda density is difficult to calculate because many of the animals spent part or most of their time outside the study area. Eighteen pandas in 35 km² gives a crude density of 1.9 km² per animal. Taking only the 12 residents within the 20 km² of bamboo of the Choushuigou and adjoining parts, the ecological density is 1.7 km² per animal. And considering only the 15 km² of *Sinarundinaria*, where the pandas spent the most time, the density is 1.25 km² per animal. In chapter 3 we showed that, at most, 0.5 km² of *Sinarundinaria* was required to support one animal on a permanent basis. In chapter 4 we noted that 4 radio-collared pandas were located on an average of 52% of the days in 92 one-hectare quadrats (see fig. 4.4). Assuming that 100 ha (1km²) can support 4 pandas for half a year, then one panda would require 0.5 km². The 2 methods of calculation provided similar results. Given conditions in that area at that time, panda density was less than half of what could be expected.

Age at sexual maturity

Compatible pairs are rare in zoos, with the result that few captive females conceive naturally when first physiologically able to do so. Washington's Ling-Ling had her first heat, as deduced from her behavior, at the probable age of 3.5 years, but Kleiman et al. (1979) did not consider her fully mature until 2 to 3 years later. At the London zoo, Chi-Chi first came into estrus at about 4 years of age, and Ching-Ching had a weak estrus at 2.5 years and a strong one at 4.5 years (Morris and Morris 1966,1981). Tokyo's Lan-Lan first showed signs of estrus at 5.5 years.* Of 2 females obtained as infants from the wild by the Beijing zoo, one came into estrus at 5.5 years and the other at 7.5 years. One female born in 1964 at the Beijing zoo had her first heat at 6.5 years. Ja-Jia at Yingxionggou had a weak estrous period at an estimated age of 4.5 years. Of 6 females at the Chongqing zoo, 5 had their first heat at about 5.5 years of age and one at 6.5 years (Shi 1982). The Chapultepec female Ying-Ying conceived when both she and her partner were 5.5 years old, and one female at the Beijing zoo also conceived at 5.5 years. Chengdu's Mei-Mei and Madrid's Shao-Shao became pregnant when artificially inseminated at 6.5 years.

The testes of young males are not evident externally. At the age of 2.5 years, No. 81 had testes about 4 cm long, as determined by feeling the lower abdomen. Long's testes at 3.5 years were approximately 7 cm long, about adult size, but they still had not descended into the scrotum. The testes of 7 adults, measured within the scrotum during March and April at the Chengdu zoo and at Yingxionggou, were 6.6 ± 0.4 cm in length and 3.4 ± 0.3 cm in width (S. Seager, pers. comm). The Chapultepec male was adult at 5.5 years; the Washington male probably was too, although production of viable sperm was not confirmed by electroejaculation until he was 8.5 years old (Kleiman 1983).

On the basis of this evidence, we conclude that both sexes usually reach maturity at 5.5–6.5 years.

For purposes of interpreting our data, we can recognize 3 age classes: (1) infants, from birth to the age of 1.5 years, when they become independent of their mothers (see below); (2) subadults, from 1.5 to about 5 years; and (3) adults, animals older than about 5 years.

Reproductive rate

The panda gives birth to single young or to twins, and exceptionally to triplets, one litter of three having been reported from the Shanghai zoo (Peking zoo 1974a). Thirty-seven litters have been born in captivity between 1963 and 1983. The number of young in 30 of these litters was 1–2, with an average of 1.7 (table 6.3). If twins are born, captive females raise only one of the young, leaving the other unattended, as described for Beijing's Juan-Juan (Anon. 1981a):

> When the yellowish pink cub touched the ground, Juan Juan picked it up in her front paws and began licking it.
> She gave birth to another newborn after about 30 minutes, but the second panda died, apparently because the mother had to choose which baby to care for.
> The latter newborn slipped to the ground, since Juan Juan was unable to hold

---

*When she died 4 September 1979, at an estimated age of 11 years, she carried a 42.6 g fetus (Brambell 1983).

TABLE 6.3

PANDAS BORN IN CAPTIVITY, 1963–83

Zoo	Year	Name of Mother	Conception date	Birth date	Gestation period (days)	Litters	Young	Young surviving 2 months +	Sex of surviving infant
Beijing	1963	Li-Li	14 April	9 Sept.	148	1	1	1	M
	1964	Li-Li	7 May	4 Sept.	120	1	2	1	F
	1965–77	—		—	—	8	15	5	—
	1978	Juan-Juan	24–27 April*	8 Sept.	134–137	1	2	1	F
	1980	Yuan-Yuan	4±4 May*	14 Sept.	133±	1	2	1	F
	1980	Dai-Dai	8±3 May*	25 Sept.	140±	1	2	0	—
	1981	Juan-Juan	27±2 April*	14 Sept.	140±	1	2	1	F
	1981	Dai-Dai	21±8 April*	21 Sept.	153±	1	2	0	—
	1982	Dai-Dai	15±3 April*	30 Aug.	137±	1	2	1	F
	1983	Yuan-Yuan	28±3 April*	14 Sept.	139±	1	2	1	M
	1983	Juan-Juan	17–19 April*	16 Sept.	150–152	1	2	0	—
Shanghai	1965–74	—		—	—	7	?	0	—
	1981	Bai Mei	2± April**	—	—	1	2	0	—
	1982	Bai Mei	17 May**	23 Aug.	98	1	1	1	F
Chengdu	1980	Mei-Mei	14–16 April**	20 Sept.	157–159	1	2	1	M
	1981	Mei-Mei	12 May**	18 Sept.	129	1	1	1	M
	1983	Mei-Mei	15–16 April**	20 Sept.	157–158	1	2	1	M
Hangzhou	1979	—	—*	11 Sept.	—	1	2	0	—
Kunming	1965	—	—	—	—	1	1	0	—
Chapultepec	1980	Ying-Ying	6 April	11 Aug.	127	1	1	0	—
	1981	Ying-Ying	17 March	21 July	126	1	1	1	M
	1983	Ying-Ying	16 April	22 June	97	1	1	1	?
Madrid	1982	Shao-Shao	27–29 March*	4 Sept.	159–161	1	2	1	?
Washington	1983	Ling-Ling	18–20 March**	21 July	123–125	1	1	0	—

*Artificial insemination.

**Artificial insemination and natural.

The precise length of gestation periods cannot be given at times because the animals were inseminated repeatedly over a period of days. The approximate midpoint of this period is arbitrarily taken as the conception day.

them both at the same time. Attendants rushed to take it away and tried to feed it in an incubator, but it died after five hours.

Although females in captivity have not cared for the second offspring, those in the wild occasionally try to rear both. Two small infants were found in a den in the Liang Mountains in July 1981 (Jilin Zhiha, pers. comm.) and several instances of a female accompanied by 2 young, both presumably her own, have been reported from the Min and Qionglai mountains.

Captives may have young in consecutive years if an infant dies or is removed before it is 6 months old. For instance, the Beijing and Chengdu zoos take surviving young from their mothers in March. Although the female's heat may be delayed until May, conception can occur, and young are then born at the usual time (table 6.3). The situation in the wild appears to be similar, although we lack detailed observations on this point. Zhen gave birth in September 1981, lost her young before the end of the year, and gave birth again in September 1982. Han followed a similar pattern, judging by circumstantial evidence. If, however, a young remains with its mother, she apparently continues to lactate through the spring mating season, and estrus is suppressed until the following year, by which time her young has become independent. Therefore, the maximum reproductive rate is about one young per female every 2 years.

Longevity of pandas in zoos outside China has been poor, seldom as much as 14 years (table B.1). One female in the Beijing zoo was an estimated 28 years old in 1980 (Xu 1981) and died in July 1982 at the age of 30; another female in the Nanjing zoo lived for 29 years. Such a life span is expected of an animal as large as a panda, and corresponds to that of captive bears (Crandall 1964). Craighead et al. (1974) found that the reproductive life of grizzly bears in the wild is as long as their longevity, about 25 years. If a panda female had her first young at the age of 6 years and reared one young every 2 years, she would by the age of 24 years have been able to raise at most about 9 young.

Mortality

In May 1979, tracks of an adult and a small young were seen above Erdaoping; we presume they belonged to Zhen and her offspring. Zhen had no surviving young in 1980. She gave birth in 1981, but her infant vanished soon after she left the den with it; she gave birth again in 1982, but the fate of this young remains uncertain (see below). She was therefore known to have reared at most one young during a 4-year period, from autumn 1978 to autumn 1982. When we caught Han in January 1982, her nipples were pink and enlarged, and we could squeeze a clear liquid from them, indicating that she may have lactated until recently; yet we found no other evidence of a young in subsequent months. Various factors may contribute to the death of small young. The Chapultepec female accidentally crushed her 7-day-old (Castillo 1982). In 1983, Beijing's Juan-Juan partially ate one of her young soon after birth. If a female leaves her young unattended in the den, even for a short period, it becomes vulnerable to such predators as golden cat, yellow-throated marten, and weasel.

TABLE 6.4
FREQUENCY OF OCCURRENCE OF FOOD ITEMS IN 168 LEOPARD DROPPINGS

Species eaten	%
Tufted deer	85.1
Musk deer	4.2
Other wild ungulates (serow, sambar, etc.)	6.5
Livestock	1.2
Golden monkey	1.7
Hog badger	1.2
Giant panda	0.6
Flying squirrel	0.6
Grass and bamboo leaves	5.4
Unknown	0.6

Mobile young sometimes become separated from their mother in dense bamboo and ultimately starve, according to local people.

One or two leopards occasionally traveled through the study area. Their main prey was tufted deer, but they also captured golden monkeys, hog badgers, and other mammals, as revealed by droppings (table 6.4). The following evidence for leopard predation on pandas has been collected in the study area since the project began in 1978: (1) leopard droppings with bone and hair of infant, April 1979; (2) dropping with panda hair, as well as a skull and other remains of a panda nearly 2 years old, July 1979; and (3) leopard dropping with two claws, bones, and hair of infant, July 1981. With the hunting ranges of local leopards unknown, we have no idea whether all three animals were killed within the Choushuigou. Nevertheless, leopards obviously have an impact on the panda population in the area.

After reaching an age of 2.5 years and weighing 50 kg or more, pandas probably become almost immune to predation. In the Pingwu area of the Min Mountains a brown bear is said to have killed a panda. On 6 February 1981, four dhole or Asiatic wild dog drove an adult female panda into a valley east of the Choushuigou. Rather than escape into a tree, she crossed a stream and entered a village, where residents herded her into a sheep pen. She was old and emaciated. On 18 February two dhole were observed in the study area, and tracks indicated two others—our only sighting of this species in 1.5 years. In Tangjiahe, dhole killed and partially ate an old panda, according to the reserve staff.

Pandas were much hunted by local people before 1949. A common method of killing in some areas, though not in Wolong, was with a spear trap, as described by Carter (1937):

A spear with an iron head and a wooden shaft is placed horizontally, at the required height, between two upright sticks. To the end of the shaft is attached a sapling which is pulled back and caught with a trigger. This sapling forms the spring. A cord runs from the trigger across the trail upon which the panda is supposed to travel. When the cord is tampered with the spear is driven forward with tremendous speed, guided by the upright stakes. The spear is so set as to strike near the animal's heart.

In recent years, however, most people have been educated regarding the rarity and value of the panda; realizing now that it represents a national treasure, they help rather than kill it. When, for example, a sick adult panda went to a commune in October 1978, a family fed it on sugar cane and rice porridge until it left three days later. Similarly, on 31 March 1981, a sick panda was cared for by a village family for 2 days before it was taken into captivity.

The Peking zoo (1974b), Liu (1978), Wang (1979), Liang (1979), Chen (1979), and the Chengdu zoo (1980) discuss ailments of captives. The Peking zoo (1974b) also noted that all wild-caught pandas except small young have round-worm (*Ascaris schroederi*). Infestations in stomach and intestine may be heavy in animals physically below par (Zhu and Li 1980), but whether these worms cause debility or merely contribute to it remains unknown. The droppings of Zhen and Pi contained few ascarid eggs (E. Dolensek, pers. comm.), and the digestive tract of an autopsied female from the Choushuigou contained only two *Ascaris* worms. Infestations possibly are heavier in other areas. We checked sedated pandas for ectoparasites but found none; however, Yong (1981) and Hu Jinchu noted that animals may have ticks and fleas.

Communication

Pandas communicate by sight, sound, and smell, but, since they seldom meet, they depend mainly on olfactory signals to maintain contact with other members of their society. The panda's perceptual world, therefore, differs vastly from our own: that which is most important to them is not detectible by us.

Visual signals

The panda is among the most strikingly colored of all mammals. There is a story to explain the panda's black and white pattern, as told to Nash (1981) by a Chinese friend:

> One day many, many years ago a young Chinese girl saw a leopard fighting with a panda. The girl knew that the panda was going to be killed, so she tried to pull the leopard away. The leopard turned on the girl and killed her instead. And the panda escaped.
> Later, when the panda found out the girl had been killed trying to save his life, he was stricken with grief. So he called together all the pandas in the world and they held a funeral for the young girl. As was the custom at panda funerals, they all wore black armbands. And they were so sad that they cried and cried. They rubbed their eyes with their black armbands and their eyes became black. To block out the sound of wailing, they held their arms to their ears, and they hugged their bodies in their grief. Soon the black armbands had made black patches on the fur of all the pandas.

Other explanations are more prosaic. The contrasting pattern is said both to be cryptic in order to warn off predators, and to serve a thermoregulatory role (Morris and Morris 1966; Lazell 1974). There is no question that pandas blend well into a snow-bound forest. But snow covers the ground for only two to three months of the year at the the upper limit of the panda's range, and it may fall only rarely or not at all lower down; for much of the year the panda's pelage is highly conspicuous. Because of their size, adult pandas are almost immune to predators, except perhaps to tigers in former lowland habitats. A predator probably would be no more deterred by a black-and-white pelage than by a predominantly black one, such as that of Asiatic black bear—an animal similar in size to the panda. While a possible thermoregulatory function cannot be denied, since black ears, for instance, probably lose less heat than would white ones, it does not help to explain the distinctive color pattern.

Striking colors send complex signals to other members of a species, and it is in this context that the adaptive value of the pelage must lie. Pandas generally avoid contact, they are silent, their habitat is dense, and their vision is not acute. In such a situation a conspicuous coat may help prevent too close an encounter. In many species, color markings on the head emphasize facial expressions. Here the panda is an anomaly. Its black ears stand prominently above the white crown; yet, as Kleiman (1983) noted, the ears move little, regardless of the emotional state of the animal. Although the black lips and nose are prominent, the panda's face, with its short muzzle, seems quite expressionless, without conspicuous snarl or tooth display during agonistic encounters. The eye patches enlarge the panda's small, dark eyes tenfold, but the eyes also lack subtlety. Pelage is short, without erectile crest or other special feature except color, and the tail is not a visual display organ either. It appears that color markings outrank other visual signals in importance.

During direct confrontations, pandas communicate with body postures and, conspicuously, with vocalizations, the latter in effect taking the place of the fine gradation of signals found in the mouth and ear movements of some other carnivores. In pandas, as in many mammals, a stare represents a threatening gesture. One panda may face another with neck held obliquely down, a position that not only presents the eye patches but also duplicates their effect by outlining the black ears against the white neck; the animal may then bob its head slowly up and down. Conversely, to convey lack of aggressive intent, an animal may avert its head or, in a more extreme gesture, drop it far down and cover eye patches and muzzle with the forepaws. Sometimes an animal tucks its head so far between its forelegs that the top rests on the ground (see fig. 5.13); copulating females may assume a similar position. This neutralizes the effect of the black eyes and ears.

Kleiman (1983) mentioned a lateral display during which pandas approach each other broadside, circle, and finally make contact by pushing with their bodies. Aggressive actions, as observed by us both in the wild and in captivity, include swatting with forepaws, lunging, and mutual grappling with paws and muzzle, the animals standing, squatting, or leaning into each other while up on the hindlegs. If one turns away, the other may bite nape or shoulder and shake its head while doing so. The attacked animal may be pushed or roll onto its side or back, all four legs flailing, while the other straddles or drapes itself over the fallen opponent, mouthing and pawing, and sometimes biting with or without a head shake. During nonaggressive contacts, a panda may roll on its back as if in invitation to play.

Vocal signals

Pandas vocalize infrequently except when courting and during certain social interactions, when the sounds they produce are notable in variety and volume. We tape-recorded vocalizations and nonvocal sounds of Zhen while she was courting and of captives at Yingxionggou. These tapes, together with written notes on vocal behavior in the wild and in captivity, augmented by D. Kleiman's recordings at Yingxionggou and G. Peters' at the National Zoological Park in Washington, form the basis of our description of the panda's repertoire (see Peters et al., in prep.). Sound spectrograms of a sample of sounds were made on a KAY sonagraph, model 7029, at the National Zoological Park. Peters (1982) and Kleiman (1983) reported on the vocalizations of the Washington pandas and also contributed comments and ideas to the present discussion, which follows their terminology to make our studies comparable.

The repertoire of adults consists of about 11 discernible sounds, for each of which we describe structure, context, and possible function. Since infant vocalizations have not yet been studied, that repertoire remains unknown.

Huff

A huffing panda exhales air audibly through its open mouth to produce a basically nonvocal sound varying from a soft panting, like heavy breathing, to loud coughing. There may be successive huffs at different intensities, some with a rasping, gutteral sound that shows tonal bands in an otherwise noisy structure. Huffs range from about 0.3 to 1.5 seconds in duration and 1 to 2 kHz in main frequency (fig. 6.1 A, B). Wild or trapped pandas huffed when they sensed the proximity of a person or when they fled after an inadvertent encounter; captives huffed when approached by us or another panda. The sound apparently denotes apprehension and seems to be somewhat threatening.

Snort

A snort is similar to a huff except that the animal expels most or all air through the nose either softly or forcefully. The sound lasts up to a second, and most of its frequency lies below 2 kHz (fig. 6.1 C). Snorts differ from huffs structurally in the basal range, almost lacking frequencies there. Pandas snort in the same contexts as they huff. A soft snort also may precede or follow a honk (fig. 6.2 A), and an explosive snort sometimes precedes a chomp (fig. 6.1 D). Once, Zhen trotted toward us snorting and roaring when we approached the den tree in which she had her infant. The snort, like the huff, is a threat, though occasionally at higher intensity.

Chomp

A panda may open and close its mouth rapidly up to six or more times to produce a repetitive sound with two components—one a click as the teeth are brought together sharply, and the other a smack, apparently made in part by vibrating lips as the animal expels air through the mouth and moves its jaws. Kleiman (1983) termed this

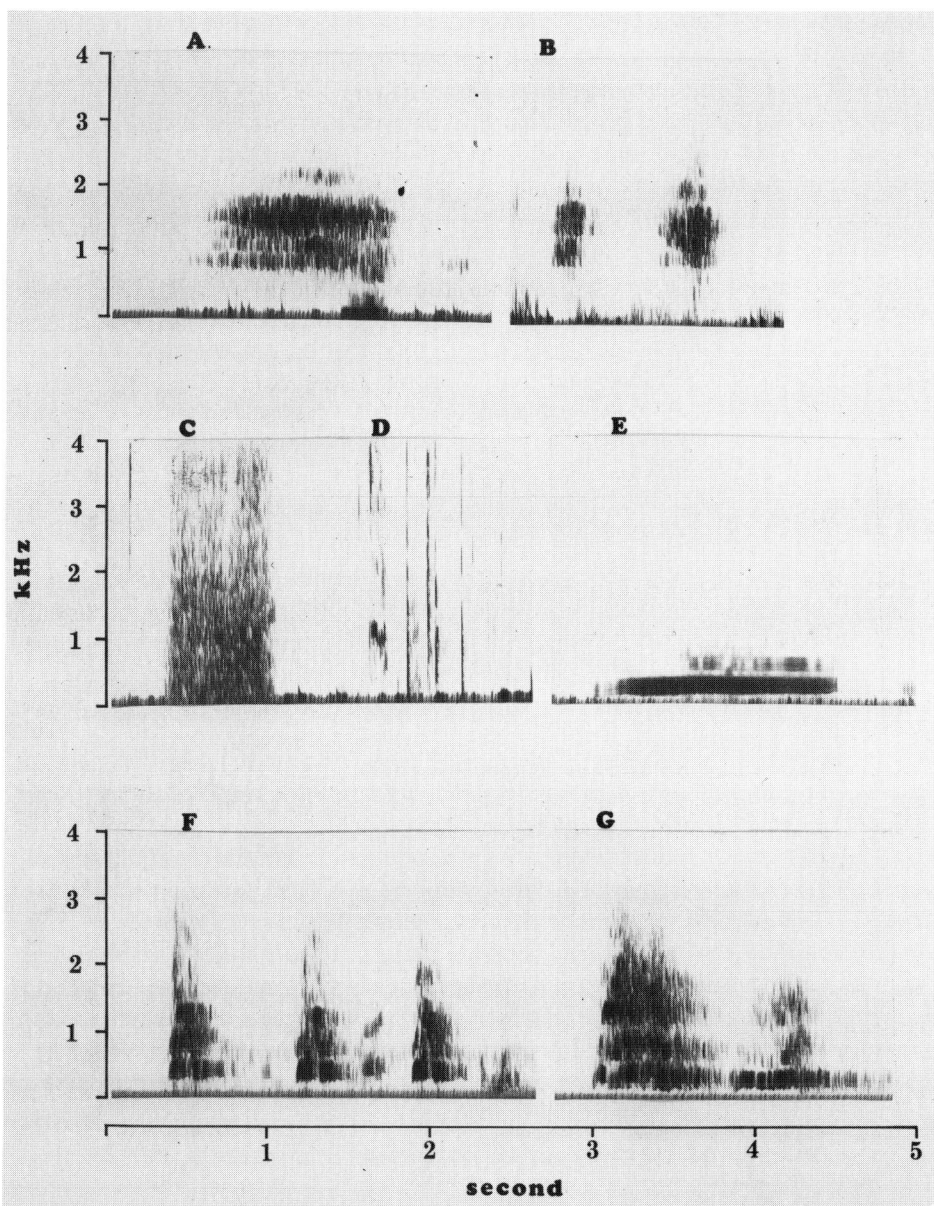

FIGURE 6.1 Vocal and nonvocal sounds of giant panda: (A) huff; (B) huff with throat rasp; (C) snort followed by (D) chomp; (E) moan; (F) barks, and (G) squealing roar. C, D, and E were recorded at Yinxionggou, the rest in the wild. (Spectrograms prepared by G. Peters.)

sound jaw-clapping. Occasionally a panda only smacks or clicks its teeth, but usually both sounds appear to be produced, although they cannot be distinguished clearly on the spectrograms. The sound sometimes lasts 1–2 seconds (fig. 6.1 D). Zhen chomped when she sensed our presence in the wild, and trapped animals occasionally chomped when we approached them. One male at Yingxionggou characteristically withdrew into a corner and snorted and chomped repeatedly when a female entered his cage, especially when she approached or faced him; other captives chomped in similar contexts. In the wild, males chomped occasionally when near an estrous female. A panda emits the sound in situations eliciting anxiety; it seems ambivalent, threatening lightly yet conveying a lack of aggressive intent.

Honk

The honk is like a resonant nasal grunt, a short, stereotyped call emitted singly or repeated every 1–3 seconds in a long series. The duration of the honk is about 0.25 to 0.50 seconds, and its main frequency lies between 0.2 and 2.7 kHz; the vocalization is tonal with one or more harmonics (fig. 6.2 A). Various situations elicit the honk. When resting, a panda sometimes honks softly in no particular context; one vocalized while defecating. Trapped individuals honk, as do captives denied access to or retreat from another animal or area. In the wild, a panda sometimes huffs and honks on perceiving a person. The vocalization appears to indicate mild distress. More detailed work may reveal other functions as well.

Bleat

The bleat of a panda is closer to that of a goat than to that of a sheep, "a tonal call of medium intensity with a rapid frequency and amplitude modulation" (Peters 1982). Consisting usually of a rapidly modulated or phased sound, the bleat lasts 0.5 to 3.0 seconds, with a main frequency range of up to 3 kHz and several harmonics (fig. 6.2 F). Pandas bleat mainly during the mating season (Kleiman et al. 1979), either while alone or when male and female associate; Zhen and a male bleated often as they followed each other between copulations (see "Reproductive Behavior," below). The vocalization is not loud enough to serve as a long-distance contact call, but, once a pair has met, the bleat may signify that overtures are friendly, providing reassurance on close approach. Listening to the sound tapes, one can distinguish the bleats of certain animals by pitch and other idiosynchrasies. It is thus possible that the vocalization assists in individual recognition.

Moan

The moan is a highly variable vocalization, ranging from a sharp hoot and softly repeated bu-bu-bu to a low-pitched moo, whiny groan, and long-drawn moan rising and falling in pitch, some plaintive, others harsh. Sitting or standing with head lowered, usually facing the other animal, a panda moans with mouth open, closed, or alternately opened or closed, a partial reason for the differences in vocalization. Given singly or repetitively, moans vary in duration from 0.2 to 2.5 seconds, and their main frequency lies below 1 kHz (fig. 6.1 E). The moan was the most common

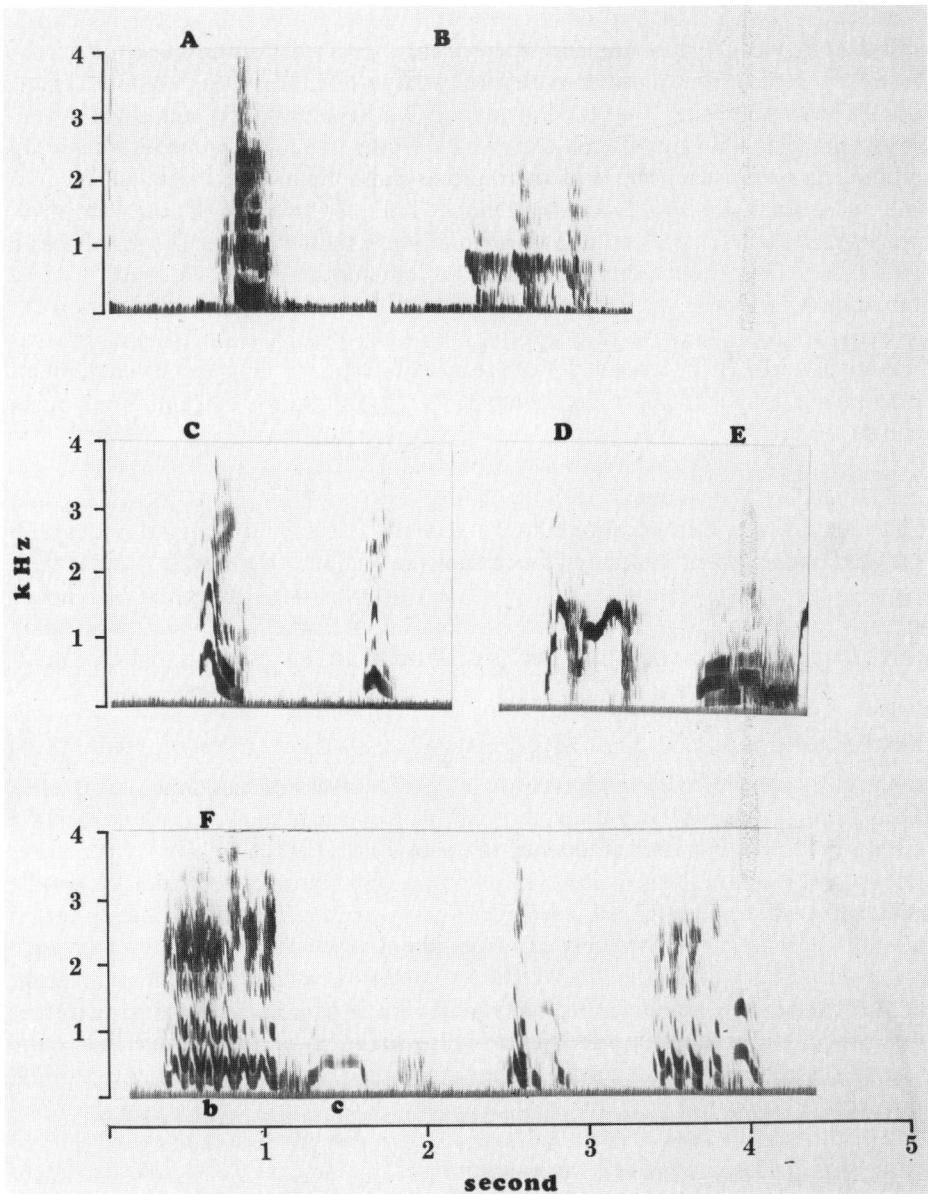

FIGURE 6.2   Vocal signals of giant panda: (A) honk preceded by soft snort; (B) chirp (yip); (C) chirp; (D) squeal; (E) roar; and (F) bleats (b) followed by chirp (c). B, D, and E were recorded in the wild, A at Yinxionggou, and C and F at the Washington Zoo by D. Kleiman and G. Peters. (Spectrograms prepared by G. Peters.)

vocalization when a male and Zhen courted. Wei and a subadult roared, squealed, yipped, and especially moaned during a meeting, and a treed subadult moaned from the top of a spruce while an adult waited below. One night, 2 pandas apparently met; from 0130 to 0330 they barked and yipped, and one moaned softly and often. Captives at Yingxionggou, unfamiliar with each other, usually moaned when placed into the same enclosure. The Washington female also moaned, chirped, and bleated while masturbating with a forepaw (Kleiman 1983). In general, the moan by itself appears to be a defensive threat of low intensity, a mild warning. However, on 12 April 1981, a large male emitted moans, yips, and barks while alone, loud vocalizations audible for one kilometer or more; another lone animal, its sex undetermined, was heard to moan, bark, squeal, and roar on 8 May 1983 in the Jiuzhaigou Reserve. The calls appeared to be associated with the mating season and, in this context, might function as a long-distance advertisement.

Bark

The panda's bark is reminiscent of that of a dog, a loud, atonal or moderately tonal sound with a duration of about 0.5 seconds and a main frequency below 1.5 kHz, emitted singly or several in succession (fig. 6.1 F). In the wild, pandas bark when courting or meeting casually, when startled, or as noted earlier, when apparently advertising their presence during the mating season. The vocalization seems to express excitement and conveys either a warning or the animal's location, depending on the situation.

Chirp (yip)

The chirp appears to be emitted at two levels of intensity. The chirp, as Kleiman et al. (1979) and Peters (1982) called it, is a tonal call surprisingly high-pitched for a sound produced by an animal the size of a panda. Its frequencies may reach 8 kHz (Peters 1982), although most energy lies below 1 kHz; the call often descends rapidly in pitch toward the end (fig. 6.2 C,F). At a lower intensity, the call resembles a short (about 0.3 seconds), high-pitched bark or squeal, given singly or in a series, with most energy below 1 kHz (fig. 6.2 B). We termed this lower-intensity call a yip. Since the chirp and the yip appear to be merely parts of one graded signal, with the former conveying a higher level of emotion, the calls were at times difficult to classify, and both are therefore combined into one category. The contexts and functions of the chirp appear to be similar to those of the bark; indeed, an animal readily switches from one to the other as its emotional level changes. The Washington female chirped during sexual presentation and when mounted (Kleiman et al. 1979). We also heard the sound during the mating season at Yingxionggou, when animals were either alone or together, and in the wild. In this context, chirps are emitted in the same situations as bleats, suggesting that the vocalization may help to promote social contact.

Squeal

The squeal is high-pitched, about 0.2–1.0 second or more in duration with a main frequency lying below 2 kHz (fig. 6.2 D). "The noisy beginning and end of the call are

lower in pitch than its more middle section which is rapidly frequency modulated"
and tonal in quality (Peters 1982). A panda usually squeals when threatened or
attacked by another, the vocalization apparently signifying apprehension and lack of
aggressive intent.

Growl

The panda's growl resembles a dog's, a low-pitched, pulsed vocalization usually
only a second or two in duration. We lack spectrograms of the growl. The more
assertive of 2 squabbling or fighting animals usually emits a growl, as when, for
example, Zhen once turned and growled at a male who followed her closely, or when
one male at the Chendgu zoo stood over another that had just rolled on his side in
submission. The growl represents an aggressive threat. Pure growls were infrequent,
however, a panda often combining the growl with a moan to produce an intermediate
sound.

Roar

Sometimes a roar is growly and harsh (fig. 6.2 E); at other times it seems to have
overtones of a squeal (fig. 6.1 G). In all cases its structural quality is masked by the
volume of noise that is so forcefully and intensely ejected one or more times, each
lasting a second or so, that those hearing it, whether field workers or pandas, are
momentarily startled. Zhen roared when we approached her den tree, and trapped
pandas sometimes roared as we drew near; males roared during disputes over a
female, and females roared at persistently courting males; Wei and a subadult roared
a number of times during a quarrel. In such situations a roar represents an aggressive
threat of the highest level. In addition, lone individuals may roar during the mating
season. At 1300 hours on 26 April 1983 near the Fengtongzhai Reserve, we heard
two squealing roars. Creeping toward the sound, we saw bamboo sway 10 m ahead.
A panda bleated, then gave a long-drawn roar. Another individual, in the Jiuzhaigou
Reserve, called repeatedly between 1120 and 1210 hours, one series consisting
of the following sounds: moan—squealing bark—moan—moan—squealing bark—
moan—moan—squealing bark—roar—squeal.

Squawk

During the first month or so of life, young emit a loud squawk or squall, either
short or long-drawn, low- or high-pitched. The young vocalizes when apparently
cold or otherwise uncomfortable; the greater the distress, the higher the pitch of its
call. The female then adjusts the position of the young until the sound subsides.
Lacking spectrograms of the squawk, we are unable to analyze its structure as a basis
for determining its relation to the structure of the squeal or other vocalizations.
Young vocalize less often, and the squawk apparently alters, with age; a 3-month-old
produced sounds that we characterized in our notes as whines and squeals. It may be
that the squawk is a precursor of the squeal.

Adult pandas emit a total of 11 auditory signals, the repertoires of males and
females being similar (see table 8.3). Three of the signals—huff, snort, chomp—are

basically nonvocal; the rest are vocal, most of them of low frequency with main energy below 1 kHz. Compared with other carnivores of comparable body size, most of the panda's vocal sounds, especially the bleat and chirp, are relatively high in their main frequencies (Peters et al., in prep.). Our understanding of the panda's vocal repertoire is still rudimentary; and the functions of the chomp, honk, and chirp, among others, need clarification. The repertoire can for convenience be divided into five provisional categories based on the presumed function or functions of the signals. These categories are not exclusive, for an animal may combine vocalizations depending on its motivational state.

1. Only one vocalization, the bleat, is purely social in that it promotes friendly interactions without ambivalence.

2. The huff, snort, and chomp convey apprehension. The first two possibly function as an aggressive threat and the last as a defensive threat, judging by the contexts in which they are emitted. All are of low intensity. The honk, a vocalization usually denoting anxiety and distress without a threat component, belongs in category 3 but is often associated with the huff, snort, and chomp. Although a panda may emit each of the four calls by itself, two or more often follow each other closely, as, for instance, snort-honk, snort-chomp-honk, and huff-snort-chomp-honk.

3. The honk and squeal convey distress and lack of aggressive intent, although at different levels of intensity.

4. The growl and roar are aggressive vocalizations, unambivalent in their offensive threat.

5. In order of increasing intensity, the moan, bark, yip, and chirp appear to represent a graded system of emotional levels. A panda may emit these vocalizations in no particular sequence; it may also combine vocalizations, with one flowing into another, and produce intermediate ones difficult to classify. The function of these signals varies with the circumstances. During direct interaction, the moan, bark, and yip may signify a warning, a defensive threat. The chirp possibly also functions as a social signal mainly during courtship. In addition, snorts, squeals, and bleats are sometimes associated with moans, barks, and chirps, producing a highly complex combination of signals, which defies easy classification.

During the mating season, a solitary panda may moan, bark, chirp, squeal, and roar, using these vocalizations alone, in a sequence, or in combination apparently as a long-distance advertisement. It is not coincidental that all are loud and easily audible. We are uncertain if both sexes call or only males. Rather than evolving a specific long-distance call, the panda apparently uses any loud signal in its repertoire to draw attention to itself.

The variation in the vocalizations suggest that a panda's emotions change constantly during an encounter. Some calls are intermediate, such as a moan with the harshness of a growl, or a roar with the tones of a squeal. Some calls are combined into a continuous signal, a bark turning into a squeal, or a moan into a roar. And different calls may follow each other in a bewildering sequence as the animal shifts between excitement, apprehension, offensive threat, and defensive threat. One function of short-distance vocal signals in mammals is to focus attention on the performer, who then conveys further information by means of facial expressions, postures, and movements. The panda's face is not expressive, and the dense environment does not promote efficient signaling through postures. Sound seems to be the primary method by which two pandas can communicate subtle shifts in emotions (Kleiman 1983). Interacting pandas are often extraordinarily vocal when compared to other carnivores. The variety of their sounds, emitted in different combinations at different intensities, provide an intricate system of signals by which the animals convey their fluctuating motivational states, a needed predictability in communication during the infrequent meetings.

Olfactory and visual signals left in the environment

A panda leaves much visible evidence of its passing in the form of food remnants and droppings. Its individual odor probably permeates the route as well. In addition, it marks the environment in several distinct ways.

Bark stripping

On 3 occasions, Zhen bit and clawed a large piece of bark from a conifer, twice in May and once in autumn. On 28 May 1981, for example, Zhen first fed on new *Fargesia* shoots, then stripped a piece of bark 75 cm long and 15–20 cm wide from a hemlock.

Tree biting

On 16 occasions a panda took a bite out of a sapling or bit it off completely. Such trees were 3–14 cm in diameter, 87.5% of them conifers. Mean height of the bites was 92.4 ± 36.4 cm, with the highest 196 cm up the trunk. Excluding saplings bitten off by Zhen and taken to a maternity den, 5 of the 7 freshly damaged trees were found in April and one each in December and January. We also found several rotten tree stumps which had been much bitten and clawed.

Tree clawing

Many large trees had faint claw marks—a few chips of bark raked off—and some were deeply scarred. Most marks were within 1.5 m of the base; if, however, an animal had climbed the tree, the bark was scuffed and cut for several meters.

Ground pawing

We noted 6 spots where a panda had raked sod or snow away with a few sweeps of its paw, clearing an area 30–40 cm in diameter, usually on a rise or base of a large fir.

Rubbing and rolling

As Kleiman et al. (1979) noted, captives may rub cheeks, neck, shoulders, sides and rump against rocks and other surfaces; they may roll and writhe on the ground and pick up sod to rub over the body. We occasionally found a site with vegetation squashed and logs scuffed where a panda apparently had rolled and rubbed; on one occasion an animal rolled on a wire screen we had placed on the ground to collect falling leaves.

Tree scenting

Both sexes have a large glandular area in the anogenital region that exudes a dark secretion. Pandas deposit this secretion on horizontal or vertical surfaces, using various marking postures (Morris and Morris 1966; Kleiman et al. 1979). To scent the ground, the edge of a log, a stump, or some other low object, a panda squats and, with a back and forth or circular motion, rubs the surface with the glandular area, its bushy tail helping to spread scent. To mark a tree or wall, a panda turns, backs up to the surface, raises its tail and rubs. While marking, the animal may bob or shake its head and open its mouth (Morris and Morris 1966). As noted by Haas (1958), a panda may also place a hindpaw or a whole hindleg vertically against the surface, in what Kleiman (1983) called a legcock, and twist its body slightly in the direction of the raised leg, bringing the glandular area into contact with tree or wall. Yingxiong-gou's female Qing-Qing, 3.5 years old, marked to a height of 52 cm in this manner. Rarely used is a handstand, in which the panda backs up as if to rub but then walks up the vertical surface with its hindpaws until it stands on its forepaws (fig. 6.3). One wild male backed to a conifer and walked up the trunk a few steps until his body was at a steep pitch, then marked at an estimated height of 110 cm. A captive male in a complete handstand marked at a height of 153 cm.

Urine is also part of the marking ritual, as suspected by Schneider (1939). While rubbing its anogenital area, a panda sometimes urinates, a few drops to a considerable trickle. In fact, the anogenital rub may be discarded in favor of urine marking; for example, one captive male twice legcocked and squirted urine against a wall without touching it with his body.

The Washington pair already marked as subadults, the male actually doing so more often at 2.5 years of age than after reaching maturity. The animals marked throughout the year, the male always with higher frequency than the female, but with an annual peak during the mating season in April. Only the male exhibited a handstand; the female seldom urine-marked. While in their outdoor enclosure, the animals usually marked well-traveled routes, commonly going to previously scented sites (Kleiman et al. 1979; Kleiman 1983).

During our first winter, we tracked pandas mainly low on the slopes, where, as we discovered later, the animals seldom marked. On 6 March 1981, tracks in the snow showed where a panda had backed to a tree, and we could smell a faintly acidic odor on the bark. The next winter, on 27 December, we tracked an animal to a scent post that had often been used. Once aware of how such posts looked, we discovered many, most of them above 2700 m. A scent post consists of two distinct portions. The side of the tree facing a ridge crest or trail has the lower part slightly darkened by secretions and smoothed by rubbing; sometimes a few hairs adhere to the bark. Bright green algae cover the scented area of posts long out of use. Above the scented area are claw marks, many of them light, as if the animal has merely flicked off bits of bark (plate 6.1).

FIGURE 6.3   Postures of giant pandas when scent marking the ground, a stump, and a tree while in a handstand.

Of the 162 scent posts we examined, 94% were conifers, mostly fir; the rest included 4 birches, 2 hardwoods, 1 rhododendron, and 2 stumps. To find out whether conifers were marked disproportionately often, we counted all trees with a diameter of 15 cm or more (DBH) along two ridges with many scent posts. Pandas selected conifers significantly more often, perhaps because scent adheres better to, and persists longer on, rough bark (table 6.5). The average DBH of marked conifers was 44.3 ± 19.7 (range 13–105) cm; only two posts had a DBH of less than 15 cm. The maximum height of the scent mark in a sample of 80 trees averaged 70.3 ± 12.0 (50–107) cm. Average scent height equalled a panda's shoulder height, indicating that an animal seldom used a full handstand. Claw marks reached an average height of 115.6 ± 17.3 (83–162 cm), with some up to 250 cm on trees that were not posts. There was no indication that pandas habitually reared up on their hindlegs to rake the trunk as high as possible; rather, they stood or raised themselves only partially in most instances. On the basis of the amount of scent deposited and bark clawed, we judged that 19% of the posts were used heavily, 69% moderately, and the rest

TABLE 6.5

KINDS OF TREES AVAILABLE FOR SCENT MARKING AND PERCENTAGE USED AS SCENT POSTS ALONG TWO RIDGES

	Ridge 1		Ridge 2	
	Number available	% scent post	Number available	% scent post
Conifer	271	11.8	112	29.5
Birch	59	1.7	52	3.8
Other trees	10	0	9	0
Stump	29	3.4	30	3.3
Totals	369	9.2	203	17.7

lightly. By definition we counted as posts only those trees that had easily visible scent deposits; we did not include trees with claw marks only. Ninety-three percent of those trees with scent had also been clawed, the exceptions being 4 thin conifers and several hardwoods.

Many posts clustered along ridges; they were rare along streams (fig. 6.4). There were fewer posts at Fanzipeng than at Erdaoping, something that can in part but not wholly be attributed to timber cutting in the former area. To be effective in communication, a post must be located along a route normally traveled by residents as well as by pandas in transit. Consequently, posts tended to cluster around knolls on high ridges, in low passes, and along spurs projecting into valleys. The heavy marking of the Eradoping area probably reflected heavy panda use both in number of animals, especially males, and in amount of time spent by them there.

While tracking pandas, we took note of every newly marked tree. Fresh bark chips on the snow indicated clawing; and the position of tracks in relation to the tree, as well as odor on the bark, revealed whether the animal had rubbed scent. Wet bark or yellow drops in the snow pointed to urine marking. Such urine had a powerful musky odor, quite unlike normal urine; we could detect it from as far as 5 m. The male urogenital system of the panda lacks accessory glands, except for glandular tissue at the distal ends of the vasa deferentia just before these ducts unite and enter the urethra (Davis 1964). It is possible that this tissue produces a secretion that mixes with urine to give it the strong odor. The urine masked any odor from the anogenital area, at least to us, and we were on occasion uncertain whether a panda had rubbed as well as urinated. A complete marking sequence included urine and anogenital marking and clawing, but pandas used all three patterns probably in fewer than 10% of the instances, usually confining themselves to urinating or rubbing (table 6.6).

Pandas marked other trees as often and with a similar frequency of method as they did scent posts (table 6.6), the main difference being that posts were marked so often that secretions accumulated. Casually marked trees tended to be away from usual travel routes, or they happened to be conveniently located. For instance, pandas sometimes scented on reaching a trail or on veering from it, using the nearest tree. The average DBH of 48 such trees was 50.15 ± 20.5 cm, a figure similar to that for posts. However, only 64.9% of the trees were conifers, as compared to 94% for posts, suggesting that pandas were less selective in choosing such a tree.

Droppings could be used to advertise a scent-marked tree by sight and smell, but only 26 of the trees had old or recent droppings at their base. The average number of droppings was 1.3, fewer than the average of 1.9 found along trails (fig. 5.10).

During the 1981–82 winter, we counted the number of trees freshly marked along 31.5 km of panda trail. Trees were marked on the average of one every 222 m. Over a period of 5.5 days, Wei traveled 7113 m (see fig. 4.7) and in that distance marked 47 trees (one every 151 m), of which 19 were scent posts; he also passed by 5 posts without marking them, though he stopped at one, perhaps to sniff. Once he walked to the end of a fallen tree and there dribbled a little urine, behavior also noted on several other occasions. Pandas seldom urinated in winter, except in the context of scenting, and it seems likely that it represented marking behavior.

Often we did not know the sex of an animal we were tracking. However, adult females were sedentary in winter, whereas adult males and some subadults traveled widely; some of the animals we followed moved considerable distances (fig. 4.6). We

PLATE 6.1 Pandas used this fir as a scent post. The lower part of the trunk is dark from being rubbed with anal secretions. Above that is a clawed area with bark chips and moss removed.

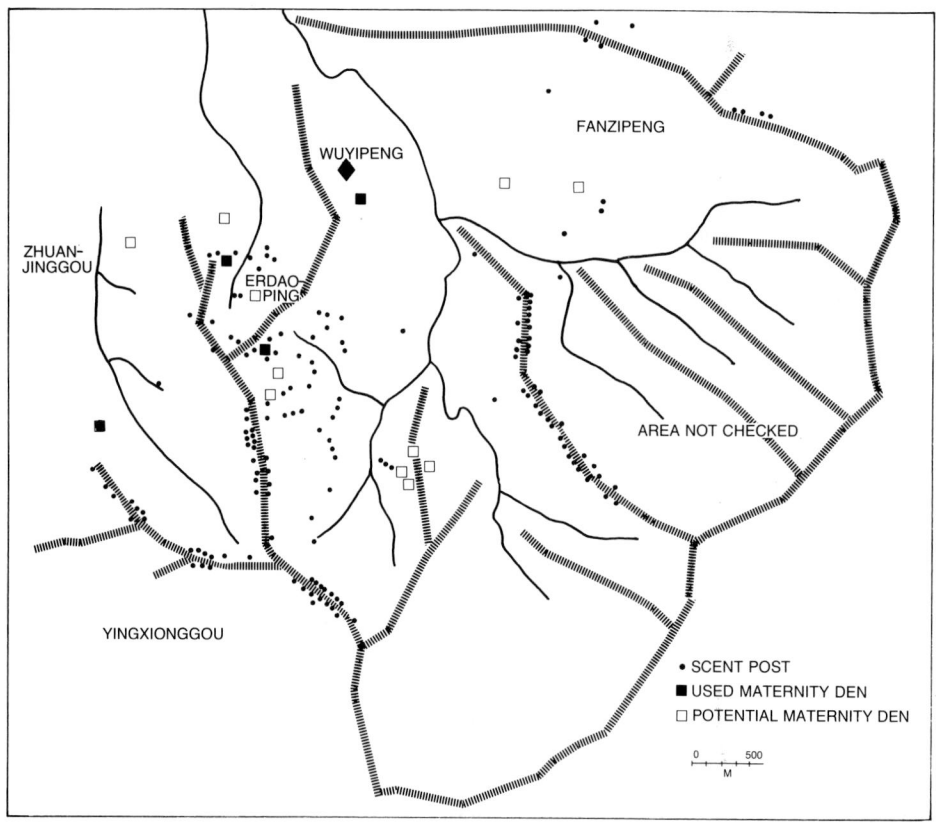

FIGURE 6.4   Distribution of scent posts in the study area, revealing concentrations along certain ridges. Definitely used and potential maternity dens are also indicated.

tracked Zhen for 1868 m without finding evidence of marking; one animal, which might have been Han, urine-marked two trees in 484 m. Excluding these two females, we tracked pandas for 300 m or more on 17 occasions during the 1981–82 winter and found marking along 14 of the routes. The evidence suggests that most marking was done by adult males. One further detail pointed to males: many trees were marked with a precise squirt.

Many scent posts looked as if they were rarely used, even along well-traveled routes. We checked 34 posts at frequent intervals along one ridge between late December 1981 and early March 1982. Of these, 62% were marked at least once that season, and, to our knowledge, none was marked more than 3 times. Marking intervals varied from a few days to over 2 months (table 6.7). At least 3 males frequented that ridge. All seemed to share the same posts, although they did not necessarily cover their own or each other's scent. For example, Wei marked one post on 6 January; 10 days later another panda stopped at that post, then continued without marking. Conversely, on 20 January Wei did not mark a tree that had

TABLE 6.6
PANDA'S MARKING OF SCENT POSTS AND OTHER TREES BY VARIOUS METHODS

Marking method	Number of times marked	
	Scent post	Other tree
Claw only	1	8
Urine only	26	32
Anogenital scent only	18	13
Claw and anogenital scent	5	4
Claw, urine (and anogenital scent?)	18	17
Total no. trees	74	68

previously been scented on 6 and 16 January, once probably by himself. On 23 February, however, he marked a tree that he had visited on 21 January (fig. 6.5).

We detected no instances of marking between June and November and do not know whether pandas scent trees during this rainy period.

Bark stripping, tree biting, ground pawing, and rolling are relatively rare behavior patterns, their functions open to speculation and their roles in communication minor and probably inadvertent. By contrast, clawing, anogenital rubbing, and urine-marking of trees are important to pandas in that the patterns are often used, singly or in combination, both at specific sites and casually. There is a seeming redundancy in the panda's marking system. With several methods available, pandas readily switch from one to another, sometimes on successive trees. Each signal, however, varies in the length of time during which it can communicate something: urine soon loses its strong odor, and rain washes it off trunks; sticky glandular secretions adhere well, and, even after smell is gone, the rubbed site remains; and claw marks can persist as visual markers for months and years. But just what specific message is communicated by each method remains wholly unknown.

It is generally accepted that scent marking is an efficient means of integrating social behavior by conveying messages about the reproductive state and individual identity of the sender long after he or she has passed a particular site (Ralls 1971). The response of the receiver of this message depends entirely on his or her sex, dominance position in the society, reproductive condition, and previous contacts

TABLE 6.7
FREQUENCY OF MARKING SELECTED SCENT POSTS DURING THE WINTER 1981–82

Post	24 Dec.	27 Dec.	6 Jan.	7 Jan.	16 Jan.	8 Feb.	23 Feb.	2 March
A	x			x				x
B	x						x	x
C		x	x					x
D							x	x
E	x							x
K					x		x	
R			x		x	x		
S			x		x			

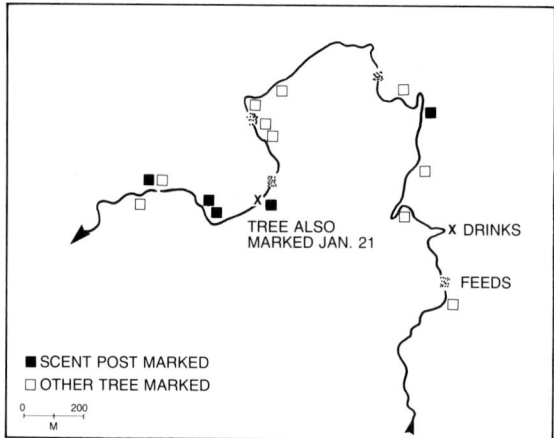

TREE ALSO
MARKED JAN. 21

X DRINKS

FEEDS

■ SCENT POST MARKED
□ OTHER TREE MARKED

0   200
         M

FIGURE 6.5   Route of the male Wei near Erdaoping on 23 February 1982, showing various activities.

with the sender, if any. Female pandas appear to mark little except during estrus, when contact with a mate is imperative. By sniffing her scent, a male can no doubt evaluate a female's potential receptivity, knowledge that may help him decide whether or not he should seek closer contact at that time. A female smelling the scent of a male might not only learn which individual is in her area but also, through repeated olfactory contact, become familiar enough with him to accept more amicably his overtures during estrus.

The fact that males do most marking and that they do so for at least 6 months of the year, during months far removed from the normal mating season, suggests that the scent signals are directed mainly at other males. Males of various carnivore species are intolerant of one another, and their marking serves as a distance-increasing message to prevent encounters (Ewer 1973). Scent marking in panda males appears to have a similar function.

Reproductive behavior

Although 37 litters have been born in captivity between 1963 and 1983, the literature contains few details about reproductive behavior. Notable exceptions are articles published by the Peking zoo (1974a), Kleiman et al. (1979), Yu (1980), Shi (1981), Xu et al. (1981), and Kleiman (1983). We summarize this knowledge here and add our own data collected from zoos and in the wild.

Courtship and mating

Reproduction in pandas is seasonal, the animals possibly being monoestrous. Conceptions in captivity generally occur between mid-March and mid-May, with a peak in April and early May (table 6.3), and periods of estrus follow the same pattern (Xu et al. 1981; Shi 1981; Kleiman 1983). Captives may show signs of estrous behavior during other months as well, as did London's Chi-Chi, for example, once in February (Morris and Morris 1966), and Tokyo's Lan-Lan once in June (Kleiman 1983). In addition, females that fail to conceive in spring may show a weak heat in September or October (Morris and Morris 1966, Peking zoo 1974a, Shi 1981). The keepers at Yingxionggou told us that testes size of all adult males there is larger in spring than at other times of year; and Platz et al. (1983), working with the Washington male, showed that testes size and ejaculate volume decrease between June and October.

The behavior of pandas changes markedly during estrus (Morris and Morris 1966; Peking zoo 1974a, Kleiman et al. 1979). One to two weeks before peak receptivity the female loses appetite, increases frequency of scent marking, becomes restless, bleats often, and chirps occasionally; her vulva swells and reddens, and she rubs it against objects or with her paw. Estrogen levels rise, peaking just prior to maximum receptivity (Bonney et al. 1982). Levels of estrone, an estrogen metabolite, in urine increase with the onset of behavioral estrus and reach a peak at the midpoint of the period, then decline sharply (Hearn, 1982) (see fig. 6.6). The level of N-acetyl-β-D-aminoglucosidase, a plasma protein, also peaks in urine at the estimated time of ovulation (Li et al. 1983). By measuring these constituents in the laboratory it is possible to pinpoint the day of ovulation more precisely than by observing behavior, thus helping to improve the conception rate of pandas through artificial insemination in captivity. Between 1978 and 1982, at least 40 females were artificially inseminated, though only 11 subsequently gave birth; of the 22 cubs born, 7 survived (Liu 1981; Tan 1983). The urinary androgen levels of the male increase when he is with the receptive female, then decrease suddenly after apparent ejaculation, as determined in the Washington male (Bonney et al. 1982).

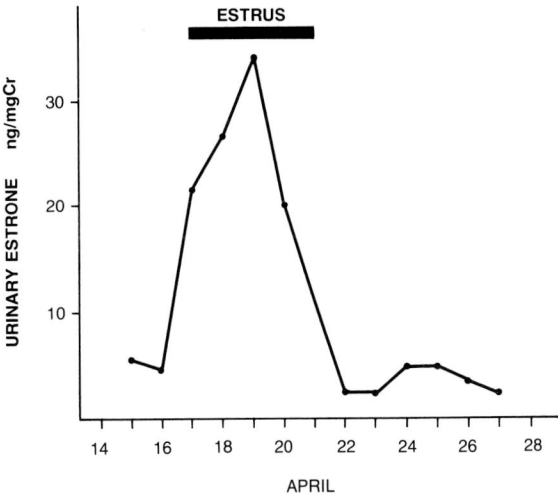

FIGURE 6.6   Urine estrone levels (in ng/mg creatinine) of the London female Ching-Ching before, during, and after the peak of behavioral estrus. (From Hearn 1982.)

Comparing the Washington pair's behavior before, during, and after estrus, Kleiman (1983) found that the female became inactive, though restless, whereas the male became more active than usual. The male also bleated more than the female. Before full estrus, interactions between the pair consisted of wrestling, swatting, and biting, with the female initiating significantly more contacts than the rather passive male. "As peak receptivity approaches, the nature of the encounter changes. The ♀ becomes less assertive and allows the ♂ to mount. While he does so, she will stand quietly and may periodically lift the tail and depress the back. Lordosis is displayed more commonly when the ♂ has the forepaws extended and placed on the centre of the ♀'s back. During peak oestrus, the ♀ may stand for periods of up to several minutes allowing multiple mounts by the ♂. At this point it is the ♂ who is essentially responsible for initiating and terminating physical contact" (Kleiman et al. 1979). The female, in fact, acts submissive to the male. As observed at Yingxionggou, she may back up to him, presenting her rump, and she may roll on her back, squirming and writhing, as she reaches for him gently with her forepaws.

When copulating, the male stands or squats behind the female with his forelegs propped on her back (Zhu and Li 1980; Kleiman 1983), a position perhaps necessary because his penis is short, 7–10 cm long (Davis 1964). He mounts often but briefly before ejaculation; mounting time lasts 0.5 to 2.5 minutes with a maximum of 4.7 minutes (Peking zoo 1974a). One Yingxionggou male grasped the back of the female's neck with his teeth during attempted copulation as if to hold her (E. Dolensek, pers. comm.); and the Washington male mouthed the female's back on occasion (Kleiman 1983). After copulating, the female may bite the male or run from him.

The whole estrus period lasts for about 12–25 days, but the period of peak receptivity only about 2–7 days (Shi 1981; Xu et al. 1981, Liu 1981). Between 1973 and 1982, Ling-Ling's annual period of receptivity varied from 2 to 5 days with an average of 3 days (Kleiman 1983).

Do these observations on captives apply to free-living animals? Pandas in the wild are generally said to mate between March and May (Giant Panda Expedition 1974; Hu et al. 1980; Yong 1981), and our observations agree. In the Qinling Mountains an occasional female is thought to come into estrus in October and November (Yong 1981), as well as in January (Liu 1983), judging by trampled sites where males supposedly fought over a mate and the sighting of 3 adults together, an unusual occurrence at that time of year. On 26 July 1981, Jilin Zhiha (pers. comm.) observed two young weighing an estimated 3.5 kg each in a hollow tree in the Liang Mountains. At that weight, the young were about 2 months old, born in late May or early June and conceived in January or February, assuming a period of delayed implantation (see below). In April 1981, an infant weighing 7 kg was captured in the Min Mountains. It was about 3.5 months old, probably born in late December or January and presumably conceived in September or October. Both records lie outside the usual range of birth dates in captivity, which extends from 22 June to 25 September with a peak in late August and the first half of September (table 6.3). The one birth points to autumn estrus, as noted in several captives, and the other illustrates the

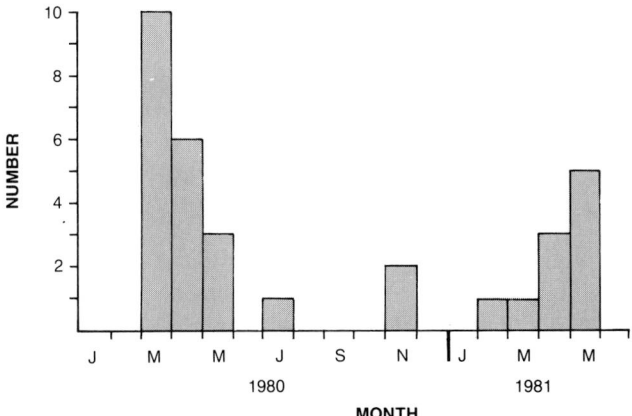

FIGURE 6.7 The number of instances pandas in the study area were heard to vocalize each month.

panda's flexibility in reproduction. This may, as Kleiman (1983) suggested, represent the vestige of a longer season in those animals that once inhabited a more equitable climate at low altitudes.

Since pandas are said to be vocal during the mating season (Giant Panda Expedition 1974), we took note of all vocalizations during the year. Excluding calls in response to an observer, we heard pandas on 32 occasions, of which 87.5% fell between March and May (fig. 6.7). Some of these calls were not related to reproduction, as when, for example, on 27 February a tree crashed and immediately afterward a panda barked, apparently startled. Of the vocalizations between March and May, at least 39% involved 2 animals during an encounter. We seldom knew which animals were together. On two occasions an adult and subadult had met, once Wei and Zhen associated, and once two males courted Zhen. Such direct contacts, for whatever reason, were significant because for most of the year they were uncommon, judging by the few calls. Pandas seemed adept at avoiding each other, except from March to May, when they probably sought meetings.

Radio locations of Wei and Zhen revealed that a male may remain near but not necessarily in direct contact with a female (fig. 6.8). For several days in 1982, Zhen had foraged on the slope between Wuyipeng and Erdaoping. On 28 April an uncollared male was near her and on 30 April Wei arrived in her vicinity. That night Zhen walked 1 km up and over a ridge. On 1 May, Wei was where Zhen had been the previous day, then followed her over the ridge so that on 2 and 3 May they were again on the same slope. By the next day both had moved over a ridge into yet another valley, but then returned to their former area for two days. Once more they crossed the ridge to where they had been on 4 May, and finally, on 9 May, they moved to where they had been 10 days earlier. There the association ended. We are unaware when or even whether they mated; vocalizations indicated only once that they were together, on 7 May between 1013 and 1124 hours. Such coordination of movement even when the animals are not together implies that pandas are able to track each other by scent.

On 13 April 1981 we observed Zhen mate with a large male. Fortunately we had begun to radio-monitor Zhen on a 24-hour basis at 1030 on 10 April, and we continued to record her activity until 1900 on 14 April and again from 0835 to 1755 on 15 April. We describe here the behavior of both animals in detail, for it places the fragmentary observations on captives into a natural context. Minutes sometimes elapsed without a glimpse of the courting animals because they were in dense bamboo.

—10 April. Zhen is on a steep slope in an area into which she moved on 6 April (fig. 6.9). She is relatively inactive but very restless, often changing position (fig. 6.10).

—11 April. Zhen remains in the same area, still restless. At 1845 and 2315 hours a panda calls from a ridge about 450 m from Zhen.

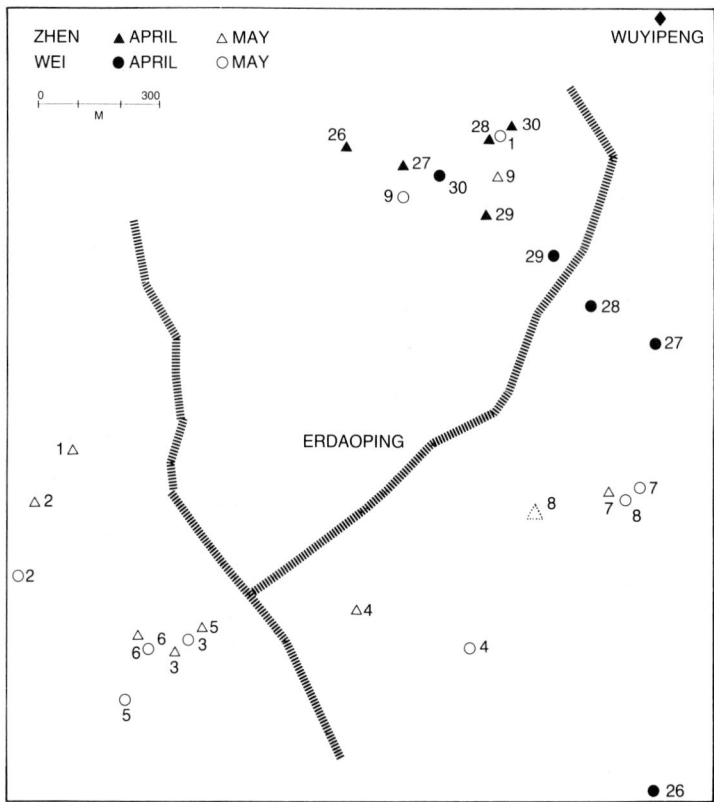

FIGURE 6.8   Daily radio locations of Zhen and Wei between 26 April and 9 May 1982, showing Wei's tendency to remain near Zhen for a number of days during the mating season.

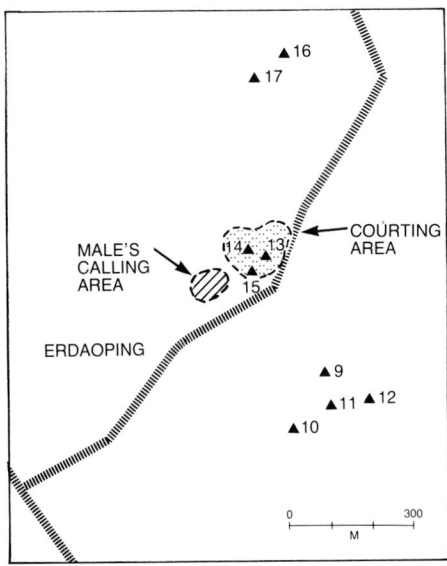

FIGURE 6.9   Daily radio locations of Zhen between 9 and 17 April 1981, before, during, and after mating.

—12 April. At 0900, a large panda is seen near the area from which the calls emanated the previous evening. On 11 occasions, between 1745 and 2325, a panda calls again, chirps, growly barks, and moans. He is observed at 1910 as he climbs 7 m up the trunk of a massive fir, sits 15 seconds on the lowest limb, then descends, possibly because he may have spotted the observer. (Later examination of the site showed that the tree had been climbed repeatedly and the bamboo around the base much trampled.) Zhen is still in her usual area, more active than on previous days. Since we could hear the male's calls clearly at a distance of 750 m, she surely has been aware of him at only 400 m.

—13 April. At 1525 hours, 2 pandas begin to bark, roar, and moan, calling almost continuously from dense bamboo growing on the opposite slope of a small, shallow valley. At 1555, a large male angles into the valley, stopping to drink from a seepage. Downhill, soft moans come from a third animal, and the large male replies similarly. He sits, head lowered. Turning abruptly, he moves back uphill toward Zhen, followed at 10 m by a second male, visibly smaller. At 1605, the two males trot across a small clearing, the smaller in the lead. Uphill Zhen bleats. Five minutes later the large male mounts her, but she steps out from under him. As he follows, the other male approaches, moaning. There is much barking and roaring, and the bamboo is being violently agitated. When next visible, the large male has mounted; he chirps, she bleats. Twice the other male walks to within 10 m of the pair, then retreats. Once the large male walks toward the other, driving him off; both growl and moan. The smaller male drinks at 1630. Next we glimpse the large male following the female, and, tagging 5 m behind, the other male. All remain out of sight until 1715.

Zhen climbs a hemlock to a height of about 4 m and sits there, one leg dangling, about 18 m from where two of us stand. Deep and resonant, she moans and bleats while the large male circles the tree, also vocalizing. Once he sprawls for 30 seconds on a patch of moss, panting heavily. Walking uphill to where we are, he stops 2.5 m from us and looks without sound or expression. Turning his attention back to Zhen, he rears on his hindlegs as if to climb her tree, but she leans down facing him and moans. At 1750 she descends. He mounts briefly 4 times in rapid succession. Both squeal, chirp, and bleat, and the male pants. The other male has moved close to the pair and bleats too. But at 1755 he leaves and we do not see him again.

By 1805 the two animals have moved to within 5 m of us. Zhen crouches, nose tucked under, forepaws covering her eyes, while the large male squats behind her, his forelegs stiff, forepaws resting on her lower back (plate 6.2). He thrusts for about 2.5 minutes before she moves away from him. After meander-

PLATE 6.2   During copulation, the male characteristically squats behind the female while she crouches, her muzzle tucked to her chest. This photo shows Zhen and the male mating on 13 April 1981.

ing through bamboo for 4 minutes, the male at her heels, Zhen crouches and he mounts. Rolling off, he lies on his side and gently mouths her tail. Zhen ambles to within 2.5 m and stares at us blankly, as if in a trance, before lying down, her back to us. When the male steps from the bamboo, Zhen goes 7 m toward him. Crouching, her rump presented, muzzle tucked under so far that the top of her head rests on the ground, she waits. He mounts. She remains immobile as he circles her slowly, then mounts again, and once more. After 3 more mounts, some with thrusts and some without, both walk for several minutes, Zhen in the lead. Once she waits for him, and, as he draws near, she crouches but with head raised. For some reason she squeals and he chirps, and both then bleat. He mounts but slumps backward and sits and paws her back softly; she raises herself and he leans over her, holding her side, while his chin rests on her shoulder and he pants loudly, perhaps tired.

At 1835, Zhen climbs a spruce to a height of 6 m, seemingly as a means of escaping his attentions. He circles the tree several times as if to keep potential competitors away. After 5 minutes she scrambles down and crouches. He mounts 20 seconds, gets off, and immediately mounts for another 40 seconds until she stands up; he sniffs her anogenital area; she crouches again, and he mounts, this time standing on his hindlegs rather than in a squat. He dismounts, as he sometimes does, by climbing up over her back and sliding off to one side, trying, it seems, to maintain contact. He circles her within 10 m, mounts, circles, mounts, again and again, as long as she remains immobile. Both bleat. When she walks off, he tries to grab one of her hindlegs with his forepaws, but she whirls around, emitting harsh barks, then sits. He reaches out and touches her side gently with a paw. She walks off, heading toward us. Only 3.5 m from us she turns to face him; he steps behind her and mounts. Zhen has by 1900 become less receptive to his overtures. Once, as he tries to mount, she turns on him with open mouth and deep growls. It is nearly dark at 1915. They move from sight, into the valley and up the other slope.

We saw 6 mountings between 1610 and 1805, but no doubt missed others; we observed 42 mountings between 1805 and 1915, one every 1.7 minutes. Average mounting time in 39 recorded instances was 35.3 ± 33.8 (range 10–150) seconds. We do not know whether the male ejaculated.

The pair headed toward a stand of fir when we last saw it, and that night Zhen remained active until 2200 hours (fig. 6.10). On examining the area later, we found trampled bamboo, scuffed logs, and a tuft of hair—signs of vigorous activity.

On 14 April, Zhen was where we had left her the previous evening; on 15 April she was still in the courting area, resting and foraging; and on 16 April she had moved off downhill. No males appeared to be near her during those days.

This sequence of events shows some features that pandas do not or cannot express in captivity. The large male called loudly, sometimes from up in a tree, behavior also reported by the Giant Panda Expedition (1974). Such calls can be heard for over 1 km, advertising the male's presence and probably his readiness to mate. Although certainly aware of him, Zhen did not join the male immediately; conversely, he did not seek her out, even though he presumably could have found her by tracking. By

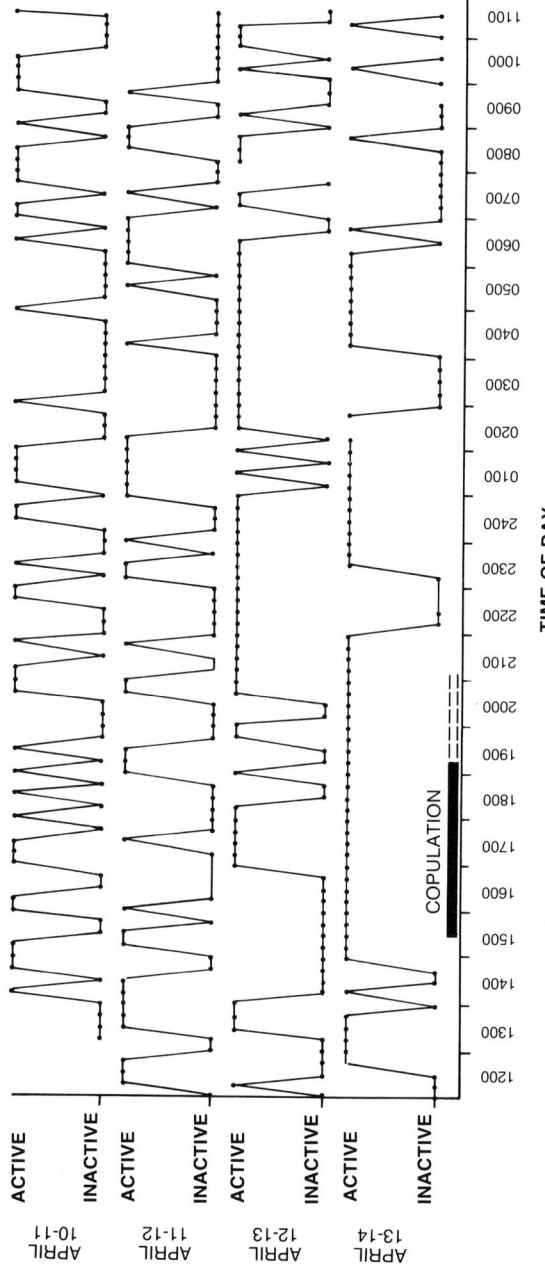

FIGURE 6.10 Activity recordings of Zhen at 15-minute intervals during 3 days prior to copulation and on the day of copulation. Zhen was restless on the first 2 days but not on the subsequent 2 days.

remaining apart, but near each other, until the female is fully receptive and subordinate to the male, a pair is likely to have less quarrelsome interactions. Both sexes change behaviorally and physiologically during the seasonal reproductive period. To be acceptable to each other, they must be responsive to each other's condition; they must initiate, maintain, and synchronize their courtship. Such synchronization, through scenting, calling, and other means, leading to compatibility, appears essential to successful mating; in any event, the failure of many captive pairs to copulate can be traced to a seeming indifference or aggressiveness on the part of the male, even when the female is in heat and solicits his attention.

The calls of a male and later vocalizations of a pair may attract one or more other males in the vicinity, causing a competitive situation. Yong (1981) and Wang Menghu (pers. comm.) report seeing 2 or 3 males with an estrous female. The large male in our observations easily drove his smaller competitor away without serious altercation, but dominance may be less easily asserted if two males are closer in size.

In 1983 we witnessed a courtship that was not only more prolonged but also more competitive than the one in 1981. We received a report that on 11 and 12 April, pandas had called along a ridge dividing the Zhuanjinggou and Yingxionggou. Searching the area on 13 April, we found on a knoll two hemlocks that pandas had climbed repeatedly; these and other trees nearby had been scent-marked. Calls were heard that night between 2300 and 0100 and again between 0500 and 0700 hours. Zhao Cannan and Wang Xueqing observed courting animals between 0920 and 1057 on 14 April in heavy rain and fog:

PLATE 6.3 An estrous female sits in a tree while the male Pi ascends; he later mounted her there. (Photo courtesy of Zhao Cannan.)

A female sits in a fir about 10 m above ground. Wei bleats near the base of the tree. He climbs 3 m up the tree, but 5 minutes later descends and, in walking away, passes the observers at 2 m. Another male, large and uncollared and with blood on forehead and ear, approaches then chases Wei a short distance. Wei, however, returns and once more climbs the tree in which the female sits; he bleats, she moans. Two minutes later Wei descends. An uncollared male is now near the tree too, as is the male Pi. The latter 2 face each other, moan, roar, and tussle until the uncollared male withdraws. At 0945, Pi ascends the fir (plate 6.3) and mounts the female, she crouched, bridging two branches, he balanced by her rump. Wei and the other male moan below. At 0956, Pi mounts the female for a minute, and then once more briefly;

at 0959, he places a forepaw on her back, sniffs her anal area and mounts as she chirps. Meanwhile, yet another male has appeared, and the three squabble around the base of the tree. Pi and the female descend, mill around with the others, then climb back up and sit 1–3 m apart. Once the female roars at Pi. At 1035 they mate. Later he first seems to embrace her without trying to copulate, then reclines, gently pawing her back while she squats by his legs. A fifth male arrives. (Long, now 4.5 years old, is in the valley nearby but does not join the group.) At 1054, Pi descends and walks out of sight, and 3 minutes later the female does so too.

One of us (GBS) returned to the area and observed the pandas between 1405 and 1515 hours. They were in dense bamboo about 300 m downslope from the ridge in the Zhuanjinggou.

A medium-sized male ambles down a path, and 25 m away, lying at the base of a fir, is another medium-sized male moaning softly and chomping. Twenty meters ahead is a large male, as large as Pi. He is alert: when a branch breaks under the observer's foot, he snorts and moves toward the sound, probably assuming that a competitor is approaching. The female lies near him. He moves in a semicircle around her, moaning and chomping. Whenever he draws close, she moans and emits squealing barks. Wei and Pi are out of sight.

The following day, observations were continued from 1125 to 1325 hours, but snowfall was so heavy and fog so dense that the animals were at times invisible.

The pandas are on a steep, logged slope. The bamboo around the base of a lone fir has been trampled. Crouched at the very top of the tree, 25 m up, is the female. At the base of the fir, facing uphill, is the large male. Pi appears and trots downhill at the other male, who roars and backs away. They make contact, both roaring, growling, and swatting as they spar with their muzzles, mouths open, trying to bite each other. The large male breaks away, hurries to the fir, and scent-marks it. Pi has circled uphill and once more approaches from above and confronts the male; when the latter turns, Pi bites his shoulder, then chases him. Being persistent, the large male returns to the fir and, as before, retreats when Pi advances from uphill. Pi climbs the fir rapidly to 8 m, but descends after a minute to battle the other male. Twice more they tussle, Pi always driving the other downhill with much roaring and swatting; once the male slides over a 6 m high precipice, but immediately returns and confronts Pi, the two rearing up and emitting screaming roars while leaning into each other. Pi climbs the fir to 12 m. Restless, he soon comes down; first he chases a medium-sized male that walks by, and then attacks the large male, biting him in the shoulder.

A few moments of peace: the female descends to a lower branch and lies, the large male forages, Pi is out sight. Suddenly one medium-sized male chases another of similar size downhill. Squealing, the one in the lead tumbles over the same precipice that had claimed the large male earlier, his body turning completely in midair before crashing into the bamboo.

The female descends at 1235 hours. She sits, bleating and chirping. The two large males are out of sight; the two medium-sized ones squabble nearby. A medium-sized male then approaches the female and mounts her; she continues to sit, ignoring him. Finally he pushes her down with a forepaw until she crouches. After mounting briefly, he climbs on her back, balancing there on all fours, then drapes himself sideways over her shoulders; she chirps. When Pi appears, the male rushes at his larger rival, and Pi retreats, apparently uninterested in the female and unwilling to assert himself. The male trots back to the female, gives a cursory mount, and then for the next 7 minutes circles her closely, slides over her, drapes himself across her, paws, rolls sideways over her back, maintaining almost playful body contact, all the while bleating and chirping; she remains crouched, muzzle tucked to her chest. In the next few minutes, the male mounts 5 times for a few seconds to a minute each. Twice he rushes at the other medium-sized male, driving him away, then returns to the female. While he is on a third pursuit, the female rises; when he comes back, she swats him. All three face each other, 1.5 m apart, the two males pawing each other, the female chirping. Suddenly the female hits one squabbling male and roars at the other, and, when he turns aside, swats his rump. He bites a stick lying on the ground. After more such strife, one male mounts the female, unmolested by the other 2 m away, and rubs himself against her. After that the animals are silent and invisible in the fog.

These observations raise several points of note with respect to dominance among males. Pi was clearly the dominant male among the five. In the morning of 14 April, he claimed priority of access to the female. Yet, after mating, he appeared to relinquish his rights to the other large male. And on the following day, a medium-sized male mounted the female with impunity in the presence of Pi. It therefore appears that any adult male may have an opportunity to mate. On evolutionary grounds one can postulate that there is selective advantage in having the dominant male impregnate a female. Presumably aware when ovulation occurred, Pi showed much interest in the female for a short time only. Still, Pi's sperm must somehow achieve priority over other sperm, which may have been deposited before or after ovulation. Unfortunately we do not know whether the female had copulated before our observations began. On 15 April, Pi and the other large male fought repeatedly in the presence of the female, giving the impression that she was the immediate reason for the strife. But neither male subsequently displayed any interest in her. It seemed that they fought not for that female but for their hierarchical position, which would in the future give them prior access to other estrous females. For instance, most of these males were together again on 28 April, at Erdaoping, around a female of uncertain identity. Present were Pi, Wei, the large male, and a medium-sized male. When first observed at 1040, the female was up in a tree, where she remained until 1600, descending only to climb another tree, where she stayed until 2400 hours. The males waited below without much squabbling; apparently the female was not fully in heat. When she moved off at midnight, the males followed.

The two courtship sequences differed greatly in duration. Zhen was, to our knowledge, with males for less than half a day, whereas the other female was seen with males on 14 and 15 April and may still have been with them on 16 April, to judge by distant calls from the Zhuanjinggou.

Panda males mount often but briefly before ejaculation occurs, behavior different from the prolonged mountings of bears and some other carnivores (see table 8.1). Frequent mountings are characteristic of species with induced ovulation, such as cats, which need the stimulation of repeated copulation before ovulation can occur. Since the interval between copulation and ovulation may be 1–2 days, it would seem desirable for a male to remain with and defend a female for a while; otherwise, another male might inseminate her too and produce young. Pandas apparently do not tend a female after copulation, which suggests that, in spite of the males' multiple mountings, the females are spontaneous ovulators.

Gestation period

The Peking zoo (1974a) reported gestation periods ranging from 122 to 163 days; and our table 6.3, based on recent records, shows periods ranging from 97 to 161 days, with an average of about 135 days. The young at birth is rat-sized, about 15–17 cm long, and weighs about 90–130 g (Peking zoo 1974a; Xu et al. 1981; Tan 1983), but occasionally as little as 60 g (Anon. 1982b) and as much as 170 g (Anon. 1981b), only about 1/900 the weight of its mother. Blind, nearly naked, and almost helpless, newborns are so undeveloped physically, as well as anatomically (Wang et al. 1981), that a gestation period of 45–60 days would seem sufficient to produce such a

PLATE 6.4   Wang Xuequan emerges from a rock cleft used as a maternity den by a panda.

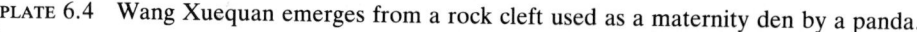

TABLE 6.8
DIMENSIONS OF ACTUAL AND POTENTIAL MATERNITY DENS IN FIR TREES

Size of entrance. Greatest width × height	Exposure of entrance	Floor space. Greatest length × width	Comments
67 × 87	NE	72 × 62	Several old droppings; no recent use
33 × 63	SE	73 × 95	No recent use
34 × 121	SE	83 × 98	One dropping inside; no recent use
46 × 79	W	85 × 81	Claw marks inside; no recent use
36 × 148	NW	90 × 105	Claw marks inside; many old droppings
48 × 186	N	98 × 110	Zhen's 1982 den
74 × 190	S	90 × 95	Zhen's 1981 den
35 × 70	SE	—	Floor space not measured; black bear in den
44 × 87	NW	56 × 45	Zhen cached month-old young in hollow

young. Analysis of progesterone levels in the urine of pregnant pandas suggests that there is delayed implantation, in which the fertilized egg develops only to the blastocyst stage and then floats free in the uterus for some time before implanting. Progesterone, a hormone responsible for preparing the uterus for implantation of the embryo, shows a sharp rise at the onset of pregnancy in most mammals, but in pandas the hormone cannot be detected until after the third month of pregnancy (Mills 1983). Similarly, the black bear has a gestation period of around 7 months. After its formation in June or July, the blastocyst does not implant and grow until about 5 months later, and births then occur mainly in January. Implantation in bears apparently occurs at about the same time of year regardless of when the female conceives (Rieffenberger et al. 1981). A similar system in the panda would help explain the 2-month variation in gestation and the birth of a highly altricial young in spite of a gestation period of 3.2–5.4 months. The delay in implantation could vary from 1.5 to 4.0 months.

Maternity dens

Pandas give birth to young in a den, usually a rock cave or tree with a hollow base (Hu et al. 1980; Zhu and Li 1980; Yong 1981). This den becomes the focal point of the female's activity until the young is about one month old. We found 2 fresh dens in firs and an old one in a cave, and, in addition, noted 12 firs with hollows of a size that made them potential dens; 8 of the 15 sites were within Zhen's range (fig. 6.4). A tree suitable for a den must be 90–100 cm or more in diameter (DBH), and have a hollow base high enough for a panda to be able to sit upright (table 6.8). The entrance to one recently used den near the Fengtongzhai Reserve measured 39 × 35 cm, probably a minimum, for the panda seemed to have enlarged the hole by biting to enable her to squeeze inside (see plate 6.10). Few trees have this combination of characteristics, especially in young forests or logged ones; trees of a size suitable for dens are probably at least 200 years old.

One den was inside the cleft of a small cliff at an altitude of 2600 m in steep terrain with little bamboo near the site (plate 6.4). After slanting in for 6 m, the ground leveled, providing about 100 × 85 cm of suitable floor space with a ceiling 2 m high. There was a nest of conifer, rhododendron, and spiny *Berberis* twigs, none thicker than 1 cm, and two pieces of dead wood from which the female had bitten chips before placing them in the nest cup. The equivalent of one day's production of droppings was to one side of the nest. Yong (1981) reported a rock den 5.7 m deep in the Qinling Mountains.

PLATE 6.5 Hu Jinchu examines a log that the female Zhen dragged to her 1981 maternity den in a hollow fir. There is a pile of droppings at the den entrance.

Zhen's 1981 den was in dense bamboo. Its wide entrance made it less cozy than other dens within her range. Piled at the entrance, like a high step, were droppings 75 cm deep, though the nest itself, composed of wood dust, was clean. Zhen had carried in various pieces of wood. At least four birch and fir saplings had been bitten off within 10 m of the den and placed at the entrance, the ends projecting inward (plate 6.5). Standing upright in the den was the top of a fir, 155 cm tall, and leaning against a wall was a log, 1 m long and 5 cm in diameter, from which Zhen had bitten chunks. Another bitten log, 220 cm long, and several branches were piled outside, close to the entrance.

Zhen's 1982 den was 650 m from her 1981 den, also in dense bamboo. She had dragged in 11 saplings and branches, mostly of birch and rhododendron, which she had collected within 3 m of the den; several branches were bitten off 2–3 m above ground. The branches were up to 5 m long and 3.5 cm in diameter. She had piled them at the entrance, the large ends facing inward. The nest consisted of rotten wood fragments, which she had raked from the inside walls to a height of 128 cm; about a dozen short twigs lined the nest cup. Just outside the entrance was a compacted mass of droppings about 100 cm wide and 40 cm high.

The three dens we examined in the Choushuigou each had a rivulet within 150 m.

We cannot explain why Zhen collected large branches, for they served no obvious function, and other nests we examined lacked such accumulations at the den entrance. Near the Fengtongzhai Reserve, one nest in a tree den consisted of debris clawed from the walls, 2 short pieces of wood, and bamboo; Yong (1981) also found a nest of bamboo in a den tree. Possibly Zhen's behavior represented incipient nest building in a situation where actual nest material was not needed.

When defecating, pandas either leaned out of the den entrance or left the site entirely, keeping the nest clean. This represented a change in their usual behavior. Normally a resting panda barely moves to defecate, with the result that after a few hours the animal is closely surrounded by droppings, on which it lies. When with young, Chengdu's Mei-Mei usually left her nest and walked to the other side of the cage to urinate and defecate.

Interactions between mother and young

Two days before giving birth, Chapultepec's Yin-Yin pawed straw around in a corner as if preparing a nest (Castillo 1982). As parturition approaches, a captive female neither eats nor drinks, her nipples and vulva become swollen, and she often squats slightly as if to defecate. At birth she sits, leaning against a wall; when the head of the young appears, she may assist the infant by picking it up with the mouth directly from the vulva, and, lifting it, press it to her breast with a forepaw. Any second young is born 20 to 30 minutes after the first (Peking zoo 1974a). One birth proceeded as follows: "At 3:20 AM on 21 July, 1983, Washington Zoo's giant panda Ling-Ling finally gave birth . . . At birth, the 130 g cub shot across his mother's abdomen and landed on the concrete floor. He lay inert for several minutes until Ling-Ling's paw accidentally touched him. When he began to squeal loudly, she picked him up and nursed him" (Mills 1983). Zhu and Li (1980), the Peking zoo

(1974a), and Schoch (1981) describe the physical and behavioral development of infants, and their data are summarized in table 6.9; the tooth eruption sequence of one infant is shown in table B.14.

To become familiar with the interactions between mother and young, we observed Chengdu's Mei-Mei and her offspring for 2 periods of a week each, one in December 1980 when her first young was 2.5 months old, and the other in September 1981 from the day of birth of her second young.

Mei-Mei's male young Jin-Jin was born at 0200 hours on 18 September 1981. Our notes between 1130 and 1630 hours on September 22 describe typical behavior (plate 6.6):

—1130. Mei sits in the corner of her cage on a bed of hay, Jin completely hidden beneath one paw and forearm, which she holds flexed to her chest. When Jin gives a harsh, penetrating squawk, she shifts her arm somewhat.

—1145. Grasping Jin lightly with her jaws, mouth over his back, Mei picks up her young and leans forward until her head rests on her hindleg (fig. 6.11), with the young tucked beneath her chin, lying apparently on her hindleg and covered and supported by her forepaw.

—1232. Mei sits up, lifting Jin with her jaws and then holding him close to her neck with one paw. She licks his lower back briefly (fig. 6.11).

PLATE 6.6 Chengdu's Mei-Mei holds her 1981 offspring Jin-Jin in her mouth. The young is about 10 days old. (Photo courtesy of Jin Xuqi.)

—1239. Jin emits a high-pitched squawk, and Mei adjusts her arm. He is lengthwise in her paw, partly held in place by the pseudothumb. She brings up her other arm too and rests her muzzle beneath crossed paws.

—1243. Holding Jin to her chest, Mei rolls on her side, the young silent and out of sight.

FIGURE 6.11   Postures of a female giant panda with a small young. Top left: she sits, holding her young in a forepaw, and licks it. Top right: she rests, using a hindleg as a pillow, the young tucked out of sight against her chest. Bottom: she walks, carrying the young in her mouth.

—1300. As Mei shifts Jin he emits a sharp squawk. Then, after pushing him into her mouth with a paw, she sits up, and licks him intensively until 1315, only a little of him visible behind her massive forearm.

—1325. Mei reclines on her belly in her usual position, head pillowed on hindleg.

—1408. She sits back up and licks his back, chest, and anal region for 4 minutes.

—1425. Mei hunches far over, top of head in the hay, her young to her chest, engulfed by both arms. As she shifts to her side 25 minutes later, Jin calls. His pink forelegs are visible, scrabbling at her muzzle, and his head is raised shakily.

—1608. Mei sits once more and, holding Jin belly up, licks him for 2 minutes. After that she just sits, the young hidden in her arms. From 1622 to 1625 she licks him again and soon thereafter reclines.

These notes do not mention suckling. Young are said to suckle 6–14 times per day early in life (table 6.9), starting 4–5 hours after birth. But we were unable to quantify this behavior because Jin-Jin was usually invisible beneath Mei-Mei's paw or forearm, close to her chest, and we had no way of judging when or how often he was at a nipple.

Mei-Mei was restless, often shifting her position. On the day of birth and the one following, she averaged 5–6 shifts per hour, a rate that subsequently was almost

TABLE 6.9

PHYSICAL AND BEHAVIORAL DEVELOPMENT OF GIANT PANDA YOUNG DURING THE FIRST 6 MONTHS OF LIFE

Day	
1–2	Young pink and naked except for white sheen of sparse hair; eyes closed; tail 1/5 to 1/3 the length of body, proportionately much longer than that of adult. Squalls loudly and often. Makes crawling movements with legs. Suckles 6–14 times per day for up to 30 minutes each time.
6–7	Black visible on eye patch, ears, and shoulders, and a day or two later on forelegs.
10–12	Black visible on hindlegs and black on other parts has darkened; hair covers body more densely.
25	Young looks like a miniature adult, except for tail, which is still disproportionately long. It squalls less often.
35–40	Eyes usually open halfway, but young keeps them closed much of the time.
45–48	Eyes usually fully open. Young suckles about 8 times per day. It can raise its head and hold it steady and it can crawl, but coordination is still poor.
60	Young suckles 3–4 times a day.
75–80	Young can stand shakily and take a step or two. The first deciduous incisors or canines appear, tooth eruption being somewhat variable.
90	Young is alert and can take several coordinated steps. It suckles 2–3 times a day.
120	Young has become active but remains clumsy: it walks, rolls over playfully, and climbs up on its mother's back.
150	Young can trot well and, in general, moves freely. It suckles now only once or twice a day.
180	Young has 26–28 teeth—canines, incisors, premolars. Begins to eat solids.

Source: Peking zoo 1974a; Zhu and Li 1980; Schoch 1981.

TABLE 6.10

BEHAVIOR OF GIANT PANDA MEI-MEI WITH NEWBORN FROM DAY OF PARTURITION, CHENGDU ZOO, SEPTEMBER 1981

Date	Observation time (hours)	% time female sitting	Major position changes by female (av. no. per hour)[a]	Female licking newborn (av. no. bouts per hour)	Latrine trips (av. no. per hour)
18	10.1	41.4	4.7	1.1+[b]	0
19	11.8	30.4	5.8	1.1+[b]	.08
20	10.5	31.3	3.2	1.0	.1
21	11.3	30.1	3.4	1.0	.09
22	10.8	36.9	2.2	.7	.09
23	10.8	43.4	3.5	1.3	.09
24	5.4	39.1	3.0	1.1	.4
27	7.4	28.2	3.0	.5+	0

Data collected by J. Stover.
[a]Changes from standing to sitting to lying in any sequence.
[b]Not all instances recorded.

halved (see table 6.11). She frequently licked her offspring, especially its anal region, on the average once an hour (table 6.10). Sometimes licking lasted a few seconds, at other times 3 minutes or more. Aside from cleaning the young, such licking stimulated it to urinate and defecate, and Mei-Mei then ingested the wastes as they were eliminated.

Jin-Jin had a loud, high-pitched squawk out of all proportion to his size. He emitted that call whenever he seemed uncomfortable, which was quite often, as when his mother held him too loosely, letting legs dangle in air, when upside down, and when picked up with the teeth. The calls alerted his mother, and she responded by shifting him. A young is so tiny and fragile that it needs an emphatic signal to communicate stress to its bulky mother.

Mei-Mei never placed her young into the nest or otherwise let it away from her body. The great dexterity of her forepaws was in this situation as important in her handling of the young as it usually is in the manipulating of bamboo. When she left the nest to go to the latrine at the other side of the cage, something she seldom had to do (table 6.10), she carried Jin-Jin with her, holding him in her mouth, her muzzle pointing in an unusual position straight at the ground (fig. 6.11). She left him unattended in the nest for the first time when he was 26 days old; the previous year she had treated her young similarly at about the same age. A young undergoes a marked developmental change between 25 and 30 days of age. Weighing now about 1 kg, it is less likely to be accidentally injured, and, being well furred, it does not need the warmth of its mother's arms. When left exposed, it now seldom gives the piercing squawk, and the call seems to disappear gradually or become modified. A mother's behavior changes too in that she forgoes the continuous contact with her offspring (plates 6.7 and 6.8).

The behavior of Mei-Mei toward one of her large offspring, the 2.5-month-old male Ronshun, was somewhat different from that toward a newborn, as observations on 2 December 1980 illustrate.

TABLE 6.11

Behavior of giant panda Mei-Mei with young, 2½ months old (born 20 September), Chengdu zoo, December 1980

Date	Observation time (hours)	% time female sitting	Major position changes by female (av. no. per hour)	Female licking young (av. no. bouts per hour)	Suckling Starting time	Suckling Duration/ min.	Latrine trips (av. no. per hour)
3	5.0	69.3	1.0	2.8	1218	10	.2
4	5.3	66.9	2.6	1.9	1427	10.5	.4
					1647	4.5	
5	3.2	31.1	.9	.9	—	—	0
6	1.8	41.9	1.1	2.8	1549	15	0
7	3.1	19.5	.6	1.0	1536	12	0
8	2.3	46.7	2.6	2.6	—	—	.4
9	3.5	36.2	2.3	2.3	—	—	.3
16	.9	47.2	3.3	2.2	1243	12.5	1.1

PLATE 6.7 Chengdu's Mei-Mei nuzzles her 1981 offspring Jin-Jin, 53 days old. (Photo courtesy of Jin Xuqi.)

PLATE 6.8 Chengdu's Mei-Mei sits by her 1983 offspring Chuan-Chuan, 3 months old.

—1040. Mei lies on her side, Ronshun before her. Reaching out with both forepaws, she pulls him in and nuzzles his head, then lies cuddling him to her chest.

—1042. She stands, takes Ronshun's forearm into her mouth, and with the same motion scoops him into her arms and sits, cradling him, biting him lightly in the leg, as if in play. After licking his anal area, she releases him, and he slides down her sloping abdomen into the hay.

—1059. Mei reclines on her side. The young lies on his back, mouth open, waving his legs; he rolls over, tucks his head by his mother's neck, and sleeps, as does she.

—1331. Waking up, Mei licks Ronshun's head, gently bites one of his forepaws; then, taking one of his forelegs into her mouth, she picks him up with her paws as well and lifts him to her chest as she sits. Ronshun weighs 4 kg and seems somewhat awkward to handle. She holds him belly up and licks his anal area. Five minutes later she sags onto her side, Ronshun in her arms.

—1406. Still lying, Mei pulls Ronshun close and nuzzles his head and chest; he opens his mouth and paws her face; she nuzzles him again, on forearm, neck, and head, and mouths him and paws—not grooming, it seems, but stimulating him—for 11 minutes.

—1421. Mei grasps Ronshun by the throat and, assisted by her forepaws, lifts him to her chest. She apparently lacks a specifically oriented bite for picking up young. Sitting now, she holds him head down as she licks his anal area. Then she turns him so that his face is by her left upper nipple. All her nipples are pink and extended. Ronshun suckles, held in position by her arms. Once he slides down, but she grasps his nape with her teeth and pulls him back up. Five minutes later she shifts him to her right upper nipple, and he suckles there for 6 minutes.

—1438. Ronshun stops suckling and struggles in her arms; she licks his face and cuddles him, but he squirms until she frees him, and he crawls down her. But she grasps his hindleg with her teeth and pulls him back into her arms. She reclines with him and then releases him into the hay. Her nipples are withdrawn, barely visible.

Compared to when she had a newborn, Mei-Mei was not as restless, the average number of major position changes per hour dropping from 3.7 to 1.8. She ate more and consequently went to the latrine more often. A main change was in the amount of attention she devoted to her offspring. Although she averaged only a little more sitting time (44.8 versus 35.1%), she licked her young twice as often (tables 6.10 and 6.11). About 7.4% of her time was spent in licking Ronshun; in addition, she mouthed and pawed him in a playful manner; she still consumed his feces and urine. Ronshun, in turn, was quite active and began to reciprocate his mother's overtures.

Ronshun suckled only once or twice in daytime, usually in the afternoon, for a total of 10 to 15 minutes. As a young grows larger, it can suckle while squatting in front of its sitting mother (plate 6.9; Zhu and Li 1980). On 30 March 1981, at the age of 6.5 months, Ronshun was removed from Mei-Mei and bottle fed. His transition

PLATE 6.9 Chengdu's Mei-Mei cuddles her large 1981 offspring Jin-Jin, aged 6 months. (Photo courtesy of Jin Xuqi.)

from milk to bamboo occurred at the age of 7 to 8 months. By August, at the age of 11 months, Ronshun readily ate bamboo leaves but seldom stem.

We have few observations on interactions between mother and young in the wild. Zhen mated on 13 April 1981, and her young was therefore expected between mid-August and mid-September. Continuous monitoring between 3 and 8 August revealed that Zhen had a normal activity pattern (fig. 6.12). On 13 August, Zhen moved across a ridge and for the rest of the month remained within 300 m of, but not consistently close to, a den tree. Beginning 1 September, she was at or near the den site, suggesting that she gave birth on about 2 or 3 September after a gestation period of 142–143 days. We monitored her continuously from 4 to 24 September.

During this period, Zhen's activity pattern was different from that of the previous month: her active readings decreased from an average of 50% in August to 38% in September, whereas the average number of activity changes increased from 23 to 35. That Zhen was relatively inactive but restless is shown in figure 6.12. Zhen remained within a radius of 200 m of the den throughout September, apparently making short excursions to forage and drink. Monitoring between 14 and 19 October showed that Zhen's activity was normal again, the restlessness gone (fig. 6.12); she was active on 62% of the radio contacts and averaged 17.4 activity changes per day. These changes in activity appear to be typical of females with newborns. Monitored in 1982, Zhen revealed a similar pattern after giving birth. Han's signals between 13 and 17 September 1982 also suggested that she had a young: she was active on only 35% of the radio contacts and averaged 24 activity changes per day. The general changes in the activity patterns of wild females resembled those of the captive Mei-Mei (tables 6.10 and 6.11).

Although Zhen was still around her den in mid-October, she now traveled farther afield, and on 19 October she was on the other side of a ridge nearly 400 m from the den. So far we had refrained from approaching the den for fear of disturbing her. Now we wondered whether she had abandoned the site or whether the young was ill or dead. We decided to investigate.

—20 October, 1420 hours. HJC and GBS approach the den tree through head-high bamboo, the former in the lead. The tree is about 40 m downhill and off to one side of them when Zhen suddenly appears by a fallen tree 10 m ahead. First she steps closer and then, from a distance of 6 m, breaks into a trot, roaring twice and snorting. GBS climbs a nearby *Sorbus* tree to a height of 2.5 m, and HJC goes rapidly back uphill. Zhen begins to follow HJC, then veers sharply toward the tree to which GBS clings. Having passed beneath this tree, she turns, snorts, and for about a minute stands and looks around as if trying to locate the source of disturbance. Abruptly she moves at a fast walk about 20 m closer to her den and there stands in the bamboo, motionless; she moves yet closer to the den and waits silently, as if listening. A young in the den squawks several times. Zhen does not move.

Zhen remained near the den until 24 October. After that, she moved across a nearby ridge and remained there much of the time until mid-November. The den tree had been abandoned when we examined it on 8 November. In general, Zhen

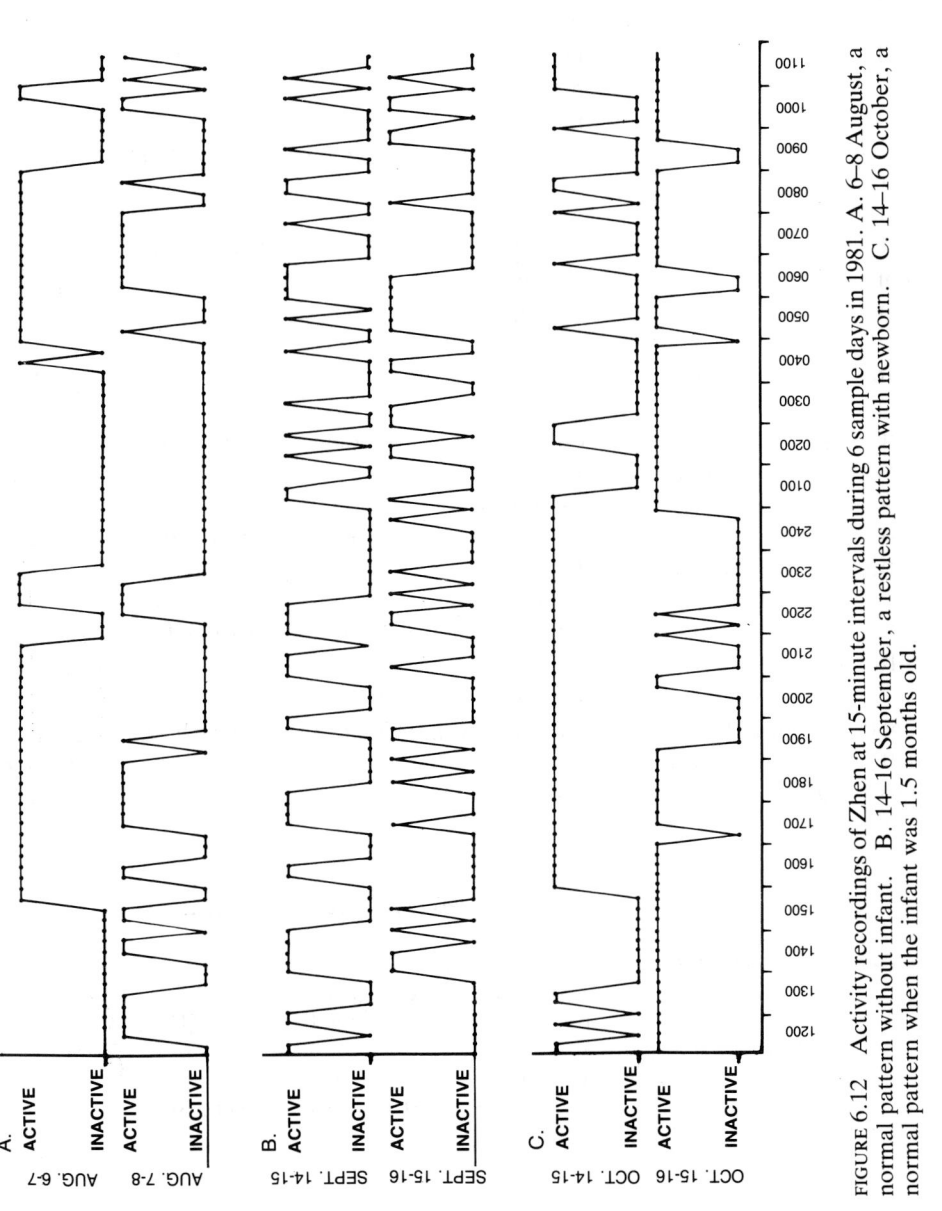

FIGURE 6.12   Activity recordings of Zhen at 15-minute intervals during 6 sample days in 1981. A. 6–8 August, a normal pattern without infant.   B. 14–16 September, a restless pattern with newborn.   C. 14–16 October, a normal pattern when the infant was 1.5 months old.

traveled little but had no particular focus of activity; presumably she carried her young with her until she somehow lost it.

In 1982, Zhen probably mated between 28 April and 7 May. On 28 August she was radio-located near a den tree, and by 30 August she had deposited 5 twigs in the den. She was observed in the den on 1 and 2 September, and an infant was heard calling on 7, 8, and 9 September. On 17 September, the radio signal remained inactive, and, thinking that something may have happened to Zhen, several members of the research staff investigated. Zhen sat motionless in her den, her back to the entrance. Shouting from a distance of 5 m elicited no response, except that she looked up, her placid behavior in strong contrast to that shown the previous year when we approached her den. It was noted then that she had removed her collar. Unable to monitor her closely, we are unaware on what day she abandoned the den. On 15 October, her young, large as a cat, was accidentally discovered in a hollow tree nearby, but, since Zhen was approaching, no further observations were made. Zhen descended from Erdaoping to Wuyipeng on 10 November and there ate some mutton put out for her by the camp staff; she returned to Erdaoping within 21 hours of leaving it. She did not have her young with her, nor was any sign of it found in subsequent months. We saw Zhen on several occasions in May and June 1983, both in daytime and at night. No young accompanied her, she was not lactating, and there were no droppings of a young at her feeding sites. Yet on 7 September and again on 13 and 15 September a female presumed to be Zhen was observed with a year-old young, and Zhen was lactating when trapped on 5 December. We consider it unlikely that this was her own young. Possibly she had a newborn that died and then adopted a stray young, at least temporarily. One such stray may have been in the area, its mother killed by poachers (see below). This would explain why Zhen had milk long after her 1982 young would have been weaned.

On 23 September 1982, loggers near the Fengtongzhai Reserve observed a panda circling a den tree on a steep slope at 2730 m. Although the tree was within 50 m of a logging operation and a footpath passed within 6 m, the panda entered the den and gave birth the following day. Loggers saw her daily and sometimes gave her meat and bones. Gao Huahang of the forest department in Baoxing took notes on her behavior (plate 6.10). The female usually stayed in the den when people were near, although she occasionally left for 2–3 hours to feed. She licked her infant before departing. Left behind unattended in the nest, the infant did not squawk or otherwise call. On leaving the den, the female first defecated, then usually drank at a nearby rivulet before beginning to forage. Female and young moved out of the den on 24 October.

This female and young behaved somewhat differently from the animals we observed in captivity. The mother readily left her young alone in the nest instead of holding it in her forepaws almost continuously, and the young remained silent when unattended instead of vocalizing loudly when not securely held.

After remaining at a den with her young until it is 4–7 weeks old, a female abandons the site. Still helpless, the young must be carried by its mother (see table 6.9). A female transports a small young in her mouth for short distances. Villagers also once saw a female walk awkwardly with a young tucked into her armpit.

Disturbed, she dropped the young and fled. It was a male weighing 1.2 kg. Hand-reared successfully, he was sent to Washington in 1972. A large young is probably held to the chest with a forepaw while the female travels, then is cached somewhere while she forages in the vicinity.

Young are fully dependent on their mothers until they can subsist on bamboo. They begin to eat bamboo leaves at 5–6 months of age and appear to be essentially weaned at 8–9 months. One female was found dead in the study area in early April. She had 2 uterine scars, one in each horn, and she was still lactating. Her young was

PLATE 6.10   Gao Huahang takes notes on a wild female in a maternity den near the Fengtong-zhai Reserve. (Photo courtesy of Forest Department, Baoxing.)

probably about 7 months old at the time of her death. In late May, three village dogs treed a young in the area where the female had died; if this was the orphan, then a young could survive on its own from the age of about 7 months. Normally, young remain with their mother until the second spring after their birth, when they are about 1.5 years old. On 13 March 1981 we saw a young of that age alone. We have no record of a female accompanied by a young older than 1.5 years.

Social interactions between pandas

Three or four adult pandas were sometimes in the same enclosure at the Chengdu zoo. The animals occasionally quarreled or came into contact as they gathered around the door at which they received food, but they usually wandered and rested alone, without attempting to socialize; they gave the impression of being alone together. In the wild, we tracked pandas in snow for many kilometers without evidence that they sought company, confirming reports (Giant Panda Expedition 1974; Sheldon 1975; Hu 1981c) that the animals are rather solitary. There was, however, occasional evidence that pandas have a limited social life, other than during courtship and in infancy.

When two pandas meet, they often vocalize vigorously. Between January 1981 and June 1982, we noted 12 such occasions, excluding one courtship, all between 2 March and 21 May, but on only 2 of these occasions were we able to observe the animals. Consequently, we seldom knew which pandas were involved. Contacts were occasionally brief, a few barks, before the animals drifted apart. At other times, interactions lasted for an hour or more, the meeting characterized by moans, barks, squeals, and other vocalizations. On one occasion, Zhen and Wei interacted between 1013 and 1124, judging by duration of calls; another time, Zhen and an unidentified panda were in contact between 0130 and 0330; and on a third occasion 2 unidentified individuals vocalized between 0830 and 1522. Although most meetings occurred during the mating season, there was no indication that they involved sexual activity. Some contacts may have been inadvertent, especially when in late April the animals concentrated in *Fargesia*, whereas others were probably deliberate. The fact that interactions may continue noisily for several hours even though one or both animals could sever contact suggests a certain social attraction. We observed the behavior of animals during two such interactions, each involving a subadult and adult.

—2 March 1981. An adult bedded near the river for part of the night, then passed Wuyipeng before dawn and angled uphill along the contours of the slope. That same night a subadult crossed the river from the opposite slope and followed a route parallel to that of the adult (fig. 6.13). Lack of snow prevented us from tracking the animals farther.

At 1535 hours a panda moans; at 1550 we spot a subadult (probably Long before he was radio-collared) about 15 m up in a spruce, crouched near the tip of a bough. The tree is below us on the slope about 150 m away. The subadult moans twice more around 1715. As he moans once more at 1730, we see an

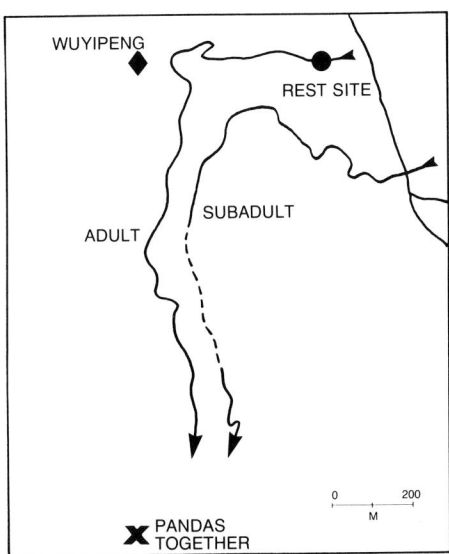

FIGURE 6.13   Routes traveled by an adult and a subadult panda before interacting, 2 March 1981.

adult descend slowly, hindlegs first, among the dense lower branches of the spruce and vanish into the bamboo. At 1740 the subadult moves close to the main trunk, and at 1805 we leave, unable to see in fog and gathering darkness.

A large panda was seen on a trail down-slope from the spruce at 1830, presumably the same adult we observed earlier. We could not determine its sex, but it was probably a male, to judge by the ranges of residents as determined later by radio-tracking. The subadult remained near the spruce for part of the night. There was a rest site with 23 droppings at the base of the tree, and 115 *Sinarundinaria* stems had been eaten there.

—8 May 1982. We hear a moan at 0850 and another at 0857. Two animals bark and moan at 0952; and, after 25 minutes of silence, noise erupts again, the animals moaning, roaring, and squealing. By this time we have crept to within 80 m of the pandas. A subadult of unknown sex, probably a stranger, crouches among the branches of a shrubby tree about 4 m above ground. Standing balanced on his hindlegs below on a swaying branch is Wei. With one forepaw he grips the tree and with the other he swats at the subadult, who slaps back and squeals. Both then bark, squeal, and yip for 25 minutes before subsiding into occasional moans and finally silence. Both squat on their respective branches. The subadult ascends another 2 m at 1130. Both rest. The subadult first sits hunched, forepaws over nose, then crouches, head hanging over the side of the branch; Wei has settled at the tree's base. Both moan at 1245. At 1420, the subadult descends suddenly and moves from sight while Wei remains briefly, moaning. The two make contact again at 1500 with much yipping and moaning, then separate.

We saw the subadult walking away rapidly at 1510. Wei stayed in the area.

Zhen was within about 300 m during the whole interaction without approaching, as revealed by her radio signals.

An indirect method of determining potential contacts is to measure the linear distance between radio-collared pandas on the same day (table 6.12). If the ranges of two pandas overlap, the average distance between the animals gives an indication of whether they tend to remain near each other. All pandas remained, on the average, 1.0 km or more apart, with the exception of Long and Ning, who were only 0.4 km apart. Long, Ning, Zhen, and Wei shared ranges; yet Long and Ning were significantly ($p < 0.001$) closer than either was to the others, suggesting affinity.

To obtain an idea how often pandas interact, we determined the number of days when two animals were radio-located within 100 and 200 m of each other (table 6.12). While proximity does not signify that the animals are aware of each other, it does at least indicate a potential for contact. The ranges of Han and Long were distinct, as were those of Han and Ning. Potential meetings between Zhen and Han and between Wei and Han were confined to spring, when all three descended into *Fargesia*. Long and Zhen were within 200 m on only 1.7% of the days and Ning and Zhen on 2.8%, indicating that the subadults had little contact with the female in spite of much range overlap. Wei was near Long on 9.6% of the days, Zhen 4.7%, and Ning 4.5%. These presumed contacts were most common (61%) during the mating season from March to May, and we surmise that an adult male monitors other pandas within his range at that season by approaching them. Excluding contacts between Long and Ning, two pandas were within 200 m on 43 occasions, 90.7% from March to August, and 9.3% from September to February—figures indicating a seasonal trend in sociability.

Long and Ning were within 200 m of each other 29.4% of the days during every month of the year but most often (60%) in August–October and December. The two tended to shift to different parts of their overlapping ranges at about the same time. For example, Ning crossed a ridge from the Zhuanjinggou into the Choushuigou on 27 April, settling into an area both rarely visited. Long followed on 3 May. By the

TABLE 6.12

DISTANCES BETWEEN PANDAS ON SAME DAY, BASED ON RADIO LOCATIONS

		Average distance apart (in m)		Days within <100m		Days within 101–200m	
	N	x̄	± SD(range)	N	%	N	%
Long-Zhen	424	1136	± 718(133–3522)	0		7	1.7
Long-Ning	289	407	± 343(40–1966)	26	9.0	59	20.4
Long-Wei	167	938	± 597(99–3051)	1	.6	15	9.0
Long-Han	75	3568	± 757(1568–5133)	0		0	
Zhen-Ning	284	982	± 649(100–3441)	1	.4	7	2.5
Zhen-Wei	169	1367	± 790(30–3111)	5	3.0	3	1.8
Zhen-Han	82	2397	± 1247(238–4338)	0		0	
Ning-Wei	67	1002	± 512(100–1912)	1	1.5	2	3.0
Ning-Han	19	4217	± 453(3280–5084)	0		0	
Wei-Han	79	2967	± 1195(184–5263)	0		1	1.3

next day both had returned to the Zhuanjinggou. We suspect that the two maintained a loose association, preferring proximity, not necessarily direct contact.

Two large aggregations of pandas were reported in 1983 by the staff of Tangjiahe Reserve. On 26 April, visitors saw between 9 and 14 pandas together, a precise figure being difficult to obtain because of dense vegetation. And on 2 May, in another valley, there were 8 in a group. Two circumstances may be responsible for these aggregations. Much bamboo flowered in the reserve during the past decade. Most of it died on the upper slopes above 2300 m, whereas on the lower ones, especially near the mouth of several valleys, it survived in patches of varying size. Pandas may have congregated at such food sources. During the mating season, moreover, a number of males may be attracted to an estrous female.

The infrequent social contacts no doubt supplement scent marking as an important means by which individuals can become acquainted, establish rank, reinforce past associations, and, in general, maintain the community structure.

Summary

1. At the end of 1981, the panda population in the 35 km^2 study area comprised 2 large infants, 4 independent subadults, 7 adult males, and 5 or 6 adult females—a total of 18–19, with a crude density of about 1.9 km^2 per animal.

2. In captivity, both sexes usually reach maturity at the age of 5.5 or 6.5 years. Thirty-seven litters were born in zoos between 1963 and 1983; average litter size was 1.7. A captive female raises only one young if twins are born, although a wild female may on rare occasions attempt to rear both. If her infant dies, a female may have young in consecutive years; if it survives, the birth interval is 2 years.

3. A panda's face is relatively expressionless, the animal depending mostly on vocalizations to communicate subtle shifts in emotions. The vocal repertoire of adults consists of about 11 distinct sounds. Pandas seldom use vocal signals, however, except during the mating season, depending mainly on olfactory cues to maintain their society. The most common marking methods consist of clawing tree trunks, rubbing the glandular area around the anus against objects, and spraying urine. Conifers are favored scent posts. Males do most marking, the scent probably conveying messages that help to prevent encounters. Scent posts are located primarily along main travel routes rather than along range boundaries.

4. Most mating occurs between mid-March and mid-May, though an occasional animal conceives in autumn or winter. The peak of estrus lasts about 1–3 days. During this period, 2–5 males may compete for access to a female, priority being based on rank; nonetheless, subordinate individuals may also copulate. Although a male may mount repeatedly, there is no evidence that female pandas are induced ovulators. The gestation period ranges from 97 to 163 days. Newborns weigh about 90–130 g and are so altricial that a gestation period of 45 days would seem sufficient to reach that stage of development. There appears to be a delay in implantation of 1.5–4.0 months.

5. A female usually gives birth in a cave or hollow tree. In captivity, a female holds her newborn almost continuously in a forepaw for the first three weeks of its life. The den is used until the young is 4–7 weeks old. The female then leaves the site carrying the offspring with her until it can walk at the age of 3–4 months. Young begin to eat bamboo at 5–6 months, are fully weaned at 8–9 months, and leave their mothers at about 18 months.

6. Several inferences about the frequency of social contacts among pandas in our study area can be made: adult pandas are essentially solitary, contacts with others being only intermittent; pandas, especially adult males, are socially most active between March and late summer with a peak during the mating season; and two subadults may form a loose social bond.

7

The Relationship
between Nutrition
and Behavior

Behavior is molded by environmental conditions and ecological pressures; it is an adaptive response, enabling an animal to survive and reproduce. The giant panda has long been associated with bamboo. Indeed, natural selection has so tied it to this food source that many aspects of its life, from body size and digestive rates to activity patterns, have been influenced by it. Earlier we posed the question, How is the panda adapted to bamboo? An adaptation is the result of a change in the animal's genotype. To what extent is the panda bound by such genetically determined adaptations? Some of its distinctive traits may not have a genetic base. Behavior may also be variable, depending on local conditions and traditions. And a trait may not be the only possible one in a given situation, or even the optimal one. As Rowell (1979) stressed, every trait need not be ideally adaptive, only tolerably so, in order to persist. The panda's dependence on bamboo is absolute under current conditions, a food specialization that permits only a slight flexibility in behavior. This chapter provides an overview of previous chapters by considering how nutrition and behavior in the panda are related, how the animal's life style has been affected by its dependence on bamboo. But the plasticity of behavior as it was expressed both in the past, when the animal's range was large and habitat diverse, and at present still needs investigation.

To refine one's ideas about the adaptiveness of certain traits, it is sometimes useful to compare the behavior of two related species living under comparable conditions. The Asiatic black bear, similar in size to and sympatric with the panda, would be the ideal choice for such a comparison, but little is as yet known about the species (Bromlei 1973). However, the American black bear living in the Great Smoky Mountains of Tennessee (35°30N, 83°30W) presents a good alternative. Its habitat is rugged, with sharp ridges and steep valleys at elevations of up to 2000 m. The seasons are similar to Wolong in that summers are wet and warm (mean monthly temperatures 20–23°C), and winters moderately cold (4–5°C). Snow at high elevations may persist for several months, especially on north-facing slopes. The vegetation is dense and diverse, floristically similar to that of eastern Asia (Wang 1961). Dominant trees include spruce, fir, hemlock, beech, birch, oak, maple, and cherry; the understory has much rhododendron; there is no bamboo. M. Pelton and his associates have studied the black bear there in detail (Johnson and Pelton 1980; Quigley 1982; Eagle 1979; Eiler 1981; Garshelis and Pelton 1980, 1981), and their findings provide valuable material for comparison with ours on the panda.

A mammal's most immediate task each day is to obtain enough energy to fuel basic metabolic functions, maintain homeothermy, and supply calories for various kinds of behavior. Although pandas retain the potential for omnivory, eating meat when possible, they have specialized on a plant resource that is readily available in unlimited amount at all seasons. But by adapting to an herbivorous diet of bamboo while retaining the unspecialized digestive tract of a carnivore, the panda has had to confront three related nutritional problems: (1) it is unable to digest bamboo leaves and stems efficiently because it lacks the microbes necessary to break down structural carbohydrates, mainly cellulose; (2) it obtains a low nutritional return for the amount eaten because leaves and stems consist primarily of water and structural carbohydrates; and (3) it derives nutrients primarily from the easily digestible cellular content rather than from the cell wall constituents. To subsist on bamboo, a panda must have developed an efficient feeding strategy; that is, it must have adapted in such a way morphologically, physiologically, and behaviorally that it obtains the greatest return in nutrients for the effort spent foraging.

A herbivore is usually limited not by the amount of time it can devote to eating but by the capacity of its digestive tract, the digestion time, and the rate of food passage (Westoby 1974). This being so, it must be selective in what it eats; it must choose foods with a certain nutritive value to prevent the digestive tract from merely being stuffed with useless bulk. Different bamboo parts vary in nutritive quality. Viewed in terms of high protein and low cellulose and lignin levels, leaves prove by far the most nutritious parts, followed by branches, old shoots and other stems (table 3.8). Nutritive values remain remarkably constant throughout the year, freeing pandas from the pressures of having to adapt to marked fluctuations in energy sources. New shoots are for a short period even more nutritious than leaves, but they are seasonal, limited in availability to May and June in the Choushuigou.

The panda's constant food supply, both in amount and quality, presents an unusual situation. Herbivores living in environments with marked seasonal changes characteristically have a fluctuating food supply (fig 7.1). For example, African buffalo, wildebeest, and other ungulates living in the Serengeti National Park of Tanzania may at the height of the annual dry season have to eat such low-quality forage that it is below minimum maintenance level (Sinclair 1975, 1977). Similarly, grass and browse eaten by North American deer and elk in winter are of conspicuously lower quality than in summer (Wallmo et al. 1977; Houston 1982). Given the constraints imposed by its digestive system, a panda would be unlikely to survive on bamboo if the nutritive value of this grass, like that of other grasses, declined greatly for part of the year.

Leaves being high in protein, as well as abundant and easy to collect, we would expect pandas to favor them. This was not always the case. As described in chapter 3, pandas have three ecological seasons, based on their food selecting: spring, from April to June, when they eat either *Sinarundinaria* stems or new *Fargesia* shoots;

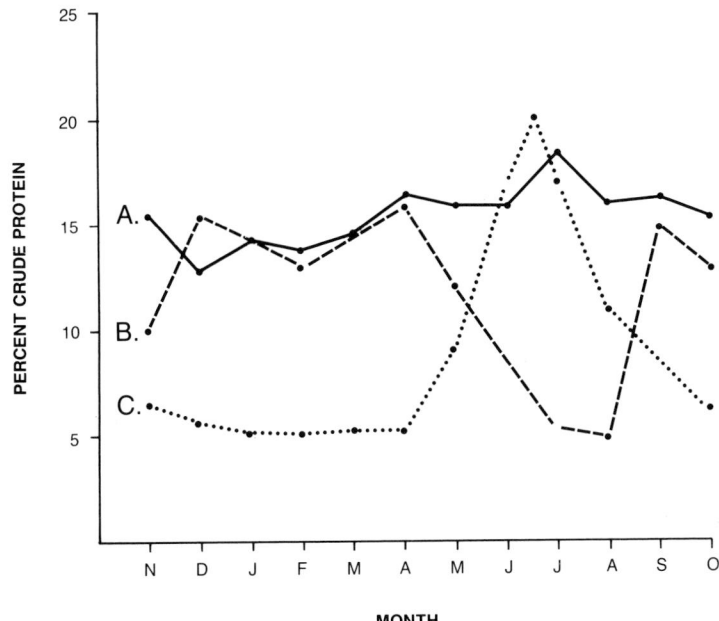

FIGURE 7.1   The percentage of crude protein available in the principal foods of three herbivores at various times of year.   A. *Sinarundinaria* leaves eaten by giant panda have a fairly constant and high protein level all year.   B. grass consumed by wildebeest in the Serengeti plains of Tanzania shows a marked drop in protein level at the height of the dry season (Sinclair 1975).   C. browse foraged by mule deer in Colorado has a low protein level in winter (Wallmo et al. 1977).

summer–autumn, from July to October, when they subsist mainly on leaves; and winter, from November to March, when they concentrate on old *Sinarundinaria* shoots and leaves. Why are leaves not eaten in spring? We have no evidence that alkaloids or tannins affect palatability, or that amino acid and mineral levels influence selection against leaves. Silica, however, which is known to inhibit digestion, may be involved.

Crude protein content varies from about 2.5% in stem to 15.5% in leaves, and most is digestible. At all seasons, pandas consume so much bamboo per day—between 10 and 18 kg—that their protein intake is considerably higher than the calculated minimum of 92 g required for basic maintenance; additional protein is needed for body growth and reproduction. On an assumed 90% protein digestibility, the estimated intake ranged from a low of 242 g/day in spring to a high of 646 g/day in summer–autumn. Even if digestibility were to drop as low as 60–75%, a panda would obtain ample protein from its food, except perhaps in spring (fig 7.2). It appears, therefore, that pandas eat so much mainly to obtain calories for energy—in the form of both soluble carbohydrates and deaminated protein—rather than to fulfill basic protein requirements. Pandas also obtain carbohydrates from the breakdown of

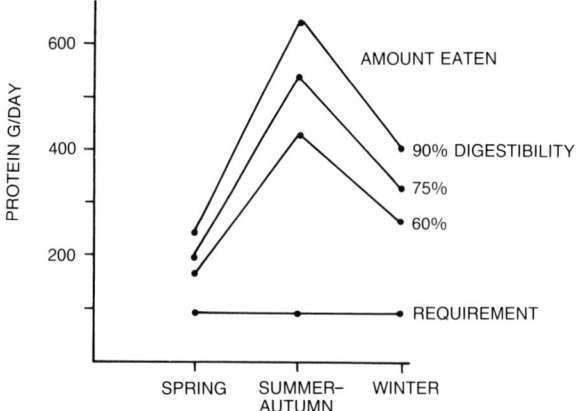

FIGURE 7.2   Daily protein intake comparing the calculated amount eaten at different levels of digestibility with the approximate minimum daily amount needed for maintenance by a 100 kg panda subsisting on *Sinarundinaria*.

hemicelluloses, the only constituent of the cell wall they can digest in part. Average hemicellulose digestibility is about 22%. On the whole, pandas can assimilate only a small fraction of their total diet. Dry matter digestibility is about 12% in spring, 23% in summer, and 19% in winter, an average of 17%. This exceptionally low level of digestibility emphasizes the panda's need to pass much bulk through its digestive tract quickly to obtain its daily requirements of nutrients. For comparison, ungulates subsisting on green grass assimilate about 80% of their food (Sinclair 1975), including 40–60% or more of the cellulose and hemicelluloses (Van Soest 1982). Among grass-eating animals, geese probably resemble pandas most closely with their low digestive efficiency of 23–34% (Drent et al. 1978–79; Summers and Grieve 1982).

Inefficient at digesting cell wall constituents, the panda has instead become adapted for rapid extraction and assimilation of cell content. Stems and leaves are quickly crushed, slightly chewed, swallowed, and passed little altered through the digestive tract within 5–13 hours. Such a short retention time allows the panda to increase its food intake. Passage time in black bear is also short, about 8 hours (D. Graber, pers. comm.), whereas in deer (Short 1981) and horses (Van Soest 1982) it is 24 hours or more, although it varies with type and amount of forage eaten.

Rate of passage is one important constraint on the amount that a panda can eat. The time factor is another. An animal can bite off leaves by the mouthful, consuming several kilograms in a relatively short time. But stems must be selected, detached, and then eaten bite by bite, a time-consuming task. Thick *Fargesia* stems can provide much bulk fairly quickly, but they were little favored in our study area. Instead pandas selected *Sinarundinaria* stems, thin stems which provided only a few grams of food each. Animals were active for 65% of the day in spring, 52% in summer, and 62% in winter, the difference probably due to the little effort needed to forage on leaves in summer. Viewed from the perspective of time, a panda's feeding behavior becomes understandable. A stem is not detached at ground level, the animal saving time by not bending over more; and the top of a leafy stem is usually not eaten in spring, the animal conserving time by not biting off branches. Young leaves, those richest in nutrients, are not laboriously selected, nor are dead leaves discarded even though these lower food quality in winter.

In spring, a panda may eat in one day a total of 650 new *Fargesia* shoots weighing 38 kg. At 60 seconds per shoot, an animal would require 10.8 hours to eat this number. However, the calculation is based on shoots of a size preferred by pandas, shoots taller than 25 cm and thicker than 0.9 cm. The panda selects for such large shoots probably because it could not, within its activity budget, consume enough small ones to meet nutritional needs. In general, a panda must be selective but not too selective in what it eats, balancing food size and quality aganst the time required to process an item.

Time also influences other aspects of feeding behavior. Pandas select, prepare, and eat food without wasted motion, and they do so with a seeming urgency, biting rapidly, chewing little, forepaws often reaching for more before the last bite has been swallowed. They usually sit while foraging, able to harvest stems all around without much shifting, and they efficiently bring food to the mouth with their forepaws.

Some of the panda's morphological adaptations for recycling bamboo are well known. Such adaptations, most of them designed for processing stems, include the broad head with the wide, flat molars and posterior premolars built to crush stems; the dexterous forepaw with the enlarged radial sesamoid, which acts like a thumb to hold stems; and the sharply curved claws, used not for digging as in most bears but to hook in stems. The thick-walled pylorus of the stomach is "almost gizzard-like," as Davis (1964) called it, an adaptation for kneading the coarse contents. Natural selection operates on the entire body, not just a few specialized traits; the panda's large size, in fact, can be viewed as an adaptation to a low-nutrient stem diet for the following reasons:

1. Larger animals with a relatively low ratio of body surface to body volume have lower metabolic rates and lower food requirements per unit weight than do smaller animals (Moen 1973). With a lower metabolic rate, a larger animal can more easily subsist on a poor diet, such as bamboo stems.

2. The energy cost of level locomotion per unit weight is lower in large animals (Schmidt-Nielsen 1975). While large animals have a relatively lower cost than small ones, the absolute cost is higher; but to compensate for this an animal can reduce travel distances.

3. Larger nonruminants have a greater digestive capacity because of longer retention time (Van Soest 1982).

4. A large body size allows an animal access to resources, namely bamboo stems, that it would otherwise not be able to harvest and process.

5. Large body size increases an animal's capacity to store energy in the form of fat and to better withstand periods of deprivation (Bourlière 1979).

Since pandas in the wild have a diet of low quality, they probably cannot store nutrients in large amounts. Sheldon (1975) found no evidence of fat deposits in an adult female he shot on 8 December 1934. We autopsied a lactating female on 8 April

1983. She lacked subcutaneous fat, but there were deposits in the mesenteries (3.6 kg) and around the kidneys (0.5 kg), totaling 4.6% of her total body weight, a low figure. That pandas can store much fat is evident from obese zoo animals. With its relatively stable food supply, a panda might need reserves only for exceptional occasions, as when lactating or traveling in deep snow.

An animal living on a constant low-quality diet must be not only sparing in its energy expenditure but also careful how calories are allocated to meet conflicting demands. In a climate with cold winters, it is essential that energy is not wasted to conserve body heat. The panda's short, thick coat provides excellent insulation; the animal readily sleeps on snow. The density and oily texture of the hairs probably prevent moisture from penetrating to the skin, an important adaptation in a damp, cool environment. And the hairs have a springy quality; they are resistent to compaction, which reduces heat loss when the panda lies on snow or cold ground. A panda has, of course, only limited control over the energy it needs for temperature regulation and other body functions, but it can regulate many expenditures by adjusting behavior. From an ecological viewpoint, an important role of behavior "appears to be the saving of energy" (Bourlière 1979).

Inactivity being a major form of energy conservation, a panda spends an average of 41% of the day at rest. When an animal's basal metabolism is measured, the animal should ideally be lying down with an empty stomach at an equitable temperature. Although, in winter, a resting panda does need extra energy to digest food and keep warm, its expenditure then probably does not far exceed that needed for basal metabolism, especially when it lies curled up, legs tucked in, reducing its body surface to prevent convective heat loss.

A panda is active for about 59% of the day, a high percentage in view of, or rather because of, its low-quality food. Since a panda has to eat much bamboo at frequent intervals, its average activity level remains quite constant and above 50% during every month of the year, except for a drop in September. The daily cycle is characterized by much activity, usually above 50%, at all hours. Discarding slight seasonal variation, a panda is most active before and around dawn, followed by a drop until about 0900 hours, then a rise until dusk, and then another decline.

The black bear provides a striking contrast to the panda. It forages on a wide variety of berries, acorns, roots, and herbs (Poelker and Hartwell 1973; Eagle 1979)—foods rich in soluble carbohydrates and fats, and seasonally so abundant that the bear with little effort can consume enough extra calories daily to deposit large stores of fat. Although 80% or more of a bear's diet usually consists of plant material, an animal also eats whatever invertebrates and vertebrates it can obtain, both good sources of protein. With high-quality food available, activity levels are similar to those of the panda only from June to October and considerably lower during the other months (Quigley 1982), as shown in figure 7.3. Stored fat enables bears in the Great Smoky Mountains to hibernate from late December or early January until the first week of April (Johnson and Pelton 1980). The need to store winter fat does not deprive a bear of leisure during its daily routine: from 2200 to 0600, while a panda typically forages, a bear is usually at rest (fig. 7.3). Different foraging strategies

obviously resulted in different life styles in panda and bear. A similar comparison
between the bamboo-eating red panda and, for example, the omnivorous raccoon
might provide further insights on this topic.

We can postulate that a panda will use the most energy-expensive activites, in
terms of calories, most sparingly. Figure 7.4 presents the energy costs of several
activities to an adult panda. Although feeding and moving are essential to survival,

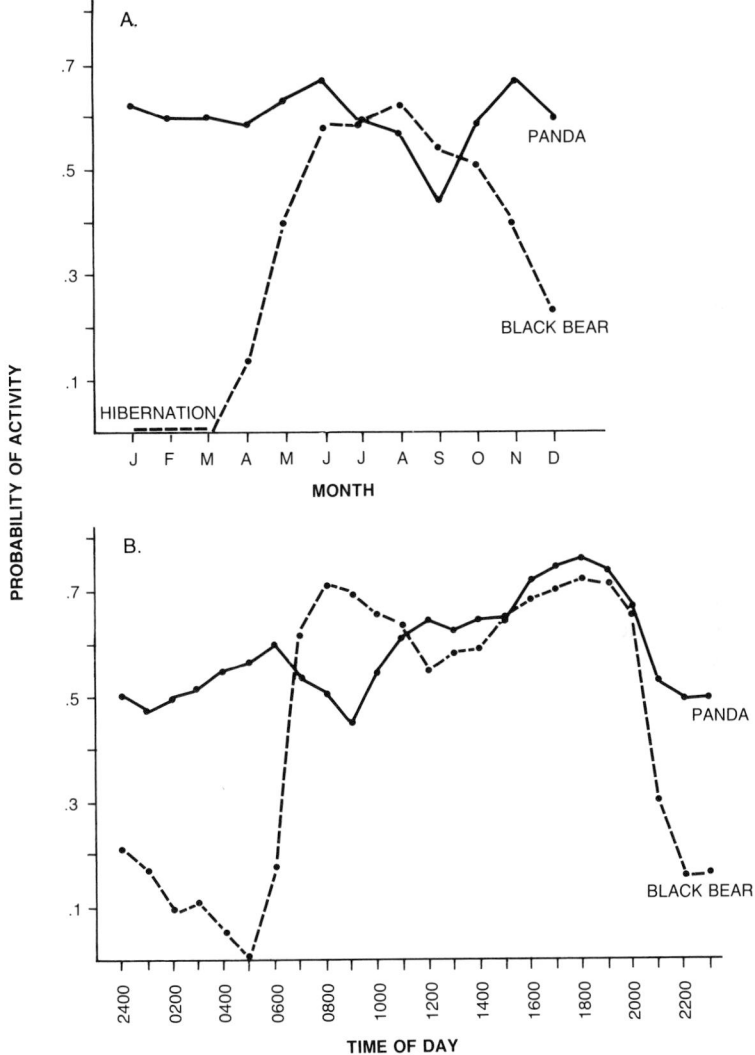

FIGURE 7.3   Probability of activity comparing black bear in the Great Smoky Mountains and
giant panda.   A. Activity by month.   B. Activity by time of day (spring and summer only).
Black bear data are from Quigley (1982).

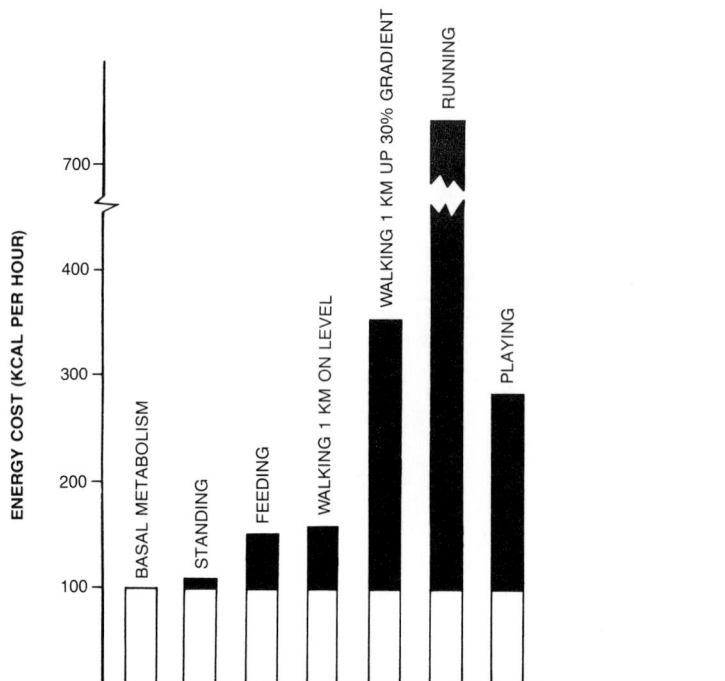

FIGURE 7.4   Energy costs of several activities to a 100 kg giant panda (calculations based on formulas in Moen, 1973).

costs can be reduced by, for instance, not climbing steep gradients. Running, the most costly of all activities, should be avoided, as should other vigorous actions such as playing and fighting. How does the panda conform to expectations?

FEEDING. A panda spends most of its active hours, or about 55% of the day, feeding, with some individuals devoting even more time on occasion. Ning's average activity in June 1981 was 74%, and Zhen's in November 1981 about 77%, most of it probably used to forage. Were a panda able to obtain meat—lean meat is 88% digestible (Graber 1982)—it would require only 2–3% of the day to feed, as is the case in polar bear and lion; instead, a panda's activity budget resembles that of zebra and other nonruminant herbivores, which, on an annual basis, spend more than 50% of the day foraging (table 5.6). Pandas can reduce the energy expenditure of feeding by saving time, both by what they select to eat and by the efficiency with which they eat it, as noted earlier.

TRAVELING. With food all around, a panda has little need to move far in search of it; indeed, animals either eat a swath through a thicket or shift only a few meters from one site to the next. Linear distances between consecutive daily radio locations were generally no more than 0.5 km (table 4.4), considerably less than the average of 2–3 km reported for black bear in Pennsylvania between April and October (Alt et al. 1980). Travel up a 30° gradient, a pitch not uncommon in the Choushuigou, expends about 4 times as much energy as travel on the level. An animal should avoid needless descents or ascents. In this context, it is significant that pandas foraged relatively little on slopes with gradients of more than 30°–40° even though bamboo often grows well there, and that Han and Zhen centered their activity on moderately sloping ridges and plateaus. Traveling pandas often follow ridge crests and contours, ambling along, except when disturbed. Tree climbing, which represents movement up a very steep gradient, is rare.

Home range size among mammals increases with metabolic needs and reflects the diet of the species (Gittleman and Harvey 1982). The ranges of pandas are relatively small, about 3.9–6.4 km², and overlap to varying degrees, animals of all ages and both sexes using certain areas communally. These ranges are larger than an animal needs to sustain itself nutritionally, even when the seasonal descent into *Fargesia* to eat new shoots is ignored. We calculated that the carrying capacity of optimum *Sinarundinaria* habitat was at least one animal per 0.5 km² during the period of study, one-third the actual density of one animal per 1.7 km². Wei's annual range was somewhat larger than the ranges of the two adult females, probably for social reasons: the more females within his range, the greater his chances of mating successfully in spring. On the whole, however, his travels were surprisingly circumscribed in spite of the fact that few females shared his range. A 2-hour walk would have taken him to the center of Han's range. Energetic limits on the number of females he can monitor may be one factor preventing such exploratory visits. Wei's range was 6.4 km², whereas the average of the two adult females was 4.7 km². Since home range size is related to body weight (Harestad and Bunnell 1979), part of this difference can be ascribed to sexual dimorphism. Males average about 1.2 times the weight of females (table 8.1), and Wei's range was about 1.4 times that of the two females, a small difference.

Black bear in the Great Smoky Mountains have a land tenure system similar to that of pandas. Adult males, females, and subadults share ranges, with overlap between female ranges considerably less than between male ranges. Animals shift seasonally to certain feeding areas, especially in autumn (Garshelis and Pelton 1981; Quigley 1982). With food resources dispersed and seasonal, bears must roam rather widely. But, even so, average female range size in one population was only 5.2 km², similar to that of pandas, and male size 32.1 km² (Quigley 1982); in another population, female range size was 15 km² and male 42 km² (Garshelis and Pelton 1981). In Pennsylvania, Alt et al. (1980) reported average ranges of 41 km² for females and 173 km² for males; and, in Alberta, Pelchat and Ruff (1983) noted ranges of 51 km² for females and 116 km² for males during a year when food was scarce. In general, male ranges are at least 2 to 3 times larger than female ranges, a situation different from that of the pandas we studied in spite of basic similarities in the land tenure systems.

SOCIALIZING. The panda is essentially solitary. With food quite evenly distributed and easy to harvest, an animal would not benefit nutritionally by having companions. Predators can be spotted more efficiently in open terrain by a group than by an animal alone, but no such benefit would accrue a panda in its bamboo thicket, and, besides, adults are virtually immune from predation. Young pandas will not lead a life in which adaptability and tradition are important requisites for survival; they need only the brief education of a mother, not that of a group. Ecological pressures have not encouraged togetherness.

Since social interactions are often costly in terms of energy, pandas regulate themselves with a minimum of direct contact. In order to monitor the activities of a neighbor, a panda has three options. It could use visual signals, but these are not practical in dense vegetation and at night, except at very close range, and they would involve much travel. It could use vocal signals, and it may in fact do so during the mating season, but sounds are transitory and must often be repeated, not only to keep information current but also to reach whatever panda might be within hearing distance. And it could use olfactory signals. Such signals have great advantages in that they are long-lasting and require only intermittent reinforcement. While olfactory signals cannot transmit emotional states with great subtlety, they can serve several functions, among them delineating ranges, preventing or initiating encounters, and providing information about individual identity and reproductive condition. The scent posts of pandas—with their scratches, glandular secretions, and urine marks—serve such functions, all accomplished with a minimum energy expenditure.

A panda can traverse its range in two hours or less. Such a range is small enough that it can, at least in part, be maintained as a territory, an area that all or certain other pandas are discouraged from entering. With bamboo abundant, it would be an energetic waste to defend a food supply. Females being sexually receptive for one short period in spring, it would not be adaptive for males to defend an area for a whole year to insure themselves priority of access. Instead, they depend mainly on olfactory signals to space themselves out and on asserting themselves should a competitive situation develop in the presence of an estrous female. The ranges of Zhen and Han overlapped only a little, each concentrating her activity within a relatively discrete core area, which males visited but other females and subadults usually did not; other adult females in the study area appeared to be spaced similarly. Males, by contrast, seemed to lack stable core areas; the ranges of several males may overlap almost completely. One potential limiting factor, one resource worth defending by a female, is a den site.

Black bear females in Minnesota apparently are territorial, chasing away intruding females but not males (Rogers 1977). Although the ranges of grizzly bear females in the Yukon overlap at certain seasons, the core areas are quite discrete (Pearson 1975). Land tenure is malleable, however, animals responding to local circumstances, to the availability of critical resources. Populations of the same species may or may not maintain exclusive ranges, as reported for female tigers (Sunquist 1981).

REPRODUCING. Female pandas appear to be exceptionally frugal in expending energy for reproduction. They do not conceive until they are 5.5 or 6.5 years old; courtship may take less than a day; implantation is delayed; and, after a short true gestation period, 1 or 2 tiny, altricial young are born—all at a very low nutritional cost to the mother (see chapter 8). One young out of a litter of 2 is often abandoned or at least does not survive the first weeks of life. It is no doubt difficult for a female to hold, suckle, and carry 2 young. Furthermore, lactation greatly increases the energy requirement of a female (Moen 1973). With a lowered feeding efficiency while transporting young and an additional energy drain due to lactation, it may not be adaptive for a female to care for two young during the six months or more until both are old enough to forage for themselves. To a panda, the birth of a second young usually represents little more than insurance at a very low premium in the event that the firstborn is not viable—a panda female tends to leave herself only one chance for success during the year. Although she has invested little energy if her young dies within a month after birth, she has lost one year of her reproductive life, an indication that the cost of raising twins may generally be too high.

Black bears have more reproductive flexibility and a higher reproductive potential than do pandas. Minimum breeding age varies throughout North America, and appears to be related to abundance and quality of food, which in turn has an impact on growth rate and onset of maturity. In areas of low food productivity, as in Montana, bears may not breed until an age of 6.5–7.5 years (Jonkel and Cowan 1971), whereas in areas with a good nutritional base, as in Pennsylvania, they usually conceive at 3.5–4.5 years, and even at 2.5 years (Alt 1982). Litter size varies from 1 to 5 with an average of 1.7 to 2.9, depending on the nutritional status of the population. Females aged 8 years or more generally have larger litters than do young females (Alt 1982). Mortality during the first 12 months of life is about 25–30% (Bunnell and Tait, in press). Well-nourished captive pandas have an average litter size of 1.7, similar to black bears from low-quality habitat, an indication of a low reproductive capacity. And, unlike a bear mother which commonly raises litters of 2 to 3 young, a panda usually attempts to raise only 1 young, an immediate mortality of 44%. We lack data on average litter size of pandas in the wild, but, if it is similar to that of captives, then total mortality during the panda's infancy may be considerable. With other losses, such as those experienced by Zhen in 1981, added to the 44%, possibly as few as one-third of the young born reach independence at 18 months. This translates into a reproductive success rate of about 1 young per female every 3 years, a figure lower than that for black bear but similar to that for some grizzly and polar bear populations (Bunnell and Tait 1981).

Selective processes have favored two broad reproductive strategies in animals. "K-strategists" have a low rate of increase and small litter size, and breed repeatedly during a long lifetime, all traits that promote population stability. They are best adapted to predictable climates and stable habitats. By contrast, "r-strategists" reproduce at an early age but sometimes only once or twice in a lifetime, and they have large litters and a short life. They are often found in unstable habitats where, by reproducing rapidly, they can take advantage of favorable but transitory situations (see Pianka 1980). Bamboo is frequently considered to be a successional or secondary growth, invading cultivated and burned areas (Wang 1961; Numata 1979). It also mass-flowers and dies at intervals, suggesting a rather unstable vegetation type favoring an r-strategy in an animal depending on it. Yet the panda is an extreme

K-strategist with little dietary and reproductive flexibility in times of environmental change. Kleiman (1983) speculated that it has only recently become an extreme K-strategist, and that in the past, when it occupied a wide variety of habitats and climates, it was a more opportunistic forager and reproductively more successful. While it is possible that the panda's reproductive season was more flexible in the past, attuned to local environmental conditions, as is true for many species, and that productivity was somewhat higher, if climate and food quality favored better young survival and a more frequent raising of twins, fossil remains give no indication that the panda's basic diet ever consisted of anything other than bamboo, much as today.

The question is not whether the panda was once less of a K-strategist but how it interacts with bamboo. Is bamboo mainly a secondary growth or is it part of the climax forest community? For each a different survival strategy in needed. If bamboo is primarily a secondary growth, the panda would in the past have had to depend on scattered food patches for sustenance with concomitant changes in many aspects of its behavior and in its energy budget; if bamboo is a common component of stable habitats, the panda would have had a widespread food source available and subsisted much as today. Bamboo unquestionably invades disturbed areas, such as landslips, and grows most densely in areas where the forest canopy has been opened, but it also exists in the interior of primary conifer and broad-leafed forests. For instance, in the Liang Mountains we made a transect at 1800 m in a stand of evergreen and deciduous broad-leafed forest composed of *Castanopsis, Lithocarpus*, and other trees. The stand had never been logged, canopy coverage was over 90%, and most trees were tall and massive, two-thirds of them over 50 cm DBH; once, much of the panda's lowland habitat must have resembled that forest. *Chimonobambusa szechuanensis*, 5–6 m tall, grew sparsely throughout the interior of the stand with an average density of two stems per m². Rather than define bamboo as a successional or primary forest component, it would be best to view it as disturbance-adapted—to use White's (1979) term—a component of forests in all successional stages. Panda habitat consists now, as it probably did in the past, of a dynamic mosaic of bamboo, with stands extensive or patchy, dense or open, homogeneous or composed of two or more species, flowering with variable synchrony at intervals, depending on soil conditions, canopy density, altitude, and other factors (see chapter 9). It is probable that the panda has always been an extreme K-strategist, investing little energy in reproduction. Only humankind has in the past 2000 years turned this successful adaptation into a liability.

The panda has reduced its energy expenditures to a minimum. It rests much, travels little, and rarely indulges in anything other than foraging. Leaving aside energy invested in reproduction and growth, what does it cost a panda in kilocalories to live each day? We calculated that the digestible energy in spring on a diet of *Sinarundinaria* is 4354 kcal/day, and on a diet of new *Fargesia* shoots it is 6741 kcal/day. Summer provided 5488 kcal/day and winter 5542 kcal/day. These are rough values, based on several assumptions, but they at least convey an order of magnitude. Given the characteristics of the panda's food supply and feeding strategy, it is not unexpected that caloric intake is relatively low and remains quite constant throughout the year.

To calculate energy expenditures we used Moen's (1973) formulas as presented in table 7.1. A 100 kg panda has a basal metabolism of 2214 kcal/day. Average annual resting and feeding times were used to derive costs, even though activity varies somewhat by season. Resting requires energy above basal metabolism. By using the formula for a standing animal we hoped to approximate the cost of resting. Because traveling may be an activity in itself or a part of foraging, we arbitrarily used 1 km per day in 1 hour, of which 40 minutes is on the level or downhill and 20 minutes up a 30% gradient. Other activities, such as scent marking, probably require no more energy than feeding. The total calculated energy cost is 3132 kcal/day or, expressed as a multiple of basal metabolism, 1.41. This represents the cost of maintenance to an average adult on an average day without extra travel, social contacts, or anything that disrupts the even tenor of life. Zhen foraging for unusually long hours in winter, or Wei cruising through his range in spring, would increase expenditures by several hundred kilocalories. Nor do our figures include energy needed for growth and reproduction. With such expenditures added, an adult may require at least 3500–4000 kcal/day.

The panda's average daily energy intake of 4300–5500 kcal/day, depending on season, is not much higher than the expenditure. The gap may be narrower than the calculations show, because we may, for example, have overestimated the amount of *Sinarundinaria* a panda consumes in spring. The evidence suggests that the panda's nutritional margin of safety is relatively narrow. Constrained by food quality and its digestive system, the animal can store only small amounts of fat to carry it through lean periods. Such periods may occur in spring for those animals that do not supplement the diet with new *Fargesia* shoots and, more drastically, for those whose bamboo mass-flowers and dies.

TABLE 7.1
ENERGY EXPENDITURE IN KCAL/DAY BY A 100 KG PANDA

Activity	Rate per hour[a]	Cost in kcal/hour above basal metabolism	No. hours activity/day	Total activity cost in kcal/day
Basal metabolism	$(70)(W_{kg}^{0.75})/24$	0	24	2214
Resting	$(70)(W_{kg}^{0.75})(1.1)/24$	9	9.8	88
Feeding	$(0.54)(W_{kg})$	54	13.2	713
Traveling		90	1.0	
		(.66 hour on level .33 on gradient)	(0.5 while feeding 0.5 travel only)	
.7 km on level or down	$(0.59)(W_{kg})(Dkm)$			27
.3 km up 30% gradient	(sum of walking) + $(6.45)(W_{kg})(Dkm)$			63
Other	(as feeding)	54	(while traveling)	27
Total				3132

[a]Formulas based on Moen (1973).

Many bears have opted for a foraging strategy that is dependent on a nutritional boom-or-bust economy. They stuff themselves on a variety of high-energy but seasonal foods, storing as much fat as they can in times of plenty, then hibernating during seasons of scarcity. In one day of feeding, a bear may consume 20,000 kcal, enough extra to provide it with at least 5 days of energy during hibernation (Nelson 1980). With their food unpredictable and transitory, bears have responded by being opportunistic and adaptable, evolving a life style that has enabled them to settle in many habitats on several continents.

The panda, by contrast, has become a specialist; dependent on a low-quality but constant and abundant food source, it has chosen security over uncertainty. Its mode of life gives the impression of being a durable triumph of evolution. But by losing its sense of struggle, its curiosity, its need to explore and be observant and try something new, by tying itself to a fate without horizon, it has become defenseless, it has lost the adaptability that it now must have to survive.

Summary

1. One of the basic questions this study has tried to answer is how the panda is adapted to bamboo. Pandas have specialized on a plant resource available in unlimited amounts at all seasons. But this has created 3 related nutritional problems for the animal: (a) it cannot digest bamboo efficiently because it lacks the microbes to break down cellulose; (b) it obtains a low nutritional return for the amount eaten; and (c) it obtains nutrients mainly from cell content. To subsist, it must have developed an efficient feeding strategy. Limited by the capacity of its digestive tract and rate of food passage, a panda must be selective in what it eats. It generally selects the most nutritious bamboo parts, it eats rapidly with little wasted motion, saving time and energy, and it passes food quickly and little altered through the tract, enabling it to eat much bulk. With a diet low in nutrients, a panda cannot eat enough to accumulate large fat deposits, in contrast to a bear, whose food is so rich it can store sufficient energy to survive several months of hibernation. The panda's large size can be viewed as an adapation to a low-quality stem diet, from the perspective both of energetics and of the animal's physical ability to handle such food.

2. To conserve energy, a panda must use calory-expensive activities sparingly. It prefers, for example, to travel over moderate terrain rather than up and down steep slopes, and it uses scent to communicate rather than involve itself in direct social interactions. Males conserve energy by not defending territorial boundaries and remaining within small ranges. A female is an extreme K-strategist, investing little energy in reproduction.

3. The basal metabolism of a 100 kg panda is 2214 kcal/day. Other activities, as well as energy used for growth and reproduction, may raise total expenditure to at least 3500–4000 kcal/day. Average daily intake was 4300–5500 kcal/day. Although these figures are only estimates, they do show that an animal's nutritional margin of safety is quite narrow.

8

The Giant Panda—
Bear or Raccoon?

In 1869, Père David gave the giant panda the scientific name *Ursus melanoleucus* on the assumption that the animal belonged in the bear family, the Ursidae. The following year, Milne-Edwards (1870), after examining David's material, concluded that the panda's bones and teeth were certainly not those of a bear but related to those of raccoons, the Procyonidae, a family of New World origin containing such animals as the raccoon, coati, kinkajou, olingo, and ringtail (fig 8.1). That same year, Gervais (1870) decided after studying the braincase that the panda was a bear. He was followed by Mivart (1885), who asserted that the panda was really allied to raccoons, and by Bardenfleth (1913), who, on the basis of studying teeth, placed the panda with the bears. Raven (1936) examined viscera and found that these were similar to those of raccoons, any resemblance to bears being "an expression of convergence in size and food habits." After studying the comparative anatomy of the panda in detail, Davis (1964) concluded: "Every morphological feature examined indicated that the giant panda is nothing more than a highly specialized bear . . . of this there can be no reasonable doubt." But, as Ewer (1973) noted, Davis "appears simply to brush aside the features which do not support this opinion"; Davis's (1964) monograph therefore did little to settle the controversy. We have not listed all players in this game of taxonomic ping-pong, but it is obvious that traditional systematics based on gross anatomical structures cannot decide the affinities of the giant panda; in any case, the animal cannot be forcefully relegated either to the raccoons or to the bears.

The controversy inextricably links the giant and the red pandas. "There is little doubt that, if the red panda had occurred in South America instead of in Asia, it would be regarded as a somewhat aberrant procyonid, with teeth adapted to an unusually specialized vegetarian diet" (Ewer 1973). The red panda's resemblance to the procyonids was recognized by Milne-Edwards (1870) and influenced his decision to place the giant panda in the same family, for the similarities between the two—especially in tooth structure—are obvious. Later, adherents of this view placed the two in the subfamily Ailurinae of the family Procyonidae, whereas opponents left the red panda with the raccoons and moved the giant panda into the family Ursidae.

At the heart of the controversy lies a fundamental evolutionary problem in systematics, that of deciding whether a similarity indicates phylogenetic relationship or convergence. The theory of natural selection unfortunately does not discriminate between the two. The giant panda looks like a bear, about that there is no disagreement; but the basic question remains whether it is a bear pure and simple, or whether the animal's many similarities to a bear are due to its having grown large, its size requiring such structural supports as heavy legs. The skull and teeth, together with the forepaws, present a specialized functional unit, evolved to process bamboo. Again, there is no argument that giant and red pandas resemble each other. The raccoon school claims relationship, the bear school convergent evolution based on similarity of diet. The problem resolves itself into two questions: (1) How closely are giant and red pandas related to each other? and (2) how closely are the two pandas related either to raccoons or to bears?

Each school of thought can point to specific features to reinforce its claims. The bear school stresses the giant panda's bearlike body proportions and such details of resemblance to bears as the brain, ear ossicles, and respiratory tract (Thenius 1979). The raccoon school counters with the fact that the giant panda's skeleton is unusually heavy-boned, giving "the impression of being the skeleton of a 'fake' bear" (Morris and Morris 1966) only recently and rapidly evolved, without refinements. If the giant panda is merely a bear adapted to eat bamboo, why has the whole skeleton been modified, rather than just forepaws and skull? Although the red panda, with its ringed tail and small size, superficially resembles a procyonid, it would require little to transform it into a miniature giant panda: change the rust-red coat to white and shorten the tail (Morris and Morris 1966). Both pandas are stoutly built and walk with toes turned in—the red panda, like the bears, forepaws only, and the giant panda all paws. One feature shared by the two pandas is the shape of the penis, short, S-curved, and directed posteriorly. The giant and the red panda also grip and pluck bamboo leaves in much the same way with a morphologically similar forepaw, except that the former has devoloped a large pseudothumb, an elaboration on the basic hand pattern that enables the animal to handle bamboo stems efficiently. The bears and the procyonids also have paws well adapted, each in its own way, to handling food, but all differ markedly from those of pandas. Morphologically the giant panda is obviously linked to two rather unspecialized lineages, the ursids and the procyonids, as well as to the specialized red panda. In addition, it has several puzzling features, among them the rhinarium or nose pad, which resembles that of cats (Davis 1973).

Molecular studies in recent years have provided additional information on the systematic position of pandas. Since protein macromolecules are an integral part of DNA, they closely reflect the hereditary and hence evolutionary history of an organism. The number of differences between the amino acids of any two proteins should, it was reasoned, be proportional to the time elasped since they diverged from a common ancestor. This is a potentially powerful method for reconstructing phylogenies, because, freed from environmental impact, molecular evolution seems regular enough to be used as a "molecular clock," one that provides precise information about the amount of genetic change (Ayala 1982).

FIGURE 8.1   The giant panda with its relatives, showing three members of the raccoon family (Procyonidae), one member of the bear family (Ursidae), and the red panda. Top row: ringtail (left), raccoon (right). Second row: red panda (left), coati (right). Third row: giant panda. Bottom row: American black bear.

"The serological affinities of the giant panda are with the bears rather than the raccoons," concluded Leone and Wiens (1956). Using advanced immunological techniques, Sarich (1976) compared two giant panda blood proteins—albumin and transferrin—to those of bears, raccoons, and red panda. In this method, albumins and transferrins of a species are injected into rabbits, producing antibodies, which then react strongly against the proteins for which they were prepared and progressively more weakly against proteins in species more distantly related. Sarich's (1976) results seen in figure 8.2 show that "the association of the Giant Panda and other bears is clear and unequivocal . . . The one rather unexpected result there is the fact that the Lesser Panda, *Ailurus*, does not group with the other procyonids," that it seems to have started a separate lineage before the giant panda and bears. Similarly, Pan et al. (1981) found that the giant panda is serologically closer to the Asiatic black bear than to the red panda.

The diploid chromosome number in giant panda is 42, in red panda 36, in procyonids 38, and in all bears 74, except for the spectacled bear with 52 (Ewer 1973). Such numbers must be used with caution in drawing taxonomic conclusions, for centric fusion and karyotypic fission can alter chromosome numbers; but it is noteworthy that pandas resemble procyonids more than they resemble bears in this respect. Looking at the pattern of heterochromatin banding in chromosomes, Wurster-Hill and Bush (1980) concluded that the giant panda belongs neither with the bears nor with the raccoons, and that "the giant panda diverged from primitive carnivore stock earlier than the lesser panda, the canids, the viverrids, and the procyonids," and contend that the giant panda should be placed "either in a family alone or with the lesser panda."

And so the confusion continues. One problem is that single characters, whether chromosome banding or tooth cusp structure, may not provide a sufficient basis for reconstructing the past of an animal, especially one that may in certain features have remained conservative and in others not. For example, Seal et al. (1970) suggested on the basis of albumin sera analysis that bears have an "immediate procyonid

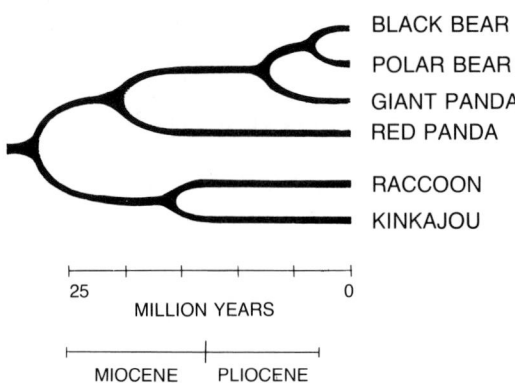

FIGURE 8.2 The phylogeny of Ursidae, Procyonidae, and pandas, based on immunological analyses of albumin and transferrin in blood serum. (After Sarich 1976.)

ancestry," which, if true, would certainly simplify the interpretation of the systematic position of the giant panda. The fossil evidence, however, indicates that the Ursidae evolved from the Canidae.

The modern families of carnivores comprise two assemblages, derived from the Miacidae in the Eocene, one including the Felidae, Hyaenidae, and Viverridae, and the other the Mustelidae, Procyonidae, Canidae, and Ursidae. Of the latter, the canids and mustelids had already appeared in the late Eocene and early Oligocene. The Procyonidae developed in North America probably from canid stock in the early Oligocene (Kurtén 1971); the modern genus *Bassariscus* was already present by the late Miocene and the other genera had appeared by the Pliocene. Some procyonids penetrated Asia via the Bering land bridge and extended their range to Europe, where, in the Miocene, the raccoonlike *Sivanasua* was found (Thenius 1979). The bears also represent a branch of the Canidae, appearing in the early Miocene in the form of *Ursavus*, a bearlike animal the size of a dog or fox, whose descendants in the Old World—*Ursus minimus* of the Pliocene and *Ursus etruscus* of the Pleistocene—increased in size until they resembled a present-day brown bear. A bear similar to *Ursus etruscus* occurred in China and probably gave rise to the Asiatic black bear (Kurtén 1968).

The two pandas unfortunately do not appear in the palaeontological record until the Pleistocene. *Parailurus*, however, a small panda related to today's red panda, occurred in the early Pliocene in central and southern Europe (Thenius 1979), as well as in North America (Tedford and Gustafson 1977). *Parailurus anglicus* persisted into the Pleistocene in Europe, where it was quite common in the temperate forests at a time when procyonids, once widespread, appear to have vanished from that continent. Fossils of modern red panda have been discovered in mid-Pleistocene beds of Yunnan (Kurtén 1968). On the basis of tooth morphology, Thenius (1979) suggested that *Agriarctos*, a small, bearlike animal of *Ursavus* lineage from the mid-Miocene in Europe, was ancestral to the giant panda. And Hendey (1980) considered the giant panda to be the only surviving member of the subfamily Agriotheriinae, family Ursidae (fig. 8.3).

A detailed discussion concerning possible taxonomic affinities of the giant panda can be found in Davis (1964), Morris and Morris (1966), Chu (1974), Goodwin (1976), and Thenius (1979), among others. Suffice it to say that on the basis of anatomical, biochemical, and palaeontological evidence the animal's systematic position remains equivocal. Behavioral observations can provide useful insights into evolutionary relationships, as Morris and Morris (1966) first tried to show for the giant panda. Unless a behavior pattern is under strong selection pressure, it may persist even after an animal's habitat has changed and morphological characters have been modified. However, species living in similar habitats may evolve similar societies and similar physical structures, which, in turn, may promote the appearance of similar behavior patterns without there being a close relationship. When comparing giant panda with red panda, bears, and raccoons, one must decide, first, which aspects correlate with ecological conditions, and second, which traits the giant panda shares with other species.

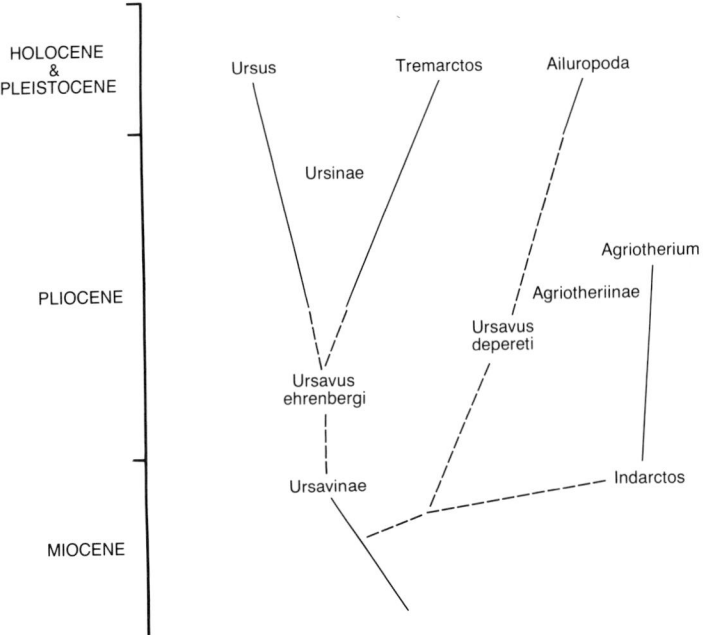

FIGURE 8.3   Hendey's (1980) suggested relationship among Ursidae, including the giant panda, based on morphological studies of fossils.

To compare the entire behavioral repertoire of all bears and procyonids with those of the two pandas is beyond the scope of this report. We have, therefore limited ourselves to describing certain similarities and differences of a few species. Among bears, we selected the black bear and the grizzly, species with different habitat preferences, the former being a forest dweller and the latter essentially an animal of open country (Herrero 1978). Among procyonids, we selected the solitary, nocturnal raccoon and the social, diurnal coati, both comparable in size to the red panda. Details concerning small procyonids—kinkajou (3.0 kg), olingo (1.2 kg), and ringtail (.8 kg)—can be found in the papers of Poglayen-Neuwall (1962, 1965, 1967, 1976a, 1976b, 1980).

Ecological conditions may have an influence on behavior patterns, on some more than on others. For instance, food availability affects feeding strategy, which in turn has an impact on movements, activity cycles, and social systems. Consequently, two populations of the same species may behave differently (see chapter 7). Such malleability makes comparisons between species difficult. Reproduction and communication are variable traits too, responding to the exigencies of habitat, climate, and other factors. For example, raccoons have, on the average, larger litters in the northern United States than in the southern (Rabinowitz 1981). And the length of winter dormancy in bears varies considerably; in one species, the polar bear, it is mainly pregnant females that enter dens, others often failing to hibernate (Harrington 1968). However, some patterns, such as courtship postures, scent marking, and vocalizations can function in a wide variety of conditions; we therefore presume that ecological pressures have had a less immediate impact on them. Here we compare only certain aspects of giant panda reproduction and communication with those of other species.

Comparisons between any such large mammal as the giant panda and such small mammal as the red panda can be made only if the consequences of certain consistent trends in evolution are taken into account. Length of life is correlated with body size, large animals living longer, and inversely correlated with metabolic rate, small mammals with a high rate having a short life span. With an increase in longevity there is generally a decrease in relative milk production, litter size, and weight of litters, and an increase in development time of young and in interval between births. These factors then affect the lifetime productivity of a female (Eisenberg 1981).

Reproduction

Table 8.1 compares certain aspects of reproduction of the giant panda with those of selected bears and procyonids and the red panda. In addition, several topics need elaboration.

Size dimorphism

Size dimorphism is the expected result of reproductive competition in polygynous mating systems, the male usually being larger than the female. Dimorphism in adult bears is relatively large, the male being, on the average, at least 36% heavier in polar bears, 34–38% in grizzlies, and 29–41% in black bears (table 8.1). Bunnell and Tait (1981) have shown that in some bear populations males may even be 60–100% heavier than females. By comparison, sex dimorphism in giant panda is about 18%, in red panda 8%, and in raccoon 17%; for coati the figure is 34%, probably reflecting a high incidence of male aggression in social groups. While not much emphasis can be placed on these differences, the giant panda shows much less dimorphism than do the bears.

Courtship and mating

So far as is known, the giant panda is monoestrus, although it is possible that some females have an autumn heat if they fail to conceive in spring. Raccoons may ovulate a second time after 80–140 days (Sanderson and Nalbandov 1973). Some red panda pairs copulate 15–21 days apart, suggesting a second estrus period (Roberts and Kessler 1979); and the grizzly may have two periods 4–18 days apart (Pearson 1975).

A male giant panda usually mounts in a squat behind the female, his forelegs resting stiffly on her back; he may also lean over and mouth her. Males of other carnivore species generally clasp the female on the sides or pelvic region with the forelegs and rest the neck and head near her shoulders. A black bear male may bite the female in the neck during copulation (Ludlow 1976), whereas raccoon (Stains 1956) and red panda males (Roberts and Kessler 1979) apparently do not. During copulation, the female giant panda crouches, her back either flat or arched, and

TABLE 8.1

SOME COMPARISONS BETWEEN PANDAS, PROCYONIDS, AND BEARS

	Giant panda	Red panda	Raccoon	Coati	Black Bear	Grizzly bear
Av. weight/kg	male 118 female 97 (captive)	male 6.2 female 5.7 (captive)	male 4.2 female 3.5 (Tenn.)	male 6.4 female 4.2 (Arizona)	male 124 female 89(NY) male 98 female 58(Cal)	male 143 female 95(Yukon) male 245 female 152(Wyoming)
Approx. maximum longevity (years)	30	13	17	15	32	34
Main activity period	Diurnal-nocturnal	Crepuscular-nocturnal	Nocturnal	Diurnal	Diurnal-nocturnal	Diurnal-nocturnal
Winter dormancy	no	no	yes	no	yes	yes
Sexual maturity (months)	66–78	18–20	male 14–22 female 10–22	male 24 female 20	30–78	66–90
Mating season	March–May	Jan.–Feb.	Feb.–April	Jan.–April	June–July	May–July
Female peak receptivity (days)	1–3	1–3	1–3	—	4	—
Duration of mount (min.)	0.6 (0.2–2.5)	23.3 (2–39)	75 (6–130)	.08	0.5–29	4–43
Gestation period (days)	135 (97–163)	131 (90–145)	63–66	70–77	235 ±	235 ±
Delayed implantation	yes	yes(?)	no	no	yes	yes
Usual type of nest	hollow tree; rock cave	hollow tree	hollow tree; ground cavity	tree nest of branches; rock cave	hollow tree; ground cavity	ground cavity
Birth season	Aug.–Sept.	June–July	April–June	March–June	Jan.–Feb.	Jan.–Feb.
Birth weight (g)	104 (75–170)	118	62	100–180	294 (255–362)	632 (510–680)

	1.7 (1–3)	1.7 (1–4)	3.4 (1–7)	3–5	1.7–2.9 (1–5)	1.7–2.5 (1–4)
Av. litter size						
Young open eyes (days)	40–48	17–18	18–20	4–8	28–40	21±
Pairs of nipples	2	2	3	3	3	3
Young first emerge from den (days)	— (carried by female)	88	50–70	40	80–120	90–120
Complete nutritional dependence on female (weeks)	30±	14	8–10	7	22	24
Weaning (weeks)	46±	20	14–16	16	30+	82+
Social independence of young (months)	18	8	6–12	24 (males only)	17–18	17–29+

Sources
Giant panda: this study.
Red panda: Roberts (1975); Roberts and Kessler (1979); Roberts 1981.
Coati: Kaufmann (1962); Gilbert (1973).
Raccoon: Rabinowitz (1981); Stuewer (1943); Montgomery (1969); Garrett and Goertz (1975); Schneider et al. (1971); Ricard and Dore (1977).
Bears: Crandall (1964); Schoonmaker (1968); Ludlow (1976); Matson (1954); Murie (1981); Pearson (1975); Piekielek (1973); Hamilton (1978); Rogers (1977); Craighead et al. (1969); Craighead et al. (1976); Butterworth (1969); Hamer et al. (1977); Bunnell and Tait (1981).

often tucks her head in so that the top rests on the ground; this head position is reminiscent of that of red panda: "she stood with hindquarters elevated, forequarters and head depressed to the ground, back arched" (Roberts and Kessler 1979).

These and other patterns reveal little concerning the giant panda's systematic position. Why is mounting generally prolonged except in coati, which copulates within 5 seconds, and in the giant panda, which mounts briefly but often? Why do males and females of most of these species court, mate, and part within minutes or hours, whereas a grizzly male may become the female's consort for 2–3 weeks (Murie 1981)?

Bears are induced ovulators, procyonids are spontaneous ovulators (Ewer 1973), and the situation in pandas remains unknown, although evidence suggests that ovulation is spontaneous.

Delayed implantation and dormancy

Reproduction is influenced by ecological conditions, specifically by the level of nutrition available to mother and young at various seasons, an important factor in tropical as well as temperate environments. For example, coatis in Panama rear young during the dry season when fruit, a main food, is most abundant (Kaufman 1962). Two conspicuous and related traits of bears in temperate climates are delayed implantation and winter dormancy. Nutritious plant food is scarce when bears emerge from hibernation and the animals lose weight. But from June to October there are berries, acorns, and other concentrated energy sources that enable bears to deposit fat rapidly, 0.4–1.0 kg or more per day in black bear (Jonkel and Cowan 1971). Then, sometime between October and December, when food becomes unavailable and weather deteriorates, bears enter dens and remain in them for 90 days or more, up to 220 days in some Yukon grizzlies (Pearson 1975). Dormant bears do not eat, drink, defecate, or urinate. Heart rate decreases, body temperature drops somewhat, metabolic activity is reduced by about 25%. For several months, bears live entirely on their stored fat reserves. Fat produces not only the most energy in terms of Kcal/g but also the most water. Combustion of fat furnishes energy for metabolism as well as metabolic water for maintaining blood and other fluid levels. The bear's muscle mass remains constant, for urea, a metabolic waste, is hydrolyzed and the nitrogen combined with glycerol to form amino acids needed for tissue formation (Nelson 1973). These adaptations for conserving energy are extraordinary, especially in view of the fact that the bear does not sleep deeply but remains alert enough to give birth and care for its offspring. The bear emerges from its den in March or April at least 25% lighter.

One can speculate on the advantages of this system in terms of the nutritional demand made on the female by her offspring. To store enough fat to survive dormancy, a female needs an unencumbered late summer and autumn for feeding, something a June mating period provides. If a fetus began to grow normally in June, it would be born prior to winter denning, an unsuitable situation; if a female gave birth to precocial young, they would be born during denning, but, being larger, their milk demands might create an excessive energy drain on the female. It may also be important for young to be born early in the year so that the female is partly relieved of the stress of lactation in time to fatten up for the following winter. And the young, too, have energy-rich food available at that time. That ample fat deposits may be essential to the survival of young in a species with dormancy was shown by Mech et al. (1968), who found that young raccoons often died from starvation during long winters. Thus, a June mating with delayed implantation and a winter birth of altricial young seems a good nutritional strategy for a female bear. Whether our reasoning applies to tropical bears, which do not hibernate but still give birth to altricial young, remains to be investigated. It is possible that altricial young in such species as the sun bear represent a conservative trait in a family whose origin was in a temperate environment (Ewer 1973).

Giant pandas resemble bears in their delayed implantation and highly altricial young, although the two differ in the duration of the blastocyst stage, the season of fetal growth, and relative size of newborn (table 8.1). Procyonids and the red panda give birth to heavy young in relation to female weight, bears to light young, and the giant panda to such light young that they are proportionately the smallest of all eutherian mammals (table 8.2).

Having a constant food supply, giant pandas lack a need to become dormant in winter; thus the speculations we advanced to account for the altricial state of bear young do not apply to this species. If it is accepted that birth seasons tend to coincide with an abundance of nutritious food to pay for the high energy cost of lactation, a possible explanation for the giant panda's reproductive cycle exists. As noted in chapter 3, the giant panda has a diet fairly low in nutrients, and these fluctuate little during the year. Limited by the time required to collect and eat its food and the rate

TABLE 8.2

FEMALE/NEWBORN WEIGHT RATIOS AND WEIGHT GAIN OF YOUNG DURING GESTATION AND LACTATION IN PANDAS AND SELECTED PROCYONIDS AND URSIDS

	Female/ newborn weight ratio	Weight gain of young in g per day					
		During gestation[a]			During lactation[c]		
		1 yg.	Litter size	Index[b]	1 yg.	Litter size	Index[b]
Giant panda	1/933	2.3	2	.005	78.8	1	.08
Red panda	1/48	1.7	2	.060	12.2	2	.43
Raccoon	1/56	1.0	3	.086	15.6	3	1.34
Coati	1/30	1.9	3	.136		3	
Black bear	1/193–297	4.9	2	.012–.017	58.0	2	.13–.20
Grizzly bear	1/152–244	9.6	2	.013–.020		2	
Polar bear	1/311	8.7	2	.010	120.2	2	.14

Based on sources in table 8.1 and also on Stirling et al. (1977); Stickley (1957); Jonkel and Cowan (1971); Seitz (1973).

[a]Assumed actual gestation of 45 days for giant panda, 60 days for black bear, 65 days for grizzly and polar bear, and 70 days for red panda.

[b]Index: $\dfrac{\text{Weight gain of litter in g/day}}{\text{Female weight}} \times 100.$

[c]Measured to end of complete nutritional dependence on female when giant panda weighs 18 kg, red panda 1.4 kg, raccoon 1 kg, black bear 9 kg, polar bear 15 kg.

of passage through the digestive tract, the panda cannot increase consumption to a level where it would deposit the large fat stores needed for dormancy. Given a low but fairly constant energy intake, it would seem that energy output must also remain low during gestation and lactation. This can be achieved by small litter size and slow development of young. The growth rate of the fetus and of the nutritionally dependent young provide a relative measure of the energy drain to which a female is subjected. As shown in table 8.2, the average daily weight gain of a giant panda fetus is similar to that of the red panda and procyonids rather than that of bears. Since the giant panda female is so large, compared to the others, her energy investment in her one or two fetuses is extremely small. The growth rate in g/day of a giant panda young during lactation is quite high, more similar to that of bears than to that of red panda and raccoon. Since a female usually raises only one young, instead of 2 or 3, however, her total investment remains low (table 8.2). A giant panda female stops lactating before her offspring is a year old, whereas a bear mother may provide supplementary milk for 1.5 and even 2.5 years (Murie 1981). It is not clear why bears provision young for so long, for food finding does not require much parental guidance except in polar bear; perhaps the extra milk insures a nutritional base for the rapidly growing young, which otherwise might not be able to store enough fat for dormancy. Early complete weaning by a giant panda female reduces the energy cost of rearing young.

Although the selective value of seasonal reproduction in the giant panda still needs explanation, our comments on this point, based on research in the Choushuigou, may not be applicable to the animal's whole range. Mating occurs in spring, when pandas subsist either on bamboo stem low in nutrients or on new shoots high in nutrients. Females give birth in August and September, when they forage almost wholly on bamboo leaves, which at that time are both palatable and nutritious. For the first month of a newborn's life, the female remains around her den, a period when she needs an abundant, easily available, and nutritious food source. Leaves represent such a source. Being born in early autumn, the young has time to grow a thick coat before cold weather begins.

We do not know why giant pandas have a delay in implantation, why selection favored a March–May rather than May–July mating season. The amount of daylight controls time of implantation in various carnivores (Sadleir 1969); if true for giant panda, this would account for the discrete birth season. Delayed implantation may be of advantage to a species in allowing flexibility, with growth of the blastocyst adapting to latitudinal and possible nutritional factors. During the Pleistocene, when pandas extended over at least 16° of latitude, such flexibility may have been important. For example, the tropical sun bear has a gestation period of only 95 days (Dathe 1970), the blastocyst apparently implanting soon after conception, quite unlike the 5-month delay in temperate bears. It may be significant that the delay in implantation occurs during the season when the panda's food is of low quality and the animal obtains fewer nutrients in terms of kcal/day than at any other time of the year; implantation occurs at nutritionally the most favorable time. If a female's food quality were for some reason to remain low, the blastocyst might fail to implant, preventing the energy drain of an undesirable pregnancy.

The red panda's bamboo diet resembles that of the giant panda rather than that of the more omnivorous bears and procyonids. The mating season is in January and February, earlier than that of giant panda. Since gestation lengths, including probable delayed implantation, are remarkably similar in the two pandas in spite of differences in body size, the birth season of the red panda is earlier too, in June and July (Roberts and Kessler 1979). Although these reproductive data are based on captives, they appear to apply to wild animals in Sichuan as well. The fact that the two pandas have different reproductive cycles in the same area while dependent on the same food source indicates different energy budgets. Red panda young become nutritionally independent of their mother in September, when bamboo leaves are still tender and have a high protein content. They are fully weaned at the onset of winter, ceasing at that time to be an energy drain on the female, a strategy similar to that of raccoons. The red panda resembles the giant panda, as well as the kinkajou (Poglayen-Neuwall 1962), in having only 1–2 young per litter. As noted, the weight gain of fetus and lactating young is similar to that of procyonids, in spite of a bamboo leaf diet, suggesting that the female may mobilize body reserves to ensure rapid prenatal and postnatal growth.

What conclusions can be drawn from these facts and suppositions? From large size and consequently decreased metabolic rate one expects a long gestation period and precocial young, especially in an animal with a predictable food source (Eisenberg 1981). The bears present an exception to this trend, which we attempted to explain in terms of great seasonal fluctuations in food availability and energy demands on the female. The giant panda is another exception, but the same reasoning cannot be applied, indicating that the similar traits are the result of different selection pressures. The red panda resembles the giant panda in some aspects and the procyonids in others. Its altricial young and short true gestation period are typical of mammals with relatively small body size, whereas its probable delayed implantation and litter size are like those of giant panda. In general, the giant panda's reproductive strategy seems more typical of a small mammal than of a large one; it resembles that of an overgrown red panda but with certain emendations related to body size. For example, the long developmental time and extended period of care required by a young extends lactation into the next mating season, which interferes with ovulation, precluding annual reproduction. Thus, the basic reproductive strategy of bears may represent an adaptation to a seasonal food supply and winter dormancy, whereas that of the giant panda may indicate a conservative condition, retained from a small, pandalike ancestor. This conclusion takes into account the fact that leaf eaters tend to have a depressed metabolic rate, regardless of body size, and with it a shortening of the gestation period, a reduction in litter size, and slow postnatal development (Eisenberg 1981). Assuming that pandas do have a relatively low metabolism, diet could have an influence on the similarities between the two species but could not explain the extent of these similarities.

Maternal care

Female pandas, bears, and procyonids are alike in selecting a cavity or other retreat for giving birth to altricial young. These are raised by the female without paternal assistance, except perhaps in the ringtail (Poglayen-Neuwall 1980). A giant panda female may build a nest of branches in the maternal den. Similarly, red panda collect branches and leaves (Roberts 1975); and black bear may break off and drag in branches, rake in leaves, and claw the walls of tree dens, adding debris as bedding material (Johnson 1978). The giant panda is unique in that it holds its infant in its forepaws for much of the time during the first weeks of life, an adaptation providing warmth and protection. Red panda and procyonid young do not require constant maternal attendance because dens tend to be less exposed to weather and less accessible to predators than those of giant pandas, and the young are quite furred. Still, a red panda female remains close to her young for the first 10 days, leaving them mainly to eat, drink, and defecate (Roberts 1975). Bear mothers are constantly with their young in the winter den; "she keeps them warm by lying on her side with her hindlegs well forward, forelegs, head and neck over the hindlegs" (Matson 1954). Dens must remain clean: a black bear female licks her young to stimulate defecation and then eats the emerging feces (Alt 1977), much as does a red panda (Roberts 1981), giant panda, and many other carnivore females. A giant panda typically sits and holds her young to her chest for suckling, rarely assuming any other position for the first months after birth. Other species may lie, sit or stand to suckle their young, depending on circumstances. Among polar bears, "by the time the cubs are a month old and their eyes are open, the mother assumes a sitting position while feeding them. Placing the cubs between her hindlegs, she holds them to her breast with her large forepaws" (Harrington 1968).

Milk composition is important in determining growth rates of young and energy cost to the female. Bear milk has 22–33% fat, 11–15% protein, and 0.3–0.6% carbohydrates (Jenness et al. 1972), in contrast to that of raccoons, for which the figures are 3.9% fat, 4.0% protein, and 4.7% carbohydrates (Ewer 1973). No analysis of giant panda milk has been published, but a secretion from the mammary gland of London's Chi-Chi at death had a composition of 24.5% fat, 14.5% protein, and 0.4% carbohydrate (Lyster 1976)—figures similar to the fat- and protein-rich milk of bears. However, since milk composition may change considerably during lactation, figures such as these cannot be used to make wholly valid comparisons.

Communication

To be efficient, communication should involve minimum energy expenditure by the sender while achieving maximum response by the receiver (Wilson 1975). With this premise, one might argue that communicatory patterns would tend to be conservative in evolution, for there is little selective pressure to change them much as long as they signal messages unambiguously to another member of the species. On the one hand, this conservative pattern should make them particularly suitable for tracing relationships, but, on the other, such relationships might be obscured by the widespread nature of conservative traits within a taxonomic unit. Furthermore, a mammal has only a few options of expressing itself, given a basic morphological plan. The fact that, for example, pandas, bears, and cats swat aggressively with a forepaw reveals little of their phylogenetic affinities. Although other factors also influence the form and use of communicatory patterns, it is still instructive to note similarities and differences between species.

Visual signals

Postures, gestures, and facial expressions tend to be similar in a wide variety of carnivores; where differences exist, clear phylogenetic trends are usually not apparent. When threatening, one giant panda faces another and lowers its neck obliquely, a position also found in black bear (Jordan 1976), brown bear (Egbert and Stokes 1976), and raccoon; a coati in a similar situation raises its muzzle (Kaufmann 1962). A threatening giant panda may bob its head up and down, a gesture also found in red panda (Roberts 1981). Many mammals avert their head as a sign of appeasement, but giant panda and coati (Kaufmann 1962) also hunch up, tucking muzzle between forelegs. In addition, giant panda and raccoon (A. Rabinowitz, pers. comm.) may cover their black eye patches with forepaws when intimidated. Facial expressions, important as signals on close contact, are poorly developed in giant panda, and somewhat better developed in the red panda; bears have mobile ears and lips, as do coati and raccoon. Giant panda, grizzly, and black bear have a lateral display during which opponents may circle each other, bears doing so stiff-legged (Kleiman 1983; Pearson, 1975; Jordan 1976). During aggressive contacts, giant pandas and bears swat, rear on hindlegs, lunge, and grab opponents with the forepaws, mouth open; red pandas behave similarly, and also threaten with arched tail and back, and rise up, holding forepaws above the head, before lunging.

Vocal signals

Peters et al. (in prep.) compare the vocal repertoire of giant pandas with that of bears and procyonids; their work forms the basis of the following discussion. Adult giant pandas emit about 11 vocal and unvoiced sounds. To compare this repertoire with that of other species we should ideally examine both the structural components, as analyzed on a sound spectrograph, and the functional contexts of every sound. However, knowledge of panda vocalizations is still rudimentary, and this is just as true of other species. The preliminary work of Jordan (1979) on black bear, Roberts (1981) on red panda, O. Sieber (pers. comm.) on raccoon, and Willey and Richards (1981) on ringtail provides the most detailed information, with vocal repertoires based on an analysis of spectrograms; other reports consist primarily of verbal descriptions and incidental observations, making direct comparisons with the giant panda difficult. Table 8.3 compares the sounds of giant panda, red panda, black bear, and five procyonids. We use black bear as representative of the bears since it has been studied more thoroughly than other bears. The fragmentary information on others, especially brown and polar bears (Meyer-Holzapfel 1957; Egbert and Stokes 1976) indicates that most vocalizations are similar to those of black bear, one exception being a trilling sound produced by spectacled bear (Peters 1978).

There are several problems in preparing a comparative table, even if we had adequate data for all species. Sounds that are structurally similar may or may not be

TABLE 8.3

Comparisons of adult panda, red panda, black bear and procyonid vocalizations

Vocal Signals	Giant panda	Red panda	Black bear	Raccoon	Coati	Kinkajou	Olingo	Ringtail	Comment
Huff (hiss, puff, spit)	++	++	++			+	+	+	
Snort	++	++	++	++		+	+		
Chomp (jaw-pop, chop, cluck, chuff)	++	+	++	−	+				
Bleat (twitter, chitter, chirp)	++	++	−	++	++	+	+	++	
Chirp (yip)	++	+?	−	−					
Squeal (screech, bawl)	++	++	+	++	+			++	
Honk (grunt, snore)	++	−	++	++	++	+		++	
Growl (snarl)	+	−	+?	++	++	+	+	++	
Moan (bellow?)	++	−	++	−					
Bark (grunt)	++	+	−	++	+			++	
Roar (scream)	++	−	++	−		+?	+		
Purr				++					Contentment
Quack-snort		+							Surprise
Whistle				++					Surprise
Loud contact call		+?		−			+	+?	Long-distance call
Gecker			−	++					Appeasement
Chuckle					+				Mainly in mating season
Chuck								++	Fright

Notes

Parentheses indicate names given in various sources.
++ Good comparisons between species, based mainly on spectograms.
+ Probably similarity in vocalizations, based mainly on verbal descriptions.
− Vocal form apparently absent.
No symbol indicates lack of definite data.

Sources

Giant panda: Peters (1982); G. Peters, pers. comm.; Kleiman (1983); this study.
Red panda: Roberts (1981); Roberts, pers. comm.
Black bear: Jordan (1979).
Raccoon: Fritzell (1978); O. Sieber, pers. comm.
Coati: Kaufman (1962).
Kinkajou: Poglayen-Neuwall (1976a).
Olingo: Poglayen-Neuwall (1976b).
Ringtail: Willey and Richards (1981).

functionally different in two species, or, if structurally different, they may or may not be functionally equivalent. For instance, the giant panda's honk structurally resembles the grunt of bears and procyonids. In the former it denotes light distress and in the latter social contact, especially in a female calling her young. Is there a functional difference, or is our knowledge of pandas incomplete on this point? Another problem lies in deciding whether two calls are related or not. The scream of kinkajou and the roar of giant panda sound different to the human ear, yet they appear to be stucturally and functionally alike; in other situations of this type it is difficult to decide from the available evidence if a relationship exists. In our search of phylogenetic affinities, only homologous vocalizations are of significance. The table was prepared with the assumption that such homology exists among similar signals, and that the presence and absence of certain ones provide an indication of relationship.

The actual size of a species's repertoire may be open to interpretation, for if a signal is graded, as from a moan to a roar in giant panda, or if there are variations in the same signal, as in a hiss or a spit, one has to decide whether to split or lump. No special trend in repertoire size is evident. Giant panda, black bear, raccoon, and ringtail are about equal, and red panda and several procyonids may have fewer signals than the others, but repertoire size in itself reveals little about potential for communication.

Various agonistic signals—huff, snort, growl, roar, squeal—are widespread. The chomp of giant panda has a counterpart in black bear, though it remains unclear if the two sounds are homologous. The chomp of bears has two distinct components, a pop followed by a chuffing noise as the animal clacks its teeth and vibrates its lips (Peters 1978); a huff or a snort may precede chomps. Coatis produce a sound resembling the chomp "by opening and closing the mouth rapidly 2 or 3 times in rapid succession" (Kaufman 1962), and red pandas cluck as they open and close the mouth slowly 1–4 times (M. Roberts, pers. comm.). Giant pandas and some procyonids bark; a comparable sound has not been reported for bears.

The bleat of the giant panda has its equivalent in the twitter of red panda and procyonids—but in no vocalization of black bear. Vocalizations with the structural pattern of a twitter in the functional context of appeasement and friendly contact are uncommon in carnivores (Peters 1982); thus the fact that the giant panda and the black bear do not share this relatively high-pitched call is significant. By contrast, giant panda and black bear share the moan as a signal of light aggression, a vocalization seemingly absent in red panda and procyonids.

The giant panda's chirp (yip) is of surprisingly high pitch for a large carnivore; it has a possible counterpart only in red panda.

As noted earlier, the honk of the giant panda is structurally but apparently not functionally similar to the grunt as emitted by black bear and several procyonids in a social context. In giant panda the honk denotes light distress, whereas in other species it is a short-distance contact call. More observations on giant pandas may reveal a similar function. The olingo and possibly the ringtail also have a loud, long-distance contact call, and the red panda may possess one too, for Hardwicke (1827, quoted in Morris and Morris 1966) noted that the animal "is frequently discovered by its loud cry or call, resembling the word Wha, often repeating the same." A lone giant panda male may moan, chirp (yip), bark, and roar during the mating season. Animals usually emit these vocalizations as they interact, but in this situation they seem to use them as advertisement calls.

Vocalizations of young have not been included in table 8.3 because so little is known about them. Young of all species have a squawk or similar signal to indicate distress, and young of certain species have other discernible calls, such as the churr of contented raccoons (O. Sieber, pers. comm.). Nursing ringtails and bear young emit a distinct vocalization, the former "high pitched, rapidly delivered grunts" (Willey and Richards 1981), and the latter a continuous keckering sound reminiscent of a harsh, loud purr; on rare occasions an adult bear may kecker while sucking its paw (G. Peters, pers. comm.). Although the precise function of this vocalization is unknown, in bears it is so loud—it can readily be heard outside a black bear denning tree (Eiler 1981)—that it must convey important information to the mother. Perhaps the sound signals the lethargic female to release milk and retain her body position. A loud nursing call is found in all bears (Meyer-Holzapfel 1957), but not in the giant panda. If the giant panda were nothing but a bear, it would be difficult to visualize an adaptive advantage in losing this call.

To sum up, the giant panda's vocal repertoire differs importantly from that of black bear in the presence of the bleat, a vocalization also found in red panda and the procyonids, and in the absence of a loud nursing call by the young; the moan appears to be the only vocalization shared by giant panda and black bear to the exclusion of red panda and the procyonids. The chirp (yip) may be an exclusive giant panda signal.

Olfactory and visual signals in the environment

The giant panda urinates, claws trees, and rubs its anogenital area on objects, to mention the three most common olfactory and visual signals, using these methods alone or in combination. Taken individually, they reveal little regarding the panda's affinity, for they are widespread among carnivores. For instance, anogenital rubbing is found in viverrids; urinating is found with or without legcock in canids; and tree clawing is found in cats; even the handstand of scenting male pandas has a counterpart in the kusimanse, a viverrid (Ewer 1973). Nonetheless, it is useful to compare the giant panda's whole repertoire with that of red panda, bears, and procyonids.

Marking behavior depends on the type of gland available to the animal and on the location of the gland. Ewer (1973) describes this aspect: "Most of the Procyonidae have normal anal sacs, much like those of the Canidae, but the kinkajou and coati are exceptional in lacking them. In the kinkajou their function has presumably been taken over by the sternal and abdominal glands. In the coati there is a glandular area situated along the dorsal margin of the anus, consisting of a series of pouches opening by four or five slits on either side. No other carnivore has exactly comparable glands . . . In the red panda the sacs are of normal type and open on an area of naked slightly invaginated skin around the anus." Anal sacs in bears "are very reduced and are said to be completely absent in some bears."

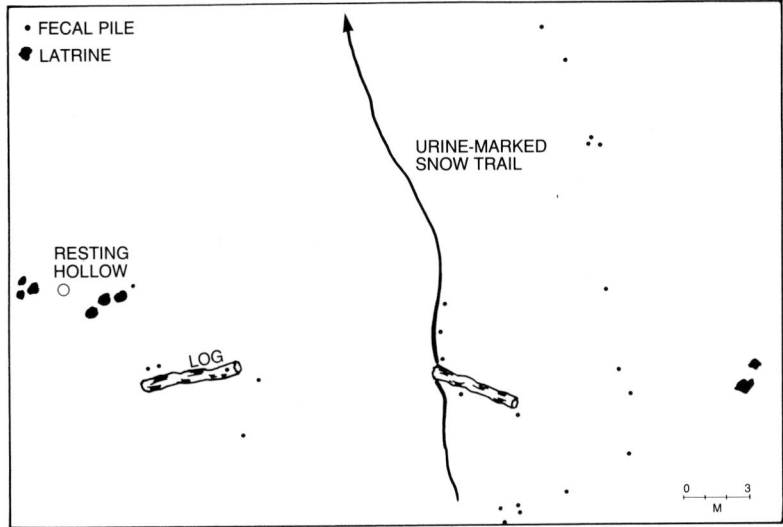

FIGURE 8.4   Latrine site of red panda at Erdaoping, 8 January 1982.

Red panda

A male red panda straddles a small stump or other protuberance, squats, squirts urine several times with lateral movements of his rump, and then deposits scent with circular rubbing motions. On occasion, a male legcocks, resting a hind paw on a vertical surface, while he marks. Females also deposit scent from the anal glands but apparently do not sprinkle urine. Males mark more often than do females, and marking frequency increases in both sexes during the mating season (Roberts 1981). The behavior closely resembles that of the giant panda. In addition, Roberts (1981) found that red pandas have several small pores on the palms that are associated with long, thickened hairs and secrete a clear, colorless fluid, no doubt a means of conveying olfactory information by the walking animal. (We found no such glands on the palms of a female giant panda).

Red pandas inspect scent posts not only by sniffing but also by touching them with the ventral surface of the tongue. Near the tip of the tongue is a cluster of special elongated papillae, which somehow enable the animal to receive olfactory signals, especially on cold days when the chemicals in scents become less volatile (Roberts 1981).

In the wild, we examined two winter sites, much used by red pandas, which had been marked in several characteristic ways (fig. 8.4). (1) Scattered around the feeding area were individual fecal deposits with an average of 8.8 ± 3.1 (n = 25, range 3–14) droppings per pile. There were, in addition, 5–8 latrines, large piles of droppings where one or more pandas had defecated repeatedly; the most-used latrines contained over 200 droppings, indicating 20 or more visits. (2) By the main latrine site was a depression, about 50 × 40 cm in length and width and 20 cm in depth, apparently excavated by the red panda and used for resting, judging by the well-packed snow and earth. (3) Each site had one much-used trail transecting the area, and this trail was heavily sprinkled with urine. (4) Logs at the site had been marked with urine and the snow on and beside them had been trampled as if by many visits.

Unlike the giant panda, the red panda concentrates scent marks in a particular area, probably reflecting its sedentary habits. Although no information on home range size exists, an animal remains localized for days, if the many feeding trails radiating from the latrine area are an indication. Evidence at one site suggested that two animals used the latrines. The giant panda does not defecate at a latrine, but its huge fecal deposits at rest sites are, in effect, analagous. The red and giant pandas also share the habit of sprinkling urine on logs. We found no indication that the red panda claws or bites trees, nor has Roberts (1981) observed that behavior.

Bears

Black, brown, and grizzly bears select isolated trees, stand on their hind legs, and rub shoulders, neck, and head against the trunk; while doing so, they may twist the head and bite into the bark. Some only rub their rumps, whereas others, biting and clawing, strip the bark completely off the lower part of a tree. Most such rubbing and clawing marks of black bear center about 1.6 m above ground. Some black bear push aspen saplings over with the chest and rub their undersides along them. Bears also lie on their back in front of a tree, rolling and squirming. Captive male brown bear sometimes urinate on themselves before rubbing. Most marked trees are conspicuously located along trails, and many are conifers, though in some areas hardwoods are much used. Marking, especially common during the mating season, appears to be mainly an activity of males. These observations by Tschanz et al. (1970), Rogers (1977), and Burst (1979) indicate that marking in bears is a prominent and variable behavior. "It is concluded that scents emanating from rubbing places, urine and faeces have a social communication function in bears" (Tschanz et al. 1970).

Giant pandas may rub their pelage against trees but do so less frequently than bears and, unlike bears, usually do not stand on their hindlegs. Both bears and giant pandas also claw and bite trees, the latter, however, rarely debarking them. Since giant pandas have a glandular anogenital area and bears do not, a different emphasis in marking is evident: giant pandas favor glandular scent, whereas bears concentrate on clawing bark and rubbing pelage. Urine features much more prominently in the marking behavior of giant pandas than in that of bears.

Procyonids

Procyonids mark in various ways. In the coati, "urine is rubbed on trees, logs, and vines by adult males in the breeding season. They emit the urine while they rub their abdomens up and down on the stems . . . by alternately extending and flexing the hindlegs" (Kaufmann 1962). Olingo and ringtail also mark with urine (Poglayen-Neuwall 1965, 1980) and, at the same time, presumably deposit scent from the anal glands; the latter also defecates at localized sites (Poglayen-Neuwall 1973). The raccoon rubs its anal area on objects (J. Seidensticker, pers, comm.), and the kinkajou has paired mandibular glands, a throat gland, and an abdominal gland, all of which it uses to mark the environment (Poglayen-Neuwall 1967). Except for the kinkajou, procyonids mark with urine or anal glands or both, rubbing the glandular area on objects—behavior similar to that of pandas.

In conclusion, red and giant pandas resemble each other closely in their scent marking, more closely than they do any procyonid. Lacking a specific glandular area, bears rub themselves against trees and claw and bite bark, behavior similar to that of the giant pandas but differing in detail.

Discussion

Before the affinities of the two pandas to each other and to the bears and procyonids can become clear, a good taxonomic system is necessary—and such a system is not yet available. For example, the Procyonidae include the specialized kinkajou with its prehensile tail; the conservative ringtail, a "living fossil" closely resembling its Oligocene ancestor; and several other miscellaneous genera that are similar to mustelids and bears but fit into neither of these taxa (Thenius and Hofer 1960). Some family members have little in common except that they are of rather generalized primitive stock of canid ancestry secondarily adapted to an omnivorous diet; they are lumped not because of known true relationships (Pocock 1921; Schmidt-Kittler 1981) but for convenience. Indeed, on the basis of middle ear morphology, Schmidt-Kittler (1981) considers the procyonids and the red panda to represent similarly specialized descendants derived independently not from the canid branch but from the mustelid one. Although today's bears are distinctive, members of the genus *Ursavus*,—the fox-sized, short-muzzled progenitors of the lineage—are superficially similar to the red panda. Unquestioned ursids are unknown before the Pliocene. It is obviously difficult to know whether a fossil had descendants.

When dealing with immunological techniques we at least have the advantage of knowing that the proteins being studied have an ancestral lineage (Sarich 1976). Yet different proteins in an organism evolve at different rates, leading to potential errors in interpretation unless analyses of many proteins are combined. Protein changes in a lineage may increase or decrease in speed, though tending to average out over long periods; lineage-specific variation in rate of evolution has also been reported (Selander 1982). So far, immunological studies provide only one more line of evidence, not an answer, concerning the giant panda's affinities. But the results are useful in reducing the number of viable alternatives that need to be considered.

We have tried to add a solution to the giant panda dilemma by comparing certain aspects of behavior, and, where pertinent, by speculating about the possible adaptive significance of a behavior pattern. This approach has its problems, for many patterns are widespread or are influenced by ecological conditions; where a difference does exist, its reason often remains obscure. Other considerations aside, our findings are resistant to neat summary because convergent evolution and plesiomor-phy—the retention of a character with little modification from an ancestral condi-tion—can be invoked to explain virtually all similarities. Comparative behavior, like comparative anatomy, has obvious limitations as a method for reconstructing phy-logenies. "In order to establish phylogenetic relationships, data obtained from the immunological study of a given protein should be combined with immunological studies of other proteins, with other biochemical evidence, as well as with morpho-logical, behavioral, and any other relevant information" (Ayala 1982). Heeding this advice, we have considered diverse evidence from several fields of inquiry.

Earlier we posed two questions. The first one was, How closely are giant and red panda related? The two animals resemble each other morphologically in many ways; and there are other similarities, from the shape of droppings to the copulatory posture of females. The following 5 characteristics, not shared by bears or, with the exception of number 4, by procyonids, seem particularly significant in pointing to an affinity between the two pandas:

1) the specialized structure of skull, teeth, and forepaws;
2) the distinctive morphology of the male reproductive organ;
3) the combination of delayed implantation and similar gestation length, weight of newborn, and litter size;
4) the high-pitched twitter/bleat vocalization, and the generally high frequency of several other vocalizations;
5) the scent glands and associated marking behavior.

It is, of course, possible to ascribe all these characteristics either to convergence or to plesiomorphy. But to argue on behalf of the former implies that the adaptive significance of the characteristic in the pandas is different from that of a functionally equivalent characteristic in bears and procyonids; and to argue for the retention of ancestral features requires an explanation of why these were retained in the pandas but not in the other related carnivores (Peters 1982). For example, the penis of the two pandas, though different in some respects, resembles that of some viverrids and felids more than it does that of procyonids and ursids, but to ascribe any similarity simply to some common Eocene ancestor (Thenius 1979) is not convincing. The bleats of the giant panda are high-pitched for an animal of that size, no similar vocalization exists in bears, and the structural pattern of the call resembles that of the red panda, as well as that of procyonids (Peters 1982). To infer possible taxonomic affinity with the red panda seems to us more plausible than to assume that the giant panda is the only bear that retained some ancestral call without apparent functional or anatomical reason. Felsenstein's (1982) principle of maximum-likelihood phy-logeny might be invoked in such situations even if the requisite numerical data are lacking. The red and giant pandas resemble each other not just in one or two but in several characteristics, and we agree with many previous investigators that the two animals are related. Most likely a small, pandalike animal became adapted to eating bamboo leaves and subsequently gave rise to two surviving genera: one, the red panda, retained the original diet; and the other, the giant panda, added bamboo stems to its diet, in the process attaining large size in part as an adaptation to handling and eating this tough food. The fact that blood protein analysis shows red and giant pandas are related somewhat distantly (fig. 8.1) suggests that the two diverged early in their evolutionary association. Such divergence could have been rapid, initiated by a major chromosomal rearrangement that simultaneously caused reproductive isolation and speciation (Bush 1981), and resulted in the adaptations peculiar to the two pandas existing today.

The second question was, How closely are the two pandas related to either raccoons or bears? The red panda has generally been lumped with the procyonids on morphological grounds, and behaviorally it also shows affinities to this diverse family, which, as noted earlier, might consist of two or more independent lineages. However, the red panda's blood proteins and chromosome banding patterns reveal only a quite distant relationship to procyonids. In our view, the giant panda is a small, pandalike animal that has grown large and secondarily evolved certain bear-like physical and behavioral attributes. Although the reproductive strategies of giant pandas and bears appear similar, especially in the birth of altricial young, we conclude that they represent different adaptations, that of the giant panda being a historical vestige modified to meet current circumstances, and that of bears a direct ecological response. Chromosome banding shows no close affinity to bears, but a few other characteristics do, notably the blood proteins and the moaning vocalization. The varied evidence suggests that the two pandas are related both to the bears and to the procyonids, but much more closely to the former.

Various taxonomic homes have in recent years been proposed for the two pandas:

Procyonidae	Ursidae	Ailuridae	Ailuropodidae	Source
Giant, red				Morris and Morris 1966, Ewer 1973
Red	Giant			Walker 1975
Red			Giant	Chu 1974, Thenius 1979
		Red	Giant	Pocock 1921, Eisenberg 1981
			Giant, red	Collins and Page 1973
		Giant, red		Thenius and Hofer 1960, Corbet and Hill 1980

To place *Ailurus* and *Ailuropoda* with the Ursidae "disturbs [the] homogeneity of that family," as Pocock (1921) phrased it, and the two are not just procyonids. We do not wish to debate taxonomic philosophies, but the diverse evidence suggests either that the red and giant pandas belong in separate but closely related families of their own, or that both belong to the same family, the Ailuridae (Ailuridae has nomenclatural priority over Ailuropodidae). We favor the latter classification.

Eisenberg and Setzer (in Collins and Page 1973) and Wurster-Hill and Bush

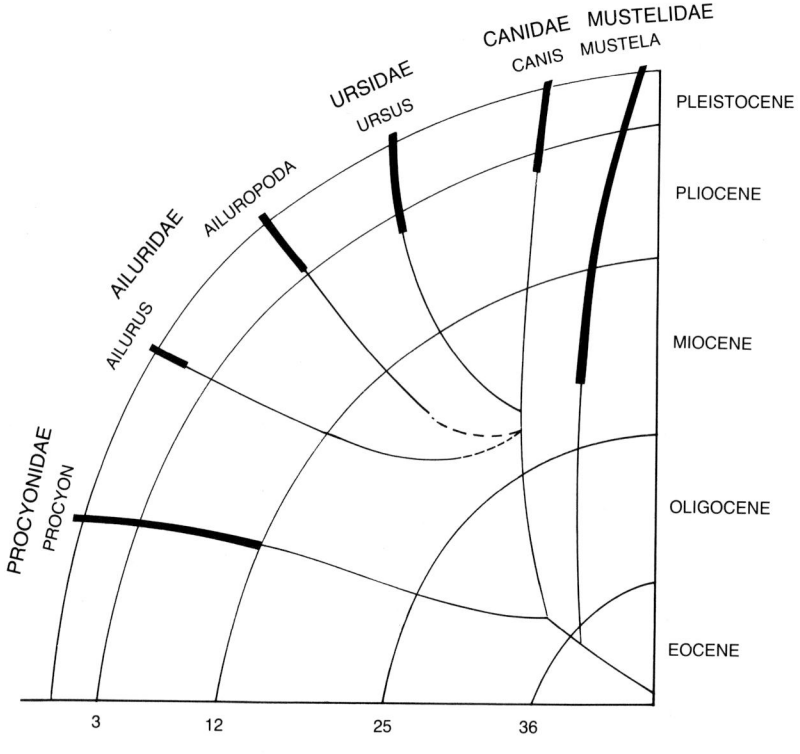

FIGURE 8.5   Presumed relationship of families in the Canoidea. Only one representative living genus is shown with most families. The heavily marked part of a branch indicates the time span during which a living genus in that family has been known from the fossil record. The Procyonidae are shown with only one branch even though several may be involved. Epoch dates are from Kurtén (1971).

(1980) suggested that pandas diverged from primitive Eocene stock prior to the viverrid and procyonid radiation. We have a different view. During the Oligocene and early Miocene a number of lineages derived from primitive canid stock became secondarily adapted to an omnivorous life—small, short-legged animals physically and behaviorally resembling the ringtail and red panda of today. One or more radiations during the Oligocene gave rise to that least some of the animals now classified with the Procyonidae. During another radiation early in the Miocene, several other lineages became distinctive, among them the Ailuridae and Ursidae (fig. 8.5).

Although we have presented new data concerning the phylogenetic position of the giant panda, we have not resolved the enigma with intellectually satisfying finality. As with any problem when looked at in the right way, the panda problem becomes ever more complicated. But the search for a more complete answer will continue "with the bear proponents and the raccoon adherents and the middle-of-the-road group advancing their several arguments with the clearest logic, while in the meantime the giant panda lives serenely in the mountains of Szechuan with never a thought about the zoological controversies he is causing by just being himself" (Colbert 1938).

Summary

1. The systematic affinity of the giant panda has been debated for over a century, but on the basis of anatomical, biochemical, and palaeontological evidence, the animal's position remains equivocal. Although behavioral observations can provide insights into evolutionary relationships, it must be decided, first, which traits correlate with ecological conditions and, second, which traits are shared by the giant panda's supposed relatives—the red panda, bears, and raccoons.

2. In bears, summer mating, delay in implantation, and birth of altricial young during hibernation is a good nutritional strategy. Pandas share some of these features, although seasonal patterns differ and there is no hibernation, indicating that different selection pressures influence their behavior. The giant panda's reproductive strategy resembles that of the red panda, with certain emendations related to body size, and may represent a conservative condition retained from a small, pandalike ancestor.

3. Giant pandas share certain vocalizations, scent-marking techniques, and other behavior patterns with bears, raccoons, and red panda. Five features point to a phylogenetic affinity between the red and the giant panda: specialized structure of teeth and forepaws, morphology of the penis, various aspects of reproduction, a bleating call and other high-pitched vocalizations, and marking behavior. The two pandas are related both to bears and to raccoons but more closely to the former; they belong either in separate but closely related families of their own, or in the same family, the Ailuridae.

9

Conservation

We have presented many facts and some conclusions about the natural history of pandas. An understanding of the evolutionary forces that shaped the animal, the vicissitudes that buffeted it over the millennia, the behavioral traits that enabled it to survive in cold and rugged mountains in spite of a diet low in nutrients, all foster admiration for the panda beyond its unique physical appeal. By tying its existence to bamboo, the panda has excluded other options. But it is nonetheless a survivor, for it was present over 3 million years ago before man became man, and it has outlived hundreds of other large mammals that vanished during the climatic upheavals of the Pleistocene. Today, with most of its habitat usurped by humankind, the panda remains in only a fraction of its former range. About 1000 survive in small, isolated populations scattered over an area of 29,500 km^2; the panda's existence depends now not on natural forces but solely on our good will. Since the animal is confined to China, the ultimate responsibility for preserving the panda rests with that country. Fully aware of its obligations to the panda and the people of the world who have taken the animal to their hearts, the government of China has expended much effort, time, and money to establish reserves, to pass and enforce protective legislation, to conduct research, and to educate the public. Still, the task of ensuring the panda a future remains immense. In a country with one billion people the demand for agricultural land, timber, and other resources is so great that the panda's wilderness home continues to shrink. As if the human threat were not enough, nature also seems to conspire against the panda. Periodic die-off of bamboo threatens populations with starvation, and inbreeding may reduce fitness in terms of the genetic contribution of animals to succeeding generations. In the past, such problems were relatively minor, local in effect; but they became serious when habitat destruction isolated the animals into small, widely spaced populations with little room to expand.

The goal of our research is to preserve the existing populations and, ultimately, to reestablish the species in other suitable habitats. For this goal to be accomplished, areas considered essential for the panda's preservation and recovery must be delineated, and the minimum viable population size—to use Shaffer's (1981) words—needed for the panda's survival must be determined. Highly specialized and highly localized, the panda provides a living blueprint for extinction. We face now the scientific and moral challenge of producing a blueprint for its survival.

Since we shall treat panda conservation and management as a whole in a later report, the discussion here concentrates on Wolong; threats to the panda in Wolong, however, are typical of those in the animal's overall range.

Direct human impact

About 3000 people, many of them Qiang of Tibetan stock, inhabit the main valley in Wolong, where, divided into two communes, they grow potatoes, maize, beans, and other crops. Many mountainsides have been denuded below an elevation of 2400 m, the forest converted into fields and pasture or reduced to scrub. Villagers penetrate ever higher up the slopes to collect wood for fuel and to cut timber for house beams and roof shingles. Their advance deprives pandas of food at low elevations and may ultimately confine animals to the upper altitudinal limit of bamboo. Even though the panda "is a rare and precious animal protected by the government," as stated in a 1962 State Council directive, it is occasionally still caught in snares set for muskdeer, or killed in some other manner. Since a panda female may not produce her first offspring until the age of 7 years and probably raises only one young successfully every 3 years (a rate of 0.3 young/year), the population can sustain an annual mortality rate no greater than about 8% per year (see Bunnell and Tait 1981). Natural mortality eliminates some individuals every year, so that any extra deaths through human actions can have a serious effect on population dynamics.

Ideally a reserve should be free of human impact. This is especially true of Wolong, which has been designated as a World Biosphere Reserve, an area of international importance for the preservation of natural habitats. Between 1984 and 1986, one commune, totaling about 1500 people, will be moved out of the upper Pitiao valley and resettled downstream in the reserve in the Gengda valley, and former fields and pastures will be replanted with trees and bamboo. In addition to this conservation initiative, the government plans to reduce adverse impact on the reserve by providing villagers with incentives to change life styles. For example, by increasing the availablity of electric power and subsidizing the insulation of homes, electricity rather than wood can be used to heat and cook. Communes may also be given monetary and other incentives to preserve forests and wildlife within their sphere of activity. Such initiatives are costly, applicable only in special circumstances, but they reveal the concern with which both the provincial and central government view the preservation of pandas.

Most forests within the panda's range have been logged during this century, some selectively, others clear-felled. In Wolong, logging began in 1916 and reached a peak between 1961 and 1975; it was stopped abruptly in 1975 to preserve panda habitat. Bamboo usually survives logging, though its growth form is affected by removal of the forest canopy. *Sinarundinaria* in our study area was denser, shorter, and seemingly drier on clear-felled than on forest-covered slopes and in winter had more dead leaves. Pandas seemed to spend little time in heavily logged areas, perhaps because bamboo there is less palatable or nutritious or because stems are more difficult to select and manipulate. Even the partial removal of the canopy by selective logging may have a long-term impact on *Sinarundinaria*. The species normally grows so densely that tree seedlings cannot establish themselves, probably because of shading and competition for space and other resources. Only where the continuity of bamboo is broken, as in the opening created by a fallen tree, do seedlings regenerate. That dense bamboo impedes growth of seedlings has also been noted for *Chusquea* bamboo in Chile (Veblen 1982) and for *Sasa* bamboo in Japan (Shidea 1974). Logging crews concentrate on conifers, often leaving birch and other broad-leafed trees. Such selective logging may initiate the following series of events:

(1) The disturbance created by loggers at first promotes growth of seedlings; reproduction is almost limited to broad-leafed trees because conifers have been cut and the seeds of some species, such as those of birch (White 1979), are well adapted for rapidly colonizing gaps in the forest canopy. (2) After an initial growth spurt, regeneration of seedlings almost ceases as bamboo grows even more densely than it did before logging. (3) Since birches and some other hardwoods are relatively short-lived, the forests become increasingly more open as trees die. (4) Synchronous flowering and death of bamboo permits sudden widespread tree regeneration, as reported when *Sasa* bamboo died in conifer forests on Honshu, Japan (Shidei 1974). This sequence of events may have occurred in our study area at Fanzipeng. Conifers on the plateau were apparently logged in the 1930s, and mostly birch remained; *Sinarundinaria* flowered during the same decade. As figure 2.9 shows, there are now few young trees but many with a DBH of 11–30 cm. Birch of that size tends to be about 40–60 years old, as determined by counting growth rings of 16 trees. Conifers have not reestablished themselves in the logged portions (Table 2.2). *Sinarundinaria* at Fanzipeng having flowered in 1983, it will be instructive to observe the responses of tree seedlings in coming years. *Fargesia* in the Choushuigou grows in the low, steep parts of the valley, where recurrent natural disturbances, especially landslips and other kinds of soil instability, provide openings in which seedlings can regenerate. The density of trees there is over twice that at Fanzipeng (table 2.2), even though the slopes were once selectively logged and partly cultivated. The relationship between forests and bamboo is a dynamic one—a function of topography, the frequency and amount of natural disturbances to the vegetation, and the colonizing ability and flowering interval of the bamboo species, to mention just a few variables. To gain an understanding of the cyclic changes in the forest community is an essential component of any panda conservation program. Even without further research, it is clear that any tampering with the forest may have an adverse impact on the pandas.

Bamboo flowering

The periodic synchronous flowering and death of bamboo is such a spectacular phenomenon that it has elicited comment in China for over 2000 years. The *Classics of Seas and Mountains*, a geography book dating from 770–256 BC, recorded flowering in a 60-year cycle (Investigation Team 1977); and later chronicles noted that a bamboo (*Phyllostachys bambusoides*) seeded in the years AD 919 and 1114 in a cycle of about 120 years (Janzen 1976). The genetic and environmental factors causing such synchrony remain unknown. Many bamboo species grow within the panda's range, and one or more of these may be in flower during any year, usually just locally—a few clumps, a patch, a whole mountainside or drainage. The 1970s and early 1980s have been notable in that flowering was widespread in several species. Various bamboos bloomed extensively during this period in the Min Mountains (see below), and *Sinarundinaria fangiana* in the Qionglai Mountains. *Phyllostachys* (?) flowered in the Qinling Mountains in 1981, *Chimonobambusa* sp. in the Liang Mountains in 1975–76 and 1980, and *Sinarundinaria* sp. in the Xiaoxianling Mountains in 1982, to name a few instances. Because *Fargesia spathacea* and *Sinarundinaria fangiana* are the two principal food species of pandas in Wolong, and also contribute importantly to the animal's diet in other parts of the range, we confine our comments to these genera.

Fargesia

Fargesia is said to have flowered during the past decades in various parts of the Min Mountains, among them: the Xiao drainage, Songpan County, during the 1930s; the southwestern corner of Pingwu County during the 1940s; another area of Pingwu County in 1956–57; Qingchuan County in 1959; and parts of Wen County in 1968–69. Then, between 1974 and 1976, an area of 5250 km² of *Fargesia spathacea*, or 40% of the pandas' total range in the Min Mountains, flowered according to the Investigation Team (1977). This publication, as well as others describing the bamboo die-off in the Min Mountains, give the impression that only one species flowered at that time. However, our surveys in 1984 showed that at least three species flowered, principally *Sinarundinaria nitida*. It is possible that the major die-off of this species went unnoticed because its flowers and those of *Fargesia spathacea* look similar. We agree with the recent taxonomic revision changing *Sinarundinaria nitida* (Mitford) Nakai to *Fargesia nitida* (Mitford) Keng f. In 1984, Yi Tongpei and Qin Zisheng investigated bamboos in the Min Mountains and noted that, in addition to *Fargesia nitida*, several other *Fargesia* species occur there. In the Tangjiahe Natural Reserve, for example, they found two species, named *Fargesia acabrida* and *F. denudata* by Yi, both of which flowered mainly in the mid-1970s. In the Wanglang Natural Reserve and adjoining areas, *Fargesia nitida* flowered widely below an elevation of 2900 m in 1975 and 1976, and locally above 2900 m in 1982; another *Fargesia* species also bloomed in some valleys there during the 1970s. The distribution of these and other species in the Min Mountains has not yet been adequately mapped.

The synchrony with which a species flowers in an area varies considerably, as illustrated by the bamboos in two panda reserves. In Wanglang, bamboo bloomed in a few patches every year between 1969 and 1974, then mass-flowered in over 80% of the reserve in 1975 and 1976; a few patches also flowered in 1982. Three small valleys remained almost unaffected, as did scattered patches in other valleys. By contrast, *F. nitida* in the Jiuzhaigou flowered mainly during two periods, above an elevation of 2600 m in 1976, and below 2600 m in 1983. Some patches bloomed in the years between these peaks, and others have not yet flowered.

F. nitida loses all its leaves during the winter prior to flowering, blossoms appear in spring, and the plant dies the same year. Flowering can be predicted a year in advance by the failure of the plants to grow new shoots; in the Jiuzhaigou, this species produced no new shoots in 1982, except for an occasional one, and flowered in 1983.

The precise flowering intervals of *Fargesia* bamboos remains unclear. On the basis of interviews with local people, the Investigation Team (1977) reported a time span of about 70–80 years, though some records are as short as 46 years or as long as 99 years. Botanical collections show that this genus flowered widely in the late 1880s and early 1890s (Soderstrom 1979).

Sinarundinaria

A few small patches of *Sinarundinaria fangiana* flowered in our study area every year in the late 1970s and in 1980. Over a dozen patches were in bloom in 1981. The following year, many small patches burst into flower, and, in addition, individual stems blossomed throughout the area. Nevertheless, probably fewer than 5% of the stems had flowered by the end of the year. Then, in May 1983, most of the remaining stems bloomed. A transect along 1 km of slope at Erdaoping in June showed that 96.8% of 715 2-year and old stems and 89.5% of 95 old shoots were in flower. The species blossomed not only throughout Wolong but also in Baoxing County and other parts of the Qionglai Mountains. Surveys in late 1983 showed that 90% or more of the bamboo had died in the affected areas, leaving only isolated patches, varying in size from a fraction of a hectare to several hectares, as food for pandas.

Twelve 1 m^2 plots sampled in June 1983 at Erdaoping revealed an average of 7.9 old shoots per m^2, a figure similar to that of previous years (table 3.14), indicating that, unlike *F. nitida*, the species produces new shoots during the year prior to flowering. Blooming *Sinarundinaria* retains its leaves until the whole plant dies in late September and October.

According to local reports, the species also bloomed widely in Wolong in 1893 and 1935, flowering intervals of about 42 and 48 years.

F. nitida and *Sinarundinaria* differ in the amount of time that elapses between flowering and a marked decline in the nutritive quality of the plant. A year prior to blooming, *F. nitida* fails to produce shoots, depriving pandas of a valuable dietary supplement during the late spring season. It also sheds all leaves several months before flowering, thus eliminating the panda's most nutritious food source in late winter and summer. Stems, however, remain palatable, and flowers represent an addition to the diet; in the Jiuzhaigou, pandas occasionally ate flowers and dying stems in early May even though other bamboo was available. *Sinarundinaria* retains leaves while in flower, although it does not replace those lost the previous winter. Pandas find the leaves, as well as the seed heads, palatable until the plant dies. Such leaves are nutritionally as good as at other times (table B.5). Pandas foraging on *Sinarundinaria* possibly enter the critical phase of bamboo die-off in better physical condition than those dependent solely on *Fargesia*.

If an area supports only one bamboo species, the effect of flowering on the panda depends on how much habitat remains unaffected at any one time. Patchy flowering over a period of years or mass-flowering at certain altitudes only, as happened in the Jiuzhaigou, enables animals to obtain food with only minor adjustments in their movements. The pandas survived the bamboo die-off in the Jiuzhaigou well, whereas at Wanglang, where most bamboo bloomed in synchrony, 13 starved animals were found. At Wanglang and in the Jiuzhaigou, where pandas live near their northern and altitudinal limit in distribution and may subsist on only one bamboo species, the animals are especially vulnerable to erratic patterns in flowering. Indeed, it is possible that in the past the vagaries in the death of bamboo determined the panda's distribution along the periphery of the range, or at least caused drastic fluctuations in numbers. In most areas, however, 2 or more bamboo species—as many as 13 in the Liang Mountains—grow at the same or different elevations. By shifting at most a kilometer or two, pandas once had access to an alternative bamboo species in the event that one died (fig. 2.1). With the expansion of agriculture, most bamboo habitat at low altitudes has been converted into fields, often leaving only one species capping the highest ridges. And when this species flowers, pandas may be deprived of food until the bamboo regenerates.

Seedlings grow slowly at elevations of 2000 m and above, attaining a height of only about 10 cm by the end of the first year and 50 cm by the fifth year; stems may require 10–15 years to attain full height and diameter. Covered by snow, such seedlings may be virtually unavailable to pandas for several months. The widespread starvation of pandas in the Min Mountains during the mid-1970s was largely due to destruction of low-altitude bamboo by agriculturalists. Excluding the deaths at Wanglang, 41 starved pandas were found in Pingwu County in 1974 and 1975, primarily in areas where *Sinarundinaria ferax* and other species have been eliminated low on the slopes. As noted in the Jiuzhaigou, a species may bloom at different altitudes in different years, and its destruction at low elevations may affect pandas just as adversely as the elimination of an alternative bamboo species.

Since two or more bamboo species grow in most Wolong valleys, it is unlikely that the mass-flowering of *Sinarundinaria* there in 1983 will cause widespread starvation among pandas. Studies on the flowering, death, and regeneration of this species, as well as on the nutritional and behavioral responses of pandas to these progressive changes in their food supply, are now in progress. In certain other areas, such as in parts of Baoxing County, pandas do not have an alternative food source available, so that the mass-flowering threatens their survival. Surveys in 1983 indicated that pandas in several localities face starvation.

Deeply concerned, the Chinese government prepared an emergency plan which includes various measures to help the pandas, among them:

1. Construction of holding stations at which starving pandas can be rehabilitated for eventual release back into the wild.
2. Formation in every affected county of a committee, led by the deputy magistrate, to supervise rescue work.
3. Mobilization of monitoring and rescue teams, consisting of 4–6 persons each,

whose duties include locating starving pandas and moving them to holding stations; providing supplementary food, such as meat, maize, and sugarcane, to pandas near human habitations, making it unnecessary to capture them; and transferring pandas from affected areas into new habitats with ample bamboo. Each county has at least one team, and potentially critical areas, such as Baoxing, Wolong, and Pingwu, have several teams.

4. Widespread publicity on behalf of the panda among communes, and payment of a reward to any person who finds a starving panda and helps in its rescue.

5. Prohibition of bamboo cutting by local people in or near panda habitat.

The problems caused by the mass-flowering in 1983 will persist for several years. More bamboo in various localities will bloom and die, and seedlings need time to grow tall enough to provide pandas with food. Consequently, the government is prepared for a long, sustained conservation effort.

Although the emergency program may help most pandas through the current crisis, it will neither eliminate the basic problem nor prevent future disasters. The lesson from the panda deaths in the Min Mountains during the 1970s is unambiguous: every panda population must, if possible, have at least 2 easily accessible bamboo species available. Every effort must be made to preserve bamboo at low elevations. Where such bamboo is already gone, it can be reestablished on the slopes by seeding or planting rhizomes, using the same species that once grew there. The introduction of exotic bamboos should generally be avoided, for these could affect the dynamic relationship between the native forest and bamboo in an area. Since our preliminary calculations show that panda density in favorable habitat may reach only 2 animals per km^2, bamboo plantings must be large to be effective.

Conservation genetics

Most panda populations are isolated, confined to high ridges, and hemmed in by cultivation. These populations tend to be small, many numbering fewer than 50 individuals, even in reserves (table 1.1). The 130–150 animals in Wolong constitute perhaps the largest remaining population; yet even this one has become fragmented (fig 2.4). The reserves were established to preserve the panda and its habitat in perpetuity. As Shaffer (1981) noted, however, a population must not only be able to maintain itself under normal conditions but must also be large enough to endure environmental stresses, natural disasters, changes in gene frequency, and other upheavals. Recent insights into the genetics of small populations indicate that the panda's future may depend as much on careful management of each population as on protection in reserves.

It is now realized that the survival of a species ultimately depends on its genetic diversity. A small population will, with time, lose its genetic variation through inbreeding. Such inbreeding may produce gene frequency changes that reduce fitness, both of the individual, as measured most commonly by reproductive success (Frankel and Soulé 1981), and of the population, as measured by adaptability to changing environmental conditions. Small populations can escape such deleterious effects by increasing rapidly (Frankel and Soulé 1981), but pandas lack this option. Their reproductive rate is low, their habitat circumscribed, and their populations small—conditions that have existed for over a century, judging by early accounts. Even where pandas have ample space and food and are little affected by human intrusion, as in the Dafending (Mabian) Reserve, they may for unknown reasons be sparse. The task, then, is to preserve genetic variability and evolutionary flexibility in these perennially small populations.

In the short term, inbreeding may have its most obvious impact on reproduction—on fertility, litter size, and viability of young. A drop in fertility can lead to extinction. "The basic rule of conservation genetics, based on the experience of animal breeders, is that the maximum tolerable rate of inbreeding is 1%. This translates into an effective population size of fifty" (Frankel and Soulé 1981). This number is based on the premises that breeding is random, that the sex ratio is equal, and that generations do not overlap. Among pandas, the largest, dominant males in an area claim priority of access to estrous females, and generations obviously overlap. In such a situation, the minimum viable population size to preserve short-term fitness might be as high as 100 (Soulé 1980). Long-term survival—for 100 generations or more—requires a capacity to respond to environmental change, often in seemingly minor ways: if, for example, the panda had a genetic inability to grow a dense coat against the severe cold of high altitudes, it might already be extinct. It is not known how large a population is necessary for continuing evolution. Franklin (1980) suggested that in a population of at least 500 randomly breeding individuals the loss of genetic variation is roughly balanced by the gain from mutation. Whatever the minimum viable size, panda populations are now so small that without management they may be unable to retain either their long-term or, in many instances, even their short-term fitness.

With demand for land and resources increasing, it is inevitable that panda habitat will become ever more fragmented, the populations more isolated. We need an estimate for minimum viable population size, we need information on the amount of habitat required by populations, and we must have data on birth and death rates before it is possible to calculate, for example, the number of pandas needed for successful introduction into new areas and the relationship between the size of a population and the probability of its becoming extinct. To collect such information takes time—but conservation action is required now before more habitat is lost. All extensive bamboo tracts within the panda's range should be given some measure of protection. About one-half of all pandas are already in reserves; more animals need such security. Some existing reserves can be expanded, and new ones can be created with the guiding principle that both they and the panda populations within them should be as large as possible. The government is considering an addition to Wolong as well as the creation of one large reserve in the Min Mountains by connecting the Tangjiahe, Baishuaijiang, Wanglang, and Jiuzhaigou reserves. Where expansion is not feasible, the preservation or reestablishment of corridors of habitat can in some instances prevent neighboring but noncontiguous populations from becoming isolated. A short bamboo corridor through cultivated land enables an animal to move from one side of a valley to another, providing at least occasional genetic interchange. Such measures might reduce the rate of genetic erosion in some populations. To preserve both short-term fitness and evolutionary potential of all populations may require a complex management plan, including the periodic shifting of animals from one population to another and subsequent monitoring of such animals.

Some survival problems are unique to the panda, the result of the animal's evolutionary compact with bamboo; others affect all living species. The future of humankind is threatened less by pollution, food shortages, depletion of oil and minerals, or the many other serious conservation issues than by the exponential destruction of the earth's natural environments, by the extermination of species. Each death of an animal or plant represents another broken link in the chain of life, a glorious and irreplaceable past not only slipping away and depriving generations to come of their heritage but also creating a downward spiral in the diversity of life that may ultimately have disastrous consequences. Some day, humankind will want to rebuild what our century has squandered with such shortsightedness. It may need the full complement of species to make new drugs, grow new foods, gain new knowledge in order to persist on this small planet. Without the biological endowment, the genetic diversity represented by each species, future generations will know only the poverty that is inextricably linked to a degraded environment. Extinction has a finality that knows no reprieve.

There are many reasons for saving a species—scientific, economic, cultural, aesthetic, and ethical, based on the moral premise that every kind of being has its rightful place in the natural community. By saving the panda in its habitat, we also assure the existence of thousands of other plants and animals there, as well as protecting watersheds upon which the lives of millions of people in the lowland ultimately depend. The panda is, however, more than an animal, more than mere muscle, bone, and skin. It is a symbol—a symbol of China's conservation effort and of the world's. By saving the panda we create an awareness that a species is valuable, worthy of preservation, no matter how great the problems. By saving the panda we emphasize that constant vigilance and long-term efforts are essential in conservation, for no rare species is ever safe; all endeavors, no matter how immediately effective, are only transitory in a changing world. With collective wisdom and dedication we must assure the panda a future. We can only hope that the choices made today are the correct ones, that the research and conservation efforts will forever preserve the animal in its mist-shrouded mountain home.

Summary

1. The panda clings to a small vestige of its former range. The ultimate responsibility for preserving the species in the wild rests with China.

2. China's goal is to preserve existing populations and to reestablish the species in suitable habitats. To accomplish this goal, it is necessary (a) to delineate areas that are essential to the animal's preservation and recovery; (b) to determine the mini-

mum viable population size needed for survival in an area; (c) to ascertain the amount of habitat required by a population of a given size under differing habitat conditions; and (d) to collect data on birth and death rates as a basis for calculating, for example, the number of pandas needed for successful reintroductions.

3. Although the panda is legally protected, an expanding human population continues to threaten its habitat. Removal of the forest canopy by logging may affect the density and palatability of bamboo; this in turn may have an adverse impact on pandas.

4. The periodic synchronous flowering and death of bamboo is a complex phenomenon whose negative impact on the panda depends on the extent of flowering in an area and on the presence of an alternative bamboo species that could serve as food. Every panda population must, if possible, have at least two bamboo species available; where only one now exists as a result of habitat destruction, others should be reestablished.

5. Most panda populations are small and isolated, many numbering fewer than 50 individuals. The loss of genetic variability and evolutionary flexibility due to inbreeding may threaten the survival of such populations. Large new reserves need to be established and existing ones enlarged, and there should be corridors of bamboo between neighboring but noncontiguous populations. Long-term management may have to include the shifting of individuals from one population to another.

Appendix A

Wild plants, mammals and birds mentioned in the text

PLANTS*

Common English name	Scientific name
Trees	
Basswood	*Tilia chinensis*
Beech	*Fagus longipetiolata*
Birch	*Betula utilis; B. alba-sinensis*
Cherry	*Prunus diehlsiana; P. brachypoda*
Dogwood	*Cornus controversa*
Dove tree	*Davidia involucrata*
False spirea	*Sorbaria arborea*
Fir	*Abies faxoniana; A. fabri*
Hazelnut	*Corylus thibetica; C. ferax*
Hawthorn	*Malus prattii*
Hemlock	*Tsuga yunnanensis; T. chinensis*
Hydrangea	*Hydrangea strigosa; H. xanthoneura*
Juniper	*Juniperus squamata*
Larch	*Larix mastersiana*
Maple	*Acer caudatum; A. flabellatum; A. tetramerum; A. laxiflorum*
Oak	*Quercus spinosa; Q. aquifolioides*
Pine	*Pinus armandii*
Poplar	*Populus lasiocarpa*
Rhododendron	*Rhododendron asterochnoum; R. pachytrichum; R. oreodoxa; R. watsonii; R. faberi*
Spruce	*Picea asperata; P. brachytyla*
Viburnum	*Viburnum cordifolium; V. mullaha; V. betulifolium*

*Only those plants which are referred to by common name in the text are noted here. Not all species within a genus in the study area are listed.

261

Walnut	*Juglans cathayensis*
Willow	*Salix magnifica; S. luctuosa; S. dissa*

Shrubs

Alder	*Ulmus* sp.
Barberry	*Berberis verruculosa*
Bramble	*Rubus amabilis*
Daphne	*Daphne retusa*
Gooseberry	*Ribes glaciale; R. meyri; R. moupinense*
Holly	*Ilex yunnanensis; I. franchetiana*
Honeysuckle	*Lonicera tangutica; L. gynochlamydea*
Rhododendron	*Rhododendron polylepis; R. bracteatum; R. lutescens*
Wild rose	*Rosa omeiensis*

Herbs and Ferns

Anemone	*Anemona alba*
Bedstraw	*Galium asperuloides*
Cowslip	*Caltha elata*
False Solomon's-seal	*Smilacina japonica*
Fern	*Ctenitis mariformis; Dryopteris uniformis*
Gentian	*Gentiana napulifera; G. rubicunda*
Iris	*Iris* sp.
Jack-in-the-pulpit	*Arisaema* sp.
Lousewort	*Pedicularis remitorta; P. pedicularis*
Nettle	*Urtica* sp.
Orchid	*Calanthe tricarinata; Epipactis* sp.
Primrose	*Primula moupinensis; P. flava*
Pyrola	*Pyrola rotundifolia*
Ragwort	*Senecio winklerianus*
Snakeroot	*Cimicifuga foetida*
Touch-me-not	*Impatiens noli-me-tangere*
Trillium	*Trillium tschonoskii*
Violet	*Viola alata*
Wild parsnip	*Angelica viridiflora; Heracleum candicans*
Wood sorrel	*Oxalis griffithii*

MAMMALS

Order Marsupialia

Koala	*Phascolarctos cinereus*

Order Primata

Golden monkey	*Rhinopithecus roxellanae*
Mountain gorilla	*Gorilla gorilla beringei*
Stump-tailed macaque	*Macaca thibetana*

Order Edentata
    Three-toed sloth   *Bradypus griseus*

Order Lagomorpha
    Hare   *Lepus* sp.
    Pika   *Ochotona thibetana*

Order Rodentia
    Bamboo rat   *Rhizomys sinense*
    Flying squirrel   *Trogopterus xanthipes*
    Marmot   *Marmota himalayana*
    Porcupine   *Hystrix hodgsoni*
    Rock squirrel   *Sciurotamias davidianus*
    Striped squirrel   *Tamiops swinhoei*

Order Carnivora
    American black bear   *Ursus americanus*
    Asiatic black bear   *Ursus (Selenarctos) thibetanus*
    Badger   *Meles meles*
    Brown and grizzly bear   *Ursus arctos*
    Civet   *Viverra zibetha*
    Clouded leopard   *Neofelis nebulosa*
    Coati   *Nasua nasua*
    Dhole or wild dog   *Cuon alpinus*
    Fox   *Vulpes* sp.
    Golden cat   *Felis temmincki*
    Giant panda   *Ailuropoda melanoleuca*
    Hog badger   *Arctonyx collaris*
    Kinkajou   *Potos flavus*
    Kusimanse   *Crossarchus obscurus*
    Leopard   *Panthera pardus*
    Lion   *Panthera leo*
    Malayan sun bear   *Helarctos malayanus*
    Masked palm civet   *Paguma larvata*
    Olingo   *Bassaricyon gabbii*
    Polar bear   *Ursus maritimus*
    Raccoon   *Procyon lotor*
    Red panda   *Ailurus fulgens*
    Ringtail   *Bassariscus astutus*
    Snow leopard   *Panthera uncia*
    Spectacled bear   *Tremarctos ornatus*
    Steppe cat   *Felis manul*
    Tiger   *Panthera tigris*
    Weasel   *Mustela sibirica*
    Wolf   *Canis lupus*
    Yellow-throated marten   *Martes flavigula*

Order Proboscidea
    African elephant   *Loxodonta africana*
    Asian elephant   *Elephas maximus*

Order Perissodactyla
    Malayan tapir   *Tapirus indicus*
    Plains zebra   *Equus burchelli*

Order Artiodactyla
    African buffalo   *Syncerus caffer*
    Elk   *Cervus elaphus (canadensis)*
    Impala   *Aepyceros melampus*
    Mule deer   *Odocoileus hemionus*
    Musk deer   *Moschus berezovski*
    Sambar deer   *Cervus unicolor*
    Serow   *Capricornis sumatraensis*
    Takin   *Budorcas taxicolor*
    Tufted deer   *Elaphodus cephalophus*
    White-lipped deer   *Cervus albirostris*
    Wildebeest   *Connochaetes taurinus*
    Wild pig   *Sus scrofa*

BIRDS

Order Charadriiformes
    Eurasean woodcock   *Scolopax rusticola*

Order Galliformes
    Blood pheasant   *Ithaginis cruentus*
    Golden pheasant   *Chrysolophus pictus*
    Green-tailed or Chinese   *Lophophorus lhuysii*
    monal
    Snowcock   *Tetraogallus tibetanus*
    Temminck's tragopan   *Tragopan temminckii*

Order Cuculiformes
    Large hawk-cuckoo   *Cuculus sparveriodes*

Order Passeriformes
    Chestnut-vented nuthatch   *Sitta europaea*
    Gould's sunbird   *Aethopyga gouldiae*
    Great parrotbill   *Conostoma oemodium*
    Japanese white-eye   *Zosterops japonica*
    Streak-throated   *Alcippe cinereiceps*
    tit-babbler
    Tit   *Parus ater; P. monticolus; P. dichrous*

Appendix B

Supplementary Tables

GIANT PANDAS TAKEN PERMANENTLY OUT OF CHINA TO FOREIGN ZOOS, 1937–83

Name	Sex	Zoo and date of arrival at zoo	Weight on arrival (kg)	Life span at zoo
Su Lin	M	Chicago, Feb. 1937	6.4	1 yr. 2 mos.
Mei-Mei	M	Chicago, Feb. 1938	22.7	4 yrs. 6 mos.
Pandora	F	New York, June 1938	16.0	2 yrs.11 mos.
Ming	F	London, Dec. 1938	25.4	6 yrs.
Tang	M	London, Dec. 1938	68.1?	1 yr. 4 mos.
Sung	M	London, Dec. 1938	68.1?	1 yr.
Grandma	F	London, Dec. 1938	72.6?	1 mo.
Happy	M	London-St. Louis, June 1939	109.0	6 yrs. 9 mos.
Pan	M	New York, May 1939	32.7	1 yr.
Pao Pei	F	New York, Sept. 1939	27.2	12 yrs. 9 mos.
Mei Lan	M	Chicago, Nov. 1939	29.5	13 yrs.10 mos.
Pandee	F	New York, Dec. 1941	28.6	3 yrs. 9 mos.
Pandah	F	New York, Dec. 1941	25.9	9 yrs.10 mos.
Lien Ho	M	London, May 1946	18.2	3 yrs. 9 mos.
Ping-Ping	M	Moscow, May 1957	—	4 yrs.
Chi-Chi	F	London, Sept. 1958	55.4	13 yrs.10 mos.
An-An	M	Moscow, Aug. 1959	104.9	13 yrs. 2 mos.
San Xing	F	Pyongyang, June 1965	—	living
Lin-Lin	M	Pyongyang, June 1965	—	dead
—	F	Pyongyang, Oct. 1971	—	dead
—	M	Pyongyang, Oct. 1971	—	dead
Ling-Ling	F	Washington, April 1972	61.8	living
Hsing-Hsing	M	Washington, April 1972	33.6	living
Lan-Lan	F	Tokyo, Oct. 1972	89.0	6 yrs.10 mos.
Kang-Kang	M	Tokyo, Oct. 1972	60.4	7 yrs. 8 mos.
Yen-Yen	M	Paris, Dec. 1973	40.0	living
Li-Li	M	Paris, Dec. 1973	20.0	4 mos.
Ching-Ching	F	London, Sept. 1974	51.2	living
Chia-Chia	M	London, Sept. 1974	50.2	living
Ying-Ying	F	Mexico, Sept. 1975	26.0	living
Pe-Pe	M	Mexico, Sept. 1975	21.0	living
Shao-Shao	F	Madrid, Dec. 1978	71.0	4 yrs.10 mos.

TABLE B.1 *continued*

GIANT PANDAS TAKEN PERMANENTLY OUT OF CHINA TO FOREIGN ZOOS, 1937–83

Name	Sex	Zoo and date of arrival at zoo	Weight on arrival (kg)	Life span at zoo
Chiang-Chiang	M	Madrid, Dec. 1978	91.5	living
Dan-Dan	M	Pyongyang, March 1979	—	living
Huan-Huan	F	Tokyo, Jan. 1980	95.5	living
Bao-Bao	M	West Berlin, Nov. 1980	60.0	living
Tian-Tian	F	West Berlin, Nov. 1980	50.0	3 yrs. 3 mos.
Fei-Fei	M	Tokyo, Nov. 1982	122.0	living

Sources: Morris and Morris (1966); Zhu and Li (1980); Kleiman (1983); Frädrich (1981).

TABLE B.2

WATER CONTENT OF *Sinarundinaria* DROPPINGS

Month	N	% Water	± SD	(range)
January 1982	24	70.1	±4.6	(59.9–77.2)
February 1981 and 1982	58	67.8	±3.9	(58.7–77.9)
March 1981 and 1982	33	68.4	±3.4	(62.1–75.7)
April 1981 and 1982	49	63.6	±5.0	(47.4–74.1)
May 1982	14	60.3	±5.6	(46.2–67.6)
June	—	—	—	—
July 1981	30	74.5	±6.3	(60.6–84.8)
August 1981	29	76.3	±4.6	(65.5–83.3)
September 1981	22	73.3	±2.4	(67.1–78.5)
October 1981	13	73.8	±2.6	(69.8–79.3)
November 1981	24	69.1	±6.7	(59.6–78.8)
December 1981	40	72.1	±2.6	(67.9–77.1)

An angular sine transformation followed by 1-way analysis of variance with Duncan's multiple-range test (Steel and Torrie 1960) showed that water content in August was significantly greater than in January, and that content in August and January were significantly greater than in April ($p < 0.05$).

TABLE B.3

PERCENT WATER IN DIFFERENT PARTS OF *Sinarundinaria*

Age	Plant part	J	F	M	A	M	J	J	A*	S	O	N	D
New shoot	Whole					84.6							
Old shoot	Stem top	50.0	50.9	52.1	53.2	50.7	49.2		69.7	68.2	62.5	57.4	53.8
	Stem middle	50.0	49.1	60.4	50.0	50.0	48.1	49.4	72.1	62.8	60.0	57.7	51.4
	Stem bottom	52.6	57.9	52.5	54.2	50.9	30.8	51.2	72.3	67.6	63.1	57.9	53.8
Two-year stem	Stem top	43.7	40.9	40.2	42.1	31.3	28.1	40.5	48.3	53.2	47.9	47.1	39.5
	Stem middle	45.9	43.3	42.9	43.1	40.3	34.0	41.8	47.7	53.3	50.0	50.0	43.5
	Stem bottom	39.8	43.6	45.4	43.7	44.4	35.2	44.2	52.8	53.2	51.9	48.9	47.3
	Branches	42.9	46.7	43.1	47.2	53.0	61.5	59.1	62.5	71.7	60.7	46.7	45.7
	Leaves	41.0	41.4	43.6	52.1	54.5	49.0	61.8	62.2	65.6	59.1	53.1	40.7
Old stem	Stem top	48.4	34.8	42.5	37.7	38.7	31.4	39.2	35.9	44.3	45.5	42.9	43.5
	Stem middle	42.9	37.3	43.4	40.0	36.5	32.6		40.4	42.0	47.5	46.9	40.3
	Stem bottom	43.6	44.8	44.4	39.8	41.7	36.9	43.5	41.7	43.3	45.9	46.2	38.3
	Branches	37.8	39.7	36.2	39.2	45.7	35.0	56.7	54.8	65.6	63.3	57.1	40.5
	Leaves	37.8	43.4	42.9	50.5	56.1	42.0	63.4	61.3	68.1	59.1	57.1	34.6
Average		44.3	44.1	45.4	45.6	45.7	39.5	52.5	55.5	58.4	55.1	51.5	44.1

*New shoots become old shoots in August.

TABLE B.4
PERCENT WATER IN DIFFERENT PARTS OF *Fargesia*

Age	Plant part	J	F	M	A	M	J	J*	A	S	O	N	D
New shoot	Whole				81.7								
Old shoot	Stem top	50.0	55.7	40.0	47.2	46.2	46.3	69.2	61.6	60.8	57.1	55.8	51.9
	Stem middle	53.1	56.6	51.5	51.7	46.3	49.2	69.4	62.4	62.1	60.3	55.5	54.9
	Stem bottom	53.8	59.5	51.1	51.5	48.2	49.3	69.9	71.4	59.3	62.0	56.4	55.7
	Branches	51.2	53.7	50.0	48.6	54.5	56.6	75.2	67.9	68.6	60.7	58.5	54.0
	Leaves	50.0	50.0	48.9	49.5	55.2	65.2		59.1	64.0	60.0	57.9	51.1
Two-year stem	Stem top	38.1	39.0	37.7	37.1	33.6	33.1	35.9	40.7	41.8	46.0	42.4	40.6
	Stem middle	39.1	40.1	40.4	31.0	32.5	34.9	42.9	46.1	42.7	45.6	45.7	43.7
	Stem bottom	44.1	42.7	44.2	35.6	38.1	36.4	42.3	43.6	44.3	55.3	45.5	48.9
	Branches	44.2	43.1	42.4	36.3	43.0	38.0	47.4	50.4	57.4	57.1	51.3	56.0
	Leaves	47.9	49.1	45.2	41.0	51.6	50.0	53.4	55.6	59.6	56.9	55.3	49.2
Old stem	Stem top	46.7	41.3	33.0	31.3	33.9	32.7	28.1	—	40.0	45.6	40.0	43.6
	Stem middle	37.3	42.7	31.0	31.8	31.4	31.4	24.3	—	39.8	40.4	41.7	42.5
	Stem bottom	40.3	39.8	36.7	34.4	34.4	36.2	31.5	—	40.3	39.5	40.4	42.5
	Branches	35.9	42.9	32.6	31.3	44.9	37.7	39.8	—	57.1	51.6	47.6	43.3
	Leaves	40.0	45.7	38.8	37.8	49.0	48.5	47.7	—	71.4	50.0	51.2	47.9
Average		44.8	46.8	41.5	42.5	42.9	43.0	48.4	42.5	53.9	52.5	49.7	48.4

*New shoots become old shoots in July.

TABLE B.5

Chemical composition of *Sinarundinaria*, expressed as % dry matter, based on average of all monthly samples

		Crude protein	Hemi-cellulose	Cellulose	Lignin	Total ash	Silica
Leaf	Two-year stem	15.74 ±1.36	35.96 ±2.79	28.07 ±1.47	8.37 ±1.95	7.89 ±0.52	1.31 ±1.69
	Old stem	15.21 ±1.58	34.93 ±3.02	27.45 ±1.32	8.73 ±1.52	8.75 ±0.95	2.32 ±2.63
Branch	Two-year stem	7.06 ±0.71	31.59 ±2.30	34.66 ±1.65	12.07 ±0.92	7.06 ±0.71	0.83 ±0.92
	Old stem	6.15 ±0.87	28.47 ±2.00	35.80 ±1.94	13.84 ±1.07	5.97 ±0.75	1.65 ±1.81
Stem top	Old shoot	5.91 ±1.00	25.97 ±3.11	43.37 ±2.82	12.57 ±1.91	3.10 ±0.56	0.21 ±0.16
	Two-year stem	2.85 ±0.43	25.02 ±2.39	44.27 ±2.54	15.27 ±1.41	1.84 ±0.34	0.32 ±0.26
	Old stem	2.51 ±0.27	24.70 ±2.48	43.36 ±2.33	15.68 ±1.30	2.34 ±0.39	0.60 ±0.64
Stem middle	Old shoot	3.71 ±0.88	23.00 ±2.68	47.97 ±2.80	13.58 ±1.60	2.47 ±0.45	0.16 ±0.16
	Two-year stem	2.49 ±0.39	22.05 ±2.38	46.93 ±2.34	16.32 ±1.33	2.14 ±0.27	0.20 ±0.15
	Old stem	2.08 ±0.21	22.90 ±2.76	45.96 ±2.81	16.16 ±1.47	1.86 ±0.41	0.42 ±0.37
Stem bottom	Old shoot	3.62 ±0.65	21.78 ±2.09	48.62 ±2.99	14.56 ±1.47	2.64 ±0.65	0.21 ±0.14
	Two-year stem	2.30 ±0.22	22.70 ±2.60	47.12 ±2.47	16.44 ±1.07	2.16 ±0.31	0.16 ±0.14
	Old stem	2.12 ±0.34	21.33 ±1.78	46.66 ±2.32	16.73 ±1.37	1.85 ±0.61	0.35 ±0.32
Rhizome*		3.95	23.33	34.06	18.42	3.83	1.87
New shoot*	Whole	14.82	33.90	35.95	5.95	6.41	.83
In flower*	Old stem, leaf	15.39	34.48	27.47	4.42	11.32	7.83
	Old stem branch	7.94	28.67	35.76	15.45	5.70	2.65
	Old stem, stem	1.91	26.88	41.56	15.72	2.33	.65

*Only 1 sample collected in May.

TABLE B.6

CHEMICAL COMPOSITION OF *Fargesia*, EXPRESSED AS % DRY MATTER, BASED ON AVERAGE OF ALL MONTHLY SAMPLES

		Crude protein	Hemi-cellulose	Cellulose	Lignin	Total ash	Silica
Leaf	Old shoot	15.79 ± 1.04	34.74 ± 3.19	29.07 ± 2.42	8.57 ± 1.54	7.76 ± 0.82	2.08 ± 1.91
	Two-year stem	13.65 ± 1.09	32.31 ± 4.26	28.79 ± 2.05	10.52 ± 2.80	9.03 ± 1.16	2.55 ± 2.56
	Old stem	12.72 ± 1.31	31.95 ± 3.03	27.71 ± 1.36	9.88 ± 1.41	9.62 ± 1.10	2.33 ± 2.71
Branch	Old shoot	5.27 ± 1.25	28.53 ± 3.07	38.56 ± 2.42	13.41 ± 2.58	4.53 ± 1.46	0.81 ± 0.66
	Two-year stem	3.66 ± 0.39	29.85 ± 2.84	37.38 ± 2.42	14.14 ± 1.33	4.28 ± 1.05	1.10 ± 1.06
	Old stem	3.89 ± 0.46	28.80 ± 2.39	35.71 ± 3.62	15.62 ± 3.23	4.76 ± 0.64	1.08 ± 1.17
Stem top	Old shoot	2.62 ± 0.49	23.76 ± 3.52	46.45 ± 3.66	15.27 ± 2.04	2.21 ± 0.72	0.09 ± 0.06
	Two-year stem	1.45 ± 0.26	23.44 ± 2.96	47.01 ± 4.10	15.88 ± 1.48	1.27 ± 0.35	0.19 ± 0.20
	Old stem	1.36 ± 0.28	23.39 ± 2.98	45.73 ± 3.06	16.16 ± 1.44	0.98 ± 0.30	0.22 ± 0.18
Stem middle	Old shoot	2.27 ± 0.40	23.40 ± 8.17	47.50 ± 6.81	15.09 ± 2.82	2.48 ± 0.38	0.55 ± 1.43
	Two-year stem	1.14 ± 0.21	22.22 ± 3.10	48.70 ± 4.00	15.92 ± 1.52	1.43 ± 0.53	0.21 ± 0.19
	Old stem	1.09 ± 0.25	22.22 ± 2.40	47.75 ± 2.67	16.77 ± 1.41	0.97 ± 0.25	0.19 ± 0.19
Stem bottom	Old shoot	2.54 ± 0.50	21.42 ± 1.89	48.75 ± 2.58	15.45 ± 1.87	2.57 ± 0.56	0.18 ± 0.13
	Two-year stem	1.20 ± 0.22	20.70 ± 2.56	49.20 ± 3.30	16.67 ± 1.07	1.81 ± 0.62	0.14 ± 0.13
	Old stem	1.04 ± 0.24	21.84 ± 2.63	48.17 ± 2.75	16.73 ± 1.22	0.91 ± 0.32	0.16 ± 0.13
Rhizome*		4.56	22.58	33.35	12.29	2.89	0.49
New shoot*	Sheath	10.93	36.60	38.49	3.28	5.26	0.09
	Core	17.57	32.48	31.45	4.74	8.66	0.51

*Only 1 or 2 samples collected in April and May.

TABLE B.7

CHEMICAL ANALYSIS OF WATER IN THE CHOUSHUIGOU

	Location			
	Erdaoping	Huishishu	Choushuigou	Jinguashugou
Source	rivulet	pool	stream	stream
pH	6.8	5.9	7.0	7.4
Hardness[a]	3.46	.67	16.14	10.93
Main ion content (mg/l)				
HCO_3^-	49.92	10.09	293.98	141.44
Cl^-	1.40	2.79	9.77	3.49
SO_4^{-2}	7.17	.79	71.69	46.45
Ca^{+2}	20.81	4.29	16.33	55.67
Mg^{+2}	2.60	.39	29.73	13.51
K^+	0	.08	19.07	0
Na^+	—	—	—	0
Trace elements (ppb.)				
Fe	.14	.33	.03	.01
Mn	.03	.21	.003	.003
Zn	.04	.08	.02	.01
Cu	0	0	0	0
Pb	0	0	.01	0

[a]German system.

TABLE B.8

CHEMICAL COMPOSITION (EXPRESSED IN % DRY MATTER) OF BAMBOO IN THE DROPPINGS OF GIANT PANDA AND OTHER SPECIES

| | Giant panda | | | | | Black bear | Red panda | Bamboo rat |
| | *Sinarundinaria* (all year) | | *Fargesia* (Jan.–May) | | | *Fargesia* (May) | *Sinarundinaria* (Jan.) | *Sinarundinaria* (May) |
	Leaf n=13	Stem n=13	Leaf n=3	Stem n=3	New shoot n=3	New shoot n=1	Leaf n=1	Stem n=1
Crude protein	9.30 ±1.55	2.87 ±0.92	9.29 ±0.18	2.01 ±0.65	5.71 ±0.76	6.53	8.91	2.71
Hemicellulose	32.92 ±2.53	23.95 ±2.28	32.37 ±0.52	25.20 ±3.49	31.40 ±2.26	10.34	31.13	23.97
Cellulose	33.43 ±1.76	48.33 ±2.15	30.49 ±0.71	45.46 ±3.39	40.86 ±0.97	26.08	32.88	42.29
Lignin	10.58 ±1.00	16.05 ±1.23	10.22 ±0.27	14.34 ±1.66	2.41 ±0.51	2.98	7.06	16.48
Total ash	7.48 ±0.97	2.24 ±0.56	9.90 ±0.46	1.82 ±0.63	8.84 ±1.36	—	9.24	8.30
Silica	1.86 ±1.92	0.49 ±0.48	2.17 ±2.62	0.32 ±0.08	0.20 ±0.08	0.23	5.05	5.19

Leaf includes branch tips; stem includes all ages.

TABLE B.9

STANDARD PROXIMATE ANALYSES COMPARING SELECTED BAMBOO PARTS AND DROPPINGS, ON A DRY MATTER BASIS

	Sinarundinaria		*Fargesia* (New shoot)
	Leaf	Old shoot	
Season	Summer-Autumn	Winter	Spring
Sample size	7	4	4
Crude protein			
Bamboo	17.39	4.07	10.53
Dropping	9.86	1.60	4.48
Crude fat			
Bamboo	3.53	0.56	1.27
Dropping	3.02	0.36	0.80
Crude fiber			
Bamboo	26.37	47.40	30.83
Dropping	27.56	49.60	35.97
NFE			
Bamboo	—	45.73	52.20
Dropping	—	46.49	51.20
Total ash			
Bamboo	7.15	2.46	5.18
Dropping	6.92	2.07	7.55

TABLE B.10

AMINO ACID CONTENT OF LEAVES VERSUS OLD SHOOTS IN *Sinarundinaria* AND IN DROPPINGS

	Leaf		Old shoot	
Amino Acid	Bamboo	Dropping	Bamboo	Dropping
Aspartic acid	1.181	0.708	1.262	0.833
Threonine	0.473	0.385	0.145	0.135
Serine	0.729	0.434	0.226	0.222
Glutamic acid	0.934	0.475	0.336	0.237
Proline	0.186	0.096	0.076	0
Glycine	0.510	0.446	0.184	0.138
Alanine	0.715	0.535	0.230	0.116
Valine	0.607	0.303	0.156	0.102
Methionine	0.105	0.051	0.044	0.028
Leucine	0.398	0.293	0.166	0.173
Isoleucine	0.729	0.567	0.302	0.277
Tyrosine	0.276	0.209	0.077	0.067
Phenylalanine	0.410	0.303	0.075	0.080
Lysine	0.512	0.327	0.220	0.172
Histidine	0.452	0.106	0.074	0.050
Arginine	0.614	0.499	0.212	0.163

Averages of 3–5 samples collected in late spring and summer; in mg/100g.

TABLE B.11

Sinarundinaria STEMS AND LEAVES EATEN MONTHLY BY A GIANT PANDA, ASSUMING A 12.5 KG DAILY FOOD INTAKE

Month	Droppings sampled (N)	% stem in dropping	Calculated intake (kg)	
			Stem	Leaf and branchtip
January	29	60.1	232.9	154.6
February	69	76.0	266.0	84.0
March	36	75.5	292.6	94.9
April	61	93.5	350.6	24.4
May	30	93.2	361.2	27.9
June	—	93.0 est.	348.8	26.3
July	31	47.7	184.8	202.7
August	30	0.2	0.9	386.7
September	22	0	0	375.0
October	13	9.1	35.3	352.2
November	42	71.0	266.3	108.8
December	36	70.4	272.8	114.7

TABLE B.12

PROBABILITY OF ACTIVITY OF PANDAS BY MONTH*

		Long	Ning	Zhen	Han	Wei
1981	March	.56*	—	.66**		
	April	.65*	.51**	.57**		
	May	.68*	.57**	.68*		
	June	.65*	.75**	.60*		
	July	.64*	.54**	.61*		
	August	.61*	.61*	.50**		
	September	.50*	.46**	.38***		
	October	.58*	.60*	.62*		
	November	.63*	.64*	.77**		
	December	.52*	.56*	.73**		
1982	January	.61*	.57*	.79**	.47***	.63*
	February	.56*	.53*	.68**	.61***	.60***
	March	.63*	.64*	.73**	.67*	.56***
	April	.62*	—	.70**	.63*	.69**
	May	.61*	—	.62*	.62*	.77**
	June	.73	—	—	—	—
	July	—	—	.66*	.66*	.71*

*Within each month, activity levels of animals with different number of asterisks are significantly ($p < 0.05$) different from each other.

TABLE B.13

Probability of activity by hour during spring, summer-autumn, and winter

Hour		Spring	Summer-autumn	Winter
Midnight	2400	.57*	.43**	.62*
	0100	.53*	.42**	.63***
	0200	.57*	.43**	.64***
	0300	.60*	.43**	.67***
	0400	.62*	.47**	.70***
	0500	.71*	.42**	.64***
	0600	.73*	.47**	.56***
	0700	.64*	.43**	.47**
	0800	.60*	.41**	.44**
	0900	.53*	.36**	.45***
	1000	.62*	.46**	.50**
	1100	.66*	.56**	.59**
Noon	1200	.69*	.60**	.63
	1300	.63*	.62*	.66*
	1400	.60*	.69**	.69**
	1500	.63*	.67	.72**
	1600	.70*	.74*	.69*
	1700	.76*	.73	.69*
	1800	.78*	.74*	.74*
	1900	.84*	.63**	.71***
	2000	.76*	.57**	.66***
	2100	.64*	.42**	.64*
	2200	.57*	.41**	.61*
	2300	.59*	.41**	.61*

*Within each hour, activity levels with different number of asterisks are significantly ($p < 0.05$) different from each other. Levels without asterisks indicate lack of significance from the other two.

TABLE B.14

Tooth eruption of the male panda Ronshun at the Chengdu Zoo during the first year of life

Age (days)	Part of jaw	Incisor	Canine	Premolar	Molar
65–85	Upper	0	0	0	0
	Lower	0	1	0	0
90	Upper	0	1	0	0
	Lower	0	1	0	0
106	Upper	0	1	0	0
	Lower	0	1	1	0
110	Upper	0	1	1	0
	Lower	0	1	1	0
114	Upper	2	1	2	0
	Lower	2	1	2	0
120	Upper	3	1	2	0
	Lower	3	1	2	0
365	Upper	3	1	2	2
	Lower	3	1	2	2

Source: Xu et al. (1981).

References

Allen, G. 1940. *The mammals of China and Mongolia*. Natural History of Central Asia, vol. 11, no. 2. New York: Am. Mus. Nat. Hist.

Alt, G. 1977. Home range, annual activity patterns, and movements of black bears in northeastern Pennsylvania. Master's thesis, Penn. State Univ.

———. 1978. Dispersal patterns of black bears in northeastern Pennsylvania. Fourth Eastern Black Bear Workshop, Greenville, Maine. Mimeo.

———. 1982. Reproductive biology of Pennsylvania black bear. *Game News* (PA.), Feb., pp. 9–15.

Alt, G., G. Matula, F. Alt, and J. Lindzey. 1980. Dynamics of home range and movements of adult black bears in northeastern Pennsylvania. In *Bears — their biology and management*, ed. C. Martinka and K. McArthur, pp. 131–36. Washington, D.C.: U.S. Govt. Printing Office.

Anon. 1974. *The cultivation of bamboo forests*. Xian: Agr. Publ. House. 278 pp. (In Chinese.)

———. 1980 *Vegetation of Sichuan*. Chengdu: Sichuan People's Press. (In Chinese.)

Anon. 1981*a*. Beijing zoo's prize panda gives birth again. *China Daily*, 20 Sept.

———. 1981b. Dan Dan a female panda. *South China Morning Post*, 19 Dec.

———. 1981c. Panda skull found in Han royal tomb. *China Daily*, 8 Dec.

———. 1982a. *SAS user's guide: statistics*. Cary, N.C.: SAS Inst. Stat. Anal. Syst.

———. 1982b. Twin pandas born in Madrid. *New York Times*, 5 Sept.

Ayala, F. 1982. Of clocks and clades, or a story of old told by genes now. In *Biochemical aspects of evolutionary biology*, ed. M. Nitecki, pp. 257–301. Chicago: Univ. Chicago Press.

Bai Juyi. 1983. *Bai Juyi, 200 selected poems*, trans. Rewi Alley. Beijing: New World Press.

Bardenfleth, K. 1913. On the systematic position of *Aeluropus melanoleucus*. *Mindeskr. Jaetus Steenstrup* 17:1–15.

Berner, A., and L. Gysel. 1967. Raccoon use of large tree cavities and ground burrows. *J. Wildl. Manage.* 31(4):706–14.

Bonney, R., D. Wood, and D. Kleiman. 1982. Endocrine correlates of behavioural oestrus in the female giant panda (*Ailuropoda melanoleuca*) and associated hormonal changes in the male. *J. Reprod. Fert.* 64:209–15.

Bourlière, F. 1979. Significant parameters of environmental quality for nonhuman primates. In *Primate ecology and human origins*, ed. I. Bernstein and E. Smith, pp. 23–46. New York: Garland STPM Press.

Brambell, M. 1976. The giant panda (*Ailuropoda melanoleuca*). *Trans. Zool. Soc. London* 33:85–92.

———. 1978. Register of giant pandas. Zool. Soc. London. Mimeo.

———. 1983. Register of giant pandas up to 31st December, 1982. Chester Zoo, England. Mimeo.

Brinker, R. 1969. Elementary surveying. Scranton, PA: Int. Textbook Co.

Bromlei, G. 1973. *Bears of the south far-eastern USSR*. Indian Nat. Scient. Doc. Centre.

Bunnell, F., and D. Tait. 1981. Population dynamics of bears—implications. In *Dynamics of large mammal populations*, ed. C. Fowler and T. Smith, pp. 75–98. New York: John Wiley.

———. In press. Mortality rates of bears. *J. Wildl. Manage.*

Burst, T. 1979. An analysis of trees marked by black bears in the Great Smoky Mountains National Park. Master's thesis, Univ. Tennessee.

Bush, G. 1981. Stasipatric speciation and rapid evolution in animals. In *Evolution and speciation*, ed. W. Atchley and D. Woodruff, pp. 201–18. Cambridge: Cambridge Univ. Press.

Butterworth, B. 1969. Postnatal growth and development of *Ursus americanus*. *J. Mammal.* 50:615–16.

Campbell, J., Qin Zisheng, and Zhang Xianti. 1983. Flowering and population dynamics of bamboo stems in the range of giant pandas, China. World Wildlife Fund, mimeo report.

Carr, P. 1983. Habitat utilization and seasonal movements of black bears in the Great Smoky Mountains National Park. Master's thesis, Univ. Tennessee.

Carter, T. 1937. The giant panda. *Animal Kingdom* 40(1):6–14.

Castillo, E. 1982. Mexico's baby panda. *Caminos de aire, Mexicana de Aviacion*, March–April, 14–24.

Chao Chison, Chu Chengde, and Hsiung Wenyue. 1980. A revision of some genera and species of Chinese bamboos. *Acta Phytotaxonomica Sinica* 18:20–36. (In Chinese.)

Chen Dongyang. 1979. Epilepsy of the giant panda. *China Zoo Yearbook* 2:147–53. (In Chinese.)

Chengdu Zoo. 1980. Clinical observations of and experiments on ringworm in the giant panda. *China Zoo Yearbook* 3:124–25. (In Chinese.)

Chiang Shu. 1960. The meadows and forests of western mountains in Szechuan Province. *Acta Botanica Sinica* 9(2):125–36. (In Chinese.)

Chu Ching. 1974. On the systematic position of the giant panda, *Ailuropoda melanoleuca* (David). *Acta Zoologica Sinica* 20(2):191–200. (In Chinese.)

Chu Ching and Long Zhi. 1983. The vicissitudes of the giant panda. Acta Zoologica Sinica 29(1):93–104. (In Chinese.)

Clutton-Brock, T., S. Albon, R. Gibson, and F. Guinness. 1979. The logical stag: Adaptive aspects of fighting behavior in red deer (*Cervus elaphus* L.). *Anim. Behav.* 27:211–25.

Colbert, E. 1938. The panda: A study in emigration. *Nat. Hist.* 42:33–39.

Collins, L. and J. Page. 1973. Ling-Ling and Hsing-Hsing: Year of the panda. Garden City, N.Y.: Anchor Press–Doubleday.

Corbet, G. and J. Hill. 1980. *A world list of mammalian species*. London and Ithaca: Brit. Mus. (Nat. Hist.) and Cornell Univ. Press.

Craighead, J. 1980. A proposed delineation of critical grizzly bear habitat in the Yellowstone region. *Bear Biol. Assn. Monogr.*, no. 1. (20 pp.)

Craighead, J., F. Craighead, and J. Sumner. 1976. Reproductive cycles and rates in the grizzly bear, *Ursus arctos horribilis* of the Yellowstone ecosystem. In *Bears: Their biology and management*, ed. M. Pelton, J. Lentfer, and G. Folk, pp. 337–56. Morges: IUCN Publ. no. 40.

Craighead, J., M. Hornocker, and F. Craighead. 1969. Reproductive biology of young female grizzly bears. *J. Reprod. Fert. Suppl.* 6:447–75.

Craighead, J., J. Varney, and F. Craighead. 1974. *A population analysis of the Yellowstone grizzly bears*. Forest. and Cons. Exp. Station, Bull. no. 40. Univ. Montana, Missoula.

Crampton, E. and L. Harris. 1969. *Applied animal nutrition*. San Francisco: W. Freeman.

Crandall, L. 1964. *The management of wild mammals in captivity*. Chicago: Univ. of Chicago Press.

Dathe, H. 1970. A second generation birth of captive sun bears. *Int. Zoo Yearbook* 10:79.

David, A. 1874. Journal d'un voyage dans le centre de la Chine et dans le Thibet oriental. *Bull. Nouv. Arch. Mus. Hist. Nat. Paris* 10:3–82.

Davis, D. 1964. The giant panda: A morphological study of evolutionary mechanisms. *Fieldiana: Zoology Memoirs* 3:1–339.

Davis, J. 1973. Pandas. New York: Curtis Books.

Dierenfeld, E. 1981. The nutritional composition of bamboo and its utilization by the giant panda. Master's thesis, Cornell Univ.

Dierenfeld, E., H. Hintz, J. Robertson, P. Van Soest, and O. Oftedal. 1982. Utilization of bamboo by the giant panda. *J. Nutrition* 112(4):636–41.

Doe, R. 1978. Sexual behavior in the raccoon (*Procyon lotor lotor*). *Animal Behaviour Abst.*, p. 93.

Drent, R., B. Ebbing, and B. Weijand. 1978–79. Balancing the energy budgets of arctic-breeding geese throughout the annual cycle: A progress report. *Verh. orn. Ges. Bayern* 23:239–64.

Eagle, T. 1979. Foods of black bears in the Great Smoky Mountains National Park. Master's thesis, Univ. Tennessee.

Eberhard, I. 1978. Ecology of the koala, *Phascolarctos cinereus* (Goldfuss). Marsupialia: Phascolarctidae, in Australia. In *The ecology of arboreal folivores*, ed. G. Montgomery, pp. 315–27. Washington: Smith. Inst. Press.

Egbert, A. and A. Stokes. 1976. The social behaviour of brown bears on an Alaskan salmon stream. In *Bears—Their biology and management*, ed. M. Pelton, J. Lentfer, and G. Folk, pp 41–56. Morges: IUCN Publ., no. 40.

Eiler, J. 1981. Reproductive biology of black bears in the Smoky Mountains of Tennessee. Master's thesis, Univ. Tennessee.

Eisenberg, J. 1981. *The mammalian radiations*. Chicago: Univ. Chicago Press.

Ewer, R. 1973. *The carnivores*. Ithaca: Cornell Univ. Press.

Expedition of rare animal species in Sichuan. 1977. *A report on the rare animal species in Sichuan*. The Sichuan Forest Bureau. (In Chinese.)

Felsenstein, J. 1982. Numerical methods for inferring evolutionary trees. *Quart. Rev. Biol.* 57(4):379–404.

Fossey, D. and A. Harcourt. 1977. Feeding ecology of free-ranging mountain gorilla (*Gorilla gorilla beringei*). In *Primate ecology*, ed. T. Clutton-Brock, pp. 415–47. New York: Academic Press.

Frädrich, H. 1981. Nach Sichuan der Pandas wegen—ein Reisetagebuch. Bongo (Berlin) 5:41–56.

Frankel, O. and M. Soulé. 1981. *Conservation and evolution*. Cambridge: Cambridge University Press.

Franklin, I. 1980. Evolutionary change in small populations. pp. 135–150. In *Conservation biology: An evolutionary-ecological approach*, ed. M. Soulé and B. Wilcox, pp. 135–50. Sunderland, Mass.: Sinauer Ass.

Frenzel, B. 1968. The Pleistocene vegetation of northern Eurasia. *Science* 161 (3842):637–49.

Fritzell, E. 1978. Aspects of raccoon (*Procyon lotor*) social organization. *Can. J. Zool.* 56:260–71.

Gansu Forest and Agriculture Bureau. 1976. Rare animals in Gansu. *Gansu Forest and Agriculture Bureau*, pp. 2–4. (In Chinese.)

Gao Yaoting. 1973. Records of the giant panda in Chinese ancient literature. *Animal use and control* 4:31–33. (In Chinese.)

Garrett, H., and J. Goertz. 1975. Longevity record for a captive raccoon (*Procyon lotor*). *Trans. Missouri Acad. Science* 9:44–45.

Garshelis, D., and M. Pelton. 1980. Activity of black bears in the Great Smoky Mountains National Park. *J. Mammal.* 61(1):8–19.

―――. 1981. Movements of black bears in the Great Smoky Mountains National Park. *J. Wildl. Manage.* 45(4):912–25.

Gebhard, J. 1983. Annual activities and behavior of a grizzly bear family. *Proc. Sixth Int. Conf. on Bear Research and Management* (Grand Canyon, AZ.), Abstract, p. 23.

Gervais, P. 1870. Mémoire sur les formes cérébrales propres au carnivores vivants et fossiles. *Nouv. Arch. Mus. Hist. Nat. Paris* 6:103–62.

Giant Panda Expedition. 1974. A survey of the giant panda (*Ailuropoda melanoleuca*) in the Wanglang Natural Reserve, Pingwu, northern Szechuan, China. *Acta Zoologica Sinica* 20(2):162–73. (In Chinese.)

Gilbert, B. 1973. *Chulo*. New York: Knopf.

Giron, J. 1980. Giant pandas *Ailuropoda melanoleuca* in Chapultepec Park Zoo, Mexico City. *Int. Zoo Yearbook* 20:264–69.

Gittleman, J., and P. Harvey. 1982. Carnivore home-range size, metabolic needs and ecology. *Behav. Ecol. Sociobiol.* 10:57–63.

Goering, H., and P. Van Soest. 1970. Forage fiber analyses. In *Agricultural Handbook*, no. 379, pp. 1–20. U.S. Dept. Agri.

Gogan, P. 1973. Some aspects of nutrient utilization by Burchell's zebra *Equus burchelli boehmi* (Matschie) in the Serengeti-Mara region East Africa. Master's thesis, Texas A and M Univ.

Goodwin, L. ed. 1976. 'Chi-Chi' the giant panda *Ailuropoda melanoleuca* at the London Zoo 1958–1972: A scientific study. *Trans. Zool. Soc. London* 33:77–171.

Graber, D. 1982. *Ecology and management of black bears in Yosemite National Park*. Coop. Nat. Park Resources Studies Unit, no. 5.

Haas, G. 1958. Beitrag zum Verhalten des Bambusbären (*Ailuropus melanoleucus*). *Zool. Gart.* 27:225–33.

Hamer, D., S. Herrero, and R. Ogilvie. 1977. *Ecological studies of the Banff National Park*. Parks Canada.

Hamilton, R. 1978. Ecology of the black bear in southeastern North Carolina. Master's thesis, Univ. Georgia.

Harestad, A., and F. Bunnell. 1979. Home range and body weight—a reevaluation. *Ecology* 60:389–402.

Harkness, R. 1938. *The lady and the panda*. London: Nicholson and Watson.

Harrington, C. 1968. Denning habits of the polar bear (*Ursus maritimus* Phipps). *Can. Wildl. Serv. Rep.* (Ottawa), no. 5.

Hearn, J. 1982. Research progress report 1979–1981: Giant panda. pp. 31–33. In Scientific report 1979–1981, The Zoological Society of London. *J. Zool.* (London) 197:1–123.

Hendey, Q. 1980. *Agriotherium* (Mammalia, Ursidae) from Langebaanweg, South Africa, and relationships of the genus. *Ann. S. Afr. Mus.* 81(1):1–109.

Herrero, S. 1978. A comparison of some features of the evolution, ecology and behavior of black and grizzly/brown bears. *Carnivore* 1(1):7–17.

Hladik, C. 1978. Adaptive strategies of primates in relation to leaf-eating. In *The ecology of arboreal folivores*, ed. G. Montgomery, pp. 373–95. Washington: Smith. Inst. Press.

Houston, D. 1982. *The northern Yellowstone elk*. New York: Macmillan.

Hu Jinchu. 1981a. The names of the giant panda in history. *Sichuan Scientific Newspaper*, 1 Jan. 1981. (In Chinese.)

———. 1981b. Panda today and yesterday. *Wildlife* 1:6–7. (In Chinese.)

———. 1981c. *Ecology and biology of the giant panda, golden monkey, and takin*. Sichuan People's Publ. House. (In Chinese.)

———. 1982. The giant panda. *Nature Explored* 1:76–86. (In Chinese.)

Hu Jinchu, Deng Qixang, Yu Zhiwei, Zhou Shoude, and Tian Zhixiang. 1980. Biological studies of giant panda, golden monkey, and some other rare and prized animals. *Nanchong Teacher's College Journal* 2:1–39. (In Chinese.)

Investigation Team. 1977. *Giant panda and the bamboo species in the Min Mountains*. Sichuan Forest Bureau. (In Chinese.)

Jacobi, A. 1923. Zoologische Ergebnisse der Walter Stötznerschen Expedition nach Szetschwan, Osttibet und Tschili auf Grund der Sammlungen Dr. Hugo Weigolds. II. Mammalia. *Abh. Ber. Mus. Tierk. u. Völkerk., Dresden* 16(1):1–22.

Jaczewski, Z., J. Gill, and S. Kozniewski. 1960. Capacity of the different parts of the digestive tract in the brown bear. *Int. Cong. Game Biol.* 4:146–54.

Janzen, D. 1976. Why bamboos wait so long to flower. *Ann. Rev. Ecol. Syst.* 7:347–91.

Jarman, M., and P. Jarman. 1973. Daily activity of impala. *E. Afr. Wildl. J.* 11:75–92.

Jenness, R., A. Erickson, and J. Craighead. 1972. Some comparative aspects of milk from four species of bears. *J. Mammal.* 53(1):34–47.

Jian Lanpo. 1977. Faunal remains in the Xia Wanh Gang site, Henan. *Cultural relic.* 6:41–49. (In Chinese.)

Johnson, K. 1978. Den ecology of black bears (*Ursus americanus*) in the Great Smoky Mountains National Park. Master's thesis, Univ. Tennessee.

Johnson, K., and M. Pelton. 1980. Environmental relationships and the denning period of black bears in Tennessee. *J. Mammal.* 61(4):653–60.

Jonkel, C., and I. Cowan. 1971. The black bear in the spruce-fir forest. *Wildl. Monogr.* 27.

Jordan, R. 1976. Threat behavior of the black bear (*Ursus americanus*). In *Bears—their biology and management,* ed. M. Pelton, J. Lentfer, and G. Folk, pp. 57–63. Morges: IUCN Publ. no. 40.

———. 1979. An observational study of the American black bear (*Ursus americanus*). Ph.D. thesis, Univ. Tennessee.

Kaufmann, J. 1962. Ecology and social behavior of the coati, *Nasua narica*, on Barro Colorado Island, Panama. *Univ. Cal. Publ. Zool.* 60(3):95–222.

Kleiman, D. 1983. Ethology and reproduction of captive giant pandas (*Ailuropoda melanoleuca*). *Z. Tierpsych.* 62:1–46.

Kleiman, D., W. Karesh, and P. Chu. 1979. Behavioural changes associated with oestrus in the giant panda (*Ailuropoda melanoleuca*) with comments on female proceptive behaviour. *Int. Zoo Yearbook* 19:217–23.

Krebs, J. 1978. Optimal foraging: Decision rules for predators. In *Behavioural ecology*, ed. J. Krebs and N. Davies, pp. 23–63. Sunderland, Mass.: Sinauer Ass.

Kurtén, B. 1968. *Pleistocene mammals of Europe*. London: Weidenfeld and Nicolson.

————. 1971. *The age of mammals.* New York: Columbia Univ. Press.

Lanning, F., B. Ponnaiya, and C. Crumpton. 1958. The chemical nature of silica in plants. *Plant. Phys.* 33(1):339–43.

Lazell, J. 1974. *Color patterns of the "panda" bear (Ailuropoda melanoleuca) and the true panda (Ailurus fulgens).* Mississippi Wildl. Fed. (4 pp.)

Lechowicz, M. 1982. The sampling characteristics of electivity indices. *Oecologia* 52:22–30.

Leone, C., and C. Wiens. 1956. Comparative serology of carnivores. *J. Mammal.* 37(1):11–23.

Li Huifu, Chen Yuanfei, Zhong Ketin, Ying Xing, Chen Keli, Zhu Benren, Zhang Anjui, and He Guangxi. 1983. Studies on the relationship between NAG specific changes and ovulation in behavioural oestrum of the giant panda (*Ailuropoda melanoleuca*). *Nature J.* 6(4):256–58. (In Chinese.)

Liang Pianpian. 1979. Ascite diseases of giant panda. *China Zoo Yearbook* 2:157–58. (In Chinese.)

Liu Weixin. 1981. A note on the artificial insemination of giant panda. *Acta Veterinaria et Zootechnica Sinica* 12(2):73–76. (In Chinese.)

Liu Wensheng. 1978. One example of the cure of epilepsy in the giant panda. *China Zoo Yearbook* 1:127–31. (In Chinese.)

Liu Yong. 1983. Conjectures regarding activity patterns and mating of giant panda in winter. *Wildlife* 1:3–4. (In Chinese.)

Ludlow, J. 1976. Observations on the breeding of captive black bears, *Ursus americanus.* In *Bears—their biology and managements*, ed. M. Pelton, J. Lentfer, and G. Folk, pp. 65–69. IUCN Publ. no. 40. Morges.

Lyster, R. 1976. Mammary gland secretion. pp. 141–145. In 'Chi-Chi' the giant panda *Ailuropoda melanoleuca* at the London zoo 1958–1972: a scientific study, ed. L. Goodwin. *Trans. Zool. Soc. London* 33:77–171.

Matson, J. 1954. Observations on the dormant phase of a female black bear. *J. Mammal.* 35(1):28–35.

McClure, F. 1943. Bamboo as panda food. *J. Mammal.* 24:267–68.

————. 1966. *The bamboos—a fresh perspective.* Cambridge: Harvard Univ. Press.

McNab, B. 1978. Energetics of arboreal folivores: Physiological problems and ecological consequences of feeding on an ubiquitous food supply. In *The ecology of arboreal folivores*, ed. G. Montgomery, pp. 153–62. Washington: Smith. Inst. Press.

Mech, L., D. Barnes, and J. Tester. 1968. Seasonal weight changes, mortality, and population structure of raccoons in Minnesota. *J. Mammal.* 49(1):63–73.

Meyer-Holzapfel, M. 1957. Das Verhalten der Bären (Ursiden). *Handb. Zool.* 8(10):1–28.

Miller, B., R. Robinson, J. Johnson, E. Jones, and B. Ponnaiya. 1960. Studies on the relation between silica in wheat plants and resistance to Hessian fly attack. *J. Economic Ent.* 53(6):995–99.

Mills, S. 1983. The panda puzzle. *BBC Wildlife* 1(1):8–13.

Milne-Edwards, A. 1870. Note sur quelques mammifères du Thibet oriental. *Ann. Sci. Nat., Zool.* Ser. 5, Art. 10. (1 p.)

Milton, K. 1980. *The foraging strategy of howler monkeys.* New York: Columbia Univ. Press.

Minson, D., and M. McLeod. 1970. The digestibility of temperate and tropical grasses. *Proc. XI Internat. Grasslands Congress*, p. 719.

Mivart, S. 1885. On the anatomy, classification, and distribution of the Arctoidea. *Proc. Zool. Soc. London*, pp. 340–404.

Moen, A. 1973. *Wildlife ecology: An analytical approach.* San Francisco: W. H. Freeman.

Montgomery, G. 1969. Weaning of captive raccoons. *J. Wildl. Manage.* 33(1):154–58.

Morris, R., and Morris, D. 1966. *Men and pandas.* New York: McGraw-Hill. (Rev. ed. 1981, J. Barzdo. London: Kogan Page.)

Murie, A. 1981. *The grizzlies of Mount McKinley.* U.S. Dept. Int., Nat. Park Serv. Monogr. no. 14.

Musser, G. 1972. The species of *Hapalomys* (Rodentia, Muridae). *Am. Mus. Novitates.* 2503:1–27.

Nash, N. 1981. How the panda got its patches. *Young discoverer, Cathay Pacific* 4(4):4–7.

Nelson, R. 1973. Winter sleep in the black bear. *Mayo Clin. Proc.* 48:734–37.

———. 1980. Protein and fat metabolism in hibernating bears. *Am. Physiol. Soc. Fed. Proc.* 39(12):2955–58.

Numata, M. 1979. The relationship of limiting factors to the distribution and growth of bamboo. In *Ecology of grasslands and bamboolands in the world*, ed. M. Numata, pp. 258–75. Jena: Gustav Fischer.

Pan Wenshi, Chen Lirong, and Xiao Nengqing. 1981. Serological study of giant panda and various mammalians. *Acta Scien. Nat. Univ. Pekinensis.* 1:79–88. (In Chinese.)

Parra, R. 1978. Comparison of foregut and hindgut fermentation in herbivores. In *The ecology of arboreal folivores*, ed. G. Montgomery, pp. 205–29. Washington D.C.: Smith. Inst. Press.

Pearson, A. 1975. The northern interior grizzly bear *Ursus arctos L.* Can. Wildl. Series Rep. no. 34.

Peking zoo. 1974a. Observations on the breeding of the giant panda and the raising of its young. *Acta Zoologica Sinica* 20:139–47. (In Chinese.)

———. 1974b. On the diseases of the giant panda and their preventive and curative measures. *Acta Zoologica Sinica* 20:154–61. (In Chinese.)

Pelchat, B., and R. Ruff. 1983. Habitat and spatial relationships of black bears in boreal mixedwood forest of Alberta. Sixth Int. Conf. on bear research and management (Grand Canyon, AZ.). Abstract, p. 39.

Pen Hongshou. 1943. Some notes on the giant panda. *Bull. Fan. Mem. Inst. Biol. Peiping* 1(1):64–71.

———, Kao Yuenting, Lu Changkun, Feng Tsochien, and Chen Qinghsing. 1962. Report on mammals in southwestern Sichuan and northwestern Yunnan. *Acta Zoologica Sinica.* 14:105–32. (In Chinese.)

Peters, G. 1978. Einige Beobachtungen zur Lautgebung der Bären. *Z. des Kölner Zoo.* 21(2):45–51.

———. 1982. A note on the vocal behaviour of the giant panda. *Ailuropoda melanoleuca* (David, 1869). *Z. f. Säugetierk.* 47(4):236–46.

Peters, G., D. Kleiman, and G. Schaller. In prep. Vocalizations of the giant panda.

Peters, R., and L. Mech. 1975. Scent-marking in wolves. *Am. Scientist* 63:628–37.

Petter, J., and A. Peyrieras. 1975. Preliminary notes on the behavior and ecology of *Hapalemur griseus.* In *Lemur biology*, ed. I. Tattersall and R. Sussman, pp. 281–86. New York: Plenum Press.

Pianka, E. 1980. On r and K selection. *Am. Nat.* 104:592–97.

Piekielek, W. 1973. A black bear population study in northern California. Master's thesis, Univ. California.

Platz, C., D. Wildt, S. Seager, J. Howard, and M. Bush. 1983. Electroejaculation, semen analysis and freezing in the giant panda (*Ailuropoda melanoleuca*). *J. Reprod. Fert.* 67:9–12.

Pocock, R. 1921. On the external characters and classification of the Procyonidae. *Proc. Zool. Soc. London*, pp. 389–422.

Poelker, R. and Hartwell, H. 1973. *Black bear in Washington*. Wash. State Game Dept. Bull. no. 14.

Poglayen-Neuwall, I. 1962. Beiträge zu einem Ethogram des Wickelbären (*Potos flavus* Schreber). *Z. Säugetierk*. 27:1–44.

———. 1967. On the marking behavior of the Kinkajou (*Potos flavus* Schreber). *Zoologica* 51:137–41.

———. 1973. Preliminary notes on maintenance and behavior of the Central American cacomistle *Bassariscus sumichrasti* at Louisville Zoo. *Int. Zoo Yearbook* 13:207–11.

———. 1976a. Zur Fortpflanzungsbiologie und Jugendentwicklung von *Potos flavus* (Schreber 1774). *Zool. Gart*. 46(4–5):237–83.

———. 1976b. Fortpflanzung, Geburt und Aufzucht, nebst anderen Beobachtungen von Makibären (*Bassaricyon* Allen 1876). *Zool. Beiträge* 22:179–33.

———. 1980. Gestation period and parturition of the ringtail *Bassariscus astutus* (Liechtenstein, 1830). *Z. Säugetierk*. 45(2):73–81.

Poglayen-Neuwall, I., and I. Poglayen-Neuwall. 1965. Gefangenschaftsbeobachtungen an Makibären (*Bassaricyon* Allen 1876). *Z. Säugetierk*. 30(6):321–66.

Qing Song. 1977. Bamboos and the giant panda in the Min Mountains. *Bot. J*. 3:38–39. (In Chinese.)

Quigley, H. 1982. Activity patterns, movement ecology, and habitat utilization of black bears in the Great Smoky Mountains National Park, Tennessee. Master's thesis, Univ. Tennessee.

Rabinowitz, A. 1981. The ecology of the raccoon (*Procyon lotor*) in Cades Cove, Great Smoky Mountains National Park. Doctoral thesis, Univ. Tennessee.

Ralls, K. 1971. Mammalian scent marking. *Science* 171:443–49.

Raven, H. 1936. Notes on the anatomy of the viscera of the giant panda (*Ailuropoda melanoleuca*). *Am. Mus. Nov*. 877:1–23.

Rhoades, D., and R. Cates. 1976. Toward a general theory of plant antiherbivore chemistry. In *Biochemical interaction between plants and insects*, ed. J. Wallace and R. Mansell, pp. 168–213. New York: Plenum.

Ricard, L., and F. Dore. 1977. Le comportement sexuel du raton laveur (*Procyon lotor lotor*). *Biol. Behav*. 2:239–48.

Rieffenberger, J., R. Anderson, W. Brown, K. Knight, and J. Cromer. 1981. *West Virginia black bear*. W. Virg. Dept. Nat. Res. Bull. no. 9.

Roberts, M. 1975. Growth and development of mother-reared red pandas, *Ailurus fulgens*. *Int. Zoo Yearbook* 15:57–63.

———. 1981. The reproductive biology of the red panda, *Ailurus fulgens*, in captivity. Master's thesis, Univ. Maryland.

Roberts, M., and D. Kessler. 1979. Reproduction in red pandas, *Ailurus fulgens* (Carnivora: Ailuropodidae). *J. Zool*. (London) 188:235–49.

Rogers, L. 1977. Social relationships, movements, and population dynamics of black bears in northeastern Minnesota. Doctoral thesis, Univ. Minnesota.

Roosevelt, T., and K. Roosevelt. 1929. Trailing the giant panda. New York: Scribner's.

Rowell, T. 1979. How would we know if social organization were not adaptive? In *Primate ecology and human origins*, ed. I. Bernstein and E. Smith, pp. 1–22. New York: Garland STPM Press.

Ruan Shiju and Yong Yange. 1983. Observations on feeding and search for food of giant panda in the wild. *Wildlife* 1:5–8. (In Chinese.)

Sadleir, R. 1969. *The ecology of reproduction in wild and domestic mammals*. London: Methuen.

Sanderson, G. and A. Nalbandov. 1973. The reproductive cycle of the raccoon in Illinois. *Ill. Nat. Hist. Survey Bull.* 31(2):1–85.

Sarich, V. 1976. Transferrin. pp. 165–171. In "Chi-Chi", the giant panda *Ailuropoda melanoleuca* at the London Zoo 1958–1972: A scientific study, ed. L. Goodwin. *Trans. Zool. Soc. London* 33:77–171.

Schäfer, E. 1938. Der Bambusbär (*Ailuropus melanoleucus* A. M.-Edw.). *Zool. Garten* 10:21–31.

Schaller, G. 1963. *The mountain gorilla*. Chicago: Univ. Chicago Press.

———. 1972. *The Serengeti lion*. Chicago: Univ. Chicago Press.

Schmidt-Kittler, N. 1981. Zur Stammesgeschichte der marderverwandten Raubtiergruppen (Musteloidea, Carnivora). *Ecologae geol. Helv.* 74(3):753–801.

Schmidt-Nielsen, K. 1975. *Animal physiology: Adaptation and environment*. London: Cambridge Univ. Press.

Schneider, D., L. Mech, and J. Tester. 1971. Movements of female raccoons and their young as determined by radio-tracking. *Animal Behaviour. Monogr.* 4(1):1–43.

Schneider, K. 1939. Einiges vom grossen und kleinen Panda. *Zool. Garten* 11:203–32.

Schoch, J. 1981. Current status of baby panda. Videotape presented at I.U.D.Z.G. meeting, Washington, D.C.

Schoener, T. 1971. Theory of feeding strategies. *Ann. Rev. Ecol. and System* 2:369–403.

Schoonmaker, W. 1968. *The world of the grizzly bear*. Philadelphia: J. Lippincott.

Seal, U., N. Phillips, and A. Erickson. 1970. Carnivora systematics: Immunological relationships of bear serum albumins. *Comp. Biochem. Physiol.* 31:799–811.

Seitz, A. 1973. Beitrag zur Zucht des Eisbären (*Thalarctos maritimus*) *Zool. Garten* 43(6):293–304.

Selander, R. 1982. Phylogeny. In *Perspectives on evolution*, ed. R. Milkman, pp. 32–59. Sunderland, MA: Sinauer Associates.

Shaanxi Biological Resources Expedition. 1976. Preliminary studies on the giant pandas in Qinling Mountains in Shaanxi Province. *Biology Exploration* 3(1):91–104. (In Chinese.)

Shaffer, M. 1981. Minimum population sizes for species conservation. *Bioscience* 31:131–34.

Sheldon, W. 1937. Notes on the giant panda. *J. Mammal.* 18:13–19.

———. 1975. *The wilderness home of the giant panda*. Amherst: Univ. Massachusetts Press.

Shen Wenxiong. 1974. The vicissitudes of the climate in China. *China Pictorial* 4:30–33.

Shi Chengying. 1981. Reproductive ecology of the giant panda. *China Zoo Yearbook* 4:17–19. (In Chinese.)

Shidea, T. 1974. Forest vegetation zones. In *The flora and vegetation of Japan*, ed. M. Numata, pp. 87–124. Amsterdam: Elsevier.

Short, H. 1981. Nutrition and metabolism. In *Mule and black-tailed deer of North America*, ed. O. Wallmo, pp. 99–127. Lincoln: Univ. Nebraska Press.

Sinclair, A. 1975. The resource limitation of trophic levels in tropical grassland ecosystems. *J. Animal Ecol.* 44:497–520.

———. 1977. *The African buffalo*. Chicago: Univ. Chicago Press.

Sizemore, D. 1980. Foraging strategies of the grizzly bear as related to its ecological energetics. Master's thesis, Univ. Montana.

Smil, V. 1983. Deforestation in China. *Ambio* 7(5):226–31.

Soderstrom, T. 1979. The bamboozling *Thamnocalamus*. *Garden* 3(4):22–27.

Soulé, M. 1980. Threshholds for survival: maintaining fitness and evolutionary potential. In *Conservation biology: An evolutionary-ecological perspective*, ed. M. Soulé and B. Wilcox, pp. 159–61. Sunderland, MA: Sinauer Associates.

Stains, H. 1956. The raccoon in Kansas, natural history, management, and economic importance. *Univ. Kansas Misc. Publ.* 10:1–76.

Steel, R., and J. Torrie. 1960. *Principles and procedures of statistics.* New York: McGraw-Hill.

Stickley, A. 1957. Status and characteristics of the black bear in Virginia. Master's thesis, Virginia Polytechnic Institute, Blacksburg.

Stirling, I. 1974. Midsummer observations on the behavior of wild polar bears (*Ursus maritimus*). *Can. J. Zool.* 52:1191–29.

Stirling, I., C. Jonkel, P. Smith, R. Robertson, and D. Cross. 1977. *The ecology of the polar bear (Ursus maritimus) along the western coast of Hudson Bay.* Can. Wildl. Service Occ. Paper no. 33. Ottawa.

Stuewer, F. 1943. Reproduction of raccoons in Michigan. *J. Wildl. Manage.* 7(1):60–73.

Summers, R., and A. Grieve. 1982. Diet, feeding behaviour and food intake of the upland goose (*Chloëphaga picta*) and ruddy-headed goose (*C. rubidiceps*) in the Falkland islands. *J. Applied Ecol.* 19:783–804.

Sunquist, M. 1981. The social organization of tigers (*Panthera tigris*) in Royal Chitawan National Park, Nepal. *Smith. Contr. Zool.* 336:1–98.

Tan Bangjie. 1983. An inquiry into the mystery of artificial breeding of the giant panda. *Nature* 12:20–23. (In Chinese.)

Tang Xiyang. 1983. Inquiry of the giant panda. *Wildlife* 1:39–41. (In Chinese.)

Tang Zhiying, Chen Tongxing, Sun Zhongwu, Han Yin, and Su Hanying. 1983. Bamboo and nutrition of giant panda. *Wildlife* 5:1–4. (In Chinese.)

Tedford, R., and E. Gustafson. 1977. First North American record of the extinct panda *Parailurus*. *Nature* 265:621–23.

Thenius, E. 1979. Zur systematischen und phylogenetischen Stellung des Bambusbären: *Ailuropoda melanoleuca* David (Carnivora, Mammalia). *Z. Säugetierk.* 44(5):286–305.

Thenius, E., and H. Hofer. 1960. *Stammesgeschichte der Säugetiere.* Berlin: Springer Verlag.

Trapp, G. 1978. Comparative behavioral ecology of the ringtail and gray fox in southwestern Utah. *Carnivore* 1(2):3–31.

Tschanz, B., M. Meyer-Holzapfel, and S. Bachmann. 1970. Das Informationssystem bei Braunbären. *Z. Tierpsych.* 27:47–72.

Van Soest, P. 1975. Physico-chemical aspects of fibre digestion. In *Digestion and metabolism in the ruminant*, ed. I. McDonald and A. Warner, pp. 351–65. Sydney: Univ. New England.

———. 1977. Plant fiber and its role in herbivore nutrition. *Cornell Vet.* 67(3):307–26.

———. 1980. Impact of feeding behavior and digestive capacity on nutritional response. Paper presented at Technical Consultation on Animal Genetic Resources Conservation and Management, Rome. Mimeo.

———. 1982. *Nutritional ecology of the ruminant.* Corvallis, OR: O and B Books.

Veblen, T. 1982. Growth patterns of *Chusquea* bamboos in the understory of Chilean *Nothofagus* forests and their influences in forest dynamics. *Bull. Torrey Bot. Club* 109(4):474–87.

Walker, E. 1975. *Mammals of the world*, 3d ed. Baltimore: Johns Hopkins Univ. Press.

Wallmo, O., L. Carpenter, W. Regelin, B. Gill and D. Baker. 1977. Evaluation of deer habitat on a nutritional basis. *J. Range Manage.* 30(2):122–27.

Wang Baoqiang. 1978. Twenty examples of panda tranquilizations with Ketamine. *China Zoo Yearbook* 1:182–86.

Wang Chiwu. 1961. *The forests of China.* Maria Moors Cabot Foundation Publ. no. 5 (Harvard Univ. Press).

Wang Huenpu, 1980. Nature conservation in China: The present situation. *Parks* 5(1):1–10.

Wang Jie. 1979. One example of intestinal obstruction by a large intestinal ulcer in the giant panda "Fang-Fang," *J. Southwest Normal College* 1:1–7. (In Chinese.)

Wang Ping, Cao Chuo, and Chen Maosheng. 1982. Histological survey of the alimentary tract of giant panda. *Zoological Research.* 3 (Supplement): 27–28. (In Chinese.)

Wang Ping, Chen Maosheng, Cao Chuo, Liu Weixin, and Yie Jüqun. 1981. Histological observations of newborn giant panda, *Ailuropoda melanoleuca. Kexue Tongbao* 26(3):23.

Wang Sung and Lu Changkun. 1973. Giant pandas in the wild. *Nat. Hist.* 82(10):70–71.

Wang Tsiangke. 1974. On the taxonomic status of species, geological distribution and evolutionary history of *Ailuropoda. Acta Zoologica Sinica* 20(2):191–201. (In Chinese.)

Wemmer, C., M. von Ebers, and K. Scow. 1976. An analysis of the chuffing vocalization in the Polar bear (*Ursus maritimus*). *J. Zool.* (London) 180:425–39.

Wen Huanran. 1981. Pandas in Henan, Hubei, Hunan, and Sichuan during the past 5000 years. *J. Southwest Normal College* 1:1–7. (In Chinese.)

———— and He Yeheng. 1980. China's wildlife yesterday and today. *China Reconstructs,* October, 49–51.

Wen Zhe and Wang Menghu. 1980. Giant pandas and bamboo. *Nature* 1(1):12–15. (In Chinese.)

Westoby, M. 1974. An analysis of diet selection by large generalist herbivores. *Am. Nat.* 108:290–304.

White, P. 1979. Pattern, process, and natural disturbances in vegetation. *Bot. Rev.* 45(3):229–99.

Willey, R., and R. Richards. 1981. Vocalizations of the ringtail (*Bassariscus astutus*). *S.W. Nat.* 26:23–30.

Wilson, E. 1929. *China: Mother of gardens.* Boston: Stratford Co.

Wilson, E. O. 1975. *Sociobiology: The new synthesis.* Cambridge: Harvard Univ. Press.

Wilson, S., and D. Kleiman. 1974. Eliciting play: A comparative study. *Am. Zool.* 14:341–70.

Woodward, A. 1915. On the skull of an extinct carnivore related to *Aeluropus* from a cave in the Ruby Mines at Mogok, Burma. *Proc. Zool. Soc. London*, pp. 425–28.

Wu Jiayan. 1981. The brief history of research on giant panda of Qinling. *Wildlife* 4:8–9. (In Chinese.)

Wurster-Hill D., and M. Bush. 1980. The interrelationship of chromosome banding patterns in the giant panda (*Ailuropoda melanoleuca*), hybrid bear (*Ursus middendorfi* × *Thalarctos maritimus*), and other carnivores. *Cytogenet. Cell Genet.* 27:147–54.

Wyatt, J., and S. Eltringham. 1974. The daily activity of the elephant in the Ruwenzori National Park, Uganda. *E. Afr. Wildl. J.* 12:273–89.

Xu Giming, He Guangjing, and Ye Zhiyong. 1981. Reproduction and hand-rearing of the giant panda. *China Zoo Yearbook* 4:10–16. (In Chinese.)

Xu Linmu. 1981. On the longevity of the giant panda. *Nature* 3:88. (In Chinese.)

Yong Yange. 1981. The preliminary observations on giant panda in Foping Natural Reserve. *Wildlife* 4:10–16. (In Chinese.)

Yu Yongjiu. 1980. Observations on the rearing of the giant panda. *China Zoo Yearbook* 3:12–14. (In Chinese.)

Zhang Yongzu and Zheng Changlin. 1981. The geographical distribution of mammals and the evolution of mammalian fauna in Qinghai-Xizang Plateau. In *Geological and ecological studies of Qinghai-Xizang-Plateau*, ed. Liu Dongsheng, 2:1006–11. Beijing: Science Press.

Zheng Guangmei and Xu Pingyu. 1964. Pandas discovered on the south slope of Qinling. *Acta Zoologica Sinica* 6:3. (In Chinese.)

Zheng Jinzhang. 1980. Twenty examples of panda tranquilizations with Ketamine. *J. Zool.* 1:30–32. (In Chinese.)

Zheng Zuoxin, Feng Zuojian, Zhang Yongzu, and Hu Shuqin. 1981. On the land-vertebrate fauna of Qinghai-Xizang Plateau with considerations concerning its history and transformation. In *Geological and ecological studies of Qinghai-Xizang Plateau*, ed. Liu Dongsheng, 2:975–87. Beijing: Science Press.

Zhou Jianren. 1956. On pandas. *People's Daily*, 6 July, p. 8. (In Chinese.)

Zhou Mingzhen. 1964. The evolution of China Quaternary fauna. *J. Zool.* 9(6):274–278. (In Chinese.)

Zhu Jing and Li Yangwen. 1980. *The giant panda.* Beijing: Science Press.

Zhu Keshen. 1973. A preliminary study on the vicissitudes of the climate in China in the past 5000 years. *People's Daily*, 19 June. (In Chinese.)

Index